eXtreme
Teen Bible

This Bible belongs to: _____

Given by: _____

Date: _____

Occasion: _____

_____

eXtreme TEEN BiBLe ™

eXtreme Teen Bible ™

NEW KING JAMES VERSION

THOMAS NELSON PUBLISHERS
Nashville

Contents

THE OLD TESTAMENT

THE NEW TESTAMENT

Welcome
Extreme Teen™ Bible: Introduction

THIS IS A BOOK OF RISK-TAKERS

This Bible is about radical devotion and revolutionary people. It is a book that God breathed into the hearts and minds of people who were grappling with life and rising to the challenge of faith in the extreme.

The stories were written by and about dreamers and risk-takers—people who bet their lives on what they could only see through faith. They were people who took a chance on God and dared to believe that this world we live in is a *virtual world* compared to the reality of who God is and how He wants to connect with us.

They didn't pretty-up their lives. They told the truth even when it was raw. They admitted their mistakes. God inspired a book that reveals life with all its problems and all of humankind's frailties. He gave us a picture of the out-on-limb-life that is the life of faith.

THIS IS A BOOK ABOUT A REVOLUTIONARY

This whole Bible is really about God connecting to us through Jesus Christ. The Old Testament is the story of Jesus' ancestors and how they lived their lives while waiting for the Messiah to come. The New Testament is about Jesus' life and the universal shock waves from His death and resurrection.

Jesus was all-the-way man and all-the-way God. He was the truest revolutionary of all time. He wasn't afraid to blast the hypocritical religious leaders or to cry when His friend died. He lived through a life just like ours with its frustrations and hard times to do something no one else has done: die as a sacrifice for our sins. The truth He spoke and the fact that He beat death turned the world upside down.

WHAT MAKES READING THE BIBLE A CHALLENGE?

It was written for a different culture.

That's why some of the concepts and behaviors seem foreign to us. We have to figure out the feelings and convictions behind those concepts and behaviors and how they might work today.

It was translated from a different language.

That's why there are so many "versions" or "translations." As our language changes we interpret the original Bible into our language again and again.

It was written in a different time.

That means different customs and attitudes. That means different names for the same things. That means understanding how faith worked in *that* time and *from that* figuring out how it should work today.

All of this means that we have to work a little harder to "translate" what the Bible says into our day and time. That's why we need extra notes and Bible helps. So take the plunge into all the great stuff packed in this Bible. It's worth it.

THIS BIBLE IS A SURVIVAL GUIDE

The Bible is a lot of books strapped together. They are inspired by God, but written by all kinds of different people in all kinds of different circumstances and for all kinds of different reasons. These people weren't setting out to write a book of the Bible. They were facing life and surviving as best they could. Their stories teach us to survive as well by God's power. Because God inspired them, they're one hundred percent accurate and reliable.

Some of these books are stories, listings of events. Some of them are poetry. Some of them are song lyrics. Some are sermons. Some are biographies. Others are letters of introduction. One is a letter of reference. Another is a thank-you note. Some books were written to show God's presence in history. One book is a passionate love poem. Another is a health manual and a textbook for priests. Still another is a war saga. Several are heated letters written to set somebody straight. A few of them are visions of the future.

When you read the Bible, any part of it, understand the big picture. Understand why that book was written, what that writer was trying to accomplish. What were the people involved struggling with? What were they trying to make sense of? Each book has an **Introduction** written specifically to help answer these kinds of questions.

There are other special features to help you get as deep inside the Bible as you can.

People Profiles give you information about specific people who stood a head above the rest to change their world.

What's It Mean? notes give you byte-sized information on specific words or phrases you read about that might not be as obvious today as they were in the culture of Bible times.

Other notes point out **Promises** that God makes in the Bible and ways that He calls us to live **On the Edge** through faith that pushes us to trust God in the extreme.

The **Quick Reference Index** is the place to turn when you need God's answers to your questions. Look up your question by topic in the front of the Bible; then find the answer at the Bible book, chapter, verse location listed. The questions are also repeated in the Bible text next to their answer.

There are also **Reading Plans** in the back. These plans give you suggestions for what to read every day to cover the Bible in a year.

It's all here—truth, inspiration, bottom-line *actual reality*. Are you up for the challenge?

Production Design and Editorial Team

The Livingstone Corporation
Bruce B. Barton
Christopher D. Hudson
David R. Veerman

Associate Editors

Katie Gieser
Carol Ochs

Contributors

Ron Luce
Linda Washington
Randy Southern
Carol Smith
Neil Wilson

Quick Reference Finder

EMOTIONS
How does it feel when we follow God? . . . . Joshua 2:12, 13
Where can we find healing for a broken heart? . . . . Psalm 34:18
Did Jesus experience emotions? . . . . John 11:35
Are emotions reliable guides? . . . . Galatians 5:1–17

ENCOURAGEMENT
How should we stand up for those who need help? Nehemiah 5:7–11
How can we encourage others? . . . . Job 4:4
Are we ever helpless? . . . . Habakkuk 3:17–19
Is God close to us? . . . . Zechariah 2:10
Who is our source of encouragement? . . . . Acts 9:31

ENEMIES
Who can defeat our enemies? . . . . Joshua 10:25
Should we be afraid of our enemies? . . . . Nehemiah 4:14
How can we avoid making enemies? . . . . Proverbs 17:9

ENVY
What kind of actions can envy lead to? . . . . Acts 7:9

ETERNAL LIFE
Who is eternal life reserved for? . . . . Matthew 7:21
What is required for eternal life? . . . . John 3:15, 16
Who receives eternal punishment? . . . . John 5:28, 29
What does Jesus give? . . . . John 11:25
Where can eternal life be found? . . . . John 14:6
What does eternal life give us? . . . . Titus 3:7

FAITH
What's a good example of faith? . . . . 2 Kings 4:1–7
How much faith is needed? . . . . Luke 17:6
What is the definition of faith? . . . . Hebrews 11:1

FAMILY
What can the members of a family do
for each other? . . . . Deuteronomy 6:4–9
What should my family be like? . . . . Joshua 24:15
What's a good example of family? . . . . Ruth 1:16
Where do kids come from? . . . . Ruth 4:13
What's more important: family or work? . . . . 1 Kings 5:13, 14
What's a good legacy parents can leave
their children? . . . . 1 Chronicles 28:8
What's a good example of love for family? . . . . Esther 2:11
Can children break the chain of sin and disobedience
in a family? . . . . Ezekiel 18:14–19
Is there anything that is more important than the family?   Luke 12:51–53

FEAR

Why should we not be afraid? . . . . 2 Chronicles 20:15	
Should Christians ever be afraid of God? . . . . .Psalm 25:12–15	
What two things does God tell us that we do not need to fear? Psalm 91:5	
Should we fear bad news? . . . . Psalm 112:7	
Who can conquer our fears? . . . . Jeremiah 46:27	

FEELINGS

What should we do when we are sad? . . . . . 1 Samuel 1:10; Nehemiah 1:4
Does God care when we hurt? . . . . Nehemiah 9:27

FOLLOWING GOD

What happens if we forget to follow God? . . . . Joshua 9:3–18
How should we follow God?   . . . . . Joshua 22:5; 2 Chronicles 15:15;
                                               Job 23:11, 12
What are Christians like? . . . . Judges 5:31
Who should we listen to? .1 Samuel 3:10
Does God put conditions on our obedience? . . . . .2 Chronicles 7:17
Who will teach us to follow God? . . . . Nehemiah 9:20
What's the hope of a righteous person? . . . . . . .Proverbs 10:24, 25
Where will following God lead us? . . . . Isaiah 35:10
How can we have a changed life? . . . . Ezekiel 11:19

FORGIVENESS

What is God known for? . . . . Nehemiah 9:17
Why does God forgive us? . . . . Psalm 86:5
Is God's forgiveness possible? . . . . Ezekiel 37:23
How many times should I forgive someone
before I stop? . . . . .Matthew 18:21–35
Who can receive forgiveness? . . . . Acts 13:38, 39

FRIENDSHIP

What's an example of good friendship? . . . . 1 Samuel 19:1–7
How can friendship outlast death? . . . . .2 Samuel 9:1
How should we care for our friends? . . . . 2 Samuel 19:33
How can friends pull you down? . . . . 2 Chronicles 10:1–14
What should we do to help hurting friends? . . . . Job 2:11
Can friends cause us pain? .Psalm 55:12–14
Can standing up for a friend make a difference? . . . . . . Jeremiah 26:24
What is friendship marked by?   . . . . John 15:13–15

FUTURE

How can our future be blessed? . . . . Deuteronomy 5:29
Does God put us in situations to make a difference? . . . . .Esther 4:14
What's the future of someone who doesn't turn from sin?   . Jeremiah 18:11
Is the future of Christians bright? . . . . .Jeremiah 31:6

HOMOSEXUALITY

What does God say about homosexual behavior? . . . Leviticus 18:22
When is sex perverted? . . . . Judges 19:22
Will homosexuals be held accountable for
their actions? . . . . Romans 1:18–32

HONESTY

Is honesty a command from God? . . . . Exodus 20:16
What does God require of us? . . . . Ezekiel 45:9–11
What do lies do to our position before God? . . . . Matthew 15:18–20

HOPE

Why can we be hopeful? . . . . 2 Samuel 22:7
What should you do when the situation is hopeless? . . 2 Kings 19:14–19
Will God still love us even if we sin? . . . . Ezra 10:2
Who does God give hope? . . . . Psalm 9:18
When is our hope misplaced? . . . . Jeremiah 23:16
Can we have hope in bad situations? . . . . Lamentations 3:21, 22

HUMILITY

How do people compare to God? . . . . Job 25:6
Does God bless a humble person? . . . . Proverbs 22:4
Is humility important? . . . . Zephaniah 2:3

HYPOCRISY

What effect does the hypocrite have on those around him? . Proverbs 11:9
What does God think of a person with double standards? . Proverbs 20:10
What is hypocrisy? . . . . Isaiah 29:13
How is religion more than occasional actions? . . . . Isaiah 58:5–7

IDOLATRY

Is it okay to be more devoted to something
than we are to God? . . . . Deuteronomy 4:23
In what circumstances are we prone to give in to idolatry? . Psalm 106:19
What does God condemn? . . . . Ezekiel 12:24

INTEGRITY

What's better: image or integrity? . . . . 1 Samuel 16:7
What's someone look like who has integrity? . . . . 2 Chronicles 26:4
Is it important for leaders to have integrity? . . . . Psalm 78:72
Does integrity take effort? . . . . Psalm 101:3–8
How does integrity help us? . . . . Daniel 6:4, 5

JEALOUSY

Does God want to share our devotion?	Deuteronomy 4:24
Can we ever envy evil people?	Psalm 37:1
Is it right to envy the prosperity of the wicked?	Psalm 73:2, 3
What can jealousy cause?	Acts 7:9
Is envying other Christians wise?	Galatians 2:6

JESUS

Was Jesus born of a virgin?	Isaiah 7:14
What is Jesus known for?	Isaiah 9:6
Will the Messiah come again?	Mark 14:61, 62
What role does Jesus have in the Trinity?	Luke 1:35
Is Jesus God?	John 1:1–5
Is Jesus the Messiah?	John 4:21–26
What is Jesus the Prince of?	Acts 3:15
Did Jesus create the world?	Colossians 1:15, 16
Has Jesus ever sinned?	Hebrews 4:15

JUDGMENT

Who is the ultimate authority?	Psalm 9:7, 8
Does God judge motives?	Jeremiah 20:12
Who will judge us?	Ezekiel 7:3, 4
Will we reap what we sow?	Obadiah 15
What does God condemn?	Malachi 3:5
Will God judge the words we speak?	Matthew 12:36
Does God ever judge by appearances?	John 7:24
Will Christians be judged for their actions?	2 Corinthians 5:10

KINDNESS

What should we do to those who have been kind to us?	1 Kings 2:7

LAZINESS

If diligence brings wealth, what does laziness bring?	Proverbs 13:4
If you are lazy, what can you expect?	Proverbs 19:15
Who should we encourage to work?	1 Thessalonians 5:12–14
Should lazy people be allowed to take advantage of other people?	2 Thessalonians 3:10

LEADERSHIP

What makes a good leader?	Exodus 18:21
Whose best should leaders look out for?	Numbers 27:16, 17
Why should we respect leaders?	1 Samuel 24:1–6
Are leaders ordained by God?	2 Samuel 1:16

Quick Reference Finder

SICKNESS
Does God care for the sick? . . . . Psalm 41:1–13
Who should believers show compassion? . . . . Matthew 25:34–40
Who had sickness that God would not heal? . . . . . 2 Corinthians 12:7–10

SIN
Does sin have consequences? . . . . Exodus 32:34; Joshua 7:25;
2 Samuel 12:9–12
How might God severely judge sin? . . . . 1 Chronicles 2:3
How should we feel about our own sin? . . . . 1 Chronicles 21:7, 8
Do we really need to confess sin to God? . . . . 2 Chronicles 6:24
What should we do when we realize that we've sinned? . . . . Ezra 9:6
What should we do about sin in our lives? . . . . Isaiah 1:16–18
What happens to the sin of Christians? . . . . Isaiah 53:6
Can we hide sin from God? . . . . Jeremiah 16:17
What does God think of our sin? . . . . Hosea 7:13
Can God tolerate sin? . . . . Romans 3:23

STRENGTH
Will God help us soar to new heights? . . . . Isaiah 40:29–31

SUCCESS
Who gives us success? . . . . Joshua 6:27
Can we trust God for our success? . . . . 1 Chronicles 11:14
How should we pray to obtain success? . . . . 2 Chronicles 7:14
When can success be bad for us? . . . . 2 Chronicles 12:1

TALENTS
How can our gifts work against us? . . . . Ezekiel 28:5
Who gives us our gifts? . . . . Daniel 1:17

TEMPTATION
What can you do to avoid temptation? . . . . 2 Kings 21:8, 9
How do we guard against temptation? . . . . Proverbs 2:10–14
What should we do when faced with temptation? . . . . . 2 Timothy 2:22

THANKFULNESS
What should we do when we are thankful? . . . 1 Chronicles 16:4–36
Why should we thank the Lord? . . . . Psalm 107:1–3
What should we be thankful for? . . . . Psalm 138:1–8
Is God thankful for you? . . . . Isaiah 62:5
Who should we thank for what we have? . . . . Acts 27:35

TRIALS

Where can we find strength? . . . . 1 Samuel 17:37
Where can we find rest? . . . . 2 Chronicles 14:11
Will we have problems in life? . . . . Job 14:1
Who will help us overcome our problems? . . . . Isaiah 37:20
What causes some trials? . . . . Lamentations 5:16
Where can we find protection? . . . . Nahum 1:7
What does Christ promise us when we're dealing
with trials? . . . . Matthew 11:25–30
Does God know what He is doing with our lives? . . . . Romans 8:28

TRUST

Whose promises always come true? . . . . 1 Chronicles 17:26, 27
How are we to trust God? . . . . Proverbs 3:5, 6
What is a result of trusting God? . . . . Proverbs 16:3
How does the Lord bless those who trust Him? . . . . . . Proverbs 28:25, 26
Why can we trust God? . . . . Isaiah 40:25–28

TRUTH

How does following truth help us? . . . . 1 Samuel 7:3
How are we to serve God? . . . . 1 Samuel 12:24
How does God want us to live? . . . . Psalm 51:1–6
What does the truth do for us? . . . . John 8:31, 32
Is God's word truth? . . . . John 17:17

VALUES

Are our values important? . . . . Jeremiah 9:7–9
How do our values affect our decisions? . . . . Jeremiah 13:23

VANITY

What does God think about vanity? . . . . Isaiah 3:16–18

VICTORY

Who should we dedicate our victory to? . . . . Nehemiah 12:27, 43

WISDOM

Where can I find wisdom? . . . . Genesis 41:16
What comes with wisdom? . . . . Proverbs 8:12–14
Why is wisdom important? . . . . Proverbs 24:3, 4
How is God's wisdom different from human wisdom? . . 1 Corinthians 2:1–16

Preface to the New King James Version

PURPOSE

In the preface to the 1611 edition, the translators of the Authorized Version, known popularly as the King James Bible, state that it was not their purpose "to make a new translation . . . but to make a good one better." Indebted to the earlier work of William Tyndale and others, they saw their best contribution to consist in revising and enhancing the excellence of the English versions which had sprung from the Reformation of the sixteenth century. In harmony with the purpose of the King James scholars, the translators and editors of the present work have not pursued a goal of innovation. They have perceived the Holy Bible, New King James Version, as a continuation of the labors of the earlier translators, thus unlocking for today's readers the spiritual treasures found especially in the Authorized Version of the Holy Scriptures.

A LIVING LEGACY

For nearly four hundred years, and throughout several revisions of its English form, the King James Bible has been deeply revered among the English-speaking peoples of the world. The precision of translation for which it is historically renowned, and its majesty of style, have enabled that monumental version of the Word of God to become the mainspring of the religion, language, and legal foundations of our civilization.

Although the Elizabethan period and our own era share in zeal for technical advance, the former period was more aggressively devoted to classical learning. Along with this awakened concern for the classics came a flourishing companion interest in the Scriptures, an interest that was enlivened by the conviction that the manuscripts were providentially handed down and were a trustworthy record of the inspired Word of God. The King James translators were committed to producing an English Bible that would be a precise translation, and by no means a paraphrase or a broadly approximate rendering. On the one hand, the scholars were almost as familiar with the original languages of the Bible as with their native English. On the other hand, their reverence for the divine Author and His Word assured a translation of the Scriptures in which only a principle of utmost accuracy could be accepted.

In 1786 Catholic scholar Alexander Geddes said of the King James Bible, "If accuracy and strictest attention to the letter of the text be supposed to constitute an excellent version, this is of all versions the most excellent." George Bernard Shaw became a literary legend in our century because of his severe and often humorous criticisms of our most cherished values. Surprisingly, however, Shaw pays the following tribute to the scholars commissioned by King James: "The translation was extraordinarily well done because to the translators what they were translating was not merely a curious collection of ancient books written by different authors in different stages of culture, but the Word of God divinely revealed through His chosen and expressly inspired scribes. In this conviction they carried out their work with boundless reverence and care and achieved a beautifully artistic result." History agrees with these estimates. Therefore, while seeking to unveil the excellent *form* of the traditional English Bible, special care has also been taken in the present edition to preserve the work of *precision* which is the legacy of the 1611 translators.

COMPLETE EQUIVALENCE IN TRANSLATION

Where new translation has been necessary in the New King James Version, the most complete representation of the original has been rendered by considering the history of usage and etymology of words in their contexts. This principle of complete equivalence seeks to preserve *all* of the information in the text, while presenting it in good literary form. Dynamic equivalence, a recent procedure in Bible translation, commonly results in paraphrasing where a more literal rendering is needed to reflect a specific and vital sense. For example, complete equivalence truly renders the original text in expressions such as "lifted her voice and wept" (Gen. 21:16); "I gave you cleanness of teeth" (Amos 4:6); "Jesus met them, saying, 'Rejoice!' " (Matt. 28:9); and " 'Woman, what does your concern have to do with Me?' " (John 2:4). Complete equivalence translates fully, in order to provide an English text that is both accurate and readable.

In keeping with the principle of complete equivalence, it is the policy to translate interjections which are commonly omitted in modern language renderings of the Bible. As an example, the interjection *behold*, in the older King James editions, continues to have a place in English usage, especially in dramatically calling attention to a spectacular scene, or an event of profound importance such as the Immanuel prophecy of Isaiah 7:14. Consequently, *behold* is retained for these occasions in the present edition. However, the Hebrew and Greek originals for this word can be translated variously, depending on the circumstances in the passage. Therefore, in addition to *behold*, words such as *indeed, look, see,* and *surely* are also rendered to convey the appropriate sense suggested by the context in each case.

In faithfulness to God and to our readers, it was deemed appropriate that all participating scholars sign a statement affirming their belief in the verbal and plenary inspiration of Scripture, and in the inerrancy of the original autographs.

DEVOTIONAL QUALITY

The King James scholars readily appreciated the intrinsic beauty of divine revelation. They accordingly disciplined their talents to render well-chosen English words of their time, as well as a graceful, often musical arrangement of language, which has stirred the hearts of Bible readers through the years. The translators, the committees, and the editors of the present edition, while sensitive to the late-twentieth-century English idiom, and while adhering faithfully to the Hebrew, Aramaic, and Greek texts, have sought to maintain those lyrical and devotional qualities that are so highly regarded in the Authorized Version. This devotional quality is especially apparent in the poetic and prophetic books, although even the relatively plain style of the Gospels and Epistles cannot strictly be likened, as sometimes suggested, to modern newspaper style. The Koine Greek of the New Testament is influenced by the Hebrew background of the writers, for whom even the Gospel narratives were not merely flat utterance, but often song in various degrees of rhythm.

THE STYLE

Students of the Bible applaud the timeless devotional character of our historic Bible. Yet it is also universally understood that our language, like all living languages, has undergone profound change since 1611. Subsequent revisions of the King James Bible have sought to keep abreast of changes in English speech. The present work is a further step toward this objective. Where obsolescence and other reading difficulties exist, present-day vocabulary, punctuation, and grammar have been carefully integrated. Words representing ancient objects, such as *chariot* and *phylactery*, have no modern substitutes and are therefore retained.

A special feature of the New King James Version is its conformity to the thought flow of the 1611 Bible. The reader discovers that the sequence and selection of words, phrases, and clauses of the new edition, while much clearer, are so close to the traditional that there is remarkable ease in listening to the reading of either edition while following with the other.

In the discipline of translating biblical and other ancient languages, a standard method of transliteration, that is, the English spelling of untranslated words, such as names of persons and places, has never been commonly adopted. In keeping with the design of the present work, the King James spelling of untranslated words is retained, although made uniform throughout. For example, instead of the spellings *Isaiah* and *Elijah* in the Old Testament, and *Esaias* and *Elias* in the New Testament, *Isaiah* and *Elijah* now appear in both Testaments.

King James doctrinal and theological terms, for example, *propitiation, justification,* and *sanctifica-*

tion, are generally familiar to English-speaking peoples. Such terms have been retained except where the original language indicates need for a more precise translation.

Readers of the Authorized Version will immediately be struck by the absence of several pronouns: *thee, thou,* and *ye* are replaced by the simple *you,* while *your* and *yours* are substituted for *thy* and *thine* as applicable. *Thee, thou, thy,* and *thine* were once forms of address to express a special relationship to human as well as divine persons. These pronouns are no longer part of our language. However, reverence for God in the present work is preserved by capitalizing pronouns, including *You, Your,* and *Yours,* which refer to Him. Additionally, capitalization of these pronouns benefits the reader by clearly distinguishing divine and human persons referred to in a passage. Without such capitalization the distinction is often obscure, because the antecedent of a pronoun is not always clear in the English translation.

In addition to the pronoun usages of the seventeenth century, the *-eth* and *-est* verb endings, so familiar in the earlier King James editions, are now obsolete. Unless a speaker is schooled in these verb endings, there is common difficulty in selecting the correct form to be used with a given subject of the verb in vocal prayer. That is, should we use *love, loveth,* or *lovest? do, doeth, doest,* or *dost? have, hath,* or *hast?* Because these forms are obsolete, contemporary English usage has been substituted for the previous verb endings.

In older editions of the King James Version, the frequency of the connective *and* far exceeded the limits of present English usage. Also, biblical linguists agree that the Hebrew and Greek original words for this conjunction may commonly be translated otherwise, depending on the immediate context. Therefore, instead of *and,* alternatives such as *also, but, however, now, so, then,* and *thus* are accordingly rendered in the present edition, when the original language permits.

The real character of the Authorized Version does not reside in its archaic pronouns or verbs or other grammatical forms of the seventeenth century, but rather in the care taken by its scholars to impart the letter and spirit of the original text in a majestic and reverent style.

THE FORMAT

The format of the New King James Version is designed to enhance the vividness and devotional quality of the Holy Scriptures:

—Subject headings assist the reader to identify topics and transitions in the biblical content.
—Words or phrases in *italics* indicate expressions in the original language which require clarification by additional English words, as also done throughout the history of the King James Bible.
—*Oblique type* in the New Testament indicates a quotation from the Old Testament.
—Prose is divided into paragraphs to indicate the structure of thought.
—Poetry is structured as contemporary verse to reflect the poetic form and beauty of the passage in the original language.
—The covenant name of God was usually translated from the Hebrew as "LORD" or "GOD" (using capital letters as shown) in the King James Old Testament. This tradition is maintained. In the present edition the name is so capitalized whenever the covenant name is quoted in the New Testament from a passage in the Old Testament.

THE OLD TESTAMENT TEXT

The Hebrew Bible has come down to us through the scrupulous care of ancient scribes who copied the original text in successive generations. By the sixth century A.D. the scribes were succeeded by a group known as the Masoretes, who continued to preserve the sacred Scriptures for another five hundred years in a form known as the Masoretic Text. Babylonia, Palestine, and Tiberias were the main centers of Masoretic activity; but by the tenth century A.D. the Masoretes of Tiberias, led by the family of ben Asher, gained the ascendancy. Through subsequent editions, the ben Asher text became in the twelfth century the only recognized form of the Hebrew Scriptures.

Daniel Bomberg printed the first Rabbinic Bible in 1516–17; that work was followed in 1524–25 by a second edition prepared by Jacob ben Chayyim and also published by Bomberg. The text of ben Chayyim was adopted in most subsequent Hebrew Bibles, including those used by the King James translators. The ben Chayyim text was also used for the first two editions of Rudolph Kittel's *Biblia Hebraica* of 1906 and 1912. In 1937 Paul Kahle published a third edition of *Biblia Hebraica.* This edition was based on the oldest dated manuscript of the ben Asher text, the

Leningrad Manuscript B19a (A.D. 1008), which Kahle regarded as superior to that used by ben Chayyim.

For the New King James Version the text used was the 1967/1977 Stuttgart edition of the *Biblia Hebraica*, with frequent comparisons being made with the Bomberg edition of 1524–25. The Septuagint (Greek) Version of the Old Testament and the Latin Vulgate also were consulted. In addition to referring to a variety of ancient versions of the Hebrew Scriptures, the New King James Version draws on the resources of relevant manuscripts from the Dead Sea caves. In the few places where the Hebrew was so obscure that the 1611 King James was compelled to follow one of the versions, but where information is now available to resolve the problems, the New King James Version follows the Hebrew text. Significant variations are recorded in footnotes.

THE NEW TESTAMENT TEXT

There is more manuscript support for the New Testament than for any other body of ancient literature. Over five thousand Greek, eight thousand Latin, and many more manuscripts in other languages attest the integrity of the New Testament. There is only one basic New Testament used by Protestants, Roman Catholics, and Orthodox, by conservatives and liberals. Minor variations in hand copying have appeared through the centuries, before mechanical printing began about A.D. 1450.

Some variations exist in the spelling of Greek words, in word order, and in similar details. These ordinarily do not show up in translation and do not affect the sense of the text in any way.

Other manuscript differences such as omission or inclusion of a word or a clause, and two paragraphs in the Gospels, should not overshadow the overwhelming degree of *agreement* which exists among the ancient records. Bible readers may be assured that the most important differences in English New Testaments of today are due, not to manuscript divergence, but to the way in which translators view the task of translation: How literally should the text be rendered? How does the translator view the matter of biblical inspiration? Does the translator adopt a paraphrase when a literal rendering would be quite clear and more to the point? The New King James Version follows the historic precedent of the Authorized Version in maintaining a literal approach to translation, except where the idiom of the original language cannot be translated directly into our tongue.

The King James New Testament was based on the traditional text of the Greek-speaking churches, first published in 1516, and later called the Textus Receptus or Received Text. Although based on the relatively few available manuscripts, these were representative of many more which existed at the time but only became known later. In the late nineteenth century, B. Westcott and F. Hort taught that this text had been officially edited by the fourth-century church, but a total lack of historical evidence for this event has forced a revision of the theory. It is now widely held that the Byzantine Text that largely supports the Textus Receptus has as much right as the Alexandrian or any other tradition to be weighed in determining the text of the New Testament.

Since the 1880s most contemporary translations of the New Testament have relied upon a relatively few manuscripts discovered chiefly in the late nineteenth and early twentieth centuries. Such translations depend primarily on two manuscripts, Codex Vaticanus and Codex Sinaiticus, because of their greater age. The Greek text obtained by using these sources and the related papyri (our most ancient manuscripts) is known as the Alexandrian Text. However, some scholars have grounds for doubting the faithfulness of Vaticanus and Sinaiticus, since they often disagree with one another, and Sinaiticus exhibits excessive omission.

A third viewpoint of New Testament scholarship holds that the best text is based on the consensus of the majority of existing Greek manuscripts. The text is called the Majority Text. Most of these manuscripts are in substantial agreement. Even though many are late, and none is earlier than the fifth century, usually their readings are verified by papyri, ancient versions, quotations from the early church fathers, or a combination of these. The Majority Text is similar to the Textus Receptus, but it corrects those readings which have little or no support in the Greek manuscript tradition.

Today, scholars agree that the science of New Testament textual criticism is in a state of flux. Very few scholars still favor the Textus Receptus as such, and then often for its historical prestige as the text of Luther, Calvin, Tyndale, and the King James Version. For about a century most have followed a Critical Text (so called because it is edited according to specific principles of textual criticism) which depends heavily upon the Alexandrian type of text. More recently many have abandoned this Critical Text (which is quite similar to the one edited by Westcott and Hort) for one that is more eclectic. Finally, a small but growing number of scholars prefer the Majority Text, which is close to the traditional text except in the Revelation.

In light of these facts, and also because the New King James Version is the fifth revision of a historic document translated from specific Greek texts, the editors decided to retain the traditional text in the body of the New Testament. It is most important to emphasize that fully eighty-five percent of the New Testament text is the same in the Textus Receptus, the Alexandrian Text, and the Majority Text.

NEW KING JAMES FOOTNOTES

Significant explanatory notes, alternate translations, and cross-references, as well as New Testament citations of Old Testament passages, are supplied in the footnotes.

Important textual variants in the Old Testament are identified in a standard form.

The textual notes in the present edition of the New Testament make no evaluation of readings, but do clearly indicate the manuscript sources of readings. They objectively present the facts without such tendentious remarks as "the best manuscripts omit" or "the most reliable manuscripts read." Such notes are value judgments that differ according to varying viewpoints on the text. By giving a clearly defined set of variants the New King James Version benefits readers of all textual persuasions.

Where significant variations occur in the New Testament Greek manuscripts, textual notes are classified as follows:

1. NU-Text
   These variations from the traditional text generally represent the Alexandrian or Egyptian type of text described previously in "The New Testament Text." They are found in the Critical Text published in the twenty-sixth edition of the Nestle-Aland Greek New Testament (N) and in the United Bible Societies' third edition (U), hence the acronym, "NU-Text."
2. M-Text
   This symbol indicates points of variation in the Majority Text from the traditional text, as also previously discussed in "The New Testament Text." It should be noted the M stands for whatever reading is printed in the published *Greek New Testament According to the Majority Text*, whether supported by overwhelming, strong, or only a divided majority textual tradition.

The textual notes reflect the scholarship of the past 150 years and will assist the reader to observe the variations between the different manuscript traditions of the New Testament. Such information is generally not available in English translations of the New Testament.

THE
OLD TESTAMENT

genesis

CONTENT   Genesis is a bottom-line, this-is-how-it-is, no-sugarcoating kind of book. When we ask the big question, "Where do we come from?" Genesis gives the big answer, "We come from God. He made us and wants to be in relationship with us." When we ask the big question, "Who do we come from?" Genesis gives the honest answer, "This is who they are, but you might not like everything you see."

Genesis has loads of famous stories and people, from Adam to Noah to Abraham to Joseph. It's a who's who of the lightly populated days of the earth. What's amazing about this book though is that, unlike a who's who, Genesis tells us the real scoop on these people who established the original cultures of the world. We read about their failures, not just their successes. We read about their mess-ups and their doubts and their . . . well . . . flops.

From this very first book of the Bible, God lays a foundation. We are what He created when He chose to love and be loved. He is the God who embraces us humans, "warts" and all, and even uses us to make the world a better place.

Purpose   A living Being—God—is the Source of all things. He wants a personal relationship with us, based on our trust in His promises.

Themes   Beginnings

Date of writing   About 1445–1400 B.C.

> "I will bless those who bless you, and I will curse him who curses you; and in you all the families of the earth shall be blessed" (12:3).

Bible Talk

Creation

The story of creation, as simple and clear-cut as it is, has been the subject of a LOT of dispute. Was it literally seven days? Did God create everything as full-grown? If God created just one family, where did all the other families come from? Was it really an apple that Adam and Eve ate that ruined paradise for all of us?

No matter how much people disagree about all the things we *don't* know about how God created the world, Genesis gives us concrete information about what we *do* know. God did create the world from nothing. He did it miraculously through a process only He can understand or re-create. He did it with a plan and a purpose that we are now living out.

TOTAL TRUTH

What's up with all the wives?

If you've noticed any married couples around you lately, you're probably aware that one husband and one wife seems to be a challenge in terms of any long-term commitment. In Genesis things are even more complicated. Men often had more than one wife and some-times had children by many wives and servants of those wives. Genesis gives us a window into an ancient world that can be wacky to say the least. Remember, though, that God never encouraged polygamy (multiple spouses) or commanded it or even honored it. Before Sarah died, Abraham had no other wives. As far as we know, Isaac only had one wife. And there seemed to be only one Mrs. Noah on the ark.

THE HISTORY OF CREATION

[1]In the beginning God created the heavens and the earth. [2]The earth was without form, and void; and darkness *was*[a] on the face of the deep. And the Spirit of God was hovering over the face of the waters.

[3]Then God said, "Let there be light"; and there was light. [4]And God saw the light, that *it was* good; and God divided the light from the darkness. [5]God called the light Day, and the darkness He called Night. So the evening and the morning were the first day.

[6]Then God said, "Let there be a firmament in the midst of the waters, and let it divide the waters from the waters." [7]Thus God made the firmament, and divided the waters which *were* under the firmament from the waters which *were* above the firmament; and it was so. [8]And God called the firmament Heaven. So the evening and the morning were the second day.

[9]Then God said, "Let the waters under the heavens be gathered together into one place, and let the dry *land* appear"; and it was so. [10]And God called the dry *land* Earth, and the gathering together of the waters He called Seas. And God saw that *it was* good.

WHAT'S IT MEAN?

Do you think it seems a little odd to single out the sky and the ground for mention in the first verse of the Bible? Actually, the phrase "the heavens and the earth" is a way of summarizing everything God made. It's another way of saying, "In the beginning God created the universe."

Genesis 1:1

[11]Then God said, "Let the earth bring forth grass, the herb *that* yields seed, *and* the fruit tree *that* yields fruit according to its kind, whose seed *is* in itself, on the earth"; and it was so. [12]And the earth brought forth grass, the herb *that* yields seed according to its kind, and the tree *that* yields fruit, whose seed *is* in itself according to its kind. And God saw that *it was* good. [13]So the evening and the morning were the third day.

[14]Then God said, "Let there be lights in the firmament of the heavens to divide the day from the night; and let them be for signs and seasons, and for days and years; [15]and let them be for lights in the firmament of the heavens to give light on the earth"; and it was so. [16]Then God made two great lights: the greater light to rule the day, and the lesser light to rule the night. *He made* the stars also. [17]God set them in the firmament of the heavens to give light on the earth, [18]and to rule over the day and over the night, and to divide the light from the darkness. And God saw that *it was* good. [19]So the evening and the morning were the fourth day.

[20]Then God said, "Let the waters abound with an abundance of living creatures, and let birds fly above the earth across the face of the firmament of the heavens." [21]So God created great sea creatures and every living thing that moves, with which the waters abounded, according to their kind, and every winged bird according to its kind. And God saw that *it was* good. [22]And God blessed them, saying, "Be fruitful and multiply, and fill the waters in the seas, and let birds multiply on the earth."

On the Edge

In the beginning God created the heavens and the earth (Gen. 1:1).

A common definition of the word *create* is "to make something out of nothing." That's exactly what God did when He created this world. He made this incredible planet out of absolutely nothing! That's what He did when He made you.

Thirty years ago you didn't exist. Now you do. Just because the earth and lots of people have been created, it doesn't mean God is finished. He's still creating. He can create something out of nothing. You may look for confidence in your life and see nothing. You may look for joy in your life and see nothing. You may look for just one good thing anywhere in your life and see nothing. When you're looking at nothing, remember that God is the supreme Creator. Ask Him to make something out of nothing for you.

SEE FOR YOURSELF:
Neh. 9:6;
Ps. 8; 93:1; 104

1:2 [a]Words in italic type have been added for clarity. They are not found in the original Hebrew or Aramaic.

²³So the evening and the morning were the fifth day. ²⁴Then God said, "Let the earth bring forth the living creature according to its kind: cattle and creeping thing and beast of the earth, *each* according to its kind"; and it was so. ²⁵And God made the beast of the earth according to its kind, cattle according to its kind, and everything that creeps on the earth according to its kind. And God saw that *it was* good.

²⁶Then God said, "Let Us make man in Our image, according to Our likeness; let them have dominion over the fish of the sea, over the birds of the air, and over the cattle, over all*ᵃ* the earth and over every creeping thing that creeps on the earth." ²⁷So God created man in His *own* image; in the image of God He created him; male and female He created them. ²⁸Then God blessed them, and God said to them, "Be fruitful and multiply; fill the earth and subdue it; have dominion over the fish of the sea, over the birds of the air, and over every living thing that moves on the earth."

²⁹And God said, "See, I have given you every herb *that* yields seed which *is* on the face of all the earth, and every tree whose fruit yields seed; to you it shall be for food. ³⁰Also, to every beast of the earth, to every bird of the air, and to everything that creeps on the earth, in which *there is* life, I have given every green herb for food"; and it was so. ³¹Then God saw everything that He had made, and indeed *it was* very good. So the evening and the morning were the sixth day.

WHAT'S IT MEAN?

Nobody knows for sure what these great sea creatures looked like. It's possible, though, that some of the dinosaur fossils scientists have uncovered belong to the underwater giants described here.

Genesis 1:21

¹Thus the heavens and the earth, and all the host of them, were finished. ²And on the seventh day God ended His work which He had done, and He rested on the seventh day from all His work which He had done. ³Then God blessed the seventh day and sanctified it, because in it He rested from all His work which God had created and made.

⁴This *is* the history*ᵃ* of the heavens and the earth when they were created, in the day that the LORD God made the earth and the heavens, ⁵before any plant of the field was in the earth and before any herb of the field had grown. For the LORD God had not caused it to rain on the earth, and *there was* no man to till the ground; ⁶but a mist went up from the earth and watered the whole face of the ground.

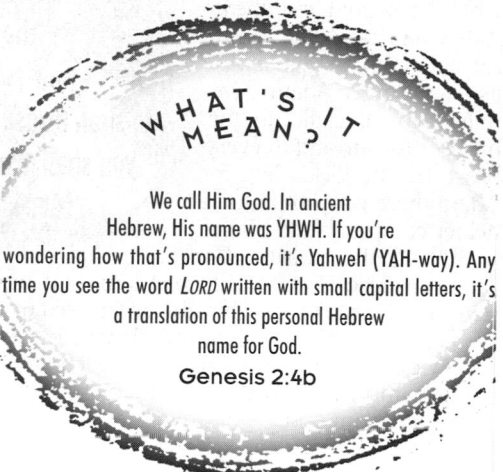

WHAT'S IT MEAN?

We call Him God. In ancient Hebrew, His name was YHWH. If you're wondering how that's pronounced, it's Yahweh (YAH-way). Any time you see the word *LORD* written with small capital letters, it's a translation of this personal Hebrew name for God.

Genesis 2:4b

⁷And the LORD God formed man *of* the dust of the ground, and breathed into his nostrils the breath of life; and man became a living being.

LIFE IN GOD'S GARDEN

⁸The LORD God planted a garden eastward in Eden, and there He put the man whom He had formed. ⁹And out of the ground the LORD God made every tree grow that is pleasant to the sight and good for food. The tree of life *was* also in the midst of the garden, and the tree of the knowledge of good and evil.

¹⁰Now a river went out of Eden to water the garden, and from there it parted and became four riverheads. ¹¹The name of the first *is* Pishon; it *is* the one which skirts the whole land of Havilah, where *there is* gold. ¹²And the gold of that land *is* good. Bdellium and the onyx stone *are* there. ¹³The name of the second river *is* Gihon; it *is* the one which goes around the whole land of Cush. ¹⁴The name of the third river *is* Hiddekel;*ᵃ* it *is* the one which goes toward the east of Assyria. The fourth river *is* the Euphrates.

¹⁵Then the LORD God took the man and put

1:26 *ᵃ*Syriac reads *all the wild animals of.*   **2:4** *ᵃ*Hebrew *toledoth,* literally *generations*   **2:14** *ᵃ*Or *Tigris* him in the garden of Eden to tend and keep it. ¹⁶And the LORD God commanded the man, saying, "Of every tree of the garden you may freely eat; ¹⁷but of the tree of the knowledge of good and evil you shall not eat, for in the day that you eat of it you shall surely die."

¹⁸And the LORD God said, "*It is* not good that man should be alone; I will make him a helper comparable to him." ¹⁹Out of the ground the LORD God formed every beast of the field and every bird of the air, and brought *them* to Adam to see what he would call them. And whatever Adam called each living creature, that *was* its name. ²⁰So Adam gave names to all cattle, to the birds of the air, and to every beast of the field. But for Adam there was not found a helper comparable to him.

²¹And the LORD God caused a deep sleep to fall on Adam, and he slept; and He took one of his ribs, and closed up the flesh in its place. ²²Then the rib which the LORD God had taken from man He made into a woman, and He brought her to the man. ²³And Adam said:

"This *is* now bone of my bones
And flesh of my flesh;
She shall be called Woman,
Because she was taken out of Man."

²⁴Therefore a man shall leave his father and mother and be joined to his wife, and they shall become one flesh. ²⁵And they were both naked, the man and his wife, and were not ashamed.

THE TEMPTATION AND FALL OF MAN

¹Now the serpent was more cunning than any beast of the field which the LORD God had made. And he said to the woman, "Has God indeed said, 'You shall not eat of every tree of the garden'?"

²And the woman said to the serpent, "We may eat the fruit of the trees of the garden; ³but of the fruit of the tree which *is* in the midst of the garden, God has said, 'You shall not eat it, nor shall you touch it, lest you die.' "

⁴Then the serpent said to the woman, "You will not surely die. ⁵For God knows that in the day you eat of it your eyes will be opened, and you will be like God, knowing good and evil." ⁶So when the woman saw that the tree *was* good for food, that it *was* pleasant to the eyes, and a tree desirable to make *one* wise, she took of its fruit and ate. She also gave to her husband with her, and he ate. ⁷Then the eyes of both of them were opened, and they knew that they *were* naked; and they sewed fig leaves together and made themselves coverings.

⁸And they heard the sound of the LORD God walking in the garden in the cool of the day, and Adam and his wife hid themselves from the presence of the LORD God among the trees of the garden. ⁹Then the LORD God called to Adam and said to him, "Where *are* you?"

¹⁰So he said, "I heard Your voice in the garden, and I was afraid because I was naked; and I hid myself."

¹¹And He said, "Who told you that you *were* naked? Have you eaten from the tree of which I commanded you that you should not eat?"

¹²Then the man said, "The woman whom You gave *to be* with me, she gave me of the tree, and I ate."

¹³And the LORD God said to the woman, "What *is* this you have done?"

The woman said, "The serpent deceived me, and I ate."

¹⁴So the LORD God said to the serpent:

"Because you have done this,
You *are* cursed more than all cattle,
And more than every beast of the field;
On your belly you shall go,
And you shall eat dust
All the days of your life.
¹⁵ And I will put enmity
Between you and the woman,
And between your seed and her Seed;
He shall bruise your head,
And you shall bruise His heel."

¹⁶To the woman He said:

"I will greatly multiply your sorrow and
    your conception;
In pain you shall bring forth children;
Your desire *shall be* for your husband,
And he shall rule over you."

¹⁷Then to Adam He said, "Because you have heeded the voice of your wife, and have eaten from the tree of which I commanded you, saying, 'You shall not eat of it':

"I will put enmity between you and the woman, and between your seed and her Seed; He shall bruise your head, and you shall bruise His heel."
(Genesis 3:15)

"Cursed *is* the ground for your sake;
In toil you shall eat *of* it
All the days of your life.
18 Both thorns and thistles it shall bring
forth for you,
And you shall eat the herb of the field.
19 In the sweat of your face you shall eat
bread
Till you return to the ground,
For out of it you were taken;
For dust you *are*,
And to dust you shall return."

20And Adam called his wife's name Eve, because she was the mother of all living.
21Also for Adam and his wife the LORD God made tunics of skin, and clothed them.
22Then the LORD God said, "Behold, the man has become like one of Us, to know good and evil. And now, lest he put out his hand and take also of the tree of life, and eat, and live forever"— 23therefore the LORD God sent him out of the garden of Eden to till the ground from which he was taken. 24So He drove out the man; and He placed cherubim at the east of the garden of Eden, and a flaming sword which turned every way, to guard the way to the tree of life.

CAIN MURDERS ABEL

1Now Adam knew Eve his wife, and she conceived and bore Cain, and said, "I have acquired a man from the LORD." 2Then she bore again, this time his brother Abel. Now Abel was a keeper of sheep, but Cain was a tiller of the ground. 3And in the process of time it came to pass that Cain brought an offering of the fruit of the ground to the LORD. 4Abel also brought of the firstborn of his flock and of their fat. And the LORD respected Abel and his offering, 5but He did not respect Cain and his offering. And Cain was very angry, and his countenance fell.

6So the LORD said to Cain, "Why are you angry? And why has your countenance fallen? 7If you do well, will you not be accepted? And if you do not do well, sin lies at the door. And its desire *is* for you, but you should rule over it."

8Now Cain talked with Abel his brother;*a* and it came to pass, when they were in the field, that Cain rose up against Abel his brother and killed him.

9Then the LORD said to Cain, "Where *is* Abel your brother?"

He said, "I do not know. *Am* I my brother's keeper?"

10And He said, "What have you done? The voice of your brother's blood cries out to Me from the ground. 11So now you *are* cursed from the earth, which has opened its mouth to receive your brother's blood from your hand. 12When you till the ground, it shall no longer yield its strength to you. A fugitive and a vagabond you shall be on the earth."

13And Cain said to the LORD, "My punishment *is* greater than I can bear! 14Surely You have driven me out this day from the face of the ground; I shall be hidden from Your face; I shall be a fugitive and a vagabond on the earth, and it will happen *that* anyone who finds me will kill me."

15And the LORD said to him, "Therefore,*a* whoever kills Cain, vengeance shall be taken on him sevenfold." And the LORD set a mark on Cain, lest anyone finding him should kill him.

THE FAMILY OF CAIN

16Then Cain went out from the presence of the LORD and dwelt in the land of Nod on the east of Eden. 17And Cain knew his wife, and she conceived and bore Enoch. And he built a city, and called the name of the city after the name of his son—Enoch. 18To Enoch was born Irad; and Irad begot Mehujael, and Mehujael begot Methushael, and Methushael begot Lamech.

19Then Lamech took for himself two wives: the name of one *was* Adah, and the name of the second *was* Zillah. 20And Adah bore Jabal. He was the father of those who dwell in tents and have livestock. 21His brother's name *was* Jubal.

WHAT'S IT MEAN?

The Bible doesn't tell us
exactly when or where animal sacrifice began.
We do know that the practice has been going on since the earliest
days of human history. The sacrifice ritual usually included killing
the animal in a specific way, praying out loud, and burning incense.
Jesus' death on the cross ended the need for
animal sacrifice once and for all.

Genesis 4:4

4:8 *a*Samaritan Pentateuch, Septuagint, Syriac, and Vulgate add *"Let us go out to the field."*   **4:15** *a*Following Masoretic Text and Targum; Septuagint, Syriac, and Vulgate read *Not so.*

ABEL made a difference

Abel compiled some unique "firsts" in his short lifetime: member of the first family, first little brother, first rancher. Other "firsts" were more tragic than unique: part of the first sibling rivalry; first to do something better than his big brother; first to die at his brother's hand.

While these facts make Abel interesting, they are not the way in which he made a difference. Abel invented worship. Because his parents Adam and Eve had turned away from God, Abel had to think about some way to approach God. Apparently Cain and Abel talked it over and both decided to offer God a sacrifice. Cain the farmer brought "an offering of the fruit of the ground"; Abel brought the best he had. He took "the firstborn of his flock" and created a fat sacrifice. God accepted the attitude of Abel's worship. Jesus later called him righteous.

It doesn't seem as if Abel suspected his brother's intense jealousy and anger. He followed Cain out to a field where the older killed the younger. Though it ended unfairly and too soon, Abel's life left a legacy of faith. When the writer of Hebrews listed the Hall of Faith in the New Testament, the first inductee was Abel:

Cutting Edge

"By faith Abel offered to God a more excellent sacrifice" (Heb. 11:4a).

YOU can, too!

If you've got brothers and/or sisters, here's a warning: don't try to make a difference by competing with them. That wasn't Abel's example. There's enough natural competition between siblings as it is. The question you can answer like Abel is, "How will I approach God?"

Cain and Abel "attended church" together, but their attitude was miles apart. One was there; the other was all there. Clarifying and participating in your relationship with God, not just going through the motions, will make a huge difference in your life . . . and in the lives of others.

Want to know more? Read about Abel's life in

Genesis 4:1–8; Matthew 23:35; Hebrews 11:4; 12:24.

He was the father of all those who play the harp and flute. [22]And as for Zillah, she also bore Tubal-Cain, an instructor of every craftsman in bronze and iron. And the sister of Tubal-Cain *was* Naamah.

[23]Then Lamech said to his wives:

"Adah and Zillah, hear my voice;
Wives of Lamech, listen to my speech!
For I have killed a man for wounding me,
Even a young man for hurting me.
[24] If Cain shall be avenged sevenfold,
Then Lamech seventy-sevenfold."

A NEW SON

[25]And Adam knew his wife again, and she bore a son and named him Seth, "For God has appointed another seed for me instead of Abel, whom Cain killed." [26]And as for Seth, to him also a son was born; and he named him Enosh.[a] Then *men* began to call on the name of the LORD.

THE FAMILY OF ADAM

[1]This is the book of the genealogy of Adam. In the day that God created man, He made him in the likeness of God. [2]He created them male and female, and blessed them and called them Mankind in the day they were created. [3]And Adam lived one hundred and thirty years, and begot *a son* in his own likeness, after his image, and named him Seth. [4]After he begot Seth, the days of Adam were eight hundred years; and he had sons and daughters. [5]So all the days that Adam lived were nine hundred and thirty years; and he died.

[6]Seth lived one hundred and five years, and begot Enosh. [7]After he begot Enosh, Seth lived eight hundred and seven years, and had sons and daughters. [8]So all the days of Seth were nine hundred and twelve years; and he died.

[9]Enosh lived ninety years, and begot Cainan.[a] [10]After he begot Cainan, Enosh lived eight hundred and fifteen years, and had sons and daughters. [11]So all the days of Enosh were nine hundred and five years; and he died.

[12]Cainan lived seventy years, and begot Mahalalel. [13]After he begot Mahalalel, Cainan lived eight hundred and forty years, and had sons and daughters. [14]So all the days of Cainan were nine hundred and ten years; and he died.

[15]Mahalalel lived sixty-five years, and begot Jared. [16]After he begot Jared, Mahalalel lived eight hundred and thirty years, and had sons and daughters. [17]So all the days of Mahalalel were eight hundred and ninety-five years; and he died.

[18]Jared lived one hundred and sixty-two years, and begot Enoch. [19]After he begot Enoch, Jared lived eight hundred years, and had sons and daughters. [20]So all the days of Jared were nine hundred and sixty-two years; and he died.

[21]Enoch lived sixty-five years, and begot Methuselah. [22]After he begot Methuselah, Enoch walked with God three hundred years, and had sons and daughters. [23]So all the days of Enoch were three hundred and sixty-five years. [24]And Enoch walked with God; and he *was* not, for God took him.

[25]Methuselah lived one hundred and eighty-seven years, and begot Lamech. [26]After he begot Lamech, Methuselah lived seven hundred and eighty-two years, and had sons and daughters. [27]So all the days of Methuselah were nine hundred and sixty-nine years; and he died.

WHAT'S IT MEAN?

Even by early biblical standards, where it was not unusual for people to live for hundreds of years, Methuselah was an old guy. At 969 years, he lived longer than anyone else mentioned in the Bible. Assuming his descendants all had children by their thirtieth birthday, Methuselah lived long enough to see his great-grandson!

Genesis 5:27

[28]Lamech lived one hundred and eighty-two years, and had a son. [29]And he called his name Noah, saying, "This *one* will comfort us concerning our work and the toil of our hands, because of the ground which the LORD has cursed." [30]After he begot Noah, Lamech lived five hundred and ninety-five years, and had sons and daughters. [31]So all the days of Lamech were seven hundred and seventy-seven years; and he died.

[32]And Noah was five hundred years old, and Noah begot Shem, Ham, and Japheth.

4:26 [a]Greek *Enos*   **5:9** [a]Hebrew *Qenan*

THE WICKEDNESS AND JUDGMENT OF MAN

¹Now it came to pass, when men began to multiply on the face of the earth, and daughters were born to them, ²that the sons of God saw the daughters of men, that they *were* beautiful; and they took wives for themselves of all whom they chose.

³And the LORD said, "My Spirit shall not strive*ᵃ* with man forever, for he *is* indeed flesh; yet his days shall be one hundred and twenty years." ⁴There were giants on the earth in those days, and also afterward, when the sons of God came in to the daughters of men and they bore *children* to them. Those *were* the mighty men who *were* of old, men of renown.

⁵Then the LORD*ᵃ* saw that the wickedness of man *was* great in the earth, and *that* every intent of the thoughts of his heart *was* only evil continually. ⁶And the LORD was sorry that He had made man on the earth, and He was grieved in His heart. ⁷So the LORD said, "I will destroy man whom I have created from the face of the earth, both man and beast, creeping thing and birds of the air, for I am sorry that I have made them." ⁸But Noah found grace in the eyes of the LORD.

NOAH PLEASES GOD

⁹This is the genealogy of Noah. Noah was a just man, perfect in his generations. Noah walked with God. ¹⁰And Noah begot three sons: Shem, Ham, and Japheth.

¹¹The earth also was corrupt before God, and the earth was filled with violence. ¹²So God looked upon the earth, and indeed it was corrupt; for all flesh had corrupted their way on the earth.

THE ARK PREPARED

¹³And God said to Noah, "The end of all flesh has come before Me, for the earth is filled with violence through them; and behold, I will destroy them with the earth. ¹⁴Make yourself an ark of gopherwood; make rooms in the ark, and cover it inside and outside with pitch. ¹⁵And this is how you shall make it: The length of the ark *shall be* three hundred cubits, its width fifty cubits, and its height thirty cubits. ¹⁶You shall make a window for the ark, and you shall finish it to a cubit from above; and set the door of the ark in its side. You shall make it *with* lower, second, and third *decks*. ¹⁷And behold, I Myself am bringing floodwaters on the earth, to destroy from under heaven all flesh in which *is* the breath of life; everything that *is* on the earth

shall die. ¹⁸But I will establish My covenant with you; and you shall go into the ark—you, your sons, your wife, and your sons' wives with you. ¹⁹And of every living thing of all flesh you shall bring two of every *sort* into the ark, to keep *them* alive with you; they shall be male and female. ²⁰Of the birds after their kind, of animals after their kind, and of every creeping thing of the earth after its kind, two of every *kind* will come to you to keep *them* alive. ²¹And you shall take for yourself of all food that is eaten, and you shall gather *it* to yourself; and it shall be food for you and for them."

²²Thus Noah did; according to all that God commanded him, so he did.

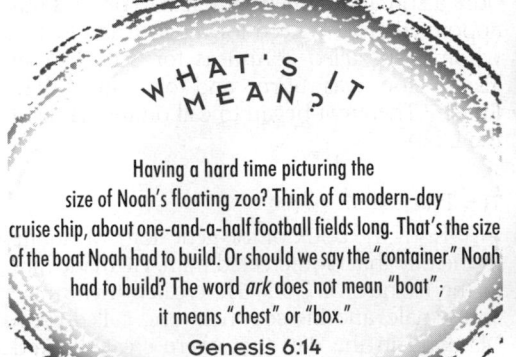

WHAT'S IT MEAN?

Having a hard time picturing the size of Noah's floating zoo? Think of a modern-day cruise ship, about one-and-a-half football fields long. That's the size of the boat Noah had to build. Or should we say the "container" Noah had to build? The word *ark* does not mean "boat"; it means "chest" or "box."

Genesis 6:14

THE GREAT FLOOD

¹Then the LORD said to Noah, "Come into the ark, you and all your household, because I have seen *that* you *are* righteous before Me in this generation. ²You shall take with you seven each of every clean animal, a male and his female; two each of animals that *are* unclean, a male and his female; ³also seven each of birds of the air, male and female, to keep the species alive on the face of all the earth. ⁴For after seven more days I will cause it to rain on the earth forty days and forty nights, and I will destroy from the face of the earth all living things that I have made." ⁵And Noah did according to all that the LORD commanded him. ⁶Noah *was* six hundred years old when the floodwaters were on the earth.

⁷So Noah, with his sons, his wife, and his sons' wives, went into the ark because of the waters of the flood. ⁸Of clean animals, of ani-

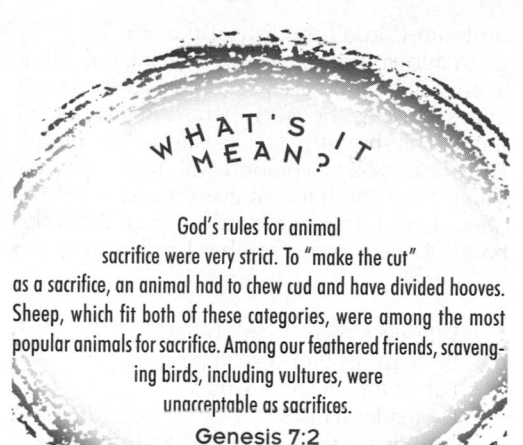

mals that *are* unclean, of birds, and of every-thing that creeps on the earth, [9]two by two they went into the ark to Noah, male and female, as God had commanded Noah. [10]And it came to pass after seven days that the waters of the flood were on the earth. [11]In the six hundredth year of Noah's life, in the second month, the seventeenth day of the month, on that day all the fountains of the great deep were broken up, and the windows of heaven were opened. [12]And the rain was on the earth forty days and forty nights.

[13]On the very same day Noah and Noah's sons, Shem, Ham, and Japheth, and Noah's wife and the three wives of his sons with them, en-tered the ark— [14]they and every beast after its kind, all cattle after their kind, every creeping thing that creeps on the earth after its kind, and every bird after its kind, every bird of every sort. [15]And they went into the ark to Noah, two by two, of all flesh in which *is* the breath of life. [16]So those that entered, male and female of all flesh, went in as God had commanded him; and the LORD shut him in.

[17]Now the flood was on the earth forty days. The waters increased and lifted up the ark, and it rose high above the earth. [18]The waters pre-vailed and greatly increased on the earth, and the ark moved about on the surface of the wa-ters. [19]And the waters prevailed exceedingly on the earth, and all the high hills under the whole heaven were covered. [20]The waters prevailed fifteen cubits upward, and the mountains were covered. [21]And all flesh died that moved on the earth: birds and cattle and beasts and every creeping thing that creeps on the earth, and

every man. [22]All in whose nostrils *was* the breath of the spirit[a] of life, all that *was* on the dry *land*, died. [23]So He destroyed all living things which were on the face of the ground: both man and cattle, creeping thing and bird of the air. They were destroyed from the earth. Only Noah and those who *were* with him in the ark remained *alive*. [24]And the waters prevailed on the earth one hundred and fifty days.

NOAH'S DELIVERANCE

[1]Then God remembered Noah, and every living thing, and all the animals that *were* with him in the ark. And God made a wind to pass over the earth, and the waters subsided. [2]The fountains of the deep and the windows of heaven were also stopped, and the rain from heaven was restrained. [3]And the waters receded continually from the earth. At the end of the hundred and fifty days the wa-ters decreased. [4]Then the ark rested in the sev-enth month, the seventeenth day of the month, on the mountains of Ararat. [5]And the waters decreased continually until the tenth month. In the tenth *month,* on the first *day* of the month, the tops of the mountains were seen.

[6]So it came to pass, at the end of forty days, that Noah opened the window of the ark which he had made. [7]Then he sent out a raven, which kept going to and fro until the waters had dried up from the earth. [8]He also sent out from him-self a dove, to see if the waters had receded from the face of the ground. [9]But the dove found no resting place for the sole of her foot, and she returned into the ark to him, for the

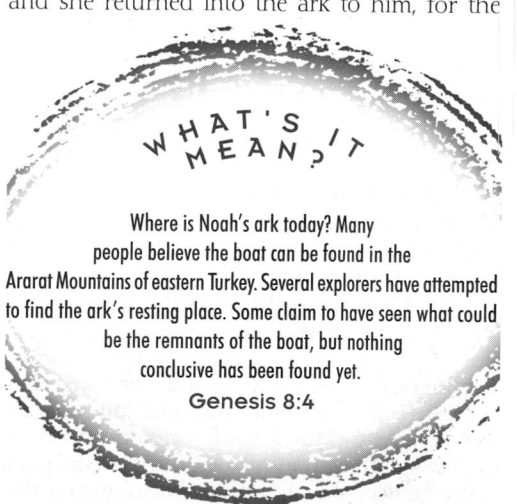

7:22 [a]Septuagint and Vulgate omit *of the spirit.*

waters *were* on the face of the whole earth. So he put out his hand and took her, and drew her into the ark to himself. ¹⁰And he waited yet another seven days, and again he sent the dove out from the ark. ¹¹Then the dove came to him in the evening, and behold, a freshly plucked olive leaf *was* in her mouth; and Noah knew that the waters had receded from the earth. ¹²So he waited yet another seven days and sent out the dove, which did not return again to him anymore.

¹³And it came to pass in the six hundred and first year, in the first *month*, the first *day* of the month, that the waters were dried up from the earth; and Noah removed the covering of the ark and looked, and indeed the surface of the ground was dry. ¹⁴And in the second month, on the twenty-seventh day of the month, the earth was dried.

¹⁵Then God spoke to Noah, saying, ¹⁶"Go out of the ark, you and your wife, and your sons and your sons' wives with you. ¹⁷Bring out with you every living thing of all flesh that *is* with you: birds and cattle and every creeping thing that creeps on the earth, so that they may abound on the earth, and be fruitful and multiply on the earth." ¹⁸So Noah went out, and his sons and his wife and his sons' wives with him. ¹⁹Every animal, every creeping thing, every bird, *and* whatever creeps on the earth, according to their families, went out of the ark.

GOD'S COVENANT WITH CREATION

²⁰Then Noah built an altar to the LORD, and took of every clean animal and of every clean bird, and offered burnt offerings on the altar. ²¹And the LORD smelled a soothing aroma. Then the LORD said in His heart, "I will never again curse the ground for man's sake, although the imagination of man's heart *is* evil from his youth; nor will I again destroy every living thing as I have done.

22 "While the earth remains,
    Seedtime and harvest,
    Cold and heat,
    Winter and summer,
    And day and night
    Shall not cease."

¹So God blessed Noah and his sons, and said to them: "Be fruitful and multiply, and fill the earth.ᵃ ²And the fear of you and the dread of you shall be on every beast of the earth, on every bird of the air, on all that move *on* the

earth, and on all the fish of the sea. They are given into your hand. ³Every moving thing that lives shall be food for you. I have given you all things, even as the green herbs. ⁴But you shall not eat flesh with its life, *that is*, its blood. ⁵Surely for your lifeblood I will demand *a reckoning;* from the hand of every beast I will require it, and from the hand of man. From the hand of every man's brother I will require the life of man.

6 "Whoever sheds man's blood,
    By man his blood shall be shed;
    For in the image of God
    He made man.
7   And as for you, be fruitful and multiply;
    Bring forth abundantly in the earth
    And multiply in it."

⁸Then God spoke to Noah and to his sons with him, saying: ⁹"And as for Me, behold, I establish My covenant with you and with your descendantsᵃ after you, ¹⁰and with every living creature that *is* with you: the birds, the cattle, and every beast of the earth with you, of all that go out of the ark, every beast of the earth. ¹¹Thus I establish My covenant with you: Never again shall all flesh be cut off by the waters of the flood; never again shall there be a flood to destroy the earth."

WHAT'S IT MEAN?

Ever wonder what causes rainbows? It's sunlight being reflected into different colors by droplets of water in the air. The angle at which we see the colors makes it appear as though they form an arch. Even today the rainbow is a reminder of God's promise to Noah. Never again will we have to worry about the world being destroyed by a flood.
Genesis 9:12, 13

¹²And God said: "This *is* the sign of the covenant which I make between Me and you, and every living creature that *is* with you, for perpetual generations: ¹³I set My rainbow in the cloud, and it shall be for the sign of the covenant between Me and the earth. ¹⁴It shall be,

when I bring a cloud over the earth, that the rainbow shall be seen in the cloud; [15]and I will remember My covenant which *is* between Me and you and every living creature of all flesh; the waters shall never again become a flood to destroy all flesh. [16]The rainbow shall be in the cloud, and I will look on it to remember the everlasting covenant between God and every living creature of all flesh that *is* on the earth." [17]And God said to Noah, "This *is* the sign of the covenant which I have established between Me and all flesh that *is* on the earth."

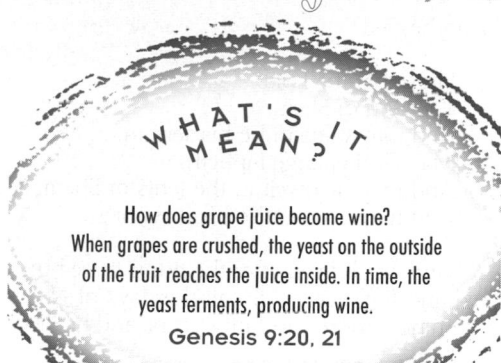

WHAT'S IT MEAN?

How does grape juice become wine? When grapes are crushed, the yeast on the outside of the fruit reaches the juice inside. In time, the yeast ferments, producing wine.
Genesis 9:20, 21

NOAH AND HIS SONS

[18]Now the sons of Noah who went out of the ark were Shem, Ham, and Japheth. And Ham *was* the father of Canaan. [19]These three *were* the sons of Noah, and from these the whole earth was populated.

[20]And Noah began *to be* a farmer, and he planted a vineyard. [21]Then he drank of the wine and was drunk, and became uncovered in his tent. [22]And Ham, the father of Canaan, saw the nakedness of his father, and told his two brothers outside. [23]But Shem and Japheth took a garment, laid *it* on both their shoulders, and went backward and covered the nakedness of their father. Their faces *were* turned away, and they did not see their father's nakedness.

[24]So Noah awoke from his wine, and knew what his younger son had done to him. [25]Then he said:

"Cursed *be* Canaan;
A servant of servants
He shall be to his brethren."

Promise   HE PROMISES THE RAINBOW AS HIS SIGN.

I set My rainbow in the cloud, and it shall be for the sign of the covenant between Me and the earth. It shall be, when I bring a cloud over the earth, that the rainbow shall be seen in the cloud; and I will remember My covenant which is between Me and you and every living creature of all flesh; the waters shall never again become a flood to destroy all flesh (Gen. 9:13–15).

God had just done something pretty amazing and probably pretty scary. He was so angry that He wiped out the whole world with a huge flood. Every person and every animal on earth drowned. Only the people and the animals on Noah's ark were saved. You can imagine what they might have been thinking. *Will He ever do this again? Maybe next time we won't live through it.* God calmed them down by promising that He would never destroy the world by flood again. To help them understand, He gave them something they could see. He put the rainbow in the sky as the sign of that promise.

Did God need the rainbow so He could remember what He'd said? No, the rainbow was for Noah and his family. It was for all his descendants who would live after him (Gen. 9:9). Today, it's for you. It lets you know that God does remember what He said. After all these millions of years, God still remembers a promise He made to a group of people on an ark. He knew that as long as the sunlight hits the raindrops, people could see the rainbow and know that He remembers His promise.

SEE FOR YOURSELF:
Gen. 9:13–15

²⁶And he said:

> "Blessed *be* the LORD,
> The God of Shem,
> And may Canaan be his servant.
> ²⁷ May God enlarge Japheth,
> And may he dwell in the tents of Shem;
> And may Canaan be his servant."

²⁸And Noah lived after the flood three hundred and fifty years. ²⁹So all the days of Noah were nine hundred and fifty years; and he died.

NATIONS DESCENDED FROM NOAH

¹Now this *is* the genealogy of the sons of Noah: Shem, Ham, and Japheth. And sons were born to them after the flood.
²The sons of Japheth *were* Gomer, Magog, Madai, Javan, Tubal, Meshech, and Tiras. ³The sons of Gomer *were* Ashkenaz, Riphath,ᵃ and Togarmah. ⁴The sons of Javan *were* Elishah, Tarshish, Kittim, and Dodanim.ᵃ ⁵From these the coastland *peoples* of the Gentiles were separated into their lands, everyone according to his language, according to their families, into their nations.

Japheth and his descendants lived near the eastern shore of the Mediterranean Sea, the area that is now southern Turkey and Syria.
Genesis 10:2–5

⁶The sons of Ham *were* Cush, Mizraim, Put,ᵃ and Canaan. ⁷The sons of Cush *were* Seba, Havilah, Sabtah, Raamah, and Sabtechah; and the sons of Raamah *were* Sheba and Dedan.
⁸Cush begot Nimrod; he began to be a mighty one on the earth. ⁹He was a mighty hunter before the LORD; therefore it is said, "Like Nimrod the mighty hunter before the LORD." ¹⁰And the beginning of his kingdom was Babel, Erech, Accad, and Calneh, in the land of Shinar. ¹¹From that land he went to Assyria and built Nineveh, Rehoboth Ir, Calah, ¹²and Resen between Nineveh and Calah (that *is* the principal city).

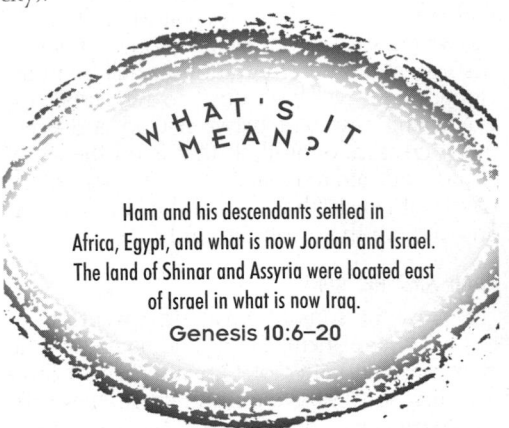

Ham and his descendants settled in Africa, Egypt, and what is now Jordan and Israel. The land of Shinar and Assyria were located east of Israel in what is now Iraq.
Genesis 10:6–20

¹³Mizraim begot Ludim, Anamim, Lehabim, Naphtuhim, ¹⁴Pathrusim, and Casluhim (from whom came the Philistines and Caphtorim).
¹⁵Canaan begot Sidon his firstborn, and Heth; ¹⁶the Jebusite, the Amorite, and the Girgashite; ¹⁷the Hivite, the Arkite, and the Sinite; ¹⁸the Arvadite, the Zemarite, and the Hamathite. Afterward the families of the Canaanites were dispersed. ¹⁹And the border of the Canaanites was from Sidon as you go toward Gerar, as far as Gaza; then as you go toward Sodom, Gomorrah, Admah, and Zeboiim, as far as Lasha. ²⁰These *were* the sons of Ham, according to their families, according to their languages, in their lands *and* in their nations.
²¹And *children* were born also to Shem, the father of all the children of Eber, the brother of Japheth the elder. ²²The sons of Shem *were* Elam, Asshur, Arphaxad, Lud, and Aram. ²³The sons of Aram *were* Uz, Hul, Gether, and Mash.ᵃ ²⁴Arphaxad begot Salah,ᵃ and Salah begot Eber. ²⁵To Eber were born two sons: the name of one *was* Peleg, for in his days the earth was divided; and his brother's name *was* Joktan. ²⁶Joktan begot Almodad, Sheleph, Hazarmaveth, Jerah, ²⁷Hadoram, Uzal, Diklah, ²⁸Obal,ᵃ Abimael, Sheba, ²⁹Ophir, Havilah, and Jobab. All these *were* the sons of Joktan. ³⁰And their dwelling place was from Mesha as you go toward Sephar, the mountain of the east. ³¹These *were* the sons of Shem, according to their families, according to their languages, in their lands, according to their nations.

10:3 ᵃSpelled *Diphath* in 1 Chronicles 1:6   **10:4** ᵃSpelled *Rodanim* in Samaritan Pentateuch and 1 Chronicles 1:7   **10:6** ᵃOr *Phut*   **10:23** ᵃCalled *Meshech* in Septuagint and 1 Chronicles 1:17
10:24 ᵃFollowing Masoretic Text, Vulgate, and Targum; Septuagint reads *Arphaxad begot Cainan, and Cainan begot Salah* (compare Luke 3:35, 36).   **10:28** ᵃSpelled *Ebal* in 1 Chronicles 1:22

³²These *were* the families of the sons of Noah, according to their generations, in their nations; and from these the nations were divided on the earth after the flood.

THE TOWER OF BABEL

¹Now the whole earth had one language and one speech. ²And it came to pass, as they journeyed from the east, that they found a plain in the land of Shinar, and they dwelt there. ³Then they said to one another, "Come, let us make bricks and bake *them* thoroughly." They had brick for stone, and they had asphalt for mortar. ⁴And they said, "Come, let us build ourselves a city, and a tower whose top *is* in the heavens; let us make a name for ourselves, lest we be scattered abroad over the face of the whole earth."

⁵But the LORD came down to see the city and the tower which the sons of men had built. ⁶And the LORD said, "Indeed the people *are* one and they all have one language, and this is what they begin to do; now nothing that they propose to do will be withheld from them. ⁷Come, let Us go down and there confuse their language, that they may not understand one another's speech." ⁸So the LORD scattered them abroad from there over the face of all the earth, and they ceased building the city. ⁹Therefore its name is called Babel, because there the LORD confused the language of all the earth; and from there the LORD scattered them abroad over the face of all the earth.

> "Therefore its name is called Babel, because there the LORD confused the language of all the earth."
> (Genesis 11:9a)

SHEM'S DESCENDANTS

¹⁰This *is* the genealogy of Shem: Shem *was* one hundred years old, and begot Arphaxad two years after the flood. ¹¹After he begot Arphaxad, Shem lived five hundred years, and begot sons and daughters.

¹²Arphaxad lived thirty-five years, and begot Salah. ¹³After he begot Salah, Arphaxad lived four hundred and three years, and begot sons and daughters.

¹⁴Salah lived thirty years, and begot Eber. ¹⁵After he begot Eber, Salah lived four hundred and three years, and begot sons and daughters.

¹⁶Eber lived thirty-four years, and begot Peleg. ¹⁷After he begot Peleg, Eber lived four hundred and thirty years, and begot sons and daughters.

¹⁸Peleg lived thirty years, and begot Reu.

¹⁹After he begot Reu, Peleg lived two hundred and nine years, and begot sons and daughters. ²⁰Reu lived thirty-two years, and begot Serug. ²¹After he begot Serug, Reu lived two hundred and seven years, and begot sons and daughters. ²²Serug lived thirty years, and begot Nahor. ²³After he begot Nahor, Serug lived two hundred years, and begot sons and daughters. ²⁴Nahor lived twenty-nine years, and begot Terah. ²⁵After he begot Terah, Nahor lived one hundred and nineteen years, and begot sons and daughters. ²⁶Now Terah lived seventy years, and begot Abram, Nahor, and Haran.

TERAH'S DESCENDANTS

²⁷This *is* the genealogy of Terah: Terah begot Abram, Nahor, and Haran. Haran begot Lot. ²⁸And Haran died before his father Terah in his native land, in Ur of the Chaldeans. ²⁹Then Abram and Nahor took wives: the name of Abram's wife *was* Sarai, and the name of Nahor's wife, Milcah, the daughter of Haran the father of Milcah and the father of Iscah. ³⁰But Sarai was barren; she had no child.

WHAT'S IT MEAN?

Ever heard of the Promised Land? That's Canaan. The land was located east of the Mediterranean Sea, where Syria, Lebanon, and Israel are today.
Genesis 11:31

³¹And Terah took his son Abram and his grandson Lot, the son of Haran, and his daughter-in-law Sarai, his son Abram's wife, and they went out with them from Ur of the Chaldeans to go to the land of Canaan; and they came to Haran and dwelt there. ³²So the days of Terah were two hundred and five years, and Terah died in Haran.

PROMISES TO ABRAM

¹Now the LORD had said to Abram:

"Get out of your country,
From your family
And from your father's house,
To a land that I will show you.
2   I will make you a great nation;
I will bless you
And make your name great;
And you shall be a blessing.
3   I will bless those who bless you,
And I will curse him who curses you;
And in you all the families of the earth
shall be blessed."

⁴So Abram departed as the LORD had spoken to him, and Lot went with him. And Abram *was* seventy-five years old when he departed from Haran. ⁵Then Abram took Sarai his wife and Lot his brother's son, and all their possessions that they had gathered, and the people whom they had acquired in Haran, and they departed to go to the land of Canaan. So they came to the land of Canaan. ⁶Abram passed through the land to the place of Shechem, as far as the tere-binth tree of Moreh.ᵃ And the Canaanites *were* then in the land.

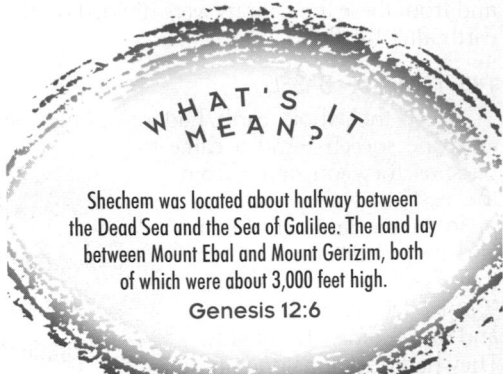

WHAT'S IT MEAN?

Shechem was located about halfway between the Dead Sea and the Sea of Galilee. The land lay between Mount Ebal and Mount Gerizim, both of which were about 3,000 feet high.

Genesis 12:6

⁷Then the LORD appeared to Abram and said, "To your descendants I will give this land." And there he built an altar to the LORD, who had appeared to him. ⁸And he moved from there to the mountain east of Bethel, and he pitched his tent *with* Bethel on the west and Ai on the east; there he built an altar to the LORD and called on the name of the LORD. ⁹So Abram journeyed, going on still toward the South.ᵃ

12:6 ᵃHebrew *Alon Moreh*   **12:9** ᵃHebrew *Negev*

Promise   HE PROMISES THAT EVERYONE ON EARTH WILL BE BLESSED.

I will make you a great nation; I will bless you and make your name great; and you shall be a blessing. I will bless those who bless you, and I will curse him who curses you; and in you all the families of the earth shall be blessed (Gen. 12:2, 3).

God had a plan for a man named Abram. God knew that Abram would believe Him, and that Abram would live out his faith by his actions. Because God knew that, He promised Abram that the world would be blessed because of him.

God blessed the world through Abram in two ways. First, Abraham (the name God gave Abram later) became the prime example for everyone who would ever put their faith in God. His descendants were honored and proud to be called the "children of Abraham." Paul said that anyone who has the same kind of faith that Abraham did is a child of Abraham.

But the greatest blessing that God gave through Abraham—the thing God was specifically talking about here—is Jesus. Jesus was born on earth as a part of God's chosen nation—the children of Abraham. God redeemed all of the sin in your life through Jesus, a descendant of the man whose greatest claim to fame was the simple fact that "he believed in the LORD" (Gen. 15:6).

SEE FOR YOURSELF:
Gen. 15:4, 5; 17:4–8; Luke 1:54, 55;
Gal. 3:14, 29

ABRAM IN EGYPT

[10]Now there was a famine in the land, and Abram went down to Egypt to dwell there, for the famine *was* severe in the land. [11]And it came to pass, when he was close to entering Egypt, that he said to Sarai his wife, "Indeed I know that you *are* a woman of beautiful countenance. [12]Therefore it will happen, when the Egyptians see you, that they will say, 'This *is* his wife'; and they will kill me, but they will let you live. [13]Please say you *are* my sister, that it may be well with me for your sake, and that I[a] may live because of you."

[14]So it was, when Abram came into Egypt, that the Egyptians saw the woman, that she *was* very beautiful. [15]The princes of Pharaoh also saw her and commended her to Pharaoh. And the woman was taken to Pharaoh's house. [16]He treated Abram well for her sake. He had sheep, oxen, male donkeys, male and female servants, female donkeys, and camels.

[17]But the LORD plagued Pharaoh and his house with great plagues because of Sarai, Abram's wife. [18]And Pharaoh called Abram and said, "What *is* this you have done to me? Why did you not tell me that she *was* your wife? [19]Why did you say, 'She *is* my sister'? I might have taken her as my wife. Now therefore, here is your wife; take *her* and go your way." [20]So Pharaoh commanded *his* men concerning him; and they sent him away, with his wife and all that he had.

ABRAM INHERITS CANAAN

[1]Then Abram went up from Egypt, he and his wife and all that he had, and Lot with him, to the South.[a] [2]Abram *was* very rich in livestock, in silver, and in gold. [3]And he went on his journey from the South as far as Bethel, to the place where his tent had been at the beginning, between Bethel and Ai, [4]to the place of the altar which he had made there at first. And there Abram called on the name of the LORD.

[5]Lot also, who went with Abram, had flocks and herds and tents. [6]Now the land was not able to support them, that they might dwell together, for their possessions were so great that they could not dwell together. [7]And there was strife between the herdsmen of Abram's livestock and the herdsmen of Lot's livestock. The Canaanites and the Perizzites then dwelt in the land.

[8]So Abram said to Lot, "Please let there be no strife between you and me, and between my herdsmen and your herdsmen; for we *are* brethren. [9]*Is* not the whole land before you? Please separate from me. If *you take* the left, then I will go to the right; or, if *you go* to the right, then I will go to the left."

[10]And Lot lifted his eyes and saw all the plain of Jordan, that it *was* well watered everywhere (before the LORD destroyed Sodom and Gomorrah) like the garden of the LORD, like the land of Egypt as you go toward Zoar. [11]Then Lot chose for himself all the plain of Jordan, and Lot journeyed east. And they separated from each other. [12]Abram dwelt in the land of Canaan, and Lot dwelt in the cities of the plain and pitched *his* tent even as far as Sodom. [13]But the men of Sodom *were* exceedingly wicked and sinful against the LORD.

[14]And the LORD said to Abram, after Lot had separated from him: "Lift your eyes now and look from the place where you are—northward, southward, eastward, and westward; [15]for all the land which you see I give to you and your descendants[a] forever. [16]And I will make your descendants as the dust of the earth; so that if a man could number the dust of the earth, *then* your descendants also could be numbered. [17]Arise, walk in the land through its length and its width, for I give it to you."

[18]Then Abram moved *his* tent, and went and dwelt by the terebinth trees of Mamre,[a] which *are* in Hebron, and built an altar there to the LORD.

WHAT'S IT MEAN?

Hebron, which lies about twenty miles south of Jerusalem, was a very important city in Old Testament times. It is the final resting place of Abraham's wife Sarah.
Genesis 13:18

LOT'S CAPTIVITY AND RESCUE

[1]And it came to pass in the days of Amraphel king of Shinar, Arioch king of Ellasar, Chedorlaomer king of Elam, and Tidal king of nations,[a] [2]*that* they made war with Bera king of Sodom, Birsha king of Gomorrah, Shinab king

12:13 [a]Literally *my soul*   **13:1** [a]Hebrew *Negev*   **13:15** [a]Literally *seed,* and so throughout the book
13:18 [a]Hebrew *Alon Mamre*   **14:1** [a]Hebrew *goyim*

of Admah, Shemeber king of Zeboiim, and the king of Bela (that is, Zoar). [3]All these joined together in the Valley of Siddim (that is, the Salt Sea). [4]Twelve years they served Chedorlaomer, and in the thirteenth year they rebelled.

[5]In the fourteenth year Chedorlaomer and the kings that were with him came and attacked the Rephaim in Ashteroth Karnaim, the Zuzim in Ham, the Emim in Shaveh Kiriathaim, [6]and the Horites in their mountain of Seir, as far as El Paran, which is by the wilderness. [7]Then they turned back and came to En Mishpat (that is, Kadesh), and attacked all the country of the Amalekites, and also the Amorites who dwelt in Hazezon Tamar.

[8]And the king of Sodom, the king of Gomorrah, the king of Admah, the king of Zeboiim, and the king of Bela (that is, Zoar) went out and joined together in battle in the Valley of Siddim [9]against Chedorlaomer king of Elam, Tidal king of nations,[a] Amraphel king of Shinar, and Arioch king of Ellasar—four kings against five. [10]Now the Valley of Siddim was full of asphalt pits; and the kings of Sodom and Gomorrah fled; some fell there, and the remainder fled to the mountains. [11]Then they took all the goods of Sodom and Gomorrah, and all their provisions, and went their way. [12]They also took Lot, Abram's brother's son who dwelt in Sodom, and his goods, and departed.

[13]Then one who had escaped came and told Abram the Hebrew, for he dwelt by the terebinth trees of Mamre[a] the Amorite, brother of Eshcol and brother of Aner; and they were allies with Abram. [14]Now when Abram heard that his brother was taken captive, he armed his three hundred and eighteen trained servants

WHAT'S IT MEAN?

Think of Abram (who later became Abraham) as a tribal chief. The people under his command weren't all his immediate relatives, but they were loyal to him. Some of the men in Abram's "tribe" were trained warriors.

Genesis 14:14

who were born in his own house, and went in pursuit as far as Dan. [15]He divided his forces against them by night, and he and his servants attacked them and pursued them as far as Hobah, which is north of Damascus. [16]So he brought back all the goods, and also brought back his brother Lot and his goods, as well as the women and the people.

[17]And the king of Sodom went out to meet him at the Valley of Shaveh (that is, the King's Valley), after his return from the defeat of Chedorlaomer and the kings who were with him.

WHAT'S IT MEAN?

Melchizedek, whose name means "King of Righteousness," is mentioned only two other times in the Bible—once in Psalms and once in Hebrews. Take away the first four letters of Jerusalem and you have Melchizedek's hometown. Salem is another name for Jerusalem.

Genesis 14:18

ABRAM AND MELCHIZEDEK

[18]Then Melchizedek king of Salem brought out bread and wine; he was the priest of God Most High. [19]And he blessed him and said:

"Blessed be Abram of God Most High,
Possessor of heaven and earth;
[20]   And blessed be God Most High,
Who has delivered your enemies into your hand."

And he gave him a tithe of all.

[21]Now the king of Sodom said to Abram, "Give me the persons, and take the goods for yourself."

[22]But Abram said to the king of Sodom, "I have raised my hand to the LORD, God Most High, the Possessor of heaven and earth, [23]that I will take nothing, from a thread to a sandal strap, and that I will not take anything that is yours, lest you should say, 'I have made Abram rich'— [24]except only what the young men have eaten, and the portion of the men who went

14:9 [a]Hebrew goyim   **14:13** [a]Hebrew Alon Mamre

with me: Aner, Eshcol, and Mamre; let them take their portion."

GOD'S COVENANT WITH ABRAM

[1]After these things the word of the LORD came to Abram in a vision, saying, "Do not be afraid, Abram. I *am* your shield, your exceedingly great reward."

[2]But Abram said, "Lord GOD, what will You give me, seeing I go childless, and the heir of my house *is* Eliezer of Damascus?" [3]Then Abram said, "Look, You have given me no offspring; indeed one born in my house is my heir!"

PROTECTION

Who will protect me? (15.1)

[4]And behold, the word of the LORD *came* to him, saying, "This one shall not be your heir, but one who will come from your own body shall be your heir." [5]Then He brought him outside and said, "Look now toward heaven, and count the stars if you are able to number them." And He said to him, "So shall your descendants be."

[6]And he believed in the LORD, and He accounted it to him for righteousness.

[7]Then He said to him, "I *am* the LORD, who brought you out of Ur of the Chaldeans, to give you this land to inherit it."

[8]And he said, "Lord GOD, how shall I know that I will inherit it?"

[9]So He said to him, "Bring Me a three-year-old heifer, a three-year-old female goat, a three-year-old ram, a turtledove, and a young pigeon." [10]Then he brought all these to Him and cut them in two, down the middle, and placed each piece opposite the other; but he did not cut the birds in two. [11]And when the vultures came down on the carcasses, Abram drove them away.

[12]Now when the sun was going down, a deep sleep fell upon Abram; and behold, horror *and* great darkness fell upon him. [13]Then He said to Abram: "Know certainly that your descendants will be strangers in a land *that is* not theirs, and will serve them, and they will afflict them four hundred years. [14]And also the nation whom they serve I will judge; afterward they shall come out with great possessions. [15]Now as for you, you shall go to your fathers in peace; you shall be buried at a good old age. [16]But in the fourth generation they shall return here, for the iniquity of the Amorites *is* not yet complete."

[17]And it came to pass, when the sun went down and it was dark, that behold, there appeared a smoking oven and a burning torch

that passed between those pieces. [18]On the same day the LORD made a covenant with Abram, saying:

"To your descendants I have given this land, from the river of Egypt to the great river, the River Euphrates— [19]the Kenites, the Kenezzites, the Kadmonites, [20]the Hittites, the Perizzites, the Rephaim, [21]the Amorites, the Canaanites, the Girgashites, and the Jebusites."

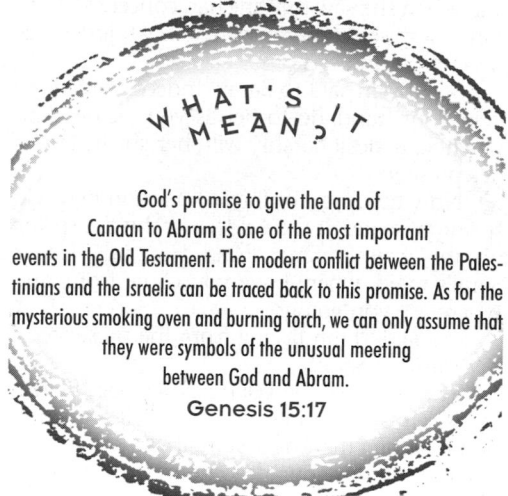

WHAT'S IT MEAN?

God's promise to give the land of Canaan to Abram is one of the most important events in the Old Testament. The modern conflict between the Palestinians and the Israelis can be traced back to this promise. As for the mysterious smoking oven and burning torch, we can only assume that they were symbols of the unusual meeting between God and Abram.
Genesis 15:17

HAGAR AND ISHMAEL

[1]Now Sarai, Abram's wife, had borne him no *children*. And she had an Egyptian maidservant whose name was Hagar. [2]So Sarai said to Abram, "See now, the LORD has restrained me from bearing *children*. Please, go in to my maid; perhaps I shall obtain children by her." And Abram heeded the voice of Sarai. [3]Then Sarai,

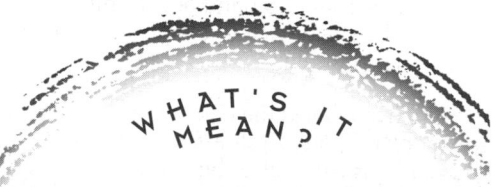

WHAT'S IT MEAN?

For a couple to be childless in Old Testament times was considered a tragedy. Children were seen as a sign of God's blessing. Without a son, there would be no one to carry on the family's name or take care of the family's property and possessions. Sarai's (Sarah's) servant could not have refused the "sleeping arrangement." Female servants were expected to bear their master's children if the master's wife could not.
Genesis 16:2

Abram's wife, took Hagar her maid, the Egyptian, and gave her to her husband Abram to be his wife, after Abram had dwelt ten years in the land of Canaan. ⁴So he went in to Hagar, and she conceived. And when she saw that she had conceived, her mistress became despised in her eyes.

⁵Then Sarai said to Abram, "My wrong *be* upon you! I gave my maid into your embrace; and when she saw that she had conceived, I became despised in her eyes. The LORD judge between you and me."

⁶So Abram said to Sarai, "Indeed your maid *is* in your hand; do to her as you please." And when Sarai dealt harshly with her, she fled from her presence.

⁷Now the Angel of the LORD found her by a spring of water in the wilderness, by the spring on the way to Shur. ⁸And He said, "Hagar, Sarai's maid, where have you come from, and where are you going?"

She said, "I am fleeing from the presence of my mistress Sarai."

⁹The Angel of the LORD said to her, "Return to your mistress, and submit yourself under her hand." ¹⁰Then the Angel of the LORD said to her, "I will multiply your descendants exceedingly, so that they shall not be counted for multitude." ¹¹And the Angel of the LORD said to her:

> "Behold, you *are* with child,
> And you shall bear a son.
> You shall call his name Ishmael,
> Because the LORD has heard your
>   affliction.
> 12 He shall be a wild man;
> His hand *shall be* against every man,
> And every man's hand against him.
> And he shall dwell in the presence of all
>   his brethren."

¹³Then she called the name of the LORD who spoke to her, You-Are-the-God-Who-Sees; for she said, "Have I also here seen Him who sees me?" ¹⁴Therefore the well was called Beer Lahai Roi;*ᵃ* observe, *it is* between Kadesh and Bered.

¹⁵So Hagar bore Abram a son; and Abram named his son, whom Hagar bore, Ishmael. ¹⁶Abram *was* eighty-six years old when Hagar bore Ishmael to Abram.

THE SIGN OF THE COVENANT

¹When Abram was ninety-nine years old, the LORD appeared to Abram and said to him, "I am Almighty God; walk before Me and be blameless. ²And I will make My covenant between Me and you, and will multiply you exceedingly." ³Then Abram fell on his face, and God talked with him, saying: ⁴"As for Me, behold, My covenant is with you, and you shall be a father of many nations. ⁵No longer shall your name be called Abram, but your name shall be Abraham; for I have made you a father of many nations. ⁶I will make you exceedingly fruitful; and I will make nations of you, and kings shall come from you. ⁷And I will establish My covenant between Me and you and your descendants after you in their generations, for an everlasting covenant, to be God to you and your descendants after you. ⁸Also I give to you and your descendants after you the land in which you are a stranger, all the land of Canaan, as an everlasting possession; and I will be their God."

⁹And God said to Abraham: "As for you, you shall keep My covenant, you and your descendants after you throughout their generations. ¹⁰This *is* My covenant which you shall keep, between Me and you and your descendants after you: Every male child among you shall be circumcised; ¹¹and you shall be circumcised in the flesh of your foreskins, and it shall be a sign of the covenant between Me and you. ¹²He who is eight days old among you shall be circumcised, every male child in your generations, he who is born in your house or bought with money from any foreigner who is not your descendant. ¹³He who is born in your house and he who is bought with your money must be circumcised, and My covenant shall be in your flesh for an everlasting covenant. ¹⁴And the un-

WHAT'S IT MEAN?

Names were a very big deal in ancient times. The meaning of a person's name often revealed a very important characteristic about him. In many cases, it was a symbol of what he stood for. In Hebrew, *Ab* means "father" and *raham* means "many."

Genesis 17:4, 5

circumcised male child, who is not circumcised in the flesh of his foreskin, that person shall be cut off from his people; he has broken My covenant."

¹⁵Then God said to Abraham, "As for Sarai your wife, you shall not call her name Sarai, but Sarah *shall be* her name. ¹⁶And I will bless her and also give you a son by her; then I will bless her, and she shall be *a mother of* nations; kings of peoples shall be from her."

¹⁷Then Abraham fell on his face and laughed, and said in his heart, "Shall *a child* be born to a man who is one hundred years old? And shall Sarah, who is ninety years old, bear *a child?*" ¹⁸And Abraham said to God, "Oh, that Ishmael might live before You!"

¹⁹Then God said: "No, Sarah your wife shall bear you a son, and you shall call his name Isaac; I will establish My covenant with him for an everlasting covenant, *and* with his descendants after him. ²⁰And as for Ishmael, I have heard you. Behold, I have blessed him, and will make him fruitful, and will multiply him exceedingly. He shall beget twelve princes, and I will make him a great nation. ²¹But My covenant I will establish with Isaac, whom Sarah shall bear to you at this set time next year." ²²Then He finished talking with him, and God went up from Abraham.

²³So Abraham took Ishmael his son, all who were born in his house and all who were bought with his money, every male among the men of Abraham's house, and circumcised the flesh of their foreskins that very same day, as God had said to him. ²⁴Abraham *was* ninety-nine years old when he was circumcised in the flesh of his foreskin. ²⁵And Ishmael his son *was* thirteen years old when he was circumcised in the flesh of his foreskin. ²⁶That very same day Abraham was circumcised, and his son Ishmael; ²⁷and all the men of his house, born in the house or bought with money from a foreigner, were circumcised with him.

THE SON OF PROMISE

¹Then the LORD appeared to him by the terebinth trees of Mamre,ᵃ as he was sitting in the tent door in the heat of the day. ²So he lifted his eyes and looked, and behold, three men were standing by him; and when he saw *them,* he ran from the tent door to meet them, and bowed himself to the ground, ³and said, "My Lord, if I have now found favor in Your sight, do not pass on by Your servant. ⁴Please let a little water be brought, and wash your feet, and rest your-

selves under the tree. ⁵And I will bring a morsel of bread, that you may refresh your hearts. After that you may pass by, inasmuch as you have come to your servant."

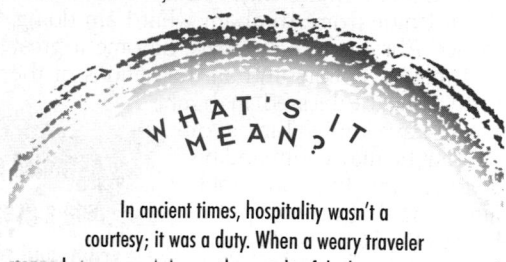

WHAT'S IT MEAN?

In ancient times, hospitality wasn't a courtesy; it was a duty. When a weary traveler stopped at someone's home, the people of the house were expected to welcome the stranger with open arms and care for his needs. It was considered rude for a host to ask his guests questions or carry on a conversation with them before they were given a chance to clean up and eat.

Genesis 18:1–5

They said, "Do as you have said."

⁶So Abraham hurried into the tent to Sarah and said, "Quickly, make ready three measures of fine meal; knead *it* and make cakes." ⁷And Abraham ran to the herd, took a tender and good calf, gave *it* to a young man, and he hastened to prepare it. ⁸So he took butter and milk and the calf which he had prepared, and set *it* before them; and he stood by them under the tree as they ate.

⁹Then they said to him, "Where *is* Sarah your wife?"

So he said, "Here, in the tent."

¹⁰And He said, "I will certainly return to you according to the time of life, and behold, Sarah your wife shall have a son."

(Sarah was listening in the tent door which *was* behind him.) ¹¹Now Abraham and Sarah were old, well advanced in age; *and* Sarah had passed the age of childbearing.ᵃ ¹²Therefore Sarah laughed within herself, saying, "After I have grown old, shall I have pleasure, my lord being old also?"

¹³And the LORD said to Abraham, "Why did Sarah laugh, saying, 'Shall I surely bear *a child,* since I am old?' ¹⁴Is anything too hard for the LORD? At the appointed time I will return to you, according to the time of life, and Sarah shall have a son."

¹⁵But Sarah denied *it,* saying, "I did not laugh," for she was afraid.

And He said, "No, but you did laugh!"

18:1 ᵃHebrew *Alon Mamre* **18:11** ᵃLiterally *the manner of women had ceased to be with Sarah*

ABRAHAM INTERCEDES FOR SODOM

¹⁶Then the men rose from there and looked toward Sodom, and Abraham went with them to send them on the way. ¹⁷And the LORD said, "Shall I hide from Abraham what I am doing, ¹⁸since Abraham shall surely become a great and mighty nation, and all the nations of the earth shall be blessed in him? ¹⁹For I have known him, in order that he may command his children and his household after him, that they keep the way of the LORD, to do righteousness and justice, that the LORD may bring to Abraham what He has spoken to him." ²⁰And the LORD said, "Because the outcry against Sodom and Gomorrah is great, and because their sin is very grave, ²¹I will go down now and see whether they have done altogether according to the outcry against it that has come to Me; and if not, I will know."

²²Then the men turned away from there and went toward Sodom, but Abraham still stood before the LORD. ²³And Abraham came near and said, "Would You also destroy the righteous with the wicked? ²⁴Suppose there were fifty righteous within the city; would You also destroy the place and not spare it for the fifty righteous that were in it? ²⁵Far be it from You to do such a thing as this, to slay the righteous with the wicked, so that the righteous should be as the wicked; far be it from You! Shall not the Judge of all the earth do right?"

²⁶So the LORD said, "If I find in Sodom fifty righteous within the city, then I will spare all the place for their sakes."

²⁷Then Abraham answered and said, "Indeed now, I who am but dust and ashes have taken it upon myself to speak to the Lord: ²⁸Suppose there were five less than the fifty righteous; would You destroy all of the city for lack of five?"

So He said, "If I find there forty-five, I will not destroy it."

²⁹And he spoke to Him yet again and said, "Suppose there should be forty found there?"

So He said, "I will not do it for the sake of forty."

³⁰Then he said, "Let not the Lord be angry, and I will speak: Suppose thirty should be found there?"

So He said, "I will not do it if I find thirty there."

³¹And he said, "Indeed now, I have taken it upon myself to speak to the Lord: Suppose twenty should be found there?"

So He said, "I will not destroy it for the sake of twenty."

> "Abraham shall surely become a great and mighty nation, and all the nations of the earth shall be blessed in him." (Genesis 18:18)

Promise — HE PROMISES NOTHING IS TOO HARD FOR HIM.

And the LORD said to Abraham, "Why did Sarah laugh, saying, 'Shall I surely bear a child, since I am old?' Is anything too hard for the LORD? At the appointed time I will return to you, according to the time of life, and Sarah shall have a son" (Gen. 18:13, 14).

Hard. You know all about *hard*. It's hard to juggle school, a part-time job, and chores at home. It's hard when the game is tied and you miss a free throw. It's hard when you sit down to take a final and realize you should have paid attention in class all year. It's hard when a grandparent dies.

Sometimes, when things are hard for us, we assume they're hard for God, too. They aren't. Nothing is too hard for God. His best stuff happens when all hope is gone. He parts the sea for people who don't have a way out. He gives babies to women who can't have any. He saves the souls of people who deserve death. Think about the hard times, the last second, the darkest hour, the deepest hole. They are "mission impossible" for us. Invite Him into your hard stuff. Every bit of it is "mission possible" for Him.

SEE FOR YOURSELF:
Num. 11:23; Matt. 19:26; Mark 10:27

[32]Then he said, "Let not the Lord be angry, and I will speak but once more: Suppose ten should be found there?"

And He said, "I will not destroy *it* for the sake of ten." [33]So the LORD went His way as soon as He had finished speaking with Abraham; and Abraham returned to his place.

SODOM'S DEPRAVITY

[1]Now the two angels came to Sodom in the evening, and Lot was sitting in the gate of Sodom. When Lot saw *them*, he rose to meet them, and he bowed himself with his face toward the ground. [2]And he said, "Here now, my lords, please turn in to your servant's house and spend the night, and wash your feet; then you may rise early and go on your way."

And they said, "No, but we will spend the night in the open square."

WHAT'S IT MEAN?

The city gate was like a commerce center and a courthouse rolled into one. It's where people conducted their business, judicial, and political matters. Judging by his position at the city gate, Lot apparently was an important man in Sodom. He saw it as his responsibility to welcome the two strangers to the city.

Genesis 19:1, 2

[3]But he insisted strongly; so they turned in to him and entered his house. Then he made them a feast, and baked unleavened bread, and they ate.

[4]Now before they lay down, the men of the city, the men of Sodom, both old and young, all the people from every quarter, surrounded the house. [5]And they called to Lot and said to him, "Where are the men who came to you tonight? Bring them out to us that we may know them *carnally*."

[6]So Lot went out to them through the doorway, shut the door behind him, [7]and said, "Please, my brethren, do not do so wickedly! [8]See now, I have two daughters who have not known a man; please, let me bring them out to you, and you may do to them as you wish;

only do nothing to these men, since this is the reason they have come under the shadow of my roof."

[9]And they said, "Stand back!" Then they said, "This one came in to stay *here*, and he keeps acting as a judge; now we will deal worse with you than with them." So they pressed hard against the man Lot, and came near to break down the door. [10]But the men reached out their hands and pulled Lot into the house with them, and shut the door. [11]And they struck the men who *were* at the doorway of the house with blindness, both small and great, so that they became weary *trying* to find the door.

SODOM AND GOMORRAH DESTROYED

[12]Then the men said to Lot, "Have you anyone else here? Son-in-law, your sons, your daughters, and whomever you have in the city—take *them* out of this place! [13]For we will destroy this place, because the outcry against them has grown great before the face of the LORD, and the LORD has sent us to destroy it."

[14]So Lot went out and spoke to his sons-in-law, who had married his daughters, and said, "Get up, get out of this place; for the LORD will destroy this city!" But to his sons-in-law he seemed to be joking.

[15]When the morning dawned, the angels urged Lot to hurry, saying, "Arise, take your wife and your two daughters who are here, lest you be consumed in the punishment of the city." [16]And while he lingered, the men took hold of his hand, his wife's hand, and the hands of his two daughters, the LORD being merciful to him, and they brought him out and set him outside the city. [17]So it came to pass, when they had brought them outside, that he[a] said, "Escape for your life! Do not look behind you nor stay anywhere in the plain. Escape to the mountains, lest you be destroyed."

[18]Then Lot said to them, "Please, no, my lords! [19]Indeed now, your servant has found favor in your sight, and you have increased your mercy which you have shown me by saving my life; but I cannot escape to the mountains, lest some evil overtake me and I die. [20]See now, this city *is* near *enough* to flee to, and it *is* a little one; please let me escape there (*is* it not a little one?) and my soul shall live."

[21]And he said to him, "See, I have favored you concerning this thing also, in that I will not overthrow this city for which you have spoken. [22]Hurry, escape there. For I cannot do anything until you arrive there."

19:17 [a]Septuagint, Syriac, and Vulgate read *they*.

Therefore the name of the city was called Zoar.

²³The sun had risen upon the earth when Lot entered Zoar. ²⁴Then the LORD rained brimstone and fire on Sodom and Gomorrah, from the LORD out of the heavens. ²⁵So He overthrew those cities, all the plain, all the inhabitants of the cities, and what grew on the ground.

²⁶But his wife looked back behind him, and she became a pillar of salt.

²⁷And Abraham went early in the morning to the place where he had stood before the LORD. ²⁸Then he looked toward Sodom and Gomorrah, and toward all the land of the plain; and he saw, and behold, the smoke of the land which went up like the smoke of a furnace. ²⁹And it came to pass, when God destroyed the cities of the plain, that God remembered Abraham, and sent Lot out of the midst of the overthrow, when He overthrew the cities in which Lot had dwelt.

THE DESCENDANTS OF LOT

³⁰Then Lot went up out of Zoar and dwelt in the mountains, and his two daughters were with him; for he was afraid to dwell in Zoar. And he and his two daughters dwelt in a cave. ³¹Now the firstborn said to the younger, "Our father *is* old, and *there is* no man on the earth to come in to us as is the custom of all the earth. ³²Come, let us make our father drink wine, and we will lie with him, that we may preserve the lineage of our father." ³³So they made their father drink wine that night. And the firstborn went in and lay with her father, and he did not know when she lay down or when she arose.

³⁴It happened on the next day that the firstborn said to the younger, "Indeed I lay with my father last night; let us make him drink wine tonight also, and you go in *and* lie with him, that we may preserve the lineage of our father." ³⁵Then they made their father drink wine that night also. And the younger arose and lay with him, and he did not know when she lay down or when she arose.

³⁶Thus both the daughters of Lot were with child by their father. ³⁷The firstborn bore a son and called his name Moab; he *is* the father of the Moabites to this day. ³⁸And the younger, she also bore a son and called his name Ben-Ammi; he *is* the father of the people of Ammon to this day.

ABRAHAM AND ABIMELECH

¹And Abraham journeyed from there to the South, and dwelt between Kadesh and Shur, and stayed in Gerar. ²Now Abraham said of Sarah his wife, "She *is* my sister." And Abimelech king of Gerar sent and took Sarah.

³But God came to Abimelech in a dream by night, and said to him, "Indeed you *are* a dead man because of the woman whom you have taken, for she *is* a man's wife."

⁴But Abimelech had not come near her; and he said, "Lord, will You slay a righteous nation also? ⁵Did he not say to me, 'She *is* my sister'? And she, even she herself said, 'He *is* my brother.' In the integrity of my heart and innocence of my hands I have done this."

⁶And God said to him in a dream, "Yes, I know that you did this in the integrity of your heart. For I also withheld you from sinning against Me; therefore I did not let you touch her. ⁷Now therefore, restore the man's wife; for he *is* a prophet, and he will pray for you and you shall live. But if you do not restore *her,* know that you shall surely die, you and all who *are* yours."

WHAT'S IT MEAN?

A prophet is a person who receives messages from God and then passes them along to others. Many of the prophet's messages involved teaching or correcting people, and some of them had to do with the future.

Genesis 20:7

⁸So Abimelech rose early in the morning, called all his servants, and told all these things in their hearing; and the men were very much afraid. ⁹And Abimelech called Abraham and said to him, "What have you done to us? How have I offended you, that you have brought on me and on my kingdom a great sin? You have done deeds to me that ought not to be done." ¹⁰Then Abimelech said to Abraham, "What did you have in view, that you have done this thing?"

¹¹And Abraham said, "Because I thought, surely the fear of God *is* not in this place; and they will kill me on account of my wife. ¹²But indeed *she is* truly my sister. She *is* the daughter of my father, but not the daughter of my mother; and she became my wife. ¹³And it came to pass, when God caused me to wander from

my father's house, that I said to her, 'This *is* your kindness that you should do for me: in every place, wherever we go, say of me, "He *is* my brother." ' "

¹⁴Then Abimelech took sheep, oxen, and male and female servants, and gave *them* to Abraham; and he restored Sarah his wife to him. ¹⁵And Abimelech said, "See, my land *is* before you; dwell where it pleases you." ¹⁶Then to Sarah he said, "Behold, I have given your brother a thousand *pieces* of silver; indeed this vindicates you*ᵃ* before all who *are* with you and before everybody." Thus she was rebuked.

¹⁷So Abraham prayed to God; and God healed Abimelech, his wife, and his female servants. Then they bore *children;* ¹⁸for the LORD had closed up all the wombs of the house of Abimelech because of Sarah, Abraham's wife.

ISAAC IS BORN

¹And the LORD visited Sarah as He had said, and the LORD did for Sarah as He had spoken. ²For Sarah conceived and bore Abraham a son in his old age, at the set time of which God had spoken to him. ³And Abraham called the name of his son who was born to him—whom Sarah bore to him—Isaac. ⁴Then Abraham circumcised his son Isaac when he was eight days old, as God had commanded him. ⁵Now Abraham was one hundred years old when his son Isaac was born to him. ⁶And Sarah said, "God has made me laugh, *and* all who hear will laugh with me." ⁷She also said, "Who would have said to Abraham that Sarah would nurse children? For I have borne *him* a son in his old age."

HAGAR AND ISHMAEL DEPART

⁸So the child grew and was weaned. And Abraham made a great feast on the same day that Isaac was weaned.

⁹And Sarah saw the son of Hagar the Egyptian, whom she had borne to Abraham, scoffing. ¹⁰Therefore she said to Abraham, "Cast out this bondwoman and her son; for the son of this bondwoman shall not be heir with my son, *namely* with Isaac." ¹¹And the matter was very displeasing in Abraham's sight because of his son.

¹²But God said to Abraham, "Do not let it be displeasing in your sight because of the lad or because of your bondwoman. Whatever Sarah has said to you, listen to her voice; for in Isaac your seed shall be called. ¹³Yet I will also make a nation of the son of the bondwoman, because he *is* your seed."

¹⁴So Abraham rose early in the morning, and took bread and a skin of water; and putting *it* on her shoulder, he gave *it* and the boy to Hagar, and sent her away. Then she departed and wandered in the Wilderness of Beersheba. ¹⁵And the water in the skin was used up, and she placed the boy under one of the shrubs. ¹⁶Then she went and sat down across from *him* at a distance of about a bowshot; for she said to herself, "Let me not see the death of the boy." So she sat opposite *him,* and lifted her voice and wept.

¹⁷And God heard the voice of the lad. Then the angel of God called to Hagar out of heaven, and said to her, "What ails you, Hagar? Fear not, for God has heard the voice of the lad where he *is.* ¹⁸Arise, lift up the lad and hold him with your hand, for I will make him a great nation."

¹⁹Then God opened her eyes, and she saw a well of water. And she went and filled the skin with water, and gave the lad a drink. ²⁰So God was with the lad; and he grew and dwelt in the wilderness, and became an archer. ²¹He dwelt in the Wilderness of Paran; and his mother took a wife for him from the land of Egypt.

A COVENANT WITH ABIMELECH

²²And it came to pass at that time that Abimelech and Phichol, the commander of his army, spoke to Abraham, saying, "God *is* with you in all that you do. ²³Now therefore, swear to me by God that you will not deal falsely with me, with my offspring, or with my posterity; but that according to the kindness that I have done to you, you will do to me and to the land in which you have dwelt."

²⁴And Abraham said, "I will swear."

²⁵Then Abraham rebuked Abimelech because of a well of water which Abimelech's servants had seized. ²⁶And Abimelech said, "I do not know who has done this thing; you did not tell me, nor had I heard *of it* until today." ²⁷So Abraham took sheep and oxen and gave them to Abimelech, and the two of them made a covenant. ²⁸And Abraham set seven ewe lambs of the flock by themselves.

²⁹Then Abimelech asked Abraham, "What *is the meaning of* these seven ewe lambs which you have set by themselves?"

³⁰And he said, "You will take *these* seven ewe lambs from my hand, that they may be my witness that I have dug this well." ³¹Therefore he called that place Beersheba,*ᵃ* because the two of them swore an oath there.

³²Thus they made a covenant at Beersheba.

20:16 *ᵃLiterally it is a covering of the eyes for you* **21:31** *ᵃLiterally Well of the Oath or Well of the Seven*

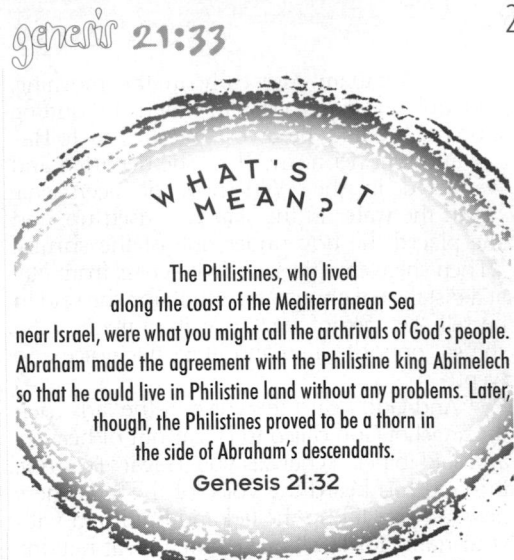

W H A T ' S   I T
M E A N ?

The Philistines, who lived
along the coast of the Mediterranean Sea
near Israel, were what you might call the archrivals of God's people.
Abraham made the agreement with the Philistine king Abimelech
so that he could live in Philistine land without any problems. Later,
though, the Philistines proved to be a thorn in
the side of Abraham's descendants.
Genesis 21:32

So Abimelech rose with Phichol, the commander of his army, and they returned to the land of the Philistines. ³³Then *Abraham* planted a tamarisk tree in Beersheba, and there called on the name of the LORD, the Everlasting God. ³⁴And Abraham stayed in the land of the Philistines many days.

ABRAHAM'S FAITH CONFIRMED

¹Now it came to pass after these things that God tested Abraham, and said to him, "Abraham!"

And he said, "Here I am."

²Then He said, "Take now your son, your only *son* Isaac, whom you love, and go to the land of Moriah, and offer him there as a burnt offering on one of the mountains of which I shall tell you."

³So Abraham rose early in the morning and saddled his donkey, and took two of his young men with him, and Isaac his son; and he split the wood for the burnt offering, and arose and went to the place of which God had told him. ⁴Then on the third day Abraham lifted his eyes and saw the place afar off. ⁵And Abraham said to his young men, "Stay here with the donkey; the lad*ᵃ* and I will go yonder and worship, and we will come back to you."

⁶So Abraham took the wood of the burnt offering and laid *it* on Isaac his son; and he took the fire in his hand, and a knife, and the two of them went together. ⁷But Isaac spoke to Abraham his father and said, "My father!"

And he said, "Here I am, my son."

Then he said, "Look, the fire and the wood, but where *is* the lamb for a burnt offering?"

⁸And Abraham said, "My son, God will provide for Himself the lamb for a burnt offering." So the two of them went together.

⁹Then they came to the place of which God had told him. And Abraham built an altar there and placed the wood in order; and he bound Isaac his son and laid him on the altar, upon the wood. ¹⁰And Abraham stretched out his hand and took the knife to slay his son.

¹¹But the Angel of the LORD called to him from heaven and said, "Abraham, Abraham!"

So he said, "Here I am."

W H A T ' S   I T
M E A N ?

In ancient times, when a servant
was called by his master, the proper response
was "Here I am." The fact that Abraham used
these words in responding to God shows
that he was ready to serve.
Genesis 22:11

¹²And He said, "Do not lay your hand on the lad, or do anything to him; for now I know that you fear God, since you have not withheld your son, your only *son*, from Me."

¹³Then Abraham lifted his eyes and looked, and there behind *him was* a ram caught in a thicket by its horns. So Abraham went and took the ram, and offered it up for a burnt offering instead of his son. ¹⁴And Abraham called the name of the place, The-LORD-Will-Provide;*ᵃ* as it is said *to* this day, "In the Mount of the LORD it shall be provided."

¹⁵Then the Angel of the LORD called to Abraham a second time out of heaven, ¹⁶and said: "By Myself I have sworn, says the LORD, because you have done this thing, and have not withheld your son, your only *son*— ¹⁷blessing I will bless you, and multiplying I will multiply your descendants as the stars of the heaven and as the sand which *is* on the seashore; and your descendants shall possess the gate of their enemies. ¹⁸In your seed all the nations of the earth shall be blessed, because you have obeyed My voice." ¹⁹So Abraham returned to his young men, and they rose and went together to Beersheba; and Abraham dwelt at Beersheba.

22:5 *ᵃ*Or *young man*   **22:14** *ᵃ*Hebrew *YHWH Yireh*

THE FAMILY OF NAHOR

20Now it came to pass after these things that it was told Abraham, saying, "Indeed Milcah also has borne children to your brother Nahor: 21Huz his firstborn, Buz his brother, Kemuel the father of Aram, 22Chesed, Hazo, Pildash, Jidlaph, and Bethuel." 23And Bethuel begot Rebekah.*a* These eight Milcah bore to Nahor, Abraham's brother. 24His concubine, whose name was Reumah, also bore Tebah, Gaham, Thahash, and Maachah.

SARAH'S DEATH AND BURIAL

1Sarah lived one hundred and twenty-seven years; *these were* the years of the life of Sarah. 2So Sarah died in Kirjath Arba (that *is*, Hebron) in the land of Canaan, and Abraham came to mourn for Sarah and to weep for her. 3Then Abraham stood up from before his dead, and spoke to the sons of Heth, saying, 4"I *am* a foreigner and a visitor among you. Give me property for a burial place among you, that I may bury my dead out of my sight."

5And the sons of Heth answered Abraham, saying to him, 6"Hear us, my lord: You *are* a mighty prince among us; bury your dead in the choicest of our burial places. None of us will withhold from you his burial place, that you may bury your dead."

7Then Abraham stood up and bowed himself to the people of the land, the sons of Heth. 8And he spoke with them, saying, "If it is your wish that I bury my dead out of my sight, hear me, and meet with Ephron the son of Zohar for me, 9that he may give me the cave of Machpelah which he has, which *is* at the end of his field. Let him give it to me at the full price, as property for a burial place among you."

10Now Ephron dwelt among the sons of Heth; and Ephron the Hittite answered Abraham in the presence of the sons of Heth, all who entered at the gate of his city, saying, 11"No, my lord, hear me: I give you the field and the cave that *is* in it; I give it to you in the presence of the sons of my people. I give it to you. Bury your dead!"

12Then Abraham bowed himself down before the people of the land; 13and he spoke to Ephron in the hearing of the people of the land, saying, "If you *will give it,* please hear me. I will give you money for the field; take *it* from me and I will bury my dead there."

14And Ephron answered Abraham, saying to him, 15"My lord, listen to me; the land *is worth* four hundred shekels of silver. What *is* that

between you and me? So bury your dead." 16And Abraham listened to Ephron; and Abraham weighed out the silver for Ephron which he had named in the hearing of the sons of Heth, four hundred shekels of silver, currency of the merchants.

17So the field of Ephron which *was* in Machpelah, which *was* before Mamre, the field and the cave which *was* in it, and all the trees that *were* in the field, which *were* within all the surrounding borders, were deeded 18to Abraham as a possession in the presence of the sons of Heth, before all who went in at the gate of his city.

19And after this, Abraham buried Sarah his wife in the cave of the field of Machpelah, before Mamre (that *is*, Hebron) in the land of Canaan. 20So the field and the cave that *is* in it were deeded to Abraham by the sons of Heth as property for a burial place.

A BRIDE FOR ISAAC

1Now Abraham was old, well advanced in age; and the LORD had blessed Abraham in all things. 2So Abraham said to the oldest servant of his house, who ruled over all that he had, "Please, put your hand under my thigh, 3and I will make you swear by the LORD, the God of heaven and the God of the earth, that you will not take a wife for my son from the daughters of the Canaanites, among whom I dwell; 4but you shall go to my country and to my family, and take a wife for my son Isaac."

WHAT'S IT MEAN?

How do you feel about large families? In Old Testament times, the family unit included everyone from grandparents to multiple wives, from widowed daughters to servants. God used the family structure to spread His message from generation to generation. Abraham wanted Isaac's wife chosen from among his family in order to keep his family unified.

Genesis 24:4

5And the servant said to him, "Perhaps the woman will not be willing to follow me to this land. Must I take your son back to the land from which you came?"

⁶But Abraham said to him, "Beware that you do not take my son back there. ⁷The LORD God of heaven, who took me from my father's house and from the land of my family, and who spoke to me and swore to me, saying, 'To your descendants*ᵃ* I give this land', He will send His angel before you, and you shall take a wife for my son from there. ⁸And if the woman is not willing to follow you, then you will be released from this oath; only do not take my son back there." ⁹So the servant put his hand under the thigh of Abraham his master, and swore to him concerning this matter.

¹⁰Then the servant took ten of his master's camels and departed, for all his master's goods *were in* his hand. And he arose and went to Mesopotamia, to the city of Nahor. ¹¹And he made his camels kneel down outside the city by a well of water at evening time, the time when women go out to draw *water.* ¹²Then he said, "O LORD God of my master Abraham, please give me success this day, and show kindness to my master Abraham. ¹³Behold, *here* I stand by the well of water, and the daughters of the men of the city are coming out to draw water. ¹⁴Now let it be that the young woman to whom I say, 'Please let down your pitcher that I may drink', and she says, 'Drink, and I will also give your camels a drink'—*let* her *be the one* You have appointed for Your servant Isaac. And by this I will know that You have shown kindness to my master."

¹⁵And it happened, before he had finished speaking, that behold, Rebekah, who was born to Bethuel, son of Milcah, the wife of Nahor, Abraham's brother, came out with her pitcher on her shoulder. ¹⁶Now the young woman *was* very beautiful to behold, a virgin; no man had known her. And she went down to the well, filled her pitcher, and came up. ¹⁷And the servant ran to meet her and said, "Please let me drink a little water from your pitcher."

¹⁸So she said, "Drink, my lord." Then she quickly let her pitcher down to her hand, and gave him a drink. ¹⁹And when she had finished giving him a drink, she said, "I will draw *water* for your camels also, until they have finished drinking." ²⁰Then she quickly emptied her pitcher into the trough, ran back to the well to draw *water,* and drew for all his camels. ²¹And the man, wondering at her, remained silent so as to know whether the LORD had made his journey prosperous or not.

²²So it was, when the camels had finished drinking, that the man took a golden nose ring weighing half a shekel, and two bracelets for her wrists weighing ten *shekels* of gold, ²³and said, "Whose daughter *are* you? Tell me, please, is there room *in* your father's house for us to lodge?"

²⁴So she said to him, "I *am* the daughter of Bethuel, Milcah's son, whom she bore to Nahor." ²⁵Moreover she said to him, "We have both straw and feed enough, and room to lodge."

²⁶Then the man bowed down his head and worshiped the LORD. ²⁷And he said, "Blessed *be* the LORD God of my master Abraham, who has not forsaken His mercy and His truth toward my master. As for me, being on the way, the LORD led me to the house of my master's brethren." ²⁸So the young woman ran and told her mother's household these things.

²⁹Now Rebekah had a brother whose name *was* Laban, and Laban ran out to the man by the well. ³⁰So it came to pass, when he saw the nose ring, and the bracelets on his sister's wrists, and when he heard the words of his sister Rebekah, saying, "Thus the man spoke to me," that he went to the man. And there he stood by the camels at the well. ³¹And he said, "Come in, O blessed of the LORD! Why do you stand outside? For I have prepared the house, and a place for the camels."

³²Then the man came to the house. And he unloaded the camels, and provided straw and feed for the camels, and water to wash his feet and the feet of the men who *were* with him. ³³*Food* was set before him to eat, but he said, "I will not eat until I have told about my errand."

And he said, "Speak on."

³⁴So he said, "I *am* Abraham's servant. ³⁵The LORD has blessed my master greatly, and he has become great; and He has given him flocks and herds, silver and gold, male and female servants, and camels and donkeys. ³⁶And Sarah my master's wife bore a son to my master when she was old; and to him he has given all that he has. ³⁷Now my master made me swear, saying, 'You shall not take a wife for my son from the daughters of the Canaanites, in whose land I dwell; ³⁸but you shall go to my father's house and to my family, and take a wife for my son.' ³⁹And I said to my master, 'Perhaps the woman will not follow me.' ⁴⁰But he said to me, 'The LORD, before whom I walk, will send His angel with you and prosper your way; and you shall take a wife for my son from my family

24:7 *ᵃLiterally seed*

and from my father's house. ⁴¹You will be clear from this oath when you arrive among my family; for if they will not give *her* to you, then you will be released from my oath.'

⁴²"And this day I came to the well and said, 'O LORD God of my master Abraham, if You will now prosper the way in which I go, ⁴³behold, I stand by the well of water; and it shall come to pass that when the virgin comes out to draw *water,* and I say to her, "Please give me a little water from your pitcher to drink," ⁴⁴and she says to me, "Drink, and I will draw for your camels also,"—let her *be* the woman whom the LORD has appointed for my master's son.'

⁴⁵"But before I had finished speaking in my heart, there was Rebekah, coming out with her pitcher on her shoulder; and she went down to the well and drew *water.* And I said to her, 'Please let me drink.' ⁴⁶And she made haste and let her pitcher down from her *shoulder,* and said, 'Drink, and I will give your camels a drink also.' So I drank, and she gave the camels a drink also. ⁴⁷Then I asked her, and said, 'Whose daughter *are* you?' And she said, 'The daughter of Bethuel, Nahor's son, whom Milcah bore to him.' So I put the nose ring on her nose and the bracelets on her wrists. ⁴⁸And I bowed my head and worshiped the LORD, and blessed the LORD God of my master Abraham, who had led me in the way of truth to take the daughter of my master's brother for his son. ⁴⁹Now if you will deal kindly and truly with my master, tell me. And if not, tell me, that I may turn to the right hand or to the left."

⁵⁰Then Laban and Bethuel answered and said, "The thing comes from the LORD; we cannot speak to you either bad or good. ⁵¹Here *is* Rebekah before you; take *her* and go, and let her be your master's son's wife, as the LORD has spoken."

⁵²And it came to pass, when Abraham's servant heard their words, that he worshiped the LORD, *bowing himself* to the earth. ⁵³Then the servant brought out jewelry of silver, jewelry of gold, and clothing, and gave *them* to Rebekah. He also gave precious things to her brother and to her mother.

⁵⁴And he and the men who *were* with him ate and drank and stayed all night. Then they arose in the morning, and he said, "Send me away to my master."

⁵⁵But her brother and her mother said, "Let the young woman stay with us *a few* days, at least ten; after that she may go."

⁵⁶And he said to them, "Do not hinder me, since the LORD has prospered my way; send me away so that I may go to my master."

⁵⁷So they said, "We will call the young woman and ask her personally." ⁵⁸Then they called Rebekah and said to her, "Will you go with this man?"

And she said, "I will go."

WHAT'S IT MEAN?

Asking Rebekah's opinion about the marriage plans was an unusual courtesy. Marriages were generally arranged by young people's families. Very few women (and few men, for that matter) had the authority to go against their family's wishes.
Genesis 24:57

⁵⁹So they sent away Rebekah their sister and her nurse, and Abraham's servant and his men. ⁶⁰And they blessed Rebekah and said to her:

"Our sister, *may* you *become*
The mother of thousands of ten thousands,
And may your descendants possess
The gates of those who hate them."

⁶¹Then Rebekah and her maids arose, and they rode on the camels and followed the man. So the servant took Rebekah and departed.

⁶²Now Isaac came from the way of Beer Lahai Roi, for he dwelt in the South. ⁶³And Isaac went out to meditate in the field in the evening; and he lifted his eyes and looked, and there, the camels *were* coming. ⁶⁴Then Rebekah lifted her eyes, and when she saw Isaac she dismounted from her camel; ⁶⁵for she had said to the servant, "Who *is* this man walking in the field to meet us?"

The servant said, "It *is* my master." So she took a veil and covered herself.

⁶⁶And the servant told Isaac all the things that he had done. ⁶⁷Then Isaac brought her into his mother Sarah's tent; and he took Rebekah and she became his wife, and he loved her. So Isaac was comforted after his mother's *death.*

ABRAHAM AND KETURAH

¹Abraham again took a wife, and her name *was* Keturah. ²And she bore him Zimran, Jokshan, Medan, Midian, Ishbak, and Shuah. ³Jokshan begot Sheba and Dedan. And the sons of Dedan were Asshurim, Letushim, and

Leummim. [4]And the sons of Midian *were* Ephah, Epher, Hanoch, Abidah, and Eldaah. All these *were* the children of Keturah.

[5]And Abraham gave all that he had to Isaac. [6]But Abraham gave gifts to the sons of the concubines which Abraham had; and while he was still living he sent them eastward, away from Isaac his son, to the country of the east.

ABRAHAM'S DEATH AND BURIAL

[7]This *is* the sum of the years of Abraham's life which he lived: one hundred and seventy-five years. [8]Then Abraham breathed his last and died in a good old age, an old man and full *of years*, and was gathered to his people. [9]And his sons Isaac and Ishmael buried him in the cave of Machpelah, which *is* before Mamre, in the field of Ephron the son of Zohar the Hittite, [10]the field which Abraham purchased from the sons of Heth. There Abraham was buried, and Sarah his wife. [11]And it came to pass, after the death of Abraham, that God blessed his son Isaac. And Isaac dwelt at Beer Lahai Roi.

THE FAMILIES OF ISHMAEL AND ISAAC

[12]Now this *is* the genealogy of Ishmael, Abraham's son, whom Hagar the Egyptian, Sarah's maidservant, bore to Abraham. [13]And these *were* the names of the sons of Ishmael, by their names, according to their generations: The firstborn of Ishmael, Nebajoth; then Kedar, Adbeel, Mibsam, [14]Mishma, Dumah, Massa, [15]Hadar,[a] Tema, Jetur, Naphish, and Kedemah. [16]These *were* the sons of Ishmael and these *were* their names, by their towns and their settlements, twelve princes according to their nations. [17]These *were* the years of the life of Ishmael: one hundred and thirty-seven years; and he breathed his last and died, and was gathered to his people. [18](They dwelt from Havilah as far as Shur, which *is* east of Egypt as you go toward Assyria.) He died in the presence of all his brethren.

[19]This *is* the genealogy of Isaac, Abraham's son. Abraham begot Isaac. [20]Isaac was forty years old when he took Rebekah as wife, the daughter of Bethuel the Syrian of Padan Aram, the sister of Laban the Syrian. [21]Now Isaac pleaded with the LORD for his wife, because she *was* barren; and the LORD granted his plea, and Rebekah his wife conceived. [22]But the children struggled together within her; and she said, "If all *is* well, why *am* I like this?" So she went to inquire of the LORD.

[23]And the LORD said to her:

"Two nations *are* in your womb,
Two peoples shall be separated from your body;
One people shall be stronger than the other,
And the older shall serve the younger."

WHAT'S IT MEAN?

The idea of a younger son ruling over his older brother was almost unheard of. Ancient customs and laws required that the oldest son have the first claim to property and the leadership role in the family.

Genesis 25:23

[24]So when her days were fulfilled *for her* to give birth, indeed *there were* twins in her womb. [25]And the first came out red. *He was* like a hairy garment all over; so they called his name Esau.[a] [26]Afterward his brother came out, and his hand took hold of Esau's heel; so his name was called Jacob.[a] Isaac *was* sixty years old when she bore them.

[27]So the boys grew. And Esau was a skillful hunter, a man of the field; but Jacob was a mild man, dwelling in tents. [28]And Isaac loved Esau because he ate *of his* game, but Rebekah loved Jacob.

ESAU SELLS HIS BIRTHRIGHT

[29]Now Jacob cooked a stew; and Esau came in from the field, and he *was* weary. [30]And Esau said to Jacob, "Please feed me with that same red *stew*, for I *am* weary." Therefore his name was called Edom.[a]

[31]But Jacob said, "Sell me your birthright as of this day."

[32]And Esau said, "Look, I *am* about to die; so what *is* this birthright to me?"

[33]Then Jacob said, "Swear to me as of this day."

So he swore to him, and sold his birthright to Jacob. [34]And Jacob gave Esau bread and stew of lentils; then he ate and drank, arose, and went his way. Thus Esau despised *his* birthright.

25:15 [a]Masoretic Text reads *Hadad*.   **25:25** [a]Literally *Hairy*   **25:26** [a]Literally *Supplanter*   **25:30** [a]Literally *Red*

CAIN made a difference

Opportunities to make a positive difference are also opportunities to make a negative difference. The Bible includes many people who made a negative difference. There are two reasons for this: (1) we can learn from other's mistakes; and (2) we are more likely to recognize ourselves making negative differences than positive. Cain made a difference in the wrong way. As is true of many people in Scripture, God included their stories to help us learn from their mistakes. But even Cain had that opportunity. God warned him when danger approached. Cain chose not to listen.

When Abel and Cain agreed to worship God, they each had something different in mind. Their personal sacrifices came from their lives. But the Bible indicates a significant difference in their attitudes. Abel brought the best; Cain brought whatever. It was a careless mistake that Cain compounded by getting angry and jealous at his younger brother. Until this point, the sin was between Cain and God. God warned Cain that he was quickly approaching a point of no return. God graciously granted Cain a second chance to get it right.

Cutting Edge

Attitudes like jealousy and anger can be rebuked and corrected. Murder cannot be undone. Cain chose to follow the guidance of his anger rather than to follow God. He killed his brother Abel and then offered God an arrogant denial—"Am I my brother's keeper?" Cain became a vivid example of the mess we create when anger is out of control.

YOU can, too!

What you do with anger will affect your life in many ways. It will also make a big difference to others. As God pointed out to Cain, anger is like a huge billboard in our path which warns: What you do next matters! Anger is a reaction looking for a way to express itself. Anger doesn't think. That's why you have to think for it when you get angry. Without a master, anger hurts and destroys. Mastered, anger offers a forceful response to wrong.

If you have a problem with anger, listen carefully to God's warning to Cain. Letting God master your anger will make a difference for you and others.

Want to know more? Read about Cain's sin and the lessons the Bible teaches from it in Genesis 4:1–17; Hebrews 11:4; 1 John 3:12; Jude 11.

ISAAC made a difference

Isaac was the only child of Abraham and Sarah. Growing up as an only child carries with it certain benefits. For one thing, sharing is just a concept you learn, not a life-and-death struggle as in most families. Only childhood also includes special challenges. You get all the attention—sometimes too much. Isaac had the added factor of parents who were old enough to be his great-grandparents. No wonder he had some special problems later when he became father of twins.

Isaac was a promise as well as a person. He had to learn to live with that fact. He was the first installment in God's promise to create a nation through Abraham. For instance, one day his father told him they were going on a camping trip. The next thing he knew, Isaac found himself tied up on an altar about to be sacrificed as a burnt offering. Fortunately, this was only a test—a test of Abraham's trust in God. An alternative sacrifice was provided.

Cutting Edge

If Isaac didn't learn anything else about God while under the knife, he certainly realized faith was serious business. His life wasn't full of accomplishments, but he kept the faith, and he passed it on. He gave God's special blessing to Jacob and continued the generations, which became God's people, Israel.

YOU can, too!

making a difference may not lead to greatness. Perhaps you will seem to do little more than be a faithful spouse, caring parent, growing disciple of Jesus—but these are the stuff from which God makes a difference in other people's lives. In God's hands, little differences become big.

Want to know more? Read about Isaac's life in Genesis 17:15—35:29. Romans 9:7–10; Hebrews 11:17–20; and James 2:21–24 also describe his significance.

REBEKAH made a difference

Even today in some cultures, marriages are arranged. Brides and grooms don't get to choose each other. We who see these choices as absolute rights find it hard to imagine a time when arranged marriages were the norm. Rebekah grew up in such a world. She lived in a large household ruled by her father and brother. They had the power to decide her marital fate. But God was also working in the background in her life.

One day when she went to the city well for water she met an old man named Eliezer, a servant of Abraham. Eliezer had just prayed for guidance in finding a suitable wife for Abraham's son Isaac. Rebekah turned out to be the answer to that prayer. Both Rebekah's timing and her attitude fit Eliezer's expectations. She didn't hesitate to be helpful, even before she found out he represented a distant relative.

Cutting Edge

After Eliezer met her family and explained his mission and the events at the well, Rebekah's father and brother realized God was arranging these events. They agreed to release Rebekah for marriage with Isaac. Gifts were presented. Return travel arrangements were made. Then, Rebekah was honored with final veto, "Will you go with this man?" (Gen. 24:58). Her simple affirmation took God's plan for the world another step. She made a difference. YOU can, too!

Rebekah had a lot to learn. She made some major mistakes as a wife and mother. But her early and beautiful cooperation with God's work in her life was never undone. If we are going to make a difference in our tomorrows and if we are going to cooperate with the difference God wants to make through us, it will hinge on what we do with our nows. What decisions and opportunities are before you now? In what ways are you seeking God's guidance about the choices you have? How ready are you to respond to His direction?

Want to know more? Read Rebekah's story in Genesis 24—27.

JOSEPH made a difference

Some young people seem to know exactly what they will accomplish in life. In Joseph's case, God gave him a vivid set of dreams that cast him in the role of ruler over his father and eleven brothers. The brothers, of course, thought their younger brother was being arrogant, rude, and silly. They were already upset by the fact that their father treated Joseph with special attention. Their jealousy and anger escalated to the point where they considered killing him but decided to sell him into slavery.

Little did the brothers know that they were working out God's plan. Still a teenager, Joseph found himself a slave in Egypt. His integrity, work ethic, and efforts earned him the trust of others. No matter where life landed him, Joseph immediately found a place to make a difference and worked at it. He practiced his considerable gifts and abilities. He made a difference in his master's home. Unfairly imprisoned, he made a difference in prison. Given an opportunity, he made a difference in a nation. With God's help he set up a massive preparation for famine, which would save Egypt and her neighbors. Later, his dream came true when his entire family bowed before him, not recognizing him as a brother but appreciating his generosity as the manager of Egypt.

Cutting Edge

Joseph knew God's hand was on his life. He apparently never wavered in his confidence of that fact. He never let the immediate circumstances determine his view of God's power and ability to make a difference through his life. **YOU can, too!**

Your vision of your future may not be as clear as Joseph's. That doesn't mean your confidence in God has to be less than his. The key is to remember that faith doesn't rest on a vision but on God. Your God must be big enough to work out His plans in your life, no matter what the obstacles. Trust in such a God, and your life will make a difference.

Want to know more? Read about Joseph's amazing riches to rags to riches to rags to riches life in (Genesis 37—50) and his listing in Hebrews 11:21, 22.

ISAAC AND ABIMELECH

¹There was a famine in the land, besides the first famine that was in the days of Abraham. And Isaac went to Abimelech king of the Philistines, in Gerar. ²Then the LORD appeared to him and said: "Do not go down to Egypt; live in the land of which I shall tell you. ³Dwell in this land, and I will be with you and bless you; for to you and your descendants I give all these lands, and I will perform the oath which I swore to Abraham your father. ⁴And I will make your descendants multiply as the stars of heaven; I will give to your descendants all these lands; and in your seed all the nations of the earth shall be blessed; ⁵because Abraham obeyed My voice and kept My charge, My commandments, My statutes, and My laws."

⁶So Isaac dwelt in Gerar. ⁷And the men of the place asked about his wife. And he said, "She *is* my sister"; for he was afraid to say, "*She is* my wife," *because he thought,* "lest the men of the place kill me for Rebekah, because she *is* beautiful to behold." ⁸Now it came to pass, when he had been there a long time, that Abimelech king of the Philistines looked through a window, and saw, and there was Isaac, showing endearment to Rebekah his wife. ⁹Then Abimelech called Isaac and said, "Quite obviously she *is* your wife; so how could you say, 'She *is* my sister'?"

Isaac said to him, "Because I said, 'Lest I die on account of her.' "

¹⁰And Abimelech said, "What *is* this you have done to us? One of the people might soon have lain with your wife, and you would have brought guilt on us." ¹¹So Abimelech charged all *his* people, saying, "He who touches this man or his wife shall surely be put to death."

¹²Then Isaac sowed in that land, and reaped in the same year a hundredfold; and the LORD blessed him. ¹³The man began to prosper, and continued prospering until he became very prosperous; ¹⁴for he had possessions of flocks and possessions of herds and a great number of servants. So the Philistines envied him. ¹⁵Now the Philistines had stopped up all the wells which his father's servants had dug in the days of Abraham his father, and they had filled them with earth. ¹⁶And Abimelech said to Isaac, "Go away from us, for you are much mightier than we."

¹⁷Then Isaac departed from there and pitched his tent in the Valley of Gerar, and dwelt there. ¹⁸And Isaac dug again the wells of water which they had dug in the days of Abraham his father, for the Philistines had stopped them up after the death of Abraham. He called them by the names which his father had called them.

¹⁹Also Isaac's servants dug in the valley, and found a well of running water there. ²⁰But the herdsmen of Gerar quarreled with Isaac's herdsmen, saying, "The water *is* ours." So he called the name of the well Esek,ᵃ because they quarreled with him. ²¹Then they dug another well, and they quarreled over that *one* also. So he called its name Sitnah.ᵃ ²²And he moved from there and dug another well, and they did not quarrel over it. So he called its name Rehoboth,ᵃ because he said, "For now the LORD has made room for us, and we shall be fruitful in the land."

WHAT'S IT MEAN?

When you consider the work
that went into digging wells in ancient times,
it's easy to understand why people argued over them. These wells
weren't dug in soft dirt, or even clay. They were dug in solid limestone, using primitive tools. The job was time-consuming and back-breaking. With water in short supply in that region, it's no wonder
that the diggers were eager to protect
what they had worked for.
Genesis 26:17–20

²³Then he went up from there to Beersheba. ²⁴And the LORD appeared to him the same night and said, "I *am* the God of your father Abraham; do not fear, for I *am* with you. I will bless you and multiply your descendants for My servant Abraham's sake." ²⁵So he built an altar there and called on the name of the LORD, and he pitched his tent there; and there Isaac's servants dug a well.

²⁶Then Abimelech came to him from Gerar with Ahuzzath, one of his friends, and Phichol the commander of his army. ²⁷And Isaac said to them, "Why have you come to me, since you hate me and have sent me away from you?" ²⁸But they said, "We have certainly seen that the LORD is with you. So we said, 'Let there now be an oath between us, between you and us; and let us make a covenant with you, ²⁹that

26:20 ᵃLiterally *Quarrel*   **26:21** ᵃLiterally *Enmity*   **26:22** ᵃLiterally *Spaciousness*

you will do us no harm, since we have not touched you, and since we have done nothing to you but good and have sent you away in peace. You *are* now the blessed of the LORD.' "

³⁰So he made them a feast, and they ate and drank. ³¹Then they arose early in the morning and swore an oath with one another; and Isaac sent them away, and they departed from him in peace.

³²It came to pass the same day that Isaac's servants came and told him about the well which they had dug, and said to him, "We have found water." ³³So he called it Shebah.ᵃ Therefore the name of the city *is* Beershebaᵇ to this day.

³⁴When Esau was forty years old, he took as wives Judith the daughter of Beeri the Hittite, and Basemath the daughter of Elon the Hittite. ³⁵And they were a grief of mind to Isaac and Rebekah.

ISAAC BLESSES JACOB

¹Now it came to pass, when Isaac was old and his eyes were so dim that he could not see, that he called Esau his older son and said to him, "My son."

And he answered him, "Here I am."

²Then he said, "Behold now, I am old. I do not know the day of my death. ³Now therefore, please take your weapons, your quiver and your bow, and go out to the field and hunt game for me. ⁴And make me savory food, such as I love, and bring *it* to me that I may eat, that my soul may bless you before I die."

WHAT'S IT MEAN?

Blessings were taken very seriously in Old Testament times. To bless someone was to call for God's favor and goodness in his life. What's more, the act of blessing someone somehow carried with it the power to make the blessing a reality. Once a blessing was spoken, it couldn't be taken back or changed.

Genesis 27:4

⁵Now Rebekah was listening when Isaac spoke to Esau his son. And Esau went to the field to hunt game and to bring *it*. ⁶So Rebekah spoke to Jacob her son, saying, "Indeed I heard your father speak to Esau your brother, saying, ⁷'Bring me game and make savory food for me, that I may eat it and bless you in the presence of the LORD before my death.' ⁸Now therefore, my son, obey my voice according to what I command you. ⁹Go now to the flock and bring me from there two choice kids of the goats, and I will make savory food from them for your father, such as he loves. ¹⁰Then you shall take *it* to your father, that he may eat *it*, and that he may bless you before his death."

¹¹And Jacob said to Rebekah his mother, "Look, Esau my brother *is* a hairy man, and I *am* a smooth-*skinned* man. ¹²Perhaps my father will feel me, and I shall seem to be a deceiver to him; and I shall bring a curse on myself and not a blessing."

¹³But his mother said to him, "*Let* your curse *be* on me, my son; only obey my voice, and go, get *them* for me." ¹⁴And he went and got *them* and brought *them* to his mother, and his mother made savory food, such as his father loved. ¹⁵Then Rebekah took the choice clothes of her elder son Esau, which *were* with her in the house, and put them on Jacob her younger son. ¹⁶And she put the skins of the kids of the goats on his hands and on the smooth part of his neck. ¹⁷Then she gave the savory food and the bread, which she had prepared, into the hand of her son Jacob.

¹⁸So he went to his father and said, "My father."

And he said, "Here I am. Who *are* you, my son?"

¹⁹Jacob said to his father, "I *am* Esau your firstborn; I have done just as you told me; please arise, sit and eat of my game, that your soul may bless me."

²⁰But Isaac said to his son, "How *is it* that you have found *it* so quickly, my son?"

And he said, "Because the LORD your God brought *it* to me."

²¹Isaac said to Jacob, "Please come near, that I may feel you, my son, whether you *are* really my son Esau or not." ²²So Jacob went near to Isaac his father, and he felt him and said, "The voice *is* Jacob's voice, but the hands *are* the hands of Esau." ²³And he did not recognize him, because his hands were hairy like his brother Esau's hands; so he blessed him.

²⁴Then he said, "*Are* you really my son Esau?"

He said, "I *am*."

²⁵He said, "Bring *it* near to me, and I will eat of my son's game, so that my soul may bless

you." So he brought *it* near to him, and he ate; and he brought him wine, and he drank. ²⁶Then his father Isaac said to him, "Come near now and kiss me, my son." ²⁷And he came near and kissed him; and he smelled the smell of his clothing, and blessed him and said:

"Surely, the smell of my son
    Is like the smell of a field
    Which the LORD has blessed.
²⁸ Therefore may God give you
    Of the dew of heaven,
    Of the fatness of the earth,
    And plenty of grain and wine.
²⁹ Let peoples serve you,
    And nations bow down to you.
    Be master over your brethren,
    And let your mother's sons bow down to
        you.
    Cursed *be* everyone who
        curses you,
    And blessed *be* those
        who bless you!"

ESAU'S LOST HOPE

³⁰Now it happened, as soon as Isaac had finished blessing Jacob, and Jacob had scarcely gone out from the presence of Isaac his father, that Esau his brother came in from his hunting. ³¹He also had made savory food, and brought it to his father, and said to his father, "Let my father arise and eat of his son's game, that your soul may bless me."

³²And his father Isaac said to him, "Who *are* you?"

So he said, "I *am* your son, your firstborn, Esau."

³³Then Isaac trembled exceedingly, and said, "Who? Where *is* the one who hunted game and brought *it* to me? I ate all *of it* before you came, and I have blessed him—*and* indeed he shall be blessed."

³⁴When Esau heard the words of his father, he cried with an exceedingly great and bitter cry, and said to his father, "Bless me—me also, O my father!"

³⁵But he said, "Your brother came with deceit and has taken away your blessing."

³⁶And *Esau* said, "Is he not rightly named Jacob? For he has supplanted me these two times. He took away my birthright, and now look, he has taken away my blessing!" And he said, "Have you not reserved a blessing for me?"

³⁷Then Isaac answered and said to Esau, "Indeed I have made him your master, and all his brethren I have given to him as servants; with grain and wine I have sustained him. What shall I do now for you, my son?"

³⁸And Esau said to his father, "Have you only one blessing, my father? Bless me—me also, O my father!" And Esau lifted up his voice and wept.

³⁹Then Isaac his father answered and said to him:

"Behold, your dwelling shall be of the
        fatness of the earth,
    And of the dew of heaven from above.
⁴⁰ By your sword you shall live,
    And you shall serve your brother;
    And it shall come to pass, when you
        become restless,
    That you shall break his yoke from your
        neck."

JACOB ESCAPES FROM ESAU

⁴¹So Esau hated Jacob because of the blessing with which his father blessed him, and Esau said in his heart, "The days of mourning for my father are at hand; then I will kill my brother Jacob."

⁴²And the words of Esau her older son were told to Rebekah. So she sent and called Jacob her younger son, and said to him, "Surely your brother Esau comforts himself concerning you *by intending* to kill you. ⁴³Now therefore, my son, obey my voice: arise, flee to my brother Laban in Haran. ⁴⁴And stay with him a few days, until your brother's fury turns away, ⁴⁵until your brother's anger turns away from you, and he forgets what you have done to him; then I will send and bring you from there. Why should I be bereaved also of you both in one day?"

⁴⁶And Rebekah said to Isaac, "I am weary of my life because of the daughters of Heth; if Jacob takes a wife of the daughters of Heth, like these *who are* the daughters of the land, what good will my life be to me?"

¹Then Isaac called Jacob and blessed him, and charged him, and said to him: "You shall not take a wife from the daughters of Canaan. ²Arise, go to Padan Aram, to the house of Bethuel your mother's father; and take yourself a wife from there of the daughters of Laban your mother's brother.

³ "May God Almighty bless you,
    And make you fruitful and multiply you,

> "May God Almighty bless you, and make you fruitful and multiply you, . . . and give you the blessing of Abraham . . ." (Genesis 28:3, 4)

That you may be an assembly of peoples;
4 And give you the blessing of Abraham,
To you and your descendants with you,
That you may inherit the land
In which you are a stranger,
Which God gave to Abraham."

5So Isaac sent Jacob away, and he went to Padan Aram, to Laban the son of Bethuel the Syrian, the brother of Rebekah, the mother of Jacob and Esau.

ESAU MARRIES MAHALATH

6Esau saw that Isaac had blessed Jacob and sent him away to Padan Aram to take himself a wife from there, *and that* as he blessed him he gave him a charge, saying, "You shall not take a wife from the daughters of Canaan," 7and that Jacob had obeyed his father and his mother and had gone to Padan Aram. 8Also Esau saw that the daughters of Canaan did not please his father Isaac. 9So Esau went to Ishmael and took Mahalath the daughter of Ishmael, Abraham's son, the sister of Nebajoth, to be his wife in addition to the wives he had.

JACOB'S VOW AT BETHEL

10Now Jacob went out from Beersheba and went toward Haran. 11So he came to a certain place and stayed there all night, because the sun had set. And he took one of the stones of that place and put it at his head, and he lay down in that place to sleep. 12Then he dreamed, and behold, a ladder *was* set up on the earth, and its top reached to heaven; and there the angels of God were ascending and descending on it. 13And behold, the LORD stood above it and said: "I *am* the LORD God of Abraham your father and the God of Isaac; the land on which you lie I will give to you and your descendants. 14Also your descendants shall be as the dust of the earth; you shall spread abroad to the west and the east, to the north and the south; and in you and in your seed all the families of the earth shall be blessed. 15Behold, I *am* with you and will keep you wherever you go, and will bring you back to this land; for I will not leave you until I have done what I have spoken to you."

16Then Jacob awoke from his sleep and said, "Surely the LORD is in this place, and I did

Promise HE PROMISES TO KEEP HIS PROMISES.

"I am the LORD God of Abraham your father and the God of Isaac; the land on which you lie I will give to you and your descendants. Also your descendants shall be as the dust of the earth; you shall spread abroad to the west and the east, to the north and the south; and in you and in your seed all the families of the earth shall be blessed.

Behold, I am with you and will keep you wherever you go, and will bring you back to this land; for I will not leave you until I have done what I have spoken to you (Gen. 28:13–15).

Jacob got off to a bad start in his spiritual life. First, he talked his older brother, Esau, out of the inheritance he was supposed to get as the firstborn. Later, he tricked his father, Isaac, into thinking he was Esau so that he could get the special blessing that Isaac wanted to give Esau.

It didn't look like Jacob had much of a chance to do anything great for God. In fact, we might think his belief in God was kind of flimsy. But God had chosen Jacob. In spite of the sneaky things he'd done, the Lord appeared to Jacob in a dream and said, "I will not leave you until I have done what I have spoken to you."

There may be times when God's promises seem really out there—way beyond the realm of possibility—especially when you know you haven't kept up your end of the deal. Even when your faith is a lot stronger than Jacob's was, there may be days when you want to say, "No way. God isn't going to do *that*—not for me." Don't give in. Instead, listen with all your heart, with every ounce of your faith to hear God say, "I will not leave you until I have done what I have spoken to you."

SEE FOR YOURSELF:
2 Sam. 23:5; 1 Kin. 8:56; 2 Kin. 20:9

WHAT'S IT MEAN?

Jacob took his dream seriously—and for good reason. The vision of the ladder, the bridge between heaven and earth, came straight from God. Jacob left his rock pillow behind as a memorial to God. To emphasize the point, he poured oil on the rock to symbolize that the land belonged to God in a special way.

Genesis 28:12–18

not know *it*." ¹⁷And he was afraid and said, "How awesome *is* this place! This *is* none other than the house of God, and this *is* the gate of heaven!"

¹⁸Then Jacob rose early in the morning, and took the stone that he had put at his head, set it up as a pillar, and poured oil on top of it. ¹⁹And he called the name of that place Bethel;ᵃ but the name of that city had been Luz previously. ²⁰Then Jacob made a vow, saying, "If God will be with me, and keep me in this way that I am going, and give me bread to eat and clothing to put on, ²¹so that I come back to my father's house in peace, then the LORD shall be my God. ²²And this stone which I have set as a pillar shall be God's house, and of all that You give me I will surely give a tenth to You."

JACOB MEETS RACHEL

¹So Jacob went on his journey and came to the land of the people of the East. ²And he looked, and saw a well in the field; and behold, there *were* three flocks of sheep lying by it; for out of that well they watered the flocks. A large stone *was* on the well's mouth. ³Now all the flocks would be gathered there; and they would roll the stone from the well's mouth, water the sheep, and put the stone back in its place on the well's mouth.

⁴And Jacob said to them, "My brethren, where *are* you from?"

And they said, "We *are* from Haran."

⁵Then he said to them, "Do you know Laban the son of Nahor?"

And they said, "We know him."

⁶So he said to them, "Is he well?"

And they said, "*He is* well. And look, his daughter Rachel is coming with the sheep."

⁷Then he said, "Look, *it is* still high day; *it is* not time for the cattle to be gathered together. Water the sheep, and go and feed *them*."

⁸But they said, "We cannot until all the flocks are gathered together, and they have rolled the stone from the well's mouth; then we water the sheep."

⁹Now while he was still speaking with them, Rachel came with her father's sheep, for she was a shepherdess. ¹⁰And it came to pass, when Jacob saw Rachel the daughter of Laban his mother's brother, and the sheep of Laban his mother's brother, that Jacob went near and rolled the stone from the well's mouth, and watered the flock of Laban his mother's brother. ¹¹Then Jacob kissed Rachel, and lifted up his voice and wept. ¹²And Jacob told Rachel that he *was* her father's relative and that he *was* Rebekah's son. So she ran and told her father.

¹³Then it came to pass, when Laban heard the report about Jacob his sister's son, that he ran to meet him, and embraced him and kissed him, and brought him to his house. So he told Laban all these things. ¹⁴And Laban said to him, "Surely you *are* my bone and my flesh." And he stayed with him for a month.

JACOB MARRIES LEAH AND RACHEL

¹⁵Then Laban said to Jacob, "Because you *are* my relative, should you therefore serve me for nothing? Tell me, what *should* your wages *be*?" ¹⁶Now Laban had two daughters: the name of the elder *was* Leah, and the name of the younger *was* Rachel. ¹⁷Leah's eyes *were* delicate, but Rachel was beautiful of form and appearance. ¹⁸Now Jacob loved Rachel; so he said, "I will serve you seven years for Rachel your younger daughter."

WHAT'S IT MEAN?

Jacob gave himself as dowry to Rachel's father. He wasn't trying to buy Rachel from her father. He worked seven years for Laban to make up for the help that would be lost in Laban's family when Rachel left.

Genesis 29:18

28:19 ᵃLiterally *House of God*

¹⁹And Laban said, "*It is* better that I give her to you than that I should give her to another man. Stay with me." ²⁰So Jacob served seven years for Rachel, and they seemed *only* a few days to him because of the love he had for her. ²¹Then Jacob said to Laban, "Give *me* my wife, for my days are fulfilled, that I may go in to her." ²²And Laban gathered together all the men of the place and made a feast. ²³Now it came to pass in the evening, that he took Leah his daughter and brought her to Jacob; and he went in to her. ²⁴And Laban gave his maid Zilpah to his daughter Leah *as* a maid. ²⁵So it came to pass in the morning, that behold, it *was* Leah. And he said to Laban, "What is this you have done to me? Was it not for Rachel that I served you? Why then have you deceived me?"

²⁶And Laban said, "It must not be done so in our country, to give the younger before the firstborn. ²⁷Fulfill her week, and we will give you this one also for the service which you will serve with me still another seven years."

²⁸Then Jacob did so and fulfilled her week. So he gave him his daughter Rachel as wife also. ²⁹And Laban gave his maid Bilhah to his daughter Rachel as a maid. ³⁰Then *Jacob* also went in to Rachel, and he also loved Rachel more than Leah. And he served with Laban still another seven years.

THE CHILDREN OF JACOB

³¹When the LORD saw that Leah *was* unloved, He opened her womb; but Rachel *was* barren. ³²So Leah conceived and bore a son, and she called his name Reuben;*a* for she said, "The LORD has surely looked on my affliction. Now therefore, my husband will love me." ³³Then she conceived again and bore a son, and said, "Because the LORD has heard that I *am* unloved, He has therefore given me this *son* also." And she called his name Simeon.*a* ³⁴She conceived again and bore a son, and said, "Now this time my husband will become attached to me, because I have borne him three sons." Therefore his name was called Levi.*a* ³⁵And she conceived again and bore a son, and said, "Now I will praise the LORD." Therefore she called his name Judah.*a* Then she stopped bearing.

¹Now when Rachel saw that she bore Jacob no children, Rachel envied her sister, and said to Jacob, "Give me children, or else I die!"

²And Jacob's anger was aroused against Rachel, and he said, "*Am* I in the place of God, who has withheld from you the fruit of the womb?"

³So she said, "Here is my maid Bilhah; go in to her, and she will bear *a child* on my knees, that I also may have children by her." ⁴Then she gave him Bilhah her maid as wife, and Jacob went in to her. ⁵And Bilhah conceived and bore Jacob a son. ⁶Then Rachel said, "God has judged my case; and He has also heard my voice and given me a son." Therefore she called his name Dan.*a* ⁷And Rachel's maid Bilhah conceived again and bore Jacob a second son. ⁸Then Rachel said, "With great wrestlings I have wrestled with my sister, *and* indeed I have prevailed." So she called his name Naphtali.*a*

⁹When Leah saw that she had stopped bearing, she took Zilpah her maid and gave her to Jacob as wife. ¹⁰And Leah's maid Zilpah bore Jacob a son. ¹¹Then Leah said, "A troop comes!"*a* So she called his name Gad.*b* ¹²And Leah's maid Zilpah bore Jacob a second son. ¹³Then Leah said, "I am happy, for the daughters will call me blessed." So she called his name Asher.*a*

¹⁴Now Reuben went in the days of wheat harvest and found mandrakes in the field, and brought them to his mother Leah. Then Rachel said to Leah, "Please give me *some* of your son's mandrakes."

¹⁵But she said to her, "*Is it* a small matter that you have taken away my husband? Would you take away my son's mandrakes also?"

WHAT'S IT MEAN?

Fertility specialists in Old Testament times weren't what you would call advanced in their treatments. Mandrakes, also known as "love flowers," were prescribed to increase fertility. In case you're wondering, a mandrake is a fruit-producing plant with dark green leaves and small blue flowers. The yellow fruit of this plant is small, sweet, and fragrant.

Genesis 30:14–16

And Rachel said, "Therefore he will lie with you tonight for your son's mandrakes."

¹⁶When Jacob came out of the field in the evening, Leah went out to meet him and said,

"You must come in to me, for I have surely hired you with my son's mandrakes." And he lay with her that night.

[17]And God listened to Leah, and she conceived and bore Jacob a fifth son. [18]Leah said, "God has given me my wages, because I have given my maid to my husband." So she called his name Issachar.[a] [19]Then Leah conceived again and bore Jacob a sixth son. [20]And Leah said, "God has endowed me *with* a good endowment; now my husband will dwell with me, because I have borne him six sons." So she called his name Zebulun.[a] [21]Afterward she bore a daughter, and called her name Dinah.

[22]Then God remembered Rachel, and God listened to her and opened her womb. [23]And she conceived and bore a son, and said, "God has taken away my reproach." [24]So she called his name Joseph,[a] and said, "The LORD shall add to me another son."

JACOB'S AGREEMENT WITH LABAN

[25]And it came to pass, when Rachel had borne Joseph, that Jacob said to Laban, "Send me away, that I may go to my own place and to my country. [26]Give *me* my wives and my children for whom I have served you, and let me go; for you know my service which I have done for you."

[27]And Laban said to him, "Please *stay*, if I have found favor in your eyes, *for* I have learned by experience that the LORD has blessed me for your sake." [28]Then he said, "Name me your wages, and I will give *it*."

[29]So *Jacob* said to him, "You know how I have served you and how your livestock has been with me. [30]For what you had before I *came was* little, and it has increased to a great amount; the LORD has blessed you since my coming. And now, when shall I also provide for my own house?"

[31]So he said, "What shall I give you?"

And Jacob said, "You shall not give me anything. If you will do this thing for me, I will again feed and keep your flocks: [32]Let me pass through all your flock today, removing from there all the speckled and spotted sheep, and all the brown ones among the lambs, and the spotted and speckled among the goats; and *these* shall be my wages. [33]So my righteousness will answer for me in time to come, when the subject of my wages comes before you: every one that *is* not speckled and spotted among the goats, and brown among the lambs, will be considered stolen, if *it is* with me."

[34]And Laban said, "Oh, that it were according to your word!" [35]So he removed that day the male goats that were speckled and spotted, all the female goats that were speckled and spotted, every one that had *some* white in it, and all the brown ones among the lambs, and gave *them* into the hand of his sons. [36]Then he put three days' journey between himself and Jacob, and Jacob fed the rest of Laban's flocks.

[37]Now Jacob took for himself rods of green poplar and of the almond and chestnut trees, peeled white strips in them, and exposed the white which *was* in the rods. [38]And the rods which he had peeled, he set before the flocks in the gutters, in the watering troughs where the flocks came to drink, so that they should conceive when they came to drink. [39]So the flocks conceived before the rods, and the flocks brought forth streaked, speckled, and spotted. [40]Then Jacob separated the lambs, and made the flocks face toward the streaked and all the brown in the flock of Laban; but he put his own flocks by themselves and did not put them with Laban's flock.

[41]And it came to pass, whenever the stronger livestock conceived, that Jacob placed the rods before the eyes of the livestock in the gutters, that they might conceive among the rods. [42]But when the flocks were feeble, he did not put *them* in; so the feebler were Laban's and the stronger Jacob's. [43]Thus the man became exceedingly prosperous, and had large flocks, female and male servants, and camels and donkeys.

JACOB FLEES FROM LABAN

[1]Now *Jacob* heard the words of Laban's sons, saying, "Jacob has taken away all that was our father's, and from what was our father's he has acquired all this wealth." [2]And Jacob saw the countenance of Laban, and indeed it *was* not *favorable* toward him as before. [3]Then the LORD said to Jacob, "Return to the land of your fathers and to your family, and I will be with you."

[4]So Jacob sent and called Rachel and Leah to the field, to his flock, [5]and said to them, "I see your father's countenance, that it *is* not *favorable* toward me as before; but the God of my father has been with me. [6]And you know that with all my might I have served your father. [7]Yet your father has deceived me and changed my wages ten times, but God did not allow him to hurt me. [8]If he said thus: 'The speckled shall be your wages,' then all the flocks bore speckled. And if he said thus: 'The streaked shall be your

30:18 [a]Literally *Wages*   **30:20** [a]Literally *Dwelling*   **30:24** [a]Literally *He Will Add*

wages', then all the flocks bore streaked. ⁹So God has taken away the livestock of your father and given *them* to me.

¹⁰"And it happened, at the time when the flocks conceived, that I lifted my eyes and saw in a dream, and behold, the rams which leaped upon the flocks *were* streaked, speckled, and gray-spotted. ¹¹Then the Angel of God spoke to me in a dream, saying, 'Jacob'. And I said, 'Here I am'. ¹²And He said, 'Lift your eyes now and see, all the rams which leap on the flocks *are* streaked, speckled, and gray-spotted; for I have seen all that Laban is doing to you. ¹³I *am* the God of Bethel, where you anointed the pillar *and* where you made a vow to Me. Now arise, get out of this land, and return to the land of your family.' "

¹⁴Then Rachel and Leah answered and said to him, "Is there still any portion or inheritance for us in our father's house? ¹⁵Are we not considered strangers by him? For he has sold us, and also completely consumed our money. ¹⁶For all these riches which God has taken from our father are *really* ours and our children's; now then, whatever God has said to you, do it."

¹⁷Then Jacob rose and set his sons and his wives on camels. ¹⁸And he carried away all his livestock and all his possessions which he had gained, his acquired livestock which he had gained in Padan Aram, to go to his father Isaac in the land of Canaan. ¹⁹Now Laban had gone to shear his sheep, and Rachel had stolen the household idols that were her father's. ²⁰And Jacob stole away, unknown to Laban the Syrian, in that he did not tell him that he intended to flee. ²¹So he fled with all that he had. He arose and crossed the river, and headed toward the mountains of Gilead.

LABAN PURSUES JACOB

²²And Laban was told on the third day that Jacob had fled. ²³Then he took his brethren with him and pursued him for seven days' journey, and he overtook him in the mountains of Gilead. ²⁴But God had come to Laban the Syrian in a dream by night, and said to him, "Be careful that you speak to Jacob neither good nor bad."

²⁵So Laban overtook Jacob. Now Jacob had pitched his tent in the mountains, and Laban with his brethren pitched in the mountains of Gilead.

²⁶And Laban said to Jacob: "What have you done, that you have stolen away unknown to me, and carried away my daughters like cap-tives *taken* with the sword? ²⁷Why did you flee away secretly, and steal away from me, and not tell me; for I might have sent you away with joy and songs, with timbrel and harp? ²⁸And you did not allow me to kiss my sons and my daughters. Now you have done foolishly in *so* doing. ²⁹It is in my power to do you harm, but the God of your father spoke to me last night, saying, 'Be careful that you speak to Jacob neither good nor bad.' ³⁰And now you have surely gone because you greatly long for your father's house, *but* why did you steal my gods?"

³¹Then Jacob answered and said to Laban, "Because I was afraid, for I said, 'Perhaps you would take your daughters from me by force.' ³²With whomever you find your gods, do not let him live. In the presence of our brethren, identify what I have of yours and take *it* with you." For Jacob did not know that Rachel had stolen them.

³³And Laban went into Jacob's tent, into Leah's tent, and into the two maids' tents, but he did not find *them*. Then he went out of Leah's tent and entered Rachel's tent. ³⁴Now Rachel had taken the household idols, put them in the camel's saddle, and sat on them. And Laban searched all about the tent but did not find *them*. ³⁵And she said to her father, "Let it not displease my lord that I cannot rise before you, for the manner of women *is* with me." And he searched but did not find the household idols.

³⁶Then Jacob was angry and rebuked Laban, and Jacob answered and said to Laban: "What *is* my trespass? What *is* my sin, that you have so hotly pursued me? ³⁷Although you have searched all my things, what part of your household things have you found? Set *it* here before my brethren and your brethren, that they may judge between us both! ³⁸These twenty years I *have been* with you; your ewes and your female goats have not miscarried their young, and I have not eaten the rams of your flock. ³⁹That which was torn *by beasts* I did not bring to you; I bore the loss of it. You required it from my hand, *whether* stolen by day or stolen by night. ⁴⁰*There* I was! In the day the drought consumed me, and the frost by night, and my sleep departed from my eyes. ⁴¹Thus I have been in your house twenty years; I served you fourteen years for your two daughters, and six years for your flock, and you have changed my wages ten times. ⁴²Unless the God of my father, the God of Abraham and the Fear of Isaac, had been with me, surely now you would have sent me away empty-handed. God has seen my affliction and the labor of my hands, and rebuked *you* last night."

LABAN'S COVENANT WITH JACOB

⁴³And Laban answered and said to Jacob, "*These* daughters *are* my daughters, and *these* children *are* my children, and *this* flock *is* my flock; all that you see *is* mine. But what can I do this day to these my daughters or to their children whom they have borne? ⁴⁴Now therefore, come, let us make a covenant, you and I, and let it be a witness between you and me."

⁴⁵So Jacob took a stone and set it up *as* a pillar. ⁴⁶Then Jacob said to his brethren, "Gather stones." And they took stones and made a heap, and they ate there on the heap. ⁴⁷Laban called it Jegar Sahadutha,*ª* but Jacob called it Galeed.*ᵇ* ⁴⁸And Laban said, "This heap *is* a witness between you and me this day." Therefore its name was called Galeed, ⁴⁹also Mizpah,*ª* because he said, "May the LORD watch between you and me when we are absent one from another. ⁵⁰If you afflict my daughters, or if you take *other* wives besides my daughters, *although* no man *is* with us—see, God *is* witness between you and me!"

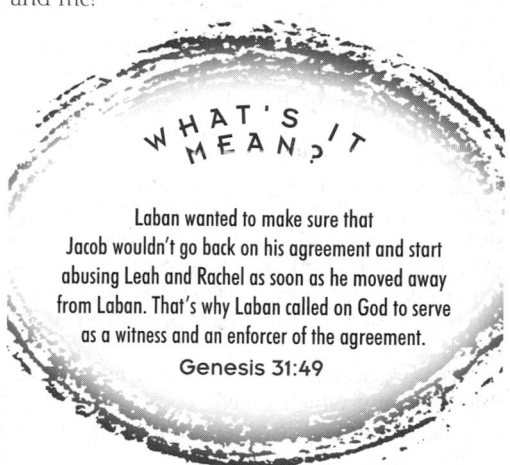

W H A T ' S
M E A N ?   **I T**

Laban wanted to make sure that Jacob wouldn't go back on his agreement and start abusing Leah and Rachel as soon as he moved away from Laban. That's why Laban called on God to serve as a witness and an enforcer of the agreement.

Genesis 31:49

⁵¹Then Laban said to Jacob, "Here is this heap and here is *this* pillar, which I have placed between you and me. ⁵²This heap *is* a witness, and *this* pillar *is* a witness, that I will not pass beyond this heap to you, and you will not pass beyond this heap and this pillar to me, for harm. ⁵³The God of Abraham, the God of Nahor, and the God of their father judge between us." And Jacob swore by the Fear of his father Isaac. ⁵⁴Then Jacob offered a sacrifice on the mountain, and called his brethren to eat bread. And they ate bread and stayed all night on the mountain. ⁵⁵And early in the morning Laban arose, and kissed his sons and daughters and blessed them. Then Laban departed and returned to his place.

ESAU COMES TO MEET JACOB

¹So Jacob went on his way, and the angels of God met him. ²When Jacob saw them, he said, "This *is* God's camp." And he called the name of that place Mahanaim.*ª*

³Then Jacob sent messengers before him to Esau his brother in the land of Seir, the country of Edom. ⁴And he commanded them, saying, "Speak thus to my lord Esau, 'Thus your servant Jacob says: "I have dwelt with Laban and stayed there until now. ⁵I have oxen, donkeys, flocks, and male and female servants; and I have sent to tell my lord, that I may find favor in your sight." ' "

⁶Then the messengers returned to Jacob, saying, "We came to your brother Esau, and he also is coming to meet you, and four hundred men *are* with him." ⁷So Jacob was greatly afraid and distressed; and he divided the people that *were* with him, and the flocks and herds and camels, into two companies. ⁸And he said, "If Esau comes to the one company and attacks it, then the other company which is left will escape."

⁹Then Jacob said, "O God of my father Abraham and God of my father Isaac, the LORD who said to me, 'Return to your country and to your family, and I will deal well with you': ¹⁰I am not worthy of the least of all the mercies and of all the truth which You have shown Your servant; for I crossed over this Jordan with my staff, and now I have become two companies. ¹¹Deliver me, I pray, from the hand of my brother, from the hand of Esau; for I fear him, lest he come and attack me *and* the mother with the children. ¹²For You said, 'I will surely treat you well, and make your descendants as the sand of the sea, which cannot be numbered for multitude.' "

¹³So he lodged there that same night, and took what came to his hand as a present for Esau his brother: ¹⁴two hundred female goats and twenty male goats, two hundred ewes and twenty rams, ¹⁵thirty milk camels with their colts, forty cows and ten bulls, twenty female donkeys and ten foals. ¹⁶Then he delivered *them* to the hand of his servants, every drove by itself, and said to his servants, "Pass over before me, and put some distance between successive droves." ¹⁷And he commanded the first one,

ANGELS

Do angels work among people? (32:1)

31:47 *ª*Literally, in Aramaic, *Heap of Witness* *ᵇ*Literally, in Hebrew, *Heap of Witness*   **31:49** *ª*Literally *Watch*   **32:2** *ª*Literally *Double Camp*

saying, "When Esau my brother meets you and asks you, saying, 'To whom do you belong, and where are you going? Whose *are* these in front of you?' ¹⁸then you shall say, 'They *are* your servant Jacob's. It *is* a present sent to my lord Esau; and behold, he also *is* behind us.' " ¹⁹So he commanded the second, the third, and all who followed the droves, saying, "In this manner you shall speak to Esau when you find him; ²⁰and also say, 'Behold, your servant Jacob *is* behind us.' " For he said, "I will appease him with the present that goes before me, and afterward I will see his face; perhaps he will accept me." ²¹So the present went on over before him, but he himself lodged that night in the camp.

WRESTLING WITH GOD

²²And he arose that night and took his two wives, his two female servants, and his eleven sons, and crossed over the ford of Jabbok. ²³He took them, sent them over the brook, and sent over what he had. ²⁴Then Jacob was left alone; and a Man wrestled with him until the breaking of day. ²⁵Now when He saw that He did not prevail against him, He touched the socket of his hip; and the socket of Jacob's hip was out of joint as He wrestled with him. ²⁶And He said, "Let Me go, for the day breaks."

But he said, "I will not let You go unless You bless me!"

²⁷So He said to him, "What *is* your name?"

He said, "Jacob."

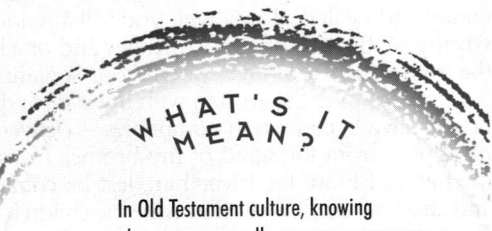

WHAT'S IT MEAN?

In Old Testament culture, knowing someone's name supposedly gave you power over that person. Being able to rename that person gave you even more power. With this in mind, notice how Jacob answers immediately when he's asked his name. Notice also how Jacob's opponent doesn't feel the need to reveal His name.

Genesis 32:27–29

²⁸And He said, "Your name shall no longer be called Jacob, but Israel;ᵃ for you have struggled with God and with men, and have prevailed."

²⁹Then Jacob asked, saying, "Tell *me* Your name, I pray."

And He said, "Why *is* it *that* you ask about My name?" And He blessed him there.

³⁰So Jacob called the name of the place Peniel:ᵃ "For I have seen God face to face, and my life is preserved." ³¹Just as he crossed over Penuelᵃ the sun rose on him, and he limped on his hip. ³²Therefore to this day the children of Israel do not eat the muscle that shrank, which *is* on the hip socket, because He touched the socket of Jacob's hip in the muscle that shrank.

JACOB AND ESAU MEET

¹Now Jacob lifted his eyes and looked, and there, Esau was coming, and with him were four hundred men. So he divided the children among Leah, Rachel, and the two maidservants. ²And he put the maidservants and their children in front, Leah and her children behind, and Rachel and Joseph last. ³Then he crossed over before them and bowed himself to the ground seven times, until he came near to his brother.

⁴But Esau ran to meet him, and embraced him, and fell on his neck and kissed him, and they wept. ⁵And he lifted his eyes and saw the women and children, and said, "Who *are* these with you?"

So he said, "The children whom God has graciously given your servant." ⁶Then the maidservants came near, they and their children, and bowed down. ⁷And Leah also came near with her children, and they bowed down. Afterward Joseph and Rachel came near, and they bowed down.

⁸Then Esau said, "What *do* you *mean by* all this company which I met?"

And he said, "*These are* to find favor in the sight of my lord."

⁹But Esau said, "I have enough, my brother; keep what you have for yourself."

¹⁰And Jacob said, "No, please, if I have now found favor in your sight, then receive my present from my hand, inasmuch as I have seen your face as though I had seen the face of God, and you were pleased with me. ¹¹Please, take my blessing that is brought to you, because God has dealt graciously with me, and because I have enough." So he urged him, and he took *it*.

¹²Then Esau said, "Let us take our journey; let us go, and I will go before you."

¹³But Jacob said to him, "My lord knows that the children *are* weak, and the flocks and herds which are nursing *are* with me. And if the men

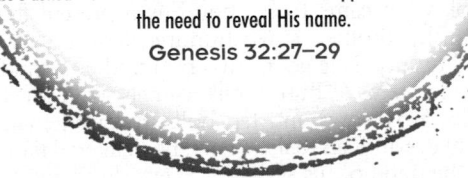

32:28 ᵃLiterally *Prince with God* **32:30** ᵃLiterally *Face of God* **32:31** ᵃSame as *Peniel*, verse 30

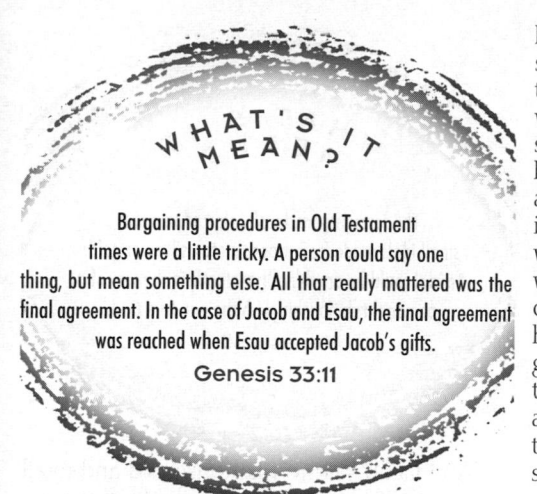

his daughter. Now his sons were with his livestock in the field; so Jacob held his peace until they came. ⁶Then Hamor the father of Shechem went out to Jacob to speak with him. ⁷And the sons of Jacob came in from the field when they heard *it;* and the men were grieved and very angry, because he had done a disgraceful thing in Israel by lying with Jacob's daughter, a thing which ought not to be done. ⁸But Hamor spoke with them, saying, "The soul of my son Shechem longs for your daughter. Please give her to him as a wife. ⁹And make marriages with us; give your daughters to us, and take our daughters to yourselves. ¹⁰So you shall dwell with us, and the land shall be before you. Dwell and trade in it, and acquire possessions for yourselves in it."

should drive them hard one day, all the flock will die. ¹⁴Please let my lord go on ahead before his servant. I will lead on slowly at a pace which the livestock that go before me, and the children, are able to endure, until I come to my lord in Seir."

¹⁵And Esau said, "Now let me leave with you *some* of the people who *are* with me."

But he said, "What need is there? Let me find favor in the sight of my lord." ¹⁶So Esau returned that day on his way to Seir. ¹⁷And Jacob journeyed to Succoth, built himself a house, and made booths for his livestock. Therefore the name of the place is called Succoth.ᵃ

JACOB COMES TO CANAAN

¹⁸Then Jacob came safely to the city of Shechem, which *is* in the land of Canaan, when he came from Padan Aram; and he pitched his tent before the city. ¹⁹And he bought the parcel of land, where he had pitched his tent, from the children of Hamor, Shechem's father, for one hundred pieces of money. ²⁰Then he erected an altar there and called it El Elohe Israel.ᵃ

THE DINAH INCIDENT

¹Now Dinah the daughter of Leah, whom she had borne to Jacob, went out to see the daughters of the land. ²And when Shechem the son of Hamor the Hivite, prince of the country, saw her, he took her and lay with her, and violated her. ³His soul was strongly attracted to Dinah the daughter of Jacob, and he loved the young woman and spoke kindly to the young woman. ⁴So Shechem spoke to his father Hamor, saying, "Get me this young woman as a wife."

⁵And Jacob heard that he had defiled Dinah

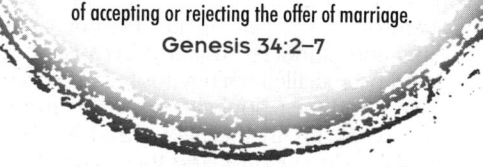

¹¹Then Shechem said to her father and her brothers, "Let me find favor in your eyes, and whatever you say to me I will give. ¹²Ask me ever so much dowry and gift, and I will give according to what you say to me; but give me the young woman as a wife."

¹³But the sons of Jacob answered Shechem and Hamor his father, and spoke deceitfully, because he had defiled Dinah their sister. ¹⁴And they said to them, "We cannot do this thing, to give our sister to one who is uncircumcised, for that *would be* a reproach to us. ¹⁵But on this *condition* we will consent to you: If you will become as we *are,* if every male of you is circumcised, ¹⁶then we will give our daughters to you, and we will take your daughters to us; and we will dwell with you, and we will become one

---

33:17 ᵃLiterally *Booths*   **33:20** ᵃLiterally *God, the God of Israel*

people. ¹⁷But if you will not heed us and be circumcised, then we will take our daughter and be gone."

¹⁸And their words pleased Hamor and Shechem, Hamor's son. ¹⁹So the young man did not delay to do the thing, because he delighted in Jacob's daughter. He *was* more honorable than all the household of his father.

²⁰And Hamor and Shechem his son came to the gate of their city, and spoke with the men of their city, saying: ²¹"These men *are* at peace with us. Therefore let them dwell in the land and trade in it. For indeed the land *is* large enough for them. Let us take their daughters to us as wives, and let us give them our daughters. ²²Only on this *condition* will the men consent to dwell with us, to be one people: if every male among us is circumcised as they *are* circumcised. ²³*Will* not their livestock, their property, and every animal of theirs *be* ours? Only let us consent to them, and they will dwell with us." ²⁴And all who went out of the gate of his city heeded Hamor and Shechem his son; every male was circumcised, all who went out of the gate of his city.

²⁵Now it came to pass on the third day, when they were in pain, that two of the sons of Jacob, Simeon and Levi, Dinah's brothers, each took his sword and came boldly upon the city and killed all the males. ²⁶And they killed Hamor and Shechem his son with the edge of the sword, and took Dinah from Shechem's house, and went out. ²⁷The sons of Jacob came upon the slain, and plundered the city, because their sister had been defiled. ²⁸They took their sheep, their oxen, and their donkeys, what *was* in the city and what *was* in the field, ²⁹and all their wealth. All their little ones and their wives they took captive; and they plundered even all that *was* in the houses.

³⁰Then Jacob said to Simeon and Levi, "You have troubled me by making me obnoxious among the inhabitants of the land, among the Canaanites and the Perizzites; and since I *am* few in number, they will gather themselves together against me and kill me. I shall be destroyed, my household and I."

³¹But they said, "Should he treat our sister like a harlot?"

JACOB'S RETURN TO BETHEL

¹Then God said to Jacob, "Arise, go up to Bethel and dwell there; and make an altar there to God, who appeared to you when you fled from the face of Esau your brother."

WHAT'S IT MEAN?

The foreign gods Jacob referred to were small idols made from wood, metal, silver, or gold. An idol could be anything that stands in the way of a personal relationship with the one true God.

Genesis 35:2

²And Jacob said to his household and to all who *were* with him, "Put away the foreign gods that *are* among you, purify yourselves, and change your garments. ³Then let us arise and go up to Bethel; and I will make an altar there to God, who answered me in the day of my distress and has been with me in the way which I have gone." ⁴So they gave Jacob all the foreign gods which *were* in their hands, and the earrings which *were* in their ears; and Jacob hid them under the terebinth tree which *was* by Shechem.

⁵And they journeyed, and the terror of God was upon the cities that *were* all around them, and they did not pursue the sons of Jacob. ⁶So Jacob came to Luz (that *is*, Bethel), which *is* in the land of Canaan, he and all the people who *were* with him. ⁷And he built an altar there and called the place El Bethel,ª because there God appeared to him when he fled from the face of his brother.

⁸Now Deborah, Rebekah's nurse, died, and she was buried below Bethel under the terebinth tree. So the name of it was called Allon Bachuth.ª

⁹Then God appeared to Jacob again, when he came from Padan Aram, and blessed him. ¹⁰And God said to him, "Your name *is* Jacob; your name shall not be called Jacob anymore, but Israel shall be your name." So He called his name Israel. ¹¹Also God said to him: "I *am* God Almighty. Be fruitful and multiply; a nation and a company of nations shall proceed from you, and kings shall come from your body. ¹²The land which I gave Abraham and Isaac I give to you; and to your descendants after you I give this land." ¹³Then God went up from him in the place where He talked with him. ¹⁴So Jacob set up a pillar in the place where He talked with him, a pillar of stone; and he poured a drink

35:7 ªLiterally *God of the House of God*   **35:8** ªLiterally *Terebinth of Weeping*

offering on it, and he poured oil on it. ¹⁵And Jacob called the name of the place where God spoke with him, Bethel.

DEATH OF RACHEL

¹⁶Then they journeyed from Bethel. And when there was but a little distance to go to Ephrath, Rachel labored *in childbirth,* and she had hard labor. ¹⁷Now it came to pass, when she was in hard labor, that the midwife said to her, "Do not fear; you will have this son also." ¹⁸And so it was, as her soul was departing (for she died), that she called his name Ben-Oni;ᵃ but his father called him Benjamin.ᵇ ¹⁹So Rachel died and was buried on the way to Ephrath (that *is,* Bethlehem). ²⁰And Jacob set a pillar on her grave, which *is* the pillar of Rachel's grave to this day.

²¹Then Israel journeyed and pitched his tent beyond the tower of Eder. ²²And it happened, when Israel dwelt in that land, that Reuben went and lay with Bilhah his father's concubine; and Israel heard *about it.*

JACOB'S TWELVE SONS

Now the sons of Jacob were twelve: ²³the sons of Leah *were* Reuben, Jacob's firstborn, and Simeon, Levi, Judah, Issachar, and Zebulun; ²⁴the sons of Rachel *were* Joseph and Benjamin; ²⁵the sons of Bilhah, Rachel's maidservant, *were* Dan and Naphtali; ²⁶and the sons of Zilpah, Leah's maidservant, *were* Gad and Asher. These *were* the sons of Jacob who were born to him in Padan Aram.

DEATH OF ISAAC

²⁷Then Jacob came to his father Isaac at Mamre, or Kirjath Arbaᵃ (that *is,* Hebron), where Abraham and Isaac had dwelt. ²⁸Now the days of Isaac were one hundred and eighty years. ²⁹So Isaac breathed his last and died, and was gathered to his people, *being* old and full of days. And his sons Esau and Jacob buried him.

THE FAMILY OF ESAU

¹Now this *is* the genealogy of Esau, who is Edom. ²Esau took his wives from the daughters of Canaan: Adah the daughter of Elon the Hittite; Aholibamah the daughter of Anah, the daughter of Zibeon the Hivite; ³and Basemath, Ishmael's daughter, sister of Nebajoth. ⁴Now Adah bore Eliphaz to Esau, and Basemath bore Reuel. ⁵And Aholibamah bore Jeush, Jaalam,

and Korah. These *were* the sons of Esau who were born to him in the land of Canaan.

⁶Then Esau took his wives, his sons, his daughters, and all the persons of his household, his cattle and all his animals, and all his goods which he had gained in the land of Canaan, and went to a country away from the presence of his brother Jacob. ⁷For their possessions were too great for them to dwell together, and the land where they were strangers could not support them because of their livestock. ⁸So Esau dwelt in Mount Seir. Esau *is* Edom.

WHAT'S IT MEAN?

The land of Seir included the area from the Dead Sea to the Red Sea. Because Seir was located so close to Canaan, there were often military and political skirmishes between the people of the two regions.
Genesis 36:8

⁹And this *is* the genealogy of Esau the father of the Edomites in Mount Seir. ¹⁰These *were* the names of Esau's sons: Eliphaz the son of Adah the wife of Esau, and Reuel the son of Basemath the wife of Esau. ¹¹And the sons of Eliphaz were Teman, Omar, Zepho,ᵃ Gatam, and Kenaz. ¹²Now Timna was the concubine of Eliphaz, Esau's son, and she bore Amalek to Eliphaz. These *were* the sons of Adah, Esau's wife. ¹³These *were* the sons of Reuel: Nahath, Zerah, Shammah, and Mizzah. These were the sons of Basemath, Esau's wife. ¹⁴These were the sons of Aholibamah, Esau's wife, the daughter of Anah, the daughter of Zibeon. And she bore to Esau: Jeush, Jaalam, and Korah.

THE CHIEFS OF EDOM

¹⁵These *were* the chiefs of the sons of Esau. The sons of Eliphaz, the firstborn *son* of Esau, were Chief Teman, Chief Omar, Chief Zepho, Chief Kenaz, ¹⁶Chief Korah,ᵃ Chief Gatam, *and* Chief Amalek. These *were* the chiefs of Eliphaz in the land of Edom. They *were* the sons of Adah. ¹⁷These *were* the sons of Reuel, Esau's son:

Chief Nahath, Chief Zerah, Chief Shammah, and Chief Mizzah. These *were* the chiefs of Reuel in the land of Edom. These *were* the sons of Basemath, Esau's wife.

18And these *were* the sons of Aholibamah, Esau's wife: Chief Jeush, Chief Jaalam, and Chief Korah. These *were* the chiefs *who descended* from Aholibamah, Esau's wife, the daughter of Anah. 19These *were* the sons of Esau, who is Edom, and these *were* their chiefs.

THE SONS OF SEIR

20These *were* the sons of Seir the Horite who inhabited the land: Lotan, Shobal, Zibeon, Anah, 21Dishon, Ezer, and Dishan. These *were* the chiefs of the Horites, the sons of Seir, in the land of Edom.

22And the sons of Lotan were Hori and Hemam.*a* Lotan's sister *was* Timna.

23These *were* the sons of Shobal: Alvan,*a* Manahath, Ebal, Shepho,*b* and Onam.

24These *were* the sons of Zibeon: both Ajah and Anah. This *was the* Anah who found the water*a* in the wilderness as he pastured the donkeys of his father Zibeon. 25These *were* the children of Anah: Dishon and Aholibamah the daughter of Anah.

26These *were* the sons of Dishon:*a* Hemdan,*b* Eshban, Ithran, and Cheran. 27These *were* the sons of Ezer: Bilhan, Zaavan, and Akan.*a* 28These *were* the sons of Dishan: Uz and Aran.

29These *were* the chiefs of the Horites: Chief Lotan, Chief Shobal, Chief Zibeon, Chief Anah, 30Chief Dishon, Chief Ezer, and Chief Dishan. These *were* the chiefs of the Horites, according to their chiefs in the land of Seir.

THE KINGS OF EDOM

31Now these *were* the kings who reigned in the land of Edom before any king reigned over the children of Israel: 32Bela the son of Beor reigned in Edom, and the name of his city *was* Dinhabah. 33And when Bela died, Jobab the son of Zerah of Bozrah reigned in his place. 34When Jobab died, Husham of the land of the Temanites reigned in his place. 35And when Husham died, Hadad the son of Bedad, who attacked Midian in the field of Moab, reigned in his place. And the name of his city *was* Avith. 36When Hadad died, Samlah of Masrekah reigned in his place. 37And when Samlah died, Saul of Rehoboth-*by*-the-River reigned in his place. 38When Saul died, Baal-Hanan the son of Achbor reigned in his place. 39And when Baal-Hanan the son of Achbor died, Hadar*a* reigned in his place; and the name of his city *was* Pau.*b* His wife's name *was* Mehetabel, the daughter of Matred, the daughter of Mezahab.

THE CHIEFS OF ESAU

40And these *were* the names of the chiefs of Esau, according to their families and their places, by their names: Chief Timnah, Chief Alvah,*a* Chief Jetheth, 41Chief Aholibamah, Chief Elah, Chief Pinon, 42Chief Kenaz, Chief Teman, Chief Mibzar, 43Chief Magdiel, and Chief Iram. These *were* the chiefs of Edom, according to their dwelling places in the land of their possession. Esau *was* the father of the Edomites.

JOSEPH DREAMS OF GREATNESS

1Now Jacob dwelt in the land where his father was a stranger, in the land of Canaan. 2This *is* the history of Jacob.

Joseph, *being* seventeen years old, was feeding the flock with his brothers. And the lad *was* with the sons of Bilhah and the sons of Zilpah, his father's wives; and Joseph brought a bad report of them to his father.

3Now Israel loved Joseph more than all his children, because he *was* the son of his old age. Also he made him a tunic of *many* colors. 4But when his brothers saw that their father loved him more than all his brothers, they hated him and could not speak peaceably to him.

5Now Joseph had a dream, and he told *it* to his brothers; and they hated him even more. 6So he said to them, "Please hear this dream which I have dreamed: 7There we were, binding sheaves in the field. Then behold, my sheaf arose and also stood upright; and indeed your sheaves stood all around and bowed down to my sheaf."

> "Behold, my sheaf arose and also stood upright; and indeed your sheaves stood all around and bowed down to my sheaf."
> (Genesis 37:7b)

36:22 *a*Spelled *Homam* in 1 Chronicles 1:39   **36:23** *a*Spelled *Alian* in 1 Chronicles 1:40 *b*Spelled *Shephi* in 1 Chronicles 1:40   **36:24** *a*Following Masoretic Text and Vulgate (*hot springs*); Septuagint reads *Jamin*; Targum reads *mighty men*; Talmud interprets as *mules*.   **36:26** *a*Hebrew *Dishan* *b*Spelled *Hamran* in 1 Chronicles 1:41 **36:27** *a*Spelled *Jaakan* in 1 Chronicles 1:42   **36:39** *a*Spelled *Hadad* in Samaritan Pentateuch, Syriac, and 1 Chronicles 1:50 *b*Spelled *Pai* in 1 Chronicles 1:50   **36:40** *a*Spelled *Aliah* in 1 Chronicles 1:51

⁸And his brothers said to him, "Shall you indeed reign over us? Or shall you indeed have dominion over us?" So they hated him even more for his dreams and for his words.

⁹Then he dreamed still another dream and told it to his brothers, and said, "Look, I have dreamed another dream. And this time, the sun, the moon, and the eleven stars bowed down to me."

¹⁰So he told it to his father and his brothers; and his father rebuked him and said to him, "What is this dream that you have dreamed? Shall your mother and I and your brothers indeed come to bow down to the earth before you?" ¹¹And his brothers envied him, but his father kept the matter in mind.

JOSEPH SOLD BY HIS BROTHERS

¹²Then his brothers went to feed their father's flock in Shechem. ¹³And Israel said to Joseph, "Are not your brothers feeding the flock in Shechem? Come, I will send you to them."

So he said to him, "Here I am."

¹⁴Then he said to him, "Please go and see if it is well with your brothers and well with the flocks, and bring back word to me." So he sent him out of the Valley of Hebron, and he went to Shechem.

¹⁵Now a certain man found him, and there he was, wandering in the field. And the man asked him, saying, "What are you seeking?"

¹⁶So he said, "I am seeking my brothers. Please tell me where they are feeding their flocks."

WHAT'S IT MEAN?

If you're looking for Dothan on a modern map, try Tell Dotha. That's what it's called now. The land was located about fifteen miles north of Shechem, halfway between the Jordan River and the Mediterranean Sea.
Genesis 37:17

¹⁷And the man said, "They have departed from here, for I heard them say, 'Let us go to Dothan.'" So Joseph went after his brothers and found them in Dothan.

¹⁸Now when they saw him afar off, even before he came near them, they conspired against him to kill him. ¹⁹Then they said to one another, "Look, this dreamer is coming! ²⁰Come therefore, let us now kill him and cast him into some pit; and we shall say, 'Some wild beast has devoured him.' We shall see what will become of his dreams!"

²¹But Reuben heard it, and he delivered him out of their hands, and said, "Let us not kill him." ²²And Reuben said to them, "Shed no blood, but cast him into this pit which is in the wilderness, and do not lay a hand on him"—that he might deliver him out of their hands, and bring him back to his father.

²³So it came to pass, when Joseph had come to his brothers, that they stripped Joseph of his tunic, the tunic of many colors that was on him. ²⁴Then they took him and cast him into a pit. And the pit was empty; there was no water in it.

²⁵And they sat down to eat a meal. Then they lifted their eyes and looked, and there was a company of Ishmaelites, coming from Gilead with their camels, bearing spices, balm, and myrrh, on their way to carry them down to Egypt. ²⁶So Judah said to his brothers, "What profit is there if we kill our brother and conceal his blood? ²⁷Come and let us sell him to the Ishmaelites, and let not our hand be upon him, for he is our brother and our flesh." And his brothers listened. ²⁸Then Midianite traders passed by; so the brothers pulled Joseph up and lifted him out of the pit, and sold him to the Ishmaelites for twenty shekels of silver. And they took Joseph to Egypt.

²⁹Then Reuben returned to the pit, and indeed Joseph was not in the pit; and he tore his clothes. ³⁰And he returned to his brothers and said, "The lad is no more; and I, where shall I go?"

³¹So they took Joseph's tunic, killed a kid of the goats, and dipped the tunic in the blood. ³²Then they sent the tunic of many colors, and they brought it to their father and said, "We have found this. Do you know whether it is your son's tunic or not?"

³³And he recognized it and said, "It is my son's tunic. A wild beast has devoured him. Without doubt Joseph is torn to pieces." ³⁴Then Jacob tore his clothes, put sackcloth on his waist, and mourned for his son many days. ³⁵And all his sons and all his daughters arose to comfort him; but he refused to be comforted, and he said, "For I shall go down into the grave to my son in mourning." Thus his father wept for him.

³⁶Now the Midianites[a] had sold him in Egypt to Potiphar, an officer of Pharaoh *and* captain of the guard.

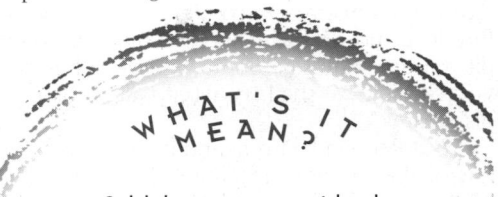

WHAT'S IT MEAN?

Sackcloth was a coarse material made from camel or goat hair. Because no one would wear such an uncomfortable cloth under normal conditions, it was an obvious sign of mourning. If you saw someone wearing sackcloth, you knew that someone had died or that something bad had happened.

Genesis 37:34

JUDAH AND TAMAR

¹It came to pass at that time that Judah departed from his brothers, and visited a certain Adullamite whose name *was* Hirah. ²And Judah saw there a daughter of a certain Canaanite whose name *was* Shua, and he married her and went in to her. ³So she conceived and bore a son, and he called his name Er. ⁴She conceived again and bore a son, and she called his name Onan. ⁵And she conceived yet again and bore a son, and called his name Shelah. He was at Chezib when she bore him.

WHAT'S IT MEAN?

If a man died before having children, it was his brother's personal responsibility to make sure that his widow would have a child. In other words, siblings were required to marry their own ex-sisters-in-law! The good news is that it helped continue the family bloodline. A child born of such a union was counted as a member of the family of the woman and her first husband.

Genesis 38:8

⁶Then Judah took a wife for Er his firstborn, and her name *was* Tamar. ⁷But Er, Judah's firstborn, was wicked in the sight of the LORD, and

the LORD killed him. ⁸And Judah said to Onan, "Go in to your brother's wife and marry her, and raise up an heir to your brother." ⁹But Onan knew that the heir would not be his; and it came to pass, when he went in to his brother's wife, that he emitted on the ground, lest he should give an heir to his brother. ¹⁰And the thing which he did displeased the LORD; therefore He killed him also.

¹¹Then Judah said to Tamar his daughter-in-law, "Remain a widow in your father's house till my son Shelah is grown." For he said, "Lest he also die like his brothers." And Tamar went and dwelt in her father's house.

¹²Now in the process of time the daughter of Shua, Judah's wife, died; and Judah was comforted, and went up to his sheepshearers at Timnah, he and his friend Hirah the Adullamite. ¹³And it was told Tamar, saying, "Look, your father-in-law is going up to Timnah to shear his sheep." ¹⁴So she took off her widow's garments, covered *herself* with a veil and wrapped herself, and sat in an open place which *was* on the way to Timnah; for she saw that Shelah was grown, and she was not given to him as a wife. ¹⁵When Judah saw her, he thought she *was* a harlot, because she had covered her face. ¹⁶Then he turned to her by the way, and said, "Please let me come in to you"; for he did not know that she *was* his daughter-in-law.

So she said, "What will you give me, that you may come in to me?"

¹⁷And he said, "I will send a young goat from the flock."

So she said, "Will you give *me* a pledge till you send *it*?"

¹⁸Then he said, "What pledge shall I give you?"

So she said, "Your signet and cord, and your staff that *is* in your hand." Then he gave *them* to her, and went in to her, and she conceived by him. ¹⁹So she arose and went away, and laid aside her veil and put on the garments of her widowhood.

²⁰And Judah sent the young goat by the hand of his friend the Adullamite, to receive *his* pledge from the woman's hand, but he did not find her. ²¹Then he asked the men of that place, saying, "Where is the harlot who *was* openly by the roadside?"

And they said, "There was no harlot in this *place*."

²²So he returned to Judah and said, "I cannot find her. Also, the men of the place said there was no harlot in this *place*."

37:36 [a]Masoretic Text reads *Medanites*.

²³Then Judah said, "Let her take *them* for herself, lest we be shamed; for I sent this young goat and you have not found her."

²⁴And it came to pass, about three months after, that Judah was told, saying, "Tamar your daughter-in-law has played the harlot; furthermore she *is* with child by harlotry."

WHAT'S IT MEAN?

Judah's signet, or ring, had a unique design carved into it. No other ring was quite like it. It was like personalized stationery. If you received a document with Judah's ring design pressed into it, you knew it came from Judah.

Genesis 38:18

So Judah said, "Bring her out and let her be burned!"

²⁵When she *was* brought out, she sent to her father-in-law, saying, "By the man to whom these belong, I *am* with child." And she said, "Please determine whose these *are*—the signet and cord, and staff."

²⁶So Judah acknowledged *them* and said, "She has been more righteous than I, because I did not give her to Shelah my son." And he never knew her again.

²⁷Now it came to pass, at the time for giving birth, that behold, twins *were* in her womb. ²⁸And so it was, when she was giving birth, that *the one* put out *his* hand; and the midwife took a scarlet *thread* and bound it on his hand, saying, "This one came out first." ²⁹Then it happened, as he drew back his hand, that his brother came out unexpectedly; and she said, "How did you break through? *This* breach *be* upon you!" Therefore his name was called Perez.ᵃ ³⁰Afterward his brother came out who had the scarlet *thread* on his hand. And his name was called Zerah.

JOSEPH A SLAVE IN EGYPT

¹Now Joseph had been taken down to Egypt. And Potiphar, an officer of Pharaoh, captain of the guard, an Egyptian, bought him from the Ishmaelites who had taken him down there. ²The LORD was with Joseph, and he was a successful man; and he was in the house of his master the Egyptian. ³And his master saw that the LORD *was* with him and that the LORD made all he did to prosper in his hand. ⁴So Joseph found favor in his sight, and served him. Then he made him overseer of his house, and all *that* he had he put under his authority. ⁵So it was, from the time *that* he had made him overseer of his house and all that he had, that the LORD blessed the Egyptian's house for Joseph's sake; and the blessing of the LORD was on all that he had in the house and in the field. ⁶Thus he left all that he had in Joseph's hand, and he did not know what he had except for the bread which he ate.

Now Joseph was handsome in form and appearance.

⁷And it came to pass after these things that his master's wife cast longing eyes on Joseph, and she said, "Lie with me."

⁸But he refused and said to his master's wife, "Look, my master does not know what *is* with me in the house, and he has committed all that he has to my hand. ⁹*There is* no one greater in this house than I, nor has he kept back anything from me but you, because you *are* his wife. How then can I do this great wickedness, and sin against God?"

¹⁰So it was, as she spoke to Joseph day by day, that he did not heed her, to lie with her *or* to be with her.

¹¹But it happened about this time, when Joseph went into the house to do his work, and none of the men of the house *was* inside, ¹²that she caught him by his garment, saying, "Lie with me." But he left his garment in her hand, and fled and ran outside. ¹³And so it was, when she saw that he had left his garment in her hand and fled outside, ¹⁴that she called to the men of her house and spoke to them, saying, "See, he has brought in to us a Hebrew to mock us. He came in to me to lie with me, and I cried out with a loud voice. ¹⁵And it happened, when he heard that I lifted my voice and cried out, that he left his garment with me, and fled and went outside."

¹⁶So she kept his garment with her until his master came home. ¹⁷Then she spoke to him with words like these, saying, "The Hebrew servant whom you brought to us came in to me to mock me; ¹⁸so it happened, as I lifted my voice and cried out, that he left his garment with me and fled outside."

¹⁹So it was, when his master heard the words which his wife spoke to him, saying,

38:29 ᵃLiterally *Breach* or *Breakthrough*

"Your servant did to me after this manner," that his anger was aroused. ²⁰Then Joseph's master took him and put him into the prison, a place where the king's prisoners *were* confined. And he was there in the prison. ²¹But the LORD was with Joseph and showed him mercy, and He gave him favor in the sight of the keeper of the prison. ²²And the keeper of the prison committed to Joseph's hand all the prisoners who *were* in the prison; whatever they did there, it was his doing. ²³The keeper of the prison did not look into anything *that was* under *Joseph's* authority,ᵃ because the LORD was with him; and whatever he did, the LORD made *it* prosper.

THE PRISONERS' DREAMS

¹It came to pass after these things *that* the butler and the baker of the king of Egypt offended their lord, the king of Egypt. ²And Pharaoh was angry with his two officers, the chief butler and the chief baker. ³So he put them in custody in the house of the captain of the guard, in the prison, the place where Joseph *was* confined. ⁴And the captain of the guard charged Joseph with them, and he served them; so they were in custody for a while.

⁵Then the butler and the baker of the king of Egypt, who *were* confined in the prison, had a dream, both of them, each man's dream in one night *and* each man's dream with its *own* interpretation. ⁶And Joseph came in to them in the morning and looked at them, and saw that they *were* sad. ⁷So he asked Pharaoh's officers who *were* with him in the custody of his lord's house, saying, "Why do you look *so* sad today?"

WHAT'S IT MEAN?

In biblical times, God often spoke to people through dreams. Rarely, though, were His messages obvious. Most of His dreams involved odd creatures and strange symbols, things that could only be explained by someone who knew God's plans.

Genesis 40:8

⁸And they said to him, "We each have had a dream, and *there is* no interpreter of it."

So Joseph said to them, "Do not interpre-

tations belong to God? Tell *them* to me, please."

⁹Then the chief butler told his dream to Joseph, and said to him, "Behold, in my dream a vine *was* before me, ¹⁰and in the vine *were* three branches; it *was* as though it budded, its blossoms shot forth, and its clusters brought forth ripe grapes. ¹¹Then Pharaoh's cup *was* in my hand; and I took the grapes and pressed them into Pharaoh's cup, and placed the cup in Pharaoh's hand."

¹²And Joseph said to him, "This *is* the interpretation of it: The three branches *are* three days. ¹³Now within three days Pharaoh will lift up your head and restore you to your place, and you will put Pharaoh's cup in his hand according to the former manner, when you were his butler. ¹⁴But remember me when it is well with you, and please show kindness to me; make mention of me to Pharaoh, and get me out of this house. ¹⁵For indeed I was stolen away from the land of the Hebrews; and also I have done nothing here that they should put me into the dungeon."

¹⁶When the chief baker saw that the interpretation was good, he said to Joseph, "I also *was* in my dream, and there *were* three white baskets on my head. ¹⁷In the uppermost basket *were* all kinds of baked goods for Pharaoh, and the birds ate them out of the basket on my head."

¹⁸So Joseph answered and said, "This *is* the interpretation of it: The three baskets *are* three days. ¹⁹Within three days Pharaoh will lift off your head from you and hang you on a tree; and the birds will eat your flesh from you."

²⁰Now it came to pass on the third day, *which was* Pharaoh's birthday, that he made a feast for all his servants; and he lifted up the head of the chief butler and of the chief baker among his servants. ²¹Then he restored the chief butler to his butlership again, and he placed the cup in Pharaoh's hand. ²²But he hanged the chief baker, as Joseph had interpreted to them. ²³Yet the chief butler did not remember Joseph, but forgot him.

PHARAOH'S DREAMS

¹Then it came to pass, at the end of two full years, that Pharaoh had a dream; and behold, he stood by the river. ²Suddenly there came up out of the river seven cows, fine looking and fat; and they fed in the meadow. ³Then behold, seven other cows came up after them out of the river, ugly and gaunt, and stood by the *other* cows on the bank of the river. ⁴And the ugly and gaunt cows ate up the seven fine looking

39:23 ᵃLiterally *his hand*

and fat cows. So Pharaoh awoke. ⁵He slept and dreamed a second time; and suddenly seven heads of grain came up on one stalk, plump and good. ⁶Then behold, seven thin heads, blighted by the east wind, sprang up after them. ⁷And the seven thin heads devoured the seven plump and full heads. So Pharaoh awoke, and indeed, *it was* a dream. ⁸Now it came to pass in the morning that his spirit was troubled, and he sent and called for all the magicians of Egypt and all its wise men. And Pharaoh told them his dreams, but *there was* no one who could interpret them for Pharaoh.

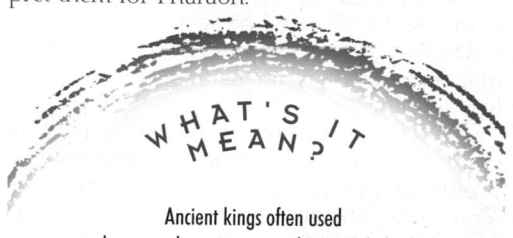

WHAT'S IT MEAN?

Ancient kings often used astrologers and magicians as advisors to help them make important decisions. Believe it or not, they tried to predict the future by "reading" the body parts of the animals they used for sacrifice. Can you imagine basing a major decision in your life on the way a sheep's liver looks?
Genesis 41:8

⁹Then the chief butler spoke to Pharaoh, saying: "I remember my faults this day. ¹⁰When Pharaoh was angry with his servants, and put me in custody in the house of the captain of the guard, *both* me and the chief baker, ¹¹we each had a dream in one night, he and I. Each of us dreamed according to the interpretation of his *own* dream. ¹²Now there *was* a young Hebrew man with us there, a servant of the captain of the guard. And we told him, and he interpreted our dreams for us; to each man he interpreted according to his *own* dream. ¹³And it came to pass, just as he interpreted for us, so it happened. He restored me to my office, and he hanged him."

¹⁴Then Pharaoh sent and called Joseph, and they brought him quickly out of the dungeon; and he shaved, changed his clothing, and came to Pharaoh. ¹⁵And Pharaoh said to Joseph, "I have had a dream, and *there is* no one who can interpret it. But I have heard it said of you *that* you can understand a dream, to interpret it."

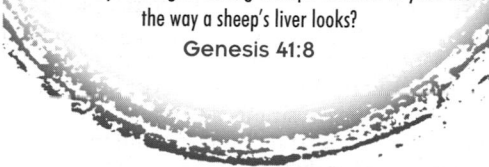

WISDOM
Where can I find wisdom? (41:16)

¹⁶So Joseph answered Pharaoh, saying, "*It is* not in me; God will give Pharaoh an answer of peace."

¹⁷Then Pharaoh said to Joseph: "Behold, in my dream I stood on the bank of the river. ¹⁸Suddenly seven cows came up out of the river, fine looking and fat; and they fed in the meadow. ¹⁹Then behold, seven other cows came up after them, poor and very ugly and gaunt, such ugliness as I have never seen in all the land of Egypt. ²⁰And the gaunt and ugly cows ate up the first seven, the fat cows. ²¹When they had eaten them up, no one would have known that they had eaten them, for they *were* just as ugly as at the beginning. So I awoke. ²²Also I saw in my dream, and suddenly seven heads came up on one stalk, full and good. ²³Then behold, seven heads, withered, thin, *and* blighted by the east wind, sprang up after them. ²⁴And the thin heads devoured the seven good heads. So I told *this* to the magicians, but *there* was no one who could explain *it* to me."

²⁵Then Joseph said to Pharaoh, "The dreams of Pharaoh *are* one; God has shown Pharaoh what He *is* about to do: ²⁶The seven good cows *are* seven years, and the seven good heads *are* seven years; the dreams *are* one. ²⁷And the seven thin and ugly cows which came up after them *are* seven years, and the seven empty heads blighted by the east wind are seven years of famine. ²⁸This *is* the thing which I have spoken to Pharaoh. God has shown Pharaoh what He *is* about to do. ²⁹Indeed seven years of great plenty will come throughout all the land of Egypt; ³⁰but after them seven years of famine will arise, and all the plenty will be forgotten in the land of Egypt; and the famine will deplete the land. ³¹So the plenty will not be known in the land because of the famine following, for it *will be* very severe. ³²And the dream was repeated to Pharaoh twice because the thing *is* established by God, and God will shortly bring it to pass.

³³"Now therefore, let Pharaoh select a discerning and wise man, and set him over the land of Egypt. ³⁴Let Pharaoh do *this*, and let him appoint officers over the land, to collect one-fifth *of the produce* of the land of Egypt in the seven plentiful years. ³⁵And let them gather all the food of those good years that are coming, and store up grain under the authority of Pharaoh, and let them keep food in the cities. ³⁶Then that food shall be as a reserve for the land for the seven years of famine which shall be in the land of Egypt, that the land may not perish during the famine."

JOSEPH'S RISE TO POWER

³⁷So the advice was good in the eyes of Pharaoh and in the eyes of all his servants.

³⁸And Pharaoh said to his servants, "Can we find *such a one* as this, a man in whom *is* the Spirit of God?"

³⁹Then Pharaoh said to Joseph, "Inasmuch as God has shown you all this, *there is* no one as discerning and wise as you. ⁴⁰You shall be over my house, and all my people shall be ruled according to your word; only in regard to the throne will I be greater than you." ⁴¹And Pharaoh said to Joseph, "See, I have set you over all the land of Egypt."

⁴²Then Pharaoh took his signet ring off his hand and put it on Joseph's hand; and he clothed him in garments of fine linen and put a gold chain around his neck. ⁴³And he had him ride in the second chariot which he had; and they cried out before him, "Bow the knee!" So he set him over all the land of Egypt. ⁴⁴Pharaoh also said to Joseph, "I *am* Pharaoh, and without your consent no man may lift his hand or foot in all the land of Egypt." ⁴⁵And Pharaoh called Joseph's name Zaphnath-Paaneah. And he gave him as a wife Asenath, the daughter of Poti-Pherah priest of On. So Joseph went out over *all* the land of Egypt.

⁴⁶Joseph was thirty years old when he stood before Pharaoh king of Egypt. And Joseph went out from the presence of Pharaoh, and went throughout all the land of Egypt. ⁴⁷Now in the seven plentiful years the ground brought forth abundantly. ⁴⁸So he gathered up all the food of the seven years which were in the land of Egypt, and laid up the food in the cities; he laid up in every city the food of the fields which surrounded them. ⁴⁹Joseph gathered very much grain, as the sand of the sea, until he stopped counting, for *it was* immeasurable.

⁵⁰And to Joseph were born two sons before the years of famine came, whom Asenath, the daughter of Poti-Pherah priest of On, bore to him. ⁵¹Joseph called the name of the firstborn Manasseh:ᵃ "For God has made me forget all my toil and all my father's house." ⁵²And the name of the second he called Ephraim:ᵃ "For God has caused me to be fruitful in the land of my affliction."

⁵³Then the seven years of plenty which were in the land of Egypt ended, ⁵⁴and the seven years of famine began to come, as Joseph had said. The famine was in all lands, but in all the land of Egypt there was bread. ⁵⁵So when all the land of Egypt was famished, the people cried to Pharaoh for bread. Then Pharaoh said to all the Egyptians, "Go to Joseph; whatever he says to you, do." ⁵⁶The famine was over all the face of the earth, and Joseph opened all the storehousesᵃ and sold to the Egyptians. And the famine became severe in the land of Egypt. ⁵⁷So all countries came to Joseph in Egypt to buy *grain*, because the famine was severe in all lands.

JOSEPH'S BROTHERS GO TO EGYPT

¹When Jacob saw that there was grain in Egypt, Jacob said to his sons, "Why do you look at one another?" ²And he said, "Indeed I have heard that there is grain in Egypt; go down to that place and buy for us there, that we may live and not die."

³So Joseph's ten brothers went down to buy grain in Egypt. ⁴But Jacob did not send Joseph's brother Benjamin with his brothers, for he said, "Lest some calamity befall him." ⁵And the sons of Israel went to buy *grain* among those who journeyed, for the famine was in the land of Canaan.

⁶Now Joseph *was* governor over the land; and it was he who sold to all the people of the land. And Joseph's brothers came and bowed down before him with *their* faces to the earth. ⁷Joseph saw his brothers and recognized them, but he acted as a stranger to them and spoke roughly to them. Then he said to them, "Where do you come from?"

And they said, "From the land of Canaan to buy food."

⁸So Joseph recognized his brothers, but they did not recognize him. ⁹Then Joseph remembered the dreams which he had dreamed about them, and said to them, "You *are* spies! You have come to see the nakedness of the land!"

¹⁰And they said to him, "No, my lord, but your servants have come to buy food. ¹¹We *are* all one man's sons; we *are* honest *men*; your servants are not spies."

¹²But he said to them, "No, but you have come to see the nakedness of the land."

¹³And they said, "Your servants *are* twelve brothers, the sons of one man in the land of Canaan; and in fact, the youngest *is* with our father today, and one *is* no more."

¹⁴But Joseph said to them, "It *is* as I spoke to

> "Can we find such a one as this, a man in whom is the Spirit of God?"
> (Genesis 41:38)

41:51 ᵃLiterally *Making Forgetful*   **41:52** ᵃLiterally *Fruitfulness*   **41:56** ᵃLiterally *all that was in them* you, saying, 'You *are* spies!' ¹⁵In this *manner* you shall be tested: By the life of Pharaoh, you shall not leave this place unless your youngest brother comes here. ¹⁶Send one of you, and let him bring your brother; and you shall be kept in prison, that your words may be tested to see whether *there is* any truth in you; or else, by the life of Pharaoh, surely you *are* spies!" ¹⁷So he put them all together in prison three days.

¹⁸Then Joseph said to them the third day, "Do this and live, *for* I fear God: ¹⁹If you *are* honest *men*, let one of your brothers be confined to your prison house; but you, go and carry grain for the famine of your houses. ²⁰And bring your youngest brother to me; so your words will be verified, and you shall not die."

And they did so. ²¹Then they said to one another, "We *are* truly guilty concerning our brother, for we saw the anguish of his soul when he pleaded with us, and we would not hear; therefore this distress has come upon us." ²²And Reuben answered them, saying, "Did I not speak to you, saying, 'Do not sin against the boy'; and you would not listen? Therefore behold, his blood is now required of us." ²³But they did not know that Joseph understood *them*, for he spoke to them through an interpreter. ²⁴And he turned himself away from them and wept. Then he returned to them again, and talked with them. And he took Simeon from them and bound him before their eyes.

THE BROTHERS RETURN TO CANAAN

²⁵Then Joseph gave a command to fill their sacks with grain, to restore every man's money to his sack, and to give them provisions for the journey. Thus he did for them. ²⁶So they loaded their donkeys with the grain and departed from there. ²⁷But as one *of them* opened his sack to give his donkey feed at the encampment, he saw his money; and there it was, in the mouth of his sack. ²⁸So he said to his brothers, "My money has been restored, and there it is, in my sack!" Then their hearts failed *them* and they were afraid, saying to one another, "What *is* this *that* God has done to us?"

²⁹Then they went to Jacob their father in the land of Canaan and told him all that had happened to them, saying: ³⁰"The man *who is* lord of the land spoke roughly to us, and took us for spies of the country. ³¹But we said to him, 'We *are* honest *men*; we are not spies. ³²We *are* twelve brothers, sons of our father; one *is* no *more,* and the youngest *is* with our father this day in the land of Canaan.' ³³Then the man, the lord of the country, said to us, 'By this I will know that you

are honest *men:* Leave one of your brothers *here* with me, take *food for* the famine of your households, and be gone. ³⁴And bring your youngest brother to me; so I shall know that you *are* not spies, but *that* you *are* honest *men.* I will grant your brother to you, and you may trade in the land.' "

³⁵Then it happened as they emptied their sacks, that surprisingly each man's bundle of money *was* in his sack; and when they and their father saw the bundles of money, they were afraid. ³⁶And Jacob their father said to them, "You have bereaved me: Joseph is no *more,* Simeon is no *more,* and you want to take Benjamin. All these things are against me."

³⁷Then Reuben spoke to his father, saying, "Kill my two sons if I do not bring him *back* to you; put him in my hands, and I will bring him back to you." ³⁸But he said, "My son shall not go down with you, for his brother is dead, and he is left alone. If any calamity should befall him along the way in which you go, then you would bring down my gray hair with sorrow to the grave."

JOSEPH'S BROTHERS RETURN WITH BENJAMIN

¹Now the famine *was* severe in the land. ²And it came to pass, when they had eaten up the grain which they had brought from Egypt, that their father said to them, "Go back, buy us a little food." ³But Judah spoke to him, saying, "The man solemnly warned us, saying, 'You shall not see my face unless your brother *is* with you.' ⁴If you send our brother with us, we will go down and buy you food. ⁵But if you will not send *him,* we will not go down; for the man said to us, 'You shall not see my face unless your brother *is* with you.' "

⁶And Israel said, "Why did you deal *so* wrongfully with me *as* to tell the man whether you had still *another* brother?"

⁷But they said, "The man asked us pointedly about ourselves and our family, saying, 'Is your father still alive? Have you *another* brother?' And we told him according to these words. Could we possibly have known that he would say, 'Bring your brother down'?"

⁸Then Judah said to Israel his father, "Send the lad with me, and we will arise and go, that we may live and not die, both we and you *and* also our little ones. ⁹I myself will be surety for him; from my hand you shall require him. If I do not bring him *back* to you and set him before you, then let me bear the blame forever. ¹⁰For if we had not lingered, surely by now we would have returned this second time."

¹¹And their father Israel said to them, "If *it must be* so, then do this: Take some of the best fruits of the land in your vessels and carry down a present for the man—a little balm and a little honey, spices and myrrh, pistachio nuts and almonds. ¹²Take double money in your hand, and take back in your hand the money that was returned in the mouth of your sacks; perhaps it was an oversight. ¹³Take your brother also, and arise, go back to the man. ¹⁴And may God Almighty give you mercy before the man, that he may release your other brother and Benjamin. If I am bereaved, I am bereaved!"

¹⁵So the men took that present and Benjamin, and they took double money in their hand, and arose and went down to Egypt; and they stood before Joseph. ¹⁶When Joseph saw Benjamin with them, he said to the steward of his house, "Take *these* men to my home, and slaughter an animal and make ready; for *these* men will dine with me at noon." ¹⁷Then the man did as Joseph ordered, and the man brought the men into Joseph's house.

¹⁸Now the men were afraid because they were brought into Joseph's house; and they said, "*It is* because of the money, which was returned in our sacks the first time, that we are brought in, so that he may make a case against us and seize us, to take us as slaves with our donkeys."

¹⁹When they drew near to the steward of Joseph's house, they talked with him at the door of the house, ²⁰and said, "O sir, we indeed came down the first time to buy food; ²¹but it happened, when we came to the encampment, that we opened our sacks, and there, *each* man's money *was* in the mouth of his sack, our money in full weight; so we have brought it back in our hand. ²²And we have brought down other money in our hands to buy food. We do not know who put our money in our sacks."

²³But he said, "Peace *be* with you, do not be afraid. Your God and the God of your father has given you treasure in your sacks; I had your money." Then he brought Simeon out to them.

²⁴So the man brought the men into Joseph's house and gave *them* water, and they washed their feet; and he gave their donkeys feed. ²⁵Then they made the present ready for Joseph's coming at noon, for they heard that they would eat bread there.

²⁶And when Joseph came home, they brought him the present which *was* in their hand into the house, and bowed down before him to the earth. ²⁷Then he asked them about their well-being, and said, "*Is* your father well, the old man of whom you spoke? *Is* he still alive?"

²⁸And they answered, "Your servant our father *is* in good health; he *is* still alive." And they bowed their heads down and prostrated themselves.

²⁹Then he lifted his eyes and saw his brother Benjamin, his mother's son, and said, "*Is* this your younger brother of whom you spoke to me?" And he said, "God be gracious to you, my son." ³⁰Now his heart yearned for his brother; so Joseph made haste and sought *somewhere* to weep. And he went into *his* chamber and wept there. ³¹Then he washed his face and came out; and he restrained himself, and said, "Serve the bread."

WHAT'S IT MEAN?

In biblical times, eating with another person was considered to be one of the highest forms of hospitality. The Egyptians, however, refused to eat at the same table as the Israelites because they saw the Israelites as a lower class of people. Notice that Joseph was following Egyptian custom by eating separately from his brothers. After all, his brothers still believed that he was an Egyptian.

Genesis 43:32

³²So they set him a place by himself, and them by themselves, and the Egyptians who ate with him by themselves; because the Egyptians could not eat food with the Hebrews, for that *is* an abomination to the Egyptians. ³³And they sat before him, the firstborn according to his birthright and the youngest according to his youth; and the men looked in astonishment at one another. ³⁴Then he took servings to them from before him, but Benjamin's serving was five times as much as any of theirs. So they drank and were merry with him.

JOSEPH'S CUP

¹And he commanded the steward of his house, saying, "Fill the men's sacks with food, as much as they can carry, and put each man's money in the mouth of his sack. ²Also put my cup, the silver cup, in the mouth of the sack of the youngest, and his grain money." So he did

according to the word that Joseph had spoken. [3]As soon as the morning dawned, the men were sent away, they and their donkeys. [4]When they had gone out of the city, *and* were not *yet* far off, Joseph said to his steward, "Get up, follow the men; and when you overtake them, say to them, 'Why have you repaid evil for good? [5]*Is* not this *the one* from which my lord drinks, and with which he indeed practices divination? You have done evil in so doing.'"

[6]So he overtook them, and he spoke to them these same words. [7]And they said to him, "Why does my lord say these words? Far be it from us that your servants should do such a thing. [8]Look, we brought back to you from the land of Canaan the money which we found in the mouth of our sacks. How then could we steal silver or gold from your lord's house? [9]With whomever of your servants it is found, let him die, and we also will be my lord's slaves."

[10]And he said, "Now also *let it be* according to your words; he with whom it is found shall be my slave, and you shall be blameless." [11]Then each man speedily let down his sack to the ground, and each opened his sack. [12]So he searched. He began with the oldest and left off with the youngest; and the cup was found in Benjamin's sack. [13]Then they tore their clothes, and each man loaded his donkey and returned to the city.

[14]So Judah and his brothers came to Joseph's house, and he *was* still there; and they fell before him on the ground. [15]And Joseph said to them, "What deed *is* this you have done? Did you not know that such a man as I can certainly practice divination?"

[16]Then Judah said, "What shall we say to my lord? What shall we speak? Or how shall we clear ourselves? God has found out the iniquity of your servants; here we are, my lord's slaves, both we and *he* also with whom the cup was found."

[17]But he said, "Far be it from me that I should do so; the man in whose hand the cup was found, he shall be my slave. And as for you, go up in peace to your father."

JUDAH INTERCEDES FOR BENJAMIN

[18]Then Judah came near to him and said: "O my lord, please let your servant speak a word in my lord's hearing, and do not let your anger burn against your servant; for you *are* even like Pharaoh. [19]My lord asked his servants, saying, 'Have you a father or a brother?' [20]And we said to my lord, 'We have a father, an old man, and a child of *his* old age, *who is* young; his brother is dead, and he alone is left of his mother's children, and his father loves him.' [21]Then you said to your servants, 'Bring him down to me, that I may set my eyes on him.' [22]And we said to my lord, 'The lad cannot leave his father, for *if* he should leave his father, *his father* would die.' [23]But you said to your servants, 'Unless your youngest brother comes down with you, you shall see my face no more.'

[24]"So it was, when we went up to your servant my father, that we told him the words of my lord. [25]And our father said, 'Go back *and* buy us a little food.' [26]But we said, 'We cannot go down; if our youngest brother is with us, then we will go down; for we may not see the man's face unless our youngest brother *is* with us.' [27]Then your servant my father said to us, 'You know that my wife bore me two sons; [28]and the one went out from me, and I said, "Surely he is torn to pieces"; and I have not seen him since. [29]But if you take this one also from me, and calamity befalls him, you shall bring down my gray hair with sorrow to the grave.'

[30]"Now therefore, when I come to your servant my father, and the lad *is* not with us, since his life is bound up in the lad's life, [31]it will happen, when he sees that the lad *is* not *with us*, that he will die. So your servants will bring down the gray hair of your servant our father with sorrow to the grave. [32]For your servant became surety for the lad to my father, saying, 'If I do not bring him *back* to you, then I shall bear the blame before my father forever.' [33]Now therefore, please let your servant remain instead of the lad as a slave to my lord, and let the lad go up with his brothers. [34]For how shall I go up to my father if the lad *is* not with me, lest perhaps I see the evil that would come upon my father?"

JOSEPH REVEALED TO HIS BROTHERS

[1]Then Joseph could not restrain himself before all those who stood by him, and he cried out, "Make everyone go out from me!" So no one stood with him while Joseph made himself known to his brothers. [2]And he wept aloud, and the Egyptians and the house of Pharaoh heard *it.*

[3]Then Joseph said to his brothers, "I *am* Joseph; does my father still live?" But his brothers could not answer him, for they were dismayed in his presence. [4]And Joseph said to his brothers, "Please come near to me." So they came near. Then he said: "I *am* Joseph your brother, whom you sold into Egypt. [5]But now, do not therefore be grieved or angry with yourselves because you sold me here; for God sent me before you to preserve life. [6]For these two years the famine

has been in the land, and there are still five years in which there will be neither plowing nor harvesting. ⁷And God sent me before you to preserve a posterity for you in the earth, and to save your lives by a great deliverance. ⁸So now it was not you who sent me here, but God; and He has made me a father to Pharaoh, and lord of all his house, and a ruler throughout all the land of Egypt.

⁹"Hurry and go up to my father, and say to him, 'Thus says your son Joseph: "God has made me lord of all Egypt; come down to me, do not tarry. ¹⁰You shall dwell in the land of Goshen, and you shall be near to me, you and your children, your children's children, your flocks and your herds, and all that you have. ¹¹There I will provide for you, lest you and your household, and all that you have, come to poverty; for there are still five years of famine." '

¹²"And behold, your eyes and the eyes of my brother Benjamin see that it is my mouth that speaks to you. ¹³So you shall tell my father of all my glory in Egypt, and of all that you have seen; and you shall hurry and bring my father down here."

¹⁴Then he fell on his brother Benjamin's neck and wept, and Benjamin wept on his neck. ¹⁵Moreover he kissed all his brothers and wept over them, and after that his brothers talked with him.

¹⁶Now the report of it was heard in Pharaoh's house, saying, "Joseph's brothers have come." So it pleased Pharaoh and his servants well. ¹⁷And Pharaoh said to Joseph, "Say to your brothers, 'Do this: Load your animals and depart; go to the land of Canaan. ¹⁸Bring your father and your households and come to me; I will give you the best of the land of Egypt, and you will eat the fat of the land. ¹⁹Now you are commanded—do this: Take carts out of the land of Egypt for your little ones and your wives; bring your father and come. ²⁰Also do not be concerned about your goods, for the best of all the land of Egypt is yours.' "

²¹Then the sons of Israel did so; and Joseph gave them carts, according to the command of Pharaoh, and he gave them provisions for the journey. ²²He gave to all of them, to each man, changes of garments; but to Benjamin he gave three hundred pieces of silver and five changes of garments. ²³And he sent to his father these things: ten donkeys loaded with the good things of Egypt, and ten female donkeys loaded with grain, bread, and food for his father for the journey. ²⁴So he sent his brothers away, and they departed; and he said to them, "See that you do not become troubled along the way."

²⁵Then they went up out of Egypt, and came to the land of Canaan to Jacob their father. ²⁶And they told him, saying, "Joseph is still alive, and he is governor over all the land of Egypt." And Jacob's heart stood still, because he did not believe them. ²⁷But when they told him all the words which Joseph had said to them, and when he saw the carts which Joseph had sent to carry him, the spirit of Jacob their father revived. ²⁸Then Israel said, "It is enough. Joseph my son is still alive. I will go and see him before I die."

JACOB'S JOURNEY TO EGYPT

¹So Israel took his journey with all that he had, and came to Beersheba, and offered sacrifices to the God of his father Isaac. ²Then God spoke to Israel in the visions of the night, and said, "Jacob, Jacob!"

And he said, "Here I am."

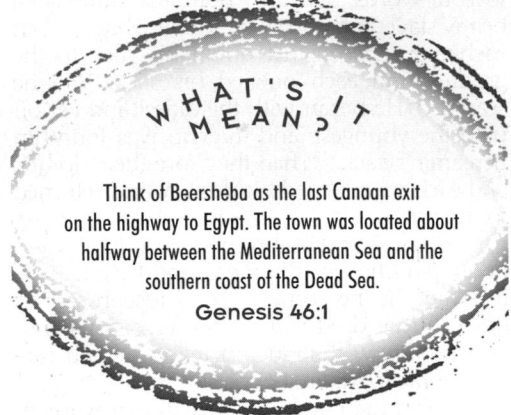

WHAT'S IT MEAN?

Think of Beersheba as the last Canaan exit on the highway to Egypt. The town was located about halfway between the Mediterranean Sea and the southern coast of the Dead Sea.

Genesis 46:1

³So He said, "I am God, the God of your father; do not fear to go down to Egypt, for I will make of you a great nation there. ⁴I will go down with you to Egypt, and I will also surely bring you up again; and Joseph will put his hand on your eyes."

⁵Then Jacob arose from Beersheba; and the sons of Israel carried their father Jacob, their little ones, and their wives, in the carts which Pharaoh had sent to carry him. ⁶So they took their livestock and their goods, which they had acquired in the land of Canaan, and went to Egypt, Jacob and all his descendants with him. ⁷His sons and his sons' sons, his daughters and his sons' daughters, and all his descendants he brought with him to Egypt.

⁸Now these were the names of the children of Israel, Jacob and his sons, who went to Egypt: Reuben was Jacob's firstborn. ⁹The sons of Reuben were Hanoch, Pallu, Hezron, and Carmi.

[10]The sons of Simeon *were* Jemuel,[a] Jamin, Ohad, Jachin,[b] Zohar,[c] and Shaul, the son of a Canaanite woman. [11]The sons of Levi *were* Gershon, Kohath, and Merari. [12]The sons of Judah *were* Er, Onan, Shelah, Perez, and Zerah (but Er and Onan died in the land of Canaan). The sons of Perez were Hezron and Hamul. [13]The sons of Issachar *were* Tola, Puvah,[a] Job,[b] and Shimron. [14]The sons of Zebulun *were* Sered, Elon, and Jahleel. [15]These *were* the sons of Leah, whom she bore to Jacob in Padan Aram, with his daughter Dinah. All the persons, his sons and his daughters, *were* thirty-three.

[16]The sons of Gad *were* Ziphion,[a] Haggi, Shuni, Ezbon,[b] Eri, Arodi,[c] and Areli. [17]The sons of Asher *were* Jimnah, Ishuah, Isui, Beriah, and Serah, their sister. And the sons of Beriah *were* Heber and Malchiel. [18]These *were* the sons of Zilpah, whom Laban gave to Leah his daughter; and these she bore to Jacob: sixteen persons.

[19]The sons of Rachel, Jacob's wife, *were* Joseph and Benjamin. [20]And to Joseph in the land of Egypt were born Manasseh and Ephraim, whom Asenath, the daughter of Poti-Pherah priest of On, bore to him. [21]The sons of Benjamin *were* Belah, Becher, Ashbel, Gera, Naaman, Ehi, Rosh, Muppim, Huppim,[a] and Ard. [22]These *were* the sons of Rachel, who were born to Jacob: fourteen persons in all.

[23]The son of Dan *was* Hushim.[a] [24]The sons of Naphtali *were* Jahzeel,[a] Guni, Jezer, and Shillem.[b] [25]These *were* the sons of Bilhah, whom Laban gave to Rachel his daughter, and she bore these to Jacob: seven persons in all.

[26]All the persons who went with Jacob to Egypt, who came from his body, besides Jacob's sons' wives, *were* sixty-six persons in all. [27]And the sons of Joseph who were born to him in Egypt *were* two persons. All the persons of the house of Jacob who went to Egypt were seventy.

JACOB SETTLES IN GOSHEN

[28]Then he sent Judah before him to Joseph, to point out before him *the way* to Goshen. And they came to the land of Goshen. [29]So Joseph made ready his chariot and went up to Goshen to meet his father Israel; and he presented himself to him, and fell on his neck and wept on his neck a good while. [30]And Israel said to Joseph, "Now let me die, since I have seen your face, because you *are* still alive."

[31]Then Joseph said to his brothers and to his father's household, "I will go up and tell Pharaoh, and say to him, 'My brothers and those of my father's house, who *were* in the land of Canaan, have come to me. [32]And the men *are* shepherds, for their occupation has been to feed livestock; and they have brought their flocks, their herds, and all that they have.' [33]So it shall be, when Pharaoh calls you and says, 'What is your occupation?' [34]that you shall say, 'Your servants' occupation has been with livestock from our youth even till now, both we *and* also our fathers,' that you may dwell in the land of Goshen; for every shepherd *is* an abomination to the Egyptians."

[1]Then Joseph went and told Pharaoh, and said, "My father and my brothers, their flocks and their herds and all that they possess, have come from the land of Canaan; and indeed they *are* in the land of Goshen." [2]And he took five men from among his brothers and presented them to Pharaoh. [3]Then Pharaoh said to his brothers, "What *is* your occupation?"

And they said to Pharaoh, "Your servants *are* shepherds, both we *and* also our fathers." [4]And they said to Pharaoh, "We have come to dwell in the land, because your servants have no pasture for their flocks, for the famine *is* severe in the land of Canaan. Now therefore, please let your servants dwell in the land of Goshen."

[5]Then Pharaoh spoke to Joseph, saying, "Your father and your brothers have come to you. [6]The land of Egypt *is* before you. Have your father and brothers dwell in the best of the land; let them dwell in the land of Goshen. And if you know *any* competent men among them, then make them chief herdsmen over my livestock."

[7]Then Joseph brought in his father Jacob and set him before Pharaoh; and Jacob blessed Pharaoh. [8]Pharaoh said to Jacob, "How old *are* you?"

[9]And Jacob said to Pharaoh, "The days of the years of my pilgrimage *are* one hundred and thirty years; few and evil have been the days of the years of my life, and they have not attained to the days of the years of the life of my fathers in the days of their pilgrimage." [10]So Jacob

---

46:10 [a]Spelled *Nemuel* in 1 Chronicles 4:24 [b]Called *Jarib* in 1 Chronicles 4:24 [c]Called *Zerah* in 1 Chronicles 4:24   **46:13** [a]Spelled *Puah* in 1 Chronicles 7:1 [b]Same as *Jashub* in Numbers 26:24 and 1 Chronicles 7:1   **46:16** [a]Spelled *Zephon* in Samaritan Pentateuch, Septuagint, and Numbers 26:15 [b]Called *Ozni* in Numbers 26:16 [c]Spelled *Arod* in Numbers 26:17   **46:21** [a]Called *Hupham* in Numbers 26:39   **46:23** [a]Called *Shuham* in Numbers 26:42   **46:24** [a]Spelled *Jahziel* in 1 Chronicles 7:13 [b]Spelled *Shallum* in 1 Chronicles 7:13

blessed Pharaoh, and went out from before Pharaoh.

¹¹And Joseph situated his father and his brothers, and gave them a possession in the land of Egypt, in the best of the land, in the land of Rameses, as Pharaoh had commanded. ¹²Then Joseph provided his father, his brothers, and all his father's household with bread, according to the number in *their* families.

JOSEPH DEALS WITH THE FAMINE

¹³Now *there was* no bread in all the land; for the famine *was* very severe, so that the land of Egypt and the land of Canaan languished because of the famine. ¹⁴And Joseph gathered up all the money that was found in the land of Egypt and in the land of Canaan, for the grain which they bought; and Joseph brought the money into Pharaoh's house.

¹⁵So when the money failed in the land of Egypt and in the land of Canaan, all the Egyptians came to Joseph and said, "Give us bread, for why should we die in your presence? For the money has failed."

¹⁶Then Joseph said, "Give your livestock, and I will give you *bread* for your livestock, if the money is gone." ¹⁷So they brought their livestock to Joseph, and Joseph gave them bread *in exchange* for the horses, the flocks, the cattle of the herds, and for the donkeys. Thus he fed them with bread *in exchange* for all their livestock that year.

¹⁸When that year had ended, they came to him the next year and said to him, "We will not hide from my lord that our money is gone; my lord also has our herds of livestock. There is nothing left in the sight of my lord but our bodies and our lands. ¹⁹Why should we die before your eyes, both we and our land? Buy us and our land for bread, and we and our land will be servants of Pharaoh; give *us* seed, that we may live and not die, that the land may not be desolate."

²⁰Then Joseph bought all the land of Egypt for Pharaoh; for every man of the Egyptians sold his field, because the famine was severe upon them. So the land became Pharaoh's. ²¹And as for the people, he moved them into the cities,ᵃ from *one* end of the borders of Egypt to the *other* end. ²²Only the land of the priests he did not buy; for the priests had rations *allotted to them* by Pharaoh, and they ate their rations which Pharaoh gave them; therefore they did not sell their lands.

²³Then Joseph said to the people, "Indeed I have bought you and your land this day for Pharaoh. Look, *here is* seed for you, and you shall sow the land. ²⁴And it shall come to pass in the harvest that you shall give one-fifth to Pharaoh. Four-fifths shall be your own, as seed for the field and for your food, for those of your households and as food for your little ones."

²⁵So they said, "You have saved our lives; let us find favor in the sight of my lord, and we will be Pharaoh's servants." ²⁶And Joseph made it a law over the land of Egypt to this day, *that* Pharaoh should have one-fifth, except for the land of the priests only, *which* did not become Pharaoh's.

JOSEPH'S VOW TO JACOB

²⁷So Israel dwelt in the land of Egypt, in the country of Goshen; and they had possessions there and grew and multiplied exceedingly. ²⁸And Jacob lived in the land of Egypt seventeen years. So the length of Jacob's life was one hundred and forty-seven years. ²⁹When the time drew near that Israel must die, he called his son Joseph and said to him, "Now if I have found favor in your sight, please put your hand under my thigh, and deal kindly and truly with me. Please do not bury me in Egypt, ³⁰but let me lie with my fathers; you shall carry me out of Egypt and bury me in their burial place."

WHAT'S IT MEAN?

The family burial ground was considered sacred, so you can understand why it was so important to Jacob to have his body returned to Canaan. He did not want Egypt to be his final resting place.
Genesis 47:29

And he said, "I will do as you have said." ³¹Then he said, "Swear to me." And he swore to him. So Israel bowed himself on the head of the bed.

47:21 ᵃFollowing Masoretic Text and Targum; Samaritan Pentateuch, Septuagint, and Vulgate read *made the people virtual slaves.*

JACOB BLESSES JOSEPH'S SONS

¹Now it came to pass after these things that Joseph was told, "Indeed your father *is* sick"; and he took with him his two sons, Manasseh and Ephraim. ²And Jacob was told, "Look, your son Joseph is coming to you"; and Israel strengthened himself and sat up on the bed. ³Then Jacob said to Joseph: "God Almighty appeared to me at Luz in the land of Canaan and blessed me, ⁴and said to me, 'Behold, I will make

---

WHAT'S IT MEAN?

Luz is another name for the town of Bethel. If that name sounds familiar to you, it should. Bethel is the place where Jacob's life changed forever. It's where he dreamed of the ladder that reached to heaven and where God promised to give the land to his descendants (Gen. 28:10–22). Jacob changed the name of the town from Luz to Bethel in honor of his dream. *Bethel* means "House of God."

Genesis 48:3

---

you fruitful and multiply you, and I will make of you a multitude of people, and give this land to your descendants after you *as* an everlasting possession.' ⁵And now your two sons, Ephraim and Manasseh, who were born to you in the land of Egypt before I came to you in Egypt, *are* mine; as Reuben and Simeon, they shall be mine. ⁶Your offspring whom you beget after them shall be yours; they will be called by the name of their brothers in their inheritance. ⁷But as for me, when I came from Padan, Rachel died beside me in the land of Canaan on the way, when *there was* but a little distance to go to Ephrath; and I buried her there on the way to Ephrath (that is, Bethlehem)."

⁸Then Israel saw Joseph's sons, and said, "Who *are* these?"

⁹Joseph said to his father, "They *are* my sons, whom God has given me in this *place.*"

And he said, "Please bring them to me, and I will bless them." ¹⁰Now the eyes of Israel were dim with age, *so that* he could not see. Then Joseph brought them near him, and he kissed them and embraced them. ¹¹And Israel said to Joseph, "I had not thought to see your face; but in fact, God has also shown me your off-spring!"

¹²So Joseph brought them from beside his

knees, and he bowed down with his face to the earth. ¹³And Joseph took them both, Ephraim with his right hand toward Israel's left hand, and Manasseh with his left hand toward Israel's right hand, and brought *them* near him. ¹⁴Then Israel stretched out his right hand and laid *it* on Ephraim's head, who *was* the younger, and his left hand on Manasseh's head, guiding his hands knowingly, for Manasseh *was* the firstborn. ¹⁵And he blessed Joseph, and said:

> "God, before whom my fathers Abraham
> and Isaac walked,
> The God who has fed me all my life long
> to this day,
> ¹⁶ The Angel who has redeemed me from all
> evil,
> Bless the lads;
> Let my name be named upon them,
> And the name of my fathers Abraham
> and Isaac;
> And let them grow into a multitude in the
> midst of the earth."

¹⁷Now when Joseph saw that his father laid his right hand on the head of Ephraim, it displeased him; so he took hold of his father's hand to remove it from Ephraim's head to Manasseh's head. ¹⁸And Joseph said to his father, "Not so, my father, for this *one is* the firstborn; put your right hand on his head." ¹⁹But his father refused and said, "I know, my son, I know. He also shall become a people, and he also shall be great; but truly his younger brother shall be greater than he, and his descendants shall become a multitude of nations." ²⁰So he blessed them that day, saying, "By you Israel will bless, saying, 'May God make you as Ephraim and as Manasseh!' " And thus he set Ephraim before Manasseh.

²¹Then Israel said to Joseph, "Behold, I am dying, but God will be with you and bring you back to the land of your fathers. ²²Moreover I have given to you one portion above your brothers, which I took from the hand of the Amorite with my sword and my bow."

JACOB'S LAST WORDS TO HIS SONS

¹And Jacob called his sons and said, "Gather together, that I may tell you what shall befall you in the last days:

> ² "Gather together and hear, you sons of
> Jacob,
> And listen to Israel your father.

3 "Reuben, you are my firstborn,
My might and the beginning of my strength,
The excellency of dignity and the excellency of power.

4 Unstable as water, you shall not excel,
Because you went up to your father's bed;
Then you defiled *it*—
He went up to my couch.

5 "Simeon and Levi *are* brothers;
Instruments of cruelty *are in* their dwelling place.

6 Let not my soul enter their council;
Let not my honor be united to their assembly;
For in their anger they slew a man,
And in their self-will they hamstrung an ox.

7 Cursed *be* their anger, for *it is* fierce;
And their wrath, for it is cruel!
I will divide them in Jacob
And scatter them in Israel.

8 "Judah, you *are he* whom your brothers shall praise;
Your hand *shall be* on the neck of your enemies;
Your father's children shall bow down before you.

9 Judah *is* a lion's whelp;
From the prey, my son, you have gone up.
He bows down, he lies down as a lion;
And as a lion, who shall rouse him?

10 The scepter shall not depart from Judah,
Nor a lawgiver from between his feet,
Until Shiloh comes;
And to Him *shall be* the obedience of the people.

11 Binding his donkey to the vine,
And his donkey's colt to the choice vine,
He washed his garments in wine,
And his clothes in the blood of grapes.

12 His eyes *are* darker than wine,
And his teeth whiter than milk.

13 "Zebulun shall dwell by the haven of the sea;
He *shall become* a haven for ships,
And his border shall adjoin Sidon.

14 "Issachar is a strong donkey,
Lying down between two burdens;

15 He saw that rest *was* good,
And that the land *was* pleasant;

He bowed his shoulder to bear *a burden,*
And became a band of slaves.

16 "Dan shall judge his people
As one of the tribes of Israel.

17 Dan shall be a serpent by the way,
A viper by the path,
That bites the horse's heels
So that its rider shall fall backward.

18 I have waited for your salvation,
O LORD!

19 "Gad, a troop shall tramp upon him,
But he shall triumph at last.

20 "Bread from Asher *shall be* rich,
And he shall yield royal dainties.

21 "Naphtali *is* a deer let loose;
He uses beautiful words.

HELP

Who will help me?
(49:25)

22 "Joseph *is* a fruitful bough,
A fruitful bough by a well;
His branches run over the wall.

23 The archers have bitterly grieved him,
Shot *at him* and hated him.

24 But his bow remained in strength,
And the arms of his hands were made strong
By the hands of the Mighty *God* of Jacob
(From there *is* the Shepherd, the Stone of Israel),

25 By the God of your father who will help you,
And by the Almighty who will bless you
With blessings of heaven above,
Blessings of the deep that lies beneath,
Blessings of the breasts and of the womb.

26 The blessings of your father
Have excelled the blessings of my ancestors,
Up to the utmost bound of the everlasting hills.
They shall be on the head of Joseph,
And on the crown of the head of him who was separate from his brothers.

27 "Benjamin is a ravenous wolf;
In the morning he shall devour the prey,
And at night he shall divide the spoil."

28 All these *are* the twelve tribes of Israel, and this *is* what their father spoke to them. And he blessed them; he blessed each one according to his own blessing.

JACOB'S DEATH AND BURIAL

²⁹Then he charged them and said to them: "I am to be gathered to my people; bury me with my fathers in the cave that *is* in the field of Ephron the Hittite, ³⁰in the cave that *is* in the field of Machpelah, which *is* before Mamre in the land of Canaan, which Abraham bought with the field of Ephron the Hittite as a possession for a burial place. ³¹There they buried Abraham and Sarah his wife, there they buried Isaac and Rebekah his wife, and there I buried Leah. ³²The field and the cave that *is* there *were* purchased from the sons of Heth." ³³And when Jacob had finished commanding his sons, he drew his feet up into the bed and breathed his last, and was gathered to his people.

¹Then Joseph fell on his father's face and wept over him, and kissed him. ²And Joseph commanded his servants the physicians to embalm his father. So the physicians embalmed Israel. ³Forty days were required for him, for such are the days required for those who are embalmed; and the Egyptians mourned for him seventy days.

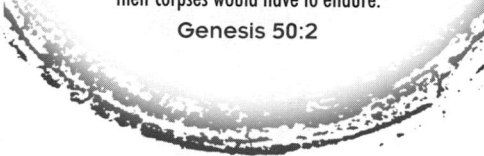

WHAT'S IT MEAN?

The Israelites had strict laws about touching dead bodies, so they rarely performed embalmings. In fact, Jacob and Joseph are the only two Old Testament people we know of who were embalmed. It may be that embalming was necessary for them because of the long journey back to Canaan that their corpses would have to endure.

Genesis 50:2

⁴Now when the days of his mourning were past, Joseph spoke to the household of Pharaoh, saying, "If now I have found favor in your eyes, please speak in the hearing of Pharaoh, saying, ⁵'My father made me swear, saying, "Behold, I am dying; in my grave which I dug for myself in the land of Canaan, there you shall bury me." Now therefore, please let me go up and bury my father, and I will come back.' "

⁶And Pharaoh said, "Go up and bury your father, as he made you swear."

⁷So Joseph went up to bury his father; and with him went up all the servants of Pharaoh, the elders of his house, and all the elders of the land of Egypt, ⁸as well as all the house of Joseph, his brothers, and his father's house. Only their little ones, their flocks, and their herds they left in the land of Goshen. ⁹And there went up with him both chariots and horsemen, and it was a very great gathering.

¹⁰Then they came to the threshing floor of Atad, which *is* beyond the Jordan, and they mourned there with a great and very solemn lamentation. He observed seven days of mourning for his father. ¹¹And when the inhabitants of the land, the Canaanites, saw the mourning at the threshing floor of Atad, they said, "This *is* a deep mourning of the Egyptians." Therefore its name was called Abel Mizraim,^a which *is* beyond the Jordan.

¹²So his sons did for him just as he had commanded them. ¹³For his sons carried him to the land of Canaan, and buried him in the cave of the field of Machpelah, before Mamre, which Abraham bought with the field from Ephron the Hittite as property for a burial place. ¹⁴And after he had buried his father, Joseph returned to Egypt, he and his brothers and all who went up with him to bury his father.

JOSEPH REASSURES HIS BROTHERS

¹⁵When Joseph's brothers saw that their father was dead, they said, "Perhaps Joseph will hate us, and may actually repay us for all the evil which we did to him." ¹⁶So they sent *messengers* to Joseph, saying, "Before your father died he commanded, saying, ¹⁷'Thus you shall say to Joseph: "I beg you, please forgive the trespass of your brothers and their sin; for they did evil to you." ' Now, please, forgive the trespass of the servants of the God of your father." And Joseph wept when they spoke to him.

¹⁸Then his brothers also went and fell down before his face, and they said, "Behold, we *are* your servants."

¹⁹Joseph said to them, "Do not be afraid, for *am* I in the place of God? ²⁰But as for you, you meant evil against me; *but* God meant it for good, in order to bring it about as *it is* this day, to save many people alive. ²¹Now therefore, do not be afraid; I will provide for you and your little ones." And he comforted them and spoke kindly to them.

DEATH OF JOSEPH

²²So Joseph dwelt in Egypt, he and his father's household. And Joseph lived one

hundred and ten years. ²³Joseph saw Ephraim's children to the third *generation*. The children of Machir, the son of Manasseh, were also brought up on Joseph's knees.

²⁴And Joseph said to his brethren, "I am dying; but God will surely visit you, and bring you out of this land to the land of which He swore to Abraham, to Isaac, and to Jacob." ²⁵Then Joseph took an oath from the children of Israel, saying, "God will surely visit you, and you shall carry up my bones from here." ²⁶So Joseph died, *being* one hundred and ten years old; and they embalmed him, and he was put in a coffin in Egypt.

exodus

CONTENT

If Exodus was a movie, it would be action-adventure. You've got your miracles. You've got your spectacular events. You've got your special effects. You've got plenty of extras standing around with their mouths hanging open at the amazing things God does. And it's all true!

The bad guys in this scenario are the Egyptians, particularly Pharaoh, who (for longer than you would imagine) would *not* let those Hebrew people go, no matter what God did through Moses.

The good guys—well, the favored guys—are the Hebrews, led by Moses. After being enslaved by the Egyptians for generations, they were freed only to wander around in a desert, no—a *wilderness*. After reading about their travels, you may not be surprised that they sometimes wished for the comforts of captivity.

All through this adventure God does amazing things—more amazing than anything you've seen in a theater. Seas split in two. Food falls like dew. Boulders sprout fountains. The glory of God's presence becomes visible. Moses' face actually GLOWS.

So buckle your seat belts and prepare for a ride of a read.

Outline

Purpose

God breaks our chains, then draws us to Himself by teaching us wise ways and worship.

Theme

Deliverance

Date of writing

1445–1440 B.C.

Bible Talk

Passover

Have you heard of a Passover meal? It's a meal of very specific foods prepared a very specific way and eaten in a very specific order. When people eat a Passover meal, they are actually remembering the last plague the Egyptians experienced because Pharaoh would not let the Hebrews leave.

On that last night, the Lord passed through Egypt and the oldest son of each household died as He passed . . . unless the family had spread the blood of a lamb on their doorpost. If the blood was on the doorpost, then the Lord *passed over* that home and the firstborn lived.

The Passover was a picture for the Hebrews, and anyone else watching, of what Jesus would do one day for all of us. He would spill His blood on a wooden cross to save us from certain death.

THE TEN COMMANDMENTS

Did you know that the first time the Ten Commandments were written, they were written by God Himself? Did you know they had to be rewritten? Do you know why?

After Moses spent time up on Mt. Sinai with God, he came down the mountain carrying the stone tablets that God Himself had written on. But when Moses saw that in his absence the people had *already* started worshiping idols, he basically pitched a fit. He threw down and broke the tablets that God had made and that God had written on.

It's amazing to think Moses would have done that, isn't it? There's no telling how many important things are lost when good men pitch fits.

ISRAEL'S SUFFERING IN EGYPT

¹Now these *are* the names of the children of Israel who came to Egypt; each man and his household came with Jacob: ²Reuben, Simeon, Levi, and Judah; ³Issachar, Zebulun, and Benjamin; ⁴Dan, Naphtali, Gad, and Asher. ⁵All those who were descendants*ᵃ* of Jacob were seventy*ᵇ* persons (for Joseph was in Egypt *already*). ⁶And

WHAT'S IT MEAN?

Don't overlook numbers in Scripture. Sometimes they can tell us quite a bit. Seventy was a significant number for Israel because it was a multiple of seven, the sacred number. To the Israelites, seven symbolized completion, abundance, and rest. (Consider the seven days of creation in Genesis 1.)

Exodus 1:1–5

Joseph died, all his brothers, and all that generation. ⁷But the children of Israel were fruitful and increased abundantly, multiplied and grew exceedingly mighty; and the land was filled with them.

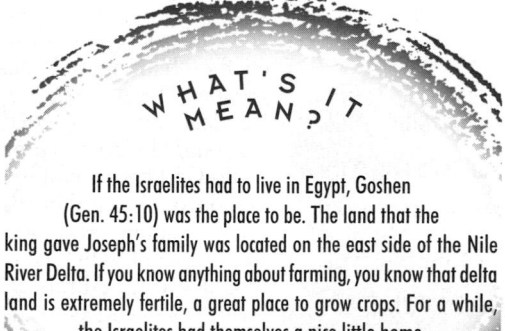

WHAT'S IT MEAN?

If the Israelites had to live in Egypt, Goshen (Gen. 45:10) was the place to be. The land that the king gave Joseph's family was located on the east side of the Nile River Delta. If you know anything about farming, you know that delta land is extremely fertile, a great place to grow crops. For a while, the Israelites had themselves a nice little home away from home.

Exodus 1:7

⁸Now there arose a new king over Egypt, who did not know Joseph. ⁹And he said to his people, "Look, the people of the children of Israel *are* more and mightier than we; ¹⁰come, let

us deal shrewdly with them, lest they multiply, and it happen, in the event of war, that they also join our enemies and fight against us, and *so* go up out of the land." ¹¹Therefore they set taskmasters over them to afflict them with their burdens. And they built for Pharaoh supply cities, Pithom and Raamses. ¹²But the more they afflicted them, the more they multiplied and grew. And they were in dread of the children of Israel. ¹³So the Egyptians made the children of Israel serve with rigor. ¹⁴And they made their lives bitter with hard bondage—in mortar, in brick, and in all manner of service in the field. All their service in which they made them serve *was* with rigor.

¹⁵Then the king of Egypt spoke to the Hebrew midwives, of whom the name of one *was* Shiphrah and the name of the other Puah; ¹⁶and he said, "When you do the duties of a midwife for the Hebrew women, and see *them* on the birthstools, if it *is* a son, then you shall kill him; but if it *is* a daughter, then she shall live." ¹⁷But the midwives feared God, and did not do as the king of Egypt commanded them, but saved the male children alive. ¹⁸So the king of Egypt called for the midwives and said to them, "Why have you done this thing, and saved the male children alive?"

¹⁹And the midwives said to Pharaoh, "Because the Hebrew women *are* not like the Egyptian women; for they *are* lively and give birth before the midwives come to them." ²⁰Therefore God dealt well with the midwives, and the people multiplied and grew very mighty. ²¹And so it was, because the midwives feared God, that He provided households for them.

²²So Pharaoh commanded all his people, saying, "Every son who is born*ᵃ* you shall cast into the river, and every daughter you shall save alive."

MOSES IS BORN

¹And a man of the house of Levi went and took *as wife* a daughter of Levi. ²So the woman conceived and bore a son. And when she saw that he *was* a beautiful *child*, she hid him three months. ³But when she could no longer hide him, she took an ark of bulrushes for him, daubed it with asphalt and pitch, put the child in it, and laid *it* in the reeds by the river's bank. ⁴And his sister stood afar off, to know what would be done to him.

⁵Then the daughter of Pharaoh came down

1:5 *ᵃ*Literally *who came from the loins of* *ᵇ*Dead Sea Scrolls and Septuagint read *seventy-five* (compare Acts 7:14). **1:22** *ᵃ*Samaritan Pentateuch, Septuagint, and Targum add *to the Hebrews.*

to bathe at the river. And her maidens walked along the riverside; and when she saw the ark among the reeds, she sent her maid to get it. ⁶And when she opened *it*, she saw the child, and behold, the baby wept. So she had compassion on him, and said, "This is one of the Hebrews' children."

⁷Then his sister said to Pharaoh's daughter, "Shall I go and call a nurse for you from the Hebrew women, that she may nurse the child for you?"

⁸And Pharaoh's daughter said to her, "Go." So the maiden went and called the child's mother. ⁹Then Pharaoh's daughter said to her, "Take this child away and nurse him for me, and I will give *you* your wages." So the woman took the child and nursed him. ¹⁰And the child grew, and she brought him to Pharaoh's daughter, and he became her son. So she called his name Moses,ᵃ saying, "Because I drew him out of the water."

MOSES FLEES TO MIDIAN

¹¹Now it came to pass in those days, when Moses was grown, that he went out to his brethren and looked at their burdens. And he saw an Egyptian beating a Hebrew, one of his brethren. ¹²So he looked this way and that way, and when he saw no one, he killed the Egyptian and hid him in the sand. ¹³And when he went out the second day, behold, two Hebrew men were fighting, and he said to the one who did the wrong, "Why are you striking your companion?"

¹⁴Then he said, "Who made you a prince and a judge over us? Do you intend to kill me as you killed the Egyptian?"

So Moses feared and said, "Surely this thing is known!" ¹⁵When Pharaoh heard of this matter, he sought to kill Moses. But Moses fled from the face of Pharaoh and dwelt in the land of Midian; and he sat down by a well.

¹⁶Now the priest of Midian had seven daughters. And they came and drew water, and they filled the troughs to water their father's flock. ¹⁷Then the shepherds came and drove them away; but Moses stood up and helped them, and watered their flock.

¹⁸When they came to Reuel their father, he said, "How *is it that* you have come so soon today?"

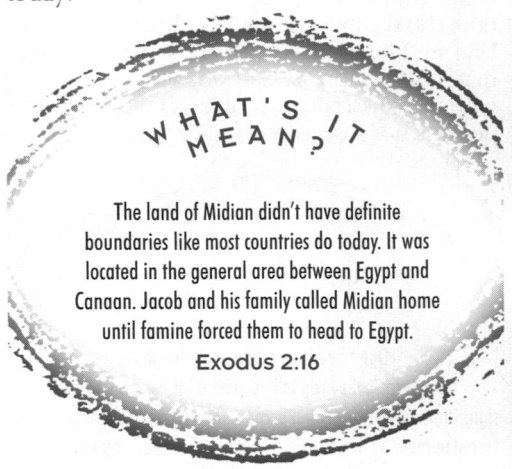

¹⁹And they said, "An Egyptian delivered us from the hand of the shepherds, and he also drew enough water for us and watered the flock."

²⁰So he said to his daughters, "And where *is* he? Why *is it that* you have left the man? Call him, that he may eat bread."

²¹Then Moses was content to live with the man, and he gave Zipporah his daughter to Moses. ²²And she bore *him* a son. He called his name Gershom,ᵃ for he said, "I have been a stranger in a foreign land."

²³Now it happened in the process of time that the king of Egypt died. Then the children of Israel groaned because of the bondage, and they cried out; and their cry came up to God because of the bondage. ²⁴So God heard their groaning, and God remembered His covenant with Abraham, with Isaac, and with Jacob. ²⁵And God looked upon the children of Israel, and God acknowledged *them.*

> "So God heard their groaning, and God remembered His covenant with Abraham, with Isaac, and with Jacob. And God looked upon the children of Israel, and God acknowledged them." (Exodus 2:24, 25)

MOSES AT THE BURNING BUSH

¹Now Moses was tending the flock of Jethro his father-in-law, the priest of Midian. And he led the flock to the back of the desert, and came to Horeb, the mountain of God. ²And the Angel of the LORD appeared to him in a flame of fire

---

from the midst of a bush. So he looked, and behold, the bush was burning with fire, but the bush *was* not consumed. ³Then Moses said, "I will now turn aside and see this great sight, why the bush does not burn."

⁴So when the LORD saw that he turned aside to look, God called to him from the midst of the bush and said, "Moses, Moses!"

And he said, "Here I am."

⁵Then He said, "Do not draw near this place. Take your sandals off your feet, for the place where you stand *is* holy ground." ⁶Moreover He said, "I *am* the God of your father—the God of Abraham, the God of Isaac, and the God of Jacob." And Moses hid his face, for he was afraid to look upon God.

⁷And the LORD said: "I have surely seen the oppression of My people who *are* in Egypt, and have heard their cry because of their taskmasters, for I know their sorrows. ⁸So I have come down to deliver them out of the hand of the Egyptians, and to bring them up from that land to a good and large land, to a land flowing with milk and honey, to the place of the Canaanites and the Hittites and the Amorites and the Perizzites and the Hivites and the Jebusites. ⁹Now therefore, behold, the cry of the children of Israel has come to Me, and I have also seen the oppression with which the Egyptians oppress them.

RESPECT

Is God worthy of our respect? (3:5)

WORSHIP

Where is God during worship? (3:5, 6)

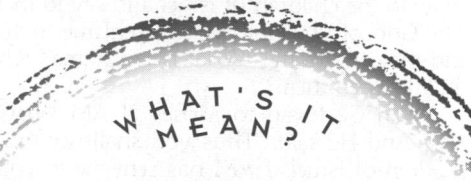

WHAT'S IT MEAN?

Horeb (also called Sinai) is a mountain in the peninsula of Sinai, which sits between Egypt and Arabia and is shaped like a triangle. Sinai Peninsula stretches from the Mediterranean Sea on the north to the Red Sea on the south. It is a dry, barren place, covered mostly by desert and mountains.

Exodus 3:1

¹⁰Come now, therefore, and I will send you to Pharaoh that you may bring My people, the children of Israel, out of Egypt."

¹¹But Moses said to God, "Who *am* I that I should go to Pharaoh, and that I should bring the children of Israel out of Egypt?"

Promise   HE PROMISES TO DELIVER HIS PEOPLE OUT OF EGYPT.

So I have come down to deliver them out of the hand of the Egyptians, and to bring them up from that land to a good and large land, to a land flowing with milk and honey . . . (Ex. 3:8).

The children of Israel had been delivered from Egypt and wandered in the desert for 40 years before entering the land God had promised them.

But you know what? Year number 41 came, and they didn't wander anymore. They entered into the land of milk and honey! Maybe it seems that you are in a desert period in your life. Maybe you feel like you've been stumbling around for 40 years. Don't worry, number 41 is on its way!

Look at these examples: Noah and his family were on the ark while it rained for 40 days and 40 nights—41 came, and the rain stopped. For 40 days Goliath showed up every morning and taunted Israel—41 came, and David slew him!

God has promised to bring you out of your Egypt as well—if you will hold on to your faith in Him. Whatever situation you are going through right now, don't give up. God is on your side! So if it seems like trouble has been raining down on you, don't worry because 41 is on the way. The rain is going to stop. Whatever giant is in your life, 41 is coming and that giant's coming down! You are more than a conquerer through Christ Jesus (see Rom. 8:37). He will deliver you out of Egypt.

SEE FOR YOURSELF:
Gen. 7; 8; 1 Sam. 17; Ps. 34:17, 19

¹²So He said, "I will certainly be with you. And this *shall be* a sign to you that I have sent you: When you have brought the people out of Egypt, you shall serve God on this mountain."

¹³Then Moses said to God, "Indeed, *when* I come to the children of Israel and say to them, 'The God of your fathers has sent me to you,' and they say to me, 'What *is* His name?' what shall I say to them?"

¹⁴And God said to Moses, "I AM WHO I AM." And He said, "Thus you shall say to the children of Israel, 'I AM has sent me to you.' " ¹⁵Moreover God said to Moses, "Thus you shall say to the children of Israel: 'The LORD God of your fathers, the God of Abraham, the God of Isaac, and the God of Jacob, has sent me to you. This *is* My name forever, and this *is* My memorial to all generations.' ¹⁶Go and gather the elders of Israel together, and say to them, 'The LORD God of your fathers, the God of Abraham, of Isaac, and of Jacob, appeared to me, saying, "I have surely visited you and *seen* what is done to you in Egypt; ¹⁷and I have said I will bring you up out of the affliction of Egypt to the land of the Canaanites and the Hittites and the Amorites and the Perizzites and the Hivites and the Jebusites, to a land flowing with milk and honey." ' ¹⁸Then they will heed your voice; and you shall come, you and the elders of Israel, to the king of Egypt; and you shall say to him, 'The LORD God of the Hebrews has met with us; and now, please, let us go three days' journey into the wilderness, that we may sacrifice to the LORD our God.' ¹⁹But I am sure that the king of Egypt will not let you go, no, not even by a mighty hand. ²⁰So I will stretch out My hand and strike Egypt with all My wonders which I will do in its midst; and after that he will let you go. ²¹And I will give this people favor in the sight of the Egyptians; and it shall be, when you go, that you shall not go empty-handed. ²²But every woman shall ask of her neighbor, namely, of her who dwells near her house, articles of silver, articles of gold, and clothing; and you shall put *them* on your sons and on your daughters. So you shall plunder the Egyptians."

MIRACULOUS SIGNS FOR PHARAOH

¹Then Moses answered and said, "But suppose they will not believe me or listen to my voice; suppose they say, 'The LORD has not appeared to you.' "

²So the LORD said to him, "What *is* that in your hand?"

He said, "A rod."

³And He said, "Cast it on the ground." So he cast it on the ground, and it became a serpent; and Moses fled from it. ⁴Then the LORD said to Moses, "Reach out your hand and take *it* by the tail" (and he reached out his hand and caught it, and it became a rod in his hand), ⁵"that they may believe that the LORD God of their fathers, the God of Abraham, the God of Isaac, and the God of Jacob, has appeared to you."

⁶Furthermore the LORD said to him, "Now put your hand in your bosom." And he put his hand in his bosom, and when he took it out, behold, his hand *was* leprous, like snow. ⁷And He said, "Put your hand in your bosom again." So he put his hand in his bosom again, and drew it out of his bosom, and behold, it was restored like his *other* flesh. ⁸"Then it will be, if they do not believe you, nor heed the message of the first sign, that they may believe the message of the latter sign. ⁹And it shall be, if they do not believe even these two signs, or listen to your voice, that you shall take water from the river*ᵃ* and pour *it* on the dry *land*. The water which you take from the river will become blood on the dry *land*."

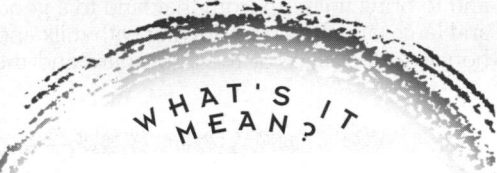

WHAT'S IT MEAN?

Without the river (which NKJV note on v. 9 identifies as the Nile), there would have been no Egypt. If you were an Egyptian and you needed water to drink, you went to the Nile. If you needed transportation, you hopped a boat on the Nile. If you wanted prime real estate, you built your house along the banks of the river. The Nile was so important to life in Egypt that many Egyptians thought of it as a god.
Exodus 4:8, 9

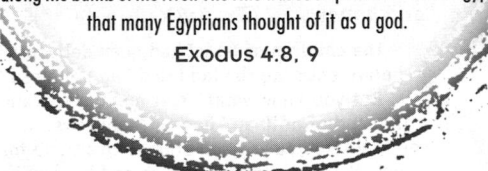

¹⁰Then Moses said to the LORD, "O my Lord, I *am* not eloquent, neither before nor since You have spoken to Your servant; but I *am* slow of speech and slow of tongue."

¹¹So the LORD said to him, "Who has made man's mouth? Or who makes the mute, the deaf, the seeing, or the blind? *Have* not I, the LORD? ¹²Now therefore, go, and I will be with your mouth and teach you what you shall say."

4:9 *ᵃ*That is, the Nile

[13]But he said, "O my Lord, please send by the hand of whomever *else* You may send."

[14]So the anger of the LORD was kindled against Moses, and He said: "Is not Aaron the Levite your brother? I know that he can speak well. And look, he is also coming out to meet you. When he sees you, he will be glad in his heart. [15]Now you shall speak to him and put the words in his mouth. And I will be with your mouth and with his mouth, and I will teach you what you shall do. [16]So he shall be your spokesman to the people. And he himself shall be as a mouth for you, and you shall be to him as God. [17]And you shall take this rod in your hand, with which you shall do the signs."

MOSES GOES TO EGYPT

[18]So Moses went and returned to Jethro his father-in-law, and said to him, "Please let me go and return to my brethren who *are* in Egypt, and see whether they are still alive."

And Jethro said to Moses, "Go in peace."

[19]Now the LORD said to Moses in Midian, "Go, return to Egypt; for all the men who sought your life are dead." [20]Then Moses took his wife and his sons and set them on a donkey, and he returned to the land of Egypt. And Moses took the rod of God in his hand.

[21]And the LORD said to Moses, "When you go back to Egypt, see that you do all those wonders before Pharaoh which I have put in your hand. But I will harden his heart, so that he will not let the people go. [22]Then you shall say to Pharaoh, 'Thus says the LORD: "Israel *is* My son, My firstborn. [23]So I say to you, let My son go that he may serve Me. But if you refuse to let him go, indeed I will kill your son, your firstborn." ' "

The firstborn son had extra responsibilities and privileges. When the father of a family died, the firstborn son was responsible for taking care of the family. When it came time to divide up the family's inheritance, though, the firstborn son received twice as much as everyone else.

Exodus 4:22

[24]And it came to pass on the way, at the encampment, that the LORD met him and sought to kill him. [25]Then Zipporah took a sharp stone and cut off the foreskin of her son and cast *it* at Moses'[a] feet, and said, "Surely you *are* a husband of blood to me!" [26]So He let him go. Then she said, "*You are* a husband of blood!"—because of the circumcision.

[27]And the LORD said to Aaron, "Go into the wilderness to meet Moses." So he went and met him on the mountain of God, and kissed him.

When friends or family members hadn't seen each other for a day or so, it was common for them to kiss when they met. It was also a common gesture for when two acquaintances said good-bye. Rarely is romantic kissing mentioned in the Bible.

Exodus 4:27

[28]So Moses told Aaron all the words of the LORD who had sent him, and all the signs which He had commanded him. [29]Then Moses and Aaron went and gathered together all the elders of the children of Israel. [30]And Aaron spoke all the words which the LORD had spoken to Moses. Then he did the signs in the sight of the people. [31]So the people believed; and when they heard that the LORD had visited the children of Israel and that He had looked on their affliction, then they bowed their heads and worshiped.

FIRST ENCOUNTER WITH PHARAOH

[1]Afterward Moses and Aaron went in and told Pharaoh, "Thus says the LORD God of Israel: 'Let My people go, that they may hold a feast to Me in the wilderness.' "

[2]And Pharaoh said, "Who *is* the LORD, that I should obey His voice to let Israel go? I do not know the LORD, nor will I let Israel go."

[3]So they said, "The God of the Hebrews has met with us. Please, let us go three days' journey into the desert and sacrifice to the LORD our God, lest He fall upon us with pestilence or with the sword."

[4]Then the king of Egypt said to them, "Moses and Aaron, why do you take the people from

4:25 [a]Literally *his*

their work? Get *back* to your labor." ⁵And Pharaoh said, "Look, the people of the land *are* many now, and you make them rest from their labor!"

⁶So the same day Pharaoh commanded the taskmasters of the people and their officers, saying, ⁷"You shall no longer give the people straw to make brick as before. Let them go and gather straw for themselves. ⁸And you shall lay on them the quota of bricks which they made before. You shall not reduce it. For they are idle; therefore they cry out, saying, 'Let us go *and* sacrifice to our God'. ⁹Let more work be laid on the men, that they may labor in it, and let them not regard false words."

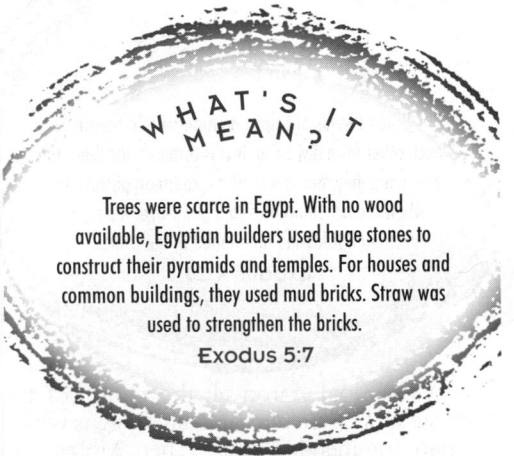

WHAT'S IT MEAN?

Trees were scarce in Egypt. With no wood available, Egyptian builders used huge stones to construct their pyramids and temples. For houses and common buildings, they used mud bricks. Straw was used to strengthen the bricks.

Exodus 5:7

¹⁰And the taskmasters of the people and their officers went out and spoke to the people, saying, "Thus says Pharaoh: 'I will not give you straw. ¹¹Go, get yourselves straw where you can find it; yet none of your work will be reduced.' " ¹²So the people were scattered abroad throughout all the land of Egypt to gather stubble instead of straw. ¹³And the taskmasters forced *them* to hurry, saying, "Fulfill your work, *your* daily quota, as when there was straw." ¹⁴Also the officers of the children of Israel, whom Pharaoh's taskmasters had set over them, were beaten *and* were asked, "Why have you not fulfilled your task in making brick both yesterday and today, as before?"

¹⁵Then the officers of the children of Israel came and cried out to Pharaoh, saying, "Why are you dealing thus with your servants? ¹⁶There is no straw given to your servants, and they say to us, 'Make brick!' And indeed your servants *are* beaten, but the fault *is* in your *own* people."

¹⁷But he said, "You *are* idle! Idle! Therefore you say, 'Let us go *and* sacrifice to the Lord.'

¹⁸Therefore go now *and* work; for no straw shall be given you, yet you shall deliver the quota of bricks." ¹⁹And the officers of the children of Israel saw *that* they *were* in trouble after it was said, "You shall not reduce *any* bricks from your daily quota."

²⁰Then, as they came out from Pharaoh, they met Moses and Aaron who stood there to meet them. ²¹And they said to them, "Let the Lord look on you and judge, because you have made us abhorrent in the sight of Pharaoh and in the sight of his servants, to put a sword in their hand to kill us."

ISRAEL'S DELIVERANCE ASSURED

²²So Moses returned to the Lord and said, "Lord, why have You brought trouble on this people? Why *is* it You have sent me? ²³For since I came to Pharaoh to speak in Your name, he has done evil to this people; neither have You delivered Your people at all."

¹Then the Lord said to Moses, "Now you shall see what I will do to Pharaoh. For with a strong hand he will let them go, and with a strong hand he will drive them out of his land."

²And God spoke to Moses and said to him: "I *am* the Lord. ³I appeared to Abraham, to Isaac, and to Jacob, as God Almighty, but *by* My name Lordᵃ I was not known to them. ⁴I have also established My covenant with them, to give them the land of Canaan, the land of their pilgrimage, in which they were strangers. ⁵And I have also heard the groaning of the children of Israel whom the Egyptians keep in bondage, and I have remembered My covenant. ⁶Therefore say to the children of Israel: 'I *am* the Lord; I will bring you out from under the burdens of the Egyptians, I will rescue you from their bondage, and I will redeem you with an outstretched arm and with great judgments. ⁷I will take you as My people, and I will be your God. Then you shall know that I *am* the Lord your God who brings you out from under the burdens of the Egyptians. ⁸And I will bring you into the land which I swore to give to Abraham, Isaac, and Jacob; and I will give it to you *as* a heritage: I *am* the Lord.' " ⁹So Moses spoke thus to the children of Israel; but they did not heed Moses, because of anguish of spirit and cruel bondage.

¹⁰And the Lord spoke to Moses, saying, ¹¹"Go in, tell Pharaoh king of Egypt to let the children of Israel go out of his land."

¹²And Moses spoke before the Lord, saying, "The children of Israel have not heeded me.

6:3 ᵃHebrew *YHWH*, traditionally *Jehovah*

How then shall Pharaoh heed me, for I *am* of uncircumcised lips?"

[13]Then the LORD spoke to Moses and Aaron, and gave them a command for the children of Israel and for Pharaoh king of Egypt, to bring the children of Israel out of the land of Egypt.

THE FAMILY OF MOSES AND AARON

[14]These *are* the heads of their fathers' houses: The sons of Reuben, the firstborn of Israel, *were* Hanoch, Pallu, Hezron, and Carmi. These are the families of Reuben. [15]And the sons of Simeon *were* Jemuel,[a] Jamin, Ohad, Jachin, Zohar, and Shaul the son of a Canaanite woman. These *are* the families of Simeon. [16]These *are* the names of the sons of Levi according to their generations: Gershon, Kohath, and Merari. And the years of the life of Levi *were* one hundred and thirty-seven. [17]The sons of Gershon *were* Libni and Shimi according to their families. [18]And the sons of Kohath *were* Amram, Izhar, Hebron, and Uzziel. And the years of the life of Kohath *were* one hundred and thirty-three. [19]The sons of Merari *were* Mahli and Mushi. These *are* the families of Levi according to their generations.

[20]Now Amram took for himself Jochebed, his father's sister, as wife; and she bore him Aaron and Moses. And the years of the life of Amram *were* one hundred and thirty-seven. [21]The sons of Izhar *were* Korah, Nepheg, and Zichri. [22]And the sons of Uzziel *were* Mishael, Elzaphan, and Zithri. [23]Aaron took to himself Elisheba, daughter of Amminadab, sister of Nahshon, as wife; and she bore him Nadab, Abihu, Eleazar, and Ithamar. [24]And the sons of Korah *were* Assir, Elkanah, and Abiasaph. These are the families of the Korahites. [25]Eleazar, Aaron's son, took for himself one of the daughters of Putiel as wife; and she bore him Phinehas. These *are* the heads of the fathers' houses of the Levites according to their families.

[26]These *are the same* Aaron and Moses to whom the LORD said, "Bring out the children of Israel from the land of Egypt according to their armies." [27]These *are* the ones who spoke to Pharaoh king of Egypt, to bring out the children of Israel from Egypt. These *are the same* Moses and Aaron.

AARON IS MOSES' SPOKESMAN

[28]And it came to pass, on the day the LORD spoke to Moses in the land of Egypt, [29]that the LORD spoke to Moses, saying, "I *am* the LORD. Speak to Pharaoh king of Egypt all that I say to you."

[30]But Moses said before the LORD, "Behold, I *am* of uncircumcised lips, and how shall Pharaoh heed me?"

6:15 [a]Spelled *Nemuel* in Numbers 26:12

Promise   HE PROMISES TO TAKE YOU AS HIS OWN.

I will take you as My people, and I will be your God. Then you shall know that I am the LORD your God who brings you out from under the burdens of the Egyptians (Ex. 6:7).

In many ways, Israel's history is a symbol of the journey that all of Jesus' followers are making. That's one reason the Old Testament is still so important to Christians. You can look in the Old Testament to find wisdom for whatever you're going through and to find out what's coming next. When God said, "I will take you as My people," He wasn't just talking to the Israelites. He was also looking out through time and speaking to Christians today. He knew you would be on earth at this moment and He wanted to be sure you knew that He accepted you as His own. The nation of Israel was God's own because of the faith and obedience of their father, Abraham. Today, you are a chosen person because of the love and obedience of Jesus.

Belonging to God makes you worth something. Your brains, your talent, your awesome sports ability—none of it impresses God. Even without all the cool things about you, you'd be worth something because God accepts you as His own.

SEE FOR YOURSELF:
Rom. 1:17; 3:10

¹So the LORD said to Moses: "See, I have made you *as* God to Pharaoh, and Aaron your brother shall be your prophet. ²You shall speak all that I command you. And Aaron your brother shall tell Pharaoh to send the children of Israel out of his land. ³And I will harden Pharaoh's heart, and multiply My signs and My wonders in the land of Egypt. ⁴But Pharaoh will not heed you, so that I may lay My hand on Egypt and bring My armies *and* My people, the children of Israel, out of the land of Egypt by great judgments. ⁵And the Egyptians shall know that I *am* the LORD, when I stretch out My hand on Egypt and bring out the children of Israel from among them."

⁶Then Moses and Aaron did *so*; just as the LORD commanded them, so they did. ⁷And Moses *was* eighty years old and Aaron eighty-three years old when they spoke to Pharaoh.

AARON'S MIRACULOUS ROD

⁸Then the LORD spoke to Moses and Aaron, saying, ⁹"When Pharaoh speaks to you, saying, 'Show a miracle for yourselves', then you shall say to Aaron, 'Take your rod and cast *it* before Pharaoh, *and* let it become a serpent.' " ¹⁰So Moses and Aaron went in to Pharaoh, and they did so, just as the LORD commanded. And Aaron cast down his rod before Pharaoh and before his servants, and it became a serpent.

WHAT'S IT MEAN?

Ancient kings often followed the advice of magicians and fortune-tellers. These "wise men" read the future and told the king when would be a good time to take action. The Israelites, on the other hand, were not allowed to be involved in occult practices like magic and fortune-telling.

Exodus 7:11

¹¹But Pharaoh also called the wise men and the sorcerers; so the magicians of Egypt, they also did in like manner with their enchantments. ¹²For every man threw down his rod, and they became serpents. But Aaron's rod swallowed up their rods. ¹³And Pharaoh's heart grew hard, and he did not heed them, as the LORD had said.

THE FIRST PLAGUE: WATERS BECOME BLOOD

¹⁴So the LORD said to Moses: "Pharaoh's heart *is* hard; he refuses to let the people go. ¹⁵Go to Pharaoh in the morning, when he goes out to the water, and you shall stand by the river's bank to meet him; and the rod which was turned to a serpent you shall take in your hand. ¹⁶And you shall say to him, 'The LORD God of the Hebrews has sent me to you, saying, "Let My people go, that they may serve Me in the wilderness"; but indeed, until now you would not hear! ¹⁷Thus says the LORD: "By this you shall know that I *am* the LORD. Behold, I will strike the waters which *are* in the river with the rod that *is* in my hand, and they shall be turned to blood. ¹⁸And the fish that *are* in the river shall die, the river shall stink, and the Egyptians will loathe to drink the water of the river." ' "

¹⁹Then the LORD spoke to Moses, "Say to Aaron, 'Take your rod and stretch out your hand over the waters of Egypt, over their streams, over their rivers, over their ponds, and over all their pools of water, that they may become blood. And there shall be blood throughout all the land of Egypt, both in *buckets of* wood and *pitchers of* stone.' " ²⁰And Moses and Aaron did so, just as the LORD commanded. So he lifted up the rod and struck the waters that *were* in the river, in the sight of Pharaoh and in the sight of his servants. And all the waters that *were* in the river were turned to blood. ²¹The fish that *were* in the river died, the river stank, and the Egyptians could not drink the water of the river. So there was blood throughout all the land of Egypt.

²²Then the magicians of Egypt did so with their enchantments; and Pharaoh's heart grew hard, and he did not heed them, as the LORD had said. ²³And Pharaoh turned and went into his house. Neither was his heart moved by this. ²⁴So all the Egyptians dug all around the river for water to drink, because they could not drink the water of the river. ²⁵And seven days passed after the LORD had struck the river.

THE SECOND PLAGUE: FROGS

¹And the LORD spoke to Moses, "Go to Pharaoh and say to him, 'Thus says the LORD: "Let My people go, that they may serve Me. ²But if you refuse to let *them* go, behold, I will smite all your territory with frogs. ³So the river shall bring forth frogs abundantly, which shall go up and come into your house, into your bedroom, on your bed, into the houses of your servants, on your people, into your ovens, and into your kneading bowls. ⁴And the frogs shall come up

on you, on your people, and on all your servants.' ' "

⁵Then the LORD spoke to Moses, "Say to Aaron, 'Stretch out your hand with your rod over the streams, over the rivers, and over the ponds, and cause frogs to come up on the land of Egypt.' " ⁶So Aaron stretched out his hand over the waters of Egypt, and the frogs came up and covered the land of Egypt. ⁷And the magicians did so with their enchantments, and brought up frogs on the land of Egypt.

⁸Then Pharaoh called for Moses and Aaron, and said, "Entreat the LORD that He may take away the frogs from me and from my people; and I will let the people go, that they may sacrifice to the LORD."

⁹And Moses said to Pharaoh, "Accept the honor of saying when I shall intercede for you, for your servants, and for your people, to destroy the frogs from you and your houses, *that* they may remain in the river only."

¹⁰So he said, "Tomorrow." And he said, "*Let it be* according to your word, that you may know that *there is* no one like the LORD our God. ¹¹And the frogs shall depart from you, from your houses, from your servants, and from your people. They shall remain in the river only."

> "And the LORD spoke to Moses, 'Go to Pharaoh and say to him, "Thus says the LORD: 'Let My people go, that they may serve Me.' " ' "
> (Exodus 8:1)

WHAT'S IT MEAN?

Frogs were considered sacred in ancient Egypt, as signs of fertility. You can imagine how confused and alarmed the people became when they saw their land covered with the amphibians.
Exodus 8:1–5

¹²Then Moses and Aaron went out from Pharaoh. And Moses cried out to the LORD concerning the frogs which He had brought against Pharaoh. ¹³So the LORD did according to the word of Moses. And the frogs died out of the houses, out of the courtyards, and out of the fields. ¹⁴They gathered them together in heaps, and the land stank. ¹⁵But when Pharaoh saw that there was relief, he hardened his heart and did not heed them, as the LORD had said.

THE THIRD PLAGUE: LICE

¹⁶So the LORD said to Moses, "Say to Aaron, 'Stretch out your rod, and strike the dust of the land, so that it may become lice throughout all the land of Egypt.' " ¹⁷And they did so. For Aaron stretched out his hand with his rod and struck the dust of the earth, and it became lice on man and beast. All the dust of the land became lice throughout all the land of Egypt. ¹⁸Now the magicians so worked with their enchantments to bring forth lice, but they could not. So there were lice on man and beast. ¹⁹Then the magicians said to Pharaoh, "This *is* the finger of God." But Pharaoh's heart grew hard, and he did not heed them, just as the LORD had said.

THE FOURTH PLAGUE: FLIES

²⁰And the LORD said to Moses, "Rise early in the morning and stand before Pharaoh as he comes out to the water. Then say to him, 'Thus says the LORD: "Let My people go, that they may serve Me. ²¹Or else, if you will not let My people go, behold, I will send swarms *of flies* on you and your servants, on your people and into your houses. The houses of the Egyptians shall be full of swarms *of flies*, and also the ground on which they *stand*. ²²And in that day I will set apart the land of Goshen, in which My people dwell, that no swarms *of flies* shall be there, in order that you may know that I *am* the LORD in the midst of the land. ²³I will make a difference*a* between My people and your people. Tomorrow this sign shall be." ' " ²⁴And the LORD did so. Thick swarms *of flies* came into the house of Pharaoh, *into* his servants' houses, and into all the land of Egypt. The land was corrupted because of the swarms *of flies*.

²⁵Then Pharaoh called for Moses and Aaron, and said, "Go, sacrifice to your God in the land."

²⁶And Moses said, "It is not right to do so, for we would be sacrificing the abomination of the Egyptians to the LORD our God. If we sacrifice the abomination of the Egyptians before

---

8:23 *a*Literally *set a ransom* (compare Exodus 9:4 and 11:7)

their eyes, then will they not stone us? [27]We will go three days' journey into the wilderness and sacrifice to the LORD our God as He will command us."

[28]So Pharaoh said, "I will let you go, that you may sacrifice to the LORD your God in the wilderness; only you shall not go very far away. Intercede for me."

[29]Then Moses said, "Indeed I am going out from you, and I will entreat the LORD, that the swarms *of flies* may depart tomorrow from Pharaoh, from his servants, and from his people. But let Pharaoh not deal deceitfully anymore in not letting the people go to sacrifice to the LORD."

[30]So Moses went out from Pharaoh and entreated the LORD. [31]And the LORD did according to the word of Moses; He removed the swarms *of flies* from Pharaoh, from his servants, and from his people. Not one remained. [32]But Pharaoh hardened his heart at this time also; neither would he let the people go.

THE FIFTH PLAGUE: LIVESTOCK DISEASED

[1]Then the LORD said to Moses, "Go in to Pharaoh and tell him, 'Thus says the LORD God of the Hebrews: "Let My people go, that they may serve Me. [2]For if you refuse to let *them* go, and still hold them, [3]behold, the hand of the LORD will be on your cattle in the field, on the horses, on the donkeys, on the camels, on the oxen, and on the sheep—a very severe pestilence. [4]And the LORD will make a difference between the livestock of Israel and the livestock of Egypt. So nothing shall die of all *that* belongs to the children of Israel."'" [5]Then the LORD appointed a set time, saying, "Tomorrow the LORD will do this thing in the land."

[6]So the LORD did this thing on the next day, and all the livestock of Egypt died; but of the livestock of the children of Israel, not one died. [7]Then Pharaoh sent, and indeed, not even one of the livestock of the Israelites was dead. But the heart of Pharaoh became hard, and he did not let the people go.

THE SIXTH PLAGUE: BOILS

[8]So the LORD said to Moses and Aaron, "Take for yourselves handfuls of ashes from a furnace, and let Moses scatter it toward the heavens in the sight of Pharaoh. [9]And it will become fine dust in all the land of Egypt, and it will cause boils that break out in sores on man and beast throughout all the land of Egypt." [10]Then they took ashes from the furnace and stood before Pharaoh, and Moses scattered them toward heaven. And *they* caused boils that break out in sores on man and beast. [11]And the magicians could not stand before Moses because of the boils, for the boils were on the magicians and on all the Egyptians. [12]But the LORD hardened the heart of Pharaoh; and he did not heed them, just as the LORD had spoken to Moses.

THE SEVENTH PLAGUE: HAIL

[13]Then the LORD said to Moses, "Rise early in the morning and stand before Pharaoh, and say to him, 'Thus says the LORD God of the Hebrews: "Let My people go, that they may serve Me, [14]for at this time I will send all My plagues to your very heart, and on your servants and on your people, that you may know that *there is* none like Me in all the earth. [15]Now if I had stretched out My hand and struck you and your people with pestilence, then you would have been cut off from the earth. [16]But indeed for this *purpose* I have raised you up, that I may show My power *in* you, and that My name may be declared in all the earth. [17]As yet you exalt yourself against My people in that you will not let them go. [18]Behold, tomorrow about this time I will cause very heavy hail to rain down, such as has not been in Egypt since its founding until now. [19]Therefore send now *and* gather your livestock and all that you have in the field, for the hail shall come down on every man and every animal which is found in the field and is not brought home; and they shall die."'"

[20]He who feared the word of the LORD among the servants of Pharaoh made his servants and his livestock flee to the houses. [21]But he who did not regard the word of the LORD left his servants and his livestock in the field.

[22]Then the LORD said to Moses, "Stretch out your hand toward heaven, that there may be hail in all the land of Egypt—on man, on beast, and on every herb of the field, throughout the land of Egypt." [23]And Moses stretched out his rod toward heaven; and the LORD sent thunder and hail, and fire darted to the ground. And the LORD rained hail on the land of Egypt. [24]So there was hail, and fire mingled with the hail, so very heavy that there was none like it in all the land of Egypt since it became a nation. [25]And the hail struck throughout the whole land of Egypt, all that *was* in the field, both man and beast; and the hail struck every herb of the field and broke every tree of the field. [26]Only in the land of Goshen, where the children of Israel *were*, there was no hail.

[27]And Pharaoh sent and called for Moses

and Aaron, and said to them, "I have sinned this time. The LORD *is* righteous, and my people and I *are* wicked. [28]Entreat the LORD, that there may be no *more* mighty thundering and hail, for *it is* enough. I will let you go, and you shall stay no longer."

[29]So Moses said to him, "As soon as I have gone out of the city, I will spread out my hands to the LORD; the thunder will cease, and there will be no more hail, that you may know that the earth *is* the LORD's. [30]But as for you and your servants, I know that you will not yet fear the LORD God."

[31]Now the flax and the barley were struck, for the barley *was* in the head and the flax *was* in bud. [32]But the wheat and the spelt were not struck, for they *are* late crops.

[33]So Moses went out of the city from Pharaoh and spread out his hands to the LORD; then the thunder and the hail ceased, and the rain was not poured on the earth. [34]And when Pharaoh saw that the rain, the hail, and the thunder had ceased, he sinned yet more; and he hardened his heart, he and his servants. [35]So the heart of Pharaoh was hard; neither would he let the children of Israel go, as the LORD had spoken by Moses.

THE EIGHTH PLAGUE: LOCUSTS

[1]Now the LORD said to Moses, "Go in to Pharaoh; for I have hardened his heart and the hearts of his servants, that I may show these signs of Mine before him, [2]and that you may tell in the hearing of your son and your son's son the mighty things I have done in Egypt, and My signs which I have done among them, that you may know that I *am* the LORD."

[3]So Moses and Aaron came in to Pharaoh and said to him, "Thus says the LORD God of the Hebrews: 'How long will you refuse to humble yourself before Me? Let My people go, that they may serve Me. [4]Or else, if you refuse to let My people go, behold, tomorrow I will bring locusts into your territory. [5]And they shall cover the face of the earth, so that no one will be able to see the earth; and they shall eat the residue of what is left, which remains to you from the hail, and they shall eat every tree which grows up for you out of the field. [6]They shall fill your houses, the houses of all your servants, and the houses of all the Egyptians— which neither your fathers nor your fathers' fathers have seen, since the day that they were on the earth to this day.' " And he turned and went out from Pharaoh.

[7]Then Pharaoh's servants said to him, "How long shall this man be a snare to us? Let the men go, that they may serve the LORD their God. Do you not yet know that Egypt is destroyed?"

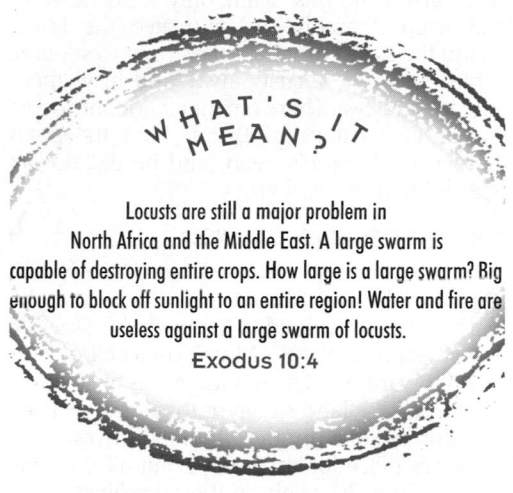

WHAT'S IT MEAN?

Locusts are still a major problem in North Africa and the Middle East. A large swarm is capable of destroying entire crops. How large is a large swarm? Big enough to block off sunlight to an entire region! Water and fire are useless against a large swarm of locusts.

Exodus 10:4

[8]So Moses and Aaron were brought again to Pharaoh, and he said to them, "Go, serve the LORD your God. Who *are* the ones that are going?"

[9]And Moses said, "We will go with our young and our old; with our sons and our daughters, with our flocks and our herds we will go, for we must hold a feast to the LORD."

[10]Then he said to them, "The LORD had better be with you when I let you and your little ones go! Beware, for evil is ahead of you. [11]Not so! Go now, you *who are* men, and serve the LORD, for that is what you desired." And they were driven out from Pharaoh's presence.

[12]Then the LORD said to Moses, "Stretch out your hand over the land of Egypt for the locusts, that they may come upon the land of Egypt, and eat every herb of the land—all that the hail has left." [13]So Moses stretched out his rod over the land of Egypt, and the LORD brought an east wind on the land all that day and all *that* night. When it was morning, the east wind brought the locusts. [14]And the locusts went up over all the land of Egypt and rested on all the territory of Egypt. *They were* very severe; previously there had been no such locusts as they, nor shall there be such after them. [15]For they covered the face of the whole earth, so that the land was darkened; and they ate every herb of the land and all the fruit of the trees which the hail had left. So there remained nothing green on the trees or on the plants of the field throughout all the land of Egypt.

[16]Then Pharaoh called for Moses and Aaron in haste, and said, "I have sinned against the

LORD your God and against you. ¹⁷Now there-fore, please forgive my sin only this once, and entreat the LORD your God, that He may take away from me this death only." ¹⁸So he went out from Pharaoh and entreated the LORD. ¹⁹And the LORD turned a very strong west wind, which took the locusts away and blew them into the Red Sea. There remained not one locust in all the territory of Egypt. ²⁰But the LORD hardened Pharaoh's heart, and he did not let the children of Israel go.

THE NINTH PLAGUE: DARKNESS

²¹Then the LORD said to Moses, "Stretch out your hand toward heaven, that there may be darkness over the land of Egypt, darkness *which* may even be felt." ²²So Moses stretched out his hand toward heaven, and there was thick dark-ness in all the land of Egypt three days. ²³They did not see one another; nor did anyone rise from his place for three days. But all the chil-dren of Israel had light in their dwellings.

²⁴Then Pharaoh called to Moses and said, "Go, serve the LORD; only let your flocks and your herds be kept back. Let your little ones also go with you."

²⁵But Moses said, "You must also give us sacrifices and burnt offerings, that we may sac-rifice to the LORD our God. ²⁶Our livestock also shall go with us; not a hoof shall be left behind. For we must take some of them to serve the LORD our God, and even we do not know with what we must serve the LORD until we arrive there."

²⁷But the LORD hardened Pharaoh's heart, and he would not let them go. ²⁸Then Pharaoh said to him, "Get away from me! Take heed to yourself and see my face no more! For in the day you see my face you shall die!"

²⁹So Moses said, "You have spoken well. I will never see your face again."

DEATH OF THE FIRSTBORN ANNOUNCED

¹And the LORD said to Moses, "I will bring one more plague on Pharaoh and on Egypt. Afterward he will let you go from here. When he lets *you* go, he will surely drive you out of here altogether. ²Speak now in the hearing of the people, and let every man ask from his neighbor and every woman from her neighbor, articles of silver and articles of gold." ³And the LORD gave the people favor in the sight of the Egyptians. Moreover the man Moses *was* very great in the land of Egypt, in the sight of Pharaoh's servants and in the sight of the people.

⁴Then Moses said, "Thus says the LORD:

'About midnight I will go out into the midst of Egypt; ⁵and all the firstborn in the land of Egypt shall die, from the firstborn of Pharaoh who sits on his throne, even to the firstborn of the female servant who *is* behind the handmill, and all the firstborn of the animals. ⁶Then there shall be a great cry throughout all the land of Egypt, such as was not like it *before,* nor shall be like it again. ⁷But against none of the children of Israel shall a dog move its tongue, against man or beast, that you may know that the LORD does make a difference between the Egyptians and Israel.' ⁸And all these your servants shall come down to me and bow down to me, saying, 'Get out, and all the people who follow you!' After that I will go out." Then he went out from Pha-raoh in great anger.

⁹But the LORD said to Moses, "Pharaoh will not heed you, so that My wonders may be multiplied in the land of Egypt." ¹⁰So Moses and Aaron did all these wonders before Pharaoh; and the LORD hardened Pharaoh's heart, and he did not let the children of Israel go out of his land.

THE PASSOVER INSTITUTED

¹Now the LORD spoke to Moses and Aaron in the land of Egypt, saying, ²"This month *shall be* your beginning of months; it *shall be* the first month of the year to you. ³Speak to all the con-gregation of Israel, saying: 'On the tenth of this month every man shall take for himself a lamb, according to the house of *his* father, a lamb for a household. ⁴And if the household is too small for the lamb, let him and his neighbor next to his house take *it* according to the number of the persons; according to each man's need you shall make your count for the lamb. ⁵Your lamb shall be without blemish, a male of the first year. You may take *it* from the sheep or from the goats. ⁶Now you shall keep it until the four-teenth day of the same month. Then the whole assembly of the congregation of Israel shall kill it at twilight. ⁷And they shall take *some* of the blood and put *it* on the two doorposts and on the lintel of the houses where they eat it. ⁸Then they shall eat the flesh on that night; roasted in fire, with unleavened bread *and* with bitter *herbs* they shall eat it. ⁹Do not eat it raw, nor boiled at all with water, but roasted in fire—its head with its legs and its entrails. ¹⁰You shall let none of it remain until morning, and what remains of it until morning you shall burn with fire. ¹¹And thus you shall eat it: *with* a belt on your waist, your sandals on your feet, and your staff in your hand. So you shall eat it in haste. It *is* the LORD's Passover.

¹²'For I will pass through the land of Egypt on that night, and will strike all the firstborn in the land of Egypt, both man and beast; and against all the gods of Egypt I will execute judgment: I *am* the LORD. ¹³Now the blood shall be a sign for you on the houses where you *are*. And when I see the blood, I will pass over you; and the plague shall not be on you to destroy *you* when I strike the land of Egypt.

WHAT'S IT MEAN?

Hyssop plants were fragrant shrubs with yellow flowers that grew to about three feet high. Their branches were used for brushing or sprinkling liquids.
Exodus 12:22

¹⁴'So this day shall be to you a memorial; and you shall keep it as a feast to the LORD throughout your generations. You shall keep it as a feast by an everlasting ordinance. ¹⁵Seven days you shall eat unleavened bread. On the first day you shall remove leaven from your houses. For whoever eats leavened bread from the first day until the seventh day, that person shall be cut off from Israel. ¹⁶On the first day *there shall be* a holy convocation, and on the seventh day there shall be a holy convocation for you. No manner of work shall be done on them; but *that* which everyone must eat—that only may be prepared by you. ¹⁷So you shall observe *the Feast of* Unleavened Bread, for on this same day I will have brought your armies out of the land of Egypt. Therefore you shall observe this day throughout your generations as an everlasting ordinance. ¹⁸In the first *month*, on the fourteenth day of the month at evening, you shall eat unleavened bread, until the twenty-first day of the month at evening. ¹⁹For seven days no leaven shall be found in your houses, since whoever eats what is leavened, that same person shall be cut off from the congregation of Israel, whether *he is* a stranger or a native of the land. ²⁰You shall eat nothing leavened; in all your dwellings you shall eat unleavened bread.' "

²¹Then Moses called for all the elders of Israel and said to them, "Pick out and take lambs for yourselves according to your families, and kill the Passover *lamb*. ²²And you shall take a bunch of hyssop, dip *it* in the blood that *is* in the basin, and strike the lintel and the two doorposts with the blood that *is* in the basin. And none of you shall go out of the door of his house until morning. ²³For the LORD will pass through to strike the Egyptians; and when He sees the blood on the lintel and on the two doorposts, the LORD will pass over the door and not allow the destroyer to come into your houses to strike *you*. ²⁴And you shall observe this thing as an ordinance for you and your sons forever. ²⁵It will come to pass when you come to the land which the LORD will give you, just as He promised, that you shall keep this service. ²⁶And it shall be, when your children say to you, 'What do you mean by this service?' ²⁷that you shall say, 'It *is* the Passover sacrifice of the LORD, who passed over the houses of the children of Israel in Egypt when He struck the Egyptians and delivered our households.' " So the people bowed their heads and worshiped. ²⁸Then the children of Israel went away and did *so*; just as the LORD had commanded Moses and Aaron, so they did.

WHAT'S IT MEAN?

The Passover is one of the most important events in Jewish history. One of the key parts of modern Passover celebrations is the retelling of the story of the Israelites' escape from Egypt. Traditionally the story is told as parents reply to questions asked by the youngest child in the family.
Exodus 12:26, 27

THE TENTH PLAGUE: DEATH OF THE FIRSTBORN

²⁹And it came to pass at midnight that the LORD struck all the firstborn in the land of Egypt, from the firstborn of Pharaoh who sat on his throne to the firstborn of the captive who *was* in the dungeon, and all the firstborn of livestock. ³⁰So Pharaoh rose in the night, he, all his servants, and all the Egyptians; and there was a great cry in Egypt, for *there was* not a house where *there was* not one dead.

THE EXODUS

[31]Then he called for Moses and Aaron by night, and said, "Rise, go out from among my people, both you and the children of Israel. And go, serve the LORD as you have said. [32]Also take your flocks and your herds, as you have said, and be gone; and bless me also."

[33]And the Egyptians urged the people, that they might send them out of the land in haste. For they said, "We *shall* all *be* dead." [34]So the people took their dough before it was leavened, having their kneading bowls bound up in their clothes on their shoulders. [35]Now the children of Israel had done according to the word of Moses, and they had asked from the Egyptians articles of silver, articles of gold, and clothing. [36]And the LORD had given the people favor in the sight of the Egyptians, so that they granted them *what they requested*. Thus they plundered the Egyptians.

[37]Then the children of Israel journeyed from Rameses to Succoth, about six hundred thousand men on foot, besides children. [38]A mixed multitude went up with them also, and flocks and herds—a great deal of livestock. [39]And they baked unleavened cakes of the dough which they had brought out of Egypt; for it was not leavened, because they were driven out of Egypt and could not wait, nor had they prepared provisions for themselves.

[40]Now the sojourn of the children of Israel who lived in Egypt[a] *was* four hundred and thirty years. [41]And it came to pass at the end of the four hundred and thirty years—on that very same day—it came to pass that all the armies of the LORD went out from the land of Egypt. [42]It *is* a night of solemn observance to the LORD for bringing them out of the land of Egypt. This *is* that night of the LORD, a solemn observance for all the children of Israel throughout their generations.

PASSOVER REGULATIONS

[43]And the LORD said to Moses and Aaron, "This *is* the ordinance of the Passover: No foreigner shall eat it. [44]But every man's servant who is bought for money, when you have circumcised him, then he may eat it. [45]A sojourner and a hired servant shall not eat it. [46]In one house it shall be eaten; you shall not carry any of the flesh outside the house, nor shall you break one of its bones. [47]All the congregation of Israel shall keep it. [48]And when a stranger dwells with you *and wants* to keep the Passover to the LORD, let all his males be circumcised, and then let him come near and keep it; and he shall be as a native of the land. For no uncircumcised person shall eat it. [49]One law shall be for the native-born and for the stranger who dwells among you."

[50]Thus all the children of Israel did; as the LORD commanded Moses and Aaron, so they did. [51]And it came to pass, on that very same day, that the LORD brought the children of Israel out of the land of Egypt according to their armies.

THE FIRSTBORN CONSECRATED

[1]Then the LORD spoke to Moses, saying, [2]"Consecrate to Me all the firstborn, whatever opens the womb among the children of Israel, *both* of man and beast; it is Mine."

THE FEAST OF UNLEAVENED BREAD

[3]And Moses said to the people: "Remember this day in which you went out of Egypt, out of the house of bondage; for by strength of hand the LORD brought you out of this *place*. No leavened bread shall be eaten. [4]On this day you are going out, in the month Abib. [5]And it shall be, when the LORD brings you into the land of the Canaanites and the Hittites and the Amorites and the Hivites and the Jebusites, which He swore to your fathers to give you, a land flowing with milk and honey, that you shall keep this service in this month. [6]Seven days you shall eat unleavened bread, and on the seventh day *there shall be* a feast to the LORD. [7]Unleavened bread shall be eaten seven days. And no leavened bread shall be seen among you, nor shall leaven be seen among you in all your quarters. [8]And you shall tell your son in that day, saying, 'This is done because of what the LORD did for me when I came up from Egypt.' [9]It shall be as a sign to you on your hand and as a memorial between your eyes, that the LORD's law may be in your mouth; for with a

> "And Moses said to the people: 'Remember this day in which you went out of Egypt, out of the house of bondage; for by strength of hand the LORD brought you out of this place. No leavened bread shall be eaten.' " (Exodus 13:3)

12:40 [a]Samaritan Pentateuch and Septuagint read *Egypt and Canaan*.

strong hand the LORD has brought you out of Egypt. [10]You shall therefore keep this ordinance in its season from year to year.

THE LAW OF THE FIRSTBORN

[11]"And it shall be, when the LORD brings you into the land of the Canaanites, as He swore to you and your fathers, and gives it to you, [12]that you shall set apart to the LORD all that open the womb, that is, every firstborn that comes from an animal which you have; the males *shall be* the LORD's. [13]But every firstborn of a donkey you shall redeem with a lamb; and if you will not redeem *it*, then you shall break its neck. And all the firstborn of man among your sons you shall redeem. [14]So it shall be, when your

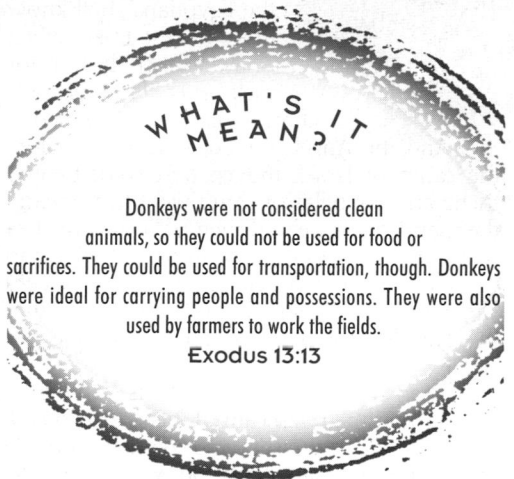

Donkeys were not considered clean animals, so they could not be used for food or sacrifices. They could be used for transportation, though. Donkeys were ideal for carrying people and possessions. They were also used by farmers to work the fields.

Exodus 13:13

son asks you in time to come, saying, 'What *is* this?' that you shall say to him, 'By strength of hand the LORD brought us out of Egypt, out of the house of bondage. [15]And it came to pass, when Pharaoh was stubborn about letting us go, that the LORD killed all the firstborn in the land of Egypt, both the firstborn of man and the firstborn of beast. Therefore I sacrifice to the LORD all males that open the womb, but all the firstborn of my sons I redeem.' [16]It shall be as a sign on your hand and as frontlets between your eyes, for by strength of hand the LORD brought us out of Egypt."

THE WILDERNESS WAY

[17]Then it came to pass, when Pharaoh had let the people go, that God did not lead them *by* way of the land of the Philistines, although that *was* near; for God said, "Lest perhaps the people change their minds when they see war, and return to Egypt." [18]So God led the people around

by way of the wilderness of the Red Sea. And the children of Israel went up in orderly ranks out of the land of Egypt.

[19]And Moses took the bones of Joseph with him, for he had placed the children of Israel under solemn oath, saying, "God will surely visit you, and you shall carry up my bones from here with you."[a]

[20]So they took their journey from Succoth and camped in Etham at the edge of the wilderness. [21]And the LORD went before them by day in a pillar of cloud to lead the way, and by night in a pillar of fire to give them light, so as to go by day and night. [22]He did not take away the pillar of cloud by day or the pillar of fire by night *from* before the people.

THE RED SEA CROSSING

[1]Now the LORD spoke to Moses, saying: [2]"Speak to the children of Israel, that they turn and camp before Pi Hahiroth, between Migdol and the sea, opposite Baal Zephon; you shall camp before it by the sea. [3]For Pharaoh will say of the children of Israel, 'They *are* bewildered by the land; the wilderness has closed them in.' [4]Then I will harden Pharaoh's heart, so that he will pursue them; and I will gain honor over Pharaoh and over all his army, that the Egyptians may know that I *am* the LORD." And they did so.

[5]Now it was told the king of Egypt that the people had fled, and the heart of Pharaoh and his servants was turned against the people; and they said, "Why have we done this, that we have let Israel go from serving us?" [6]So he made

The chariot was the vehicle of choice in ancient Egypt for good reason. The Egyptians were the Ferrari of chariot makers. Their models were built from wood held together by leather strips. This made the chariots light and gave them excellent shock absorbency. Chariots were designed to carry at least two people—one person to drive and one person, armed with a bow, to fight the enemy.

Exodus 14:6

13:19 [a]Genesis 50:25

ready his chariot and took his people with him. [7]Also, he took six hundred choice chariots, and all the chariots of Egypt with captains over every one of them. [8]And the LORD hardened the heart of Pharaoh king of Egypt, and he pursued the children of Israel; and the children of Israel went out with boldness. [9]So the Egyptians pursued them, all the horses *and* chariots of Pharaoh, his horsemen and his army, and overtook them camping by the sea beside Pi Hahiroth, before Baal Zephon.

[10]And when Pharaoh drew near, the children of Israel lifted their eyes, and behold, the Egyptians marched after them. So they were very afraid, and the children of Israel cried out to the LORD. [11]Then they said to Moses, "Because *there were* no graves in Egypt, have you taken us away to die in the wilderness? Why have you so dealt with us, to bring us up out of Egypt? [12]*Is* this not the word that we told you in Egypt, saying, 'Let us alone that we may serve the Egyptians'? For *it would have been* better for us to serve the Egyptians than that we should die in the wilderness."

[13]And Moses said to the people, "Do not be afraid. Stand still, and see the salvation of the LORD, which He will accomplish for you today. For the Egyptians whom you see today, you shall see again no more forever. [14]The LORD will fight for you, and you shall hold your peace."

[15]And the LORD said to Moses, "Why do you cry to Me? Tell the children of Israel to go forward. [16]But lift up your rod, and stretch out your hand over the sea and divide it. And the children of Israel shall go on dry *ground* through the midst of the sea. [17]And I indeed will harden the hearts of the Egyptians, and they shall follow them. So I will gain honor over Pharaoh and over all his army, his chariots, and his horsemen. [18]Then the Egyptians shall know that I *am* the LORD, when I have gained honor for Myself over Pharaoh, his chariots, and his horsemen."

[19]And the Angel of God, who went before the camp of Israel, moved and went behind them; and the pillar of cloud went from before them and stood behind them. [20]So it came between the camp of the Egyptians and the camp of Israel. Thus it was a cloud and darkness *to the one*, and it gave light by night *to the other*, so that the one did not come near the other all that night.

[21]Then Moses stretched out his hand over the sea; and the LORD caused the sea to go *back* by a strong east wind all that night, and made the sea into dry *land*, and the waters were divided. [22]So the children of Israel went into the

> "The LORD is my strength and song, and He has become my salvation; He is my God, and I will praise Him; my father's God, and I will exalt Him."
> (Exodus 15:2)

Promise   HE PROMISES TO FIGHT FOR YOU.

The LORD will fight for you, and you shall hold your peace (Ex. 14:14).

Just as God fought for the Israelites when they were stuck between the raging Red Sea and the advancing Egyptian army, Jesus has fought for you. He fought and defeated the power of sin in your life. Big deal, right? Right—that means you can do the right thing even when it's hard.

Even the apostle Paul said that he had a hard time doing the right thing because his selfish desires kept urging him to do something else. Everyone who wants to please God faces this problem. But Jesus went up against all of your selfishness and temptations. He went smack up against all the right things that you don't want to do. And He won.

Moses told the Israelites, "You shall hold your peace." That's true for you. You don't have to fight because Jesus has already won your battle. Does that mean you just sit around like mush? No, you just have to stay strong, stay close to Him, and keep believing that He's already won.

SEE FOR YOURSELF:
Deut. 1:30, 31; 2 Chr. 32:8; Neh. 4:20

midst of the sea on the dry *ground*, and the waters *were* a wall to them on their right hand and on their left. ²³And the Egyptians pursued and went after them into the midst of the sea, all Pharaoh's horses, his chariots, and his horsemen.

²⁴Now it came to pass, in the morning watch, that the LORD looked down upon the army of the Egyptians through the pillar of fire and cloud, and He troubled the army of the Egyptians. ²⁵And He took off*ᵃ* their chariot wheels, so that they drove them with difficulty; and the Egyptians said, "Let us flee from the face of Israel, for the LORD fights for them against the Egyptians."

²⁶Then the LORD said to Moses, "Stretch out your hand over the sea, that the waters may come back upon the Egyptians, on their chariots, and on their horsemen." ²⁷And Moses stretched out his hand over the sea; and when the morning appeared, the sea returned to its full depth, while the Egyptians were fleeing into it. So the LORD overthrew the Egyptians in the midst of the sea. ²⁸Then the waters returned and covered the chariots, the horsemen, *and* all the army of Pharaoh that came into the sea after them. Not so much as one of them remained. ²⁹But the children of Israel had walked on dry *land* in the midst of the sea, and the waters *were* a wall to them on their right hand and on their left.

³⁰So the LORD saved Israel that day out of the hand of the Egyptians, and Israel saw the Egyptians dead on the seashore. ³¹Thus Israel saw the great work which the LORD had done in Egypt; so the people feared the LORD, and believed the LORD and His servant Moses.

THE SONG OF MOSES

¹Then Moses and the children of Israel sang this song to the LORD, and spoke, saying:

> "I will sing to the LORD,
> For He has triumphed
>   gloriously!
> The horse and its rider
> He has thrown into the
>   sea!

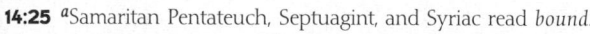

MUSIC
What can music be used for? (15:1)

2
> The LORD *is* my strength and
>   song,
> And He has become my salvation;
> He *is* my God, and I will praise Him;
> My father's God, and I will exalt Him.

3
> The LORD *is* a man of war;
> The LORD *is* His name.

4
> Pharaoh's chariots and his army
>   He has cast into the sea;
> His chosen captains also
>   are drowned in the
>   Red Sea.

5
> The depths have covered
>   them;
> They sank to the bottom
>   like a stone.

GOD
What is God like? (15:3, 4)

6
> "Your right hand, O LORD, has become
>   glorious in power;
> Your right hand, O LORD, has dashed the
>   enemy in pieces.

7
> And in the greatness of Your excellence
> You have overthrown those who rose
>   against You;
> You sent forth Your wrath;
> It consumed them like stubble.

8
> And with the blast of Your nostrils
> The waters were gathered together;
> The floods stood upright like a heap;
> The depths congealed in the heart of the
>   sea.

9
> The enemy said, 'I will pursue,
> I will overtake,
> I will divide the spoil;
> My desire shall be satisfied on them.
> I will draw my sword,
> My hand shall destroy them.'

10
> You blew with Your wind,
> The sea covered them;
> They sank like lead in the mighty waters.

11
> "Who *is* like You, O LORD, among the
>   gods?
> Who *is* like You, glorious in holiness,
> Fearful in praises, doing wonders?

12
> You stretched out Your right hand;
> The earth swallowed them.

13
> You in Your mercy have led forth
> The people whom You have redeemed;
> You have guided *them* in Your strength
> To Your holy habitation.

14
> "The people will hear *and* be afraid;
> Sorrow will take hold of the inhabitants
>   of Philistia.

15
> Then the chiefs of Edom will be dismayed;
> The mighty men of Moab,
> Trembling will take hold of them;
> All the inhabitants of Canaan will melt
>   away.

16
> Fear and dread will fall on them;
> By the greatness of Your arm

14:25 *ᵃ*Samaritan Pentateuch, Septuagint, and Syriac read *bound*.

WHAT'S IT MEAN?

The Philistines happened to be living in the very place God had promised to the Israelites. In order to claim their land, the Israelites would have to "evict" the Philistines. The job would not be easy, though. The Philistines were known for making advanced weapons out of iron. Edom and Moab were the countries on the other side of the Jordan River, which ran to the east of the Philistines' land.

Exodus 15:14, 15

They will be *as* still as a stone,
Till Your people pass over, O LORD,
Till the people pass over
Whom You have purchased.
17 You will bring them in and plant them
In the mountain of Your inheritance,
In the place, O LORD, *which* You have made
For Your own dwelling,
The sanctuary, O LORD, *which* Your hands have established.

18 "The LORD shall reign forever and ever."

19For the horses of Pharaoh went with his chariots and his horsemen into the sea, and the LORD brought back the waters of the sea upon them. But the children of Israel went on dry *land* in the midst of the sea.

THE SONG OF MIRIAM

20Then Miriam the prophetess, the sister of Aaron, took the timbrel in her hand; and all the women went out after her with timbrels and with dances. 21And Miriam answered them:

"Sing to the LORD,
For He has triumphed gloriously!
The horse and its rider
He has thrown into the sea!"

BITTER WATERS MADE SWEET

22So Moses brought Israel from the Red Sea; then they went out into the Wilderness of Shur. And they went three days in the wilderness and found no water. 23Now when they came to Marah, they could not drink the waters of Marah, for they *were* bitter. Therefore the name of it was called Marah.*a* 24And the people complained against Moses, saying, "What shall we drink?" 25So he cried out to the LORD, and the LORD showed him a tree. When he cast *it* into the waters, the waters were made sweet.

There He made a statute and an ordinance for them, and there He tested them, 26and said, "If you diligently heed the voice of the LORD your God and do what is right in His sight, give ear to His commandments and keep all His statutes, I will put none of the diseases on you which I have brought on the Egyptians. For I *am* the LORD who heals you."

27Then they came to Elim, where there *were* twelve wells of water and seventy palm trees; so they camped there by the waters.

BREAD FROM HEAVEN

1And they journeyed from Elim, and all the congregation of the children of Israel came to the Wilderness of Sin, which is between Elim and Sinai, on the fifteenth day of the second month after they departed from the land of Egypt. 2Then the whole congregation of the children of Israel complained against Moses and Aaron in the wilderness. 3And the children of Israel said to them, "Oh, that we had died by the hand of the LORD in the land of Egypt, when we sat by the pots of meat *and* when we ate bread to the full! For you have brought us out into this wilderness to kill this whole assembly with hunger."

4Then the LORD said to Moses, "Behold, I will rain bread from heaven for you. And the people shall go out and gather a certain quota every

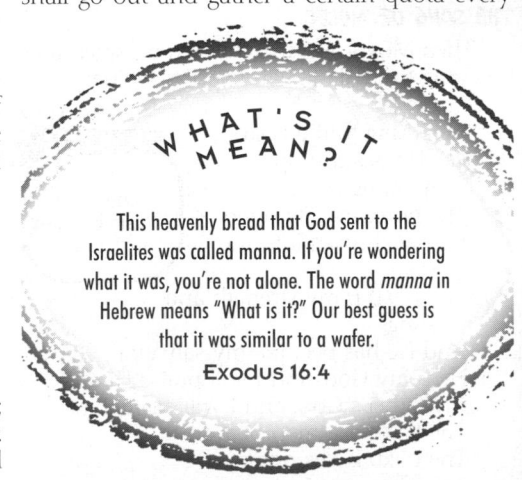

WHAT'S IT MEAN?

This heavenly bread that God sent to the Israelites was called manna. If you're wondering what it was, you're not alone. The word *manna* in Hebrew means "What is it?" Our best guess is that it was similar to a wafer.

Exodus 16:4

15:23 *a*Literally *Bitter*

day, that I may test them, whether they will walk in My law or not. [5]And it shall be on the sixth day that they shall prepare what they bring in, and it shall be twice as much as they gather daily."

[6]Then Moses and Aaron said to all the children of Israel, "At evening you shall know that the LORD has brought you out of the land of Egypt. [7]And in the morning you shall see the glory of the LORD; for He hears your complaints against the LORD. But what *are* we, that you complain against us?" [8]Also Moses said, "*This shall be seen* when the LORD gives you meat to eat in the evening, and in the morning bread to the full; for the LORD hears your complaints which you make against Him. And what *are* we? Your complaints *are* not against us but against the LORD."

[9]Then Moses spoke to Aaron, "Say to all the congregation of the children of Israel, 'Come near before the LORD, for He has heard your complaints.'" [10]Now it came to pass, as Aaron spoke to the whole congregation of the children of Israel, that they looked toward the wilderness, and behold, the glory of the LORD appeared in the cloud.

[11]And the LORD spoke to Moses, saying, [12]"I have heard the complaints of the children of Israel. Speak to them, saying, 'At twilight you shall eat meat, and in the morning you shall be filled with bread. And you shall know that I *am* the LORD your God.'"

[13]So it was that quails came up at evening and covered the camp, and in the morning the dew lay all around the camp. [14]And when the layer of dew lifted, there, on the surface of the wilderness, was a small round substance, *as* fine as frost on the ground. [15]So when the children of Israel saw *it,* they said to one another, "What is it?" For they did not know what it *was.*

And Moses said to them, "This *is* the bread which the LORD has given you to eat. [16]This is the thing which the LORD has commanded: 'Let every man gather it according to each one's need, one omer for each person, *according to the* number of persons; let every man take for *those* who *are* in his tent.'"

[17]Then the children of Israel did so and gathered, some more, some less. [18]So when they measured *it* by omers, he who gathered much had nothing left over, and he who gathered little had no lack. Every man had gathered according to each one's need. [19]And Moses said, "Let no one leave any of it till morning." [20]Notwithstanding they did not heed Moses. But some of

them left part of it until morning, and it bred worms and stank. And Moses was angry with them. [21]So they gathered it every morning, every man according to his need. And when the sun became hot, it melted.

[22]And so it was, on the sixth day, *that* they gathered twice as much bread, two omers for each one. And all the rulers of the congregation came and told Moses. [23]Then he said to them, "This *is what* the LORD has said: 'Tomorrow *is* a Sabbath rest, a holy Sabbath to the LORD. Bake what you will bake *today,* and boil what you will boil; and lay up for yourselves all that remains, to be kept until morning.'" [24]So they laid it up till morning, as Moses commanded; and it did not stink, nor were there any worms in it. [25]Then Moses said, "Eat that today, for today *is* a Sabbath to the LORD; today you will not find it in the field. [26]Six days you shall gather it, but on the seventh day, the Sabbath, there will be none."

[27]Now it happened *that some* of the people went out on the seventh day to gather, but they found none. [28]And the LORD said to Moses, "How long do you refuse to keep My commandments and My laws? [29]See! For the LORD has given you the Sabbath; therefore He gives you on the sixth day bread for two days. Let every man remain in his place; let no man go out of his place on the seventh day." [30]So the people rested on the seventh day.

[31]And the house of Israel called its name Manna.[a] And it *was* like white coriander seed, and the taste of it *was* like wafers *made* with honey.

[32]Then Moses said, "This *is* the thing which the LORD has commanded: 'Fill an omer with it, to be kept for your generations, that they may see the bread with which I fed you in the wilderness, when I brought you out of the land of Egypt.'" [33]And Moses said to Aaron, "Take a pot and put an omer of manna in it, and lay it up before the LORD, to be kept for your generations." [34]As the LORD commanded Moses, so Aaron laid it up before the Testimony, to be kept. [35]And the children of Israel ate manna forty years, until they came to an inhabited land; they ate manna until they came to the border of the land of Canaan. [36]Now an omer *is* one-tenth of an ephah.

WATER FROM THE ROCK

[1]Then all the congregation of the children of Israel set out on their journey from the Wilderness of Sin, according to the commandment of

16:31 [a]Literally *What?* (compare Exodus 16:15)

the LORD, and camped in Rephidim; but *there was* no water for the people to drink. ²Therefore the people contended with Moses, and said, "Give us water, that we may drink."

So Moses said to them, "Why do you contend with me? Why do you tempt the LORD?"

³And the people thirsted there for water, and the people complained against Moses, and said, "Why *is* it you have brought us up out of Egypt, to kill us and our children and our livestock with thirst?"

⁴So Moses cried out to the LORD, saying, "What shall I do with this people? They are almost ready to stone me!"

⁵And the LORD said to Moses, "Go on before the people, and take with you some of the elders of Israel. Also take in your hand your rod with which you struck the river, and go. ⁶Behold, I will stand before you there on the rock in Horeb; and you shall strike the rock, and water will come out of it, that the people may drink."

And Moses did so in the sight of the elders of Israel. ⁷So he called the name of the place Massah*ᵃ* and Meribah,*ᵇ* because of the contention of the children of Israel, and because they tempted the LORD, saying, "Is the LORD among us or not?"

VICTORY OVER THE AMALEKITES

⁸Now Amalek came and fought with Israel in Rephidim. ⁹And Moses said to Joshua, "Choose us some men and go out, fight with Amalek. Tomorrow I will stand on the top of the hill with the rod of God in my hand." ¹⁰So Joshua did as Moses said to him, and fought with Amalek. And Moses, Aaron, and Hur went up to the top of the hill. ¹¹And so it was, when

WHAT'S IT MEAN?

The Amalekites were desert dwellers who wandered between Egypt and Canaan. They were a thorn in the side of Israel throughout the Old Testament, but were eventually defeated.

Exodus 17:8

Moses held up his hand, that Israel prevailed; and when he let down his hand, Amalek prevailed. ¹²But Moses' hands *became* heavy; so they took a stone and put *it* under him, and he sat on it. And Aaron and Hur supported his hands, one on one side, and the other on the other side; and his hands were steady until the going down of the sun. ¹³So Joshua defeated Amalek and his people with the edge of the sword.

¹⁴Then the LORD said to Moses, "Write this *for* a memorial in the book and recount *it* in the hearing of Joshua, that I will utterly blot out the remembrance of Amalek from under heaven." ¹⁵And Moses built an altar and called its name, The-LORD-Is-My-Banner;*ᵃ* ¹⁶for he said, "Because the LORD has sworn: the LORD *will have* war with Amalek from generation to generation."

WHAT'S IT MEAN?

If you know where the Sinai Peninsula is, you know where Midian was located. Moses was familiar with the place because he had stayed there as a young man while he was on the run after killing an Egyptian.

Exodus 18:1

JETHRO'S ADVICE

¹And Jethro, the priest of Midian, Moses' father-in-law, heard of all that God had done for Moses and for Israel His people—that the LORD had brought Israel out of Egypt. ²Then Jethro, Moses' father-in-law, took Zipporah, Moses' wife, after he had sent her back, ³with her two sons, of whom the name of one *was* Gershom (for he said, "I have been a stranger in a foreign land")*ᵃ* ⁴and the name of the other *was* Eliezer*ᵃ* (for *he said,* "The God of my father *was* my help, and delivered me from the sword of Pharaoh"); ⁵and Jethro, Moses' father-in-law, came with his sons and his wife to Moses in the wilderness, where he was encamped at the mountain of God. ⁶Now he had said to Moses, "I, your father-in-law Jethro, am coming to you with your wife and her two sons with her."

17:7 *ᵃ*Literally *Tempted* *ᵇ*Literally *Contention*   **17:15** *ᵃ*Hebrew *YHWH Nissi*   **18:3** *ᵃ*Compare Exodus 2:22
18:4 *ᵃ*Literally *My God Is Help*

[7]So Moses went out to meet his father-in-law, bowed down, and kissed him. And they asked each other about *their* well-being, and they went into the tent. [8]And Moses told his father-in-law all that the LORD had done to Pharaoh and to the Egyptians for Israel's sake, all the hardship that had come upon them on the way, and *how* the LORD had delivered them. [9]Then Jethro rejoiced for all the good which the LORD had done for Israel, whom He had delivered out of the hand of the Egyptians. [10]And Jethro said, "Blessed *be* the LORD, who has delivered you out of the hand of the Egyptians and out of the hand of Pharaoh, *and* who has delivered the people from under the hand of the Egyptians. [11]Now I know that the LORD *is* greater than all the gods; for in the very thing in which they behaved proudly, *He was* above them." [12]Then Jethro, Moses' father-in-law, took[a] a burnt offering and *other* sacrifices *to offer* to God. And Aaron came with all the elders of Israel to eat bread with Moses' father-in-law before God.

[13]And so it was, on the next day, that Moses sat to judge the people; and the people stood before Moses from morning until evening. [14]So when Moses' father-in-law saw all that he did for the people, he said, "What *is* this thing that you are doing for the people? Why do you alone sit, and all the people stand before you from morning until evening?"

WHAT'S IT MEAN?

It would have been tough to argue with Moses' rulings as a judge, since he was appointed by God. His responsibility included not only making sure that justice was done, but also protecting the people he served.

Exodus 18:13, 14

[15]And Moses said to his father-in-law, "Because the people come to me to inquire of God. [16]When they have a difficulty, they come to me, and I judge between one and another; and I make known the statutes of God and His laws." [17]So Moses' father-in-law said to him, "The thing that you do *is* not good. [18]Both you and these people who *are* with you will surely wear yourselves out. For this thing *is* too much for you; you are not able to perform it by yourself. [19]Listen now to my voice; I will give you counsel, and God will be with you: Stand before God for the people, so that you may bring the difficulties to God. [20]And you shall teach them the statutes and the laws, and show them the way in which they must walk and the work they must do. [21]Moreover you shall select from all the people able men, such as fear God, men of truth, hating covetousness; and place *such* over them *to* be rulers of thousands, rulers of hundreds, rulers of fifties, and rulers of tens. [22]And let them judge the people at all times. Then it will be *that* every great matter they shall bring to you, but every small matter they themselves shall judge. So it will be easier for you, for they will bear *the* burden with you. [23]If you do this thing, and God *so* commands you, then you will be able to endure, and all this people will also go to their place in peace."

LEADERSHIP

What makes a good leader? (18:21)

[24]So Moses heeded the voice of his father-in-law and did all that he had said. [25]And Moses chose able men out of all Israel, and made them heads over the people: rulers of thousands, rulers of hundreds, rulers of fifties, and rulers of tens. [26]So they judged the people at all times; the hard cases they brought to Moses, but they judged every small case themselves.

[27]Then Moses let his father-in-law depart, and he went his way to his own land.

ISRAEL AT MOUNT SINAI

[1]In the third month after the children of Israel had gone out of the land of Egypt, on the same day, they came *to* the Wilderness of Sinai. [2]For they had departed from Rephidim, had come *to* the Wilderness of Sinai, and camped in the wilderness. So Israel camped there before the mountain.

[3]And Moses went up to God, and the LORD called to him from the mountain, saying, "Thus you shall say to the house of Jacob, and tell the children of Israel: [4]You have seen what I did to the Egyptians, and *how* I bore you on eagles' wings and brought you to Myself. [5]Now therefore, if you will indeed obey My voice and keep My covenant, then you shall be a special treasure to Me above all people; for all the earth *is* Mine. [6]And you shall be to Me a kingdom of

18:12 [a]Following Masoretic Text and Septuagint; Syriac, Targum, and Vulgate read *offered*.

On the Edge

You shall be a special treasure to Me above all people; for all the earth is Mine. And you shall be to Me a kingdom of priests and a holy nation (Ex. 19:5, 6).

When you hear the word *priest,* what do you think of? Maybe you picture a person standing before a congregation wearing a robe or a special collar—something that identifies the person as holy. You probably think of that person as someone who has a hotline to God. You may even think that person loves God more than you do.

Since most people have this exalted idea of what a priest is, it's kind of a shock that God told Moses to tell the whole nation of Israel that they would serve Him as priests. Later God appointed men to wear special clothes and to lead religious ceremonies. But He didn't leave the rest of the population to be just "regular" people. In some way, God wanted every one of the Israelites to serve Him as a priest.

Because much of what happens to Israel is a shadow, or a picture, of what God intends for all Christians, what God told Moses applies to you, too. In fact, 1 Peter 2:9 says, "You are a chosen generation, a royal priesthood." But don't think you have to go to seminary just yet. Being a priest isn't about wearing special clothes or conducting a religious service. It's about dedicating your whole life and heart to God, no matter what you decide to do for a living. It's about serving Him out of a pure heart. It's about knowing that—because of Jesus—you've got your own hotline to heaven. So even if you don't become a pastor or a missionary, you still have the privilege of serving God as a priest.

SEE FOR YOURSELF:
1 Pet. 2:5, 9;
Rev. 1:6

LORD has spoken we will do." So Moses brought back the words of the people to the LORD. [9]And the LORD said to Moses, "Behold, I come to you in the thick cloud, that the people may hear when I speak with you, and believe you forever."

So Moses told the words of the people to the LORD.

[10]Then the LORD said to Moses, "Go to the people and consecrate them today and tomorrow, and let them wash their clothes. [11]And let them be ready for the third day. For on the third day the LORD will come down upon Mount Sinai in the sight of all the people. [12]You shall set bounds for the people all around, saying, 'Take heed to yourselves *that* you do *not* go up to the mountain or touch its base. Whoever touches the mountain shall surely be put to death. [13]Not a hand shall touch him, but he shall surely be stoned or shot *with an arrow;* whether man or beast, he shall not live.' When the trumpet sounds long, they shall come near the mountain."

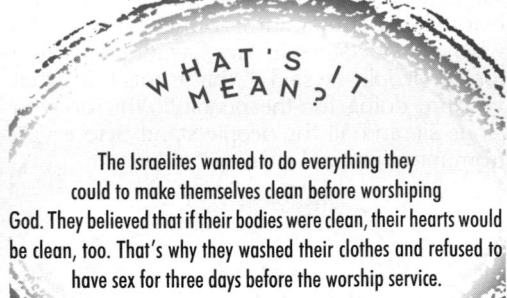

WHAT'S IT MEAN?

The Israelites wanted to do everything they could to make themselves clean before worshiping God. They believed that if their bodies were clean, their hearts would be clean, too. That's why they washed their clothes and refused to have sex for three days before the worship service.
Exodus 19:14, 15

[14]So Moses went down from the mountain to the people and sanctified the people, and they washed their clothes. [15]And he said to the people, "Be ready for the third day; do not come near *your* wives."

[16]Then it came to pass on the third day, in the morning, that there were thunderings and lightnings, and a thick cloud on the mountain; and the sound of the trumpet was very loud, so that all the people who *were* in the camp trembled. [17]And Moses brought the people out of the camp to meet with God, and they stood at the foot of the mountain. [18]Now Mount Sinai *was* completely in smoke, because the LORD descended upon it in fire. Its smoke ascended like the smoke of a furnace, and the whole moun-

priests and a holy nation.' These *are* the words which you shall speak to the children of Israel."

[7]So Moses came and called for the elders of the people, and laid before them all these words which the LORD commanded him. [8]Then all the people answered together and said, "All that the

tain[a] quaked greatly. [19]And when the blast of the trumpet sounded long and became louder and louder, Moses spoke, and God answered him by voice. [20]Then the LORD came down upon Mount Sinai, on the top of the mountain. And the LORD called Moses to the top of the mountain, and Moses went up.

[21]And the LORD said to Moses, "Go down and warn the people, lest they break through to gaze at the LORD, and many of them perish. [22]Also let the priests who come near the LORD consecrate themselves, lest the LORD break out against them."

[23]But Moses said to the LORD, "The people cannot come up to Mount Sinai; for You warned us, saying, 'Set bounds around the mountain and consecrate it.'"

[24]Then the LORD said to him, "Away! Get down and then come up, you and Aaron with you. But do not let the priests and the people break through to come up to the LORD, lest He break out against them." [25]So Moses went down to the people and spoke to them.

THE TEN COMMANDMENTS

[1]And God spoke all these words, saying:

[2] "I *am* the LORD your God, who brought you out of the land of Egypt, out of the house of bondage.

[3] "You shall have no other gods before Me.

[4] "You shall not make for yourself a carved image—any likeness *of anything* that *is* in heaven above, or that *is* in the earth beneath, or that *is* in the water under the earth; [5]you shall not bow down to them nor serve them. For I, the LORD your God, *am* a jealous God, visiting the iniquity of the fathers upon the children to the third and fourth *generations* of those who hate Me, [6]but showing mercy to thousands, to those who love Me and keep My commandments.

[7] "You shall not take the name of the LORD your God in vain, for the LORD will not hold *him* guiltless who takes His name in vain.

[8] "Remember the Sabbath day, to keep it holy. [9]Six days you shall labor and do all your work, [10]but the seventh day *is* the Sabbath of the LORD your God. *In it* you shall do no work: you, nor your son, nor your daughter, nor your male servant, nor your female servant, nor your cattle, nor your stranger who *is* within your gates. [11]For *in* six days the LORD made the heavens and the earth, the sea, and all that *is* in them, and rested the seventh day. Therefore the LORD blessed the Sabbath day and hallowed it.

[12] "Honor your father and your mother, that your days may be long upon the land which the LORD your God is giving you.

[13] "You shall not murder.

[14] "You shall not commit adultery.

[15] "You shall not steal.

[16] "You shall not bear false witness against your neighbor.

> **HONESTY**
> Is honesty a command from God? (20:16)

[17] "You shall not covet your neighbor's house; you shall not covet your neighbor's wife, nor his male servant, nor his female servant, nor his ox, nor his donkey, nor anything that *is* your neighbor's."

WHAT'S IT MEAN?

The Ten Commandments are God's laws for living. They apply to us today every bit as much as they applied to the Israelites in the wilderness. God's morals do not change. As if the Israelites needed a reminder, God began the commandments with an announcement of who He is and what He had done for them.

Exodus 20:2–17

THE PEOPLE AFRAID OF GOD'S PRESENCE

[18]Now all the people witnessed the thunderings, the lightning flashes, the sound of the trumpet, and the mountain smoking; and when the people saw *it*, they trembled and stood afar off. [19]Then they said to Moses, "You speak with us, and we will hear; but let not God speak with us, lest we die."

[20]And Moses said to the people, "Do not fear; for God has come to test you, and that His fear may be before you, so that you may not sin." [21]So the people stood afar off, but Moses drew near the thick darkness where God *was*.

THE LAW OF THE ALTAR

²²Then the LORD said to Moses, "Thus you shall say to the children of Israel: 'You have seen that I have talked with you from heaven. ²³You shall not make *anything to be* with Me— gods of silver or gods of gold you shall not make for yourselves. ²⁴An altar of earth you shall make for Me, and you shall sacrifice on it your burnt offerings and your peace offerings, your sheep and your oxen. In every place where I record My name I will come to you, and I will bless you. ²⁵And if you make Me an altar of stone, you shall not build it of hewn stone; for if you use your tool on it, you have profaned it. ²⁶Nor shall you go up by steps to My altar, that your nakedness may not be exposed on it.'

WHAT'S IT MEAN?

If you had to be a slave in ancient times, your best bet was to be a slave of the Israelites. Unlike, say, the Romans, who had the power to kill disobedient slaves, the Israelites had strict rules regarding the treatment of their slaves.

Exodus 21:2–6

On the Edge

Honor your father and your mother, that your days may be long upon the land which the LORD your God is giving you (Ex. 20:12).

What do I do if my mom is always on my case about the way I dress? The answer to this question lies in the big principle of Exodus 20:12—honor your father and your mother. It's amazing how rational parents can be when you confront them with respect and honor instead of rebellion. The next time the clothes thing comes up with your mom, try something like this: "Mom, I know you don't like this outfit. This is what I like to wear when I'm around my friends. I want to honor you even with my clothes, so when we're going somewhere and it's really important to you that I dress less weird, just let me know." Major life events like weddings and funerals will probably rate pretty high on the "please dress less weird" list. Growing in your faith means that you're always trying to live your life according to the truth in the Bible. Go ahead and talk it through with your mom. You'll be surprised by the respect she'll give you when you give it to her. God will be honored because you honored her.

SEE FOR YOURSELF:
   Eph. 6:1–3;
   Col. 3:20

THE LAW CONCERNING SERVANTS

¹"Now these *are* the judgments which you shall set before them: ²If you buy a Hebrew servant, he shall serve six years; and in the seventh he shall go out free and pay nothing. ³If he comes in by himself, he shall go out by himself; if he *comes in* married, then his wife shall go out with him. ⁴If his master has given him a wife, and she has borne him sons or daughters, the wife and her children shall be her master's, and he shall go out by himself. ⁵But if the servant plainly says, 'I love my master, my wife, and my children; I will not go out free,' ⁶then his master shall bring him to the judges. He shall also bring him to the door, or to the doorpost, and his master shall pierce his ear with an awl; and he shall serve him forever.

⁷"And if a man sells his daughter to be a female slave, she shall not go out as the male slaves do. ⁸If she does not please her master, who has betrothed her to himself, then he shall let her be redeemed. He shall have no right to sell her to a foreign people, since he has dealt deceitfully with her. ⁹And if he has betrothed her to his son, he shall deal with her according to the custom of daughters. ¹⁰If he takes another *wife*, he shall not diminish her food, her clothing, and her marriage rights. ¹¹And if he does not do these three for her, then she shall go out free, without *paying* money.

THE LAW CONCERNING VIOLENCE

¹²"He who strikes a man so that he dies shall surely be put to death. ¹³However, if he did not lie in wait, but God delivered *him* into his hand, then I will appoint for you a place where he may flee.

[14] "But if a man acts with premeditation against his neighbor, to kill him by treachery, you shall take him from My altar, that he may die.

[15] "And he who strikes his father or his mother shall surely be put to death.

[16] "He who kidnaps a man and sells him, or if he is found in his hand, shall surely be put to death.

[17] "And he who curses his father or his mother shall surely be put to death.

[18] "If men contend with each other, and one strikes the other with a stone or with *his* fist, and he does not die but is confined to *his* bed, [19] if he rises again and walks about outside with his staff, then he who struck *him* shall be acquitted. He shall only pay *for* the loss of his time, and shall provide *for him* to be thoroughly healed.

[20] "And if a man beats his male or female servant with a rod, so that he dies under his hand, he shall surely be punished. [21] Notwithstanding, if he remains alive a day or two, he shall not be punished; for he *is* his property.

[22] "If men fight, and hurt a woman with child, so that she gives birth prematurely, yet no harm follows, he shall surely be punished accordingly as the woman's husband imposes on him; and he shall pay as the judges *determine.* [23] But if *any* harm follows, then you shall give life for life, [24] eye for eye, tooth for tooth, hand for hand, foot for foot, [25] burn for burn, wound for wound, stripe for stripe.

[26] "If a man strikes the eye of his male or female servant, and destroys it, he shall let him go free for the sake of his eye. [27] And if he knocks out the tooth of his male or female servant, he shall let him go free for the sake of his tooth.

ANIMAL CONTROL LAWS

[28] "If an ox gores a man or a woman to death, then the ox shall surely be stoned, and its flesh shall not be eaten; but the owner of the ox *shall be* acquitted. [29] But if the ox tended to thrust with its horn in times past, and it has been made known to his owner, and he has not kept it confined, so that it has killed a man or a woman, the ox shall be stoned and its owner also shall be put to death. [30] If there is imposed on him a sum of money, then he shall pay to redeem his life, whatever is imposed on him. [31] Whether it has gored a son or gored a daughter, according to this judgment it shall be done to him. [32] If the ox gores a male or female servant, he shall give to their master thirty shekels of silver, and the ox shall be stoned.

[33] "And if a man opens a pit, or if a man digs a pit and does not cover it, and an ox or a donkey falls in it, [34] the owner of the pit shall make *it* good; he shall give money to their owner, but the dead *animal* shall be his.

[35] "If one man's ox hurts another's, so that it dies, then they shall sell the live ox and divide the money from it; and the dead *ox* they shall also divide. [36] Or if it was known that the ox tended to thrust in time past, and its owner has not kept it confined, he shall surely pay ox for ox, and the dead animal shall be his own.

RESPONSIBILITY FOR PROPERTY

[1] "If a man steals an ox or a sheep, and slaughters it or sells it, he shall restore five oxen for an ox and four sheep for a sheep. [2] If the thief is found breaking in, and he is struck so that he dies, *there shall be* no guilt for his bloodshed. [3] If the sun has risen on him, *there shall be* guilt for his bloodshed. He should make full restitution; if he has nothing, then he shall be sold for his theft. [4] If the theft is certainly found alive in his hand, whether it is an ox or donkey or sheep, he shall restore double.

[5] "If a man causes a field or vineyard to be grazed, and lets loose his animal, and it feeds in another man's field, he shall make restitution from the best of his own field and the best of his own vineyard.

[6] "If fire breaks out and catches in thorns, so that stacked grain, standing grain, or the field is consumed, he who kindled the fire shall surely make restitution.

[7] "If a man delivers to his neighbor money or articles to keep, and it is stolen out of the man's house, if the thief is found, he shall pay double. [8] If the thief is not found, then the master of the house shall be brought to the judges *to see* whether he has put his hand into his neighbor's goods.

[9] "For any kind of trespass, *whether it concerns* an ox, a donkey, a sheep, or clothing, *or* for any kind of lost thing which *another* claims to be his, the cause of both parties shall come before the

---

"You shall not make anything to be with Me— gods of silver or gods of gold you shall not make for yourselves." (Exodus 20:23)

ABORTION

Does God care for the unborn? (21:22–25)

judges; *and* whomever the judges condemn shall pay double to his neighbor. [10]If a man delivers to his neighbor a donkey, an ox, a sheep, or any animal to keep, and it dies, is hurt, or driven away, no one seeing *it*, [11]*then* an oath of the LORD shall be between them both, that he has not put his hand into his neighbor's goods; and the owner of it shall accept *that*, and he shall not make *it* good. [12]But if, in fact, it is stolen from him, he shall make restitution to the owner of it. [13]If it is torn to pieces *by a beast, then* he shall bring it as evidence, *and* he shall not make good what was torn.

[14]"And if a man borrows *anything* from his neighbor, and it becomes injured or dies, the owner of it not *being* with it, he shall surely make *it* good. [15]If its owner *was* with it, he shall not make *it* good; if it *was* hired, it came for its hire.

WHAT'S IT MEAN?

The law was serious business among the Israelites, who considered all crimes to be against God. The people were responsible for treating each other fairly. Those who didn't were punished publicly.
Exodus 22:21–24

MORAL AND CEREMONIAL PRINCIPLES

[16]"If a man entices a virgin who is not betrothed, and lies with her, he shall surely pay the bride-price for her *to be* his wife. [17]If her father utterly refuses to give her to him, he shall pay money according to the bride-price of virgins.

[18]"You shall not permit a sorceress to live.

[19]"Whoever lies with an animal shall surely be put to death.

[20]"He who sacrifices to *any* god, except to the LORD only, he shall be utterly destroyed.

[21]"You shall neither mistreat a stranger nor oppress him, for you were strangers in the land of Egypt.

[22]"You shall not afflict any widow or fatherless child. [23]If you afflict them in any way, *and* they cry at all to Me, I will surely hear their cry; [24]and My wrath will become hot, and I will kill you with the sword; your wives shall be widows, and your children fatherless.

[25]"If you lend money to *any of* My people *who are* poor among you, you shall not be like a moneylender to him; you shall not charge him interest. [26]If you ever take your neighbor's garment as a pledge, you shall return it to him before the sun goes down. [27]For that *is* his only covering, it *is* his garment for his skin. What will he sleep in? And it will be that when he cries to Me, I will hear, for I *am* gracious.

[28]"You shall not revile God, nor curse a ruler of your people.

[29]"You shall not delay *to offer* the first of your ripe produce and your juices. The firstborn of your sons you shall give to Me. [30]Likewise you shall do with your oxen *and* your sheep. It shall

be with its mother seven days; on the eighth day you shall give it to Me. ³¹"And you shall be holy men to Me: you shall not eat meat torn *by beasts* in the field; you shall throw it to the dogs.

JUSTICE FOR ALL

¹"You shall not circulate a false report. Do not put your hand with the wicked to be an unrighteous witness. ²You shall not follow a crowd to do evil; nor shall you testify in a dispute so as to turn aside after many to pervert *justice.* ³You shall not show partiality to a poor man in his dispute.

GOSSIP
Does God command us not to gossip? (23:1)

⁴"If you meet your enemy's ox or his donkey going astray, you shall surely bring it back to him again. ⁵If you see the donkey of one who hates you lying under its burden, and you would refrain from helping it, you shall surely help him with it.

⁶"You shall not pervert the judgment of your poor in his dispute. ⁷Keep yourself far from a false matter; do not kill the innocent and righteous. For I will not justify the wicked. ⁸And you shall take no bribe, for a bribe blinds the discerning and perverts the words of the righteous.

⁹"Also you shall not oppress a stranger, for you know the heart of a stranger, because you were strangers in the land of Egypt.

THE LAW OF SABBATHS

¹⁰"Six years you shall sow your land and gather in its produce, ¹¹but the seventh *year* you shall let it rest and lie fallow, that the poor of your people may eat; and what they leave, the beasts of the field may eat. In like manner you shall do with your vineyard *and* your olive grove. ¹²Six days you shall do your work, and on the seventh day you shall rest, that your ox and your donkey may rest, and the son of your female servant and the stranger may be refreshed.

¹³"And in all that I have said to you, be circumspect and make no mention of the name of other gods, nor let it be heard from your mouth.

THREE ANNUAL FEASTS

¹⁴"Three times you shall keep a feast to Me in the year: ¹⁵You shall keep the Feast of Unleavened Bread (you shall eat unleavened bread seven days, as I commanded you, at the time appointed in the month of Abib, for in it you came out of Egypt; none shall appear before Me empty); ¹⁶and the Feast of Harvest, the first-fruits of your labors which you have sown in the field; and the Feast of Ingathering at the end of the year, when you have gathered in *the fruit of* your labors from the field.

¹⁷"Three times in the year all your males shall appear before the Lord GOD.*a*

¹⁸"You shall not offer the blood of My sacrifice with leavened bread; nor shall the fat of My sacrifice remain until morning. ¹⁹The first of the firstfruits of your land you shall bring into the house of the LORD your God. You shall not boil a young goat in its mother's milk.

THE ANGEL AND THE PROMISES

²⁰"Behold, I send an Angel before you to keep you in the way and to bring you into the place which I have prepared. ²¹Beware of Him and obey His voice; do not provoke Him, for He will not pardon your transgressions; for My name *is* in Him. ²²But if you indeed obey His voice and do all that I speak, then I will be an enemy to your enemies and an adversary to your adversaries. ²³For My Angel will go before you and bring you in to the Amorites and the Hittites and the Perizzites and the Canaanites and the Hivites and the Jebusites; and I will cut them off. ²⁴You shall not bow down to their gods, nor serve them, nor do according to their works; but you shall utterly overthrow them and completely break down their *sacred* pillars.

²⁵"So you shall serve the LORD your God, and He will bless your bread and your water. And I will take sickness away from the midst of

WHAT'S IT MEAN?

The Amorites, Hittites, Perizzites, Canaanites, Hivites, and Jebusites all lived in the land God had promised to Abraham and his descendants. The Hittites lived as far north as modern-day Turkey. The Canaanites lived between the Jordan River and the Mediterranean Sea. The Jebusites could be found in what is now Jerusalem.

Exodus 23:23

23:17 *a*Hebrew *YHWH,* usually translated *LORD*

you. ²⁶No one shall suffer miscarriage or be barren in your land; I will fulfill the number of your days.

²⁷"I will send My fear before you, I will cause confusion among all the people to whom you come, and will make all your enemies turn *their* backs to you. ²⁸And I will send hornets before you, which shall drive out the Hivite, the Canaanite, and the Hittite from before you. ²⁹I will not drive them out from before you in one year, lest the land become desolate and the beasts of the field become too numerous for you. ³⁰Little by little I will drive them out from before you, until you have increased, and you inherit the land. ³¹And I will set your bounds from the Red Sea to the sea, Philistia, and from the desert to the River.^a For I will deliver the inhabitants of the land into your hand, and you shall drive them out before you. ³²You shall make no covenant with them, nor with their gods. ³³They shall not dwell in your land, lest they make you sin against Me. For *if* you serve their gods, it will surely be a snare to you."

ISRAEL AFFIRMS THE COVENANT

¹Now He said to Moses, "Come up to the LORD, you and Aaron, Nadab and Abihu, and seventy of the elders of Israel, and worship from afar. ²And Moses alone shall come near the LORD, but they shall not come near; nor shall the people go up with him."

³So Moses came and told the people all the words of the LORD and all the judgments. And all the people answered with one voice and said, "All the words which the LORD has said we will do." ⁴And Moses wrote all the words of the LORD. And he rose early in the morning, and built an altar at the foot of the mountain, and twelve pillars according to the twelve tribes of Israel. ⁵Then he sent young men of the children of Israel, who offered burnt offerings and sacrificed peace offerings of oxen to the LORD. ⁶And Moses took half the blood and put *it* in basins, and half the blood he sprinkled on the altar. ⁷Then he took the Book of the Covenant and read in the hearing of the people. And they said, "All that the LORD has said we will do, and be obedient." ⁸And Moses took the blood, sprinkled *it* on the people, and said, "This is the blood of the covenant which the LORD has made with you according to all these words."

ON THE MOUNTAIN WITH GOD

⁹Then Moses went up, also Aaron, Nadab, and Abihu, and seventy of the elders of Israel,

¹⁰and they saw the God of Israel. And *there was* under His feet as it were a paved work of sapphire stone, and it was like the very heavens in *its* clarity. ¹¹But on the nobles of the children of Israel He did not lay His hand. So they saw God, and they ate and drank.

WHAT'S IT MEAN?

The sprinkling of blood was serious business. The people making the covenant were literally saying, "We would rather die than break our promise." The blood of this particular covenant indicated that the Israelites agreed to obey God's covenant.
Exodus 24:8

¹²Then the LORD said to Moses, "Come up to Me on the mountain and be there; and I will give you tablets of stone, and the law and commandments which I have written, that you may teach them."

¹³So Moses arose with his assistant Joshua, and Moses went up to the mountain of God. ¹⁴And he said to the elders, "Wait here for us until we come back to you. Indeed, Aaron and Hur *are* with you. If any man has a difficulty, let him go to them." ¹⁵Then Moses went up into the mountain, and a cloud covered the mountain. ¹⁶Now the glory of the LORD rested on Mount Sinai, and the cloud covered it six days. And on the seventh day He called to Moses out of the midst of the cloud. ¹⁷The sight of the glory of the LORD *was* like a consuming fire on the top of the mountain in the eyes of the children of Israel. ¹⁸So Moses went into the midst of the cloud and went up into the mountain. And Moses was on the mountain forty days and forty nights.

OFFERINGS FOR THE SANCTUARY

¹Then the LORD spoke to Moses, saying: ²"Speak to the children of Israel, that they bring Me an offering. From everyone who gives it willingly with his heart you shall take My offering. ³And this *is* the offering which you shall take from them: gold, silver, and bronze; ⁴blue, purple, and scarlet *thread*, fine linen, and goats'

23:31 ^aHebrew *Nahar,* the Euphrates

hair; ⁵ram skins dyed red, badger skins, and acacia wood; ⁶oil for the light, and spices for the anointing oil and for the sweet incense; ⁷onyx stones, and stones to be set in the ephod and in the breastplate. ⁸And let them make Me a sanctuary, that I may dwell among them. ⁹According to all that I show you, *that is,* the pattern of the tabernacle and the pattern of all its furnishings, just so you shall make *it.*

THE ARK OF THE TESTIMONY

¹⁰"And they shall make an ark of acacia wood; two and a half cubits *shall be* its length, a cubit and a half its width, and a cubit and a half its height. ¹¹And you shall overlay it with pure gold, inside and out you shall overlay it, and shall make on it a molding of gold all around. ¹²You shall cast four rings of gold for it, and put *them* in its four corners; two rings *shall be* on one side, and two rings on the other side. ¹³And you shall make poles *of* acacia wood, and overlay them with gold. ¹⁴You shall put the poles into the rings on the sides of the ark, that the ark may be carried by them. ¹⁵The poles shall be in the rings of the ark; they shall not be taken from it. ¹⁶And you shall put into the ark the Testimony which I will give you.

WHAT'S IT MEAN?

Acacia wood was used because it's strong enough to withstand hungry insects and preserve the contents of the chest. If you'd like some acacia wood for your next building project, head for the Sinai Desert, southern Palestine, or Egypt. That's where the trees grow.

Exodus 25:10

¹⁷"You shall make a mercy seat of pure gold; two and a half cubits *shall be* its length and a cubit and a half its width. ¹⁸And you shall make two cherubim of gold; of hammered work you shall make them at the two ends of the mercy seat. ¹⁹Make one cherub at one end, and the other cherub at the other end; you shall make the cherubim at the two ends of it *of one piece* with the mercy seat. ²⁰And the cherubim shall stretch out *their* wings above, covering the mercy seat with their wings, and they shall face one another; the faces of the cherubim *shall*

be toward the mercy seat. ²¹You shall put the mercy seat on top of the ark, and in the ark you shall put the Testimony that I will give you. ²²And there I will meet with you, and I will speak with you from above the mercy seat, from between the two cherubim which *are* on the ark of the Testimony, about everything which I will give you in commandment to the children of Israel.

THE TABLE FOR THE SHOWBREAD

²³"You shall also make a table of acacia wood; two cubits *shall be* its length, a cubit its width, and a cubit and a half its height. ²⁴And you shall overlay it with pure gold, and make a molding of gold all around. ²⁵You shall make for it a frame of a handbreadth all around, and you shall make a gold molding for the frame all around. ²⁶And you shall make for it four rings of gold, and put the rings on the four corners that *are* at its four legs. ²⁷The rings shall be close to the frame, as holders for the poles to bear the table. ²⁸And you shall make the poles of acacia wood, and overlay them with gold, that the table may be carried with them. ²⁹You shall make its dishes, its pans, its pitchers, and its bowls for pouring. You shall make them of pure gold. ³⁰And you shall set the showbread on the table before Me always.

THE GOLD LAMPSTAND

³¹"You shall also make a lampstand of pure gold; the lampstand shall be of hammered work. Its shaft, its branches, its bowls, its *ornamental* knobs, and flowers shall be *of one piece.* ³²And six branches shall come out of its sides: three branches of the lampstand out of one side, and three branches of the lampstand out of the other side. ³³Three bowls *shall be* made like almond *blossoms* on one branch, *with an ornamental* knob and a flower, and three bowls made like almond *blossoms* on the other branch, *with an ornamental* knob and a flower—and so for the six branches that come out of the lampstand. ³⁴On the lampstand itself four bowls *shall be* made like almond *blossoms, each with* its *ornamental* knob and flower. ³⁵And *there shall be* a knob under the *first* two branches of the same, a knob under the *second* two branches of the same, and a knob under the *third* two branches of the same, according to the six branches that extend from the lampstand. ³⁶Their knobs and their branches *shall be of one piece;* all of it *shall be* one hammered piece of pure gold. ³⁷You shall make seven lamps for it, and they shall arrange its lamps so that they give light in front of it. ³⁸And its wick-trimmers

and their trays *shall be* of pure gold. ³⁹It shall be made of a talent of pure gold, with all these utensils. ⁴⁰And see to it that you make *them* according to the pattern which was shown you on the mountain.

THE TABERNACLE

¹"Moreover you shall make the tabernacle *with* ten curtains *of* fine woven linen and blue, purple, and scarlet *thread;* with artistic designs of cherubim you shall weave them. ²The length of each curtain *shall be* twenty-eight cubits, and the width of each curtain four cubits. And every one of the curtains shall have the same measurements. ³Five curtains shall be coupled to one another, and *the other* five curtains *shall be* coupled to one another. ⁴And you shall make loops of blue *yarn* on the edge of the curtain on the selvedge of *one* set, and likewise you shall do on the outer edge of *the other* curtain of the second set. ⁵Fifty loops you shall make in the one curtain, and fifty loops you shall make on the edge of the curtain that *is* on the end of the second set, that the loops may be clasped to one another. ⁶And you shall make fifty clasps of gold, and couple the curtains together with the clasps, so that it may be one tabernacle.

⁷"You shall also make curtains of goats' *hair*, to be a tent over the tabernacle. You shall make eleven curtains. ⁸The length of each curtain *shall be* thirty cubits, and the width of each curtain four cubits; and the eleven curtains shall all have the same measurements. ⁹And you shall couple five curtains by themselves and six curtains by themselves, and you shall double over the sixth curtain at the forefront of the tent. ¹⁰You shall make fifty loops on the edge of the curtain that is outermost in *one* set, and fifty loops on the edge of the curtain of the second set. ¹¹And you shall make fifty bronze clasps, put the clasps into the loops, and couple the tent together, that it may be one. ¹²The remnant that remains of the curtains of the tent, the half curtain that remains, shall hang over the back of the tabernacle. ¹³And a cubit on one side and a cubit on the other side, of what remains of the length of the curtains of the tent, shall hang over the sides of the tabernacle, on this side and on that side, to cover it.

¹⁴"You shall also make a covering of ram skins dyed red for the tent, and a covering of badger skins above that.

¹⁵"And for the tabernacle you shall make the boards of acacia wood, standing upright. ¹⁶Ten cubits *shall be* the length of a board, and a cubit and a half *shall be* the width of each board. ¹⁷Two tenons *shall be* in each board for binding one to another. Thus you shall make for all the boards of the tabernacle. ¹⁸And you shall make the boards for the tabernacle, twenty boards for the south side. ¹⁹You shall make forty sockets of silver under the twenty boards: two sockets under each of the boards for its two tenons. ²⁰And for the second side of the tabernacle, the north side, *there shall be* twenty boards ²¹and their forty sockets of silver: two sockets under each of the boards. ²²For the far side of the tabernacle, westward, you shall make six boards. ²³And you shall also make two boards for the two back corners of the tabernacle. ²⁴They shall be coupled together at the bottom and they shall be coupled together at the top by one ring. Thus it shall be for both of them. They shall be for the two corners. ²⁵So there shall be eight boards with their sockets of silver—sixteen sockets—two sockets under each of the boards.

²⁶"And you shall make bars of acacia wood: five for the boards on one side of the tabernacle, ²⁷five bars for the boards on the other side of the tabernacle, and five bars for the boards of the side of the tabernacle, for the far side westward. ²⁸The middle bar shall pass through the midst of the boards from end to end. ²⁹You shall overlay the boards with gold, make their rings of gold *as* holders for the bars, and overlay the bars with gold. ³⁰And you shall raise up the tabernacle according to its pattern which you were shown on the mountain.

WHAT'S IT MEAN?

The tabernacle, or sacred tent, was the place where the Israelites would go to worship the Lord. It was important that it be built exactly according to the Lord's instructions: five feet wide, fifteen feet long, and fifteen feet high. That's an area of seventy-five square feet. The inner room, which only the high priest was allowed to enter, was five feet square.
Exodus 26:30

³¹"You shall make a veil woven of blue, purple, and scarlet *thread*, and fine woven linen. It shall be woven with an artistic design of cherubim. ³²You shall hang it upon the four pillars of acacia *wood* overlaid with gold. Their hooks *shall be* gold, upon four sockets of silver. ³³And you shall hang the veil from the clasps. Then

you shall bring the ark of the Testimony in there, behind the veil. The veil shall be a divider for you between the holy *place* and the Most Holy. ³⁴You shall put the mercy seat upon the ark of the Testimony in the Most Holy. ³⁵You shall set the table outside the veil, and the lampstand across from the table on the side of the tabernacle toward the south; and you shall put the table on the north side.

³⁶"You shall make a screen for the door of the tabernacle, *woven of* blue, purple, and scarlet *thread,* and fine woven linen, made by a weaver. ³⁷And you shall make for the screen five pillars of acacia *wood,* and overlay them with gold; their hooks *shall be* gold, and you shall cast five sockets of bronze for them.

THE ALTAR OF BURNT OFFERING

¹"You shall make an altar of acacia wood, five cubits long and five cubits wide—the altar shall be square—and its height *shall be* three cubits. ²You shall make its horns on its four corners; its horns shall be of one piece with it. And you shall overlay it with bronze. ³Also you shall make its pans to receive its ashes, and its shovels and its basins and its forks and its firepans; you shall make all its utensils of bronze. ⁴You shall make a grate for it, a network of bronze; and on the network you shall make four bronze rings at its four corners. ⁵You shall put it under the rim of the altar beneath, that the network may be midway up the altar. ⁶And you shall make poles for the altar, poles of acacia wood, and overlay them with bronze. ⁷The poles shall be put in the rings, and the poles shall be on the two sides of the altar to bear it. ⁸You shall make it hollow with boards; as it was shown you on the mountain, so shall they make *it.*

THE COURT OF THE TABERNACLE

⁹"You shall also make the court of the tabernacle. For the south side *there shall be* hangings for the court *made of* fine woven linen, one hundred cubits long for one side. ¹⁰And its twenty pillars and their twenty sockets *shall be* bronze. The hooks of the pillars and their bands *shall be* silver. ¹¹Likewise along the length of the north side *there shall be* hangings one hundred *cubits* long, with its twenty pillars and their twenty sockets of bronze, and the hooks of the pillars and their bands of silver. ¹²And along the width of the court on the west side *shall be* hangings of fifty cubits, with their ten pillars and their ten sockets. ¹³The

width of the court on the east side *shall be* fifty cubits. ¹⁴The hangings on *one* side *of the gate shall be* fifteen cubits, *with* their three pillars and their three sockets. ¹⁵And on the other side *shall be* hangings of fifteen *cubits, with* their three pillars and their three sockets.

¹⁶"For the gate of the court *there shall be* a screen twenty cubits long, *woven of* blue, purple, and scarlet *thread,* and fine woven linen, made by a weaver. It *shall have* four pillars and four sockets. ¹⁷All the pillars around the court shall have bands of silver; their hooks *shall be* of silver and their sockets of bronze. ¹⁸The length of the court *shall be* one hundred cubits, the width fifty throughout, and the height five cubits, *made of* fine woven linen, and its sockets of bronze. ¹⁹All the utensils of the tabernacle for all its service, all its pegs, and all the pegs of the court, *shall be* of bronze.

THE CARE OF THE LAMPSTAND

²⁰"And you shall command the children of Israel that they bring you pure oil of pressed olives for the light, to cause the lamp to burn continually. ²¹In the tabernacle of meeting, outside the veil which *is* before the Testimony, Aaron and his sons shall tend it from evening until morning before the LORD. *It shall be a* statute forever to their generations on behalf of the children of Israel.

GARMENTS FOR THE PRIESTHOOD

¹"Now take Aaron your brother, and his sons with him, from among the children of Israel, that he may minister to Me as priest, Aaron *and* Aaron's sons: Nadab, Abihu, Eleazar, and Ithamar. ²And you shall make holy garments for Aaron your brother, for glory and for beauty. ³So you shall speak to all *who are* gifted artisans, whom I have filled with the spirit of wisdom, that they may make Aaron's garments, to consecrate him, that he may minister to Me as priest. ⁴And these *are* the garments which they shall make: a breastplate, an ephod,ᵃ a robe, a skillfully woven tunic, a turban, and a sash. So they shall make holy garments for Aaron your brother and his sons, that he may minister to Me as priest.

THE EPHOD

⁵"They shall take the gold, blue, purple, and scarlet *thread,* and the fine linen, ⁶and they shall make the ephod of gold, blue, purple, *and* scarlet *thread,* and fine woven linen, artistically worked. ⁷It shall have two shoulder straps

28:4 ᵃThat is, an ornamented vest

joined at its two edges, and *so* it shall be joined together. [8]And the intricately woven band of the ephod, which *is* on it, shall be of the same workmanship, *made of* gold, blue, purple, and scarlet *thread,* and fine woven linen.

[9]"Then you shall take two onyx stones and engrave on them the names of the sons of Israel: [10]six of their names on one stone and six names on the other stone, in order of their birth. [11]With the work of an engraver in stone, *like* the engravings of a signet, you shall engrave the two stones with the names of the sons of Israel. You shall set them in settings of gold. [12]And you shall put the two stones on the shoulders of the ephod *as* memorial stones for the sons of Israel. So Aaron shall bear their names before the LORD on his two shoulders as a memorial. [13]You shall also make settings of gold, [14]and you shall make two chains of pure gold like braided cords, and fasten the braided chains to the settings.

THE BREASTPLATE

[15]"You shall make the breastplate of judgment. Artistically woven according to the workmanship of the ephod you shall make it: of gold, blue, purple, and scarlet *thread,* and fine woven linen, you shall make it. [16]It shall be doubled into a square: a span *shall be* its length, and a span *shall be* its width. [17]And you shall put settings of stones in it, four rows of stones: *The first* row *shall be* a sardius, a topaz, and an emerald; *this shall be* the first row; [18]the second row *shall be* a turquoise, a sapphire, and a diamond; [19]the third row, a jacinth, an agate, and an amethyst; [20]and the fourth row, a beryl, an onyx, and a jasper. They shall be set in gold settings. [21]And the stones shall have the names of the sons of Israel, twelve according to their names, *like* the engravings of a signet, each one with its own name; they shall be according to the twelve tribes.

[22]"You shall make chains for the breastplate at the end, like braided cords of pure gold. [23]And you shall make two rings of gold for the breastplate, and put the two rings on the two ends of the breastplate. [24]Then you shall put the two braided *chains* of gold in the two rings which are on the ends of the breastplate; [25]and the *other* two ends of the two braided *chains* you shall fasten to the two settings, and put them on the shoulder straps of the ephod in the front.

[26]"You shall make two rings of gold, and put them on the two ends of the breastplate, on the edge of it, which is on the inner side of the ephod. [27]And two *other* rings of gold you shall make, and put them on the two shoulder straps, underneath the ephod toward its front, right at the seam above the intricately woven band of the ephod. [28]They shall bind the breastplate by means of its rings to the rings of the ephod, using a blue cord, so that it is above the intricately woven band of the ephod, and so that the breastplate does not come loose from the ephod.

[29]"So Aaron shall bear the names of the sons of Israel on the breastplate of judgment over his heart, when he goes into the holy *place,* as a memorial before the LORD continually. [30]And you shall put in the breastplate of judgment the Urim and the Thummim,[a] and they shall be over Aaron's heart when he goes in before the LORD. So Aaron shall bear the judgment of the children of Israel over his heart before the LORD continually.

OTHER PRIESTLY GARMENTS

[31]"You shall make the robe of the ephod all of blue. [32]There shall be an opening for his head in the middle of it; it shall have a woven binding all around its opening, like the opening in a coat of mail, so that it does not tear. [33]And upon its hem you shall make pomegranates of blue, purple, and scarlet, all around its hem, and bells of gold between them all around: [34]a golden bell and a pomegranate, a golden bell and a pomegranate, upon the hem of the robe all around. [35]And it shall be upon Aaron when he ministers, and its sound will be heard when he goes into the holy *place* before the LORD and when he comes out, that he may not die.

[36]"You shall also make a plate of pure gold and engrave on it, *like* the engraving of a signet:

HOLINESS TO THE LORD.

[37]And you shall put it on a blue cord, that it may be on the turban; it shall be on the front of the turban. [38]So it shall be on Aaron's forehead, that Aaron may bear the iniquity of the holy things which the children of Israel hallow in all their holy gifts; and it shall always be on his forehead, that they may be accepted before the LORD.

[39]"You shall skillfully weave the tunic of fine linen *thread,* you shall make the turban of fine linen, and you shall make the sash of woven work.

[40]"For Aaron's sons you shall make tunics,

28:30 [a]Literally *the Lights and the Perfections* (compare Leviticus 8:8)

W H A T ' S
MEAN?IT

Pouring oil on a person's head was a
common way of preparing someone for a new job or
a promotion. This anointing ceremony, as it was also
called, was performed by a person acting
with God's authority.

Exodus 28:41

and you shall make sashes for them. And you shall make hats for them, for glory and beauty. [41]So you shall put them on Aaron your brother and on his sons with him. You shall anoint them, consecrate them, and sanctify them, that they may minister to Me as priests. [42]And you shall make for them linen trousers to cover their nakedness; they shall reach from the waist to the thighs. [43]They shall be on Aaron and on his sons when they come into the tabernacle of meeting, or when they come near the altar to minister in the holy *place*, that they do not incur iniquity and die. *It shall be* a statute forever to him and his descendants after him.

AARON AND HIS SONS CONSECRATED

[1]"And this is what you shall do to them to hallow them for ministering to Me as priests: Take one young bull and two rams without blemish, [2]and unleavened bread, unleavened cakes mixed with oil, and unleavened wafers anointed with oil (you shall make them of wheat flour). [3]You shall put them in one basket and bring them in the basket, with the bull and the two rams.

[4]"And Aaron and his sons you shall bring to the door of the tabernacle of meeting, and you shall wash them with water. [5]Then you shall take the garments, put the tunic on Aaron, and the robe of the ephod, the ephod, and the breastplate, and gird him with the intricately woven band of the ephod. [6]You shall put the turban on his head, and put the holy crown on the turban. [7]And you shall take the anointing oil, pour *it* on his head, and anoint him. [8]Then you shall bring his sons and put tunics on them. [9]And you shall gird them with sashes, Aaron and his sons, and put the hats on them. The priesthood shall be theirs for a perpetual

statute. So you shall consecrate Aaron and his sons.

[10]"You shall also have the bull brought before the tabernacle of meeting, and Aaron and his sons shall put their hands on the head of the bull. [11]Then you shall kill the bull before the LORD, *by* the door of the tabernacle of meeting. [12]You shall take *some* of the blood of the bull and put *it* on the horns of the altar with your finger, and pour all the blood beside the base of the altar. [13]And you shall take all the fat that covers the entrails, the fatty lobe *attached* to the liver, and the two kidneys and the fat that *is* on them, and burn *them* on the altar. [14]But the flesh of the bull, with its skin and its offal, you shall burn with fire outside the camp. It *is* a sin offering.

[15]"You shall also take one ram, and Aaron and his sons shall put their hands on the head of the ram; [16]and you shall kill the ram, and you shall take its blood and sprinkle *it* all around on the altar. [17]Then you shall cut the ram in pieces, wash its entrails and its legs, and put *them* with its pieces and with its head. [18]And you shall burn the whole ram on the altar. It *is* a burnt offering to the LORD; it *is* a sweet aroma, an offering made by fire to the LORD.

[19]"You shall also take the other ram, and Aaron and his sons shall put their hands on the head of the ram. [20]Then you shall kill the ram, and take some of its blood and put *it* on the tip of the right ear of Aaron and on the tip of the right ear of his sons, on the thumb of their right hand and on the big toe of their right foot, and sprinkle the blood all around on the altar. [21]And you shall take some of the blood that is on the altar, and some of the anointing oil, and sprinkle *it* on Aaron and on his garments, on his sons and on the garments of his sons with him; and he and his garments shall be hallowed, and his sons and his sons' garments with him.

[22]"Also you shall take the fat of the ram, the fat tail, the fat that covers the entrails, the fatty lobe *attached to* the liver, the two kidneys and the fat on them, the right thigh (for it *is* a ram of consecration), [23]one loaf of bread, one cake *made with* oil, and one wafer from the basket of the unleavened bread that *is* before the LORD; [24]and you shall put all these in the hands of Aaron and in the hands of his sons, and you shall wave them *as* a wave offering before the LORD. [25]You shall receive them back from their hands and burn *them* on the altar as a burnt offering, as a sweet aroma before the LORD. It *is* an offering made by fire to the LORD.

[26]"Then you shall take the breast of the ram

of Aaron's consecration and wave it *as* a wave offering before the LORD; and it shall be your portion. ²⁷And from the ram of the consecration you shall consecrate the breast of the wave offering which is waved, and the thigh of the heave offering which is raised, of *that* which *is* for Aaron and of *that* which is for his sons. ²⁸It shall be from the children of Israel *for* Aaron and his sons by a statute forever. For it is a heave offering; it shall be a heave offering from the children of Israel from the sacrifices of their peace offerings, *that is*, their heave offering to the LORD.

²⁹"And the holy garments of Aaron shall be his sons' after him, to be anointed in them and to be consecrated in them. ³⁰That son who becomes priest in his place shall put them on for seven days, when he enters the tabernacle of meeting to minister in the holy *place.*

³¹"And you shall take the ram of the consecration and boil its flesh in the holy place. ³²Then Aaron and his sons shall eat the flesh of the ram, and the bread that *is* in the basket, *by* the door of the tabernacle of meeting. ³³They shall eat those things with which the atonement was made, to consecrate *and* to sanctify them; but an outsider shall not eat *them,* because they *are* holy. ³⁴And if any of the flesh of the consecration offerings, or of the bread, remains until the morning, then you shall burn the remainder with fire. It shall not be eaten, because it *is* holy.

³⁵"Thus you shall do to Aaron and his sons, according to all that I have commanded you. Seven days you shall consecrate them. ³⁶And you shall offer a bull every day *as* a sin offering for atonement. You shall cleanse the altar when you make atonement for it, and you shall anoint it to sanctify it. ³⁷Seven days you shall make atonement for the altar and sanctify it. And the altar shall be most holy. Whatever touches the altar must be holy.ᵃ

THE DAILY OFFERINGS

³⁸"Now this *is* what you shall offer on the altar: two lambs of the first year, day by day continually. ³⁹One lamb you shall offer in the morning, and the other lamb you shall offer at twilight. ⁴⁰With the one lamb shall be one-tenth *of an ephah* of flour mixed with one-fourth of a hin of pressed oil, and one-fourth of a hin of wine *as* a drink offering. ⁴¹And the other lamb you shall offer at twilight; and you shall offer with it the grain offering and the drink offering, as in the morning, for a sweet aroma, an offering made by fire to the LORD. ⁴²This *shall be* a continual burnt offering throughout your generations *at* the door of the tabernacle of meeting before the LORD, where I will meet you to speak with you. ⁴³And there I will meet with the children of Israel, and *the tabernacle* shall be sanctified by My glory. ⁴⁴So I will consecrate the tabernacle of meeting and the altar. I will also consecrate both Aaron and his sons to minister to Me as priests. ⁴⁵I will dwell among the children of Israel and will be their God. ⁴⁶And they shall know that I *am* the LORD their God, who brought them up out of the land of Egypt, that I may dwell among them. I *am* the LORD their God.

THE ALTAR OF INCENSE

¹"You shall make an altar to burn incense on; you shall make it of acacia wood. ²A cubit *shall be* its length and a cubit its width—it shall be square—and two cubits *shall be* its height. Its horns *shall be* of one piece with it. ³And you shall overlay its top, its sides all around, and its horns with pure gold; and you shall make for it a molding of gold all around. ⁴Two gold rings you shall make for it, under the molding on both its sides. You shall place *them* on its two sides, and they will be holders for the poles with which to bear it. ⁵You shall make the poles of acacia wood, and overlay them with gold. ⁶And you shall put it before the veil that *is* before the ark of the Testimony, before the mercy seat that *is* over the Testimony, where I will meet with you.

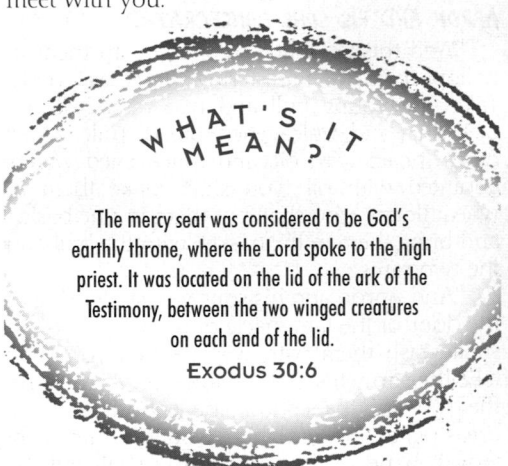

WHAT'S IT MEAN?

The mercy seat was considered to be God's earthly throne, where the Lord spoke to the high priest. It was located on the lid of the ark of the Testimony, between the two winged creatures on each end of the lid.
Exodus 30:6

⁷"Aaron shall burn on it sweet incense every morning; when he tends the lamps, he shall burn incense on it. ⁸And when Aaron lights the lamps at twilight, he shall burn incense on it, a perpetual incense before the LORD throughout

29:37 ᵃCompare Numbers 4:15 and Haggai 2:11–13

your generations. ⁹You shall not offer strange incense on it, or a burnt offering, or a grain offering; nor shall you pour a drink offering on it. ¹⁰And Aaron shall make atonement upon its horns once a year with the blood of the sin offering of atonement; once a year he shall make atonement upon it throughout your generations. It *is* most holy to the LORD."

THE RANSOM MONEY

¹¹Then the LORD spoke to Moses, saying: ¹²"When you take the census of the children of Israel for their number, then every man shall give a ransom for himself to the LORD, when you number them, that there may be no plague among them when *you* number them. ¹³This is what everyone among those who are numbered shall give: half a shekel according to the shekel of the sanctuary (a shekel *is* twenty gerahs). The half-shekel *shall be* an offering to the LORD. ¹⁴Everyone included among those who are numbered, from twenty years old and above, shall give an offering to the LORD. ¹⁵The rich shall not give more and the poor shall not give less than half a shekel, when *you* give an offering to the LORD, to make atonement for yourselves. ¹⁶And you shall take the atonement money of the children of Israel, and shall appoint it for the service of the tabernacle of meeting, that it may be a memorial for the children of Israel before the LORD, to make atonement for yourselves."

THE BRONZE LAVER

¹⁷Then the LORD spoke to Moses, saying: ¹⁸"You shall also make a laver of bronze, with its base also of bronze, for washing. You shall put it between the tabernacle of meeting and the altar. And you shall put water in it, ¹⁹for Aaron and his sons shall wash their hands and their feet in water from it. ²⁰When they go into the tabernacle of meeting, or when they come near the altar to minister, to burn an offering made by fire to the LORD, they shall wash with water, lest they die. ²¹So they shall wash their hands and their feet, lest they die. And it shall be a statute forever to them—to him and his descendants throughout their generations."

THE HOLY ANOINTING OIL

²²Moreover the LORD spoke to Moses, saying: ²³"Also take for yourself quality spices—five hundred *shekels* of liquid myrrh, half as much sweet-smelling cinnamon (two hundred and fifty *shekels*), two hundred and fifty *shekels* of sweet-smelling cane, ²⁴five hundred *shekels* of cassia, according to the shekel of the sanctuary, and a hin of olive oil. ²⁵And you shall make from these a holy anointing oil, an ointment compounded according to the art of the perfumer. It shall be a holy anointing oil. ²⁶With it you shall anoint the tabernacle of meeting and the ark of the Testimony; ²⁷the table and all its utensils, the lampstand and its utensils, and the altar of incense; ²⁸the altar of burnt offering with all its utensils, and the laver and its base. ²⁹You shall consecrate them, that they may be most holy; whatever touches them must be holy.ᵃ ³⁰And you shall anoint Aaron and his sons, and consecrate them, that *they* may minister to Me as priests.

³¹"And you shall speak to the children of Israel, saying: 'This shall be a holy anointing oil to Me throughout your generations. ³²It shall not be poured on man's flesh; nor shall you make *any other* like it, according to its composition. It *is* holy, *and* it shall be holy to you. ³³Whoever compounds *any* like it, or whoever puts *any* of it on an outsider, shall be cut off from his people.' "

THE INCENSE

³⁴And the LORD said to Moses: "Take sweet spices, stacte and onycha and galbanum, and pure frankincense with *these* sweet spices; there shall be equal amounts of each. ³⁵You shall make of these an incense, a compound according to the art of the perfumer, salted, pure, *and* holy. ³⁶And you shall beat *some* of it very fine, and put some of it before the Testimony in the tabernacle of meeting where I will meet with

WHAT'S IT MEAN?

The subject is Biblical Botany 101. Here's what you will need to know for the test. Stacte gum comes from the storax tree, a small shrub that can be found throughout Palestine. Onycha comes from the sweet-smelling rockrose or ladanum. Galbanum is a milky gum that comes from an herb. Frankincense comes from the Boswellia tree, with its white, star-shaped flowers.

Exodus 30:34, 35

30:29 ᵃCompare Numbers 4:15 and Haggai 2:11–13

you. It shall be most holy to you. [37]But *as for* the incense which you shall make, you shall not make any for yourselves, according to its composition. It shall be to you holy for the LORD. [38]Whoever makes *any* like it, to smell it, he shall be cut off from his people."

ARTISANS FOR BUILDING THE TABERNACLE

[1]Then the LORD spoke to Moses, saying: [2]"See, I have called by name Bezalel the son of Uri, the son of Hur, of the tribe of Judah. [3]And I have filled him with the Spirit of God, in wisdom, in understanding, in knowledge, and in all *manner of* workmanship, [4]to design artistic works, to work in gold, in silver, in bronze, [5]in cutting jewels for setting, in carving wood, and to work in all *manner of* workmanship.

[6]"And I, indeed I, have appointed with him Aholiab the son of Ahisamach, of the tribe of Dan; and I have put wisdom in the hearts of all the gifted artisans, that they may make all that I have commanded you: [7]the tabernacle of meeting, the ark of the Testimony and the mercy seat that *is* on it, and all the furniture of the tabernacle— [8]the table and its utensils, the pure *gold* lampstand with all its utensils, the altar of incense, [9]the altar of burnt offering with all its utensils, and the laver and its base— [10]the garments of ministry,[a] the holy garments for Aaron the priest and the garments of his sons, to minister as priests, [11]and the anointing oil and sweet incense for the holy *place*. According to all that I have commanded you they shall do."

THE SABBATH LAW

[12]And the LORD spoke to Moses, saying, [13]"Speak also to the children of Israel, saying: 'Surely My Sabbaths you shall keep, for it *is* a sign between Me and you throughout your generations, that *you* may know that I *am* the LORD who sanctifies you. [14]You shall keep the Sabbath, therefore, for *it is* holy to you. Everyone who profanes it shall surely be put to death; for whoever does *any* work on it, that person shall be cut off from among his people. [15]Work shall be done for six days, but the seventh *is* the Sabbath of rest, holy to the LORD. Whoever does *any* work on the Sabbath day, he

shall surely be put to death. [16]Therefore the children of Israel shall keep the Sabbath, to observe the Sabbath throughout their generations *as* a perpetual covenant. [17]It *is* a sign between Me and the children of Israel forever; for *in* six days the LORD made the heavens and the earth, and on the seventh day He rested and was refreshed.' "

[18]And when He had made an end of speaking with him on Mount Sinai, He gave Moses two tablets of the Testimony, tablets of stone, written with the finger of God.

THE GOLD CALF

[1]Now when the people saw that Moses delayed coming down from the mountain, the people gathered together to Aaron, and said to him, "Come, make us gods that shall go before us; for *as for* this Moses, the man who brought us up out of the land of Egypt, we do not know what has become of him." [2]And Aaron said to them, "Break off the golden earrings which *are* in the ears of your wives, your sons, and your daughters, and bring *them* to me." [3]So all the people broke off the golden earrings which *were* in their ears, and brought *them* to Aaron. [4]And he received *the gold* from their hand, and he fashioned it with an engraving tool, and made a molded calf.

Then they said, "This *is* your god, O Israel, that brought you out of the land of Egypt!"

[5]So when Aaron saw *it*, he built an altar

> "And when He had made an end of speaking with him on Mount Sinai, He gave Moses two tablets of the Testimony, tablets of stone, written with the finger of God."
> (Exodus 31:18)

WHAT'S IT MEAN?

Bulls were popular worship objects in the ancient world. Centuries-old images of bulls have been found everywhere from the palaces of Crete, an island in the Mediterranean Sea, to the temples of Egypt.
Exodus 32:2–4

BEZALEL made a difference

God creates creators. That's why God is the original Creator. The rest of us, creatures all, in one way or another simply imitate the One who made us. To make this point very clear, God sometimes fills a person with special abilities and calls them to do special work for Him. Those people make a difference. One of them was a Bezalel.

God gave Moses, who may not have had an artistic bone in his body, the exact details of the portable worship center the people of Israel would use in the wilderness. Then God gave Moses someone to do the work—Bezalel. God filled Bezalel with the Holy Spirit. The results in this case meant two things in Bezalel's life: (1)he could do; (2)he could teach others to do. Bezalel was an artist's artist. He could cast, cut, shape, build, paint, design, sew, weave objects of exquisite beauty. He helped others do the same. Imagine building a place in which God's presence would be so real that it would take on the form of a cloud or pillar of fire. So, how did Bezalel make a difference? He built a house for God. He helped create a beautiful space in which people could worship. His work touched the spiritual life of an entire nation.

Cutting Edge

YOU can, too!

Perhaps you are a Michelangelo, a da Vinci, a Bezalel in the wings—go for it! In any case, the most important lessons from Bezalel's life are not limited to artists. He was available to God. He was called by God. Bezalel was equipped by God; and he was filled by God's Spirit. How many of these facts are already true in your life? Notice that most of Bezalel's portfolio was up to God. The only aspect under his control was availability. Are you available to God? Do you remind yourself and God regularly that you want to serve Him in the world? "For we are His workmanship, created in Christ Jesus for good works, which God prepared beforehand that we should walk in them" (Eph. 2:10).

Want to know more? Read about Bezalel's gifted work in

Exodus 31:1–11; 35:30—36:3.

before it. And Aaron made a proclamation and said, "Tomorrow *is* a feast to the LORD." ⁶Then they rose early on the next day, offered burnt offerings, and brought peace offerings; and the people sat down to eat and drink, and rose up to play.

⁷And the LORD said to Moses, "Go, get down! For your people whom you brought out of the land of Egypt have corrupted *themselves.* ⁸They have turned aside quickly out of the way which I commanded them. They have made themselves a molded calf, and worshiped it and sacrificed to it, and said, 'This *is* your god, O Israel, that brought you out of the land of Egypt!' " ⁹And the LORD said to Moses, "I have seen this people, and indeed it *is* a stiff-necked people! ¹⁰Now therefore, let Me alone, that My wrath may burn hot against them and I may consume them. And I will make of you a great nation."

¹¹Then Moses pleaded with the LORD his God, and said: "LORD, why does Your wrath burn hot against Your people whom You have brought out of the land of Egypt with great power and with a mighty hand? ¹²Why should the Egyptians speak, and say, 'He brought them out to harm them, to kill them in the mountains, and to consume them from the face of the earth'? Turn from Your fierce wrath, and relent from this harm to Your people. ¹³Remember Abraham, Isaac, and Israel, Your servants, to whom You swore by Your own self, and said to them, 'I will multiply your descendants as the stars of heaven; and all this land that I have spoken of I give to your descendants, and they shall inherit *it* forever.' "ᵃ ¹⁴So the LORD relented from the harm which He said He would do to His people.

¹⁵And Moses turned and went down from the mountain, and the two tablets of the Testimony *were* in his hand. The tablets *were* written on both sides; on the one *side* and on the other they were written. ¹⁶Now the tablets *were* the work of God, and the writing *was* the writing of God engraved on the tablets.

¹⁷And when Joshua heard the noise of the people as they shouted, he said to Moses, "*There is* a noise of war in the camp."

¹⁸But he said:

"*It is* not the noise of the shout of victory,
    Nor the noise of the cry of defeat,
    But the sound of singing I hear."

¹⁹So it was, as soon as he came near the camp, that he saw the calf *and* the dancing. So Moses' anger became hot, and he cast the tablets out of his hands and broke them at the foot of the mountain. ²⁰Then he took the calf which they had made, burned *it* in the fire, and ground *it* to powder; and he scattered *it* on the water and made the children of Israel drink *it.* ²¹And Moses said to Aaron, "What did this people do to you that you have brought *so* great a sin upon them?"

²²So Aaron said, "Do not let the anger of my lord become hot. You know the people, that they *are set* on evil. ²³For they said to me, 'Make us gods that shall go before us; *as for* this Moses, the man who brought us out of the land of Egypt, we do not know what has become of him.' ²⁴And I said to them, 'Whoever has any gold, let them break *it* off.' So they gave *it* to me, and I cast it into the fire, and this calf came out."

²⁵Now when Moses saw that the people *were* unrestrained (for Aaron had not restrained them, to *their* shame among their enemies), ²⁶then Moses stood in the entrance of the camp, and said, "Whoever *is* on the LORD's side—*come* to me!" And all the sons of Levi gathered themselves together to him. ²⁷And he said to them, "Thus says the LORD God of Israel: 'Let every man put his sword on his side, and go in and out from entrance to entrance throughout the camp, and let every man kill his brother, every man his companion, and every man his neighbor.' " ²⁸So the sons of Levi did according to the word of Moses. And about three thousand men of the people fell that day. ²⁹Then Moses said, "Consecrate yourselves today to the LORD, that He may bestow on you a blessing this day, for every man has opposed his son and his brother."

³⁰Now it came to pass on the next day that Moses said to the people, "You have committed a great sin. So now I will go up to the LORD; perhaps I can make atonement for your sin." ³¹Then Moses returned to the LORD and said, "Oh, these people have committed a great sin, and have made for themselves a god of gold! ³²Yet now, if You will forgive their sin—but if not, I pray, blot me out of Your book which You have written."

³³And the LORD said to Moses, "Whoever has sinned against Me, I will blot him out of My book. ³⁴Now therefore, go, lead the people to *the place* of which I have spoken to you. Behold, My Angel shall go before you. Nevertheless, in the day when I

Does sin have consequences? (32:34)

visit for punishment, I will visit punishment upon them for their sin."

35So the LORD plagued the people because of what they did with the calf which Aaron made.

THE COMMAND TO LEAVE SINAI

1Then the LORD said to Moses, "Depart *and* go up from here, you and the people whom you have brought out of the land of Egypt, to the land of which I swore to Abraham, Isaac, and Jacob, saying, 'To your descendants I will give it.' 2And I will send *My* Angel before you, and I will drive out the Canaanite and the Amorite and the Hittite and the Perizzite and the Hivite and the Jebusite. 3*Go up* to a land flowing with milk and honey; for I will not go up in your midst, lest I consume you on the way, for you *are* a stiff-necked people."

4And when the people heard this bad news, they mourned, and no one put on his ornaments. 5For the LORD had said to Moses, "Say to the children of Israel, 'You *are* a stiff-necked people. I could come up into your midst in one moment and consume you. Now therefore, take off your ornaments, that I may know what to do to you.'" 6So the children of Israel stripped themselves of their ornaments by Mount Horeb.

MOSES MEETS WITH THE LORD

7Moses took his tent and pitched it outside the camp, far from the camp, and called it the tabernacle of meeting. And it came to pass *that* everyone who sought the LORD went out to the tabernacle of meeting which *was* outside the camp. 8So it was, whenever Moses went out to the tabernacle, *that* all the people rose, and each man stood *at* his tent door and watched Moses until he had gone into the tabernacle. 9And it came to pass, when Moses entered the tabernacle, that the pillar of cloud descended and stood *at* the door of the tabernacle, and *the* LORD

talked with Moses. 10All the people saw the pillar of cloud standing *at* the tabernacle door, and all the people rose and worshiped, each man *in* his tent door. 11So the LORD spoke to Moses face to face, as a man speaks to his friend. And he would return to the camp, but his servant Joshua the son of Nun, a young man, did not depart from the tabernacle.

THE PROMISE OF GOD'S PRESENCE

12Then Moses said to the LORD, "See, You say to me, 'Bring up this people.' But You have not let me know whom You will send with me. Yet You have said, 'I know you by name, and you have also found grace in My sight.' 13Now therefore, I pray, if I have found grace in Your sight, show me now Your way, that I may know You and that I may find grace in Your sight. And consider that this nation *is* Your people."

14And He said, "My Presence will go *with you,* and I will give you rest."

15Then he said to Him, "If Your Presence does not go *with us,* do not bring us up from here. 16For how then will it be known that Your people and I have found grace in Your sight, except You go with us? So we shall be separate, Your people and I, from all the people who *are* upon the face of the earth."

17So the LORD said to Moses, "I will also do this thing that you have spoken; for you have found grace in My sight, and I know you by name."

18And he said, "Please, show me Your glory."

19Then He said, "I will make all My goodness pass before you, and I will proclaim the name of the LORD before you. I will be gracious to whom I will be gracious, and I will have compassion on whom I will have compassion." 20But He said, "You cannot see My face; for no man shall see Me, and live." 21And the LORD said, "Here is a place by Me, and you shall stand on the rock. 22So it shall be, while My glory passes by, that I will put you in the cleft of the rock, and will cover you with My hand while I pass by. 23Then I will take away My hand, and you shall see My back; but My face shall not be seen."

MOSES MAKES NEW TABLETS

1And the LORD said to Moses, "Cut two tablets of stone like the first *ones,* and I will write on *these* tablets the words that were on the first tablets which you broke. 2So be ready in the morning, and come up in the morning to Mount Sinai, and present yourself to Me there on the top of the mountain. 3And no man shall come up with you, and let no man be seen

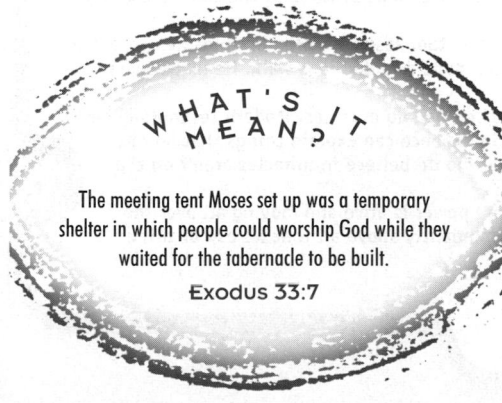

WHAT'S IT MEAN?

The meeting tent Moses set up was a temporary shelter in which people could worship God while they waited for the tabernacle to be built.

Exodus 33:7

throughout all the mountain; let neither flocks nor herds feed before that mountain."

[4]So he cut two tablets of stone like the first *ones.* Then Moses rose early in the morning and went up Mount Sinai, as the LORD had commanded him; and he took in his hand the two tablets of stone.

[5]Now the LORD descended in the cloud and stood with him there, and proclaimed the name of the LORD. [6]And the LORD passed before him and proclaimed, "The LORD, the LORD God, merciful and gracious, longsuffering, and abounding in goodness and truth, [7]keeping mercy for thousands, forgiving iniquity and transgression and sin, by no means clearing *the guilty,* visiting the iniquity of the fathers upon the children and the children's children to the third and the fourth generation."

[8]So Moses made haste and bowed his head toward the earth, and worshiped. [9]Then he said, "If now I have found grace in Your sight, O Lord, let my Lord, I pray, go among us, even though we *are* a stiff-necked people; and pardon our iniquity and our sin, and take us as Your inheritance."

THE COVENANT RENEWED

[10]And He said: "Behold, I make a covenant. Before all your people I will do marvels such as

WHAT'S IT MEAN?

The wooden images were used in the worship of Asherah, who was similar to Venus, the Roman goddess of love. The Canaanites believed that Asherah, the wife of the fertility god Baal, had some special powers over fertility herself.

Exodus 34:13

have not been done in all the earth, nor in any nation; and all the people among whom you *are* shall see the work of the LORD. For it *is* an awesome thing that I will do with you. [11]Observe what I command you this day. Behold, I am driving out from before you the Amorite and the Canaanite and the Hittite and the Perizzite and the Hivite and the Jebusite. [12]Take heed to yourself, lest you make a covenant with the inhabitants of the land where you are going, lest it be a snare in your midst. [13]But you shall destroy their altars, break their *sacred* pillars,

Promise   HE PROMISES TO DO MIRACLES.

Behold, I make a covenant. Before all your people I will do marvels such as have not been done in all the earth (Ex. 34:10).

God said that He would do things "such as have not been done in all the earth." He sure kept that promise to the Israelites. He cut a path for them through the Jordan River. He made the walls of Jericho fall down when the priests blew their trumpets. He kept the sun from going down one day. And that was just the beginning.

God did a lot of miracles in New Testament times, too. Jesus and His disciples healed people almost all the time. Jesus made blind eyes see. He made crippled legs walk. He made lepers whole. He even raised people from the dead.

Today, a lot of people have just quit expecting to see God do miracles. Modern technology has been able to do things that used to require a miracle. Science can explain things that no one understood many years ago. Sometimes even people who do believe in miracles aren't on the lookout for them anymore.

We live in a day of miracles. God's miracle-working power is alive and moving all over the world. Be on the lookout. He can do "exceedingly abundantly above all that we ask or think" (Eph. 3:20). He'll do miracles.

SEE FOR YOURSELF:
Ex. 11:9; Ps. 77:14; Dan. 6:27; Mic. 7:15;
Gal. 3:5

and cut down their wooden images [14](for you shall worship no other god, for the LORD, whose name *is* Jealous, *is* a jealous God), [15]lest you make a covenant with the inhabitants of the land, and they play the harlot with their gods and make sacrifice to their gods, and *one of them* invites you and you eat of his sacrifice, [16]and you take of his daughters for your sons, and his daughters play the harlot with their gods and make your sons play the harlot with their gods.

WORSHIP

Is worship meant for anyone else except God? (34:14)

[17]"You shall make no molded gods for yourselves.

[18]"The Feast of Unleavened Bread you shall keep. Seven days you shall eat unleavened bread, as I commanded you, in the appointed time of the month of Abib; for in the month of Abib you came out from Egypt.

[19]"All that open the womb *are* Mine, and every male firstborn among your livestock, *whether* ox or sheep. [20]But the firstborn of a donkey you shall redeem with a lamb. And if you will not redeem *him*, then you shall break his neck. All the firstborn of your sons you shall redeem.

"And none shall appear before Me empty-handed.

[21]"Six days you shall work, but on the seventh day you shall rest; in plowing time and in harvest you shall rest.

[22]"And you shall observe the Feast of Weeks, of the firstfruits of wheat harvest, and the Feast of Ingathering at the year's end.

[23]"Three times in the year all your men shall appear before the Lord, the LORD God of Israel. [24]For I will cast out the nations before you and enlarge your borders; neither will any man covet your land when you go up to appear before the LORD your God three times in the year.

[25]"You shall not offer the blood of My sacrifice with leaven, nor shall the sacrifice of the Feast of the Passover be left until morning.

[26]"The first of the firstfruits of your land you shall bring to the house of the LORD your God. You shall not boil a young goat in its mother's milk."

[27]Then the LORD said to Moses, "Write these words, for according to the tenor of these words I have made a covenant with you and with Israel." [28]So he was there with the LORD forty days and forty nights; he neither ate bread nor drank water. And He wrote on the tablets the words of the covenant, the Ten Commandments.[a]

THE SHINING FACE OF MOSES

[29]Now it was so, when Moses came down from Mount Sinai (and the two tablets of the Testimony *were* in Moses' hand when he came down from the mountain), that Moses did not know that the skin of his face shone while he talked with Him. [30]So when Aaron and all the children of Israel saw Moses, behold, the skin of his face shone, and they were afraid to come near him. [31]Then Moses called to them, and Aaron and all the rulers of the congregation returned to him; and Moses talked with them. [32]Afterward all the children of Israel came near, and he gave them as commandments all that the LORD had spoken with him on Mount Sinai. [33]And when Moses had finished speaking with them, he put a veil on his face. [34]But whenever Moses went in before the LORD to speak with Him, he would take the veil off until he came out; and he would come out and speak to the children of Israel whatever he had been commanded. [35]And whenever the children of Israel saw the face of Moses, that the skin of Moses' face shone, then Moses would put the veil on his face again, until he went in to speak with Him.

SABBATH REGULATIONS

[1]Then Moses gathered all the congregation of the children of Israel together, and said to them, "These *are* the words which the LORD has commanded *you* to do: [2]Work shall be done for six days, but the seventh day shall be a holy day for you, a Sabbath of rest to the LORD. Whoever does any work on it shall be put to death. [3]You shall kindle no fire throughout your dwellings on the Sabbath day."

OFFERINGS FOR THE TABERNACLE

[4]And Moses spoke to all the congregation of the children of Israel, saying, "This *is* the thing which the LORD commanded, saying: [5]'Take from among you an offering to the LORD. Whoever *is* of a willing heart, let him bring it as an offering to the LORD: gold, silver, and bronze; [6]blue, purple, and scarlet *thread*, fine linen, and goats' *hair*; [7]ram skins dyed red, badger skins, and acacia wood; [8]oil for the light, and spices for the anointing oil and for the sweet incense; [9]onyx stones, and stones to be set in the ephod and in the breastplate.

34:28 [a]Literally *Ten Words*

ARTICLES OF THE TABERNACLE

10'All *who are* gifted artisans among you shall come and make all that the LORD has commanded: 11the tabernacle, its tent, its covering, its clasps, its boards, its bars, its pillars, and its sockets; 12the ark and its poles, *with* the mercy seat, and the veil of the covering; 13the table and its poles, all its utensils, and the showbread; 14also the lampstand for the light, its utensils, its lamps, and the oil for the light; 15the incense altar, its poles, the anointing oil, the sweet incense, and the screen for the door at the entrance of the tabernacle; 16the altar of burnt offering with its bronze grating, its poles, all its utensils, *and* the laver and its base; 17the hangings of the court, its pillars, their sockets, and the screen for the gate of the court; 18the pegs of the tabernacle, the pegs of the court, and their cords; 19the garments of ministry,*a* for ministering in the holy *place*—the holy garments for Aaron the priest and the garments of his sons, to minister as priests'. "

THE TABERNACLE OFFERINGS PRESENTED

20And all the congregation of the children of Israel departed from the presence of Moses. 21Then everyone came whose heart was stirred, and everyone whose spirit was willing, *and* they brought the LORD's offering for the work of the tabernacle of meeting, for all its service, and for the holy garments. 22They came, both men and women, as many as had a willing heart, *and* brought earrings and nose rings, rings and necklaces, all jewelry of gold, that is, every man who *made* an offering of gold to the LORD. 23And every man, with whom was found blue, purple, and scarlet *thread*, fine linen, goats' *hair*, red skins of rams, and badger skins, brought *them*. 24Everyone who offered an offering of silver or bronze brought the LORD's offering. And everyone with whom was found acacia wood for any work of the service, brought *it*. 25All the women *who were* gifted artisans spun yarn with their hands,

> GIVING
> What kind of attitude should we have?
> (35:22)

and brought what they had spun, of blue, purple, *and* scarlet, and fine linen. 26And all the women whose hearts stirred with wisdom spun yarn of goats' hair. 27The rulers brought onyx stones, and the stones to be set in the ephod and in the breastplate, 28and spices and oil for the light, for the anointing oil, and for the sweet incense. 29The children of Israel brought a freewill offering to the LORD, all the men and women whose hearts were willing to bring *material* for all kinds of work which the LORD, by the hand of Moses, had commanded to be done.

THE ARTISANS CALLED BY GOD

30And Moses said to the children of Israel, "See, the LORD has called by name Bezalel the son of Uri, the son of Hur, of the tribe of Judah; 31and He has filled him with the Spirit of God, in wisdom and understanding, in knowledge and all manner of workmanship, 32to design artistic works, to work in gold and silver and bronze, 33in cutting jewels for setting, in carving wood, and to work in all manner of artistic workmanship. 34"And He has put in his heart the ability to teach, *in* him and Aholiab the son of Ahisamach, of the tribe of Dan. 35He has filled them with skill to do all manner of work of the engraver and the designer and the tapestry maker, in blue, purple, and scarlet *thread*, and fine linen, and of the weaver—those who do every work and those who design artistic works.

1"And Bezalel and Aholiab, and every gifted artisan in whom the LORD has put wisdom and understanding, to know how to do all manner of work for the service of the sanctuary, shall do according to all that the LORD has commanded."

THE PEOPLE GIVE MORE THAN ENOUGH

2Then Moses called Bezalel and Aholiab, and every gifted artisan in whose heart the LORD had put wisdom, everyone whose heart was stirred, to come and do the work. 3And they received from Moses all the offering which the children of Israel had brought for the work of the service of making the sanctuary. So they

"Then everyone came whose heart was stirred, and everyone whose spirit was willing, and they brought the LORD's offering for the work of the tabernacle of meeting, for all its service, and for the holy garments."
(Exodus 35:21)

35:19 *a*Or *woven garments*

continued bringing to him freewill offerings every morning. ⁴Then all the craftsmen who were doing all the work of the sanctuary came, each from the work he was doing, ⁵and they spoke to Moses, saying, "The people bring much more than enough for the service of the work which the LORD commanded *us* to do."

⁶So Moses gave a commandment, and they caused it to be proclaimed throughout the camp, saying, "Let neither man nor woman do any more work for the offering of the sanctuary." And the people were restrained from bringing, ⁷for the material they had was sufficient for all the work to be done—indeed too much.

BUILDING THE TABERNACLE

⁸Then all the gifted artisans among them who worked on the tabernacle made ten curtains woven of fine linen, and of blue, purple, and scarlet *thread; with* artistic designs of cherubim they made them. ⁹The length of each curtain *was* twenty-eight cubits, and the width of each curtain four cubits; the curtains *were* all the same size. ¹⁰And he coupled five curtains to one another, and *the other* five curtains he coupled to one another. ¹¹He made loops of blue *yarn* on the edge of the curtain on the selvedge of one set; likewise he did on the outer edge of *the other* curtain of the second set. ¹²Fifty loops he made on one curtain, and fifty loops he made on the edge of the curtain on the end of the second set; the loops held one *curtain* to another. ¹³And he made fifty clasps of gold, and coupled the curtains to one another with the clasps, that it might be one tabernacle.

¹⁴He made curtains of goats' *hair* for the tent over the tabernacle; he made eleven curtains. ¹⁵The length of each curtain *was* thirty cubits, and the width of each curtain four cubits; the eleven curtains *were* the same size. ¹⁶He coupled five curtains by themselves and six curtains by themselves. ¹⁷And he made fifty loops on the edge of the curtain that is outermost in one set, and fifty loops he made on the edge of the curtain of the second set. ¹⁸He also made fifty bronze clasps to couple the tent together, that it might be one. ¹⁹Then he made a covering for the tent of ram skins dyed red, and a covering of badger skins above *that.*

²⁰For the tabernacle he made boards of acacia wood, standing upright. ²¹The length of each board *was* ten cubits, and the width of each board a cubit and a half. ²²Each board had two tenons for binding one to another. Thus he made for all the boards of the tabernacle. ²³And he made boards for the tabernacle, twenty boards for the south side. ²⁴Forty sockets of silver he made to go under the twenty boards: two sockets under each of the boards for its two tenons. ²⁵And for the other side of the tabernacle, the north side, he made twenty boards ²⁶and their forty sockets of silver: two sockets under each of the boards. ²⁷For the west side of the tabernacle he made six boards. ²⁸He also made two boards for the two back corners of the tabernacle. ²⁹And they were coupled at the bottom and coupled together at the top by one ring. Thus he made both of them for the two corners. ³⁰So there were eight boards and their sockets—sixteen sockets of silver—two sockets under each of the boards.

³¹And he made bars of acacia wood: five for the boards on one side of the tabernacle, ³²five bars for the boards on the other side of the tabernacle, and five bars for the boards of the tabernacle on the far side westward. ³³And he made the middle bar to pass through the boards from one end to the other. ³⁴He overlaid the boards with gold, made their rings of gold *to be* holders for the bars, and overlaid the bars with gold.

³⁵And he made a veil of blue, purple, and scarlet *thread,* and fine woven linen; it was worked *with* an artistic design of cherubim. ³⁶He made for it four pillars of acacia *wood,* and overlaid them with gold, with their hooks of gold; and he cast four sockets of silver for them. ³⁷He also made a screen for the tabernacle door, of blue, purple, and scarlet *thread,* and fine woven linen, made by a weaver, ³⁸and its five pillars with their hooks. And he overlaid their capitals and their rings with gold, but their five sockets *were* bronze.

MAKING THE ARK OF THE TESTIMONY

¹Then Bezalel made the ark of acacia wood; two and a half cubits *was* its length, a cubit and a half its width, and a cubit and a half its height.

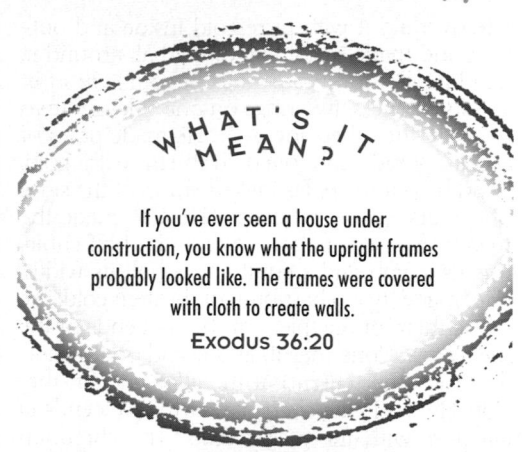

WHAT'S IT MEAN?

If you've ever seen a house under construction, you know what the upright frames probably looked like. The frames were covered with cloth to create walls.

Exodus 36:20

²He overlaid it with pure gold inside and out-side, and made a molding of gold all around it. ³And he cast for it four rings of gold *to be set* in its four corners: two rings on one side, and two rings on the other side of it. ⁴He made poles of acacia wood, and overlaid them with gold. ⁵And he put the poles into the rings at the sides of the ark, to bear the ark. ⁶He also made the mercy seat of pure gold; two and a half cubits *was* its length and a cubit and a half its width. ⁷He made two cherubim of beaten gold; he made them of one piece at the two ends of the mercy seat: ⁸one cherub at one end on this side, and the other cherub at the *other* end on that side. He made the cherubim at the two ends *of one piece* with the mercy seat. ⁹The cherubim spread out *their* wings above, *and* covered the mercy seat with their wings. They faced one another; the faces of the cherubim were toward the mercy seat.

MAKING THE TABLE FOR THE SHOWBREAD

¹⁰He made the table of acacia wood; two cu-bits *was* its length, a cubit its width, and a cubit and a half its height. ¹¹And he overlaid it with pure gold, and made a molding of gold all around it. ¹²Also he made a frame of a hand-breadth all around it, and made a molding of gold for the frame all around it. ¹³And he cast for it four rings of gold, and put the rings on the four corners that *were* at its four legs. ¹⁴The rings were close to the frame, as holders for the poles to bear the table. ¹⁵And he made the poles of acacia wood to bear the table, and overlaid them with gold. ¹⁶He made of pure gold the utensils which were on the table: its dishes, its cups, its bowls, and its pitchers for pouring.

MAKING THE GOLD LAMPSTAND

¹⁷He also made the lampstand of pure gold; of hammered work he made the lampstand. Its shaft, its branches, its bowls, its *ornamental* knobs, and its flowers were of the same piece. ¹⁸And six branches came out of its sides: three branches of the lampstand out of one side, and three branches of the lampstand out of the other side. ¹⁹There were three bowls made like almond *blossoms* on one branch, with an *orna-mental* knob and a flower, and three bowls made like almond *blossoms* on the other branch, with an *ornamental* knob and a flower—and so for the six branches coming out of the lamp-stand. ²⁰And on the lampstand itself *were* four bowls made like almond *blossoms, each with its* ornamental knob and flower. ²¹*There was* a knob under the *first* two branches of the same, a

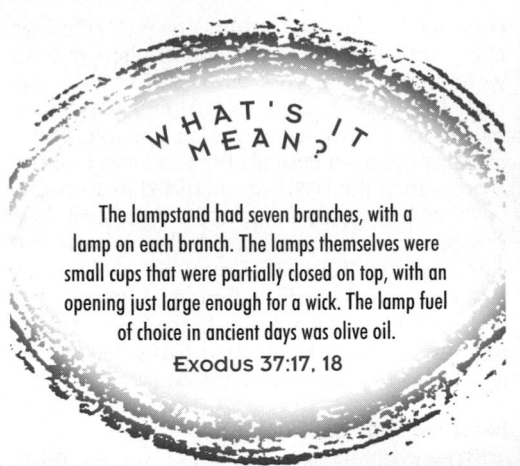

WHAT'S IT MEAN?

The lampstand had seven branches, with a lamp on each branch. The lamps themselves were small cups that were partially closed on top, with an opening just large enough for a wick. The lamp fuel of choice in ancient days was olive oil.

Exodus 37:17, 18

knob under the *second* two branches of the same, and a knob under the *third* two branches of the same, according to the six branches extending from it. ²²Their knobs and their branches were of one piece; all of it *was* one hammered piece of pure gold. ²³And he made its seven lamps, its wick-trimmers, and its trays of pure gold. ²⁴Of a talent of pure gold he made it, with all its utensils.

MAKING THE ALTAR OF INCENSE

²⁵He made the incense altar of acacia wood. Its length *was* a cubit and its width a cubit—*it was* square—and two cubits *was* its height. Its horns were *of one piece* with it. ²⁶And he overlaid it with pure gold: its top, its sides all around, and its horns. He also made for it a molding of gold all around it. ²⁷He made two rings of gold for it under its molding, by its two corners on both sides, as holders for the poles with which to bear it. ²⁸And he made the poles of acacia wood, and overlaid them with gold.

MAKING THE ANOINTING OIL AND THE INCENSE

²⁹He also made the holy anointing oil and the pure incense of sweet spices, according to the work of the perfumer.

MAKING THE ALTAR OF BURNT OFFERING

¹He made the altar of burnt offering of aca-cia wood; five cubits *was* its length and five cu-bits its width—*it was* square—and its height *was* three cubits. ²He made its horns on its four cor-ners; the horns were *of one piece* with it. And he overlaid it with bronze. ³He made all the uten-sils for the altar: the pans, the shovels, the ba-sins, the forks, and the firepans; all its utensils he made of bronze. ⁴And he made a grate of bronze network for the altar, under its rim,

midway from the bottom. ⁵He cast four rings for the four corners of the bronze grating, *as* holders for the poles. ⁶And he made the poles of acacia wood, and overlaid them with bronze. ⁷Then he put the poles into the rings on the sides of the altar, with which to bear it. He made the altar hollow with boards.

MAKING THE BRONZE LAVER

⁸He made the laver of bronze and its base of bronze, from the bronze mirrors of the serving women who assembled at the door of the tabernacle of meeting.

MAKING THE COURT OF THE TABERNACLE

⁹Then he made the court on the south side; the hangings of the court *were of* fine woven linen, one hundred cubits long. ¹⁰There *were* twenty pillars for them, with twenty bronze sockets. The hooks of the pillars and their bands *were* silver. ¹¹On the north side *the hangings were* one hundred cubits *long*, with twenty pillars and their twenty bronze sockets. The hooks of the pillars and their bands *were* silver. ¹²And on the west side *there were* hangings of fifty cubits, with ten pillars and their ten sockets. The hooks of the pillars and their bands *were* silver. ¹³For the east side *the hangings were* fifty cubits. ¹⁴The hangings of one side *of the gate were* fifteen cubits *long, with* their three pillars and their three sockets, ¹⁵and the same for the other side of the court gate; on this side and that *were* hangings of fifteen cubits, *with* their three pillars and their three sockets. ¹⁶All the hangings of the court all around *were of* fine woven linen. ¹⁷The sockets for the pillars *were* bronze, the hooks of the pillars and their bands *were* silver, and the overlay of their capitals *was* silver; and all the pillars of the court had bands of silver. ¹⁸The screen for the gate of the court *was* woven of blue, purple, and scarlet *thread,* and of fine woven linen. The length *was* twenty cubits, and the height along its width *was* five cubits, corresponding to the hangings of the court. ¹⁹And *there were* four pillars *with* their four sockets of bronze; their hooks *were* silver, and the overlay of their capitals and their bands *was* silver. ²⁰All the pegs of the tabernacle, and of the court all around, *were* bronze.

MATERIALS OF THE TABERNACLE

²¹This is the inventory of the tabernacle, the tabernacle of the Testimony, which was counted according to the commandment of Moses, for the service of the Levites, by the hand of Ithamar, son of Aaron the priest. ²²Bezalel the son of Uri, the son of Hur, of the tribe of Judah, made all that the LORD had commanded Moses. ²³And with him *was* Aholiab the son of Ahisamach, of the tribe of Dan, an engraver and designer, a weaver of blue, purple, and scarlet *thread,* and of fine linen. ²⁴All the gold that was used in all the work of the holy *place,* that is, the gold of the offering, was twenty-nine talents and seven hundred and thirty shekels, according to the shekel of the sanctuary. ²⁵And the silver from those who were numbered of the congregation *was* one hundred talents and one thousand seven hundred and seventy-five shekels, according to the shekel of the sanctuary: ²⁶a bekah for each man (*that is,* half a shekel, according to the shekel of the sanctuary), for everyone included in the numbering from twenty years old and above, for six hundred and three thousand, five hundred and fifty *men.* ²⁷And from the hundred talents of silver were cast the sockets of the sanctuary and the bases of the veil: one hundred sockets from the hundred talents, one talent for each socket. ²⁸Then from the one thousand seven hundred and seventy-five *shekels* he made hooks for the pillars, overlaid their capitals, and made bands for them.

²⁹The offering of bronze *was* seventy talents and two thousand four hundred shekels. ³⁰And with it he made the sockets for the door of the tabernacle of meeting, the bronze altar, the bronze grating for it, and all the utensils for the altar, ³¹the sockets for the court all around, the bases for the court gate, all the pegs for the tabernacle, and all the pegs for the court all around.

WHAT'S IT MEAN?

The inner part of the tabernacle was the worship area. Only gold and silver, the finest and most expensive metals, were good enough to be used as decorations for the holy area. The outer area of the tabernacle was decorated with bronze, a less expensive metal.

Exodus 38:21–31

MAKING THE GARMENTS OF THE PRIESTHOOD

¹Of the blue, purple, and scarlet *thread* they made garments of ministry,ᵃ for ministering in the holy *place*, and made the holy garments for Aaron, as the LORD had commanded Moses.

MAKING THE EPHOD

²He made the ephod of gold, blue, purple, and scarlet *thread*, and of fine woven linen. ³And they beat the gold into thin sheets and cut *it into* threads, to work *it in with* the blue, purple, and scarlet *thread*, and the fine linen, *into* artistic designs. ⁴They made shoulder straps for it to couple *it* together; it was coupled together at its two edges. ⁵And the intricately woven band of his ephod that *was* on it *was* of the same workmanship, *woven of* gold, blue, purple, and scarlet *thread*, and of fine woven linen, as the LORD had commanded Moses.

⁶And they set onyx stones, enclosed in settings of gold; they were engraved, as signets are engraved, with the names of the sons of Israel. ⁷He put them on the shoulders of the ephod *as* memorial stones for the sons of Israel, as the LORD had commanded Moses.

MAKING THE BREASTPLATE

⁸And he made the breastplate, artistically woven like the workmanship of the ephod, of gold, blue, purple, and scarlet *thread*, and of fine woven linen. ⁹They made the breastplate square by doubling it; a span *was* its length and a span its width when doubled. ¹⁰And they set in it four rows of stones: a row with a sardius, a topaz, and an emerald was the first row; ¹¹the second row, a turquoise, a sapphire, and a diamond; ¹²the third row, a jacinth, an agate, and an amethyst; ¹³the fourth row, a beryl, an onyx, and a jasper. *They were* enclosed in settings of gold in their mountings. ¹⁴*There were* twelve stones according to the names of the sons of Israel: according to their names, *engraved like* a signet, each one with its own name according to the twelve tribes. ¹⁵And they made chains for the breastplate at the ends, like braided cords of pure gold. ¹⁶They also made two settings of gold and two gold rings, and put the two rings on the two ends of the breastplate. ¹⁷And they put the two braided *chains* of gold in the two rings on the ends of the breastplate. ¹⁸The two ends of the two braided *chains* they fastened in the two settings, and put them on the shoulder straps of the ephod in the front. ¹⁹And they made two rings of gold and put *them* on the two ends of the breastplate, on the edge of it,

which *was* on the inward side of the ephod. ²⁰They made two *other* gold rings and put them on the two shoulder straps, underneath the ephod toward its front, right at the seam above the intricately woven band of the ephod. ²¹And they bound the breastplate by means of its rings to the rings of the ephod with a blue cord, so that it would be above the intricately woven band of the ephod, and that the breastplate would not come loose from the ephod, as the LORD had commanded Moses.

MAKING THE OTHER PRIESTLY GARMENTS

²²He made the robe of the ephod of woven work, all of blue. ²³And *there was* an opening in the middle of the robe, like the opening in a coat of mail, *with* a woven binding all around the opening, so that it would not tear. ²⁴They made on the hem of the robe pomegranates of blue, purple, and scarlet, and of fine woven linen. ²⁵And they made bells of pure gold, and put the bells between the pomegranates on the hem of the robe all around between the pomegranates: ²⁶a bell and a pomegranate, a bell and a pomegranate, all around the hem of the robe to minister in, as the LORD had commanded Moses.

WHAT'S IT MEAN?

Only big shots wore purple dye in ancient times. The dye came from a shellfish that lived in the Mediterranean Sea. Preparing it was difficult and expensive. Only royalty and other important people could afford it. Purple wasn't the only expensive dye, though. Red and blue dyes were also very valuable.

Exodus 39:24–26

²⁷They made tunics, artistically woven of fine linen, for Aaron and his sons, ²⁸a turban of fine linen, exquisite hats of fine linen, short trousers of fine woven linen, ²⁹and a sash of fine woven linen with blue, purple, and scarlet *thread*, made by a weaver, as the LORD had commanded Moses.

³⁰Then they made the plate of the holy crown of pure gold, and wrote on it an inscription *like* the engraving of a signet:

39:1 ᵃOr *woven garments*

HOLINESS TO THE LORD.

³¹And they tied to it a blue cord, to fasten *it* above on the turban, as the LORD had commanded Moses.

THE WORK COMPLETED

³²Thus all the work of the tabernacle of the tent of meeting was finished. And the children of Israel did according to all that the LORD had commanded Moses; so they did. ³³And they brought the tabernacle to Moses, the tent and all its furnishings: its clasps, its boards, its bars, its pillars, and its sockets; ³⁴the covering of ram skins dyed red, the covering of badger skins, and the veil of the covering; ³⁵the ark of the Testimony with its poles, and the mercy seat; ³⁶the table, all its utensils, and the showbread; ³⁷the pure *gold* lampstand with its lamps (the lamps set in order), all its utensils, and the oil for light; ³⁸the gold altar, the anointing oil, and the sweet incense; the screen for the tabernacle door; ³⁹the bronze altar, its grate of bronze, its poles, and all its utensils; the laver with its base; ⁴⁰the hangings of the court, its pillars and its sockets, the screen for the court gate, its cords, and its pegs; all the utensils for the service of the tabernacle, for the tent of meeting; ⁴¹and the garments of ministry,ᵃ to minister in the holy *place:* the holy garments for Aaron the priest, and his sons' garments, to minister as priests.

⁴²According to all that the LORD had commanded Moses, so the children of Israel did all the work. ⁴³Then Moses looked over all the work, and indeed they had done it; as the LORD had commanded, just so they had done it. And Moses blessed them.

THE TABERNACLE ERECTED AND ARRANGED

¹Then the LORD spoke to Moses, saying: ²"On the first day of the first month you shall set up the tabernacle of the tent of meeting. ³You shall put in it the ark of the Testimony, and partition off the ark with the veil. ⁴You shall bring in the table and arrange the things that are to be set in order on it; and you shall bring in the lampstand and light its lamps. ⁵You shall also set the altar of gold for the incense before the ark of the Testimony, and put up the screen for the door of the tabernacle. ⁶Then you shall set the altar of the burnt offering before the door of the tabernacle of the tent of meeting. ⁷And you shall set the laver between the tabernacle of meeting and the altar, and put water in it. ⁸You shall set up the court all around, and hang up the screen at the court gate.

⁹"And you shall take the anointing oil, and anoint the tabernacle and all that *is* in it; and you shall hallow it and all its utensils, and it shall be holy. ¹⁰You shall anoint the altar of the burnt offering and all its utensils, and consecrate the altar. The altar shall be most holy. ¹¹And you shall anoint the laver and its base, and consecrate it.

¹²"Then you shall bring Aaron and his sons to the door of the tabernacle of meeting and wash them with water. ¹³You shall put the holy garments on Aaron, and anoint him and consecrate him, that he may minister to Me as priest. ¹⁴And you shall bring his sons and clothe them with tunics. ¹⁵You shall anoint them, as you anointed their father, that they may minister to Me as priests; for their anointing shall surely be an everlasting priesthood throughout their generations."

¹⁶Thus Moses did; according to all that the LORD had commanded him, so he did.

¹⁷And it came to pass in the first month of the second year, on the first *day* of the month, *that* the tabernacle was raised up. ¹⁸So Moses raised up the tabernacle, fastened its sockets, set up its boards, put in its bars, and raised up its pillars. ¹⁹And he spread out the tent over the tabernacle and put the covering of the tent on top of it, as the LORD had commanded Moses. ²⁰He took the Testimony and put *it* into the ark, inserted the poles through the rings of the ark, and put the mercy seat on top of the ark. ²¹And he brought the ark into the tabernacle, hung up the veil of the covering, and partitioned off the ark of the Testimony, as the LORD had commanded Moses.

²²He put the table in the tabernacle of meeting, on the north side of the tabernacle, outside the veil; ²³and he set the bread in order upon it before the LORD, as the LORD had commanded Moses. ²⁴He put the lampstand in the tabernacle of meeting, across from the table, on the south side of the tabernacle; ²⁵and he lit the

> "Then the cloud covered the tabernacle of meeting, and the glory of the LORD filled the tabernacle."
> (Exodus 40:34)

39:41 ᵃOr *woven garments*

lamps before the LORD, as the LORD had commanded Moses. [26]He put the gold altar in the tabernacle of meeting in front of the veil; [27]and he burned sweet incense on it, as the LORD had commanded Moses. [28]He hung up the screen *at* the door of the tabernacle. [29]And he put the altar of burnt offering *before* the door of the tabernacle of the tent of meeting, and offered upon it the burnt offering and the grain offering, as the LORD had commanded Moses. [30]He set the laver between the tabernacle of meeting and the altar, and put water there for washing; [31]and Moses, Aaron, and his sons would wash their hands and their feet *with water* from it. [32]Whenever they went into the tabernacle of meeting, and when they came near the altar, they washed, as the LORD had commanded Moses. [33]And he raised up the court all around the tabernacle and the altar, and hung up the screen of the court gate. So Moses finished the work.

THE CLOUD AND THE GLORY

[34]Then the cloud covered the tabernacle of meeting, and the glory of the LORD filled the tabernacle. [35]And Moses was not able to enter the tabernacle of meeting, because the cloud rested above it, and the glory of the LORD filled the tabernacle. [36]Whenever the cloud was taken up from above the tabernacle, the children of Israel would go onward in all their journeys. [37]But if the cloud was not taken up, then they did not journey till the day that it was taken up. [38]For the cloud of the LORD *was* above the tabernacle by day, and fire was over it by night, in the sight of all the house of Israel, throughout all their journeys.

CONTENT

When you hear someone say, "I never knew *that* was in the Bible!" they could very well be talking about the Book of Leviticus. Leviticus was a "Basic Holiness & Survival Guide" for the Hebrews as they wandered through the wilderness. It was an instruction manual for the priests. It discussed everything from mildew to baldness to skin disease to sacrifices to holiness.

Think about it. This group of people was living like gypsies. It was a forty-year camping trip. Who took out the garbage? How did they keep from passing around colds and infections? What about food poisoning? Just staying alive and well was a huge task, not to mention maintaining their faith and a right relationship with God.

So, God introduced the concept of clean and unclean. He applied it to their lifestyle and their lives. The Book of Leviticus is a housekeeping/faith-keeping kind of book. To us it can seem a bit nit-picky and a little pretentious, but to them it was new news.

Put yourself in the Hebrews' sandals before you read the Book of Leviticus. A little mildew on the bathroom wall might look different to you if your whole family could get exiled because of it.

Outline

Purpose

We worship God by the way we live as well as by celebrating His goodness.

Theme

The Sanctity of God and Holiness in Everyday Life

Date of writing

1445–1440 B.C.

Bible Talk

Sacrifices

You read a lot about sacrifices in the Old Testament books. In fact, the tabernacle and the temple were both built around places where people slaughtered and then barbecued animals, sacrificing them to God. Seem a little barbaric in a world filled with vegetarian bumper stickers, not to mention vegetarians?

There are two things you might consider—

First, the sacrifices in the temple were a picture of the sacrifice that Jesus eventually made for all of us. He basically put Himself on that wooden altar that was a cross and spilled His blood and gave His life.

Second, as gross as a sacrifice might seem to you—that's how gross our sin is to a holy God. We should be just that repulsed by our own sin. It's something to think about.

KEEPING KOSHER

The laws in Leviticus regarding food are the very laws that people follow even today when they are "keeping Kosher." That means they are eating according to the Jewish laws. You can see items on almost every grocery store aisle that are kosher. Look for a *U* on the label or a *K*. (The letters may be in a circle as well.)

When you see those symbols, it means that food is considered clean and was prepared in a way that is considered clean according to the laws that originated in Leviticus.

Amazing, isn't it, that an ancient law in the Bible affects our food labels today?

THE BURNT OFFERING

¹Now the LORD called to Moses, and spoke to him from the tabernacle of meeting, saying, ²"Speak to the children of Israel, and say to them: 'When any one of you brings an offering to the LORD, you shall bring your offering of the livestock—of the herd and of the flock.

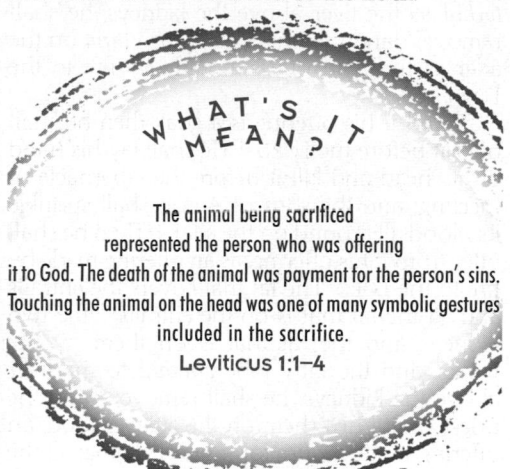

WHAT'S IT MEAN?

The animal being sacrificed represented the person who was offering it to God. The death of the animal was payment for the person's sins. Touching the animal on the head was one of many symbolic gestures included in the sacrifice.

Leviticus 1:1–4

³'If his offering is a burnt sacrifice of the herd, let him offer a male without blemish; he shall offer it of his own free will at the door of the tabernacle of meeting before the LORD. ⁴Then he shall put his hand on the head of the burnt offering, and it will be accepted on his behalf to make atonement for him. ⁵He shall kill the bull before the LORD; and the priests, Aaron's sons, shall bring the blood and sprinkle the blood all around on the altar that is by the door of the tabernacle of meeting. ⁶And he shall skin the burnt offering and cut it into its pieces. ⁷The sons of Aaron the priest shall put fire on the altar, and lay the wood in order on the fire. ⁸Then the priests, Aaron's sons, shall lay the parts, the head, and the fat in order on the wood that is on the fire upon the altar; ⁹but he shall wash its entrails and its legs with water. And the priest shall burn all on the altar as a burnt sacrifice, an offering made by fire, a sweet aroma to the LORD.

¹⁰'If his offering is of the flocks—of the sheep or of the goats—as a burnt sacrifice, he shall bring a male without blemish. ¹¹He shall kill it on the north side of the altar before the LORD; and the priests, Aaron's sons, shall sprinkle its blood all around on the altar. ¹²And he shall cut it into its pieces, with its head and its fat; and the priest shall lay them in order on the wood that is on the fire upon the altar; ¹³but he shall wash the entrails and the legs with water. Then the priest shall bring it all and burn it on the altar; it is a burnt sacrifice, an offering made by fire, a sweet aroma to the LORD.

¹⁴'And if the burnt sacrifice of his offering to the LORD is of birds, then he shall bring his offering of turtledoves or young pigeons. ¹⁵The priest shall bring it to the altar, wring off its head, and burn it on the altar; its blood shall be drained out at the side of the altar. ¹⁶And he shall remove its crop with its feathers and cast it beside the altar on the east side, into the place for ashes. ¹⁷Then he shall split it at its wings, but shall not divide it completely; and the priest shall burn it on the altar, on the wood that is on the fire. It is a burnt sacrifice, an offering made by fire, a sweet aroma to the LORD.

THE GRAIN OFFERING

¹'When anyone offers a grain offering to the LORD, his offering shall be of fine flour. And he shall pour oil on it, and put frankincense on it. ²He shall bring it to Aaron's sons, the priests, one of whom shall take from it his handful of fine flour and oil with all the frankincense. And the priest shall burn it as a memorial on the altar, an offering made by fire, a sweet aroma to the LORD. ³The rest of the grain offering shall be Aaron's and his sons'. It is most holy of the offerings to the LORD made by fire.

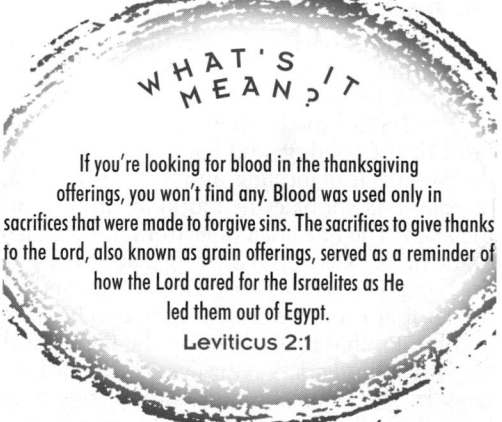

WHAT'S IT MEAN?

If you're looking for blood in the thanksgiving offerings, you won't find any. Blood was used only in sacrifices that were made to forgive sins. The sacrifices to give thanks to the Lord, also known as grain offerings, served as a reminder of how the Lord cared for the Israelites as He led them out of Egypt.

Leviticus 2:1

⁴'And if you bring as an offering a grain offering baked in the oven, it shall be unleavened cakes of fine flour mixed with oil, or unleavened wafers anointed with oil. ⁵But if your offering is a grain offering baked in a pan, it shall be of fine flour, unleavened, mixed with oil. ⁶You shall break it in pieces and pour oil on it; it is a grain offering.

⁷'If your offering is a grain offering baked in a covered pan, it shall be made of fine flour with oil. ⁸You shall bring the grain offering that is

made of these things to the LORD. And when it is presented to the priest, he shall bring it to the altar. ⁹Then the priest shall take from the grain offering a memorial portion, and burn *it* on the altar. *It is* an offering made by fire, a sweet aroma to the LORD. ¹⁰And what is left of the grain offering *shall be* Aaron's and his sons'. *It is* most holy of the offerings to the LORD made by fire.

¹¹'No grain offering which you bring to the LORD shall be made with leaven, for you shall burn no leaven nor any honey in any offering to the LORD made by fire. ¹²As for the offering of the firstfruits, you shall offer them to the LORD, but they shall not be burned on the altar for a sweet aroma. ¹³And every offering of your grain offering you shall season with salt; you shall not allow the salt of the covenant of your God to be lacking from your grain offering. With all your offerings you shall offer salt.

¹⁴'If you offer a grain offering of your firstfruits to the LORD, you shall offer for the grain offering of your firstfruits green heads of grain roasted on the fire, grain beaten from full heads. ¹⁵And you shall put oil on it, and lay frankincense on it. It *is* a grain offering. ¹⁶Then the priest shall burn the memorial portion: *part of* its beaten grain and *part* of its oil, with all the frankincense, as an offering made by fire to the LORD.

THE PEACE OFFERING

¹'When his offering *is* a sacrifice of a peace offering, if he offers *it* of the herd, whether male or female, he shall offer it without blemish before the LORD. ²And he shall lay his hand on the head of his offering, and kill it *at* the door of the tabernacle of meeting; and Aaron's sons, the priests, shall sprinkle the blood all around on the altar. ³Then he shall offer from the sacrifice of the peace offering an offering made by fire to the LORD. The fat that covers the entrails and all the fat that *is* on the entrails, ⁴the two kidneys and the fat that *is* on them by the flanks, and the fatty lobe *attached* to the liver above the kidneys, he shall remove; ⁵and Aaron's sons shall burn it on the altar upon the burnt sacrifice, which *is* on the wood that *is* on the fire, *as* an offering made by fire, a sweet aroma to the LORD.

⁶'If his offering as a sacrifice of a peace offering to the LORD *is* of the flock, *whether* male or female, he shall offer it without blemish. ⁷If he offers a lamb as his offering, then he shall offer it before the LORD. ⁸And he shall lay his hand on the head of his offering, and kill it before the tabernacle of meeting; and Aaron's sons shall sprinkle its blood all around on the altar.

⁹Then he shall offer from the sacrifice of the peace offering, as an offering made by fire to the LORD, its fat *and* the whole fat tail which he shall remove close to the backbone. And the fat that covers the entrails and all the fat that *is* on the entrails, ¹⁰the two kidneys and the fat that *is* on them by the flanks, and the fatty lobe *attached* to the liver above the kidneys, he shall remove; ¹¹and the priest shall burn *them* on the altar *as* food, an offering made by fire to the LORD.

¹²'And if his offering *is* a goat, then he shall offer it before the LORD. ¹³He shall lay his hand on its head and kill it before the tabernacle of meeting; and the sons of Aaron shall sprinkle its blood all around on the altar. ¹⁴Then he shall offer from it his offering, as an offering made by fire to the LORD. The fat that covers the entrails and all the fat that *is* on the entrails, ¹⁵the two kidneys and the fat that *is* on them by the flanks, and the fatty lobe *attached* to the liver above the kidneys, he shall remove; ¹⁶and the priest shall burn them on the altar *as* food, an offering made by fire for a sweet aroma; all the fat *is* the LORD's.

¹⁷'This shall be a perpetual statute throughout your generations in all your dwellings: you shall eat neither fat nor blood.' "

THE SIN OFFERING

¹Now the LORD spoke to Moses, saying, ²"Speak to the children of Israel, saying: 'If a person sins unintentionally against any of the commandments of the LORD *in anything* which ought not to be done, and does any of them, ³if the anointed priest sins, bringing guilt on the people, then let him offer to the LORD for his sin which he has sinned a young bull without blemish as a sin offering. ⁴He shall bring the bull to the door of the tabernacle of meeting before the LORD, lay his hand on the bull's head,

WHAT'S IT MEAN?

High priest was a demanding position. As the moral leader of the Israelites, he was supposed to reflect God's holiness in the way he lived. When he sinned, all of the Israelites were affected.

Leviticus 4:3–7

and kill the bull before the LORD. ⁵Then the anointed priest shall take some of the bull's blood and bring it to the tabernacle of meeting. ⁶The priest shall dip his finger in the blood and sprinkle some of the blood seven times before the LORD, in front of the veil of the sanctuary. ⁷And the priest shall put some of the blood on the horns of the altar of sweet incense before the LORD, which is in the tabernacle of meeting; and he shall pour the remaining blood of the bull at the base of the altar of the burnt offering, which is at the door of the tabernacle of meeting. ⁸He shall take from it all the fat of the bull as the sin offering. The fat that covers the entrails and all the fat which is on the entrails, ⁹the two kidneys and the fat that is on them by the flanks, and the fatty lobe attached to the liver above the kidneys, he shall remove, ¹⁰as it was taken from the bull of the sacrifice of the peace offering; and the priest shall burn them on the altar of the burnt offering. ¹¹But the bull's hide and all its flesh, with its head and legs, its entrails and offal— ¹²the whole bull he shall carry outside the camp to a clean place, where the ashes are poured out, and burn it on wood with fire; where the ashes are poured out it shall be burned.

¹³'Now if the whole congregation of Israel sins unintentionally, and the thing is hidden from the eyes of the assembly, and they have done something against any of the commandments of the LORD in anything which should not be done, and are guilty; ¹⁴when the sin which they have committed becomes known, then the assembly shall offer a young bull for the sin, and bring it before the tabernacle of meeting. ¹⁵And the elders of the congregation shall lay their hands on the head of the bull before the LORD. Then the bull shall be killed before the LORD. ¹⁶The anointed priest shall bring some of the bull's blood to the tabernacle of meeting. ¹⁷Then the priest shall dip his finger in the blood and sprinkle it seven times before the LORD, in front of the veil. ¹⁸And he shall put some of the blood on the horns of the altar which is before the LORD, which is in the tabernacle of meeting; and he shall pour the remaining blood at the base of the altar of burnt offering, which is at the door of the tabernacle of meeting. ¹⁹He shall take all the fat from it and burn it on the altar. ²⁰And he shall do with the bull as he did with the bull as a sin offering; thus he shall do with it. So the priest shall make

atonement for them, and it shall be forgiven them. ²¹Then he shall carry the bull outside the camp, and burn it as he burned the first bull. It is a sin offering for the assembly.

²²'When a ruler has sinned, and done something unintentionally against any of the commandments of the LORD his God in anything which should not be done, and is guilty, ²³or if his sin which he has committed comes to his knowledge, he shall bring as his offering a kid of the goats, a male without blemish. ²⁴And he shall lay his hand on the head of the goat, and kill it at the place where they kill the burnt offering before the LORD. It is a sin offering. ²⁵The priest shall take some of the blood of the sin offering with his finger, put it on the horns of the altar of burnt offering, and pour its blood at the base of the altar of burnt offering. ²⁶And he shall burn all its fat on the altar, like the fat of the sacrifice of the peace offering. So the priest shall make atonement for him concerning his sin, and it shall be forgiven him.

²⁷'If anyone of the common people sins unintentionally by doing something against any of the commandments of the LORD in anything which ought not to be done, and is guilty, ²⁸or if his sin which he has committed comes to his knowledge, then he shall bring as his offering a kid of the goats, a female without blemish, for his sin which he has committed. ²⁹And he shall lay his hand on the head of the sin offering, and kill the sin offering at the place of the burnt offering. ³⁰Then the priest shall take some of its blood with his finger, put it on the horns of the altar of burnt offering, and pour all the remaining blood at the base of the altar. ³¹He shall remove all its fat, as fat is removed from the sacrifice of the peace offering; and the priest shall burn it on the altar for a sweet aroma to the LORD. So the priest shall make atonement for him, and it shall be forgiven him.

³²'If he brings a lamb as his sin offering, he shall bring a female without blemish. ³³Then he shall lay his hand on the head of the sin offering, and kill it as a sin offering at the place where they kill the burnt offering. ³⁴The priest shall take some of the blood of the sin offering with his finger, put it on the horns of the altar of burnt offering, and pour all the remaining blood at the base of the altar. ³⁵He shall remove all its fat, as the fat of the lamb is removed from the sacrifice of the peace offering. Then the priest

"So the priest shall make atonement for his sin that he has committed, and it shall be forgiven him."
(Leviticus 4:35b)

shall burn it on the altar, according to the offerings made by fire to the LORD. So the priest shall make atonement for his sin that he has committed, and it shall be forgiven him.

THE TRESPASS OFFERING

[1]'If a person sins in hearing the utterance of an oath, and *is* a witness, whether he has seen or known *of the matter*—if he does not tell *it*, he bears guilt.

[2]'Or if a person touches any unclean thing, whether *it is* the carcass of an unclean beast, or the carcass of unclean livestock, or the carcass of unclean creeping things, and he is unaware of it, he also shall be unclean and guilty. [3]Or if he touches human uncleanness—whatever uncleanness with which a man may be defiled, and he is unaware of it—when he realizes *it*, then he shall be guilty.

[4]'Or if a person swears, speaking thoughtlessly with *his* lips to do evil or to do good, whatever *it is* that a man may pronounce by an oath, and he is unaware of it—when he realizes *it*, then he shall be guilty in any of these *matters*.

[5]And it shall be, when he is guilty in any of these *matters*, that he shall confess that he has sinned in that *thing*; [6]and he shall bring his trespass offering to the LORD for his sin which he has committed, a female from the flock, a lamb or a kid of the goats as a sin offering. So the priest shall make atonement for him concerning his sin.

[7]If he is not able to bring a lamb, then he shall bring to the LORD, for his trespass which he has committed, two turtledoves or two young pigeons: one as a sin offering and the other as a burnt offering. [8]And he shall bring them to the priest, who shall offer *that* which *is* for the sin offering first, and wring off its head from its neck, but shall not divide *it* completely. [9]Then he shall sprinkle *some* of the blood of the sin offering on the side of the altar, and the rest of the blood shall be drained out at the base of the altar. It *is* a sin offering. [10]And he shall offer the second *as* a burnt offering according to the prescribed manner. So the priest shall make atonement on his behalf for his sin which he has committed, and it shall be forgiven him.

[11]'But if he is not able to bring two turtledoves or two young pigeons, then he who sinned shall bring for his offering one-tenth of an ephah of fine flour as a sin offering. He shall put no oil on it, nor shall he put frankincense on it, for it *is* a sin offering. [12]Then he shall bring it to the priest, and the priest shall take his handful of it as a memorial portion, and burn *it* on the altar according to the offerings made by fire to the LORD. It *is* a sin offering. [13]The priest shall make atonement for him, for his sin that he has committed in any of these matters; and it shall be forgiven him. *The rest* shall be the priest's as a grain offering.' "

OFFERINGS WITH RESTITUTION

[14]Then the LORD spoke to Moses, saying: [15]"If a person commits a trespass, and sins unintentionally in regard to the holy things of the LORD, then he shall bring to the LORD as his trespass offering a ram without blemish from the flocks, with your valuation in shekels of silver according to the shekel of the sanctuary, as a trespass offering. [16]And he shall make restitution for the harm that he has done in regard to the holy thing, and shall add one-fifth to it and give it to the priest. So the priest shall make atonement for him with the ram of the trespass offering, and it shall be forgiven him.

WHAT'S IT MEAN?

Raising sheep was an obvious career choice for the wandering Israelites. Sheep were used for food and clothes. The meat of the animals was especially important, since it could be preserved and stored for winter. Male sheep, also known as rams, were especially valuable to the Israelites.
Leviticus 5:14, 15

[17]"If a person sins, and commits any of these things which are forbidden to be done by the commandments of the LORD, though he does not know *it*, yet he is guilty and shall bear his iniquity. [18]And he shall bring to the priest a ram without blemish from the flock, with your valuation, as a trespass offering. So the priest shall make atonement for him regarding his ignorance in which he erred and did not know *it*, and it shall be forgiven him. [19]It is a trespass offering; he has certainly trespassed against the LORD."

[1]And the LORD spoke to Moses, saying: [2]"If a person sins and commits a trespass against the LORD by lying to his neighbor about what was delivered to him for safekeeping, or about a pledge, or about a robbery, or if he has extorted from his neighbor, [3]or if he has found what was

lost and lies concerning it, and swears falsely—in any one of these things that a man may do in which he sins: [4]then it shall be, because he has sinned and is guilty, that he shall restore what he has stolen, or the thing which he has extorted, or what was delivered to him for safekeeping, or the lost thing which he found, [5]or all that about which he has sworn falsely. He shall restore its full value, add one-fifth more to it, *and* give it to whomever it belongs, on the day of his trespass offering. [6]And he shall bring his trespass offering to the LORD, a ram without blemish from the flock, with your valuation, as a trespass offering, to the priest. [7]So the priest shall make atonement for him before the LORD, and he shall be forgiven for any one of these things that he may have done in which he trespasses."

THE LAW OF THE BURNT OFFERING

[8]Then the LORD spoke to Moses, saying, [9]"Command Aaron and his sons, saying, 'This *is* the law of the burnt offering: The burnt offering *shall be* on the hearth upon the altar all night until morning, and the fire of the altar shall be kept burning on it. [10]And the priest shall put on his linen garment, and his linen trousers he shall put on his body, and take up the ashes of the burnt offering which the fire has consumed on the altar, and he shall put them beside the altar. [11]Then he shall take off his garments, put on other garments, and carry the ashes outside the camp to a clean place. [12]And the fire on the altar shall be kept burning on it; it shall not be put out. And the priest shall burn wood on it every morning, and lay the burnt offering in order on it; and he shall burn on it the fat of the peace offerings. [13]A fire shall always be burning on the altar; it shall never go out.

THE LAW OF THE GRAIN OFFERING

[14]'This *is* the law of the grain offering: The sons of Aaron shall offer it on the altar before the LORD. [15]He shall take from it his handful of the fine flour of the grain offering, with its oil, and all the frankincense which *is* on the grain offering, and shall burn *it* on the altar *for* a sweet aroma, as a memorial to the LORD. [16]And the remainder of it Aaron and his sons shall eat; with unleavened bread it shall be eaten in a holy place; in the court of the tabernacle of meeting they shall eat it. [17]It shall not be baked with leaven. I have given it *as* their portion of My offerings made by fire; it *is* most holy, like the sin offering and the trespass offering. [18]All

the males among the children of Aaron may eat it. *It shall be* a statute forever in your generations concerning the offerings made by fire to the LORD. Everyone who touches them must be holy.' "[a]

[19]And the LORD spoke to Moses, saying, [20]"This *is* the offering of Aaron and his sons, which they shall offer to the LORD, *beginning* on the day when he is anointed: one-tenth of an ephah of fine flour as a daily grain offering, half of it in the morning and half of it at night. [21]It shall be made in a pan with oil. *When it is* mixed, you shall bring it in. The baked pieces of the grain offering you shall offer *for* a sweet aroma to the LORD. [22]The priest from among his sons, who is anointed in his place, shall offer it. *It is* a statute forever to the LORD. It shall be wholly burned. [23]For every grain offering for the priest shall be wholly burned. It shall not be eaten."

THE LAW OF THE SIN OFFERING

[24]Also the LORD spoke to Moses, saying, [25]"Speak to Aaron and to his sons, saying, 'This *is* the law of the sin offering: In the place where the burnt offering is killed, the sin offering shall be killed before the LORD. It *is* most holy. [26]The priest who offers it for sin shall eat it. In a holy place it shall be eaten, in the court of the tabernacle of meeting. [27]Everyone who touches its flesh must be holy.[a] And when its blood is sprinkled on any garment, you shall wash that on which it was sprinkled, in a holy place. [28]But the earthen vessel in which it is boiled shall be broken. And if it is boiled in a bronze pot, it shall be both scoured and rinsed in water. [29]All the males among the priests may eat it. It *is*

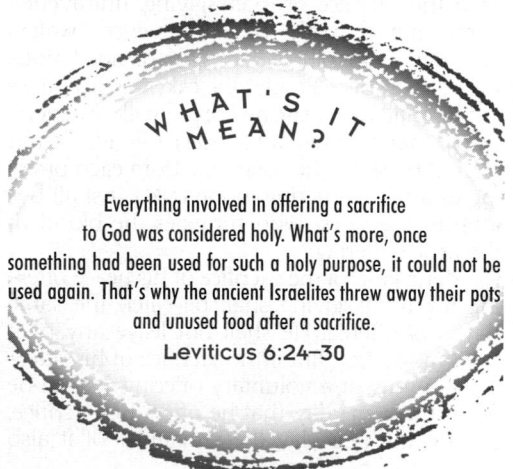

WHAT'S IT MEAN?

Everything involved in offering a sacrifice to God was considered holy. What's more, once something had been used for such a holy purpose, it could not be used again. That's why the ancient Israelites threw away their pots and unused food after a sacrifice.

Leviticus 6:24–30

6:18 [a]Compare Numbers 4:15 and Haggai 2:11–13   **6:27** [a]Compare Numbers 4:15 and Haggai 2:11–13 most holy. [30]But no sin offering from which *any* of the blood is brought into the tabernacle of meeting, to make atonement in the holy *place*,[a] shall be eaten. It shall be burned in the fire.

THE LAW OF THE TRESPASS OFFERING

[1]Likewise this *is* the law of the trespass offering (it *is* most holy): [2]In the place where they kill the burnt offering they shall kill the trespass offering. And its blood he shall sprinkle all around on the altar. [3]And he shall offer from it all its fat. The fat tail and the fat that covers the entrails, [4]the two kidneys and the fat that *is* on them by the flanks, and the fatty lobe *attached* to the liver above the kidneys, he shall remove; [5]and the priest shall burn them on the altar *as* an offering made by fire to the LORD. It *is* a trespass offering. [6]Every male among the priests may eat it. It shall be eaten in a holy place. It *is* most holy. [7]The trespass offering *is* like the sin offering; *there is* one law for them both: the priest who makes atonement with it shall have *it.* [8]And the priest who offers anyone's burnt offering, that priest shall have for himself the skin of the burnt offering which he has offered. [9]Also every grain offering that is baked in the oven and all that is prepared in the covered pan, or in a pan, shall be the priest's who offers it. [10]Every grain offering, *whether* mixed with oil or dry, shall belong to all the sons of Aaron, to one *as much* as the other.

THE LAW OF PEACE OFFERINGS

[11]This *is* the law of the sacrifice of peace offerings which he shall offer to the LORD: [12]If he offers it for a thanksgiving, then he shall offer, with the sacrifice of thanksgiving, unleavened cakes mixed with oil, unleavened wafers anointed with oil, or cakes of blended flour mixed with oil. [13]Besides the cakes, *as* his offering he shall offer leavened bread with the sacrifice of thanksgiving of his peace offering. [14]And from it he shall offer one cake from each offering *as* a heave offering to the LORD. It shall belong to the priest who sprinkles the blood of the peace offering.

[15]The flesh of the sacrifice of his peace offering for thanksgiving shall be eaten the same day it is offered. He shall not leave any of it until morning. [16]But if the sacrifice of his offering *is* a vow or a voluntary offering, it shall be eaten the same day that he offers his sacrifice; but on the next day the remainder of it also

WHAT'S IT MEAN?

The bread with leavening to lighten the batter was a change of pace for the Israelites. Most of the time they were instructed to make bread without leavening because that was the kind of bread served at the first Passover meal. Continuing to eat bread without leavening reminded them of how God had rescued and protected them.

Leviticus 7:13, 14

may be eaten; [17]the remainder of the flesh of the sacrifice on the third day must be burned with fire. [18]And if *any* of the flesh of the sacrifice of his peace offering is eaten at all on the third day, it shall not be accepted, nor shall it be imputed to him; it shall be an abomination *to* him who offers it, and the person who eats of it shall bear guilt.

[19]The flesh that touches any unclean thing shall not be eaten. It shall be burned with fire. And as for the *clean* flesh, all who are clean may eat of it. [20]But the person who eats the flesh of the sacrifice of the peace offering that *belongs* to the LORD, while he is unclean, that person shall be cut off from his people. [21]Moreover the person who touches any unclean thing, *such as* human uncleanness, *an* unclean animal, or any abominable unclean thing,[a] and who eats the flesh of the sacrifice of the peace offering that *belongs* to the LORD, that person shall be cut off from his people.' "

FAT AND BLOOD MAY NOT BE EATEN

[22]And the LORD spoke to Moses, saying, [23]"Speak to the children of Israel, saying: 'You shall not eat any fat, of ox or sheep or goat. [24]And the fat of an animal that dies *naturally*, and the fat of what is torn by wild beasts, may be used in any other way; but you shall by no means eat it. [25]For whoever eats the fat of the animal of which men offer an offering made by fire to the LORD, the person who eats *it* shall be cut off from his people. [26]Moreover you shall not eat any blood in any of your dwellings, *whether* of bird or beast. [27]Whoever eats

---

6:30 [a]The Most Holy Place when capitalized   **7:21** [a]Following Masoretic Text, Septuagint, and Vulgate; Samaritan Pentateuch, Syriac, and Targum read *swarming thing* (compare 5:2).

any blood, that person shall be cut off from his people.' "

THE PORTION OF AARON AND HIS SONS

²⁸Then the LORD spoke to Moses, saying, ²⁹"Speak to the children of Israel, saying: 'He who offers the sacrifice of his peace offering to the LORD shall bring his offering to the LORD from the sacrifice of his peace offering. ³⁰His own hands shall bring the offerings made by fire to the LORD. The fat with the breast he shall bring, that the breast may be waved *as* a wave offering before the LORD. ³¹And the priest shall burn the fat on the altar, but the breast shall be Aaron's and his sons'. ³²Also the right thigh you shall give to the priest *as* a heave offering from the sacrifices of your peace offerings. ³³He among the sons of Aaron, who offers the blood of the peace offering and the fat, shall have the right thigh for *his* part. ³⁴For the breast of the wave offering and the thigh of the heave offering I have taken from the children of Israel, from the sacrifices of their peace offerings, and I have given them to Aaron the priest and to his sons from the children of Israel by a statute forever.' "

³⁵This *is* the consecrated portion for Aaron and his sons, from the offerings made by fire to the LORD, on the day when *Moses* presented them to minister to the LORD as priests. ³⁶The LORD commanded this to be given to them by the children of Israel, on the day that He anointed them, *by* a statute forever throughout their generations.

³⁷This *is* the law of the burnt offering, the grain offering, the sin offering, the trespass offering, the consecrations, and the sacrifice of the peace offering, ³⁸which the LORD commanded Moses on Mount Sinai, on the day when He commanded the children of Israel to offer their offerings to the LORD in the Wilderness of Sinai.

AARON AND HIS SONS CONSECRATED

¹And the LORD spoke to Moses, saying: ²"Take Aaron and his sons with him, and the garments, the anointing oil, a bull as the sin offering, two rams, and a basket of unleavened bread; ³and gather all the congregation together at the door of the tabernacle of meeting."

⁴So Moses did as the LORD commanded him. And the congregation was gathered together at the door of the tabernacle of meeting. ⁵And Moses said to the congregation, "This *is* what the LORD commanded to be done."

⁶Then Moses brought Aaron and his sons and washed them with water. ⁷And he put the tunic on him, girded him with the sash, clothed him with the robe, and put the ephod on him; and he girded him with the intricately woven band of the ephod, and with it tied *the ephod* on him. ⁸Then he put the breastplate on him, and he put the Urim and the Thummim^a in the breastplate. ⁹And he put the turban on his head. Also on the turban, on its front, he put the golden plate, the holy crown, as the LORD had commanded Moses.

WHAT'S IT MEAN?

The priest's elaborate outfit symbolized his role as a go-between for the Israelites and God. Each piece of clothing represented the beauty and magnificence of God.
Leviticus 8:6–9

¹⁰Also Moses took the anointing oil, and anointed the tabernacle and all that *was* in it, and consecrated them. ¹¹He sprinkled some of it on the altar seven times, anointed the altar and all its utensils, and the laver and its base, to consecrate them. ¹²And he poured some of the anointing oil on Aaron's head and anointed him, to consecrate him.

¹³Then Moses brought Aaron's sons and put tunics on them, girded them with sashes, and put hats on them, as the LORD had commanded Moses.

¹⁴And he brought the bull for the sin offering. Then Aaron and his sons laid their hands on the head of the bull for the sin offering, ¹⁵and Moses killed *it*. Then he took the blood, and put *some* on the horns of the altar all around with his finger, and purified the altar. And he poured the blood at the base of the altar, and consecrated it, to make atonement for it. ¹⁶Then he took all the fat that *was* on the entrails, the fatty lobe *attached to* the liver, and the two kidneys with their fat, and Moses burned *them* on the altar. ¹⁷But the bull, its hide, its flesh, and its offal, he burned with fire outside the camp, as the LORD had commanded Moses.

¹⁸Then he brought the ram as the burnt offering. And Aaron and his sons laid their hands

8:8 ^aLiterally *the Lights and the Perfections* (compare Exodus 28:30) on the head of the ram, ¹⁹and Moses killed *it.* Then he sprinkled the blood all around on the altar. ²⁰And he cut the ram into pieces; and Moses burned the head, the pieces, and the fat. ²¹Then he washed the entrails and the legs in water. And Moses burned the whole ram on the altar. It *was* a burnt sacrifice for a sweet aroma, an offering made by fire to the LORD, as the LORD had commanded Moses.

²²And he brought the second ram, the ram of consecration. Then Aaron and his sons laid their hands on the head of the ram, ²³and Moses killed *it.* Also he took *some* of its blood and put it on the tip of Aaron's right ear, on the thumb of his right hand, and on the big toe of his right foot. ²⁴Then he brought Aaron's sons. And Moses put *some* of the blood on the tips of their right ears, on the thumbs of their right hands, and on the big toes of their right feet. And Moses sprinkled the blood all around on the altar. ²⁵Then he took the fat and the fat tail, all the fat that *was* on the entrails, the fatty lobe *attached to* the liver, the two kidneys and their fat, and the right thigh; ²⁶and from the basket of unleavened bread that was before the LORD he took one unleavened cake, a cake of bread *anointed with* oil, and one wafer, and put *them* on the fat and on the right thigh; ²⁷and he put all *these* in Aaron's hands and in his sons' hands, and waved them *as* a wave offering before the LORD. ²⁸Then Moses took them from their hands and burned *them* on the altar, on the burnt offering. They *were* consecration offerings for a sweet aroma. That *was* an offering made by fire to the LORD. ²⁹And Moses took the breast and waved it *as* a wave offering before the LORD. It was Moses' part of the ram of consecration, as the LORD had commanded Moses.

³⁰Then Moses took some of the anointing oil and some of the blood which *was* on the altar, and sprinkled *it* on Aaron, on his garments, on his sons, and on the garments of his sons with him; and he consecrated Aaron, his garments, his sons, and the garments of his sons with him.

³¹And Moses said to Aaron and his sons, "Boil the flesh *at* the door of the tabernacle of meeting, and eat it there with the bread that *is* in the basket of consecration offerings, as I commanded, saying, 'Aaron and his sons shall eat it.' ³²What remains of the flesh and of the bread you shall burn with fire. ³³And you shall not go outside the door of the tabernacle of meeting *for* seven days, until the days of your consecration are ended. For seven days he shall consecrate you. ³⁴As he has done this day, *so* the LORD has commanded to do, to make atonement for you. ³⁵Therefore you shall stay *at* the door of the tabernacle of meeting day and night for seven days, and keep the charge of the LORD, so that you may not die; for so I have been commanded." ³⁶So Aaron and his sons did all the things that the LORD had commanded by the hand of Moses.

THE PRIESTLY MINISTRY BEGINS

¹It came to pass on the eighth day that Moses called Aaron and his sons and the elders of Israel. ²And he said to Aaron, "Take for yourself a young bull as a sin offering and a ram as a burnt offering, without blemish, and offer *them* before the LORD. ³And to the children of Israel you shall speak, saying, 'Take a kid of the goats as a sin offering, and a calf and a lamb, *both* of the first year, without blemish, as a burnt offering, ⁴also a bull and a ram as peace offerings, to sacrifice before the LORD, and a grain offering mixed with oil; for today the LORD will appear to you.' "

⁵So they brought what Moses commanded before the tabernacle of meeting. And all the congregation drew near and stood before the LORD. ⁶Then Moses said, "This *is* the thing which the LORD commanded you to do, and the glory of the LORD will appear to you." ⁷And Moses said to Aaron, "Go to the altar, offer your sin offering and your burnt offering, and make atonement for yourself and for the people. Offer the offering of the people, and make atonement for them, as the LORD commanded."

⁸Aaron therefore went to the altar and killed the calf of the sin offering, which *was* for himself. ⁹Then the sons of Aaron brought the blood to him. And he dipped his finger in the blood, put *it* on the horns of the altar, and poured the blood at the base of the altar. ¹⁰But the fat, the kidneys, and the fatty lobe from the liver of the sin offering he burned on the altar, as the LORD had commanded Moses. ¹¹The flesh and the hide he burned with fire outside the camp.

¹²And he killed the burnt offering; and Aaron's sons presented to him the blood, which he sprinkled all around on the altar.

> "It was a burnt sacrifice for a sweet aroma, an offering made by fire to the LORD, as the LORD had commanded Moses."
> (Leviticus 8:21b)

[13]Then they presented the burnt offering to him, with its pieces and head, and he burned *them* on the altar. [14]And he washed the entrails and the legs, and burned *them* with the burnt offering on the altar.

[15]Then he brought the people's offering, and took the goat, which *was* the sin offering for the people, and killed it and offered it for sin, like the first one. [16]And he brought the burnt offering and offered it according to the prescribed manner. [17]Then he brought the grain offering, took a handful of it, and burned *it* on the altar, besides the burnt sacrifice of the morning.

[18]He also killed the bull and the ram *as* sacrifices of peace offerings, which *were* for the people. And Aaron's sons presented to him the blood, which he sprinkled all around on the altar, [19]and the fat from the bull and the ram—the fatty tail, what covers *the entrails* and the kidneys, and the fatty lobe *attached to* the liver; [20]and they put the fat on the breasts. Then he burned the fat on the altar; [21]but the breasts and the right thigh Aaron waved *as* a wave offering before the LORD, as Moses had commanded.

[22]Then Aaron lifted his hand toward the people, blessed them, and came down from offering the sin offering, the burnt offering, and peace offerings. [23]And Moses and Aaron went into the tabernacle of meeting, and came out and blessed the people. Then the glory of the LORD appeared to all the people, [24]and fire came out from before the LORD and consumed the burnt offering and the fat on the altar. When all the people saw *it*, they shouted and fell on their faces.

THE PROFANE FIRE OF NADAB AND ABIHU

[1]Then Nadab and Abihu, the sons of Aaron, each took his censer and put fire in it, put incense on it, and offered profane fire before the LORD, which He had not commanded them. [2]So fire went out from the LORD and devoured them, and they died before the LORD. [3]And Moses said to Aaron, "This is what the LORD spoke, saying:

'By those who come near Me
I must be regarded as holy;
And before all the people
I must be glorified.' "

So Aaron held his peace.

[4]Then Moses called Mishael and Elzaphan, the sons of Uzziel the uncle of Aaron, and said to them, "Come near, carry your brethren from before the sanctuary out of the camp." [5]So they went near and carried them by their tunics out of the camp, as Moses had said.

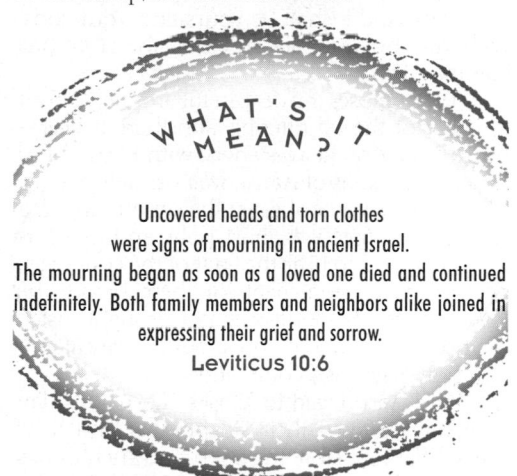

WHAT'S IT MEAN?

Uncovered heads and torn clothes
were signs of mourning in ancient Israel.
The mourning began as soon as a loved one died and continued indefinitely. Both family members and neighbors alike joined in expressing their grief and sorrow.
Leviticus 10:6

[6]And Moses said to Aaron, and to Eleazar and Ithamar, his sons, "Do not uncover your heads nor tear your clothes, lest you die, and wrath come upon all the people. But let your brethren, the whole house of Israel, bewail the burning which the LORD has kindled. [7]You shall not go out from the door of the tabernacle of meeting, lest you die, for the anointing oil of the LORD *is* upon you." And they did according to the word of Moses.

CONDUCT PRESCRIBED FOR PRIESTS

[8]Then the LORD spoke to Aaron, saying: [9]"Do not drink wine or intoxicating drink, you, nor your sons with you, when you go into the tabernacle of meeting, lest you die. *It shall be* a statute forever throughout your generations, [10]that you may distinguish between holy and unholy, and between unclean and clean, [11]and that you may teach the children of Israel all the statutes which the LORD has spoken to them by the hand of Moses."

[12]And Moses spoke to Aaron, and to Eleazar and Ithamar, his sons who were left: "Take the grain offering that remains of the offerings made by fire to the LORD, and eat it without leaven beside the altar; for it *is* most holy. [13]You shall eat it in a holy place, because it *is* your due and your sons' due, of the sacrifices made by fire to the LORD; for so I have been commanded. [14]The breast of the wave offering and the thigh of the heave offering you shall eat in a clean place, you, your sons, and your daughters with you; for *they are* your due and your sons' due, *which* are given from the sacrifices of peace offerings of the children of Israel. [15]The thigh of the heave offering and the breast of the wave

offering they shall bring with the offerings of fat made by fire, to offer *as* a wave offering before the LORD. And it shall be yours and your sons' with you, by a statute forever, as the LORD has commanded."

[16]Then Moses made careful inquiry about the goat of the sin offering, and there it was—burned up. And he was angry with Eleazar and Ithamar, the sons of Aaron *who were* left, saying, [17]"Why have you not eaten the sin offering in a holy place, since it *is* most holy, and *God* has given it to you to bear the guilt of the congregation, to make atonement for them before the LORD? [18]See! Its blood was not brought inside the holy *place;*[a] indeed you should have eaten it in a holy *place,* as I commanded."

[19]And Aaron said to Moses, "Look, this day they have offered their sin offering and their burnt offering before the LORD, and such things have befallen me! *If* I had eaten the sin offering today, would it have been accepted in the sight of the LORD?" [20]So when Moses heard *that,* he was content.

FOODS PERMITTED AND FORBIDDEN

[1]Now the LORD spoke to Moses and Aaron, saying to them, [2]"Speak to the children of Israel, saying, 'These *are* the animals which you may eat among all the animals that *are* on the earth: [3]Among the animals, whatever divides the hoof, having cloven hooves *and* chewing the cud—that you may eat. [4]Nevertheless these you shall not eat among those that chew the cud or those that have cloven hooves: the camel, because it chews the cud but does not have cloven hooves, is unclean to you; [5]the rock hyrax,

WHAT'S IT MEAN?

Rock hyraxes look a lot like guinea pigs. They do not chew cud like cows do, but their mouths are moving all the time, giving the impression that they're chewing cud. The rock hyraxes have a suctionlike grip that allows them to maneuver on rocks.

Leviticus 11:4–8

because it chews the cud but does not have cloven hooves, *is* unclean to you; [6]the hare, because it chews the cud but does not have cloven hooves, *is* unclean to you; [7]and the swine, though it divides the hoof, having cloven hooves, yet does not chew the cud, *is* unclean to you. [8]Their flesh you shall not eat, and their carcasses you shall not touch. They *are* unclean to you.

[9]These you may eat of all that *are* in the water: whatever in the water has fins and scales, whether in the seas or in the rivers—that you may eat. [10]But all in the seas or in the rivers that do not have fins and scales, all that move in the water or any living thing which *is* in the water, they *are* an abomination to you. [11]They shall be an abomination to you; you shall not eat their flesh, but you shall regard their carcasses as an abomination. [12]Whatever in the water does not have fins or scales—that *shall be* an abomination to you.

[13]And these you shall regard as an abomination among the birds; they shall not be eaten, they *are* an abomination: the eagle, the vulture, the buzzard, [14]the kite, and the falcon after its kind; [15]every raven after its kind, [16]the ostrich, the short-eared owl, the sea gull, and the hawk after its kind; [17]the little owl, the fisher owl, and the screech owl; [18]the white owl, the jackdaw, and the carrion vulture; [19]the stork, the heron after its kind, the hoopoe, and the bat.

[20]All flying insects that creep on *all* fours *shall be* an abomination to you. [21]Yet these you may eat of every flying insect that creeps on *all* fours: those which have jointed legs above their feet with which to leap on the earth. [22]These you may eat: the locust after its kind, the destroying locust after its kind, the cricket after its kind, and the grasshopper after its kind. [23]But all *other* flying insects which have four feet *shall be* an abomination to you.

UNCLEAN ANIMALS

[24]By these you shall become unclean; whoever touches the carcass of any of them shall be unclean until evening; [25]whoever carries part of the carcass of any of them shall wash his clothes and be unclean until evening: [26]The carcass of any animal which divides the foot, but is not cloven-hoofed or does not chew the cud, *is* unclean to you. Everyone who touches it shall be unclean. [27]And whatever goes on its paws, among all kinds of animals that go on *all* fours, those *are* unclean to you. Whoever touches any such carcass shall be unclean until evening.

10:18 [a]The Most Holy Place when capitalized

²⁸Whoever carries *any such* carcass shall wash his clothes and be unclean until evening. It *is* unclean to you.

²⁹These also *shall be* unclean to you among the creeping things that creep on the earth: the mole, the mouse, and the large lizard after its kind; ³⁰the gecko, the monitor lizard, the sand reptile, the sand lizard, and the chameleon. ³¹These *are* unclean to you among all that creep. Whoever touches them when they are dead shall be unclean until evening. ³²Anything on which *any* of them falls, when they are dead shall be unclean, whether *it is* any item of wood or clothing or skin or sack, whatever item *it is*, in which *any* work is done, it must be put in water. And it shall be unclean until evening; then it shall be clean. ³³Any earthen vessel into which *any* of them falls you shall break; and whatever *is* in it shall be unclean: ³⁴in such a vessel, any edible food upon which water falls becomes unclean, and any drink that may be drunk from it becomes unclean. ³⁵And everything on which *a part* of *any such* carcass falls shall be unclean; *whether it is* an oven or cooking stove, it shall be broken down; *for* they *are* unclean, and shall be

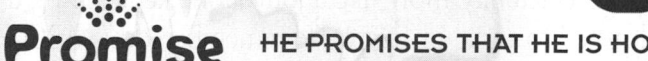

"I am the LORD your God. You shall therefore consecrate yourselves, and you shall be holy; for I am holy." (Leviticus 11:44)

unclean to you. ³⁶Nevertheless a spring or a cistern, *in which there is* plenty of water, shall be clean, but whatever touches any such carcass becomes unclean. ³⁷And if a part of *any such* carcass falls on any planting seed which is to be sown, it *remains* clean. ³⁸But if water is put on the seed, and if *a part of any such* carcass falls on it, it *becomes* unclean to you.

³⁹And if any animal which you may eat dies, he who touches its carcass shall be unclean until evening. ⁴⁰He who eats of its carcass shall wash his clothes and be unclean until evening. He also who carries its carcass shall wash his clothes and be unclean until evening.

⁴¹And every creeping thing that creeps on the earth *shall be* an abomination. It shall not be eaten. ⁴²Whatever crawls on its belly, whatever goes on *all* fours, or whatever has many feet among all creeping things that creep on the earth—these you shall not eat, for they *are* an abomination. ⁴³You shall not make yourselves abominable with any creeping thing that creeps; nor shall you make yourselves unclean with them, lest you be defiled by them. ⁴⁴For I *am* the LORD your God. You shall therefore

---

Promise HE PROMISES THAT HE IS HOLY.

I am the LORD your God. You shall therefore consecrate yourselves, and you shall be holy; for I am holy (Lev. 11:44).

It's the bottom of the ninth inning, bases loaded, and your team's down 4—1. The best hitter's at bat with two outs and two strikes. The pitch . . . grand slam! Your team wins 5—4. "HOLY COW!" screams the announcer. "Holy cow!"

Holiness is taken lightly by a lot of people—not just sports announcers. Let's find out what God says about being holy.

First, we must know that we serve a holy God. Psalm 111:9 says, "He has sent redemption to His people; He has commanded His covenant forever: Holy and awesome is His name." Psalm 99:5 tells us that the Lord is a God of holiness. Second, He wants us to strive to be holy as well, so we can be like Him (Eph. 5:1). Do you want to be like Jesus? Live like Him? Talk like Him? Act like Him? Think like Him? That's what being holy is: being devoted to God and obeying His Word.

As you spend time with God, He will make Himself known to you. There's nothing greater than spending time in the presence of Almighty God! Spend time today praising Him because He is the One who is holy (Ps. 71:22).

SEE FOR YOURSELF:
Lev. 20:7; 1 Pet. 1:15, 16

MOSES made a difference

Few doubt the amazing difference Moses made in his lifetime. Or in the millennia since. His is one of the few almost universally known names in history. But what about his youth? Were there signs of his later greatness in the events of his early years?

We don't know when Moses discovered his unique background, but perhaps his mother cared for him long enough to instill a strong sense of his heritage. Apparently his training in all the wisdom and knowledge of Egypt couldn't drive out of Moses his early education. He knew himself to be a Hebrew, and the Book of Hebrews describes Moses: "choosing rather to suffer affliction with the people of God than to enjoy the passing pleasures of sin" (Heb. 11:25).

Moses was loyal to his people. When faced with an Egyptian guard beating a Hebrew slave, Moses did not hesitate. He intervened, killing the guard. This led to his escape into the wilderness and the second long phase of training in his life. When he eventually led his people out of Egypt, he led them into a desert that had become his backyard in the previous forty years.

Cutting Edge

Two large lessons from Moses' youth lurk behind the events of his life: (1) His faith in God and (2) his ability to write. He did not record the first five books of the Bible in his youth. They were actually more like a journal he kept during the years of travel. But he learned to write in Egypt. He remembered his ABCs. His elementary school tutors taught him well. And Moses made a difference for the world with the way he used the tools of faith and knowledge he was given as a child.

YOU can, too!

Don't fall into the trap of thinking of your youthful years as marking time until you arrive at adulthood. Much of what you accomplish as an adult will be shaped by what you learn as a kid. You don't know what God will use from your past when you get older. Give Him lots to work with.

Make the most of your opportunities to know God better. Pay attention in church. Read your Bible on your own. Take your educational opportunities seriously, but enjoy learning. Let God make a difference in your life. He will take care of most of the rest.

Want to know more?
Read about Moses' life in
Exodus, Leviticus, Numbers, and Deuteronomy.

consecrate yourselves, and you shall be holy; for I *am* holy. Neither shall you defile yourselves with any creeping thing that creeps on the earth. ⁴⁵For I *am* the LORD who brings you up out of the land of Egypt, to be your God. You shall therefore be holy, for I *am* holy. ⁴⁶This *is* the law of the animals and the birds and every living creature that moves in the waters, and of every creature that creeps on the earth, ⁴⁷to distinguish between the unclean and the clean, and between the animal that may be eaten and the animal that may not be eaten.' "

THE RITUAL AFTER CHILDBIRTH

¹Then the LORD spoke to Moses, saying, ²"Speak to the children of Israel, saying: 'If a woman has conceived, and borne a male child, then she shall be unclean seven days; as in the days of her customary impurity she shall be unclean. ³And on the eighth day the flesh of his foreskin shall be circumcised. ⁴She shall then continue in the blood of *her* purification thirty-three days. She shall not touch any hallowed thing, nor come into the sanctuary until the days of her purification are fulfilled.

WHAT'S IT MEAN?

To be clean meant to be acceptable before God. It required more than just a bath. Although giving birth was a joyous event, according to God's law, it caused a woman's body to be unclean.

Leviticus 12:2–4

⁵'But if she bears a female child, then she shall be unclean two weeks, as in her customary impurity, and she shall continue in the blood of *her* purification sixty-six days. ⁶'When the days of her purification are fulfilled, whether for a son or a daughter, she shall bring to the priest a lamb of the first year as a burnt offering, and a young pigeon or a turtledove as a sin offering, to the door of the tabernacle of meeting. ⁷Then he shall offer it before the LORD, and make atonement for her. And she shall be clean from the flow of her blood. This *is* the law for her who has borne a male or a female.

⁸'And if she is not able to bring a lamb, then she may bring two turtledoves or two young pigeons—one as a burnt offering and the other as a sin offering. So the priest shall make atonement for her, and she will be clean.' "

THE LAW CONCERNING LEPROSY

¹And the LORD spoke to Moses and Aaron, saying: ²"When a man has on the skin of his body a swelling, a scab, or a bright spot, and it becomes on the skin of his body *like* a leprous*ᵃ* sore, then he shall be brought to Aaron the priest or to one of his sons the priests. ³The priest shall examine the sore on the skin of the body; and if the hair on the sore has turned white, and the sore appears *to be* deeper than the skin of his body, it *is* a leprous sore. Then the priest shall examine him, and pronounce him unclean. ⁴But if the bright spot *is* white on the skin of his body, and does not appear *to be* deeper than the skin, and its hair has not turned white, then the priest shall isolate *the one who has* the sore seven days. ⁵And the priest shall examine him on the seventh day; and indeed *if* the sore appears to be as it was, *and* the sore has not spread on the skin, then the priest shall isolate him another seven days. ⁶Then the priest shall examine him again on the seventh day; and indeed *if* the sore has faded, *and* the sore has not spread on the skin, then the priest shall pronounce him clean; it *is only* a scab, and he shall wash his clothes and be clean. ⁷But if the scab should at all spread over the skin, after he has been seen by the priest for his cleansing, he shall be seen by the priest again. ⁸And *if* the priest sees that the scab has indeed spread on the skin, then the priest shall pronounce him unclean. It *is* leprosy.

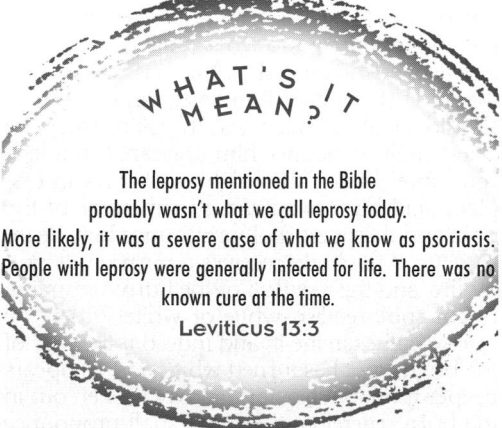

WHAT'S IT MEAN?

The leprosy mentioned in the Bible probably wasn't what we call leprosy today. More likely, it was a severe case of what we know as psoriasis. People with leprosy were generally infected for life. There was no known cure at the time.

Leviticus 13:3

13:2 *ᵃ*Hebrew *saraath*, disfiguring skin diseases, including leprosy, and so in verses 2–46 and 14:1–32

⁹"When the leprous sore is on a person, then he shall be brought to the priest. ¹⁰And the priest shall examine *him;* and indeed *if* the swelling on the skin *is* white, and it has turned the hair white, and *there is* a spot of raw flesh in the swelling, ¹¹it *is* an old leprosy on the skin of his body. The priest shall pronounce him unclean, and shall not isolate him, for he *is* unclean.

¹²"And if leprosy breaks out all over the skin, and the leprosy covers all the skin of *the one who has* the sore, from his head to his foot, wherever the priest looks, ¹³then the priest shall consider; and indeed *if* the leprosy has covered all his body, he shall pronounce *him* clean *who has* the sore. It has all turned white. He *is* clean. ¹⁴But when raw flesh appears on him, he shall be unclean. ¹⁵And the priest shall examine the raw flesh and pronounce him to be unclean; *for the* raw flesh *is* unclean. It *is* leprosy. ¹⁶Or if the raw flesh changes and turns white again, he shall come to the priest. ¹⁷And the priest shall examine him; and indeed *if* the sore has turned white, then the priest shall pronounce *him* clean *who has* the sore. He *is* clean.

¹⁸"If the body develops a boil in the skin, and it is healed, ¹⁹and in the place of the boil there comes a white swelling or a bright spot, reddish-white, then it shall be shown to the priest; ²⁰and *if,* when the priest sees it, it indeed *appears* deeper than the skin, and its hair has turned white, the priest shall pronounce him unclean. It *is* a leprous sore which has broken out of the boil. ²¹But if the priest examines it, and indeed *there are* no white hairs in it, and it *is* not deeper than the skin, but has faded, then the priest shall isolate him seven days; ²²and if it should at all spread over the skin, then the priest shall pronounce him unclean. It *is* a leprous sore. ²³But if the bright spot stays in one place, *and* has not spread, it *is* the scar of the boil; and the priest shall pronounce him clean.

²⁴"Or if the body receives a burn on its skin by fire, and the raw *flesh* of the burn becomes a bright spot, reddish-white or white, ²⁵then the priest shall examine it; and indeed *if* the hair of the bright spot has turned white, and it appears deeper than the skin, it *is* leprosy broken out in the burn. Therefore the priest shall pronounce him unclean. It *is* a leprous sore. ²⁶But if the priest examines it, and indeed *there are* no white hairs in the bright spot, and it *is* not deeper than the skin, but has faded, then the priest shall isolate him seven days. ²⁷And the priest shall examine him on the seventh day. If it has at all spread over the skin, then the priest shall pronounce him unclean. It *is* a leprous sore. ²⁸But if the bright spot stays in one place, *and* has not spread on the skin, but has faded, it *is* a swelling from the burn. The priest shall pronounce him clean, for it *is* the scar from the burn.

²⁹"If a man or woman has a sore on the head or the beard, ³⁰then the priest shall examine the sore; and indeed if it appears deeper than the skin, *and there is* in it thin yellow hair, then the priest shall pronounce him unclean. It *is* a scaly leprosy of the head or beard. ³¹But if the priest examines the scaly sore, and indeed it does not appear deeper than the skin, and *there is* no black hair in it, then the priest shall isolate *the one who has* the scale seven days. ³²And on the seventh day the priest shall examine the sore; and indeed *if* the scale has not spread, and there is no yellow hair in it, and the scale does not appear deeper than the skin, ³³he shall shave himself, but the scale he shall not shave. And the priest shall isolate *the one who has* the scale another seven days. ³⁴On the seventh day the priest shall examine the scale; and indeed *if* the scale has not spread over the skin, and does not appear deeper than the skin, then the priest shall pronounce him clean. He shall wash his clothes and be clean. ³⁵But if the scale should at all spread over the skin after his cleansing, ³⁶then the priest shall examine him; and indeed *if* the scale has spread over the skin, the priest need not seek for yellow hair. He *is* unclean. ³⁷But if the scale appears to be at a standstill, and there is black hair grown up in it, the scale has healed. He *is* clean, and the priest shall pronounce him clean.

³⁸"If a man or a woman has bright spots on the skin of the body, *specifically* white bright spots, ³⁹then the priest shall look; and indeed *if* the bright spots on the skin of the body *are* dull white, it *is* a white spot *that* grows on the skin. He *is* clean.

⁴⁰"As for the man whose hair has fallen from his head, he *is* bald, *but* he *is* clean. ⁴¹He whose hair has fallen from his forehead, he *is* bald on the forehead, *but* he *is* clean. ⁴²And if there is on

> "Thus you shall separate the children of Israel from their uncleanness, lest they die in their uncleanness when they defile My tabernacle that is among them."
> (Leviticus 15:31)

the bald head or bald forehead a reddish-white sore, it *is* leprosy breaking out on his bald head or his bald forehead. ⁴³Then the priest shall examine it; and indeed *if* the swelling of the sore *is* reddish-white on his bald head or on his bald forehead, as the appearance of leprosy on the skin of the body, ⁴⁴he is a leprous man. He *is* unclean. The priest shall surely pronounce him unclean; his sore *is* on his head.

⁴⁵"Now the leper on whom the sore *is*, his clothes shall be torn and his head bare; and he shall cover his mustache, and cry, 'Unclean! Unclean!' ⁴⁶He shall be unclean. All the days he has the sore he shall be unclean. He *is* unclean, and he shall dwell alone; his dwelling *shall be* outside the camp.

THE LAW CONCERNING LEPROUS GARMENTS

⁴⁷"Also, if a garment has a leprous plague*ᵃ* in it, *whether it is* a woolen garment or a linen garment, ⁴⁸whether *it is* in the warp or woof of linen or wool, whether in leather or in anything made of leather, ⁴⁹and if the plague is greenish or reddish in the garment or in the leather, whether in the warp or in the woof, or in anything made of leather, it *is* a leprous plague and shall be shown to the priest. ⁵⁰The priest shall examine the plague and isolate *that which has* the plague seven days. ⁵¹And he shall examine the plague on the seventh day. If the plague has spread in the garment, either in the warp or in the woof, in the leather *or* in anything made of leather, the plague *is* an active leprosy. It *is* unclean. ⁵²He shall therefore burn that garment in which is the plague, whether warp or woof, in wool or in linen, or anything of leather, for it *is* an active leprosy; *the garment* shall be burned in the fire.

⁵³"But if the priest examines *it*, and indeed the plague has not spread in the garment, either in the warp or in the woof, or in anything made of leather, ⁵⁴then the priest shall command that they wash *the thing* in which *is* the plague; and he shall isolate it another seven days. ⁵⁵Then the priest shall examine the plague after it has been washed; and indeed *if* the plague has not changed its color, though the plague has not spread, it *is* unclean, and you shall burn it in the fire; it continues eating away, *whether* the damage *is* outside or inside. ⁵⁶If the priest examines *it*, and indeed the plague has faded after washing it, then he shall tear it out of the garment, whether out of the warp or out of the woof, or out of the leather. ⁵⁷But if it appears again in the garment, either in the warp or in the woof, or in anything made of leather, it *is* a spreading *plague;* you shall burn with fire that in which is the plague. ⁵⁸And if you wash the garment, either warp or woof, or whatever is made of leather, if the plague has disappeared from it, then it shall be washed a second time, and shall be clean.

⁵⁹"This *is* the law of the leprous plague in a garment of wool or linen, either in the warp or woof, or in anything made of leather, to pronounce it clean or to pronounce it unclean."

THE RITUAL FOR CLEANSING HEALED LEPERS

¹Then the LORD spoke to Moses, saying, ²"This shall be the law of the leper for the day of his cleansing: He shall be brought to the priest. ³And the priest shall go out of the camp, and the priest shall examine *him;* and indeed, *if* the leprosy is healed in the leper, ⁴then the priest shall command to take for him who is to be cleansed two living *and* clean birds, cedar wood, scarlet, and hyssop. ⁵And the priest shall command that one of the birds be killed in an earthen vessel over running water. ⁶As for the living bird, he shall take it, the cedar wood and the scarlet and the hyssop, and dip them and the living bird in the blood of the bird *that was* killed over the running water. ⁷And he shall sprinkle it seven times on him who is to be cleansed from the leprosy, and shall pronounce him clean, and shall let the living bird loose in the open field. ⁸He who is to be cleansed shall wash his clothes, shave off all his hair, and wash himself in water, that he may be clean. After that he shall come into the camp, and shall stay outside his tent seven days. ⁹But on the seventh day he shall shave all the hair off his head and his beard and his eyebrows—all his hair he shall shave off. He shall wash his clothes and wash his body in water, and he shall be clean.

¹⁰"And on the eighth day he shall take two male lambs without blemish, one ewe lamb of the first year without blemish, three-tenths *of an ephah* of fine flour mixed with oil as a grain offering, and one log of oil. ¹¹Then the priest who makes *him* clean shall present the man who is to be made clean, and those things, before the LORD, *at* the door of the tabernacle of meeting. ¹²And the priest shall take one male lamb and offer it as a trespass offering, and the log of oil, and wave them *as* a wave offering before the LORD. ¹³Then he shall kill the lamb in the place where he kills the sin offering and the burnt offering, in a holy place; for as the sin offering *is*

WHAT'S IT MEAN?

After making his sacrifice, the unclean person received a dab of blood on his ear, his thumb, and his toe. These three places symbolized the three main activities of life: thinking, working, and walking.

Leviticus 14:14

the priest's, so *is* the trespass offering. It *is* most holy. [14]The priest shall take *some* of the blood of the trespass offering, and the priest shall put *it* on the tip of the right ear of him who is to be cleansed, on the thumb of his right hand, and on the big toe of his right foot. [15]And the priest shall take *some* of the log of oil, and pour *it* into the palm of his own left hand. [16]Then the priest shall dip his right finger in the oil that *is* in his left hand, and shall sprinkle some of the oil with his finger seven times before the LORD. [17]And of the rest of the oil in his hand, the priest shall put *some* on the tip of the right ear of him who is to be cleansed, on the thumb of his right hand, and on the big toe of his right foot, on the blood of the trespass offering. [18]The rest of the oil that *is* in the priest's hand he shall put on the head of him who is to be cleansed. So the priest shall make atonement for him before the LORD.

[19]"Then the priest shall offer the sin offering, and make atonement for him who is to be cleansed from his uncleanness. Afterward he shall kill the burnt offering. [20]And the priest shall offer the burnt offering and the grain offering on the altar. So the priest shall make atonement for him, and he shall be clean.

[21]"But if he *is* poor and cannot afford it, then he shall take one male lamb *as* a trespass offering to be waved, to make atonement for him, one-tenth *of an ephah* of fine flour mixed with oil as a grain offering, a log of oil, [22]and two turtledoves or two young pigeons, such as he is able to afford: one shall be a sin offering and the other a burnt offering. [23]He shall bring them to the priest on the eighth day for his cleansing, to the door of the tabernacle of meeting, before the LORD. [24]And the priest shall take the lamb of the trespass offering and the log of oil, and the

priest shall wave them *as* a wave offering before the LORD. [25]Then he shall kill the lamb of the trespass offering, and the priest shall take *some* of the blood of the trespass offering and put *it* on the tip of the right ear of him who is to be cleansed, on the thumb of his right hand, and on the big toe of his right foot. [26]And the priest shall pour some of the oil into the palm of his own left hand. [27]Then the priest shall sprinkle with his right finger *some* of the oil that *is* in his left hand seven times before the LORD. [28]And the priest shall put *some* of the oil that *is* in his hand on the tip of the right ear of him who is to be cleansed, on the thumb of the right hand, and on the big toe of his right foot, on the place of the blood of the trespass offering. [29]The rest of the oil that *is* in the priest's hand he shall put on the head of him who is to be cleansed, to make atonement for him before the LORD. [30]And he shall offer one of the turtledoves or young pigeons, such as he can afford— [31]such as he is able to afford, the one *as* a sin offering and the other *as* a burnt offering, with the grain offering. So the priest shall make atonement for him who is to be cleansed before the LORD. [32]This *is* the law *for one* who had a leprous sore, who cannot afford the usual cleansing."

THE LAW CONCERNING LEPROUS HOUSES

[33]And the LORD spoke to Moses and Aaron, saying: [34]"When you have come into the land of Canaan, which I give you as a possession, and I put the leprous plague[a] in a house in the land of your possession, [35]and he who owns the house comes and tells the priest, saying, 'It seems to me that *there is* some plague in the house', [36]then the priest shall command that they empty the house, before the priest goes *into it* to examine the plague, that all that *is* in the house may not be made unclean; and afterward the priest shall go in to examine the house. [37]And he shall examine the plague; and indeed *if* the plague *is* on the walls of the house with ingrained streaks, greenish or reddish, which appear to be deep in the wall, [38]then the priest shall go out of the house, to the door of the house, and shut up the house seven days. [39]And the priest shall come again on the seventh day and look; and indeed *if* the plague has spread on the walls of the house, [40]then the priest shall command that they take away the stones in which *is* the plague, and they shall cast them into an unclean place outside the city. [41]And he shall cause the house to be scraped inside, all around, and the dust that they scrape

14:34 [a]Decomposition by mildew, mold, dry rot, etc., and so in verses 34–53

off they shall pour out in an unclean place outside the city. ⁴²Then they shall take other stones and put *them* in the place of *those* stones, and he shall take other mortar and plaster the house.

⁴³"Now if the plague comes back and breaks out in the house, after he has taken away the stones, after he has scraped the house, and after it is plastered, ⁴⁴then the priest shall come and look; and indeed *if* the plague has spread in the house, it *is* an active leprosy in the house. It *is* unclean. ⁴⁵And he shall break down the house, its stones, its timber, and all the plaster of the house, and he shall carry *them* outside the city to an unclean place. ⁴⁶Moreover he who goes into the house at all while it is shut up shall be unclean until evening. ⁴⁷And he who lies down in the house shall wash his clothes, and he who eats in the house shall wash his clothes.

⁴⁸"But if the priest comes in and examines *it,* and indeed the plague has not spread in the house after the house was plastered, then the priest shall pronounce the house clean, because the plague is healed. ⁴⁹And he shall take, to cleanse the house, two birds, cedar wood, scarlet, and hyssop. ⁵⁰Then he shall kill one of the birds in an earthen vessel over running water; ⁵¹and he shall take the cedar wood, the hyssop, the scarlet, and the living bird, and dip them in the blood of the slain bird and in the running water, and sprinkle the house seven times. ⁵²And he shall cleanse the house with the blood of the bird and the running water and the living bird, with the cedar wood, the hyssop, and the scarlet. ⁵³Then he shall let the living bird loose outside the city in the open field, and make atonement for the house, and it shall be clean.

⁵⁴"This *is* the law for any leprous sore and scale, ⁵⁵for the leprosy of a garment and of a house, ⁵⁶for a swelling and a scab and a bright spot, ⁵⁷to teach when *it is* unclean and when *it is* clean. This *is* the law of leprosy."

THE LAW CONCERNING BODILY DISCHARGES

¹And the LORD spoke to Moses and Aaron, saying, ²"Speak to the children of Israel, and say to them: 'When any man has a discharge from his body, his discharge *is* unclean. ³And this shall be his uncleanness in regard to his discharge—whether his body runs with his discharge, or his body is stopped up by his discharge, it *is* his uncleanness. ⁴Every bed is unclean on which he who has the discharge lies, and everything on which he sits shall be unclean. ⁵And whoever touches his bed shall wash his clothes and bathe in water, and be unclean until evening. ⁶He who sits on any-

thing on which he who has the discharge sat shall wash his clothes and bathe in water, and be unclean until evening. ⁷And he who touches the body of him who has the discharge shall wash his clothes and bathe in water, and be unclean until evening. ⁸If he who has the discharge spits on him who is clean, then he shall wash his clothes and bathe in water, and be unclean until evening. ⁹Any saddle on which he who has the discharge rides shall be unclean. ¹⁰Whoever touches anything that was under him shall be unclean until evening. He who carries *any of* those things shall wash his clothes and bathe in water, and be unclean until evening. ¹¹And whomever the one who has the discharge touches, and has not rinsed his hands in water, he shall wash his clothes and bathe in water, and be unclean until evening. ¹²The vessel of earth that he who has the discharge touches shall be broken, and every vessel of wood shall be rinsed in water.

¹³'And when he who has a discharge is cleansed of his discharge, then he shall count for himself seven days for his cleansing, wash his clothes, and bathe his body in running water; then he shall be clean. ¹⁴On the eighth day he shall take for himself two turtledoves or two young pigeons, and come before the LORD, to the door of the tabernacle of meeting, and give them to the priest. ¹⁵Then the priest shall offer them, the one *as* a sin offering and the other *as* a burnt offering. So the priest shall make atonement for him before the LORD because of his discharge.

¹⁶'If any man has an emission of semen, then he shall wash all his body in water, and be unclean until evening. ¹⁷And any garment and any leather on which there is semen, it shall be washed with water, and be unclean until evening. ¹⁸Also, when a woman lies with a man, and *there is* an emission of semen, they shall bathe in water, and be unclean until evening.

¹⁹'If a woman has a discharge, *and* the discharge from her body is blood, she shall be set apart seven days; and whoever touches her shall be unclean until evening. ²⁰Everything that she lies on during her impurity shall be unclean; also everything that she sits on shall be unclean. ²¹Whoever touches her bed shall wash his clothes and bathe in water, and be unclean until evening. ²²And whoever touches anything that she sat on shall wash his clothes and bathe in water, and be unclean until evening. ²³If *anything* is on *her* bed or on anything on which she sits, when he touches it, he shall be unclean until evening. ²⁴And if any man lies with her at all, so that her impurity is on him,

he shall be unclean seven days; and every bed on which he lies shall be unclean.

25"If a woman has a discharge of blood for many days, other than at the time of her *customary* impurity, or if it runs beyond her *usual time of* impurity, all the days of her unclean discharge shall be as the days of her *customary* impurity. She *shall be* unclean. 26Every bed on which she lies all the days of her discharge shall be to her as the bed of her impurity; and whatever she sits on shall be unclean, as the uncleanness of her impurity. 27Whoever touches those things shall be unclean; he shall wash his clothes and bathe in water, and be unclean until evening.

28But if she is cleansed of her discharge, then she shall count for herself seven days, and after that she shall be clean. 29And on the eighth day she shall take for herself two turtledoves or two young pigeons, and bring them to the priest, to the door of the tabernacle of meeting. 30Then the priest shall offer the one *as* a sin offering and the other *as* a burnt offering, and the priest shall make atonement for her before the LORD for the discharge of her uncleanness.

31Thus you shall separate the children of Israel from their uncleanness, lest they die in their uncleanness when they defile My tabernacle that *is* among them. 32This *is* the law for one who has a discharge, and *for him* who emits semen and is unclean thereby, 33and for her who is indisposed because of her *customary* impurity, and for one who has a discharge, either man or woman, and for him who lies with her who is unclean.' "

THE DAY OF ATONEMENT

1Now the LORD spoke to Moses after the death of the two sons of Aaron, when they offered *profane fire* before the LORD, and died; 2and the LORD said to Moses: "Tell Aaron your brother not to come at *just* any time into the Holy *Place* inside the veil, before the mercy seat which *is* on the ark, lest he die; for I will appear in the cloud above the mercy seat.

3Thus Aaron shall come into the Holy *Place:* with *the blood of* a young bull as a sin offering, and *of* a ram as a burnt offering. 4He shall put the holy linen tunic and the linen trousers on his body; he shall be girded with a linen sash, and with the linen turban he shall be attired. These *are* holy garments. Therefore he shall wash his body in water, and put them on. 5And he shall take from the congregation of the children of Israel two kids of the goats as a sin offering, and one ram as a burnt offering.

6"Aaron shall offer the bull as a sin offering, which *is* for himself, and make atonement for himself and for his house. 7He shall take the two goats and present them before the LORD *at* the door of the tabernacle of meeting. 8Then Aaron shall cast lots for the two goats: one lot for the LORD and the other lot for the scapegoat. 9And Aaron shall bring the goat on which the LORD's lot fell, and offer it *as* a sin offering. 10But the goat on which the lot fell to be the scapegoat shall be presented alive before the LORD, to make atonement upon it, *and* to let it go as the scapegoat into the wilderness.

WHAT'S IT MEAN?

Goats were all-purpose animals, as far as the ancient Israelites were concerned. The milk the Israelites drank, the clothes they wore, and the containers they used to hold their water and wine all came from goats. And if that weren't enough, goats were also used as sacrifices in burnt offerings and in sin offerings.
Leviticus 16:7–10

11"And Aaron shall bring the bull of the sin offering, which is for himself, and make atonement for himself and for his house, and shall kill the bull as the sin offering which *is* for himself. 12Then he shall take a censer full of burning coals of fire from the altar before the LORD, with his hands full of sweet incense beaten fine, and bring *it* inside the veil. 13And he shall put the incense on the fire before the LORD, that the cloud of incense may cover the mercy seat that *is* on the Testimony, lest he die. 14He shall take some of the blood of the bull and sprinkle *it* with his finger on the mercy seat on the east *side;* and before the mercy seat he shall sprinkle some of the blood with his finger seven times.

15"Then he shall kill the goat of the sin offering, which *is* for the people, bring its blood inside the veil, do with that blood as he did with the blood of the bull, and sprinkle it on the mercy seat and before the mercy seat. 16So he shall make atonement for the Holy *Place,* because of the uncleanness of the children of Israel, and because of their transgressions, for all their sins; and so he shall do for the tabernacle of meeting which remains among them in the midst of their uncleanness. 17There shall be no man in the tabernacle of meeting when he goes in to make atonement in the Holy *Place*, until he comes out, that he may make atonement for himself, for his household, and for all the assembly of Israel. [18]And he shall go out to the altar that *is* before the LORD, and make atonement for it, and shall take some of the blood of the bull and some of the blood of the goat, and put it on the horns of the altar all around. [19]Then he shall sprinkle some of the blood on it with his finger seven times, cleanse it, and consecrate it from the uncleanness of the children of Israel.

[20]"And when he has made an end of atoning for the Holy *Place*, the tabernacle of meeting, and the altar, he shall bring the live goat. [21]Aaron shall lay both his hands on the head of the live goat, confess over it all the iniquities of the children of Israel, and all their transgressions, concerning all their sins, putting them on the head of the goat, and shall send *it* away into the wilderness by the hand of a suitable man. [22]The goat shall bear on itself all their iniquities to an uninhabited land; and he shall release the goat in the wilderness.

[23]"Then Aaron shall come into the tabernacle of meeting, shall take off the linen garments which he put on when he went into the Holy *Place*, and shall leave them there. [24]And he shall wash his body with water in a holy place, put on his garments, come out and offer his burnt offering and the burnt offering of the people, and make atonement for himself and for the people. [25]The fat of the sin offering he shall burn on the altar. [26]And he who released the goat as the scapegoat shall wash his clothes and bathe his body in water, and afterward he may come into the camp. [27]The bull *for* the sin offering and the goat *for* the sin offering, whose blood was brought in to make atonement in the Holy *Place*, shall be carried outside the camp. And they shall burn in the fire their skins, their flesh, and their offal. [28]Then he who burns them shall wash his clothes and bathe his body in water, and afterward he may come into the camp.

[29]"*This* shall be a statute forever for you: In the seventh month, on the tenth *day* of the month, you shall afflict your souls, and do no work at all, *whether* a native of your own country or a stranger who dwells among you. [30]For on that day *the priest* shall make atonement for you, to cleanse you, *that* you may be clean from all your sins before the LORD. [31]It *is* a sabbath of solemn rest for you, and you shall afflict your souls. *It is* a statute forever. [32]And the priest,

who is anointed and consecrated to minister as priest in his father's place, shall make atonement, and put on the linen clothes, the holy garments; [33]then he shall make atonement for the Holy Sanctuary,[a] and he shall make atonement for the tabernacle of meeting and for the altar, and he shall make atonement for the priests and for all the people of the assembly. [34]This shall be an everlasting statute for you, to make atonement for the children of Israel, for all their sins, once a year." And he did as the LORD commanded Moses.

THE SANCTITY OF BLOOD

[1]And the LORD spoke to Moses, saying, [2]"Speak to Aaron, to his sons, and to all the children of Israel, and say to them, 'This *is* the thing which the LORD has commanded, saying: [3]"Whatever man of the house of Israel who kills an ox or lamb or goat in the camp, or who kills *it* outside the camp, [4]and does not bring it to the door of the tabernacle of meeting to offer an offering to the LORD before the tabernacle of the LORD, the guilt of bloodshed shall be imputed to that man. He has shed blood; and that man shall be cut off from among his people, [5]to the end that the children of Israel may bring their sacrifices which they offer in the open field, that they may bring them to the LORD at the door of the tabernacle of meeting, to the priest, and offer them *as* peace offerings to the LORD. [6]And the priest shall sprinkle the blood on the altar of the LORD *at* the door of the tabernacle of meeting, and burn the fat for a sweet aroma to the LORD. [7]They shall no more offer their sacrifices to demons, after whom they have played the harlot. This shall be a statute forever for them throughout their generations." '

[8]"Also you shall say to them: 'Whatever man of the house of Israel, or of the strangers who dwell among you, who offers a burnt offering or sacrifice, [9]and does not bring it to the door of the tabernacle of meeting, to offer it to the LORD, that man shall be cut off from among his people.

[10]'And whatever man of the house of Israel, or of the strangers who dwell among you, who eats any blood, I will set My face against that person who eats blood, and will cut him off from among his people. [11]For the life of the flesh *is* in the blood, and I have given it to you upon the altar to make atonement for your souls; for it *is* the blood *that* makes atonement for the soul.' [12]Therefore I said to the children of Israel, 'No one among you shall eat blood, nor

shall any stranger who dwells among you eat blood.'

13"Whatever man of the children of Israel, or of the strangers who dwell among you, who hunts and catches any animal or bird that may be eaten, he shall pour out its blood and cover it with dust; 14for *it is* the life of all flesh. Its blood sustains its life. Therefore I said to the children of Israel, 'You shall not eat the blood of any flesh, for the life of all flesh is its blood. Whoever eats it shall be cut off.'

15"And every person who eats what died *naturally* or what was torn *by beasts, whether he is* a native of your own country or a stranger, he shall both wash his clothes and bathe in water, and be unclean until evening. Then he shall be clean. 16But if he does not wash *them* or bathe his body, then he shall bear his guilt."

LAWS OF SEXUAL MORALITY

1Then the LORD spoke to Moses, saying, 2"Speak to the children of Israel, and say to them: 'I am the LORD your God. 3According to the doings of the land of Egypt, where you dwelt, you shall not do; and according to the doings of the land of Canaan, where I am bringing you, you shall not do; nor shall you walk in their ordinances. 4You shall observe My judgments and keep My ordinances, to walk in them: I *am* the LORD your God. 5You shall therefore keep My statutes and My judgments, which if a man does, he shall live by them: I *am* the LORD.

6'None of you shall approach anyone who is near of kin to him, to uncover his nakedness: I *am* the LORD. 7The nakedness of your father or the nakedness of your mother you shall not uncover. She *is* your mother; you shall not uncover her nakedness. 8The nakedness of your father's wife you shall not uncover; it *is* your father's nakedness. 9The nakedness of your sister, the daughter of your father, or the daughter of your mother, *whether* born at home or elsewhere, their nakedness you shall not uncover. 10The nakedness of your son's daughter or your daughter's daughter, their nakedness you shall not uncover; for theirs *is* your own nakedness. 11The nakedness of your father's wife's daughter, begotten by your father—she *is* your sister—you shall not uncover her nakedness. 12You shall not uncover the nakedness of your father's sister; she *is* near of kin to your father. 13You shall not uncover the nakedness of your mother's sister, for she *is* near of kin to your mother. 14You shall not uncover the nakedness of your father's brother. You shall not approach his wife; she *is* your aunt. 15You shall not un-

cover the nakedness of your daughter-in-law—she *is* your son's wife—you shall not uncover her nakedness. 16You shall not uncover the nakedness of your brother's wife; it *is* your brother's nakedness. 17You shall not uncover the nakedness of a woman and her daughter, nor shall you take her son's daughter or her daughter's daughter, to uncover her nakedness. They *are* near of kin to her. It *is* wickedness. 18Nor shall you take a woman as a rival to her sister, to uncover her nakedness while the other is alive.

19'Also you shall not approach a woman to uncover her nakedness as long as she is in her *customary* impurity. 20Moreover you shall not lie carnally with your neighbor's wife, to defile yourself with her. 21And you shall not let any of your descendants pass through *the fire* to Molech, nor shall you profane the name of your God: I *am* the LORD. 22You shall not lie with a male as with a woman. It *is* an abomination. 23Nor shall you mate with any animal, to defile yourself with it. Nor shall any woman stand before an animal to mate with it. It *is* perversion.

24'Do not defile yourselves with any of these things; for by all these the nations are defiled, which I am casting out before you. 25For the land is defiled; therefore I visit the punishment of its iniquity upon it, and the land vomits out its inhabitants. 26You shall therefore keep My statutes and My judgments, and shall not commit *any* of these abominations, *either* any of your own nation or any stranger who dwells

WHAT'S IT MEAN?

The Canaanites worshiped a fertility god named Baal. Male and female prostitutes lived in Baal's temple. Both the Egyptians and Canaanites believed that if they had sex with the temple prostitutes, they would be blessed with more children, animals, and crops. God wanted His people to have nothing to do with those kinds of practices.
Leviticus 18:3

HOMOSEXUALITY
What does God say about homosexual behavior? (18:22)

On the Edge

You shall not lie with a male as with a woman. It is an abomination (Lev. 18:22).

In the Old Testament and again in the New Testament, God calls homosexuality a sin that is disgusting to Him. Sin always has its consequences. With homosexuality comes guilt, emotional scars, condemnation, and possibly disease and death—not to mention how it can impact the people around a person. If your friend does not know Jesus, that's the first step. Introduce him or her to Him. Let your friend know that Jesus loves us *no matter what we do.* People who don't know Jesus often live according to what *feels* right. Most of the time that gets folks in trouble. If your friend does know Jesus, remind him or her of some things. Remind him or her that our purpose is to live a life that pleases God and to do our best to stay away from sin. Remind him or her that in Jesus there is the power to break any bondage. Your friend may need counseling or other help. For sure he or she will need a good friend. Hang in there. God can do anything!

SEE FOR YOURSELF:
Lev. 20:13;
1 Cor. 6:9

3'Every one of you shall revere his mother and his father, and keep My Sabbaths: I *am* the LORD your God.

4'Do not turn to idols, nor make for yourselves molded gods: I *am* the LORD your God.

RESPECT
Do we need to respect our parents? (19:3)

5'And if you offer a sacrifice of a peace offering to the LORD, you shall offer it of your own free will. 6It shall be eaten the same day you offer *it,* and on the next day. And if any remains until the third day, it shall be burned in the fire. 7And if it is eaten at all on the third day, it *is* an abomination. It shall not be accepted. 8Therefore *everyone* who eats it shall bear his iniquity, because he has profaned the hallowed *offering* of the LORD; and that person shall be cut off from his people.

9'When you reap the harvest of your land, you shall not wholly reap the corners of your field, nor shall you gather the gleanings of your harvest. 10And you shall not glean your vineyard, nor shall you gather *every* grape of your vineyard; you shall leave them for the poor and the stranger: I *am* the LORD your God.

11'You shall not steal, nor deal falsely, nor lie to one another. 12And you shall not swear by My name falsely, nor shall you profane the name of your God: I *am* the LORD.

13'You shall not cheat your neighbor, nor rob *him.* The wages of him who is hired shall not remain with you all night until morning. 14You shall not curse the deaf, nor put a stumbling block before the blind, but shall fear your God: I *am* the LORD.

15'You shall do no injustice in judgment. You shall not be partial to the poor, nor honor the person of the mighty. In righteousness you shall judge your neighbor. 16You shall not go about *as* a talebearer among your people; nor shall you take a stand against the life of your neighbor: I *am* the LORD.

GOSSIP
What should we be careful of when we're talking about other people? (19:16)

17'You shall not hate your brother in your heart. You shall surely rebuke your neighbor, and not bear sin because of him. 18You shall not take vengeance, nor bear any grudge against the children of your people, but you shall love your neighbor as yourself: I *am* the LORD.

REVENGE
Should God's people seek revenge? (19:18)

19'You shall keep My statutes. You shall not let your livestock breed with another kind. You shall not sow your field with mixed seed. Nor shall a

among you 27(for all these abominations the men of the land have done, who *were* before you, and thus the land is defiled), 28lest the land vomit you out also when you defile it, as it vomited out the nations that *were* before you. 29For whoever commits any of these abominations, the persons who commit *them* shall be cut off from among their people.

30'Therefore you shall keep My ordinance, so that *you* do not commit *any* of these abominable customs which were committed before you, and that you do not defile yourselves by them: I *am* the LORD your God.' "

MORAL AND CEREMONIAL LAWS

1And the LORD spoke to Moses, saying, 2"Speak to all the congregation of the children of Israel, and say to them: 'You shall be holy, for I the LORD your God *am* holy.

garment of mixed linen and wool come upon you.

^{20}'Whoever lies carnally with a woman who *is* betrothed to a man as a concubine, and who has not at all been redeemed nor given her freedom, for this there shall be scourging; *but* they shall not be put to death, because she was not free. ^{21}And he shall bring his trespass offering to the LORD, to the door of the tabernacle of meeting, a ram as a trespass offering. ^{22}The priest shall make atonement for him with the ram of the trespass offering before the LORD for his sin which he has committed. And the sin which he has committed shall be forgiven him.

^{23}'When you come into the land, and have planted all kinds of trees for food, then you shall count their fruit as uncircumcised. Three years it shall be as uncircumcised to you. *It* shall not be eaten. ^{24}But in the fourth year all its fruit shall be holy, a praise to the LORD. ^{25}And in the fifth year you may eat its fruit, that it may yield to you its increase: I *am* the LORD your God.

^{26}'You shall not eat *anything* with the blood, nor shall you practice divination or soothsaying. ^{27}You shall not shave around the sides of your head, nor shall you disfigure the edges of your beard. ^{28}You shall not make any cuttings in your flesh for the dead, nor tattoo any marks on you: I *am* the LORD.

^{29}'Do not prostitute your daughter, to cause her to be a harlot, lest the land fall into harlotry, and the land become full of wickedness.

^{30}'You shall keep My Sabbaths and reverence My sanctuary: I *am* the LORD.

^{31}'Give no regard to mediums and familiar spirits; do not seek after them, to be defiled by them: I *am* the LORD your God.

^{32}'You shall rise before the gray headed and honor the presence of an old man, and fear your God: I *am* the LORD.

^{33}'And if a stranger dwells with you in your land, you shall not mistreat him. ^{34}The stranger who dwells among you shall be to you as one born among you, and you shall love him as yourself; for you were strangers in the land of Egypt: I *am* the LORD your God.

^{35}'You shall do no injustice in judgment, in measurement of length, weight, or volume. ^{36}You shall have honest scales, honest weights, an honest ephah, and an honest hin: I *am* the LORD your God, who brought you out of the land of Egypt.

^{37}'Therefore you shall observe all My statutes and all My judgments, and perform them: I *am* the LORD.' "

PENALTIES FOR BREAKING THE LAW

^{1}Then the LORD spoke to Moses, saying, ^{2}"Again, you shall say to the children of Israel: 'Whoever of the children of Israel, or of the strangers who dwell in Israel, who gives *any* of his descendants to Molech, he shall surely be put to death. The people of the land shall stone

WHAT'S IT MEAN?

Intentionally disobeying God was a capital offense in ancient Israel. Death by stoning was the normal sentence. Offenders were taken outside the camp, where the men of the community threw rocks at them until they died.

Leviticus 20:2

him with stones. [3]I will set My face against that man, and will cut him off from his people, because he has given *some* of his descendants to Molech, to defile My sanctuary and profane My holy name. [4]And if the people of the land should in any way hide their eyes from the man, when he gives *some* of his descendants to Molech, and they do not kill him, [5]then I will set My face against that man and against his family; and I will cut him off from his people, and all who prostitute themselves with him to commit harlotry with Molech.

[6]And the person who turns to mediums and familiar spirits, to prostitute himself with them, I will set My face against that person and cut him off from his people. [7]Consecrate yourselves therefore, and be holy, for I *am* the LORD your God. [8]And you shall keep My statutes, and perform them: I *am* the LORD who sanctifies you.

[9]For everyone who curses his father or his mother shall surely be put to death. He has cursed his father or his mother. His blood *shall be* upon him.

[10]The man who commits adultery with *another* man's wife, *he* who commits adultery with his neighbor's wife, the adulterer and the adulteress, shall surely be put to death. [11]The man who lies with his father's wife has uncovered his father's nakedness; both of them shall surely be put to death. Their blood *shall be* upon them. [12]If a man lies with his daughter-in-law, both of them shall surely be put to death. They have committed perversion. Their blood *shall be*

upon them. [13]If a man lies with a male as he lies with a woman, both of them have committed an abomination. They shall surely be put to death. Their blood *shall be* upon them. [14]If a man marries a woman and her mother, it *is* wickedness. They shall be burned with fire, both he and they, that there may be no wickedness among you. [15]If a man mates with an animal, he shall surely be put to death, and you shall kill the animal. [16]If a woman approaches any animal and mates with it, you shall kill the woman and the animal. They shall surely be put to death. Their blood *is* upon them.

[17]If a man takes his sister, his father's daughter or his mother's daughter, and sees her nakedness and she sees his nakedness, it *is* a wicked thing. And they shall be cut off in the sight of their people. He has uncovered his sister's nakedness. He shall bear his guilt. [18]If a man lies with a woman during her sickness and uncovers her nakedness, he has exposed her flow, and she has uncovered the flow of her blood. Both of them shall be cut off from their people.

[19]You shall not uncover the nakedness of your mother's sister nor of your father's sister, for that would uncover his near of kin. They shall bear their guilt. [20]If a man lies with his uncle's wife, he has uncovered his uncle's nakedness. They shall bear their sin; they shall die childless. [21]If a man takes his brother's wife, it *is* an unclean thing. He has uncovered his brother's nakedness. They shall be childless.

[22]You shall therefore keep all My statutes and all My judgments, and perform them, that the land where I am bringing you to dwell may not vomit you out. [23]And you shall not walk in the statutes of the nation which I am casting out before you; for they commit all these things, and therefore I abhor them. [24]But I have said to you, "You shall inherit their land, and I will give it to you to possess, a land flowing with milk and honey." I *am* the LORD your God, who has separated you from the peoples. [25]You shall therefore distinguish between clean animals and unclean, between unclean birds and clean, and you shall not make yourselves abominable by beast or by bird, or by any kind of living thing that creeps on the ground, which I have separated

> "But I have said to you, 'You shall inherit their land, and I will give it to you to possess, a land flowing with milk and honey.' I am the LORD your God, who has separated you from the peoples."
> (Leviticus 20:24)

from you as unclean. ²⁶And you shall be holy to Me, for I the LORD *am* holy, and have separated you from the peoples, that you should be Mine.

On the Edge

And the person who turns to mediums and familiar spirits, to prostitute himself with them, I will set My face against that person and cut him off from his people (Lev. 20:6).

How many times have you flipped through the channels to see somebody trying to convince you to call a 1-900 number that will put you in touch with your very own psychic?

We live in a world today that is fascinated with the supernatural, but rather than turning to God or His Word for answers, a lot of people want to turn to "mediums and familiar spirits," that is, to psychics, fortune-tellers, witches, channelers, and others. God's Word calls this kind of stuff an abomination; and in this particular verse, He says that He is against (the enemy of) those who even visit someone like this. Don't even associate with such people. Instead, turn to Jesus. He really is the *only* answer!

You don't need to go looking to someone else for answers about your future. God speaks to you through His Word and through His Holy Spirit. Don't settle for a cheap imitation. All the answers you need are in the Bible, and if you read the end of it you'll see that you are a winner. In fact, you're more than a conquerer (Rom. 8:37), and God is on your side. Your power isn't counterfeit. It's real. "He who is in you is greater than he who is in the world" (1 John 4:4).

SEE FOR YOURSELF:
   2 Chr. 33:6;
   Gal. 5:19–21

²⁷'A man or a woman who is a medium, or who has familiar spirits, shall surely be put to death; they shall stone them with stones. Their blood *shall be* upon them.' "

REGULATIONS FOR CONDUCT OF PRIESTS

¹And the LORD said to Moses, "Speak to the priests, the sons of Aaron, and say to them: 'None shall defile himself for the dead among his people, ²except for his relatives who are nearest to him: his mother, his father, his son, his daughter, and his brother; ³also his virgin sister who is near to him, who has had no husband, for her he may defile himself. ⁴*Otherwise* he shall not defile himself, *being* a chief man among his people, to profane himself.

⁵'They shall not make any bald *place* on their heads, nor shall they shave the edges of their beards nor make any cuttings in their flesh. ⁶They shall be holy to their God and not profane the name of their God, for they offer the offerings of the LORD made by fire, *and* the bread of their God; therefore they shall be holy. ⁷They shall not take a wife *who is* a harlot or a defiled woman, nor shall they take a woman divorced from her husband; for *the priest*ᵃ is holy to his God. ⁸Therefore you shall consecrate him, for he offers the bread of your God. He shall be holy to you, for I the LORD, who sanctify you, *am* holy. ⁹The daughter of any priest, if she profanes herself by playing the harlot, she profanes her father. She shall be burned with fire.

¹⁰'*He who is* the high priest among his brethren, on whose head the anointing oil was poured and who is consecrated to wear the garments, shall not uncover his head nor tear his clothes; ¹¹nor shall he go near any dead body, nor defile himself for his father or his mother; ¹²nor shall he go out of the sanctuary, nor profane the sanctuary of his God; for the consecration of the anointing oil of his God *is* upon him: I *am* the LORD. ¹³And he shall take a wife in her virginity. ¹⁴A widow or a divorced woman or a defiled woman *or* a harlot—these he shall not marry; but he shall take a virgin of his own people as wife. ¹⁵Nor shall he profane his posterity among his people, for I the LORD sanctify him.' "

¹⁶And the LORD spoke to Moses, saying, ¹⁷"Speak to Aaron, saying: 'No man of your descendants in *succeeding* generations, who has *any* defect, may approach to offer the bread of his God. ¹⁸For any man who has a defect shall not approach: a man blind or lame, who has a marred *face* or any *limb* too long, ¹⁹a man who has a broken foot or broken hand, ²⁰or is a hunchback or a dwarf, or *a man* who has a defect in his eye, or eczema or scab, or is a eunuch. ²¹No man of the descendants of Aaron

21:7 ᵃLiterally *he*

WHAT'S IT MEAN?

Because the priests' work was holy, it was important for them to be pure and clean in every area of their lives. That's why they could marry only virgins, who were sexually pure.

Leviticus 21:13

the priest, who has a defect, shall come near to offer the offerings made by fire to the LORD. He has a defect; he shall not come near to offer the bread of his God. ²²He may eat the bread of his God, *both* the most holy and the holy; ²³only he shall not go near the veil or approach the altar, because he has a defect, lest he profane My sanctuaries; for I the LORD sanctify them.' "

²⁴And Moses told *it* to Aaron and his sons, and to all the children of Israel.

¹Then the LORD spoke to Moses, saying, ²"Speak to Aaron and his sons, that they separate themselves from the holy things of the children of Israel, and that they do not profane My holy name *by* what they dedicate to Me: I *am* the LORD. ³Say to them: 'Whoever of all your descendants throughout your generations, who goes near the holy things which the children of Israel dedicate to the LORD, while he has uncleanness upon him, that person shall be cut off from My presence: I *am* the LORD.

⁴'Whatever man of the descendants of Aaron, who *is* a leper or has a discharge, shall not eat the holy offerings until he is clean. And whoever touches anything made unclean *by* a corpse, or a man who has had an emission of semen, ⁵or whoever touches any creeping thing by which he would be made unclean, or any person by whom he would become unclean, whatever his uncleanness may be— ⁶the person who has touched any such thing shall be unclean until evening, and shall not eat the holy *offerings* unless he washes his body with water. ⁷And when the sun goes down he shall be clean; and afterward he may eat the holy *offerings*, because it *is* his food. ⁸Whatever dies *naturally* or is torn *by beasts* he shall not eat, to defile himself with it: I *am* the LORD.

⁹'They shall therefore keep My ordinance, lest they bear sin for it and die thereby, if they profane it: I the LORD sanctify them.

¹⁰'No outsider shall eat the holy *offering*; one who dwells with the priest, or a hired servant, shall not eat the holy thing. ¹¹But if the priest buys a person with his money, he may eat it; and one who is born in his house may eat his food. ¹²If the priest's daughter is married to an outsider, she may not eat of the holy offerings. ¹³But if the priest's daughter is a widow or divorced, and has no child, and has returned to her father's house as in her youth, she may eat her father's food; but no outsider shall eat it.

¹⁴'And if a man eats the holy *offering* unintentionally, then he shall restore a holy *offering* to the priest, and add one-fifth to it. ¹⁵They shall not profane the holy *offerings* of the children of Israel, which they offer to the LORD, ¹⁶or allow them to bear the guilt of trespass when they eat their holy *offerings*; for I the LORD sanctify them.' "

OFFERINGS ACCEPTED AND NOT ACCEPTED

¹⁷And the LORD spoke to Moses, saying, ¹⁸"Speak to Aaron and his sons, and to all the children of Israel, and say to them: 'Whatever man of the house of Israel, or of the strangers in Israel, who offers his sacrifice for any of his vows or for any of his freewill offerings, which they offer to the LORD as a burnt offering— ¹⁹*you shall offer* of your own free will a male without blemish from the cattle, from the sheep, or from the goats. ²⁰Whatever has a defect, you shall not offer, for it shall not be acceptable on your behalf. ²¹And whoever offers a sacrifice of a peace offering to the LORD, to fulfill *his* vow, or a freewill offering from the cattle or the sheep, it must be perfect to be accepted; there shall be no defect in it. ²²Those *that are* blind or broken or maimed, or have an ulcer or eczema or scabs, you shall not offer to the LORD, nor make an offering by fire of them on the altar to the LORD. ²³Either a bull or a lamb that has any limb too long or too short you may offer *as* a freewill offering, but for a vow it shall not be accepted.

²⁴'You shall not offer to the LORD what is bruised or crushed, or torn or cut; nor shall you make *any offering of them* in your land. ²⁵Nor from a foreigner's hand shall you offer any of these as the bread of your God, because their corruption *is* in them, *and* defects *are* in them. They shall not be accepted on your behalf.' "

²⁶And the LORD spoke to Moses, saying: ²⁷"When a bull or a sheep or a goat is born, it shall be seven days with its mother; and from the eighth day and thereafter it shall be

accepted as an offering made by fire to the LORD. [28]*Whether it is* a cow or ewe, do not kill both her and her young on the same day. [29]And when you offer a sacrifice of thanksgiving to the LORD, offer *it* of your own free will. [30]On the same day it shall be eaten; you shall leave none of it until morning: I *am* the LORD.

[31]"Therefore you shall keep My commandments, and perform them: I *am* the LORD. [32]You shall not profane My holy name, but I will be hallowed among the children of Israel. I *am* the LORD who sanctifies you, [33]who brought you out of the land of Egypt, to be your God: I *am* the LORD."

FEASTS OF THE LORD

[1]And the LORD spoke to Moses, saying, [2]"Speak to the children of Israel, and say to them: 'The feasts of the LORD, which you shall proclaim *to be* holy convocations, these *are* My feasts.

THE SABBATH

[3]'Six days shall work be done, but the seventh day *is* a Sabbath of solemn rest, a holy convocation. You shall do no work *on it;* it *is* the Sabbath of the LORD in all your dwellings.

WHAT'S IT MEAN?

Before leaving Egypt, every Israelite household sacrificed a lamb and painted their doorframe with its blood. When the angel of death came for every firstborn son in the country, he passed over those houses with the lamb's blood on their doors. The Israelites then ate a special Passover meal that included bread made without leavening. Jews still celebrate Passover every spring as a reminder of how God rescued their people from slavery.

Leviticus 23:4, 5

THE PASSOVER AND UNLEAVENED BREAD

[4]'These *are* the feasts of the LORD, holy convocations which you shall proclaim at their appointed times. [5]On the fourteenth *day* of the first month at twilight *is* the LORD's Passover. [6]And on the fifteenth day of the same month *is* the Feast of Unleavened Bread to the LORD;

seven days you must eat unleavened bread. [7]On the first day you shall have a holy convocation; you shall do no customary work on it. [8]But you shall offer an offering made by fire to the LORD for seven days. The seventh day *shall be* a holy convocation; you shall do no customary work *on it.*' "

THE FEAST OF FIRSTFRUITS

[9]And the LORD spoke to Moses, saying, [10]"Speak to the children of Israel, and say to them: 'When you come into the land which I give to you, and reap its harvest, then you shall bring a sheaf of the firstfruits of your harvest to the priest. [11]He shall wave the sheaf before the LORD, to be accepted on your behalf; on the day after the Sabbath the priest shall wave it. [12]And you shall offer on that day, when you wave the sheaf, a male lamb of the first year, without blemish, as a burnt offering to the LORD. [13]Its grain offering *shall be* two-tenths *of an ephah* of fine flour mixed with oil, an offering made by fire to the LORD, for a sweet aroma; and its drink offering *shall be* of wine, one-fourth of a hin. [14]You shall eat neither bread nor parched grain nor fresh grain until the same day that you have brought an offering to your God; *it shall be* a statute forever throughout your generations in all your dwellings.

THE FEAST OF WEEKS

[15]'And you shall count for yourselves from the day after the Sabbath, from the day that you brought the sheaf of the wave offering: seven Sabbaths shall be completed. [16]Count fifty days to the day after the seventh Sabbath; then you shall offer a new grain offering to the LORD. [17]You shall bring from your dwellings two wave *loaves* of two-tenths *of an ephah.* They shall be of fine flour; they shall be baked with leaven. *They are* the firstfruits to the LORD. [18]And you shall offer with the bread seven lambs of the first year, without blemish, one young bull, and two rams. They shall be *as* a burnt offering to the LORD, with their grain offering and their drink offerings, an offering made by fire for a sweet aroma to the LORD. [19]Then you shall sacrifice one kid of the goats as a sin offering, and two male lambs of the first year as a sacrifice of a peace offering. [20]The priest shall wave them with the bread of the firstfruits *as* a wave offering before the LORD, with the two lambs. They shall be holy to the LORD for the priest. [21]And you shall proclaim on the same day *that* it is a holy convocation to you. You shall do no customary work *on it. It shall be* a statute forever in all your dwellings throughout your generations.

²²'When you reap the harvest of your land, you shall not wholly reap the corners of your field when you reap, nor shall you gather any gleaning from your harvest. You shall leave them for the poor and for the stranger: I *am* the LORD your God.' "

THE FEAST OF TRUMPETS

²³Then the LORD spoke to Moses, saying, ²⁴"Speak to the children of Israel, saying: 'In the seventh month, on the first *day* of the month, you shall have a sabbath-*rest*, a memorial of blowing of trumpets, a holy convocation. ²⁵You shall do no customary work *on it;* and you shall offer an offering made by fire to the LORD.' "

THE DAY OF ATONEMENT

²⁶And the LORD spoke to Moses, saying: ²⁷"Also the tenth *day* of this seventh month *shall be* the Day of Atonement. It shall be a holy convocation for you; you shall afflict your souls, and offer an offering made by fire to the LORD. ²⁸And you shall do no work on that same day, for it *is* the Day of Atonement, to make atonement for you before the LORD your God. ²⁹For any person who is not afflicted *in soul* on that same day shall be cut off from his people. ³⁰And any person who does any work on that same day, that person I will destroy from among his people. ³¹You shall do no manner of work; *it shall be* a statute forever throughout your generations in all your dwellings. ³²It *shall be* to you a sabbath of *solemn* rest, and you shall afflict your souls; on the ninth *day* of the month at evening, from evening to evening, you shall celebrate your sabbath."

THE FEAST OF TABERNACLES

³³Then the LORD spoke to Moses, saying, ³⁴"Speak to the children of Israel, saying: 'The fifteenth day of this seventh month *shall be* the Feast of Tabernacles *for* seven days to the LORD. ³⁵On the first day *there shall be* a holy convocation. You shall do no customary work *on it.* ³⁶*For* seven days you shall offer an offering made by fire to the LORD. On the eighth day you shall have a holy convocation, and you shall offer an offering made by fire to the LORD. It *is* a sacred assembly, *and* you shall do no customary work *on it.*

³⁷'These *are* the feasts of the LORD which you shall proclaim *to be* holy convocations, to offer an offering made by fire to the LORD, a burnt offering and a grain offering, a sacrifice and drink offerings, everything on its day— ³⁸besides the Sabbaths of the LORD, besides your gifts, besides all your vows, and besides all your freewill offerings which you give to the LORD.

³⁹'Also on the fifteenth day of the seventh month, when you have gathered in the fruit of the land, you shall keep the feast of the LORD *for* seven days; on the first day *there shall be* a sabbath-*rest,* and on the eighth day a sabbath-*rest.* ⁴⁰And you shall take for yourselves on the first day the fruit of beautiful trees, branches of palm trees, the boughs of leafy trees, and willows of the brook; and you shall rejoice before the LORD your God for seven days. ⁴¹You shall keep it as a feast to the LORD for seven days in the year. *It shall be* a statute forever in your generations. You shall celebrate it in the seventh month. ⁴²You shall dwell in booths for seven days. All who are native Israelites shall dwell in booths, ⁴³that your generations may know that I made the children of Israel dwell in booths when I brought them out of the land of Egypt: I *am* the LORD your God.' "

⁴⁴So Moses declared to the children of Israel the feasts of the LORD.

CARE OF THE TABERNACLE LAMPS

¹Then the LORD spoke to Moses, saying: ²"Command the children of Israel that they bring to you pure oil of pressed olives for the light, to make the lamps burn continually. ³Outside the veil of the Testimony, in the tabernacle of meeting, Aaron shall be in charge of it from evening until morning before the LORD continually; *it shall be* a statute forever in your generations. ⁴He shall be in charge of the lamps on the pure *gold* lampstand before the LORD continually.

WHAT'S IT MEAN?

The best and purest olive oil came from green olives. Not only was olive oil used to anoint kings and priests; it was also used to treat wounds.
Leviticus 24:2

THE BREAD OF THE TABERNACLE

⁵"And you shall take fine flour and bake twelve cakes with it. Two-tenths *of an ephah* shall be in each cake. ⁶You shall set them in two

rows, six in a row, on the pure *gold* table before the LORD. [7]And you shall put pure frankincense on *each* row, that it may be on the bread for a memorial, an offering made by fire to the LORD. [8]Every Sabbath he shall set it in order before the LORD continually, *being taken* from the children of Israel by an everlasting covenant. [9]And it shall be for Aaron and his sons, and they shall eat it in a holy place; for it *is* most holy to him from the offerings of the LORD made by fire, by a perpetual statute."

THE PENALTY FOR BLASPHEMY

[10]Now the son of an Israelite woman, whose father *was* an Egyptian, went out among the children of Israel; and this Israelite *woman's* son and a man of Israel fought each other in the camp. [11]And the Israelite woman's son blasphemed the name *of the* LORD and cursed; and so they brought him to Moses. (His mother's name *was* Shelomith the daughter of Dibri, of the tribe of Dan.) [12]Then they put him in custody, that the mind of the LORD might be shown to them.

[13]And the LORD spoke to Moses, saying, [14]"Take outside the camp him who has cursed; then let all who heard *him* lay their hands on his head, and let all the congregation stone him. [15]"Then you shall speak to the children of Israel, saying: 'Whoever curses his God shall bear his sin. [16]And whoever blasphemes the name of the LORD shall surely be put to death. All the congregation shall certainly stone him, the stranger as well as him who is born in the land. When he blasphemes the name *of the* LORD, he shall be put to death.

[17]'Whoever kills any man shall surely be put to death. [18]Whoever kills an animal shall make it good, animal for animal.

[19]'If a man causes disfigurement of his neighbor, as he has done, so shall it be done to him— [20]fracture for fracture, eye for eye, tooth for tooth; as he has caused disfigurement of a man, so shall it be done to him. [21]And whoever kills an animal shall restore it; but whoever kills a man shall be put to death. [22]You shall have the same law for the stranger and for one from your own country; for I *am* the LORD your God.' "

[23]Then Moses spoke to the children of Israel; and they took outside the camp him who had cursed, and stoned him with stones. So the children of Israel did as the LORD commanded Moses.

> "So the children of Israel did as the LORD commanded Moses."
> (Leviticus 24:23b)

THE SABBATH OF THE SEVENTH YEAR

[1]And the LORD spoke to Moses on Mount Sinai, saying, [2]"Speak to the children of Israel, and say to them: 'When you come into the land which I give you, then the land shall keep a sabbath to the LORD. [3]Six years you shall sow your field, and six years you shall prune your vineyard, and gather its fruit; [4]but in the seventh year there shall be a sabbath of solemn rest for the land, a sabbath to the LORD. You shall neither sow your field nor prune your vineyard. [5]What grows of its own accord of your harvest you shall not reap, nor gather the grapes of your untended vine, *for* it is a year of rest for the land. [6]And the sabbath *produce* of the land shall be food for you: for you, your male and female servants, your hired man, and the stranger who dwells with you, [7]for your livestock and the beasts that *are* in your land—all its produce shall be for food.

THE YEAR OF JUBILEE

[8]'And you shall count seven sabbaths of years for yourself, seven times seven years; and the time of the seven sabbaths of years shall be to you forty-nine years. [9]Then you shall cause the trumpet of the Jubilee to sound on the tenth *day* of the seventh month; on the Day of Atonement you shall make the trumpet to sound throughout all your land. [10]And you shall consecrate the fiftieth year, and proclaim liberty throughout *all* the land to all its inhabitants. It shall be a Jubilee for you; and each of you shall return to his possession, and each of you shall return to his family. [11]That fiftieth year shall be a Jubilee to you; in it you shall neither sow nor reap what grows of its own accord, nor gather *the grapes* of your untended vine. [12]For it *is* the Jubilee; it shall be holy to you; you shall eat its produce from the field.

[13]'In this Year of Jubilee, each of you shall return to his possession. [14]And if you sell anything to your neighbor or buy from your neighbor's hand, you shall not oppress one another. [15]According to the number of years after the Jubilee you shall buy from your neighbor, and according to the number of years of crops he shall sell to you. [16]According to the multitude of years you shall increase its price, and according to the fewer number of years you shall diminish its price; for he sells to you *according* to the number *of the years* of the crops. [17]Therefore you shall not oppress one another,

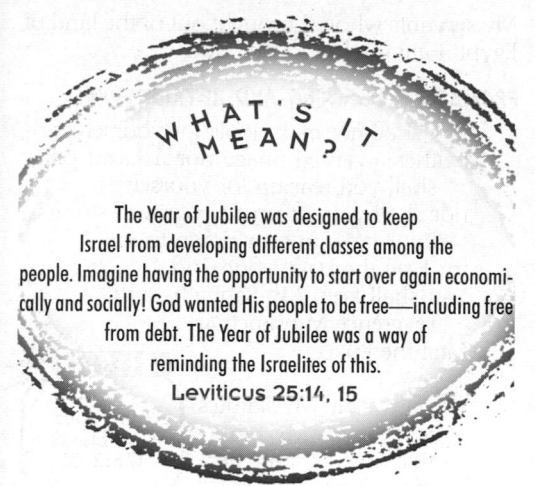

WHAT'S IT MEAN?

The Year of Jubilee was designed to keep Israel from developing different classes among the people. Imagine having the opportunity to start over again economically and socially! God wanted His people to be free—including free from debt. The Year of Jubilee was a way of reminding the Israelites of this.
Leviticus 25:14, 15

but you shall fear your God; for I *am* the LORD your God.

PROVISIONS FOR THE SEVENTH YEAR

[18]'So you shall observe My statutes and keep My judgments, and perform them; and you will dwell in the land in safety. [19]Then the land will yield its fruit, and you will eat your fill, and dwell there in safety.

[20]And if you say, "What shall we eat in the seventh year, since we shall not sow nor gather in our produce?" [21]Then I will command My blessing on you in the sixth year, and it will bring forth produce enough for three years. [22]And you shall sow in the eighth year, and eat old produce until the ninth year; until its produce comes in, you shall eat *of* the old *harvest*.

REDEMPTION OF PROPERTY

[23]'The land shall not be sold permanently, for the land *is* Mine; for you *are* strangers and sojourners with Me. [24]And in all the land of your possession you shall grant redemption of the land.

[25]'If one of your brethren becomes poor, and has sold *some* of his possession, and if his redeeming relative comes to redeem it, then he may redeem what his brother sold. [26]Or if the man has no one to redeem it, but he himself becomes able to redeem it, [27]then let him count the years since its sale, and restore the remainder to the man to whom he sold it, that he may return to his possession. [28]But if he is not able to have *it* restored to himself, then what was sold shall remain in the hand of him who bought it until the Year of Jubilee; and in the Jubilee it shall be released, and he shall return to his possession.

[29]'If a man sells a house in a walled city, then he may redeem it within a whole year after it is sold; *within* a full year he may redeem it. [30]But if it is not redeemed within the space of a full year, then the house in the walled city shall belong permanently to him who bought it, throughout his generations. It shall not be released in the Jubilee. [31]However the houses of villages which have no wall around them shall be counted as the fields of the country. They may be redeemed, and they shall be released in the Jubilee. [32]Nevertheless the cities of the Levites, *and* the houses in the cities of their possession, the Levites may redeem at any time. [33]And if a man purchases a house from the Levites, then the house that was sold in the city of his possession shall be released in the Jubilee; for the houses in the cities of the Levites *are* their possession among the children of Israel. [34]But the field of the common-land of their cities may not be sold, for it *is* their perpetual possession.

LENDING TO THE POOR

[35]'If one of your brethren becomes poor, and falls into poverty among you, then you shall help him, like a stranger or a sojourner, that he may live with you. [36]Take no usury or interest from him; but fear your God, that your brother may live with you. [37]You shall not lend him your money for usury, nor lend him your food at a profit. [38]I *am* the LORD your God, who brought you out of the land of Egypt, to give you the land of Canaan *and* to be your God.

THE LAW CONCERNING SLAVERY

[39]'And if *one* of your brethren *who dwells* by you becomes poor, and sells himself to you, you shall not compel him to serve as a slave. [40]As a hired servant *and* a sojourner he shall be with you, *and* shall serve you until the Year of Jubilee. [41]And *then* he shall depart from you— he and his children with him—and shall return to his own family. He shall return to the possession of his fathers. [42]For they *are* My servants, whom I brought out of the land of Egypt; they shall not be sold as slaves. [43]You shall not rule over him with rigor, but you shall fear your God. [44]And as for your male and female slaves whom you may have—from the nations that are around you, from them you may buy male and female slaves. [45]Moreover you may buy the children of the strangers who dwell among you, and their families who are with you, which they beget in your land; and they shall become your property. [46]And you may take them as an inheritance for your children after you, to inherit *them as* a possession; they shall be your permanent slaves. But regarding your brethren,

the children of Israel, you shall not rule over one another with rigor.

⁴⁷'Now if a sojourner or stranger close to you becomes rich, and *one of* your brethren *who dwells* by him becomes poor, and sells himself to the stranger *or* sojourner close to you, or to a member of the stranger's family, ⁴⁸after he is sold he may be redeemed again. One of his brothers may redeem him; ⁴⁹or his uncle or his uncle's son may redeem him; or *anyone* who is near of kin to him in his family may redeem him; or if he is able he may redeem himself. ⁵⁰Thus he shall reckon with him who bought him: The price of his release shall be according to the number of years, from the year that he was sold to him until the Year of Jubilee; *it shall be* according to the time of a hired servant for him. ⁵¹If *there are* still many years *remaining*, according to them he shall repay the price of his redemption from the money with which he was bought. ⁵²And if there remain but a few years until the Year of Jubilee, then he shall reckon with him, *and* according to his years he shall repay him the price of his redemption. ⁵³He shall be with him as a yearly hired servant, and he shall not rule with rigor over him in your sight. ⁵⁴And if he is not redeemed in these *years*, then he shall be released in the Year of Jubilee—he and his children with him. ⁵⁵For the children of Israel *are* servants to Me; they *are* My servants whom I brought out of the land of Egypt: I *am* the LORD your God.

PROMISE OF BLESSING AND RETRIBUTION

1 'You shall not make idols for yourselves;
neither a carved image nor a *sacred* pillar shall you rear up for yourselves;
nor shall you set up an engraved stone in your land, to bow down to it;
for I *am* the LORD your God.

2 You shall keep My Sabbaths and reverence My sanctuary:
I *am* the LORD.

BLESSING
Who does God bless? (26:3–5)

3 'If you walk in My statutes and keep My commandments, and perform them,

4 then I will give you rain in its season, the land shall yield its produce, and the trees of the field shall yield their fruit.

5 Your threshing shall last till the time of vintage, and the vintage shall last till the time of sowing;
you shall eat your bread to the full, and dwell in your land safely.

6 I will give peace in the land, and you shall lie down, and none will make *you* afraid;

Promise   HE PROMISES TO WALK ALONG WITH YOU.

I will walk among you and be your God, and you shall be My people (Lev. 26:12).

You may have heard the story called "Footprints." It's the story of a man who had a dream. In his dream he was walking along the beach with the Lord. Scenes from his life flashed across the sky. For each scene, he noticed two sets of footprints in the sand—one belonging to him and the other to the Lord. When the last scene of his life flashed before him, he looked back at the footprints in the sand. He noticed that many times along the path of his life there was only one set of footprints. He also noticed that only one set appeared during the lowest and saddest times in his life. This really bothered him, and he questioned the Lord about it. "Lord, You said that once I decided to follow You, You'd walk with me all the way. But I have noticed that during the most troublesome times in my life, there is only one set of footprints. I don't understand why You weren't there when I needed You most. You said You would never leave me."

The Lord replied, "My son, My precious child, I love you and I would never leave you. During your times of trial and suffering, when you see only one set of footprints, it was then that I carried you."

Can you catch what this story is saying? No matter what kind of situation you go through, the Lord is going to be right there with you. Don't forget it. You never have to walk alone again. He's the One who walks with you.

SEE FOR YOURSELF:
Ps. 23:4; Prov. 3:23–26; Heb. 13:5b

I will rid the land of evil beasts,
and the sword will not go through your land.

7 You will chase your enemies, and they shall fall by the sword before you.

8 Five of you shall chase a hundred, and a hundred of you shall put ten thousand to flight;
your enemies shall fall by the sword before you.

9 'For I will look on you favorably and make you fruitful, multiply you and confirm My covenant with you.

10 You shall eat the old harvest, and clear out the old because of the new.

11 I will set My tabernacle among you, and My soul shall not abhor you.

12 I will walk among you and be your God, and you shall be My people.

13 I *am* the LORD your God, who brought you out of the land of Egypt, that *you* should not be their slaves;
I have broken the bands of your yoke and made you walk upright.

14 'But if you do not obey Me, and do not observe all these commandments,

15 and if you despise My statutes, or if your soul abhors My judgments, so that you do not perform all My commandments, *but* break My covenant,

16 I also will do this to you:
I will even appoint terror over you, wasting disease and fever which shall consume the eyes and cause sorrow of heart.
And you shall sow your seed in vain, for your enemies shall eat it.

17 I will set My face against you, and you shall be defeated by your enemies.
Those who hate you shall reign over you, and you shall flee when no one pursues you.

18 'And after all this, if you do not obey Me, then I will punish you seven times more for your sins.

19 I will break the pride of your power;
I will make your heavens like iron and your earth like bronze.

20 And your strength shall be spent in vain;
for your land shall not yield its produce, nor shall the trees of the land yield their fruit.

21 'Then, if you walk contrary to Me, and are not willing to obey Me, I will bring on you seven times more plagues, according to your sins.

Promise HE PROMISES TO PUNISH SIN.

But if you do not obey Me, and do not observe all these commandments, and if you despise My statutes, or if your soul abhors My judgments, so that you do not perform all My commandments, but break My covenant, I also will do this to you: I will even appoint terror over you, wasting disease and fever which shall consume the eyes and cause sorrow of heart . . . And after all this, if you do not obey Me, then I will punish you seven times more for your sins (Lev. 26:14–18).

Wow! God really means business. He intends for us to obey His laws. He gave us laws in order to give us guidance and boundaries. God designed our lives, so He knows better than anyone how they need to operate. Think of Him as the "manufacturer." The manufacturer has set the limits, knowing at what point the whole system will crash and burn. Breaking God's law is sin. God punishes sin for the same reason that a parent fairly punishes a child for disobedience. Sometimes, the consequence of the sin is the punishment. Other times, punishment may come in another form. The promise of punishment is enough to encourage some people to try to stay out of sin. For others, once they've been punished, they know they never want to make the same mistake again. Been there, done that, no thanks.

SEE FOR YOURSELF:
Ps. 89:32; Lam. 4:22; Hos. 9:9

22 I will also send wild beasts among you, which shall rob you of your children, destroy your livestock, and make you few in number;
and your highways shall be desolate.

23 'And if by these things you are not reformed by Me, but walk contrary to Me,
24 then I also will walk contrary to you, and I will punish you yet seven times for your sins.
25 And I will bring a sword against you that will execute the vengeance of the covenant;
when you are gathered together within your cities I will send pestilence among you;
and you shall be delivered into the hand of the enemy.
26 When I have cut off your supply of bread, ten women shall bake your bread in one oven, and they shall bring back your bread by weight, and you shall eat and not be satisfied.

27 'And after all this, if you do not obey Me, but walk contrary to Me,
28 then I also will walk contrary to you in fury;
and I, even I, will chastise you seven times for your sins.
29 You shall eat the flesh of your sons, and you shall eat the flesh of your daughters.
30 I will destroy your high places, cut down your incense altars, and cast your carcasses on the lifeless forms of your idols;
and My soul shall abhor you.
31 I will lay your cities waste and bring your sanctuaries to desolation, and I will not smell the fragrance of your sweet aromas.
32 I will bring the land to desolation, and your enemies who dwell in it shall be astonished at it.
33 I will scatter you among the nations and draw out a sword after you;
your land shall be desolate and your cities waste.
34 Then the land shall enjoy its sabbaths as long as it lies desolate and you *are* in your enemies' land;
then the land shall rest and enjoy its sabbaths.
35 As long as *it* lies desolate it shall rest—
for the time it did not rest on your sabbaths when you dwelt in it.

36 'And as for those of you who are left, I will send faintness into their hearts in the lands of their enemies;
the sound of a shaken leaf shall cause them to flee;
they shall flee as though fleeing from a sword, and they shall fall when no one pursues.
37 They shall stumble over one another, as it were before a sword, when no one pursues;
and you shall have no *power* to stand before your enemies.
38 You shall perish among the nations, and the land of your enemies shall eat you up.
39 And those of you who are left shall waste away in their iniquity in your enemies' lands;
also in their fathers' iniquities, which are with them, they shall waste away.

40 'But if they confess their iniquity and the iniquity of their fathers, with their unfaithfulness in which they were unfaithful to Me, and that they also have walked contrary to Me,
41 and *that* I also have walked contrary to them and have brought them into the land of their enemies;
if their uncircumcised hearts are humbled, and they accept their guilt—
42 then I will remember My covenant with Jacob, and My covenant with Isaac and My covenant with Abraham I will remember;
I will remember the land.
43 The land also shall be left empty by them, and will enjoy its sabbaths while it lies desolate without them;
they will accept their guilt, because they despised My judgments and because their soul abhorred My statutes.
44 Yet for all that, when they are in the land of their enemies, I will not cast them away, nor shall I abhor them, to utterly destroy them and break My covenant with them;
for I *am* the LORD their God.
45 But for their sake I will remember the covenant of their ancestors, whom I brought out of the land of Egypt in the sight of the nations, that I might be their God:
I *am* the LORD.' "

46 These *are* the statutes and judgments and laws which the LORD made between Himself

and the children of Israel on Mount Sinai by the hand of Moses.

REDEEMING PERSONS AND PROPERTY DEDICATED TO GOD

[1]Now the LORD spoke to Moses, saying, [2]"Speak to the children of Israel, and say to them: 'When a man consecrates by a vow certain persons to the LORD, according to your valuation, [3]if your valuation is of a male from twenty years old up to sixty years old, then your valuation shall be fifty shekels of silver, according to the shekel of the sanctuary. [4]If it is a female, then your valuation shall be thirty shekels; [5]and if from five years old up to twenty years old, then your valuation for a male shall be twenty shekels, and for a female ten shekels; [6]and if from a month old up to five years old, then your valuation for a male shall be five shekels of silver, and for a female your valuation shall be three shekels of silver; [7]and if from sixty years old and above, if it is a male, then your valuation shall be fifteen shekels, and for a female ten shekels.

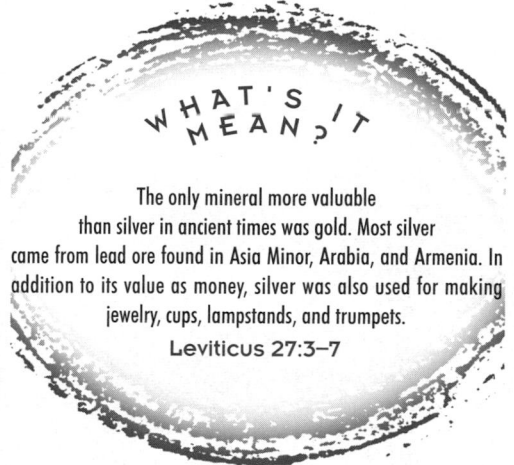

WHAT'S IT MEAN?

The only mineral more valuable than silver in ancient times was gold. Most silver came from lead ore found in Asia Minor, Arabia, and Armenia. In addition to its value as money, silver was also used for making jewelry, cups, lampstands, and trumpets.

Leviticus 27:3–7

[8]'But if he is too poor to pay your valuation, then he shall present himself before the priest, and the priest shall set a value for him; according to the ability of him who vowed, the priest shall value him.

[9]If it is an animal that men may bring as an offering to the LORD, all that anyone gives to the LORD shall be holy. [10]He shall not substitute it or exchange it, good for bad or bad for good; and if he at all exchanges animal for animal, then both it and the one exchanged for it shall be holy. [11]If it is an unclean animal which they do not offer as a sacrifice to the LORD, then he shall present the animal before the priest; [12]and the priest shall set a value for it, whether it is good or bad; as you, the priest, value it, so it shall be. [13]But if he wants at all to redeem it, then he must add one-fifth to your valuation.

[14]And when a man dedicates his house to be holy to the LORD, then the priest shall set a value for it, whether it is good or bad; as the priest values it, so it shall stand. [15]If he who dedicated it wants to redeem his house, then he must add one-fifth of the money of your valuation to it, and it shall be his.

[16]If a man dedicates to the LORD part of a field of his possession, then your valuation shall be according to the seed for it. A homer of barley seed shall be valued at fifty shekels of silver. [17]If he dedicates his field from the Year of Jubilee, according to your valuation it shall stand. [18]But if he dedicates his field after the Jubilee, then the priest shall reckon to him the money due according to the years that remain till the Year of Jubilee, and it shall be deducted from your valuation. [19]And if he who dedicates the field ever wishes to redeem it, then he must add one-fifth of the money of your valuation to it, and it shall belong to him. [20]But if he does not want to redeem the field, or if he has sold the field to another man, it shall not be redeemed anymore; [21]but the field, when it is released in the Jubilee, shall be holy to the LORD, as a devoted field; it shall be the possession of the priest.

[22]'And if a man dedicates to the LORD a field which he has bought, which is not the field of his possession, [23]then the priest shall reckon to him the worth of your valuation, up to the Year of Jubilee, and he shall give your valuation on that day as a holy offering to the LORD. [24]In the Year of Jubilee the field shall return to him from whom it was bought, to the one who owned the land as a possession. [25]And all your valuations shall be according to the shekel of the sanctuary: twenty gerahs to the shekel.

[26]'But the firstborn of the animals, which should be the LORD's firstborn, no man shall dedicate; whether it is an ox or sheep, it is the LORD's. [27]And if it is an unclean animal, then he shall redeem it according to your valuation, and shall add one-fifth to it; or if it is not redeemed, then it shall be sold according to your valuation.

[28]'Nevertheless no devoted offering that a man may devote to the LORD of all that he has, both man and beast, or the field of his possession, shall be sold or redeemed; every devoted offering is most holy to the LORD. [29]No person under the ban, who may become doomed to destruction among men, shall be redeemed, but shall surely be put to death. [30]And all the tithe

of the land, *whether* of the seed of the land *or of the fruit of the tree, is* the LORD's. It *is* holy to the LORD. [31]If a man wants at all to redeem *any of* his tithes, he shall add one-fifth to it. [32]And concerning the tithe of the herd or the flock, of whatever passes under the rod, the tenth one shall be holy to the LORD. [33]He shall not in- quire whether it is good or bad, nor shall he exchange it; and if he exchanges it at all, then both it and the one exchanged for it shall be holy; it shall not be redeemed.' "

[34]These *are* the commandments which the LORD commanded Moses for the children of Israel on Mount Sinai.

"These are the commandments which the LORD commanded Moses for the children of Israel on Mount Sinai." (Leviticus 27:34)

numbers

CONTENT First of all, this isn't just a book of numerals, Roman or otherwise. The book title refers to the two times that Moses took a census of the people (counted them). The book itself is really about the time period in between the two censuses.

The awful truth is this: After God miraculously brought the Hebrews out of slavery in Egypt, they went directly to the Promised Land without delay. It took about twenty-four months, but they were about to pass "go" and collect their heritage when—they freaked out and got afraid. After all God had done to get them there, they basically wimped out. The consequence for their lack of faith was that they put the camels in reverse and cruised the wilderness for almost forty long, hot, dry years.

The Book of Numbers is about the yucky parts of life that we bring on ourselves when we refuse to believe that God will come through for us. It's about the weak parts of our selves that don't believe even when God has been faithful. It's about the part of us that grumbles because we want God's blessings, but we want them the easy way; we don't want to work to keep our part of our agreement to worship Him. It's about us learning from the Hebrews' mistakes so that maybe we won't make the same ones.

Outline

Purpose Actions have consequences that even the forgiven cannot escape.

Theme God's Guiding Presence for the Journey from Sinai Across the Jordan River

Date of writing 1445–1440 B.C.

Bible Talk

Complaining

You know what one of the main themes of Numbers is about? Plain old complaining. Mere grumbling. Simple crankiness.

The people had been under horrible stress in Egypt. They were literally worked to death! There was one period of time when a baby boy could be killed, just because he was a Hebrew. Make no mistake—the Hebrews wanted out.

Yet, when they ended up in the desert, they complained and grumbled. It wasn't that they were hungry. God sent manna every day. It wasn't that they needed new clothes. In forty years their shoes never even wore out! No, it was the inconvenience of it all. It was the boredom.

So they complained. We wouldn't be that way—would we?

CIVIL WARS AND FAMILY CONFLICTS

Sometimes when we retell the ancient stories, we gloss over them. Moses led the people out. . . . It was hard. . . . They finally got there. . . . End of story.

We forget that these were people, in many ways just like us. They had opinions. They had family loyalties. They got ticked off. They wanted their way. They wanted control. Have you ever known a group of people *not* to have conflicts? Is there any way a group of 600,000+ wouldn't?

A man named Korah led a rebellion. Moses' own sister and brother picked a fight with him.

When you read these stories, remember that these are people like you and the guy who made you angry last week. Their stories are as true to life as your own.

THE FIRST CENSUS OF ISRAEL

¹Now the LORD spoke to Moses in the Wilderness of Sinai, in the tabernacle of meeting, on the first *day* of the second month, in the second year after they had come out of the land of Egypt, saying: ²"Take a census of all the congregation of the children of Israel, by their families, by their fathers' houses, according to the number of names, every male individually, ³from twenty years old and above—all who *are able to* go to war in Israel. You and Aaron shall number them by their armies. ⁴And with you there shall be a man from every tribe, each one the head of his father's house.

⁵"These are the names of the men who shall stand with you: from Reuben, Elizur the son of Shedeur; ⁶from Simeon, Shelumiel the son of Zurishaddai; ⁷from Judah, Nahshon the son of Amminadab; ⁸from Issachar, Nethanel the son of Zuar; ⁹from Zebulun, Eliab the son of Helon; ¹⁰from the sons of Joseph: from Ephraim, Elishama the son of Ammihud; from Manasseh, Gamaliel the son of Pedahzur; ¹¹from Benjamin, Abidan the son of Gideoni; ¹²from Dan, Ahiezer the son of Ammishaddai; ¹³from Asher, Pagiel the son of Ocran; ¹⁴from Gad, Eliasaph the son of Deuel;ᵃ ¹⁵from Naphtali, Ahira the son of Enan." ¹⁶These *were* chosen from the congregation, leaders of their fathers' tribes, heads of the divisions in Israel.

¹⁷Then Moses and Aaron took these men who had been mentioned by name, ¹⁸and they assembled all the congregation together on the first *day* of the second month; and they recited their ancestry by families, by their fathers' houses, according to the number of names, from twenty years old and above, each one individually. ¹⁹As the LORD commanded Moses, so he numbered them in the Wilderness of Sinai.

²⁰Now the children of Reuben, Israel's oldest son, their genealogies by their families, by their fathers' house, according to the number of names, every male individually, from twenty years old and above, all who *were able to* go to war: ²¹those who were numbered of the tribe of Reuben *were* forty-six thousand five hundred.

²²From the children of Simeon, their genealogies by their families, by their fathers' house, of those who were numbered, according to the number of names, every male individually, from twenty years old and above, all who *were able to* go to war: ²³those who were numbered of the tribe of Simeon *were* fifty-nine thousand three hundred.

²⁴From the children of Gad, their genealogies by their families, by their fathers' house, according to the number of names, from twenty years old and above, all who *were able to* go to war: ²⁵those who were numbered of the tribe of Gad *were* forty-five thousand six hundred and fifty.

WHAT'S IT MEAN?

Don't underestimate the size of the Israelite nation. The 603,550 people counted in the census were all men. Throw in the women and children, and you probably had a total population of two million or more! That's quite a population growth from the seventy people who first settled in Egypt.

Numbers 1:20–46

²⁶From the children of Judah, their genealogies by their families, by their fathers' house, according to the number of names, from twenty years old and above, all who *were able to* go to war: ²⁷those who were numbered of the tribe of Judah *were* seventy-four thousand six hundred.

²⁸From the children of Issachar, their genealogies by their families, by their fathers' house, according to the number of names, from twenty years old and above, all who *were able to* go to war: ²⁹those who were numbered of the tribe of Issachar *were* fifty-four thousand four hundred.

³⁰From the children of Zebulun, their genealogies by their families, by their fathers' house, according to the number of names, from twenty years old and above, all who *were able to* go to war: ³¹those who were numbered of the tribe of Zebulun *were* fifty-seven thousand four hundred.

³²From the sons of Joseph, the children of Ephraim, their genealogies by their families, by their fathers' house, according to the number of names, from twenty years old and above, all who *were able to* go to war: ³³those who were numbered of the tribe of Ephraim *were* forty thousand five hundred.

³⁴From the children of Manasseh, their genealogies by their families, by their fathers' house, according to the number of names, from

---

1:14 ᵃSpelled *Reuel* in 2:14

twenty years old and above, all who *were able to* go to war: ³⁵those who were numbered of the tribe of Manasseh *were* thirty-two thousand two hundred.

³⁶From the children of Benjamin, their genealogies by their families, by their fathers' house, according to the number of names, from twenty years old and above, all who *were able to* go to war: ³⁷those who were numbered of the tribe of Benjamin *were* thirty-five thousand four hundred.

³⁸From the children of Dan, their genealogies by their families, by their fathers' house, according to the number of names, from twenty years old and above, all who *were able to* go to war: ³⁹those who were numbered of the tribe of Dan *were* sixty-two thousand seven hundred.

⁴⁰From the children of Asher, their genealogies by their families, by their fathers' house, according to the number of names, from twenty years old and above, all who *were able to* go to war: ⁴¹those who were numbered of the tribe of Asher *were* forty-one thousand five hundred.

⁴²From the children of Naphtali, their genealogies by their families, by their fathers' house, according to the number of names, from twenty years old and above, all who *were able to* go to war: ⁴³those who were numbered of the tribe of Naphtali *were* fifty-three thousand four hundred.

⁴⁴These are the ones who were numbered, whom Moses and Aaron numbered, with the leaders of Israel, twelve men, each one representing his father's house. ⁴⁵So all who were numbered of the children of Israel, by their fathers' houses, from twenty years old and above, all who *were able to* go to war in Israel— ⁴⁶all who were numbered were six hundred and three thousand five hundred and fifty.

⁴⁷But the Levites were not numbered among them by their fathers' tribe; ⁴⁸for the LORD had spoken to Moses, saying: ⁴⁹"Only the tribe of Levi you shall not number, nor take a census of them among the children of Israel; ⁵⁰but you shall appoint the Levites over the tabernacle of the Testimony, over all its furnishings, and over all things that belong to it; they shall carry the tabernacle and all its furnishings; they shall attend to it and camp around the tabernacle. ⁵¹And when the tabernacle is to go forward, the Levites shall take it down; and when the tabernacle is to be set up, the Levites shall set it up. The outsider who comes near shall be put to death. ⁵²The children of Israel shall pitch their tents, everyone by his own camp, everyone by his own standard, according to their armies;

⁵³but the Levites shall camp around the tabernacle of the Testimony, that there may be no wrath on the congregation of the children of Israel; and the Levites shall keep charge of the tabernacle of the Testimony."

⁵⁴Thus the children of Israel did; according to all that the LORD commanded Moses, so they did.

THE TRIBES AND LEADERS BY ARMIES

¹And the LORD spoke to Moses and Aaron, saying: ²"Everyone of the children of Israel shall camp by his own standard, beside the emblems of his father's house; they shall camp some distance from the tabernacle of meeting. ³On the east side, toward the rising of the sun, those of the standard of the forces with Judah shall camp according to their armies; and Nahshon the son of Amminadab *shall be* the leader of the children of Judah." ⁴And his army was numbered at seventy-four thousand six hundred.

WHAT'S IT MEAN?

The twelve tribes of Israel were divided into four groups of three tribes each. Judah, Issachar, and Zebulun camped on the east side of the tabernacle of meeting. Reuben, Simeon, and Gad camped on the south side. Ephraim, Manasseh, and Benjamin camped on the west side. Dan, Asher, and Naphtali camped on the north side.
Numbers 2:2

⁵"Those who camp next to him *shall be* the tribe of Issachar, and Nethanel the son of Zuar *shall be* the leader of the children of Issachar." ⁶And his army was numbered at fifty-four thousand four hundred.

⁷"Then *comes* the tribe of Zebulun, and Eliab the son of Helon *shall be* the leader of the children of Zebulun." ⁸And his army was numbered at fifty-seven thousand four hundred. ⁹All who were numbered according to their armies of the forces with Judah, one hundred and eighty-six thousand four hundred—these shall break camp first.

¹⁰"On the south side *shall be* the standard of the forces with Reuben according to their armies, and the leader of the children of Reuben *shall be* Elizur the son of Shedeur." ¹¹And his army was numbered at forty-six thousand five hundred.

¹²"Those who camp next to him *shall be* the tribe of Simeon, and the leader of the children of Simeon *shall be* Shelumiel the son of Zurishaddai." ¹³And his army was numbered at fifty-nine thousand three hundred.

¹⁴"Then *comes* the tribe of Gad, and the leader of the children of Gad *shall be* Eliasaph the son of Reuel."[a] ¹⁵And his army was numbered at forty-five thousand six hundred and fifty. ¹⁶All who were numbered according to their armies of the forces with Reuben, one hundred and fifty-one thousand four hundred and fifty—they shall be the second to break camp.

¹⁷"And the tabernacle of meeting shall move out with the camp of the Levites in the middle of the camps; as they camp, so they shall move out, everyone in his place, by their standards.

¹⁸"On the west side *shall be* the standard of the forces with Ephraim according to their armies, and the leader of the children of Ephraim *shall be* Elishama the son of Ammihud." ¹⁹And his army was numbered at forty thousand five hundred.

²⁰"Next to him *comes* the tribe of Manasseh, and the leader of the children of Manasseh *shall be* Gamaliel the son of Pedahzur." ²¹And his army was numbered at thirty-two thousand two hundred.

²²"Then *comes* the tribe of Benjamin, and the leader of the children of Benjamin *shall be* Abidan the son of Gideoni." ²³And his army was numbered at thirty-five thousand four hundred. ²⁴"All who were numbered according to their armies of the forces with Ephraim, one hundred and eight thousand one hundred—they shall be the third to break camp.

²⁵"The standard of the forces with Dan *shall be* on the north side according to their armies, and the leader of the children of Dan *shall be* Ahiezer the son of Ammishaddai." ²⁶And his army was numbered at sixty-two thousand seven hundred.

²⁷"Those who camp next to him *shall be* the tribe of Asher, and the leader of the children of Asher *shall be* Pagiel the son of Ocran." ²⁸And his army was numbered at forty-one thousand five hundred.

²⁹"Then *comes* the tribe of Naphtali, and the leader of the children of Naphtali *shall be* Ahira the son of Enan." ³⁰And his army was numbered at fifty-three thousand four hundred.

³¹"All who were numbered of the forces with Dan, one hundred and fifty-seven thousand six hundred—they shall break camp last, with their standards."

³²These *are* the ones who were numbered of the children of Israel by their fathers' houses. All who were numbered according to their armies of the forces *were* six hundred and three thousand five hundred and fifty. ³³But the Levites were not numbered among the children of Israel, just as the LORD commanded Moses.

³⁴Thus the children of Israel did according to all that the LORD commanded Moses; so they camped by their standards and so they broke camp, each one by his family, according to their fathers' houses.

> "Thus the children of Israel did according to all that the LORD commanded Moses."
> (Numbers 2:34a)

THE SONS OF AARON

¹Now these *are* the records of Aaron and Moses when the LORD spoke with Moses on Mount Sinai. ²And these *are* the names of the sons of Aaron: Nadab, the firstborn, and Abihu, Eleazar, and Ithamar. ³These *are* the names of the sons of Aaron, the anointed priests, whom he consecrated to minister as priests. ⁴Nadab and Abihu had died before the LORD when they offered profane fire before the LORD in the Wilderness of Sinai; and they had no children. So Eleazar and Ithamar ministered as priests in the presence of Aaron their father.

THE LEVITES SERVE IN THE TABERNACLE

⁵And the LORD spoke to Moses, saying: ⁶"Bring the tribe of Levi near, and present them before Aaron the priest, that they may serve him. ⁷And they shall attend to his needs and the needs of the whole congregation before the tabernacle of meeting, to do the work of the tabernacle. ⁸Also they shall attend to all the furnishings of the tabernacle of meeting, and to the needs of the children of Israel, to do the work of the tabernacle. ⁹And you shall give the Levites to Aaron and his sons; they *are* given entirely to him[a] from among the children of Israel. ¹⁰So you shall appoint Aaron and his sons, and they shall attend to their priesthood; but the outsider who comes near shall be put to death."

¹¹Then the LORD spoke to Moses, saying: ¹²"Now behold, I Myself have taken the Levites from among the children of Israel instead of

2:14 [a]Spelled *Deuel* in 1:14 and 7:42   **3:9** [a]Samaritan Pentateuch and Septuagint read *Me.*

every firstborn who opens the womb among the children of Israel. Therefore the Levites shall be Mine, ¹³because all the firstborn *are* Mine. On the day that I struck all the firstborn in the land of Egypt, I sanctified to Myself all the firstborn in Israel, both man and beast. They shall be Mine: I *am* the LORD."

CENSUS OF THE LEVITES COMMANDED

¹⁴Then the LORD spoke to Moses in the Wilderness of Sinai, saying: ¹⁵"Number the children of Levi by their fathers' houses, by their families; you shall number every male from a month old and above."

¹⁶So Moses numbered them according to the word of the LORD, as he was commanded. ¹⁷These were the sons of Levi by their names: Gershon, Kohath, and Merari. ¹⁸And these *are* the names of the sons of Gershon by their families: Libni and Shimei. ¹⁹And the sons of Kohath by their families: Amram, Izehar, Hebron, and Uzziel. ²⁰And the sons of Merari by their families: Mahli and Mushi. These *are* the families of the Levites by their fathers' houses.

²¹From Gershon *came* the family of the Libnites and the family of the Shimites; these *were* the families of the Gershonites. ²²Those who were numbered, according to the number of all the males from a month old and above—of those who were numbered *there were* seven thousand five hundred. ²³The families of the Gershonites were to camp behind the tabernacle westward. ²⁴And the leader of the father's house of the Gershonites *was* Eliasaph the son of Lael. ²⁵The duties of the children of Gershon in the tabernacle of meeting *included* the tabernacle, the tent with its covering, the screen for the door of the tabernacle of meeting, ²⁶the screen for the door of the court, the hangings of the court which *are* around the tabernacle and the altar, and their cords, according to all the work relating to them.

²⁷From Kohath *came* the family of the Amramites, the family of the Izharites, the family of the Hebronites, and the family of the Uzzielites; these *were* the families of the Kohathites. ²⁸According to the number of all the males, from a month old and above, *there were* eight thousand six*ᵃ* hundred keeping charge of the sanctuary. ²⁹The families of the children of Kohath were to camp on the south side of the tabernacle. ³⁰And the leader of the fathers' house of the families of the Kohathites *was* Elizaphan the son of Uzziel. ³¹Their duty *included* the ark, the table, the lampstand, the altars, the utensils of the sanctu-

ary with which they ministered, the screen, and all the work relating to them.

³²And Eleazar the son of Aaron the priest *was to be* chief over the leaders of the Levites, *with* oversight of those who kept charge of the sanctuary.

³³From Merari *came* the family of the Mahlites and the family of the Mushites; these *were* the families of Merari. ³⁴And those who were numbered, according to the number of all the males from a month old and above, *were* six thousand two hundred. ³⁵The leader of the fathers' house of the families of Merari *was* Zuriel the son of Abihail. These *were* to camp on the north side of the tabernacle. ³⁶And the appointed duty of the children of Merari *included* the boards of the tabernacle, its bars, its pillars, its sockets, its utensils, all the work relating to them, ³⁷and the pillars of the court all around, with their sockets, their pegs, and their cords.

³⁸Moreover those who were to camp before the tabernacle on the east, before the tabernacle of meeting, *were* Moses, Aaron, and his sons, keeping charge of the sanctuary, to meet the needs of the children of Israel; but the outsider who came near was to be put to death. ³⁹All who were numbered of the Levites, whom Moses and Aaron numbered at the commandment of the LORD, by their families, all the males from a month old and above, *were* twenty-two thousand.

LEVITES DEDICATED INSTEAD OF THE FIRSTBORN

⁴⁰Then the LORD said to Moses: "Number all the firstborn males of the children of Israel from a month old and above, and take the number of their names. ⁴¹And you shall take the Levites for Me—I *am* the LORD—instead of all the firstborn among the children of Israel, and the livestock of the Levites instead of all the firstborn among the livestock of the children of Israel." ⁴²So Moses numbered all the firstborn among the children of Israel, as the LORD commanded him. ⁴³And all the firstborn males, according to the number of names from a month old and above, of those who were numbered of them, were twenty-two thousand two hundred and seventy-three.

⁴⁴Then the LORD spoke to Moses, saying: ⁴⁵"Take the Levites instead of all the firstborn among the children of Israel, and the livestock of the Levites instead of their livestock. The Levites shall be Mine: I *am* the LORD. ⁴⁶And for the redemption of the two hundred and

3:28 *ᵃ*Some manuscripts of the Septuagint read *three.*

seventy-three of the firstborn of the children of Israel, who are more than the number of the Levites, ⁴⁷you shall take five shekels for each one individually; you shall take *them* in the currency of the shekel of the sanctuary, the shekel of twenty gerahs. ⁴⁸And you shall give the money, with which the excess number of them is redeemed, to Aaron and his sons."

⁴⁹So Moses took the redemption money from those who were over and above those who were redeemed by the Levites. ⁵⁰From the firstborn of the children of Israel he took the money, one thousand three hundred and sixty-five *shekels*, according to the shekel of the sanctuary. ⁵¹And Moses gave their redemption money to Aaron and his sons, according to the word of the LORD, as the LORD commanded Moses.

DUTIES OF THE SONS OF KOHATH

¹Then the LORD spoke to Moses and Aaron, saying: ²"Take a census of the sons of Kohath from among the children of Levi, by their families, by their fathers' house, ³from thirty years old and above, even to fifty years old, all who enter the service to do the work in the tabernacle of meeting.

⁴"This *is* the service of the sons of Kohath in the tabernacle of meeting, *relating to* the most holy things: ⁵When the camp prepares to journey, Aaron and his sons shall come, and they shall take down the covering veil and cover the ark of the Testimony with it. ⁶Then they shall put on it a covering of badger skins, and spread over *that* a cloth entirely of blue; and they shall insert its poles.

⁷"On the table of showbread they shall spread a blue cloth, and put on it the dishes, the pans, the bowls, and the pitchers for pouring; and the showbread*ᵃ* shall be on it. ⁸They shall spread over them a scarlet cloth, and cover the same with a covering of badger skins; and they shall insert its poles. ⁹And they shall take a blue cloth and cover the lampstand of the light, with its lamps, its wick-trimmers, its trays, and all its oil vessels, with which they service it. ¹⁰Then they shall put it with all its utensils in a covering of badger skins, and put *it* on a carrying beam.

¹¹"Over the golden altar they shall spread a blue cloth, and cover it with a covering of badger skins; and they shall insert its poles. ¹²Then they shall take all the utensils of service with which they minister in the sanctuary, put *them* in a blue cloth, cover them with a covering of badger skins, and put *them* on a carrying beam.

¹³Also they shall take away the ashes from the altar, and spread a purple cloth over it. ¹⁴They shall put on it all its implements with which they minister there—the firepans, the forks, the shovels, the basins, and all the utensils of the altar—and they shall spread on it a covering of badger skins, and insert its poles. ¹⁵And when Aaron and his sons have finished covering the sanctuary and all the furnishings of the sanctuary, when the camp is set to go, then the sons of Kohath shall come to carry *them;* but they shall not touch any holy thing, lest they die.

"These *are* the things in the tabernacle of meeting which the sons of Kohath are to carry.

¹⁶"The appointed duty of Eleazar the son of Aaron the priest *is* the oil for the light, the sweet incense, the daily grain offering, the anointing oil, the oversight of all the tabernacle, of all that *is* in it, with the sanctuary and its furnishings."

¹⁷Then the LORD spoke to Moses and Aaron, saying: ¹⁸"Do not cut off the tribe of the families of the Kohathites from among the Levites; ¹⁹but do this in regard to them, that they may live and not die when they approach the most holy things: Aaron and his sons shall go in and appoint each of them to his service and his task. ²⁰But they shall not go in to watch while the holy things are being covered, lest they die."

DUTIES OF THE SONS OF GERSHON

²¹Then the LORD spoke to Moses, saying: ²²"Also take a census of the sons of Gershon, by their fathers' house, by their families. ²³From thirty years old and above, even to fifty years old, you shall number them, all who enter to perform the service, to do the work in the tabernacle of meeting. ²⁴This *is* the service of the families of the Gershonites, in serving and carrying: ²⁵They shall carry the curtains of the tabernacle and the tabernacle of meeting *with* its covering, the covering of badger skins that *is* on it, the screen for the door of the tabernacle of meeting, ²⁶the screen for the door of the gate of the court, the hangings of the court which *are* around the tabernacle and altar, and their cords, all the furnishings for their service and all that is made for these things: so shall they serve.

²⁷"Aaron and his sons shall assign all the service of the sons of the Gershonites, all their tasks and all their service. And you shall appoint to them all their tasks as their duty. ²⁸This *is* the service of the families of the sons of Gershon in the tabernacle of meeting. And their duties *shall be* under the authority*ᵃ* of Ithamar the son of Aaron the priest.

4:7 *ᵃLiterally the continual bread*   **4:28** *ᵃLiterally hand*

DUTIES OF THE SONS OF MERARI

29"As for the sons of Merari, you shall number them by their families and by their fathers' house. 30From thirty years old and above, even to fifty years old, you shall number them, everyone who enters the service to do the work of the tabernacle of meeting. 31And this is what they must carry as all their service for the tabernacle of meeting: the boards of the tabernacle, its bars, its pillars, its sockets, 32and the pillars around the court with their sockets, pegs, and cords, with all their furnishings and all their service; and you shall assign to each man by name the items he must carry. 33This is the service of the families of the sons of Merari, as all their service for the tabernacle of meeting, under the authority*a* of Ithamar the son of Aaron the priest."

CENSUS OF THE LEVITES

34And Moses, Aaron, and the leaders of the congregation numbered the sons of the Kohathites by their families and by their fathers' house, 35from thirty years old and above, even to fifty years old, everyone who entered the service for work in the tabernacle of meeting; 36and those who were numbered by their families were two thousand seven hundred and fifty. 37These were the ones who were numbered of the families of the Kohathites, all who might serve in the tabernacle of meeting, whom Moses and Aaron numbered according to the commandment of the LORD by the hand of Moses.

38And those who were numbered of the sons of Gershon, by their families and by their fathers' house, 39from thirty years old and above, even to fifty years old, everyone who entered the service for work in the tabernacle of meeting— 40those who were numbered by their families, by their fathers' house, were two thousand six hundred and thirty. 41These are the ones who were numbered of the families of the sons of Gershon, of all who might serve in the tabernacle of meeting, whom Moses and Aaron numbered according to the commandment of the LORD.

42Those of the families of the sons of Merari who were numbered, by their families, by their fathers' house, 43from thirty years old and above, even to fifty years old, everyone who entered the service for work in the tabernacle of meeting— 44those who were numbered by their families were three thousand two hundred. 45These are the ones who were numbered of the families of the sons of Merari, whom Moses and Aaron numbered according to the word of the LORD by the hand of Moses.

46All who were numbered of the Levites, whom Moses, Aaron, and the leaders of Israel numbered, by their families and by their fathers' houses, 47from thirty years old and above, even to fifty years old, everyone who came to do the work of service and the work of bearing burdens in the tabernacle of meeting— 48those who were numbered were eight thousand five hundred and eighty.

49According to the commandment of the LORD they were numbered by the hand of Moses, each according to his service and according to his task; thus were they numbered by him, as the LORD commanded Moses.

CEREMONIALLY UNCLEAN PERSONS ISOLATED

1And the LORD spoke to Moses, saying: 2"Command the children of Israel that they put out of the camp every leper, everyone who has a discharge, and whoever becomes defiled by a corpse. 3You shall put out both male and female; you shall put them outside the camp, that they may not defile their camps in the midst of which I dwell." 4And the children of Israel did so, and put them outside the camp; as the LORD spoke to Moses, so the children of Israel did.

CONFESSION AND RESTITUTION

5Then the LORD spoke to Moses, saying, 6"Speak to the children of Israel: 'When a man or woman commits any sin that men commit in unfaithfulness against the LORD, and that person is guilty, 7then he shall confess the sin which he has committed. He shall make restitution for his trespass in full, plus one-fifth of it, and give it to the one he has wronged. 8But if the man has no relative to whom restitution may be made for the wrong, the restitution for the wrong must go to the LORD for the priest, in addition to the ram of the atonement with which atonement is made for him. 9Every offering of all the holy things of the children of Israel, which they bring to the priest, shall be his. 10And every man's holy things shall be his; whatever any man gives the priest shall be his.' "

CONCERNING UNFAITHFUL WIVES

11And the LORD spoke to Moses, saying, 12"Speak to the children of Israel, and say to them: 'If any man's wife goes astray and behaves unfaithfully toward him, 13and a man lies with her carnally, and it is hidden from the eyes of her husband, and it is concealed that she has defiled herself, and *there was* no witness against her, nor was she caught— [14]if the spirit of jealousy comes upon him and he becomes jealous of his wife, who has defiled herself; or if the spirit of jealousy comes upon him and he becomes jealous of his wife, although she has not defiled herself— [15]then the man shall bring his wife to the priest. He shall bring the offering required for her, one-tenth of an ephah of barley meal; he shall pour no oil on it and put no frankincense on it, because it *is* a grain offering of jealousy, an offering for remembering, for bringing iniquity to remembrance.

WHAT'S IT MEAN?

This unusual testing process, also known as an "ordeal," was commonly used in ancient times to determine whether a person was innocent or guilty. The outcome of the ordeal was considered to be God's judgment.

Numbers 5:11–22

[16]'And the priest shall bring her near, and set her before the LORD. [17]The priest shall take holy water in an earthen vessel, and take some of the dust that is on the floor of the tabernacle and put *it* into the water. [18]Then the priest shall stand the woman before the LORD, uncover the woman's head, and put the offering for remembering in her hands, which *is* the grain offering of jealousy. And the priest shall have in his hand the bitter water that brings a curse. [19]And the priest shall put her under oath, and say to the woman, "If no man has lain with you, and if you have not gone astray to uncleanness *while* under your husband's *authority*, be free from this bitter water that brings a curse. [20]But if you have gone astray *while* under your husband's *authority*, and if you have defiled yourself and some man other than your husband has lain with you"— [21]then the priest shall put the woman under the oath of the curse, and he shall say to the woman—"the LORD make you a curse and an oath among your people, when the LORD makes your thigh rot and your belly swell; [22]and may this water that causes the curse go into your stomach, and make *your* belly swell and *your* thigh rot."

Then the woman shall say, "Amen, so be it." [23]Then the priest shall write these curses in a book, and he shall scrape *them* off into the bitter water. [24]And he shall make the woman drink the bitter water that brings a curse, and the water that brings the curse shall enter her *to become* bitter. [25]Then the priest shall take the grain offering of jealousy from the woman's hand, shall wave the offering before the LORD, and bring it to the altar; [26]and the priest shall take a handful of the offering, as its memorial portion, burn *it* on the altar, and afterward make the woman drink the water. [27]When he has made her drink the water, then it shall be, if she has defiled herself and behaved unfaithfully toward her husband, that the water that brings a curse will enter her *and become* bitter, and her belly will swell, her thigh will rot, and the woman will become a curse among her people. [28]But if the woman has not defiled herself, and is clean, then she shall be free and may conceive children.

[29]'This *is* the law of jealousy, when a wife, *while* under her husband's *authority*, goes astray and defiles herself, [30]or when the spirit of jealousy comes upon a man, and he becomes jealous of his wife; then he shall stand the woman before the LORD, and the priest shall execute all this law upon her. [31]Then the man shall be free from iniquity, but that woman shall bear her guilt.' "

THE LAW OF THE NAZIRITE

[1]Then the LORD spoke to Moses, saying, [2]"Speak to the children of Israel, and say to them: 'When either a man or woman consecrates an offering to take the vow of a Nazirite, to separate himself to the LORD, [3]he shall separate himself from wine and *similar* drink; he shall drink neither vinegar made from wine nor vinegar made from *similar* drink; neither shall he drink any grape juice, nor eat fresh grapes or raisins. [4]All the days of his separation he shall eat nothing that is produced by the grapevine, from seed to skin.

[5]'All the days of the vow of his separation no razor shall come upon his head; until the days are fulfilled for which he separated himself to the LORD, he shall be holy. *Then* he shall let the locks of the hair of his head grow. [6]All the days that he separates himself to the LORD he shall not go near a dead body. [7]He shall not make himself unclean even for his father or his mother, for his brother or his sister, when they die, because his separation to God *is* on his head. [8]All the days of his separation he shall be holy to the LORD.

⁹"And if anyone dies very suddenly beside him, and he defiles his consecrated head, then he shall shave his head on the day of his cleansing; on the seventh day he shall shave it. ¹⁰Then on the eighth day he shall bring two turtledoves or two young pigeons to the priest, to the door of the tabernacle of meeting; ¹¹and the priest shall offer one as a sin offering and *the* other as a burnt offering, and make atonement for him, because he sinned in regard to the corpse; and he shall sanctify his head that same day. ¹²He shall consecrate to the LORD the days of his separation, and bring a male lamb in its first year as a trespass offering; but the former days shall be lost, because his separation was defiled.

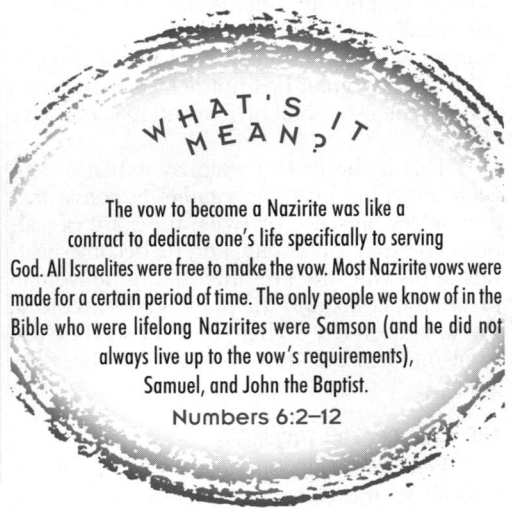

WHAT'S IT MEAN?

The vow to become a Nazirite was like a contract to dedicate one's life specifically to serving God. All Israelites were free to make the vow. Most Nazirite vows were made for a certain period of time. The only people we know of in the Bible who were lifelong Nazirites were Samson (and he did not always live up to the vow's requirements), Samuel, and John the Baptist.

Numbers 6:2–12

¹³'Now this *is* the law of the Nazirite: When the days of his separation are fulfilled, he shall be brought to the door of the tabernacle of meeting. ¹⁴And he shall present his offering to the LORD: one male lamb in its first year without blemish as a burnt offering, one ewe lamb in its first year without blemish as a sin offering, one ram without blemish as a peace offering, ¹⁵a basket of unleavened bread, cakes of fine flour mixed with oil, unleavened wafers anointed with oil, and their grain offering with their drink offerings.

¹⁶'Then the priest shall bring *them* before the LORD and offer his sin offering and his burnt offering; ¹⁷and he shall offer the ram as a sacrifice of a peace offering to the LORD, with the basket of unleavened bread; the priest shall also offer its grain offering and its drink offering. ¹⁸Then the Nazirite shall shave his consecrated head *at* the door of the tabernacle of meeting, and shall take the hair from his consecrated

head and put *it* on the fire which is under the sacrifice of the peace offering.

¹⁹'And the priest shall take the boiled shoulder of the ram, one unleavened cake from the basket, and one unleavened wafer, and put *them* upon the hands of the Nazirite after he has shaved his consecrated *hair*, ²⁰and the priest shall wave them as a wave offering before the LORD; they *are* holy for the priest, together with the breast of the wave offering and the thigh of the heave offering. After that the Nazirite may drink wine.'

²¹"This is the law of the Nazirite who vows to the LORD the offering for his separation, and besides that, whatever else his hand is able to provide; according to the vow which he takes, so he must do according to the law of his separation."

THE PRIESTLY BLESSING

²²And the LORD spoke to Moses, saying: ²³"Speak to Aaron and his sons, saying, 'This is the way you shall bless the children of Israel. Say to them:

24   "The LORD bless you and keep you;
25   The LORD make His face shine upon you,
       And be gracious to you;
26   The LORD lift up His countenance upon
          you,
       And give you peace." '

²⁷"So they shall put My name on the children of Israel, and I will bless them."

OFFERINGS OF THE LEADERS

¹Now it came to pass, when Moses had finished setting up the tabernacle, that he anointed it and consecrated it and all its furnishings, and the altar and all its utensils; so he anointed them and consecrated them. ²Then the leaders of Israel, the heads of their fathers' houses, who *were* the leaders of the tribes and over those who were numbered, made an offering. ³And they brought their offering before the LORD, six covered carts and twelve oxen, a cart for *every* two of the leaders, and for each one an ox; and they presented them before the tabernacle.

⁴Then the LORD spoke to Moses, saying, ⁵"Accept *these* from them, that they may be used in doing the work of the tabernacle of meeting; and you shall give them to the Levites, *to* every man according to his service." ⁶So Moses took the carts and the oxen, and gave them to the Levites. ⁷Two carts and four oxen he gave to the sons of Gershon, according to their service; ⁸and four carts and eight oxen he gave to the

sons of Merari, according to their service, under the authority[a] of Ithamar the son of Aaron the priest. [9]But to the sons of Kohath he gave none, because theirs *was* the service of the holy things, *which* they carried on their shoulders.

[10]Now the leaders offered the dedication *offering* for the altar when it was anointed; so the leaders offered their offering before the altar. [11]For the LORD said to Moses, "They shall offer their offering, one leader each day, for the dedication of the altar."

[12]And the one who offered his offering on the first day *was* Nahshon the son of Amminadab, from the tribe of Judah. [13]His offering *was* one silver platter, the weight of which *was* one hundred and thirty *shekels*, and one silver bowl of seventy shekels, according to the shekel of the sanctuary, both of them full of fine flour mixed with oil as a grain offering; [14]one gold pan of ten *shekels*, full of incense; [15]one young bull, one ram, and one male lamb in its first year, as a burnt offering; [16]one kid of the goats as a sin offering; [17]and for the sacrifice of peace offerings: two oxen, five rams, five male goats, and five male lambs in their first year. This *was* the offering of Nahshon the son of Amminadab.

[18]On the second day Nethanel the son of Zuar, leader of Issachar, presented *an offering*. [19]*For* his offering he offered one silver platter, the weight of which *was* one hundred and thirty *shekels*, and one silver bowl of seventy shekels, according to the shekel of the sanctuary, both of them full of fine flour mixed with oil as a grain offering; [20]one gold pan of ten *shekels*, full of incense; [21]one young bull, one ram, and one male lamb in its first year, as a burnt offering; [22]one kid of the goats as a sin offering; [23]and as the sacrifice of peace offerings: two oxen, five rams, five male goats, and five male lambs in their first year. This *was* the offering of Nethanel the son of Zuar.

[24]On the third day Eliab the son of Helon, leader of the children of Zebulun, *presented an offering*. [25]His offering *was* one silver platter, the weight of which *was* one hundred and thirty *shekels*, and one silver bowl of seventy shekels, according to the shekel of the sanctuary, both of them full of fine flour mixed with oil as a grain offering; [26]one gold pan of ten *shekels*, full of incense; [27]one young bull, one ram, and one male lamb in its first year, as a burnt offering;

"The LORD bless you and keep you; . . ."
(Numbers 6:24–26)

[28]one kid of the goats as a sin offering; [29]and for the sacrifice of peace offerings: two oxen, five rams, five male goats, and five male lambs in their first year. This *was* the offering of Eliab the son of Helon.

[30]On the fourth day Elizur the son of Shedeur, leader of the children of Reuben, *presented an offering*. [31]His offering *was* one silver platter, the weight of which *was* one hundred and thirty *shekels*, and one silver bowl of seventy shekels, according to the shekel of the sanctuary, both of them full of fine flour mixed with oil as a grain offering; [32]one gold pan of ten *shekels*, full of incense; [33]one young bull, one ram, and one male lamb in its first year, as a burnt offering; [34]one kid of the goats as a sin offering; [35]and as the sacrifice of peace offerings: two oxen, five rams, five male goats, and five male lambs in their first year. This *was* the offering of Elizur the son of Shedeur.

[36]On the fifth day Shelumiel the son of Zurishaddai, leader of the children of Simeon, *presented an offering*. [37]His offering *was* one silver platter, the weight of which *was* one hundred and thirty *shekels*, and one silver bowl of seventy shekels, according to the shekel of the sanctuary, both of them full of fine flour mixed with oil as a grain offering; [38]one gold pan of ten *shekels*, full of incense; [39]one young bull, one ram, and one male lamb in its first year, as a burnt offering; [40]one kid of the goats as a sin offering; [41]and as the sacrifice of peace offerings: two oxen, five rams, five male goats, and five male lambs in their first year. This *was* the offering of Shelumiel the son of Zurishaddai.

[42]On the sixth day Eliasaph the son of Deuel,[a] leader of the children of Gad, *presented an offering*. [43]His offering *was* one silver platter, the weight of which *was* one hundred and thirty *shekels*, and one silver bowl of seventy shekels, according to the shekel of the sanctuary, both of them full of fine flour mixed with oil as a grain offering; [44]one gold pan of ten *shekels*, full of incense; [45]one young bull, one ram, and one male lamb in its first year, as a burnt offering; [46]one kid of the goats as a sin offering; [47]and as the sacrifice of peace offerings: two oxen, five rams, five male goats, and five male lambs in their first year. This *was* the offering of Eliasaph the son of Deuel.

[48]On the seventh day Elishama the son of

7:8 [a]Literally *hand*   **7:42** [a]Spelled *Reuel* in 2:14

Ammihud, leader of the children of Ephraim, *presented an offering.* [49]His offering *was* one silver platter, the weight of which *was* one hundred and thirty *shekels,* and one silver bowl of seventy shekels, according to the shekel of the sanctuary, both of them full of fine flour mixed with oil as a grain offering; [50]one gold pan of ten *shekels,* full of incense; [51]one young bull, one ram, and one male lamb in its first year, as a burnt offering; [52]one kid of the goats as a sin offering; [53]and as the sacrifice of peace offerings: two oxen, five rams, five male goats, and five male lambs in their first year. This *was* the offering of Elishama the son of Ammihud.

[54]On the eighth day Gamaliel the son of Pedahzur, leader of the children of Manasseh, *presented an offering.* [55]His offering *was* one silver platter, the weight of which *was* one hundred and thirty *shekels,* and one silver bowl of seventy shekels, according to the shekel of the sanctuary, both of them full of fine flour mixed with oil as a grain offering; [56]one gold pan of ten *shekels,* full of incense; [57]one young bull, one ram, and one male lamb in its first year, as a burnt offering; [58]one kid of the goats as a sin offering; [59]and as the sacrifice of peace offerings: two oxen, five rams, five male goats, and five male lambs in their first year. This *was* the offering of Gamaliel the son of Pedahzur.

[60]On the ninth day Abidan the son of Gideoni, leader of the children of Benjamin, *presented an offering.* [61]His offering *was* one silver platter, the weight of which *was* one hundred and thirty *shekels,* and one silver bowl of seventy shekels, according to the shekel of the sanctuary, both of them full of fine flour mixed with oil as a grain offering; [62]one gold pan of ten *shekels,* full of incense; [63]one young bull, one ram, and one male lamb in its first year, as a burnt offering; [64]one kid of the goats as a sin offering; [65]and as the sacrifice of peace offerings: two oxen, five rams, five male goats, and five male lambs in their first year. This *was* the offering of Abidan the son of Gideoni.

[66]On the tenth day Ahiezer the son of Ammishaddai, leader of the children of Dan, *presented an offering.* [67]His offering *was* one silver platter, the weight of which *was* one hundred and thirty *shekels,* and one silver bowl of seventy shekels, according to the shekel of the sanctuary, both of them full of fine flour mixed with oil as a grain offering; [68]one gold pan of ten *shekels,* full of incense; [69]one young bull, one ram, and one male lamb in its first year, as a burnt offering; [70]one kid of the goats as a sin offering; [71]and as the sacrifice of peace offerings: two oxen, five rams, five male goats, and five male lambs in their first year. This *was* the offering of Ahiezer the son of Ammishaddai.

[72]On the eleventh day Pagiel the son of Ocran, leader of the children of Asher, *presented an offering.* [73]His offering *was* one silver platter, the weight of which *was* one hundred and thirty *shekels,* and one silver bowl of seventy shekels, according to the shekel of the sanctuary, both of them full of fine flour mixed with oil as a grain offering; [74]one gold pan of ten *shekels,* full of incense; [75]one young bull, one ram, and one male lamb in its first year, as a burnt offering; [76]one kid of the goats as a sin offering; [77]and as the sacrifice of peace offerings: two oxen, five rams, five male goats, and five male lambs in their first year. This *was* the offering of Pagiel the son of Ocran.

[78]On the twelfth day Ahira the son of Enan, leader of the children of Naphtali, *presented an offering.* [79]His offering *was* one silver platter, the weight of which *was* one hundred and thirty *shekels,* and one silver bowl of seventy shekels, according to the shekel of the sanctuary, both of them full of fine flour mixed with oil as a grain offering; [80]one gold pan of ten *shekels,* full of incense; [81]one young bull, one ram, and one male lamb in its first year, as a burnt offering; [82]one kid of the goats as a sin offering; [83]and as the sacrifice of peace offerings: two oxen, five rams, five male goats, and five male lambs in their first year. This *was* the offering of Ahira the son of Enan.

[84]This *was* the dedication *offering* for the altar from the leaders of Israel, when it was anointed: twelve silver platters, twelve silver bowls, and twelve gold pans. [85]Each silver platter *weighed* one hundred and thirty *shekels* and each bowl seventy *shekels.* All the silver of the vessels *weighed* two thousand four hundred *shekels,* according to the shekel of the sanctuary. [86]The twelve gold pans full of incense *weighed* ten *shekels* apiece, according to the shekel of the sanctuary; all the gold of the pans *weighed* one hundred and twenty *shekels.* [87]All the oxen for the burnt offering *were* twelve young bulls, the rams twelve, the male lambs in their first year twelve, with their grain offering, and the kids of the goats as a sin offering twelve. [88]And all the oxen for the sacrifice of peace offerings were twenty-four bulls, the rams sixty, the male goats sixty, and the lambs in their first year sixty. This *was* the dedication *offering* for the altar after it was anointed.

[89]Now when Moses went into the tabernacle of meeting to speak with Him, he heard the voice of One speaking to him from above the mercy seat that *was* on the ark of the Testi-

mony, from between the two cherubim; thus He spoke to him.

WHAT'S IT MEAN?

God spoke to Moses from His earthly throne, which was located between the two winged figures (cherubim) on the lid of the ark of the Testimony. The "mercy seat" is another name for God's throne.

Numbers 7:89

ARRANGEMENT OF THE LAMPS

¹And the LORD spoke to Moses, saying: ²"Speak to Aaron, and say to him, 'When you arrange the lamps, the seven lamps shall give light in front of the lampstand.' " ³And Aaron did so; he arranged the lamps to face toward the front of the lampstand, as the LORD commanded Moses. ⁴Now this workmanship of the lampstand *was* hammered gold; from its shaft to its flowers it *was* hammered work. According to the pattern which the LORD had shown Moses, so he made the lampstand.

CLEANSING AND DEDICATION OF THE LEVITES

⁵Then the LORD spoke to Moses, saying: ⁶"Take the Levites from among the children of Israel and cleanse them *ceremonially.* ⁷Thus you shall do to them to cleanse them: Sprinkle water of purification on them, and let them shave all their body, and let them wash their clothes, and *so* make themselves clean. ⁸Then let them take a young bull with its grain offering of fine flour mixed with oil, and you shall take another young bull as a sin offering. ⁹And you shall bring the Levites before the tabernacle of meeting, and you shall gather together the whole congregation of the children of Israel. ¹⁰So you shall bring the Levites before the LORD, and the children of Israel shall lay their hands on the Levites; ¹¹and Aaron shall offer the Levites before the LORD *like* a wave offering from the children of Israel, that they may perform the work of the LORD. ¹²Then the Levites shall lay their hands on the heads of the young bulls, and you

shall offer one as a sin offering and the other as a burnt offering to the LORD, to make atonement for the Levites.

¹³"And you shall stand the Levites before Aaron and his sons, and then offer them *like* a wave offering to the LORD. ¹⁴Thus you shall separate the Levites from among the children of Israel, and the Levites shall be Mine. ¹⁵After that the Levites shall go in to service the tabernacle of meeting. So you shall cleanse them and offer them *like* a wave offering. ¹⁶For they *are* wholly given to Me from among the children of Israel; I have taken them for Myself instead of all who open the womb, the firstborn of all the children of Israel. ¹⁷For all the firstborn among the children of Israel *are* Mine, *both* man and beast; on the day that I struck all the firstborn in the land of Egypt I sanctified them to Myself. ¹⁸I have taken the Levites instead of all the firstborn of the children of Israel. ¹⁹And I have given the Levites as a gift to Aaron and his sons from among the children of Israel, to do the work for the children of Israel in the tabernacle of meeting, and to make atonement for the children of Israel, that there be no plague among the children of Israel when the children of Israel come near the sanctuary."

²⁰Thus Moses and Aaron and all the congregation of the children of Israel did to the Levites; according to all that the LORD commanded Moses concerning the Levites, so the children of Israel did to them. ²¹And the Levites purified themselves and washed their clothes; then Aaron presented them *like* a wave offering before the LORD, and Aaron made atonement for them to cleanse them. ²²After that the Levites went in to do their work in the tabernacle of meeting before Aaron and his sons; as the LORD commanded Moses concerning the Levites, so they did to them.

²³Then the LORD spoke to Moses, saying, ²⁴"This *is* what *pertains* to the Levites: From twenty-five years old and above one may enter to perform service in the work of the tabernacle of meeting; ²⁵and at the age of fifty years they must cease performing this work, and shall work no more. ²⁶They may minister with their brethren in the tabernacle of meeting, to attend to needs, but they *themselves* shall do no work. Thus you shall do to the Levites regarding their duties."

THE SECOND PASSOVER

¹Now the LORD spoke to Moses in the Wilderness of Sinai, in the first month of the second year after they had come out of the land of Egypt, saying: ²"Let the children of Israel keep

the Passover at its appointed time. ³On the fourteenth day of this month, at twilight, you shall keep it at its appointed time. According to all its rites and ceremonies you shall keep it." ⁴So Moses told the children of Israel that they should keep the Passover. ⁵And they kept the Passover on the fourteenth day of the first month, at twilight, in the Wilderness of Sinai; according to all that the LORD commanded Moses, so the children of Israel did.

⁶Now there were *certain* men who were defiled by a human corpse, so that they could not keep the Passover on that day; and they came before Moses and Aaron that day. ⁷And those men said to him, "We *became* defiled by a human corpse. Why are we kept from presenting the offering of the LORD at its appointed time among the children of Israel?"

⁸And Moses said to them, "Stand still, that I may hear what the LORD will command concerning you."

⁹Then the LORD spoke to Moses, saying, ¹⁰"Speak to the children of Israel, saying: 'If anyone of you or your posterity is unclean because of a corpse, or *is* far away on a journey, he may still keep the LORD's Passover. ¹¹On the fourteenth day of the second month, at twilight, they may keep it. They shall eat it with unleavened bread and bitter herbs. ¹²They shall leave none of it until morning, nor break one of its bones. According to all the ordinances of the Passover they shall keep it. ¹³But the man who *is* clean and is not on a journey, and ceases to keep the Passover, that same person shall be cut off from among his people, because he did not bring the offering of the LORD at its appointed time; that man shall bear his sin.

¹⁴'And if a stranger dwells among you, and would keep the LORD's Passover, he must do so according to the rite of the Passover and according to its ceremony; you shall have one ordinance, both for the stranger and the native of the land.' "

THE CLOUD AND THE FIRE

¹⁵Now on the day that the tabernacle was raised up, the cloud covered the tabernacle, the tent of the Testimony; from evening until morning it was above the tabernacle like the appearance of fire. ¹⁶So it was always: the cloud covered it *by day*, and the appearance of fire by night. ¹⁷Whenever the cloud was taken up from above the tabernacle, after that the children of Israel would journey; and in the place where the cloud settled, there the children of Israel would pitch their tents. ¹⁸At the command of the LORD the children of Israel would journey,

and at the command of the LORD they would camp; as long as the cloud stayed above the tabernacle they remained encamped. ¹⁹Even when the cloud continued long, many days above the tabernacle, the children of Israel kept the charge of the LORD and did not journey. ²⁰So it was, when the cloud was above the tabernacle a few days: according to the command of the LORD they would remain encamped, and according to the command of the LORD they would journey. ²¹So it was, when the cloud remained only from evening until morning: when the cloud was taken up in the morning, then they would journey; whether by day or by night, whenever the cloud was taken up, they would journey. ²²Whether *it was* two days, a month, or a year that the cloud remained above the tabernacle, the children of Israel would remain encamped and not journey; but when it was taken up, they would journey. ²³At the command of the LORD they remained encamped, and at the command of the LORD they journeyed; they kept the charge of the LORD, at the command of the LORD by the hand of Moses.

TWO SILVER TRUMPETS

¹And the LORD spoke to Moses, saying: ²"Make two silver trumpets for yourself; you shall make them of hammered work; you shall use them for calling the congregation and for directing the movement of the camps. ³When they blow both of them, all the congregation shall gather before you at the door of the tabernacle of meeting. ⁴But if they blow *only* one, then the leaders, the heads of the divisions of Israel, shall gather to you. ⁵When you sound the advance, the camps that lie on the east side shall then begin their journey. ⁶When you

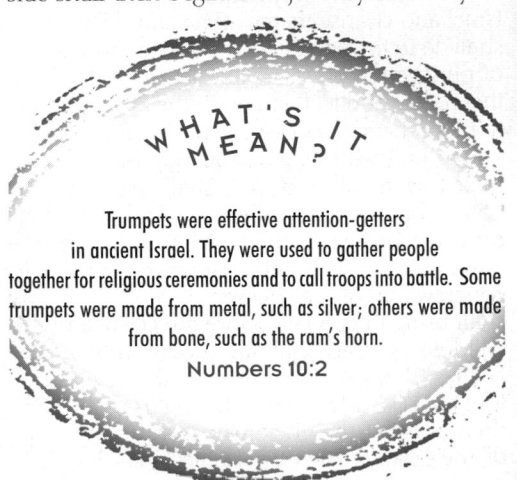

WHAT'S IT MEAN?

Trumpets were effective attention-getters in ancient Israel. They were used to gather people together for religious ceremonies and to call troops into battle. Some trumpets were made from metal, such as silver; others were made from bone, such as the ram's horn.

Numbers 10:2

sound the advance the second time, then the camps that lie on the south side shall begin their journey; they shall sound the call for them to begin their journeys. [7]And when the assembly is to be gathered together, you shall blow, but not sound the advance. [8]The sons of Aaron, the priests, shall blow the trumpets; and these shall be to you as an ordinance forever throughout your generations.

[9]"When you go to war in your land against the enemy who oppresses you, then you shall sound an alarm with the trumpets, and you will be remembered before the LORD your God, and you will be saved from your enemies. [10]Also in the day of your gladness, in your appointed feasts, and at the beginning of your months, you shall blow the trumpets over your burnt offerings and over the sacrifices of your peace offerings; and they shall be a memorial for you before your God: I am the LORD your God."

DEPARTURE FROM SINAI

[11]Now it came to pass on the twentieth day of the second month, in the second year, that the cloud was taken up from above the tabernacle of the Testimony. [12]And the children of Israel set out from the Wilderness of Sinai on their journeys; then the cloud settled down in the Wilderness of Paran. [13]So they started out for the first time according to the command of the LORD by the hand of Moses.

[14]The standard of the camp of the children of Judah set out first according to their armies; over their army was Nahshon the son of Amminadab. [15]Over the army of the tribe of the children of Issachar was Nethanel the son of Zuar. [16]And over the army of the tribe of the children of Zebulun was Eliab the son of Helon.

[17]Then the tabernacle was taken down; and the sons of Gershon and the sons of Merari set out, carrying the tabernacle.

[18]And the standard of the camp of Reuben set out according to their armies; over their army was Elizur the son of Shedeur. [19]Over the army of the tribe of the children of Simeon was Shelumiel the son of Zurishaddai. [20]And over the army of the tribe of the children of Gad was Eliasaph the son of Deuel.

[21]Then the Kohathites set out, carrying the holy things. (The tabernacle would be prepared for their arrival.)

[22]And the standard of the camp of the children of Ephraim set out according to their armies; over their army was Elishama the son of Ammihud. [23]Over the army of the tribe of the children of Manasseh was Gamaliel the son of Pedahzur. [24]And over the army of the tribe of the children of Benjamin was Abidan the son of Gideoni.

[25]Then the standard of the camp of the children of Dan (the rear guard of all the camps) set out according to their armies; over their army was Ahiezer the son of Ammishaddai. [26]Over the army of the tribe of the children of Asher was Pagiel the son of Ocran. [27]And over the army of the tribe of the children of Naphtali was Ahira the son of Enan.

[28]Thus was the order of march of the children of Israel, according to their armies, when they began their journey.

[29]Now Moses said to Hobab the son of Reuel[a] the Midianite, Moses' father-in-law, "We are setting out for the place of which the LORD said, 'I will give it to you.' Come with us, and we will treat you well; for the LORD has promised good things to Israel."

[30]And he said to him, "I will not go, but I will depart to my own land and to my relatives."

[31]So Moses said, "Please do not leave, inasmuch as you know how we are to camp in the wilderness, and you can be our eyes. [32]And it shall be, if you go with us—indeed it shall be—that whatever good the LORD will do to us, the same we will do to you."

[33]So they departed from the mountain of the LORD on a journey of three days; and the ark of the covenant of the LORD went before them for the three days' journey, to search out a resting place for them. [34]And the cloud of the LORD was above them by day when they went out from the camp.

[35]So it was, whenever the ark set out, that Moses said:

> "Rise up, O LORD!
> Let Your enemies be scattered,
> And let those who hate You flee before You."

[36]And when it rested, he said:

"Rise up, O LORD! Let Your enemies be scattered, and let those who hate You flee before You."
(Numbers 10:35b)

10:29 [a]Septuagint reads Raguel (compare Exodus 2:18).

"Return, O LORD,
To the many thousands of Israel."

THE PEOPLE COMPLAIN

[1]Now *when* the people complained, it displeased the LORD; for the LORD heard *it*, and His anger was aroused. So the fire of the LORD burned among them, and consumed *some* in the outskirts of the camp. [2]Then the people cried out to Moses, and when Moses prayed to the LORD, the fire was quenched. [3]So he called the name of the place Taberah,[a] because the fire of the LORD had burned among them.

[4]Now the mixed multitude who were among them yielded to intense craving; so the children of Israel also wept again and said: "Who will give us meat to eat? [5]We remember the fish which we ate freely in Egypt, the cucumbers, the melons, the leeks, the onions, and the garlic; [6]but now our whole being *is* dried up; *there is* nothing at all except this manna *before* our eyes!"

[7]Now the manna *was* like coriander seed, and its color like the color of bdellium. [8]The people went about and gathered *it*, ground *it* on millstones or beat *it* in the mortar, cooked *it* in pans, and made cakes of it; and its taste was like the taste of pastry prepared with oil. [9]And when the dew fell on the camp in the night, the manna fell on it.

[10]Then Moses heard the people weeping throughout their families, everyone at the door of his tent; and the anger of the LORD was greatly aroused; Moses also was displeased. [11]So Moses said to the LORD, "Why have You afflicted Your servant? And why have I not found favor in Your sight, that You have laid the burden of all these people on me? [12]Did I conceive all these people? Did I beget them, that You should say to me, 'Carry them in your bosom, as a guardian carries a nursing child', to the land which You swore to their fathers? [13]Where am I to get meat to give to all these people? For they weep all over me, saying, 'Give us meat, that we may eat'. [14]I am not able to bear all these people alone, because the burden *is* too heavy for me. [15]If You treat me like this, please kill me here and now—if I have found favor in Your sight—and do not let me see my wretchedness!"

11:3 [a]Literally *Burning*

·:·: Promise   HE PROMISES THAT HE CAN DO ANYTHING.

And the LORD said to Moses, "Has the LORD's arm been shortened? Now you shall see whether what I say will happen to you or not" (Num. 11:23).

This is a powerful chapter! It starts out with the Israelites complaining about their troubles. They were grumbling to Moses that they didn't have any meat to eat. They complained that they had all the fish they wanted in Egypt and that they were sick of having only manna to eat. God heard their cry and told Moses to tell them to purify themselves because He was going to send meat. Moses replied by asking God how such a feat was possible because there were 600,000 men alone to feed. Moses knew that all the meat from their animals wouldn't be enough to feed them. That's when the Lord replied, "Has the LORD's arm been shortened? " In other words, "I can do anything!"

Let this verse encourage you today. Nothing is beyond reach with God on your side, because He is the One who can do anything. What's your need today? Do you need a miracle? He's just waiting for you to bring that need to Him.

In 2 Peter 1:3 God promises to give us "all things that pertain to life and godliness" to live a life that pleases Him. That includes things that pertain to our spiritual, physical, emotional, financial, and other needs. In fact, if something affects you, God wants to be right there. He is El Shaddai—the God who is more than enough! He is bigger than any problem you can encounter. Begin to seek Him first and watch Him give you everything you need. He promises that He can do anything!

SEE FOR YOURSELF:
Matt. 19:26; Mark 9:23; 10:27; Luke 18:27;
Rom. 8:32

THE SEVENTY ELDERS

16So the LORD said to Moses: "Gather to Me seventy men of the elders of Israel, whom you know to be the elders of the people and officers over them; bring them to the tabernacle of meeting, that they may stand there with you. 17Then I will come down and talk with you there. I will take of the Spirit that *is* upon you and will put *the same* upon them; and they shall bear the burden of the people with you, that you may not bear *it* yourself alone. 18Then you shall say to the people, 'Consecrate yourselves for tomorrow, and you shall eat meat; for you have wept in the hearing of the LORD, saying, "Who will give us meat to eat? For *it was* well with us in Egypt." Therefore the LORD will give you meat, and you shall eat. 19You shall eat, not one day, nor two days, nor five days, nor ten days, nor twenty days, 20but *for* a whole month, until it comes out of your nostrils and becomes loathsome to you, because you have despised the LORD who is among you, and have wept before Him, saying, "Why did we ever come up out of Egypt?" ' "

21And Moses said, "The people whom I *am* among *are* six hundred thousand men on foot; yet You have said, 'I will give them meat, that they may eat *for* a whole month.' 22Shall flocks and herds be slaughtered for them, to provide enough for them? Or shall all the fish of the sea be gathered together for them, to provide enough for them?"

23And the LORD said to Moses, "Has the LORD's arm been shortened? Now you shall see whether what I say will happen to you or not."

24So Moses went out and told the people the words of the LORD, and he gathered the seventy men of the elders of the people and placed them around the tabernacle. 25Then the LORD came down in the cloud, and spoke to him, and took of the Spirit that *was* upon him, and placed *the same* upon the seventy elders; and it happened, when the Spirit rested upon them, that they prophesied, although they never did *so* again.*a*

26But two men had remained in the camp: the name of one *was* Eldad, and the name of the other Medad. And the Spirit rested upon them. Now they *were* among those listed, but who had not gone out to the tabernacle; yet they prophesied in the camp. 27And a young man ran and told Moses, and said, "Eldad and Medad are prophesying in the camp."

28So Joshua the son of Nun, Moses' assistant, *one* of his choice men, answered and said, "Moses my lord, forbid them!"

29Then Moses said to him, "Are you zealous for my sake? Oh, that all the LORD's people were prophets *and* that the LORD would put His Spirit upon them!" 30And Moses returned to the camp, he and the elders of Israel.

WHAT'S IT MEAN?

A prophet was a person who received messages from God and passed them along to the people. Sometimes those messages told of future events. There was no use in arguing with a prophet, since his authority came directly from God. Rich people, poor people, young people, and old people alike delivered God's messages. No special training was necessary to become a prophet.

Numbers 11:26

THE LORD SENDS QUAIL

31Now a wind went out from the LORD, and it brought quail from the sea and left *them* fluttering near the camp, about a day's journey on this side and about a day's journey on the other side, all around the camp, and about two cubits above the surface of the ground. 32And the people stayed up all that day, all night, and all the next day, and gathered the quail (he who gathered least gathered ten homers); and they spread *them* out for themselves all around the camp. 33But while the meat *was* still between their teeth, before it was chewed, the wrath of the LORD was aroused against the people, and the LORD struck the people with a very great plague. 34So he called the name of that place Kibroth Hattaavah,*a* because there they buried the people who had yielded to craving.

35From Kibroth Hattaavah the people moved to Hazeroth, and camped at Hazeroth.

DISSENSION OF AARON AND MIRIAM

1Then Miriam and Aaron spoke against Moses because of the Ethiopian woman whom he had married; for he had married an Ethiopian woman. 2So they said, "Has the LORD indeed spoken only through Moses? Has He not spoken through us also?" And the LORD heard *it.*
3(Now the man Moses *was* very humble, more than all men who *were* on the face of the earth.)

⁴Suddenly the LORD said to Moses, Aaron, and Miriam, "Come out, you three, to the tabernacle of meeting!" So the three came out. ⁵Then the LORD came down in the pillar of cloud and stood *in* the door of the tabernacle, and called Aaron and Miriam. And they both went forward. ⁶Then He said,

"Hear now My words:
If there is a prophet among you,
I, the LORD, make Myself known to him
    in a vision;
I speak to him in a dream.
⁷ Not so with My servant Moses;
He *is* faithful in all My house.
⁸ I speak with him face to face,
Even plainly, and not in dark sayings;
And he sees the form of the LORD.
Why then were you not afraid
To speak against My servant Moses?"

⁹So the anger of the LORD was aroused against them, and He departed. ¹⁰And when the cloud departed from above the tabernacle, suddenly Miriam *became* leprous, as *white as* snow. Then Aaron turned toward Miriam, and there she was, a leper. ¹¹So Aaron said to Moses, "Oh, my lord! Please do not lay *this* sin on us, in which we have done foolishly and in which we have sinned. ¹²Please do not let her be as one dead, whose flesh is half consumed when he comes out of his mother's womb!"

¹³So Moses cried out to the LORD, saying, "Please heal her, O God, I pray!"

¹⁴Then the LORD said to Moses, "If her father had but spit in her face, would she not be shamed seven days? Let her be shut out of the camp seven days, and afterward she may be received *again*." ¹⁵So Miriam was shut out of the camp seven days, and the people did not journey till Miriam was brought in *again*. ¹⁶And afterward the people moved from Hazeroth and camped in the Wilderness of Paran.

SPIES SENT INTO CANAAN

¹And the LORD spoke to Moses, saying, ²"Send men to spy out the land of Canaan, which I am giving to the children of Israel; from each tribe of their fathers you shall send a man, every one a leader among them."

³So Moses sent them from the Wilderness of Paran according to the command of the LORD, all of them men who *were* heads of the children of Israel. ⁴Now these *were* their names: from the tribe of Reuben, Shammua the son of Zaccur;

⁵from the tribe of Simeon, Shaphat the son of Hori; ⁶from the tribe of Judah, Caleb the son of Jephunneh; ⁷from the tribe of Issachar, Igal the son of Joseph; ⁸from the tribe of Ephraim, Hoshea*ᵃ* the son of Nun; ⁹from the tribe of Benjamin, Palti the son of Raphu; ¹⁰from the tribe of Zebulun, Gaddiel the son of Sodi; ¹¹from the tribe of Joseph, *that is,* from the tribe of Manasseh, Gaddi the son of Susi; ¹²from the tribe of Dan, Ammiel the son of Gemalli; ¹³from the tribe of Asher, Sethur the son of Michael; ¹⁴from the tribe of Naphtali, Nahbi the son of Vophsi; ¹⁵from the tribe of Gad, Geuel the son of Machi.

¹⁶These *are* the names of the men whom Moses sent to spy out the land. And Moses called Hoshea*ᵃ* the son of Nun, Joshua.

¹⁷Then Moses sent them to spy out the land of Canaan, and said to them, "Go up this *way* into the South, and go up to the mountains, ¹⁸and see what the land is like: whether the people who dwell in it *are* strong or weak, few or many; ¹⁹whether the land they dwell in *is* good or bad; whether the cities they inhabit *are* like camps or strongholds; ²⁰whether the land *is* rich or poor; and whether there are forests there or not. Be of good courage. And bring some of the fruit of the land." Now the time *was* the season of the first ripe grapes.

WHAT'S IT MEAN?

What was the difference between a city and a camp? Generally, a city was larger than a camp. Some camps were simply clusters of homes and buildings. What's more, a city was usually surrounded by walls for protection against enemy attacks. A camp usually did not have protective walls and could be captured easily.
Numbers 13:19, 20

²¹So they went up and spied out the land from the Wilderness of Zin as far as Rehob, near the entrance of Hamath. ²²And they went up through the South and came to Hebron; Ahiman, Sheshai, and Talmai, the descendants of Anak, *were* there. (Now Hebron was built seven years before Zoan in Egypt.) ²³Then they came to the Valley of Eshcol, and there cut down a

13:8 *ᵃ*Septuagint and Vulgate read *Oshea*.   **13:16** *ᵃ*Septuagint and Vulgate read *Oshea*.

MIRIAM made a difference

Older brothers or sisters find out sooner or later that they have an automatic job—watching younger brothers or sisters! Miriam lived during a time when the children of Israel were slaves in Egypt. As if that wasn't bad enough, the government decided that male children were to be killed at birth. That's when Miriam's little brother Moses was born.

Miriam and her mother worked out a plan they hoped would keep Moses alive. They put the baby in a floating basket near a place in the Nile River where wealthy Egyptian women came to bathe. As it turned out, as Miriam watched from the reeds, Moses was fished out and adopted by a princess of Egypt. Thinking quickly, Miriam approached the princess and offered to get a nanny for the baby. She brought her mother, of course.

Cutting Edge

Miriam was part of God's plan to keep Moses alive. She made a difference by following through on her responsibilities. How could she have known her little brother would turn out to be such a large figure in history? She didn't have to know. She only had to do what she was asked to do.

YOU can, too!

The younger you are, the less important your duties may seem sometimes. Don't worry about it. The shortest road to bigger jobs is doing little jobs very well. In fact, God tells us that those who show Him they can be trusted with small things will be trusted with large ones. Besides, like Miriam, you probably won't know ahead of time what tasks in your life will make the biggest difference. Your job is to carry out your responsibilities—whatever their size!

Want to know more? You can read this adventure in babysitting in Exodus 1:15—2:10.

branch with one cluster of grapes; they carried it between two of them on a pole. *They* also *brought* some of the pomegranates and figs. ²⁴The place was called the Valley of Eshcol,*a* because of the cluster which the men of Israel cut down there. ²⁵And they returned from spying out the land after forty days.

²⁶Now they departed and came back to Moses and Aaron and all the congregation of the children of Israel in the Wilderness of Paran, at Kadesh; they brought back word to them and to all the congregation, and showed them the fruit of the land. ²⁷Then they told him, and said: "We went to the land where you sent us. It truly flows with milk and honey, and this *is* its fruit. ²⁸Nevertheless the people who dwell in the land *are* strong; the cities *are* fortified *and* very large; moreover we saw the descendants of Anak there. ²⁹The Amalekites dwell in the land of the South; the Hittites, the Jebusites, and the Amorites dwell in the mountains; and the Canaanites dwell by the sea and along the banks of the Jordan."

³⁰Then Caleb quieted the people before Moses, and said, "Let us go up at once and take possession, for we are well able to overcome it."

³¹But the men who had gone up with him said, "We are not able to go up against the people, for they *are* stronger than we." ³²And they gave the children of Israel a bad report of the land which they had spied out, saying, "The land through which we have gone as spies *is* a land that devours its inhabitants, and all the people whom we saw in it *are* men of *great* stature. ³³There we saw the giants*a* (the descendants of Anak came from the giants); and we were like grasshoppers in our own sight, and so we were in their sight."

ISRAEL REFUSES TO ENTER CANAAN

¹So all the congregation lifted up their voices and cried, and the people wept that night. ²And all the children of Israel complained against Moses and Aaron, and the whole congregation said to them, "If only we had died in the land of Egypt! Or if only we had died in this wilderness! ³Why has the LORD brought us to this land to fall by the sword, that our wives and children should become victims? Would it not be better

for us to return to Egypt?" ⁴So they said to one another, "Let us select a leader and return to Egypt."

⁵Then Moses and Aaron fell on their faces before all the assembly of the congregation of the children of Israel.

⁶But Joshua the son of Nun and Caleb the son of Jephunneh, *who were* among those who had spied out the land, tore their clothes; ⁷and they spoke to all the congregation of the children of Israel, saying: "The land we passed through to spy out *is* an exceedingly good land. ⁸If the LORD delights in us, then He will bring us into this land and give it to us, 'a land which flows with milk and honey.'*a* ⁹Only do not rebel against the LORD, nor fear the people of the land, for they *are* our bread; their protection has departed from them, and the LORD *is* with us. Do not fear them."

¹⁰And all the congregation said to stone them with stones. Now the glory of the LORD appeared in the tabernacle of meeting before all the children of Israel.

MOSES INTERCEDES FOR THE PEOPLE

¹¹Then the LORD said to Moses: "How long will these people reject Me? And how long will they not believe Me, with all the signs which I have performed among them? ¹²I will strike them with the pestilence and disinherit them, and I will make of you a nation greater and mightier than they."

¹³And Moses said to the LORD: "Then the Egyptians will hear *it,* for by Your might You brought these people up from among them, ¹⁴and they will tell *it* to the inhabitants of this land. They have heard that You, LORD, *are* among these people; that You, LORD, are seen face to face and Your cloud stands above them, and You go before them in a pillar of cloud by day and in a pillar of fire by night. ¹⁵Now if You kill these people as one man, then the nations which have heard of Your fame will speak, saying, ¹⁶'Because the LORD was not able to bring this people to the land which He swore to give them, therefore He killed them in the wilderness.' ¹⁷And now, I pray, let the power of my

---

> **ATTITUDE**
> Where do poor decisions come from?
> (14:1–4)

> "The LORD is longsuffering and abundant in mercy, forgiving iniquity and transgression; but He by no means clears the guilty."
> (Numbers 14:18a)

13:24 *a*Literally *Cluster*   **13:33** *a*Hebrew *nephilim*   **14:8** *a*Exodus 3:8

Lord be great, just as You have spoken, saying, [18]The LORD is longsuffering and abundant in mercy, forgiving iniquity and transgression; but He by no means clears *the guilty*, visiting the iniquity of the fathers on the children to the third and fourth *generation.'ª* [19]Pardon the iniquity of this people, I pray, according to the greatness of Your mercy, just as You have forgiven this people, from Egypt even until now."

[20]Then the LORD said: "I have pardoned, according to your word; [21]but truly, as I live, all the earth shall be filled with the glory of the LORD— [22]because all these men who have seen My glory and the signs which I did in Egypt and in the wilderness, and have put Me to the test now these ten times, and have not heeded My voice, [23]they certainly shall not see the land of which I swore to their fathers, nor shall any of those who rejected Me see it. [24]But My servant Caleb, because he has a different spirit in him and has followed Me fully, I will bring into the land where he went, and his descendants shall inherit it. [25]Now the Amalekites and the Canaanites dwell in the valley; tomorrow turn and move out into the wilderness by the Way of the Red Sea."

DEATH SENTENCE ON THE REBELS

[26]And the LORD spoke to Moses and Aaron, saying, [27]"How long *shall I bear with* this evil congregation who complain against Me? I have heard the complaints which the children of Israel make against Me. [28]Say to them, 'As I live,' says the LORD, 'just as you have spoken in My hearing, so I will do to you: [29]The carcasses of you who have complained against Me shall fall in this wilderness, all of you who were numbered, according to your entire number, from twenty years old and above. [30]Except for Caleb the son of Jephunneh and Joshua the son of Nun, you shall by no means enter the land which I swore I would make you dwell in. [31]But your little ones, whom you said would be victims, I will bring in, and they shall know the land which you have despised. [32]But *as for you,* your carcasses shall fall in this wilderness. [33]And your sons shall be shepherds in the wilderness forty years, and bear the brunt of your infidelity, until your carcasses are consumed in the wilderness. [34]According to the number of the days in which you spied out the land, forty days, for each day you shall bear your guilt one year, *namely* forty years, and you shall know My rejection. [35]I the LORD have spoken this. I will surely do so to all this evil congregation

who are gathered together against Me. In this wilderness they shall be consumed, and there they shall die.' "

[36]Now the men whom Moses sent to spy out the land, who returned and made all the congregation complain against him by bringing a bad report of the land, [37]those very men who brought the evil report about the land, died by the plague before the LORD. [38]But Joshua the son of Nun and Caleb the son of Jephunneh remained alive, of the men who went to spy out the land.

A FUTILE INVASION ATTEMPT

[39]Then Moses told these words to all the children of Israel, and the people mourned greatly. [40]And they rose early in the morning and went up to the top of the mountain, saying, "Here we are, and we will go up to the place which the LORD has promised, for we have sinned!"

[41]And Moses said, "Now why do you transgress the command of the LORD? For this will not succeed. [42]Do not go up, lest you be defeated by your enemies, for the LORD *is* not among you. [43]For the Amalekites and the Canaanites *are* there before you, and you shall fall by the sword; because you have turned away from the LORD, the LORD will not be with you."

[44]But they presumed to go up to the mountaintop. Nevertheless, neither the ark of the covenant of the LORD nor Moses departed from the camp. [45]Then the Amalekites and the Canaanites who dwelt in that mountain came down and attacked them, and drove them back as far as Hormah.

LAWS OF GRAIN AND DRINK OFFERINGS

[1]And the LORD spoke to Moses, saying, [2]"Speak to the children of Israel, and say to them: 'When you have come into the land you are to inhabit, which I am giving to you, [3]and you make an offering by fire to the LORD, a burnt offering or a sacrifice, to fulfill a vow or as a freewill offering or in your appointed feasts, to make a sweet aroma to the LORD, from the herd or the flock, [4]then he who presents his offering to the LORD shall bring a grain offering of one-tenth *of an ephah* of fine flour mixed with one-fourth of a hin of oil; [5]and one-fourth of a hin of wine as a drink offering you shall prepare with the burnt offering or the sacrifice, for each lamb. [6]Or for a ram you shall prepare as a grain offering two-tenths *of an ephah* of fine

14:18 ªExodus 34:6, 7

flour mixed with one-third of a hin of oil; ⁷and as a drink offering you shall offer one-third of a hin of wine as a sweet aroma to the LORD. ⁸And when you prepare a young bull as a burnt offering, or as a sacrifice to fulfill a vow, or as a peace offering to the LORD, ⁹then shall be offered with the young bull a grain offering of three-tenths *of an ephah* of fine flour mixed with half a hin of oil; ¹⁰and you shall bring as the drink offering half a hin of wine as an offering made by fire, a sweet aroma to the LORD.

¹¹Thus it shall be done for each young bull, for each ram, or for each lamb or young goat. ¹²According to the number that you prepare, so you shall do with everyone according to their number. ¹³All who are native-born shall do these things in this manner, in presenting an offering made by fire, a sweet aroma to the LORD. ¹⁴And if a stranger dwells with you, or whoever *is* among you throughout your generations, and would present an offering made by fire, a sweet aroma to the LORD, just as you do, so shall he do. ¹⁵One ordinance *shall be* for you of the assembly and for the stranger who dwells *with you*, an ordinance forever throughout your generations; as you are, so shall the stranger be before the LORD. ¹⁶One law and one custom shall be for you and for the stranger who dwells with you.' "ᵃ

¹⁷Again the LORD spoke to Moses, saying, ¹⁸"Speak to the children of Israel, and say to them: 'When you come into the land to which I bring you, ¹⁹then it will be, when you eat of the bread of the land, that you shall offer up a heave offering to the LORD. ²⁰You shall offer up a cake of the first of your ground meal *as* a heave offering; as a heave offering of the threshing floor, so shall you offer it up. ²¹Of the first of your ground meal you shall give to the LORD a heave offering throughout your generations.

LAWS CONCERNING UNINTENTIONAL SIN

²²'If you sin unintentionally, and do not observe all these commandments which the LORD has spoken to Moses— ²³all that the LORD has commanded you by the hand of Moses, from the day the LORD gave commandment and onward throughout your generations— ²⁴then it will be, if it is unintentionally committed, without the knowledge of the congregation, that the whole congregation shall offer one young bull as a burnt offering, as a sweet aroma to the LORD, with its grain offering and its drink offering, according to the ordinance, and one kid of the goats as a sin offering. ²⁵So the priest shall make atonement for the whole congregation of the children of Israel, and it shall be forgiven them, for it was unintentional; they shall bring their offering, an offering made by fire to the LORD, and their sin offering before the LORD, for their unintended sin. ²⁶It shall be forgiven the whole congregation of the children of Israel and the stranger who dwells among them, because all the people *did it* unintentionally.

²⁷'And if a person sins unintentionally, then he shall bring a female goat in its first year as a sin offering. ²⁸So the priest shall make atonement for the person who sins unintentionally, when he sins unintentionally before the LORD, to make atonement for him; and it shall be forgiven him. ²⁹You shall have one law for him who sins unintentionally, *for* him who is native-born among the children of Israel and for the stranger who dwells among them.

LAW CONCERNING PRESUMPTUOUS SIN

³⁰'But the person who does *anything* presumptuously, *whether he is* native-born or a stranger, that one brings reproach on the LORD, and he shall be cut off from among his people. ³¹Because he has despised the word of the LORD, and has broken His commandment, that person shall be completely cut off; his guilt *shall be* upon him.' "

PENALTY FOR VIOLATING THE SABBATH

³²Now while the children of Israel were in the wilderness, they found a man gathering sticks on the Sabbath day. ³³And those who found him gathering sticks brought him to Moses and Aaron, and to all the congregation.

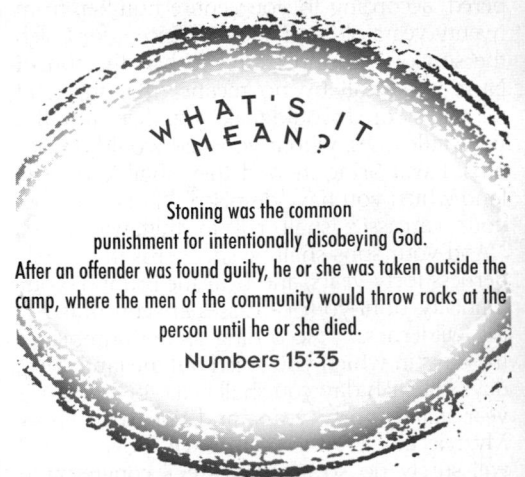

WHAT'S IT MEAN?

Stoning was the common punishment for intentionally disobeying God. After an offender was found guilty, he or she was taken outside the camp, where the men of the community would throw rocks at the person until he or she died.

Numbers 15:35

15:16 ᵃCompare Exodus 12:49

³⁴They put him under guard, because it had not been explained what should be done to him.

³⁵Then the LORD said to Moses, "The man must surely be put to death; all the congregation shall stone him with stones outside the camp." ³⁶So, as the LORD commanded Moses, all the congregation brought him outside the camp and stoned him with stones, and he died.

TASSELS ON GARMENTS

³⁷Again the LORD spoke to Moses, saying, ³⁸"Speak to the children of Israel: Tell them to make tassels on the corners of their garments throughout their generations, and to put a blue thread in the tassels of the corners. ³⁹And you shall have the tassel, that you may look upon it and remember all the commandments of the LORD and do them, and that you *may* not follow the harlotry to which your own heart and your own eyes are inclined, ⁴⁰and that you may remember and do all My commandments, and be holy for your God. ⁴¹I *am* the LORD your God, who brought you out of the land of Egypt, to be your God: I *am* the LORD your God."

REBELLION AGAINST MOSES AND AARON

¹Now Korah the son of Izhar, the son of Kohath, the son of Levi, with Dathan and Abiram the sons of Eliab, and On the son of Peleth, sons of Reuben, took *men;* ²and they rose up before Moses with some of the children of Israel, two hundred and fifty leaders of the congregation, representatives of the congregation, men of renown. ³They gathered together against Moses and Aaron, and said to them, "*You take* too much upon yourselves, for all the congregation *is* holy, every one of them, and the LORD *is* among them. Why then do you exalt yourselves above the assembly of the LORD?"

⁴So when Moses heard *it,* he fell on his face; ⁵and he spoke to Korah and all his company, saying, "Tomorrow morning the LORD will show who *is* His and *who is* holy, and will cause *him* to come near to Him. That one whom He chooses He will cause to come near to Him. ⁶Do this: Take censers, Korah and all your company; ⁷put fire in them and put incense in them before the LORD tomorrow, and it shall be *that* the man whom the LORD chooses *is* the holy one. *You take* too much upon yourselves, you sons of Levi!"

⁸Then Moses said to Korah, "Hear now, you sons of Levi: ⁹*Is* it a small thing to you that the God of Israel has separated you from the congregation of Israel, to bring you near to Himself, to do the work of the tabernacle of the LORD, and to stand before the congregation to serve

them; ¹⁰and that He has brought you near *to Himself,* you and all your brethren, the sons of Levi, with you? And are you seeking the priesthood also? ¹¹Therefore you and all your company *are* gathered together against the LORD. And what *is* Aaron that you complain against him?"

¹²And Moses sent to call Dathan and Abiram the sons of Eliab, but they said, "We will not come up! ¹³*Is it* a small thing that you have brought us up out of a land flowing with milk and honey, to kill us in the wilderness, that you should keep acting like a prince over us? ¹⁴Moreover you have not brought us into a land flowing with milk and honey, nor given us inheritance of fields and vineyards. Will you put out the eyes of these men? We will not come up!"

¹⁵Then Moses was very angry, and said to the LORD, "Do not respect their offering. I have not taken one donkey from them, nor have I hurt one of them."

¹⁶And Moses said to Korah, "Tomorrow, you and all your company be present before the LORD—you and they, as well as Aaron. ¹⁷Let each take his censer and put incense in it, and each of you bring his censer before the LORD, two hundred and fifty censers; both you and Aaron, each *with* his censer." ¹⁸So every man took his censer, put fire in it, laid incense on it, and stood at the door of the tabernacle of meeting with Moses and Aaron. ¹⁹And Korah gathered all the congregation against them at the door of the tabernacle of meeting. Then the glory of the LORD appeared to all the congregation.

²⁰And the LORD spoke to Moses and Aaron, saying, ²¹"Separate yourselves from among this congregation, that I may consume them in a moment."

²²Then they fell on their faces, and said, "O God, the God of the spirits of all flesh, shall one man sin, and You be angry with all the congregation?"

²³So the LORD spoke to Moses, saying, ²⁴"Speak to the congregation, saying, 'Get away from the tents of Korah, Dathan, and Abiram.' "

²⁵Then Moses rose and went to Dathan and Abiram, and the elders of Israel followed him. ²⁶And he spoke to the congregation, saying, "Depart now from the tents of these wicked men! Touch nothing of theirs, lest you be consumed in all their sins." ²⁷So they got away from around the tents of Korah, Dathan, and Abiram; and Dathan and Abiram came out and stood at the door of their tents, with their wives, their sons, and their little children.

28And Moses said: "By this you shall know that the LORD has sent me to do all these works, for *I have* not *done them* of my own will. 29If these men die naturally like all men, or if they are visited by the common fate of all men, *then* the LORD has not sent me. 30But if the LORD creates a new thing, and the earth opens its mouth and swallows them up with all that belongs to them, and they go down alive into the pit, then you will understand that these men have rejected the LORD."

31Now it came to pass, as he finished speaking all these words, that the ground split apart under them, 32and the earth opened its mouth and swallowed them up, with their households and all the men with Korah, with all *their* goods. 33So they and all those with them went down alive into the pit; the earth closed over them, and they perished from among the assembly. 34Then all Israel who *were* around them fled at their cry, for they said, "Lest the earth swallow us up *also!*"

35And a fire came out from the LORD and consumed the two hundred and fifty men who were offering incense.

36Then the LORD spoke to Moses, saying: 37"Tell Eleazar, the son of Aaron the priest, to pick up the censers out of the blaze, for they are holy, and scatter the fire some distance away. 38The censers of these men who sinned against their own souls, let them be made into hammered plates as a covering for the altar. Because they presented them before the LORD, therefore they are holy; and they shall be a sign to the children of Israel." 39So Eleazar the priest took the bronze censers, which those who were burned up had presented, and they were hammered out as a covering on the altar, 40*to be* a memorial to the children of Israel that no outsider, who *is* not a descendant of Aaron, should come near to offer incense before the LORD, that he might not become like Korah and his companions, just as the LORD had said to him through Moses.

COMPLAINTS OF THE PEOPLE

41On the next day all the congregation of the children of Israel complained against Moses and Aaron, saying, "You have killed the people of the LORD." 42Now it happened, when the congregation had gathered against Moses and Aaron, that they turned toward the tabernacle of meeting; and suddenly the cloud covered it, and the glory of the LORD appeared. 43Then Moses and Aaron came before the tabernacle of meeting.

44And the LORD spoke to Moses, saying,

45"Get away from among this congregation, that I may consume them in a moment."

And they fell on their faces.

46So Moses said to Aaron, "Take a censer and put fire in it from the altar, put incense *on it,* and take it quickly to the congregation and make atonement for them; for wrath has gone out from the LORD. The plague has begun." 47Then Aaron took *it* as Moses commanded, and ran into the midst of the assembly; and already the plague had begun among the people. So he put in the incense and made atonement for the people. 48And he stood between the dead and the living; so the plague was stopped. 49Now those who died in the plague were fourteen thousand seven hundred, besides those who died in the Korah incident. 50So Aaron returned to Moses at the door of the tabernacle of meeting, for the plague had stopped.

THE BUDDING OF AARON'S ROD

1And the LORD spoke to Moses, saying: 2"Speak to the children of Israel, and get from them a rod from each father's house, all their leaders according to their fathers' houses—twelve rods. Write each man's name on his rod. 3And you shall write Aaron's name on the rod of Levi. For there shall be one rod for the head of *each* father's house. 4Then you shall place them in the tabernacle of meeting before the Testimony, where I meet with you. 5And it shall be *that* the rod of the man whom I choose will blossom; thus I will rid Myself of the complaints of the children of Israel, which they make against you."

WHAT'S IT MEAN?

Almond trees were popular with the Israelites because almonds were used to make medicine. The Hebrew word for almond means "awakening," probably due to the fact that the almond tree is the first to bloom in the spring. For the Israelites, the almond was a symbol of God's dependability.

Numbers 17:8

6So Moses spoke to the children of Israel, and each of their leaders gave him a rod apiece, for each leader according to their fathers' houses, twelve rods; and the rod of Aaron *was* among their rods. [7]And Moses placed the rods before the LORD in the tabernacle of witness.

[8]Now it came to pass on the next day that Moses went into the tabernacle of witness, and behold, the rod of Aaron, of the house of Levi, had sprouted and put forth buds, had produced blossoms and yielded ripe almonds. [9]Then Moses brought out all the rods from before the LORD to all the children of Israel; and they looked, and each man took his rod.

[10]And the LORD said to Moses, "Bring Aaron's rod back before the Testimony, to be kept as a sign against the rebels, that you may put their complaints away from Me, lest they die." [11]Thus did Moses; just as the LORD had commanded him, so he did.

[12]So the children of Israel spoke to Moses, saying, "Surely we die, we perish, we all perish! [13]Whoever even comes near the tabernacle of the LORD must die. Shall we all utterly die?"

DUTIES OF PRIESTS AND LEVITES

[1]Then the LORD said to Aaron: "You and your sons and your father's house with you shall bear the iniquity *related to* the sanctuary, and you and your sons with you shall bear the iniquity *associated with* your priesthood. [2]Also bring with you your brethren of the tribe of Levi, the tribe of your father, that they may be joined with you and serve you while you and your sons *are* with you before the tabernacle of witness. [3]They shall attend to your needs and all the needs of the tabernacle; but they shall not come near the articles of the sanctuary and the altar, lest they die—they and you also. [4]They shall be joined with you and attend to the needs of the tabernacle of meeting, for all the work of the tabernacle; but an outsider shall not come near you. [5]And you shall attend to the duties of the sanctuary and the duties of the altar, that there *may* be no more wrath on the children of Israel. [6]Behold, I Myself have taken your brethren the Levites from among the children of Israel; *they are* a gift to you, given by the LORD, to do the work of the tabernacle of meeting. [7]Therefore you and your sons with you shall attend to your priesthood for everything at the altar and behind the veil; and you shall serve. I give your priesthood *to you* as a gift for service, but the outsider who comes near shall be put to death."

OFFERINGS FOR SUPPORT OF THE PRIESTS

[8]And the LORD spoke to Aaron: "Here, I Myself have also given you charge of My heave offerings, all the holy gifts of the children of Israel; I have given them as a portion to you and your sons, as an ordinance forever. [9]This shall be yours of the most holy things *reserved* from the fire: every offering of theirs, every grain offering and every sin offering and every trespass offering which they render to Me, *shall be* most holy for you and your sons. [10]In a most holy *place* you shall eat it; every male shall eat it. It shall be holy to you.

[11]"This also *is* yours: the heave offering of their gift, with all the wave offerings of the children of Israel; I have given them to you, and your sons and daughters with you, as an ordinance forever. Everyone who is clean in your house may eat it.

[12]"All the best of the oil, all the best of the new wine and the grain, their firstfruits which they offer to the LORD, I have given them to you. [13]Whatever first ripe fruit is in their land, which they bring to the LORD, shall be yours. Everyone who is clean in your house may eat it.

[14]"Every devoted thing in Israel shall be yours.

[15]"Everything that first opens the womb of all flesh, which they bring to the LORD, whether man or beast, shall be yours; nevertheless the firstborn of man you shall surely redeem, and the firstborn of unclean animals you shall redeem. [16]And those redeemed of the devoted things you shall redeem when one month old, according to your valuation, for five shekels of silver, according to the shekel of the sanctuary, which *is* twenty gerahs. [17]But the firstborn of a cow, the firstborn of a sheep, or the firstborn of a goat you shall not redeem; they *are* holy. You shall sprinkle their blood on the altar, and burn their fat *as* an offering made by fire for a sweet aroma to the LORD. [18]And their flesh shall be yours, just as the wave breast and the right thigh are yours.

[19]"All the heave offerings of the holy things, which the children of Israel offer to the LORD, I have given to you and your sons and daughters with you as an ordinance forever; it *is* a covenant of salt forever before the LORD with you and your descendants with you."

> "All the best of the oil, all the best of the new wine and the grain, their firstfruits which they offer to the LORD, I have given them to you."
> (Numbers 18:12)

20Then the LORD said to Aaron: "You shall have no inheritance in their land, nor shall you have any portion among them; I *am* your portion and your inheritance among the children of Israel.

TITHES FOR SUPPORT OF THE LEVITES

21"Behold, I have given the children of Levi all the tithes in Israel as an inheritance in return for the work which they perform, the work of the tabernacle of meeting. 22Hereafter the children of Israel shall not come near the tabernacle of meeting, lest they bear sin and die. 23But the Levites shall perform the work of the tabernacle of meeting, and they shall bear their iniquity; *it shall be* a statute forever, throughout your generations, that among the children of Israel they shall have no inheritance. 24For the tithes of the children of Israel, which they offer up *as* a heave offering to the LORD, I have given to the Levites as an inheritance; therefore I have said to them, 'Among the children of Israel they shall have no inheritance.' "

THE TITHE OF THE LEVITES

25Then the LORD spoke to Moses, saying, 26"Speak thus to the Levites, and say to them: 'When you take from the children of Israel the tithes which I have given you from them as your inheritance, then you shall offer up a heave offering of it to the LORD, a tenth of the tithe. 27And your heave offering shall be reckoned to you as though *it were* the grain of the threshing floor and as the fullness of the winepress. 28Thus you shall also offer a heave offering to the LORD from all your tithes which you receive from the children of Israel, and you shall give the LORD's heave offering from it to Aaron the priest. 29Of all your gifts you shall offer up every heave offering due to the LORD, from all the best of them, the consecrated part of them.' 30Therefore you shall say to them: 'When you have lifted up the best of it, then *the rest* shall be accounted to the Levites as the produce of the threshing floor and as the produce of the winepress. 31You may eat it in any place, you and your households, for it *is* your reward for your work in the tabernacle of meeting. 32And you shall bear no sin because of it, when you have lifted up the best of it. But you shall not profane the holy gifts of the children of Israel, lest you die.' "

LAWS OF PURIFICATION

1Now the LORD spoke to Moses and Aaron, saying, 2"This *is* the ordinance of the law which the LORD has commanded, saying: 'Speak to the children of Israel, that they bring you a red heifer without blemish, in which there *is* no defect *and* on which a yoke has never come. 3You shall give it to Eleazar the priest, that he may take it outside the camp, and it shall be slaughtered before him; 4and Eleazar the priest shall take some of its blood with his finger, and sprinkle some of its blood seven times directly in front of the tabernacle of meeting. 5Then the heifer shall be burned in his sight: its hide, its flesh, its blood, and its offal shall be burned. 6And the priest shall take cedar wood and hyssop and scarlet, and cast *them* into the midst of

Promise   HE PROMISES TO GIVE YOU EVERYTHING YOU NEED.

I am your portion and your inheritance among the children of Israel (Num. 18:20b).

God is faithful. You can count on Him. God has always been faithful to keep His Word. He has supplied all of our needs. Most of the time we have much more than we could ever use or appreciate. We doubt God's provision when we confuse our needs with our wants. Need says that you need clothes. Want says that you can only put the hippest, coolest things on your body. Need says that you need to eat lunch every day. Want says that you have to go out with your friends because they'd laugh if you ate in the cafeteria. We live in abundant times. A lot of people have a lot of stuff, and they want more. Think about your needs. Learn to separate them from the things you want. What do you really need in order to live? Has God provided? Take some time to thank Him. He's given you all you need.

SEE FOR YOURSELF:
Matt. 6:31–33; Luke 12:29, 30; Phil. 4:19

the fire burning the heifer. ⁷Then the priest shall wash his clothes, he shall bathe in water, and afterward he shall come into the camp; the priest shall be unclean until evening. ⁸And the one who burns it shall wash his clothes in water, bathe in water, and shall be unclean until evening. ⁹Then a man *who is* clean shall gather up the ashes of the heifer, and store *them* outside the camp in a clean place; and they shall be kept for the congregation of the children of Israel for the water of purification;ᵃ it *is* for purifying from sin. ¹⁰And the one who gathers the ashes of the heifer shall wash his clothes, and be unclean until evening. It shall be a statute forever to the children of Israel and to the stranger who dwells among them.

¹¹'He who touches the dead body of anyone shall be unclean seven days. ¹²He shall purify himself with the water on the third day and on the seventh day; *then* he will be clean. But if he does not purify himself on the third day and on the seventh day, he will not be clean. ¹³Whoever touches the body of anyone who has died, and does not purify himself, defiles the tabernacle of the LORD. That person shall be cut off from Israel. He shall be unclean, because the water of purification was not sprinkled on him; his uncleanness *is* still on him.

WHAT'S IT MEAN?

An unclean person was not allowed to participate in the Israelites' normal religious activities and worship services. One of the most extreme forms of uncleanness came from touching a dead body.
Numbers 19:11

¹⁴'This *is* the law when a man dies in a tent: All who come into the tent and all who *are* in the tent shall be unclean seven days; ¹⁵and every open vessel, which has no cover fastened on it, *is* unclean. ¹⁶Whoever in the open field touches one who is slain by a sword or who has died, or a bone of a man, or a grave, shall be unclean seven days.

¹⁷'And for an unclean *person* they shall take some of the ashes of the heifer burnt for purifi-

cation from sin, and running water shall be put on them in a vessel. ¹⁸A clean person shall take hyssop and dip *it* in the water, sprinkle *it* on the tent, on all the vessels, on the persons who were there, or on the one who touched a bone, the slain, the dead, or a grave. ¹⁹The clean *person* shall sprinkle the unclean on the third day and on the seventh day; and on the seventh day he shall purify himself, wash his clothes, and bathe in water; and at evening he shall be clean.

²⁰But the man who is unclean and does not purify himself, that person shall be cut off from among the assembly, because he has defiled the sanctuary of the LORD. The water of purification has not been sprinkled on him; he *is* unclean. ²¹It shall be a perpetual statute for them. He who sprinkles the water of purification shall wash his clothes; and he who touches the water of purification shall be unclean until evening. ²²Whatever the unclean *person* touches shall be unclean; and the person who touches *it* shall be unclean until evening.' "

MOSES' ERROR AT KADESH

¹Then the children of Israel, the whole congregation, came into the Wilderness of Zin in the first month, and the people stayed in Kadesh; and Miriam died there and was buried there.

²Now there was no water for the congregation; so they gathered together against Moses and Aaron. ³And the people contended with Moses and spoke, saying: "If only we had died when our brethren died before the LORD! ⁴Why have you brought up the assembly of the LORD into this wilderness, that we and our animals should die here? ⁵And why have you made us come up out of Egypt, to bring us to this evil place? It *is* not a place of grain or figs or vines or pomegranates; nor *is* there any water to drink." ⁶So Moses and Aaron went from the presence of the assembly to the door of the tabernacle of meeting, and they fell on their faces. And the glory of the LORD appeared to them.

⁷Then the LORD spoke to Moses, saying, ⁸"Take the rod; you and your brother Aaron gather the congregation together. Speak to the rock before their eyes, and it will yield its water; thus you shall bring water for them out of the rock, and give drink to the congregation and their animals." ⁹So Moses took the rod from before the LORD as He commanded him.

¹⁰And Moses and Aaron gathered the assembly together before the rock; and he said to them, "Hear now, you rebels! Must we bring

19:9 ᵃLiterally *impurity*

water for you out of this rock?" ¹¹Then Moses lifted his hand and struck the rock twice with his rod; and water came out abundantly, and the congregation and their animals drank.

¹²Then the LORD spoke to Moses and Aaron, "Because you did not believe Me, to hallow Me in the eyes of the children of Israel, therefore you shall not bring this assembly into the land which I have given them."

¹³This *was* the water of Meribah,ᵃ because the children of Israel contended with the LORD, and He was hallowed among them.

PASSAGE THROUGH EDOM REFUSED

¹⁴Now Moses sent messengers from Kadesh to the king of Edom. "Thus says your brother Israel: 'You know all the hardship that has befallen us, ¹⁵how our fathers went down to Egypt, and we dwelt in Egypt a long time, and the Egyptians afflicted us and our fathers. ¹⁶When we cried out to the LORD, He heard our voice and sent the Angel and brought us up out of Egypt; now here we are in Kadesh, a city on the edge of your border. ¹⁷Please let us pass through your country. We will not pass through fields or vineyards, nor will we drink water from wells; we will go along the King's Highway; we will not turn aside to the right hand or to the left until we have passed through your territory.' "

¹⁸Then Edom said to him, "You shall not pass through my *land,* lest I come out against you with the sword."

¹⁹So the children of Israel said to him, "We will go by the Highway, and if I or my livestock drink any of your water, then I will pay for it; let me only pass through on foot, nothing *more.*"

²⁰Then he said, "You shall not pass through." So Edom came out against them with many men and with a strong hand. ²¹Thus Edom refused to give Israel passage through his territory; so Israel turned away from him.

DEATH OF AARON

²²Now the children of Israel, the whole congregation, journeyed from Kadesh and came to Mount Hor. ²³And the LORD spoke to Moses and Aaron in Mount Hor by the border of the land of Edom, saying: ²⁴"Aaron shall be gathered to his people, for he shall not enter the land which I have given to the children of Israel, because you rebelled against My word at the water of Meribah. ²⁵Take Aaron and Eleazar his son, and bring them up to Mount Hor; ²⁶and strip Aaron of his garments and put them

WHAT'S IT MEAN?

Aaron's robe did not have any magical powers. It was just a symbol of authority, like a king's crown. God wanted to show the Israelites that Aaron's power was being transferred to Eleazar.

Numbers 20:26

on Eleazar his son; for Aaron shall be gathered *to his people* and die there." ²⁷So Moses did just as the LORD commanded, and they went up to Mount Hor in the sight of all the congregation. ²⁸Moses stripped Aaron of his garments and put them on Eleazar his son; and Aaron died there on the top of the mountain. Then Moses and Eleazar came down from the mountain. ²⁹Now when all the congregation saw that Aaron was dead, all the house of Israel mourned for Aaron thirty days.

CANAANITES DEFEATED AT HORMAH

¹The king of Arad, the Canaanite, who dwelt in the South, heard that Israel was coming on the road to Atharim. Then he fought against Israel and took *some* of them prisoners. ²So Israel made a vow to the LORD, and said, "If You will indeed deliver this people into my hand, then I will utterly destroy their cities." ³And the LORD listened to the voice of Israel and delivered up the Canaanites, and they utterly destroyed them and their cities. So the name of that place was called Hormah.ᵃ

THE BRONZE SERPENT

⁴Then they journeyed from Mount Hor by the Way of the Red Sea, to go around the land of Edom; and the soul of the people became very discouraged on the way. ⁵And the people spoke against God and against Moses: "Why have you brought us up out of Egypt to die in the wilderness? For *there is* no food and no water, and our soul loathes this worthless bread." ⁶So the LORD sent fiery serpents among the people, and they bit the people; and many of the people of Israel died.

⁷Therefore the people came to Moses, and said, "We have sinned, for we have spoken

20:13 ᵃLiterally *Contention*   **21:3** ᵃLiterally *Utter Destruction*

against the LORD and against you; pray to the LORD that He take away the serpents from us." So Moses prayed for the people.

WHAT'S IT MEAN?

Are you afraid of snakes? The Israelites were. It didn't matter whether they were poisonous ("fiery serpents") or not. In the Bible, snakes represented evil and sin. In some cultures, though, the snake was a symbol of life and health.
Numbers 21:6

⁸Then the LORD said to Moses, "Make a fiery *serpent*, and set it on a pole; and it shall be that everyone who is bitten, when he looks at it, shall live." ⁹So Moses made a bronze serpent, and put it on a pole; and so it was, if a serpent had bitten anyone, when he looked at the bronze serpent, he lived.

FROM MOUNT HOR TO MOAB

¹⁰Now the children of Israel moved on and camped in Oboth. ¹¹And they journeyed from Oboth and camped at Ije Abarim, in the wilderness which *is* east of Moab, toward the sunrise. ¹²From there they moved and camped in the Valley of Zered. ¹³From there they moved and camped on the other side of the Arnon, which *is* in the wilderness that extends from the border of the Amorites; for the Arnon *is* the border of Moab, between Moab and the Amorites. ¹⁴Therefore it is said in the Book of the Wars of the LORD:

"Waheb in Suphah,ᵃ
The brooks of the Arnon,
15 And the slope of the brooks
That reaches to the dwelling of Ar,
And lies on the border of Moab."

¹⁶From there *they went* to Beer, which *is* the well where the LORD said to Moses, "Gather the people together, and I will give them water." ¹⁷Then Israel sang this song:

"Spring up, O well!
All of you sing to it—

18 The well the leaders sank,
Dug by the nation's nobles,
By the lawgiver, with their staves."

And from the wilderness *they went* to Mattanah, ¹⁹from Mattanah to Nahaliel, from Nahaliel to Bamoth, ²⁰and from Bamoth, *in* the valley that *is* in the country of Moab, to the top of Pisgah which looks down on the wasteland.ᵃ

KING SIHON DEFEATED

²¹Then Israel sent messengers to Sihon king of the Amorites, saying, ²²"Let me pass through your land. We will not turn aside into fields or vineyards; we will not drink water from wells. We will go by the King's Highway until we have passed through your territory." ²³But Sihon would not allow Israel to pass through his territory. So Sihon gathered all his people together and went out against Israel in the wilderness, and he came to Jahaz and fought against Israel. ²⁴Then Israel defeated him with the edge of the sword, and took possession of his land from the Arnon to the Jabbok, as far as the people of Ammon; for the border of the people of Ammon *was* fortified. ²⁵So Israel took all these cities, and Israel dwelt in all the cities of the Amorites, in Heshbon and in all its villages.

WHAT'S IT MEAN?

Sticking close to the water, the Israelites were traveling up the eastern side of the Dead Sea when they reached Heshbon. Twenty-five miles to the west of Heshbon was Jericho, the first city the Israelites came to when they entered Canaan.
Numbers 21:25

²⁶For Heshbon *was* the city of Sihon king of the Amorites, who had fought against the former king of Moab, and had taken all his land from his hand as far as the Arnon. ²⁷Therefore those who speak in proverbs say:

"Come to Heshbon, let it be built;
Let the city of Sihon be repaired.

21:14 ᵃAncient unknown places; Vulgate reads *What He did in the Red Sea.* **21:20** ᵃHebrew *Jeshimon*

28 "For fire went out from Heshbon,
A flame from the city of Sihon;
It consumed Ar of Moab,
The lords of the heights of the Arnon.
29 Woe to you, Moab!
You have perished, O people of Chemosh!
He has given his sons as fugitives,
And his daughters into captivity,
To Sihon king of the Amorites.

30 "But we have shot at them;
Heshbon has perished as far as Dibon.
Then we laid waste as far as Nophah,
Which *reaches* to Medeba."

31Thus Israel dwelt in the land of the Amorites. 32Then Moses sent to spy out Jazer; and they took its villages and drove out the Amorites who *were* there.

KING OG DEFEATED

33And they turned and went up by the way to Bashan. So Og king of Bashan went out against them, he and all his people, to battle at Edrei. 34Then the LORD said to Moses, "Do not fear him, for I have delivered him into your hand, with all his people and his land; and you shall do to him as you did to Sihon king of the Amorites, who dwelt at Heshbon." 35So they defeated him, his sons, and all his people, until there was no survivor left him; and they took possession of his land.

BALAK SENDS FOR BALAAM

1Then the children of Israel moved, and camped in the plains of Moab on the side of the Jordan *across from* Jericho.
2Now Balak the son of Zippor saw all that Israel had done to the Amorites. 3And Moab was exceedingly afraid of the people because they *were* many, and Moab was sick with dread because of the children of Israel. 4So Moab said to the elders of Midian, "Now this company will lick up everything around us, as an ox licks up the grass of the field." And Balak the son of Zippor *was* king of the Moabites at that time. 5Then he sent messengers to Balaam the son of Beor at Pethor, which *is* near the River[a] in the land of the sons of his people,[b] to call him, saying: "Look, a people has come from Egypt. See, they cover the face of the earth, and are settling

next to me! 6Therefore please come at once, curse this people for me, for they *are* too mighty for me. Perhaps I shall be able to defeat them and drive them out of the land, for I know that he whom you bless *is* blessed, and he whom you curse is cursed."

7So the elders of Moab and the elders of Midian departed with the diviner's fee in their hand, and they came to Balaam and spoke to him the words of Balak. 8And he said to them, "Lodge here tonight, and I will bring back word to you, as the LORD speaks to me." So the princes of Moab stayed with Balaam.

9Then God came to Balaam and said, "Who *are* these men with you?"

10So Balaam said to God, "Balak the son of Zippor, king of Moab, has sent to me, *saying*, 11'Look, a people has come out of Egypt, and they cover the face of the earth. Come now, curse them for me; perhaps I shall be able to overpower them and drive them out.' "

12And God said to Balaam, "You shall not go with them; you shall not curse the people, for they *are* blessed."

13So Balaam rose in the morning and said to the princes of Balak, "Go back to your land, for the LORD has refused to give me permission to go with you."

14And the princes of Moab rose and went to Balak, and said, "Balaam refuses to come with us."

15Then Balak again sent princes, more numerous and more honorable than they. 16And they came to Balaam and said to him, "Thus says Balak the son of Zippor: 'Please let nothing hinder you from coming to me; 17for I will certainly honor you greatly, and I will do whatever you say to me. Therefore please come, curse this people for me.' "

18Then Balaam answered and said to the servants of Balak, "Though Balak were to give me his house full of silver and gold, I could not go beyond the word of the LORD my God, to do less or more. 19Now therefore, please, you also stay here tonight, that I may know what more the LORD will say to me."

20And God came to Balaam at night and said to him, "If the men come to call you, rise *and* go with them; but only the word which I speak to you—that you shall do." 21So Balaam rose in

"Then the LORD said to Moses, 'Do not fear him, for I have delivered him into your hand, with all his people and his land.' " (Numbers 21:34a)

the morning, saddled his donkey, and went with the princes of Moab.

BALAAM, THE DONKEY, AND THE ANGEL

²²Then God's anger was aroused because he went, and the Angel of the LORD took His stand in the way as an adversary against him. And he was riding on his donkey, and his two servants *were* with him. ²³Now the donkey saw the Angel of the LORD standing in the way with His drawn sword in His hand, and the donkey turned aside out of the way and went into the field. So Balaam struck the donkey to turn her back onto the road. ²⁴Then the Angel of the LORD stood in a narrow path between the vineyards, *with* a wall on this side and a wall on that side. ²⁵And when the donkey saw the Angel of the LORD, she pushed herself against the wall and crushed Balaam's foot against the wall; so he struck her again. ²⁶Then the Angel of the LORD went further, and stood in a narrow place where there *was* no way to turn either to the right hand or to the left. ²⁷And when the donkey saw the Angel of the LORD, she lay down under Balaam; so Balaam's anger was aroused, and he struck the donkey with his staff.

WHAT'S IT MEAN?

Standing only about four feet high, donkeys pack a lot of strength in their small bodies. These powerful creatures were useful for work in the fields and also for transportation. Here's one more piece of donkey trivia for you: The donkey was one of the first animals tamed and put to use by humans.

Numbers 22:23

²⁸Then the LORD opened the mouth of the donkey, and she said to Balaam, "What have I done to you, that you have struck me these three times?"

²⁹And Balaam said to the donkey, "Because you have abused me. I wish there were a sword in my hand, for now I would kill you!"

³⁰So the donkey said to Balaam, "*Am* I not your donkey on which you have ridden, ever since *I became* yours, to this day? Was I ever disposed to do this to you?"

And he said, "No."

³¹Then the LORD opened Balaam's eyes, and he saw the Angel of the LORD standing in the way with His drawn sword in His hand; and he bowed his head and fell flat on his face. ³²And the Angel of the LORD said to him, "Why have you struck your donkey these three times? Behold, I have come out to stand against you, because *your* way is perverse before Me. ³³The donkey saw Me and turned aside from Me these three times. If she had not turned aside from Me, surely I would also have killed you by now, and let her live."

³⁴And Balaam said to the Angel of the LORD, "I have sinned, for I did not know You stood in the way against me. Now therefore, if it displeases You, I will turn back."

³⁵Then the Angel of the LORD said to Balaam, "Go with the men, but only the word that I speak to you, that you shall speak." So Balaam went with the princes of Balak.

³⁶Now when Balak heard that Balaam was coming, he went out to meet him at the city of Moab, which *is* on the border at the Arnon, the boundary of the territory. ³⁷Then Balak said to Balaam, "Did I not earnestly send to you, calling for you? Why did you not come to me? Am I not able to honor you?"

³⁸And Balaam said to Balak, "Look, I have come to you! Now, have I any power at all to say anything? The word that God puts in my mouth, that I must speak." ³⁹So Balaam went with Balak, and they came to Kirjath Huzoth. ⁴⁰Then Balak offered oxen and sheep, and he sent *some* to Balaam and to the princes who *were* with him.

BALAAM'S FIRST PROPHECY

⁴¹So it was, the next day, that Balak took Balaam and brought him up to the high places of Baal, that from there he might observe the extent of the people.

¹Then Balaam said to Balak, "Build seven altars for me here, and prepare for me here seven bulls and seven rams."

²And Balak did just as Balaam had spoken, and Balak and Balaam offered a bull and a ram on *each* altar. ³Then Balaam said to Balak, "Stand by your burnt offering, and I will go; perhaps the LORD will come to meet me, and whatever He shows me I will tell you." So he went to a desolate height. ⁴And God met Balaam, and he said to Him, "I have prepared the seven altars, and I have offered on *each* altar a bull and a ram."

⁵Then the LORD put a word in Balaam's mouth, and said, "Return to Balak, and thus you shall speak." ⁶So he returned to him, and there he was, standing by his burnt offering, he and all the princes of Moab.

⁷And he took up his oracle and said:

"Balak the king of Moab has brought me
    from Aram,
  From the mountains of the east.
  'Come, curse Jacob for me,
  And come, denounce Israel!'

8 "How shall I curse whom God has not
        cursed?
    And how shall I denounce *whom* the
        LORD has not denounced?
9 For from the top of the rocks I see him,
    And from the hills I behold him;
    There! A people dwelling alone,
    Not reckoning itself among the nations.

10 "Who can count the dust*a* of Jacob,
    Or number one-fourth of Israel?
    Let me die the death of the righteous,
    And let my end be like his!"

¹¹Then Balak said to Balaam, "What have
you done to me? I took you to curse my enemies, and look, you have blessed *them* bountifully!"
¹²So he answered and said, "Must I not take
heed to speak what the LORD has put in my
mouth?"

BALAAM'S SECOND PROPHECY

¹³Then Balak said to him, "Please come with
me to another place from which you may see
them; you shall see only the outer part of them,
and shall not see them all; curse them for me
from there." ¹⁴So he brought him to the field of
Zophim, to the top of Pisgah, and built seven
altars, and offered a bull and a ram on *each* altar.
¹⁵And he said to Balak, "Stand here by your
burnt offering while I meet*a* the LORD over there."
¹⁶Then the LORD met Balaam, and put a
word in his mouth, and said, "Go back to Balak,
and thus you shall speak." ¹⁷So he came to him,
and there he was, standing by his burnt offering, and the princes of Moab were with him.
And Balak said to him, "What has the LORD
spoken?"
¹⁸Then he took up his oracle and said:

"Rise up, Balak, and hear!
  Listen to me, son of Zippor!

19 "God *is* not a man, that He should lie,
    Nor a son of man, that He should repent.
    Has He said, and will He not do?
    Or has He spoken, and will He not make
      it good?
20 Behold, I have received *a command* to bless;
    He has blessed, and I cannot reverse it.

23:10 *a*Or *dust cloud*   **23:15** *a*Following Masoretic Text, Targum, and Vulgate; Syriac reads *call*; Septuagint
reads *go and ask God.*

∴ Promise   HE PROMISES NOT TO BE LIKE PEOPLE.

*God is not a man, that He should lie, nor a son of man, that He should repent.
Has He said, and will He not do? Or has He spoken, and will He not make it good?*
(Num. 23:19).

Do you know anyone who has *never* broken a promise? It's a fact: Somewhere along the line,
everyone is going to break a promise. Maybe they didn't mean to and they're terribly sorry, but
for some reason they just couldn't keep their word. That can hurt. The Bible tells us that God is
not like people. Aren't you glad that He doesn't break any of His promises?
God's Word tells us that Christ says yes to *all* His promises for you. And all we have to do is say
Amen (or, literally, "Let it be") to that promise. If God said it, He'll do it. If He spoke it, He'll
bring it to pass. God cannot lie. He is not human. He's not going to lie, and He's not going to
change His mind. Do you know what that means? All the promises of the Bible are for you.
He's not going to forget one of them. You've been promised not only eternal life, but also "all
things that pertain to life and godliness" here on earth (2 Pet. 1:3). Personalize every one of
His promises for yourself because He is the One who always keeps His promises!
   SEE FOR YOURSELF:
   Josh. 23:15; 1 Kin. 8:56; 2 Cor. 1:20

21 "He has not observed iniquity in Jacob,
Nor has He seen wickedness in Israel.
The LORD his God *is* with him,
And the shout of a King *is* among them.
22 God brings them out of Egypt;
He has strength like a wild ox.

23 "For *there is* no sorcery against Jacob,
Nor any divination against Israel.
It now must be said of Jacob
And of Israel, 'Oh, what God has done!'
24 Look, a people rises like a lioness,
And lifts itself up like a lion;
It shall not lie down until it devours the prey,
And drinks the blood of the slain."

25Then Balak said to Balaam, "Neither curse them at all, nor bless them at all!"
26So Balaam answered and said to Balak, "Did I not tell you, saying, 'All that the LORD speaks, that I must do'?"

BALAAM'S THIRD PROPHECY

27Then Balak said to Balaam, "Please come, I will take you to another place; perhaps it will please God that you may curse them for me from there." 28So Balak took Balaam to the top of Peor, that overlooks the wasteland.*a* 29Then Balaam said to Balak, "Build for me here seven altars, and prepare for me here seven bulls and seven rams." 30And Balak did as Balaam had said, and offered a bull and a ram on *every* altar.
1Now when Balaam saw that it pleased the LORD to bless Israel, he did not go as at other times, to seek to use sorcery, but he set his face toward the wilderness. 2And Balaam raised his eyes, and saw Israel encamped according to their tribes; and the Spirit of God came upon him.
3Then he took up his oracle and said:

"The utterance of Balaam the son of Beor,
The utterance of the man whose eyes are opened,
4 The utterance of him who hears the words of God,
Who sees the vision of the Almighty,
Who falls down, with eyes wide open:

5 "How lovely are your tents, O Jacob!
Your dwellings, O Israel!
6 Like valleys that stretch out,
Like gardens by the riverside,
Like aloes planted by the LORD,

Like cedars beside the waters.
7 He shall pour water from his buckets,
And his seed *shall be* in many waters.

"His king shall be higher than Agag,
And his kingdom shall be exalted.

8 "God brings him out of Egypt;
He has strength like a wild ox;
He shall consume the nations, his enemies;
He shall break their bones
And pierce *them* with his arrows.
9 'He bows down, he lies down as a lion;
And as a lion, who shall rouse him?'*a*

"Blessed *is* he who blesses you,
And cursed *is* he who curses you."

10Then Balak's anger was aroused against Balaam, and he struck his hands together; and Balak said to Balaam, "I called you to curse my enemies, and look, you have bountifully blessed *them* these three times! 11Now therefore, flee to your place. I said I would greatly honor you, but in fact, the LORD has kept you back from honor."
12So Balaam said to Balak, "Did I not also speak to your messengers whom you sent to me, saying, 13'If Balak were to give me his house full of silver and gold, I could not go beyond the word of the LORD, to do good or bad of my own will. What the LORD says, that I must speak'? 14And now, indeed, I am going to my people. Come, I will advise you what this people will do to your people in the latter days."

BALAAM'S FOURTH PROPHECY

15So he took up his oracle and said:

"The utterance of Balaam the son of Beor,
And the utterance of the man whose eyes are opened;
16 The utterance of him who hears the words of God,
And has the knowledge of the Most High,
Who sees the vision of the Almighty,
Who falls down, with eyes wide open:

17 "I see Him, but not now;
I behold Him, but not near;
A Star shall come out of Jacob;
A Scepter shall rise out of Israel,
And batter the brow of Moab,
And destroy all the sons of tumult.*a*

23:28 *a*Hebrew *Jeshimon* 24:9 *a*Genesis 49:9 24:17 *a*Hebrew *Sheth* (compare Jeremiah 48:45)

18 "And Edom shall be a possession;
     Seir also, his enemies, shall be a
          possession,
     While Israel does valiantly.
19   Out of Jacob One shall have
          dominion,
     And destroy the remains of the city."

²⁰Then he looked on Amalek, and he took up his oracle and said:

"Amalek *was* first among the nations,
 But *shall be* last until he perishes."

²¹Then he looked on the Kenites, and he took up his oracle and said:

"Firm is your dwelling place,
 And your nest is set in the rock;
22   Nevertheless Kain shall be burned.
     How long until Asshur carries you away
          captive?"

²³Then he took up his oracle and said:

"Alas! Who shall live when God does this?
24   But ships *shall come* from the coasts of
          Cyprus,ᵃ
     And they shall afflict Asshur and afflict
          Eber,
     And so shall *Amalek,*ᵇ until he perishes."

²⁵So Balaam rose and departed and returned to his place; Balak also went his way.

ISRAEL'S HARLOTRY IN MOAB

¹Now Israel remained in Acacia Grove,ᵃ and the people began to commit harlotry with the women of Moab. ²They invited the people to the sacrifices of their gods, and the people ate and bowed down to their gods. ³So Israel was joined to Baal of Peor, and the anger of the LORD was aroused against Israel.

⁴Then the LORD said to Moses, "Take all the leaders of the people and hang the offenders before the LORD, out in the sun, that the fierce anger of the LORD may turn away from Israel."

⁵So Moses said to the judges of Israel, "Every one of you kill his men who were joined to Baal of Peor."

⁶And indeed, one of the children of Israel came and presented to his brethren a Midianite woman in the sight of Moses and in the sight of all the congregation of the children of Israel,

WHAT'S IT MEAN?

Baal, whose name means "lord" or "master," was a fertility god worshiped by the Canaanites. The Canaanites had an odd way of "personalizing" Baal. Because Baal was worshiped throughout Canaan, the Canaanites added the names of their towns to his name. Baal-Peor is an example of this. To make things even more complicated, sometimes Baal was referred to as simply Peor.

Numbers 25:3–5

who *were* weeping at the door of the tabernacle of meeting. ⁷Now when Phinehas the son of Eleazar, the son of Aaron the priest, saw *it,* he rose from among the congregation and took a javelin in his hand; ⁸and he went after the man of Israel into the tent and thrust both of them through, the man of Israel, and the woman through her body. So the plague was stopped among the children of Israel. ⁹And those who died in the plague were twenty-four thousand.

¹⁰Then the LORD spoke to Moses, saying: ¹¹"Phinehas the son of Eleazar, the son of Aaron the priest, has turned back My wrath from the children of Israel, because he was zealous with My zeal among them, so that I did not consume the children of Israel in My zeal. ¹²Therefore say, 'Behold, I give to him My covenant of peace; ¹³and it shall be to him and his descendants after him a covenant of an everlasting priesthood, because he was zealous for his God, and made atonement for the children of Israel.' "

¹⁴Now the name of the Israelite who was killed, who was killed with the Midianite woman, *was* Zimri the son of Salu, a leader of a father's house among the Simeonites. ¹⁵And the name of the Midianite woman who was killed *was* Cozbi the daughter of Zur; he *was* head of the people of a father's house in Midian.

¹⁶Then the LORD spoke to Moses, saying: ¹⁷"Harass the Midianites, and attack them; ¹⁸for they harassed you with their schemes by which they seduced you in the matter of Peor and in the matter of Cozbi, the daughter of a leader of Midian, their sister, who was killed in the day of the plague because of Peor."

24:24 ᵃHebrew *Kittim* ᵇLiterally *he* or *that one*   **25:1** ᵃHebrew *Shittim*

THE SECOND CENSUS OF ISRAEL

[1]And it came to pass, after the plague, that the LORD spoke to Moses and Eleazar the son of Aaron the priest, saying: [2]"Take a census of all the congregation of the children of Israel from twenty years old and above, by their fathers' houses, all who are able to go to war in Israel." [3]So Moses and Eleazar the priest spoke with them in the plains of Moab by the Jordan, *across from* Jericho, saying: [4]*"Take a census of the people* from twenty years old and above, just as the LORD commanded Moses and the children of Israel who came out of the land of Egypt."

[5]Reuben *was* the firstborn of Israel. The children of Reuben *were: of* Hanoch, the family of the Hanochites; *of* Pallu, the family of the Palluites; [6]*of* Hezron, the family of the Hezronites; *of* Carmi, the family of the Carmites. [7]These *are* the families of the Reubenites: those who were numbered of them were forty-three thousand seven hundred and thirty. [8]And the son of Pallu *was* Eliab. [9]The sons of Eliab *were* Nemuel, Dathan, and Abiram. These *are* the Dathan and Abiram, representatives of the congregation, who contended against Moses and Aaron in the company of Korah, when they contended against the LORD; [10]and the earth opened its mouth and swallowed them up together with Korah when that company died, when the fire devoured two hundred and fifty men; and they became a sign. [11]Nevertheless the children of Korah did not die.

[12]The sons of Simeon according to their families *were: of* Nemuel,[a] the family of the Nemuelites; *of* Jamin, the family of the Jaminites; *of* Jachin,[b] the family of the Jachinites; [13]*of* Zerah,[a] the family of the Zarhites; *of* Shaul, the family of the Shaulites. [14]These *are* the families of the Simeonites: twenty-two thousand two hundred.

[15]The sons of Gad according to their families *were: of* Zephon,[a] the family of the Zephonites; *of* Haggi, the family of the Haggites; *of* Shuni, the family of the Shunites; [16]*of* Ozni,[a] the family of the Oznites; *of* Eri, the family of the Erites; [17]*of* Arod,[a] the family of the Arodites; *of* Areli, the family of the Arelites. [18]These *are* the families of the sons of Gad according to those who were numbered of them: forty thousand five hundred.

[19]The sons of Judah *were* Er and Onan; and Er and Onan died in the land of Canaan. [20]And the sons of Judah according to their families were: *of* Shelah, the family of the Shelanites; *of* Perez, the family of the Parzites; *of* Zerah, the family of the Zarhites. [21]And the sons of Perez were: *of* Hezron, the family of the Hezronites; *of* Hamul, the family of the Hamulites. [22]These *are* the families of Judah according to those who were numbered of them: seventy-six thousand five hundred.

[23]The sons of Issachar according to their families *were: of* Tola, the family of the Tolaites; *of* Puah,[a] the family of the Punites;[b] [24]*of* Jashub, the family of the Jashubites; *of* Shimron, the family of the Shimronites. [25]These *are* the families of Issachar according to those who were numbered of them: sixty-four thousand three hundred.

[26]The sons of Zebulun according to their families *were: of* Sered, the family of the Sardites; *of* Elon, the family of the Elonites; *of* Jahleel, the family of the Jahleelites. [27]These *are* the families of the Zebulunites according to those who were numbered of them: sixty thousand five hundred.

[28]The sons of Joseph according to their families, by Manasseh and Ephraim, *were:* [29]The sons of Manasseh: of Machir, the family of the Machirites; and Machir begot Gilead; of Gilead, the family of the Gileadites. [30]These *are* the sons of Gilead: *of* Jeezer,[a] the family of the Jeezerites; of Helek, the family of the Helekites; [31]*of* Asriel, the family of the Asrielites; *of* Shechem, the family of the Shechemites; [32]*of* Shemida, the family of the Shemidaites; *of* Hepher, the family of the Hepherites. [33]Now Zelophehad the son of Hepher had no sons, but daughters; and the names of the daughters of Zelophehad *were*

> "Behold, I give to him My covenant of peace; and it shall be to him and his descendants after him a covenant of an everlasting priesthood, because he was zealous for his God."
> (Numbers 25:12, 13a)

26:12 [a]Spelled *Jemuel* in Genesis 46:10 and Exodus 6:15 [b]Called *Jarib* in 1 Chronicles 4:24 **26:13** [a]Called *Zohar* in Genesis 46:10 **26:15** [a]Called *Ziphion* in Genesis 46:16 **26:16** [a]Called *Ezbon* in Genesis 46:16 **26:17** [a]Spelled *Arodi* in Samaritan Pentateuch, Syriac, and Genesis 46:16 **26:23** [a]Hebrew *Puvah* (compare Genesis 46:13 and 1 Chronicles 7:1); Samaritan Pentateuch, Septuagint, Syriac, and Vulgate read *Puah.* [b]Samaritan Pentateuch, Septuagint, Syriac, and Vulgate read *Puaites.* **26:30** [a]Called *Abiezer* in Joshua 17:2

Mahlah, Noah, Hoglah, Milcah, and Tirzah. ³⁴These *are* the families of Manasseh; and those who were numbered of them *were* fifty-two thousand seven hundred.

³⁵These *are* the sons of Ephraim according to their families: of Shuthelah, the family of the Shuthalhites; of Becher,^a the family of the Bachrites; of Tahan, the family of the Tahanites. ³⁶And these *are* the sons of Shuthelah: of Eran, the family of the Eranites. ³⁷These *are* the families of the sons of Ephraim according to those who were numbered of them: thirty-two thousand five hundred.

These *are* the sons of Joseph according to their families.

³⁸The sons of Benjamin according to their families were: of Bela, the family of the Belaites; of Ashbel, the family of the Ashbelites; of Ahiram, the family of the Ahiramites; ³⁹of Shupham,^a the family of the Shuphamites; of Hupham,^b the family of the Huphamites. ⁴⁰And the sons of Bela were Ard^a and Naaman: *of Ard*, the family of the Ardites; of Naaman, the family of the Naamites. ⁴¹These *are* the sons of Benjamin according to their families; and those who were numbered of them *were* forty-five thousand six hundred.

⁴²These *are* the sons of Dan according to their families: of Shuham,^a the family of the Shuhamites. These *are* the families of Dan according to their families. ⁴³All the families of the Shuhamites, according to those who were numbered of them, *were* sixty-four thousand four hundred.

⁴⁴The sons of Asher according to their families *were:* of Jimna, the family of the Jimnites; of Jesui, the family of the Jesuites; of Beriah, the family of the Beriites. ⁴⁵Of the sons of Beriah: of Heber, the family of the Heberites; of Malchiel, the family of the Malchielites. ⁴⁶And the name of the daughter of Asher *was* Serah. ⁴⁷These *are* the families of the sons of Asher according to those who were numbered of them: fifty-three thousand four hundred.

⁴⁸The sons of Naphtali according to their families *were:* of Jahzeel,^a the family of the Jahzeelites; of Guni, the family of the Gunites; ⁴⁹of Jezer, the family of the Jezerites; of Shillem, the family of the Shillemites. ⁵⁰These *are* the families of Naphtali according to their families; and those who were numbered of them *were* forty-five thousand four hundred.

⁵¹These *are* those who were numbered of the children of Israel: six hundred and one thousand seven hundred and thirty.

⁵²Then the Lord spoke to Moses, saying: ⁵³"To these the land shall be divided as an inheritance, according to the number of names. ⁵⁴To a large *tribe* you shall give a larger inheritance, and to a small *tribe* you shall give a smaller inheritance. Each shall be given its inheritance according to those who were numbered of them. ⁵⁵But the land shall be divided by lot; they shall inherit according to the names of the tribes of their fathers. ⁵⁶According to the lot their inheritance shall be divided between the larger and the smaller."

⁵⁷And these *are* those who were numbered of the Levites according to their families: of Gershon, the family of the Gershonites; of Kohath, the family of the Kohathites; of Merari, the family of the Merarites. ⁵⁸These *are* the families of the Levites: the family of the Libnites, the family of the Hebronites, the family of the Mahlites, the family of the Mushites, and the family of the Korathites. And Kohath begot Amram. ⁵⁹The name of Amram's wife *was* Jochebed the daughter of Levi, who was born to Levi in Egypt; and to Amram she bore Aaron and Moses and their sister Miriam. ⁶⁰To Aaron were born Nadab and Abihu, Eleazar and Ithamar. ⁶¹And Nadab and Abihu died when they offered profane fire before the Lord.

⁶²Now those who were numbered of them were twenty-three thousand, every male from a month old and above; for they were not numbered among the other children of Israel, because there was no inheritance given to them among the children of Israel.

⁶³These *are* those who were numbered by Moses and Eleazar the priest, who numbered the children of Israel in the plains of Moab by the Jordan, *across from* Jericho. ⁶⁴But among these there was not a man of those who were numbered by Moses and Aaron the priest when they numbered the children of Israel in the Wilderness of Sinai. ⁶⁵For the Lord had said of them, "They shall surely die in the wilderness." So there was not left a man of them, except Caleb the son of Jephunneh and Joshua the son of Nun.

INHERITANCE LAWS

¹Then came the daughters of Zelophehad the son of Hepher, the son of Gilead, the son of Machir, the son of Manasseh, from the families

---

26:35 ^aCalled *Bered* in 1 Chronicles 7:20   **26:39** ^aMasoretic Text reads *Shephupham*, spelled *Shephuphan* in 1 Chronicles 8:5.   ^bCalled *Huppim* in Genesis 46:21   **26:40** ^aCalled *Addar* in 1 Chronicles 8:3   **26:42** ^aCalled *Hushim* in Genesis 46:23   **26:48** ^aSpelled *Jahziel* in 1 Chronicles 7:13

of Manasseh the son of Joseph; and these *were* the names of his daughters: Mahlah, Noah, Hoglah, Milcah, and Tirzah. ²And they stood before Moses, before Eleazar the priest, and before the leaders and all the congregation, *by* the doorway of the tabernacle of meeting, saying: ³"Our father died in the wilderness; but he was not in the company of those who gathered together against the LORD, in company with Korah, but he died in his own sin; and he had no sons. ⁴Why should the name of our father be removed from among his family because he had no son? Give us a possession among our father's brothers."

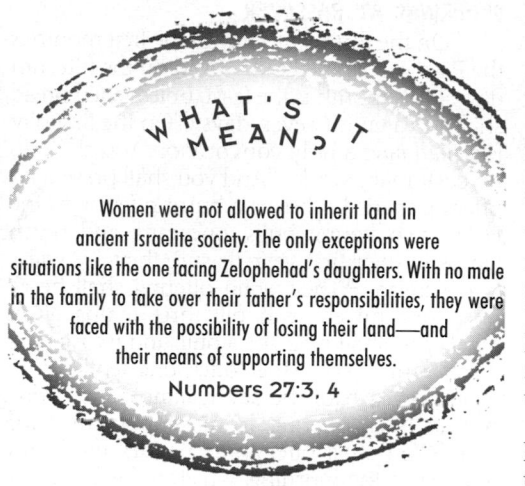

WHAT'S IT MEAN?

Women were not allowed to inherit land in ancient Israelite society. The only exceptions were situations like the one facing Zelophehad's daughters. With no male in the family to take over their father's responsibilities, they were faced with the possibility of losing their land—and their means of supporting themselves.

Numbers 27:3, 4

⁵So Moses brought their case before the LORD.

⁶And the LORD spoke to Moses, saying: ⁷"The daughters of Zelophehad speak *what is* right; you shall surely give them a possession of inheritance among their father's brothers, and cause the inheritance of their father to pass to them. ⁸And you shall speak to the children of Israel, saying: 'If a man dies and has no son, then you shall cause his inheritance to pass to his daughter. ⁹If he has no daughter, then you shall give his inheritance to his brothers. ¹⁰If he has no brothers, then you shall give his inheritance to his father's brothers. ¹¹And if his father has no brothers, then you shall give his inheritance to the relative closest to him in his family, and he shall possess it.'" And it shall be to the children of Israel a statute of judgment, just as the LORD commanded Moses.

JOSHUA THE NEXT LEADER OF ISRAEL

¹²Now the LORD said to Moses: "Go up into this Mount Abarim, and see the land which I have given to the children of Israel. ¹³And when you have seen it, you also shall be gathered to your people, as Aaron your brother was gathered. ¹⁴For in the Wilderness of Zin, during the strife of the congregation, you rebelled against My command to hallow Me at the waters before their eyes." (These *are* the waters of Meribah, at Kadesh in the Wilderness of Zin.)

¹⁵Then Moses spoke to the LORD, saying: ¹⁶"Let the LORD, the God of the spirits of all flesh, set a man over the congregation, ¹⁷who may go out before them and go in before them, who may lead them out and bring them in, that the congregation of the LORD may not be like sheep which have no shepherd."

LEADERSHIP
Who should leaders look out for? (27:16, 17)

¹⁸And the LORD said to Moses: "Take Joshua the son of Nun with you, a man in whom *is* the Spirit, and lay your hand on him; ¹⁹set him before Eleazar the priest and before all the congregation, and inaugurate him in their sight. ²⁰And you shall give *some* of your authority to him, that all the congregation of the children of Israel may be obedient. ²¹He shall stand before Eleazar the priest, who shall inquire before the LORD for him by the judgment of the Urim. At his word they shall go out, and at his word they shall come in, he and all the children of Israel with him—all the congregation."

²²So Moses did as the LORD commanded him. He took Joshua and set him before Eleazar the priest and before all the congregation. ²³And he laid his hands on him and inaugurated him, just as the LORD commanded by the hand of Moses.

DAILY OFFERINGS

¹Now the LORD spoke to Moses, saying, ²"Command the children of Israel, and say to them, 'My offering, My food for My offerings made by fire as a sweet aroma to Me, you shall be careful to offer to Me at their appointed time.'

³"And you shall say to them, 'This *is* the offering made by fire which you shall offer to the LORD: two male lambs in their first year without blemish, day by day, as a regular burnt offering. ⁴The one lamb you shall offer in the morning, the other lamb you shall offer in the evening, ⁵and one-tenth of an ephah of fine flour as a grain offering mixed with one-fourth of a hin of pressed oil. ⁶*It is* a regular burnt offering which was ordained at Mount Sinai for a sweet aroma, an offering made by fire to the LORD. ⁷And its drink offering *shall be* one-fourth of a hin for each lamb; in a holy *place* you shall pour out the drink to the LORD as an offering. ⁸The other lamb you shall offer in the evening;

On the Edge

Now the LORD spoke to Moses, saying, "Command the children of Israel, and say to them . . ." (Num. 28:1, 2).

God told Moses to give lots of laws to the people of Israel. He did that because He wanted to bless the people. You're thinking *What? Why would He make them do all that stuff if all He wanted was to bless them? Why didn't He just bless them anyway?* Think about it. God is holy. He has rules for living. He will not bless sin. He could not have a bunch of people running around doing whatever they wanted and then bless them in spite of it. The laws don't exist so that God can play "boss" and bark orders to people. They were necessary conditions for the blessing that comes from holy living. Jewish law had 613 points, or rules, that had to be obeyed before a person could approach God. Imagine that. It would be impossible for anybody to meet all those demands. When Jesus came, He fulfilled the law—all 613 points. When Jesus lives in you, every rule is obeyed. The law is satisfied and you can approach God. You are free from having to live up to all those rules. Jesus has done it for you.

SEE FOR YOURSELF:

Ex. 20; Deut. 5:1–22; 1 Chr. 22:13; Rom. 10:4; Gal. 3—5

---

fine flour as a grain offering, mixed with oil, for the one ram; ¹³and one-tenth *of an ephah* of fine flour, mixed with oil, as a grain offering for each lamb, as a burnt offering of sweet aroma, an offering made by fire to the LORD. ¹⁴Their drink offering shall be half a hin of wine for a bull, one-third of a hin for a ram, and one-fourth of a hin for a lamb; this *is* the burnt offering for each month throughout the months of the year. ¹⁵Also one kid of the goats as a sin offering to the LORD shall be offered, besides the regular burnt offering and its drink offering.

OFFERINGS AT PASSOVER

¹⁶'On the fourteenth day of the first month *is* the Passover of the LORD. ¹⁷And on the fifteenth day of this month *is* the feast; unleavened bread shall be eaten for seven days. ¹⁸On the first day *you shall have* a holy convocation. You shall do no customary work. ¹⁹And you shall present an offering made by fire as a burnt offering to the LORD: two young bulls, one ram, and seven lambs in their first year. Be sure they are without blemish. ²⁰Their grain offering shall be of fine flour mixed with oil: three-tenths *of an ephah* you shall offer for a bull, and two-tenths for a ram; ²¹you shall offer one-tenth *of an ephah* for each of the seven lambs; ²²also one goat *as* a sin offering, to make atonement for you. ²³You shall offer these besides the burnt offering of the morning, which *is* for a regular burnt offering. ²⁴In this manner you shall offer the food of the offering made by fire daily for seven days, as a sweet aroma to the LORD; it shall be offered besides the regular burnt offering and its drink offering. ²⁵And on the seventh day you shall have a holy convocation. You shall do no customary work.

---

as the morning grain offering and its drink offering, you shall offer *it* as an offering made by fire, a sweet aroma to the LORD.

SABBATH OFFERINGS

⁹And on the Sabbath day two lambs in their first year, without blemish, and two-tenths *of an ephah* of fine flour as a grain offering, mixed with oil, with its drink offering— ¹⁰*this is* the burnt offering for every Sabbath, besides the regular burnt offering with its drink offering.

MONTHLY OFFERINGS

¹¹'At the beginnings of your months you shall present a burnt offering to the LORD: two young bulls, one ram, and seven lambs in their first year, without blemish; ¹²three-tenths *of an ephah* of fine flour as a grain offering, mixed with oil, for each bull; two-tenths *of an ephah* of

---

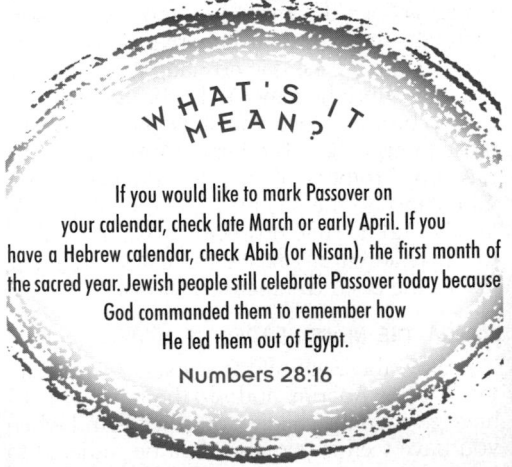

WHAT'S IT MEAN?

If you would like to mark Passover on your calendar, check late March or early April. If you have a Hebrew calendar, check Abib (or Nisan), the first month of the sacred year. Jewish people still celebrate Passover today because God commanded them to remember how He led them out of Egypt.

Numbers 28:16

OFFERINGS AT THE FEAST OF WEEKS

²⁶'Also on the day of the firstfruits, when you bring a new grain offering to the LORD at your *Feast of Weeks*, you shall have a holy convocation. You shall do no customary work. ²⁷You shall present a burnt offering as a sweet aroma to the LORD: two young bulls, one ram, and seven lambs in their first year, ²⁸with their grain offering of fine flour mixed with oil: three-tenths *of an ephah* for each bull, two-tenths for the one ram, ²⁹and one-tenth for each of the seven lambs; ³⁰*also* one kid of the goats, to make atonement for you. ³¹Be sure they are without blemish. You shall present *them* with their drink offerings, besides the regular burnt offering with its grain offering.

OFFERINGS AT THE FEAST OF TRUMPETS

¹'And in the seventh month, on the first *day* of the month, you shall have a holy convocation. You shall do no customary work. For you it is a day of blowing the trumpets. ²You shall offer a burnt offering as a sweet aroma to the LORD: one young bull, one ram, *and* seven lambs in their first year, without blemish. ³Their grain offering *shall be* fine flour mixed with oil: three-tenths *of an ephah* for the bull, two-tenths for the ram, ⁴and one-tenth for each of the seven lambs; ⁵also one kid of the goats *as a sin* offering, to make atonement for you; ⁶besides the burnt offering with its grain offering for the New Moon, the regular burnt offering with its grain offering, and their drink offerings, according to their ordinance, as a sweet aroma, an offering made by fire to the LORD.

OFFERINGS ON THE DAY OF ATONEMENT

⁷'On the tenth *day* of this seventh month you shall have a holy convocation. You shall afflict your souls; you shall not do any work. ⁸You shall present a burnt offering to the LORD *as* a sweet aroma: one young bull, one ram, *and* seven lambs in their first year. Be sure they are without blemish. ⁹Their grain offering *shall be of* fine flour mixed with oil: three-tenths *of an ephah* for the bull, two-tenths for the one ram, ¹⁰and one-tenth for each of the seven lambs; ¹¹also one kid of the goats *as a* sin offering, besides the sin offering for atonement, the regular burnt offering with its grain offering, and their drink offerings.

OFFERINGS AT THE FEAST OF TABERNACLES

¹²'On the fifteenth day of the seventh month you shall have a holy convocation. You shall do no customary work, and you shall keep a feast to the LORD seven days. ¹³You shall present a burnt offering, an offering made by fire as a sweet aroma to the LORD: thirteen young bulls, two rams, *and* fourteen lambs in their first year. They shall be without blemish. ¹⁴Their grain offering *shall be of* fine flour mixed with oil: three-tenths *of an ephah* for each of the thirteen bulls, two-tenths for each of the two rams, ¹⁵and one-tenth for each of the fourteen lambs; ¹⁶also one kid of the goats *as* a sin offering, besides the regular burnt offering, its grain offering, and its drink offering.

¹⁷'On the second day *present* twelve young bulls, two rams, fourteen lambs in their first year without blemish, ¹⁸and their grain offering and their drink offerings for the bulls, for the rams, and for the lambs, by their number, according to the ordinance; ¹⁹also one kid of the goats *as* a sin offering, besides the regular burnt offering with its grain offering, and their drink offerings.

²⁰'On the third day *present* eleven bulls, two rams, fourteen lambs in their first year without blemish, ²¹and their grain offering and their drink offerings for the bulls, for the rams, and for the lambs, by their number, according to the ordinance; ²²also one goat *as* a sin offering, besides the regular burnt offering, its grain offering, and its drink offering.

²³'On the fourth day *present* ten bulls, two rams, *and* fourteen lambs in their first year, without blemish, ²⁴and their grain offering and their drink offerings for the bulls, for the rams, and for the lambs, by their number, according to the ordinance; ²⁵also one kid of the goats *as* a sin offering, besides the regular burnt offering, its grain offering, and its drink offering.

²⁶'On the fifth day *present* nine bulls, two rams, *and* fourteen lambs in their first year without blemish, ²⁷and their grain offering and their drink offerings for the bulls, for the rams, and for the lambs, by their number, according to the ordinance; ²⁸also one goat *as* a sin offering, besides the regular burnt offering, its grain offering, and its drink offering.

²⁹'On the sixth day *present* eight bulls, two rams, *and* fourteen lambs in their first year without blemish, ³⁰and their grain offering and their drink offerings for the bulls, for the rams, and for the lambs, by their number, according to the ordinance; ³¹also one goat *as* a sin offering, besides the regular burnt offering, its grain offering, and its drink offering.

³²'On the seventh day *present* seven bulls, two rams, *and* fourteen lambs in their first year without blemish, ³³and their grain offering and their drink offerings for the bulls, for the rams, and for the lambs, by their number, according

to the ordinance; ³⁴also one goat *as* a sin offering, besides the regular burnt offering, its grain offering, and its drink offering.

³⁵'On the eighth day you shall have a sacred assembly. You shall do no customary work. ³⁶You shall present a burnt offering, an offering made by fire as a sweet aroma to the LORD: one bull, one ram, seven lambs in their first year without blemish, ³⁷and their grain offering and their drink offerings for the bull, for the ram, and for the lambs, by their number, according to the ordinance; ³⁸also one goat *as* a sin offering, besides the regular burnt offering, its grain offering, and its drink offering.

³⁹'These you shall present to the LORD at your appointed feasts (besides your vowed offerings and your freewill offerings) as your burnt offerings and your grain offerings, as your drink offerings and your peace offerings.' "

⁴⁰So Moses told the children of Israel everything, just as the LORD commanded Moses.

> "So Moses told the children of Israel everything, just as the LORD commanded Moses."
> (Numbers 29:40)

THE LAW CONCERNING VOWS

¹Then Moses spoke to the heads of the tribes concerning the children of Israel, saying, "This *is* the thing which the LORD has commanded: ²If a man makes a vow to the LORD, or swears an oath to bind himself by some agreement, he shall not break his word; he shall do according to all that proceeds out of his mouth.

³"Or if a woman makes a vow to the LORD, and binds *herself* by some agreement while in her father's house in her youth, ⁴and her father hears her vow and the agreement by which she has bound herself, and her father holds his peace, then all her vows shall stand, and every agreement with which she has bound herself shall stand. ⁵But if her father overrules her on the day that he hears, then none of her vows nor her agreements by which she has bound herself shall stand; and the LORD will release her, because her father overruled her.

⁶"If indeed she takes a husband, while bound by her vows or by a rash utterance from her lips by which she bound herself, ⁷and her husband hears *it*, and makes no response to her on the day that he hears, then her vows shall stand, and her agreements by which she bound herself shall stand. ⁸But if her husband overrules her on the day that he hears *it*, he shall make void her vow which she took and what she uttered with her lips, by which she bound herself, and the LORD will release her.

⁹"Also any vow of a widow or a divorced woman, by which she has bound herself, shall stand against her.

¹⁰"If she vowed in her husband's house, or bound herself by an agreement with an oath, ¹¹and her husband heard *it*, and made no response to her *and* did not overrule her, then all her vows shall stand, and every agreement by which she bound herself shall stand. ¹²But if her husband truly made them void on the day he heard *them*, then whatever proceeded from her lips concerning her vows or concerning the agreement binding her, it shall not stand; her husband has made them void, and the LORD will release her. ¹³Every vow and every binding oath to afflict her soul, her husband may confirm it, or her husband may make it void. ¹⁴Now if her husband makes no response whatever to her from day to day, then he confirms all her vows or all the agreements that bind her; he confirms them, because he made no response to her on the day that he heard *them*. ¹⁵But if he does make them void after he has heard *them*, then he shall bear her guilt."

¹⁶These *are* the statutes which the LORD commanded Moses, between a man and his wife, and between a father and his daughter in her youth in her father's house.

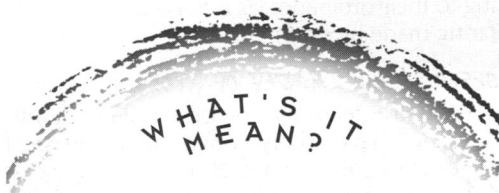

WHAT'S IT MEAN?

Among the Israelites, the men were responsible for the women in their family. In many cases, the men had the power to make decisions for the women. Widows and divorced women were not under the authority of a man, so they were responsible for themselves.

Numbers 30:9

VENGEANCE ON THE MIDIANITES

¹And the LORD spoke to Moses, saying: ²"Take vengeance on the Midianites for the children of Israel. Afterward you shall be gathered to your people."

³So Moses spoke to the people, saying, "Arm some of yourselves for war, and let them go against the Midianites to take vengeance for the LORD on Midian. ⁴A thousand from each tribe of all the tribes of Israel you shall send to the war."

⁵So there were recruited from the divisions of Israel one thousand from *each* tribe, twelve thousand armed for war. ⁶Then Moses sent them to the war, one thousand from *each* tribe; he sent them to the war with Phinehas the son of Eleazar the priest, with the holy articles and the signal trumpets in his hand. ⁷And they warred against the Midianites, just as the LORD commanded Moses, and they killed all the males. ⁸They killed the kings of Midian with *the rest of* those who were killed—Evi, Rekem, Zur, Hur, and Reba, the five kings of Midian. Balaam the son of Beor they also killed with the sword.

⁹And the children of Israel took the women of Midian captive, with their little ones, and took as spoil all their cattle, all their flocks, and all their goods. ¹⁰They also burned with fire all the cities where they dwelt, and all their forts. ¹¹And they took all the spoil and all the booty—of man and beast.

RETURN FROM THE WAR

¹²Then they brought the captives, the booty, and the spoil to Moses, to Eleazar the priest, and to the congregation of the children of Israel, to the camp in the plains of Moab by the Jordan, *across from* Jericho. ¹³And Moses, Eleazar the priest, and all the leaders of the congregation, went to meet them outside the camp. ¹⁴But Moses was angry with the officers of the army, *with* the captains over thousands and captains over hundreds, who had come from the battle.

¹⁵And Moses said to them: "Have you kept all the women alive? ¹⁶Look, these *women* caused the children of Israel, through the counsel of Balaam, to trespass against the LORD in the incident of Peor, and there was a plague among the congregation of the LORD. ¹⁷Now therefore, kill every male among the little ones, and kill every woman who has known a man intimately. ¹⁸But keep alive for yourselves all the young girls who have not known a man intimately. ¹⁹And as for you, remain outside the camp seven days; whoever has killed any person, and whoever has touched any slain, purify yourselves and your captives on the third day and on the seventh day. ²⁰Purify every garment, everything made of leather, everything woven of goats' *hair*, and everything made of wood."

²¹Then Eleazar the priest said to the men of war who had gone to the battle, "This *is* the or-

WHAT'S IT MEAN?

God's orders to kill the women who had had sex may seem extreme, but remember, the Midianites used sex as part of their idol worship. The people who had been exposed to this type of "religious" ceremony might have brought those influences to the Israelites' worship of God.

Numbers 31:17, 18

dinance of the law which the LORD commanded Moses: ²²"Only the gold, the silver, the bronze, the iron, the tin, and the lead, ²³everything that can endure fire, you shall put through the fire, and it shall be clean; and it shall be purified with the water of purification. But all that cannot endure fire you shall put through water. ²⁴And you shall wash your clothes on the seventh day and be clean, and afterward you may come into the camp."

DIVISION OF THE PLUNDER

²⁵Now the LORD spoke to Moses, saying: ²⁶"Count up the plunder that was taken—of man and beast—you and Eleazar the priest and the chief fathers of the congregation; ²⁷and divide the plunder into two parts, between those who took part in the war, who went out to battle, and all the congregation. ²⁸And levy a tribute for the LORD on the men of war who went out to battle: one of every five hundred of the persons, the cattle, the donkeys, and the sheep; ²⁹take *it* from their half, and give *it* to Eleazar the priest as a heave offering to the LORD. ³⁰And from the children of Israel's half you shall take one of every fifty, drawn from the persons, the cattle, the donkeys, and the sheep, from all the livestock, and give them to the Levites who keep charge of the tabernacle of the LORD." ³¹So Moses and Eleazar the priest did as the LORD commanded Moses.

³²The booty remaining from the plunder, which the men of war had taken, was six hundred and seventy-five thousand sheep, ³³seventy-two thousand cattle, ³⁴sixty-one thousand donkeys, ³⁵and thirty-two thousand persons in all, of women who had not known a man intimately. ³⁶And the half, the portion for those who had gone out to war, was in number three hundred

and thirty-seven thousand five hundred sheep; [37]and the LORD's tribute of the sheep was six hundred and seventy-five. [38]The cattle *were* thirty-six thousand, of which the LORD's tribute *was* seventy-two. [39]The donkeys *were* thirty thousand five hundred, of which the LORD's tribute *was* sixty-one. [40]The persons *were* sixteen thousand, of which the LORD's tribute *was* thirty-two persons. [41]So Moses gave the tribute *which was* the LORD's heave offering to Eleazar the priest, as the LORD commanded Moses.

[42]And from the children of Israel's half, which Moses separated from the men who fought— [43]now the half belonging to the congregation was three hundred and thirty-seven thousand five hundred sheep, [44]thirty-six thousand cattle, [45]thirty thousand five hundred donkeys, [46]and sixteen thousand persons— [47]and from the children of Israel's half Moses took one of every fifty, drawn from man and beast, and gave them to the Levites, who kept charge of the tabernacle of the LORD, as the LORD commanded Moses.

[48]Then the officers who *were* over thousands of the army, the captains of thousands and captains of hundreds, came near to Moses; [49]and they said to Moses, "Your servants have taken a count of the men of war who *are* under our command, and not a man of us is missing. [50]Therefore we have brought an offering for the LORD, what every man found of ornaments of gold: armlets and bracelets and signet rings and earrings and necklaces, to make atonement for ourselves before the LORD." [51]So Moses and Eleazar the priest received the gold from them, all the fashioned ornaments. [52]And all the gold of the offering that they offered to the LORD, from the captains of thousands and captains of hundreds, was sixteen thousand seven hundred and fifty shekels. [53](The men of war had taken spoil, every man for himself.) [54]And Moses and Eleazar the priest received the gold from the captains of thousands and of hundreds, and brought it into the tabernacle of meeting as a memorial for the children of Israel before the LORD.

THE TRIBES SETTLING EAST OF THE JORDAN

[1]Now the children of Reuben and the children of Gad had a very great multitude of livestock; and when they saw the land of Jazer and the land of Gilead, that indeed the region *was* a place for livestock, [2]the children of Gad and the children of Reuben came and spoke to Moses, to Eleazar the priest, and to the leaders of the congregation, saying, [3]"Ataroth, Dibon, Jazer, Nimrah, Heshbon, Elealeh, Shebam, Nebo, and Beon, [4]the country which the LORD defeated before the congregation of Israel, *is* a land for livestock, and your servants have livestock." [5]Therefore they said, "If we have found favor in your sight, let this land be given to your servants as a possession. Do not take us over the Jordan."

[6]And Moses said to the children of Gad and to the children of Reuben: "Shall your brethren go to war while you sit here? [7]Now why will you discourage the heart of the children of Israel from going over into the land which the LORD has given them? [8]Thus your fathers did when I sent them away from Kadesh Barnea to see the land. [9]For when they went up to the Valley of Eshcol and saw the land, they discouraged the heart of the children of Israel, so that they did not go into the land which the LORD had given them. [10]So the LORD's anger was aroused on that day, and He swore an oath, saying, [11]'Surely none of the men who came up from Egypt, from twenty years old and above, shall see the land of which I swore to Abraham, Isaac, and Jacob, because they have not wholly followed Me, [12]except Caleb the son of Jephunneh, the Kenizzite, and Joshua the son of Nun, for they have wholly followed the LORD.' [13]So the LORD's anger was aroused against Israel, and He made them wander in the wilderness forty years, until all the generation that had done evil in the sight of the LORD was gone. [14]And look! You have risen in your fathers' place, a brood of sinful men, to increase still more the fierce anger of the LORD against Israel. [15]For if you turn away from following Him, He will once again leave them in the wilderness, and you will destroy all these people."

[16]Then they came near to him and said: "We will build sheepfolds here for our livestock, and cities for our little ones, [17]but we ourselves will be armed, ready *to go* before the children of Israel until we have brought them to their place; and our little ones will dwell in the fortified cities because of the inhabitants of the land. [18]We will not return to our homes until every one of the children of Israel has received his inheritance. [19]For we will not inherit with them on the other side of the Jordan and beyond, because our inheritance has fallen to us on this eastern side of the Jordan."

[20]Then Moses said to them: "If you do this thing, if you arm yourselves before the LORD for the war, [21]and all your armed men cross over the Jordan before the LORD until He has driven out His enemies from before Him, [22]and the land is subdued before the LORD, then after-

ward you may return and be blameless before the LORD and before Israel; and this land shall be your possession before the LORD. ²³But if you do not do so, then take note, you have sinned against the LORD; and be sure your sin will find you out. ²⁴Build cities for your little ones and folds for your sheep, and do what has proceeded out of your mouth."

²⁵And the children of Gad and the children of Reuben spoke to Moses, saying: "Your servants will do as my lord commands. ²⁶Our little ones, our wives, our flocks, and all our livestock will be there in the cities of Gilead; ²⁷but your servants will cross over, every man armed for war, before the LORD to battle, just as my lord says."

²⁸So Moses gave command concerning them to Eleazar the priest, to Joshua the son of Nun, and to the chief fathers of the tribes of the children of Israel. ²⁹And Moses said to them: "If the children of Gad and the children of Reuben cross over the Jordan with you, every man armed for battle before the LORD, and the land is subdued before you, then you shall give them the land of Gilead as a possession. ³⁰But if they do not cross over armed with you, they shall have possessions among you in the land of Canaan."

³¹Then the children of Gad and the children of Reuben answered, saying: "As the LORD has said to your servants, so we will do. ³²We will cross over armed before the LORD into the land of Canaan, but the possession of our inheritance *shall remain* with us on this side of the Jordan."

³³So Moses gave to the children of Gad, to the children of Reuben, and to half the tribe of Manasseh the son of Joseph, the kingdom of Sihon king of the Amorites and the kingdom of Og king of Bashan, the land with its cities within the borders, the cities of the surrounding country. ³⁴And the children of Gad built Dibon and Ataroth and Aroer, ³⁵Atroth and Shophan and Jazer and Jogbehah, ³⁶Beth Nimrah and Beth Haran, fortified cities, and folds for sheep. ³⁷And the children of Reuben built Heshbon and Elealeh and Kirjathaim, ³⁸Nebo and Baal Meon (*their* names being changed) and Shibmah; and they gave *other* names to the cities which they built.

³⁹And the children of Machir the son of Manasseh went to Gilead and took it, and dispossessed the Amorites who *were* in it. ⁴⁰So Moses gave Gilead to Machir the son of Manasseh, and he dwelt in it. ⁴¹Also Jair the son of Manasseh went and took its small towns, and called them Havoth Jair.[a] ⁴²Then Nobah went and took Kenath and its villages, and he called it Nobah, after his own name.

ISRAEL'S JOURNEY FROM EGYPT REVIEWED

¹These *are* the journeys of the children of Israel, who went out of the land of Egypt by their armies under the hand of Moses and Aaron. ²Now Moses wrote down the starting points of their journeys at the command of the LORD. And these *are* their journeys according to their starting points:

³They departed from Rameses in the first month, on the fifteenth day of the first month; on the day after the Passover the children of Israel went out with boldness in the sight of all the Egyptians. ⁴For the Egyptians were burying all *their* firstborn, whom the LORD had killed among them. Also on their gods the LORD had executed judgments.

⁵Then the children of Israel moved from Rameses and camped at Succoth. ⁶They departed from Succoth and camped at Etham, which *is* on the edge of the wilderness. ⁷They moved from Etham and turned back to Pi Hahiroth, which *is* east of Baal Zephon; and they camped near Migdol. ⁸They departed from before Hahiroth[a] and passed through the midst of the sea into the wilderness, went three days' journey in the Wilderness of Etham, and camped at Marah. ⁹They moved from Marah and came to Elim. At Elim *were* twelve springs of water and seventy palm trees; so they camped there.

¹⁰They moved from Elim and camped by the Red Sea. ¹¹They moved from the Red Sea and camped in the Wilderness of Sin. ¹²They journeyed from the Wilderness of Sin and camped at Dophkah. ¹³They departed from Dophkah and camped at Alush. ¹⁴They moved from Alush and camped at Rephidim, where there was no water for the people to drink.

¹⁵They departed from Rephidim and camped in the Wilderness of Sinai. ¹⁶They moved from the Wilderness of Sinai and camped at Kibroth Hattaavah. ¹⁷They departed from Kibroth Hattaavah and camped at Hazeroth. ¹⁸They departed from Hazeroth and camped at Rithmah. ¹⁹They departed from Rithmah and camped at Rimmon Perez. ²⁰They departed from Rimmon Perez and camped at Libnah. ²¹They moved from Libnah and

32:41 [a]Literally *Towns of Jair*   **33:8** [a]Many Hebrew manuscripts, Samaritan Pentateuch, Syriac, Targum, and Vulgate read *from Pi Hahiroth* (compare verse 7).

camped at Rissah. ²²They journeyed from Rissah and camped at Kehelathah. ²³They went from Kehelathah and camped at Mount Shepher. ²⁴They moved from Mount Shepher and camped at Haradah. ²⁵They moved from Haradah and camped at Makheloth. ²⁶They moved from Makheloth and camped at Tahath. ²⁷They departed from Tahath and camped at Terah. ²⁸They moved from Terah and camped at Mithkah. ²⁹They went from Mithkah and camped at Hashmonah. ³⁰They departed from Hashmonah and camped at Moseroth. ³¹They departed from Moseroth and camped at Bene Jaakan. ³²They moved from Bene Jaakan and camped at Hor Hagidgad. ³³They went from Hor Hagidgad and camped at Jotbathah. ³⁴They moved from Jotbathah and camped at Abronah. ³⁵They departed from Abronah and camped at Ezion Geber. ³⁶They moved from Ezion Geber and camped in the Wilderness of Zin, which is Kadesh. ³⁷They moved from Kadesh and camped at Mount Hor, on the boundary of the land of Edom.

³⁸Then Aaron the priest went up to Mount Hor at the command of the LORD, and died there in the fortieth year after the children of Israel had come out of the land of Egypt, on the first day of the fifth month. ³⁹Aaron was one hundred and twenty-three years old when he died on Mount Hor.

⁴⁰Now the king of Arad, the Canaanite, who dwelt in the South in the land of Canaan, heard of the coming of the children of Israel.

⁴¹So they departed from Mount Hor and camped at Zalmonah. ⁴²They departed from Zalmonah and camped at Punon. ⁴³They departed from Punon and camped at Oboth. ⁴⁴They departed from Oboth and camped at Ije Abarim, at the border of Moab. ⁴⁵They departed from Ijim^a and camped at Dibon Gad. ⁴⁶They moved from Dibon Gad and camped at Almon Diblathaim. ⁴⁷They moved from Almon Diblathaim and camped in the mountains of Abarim, before Nebo. ⁴⁸They departed from the mountains of Abarim and camped in the plains of Moab by the Jordan, across from Jericho. ⁴⁹They camped by the Jordan, from Beth Jesimoth as far as the Abel Acacia Grove^a in the plains of Moab.

INSTRUCTIONS FOR THE CONQUEST OF CANAAN

⁵⁰Now the LORD spoke to Moses in the plains of Moab by the Jordan, across from Jericho, saying, ⁵¹"Speak to the children of Israel, and say to them: 'When you have crossed the Jordan into the land of Canaan, ⁵²then you shall drive out all the inhabitants of the land from before you, destroy all their engraved stones, destroy all their molded images, and demolish all their high places; ⁵³you shall dispossess the inhabitants of the land and dwell in it, for I have given you the land to possess. ⁵⁴And you shall divide the land by lot as an inheritance among your families; to the larger you shall give a larger inheritance, and to the smaller you shall give a smaller inheritance; there everyone's inheritance shall be whatever falls to him by lot. You shall inherit according to the tribes of your fathers. ⁵⁵But if you do not drive out the inhabitants of the land from before you, then it shall be that those whom you let remain shall be irritants in your eyes and thorns in your sides, and they shall harass you in the land where you dwell. ⁵⁶Moreover it shall be that I will do to you as I thought to do to them.' "

THE APPOINTED BOUNDARIES OF CANAAN

¹Then the LORD spoke to Moses, saying, ²"Command the children of Israel, and say to them: 'When you come into the land of Canaan, this is the land that shall fall to you as an inheritance—the land of Canaan to its boundaries. ³Your southern border shall be from the Wilderness of Zin along the border of Edom; then your southern border shall extend eastward to the end of the Salt Sea; ⁴your border shall turn from the southern side of the Ascent of Akrabbim, continue to Zin, and be on the south of Kadesh Barnea; then it shall go on to Hazar Addar, and continue to Azmon; ⁵the border shall turn from Azmon to the Brook of Egypt, and it shall end at the Sea.

⁶As for the western border, you shall have

> "Speak to the children of Israel, and say to them: 'When you have crossed the Jordan into the land of Canaan, then you shall drive out all the inhabitants of the land from before you.' "
> (Numbers 33:51, 52a)

33:45 ^aSame as Ije Abarim, verse 44   **33:49** ^aHebrew Abel Shittim the Great Sea for a border; this shall be your western border.

7And this shall be your northern border: From the Great Sea you shall mark out your *border* line to Mount Hor; 8from Mount Hor you shall mark out *your border* to the entrance of Hamath; then the direction of the border shall be toward Zedad; 9the border shall proceed to Ziphron, and it shall end at Hazar Enan. This shall be your northern border.

10"You shall mark out your eastern border from Hazar Enan to Shepham; 11the border shall go down from Shepham to Riblah on the east side of Ain; the border shall go down and reach to the eastern side of the Sea of Chinnereth; 12the border shall go down along the Jordan, and it shall end at the Salt Sea. This shall be your land with its surrounding boundaries.' "

13Then Moses commanded the children of Israel, saying: "This *is* the land which you shall inherit by lot, which the LORD has commanded to give to the nine tribes and to the half-tribe. 14For the tribe of the children of Reuben according to the house of their fathers, and the tribe of the children of Gad according to the house of their fathers, have received *their inheritance;* and the half-tribe of Manasseh has received its inheritance. 15The two tribes and the half-tribe have received their inheritance on this side of the Jordan, *across from* Jericho eastward, toward the sunrise."

THE LEADERS APPOINTED TO DIVIDE THE LAND

16And the LORD spoke to Moses, saying, 17"These *are* the names of the men who shall divide the land among you as an inheritance: Eleazar the priest and Joshua the son of Nun. 18And you shall take one leader of every tribe to divide the land for the inheritance. 19These *are* the names of the men: from the tribe of Judah, Caleb the son of Jephunneh; 20from the tribe of the children of Simeon, Shemuel the son of Ammihud; 21from the tribe of Benjamin, Elidad the son of Chislon; 22a leader from the tribe of the children of Dan, Bukki the son of Jogli; 23from the sons of Joseph: a leader from the tribe of the children of Manasseh, Hanniel the son of Ephod, 24and a leader from the tribe of the children of Ephraim, Kemuel the son of Shiphtan; 25a leader from the tribe of the children of Zebulun, Elizaphan the son of Parnach; 26a leader from the tribe of the children of Issachar, Paltiel the son of Azzan; 27a leader from the tribe of the children of Asher, Ahihud the son of Shelomi; 28and a leader from the tribe of the children of Naphtali, Pedahel the son of Ammihud."

29These *are* the ones the LORD commanded to divide the inheritance among the children of Israel in the land of Canaan.

CITIES FOR THE LEVITES

1And the LORD spoke to Moses in the plains of Moab by the Jordan *across from* Jericho, saying: 2"Command the children of Israel that they give the Levites cities to dwell in from the inheritance of their possession, and you shall *also* give the Levites common-land around the cities. 3They shall have the cities to dwell in; and their common-land shall be for their cattle, for their herds, and for all their animals. 4The common-land of the cities which you will give the Levites *shall extend* from the wall of the city outward a thousand cubits all around. 5And you shall measure outside the city on the east side two thousand cubits, on the south side two thousand cubits, on the west side two thousand cubits, and on the north side two thousand cubits. The city *shall be* in the middle. This shall belong to them as common-land for the cities.

6"Now among the cities which you will give to the Levites *you shall appoint* six cities of refuge, to which a manslayer may flee. And to these you shall add forty-two cities. 7So all the cities you will give to the Levites *shall be* forty-eight; these *you shall give* with their common-land. 8And the cities which you will give *shall be* from the possession of the children of Israel; from the larger *tribe* you shall give many, from the smaller you shall give few. Each shall give some of its cities to the Levites, in proportion to the inheritance that each receives."

CITIES OF REFUGE

9Then the LORD spoke to Moses, saying, 10"Speak to the children of Israel, and say to them: 'When you cross the Jordan into the land of Canaan, 11then you shall appoint cities to be cities of refuge for you, that the manslayer who kills any person accidentally may flee there. 12They shall be cities of refuge for you from the avenger, that the manslayer may not die until he stands before the congregation in judgment. 13And of the cities which you give, you shall have six cities of refuge. 14You shall appoint three cities on this side of the Jordan, and three cities you shall appoint in the land of Canaan, *which* will be cities of refuge. 15These six cities shall be for refuge for the children of Israel, for the stranger, and for the sojourner among them, that anyone who kills a person accidentally may flee there.

16'But if he strikes him with an iron implement, so that he dies, he *is* a murderer; the murderer shall surely be put to death. ¹⁷And if he strikes him with a stone in the hand, by which one could die, and he does die, he *is* a murderer; the murderer shall surely be put to death. ¹⁸Or *if* he strikes him with a wooden hand weapon, by which one could die, and he does die, he *is* a murderer; the murderer shall surely be put to death. ¹⁹The avenger of blood himself shall put the murderer to death; when he meets him, he shall put him to death. ²⁰If he pushes him out of hatred or, while lying in wait, hurls something at him so that he dies, ²¹or in enmity he strikes him with his hand so that he dies, the one who struck *him* shall surely be put to death. He *is* a murderer. The avenger of blood shall put the murderer to death when he meets him.

²²However, if he pushes him suddenly without enmity, or throws anything at him without lying in wait, ²³or uses a stone, by which a man could die, throwing *it* at him without seeing *him*, so that he dies, while he was not his enemy or seeking his harm, ²⁴then the congregation shall judge between the manslayer and the avenger of blood according to these judgments. ²⁵So the congregation shall deliver the manslayer from the hand of the avenger of blood, and the congregation shall return him to the city of refuge where he had fled, and he shall remain there until the death of the high priest who was anointed with the holy oil. ²⁶But if the manslayer at any time goes outside the limits of the city of refuge where he fled, ²⁷and the avenger of blood finds him outside the limits of his city of refuge, and the avenger of blood kills the manslayer, he shall not be guilty of blood, ²⁸because he should have remained in his city of refuge until the death of the high priest. But after the death of the high priest the manslayer may return to the land of his possession.

²⁹And these *things* shall be a statute of judgment to you throughout your generations in all your dwellings. ³⁰Whoever kills a person, the murderer shall be put to death on the testimony of witnesses; but one witness is not *sufficient* testimony against a person for the death *penalty.* ³¹Moreover you shall take no ransom for the life of a murderer who *is* guilty of death, but he shall surely be put to death. ³²And you shall take no ransom for him who has fled to his city of refuge, that he may return to dwell in the land before the death of the priest.

³³So you shall not pollute the land where you *are;* for blood defiles the land, and no atonement can be made for the land, for the blood that is shed on it, except by the blood of him who shed it. ³⁴Therefore do not defile the land which you inhabit, in the midst of which I dwell; for I the LORD dwell among the children of Israel.' "

MARRIAGE OF FEMALE HEIRS

¹Now the chief fathers of the families of the children of Gilead the son of Machir, the son of Manasseh, of the families of the sons of Joseph, came near and spoke before Moses and before the leaders, the chief fathers of the children of Israel. ²And they said: "The LORD commanded my lord *Moses* to give the land as an inheritance by lot to the children of Israel, and my lord was commanded by the LORD to give the inheritance of our brother Zelophehad to his daughters. ³Now if they are married to any of the sons of the *other* tribes of the children of Israel, then their inheritance will be taken from the inheritance of our fathers, and it will be added to the inheritance of the tribe into which they marry; so it will be taken from the lot of our inheritance. ⁴And when the Jubilee of the children of Israel comes, then their inheritance will be added to the inheritance of the tribe into which they marry; so their inheritance will be taken away from the inheritance of the tribe of our fathers."

⁵Then Moses commanded the children of Israel according to the word of the LORD, saying: "What the tribe of the sons of Joseph speaks is right. ⁶This *is* what the LORD commands concerning the daughters of Zelophehad, saying, 'Let them marry whom they think best, but they may marry only within the family of their father's tribe.' ⁷So the inheritance of the children of Israel shall not change hands from tribe to tribe, for every one of the children of Israel shall keep the inheritance of the tribe of his fathers. ⁸And every daughter who possesses an inheritance in any tribe of the children of Israel shall be the wife of one of the family of her father's tribe, so that the children of Israel each may possess the inheritance of his fathers. ⁹Thus no inheritance shall change hands from *one* tribe to another, but every tribe of the children of Israel shall keep its own inheritance."

"These are the commandments and the judgments which the LORD commanded the children of Israel by the hand of Moses."
(Numbers 36:13)

¹⁰Just as the LORD commanded Moses, so did the daughters of Zelophehad; ¹¹for Mahlah, Tirzah, Hoglah, Milcah, and Noah, the daughters of Zelophehad, were married to the sons of their father's brothers. ¹²They were married into the families of the children of Manasseh the son of Joseph, and their inheritance remained in the tribe of their father's family.

¹³These *are* the commandments and the judgments which the LORD commanded the children of Israel by the hand of Moses in the plains of Moab by the Jordan, *across from* Jericho.

Deuteronomy

CONTENT You don't really understand Deuteronomy unless you understand that this book is really a dying man's last words. Let's recap. Moses had just led the Hebrews out of Egypt and then wandered around the desert for forty years, trying to get up the courage and the faith to cross the border.

By the time they finally get to the border, only three of the adults who had left Egypt survived. To make it worse, one of them was about to die—Moses.

So Moses did what any leader would do. He gathered all the people together and he told them the story all over again. But he didn't just tell them the story, he told them why the story mattered and what they should do about it. It was his last chance, so he talked to them about *real stuff*, the *real-est*.

Imagine if your country had had the same president your whole life and he was a great and wonderful leader. Imagine your leader said, "You go the rest of the way without me. But before you leave, let me tell you one last thing . . ."

You'd listen to him, wouldn't you? Listen to Deuteronomy like that.

Purpose Love is expressed in God's Word and in our response to God's Word.

Themes Obedience Brings Blessing; Disobedience Brings Cursing

Date of writing 1445–1440 B.C.

> "And now, Israel, what does the LORD your God require of you, but to fear the LORD your God, to walk in all His ways and to love Him, to serve the LORD your God with all your heart and with all your soul, and to keep the commandments of the LORD and His statutes which I command you today for your good?" (10:12, 13).

Bible Talk

Biblical Welfare

There are a lot of directions in Deuteronomy about taking care of people who have less than you do. Sometimes those people were homeless. Sometimes they were poor. Every time they were less fortunate.

Deuteronomy doesn't let us off the hook by passing people's needs over to a church or an agency. Instead, Deuteronomy teaches us that if we pass someone in need we're responsible to at least help. Deuteronomy also has practical tips for helping people help themselves.

We think that's a modern lesson today—being a community. But it's not new. We just forgot that God had said it.

MOSES DIDN'T GO IN?

After all the effort Moses put into caring for the Hebrew people, he never got to set a foot into the land of Israel. Think about all he had done. He confronted Pharaoh even when it gave him the shivers. He wandered around for forty years with the worst grumblers he'd probably ever known. He faced God Himself on several occasions. But, in the end, he only got to hike to the top of a mountain and look over the other side.

If you want the whole sad tale, check out Numbers 20:6–12 and Deuteronomy 32:48–52.

THE PREVIOUS COMMAND TO ENTER CANAAN

¹These *are* the words which Moses spoke to all Israel on this side of the Jordan in the wilderness, in the plain*ᵃ* opposite Suph,*ᵇ* between Paran, Tophel, Laban, Hazeroth, and Dizahab. ²*It is* eleven days' *journey* from Horeb by way of Mount Seir to Kadesh Barnea. ³Now it came to pass in the fortieth year, in the eleventh month, on the first *day* of the month, *that* Moses spoke to the children of Israel according to all that the LORD had given him as commandments to them, ⁴after he had killed Sihon king of the Amorites, who dwelt in Heshbon, and Og king of Bashan, who dwelt at Ashtaroth in*ᵃ* Edrei.

⁵On this side of the Jordan in the land of Moab, Moses began to explain this law, saying, ⁶"The LORD our God spoke to us in Horeb, saying: 'You have dwelt long enough at this mountain. ⁷Turn and take your journey, and go to the mountains of the Amorites, to all the neighboring *places* in the plain,*ᵃ* in the mountains and in the lowland, in the South and on the seacoast, to the land of the Canaanites and to Lebanon, as far as the great river, the River Euphrates. ⁸See, I have set the land before you; go in and possess the land which the LORD swore to your fathers—to Abraham, Isaac, and Jacob—to give to them and their descendants after them.'

TRIBAL LEADERS APPOINTED

⁹"And I spoke to you at that time, saying: 'I alone am not able to bear you. ¹⁰The LORD your God has multiplied you, and here you *are* today, as the stars of heaven in multitude. ¹¹May the LORD God of your fathers make you a thousand times more numerous than you are, and bless you as He has promised you! ¹²How can I alone bear your problems and your burdens and your complaints? ¹³Choose wise, understanding, and knowledgeable men from among your tribes, and I will make them heads over you.' ¹⁴And you answered me and said, 'The thing which you have told *us* to do *is* good.' ¹⁵So I took the heads of your tribes, wise and knowledgeable men, and made them heads over you, leaders of thousands, leaders of hundreds, leaders of fifties, leaders of tens, and officers for your tribes.

¹⁶"Then I commanded your judges at that time, saying, 'Hear *the cases* between your brethren, and judge righteously between a man and his brother or the stranger who is with him. ¹⁷You shall not show partiality in judgment; you shall hear the small as well as the great; you shall not be afraid in any man's presence, for the judgment is God's. The case that is too hard for you, bring to me, and I will hear it.' ¹⁸And I commanded you at that time all the things which you should do.

ISRAEL'S REFUSAL TO ENTER THE LAND

¹⁹"So we departed from Horeb, and went through all that great and terrible wilderness which you saw on the way to the mountains of the Amorites, as the LORD our God had commanded us. Then we came to Kadesh Barnea. ²⁰And I said to you, 'You have come to the mountains of the Amorites, which the LORD our God is giving us. ²¹Look, the LORD your God has set the land before you; go up *and* possess *it*, as the LORD God of your fathers has spoken to you; do not fear or be discouraged.'

²²"And every one of you came near to me and said, 'Let us send men before us, and let them search out the land for us, and bring back

> "See, I have set the land before you; go in and possess the land which the LORD swore to your fathers—to Abraham, Isaac, and Jacob—to give to them and their descendants after them."
> (Deuteronomy 1:8)

WHAT'S IT MEAN?

In most places in the ancient world, a foreigner ("stranger") had no legal rights. The land of the Israelites, however, was different. God's people were expected to treat foreigners just as they would treat each other. They were to show that God's law applied to everyone.

Deuteronomy 1:16

1:1 *ᵃ*Hebrew *arabah* *ᵇ*One manuscript of the Septuagint, also Targum and Vulgate, read *Red Sea*. **1:4** *ᵃ*Septuagint, Syriac, and Vulgate read *and* (compare Joshua 12:4). **1:7** *ᵃ*Hebrew *arabah* word to us of the way by which we should go up, and of the cities into which we shall come.'

23"The plan pleased me well; so I took twelve of your men, one man from *each* tribe. 24And they departed and went up into the mountains, and came to the Valley of Eshcol, and spied it out. 25They also took *some* of the fruit of the land in their hands and brought *it* down to us; and they brought back word to us, saying, 'It *is* a good land which the LORD our God is giving us.'

26"Nevertheless you would not go up, but rebelled against the command of the LORD your God; 27and you complained in your tents, and said, 'Because the LORD hates us, He has brought us out of the land of Egypt to deliver us into the hand of the Amorites, to destroy us. 28Where can we go up? Our brethren have discouraged our hearts, saying, "The people *are* greater and taller than we; the cities *are* great and fortified up to heaven; moreover we have seen the sons of the Anakim there." '

29"Then I said to you, 'Do not be terrified, or afraid of them. 30The LORD your God, who goes before you, He will fight for you, according to all He did for you in Egypt before your eyes, 31and in the wilderness where you saw how the LORD your God carried you, as a man carries his son, in all the way that you went until you came to this place.' 32Yet, for all that, you did not believe the LORD your God, 33who went in the way before you to search out a place for you to pitch your tents, to show you the way you should go, in the fire by night and in the cloud by day.

THE PENALTY FOR ISRAEL'S REBELLION

34"And the LORD heard the sound of your words, and was angry, and took an oath, saying, 35'Surely not one of these men of this evil generation shall see that good land of which I swore to give to your fathers, 36except Caleb the son of Jephunneh; he shall see it, and to him and his children I am giving the land on which he walked, because he wholly followed the LORD.' 37The LORD was also angry with me for your sakes, saying, 'Even you shall not go in there. 38Joshua the son of Nun, who stands before you, he shall go in there. Encourage him, for he shall cause Israel to inherit it.

39'Moreover your little ones and your children, who you say will be victims, who today have no knowledge of good and evil, they shall go in there; to them I will give it, and they shall possess it. 40But *as for* you, turn and take your journey into the wilderness by the Way of the Red Sea.'

41"Then you answered and said to me, 'We have sinned against the LORD; we will go up and fight, just as the LORD our God commanded us.' And when everyone of you had girded on his weapons of war, you were ready to go up into the mountain.

42"And the LORD said to me, 'Tell them, "Do not go up nor fight, for I *am* not among you; lest you be defeated before your enemies." ' 43So I spoke to you; yet you would not listen, but rebelled against the command of the LORD, and presumptuously went up into the mountain. 44And the Amorites who dwelt in that mountain came out against you and chased you as bees do, and drove you back from Seir to Hormah. 45Then you returned and wept before the LORD, but the LORD would not listen to your voice nor give ear to you.

46"So you remained in Kadesh many days, according to the days that you spent *there*.

THE DESERT YEARS

1"Then we turned and journeyed into the wilderness of the Way of the Red Sea, as the LORD spoke to me, and we skirted Mount Seir for many days.

2"And the LORD spoke to me, saying: 3'You have skirted this mountain long enough; turn northward. 4And command the people, saying, "You *are about to* pass through the territory of your brethren, the descendants of Esau, who live in Seir; and they will be afraid of you. Therefore watch yourselves carefully. 5Do not meddle with them, for I will not give you *any* of their land, no, not so much as one footstep, because I have given Mount Seir to Esau *as* a possession. 6You shall buy food from them with money, that you may eat; and you shall also buy water from them with money, that you may drink.

7"For the LORD your God has blessed you in all the work of your hand. He knows your trudging through this great wilderness. These forty years the LORD your God *has been* with you; you have lacked nothing." '

8"And when we passed beyond our brethren, the descendants of Esau who dwell in Seir, away from the road of the plain, away from Elath and Ezion Geber, we turned and passed by way of the Wilderness of Moab. 9Then the LORD said to me, 'Do not harass Moab, nor contend with them in battle, for I will not give you *any* of their land *as* a possession, because I have given Ar to the descendants of Lot *as* a possession.' "

10(The Emim had dwelt there in times past, a people as great and numerous and tall as the

Anakim. [11]They were also regarded as giants,[a] like the Anakim, but the Moabites call them Emim. [12]The Horites formerly dwelt in Seir, but the descendants of Esau dispossessed them and destroyed them from before them, and dwelt in their place, just as Israel did to the land of their possession which the LORD gave them.)

[13]" 'Now rise and cross over the Valley of the Zered.' So we crossed over the Valley of the Zered. [14]And the time we took to come from Kadesh Barnea until we crossed over the Valley of the Zered was thirty-eight years, until all the generation of the men of war was consumed from the midst of the camp, just as the LORD had sworn to them. [15]For indeed the hand of the LORD was against them, to destroy them from the midst of the camp until they were consumed.

[16]"So it was, when all the men of war had finally perished from among the people, [17]that the LORD spoke to me, saying: [18]This day you are to cross over at Ar, the boundary of Moab. [19]And when you come near the people of Ammon, do not harass them or meddle with them, for I will not give you any of the land of the people of Ammon as a possession, because I have given it to the descendants of Lot as a possession.' "

[20](That was also regarded as a land of giants;[a] giants formerly dwelt there. But the Ammonites call them Zamzummim, [21]a people as great and numerous and tall as the Anakim. But the LORD destroyed them before them, and they dispossessed them and dwelt in their place, [22]just as He had done for the descendants of Esau, who dwelt in Seir, when He destroyed the Horites from before them. They dispossessed them and dwelt in their place, even to this day. [23]And the Avim, who dwelt in villages as far as Gaza—the Caphtorim, who came from Caphtor, destroyed them and dwelt in their place.)

[24]" 'Rise, take your journey, and cross over the River Arnon. Look, I have given into your hand Sihon the Amorite, king of Heshbon, and his land. Begin to possess it, and engage him in battle. [25]This day I will begin to put the dread and fear of you upon the nations under the whole heaven, who shall hear the report of you, and shall tremble and be in anguish because of you.'

KING SIHON DEFEATED

[26]"And I sent messengers from the Wilderness of Kedemoth to Sihon king of Heshbon, with words of peace, saying, [27]'Let me pass through your land; I will keep strictly to the road, and I will turn neither to the right nor to the left. [28]You shall sell me food for money, that I may eat, and give me water for money, that I may drink; only let me pass through on foot, [29]just as the descendants of Esau who dwell in Seir and the Moabites who dwell in Ar did for me, until I cross the Jordan to the land which the LORD our God is giving us.'

[30]"But Sihon king of Heshbon would not let us pass through, for the LORD your God hardened his spirit and made his heart obstinate, that He might deliver him into your hand, as it is this day.

[31]"And the LORD said to me, 'See, I have begun to give Sihon and his land over to you. Begin to possess it, that you may inherit his land.' [32]Then Sihon and all his people came out against us to fight at Jahaz. [33]And the LORD our God delivered him over to us; so we defeated him, his sons, and all his people. [34]We took all his cities at that time, and we utterly destroyed the men, women, and little ones of every city; we left none remaining. [35]We took only the livestock as plunder for ourselves, with the spoil of the cities which we took. [36]From Aroer, which is on the bank of the River Arnon, and from the city that is in the ravine, as far as Gilead, there was not one city too strong for us; the LORD our God delivered all to us. [37]Only you did not go near the land of the people of Ammon— anywhere along the River Jabbok, or to the cities of the mountains, or wherever the LORD our God had forbidden us.

KING OG DEFEATED

[1]"Then we turned and went up the road to Bashan; and Og king of Bashan came out against us, he and all his people, to battle at Edrei. [2]And the LORD said to me, 'Do not fear him, for I have delivered him and all his people and his land into your hand; you shall do to him as you did to Sihon king of the Amorites, who dwelt at Heshbon.'

[3]"So the LORD our God also delivered into our hands Og king of Bashan, with all his people, and we attacked him until he had no survivors remaining. [4]And we took all his cities at that time; there was not a city which we did not take from them: sixty cities, all the region of Argob, the kingdom of Og in Bashan. [5]All these cities were fortified with high walls, gates, and bars, besides a great many rural towns. [6]And we utterly destroyed them, as we did to Sihon king of Heshbon, utterly destroying the men,

women, and children of every city. ⁷But all the livestock and the spoil of the cities we took as booty for ourselves.

⁸"And at that time we took the land from the hand of the two kings of the Amorites who *were* on this side of the Jordan, from the River Arnon to Mount Hermon ⁹(the Sidonians call Hermon Sirion, and the Amorites call it Senir), ¹⁰all the cities of the plain, all Gilead, and all Bashan, as far as Salcah and Edrei, cities of the kingdom of Og in Bashan.

¹¹"For only Og king of Bashan remained of the remnant of the giants.ᵃ Indeed his bedstead *was* an iron bedstead. (*Is* it not in Rabbah of the people of Ammon?) Nine cubits *is* its length and four cubits its width, according to the standard cubit.

King Og was a big guy, both in his power and his size. This giant of a man ruled over sixty cities. Defeating him was like knocking out the heavyweight champ.

Deuteronomy 3:11

THE LAND EAST OF THE JORDAN DIVIDED

¹²"And this land, *which* we possessed at that time, from Aroer, which *is* by the River Arnon, and half the mountains of Gilead and its cities, I gave to the Reubenites and the Gadites. ¹³The rest of Gilead, and all Bashan, the kingdom of Og, I gave to half the tribe of Manasseh. (All the region of Argob, with all Bashan, was called the land of the giants.ᵃ ¹⁴Jair the son of Manasseh took all the region of Argob, as far as the border of the Geshurites and the Maachathites, and called Bashan after his own name, Havoth Jair,ᵃ to this day.)

¹⁵"Also I gave Gilead to Machir. ¹⁶And to the Reubenites and the Gadites I gave from Gilead as far as the River Arnon, the middle of the river as *the* border, as far as the River Jabbok, the border of the people of Ammon; ¹⁷the plain also, with the Jordan as *the* border, from Chinnereth as far as the east side of the Sea of the Arabah (the Salt Sea), below the slopes of Pisgah.

WHAT'S IT MEAN?

The land that each tribe received was supposed to be held by that tribe for always. Each tribe was responsible for protecting its territory, maintaining control over its region, and passing the land down from generation to generation.

Deuteronomy 3:12–17

¹⁸"Then I commanded you at that time, saying: 'The LORD your God has given you this land to possess. All you men of valor shall cross over armed before your brethren, the children of Israel. ¹⁹But your wives, your little ones, and your livestock (I know that you have much livestock) shall stay in your cities which I have given you, ²⁰until the LORD has given rest to your brethren as to you, and they also possess the land which the LORD your God is giving them beyond the Jordan. Then each of you may return to his possession which I have given you.'

²¹"And I commanded Joshua at that time, saying, 'Your eyes have seen all that the LORD your God has done to these two kings; so will the LORD do to all the kingdoms through which you pass. ²²You must not fear them, for the LORD your God Himself fights for you.'

MOSES FORBIDDEN TO ENTER THE LAND

²³"Then I pleaded with the LORD at that time, saying: ²⁴'O Lord GOD, You have begun to show Your servant Your greatness and Your mighty hand, for what god *is there* in heaven or on earth who can do *anything* like Your works and Your mighty *deeds*? ²⁵I pray, let me cross over and see the good land beyond the Jordan, those pleasant mountains, and Lebanon.'

²⁶"But the LORD was angry with me on your account, and would not listen to me. So the LORD said to me: 'Enough of that! Speak no more to Me of this matter. ²⁷Go up to the top of Pisgah, and lift your eyes toward the west, the north, the south, and the east; behold *it* with your eyes, for you shall not cross over this Jordan. ²⁸But command Joshua, and encourage

3:11 ᵃHebrew *rephaim*   **3:13** ᵃHebrew *rephaim*   **3:14** ᵃLiterally *Towns of Jair*

him and strengthen him; for he shall go over before this people, and he shall cause them to inherit the land which you will see.'

²⁹"So we stayed in the valley opposite Beth Peor.

MOSES COMMANDS OBEDIENCE

¹"Now, O Israel, listen to the statutes and the judgments which I teach you to observe, that you may live, and go in and possess the land which the LORD God of your fathers is giving you. ²You shall not add to the word which I command you, nor take from it, that you may keep the commandments of the LORD your God which I command you. ³Your eyes have seen

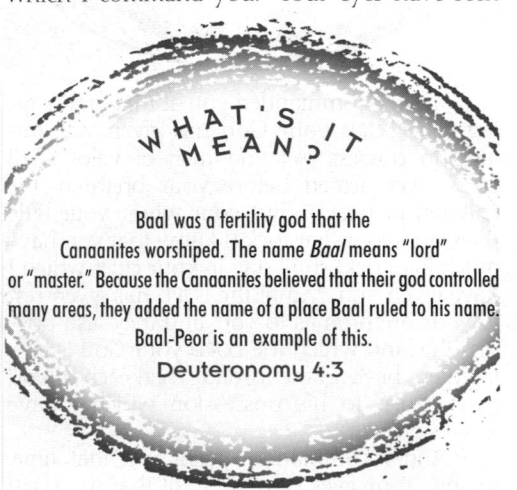

Baal was a fertility god that the Canaanites worshiped. The name *Baal* means "lord" or "master." Because the Canaanites believed that their god controlled many areas, they added the name of a place Baal ruled to his name. Baal-Peor is an example of this.

Deuteronomy 4:3

what the LORD did at Baal Peor; for the LORD your God has destroyed from among you all the men who followed Baal of Peor. ⁴But you who held fast to the LORD your God *are* alive today, every one of you.

⁵"Surely I have taught you statutes and judgments, just as the LORD my God commanded me, that you should act according *to them* in the land which you go to possess. ⁶Therefore be careful to observe *them;* for this *is* your wisdom and your understanding in the sight of the peoples who will hear all these statutes, and say, 'Surely this great nation *is* a wise and understanding people'.

⁷"For what great nation *is there* that has God so near to it, as the LORD our God *is* to us, for

whatever *reason* we may call upon Him? ⁸And what great nation *is there* that has *such* statutes and righteous judgments as are in all this law which I set before you this day? ⁹Only take heed to yourself, and diligently keep yourself, lest you forget the things your eyes have seen, and lest they depart from your heart all the days of your life. And teach them to your children and your grandchildren, ¹⁰*especially concerning* the day you stood before the LORD your God in Horeb, when the LORD said to me, 'Gather the people to Me, and I will let them hear My words, that they may learn to fear Me all the days they live on the earth, and *that* they may teach their children'.

¹¹"Then you came near and stood at the foot of the mountain, and the mountain burned with fire to the midst of heaven, with darkness, cloud, and thick darkness. ¹²And the LORD spoke to you out of the midst of the fire. You heard the sound of the words, but saw no form; *you* only *heard* a voice. ¹³So He declared to you His covenant which He commanded you to perform, the Ten Commandments; and He wrote them on two tablets of stone. ¹⁴And the LORD commanded me at that time to teach you statutes and judgments, that you might observe them in the land which you cross over to possess.

REPUTATION
How is a good reputation built? (4:1–14)

BEWARE OF IDOLATRY

¹⁵"Take careful heed to yourselves, for you saw no form when the LORD spoke to you at Horeb out of the midst of the fire, ¹⁶lest you act corruptly and make for yourselves a carved image in the form of any figure: the likeness of male or female, ¹⁷the likeness of any animal that *is* on the earth or the likeness of any winged bird that flies in the air, ¹⁸the likeness of anything that creeps on the ground or the likeness of any fish that *is* in the water beneath the earth. ¹⁹And *take heed,* lest you lift your eyes to heaven, and *when* you see the sun, the moon, and the stars, all the host of heaven, you feel driven to worship them and serve them, which the LORD

"Only take heed to yourself, and diligently keep yourself, lest you forget the things your eyes have seen, and lest they depart from your heart all the days of your life. And teach them to your children and your grandchildren."
(Deuteronomy 4:9)

your God has given to all the peoples under the whole heaven as a heritage. [20]But the LORD has taken you and brought you out of the iron furnace, out of Egypt, to be His people, an inheritance, as you are this day. [21]Furthermore the LORD was angry with me for your sakes, and swore that I would not cross over the Jordan, and that I would not enter the good land which the LORD your God is giving you as an inheritance. [22]But I must die in this land, I must not cross over the Jordan; but you shall cross over and possess that good land. [23]Take heed to yourselves, lest you forget the covenant of the LORD your God which He made with you, and make for yourselves a carved image in the form of anything which the LORD your God has forbidden you. [24]For the LORD your God *is* a consuming fire, a jealous God.

IDOLATRY
Is it okay to be more devoted to something than we are to God?
(4:23)

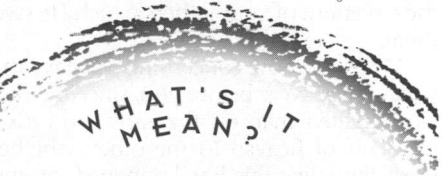

[25]"When you beget children and grandchildren and have grown old in the land, and act corruptly and make a carved image in the form of anything, and do evil in the sight of the LORD your God to provoke Him to anger, [26]I call heaven and earth to witness against you this day, that you will soon utterly perish from the land which you cross over the Jordan to possess; you will not prolong *your* days in it, but will be utterly destroyed. [27]And the LORD will scatter you

JEALOUSY
Does God want to share our devotion?
(4:24)

among the peoples, and you will be left few in number among the nations where the LORD will drive you. [28]And there you will serve gods, the work of men's hands, wood and stone, which neither see nor hear nor eat nor smell. [29]But from there you will seek the LORD your God, and you will find *Him* if you seek Him with all your heart and with all your soul. [30]When you are in distress, and all these things come upon you in the latter days, when you turn to the LORD your God and obey His voice [31](for the LORD your God *is* a merciful God), He will not forsake you nor destroy you, nor forget

Promise

HE PROMISES TO REMEMBER HIS COVENANT.

(For the LORD your God is a merciful God), He will not forsake you nor destroy you, nor forget the covenant of your fathers which He swore to them (Deut. 4:31).

You promise to meet your friend for breakfast a week from Saturday. A family emergency takes you out of town until late Friday night. You remember that you've got a breakfast date, but will your friend remember? You decide to chance it and show up. Pulling into the restaurant parking lot, you see her. She remembered. Wow. No phone calls to say, "We're still on." You were so important to her that she couldn't forget. It made you feel special that she remembered this time with you.

You're even more important to God. Trust Him when He promises to remember His promises. He won't lose His calendar or forget your phone number. He will never stand you up. It's a promise.

SEE FOR YOURSELF:
Josh. 23:15, 16; 2 Sam. 23:5; 1 Kin. 8:56;
Neh. 1:5

the covenant of your fathers which He swore to them.

³²"For ask now concerning the days that are past, which were before you, since the day that God created man on the earth, and *ask* from one end of heaven to the other, whether *any* great *thing* like this has happened, or *anything* like it has been heard. ³³Did *any* people *ever* hear the voice of God speaking out of the midst of the fire, as you have heard, and live? ³⁴Or did God *ever* try to go *and* take for Himself a nation from the midst of *another* nation, by trials, by signs, by wonders, by war, by a mighty hand and an outstretched arm, and by great terrors, according to all that the LORD your God did for you in Egypt before your eyes? ³⁵To you it was shown, that you might know that the LORD Himself *is* God; *there is* none other besides Him. ³⁶Out of heaven He let you hear His voice, that He might instruct you; on earth He showed you His great fire, and you heard His words out of the midst of the fire. ³⁷And because He loved your fathers, therefore He chose their descendants after them; and He brought you out of Egypt with His Presence, with His mighty power, ³⁸driving out from before you nations greater and mightier than you, to bring you in, to give you their land *as* an inheritance, as *it is* this day. ³⁹Therefore know this day, and consider *it* in your heart, that the LORD Himself *is* God in heaven above and on the earth beneath; *there is* no other. ⁴⁰You shall therefore keep His statutes and His commandments which I command you today, that it may go well with you and with your children after you, and that you may prolong *your* days in the land which the LORD your God is giving you for all time."

CITIES OF REFUGE EAST OF THE JORDAN

⁴¹Then Moses set apart three cities on this side of the Jordan, toward the rising of the sun, ⁴²that the manslayer might flee there, who kills his neighbor unintentionally, without having hated him in time past, and that by fleeing to one of these cities he might live: ⁴³Bezer in the wilderness on the plateau for the Reubenites, Ramoth in Gilead for the Gadites, and Golan in Bashan for the Manassites.

INTRODUCTION TO GOD'S LAW

⁴⁴Now this *is* the law which Moses set before the children of Israel. ⁴⁵These *are* the testimonies, the statutes, and the judgments which Moses spoke to the children of Israel after they came out of Egypt, ⁴⁶on this side of the Jordan,

in the valley opposite Beth Peor, in the land of Sihon king of the Amorites, who dwelt at Heshbon, whom Moses and the children of Israel defeated after they came out of Egypt. ⁴⁷And they took possession of his land and the land of Og king of Bashan, two kings of the Amorites, who *were* on this side of the Jordan, toward the rising of the sun, ⁴⁸from Aroer, which *is* on the bank of the River Arnon, even to Mount Sion*ᵃ* (that is, Hermon), ⁴⁹and all the plain on the east side of the Jordan as far as the Sea of the Arabah, below the slopes of Pisgah.

THE TEN COMMANDMENTS REVIEWED

¹And Moses called all Israel, and said to them: "Hear, O Israel, the statutes and judgments which I speak in your hearing today, that you may learn them and be careful to observe them. ²The LORD our God made a covenant with us in Horeb. ³The LORD did not make this covenant with our fathers, but with us, those who *are* here today, all of us who *are* alive. ⁴The LORD talked with you face to face on the mountain from the midst of the fire. ⁵I stood between the LORD and you at that time, to declare to you the word of the LORD; for you were afraid because of the fire, and you did not go up the mountain. *He* said:

6   'I *am* the LORD your God who brought you out of the land of Egypt, out of the house of bondage.

7   'You shall have no other gods before Me.

8   'You shall not make for yourself a carved image—any likeness *of anything* that is

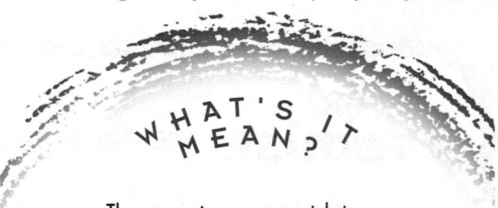

WHAT'S IT MEAN?

The covenant, or agreement, between
God and His people was very similar to a treaty
between two political leaders. In ancient times, a leader seeking a
treaty would identify himself, describe some of the things he had
done, and then present a list of regulations to be followed. After a
treaty had been established, the two leaders would agree on how it
would be written down and where
copies of it would be kept.
Deuteronomy 5:2

in heaven above, or that *is* in the earth beneath, or that *is* in the water under the earth; ⁹you shall not bow down to them nor serve them. For I, the LORD your God, *am* a jealous God, visiting the iniquity of the fathers upon the children to the third and fourth *generations* of those who hate Me, ¹⁰but showing mercy to thousands, to those who love Me and keep My commandments.

¹¹ 'You shall not take the name of the LORD your God in vain, for the LORD will not hold *him* guiltless who takes His name in vain.

¹² 'Observe the Sabbath day, to keep it holy, as the LORD your God commanded you. ¹³Six days you shall labor and do all your work, ¹⁴but the seventh day *is* the Sabbath of the LORD your God. *In it* you shall do no work: you, nor your son, nor your daughter, nor your male servant, nor your female servant, nor your ox, nor your donkey, nor any of your cattle, nor your stranger who *is* within your gates, that your male servant and your female servant may rest as well as you. ¹⁵And remember that you were a slave in the land of Egypt, and the LORD your God brought you out from there

by a mighty hand and by an outstretched arm; therefore the LORD your God commanded you to keep the Sabbath day.

¹⁶ 'Honor your father and your mother, as the LORD your God has commanded you, that your days may be long, and that it may be well with you in the land which the LORD your God is giving you.

¹⁷ 'You shall not murder.

¹⁸ 'You shall not commit adultery.

¹⁹ 'You shall not steal.

²⁰ 'You shall not bear false witness against your neighbor.

²¹ 'You shall not covet your neighbor's wife; and you shall not desire your neighbor's house, his field, his male servant, his female servant, his ox, his donkey, or anything that *is* your neighbor's.'

²²"These words the LORD spoke to all your assembly, in the mountain from the midst of the fire, the cloud, and the thick darkness, with a loud voice; and He added no more. And He wrote them on two tablets of stone and gave them to me.

MURDER — Does God allow murder? (5:17)

Promise — HE PROMISES TO BE JEALOUS FOR YOU.

You shall not bow down to [carved images] nor serve them. For I, the LORD your God, am a jealous God, visiting the iniquity of the fathers upon the children to the third and fourth generations of those who hate Me (Deut. 5:9).

God is a jealous God—that's the bottom line. He wants to be number one in your life above everything: your boyfriend/girlfriend, your job, your family, TV, music, your friends—the list goes on.

There's nothing wrong with having things, but *don't allow things to have you!* You may not bow down and worship a physical idol you've constructed in your bedroom, but once you've placed someone or something above God, that person, place, or thing becomes an article of worship—an idol. Be careful. That idol will eventually let you down. Nothing can fill the place of God in your life.

Remember the story of Abraham and how he put God first in his life. God was so important to him that he was willing to kill Isaac and sacrifice him to the Lord. God has that kind of love for you. You're that important to Him.

Where is God on your priority list? Check your heart and make Him first in your life today. He wants to be close to you. In fact, He created you to have fellowship with Him. And His Word says that if you seek Him first, He'll bless you. Be blessed today!

SEE FOR YOURSELF:
Gen. 22:1–18; Deut. 4:24; 5:9; Josh. 24:19, 20; Matt. 6:33; Mark 12:30

THE PEOPLE AFRAID OF GOD'S PRESENCE

23"So it was, when you heard the voice from the midst of the darkness, while the mountain was burning with fire, that you came near to me, all the heads of your tribes and your elders. 24And you said: 'Surely the LORD our God has shown us His glory and His greatness, and we have heard His voice from the midst of the fire. We have seen this day that God speaks with man; yet he *still* lives. 25Now therefore, why should we die? For this great fire will consume us; if we hear the voice of the LORD our God anymore, then we shall die. 26For who *is there* of all flesh who has heard the voice of the living God speaking from the midst of the fire, as we *have*, and lived? 27You go near and hear all that the LORD our God may say, and tell us all that the LORD our God says to you, and we will hear and do *it*.'

FUTURE

How can our future be blessed? (5:29)

28"Then the LORD heard the voice of your words when you spoke to me, and the LORD said to me: 'I have heard the voice of the words of this people which they have spoken to you. They are right *in* all that they have spoken. 29Oh, that they had such a heart in them that they would fear Me and always keep all My commandments, that it might be well with them and with their children forever! 30Go and say to them, "Return to your tents." 31But as for you, stand here by Me, and I will speak to you all the commandments, the statutes, and the judgments which you shall teach them, that they may observe *them* in the land which I am giving them to possess.'

32"Therefore you shall be careful to do as the LORD your God has commanded you; you shall not turn aside to the right hand or to the left. 33You shall walk in all the ways which the LORD your God has commanded you, that you may live and *that it may be* well with you, and *that* you may prolong *your* days in the land which you shall possess.

THE GREATEST COMMANDMENT

1"Now this *is* the commandment, *and these are* the statutes and judgments which the LORD your God has commanded to teach you, that you may observe *them* in the land which you are crossing over to possess, 2that you may fear the LORD your God,

EDUCATION

Who is responsible for teaching children? (6:1–9)

Promise HE PROMISES TO PUNISH THOSE WHO WORSHIP FALSE GODS.

You shall not go after other gods, the gods of the peoples who are all around you (for the LORD your God is a jealous God among you), lest the anger of the LORD your God be aroused against you and destroy you from the face of the earth (Deut. 6:14, 15).

There are a lot of other religions out there and a lot of people who worship other gods, but you worship the only true God! You serve the Great I Am. You have something that isn't a fairy tale, that isn't phony, that isn't fake. You have the truth that will cause blinders to fall from the eyes of those who don't know God.

Why are so many people wrapped up in false religions and worshiping false gods? Because they want to live for a cause. They are searching for power. Because you are living for Jesus, you have the same power living in you that raised Him from the dead (see Rom. 8:11). Now that's power! That's someone and something to live for! Don't settle for boring religion with a bunch of rules and regulations. You can have a radical relationship with Christ! You want to do the right thing because of your relationship with Him. It's a relationship that brings freedom, a relationship that brings life, a relationship that brings power, and a relationship that brings every other good thing. Only Jesus will give you what you're looking for.

Embrace the true Christianity you have. You'll have everything you need, and you'll escape the punishment of those who worship false gods.

SEE FOR YOURSELF:
Ex. 3:14; Ezek. 23:49; Matt. 5:16; Rom. 1:19

to keep all His statutes and His commandments which I command you, you and your son and your grandson, all the days of your life, and that your days may be prolonged. ³Therefore hear, O Israel, and be careful to observe it, that it may be well with you, and that you may multiply greatly as the LORD God of your fathers has promised you—'a land flowing with milk and honey.'ᵃ

GOD

Is God one? (6:4)

⁴"Hear, O Israel: The LORD our God, the LORD is one!ᵃ ⁵You shall love the LORD your God with all your heart, with all your soul, and with all your strength.

⁶"And these words which I command you today shall be in your heart. ⁷You shall teach them diligently to your children, and shall talk of them when you sit in your house, when you walk by the way, when you lie down, and when you rise up. ⁸You shall bind them as a sign on your hand, and they shall be as frontlets between your eyes. ⁹You shall write them on the doorposts of your house and on your gates.

FAMILY

What can the members of a family do for each other? (6:4–9)

> "Hear, O Israel: The LORD our God, the LORD is one! You shall love the LORD your God with all your heart, with all your soul, and with all your strength."
> (Deuteronomy 6:4, 5)

CAUTION AGAINST DISOBEDIENCE

¹⁰"So it shall be, when the LORD your God brings you into the land of which He swore to your fathers, to Abraham, Isaac, and Jacob, to give you large and beautiful cities which you did not build, ¹¹houses full of all good things, which you did not fill, hewn-out wells which you did not dig, vineyards and olive trees which you did not plant—when you have eaten and are full— ¹²then beware, lest you forget the LORD who brought you out of the land of Egypt, from the house of bondage. ¹³You shall fear the LORD your God and serve Him, and shall take oaths in His name. ¹⁴You shall not go after other gods, the gods of the peoples who are all around you ¹⁵(for the LORD your God is a jealous God among you), lest the anger of the LORD your God be aroused against you and destroy you from the face of the earth.

¹⁶"You shall not tempt the LORD your God as you tempted Him in Massah. ¹⁷You shall diligently keep the commandments of the LORD your God, His testimonies, and His statutes which He has commanded you. ¹⁸And you shall do what is right and good in the sight of the LORD, that it may be well with you, and that you may go in and possess the good land of which the LORD swore to your fathers, ¹⁹to cast out all your enemies from before you, as the LORD has spoken.

²⁰"When your son asks you in time to come, saying, 'What is the meaning of the testimonies, the statutes, and the judgments which the LORD our God has commanded you?' ²¹then you shall say to your son: 'We were slaves of Pharaoh in Egypt, and the LORD brought us out of Egypt with a mighty hand; ²²and the LORD showed signs and wonders before our eyes, great and severe, against Egypt, Pharaoh, and all his household. ²³Then He brought us out from there, that He might bring us in, to give us the land of which He swore to our fathers. ²⁴And the LORD commanded us to observe all these statutes, to fear the LORD our God, for our good always, that He might preserve us alive, as it is this day. ²⁵Then it will be righteousness for us, if we are careful to observe all these commandments before the LORD our God, as He has commanded us.'

A CHOSEN PEOPLE

¹"When the LORD your God brings you into the land which you go to possess, and has cast out many nations before you, the Hittites and the Girgashites and the Amorites and the Canaanites and the Perizzites and the Hivites and the Jebusites, seven nations greater and mightier than you, ²and when the LORD your God delivers them over to you, you shall conquer them and utterly destroy them. You shall make no covenant with them nor show mercy to them. ³Nor shall you make marriages with them. You shall not give your daughter to their son, nor take their daughter for your son. ⁴For they will turn your sons away from following Me, to serve other gods; so the anger of the LORD will

6:3 ᵃExodus 3:8   **6:4** ᵃOr The LORD is our God, the LORD alone (that is, the only one)

be aroused against you and destroy you suddenly. [5]But thus you shall deal with them: you shall destroy their altars, and break down their *sacred* pillars, and cut down their wooden images,[a] and burn their carved images with fire.

[6]"For you *are* a holy people to the LORD your God; the LORD your God has chosen you to be a people for Himself, a special treasure above all the peoples on the face of the earth. [7]The LORD did not set His love on you nor choose you because you were more in number than any other people, for you were the least of all peoples; [8]but because the LORD loves you, and because He would keep the oath which He swore to your fathers, the LORD has brought you out with a mighty hand, and redeemed you from the house of bondage, from the hand of Pharaoh king of Egypt.

[9]"Therefore know that the LORD your God, He *is* God, the faithful God who keeps covenant and mercy for a thousand generations with those who love Him and keep His commandments; [10]and He repays those who hate Him to their face, to destroy them. He will not be slack with him who hates Him; He will repay him to his face. [11]Therefore you shall keep the commandment, the statutes, and the judgments which I command you today, to observe them.

CARING
Who does God care for? (7:9)

GOD
Is God trustworthy? (7:9)

PAIN
Does God care for His people? (7:9)

BLESSINGS OF OBEDIENCE

[12]"Then it shall come to pass, because you listen to these judgments, and keep and do them, that the LORD your God will keep with you the covenant and the mercy which He swore to your fathers. [13]And He will love you and bless you and multiply you; He will also bless the fruit of your womb and the fruit of your land, your grain and your new wine and your oil, the increase of your cattle and the offspring of your flock, in the land of which He swore to your fathers to give you. [14]You shall be blessed above all peoples; there shall not be a male or female barren among you or among your livestock. [15]And the LORD will take away from you all sickness, and will afflict you with none of the terrible diseases of Egypt which you have known, but will lay *them* on all those who hate you. [16]Also you shall destroy all the peoples whom the LORD your God delivers over to you; your eye shall have no pity on them; nor shall you serve their gods, for that *will be* a snare to you.

WHAT'S IT MEAN?

Farming and shepherding were the two major career options for Canaanites. Olive oil, a product of Canaanite agriculture, was a vital part of everyday life. It was used for everything from fueling lamps to anointing kings to treating wounds.

Deuteronomy 7:13

[17]"If you should say in your heart, 'These nations are greater than I; how can I dispossess them?'— [18]you shall not be afraid of them, *but* you shall remember well what the LORD your God did to Pharaoh and to all Egypt: [19]the great trials which your eyes saw, the signs and the wonders, the mighty hand and the outstretched arm, by which the LORD your God brought you out. So shall the LORD your God do to all the peoples of whom you are afraid. [20]Moreover the LORD your God will send the hornet among them until those who are left, who hide themselves from you, are destroyed. [21]You shall not be terrified of them; for the LORD your God, the great and awesome God, *is* among you. [22]And the LORD your God will drive out those nations before you little by little; you will be unable to destroy them at once, lest the beasts of the field become *too* numerous for you. [23]But the LORD your God will deliver them over to you, and will inflict defeat upon them until they are destroyed. [24]And He will deliver their kings into your hand, and you will destroy their name from under heaven; no one shall be able to stand against you until you have destroyed them. [25]You shall burn the carved images of their gods with fire; you shall not covet the silver or gold *that is* on them, nor take *it* for yourselves, lest you be snared by it; for it *is* an abomination to the LORD your God. [26]Nor shall you bring an abomination into your house, lest you be doomed to destruction like it. You shall

7:5 [a]Hebrew *Asherim*, Canaanite deities

utterly detest it and utterly abhor it, for it *is* an accursed thing.

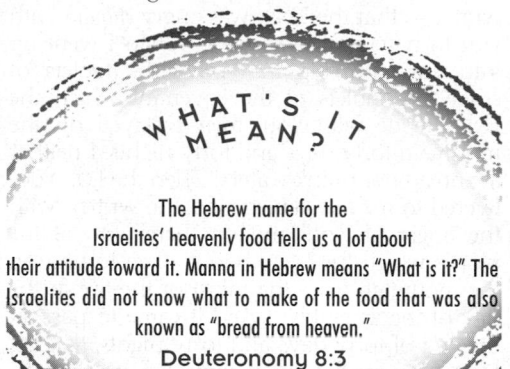

WHAT'S IT MEAN?

The Hebrew name for the Israelites' heavenly food tells us a lot about their attitude toward it. Manna in Hebrew means "What is it?" The Israelites did not know what to make of the food that was also known as "bread from heaven."

Deuteronomy 8:3

REMEMBER THE LORD YOUR GOD

[1]"Every commandment which I command you today you must be careful to observe, that you may live and multiply, and go in and possess the land of which the LORD swore to your fathers. [2]And you shall remember that the LORD your God led you all the way these forty years in the wilderness, to humble you *and* test you, to know what *was* in your heart, whether you would keep His commandments or not. [3]So He humbled you, allowed you to hunger, and fed you with manna which you did not know nor did your fathers know, that He might make you know that man shall not live by bread alone; but man lives by every *word* that proceeds from the mouth of the LORD. [4]Your garments did not wear out on you, nor did your foot swell these forty years. [5]You should know in your heart that as a man chastens his son, *so* the LORD your God chastens you.

ADOPTION

Does God help His children grow? (8:5)

[6]"Therefore you shall keep the commandments of the LORD your God, to walk in His ways and to fear Him. [7]For the LORD your God is bringing you into a good land, a land of brooks of water, of fountains and springs, that flow out of valleys and hills; [8]a land of wheat and barley, of vines and fig trees and pomegranates, a land of olive oil and honey; [9]a land in which you will eat bread without scarcity, in which you will lack nothing; a land whose stones *are* iron and out of whose hills you can dig copper. [10]When you have eaten and are full, then you shall bless the LORD your God for the good land which He has given you.

On the Edge

And you shall remember the LORD your God, for it is He who gives you power to get wealth, that He may establish His covenant which He swore to your fathers, as it is this day (Deut. 8:18).

We serve an awesome God! He is so practical. There's nothing that He will not or cannot do for you. It's a fact. God is concerned with every area of your life. Every area? Yes, every area. He's so concerned that He will even give you strength to make a living. He wants to give you creative ideas that will cause you to turn the corner financially. If anybody should be blessed, it should be God's children. Remember, God wants you blessed so you can be a blessing! You are His child, and He gets pleasure when His people prosper. Don't settle for second best. God has equipped you with the goods that you need to make a living.

We can learn from Solomon's example. God told Solomon that he could ask for whatever he wanted, and it would be granted. What did Solomon ask for? Money, wealth, power, fame? No! He asked for wisdom; and, boy, did he get it! He received the wisdom of God and this wisdom brought the money, wealth, fame, and the admiration of others. One thing is certain: Solomon didn't have a problem making a living, and neither should you. Begin asking God for godly wisdom today—and meaning it from your heart. He promises to give you the strength to make a living!

SEE FOR YOURSELF:
1 Kin. 3:5–14; Job 12:13;
Ps. 35:27; Prov. 8:12;
Phil. 4:19

[11]"Beware that you do not forget the LORD your God by not keeping His commandments, His judgments, and His statutes which I command you today, [12]lest—*when* you have eaten and are full, and have built beautiful houses and dwell *in them;* [13]and *when* your herds and your flocks multiply, and your silver and your gold are multiplied, and all that you have is multiplied; [14]when your heart is lifted up, and you forget the LORD your God who brought you out of the land of Egypt, from the house of bondage; [15]who led you through that great and

terrible wilderness, *in which were* fiery serpents and scorpions and thirsty land where there was no water; who brought water for you out of the flinty rock; [16]who fed you in the wilderness with manna, which your fathers did not know, that He might humble you and that He might test you, to do you good in the end— [17]then you say in your heart, 'My power and the might of my hand have gained me this wealth.'

[18]"And you shall remember the LORD your God, for *it is* He who gives you power to get wealth, that He may establish His covenant which He swore to your fathers, as *it is* this day. [19]Then it shall be, if you by any means forget the LORD your God, and follow other gods, and serve them and worship them, I testify against you this day that you shall surely perish. [20]As the nations which the LORD destroys before you, so you shall perish, because you would not be obedient to the voice of the LORD your God.

ISRAEL'S REBELLIONS REVIEWED

[1]"Hear, O Israel: You *are* to cross over the Jordan today, and go in to dispossess nations greater and mightier than yourself, cities great and fortified up to heaven, [2]a people great and tall, the descendants of the Anakim, whom you know, and *of whom* you heard *it said,* 'Who can stand before the descendants of Anak?' [3]Therefore understand today that the LORD your God *is* He who goes over before you *as* a consuming fire. He will destroy them and bring them down before you; so you shall drive them out and destroy them quickly, as the LORD has said to you.

[4]"Do not think in your heart, after the LORD your God has cast them out before you, saying, 'Because of my righteousness the LORD has brought me in to possess this land'; but *it is* because of the wickedness of these nations *that* the LORD is driving them out from before you. [5]*It is* not because of your righteousness or the uprightness of your heart *that* you go in to possess their land, but because of the wickedness of these nations *that* the LORD your God drives them out from before you, and that He may fulfill the word which the LORD swore to your fathers, to Abraham, Isaac, and Jacob. [6]Therefore understand that the LORD your God is not giving you this good land to possess because of your righteousness, for you *are* a stiff-necked people.

[7]"Remember! Do not forget how you provoked the LORD your God to wrath in the wilderness. From the day that you departed from the land of Egypt until you came to this place,

you have been rebellious against the LORD. [8]Also in Horeb you provoked the LORD to wrath, so that the LORD was angry *enough* with you to have destroyed you. [9]When I went up into the mountain to receive the tablets of stone, the tablets of the covenant which the LORD made with you, then I stayed on the mountain forty days and forty nights. I neither ate bread nor drank water. [10]Then the LORD delivered to me two tablets of stone written with the finger of God, and on them *were* all the words which the LORD had spoken to you on the mountain from the midst of the fire in the day of the assembly. [11]And it came to pass, at the end of forty days and forty nights, *that* the LORD gave me the two tablets of stone, the tablets of the covenant.

[12]"Then the LORD said to me, 'Arise, go down quickly from here, for your people whom you brought out of Egypt have acted corruptly; they have quickly turned aside from the way which I commanded them; they have made themselves a molded image.'

[13]"Furthermore the LORD spoke to me, saying, 'I have seen this people, and indeed they are a stiff-necked people. [14]Let Me alone, that I may destroy them and blot out their name from under heaven; and I will make of you a nation mightier and greater than they.'

[15]"So I turned and came down from the mountain, and the mountain burned with fire; and the two tablets of the covenant *were* in my two hands. [16]And I looked, and behold, you had sinned against the LORD your God—had made for yourselves a molded calf! You had turned aside quickly from the way which the LORD had commanded you. [17]Then I took the two tablets and threw them out of my two hands and broke them before your eyes. [18]And I fell down before the LORD, as at the first, forty days and forty nights; I neither ate bread nor drank water, because of all your sin which you committed in doing wickedly in the sight of the LORD, to provoke Him to anger. [19]For I was afraid of the anger and hot displeasure with which the LORD was angry with you, to destroy you. But the LORD listened to me at that time also. [20]And the LORD was very angry with Aaron *and* would have destroyed him; so I prayed for Aaron also at the same time. [21]Then I took your sin, the calf which you had made, and burned it with fire and crushed it *and* ground *it* very small, until it was as fine as dust; and I threw its dust into the brook that descended from the mountain.

[22]"Also at Taberah and Massah and Kibroth Hattaavah you provoked the LORD to wrath.

²³Likewise, when the LORD sent you from Kadesh Barnea, saying, 'Go up and possess the land which I have given you', then you rebelled against the commandment of the LORD your God, and you did not believe Him nor obey His voice. ²⁴You have been rebellious against the LORD from the day that I knew you.

²⁵"Thus I prostrated myself before the LORD; forty days and forty nights I kept prostrating myself, because the LORD had said He would destroy you. ²⁶Therefore I prayed to the LORD, and said: 'O Lord GOD, do not destroy Your people and Your inheritance whom You have redeemed through Your greatness, whom You have brought out of Egypt with a mighty hand. ²⁷Remember Your servants, Abraham, Isaac, and Jacob; do not look on the stubbornness of this people, or on their wickedness or their sin, ²⁸lest the land from which You brought us should say, "Because the LORD was not able to bring them to the land which He promised them, and because He hated them, He has brought them out to kill them in the wilderness." ²⁹Yet they *are* Your people and Your inheritance, whom You brought out by Your mighty power and by Your outstretched arm.'

THE SECOND PAIR OF TABLETS

¹"At that time the LORD said to me, 'Hew for yourself two tablets of stone like the first, and come up to Me on the mountain and make yourself an ark of wood. ²And I will write on the tablets the words that were on the first tablets, which you broke; and you shall put them in the ark.'

WHAT'S IT MEAN?

The acacia was a thorn tree that grew in the Sinai Desert, southern Canaan, and Egypt. Because its wood was hard enough to withstand insects, it was used to preserve the contents of the ark of the Testimony. The ark, or chest, itself was about the size of a small desk.
Deuteronomy 10:3

³"So I made an ark of acacia wood, hewed two tablets of stone like the first, and went up the mountain, having the two tablets in my hand. ⁴And He wrote on the tablets according to the first writing, the Ten Commandments, which the LORD had spoken to you in the mountain from the midst of the fire in the day of the assembly; and the LORD gave them to me. ⁵Then I turned and came down from the mountain, and put the tablets in the ark which I had made; and there they are, just as the LORD commanded me."

On the Edge

And now, Israel, what does the LORD your God require of you, but to fear the LORD your God, to walk in all His ways and to love Him, to serve the LORD your God with all your heart and with all your soul, and to keep the commandments of the LORD and His statutes which I command you today for your good? (Deut. 10:12, 13).

Your teacher gave you a final exam. One question—"What is the meaning of life?" You read it and feel sick. What does she want? An essay? A word? A drawing? You hate stuff like this. You look at the teacher for some kind of direction. She just gives you that "do your best" look.

God is not like that teacher. Life is not a test on which you just hope you get the right answer. God gives you the answers Himself. He gives them over and over again. He even reminds you when you forget. Everybody wonders *What does He want?* What does God require from me? Read Deuteronomy 10:12, 13 for yourself. He gives you the answer.

SEE FOR YOURSELF:
Mic. 6:8;
John 13:34, 35

⁶(Now the children of Israel journeyed from the wells of Bene Jaakan to Moserah, where Aaron died, and where he was buried; and Eleazar his son ministered as priest in his stead. ⁷From there they journeyed to Gudgodah, and from Gudgodah to Jotbathah, a land of rivers of water. ⁸At that time the LORD separated the tribe of Levi to bear the ark of the covenant of the LORD, to stand before the LORD to minister to Him and to bless in His name, to this day. ⁹Therefore Levi has no portion nor inheritance with his brethren; the LORD *is* his inheritance, just as the LORD your God promised him.)

10"As at the first time, I stayed in the mountain forty days and forty nights; the LORD also heard me at that time, *and* the LORD chose not to destroy you. 11Then the LORD said to me, 'Arise, begin *your* journey before the people, that they may go in and possess the land which I swore to their fathers to give them.'

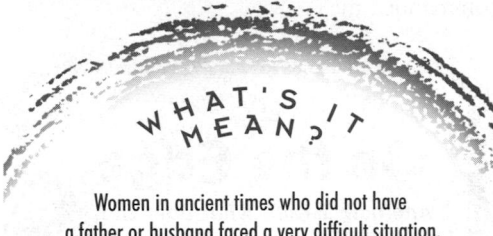

WHAT'S IT MEAN?

Women in ancient times who did not have a father or husband faced a very difficult situation. They had no one to protect them, no one to provide for them, and very few rights. Fortunately for them, the Lord cares about the well-being of widows and orphans. What's more, He ordered His people to do the same.

Deuteronomy 10:18

THE ESSENCE OF THE LAW

12"And now, Israel, what does the LORD your God require of you, but to fear the LORD your God, to walk in all His ways and to love Him, to serve the LORD your God with all your heart and with all your soul, 13and to keep the commandments of the LORD and His statutes which I command you today for your good? 14Indeed heaven and the highest heavens belong to the LORD your God, *also* the earth with all that *is* in it. 15The LORD delighted only in your fathers, to love them; and He chose their descendants after them, you above all peoples, as *it is* this day. 16Therefore circumcise the foreskin of your heart, and be stiff-necked no longer. 17For the LORD your God *is* God of gods and Lord of lords, the great God, mighty and awesome, who shows no partiality nor takes a bribe. 18He administers justice for the fatherless and the widow, and loves the stranger, giving him food and clothing. 19Therefore love the stranger, for you were strangers in the land of Egypt. 20You shall fear the LORD your God; you shall serve Him, and to Him you shall hold fast, and take oaths in His name. 21He *is* your praise,

> "You shall fear the LORD your God; you shall serve Him, and to Him you shall hold fast, and take oaths in His name."
> (Deuteronomy 10:20)

and He *is* your God, who has done for you these great and awesome things which your eyes have seen. 22Your fathers went down to Egypt with seventy persons, and now the LORD your God has made you as the stars of heaven in multitude.

LOVE AND OBEDIENCE REWARDED

1"Therefore you shall love the LORD your God, and keep His charge, His statutes, His judgments, and His commandments always. 2Know today that I *do* not *speak* with your children, who have not known and who have not seen the chastening of the LORD your God, His greatness and His mighty hand and His outstretched arm— 3His signs and His acts which He did in the midst of Egypt, to Pharaoh king of Egypt, and to all his land; 4what He did to the army of Egypt, to their horses and their chariots: how He made the waters of the Red Sea overflow them as they pursued you, and *how* the LORD has destroyed them to this day; 5what He did for you in the wilderness until you came to this place; 6and what He did to Dathan and Abiram the sons of Eliab, the son of Reuben: how the earth opened its mouth and swallowed them up, their households, their tents, and all the substance that *was* in their possession, in the midst of all Israel— 7but your eyes have seen every great act of the LORD which He did.

8"Therefore you shall keep every commandment which I command you today, that you may be strong, and go in and possess the land which you cross over to possess, 9and that you may prolong *your* days in the land which the LORD swore to give your fathers, to them and their descendants, 'a land flowing with milk and honey.'ª 10For the land which you go to possess *is* not like the land of Egypt from which you have come, where you sowed your seed and watered *it* by foot, as a vegetable garden; 11but the land which you cross over to possess *is* a land of hills and valleys, which drinks water from the rain of heaven, 12a land for which the LORD your God cares; the eyes of the LORD your God *are* always on it, from the beginning of the year to the very end of the year.

13"And it shall be that if you earnestly obey

11:9 ªExodus 3:8

My commandments which I command you today, to love the LORD your God and serve Him with all your heart and with all your soul, [14]then I[a] will give *you* the rain for your land in its season, the early rain and the latter rain, that you may gather in your grain, your new wine, and your oil. [15]And I will send grass in your fields for your livestock, that you may eat and be filled. [16]Take heed to yourselves, lest your heart be deceived, and you turn aside and serve other gods and worship them, [17]lest the LORD's anger be aroused against you, and He shut up the heavens so that there be no rain, and the land yield no produce, and you perish quickly from the good land which the LORD is giving you.

[18]"Therefore you shall lay up these words of mine in your heart and in your soul, and bind them as a sign on your hand, and they shall be as frontlets between your eyes. [19]You shall teach them to your children, speaking of them when you sit in your house, when you walk by the way, when you lie down, and when you rise up. [20]And you shall write them on the doorposts of your house and on your gates, [21]that your days and the days of your children may be multiplied in the land of which the LORD swore to your fathers to give them, like the days of the heavens above the earth.

WHAT'S IT MEAN?

Today it is customary for Jewish people to make handwritten copies of certain parts of Deuteronomy. The copied passages are rolled up or folded and placed in cases that are worn around the wrist during prayer. Sometimes they are fastened beside the front door of a house to remind all who live there of God's law.
Deuteronomy 11:18–21

[22]"For if you carefully keep all these commandments which I command you to do—to love the LORD your God, to walk in all His ways, and to hold fast to Him— [23]then the LORD will drive out all these nations from before you, and you will dispossess greater and mightier nations than yourselves. [24]Every place

on which the sole of your foot treads shall be yours: from the wilderness and Lebanon, from the river, the River Euphrates, even to the Western Sea,[a] shall be your territory. [25]No man shall be able to stand against you; the LORD your God will put the dread of you and the fear of you upon all the land where you tread, just as He has said to you.

[26]"Behold, I set before you today a blessing and a curse: [27]the blessing, if you obey the commandments of the LORD your God which I command you today; [28]and the curse, if you do not obey the commandments of the LORD your God, but turn aside from the way which I command you today, to go after other gods which you have not known. [29]Now it shall be, when the LORD your God has brought you into the land which you go to possess, that you shall put the blessing on Mount Gerizim and the curse on Mount Ebal. [30]*Are* they not on the other side of the Jordan, toward the setting sun, in the land of the Canaanites who dwell in the plain opposite Gilgal, beside the terebinth trees of Moreh? [31]For you will cross over the Jordan and go in to possess the land which the LORD your God is giving you, and you will possess it and dwell in it. [32]And you shall be careful to observe all the statutes and judgments which I set before you today.

A PRESCRIBED PLACE OF WORSHIP

[1]"These *are* the statutes and judgments which you shall be careful to observe in the land which the LORD God of your fathers is giving you to possess, all the days that you live on the earth. [2]You shall utterly destroy all the places where the nations which you shall dispossess served their gods, on the high mountains and on the hills and under every green tree. [3]And you shall destroy their altars, break their *sacred* pillars, and burn their wooden images with fire; you shall cut down the carved images of their gods and destroy their names from that place. [4]You shall not worship the LORD your God *with* such *things.*

[5]"But you shall seek the place where the LORD your God chooses, out of all your tribes, to put His name for His dwelling place; and there you shall go. [6]There you shall take your burnt offerings, your sacrifices, your tithes, the heave offerings of your hand, your vowed offerings, your freewill offerings, and the firstborn of your herds and flocks. [7]And there you shall eat before the LORD your God, and you

shall rejoice in all to which you have put your hand, you and your households, in which the LORD your God has blessed you.

8"You shall not at all do as we are doing here today—every man doing whatever *is* right in his own eyes— 9for as yet you have not come to the rest and the inheritance which the LORD your God is giving you. 10But *when* you cross over the Jordan and dwell in the land which the LORD your God is giving you to inherit, and He gives you rest from all your enemies round about, so that you dwell in safety, 11then there will be the place where the LORD your God chooses to make His name abide. There you shall bring all that I command you: your burnt offerings, your sacrifices, your tithes, the heave offerings of your hand, and all your choice offerings which you vow to the LORD. 12And you shall rejoice before the LORD your God, you and your sons and your daughters, your male and female servants, and the Levite who *is* within your gates, since he has no portion nor inheritance with you. 13Take heed to yourself that you do not offer your burnt offerings in every place that you see; 14but in the place which the LORD chooses, in one of your tribes, there you shall offer your burnt offerings, and there you shall do all that I command you.

15"However, you may slaughter and eat meat within all your gates, whatever your heart desires, according to the blessing of the LORD your God which He has given you; the unclean and the clean may eat of it, of the gazelle and the deer alike. 16Only you shall not eat the blood; you shall pour it on the earth like water. 17You may not eat within your gates the tithe of your grain or your new wine or your oil, of the first-born of your herd or your flock, of any of your offerings which you vow, of your freewill offerings, or of the heave offering of your hand. 18But you must eat them before the LORD your God in the place which the LORD your God chooses, you and your son and your daughter, your male servant and your female servant, and the Levite who *is* within your gates; and you shall rejoice before the LORD your God in all to which you put your hands. 19Take heed to yourself that you do not forsake the Levite as long as you live in your land.

20"When the LORD your God enlarges your border as He has promised you, and you say, 'Let me eat meat,' because you long to eat meat, you may eat as much meat as your heart desires. 21If the place where the LORD your God chooses to put His name is too far from you, then you may slaughter from your herd and from your flock which the LORD has given you,

just as I have commanded you, and you may eat within your gates as much as your heart desires. 22Just as the gazelle and the deer are eaten, so you may eat them; the unclean and the clean alike may eat them. 23Only be sure that you do not eat the blood, for the blood *is* the life; you may not eat the life with the meat. 24You shall not eat it; you shall pour it on the earth like water. 25You shall not eat it, that it may go well with you and your children after you, when you do *what is* right in the sight of the LORD. 26Only the holy things which you have, and your vowed offerings, you shall take and go to the place which the LORD chooses. 27And you shall offer your burnt offerings, the meat and the blood, on the altar of the LORD your God; and the blood of your sacrifices shall be poured out on the altar of the LORD your God, and you shall eat the meat. 28Observe and obey all these words which I command you, that it may go well with you and your children after you forever, when you do *what is* good and right in the sight of the LORD your God.

WHAT'S IT MEAN?

The Canaanites, like many other pagan cultures in the ancient world, offered human sacrifices to their god. Often the required sacrifice was a family's firstborn child. The Canaanites believed that sacrificing a human life earned them forgiveness for their sins and the favor of their god.

Deuteronomy 12:31

BEWARE OF FALSE GODS

29"When the LORD your God cuts off from before you the nations which you go to dispossess, and you displace them and dwell in their land, 30take heed to yourself that you are not ensnared to follow them, after they are destroyed from before you, and that you do not inquire after their gods, saying, 'How did these nations serve their gods? I also will do likewise.' 31You shall not worship the LORD your God in that way; for every abomination to the LORD which He hates they have done to their gods; for they burn even their sons and daughters in the fire to their gods.

32"Whatever I command you, be careful to

observe it; you shall not add to it nor take away from it.

PUNISHMENT OF APOSTATES

[1]"If there arises among you a prophet or a dreamer of dreams, and he gives you a sign or a wonder, [2]and the sign or the wonder comes to pass, of which he spoke to you, saying, 'Let us go after other gods'—which you have not known—'and let us serve them,' [3]you shall not listen to the words of that prophet or that dreamer of dreams, for the LORD your God is testing you to know whether you love the LORD your God with all your heart and with all your soul. [4]You shall walk after the LORD your God and fear Him, and keep His commandments and obey His voice; you shall serve Him and hold fast to Him. [5]But that prophet or that dreamer of dreams shall be put to death, because he has spoken in order to turn *you* away from the LORD your God, who brought you out of the land of Egypt and redeemed you from the house of bondage, to entice you from the way in which the LORD your God commanded you to walk. So you shall put away the evil from your midst.

[6]"If your brother, the son of your mother, your son or your daughter, the wife of your bosom, or your friend who is as your own soul, secretly entices you, saying, 'Let us go and serve other gods,' which you have not known, neither you nor your fathers, [7]of the gods of the people which *are* all around you, near to you or far off from you, from *one* end of the earth to the *other* end of the earth, [8]you shall not consent to him or listen to him, nor shall your eye pity him, nor shall you spare him or conceal him; [9]but you shall surely kill him; your hand shall be first against him to put him to death, and afterward the hand of all the people. [10]And you shall stone him with stones until he dies, because he sought to entice you away from the LORD your God, who brought you out of the land of Egypt, from the house of bondage. [11]So all Israel shall hear and fear, and not again do such wickedness as this among you.

[12]"If you hear someone in one of your cities, which the LORD your God gives you to dwell in, saying, [13]'Corrupt men have gone out from among you and enticed the inhabitants of their city, saying, "Let us go and serve other gods" '—which you have not known— [14]then you shall inquire, search out, and ask diligently. And *if it is* indeed true *and* certain *that* such an abomination was committed among you, [15]you shall surely strike the inhabitants of that city with the edge of the sword, utterly destroying it, all that is in it and its livestock—with the edge of the sword. [16]And you shall gather all its plunder into the middle of the street, and completely burn with fire the city and all its plunder, for the LORD your God. It shall be a heap forever; it shall not be built again. [17]So none of the accursed things shall remain in your hand, that

On the Edge

If your brother, the son of your mother, your son or your daughter, the wife of your bosom, or your friend who is as your own soul, secretly entices you, saying, "Let us go and serve other gods," which you have not known, neither you nor your fathers, of the gods of the people which are all around you, near to you or far off from you, from one end of the earth to the other end of the earth, you shall not consent to him or listen to him, nor shall your eye pity him, nor shall you spare him or conceal him; but you shall surely kill him . . . (Deut. 13:6–9).

Most Christians who experiment with other religions (Hinduism, Buddhism, the New Age, etc.) lack the maturity needed to learn about other faiths. When you're spiritually immature, you can easily get confused and "sucked in" to the deception of other religions. This can be especially true when those other religions claim to be "Christian based" or claim to believe in Jesus.

It takes maturity to discern spiritual things. Maturity comes from consistently walking with the Lord, communicating with Him, growing in the knowledge of Him and of His Word, and knowing that areas of your life are different because He is changing you. Some people have fallen into false religions because they weren't mature enough to tell good from "evil in disguise." Satan is the master of trickery. He is more than happy to make other religions look good to you, because he wants to pull you away from the truth. Do not experiment with other religions. You may fall into a well-set trap.

SEE FOR YOURSELF:
Ex. 20:3; Deut. 6:14; 1 Kin. 9:6–9; Jer. 35:15; John 14:6

the LORD may turn from the fierceness of His anger and show you mercy, have compassion on you and multiply you, just as He swore to your fathers, [18]because you have listened to the voice of the LORD your God, to keep all His commandments which I command you today, to do *what is* right in the eyes of the LORD your God.

IMPROPER MOURNING

[1]"You *are* the children of the LORD your God; you shall not cut yourselves nor shave the front of your head for the dead. [2]For you *are* a holy people to the LORD your God, and the LORD has chosen you to be a people for Himself, a special treasure above all the peoples who *are* on the face of the earth.

roe deer, the wild goat, the mountain goat,[a] the antelope, and the mountain sheep. [6]And you may eat every animal with cloven hooves, having the hoof split into two parts, *and that* chews the cud, among the animals. [7]Nevertheless, of those that chew the cud or have cloven hooves, you shall not eat, *such as* these: the camel, the hare, and the rock hyrax; for they chew the cud but do not have cloven hooves; they *are* unclean for you. [8]Also the swine is unclean for you, because it has cloven hooves, yet *does* not *chew* the cud; you shall not eat their flesh or touch their dead carcasses.

[9]"These you may eat of all that *are* in the waters: you may eat all that have fins and scales. [10]And whatever does not have fins and scales you shall not eat; it *is* unclean for you.

[11]"All clean birds you may eat. [12]But these you shall not eat: the eagle, the vulture, the buzzard, [13]the red kite, the falcon, and the kite after their kinds; [14]every raven after its kind; [15]the ostrich, the short-eared owl, the sea gull, and the hawk after their kinds; [16]the little owl, the screech owl, the white owl, [17]the jackdaw, the carrion vulture, the fisher owl, [18]the stork, the heron after its kind, and the hoopoe and the bat.

On the Edge

For you are a holy people to the LORD your God, and the LORD has chosen you to be a people for Himself, a special treasure above all the peoples who are on the face of the earth (Deut. 14:2).

You know what it feels like to be chosen. Remember in grade school when your gym class picked teams for sports? Remember when you got chosen pretty close to the beginning? Or maybe you were the last one chosen and you remember that sting. Regardless of what happened to you then, God chose you. And He chose you first. He chose you for just one reason—He loves you. He's crazy about you. He wants you on His team because He doesn't want to be apart from you.

That's cool! It's awesome that God chose you. He can choose anybody He wants and He chose you. This shows you how much He wants you with Him. He wants to be with you, too.

SEE FOR YOURSELF:
Ex. 22:31; 1 Chr. 16;
Is. 49:7; 1 Pet. 2:9

WHAT'S IT MEAN?

The birds listed in this passage were considered unclean because of their eating habits. All are birds of prey or scavengers. In case you were wondering, the hoopoe is known for hunting insects in unclean places and picking up a terrible odor in the process. If you would like to study the bird for yourself, head for Israel, where it can still be seen today.
Deuteronomy 14:11–18

[19]"Also every creeping thing that flies is unclean for you; they shall not be eaten.

[20]"You may eat all clean birds.

[21]"You shall not eat anything that dies *of itself*; you may give it to the alien who *is* within your gates, that he may eat it, or you may sell it to a foreigner; for you *are* a holy people to the LORD your God.

"You shall not boil a young goat in its mother's milk.

CLEAN AND UNCLEAN MEAT

[3]"You shall not eat any detestable thing. [4]These *are* the animals which you may eat: the ox, the sheep, the goat, [5]the deer, the gazelle, the

14:5 [a]Or *addax*

TITHING PRINCIPLES

22"You shall truly tithe all the increase of your grain that the field produces year by year. 23And you shall eat before the LORD your God, in the place where He chooses to make His name abide, the tithe of your grain and your new wine and your oil, of the firstborn of your herds and your flocks, that you may learn to fear the LORD your God always. 24But if the journey is too long for you, so that you are not able to carry the tithe, or if the place where the LORD your God chooses to put His name is too far from you, when the LORD your God has blessed you, 25then you shall exchange it for money, take the money in your hand, and go to the place which the LORD your God chooses. 26And you shall spend that money for whatever your heart desires: for oxen or sheep, for wine or similar drink, for whatever your heart desires; you shall eat there before the LORD your God, and you shall rejoice, you and your household. 27You shall not forsake the Levite who is within your gates, for he has no part nor inheritance with you.

28"At the end of every third year you shall bring out the tithe of your produce of that year and store it up within your gates. 29And the Levite, because he has no portion nor inheritance with you, and the stranger and the fatherless and the widow who are within your gates, may come and eat and be satisfied, that the LORD your God may bless you in all the work of your hand which you do.

DEBTS CANCELED EVERY SEVEN YEARS

1"At the end of every seven years you shall grant a release of debts. 2And this is the form of the release: Every creditor who has lent anything to his neighbor shall release it; he shall not require it of his neighbor or his brother, because it is called the LORD's release. 3Of a foreigner you may require it; but you shall give up your claim to what is owed by your brother, 4except when there may be no poor among you; for the LORD will greatly bless you in the land which the LORD your God is giving you to possess as an inheritance— 5only if you carefully obey the voice of the LORD your God, to observe with care all these commandments which I command you today. 6For the LORD your God will bless you just as He promised you; you shall lend to many nations, but you shall not borrow; you shall reign over many nations, but they shall not reign over you.

"For the LORD your God will bless you just as He promised you." (Deuteronomy 15:6a)

GENEROSITY TO THE POOR

7"If there is among you a poor man of your brethren, within any of the gates in your land which the LORD your God is giving you, you shall not harden your heart nor shut your hand from your poor brother, 8but you shall open your hand wide to him and willingly lend him sufficient for his need, whatever he needs. 9Beware lest there be a wicked thought in your heart, saying, 'The seventh year, the year of release, is at hand,' and your eye be evil against your poor brother and you give him nothing, and he cry out to the LORD against you, and it become sin among you. 10You shall surely give to him, and your heart should not be grieved when you give to him, because for this thing the LORD your God will bless you in all your works and in all to which you put your hand. 11For the poor will never cease from the land; therefore I command you, saying, 'You shall open your hand wide to your brother, to your poor and your needy, in your land.'

THE LAW CONCERNING BONDSERVANTS

12"If your brother, a Hebrew man, or a Hebrew woman, is sold to you and serves you six years, then in the seventh year you shall let him go free from you. 13And when you send him away free from you, you shall not let him go away empty-handed; 14you shall supply him liberally from your flock, from your threshing floor, and from your winepress. From what the LORD has blessed you with, you shall give to him. 15You shall remember that you were a slave in the land of Egypt, and the LORD your God redeemed you; therefore I command

WHAT'S IT MEAN?

Israelites were allowed to keep other Israelites as slaves, but only for six years. God's law required that all slaves be set free in the seventh year. The law was intended to prevent a class system from developing among the Israelites.
Deuteronomy 15:12

you this thing today. [16]And if it happens that he says to you, 'I will not go away from you', because he loves you and your house, since he prospers with you, [17]then you shall take an awl and thrust *it* through his ear to the door, and he shall be your servant forever. Also to your female servant you shall do likewise. [18]It shall not seem hard to you when you send him away free from you; for he has been worth a double hired servant in serving you six years. Then the LORD your God will bless you in all that you do.

THE LAW CONCERNING FIRSTBORN ANIMALS

[19]"All the firstborn males that come from your herd and your flock you shall sanctify to the LORD your God; you shall do no work with the firstborn of your herd, nor shear the firstborn of your flock. [20]You and your household shall eat *it* before the LORD your God year by year in the place which the LORD chooses. [21]But if there is a defect in it, *if it is* lame or blind *or has* any serious defect, you shall not sacrifice it to the LORD your God. [22]You may eat it within your gates; the unclean and the clean *person* alike *may eat it,* as *if it were* a gazelle or a deer. [23]Only you shall not eat its blood; you shall pour it on the ground like water.

WHAT'S IT MEAN?

The Hebrew calendar is based on a week of seven days and a month of about four weeks, just like our calendar. The only difference is the names of the months. Passover is celebrated in the first month of the Hebrew calendar (sacred year) and the third or fourth month of ours.
Deuteronomy 16:1

THE PASSOVER REVIEWED

[1]"Observe the month of Abib, and keep the Passover to the LORD your God, for in the month of Abib the LORD your God brought you out of Egypt by night. [2]Therefore you shall sacrifice the Passover to the LORD your God, from the flock and the herd, in the place where the LORD chooses to put His name. [3]You shall eat no leavened bread with it; seven days you shall eat unleavened bread with it, *that is,* the bread of affliction (for you came out of the land

of Egypt in haste), that you may remember the day in which you came out of the land of Egypt all the days of your life. [4]And no leaven shall be seen among you in all your territory for seven days, nor shall *any* of the meat which you sacrifice the first day at twilight remain overnight until morning.

[5]"You may not sacrifice the Passover within any of your gates which the LORD your God gives you; [6]but at the place where the LORD your God chooses to make His name abide, there you shall sacrifice the Passover at twilight, at the going down of the sun, at the time you came out of Egypt. [7]And you shall roast and eat *it* in the place which the LORD your God chooses, and in the morning you shall turn and go to your tents. [8]Six days you shall eat unleavened bread, and on the seventh day there *shall be* a sacred assembly to the LORD your God. You shall do no work *on it.*

THE FEAST OF WEEKS REVIEWED

[9]"You shall count seven weeks for yourself; begin to count the seven weeks from *the time* you begin *to put* the sickle to the grain. [10]Then you shall keep the Feast of Weeks to the LORD your God with the tribute of a freewill offering from your hand, which you shall give as the LORD your God blesses you. [11]You shall rejoice before the LORD your God, you and your son and your daughter, your male servant and your female servant, the Levite who *is* within your gates, the stranger and the fatherless and the widow who *are* among you, at the place where the LORD your God chooses to make His name abide. [12]And you shall remember that you were a slave in Egypt, and you shall be careful to observe these statutes.

THE FEAST OF TABERNACLES REVIEWED

[13]"You shall observe the Feast of Tabernacles seven days, when you have gathered from your threshing floor and from your winepress. [14]And you shall rejoice in your feast, you and your son and your daughter, your male servant and your female servant and the Levite, the stranger and the fatherless and the widow, who *are* within your gates. [15]Seven days you shall keep a sacred feast to the LORD your God in the place which the LORD chooses, because the LORD your God will bless you in all your produce and in all the work of your hands, so that you surely rejoice.

[16]"Three times a year all your males shall appear before the LORD your God in the place which He chooses: at the Feast of Unleavened Bread, at the Feast of Weeks, and at the Feast of

Tabernacles; and they shall not appear before the LORD empty-handed. [17]Every man *shall give* as he is able, according to the blessing of the LORD your God which He has given you.

JUSTICE MUST BE ADMINISTERED

[18]"You shall appoint judges and officers in all your gates, which the LORD your God gives you, according to your tribes, and they shall judge the people with just judgment. [19]You shall not pervert justice; you shall not show partiality, nor take a bribe, for a bribe blinds the eyes of the wise and twists the words of the righteous. [20]You shall follow what is altogether just, that you may live and inherit the land which the LORD your God is giving you.

[21]"You shall not plant for yourself any tree, as a wooden image, near the altar which you build for yourself to the LORD your God. [22]You shall not set up a sacred pillar, which the LORD your God hates.

[1]"You shall not sacrifice to the LORD your God a bull or sheep which has any blemish *or* defect, for that *is* an abomination to the LORD your God.

[2]"If there is found among you, within any of your gates which the LORD your God gives you, a man or a woman who has been wicked in the sight of the LORD your God, in transgressing His covenant, [3]who has gone and served other gods and worshiped them, either the sun or moon or any of the host of heaven, which I have not commanded, [4]and it is told you, and you hear *of it*, then you shall inquire diligently. And if *it is* indeed true *and* certain that such an abomination has been committed in Israel, [5]then you shall bring out to your gates that man or woman who has committed that wicked thing, and shall stone to death that man or woman with stones. [6]Whoever is deserving of death shall be put to death on the testimony of two or three witnesses; he shall not be put to death on the testimony of one witness. [7]The hands of the witnesses shall be the first against him to put him to death, and afterward the hands of all the people. So you shall put away the evil from among you.

[8]"If a matter arises which is too hard for you to judge, between degrees of guilt for bloodshed, between one judgment or another, or between one punishment or another, matters of controversy within your gates, then you shall arise and go up to the place which the LORD your God chooses. [9]And you shall come to the priests, the Levites, and to the judge *there* in those days, and inquire *of them;* they shall pronounce upon you the sentence of judgment.

[10]You shall do according to the sentence which they pronounce upon you in that place which the LORD chooses. And you shall be careful to do according to all that they order you. [11]According to the sentence of the law in which they instruct you, according to the judgment which they tell you, you shall do; you shall not turn aside *to* the right hand or *to* the left from the sentence which they pronounce upon you. [12]Now the man who acts presumptuously and will not heed the priest who stands to minister there before the LORD your God, or the judge, that man shall die. So you shall put away the evil from Israel. [13]And all the people shall hear and fear, and no longer act presumptuously.

Stoning was the ancient equivalent of the electric chair or lethal injection. It was the death penalty handed down to convicted murderers. The only difference is there was no death row in ancient Israel. When a person was convicted, he was immediately taken outside the camp, where the men of the community threw rocks at him until he died.
Deuteronomy 17:5–7

PRINCIPLES GOVERNING KINGS

[14]"When you come to the land which the LORD your God is giving you, and possess it and dwell in it, and say, 'I will set a king over me like all the nations that *are* around me', [15]you shall surely set a king over you whom the LORD your God chooses; *one* from among your brethren you shall set as king over you; you may not set a foreigner over you, who *is* not your brother. [16]But he shall not multiply horses for himself, nor cause the people to return to Egypt to multiply horses, for the LORD has said to you, 'You shall not return that way again'. [17]Neither shall he multiply wives for himself, lest his heart turn away; nor shall he greatly multiply silver and gold for himself.

[18]"Also it shall be, when he sits on the throne of his kingdom, that he shall write for himself a copy of this law in a book, from *the one* before the priests, the Levites. [19]And it shall be with him, and he shall read it all the days of his life, that he may learn to fear the LORD his God and

WHAT'S IT MEAN?

For some reason, the Israelites considered horses to be war animals and did not use them much for everyday travel and work. The Egyptians used horses quite often—usually to pull chariots.

Deuteronomy 17:16

be careful to observe all the words of this law and these statutes, [20]that his heart may not be lifted above his brethren, that he may not turn aside from the commandment *to* the right hand or *to* the left, and that he may prolong *his* days in his kingdom, he and his children in the midst of Israel.

THE PORTION OF THE PRIESTS AND LEVITES

[1]"The priests, the Levites—all the tribe of Levi—shall have no part nor inheritance with Israel; they shall eat the offerings of the LORD made by fire, and His portion. [2]Therefore they shall have no inheritance among their brethren; the LORD is their inheritance, as He said to them.

[3]"And this shall be the priest's due from the people, from those who offer a sacrifice, whether *it is* bull or sheep: they shall give to the priest the shoulder, the cheeks, and the stomach. [4]The firstfruits of your grain and your new wine and your oil, and the first of the fleece of your sheep, you shall give him. [5]For the LORD your God has chosen him out of all your tribes to stand to minister in the name of the LORD, him and his sons forever.

[6]"So if a Levite comes from any of your gates, from where he dwells among all Israel, and comes with all the desire of his mind to the place which the LORD chooses, [7]then he may serve in the name of the LORD his God as all his brethren the Levites *do*, who stand there before the LORD. [8]They shall have equal portions to eat, besides what comes from the sale of his inheritance.

AVOID WICKED CUSTOMS

[9]"When you come into the land which the LORD your God is giving you, you shall not learn to follow the abominations of those nations. [10]There shall not be found among you *anyone* who makes his son or his daughter pass through the fire, *or one* who practices witchcraft, *or* a soothsayer, or one who interprets omens, or a sorcerer, [11]or one who conjures spells, or a medium, or a spiritist, or one who calls up the dead. [12]For all who do these things *are* an abomination to the LORD, and because of these abominations the LORD your God drives them out from before you. [13]You shall be blameless before the LORD your God. [14]For these nations which you will dispossess listened to soothsayers and diviners; but as for you, the LORD your God has not appointed such for you.

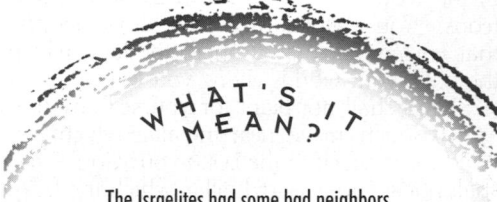

WHAT'S IT MEAN?

The Israelites had some bad neighbors, most of whom practiced witchcraft and magic. Witchcraft involved trying to see the future with the help of a pagan god. Magic involved trying to expand one's knowledge through mind-altering drugs. All forms of witchcraft, magic, and fortune-telling were strictly forbidden by God.

Deuteronomy 18:10, 11

A NEW PROPHET LIKE MOSES

[15]"The LORD your God will raise up for you a Prophet like me from your midst, from your brethren. Him you shall hear, [16]according to all you desired of the LORD your God in Horeb in the day of the assembly, saying, 'Let me not hear again the voice of the LORD my God, nor let me see this great fire anymore, lest I die.'

[17]"And the LORD said to me: 'What they have spoken is good. [18]I will raise up for them a Prophet like you from among their brethren, and will put My words in His mouth, and He shall speak to them all that I command Him. [19]And it shall be *that* whoever will not hear My words, which He speaks in My name, I will require *it of* him. [20]But the prophet who presumes to speak a word in My name, which I have not commanded him to speak, or who speaks in the name of other gods, that prophet shall die.' [21]And if you say in your heart, 'How shall we know the word which the LORD has not spo-

CULT

How does God feel about people who wrongly claim to be speaking for Him? (18:20–22) ken?'— ²²when a prophet speaks in the name of the LORD, if the thing does not happen or come to pass, that *is* the thing which the LORD has not spoken; the prophet has spoken it presumptuously; you shall not be afraid of him.

On the Edge

There shall not be found among you anyone who makes his son or his daughter pass through the fire, or one who practices witchcraft, or a soothsayer, or one who interprets omens, or a sorcerer, or one who conjures spells, or a medium, or a spiritist, or one who calls up the dead. For all who do these things are an abomination to the LORD . . . You shall be blameless before the LORD your God (Deut. 18:10–13).

God calls those things an abomination. As a believer, it's your job to imitate God and to think His kind of thoughts. So the next time you're at a slumber party or sleep-over and someone wants to turn off the lights and levitate somebody or contact a dead person, be the brave one who says, "No. That's disgusting and stupid. It's fooling around with Satan; and if he's invited to this party, I'm outta here." That's what séances are—an invitation for Satan to come in and use his power on a game board or whatever else you ask him for. He'd love to come to your party and play tricks with a bunch of young people and hang out all night messing with you. Come on, there are plenty of other fun, innocent things to do at slumber parties. (We don't need to give you any ideas!)

SEE FOR YOURSELF:
Ex. 22:18;
Lev. 19:31; 20:6, 27

THREE CITIES OF REFUGE

¹"When the LORD your God has cut off the nations whose land the LORD your God is giving you, and you dispossess them and dwell in their cities and in their houses, ²you shall separate three cities for yourself in the midst of your land which the LORD your God is giving you to possess. ³You shall prepare roads for yourself, and divide into three parts the territory of your land which the LORD your God is giving you to inherit, that any manslayer may flee there.

⁴"And this *is* the case of the manslayer who flees there, that he may live: Whoever kills his neighbor unintentionally, not having hated him in time past— ⁵as when *a man* goes to the woods with his neighbor to cut timber, and his hand swings a stroke with the ax to cut down the tree, and the head slips from the handle and strikes his neighbor so that he dies—he shall flee to one of these cities and live; ⁶lest the avenger of blood, while his anger is hot, pursue the manslayer and overtake him, because the way is long, and kill him, though he *was* not deserving of death, since he had not hated the victim in time past. ⁷Therefore I command you, saying, 'You shall separate three cities for yourself.'

⁸"Now if the LORD your God enlarges your territory, as He swore to your fathers, and gives you the land which He promised to give to your fathers, ⁹and if you keep all these commandments and do them, which I command you today, to love the LORD your God and to walk always in His ways, then you shall add three more cities for yourself besides these three, ¹⁰lest innocent blood be shed in the midst of your land which the LORD your God is giving you *as* an inheritance, and *thus* guilt of bloodshed be upon you.

¹¹"But if anyone hates his neighbor, lies in wait for him, rises against him and strikes him mortally, so that he dies, and he flees to one of these cities, ¹²then the elders of his city shall send and bring him from there, and deliver him over to the hand of the avenger of blood, that he may die. ¹³Your eye shall not pity him, but you shall put away *the guilt of* innocent blood from Israel, that it may go well with you.

PROPERTY BOUNDARIES

¹⁴"You shall not remove your neighbor's landmark, which the men of old have set, in your inheritance which you will inherit in the land that the LORD your God is giving you to possess.

THE LAW CONCERNING WITNESSES

¹⁵"One witness shall not rise against a man concerning any iniquity or any sin that he commits; by the mouth of two or three witnesses the matter shall be established. ¹⁶If a false witness rises against any man to testify against him of wrongdoing, ¹⁷then both men in the controversy shall stand before the LORD, before the priests and the judges who serve in those days. ¹⁸And the judges shall make careful

inquiry, and indeed, *if* the witness *is* a false witness, who has testified falsely against his brother, ¹⁹then you shall do to him as he thought to have done to his brother; so you shall put away the evil from among you. ²⁰And those who remain shall hear and fear, and hereafter they shall not again commit such evil among you. ²¹Your eye shall not pity: life *shall be* for life, eye for eye, tooth for tooth, hand for hand, foot for foot.

PRINCIPLES GOVERNING WARFARE

¹"When you go out to battle against your enemies, and see horses and chariots *and* people more numerous than you, do not be afraid of them; for the LORD your God *is* with you, who brought you up from the land of Egypt. ²So it shall be, when you are on the verge of battle, that the priest shall approach and speak to the people. ³And he shall say to them, 'Hear, O Israel: Today you are on the verge of battle with your enemies. Do not let your heart faint, do not be afraid, and do not tremble or be terrified because of them; ⁴for the LORD your God *is* He who goes with you, to fight for you against your enemies, to save you.'

⁵"Then the officers shall speak to the people, saying: 'What man *is there* who has built a new house and has not dedicated it? Let him go and return to his house, lest he die in the battle and another man dedicate it. ⁶Also what man *is there* who has planted a vineyard and has not eaten of it? Let him go and return to his house, lest he die in the battle and another man eat of it. ⁷And what man *is there* who is betrothed to a woman and has not married her? Let him go and return to his house, lest he die in the battle and another man marry her.' ⁸"The officers shall speak further to the people, and say, 'What man *is there who is* fearful and fainthearted? Let him go and return to his house, lest the heart of his brethren faint[a] like his heart.' ⁹And so it shall be, when the officers have finished speaking to the people, that they shall make captains of the armies to lead the people.

¹⁰"When you go near a city to fight against it, then proclaim an offer of peace to it. ¹¹And it shall be that if they accept your offer of peace,

and open to you, then all the people *who are* found in it shall be placed under tribute to you, and serve you. ¹²Now if *the city* will not make peace with you, but war against you, then you shall besiege it. ¹³And when the LORD your God delivers it into your hands, you shall strike every male in it with the edge of the sword. ¹⁴But the women, the little ones, the livestock, and all that is in the city, all its spoil, you shall plunder for yourself; and you shall eat the enemies' plunder which the LORD your God gives you. ¹⁵Thus you shall do to all the cities *which are* very far from you, which *are* not of the cities of these nations.

¹⁶"But of the cities of these peoples which the LORD your God gives you *as* an inheritance, you shall let nothing that breathes remain alive, ¹⁷but you shall utterly destroy them: the Hittite and the Amorite and the Canaanite and the Perizzite and the Hivite and the Jebusite, just as the LORD your God has commanded you, ¹⁸lest they teach you to do according to all their abominations which they have done for their gods, and you sin against the LORD your God.

¹⁹"When you besiege a city for a long time, while making war against it to take it, you shall not destroy its trees by wielding an ax against them; if you can eat of them, do not cut them down to use in the siege, for the tree of the field *is* man's food. ²⁰Only the trees which you know *are* not trees for food you may destroy and cut down, to build siegeworks against the city that makes war with you, until it is subdued.

> "For the LORD your God is with you, who brought you up from the land of Egypt."
> (Deuteronomy 20:1b)

THE LAW CONCERNING UNSOLVED MURDER

¹"If *anyone* is found slain, lying in the field in the land which the LORD your God is giving you to possess, *and* it is not known who killed him, ²then your elders and your judges shall go out and measure *the distance* from the slain man to the surrounding cities. ³And it shall be *that* the elders of the city nearest to the slain man will take a heifer which has not been worked *and* which has not pulled with a yoke. ⁴The elders of that city shall bring the heifer down to a valley with flowing water, which is neither plowed nor sown, and they shall break the heifer's neck there in the valley. ⁵Then the

20:8 ᵃFollowing Masoretic Text and Targum; Samaritan Pentateuch, Septuagint, Syriac, and Vulgate read *lest he make his brother's heart faint.*

priests, the sons of Levi, shall come near, for the LORD your God has chosen them to minister to Him and to bless in the name of the LORD; by their word every controversy and every assault shall be *settled.* [6]And all the elders of that city nearest to the slain *man* shall wash their hands over the heifer whose neck was broken in the valley. [7]Then they shall answer and say, 'Our hands have not shed this blood, nor have our eyes seen *it.* [8]Provide atonement, O LORD, for Your people Israel, whom You have redeemed, and do not lay innocent blood to the charge of Your people Israel.' And atonement shall be provided on their behalf for the blood. [9]So you shall put away the *guilt of* innocent blood from among you when you do *what is* right in the sight of the LORD.

FEMALE CAPTIVES

[10]"When you go out to war against your enemies, and the LORD your God delivers them into your hand, and you take them captive, [11]and you see among the captives a beautiful woman, and desire her and would take her for your wife, [12]then you shall bring her home to your house, and she shall shave her head and trim her nails. [13]She shall put off the clothes of her captivity, remain in your house, and mourn her father and her mother a full month; after that you may go in to her and be her husband, and she shall be your wife. [14]And it shall be, if you have no delight in her, then you shall set her free, but you certainly shall not sell her for money; you shall not treat her brutally, because you have humbled her.

FIRSTBORN INHERITANCE RIGHTS

[15]"If a man has two wives, one loved and the other unloved, and they have borne him children, *both* the loved and the unloved, and *if* the firstborn son is of her who is unloved, [16]then it shall be, on the day he bequeaths his possessions to his sons, *that* he must not bestow firstborn status on the son of the loved wife in preference to the son of the unloved, the *true* firstborn. [17]But he shall acknowledge the son of the unloved wife *as* the firstborn by giving him a double portion of all that he has, for he *is* the beginning of his strength; the right of the firstborn *is* his.

THE REBELLIOUS SON

[18]"If a man has a stubborn and rebellious son who will not obey the voice of his father or the voice of his mother, and *who,* when they have chastened him, will not heed them, [19]then his father and his mother shall take hold of him and bring him out to the elders of his city, to the gate of his city. [20]And they shall say to the elders of his city, 'This son of ours is stubborn and rebellious; he will not obey our voice; he is a glutton and a drunkard.' [21]Then all the men of his city shall stone him to death with stones; so you shall put away the evil from among you, and all Israel shall hear and fear.

MISCELLANEOUS LAWS

[22]"If a man has committed a sin deserving of death, and he is put to death, and you hang him on a tree, [23]his body shall not remain overnight on the tree, but you shall surely bury him that day, so that you do not defile the land which the LORD your God is giving you *as* an inheritance; for he who is hanged *is* accursed of God.

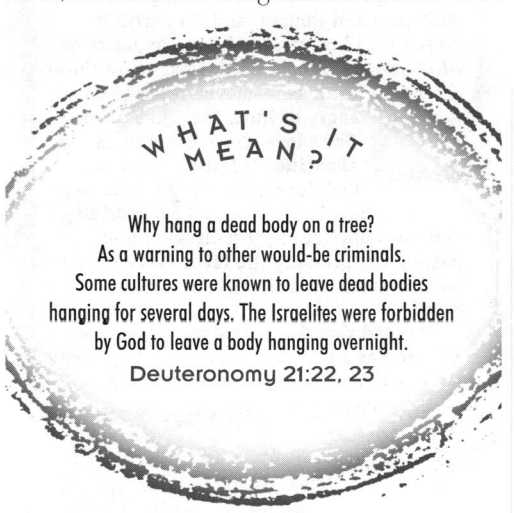

WHAT'S IT MEAN?

Why hang a dead body on a tree?
As a warning to other would-be criminals.
Some cultures were known to leave dead bodies
hanging for several days. The Israelites were forbidden
by God to leave a body hanging overnight.
Deuteronomy 21:22, 23

[1]"You shall not see your brother's ox or his sheep going astray, and hide yourself from them; you shall certainly bring them back to your brother. [2]And if your brother *is* not near you, or if you do not know him, then you shall bring it to your own house, and it shall remain with you until your brother seeks it; then you shall restore it to him. [3]You shall do the same with his donkey, and so shall you do with his garment; with any lost thing of your brother's, which he has lost and you have found, you shall do likewise; you must not hide yourself.

[4]"You shall not see your brother's donkey or his ox fall down along the road, and hide yourself from them; you shall surely help him lift *them* up again.

[5]"A woman shall not wear anything that pertains to a man, nor shall a man put on a woman's garment, for all who do so *are* an abomination to the LORD your God.

On the Edge

A woman shall not wear anything that pertains to a man, nor shall a man put on a woman's garment, for all who do so are an abomination to the LORD your God (Deut. 22:5).

God made two types of people—men and women. He made us with different body shapes, different emotional makeups, and different strengths and weaknesses. He is disgusted when someone tries to go against His design. He has a plan and a purpose for both men and women, and it's sinful to dress up and pretend to be the opposite of what you are. People do it. Most often these people are confused—maybe rejected or angry or hurt, too. They need God's love. Cross-dressing is like shouting, "I know more than God does. I look better this way!" Read Deuteronomy 22:5 carefully. God does not hate a cross-dresser. God hates cross-dressing. He loves every person on this earth. It is sin that He cannot stand.

Be glad that God made you the way you are. He has a plan for you as a strong, godly man or woman. He makes no mistakes.

SEE FOR YOURSELF:
1 Cor. 6:9

⁶"If a bird's nest happens to be before you along the way, in any tree or on the ground, with young ones or eggs, with the mother sitting on the young or on the eggs, you shall not take the mother with the young; ⁷you shall surely let the mother go, and take the young for yourself, that it may be well with you and *that* you may prolong *your* days.

⁸"When you build a new house, then you shall make a parapet for your roof, that you may not bring guilt of bloodshed on your household if anyone falls from it.

⁹"You shall not sow your vineyard with different kinds of seed, lest the yield of the seed which you have sown and the fruit of your vineyard be defiled.

¹⁰"You shall not plow with an ox and a donkey together.

¹¹"You shall not wear a garment of different sorts, *such as* wool and linen mixed together.

¹²"You shall make tassels on the four corners of the clothing with which you cover *yourself.*

LAWS OF SEXUAL MORALITY

¹³"If any man takes a wife, and goes in to her, and detests her, ¹⁴and charges her with shameful conduct, and brings a bad name on her, and says, 'I took this woman, and when I came to her I found she *was* not a virgin,' ¹⁵then the father and mother of the young woman shall take and bring out *the evidence of* the young woman's virginity to the elders of the city at the gate. ¹⁶And the young woman's father shall say to the elders, 'I gave my daughter to this man as wife, and he detests her. ¹⁷Now he has charged her with shameful conduct, saying, "I found your daughter *was* not a virgin," and yet these *are the evidences of* my daughter's virginity.' And they shall spread the cloth before the elders of the city. ¹⁸Then the elders of that city shall take that man and punish him; ¹⁹and they shall fine him one hundred *shekels* of silver and give *them* to the father of the young woman, because he has brought a bad name on a virgin of Israel. And she shall be his wife; he cannot divorce her all his days.

²⁰"But if the thing is true, *and evidences of* virginity are not found for the young woman, ²¹then they shall bring out the young woman to the door of her father's house, and the men of her city shall stone her to death with stones, because she has done a disgraceful thing in Israel, to play the harlot in her father's house. So you shall put away the evil from among you.

²²"If a man is found lying with a woman married to a husband, then both of them shall die—the man that lay with the woman, and the woman; so you shall put away the evil from Israel.

²³"If a young woman *who is* a virgin is betrothed to a husband, and a man finds her in the city and lies with her, ²⁴then you shall bring them both out to the gate of that city, and you shall stone them to death with stones, the young woman because she did not cry out in the city, and the man because he humbled his neighbor's wife; so you shall put away the evil from among you.

²⁵"But if a man finds a betrothed young woman in the countryside, and the man forces her and lies with her, then only the man who lay with her shall die. ²⁶But you shall do nothing to the young woman; *there is* in the young woman no sin *deserving* of death, for just as when a man rises against his neighbor and kills him, even so *is* this matter. ²⁷For he found her in the countryside, *and* the betrothed young woman cried out, but *there was* no one to save her.

²⁸"If a man finds a young woman *who is* a

virgin, who is not betrothed, and he seizes her and lies with her, and they are found out, ²⁹then the man who lay with her shall give to the young woman's father fifty *shekels* of silver, and she shall be his wife because he has humbled her; he shall not be permitted to divorce her all his days.

³⁰"A man shall not take his father's wife, nor uncover his father's bed.

THOSE EXCLUDED FROM THE CONGREGATION

¹"He who is emasculated by crushing or mutilation shall not enter the assembly of the LORD.

²"One of illegitimate birth shall not enter the assembly of the LORD; even to the tenth generation none of his *descendants* shall enter the assembly of the LORD.

³"An Ammonite or Moabite shall not enter the assembly of the LORD; even to the tenth generation none of his *descendants* shall enter the assembly of the LORD forever, ⁴because they did not meet you with bread and water on the road when you came out of Egypt, and because they hired against you Balaam the son of Beor from Pethor of Mesopotamia,ᵃ to curse you. ⁵Nevertheless the LORD your God would not listen to Balaam, but the LORD your God turned the curse into a blessing for you, because the LORD your God loves you. ⁶You shall not seek their peace nor their prosperity all your days forever.

⁷"You shall not abhor an Edomite, for he *is* your brother. You shall not abhor an Egyptian, because you were an alien in his land. ⁸The children of the third generation born to them may enter the assembly of the LORD.

CLEANLINESS OF THE CAMPSITE

⁹"When the army goes out against your enemies, then keep yourself from every wicked thing. ¹⁰If there is any man among you who becomes unclean by some occurrence in the night, then he shall go outside the camp; he shall not come inside the camp. ¹¹But it shall be, when evening comes, that he shall wash with water; and when the sun sets, he may come into the camp.

¹²"Also you shall have a place outside the camp, where you may go out; ¹³and you shall have an implement among your equipment, and when you sit down outside, you shall dig with it and turn and cover your refuse. ¹⁴For the LORD your God walks in the midst of your camp, to deliver you and give your enemies over to you; therefore your camp shall be holy, that He may see no unclean thing among you, and turn away from you.

WHAT'S IT MEAN?

Running away was one of the worst crimes a slave could commit. Most cultures allowed masters to kill their runaway slaves. You can see God's respect for human life in His command to the Israelites to protect runaway slaves.

Deuteronomy 23:15

MISCELLANEOUS LAWS

¹⁵"You shall not give back to his master the slave who has escaped from his master to you. ¹⁶He may dwell with you in your midst, in the place which he chooses within one of your gates, where it seems best to him; you shall not oppress him.

¹⁷"There shall be no *ritual* harlotᵃ of the daughters of Israel, or a *perverted*ᵇ one of the sons of Israel. ¹⁸You shall not bring the wages of a harlot or the price of a dog to the house of the LORD your God for any vowed offering, for both of these *are* an abomination to the LORD your God.

¹⁹"You shall not charge interest to your brother—interest on money *or* food *or* anything that is lent out at interest. ²⁰To a foreigner you may charge

"For the LORD your God walks in the midst of your camp, to deliver you and give your enemies over to you; therefore your camp shall be holy, that He may see no unclean thing among you, and turn away from you." (Deuteronomy 23:14)

23:4 ᵃHebrew *Aram Naharaim*   **23:17** ᵃHebrew *qedeshah*, feminine of *qadesh* (see note b)   ᵇHebrew *qadesh*, that is, one practicing sodomy and prostitution in religious rituals interest, but to your brother you shall not charge interest, that the LORD your God may bless you in all to which you set your hand in the land which you are entering to possess.

21"When you make a vow to the LORD your God, you shall not delay to pay it; for the LORD your God will surely require it of you, and it would be sin to you. 22But if you abstain from vowing, it shall not be sin to you. 23That which has gone from your lips you shall keep and perform, for you voluntarily vowed to the LORD your God what you have promised with your mouth.

24"When you come into your neighbor's vineyard, you may eat your fill of grapes at your pleasure, but you shall not put *any* in your container. 25When you come into your neighbor's standing grain, you may pluck the heads with your hand, but you shall not use a sickle on your neighbor's standing grain.

LAW CONCERNING DIVORCE

1"When a man takes a wife and marries her, and it happens that she finds no favor in his eyes because he has found some uncleanness in her, and he writes her a certificate of divorce, puts *it* in her hand, and sends her out of his house, 2when she has departed from his house, and goes and becomes another man's *wife*, 3if the latter husband detests her and writes her a certificate of divorce, puts *it* in her hand, and sends her out of his house, or if the latter husband dies who took her as his wife, 4then her former husband who divorced her must not take her back to be his wife after she has been defiled; for that *is* an abomination before the LORD, and you shall not bring sin on the land which the LORD your God is giving you *as* an inheritance.

MISCELLANEOUS LAWS

5"When a man has taken a new wife, he shall not go out to war or be charged with any business; he shall be free at home one year, and bring happiness to his wife whom he has taken.

6"No man shall take the lower or the upper millstone in pledge, for he takes *one's* living in pledge.

7"If a man is found kidnapping any of his brethren of the children of Israel, and mistreats him or sells him, then that kidnapper shall die; and you shall put away the evil from among you.

8"Take heed in an outbreak of leprosy, that you carefully observe and do according to all that the priests, the Levites, shall teach you; just as I commanded them, *so* you shall be careful

to do. 9Remember what the LORD your God did to Miriam on the way when you came out of Egypt!

10"When you lend your brother anything, you shall not go into his house to get his pledge. 11You shall stand outside, and the man to whom you lend shall bring the pledge out to you. 12And if the man *is* poor, you shall not keep his pledge overnight. 13You shall in any case return the pledge to him again when the sun goes down, that he may sleep in his own garment and bless you; and it shall be righteousness to you before the LORD your God.

On the Edge

And if the man is poor, you shall not keep his pledge overnight. You shall in any case return the pledge to him again when the sun goes down, that he may sleep in his own garment and bless you; and it shall be righteousness to you before the LORD your God (Deut. 24:12, 13).

We live in a society that notices everything that's wrong. The 6:00 o'clock news, organized protests, flyers on your windshield, newspapers, magazines—everything seems to highlight things that are bad. The world doesn't notice much when something really good happens.

Lots of times, kids in school say they act up just to get some attention. You can bet someone will notice when they break the rules, but there are few rewards for kids who do the right thing. We've forgotten that God promises to notice (see Heb. 6:10). He doesn't miss a thing. He isn't sleeping through your sacrifice. He isn't watching the bad kids when you're off doing good. He is pleased to watch you do the right thing. He's faithful to notice every good move you make.

SEE FOR YOURSELF:
   Ps. 33:13–15;
Matt. 13:43; Mark 9:41

14"You shall not oppress a hired servant *who is* poor and needy, *whether* one of your brethren or one of the aliens who *is* in your land within your gates. 15Each day you shall give *him* his wages, and not let the sun go down on it, for he *is* poor and has set his heart on it; lest he cry out against you to the LORD, and it be sin to you.

¹⁶"Fathers shall not be put to death for *their* children, nor shall children be put to death for *their* fathers; a person shall be put to death for his own sin.

¹⁷"You shall not pervert justice due the stranger or the fatherless, nor take a widow's garment as a pledge. ¹⁸But you shall remember that you were a slave in Egypt, and the LORD your God redeemed you from there; therefore I command you to do this thing.

¹⁹"When you reap your harvest in your field, and forget a sheaf in the field, you shall not go back to get it; it shall be for the stranger, the fatherless, and the widow, that the LORD your God may bless you in all the work of your hands. ²⁰When you beat your olive trees, you shall not go over the boughs again; it shall be for the stranger, the fatherless, and the widow. ²¹When you gather the grapes of your vineyard, you shall not glean *it* afterward; it shall be for the stranger, the fatherless, and the widow. ²²And you shall remember that you were a slave in the land of Egypt; therefore I command you to do this thing.

¹"If there is a dispute between men, and they come to court, that *the judges* may judge them, and they justify the righteous and condemn the wicked, ²then it shall be, if the wicked man deserves to be beaten, that the judge will cause him to lie down and be beaten in his presence, according to his guilt, with a certain number of blows. ³Forty blows he may give him *and* no more, lest he should exceed this and beat him with many blows above these, and your brother be humiliated in your sight.

⁴"You shall not muzzle an ox while it treads out *the grain.*

WHAT'S IT MEAN?

Forty lashes with a whip
was the maximum number God allowed
as punishment for a crime. The Israelites were so careful not to
exceed that number that they stopped at thirty-nine lashes, just in
case they made a mistake in counting.
Deuteronomy 25:3

WHAT'S IT MEAN?

Wheat and other grains had to be crushed
so that the grain could be separated from the leaves
and stems of the plant. One of the best crushing methods was to
spread the grain on the ground and have an ox pull a heavy piece of
wood over it. As a reward for its hard work, the ox's mouth was left
unmuzzled so that the animal could eat
some of the grain while it worked.
Deuteronomy 25:4

MARRIAGE DUTY OF THE SURVIVING BROTHER

⁵"If brothers dwell together, and one of them dies and has no son, the widow of the dead man shall not be *married* to a stranger outside *the family;* her husband's brother shall go in to her, take her as his wife, and perform the duty of a husband's brother to her. ⁶And it shall be *that* the firstborn son which she bears will succeed to the name of his dead brother, that his name may not be blotted out of Israel. ⁷But if the man does not want to take his brother's wife, then let his brother's wife go up to the gate to the elders, and say, 'My husband's brother refuses to raise up a name to his brother in Israel; he will not perform the duty of my husband's brother.' ⁸Then the elders of his city shall call him and speak to him. But *if* he stands firm and says, 'I do not want to take her,' ⁹then his brother's wife shall come to him in the presence of the elders, remove his sandal from his foot, spit in his face, and answer and say, 'So shall it be done to the man who will not build up his brother's house.' ¹⁰And his name shall be called in Israel, 'The house of him who had his sandal removed.'

MISCELLANEOUS LAWS

¹¹"If *two* men fight together, and the wife of one draws near to rescue her husband from the hand of the one attacking him, and puts out her hand and seizes him by the genitals, ¹²then you shall cut off her hand; your eye shall not pity *her.*

¹³"You shall not have in your bag differing weights, a heavy and a light. ¹⁴You shall not have in your house differing measures, a large and a small. ¹⁵You shall have a perfect and just

weight, a perfect and just measure, that your days may be lengthened in the land which the LORD your God is giving you. ¹⁶For all who do such things, all who behave unrighteously, *are* an abomination to the LORD your God.

DESTROY THE AMALEKITES

¹⁷"Remember what Amalek did to you on the way as you were coming out of Egypt, ¹⁸how he met you on the way and attacked your rear ranks, all the stragglers at your rear, when you *were* tired and weary; and he did not fear God. ¹⁹Therefore it shall be, when the LORD your God has given you rest from your enemies all around, in the land which the LORD your God is giving you to possess *as* an inheritance, *that* you will blot out the remembrance of Amalek from under heaven. You shall not forget.

OFFERINGS OF FIRSTFRUITS AND TITHES

¹"And it shall be, when you come into the land which the LORD your God is giving you *as* an inheritance, and you possess it and dwell in it, ²that you shall take some of the first of all the produce of the ground, which you shall bring from your land that the LORD your God is giving you, and put *it* in a basket and go to the place where the LORD your God chooses to make His name abide. ³And you shall go to the one who is priest in those days, and say to him, 'I declare today to the LORD your^a God that I have come to the country which the LORD swore to our fathers to give us.'

WHAT'S IT MEAN?

This prayer is actually a poem about Jacob, Moses' ancestor, who moved to Egypt to live with his son Joseph. Leah and Rachel, Jacob's wives, were Syrians by birth.
Deuteronomy 26:5–10

⁴"Then the priest shall take the basket out of your hand and set it down before the altar of the LORD your God. ⁵And you shall answer and say before the LORD your God: 'My father *was* a Syrian,^a about to perish, and he went down to

Egypt and dwelt there, few in number; and there he became a nation, great, mighty, and populous. ⁶But the Egyptians mistreated us, afflicted us, and laid hard bondage on us. ⁷Then we cried out to the LORD God of our fathers, and the LORD heard our voice and looked on our affliction and our labor and our oppression. ⁸So the LORD brought us out of Egypt with a mighty hand and with an outstretched arm, with great terror and with signs and wonders. ⁹He has brought us to this place and has given us this land, "a land flowing with milk and honey";^a ¹⁰and now, behold, I have brought the firstfruits of the land which you, O LORD, have given me.'

"Then you shall set it before the LORD your God, and worship before the LORD your God. ¹¹So you shall rejoice in every good *thing* which the LORD your God has given to you and your house, you and the Levite and the stranger who *is* among you.

¹²"When you have finished laying aside all the tithe of your increase in the third year—the year of tithing—and have given *it* to the Levite, the stranger, the fatherless, and the widow, so that they may eat within your gates and be filled, ¹³then you shall say before the LORD your God: 'I have removed the holy *tithe* from *my* house, and also have given them to the Levite, the stranger, the fatherless, and the widow, according to all Your commandments which You have commanded me; I have not transgressed Your commandments, nor have I forgotten *them.* ¹⁴I have not eaten any of it when in mourning, nor have I removed *any* of it for an unclean *use,* nor given *any* of it for the dead. I have obeyed the voice of the LORD my God, and have done according to all that You have commanded me. ¹⁵Look down from Your holy habitation, from heaven, and bless Your people Israel and the land which You have given us, just as You swore to our fathers, "a land flowing with milk and honey." '^a

A SPECIAL PEOPLE OF GOD

¹⁶"This day the LORD your God commands you to observe these statutes and judgments; therefore you shall be careful to observe them with all your heart and with all your soul. ¹⁷Today you have proclaimed the LORD to be your God, and that you will walk in His ways and keep His statutes, His commandments, and His judgments, and that you will obey His voice. ¹⁸Also today the LORD has proclaimed you to be His special people, just as He promised you,

26:3 ^aSeptuagint reads *my.* **26:5** ^aOr *Aramean* **26:9** ^aExodus 3:8 **26:15** ^aExodus 3:8

that *you* should keep all His commandments, [19]and that He will set you high above all nations which He has made, in praise, in name, and in honor, and that you may be a holy people to the LORD your God, just as He has spoken."

ADOPTION

What are God's children called to do? (26:18)

THE LAW INSCRIBED ON STONES

[1]Now Moses, with the elders of Israel, commanded the people, saying: "Keep all the commandments which I command you today. [2]And it shall be, on the day when you cross over the Jordan to the land which the LORD your God is giving you, that you shall set up for yourselves large stones, and whitewash them with lime. [3]You shall write on them all the words of this law, when you have crossed over, that you may enter the land which the LORD your God is giving you, 'a land flowing with milk and honey,'[a] just as the LORD God of your fathers promised you. [4]Therefore it shall be, when you have crossed over the Jordan, *that* on Mount Ebal you shall set up these stones, which I command you today, and you shall whitewash them with lime. [5]And there you shall build an altar to the LORD your God, an altar of stones; you shall not use an iron *tool* on them. [6]You shall build with whole stones the altar of the LORD your God, and offer burnt offerings on it to the LORD your God. [7]You shall offer peace offerings, and shall eat there, and rejoice before the LORD your God. [8]And you shall write very plainly on the stones all the words of this law."

[9]Then Moses and the priests, the Levites, spoke to all Israel, saying, "Take heed and listen, O Israel: This day you have become the people of the LORD your God. [10]Therefore you shall obey the voice of the LORD your God, and observe His commandments and His statutes which I command you today."

BELIEF

What should accompany belief in God? (27:10)

CURSES PRONOUNCED FROM MOUNT EBAL

[11]And Moses commanded the people on the same day, saying, [12]"These shall stand on Mount Gerizim to bless the people, when you have crossed over the Jordan: Simeon, Levi, Judah, Issachar, Joseph, and Benjamin; [13]and these shall stand on Mount Ebal to curse: Reuben, Gad, Asher, Zebulun, Dan, and Naphtali.

[14]"And the Levites shall speak with a loud voice and say to all the men of Israel: [15]'Cursed *is* the one who makes a carved or molded image, an abomination to the LORD, the work of the hands of the craftsman, and sets *it* up in secret.'

"And all the people shall answer and say, 'Amen!'

[16]'Cursed *is* the one who treats his father or his mother with contempt.'

"And all the people shall say, 'Amen!'

[17]'Cursed *is* the one who moves his neighbor's landmark.'

"And all the people shall say, 'Amen!'

[18]'Cursed *is* the one who makes the blind to wander off the road.'

"And all the people shall say, 'Amen!'

[19]'Cursed *is* the one who perverts the justice due the stranger, the fatherless, and widow.'

"And all the people shall say, 'Amen!'

[20]'Cursed *is* the one who lies with his father's wife, because he has uncovered his father's bed.'

"And all the people shall say, 'Amen!'

[21]'Cursed *is* the one who lies with any kind of animal.'

"And all the people shall say, 'Amen!'

[22]'Cursed *is* the one who lies with his sister, the daughter of his father or the daughter of his mother.'

"And all the people shall say, 'Amen!'

[23]'Cursed *is* the one who lies with his mother-in-law.'

"And all the people shall say, 'Amen!'

[24]'Cursed *is* the one who attacks his neighbor secretly.'

"And all the people shall say, 'Amen!'

[25]'Cursed *is* the one who takes a bribe to slay an innocent person.'

"And all the people shall say, 'Amen!'

[26]'Cursed *is* the one who does not confirm *all* the words of this law by observing them.'

"And all the people shall say, 'Amen!' "

BLESSINGS ON OBEDIENCE

[1]"Now it shall come to pass, if you diligently obey the voice of the LORD your God, to observe carefully all His commandments which I command you today, that the LORD your God will set you high above all nations of the earth. [2]And all these blessings shall come upon you and overtake you, because you obey the voice of the LORD your God:

[3]"Blessed *shall* you *be* in the city, and blessed *shall* you *be* in the country.

[4]"Blessed *shall be* the fruit of your body, the

produce of your ground and the increase of your herds, the increase of your cattle and the offspring of your flocks.

⁵"Blessed *shall be* your basket and your kneading bowl.

⁶"Blessed *shall* you *be* when you come in, and blessed *shall* you *be* when you go out.

⁷"The LORD will cause your enemies who rise against you to be defeated before your face; they shall come out against you one way and flee before you seven ways.

⁸"The LORD will command the blessing on you in your storehouses and in all to which you set your hand, and He will bless you in the land which the LORD your God is giving you.

⁹"The LORD will establish you as a holy people to Himself, just as He has sworn to you, if you keep the commandments of the LORD your God and walk in His ways. ¹⁰Then all peoples of the earth shall see that you are called by the name of the LORD, and they shall be afraid of you. ¹¹And the LORD will grant you plenty of goods, in the fruit of your body, in the increase of your livestock, and in the produce of your ground, in the land of which the LORD swore to your fathers to give you. ¹²The LORD will open to you His good treasure, the heavens, to give the rain to your land in its season, and to bless all the work of your hand. You shall lend to many nations, but you shall not borrow. ¹³And the LORD will make you the head and not the tail; you shall be above only, and not be beneath, if you heed the commandments of the LORD your God, which I command you today,

and are careful to observe *them.* ¹⁴So you shall not turn aside from any of the words which I command you this day, *to* the right or the left, to go after other gods to serve them.

WHAT'S IT MEAN?

While they were traveling, most Israelites made their living as farmers and shepherds—skills that were necessary for their mobile lifestyle. After settling in Canaan, they were free to learn new skills and pursue other careers, such as carpentry, metalworking, weaving, masonry, and making pottery.

Deuteronomy 28:12

CURSES ON DISOBEDIENCE

¹⁵"But it shall come to pass, if you do not obey the voice of the LORD your God, to observe carefully all His commandments and His statutes which I command you today, that all these curses will come upon you and overtake you:

¹⁶"Cursed *shall* you *be* in the city, and cursed *shall* you *be* in the country.

¹⁷"Cursed *shall be* your basket and your kneading bowl.

Promise

HE PROMISES TO MAKE YOU SUCCESSFUL IN YOUR WORK.

Blessed shall you be when you come in, and blessed shall you be when you go out (Deut. 28:6).

One of the blessings of obedience is that God will make you successful in your work (see Deut. 28:3–6). But be careful not to confuse God's kind of success with the world's version of success. The world deceives us into believing that we're successful if we wear the right clothes, drive an expensive car, live in a big house, have lots of people working for us, and carry a gold card. God says we have been successful in our work if we have been pleasing to Him (see 2 Cor. 5:9). You've been successful to God today if you've brought glory to Him. It's that simple. Rest easy tonight, knowing that you've been obedient to Him. He'll make you successful in your work. You don't have to worry or wonder what He's going to do to make you look successful. He'll make you successful in His eyes.

SEE FOR YOURSELF:
Deut. 2:7; 15:10; 1 Chr. 28:20; Neh. 2:20; Ps. 1:3

18"Cursed *shall be* the fruit of your body and the produce of your land, the increase of your cattle and the offspring of your flocks.

19"Cursed *shall* you *be* when you come in, and cursed *shall* you *be* when you go out.

20"The LORD will send on you cursing, confusion, and rebuke in all that you set your hand to do, until you are destroyed and until you perish quickly, because of the wickedness of your doings in which you have forsaken Me. 21The LORD will make the plague cling to you until He has consumed you from the land which you are going to possess. 22The LORD will strike you with consumption, with fever, with inflammation, with severe burning fever, with the sword, with scorching, and with mildew; they shall pursue you until you perish. 23And your heavens which *are* over your head shall be bronze, and the earth which is under you *shall be* iron. 24The LORD will change the rain of your land to powder and dust; from the heaven it shall come down on you until you are destroyed.

25"The LORD will cause you to be defeated before your enemies; you shall go out one way against them and flee seven ways before them; and you shall become troublesome to all the kingdoms of the earth. 26Your carcasses shall be food for all the birds of the air and the beasts of the earth, and no one shall frighten *them* away. 27The LORD will strike you with the boils of Egypt, with tumors, with the scab, and with the itch, from which you cannot be healed. 28The LORD will strike you with madness and blindness and confusion of heart. 29And you shall grope at noonday, as a blind man gropes in darkness; you shall not prosper in your ways; you shall be only oppressed and plundered continually, and no one shall save *you*.

30"You shall betroth a wife, but another man shall lie with her; you shall build a house, but you shall not dwell in it; you shall plant a vineyard, but shall not gather its grapes. 31Your ox *shall be* slaughtered before your eyes, but you shall not eat of it; your donkey *shall be* violently taken away from before you, and shall not be restored to you; your sheep *shall be* given to your enemies, and you shall have no one to rescue *them*. 32Your sons and your daughters *shall be* given to another people, and your eyes shall look and fail *with longing* for them all day long; and *there shall be* no strength in your hand. 33A nation whom you have not known shall eat the fruit of your land and the produce of your labor, and you shall be only oppressed and crushed continually. 34So you shall be driven mad because of the sight which your eyes see. 35The LORD will strike you in the knees and on the legs with severe boils which cannot be healed, and from the sole of your foot to the top of your head.

36"The LORD will bring you and the king whom you set over you to a nation which neither you nor your fathers have known, and there you shall serve other gods—wood and stone. 37And you shall become an astonishment, a proverb, and a byword among all nations where the LORD will drive you.

38"You shall carry much seed out to the field but gather little in, for the locust shall consume it. 39You shall plant vineyards and tend *them*, but you shall neither drink *of* the wine nor gather the *grapes*; for the worms shall eat them. 40You shall have olive trees throughout all your territory, but you shall not anoint *yourself* with the oil; for your olives shall drop off. 41You shall beget sons and daughters, but they shall not be yours; for they shall go into captivity. 42Locusts shall consume all your trees and the produce of your land.

43"The alien who *is* among you shall rise higher and higher above you, and you shall come down lower and lower. 44He shall lend to you, but you shall not lend to him; he shall be the head, and you shall be the tail.

45"Moreover all these curses shall come upon you and pursue and overtake you, until you are destroyed, because you did not obey the voice of the LORD your God, to keep His commandments and His statutes which He commanded you. 46And they shall be upon you for a sign and a wonder, and on your descendants forever.

47"Because you did not serve the LORD your God with joy and gladness of heart, for the abundance of everything, 48therefore you shall serve your enemies, whom the LORD will send

"Now it shall come to pass, if you diligently obey the voice of the LORD your God, to observe carefully all His commandments which I command you today, that the LORD your God will set you high above all nations of the earth."
(Deuteronomy 28:1)

against you, in hunger, in thirst, in nakedness, and in need of everything; and He will put a yoke of iron on your neck until He has destroyed you. ⁴⁹The LORD will bring a nation against you from afar, from the end of the earth, *as swift* as the eagle flies, a nation whose language you will not understand, ⁵⁰a nation of fierce countenance, which does not respect the elderly nor show favor to the young. ⁵¹And they shall eat the increase of your livestock and the produce of your land, until you are destroyed; they shall not leave you grain or new wine or oil, *or* the increase of your cattle or the offspring of your flocks, until they have destroyed you.

WHAT'S IT MEAN?

Ancient armies did not always use violence to conquer their enemies. One particularly cruel, but effective, strategy was to surround an enemy's town and not allow food or water to be brought inside. If the people of the town could not break through the enemy lines, or if no one came to their rescue, they would die slowly of thirst and starvation.

Deuteronomy 28:52, 53

⁵²"They shall besiege you at all your gates until your high and fortified walls, in which you trust, come down throughout all your land; and they shall besiege you at all your gates throughout all your land which the LORD your God has given you. ⁵³You shall eat the fruit of your own body, the flesh of your sons and your daughters whom the LORD your God has given you, in the siege and desperate straits in which your enemy shall distress you. ⁵⁴The sensitive and very refined man among you will be hostile toward his brother, toward the wife of his bosom, and toward the rest of his children whom he leaves behind, ⁵⁵so that he will not give any of them the flesh of his children whom he will eat, because he has nothing left in the siege and desperate straits in which your enemy shall distress you at all your gates. ⁵⁶The tender and delicate woman among you, who would not venture to set the sole of her foot on the ground because of her delicateness and sensitivity, will refuse*ᵃ* to the husband of her bo-

som, and to her son and her daughter, ⁵⁷her placenta which comes out from between her feet and her children whom she bears; for she will eat them secretly for lack of everything in the siege and desperate straits in which your enemy shall distress you at all your gates.

⁵⁸"If you do not carefully observe all the words of this law that are written in this book, that you may fear this glorious and awesome name, THE LORD YOUR GOD, ⁵⁹then the LORD will bring upon you and your descendants extraordinary plagues—great and prolonged plagues—and serious and prolonged sicknesses. ⁶⁰Moreover He will bring back on you all the diseases of Egypt, of which you were afraid, and they shall cling to you. ⁶¹Also every sickness and every plague, which *is* not written in this Book of the Law, will the LORD bring upon you until you are destroyed. ⁶²You shall be left few in number, whereas you were as the stars of heaven in multitude, because you would not obey the voice of the LORD your God. ⁶³And it shall be, *that* just as the LORD rejoiced over you to do you good and multiply you, so the LORD will rejoice over you to destroy you and bring you to nothing; and you shall be plucked from off the land which you go to possess.

⁶⁴"Then the LORD will scatter you among all peoples, from one end of the earth to the other, and there you shall serve other gods, which neither you nor your fathers have known— wood and stone. ⁶⁵And among those nations you shall find no rest, nor shall the sole of your foot have a resting place; but there the LORD will give you a trembling heart, failing eyes, and anguish of soul. ⁶⁶Your life shall hang in doubt before you; you shall fear day and night, and have no assurance of life. ⁶⁷In the morning you shall say, 'Oh, that it were evening!' And at evening you shall say, 'Oh, that it were morning!' because of the fear which terrifies your heart, and because of the sight which your eyes see.

⁶⁸"And the LORD will take you back to Egypt in ships, by the way of which I said to you, 'You shall never see it again.' And there you shall be offered for sale to your enemies as male and female slaves, but no one will buy *you.*"

THE COVENANT RENEWED IN MOAB

¹These *are* the words of the covenant which the LORD commanded Moses to make with the children of Israel in the land of Moab, besides the covenant which He made with them in Horeb.

28:56 *ᵃLiterally her eye shall be evil toward*

²Now Moses called all Israel and said to them: "You have seen all that the LORD did before your eyes in the land of Egypt, to Pharaoh and to all his servants and to all his land— ³the great trials which your eyes have seen, the signs, and those great wonders. ⁴Yet the LORD has not given you a heart to perceive and eyes to see and ears to hear, to this *very* day. ⁵And I have led you forty years in the wilderness. Your clothes have not worn out on you, and your sandals have not worn out on your feet. ⁶You have not eaten bread, nor have you drunk wine or *similar* drink, that you may know that I *am* the LORD your God. ⁷And when you came to this place, Sihon king of Heshbon and Og king of Bashan came out against us to battle, and we conquered them. ⁸We took their land and gave it as an inheritance to the Reubenites, to the Gadites, and to half the tribe of Manasseh. ⁹Therefore keep the words of this covenant, and do them, that you may prosper in all that you do.

WHAT'S IT MEAN?

Heshbon and Bashan were located east of the Jordan River. Most of the land the Israelites had been promised lay west of the Jordan.
Deuteronomy 29:7

¹⁰"All of you stand today before the LORD your God: your leaders and your tribes and your elders and your officers, all the men of Israel, ¹¹your little ones and your wives—also the stranger who *is* in your camp, from the one who cuts your wood to the one who draws your water— ¹²that you may enter into covenant with the LORD your God, and into His oath, which the LORD your God makes with you today, ¹³that He may establish you today as a people for Himself, and *that* He may be God to you, just as He has spoken to you, and just as He has sworn to your fathers, to Abraham, Isaac, and Jacob.

¹⁴"I make this covenant and this oath, not with you alone, ¹⁵but with *him* who stands here with us today before the LORD our God, as well as with *him* who *is* not here with us today

WHAT'S IT MEAN?

Many Egyptian idols were strange combinations of animals and humans. For example, Anubis, the Egyptian god of tombs, had the body of a man and the head of a jackal.
Deuteronomy 29:16, 17

¹⁶(for you know that we dwelt in the land of Egypt and that we came through the nations which you passed by, ¹⁷and you saw their abominations and their idols which *were* among them—wood and stone and silver and gold); ¹⁸so that there may not be among you man or woman or family or tribe, whose heart turns away today from the LORD our God, to go *and* serve the gods of these nations, and that there may not be among you a root bearing bitterness or wormwood; ¹⁹and so it may not happen, when he hears the words of this curse, that he blesses himself in his heart, saying, 'I shall have peace, even though I follow the dictates[a] of my heart'—as though the drunkard could be included with the sober.

²⁰"The LORD would not spare him; for then the anger of the LORD and His jealousy would burn against that man, and every curse that is written in this book would settle on him, and the LORD would blot out his name from under heaven. ²¹And the LORD would separate him from all the tribes of Israel for adversity, according to all the curses of the covenant that are written in this Book of the Law, ²²so that the coming generation of your children who rise up after you, and the foreigner who comes from a far land, would say, when they see the plagues of that land and the sicknesses which the LORD has laid on it:

²³'The whole land *is* brimstone, salt, and burning; it is not sown, nor does it bear, nor does any grass grow there, like the overthrow of Sodom and Gomorrah, Admah, and Zeboiim, which the LORD overthrew in His anger and His wrath.' ²⁴All nations would say, 'Why has the LORD done so to this land? What does the heat of this great anger mean?' ²⁵Then *people* would say: 'Because they have forsaken the

29:19 *a*Or *stubbornness*

covenant of the LORD God of their fathers, which He made with them when He brought them out of the land of Egypt; [26]for they went and served other gods and worshiped them, gods that they did not know and that He had not given to them. [27]Then the anger of the LORD was aroused against this land, to bring on it every curse that is written in this book. [28]And the LORD uprooted them from their land in anger, in wrath, and in great indignation, and cast them into another land, as *it is* this day.'

[29]"The secret *things belong* to the LORD our God, but those *things which are* revealed *belong* to us and to our children forever, that *we* may do all the words of this law.

THE BLESSING OF RETURNING TO GOD

[1]"Now it shall come to pass, when all these things come upon you, the blessing and the curse which I have set before you, and you call *them* to mind among all the nations where the LORD your God drives you, [2]and you return to the LORD your God and obey His voice, according to all that I command you today, you and your children, with all your heart and with all your soul, [3]that the LORD your God will bring you back from captivity, and have compassion on you, and gather you again from all the nations where the LORD your God has scattered you. [4]If *any* of you are driven out to the farthest *parts* under heaven, from there the LORD your God will gather you, and from there He will bring you. [5]Then the LORD your God will bring you to the land which your fathers possessed, and you shall possess it. He will prosper you and multiply you more than your fathers. [6]And the LORD your God will circumcise your heart and the heart of your descendants, to love the LORD your God with all your heart and with all your soul, that you may live. [7]"Also the LORD your God will put all these curses on your enemies and on those who hate you, who persecuted you. [8]And you will again obey the voice of the LORD and do all His commandments which I command you today. [9]The LORD your God will make you abound in all the work of your hand, in the fruit of your body, in the increase of your livestock, and in the produce of your land for good. For the LORD will again rejoice over you for good as He rejoiced over your fathers, [10]if you obey the voice of the LORD your God, to keep His com-

mandments and His statutes which are written in this Book of the Law, *and* if you turn to the LORD your God with all your heart and with all your soul.

THE CHOICE OF LIFE OR DEATH

[11]"For this commandment which I command you today *is* not *too* mysterious for you, nor *is* it far off. [12]It *is* not in heaven, that you should say, 'Who will ascend into heaven for us and bring it to us, that we may hear it and do it?' [13]Nor *is* it beyond the sea, that you should say, 'Who will go over the sea for us and bring it to us, that we may hear it and do it?' [14]But the word *is* very near you, in your mouth and in your heart, that you may do it.

[15]"See, I have set before you today life and good, death and evil, [16]in that I command you today to love the LORD your God, to walk in His ways, and to keep His commandments, His statutes, and His judgments, that you may live and multiply; and the LORD your God will bless you in the land which you go to possess. [17]But if your heart turns away so that you do not hear, and are drawn away, and worship other gods and serve them, [18]I announce to you today that you shall surely perish; you shall not prolong *your* days in the land which you cross over the Jordan to go in and possess. [19]I call heaven and earth as witnesses today against you, *that* I have set before you life and death, blessing and cursing; therefore choose life, that both you and your descendants may live; [20]that you may love the LORD your God, that you may obey His voice, and that you may cling to Him, for He *is* your life and the length of your days; and that you may dwell in the land which the LORD swore to your fathers, to Abraham, Isaac, and Jacob, to give them."

JOSHUA THE NEW LEADER OF ISRAEL

[1]Then Moses went and spoke these words to all Israel. [2]And he said to them: "I *am* one hundred and twenty years old today. I can no longer go out and come in. Also the LORD has said to me, 'You shall not cross over this Jordan.' [3]The LORD your God Himself crosses over before you; He will destroy these nations from before you, and you shall dispossess them. Joshua himself crosses over before you, just as the LORD has said. [4]And the LORD will do to

> "For the LORD will again rejoice over you for good as He rejoiced over your fathers."
> (Deuteronomy 30:9b)

them as He did to Sihon and Og, the kings of the Amorites and their land, when He destroyed them. ⁵The LORD will give them over to you, that you may do to them according to every commandment which I have commanded you. ⁶Be strong and of good courage, do not fear nor be afraid of them; for the LORD your God, He *is* the One who goes with you. He will not leave you nor forsake you."

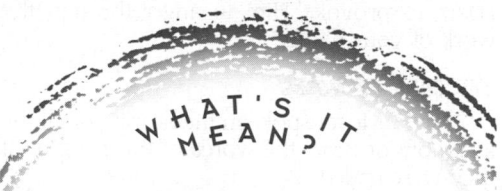

WHAT'S IT MEAN?

Joshua had experienced it all as an Israelite. He was born in Egypt while the Israelites were still captives, so he knew what it was like to be a slave. He was around for the first Passover, so he saw God's protection firsthand. He was one of the twelve spies Moses sent to check out the land of Canaan, so he knew what the Lord had waiting for the Israelites. He had faithfully served the Lord and followed Moses' instruction, and now he was going to be the new leader of Israel.

Deuteronomy 31:7

⁷Then Moses called Joshua and said to him in the sight of all Israel, "Be strong and of good courage, for you must go with this people to the land which the LORD has sworn to their fathers to give them, and you shall cause them to inherit it. ⁸And the LORD, He *is* the One who goes before you. He will be with you, He will not leave you nor forsake you; do not fear nor be dismayed."

THE LAW TO BE READ EVERY SEVEN YEARS

⁹So Moses wrote this law and delivered it to the priests, the sons of Levi, who bore the ark of the covenant of the LORD, and to all the elders of Israel. ¹⁰And Moses commanded them, saying: "At the end of *every* seven years, at the appointed time in the year of release, at the Feast of Tabernacles, ¹¹when all Israel comes to appear before the LORD your God in the place which He chooses, you shall read this law before all Israel in their hearing. ¹²Gather the people together, men and women and little ones, and the stranger who *is* within your gates, that they may hear and that they may learn to fear the LORD your God and carefully observe all the words of this law, ¹³and *that* their children, who have not known it, may hear and learn to fear the LORD your God as long as you live in the land which you cross the Jordan to possess."

PREDICTION OF ISRAEL'S REBELLION

¹⁴Then the LORD said to Moses, "Behold, the days approach when you must die; call Joshua,

Promise
HE PROMISES NEVER TO LEAVE OR FORSAKE YOU.

And the LORD, He is the One who goes before you. He will be with you, He will not leave you nor forsake you; do not fear nor be dismayed (Deut. 31:8).

When you're about to go into unfamiliar territory—a new school, your first date, standing up for yourself for the first time—you probably feel a little shaky. Everyone understands that new situations can be a little scary. But if God told the Israelites not to be afraid of their enemies, you can bet He doesn't want you to be afraid of anything either. He certainly doesn't want you to be afraid of something just because you're not used to it.

He is with you all the time. You can't get rid of Him. In these days of convenient relationships, children disowning their parents, divorce everywhere, it's easy to think that no one will ever be truly committed to you. God will. In the good times and the bad, in the familiar time and the new experiences, God is totally with you. No matter what you do or where you go, He is there. He doesn't take a break, doesn't blink for a split second. When God says He will not leave you nor forsake you, He is telling you He is with you all the time. You are never alone.

SEE FOR YOURSELF:
Josh. 1:5; Matt. 28:20; Heb. 13:5

and present yourselves in the tabernacle of meeting, that I may inaugurate him."

So Moses and Joshua went and presented themselves in the tabernacle of meeting. ¹⁵Now the LORD appeared at the tabernacle in a pillar of cloud, and the pillar of cloud stood above the door of the tabernacle.

¹⁶And the LORD said to Moses: "Behold, you will rest with your fathers; and this people will rise and play the harlot with the gods of the foreigners of the land, where they go *to be* among them, and they will forsake Me and break My covenant which I have made with them. ¹⁷Then My anger shall be aroused against them in that day, and I will forsake them, and I will hide My face from them, and they shall be devoured. And many evils and troubles shall befall them, so that they will say in that day, 'Have not these evils come upon us because our God *is* not among us?' ¹⁸And I will surely hide My face in that day because of all the evil which they have done, in that they have turned to other gods.

¹⁹"Now therefore, write down this song for yourselves, and teach it to the children of Israel; put it in their mouths, that this song may be a witness for Me against the children of Israel. ²⁰When I have brought them to the land flowing with milk and honey, of which I swore to their fathers, and they have eaten and filled themselves and grown fat, then they will turn to other gods and serve them; and they will provoke Me and break My covenant. ²¹Then it shall be, when many evils and troubles have come upon them, that this song will testify against them as a witness; for it will not be forgotten in the mouths of their descendants, for I know the inclination of their behavior today, even before I have brought them to the land of which I *swore to give them*."

²²Therefore Moses wrote this song the same day, and taught it to the children of Israel. ²³Then He inaugurated Joshua the son of Nun, and said, "Be strong and of good courage; for you shall bring the children of Israel into the land of which I swore to them, and I will be with you."

²⁴So it was, when Moses had completed writing the words of this law in a book, when they were finished, ²⁵that Moses commanded the Levites, who bore the ark of the covenant of the LORD, saying: ²⁶"Take this Book of the Law, and put it beside the ark of the covenant of the LORD your God, that it may be there as a witness against you; ²⁷for I know your rebellion and your stiff neck. *If* today, while I am yet alive with you, you have been rebellious against the

LORD, then how much more after my death? ²⁸Gather to me all the elders of your tribes, and your officers, that I may speak these words in their hearing and call heaven and earth to witness against them. ²⁹For I know that after my death you will become utterly corrupt, and turn aside from the way which I have commanded you. And evil will befall you in the latter days, because you will do evil in the sight of the LORD, to provoke Him to anger through the work of your hands."

THE SONG OF MOSES

³⁰Then Moses spoke in the hearing of all the assembly of Israel the words of this song until they were ended:

1   "Give ear, O heavens, and I will speak;
     And hear, O earth, the words of my
          mouth.
2   Let my teaching drop as the rain,
     My speech distill as the dew,
     As raindrops on the tender herb,
     And as showers on the grass.
3   For I proclaim the name of the LORD:
     Ascribe greatness to our God.
4   *He is* the Rock, His work *is* perfect;
     For all His ways *are* justice,
     A God of truth and without injustice;
     Righteous and upright *is* He.

5   "They have corrupted themselves;
     They are not His children,
     Because of their blemish:
     A perverse and crooked generation.
6   Do you thus deal with the LORD,
     O foolish and unwise people?
     Is He not your Father, *who* bought you?
     Has He not made you and established
          you?

7   "Remember the days of old,
     Consider the years of many generations.
     Ask your father, and he will show you;
     Your elders, and they will tell you:
8   When the Most High divided their
          inheritance to the nations,
     When He separated the sons of Adam,
     He set the boundaries of the peoples
     According to the number of the children
          of Israel.
9   For the LORD's portion *is* His people;
     Jacob *is* the place of His inheritance.

10   "He found him in a desert land
     And in the wasteland, a howling
          wilderness;

He encircled him, He instructed him,
He kept him as the apple of His eye.
11 As an eagle stirs up its nest,
Hovers over its young,
Spreading out its wings, taking them up,
Carrying them on its wings,
12 *So* the LORD alone led him,
And *there was* no foreign god with him.

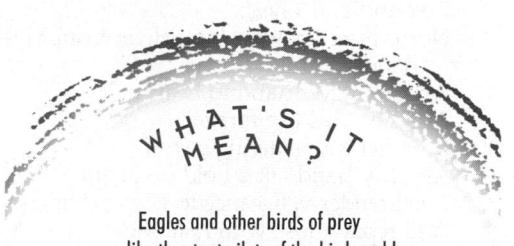

WHAT'S IT MEAN?

Eagles and other birds of prey
are like the stunt pilots of the bird world.
If a young eagle falls out of its nest, the adult is capable of swoop-
ing down, catching the falling bird on its back before it hits
the ground, and returning it to the nest.
Deuteronomy 32:11

13 "He made him ride in the heights of the
earth,
That he might eat the produce of the
fields;
He made him draw honey from the
rock,
And oil from the flinty rock;
14 Curds from the cattle, and milk of the
flock,
With fat of lambs;
And rams of the breed of Bashan, and
goats,
With the choicest wheat;
And you drank wine, the blood of the
grapes.

15 "But Jeshurun grew fat and kicked;
You grew fat, you grew thick,
You are obese!
Then he forsook God *who* made him,
And scornfully esteemed the Rock of his
salvation.
16 They provoked Him to jealousy with
foreign *gods*;
With abominations they provoked Him
to anger.
17 They sacrificed to demons, not to God,
To gods they did not know,
To new *gods*, new arrivals
That your fathers did not fear.

18 Of the Rock *who* begot you, you are
unmindful,
And have forgotten the God who
fathered you.

19 "And when the LORD saw *it*, He spurned
them,
Because of the provocation of His sons
and His daughters.
20 And He said: 'I will hide My face from
them,
I will see what their end *will be*,
For they *are* a perverse generation,
Children in whom *is* no faith.
21 They have provoked Me to jealousy by
what is not God;
They have moved Me to anger by their
foolish idols.
But I will provoke them to jealousy by
those who are not a nation;
I will move them to anger by a foolish
nation.
22 For a fire is kindled in My anger,
And shall burn to the lowest hell;
It shall consume the earth with her
increase,
And set on fire the foundations of the
mountains.

23 'I will heap disasters on them;
I will spend My arrows on them.
24 *They shall be* wasted with hunger,
Devoured by pestilence and bitter
destruction;
I will also send against them the teeth of
beasts,
With the poison of serpents of the dust.
25 The sword shall destroy outside;
There shall be terror within
For the young man and virgin,
The nursing child with the man of gray
hairs.
26 I would have said, "I will dash them in
pieces,
I will make the memory of them to cease
from among men,"
27 Had I not feared the wrath of the enemy,
Lest their adversaries should
misunderstand,
Lest they should say, "Our hand *is* high;
And it is not the LORD who has done all
this." '

28 "For they *are* a nation void of counsel,
Nor *is there any* understanding in them.
29 Oh, that they were wise, *that* they
understood this,

That they would consider their latter end!

30 How could one chase a thousand,
And two put ten thousand to flight,
Unless their Rock had sold them,
And the LORD had surrendered them?

31 For their rock *is* not like our Rock,
Even our enemies themselves *being* judges.

32 For their vine *is* of the vine of Sodom
And of the fields of Gomorrah;
Their grapes *are* grapes of gall,
Their clusters *are* bitter.

33 Their wine *is* the poison of serpents,
And the cruel venom of cobras.

34 'Is this not laid up in store with Me,
Sealed up among My treasures?

35 Vengeance is Mine, and recompense;
Their foot shall slip in *due* time;
For the day of their calamity *is* at hand,
And the things to come hasten upon
them'.

36 "For the LORD will judge His people
And have compassion on His servants,
When He sees that *their* power is gone,
And *there is* no one *remaining*, bond or
free.

37 He will say: 'Where *are* their gods,
The rock in which they sought refuge?

38 Who ate the fat of their sacrifices,
And drank the wine of their drink
offering?
Let them rise and help you,
And be your refuge.

39 'Now see that I, *even* I, *am* He,
And *there is* no God besides Me;
I kill and I make alive;
I wound and I heal;
Nor *is there any* who can deliver from My
hand.

40 For I raise My hand to heaven,
And say, "*As* I live forever,

41 If I whet My glittering sword,
And My hand takes hold on judgment,
I will render vengeance to My enemies,
And repay those who hate Me.

42 I will make My arrows drunk with blood,
And My sword shall devour flesh,
With the blood of the slain and the
captives,
From the heads of the leaders of the
enemy." '

43 "Rejoice, O Gentiles, *with* His people;[a]
For He will avenge the blood of His
servants,
And render vengeance to His adversaries;
He will provide atonement for His land
and His people."

32:43 [a]A Dead Sea Scroll fragment adds *And let all the gods (angels) worship Him* (compare Septuagint and Hebrews 1:6).

Promise — HE PROMISES TO TAKE REVENGE ON HIS ENEMIES.

For I raise My hand to heaven, and say, "As I live forever, if I whet My glittering sword, and My hand takes hold on judgment, I will render vengeance to My enemies . . ." (Deut. 32:40, 41).

Sometimes it seems like people can get away with anything. They cheat and steal and lie and curse God. They get other people to go along with them. Sometimes it goes on for years, and they just seem to be getting richer and more powerful by the minute. You look at them and think, *What good is it to obey God? I'm over here trying to live the Christian life, and I'm struggling day by day, and that guy is doing great!* Then BOOM, God takes revenge on His enemies. Everything goes to pieces for the other guy. You realize that God calls us to make choices for Him. God calls us to be responsible for living His way. You see that He may tolerate stuff from His enemies for a while, but not forever. Read the Book of Revelation. You'll see that He will take revenge on His enemies. It *is* worth it to be on His side. He wins.

SEE FOR YOURSELF:
Is. 1:24; Ezek. 25:17; Nah. 1:2

[44]So Moses came with Joshua[a] the son of Nun and spoke all the words of this song in the hearing of the people. [45]Moses finished speaking all these words to all Israel, [46]and he said to them: "Set your hearts on all the words which I testify among you today, which you shall command your children to be careful to observe— all the words of this law. [47]For it *is* not a futile thing for you, because it *is* your life, and by this word you shall prolong *your* days in the land which you cross over the Jordan to possess."

MOSES TO DIE ON MOUNT NEBO

[48]Then the LORD spoke to Moses that very same day, saying: [49]"Go up this mountain of the Abarim, Mount Nebo, which *is* in the land of Moab, across from Jericho; view the land of Canaan, which I give to the children of Israel as a possession; [50]and die on the mountain which you ascend, and be gathered to your people, just as Aaron your brother died on Mount Hor and was gathered to his people; [51]because you trespassed against Me among the children of Israel at the waters of Meribah Kadesh, in the Wilderness of Zin, because you did not hallow Me in the midst of the children of Israel. [52]Yet you shall see the land before *you*, though you shall not go there, into the land which I am giving to the children of Israel."

WHAT'S IT MEAN?

In ancient times, when a man reached the end of his life, it was common for him to pass along his visions or hopes for the future. In chapter 33's long poem, Moses shares his blessings for each of the twelve tribes of Israel.
Deuteronomy 33:1

MOSES' FINAL BLESSING ON ISRAEL

[1]Now this *is* the blessing with which Moses the man of God blessed the children of Israel before his death. [2]And he said:

"The LORD came from Sinai,
  And dawned on them from Seir;
  He shone forth from Mount Paran,

And He came with ten thousands of saints;
  From His right hand
  Came a fiery law for them.
[3]Yes, He loves the people;
  All His saints *are* in Your hand;
  They sit down at Your feet;
  Everyone receives Your words.
[4]Moses commanded a law for us,
  A heritage of the congregation of Jacob.
[5]And He was King in Jeshurun,
  When the leaders of the people were gathered,
  All the tribes of Israel together.

[6]"Let Reuben live, and not die,
  Nor let his men be few."

WHAT'S IT MEAN?

Massah and Meribah weren't what you would call happy memories for the Israelites. These were the places God gave the Israelites water to stop their grumbling and complaining. They were remembered as places where the people of Israel had gone too far in questioning and challenging God.
Deuteronomy 33:8

[7]And this he said of Judah:

"Hear, LORD, the voice of Judah,
  And bring him to his people;
  Let his hands be sufficient for him,
  And may You be a help against his enemies."

[8]And of Levi he said:

"*Let* Your Thummim and Your Urim *be* with Your holy one,
  Whom You tested at Massah,
  And with whom You contended at the waters of Meribah,
[9]Who says of his father and mother,
  'I have not seen them';
  Nor did he acknowledge his brothers,
  Or know his own children;

For they have observed Your word
And kept Your covenant.
10 They shall teach Jacob Your judgments,
And Israel Your law.
They shall put incense before You,
And a whole burnt sacrifice on Your altar.
11 Bless his substance, LORD,
And accept the work of his hands;
Strike the loins of those who rise against
him,
And of those who hate him, that they rise
not again."

12Of Benjamin he said:

"The beloved of the LORD shall dwell in
safety by Him,
Who shelters him all the day long;
And he shall dwell between His
shoulders."

13And of Joseph he said:

"Blessed of the LORD *is* his land,
With the precious things of heaven, with
the dew,
And the deep lying beneath,
14 With the precious fruits of the sun,
With the precious produce of the months,
15 With the best things of the ancient
mountains,
With the precious things of the everlasting
hills,
16 With the precious things of the earth and
its fullness,
And the favor of Him who dwelt in the
bush.
Let *the blessing* come 'on the head of
Joseph,
And on the crown of the head of him
who was separate from his brothers.'*a*
17 His glory *is like* a firstborn bull,
And his horns *like* the horns of the wild
ox;
Together with them
He shall push the peoples
To the ends of the earth;
They *are* the ten thousands of Ephraim,
And they *are* the thousands of
Manasseh."

18And of Zebulun he said:

"Rejoice, Zebulun, in your going out,
And Issachar in your tents!

19 They shall call the peoples *to* the
mountain;
There they shall offer sacrifices of
righteousness;
For they shall partake *of* the abundance
of the seas
And *of* treasures hidden in the sand."

20And of Gad he said:

"Blessed *is* he who enlarges Gad;
He dwells as a lion,
And tears the arm and the crown of his
head.
21 He provided the first *part* for himself,
Because a lawgiver's portion was reserved
there.
He came *with* the heads of the people;
He administered the justice of the LORD,
And His judgments with Israel."

22And of Dan he said:

"Dan *is* a lion's whelp;
He shall leap from Bashan."

23And of Naphtali he said:

"O Naphtali, satisfied with favor,
And full of the blessing of the LORD,
Possess the west and the south."

WHAT'S IT MEAN?

Jericho is one of the oldest inhabited cities in the
world. Because the city lies almost 800 feet below sea
level, Jericho enjoys a tropical climate.
Deuteronomy 34:1

24And of Asher he said:

"Asher *is* most blessed of sons;
Let him be favored by his brothers,
And let him dip his foot in oil.
25 Your sandals *shall be* iron and bronze;
As your days, *so shall* your strength *be*.

33:16 *a*Genesis 49:26

26 "*There is* no one like the God of Jeshurun,
Who rides the heavens to help you,
And in His excellency on the clouds.

27 The eternal God *is your* refuge,
And underneath *are* the everlasting arms;
He will thrust out the enemy from before you,
And will say, 'Destroy!'

28 Then Israel shall dwell in safety,
The fountain of Jacob alone,
In a land of grain and new wine;
His heavens shall also drop dew.

29 Happy *are* you, O Israel!
Who *is* like you, a people saved by the LORD,
The shield of your help
And the sword of your majesty!
Your enemies shall submit to you,
And you shall tread down their high places."

MOSES DIES ON MOUNT NEBO

1 Then Moses went up from the plains of Moab to Mount Nebo, to the top of Pisgah, which is across from Jericho. And the LORD showed him all the land of Gilead as far as Dan, 2all Naphtali and the land of Ephraim and Manasseh, all the land of Judah as far as the Western Sea,*a* 3the South, and the plain of the Valley of Jericho, the city of palm trees, as far as Zoar. 4Then the LORD said to him, "This *is* the land of which I swore to give Abraham, Isaac, and Jacob, saying, 'I will give it to your descendants.' I have caused you to see *it* with your eyes, but you shall not cross over there."

5So Moses the servant of the LORD died there in the land of Moab, according to the word of the LORD. 6And He buried him in a valley in the land of Moab, opposite Beth Peor; but no one knows his grave to this day. 7Moses *was* one hundred and twenty years old when he died. His eyes were not dim nor his natural vigor diminished. 8And the children of Israel wept for Moses in the plains of Moab thirty days. So the days of weeping *and* mourning for Moses ended.

9Now Joshua the son of Nun was full of the spirit of wisdom, for Moses had laid his hands on him; so the children of Israel heeded him, and did as the LORD had commanded Moses.

10But since then there has not arisen in Israel a prophet like Moses, whom the LORD knew face to face, 11in all the signs and wonders which the LORD sent him to do in the land of Egypt, before Pharaoh, before all his servants, and in all his land, 12and by all that mighty power and all the great terror which Moses performed in the sight of all Israel.

34:2 *a*That is, the Mediterranean

> "The beloved of the LORD shall dwell in safety by Him, who shelters him all the day long; and he shall dwell between His shoulders."
> (Deuteronomy 33:12)

CONTENT If you want to read a war epic, Joshua is a book you'll enjoy. It's a "blood-and-guts" kind of story, too violent for a G-rating but too inspiring to pass up. Basically, while the Hebrews were slaves in Egypt, other people settled on their land. That meant the homeland was home to more than one inhabitant. That's never good news. So the Hebrews had to fight to get their land back. The Book of Joshua is the record of those battles.

Joshua was actually the name of the man who led the Hebrews into battles. He was a soldier, a diplomat, a negotiator, and a strategist. He was a good man who believed God even when the odds were stacked up so high against his people that almost everyone else chickened out. He was a real hero.

Over and over God showed the Hebrews that it takes as much courage to believe in the power of God as it does to fight under your own power. But when you believe, the results are better every time.

Outline

Purpose Obedience to God is the key to a success-filled life.

Theme Possessing the Inheritance

Date of writing 1405–1390 B.C.

> "This Book of the Law shall not depart from your mouth, but you shall meditate in it day and night, that you may observe to do according to all that is written in it. For then you will make your way prosperous, and then you will have good success" (1:8).

Bible Talk

Jericho

One of the most famous battles that Joshua faced was the battle of Jericho. This was the battle where the people marched around the city of Jericho for seven days. Just marched. That's all they did. On the seventh day, they marched seven times and then shouted. At this point, to everyone's amazement, the walls of the city fell right down. In went the Hebrews and down went the city.

God did these kinds of miracles for the Hebrews all the time as long as they were faithful. He did this because He wanted it to be oh so obvious that it was God's strength that won the battles, not the people's strength. Sometimes they got it and sometimes they didn't.

LIKE BATTLES WE FACE

The Book of Joshua matters to us today for several reasons. One of those reasons is because we face the same kind of battles that they faced. We face temptations that are too big for us to conquer alone. We face difficult times that feel like they are going to overwhelm us.

The lesson for us in our battles is the same as the lesson for the Hebrews. *Trust God to do your fighting for you. Keep your life clean and take it one step at a time.*

Joshua was pretty good at following this lesson. That's why he was known as a mighty warrior. He really and truly knew that it was God's strength that made the difference in the battles of life.

GOD'S COMMISSION TO JOSHUA

¹After the death of Moses the servant of the LORD, it came to pass that the LORD spoke to Joshua the son of Nun, Moses' assistant, saying: ²"Moses My servant is dead. Now therefore, arise, go over this Jordan, you and all this people, to the land which I am giving to them—the children of Israel. ³Every place that the sole of your foot will tread upon I have given you, as I said to Moses. ⁴From the wilderness and this Lebanon as far as the great river, the River Euphrates, all the land of the Hittites, and to the Great Sea toward the going down of the sun, shall be your territory. ⁵No man shall *be able to* stand before you all the days of your life; as I was with Moses, *so* I will be with you. I will not leave you nor forsake you. ⁶Be strong and of good courage, for to this people you shall divide as an inheritance the land which I swore to their fathers to give them. ⁷Only be strong and very courageous, that you may observe to do according to all the law which Moses My servant commanded you; do not turn from it to the right hand or to the left, that you may prosper wherever you go. ⁸This Book of the Law shall not depart from your mouth, but you shall meditate in it day and night, that you may observe to do according to all that is written in it. For then you will make your way prosperous, and then you will have good success. ⁹Have I not commanded you? Be strong and of good courage; do not be afraid, nor be dis-

COURAGE

Why should we have courage? (1:9)

mayed, for the LORD your God *is* with you wherever you go."

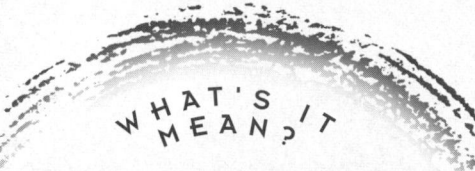

Just in case you were wondering . . .
The Euphrates River is located 350 to 400 miles northeast of Jerusalem. At almost 1,780 miles, it is the longest river in western Asia. The Euphrates begins in Turkey, or Armenia, as the ancient Israelites called it. The ruins of the ancient cities of Babylon, Kish, and Ur can be found on the banks of the Euphrates.
Joshua 1:4

THE ORDER TO CROSS THE JORDAN

¹⁰Then Joshua commanded the officers of the people, saying, ¹¹"Pass through the camp and command the people, saying, 'Prepare provisions for yourselves, for within three days you will cross over this Jordan, to go in to possess the land which the LORD your God is giving you to possess.' "

¹²And to the Reubenites, the Gadites, and half the tribe of Manasseh Joshua spoke, saying, ¹³"Remember the word which Moses the servant of the LORD commanded you, saying, 'The LORD your God is giving you rest and is giving you this land.' ¹⁴Your wives, your little

Promise — HE PROMISES TO HELP YOU WHEREVER YOU GO.

Have I not commanded you? Be strong and of good courage; do not be afraid, nor be dismayed, for the LORD your God is with you wherever you go (Josh. 1:9).

Remember the last time you needed help? Not just help with your homework, but HELP. You were at the end of your rope, no more options; you'd done everything and nothing worked. You were confused, afraid, and lonely all at the same time. What do you do when the answers just don't seem to come? Joshua 1:9. God gives two positive commands here—be strong and be of courage. Don't be afraid. Don't be discouraged. And then, the promise, "The LORD your God *is* with you wherever you go." That promise gives you strength to obey the two commands. You can rest in the fact that God promises to help. You are not alone. You may not get help at the exact second you think you need it, but He will help you. He knows exactly how much you can take. He'll be right on time.

SEE FOR YOURSELF:
Ps. 54:4; Zech. 1:2, 3; John 14:16; Heb. 13:6

ones, and your livestock shall remain in the land which Moses gave you on this side of the Jordan. But you shall pass before your brethren armed, all your mighty men of valor, and help them, ¹⁵until the LORD has given your brethren rest, as He *gave* you, and they also have taken possession of the land which the LORD your God is giving them. Then you shall return to the land of your possession and enjoy it, which Moses the LORD's servant gave you on this side of the Jordan toward the sunrise."

¹⁶So they answered Joshua, saying, "All that you command us we will do, and wherever you send us we will go. ¹⁷Just as we heeded Moses in all things, so we will heed you. Only the LORD your God be with you, as He was with Moses. ¹⁸Whoever rebels against your command and does not heed your words, in all that you command him, shall be put to death. Only be strong and of good courage."

RAHAB HIDES THE SPIES

¹Now Joshua the son of Nun sent out two men from Acacia Grove*ᵃ* to spy secretly, saying, "Go, view the land, especially Jericho."

So they went, and came to the house of a harlot named Rahab, and lodged there. ²And it was told the king of Jericho, saying, "Behold, men have come here tonight from the children of Israel to search out the country."

³So the king of Jericho sent to Rahab, saying, "Bring out the men who have come to you, who have entered your house, for they have come to search out all the country."

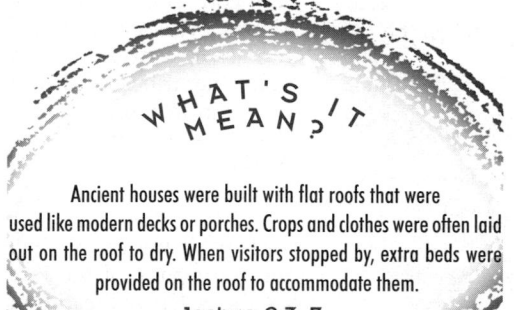

WHAT'S IT MEAN?

Ancient houses were built with flat roofs that were used like modern decks or porches. Crops and clothes were often laid out on the roof to dry. When visitors stopped by, extra beds were provided on the roof to accommodate them.

Joshua 2:3–7

⁴Then the woman took the two men and hid them. So she said, "Yes, the men came to me, but I did not know where they *were* from. ⁵And it happened as the gate was being shut, when it was dark, that the men went out. Where the men went I do not know; pursue them quickly, for you may overtake them." ⁶(But she had brought them up to the roof and hidden them with the stalks of flax, which she had laid in order on the roof.) ⁷Then the men pursued them by the road to the Jordan, to the fords. And as soon as those who pursued them had gone out, they shut the gate.

⁸Now before they lay down, she came up to them on the roof, ⁹and said to the men: "I know that the LORD has given you the land, that the terror of you has fallen on us, and that all the inhabitants of the land are fainthearted because of you. ¹⁰For we have heard how the LORD dried up the water of the Red Sea for you when you came out of Egypt, and what you did to the two kings of the Amorites who *were* on the other side of the Jordan, Sihon and Og, whom you utterly destroyed. ¹¹And as soon as we heard *these things*, our hearts melted; neither did there remain any more courage in anyone because of you, for the LORD your God, He *is* God in heaven above and on earth beneath. ¹²Now therefore, I beg you, swear to me by the LORD, since I have shown you kindness, that you also will show kindness to my father's house, and give me a true token, ¹³and spare my father, my mother, my brothers, my sisters, and all that they have, and deliver our lives from death."

> **EMOTIONS**
> How does it feel when we follow God? (2:12,13)

¹⁴So the men answered her, "Our lives for yours, if none of you tell this business of ours. And it shall be, when the LORD has given us the land, that we will deal kindly and truly with you."

¹⁵Then she let them down by a rope through the window, for her house *was* on the city wall; she dwelt on the wall. ¹⁶And she said to them, "Get to the mountain, lest the pursuers meet you. Hide there three days, until the pursuers have returned. Afterward you may go your way."

¹⁷So the men said to her: "We *will be* blameless of this oath of yours which you have made us swear, ¹⁸unless, *when* we come into the land, you bind this line of scarlet cord in the window through which you let us down, and unless you bring your father, your mother, your brothers, and all your father's household to your own home. ¹⁹So it shall be *that* whoever goes outside the doors of your house into the street, his blood *shall be* on his own head, and

2:1 *ᵃ*Hebrew *Shittim*

we *will be* guiltless. And whoever is with you in the house, his blood *shall be* on our head if a hand is laid on him. ²⁰And if you tell this business of ours, then we will be free from your oath which you made us swear."

²¹Then she said, "According to your words, so *be* it." And she sent them away, and they departed. And she bound the scarlet cord in the window.

²²They departed and went to the mountain, and stayed there three days until the pursuers returned. The pursuers sought *them* all along the way, but did not find *them.* ²³So the two men returned, descended from the mountain, and crossed over; and they came to Joshua the son of Nun, and told him all that had befallen them. ²⁴And they said to Joshua, "Truly the LORD has delivered all the land into our hands, for indeed all the inhabitants of the country are fainthearted because of us."

ISRAEL CROSSES THE JORDAN

¹Then Joshua rose early in the morning; and they set out from Acacia Grove^a and came to the Jordan, he and all the children of Israel, and lodged there before they crossed over. ²So it was, after three days, that the officers went through the camp; ³and they commanded the people, saying, "When you see the ark of the covenant of the LORD your God, and the priests, the Levites, bearing it, then you shall set out from your place and go after it. ⁴Yet there shall be a space between you and it, about two thousand cubits by measure. Do not come near it, that you may know the way by which you must go, for you have not passed *this* way before."

⁵And Joshua said to the people, "Sanctify yourselves, for tomorrow the LORD will do wonders among you." ⁶Then Joshua spoke to the priests, saying, "Take up the ark of the covenant and cross over before the people."

So they took up the ark of the covenant and went before the people.

⁷And the LORD said to Joshua, "This day I will begin to exalt you in the sight of all Israel, that they may know that, as I was with Moses, so I will be with you. ⁸You shall command the priests who bear the ark of the covenant, saying, 'When you have come to the edge of the water of the Jordan, you shall stand in the Jordan.' "

WHAT'S IT MEAN?

Carrying the ark of the covenant was no small task. It was about the size of a small desk. The ark had rings on its sides so that the priests could put poles through them and carry the sacred container without actually touching it. The Israelites carried it into battle because they believed it gave them the power of God.

Joshua 3:3, 4

⁹So Joshua said to the children of Israel, "Come here, and hear the words of the LORD your God." ¹⁰And Joshua said, "By this you shall know that the living God *is* among you, and *that* He will without fail drive out from before you the Canaanites and the Hittites and the Hivites and the Perizzites and the Girgashites and the Amorites and the Jebusites: ¹¹Behold, the ark of the covenant of the Lord of all the earth is crossing over before you into the Jordan. ¹²Now therefore, take for yourselves twelve men from the tribes of Israel, one man from every tribe. ¹³And it shall come to pass, as soon as the soles of the feet of the priests who bear the ark of the LORD, the Lord of all the earth, shall rest in the waters of the Jordan, *that* the waters of the Jordan shall be cut off, the waters that come down from upstream, and they shall stand as a heap."

ADVICE

Where should we turn for advice? (3:9)

"And Joshua said to the people, 'Sanctify yourselves, for tomorrow the LORD will do wonders among you.' " (Joshua 3:5)

¹⁴So it was, when the people set out from their camp to cross over the Jordan, with the priests bearing the ark of the covenant before the people, ¹⁵and as those who bore the ark came to the Jordan, and the feet of the priests who bore the ark dipped in the edge of the water (for the Jordan overflows all its banks

3:1 ^aHebrew *Shittim*

during the whole time of harvest), [16]that the waters which came down from upstream stood *still, and* rose in a heap very far away at Adam, the city that *is* beside Zaretan. So the waters that went down into the Sea of the Arabah, the Salt Sea, failed, *and* were cut off; and the people crossed over opposite Jericho. [17]Then the priests who bore the ark of the covenant of the LORD stood firm on dry ground in the midst of the Jordan; and all Israel crossed over on dry ground, until all the people had crossed completely over the Jordan.

THE MEMORIAL STONES

[1]And it came to pass, when all the people had completely crossed over the Jordan, that the LORD spoke to Joshua, saying: [2]"Take for yourselves twelve men from the people, one man from every tribe, [3]and command them, saying, 'Take for yourselves twelve stones from here, out of the midst of the Jordan, from the place where the priests' feet stood firm. You shall carry them over with you and leave them in the lodging place where you lodge tonight.' "

[4]Then Joshua called the twelve men whom he had appointed from the children of Israel, one man from every tribe; [5]and Joshua said to them: "Cross over before the ark of the LORD your God into the midst of the Jordan, and each one of you take up a stone on his shoulder, according to the number of the tribes of the children of Israel, [6]that this may be a sign among you when your children ask in time to come, saying, 'What do these stones *mean* to you?' [7]Then you shall answer them that the waters of the Jordan were cut off before the ark of the covenant of the LORD; when it crossed over the Jordan, the waters of the Jordan were cut off. And these stones shall be for a memorial to the children of Israel forever."

[8]And the children of Israel did so, just as Joshua commanded, and took up twelve stones from the midst of the Jordan, as the LORD had spoken to Joshua, according to the number of the tribes of the children of Israel, and carried them over with them to the place where they lodged, and laid them down there. [9]Then Joshua set up twelve stones in the midst of the Jordan, in the place where the feet of the priests who bore the ark of the covenant stood; and they are there to this day.

[10]So the priests who bore the ark stood in the midst of the Jordan until everything was finished that the LORD had commanded Joshua

to speak to the people, according to all that Moses had commanded Joshua; and the people hurried and crossed over. [11]Then it came to pass, when all the people had completely crossed over, that the ark of the LORD and the priests crossed over in the presence of the people. [12]And the men of Reuben, the men of Gad, and half the tribe of Manasseh crossed over armed before the children of Israel, as Moses had spoken to them. [13]About forty thousand prepared for war crossed over before the LORD for battle, to the plains of Jericho. [14]On that day the LORD exalted Joshua in the sight of all Israel; and they feared him, as they had feared Moses, all the days of his life.

[15]Then the LORD spoke to Joshua, saying, [16]"Command the priests who bear the ark of the Testimony to come up from the Jordan." [17]Joshua therefore commanded the priests, saying, "Come up from the Jordan." [18]And it came to pass, when the priests who bore the ark of the covenant of the LORD had come from the midst of the Jordan, *and* the soles of the priests' feet touched the dry land, that the waters of the Jordan returned to their place and overflowed all its banks as before.

[19]Now the people came up from the Jordan on the tenth *day* of the first month, and they camped in Gilgal on the east border of Jericho. [20]And those twelve stones which they took out of the Jordan, Joshua set up in Gilgal. [21]Then he spoke to the children of Israel, saying: "When your children ask their fathers in time to come, saying, 'What *are* these stones?' [22]then you shall let your children know, saying, 'Israel crossed over this Jordan on dry land'; [23]for the LORD your God dried up the waters of the Jordan before you until you had crossed over, as the LORD your God did to the Red Sea, which He dried up before us until we had crossed over, [24]that all the peoples of the earth may know the hand of the LORD, that it *is* mighty, that you may fear the LORD your God forever."

GOD

How powerful is God? (4:24)

THE SECOND GENERATION CIRCUMCISED

[1]So it was, when all the kings of the Amorites who *were* on the west side of the Jordan, and all the kings of the Canaanites who *were* by the sea, heard that the LORD had dried up the waters of the Jordan from before the children of Israel until we[a] had crossed over, that their

---

5:1 [a]Following Kethib; Qere, some Hebrew manuscripts and editions, Septuagint, Syriac, Targum, and Vulgate read *they*.

heart melted; and there was no spirit in them any longer because of the children of Israel.

[2]At that time the LORD said to Joshua, "Make flint knives for yourself, and circumcise the sons of Israel again the second time." [3]So Joshua made flint knives for himself, and circumcised the sons of Israel at the hill of the foreskins.[a] [4]And this *is* the reason why Joshua circumcised them: All the people who came out of Egypt *who were* males, all the men of war, had died in the wilderness on the way, after they had come out of Egypt. [5]For all the people who came out had been circumcised, but all the people born in the wilderness, on the way as they came out of Egypt, had not been circumcised. [6]For the children of Israel walked forty years in the wilderness, till all the people *who were* men of war, who came out of Egypt, were consumed, because they did not obey the voice of the LORD— to whom the LORD swore that He would not show them the land which the LORD had sworn to their fathers that He would give us, "a land flowing with milk and honey."[a] [7]Then Joshua circumcised their sons *whom* He raised up in their place; for they were uncircumcised, because they had not been circumcised on the way.

[8]So it was, when they had finished circumcising all the people, that they stayed in their places in the camp till they were healed. [9]Then the LORD said to Joshua, "This day I have rolled away the reproach of Egypt from you." Therefore the name of the place is called Gilgal[a] to this day.

[10]Now the children of Israel camped in Gilgal, and kept the Passover on the fourteenth day of the month at twilight on the plains of Jericho. [11]And they ate of the produce of the land on the day after the Passover, unleavened bread and parched grain, on the very same day. [12]Then the manna ceased on the day after they had eaten the produce of the land; and the children of Israel no longer had manna, but they ate the food of the land of Canaan that year.

THE COMMANDER OF THE ARMY OF THE LORD

[13]And it came to pass, when Joshua was by Jericho, that he lifted his eyes and looked, and behold, a Man stood opposite him with His sword drawn in His hand. And Joshua went to Him and said to Him, "*Are* You for us or for our adversaries?"

[14]So He said, "No, but *as* Commander of the army of the LORD I have now come."

And Joshua fell on his face to the earth and worshiped, and said to Him, "What does my Lord say to His servant?"

[15]Then the Commander of the LORD's army said to Joshua, "Take your sandal off your foot, for the place where you stand *is* holy." And Joshua did so.

WHAT'S IT MEAN?

Taking off one's shoes was a sign of respect, a lot like removing one's hat in church. Moses had been told to remove his shoes when God spoke to him from the burning bush.
Joshua 5:15

THE DESTRUCTION OF JERICHO

[1]Now Jericho was securely shut up because of the children of Israel; none went out, and none came in. [2]And the LORD said to Joshua: "See! I have given Jericho into your hand, its king, *and* the mighty men of valor. [3]You shall march around the city, all *you* men of war; you shall go all around the city once. This you shall do six days. [4]And seven priests shall bear seven trumpets of rams' horns before the ark. But the seventh day you shall march around the city seven times, and the priests shall blow the trumpets. [5]It shall come to pass, when they make a long *blast* with the ram's horn, *and* when you hear the sound of the trumpet, that all the people shall shout with a great shout; then the wall of the city will fall down flat. And the people shall go up every man straight before him."

[6]Then Joshua the son of Nun called the priests and said to them, "Take up the ark of the covenant, and let seven priests bear seven trumpets of rams' horns before the ark of the LORD." [7]And he said to the people, "Proceed, and march around the city, and let him who is armed advance before the ark of the LORD."

[8]So it was, when Joshua had spoken to the people, that the seven priests bearing the seven trumpets of rams' horns before the LORD advanced and blew the trumpets, and the ark of the covenant of the LORD followed them. [9]The armed men went before the priests who blew

the trumpets, and the rear guard came after the ark, while *the priests* continued blowing the trumpets. [10]Now Joshua had commanded the people, saying, "You shall not shout or make any noise with your voice, nor shall a word proceed out of your mouth, until the day I say to you, 'Shout!' Then you shall shout." [11]So he had the ark of the LORD circle the city, going around *it* once. Then they came into the camp and lodged in the camp.

[12]And Joshua rose early in the morning, and the priests took up the ark of the LORD. [13]Then seven priests bearing seven trumpets of rams' horns before the ark of the LORD went on continually and blew with the trumpets. And the armed men went before them. But the rear guard came after the ark of the LORD, while *the priests* continued blowing the trumpets. [14]And the second day they marched around the city once and returned to the camp. So they did six days.

[15]But it came to pass on the seventh day that they rose early, about the dawning of the day, and marched around the city seven times in the same manner. On that day only they marched around the city seven times. [16]And the seventh time it happened, when the priests blew the trumpets, that Joshua said to the people: "Shout, for the LORD has given you the city! [17]Now the city shall be doomed by the LORD to destruction, it and all who *are* in it. Only Rahab the harlot shall live, she and all who *are* with her in the house, because she hid the messengers that we sent. [18]And you, by all means abstain from the accursed things, lest you become accursed when you take of the accursed things, and make the camp of Israel a curse, and trouble it. [19]But all the silver and gold, and vessels of bronze and iron, *are* consecrated to the LORD; they shall come into the treasury of the LORD."

[20]So the people shouted when *the priests* blew the trumpets. And it happened when the people heard the sound of the trumpet, and the people shouted with a great shout, that the wall fell down flat. Then the people went up into the city, every man straight before him, and they took the city. [21]And they utterly destroyed all that *was* in the city, both man and woman, young and old, ox and sheep and donkey, with the edge of the sword.

[22]But Joshua had said to the two men who had spied out the country, "Go into the harlot's house, and from there bring out the woman and all that she has, as you swore to her." [23]And the young men who had been spies went in and brought out Rahab, her father, her mother,

her brothers, and all that she had. So they brought out all her relatives and left them outside the camp of Israel. [24]But they burned the city and all that *was* in it with fire. Only the silver and gold, and the vessels of bronze and iron, they put into the treasury of the house of the LORD. [25]And Joshua spared Rahab the harlot, her father's household, and all that she had. So she dwells in Israel to this day, because she hid the messengers whom Joshua sent to spy out Jericho.

[26]Then Joshua charged *them* at that time, saying, "Cursed *be* the man before the LORD who rises up and builds this city Jericho; he shall lay its foundation with his firstborn, and with his youngest he shall set up its gates."

[27]So the LORD was with Joshua, and his fame spread throughout all the country.

SUCCESS
Who gives us success? (6:27)

DEFEAT AT AI

[1]But the children of Israel committed a trespass regarding the accursed things, for Achan

On the Edge

So the LORD was with Joshua, and his fame spread throughout all the country (Josh. 6:27).

Jericho belonged to God, and it was time to reclaim it. So He sent Joshua and gave him the plan. "March slowly around the city every day for six days. On the seventh day, go around seven times, then blow the trumpets, and shout. The walls will fall down, and the soldiers can just walk in and take the city." Cool. What a plan! It worked. Do all good plans work? Nope. This plan worked because it was a God-plan. Joshua listened to God's plans, and God was with him to help in everything he did. The same is true for you. When you listen to God and obey His plan, He promises to help you. He will guide you every single day. His instruction will not be confusing. What wall is God calling you to conquer? Are you listening to Him? Then start marching.

SEE FOR YOURSELF:
2 Chr. 14:11;
Ps. 33:20; 46:1;
Rom. 8:26

the son of Carmi, the son of Zabdi,[a] the son of Zerah, of the tribe of Judah, took of the accursed things; so the anger of the LORD burned against the children of Israel.

WHAT'S IT MEAN?

Ai was probably smaller than Jericho, which led the spies to believe it wouldn't take many soldiers to capture it. Big mistake.
Joshua 7:2, 3

[2]Now Joshua sent men from Jericho to Ai, which is beside Beth Aven, on the east side of Bethel, and spoke to them, saying, "Go up and spy out the country." So the men went up and spied out Ai. [3]And they returned to Joshua and said to him, "Do not let all the people go up, but let about two or three thousand men go up and attack Ai. Do not weary all the people there, for the people of Ai are few." [4]So about three thousand men went up there from the people, but they fled before the men of Ai. [5]And the men of Ai struck down about thirty-six men, for they chased them from before the gate as far as Shebarim, and struck them down on the descent; therefore the hearts of the people melted and became like water.

WHAT'S IT MEAN?

Tearing one's clothes was a way of mourning a tragedy or death. Joshua and his soldiers expressed their grief over being defeated by the people of Ai by lying on the ground.
Joshua 7:6

[6]Then Joshua tore his clothes, and fell to the earth on his face before the ark of the LORD until evening, he and the elders of Israel; and they put dust on their heads. [7]And Joshua said,

"Alas, Lord GOD, why have You brought this people over the Jordan at all—to deliver us into the hand of the Amorites, to destroy us? Oh, that we had been content, and dwelt on the other side of the Jordan! [8]O Lord, what shall I say when Israel turns its back before its enemies? [9]For the Canaanites and all the inhabitants of the land will hear it, and surround us, and cut off our name from the earth. Then what will You do for Your great name?"

THE SIN OF ACHAN

[10]So the LORD said to Joshua: "Get up! Why do you lie thus on your face? [11]Israel has sinned, and they have also transgressed My covenant which I commanded them. For they have even taken some of the accursed things, and have both stolen and deceived; and they have also put it among their own stuff. [12]Therefore the children of Israel could not stand before their enemies, but turned their backs before their enemies, because they have become doomed to destruction. Neither will I be with you anymore, unless you destroy the accursed from among you. [13]Get up, sanctify the people, and say, 'Sanctify yourselves for tomorrow, because thus says the LORD God of Israel: "There is an accursed thing in your midst, O Israel; you cannot stand before your enemies until you take away the accursed thing from among you." [14]In the morning therefore you shall be brought according to your tribes. And it shall be that the tribe which the LORD takes shall come according to families; and the family which the LORD takes shall come by households; and the household which the LORD takes shall come man by man. [15]Then it shall be that he who is taken with the accursed thing shall be burned with fire, he and all that he has, because he has transgressed the covenant of the LORD, and because he has done a disgraceful thing in Israel.' "

[16]So Joshua rose early in the morning and brought Israel by their tribes, and the tribe of Judah was taken. [17]He brought the clan of Judah, and he took the family of the Zarhites; and he brought the family of the Zarhites man by man, and Zabdi was taken. [18]Then he brought his household man by man, and Achan the son of Carmi, the son of Zabdi, the son of Zerah, of the tribe of Judah, was taken.

[19]Now Joshua said to Achan, "My son, I beg you, give glory to the LORD God of Israel, and make confession to Him, and tell me now what you have done; do not hide it from me."

[20]And Achan answered Joshua and said, "In-

7:1 [a]Called Zimri in 1 Chronicles 2:6

deed I have sinned against the LORD God of Israel, and this is what I have done: ²¹When I saw among the spoils a beautiful Babylonian garment, two hundred shekels of silver, and a wedge of gold weighing fifty shekels, I coveted them and took them. And there they are, hidden in the earth in the midst of my tent, with the silver under it."

²²So Joshua sent messengers, and they ran to the tent; and there it was, hidden in his tent, with the silver under it. ²³And they took them from the midst of the tent, brought them to Joshua and to all the children of Israel, and laid them out before the LORD.

²⁴Then Joshua, and all Israel with him, took Achan the son of Zerah, the silver, the garment, the wedge of gold, his sons, his daughters, his oxen, his donkeys, his sheep, his tent, and all that he had, and they brought them to the Valley of Achor. ²⁵And Joshua said, "Why have you troubled us? The LORD will trouble you this day." So all Israel stoned him with stones; and they burned them with fire after they had stoned them with stones.

²⁶Then they raised over him a great heap of stones, still there to this day. So the LORD turned from the fierceness of His anger. Therefore the name of that place has been called the Valley of Achorᵃ to this day.

THE FALL OF AI

¹Now the LORD said to Joshua: "Do not be afraid, nor be dismayed; take all the people of war with you, and arise, go up to Ai. See, I have given into your hand the king of Ai, his people, his city, and his land. ²And you shall do to Ai and its king as you did to Jericho and its king. Only its spoil and its cattle you shall take as booty for yourselves. Lay an ambush for the city behind it."

³So Joshua arose, and all the people of war, to go up against Ai; and Joshua chose thirty thousand mighty men of valor and sent them away by night. ⁴And he commanded them, saying: "Behold, you shall lie in ambush against the city, behind the city. Do not go very far from the city, but all of you be ready. ⁵Then I and all the people who *are* with me will approach the city; and it will come about, when they come out against us as at the first, that we shall flee before them. ⁶For they will come out after us till we have drawn them from the city, for they will say, 'They *are* fleeing before us as at the first.' Therefore we will flee before them. ⁷Then you shall rise from the ambush and seize the city, for the LORD your God will deliver it into your hand. ⁸And it will be, when you have taken the city, *that* you shall set the city on fire. According to the commandment of the LORD you shall do. See, I have commanded you."

⁹Joshua therefore sent them out; and they went to lie in ambush, and stayed between Bethel and Ai, on the west side of Ai; but Joshua lodged that night among the people. ¹⁰Then Joshua rose up early in the morning and mustered the people, and went up, he and the elders of Israel, before the people to Ai. ¹¹And all the people of war who *were* with him went up and drew near; and they came before the city and camped on the north side of Ai. Now a valley *lay* between them and Ai. ¹²So he took about five thousand men and set them in ambush between Bethel and Ai, on the west side of the city. ¹³And when they had set the people, all the army that *was* on the north of the city, and its rear guard on the west of the city, Joshua went that night into the midst of the valley.

¹⁴Now it happened, when the king of Ai saw *it,* that the men of the city hurried and rose early and went out against Israel to battle, he and all his people, at an appointed place before the plain. But he did not know that *there was* an ambush against him behind the city. ¹⁵And Joshua and all Israel made as if they were beaten before them, and fled by the way of the wilderness. ¹⁶So all the people who *were* in Ai were called together to pursue them. And they pursued Joshua and were drawn away from the city. ¹⁷There was not a man left in Ai or Bethel who did not go out after Israel. So they left the city open and pursued Israel.

¹⁸Then the LORD said to Joshua, "Stretch out the spear that *is* in your hand toward Ai, for I will give it into your hand." And Joshua

> "Now the LORD said to Joshua: 'Do not be afraid, nor be dismayed; take all the people of war with you, and arise, go up to Ai.' "
> (Joshua 8:1a)

SIN
Does sin have consequences? (7:25)

DISCOURAGEMENT
Who encourages us with victories? (8:1)

7:26 ᵃLiterally *Trouble*

stretched out the spear that *was* in his hand toward the city. ¹⁹So *those in* ambush arose quickly out of their place; they ran as soon as he had stretched out his hand, and they entered the city and took it, and hurried to set the city on fire. ²⁰And when the men of Ai looked behind them, they saw, and behold, the smoke of the city ascended to heaven. So they had no power to flee this way or that way, and the people who had fled to the wilderness turned back on the pursuers.

²¹Now when Joshua and all Israel saw that the ambush had taken the city and that the smoke of the city ascended, they turned back and struck down the men of Ai. ²²Then the others came out of the city against them; so they were *caught* in the midst of Israel, some on this side and some on that side. And they struck them down, so that they let none of them remain or escape. ²³But the king of Ai they took alive, and brought him to Joshua.

²⁴And it came to pass when Israel had made an end of slaying all the inhabitants of Ai in the field, in the wilderness where they pursued them, and when they all had fallen by the edge of the sword until they were consumed, that all the Israelites returned to Ai and struck it with the edge of the sword. ²⁵So it was *that* all who fell that day, both men and women, *were* twelve thousand—all the people of Ai. ²⁶For Joshua did not draw back his hand, with which he stretched out the spear, until he had utterly destroyed all the inhabitants of Ai. ²⁷Only the livestock and the spoil of that city Israel took as booty for themselves, according to the word of the LORD which He had commanded Joshua. ²⁸So Joshua burned Ai and made it a heap forever, a desolation to this day. ²⁹And the king of Ai he hanged on a tree until evening. And as soon as the sun was down, Joshua commanded that they should take his corpse down from the tree, cast it at the entrance of the gate of the city, and raise over it a great heap of stones *that remains* to this day.

JOSHUA RENEWS THE COVENANT

³⁰Now Joshua built an altar to the LORD God of Israel in Mount Ebal, ³¹as Moses the servant of the LORD had commanded the children of Israel, as it is written in the Book of the Law of Moses: "an altar of whole stones over which no man has wielded an iron *tool.*"ᵃ And they offered on it burnt offerings to the LORD, and sacrificed peace offerings. ³²And there, in the presence of the children of Israel, he wrote on

the stones a copy of the law of Moses, which he had written. ³³Then all Israel, with their elders and officers and judges, stood on either side of the ark before the priests, the Levites, who bore the ark of the covenant of the LORD, the stranger as well as he who was born among them. Half of them *were* in front of Mount Gerizim and half of them in front of Mount Ebal, as Moses the servant of the LORD had commanded before, that they should bless the people of Israel. ³⁴And afterward he read all the words of the law, the blessings and the cursings, according to all that is written in the Book of the Law. ³⁵There was not a word of all that Moses had commanded which Joshua did not read before all the assembly of Israel, with the women, the little ones, and the strangers who were living among them.

WHAT'S IT MEAN?

The king's body was hung on a tree to show that no one had escaped the battle. Leaving the body on the tree overnight would have been against God's law. The corpse had to be buried by sunset.
Joshua 8:28, 29

THE TREATY WITH THE GIBEONITES

¹And it came to pass when all the kings who *were* on this side of the Jordan, in the hills and in the lowland and in all the coasts of the Great Sea toward Lebanon—the Hittite, the Amorite, the Canaanite, the Perizzite, the Hivite, and the Jebusite—heard *about it,* ²that they gathered together to fight with Joshua and Israel with one accord.

³But when the inhabitants of Gibeon heard what Joshua had done to Jericho and Ai, ⁴they worked craftily, and went and pretended to be ambassadors. And they took old sacks on their donkeys, old wineskins torn and mended, ⁵old and patched sandals on their feet, and old garments on themselves; and all the bread of their provision was dry *and* moldy. ⁶And they went to Joshua, to the camp at Gilgal, and said to him and to the men of Israel, "We have come from a

8:31 ᵃDeuteronomy 27:5, 6

far country; now therefore, make a covenant with us."

7Then the men of Israel said to the Hivites, "Perhaps you dwell among us; so how can we make a covenant with you?"

8But they said to Joshua, "We *are* your servants."

And Joshua said to them, "Who *are* you, and where do you come from?"

9So they said to him: "From a very far country your servants have come, because of the name of the LORD your God; for we have heard of His fame, and all that He did in Egypt, 10and all that He did to the two kings of the Amorites who *were* beyond the Jordan—to Sihon king of Heshbon, and Og king of Bashan, who was at Ashtaroth. 11Therefore our elders and all the inhabitants of our country spoke to us, saying, 'Take provisions with you for the journey, and go to meet them, and say to them, "We *are* your servants; now therefore, make a covenant with us."' 12This bread of ours we took hot *for* our provision from our houses on the day we departed to come to you. But now look, it is dry and moldy. 13And these wineskins which we filled *were* new, and see, they are torn; and these our garments and our sandals have become old because of the very long journey."

14Then the men of Israel took some of their provisions; but they did not ask counsel of the LORD. 15So Joshua made peace with them, and made a covenant with them to let them live; and the rulers of the congregation swore to them.

16And it happened at the end of three days, after they had made a covenant with them, that they heard that they *were* their neighbors who dwelt near them. 17Then the children of Israel journeyed and came to their cities on the third day. Now their cities *were* Gibeon, Chephirah, Beeroth, and Kirjath Jearim. 18But the children of Israel did not attack them, because the rulers of the congregation had sworn to them by the LORD God of Israel. And all the congregation complained against the rulers.

19Then all the rulers said to all the congregation, "We have sworn to them by the LORD God of Israel; now therefore, we may not touch them. 20This we will do to them: We will let them live, lest wrath be upon us because of the oath which we swore to them." 21And the rulers said to them, "Let them live, but let them be woodcutters and water carriers for all the congregation, as the rulers had promised them."

22Then Joshua called for them, and he spoke to them, saying, "Why have you deceived us, saying, 'We *are* very far from you', when you dwell near us? 23Now therefore, you *are* cursed, and none of you shall be freed from being slaves—woodcutters and water carriers for the house of my God."

24So they answered Joshua and said, "Because your servants were clearly told that the LORD your God commanded His servant Moses to give you all the land, and to destroy all the inhabitants of the land from before you; therefore we were very much afraid for our lives because of you, and have done this thing. 25And now, here we are, in your hands; do with us as it seems good and right to do to us." 26So he did to them, and delivered them out of the hand of the children of Israel, so that they did not kill them. 27And that day Joshua made them woodcutters and water carriers for the congregation and for the altar of the LORD, in the place which He would choose, even to this day.

THE SUN STANDS STILL

1Now it came to pass when Adoni-Zedek king of Jerusalem heard how Joshua had taken Ai and had utterly destroyed it—as he had done to Jericho and its king, so he had done to Ai and its king—and how the inhabitants of Gibeon had made peace with Israel and were among them, 2that they feared greatly, because Gibeon *was* a great city, like one of the royal cities, and because it *was* greater than Ai, and all its men *were* mighty. 3Therefore Adoni-Zedek king of Jerusalem sent to Hoham king of Hebron, Piram king of Jarmuth, Japhia king of Lachish, and Debir king of Eglon, saying, 4"Come up to me and help me, that we may attack Gibeon, for it has made peace with Joshua and with the children of Israel." 5Therefore the five kings of the Amorites, the king of Jerusalem, the king of Hebron, the king of Jarmuth, the king of Lachish, *and* the king of Eglon, gathered together and went up, they and all their armies, and camped before Gibeon and made war against it.

6And the men of Gibeon sent to Joshua at the camp at Gilgal, saying, "Do not forsake your servants; come up to us quickly, save us and help us, for all the kings of the Amorites who dwell in the mountains have gathered together against us."

7So Joshua ascended from Gilgal, he and all the people of war with him, and all the mighty men of valor. 8And the LORD said to Joshua, "Do not fear them, for I have delivered them into your hand; not a man of them shall stand

---

FOLLOWING GOD

What happens if we forget to follow God? (9:3–18)

before you." ⁹Joshua therefore came upon them suddenly, having marched all night from Gilgal. ¹⁰So the LORD routed them before Israel, killed them with a great slaughter at Gibeon, chased them along the road that goes to Beth Horon, and struck them down as far as Azekah and Makkedah. ¹¹And it happened, as they fled before Israel *and* were on the descent of Beth Horon, that the LORD cast down large hailstones from heaven on them as far as Azekah, and they died. *There were* more who died from the hailstones than the children of Israel killed with the sword.

¹²Then Joshua spoke to the LORD in the day when the LORD delivered up the Amorites before the children of Israel, and he said in the sight of Israel:

> "Sun, stand still over Gibeon;
> And Moon, in the Valley of Aijalon."
> 13   So the sun stood still,
> And the moon stopped,
> Till the people had revenge
> Upon their enemies.

Is this not written in the Book of Jasher? So the sun stood still in the midst of heaven, and did not hasten to go *down* for about a whole day. ¹⁴And there has been no day like that, before it or after it, that the LORD heeded the voice of a man; for the LORD fought for Israel. ¹⁵Then Joshua returned, and all Israel with him, to the camp at Gilgal.

THE AMORITE KINGS EXECUTED

¹⁶But these five kings had fled and hidden themselves in a cave at Makkedah. ¹⁷And it was told Joshua, saying, "The five kings have been found hidden in the cave at Makkedah." ¹⁸So Joshua said, "Roll large stones against the mouth of the cave, and set men by it to guard them. ¹⁹And do not stay *there* yourselves, *but* pursue your enemies, and attack their rear *guard.* Do not allow them to enter their cities, for the LORD your God has delivered them into your hand." ²⁰Then it happened, while Joshua and the children of Israel made an end of slaying them with a very great slaughter, till they had finished, that those who escaped entered fortified cities. ²¹And all the people returned to the camp, to Joshua at Makkedah, in peace.

No one moved his tongue against any of the children of Israel.

²²Then Joshua said, "Open the mouth of the cave, and bring out those five kings to me from the cave." ²³And they did so, and brought out those five kings to him from the cave: the king of Jerusalem, the king of Hebron, the king of Jarmuth, the king of Lachish, *and* the king of Eglon.

²⁴So it was, when they brought out those kings to Joshua, that Joshua called for all the men of Israel, and said to the captains of the men of war who went with him, "Come near, put your feet on the necks of these kings." And they drew near and put their feet on their necks. ²⁵Then Joshua said to them, "Do not be afraid, nor be dismayed; be strong and of good courage, for thus the LORD will do to all your enemies against whom you fight." ²⁶And afterward Joshua struck them and killed them, and hanged them on five trees; and they were hanging on the trees until evening. ²⁷So it was at the time of the going down of the sun *that* Joshua commanded, and they took them down from the trees, cast them into the cave where they had been hidden, and laid large stones against the cave's mouth, *which remain* until this very day.

> "Then Joshua said to them, 'Do not be afraid, nor be dismayed; be strong and of good courage.' "
> (Joshua 10:25a)

ENEMIES
Who can defeat our enemies? (10:25)

WHAT'S IT MEAN?

Stepping on the neck or body of an enemy was a way of humiliating him and showing that you had defeated him. The Israelites weren't alone in this kind of practice. The Romans made their defeated enemies crawl under a spear held low to the ground.
Joshua 10:24

CONQUEST OF THE SOUTHLAND

²⁸On that day Joshua took Makkedah, and struck it and its king with the edge of the sword.

He utterly destroyed them*—all the people who *were* in it. He let none remain. He also did to the king of Makkedah as he had done to the king of Jericho.

²⁹Then Joshua passed from Makkedah, and all Israel with him, to Libnah; and they fought against Libnah. ³⁰And the LORD also delivered it and its king into the hand of Israel; he struck it and all the people who *were* in it with the edge of the sword. He let none remain in it, but did to its king as he had done to the king of Jericho.

³¹Then Joshua passed from Libnah, and all Israel with him, to Lachish; and they encamped against it and fought against it. ³²And the LORD delivered Lachish into the hand of Israel, who took it on the second day, and struck it and all the people who *were* in it with the edge of the sword, according to all that he had done to Libnah. ³³Then Horam king of Gezer came up to help Lachish; and Joshua struck him and his people, until he left him none remaining.

³⁴From Lachish Joshua passed to Eglon, and all Israel with him; and they encamped against it and fought against it. ³⁵They took it on that day and struck it with the edge of the sword; all the people who *were* in it he utterly destroyed that day, according to all that he had done to Lachish.

³⁶So Joshua went up from Eglon, and all Israel with him, to Hebron; and they fought against it. ³⁷And they took it and struck it with the edge of the sword—its king, all its cities, and all the people who *were* in it; he left none remaining, according to all that he had done to Eglon, but utterly destroyed it and all the people who *were* in it.

³⁸Then Joshua returned, and all Israel with him, to Debir; and they fought against it. ³⁹And he took it and its king and all its cities; they struck them with the edge of the sword and utterly destroyed all the people who *were* in it. He left none remaining; as he had done to Hebron, so he did to Debir and its king, as he had done also to Libnah and its king.

⁴⁰So Joshua conquered all the land: the mountain country and the South* and the lowland and the wilderness slopes, and all their kings; he left none remaining, but utterly destroyed all that breathed, as the LORD God of Israel had commanded. ⁴¹And Joshua conquered them from Kadesh Barnea as far as Gaza, and all the country of Goshen, even as far as Gibeon. ⁴²All these kings and their land Joshua took at one time, because the LORD God of Israel fought for Israel. ⁴³Then Joshua returned, and all Israel with him, to the camp at Gilgal.

THE NORTHERN CONQUEST

¹And it came to pass, when Jabin king of Hazor heard *these things*, that he sent to Jobab king of Madon, to the king of Shimron, to the king of Achshaph, ²and to the kings who *were* from the north, in the mountains, in the plain south of Chinneroth, in the lowland, and in the heights of Dor on the west, ³to the Canaanites in the east and in the west, the Amorite, the Hittite, the Perizzite, the Jebusite in the mountains, and the Hivite below Hermon in the land of Mizpah. ⁴So they went out, they and all their armies with them, *as* many people *as* the sand that *is* on the seashore in multitude, with very many horses and chariots. ⁵And when all these kings had met together, they came and camped together at the waters of Merom to fight against Israel.

WHAT'S IT MEAN?

Hazor, which was located about ten miles northwest of Chinneroth (later called the Sea of Galilee), was one of the most important cities in Canaan because of its size and location.
Joshua 11:1

⁶But the LORD said to Joshua, "Do not be afraid because of them, for tomorrow about this time I will deliver all of them slain before Israel. You shall hamstring their horses and burn their chariots with fire." ⁷So Joshua and all the people of war with him came against them suddenly by the waters of Merom, and they attacked them. ⁸And the LORD delivered them into the hand of Israel, who defeated them and chased them to Greater Sidon, to the Brook Misrephoth,* and to the Valley of Mizpah eastward; they attacked them until they left none of them remaining. ⁹So Joshua did to them as the LORD had told him: he hamstrung their horses and burned their chariots with fire.

¹⁰Joshua turned back at that time and took

10:28 *Following Masoretic Text and most authorities; many Hebrew manuscripts, some manuscripts of the Septuagint, and some manuscripts of the Targum read *it*. **10:40** *Hebrew *Negev*, and so throughout this book **11:8** *Hebrew *Misrephoth Maim*

Hazor, and struck its king with the sword; for Hazor was formerly the head of all those kingdoms. [11]And they struck all the people who *were* in it with the edge of the sword, utterly destroying *them*. There was none left breathing. Then he burned Hazor with fire.

[12]So all the cities of those kings, and all their kings, Joshua took and struck with the edge of the sword. He utterly destroyed them, as Moses the servant of the LORD had commanded. [13]But *as for* the cities that stood on their mounds,[a] Israel burned none of them, except Hazor only, which Joshua burned. [14]And all the spoil of these cities and the livestock, the children of Israel took as booty for themselves; but they struck every man with the edge of the sword until they had destroyed them, and they left none breathing. [15]As the LORD had commanded Moses his servant, so Moses commanded Joshua, and so Joshua did. He left nothing undone of all that the LORD had commanded Moses.

SUMMARY OF JOSHUA'S CONQUESTS

[16]Thus Joshua took all this land: the mountain country, all the South, all the land of Goshen, the lowland, and the Jordan plain[a]—the mountains of Israel and its lowlands, [17]from Mount Halak and the ascent to Seir, even as far as Baal Gad in the Valley of Lebanon below Mount Hermon. He captured all their kings, and struck them down and killed them. [18]Joshua made war a long time with all those kings. [19]There was not a city that made peace with the children of Israel, except the Hivites, the inhabitants of Gibeon. All *the others* they took in battle. [20]For it was of the LORD to harden their hearts, that they should come against Israel in battle, that He might utterly destroy them, *and* that they might receive no mercy, but that He might destroy them, as the LORD had commanded Moses.

[21]And at that time Joshua came and cut off the Anakim from the mountains: from Hebron, from Debir, from Anab, from all the mountains of Judah, and from all the mountains of Israel; Joshua utterly destroyed them with their cities. [22]None of the Anakim were left in the land of the children of Israel; they remained only in Gaza, in Gath, and in Ashdod. [23]So Joshua took the whole land, according to all that the LORD had said to Moses; and Joshua gave it as an inheritance to Israel according to their divisions by their tribes. Then the land rested from war.

THE KINGS CONQUERED BY MOSES

[1]These *are* the kings of the land whom the children of Israel defeated, and whose land they possessed on the other side of the Jordan toward the rising of the sun, from the River Arnon to Mount Hermon, and all the eastern Jordan plain: [2]One king was Sihon king of the Amorites, who dwelt in Heshbon *and* ruled half of Gilead, from Aroer, which is on the bank of the River Arnon, from the middle of that river, even as far as the River Jabbok, *which is* the border of the Ammonites, [3]and the eastern Jordan plain from the Sea of Chinneroth as far as the Sea of the Arabah (the Salt Sea), the road to Beth Jeshimoth, and southward below the slopes of Pisgah. [4]The other king was Og king of Bashan and his territory, *who was* of the remnant of the giants, who dwelt at Ashtaroth and at Edrei, [5]and reigned over Mount Hermon, over Salcah, over all Bashan, as far as the border of the Geshurites and the Maachathites, and over half of Gilead *to* the border of Sihon king of Heshbon.

[6]These Moses the servant of the LORD and the children of Israel had conquered; and Moses the servant of the LORD had given it *as* a possession to the Reubenites, the Gadites, and half the tribe of Manasseh.

THE KINGS CONQUERED BY JOSHUA

[7]And these *are* the kings of the country which Joshua and the children of Israel conquered on this side of the Jordan, on the west, from Baal Gad in the Valley of Lebanon as far as Mount Halak and the ascent to Seir, which Joshua gave to the tribes of Israel *as* a possession according to their divisions, [8]in the mountain country, in the lowlands, in the *Jordan* plain, in the slopes, in the wilderness, and in the South—the Hittites, the Amorites, the Canaanites, the Perizzites, the Hivites, and the Jebusites: [9]the king of Jericho, one; the king of Ai, which *is* beside Bethel, one; [10]the king of Jerusalem, one; the king of Hebron, one; [11]the king of Jarmuth, one; the king of Lachish, one; [12]the king of Eglon, one; the king of Gezer, one; [13]the king of Debir, one; the king of Geder, one; [14]the king of Hormah, one; the king of Arad, one; [15]the king of Libnah, one; the king of Adullam, one; [16]the king of Makkedah, one; the king of Bethel, one; [17]the king of Tappuah, one; the king of Hepher, one; [18]the king of Aphek, one; the king of Lasharon, one; [19]the king of Madon, one; the king of Hazor, one; [20]the king of Shimron Meron, one; the king of Achshaph, one; [21]the king of

Taanach, one; the king of Megiddo, one; [22]the king of Kedesh, one; the king of Jokneam in Carmel, one; [23]the king of Dor in the heights of Dor, one; the king of the people of Gilgal, one; [24]the king of Tirzah, one—all the kings, thirty-one.

REMAINING LAND TO BE CONQUERED

[1]Now Joshua was old, advanced in years. And the LORD said to him: "You are old, advanced in years, and there remains very much land yet to be possessed. [2]This is the land that yet remains: all the territory of the Philistines and all *that of* the Geshurites, [3]from Sihor, which *is* east of Egypt, as far as the border of Ekron northward (*which* is counted as Canaanite); the five lords of the Philistines—the Gazites, the Ashdodites, the Ashkelonites, the Gittites, and the Ekronites; also the Avites; [4]from the south, all the land of the Canaanites, and Mearah that belongs to the Sidonians as far as Aphek, to the border of the Amorites; [5]the land of the Gebalites,[a] and all Lebanon, toward the sunrise, from Baal Gad below Mount Hermon as far as the entrance to Hamath; [6]all the inhabitants of the mountains from Lebanon as far as the Brook Misrephoth,[a] *and* all the Sidonians—them I will drive out from before the children of Israel; only divide it by lot to Israel as an inheritance, as I have commanded you. [7]Now therefore, divide this land as an inheritance to the nine tribes and half the tribe of Manasseh."

The five Philistine cities located near the Mediterranean Sea—Gaza, Ashdod, Ashkelon, Gath, and Ekron—often teamed up to fight the Israelites.
Joshua 13:2

THE LAND DIVIDED EAST OF THE JORDAN

[8]With the other half-tribe the Reubenites and the Gadites received their inheritance, which Moses had given them, beyond the Jordan eastward, as Moses the servant of the LORD had given them: [9]from Aroer which *is* on the bank of the River Arnon, and the town that *is* in the midst of the ravine, and all the plain of Medeba as far as Dibon; [10]all the cities of Sihon king of the Amorites, who reigned in Heshbon, as far as the border of the children of Ammon; [11]Gilead, and the border of the Geshurites and Maachathites, all Mount Hermon, and all Bashan as far as Salcah; [12]all the kingdom of Og in Bashan, who reigned in Ashtaroth and Edrei, who remained of the remnant of the giants; for Moses had defeated and cast out these.

[13]Nevertheless the children of Israel did not drive out the Geshurites or the Maachathites, but the Geshurites and the Maachathites dwell among the Israelites until this day.

[14]Only to the tribe of Levi he had given no inheritance; the sacrifices of the LORD God of Israel made by fire *are* their inheritance, as He said to them.

THE LAND OF REUBEN

[15]And Moses had given to the tribe of the children of Reuben *an inheritance* according to their families. [16]Their territory was from Aroer, which *is* on the bank of the River Arnon, and the city that *is* in the midst of the ravine, and all the plain by Medeba; [17]Heshbon and all its cities that *are* in the plain: Dibon, Bamoth Baal, Beth Baal Meon, [18]Jahaza, Kedemoth, Mephaath, [19]Kirjathaim, Sibmah, Zereth Shahar on the mountain of the valley, [20]Beth Peor, the slopes of Pisgah, and Beth Jeshimoth—[21]all the cities of the plain and all the kingdom of Sihon king of the Amorites, who reigned in Heshbon, whom Moses had struck with the princes of Midian: Evi, Rekem, Zur, Hur, and Reba, who *were* princes of Sihon dwelling in the country. [22]The children of Israel also killed with the sword Balaam the son of Beor, the soothsayer, among those who were killed by them. [23]And the border of the children of Reuben was the bank of the Jordan. This *was* the inheritance of the children of Reuben according to their families, the cities and their villages.

THE LAND OF GAD

[24]Moses also had given *an inheritance* to the tribe of Gad, to the children of Gad according to their families. [25]Their territory was Jazer, and all the cities of Gilead, and half the land of the Ammonites as far as Aroer, which *is* before Rabbah, [26]and from Heshbon to Ramath Mizpah and Betonim, and from Mahanaim to the

13:5 [a]Or *Giblites*   13:6 [a]Hebrew *Misrephoth Maim*

border of Debir, ²⁷and in the valley Beth Haram, Beth Nimrah, Succoth, and Zaphon, the rest of the kingdom of Sihon king of Heshbon, with the Jordan as *its* border, as far as the edge of the Sea of Chinnereth, on the other side of the Jordan eastward. ²⁸This *is* the inheritance of the children of Gad according to their families, the cities and their villages.

HALF THE TRIBE OF MANASSEH (EAST)

²⁹Moses also had given *an inheritance* to half the tribe of Manasseh; it was for half the tribe of the children of Manasseh according to their families: ³⁰Their territory was from Mahanaim, all Bashan, all the kingdom of Og king of Bashan, and all the towns of Jair which are in Bashan, sixty cities; ³¹half of Gilead, and Ashtaroth and Edrei, cities of the kingdom of Og in Bashan, *were* for the children of Machir the son of Manasseh, for half of the children of Machir according to their families.

³²These *are the areas* which Moses had distributed as an inheritance in the plains of Moab on the other side of the Jordan, by Jericho eastward. ³³But to the tribe of Levi Moses had given no inheritance; the LORD God of Israel *was* their inheritance, as He had said to them.

THE LAND DIVIDED WEST OF THE JORDAN

¹These *are the areas* which the children of Israel inherited in the land of Canaan, which Eleazar the priest, Joshua the son of Nun, and the heads of the fathers of the tribes of the children of Israel distributed as an inheritance to them. ²Their inheritance *was* by lot, as the LORD had commanded by the hand of Moses, for the nine tribes and the half-tribe. ³For Moses had given the inheritance of the two tribes and the half-tribe on the other side of the Jordan; but to the Levites he had given no inheritance among them. ⁴For the children of Joseph were two tribes: Manasseh and Ephraim. And they gave no part to the Levites in the land, except cities to dwell *in*, with their common-lands for their livestock and their property. ⁵As the LORD had commanded Moses, so the children of Israel did; and they divided the land.

CALEB INHERITS HEBRON

⁶Then the children of Judah came to Joshua in Gilgal. And Caleb the son of Jephunneh the

Kenizzite said to him: "You know the word which the LORD said to Moses the man of God concerning you and me in Kadesh Barnea. ⁷I *was* forty years old when Moses the servant of the LORD sent me from Kadesh Barnea to spy out the land, and I brought back word to him as *it was* in my heart. ⁸Nevertheless my brethren who went up with me made the heart of the people melt, but I wholly followed the LORD my God. ⁹So Moses swore on that day, saying, 'Surely the land where your foot has trodden shall be your inheritance and your children's forever, because you have wholly followed the LORD my God.' ¹⁰And now, behold, the LORD has kept me alive, as He said, these forty-five years, ever since the LORD spoke this word to Moses while Israel wandered in the wilderness; and

> "Nevertheless my brethren who went up with me made the heart of the people melt, but I wholly followed the LORD my God."
> (Joshua 14:8)

now, here I am this day, eighty-five years old. ¹¹As yet I *am as* strong this day as on the day that Moses sent me; just as my strength *was* then, so now *is* my strength for war, both for going out and for coming in. ¹²Now therefore, give me this mountain of which the LORD spoke in that day; for you heard in that day how the Anakim *were* there, and *that* the cities *were* great *and* fortified. It may be that the LORD *will be* with me, and I shall be able to drive them out as the LORD said."

LIFE

Where do we get our strength? (14:11)

WHAT'S IT MEAN?

You may recognize the name *Hebron* from biblical history. Hebron is where Abram's name was changed to Abraham, and Abraham's wife Sarah was buried near there. At 3,000 feet above sea level, Hebron is higher than any other city west of the Jordan River.

Joshua 14:13

¹³And Joshua blessed him, and gave Hebron to Caleb the son of Jephunneh as an inheritance. ¹⁴Hebron therefore became the inheritance of Caleb the son of Jephunneh the Kenizzite to this day, because he wholly followed

JOSHUA made a difference

Some shoes are impossible to fill. Think about the person who amazes you the most and then imagine what it would be like to hear you have to assume their role and responsibilities tomorrow. Joshua lived his youth in the shadow of Moses. He became Moses' military commander as well as his personal assistant. Joshua was trained and mentored more than forty years before stepping into Moses' sandals. His development demonstrates that big shoes can sometimes be grown into and sometimes have to be remade to fit new feet.

Joshua appears in the Bible story without introduction. By that point in the Exodus, Joshua was already a recognized soldier and leader. Only later (Ex. 33:11) do we discover two significant facts about Joshua: (1) he was young; (2) he spent most of his time at the tabernacle where Moses met with God. What shaped Joshua most were the times spent with his mentor, Moses, and the times he spent alone with God. When God affirmed Joshua's role as Israel's new leader, the Lord used a revealing phrase to indicate His approval: "As I was with Moses, so I will be with you" (Josh. 1:5). Joshua was also promised that "the LORD your God is with you wherever you go" (Josh. 1:9). Joshua spent enough time with God to know that God would be with him all the time throughout his life.

Cutting Edge

YOU can, too! Not a moment you spend with God is wasted. No relationship in your life will turn out to be more significant than your relationship with God. Every other relationship you have will be affected by the development of your relationship with God. Here's the big secret. What God does in you will improve every other relationship you have. There's no real choice between God and everyone else. But when you choose God truly, everyone in your life will benefit.

Want to know more? You can pick up hints of Joshua's life in
Exodus, Numbers, and Deuteronomy.
He is the central figure in the book that bears his name.

the LORD God of Israel. ¹⁵And the name of Hebron formerly was Kirjath Arba (*Arba was* the greatest man among the Anakim).

Then the land had rest from war.

THE LAND OF JUDAH

¹So *this* was the lot of the tribe of the children of Judah according to their families:

The border of Edom at the Wilderness of Zin southward *was* the extreme southern boundary. ²And their southern border began at the shore of the Salt Sea, from the bay that faces southward. ³Then it went out to the southern side of the Ascent of Akrabbim, passed along to Zin, ascended on the south side of Kadesh Barnea, passed along to Hezron, went up to Adar, and went around to Karkaa. ⁴*From there* it passed toward Azmon and went out to the Brook of Egypt; and the border ended at the sea. This shall be your southern border.

⁵The east border *was* the Salt Sea as far as the mouth of the Jordan.

And the border on the northern quarter *began* at the bay of the sea at the mouth of the Jordan. ⁶The border went up to Beth Hoglah and passed north of Beth Arabah; and the border went up to the stone of Bohan the son of Reuben. ⁷Then the border went up toward Debir from the Valley of Achor, and it turned northward toward Gilgal, which *is* before the Ascent of Adummim, which *is* on the south side of the valley. The border continued toward the waters of En Shemesh and ended at En Rogel. ⁸And the border went up by the Valley of the Son of Hinnom to the southern slope of the Jebusite *city* (which *is* Jerusalem). The border went up to the top of the mountain that *lies* before the Valley of Hinnom westward, which *is* at the end of the Valley of Rephaimᵃ northward. ⁹Then the border went around from the top of the hill to the fountain of the water of Nephtoah, and extended to the cities of Mount Ephron. And the border went around to Baalah (which *is* Kirjath Jearim). ¹⁰Then the border turned westward from Baalah to Mount Seir, passed along to the side of Mount Jearim on the north (which *is* Chesalon), went down to Beth Shemesh, and passed on to Timnah. ¹¹And the border went out to the side of Ekron northward. Then the border went around to Shicron, passed along to Mount Baalah, and extended to Jabneel; and the border ended at the sea.

¹²The west border *was* the coastline of the Great Sea. This *is* the boundary of the children of Judah all around according to their families.

CALEB OCCUPIES HEBRON AND DEBIR

¹³Now to Caleb the son of Jephunneh he gave a share among the children of Judah, according to the commandment of the LORD to Joshua, *namely,* Kirjath Arba, which *is* Hebron (*Arba was* the father of Anak). ¹⁴Caleb drove out the three sons of Anak from there: Sheshai, Ahiman, and Talmai, the children of Anak. ¹⁵Then he went up from there to the inhabitants of Debir (formerly the name of Debir *was* Kirjath Sepher).

¹⁶And Caleb said, "He who attacks Kirjath Sepher and takes it, to him I will give Achsah my daughter as wife." ¹⁷So Othniel the son of Kenaz, the brother of Caleb, took it; and he gave him Achsah his daughter as wife. ¹⁸Now it was so, when she came *to him,* that she persuaded him to ask her father for a field. So she dismounted from *her* donkey, and Caleb said to her, "What do you wish?" ¹⁹She answered, "Give me a blessing; since you have given me land in the South, give me also springs of water." So he gave her the upper springs and the lower springs.

THE CITIES OF JUDAH

²⁰This *was* the inheritance of the tribe of the children of Judah according to their families:

²¹The cities at the limits of the tribe of the children of Judah, toward the border of Edom in the South, were Kabzeel, Eder, Jagur, ²²Kinah, Dimonah, Adadah, ²³Kedesh, Hazor, Ithnan, ²⁴Ziph, Telem, Bealoth, ²⁵Hazor, Hadattah, Kerioth, Hezron (which *is* Hazor), ²⁶Amam, Shema, Moladah, ²⁷Hazar Gaddah, Heshmon, Beth Pelet, ²⁸Hazar Shual, Beersheba, Bizjothjah, ²⁹Baalah, Ijim, Ezem, ³⁰Eltolad, Chesil, Hormah, ³¹Ziklag, Madmannah, Sansannah, ³²Lebaoth, Shilhim, Ain, and Rimmon: all the cities *are* twenty-nine, with their villages.

³³In the lowland: Eshtaol, Zorah, Ashnah, ³⁴Zanoah, En Gannim, Tappuah, Enam, ³⁵Jarmuth, Adullam, Socoh, Azekah, ³⁶Sharaim, Adithaim, Gederah, and Gederothaim: fourteen cities with their villages; ³⁷Zenan, Hadashah, Migdal Gad, ³⁸Dilean, Mizpah, Joktheel, ³⁹Lachish, Bozkath, Eglon, ⁴⁰Cabbon, Lahmas,ᵃ Kithlish, ⁴¹Gederoth, Beth Dagon, Naamah, and Makkedah: sixteen cities with their villages; ⁴²Libnah, Ether, Ashan, ⁴³Jiphtah, Ashnah, Nezib, ⁴⁴Keilah, Achzib, and Mareshah: nine cities with their villages; ⁴⁵Ekron, with its towns and villages; ⁴⁶from Ekron to the sea, all that *lay* near Ashdod, with their villages; ⁴⁷Ashdod with its towns and villages, Gaza with its towns and

15:8 ᵃLiterally *Giants* **15:40** ᵃOr *Lahmam*

villages—as far as the Brook of Egypt and the Great Sea with *its* coastline.

⁴⁸And in the mountain country: Shamir, Jattir, Sochoh, ⁴⁹Dannah, Kirjath Sannah (which *is* Debir), ⁵⁰Anab, Eshtemoh, Anim, ⁵¹Goshen, Holon, and Giloh: eleven cities with their villages; ⁵²Arab, Dumah, Eshean, ⁵³Janum, Beth Tappuah, Aphekah, ⁵⁴Humtah, Kirjath Arba (which *is* Hebron), and Zior: nine cities with their villages; ⁵⁵Maon, Carmel, Ziph, Juttah, ⁵⁶Jezreel, Jokdeam, Zanoah, ⁵⁷Kain, Gibeah, and Timnah: ten cities with their villages; ⁵⁸Halhul, Beth Zur, Gedor, ⁵⁹Maarath, Beth Anoth, and Eltekon: six cities with their villages; ⁶⁰Kirjath Baal (which *is* Kirjath Jearim) and Rabbah: two cities with their villages.

⁶¹In the wilderness: Beth Arabah, Middin, Secacah, ⁶²Nibshan, the City of Salt, and En Gedi: six cities with their villages.

⁶³As for the Jebusites, the inhabitants of Jerusalem, the children of Judah could not drive them out; but the Jebusites dwell with the children of Judah at Jerusalem to this day.

EPHRAIM AND WEST MANASSEH

¹The lot fell to the children of Joseph from the Jordan, by Jericho, to the waters of Jericho on the east, to the wilderness that goes up from Jericho through the mountains to Bethel, ²then went out from Bethel to Luz,ᵃ passed along to the border of the Archites at Ataroth, ³and went down westward to the boundary of the Japhletites, as far as the boundary of Lower Beth Horon to Gezer; and it ended at the sea.

⁴So the children of Joseph, Manasseh and Ephraim, took their inheritance.

THE LAND OF EPHRAIM

⁵The border of the children of Ephraim, according to their families, was *thus:* The border of their inheritance on the east side was Ataroth Addar as far as Upper Beth Horon.

⁶And the border went out toward the sea on the north side of Michmethath; then the border went around eastward to Taanath Shiloh, and passed by it on the east of Janohah. ⁷Then it went down from Janohah to Ataroth and Naarah,ᵃ reached to Jericho, and came out at the Jordan.

⁸The border went out from Tappuah westward to the Brook Kanah, and it ended at the sea. This *was* the inheritance of the tribe of the children of Ephraim according to their families. ⁹The separate cities for the children of Ephraim

were among the inheritance of the children of Manasseh, all the cities with their villages.

¹⁰And they did not drive out the Canaanites who dwelt in Gezer; but the Canaanites dwell among the Ephraimites to this day and have become forced laborers.

THE OTHER HALF-TRIBE OF MANASSEH (WEST)

¹There was also a lot for the tribe of Manasseh, for he *was* the firstborn of Joseph: *namely* for Machir the firstborn of Manasseh, the father of Gilead, because he was a man of war; therefore he was given Gilead and Bashan. ²And there was *a* lot for the rest of the children of Manasseh according to their families: for the children of Abiezer,ᵃ the children of Helek, the children of Asriel, the children of Shechem, the children of Hepher, and the children of Shemida; these *were* the male children of Manasseh the son of Joseph according to their families.

W H A T ' S I T M E A N ?

Women were not allowed to inherit land In biblical times. The only exceptions were situations like the one facing the five daughters of Zelophehad. With no male in the family to take over their father's responsibilities, they were allowed to keep their land—and their means of supporting themselves.
Joshua 17:1–6

³But Zelophehad the son of Hepher, the son of Gilead, the son of Machir, the son of Manasseh, had no sons, but only daughters. And these *are* the names of his daughters: Mahlah, Noah, Hoglah, Milcah, and Tirzah. ⁴And they came near before Eleazar the priest, before Joshua the son of Nun, and before the rulers, saying, "The LORD commanded Moses to give us an inheritance among our brothers." Therefore, according to the commandment of the LORD, he gave them an inheritance among their father's brothers. ⁵Ten shares fell to Manasseh, besides the land of Gilead and Bashan, which *were* on the other side of the Jordan, ⁶because the daughters of Manasseh received an inheritance among his sons; and the rest of Manasseh's sons had the land of Gilead.

16:2 ᵃSeptuagint reads *Bethel* (that is, Luz).   **16:7** ᵃOr *Naaran* (compare 1 Chronicles 7:28)   **17:2** ᵃCalled *Jeezer* in Numbers 26:30

[7]And the territory of Manasseh was from Asher to Michmethath, that *lies* east of Shechem; and the border went along south to the inhabitants of En Tappuah. [8]Manasseh had the land of Tappuah, but Tappuah on the border of Manasseh *belonged* to the children of Ephraim. [9]And the border descended to the Brook Kanah, southward to the brook. These cities of Ephraim *are* among the cities of Manasseh. The border of Manasseh *was* on the north side of the brook; and it ended at the sea.

[10]Southward *it was* Ephraim's, northward *it was* Manasseh's, and the sea was its border. Manasseh's territory was adjoining Asher on the north and Issachar on the east. [11]And in Issachar and in Asher, Manasseh had Beth Shean and its towns, Ibleam and its towns, the inhabitants of Dor and its towns, the inhabitants of En Dor and its towns, the inhabitants of Taanach and its towns, and the inhabitants of Megiddo and its towns—three hilly regions. [12]Yet the children of Manasseh could not drive out *the inhabitants of* those cities, but the Canaanites were determined to dwell in that land. [13]And it happened, when the children of Israel grew strong, that they put the Canaanites to forced labor, but did not utterly drive them out.

MORE LAND FOR EPHRAIM AND MANASSEH

[14]Then the children of Joseph spoke to Joshua, saying, "Why have you given us *only* one lot and one share to inherit, since we *are* a great people, inasmuch as the LORD has blessed us until now?"

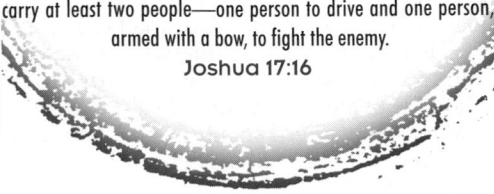

Most ancient chariots were made of wood held together by leather strips. The iron chariots mentioned here probably had iron only in strategic places on the vehicle, for extra support and durability. Chariots were designed to carry at least two people—one person to drive and one person, armed with a bow, to fight the enemy.
Joshua 17:16

[15]So Joshua answered them, "If you *are* a great people, *then* go up to the forest *country* and clear a place for yourself there in the land of the Perizzites and the giants, since the mountains of Ephraim are too confined for you."

[16]But the children of Joseph said, "The mountain country is not enough for us; and all the Canaanites who dwell in the land of the valley have chariots of iron, *both those* who *are* of Beth Shean and its towns and *those* who *are* of the Valley of Jezreel."

[17]And Joshua spoke to the house of Joseph—to Ephraim and Manasseh—saying, "You *are* a great people and have great power; you shall not have *only* one lot, [18]but the mountain country shall be yours. Although it *is* wooded, you shall cut it down, and its farthest extent shall be yours; for you shall drive out the Canaanites, though they have iron chariots *and* are strong."

THE REMAINDER OF THE LAND DIVIDED

[1]Now the whole congregation of the children of Israel assembled together at Shiloh, and set up the tabernacle of meeting there. And the land was subdued before them. [2]But there remained among the children of Israel seven tribes which had not yet received their inheritance.

Shiloh, a city located about twenty miles north of Jerusalem, became an important religious center in Canaan after the Israelites set up their tabernacle of meeting there.
Joshua 18:1

[3]Then Joshua said to the children of Israel: "How long will you neglect to go and possess the land which the LORD God of your fathers has given you? [4]Pick out from among you three men for *each* tribe, and I will send them; they shall rise and go through the land, survey it according to their inheritance, and come *back* to me. [5]And they shall divide it into seven parts. Judah shall remain in their territory on the south, and the house of Joseph shall remain in their territory on the north. [6]You shall therefore survey the land in seven parts and bring *the survey* here to me, that I may cast lots for you here before the LORD our God. [7]But the Levites have no part among you, for the priesthood of the

LORD *is* their inheritance. And Gad, Reuben, and half the tribe of Manasseh have received their inheritance beyond the Jordan on the east, which Moses the servant of the LORD gave them."

⁸Then the men arose to go away; and Joshua charged those who went to survey the land, saying, "Go, walk through the land, survey it, and come back to me, that I may cast lots for you here before the LORD in Shiloh." ⁹So the men went, passed through the land, and wrote the survey in a book in seven parts by cities; and they came to Joshua at the camp in Shiloh. ¹⁰Then Joshua cast lots for them in Shiloh before the LORD, and there Joshua divided the land to the children of Israel according to their divisions.

> "Then Joshua cast lots for them in Shiloh before the LORD, and there Joshua divided the land to the children of Israel according to their divisions."
> (Joshua 18:10)

THE LAND OF BENJAMIN

¹¹Now the lot of the tribe of the children of Benjamin came up according to their families, and the territory of their lot came out between the children of Judah and the children of Joseph. ¹²Their border on the north side began at the Jordan, and the border went up to the side of Jericho on the north, and went up through the mountains westward; it ended at the Wilderness of Beth Aven. ¹³The border went over from there toward Luz, to the side of Luz (which *is* Bethel) southward; and the border descended to Ataroth Addar, near the hill that *lies* on the south side of Lower Beth Horon.

¹⁴Then the border extended around the west side to the south, from the hill that *lies* before Beth Horon southward; and it ended at Kirjath Baal (which *is* Kirjath Jearim), a city of the children of Judah. This *was* the west side.

¹⁵The south side *began* at the end of Kirjath Jearim, and the border extended on the west and went out to the spring of the waters of Nephtoah. ¹⁶Then the border came down to the end of the mountain that *lies* before the Valley of the Son of Hinnom, which *is* in the Valley of the Rephaim^a on the north, descended to the Valley of Hinnom, to the side of the Jebusite *city* on the south, and descended to En Rogel. ¹⁷And it went around from the north, went out to En Shemesh, and extended toward Geliloth, which is before the Ascent of Adummim, and descended to the stone of Bohan the son of Reu-

ben. ¹⁸Then it passed along toward the north side of Arabah,^{a} and went down to Arabah. ¹⁹And the border passed along to the north side of Beth Hoglah; then the border ended at the north bay at the Salt Sea, at the south end of the Jordan. This *was* the southern boundary.

²⁰The Jordan was its border on the east side. This *was* the inheritance of the children of Benjamin, according to its boundaries all around, according to their families.

²¹Now the cities of the tribe of the children of Benjamin, according to their families, were Jericho, Beth Hoglah, Emek Keziz, ²²Beth Arabah, Zemaraim, Bethel, ²³Avim, Parah, Ophrah, ²⁴Chephar Haammoni, Ophni, and Gaba: twelve cities with their villages; ²⁵Gibeon, Ramah, Beeroth, ²⁶Mizpah, Chephirah, Mozah, ²⁷Rekem, Irpeel, Taralah, ²⁸Zelah, Eleph, Jebus (which *is* Jerusalem), Gibeath, *and* Kirjath: fourteen cities with their villages. This was the inheritance of the children of Benjamin according to their families.

SIMEON'S INHERITANCE WITH JUDAH

¹The second lot came out for Simeon, for the tribe of the children of Simeon according to their families. And their inheritance was within the inheritance of the children of Judah. ²They had in their inheritance Beersheba (Sheba), Moladah, ³Hazar Shual, Balah, Ezem, ⁴Eltolad, Bethul, Hormah, ⁵Ziklag, Beth Marcaboth, Hazar Susah, ⁶Beth Lebaoth, and Sharuhen: thirteen cities and their villages; ⁷Ain, Rimmon, Ether, and Ashan: four cities and their villages; ⁸and all the villages that *were* all around these cities as far as Baalath Beer, Ramah of the South. This *was* the inheritance of the tribe of the children of Simeon according to their families.

⁹The inheritance of the children of Simeon *was included* in the share of the children of Judah, for the share of the children of Judah was too much for them. Therefore the children of Simeon had *their* inheritance within the inheritance of that people.

THE LAND OF ZEBULUN

¹⁰The third lot came out for the children of Zebulun according to their families, and the

border of their inheritance was as far as Sarid. [11]Their border went toward the west and to Maralah, went to Dabbasheth, and extended along the brook that is east of Jokneam. [12]Then from Sarid it went eastward toward the sunrise along the border of Chisloth Tabor, and went out toward Daberath, bypassing Japhia. [13]And from there it passed along on the east of Gath Hepher, toward Eth Kazin, and extended to Rimmon, which borders on Neah. [14]Then the border went around it on the north side of Hannathon, and it ended in the Valley of Jiphthah El. [15]Included were Kattath, Nahallal, Shimron, Idalah, and Bethlehem: twelve cities with their villages. [16]This *was* the inheritance of the children of Zebulun according to their families, these cities with their villages.

THE LAND OF ISSACHAR

[17]The fourth lot came out to Issachar, for the children of Issachar according to their families. [18]And their territory went to Jezreel, and *included* Chesulloth, Shunem, [19]Haphraim, Shion, Anaharath, [20]Rabbith, Kishion, Abez, [21]Remeth, En Gannim, En Haddah, and Beth Pazzez. [22]And the border reached to Tabor, Shahazimah, and Beth Shemesh; their border ended at the Jordan: sixteen cities with their villages. [23]This *was* the inheritance of the tribe of the children of Issachar according to their families, the cities and their villages.

THE LAND OF ASHER

[24]The fifth lot came out for the tribe of the children of Asher according to their families. [25]And their territory included Helkath, Hali, Beten, Achshaph, [26]Alammelech, Amad, and Mishal; it reached to Mount Carmel westward, along *the Brook* Shihor Libnath. [27]It turned toward the sunrise to Beth Dagon; and it reached to Zebulun and to the Valley of Jiphthah El, then northward beyond Beth Emek and Neiel, bypassing Cabul *which was* on the left, [28]including Ebron,[a] Rehob, Hammon, and Kanah, as far as Greater Sidon. [29]And the border turned to Ramah and to the fortified city of Tyre; then the border turned to Hosah, and ended at the sea by the region of Achzib. [30]Also Ummah, Aphek, and Rehob *were included:* twenty-two cities with their villages. [31]This *was* the inheritance of the tribe of the children of Asher according to their families, these cities with their villages.

THE LAND OF NAPHTALI

[32]The sixth lot came out to the children of Naphtali, for the children of Naphtali according to their families. [33]And their border began at Heleph, enclosing the territory from the terebinth tree in Zaanannim, Adami Nekeb, and Jabneel, as far as Lakkum; it ended at the Jordan. [34]From Heleph the border extended westward to Aznoth Tabor, and went out from there toward Hukkok; it adjoined Zebulun on the south side and Asher on the west side, and ended at Judah by the Jordan toward the sunrise. [35]And the fortified cities *are* Ziddim, Zer, Hammath, Rakkath, Chinnereth, [36]Adamah, Ramah, Hazor, [37]Kedesh, Edrei, En Hazor, [38]Iron, Migdal El, Horem, Beth Anath, and Beth Shemesh: nineteen cities with their villages. [39]This *was* the inheritance of the tribe of the children of Naphtali according to their families, the cities and their villages.

THE LAND OF DAN

[40]The seventh lot came out for the tribe of the children of Dan according to their families. [41]And the territory of their inheritance was Zorah, Eshtaol, Ir Shemesh, [42]Shaalabbin, Aijalon, Jethlah, [43]Elon, Timnah, Ekron, [44]Eltekeh, Gibbethon, Baalath, [45]Jehud, Bene Berak, Gath Rimmon, [46]Me Jarkon, and Rakkon, with the region near Joppa. [47]And the border of the children of Dan went beyond these, because the children of Dan went up to fight against Leshem and took it; and they struck it with the edge of the sword, took possession of it, and dwelt in it. They called Leshem, Dan, after the name of Dan their father. [48]This *is* the inheritance of the tribe of the children of Dan according to their families, these cities with their villages.

JOSHUA'S INHERITANCE

[49]When they had made an end of dividing the land as an inheritance according to their borders, the children of Israel gave an inheritance among them to Joshua the son of Nun. [50]According to the word of the LORD they gave him the city which he asked for, Timnath Serah in the mountains of Ephraim; and he built the city and dwelt in it.

[51]These *were* the inheritances which Eleazar the priest, Joshua the son of Nun, and the heads of the fathers of the tribes of the children of Israel divided as an inheritance by lot in Shiloh before the LORD, at the door of the tabernacle of

19:28 [a]Following Masoretic Text, Targum, and Vulgate; a few Hebrew manuscripts read *Abdon* (compare 21:30 and 1 Chronicles 6:74).

meeting. So they made an end of dividing the country.

THE CITIES OF REFUGE

¹The LORD also spoke to Joshua, saying, ²"Speak to the children of Israel, saying: 'Appoint for yourselves cities of refuge, of which I spoke to you through Moses, ³that the slayer who kills a person accidentally *or* unintentionally may flee there; and they shall be your refuge from the avenger of blood. ⁴And when he flees to one of those cities, and stands at the entrance of the gate of the city, and declares his case in the hearing of the elders of that city, they shall take him into the city as one of them, and give him a place, that he may dwell among them. ⁵Then if the avenger of blood pursues him, they shall not deliver the slayer into his hand, because he struck his neighbor unintentionally, but did not hate him beforehand. ⁶And he shall dwell in that city until he stands before the congregation for judgment, *and* until the death of the one who is high priest in those days. Then the slayer may return and come to his own city and his own house, to the city from which he fled.'"

⁷So they appointed Kedesh in Galilee, in the mountains of Naphtali, Shechem in the mountains of Ephraim, and Kirjath Arba (which *is* Hebron) in the mountains of Judah. ⁸And on the other side of the Jordan, by Jericho eastward, they assigned Bezer in the wilderness on the plain, from the tribe of Reuben, Ramoth in Gilead, from the tribe of Gad, and Golan in Bashan, from the tribe of Manasseh. ⁹These were the cities appointed for all the children of Israel and for the stranger who dwelt among them, that whoever killed a person accidentally might flee there, and not die by the hand of the avenger of blood until he stood before the congregation.

CITIES OF THE LEVITES

¹Then the heads of the fathers' *houses* of the Levites came near to Eleazar the priest, to Joshua the son of Nun, and to the heads of the fathers' *houses* of the tribes of the children of Israel. ²And they spoke to them at Shiloh in the land of Canaan, saying, "The LORD commanded through Moses to give us cities to dwell in, with their common-lands for our livestock." ³So the children of Israel gave to the Levites from their inheritance, at the commandment of the LORD, these cities and their common-lands:

⁴Now the lot came out for the families of the Kohathites. And the children of Aaron the priest, *who were* of the Levites, had thirteen cities by lot from the tribe of Judah, from the tribe of Simeon, and from the tribe of Benjamin. ⁵The rest of the children of Kohath had ten cities by lot from the families of the tribe of Ephraim, from the tribe of Dan, and from the half-tribe of Manasseh.

⁶And the children of Gershon had thirteen cities by lot from the families of the tribe of Issachar, from the tribe of Asher, from the tribe of Naphtali, and from the half-tribe of Manasseh in Bashan.

⁷The children of Merari according to their families had twelve cities from the tribe of Reuben, from the tribe of Gad, and from the tribe of Zebulun.

⁸And the children of Israel gave these cities with their common-lands by lot to the Levites, as the LORD had commanded by the hand of Moses.

⁹So they gave from the tribe of the children of Judah and from the tribe of the children of Simeon these cities which are designated by name, ¹⁰which were for the children of Aaron, one of the families of the Kohathites, *who were* of the children of Levi; for the lot was theirs first. ¹¹And they gave them Kirjath Arba (*Arba was* the father of Anak), which *is* Hebron, in the mountains of Judah, with the common-land surrounding it. ¹²But the fields of the city and its villages they gave to Caleb the son of Jephunneh as his possession.

¹³Thus to the children of Aaron the priest they gave Hebron with its common-land (a city of refuge for the slayer), Libnah with its common-land, ¹⁴Jattir with its common-land, Eshtemoa with its common-land, ¹⁵Holon with its common-land, Debir with its common-land, ¹⁶Ain with its common-land, Juttah with its common-land, and Beth Shemesh with its common-land: nine cities from those two tribes; ¹⁷and from the tribe of Benjamin, Gibeon with its common-land, Geba with its common-land, ¹⁸Anathoth with its common-land, and Almon with its common-land: four cities. ¹⁹All the cities of the children of Aaron, the priests, *were* thirteen cities with their common-lands.

²⁰And the families of the children of Kohath, the Levites, the rest of the children of Kohath, even they had the cities of their lot from the tribe of Ephraim. ²¹For they gave them Shechem with its common-land in the mountains of Ephraim (a city of refuge for the slayer), Gezer with its common-land, ²²Kibzaim with its common-land, and Beth Horon with its common-land: four cities; ²³and from the tribe of Dan, Eltekeh with its common-land, Gibbethon with its common-land, ²⁴Aijalon

with its common-land, *and* Gath Rimmon with its common-land: four cities; [25]and from the half-tribe of Manasseh, Tanach with its common-land and Gath Rimmon with its common-land: two cities. [26]All the ten cities with their common-lands were for the rest of the families of the children of Kohath.

[27]Also to the children of Gershon, of the families of the Levites, from the *other* half-tribe of Manasseh, *they gave* Golan in Bashan with its common-land (a city of refuge for the slayer), and Be Eshterah with its common-land: two cities; [28]and from the tribe of Issachar, Kishion with its common-land, Daberath with its common-land, [29]Jarmuth with its common-land, *and* En Gannim with its common-land: four cities; [30]and from the tribe of Asher, Mishal with its common-land, Abdon with its common-land, [31]Helkath with its common-land, and Rehob with its common-land: four cities; [32]and from the tribe of Naphtali, Kedesh in Galilee with its common-land (a city of refuge for the slayer), Hammoth Dor with its common-land, and Kartan with its common-land: three cities. [33]All the cities of the Gershonites according to their families *were* thirteen cities with their common-lands.

[34]And to the families of the children of Merari, the rest of the Levites, from the tribe of Zebulun, Jokneam with its common-land, Kartah with its common-land, [35]Dimnah with its common-land, *and* Nahalal with its common-land: four cities; [36]and from the tribe of Reuben, Bezer with its common-land, Jahaz with its common-land, [37]Kedemoth with its common-land, and Mephaath with its common-land: four cities;[a] [38]and from the tribe of Gad, Ramoth in Gilead with its common-land (a city of refuge for the slayer), Mahanaim with its common-land, [39]Heshbon with its common-land, *and* Jazer with its common-land: four cities in all. [40]So all the cities for the children of Merari according to their families, the rest of the families of the Levites, were *by* their lot twelve cities.

[41]All the cities of the Levites within the possession of the children of Israel *were* forty-eight cities with their common-lands. [42]Every one of these cities had its common-land surrounding it; thus *were* all these cities.

THE PROMISE FULFILLED

[43]So the LORD gave to Israel all the land of which He had sworn to give to their fathers,

and they took possession of it and dwelt in it. [44]The LORD gave them rest all around, according to all that He had sworn to their fathers. And not a man of all their enemies stood against them; the LORD delivered all their enemies into their hand. [45]Not a word failed of any good thing which the LORD had spoken to the house of Israel. All came to pass.

EASTERN TRIBES RETURN TO THEIR LANDS

[1]Then Joshua called the Reubenites, the Gadites, and half the tribe of Manasseh, [2]and said to them: "You have kept all that Moses the servant of the LORD commanded you, and have obeyed my voice in all that I commanded you. [3]You have not left your brethren these many days, up to this day, but have kept the charge of the commandment of the LORD your God. [4]And now the LORD your God has given rest to your brethren, as He promised them; now therefore, return and go to your tents *and* to the land of your possession, which Moses the servant of the LORD gave you on the other side of the Jordan. [5]But take careful heed to do the commandment and the law which Moses the servant of the LORD commanded you, to love the LORD your God, to walk in all His ways, to keep His commandments, to hold fast to Him, and to serve Him with all your heart and with all your soul." [6]So Joshua blessed them and sent them away, and they went to their tents.

[7]Now to half the tribe of Manasseh Moses had given a possession in Bashan, but to the *other* half of it Joshua gave *a possession* among their brethren on this side of the Jordan, westward. And indeed, when Joshua sent them away to their tents, he blessed them, [8]and spoke to them, saying, "Return with much riches to your tents, with very much livestock, with silver, with gold, with bronze, with iron, and with very much clothing. Divide the spoil of your enemies with your brethren."

[9]So the children of Reuben, the children of Gad, and half the tribe of Manasseh returned, and departed from the children of Israel at Shiloh, which *is* in the land of Canaan, to go to the country of Gilead, to the land of their possession, which they had obtained according to the word of the LORD by the hand of Moses.

FOLLOWING GOD

How should we follow God? (22:5)

21:37 [a]Following Septuagint and Vulgate (compare 1 Chronicles 6:78, 79); Masoretic Text, Bomberg, and Targum omit verses 36 and 37.

AN ALTAR BY THE JORDAN

¹⁰And when they came to the region of the Jordan which *is* in the land of Canaan, the children of Reuben, the children of Gad, and half the tribe of Manasseh built an altar there by the Jordan— a great, impressive altar. ¹¹Now the children of Israel heard *someone* say, "Behold, the children of Reuben, the children of Gad, and half the tribe of Manasseh have built an altar on the frontier of the land of Canaan, in the region of the Jordan—on the children of Israel's side." ¹²And when the children of Israel heard *of* it, the whole congregation of the children of Israel gathered together at Shiloh to go to war against them.

> "And it shall be, if you rebel today against the LORD, that tomorrow He will be angry with the whole congregation of Israel."
> (Joshua 22:18b)

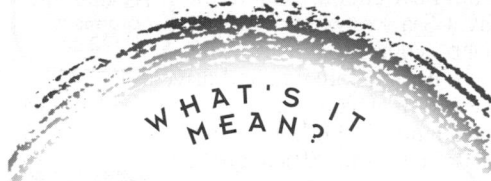

WHAT'S IT MEAN?

The word for altar in Hebrew means "a place of sacrifice." Once the tabernacle of meeting was in place, it became the official place for sacrifice in Canaan. The Israelites were not allowed to offer sacrifices to the Lord anywhere but there. When a second altar was built on the east side of the Jordan River by people who were tired of traveling to make their sacrifices, the Israelites on the west side of the river thought their neighbors were being unfaithful to God.

Joshua 22:16

¹³Then the children of Israel sent Phinehas the son of Eleazar the priest to the children of Reuben, to the children of Gad, and to half the tribe of Manasseh, into the land of Gilead, ¹⁴and with him ten rulers, one ruler each from the chief house of every tribe of Israel; and each one *was* the head of the house of his father among the divisions*a* of Israel. ¹⁵Then they came to the children of Reuben, to the children of Gad, and to half the tribe of Manasseh, to the land of Gilead, and they spoke with them, saying, ¹⁶"Thus says the whole congregation of the LORD: 'What treachery *is* this that you have committed against the God of Israel, to turn away this day from following the LORD, in that you have built for yourselves an altar, that you might rebel this day against the LORD? ¹⁷*Is* the iniquity of Peor not enough for us, from which we are not cleansed till this day, although there was a plague in the congregation of the LORD, ¹⁸but that you must turn away this day from following the LORD? And it shall be, if you rebel today against the LORD, that tomorrow He will be angry with the whole congregation of Israel. ¹⁹Nevertheless, if the land of your possession *is* unclean, *then* cross over to the land of the possession of the LORD, where the LORD's tabernacle stands, and take possession among us; but do not rebel against the LORD, nor rebel against us, by building yourselves an altar besides the altar of the LORD our God. ²⁰Did not Achan the son of Zerah commit a trespass in the accursed thing, and wrath fell on all the congregation of Israel? And that man did not perish alone in his iniquity.'"

²¹Then the children of Reuben, the children of Gad, and half the tribe of Manasseh answered and said to the heads of the divisions*a* of Israel: ²²"The LORD God of gods, the LORD God of gods, He knows, and let Israel itself know—if *it is* in rebellion, or if in treachery against the LORD, do not save us this day. ²³If we have built ourselves an altar to turn from following the LORD, or if to offer on it burnt offerings or grain offerings, or if to offer peace offerings on it, let the LORD Himself require *an account*. ²⁴But in fact we have done it for fear, for a reason, saying, 'In time to come your descendants may speak to our descendants, saying, "What have you to do with the LORD God of Israel? ²⁵For the LORD has made the Jordan a border between you and us, *you* children of Reuben and children of Gad. You have no part in the LORD." So your descendants would make our descendants cease fearing the LORD.' ²⁶Therefore we said, 'Let us now prepare to build ourselves an altar, not for burnt offering nor for sacrifice, ²⁷but *that* it *may be* a witness between you and us and our generations after us, that we may perform the service of the LORD before Him with our burnt offerings, with our sacrifices, and with our peace offerings; that

22:14 *a*Literally *thousands*   **22:21** *a*Literally *thousands*

your descendants may not say to our descendants in time to come, "You have no part in the LORD." ' ²⁸Therefore we said that it will be, when they say *this* to us or to our generations in time to come, that we may say, 'Here is the replica of the altar of the LORD which our fathers made, though not for burnt offerings nor for sacrifices; but it *is* a witness between you and us.' ²⁹Far be it from us that we should rebel against the LORD, and turn from following the LORD this day, to build an altar for burnt offerings, for grain offerings, or for sacrifices, besides the altar of the LORD our God which *is* before His tabernacle."

³⁰Now when Phinehas the priest and the rulers of the congregation, the heads of the divisions[a] of Israel who *were* with him, heard the words that the children of Reuben, the children of Gad, and the children of Manasseh spoke, it pleased them. ³¹Then Phinehas the son of Eleazar the priest said to the children of Reuben, the children of Gad, and the children of Manasseh, "This day we perceive that the LORD *is* among us, because you have not committed this treachery against the LORD. Now you have delivered the children of Israel out of the hand of the LORD."

³²And Phinehas the son of Eleazar the priest, and the rulers, returned from the children of Reuben and the children of Gad, from the land of Gilead to the land of Canaan, to the children of Israel, and brought back word to them. ³³So the thing pleased the children of Israel, and the children of Israel blessed God; they spoke no more of going against them in battle, to destroy the land where the children of Reuben and Gad dwelt.

³⁴The children of Reuben and the children of Gad[a] called the altar, *Witness*, "For *it is* a witness between us that the LORD *is* God."

JOSHUA'S FAREWELL ADDRESS

¹Now it came to pass, a long time after the LORD had given rest to Israel from all their enemies round about, that Joshua was old, advanced in age. ²And Joshua called for all Israel, for their elders, for their heads, for their judges, and for their officers, and said to them:

"I am old, advanced in age. ³You have seen all that the LORD your God has done to all these nations because of you, for the LORD your God *is* He who has fought for you. ⁴See, I have divided to you by lot these nations that remain, to be an inheritance for your tribes, from the Jordan, with all the nations that I have cut off, as far as the Great Sea westward. ⁵And the LORD your God will expel them from before you and drive them out of your sight. So you shall possess their land, as the LORD your God promised you. ⁶Therefore be very courageous to keep and to do all that is written in the Book of the Law of Moses, lest you turn aside from it to the right hand or to the left, ⁷*and* lest you go among these nations, these who remain among you. You

GOD Does He keep His promises? (23:5)

BIBLE Why should we obey the Bible? (23:6, 7)

22:30 [a]Literally *thousands*   **22:34** [a]Septuagint adds *and half the tribe of Manasseh*

Promise HE DOES WHAT HE HAS PROMISED.

Therefore it shall come to pass, that as all the good things have come upon you which the LORD your God promised you, . . . (Josh. 23:15).

All through the Bible, God models what good character is, then calls us to be like Him. Here, He promises to keep His word. You're a person of strong character if you do what you say you will do—if you keep your promises. Do you normally slide in after curfew? Do you keep people waiting for you? Do you really go where you tell your parents you'll be? If you find yourself always making excuses, it's time for a character adjustment. Look at God and imitate Him. You can be successful at almost anything if you do what you've said you will do. Be dependable, trustworthy, faithful. Those are all attributes of God. He doesn't need to make any excuses.

SEE FOR YOURSELF:
Gen. 28:15; Num. 23:19; Deut. 4:31; 1 Kin. 8:56; Neh. 1:5

shall not make mention of the name of their gods, nor cause *anyone* to swear *by them;* you shall not serve them nor bow down to them, [8]but you shall hold fast to the LORD your God, as you have done to this day. [9]For the LORD has driven out from before you great and strong nations; but *as for* you, no one has been able to stand against you to this day. [10]One man of you shall chase a thousand, for the LORD your God *is* He who fights for you, as He promised you. [11]Therefore take careful heed to yourselves, that you love the LORD your God. [12]Or else, if indeed you do go back, and cling to the remnant of these nations—these that remain among you—and make marriages with them, and go in to them and they to you, [13]know for certain that the LORD your God will no longer drive out these nations from before you. But they shall be snares and traps to you, and scourges on your sides and thorns in your eyes, until you perish from this good land which the LORD your God has given you.

[14]"Behold, this day I *am* going the way of all the earth. And you know in all your hearts and in all your souls that not one thing has failed of all the good things which the LORD your God spoke concerning you. All have come to pass for you; not one word of them has failed. [15]Therefore it shall come to pass, that as all the good things have come upon you which the LORD your God promised you, so the LORD will bring upon you all harmful things, until He has destroyed you from this good land which the LORD your God has given you. [16]When you have transgressed the covenant of the LORD your God, which He commanded you, and have gone and served other gods, and bowed down to them, then the anger of the LORD will burn against you, and you shall perish quickly from the good land which He has given you."

THE COVENANT AT SHECHEM

[1]Then Joshua gathered all the tribes of Israel to Shechem and called for the elders of Israel, for their heads, for their judges, and for their officers; and they presented themselves before God. [2]And Joshua said to all the people, "Thus says the LORD God of Israel: 'Your fathers, *including* Terah, the father of Abraham and the father of Nahor, dwelt on the other side of the River[a] in old times; and they served other gods. [3]Then I took your father Abraham from the other side of the River, led him throughout all the land of Canaan, and multiplied his descendants and gave him Isaac. [4]To Isaac I gave Jacob and Esau. To Esau I gave the mountains of Seir to possess, but Jacob and his children went down to Egypt. [5]Also I sent Moses and Aaron, and I plagued Egypt, according to what I did among them. Afterward I brought you out.

WHAT'S IT MEAN?

Shechem was a bustling city even before the Israelites lived there. Located near ancient highways and trade routes, the city drew travelers from all over. Shechem, the site of Joshua's farewell address, was located between Mount Gerizim and Mount Ebal. Mount Gerizim is the place where Moses blessed the Israelites for obeying God; Mount Ebal is where he cursed the people for their disobedience. Interestingly, today Mount Gerizim is covered with vegetation and Mount Ebal is bare, perhaps as reminders of the Lord's blessings and curses.

Joshua 24:1

[6]'Then I brought your fathers out of Egypt, and you came to the sea; and the Egyptians pursued your fathers with chariots and horsemen to the Red Sea. [7]So they cried out to the LORD; and He put darkness between you and the Egyptians, brought the sea upon them, and covered them. And your eyes saw what I did in Egypt. Then you dwelt in the wilderness a long time. [8]And I brought you into the land of the Amorites, who dwelt on the other side of the Jordan, and they fought with you. But I gave them into your hand, that you might possess their land, and I destroyed them from before you. [9]Then Balak the son of Zippor, king of Moab, arose to make war against Israel, and sent and called Balaam the son of Beor to curse you. [10]But I would not listen to Balaam; therefore he continued to bless you. So I delivered you out of his hand. [11]Then you went over the Jordan and came to Jericho. And the men of Jericho fought against you—*also* the Amorites, the Perizzites, the Canaanites, the Hittites, the Girgashites, the Hivites, and the Jebusites. But I delivered them into your hand. [12]I sent the hornet before you which drove them out from before you, *also* the two kings of the Amorites, *but* not with your sword or with your bow. [13]I have given you a land for which you did not

labor, and cities which you did not build, and you dwell in them; you eat of the vineyards and olive groves which you did not plant.'

[14]"Now therefore, fear the LORD, serve Him in sincerity and in truth, and put away the gods which your fathers served on the other side of the River and in Egypt. Serve the LORD! [15]And if it seems evil to you to serve the LORD, choose for yourselves this day whom you will serve, whether the gods which your fathers served that *were* on the other side of the River, or the gods of the Amorites, in whose land you dwell. But as for me and my house, we will serve the LORD."

DEVOTION

How should we be devoted? (24:14)

FAMILY

What should my family be like? (24:15)

[16]So the people answered and said: "Far be it from us that we should forsake the LORD to serve other gods; [17]for the LORD our God *is* He who brought us and our fathers up out of the land of Egypt, from the house of bondage, who did those great signs in our sight, and preserved us in all the way that we went and among all the people through whom we passed. [18]And the LORD drove out from before us all the people, including the Amorites who dwelt in the land. We also will serve the LORD, for He *is* our God."

[19]But Joshua said to the people, "You cannot serve the LORD, for He *is* a holy God. He *is* a jealous God; He will not forgive your transgressions nor your sins. [20]If you forsake the LORD and serve foreign gods, then He will turn and do you harm and consume you, after He has done you good."

[21]And the people said to Joshua, "No, but we will serve the LORD!"

[22]So Joshua said to the people, "You *are* witnesses against yourselves that you have chosen the LORD for yourselves, to serve Him."

And they said, "*We are* witnesses!"

[23]"Now therefore," *he said,* "put away the foreign gods which *are* among you, and incline your heart to the LORD God of Israel."

[24]And the people said to Joshua, "The LORD our God we will serve, and His voice we will obey!"

[25]So Joshua made a covenant with the peo-

> "And the people said to Joshua, 'The LORD our God we will serve, and His voice we will obey!'"
> (Joshua 24:24)

On the Edge

But Joshua said to the people, "You cannot serve the LORD, for He is a holy God. He is a jealous God; He will not forgive your transgressions nor your sins" (Josh. 24:19).

Fake is in. Phony is fashionable: bodies that are beautiful because of plastic surgery; imitation foods that taste sweet—with no sugar. Virtual realities that are only pretend. Somewhere in the world of impostors we've lost our sense of what is true. God can restore the standard. He is not a fake. He is not pretending to be God. He is real, and pure, and holy, and awesome. So if you've been feeling like you can't figure out what's true anymore, get off the stage. Get with God. Some time in the presence of His truth will bring you back to reality.

SEE FOR YOURSELF:
Deut. 6:4; John 17:3; Eph. 4:5, 6; 1 Tim. 2:5

ple that day, and made for them a statute and an ordinance in Shechem.

[26]Then Joshua wrote these words in the Book of the Law of God. And he took a large stone, and set it up there under the oak that *was* by the sanctuary of the LORD. [27]And Joshua said to all the people, "Behold, this stone shall be a witness to us, for it has heard all the words of the LORD which He spoke to us. It shall therefore be a witness to you, lest you deny your God." [28]So Joshua let the people depart, each to his own inheritance.

DEATH OF JOSHUA AND ELEAZAR

[29]Now it came to pass after these things that Joshua the son of Nun, the servant of the LORD, died, *being* one hundred and ten years old. [30]And they buried him within the border of his inheritance at Timnath Serah, which *is* in the mountains of Ephraim, on the north side of Mount Gaash.

[31]Israel served the LORD all the days of Joshua, and all the days of the elders who outlived Joshua, who had known all the works

of the LORD which He had done for Israel.

³²The bones of Joseph, which the children of Israel had brought up out of Egypt, they buried at Shechem, in the plot of ground which Jacob had bought from the sons of Hamor the father of Shechem for one hundred pieces of silver, and which had become an inheritance of the children of Joseph.

³³And Eleazar the son of Aaron died. They buried him in a hill *belonging to* Phinehas his son, which was given to him in the mountains of Ephraim.

CONTENT   In their earliest days the Hebrews were a family led by a dad named Jacob who had twelve sons. Then the descendants of those twelve sons grew to be a nation of slaves in Egypt, a country led by a Pharaoh, or king. Then they became exiles led by Moses. Then they became an army led by Joshua. Then came the Book of Judges.

The Book of Judges is about a time in the life of the Hebrews before they had a king. When they needed to make decisions, they went to a judge, a national leader. A judge was sort of like a king, but no castle or crown or bowing—just a leader.

During the time of the judges, the Hebrews went up and down like a morality yo-yo. They would obey God if they were listening to a good judge. Then that judge would die and the people would fall away again. In fact, the phrase you'll most often read about in this book is "and everyone did as he saw fit . . ." When you read that in Judges, you know that it means, "and here they go again—doing their own thing no matter what God wants." Then another judge would come into leadership and they'd clean up their act for a while.

Purpose   What we fail to learn from history we must often learn by painful experience.

Themes   Apostasy, Oppression, Repentance, Deliverance

Date of writing   1043–1004 B.C.

Bible Talk

Deborah

You hear a lot about how women were second-class citizens in the culture that you read about in the Bible. It's important to notice, though, that women were not second-class citizens in God's eyes, ever. Deborah is a great example.

Deborah was a judge, a national leader, just like any male judge that Israel recognized. She was even asked to go to battle. Know what she said? "I'll go as long as you realize that everybody is going to know that a woman did the winning."

SAMSON, NAZIRITE

Even if you've not been much of a church-goer, you probably have heard of Samson with his long hair and supernatural strength. Sometimes the story can sound like Popeye with his spinach.

It's important to remember, though, that Samson's hair wasn't made of different stuff than yours. His hair just represented a promise he had made. He was a Nazirite (like Samuel and John the Baptist). That means he kept certain traditions (like not drinking wine) that kept him close to God. When Samson let his hair be cut, it wasn't like some spell was broken. It was that a promise was broken. Samson was turning his back on a promise that he had made to God. When he did, he lost access to God's power and you probably know the rest. If not, read on . . .

THE CONTINUING CONQUEST OF CANAAN

¹Now after the death of Joshua it came to pass that the children of Israel asked the LORD, saying, "Who shall be first to go up for us against the Canaanites to fight against them?"

²And the LORD said, "Judah shall go up. Indeed I have delivered the land into his hand."

³So Judah said to Simeon his brother, "Come up with me to my allotted territory, that we may fight against the Canaanites; and I will likewise go with you to your allotted territory." And Simeon went with him. ⁴Then Judah went up, and the LORD delivered the Canaanites and the Perizzites into their hand; and they killed ten thousand men at Bezek. ⁵And they found Adoni-Bezek in Bezek, and fought against him; and they defeated the Canaanites and the Perizzites. ⁶Then Adoni-Bezek fled, and they pursued him and caught him and cut off his thumbs and big toes. ⁷And Adoni-Bezek said, "Seventy kings with their thumbs and big toes cut off used to gather *scraps* under my table; as I have done, so God has repaid me." Then they brought him to Jerusalem, and there he died.

Most chariots were made of wood and held together by leather strips. The deluxe models, the "chariots of iron," probably weren't made completely of iron. They would have been too heavy to pull. Instead, they were probably reinforced with iron in certain spots to make them sturdier or to give their riders more protection. Though some chariots could carry as many as four passengers, most combat models were built to hold two—a driver and a fighter armed with a bow and arrows.

Judges 1:18, 19

⁸Now the children of Judah fought against Jerusalem and took it; they struck it with the edge of the sword and set the city on fire. ⁹And afterward the children of Judah went down to fight against the Canaanites who dwelt in the mountains, in the South,ᵃ and in the lowland. ¹⁰Then Judah went against the Canaanites who dwelt in Hebron. (Now the name of Hebron *was* formerly Kirjath Arba.) And they killed Sheshai, Ahiman, and Talmai.

¹¹From there they went against the inhabitants of Debir. (The name of Debir *was* formerly Kirjath Sepher.)

¹²Then Caleb said, "Whoever attacks Kirjath Sepher and takes it, to him I will give my daughter Achsah as wife." ¹³And Othniel the son of Kenaz, Caleb's younger brother, took it; so he gave him his daughter Achsah as wife. ¹⁴Now it happened, when she came *to him*, that she urged himᵃ to ask her father for a field. And she dismounted from *her* donkey, and Caleb said to her, "What do you wish?" ¹⁵So she said to him, "Give me a blessing; since you have given me land in the South, give me also springs of water."

And Caleb gave her the upper springs and the lower springs.

¹⁶Now the children of the Kenite, Moses' father-in-law, went up from the City of Palms with the children of Judah into the Wilderness of Judah, which *lies* in the South *near* Arad; and they went and dwelt among the people. ¹⁷And Judah went with his brother Simeon, and they attacked the Canaanites who inhabited Zephath, and utterly destroyed it. So the name of the city was called Hormah. ¹⁸Also Judah took Gaza with its territory, Ashkelon with its territory, and Ekron with its territory. ¹⁹So the LORD was with Judah. And they drove out the mountaineers, but they could not drive out the inhabitants of the lowland, because they had chariots of iron. ²⁰And they gave Hebron to Caleb, as Moses had said. Then he expelled from there the three sons of Anak. ²¹But the children of Benjamin did not drive out the Jebusites who inhabited Jerusalem; so the Jebusites dwell with the children of Benjamin in Jerusalem to this day.

²²And the house of Joseph also went up against Bethel, and the LORD *was* with them. ²³So the house of Joseph sent men to spy out Bethel. (The name of the city *was* formerly Luz.) ²⁴And when the spies saw a man coming out of the city, they said to him, "Please show us the entrance to the city, and we will show you mercy." ²⁵So he showed them the entrance to the city, and they struck the city with the edge of the sword; but they let the man and all his family go. ²⁶And the man went to the land of the Hittites, built a city, and called its name Luz, which *is* its name to this day.

INCOMPLETE CONQUEST OF THE LAND

²⁷However, Manasseh did not drive out *the inhabitants of* Beth Shean and its villages, or Ta-

---

1:9 ᵃHebrew *Negev*, and so throughout this book   **1:14** ᵃSeptuagint and Vulgate read *he urged her.*

anach and its villages, or the inhabitants of Dor and its villages, or the inhabitants of Ibleam and its villages, or the inhabitants of Megiddo and its villages; for the Canaanites were determined to dwell in that land. ²⁸And it came to pass, when Israel was strong, that they put the Canaanites under tribute, but did not completely drive them out.

²⁹Nor did Ephraim drive out the Canaanites who dwelt in Gezer; so the Canaanites dwelt in Gezer among them.

³⁰Nor did Zebulun drive out the inhabitants of Kitron or the inhabitants of Nahalol; so the Canaanites dwelt among them, and were put under tribute.

³¹Nor did Asher drive out the inhabitants of Acco or the inhabitants of Sidon, or of Ahlab, Achzib, Helbah, Aphik, or Rehob. ³²So the Asherites dwelt among the Canaanites, the inhabitants of the land; for they did not drive them out.

³³Nor did Naphtali drive out the inhabitants of Beth Shemesh or the inhabitants of Beth Anath; but they dwelt among the Canaanites, the inhabitants of the land. Nevertheless the inhabitants of Beth Shemesh and Beth Anath were put under tribute to them.

³⁴And the Amorites forced the children of Dan into the mountains, for they would not allow them to come down to the valley; ³⁵and the Amorites were determined to dwell in Mount Heres, in Aijalon, and in Shaalbim;ᵃ yet when the strength of the house of Joseph became greater, they were put under tribute.

³⁶Now the boundary of the Amorites *was* from the Ascent of Akrabbim, from Sela, and upward.

ISRAEL'S DISOBEDIENCE

¹Then the Angel of the LORD came up from Gilgal to Bochim, and said: "I led you up from Egypt and brought you to the land of which I swore to your fathers; and I said, 'I will never break My covenant with you. ²And you shall make no covenant with the inhabitants of this land; you shall tear down their altars.' But you have not obeyed My voice. Why have you done this? ³Therefore I also said, 'I will not drive them out before you; but they shall be *thorns* in your side,ᵃ and their gods shall be a snare to

you.'" ⁴So it was, when the Angel of the LORD spoke these words to all the children of Israel, that the people lifted up their voices and wept.

⁵Then they called the name of that place Bochim;ᵃ and they sacrificed there to the LORD. ⁶And when Joshua had dismissed the people, the children of Israel went each to his own inheritance to possess the land.

DEATH OF JOSHUA

⁷So the people served the LORD all the days of Joshua, and all the days of the elders who outlived Joshua, who had seen all the great works of the LORD which He had done for Israel. ⁸Now Joshua the son of Nun, the servant of the LORD, died *when he was* one hundred and ten years old. ⁹And they buried him within the border of his inheritance at Timnath Heres, in the mountains of Ephraim, on the north side of Mount Gaash. ¹⁰When all that generation had been gathered to their fathers, another generation arose after them who did not know the LORD nor the work which He had done for Israel.

> "So the people served the LORD all the days of Joshua, and all the days of the elders who outlived Joshua, who had seen all the great works of the LORD which He had done for Israel."
> (Judges 2:7)

WHAT'S IT MEAN?

The Canaanites believed that their god Baal was responsible for making things fertile and productive, including crops, animals, and humans. In addition to Baal, they worshiped the Ashtoreths, Canaanite goddesses.
Judges 2:11–13

ISRAEL'S UNFAITHFULNESS

¹¹Then the children of Israel did evil in the sight of the LORD, and served the Baals; ¹²and they forsook the LORD God of their fathers, who

---

1:35 ᵃSpelled *Shaalabbin* in Joshua 19:42   **2:3** ᵃSeptuagint, Targum, and Vulgate read *enemies to you.*
2:5 ᵃLiterally *Weeping*

had brought them out of the land of Egypt; and they followed other gods from *among* the gods of the people who *were* all around them, and they bowed down to them; and they provoked the LORD to anger. [13]They forsook the LORD and served Baal and the Ashtoreths.*ᵃ* [14]And the anger of the LORD was hot against Israel. So He delivered them into the hands of plunderers who despoiled them; and He sold them into the hands of their enemies all around, so that they could no longer stand before their enemies. [15]Wherever they went out, the hand of the LORD was against them for calamity, as the LORD had said, and as the LORD had sworn to them. And they were greatly distressed.

[16]Nevertheless, the LORD raised up judges who delivered them out of the hand of those who plundered them. [17]Yet they would not listen to their judges, but they played the harlot with other gods, and bowed down to them. They turned quickly from the way in which their fathers walked, in obeying the commandments of the LORD; they did not do so. [18]And when the LORD raised up judges for them, the LORD was with the judge and delivered them out of the hand of their enemies all the days of the judge; for the LORD was moved to pity by their groaning because of those who oppressed them and harassed them. [19]And it came to pass, when the judge was dead, that they reverted and behaved more corruptly than their fathers, by following other gods, to serve them and bow down to them. They did not cease from their own doings nor from their stubborn way.

WHAT'S IT MEAN?

Judges were a lot more important in ancient Israel than they are today. Not only did they decide legal cases, they acted as military leaders. Judges were responsible for inspiring the Israelites when they didn't seem to care about God's plan, leading them into battle against the people who were oppressing them, and encouraging them to worship the Lord again.

Judges 2:16

[20]Then the anger of the LORD was hot against Israel; and He said, "Because this nation has transgressed My covenant which I commanded their fathers, and has not heeded My voice, [21]I also will no longer drive out before them any of the nations which Joshua left when he died, [22]so that through them I may test Israel, whether they will keep the ways of the LORD, to walk in them as their fathers kept *them,* or not." [23]Therefore the LORD left those nations, without driving them out immediately; nor did He deliver them into the hand of Joshua.

THE NATIONS REMAINING IN THE LAND

[1]Now these *are* the nations which the LORD left, that He might test Israel by them, *that is,* all who had not known any of the wars in Canaan [2](*this was* only so that the generations of the children of Israel might be taught to know war, at least those who had not formerly known it), [3]*namely,* five lords of the Philistines, all the Canaanites, the Sidonians, and the Hivites who dwelt in Mount Lebanon, from Mount Baal Hermon to the entrance of Hamath. [4]And they were *left, that He might* test Israel by them, to know whether they would obey the commandments of the LORD, which He had commanded their fathers by the hand of Moses.

[5]Thus the children of Israel dwelt among the Canaanites, the Hittites, the Amorites, the Perizzites, the Hivites, and the Jebusites. [6]And they took their daughters to be their wives, and gave their daughters to their sons; and they served their gods.

OTHNIEL

[7]So the children of Israel did evil in the sight of the LORD. They forgot the LORD their God, and served the Baals and Asherahs.*ᵃ* [8]Therefore the anger of the LORD was hot against Israel, and He sold them into the hand of Cushan-Rishathaim king of Mesopotamia; and the children of Israel served Cushan-Rishathaim eight years. [9]When the children of Israel cried out to the LORD, the LORD raised up a deliverer for the children of Israel, who delivered them: Othniel the son of Kenaz, Caleb's younger brother. [10]The Spirit of the LORD came upon him, and he judged Israel. He went out to war, and the LORD delivered Cushan-Rishathaim king of Mesopotamia into his hand; and his hand prevailed over Cushan-

GOD
What happens when we forget about God? (3:7)

HELP
Who should we call for help? (3:9)

2:13 *ᵃ*Canaanite goddesses　**3:7** *ᵃ*Name or symbol for Canaanite goddesses

Rishathaim. ¹¹So the land had rest for forty years. Then Othniel the son of Kenaz died.

EHUD

¹²And the children of Israel again did evil in the sight of the LORD. So the LORD strengthened Eglon king of Moab against Israel, because they had done evil in the sight of the LORD. ¹³Then he gathered to himself the people of Ammon and Amalek, went and defeated Israel, and took possession of the City of Palms. ¹⁴So the children of Israel served Eglon king of Moab eighteen years.

¹⁵But when the children of Israel cried out to the LORD, the LORD raised up a deliverer for them: Ehud the son of Gera, the Benjamite, a left-handed man. By him the children of Israel sent tribute to Eglon king of Moab. ¹⁶Now Ehud made himself a dagger (it was double-edged and a cubit in length) and fastened it under his clothes on his right thigh. ¹⁷So he brought the tribute to Eglon king of Moab. (Now Eglon *was* a very fat man.) ¹⁸And when he had finished presenting the tribute, he sent away the people who had carried the tribute. ¹⁹But he himself turned back from the stone images that *were* at Gilgal, and said, "I have a secret message for you, O king."

WHAT'S IT MEAN?

King Eglon was from Moab, across the Jordan River from Jericho. He used Joshua's old strategy for conquering Israel, crossing the Jordan from the east to attack and capture Jericho. Think of Gilgal as a suburb of Jericho. It was located about a mile and a half outside the city.

Judges 3:17–20

He said, "Keep silence!" And all who attended him went out from him.

²⁰So Ehud came to him (now he was sitting upstairs in his cool private chamber). Then Ehud said, "I have a message from God for you." So he arose from *his* seat. ²¹Then Ehud reached with his left hand, took the dagger from his right thigh, and thrust it into his belly. ²²Even the hilt went in after the blade, and the fat closed over the blade, for he did not draw the dagger out of his belly; and his entrails came out. ²³Then Ehud went out through the porch and shut the doors of the upper room behind him and locked them.

²⁴When he had gone out, *Eglon's*ᵃ servants came to look, and *to their* surprise, the doors of the upper room were locked. So they said, "He is probably attending to his needs in the cool chamber." ²⁵So they waited till they were embarrassed, and still he had not opened the doors of the upper room. Therefore they took the key and opened *them*. And there was their master, fallen dead on the floor.

²⁶But Ehud had escaped while they delayed, and passed beyond the stone images and escaped to Seirah. ²⁷And it happened, when he arrived, that he blew the trumpet in the mountains of Ephraim, and the children of Israel went down with him from the mountains; and he led them. ²⁸Then he said to them, "Follow *me*, for the LORD has delivered your enemies the Moabites into your hand." So they went down after him, seized the fords of the Jordan leading to Moab, and did not allow anyone to cross over. ²⁹And at that time they killed about ten thousand men of Moab, all stout men of valor; not a man escaped. ³⁰So Moab was subdued that day under the hand of Israel. And the land had rest for eighty years.

SHAMGAR

³¹After him was Shamgar the son of Anath, who killed six hundred men of the Philistines with an ox goad; and he also delivered Israel.

DEBORAH

¹When Ehud was dead, the children of Israel again did evil in the sight of the LORD. ²So the LORD sold them into the hand of Jabin king of Canaan, who reigned in Hazor. The commander of his army *was* Sisera, who dwelt in Harosheth Hagoyim. ³And the children of Israel cried out to the LORD; for Jabin had nine hundred chariots of iron, and for twenty years he had harshly oppressed the children of Israel.

⁴Now Deborah, a prophetess, the wife of Lapidoth, was judging Israel at that time. ⁵And she would sit under the palm tree of Deborah between Ramah and Bethel in the mountains of Ephraim. And the children of Israel came up to her for judgment. ⁶Then she sent and called for Barak the son of Abinoam from Kedesh in Naphtali, and said to him, "Has not the LORD

3:24 ᵃLiterally *his*

God of Israel commanded, 'Go and deploy *troops* at Mount Tabor; take with you ten thousand men of the sons of Naphtali and of the sons of Zebulun; ⁷and against you I will deploy Sisera, the commander of Jabin's army, with his chariots and his multitude at the River Kishon; and I will deliver him into your hand'?"

⁸And Barak said to her, "If you will go with me, then I will go; but if you will not go with me, I will not go!"

⁹So she said, "I will surely go with you; nevertheless there will be no glory for you in the journey you are taking, for the LORD will sell Sisera into the hand of a woman." Then Deborah arose and went with Barak to Kedesh. ¹⁰And Barak called Zebulun and Naphtali to Kedesh; he went up with ten thousand men under his command,ᵃ and Deborah went up with him.

¹¹Now Heber the Kenite, of the children of Hobab the father-in-law of Moses, had separated himself from the Kenites and pitched his tent near the terebinth tree at Zaanaim, which *is* beside Kedesh.

¹²And they reported to Sisera that Barak the son of Abinoam had gone up to Mount Tabor. ¹³So Sisera gathered together all his chariots, nine hundred chariots of iron, and all the people who *were* with him, from Harosheth Hagoyim to the River Kishon.

¹⁴Then Deborah said to Barak, "Up! For this *is* the day in which the LORD has delivered Sisera into your hand. Has not the LORD gone out before you?" So Barak went down from Mount Tabor with ten thousand men following him. ¹⁵And the LORD routed Sisera and all *his* chariots and all *his* army with the edge of the sword before Barak; and Sisera alighted from *his* chariot and fled away on foot. ¹⁶But Barak pursued the chariots and the army as far as Harosheth Hagoyim, and all the army of Sisera fell by the edge of the sword; not a man was left.

¹⁷However, Sisera had fled away on foot to the tent of Jael, the wife of Heber the Kenite; for *there was* peace between Jabin king of Hazor and the house of Heber the Kenite. ¹⁸And Jael went out to meet Sisera, and said to him, "Turn aside, my lord, turn aside to me; do not fear." And when he had turned aside with her into the tent, she covered him with a blanket.

¹⁹Then he said to her, "Please give me a little water to drink, for I am thirsty." So she opened a jug of milk, gave him a drink, and covered him. ²⁰And he said to her, "Stand at the door of the tent, and if any man comes and inquires of you,

and says, 'Is there any man here?' you shall say, 'No.'"

²¹Then Jael, Heber's wife, took a tent peg and took a hammer in her hand, and went softly to him and drove the peg into his temple, and it went down into the ground; for he was fast asleep and weary. So he died. ²²And then, as Barak pursued Sisera, Jael came out to meet him, and said to him, "Come, I will show you the man whom you seek." And when he went into her *tent*, there lay Sisera, dead with the peg in his temple.

²³So on that day God subdued Jabin king of Canaan in the presence of the children of Israel. ²⁴And the hand of the children of Israel grew stronger and stronger against Jabin king of Canaan, until they had destroyed Jabin king of Canaan.

THE SONG OF DEBORAH

¹Then Deborah and Barak the son of Abinoam sang on that day, saying:

2 "When leaders lead in Israel,
   When the people willingly offer
      themselves,
   Bless the LORD!

3 "Hear, O kings! Give ear,
      O princes!
   I, *even* I, will sing to the
      LORD;
   I will sing praise to the
      LORD God of Israel.

4 "LORD, when You went out
      from Seir,
   When You marched from the field of
      Edom,
   The earth trembled and the heavens
      poured,
   The clouds also poured water;
5 The mountains gushed before the LORD,
   This Sinai, before the LORD God of Israel.

6 "In the days of Shamgar, son of Anath,
   In the days of Jael,
   The highways were deserted,
   And the travelers walked along the
      byways.
7 Village life ceased, it ceased in Israel,
   Until I, Deborah, arose,
   Arose a mother in Israel.
8 They chose new gods;
   Then *there was* war in the gates;

WORSHIP
Who should we worship? (5:3)

4:10 ᵃLiterally *at his feet*

Not a shield or spear was seen among
   forty thousand in Israel.
9 My heart *is* with the rulers of Israel
   Who offered themselves willingly with the
     people.
   Bless the LORD!

WHAT'S IT MEAN?

Conditions in Israel were terrible at this
time. As if the outrageous taxes and evil foreign
rulers weren't enough, the crime rate was so bad that
it was impossible to live a normal life.

Judges 5:6

10 "Speak, you who ride on white donkeys,
   Who sit in judges' attire,
   And who walk along the road.
11 Far from the noise of the archers, among
    the watering places,
   There they shall recount the righteous
    acts of the LORD,
   The righteous acts *for* His villagers in
    Israel;
   Then the people of the LORD shall go
    down to the gates.

12 "Awake, awake, Deborah!
   Awake, awake, sing a song!
   Arise, Barak, and lead your captives away,
   O son of Abinoam!

13 "Then the survivors came down, the
    people against the nobles;
   The LORD came down for me against the
    mighty.
14 From Ephraim *were* those whose roots
    were in Amalek.
   After you, Benjamin, with your peoples,
   From Machir rulers came down,
   And from Zebulun those who bear the
    recruiter's staff.
15 And the princes of Issachar*a were* with
    Deborah;
   As Issachar, so *was* Barak

Sent into the valley under his command;*b*
Among the divisions of Reuben
There were great resolves of heart.
16 Why did you sit among the sheepfolds,
   To hear the pipings for the flocks?
   The divisions of Reuben have great
    searchings of heart.
17 Gilead stayed beyond the Jordan,
   And why did Dan remain on ships?*a*
   Asher continued at the seashore,
   And stayed by his inlets.
18 Zebulun *is* a people *who* jeopardized their
    lives to the point of death,
   Naphtali also, on the heights of the
    battlefield.

19 "The kings came *and* fought,
   Then the kings of Canaan fought
   In Taanach, by the waters of Megiddo;
   They took no spoils of silver.
20 They fought from the heavens;
   The stars from their courses fought
    against Sisera.
21 The torrent of Kishon swept them away,
   That ancient torrent, the torrent of
    Kishon.
   O my soul, march on in strength!
22 Then the horses' hooves pounded,
   The galloping, galloping of his steeds.
23 'Curse Meroz,' said the angel*a* of the LORD,
   'Curse its inhabitants bitterly,
   Because they did not come to the help of
    the LORD,
   To the help of the LORD against the
    mighty.'

24 "Most blessed among women is Jael,
   The wife of Heber the Kenite;
   Blessed is she among women in tents.
25 He asked for water, she gave milk;
   She brought out cream in a lordly bowl.
26 She stretched her hand to the tent peg,
   Her right hand to the workmen's
    hammer;
   She pounded Sisera, she pierced his head,
   She split and struck through his temple.
27 At her feet he sank, he fell, he lay still;
   At her feet he sank, he fell;
   Where he sank, there he fell dead.

28 "The mother of Sisera looked through the
    window,
   And cried out through the lattice,
   'Why is his chariot so long in coming?

5:15 *a*Following Septuagint, Syriac, Targum, and Vulgate; Masoretic Text reads *And my princes in Issachar.*
*b*Literally *at his feet*   **5:17** *a*Or *at ease*   **5:23** *a*Or *Angel*

Why tarries the clatter of his chariots?"
29 Her wisest ladies answered her,
Yes, she answered herself,
30 'Are they not finding and dividing the
spoil:
To every man a girl *or* two;
For Sisera, plunder of dyed garments,
Plunder of garments embroidered and
dyed,
Two pieces of dyed embroidery for the
neck of the looter?'

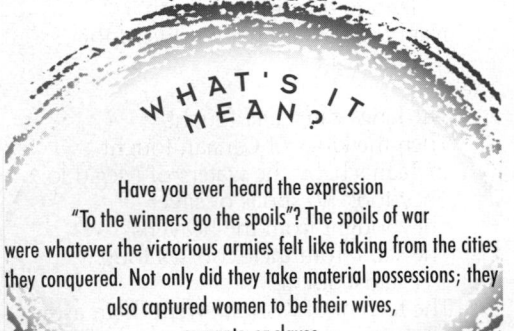

WHAT'S IT MEAN?

Have you ever heard the expression
"To the winners go the spoils"? The spoils of war
were whatever the victorious armies felt like taking from the cities
they conquered. Not only did they take material possessions; they
also captured women to be their wives,
servants, or slaves.
Judges 5:30

31 "Thus let all Your enemies perish, O LORD!
But *let* those who love Him *be* like the sun
When it comes out in full strength."

FOLLOWING GOD

What are
Christians like?
(5:31)

So the land had rest for
forty years.

MIDIANITES OPPRESS ISRAEL

1 Then the children of Israel
did evil in the sight of the
LORD. So the LORD delivered them
into the hand of Midian for seven years, 2and
the hand of Midian prevailed against Israel.
Because of the Midianites, the children of Israel
made for themselves the dens, the caves, and

DECISIONS

Do bad
decisions have
consequences?
(6:1)

the strongholds which *are* in
the mountains. 3So it was,
whenever Israel had sown,
Midianites would come up;
also Amalekites and the people
of the East would come up
against them. 4Then they
would encamp against them and destroy the
produce of the earth as far as Gaza, and leave
no sustenance for Israel, neither sheep nor ox

nor donkey. 5For they would come up with
their livestock and their tents, coming in as numerous as locusts; both they and their camels
were without number; and they would enter
the land to destroy it. 6So Israel was greatly impoverished because of the Midianites, and the
children of Israel cried out to the LORD.

7And it came to pass, when the children of
Israel cried out to the LORD because of the Midianites, 8that the LORD sent a prophet to the
children of Israel, who said to them, "Thus says
the LORD God of Israel: 'I brought you up from
Egypt and brought you out of the house of
bondage; 9and I delivered you out of the hand
of the Egyptians and out of the hand of all who
oppressed you, and drove them out before you
and gave you their land. 10Also I said to you, "I
am the LORD your God; do not fear the gods of
the Amorites, in whose land you dwell." But you
have not obeyed My voice.' "

GIDEON

11Now the Angel of the LORD came and sat
under the terebinth tree which *was* in Ophrah,
which *belonged* to Joash the Abiezrite, while his
son Gideon threshed wheat in the winepress, in
order to hide *it* from the Midianites. 12And the
Angel of the LORD appeared to him, and said to
him, "The LORD *is* with you, you mighty man of
valor!"

13Gideon said to Him, "O my lord,*a* if the
LORD is with us, why then has all this happened
to us? And where *are* all His miracles which our
fathers told us about, saying, 'Did not the LORD
bring us up from Egypt?' But now the LORD has
forsaken us and delivered us into the hands of
the Midianites."

14Then the LORD turned to him and said, "Go
in this might of yours, and you shall save Israel
from the hand of the Midianites. Have I not
sent you?"

15So he said to Him, "O my Lord,*a* how can I
save Israel? Indeed my clan *is* the weakest in
Manasseh, and I *am* the least in my father's
house."

16And the LORD said to him, "Surely I will be
with you, and you shall defeat the Midianites as
one man."

17Then he said to Him, "If now I have found
favor in Your sight, then show me a sign that it
is You who talk with me. 18Do not depart from
here, I pray, until I come to You and bring out
my offering and set *it* before You."

And He said, "I will wait until you come
back."

6:13 *a*Hebrew *adoni,* used of man   **6:15** *a*Hebrew *Adonai,* used of God

¹⁹So Gideon went in and prepared a young goat, and unleavened bread from an ephah of flour. The meat he put in a basket, and he put the broth in a pot; and he brought *them* out to Him under the terebinth tree and presented *them*. ²⁰The Angel of God said to him, "Take the meat and the unleavened bread and lay *them* on this rock, and pour out the broth." And he did so.

²¹Then the Angel of the LORD put out the end of the staff that *was* in His hand, and touched the meat and the unleavened bread; and fire rose out of the rock and consumed the meat and the unleavened bread. And the Angel of the LORD departed out of his sight.

²²Now Gideon perceived that He *was* the Angel of the LORD. So Gideon said, "Alas, O Lord GOD! For I have seen the Angel of the LORD face to face."

²³Then the LORD said to him, "Peace *be* with you; do not fear, you shall not die." ²⁴So Gideon built an altar there to the LORD, and called it The-LORD-Is-Peace.ᵃ To this day *it is* still in Ophrah of the Abiezrites.

WHAT'S IT MEAN?

The wooden images were probably idols made of carved wood, used to mark Canaanite places of worship. Most of the time these images were associated with Asherah, the goddess of fertility and the wife of Baal.

Judges 6:25

²⁵Now it came to pass the same night that the LORD said to him, "Take your father's young bull, the second bull of seven years old, and tear down the altar of Baal that your father has, and cut down the wooden imageᵃ that *is* beside it; ²⁶and build an altar to the LORD your God on top of this rock in the proper arrangement, and take the second bull and offer a burnt sacrifice with the wood of the image which you shall cut down." ²⁷So Gideon took ten men from among his servants and did as the LORD had said to

him. But because he feared his father's household and the men of the city too much to do *it* by day, he did *it* by night.

GIDEON DESTROYS THE ALTAR OF BAAL

²⁸And when the men of the city arose early in the morning, there was the altar of Baal, torn down; and the wooden image that *was* beside it was cut down, and the second bull was being offered on the altar *which had been* built. ²⁹So they said to one another, "Who has done this thing?" And when they had inquired and asked, they said, "Gideon the son of Joash has done this thing." ³⁰Then the men of the city said to Joash, "Bring out your son, that he may die, because he has torn down the altar of Baal, and because he has cut down the wooden image that *was* beside it."

³¹But Joash said to all who stood against him, "Would you plead for Baal? Would you save him? Let the one who would plead for him be put to death by morning! If he *is* a god, let him plead for himself, because his altar has been torn down!" ³²Therefore on that day he called him Jerubbaal,ᵃ saying, "Let Baal plead against him, because he has torn down his altar."

³³Then all the Midianites and Amalekites, the people of the East, gathered together; and they crossed over and encamped in the Valley of Jezreel. ³⁴But the Spirit of the LORD came upon Gideon; then he blew the trumpet, and the Abiezrites gathered behind him. ³⁵And he sent messengers throughout all Manasseh, who also gathered behind him. He also sent messengers to Asher, Zebulun, and Naphtali; and they came up to meet them.

THE SIGN OF THE FLEECE

³⁶So Gideon said to God, "If You will save Israel by my hand as You have said—³⁷look, I shall put a fleece of wool on the threshing floor; if there is dew on the fleece only, and *it is* dry on all the ground, then I shall know that You will save Israel by my hand, as You have said." ³⁸And it was so. When he rose early the next morning and squeezed the fleece together, he wrung the dew out of the fleece, a bowlful of water. ³⁹Then Gideon said to God, "Do not be angry with me, but let me speak just once more: Let me test, I pray, just once more with the

"Alas, O Lord God! For I have seen the Angel of the LORD face to face." (Judges 6:22b)

6:24 ᵃHebrew *YHWH Shalom*   **6:25** ᵃHebrew *Asherah*, a Canaanite goddess   **6:32** ᵃLiterally *Let Baal Plead*

On the Edge

But the Spirit of the LORD came upon Gideon; then he blew the trumpet, and the Abiezrites gathered behind him (Judg. 6:34).

In this passage, the Holy Spirit "came upon Gideon," giving him the divine power he needed to carry out God's plan. The assignment was big—rescue Israel. It required one faithful man and supernatural help from the Holy Spirit. One man plus God is mightier than any army and stronger than any opposition. If God is calling you for a big job, you can bet that He will also send the power of the Holy Spirit. You won't be alone. God goes before you to clear the way for you, and He sends the Holy Spirit to take control of the situation—and of you. You'll know what to do. You'll know what to say. You can run to the battle with the total confidence that the Spirit of God is in control.

SEE FOR YOURSELF:
Judg. 14:19;
1 Sam. 10:6;
Ezek. 2:2

fleece; let it now be dry only on the fleece, but on all the ground let there be dew." ⁴⁰And God did so that night. It was dry on the fleece only, but there was dew on all the ground.

GIDEON'S VALIANT THREE HUNDRED

¹Then Jerubbaal (that *is,* Gideon) and all the people who *were* with him rose early and encamped beside the well of Harod, so that the camp of the Midianites was on the north side of them by the hill of Moreh in the valley.

²And the LORD said to Gideon, "The people who *are* with you *are* too many for Me to give the Midianites into their hands, lest Israel claim glory for itself against Me, saying, 'My own hand has saved me'. ³Now therefore, proclaim in the hearing of the people, saying, 'Whoever *is* fearful and afraid, let him turn and depart at once from Mount Gilead.' " And twenty-two thousand of

the people returned, and ten thousand remained.

⁴But the LORD said to Gideon, "The people *are* still *too* many; bring them down to the water, and I will test them for you there. Then it will be, *that* of whom I say to you, 'This one shall go with you,' the same shall go with you; and of whomever I say to you, 'This one shall not go with you,' the same shall not go." ⁵So he brought the people down to the water. And the LORD said to Gideon, "Everyone who laps from the water with his tongue, as a dog laps, you shall set apart by himself; likewise everyone who gets down on his knees to drink." ⁶And the number of those who lapped, *putting* their hand to their mouth, was three hundred men; but all the rest of the people got down on their knees to drink water. ⁷Then the LORD said to Gideon, "By the three hundred men who lapped I will save you, and deliver the Midianites into your hand. Let all the *other* people go, every man to his place." ⁸So the people took provisions and their trumpets in their hands. And he sent away all *the rest of* Israel, every man to his tent, and retained those three hundred men. Now the camp of Midian was below him in the valley.

⁹It happened on the same night that the LORD said to him, "Arise, go down against the camp, for I have delivered it into your hand. ¹⁰But if you are afraid to go down, go down to the camp with Purah your servant, ¹¹and you shall hear what they say; and afterward your hands shall be strengthened to go down against the camp." Then he went down with Purah his servant to the outpost of the armed men who *were* in the camp. ¹²Now the Midianites and Amalekites, all the people of the East, were lying in the valley as numerous as locusts; and their camels *were* without number, as the sand by the seashore in multitude.

¹³And when Gideon had come, there was a man telling a dream to his companion. He said, "I have had a dream: *To my* surprise, a loaf of barley bread tumbled into the camp of Midian; it came to a tent and struck it so that it fell and overturned, and the tent collapsed."

¹⁴Then his companion answered and said, "This *is* nothing else but the sword of Gideon the son of Joash, a man of Israel! Into his hand God has delivered Midian and the whole camp."

¹⁵And so it was, when Gideon heard the tell-

"Arise, for the LORD has delivered the camp of Midian into your hand." (Judges 7:15b)

WHAT'S IT MEAN?

In ancient times, God spoke to people through their dreams, revealing His plans for them while they slept. Not all of these dreams made obvious sense at first. Sometimes the dreamers needed other people to help them understand what their nighttime visions meant.

Judges 7:13

ing of the dream and its interpretation, that he worshiped. He returned to the camp of Israel, and said, "Arise, for the LORD has delivered the camp of Midian into your hand." ¹⁶Then he divided the three hundred men *into* three companies, and he put a trumpet into every man's hand, with empty pitchers, and torches inside the pitchers. ¹⁷And he said to them, "Look at me and do likewise; watch, and when I come to the edge of the camp you shall do as I do: ¹⁸When I blow the trumpet, I and all who *are* with me, then you also blow the trumpets on every side of the whole camp, and say, '*The sword of* the LORD and of Gideon!'"

¹⁹So Gideon and the hundred men who *were* with him came to the outpost of the camp at the beginning of the middle watch, just as they had posted the watch; and they blew the trumpets and broke the pitchers that *were* in their hands. ²⁰Then the three companies blew the trumpets and broke the pitchers—they held the torches in their left hands and the trumpets in their right hands for blowing—and they cried, "The sword of the LORD and of Gideon!" ²¹And every man stood in his place all around the camp; and the whole army ran and cried out and fled. ²²When the three hundred blew the trumpets, the LORD set every man's sword against his companion throughout the whole camp; and the army fled to Beth Acacia,ᵃ toward Zererah, as far as the border of Abel Meholah, by Tabbath.

²³And the men of Israel gathered together from Naphtali, Asher, and all Manasseh, and pursued the Midianites.

²⁴Then Gideon sent messengers throughout all the mountains of Ephraim, saying, "Come

down against the Midianites, and seize from them the watering places as far as Beth Barah and the Jordan." Then all the men of Ephraim gathered together and seized the watering places as far as Beth Barah and the Jordan. ²⁵And they captured two princes of the Midianites, Oreb and Zeeb. They killed Oreb at the rock of Oreb, and Zeeb they killed at the winepress of Zeeb. They pursued Midian and brought the heads of Oreb and Zeeb to Gideon on the other side of the Jordan.

WHAT'S IT MEAN?

A winepress was a place where ripe grapes were stomped for their juice. When that juice "fermented" for a certain period of time, it became wine. Not only was wine a common drink among the Israelites, it was also used as medicine and as part of their religious ceremonies.

Judges 7:25

GIDEON SUBDUES THE MIDIANITES

¹Now the men of Ephraim said to him, "Why have you done this to us by not calling us when you went to fight with the Midianites?" And they reprimanded him sharply.

²So he said to them, "What have I done now in comparison with you? *Is* not the gleaning *of the grapes* of Ephraim better than the vintage of Abiezer? ³God has delivered into your hands the princes of Midian, Oreb and Zeeb. And what was I able to do in comparison with you?" Then their anger toward him subsided when he said that.

⁴When Gideon came to the Jordan, he and the three hundred men who *were* with him crossed over, exhausted but still in pursuit. ⁵Then he said to the men of Succoth, "Please give loaves of bread to the people who follow me, for they are exhausted, and I am pursuing Zebah and Zalmunna, kings of Midian."

⁶And the leaders of Succoth said, "*Are* the hands of Zebah and Zalmunna now in your hand, that we should give bread to your army?"

⁷So Gideon said, "For this cause, when the LORD has delivered Zebah and Zalmunna into

my hand, then I will tear your flesh with the thorns of the wilderness and with briers!" ⁸Then he went up from there to Penuel and spoke to them in the same way. And the men of Penuel answered him as the men of Succoth had answered. ⁹So he also spoke to the men of Penuel, saying, "When I come back in peace, I will tear down this tower!"

¹⁰Now Zebah and Zalmunna *were* at Karkor, and their armies with them, about fifteen thousand, all who were left of all the army of the people of the East; for one hundred and twenty thousand men who drew the sword had fallen. ¹¹Then Gideon went up by the road of those who dwell in tents on the east of Nobah and Jogbehah; and he attacked the army while the camp felt secure. ¹²When Zebah and Zalmunna fled, he pursued them; and he took the two kings of Midian, Zebah and Zalmunna, and routed the whole army.

¹³Then Gideon the son of Joash returned from battle, from the Ascent of Heres. ¹⁴And he caught a young man of the men of Succoth and interrogated him; and he wrote down for him the leaders of Succoth and its elders, seventy-seven men. ¹⁵Then he came to the men of Succoth and said, "Here are Zebah and Zalmunna, about whom you ridiculed me, saying, '*Are the hands of Zebah and Zalmunna now in your hand, that we should give bread to your weary men?*' " ¹⁶And he took the elders of the city, and thorns of the wilderness and briers, and with them he taught the men of Succoth. ¹⁷Then he tore down the tower of Penuel and killed the men of the city.

¹⁸And he said to Zebah and Zalmunna, "What kind of men *were they* whom you killed at Tabor?"

So they answered, "As you *are*, so *were* they; each one resembled the son of a king."

¹⁹Then he said, "They *were* my brothers, the sons of my mother. *As* the LORD lives, if you had let them live, I would not kill you." ²⁰And he said to Jether his firstborn, "Rise, kill them!" But the youth would not draw his sword; for he was afraid, because he *was* still a youth.

²¹So Zebah and Zalmunna said, "Rise yourself, and kill us; for as a man *is, so is* his strength." So Gideon arose and killed Zebah and Zalmunna, and took the crescent ornaments that *were* on their camels' necks.

GIDEON'S EPHOD

²²Then the men of Israel said to Gideon, "Rule over us, both you and your son, and your grandson also; for you have delivered us from the hand of Midian."

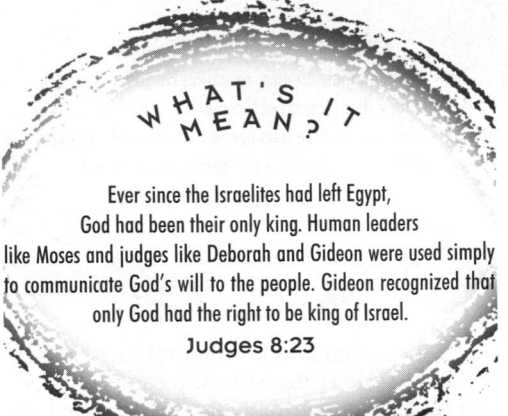

WHAT'S IT MEAN?

Ever since the Israelites had left Egypt, God had been their only king. Human leaders like Moses and judges like Deborah and Gideon were used simply to communicate God's will to the people. Gideon recognized that only God had the right to be king of Israel.

Judges 8:23

²³But Gideon said to them, "I will not rule over you, nor shall my son rule over you; the LORD shall rule over you." ²⁴Then Gideon said to them, "I would like to make a request of you, that each of you would give me the earrings from his plunder." For they had golden earrings, because they *were* Ishmaelites.

²⁵So they answered, "We will gladly give *them*." And they spread out a garment, and each man threw into it the earrings from his plunder. ²⁶Now the weight of the gold earrings that he requested was one thousand seven hundred *shekels* of gold, besides the crescent ornaments, pendants, and purple robes which *were* on the kings of Midian, and besides the chains that *were* around their camels' necks.

²⁷Then Gideon made it into an ephod and set it up in his city, Ophrah. And all Israel played the harlot with it there. It became a snare to Gideon and to his house.

²⁸Thus Midian was subdued before the children of Israel, so that they lifted their heads no more. And the country was quiet for forty years in the days of Gideon.

> "But Gideon said to them, 'I will not rule over you, nor shall my son rule over you; the LORD shall rule over you.' "
> (Judges 8:23)

DEATH OF GIDEON

²⁹Then Jerubbaal the son of Joash went and dwelt in his own house. ³⁰Gideon had seventy sons who were his own offspring, for he had many wives. ³¹And his concubine who *was* in

Shechem also bore him a son, whose name he called Abimelech. [32]Now Gideon the son of Joash died at a good old age, and was buried in the tomb of Joash his father, in Ophrah of the Abiezrites.

[33]So it was, as soon as Gideon was dead, that the children of Israel again played the harlot with the Baals, and made Baal-Berith their god. [34]Thus the children of Israel did not remember the LORD their God, who had delivered them from the hands of all their enemies on every side; [35]nor did they show kindness to the house of Jerubbaal (Gideon) in accordance with the good he had done for Israel.

ABIMELECH'S CONSPIRACY

[1]Then Abimelech the son of Jerubbaal went to Shechem, to his mother's brothers, and spoke with them and with all the family of the house of his mother's father, saying, [2]"Please speak in the hearing of all the men of Shechem: 'Which is better for you, that all seventy of the sons of Jerubbaal reign over you, or that one reign over you?' Remember that I am your own flesh and bone."

Not only were temples used as places of worship in ancient cultures, they were also used as vaults, places to store valuables for safekeeping. Using money from Baal-Berith's temple made it look as though Abimelech was getting help from Baal and not just from his human supporters.
Judges 9:4

[3]And his mother's brothers spoke all these words concerning him in the hearing of all the men of Shechem; and their heart was inclined to follow Abimelech, for they said, "He is our brother." [4]So they gave him seventy shekels of silver from the temple of Baal-Berith, with which Abimelech hired worthless and reckless men; and they followed him. [5]Then he went to his father's house at Ophrah and killed his brothers, the seventy sons of Jerubbaal, on one stone. But Jotham the youngest son of Jerubbaal was left, because he hid himself. [6]And all the men of Shechem gathered together, all of Beth Millo, and they went and made Abimelech

king beside the terebinth tree at the pillar that was in Shechem.

THE PARABLE OF THE TREES

[7]Now when they told Jotham, he went and stood on top of Mount Gerizim, and lifted his voice and cried out. And he said to them:

"Listen to me, you men of Shechem,
That God may listen to you!

[8] "The trees once went forth to anoint a king over them.
And they said to the olive tree,
'Reign over us!'
[9] But the olive tree said to them,
'Should I cease giving my oil,
With which they honor God and men,
And go to sway over trees?'

[10] "Then the trees said to the fig tree,
'You come and reign over us!'
[11] But the fig tree said to them,
'Should I cease my sweetness and my good fruit,
And go to sway over trees?'

[12] "Then the trees said to the vine,
'You come and reign over us!'
[13] But the vine said to them,
'Should I cease my new wine,
Which cheers both God and men,
And go to sway over trees?'

[14] "Then all the trees said to the bramble,
'You come and reign over us!'
[15] And the bramble said to the trees,
'If in truth you anoint me as king over you,

Jotham compared Abimelech to a bramble, a tree that was practically worthless to people. Jotham warned that Abimelech was powerless to protect the people and that making him king would only lead to disaster.
Judges 9:15

Then come *and* take shelter in my shade;
But if not, let fire come out of the
   bramble
And devour the cedars of Lebanon!'

¹⁶"Now therefore, if you have acted in truth and sincerity in making Abimelech king, and if you have dealt well with Jerubbaal and his house, and have done to him as he deserves— ¹⁷for my father fought for you, risked his life, and delivered you out of the hand of Midian; ¹⁸but you have risen up against my father's house this day, and killed his seventy sons on one stone, and made Abimelech, the son of his female servant, king over the men of Shechem, because he is your brother—¹⁹if then you have acted in truth and sincerity with Jerubbaal and with his house this day, *then* rejoice in Abimelech, and let him also rejoice in you. ²⁰But if not, let fire come from Abimelech and devour the men of Shechem and Beth Millo; and let fire come from the men of Shechem and from Beth Millo and devour Abimelech!" ²¹And Jotham ran away and fled; and he went to Beer and dwelt there, for fear of Abimelech his brother.

DOWNFALL OF ABIMELECH

²²After Abimelech had reigned over Israel three years, ²³God sent a spirit of ill will between Abimelech and the men of Shechem; and the men of Shechem dealt treacherously with Abimelech, ²⁴that the crime *done* to the seventy sons of Jerubbaal might be settled and their blood be laid on Abimelech their brother, who killed them, and on the men of Shechem, who aided him in the killing of his brothers. ²⁵And the men of Shechem set men in ambush against him on the tops of the mountains, and they robbed all who passed by them along that way; and it was told Abimelech.

²⁶Now Gaal the son of Ebed came with his brothers and went over to Shechem; and the men of Shechem put their confidence in him. ²⁷So they went out into the fields, and gathered *grapes* from their vineyards and trod *them,* and made merry. And they went into the house of their god, and ate and drank, and cursed Abimelech. ²⁸Then Gaal the son of Ebed said, "Who *is* Abimelech, and who *is* Shechem, that we should serve him? *Is he* not the son of Jerubbaal, and *is not* Zebul his officer? Serve the men of Hamor the father of Shechem; but why should we serve him? ²⁹If only this people were under my authority!ᵃ Then I would remove Abimelech." So heᵇ said to Abimelech, "Increase your army and come out!"

³⁰When Zebul, the ruler of the city, heard the words of Gaal the son of Ebed, his anger was aroused. ³¹And he sent messengers to Abimelech secretly, saying, "Take note! Gaal the son of Ebed and his brothers have come to Shechem; and here they are, fortifying the city against you. ³²Now therefore, get up by night, you and the people who *are* with you, and lie in wait in the field. ³³And it shall be, as soon as the sun is up in the morning, *that* you shall rise early and rush upon the city; and *when* he and the people who are with him come out against you, you may then do to them as you find opportunity."

³⁴So Abimelech and all the people who *were* with him rose by night, and lay in wait against Shechem in four companies. ³⁵When Gaal the son of Ebed went out and stood in the entrance to the city gate, Abimelech and the people who *were* with him rose from lying in wait. ³⁶And when Gaal saw the people, he said to Zebul, "Look, people are coming down from the tops of the mountains!"

But Zebul said to him, "You see the shadows of the mountains as *if they were* men."

³⁷So Gaal spoke again and said, "See, people are coming down from the center of the land, and another company is coming from the Diviners'ᵃ Terebinth Tree."

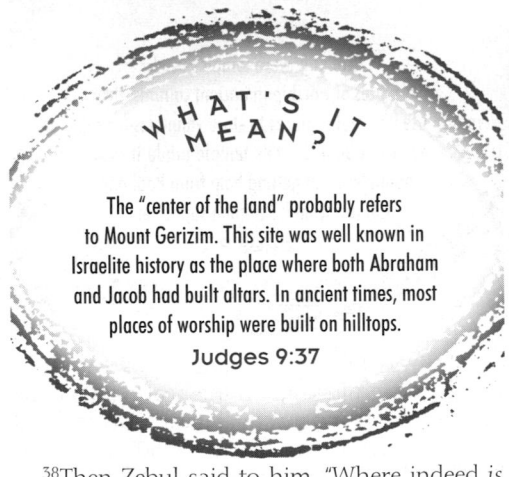

WHAT'S IT MEAN?

The "center of the land" probably refers to Mount Gerizim. This site was well known in Israelite history as the place where both Abraham and Jacob had built altars. In ancient times, most places of worship were built on hilltops.

Judges 9:37

³⁸Then Zebul said to him, "Where indeed *is* your mouth now, with which you said, 'Who *is* Abimelech, that we should serve him?' *Are* not these the people whom you despised? Go out, if you will, and fight with them now."

³⁹So Gaal went out, leading the men of Shechem, and fought with Abimelech. ⁴⁰And

9:29 ᵃLiterally *hand* ᵇFollowing Masoretic Text and Targum; Dead Sea Scrolls read *they*; Septuagint reads *I.* **9:37** ᵃHebrew *Meonenim*

Abimelech chased him, and he fled from him; and many fell wounded, to the *very* entrance of the gate. ⁴¹Then Abimelech dwelt at Arumah, and Zebul drove out Gaal and his brothers, so that they would not dwell in Shechem.

⁴²And it came about on the next day that the people went out into the field, and they told Abimelech. ⁴³So he took his people, divided them into three companies, and lay in wait in the field. And he looked, and there were the people, coming out of the city; and he rose against them and attacked them. ⁴⁴Then Abimelech and the company that *was* with him rushed forward and stood at the entrance of the gate of the city; and the *other* two companies rushed upon all who *were* in the fields and killed them. ⁴⁵So Abimelech fought against the city all that day; he took the city and killed the people who *were* in it; and he demolished the city and sowed it with salt.

WHAT'S IT MEAN?

Sowing salt was Abimelech's way of cursing the land and destroying its ability to produce crops.
Judges 9:45

⁴⁶Now when all the men of the tower of Shechem had heard *that*, they entered the stronghold of the temple of the god Berith. ⁴⁷And it was told Abimelech that all the men of the tower of Shechem were gathered together. ⁴⁸Then Abimelech went up to Mount Zalmon, he and all the people who *were* with him. And Abimelech took an ax in his hand and cut down a bough from the trees, and took it and laid *it* on his shoulder; then he said to the people who were with him, "What you have seen me do, make haste *and* do as I have done." ⁴⁹So each of the people likewise cut down his own bough and followed Abimelech, put *them* against the stronghold, and set the stronghold on fire above them, so that all the people of the tower of Shechem died, about a thousand men and women.

⁵⁰Then Abimelech went to Thebez, and he encamped against Thebez and took it. ⁵¹But there was a strong tower in the city, and all the men and women—all the people of the city—fled there and shut themselves in; then they went up to the top of the tower. ⁵²So Abimelech came as far as the tower and fought against it; and he drew near the door of the tower to burn it with fire. ⁵³But a certain woman dropped an upper millstone on Abimelech's head and crushed his skull. ⁵⁴Then he called quickly to the young man, his armorbearer, and said to him, "Draw your sword and kill me, lest men say of me, 'A woman killed him.'" So his young man thrust him through, and he died. ⁵⁵And when the men of Israel saw that Abimelech was dead, they departed, every man to his place.

⁵⁶Thus God repaid the wickedness of Abimelech, which he had done to his father by killing his seventy brothers. ⁵⁷And all the evil of the men of Shechem God returned on their own heads, and on them came the curse of Jotham the son of Jerubbaal.

TOLA

¹After Abimelech there arose to save Israel Tola the son of Puah, the son of Dodo, a man of Issachar; and he dwelt in Shamir in the mountains of Ephraim. ²He judged Israel twenty-three years; and he died and was buried in Shamir.

JAIR

³After him arose Jair, a Gileadite; and he judged Israel twenty-two years. ⁴Now he had thirty sons who rode on thirty donkeys; they also had thirty towns, which are called "Havoth Jair"*ᵃ* to this day, which *are* in the land of Gilead. ⁵And Jair died and was buried in Camon.

ISRAEL OPPRESSED AGAIN

⁶Then the children of Israel again did evil in the sight of the LORD, and served the Baals and the Ashtoreths, the gods of Syria, the gods of Sidon, the gods of Moab, the gods of the people of Ammon, and the gods of the Philistines; and they forsook the LORD and did not serve Him. ⁷So the anger of the LORD was hot against Israel; and He sold them into the hands of the Philistines and into the hands of the people of Ammon. ⁸From that year they harassed and oppressed the children of Israel for eighteen years—all the children of Israel who *were* on the other side of the Jordan in the land of the Amorites, in Gilead. ⁹Moreover the people of Ammon crossed over the Jordan to fight against Judah also, against Benjamin, and

10:4 *ᵃ*Literally *Towns of Jair* (compare Numbers 32:41 and Deuteronomy 3:14)

against the house of Ephraim, so that Israel was severely distressed.

¹⁰And the children of Israel cried out to the LORD, saying, "We have sinned against You, because we have both forsaken our God and served the Baals!"

¹¹So the LORD said to the children of Israel, "*Did I* not *deliver you* from the Egyptians and from the Amorites and from the people of Ammon and from the Philistines? ¹²Also the Sidonians and Amalekites and Maonites*ᵃ* oppressed you; and you cried out to Me, and I delivered you from their hand. ¹³Yet you have forsaken Me and served other gods. Therefore I will deliver you no more. ¹⁴Go and cry out to the gods which you have chosen; let them deliver you in your time of distress."

¹⁵And the children of Israel said to the LORD, "We have sinned! Do to us whatever seems best to You; only deliver us this day, we pray." ¹⁶So they put away the foreign gods from among them and served the LORD. And His soul could no longer endure the misery of Israel.

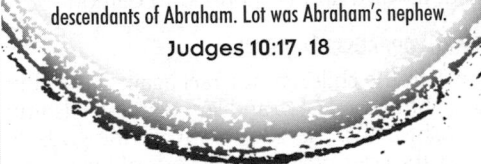

Both Gilead and Ammon were located on the east side of the Jordan River, across from Shechem. The Ammonites may have been distant relatives of the Israelites. The Ammonites were descendants of Lot. (Specifically, they were the result of Lot's drunken act of incest with his own daughter, but that's a different story.) The Israelites were descendants of Abraham. Lot was Abraham's nephew.

Judges 10:17, 18

¹⁷Then the people of Ammon gathered together and encamped in Gilead. And the children of Israel assembled together and encamped in Mizpah. ¹⁸And the people, the leaders of Gilead, said to one another, "Who *is* the man who will begin the fight against the people of Ammon? He shall be head over all the inhabitants of Gilead."

JEPHTHAH

¹Now Jephthah the Gileadite was a mighty man of valor, but he *was* the son of a harlot;

and Gilead begot Jephthah. ²Gilead's wife bore sons; and when his wife's sons grew up, they drove Jephthah out, and said to him, "You shall have no inheritance in our father's house, for you *are* the son of another woman." ³Then Jephthah fled from his brothers and dwelt in the land of Tob; and worthless men banded together with Jephthah and went out *raiding* with him.

⁴It came to pass after a time that the people of Ammon made war against Israel. ⁵And so it was, when the people of Ammon made war against Israel, that the elders of Gilead went to get Jephthah from the land of Tob. ⁶Then they said to Jephthah, "Come and be our commander, that we may fight against the people of Ammon."

⁷So Jephthah said to the elders of Gilead, "Did you not hate me, and expel me from my father's house? Why have you come to me now when you are in distress?"

⁸And the elders of Gilead said to Jephthah, "That is why we have turned again to you now, that you may go with us and fight against the people of Ammon, and be our head over all inhabitants of Gilead."

⁹So Jephthah said to the elders of Gilead, "If you take me back home to fight against the people of Ammon, and the LORD delivers them to me, shall I be your head?"

¹⁰And the elders of Gilead said to Jephthah, "The LORD will be a witness between us, if we do not do according to your words." ¹¹Then Jephthah went with the elders of Gilead, and the people made him head and commander over them; and Jephthah spoke all his words before the LORD in Mizpah.

¹²Now Jephthah sent messengers to the king of the people of Ammon, saying, "What do you have against me, that you have come to fight against me in my land?"

¹³And the king of the people of Ammon answered the messengers of Jephthah, "Because Israel took away my land when they came up out of Egypt, from the Arnon as far as the Jabbok, and to the Jordan. Now therefore, restore those *lands* peaceably."

¹⁴So Jephthah again sent messengers to the king of the people of Ammon, ¹⁵and said to him, "Thus says Jephthah: 'Israel did not take away the land of Moab, nor the land of the people of Ammon; ¹⁶for when Israel came up from Egypt, they walked through the wilderness as far as the Red Sea and came to Kadesh. ¹⁷Then Israel sent messengers to the king of

CALEB made a difference

Anyone making a list of people who have successfully resisted peer pressure would have to include Caleb. He served on a special twelve-man unit sent into the Promised Land by Moses to spy and bring back a report. When the unit returned, they had a unanimous report; but they were seriously divided in their recommendations. They all agreed that the land was fertile, wonderful, and settled by powerful peoples. Ten of the spies concluded the invasion should be called off immediately. The enemy was simply too powerful to defeat. Caleb offered a minority opinion:

Cutting Edge

> "Let us go up at once and take possession, for we are well able to overcome it" (Num. 13:30).

Short term, majorities often get their way. The people of Israel rejected Caleb and Joshua's confidence. They accepted the opinion of the ten. Then they discovered that God's plan included Caleb's perspective. The people's lack of trust led directly to forty years of wilderness wandering. Because he spoke the truth under intense pressure, Caleb was rewarded with one of only two permissions to enter the Promised Land given to his generation. From their peer group only Joshua and Caleb crossed the Jordan. The rest died in the desert.

Although they were right and were rewarded for their consistency, Caleb and Joshua shared forty years in the desert with everyone else. Even that disappointment didn't wear Caleb down. When he did receive his portion in the Promised Land (at age eighty-five!) he claimed to be fit, able, and trusting in God as he had been as a young man. **YOU can, too!**

One of the important lessons from Caleb's life has to do with the purpose of standing alone. You can probably think of several people in your life who are willing to stand alone for clothing styles, haircuts, and negative attitudes. Caleb's purpose wasn't to stand alone; it was to stand with God. Because Caleb wanted God's way, any other way didn't have much appeal to him.

Trusting in God and living for Him will create minority situations. Taking God seriously in your life will quickly show you where the majority stands. Like Caleb's, your words may not seem to make a difference to those around you. But God hears. And eventually you will find that standing with God does make a difference!

Want to know more? Read about Caleb's adventures and his faithful attitude in Numbers 13 and 14 and in Joshua 14 and 15.

GIDEON made a difference

You can learn a lot from watching kids. Some sit in their playpens and randomly handle the blocks and toys around them. Others immediately try to build a skyscraper. Those are the resourceful ones. They grow up to be natural problem solvers. Gideon was just such a kid. God made good use of Gideon's skills when He called the boy to be a judge of Israel.

The Jewish people lived under crushing oppression by the Midianites. God had allowed it because Israel had ignored their unique role as God's people. But they had been calling out to God for relief. Meanwhile, Gideon was busy providing food for his family by using a winepress to thresh his wheat ("in order to hide it from the Midianites"). This was a little like hiding a garden in a bathtub. It worked.

God called Gideon to lead the rebellion against Midian. But God used Gideon's creativity to emphasize who was behind the astounding victory. Gideon's band of three hundred—each armed with a clay pitcher, a torch, and a trumpet—routed an army of over one hundred and twenty thousand. God made a big difference! And Gideon had the wonderful honor of participating in God's plan.

Cutting Edge

YOU can, too! You may have some unusual skills, or you may be given an unusual opportunity to use what may seem like ordinary skills. Remember that God is behind the events of life. God gives us what we need and then invites us to use it in His service. When you consider and pray about what God might want to do in your life, remember this: God's plan will always include tasks that you will not be able to accomplish without His help. Making a difference isn't just about what you can do; it's even more about what God can do with you, in you, and through you!

Want to know more? Read about Gideon in (Judges 6—8.) He is also listed in the Hall of Faith (Hebrews 11:32.)

SAMSON made a difference

Samson never wore an *S* on his chest, but he was probably one of the few men who could claim the title of *superman*. His physical prowess astonished both friends and enemies. In battle, Samson proved lethal. There was little question that Samson had the basic qualifications to be a champion for his people. God had promised to give Samson unique gifts. He was designed with a special task in mind. Samson made a difference, all right, but far less than his potential promised.

Unfortunately, Samson made at least two errors in judgment early in his life and they cost him dearly. He never learned to control the connection between his eyes and his heart. He failed to see the dangers in his relation-ship with Delilah. Not until he lost his eyes did he finally see the folly of much of his life. He also did not acknowledge the source of his amazing strength or take seriously the responsibilities that came with it. Though his long hair was a reminder of the source of his strength, Samson lost sight of God's presence in his life. His hair became his strength. He thought he was revealing his secret to Delilah; but he was actually revealing his failure. Once his hair was cut, Samson was faced with his true weaknesses.

Cutting Edge

Samson never regained his sight, but he learned to see the truth. His hair did grow back, but it was God to whom he turned for his final strength. Samson learned from his losses, but late. He represents so many other lives that might have made a big difference, but fell short. Others can avoid Samson's errors and gain insight from his lessons. **YOU can, too!**

youthful mistakes are part of the learning cycle. Hopefully, we learn from them. Fortunately, few of them prove to be fatal. But most of us could benefit from paying closer attention to our youthful lessons. We don't have to repeat the mistakes of others. When we see others receive painful and sometimes permanent consequences from their behaviors, we must resist the thought that such results cannot happen to us.

The more we seek to learn from our own mistakes, as well as from others' mistakes, the more we will be able to make a difference with our lives. Continually acknowledge God for your strengths and ask for His help with your mistakes.

Want to know more? Read about Samson's life in Judges 13—16.

RUTH made a difference

Moab and Israel were neighbors and enemies. They shared a history of conflicts. But hardship and famine sometimes change attitudes; and during an extreme famine in Israel, Naomi, her husband, and two sons moved to Moab. There the boys eventually married local girls. One of those girls was Ruth.

Years later, when Naomi's husband and both boys died, she decided to return to her home in Bethlehem with her grief. Somewhat to her amazement, Ruth insisted on returning with her. They had not only become a family and friends; they had also grown to share a common faith.

The events that led up to Ruth's marriage to Boaz of Bethlehem were full of romance and excitement. God brought goodness out of grief. God grafted a foreign daughter in His own lineage. For we discover at the end of Ruth's story that she was an ancestor of King David. This fact also makes her part of the family tree of Jesus, the Savior and King.

Cutting Edge

In the relationship between Ruth and Naomi, we find a lovely example of the way young and old make a difference in each other's lives. Even mothers-in-law and daughters-in-law can be friends. They can also become sisters in their shared relationship with God. Ruth made a difference as she honored and cooperated with Naomi's wisdom. Her trust in God allowed Him to make a difference through her and in her life.

YOU can, too!

Every relationship in your life offers God an opportunity to work. Relationships are His fertile ground. When God describes His highest purposes for us, He uses relationship language: "You shall love the LORD your God with all your heart, with all your soul, with all your mind, and with all your strength" and "You shall love your neighbor as yourself" (Mark 12:30, 31). Relationships are where God wants to make a difference. Shouldn't that be our goal, too?

Want to know more? Read Ruth's delightful story in the book that bears her name.

Edom, saying, "Please let me pass through your land." But the king of Edom would not heed. And in like manner they sent to the king of Moab, but he would not *consent.* So Israel remained in Kadesh. ¹⁸And they went along through the wilderness and bypassed the land of Edom and the land of Moab, came to the east side of the land of Moab, and encamped on the other side of the Arnon. But they did not enter the border of Moab, for the Arnon *was* the border of Moab. ¹⁹Then Israel sent messengers to Sihon king of the Amorites, king of Heshbon; and Israel said to him, "Please let us pass through your land into our place." ²⁰But Sihon did not trust Israel to pass through his territory. So Sihon gathered all his people together, encamped in Jahaz, and fought against Israel. ²¹And the LORD God of Israel delivered Sihon and all his people into the hand of Israel, and they defeated them. Thus Israel gained possession of all the land of the Amorites, who inhabited that country. ²²They took possession of all the territory of the Amorites, from the Arnon to the Jabbok and from the wilderness to the Jordan.

²³"And now the LORD God of Israel has dispossessed the Amorites from before His people Israel; should you then possess it? ²⁴Will you not possess whatever Chemosh your god gives you to possess? So whatever the LORD our God takes possession of before us, we will possess. ²⁵And now, *are* you any better than Balak the son of Zippor, king of Moab? Did he ever strive against Israel? Did he ever fight against them? ²⁶While Israel dwelt in Heshbon and its villages, in Aroer and its villages, and in all the cities along the banks of the Arnon, for three hundred years, why did you not recover *them* within that time? ²⁷Therefore I have not sinned against you, but you wronged me by fighting against me. May the LORD, the Judge, render judgment this day between the children of Israel and the people of Ammon.' " ²⁸However, the king of the people of Ammon did not heed the words which Jephthah sent him.

JEPHTHAH'S VOW AND VICTORY

²⁹Then the Spirit of the LORD came upon Jephthah, and he passed through Gilead and Manasseh, and passed through Mizpah of Gilead; and from Mizpah of Gilead he advanced *toward* the people of Ammon. ³⁰And Jephthah made a vow to the LORD, and said, "If You will indeed deliver the people of Ammon into my hands, ³¹then it will be that whatever comes out of the doors of my house to meet me, when I return in peace from the people of Ammon, shall surely be the LORD's, and I will offer it up as a burnt offering."

³²So Jephthah advanced toward the people of Ammon to fight against them, and the LORD delivered them into his hands. ³³And he defeated them from Aroer as far as Minnith—twenty cities—and to Abel Keramim,ᵃ with a very great slaughter. Thus the people of Ammon were subdued before the children of Israel.

JEPHTHAH'S DAUGHTER

³⁴When Jephthah came to his house at Mizpah, there was his daughter, coming out to meet him with timbrels and dancing; and she *was his* only child. Besides her he had neither son nor daughter. ³⁵And it came to pass, when he saw her, that he tore his clothes, and said, "Alas, my daughter! You have brought me very low! You are among those who trouble me! For I have given my word to the LORD, and I cannot go back on it."

> "So Jephthah advanced toward the people of Ammon to fight against them, and the LORD delivered them into his hands."
> (Judges 11:32)

WHAT'S IT MEAN?

Did Jephthah really kill his own daughter as a sacrifice to God? Maybe not. First of all, human sacrifice was forbidden by the Law of Moses. Second, the passage seems to suggest that Jephthah may have "sacrificed" his daughter to the temple, meaning that she had to spend the rest of her life serving in God's house—never being able to marry or have a family of her own.
Judges 11:34–39

JEPHTHAH'S DAUGHTER made a difference

Jephthah was an Old Testament superhero. He had a daughter he loved. Unfortunately, Jephthah didn't always see how his job as a superhero might affect the life of his daughter. Jephthah got into trouble with a rash promise. He publicly announced he would sacrifice the first thing that came out of his house if he returned from war victorious. His great victory march came to a halt when the first thing he saw from home was his daughter.

It appears that the sacrifice Jephthah made was to commit his only daughter to lifelong virginity. Jephthah rashly sacrificed his opportunity to have grandchildren. Though his daughter grieved over her loss, she honored her father's rash vow. That honor probably stung Jephthah deeply. Little hurts a loving parent more than when their mistakes cause their children to suffer. But Jephthah's daughter made a difference with her acceptance. The dignity Jephthah's daughter displayed was so powerful that she is remembered. She offers an example of a costly obedience to the fifth commandment—to honor father and mother. She did so even when her father had made a mistake.

YOU can, too!

When parents make mistakes, children find out how difficult it is to honor and forgive. But dishonor and unforgiveness do not lead to freedom. Honoring and forgiving other people doesn't let them off the hook; it lets us off the hook. As long as we hold hurts against other people, we, too, are bound. Jephthah's daughter was free to grieve and play in the mountains because she forgave . . . because she honored. Do you have that freedom?

Want to know more? Read about Jephthah's daughter in
Judges 11:1—12:7.

³⁶So she said to him, "My father, *if* you have given your word to the LORD, do to me according to what has gone out of your mouth, because the LORD has avenged you of your enemies, the people of Ammon." ³⁷Then she said to her father, "Let this thing be done for me: let me alone for two months, that I may go and wander on the mountains and bewail my virginity, my friends and I."

³⁸So he said, "Go." And he sent her away *for* two months; and she went with her friends, and bewailed her virginity on the mountains. ³⁹And it was so at the end of two months that she returned to her father, and he carried out his vow with her which he had vowed. She knew no man.

And it became a custom in Israel ⁴⁰*that* the daughters of Israel went four days each year to lament the daughter of Jephthah the Gileadite.

JEPHTHAH'S CONFLICT WITH EPHRAIM

¹Then the men of Ephraim gathered together, crossed over toward Zaphon, and said to Jephthah, "Why did you cross over to fight against the people of Ammon, and did not call us to go with you? We will burn your house down on you with fire!"

WHAT'S IT MEAN?

Talk about a tough pop quiz! Imagine taking a one-question test to determine whether you live or die. That's the situation the Ephraimites faced when they tried to escape. The Gileadites used the word *Shibboleth* as a password. Those people who could pronounce it correctly were allowed to pass. Those who couldn't were killed on the spot. Seems easy enough, doesn't it? Not for the Ephraimites, who apparently had problems making the "sh" sound. Forty-two thousand of them were killed because of their different dialect.

Judges 12:6

²And Jephthah said to them, "My people and I were in a great struggle with the people of Ammon; and when I called you, you did not deliver me out of their hands. ³So when I saw that you would not deliver *me*, I took my life in my hands and crossed over against the people of Ammon; and the LORD delivered them into my hand. Why then have you come up to me

this day to fight against me?" ⁴Now Jephthah gathered together all the men of Gilead and fought against Ephraim. And the men of Gilead defeated Ephraim, because they said, "You Gileadites *are* fugitives of Ephraim among the Ephraimites *and* among the Manassites." ⁵The Gileadites seized the fords of the Jordan before the Ephraimites *arrived*. And when *any* Ephraimite who escaped said, "Let me cross over," the men of Gilead would say to him, "*Are* you an Ephraimite?" If he said, "No," ⁶then they would say to him, "Then say, 'Shibboleth'!" And he would say, "Sibboleth," for he could not pronounce *it* right. Then they would take him and kill him at the fords of the Jordan. There fell at that time forty-two thousand Ephraimites.

⁷And Jephthah judged Israel six years. Then Jephthah the Gileadite died and was buried among the cities of Gilead.

IBZAN, ELON, AND ABDON

⁸After him, Ibzan of Bethlehem judged Israel. ⁹He had thirty sons. And he gave away thirty daughters in marriage, and brought in thirty daughters from elsewhere for his sons. He judged Israel seven years. ¹⁰Then Ibzan died and was buried at Bethlehem.

¹¹After him, Elon the Zebulunite judged Israel. He judged Israel ten years. ¹²And Elon the Zebulunite died and was buried at Aijalon in the country of Zebulun.

¹³After him, Abdon the son of Hillel the Pirathonite judged Israel. ¹⁴He had forty sons and thirty grandsons, who rode on seventy young donkeys. He judged Israel eight years. ¹⁵Then Abdon the son of Hillel the Pirathonite died and was buried in Pirathon in the land of Ephraim, in the mountains of the Amalekites.

THE BIRTH OF SAMSON

¹Again the children of Israel did evil in the sight of the LORD, and the LORD delivered them into the hand of the Philistines for forty years.

²Now there was a certain man from Zorah, of the family of the Danites, whose name *was* Manoah; and his wife *was* barren and had no children. ³And the Angel of the LORD appeared to the woman and said to her, "Indeed now, you are barren and have borne no children, but you shall conceive and bear a son. ⁴Now therefore, please be careful not to drink wine or *similar* drink, and not to eat anything unclean. ⁵For behold, you shall conceive and bear a son. And no razor shall come upon his head, for the child shall be a Nazirite to God from the womb; and he shall begin to deliver Israel out of the hand of the Philistines."

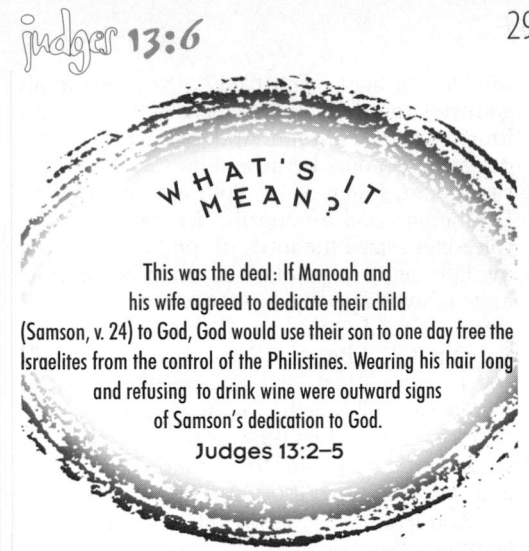

WHAT'S IT MEAN?

This was the deal: If Manoah and
his wife agreed to dedicate their child
(Samson, v. 24) to God, God would use their son to one day free the
Israelites from the control of the Philistines. Wearing his hair long
and refusing to drink wine were outward signs
of Samson's dedication to God.

Judges 13:2–5

⁶So the woman came and told her husband, saying, "A Man of God came to me, and His countenance *was* like the countenance of the Angel of God, very awesome; but I did not ask Him where He *was* from, and He did not tell me His name. ⁷And He said to me, 'Behold, you shall conceive and bear a son. Now drink no wine or *similar* drink, nor eat anything unclean, for the child shall be a Nazirite to God from the womb to the day of his death.' "

⁸Then Manoah prayed to the LORD, and said, "O my Lord, please let the Man of God whom You sent come to us again and teach us what we shall do for the child who will be born."

⁹And God listened to the voice of Manoah, and the Angel of God came to the woman again as she was sitting in the field; but Manoah her husband *was* not with her. ¹⁰Then the woman ran in haste and told her husband, and said to him, "Look, the Man who came to me the *other* day has just now appeared to me!"

¹¹So Manoah arose and followed his wife. When he came to the Man, he said to Him, "Are You the Man who spoke to this woman?"

And He said, "I *am*."

¹²Manoah said, "Now let Your words come *to pass!* What will be the boy's rule of life, and his work?"

¹³So the Angel of the LORD said to Manoah, "Of all that I said to the woman let her be careful. ¹⁴She may not eat anything that comes from the vine, nor may she drink wine or *similar* drink, nor eat anything unclean. All that I commanded her let her observe."

¹⁵Then Manoah said to the Angel of the LORD, "Please let us detain You, and we will prepare a young goat for You."

¹⁶And the Angel of the LORD said to Manoah, "Though you detain Me, I will not eat your food. But if you offer a burnt offering, you must offer it to the LORD." (For Manoah did not know He *was* the Angel of the LORD.)

¹⁷Then Manoah said to the Angel of the LORD, "What *is* Your name, that when Your words come *to pass* we may honor You?"

WHAT'S IT MEAN?

Here's an odd tradition from biblical
times. Apparently, knowing and using someone's
name gave you a certain amount of power over that person. The fact
that the angel refused to tell Manoah his name indicated that the
angel had a higher rank than Manoah.

Judges 13:18

¹⁸And the Angel of the LORD said to him, "Why do you ask My name, seeing it *is* wonderful?"

¹⁹So Manoah took the young goat with the grain offering, and offered it upon the rock to the LORD. And He did a wondrous thing while Manoah and his wife looked on—²⁰it happened as the flame went up toward heaven from the altar—the Angel of the LORD ascended in the flame of the altar! When Manoah and his wife saw *this*, they fell on their faces to the ground. ²¹When the Angel of the LORD appeared no more to Manoah and his wife, then Manoah knew that He *was* the Angel of the LORD.

²²And Manoah said to his wife, "We shall surely die, because we have seen God!"

²³But his wife said to him, "If the LORD had desired to kill us, He would not have accepted a burnt offering and a grain offering from our hands, nor would He have shown us all these *things*, nor would He have told us *such things* as these at this time."

²⁴So the woman bore a son and called his name Samson; and the child grew, and the LORD blessed him. ²⁵And the Spirit of the LORD began to move upon him at Mahaneh Dan*ᵃ* between Zorah and Eshtaol.

13:25 *ᵃ*Literally *Camp of Dan* (compare 18:12)

SAMSON'S PHILISTINE WIFE

¹Now Samson went down to Timnah, and saw a woman in Timnah of the daughters of the Philistines. ²So he went up and told his father and mother, saying, "I have seen a woman in Timnah of the daughters of the Philistines; now therefore, get her for me as a wife."

³Then his father and mother said to him, "*Is there* no woman among the daughters of your brethren, or among all my people, that you must go and get a wife from the uncircumcised Philistines?"

And Samson said to his father, "Get her for me, for she pleases me well."

⁴But his father and mother did not know that it was of the LORD—that He was seeking an occasion to move against the Philistines. For at that time the Philistines had dominion over Israel.

⁵So Samson went down to Timnah with his father and mother, and came to the vineyards of Timnah.

Now *to his* surprise, a young lion *came* roaring against him. ⁶And the Spirit of the LORD came mightily upon him, and he tore the lion apart as one would have torn apart a young goat, though *he had* nothing in his hand. But he did not tell his father or his mother what he had done.

WHAT'S IT MEAN?

Riddles weren't kids' stuff in ancient times. They were used as tests of people's wisdom. Often a great deal of pride and money rode on the outcome of a riddle.

Judges 14:12

⁷Then he went down and talked with the woman; and she pleased Samson well. ⁸After some time, when he returned to get her, he turned aside to see the carcass of the lion. And behold, a swarm of bees and honey *were* in the carcass of the lion. ⁹He took some of it in his hands and went along, eating. When he came to his father and mother, he gave *some* to them, and they also ate. But he did not tell them that he had taken the honey out of the carcass of the lion.

¹⁰So his father went down to the woman. And Samson gave a feast there, for young men used to do so. ¹¹And it happened, when they saw him, that they brought thirty companions to be with him.

¹²Then Samson said to them, "Let me pose a riddle to you. If you can correctly solve and explain it to me within the seven days of the feast, then I will give you thirty linen garments and thirty changes of clothing. ¹³But if you cannot explain *it* to me, then you shall give me thirty linen garments and thirty changes of clothing."

And they said to him, "Pose your riddle, that we may hear it."

¹⁴So he said to them:

"Out of the eater came something to eat,
  And out of the strong came something sweet."

Now for three days they could not explain the riddle.

¹⁵But it came to pass on the seventh[a] day that they said to Samson's wife, "Entice your husband, that he may explain the riddle to us, or else we will burn you and your father's house with fire. Have you invited us in order to take what is ours? *Is that* not *so?*"

¹⁶Then Samson's wife wept on him, and said, "You only hate me! You do not love me! You have posed a riddle to the sons of my people, but you have not explained *it* to me."

And he said to her, "Look, I have not explained *it* to my father or my mother; so should I explain *it* to you?" ¹⁷Now she had wept on him the seven days while their feast lasted. And it happened on the seventh day that he told her, because she pressed him so much. Then she explained the riddle to the sons of her people. ¹⁸So the men of the city said to him on the seventh day before the sun went down:

"What *is* sweeter than honey?
  And what *is* stronger than a lion?"

And he said to them:

"If you had not plowed with my heifer,
  You would not have solved my riddle!"

¹⁹Then the Spirit of the LORD came upon him mightily, and he went down to Ashkelon

14:15 ᵃFollowing Masoretic Text, Targum, and Vulgate; Septuagint and Syriac read *fourth.*

and killed thirty of their men, took their apparel, and gave the changes *of clothing* to those who had explained the riddle. So his anger was aroused, and he went back up to his father's house. ²⁰And Samson's wife was *given* to his companion, who had been his best man.

SAMSON DEFEATS THE PHILISTINES

¹After a while, in the time of wheat harvest, it happened that Samson visited his wife with a young goat. And he said, "Let me go in to my wife, into *her* room." But her father would not permit him to go in.

²Her father said, "I really thought that you thoroughly hated her; therefore I gave her to your companion. *Is* not her younger sister better than she? Please, take her instead."

³And Samson said to them, "This time I shall be blameless regarding the Philistines if I harm them!" ⁴Then Samson went and caught three hundred foxes; and he took torches, turned *the foxes* tail to tail, and put a torch between each pair of tails. ⁵When he had set the torches on fire, he let *the foxes* go into the standing grain of the Philistines, and burned up both the shocks and the standing grain, as well as the vineyards *and* olive groves.

⁶Then the Philistines said, "Who has done this?"

And they answered, "Samson, the son-in-law of the Timnite, because he has taken his wife and given her to his companion." So the Philistines came up and burned her and her father with fire.

⁷Samson said to them, "Since you would do a thing like this, I will surely take revenge on you, and after that I will cease." ⁸So he attacked them hip and thigh with a great slaughter; then he went down and dwelt in the cleft of the rock of Etam.

⁹Now the Philistines went up, encamped in Judah, and deployed themselves against Lehi. ¹⁰And the men of Judah said, "Why have you come up against us?"

So they answered, "We have come up to arrest Samson, to do to him as he has done to us."

¹¹Then three thousand men of Judah went down to the cleft of the rock of Etam, and said to Samson, "Do you not know that the Philistines rule over us? What *is* this you have done to us?"

And he said to them, "As they did to me, so I have done to them."

¹²But they said to him, "We have come down to arrest you, that we may deliver you into the hand of the Philistines."

Then Samson said to them, "Swear to me that you will not kill me yourselves."

¹³So they spoke to him, saying, "No, but we will tie you securely and deliver you into their hand; but we will surely not kill you." And they bound him with two new ropes and brought him up from the rock.

¹⁴When he came to Lehi, the Philistines came shouting against him. Then the Spirit of the LORD came mightily upon him; and the ropes that *were* on his arms became like flax that is burned with fire, and his bonds broke loose from his hands. ¹⁵He found a fresh jawbone of a donkey, reached out his hand and took it, and killed a thousand men with it. ¹⁶Then Samson said:

"With the jawbone of a donkey,
  Heaps upon heaps,
  With the jawbone of a donkey
  I have slain a thousand men!"

WHAT'S IT MEAN?

Samson was so pleased with his accomplishment that he wrote a short poem to commemorate it. He wanted to preserve what he had done and pass it on to future generations.
Judges 15:16

¹⁷And so it was, when he had finished speaking, that he threw the jawbone from his hand, and called that place Ramath Lehi.*ᵃ*

¹⁸Then he became very thirsty; so he cried out to the LORD and said, "You have given this great deliverance by the hand of Your servant; and now shall I die of thirst and fall into the hand of the uncircumcised?" ¹⁹So God split the hollow place that *is* in Lehi,*ᵃ* and water came out, and he drank; and his spirit returned, and he revived. Therefore he called its name En Hakkore,*ᵇ* which is in Lehi to this day. ²⁰And he judged Israel twenty years in the days of the Philistines.

15:17 *ᵃ*Literally *Jawbone Height*   **15:19** *ᵃ*Literally *Jawbone* (compare verse 14) *ᵇ*Literally *Spring of the Caller*

SAMSON AND DELILAH

[1]Now Samson went to Gaza and saw a harlot there, and went in to her. [2]When the Gazites *were told*, "Samson has come here!" they surrounded *the place* and lay in wait for him all night at the gate of the city. They were quiet all night, saying, "In the morning, when it is daylight, we will kill him." [3]And Samson lay *low* till midnight; then he arose at midnight, took hold of the doors of the gate of the city and the two gateposts, pulled them up, bar and all, put *them* on his shoulders, and carried them to the top of the hill that faces Hebron.

[4]Afterward it happened that he loved a woman in the Valley of Sorek, whose name *was* Delilah. [5]And the lords of the Philistines came up to her and said to her, "Entice him, and find out where his great strength *lies*, and by what *means* we may overpower him, that we may bind him to afflict him; and every one of us will give you eleven hundred *pieces* of silver."

[6]So Delilah said to Samson, "Please tell me where your great strength *lies*, and with what you may be bound to afflict you."

[7]And Samson said to her, "If they bind me with seven fresh bowstrings, not yet dried, then I shall become weak, and be like any *other* man."

[8]So the lords of the Philistines brought up to her seven fresh bowstrings, not yet dried, and she bound him with them. [9]Now *men were* lying in wait, staying with her in the room. And she said to him, "The Philistines *are* upon you, Samson!" But he broke the bowstrings as a strand of yarn breaks when it touches fire. So the secret of his strength was not known.

[10]Then Delilah said to Samson, "Look, you have mocked me and told me lies. Now, please tell me what you may be bound with."

[11]So he said to her, "If they bind me securely with new ropes that have never been used, then I shall become weak, and be like any *other* man."

[12]Therefore Delilah took new ropes and bound him with them, and said to him, "The Philistines *are* upon you, Samson!" And *men were* lying in wait, staying in the room. But he broke them off his arms like a thread.

[13]Delilah said to Samson, "Until now you have mocked me and told me lies. Tell me what you may be bound with."

And he said to her, "If you weave the seven locks of my head into the web of the loom"—

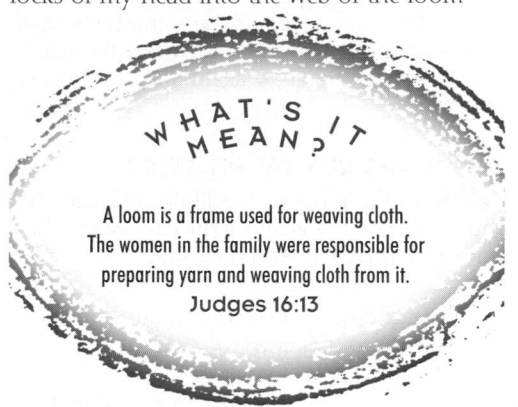

WHAT'S IT MEAN?

A loom is a frame used for weaving cloth. The women in the family were responsible for preparing yarn and weaving cloth from it.

Judges 16:13

[14]So she wove *it* tightly with the batten of the loom, and said to him, "The Philistines *are* upon you, Samson!" But he awoke from his sleep, and pulled out the batten and the web from the loom.

[15]Then she said to him, "How can you say, 'I love you,' when your heart *is* not with me? You have mocked me these three times, and have not told me where your great strength *lies*." [16]And it came to pass, when she pestered him daily with her words and pressed him, *so* that his soul was vexed to death, [17]that he told her all his heart, and said to her, "No razor has ever come upon my head, for I *have been* a Nazirite to God from my mother's womb. If I am shaven, then my strength will leave me, and I shall become weak, and be like any *other* man."

[18]When Delilah saw that he had told her all his heart, she sent and called for the lords of the Philistines, saying, "Come up once more, for he has told me all his heart." So the lords of the Philistines came up to her and brought the money in their hand. [19]Then she lulled him to sleep on her knees, and called for a man and had him shave off the seven locks of his head. Then she began to torment him,[a] and his strength left him. [20]And she said, "The Philistines *are* upon you, Samson!" So he awoke from his sleep, and said, "I will go out as before, at other times, and shake myself free!" But he did not know that the LORD had departed from him.

> "So Delilah said to Samson, 'Please tell me where your great strength lies, and with what you may be bound to afflict you.' "
> (Judges 16:6)

²¹Then the Philistines took him and put out his eyes, and brought him down to Gaza. They bound him with bronze fetters, and he became a grinder in the prison. ²²However, the hair of his head began to grow again after it had been shaven.

SAMSON DIES WITH THE PHILISTINES

²³Now the lords of the Philistines gathered together to offer a great sacrifice to Dagon their god, and to rejoice. And they said:

"Our god has delivered into our hands
   Samson our enemy!"

²⁴When the people saw him, they praised their god; for they said:

"Our god has delivered into our hands
   our enemy,
The destroyer of our land,
And the one who multiplied our
   dead."

²⁵So it happened, when their hearts were merry, that they said, "Call for Samson, that he may perform for us." So they called for Samson from the prison, and he performed for them. And they stationed him between the pillars. ²⁶Then Samson said to the lad who held him by the hand, "Let me feel the pillars which support the temple, so that I can lean on them." ²⁷Now the temple was full of men and women. All the lords of the Philistines *were* there—about three thousand men and women on the roof watching while Samson performed. ²⁸Then Samson called to the LORD, saying, "O Lord GOD, remember me, I pray! Strengthen me, I pray, just this once, O God, that I may with one *blow* take vengeance on the Philistines for my two eyes!" ²⁹And Samson took hold of the two middle pillars which supported the temple, and he braced himself against them, one on his right and the other on his left. ³⁰Then Samson said, "Let me die with the Philistines!" And he pushed with *all his* might, and the temple fell on the lords and all the people who *were* in it. So the dead that he killed at his death were more than he had killed in his life.

³¹And his brothers and all his father's household came down and took him, and brought *him* up and buried him between Zorah and Eshtaol in the tomb of his father Manoah. He had judged Israel twenty years.

MICAH'S IDOLATRY

¹Now there was a man from the mountains of Ephraim, whose name *was* Micah. ²And he said to his mother, "The eleven hundred *shekels* of silver that were taken from you, and on which you put a curse, even saying it in my ears—here *is* the silver with me; I took it."

And his mother said, "*May you be* blessed by the LORD, my son!" ³So when he had returned the eleven hundred *shekels* of silver to his mother, his mother said, "I had wholly dedicated the silver from my hand to the LORD for my son, to make a carved image and a molded image; now therefore, I will return it to you." ⁴Thus he returned the silver to his mother. Then his mother took two hundred *shekels* of silver and gave them to the silversmith, and he made it into a carved image and a molded image; and they were in the house of Micah.

WHAT'S IT MEAN?

Some offerings to God were required. People had to make them, just as they had to pay taxes. Other offerings were voluntary. People chose to make them for private reasons. The priests, who were chosen from the descendants of Levi, handled the gifts and offerings according to God's law. Micah and his family were not descendants of Levi, so they were not legally qualified to handle the gifts—not to mention the fact that using the money to create an idol violated God's law.

Judges 17:3, 4

⁵The man Micah had a shrine, and made an ephod and household idols;ᵃ and he consecrated one of his sons, who became his priest. ⁶In those days *there was* no king in Israel; everyone did *what was* right in his own eyes.

⁷Now there was a young man from Bethlehem in Judah, of the family of Judah; he *was* a Levite, and was staying there. ⁸The man departed from the city of Bethlehem in Judah to stay wherever he could find *a place.* Then he came to the mountains of Ephraim, to the house of Micah, as he journeyed. ⁹And Micah said to him, "Where do you come from?"

So he said to him, "I *am* a Levite from Beth-

17:5 ᵃHebrew *teraphim*

lehem in Judah, and I am on my way to find *a place* to stay."

¹⁰Micah said to him, "Dwell with me, and be a father and a priest to me, and I will give you ten *shekels* of silver per year, a suit of clothes, and your sustenance." So the Levite went in. ¹¹Then the Levite was content to dwell with the man; and the young man became like one of his sons to him. ¹²So Micah consecrated the Levite, and the young man became his priest, and lived in the house of Micah. ¹³Then Micah said, "Now I know that the LORD will be good to me, since I have a Levite as priest!"

THE DANITES ADOPT MICAH'S IDOLATRY

¹In those days *there was* no king in Israel. And in those days the tribe of the Danites was seeking an inheritance for itself to dwell in; for until that day *their* inheritance among the tribes of Israel had not fallen to them. ²So the children of Dan sent five men of their family from their territory, men of valor from Zorah and Eshtaol, to spy out the land and search it. They said to them, "Go, search the land." So they went to the mountains of Ephraim, to the house of Micah, and lodged there. ³While they *were* at the house of Micah, they recognized the voice of the young Levite. They turned aside and said to him, "Who brought you here? What are you doing in this *place?* What do you have here?"

⁴He said to them, "Thus and so Micah did for me. He has hired me, and I have become his priest."

⁵So they said to him, "Please inquire of God, that we may know whether the journey on which we go will be prosperous."

⁶And the priest said to them, "Go in peace. The presence of the LORD *be* with you on your way."

⁷So the five men departed and went to Laish. They saw the people who *were* there, how they dwelt safely, in the manner of the Sidonians, quiet and secure. *There were* no rulers in the land who might put *them* to shame for anything. They *were* far from the Sidonians, and they had no ties with anyone.ᵃ

⁸Then *the spies* came back to their brethren at Zorah and Eshtaol, and their brethren said to them, "What *is* your *report?"*

⁹So they said, "Arise, let us go up against them. For we have seen the land, and indeed it *is* very good. *Would* you *do* nothing? Do not hesitate to go, *and* enter to possess the land. ¹⁰When you go, you will come to a secure people and a large land. For God has given it into

your hands, a place where *there is* no lack of anything that *is* on the earth."

WHAT'S IT MEAN?

The tribe of Dan had been given land of their own when the Israelites first got to Canaan. Unfortunately, they couldn't hold on to it. That's why they were looking for somewhere else to go. Laish was located north of the Sea of Galilee. Sidon was located even further north.

Judges 18:1–7

¹¹And six hundred men of the family of the Danites went from there, from Zorah and Eshtaol, armed with weapons of war. ¹²Then they went up and encamped in Kirjath Jearim in Judah. (Therefore they call that place Mahaneh Danᵃ to this day. There it is, west of Kirjath Jearim.) ¹³And they passed from there to the mountains of Ephraim, and came to the house of Micah.

¹⁴Then the five men who had gone to spy out the country of Laish answered and said to their brethren, "Do you know that there are in these houses an ephod, household idols, a carved image, and a molded image? Now therefore, consider what you should do." ¹⁵So they turned aside there, and came to the house of the young Levite man—to the house of Micah—and greeted him. ¹⁶The six hundred men armed with their weapons of war, who *were* of the children of Dan, stood by the entrance of the gate. ¹⁷Then the five men who had gone to spy out the land went up. Entering there, they took the carved image, the ephod, the household idols, and the molded image. The priest stood at the entrance of the gate with the six hundred men *who were* armed with weapons of war.

¹⁸When these went into Micah's house and took the carved image, the ephod, the household idols, and the molded image, the priest said to them, "What are you doing?"

¹⁹And they said to him, "Be quiet, put your hand over your mouth, and come with us; be a father and a priest to us. *Is it* better for you to be a priest to the household of one man, or that

18:7 ᵃFollowing Masoretic Text, Targum, and Vulgate; Septuagint reads *with Syria.* **18:12** ᵃLiterally *Camp of Dan*

you be a priest to a tribe and a family in Israel?" ²⁰So the priest's heart was glad; and he took the ephod, the household idols, and the carved image, and took his place among the people.

²¹Then they turned and departed, and put the little ones, the livestock, and the goods in front of them. ²²When they were a good way from the house of Micah, the men who *were* in the houses near Micah's house gathered together and overtook the children of Dan. ²³And they called out to the children of Dan. So they turned around and said to Micah, "What ails you, that you have gathered such a company?"

²⁴So he said, "You have taken away my gods which I made, and the priest, and you have gone away. Now what more do I have? How can you say to me, 'What ails you?' "

²⁵And the children of Dan said to him, "Do not let your voice be heard among us, lest angry men fall upon you, and you lose your life, with the lives of your household!" ²⁶Then the children of Dan went their way. And when Micah saw that they *were* too strong for him, he turned and went back to his house.

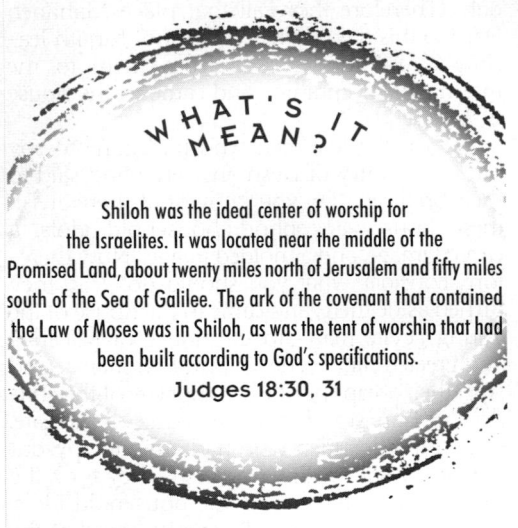

WHAT'S IT MEAN?

Shiloh was the ideal center of worship for the Israelites. It was located near the middle of the Promised Land, about twenty miles north of Jerusalem and fifty miles south of the Sea of Galilee. The ark of the covenant that contained the Law of Moses was in Shiloh, as was the tent of worship that had been built according to God's specifications.

Judges 18:30, 31

DANITES SETTLE IN LAISH

²⁷So they took *the things* Micah had made, and the priest who had belonged to him, and went to Laish, to a people quiet and secure; and they struck them with the edge of the sword and burned the city with fire. ²⁸*There was* no deliverer, because it *was* far from Sidon, and they had no ties with anyone. It was in the valley that belongs to Beth Rehob. So they rebuilt the city and dwelt there. ²⁹And they called the name of the city Dan, after the name of Dan

their father, who was born to Israel. However, the name of the city formerly *was* Laish.

³⁰Then the children of Dan set up for themselves the carved image; and Jonathan the son of Gershom, the son of Manasseh,ᵃ and his sons were priests to the tribe of Dan until the day of the captivity of the land. ³¹So they set up for themselves Micah's carved image which he made, all the time that the house of God was in Shiloh.

THE LEVITE'S CONCUBINE

¹And it came to pass in those days, when *there was* no king in Israel, that there was a certain Levite staying in the remote mountains of Ephraim. He took for himself a concubine from Bethlehem in Judah. ²But his concubine played the harlot against him, and went away from him to her father's house at Bethlehem in Judah, and was there four whole months. ³Then her husband arose and went after her, to speak kindly to her *and* bring her back, having his servant and a couple of donkeys with him. So she brought him into her father's house; and when the father of the young woman saw him, he was glad to meet him. ⁴Now his father-in-law, the young woman's father, detained him; and he stayed with him three days. So they ate and drank and lodged there.

⁵Then it came to pass on the fourth day that they arose early in the morning, and he stood to depart; but the young woman's father said to his son-in-law, "Refresh your heart with a morsel of bread, and afterward go your way."

⁶So they sat down, and the two of them ate and drank together. Then the young woman's father said to the man, "Please be content to stay all night, and let your heart be merry." ⁷And when the man stood to depart, his father-in-law urged him; so he lodged there again. ⁸Then he arose early in the morning on the fifth day to depart, but the young woman's father said, "Please refresh your heart." So they delayed until afternoon; and both of them ate.

⁹And when the man stood to depart—he and his concubine and his servant—his father-in-law, the young woman's father, said to him, "Look, the day is now drawing toward evening; please spend the night. See, the day is coming to an end; lodge here, that your heart may be merry. Tomorrow go your way early, so that you may get home."

¹⁰However, the man was not willing to spend that night; so he rose and departed, and came opposite Jebus (that *is*, Jerusalem). With

18:30 ᵃSeptuagint and Vulgate read *Moses.*

him were the two saddled donkeys; his concubine *was* also with him. [11]They *were* near Jebus, and the day was far spent; and the servant said to his master, "Come, please, and let us turn aside into this city of the Jebusites and lodge in it."

[12]But his master said to him, "We will not turn aside here into a city of foreigners, who *are* not of the children of Israel; we will go on to Gibeah." [13]So he said to his servant, "Come, let us draw near to one of these places, and spend the night in Gibeah or in Ramah." [14]And they passed by and went their way; and the sun went down on them near Gibeah, which belongs to Benjamin. [15]They turned aside there to go in to lodge in Gibeah. And when he went in, he sat down in the open square of the city, for no one would take them into *his* house to spend the night.

[16]Just then an old man came in from his work in the field at evening, who also *was* from the mountains of Ephraim; he was staying in Gibeah, whereas the men of the place *were* Benjamites. [17]And when he raised his eyes, he saw the traveler in the open square of the city; and the old man said, "Where are you going, and where do you come from?"

[18]So he said to him, "We *are* passing from Bethlehem in Judah toward the remote mountains of Ephraim; I *am* from there. I went to Bethlehem in Judah; *now* I am going to the house of the LORD. But there *is* no one who will take me into his house, [19]although we have both straw and fodder for our donkeys, and bread and wine for myself, for your female servant, and for the young man *who is* with your servant; *there is* no lack of anything."

[20]And the old man said, "Peace *be* with you! However, *let* all your needs *be* my responsibility; only do not spend the night in the open square." [21]So he brought him into his house, and gave fodder to the donkeys. And they washed their feet, and ate and drank.

GIBEAH'S CRIME

[22]As they were enjoying themselves, suddenly certain men of the city, perverted men,[a] surrounded the house *and* beat on the door. They spoke to the master of the house, the old man, saying, "Bring out the man who came to your house, that we may know him *carnally!*"

[23]But the man, the master of the house, went out to them and said to them, "No, my brethren! I beg you, do not act *so* wickedly! Seeing this man has come into my house, do not commit this outrage. [24]Look, *here is* my virgin daughter and *the man's*[a] concubine; let me bring them out now. Humble them, and do with them as you please; but to this man do not do such a vile thing!" [25]But the men would not heed him. So the man took his concubine and brought *her* out to them. And they knew her and abused her all night until morning; and when the day began to break, they let her go.

[26]Then the woman came as the day was dawning, and fell down at the door of the man's house where her master *was*, till it was light.

[27]When her master arose in the morning, and opened the doors of the house and went out to go his way, there was his concubine, fallen *at* the door of the house with her hands on the threshold. [28]And he said to her, "Get up and let us be going." But there was no answer. So the man lifted her onto the donkey; and the man got up and went to his place.

[29]When he entered his house he took a knife, laid hold of his concubine, and divided her into twelve pieces, limb by limb,[a] and sent her throughout all the territory of Israel. [30]And so it was that all who saw it said, "No such deed has been done or seen from the day that the children of Israel came up from the land of Egypt until this day. Consider it, confer, and speak up!"

ISRAEL'S WAR WITH THE BENJAMITES

[1]So all the children of Israel came out, from Dan to Beersheba, as well as from the land of Gilead, and the congregation gathered together as one man before the LORD at Mizpah. [2]And

HOMOSEXUALITY

When is sex perverted? (19:22)

WHAT'S IT MEAN?

Hospitality was serious business in ancient Israel. God commanded His people to show kindness to strangers. Often this involved offering food and shelter to travelers and their animals. Since most travelers wore open shoes, hosts were also expected to provide water so that their guests could wash their dirty feet.

Judges 19:20, 21

19:22 [a]Literally *sons of Belial*   **19:24** [a]Literally *his*   **19:29** [a]Literally *with her bones*

the leaders of all the people, all the tribes of Israel, presented themselves in the assembly of the people of God, four hundred thousand foot soldiers who drew the sword. ³(Now the children of Benjamin heard that the children of Israel had gone up to Mizpah.)

Then the children of Israel said, "Tell us, how did this wicked deed happen?"

⁴So the Levite, the husband of the woman who was murdered, answered and said, "My concubine and I went into Gibeah, which belongs to Benjamin, to spend the night. ⁵And the men of Gibeah rose against me, and surrounded the house at night because of me. They intended to kill me, but instead they ravished my concubine so that she died. ⁶So I took hold of my concubine, cut her in pieces, and sent her throughout all the territory of the inheritance of Israel, because they committed lewdness and outrage in Israel. ⁷Look! All of you are children of Israel; give your advice and counsel here and now!"

> "So all the children of Israel came out, from Dan to Beersheba, as well as from the land of Gilead, and the congregation gathered together as one man before the LORD at Mizpah." (Judges 20:1)

WHAT'S IT MEAN?

A sling was a leather strap designed to hold a rock. The strap was whirled around and around until the rock was released. Because of the whirling motion, the rock flew out of the sling much faster than if it had been thrown by hand. Most people used small clay pebbles in their slings. Some warriors, though, used baseball-sized limestone or flint rocks. You can imagine the damage they caused—assuming, of course, that they hit their target. You see, only experienced soldiers were able to use these weapons accurately.

Judges 20:16

⁸So all the people arose as one man, saying, "None of us will go to his tent, nor will any turn back to his house; ⁹but now this is the thing which we will do to Gibeah: We will go up against it by lot. ¹⁰We will take ten men out of every hundred throughout all the tribes of Israel, a hundred out of every thousand, and a thousand out of every ten thousand, to make provisions for the people, that when they come to Gibeah in Benjamin, they may repay all the vileness that they have done in Israel." ¹¹So all the men of Israel were gathered against the city, united together as one man.

¹²Then the tribes of Israel sent men through all the tribe of Benjamin, saying, "What is this wickedness that has occurred among you? ¹³Now therefore, deliver up the men, the perverted menᵃ who are in Gibeah, that we may put them to death and remove the evil from Israel!" But the children of Benjamin would not listen to the voice of their brethren, the children of Israel. ¹⁴Instead, the children of Benjamin gathered together from their cities to Gibeah, to go to battle against the children of Israel. ¹⁵And from their cities at that time the children of Benjamin numbered twenty-six thousand men who drew the sword, besides the inhabitants of Gibeah, who numbered seven hundred select men. ¹⁶Among all this people were seven hundred select men who were left-handed; every one could sling a stone at a hair's breadth and not miss. ¹⁷Now besides Benjamin, the men of Israel numbered four hundred thousand men who drew the sword; all of these were men of war.

¹⁸Then the children of Israel arose and went up to the house of Godᵃ to inquire of God. They said, "Which of us shall go up first to battle against the children of Benjamin?"

The LORD said, "Judah first!"

¹⁹So the children of Israel rose in the morning and encamped against Gibeah. ²⁰And the men of Israel went out to battle against Benjamin, and the men of Israel put themselves in battle array to fight against them at Gibeah. ²¹Then the children of Benjamin came out of Gibeah, and on that day cut down to the ground twenty-two thousand men of the Israelites. ²²And the people, that is, the men of Israel, encouraged themselves and again formed the battle line at the place where they had put themselves in array on the first day. ²³Then the children of Israel went up and wept before the

20:13 ᵃLiterally sons of Belial   **20:18** ᵃOr Bethel

LORD until evening, and asked counsel of the LORD, saying, "Shall I again draw near for battle against the children of my brother Benjamin?"

And the LORD said, "Go up against him."

[24]So the children of Israel approached the children of Benjamin on the second day. [25]And Benjamin went out against them from Gibeah on the second day, and cut down to the ground eighteen thousand more of the children of Israel; all these drew the sword.

[26]Then all the children of Israel, that is, all the people, went up and came to the house of God[a] and wept. They sat there before the LORD and fasted that day until evening; and they offered burnt offerings and peace offerings before the LORD. [27]So the children of Israel inquired of the LORD (the ark of the covenant of God *was* there in those days, [28]and Phinehas the son of Eleazar, the son of Aaron, stood before it in those days), saying, "Shall I yet again go out to battle against the children of my brother Benjamin, or shall I cease?"

And the LORD said, "Go up, for tomorrow I will deliver them into your hand."

[29]Then Israel set men in ambush all around Gibeah. [30]And the children of Israel went up against the children of Benjamin on the third day, and put themselves in battle array against Gibeah as at the other times. [31]So the children of Benjamin went out against the people, *and* were drawn away from the city. They began to strike down *and* kill some of the people, as at the other times, in the highways (one of which goes up to Bethel and the other to Gibeah) and in the field, about thirty men of Israel. [32]And the children of Benjamin said, "They *are* defeated before us, as at first."

But the children of Israel said, "Let us flee and draw them away from the city to the highways." [33]So all the men of Israel rose from their place and put themselves in battle array at Baal Tamar. Then Israel's men in ambush burst forth from their position in the plain of Geba. [34]And ten thousand select men from all Israel came against Gibeah, and the battle was fierce. But *the Benjamites*[a] did not know that disaster *was* upon them. [35]The LORD defeated Benjamin before Israel. And the children of Israel destroyed that day twenty-five thousand one hundred Benjamites; all these drew the sword.

[36]So the children of Benjamin saw that they were defeated. The men of Israel had given ground to the Benjamites, because they relied on the men in ambush whom they had set against Gibeah. [37]And the men in ambush quickly rushed upon Gibeah; the men in ambush spread out and struck the whole city with the edge of the sword. [38]Now the appointed signal between the men of Israel and the men in ambush was that they would make a great cloud of smoke rise up from the city, [39]whereupon the men of Israel would turn in battle. Now Benjamin had begun to strike *and* kill about thirty of the men of Israel. For they said, "Surely they are defeated before us, as *in* the first battle." [40]But when the cloud began to rise from the city in a column of smoke, the Benjamites looked behind them, and there was the whole city going up *in smoke* to heaven. [41]And when the men of Israel turned back, the men of Benjamin panicked, for they saw that disaster had come upon them. [42]Therefore they turned *their backs* before the men of Israel in the direction of the wilderness; but the battle overtook them, and whoever *came* out of the cities they destroyed in their midst. [43]They surrounded the Benjamites, chased them, *and* easily trampled them down as far as the front of Gibeah toward the east. [44]And eighteen thousand men of Benjamin fell; all these *were* men of valor. [45]Then they[a] turned and fled toward the wilderness to the rock of Rimmon; and they cut down five thousand of them on the highways. Then they pursued them relentlessly up to Gidom, and killed two thousand of them. [46]So all who fell of Benjamin that day were twenty-five thousand men who drew the sword; all these *were* men of valor.

[47]But six hundred men turned and fled toward the wilderness to the rock of Rimmon, and they stayed at the rock of Rimmon for four months. [48]And the men of Israel turned back against the children of Benjamin, and struck them down with the edge of the sword—from *every* city, men and beasts, all who were found. They also set fire to all the cities they came to.

WIVES PROVIDED FOR THE BENJAMITES

[1]Now the men of Israel had sworn an oath at Mizpah, saying, "None of us shall give his daughter to Benjamin as a wife." [2]Then the people came to the house of God,[a] and remained there before God till evening. They lifted up their voices and wept bitterly, [3]and said, "O LORD God of Israel, why has this come to pass in Israel, that today there should be one tribe *missing* in Israel?"

[4]So it was, on the next morning, that the people rose early and built an altar there, and offered burnt offerings and peace offerings.

20:26 [a]Or *Bethel* 20:34 [a]Literally *they* 20:45 [a]Septuagint reads *the rest.* 21:2 [a]Or *Bethel*

WHAT'S IT MEAN?

This was more than a promise the Israelites made. It was a vow, and vows were unbreakable. The men of Israel weren't required to make this pledge, but once they did, they were bound by it. It was unthinkable for people in ancient times to go back on their word.

Judges 21:1

⁵The children of Israel said, "Who *is there* among all the tribes of Israel who did not come up with the assembly to the LORD?" For they had made a great oath concerning anyone who had not come up to the LORD at Mizpah, saying, "He shall surely be put to death." ⁶And the children of Israel grieved for Benjamin their brother, and said, "One tribe is cut off from Israel today. ⁷What shall we do for wives for those who remain, seeing we have sworn by the LORD that we will not give them our daughters as wives?"

⁸And they said, "What one *is there* from the tribes of Israel who did not come up to Mizpah to the LORD?" And, in fact, no one had come to the camp from Jabesh Gilead to the assembly. ⁹For when the people were counted, indeed, not one of the inhabitants of Jabesh Gilead *was* there. ¹⁰So the congregation sent out there twelve thousand of their most valiant men, and commanded them, saying, "Go and strike the inhabitants of Jabesh Gilead with the edge of the sword, including the women and children. ¹¹And this *is* the thing that you shall do: You shall utterly destroy every male, and every woman who has known a man intimately." ¹²So they found among the inhabitants of Jabesh Gilead four hundred young virgins who had not known a man intimately; and they brought them to the camp at Shiloh, which is in the land of Canaan.

¹³Then the whole congregation sent *word* to the children of Benjamin who *were* at the rock of Rimmon, and announced peace to them. ¹⁴So Benjamin came back at that time, and they gave them the women whom they had saved alive of the women of Jabesh Gilead; and yet they had not found enough for them.

¹⁵And the people grieved for Benjamin, because the LORD had made a void in the tribes of Israel.

¹⁶Then the elders of the congregation said, "What shall we do for wives for those who remain, since the women of Benjamin have been destroyed?" ¹⁷And they said, "*There must be* an inheritance for the survivors of Benjamin, that a tribe may not be destroyed from Israel. ¹⁸However, we cannot give them wives from our daughters, for the children of Israel have sworn an oath, saying, 'Cursed *be* the one who gives a wife to Benjamin.'" ¹⁹Then they said, "In fact, *there is* a yearly feast of the LORD in Shiloh, which *is* north of Bethel, on the east side of the highway that goes up from Bethel to Shechem, and south of Lebonah."

²⁰Therefore they instructed the children of Benjamin, saying, "Go, lie in wait in the vineyards, ²¹and watch; and just when the daughters of Shiloh come out to perform their dances, then come out from the vineyards, and every man catch a wife for himself from the daughters of Shiloh; then go to the land of Benjamin. ²²Then it shall be, when their fathers or their brothers come to us to complain, that we will say to them, 'Be kind to them for our sakes, because we did not take a wife for any of them in the war; for *it is* not *as though* you have given the *women* to them at this time, making yourselves guilty of your oath.'"

²³And the children of Benjamin did so; they took enough wives for their number from those who danced, whom they caught. Then they went and returned to their inheritance, and they rebuilt the cities and dwelt in them. ²⁴So the children of Israel departed from there at that time, every man to his tribe and family; they went out from there, every man to his inheritance.

²⁵In those days *there was* no king in Israel; everyone did *what was* right in his own eyes.

AUTHORITY

Do laws help us live right? (21:25)

CONTENT   The Book of Ruth is a story about a woman and, of all people, her mother-in-law. If it were a movie, you could call it a chick-flick. It has all the elements: drama, tragedy, danger, loyalty, flirtation, a love story, brave women, an honorable man, a marriage, and a baby. But it's not a flick at all, and it's not just for chicks.

This is actually a story that, first of all, shows us something about the Jewish culture. It also reveals an important link in the genetic chain that led to Jesus Christ. Finally, it tells us a lot about the kind of people we should be: People that stick by their families and ask for the love they need and honor their cultural traditions.

The Book of Ruth is about the kind of love that draws people together and then helps them stay that way. It's about the kind of love that you need in your life. The first key to finding it is recognizing the right kind of people to ask for it from. Ruth was one.

Outline

Purpose   Faithful people live godly lives in the worst of times.

Theme   God's Sovereign Intervention Brings Universal Redemption

Date of writing   Uncertain

Bible Talk

Wheat Fields

Some important parts of this story take place in a field of wheat. When Ruth went out for groceries, a wheat field is one of the places she stopped. Boaz first noticed Ruth when she was *gleaning* in his wheat fields.

So what was Ruth actually doing when she was out *gleaning*? Basically she was walking behind the guys that were gathering the wheat. Because they didn't have automatic machines to harvest the wheat, some wheat would be left behind. Ladies would go behind the harvesters and gather up the leftovers. This was one of the ways that society took care of its poor.

Boaz saw Ruth gleaning, got a little crush on her, and told his guys to be sure and drop something extra for her to pick up. How's that for a move?

MARRIAGE CUSTOMS

Boaz was allowed, even obligated, to marry Ruth because of a particular family custom. In those days women didn't *usually* have a career outside of the home. When a woman's husband died she was up the creek. So there were a lot of provisions made for widows in Jewish customs.

If a widow was young, then she could go to the closest living relative and expect him to take care of her, even marry her. Ruth wasn't related to Boaz; but her mother-in-law, Naomi, was. This put him in line to marry Ruth with only one person standing in line before him. Read chapter 4 to find out what he did about that.

ELIMELECH'S FAMILY GOES TO MOAB

¹Now it came to pass, in the days when the judges ruled, that there was a famine in the land. And a certain man of Bethlehem, Judah, went to dwell in the country of Moab, he and his wife and his two sons. ²The name of the man *was* Elimelech, the name of his wife *was* Naomi, and the names of his two sons *were* Mahlon and Chilion—Ephrathites of Bethlehem, Judah. And they went to the country of Moab and remained there. ³Then Elimelech, Naomi's husband, died; and she was left, and her two sons. ⁴Now they took wives of the women of Moab: the name of the one *was* Orpah, and the name of the other Ruth. And they dwelt there about ten years. ⁵Then both Mahlon and Chilion also died; so the woman survived her two sons and her husband.

WHAT'S IT MEAN?

Here's what you need to know about the geography of this story: Bethlehem and Jerusalem are neighboring cities on the western side of the Dead Sea. The country of Moab was an enemy of Israel located about fifty miles away, on the eastern side of the Dead Sea.

Ruth 1:1, 2

NAOMI RETURNS WITH RUTH

⁶Then she arose with her daughters-in-law that she might return from the country of Moab, for she had heard in the country of Moab that the LORD had visited His people by giving them bread. ⁷Therefore she went out from the place where she was, and her two daughters-in-law with her; and they went on the way to return to the land of Judah. ⁸And Naomi said to her two daughters-in-law, "Go, return each to her mother's house. The LORD deal kindly with you, as you have dealt with the dead and with me. ⁹The LORD grant that you may

find rest, each in the house of her husband."

So she kissed them, and they lifted up their voices and wept. ¹⁰And they said to her, "Surely we will return with you to your people."

¹¹But Naomi said, "Turn back, my daughters; why will you go with me? *Are* there still sons in my womb, that they may be your husbands? ¹²Turn back, my daughters, go—for I am too old to have a husband. If I should say I have hope, *if* I should have a husband tonight and should also bear sons, ¹³would you wait for them till they were grown? Would you restrain yourselves from having husbands? No, my daughters; for it grieves me very much for your sakes that the hand of the LORD has gone out against me!"

¹⁴Then they lifted up their voices and wept again; and Orpah kissed her mother-in-law, but Ruth clung to her.

¹⁵And she said, "Look, your sister-in-law has gone back to her people and to her gods; return after your sister-in-law."

¹⁶But Ruth said:

> "Entreat me not to leave
>   you,
> *Or to* turn back from following after you;
> For wherever you go, I will go;
> And wherever you lodge, I will lodge;
> Your people *shall be* my people,
> And your God, my God.
> ¹⁷ Where you die, I will die,
> And there will I be buried.
> The LORD do so to me, and more also,
> If *anything but* death parts you and me."

FAMILY

What's a good example of family? (1:16)

¹⁸When she saw that she was determined to go with her, she stopped speaking to her.

¹⁹Now the two of them went until they came to Bethlehem. And it happened, when they had come to Bethlehem, that all the city was excited because of them; and the women said, "Is this Naomi?"

²⁰But she said to them, "Do not call me Naomi;ᵃ call me Mara,ᵇ for the Almighty has dealt very bitterly with me. ²¹I went out full, and the LORD has brought me home again empty. Why do you call me Naomi, since the LORD has testified against me, and the Almighty has afflicted me?"

"For wherever you go, I will go; and wherever you lodge, I will lodge; your people shall be my people, and your God, my God."
(Ruth 1:16b)

1:20 ᵃLiterally *Pleasant* ᵇLiterally *Bitter*

²²So Naomi returned, and Ruth the Moabitess her daughter-in-law with her, who returned from the country of Moab. Now they came to Bethlehem at the beginning of barley harvest.

RUTH MEETS BOAZ

¹There was a relative of Naomi's husband, a man of great wealth, of the family of Elimelech. His name *was* Boaz. ²So Ruth the Moabitess said to Naomi, "Please let me go to the field, and glean heads of grain after *him* in whose sight I may find favor."

And she said to her, "Go, my daughter."

³Then she left, and went and gleaned in the field after the reapers. And she happened to come to the part of the field *belonging* to Boaz, who *was* of the family of Elimelech.

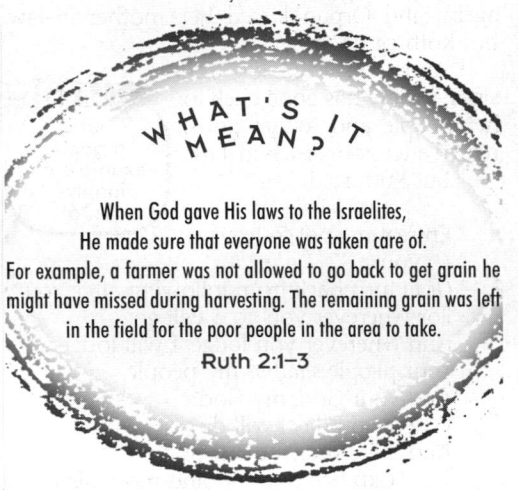

WHAT'S IT MEAN?

When God gave His laws to the Israelites, He made sure that everyone was taken care of. For example, a farmer was not allowed to go back to get grain he might have missed during harvesting. The remaining grain was left in the field for the poor people in the area to take.

Ruth 2:1–3

⁴Now behold, Boaz came from Bethlehem, and said to the reapers, "The LORD *be* with you!"

And they answered him, "The LORD bless you!"

⁵Then Boaz said to his servant who was in charge of the reapers, "Whose young woman *is* this?"

⁶So the servant who was in charge of the reapers answered and said, "It *is* the young Moabite woman who came back with Naomi from the country of Moab. ⁷And she said, 'Please let me glean and gather after the reapers among the sheaves.' So she came and has continued from morning until now, though she rested a little in the house."

⁸Then Boaz said to Ruth, "You will listen, my daughter, will you not? Do not go to glean in another field, nor go from here, but stay close by my young women. ⁹*Let* your eyes *be* on the field which they reap, and go after them. Have I not commanded the young men not to touch you? And when you are thirsty, go to the ves-

sels and drink from what the young men have drawn."

¹⁰So she fell on her face, bowed down to the ground, and said to him, "Why have I found favor in your eyes, that you should take notice of me, since I *am* a foreigner?"

¹¹And Boaz answered and said to her, "It has been fully reported to me, all that you have done for your mother-in-law since the death of your husband, and *how* you have left your father and your mother and the land of your birth, and have come to a people whom you did not know before. ¹²The LORD repay your work, and a full reward be given you by the LORD God of Israel, under whose wings you have come for refuge."

¹³Then she said, "Let me find favor in your sight, my lord; for you have comforted me, and have spoken kindly to your maidservant, though I am not like one of your maidservants."

¹⁴Now Boaz said to her at mealtime, "Come here, and eat of the bread, and dip your piece of bread in the vinegar." So she sat beside the reapers, and he passed parched *grain* to her; and she ate and was satisfied, and kept some back. ¹⁵And when she rose up to glean, Boaz commanded his young men, saying, "Let her glean even among the sheaves, and do not reproach her. ¹⁶Also let *grain* from the bundles fall purposely for her; leave *it* that she may glean, and do not rebuke her."

¹⁷So she gleaned in the field until evening, and beat out what she had gleaned, and it was about an ephah of barley. ¹⁸Then she took *it* up and went into the city, and her mother-in-law saw what she had gleaned. So she brought out and gave to her what she had kept back after she had been satisfied.

¹⁹And her mother-in-law said to her, "Where have you gleaned today? And where did you work? Blessed be the one who took notice of you."

So she told her mother-in-law with whom she had worked, and said, "The man's name with whom I worked today *is* Boaz."

²⁰Then Naomi said to her daughter-in-law, "Blessed *be* he of the LORD, who has not forsaken His kindness to the living and the dead!" And Naomi said to her, "This man *is* a relation of ours, one of our close relatives."

²¹Ruth the Moabitess said, "He also said to me, 'You shall stay close by my young men until they have finished all my harvest.' "

²²And Naomi said to Ruth her daughter-in-law, "*It is* good, my daughter, that you go out with his young women, and that people do not meet you in any other field." ²³So she stayed

close by the young women of Boaz, to glean until the end of barley harvest and wheat harvest; and she dwelt with her mother-in-law.

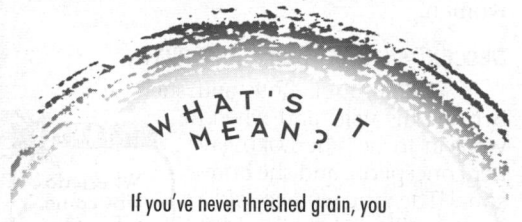

WHAT'S IT MEAN?

If you've never threshed grain, you may not know that it involves separating the grain itself from the stalk. In ancient times, this was done by beating the stalks or having animals walk over them. Afterward, the whole smashed mess was thrown into the air. The leaves and stalks were blown away by the wind, and the grain fell back to the ground. Threshing was hard work, but there was usually something special to look forward to when the work was done. Traditionally, the harvest and threshing season was a time of celebrations and fun.

Ruth 3:2

RUTH'S REDEMPTION ASSURED

[1]Then Naomi her mother-in-law said to her, "My daughter, shall I not seek security for you, that it may be well with you? [2]Now Boaz, whose young women you were with, is he not our relative? In fact, he is winnowing barley tonight at the threshing floor. [3]Therefore wash yourself and anoint yourself, put on your *best* garment and go down to the threshing floor; *but* do not make yourself known to the man until he has finished eating and drinking. [4]Then it shall be, when he lies down, that you shall notice the place where he lies; and you shall go in, uncover his feet, and lie down; and he will tell you what you should do."

[5]And she said to her, "All that you say to me I will do."

[6]So she went down to the threshing floor and did according to all that her mother-in-law instructed her. [7]And after Boaz had eaten and drunk, and his heart was cheerful, he went to lie down at the end of the heap of grain; and she came softly, uncovered his feet, and lay down.

[8]Now it happened at midnight that the man was startled, and turned himself; and there, a woman was lying at his feet. [9]And he said, "Who *are* you?"

So she answered, "I *am* Ruth, your maidservant. Take your maidservant under your wing,[a] for you are a close relative."

[10]Then he said, "Blessed *are* you of the LORD, my daughter! For you have shown more kindness at the end than at the beginning, in that you did not go after young men, whether poor or rich. [11]And now, my daughter, do not fear. I will do for you all that you request, for all the people of my town know that you *are* a virtuous woman. [12]Now it is true that I *am* a close relative; however, there is a relative closer than I. [13]Stay this night, and in the morning it shall be *that* if he will perform the duty of a close relative for you—good; let him do it. But if he does not want to perform the duty for you, then I will perform the duty for you, *as* the LORD lives! Lie down until morning."

[14]So she lay at his feet until morning, and she arose before one could recognize another. Then he said, "Do not let it be known that the woman came to the threshing floor." [15]Also he said, "Bring the shawl that *is* on you and hold it." And when she held it, he measured six *ephahs* of barley, and laid *it* on her. Then she[a] went into the city.

[16]When she came to her mother-in-law, she said, "*Is* that you, my daughter?"

Then she told her all that the man had done for her. [17]And she said, "These six *ephahs* of barley he gave me; for he said to me, 'Do not go empty-handed to your mother-in-law.' "

[18]Then she said, "Sit still, my daughter, until you know how the matter will turn out; for the man will not rest until he has concluded the matter this day."

BOAZ REDEEMS RUTH

[1]Now Boaz went up to the gate and sat down there; and behold, the close relative of whom Boaz had spoken came by. So Boaz said, "Come aside, friend,[a] sit down here." So he came aside and sat down. [2]And he took ten men of the elders of the city, and said, "Sit down here." So they sat down. [3]Then he said to the close relative, "Naomi, who has come back from the country of Moab, sold the piece of land which *belonged* to our brother Elimelech. [4]And I thought to inform you, saying, 'Buy *it* back in the presence of the inhabitants and the elders of my people. If you will redeem *it*, redeem *it*; but if you[a] will not redeem *it*, *then* tell me, that

---

3:9 [a]Or *Spread the corner of your garment over your maidservant*   **3:15** [a]Many Hebrew manuscripts, Syriac, and Vulgate read *she*; Masoretic Text, Septuagint, and Targum read *he*.   **4:1** [a]Hebrew *peloni almoni*; literally *so and so*   **4:4** [a]Following many Hebrew manuscripts, Septuagint, Syriac, Targum, and Vulgate; Masoretic Text reads *he*.

I may know; for *there is* no one but you to redeem *it,* and I *am* next after you.' "

And he said, "I will redeem *it.*"

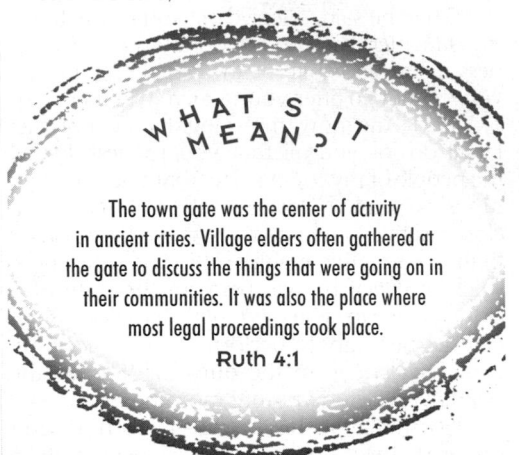

WHAT'S IT MEAN?

The town gate was the center of activity in ancient cities. Village elders often gathered at the gate to discuss the things that were going on in their communities. It was also the place where most legal proceedings took place.

Ruth 4:1

⁵Then Boaz said, "On the day you buy the field from the hand of Naomi, you must also buy *it* from Ruth the Moabitess, the wife of the dead, to perpetuate*ᵃ* the name of the dead through his inheritance."

⁶And the close relative said, "I cannot redeem *it* for myself, lest I ruin my own inheritance. You redeem my right of redemption for yourself, for I cannot redeem *it.*"

⁷Now this *was the custom* in former times in Israel concerning redeeming and exchanging, to confirm anything: one man took off his sandal and gave *it* to the other, and this *was* a confirmation in Israel.

⁸Therefore the close relative said to Boaz, "Buy *it* for yourself." So he took off his sandal. ⁹And Boaz said to the elders and all the people, "You *are* witnesses this day that I have bought all that was Elimelech's, and all that *was* Chilion's and Mahlon's, from the hand of Naomi. ¹⁰Moreover, Ruth the Moabitess, the widow of Mahlon, I have acquired as my wife, to perpetuate the name of the dead through his inheritance, that the name of the dead may not be cut off from among his brethren and from his position at the gate.*ᵃ* You *are* witnesses this day."

¹¹And all the people who *were* at the gate, and the elders, said, "*We are* witnesses. The LORD make the woman who is coming to your house like Rachel and Leah, the two who built the house of Israel; and may you prosper in Ephrathah and be famous in Bethlehem. ¹²May your house be like the house of Perez, whom Tamar bore to Judah, because of the offspring which the LORD will give you from this young woman."

DESCENDANTS OF BOAZ AND RUTH

¹³So Boaz took Ruth and she became his wife; and when he went in to her, the LORD gave her conception, and she bore a son. ¹⁴Then the women said to Naomi, "Blessed *be* the LORD, who has not left you this day without a close relative; and may his name be famous in Israel! ¹⁵And may he be to you a restorer of life and a nourisher of your old age; for your daughter-in-law, who loves you, who is better to you than seven sons, has borne him." ¹⁶Then Naomi took the child and laid him on her bosom, and became a nurse to him. ¹⁷Also the neighbor women gave him a name, saying, "There is a son born to Naomi." And they called his name Obed. He *is* the father of Jesse, the father of David.

FAMILY

Where do kids come from? (4:13)

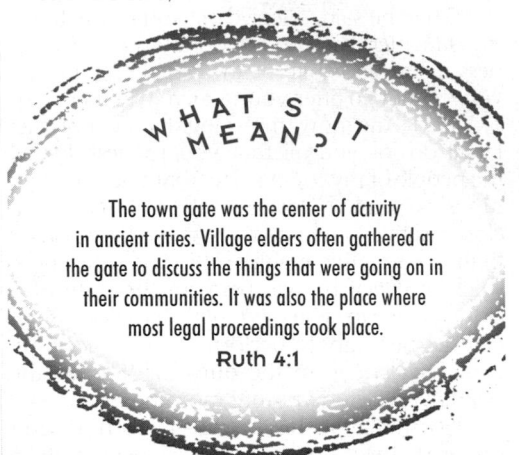

WHAT'S IT MEAN?

How would you like to be best known for the way you were born? That was the fate of Perez, an ancestor of Boaz. When it was time for Perez and his twin brother to be delivered, Perez's brother stuck his hand out first. After a few minutes, the hand disappeared back into the womb, and out popped Perez, followed by his older or younger brother (depending on how you look at it). Like Ruth, Perez's mother, Tamar, was an outsider who married into an Israelite family. Several kings of Israel, including David, descended from this family line.

Ruth 4:12

¹⁸Now this *is* the genealogy of Perez: Perez begot Hezron; ¹⁹Hezron begot Ram, and Ram begot Amminadab; ²⁰Amminadab begot Nahshon, and Nahshon begot Salmon;*ᵃ* ²¹Salmon begot Boaz, and Boaz begot Obed; ²²Obed begot Jesse, and Jesse begot David.

4:5 *ᵃ*Literally *raise up*   **4:10** *ᵃ*Probably his civic office   **4:20** *ᵃ*Hebrew *Salmah*

1 Samuel

CONTENT

Reading First Samuel is like finding a home movie or home video of the Hebrew nation. It's a family history in real-time and with the skeletons all hanging out of the family closets.

The time line of this verbal "video" starts with one of the key players, Samuel, as a child being raised by the church. He grows up to be a national leader, a judge, and a prophet. His real claim to fame, though, is that he anointed the first king of Israel, King Saul.

Saul was a warrior kind of king. He protected his territory and fought off the bad guys. This time in history would have looked a little like an *Arabian Knights* episode with shields and horses and armor. Saul's downfall began when he got violently jealous of an up-and-coming leader named David.

Saul eventually lost his mind and then his life while he was losing his kingdom. He's an example to us of someone who failed to do things God's way and lost it all.

Outline

Purpose

In leaders, character and commitment do count.

Theme

God Is Working in History

Date of writing

1050–750 B.C.

"So Samuel said, 'Has the LORD as great delight in burnt offerings and sacrifices, as in obeying the voice of the LORD? Behold, to obey is better than sacrifice, and to heed than the fat of rams' " (15:22).

Bible Talk

The First King Thing

Do you understand why this time in the Hebrews' history is so significant? The whole nation of Israel had never had a king before! That's like America not ever having had a president before. The Hebrews had been led by God through men like Moses and then Joshua and then by judges, such as Samson and Deborah, but not by an official king.

Actually this system had worked well for them, but they did exactly what we do. They looked at the other nations around them, and said, "We want a king like *they've* got." Sometimes God gives us what we want even though He knows we won't like the consequences.

That's what happened for the Hebrews.

TALK ABOUT AN INTERPERSONAL CONFLICT!

David and Saul's relationship was, at the *very* least, a difficult one. Saul was intimidated by David. He felt threatened because the people respected David. It's never a good thing for someone else in a kingdom to be respected more than the king.

Saul even put out a contract on David as if he were a criminal. David and his men had to hide out like Robin Hood's guys, but not because they had done anything wrong.

The amazing thing was that David didn't strike back at Saul. David realized that God had made Saul king and so Saul deserved respect. David also realized that in a conflict you can only control your own attitude, not the other person's.

Pretty smart guy.

THE FAMILY OF ELKANAH

[1]Now there was a certain man of Ramathaim Zophim, of the mountains of Ephraim, and his name *was* Elkanah the son of Jeroham, the son of Elihu,[a] the son of Tohu,[b] the son of Zuph, an Ephraimite. [2]And he had two wives: the name of one *was* Hannah, and the name of the other Peninnah. Peninnah had children, but Hannah had no children. [3]This man went up from his city yearly to worship and sacrifice to the LORD of hosts in Shiloh. Also the two sons of Eli, Hophni and Phinehas, the priests of the LORD, *were* there. [4]And whenever the time came for Elkanah to make an offering, he would give portions to Peninnah his wife and to all her sons and daughters. [5]But to Hannah he would give a double portion, for he loved Hannah, although the LORD had closed her womb. [6]And her rival also provoked her severely, to make her miserable, because the LORD had closed her womb. [7]So it was, year by year, when she went up to the house of the LORD, that she provoked her; therefore she wept and did not eat.

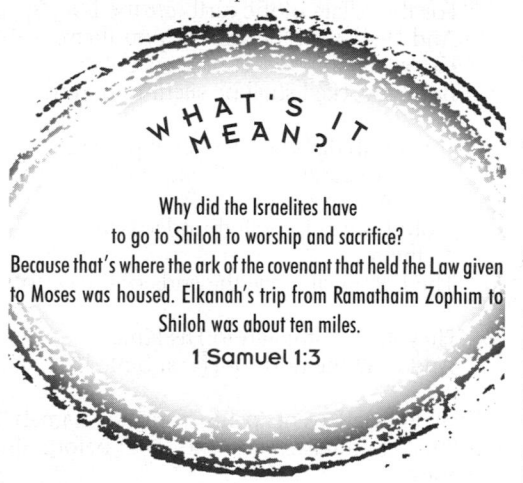

WHAT'S IT MEAN?

Why did the Israelites have to go to Shiloh to worship and sacrifice?
Because that's where the ark of the covenant that held the Law given to Moses was housed. Elkanah's trip from Ramathaim Zophim to Shiloh was about ten miles.

1 Samuel 1:3

HANNAH'S VOW

[8]Then Elkanah her husband said to her, "Hannah, why do you weep? Why do you not eat? And why is your heart grieved? *Am* I not better to you than ten sons?"

FEELINGS
What should we do when we are sad? (1:10)

[9]So Hannah arose after they had finished eating and drinking in Shiloh. Now Eli the priest was sitting on the seat by the doorpost of the tabernacle[a] of the LORD. [10]And she *was* in bitterness of soul, and

prayed to the LORD and wept in anguish. [11]Then she made a vow and said, "O LORD of hosts, if You will indeed look on the affliction of Your maidservant and remember me, and not forget Your maidservant, but will give Your maidservant a male child, then I will give him to the LORD all the days of his life, and no razor shall come upon his head."

[12]And it happened, as she continued praying before the LORD, that Eli watched her mouth. [13]Now Hannah spoke in her heart; only her lips moved, but her voice was not heard. Therefore Eli thought she was drunk. [14]So Eli said to her, "How long will you be drunk? Put your wine away from you!"

[15]But Hannah answered and said, "No, my lord, I *am* a woman of sorrowful spirit. I have drunk neither wine nor intoxicating drink, but have poured out my soul before the LORD. [16]Do not consider your maidservant a wicked woman,[a] for out of the abundance of my complaint and grief I have spoken until now."

[17]Then Eli answered and said, "Go in peace, and the God of Israel grant your petition which you have asked of Him."

PRAYER
Who answers prayer? (1:17)

[18]And she said, "Let your maidservant find favor in your sight." So the woman went her way and ate, and her face was no longer *sad*.

SAMUEL IS BORN AND DEDICATED

[19]Then they rose early in the morning and worshiped before the LORD, and returned and came to their house at Ramah. And Elkanah knew Hannah his wife, and the LORD remembered her. [20]So it came to pass in the process of time that Hannah conceived and bore a son, and called his name Samuel,[a] *saying,* "Because I have asked for him from the LORD."

[21]Now the man Elkanah and all his house went up to offer to the LORD the yearly sacrifice and his vow. [22]But Hannah did not go up, for she said to her husband, "Not until the child is weaned; then I will take him, that he may appear before the LORD and remain there forever."

[23]So Elkanah her husband said to her, "Do what seems best to you; wait until you have weaned him. Only let the LORD establish His[a] word." Then the woman stayed and nursed her son until she had weaned him.

[24]Now when she had weaned him, she took

1:1 [a]Spelled *Eliel* in 1 Chronicles 6:34 [b]Spelled *Toah* in 1 Chronicles 6:34   **1:9** [a]Hebrew *heykal*, palace or temple   **1:16** [a]Literally *daughter of Belial*   **1:20** [a]Literally *Heard by God*   **1:23** [a]Following Masoretic Text, Targum, and Vulgate; Dead Sea Scrolls, Septuagint, and Syriac read *your*.

him up with her, with three bulls,[a] one ephah of flour, and a skin of wine, and brought him to the house of the LORD in Shiloh. And the child *was* young. ²⁵Then they slaughtered a bull, and brought the child to Eli. ²⁶And she said, "O my lord! As your soul lives, my lord, I *am* the woman who stood by you here, praying to the LORD. ²⁷For this child I prayed, and the LORD has granted me my petition which I asked of Him. ²⁸Therefore I also have lent him to the LORD; as long as he lives he shall be lent to the LORD." So they worshiped the LORD there.

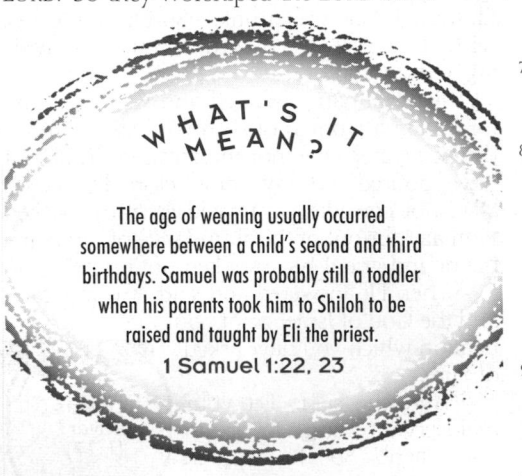

WHAT'S IT MEAN?

The age of weaning usually occurred somewhere between a child's second and third birthdays. Samuel was probably still a toddler when his parents took him to Shiloh to be raised and taught by Eli the priest.

1 Samuel 1:22, 23

HANNAH'S PRAYER

¹And Hannah prayed and said:

"My heart rejoices in the LORD;
My horn[a] is exalted in the LORD.
I smile at my enemies,
Because I rejoice in Your salvation.

HAPPINESS
Where can I find happiness?
(2:1)

² "No one is holy like the LORD,
For *there is* none besides You,
Nor *is there* any rock like our God.

GOD
Who is like God?
(2:2)

³ "Talk no more so very proudly;
Let no arrogance come from your mouth,
For the LORD *is* the God of knowledge;
And by Him actions are weighed.

⁴ "The bows of the mighty men *are* broken,
And those who stumbled are girded with strength.
⁵ *Those who were* full have hired themselves out for bread,
And the hungry have ceased *to hunger.*
Even the barren has borne seven,
And she who has many children has become feeble.

⁶ "The LORD kills and makes alive;
He brings down to the grave and brings up.
⁷ The LORD makes poor and makes rich;
He brings low and lifts up.
⁸ He raises the poor from the dust
And lifts the beggar from the ash heap,
To set *them* among princes
And make them inherit the throne of glory.

GOD
How is God sovereign?
(2:6, 7)

"For the pillars of the earth *are* the LORD's,
And He has set the world upon them.
⁹ He will guard the feet of His saints,
But the wicked shall be silent in darkness.

"For by strength no man shall prevail.
¹⁰ The adversaries of the LORD shall be broken in pieces;
From heaven He will thunder against them.
The LORD will judge the ends of the earth.

"He will give strength to His king,
And exalt the horn of His anointed."

¹¹Then Elkanah went to his house at Ramah. But the child ministered to the LORD before Eli the priest.

THE WICKED SONS OF ELI

¹²Now the sons of Eli *were* corrupt;[a] they did not know the LORD. ¹³And the priests' custom with the people *was that* when any man offered a sacrifice, the priest's servant would come with a three-pronged fleshhook in his hand while the meat was boiling. ¹⁴Then he would thrust *it* into the pan, or kettle, or caldron, or pot; and the priest would take for himself all that the fleshhook brought up. So they did in Shiloh to all the Israelites who came there. ¹⁵Also, before they burned the fat, the priest's servant would

---

1:24 [a]Dead Sea Scrolls, Septuagint, and Syriac read *a three-year-old bull.*   **2:1** [a]That is, *strength*
2:12 [a]Literally *sons of Belial*

come and say to the man who sacrificed, "Give meat for roasting to the priest, for he will not take boiled meat from you, but raw."

¹⁶And *if* the man said to him, "They should really burn the fat first; *then* you may take *as much* as your heart desires," he would then answer him, "No, but you must give *it* now; and if not, I will take *it* by force."

¹⁷Therefore the sin of the young men was very great before the LORD, for men abhorred the offering of the LORD.

SAMUEL'S CHILDHOOD MINISTRY

¹⁸But Samuel ministered before the LORD, *even as* a child, wearing a linen ephod. ¹⁹Moreover his mother used to make him a little robe, and bring *it* to him year by year when she came up with her husband to offer the yearly sacrifice. ²⁰And Eli would bless Elkanah and his wife, and say, "The LORD give you descendants from this woman for the loan that was given to the LORD." Then they would go to their own home.

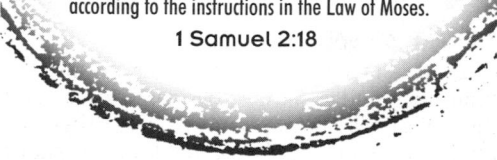

WHAT'S IT MEAN?

Linen, which was handwoven from the fibers of the hemp plant, was considered to be the highest-quality fabric in the ancient world. For the most part, only people of great wealth or power wore linen. Priests and those who served in the temple were the exception. They, too, wore linen. The white linen uniforms that the priests wore were designed according to the instructions in the Law of Moses.

1 Samuel 2:18

²¹And the LORD visited Hannah, so that she conceived and bore three sons and two daughters. Meanwhile the child Samuel grew before the LORD.

PROPHECY AGAINST ELI'S HOUSEHOLD

²²Now Eli was very old; and he heard everything his sons did to all Israel,^a and how they lay with the women who assembled at the door of the tabernacle of meeting. ²³So he said to them, "Why do you do such things? For I hear of your evil dealings from all the people. ²⁴No, my sons! For *it is* not a good report that I hear. You make the LORD's people transgress. ²⁵If one man sins against another, God will judge him. But if a man sins against the LORD, who will intercede for him?" Nevertheless they did not heed the voice of their father, because the LORD desired to kill them.

²⁶And the child Samuel grew in stature, and in favor both with the LORD and men.

²⁷Then a man of God came to Eli and said to him, "Thus says the LORD: 'Did I not clearly reveal Myself to the house of your father when they were in Egypt in Pharaoh's house? ²⁸Did I not choose him out of all the tribes of Israel *to be* My priest, to offer upon My altar, to burn incense, and to wear an ephod before Me? And did I not give to the house of your father all the offerings of the children of Israel made by fire? ²⁹Why do you kick at My sacrifice and My offering which I have commanded *in My* dwelling place, and honor your sons more than Me, to make yourselves fat with the best of all the offerings of Israel My people?' ³⁰Therefore the LORD God of Israel says: 'I said indeed *that* your house and the house of your father would walk before Me forever.' But now the LORD says: 'Far be it from Me; for those who honor Me I will honor, and those who despise Me shall be lightly esteemed. ³¹Behold, the days are coming that I will cut off your arm and the arm of your father's house, so that there will not be an old man in your house. ³²And you will see an enemy *in My* dwelling place, *despite* all the good which God does for Israel. And there shall not be an old man in your house forever. ³³But any of your men *whom* I do not cut off from My altar shall consume your eyes and grieve your heart. And all the descendants of your house shall die in the flower of their age. ³⁴Now this *shall be* a sign to you that will come upon your two sons, on Hophni and Phinehas: in one day they shall die, both of them. ³⁵Then I will raise up for Myself a faithful priest *who* shall do according to what *is* in My heart and in My mind. I will build him a sure house, and he shall walk before My anointed forever. ³⁶And it shall come

2:22 ^aFollowing Masoretic Text, Targum, and Vulgate; Dead Sea Scrolls and Septuagint omit the rest of this verse.

> "No one is holy like the LORD, for there is none besides You, nor is there any rock like our God."
> **(1 Samuel 2:2)**

to pass that everyone who is left in your house will come *and* bow down to him for a piece of silver and a morsel of bread, and say, "Please, put me in one of the priestly positions, that I may eat a piece of bread.' ' "

SAMUEL'S FIRST PROPHECY

[1]Now the boy Samuel ministered to the LORD before Eli. And the word of the LORD was rare in those days; *there was* no widespread revelation. [2]And it came to pass at that time, while Eli *was* lying down in his place, and when his eyes had begun to grow so dim that he could not see, [3]and before the lamp of God went out in the tabernacle[a] of the LORD where the ark of God *was*, and while Samuel was lying down, [4]that the LORD called Samuel. And he answered, "Here I am!" [5]So he ran to Eli and said, "Here I am, for you called me."

And he said, "I did not call; lie down again." And he went and lay down.

[6]Then the LORD called yet again, "Samuel!" So Samuel arose and went to Eli, and said, "Here I am, for you called me." He answered, "I did not call, my son; lie down again." [7](Now Samuel did not yet know the LORD, nor was the word of the LORD yet revealed to him.)

[8]And the LORD called Samuel again the third time. So he arose and went to Eli, and said, "Here I am, for you did call me."

Then Eli perceived that the LORD had called the boy. [9]Therefore Eli said to Samuel, "Go, lie down; and it shall be, if He calls you, that you must say, 'Speak, LORD, for Your servant hears.' " So Samuel went and lay down in his place.

[10]Now the LORD came and stood and called as at other times, "Samuel! Samuel!"

Who should we listen to? (3:10)

And Samuel answered, "Speak, for Your servant hears." [11]Then the LORD said to Samuel: "Behold, I will do something in Israel at which both ears of everyone who hears it will tingle. [12]In that day I will perform against Eli all that I have spoken concerning his house, from beginning to end. [13]For I have told him that I will judge his house forever for the iniquity which he knows, because his sons made themselves vile, and he did not restrain them. [14]And therefore I have sworn to the house of Eli that the iniquity of Eli's house shall not be atoned for by sacrifice or offering forever."

[15]So Samuel lay down until morning,[a] and opened the doors of the house of the LORD. And Samuel was afraid to tell Eli the vision. [16]Then Eli called Samuel and said, "Samuel, my son!"

He answered, "Here I am."

[17]And he said, "What *is* the word that *the* LORD spoke to you? Please do not hide *it* from me. God do so to you, and more also, if you hide anything from me of all the things that He said to you." [18]Then Samuel told him everything, and hid nothing from him. And he said, "It *is* the LORD. Let Him do what seems good to Him."

WHAT'S IT MEAN?

After being run out of their own land in the south, the tribe of Dan moved north. The expression "from Dan to Beersheba" was another way of saying "from one end of the country to the other."

1 Samuel 3:20

[19]So Samuel grew, and the LORD was with him and let none of his words fall to the ground. [20]And all Israel from Dan to Beersheba knew that Samuel *had been* established as a prophet of the LORD. [21]Then the LORD appeared again in Shiloh. For the LORD revealed Himself to Samuel in Shiloh by the word of the LORD.

[1]And the word of Samuel came to all Israel.[a]

THE ARK OF GOD CAPTURED

Now Israel went out to battle against the Philistines, and encamped beside Ebenezer; and the Philistines encamped in Aphek. [2]Then the Philistines put themselves in battle array against Israel. And when they joined battle, Israel was defeated by the Philistines, who killed about four thousand men of the army in the field. [3]And when the people had come into the camp, the elders of Israel said, "Why has the LORD defeated us today before the Philistines? Let us

---

3:3 [a]Hebrew *heykal*, palace or temple   **3:15** [a]Following Masoretic Text, Targum, and Vulgate; Septuagint adds *and he arose in the morning.*   **4:1** [a]Following Masoretic Text and Targum; Septuagint and Vulgate add *And it came to pass in those days that the Philistines gathered themselves together to fight;* Septuagint adds further *against Israel.*

bring the ark of the covenant of the LORD from Shiloh to us, that when it comes among us it may save us from the hand of our enemies." [4]So the people sent to Shiloh, that they might bring from there the ark of the covenant of the LORD of hosts, who dwells *between* the cherubim. And the two sons of Eli, Hophni and Phinehas, *were* there with the ark of the covenant of God.

WHAT'S IT MEAN?

The ark of the covenant was about the size of a small desk. It had rings on its sides so that the priests could run poles through them and carry the ark more easily. Once a year, the high priest would stand in front of the ark to offer a special sacrifice to the Lord. To the Israelites, the ark symbolized God's presence and power.

1 Samuel 4:3

[5]And when the ark of the covenant of the LORD came into the camp, all Israel shouted so loudly that the earth shook. [6]Now when the Philistines heard the noise of the shout, they said, "What *does* the sound of this great shout in the camp of the Hebrews *mean*?" Then they understood that the ark of the LORD had come into the camp. [7]So the Philistines were afraid, for they said, "God has come into the camp!" And they said, "Woe to us! For such a thing has never happened before. [8]Woe to us! Who will deliver us from the hand of these mighty gods? These *are* the gods who struck the Egyptians with all the plagues in the wilderness. [9]Be strong and conduct yourselves like men, you Philistines, that you do not become servants of the Hebrews, as they have been to you. Conduct yourselves like men, and fight!"

[10]So the Philistines fought, and Israel was defeated, and every man fled to his tent. There was a very great slaughter, and there fell of Israel thirty thousand foot soldiers. [11]Also the ark of God was captured; and the two sons of Eli, Hophni and Phinehas, died.

DEATH OF ELI

[12]Then a man of Benjamin ran from the battle line the same day, and came to Shiloh with his clothes torn and dirt on his head. [13]Now when he came, there was Eli, sitting on a seat by the wayside watching,[a] for his heart trembled for the ark of God. And when the man came into the city and told *it*, all the city cried out. [14]When Eli heard the noise of the outcry, he said, "What *does* the sound of this tumult *mean*?" And the man came quickly and told Eli. [15]Eli was ninety-eight years old, and his eyes were so dim that he could not see.

[16]Then the man said to Eli, "I *am* he who came from the battle. And I fled today from the battle line."

And he said, "What happened, my son?"

[17]So the messenger answered and said, "Israel has fled before the Philistines, and there has been a great slaughter among the people. Also your two sons, Hophni and Phinehas, are dead; and the ark of God has been captured."

[18]Then it happened, when he made mention of the ark of God, that Eli fell off the seat backward by the side of the gate; and his neck was broken and he died, for the man was old and heavy. And he had judged Israel forty years.

ICHABOD

[19]Now his daughter-in-law, Phinehas' wife, was with child, *due* to be delivered; and when she heard the news that the ark of God was captured, and that her father-in-law and her husband were dead, she bowed herself and gave birth, for her labor pains came upon her. [20]And about the time of her death the women who stood by her said to her, "Do not fear, for you have borne a son." But she did not answer, nor did she regard *it*. [21]Then she named the child Ichabod,[a] saying, "The glory has departed from Israel!" because the ark of God had been captured and because of her father-in-law and her husband. [22]And she said, "The glory has departed from Israel, for the ark of God has been captured."

THE PHILISTINES AND THE ARK

[1]Then the Philistines took the ark of God and brought it from Ebenezer to Ashdod. [2]When the Philistines took the ark of God, they brought it into the house of Dagon[a] and set it by Dagon. [3]And when the people of Ashdod arose early in the morning, there was Dagon, fallen on its face to the earth before the ark of the LORD. So they took Dagon and set it in its place again. [4]And when they arose early the next morning, there was Dagon, fallen on its

face to the ground before the ark of the LORD. The head of Dagon and both the palms of its hands *were* broken off on the threshold; only Dagon's torso[a] was left of it. [5]Therefore neither the priests of Dagon nor any who come into Dagon's house tread on the threshold of Dagon in Ashdod to this day.

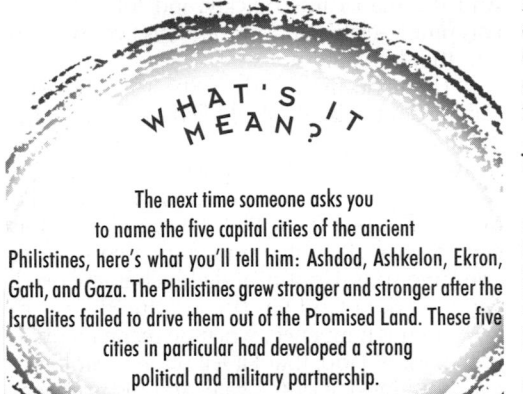

WHAT'S IT MEAN?

The next time someone asks you to name the five capital cities of the ancient Philistines, here's what you'll tell him: Ashdod, Ashkelon, Ekron, Gath, and Gaza. The Philistines grew stronger and stronger after the Israelites failed to drive them out of the Promised Land. These five cities in particular had developed a strong political and military partnership.

1 Samuel 5:1

[6]But the hand of the LORD was heavy on the people of Ashdod, and He ravaged them and struck them with tumors,[a] *both* Ashdod and its territory. [7]And when the men of Ashdod saw how *it was*, they said, "The ark of the God of Israel must not remain with us, for His hand is harsh toward us and Dagon our god." [8]Therefore they sent and gathered to themselves all the lords of the Philistines, and said, "What shall we do with the ark of the God of Israel?"

And they answered, "Let the ark of the God of Israel be carried away to Gath." So they carried the ark of the God of Israel away. [9]So it was, after they had carried it away, that the hand of the LORD was against the city with a very great destruction; and He struck the men of the city, both small and great, and tumors broke out on them.

[10]Therefore they sent the ark of God to Ek-

ron. So it was, as the ark of God came to Ekron, that the Ekronites cried out, saying, "They have brought the ark of the God of Israel to us, to kill us and our people!" [11]So they sent and gathered together all the lords of the Philistines, and said, "Send away the ark of the God of Israel, and let it go back to its own place, so that it does not kill us and our people." For there was a deadly destruction throughout all the city; the hand of God was very heavy there. [12]And the men who did not die were stricken with the tumors, and the cry of the city went up to heaven.

THE ARK RETURNED TO ISRAEL

[1]Now the ark of the LORD was in the country of the Philistines seven months. [2]And the Philistines called for the priests and the diviners, saying, "What shall we do with the ark of the LORD? Tell us how we should send it to its place."

[3]So they said, "If you send away the ark of the God of Israel, do not send it empty; but by all means return *it* to Him *with* a trespass offering. Then you will be healed, and it will be known to you why His hand is not removed from you."

[4]Then they said, "What *is* the trespass offering which we shall return to Him?"

They answered, "Five golden tumors and five golden rats, *according to* the number of the lords of the Philistines. For the same plague *was* on all of you and on your lords. [5]Therefore you shall make images of your tumors and images of your rats that ravage the land, and you shall give glory to the God of Israel; perhaps He will lighten His hand from you, from your gods, and from your land. [6]Why then do you harden your hearts as the Egyptians and Pharaoh hardened their hearts? When He did mighty things among them, did they not let the people go, that they might depart? [7]Now therefore, make a new cart, take two milk cows which have never been yoked, and hitch the cows to the cart; and take their calves home, away from them. [8]Then take the ark of

"Now the ark of the LORD was in the country of the Philistines seven months. And the Philistines called for the priests and the diviners, saying, 'What shall we do with the ark of the LORD? Tell us how we should send it to its place.'"
(1 Samuel 6:1, 2)

5:4 [a]Following Septuagint, Syriac, Targum, and Vulgate; Masoretic Text reads *Dagon*.   **5:6** [a]Probably bubonic plague. Septuagint and Vulgate add here *And in the midst of their land rats sprang up, and there was a great death panic in the city.*

the LORD and set it on the cart; and put the articles of gold which you are returning to Him *as* a trespass offering in a chest by its side. Then send it away, and let it go. [9]And watch: if it goes up the road to its own territory, to Beth Shemesh, *then* He has done us this great evil. But if not, then we shall know that *it is* not His hand *that* struck us—it happened to us by chance."

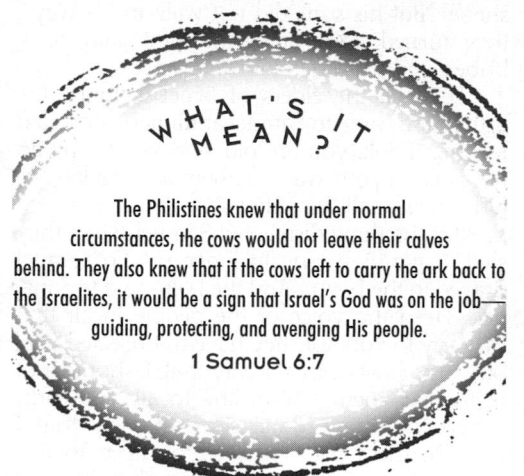

WHAT'S IT MEAN?

The Philistines knew that under normal circumstances, the cows would not leave their calves behind. They also knew that if the cows left to carry the ark back to the Israelites, it would be a sign that Israel's God was on the job—guiding, protecting, and avenging His people.

1 Samuel 6:7

[10]Then the men did so; they took two milk cows and hitched them to the cart, and shut up their calves at home. [11]And they set the ark of the LORD on the cart, and the chest with the gold rats and the images of their tumors. [12]Then the cows headed straight for the road to Beth Shemesh, *and* went along the highway, lowing as they went, and did not turn aside to the right hand or the left. And the lords of the Philistines went after them to the border of Beth Shemesh.

[13]Now *the people of* Beth Shemesh *were* reaping their wheat harvest in the valley; and they lifted their eyes and saw the ark, and rejoiced to see *it*. [14]Then the cart came into the field of Joshua of Beth Shemesh, and stood there; a large stone *was* there. So they split the wood of the cart and offered the cows as a burnt offering to the LORD. [15]The Levites took down the ark of the LORD and the chest that *was* with it, in which *were* the articles of gold, and put *them* on the large stone. Then the men of Beth Shemesh offered burnt offerings and made sacrifices the same day to the LORD. [16]So when the five lords of the Philistines had seen *it*, they returned to Ekron the same day.

[17]These *are* the golden tumors which the Philistines returned *as* a trespass offering to the LORD: one for Ashdod, one for Gaza, one for Ashkelon, one for Gath, one for Ekron; [18]and the golden rats, *according to* the number of all the cities of the Philistines *belonging* to the five lords, *both* fortified cities and country villages, even as far as the large *stone of* Abel on which they set the ark of the LORD, *which stone remains* to this day in the field of Joshua of Beth Shemesh.

[19]Then He struck the men of Beth Shemesh, because they had looked into the ark of the LORD. He struck fifty thousand and seventy men[a] of the people, and the people lamented because the LORD had struck the people with a great slaughter.

THE ARK AT KIRJATH JEARIM

[20]And the men of Beth Shemesh said, "Who is able to stand before this holy LORD God? And to whom shall it go up from us?" [21]So they sent messengers to the inhabitants of Kirjath Jearim, saying, "The Philistines have brought back the ark of the LORD; come down *and* take it up with you."

GOD — Who can stand before God? (6:20)

[1]Then the men of Kirjath Jearim came and took the ark of the LORD, and brought it into the house of Abinadab on the hill, and consecrated Eleazar his son to keep the ark of the LORD.

SAMUEL JUDGES ISRAEL

[2]So it was that the ark remained in Kirjath Jearim a long time; it was there twenty years. And all the house of Israel lamented after the LORD.

[3]Then Samuel spoke to all the house of Israel, saying, "If you return to the LORD with all your hearts, *then* put away the foreign gods and the Ashtoreths[a] from among you, and prepare your hearts for the LORD, and serve Him only; and He will deliver you from the hand of the Philistines." [4]So the children of Israel put away the Baals and the Ashtoreths,[a] and served the LORD only.

TRUTH — How does following truth help us? (7:3)

[5]And Samuel said, "Gather all Israel to Mizpah, and I will pray to the LORD for you." [6]So they gathered together at Mizpah, drew water, and poured *it* out before the LORD. And they fasted that day, and said there, "We have sinned against the LORD." And Samuel judged the children of Israel at Mizpah.

[7]Now when the Philistines heard that the

6:19 [a]Or *He struck seventy men of the people and fifty oxen of a man*   **7:3** [a]Canaanite goddesses   **7:4** [a]Canaanite goddesses children of Israel had gathered together at Mizpah, the lords of the Philistines went up against Israel. And when the children of Israel heard *of it*, they were afraid of the Philistines. [8]So the children of Israel said to Samuel, "Do not cease to cry out to the LORD our God for us, that He may save us from the hand of the Philistines."

[9]And Samuel took a suckling lamb and offered *it as* a whole burnt offering to the LORD. Then Samuel cried out to the LORD for Israel, and the LORD answered him. [10]Now as Samuel was offering up the burnt offering, the Philistines drew near to battle against Israel. But the LORD thundered with a loud thunder upon the Philistines that day, and so confused them that they were overcome before Israel. [11]And the men of Israel went out of Mizpah and pursued the Philistines, and drove them back as far as below Beth Car. [12]Then Samuel took a stone and set *it* up between Mizpah and Shen, and called its name Ebenezer,[a] saying, "Thus far the LORD has helped us."

[13]So the Philistines were subdued, and they did not come anymore into the territory of Israel. And the hand of the LORD was against the Philistines all the days of Samuel. [14]Then the cities which the Philistines had taken from Israel were restored to Israel, from Ekron to Gath; and Israel recovered its territory from the hands of the Philistines. Also there was peace between Israel and the Amorites.

WHAT'S IT MEAN?

All of the places mentioned in this passage were located between Jerusalem and Shiloh. If an ancient travel agent had booked the trip, he would have scheduled at least two to three days of travel. The journey to visit each of the cities and then return to Ramah would have covered about forty miles. Traveling on foot, Samuel probably averaged about sixteen miles a day.

1 Samuel 7:16, 17

[15]And Samuel judged Israel all the days of his life. [16]He went from year to year on a circuit to Bethel, Gilgal, and Mizpah, and judged Israel in all those places. [17]But he always returned to Ramah, for his home *was* there. There he judged Israel, and there he built an altar to the LORD.

ISRAEL DEMANDS A KING

[1]Now it came to pass when Samuel was old that he made his sons judges over Israel. [2]The name of his firstborn was Joel, and the name of his second, Abijah; *they were* judges in Beersheba. [3]But his sons did not walk in his ways; they turned aside after dishonest gain, took bribes, and perverted justice.

[4]Then all the elders of Israel gathered together and came to Samuel at Ramah, [5]and said to him, "Look, you are old, and your sons do not walk in your ways. Now make us a king to judge us like all the nations."

[6]But the thing displeased Samuel when they said, "Give us a king to judge us." So Samuel prayed to the LORD. [7]And the LORD said to Samuel, "Heed the voice of the people in all that they say to you; for they have not rejected you, but they have rejected Me, that I should not reign over them. [8]According to all the works which they have done since the day that I brought them up out of Egypt, even to this day—with which they have forsaken Me and served other gods—so they are doing to you also. [9]Now therefore, heed their voice. However, you shall solemnly forewarn them, and show them the behavior of the king who will reign over them."

[10]So Samuel told all the words of the LORD to the people who asked him for a king. [11]And he said, "This will be the behavior of the king who will reign over you: He will take your sons and appoint *them* for his own chariots and *to be* his horsemen, and *some* will run before his chariots. [12]He will appoint captains over his thousands and captains over his fifties, *will set some* to plow his ground and reap his harvest, and *some* to make his weapons of war and equipment for his chariots. [13]He will take your daughters *to be* perfumers, cooks, and bakers. [14]And he will take the best of your fields, your vineyards, and your olive groves, and give *them* to his servants. [15]He will take a tenth of your grain and your vintage, and give it to his officers and servants. [16]And he will take your male servants, your female servants, your finest young men,[a] and your donkeys, and put *them* to his work. [17]He will take a tenth of your sheep. And you will be his servants. [18]And you will cry out in that day because of your king whom you have chosen for yourselves, and the LORD will not hear you in that day."

7:12 [a]Literally *Stone of Help*   **8:16** [a]Septuagint reads *cattle*.

[19]Nevertheless the people refused to obey the voice of Samuel; and they said, "No, but we will have a king over us, [20]that we also may be like all the nations, and that our king may judge us and go out before us and fight our battles."

[21]And Samuel heard all the words of the people, and he repeated them in the hearing of the LORD. [22]So the LORD said to Samuel, "Heed their voice, and make them a king."

And Samuel said to the men of Israel, "Every man go to his city."

SAUL CHOSEN TO BE KING

[1]There was a man of Benjamin whose name was Kish the son of Abiel, the son of Zeror, the son of Bechorath, the son of Aphiah, a Benjamite, a mighty man of power. [2]And he had a choice and handsome son whose name was Saul. There was not a more handsome person than he among the children of Israel. From his shoulders upward he was taller than any of the people.

[3]Now the donkeys of Kish, Saul's father, were lost. And Kish said to his son Saul, "Please take one of the servants with you, and arise, go and look for the donkeys." [4]So he passed through the mountains of Ephraim and through the land of Shalisha, but they did not find them. Then they passed through the land of Shaalim, and they were not there. Then he passed through the land of the Benjamites, but they did not find them.

[5]When they had come to the land of Zuph, Saul said to his servant who was with him, "Come, let us return, lest my father cease caring about the donkeys and become worried about us."

[6]And he said to him, "Look now, there is in this city a man of God, and he is an honorable man; all that he says surely comes to pass. So let us go there; perhaps he can show us the way that we should go."

[7]Then Saul said to his servant, "But look, if we go, what shall we bring the man? For the bread in our vessels is all gone, and there is no present to bring to the man of God. What do we have?"

[8]And the servant answered Saul again and said, "Look, I have here at hand one-fourth of a shekel of silver. I will give that to the man of God, to tell us our way." [9](Formerly in Israel, when a man went to inquire of God, he spoke thus: "Come, let us go to the seer"; for he who is now called a prophet was formerly called a seer.)

[10]Then Saul said to his servant, "Well said; come, let us go." So they went to the city where the man of God was.

[11]As they went up the hill to the city, they met some young women going out to draw water, and said to them, "Is the seer here?"

[12]And they answered them and said, "Yes, there he is, just ahead of you. Hurry now; for today he came to this city, because there is a sacrifice of the people today on the high place. [13]As soon as you come into the city, you will surely find him before he goes up to the high place to eat. For the people will not eat until he comes, because he must bless the sacrifice; afterward those who are invited will eat. Now therefore, go up, for about this time you will find him." [14]So they went up to the city. As they were coming into the city, there was Samuel, coming out toward them on his way up to the high place.

[15]Now the LORD had told Samuel in his ear the day before Saul came, saying, [16]"Tomorrow about this time I will send you a man from the land of Benjamin, and you shall anoint him commander over My people Israel, that he may save My people from the hand of the Philistines; for I have looked upon My people, because their cry has come to Me."

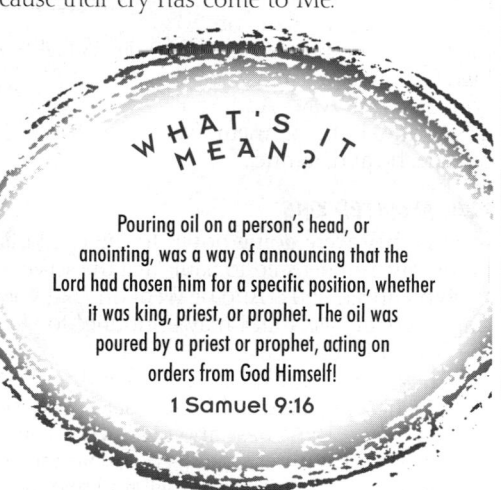

WHAT'S IT MEAN?

Pouring oil on a person's head, or anointing, was a way of announcing that the Lord had chosen him for a specific position, whether it was king, priest, or prophet. The oil was poured by a priest or prophet, acting on orders from God Himself!

1 Samuel 9:16

[17]So when Samuel saw Saul, the LORD said to him, "There he is, the man of whom I spoke to you. This one shall reign over My people."
[18]Then Saul drew near to Samuel in the gate, and said, "Please tell me, where is the seer's house?"

[19]Samuel answered Saul and said, "I am the seer. Go up before me to the high place, for you shall eat with me today; and tomorrow I will let you go and will tell you all that is in your heart. [20]But as for your donkeys that were lost three days ago, do not be anxious about them, for

they have been found. And on whom *is* all the desire of Israel? *Is it* not on you and on all your father's house?"

²¹And Saul answered and said, "*Am* I not a Benjamite, of the smallest of the tribes of Israel, and my family the least of all the families of the tribe[a] of Benjamin? Why then do you speak like this to me?"

²²Now Samuel took Saul and his servant and brought them into the hall, and had them sit in the place of honor among those who were invited; there *were* about thirty persons. ²³And Samuel said to the cook, "Bring the portion which I gave you, of which I said to you, 'Set it apart.' " ²⁴So the cook took up the thigh with its upper part and set *it* before Saul. And *Samuel* said, "Here it is, what was kept back. *It* was set apart for you. Eat; for until this time it has been kept for you, since I said I invited the people." So Saul ate with Samuel that day.

²⁵When they had come down from the high place into the city, *Samuel* spoke with Saul on the top of the house.[a] ²⁶They arose early; and it was about the dawning of the day that Samuel called to Saul on the top of the house, saying, "Get up, that I may send you on your way." And Saul arose, and both of them went outside, he and Samuel.

SAUL ANOINTED KING

²⁷As they were going down to the outskirts of the city, Samuel said to Saul, "Tell the servant to go on ahead of us." And he went on. "But you stand here awhile, that I may announce to you the word of God."

¹Then Samuel took a flask of oil and poured *it* on his head, and kissed him and said: "*Is it* not because the LORD has anointed you commander over His inheritance?[a] ²When you have departed from me today, you will find two men by Rachel's tomb in the territory of Benjamin at Zelzah; and they will say to you, 'The donkeys which you went to look for have been found. And now your father has ceased caring about the donkeys and is worrying about you, saying, "What shall I do about my son?" ' ³Then you

shall go on forward from there and come to the terebinth tree of Tabor. There three men going up to God at Bethel will meet you, one carrying three young goats, another carrying three loaves of bread, and another carrying a skin of wine. ⁴And they will greet you and give you two *loaves* of bread, which you shall receive from their hands. ⁵After that you shall come to the hill of God where the Philistine garrison *is*. And it will happen, when you have come there to the city, that you will meet a group of prophets coming down from the high place with a stringed instrument, a tambourine, a flute, and a harp before them; and they will be prophesying. ⁶Then the Spirit of the LORD will come upon you, and you will prophesy with them and be turned into another man. ⁷And let it be, when these signs come to you, *that* you do as the occasion demands; for God *is* with you.

⁸You shall go down before me to Gilgal; and surely I will come down to you to offer burnt offerings *and* make sacrifices of peace offerings. Seven days you shall wait, till I come to you and show you what you should do."

⁹So it was, when he had turned his back to go from Samuel, that God gave him another heart; and all those signs came to pass that day.

> "So it was, when he had turned his back to go from Samuel, that God gave him another heart; and all those signs came to pass that day."
> (1 Samuel 10:9)

¹⁰When they came there to the hill, there was a group of prophets to meet him; then the Spirit of God came upon him, and he prophesied among them. ¹¹And it happened, when all who knew him formerly saw that he indeed prophesied among the prophets, that the people said to one another, "What *is* this *that* has come upon the son of Kish? *Is* Saul also among the prophets?" ¹²Then a man from there answered and said, "But who *is* their father?" Therefore it became a proverb: "*Is* Saul also among the prophets?" ¹³And when he had finished prophesying, he went to the high place.

¹⁴Then Saul's uncle said to him and his servant, "Where did you go?"

So he said, "To look for the donkeys. When we saw that *they were* nowhere *to be found*, we went to Samuel."

9:21 [a]Literally *tribes*   **9:25** [a]Following Masoretic Text and Targum; Septuagint omits *He spoke with Saul on the top of the house*; Septuagint and Vulgate add *And he prepared a bed for Saul on the top of the house, and he slept.*
10:1 [a]Following Masoretic Text, Targum, and Vulgate; Septuagint reads *His people Israel; and you shall rule the people of the Lord*; Septuagint and Vulgate add *And you shall deliver His people from the hands of their enemies all around them. And this shall be a sign to you, that God has anointed you to be a prince.*

SAMUEL made a difference

What would be your first words in response if you heard God speak to you? The first time God spoke to Samuel, the young man didn't even recognize the voice. Fortunately, Samuel knew someone who steered him in the right direction. After all, having God speak to you probably isn't as important in the long run as listening to what God has to say! So old Eli told Samuel if he heard the voice again to keep the conversation going.

That was one thing Eli got right. He didn't explain God to Samuel at that point. He might not even have been sure God was speaking to Samuel. But he helped Samuel let God settle the issue. The fact that Samuel learned at a young age to give attention to God indicates the central reason why Samuel's life made such a difference.

Samuel bridged the time in history between the judges and the prophets in Israel. He anointed the first two kings of Israel (Saul and David). He conveyed God's warnings to the people that, in begging for a king, they were not only asking for trouble; they were separating themselves from God's guidance. He held kings accountable in God's name for their behavior. Samuel listened to God and, as a result, was able to speak for God. But it all began when he was still very young. The conversation he began with God lasted a lifetime.

Cutting Edge

YOU can, too! You have a tremendous spiritual advantage over Samuel. God has not only spoken; He has made His Word available in writing. Samuel had Moses' inspired writings; you have God's complete Word. Eli's wisdom still applies. God's Word will not make a difference in your life if you neither listen to nor obey it. But if you want your life to make a difference for God, pay attention to what your Creator has to say. Respond to the conversation He has begun with you!

Want to know more? Read the story of Samuel's effective life in 1 Samuel 1—28. He is also listed in the great Hall of Faith (Hebrews 11:32).

¹⁵And Saul's uncle said, "Tell me, please, what Samuel said to you."

¹⁶So Saul said to his uncle, "He told us plainly that the donkeys had been found." But about the matter of the kingdom, he did not tell him what Samuel had said.

SAUL PROCLAIMED KING

¹⁷Then Samuel called the people together to the LORD at Mizpah, ¹⁸and said to the children of Israel, "Thus says the LORD God of Israel: 'I brought up Israel out of Egypt, and delivered you from the hand of the Egyptians *and* from the hand of all kingdoms and from those who oppressed you.' ¹⁹But you have today rejected your God, who Himself saved you from all your adversities and your tribulations; and you have said to Him, 'No, set a king over us!' Now therefore, present yourselves before the LORD by your tribes and by your clans."ᵃ

²⁰And when Samuel had caused all the tribes of Israel to come near, the tribe of Benjamin was chosen. ²¹When he had caused the tribe of Benjamin to come near by their families, the family of Matri was chosen. And Saul the son of Kish was chosen. But when they sought him, he could not be found. ²²Therefore they inquired of the LORD further, "Has the man come here yet?"

And the LORD answered, "There he is, hidden among the equipment."

²³So they ran and brought him from there; and when he stood among the people, he was taller than any of the people from his shoulders upward. ²⁴And Samuel said to all the people, "Do you see him whom the LORD has chosen, that *there is* no one like him among all the people?"

So all the people shouted and said, "Long live the king!"

²⁵Then Samuel explained to the people the behavior of royalty, and wrote *it* in a book and laid *it* up before the LORD. And Samuel sent all the people away, every man to his house. ²⁶And Saul also went home to Gibeah; and valiant *men* went with him, whose hearts God had touched. ²⁷But some rebels said, "How can this man save us?" So they despised him, and brought him no presents. But he held his peace.

SAUL SAVES JABESH GILEAD

¹Then Nahash the Ammonite came up and encamped against Jabesh Gilead; and all the men of Jabesh said to Nahash, "Make a covenant with us, and we will serve you."

²And Nahash the Ammonite answered them, "On this *condition* I will make *a covenant* with you, that I may put out all your right eyes, and bring reproach on all Israel."

³Then the elders of Jabesh said to him, "Hold off for seven days, that we may send messengers to all the territory of Israel. And then, if *there is* no one to save us, we will come out to you."

WHAT'S IT MEAN?

Gibeah lies about fifty-five miles from Gilead, across the Jordan River. Saul, Israel's first human king, later made Gibeah the capital of his kingdom.

1 Samuel 11:4

⁴So the messengers came to Gibeah of Saul and told the news in the hearing of the people. And all the people lifted up their voices and wept. ⁵Now there was Saul, coming behind the herd from the field; and Saul said, "What *troubles* the people, that they weep?" And they told him the words of the men of Jabesh. ⁶Then the Spirit of God came upon Saul when he heard this news, and his anger was greatly aroused. ⁷So he took a yoke of oxen and cut them in pieces, and sent *them* throughout all the territory of Israel by the hands of messengers, saying, "Whoever does not go out with Saul and Samuel to battle, so it shall be done to his oxen."

WHAT'S IT MEAN?

Saul used the oxen as an attention-getter, not as a sacrifice. He wanted the people to understand that the situation was serious.

1 Samuel 11:7

10:19 ᵃLiterally *thousands*

And the fear of the LORD fell on the people, and they came out with one consent. [8]When he numbered them in Bezek, the children of Israel were three hundred thousand, and the men of Judah thirty thousand. [9]And they said to the messengers who came, "Thus you shall say to the men of Jabesh Gilead: 'Tomorrow, by *the time* the sun is hot, you shall have help.'" Then the messengers came and reported *it* to the men of Jabesh, and they were glad. [10]Therefore the men of Jabesh said, "Tomorrow we will come out to you, and you may do with us whatever seems good to you."

[11]So it was, on the next day, that Saul put the people in three companies; and they came into the midst of the camp in the morning watch, and killed Ammonites until the heat of the day. And it happened that those who survived were scattered, so that no two of them were left together.

[12]Then the people said to Samuel, "Who *is* he who said, 'Shall Saul reign over us?' Bring the men, that we may put them to death."

[13]But Saul said, "Not a man shall be put to death this day, for today the LORD has accomplished salvation in Israel."

WHAT'S IT MEAN?

Gilgal was the site of many major events in Israel's history. It was the first place the Israelites had stopped after crossing the Jordan River on their way into Canaan. At their campsite in Gilgal, the Israelites had left twelve stones, one for each tribe, as a memorial to the help they had received from God during their long journey. Gilgal had also been Joshua's military headquarters during Israel's battles against the Canaanites. Finally, Gilgal was the place Saul had chosen as the central location for his war against the Philistines.

1 Samuel 11:14

[14]Then Samuel said to the people, "Come, let us go to Gilgal and renew the kingdom there." [15]So all the people went to Gilgal, and there they made Saul king before the LORD in Gilgal. There they made sacrifices of peace offerings before the LORD, and there Saul and all the men of Israel rejoiced greatly.

SAMUEL'S ADDRESS AT SAUL'S CORONATION

[1]Now Samuel said to all Israel: "Indeed I have heeded your voice in all that you said to me, and have made a king over you. [2]And now here is the king, walking before you; and I am old and grayheaded, and look, my sons *are* with you. I have walked before you from my childhood to this day. [3]Here I am. Witness against me before the LORD and before His anointed: Whose ox have I taken, or whose donkey have I taken, or whom have I cheated? Whom have I oppressed, or from whose hand have I received *any* bribe with which to blind my eyes? I will restore *it* to you."

[4]And they said, "You have not cheated us or oppressed us, nor have you taken anything from any man's hand."

[5]Then he said to them, "The LORD *is* witness against you, and His anointed *is* witness this day, that you have not found anything in my hand."

And they answered, "*He is* witness."

[6]Then Samuel said to the people, "It is the LORD who raised up Moses and Aaron, and who brought your fathers up from the land of Egypt. [7]Now therefore, stand still, that I may reason with you before the LORD concerning all the righteous acts of the LORD which He did to you and your fathers: [8]When Jacob had gone into Egypt,[a] and your fathers cried out to the LORD, then the LORD sent Moses and Aaron, who brought your fathers out of Egypt and made them dwell in this place. [9]And when they forgot the LORD their God, He sold them into the hand of Sisera, commander of the army of Hazor, into the hand of the Philistines, and into the hand of the king of Moab; and they fought against them. [10]Then they cried out to the LORD, and said, 'We have sinned, because we have forsaken the LORD and served the Baals and Ashtoreths;[a] but now deliver us from the hand of our enemies, and we will serve You.' [11]And the LORD sent Jerubbaal,[a] Bedan,[b] Jephthah, and Samuel,[c] and delivered you out of the hand of your enemies on every side; and you dwelt in safety. [12]And when you saw that Nahash king of the Ammonites came against you, you said to me, 'No, but a king shall reign over us,' when the LORD your God *was* your king. [13]"Now therefore, here is the king whom you

---

12:8 [a]Following Masoretic Text, Targum, and Vulgate; Septuagint adds *and the Egyptians afflicted them.*
12:10 [a]Canaanite goddesses　　**12:11** [a]Syriac reads *Deborah*; Targum reads *Gideon.*　　[b]Septuagint and Syriac read *Barak*; Targum reads *Simson.*　　[c]Syriac reads *Simson.*

have chosen *and* whom you have desired. And take note, the LORD has set a king over you. ¹⁴If you fear the LORD and serve Him and obey His voice, and do not rebel against the commandment of the LORD, then both you and the king who reigns over you will continue following the LORD your God. ¹⁵However, if you do not obey the voice of the LORD, but rebel against the commandment of the LORD, then the hand of the LORD will be against you, as *it was* against your fathers.

¹⁶"Now therefore, stand and see this great thing which the LORD will do before your eyes: ¹⁷*Is* today not the wheat harvest? I will call to the LORD, and He will send thunder and rain, that you may perceive and see that your wickedness *is* great, which you have done in the sight of the LORD, in asking a king for yourselves."

¹⁸So Samuel called to the LORD, and the LORD sent thunder and rain that day; and all the people greatly feared the LORD and Samuel.

¹⁹And all the people said to Samuel, "Pray for your servants to the LORD your God, that we may not die; for we have added to all our sins the evil of asking a king for ourselves."

²⁰Then Samuel said to the people, "Do not fear. You have done all this wickedness; yet do not turn aside from following the LORD, but serve the LORD with all your heart. ²¹And do not turn aside; for *then you would go* after empty things which cannot profit or deliver, for they *are* nothing. ²²For the LORD will not forsake His people, for His great name's sake, because it has pleased the LORD to make you His people. ²³Moreover, as for me, far be it from me that I should sin against the LORD in ceasing to pray for you; but I will teach you the good and the right way. ²⁴Only fear the LORD, and serve Him in truth with all your heart; for consider what great things He has done for you. ²⁵But if you still do wickedly, you shall be swept away, both you and your king."

TRUTH

How are we to serve God? (12:24)

SAUL'S UNLAWFUL SACRIFICE

¹Saul reigned one year; and when he had reigned two years over Israel,ᵃ ²Saul chose for himself three thousand *men* of Israel. Two thousand were with Saul in Michmash and in the mountains of Bethel, and a thousand were with Jonathan in Gibeah of Benjamin. The rest of the people he sent away, every man to his tent.

³And Jonathan attacked the garrison of the Philistines that *was* in Geba, and the Philistines heard *of it.* Then Saul blew the trumpet throughout all the land, saying, "Let the Hebrews hear!" ⁴Now all Israel heard it said *that* Saul had attacked a garrison of the Philistines, and *that* Israel had also become an abomination to the Philistines. And the people were called together to Saul at Gilgal.

⁵Then the Philistines gathered together to fight with Israel, thirtyᵃ thousand chariots and six thousand horsemen, and people as the sand which *is* on the seashore in multitude. And they came up and encamped in Michmash, to the east of Beth Aven. ⁶When the men of Israel saw that they were in danger (for the people were distressed), then the people hid in caves, in thickets, in rocks, in holes, and in pits. ⁷And *some of* the Hebrews crossed over the Jordan to the land of Gad and Gilead.

As for Saul, he *was* still in Gilgal, and all the people followed him trembling. ⁸Then he waited seven days, according to the time set by Samuel. But Samuel did not come to Gilgal; and the people were scattered from him. ⁹So Saul said, "Bring a burnt offering and peace offerings here to me." And he offered the burnt offering. ¹⁰Now it happened, as soon as he had finished presenting the burnt offering, that Samuel came; and Saul went out to meet him, that he might greet him.

¹¹And Samuel said, "What have you done?"

Saul said, "When I saw that the people were scattered from me, and *that* you did not come within the days appointed, and *that* the Philistines gathered together at Michmash, ¹²then I said, 'The Philistines will now come down on me at Gilgal, and I have not made supplication to the LORD.' Therefore I felt compelled, and offered a burnt offering."

¹³And Samuel said to Saul, "You have done foolishly. You have not kept the commandment of the LORD your God, which He commanded you. For now the LORD would have established your kingdom over Israel forever. ¹⁴But now your kingdom shall not continue. The LORD has sought for Himself a man after His own heart, and the LORD has commanded him *to be* commander over His people, because you have not kept what the LORD commanded you."

13:1 ᵃThe Hebrew is difficult (compare 2 Samuel 5:4; 2 Kings 14:2; see also 2 Samuel 2:10; Acts 13:21).
13:5 ᵃFollowing Masoretic Text, Septuagint, Targum, and Vulgate; Syriac and some manuscripts of the Septuagint read *three.*

[15]Then Samuel arose and went up from Gilgal to Gibeah of Benjamin.[a] And Saul numbered the people present with him, about six hundred men.

NO WEAPONS FOR THE ARMY

[16]Saul, Jonathan his son, and the people present with them remained in Gibeah of Benjamin. But the Philistines encamped in Michmash. [17]Then raiders came out of the camp of the Philistines in three companies. One company turned onto the road to Ophrah, to the land of Shual, [18]another company turned to the road *to* Beth Horon, and another company turned *to* the road of the border that overlooks the Valley of Zeboim toward the wilderness. [19]Now there was no blacksmith to be found throughout all the land of Israel, for the Philistines said, "Lest the Hebrews make swords or spears." [20]But all the Israelites would go down to the Philistines to sharpen each man's plowshare, his mattock, his ax, and his sickle; [21]and the charge for a sharpening was a pim[a] for the plowshares, the mattocks, the forks, and the axes, and to set the points of the goads. [22]So it came about, on the day of battle, that there was neither sword nor spear found in the hand of any of the people who *were* with Saul and Jonathan. But they were found with Saul and Jonathan his son.

[23]And the garrison of the Philistines went out to the pass of Michmash.

JONATHAN DEFEATS THE PHILISTINES

[1]Now it happened one day that Jonathan the son of Saul said to the young man who bore his armor, "Come, let us go over to the Philistines' garrison that *is* on the other side." But he did not tell his father. [2]And Saul was sitting in the outskirts of Gibeah under a pomegranate tree which *is* in Migron. The people who *were* with him *were* about six hundred men. [3]Ahijah the son of Ahitub, Ichabod's brother, the son of Phinehas, the son of Eli, the LORD's priest in Shiloh, was wearing an ephod. But the people did not know that Jonathan had gone.

[4]Between the passes, by which Jonathan sought to go over to the Philistines' garrison, *there was* a sharp rock on one side and a sharp rock on the other side. And the name of one *was* Bozez, and the name of the other Seneh. [5]The front of one faced northward opposite Michmash, and the other southward opposite Gibeah.

WHAT'S IT MEAN?

Priests received answers from God in three different ways: through prayer, through visions and dreams, and through the use of objects called "Urim" and "Thummim." The Urim and Thummim were small gems or stones carried by the high priest. Many Bible experts believe the stones were engraved with symbols and thrown like dice to determine God's will.

1 Samuel 14:1–3

[6]Then Jonathan said to the young man who bore his armor, "Come, let us go over to the garrison of these uncircumcised; it may be that the LORD will work for us. For nothing restrains the LORD from saving by many or by few." [7]So his armorbearer said to him, "Do all that is in your heart. Go then; here I am with you, according to your heart." [8]Then Jonathan said, "Very well, let us cross over to *these* men, and we will show ourselves to them. [9]If they say thus to us, 'Wait until we come to you', then we will stand still in our place and not go up to them. [10]But if they say thus, 'Come up to us', then we will go up. For the LORD has delivered them into our hand, and this *will be* a sign to us."

[11]So both of them showed themselves to the garrison of the Philistines. And the Philistines said, "Look, the Hebrews are coming out of the holes where they have hidden." [12]Then the men of the garrison called to Jonathan and his armorbearer, and said, "Come up to us, and we will show you something."

Jonathan said to his armorbearer, "Come up after me, for the LORD has delivered them into the hand of Israel." [13]And Jonathan climbed up on his hands and knees with his armorbearer after him; and they fell before Jonathan. And as he came after him, his armorbearer killed them. [14]That first slaughter which Jonathan and his armorbearer made was about twenty men within about half an acre of land.[a]

[15]And there was trembling in the camp, in the field, and among all the people. The garrison

---

13:15 [a]Following Masoretic Text and Targum; Septuagint and Vulgate add *And the rest of the people went up after Saul to meet the people who fought against them, going from Gilgal to Gibeah in the hill of Benjamin.* **13:21** [a]About two-thirds shekel weight **14:14** [a]Literally *half the area plowed by a yoke* (of oxen in a day) and the raiders also trembled; and the earth quaked, so that it was a very great trembling. [16]Now the watchmen of Saul in Gibeah of Benjamin looked, and *there* was the multitude, melting away; and they went here and there. [17]Then Saul said to the people who *were* with him, "Now call the roll and see who has gone from us." And when they had called the roll, surprisingly, Jonathan and his armorbearer *were* not *there*. [18]And Saul said to Ahijah, "Bring the ark[a] of God here" (for at that time the ark[b] of God was with the children of Israel). [19]Now it happened, while Saul talked to the priest, that the noise which *was* in the camp of the Philistines continued to increase; so Saul said to the priest, "Withdraw your hand." [20]Then Saul and all the people who *were* with him assembled, and they went to the battle; and indeed every man's sword was against his neighbor, *and there was* very great confusion. [21]Moreover the Hebrews *who* were with the Philistines before that time, who went up with them into the camp *from the* surrounding *country*, they also joined the Israelites who *were* with Saul and Jonathan. [22]Likewise all the men of Israel who had hidden in the mountains of Ephraim, *when* they heard that the Philistines fled, they also followed hard after them in the battle. [23]So the LORD saved Israel that day, and the battle shifted to Beth Aven.

SAUL'S RASH OATH

[24]And the men of Israel were distressed that day, for Saul had placed the people under oath, saying, "Cursed *is* the man who eats *any* food until evening, before I have taken vengeance on my enemies." So none of the people tasted food. [25]Now all *the people* of the land came to a forest; and there was honey on the ground. [26]And when the people had come into the woods, there was the honey, dripping; but no one put his hand to his mouth, for the people feared the oath. [27]But Jonathan had not heard his father charge the people with the oath; therefore he stretched out the end of the rod that *was* in his hand and dipped it in a honeycomb, and put his hand to his mouth; and his countenance brightened. [28]Then one of the people said, "Your

father strictly charged the people with an oath, saying, 'Cursed *is* the man who eats food this day.'" And the people were faint. [29]But Jonathan said, "My father has troubled the land. Look now, how my countenance has brightened because I tasted a little of this honey. [30]How much better if the people had eaten freely today of the spoil of their enemies which they found! For now would there not have been a much greater slaughter among the Philistines?"

[31]Now they had driven back the Philistines that day from Michmash to Aijalon. So the people were very faint. [32]And the people rushed on the spoil, and took sheep, oxen, and calves, and slaughtered *them* on the ground; and the people ate *them* with the blood. [33]Then they told Saul, saying, "Look, the people are sinning against the LORD by eating with the blood!"

So he said, "You have dealt treacherously; roll a large stone to me this day." [34]Then Saul said, "Disperse yourselves among the people, and say to them, 'Bring me here every man's ox and every man's sheep, slaughter *them* here, and eat; and do not sin against the LORD by eating with the blood.'" So every one of the people brought his ox with him that night, and slaughtered *it* there. [35]Then Saul built an altar to the LORD. This was the first altar that he built to the LORD.

[36]Now Saul said, "Let us go down after the Philistines by night, and plunder them until the morning light; and let us not leave a man of them."

And they said, "Do whatever seems good to you."

Then the priest said, "Let us draw near to God here."

[37]So Saul asked counsel of God, "Shall I go down after the Philistines? Will You deliver them into the hand of Israel?" But He did not answer him that day. [38]And Saul said, "Come over here, all you chiefs of the people, and know and see what this sin was today. [39]For *as* the LORD lives, who saves Israel, though it be in Jonathan my son, he shall surely die." But not a man among all the people answered him. [40]Then he said to all Israel, "You be on one side,

> "Samuel also said to Saul, 'The LORD sent me to anoint you king over His people, over Israel. Now therefore, heed the voice of the words of the LORD.'"
> (1 Samuel 15:1)

14:18 [a]Following Masoretic Text, Targum, and Vulgate; Septuagint reads *ephod*. [b]Following Masoretic Text, Targum, and Vulgate; Septuagint reads *ephod*.

and my son Jonathan and I will be on the other side."

And the people said to Saul, "Do what seems good to you."

[41]Therefore Saul said to the LORD God of Israel, "Give a perfect *lot*."[a] So Saul and Jonathan were taken, but the people escaped. [42]And Saul said, "Cast *lots* between my son Jonathan and me." So Jonathan was taken. [43]Then Saul said to Jonathan, "Tell me what you have done."

And Jonathan told him, and said, "I only tasted a little honey with the end of the rod that *was* in my hand. So now I must die!"

[44]Saul answered, "God do so and more also; for you shall surely die, Jonathan."

[45]But the people said to Saul, "Shall Jonathan die, who has accomplished this great deliverance in Israel? Certainly not! *As* the LORD lives, not one hair of his head shall fall to the ground, for he has worked with God this day." So the people rescued Jonathan, and he did not die.

[46]Then Saul returned from pursuing the Philistines, and the Philistines went to their own place.

SAUL'S CONTINUING WARS

[47]So Saul established his sovereignty over Israel, and fought against all his enemies on every side, against Moab, against the people of Ammon, against Edom, against the kings of Zobah, and against the Philistines. Wherever he turned, he harassed *them*.[a] [48]And he gathered an army and attacked the Amalekites, and delivered Israel from the hands of those who plundered them.

[49]The sons of Saul were Jonathan, Jishui,[a]

The Israelites were surrounded by people who wanted them out of Canaan. Enemies on both sides of the Jordan River had been waging war against the Israelites since they arrived in the Promised Land.

1 Samuel 14:47, 48

and Malchishua. And the names of his two daughters *were these:* the name of the firstborn Merab, and the name of the younger Michal. [50]The name of Saul's wife *was* Ahinoam the daughter of Ahimaaz. And the name of the commander of his army *was* Abner the son of Ner, Saul's uncle. [51]Kish *was* the father of Saul, and Ner the father of Abner *was* the son of Abiel.

[52]Now there was fierce war with the Philistines all the days of Saul. And when Saul saw any strong man or any valiant man, he took him for himself.

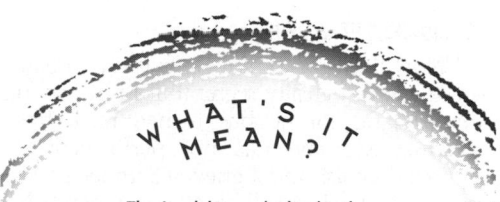

The Amalekites, who lived in the southern desert land of Canaan, had been a thorn in the Israelites' side since the tribes left Egypt for the Promised Land. During the time of the judges, the Amalekites teamed up with the Moabites and Ammonites to attack Israel, only to be defeated by Gideon and his men. God was finally sentencing the Amalekites to death.

1 Samuel 15:3

SAUL SPARES KING AGAG

[1]Samuel also said to Saul, "The LORD sent me to anoint you king over His people, over Israel. Now therefore, heed the voice of the words of the LORD. [2]Thus says the LORD of hosts: 'I will punish Amalek *for* what he did to Israel, how he ambushed him on the way when he came up from Egypt. [3]Now go and attack Amalek, and utterly destroy all that they have, and do not spare them. But kill both man and woman, infant and nursing child, ox and sheep, camel and donkey.' "

[4]So Saul gathered the people together and numbered them in Telaim, two hundred thousand foot soldiers and ten thousand men of Judah. [5]And Saul came to a city of Amalek, and lay in wait in the valley.

[6]Then Saul said to the Kenites, "Go, depart, get down from among the Amalekites, lest I

14:41 [a]Following Masoretic Text and Targum; Septuagint and Vulgate read *Why do You not answer Your servant today? If the injustice is with me or Jonathan my son, O LORD God of Israel, give proof; and if You say it is with Your people Israel, give holiness.* **14:47** [a]Septuagint and Vulgate read *prospered.* **14:49** [a]Called *Abinadab* in 1 Chronicles 8:33 and 9:39

destroy you with them. For you showed kindness to all the children of Israel when they came up out of Egypt." So the Kenites departed from among the Amalekites. 7And Saul attacked the Amalekites, from Havilah all the way to Shur, which is east of Egypt. 8He also took Agag king of the Amalekites alive, and utterly destroyed all the people with the edge of the sword. 9But Saul and the people spared Agag and the best of the sheep, the oxen, the fatlings, the lambs, and all *that was* good, and were unwilling to utterly destroy them. But everything despised and worthless, that they utterly destroyed.

SAUL REJECTED AS KING

10Now the word of the LORD came to Samuel, saying, 11"I greatly regret that I have set up Saul *as* king, for he has turned back from following Me, and has not performed My commandments." And it grieved Samuel, and he cried out to the LORD all night. 12So when Samuel rose early in the morning to meet Saul, it was told Samuel, saying, "Saul went to Carmel, and indeed, he set up a monument for himself; and he has gone on around, passed by, and gone down to Gilgal." 13Then Samuel went to Saul, and Saul said to him, "Blessed *are* you of the LORD! I have performed the commandment of the LORD."

14But Samuel said, "What then *is* this bleating of the sheep in my ears, and the lowing of the oxen which I hear?"

15And Saul said, "They have brought them from the Amalekites; for the people spared the best of the sheep and the oxen, to sacrifice to the LORD your God; and the rest we have utterly destroyed."

16Then Samuel said to Saul, "Be quiet! And I will tell you what the LORD said to me last night."

And he said to him, "Speak on."

17So Samuel said, "When you *were* little in your own eyes, *were* you not head of the tribes of Israel? And did not the LORD anoint you king over Israel? 18Now the LORD sent you on a mission, and said, 'Go, and utterly destroy the sinners, the Amalekites, and fight against them until they are consumed.' 19Why then did you not obey the voice of the LORD? Why did you swoop down on the spoil, and do evil in the sight of the LORD?"

20And Saul said to Samuel, "But I have obeyed the voice of the LORD, and gone on the mission on which the LORD sent me, and brought back Agag king of Amalek; I have utterly destroyed the Amalekites. 21But the people took of the plunder, sheep and oxen, the best of the things which should have been utterly destroyed, to sacrifice to the LORD your God in Gilgal."

22So Samuel said:

"Has the LORD *as great*
 delight in burnt
 offerings and
 sacrifices,
As in obeying the voice of
 the LORD?
Behold, to obey is better than sacrifice,
And to heed than the fat of rams.
23 For rebellion *is as* the sin of witchcraft,
 And stubbornness *is as* iniquity and
 idolatry.
Because you have rejected the word of
 the LORD,
He also has rejected you from *being* king."

24Then Saul said to Samuel, "I have sinned, for I have transgressed the commandment of the LORD and your words, because I feared the people and obeyed their voice. 25Now therefore, please pardon my sin, and return with me, that I may worship the LORD."

OBEDIENCE
Is it better to obey or to ask forgiveness? (15:22)

On the Edge

So Samuel said: "Has the LORD as great delight in burnt offerings and sacrifices, as in obeying the voice of the LORD? Behold, to obey is better than sacrifice, and to heed than the fat of rams" (1 Sam. 15:22).

The right thing is always to obey God. Saul proves in this passage that you can't just do whatever you want, even if it seems okay or harmless. God wants you to obey Him. Saul thought he could just take over and revise God's instructions to suit himself. God was really disappointed with Saul's disobedience and took away his title as king. The Bible is God's word of instruction to us. It helps us live so that we can be safe, happy, and blessed. It is not up for revision. You can't just pick the parts you like. God wants you to obey Him. All of Him and all of His Word.

SEE FOR YOURSELF:
Ex. 19:5;
Deut. 10:12, 13;
Is. 1:19

BELIEF

What happens if we reject God? (15:26)

26But Samuel said to Saul, "I will not return with you, for you have rejected the word of the LORD, and the LORD has rejected you from being king over Israel." 27And as Samuel turned around to go away, *Saul* seized the edge of his robe, and it tore. 28So Samuel said to him, "The LORD has torn the kingdom of Israel from you today, and has given it to a neighbor of yours, *who is* better than you. 29And also the Strength of Israel will not lie nor relent. For He *is* not a man, that He should relent."

30Then he said, "I have sinned; *yet* honor me now, please, before the elders of my people and before Israel, and return with me, that I may worship the LORD your God." 31So Samuel turned back after Saul, and Saul worshiped the LORD.

32Then Samuel said, "Bring Agag king of the Amalekites here to me." So Agag came to him cautiously.

And Agag said, "Surely the bitterness of death is past."

33But Samuel said, "As your sword has made women childless, so shall your mother be childless among women." And Samuel hacked Agag in pieces before the LORD in Gilgal.

34Then Samuel went to Ramah, and Saul went up to his house at Gibeah of Saul. 35And Samuel went no more to see Saul until the day of his death. Nevertheless Samuel mourned for Saul, and the LORD regretted that He had made Saul king over Israel.

DAVID ANOINTED KING

1Now the LORD said to Samuel, "How long will you mourn for Saul, seeing I have rejected him from reigning over Israel? Fill your horn with oil, and go; I am sending you to Jesse the Bethlehemite. For I have provided Myself a king among his sons."

2And Samuel said, "How can I go? If Saul hears *it*, he will kill me."

But the LORD said, "Take a heifer with you, and say, 'I have come to sacrifice to the LORD.' 3Then invite Jesse to the sacrifice, and I will show you what you shall do; you shall anoint for Me the one I name to you."

4So Samuel did what the LORD said, and went to Bethlehem. And the elders of the town trembled at his coming, and said, "Do you come peaceably?"

On the Edge

But the LORD said to Samuel, "Do not look at his appearance or at his physical stature, because I have refused him. For the LORD does not see as man sees; for man looks at the outward appearance, but the LORD looks at the heart"(1 Sam. 16:7).

First impressions. Yuck. You look. They look. You shake hands; fake a smile. Yep, you've got this one figured out, wrapped up in a box, and slapped into category A, B, or C. He's either "hip, drip," or "wanna-be." However you do it, you still label people. Everybody does, and we all do it based on the superficial. Looks determine the label—straight teeth, good haircut, right jeans—all the right stuff.

Guess what? God doesn't give a rip about jeans or haircuts. People's looks aren't even an issue for Him. His radar locks on to the heart and makes an inspection there. He wants to know who you are way down deep inside. How do you really feel? Are you really mean as a yard dog, or do you cut other people down because your heart's been broken and really hurting? God knows the truth about people—good and bad. He always looks past all your stuff and sees your heart.

SEE FOR YOURSELF:
1 Chr. 28:9;
2 Chr. 6:30; Jer. 20:12;
Acts 15:8, 9

5And he said, "Peaceably; I have come to sacrifice to the LORD. Sanctify yourselves, and come with me to the sacrifice." Then he consecrated Jesse and his sons, and invited them to the sacrifice.

6So it was, when they came, that he looked at Eliab and said, "Surely the LORD's anointed *is* before Him!"

INTEGRITY

What's better: image or integrity? (16:7)

7But the LORD said to Samuel, "Do not look at his appearance or at his physical stature, because I have refused him. For *the LORD does* not *see* as man sees;a for man looks at the outward appearance, but the LORD looks at the heart."

16:7 aSeptuagint reads *For God does not see as man sees;* Targum reads *It is not by the appearance of a man;* Vulgate reads *Nor do I judge according to the looks of a man.*

⁸So Jesse called Abinadab, and made him pass before Samuel. And he said, "Neither has the LORD chosen this one." ⁹Then Jesse made Shammah pass by. And he said, "Neither has the LORD chosen this one." ¹⁰Thus Jesse made seven of his sons pass before Samuel. And Samuel said to Jesse, "The LORD has not chosen these." ¹¹And Samuel said to Jesse, "Are all the young men here?" Then he said, "There remains yet the youngest, and there he is, keeping the sheep."

WHAT'S IT MEAN?

Sheepherding was a job often given to a son, a daughter, or a hired servant. Jesse gave this responsibility to David, his youngest son.

1 Samuel 16:11

And Samuel said to Jesse, "Send and bring him. For we will not sit down*ᵃ* till he comes here." ¹²So he sent and brought him in. Now he *was* ruddy, with bright eyes, and good-looking. And the LORD said, "Arise, anoint him; for this *is* the one!" ¹³Then Samuel took the horn of oil and anointed him in the midst of his brothers; and the Spirit of the LORD came upon David from that day forward. So Samuel arose and went to Ramah.

A DISTRESSING SPIRIT TROUBLES SAUL

¹⁴But the Spirit of the LORD departed from Saul, and a distressing spirit from the LORD troubled him. ¹⁵And Saul's servants said to him, "Surely, a distressing spirit from God is troubling you. ¹⁶Let our master now command your servants, *who are* before you, to seek out a man *who is* a skillful player on the harp. And it shall be that he will play it with his hand when the distressing spirit from God is upon you, and you shall be well." ¹⁷So Saul said to his servants, "Provide me now a man who can play well, and bring *him* to me." ¹⁸Then one of the servants answered and said, "Look, I have seen a son of Jesse the Bethlehemite, *who is* skillful in playing, a mighty man of valor, a man of war, prudent in speech,

and a handsome person; and the LORD *is* with him."

WHAT'S IT MEAN?

The distressing spirit may have been some kind of mental illness or manic depression. While David's music seemed to make Saul feel better for a while, eventually the king's mental disorder became untreatable.

1 Samuel 16:23

¹⁹Therefore Saul sent messengers to Jesse, and said, "Send me your son David, who *is* with the sheep." ²⁰And Jesse took a donkey *loaded with* bread, a skin of wine, and a young goat, and sent *them* by his son David to Saul. ²¹So David came to Saul and stood before him. And he loved him greatly, and he became his armorbearer. ²²Then Saul sent to Jesse, saying, "Please let David stand before me, for he has found favor in my sight." ²³And so it was, whenever the spirit from God was upon Saul, that David would take a harp and play *it* with his hand. Then Saul would become refreshed and well, and the distressing spirit would depart from him.

DAVID AND GOLIATH

¹Now the Philistines gathered their armies together to battle, and were gathered at Sochoh, which *belongs* to Judah; they encamped between Sochoh and Azekah, in Ephes Dammim. ²And Saul and the men of Israel were gathered together, and they encamped in the Valley of Elah, and drew up in battle array against the Philistines. ³The Philistines stood on a mountain on one side, and Israel stood on a mountain on the other side, with a valley between them.

⁴And a champion went out from the camp of the Philistines, named Goliath, from Gath, whose height *was* six cubits and a span. ⁵He had a bronze helmet on his head, and he *was* armed with a coat of mail, and the weight of the coat *was* five thousand shekels of bronze. ⁶And *he had* bronze armor on his legs and a bronze javelin between his shoulders. ⁷Now the staff of his spear *was* like a weaver's beam, and his iron

---

16:11 ᵃFollowing Septuagint and Vulgate; Masoretic Text reads *turn around;* Targum and Syriac read *turn away.*

spearhead *weighed* six hundred shekels; and a shield-bearer went before him. ⁸Then he stood and cried out to the armies of Israel, and said to them, "Why have you come out to line up for battle? *Am* I not a Philistine, and you the servants of Saul? Choose a man for yourselves, and let him come down to me. ⁹If he is able to fight with me and kill me, then we will be your servants. But if I prevail against him and kill him, then you shall be our servants and serve us." ¹⁰And the Philistine said, "I defy the armies of Israel this day; give me a man, that we may fight together." ¹¹When Saul and all Israel heard these words of the Philistine, they were dismayed and greatly afraid.

WHAT'S IT MEAN?

Occasionally, ancient armies showed efficiency in the way they fought battles. Rather than putting all of their soldiers to risk in an all-out war, each side could choose its best warrior for a one-on-one, winner-take-all, fight to the death. In such cases, the army whose representative won the fight won the battle. This particular battle took place near Gath, south of Gibeah and Jerusalem.

1 Samuel 17:1–10

¹²Now David *was* the son of that Ephrathite of Bethlehem Judah, whose name *was* Jesse, and who had eight sons. And the man was old, advanced *in years*, in the days of Saul. ¹³The three oldest sons of Jesse had gone to follow Saul to the battle. The names of his three sons who went to the battle *were* Eliab the firstborn, next to him Abinadab, and the third Shammah. ¹⁴David *was* the youngest. And the three oldest followed Saul. ¹⁵But David occasionally went and returned from Saul to feed his father's sheep at Bethlehem.

¹⁶And the Philistine drew near and presented himself forty days, morning and evening.

¹⁷Then Jesse said to his son David, "Take now for your brothers an ephah of this dried *grain* and these ten loaves, and run to your brothers at the camp. ¹⁸And carry these ten cheeses to the captain of *their* thousand, and see how your brothers fare, and bring back news of them." ¹⁹Now Saul and they and all the men of Israel *were* in the Valley of Elah, fighting with the Philistines.

²⁰So David rose early in the morning, left the sheep with a keeper, and took *the things* and went as Jesse had commanded him. And he came to the camp as the army was going out to the fight and shouting for the battle. ²¹For Israel and the Philistines had drawn up in battle array, army against army. ²²And David left his supplies in the hand of the supply keeper, ran to the army, and came and greeted his brothers. ²³Then as he talked with them, there was the champion, the Philistine of Gath, Goliath by name, coming up from the armies of the Philistines; and he spoke according to the same words. So David heard *them*. ²⁴And all the men of Israel, when they saw the man, fled from him and were dreadfully afraid. ²⁵So the men of Israel said, "Have you seen this man who has come up? Surely he has come up to defy Israel; and it shall be *that* the man who kills him the king will enrich with great riches, will give him his daughter, and give his father's house exemption *from taxes* in Israel."

²⁶Then David spoke to the men who stood by him, saying, "What shall be done for the man who kills this Philistine and takes away the reproach from Israel? For who *is* this uncircumcised Philistine, that he should defy the armies of the living God?"

²⁷And the people answered him in this manner, saying, "So shall it be done for the man who kills him."

²⁸Now Eliab his oldest brother heard when he spoke to the men; and Eliab's anger was aroused against David, and he said, "Why did you come down here? And with whom have you left those few sheep in the wilderness? I know your pride and the insolence of your heart, for you have come down to see the battle."

²⁹And David said, "What have I done now? *Is there* not a cause?" ³⁰Then he turned from him toward another and said the same thing; and these people answered him as the first ones *did*.

³¹Now when the words which David spoke were heard, they reported *them* to Saul; and he sent for him. ³²Then David said to Saul, "Let no man's heart fail because of him; your servant will go and fight with this Philistine."

³³And Saul said to David, "You are not able to go against this Philistine to fight with him; for you *are* a youth, and he a man of war from his youth."

³⁴But David said to Saul, "Your servant used to keep his father's sheep, and when a lion or a bear came and took a lamb out of the flock, ³⁵I went out after it and struck it, and delivered *the lamb* from its mouth; and when it arose against

me, I caught *it* by its beard, and struck and killed it. [36]Your servant has killed both lion and bear; and this uncircumcised Philistine will be like one of them, seeing he has defied the armies of the living God." [37]Moreover David said, "The LORD, who delivered me from the paw of the lion and from the paw of the bear, He will deliver me from the hand of this Philistine."

TRIALS

Where can we find strength? (17:37)

And Saul said to David, "Go, and the LORD be with you!"

[38]So Saul clothed David with his armor, and he put a bronze helmet on his head; he also clothed him with a coat of mail. [39]David fastened his sword to his armor and tried to walk, for he had not tested *them*. And David said to Saul, "I cannot walk with these, for I have not tested *them*." So David took them off.

WHAT'S IT MEAN?

Receiving a proper burial was very important in the Israelite culture. The thought of one's body not being buried would have been humiliating and shameful. That's why Goliath's threat to feed David's body to the birds and animals was so insulting.

1 Samuel 17:44

[40]Then he took his staff in his hand; and he chose for himself five smooth stones from the brook, and put them in a shepherd's bag, in a pouch which he had, and his sling was in his hand. And he drew near to the Philistine. [41]So the Philistine came, and began drawing near to David, and the man who bore the shield *went* before him. [42]And when the Philistine looked about and saw David, he disdained him; for he was *only* a youth, ruddy and good-looking. [43]So the Philistine said to David, "*Am* I a dog, that you come to me with sticks?" And the Philistine cursed David by his gods. [44]And the Philistine said to David, "Come to me, and I will give your flesh to the birds of the air and the beasts of the field!"

[45]Then David said to the Philistine, "You come to me with a sword, with a spear, and

with a javelin. But I come to you in the name of the LORD of hosts, the God of the armies of Israel, whom you have defied. [46]This day the LORD will deliver you into my hand, and I will strike you and take your head from you. And this day I will give the carcasses of the camp of the Philistines to the birds of the air and the wild beasts of the earth, that all the earth may know that there is a God in Israel. [47]Then all this assembly shall know that the LORD does not save with sword and spear; for the battle *is* the LORD's, and He will give you into our hands."

[48]So it was, when the Philistine arose and came and drew near to meet David, that David hurried and ran toward the army to meet the Philistine. [49]Then David put his hand in his bag and took out a stone; and he slung *it* and struck the Philistine in his forehead, so that the stone sank into his forehead, and he fell on his face to the earth. [50]So David prevailed over the Philistine with a sling and a stone, and struck the Philistine and killed him. But *there was* no sword in the hand of David. [51]Therefore David ran and stood over the Philistine, took his sword and drew it out of its sheath and killed him, and cut off his head with it.

WHAT'S IT MEAN?

A sling was a long-range weapon with a simple design: a pouch attached to long leather straps. The pouch held a rock, anywhere from the size of a pebble to the size of a baseball. When the straps were whirled around and released by an experienced warrior, the rock left the sling at an incredible speed. It took years and years of experience for a person to learn to sling rocks with any kind of accuracy. That's why David's victory against Goliath was so remarkable. David was a very young man.

1 Samuel 17:49

And when the Philistines saw that their champion was dead, they fled. [52]Now the men of Israel and Judah arose and shouted, and pursued the Philistines as far as the entrance of the valley[a] and to the gates of Ekron. And the wounded of the Philistines fell along the road to Shaaraim, even as far as Gath and Ek-

---

17:52 [a]Following Masoretic Text, Syriac, Targum, and Vulgate; Septuagint reads *Gath*.

ron. ⁵³Then the children of Israel returned from chasing the Philistines, and they plundered their tents. ⁵⁴And David took the head of the Philistine and brought it to Jerusalem, but he put his armor in his tent.

⁵⁵When Saul saw David going out against the Philistine, he said to Abner, the commander of the army, "Abner, whose son *is* this youth?"

And Abner said, "As your soul lives, O king, I do not know."

⁵⁶So the king said, "Inquire whose son this young man *is*."

⁵⁷Then, as David returned from the slaughter of the Philistine, Abner took him and brought him before Saul with the head of the Philistine in his hand. ⁵⁸And Saul said to him, "Whose son *are* you, young man?"

So David answered, "I *am* the son of your servant Jesse the Bethlehemite."

SAUL RESENTS DAVID

¹Now when he had finished speaking to Saul, the soul of Jonathan was knit to the soul of David, and Jonathan loved him as his own soul. ²Saul took him that day, and would not let him go home to his father's house anymore. ³Then Jonathan and David made a covenant, because he loved him as his own soul. ⁴And Jonathan took off the robe that *was* on him and gave it to David, with his armor, even to his sword and his bow and his belt.

Music was an important part of Israelite life. Songs were often used for honoring heroes, for celebrating victories, and for passing on the stories of those heroes and victories to future generations.

1 Samuel 18:7

⁵So David went out wherever Saul sent him, *and* behaved wisely. And Saul set him over the men of war, and he was accepted in the sight of all the people and also in the sight of Saul's servants. ⁶Now it had happened as they were coming *home*, when David was returning from the slaughter of the Philistine, that the women had come out of all the cities of Israel, singing and dancing, to meet King Saul, with tambou-

rines, with joy, and with musical instruments. ⁷So the women sang as they danced, and said:

> "Saul has slain his thousands,
> And David his ten thousands."

⁸Then Saul was very angry, and the saying displeased him; and he said, "They have ascribed to David ten thousands, and to me they have ascribed *only* thousands. Now *what* more can he have but the kingdom?" ⁹So Saul eyed David from that day forward.

¹⁰And it happened on the next day that the distressing spirit from God came upon Saul, and he prophesied inside the house. So David played *music* with his hand, as at other times; but *there was* a spear in Saul's hand. ¹¹And Saul cast the spear, for he said, "I will pin David to the wall!" But David escaped his presence twice.

¹²Now Saul was afraid of David, because the Lord was with him, but had departed from Saul. ¹³Therefore Saul removed him from his presence, and made him his captain over a thousand; and he went out and came in before the people. ¹⁴And David behaved wisely in all his ways, and the Lord *was* with him. ¹⁵Therefore, when Saul saw that he behaved very wisely, he was afraid of him. ¹⁶But all Israel and Judah loved David, because he went out and came in before them.

DAVID MARRIES MICHAL

¹⁷Then Saul said to David, "Here is my older daughter Merab; I will give her to you as a wife. Only be valiant for me, and fight the Lord's battles." For Saul thought, "Let my hand not be against him, but let the hand of the Philistines be against him."

¹⁸So David said to Saul, "Who *am* I, and what *is* my life *or* my father's family in Israel, that I should be son-in-law to the king?" ¹⁹But it happened at the time when Merab, Saul's daughter, should have been given to David, that she was given to Adriel the Meholathite as a wife.

²⁰Now Michal, Saul's daughter, loved David. And they told Saul, and the thing pleased him. ²¹So Saul said, "I will give her to him, that she may be a snare to him, and that the hand of the Philistines may be against him." Therefore Saul said to David a second time, "You shall be my son-in-law today."

²²And Saul commanded his servants, "Communicate with David secretly, and say, 'Look, the king has delight in you, and all his servants love you. Now therefore, become the king's son-in-law.' "

²³So Saul's servants spoke those words in the hearing of David. And David said, "Does it seem to you *a light thing* to be a king's son-in-law, seeing I *am* a poor and lightly esteemed man?" ²⁴And the servants of Saul told him, saying, "In this manner David spoke."

²⁵Then Saul said, "Thus you shall say to David: 'The king does not desire any dowry but one hundred foreskins of the Philistines, to take vengeance on the king's enemies.'" But Saul thought to make David fall by the hand of the Philistines. ²⁶So when his servants told David these words, it pleased David well to become the king's son-in-law. Now the days had not expired; ²⁷therefore David arose and went, he and his men, and killed two hundred men of the Philistines. And David brought their foreskins, and they gave them in full count to the king, that he might become the king's son-in-law. Then Saul gave him Michal his daughter as a wife.

> "Thus Saul saw and knew that the LORD was with David, and that Michal, Saul's daughter, loved him; and Saul was still more afraid of David. So Saul became David's enemy continually."
> (1 Samuel 18:28, 29)

WHAT'S IT MEAN?

Ouch! The bloody evidence that David gave to Saul was the foreskin—the part of the male body removed by circumcision—of every Philistine he killed. God required the Israelites to circumcise every male baby. The Philistines did not practice circumcision.

1 Samuel 18:27

²⁸Thus Saul saw and knew that the LORD *was* with David, and *that* Michal, Saul's daughter, loved him; ²⁹and Saul was still more afraid of David. So Saul became David's enemy continually. ³⁰Then the princes of the Philistines went out *to war.* And so it was, whenever they went out, *that* David behaved more wisely than all the servants of Saul, so that his name became highly esteemed.

SAUL PERSECUTES DAVID

¹Now Saul spoke to Jonathan his son and to all his servants, that they should kill David; but Jonathan, Saul's son, delighted greatly in David. ²So Jonathan told David, saying, "My father Saul seeks to kill you. Therefore please be on your guard until morning, and stay in a secret *place* and hide. ³And I will go out and stand beside my father in the field where you *are,* and I will speak with my father about you. Then what I observe, I will tell you."

⁴Thus Jonathan spoke well of David to Saul his father, and said to him, "Let not the king sin against his servant, against David, because he has not sinned against you, and because his works *have been* very good toward you. ⁵For he took his life in his hands and killed the Philistine, and the LORD brought about a great deliverance for all Israel. You saw *it* and rejoiced. Why then will you sin against innocent blood, to kill David without a cause?"

⁶So Saul heeded the voice of Jonathan, and Saul swore, "*As* the LORD lives, he shall not be killed." ⁷Then Jonathan called David, and Jonathan told him all these things. So Jonathan brought David to Saul, and he was in his presence as in times past.

⁸And there was war again; and David went out and fought with the Philistines, and struck them with a mighty blow, and they fled from him.

⁹Now the distressing spirit from the LORD came upon Saul as he sat in his house with his spear in his hand. And David was playing *music* with *his* hand. ¹⁰Then Saul sought to pin David to the wall with the spear, but he slipped away from Saul's presence; and he drove the spear into the wall. So David fled and escaped that night.

¹¹Saul also sent messengers to David's house to watch him and to kill him in the morning. And Michal, David's wife, told him, saying, "If you do not save your life tonight, tomorrow you will be killed." ¹²So Michal let David down through a window. And he went and fled and escaped. ¹³And Michal took an image and laid *it* in the bed, put a cover of goats' *hair* for his

FRIENDSHIP

What's an example of good friendship? (19:1–7)

head, and covered *it* with clothes. ¹⁴So when Saul sent messengers to take David, she said, "He *is* sick."

¹⁵Then Saul sent the messengers *back* to see David, saying, "Bring him up to me in the bed, that I may kill him." ¹⁶And when the messengers had come in, there was the image in the bed, with a cover of goats' *hair* for his head. ¹⁷Then Saul said to Michal, "Why have you deceived me like this, and sent my enemy away, so that he has escaped?"

And Michal answered Saul, "He said to me, 'Let me go! Why should I kill you?'"

¹⁸So David fled and escaped, and went to Samuel at Ramah, and told him all that Saul had done to him. And he and Samuel went and stayed in Naioth. ¹⁹Now it was told Saul, saying, "Take note, David *is* at Naioth in Ramah!" ²⁰Then Saul sent messengers to take David. And when they saw the group of prophets prophesying, and Samuel standing *as* leader over them, the Spirit of God came upon the messengers of Saul, and they also prophesied. ²¹And when Saul was told, he sent other messengers, and they prophesied likewise. Then Saul sent messengers again the third time, and they prophesied also. ²²Then he also went to Ramah, and came to the great well that *is* at Sechu. So he asked, and said, "Where *are* Samuel and David?"

And *someone* said, "Indeed *they are* at Naioth in Ramah." ²³So he went there to Naioth in Ramah. Then the Spirit of God was upon him also, and he went on and prophesied until he came to Naioth in Ramah. ²⁴And he also stripped off his clothes and prophesied before Samuel in like manner, and lay down naked all that day and all that night. Therefore they say, "*Is* Saul also among the prophets?"[a]

JONATHAN'S LOYALTY TO DAVID

¹Then David fled from Naioth in Ramah, and went and said to Jonathan, "What have I done? What *is* my iniquity, and what *is* my sin before your father, that he seeks my life?"

²So Jonathan said to him, "By no means! You shall not die! Indeed, my father will do nothing either great or small without first telling me. And why should my father hide this thing from me? It *is* not *so!*"

³Then David took an oath again, and said, "Your father certainly knows that I have found favor in your eyes, and he has said, 'Do not let Jonathan know this, lest he be grieved.' But truly, *as* the LORD lives and *as* your soul lives, *there is* but a step between me and death."

⁴So Jonathan said to David, "Whatever you yourself desire, I will do *it* for you."

⁵And David said to Jonathan, "Indeed tomorrow *is* the New Moon, and I should not fail to sit with the king to eat. But let me go, that I may hide in the field until the third *day* at evening. ⁶If your father misses me at all, then say, 'David earnestly asked *permission* of me that he might run over to Bethlehem, his city, for *there is* a yearly sacrifice there for all the family.' ⁷If he says thus: '*It is* well,' your servant will be safe. But if he is very angry, be sure that evil is determined by him. ⁸Therefore you shall deal kindly with your servant, for you have brought your servant into a covenant of the LORD with you. Nevertheless, if there is iniquity in me, kill me yourself, for why should you bring me to your father?"

⁹But Jonathan said, "Far be it from you! For if I knew certainly that evil was determined by my father to come upon you, then would I not tell you?"

¹⁰Then David said to Jonathan, "Who will tell me, or what *if* your father answers you roughly?"

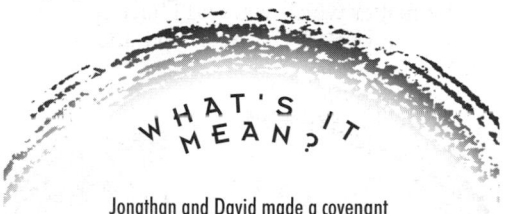

WHAT'S IT MEAN?

Jonathan and David made a covenant to fulfill certain responsibilities for each other. Not only were they bound by this contract, their descendants were bound by it as well. This kind of promise was common in Israel. Asking God to witness the agreement and hold them to it was also a common practice.
1 Samuel 20:11–16

¹¹And Jonathan said to David, "Come, let us go out into the field." So both of them went out into the field. ¹²Then Jonathan said to David: "The LORD God of Israel *is witness!* When I have sounded out my father sometime tomorrow, *or* the third *day*, and indeed *there is* good toward David, and I do not send to you and tell you, ¹³may the LORD do so and much more to Jonathan. But if it pleases my father *to do* you evil, then I will report it to you and send you away, that you may go in safety. And the LORD be with you as He has been with my father. ¹⁴And

you shall not only show me the kindness of the LORD while I still live, that I may not die; ¹⁵but you shall not cut off your kindness from my house forever, no, not when the LORD has cut off every one of the enemies of David from the face of the earth." ¹⁶So Jonathan made *a covenant* with the house of David, *saying,* "Let the LORD require *it* at the hand of David's enemies."

¹⁷Now Jonathan again caused David to vow, because he loved him; for he loved him as he loved his own soul. ¹⁸Then Jonathan said to David, "Tomorrow *is* the New Moon; and you will be missed, because your seat will be empty. ¹⁹And *when* you have stayed three days, go down quickly and come to the place where you hid on the day of the deed; and remain by the stone Ezel. ²⁰Then I will shoot three arrows to the side, as though I shot at a target; ²¹and there I will send a lad, *saying,* 'Go, find the arrows.' If I expressly say to the lad, 'Look, the arrows *are* on this side of you; get them and come'—then, as the LORD lives, *there is* safety for you and no harm. ²²But if I say thus to the young man, 'Look, the arrows *are* beyond you'—go your way, for the LORD has sent you away. ²³And as for the matter which you and I have spoken of, indeed the LORD *be* between you and me forever."

WHAT'S IT MEAN?

Not just anyone could participate in a religious sacrifice or feast. People had to meet certain requirements; they had to be ceremonially "clean." Touching a dead body, for example, made a person "unclean." That person was not allowed to join in religious ceremonies until he had followed certain procedures to become clean again.

1 Samuel 20:24–26

²⁴Then David hid in the field. And when the New Moon had come, the king sat down to eat the feast. ²⁵Now the king sat on his seat, as at other times, on a seat by the wall. And Jonathan arose,ᵃ and Abner sat by Saul's side, but David's place was empty. ²⁶Nevertheless Saul did not say anything that day, for he thought, "Something has happened to him; he *is* unclean,

surely he *is* unclean." ²⁷And it happened the next day, the second *day* of the month, that David's place was empty. And Saul said to Jonathan his son, "Why has the son of Jesse not come to eat, either yesterday or today?"

²⁸So Jonathan answered Saul, "David earnestly asked *permission* of me *to go* to Bethlehem. ²⁹And he said, 'Please let me go, for our family has a sacrifice in the city, and my brother has commanded me *to be there.* And now, if I have found favor in your eyes, please let me get away and see my brothers.' Therefore he has not come to the king's table."

WHAT'S IT MEAN?

Even today in Palestine, a kiss is a common greeting between friends and relatives who haven't seen each other in a while. The kiss between David and Jonathan was an indication of their friendship.

1 Samuel 20:41

³⁰Then Saul's anger was aroused against Jonathan, and he said to him, "You son of a perverse, rebellious *woman!* Do I not know that you have chosen the son of Jesse to your own shame and to the shame of your mother's nakedness? ³¹For as long as the son of Jesse lives on the earth, you shall not be established, nor your kingdom. Now therefore, send and bring him to me, for he shall surely die."

³²And Jonathan answered Saul his father, and said to him, "Why should he be killed? What has he done?" ³³Then Saul cast a spear at him to kill him, by which Jonathan knew that it was determined by his father to kill David.

³⁴So Jonathan arose from the table in fierce anger, and ate no food the second day of the month, for he was grieved for David, because his father had treated him shamefully.

³⁵And so it was, in the morning, that Jonathan went out into the field at the time appointed with David, and a little lad *was* with him. ³⁶Then he said to his lad, "Now run, find the arrows which I shoot." As the lad ran, he shot an arrow beyond him. ³⁷When the lad had come to the place where the arrow was which

20:25 ᵃFollowing Masoretic Text, Syriac, Targum, and Vulgate; Septuagint reads *he sat across from Jonathan.*

Jonathan had shot, Jonathan cried out after the lad and said, "*Is* not the arrow beyond you?" ³⁸And Jonathan cried out after the lad, "Make haste, hurry, do not delay!" So Jonathan's lad gathered up the arrows and came back to his master. ³⁹But the lad did not know anything. Only Jonathan and David knew of the matter. ⁴⁰Then Jonathan gave his weapons to his lad, and said to him, "Go, carry *them* to the city."

⁴¹As soon as the lad had gone, David arose from *a place* toward the south, fell on his face to the ground, and bowed down three times. And they kissed one another; and they wept together, but David more so. ⁴²Then Jonathan said to David, "Go in peace, since we have both sworn in the name of the LORD, saying, 'May the LORD be between you and me, and between your descendants and my descendants, forever.' " So he arose and departed, and Jonathan went into the city.

DAVID AND THE HOLY BREAD

¹Now David came to Nob, to Ahimelech the priest. And Ahimelech was afraid when he met David, and said to him, "Why *are* you alone, and no one is with you?"

²So David said to Ahimelech the priest, "The king has ordered me on some business, and said to me, 'Do not let anyone know anything about the business on which I send you, or what I have commanded you.' And I have directed *my* young men to such and such a place. ³Now therefore, what have you on hand? Give *me* five *loaves of* bread in my hand, or whatever can be found."

⁴And the priest answered David and said, "*There is* no common bread on hand; but there is holy bread, if the young men have at least kept themselves from women."

⁵Then David answered the priest, and said to him, "Truly, women *have been* kept from us about three days since I came out. And the vessels of the young men are holy, and *the bread is* in effect common, even though it was consecrated in the vessel this day."

⁶So the priest gave him holy *bread;* for there was no bread there but the showbread which had been taken from before the LORD, in order to put hot bread *in its place* on the day when it was taken away.

⁷Now a certain man of the servants of Saul *was* there that day, detained before the LORD. And his name *was* Doeg, an Edomite, the chief of the herdsmen who *belonged* to Saul.

⁸And David said to Ahimelech, "Is there not here on hand a spear or a sword? For I have brought neither my sword nor my weapons with me, because the king's business required haste."

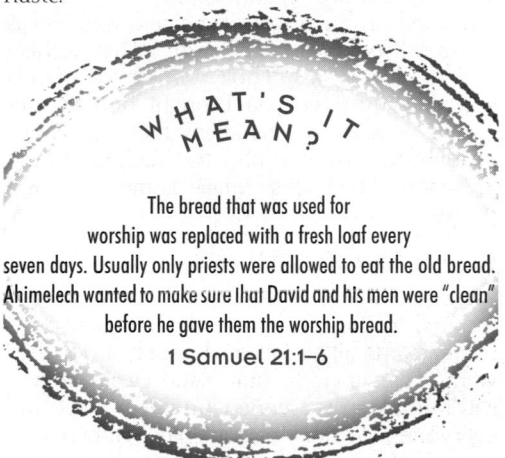

WHAT'S IT MEAN?

The bread that was used for worship was replaced with a fresh loaf every seven days. Usually only priests were allowed to eat the old bread. Ahimelech wanted to make sure that David and his men were "clean" before he gave them the worship bread.

1 Samuel 21:1–6

⁹So the priest said, "The sword of Goliath the Philistine, whom you killed in the Valley of Elah, there it is, wrapped in a cloth behind the ephod. If you will take that, take *it.* For *there is* no other except that one here."

And David said, "*There is* none like it; give it to me."

DAVID FLEES TO GATH

¹⁰Then David arose and fled that day from before Saul, and went to Achish the king of Gath. ¹¹And the servants of Achish said to him, "Is this not David the king of the land? Did they not sing of him to one another in dances, saying:

'Saul has slain his thousands,
And David his ten thousands'?"[a]

WHAT'S IT MEAN?

In his tour of one-syllable towns, David traveled about twenty-five miles from Nob to Gath. Gath was probably the last place anyone would expect to find David. Gath was one of the five capital cities of the Philistines, the enemies of Israel.

1 Samuel 21:10

21:11 [a]Compare 1 Samuel 18:7

[12]Now David took these words to heart, and was very much afraid of Achish the king of Gath. [13]So he changed his behavior before them, pretended madness in their hands, scratched on the doors of the gate, and let his saliva fall down on his beard. [14]Then Achish said to his servants, "Look, you see the man is insane. Why have you brought him to me? [15]Have I need of madmen, that you have brought this *fellow* to play the madman in my presence? Shall this *fellow* come into my house?"

DAVID'S FOUR HUNDRED MEN

[1]David therefore departed from there and escaped to the cave of Adullam. So when his brothers and all his father's house heard *it,* they went down there to him. [2]And everyone *who was* in distress, everyone who *was* in debt, and everyone *who was* discontented gathered to him. So he became captain over them. And there were about four hundred men with him.

[3]Then David went from there to Mizpah of Moab; and he said to the king of Moab, "Please let my father and mother come here with you, till I know what God will do for me." [4]So he brought them before the king of Moab, and they dwelt with him all the time that David was in the stronghold.

WHAT'S IT MEAN?

Moab was located on the far side of the Dead Sea. Like the Philistines, David's earlier "hosts," the Moabites were continually at war with the Israelites. David must have assumed that the safest places for him to hide were with Saul's enemies.

1 Samuel 22:3

[5]Now the prophet Gad said to David, "Do not stay in the stronghold; depart, and go to the land of Judah." So David departed and went into the forest of Hereth.

SAUL MURDERS THE PRIESTS

[6]When Saul heard that David and the men who *were* with him had been discovered—now Saul was staying in Gibeah under a tamarisk tree in Ramah, with his spear in his hand, and all his servants standing about him— [7]then Saul said to his servants who stood about him, "Hear now, you Benjamites! Will the son of Jesse give every one of you fields and vineyards, *and* make you all captains of thousands and captains of hundreds? [8]All of you have conspired against me, and *there is* no one who reveals to me that my son has made a covenant with the son of Jesse; and *there is* not one of you who is sorry for me or reveals to me that my son has stirred up my servant against me, to lie in wait, as *it is* this day."

[9]Then answered Doeg the Edomite, who was set over the servants of Saul, and said, "I saw the son of Jesse going to Nob, to Ahimelech the son of Ahitub. [10]And he inquired of the LORD for him, gave him provisions, and gave him the sword of Goliath the Philistine."

[11]So the king sent to call Ahimelech the priest, the son of Ahitub, and all his father's house, the priests who *were* in Nob. And they all came to the king. [12]And Saul said, "Hear now, son of Ahitub!"

He answered, "Here I am, my lord."

[13]Then Saul said to him, "Why have you conspired against me, you and the son of Jesse, in that you have given him bread and a sword, and have inquired of God for him, that he should rise against me, to lie in wait, as it is this day?"

[14]So Ahimelech answered the king and said, "And who among all your servants *is as* faithful as David, who is the king's son-in-law, who goes at your bidding, and is honorable in your house? [15]Did I then begin to inquire of God for him? Far be it from me! Let not the king impute anything to his servant, *or* to any in the house of my father. For your servant knew nothing of all this, little or much."

[16]And the king said, "You shall surely die, Ahimelech, you and all your father's house!" [17]Then the king said to the guards who stood about him, "Turn and kill the priests of the LORD, because their hand also *is* with David, and because they knew when he fled and did not tell it to me." But the servants of the king would not lift their hands to strike the priests of the LORD. [18]And the king said to Doeg, "You turn and kill the priests!" So Doeg the Edomite turned and struck the priests, and killed on that day eighty-five men who wore a linen ephod. [19]Also Nob, the city of the priests, he struck with the edge of the sword, both men and women, children and nursing infants, oxen and donkeys and sheep—with the edge of the sword.

[20]Now one of the sons of Ahimelech the son

of Ahitub, named Abiathar, escaped and fled after David. [21]And Abiathar told David that Saul had killed the LORD's priests. [22]So David said to Abiathar, "I knew that day, when Doeg the Edomite *was* there, that he would surely tell Saul. I have caused *the death* of all the persons of your father's house. [23]Stay with me; do not fear. For he who seeks my life seeks your life, but with me you *shall be* safe."

DAVID SAVES THE CITY OF KEILAH

[1]Then they told David, saying, "Look, the Philistines are fighting against Keilah, and they are robbing the threshing floors."

[2]Therefore David inquired of the LORD, saying, "Shall I go and attack these Philistines?"

And the LORD said to David, "Go and attack the Philistines, and save Keilah."

[3]But David's men said to him, "Look, we are afraid here in Judah. How much more then if we go to Keilah against the armies of the Philistines?" [4]Then David inquired of the LORD once again.

And the LORD answered him and said, "Arise, go down to Keilah. For I will deliver the Philistines into your hand." [5]And David and his men went to Keilah and fought with the Philistines, struck them with a mighty blow, and took away their livestock. So David saved the inhabitants of Keilah.

[6]Now it happened, when Abiathar the son of Ahimelech fled to David at Keilah, *that* he went down *with* an ephod in his hand.

[7]And Saul was told that David had gone to Keilah. So Saul said, "God has delivered him into my hand, for he has shut himself in by entering a town that has gates and bars." [8]Then Saul called all the people together for war, to go down to Keilah to besiege David and his men.

[9]When David knew that Saul plotted evil against him, he said to Abiathar the priest, "Bring the ephod here." [10]Then David said, "O LORD God of Israel, Your servant has certainly heard that Saul seeks to come to Keilah to destroy the city for my sake. [11]Will the men of Keilah deliver me into his hand? Will Saul come down, as Your servant has heard? O LORD God of Israel, I pray, tell Your servant."

And the LORD said, "He will come down."
[12]Then David said, "Will the men of Keilah deliver me and my men into the hand of Saul?"

And the LORD said, "They will deliver *you.*"
[13]So David and his men, about six hundred, arose and departed from Keilah and went wherever they could go. Then it was told Saul that David had escaped from Keilah; so he halted the expedition.

DAVID IN WILDERNESS STRONGHOLDS

[14]And David stayed in strongholds in the wilderness, and remained in the mountains in the Wilderness of Ziph. Saul sought him every day, but God did not deliver him into his hand. [15]So David saw that Saul had come out to seek his life. And David *was* in the Wilderness of Ziph in a forest.[a] [16]Then Jonathan, Saul's son, arose and went to David in the woods and strengthened his hand in God. [17]And he said to him, "Do not fear, for the hand of Saul my father shall not find you. You shall be king over Israel, and I shall be next to you. Even my father Saul knows that." [18]So the two of them made a covenant before the LORD. And David stayed in the woods, and Jonathan went to his own house.

> "And David stayed in strongholds in the wilderness, and remained in the mountains in the Wilderness of Ziph. Saul sought him every day, but God did not deliver him into his hand."
> (1 Samuel 23:14)

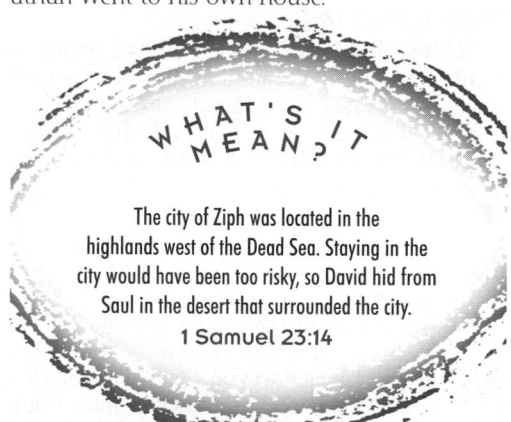

WHAT'S IT MEAN?

The city of Ziph was located in the highlands west of the Dead Sea. Staying in the city would have been too risky, so David hid from Saul in the desert that surrounded the city.
1 Samuel 23:14

[19]Then the Ziphites came up to Saul at Gibeah, saying, "Is David not hiding with us in strongholds in the woods, in the hill of Hachilah, which *is* on the south of Jeshimon? [20]Now therefore, O king, come down according to all the desire of your soul to come down; and

our part *shall be* to deliver him into the king's hand."

²¹And Saul said, "Blessed *are* you of the LORD, for you have compassion on me. ²²Please go and find out for sure, and see the place where his hideout is, *and* who has seen him there. For I am told he is very crafty. ²³See therefore, and take knowledge of all the lurking places where he hides; and come back to me with certainty, and I will go with you. And it shall be, if he is in the land, that I will search for him throughout all the clans*ᵃ* of Judah."

²⁴So they arose and went to Ziph before Saul. But David and his men *were* in the Wilderness of Maon, in the plain on the south of Jeshimon. ²⁵When Saul and his men went to seek *him,* they told David. Therefore he went down to the rock, and stayed in the Wilderness of Maon. And when Saul heard *that,* he pursued David in the Wilderness of Maon. ²⁶Then Saul went on one side of the mountain, and David and his men on the other side of the mountain. So David made haste to get away from Saul, for Saul and his men were encircling David and his men to take them.

²⁷But a messenger came to Saul, saying, "Hurry and come, for the Philistines have invaded the land!" ²⁸Therefore Saul returned from pursuing David, and went against the Philistines; so they called that place the Rock of Escape.*ᵃ* ²⁹Then David went up from there and dwelt in strongholds at En Gedi.

DAVID SPARES SAUL

¹Now it happened, when Saul had returned from following the Philistines, that it was told him, saying, "Take note! David *is* in the Wilderness of En Gedi." ²Then Saul took three thousand chosen men from all Israel, and went to seek David and his men on the Rocks of the Wild Goats. ³So he came to the sheepfolds by the road, where there *was* a cave; and Saul went in to attend to his needs. (David and his men were staying in the recesses of the cave.) ⁴Then the men of David said to him, "This is the day of which the LORD said to you, 'Behold, I will deliver your enemy into your hand, that you may do to him as it seems good to you.' " And David arose and secretly cut off a corner of Saul's robe.

⁵Now it happened afterward that David's heart troubled him because he had cut Saul's *robe.* ⁶And he said to his men, "The LORD forbid that

I should do this thing to my master, the LORD's anointed, to stretch out my hand against him, seeing he *is* the anointed of the LORD." ⁷So David restrained his servants with *these* words, and did not allow them to rise against Saul. And Saul got up from the cave and went on *his* way.

WHAT'S IT MEAN?

En Gedi, an oasis in the Negev Desert, was famous for two things: its freshwater spring and the wild goats that lived in the surrounding hills. In fact, the name *En Gedi* means "Spring of the Kid."
1 Samuel 24:1, 2

⁸David also arose afterward, went out of the cave, and called out to Saul, saying, "My lord the king!" And when Saul looked behind him, David stooped with his face to the earth, and bowed down. ⁹And David said to Saul: "Why do you listen to the words of men who say, 'Indeed David seeks your harm'? ¹⁰Look, this day your eyes have seen that the LORD delivered you today into my hand in the cave, and *some-one* urged *me* to kill you. But *my eye* spared you, and I said, 'I will not stretch out my hand against my lord, for he *is* the LORD's anointed.' ¹¹Moreover, my father, see! Yes, see the corner of your robe in my hand! For in that I cut off the corner of your robe, and did not kill you, know and see that *there is* neither evil nor rebellion in my hand, and I have not sinned against you. Yet you hunt my life to take it. ¹²Let the LORD judge between you and me, and let the LORD avenge me

> **REVENGE**
> Who is in charge of vengeance?
> (24:12)

on you. But my hand shall not be against you. ¹³As the proverb of the ancients says, 'Wickedness proceeds from the wicked.' But my hand shall not be against you. ¹⁴After whom has the king of Israel come out? Whom do you pursue? A dead dog? A flea? ¹⁵Therefore let the LORD be judge, and judge between you and me, and see and plead my case, and deliver me out of your hand."

¹⁶So it was, when David had finished speaking these words to Saul, that Saul said, "*Is* this

> **LEADERSHIP**
> Why should we respect leaders?
> (24:1–6)

your voice, my son David?" And Saul lifted up his voice and wept. ¹⁷Then he said to David: "You *are* more righteous than I; for you have rewarded me with good, whereas I have rewarded you with evil. ¹⁸And you have shown this day how you have dealt well with me; for when the LORD delivered me into your hand, you did not kill me. ¹⁹For if a man finds his enemy, will he let him get away safely? Therefore may the LORD reward you with good for what you have done to me this day. ²⁰And now I know indeed that you shall surely be king, and that the kingdom of Israel shall be established in your hand. ²¹Therefore swear now to me by the LORD that you will not cut off my descendants after me, and that you will not destroy my name from my father's house."

²²So David swore to Saul. And Saul went home, but David and his men went up to the stronghold.

DEATH OF SAMUEL

¹Then Samuel died; and the Israelites gathered together and lamented for him, and buried him at his home in Ramah. And David arose and went down to the Wilderness of Paran.*ᵃ*

DAVID AND THE WIFE OF NABAL

²Now *there was* a man in Maon whose business *was* in Carmel, and the man *was* very rich. He had three thousand sheep and a thousand goats. And he was shearing his sheep in Carmel. ³The name of the man *was* Nabal, and the name of his wife Abigail. And *she was* a woman of good understanding and beautiful appearance; but the man *was* harsh and evil in *his* doings. He *was of the house of* Caleb.

⁴When David heard in the wilderness that Nabal was shearing his sheep, ⁵David sent ten young men; and David said to the young men, "Go up to Carmel, go to Nabal, and greet him in my name. ⁶And thus you shall say to him who lives *in prosperity:* 'Peace *be* to you, peace to your house, and peace to all that you have! ⁷Now I have heard that you have shearers. Your shepherds were with us, and we did not hurt them, nor was there anything missing from them all the while they were in Carmel. ⁸Ask your young men, and they will tell you. Therefore let *my* young men find favor in your eyes, for we come on a feast day. Please give whatever comes to your hand to your servants and to your son David.' "

⁹So when David's young men came, they spoke to Nabal according to all these words in the name of David, and waited.

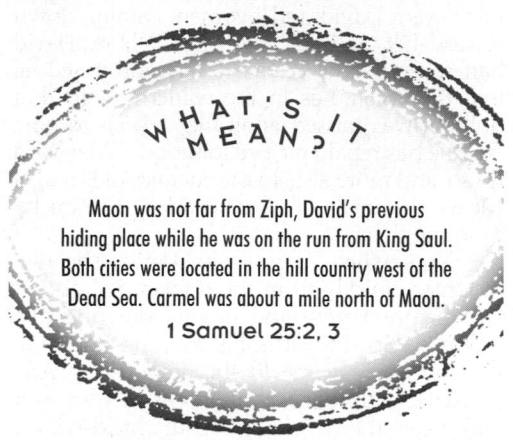

WHAT'S IT MEAN?

Maon was not far from Ziph, David's previous hiding place while he was on the run from King Saul. Both cities were located in the hill country west of the Dead Sea. Carmel was about a mile north of Maon.

1 Samuel 25:2, 3

¹⁰Then Nabal answered David's servants, and said, "Who *is* David, and who *is* the son of Jesse? There are many servants nowadays who break away each one from his master. ¹¹Shall I then take my bread and my water and my meat that I have killed for my shearers, and give *it* to men when I do not know where they *are* from?"

¹²So David's young men turned on their heels and went back; and they came and told him all these words. ¹³Then David said to his men, "Every man gird on his sword." So every man girded on his sword, and David also girded on his sword. And about four hundred men went with David, and two hundred stayed with the supplies.

¹⁴Now one of the young men told Abigail, Nabal's wife, saying, "Look, David sent messengers from the wilderness to greet our master; and he reviled them. ¹⁵But the men *were* very good to us, and we were not hurt, nor did we miss anything as long as we accompanied them, when we were in the fields. ¹⁶They were a wall to us both by night and day, all the time we were with them keeping the sheep. ¹⁷Now therefore, know and consider what you will do, for harm is determined against our master and against all his household. For he *is such* a scoundrel*ᵃ* that *one* cannot speak to him."

¹⁸Then Abigail made haste and took two hundred *loaves* of bread, two skins of wine, five sheep already dressed, five seahs of roasted *grain*, one hundred clusters of raisins, and two hundred cakes of figs, and loaded *them* on donkeys. ¹⁹And she said to her servants, "Go on before me; see, I am coming after you." But she did not tell her husband Nabal.

25:1 ᵃFollowing Masoretic Text, Syriac, Targum, and Vulgate; Septuagint reads *Maon.* 25:17 ᵃLiterally *son of Belial*

²⁰So it was, *as* she rode on the donkey, that she went down under cover of the hill; and there were David and his men, coming down toward her, and she met them. ²¹Now David had said, "Surely in vain I have protected all that this *fellow* has in the wilderness, so that nothing was missed of all that *belongs* to him. And he has repaid me evil for good. ²²May God do so, and more also, to the enemies of David, if I leave one male of all who *belong* to him by morning light."

²³Now when Abigail saw David, she dismounted quickly from the donkey, fell on her face before David, and bowed down to the ground. ²⁴So she fell at his feet and said: "On me, my lord, *on me let* this iniquity *be*! And please let your maidservant speak in your ears, and hear the words of your maidservant. ²⁵Please, let not my lord regard this scoundrel Nabal. For as his name *is*, so *is* he: Nabal^a *is* his name, and folly *is* with him! But I, your maidservant, did not see the young men of my lord whom you sent. ²⁶Now therefore, my lord, *as* the LORD lives and *as* your soul lives, since the LORD has held you back from coming to bloodshed and from avenging yourself with your own hand, now then, let your enemies and those who seek harm for my lord be as Nabal. ²⁷And now this present which your maidservant has brought to my lord, let it be given to the young men who follow my lord. ²⁸Please forgive the trespass of your maidservant. For the LORD will certainly make for my lord an enduring house, because my lord fights the battles of the LORD, and evil is not found in you throughout your days. ²⁹Yet a man has risen to pursue you and seek your life, but the life of my lord shall be bound in the bundle of the living with the LORD your God; and the lives of your enemies He shall sling out, *as from* the pocket of a sling. ³⁰And it shall come to pass, when the LORD has done for my lord according to all the good that He has spoken concerning you, and has appointed you ruler over Israel, ³¹that this will be no grief to you, nor offense of heart to my lord, either that you have shed blood without cause, or that my lord has avenged himself. But when the LORD has dealt well with my lord, then remember your maidservant."

³²Then David said to Abigail: "Blessed *is* the LORD God of Israel, who sent you this day to meet me! ³³And blessed *is* your advice and blessed *are* you, because you have kept me this day from coming to bloodshed and from avenging myself with my own hand. ³⁴For indeed, *as* the LORD God of Israel lives, who has kept me back from hurting you, unless you had hurried and come to meet me, surely by morning light no males would have been left to Nabal!" ³⁵So David received from her hand what she had brought him, and said to her, "Go up in peace to your house. See, I have heeded your voice and respected your person."

³⁶Now Abigail went to Nabal, and there he was, holding a feast in his house, like the feast of a king. And Nabal's heart *was* merry within him, for he *was* very drunk; therefore she told him nothing, little or much, until morning light. ³⁷So it was, in the morning, when the wine had gone from Nabal, and his wife had told him these things, that his heart died within him, and he became *like* a stone. ³⁸Then it happened, *after* about ten days, that the LORD struck Nabal, and he died.

³⁹So when David heard that Nabal was dead, he said, "Blessed *be* the LORD, who has pleaded the cause of my reproach from the hand of Nabal, and has kept His servant from evil! For the LORD has returned the wickedness of Nabal on his own head."

And David sent and proposed to Abigail, to take her as his wife. ⁴⁰When the servants of David had come to Abigail at Carmel, they spoke to her saying, "David sent us to you, to ask you to become his wife."

⁴¹Then she arose, bowed her face to the earth, and said, "Here is your maidservant, a servant to wash the feet of the servants of my lord." ⁴²So Abigail rose in haste and rode on a donkey, attended by five of her maidens; and she followed the messengers of David, and became his wife. ⁴³David also took Ahinoam of Jezreel, and so both of them were his wives.

⁴⁴But Saul had given Michal his daughter, David's wife, to Palti^a the son of Laish, who *was* from Gallim.

DAVID SPARES SAUL A SECOND TIME

¹Now the Ziphites came to Saul at Gibeah, saying, "Is David not hiding in the hill of Hachilah, opposite Jeshimon?" ²Then Saul arose and went down to the Wilderness of Ziph, having three thousand chosen men of Israel with him, to seek David in the Wilderness of Ziph. ³And Saul encamped in the hill of Hachilah, which *is* opposite Jeshimon, by the road. But David stayed in the wilderness, and he saw that Saul came after him into the wilderness. ⁴David therefore sent out spies, and understood that Saul had indeed come.

25:25 ^aLiterally *Fool* **25:44** ^aSpelled *Paltiel* in 2 Samuel 3:15

⁵So David arose and came to the place where Saul had encamped. And David saw the place where Saul lay, and Abner the son of Ner, the commander of his army. Now Saul lay within the camp, with the people encamped all around him. ⁶Then David answered, and said to Ahimelech the Hittite and to Abishai the son of Zeruiah, brother of Joab, saying, "Who will go down with me to Saul in the camp?"

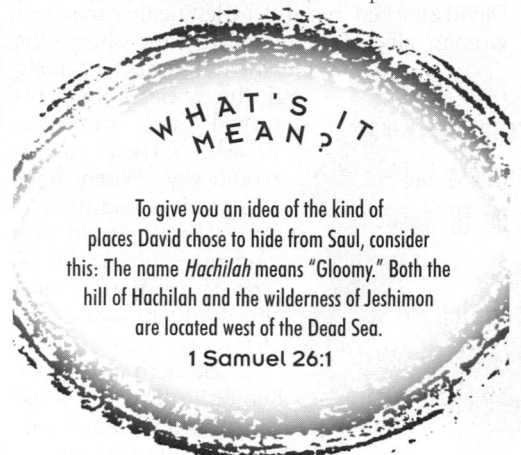

WHAT'S IT MEAN?

To give you an idea of the kind of places David chose to hide from Saul, consider this: The name *Hachilah* means "Gloomy." Both the hill of Hachilah and the wilderness of Jeshimon are located west of the Dead Sea.

1 Samuel 26:1

And Abishai said, "I will go down with you."

⁷So David and Abishai came to the people by night; and there Saul lay sleeping within the camp, with his spear stuck in the ground by his head. And Abner and the people lay all around him. ⁸Then Abishai said to David, "God has delivered your enemy into your hand this day. Now therefore, please, let me strike him at once with the spear, right to the earth; and I will not *have to strike* him a second time!"

⁹But David said to Abishai, "Do not destroy him; for who can stretch out his hand against the LORD's anointed, and be guiltless?" ¹⁰David said furthermore, "*As* the LORD lives, the LORD shall strike him, or his day shall come to die, or he shall go out to battle and perish. ¹¹The LORD forbid that I should stretch out my hand against the LORD's anointed. But please, take now the spear and the jug of water that *are* by his head, and let us go." ¹²So David took the spear and the jug of water *by* Saul's head, and they got away; and no man saw or knew *it* or awoke. For they *were* all asleep, because a deep sleep from the LORD had fallen on them.

¹³Now David went over to the other side, and stood on the top of a hill afar off, a great distance *being* between them. ¹⁴And David called out to the people and to Abner the son of Ner, saying, "Do you not answer, Abner?"

Then Abner answered and said, "Who *are* you, calling out to the king?"

¹⁵So David said to Abner, "*Are* you not a man? And who *is* like you in Israel? Why then have you not guarded your lord the king? For one of the people came in to destroy your lord the king. ¹⁶This thing that you have done *is* not good. *As* the LORD lives, you deserve to die, because you have not guarded your master, the LORD's anointed. And now see where the king's spear *is*, and the jug of water that *was* by his head."

¹⁷Then Saul knew David's voice, and said, "*Is* that your voice, my son David?"

David said, "*It is* my voice, my lord, O king." ¹⁸And he said, "Why does my lord thus pursue his servant? For what have I done, or what evil *is* in my hand? ¹⁹Now therefore, please, let my lord the king hear the words of his servant: If the LORD has stirred you up against me, let Him accept an offering. But if *it is* the children of men, *may* they *be* cursed before the LORD, for they have driven me out this day from sharing in the inheritance of the LORD, saying, 'Go, serve other gods.' ²⁰So now, do not let my blood fall to the earth before the face of the LORD. For the king of Israel has come out to seek a flea, as when one hunts a partridge in the mountains."

²¹Then Saul said, "I have sinned. Return, my son David. For I will harm you no more, because my life was precious in your eyes this day. Indeed I have played the fool and erred exceedingly."

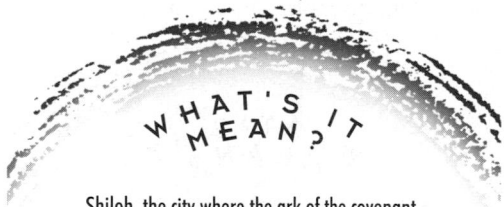

WHAT'S IT MEAN?

Shiloh, the city where the ark of the covenant was kept, was considered the official worship site of the Israelites. Kicking someone out of Israel, then, prevented that person from officially worshiping God. Because worship was so important to the Israelites, depriving someone of the opportunity to worship was considered cruel punishment and was reserved for serious criminals.

1 Samuel 26:19

²²And David answered and said, "Here is the king's spear. Let one of the young men come over and get it. ²³May the LORD repay every man *for* his righteousness and his faithfulness; for the LORD delivered you into *my* hand today, but I would not stretch out my hand against the LORD's anointed. ²⁴And indeed, as your life

was valued much this day in my eyes, so let my life be valued much in the eyes of the LORD, and let Him deliver me out of all tribulation."

25Then Saul said to David, "*May* you *be* blessed, my son David! You shall both do great things and also still prevail."

So David went on his way, and Saul returned to his place.

DAVID ALLIED WITH THE PHILISTINES

1And David said in his heart, "Now I shall perish someday by the hand of Saul. *There is* nothing better for me than that I should speedily escape to the land of the Philistines; and Saul will despair of me, to seek me anymore in any part of Israel. So I shall escape out of his hand." 2Then David arose and went over with the six hundred men who *were* with him to Achish the son of Maoch, king of Gath. 3So David dwelt with Achish at Gath, he and his men, each man with his household, *and* David with his two wives, Ahinoam the Jezreelitess, and Abigail the Carmelitess, Nabal's widow. 4And it was told Saul that David had fled to Gath; so he sought him no more.

> "May the LORD repay every man for his righteousness and his faithfulness; for the LORD delivered you into my hand today, but I would not stretch out my hand against the LORD's anointed."
> (1 Samuel 26:23)

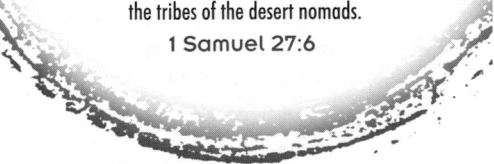

WHAT'S IT MEAN?

What's the biggest present you've ever received? David was given an entire city. Achish, the king of Gath, gave David the city of Ziklag in the south. David eventually used Ziklag as a military base for his attacks on the tribes of the desert nomads.

1 Samuel 27:6

5Then David said to Achish, "If I have now found favor in your eyes, let them give me a place in some town in the country, that I may dwell there. For why should your servant dwell in the royal city with you?" 6So Achish gave him Ziklag that day. Therefore Ziklag has belonged to the kings of Judah to this day. 7Now the time that David dwelt in the country of the Philistines was one full year and four months.

8And David and his men went up and raided the Geshurites, the Girzites,*a* and the Amalekites. For those nations were the inhabitants of the land from of old, as you go to Shur, even as far as the land of Egypt. 9Whenever David attacked the land, he left neither man nor woman alive, but took away the sheep, the oxen, the donkeys, the camels, and the apparel, and returned and came to Achish. 10Then Achish would say, "Where have you made a raid today?" And David would say, "Against the southern *area* of Judah, or against the southern *area* of the Jerahmeelites, or against the southern *area* of the Kenites." 11David would save neither man nor woman alive, to bring *news* to Gath, saying, "Lest they should inform on us, saying, 'Thus David did.' " And thus *was* his behavior all the time he dwelt in the country of the Philistines. 12So Achish believed David, saying, "He has made his people Israel utterly abhor him; therefore he will be my servant forever."

1Now it happened in those days that the Philistines gathered their armies together for war, to fight with Israel. And Achish said to David, "You assuredly know that you will go out with me to battle, you and your men."

2So David said to Achish, "Surely you know what your servant can do."

And Achish said to David, "Therefore I will make you one of my chief guardians forever."

SAUL CONSULTS A MEDIUM

3Now Samuel had died, and all Israel had lamented for him and buried him in Ramah, in his own city. And Saul had put the mediums and the spiritists out of the land.

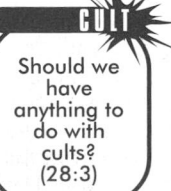

CULT

Should we have anything to do with cults? (28:3)

4Then the Philistines gathered together, and came and encamped at Shunem. So Saul gathered all Israel together, and they encamped at Gilboa. 5When Saul saw the army of the Philistines, he was afraid, and his heart trembled greatly. [6]And when Saul inquired of the LORD, the LORD did not answer him, either by dreams or by Urim or by the prophets.

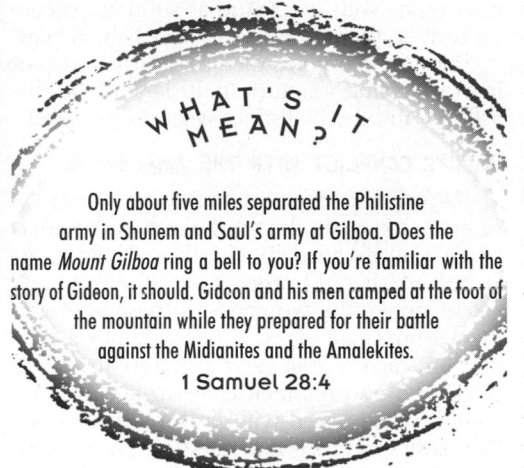

WHAT'S IT MEAN?

Only about five miles separated the Philistine army in Shunem and Saul's army at Gilboa. Does the name *Mount Gilboa* ring a bell to you? If you're familiar with the story of Gideon, it should. Gideon and his men camped at the foot of the mountain while they prepared for their battle against the Midianites and the Amalekites.

1 Samuel 28:4

[7]Then Saul said to his servants, "Find me a woman who is a medium, that I may go to her and inquire of her."

And his servants said to him, "In fact, *there is* a woman who is a medium at En Dor."

[8]So Saul disguised himself and put on other clothes, and he went, and two men with him; and they came to the woman by night. And he said, "Please conduct a séance for me, and bring up for me the one I shall name to you."

[9]Then the woman said to him, "Look, you know what Saul has done, how he has cut off the mediums and the spiritists from the land. Why then do you lay a snare for my life, to cause me to die?"

[10]And Saul swore to her by the LORD, saying, "*As* the LORD lives, no punishment shall come upon you for this thing."

[11]Then the woman said, "Whom shall I bring up for you?"

And he said, "Bring up Samuel for me."

[12]When the woman saw Samuel, she cried out with a loud voice. And the woman spoke to Saul, saying, "Why have you deceived me? For you *are* Saul!"

[13]And the king said to her, "Do not be afraid. What did you see?"

And the woman said to Saul, "I saw a spirit[a] ascending out of the earth."

[14]So he said to her, "What *is* his form?"

And she said, "An old man is coming up, and he *is* covered with a mantle." And Saul perceived that it *was* Samuel, and he stooped with *his* face to the ground and bowed down.

[15]Now Samuel said to Saul, "Why have you disturbed me by bringing me up?"

And Saul answered, "I am deeply distressed; for the Philistines make war against me, and God has departed from me and does not answer me anymore, neither by prophets nor by dreams. Therefore I have called you, that you may reveal to me what I should do."

[16]Then Samuel said: "So why do you ask me, seeing the LORD has departed from you and has become your enemy? [17]And the LORD has done for Himself[a] as He spoke by me. For the LORD has torn the kingdom out of your hand and given it to your neighbor, David. [18]Because you did not obey the voice of the LORD nor execute His fierce wrath upon Amalek, therefore the LORD has done this thing to you this day. [19]Moreover the LORD will also deliver Israel with you into the hand of the Philistines. And tomorrow you and your sons *will be* with me. The LORD will also deliver the army of Israel into the hand of the Philistines."

[20]Immediately Saul fell full length on the ground, and was dreadfully afraid because of the words of Samuel. And there was no strength in him, for he had eaten no food all day or all night.

[21]And the woman came to Saul and saw that he was severely troubled, and said to him, "Look, your maidservant has obeyed your voice, and I have put my life in my hands and heeded the words which you spoke to me. [22]Now therefore, please, heed also the voice of your maidservant, and let me set a piece of bread before you; and eat, that you may have strength when you go on *your* way."

[23]But he refused and said, "I will not eat."

So his servants, together with the woman, urged him; and he heeded their voice. Then he arose from the ground and sat on the bed. [24]Now the woman had a fatted calf in the house, and she hastened to kill it. And she took flour and kneaded *it*, and baked unleavened bread from it. [25]So she brought *it* before Saul and his servants, and they ate. Then they rose and went away that night.

THE PHILISTINES REJECT DAVID

[1]Then the Philistines gathered together all their armies at Aphek, and the Israelites encamped by a fountain which *is* in Jezreel. [2]And the lords of the Philistines passed in review by hundreds and by thousands, but David and his men passed in review at the rear with Achish.

28:13 [a]Hebrew *elohim*   **28:17** [a]Or *him,* that is, David

³Then the princes of the Philistines said, "What *are* these Hebrews *doing here?*"

And Achish said to the princes of the Philistines, "*Is* this not David, the servant of Saul king of Israel, who has been with me these days, or these years? And to this day I have found no fault in him since he defected *to me.*"

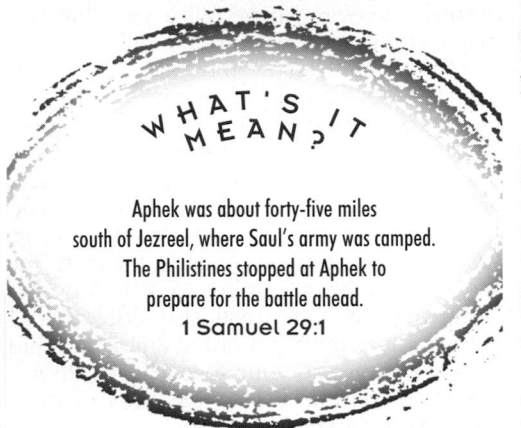

WHAT'S IT MEAN?

Aphek was about forty-five miles south of Jezreel, where Saul's army was camped. The Philistines stopped at Aphek to prepare for the battle ahead.

1 Samuel 29:1

⁴But the princes of the Philistines were angry with him; so the princes of the Philistines said to him, "Make this fellow return, that he may go back to the place which you have appointed for him, and do not let him go down with us to battle, lest in the battle he become our adversary. For with what could he reconcile himself to his master, if not with the heads of these men? ⁵*Is* this not David, of whom they sang to one another in dances, saying:

'Saul has slain his thousands,
And David his ten thousands'?"*ᵃ*

⁶Then Achish called David and said to him, "Surely, *as* the LORD lives, you have been upright, and your going out and your coming in with me in the army *is* good in my sight. For to this day I have not found evil in you since the day of your coming to me. Nevertheless the lords do not favor you. ⁷Therefore return now, and go in peace, that you may not displease the lords of the Philistines."

⁸So David said to Achish, "But what have I done? And to this day what have you found in your servant as long as I have been with you, that I may not go and fight against the enemies of my lord the king?"

⁹Then Achish answered and said to David, "I know that you *are* as good in my sight as an angel of God; nevertheless the princes of the Philistines have said, 'He shall not go up with us to battle.' ¹⁰Now therefore, rise early in the morning with your master's servants who have come with you.*ᵃ* And as soon as you are up early in the morning and have light, depart."

¹¹So David and his men rose early to depart in the morning, to return to the land of the Philistines. And the Philistines went up to Jezreel.

DAVID'S CONFLICT WITH THE AMALEKITES

¹Now it happened, when David and his men came to Ziklag, on the third day, that the Amalekites had invaded the South and Ziklag, attacked Ziklag and burned it with fire, ²and had taken captive the women and those who *were* there, from small to great; they did not kill anyone, but carried *them* away and went their way. ³So David and his men came to the city, and there it was, burned with fire; and their wives, their sons, and their daughters had been taken captive. ⁴Then David and the people who *were* with him lifted up their voices and wept, until they had no more power to weep. ⁵And David's two wives, Ahinoam the Jezreelitess, and Abigail the widow of Nabal the Carmelite, had been taken captive. ⁶Now David was greatly distressed, for the people spoke of stoning him, because the soul of all the people was grieved, every man for his sons and his daughters. But David strengthened himself in the LORD his God.

⁷Then David said to Abiathar the priest, Ahimelech's son, "Please bring the ephod here to me." And Abiathar brought the ephod to David. ⁸So David inquired of the LORD, saying, "Shall I pursue this troop? Shall I overtake them?"

And He answered him, "Pursue, for you shall surely overtake *them* and without fail recover *all.*"

⁹So David went, he and the six hundred men who *were* with him, and came to the Brook Besor, where those stayed who were left behind. ¹⁰But David pursued, he and four hundred men; for two hundred stayed *behind,* who were so weary that they could not cross the Brook Besor.

¹¹Then they found an Egyptian in the field, and brought him to David; and they gave him bread and he ate, and they let him drink water. ¹²And they gave him a piece of a cake of figs and two clusters of raisins. So when he had

---

29:5 *ᵃ*Compare 1 Samuel 18:7   **29:10** *ᵃ*Following Masoretic Text, Targum, and Vulgate; Septuagint adds *and go to the place which I have selected for you there; and set no bothersome word in your heart, for you are good before me. And rise on your way.*

eaten, his strength came back to him; for he had eaten no bread nor drunk water for three days and three nights. ¹³Then David said to him, "To whom do you *belong*, and where *are* you from?"

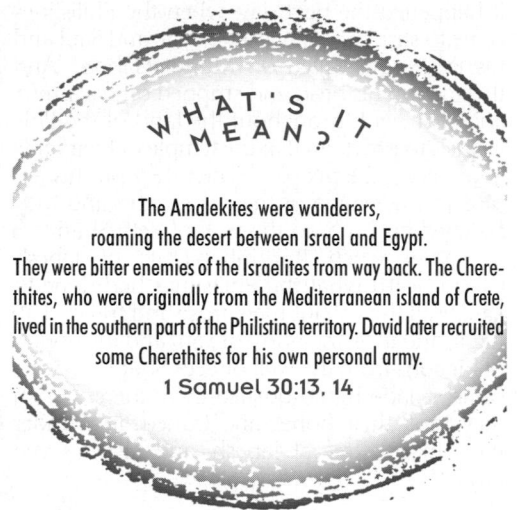

WHAT'S IT MEAN?

The Amalekites were wanderers, roaming the desert between Israel and Egypt. They were bitter enemies of the Israelites from way back. The Cherethites, who were originally from the Mediterranean island of Crete, lived in the southern part of the Philistine territory. David later recruited some Cherethites for his own personal army.

1 Samuel 30:13, 14

And he said, "I *am* a young man from Egypt, servant of an Amalekite; and my master left me behind, because three days ago I fell sick. ¹⁴We made an invasion of the southern *area* of the Cherethites, in the *territory* which *belongs* to Judah, and of the southern *area* of Caleb; and we burned Ziklag with fire."

¹⁵And David said to him, "Can you take me down to this troop?"

So he said, "Swear to me by God that you will neither kill me nor deliver me into the hands of my master, and I will take you down to this troop."

¹⁶And when he had brought him down, there they were, spread out over all the land, eating and drinking and dancing, because of all the great spoil which they had taken from the land of the Philistines and from the land of Judah. ¹⁷Then David attacked them from twilight until the evening of the next day. Not a man of them escaped, except four hundred young men who rode on camels and fled. ¹⁸So David recovered all that the Amalekites had carried away, and David rescued his two wives. ¹⁹And nothing of theirs was lacking, either small or great, sons or daughters, spoil or anything which they had taken from them; David recovered all. ²⁰Then David took all the flocks and herds they had driven before those *other* livestock, and said, "This *is* David's spoil."

²¹Now David came to the two hundred men who had been so weary that they could not follow David, whom they also had made to stay at the Brook Besor. So they went out to meet David and to meet the people who *were* with him. And when David came near the people, he greeted them. ²²Then all the wicked and worthless men[a] of those who went with David answered and said, "Because they did not go with us, we will not give them *any* of the spoil that we have recovered, except for every man's wife and children, that they may lead *them* away and depart."

²³But David said, "My brethren, you shall not do so with what the LORD has given us, who has preserved us and delivered into our hand the troop that came against us. ²⁴For who will heed you in this matter? But as his part *is* who goes down to the battle, so *shall* his part *be* who stays by the supplies; they shall share alike." ²⁵So it was, from that day forward; he made it a statute and an ordinance for Israel to this day.

²⁶Now when David came to Ziklag, he sent *some* of the spoil to the elders of Judah, to his friends, saying, "Here is a present for you from the spoil of the enemies of the LORD"—²⁷to *those* who *were* in Bethel, *those* who *were* in Ramoth of the South, *those* who *were* in Jattir, ²⁸*those* who *were* in Aroer, *those* who *were* in Siphmoth, *those* who *were* in Eshtemoa, ²⁹*those* who *were* in Rachal, *those* who *were* in the cities of the Jerahmeelites, *those* who *were* in the cities of the Kenites, ³⁰*those* who *were* in Hormah, *those* who *were* in Chorashan,[a] *those* who *were* in Athach, ³¹*those* who *were* in Hebron, and to all the places where David himself and his men were accustomed to rove.

THE TRAGIC END OF SAUL AND HIS SONS

¹Now the Philistines fought against Israel; and the men of Israel fled from before the Philistines, and fell slain on Mount Gilboa. ²Then the Philistines followed hard after Saul and his sons. And the Philistines killed Jonathan, Abinadab, and Malchishua, Saul's sons. ³The battle became fierce against Saul. The archers hit him, and he was severely wounded by the archers.

⁴Then Saul said to his armorbearer, "Draw your sword, and thrust me through with it, lest these uncircumcised men come and thrust me through and abuse me."

But his armorbearer would not, for he was greatly afraid. Therefore Saul took a sword and fell on it. ⁵And when his armorbearer saw that Saul was dead, he also fell on his sword, and died with him. ⁶So Saul, his three sons, his armorbearer, and all his men died together that same day.

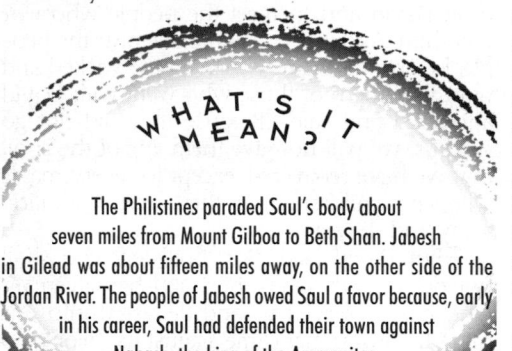

WHAT'S IT MEAN?

The Philistines paraded Saul's body about seven miles from Mount Gilboa to Beth Shan. Jabesh in Gilead was about fifteen miles away, on the other side of the Jordan River. The people of Jabesh owed Saul a favor because, early in his career, Saul had defended their town against Nahash, the king of the Ammonites.

1 Samuel 31:8–13

[7]And when the men of Israel who *were* on the other side of the valley, and *those* who *were* on the other side of the Jordan, saw that the men of Israel had fled and that Saul and his sons were dead, they forsook the cities and fled; and the Philistines came and dwelt in them. [8]So it happened the next day, when the Philistines came to strip the slain, that they found Saul and his three sons fallen on Mount Gilboa. [9]And they cut off his head and stripped off his armor, and sent *word* throughout the land of the Philistines, to proclaim *it in* the temple of their idols and among the people. [10]Then they put his armor in the temple of the Ashtoreths, and they fastened his body to the wall of Beth Shan.[a]

[11]Now when the inhabitants of Jabesh Gilead heard what the Philistines had done to Saul, [12]all the valiant men arose and traveled all night, and took the body of Saul and the bodies of his sons from the wall of Beth Shan; and they came to Jabesh and burned them there. [13]Then they took their bones and buried *them* under the tamarisk tree at Jabesh, and fasted seven days.

31:10 [a]Spelled *Beth Shean* in Joshua 17:11 and elsewhere

2 Samuel

CONTENT

As you start on the second tape of this home-grown epic called Second Samuel, King Saul's worst fears come true: David replaces Saul as king. You've probably heard of King David. He was an ancestor of Jesus. He built the first temple, and he wrote a lot of the Psalms. He was the original Renaissance man. There are more stories in the Bible about David than about anyone else except Jesus Himself.

God called David a man after His own heart. That's why David's story is such an encouragement to us. He wasn't a perfect man, but he loved God and God was pleased with that.

There are a lot of sad tales and mishaps in Second Samuel but it's a book that shows us that God's concern is not that we never foul up. His concern is that we keep coming back to Him and starting over. David was a man who understood that.

Outline

Purpose

The most committed believer can fail and constantly needs God's grace.

Theme

King David, Forerunner of the Messiah

Date of writing

1050–750 B.C.

> "When your days are fulfilled and you rest with your fathers, I will set up your seed after you, who will come from your body, and I will establish his kingdom. He shall build a house for My name, and I will establish the throne of his kingdom forever" (7:12, 13).

Bible Talk

David: A Good Man, Except for One Thing

The Bible doesn't sugarcoat the truth, even for its heroes. Look at David more closely. He was one of the best. He loved God. He was a fantastic musician and writer. He was a good king. The Bible could have left it at that. God could have swept all the rest of David's faults under a rug or into a closet.

That's not what God does, though. He accepts us and uses us as we are with all of our faults. David is famous for one *really* big blunder. He fell for a married woman. He even had her husband killed to try and clean up the mess.

David's story reminds us that the best of us make bad mistakes, but God never gives up on us.

TALK ABOUT A DYSFUNCTIONAL FAMILY

Families can be a great thing to have, but they can also be difficult. King David's family was . . . a mess. He had kids by several wives, and those kids mistreated each other. David didn't stand up to them when they did wrong, and so their wrongs got bigger and bigger.

Eventually David's own son tried to take the kingdom away from him. His daughter lived a life of shame after being raped by a half brother, who was killed by another brother in an act of retribution. David's youngest son, Solomon, did receive the kingdom from his father and, in many ways, succeeded greatly. Yet some of his most famous writings are writings of disillusionment with even the best things of life.

Families struggled in David's time, as they do now, with selfishness and greed and a lack of connection. Families needed, in David's time, what they need now—a connection to God that will heal them.

THE REPORT OF SAUL'S DEATH

¹Now it came to pass after the death of Saul, when David had returned from the slaughter of the Amalekites, and David had stayed two days in Ziklag, ²on the third day, behold, it happened that a man came from Saul's camp with his clothes torn and dust on his head. So it was, when he came to David, that he fell to the ground and prostrated himself.

³And David said to him, "Where have you come from?"

So he said to him, "I have escaped from the camp of Israel."

⁴Then David said to him, "How did the matter go? Please tell me."

And he answered, "The people have fled from the battle, many of the people are fallen and dead, and Saul and Jonathan his son are dead also."

⁵So David said to the young man who told him, "How do you know that Saul and Jonathan his son are dead?"

⁶Then the young man who told him said, "As I happened by chance *to be* on Mount Gilboa, there was Saul, leaning on his spear; and indeed the chariots and horsemen followed hard after him. ⁷Now when he looked behind him, he saw me and called to me. And I answered, 'Here I am.' ⁸And he said to me, 'Who *are* you?' So I answered him, 'I *am* an Amalekite.' ⁹He said to me again, 'Please stand over me and kill me, for anguish has come upon me, but my life still *remains* in me.' ¹⁰So I stood over him and killed him, because I was sure that he could not live after he had fallen. And I took the crown that *was* on his head and the bracelet that *was* on his arm, and have brought them here to my lord."

¹¹Therefore David took hold of his own clothes and tore them, and *so did* all the men who *were* with him. ¹²And they mourned and wept and fasted until evening for Saul and for Jonathan his son, for the people of the LORD and for the house of Israel, because they had fallen by the sword.

¹³Then David said to the young man who told him, "Where *are* you from?"

And he answered, "I *am* the son of an alien, an Amalekite."

¹⁴So David said to him, "How was it you were not afraid to put forth your hand to destroy the LORD's anointed?" ¹⁵Then David called one of the young men and said, "Go near, *and* execute him!" And he struck him so that he died. ¹⁶So David said to him, "Your blood *is* on

LEADERSHIP
Are leaders ordained by God? (1:16)

your own head, for your own mouth has testified against you, saying, 'I have killed the LORD's anointed.' "

THE SONG OF THE BOW

¹⁷Then David lamented with this lamentation over Saul and over Jonathan his son, ¹⁸and he told *them* to teach the children of Judah *the Song of* the Bow; indeed *it is* written in the Book of Jasher:

¹⁹ "The beauty of Israel is slain on your high
    places!
How the mighty have fallen!
²⁰ Tell *it* not in Gath,
Proclaim *it* not in the streets of
    Ashkelon—
Lest the daughters of the Philistines
    rejoice,
Lest the daughters of the uncircumcised
    triumph.

WHAT'S IT MEAN?

Don't bother looking for the Book of Jasher in your Bible or your local library or your nearest bookstore. You won't find it. This ancient book, which contained everything from Joshua's speech at the battle of Gibeon to David's tribute to Saul and Jonathan, has been lost for centuries. In case you're wondering, Jasher means "Upright" or "Righteous."

2 Samuel 1:18

²¹ "O mountains of Gilboa,
Let there be no dew nor rain upon you,
Nor fields of offerings.
For the shield of the mighty is cast away
    there!
The shield of Saul, not anointed with oil.
²² From the blood of the slain,
From the fat of the mighty,
The bow of Jonathan did not turn back,
And the sword of Saul did not return
    empty.

²³ "Saul and Jonathan *were* beloved and
    pleasant in their lives,
And in their death they were not divided;
They were swifter than eagles,
They were stronger than lions.

24 "O daughters of Israel, weep over Saul,
   Who clothed you in scarlet, with luxury;
   Who put ornaments of gold on your
      apparel.

25 "How the mighty have fallen in the midst
      of the battle!
   Jonathan *was* slain in your high places.
26 I am distressed for you, my brother
      Jonathan;
   You have been very pleasant to me;
   Your love to me was wonderful,
   Surpassing the love of women.

27 "How the mighty have fallen,
   And the weapons of war perished!"

DAVID ANOINTED KING OF JUDAH

¹It happened after this that David inquired of the LORD, saying, "Shall I go up to any of the cities of Judah?"

And the LORD said to him, "Go up."

David said, "Where shall I go up?"

And He said, "To Hebron."

²So David went up there, and his two wives also, Ahinoam the Jezreelitess, and Abigail the widow of Nabal the Carmelite. ³And David brought up the men who *were* with him, every man with his household. So they dwelt in the cities of Hebron. ⁴Then the men of Judah came, and there they anointed David king over the house of Judah. And they told David, saying, "The men of Jabesh Gilead *were the ones* who buried Saul." ⁵So David sent messengers to the men of Jabesh Gilead, and said to them, "You *are* blessed of the LORD, for you have shown this kindness to your lord, to Saul, and have buried him. ⁶And now may the LORD show kindness and truth to you. I also will repay you this kindness, because you have done this thing. ⁷Now therefore, let your hands be strengthened, and be valiant; for your master Saul is dead, and also the house of Judah has anointed me king over them."

ISHBOSHETH MADE KING OF ISRAEL

⁸But Abner the son of Ner, commander of Saul's army, took Ishbosheth[a] the son of Saul and brought him over to Mahanaim; ⁹and he made him king over Gilead, over the Ashurites, over Jezreel, over Ephraim, over Benjamin, and over all Israel. ¹⁰Ishbosheth, Saul's son, *was* forty years old when he began to reign over Israel, and he reigned two years. Only the house of Judah followed David. ¹¹And the time that David was king in Hebron over the house of Judah was seven years and six months.

WHAT'S IT MEAN?

When a prophet or priest anointed someone, he poured olive oil on the person's head to indicate that the Lord had chosen that person for a special purpose. The same kind of presses that were used to make wine from grapes were used to make olive oil from green olives.

2 Samuel 2:4

ISRAEL AND JUDAH AT WAR

¹²Now Abner the son of Ner, and the servants of Ishbosheth the son of Saul, went out from Mahanaim to Gibeon. ¹³And Joab the son of Zeruiah, and the servants of David, went out and met them by the pool of Gibeon. So they sat down, one on one side of the pool and the other on the other side of the pool. ¹⁴Then Abner said to Joab, "Let the young men now arise and compete before us."

And Joab said, "Let them arise."

¹⁵So they arose and went over by number, twelve from Benjamin, *followers* of Ishbosheth the son of Saul, and twelve from the servants of David. ¹⁶And each one grasped his opponent by the head and *thrust* his sword in his opponent's side; so they fell down together. Therefore that place was called the Field of Sharp Swords,[a] which *is* in Gibeon. ¹⁷So there was a very fierce battle that day, and Abner and the men of Israel were beaten before the servants of David.

> "And now may the LORD show kindness and truth to you. I also will repay you this kindness, because you have done this thing."
> (2 Samuel 2:6)

2:8 ᵃCalled *Esh-Baal* in 1 Chronicles 8:33 and 9:39   2:16 ᵃHebrew *Helkath Hazzurim*

¹⁸Now the three sons of Zeruiah were there: Joab and Abishai and Asahel. And Asahel *was* as fleet of foot as a wild gazelle. ¹⁹So Asahel pursued Abner, and in going he did not turn to the right hand or to the left from following Abner.

WHAT'S IT MEAN?

Both Saul and David believed in "keeping it in the family," when it came to appointing military leaders. Abner, the commander of Saul's army, was Saul's first cousin. Joab, the commander of David's army, was David's nephew. The gruesome game that Abner and Joab suggested was prompted by the rivalry between the tribe of Benjamin (Saul's tribe), which wanted the throne passed on to one of Saul's descendants, and the tribe of Judah (David's tribe), which had chosen David as its king.

2 Samuel 2:14–17

²⁰Then Abner looked behind him and said, "*Are* you Asahel?"

He answered, "I *am.*"

²¹And Abner said to him, "Turn aside to your right hand or to your left, and lay hold on one of the young men and take his armor for yourself." But Asahel would not turn aside from following him. ²²So Abner said again to Asahel, "Turn aside from following me. Why should I strike you to the ground? How then could I face your brother Joab?" ²³However, he refused to turn aside. Therefore Abner struck him in the stomach with the blunt end of the spear, so that the spear came out of his back; and he fell down there and died on the spot. So it was *that* as many as came to the place where Asahel fell down and died, stood still.

²⁴Joab and Abishai also pursued Abner. And the sun was going down when they came to the hill of Ammah, which *is* before Giah by the road to the Wilderness of Gibeon. ²⁵Now the children of Benjamin gathered together behind Abner and became a unit, and took their stand on top of a hill. ²⁶Then Abner called to Joab and said, "Shall the sword devour forever? Do you not know that it will be bitter in the latter end? How long will it be then until you tell the people to return from pursuing their brethren?"

²⁷And Joab said, "*As* God lives, unless you had spoken, surely then by morning all the people would have given up pursuing their brethren." ²⁸So Joab blew a trumpet; and all the people stood still and did not pursue Israel anymore, nor did they fight anymore. ²⁹Then Abner and his men went on all that night through the plain, crossed over the Jordan, and went through all Bithron; and they came to Mahanaim.

³⁰So Joab returned from pursuing Abner. And when he had gathered all the people together, there were missing of David's servants nineteen men and Asahel. ³¹But the servants of David had struck down, of Benjamin and Abner's men, three hundred and sixty men who died. ³²Then they took up Asahel and buried him in his father's tomb, which *was in* Bethlehem. And Joab and his men went all night, and they came to Hebron at daybreak.

¹Now there was a long war between the house of Saul and the house of David. But David grew stronger and stronger, and the house of Saul grew weaker and weaker.

SONS OF DAVID

²Sons were born to David in Hebron: His firstborn was Amnon by Ahinoam the Jezreelitess; ³his second, Chileab, by Abigail the widow of Nabal the Carmelite; the third, Absalom the son of Maacah, the daughter of Talmai, king of Geshur; ⁴the fourth, Adonijah the son of Haggith; the fifth, Shephatiah the son of Abital; ⁵and the sixth, Ithream, by David's wife Eglah. These were born to David in Hebron.

ABNER JOINS FORCES WITH DAVID

⁶Now it was so, while there was war between the house of Saul and the house of David, that Abner was strengthening *his hold* on the house of Saul.

⁷And Saul had a concubine, whose name *was* Rizpah, the daughter of Aiah. So *Ishbosheth* said to Abner, "Why have you gone in to my father's concubine?"

⁸Then Abner became very angry at the words of Ishbosheth, and said, "*Am* I a dog's head that belongs to Judah? Today I show loyalty to the house of Saul your father, to his brothers, and to his friends, and have not delivered you into the hand of David; and you charge me today with a fault concerning this woman? ⁹May God do so to Abner, and more also, if I do not do for David as the LORD has sworn to him—¹⁰to transfer the kingdom from the house of Saul, and set up the throne of David over Israel and over Judah, from Dan to Beersheba." ¹¹And he could not answer Abner another word, because he feared him.

¹²Then Abner sent messengers on his behalf to David, saying, "Whose is the land?" saying also, "Make your covenant with me, and indeed my hand shall be with you to bring all Israel to you."

WHAT'S IT MEAN?

The phrase "over Israel and over Judah" shows the division that was occurring among God's people. "Judah" refers to David's tribe and his followers. "Israel" here refers to the tribes that followed Saul and his descendants.

2 Samuel 3:10

¹³And David said, "Good, I will make a covenant with you. But one thing I require of you: you shall not see my face unless you first bring Michal, Saul's daughter, when you come to see my face." ¹⁴So David sent messengers to Ishbosheth, Saul's son, saying, "Give me my wife Michal, whom I betrothed to myself for a hundred foreskins of the Philistines." ¹⁵And Ishbosheth sent and took her from her husband, from Paltielᵃ the son of Laish. ¹⁶Then her husband went along with her to Bahurim, weeping behind her. So Abner said to him, "Go, return!" And he returned.

¹⁷Now Abner had communicated with the elders of Israel, saying, "In time past you were seeking for David to be king over you. ¹⁸Now then, do it! For the LORD has spoken of David, saying, 'By the hand of My servant David, Iᵃ will save My people Israel from the hand of the Philistines and the hand of all their enemies.' "

¹⁹And Abner also spoke in the hearing of Benjamin. Then Abner also went to speak in the hearing of David in Hebron all that seemed good to Israel and the whole house of Benjamin.

²⁰So Abner and twenty men with him came to David at Hebron. And David made a feast for Abner and the men who were with him. ²¹Then Abner said to David, "I will arise and go, and gather all Israel to my lord the king, that they may make a covenant with you, and that you may reign over all that your heart desires." So David sent Abner away, and he went in peace.

JOAB MURDERS ABNER

²²At that moment the servants of David and Joab came from a raid and brought much spoil with them. But Abner was not with David in Hebron, for he had sent him away, and he had gone in peace. ²³When Joab and all the troops that were with him had come, they told Joab, saying, "Abner the son of Ner came to the king, and he sent him away, and he has gone in peace." ²⁴Then Joab came to the king and said, "What have you done? Look, Abner came to you; why is it that you sent him away, and he has already gone? ²⁵Surely you realize that Abner the son of Ner came to deceive you, to know your going out and your coming in, and to know all that you are doing."

²⁶And when Joab had gone from David's presence, he sent messengers after Abner, who brought him back from the well of Sirah. But David did not know it. ²⁷Now when Abner had returned to Hebron, Joab took him aside in the gate to speak with him privately, and there stabbed him in the stomach, so that he died for the blood of Asahel his brother.

²⁸Afterward, when David heard it, he said, "My kingdom and I are guiltless before the LORD forever of the blood of Abner the son of Ner. ²⁹Let it rest on the head of Joab and on all his father's house; and let there never fail to be in the house of Joab one who has a discharge or is a leper, who leans on a staff or falls by the sword, or who lacks bread." ³⁰So Joab and Abishai his brother killed Abner, because he had killed their brother Asahel at Gibeon in the battle.

DAVID'S MOURNING FOR ABNER

³¹Then David said to Joab and to all the people who were with him, "Tear your clothes, gird yourselves with sackcloth, and mourn for Abner." And King David followed the coffin. ³²So they buried Abner in Hebron; and the king lifted up his voice and wept at the grave of Abner, and all the people wept. ³³And the king sang a lament over Abner and said:

"Should Abner die as a fool dies?
³⁴   Your hands were not bound
    Nor your feet put into fetters;
    As a man falls before wicked men, so you fell."

Then all the people wept over him again.

³⁵And when all the people came to persuade

3:15 ᵃSpelled Palti in 1 Samuel 25:44   **3:18** ᵃFollowing many Hebrew manuscripts, Septuagint, Syriac, and Targum; Masoretic Text reads he.

David to eat food while it was still day, David took an oath, saying, "God do so to me, and more also, if I taste bread or anything else till the sun goes down!" 36Now all the people took note *of it*, and it pleased them, since whatever the king did pleased all the people. 37For all the people and all Israel understood that day that it had not been the king's *intent* to kill Abner the son of Ner. 38Then the king said to his servants, "Do you not know that a prince and a great man has fallen this day in Israel? 39And I *am* weak today, though anointed king; and these men, the sons of Zeruiah, *are* too harsh for me. The LORD shall repay the evildoer according to his wickedness."

WHAT'S IT MEAN?

Grief was a much more public emotion in ancient times than it is today. People demonstrated their feelings of loss and sadness by tearing their clothes, putting ashes or dust in their hair, and wearing really uncomfortable clothes called sackcloth. These outward signs were used both for mourning a death and for repenting of sin, and they were often continued for several days.

2 Samuel 3:31

ISHBOSHETH IS MURDERED

1When Saul's son[a] heard that Abner had died in Hebron, he lost heart, and all Israel was troubled. 2Now Saul's son *had* two men *who were* captains of troops. The name of one *was* Baanah and the name of the other Rechab, the sons of Rimmon the Beerothite, of the children of Benjamin. (For Beeroth also was *part* of Benjamin, 3because the Beerothites fled to Gittaim and have been sojourners there until this day.)

4Jonathan, Saul's son, had a son *who was* lame in *his* feet. He was five years old when the news about Saul and Jonathan came from Jezreel; and his nurse took him up and fled. And it happened, as she made haste to flee, that he fell and became lame. His name *was* Mephibosheth.[a]

5Then the sons of Rimmon the Beerothite, Rechab and Baanah, set out and came at about the heat of the day to the house of Ishbosheth, who was lying on his bed at noon. 6And they

came there, all the way into the house, *as though* to get wheat, and they stabbed him in the stomach. Then Rechab and Baanah his brother escaped. 7For when they came into the house, he was lying on his bed in his bedroom; then they struck him and killed him, beheaded him and took his head, and were all night escaping through the plain. 8And they brought the head of Ishbosheth to David at Hebron, and said to the king, "Here is the head of Ishbosheth, the son of Saul your enemy, who sought your life; and the LORD has avenged my lord the king this day of Saul and his descendants."

9But David answered Rechab and Baanah his brother, the sons of Rimmon the Beerothite, and said to them, "*As* the LORD lives, who has redeemed my life from all adversity, 10when someone told me, saying, 'Look, Saul is dead', thinking to have brought good news, I arrested him and had him executed in Ziklag—the one who *thought* I would give him a reward for *his* news. 11How much more, when wicked men have killed a righteous person in his own house on his bed? Therefore, shall I not now require his blood at your hand and remove you from the earth?" 12So David commanded his young men, and they executed them, cut off their hands and feet, and hanged *them* by the pool in Hebron. But they took the head of Ishbosheth and buried *it* in the tomb of Abner in Hebron.

LIFE

Is it sacred? (4:9–12)

DAVID REIGNS OVER ALL ISRAEL

1Then all the tribes of Israel came to David at Hebron and spoke, saying, "Indeed we *are* your bone and your flesh. 2Also, in time past, when Saul was king over us, you were the one who led Israel out and brought them in; and the LORD said to you, 'You shall shepherd My people Israel, and be ruler over Israel.' " 3Therefore all the elders of Israel came to the king at Hebron, and King David made a covenant with them at Hebron before the LORD. And they anointed David king over Israel. 4David *was* thirty years old when he began to reign, *and* he reigned forty years. 5In Hebron he reigned over Judah seven years and six months, and in Jerusalem he reigned thirty-three years over all Israel and Judah.

THE CONQUEST OF JERUSALEM

6And the king and his men went to Jerusalem against the Jebusites, the inhabitants of

MEPHIBOSHETH made a difference

Not long after David became king of Israel he made inquiries about the family of Saul, the previous king. His good friend Jonathan, Saul's son, had died with his father in battle. The news came back that Saul's entire family had been killed with one exception: Jonathan's son Mephibosheth. A nurse hurrying to save the orphan had dropped him, and Mephibosheth had grown up lame.

David honored and protected Mephibosheth out of respect for Jonathan. He guaranteed Mephibosheth's family property and welcomed the young man to the royal table. Later, Mephibosheth was betrayed by his servant Ziba who convinced a fleeing David that Mephibosheth still held hopes of reclaiming the crown for his family. In his words of humble reconciliation, Mephibosheth offers as fine an example of honesty and gratitude as found anywhere in Scripture.

Cutting Edge

Lame as he was, Mephibosheth was dependent on others. Some, like Ziba, took advantage of him. Others, like David, respected him in spite of his limitations. Mephibosheth understood where gratitude was due. When he was accused, he did everything he could to make the matter right and acted with dignity and integrity.

YOU can, too!

You may be frustrated by the limitations in your life. They come in all sizes and shapes. Some are physical; others are emotional, educational, or social. It will take self-control not to lobby for fairness or demand your own way. As with Mephibosheth, limitations don't have to become excuses. In the very act of persisting in spite of your limitations, you will be an example to others. Your efforts will make a difference.

Want to know more? Read about Mephibosheth's life in
2 Samuel 4; 9:1–13; 16:1–4; 19:24–30.

the land, who spoke to David, saying, "You shall not come in here; but the blind and the lame will repel you," thinking, "David cannot come in here." [7]Nevertheless David took the stronghold of Zion (that *is*, the City of David).

[8]Now David said on that day, "Whoever climbs up by way of the water shaft and defeats the Jebusites (the lame and the blind, *who are* hated by David's soul), *he shall be chief and captain.*" [a] Therefore they say, "The blind and the lame shall not come into the house."

[9]Then David dwelt in the stronghold, and called it the City of David. And David built all around from the Millo[a] and inward. [10]So David went on and became great, and the LORD God of hosts *was* with him.

[11]Then Hiram king of Tyre sent messengers to David, and cedar trees, and carpenters and masons. And they built David a house. [12]So David knew that the LORD had established him as king over Israel, and that He had exalted His kingdom for the sake of His people Israel.

[13]And David took more concubines and wives from Jerusalem, after he had come from Hebron. Also more sons and daughters were born to David. [14]Now these *are* the names of those who were born to him in Jerusalem: Shammua,[a] Shobab, Nathan, Solomon, [15]Ibhar, Elishua,[a] Nepheg, Japhia, [16]Elishama, Eliada, and Eliphelet.

THE PHILISTINES DEFEATED

[17]Now when the Philistines heard that they had anointed David king over Israel, all the Philistines went up to search for David. And David heard *of it* and went down to the stronghold. [18]The Philistines also went and deployed themselves in the Valley of Rephaim. [19]So David inquired of the LORD, saying, "Shall I go up against the Philistines? Will You deliver them into my hand?"

And the LORD said to David, "Go up, for I will doubtless deliver the Philistines into your hand."

[20]So David went to Baal Perazim, and David defeated them there; and he said, "The LORD has broken through my enemies before me, like a breakthrough of water." Therefore he called the name of that place Baal Perazim.[a] [21]And they left their images there, and David and his men carried them away.

[22]Then the Philistines went up once again

and deployed themselves in the Valley of Rephaim. [23]Therefore David inquired of the LORD, and He said, "You shall not go up; circle around behind them, and come upon them in front of the mulberry trees. [24]And it shall be, when you hear the sound of marching in the tops of the mulberry trees, then you shall advance quickly. For then the LORD will go out before you to strike the camp of the Philistines." [25]And David did so, as the LORD commanded him; and he drove back the Philistines from Geba[a] as far as Gezer.

WHAT'S IT MEAN?

The ancient Israelites preferred stringed instruments for their worship services and percussion instruments for their parties and celebrations. The instruments the Israelites played were probably quite different from our instruments today. For example, the sistrums mentioned in this passage were probably U-shaped frames with small metal pieces or other objects strung between the parts of the U. Held by handles at the bottom, the sistrums were used to create a rattling sound.
2 Samuel 6:5

THE ARK BROUGHT TO JERUSALEM

[1]Again David gathered all *the* choice *men* of Israel, thirty thousand. [2]And David arose and went with all the people who *were* with him from Baale Judah to bring up from there the ark of God, whose name is called by the Name,[a] the LORD of Hosts, who dwells *between* the cherubim. [3]So they set the ark of God on a new cart, and brought it out of the house of Abinadab, which *was* on the hill; and Uzzah and Ahio, the sons of Abinadab, drove the new cart.[a] [4]And they brought it out of the house of Abinadab, which *was* on the hill, accompanying the ark of God; and Ahio went before the ark. [5]Then David and all the house of Israel played *music* before the LORD on all kinds of *instruments of* fir wood, on harps, on stringed instruments, on tambourines, on sistrums, and on cymbals.

5:8 [a]Compare 1 Chronicles 11:6   **5:9** [a]Literally *The Landfill*   **5:14** [a]Spelled *Shimea* in 1 Chronicles 3:5   **5:15** [a]Spelled *Elishama* in 1 Chronicles 3:6   **5:20** [a]Literally *Master of Breakthroughs*   **5:25** [a]Following Masoretic Text, Targum, and Vulgate; Septuagint reads *Gibeon.*   **6:2** [a]Septuagint, Targum, and Vulgate omit *by the Name;* many Hebrew manuscripts and Syriac read *there.*   **6:3** [a]Septuagint adds *with the ark.*

⁶And when they came to Nachon's threshing floor, Uzzah put out *his* hand to the ark of God and took hold of it, for the oxen stumbled. ⁷Then the anger of the LORD was aroused against Uzzah, and God struck him there for *his* error; and he died there by the ark of God. ⁸And David became angry because of the LORD's outbreak against Uzzah; and he called the name of the place Perez Uzzah*ᵃ* to this day.

⁹David was afraid of the LORD that day; and he said, "How can the ark of the LORD come to me?" ¹⁰So David would not move the ark of the LORD with him into the City of David; but David took it aside into the house of Obed-Edom the Gittite. ¹¹The ark of the LORD remained in the house of Obed-Edom the Gittite three months. And the LORD blessed Obed-Edom and all his household.

¹²Now it was told King David, saying, "The LORD has blessed the house of Obed-Edom and all that *belongs* to him, because of the ark of God." So David went and brought up the ark of God from the house of Obed-Edom to the City of David with gladness. ¹³And so it was, when those bearing the ark of the LORD had gone six paces, that he sacrificed oxen and fatted sheep. ¹⁴Then David danced before the LORD with all *his* might; and David *was* wearing a linen ephod. ¹⁵So David and all the house of Israel brought up the ark of the LORD with shouting and with the sound of the trumpet.

¹⁶Now as the ark of the LORD came into the City of David, Michal, Saul's daughter, looked through a window and saw King David leaping and whirling before the LORD; and she despised him in her heart. ¹⁷So they brought the ark of the LORD, and set it in its place in the midst of the tabernacle that David had erected for it. Then David offered burnt offerings and peace offerings before the LORD. ¹⁸And when David had finished offering burnt offerings and peace offerings, he blessed the people in the name of the LORD of hosts. ¹⁹Then he distributed among all the people, among the whole multitude of Israel, both the women and the men, to everyone a loaf of bread, a piece *of meat,* and a cake of raisins. So all the people departed, everyone to his house.

²⁰Then David returned to bless his household. And Michal the daughter of Saul came out to meet David, and said, "How glorious was the king of Israel today, uncovering himself today in the eyes of the maids of his servants, as one of the base fellows shamelessly uncovers himself!"

²¹So David said to Michal, "*It was* before the LORD, who chose me instead of your father and all his house, to appoint me ruler over the people of the LORD, over Israel. Therefore I will play *music* before the LORD. ²²And I will be even more undignified than this, and will be humble in my own sight. But as for the maidservants of whom you have spoken, by them I will be held in honor."

²³Therefore Michal the daughter of Saul had no children to the day of her death.

GOD'S COVENANT WITH DAVID

¹Now it came to pass when the king was dwelling in his house, and the LORD had given him rest from all his enemies all around, ²that the king said to Nathan the prophet, "See now, I dwell in a house of cedar, but the ark of God dwells inside tent curtains."

³Then Nathan said to the king, "Go, do all that *is* in your heart, for the LORD *is* with you."

⁴But it happened that night that the word of the LORD came to Nathan, saying, ⁵"Go and tell My servant David, 'Thus says the LORD: "Would you build a house for Me to dwell in? ⁶For I have not dwelt in a house since the time that I brought the children of Israel up from Egypt, even to this day, but have moved about in a tent and in a tabernacle. ⁷Wherever I have moved about with all the children of Israel, have I ever spoken a word to anyone from the tribes of Israel, whom I commanded to shepherd My people Israel, saying, 'Why have you not built Me a house of cedar?'"' ⁸Now therefore, thus shall you say to My servant David, 'Thus says the LORD of hosts: "I took you from the sheepfold, from following the sheep, to be ruler over My people, over Israel. ⁹And I have been with you wherever you have gone, and have cut off all your enemies from before you, and have made you a great name, like the name of the great men who *are* on the earth. ¹⁰Moreover I will appoint a place for My people Israel, and will plant them, that they may

WORSHIP How should we worship God? (6:21)

"Then Nathan said to the king, 'Go, do all that is in your heart, for the LORD is with you.'" (2 Samuel 7:3)

dwell in a place of their own and move no more; nor shall the sons of wickedness oppress them anymore, as previously, ¹¹since the time that I commanded judges *to be* over My people Israel, and have caused you to rest from all your enemies. Also the LORD tells you that He will make you a house.*

¹²"When your days are fulfilled and you rest with your fathers, I will set up your seed after you, who will come from your body, and I will establish his kingdom. ¹³He shall build a house for My name, and I will establish the throne of his kingdom forever. ¹⁴I will be his Father, and he shall be My son. If he commits iniquity, I will chasten him with the rod of men and with the blows of the sons of men. ¹⁵But My mercy shall not depart from him, as I took *it* from Saul, whom I removed from before you. ¹⁶And your house and your kingdom shall be established forever before you.* Your throne shall be established forever.' ' "

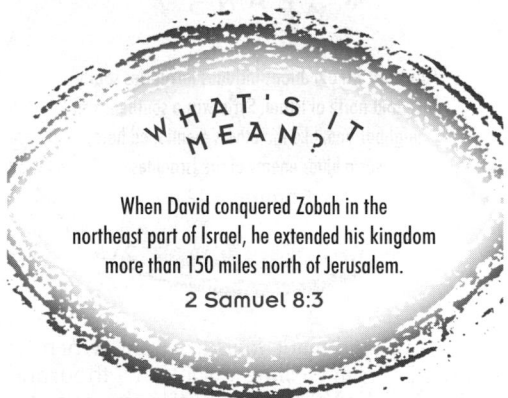

ADOPTION

Who does God discipline? (7:14)

¹⁷According to all these words and according to all this vision, so Nathan spoke to David.

DAVID'S THANKSGIVING TO GOD

¹⁸Then King David went in and sat before the LORD; and he said: "Who *am* I, O Lord GOD? And what is my house, that You have brought me this far? ¹⁹And yet this was a small thing in Your sight, O Lord GOD; and You have also spoken of Your servant's house for a great while to come. *Is* this the manner of man, O Lord GOD? ²⁰Now what more can David say to You? For You, Lord GOD, know Your servant. ²¹For Your word's sake, and according to Your own heart, You have done all these great things, to make Your servant know *them.* ²²Therefore You are great, O Lord GOD.* For *there is* none like You, nor *is there any* God besides You, according to all that we have heard with our ears. ²³And who *is* like Your people, like Israel, the one nation on the earth whom God went to redeem for Himself as a people, to make for Himself a name—and to do for Yourself great and awesome deeds for Your land—before Your people whom You redeemed for Yourself from Egypt, the nations, and their gods? ²⁴For You have made Your peo-

GOD

Is God unique? (7:22)

ple Israel Your very own people forever; and You, LORD, have become their God.

²⁵"Now, O LORD God, the word which You have spoken concerning Your servant and concerning his house, establish *it* forever and do as You have said. ²⁶So let Your name be magnified forever, saying, 'The LORD of hosts *is* the God over Israel.' And let the house of Your servant David be established before You. ²⁷For You, O LORD of hosts, God of Israel, have revealed *this* to Your servant, saying, 'I will build you a house.' Therefore Your servant has found it in his heart to pray this prayer to You.

²⁸"And now, O Lord GOD, You are God, and Your words are true, and You have promised this goodness to Your servant. ²⁹Now therefore, let it please You to bless the house of Your servant, that it may continue before You forever; for You, O Lord GOD, have spoken *it,* and with Your blessing let the house of Your servant be blessed forever."

DAVID'S FURTHER CONQUESTS

¹After this it came to pass that David attacked the Philistines and subdued them. And David took Metheg Ammah from the hand of the Philistines.

²Then he defeated Moab. Forcing them down to the ground, he measured them off with a line. With two lines he measured off those to be put to death, and with one full line those to be kept alive. So the Moabites became David's servants, *and* brought tribute.

WHAT'S IT MEAN?

When David conquered Zobah in the northeast part of Israel, he extended his kingdom more than 150 miles north of Jerusalem.

2 Samuel 8:3

³David also defeated Hadadezer the son of Rehob, king of Zobah, as he went to recover his territory at the River Euphrates. ⁴David took from him one thousand *chariots,* seven hundred* horsemen, and twenty thousand foot soldiers. Also David hamstrung all the chariot

---

7:11 *That is, a royal dynasty　**7:16** *Septuagint reads Me.　**7:22** *Targum and Syriac read O LORD God.
8:4 *Or seven thousand (compare 1 Chronicles 18:4)

horses, except that he spared *enough* of them for one hundred chariots.

[5]When the Syrians of Damascus came to help Hadadezer king of Zobah, David killed twenty-two thousand of the Syrians. [6]Then David put garrisons in Syria of Damascus; and the Syrians became David's servants, *and* brought tribute. So the LORD preserved David wherever he went. [7]And David took the shields of gold that had belonged to the servants of Hadadezer, and brought them to Jerusalem. [8]Also from Betah[a] and from Berothai, cities of Hadadezer, King David took a large amount of bronze.

[9]When Toi[a] king of Hamath heard that David had defeated all the army of Hadadezer, [10]then Toi sent Joram[a] his son to King David, to greet him and bless him, because he had fought against Hadadezer and defeated him (for Hadadezer had been at war with Toi); and *Joram* brought with him articles of silver, articles of gold, and articles of bronze. [11]King David also dedicated these to the LORD, along with the silver and gold that he had dedicated from all the nations which he had subdued—[12]from Syria,[a] from Moab, from the people of Ammon, from the Philistines, from Amalek, and from the spoil of Hadadezer the son of Rehob, king of Zobah.

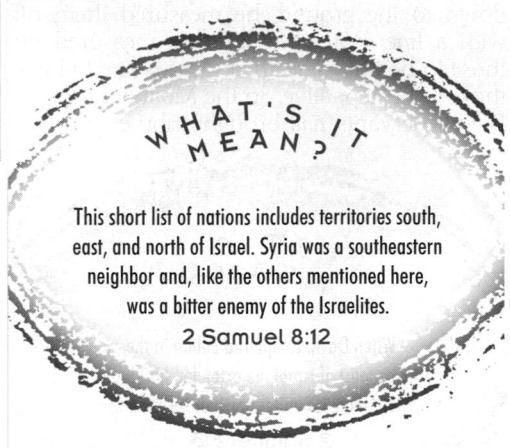

WHAT'S IT MEAN?

This short list of nations includes territories south, east, and north of Israel. Syria was a southeastern neighbor and, like the others mentioned here, was a bitter enemy of the Israelites.

2 Samuel 8:12

[13]And David made *himself* a name when he returned from killing eighteen thousand Syrians[a] in the Valley of Salt. [14]He also put garrisons in Edom; throughout all Edom he put garrisons, and all the Edomites became David's servants. And the LORD preserved David wherever he went.

DAVID'S ADMINISTRATION

[15]So David reigned over all Israel; and David administered judgment and justice to all his people. [16]Joab the son of Zeruiah *was* over the army; Jehoshaphat the son of Ahilud *was* recorder; [17]Zadok the son of Ahitub and Ahimelech the son of Abiathar *were* the priests; Seraiah[a] *was* the scribe; [18]Benaiah the son of Jehoiada *was over* both the Cherethites and the Pelethites; and David's sons were chief ministers.

LEADERSHIP
What should leaders be known for? (8:15)

DAVID'S KINDNESS TO MEPHIBOSHETH

[1]Now David said, "Is there still anyone who is left of the house of Saul, that I may show him kindness for Jonathan's sake?"

[2]And *there was* a servant of the house of Saul whose name *was* Ziba. So when they had called him to David, the king said to him, "*Are* you Ziba?"

He said, "At your service!"

[3]Then the king said, "*Is there* not still someone of the house of Saul, to whom I may show the kindness of God?"

And Ziba said to the king, "There is still a son of Jonathan *who is* lame in *his* feet."

[4]So the king said to him, "Where *is* he?"

And Ziba said to the king, "Indeed he *is* in the house of Machir the son of Ammiel, in Lo Debar."

[5]Then King David sent and brought him out of the house of Machir the son of Ammiel, from Lo Debar.

[6]Now when Mephibosheth the son of Jonathan, the son of Saul, had come to David, he fell on his face and prostrated himself. Then David said, "Mephibosheth?"

And he answered, "Here is your servant!"

[7]So David said to him, "Do not fear, for I will surely show you kindness for Jonathan your father's sake, and will restore to you all the land of Saul your grandfather; and you shall eat bread at my table continually."

[8]Then he bowed himself, and said, "What *is* your servant, that you should look upon such a dead dog as I?"

[9]And the king called to Ziba, Saul's servant, and said to him, "I have given to your master's son all that belonged to Saul and to all his

FRIENDSHIP
How can friendship outlast death? (9:1)

8:8 [a]Spelled *Tibhath* in 1 Chronicles 18:8   **8:9** [a]Spelled *Tou* in 1 Chronicles 18:9   **8:10** [a]Spelled *Hadoram* in 1 Chronicles 18:10   **8:12** [a]Septuagint, Syriac, and some Hebrew manuscripts read *Edom.*   **8:13** [a]Septuagint, Syriac, and some Hebrew manuscripts read *Edomites* (compare 1 Chronicles 18:12).   **8:17** [a]Spelled *Shavsha* in 1 Chronicles 18:16

house. ¹⁰You therefore, and your sons and your servants, shall work the land for him, and you shall bring in *the harvest,* that your master's son may have food to eat. But Mephibosheth your master's son shall eat bread at my table always." Now Ziba had fifteen sons and twenty servants.

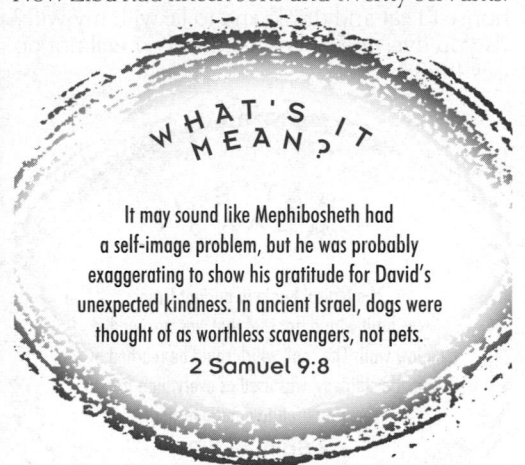

WHAT'S IT MEAN?

It may sound like Mephibosheth had a self-image problem, but he was probably exaggerating to show his gratitude for David's unexpected kindness. In ancient Israel, dogs were thought of as worthless scavengers, not pets.

2 Samuel 9:8

¹¹Then Ziba said to the king, "According to all that my lord the king has commanded his servant, so will your servant do."

"As for Mephibosheth," *said the king,* "he shall eat at my table*ᵃ* like one of the king's sons." ¹²Mephibosheth had a young son whose name *was* Micha. And all who dwelt in the house of Ziba *were* servants of Mephibosheth. ¹³So Mephibosheth dwelt in Jerusalem, for he ate continually at the king's table. And he was lame in both his feet.

THE AMMONITES AND SYRIANS DEFEATED

¹It happened after this that the king of the people of Ammon died, and Hanun his son reigned in his place. ²Then David said, "I will show kindness to Hanun the son of Nahash, as his father showed kindness to me."

So David sent by the hand of his servants to comfort him concerning his father. And David's servants came into the land of the people of Ammon. ³And the princes of the people of Ammon said to Hanun their lord, "Do you think that David really honors your father because he has sent comforters to you? Has David not *rather* sent his servants to you to search the city, to spy it out, and to overthrow it?"

⁴Therefore Hanun took David's servants, shaved off half of their beards, cut off their garments in the middle, at their buttocks, and sent them away. ⁵When they told David, he sent to meet them, because the men were greatly

ashamed. And the king said, "Wait at Jericho until your beards have grown, and *then* return."

⁶When the people of Ammon saw that they had made themselves repulsive to David, the people of Ammon sent and hired the Syrians of Beth Rehob and the Syrians of Zoba, twenty thousand foot soldiers; and from the king of Maacah one thousand men, and from Ish-Tob twelve thousand men. ⁷Now when David heard *of it,* he sent Joab and all the army of the mighty men. ⁸Then the people of Ammon came out and put themselves in battle array at the entrance of the gate. And the Syrians of Zoba, Beth Rehob, Ish-Tob, and Maacah *were* by themselves in the field.

WHAT'S IT MEAN?

When the Ammonites were looking for help in attacking Israel, they turned to their northern neighbors. The soldiers of Ish-Tob came from the land between Gilead and the Syrian Desert. The Syrians came from much further north in Zoba, which had recently been defeated by David.

2 Samuel 10:8

⁹When Joab saw that the battle line was against him before and behind, he chose some of Israel's best and put *them* in battle array against the Syrians. ¹⁰And the rest of the people he put under the command of Abishai his brother, that he might set *them* in battle array against the people of Ammon. ¹¹Then he said, "If the Syrians are too strong for me, then you shall help me; but if the people of Ammon are too strong for you, then I will come and help you. ¹²Be of good courage, and let us be strong for our people and for the cities of our God. And may the LORD do *what is* good in His sight."

¹³So Joab and the people who *were* with him drew near for the battle against the Syrians, and they fled before him. ¹⁴When the people of Ammon saw that the Syrians were fleeing, they also fled before Abishai, and entered the city. So Joab returned from the people of Ammon and went to Jerusalem.

¹⁵When the Syrians saw that they had been defeated by Israel, they gathered together,

9:11 *ᵃ*Septuagint reads *David's table.*

[16]Then Hadadezer[a] sent and brought out the Syrians who *were* beyond the River,[b] and they came to Helam. And Shobach the commander of Hadadezer's army *went* before them. [17]When it was told David, he gathered all Israel, crossed over the Jordan, and came to Helam. And the Syrians set themselves in battle array against David and fought with him. [18]Then the Syrians fled before Israel; and David killed seven hundred charioteers and forty thousand horsemen of the Syrians, and struck Shobach the commander of their army, who died there. [19]And when all the kings *who were* servants to Hadadezer[a] saw that they were defeated by Israel, they made peace with Israel and served them. So the Syrians were afraid to help the people of Ammon anymore.

DAVID, BATHSHEBA, AND URIAH

[1]It happened in the spring of the year, at the time when kings go out *to battle,* that David sent Joab and his servants with him, and all Israel; and they destroyed the people of Ammon and besieged Rabbah. But David remained at Jerusalem.

[2]Then it happened one evening that David arose from his bed and walked on the roof of the king's house. And from the roof he saw a woman bathing, and the woman *was* very beautiful to behold. [3]So David sent and inquired about the woman. And *someone* said, "*Is* this not Bathsheba, the daughter of Eliam, the wife of Uriah the Hittite?" [4]Then David sent messengers, and took her; and she came to him, and he lay with her, for she was cleansed from her impurity; and she returned to her house. [5]And the woman conceived; so she sent and told David, and said, "I *am* with child."

LUST

Where can sexual lust lead? (11:1–4)

[6]Then David sent to Joab, *saying,* "Send me Uriah the Hittite." And Joab sent Uriah to David. [7]When Uriah had come to him, David asked how Joab was doing, and how the people were doing, and how the war prospered. [8]And David said to Uriah, "Go down to your house and wash your feet." So Uriah departed from the king's house, and a gift *of food* from the king followed him. [9]But Uriah slept at the door of the king's house with all the servants of his lord, and did not go down to his house. [10]So when they told David, saying, "Uriah did not go down to his house," David said to Uriah, "Did you not come from a journey? Why did you not go down to your house?"

[11]And Uriah said to David, "The ark and Israel and Judah are dwelling in tents, and my lord Joab and the servants of my lord are encamped in the open fields. Shall I then go to my house to eat and drink, and to lie with my wife? *As* you live, and *as* your soul lives, I will not do this thing."

WHAT'S IT MEAN?

The typical home in ancient Israel was built with a flat roof that was surrounded by a low wall. The roof, which could be reached by an outside stairway, was used as everything from a sleeping area to a patio or deck.

2 Samuel 11:2

[12]Then David said to Uriah, "Wait here today also, and tomorrow I will let you depart." So Uriah remained in Jerusalem that day and the next. [13]Now when David called him, he ate and drank before him; and he made him drunk. And at evening he went out to lie on his bed with the servants of his lord, but he did not go down to his house.

[14]In the morning it happened that David wrote a letter to Joab and sent *it* by the hand of Uriah. [15]And he wrote in the letter, saying, "Set Uriah in the forefront of the hottest battle, and retreat from him, that he may be struck down and die." [16]So it was, while Joab besieged the city, that he assigned Uriah to a place where he knew there *were* valiant men. [17]Then the men of the city came out and fought with Joab. And *some* of the people of the servants of David fell; and Uriah the Hittite died also.

[18]Then Joab sent and told David all the things concerning the war, [19]and charged the messenger, saying, "When you have finished telling the matters of the war to the king, [20]if it happens that the king's wrath rises, and he says to you: 'Why did you approach so near to the city when you fought? Did you not know that they would shoot from the wall? [21]Who struck Abimelech the son of Jerubbesheth?[a] Was it not

---

10:16 [a]Hebrew *Hadarezer* [b]That is, the Euphrates   **10:19** [a]Hebrew *Hadarezer*   **11:21** [a]Same as *Jerubbaal* (Gideon), Judges 6:32ff a woman who cast a piece of a millstone on him from the wall, so that he died in Thebez? Why did you go near the wall?'—then you shall say, 'Your servant Uriah the Hittite is dead also.' "

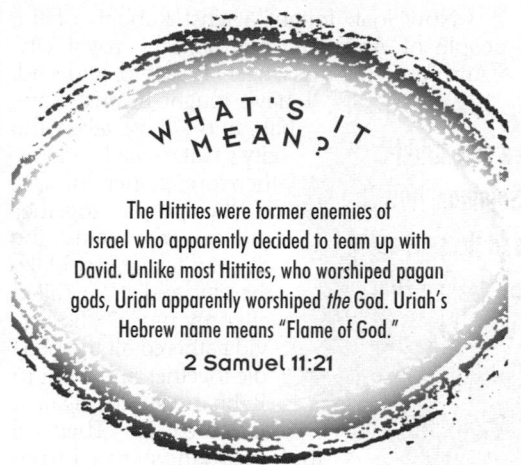

WHAT'S IT MEAN?

The Hittites were former enemies of Israel who apparently decided to team up with David. Unlike most Hittites, who worshiped pagan gods, Uriah apparently worshiped *the* God. Uriah's Hebrew name means "Flame of God."

2 Samuel 11:21

²²So the messenger went, and came and told David all that Joab had sent by him. ²³And the messenger said to David, "Surely the men prevailed against us and came out to us in the field; then we drove them back as far as the entrance of the gate. ²⁴The archers shot from the wall at your servants; and *some* of the king's servants are dead, and your servant Uriah the Hittite is dead also."

²⁵Then David said to the messenger, "Thus you shall say to Joab: 'Do not let this thing displease you, for the sword devours one as well as another. Strengthen your attack against the city, and overthrow it.' So encourage him."

²⁶When the wife of Uriah heard that Uriah her husband was dead, she mourned for her husband. ²⁷And when her mourning was over, David sent and brought her to his house, and she became his wife and bore him a son. But the thing that David had done displeased the LORD.

NATHAN'S PARABLE AND DAVID'S CONFESSION

¹Then the LORD sent Nathan to David. And he came to him, and said to him: "There were two men in one city, one rich and the other poor. ²The rich *man* had exceedingly many flocks and herds. ³But the poor *man* had nothing, except one little ewe lamb which he had bought and nourished; and it grew up together with him and with his children. It ate of his own food and drank from his own cup and lay in his bosom; and it was like a daughter to him. ⁴And a traveler came to the rich man, who refused to take from his own flock and from his own herd to prepare one for the wayfaring man who had come to him; but he took the poor man's lamb and prepared it for the man who had come to him."

⁵So David's anger was greatly aroused against the man, and he said to Nathan, "*As* the LORD lives, the man who has done this shall surely die! ⁶And he shall restore fourfold for the lamb, because he did this thing and because he had no pity."

⁷Then Nathan said to David, "You *are* the man! Thus says the LORD God of Israel: 'I anointed you king over Israel, and I delivered you from the hand of Saul. ⁸I gave you your master's house and your master's wives into your keeping, and gave you the house of Israel and Judah. And if *that had been* too little, I also would have given you much more! ⁹Why have you despised the commandment of the LORD, to do evil in His sight? You have killed Uriah the Hittite with the sword; you have taken his wife *to be* your wife, and have killed him with the sword of the people of Ammon. ¹⁰Now therefore, the sword shall never depart from your house, because you have despised Me, and have taken the wife of Uriah the Hittite to be your wife.' ¹¹Thus says the LORD: 'Behold, I will raise up adversity against you from your own house; and I will take your wives before your eyes and give *them* to your neighbor, and he shall lie with your wives in the sight of this sun. ¹²For you did *it* secretly, but I will do this thing before all Israel, before the sun.' "

SIN

Does sin have consequences? (12:9–12)

¹³So David said to Nathan, "I have sinned against the LORD."

And Nathan said to David, "The LORD also has put away your sin; you shall not die. ¹⁴However, because by this deed you have given great occasion to the enemies of the LORD to blaspheme, the child also *who is* born to you shall surely die." ¹⁵Then Nathan departed to his house.

THE DEATH OF DAVID'S SON

And the LORD struck the child that Uriah's wife bore to David, and it became ill. ¹⁶David therefore pleaded with God for the child, and David fasted and went in and lay all night on the ground. ¹⁷So the elders of his house arose *and went* to him, to raise him up from the ground. But he would not, nor did he eat food with them. ¹⁸Then on the seventh day it came to pass that the child died. And the servants of David were afraid to tell him that the child was dead. For they said, "Indeed, while the child was alive, we spoke to him, and he would not heed our voice. How can we tell him that the child is dead? He may do some harm!"

19When David saw that his servants were whispering, David perceived that the child was dead. Therefore David said to his servants, "Is the child dead?"

And they said, "He is dead."

20So David arose from the ground, washed and anointed himself, and changed his clothes; and he went into the house of the LORD and worshiped. Then he went to his own house; and when he requested, they set food before him, and he ate. 21Then his servants said to him, "What *is* this that you have done? You fasted and wept for the child *while he was* alive, but when the child died, you arose and ate food."

> "So she bore a son, and he called his name Solomon. Now the LORD loved him, and He sent word by the hand of Nathan the prophet: So he called his name Jedidiah, because of the LORD."
> (2 Samuel 12:24b, 25)

22And he said, "While the child was alive, I fasted and wept; for I said, 'Who can tell *whether* the LORD*a* will be gracious to me, that the child may live?' 23But now he is dead; why should I fast? Can I bring him back again? I shall go to him, but he shall not return to me."

SOLOMON IS BORN

24Then David comforted Bathsheba his wife, and went in to her and lay with her. So she bore a son, and he*a* called his name Solomon. Now

the LORD loved him, 25and He sent *word* by the hand of Nathan the prophet: So he*a* called his name Jedidiah,*b* because of the LORD.

RABBAH IS CAPTURED

26Now Joab fought against Rabbah of the people of Ammon, and took the royal city. 27And Joab sent messengers to David, and said, "I have fought against Rabbah, and I have taken the city's water *supply.* 28Now therefore, gather the rest of the people together and encamp against the city and take it, lest I take the city and it be called after my name." 29So David gathered all the people together and went to Rabbah, fought against it, and took it. 30Then he took their king's crown from his head. Its weight *was* a talent of gold, with precious stones. And it was *set* on David's head. Also he brought out the spoil of the city in great abundance. 31And he brought out the people who *were* in it, and put *them to work* with saws and iron picks and iron axes, and made them cross over to the brick works. So he did to all the cities of the people of Ammon. Then David and all the people returned to Jerusalem.

AMNON AND TAMAR

1After this Absalom the son of David had a lovely sister, whose name *was* Tamar; and Amnon the son of David loved her. 2Amnon was so distressed over his sister Tamar that he became sick; for she *was* a virgin. And it was improper for Amnon to do anything to her. 3But Amnon had a friend whose name *was* Jonadab the son of Shimeah, David's brother. Now Jonadab *was* a very crafty man. 4And he said to him, "Why *are* you, the king's son, becoming thinner day after day? Will you not tell me?"

Amnon said to him, "I love Tamar, my brother Absalom's sister."

5So Jonadab said to him, "Lie down on your bed and pretend to be ill. And when your father comes to see you, say to him, 'Please let my sister Tamar come and give me food, and prepare the food in my sight, that I may see *it* and eat it from her hand.' " 6Then Amnon lay down and

WHAT'S IT MEAN?

The name *Jedidiah* means "Loved by the LORD." Nathan gave Solomon this name to indicate that God had forgiven David. Not only would Solomon live—unlike his older brother—he would eventually become king of Israel.

2 Samuel 12:25

12:22 *a*A few Hebrew manuscripts and Syriac read *God.*   **12:24** *a*Following Kethib, Septuagint, and Vulgate; Qere, a few Hebrew manuscripts, Syriac, and Targum read *she.*   **12:25** *a*Qere, some Hebrew manuscripts, Syriac, and Targum read *she.* *b*Literally *Beloved of the LORD*

pretended to be ill; and when the king came to see him, Amnon said to the king, "Please let Tamar my sister come and make a couple of cakes for me in my sight, that I may eat from her hand."

[7]And David sent home to Tamar, saying, "Now go to your brother Amnon's house, and prepare food for him." [8]So Tamar went to her brother Amnon's house; and he was lying down. Then she took flour and kneaded *it*, made cakes in his sight, and baked the cakes. [9]And she took the pan and placed *them* out before him, but he refused to eat. Then Amnon said, "Have everyone go out from me." And they all went out from him. [10]Then Amnon said to Tamar, "Bring the food into the bedroom, that I may eat from your hand." And Tamar took the cakes which she had made, and brought *them* to Amnon her brother in the bedroom. [11]Now when she had brought *them* to him to eat, he took hold of her and said to her, "Come, lie with me, my sister."

[12]But she answered him, "No, my brother, do not force me, for no such thing should be done in Israel. Do not do this disgraceful thing! [13]And I, where could I take my shame? And as for you, you would be like one of the fools in Israel. Now therefore, please speak to the king; for he will not withhold me from you." [14]However, he would not heed her voice; and being stronger than she, he forced her and lay with her.

[15]Then Amnon hated her exceedingly, so that the hatred with which he hated her *was* greater than the love with which he had loved her. And Amnon said to her, "Arise, be gone!"

[16]So she said to him, "No, indeed! This evil of sending me away *is* worse than the other that you did to me."

But he would not listen to her. [17]Then he called his servant who attended him, and said, "Here! Put this *woman* out, away from me, and bolt the door behind her." [18]Now she had on a robe of many colors, for the king's virgin daughters wore such apparel. And his servant put her out and bolted the door behind her.

[19]Then Tamar put ashes on her head, and tore her robe of many colors that *was* on her, and laid her hand on her head and went away crying bitterly. [20]And Absalom her brother said to her, "Has Amnon your brother been with you? But now hold your peace, my sister. He *is* your brother; do not take this thing to heart." So Tamar remained desolate in her brother Absalom's house.

[21]But when King David heard of all these things, he was very angry. [22]And Absalom spoke to his brother Amnon neither good nor bad. For Absalom hated Amnon, because he had forced his sister Tamar.

ABSALOM MURDERS AMNON

[23]And it came to pass, after two full years, that Absalom had sheepshearers in Baal Hazor, which *is* near Ephraim; so Absalom invited all the king's sons. [24]Then Absalom came to the king and said, "Kindly note, your servant has sheepshearers; please, let the king and his servants go with your servant."

[25]But the king said to Absalom, "No, my son, let us not all go now, lest we be a burden to you." Then he urged him, but he would not go; and he blessed him.

[26]Then Absalom said, "If not, please let my brother Amnon go with us."

And the king said to him, "Why should he go with you?" [27]But Absalom urged him; so he let Amnon and all the king's sons go with him. [28]Now Absalom had commanded his servants, saying, "Watch now, when Amnon's heart is merry with wine, and when I say to you, 'Strike Amnon!' then kill him. Do not be afraid. Have I not commanded you? Be courageous and valiant." ²⁹So the servants of Absalom did to Amnon as Absalom had commanded. Then all the king's sons arose, and each one got on his mule and fled.

³⁰And it came to pass, while they were on the way, that news came to David, saying, "Absalom has killed all the king's sons, and not one of them is left!" ³¹So the king arose and tore his garments and lay on the ground, and all his servants stood by with their clothes torn. ³²Then Jonadab the son of Shimeah, David's brother, answered and said, "Let not my lord suppose they have killed all the young men, the king's sons, for only Amnon is dead. For by the command of Absalom this has been determined from the day that he forced his sister Tamar. ³³Now therefore, let not my lord the king take the thing to his heart, to think that all the king's sons are dead. For only Amnon is dead."

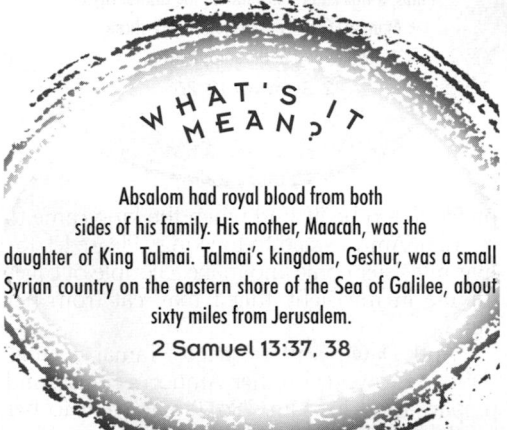

WHAT'S IT MEAN?

Entertaining a king in ancient times was a pretty expensive job. Not only did the host have to feed and house the king himself; he had to take care of all the servants and officials who traveled with the king. King David did not want his son Absalom to have to pay for such a visit.

2 Samuel 13:25

ABSALOM FLEES TO GESHUR

³⁴Then Absalom fled. And the young man who was keeping watch lifted his eyes and looked, and there, many people were coming from the road on the hillside behind him.ᵃ ³⁵And Jonadab said to the king, "Look, the king's sons are coming; as your servant said, so it is." ³⁶So it was, as soon as he had finished speaking, that the king's sons indeed came, and

they lifted up their voice and wept. Also the king and all his servants wept very bitterly.

³⁷But Absalom fled and went to Talmai the son of Ammihud, king of Geshur. And *David* mourned for his son every day. ³⁸So Absalom fled and went to Geshur, and was there three years. ³⁹And King Davidᵃ longed to go toᵇ Absalom. For he had been comforted concerning Amnon, because he was dead.

WHAT'S IT MEAN?

Absalom had royal blood from both sides of his family. His mother, Maacah, was the daughter of King Talmai. Talmai's kingdom, Geshur, was a small Syrian country on the eastern shore of the Sea of Galilee, about sixty miles from Jerusalem.

2 Samuel 13:37, 38

ABSALOM RETURNS TO JERUSALEM

¹So Joab the son of Zeruiah perceived that the king's heart *was* concerned about Absalom. ²And Joab sent to Tekoa and brought from there a wise woman, and said to her, "Please pretend to be a mourner, and put on mourning apparel; do not anoint yourself with oil, but act like a woman who has been mourning a long time for the dead. ³Go to the king and speak to him in this manner." So Joab put the words in her mouth.

⁴And when the woman of Tekoa spokeᵃ to the king, she fell on her face to the ground and prostrated herself, and said, "Help, O king!"

⁵Then the king said to her, "What troubles you?"

And she answered, "Indeed I *am* a widow, my husband is dead. ⁶Now your maidservant had two sons; and the two fought with each other in the field, and *there was* no one to part them, but the one struck the other and killed him. ⁷And now the whole family has risen up against your maidservant, and they said, 'De-

---

13:34 ᵃSeptuagint adds *And the watchman went and told the king, and said, "I see men from the way of Horonaim, from the regions of the mountains."* **13:39** ᵃFollowing Masoretic Text, Syriac, and Vulgate; Septuagint reads *the spirit of the king;* Targum reads *the soul of King David.* ᵇFollowing Masoretic Text and Targum; Septuagint and Vulgate read *ceased to pursue after.* **14:4** ᵃMany Hebrew manuscripts, Septuagint, Syriac, and Vulgate read *came.*

liver him who struck his brother, that we may execute him for the life of his brother whom he killed; and we will destroy the heir also'. So they would extinguish my ember that is left, and leave to my husband *neither* name nor remnant on the earth."

⁸Then the king said to the woman, "Go to your house, and I will give orders concerning you."

⁹And the woman of Tekoa said to the king, "My lord, O king, *let* the iniquity *be* on me and on my father's house, and the king and his throne *be* guiltless."

¹⁰So the king said, "Whoever says *anything* to you, bring him to me, and he shall not touch you anymore."

¹¹Then she said, "Please let the king remember the LORD your God, and do not permit the avenger of blood to destroy anymore, lest they destroy my son."

And he said, "*As* the LORD lives, not one hair of your son shall fall to the ground."

¹²Therefore the woman said, "Please, let your maidservant speak *another* word to my lord the king."

And he said, "Say on."

¹³So the woman said: "Why then have you schemed such a thing against the people of God? For the king speaks this thing as one who is guilty, *in that* the king does not bring his banished one home again. ¹⁴For we will surely die and *become* like water spilled on the ground, which cannot be gathered up again. Yet God does not take away a life; but He devises means, so that His banished ones are not expelled from Him. ¹⁵Now therefore, I have come to speak of this thing to my lord the king because the people have made me afraid. And your maidservant said, 'I will now speak to the king; it may be that the king will perform the request of his maidservant. ¹⁶For the king will hear and deliver his maidservant from the hand of the man *who would* destroy me and my son together from the inheritance of God'. ¹⁷Your maidservant said, 'The word of my lord the king will now be comforting; for as the angel of God, so *is* my lord the king in discerning good and evil. And may the LORD your God be with you.' "

¹⁸Then the king answered and said to the woman, "Please do not hide from me anything that I ask you."

And the woman said, "Please, let my lord the king speak."

¹⁹So the king said, "*Is* the hand of Joab with you in all this?" And the woman answered and said, "*As* you live, my lord the king, no one can turn to the right hand or to the left from any-

thing that my lord the king has spoken. For your servant Joab commanded me, and he put all these words in the mouth of your maidservant. ²⁰To bring about this change of affairs your servant Joab has done this thing; but my lord *is* wise, according to the wisdom of the angel of God, to know everything that *is* in the earth."

²¹And the king said to Joab, "All right, I have granted this thing. Go therefore, bring back the young man Absalom."

²²Then Joab fell to the ground on his face and bowed himself, and thanked the king. And Joab said, "Today your servant knows that I have found favor in your sight, my lord, O king, in that the king has fulfilled the request of his servant." ²³So Joab arose and went to Geshur, and brought Absalom to Jerusalem. ²⁴And the king said, "Let him return to his own house, but do not let him see my face." So Absalom returned to his own house, but did not see the king's face.

DAVID FORGIVES ABSALOM

²⁵Now in all Israel there was no one who was praised as much as Absalom for his good looks. From the sole of his foot to the crown of his head there was no blemish in him. ²⁶And when he cut the hair of his head—at the end of every year he cut *it* because it was heavy on him—when he cut it, he weighed the hair of his head at two hundred shekels according to the king's standard. ²⁷To Absalom were born three sons, and one daughter whose name *was* Tamar. She was a woman of beautiful appearance.

²⁸And Absalom dwelt two full years in Jerusalem, but did not see the king's face. ²⁹Therefore Absalom sent for Joab, to send him to the king, but he would not come to him. And when he sent again the second time, he would not come. ³⁰So he said to his servants, "See, Joab's field is near mine, and he has barley there; go and set it on fire." And Absalom's servants set the field on fire.

³¹Then Joab arose and came to Absalom's house, and said to him, "Why have your servants set my field on fire?"

³²And Absalom answered Joab, "Look, I sent to you, saying, 'Come here, so that I may send you to the king, to say, "Why have I come from Geshur? *It would be* better for me *to be* there still." ' Now therefore, let me see the king's face; but if there is iniquity in me, let him execute me."

³³So Joab went to the king and told him. And when he had called for Absalom, he came to the king and bowed himself on his face to the

ground before the king. Then the king kissed Absalom.

ABSALOM'S TREASON

[1]After this it happened that Absalom provided himself with chariots and horses, and fifty men to run before him. [2]Now Absalom would rise early and stand beside the way to the gate. *So* it was, whenever anyone who had a lawsuit came to the king for a decision, that Absalom would call to him and say, "What city *are* you from?" And he would say, "Your servant *is* from such and such a tribe of Israel." [3]Then Absalom would say to him, "Look, your case *is* good and right; but *there is* no deputy of the king to hear you." [4]Moreover Absalom would say, "Oh, that I were made judge in the land, and everyone who has any suit or cause would come to me; then I would give him justice." [5]And *so* it was, whenever anyone came near to bow down to him, that he would put out his hand and take him and kiss him. [6]In this manner Absalom acted toward all Israel who came to the king for judgment. So Absalom stole the hearts of the men of Israel.

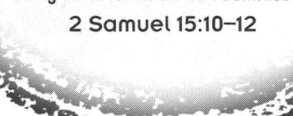

WHAT'S IT MEAN?

Hebron, a city about twenty miles southwest of Jerusalem, was important in Israel's history. Abraham, Isaac, and Jacob were all buried there. Because Absalom was a hometown boy, he found many supporters in Hebron. One of these supporters, Ahithophel, may have been related to Bathsheba. He may have supported Absalom out of his disgust with King David for his sin with Bathsheba.
2 Samuel 15:10–12

[7]Now it came to pass after forty[a] years that Absalom said to the king, "Please, let me go to Hebron and pay the vow which I made to the LORD. [8]For your servant took a vow while I dwelt at Geshur in Syria, saying, 'If the LORD indeed brings me back to Jerusalem, then I will serve the LORD.' "

[9]And the king said to him, "Go in peace." So he arose and went to Hebron.

[10]Then Absalom sent spies throughout all the tribes of Israel, saying, "As soon as you hear the sound of the trumpet, then you shall say, 'Absalom reigns in Hebron!' " [11]And with Absalom went two hundred men invited from Jerusalem, and they went along innocently and did not know anything. [12]Then Absalom sent for Ahithophel the Gilonite, David's counselor, from his city—from Giloh—while he offered sacrifices. And the conspiracy grew strong, for the people with Absalom continually increased in number.

DAVID ESCAPES FROM JERUSALEM

[13]Now a messenger came to David, saying, "The hearts of the men of Israel are with Absalom."

[14]So David said to all his servants who *were* with him at Jerusalem, "Arise, and let us flee, or we shall not escape from Absalom. Make haste to depart, lest he overtake us suddenly and bring disaster upon us, and strike the city with the edge of the sword."

[15]And the king's servants said to the king, "We *are* your servants, *ready to do* whatever my lord the king commands." [16]Then the king went out with all his household after him. But the king left ten women, concubines, to keep the house. [17]And the king went out with all the people after him, and stopped at the outskirts. [18]Then all his servants passed before him; and all the Cherethites, all the Pelethites, and all the Gittites, six hundred men who had followed him from Gath, passed before the king.

WHAT'S IT MEAN?

Gath was one of the five capital cities of the Philistines. The six hundred soldiers mentioned here had served with David while he was living with the Philistines to avoid the murderous King Saul.
2 Samuel 15:18

[19]Then the king said to Ittai the Gittite, "Why are you also going with us? Return and remain with the king. For you *are* a foreigner and also an exile from your own place. [20]In fact, you came *only* yesterday. Should I make you wander up and down with us today, since I go I

15:7 [a]Septuagint manuscripts, Syriac, and Josephus read *four.*

know not where? Return, and take your brethren back. Mercy and truth *be* with you."

²¹But Ittai answered the king and said, "*As* the LORD lives, and *as* my lord the king lives, surely in whatever place my lord the king shall be, whether in death or life, even there also your servant will be."

²²So David said to Ittai, "Go, and cross over." Then Ittai the Gittite and all his men and all the little ones who *were* with him crossed over. ²³And all the country wept with a loud voice, and all the people crossed over. The king himself also crossed over the Brook Kidron, and all the people crossed over toward the way of the wilderness.

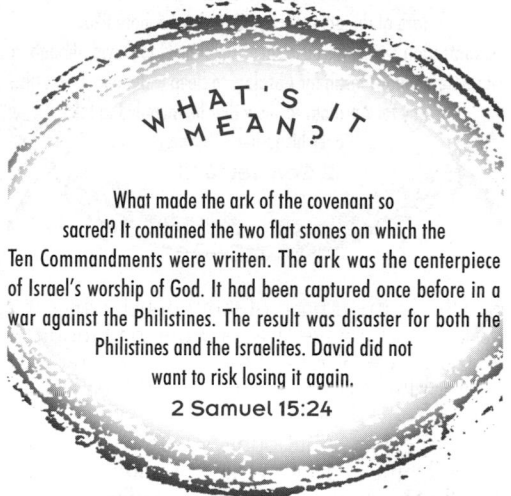

WHAT'S IT MEAN?

What made the ark of the covenant so sacred? It contained the two flat stones on which the Ten Commandments were written. The ark was the centerpiece of Israel's worship of God. It had been captured once before in a war against the Philistines. The result was disaster for both the Philistines and the Israelites. David did not want to risk losing it again.

2 Samuel 15:24

²⁴There was Zadok also, and all the Levites with him, bearing the ark of the covenant of God. And they set down the ark of God, and Abiathar went up until all the people had finished crossing over from the city. ²⁵Then the king said to Zadok, "Carry the ark of God back into the city. If I find favor in the eyes of the LORD, He will bring me back and show me *both* it and His dwelling place. ²⁶But if He says thus: 'I have no delight in you,' here I am, let Him do to me as seems good to Him." ²⁷The king also said to Zadok the priest, "*Are* you *not* a seer? Return to the city in peace, and your two sons with you, Ahimaaz your son, and Jonathan the son of Abiathar. ²⁸See, I will wait in the plains of the wilderness until word comes from you to inform me." ²⁹Therefore Zadok and Abiathar carried the ark of God back to Jerusalem. And they remained there.

³⁰So David went up by the Ascent of the *Mount of* Olives, and wept as he went up; and he had his head covered and went barefoot. And all the people who *were* with him covered their heads and went up, weeping as they went up. ³¹Then *someone* told David, saying, "Ahithophel *is* among the conspirators with Absalom." And David said, "O LORD, I pray, turn the counsel of Ahithophel into foolishness!"

³²Now it happened when David had come to the top *of the mountain*, where he worshiped God—there was Hushai the Archite coming to meet him with his robe torn and dust on his head. ³³David said to him, "If you go on with me, then you will become a burden to me. ³⁴But if you return to the city, and say to Absalom, 'I will be your servant, O king; as I *was* your father's servant previously, so I *will* now also *be* your servant,' then you may defeat the counsel of Ahithophel for me. ³⁵And *do* you not *have* Zadok and Abiathar the priests with you there? Therefore it will be *that* whatever you hear from the king's house, you shall tell to Zadok and Abiathar the priests. ³⁶Indeed *they have* there with them their two sons, Ahimaaz, Zadok's *son*, and Jonathan, Abiathar's *son*; and by them you shall send me everything you hear."

³⁷So Hushai, David's friend, went into the city. And Absalom came into Jerusalem.

MEPHIBOSHETH'S SERVANT

¹When David was a little past the top *of the mountain*, there was Ziba the servant of Mephibosheth, who met him with a couple of saddled donkeys, and on them two hundred *loaves* of bread, one hundred clusters of raisins, one hundred summer fruits, and a skin of wine. ²And the king said to Ziba, "What do you mean to do with these?"

So Ziba said, "The donkeys *are* for the king's household to ride on, the bread and summer fruit for the young men to eat, and the wine for those who are faint in the wilderness to drink."

³Then the king said, "And where *is* your master's son?"

And Ziba said to the king, "Indeed he is staying in Jerusalem, for he said, 'Today the house of Israel will restore the kingdom of my father to me.'"

⁴So the king said to Ziba, "Here, all that *belongs* to Mephibosheth *is* yours."

And Ziba said, "I humbly bow before you, *that* I may find favor in your sight, my lord, O king!"

SHIMEI CURSES DAVID

⁵Now when King David came to Bahurim, there was a man from the family of the house of Saul, whose name *was* Shimei the son of Gera, coming from there. He came out, cursing

continuously as he came. [6]And he threw stones at David and at all the servants of King David. And all the people and all the mighty men *were* on his right hand and on his left. [7]Also Shimei said thus when he cursed: "Come out! Come out! You bloodthirsty man, you rogue! [8]The LORD has brought upon you all the blood of the house of Saul, in whose place you have reigned; and the LORD has delivered the kingdom into the hand of Absalom your son. So now you *are caught* in your own evil, because you are a bloodthirsty man!"

[9]Then Abishai the son of Zeruiah said to the king, "Why should this dead dog curse my lord the king? Please, let me go over and take off his head!"

[10]But the king said, "What have I to do with you, you sons of Zeruiah? So let him curse, because the LORD has said to him, 'Curse David.' Who then shall say, 'Why have you done so?' "

[11]And David said to Abishai and all his servants, "See how my son who came from my own body seeks my life. How much more now *may this* Benjamite? Let him alone, and let him curse; for so the LORD has ordered him. [12]It may be that the LORD will look on my affliction,[a] and that the LORD will repay me with good for his cursing this day." [13]And as David and his men went along the road, Shimei went along the hillside opposite him and cursed as he went, threw stones at him and kicked up dust. [14]Now the king and all the people who *were* with him became weary; so they refreshed themselves there.

THE ADVICE OF AHITHOPHEL

[15]Meanwhile Absalom and all the people, the men of Israel, came to Jerusalem; and Ahithophel *was* with him. [16]And so it was, when Hushai the Archite, David's friend, came to Absalom, that Hushai said to Absalom, "*Long* live the king! *Long* live the king!"

[17]So Absalom said to Hushai, "*Is* this your loyalty to your friend? Why did you not go with your friend?"

[18]And Hushai said to Absalom, "No, but whom the LORD and this people and all the men of Israel choose, his I will be, and with him I will remain. [19]Furthermore, whom should I serve? *Should I* not *serve* in the presence of his son? As I have served in your father's presence, so will I be in your presence."

[20]Then Absalom said to Ahithophel, "Give advice as to what we should do."

[21]And Ahithophel said to Absalom, "Go in to your father's concubines, whom he has left to keep the house; and all Israel will hear that you are abhorred by your father. Then the hands of all who are with you will be strong." [22]So they pitched a tent for Absalom on the top of the house, and Absalom went in to his father's concubines in the sight of all Israel.

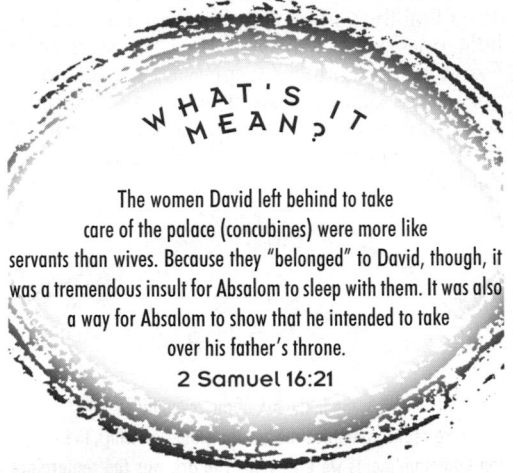

WHAT'S IT MEAN?

The women David left behind to take care of the palace (concubines) were more like servants than wives. Because they "belonged" to David, though, it was a tremendous insult for Absalom to sleep with them. It was also a way for Absalom to show that he intended to take over his father's throne.

2 Samuel 16:21

[23]Now the advice of Ahithophel, which he gave in those days, *was* as if one had inquired at the oracle of God. So *was* all the advice of Ahithophel both with David and with Absalom.

[1]Moreover Ahithophel said to Absalom, "Now let me choose twelve thousand men, and I will arise and pursue David tonight. [2]I will come upon him while he *is* weary and weak, and make him afraid. And all the people who *are* with him will flee, and I will strike only the king. [3]Then I will bring back all the people to you. When all return except the man whom you seek, all the people will be at peace." [4]And the saying pleased Absalom and all the elders of Israel.

THE ADVICE OF HUSHAI

[5]Then Absalom said, "Now call Hushai the Archite also, and let us hear what he says too." [6]And when Hushai came to Absalom, Absalom spoke to him, saying, "Ahithophel has spoken in this manner. Shall we do as he says? If not, speak up."

[7]So Hushai said to Absalom: "The advice that Ahithophel has given *is* not good at this time. [8]For," said Hushai, "you know your father and his men, that they *are* mighty men, and they *are* enraged in their minds, like a bear

---

16:12 [a]Following Kethib, Septuagint, Syriac, and Vulgate; Qere reads *my eyes*; Targum reads *tears of my eyes*.

robbed of her cubs in the field; and your father *is* a man of war, and will not camp with the people. ⁹Surely by now he is hidden in some pit, or in some *other* place. And it will be, when some of them are overthrown at the first, that whoever hears *it* will say, 'There is a slaughter among the people who follow Absalom.' ¹⁰And even he *who is* valiant, whose heart *is* like the heart of a lion, will melt completely. For all Israel knows that your father *is* a mighty man, and *those* who *are* with him *are* valiant men. ¹¹Therefore I advise that all Israel be fully gathered to you, from Dan to Beersheba, like the sand that *is* by the sea for multitude, and that you go to battle in person. ¹²So we will come upon him in some place where he may be found, and we will fall on him as the dew falls on the ground. And of him and all the men who *are* with him there shall not be left so much as one. ¹³Moreover, if he has withdrawn into a city, then all Israel shall bring ropes to that city; and we will pull it into the river, until there is not one small stone found there."

¹⁴So Absalom and all the men of Israel said, "The advice of Hushai the Archite *is* better than the advice of Ahithophel." For the LORD had purposed to defeat the good advice of Ahithophel, to the intent that the LORD might bring disaster on Absalom.

HUSHAI WARNS DAVID TO ESCAPE

¹⁵Then Hushai said to Zadok and Abiathar the priests, "Thus and so Ahithophel advised Absalom and the elders of Israel, and thus and so I have advised. ¹⁶Now therefore, send quickly and tell David, saying, 'Do not spend this night in the plains of the wilderness, but speedily cross over, lest the king and all the people who *are* with him be swallowed up.'" ¹⁷Now Jonathan and Ahimaaz stayed at En Rogel, for they dared not be seen coming into the city; so a female servant would come and tell them, and they would go and tell King David. ¹⁸Nevertheless a lad saw them, and told Absalom. But both of them went away quickly and came to a man's house in Bahurim, who had a well in his court; and they went down into it. ¹⁹Then the woman took and spread a covering over the well's mouth, and spread ground grain on it; and the thing was not known. ²⁰And when Absalom's servants came to the woman at the house, they said, "Where *are* Ahimaaz and Jonathan?"

So the woman said to them, "They have gone over the water brook."

And when they had searched and could not find *them,* they returned to Jerusalem. ²¹Now it came to pass, after they had departed, that they came up out of the well and went and told King David, and said to David, "Arise and cross over the water quickly. For thus has Ahithophel advised against you." ²²So David and all the people who *were* with him arose and crossed over the Jordan. By morning light not one of them was left who had not gone over the Jordan.

²³Now when Ahithophel saw that his advice was not followed, he saddled a donkey, and arose and went home to his house, to his city. Then he put his household in order, and hanged himself, and died; and he was buried in his father's tomb.

²⁴Then David went to Mahanaim. And Absalom crossed over the Jordan, he and all the men of Israel with him. ²⁵And Absalom made Amasa captain of the army instead of Joab. This Amasa *was* the son of a man whose name *was* Jithra,*ᵃ* an Israelite,*ᵇ* who had gone in to Abigail the daughter of Nahash, sister of Zeruiah, Joab's mother. ²⁶So Israel and Absalom encamped in the land of Gilead.

²⁷Now it happened, when David had come to Mahanaim, that Shobi the son of Nahash from Rabbah of the people of Ammon, Machir the son of Ammiel from Lo Debar, and Barzillai the Gileadite from Rogelim, ²⁸brought beds and basins, earthen vessels and wheat, barley and flour, parched *grain* and beans, lentils and parched *seeds,* ²⁹honey and curds, sheep and cheese of the herd, for David and the people who *were* with him to eat. For they said, "The people are hungry and weary and thirsty in the wilderness."

ABSALOM'S DEFEAT AND DEATH

¹And David numbered the people who *were* with him, and set captains of thousands and captains of hundreds over them. ²Then David sent out one third of the people under the hand of Joab, one third under the hand of Abishai the son of Zeruiah, Joab's brother, and one third under the hand of Ittai the Gittite. And the king said to the people, "I also will surely go out with you myself."

³But the people answered, "You shall not go out! For if we flee away, they will not care about us; nor if half of us die, will they care about us.

17:25 *ᵃ*Spelled *Jether* in 1 Chronicles 2:17 and elsewhere *ᵇ*Following Masoretic Text, some manuscripts of the Septuagint, and Targum; some manuscripts of the Septuagint read *Ishmaelite* (compare 1 Chronicles 2:17); Vulgate reads *of Jezrael.*

But *you are* worth ten thousand of us now. For you are now more help to us in the city."

⁴Then the king said to them, "Whatever seems best to you I will do." So the king stood beside the gate, and all the people went out by hundreds and by thousands. ⁵Now the king had commanded Joab, Abishai, and Ittai, saying, "*Deal* gently for my sake with the young man Absalom." And all the people heard when the king gave all the captains orders concerning Absalom.

⁶So the people went out into the field of battle against Israel. And the battle was in the woods of Ephraim. ⁷The people of Israel were overthrown there before the servants of David, and a great slaughter of twenty thousand took place there that day. ⁸For the battle there was scattered over the face of the whole countryside, and the woods devoured more people that day than the sword devoured.

⁹Then Absalom met the servants of David. Absalom rode on a mule. The mule went under the thick boughs of a great terebinth tree, and his head caught in the terebinth; so he was left hanging between heaven and earth. And the mule which *was* under him went on. ¹⁰Now a certain man saw *it* and told Joab, and said, "I just saw Absalom hanging in a terebinth tree!"

¹¹So Joab said to the man who told him, "You just saw *him*! And why did you not strike him there to the ground? I would have given you ten *shekels* of silver and a belt."

¹²But the man said to Joab, "Though I were to receive a thousand *shekels* of silver in my hand, I would not raise my hand against the king's son. For in our hearing the king commanded you and Abishai and Ittai, saying, 'Beware lest anyone *touch* the young man Absalom!'ᵃ ¹³Otherwise I would have dealt falsely against my own life. For there is nothing hidden from the king, and you yourself would have set yourself against *me*."

¹⁴Then Joab said, "I cannot linger with you." And he took three spears in his hand and thrust them through Absalom's heart, while he was *still* alive in the midst of the terebinth tree. ¹⁵And ten young men who bore Joab's armor surrounded Absalom, and struck and killed him.

¹⁶So Joab blew the trumpet, and the people returned from pursuing Israel. For Joab held back the people. ¹⁷And they took Absalom and cast him into a large pit in the woods, and laid a very large heap of stones over him. Then all Israel fled, everyone to his tent.

¹⁸Now Absalom in his lifetime had taken and set up a pillar for himself, which *is* in the King's Valley. For he said, "I have no son to keep my name in remembrance." He called the pillar after his own name. And to this day it is called Absalom's Monument.

DAVID HEARS OF ABSALOM'S DEATH

¹⁹Then Ahimaaz the son of Zadok said, "Let me run now and take the news to the king, how the LORD has avenged him of his enemies."

²⁰And Joab said to him, "You shall not take the news this day, for you shall take the news another day. But today you shall take no news, because the king's son is dead." ²¹Then Joab said to the Cushite, "Go, tell the king what you have seen." So the Cushite bowed himself to Joab and ran.

²²And Ahimaaz the son of Zadok said again to Joab, "But whatever happens, please let me also run after the Cushite."

So Joab said, "Why will you run, my son, since you have no news ready?"

²³"But whatever happens," *he* said, "let me run."

So he said to him, "Run." Then Ahimaaz ran by way of the plain, and outran the Cushite.

²⁴Now David was sitting between the two gates. And the watchman went up to the roof over the gate, to the wall, lifted his eyes and looked, and there was a man, running alone. ²⁵Then the watchman cried out and told the king. And the king said, "If he *is* alone, *there is* news in his mouth." And he came rapidly and drew near.

²⁶Then the watchman saw *another* man running, and the watchman called to the gatekeeper and said, "There is *another* man, running alone!"

And the king said, "He also brings news."

²⁷So the watchman said, "I think the running of the first is like the running of Ahimaaz the son of Zadok."

And the king said, "He *is* a good man, and comes with good news."

²⁸So Ahimaaz called out and said to the king, "All is well!" Then he bowed down with his face to the earth before the king, and said, "Blessed *be* the LORD your God, who has delivered up the men who raised their hand against my lord the king!"

²⁹The king said, "Is the young man Absalom safe?"

Ahimaaz answered, "When Joab sent the king's servant and *me* your servant, I saw a

---

18:12 ᵃThe ancient versions read 'Protect the young man Absalom for me!'

great tumult, but I did not know what *it was about.*"

³⁰And the king said, "Turn aside *and* stand here." So he turned aside and stood still.

³¹Just then the Cushite came, and the Cushite said, "There is good news, my lord the king! For the LORD has avenged you this day of all those who rose against you."

³²And the king said to the Cushite, "Is the young man Absalom safe?"

So the Cushite answered, "May the enemies of my lord the king, and all who rise against you to do harm, be like *that* young man!"

DAVID'S MOURNING FOR ABSALOM

³³Then the king was deeply moved, and went up to the chamber over the gate, and wept. And as he went, he said thus: "O my son Absalom—my son, my son Absalom—if only I had died in your place! O Absalom my son, my son!"

¹And Joab was told, "Behold, the king is weeping and mourning for Absalom." ²So the victory that day was *turned* into mourning for all the people. For the people heard it said that day, "The king is grieved for his son." ³And the people stole back into the city that day, as people who are ashamed steal away when they flee in battle. ⁴But the king covered his face, and the king cried out with a loud voice, "O my son Absalom! O Absalom, my son, my son!"

⁵Then Joab came into the house to the king, and said, "Today you have disgraced all your servants who today have saved your life, the lives of your sons and daughters, the lives of your wives and the lives of your concubines, ⁶in that you love your enemies and hate your friends. For you have declared today that you regard neither princes nor servants; for today I perceive that if Absalom had lived and all of us had died today, then it would have pleased you well. ⁷Now therefore, arise, go out and speak comfort to your servants. For I swear by the LORD, if you do not go out, not one will stay with you this night. And that will be worse for you than all the evil that has befallen you from your youth until now." ⁸Then the king arose

> **COMFORT**
> What should we do when comfort is hard to give?
> (19:7)

> "Just then the Cushite came, and the Cushite said, 'There is good news, my lord the king! For the LORD has avenged you this day of all those who rose against you.'"
> (2 Samuel 18:31)

and sat in the gate. And they told all the people, saying, "There is the king, sitting in the gate." So all the people came before the king.

For everyone of Israel had fled to his tent.

DAVID RETURNS TO JERUSALEM

⁹Now all the people were in a dispute throughout all the tribes of Israel, saying, "The king saved us from the hand of our enemies, he delivered us from the hand of the Philistines, and now he has fled from the land because of Absalom. ¹⁰But Absalom, whom we anointed over us, has died in battle. Now therefore, why do you say nothing about bringing back the king?"

¹¹So King David sent to Zadok and Abiathar the priests, saying, "Speak to the elders of Judah, saying, 'Why are you the last to bring the king back to his house, since the words of all Israel have come to the king, to his *very* house? ¹²You *are* my brethren, you *are* my bone and my flesh. Why then are you the last to bring back the king?' ¹³And say to Amasa, '*Are* you not my bone and my flesh? God do so to me, and more also, if you are not commander of the army before me continually in place of Joab.' " ¹⁴So he swayed the hearts of all the men of Judah, just as *the heart of* one man, so that they sent *this* word to the king: "Return, you and all your servants!"

¹⁵Then the king returned and came to the Jordan. And Judah came to Gilgal, to go to meet the king, to escort the king across the Jordan. ¹⁶And Shimei the son of Gera, a Benjamite, who *was* from Bahurim, hurried and came down with the men of Judah to meet King David. ¹⁷*There were* a thousand men of Benjamin with him, and Ziba the servant of the house of Saul, and his fifteen sons and his twenty servants with him; and they went over the Jordan before the king. ¹⁸Then a ferryboat went across to carry over the king's household, and to do what he thought good.

DAVID'S MERCY TO SHIMEI

Now Shimei the son of Gera fell down before the king when he had crossed the Jordan. ¹⁹Then he said to the king, "Do not let my lord impute iniquity to me, or remember what wrong your servant did on the day that my lord the king left Jerusalem, that the king should take *it* to heart. [20]For I, your servant, know that I have sinned. Therefore here I am, the first to come today of all the house of Joseph to go down to meet my lord the king."

[21]But Abishai the son of Zeruiah answered and said, "Shall not Shimei be put to death for this, because he cursed the LORD's anointed?"

[22]And David said, "What have I to do with you, you sons of Zeruiah, that you should be adversaries to me today? Shall any man be put to death today in Israel? For do I not know that today I *am* king over Israel?" [23]Therefore the king said to Shimei, "You shall not die." And the king swore to him.

DAVID AND MEPHIBOSHETH MEET

[24]Now Mephibosheth the son of Saul came down to meet the king. And he had not cared for his feet, nor trimmed his mustache, nor washed his clothes, from the day the king departed until the day he returned in peace. [25]So it was, when he had come to Jerusalem to meet the king, that the king said to him, "Why did you not go with me, Mephibosheth?"

[26]And he answered, "My lord, O king, my servant deceived me. For your servant said, 'I will saddle a donkey for myself, that I may ride on it and go to the king,' because your servant *is* lame. [27]And he has slandered your servant to my lord the king, but my lord the king *is* like the angel of God. Therefore do *what is* good in your eyes. [28]For all my father's house were but dead men before my lord the king. Yet you set your servant among those who eat at your own table. Therefore what right have I still to cry out anymore to the king?"

[29]So the king said to him, "Why do you speak anymore of your matters? I have said, 'You and Ziba divide the land.' "

[30]Then Mephibosheth said to the king, "Rather, let him take it all, inasmuch as my lord the king has come back in peace to his own house."

DAVID'S KINDNESS TO BARZILLAI

[31]And Barzillai the Gileadite came down from Rogelim and went across the Jordan with the king, to escort him across the Jordan. [32]Now Barzillai was a very aged man, eighty years old. And he had provided the king with supplies while he stayed at Mahanaim, for he was a very rich man. [33]And the king said to Barzillai, "Come across with me, and I will provide for you while you are with me in Jerusalem."

[34]But Barzillai said to the king, "How long have I to live, that I should go up with the king to Jerusalem? [35]I *am* today eighty years old. Can I discern between the good and bad? Can your servant taste what I eat or what I drink? Can I hear any longer the voice of singing men and singing women? Why then should your servant be a further burden to my lord the king? [36]Your servant will go a little way across the Jordan with the king. And why should the king repay me *with* such a reward? [37]Please let your servant turn back again, that I may die in my own city, near the grave of my father and mother. But here is your servant Chimham; let him cross over with my lord the king, and do for him what seems good to you."

[38]And the king answered, "Chimham shall cross over with me, and I will do for him what seems good to you. Now whatever you request of me, I will do for you." [39]Then all the people went over the Jordan. And when the king had crossed over, the king kissed Barzillai and blessed him, and he returned to his own place.

THE QUARREL ABOUT THE KING

[40]Now the king went on to Gilgal, and Chimham[a] went on with him. And all the people of Judah escorted the king, and also half the people of Israel. [41]Just then all the men of Israel came to the king, and said to the king, "Why have our brethren, the men of Judah, stolen you away and brought the king, his household, and all David's men with him across the Jordan?"

[42]So all the men of Judah answered the men of Israel, "Because the king *is* a close relative of ours. Why then are you angry over this matter? Have we ever eaten at the king's *expense*? Or has he given us any gift?"

[43]And the men of Israel answered the men of Judah, and said, "We have ten shares in the king; therefore we also have more *right* to David than you. Why then do you despise us— were we not the first to advise bringing back our king?"

Yet the words of the men of Judah were fiercer than the words of the men of Israel.

THE REBELLION OF SHEBA

[1]And there happened to be there a rebel,[a] whose name *was* Sheba the son of Bichri, a Benjamite. And he blew a trumpet, and said:

FRIENDSHIP

How should we care for our friends? (19:33)

19:40 [a]Masoretic Text reads *Chimhan.*   **20:1** [a]Literally *man of Belial*

"We have no share in David,
Nor do we have inheritance in the son of Jesse;
Every man to his tents, O Israel!"

²So every man of Israel deserted David, *and* followed Sheba the son of Bichri. But the men of Judah, from the Jordan as far as Jerusalem, remained loyal to their king.

³Now David came to his house at Jerusalem. And the king took the ten women, his concubines whom he had left to keep the house, and put them in seclusion and supported them, but did not go in to them. So they were shut up to the day of their death, living in widowhood.

⁴And the king said to Amasa, "Assemble the men of Judah for me within three days, and be present here yourself." ⁵So Amasa went to assemble *the men of* Judah. But he delayed longer than the set time which David had appointed him. ⁶And David said to Abishai, "Now Sheba the son of Bichri will do us more harm than Absalom. Take your lord's servants and pursue him, lest he find for himself fortified cities, and escape us." ⁷So Joab's men, with the Cherethites, the Pelethites, and all the mighty men, went out after him. And they went out of Jerusalem to pursue Sheba the son of Bichri. ⁸When they *were* at the large stone which *is* in Gibeon, Amasa came before them. Now Joab was dressed in battle armor; on it was a belt *with* a sword fastened in its sheath at his hips; and as he was going forward, it fell out. ⁹Then Joab said to Amasa, "*Are* you in health, my brother?" And Joab took Amasa by the beard with his right hand to kiss him. ¹⁰But Amasa did not notice the sword that *was* in Joab's hand. And he struck him with it in the stomach, and his entrails poured out on the ground; and he did not *strike* him again. Thus he died.

Then Joab and Abishai his brother pursued Sheba the son of Bichri. ¹¹Meanwhile one of Joab's men stood near Amasa, and said, "Whoever favors Joab and whoever *is* for David—follow Joab!" ¹²But Amasa wallowed in *his* blood in the middle of the highway. And when the man saw that all the people stood still, he moved Amasa from the highway to the field and threw a garment over him, when he saw that everyone who came upon him halted. ¹³When he was removed from the highway, all the people went on after Joab to pursue Sheba the son of Bichri.

¹⁴And he went through all the tribes of Israel to Abel and Beth Maachah and all the Berites. So they were gathered together and also went after *Sheba.ᵃ* ¹⁵Then they came and besieged him in Abel of Beth Maachah; and they cast up a siege mound against the city, and it stood by the rampart. And all the people who *were* with Joab battered the wall to throw it down.

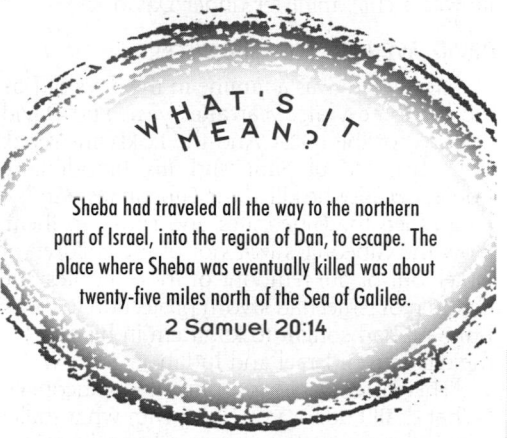

WHAT'S IT MEAN?

Sheba had traveled all the way to the northern part of Israel, into the region of Dan, to escape. The place where Sheba was eventually killed was about twenty-five miles north of the Sea of Galilee.
2 Samuel 20:14

¹⁶Then a wise woman cried out from the city, "Hear, hear! Please say to Joab, 'Come nearby, that I may speak with you.'" ¹⁷When he had come near to her, the woman said, "*Are* you Joab?"

He answered, "I *am*."

Then she said to him, "Hear the words of your maidservant."

And he answered, "I am listening."

¹⁸So she spoke, saying, "They used to talk in former times, saying, 'They shall surely seek *guidance* at Abel,' and so they would end *disputes.* ¹⁹I *am among the* peaceable *and* faithful in Israel. You seek to destroy a city and a mother in Israel. Why would you swallow up the inheritance of the LORD?"

²⁰And Joab answered and said, "Far be it, far be it from me, that I should swallow up or destroy! ²¹That *is* not so. But a man from the mountains of Ephraim, Sheba the son of Bichri by name, has raised his hand against the king, against David. Deliver him only, and I will depart from the city."

So the woman said to Joab, "Watch, his head will be thrown to you over the wall." ²²Then the woman in her wisdom went to all the people. And they cut off the head of Sheba the son of Bichri, and threw *it* out to Joab. Then he blew a trumpet, and they withdrew from the city, every man to his tent. So Joab returned to the king at Jerusalem.

DAVID'S GOVERNMENT OFFICERS

²³And Joab *was* over all the army of Israel; Benaiah the son of Jehoiada *was* over the Cherethites and the Pelethites; ²⁴Adoram *was* in charge of revenue; Jehoshaphat the son of Ahilud *was* recorder; ²⁵Sheva *was* scribe; Zadok and Abiathar *were* the priests; ²⁶and Ira the Jairite was a chief minister under David.

DAVID AVENGES THE GIBEONITES

¹Now there was a famine in the days of David for three years, year after year; and David inquired of the LORD. And the LORD answered, "*It is* because of Saul and *his* bloodthirsty house, because he killed the Gibeonites." ²So the king called the Gibeonites and spoke to them. Now the Gibeonites *were* not of the children of Israel, but of the remnant of the Amorites; the children of Israel had sworn protection to them, but Saul had sought to kill them in his zeal for the children of Israel and Judah.

³Therefore David said to the Gibeonites, "What shall I do for you? And with what shall I make atonement, that you may bless the inheritance of the LORD?"

⁴And the Gibeonites said to him, "We will have no silver or gold from Saul or from his house, nor shall you kill any man in Israel for us."

So he said, "Whatever you say, I will do for you."

⁵Then they answered the king, "As for the man who consumed us and plotted against us, *that* we should be destroyed from remaining in any of the territories of Israel, ⁶let seven men of his descendants be delivered to us, and we will hang them before the LORD in Gibeah of Saul, *whom* the LORD chose."

And the king said, "I will give *them*."

⁷But the king spared Mephibosheth the son of Jonathan, the son of Saul, because of the LORD's oath that *was* between them, between David and Jonathan the son of Saul. ⁸So the king took Armoni and Mephibosheth, the two sons of Rizpah the daughter of Aiah, whom she bore to Saul, and the five sons of Michal^a the daughter of Saul, whom she brought up for Adriel the son of Barzillai the Meholathite; ⁹and he delivered them into the hands of the Gibeonites, and they hanged them on the hill before the LORD. So they fell, *all* seven together, and were put to death in the days of harvest, in the first *days*, in the beginning of barley harvest.

¹⁰Now Rizpah the daughter of Aiah took sackcloth and spread it for herself on the rock, from the beginning of harvest until the late rains poured on them from heaven. And she did not allow the birds of the air to rest on them by day nor the beasts of the field by night.

¹¹And David was told what Rizpah the daughter of Aiah, the concubine of Saul, had done. ¹²Then David went and took the bones of Saul, and the bones of Jonathan his son, from the men of Jabesh Gilead who had stolen them from the street of Beth Shan,^a where the Philistines had hung them up, after the Philistines had struck down Saul in Gilboa. ¹³So he brought up the bones of Saul and the bones of Jonathan his son from there; and they gathered the bones of those who had been hanged. ¹⁴They buried the bones of Saul and Jonathan his son in the country of Benjamin in Zelah, in the tomb of Kish his father. So they performed all that the king commanded. And after that God heeded the prayer for the land.

WHAT'S IT MEAN?

The Israelites were very particular about their final resting place. Allowing a body to be abandoned and eaten by birds and dogs was the ultimate insult. In fact, it was considered a curse on the dead person. Rizpah prevented this from happening to the descendants of Saul (two of them were her own sons!), and David rewarded her by having the bodies buried in the family tomb.
2 Samuel 21:13, 14

PHILISTINE GIANTS DESTROYED

¹⁵When the Philistines were at war again with Israel, David and his servants with him went down and fought against the Philistines; and David grew faint. ¹⁶Then Ishbi-Benob, who *was* one of the sons of the giant, the weight of whose bronze spear *was* three hundred *shekels*, who was bearing a new *sword*, thought he could kill David. ¹⁷But Abishai the son of Zeruiah came to his aid, and struck the Philistine and killed him. Then the men of David swore to him, saying, "You shall go out no more with us to battle, lest you quench the lamp of Israel."

21:8 ^aOr *Merab* (compare 1 Samuel 18:19 and 25:44; 2 Samuel 3:14 and 6:23)   **21:12** ^aSpelled *Beth Shean* in Joshua 17:11 and elsewhere

¹⁸Now it happened afterward that there was again a battle with the Philistines at Gob. Then Sibbechai the Hushathite killed Saph,ᵃ who *was* one of the sons of the giant. ¹⁹Again there was war at Gob with the Philistines, where Elhanan the son of Jaare-Oregimᵃ the Bethlehemite killed *the brother of* Goliath the Gittite, the shaft of whose spear *was* like a weaver's beam.

²⁰Yet again there was war at Gath, where there was a man of *great* stature, who had six fingers on each hand and six toes on each foot, twenty-four in number; and he also was born to the giant. ²¹So when he defied Israel, Jonathan the son of Shimea,ᵃ David's brother, killed him.

²²These four were born to the giant in Gath, and fell by the hand of David and by the hand of his servants.

PRAISE FOR GOD'S DELIVERANCE

¹Then David spoke to the LORD the words of this song, on the day when the LORD had delivered him from the hand of all his enemies, and from the hand of Saul. ²And he said:ᵃ

"The LORD *is* my rock
  and my fortress and
  my deliverer;
3 The God of my
  strength, in whom I
  will trust;
My shield and the horn of my salvation,
My stronghold and my refuge;
My Savior, You save me from violence.
4 I will call upon the LORD, *who is worthy* to
  be praised;
So shall I be saved from
  my enemies.

5 "When the waves of death
  surrounded me,
The floods of ungodliness
  made me afraid.
6 The sorrows of Sheol surrounded
  me;
The snares of death
  confronted me.
7 In my distress I called
  upon the LORD,
And cried out to my
  God;

SALVATION
Who will
deliver us?
(22:2)

WORSHIP
Who is
worthy of
praise?
(22:4)

HOPE
Why can we
be hopeful?
(22:7)

He heard my voice from His temple,
And my cry *entered* His ears.

8 "Then the earth shook and trembled;
The foundations of heavenᵃ quaked and
  were shaken,
Because He was angry.
9 Smoke went up from His nostrils,
And devouring fire from His mouth;
Coals were kindled by it.
10 He bowed the heavens also, and came
  down
With darkness under His feet.
11 He rode upon a cherub, and flew;
And He was seenᵃ upon the wings of the
  wind.
12 He made darkness canopies around Him,
Dark waters *and* thick clouds of the skies.
13 From the brightness before Him
Coals of fire were kindled.

14 "The LORD thundered from heaven,
And the Most High uttered His voice.
15 He sent out arrows and scattered them;
Lightning bolts, and He vanquished
  them.
16 Then the channels of the sea were seen,
The foundations of the world were
  uncovered,
At the rebuke of the LORD,
At the blast of the breath of His nostrils.

17 "He sent from above, He took me,
He drew me out of many waters.
18 He delivered me from my strong enemy,

21:18 ᵃSpelled *Sippai* in 1 Chronicles 20:4 **21:19** ᵃSpelled *Jair* in 1 Chronicles 20:5 **21:21** ᵃSpelled *Shammah* in 1 Samuel 16:9 and elsewhere **22:2** ᵃCompare Psalm 18 **22:8** ᵃFollowing Masoretic Text, Septuagint, and Targum; Syriac and Vulgate read *hills* (compare Psalm 18:7). **22:11** ᵃFollowing Masoretic Text and Septuagint; many Hebrew manuscripts, Syriac, and Vulgate read *He flew* (compare Psalm 18:10); Targum reads *He spoke with power.*

From those who hated me;
For they were too strong for me.
19 They confronted me in the day of my
calamity,
But the LORD was my support.
20 He also brought me out into a broad
place;
He delivered me because He delighted in
me.

21 "The LORD rewarded me according to my
righteousness;
According to the cleanness of my hands
He has recompensed me.
22 For I have kept the ways of the LORD,
And have not wickedly departed from my
God.
23 For all His judgments *were* before me;
And *as for* His statutes, I did not depart
from them.
24 I was also blameless before Him,
And I kept myself from my iniquity.
25 Therefore the LORD has recompensed me
according to my righteousness,
According to my cleanness in His eyes.[a]

26 "With the merciful You will show Yourself
merciful;
With a blameless man You will show
Yourself blameless;
27 With the pure You will show Yourself pure;
And with the devious You will show
Yourself shrewd.
28 You will save the humble people;
But Your eyes *are* on the haughty, *that*
You may bring *them* down.

29 "For You *are* my lamp, O LORD;
The LORD shall enlighten
my darkness.
30 For by You I can run
against a troop;
By my God I can leap
over a wall.
31 *As for* God, His way *is* perfect;
The word of the LORD *is* proven;
He *is* a shield to all who trust in Him.

32 "For who *is* God, except the LORD?
And who *is* a rock, except our God?
33 God *is* my strength *and* power,[a]

WHAT'S IT MEAN?

"Merciful" and "blameless"
mean pretty much the same thing, don't
they? Was David repeating himself? Well, yes, he was—but for a
reason. David was writing a type of Hebrew poetry that used different words to make the same point.
2 Samuel 22:26

And He makes my[b] way perfect.
34 He makes my[a] feet like the *feet* of deer,
And sets me on my high places.
35 He teaches my hands to make war,
So that my arms can bend a bow of
bronze.

36 "You have also given me the shield of Your
salvation;
Your gentleness has made me great.
37 You enlarged my path under me;
So my feet did not slip.

38 "I have pursued my enemies and
destroyed them;
Neither did I turn back again till they
were destroyed.
39 And I have destroyed them and wounded
them,
So that they could not rise;
They have fallen under my feet.
40 For You have armed me with strength for
the battle;
You have subdued under me those who
rose against me.
41 You have also given me the necks of my
enemies,
So that I destroyed those who hated me.
42 They looked, but *there was* none to save;
Even to the LORD, but He did not answer
them.
43 Then I beat them as fine as the dust of
the earth;

BIBLE
Is it
trustworthy?
(22:29–31)

22:25 [a]Septuagint, Syriac, and Vulgate read *the cleanness of my hands in His sight* (compare Psalm 18:24);
Targum reads *my cleanness before His word.* **22:33** [a]Dead Sea Scrolls, Septuagint, Syriac, and Vulgate read *It is
God who arms me with strength* (compare Psalm 18:32); Targum reads *It is God who sustains me with strength.*
[b]Following Qere, Septuagint, Syriac, Targum, and Vulgate (compare Psalm 18:32); Kethib reads *His.*
22:34 [a]Following Qere, Septuagint, Syriac, Targum, and Vulgate (compare Psalm 18:33); Kethib reads *His.*

I trod them like dirt in the streets,
And I spread them out.

44 "You have also delivered me from the
strivings of my people;
You have kept me as the head of the
nations.
A people I have not known shall serve
me.
45 The foreigners submit to me;
As soon as they hear, they obey me.
46 The foreigners fade away,
And come frightened[a] from their
hideouts.

47 "The LORD lives!
Blessed be my Rock!
Let God be exalted,
The Rock of my
salvation!
48 It is God who avenges
me,
And subdues the peoples under me;
49 He delivers me from my enemies.
You also lift me up above those who rise
against me;
You have delivered me from the violent
man.
50 Therefore I will give thanks to You,
O LORD, among the Gentiles,
And sing praises to Your name.

SALVATION
Why should
we praise
God?
(22:47, 48)

51 "He is the tower of salvation to His king,
And shows mercy to His anointed,
To David and his descendants
forevermore."

DAVID'S LAST WORDS

1 Now these are the last words of David.

Thus says David the son of Jesse;
Thus says the man raised up on high,
The anointed of the God of Jacob,
And the sweet psalmist of Israel:

2 "The Spirit of the LORD spoke by me,
And His word was on my tongue.
3 The God of Israel said,
The Rock of Israel spoke to me:
'He who rules over men must be just,
Ruling in the fear of God.
4 And he shall be like the light of the
morning when the sun rises,
A morning without clouds,
Like the tender grass springing out of the
earth,
By clear shining after rain.'

5 "Although my house is not so with
God,
Yet He has made with me an everlasting
covenant,
Ordered in all things and secure.

22:46 [a]Following Septuagint, Targum, and Vulgate (compare Psalm 18:45); Masoretic Text reads *gird themselves*.

Promise HE PROMISES TO NEVER BREAK HIS PROMISES.

Although my house is not so with God, yet He has made with me an everlasting covenant, ordered in all things and secure. For this is all my salvation and all my desire; will He not make it increase? (2 Sam. 23:5).

Broken promises. Nothing stings more. They tear you up and rip your heart out. Friends who tell your deepest secrets. Being stood up by the girl you finally ask out. Dads who walk out on moms. Promise made, promise broken, heartache. When someone breaks a promise, it feels like a punch in the gut—all the wind gets knocked out of you and all your energy is drained.

Because we've felt this pain so many times, we assume that God could treat us the same way. He might pull out at any turn. He might say He didn't really mean it—we just misunderstood Him. Not a chance. He promises never to break His promise. He'll always keep your secrets, always be there when you need Him, and always do what He says He will do. You can stake your heart on it.

SEE FOR YOURSELF:
Num. 23:19; Josh. 23:15, 16; 1 Kin. 8:56

For *this is* all my salvation and all *my* desire;
    Will He not make *it* increase?
6   But *the sons* of rebellion *shall* all *be* as thorns thrust away,
    Because they cannot be taken with hands.
7   But the man *who* touches them
    Must be armed with iron and the shaft of a spear,
    And they shall be utterly burned with fire in *their* place."

DAVID'S MIGHTY MEN

[8]These *are* the names of the mighty men whom David had: Josheb-Basshebeth[a] the Tachmonite, chief among the captains.[b] He was called Adino the Eznite, because he had killed eight hundred men at one time. [9]And after him *was* Eleazar the son of Dodo,[a] the Ahohite, *one* of the three mighty men with David when they defied the Philistines *who* were gathered there for battle, and the men of Israel had retreated. [10]He arose and attacked the Philistines until his hand was weary, and his hand stuck to the sword. The LORD brought about a great victory that day; and the people returned after him only to plunder. [11]And after him *was* Shammah the son of Agee the Hararite. The Philistines had gathered together into a troop where there was a piece of ground full of lentils. So the people fled from the Philistines. [12]But he stationed himself in the middle of the field, defended it, and killed the Philistines. So the LORD brought about a great victory.

WHAT'S IT MEAN?

David used the cave of Adullam as a hiding place while he was on the run from King Saul. The cave was located just outside the city of Adullam, southwest of Jerusalem.

2 Samuel 23:13

[13]Then three of the thirty chief men went down at harvest time and came to David at the cave of Adullam. And the troop of Philistines encamped in the Valley of Rephaim. [14]David *was* then in the stronghold, and the garrison of the Philistines *was* then *in* Bethlehem. [15]And David said with longing, "Oh, that someone would give me a drink of the water from the well of Bethlehem, which *is* by the gate!" [16]So the three mighty men broke through the camp of the Philistines, drew water from the well of Bethlehem that *was* by the gate, and took it and brought *it* to David. Nevertheless he would not drink it, but poured it out to the LORD. [17]And he said, "Far be it from me, O LORD, that I should do this! Is *this not* the blood of the men who went in *jeopardy of* their lives?" Therefore he would not drink it.

These things were done by the three mighty men.

[18]Now Abishai the brother of Joab, the son of Zeruiah, was chief of *another* three.[a] He lifted his spear against three hundred *men*, killed *them*, and won a name among *these* three. [19]Was he not the most honored of three? Therefore he became their captain. However, he did not attain to the *first* three.

[20]Benaiah *was* the son of Jehoiada, the son of a valiant man from Kabzeel, who had done many deeds. He had killed two lion-like heroes of Moab. He also had gone down and killed a lion in the midst of a pit on a snowy day. [21]And he killed an Egyptian, a spectacular man. The Egyptian *had* a spear in his hand; so he went down to him with a staff, wrested the spear out of the Egyptian's hand, and killed him with his own spear. [22]These *things* Benaiah the son of Jehoiada did, and won a name among three mighty men. [23]He was more honored than the thirty, but he did not attain to the *first* three. And David appointed him over his guard.

[24]Asahel the brother of Joab *was* one of the thirty; Elhanan the son of Dodo of Bethlehem, [25]Shammah the Harodite, Elika the Harodite, [26]Helez the Paltite, Ira the son of Ikkesh the Tekoite, [27]Abiezer the Anathothite, Mebunnai the Hushathite, [28]Zalmon the Ahohite, Maharai the Netophathite, [29]Heleb the son of Baanah (the Netophathite), Ittai the son of Ribai from Gibeah of the children of Benjamin, [30]Benaiah a Pirathonite, Hiddai from the brooks of Gaash, [31]Abi-Albon the Arbathite, Azmaveth the Barhumite, [32]Eliahba the Shaalbonite (of the sons of Jashen), Jonathan, [33]Shammah the Hararite, Ahiam the son of Sharar the Hararite, [34]Eliphe-

---

23:8 [a]Literally *One Who Sits in the Seat* (compare 1 Chronicles 11:11) [b]Following Masoretic Text and Targum; Septuagint and Vulgate read *the three*.   **23:9** [a]Spelled *Dodai* in 1 Chronicles 27:4   **23:18** [a]Following Masoretic Text, Septuagint, and Vulgate; some Hebrew manuscripts and Syriac read *thirty*; Targum reads *the mighty men*.

let the son of Ahasbai, the son of the Maacha-thite, Eliam the son of Ahithophel the Gilonite, [35]Hezrai[a] the Carmelite, Paarai the Arbite, [36]Igal the son of Nathan of Zobah, Bani the Gadite, [37]Zelek the Ammonite, Naharai the Beerothite (armorbearer of Joab the son of Zeruiah), [38]Ira the Ithrite, Gareb the Ithrite, [39]and Uriah the Hittite: thirty-seven in all.

DAVID'S CENSUS OF ISRAEL AND JUDAH

[1]Again the anger of the LORD was aroused against Israel, and He moved David against them to say, "Go, number Israel and Judah."

[2]So the king said to Joab the commander of the army who was with him, "Now go throughout all the tribes of Israel, from Dan to Beersheba, and count the people, that I may know the number of the people."

[3]And Joab said to the king, "Now may the LORD your God add to the people a hundred times more than there are, and may the eyes of my lord the king see it. But why does my lord the king desire this thing?" [4]Nevertheless the king's word prevailed against Joab and against the captains of the army. Therefore Joab and the captains of the army went out from the presence of the king to count the people of Israel.

[5]And they crossed over the Jordan and camped in Aroer, on the right side of the town which is in the midst of the ravine of Gad, and toward Jazer. [6]Then they came to Gilead and to the land of Tahtim Hodshi; they came to Dan Jaan and around to Sidon; [7]and they came to the stronghold of Tyre and to all the cities of the Hivites and the Canaanites. Then they went out to South Judah as far as Beersheba. [8]So when they had gone through all the land, they came to Jerusalem at the end of nine months and twenty days. [9]Then Joab gave the sum of the number of the people to the king. And there were in Israel eight hundred thousand valiant men who drew the sword, and the men of Judah were five hundred thousand men.

THE JUDGMENT ON DAVID'S SIN

[10]And David's heart condemned him after he had numbered the people. So David said to the LORD, "I have sinned greatly in what I have done; but now, I pray, O LORD, take away the iniquity of Your servant, for I have done very foolishly."

[11]Now when David arose in the morning, the word of the LORD came to the prophet Gad, David's seer, saying, [12]"Go and tell David, 'Thus says the LORD. "I offer you three things; choose one of them for yourself, that I may do it to you." ' " [13]So Gad came to David and told him; and he said to him, "Shall seven[a] years of famine come to you in your land? Or shall you flee three months before your enemies, while they pursue you? Or shall there be three days' plague in your land? Now consider and see what answer I should take back to Him who sent me."

[14]And David said to Gad, "I am in great distress. Please let us fall into the hand of the LORD, for His mercies are great; but do not let me fall into the hand of man."

[15]So the LORD sent a plague upon Israel from the morning till the appointed time. From Dan to Beersheba seventy thousand men of the people died. [16]And when the angel[a] stretched out His hand over Jerusalem to destroy it, the LORD relented from the destruction, and said to the angel who was destroying the people, "It is enough; now restrain your hand." And the angel of the LORD was by the threshing floor of Araunah[b] the Jebusite.

ANGELS

Who carries out God's judgment? (24:16, 17)

[17]Then David spoke to the LORD when he saw the angel who was striking the people, and said, "Surely I have sinned, and I have done wickedly; but these sheep, what have they done? Let Your hand, I pray, be against me and against my father's house."

WHAT'S IT MEAN?

Threshing grain means crushing and tearing the plant to separate the edible part from the leaves and stalk. In ancient times, this was done by having animals drag heavy wooden boards over the grain. Afterward, the whole smashed mess was thrown into the air. The leaves and stalks were blown away by the wind, and the grain fell back to the ground.

2 Samuel 24:22

23:35 [a]Spelled Hezro in 1 Chronicles 11:37 **24:13** [a]Following Masoretic Text, Syriac, Targum, and Vulgate; Septuagint reads three (compare 1 Chronicles 21:12). **24:16** [a]Or Angel [b]Spelled Ornan in 1 Chronicles 21:15

THE ALTAR ON THE THRESHING FLOOR

18And Gad came that day to David and said to him, "Go up, erect an altar to the LORD on the threshing floor of Araunah the Jebusite." 19So David, according to the word of Gad, went up as the LORD commanded. 20Now Araunah looked, and saw the king and his servants coming toward him. So Araunah went out and bowed before the king with his face to the ground.

21Then Araunah said, "Why has my lord the king come to his servant?"

And David said, "To buy the threshing floor from you, to build an altar to the LORD, that the plague may be withdrawn from the people."

22Now Araunah said to David, "Let my lord the king take and offer up whatever *seems* good to him. Look, *here are* oxen for burnt sacrifice, and threshing implements and the yokes of the oxen for wood. 23All these, O king, Araunah has given to the king."

And Araunah said to the king, "May the LORD your God accept you."

24Then the king said to Araunah, "No, but I will surely buy *it* from you for a price; nor will I offer burnt offerings to the LORD my God with that which costs me nothing." So David bought the threshing floor and the oxen for fifty shekels of silver. 25And David built there an altar to the LORD, and offered burnt offerings and peace offerings. So the LORD heeded the prayers for the land, and the plague was withdrawn from Israel.

"The LORD lives! Blessed be my Rock! Let God be exalted, the Rock of my salvation!" (2 Samuel 22:47)

1 Kings

CONTENT   If reading First and Second Samuel is like watching a couple of home videos, then reading First Kings is like finding the sequel to those home videos. In fact, First Kings picks up right where Second Samuel leaves off.

In First and Second Samuel, the Hebrews got their first king, Saul, and their second king, David. In the first half of First Kings, David's son Solomon takes over the throne, and boy(!) what a throne he made of it. King Solomon was like a superstar in Israel. He was as rich as a rock star, as glamorous as a movie star, and as smart as a Wall Street millionaire. He could wheel and deal and network and schmooze with the best.

The last half of First Kings tells the other side of the story. After Solomon's reign, the kingdom started falling to pieces. What was a united kingdom became two separate kingdoms with their own kings and their own *big* mistakes.

Purpose   It is especially important for leaders to be fully committed to the Lord.

Theme   Lessons from the Dividing of the United Kingdom

Date of writing   590–570 B.C.

Bible Talk

King Solomon's reign of riches
Israel never enjoyed as much wealth or prestige as when King Solomon ruled. They also had to work way too hard to keep the riches flowing.

There was another problem as well. Solomon forgot where his wisdom and riches came from. He became disillusioned with "having it all" and failed to keep God in first place in his life. He even worshiped false gods before his life was over. (He wrote Ecclesiastes, a book of the Bible, about this very thing.) His country suffered for it. He is still known throughout the world as the person who had it all and found out that, without God, it's not good enough.

FALSE GODS AND IDOLS

The big problem with the Hebrews was always idolatry. In those days, there were temples to a lot of different gods. When the Hebrews moved back into their land (read about this in the Book of Joshua), they didn't do something that God had asked. They didn't get rid of everyone else that lived there. Instead they just moved in beside the people, their temples, and their idols.

So you can guess what happened. Slowly the Hebrews got to know these people. Eventually these people would invite their new Hebrew friends to "church" with them. Finally the Hebrews would start worshiping these fake-god-nothings.

To put it lightly, this was unacceptable to the one true God.

ADONIJAH PRESUMES TO BE KING

[1]Now King David was old, advanced in years; and they put covers on him, but he could not get warm. [2]Therefore his servants said to him, "Let a young woman, a virgin, be sought for our lord the king, and let her stand before the king, and let her care for him; and let her lie in your bosom, that our lord the king may be warm." [3]So they sought for a lovely young woman throughout all the territory of Israel, and found Abishag the Shunammite, and brought her to the king. [4]The young woman *was* very lovely; and she cared for the king, and served him; but the king did not know her.

[5]Then Adonijah the son of Haggith exalted himself, saying, "I will be king"; and he prepared for himself chariots and horsemen, and fifty men to run before him. [6](And his father had not rebuked him at any time by saying, "Why have you done so?" He *was* also very good-looking. *His mother* had borne him after Absalom.) [7]Then he conferred with Joab the son of Zeruiah and with Abiathar the priest, and they followed and helped Adonijah. [8]But Zadok the priest, Benaiah the son of Jehoiada, Nathan the prophet, Shimei, Rei, and the mighty men who *belonged* to David were not with Adonijah.

[9]And Adonijah sacrificed sheep and oxen and fattened cattle by the stone of Zoheleth, which *is* by En Rogel; he also invited all his brothers, the king's sons, and all the men of Judah, the king's servants. [10]But he did not invite Nathan the prophet, Benaiah, the mighty men, or Solomon his brother.

[11]So Nathan spoke to Bathsheba the mother of Solomon, saying, "Have you not heard that Adonijah the son of Haggith has become king, and David our lord does not know *it*? [12]Come, please, let me now give you advice, that you may save your own life and the life of your son Solomon. [13]Go immediately to King David and say to him, 'Did you not, my lord, O king, swear to your maidservant, saying, "Assuredly your son Solomon shall reign after me, and he shall sit on my throne"? Why then has Adonijah become king?' [14]Then, while you are still talking there with the king, I also will come in after you and confirm your words."

[15]So Bathsheba went into the chamber to the king. (Now the king was very old, and Abishag the Shunammite was serving the king.) [16]And Bathsheba bowed and did homage to the king. Then the king said, "What is your wish?"

[17]Then she said to him, "My lord, you swore by the LORD your God to your maidservant, *saying*, 'Assuredly Solomon your son shall reign after me, and he shall sit on my throne.' [18]So now, look! Adonijah has become king; and now, my lord the king, you do not know about *it*. [19]He has sacrificed oxen and fattened cattle and sheep in abundance, and has invited all the sons of the king, Abiathar the priest, and Joab the commander of the army; but Solomon your servant he has not invited. [20]And as for you, my lord, O king, the eyes of all Israel *are* on you, that you should tell them who will sit on the throne of my lord the king after him. [21]Otherwise it will happen, when my lord the king rests with his fathers, that I and my son Solomon will be counted as offenders."

[22]And just then, while she was still talking with the king, Nathan the prophet also came in. [23]So they told the king, saying, "Here is Nathan the prophet." And when he came in before the king, he bowed down before the king with his face to the ground. [24]And Nathan said, "My lord, O king, have you said, 'Adonijah shall reign after me, and he shall sit on my throne'? [25]For he has gone down today, and has sacrificed oxen and fattened cattle and sheep in abundance, and has invited all the king's sons, and the commanders of the army, and Abiathar the priest; and look! They are eating and drinking before him; and they say, 'Long live King Adonijah!' [26]But he has not invited me—me your servant—nor Zadok the priest, nor Benaiah the son of Jehoiada, nor your servant Solomon. [27]Has this thing been done by my lord the king, and you have not told your servant who should sit on the throne of my lord the king after him?"

DAVID PROCLAIMS SOLOMON KING

[28]Then King David answered and said, "Call Bathsheba to me." So she came into the king's presence and stood before the king. [29]And the king took an oath and said, "*As* the LORD lives, who has redeemed my life from every distress, [30]just as I swore to you by the LORD God of Israel, saying, 'Assuredly Solomon your son shall be king after me, and he shall sit on my throne in my place,' so I certainly will do this day."

[31]Then Bathsheba bowed with *her* face to the earth, and paid homage to the king, and said, "Let my lord King David live forever!"

[32]And King David said, "Call to me Zadok the priest, Nathan the prophet, and Benaiah the son of Jehoiada." So they came before the king. [33]The king also said to them, "Take with you the servants of your lord, and have Solomon my son ride on my own mule, and take him down to Gihon. [34]There let Zadok the priest and Nathan the prophet anoint him king over Israel; and blow the horn, and say, 'Long live King

Solomon!" ³⁵Then you shall come up after him, and he shall come and sit on my throne, and he shall be king in my place. For I have appointed him to be ruler over Israel and Judah."

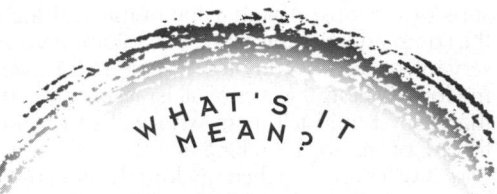

WHAT'S IT MEAN?

Gihon, which is located west of Jerusalem, still supplies water to the city today. The site had a great deal of significance to David and his family. David's soldiers had used a water shaft leading from the springs to sneak into the city and defeat the Jebusites. Years later, Gihon was the place David's son, Solomon, was declared king. Some Bible experts believe that later kings continued the tradition Solomon started by drinking from the spring during their coronation ceremonies.

1 Kings 1:33

³⁶Benaiah the son of Jehoiada answered the king and said, "Amen! May the LORD God of my lord the king say so too. ³⁷As the LORD has been with my lord the king, even so may He be with Solomon, and make his throne greater than the throne of my lord King David."

³⁸So Zadok the priest, Nathan the prophet, Benaiah the son of Jehoiada, the Cherethites, and the Pelethites went down and had Solomon ride on King David's mule, and took him to Gihon. ³⁹Then Zadok the priest took a horn of oil from the tabernacle and anointed Solomon. And they blew the horn, and all the people said, "Long live King Solomon!" ⁴⁰And all the people went up after him; and the people played the flutes and rejoiced with great joy, so that the earth *seemed to* split with their sound.

⁴¹Now Adonijah and all the guests who *were* with him heard *it* as they finished eating. And when Joab heard the sound of the horn, he said, "Why *is* the city in such a noisy uproar?" ⁴²While he was still speaking, there came Jonathan, the son of Abiathar the priest. And Adonijah said to him, "Come in, for you *are* a prominent man, and bring good news."

⁴³Then Jonathan answered and said to Adonijah, "No! Our lord King David has made Solomon king. ⁴⁴The king has sent with him Zadok the priest, Nathan the prophet, Benaiah the son of Jehoiada, the Cherethites, and the Pelethites; and they have made him ride on the king's mule. ⁴⁵So Zadok the priest and Nathan the

prophet have anointed him king at Gihon; and they have gone up from there rejoicing, so that the city is in an uproar. This *is* the noise that you have heard. ⁴⁶Also Solomon sits on the throne of the kingdom. ⁴⁷And moreover the king's servants have gone to bless our lord King David, saying, 'May God make the name of Solomon better than your name, and may He make his throne greater than your throne.' Then the king bowed himself on the bed. ⁴⁸Also the king said thus, 'Blessed *be* the LORD God of Israel, who has given *one* to sit on my throne this day, while my eyes see *it!*' "

⁴⁹So all the guests who were with Adonijah were afraid, and arose, and each one went his way.

⁵⁰Now Adonijah was afraid of Solomon; so he arose, and went and took hold of the horns of the altar. ⁵¹And it was told Solomon, saying, "Indeed Adonijah is afraid of King Solomon; for look, he has taken hold of the horns of the altar, saying, 'Let King Solomon swear to me today that he will not put his servant to death with the sword.' "

⁵²Then Solomon said, "If he proves himself a worthy man, not one hair of him shall fall to the earth; but if wickedness is found in him, he shall die." ⁵³So King Solomon sent them to bring him down from the altar. And he came and fell down before King Solomon; and Solomon said to him, "Go to your house."

DAVID'S INSTRUCTIONS TO SOLOMON

¹Now the days of David drew near that he should die, and he charged Solomon his son, saying: ²"I go the way of all the earth; be strong, therefore, and prove yourself a man. ³And keep the charge of the LORD your God: to walk in His ways, to keep His statutes, His commandments,

WHAT'S IT MEAN?

It didn't matter to Joab that Abner had killed his brother in self-defense. Joab wanted vengeance, so he murdered Abner in cold blood. Years later, Joab continued his murderous ways by killing Amasa, the man David had chosen to replace Joab as commander of the royal army.

1 Kings 2:5

His judgments, and His testimonies, as it is written in the Law of Moses, that you may prosper in all that you do and wherever you turn; [4]that the LORD may fulfill His word which He spoke concerning me, saying, 'If your sons take heed to their way, to walk before Me in truth with all their heart and with all their soul,' He said, 'you shall not lack a man on the throne of Israel.'

[5]"Moreover you know also what Joab the son of Zeruiah did to me, *and* what he did to the two commanders of the armies of Israel, to Abner the son of Ner and Amasa the son of Jether, whom he killed. And he shed the blood of war in peacetime, and put the blood of war on his belt that *was* around his waist, and on his sandals that *were* on his feet. [6]Therefore do according to your wisdom, and do not let his gray hair go down to the grave in peace.

[7]"But show kindness to the sons of Barzillai the Gileadite, and let them be among those who eat at your table, for so they came to me when I fled from Absalom your brother.

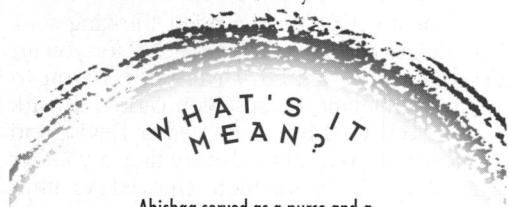

KINDNESS

What should we do to those who have been kind to us? (2:7)

[8]"And see, *you have* with you Shimei the son of Gera, a Benjamite from Bahurim, who cursed me with a malicious curse in the day when I went to Mahanaim. But he came down to meet me at the Jordan, and I swore to him by the LORD, saying, 'I will not put you to death with the sword.' [9]Now therefore, do not hold him guiltless, for you *are* a wise man and know what you ought to do to him; but bring his gray hair down to the grave with blood."

DEATH OF DAVID

[10]So David rested with his fathers, and was buried in the City of David. [11]The period that David reigned over Israel *was* forty years; seven years he reigned in Hebron, and in Jerusalem he reigned thirty-three years. [12]Then Solomon sat on the throne of his father David; and his kingdom was firmly established.

SOLOMON EXECUTES ADONIJAH

[13]Now Adonijah the son of Haggith came to Bathsheba the mother of Solomon. So she said, "Do you come peaceably?"

And he said, "Peaceably." [14]Moreover he said, "I have something *to say* to you."

And she said, "Say it."

[15]Then he said, "You know that the kingdom was mine, and all Israel had set their expectations on me, that I should reign. However, the kingdom has been turned over, and has become my brother's; for it was his from the LORD. [16]Now I ask one petition of you; do not deny me."

And she said to him, "Say it."

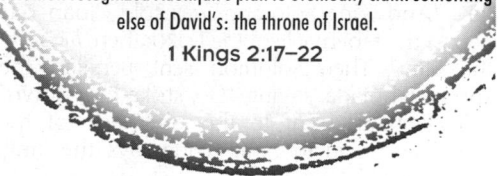

WHAT'S IT MEAN?

Abishag served as a nurse and a companion to David in his old age. Part of her responsibility was to help David stay warm at night. She slept with David, but did not have a physical relationship with him. Even so, she was considered to be one of David's concubines. Adonijah's request to marry Abishag was a way of claiming what had been David's. Solomon recognized Adonijah's plan to eventually claim something else of David's: the throne of Israel.

1 Kings 2:17–22

[17]Then he said, "Please speak to King Solomon, for he will not refuse you, that he may give me Abishag the Shunammite as wife."

[18]So Bathsheba said, "Very well, I will speak for you to the king."

[19]Bathsheba therefore went to King Solomon, to speak to him for Adonijah. And the king rose up to meet her and bowed down to her, and sat down on his throne and had a throne set for the king's mother; so she sat at his right hand. [20]Then she said, "I desire one small petition of you; do not refuse me."

And the king said to her, "Ask it, my mother, for I will not refuse you."

[21]So she said, "Let Abishag the Shunammite be given to Adonijah your brother as wife."

[22]And King Solomon answered and said to his mother, "Now why do you ask Abishag the Shunammite for Adonijah? Ask for him the kingdom also—for he *is* my older brother—for him, and for Abiathar the priest, and for Joab the son of Zeruiah." [23]Then King Solomon swore by the LORD, saying, "May God do so to me, and more also, if Adonijah has not spoken this word against his own life! [24]Now therefore, *as* the LORD lives, who has confirmed me and set me on the throne of David my father, and who has established a house[a] for me, as He promised, Adonijah shall be put to death today!"

2:24 [a]That is, a royal dynasty

²⁵So King Solomon sent by the hand of Benaiah the son of Jehoiada; and he struck him down, and he died.

ABIATHAR EXILED, JOAB EXECUTED

²⁶And to Abiathar the priest the king said, "Go to Anathoth, to your own fields, for you *are* deserving of death; but I will not put you to death at this time, because you carried the ark of the Lord GOD before my father David, and because you were afflicted every time my father was afflicted." ²⁷So Solomon removed Abiathar from being priest to the LORD, that he might fulfill the word of the LORD which He spoke concerning the house of Eli at Shiloh.

²⁸Then news came to Joab, for Joab had defected to Adonijah, though he had not defected to Absalom. So Joab fled to the tabernacle of the LORD, and took hold of the horns of the altar. ²⁹And King Solomon was told, "Joab has fled to the tabernacle of the LORD; there *he is*, by the altar." Then Solomon sent Benaiah the son of Jehoiada, saying, "Go, strike him down."
³⁰So Benaiah went to the tabernacle of the LORD, and said to him, "Thus says the king, 'Come out!' "

And he said, "No, but I will die here." And Benaiah brought back word to the king, saying, "Thus said Joab, and thus he answered me."

³¹Then the king said to him, "Do as he has said, and strike him down and bury him, that you may take away from me and from the house of my father the innocent blood which Joab shed. ³²So the LORD will return his blood on his head, because he struck down two men more righteous and better than he, and killed them with the sword— Abner the son of Ner, the commander of the army of Israel, and Amasa the son of Jether, the commander of the army of Judah—though my father David did not know *it*. ³³Their blood shall therefore return upon the head of Joab and upon the head of his descendants forever. But upon David and his descendants, upon his house and his throne, there shall be peace forever from the LORD."

³⁴So Benaiah the son of Jehoiada went up and struck and killed him; and he was buried in his own house in the wilderness. ³⁵The king put Benaiah the son of Jehoiada in his place over the army, and the king put Zadok the priest in the place of Abiathar.

SHIMEI EXECUTED

³⁶Then the king sent and called for Shimei, and said to him, "Build yourself a house in Jerusalem and dwell there, and do not go out from there anywhere. ³⁷For it shall be, on the day you go out and cross the Brook Kidron, know for certain you shall surely die; your blood shall be on your own head."

³⁸And Shimei said to the king, "The saying *is* good. As my lord the king has said, so your servant will do." So Shimei dwelt in Jerusalem many days.

³⁹Now it happened at the end of three years, that two slaves of Shimei ran away to Achish the son of Maachah, king of Gath. And they told Shimei, saying, "Look, your slaves *are* in Gath!" ⁴⁰So Shimei arose, saddled his donkey, and went to Achish at Gath to seek his slaves. And Shimei went and brought his slaves from Gath. ⁴¹And Solomon was told that Shimei had gone from Jerusalem to Gath and had come back. ⁴²Then the king sent and called for Shimei, and said to him, "Did I not make you swear by the LORD, and warn you, saying, 'Know for certain that on the day you go out and travel anywhere, you shall surely die'? And you said to me, 'The word I have heard *is* good.' ⁴³Why then have you not kept the oath of the LORD and the commandment that I gave you?" ⁴⁴The king said moreover to Shimei, "You know, as your heart acknowledges, all the wickedness that you did to my father David; therefore the LORD will return your wickedness on your own head. ⁴⁵But King Solomon *shall be* blessed, and the throne of David shall be established before the LORD forever."

⁴⁶So the king commanded Benaiah the son of Jehoiada; and he went out and struck him down, and he died. Thus the kingdom was established in the hand of Solomon.

SOLOMON REQUESTS WISDOM

¹Now Solomon made a treaty with Pharaoh king of Egypt, and married Pharaoh's daughter; then he brought her to the City of David until he had finished building his own house, and the house of the LORD, and the wall all around Jerusalem. ²Meanwhile the people sacrificed at the high places, because there was no house built for the

> "But upon David and his descendants, upon his house and his throne, there shall be peace forever from the LORD."
> (1 Kings 2:33b)

MARRIAGE
How can a spouse be a bad influence?
(3:1–3)

name of the LORD until those days. ³And Solomon loved the LORD, walking in the statutes of his father David, except that he sacrificed and burned incense at the high places.

⁴Now the king went to Gibeon to sacrifice there, for that *was* the great high place: Solomon offered a thousand burnt offerings on that altar. ⁵At Gibeon the LORD appeared to Solomon in a dream by night; and God said, "Ask! What shall I give you?"

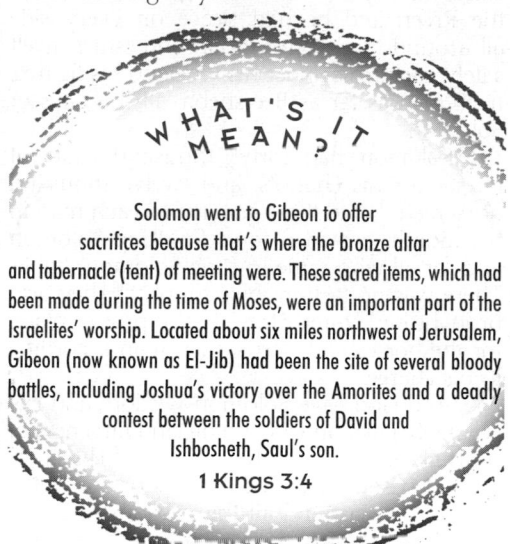

WHAT'S IT MEAN?

Solomon went to Gibeon to offer sacrifices because that's where the bronze altar and tabernacle (tent) of meeting were. These sacred items, which had been made during the time of Moses, were an important part of the Israelites' worship. Located about six miles northwest of Jerusalem, Gibeon (now known as El-Jib) had been the site of several bloody battles, including Joshua's victory over the Amorites and a deadly contest between the soldiers of David and Ishbosheth, Saul's son.

1 Kings 3:4

⁶And Solomon said: "You have shown great mercy to Your servant David my father, because he walked before You in truth, in righteousness, and in uprightness of heart with You; You have continued this great kindness for him, and You have given him a son to sit on his throne, as *it is* this day. ⁷Now, O LORD my God, You have made Your servant king instead of my father David, but I *am* a little child; I do not know *how* to go out or come in. ⁸And Your servant *is* in the midst of Your people whom You have chosen, a great people, too numerous to be numbered or counted. ⁹Therefore give to Your servant an understanding heart to judge Your people, that I may discern between good and evil. For who is able to judge this great people of Yours?"

¹⁰The speech pleased the LORD, that Solomon had asked this thing. ¹¹Then God said to him: "Because you have asked this thing, and have not asked long life for yourself, nor have asked riches for yourself, nor have asked the life of your enemies, but have asked for yourself understanding to discern justice, ¹²behold, I have done according to your words; see, I have given you a wise and understanding heart, so

that there has not been anyone like you before you, nor shall any like you arise after you. ¹³And I have also given you what you have not asked: both riches and honor, so that there shall not be anyone like you among the kings all your days. ¹⁴So if you walk in My ways, to keep My statutes and My commandments, as your father David walked, then I will lengthen your days."

¹⁵Then Solomon awoke; and indeed it had been a dream. And he came to Jerusalem and stood before the ark of the covenant of the LORD, offered up burnt offerings, offered peace offerings, and made a feast for all his servants.

SOLOMON'S WISE JUDGMENT

¹⁶Now two women *who were* harlots came to the king, and stood before him. ¹⁷And one woman said, "O my lord, this woman and I dwell in the same house; and I gave birth while she *was* in the house. ¹⁸Then it happened, the third day after I had given birth, that this woman also gave birth. And we *were* together; no one *was* with us in the house, except the two of us in the house. ¹⁹And this woman's son died in the night, because she lay on him. ²⁰So she arose in the middle of the night and took my son from my side, while your maidservant slept, and laid him in her bosom, and laid her dead child in my bosom. ²¹And when I rose in the morning to nurse my son, there he was, dead. But when I had examined him in the morning, indeed, he was not my son whom I had borne."

²²Then the other woman said, "No! But the living one *is* my son, and the dead one *is* your son."

And the first woman said, "No! But the dead one *is* your son, and the living one *is* my son."

Thus they spoke before the king.

²³And the king said, "The one says, 'This *is* my son, who lives, and your son *is* the dead one'; and the other says, 'No! But your son *is* the dead one, and my son *is* the living one.' " ²⁴Then the king said, "Bring me a sword." So they brought a sword before the king. ²⁵And the king said, "Divide the living child in two, and give half to one, and half to the other."

²⁶Then the woman whose son *was* living spoke to the king, for she yearned with compassion for her son; and she said, "O my lord, give her the living child, and by no means kill him!"

But the other said, "Let him be neither mine nor yours, *but* divide *him*."

²⁷So the king answered and said, "Give the first woman the living child, and by no means kill him; she *is* his mother."

²⁸And all Israel heard of the judgment which the king had rendered; and they feared the king, for they saw that the wisdom of God *was* in him to administer justice.

SOLOMON'S ADMINISTRATION

¹So King Solomon was king over all Israel. ²And these *were* his officials: Azariah the son of Zadok, the priest; ³Elihoreph and Ahijah, the sons of Shisha, scribes; Jehoshaphat the son of Ahilud, the recorder; ⁴Benaiah the son of Jehoiada, over the army; Zadok and Abiathar, the priests; ⁵Azariah the son of Nathan, over the officers; Zabud the son of Nathan, a priest *and* the king's friend; ⁶Ahishar, over the household; and Adoniram the son of Abda, over the labor force.

⁷And Solomon had twelve governors over all Israel, who provided food for the king and his household; each one made provision for one month of the year. ⁸These *are* their names: Ben-Hur,ᵃ in the mountains of Ephraim; ⁹Ben-Deker,ᵃ in Makaz, Shaalbim, Beth Shemesh, and Elon Beth Hanan; ¹⁰Ben-Hesed,ᵃ in Arubboth; to him *belonged* Sochoh and all the land of Hepher; ¹¹Ben-Abinadab,ᵃ *in* all the regions of Dor; he had Taphath the daughter of Solomon as wife; ¹²Baana the son of Ahilud, *in* Taanach, Megiddo, and all Beth Shean, which *is* beside Zaretan below Jezreel, from Beth Shean to Abel Meholah, as far as the other side of Jokneam; ¹³Ben-Geber,ᵃ in Ramoth Gilead; to him *belonged* the towns of Jair the son of Manasseh, in Gilead; to him *also belonged* the region of Argob in Bashan—sixty large cities with walls and bronze gate-bars; ¹⁴Ahinadab the son of Iddo, *in* Mahanaim; ¹⁵Ahimaaz, in Naphtali; he also took Basemath the daughter of Solomon as wife; ¹⁶Baanah the son of Hushai, in Asher and Aloth; ¹⁷Jehoshaphat the son of Paruah, in Issachar; ¹⁸Shimei the son of Elah, in Benjamin; ¹⁹Geber the son of Uri, in the land of Gilead, *in* the country of Sihon king of the Amorites, and of Og king of Bashan. *He was* the only governor who *was* in the land.

PROSPERITY AND WISDOM OF SOLOMON'S REIGN

²⁰Judah and Israel *were* as numerous as the sand by the sea in multitude, eating and drinking and rejoicing. ²¹So Solomon reigned over all kingdoms from the Riverᵃ *to* the land of the Philistines, as far as the border of Egypt. *They* brought tribute and served Solomon all the days of his life.

²²Now Solomon's provision for one day was thirty kors of fine flour, sixty kors of meal, ²³ten fatted oxen, twenty oxen from the pastures, and one hundred sheep, besides deer, gazelles, roebucks, and fatted fowl.

²⁴For he had dominion over all *the region* on this side of the Riverᵃ from Tiphsah even to Gaza, namely over all the kings on this side of the River; and he had peace on every side all around him. ²⁵And Judah and Israel dwelt safely, each man under his vine and his fig tree, from Dan as far as Beersheba, all the days of Solomon.

²⁶Solomon had fortyᵃ thousand stalls of horses for his chariots, and twelve thousand horsemen. ²⁷And these governors, each man in his month, provided food for King Solomon and for all who came to King Solomon's table. There was no lack in their supply. ²⁸They also brought barley and straw to the proper place, for the horses and steeds, each man according to his charge.

²⁹And God gave Solomon wisdom and exceedingly great understanding, and largeness of heart like the sand on the seashore. ³⁰Thus Solomon's wisdom excelled the wisdom of all the men of the East and all the wisdom of Egypt. ³¹For he was wiser than all men—than Ethan the Ezrahite, and Heman, Chalcol, and Darda, the sons of Mahol; and his fame was in all the surrounding nations. ³²He spoke three thousand proverbs, and his songs were one thousand and five. ³³Also he spoke of trees, from the cedar tree of Lebanon even to the hyssop that springs out of the wall; he spoke also of animals, of birds, of creeping things, and of fish. ³⁴And men of all nations, from all the kings of the earth who had heard of his wisdom, came to hear the wisdom of Solomon.

SOLOMON PREPARES TO BUILD THE TEMPLE

¹Now Hiram king of Tyre sent his servants to Solomon, because he heard that they had anointed him king in place of his father, for Hiram had always loved David. ²Then Solomon sent to Hiram, saying:

³   You know how my father David could not build a house for the name of the LORD his God because of the wars which

---

4:8 ᵃLiterally *Son of Hur* **4:9** ᵃLiterally *Son of Deker* **4:10** ᵃLiterally *Son of Hesed* **4:11** ᵃLiterally *Son of Abinadab* **4:13** ᵃLiterally *Son of Geber* **4:21** ᵃThat is, the Euphrates **4:24** ᵃThat is, the Euphrates **4:26** ᵃFollowing Masoretic Text and most other authorities; some manuscripts of the Septuagint read *four* (compare 2 Chronicles 9:25).

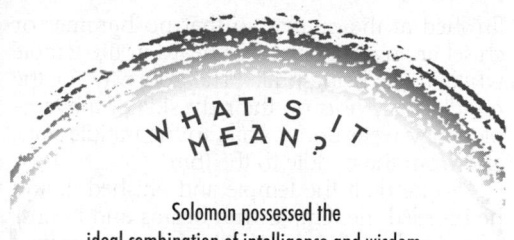

were fought against him on every side, until the LORD put *his foes*[a] under the soles of his feet.

4 But now the LORD my God has given me rest on every side; *there is* neither adversary nor evil occurrence.

5 And behold, I propose to build a house for the name of the LORD my God, as the LORD spoke to my father David, saying, "Your son, whom I will set on your throne in your place, he shall build the house for My name."

6 Now therefore, command that they cut down cedars for me from Lebanon; and my servants will be with your servants, and I will pay you wages for your servants according to whatever you say. For you know *there is* none among us who has skill to cut timber like the Sidonians.

7 So it was, when Hiram heard the words of Solomon, that he rejoiced greatly and said,

Blessed *be* the LORD this day, for He has given David a wise son over this great people!

8 Then Hiram sent to Solomon, saying:

I have considered *the message* which you sent me, *and* I will do all you desire concerning the cedar and cypress logs.

9 My servants shall bring *them* down from Lebanon to the sea; I will float them in rafts by sea to the place you indicate to me, and will have them broken apart there; then you can take *them* away. And you shall fulfill my desire by giving food for my houschold.

10 Then Hiram gave Solomon cedar and cypress logs *according to* all his desire. 11 And Solomon gave Hiram twenty thousand kors of wheat *as* food for his household, and twenty[a] kors of pressed oil. Thus Solomon gave to Hiram year by year.

12 So the LORD gave Solomon wisdom, as He had promised him; and there was peace between Hiram and Solomon, and the two of them made a treaty together.

13 Then King Solomon raised up a labor force out of all Israel; and the labor force was thirty thousand men. 14 And he sent them to Lebanon, ten thousand a month in shifts: they were one month in Lebanon *and* two months at home; Adoniram *was* in charge of the labor force. 15 Solomon had seventy thousand who carried burdens, and eighty thousand who quarried *stone* in the mountains, 16 besides three thousand three hundred[a] from the chiefs of Solomon's deputies, who supervised the people who labored in the work. 17 And the king commanded them to quarry large stones, costly stones, *and* hewn stones, to lay the foundation of the temple.[a] 18 So Solomon's builders, Hiram's builders, and the Gebalites quarried *them;* and they prepared timber and stones to build the temple.

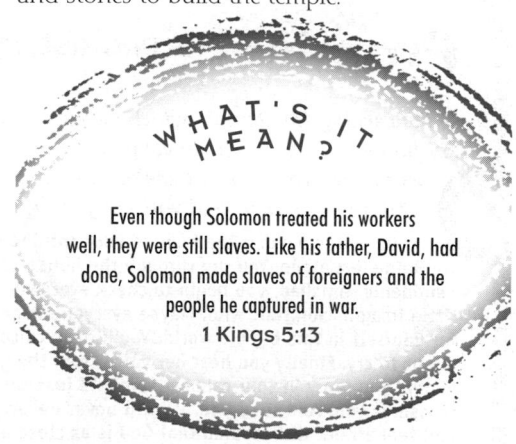

5:3 [a]Literally *them*　**5:11** [a]Following Masoretic Text, Targum, and Vulgate; Septuagint and Syriac read *twenty thousand.*　**5:16** [a]Following Masoretic Text, Targum, and Vulgate; Septuagint reads *three thousand six hundred.*　**5:17** [a]Literally *house,* and so frequently throughout this book

SOLOMON BUILDS THE TEMPLE

[1]And it came to pass in the four hundred and eightieth[a] year after the children of Israel had come out of the land of Egypt, in the fourth year of Solomon's reign over Israel, in the month of Ziv, which is the second month, that he began to build the house of the LORD. [2]Now the house which King Solomon built for the LORD, its length was sixty cubits, its width twenty, and its height thirty cubits. [3]The vestibule in front of the sanctuary[a] of the house was twenty cubits long across the width of the house, and the width of the vestibule[b] extended ten cubits from the front of the house. [4]And he made for the house windows with beveled frames.

[5]Against the wall of the temple he built chambers all around, against the walls of the temple, all around the sanctuary and the inner sanctuary.[a] Thus he made side chambers all around it. [6]The lowest chamber was five cubits wide, the middle was six cubits wide, and the third was seven cubits wide; for he made narrow ledges around the outside of the temple, so that the support beams would not be fastened into the walls of the temple. [7]And the temple, when it was being built, was built with stone finished at the quarry, so that no hammer or chisel or any iron tool was heard in the temple while it was being built. [8]The doorway for the middle story[a] was on the right side of the temple. They went up by stairs to the middle story, and from the middle to the third.

[9]So he built the temple and finished it, and he paneled the temple with beams and boards of cedar. [10]And he built side chambers against the entire temple, each five cubits high; they were attached to the temple with cedar beams.

[11]Then the word of the LORD came to Solomon, saying: [12]"Concerning this temple which you are building, if you walk in My statutes, execute My judgments, keep all My commandments, and walk in them, then I will perform My word with you, which I spoke to your father David. [13]And I will dwell among the children of Israel, and will not forsake My people Israel."

[14]So Solomon built the temple and finished it. [15]And he built the inside walls of the temple with cedar boards; from the floor of the temple to the ceiling he paneled the inside with wood; and he covered the floor of the temple with planks of cypress. [16]Then he built the twenty-cubit room at the rear of the temple, from floor

---

6:1 [a]Following Masoretic Text, Targum, and Vulgate; Septuagint reads fortieth. **6:3** [a]Hebrew heykal; here the main room of the temple, elsewhere called the holy place (compare Exodus 26:33 and Ezekiel 41:1) [b]Literally it **6:5** [a]Hebrew debir; here the inner room of the temple, elsewhere called the Most Holy Place (compare verse 16) **6:8** [a]Following Masoretic Text and Vulgate; Septuagint reads upper story; Targum reads ground story.

Promise   HE PROMISES TO NEVER FORSAKE YOU.

Concerning this temple which you are building, if you walk in My statutes, execute My judgments, keep all My commandments, and walk in them, then I will perform My word with you, which I spoke to your father David. And I will dwell among the children of Israel, and will not forsake My people Israel (1 Kin. 6:12, 13).

Do you remember the fears of your childhood? Monsters in the closet. Thunder in the night. Being left alone. You run through the house screaming, "Mommmmm!" Fearing that she has suddenly vanished, you begin to check everywhere, look in every room. Your heart is racing as your little imagination runs wild. Maybe everyone is gone. You've been deserted. You'll have to fend for yourself in this big old world. You'll have to cook and clean and earn money. Oh no. You're about to cry. Finally you hear her voice from the garage, "What is it, honey?" "Nothing, Mom," you reply in your calmest voice. "I just couldn't find you." "Well, I'm right here," she reassures you. And so is God. He will never desert you or leave you. Even when you're an adult and feel afraid, rest assured that God is as close as the air you breathe.

SEE FOR YOURSELF:
Ex. 33:14; Deut. 31:8; Ps. 37:28; Ezek. 11:16

to ceiling, with cedar boards; he built it inside as the inner sanctuary, as the Most Holy *Place*. [17]And in front of it the temple sanctuary was forty cubits *long*. [18]The inside of the temple was cedar, carved with ornamental buds and open flowers. All *was* cedar; there was no stone *to be* seen.

[19]And he prepared the inner sanctuary inside the temple, to set the ark of the covenant of the LORD there. [20]The inner sanctuary *was* twenty cubits long, twenty cubits wide, and twenty cubits high. He overlaid it with pure gold, and overlaid the altar of cedar. [21]So Solomon overlaid the inside of the temple with pure gold. He stretched gold chains across the front of the inner sanctuary, and overlaid it with gold. [22]The whole temple he overlaid with gold, until he had finished all the temple; also he overlaid with gold the entire altar that *was* by the inner sanctuary.

[23]Inside the inner sanctuary he made two cherubim *of* olive wood, *each* ten cubits high. [24]One wing of the cherub *was* five cubits, and the other wing of the cherub five cubits: ten cubits from the tip of one wing to the tip of the other. [25]And the other cherub *was* ten cubits; both cherubim *were* of the same size and shape. [26]The height of one cherub *was* ten cubits, and so *was* the other cherub. [27]Then he set the cherubim inside the inner room;[a] and they stretched out the wings of the cherubim so that the wing of the one touched *one* wall, and the wing of the

other cherub touched the other wall. And their wings touched each other in the middle of the room. [28]Also he overlaid the cherubim with gold.

[29]Then he carved all the walls of the temple all around, both the inner and outer *sanctuaries*, with carved figures of cherubim, palm trees, and open flowers. [30]And the floor of the temple he overlaid with gold, both the inner and outer *sanctuaries*.

[31]For the entrance of the inner sanctuary he made doors *of* olive wood; the lintel *and* doorposts *were* one-fifth *of the wall*. [32]The two doors *were of* olive wood; and he carved on them figures of cherubim, palm trees, and open flowers, and overlaid *them* with gold; and he spread gold on the cherubim and on the palm trees. [33]So for the door of the sanctuary he also made doorposts *of* olive wood, one-fourth *of the wall*. [34]And the two doors *were of* cypress wood; two panels *comprised* one folding door, and two panels *comprised* the other folding door. [35]Then he carved cherubim, palm trees, and open flowers *on them*, and overlaid *them* with gold applied evenly on the carved work.

[36]And he built the inner court with three rows of hewn stone and a row of cedar beams.

[37]In the fourth year the foundation of the house of the LORD was laid, in the month of Ziv. [38]And in the eleventh year, in the month of Bul, which is

"And he prepared the inner sanctuary inside the temple, to set the ark of the covenant of the LORD there." (1 Kings 6:19)

6:27 [a]Literally *house*

the eighth month, the house was finished in all its details and according to all its plans. So he was seven years in building it.

SOLOMON'S OTHER BUILDINGS

¹But Solomon took thirteen years to build his own house; so he finished all his house. ²He also built the House of the Forest of Lebanon; its length *was* one hundred cubits, its width fifty cubits, and its height thirty cubits, with four rows of cedar pillars, and cedar beams on the pillars. ³And *it was* paneled with cedar above the beams that *were* on forty-five pillars, fifteen *to* a row. ⁴*There were* windows *with beveled frames in* three rows, and window *was* opposite window *in* three tiers. ⁵And all the doorways and doorposts *had* rectangular frames; and window *was* opposite window *in* three tiers.

⁶He also made the Hall of Pillars: its length *was* fifty cubits, and its width thirty cubits; and in front of them *was* a portico with pillars, and a canopy *was* in front of them.

⁷Then he made a hall for the throne, the Hall of Judgment, where he might judge; and *it was* paneled with cedar from floor to ceiling.[a]

⁸And the house where he dwelt *had* another court inside the hall, of like workmanship. Solomon also made a house like this hall for Pharaoh's daughter, whom he had taken *as wife.*

⁹All these *were of* costly stones cut to size, trimmed with saws, inside and out, from the foundation to the eaves, and also on the outside to the great court. ¹⁰The foundation *was of* costly stones, large stones, some ten cubits and some eight cubits. ¹¹And above *were* costly stones, hewn to size, and cedar wood. ¹²The great court *was* enclosed with three rows of hewn stones and a row of cedar beams. So were the inner court of the house of the LORD and the vestibule of the temple.

HIRAM THE CRAFTSMAN

¹³Now King Solomon sent and brought Huram[a] from Tyre. ¹⁴He *was* the son of a widow from the tribe of Naphtali, and his father *was* a man of Tyre, a bronze worker; he was filled with wisdom and understanding and skill in working with all kinds of bronze work. So he came to King Solomon and did all his work.

THE BRONZE PILLARS FOR THE TEMPLE

¹⁵And he cast two pillars of bronze, each one eighteen cubits high, and a line of twelve cubits measured the circumference of each. ¹⁶Then he made two capitals *of* cast bronze, to set on the tops of the pillars. The height of one capital *was* five cubits, and the height of the other capital *was* five cubits. ¹⁷*He made* a lattice network, with wreaths of chainwork, for the capitals which *were* on top of the pillars: seven chains for one capital and seven for the other capital. ¹⁸So he made the pillars, and two rows of pomegranates above the network all around to cover the capitals that *were* on top; and thus he did for the other capital.

¹⁹The capitals which *were* on top of the pillars in the hall *were* in the shape of lilies, four cubits. ²⁰The capitals on the two pillars also *had* pomegranates above, by the convex surface which *was* next to the network; and there *were* two hundred such pomegranates in rows on each of the capitals all around.

²¹Then he set up the pillars by the vestibule of the temple; he set up the pillar on the right and called its name Jachin, and he set up the pillar on the left and called its name Boaz. ²²The tops of the pillars were in the shape of lilies. So the work of the pillars was finished.

THE SEA AND THE OXEN

²³And he made the Sea of cast bronze, ten cubits from one brim to the other; *it was* completely round. Its height *was* five cubits, and a line of thirty cubits measured its circumference. ²⁴Below its brim *were* ornamental buds encircling it all around, ten to a cubit, all the way around the Sea. The ornamental buds *were* cast in two rows when it was cast. ²⁵It stood on twelve oxen: three looking toward the north, three looking toward the west, three looking toward the south, and three looking toward the east; the Sea *was set* upon them, and all their back parts *pointed* inward. ²⁶It *was* a handbreadth thick; and its brim was shaped like the brim of a cup, *like* a lily blossom. It contained two thousand[a] baths.

THE CARTS AND THE LAVERS

²⁷He also made ten carts of bronze; four cubits *was* the length of each cart, four cubits its width, and three cubits its height. ²⁸And this *was* the design of the carts: They had panels, and the panels *were* between frames; ²⁹on the panels that *were* between the frames *were* lions, oxen, and cherubim. And on the frames *was* a pedestal on top. Below the lions and oxen *were* wreaths of plaited work. ³⁰Every cart had four

---

7:7 [a]Literally *floor*, that is, of the upper level   **7:13** [a]Hebrew *Hiram* (compare 2 Chronicles 2:13, 14)
7:26 [a]Or *three thousand* (compare 2 Chronicles 4:5)

bronze wheels and axles of bronze, and its four feet had supports. Under the laver *were* supports of cast *bronze* beside each wreath. ³¹Its opening inside the crown at the top *was* one cubit in diameter; and the opening *was* round, shaped *like* a pedestal, one and a half cubits in outside diameter; and also on the opening *were* engravings, but the panels were square, not round. ³²Under the panels *were* the four wheels, and the axles of the wheels *were joined* to the cart. The height of a wheel *was* one and a half cubits. ³³The workmanship of the wheels *was* like the workmanship of a chariot wheel; their axle pins, their rims, their spokes, and their hubs *were* all of cast *bronze.* ³⁴And *there were* four supports at the four corners of each cart; its supports *were* part of the cart itself. ³⁵On the top of the cart, at the height of half a cubit, *it was* perfectly round. And on the top of the cart, its flanges and its panels *were* of the same casting. ³⁶On the plates of its flanges and on its panels he engraved cherubim, lions, and palm trees, wherever there was a clear space on each, with wreaths all around. ³⁷Thus he made the ten carts. All of them were of the same mold, one measure, *and* one shape.

³⁸Then he made ten lavers of bronze; each laver contained forty baths, *and* each laver *was* four cubits. On each of the ten carts *was* a laver. ³⁹And he put five carts on the right side of the house, and five on the left side of the house. He set the Sea on the right side of the house, toward the southeast.

FURNISHINGS OF THE TEMPLE

⁴⁰Huram^a made the lavers and the shovels and the bowls. So Huram finished doing all the work that he was to do for King Solomon *for* the house of the LORD: ⁴¹the two pillars, the *two* bowl-shaped capitals that *were* on top of the two pillars; the two networks covering the two bowl-shaped capitals which *were* on top of the pillars; ⁴²four hundred pomegranates for the two networks (two rows of pomegranates for each network, to cover the two bowl-shaped capitals that *were* on top of the pillars); ⁴³the ten carts, and ten lavers on the carts; ⁴⁴one Sea, and twelve oxen under the Sea; ⁴⁵the pots, the shovels, and the bowls.

All these articles which Huram^a made for King Solomon *for* the house of the LORD *were of* burnished bronze. ⁴⁶In the plain of Jordan the king had them cast in clay molds, between Succoth and Zaretan. ⁴⁷And Solomon did not weigh all the articles, because *there were* so many; the weight of the bronze was not determined.

⁴⁸Thus Solomon had all the furnishings made for the house of the LORD: the altar of gold, and the table of gold on which *was* the showbread; ⁴⁹the lampstands of pure gold, five on the right *side* and five on the left in front of the inner sanctuary, with the flowers and the lamps and the wick-trimmers of gold; ⁵⁰the basins, the trimmers, the bowls, the ladles, and the censers of pure gold; and the hinges of gold, *both* for the doors of the inner room (the Most Holy *Place*) *and* for the doors of the main hall of the temple.

⁵¹So all the work that King Solomon had done for the house of the LORD was finished; and Solomon brought in the things which his father David had dedicated: the silver and the gold and the furnishings. He put them in the treasuries of the house of the LORD.

THE ARK BROUGHT INTO THE TEMPLE

¹Now Solomon assembled the elders of Israel and all the heads of the tribes, the chief fathers of the children of Israel, to King Solomon in Jerusalem, that they might bring up the ark of the covenant of the LORD from the City of David, which *is* Zion. ²Therefore all the men of Israel assembled with King Solomon at the feast in the month of Ethanim, which *is* the seventh month. ³So all the elders of Israel came, and the priests took up the ark. ⁴Then they brought up the ark of the LORD, the tabernacle of meeting, and all the holy furnishings that *were* in the tabernacle. The priests and the Levites brought them up. ⁵Also King Solomon, and all the

WHAT'S IT MEAN?

The ark of the covenant and the tabernacle (tent) of meeting had been the centerpieces of Israelite worship since the time of Moses. Solomon didn't want the Israelites to have to choose between worshiping at the tabernacle of meeting or at the new temple, so he had the ark and the tabernacle brought to the temple. The tabernacle may have been set up as a permanent display in the temple.

1 Kings 8:3, 4

congregation of Israel who were assembled with him, *were* with him before the ark, sacrificing sheep and oxen that could not be counted or numbered for multitude. [6]Then the priests brought in the ark of the covenant of the LORD to its place, into the inner sanctuary of the temple, to the Most Holy *Place*, under the wings of the cherubim. [7]For the cherubim spread *their* two wings over the place of the ark, and the cherubim overshadowed the ark and its poles. [8]The poles extended so that the ends of the poles could be seen from the holy *place*, in front of the inner sanctuary; but they could not be seen from outside. And they are there to this day. [9]Nothing *was* in the ark except the two tablets of stone which Moses put there at Horeb, when the LORD made *a covenant* with the children of Israel, when they came out of the land of Egypt.

[10]And it came to pass, when the priests came out of the holy *place*, that the cloud filled the house of the LORD, [11]so that the priests could not continue ministering because of the cloud; for the glory of the LORD filled the house of the LORD.

[12]Then Solomon spoke:

    "The LORD said He would dwell in the
       dark cloud.
[13]   I have surely built You an exalted house,
       And a place for You to dwell in forever."

SOLOMON'S SPEECH AT COMPLETION OF THE WORK

[14]Then the king turned around and blessed the whole assembly of Israel, while all the assembly of Israel was standing. [15]And he said: "Blessed *be* the LORD God of Israel, who spoke with His mouth to my father David, and with His hand has fulfilled *it*, saying, [16]'Since the day that I brought My people Israel out of Egypt, I have chosen no city from any tribe of Israel *in which* to build a house, that My name might be there; but I chose David to be over My people Israel.' [17]Now it was in the heart of my father David to build a temple[a] for the name of the LORD God of Israel. [18]But the LORD said to my father David, 'Whereas it was in your heart to build a temple for My name, you did well that it was in your heart. [19]Nevertheless you shall not build the temple, but your son who will come from your body, he shall build the temple for My name.' [20]So the LORD has fulfilled His word which He spoke; and I have filled the position of my father David, and sit on the throne of Is-

rael, as the LORD promised; and I have built a temple for the name of the LORD God of Israel. [21]And there I have made a place for the ark, in which *is* the covenant of the LORD which He made with our fathers, when He brought them out of the land of Egypt."

SOLOMON'S PRAYER OF DEDICATION

[22]Then Solomon stood before the altar of the LORD in the presence of all the assembly of Israel, and spread out his hands toward heaven; [23]and he said: "LORD God of Israel, *there is* no God in heaven above or on earth below like You, who keep *Your* covenant and mercy with Your servants who walk before You with all their hearts. [24]You have kept what You promised Your servant David my father; You have both spoken with Your mouth and fulfilled *it* with Your hand, as *it is* this day. [25]Therefore, LORD God of Israel, now keep what You promised Your servant David my father, saying, 'You shall not fail to have a man sit before Me on the throne of Israel, only if your sons take heed to their way, that they walk before Me as you have walked before Me.' [26]And now I pray, O God of Israel, let Your word come true, which You have spoken to Your servant David my father.

[27]"But will God indeed dwell on the earth? Behold, heaven and the heaven of heavens cannot contain You. How much less this temple which I have built! [28]Yet regard the prayer of Your servant and his supplication, O LORD my God, and listen to the cry and the prayer which Your servant is praying before You today: [29]that Your eyes may be open toward this temple night and day, toward the place of which You said, 'My name shall be there,' that You may hear the prayer which Your servant makes toward this place. [30]And may You hear the supplication of Your servant and of Your people Israel, when they pray toward this place. Hear in heaven Your dwelling place; and when You hear, forgive.

[31]"When anyone sins against his neighbor, and is forced to take an oath, and comes *and* takes an oath before Your altar in this temple, [32]then hear in heaven, and act, and judge Your servants, condemning the wicked, bringing his way on his head, and justifying the righteous by giving him according to his righteousness.

[33]"When Your people Israel are defeated before an enemy because they have sinned

GOD

Can we fully describe God? (8:27)

8:17 [a]Literally *house*, and so in verses 18–20

against You, and when they turn back to You and confess Your name, and pray and make supplication to You in this temple, [34]then hear in heaven, and forgive the sin of Your people Israel, and bring them back to the land which You gave to their fathers.

[35]"When the heavens are shut up and there is no rain because they have sinned against You, when they pray toward this place and confess Your name, and turn from their sin because You afflict them, [36]then hear in heaven, and forgive the sin of Your servants, Your people Israel, that You may teach them the good way in which they should walk; and send rain on Your land which You have given to Your people as an inheritance.

[37]"When there is famine in the land, pestilence or blight or mildew, locusts or grasshoppers; when their enemy besieges them in the land of their cities; whatever plague or whatever sickness there is; [38]whatever prayer, whatever supplication is made by anyone, or by all Your people Israel, when each one knows the plague of his own heart, and spreads out his hands toward this temple: [39]then hear in heaven Your dwelling place, and forgive, and act, and give to everyone according to all his ways, whose heart You know (for You alone know the hearts of all the sons of men), [40]that they may fear You all the days that they live in the land which You gave to our fathers.

[41]"Moreover, concerning a foreigner, who is not of Your people Israel, but has come from a far country for Your name's sake [42](for they will hear of Your great name and Your strong hand and Your outstretched arm), when he comes and prays toward this temple, [43]hear in heaven Your dwelling place, and do according to all for which the foreigner calls to You, that all peoples of the earth may know Your name and fear You, as do Your people Israel, and that they may know that this temple which I have built is called by Your name.

[44]"When Your people go out to battle against their enemy, wherever You send them, and when they pray to the LORD toward the city which You have chosen and the temple which I have built for Your name, [45]then hear in heaven their prayer and their supplication, and maintain their cause.

[46]"When they sin against You (for there is no one who does not sin), and You become angry with them and deliver them to the enemy, and they take them captive to the land of the enemy, far or near; [47]yet when they come to themselves in the land where they were carried captive, and repent, and make supplication to You in the land of those who took them captive, saying, 'We have sinned and done wrong, we have committed wickedness'; [48]and when they return to You with all their heart and with all their soul in the land of their enemies who led them away captive, and pray to You toward their land which You gave to their fathers, the city which You have chosen and the temple which I have built for Your name: [49]then hear in heaven Your dwelling place their prayer and their supplication, and maintain their cause, [50]and forgive Your people who have sinned against You, and all their transgressions which they have transgressed against You; and grant them compassion before those who took them captive, that they may have compassion on them [51](for they are Your people and Your inheritance, whom You brought out of Egypt, out of the iron furnace), [52]that Your eyes may be open to the supplication of Your servant and the supplication of Your people Israel, to listen to them whenever they call to You. [53]For You separated them from among all the peoples of the earth to be Your inheritance, as You spoke by Your servant Moses, when You brought our fathers out of Egypt, O Lord GOD."

WHAT'S IT MEAN?

Years later, in 586 B.C., the Israelites discovered firsthand that their king knew what he was talking about. Rejecting Solomon's earlier warnings, they turned their backs on God and openly worshiped idols. As punishment, the Lord allowed the Babylonians to invade northern Israel, destroy the temple, and haul the people away as prisoners. For seventy years the people of Israel were held captive in Babylon.

1 Kings 8:46

SOLOMON BLESSES THE ASSEMBLY

[54]And so it was, when Solomon had finished praying all this prayer and supplication to the LORD, that he arose from before the altar of the LORD, from kneeling on his knees with his hands spread up to heaven. [55]Then he stood and blessed all the assembly of Israel with a loud voice, saying: [56]"Blessed be the LORD, who has given rest to His people Israel, according to all that He promised. There has not failed one word of all His good promise, which He

promised through His servant Moses. ⁵⁷May the LORD our God be with us, as He was with our fathers. May He not leave us nor forsake us, ⁵⁸that He may incline our hearts to Himself, to walk in all His ways, and to keep His commandments and His statutes and His judgments, which He commanded our fathers. ⁵⁹And may these words of mine, with which I have made supplication before the LORD, be near the LORD our God day and night, that He may maintain the cause of His servant and the cause of His people Israel, as each day may require, ⁶⁰that all the peoples of the earth may know that the LORD *is* God; *there is* no other. ⁶¹Let your heart therefore be loyal to the LORD our God, to walk in His statutes and keep His commandments, as at this day."

SOLOMON DEDICATES THE TEMPLE

⁶²Then the king and all Israel with him offered sacrifices before the LORD. ⁶³And Solomon offered a sacrifice of peace offerings, which he offered to the LORD, twenty-two thousand bulls and one hundred and twenty thousand sheep. So the king and all the children of Israel dedicated the house of the LORD. ⁶⁴On the same day the king consecrated the middle of the court that *was* in front of the house of the LORD; for there he offered burnt offerings, grain offerings, and the fat of the peace offerings, because the bronze altar that *was* before the LORD *was* too small to receive the burnt offerings, the grain offerings, and the fat of the peace offerings.

⁶⁵At that time Solomon held a feast, and all Israel with him, a great assembly from the entrance of Hamath to the Brook of Egypt, before the LORD our God, seven days and seven *more* days—fourteen days. ⁶⁶On the eighth day he sent the people away; and they blessed the king, and went to their tents joyful and glad of heart for all the good that the LORD had done for His servant David, and for Israel His people.

WORSHIP
What should we do when God is good to us? (8:66)

GOD'S SECOND APPEARANCE TO SOLOMON

¹And it came to pass, when Solomon had finished building the house of the LORD and the king's house, and all Solomon's desire which he wanted to do, ²that the LORD appeared to Solomon the second time, as He had appeared to him at Gibeon. ³And the LORD said to him: "I have heard your prayer and your supplication that you have made before Me; I have conse-

crated this house which you have built to put My name there forever, and My eyes and My heart will be there perpetually. ⁴Now if you walk before Me as your father David walked, in integrity of heart and in uprightness, to do according to all that I have commanded you, *and* if you keep My statutes

PRAYER
Does God hear our prayers? (9:3–5)

and My judgments, ⁵then I will establish the throne of your kingdom over Israel forever, as I promised David your father, saying, 'You shall not fail to have a man on the throne of Israel.' ⁶But if you or your sons at all turn from following Me, and do not keep My commandments *and* My statutes which I have set before you, but go and serve other gods and worship them, ⁷then I will cut off Israel from the land which I have given them; and this house which I have consecrated for My name I will cast out of My sight. Israel will be a proverb and a byword among all peoples. ⁸And *as for* this house, which is exalted, everyone who passes by it will be astonished and will hiss, and say, 'Why has the LORD done thus to this land and to this house?' ⁹Then they will answer, 'Because they forsook the LORD their God, who brought their fathers out of the land of Egypt, and have embraced other gods, and worshiped them and served them; therefore the LORD has brought all this calamity on them.' "

SOLOMON AND HIRAM EXCHANGE GIFTS

¹⁰Now it happened at the end of twenty years, when Solomon had built the two houses, the house of the LORD and the king's house ¹¹(Hiram the king of Tyre had supplied Solomon with cedar and cypress and gold, as much as he desired), *that* King Solomon then gave Hiram twenty cities in the land of Galilee. ¹²Then Hiram went from Tyre to see the cities which Solomon had given him, but they did not please him. ¹³So he said, "What *kind of* cities *are* these which you have given me, my brother?" And he called them the land of Cabul,[a] as they are to this day. ¹⁴Then Hiram sent the king one hundred and twenty talents of gold.

SOLOMON'S ADDITIONAL ACHIEVEMENTS

¹⁵And this *is* the reason for the labor force which King Solomon raised: to build the house of the LORD, his own house, the Millo,[a] the wall of Jerusalem, Hazor, Megiddo, and Gezer. ¹⁶(Pharaoh king of Egypt had gone up and taken Gezer and burned it with fire, had killed

9:13 [a]Literally *Good for Nothing*   **9:15** [a]Literally *The Landfill* the Canaanites who dwelt in the city, and had given it *as* a dowry to his daughter, Solomon's wife.) [17]And Solomon built Gezer, Lower Beth Horon, [18]Baalath, and Tadmor in the wilderness, in the land *of Judah*, [19]all the storage cities that Solomon had, cities for his chariots and cities for his cavalry, and whatever Solomon desired to build in Jerusalem, in Lebanon, and in all the land of his dominion.

[20]All the people *who were* left of the Amorites, Hittites, Perizzites, Hivites, and Jebusites, who *were* not of the children of Israel—[21]that is, their descendants who were left in the land after them, whom the children of Israel had not been able to destroy completely—from these Solomon raised forced labor, as it is to this day. [22]But of the children of Israel Solomon made no forced laborers, because they *were* men of war and his servants: his officers, his captains, commanders of his chariots, and his cavalry.

[23]Others *were* chiefs of the officials who *were* over Solomon's work: five hundred and fifty, who ruled over the people who did the work.

[24]But Pharaoh's daughter came up from the City of David to her house which *Solomon*[a] had built for her. Then he built the Millo.

[25]Now three times a year Solomon offered burnt offerings and peace offerings on the altar which he had built for the LORD, and he burned incense with them *on the altar* that *was* before the LORD. So he finished the temple.

[26]King Solomon also built a fleet of ships at Ezion Geber, which *is* near Elath[a] on the shore of the Red Sea, in the land of Edom. [27]Then Hiram sent his servants with the fleet, seamen who knew the sea, to work with the servants of Solomon. [28]And they went to Ophir, and acquired four hundred and twenty talents of gold from there, and brought *it* to King Solomon.

THE QUEEN OF SHEBA'S PRAISE OF SOLOMON

[1]Now when the queen of Sheba heard of the fame of Solomon concerning the name of the LORD, she came to test him with hard questions. [2]She came to Jerusalem with a very great retinue, with camels that bore spices, very much

WHAT'S IT MEAN?

Sheba was known as an international trading center. When countries needed valuable items, such as perfumes and incense, they turned to Sheba. The queen of Sheba's visit to Solomon was probably part-personal and part-business. On a personal level, she wanted to see if the rumors she had heard about Solomon's wealth were true. On a business level, she probably wanted to add Solomon and Israel to her list of clients.

1 Kings 10:1

gold, and precious stones; and when she came to Solomon, she spoke with him about all that was in her heart. [3]So Solomon answered all her questions; there was nothing so difficult for the king that he could not explain *it* to her. [4]And when the queen of Sheba had seen all the wisdom of Solomon, the house that he had built, [5]the food on his table, the seating of his servants, the service of his waiters and their apparel, his cupbearers, and his entryway by which he went up to the house of the LORD, there was no more spirit in her. [6]Then she said to the king: "It was a true report which I heard in my own land about your words and your wisdom. [7]However I did not believe the words until I came and saw with my own eyes; and indeed the half was not told me. Your wisdom and prosperity exceed the fame of which I heard. [8]Happy *are* your men and happy *are* these your servants, who stand continually before you *and* hear your wisdom! [9]Blessed be the LORD your God, who delighted in you, setting you on the throne of Israel! Because the LORD has loved Israel forever, therefore He made you king, to do justice and righteousness." [10]Then she gave the king one hundred and twenty talents of gold, spices in great quantity,

> "Now three times a year Solomon offered burnt offerings and peace offerings on the altar which he had built for the LORD, and he burned incense with them on the altar that was before the LORD. So he finished the temple."
>
> (1 Kings 9:25)

9:24 [a]Literally *he* (compare 2 Chronicles 8:11)   9:26 [a]Hebrew *Eloth* (compare 2 Kings 14:22) and precious stones. There never again came such abundance of spices as the queen of Sheba gave to King Solomon. [11]Also, the ships of Hiram, which brought gold from Ophir, brought great *quantities* of almug[a] wood and precious stones from Ophir. [12]And the king made steps of the almug wood for the house of the LORD and for the king's house, also harps and stringed instruments for singers. There never again came such almug wood, nor has the like been seen to this day.

[13]Now King Solomon gave the queen of Sheba all she desired, whatever she asked, besides what Solomon had given her according to the royal generosity. So she turned and went to her own country, she and her servants.

WHAT'S IT MEAN?

King Hiram was from Tyre, a seaport on the Mediterranean. If you'd like to visit Tyre today, head for Lebanon. If you'd like to visit Ophir, good luck! No one knows for sure where the city was located. Some guesses put it in west Arabia or east Africa, beyond the southern end of the Dead Sea. About all that is known for sure about Ophir is that it was a supplier of gold and precious stones.

1 Kings 10:11–13

SOLOMON'S GREAT WEALTH

[14]The weight of gold that came to Solomon yearly was six hundred and sixty-six talents of gold, [15]besides *that* from the traveling merchants, from the income of traders, from all the kings of Arabia, and from the governors of the country.

[16]And King Solomon made two hundred large shields *of* hammered gold; six hundred *shekels* of gold went into each shield. [17]He also *made* three hundred shields *of* hammered gold; three minas of gold went into each shield. The king put them in the House of the Forest of Lebanon.

[18]Moreover the king made a great throne of ivory, and overlaid it with pure gold. [19]The throne had six steps, and the top of the throne *was* round at the back; *there were* armrests on ei-

ther side of the place of the seat, and two lions stood beside the armrests. [20]Twelve lions stood there, one on each side of the six steps; nothing like *this* had been made for any *other* kingdom.

[21]All King Solomon's drinking vessels *were* gold, and all the vessels of the House of the Forest of Lebanon *were* pure gold. Not *one was* silver, for this was accounted as nothing in the days of Solomon. [22]For the king had merchant ships[a] at sea with the fleet of Hiram. Once every three years the merchant ships came bringing gold, silver, ivory, apes, and monkeys.[b] [23]So King Solomon surpassed all the kings of the earth in riches and wisdom.

[24]Now all the earth sought the presence of Solomon to hear his wisdom, which God had put in his heart. [25]Each man brought his present: articles of silver and gold, garments, armor, spices, horses, and mules, at a set rate year by year.

[26]And Solomon gathered chariots and horsemen; he had one thousand four hundred chariots and twelve thousand horsemen, whom he stationed[a] in the chariot cities and with the king at Jerusalem. [27]The king made silver *as common* in Jerusalem as stones, and he made cedar trees as abundant as the sycamores which *are* in the lowland.

[28]Also Solomon had horses imported from Egypt and Keveh; the king's merchants bought them in Keveh at the *current* price. [29]Now a chariot that was imported from Egypt cost six hundred *shekels* of silver, and a horse one hundred and fifty; and thus, through their agents,[a] they exported *them* to all the kings of the Hittites and the kings of Syria.

SOLOMON'S HEART TURNS FROM THE LORD

[1]But King Solomon loved many foreign women, as well as the daughter of Pharaoh: women of the Moabites, Ammonites, Edomites, Sidonians, *and* Hittites— [2]from the nations of whom the LORD had said to the children of Israel, "You shall not intermarry with them, nor they with you. Surely they will turn away your hearts after their gods." Solomon clung to these in love.

MARRIAGE
Can a spouse lead you away from God? (11:2)

[3]And he had seven hundred wives, princesses, and three hundred concubines; and his wives turned away his heart. [4]For it was so, when Solomon was old, that his wives turned his heart

---

10:11 [a]Or *algum* (compare 2 Chronicles 9:10, 11) **10:22** [a]Literally *ships of Tarshish,* deep-sea vessels [b]Or *peacocks* **10:26** [a]Following Septuagint, Syriac, Targum, and Vulgate (compare 2 Chronicles 9:25); Masoretic Text reads *led.* **10:29** [a]Literally *by their hands*

after other gods; and his heart was not loyal to the LORD his God, as *was* the heart of his father David. ⁵For Solomon went after Ashtoreth the goddess of the Sidonians, and after Milcom the abomination of the Ammonites. ⁶Solomon did evil in the sight of the LORD, and did not fully follow the LORD, as *did* his father David. ⁷Then Solomon built a high place for Chemosh the abomination of Moab, on the hill that *is* east of Jerusalem, and for Molech the abomination of the people of Ammon. ⁸And he did likewise for all his foreign wives, who burned incense and sacrificed to their gods.

⁹So the LORD became angry with Solomon, because his heart had turned from the LORD God of Israel, who had appeared to him twice, ¹⁰and had commanded him concerning this thing, that he should not go after other gods; but he did not keep what the LORD had commanded. ¹¹Therefore the LORD said to Solomon, "Because you have done this, and have not kept My covenant and My statutes, which I have commanded you, I will surely tear the kingdom away from you and give it to your servant. ¹²Nevertheless I will not do it in your days, for the sake of your father David; I will tear it out of the hand of your son. ¹³However I will not tear away the whole kingdom; I will give one tribe to your son for the sake of My servant David, and for the sake of Jerusalem which I have chosen."

ADVERSARIES OF SOLOMON

¹⁴Now the LORD raised up an adversary against Solomon, Hadad the Edomite; he *was* a descendant of the king in Edom. ¹⁵For it happened, when David was in Edom, and Joab the commander of the army had gone up to bury the slain, after he had killed every male in Edom ¹⁶(because for six months Joab remained there with all Israel, until he had cut down every male in Edom), ¹⁷that Hadad fled to go to Egypt, he and certain Edomites of his father's servants with him. Hadad *was* still a little child. ¹⁸Then they arose from Midian and came to Paran; and they took men with them from Paran and came to Egypt, to Pharaoh king of Egypt, who gave him a house, apportioned food for him, and gave him land. ¹⁹And Hadad found great favor in the sight of Pharaoh, so that he gave him as wife the sister of his own wife, that is, the sister of Queen Tahpenes. ²⁰Then the sister of Tahpenes bore him Genubath his son, whom Tahpenes weaned in Pharaoh's house. And Genubath was in Pharaoh's household among the sons of Pharaoh.

²¹So when Hadad heard in Egypt that David rested with his fathers, and that Joab the commander of the army was dead, Hadad said to Pharaoh, "Let me depart, that I may go to my own country."

²²Then Pharaoh said to him, "But what have you lacked with me, that suddenly you seek to go to your own country?"

So he answered, "Nothing, but do let me go anyway."

²³And God raised up *another* adversary against him, Rezon the son of Eliadah, who had fled from his lord, Hadadezer king of Zobah. ²⁴So he gathered men to him and became captain over a band *of raiders*, when David killed those *of Zobah*. And they went to Damascus and dwelt there, and reigned in Damascus. ²⁵He was an adversary of Israel all the days of Solomon (besides the trouble that Hadad *caused*); and he abhorred Israel, and reigned over Syria.

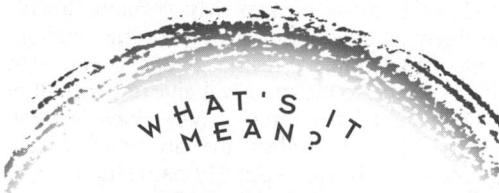

WHAT'S IT MEAN?

Damascus just happens to be one of the oldest cities in the world. The city has been occupied continuously for over 4,000 years—though not by the same people, of course. In Arabic, the city is called "The Place." It's easy to understand why Damascus has been so popular for so long: Three major caravan routes pass right through it. The city, which also happens to be the capital of Syria, is located northeast of the Sea of Galilee, about 135 miles away from Jerusalem.

1 Kings 11:24, 25

JEROBOAM'S REBELLION

²⁶Then Solomon's servant, Jeroboam the son of Nebat, an Ephraimite from Zereda, whose mother's name *was* Zeruah, a widow, also rebelled against the king.

²⁷And this *is* what caused him to rebel against the king: Solomon had built the Millo *and* repaired the damages to the City of David his father. ²⁸The man Jeroboam *was* a mighty man of valor; and Solomon, seeing that the young man was industrious, made him the officer over all the labor force of the house of Joseph.

²⁹Now it happened at that time, when Jeroboam went out of Jerusalem, that the prophet Ahijah the Shilonite met him on the way; and he had clothed himself with a new garment, and the two *were* alone in the field. ³⁰Then Ahijah took hold of the new garment that *was* on

him, and tore it *into* twelve pieces. ³¹And he said to Jeroboam, "Take for yourself ten pieces, for thus says the LORD, the God of Israel: 'Behold, I will tear the kingdom out of the hand of Solomon and will give ten tribes to you ³²(but he shall have one tribe for the sake of My servant David, and for the sake of Jerusalem, the city which I have chosen out of all the tribes of Israel), ³³because they have*ᵃ* forsaken Me, and worshiped Ashtoreth the goddess of the Sidonians, Chemosh the god of the Moabites, and Milcom the god of the people of Ammon, and have not walked in My ways to do *what is* right in My eyes and *keep* My statutes and My judgments, as *did* his father David. ³⁴However I will not take the whole kingdom out of his hand, because I have made him ruler all the days of his life for the sake of My servant David, whom I chose because he kept My commandments and My statutes. ³⁵But I will take the kingdom out of his son's hand and give it to you—ten tribes. ³⁶And to his son I will give one tribe, that My servant David may always have a lamp before Me in Jerusalem, the city which I have chosen for Myself, to put My name there. ³⁷So I will take you, and you shall reign over all your heart desires, and you shall be king over Israel. ³⁸Then it shall be, if you heed all that I command you, walk in My ways, and do *what is* right in My sight, to keep My statutes and My commandments, as My servant David did, then I will be with you and build for you an enduring house, as I built for David, and will give Israel to you. ³⁹And I will afflict the descendants of David because of this, but not forever.' "

⁴⁰Solomon therefore sought to kill Jeroboam. But Jeroboam arose and fled to Egypt, to Shishak king of Egypt, and was in Egypt until the death of Solomon.

DEATH OF SOLOMON

⁴¹Now the rest of the acts of Solomon, all that he did, and his wisdom, *are* they not written in the book of the acts of Solomon? ⁴²And the period that Solomon reigned in Jerusalem over all Israel *was* forty years. ⁴³Then Solomon rested with his fathers, and was buried in the City of David his father. And Rehoboam his son reigned in his place.

THE REVOLT AGAINST REHOBOAM

¹And Rehoboam went to Shechem, for all Israel had gone to Shechem to make him king. ²So it happened, when Jeroboam the son of Nebat heard *it* (he was still in Egypt, for he had fled from the presence of King Solomon and had been dwelling in Egypt), ³that they sent and called him. Then Jeroboam and the whole assembly of Israel came and spoke to Rehoboam, saying, ⁴"Your father made our yoke heavy; now therefore, lighten the burdensome service of your father, and his heavy yoke which he put on us, and we will serve you."

⁵So he said to them, "Depart *for* three days, then come back to me." And the people departed.

⁶Then King Rehoboam consulted the elders who stood before his father Solomon while he still lived, and he said, "How do you advise *me* to answer these people?"

⁷And they spoke to him, saying, "If you will be a servant to these people today, and serve them, and answer them, and speak good words to them, then they will be your servants forever."

⁸But he rejected the advice which the elders had given him, and consulted the young men who had grown up with him, who stood before him. ⁹And he said to them, "What advice do you give? How should we answer this people who have spoken to me, saying, 'Lighten the yoke which your father put on us'?"

¹⁰Then the young men who had grown up with him spoke to him, saying, "Thus you should speak to this people who have spoken to you, saying, 'Your father made our yoke heavy, but you make *it* lighter on us'—thus you shall say to them: 'My little *finger* shall be thicker than my father's waist! ¹¹And now, whereas my father put a heavy yoke on you, I will add to your yoke; my father chastised you with whips, but I will chastise you with scourges!' "*ᵃ*

¹²So Jeroboam and all the people came to Rehoboam the third day, as the king had directed, saying, "Come back to me the third day." ¹³Then the king answered the people roughly, and rejected the advice which the elders had given him; ¹⁴and he spoke to them according to the advice of the young men, saying, "My father made your yoke heavy, but I will add to your yoke; my father chastised you with whips, but I will chastise you with scourges!"*ᵃ* ¹⁵So the king did not listen to the people; for the turn *of events* was from the LORD, that He might fulfill His word, which the LORD had spoken by Ahijah the Shilonite to Jeroboam the son of Nebat.

¹⁶Now when all Israel saw that the king did not listen to them, the people answered the king, saying:

11:33 *ᵃ*Following Masoretic Text and Targum; Septuagint, Syriac, and Vulgate read *he has.*   **12:11** *ᵃ*Literally *scorpions*   **12:14** *ᵃ*Literally *scorpions*

"What share have we in David?
We have no inheritance in the son of Jesse.
To your tents, O Israel!
Now, see to your own house, O David!"

So Israel departed to their tents. ¹⁷But Rehoboam reigned over the children of Israel who dwelt in the cities of Judah.

¹⁸Then King Rehoboam sent Adoram, who was in charge of the revenue; but all Israel stoned him with stones, and he died. Therefore King Rehoboam mounted his chariot in haste to flee to Jerusalem. ¹⁹So Israel has been in rebellion against the house of David to this day.

²⁰Now it came to pass when all Israel heard that Jeroboam had come back, they sent for him and called him to the congregation, and made him king over all Israel. There was none who followed the house of David, but the tribe of Judah only.

²¹And when Rehoboam came to Jerusalem, he assembled all the house of Judah with the tribe of Benjamin, one hundred and eighty thousand chosen men who were warriors, to fight against the house of Israel, that he might restore the kingdom to Rehoboam the son of Solomon. ²²But the word of God came to Shemaiah the man of God, saying, ²³"Speak to Rehoboam the son of Solomon, king of Judah, to all the house of Judah and Benjamin, and to the rest of the people, saying, ²⁴'Thus says the LORD: "You shall not go up nor fight against your brethren the children of Israel. Let every man return to his house, for this thing is from Me." ' " Therefore they obeyed the word of the LORD, and turned back, according to the word of the LORD.

JEROBOAM'S GOLD CALVES

²⁵Then Jeroboam built Shechem in the mountains of Ephraim, and dwelt there. Also he went out from there and built Penuel. ²⁶And Jeroboam said in his heart, "Now the kingdom may return to the house of David: ²⁷If these people go up to offer sacrifices in the house of the LORD at Jerusalem, then the heart of this people will turn back to their lord, Rehoboam king of Judah, and they will kill me and go back to Rehoboam king of Judah."

²⁸Therefore the king asked advice, made two calves of gold, and said to the people, "It is too much for you to go up to Jerusalem. Here are your gods, O Israel, which brought you up from the land of Egypt!" ²⁹And he set up one in Bethel, and the other he put in Dan. ³⁰Now this thing became a sin, for the people went to worship before the one as far as Dan. ³¹He made shrines[a] on the high places, and made priests from every class of people, who were not of the sons of Levi.

³²Jeroboam ordained a feast on the fifteenth day of the eighth month, like the feast that was in Judah, and offered sacrifices on the altar. So he did at Bethel, sacrificing to the calves that he had made. And at Bethel he installed the priests of the high places which he had made. ³³So he made offerings on the altar which he had made at Bethel on the fifteenth day of the eighth month, in the month which he had devised in his own heart. And he ordained a feast for the children of Israel, and offered sacrifices on the altar and burned incense.

THE MESSAGE OF THE MAN OF GOD

¹And behold, a man of God went from Judah to Bethel by the word of the LORD, and Jeroboam stood by the altar to burn incense. ²Then he cried out against the altar by the word of the LORD, and said, "O altar, altar! Thus says the LORD: 'Behold, a child, Josiah by name, shall be born to the house of David; and on you he shall sacrifice the priests of the high places who burn incense on you, and men's bones shall be burned on you.' " ³And he gave a sign the same day, saying, "This is the sign which the LORD has spoken: Surely the altar shall split apart, and the ashes on it shall be poured out."

⁴So it came to pass when King Jeroboam heard the saying of the man of God, who cried out against the altar in Bethel, that he stretched out his hand from the altar, saying, "Arrest him!" Then his hand, which he stretched out toward him, withered, so that he could not pull it back to himself. ⁵The altar also was split apart, and the ashes poured out from the altar, according to the sign which the man of God had given by the word of the LORD. ⁶Then the king answered and said to the man of God, "Please entreat the favor of the LORD your God, and pray for me, that my hand may be restored to me."

So the man of God entreated the LORD, and the king's hand was restored to him, and became as before. ⁷Then the king said to the man of God, "Come home with me and refresh yourself, and I will give you a reward."

⁸But the man of God said to the king, "If you were to give me half your house, I would not go in with you; nor would I eat bread nor drink water in this place. ⁹For so it was commanded me by the word of the LORD, saying, 'You shall

12:31 [a]Literally a house

not eat bread, nor drink water, nor return by the same way you came.' " [10]So he went another way and did not return by the way he came to Bethel.

DEATH OF THE MAN OF GOD

[11]Now an old prophet dwelt in Bethel, and his sons came and told him all the works that the man of God had done that day in Bethel; they also told their father the words which he had spoken to the king. [12]And their father said to them, "Which way did he go?" For his sons had seen[a] which way the man of God went who came from Judah. [13]Then he said to his sons, "Saddle the donkey for me." So they saddled the donkey for him; and he rode on it, [14]and went after the man of God, and found him sitting under an oak. Then he said to him, "*Are* you the man of God who came from Judah?"

And he said, "I *am*."

[15]Then he said to him, "Come home with me and eat bread."

[16]And he said, "I cannot return with you nor go in with you; neither can I eat bread nor drink water with you in this place. [17]For I have been told by the word of the LORD, 'You shall not eat bread nor drink water there, nor return by going the way you came.' "

[18]He said to him, "I too *am* a prophet as you *are*, and an angel spoke to me by the word of the LORD, saying, 'Bring him back with you to your house, that he may eat bread and drink water.' " (He was lying to him.)

[19]So he went back with him, and ate bread in his house, and drank water.

[20]Now it happened, as they sat at the table, that the word of the LORD came to the prophet who had brought him back; [21]and he cried out to the man of God who came from Judah, saying, "Thus says the LORD: 'Because you have disobeyed the word of the LORD, and have not kept the commandment which the LORD your God commanded you, [22]but you came back, ate bread, and drank water in the place of which *the* LORD said to you, "Eat no bread and drink no water," your corpse shall not come to the tomb of your fathers.' "

[23]So it was, after he had eaten bread and after he had drunk, that he saddled the donkey for him, the prophet whom he had brought back. [24]When he was gone, a lion met him on the road and killed him. And his corpse was thrown on the road, and the donkey stood by it. The lion also stood by the corpse. [25]And

there, men passed by and saw the corpse thrown on the road, and the lion standing by the corpse. Then they went and told *it* in the city where the old prophet dwelt.

[26]Now when the prophet who had brought him back from the way heard *it*, he said, "It *is* the man of God who was disobedient to the word of the LORD. Therefore the LORD has delivered him to the lion, which has torn him and killed him, according to the word of the LORD which He spoke to him." [27]And he spoke to his sons, saying, "Saddle the donkey for me." So they saddled *it*. [28]Then he went and found his corpse thrown on the road, and the donkey and the lion standing by the corpse. The lion had not eaten the corpse nor torn the donkey. [29]And the prophet took up the corpse of the man of God, laid it on the donkey, and brought it back. So the old prophet came to the city to mourn, and to bury him. [30]Then he laid the corpse in his own tomb; and they mourned over him, *saying*, "Alas, my brother!" [31]So it was, after he had buried him, that he spoke to his sons, saying, "When I am dead, then bury me in the tomb where the man of God *is* buried; lay my bones beside his bones. [32]For the saying which he cried out by the word of the LORD against the altar in Bethel, and against all the shrines[a] on the high places which *are* in the cities of Samaria, will surely come to pass."

[33]After this event Jeroboam did not turn from his evil way, but again he made priests from every class of people for the high places; whoever wished, he consecrated him, and he became *one* of the priests of the high places. [34]And this thing was the sin of the house of Jeroboam, so as to exterminate and destroy *it* from the face of the earth.

JUDGMENT ON THE HOUSE OF JEROBOAM

[1]At that time Abijah the son of Jeroboam became sick. [2]And Jeroboam said to his wife, "Please arise, and disguise yourself, that they may not recognize you as the wife of Jeroboam, and go to Shiloh. Indeed, Ahijah the prophet *is* there, who told me that I *would be* king over this people. [3]Also take with you ten loaves, *some* cakes, and a jar of honey, and go to him; he will tell you what will become of the child." [4]And Jeroboam's wife did so; she arose and went to Shiloh, and came to the house of Ahijah. But Ahijah could not see, for his eyes were glazed by reason of his age.

[5]Now the LORD had said to Ahijah, "Here is the wife of Jeroboam, coming to ask you some-

---

13:12 [a]Septuagint, Syriac, Targum, and Vulgate read *showed him.*   **13:32** [a]Literally *houses* thing about her son, for he *is* sick. Thus and thus you shall say to her; for it will be, when she comes in, that she will pretend *to be* another *woman."*

⁶And so it was, when Ahijah heard the sound of her footsteps as she came through the door, he said, "Come in, wife of Jeroboam. Why do you pretend *to be* another *person?* For I *have been* sent to you *with* bad *news.* ⁷Go, tell Jeroboam, 'Thus says the LORD God of Israel: "Because I exalted you from among the people, and made you ruler over My people Israel, ⁸and tore the kingdom away from the house of David, and gave it to you; and *yet* you have not been as My servant David, who kept My commandments and who followed Me with all his heart, to do only *what was* right in My eyes; ⁹but you have done more evil than all who were before you, for you have gone and made for yourself other gods and molded images to provoke Me to anger, and have cast Me behind your back—¹⁰therefore behold! I will bring disaster on the house of Jeroboam, and will cut off from Jeroboam every male in Israel, bond and free; I will take away the remnant of the house of Jeroboam, as one takes away refuse until it is all gone. ¹¹The dogs shall eat whoever belongs to Jeroboam and dies in the city, and the birds of the air shall eat whoever dies in the field; for the LORD has spoken!" ' ¹²Arise therefore, go to your own house. When your feet enter the city, the child shall die. ¹³And all Israel shall mourn for him and bury him, for he is the only one of Jeroboam who shall come to the grave, because in him there is found something good toward the LORD God of Israel in the house of Jeroboam.

¹⁴"Moreover the LORD will raise up for Himself a king over Israel who shall cut off the house of Jeroboam; this is the day. What? Even now! ¹⁵For the LORD will strike Israel, as a reed is shaken in the water. He will uproot Israel from this good land which He gave to their fathers, and will scatter them beyond the River,ᵃ

WHAT'S IT MEAN?

The Israelites had adopted the Sidonian goddess Ashtoreth as their own deity. The places where people worshiped Ashtoreth were marked with wooden poles, which may have had symbols carved on them.
1 Kings 14:15

because they have made their wooden images,ᵇ provoking the LORD to anger. ¹⁶And He will give Israel up because of the sins of Jeroboam, who sinned and who made Israel sin."

¹⁷Then Jeroboam's wife arose and departed, and came to Tirzah. When she came to the threshold of the house, the child died. ¹⁸And they buried him; and all Israel mourned for him, according to the word of the LORD which He spoke through His servant Ahijah the prophet.

DEATH OF JEROBOAM

¹⁹Now the rest of the acts of Jeroboam, how he made war and how he reigned, indeed they *are* written in the book of the chronicles of the kings of Israel. ²⁰The period that Jeroboam reigned *was* twenty-two years. So he rested with his fathers. Then Nadab his son reigned in his place.

REHOBOAM REIGNS IN JUDAH

²¹And Rehoboam the son of Solomon reigned in Judah. Rehoboam *was* forty-one years old when he became king. He reigned seventeen years in Jerusalem, the city which the LORD had chosen out of all the tribes of Israel, to put His name there. His mother's name *was*

"I exalted you from among the people, and made you ruler over My people Israel, and tore the kingdom away from the house of David, and gave it to you; and yet you have not been as My servant David, who kept My commandments and who followed Me with all his heart, to do only what was right in My eyes."
(1 Kings 14:7b, 8)

14:15 ᵃThat is, the Euphrates ᵇHebrew *Asherim,* Canaanite deities

Naamah, an Ammonitess. ²²Now Judah did evil in the sight of the LORD, and they provoked Him to jealousy with their sins which they committed, more than all that their fathers had done. ²³For they also built for themselves high places, *sacred* pillars, and wooden images on every high hill and under every green tree. ²⁴And there were also perverted persons*ᵃ* in the land. They did according to all the abominations of the nations which the LORD had cast out before the children of Israel.

²⁵It happened in the fifth year of King Rehoboam *that* Shishak king of Egypt came up against Jerusalem. ²⁶And he took away the treasures of the house of the LORD and the treasures of the king's house; he took away everything. He also took away all the gold shields which Solomon had made. ²⁷Then King Rehoboam made bronze shields in their place, and committed *them* to the hands of the captains of the guard, who guarded the doorway of the king's house. ²⁸And whenever the king entered the house of the LORD, the guards carried them, then brought them back into the guardroom.

²⁹Now the rest of the acts of Rehoboam, and all that he did, *are* they not written in the book of the chronicles of the kings of Judah? ³⁰And there was war between Rehoboam and Jeroboam all *their* days. ³¹So Rehoboam rested with his fathers, and was buried with his fathers in the City of David. His mother's name *was* Naamah, an Ammonitess. Then Abijam*ᵃ* his son reigned in his place.

ABIJAM REIGNS IN JUDAH

¹In the eighteenth year of King Jeroboam the son of Nebat, Abijam became king over Judah. ²He reigned three years in Jerusalem. His mother's name *was* Maachah the granddaughter of Abishalom. ³And he walked in all the sins of his father, which he had done before him; his heart was not loyal to the LORD his God, as was the heart of his father David. ⁴Nevertheless for David's sake the LORD his God gave him a lamp in Jerusalem, by setting up his son after him and by establishing Jerusalem; ⁵because David did *what was* right in the eyes of the LORD, and had not turned aside from anything that He commanded him all the days of his life, except

in the matter of Uriah the Hittite. ⁶And there was war between Rehoboam*ᵃ* and Jeroboam all the days of his life. ⁷Now the rest of the acts of Abijam, and all that he did, *are* they not written in the book of the chronicles of the kings of Judah? And there was war between Abijam and Jeroboam.

⁸So Abijam rested with his fathers, and they buried him in the City of David. Then Asa his son reigned in his place.

ASA REIGNS IN JUDAH

⁹In the twentieth year of Jeroboam king of Israel, Asa became king over Judah. ¹⁰And he reigned forty-one years in Jerusalem. His grandmother's name *was* Maachah the granddaughter of Abishalom. ¹¹Asa did *what was* right in the eyes of the LORD, as *did* his father David. ¹²And he banished the perverted persons*ᵃ* from the land, and removed all the idols that his fathers had made. ¹³Also he removed Maachah his grandmother from *being* queen mother, because she had made an obscene image of Asherah.*ᵃ* And Asa cut down her obscene image and burned *it* by the Brook Kidron. ¹⁴But the high places were not removed. Nevertheless Asa's heart was loyal to the LORD all his days. ¹⁵He also brought into the house of the LORD the things which his father had dedicated, and the things which he himself had dedicated: silver and gold and utensils.

¹⁶Now there was war between Asa and Baasha king of Israel all their days. ¹⁷And Baasha king of Israel came up against Judah, and built Ramah, that he might let none go out or come in to Asa king of Judah. ¹⁸Then Asa took all the silver and gold *that was* left in the treasuries of the house of the LORD and the treasuries of the king's house, and delivered them into the hand of his servants. And King Asa sent them to Ben-Hadad the son of Tabrimmon, the son of Hezion, king of Syria, who dwelt in Damascus, saying, ¹⁹"*Let there be* a treaty between you and me, as there was between my father and your father. See, I have sent you a present of silver and gold. Come and break your treaty with Baasha king of Israel, so that he will withdraw from me."

²⁰So Ben-Hadad heeded King Asa, and sent the captains of his armies against the cities of Israel. He attacked Ijon, Dan, Abel Beth Maachah, and all Chinneroth, with all the land of

---

14:24 *ᵃ*Hebrew *qadesh*, that is, one practicing sodomy and prostitution in religious rituals **14:31** *ᵃ*Spelled *Abijah* in 2 Chronicles 12:16ff **15:6** *ᵃ*Following Masoretic Text, Septuagint, Targum, and Vulgate; some Hebrew manuscripts and Syriac read *Abijam*. **15:12** *ᵃ*Hebrew *qedeshim*, that is, those practicing sodomy and prostitution in religious rituals **15:13** *ᵃ*A Canaanite goddess

Naphtali. ²¹Now it happened, when Baasha heard *it*, that he stopped building Ramah, and remained in Tirzah.

²²Then King Asa made a proclamation throughout all Judah; none *was* exempted. And they took away the stones and timber of Ramah, which Baasha had used for building; and with them King Asa built Geba of Benjamin, and Mizpah.

²³The rest of all the acts of Asa, all his might, all that he did, and the cities which he built, *are* they not written in the book of the chronicles of the kings of Judah? But in the time of his old age he was diseased in his feet. ²⁴So Asa rested with his fathers, and was buried with his fathers in the City of David his father. Then Jehoshaphat his son reigned in his place.

NADAB REIGNS IN ISRAEL

²⁵Now Nadab the son of Jeroboam became king over Israel in the second year of Asa king of Judah, and he reigned over Israel two years. ²⁶And he did evil in the sight of the LORD, and walked in the way of his father, and in his sin by which he had made Israel sin.

²⁷Then Baasha the son of Ahijah, of the house of Issachar, conspired against him. And Baasha killed him at Gibbethon, which *belonged* to the Philistines, while Nadab and all Israel laid siege to Gibbethon. ²⁸Baasha killed him in the third year of Asa king of Judah, and reigned in his place. ²⁹And it was so, when he became king, *that* he killed all the house of Jeroboam. He did not leave to Jeroboam anyone that breathed, until he had destroyed him, according to the word of the LORD which He had spoken by His servant Ahijah the Shilonite, ³⁰because of the sins of Jeroboam, which he had sinned and by which he had made Israel sin, because of his provocation with which he had provoked the LORD God of Israel to anger.

³¹Now the rest of the acts of Nadab, and all that he did, *are* they not written in the book of the chronicles of the kings of Israel? ³²And there was war between Asa and Baasha king of Israel all their days.

BAASHA REIGNS IN ISRAEL

³³In the third year of Asa king of Judah, Baasha the son of Ahijah became king over all Israel in Tirzah, and *reigned* twenty-four years. ³⁴He did evil in the sight of the LORD, and walked in the way of Jeroboam, and in his sin by which he had made Israel sin.

¹Then the word of the LORD came to Jehu the son of Hanani, against Baasha, saying: ²"Inasmuch as I lifted you out of the dust and made you ruler over My people Israel, and you have walked in the way of Jeroboam, and have made My people Israel sin, to provoke Me to anger with their sins, ³surely I will take away the posterity of Baasha and the posterity of his house, and I will make your house like the house of Jeroboam the son of Nebat. ⁴The dogs shall eat whoever belongs to Baasha and dies in the city, and the birds of the air shall eat whoever dies in the fields."

WHAT'S IT MEAN?

The Israelites placed a high priority on proper burial for their dead. Allowing a body to be eaten by birds and animals was considered the ultimate insult to the deceased.
1 Kings 16:4

⁵Now the rest of the acts of Baasha, what he did, and his might, *are* they not written in the book of the chronicles of the kings of Israel? ⁶So Baasha rested with his fathers and was buried in Tirzah. Then Elah his son reigned in his place.

⁷And also the word of the LORD came by the prophet Jehu the son of Hanani against Baasha and his house, because of all the evil that he did in the sight of the LORD in provoking Him to anger with the work of his hands, in being like the house of Jeroboam, and because he killed them.

ELAH REIGNS IN ISRAEL

⁸In the twenty-sixth year of Asa king of Judah, Elah the son of Baasha became king over Israel, *and reigned* two years in Tirzah. ⁹Now his servant Zimri, commander of half *his* chariots, conspired against him as he was in Tirzah drinking himself drunk in the house of Arza, steward of *his* house in Tirzah. ¹⁰And Zimri went in and struck him and killed him in the twenty-seventh year of Asa king of Judah, and reigned in his place.

¹¹Then it came to pass, when he began to reign, as soon as he was seated on his throne, *that* he killed all the household of Baasha; he did not leave him one male, neither of his relatives nor of his friends. ¹²Thus Zimri destroyed all the household of Baasha, according to the

word of the LORD, which He spoke against Baasha by Jehu the prophet, [13]for all the sins of Baasha and the sins of Elah his son, by which they had sinned and by which they had made Israel sin, in provoking the LORD God of Israel to anger with their idols.

[14]Now the rest of the acts of Elah, and all that he did, *are* they not written in the book of the chronicles of the kings of Israel?

ZIMRI REIGNS IN ISRAEL

[15]In the twenty-seventh year of Asa king of Judah, Zimri had reigned in Tirzah seven days. And the people *were* encamped against Gibbethon, which *belonged* to the Philistines. [16]Now the people *who were* encamped heard it said, "Zimri has conspired and also has killed the king." So all Israel made Omri, the commander of the army, king over Israel that day in the camp. [17]Then Omri and all Israel with him went up from Gibbethon, and they besieged Tirzah. [18]And it happened, when Zimri saw that the city was taken, that he went into the citadel of the king's house and burned the king's house down upon himself with fire, and died, [19]because of the sins which he had committed in doing evil in the sight of the LORD, in walking in the way of Jeroboam, and in his sin which he had committed to make Israel sin.

[20]Now the rest of the acts of Zimri, and the treason he committed, *are* they not written in the book of the chronicles of the kings of Israel?

OMRI REIGNS IN ISRAEL

[21]Then the people of Israel were divided into two parts: half of the people followed Tibni the son of Ginath, to make him king, and half followed Omri. [22]But the people who followed Omri prevailed over the people who followed Tibni the son of Ginath. So Tibni died and Omri reigned. [23]In the thirty-first year of Asa king of Judah, Omri became king over Israel, *and reigned* twelve years. Six years he reigned in Tirzah. [24]And he bought the hill of Samaria from Shemer for two talents of silver; then he built on the hill, and called the name of the city which he built, Samaria, after the name of Shemer, owner of the hill. [25]Omri did evil in the eyes of the LORD, and did worse than all who *were* before him. [26]For he walked in all the ways of Jeroboam the son of Nebat, and in his sin by which he had made Israel sin, provoking the LORD God of Israel to anger with their idols.

[27]Now the rest of the acts of Omri which he did, and the might that he showed, *are* they not

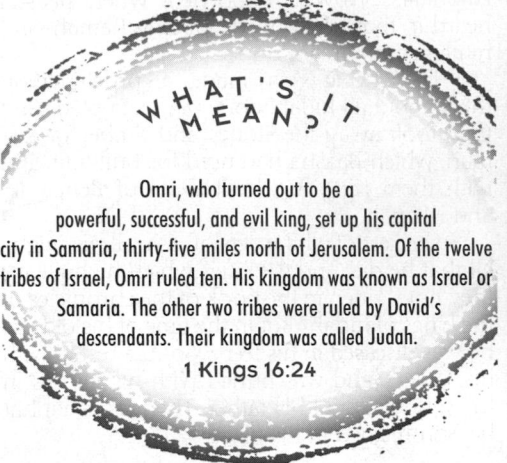

WHAT'S IT MEAN?

Omri, who turned out to be a powerful, successful, and evil king, set up his capital city in Samaria, thirty-five miles north of Jerusalem. Of the twelve tribes of Israel, Omri ruled ten. His kingdom was known as Israel or Samaria. The other two tribes were ruled by David's descendants. Their kingdom was called Judah.

1 Kings 16:24

written in the book of the chronicles of the kings of Israel?

[28]So Omri rested with his fathers and was buried in Samaria. Then Ahab his son reigned in his place.

AHAB REIGNS IN ISRAEL

[29]In the thirty-eighth year of Asa king of Judah, Ahab the son of Omri became king over Israel; and Ahab the son of Omri reigned over Israel in Samaria twenty-two years. [30]Now Ahab the son of Omri did evil in the sight of the LORD, more than all who *were* before him. [31]And it came to pass, as though it had been a trivial thing for him to walk in the sins of Jeroboam the son of Nebat, that he took as wife Jezebel the daughter of Ethbaal, king of the Sidonians; and he went and served Baal and worshiped him. [32]Then he set up an altar for Baal in the temple of Baal, which he had built in Samaria. [33]And Ahab made a wooden image.[a] Ahab did more to provoke the LORD God of Israel to anger than all the kings of Israel who were before him. [34]In his days Hiel of Bethel built Jericho. He laid its foundation with Abiram his firstborn, and with his youngest *son* Segub he set up its gates, according to the word of the LORD, which He had spoken through Joshua the son of Nun.[a]

ELIJAH PROCLAIMS A DROUGHT

[1]And Elijah the Tishbite, of the inhabitants of Gilead, said to Ahab, "*As* the LORD God of Israel lives, before whom I stand, there shall not be dew nor rain these years, except at my word."

[2]Then the word of the LORD came to him, saying, [3]"Get away from here and turn east-

16:33 [a]Hebrew *Asherah*, a Canaanite goddess   **16:34** [a]Compare Joshua 6:26

ward, and hide by the Brook Cherith, which flows into the Jordan. ⁴And it will be *that* you shall drink from the brook, and I have commanded the ravens to feed you there."

⁵So he went and did according to the word of the LORD, for he went and stayed by the Brook Cherith, which flows into the Jordan. ⁶The ravens brought him bread and meat in the morning, and bread and meat in the evening; and he drank from the brook. ⁷And it happened after a while that the brook dried up, because there had been no rain in the land.

ELIJAH AND THE WIDOW

⁸Then the word of the LORD came to him, saying, ⁹"Arise, go to Zarephath, which *belongs* to Sidon, and dwell there. See, I have commanded a widow there to provide for you." ¹⁰So he arose and went to Zarephath. And when he came to the gate of the city, indeed a widow *was* there gathering sticks. And he called to her and said, "Please bring me a little water in a cup, that I may drink." ¹¹And as she was going to get *it*, he called to her and said, "Please bring me a morsel of bread in your hand."

WHAT'S IT MEAN?

Elijah had been staying near the Brook Cherith, more than one hundred miles to the south, when God told him to head for Zarephath, which was near Jezebel's hometown of Sidon. Zarephath, Elijah's new hiding place, was a coastal town on the Mediterranean Sea (in what is now Lebanon).

1 Kings 17:9

¹²So she said, "As the LORD your God lives, I do not have bread, only a handful of flour in a bin, and a little oil in a jar; and see, I *am* gathering a couple of sticks that I may go in and prepare it for myself and my son, that we may eat it, and die."

¹³And Elijah said to her, "Do not fear; go *and* do as you have said, but make me a small cake from it first, and bring *it* to me; and afterward make *some* for yourself and your son. ¹⁴For thus says the LORD God of Israel: 'The bin of flour shall not be used up, nor

OBEDIENCE
Does God reward obedience? (17:13–16)

shall the jar of oil run dry, until the day the LORD sends rain on the earth.' "

¹⁵So she went away and did according to the word of Elijah; and she and he and her household ate for *many* days. ¹⁶The bin of flour was not used up, nor did the jar of oil run dry, according to the word of the LORD which He spoke by Elijah.

ELIJAH REVIVES THE WIDOW'S SON

¹⁷Now it happened after these things *that* the son of the woman who owned the house became sick. And his sickness was so serious that there was no breath left in him. ¹⁸So she said to Elijah, "What have I to do with you, O man of God? Have you come to me to bring my sin to remembrance, and to kill my son?"

¹⁹And he said to her, "Give me your son." So he took him out of her arms and carried him to the upper room where he was staying, and laid him on his own bed. ²⁰Then he cried out to the LORD and said, "O LORD my God, have You also brought tragedy on the widow with whom I lodge, by killing her son?" ²¹And he stretched himself out on the child three times, and cried out to the LORD and said, "O LORD my God, I pray, let this child's soul come back to him." ²²Then the LORD heard the voice of Elijah; and the soul of the child came back to him, and he revived.

²³And Elijah took the child and brought him down from the upper room into the house, and gave him to his mother. And Elijah said, "See, your son lives!"

²⁴Then the woman said to Elijah, "Now by this I know that you *are* a man of God, *and* that the word of the LORD in your mouth *is* the truth."

ELIJAH'S MESSAGE TO AHAB

¹And it came to pass *after* many days that the word of the LORD came to Elijah, in the third year, saying, "Go, present yourself to Ahab, and I will send rain on the earth."

²So Elijah went to present himself to Ahab; and *there was* a severe famine in Samaria. ³And Ahab had called Obadiah, who *was* in charge of *his* house. (Now Obadiah feared the LORD greatly. ⁴For so it was, while Jezebel massacred the prophets of the LORD, that Obadiah had taken one hundred prophets and hidden them, fifty to a cave, and had fed them with bread and water.) ⁵And Ahab had said to Obadiah, "Go into the land to all the springs of water and to all the brooks; perhaps we may find grass to keep the horses and mules alive, so that we will not have to kill any livestock." ⁶So they divided

the land between them to explore it; Ahab went one way by himself, and Obadiah went another way by himself.

⁷Now as Obadiah was on his way, suddenly Elijah met him; and he recognized him, and fell on his face, and said, "Is that you, my lord Elijah?"

⁸And he answered him, "It is I. Go, tell your master, 'Elijah is here.' "

⁹So he said, "How have I sinned, that you are delivering your servant into the hand of Ahab, to kill me? ¹⁰As the LORD your God lives, there is no nation or kingdom where my master has not sent someone to hunt for you; and when they said, 'He is not here,' he took an oath from the kingdom or nation that they could not find you. ¹¹And now you say, 'Go, tell your master, "Elijah is here" '! ¹²And it shall come to pass, as soon as I am gone from you, that the Spirit of the LORD will carry you to a place I do not know; so when I go and tell Ahab, and he cannot find you, he will kill me. But I your servant have feared the LORD from my youth. ¹³Was it not reported to my lord what I did when Jezebel killed the prophets of the LORD, how I hid one hundred men of the LORD's prophets, fifty to a cave, and fed them with bread and water? ¹⁴And now you say, 'Go, tell your master, "Elijah is here." ' He will kill me!"

¹⁵Then Elijah said, "As the LORD of hosts lives, before whom I stand, I will surely present myself to him today."

¹⁶So Obadiah went to meet Ahab, and told him; and Ahab went to meet Elijah.

¹⁷Then it happened, when Ahab saw Elijah, that Ahab said to him, "Is that you, O troubler of Israel?"

¹⁸And he answered, "I have not troubled Israel, but you and your father's house have, in that you have forsaken the commandments of the LORD and have followed the Baals. ¹⁹Now therefore, send and gather all Israel to me on Mount Carmel, the four hundred and fifty prophets of Baal, and the four hundred prophets of Asherah,ᵃ who eat at Jezebel's table."

ELIJAH'S MOUNT CARMEL VICTORY

²⁰So Ahab sent for all the children of Israel, and gathered the prophets together on Mount Carmel. ²¹And Elijah came to all the people, and said, "How long will you falter between two opinions? If the LORD is God, follow Him; but if Baal, follow him." But the people answered him not a word. ²²Then Elijah said to the people, "I alone am left a prophet of the LORD; but Baal's

prophets are four hundred and fifty men. ²³Therefore let them give us two bulls; and let them choose one bull for themselves, cut it in pieces, and lay it on the wood, but put no fire under it; and I will prepare the other bull, and lay it on the wood, but put no fire under it. ²⁴Then you call on the name of your gods, and I will call on the name of the LORD; and the God who answers by fire, He is God."

WHAT'S IT MEAN?

Let's set the scene for Elijah's contest with the prophets of Baal and Ashtoreth. Mount Carmel was a picturesque site overlooking the Mediterranean Sea. The Canaanites had built monuments to their gods of weather on the mountain.

1 Kings 18:19

So all the people answered and said, "It is well spoken."

²⁵Now Elijah said to the prophets of Baal, "Choose one bull for yourselves and prepare it first, for you are many; and call on the name of your god, but put no fire under it."

²⁶So they took the bull which was given them, and they prepared it, and called on the name of Baal from morning even till noon, saying, "O Baal, hear us!" But there was no voice; no one answered. Then they leaped about the altar which they had made.

²⁷And so it was, at noon, that Elijah mocked them and said, "Cry aloud, for he is a god; either he is meditating, or he is busy, or he is on a journey, or perhaps he is sleeping and must be awakened." ²⁸So they cried aloud, and cut themselves, as was their custom, with knives and lances, until the blood gushed out on them. ²⁹And when midday was past, they prophesied until the time of the offering of the evening sacrifice. But there was no voice; no one answered, no one paid attention.

³⁰Then Elijah said to all the people, "Come near to me." So all the people came near to him. And he repaired the altar of the LORD that was broken down. ³¹And Elijah took twelve stones, according to the number of the tribes of the sons of Jacob, to whom the word of the LORD

18:19 ᵃA Canaanite goddess

had come, saying, "Israel shall be your name."[a] ³²Then with the stones he built an altar in the name of the LORD; and he made a trench around the altar large enough to hold two seahs of seed. ³³And he put the wood in order, cut the bull in pieces, and laid *it* on the wood, and said, "Fill four waterpots with water, and pour *it* on the burnt sacrifice and on the wood." ³⁴Then he said, "Do *it* a second time," and they did *it* a second time; and he said, "Do *it* a third time," and they did *it* a third time. ³⁵So the water ran all around the altar; and he also filled the trench with water.

³⁶And it came to pass, at *the time of* the offering of the *evening* sacrifice, that Elijah the prophet came near and said, "LORD God of Abraham, Isaac, and Israel, let it be known this day that You *are* God in Israel and I *am* Your servant, and *that* I have done all these things at Your word. ³⁷Hear me, O LORD, hear me, that this people may know that You *are* the LORD God, and *that* You have turned their hearts back to You again."

³⁸Then the fire of the LORD fell and consumed the burnt sacrifice, and the wood and the stones and the dust, and it licked up the water that *was* in the trench. ³⁹Now when all the people saw *it,* they fell on their faces; and they said, "The LORD, He *is* God! The LORD, He *is* God!"

⁴⁰And Elijah said to them, "Seize the prophets of Baal! Do not let one of them escape!" So they seized them; and Elijah brought them down to the Brook Kishon and executed them there.

THE DROUGHT ENDS

⁴¹Then Elijah said to Ahab, "Go up, eat and drink; for *there is* the sound of abundance of rain." ⁴²So Ahab went up to eat and drink. And Elijah went up to the top of Carmel; then he bowed down on the ground, and put his face between his knees, ⁴³and said to his servant, "Go up now, look toward the sea."

So he went up and looked, and said, "*There is* nothing." And seven times he said, "Go again."

⁴⁴Then it came to pass the seventh *time,* that he said, "There is a cloud, as small as a man's hand, rising out of the sea!" So he said, "Go up, say to Ahab, 'Prepare *your chariot,* and go down before the rain stops you.'"

⁴⁵Now it happened in the meantime that the sky became black with clouds and wind, and there was a heavy rain. So Ahab rode away and went to Jezreel. ⁴⁶Then the hand of the LORD came upon Elijah; and he girded up his loins and ran ahead of Ahab to the entrance of Jezreel.

ELIJAH ESCAPES FROM JEZEBEL

¹And Ahab told Jezebel all that Elijah had done, also how he had executed all the prophets with the sword. ²Then Jezebel sent a messenger to Elijah, saying, "So let the gods do *to me,* and more also, if I do not make your life as the life of one of them by tomorrow about this time." ³And when he saw *that,* he arose and ran for his life, and went to Beersheba, which *belongs* to Judah, and left his servant there.

⁴But he himself went a day's journey into the wilderness, and came and sat down under a broom tree. And he prayed that he might die, and said, "It is enough! Now, LORD, take my life, for I *am* no better than my fathers!"

⁵Then as he lay and slept under a broom tree, suddenly an angel[a] touched him, and said to him, "Arise *and* eat." ⁶Then he looked, and there by his head *was* a cake baked on coals, and a jar of water. So he ate and drank, and lay down again. ⁷And the angel[a] of the LORD came back the second time, and touched him, and said, "Arise *and* eat, because the journey *is* too great for you." ⁸So he arose, and ate and drank; and he went in the strength of that food forty days and forty nights as far as Horeb, the mountain of God.

⁹And there he went into a cave, and spent

> **DEPRESSION**
> Can depression follow success?
> (19:3, 4)

> "Then the fire of the LORD fell and consumed the burnt sacrifice, and the wood and the stones and the dust, and it licked up the water that was in the trench. Now when all the people saw it, they fell on their faces; and they said, 'The LORD, He is God! The LORD, He is God!'"
> (1 Kings 18:38, 39)

18:31 [a]Genesis 32:28 **19:5** [a]Or *Angel* **19:7** [a]Or *Angel* the night in that place; and behold, the word of the LORD *came* to him, and He said to him, "What are you doing here, Elijah?"

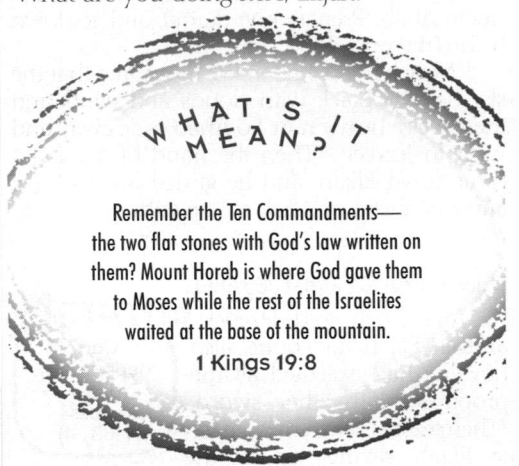

WHAT'S IT MEAN?

Remember the Ten Commandments— the two flat stones with God's law written on them? Mount Horeb is where God gave them to Moses while the rest of the Israelites waited at the base of the mountain.

1 Kings 19:8

[10]So he said, "I have been very zealous for the LORD God of hosts; for the children of Israel have forsaken Your covenant, torn down Your altars, and killed Your prophets with the sword. I alone am left; and they seek to take my life."

GOD'S REVELATION TO ELIJAH

[11]Then He said, "Go out, and stand on the mountain before the LORD." And behold, the LORD passed by, and a great and strong wind tore into the mountains and broke the rocks in pieces before the LORD, *but* the LORD *was* not in the wind; and after the wind an earthquake, *but* the LORD *was* not in the earthquake; [12]and after the earthquake a fire, *but* the LORD *was* not in the fire; and after the fire a still small voice. [13]So it was, when Elijah heard *it,* that he

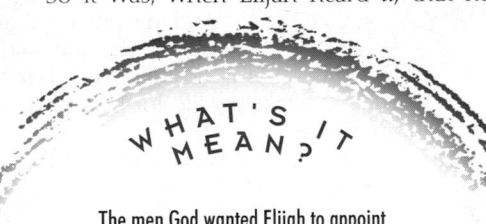

WHAT'S IT MEAN?

The men God wanted Elijah to appoint as leaders had one thing in common: They were all anti-Baal. Hazael and his fellow countrymen weren't particularly friendly toward either Israel or Judah. In fact, later in his reign, Hazael frequently attacked the Israelites. Jehu was a captain in Ahab's army when God gave these instructions to Elijah. During his reign, Jehu was responsible for many deaths, including a mass slaughter of Baal worshipers.

1 Kings 19:15

wrapped his face in his mantle and went out and stood in the entrance of the cave. Suddenly a voice *came* to him, and said, "What are you doing here, Elijah?"

[14]And he said, "I have been very zealous for the LORD God of hosts; because the children of Israel have forsaken Your covenant, torn down Your altars, and killed Your prophets with the sword. I alone am left; and they seek to take my life."

LONELINESS

What does God do for lonely people? (19:14–18)

[15]Then the LORD said to him: "Go, return on your way to the Wilderness of Damascus; and when you arrive, anoint Hazael *as* king over Syria. [16]Also you shall anoint Jehu the son of Nimshi *as* king over Israel. And Elisha the son of Shaphat of Abel Meholah you shall anoint *as* prophet in your place. [17]It shall be *that* whoever escapes the sword of Hazael, Jehu will kill; and whoever escapes the sword of Jehu, Elisha will kill. [18]Yet I have reserved seven thousand in Israel, all whose knees have not bowed to Baal, and every mouth that has not kissed him."

ELISHA FOLLOWS ELIJAH

[19]So he departed from there, and found Elisha the son of Shaphat, who *was* plowing *with* twelve yoke *of oxen* before him, and he was with the twelfth. Then Elijah passed by him and threw his mantle on him. [20]And he left the oxen and ran after Elijah, and said, "Please let me kiss my father and my mother, and *then* I will follow you."

And he said to him, "Go back again, for what have I done to you?"

[21]So *Elisha* turned back from him, and took a yoke of oxen and slaughtered them and boiled their flesh, using the oxen's equipment, and gave it to the people, and they ate. Then he arose and followed Elijah, and became his servant.

AHAB DEFEATS THE SYRIANS

[1]Now Ben-Hadad the king of Syria gathered all his forces together; thirty-two kings *were* with him, with horses and chariots. And he went up and besieged Samaria, and made war against it. [2]Then he sent messengers into the city to Ahab king of Israel, and said to him, "Thus says Ben-Hadad: [3]'Your silver and your gold *are* mine; your loveliest wives and children *are* mine.'"

[4]And the king of Israel answered and said, "My lord, O king, just as you say, I and all that I have *are* yours."

⁵Then the messengers came back and said, "Thus speaks Ben-Hadad, saying, 'Indeed I have sent to you, saying, "You shall deliver to me your silver and your gold, your wives and your children"; ⁶but I will send my servants to you tomorrow about this time, and they shall search your house and the houses of your servants. And it shall be, *that* whatever is pleasant in your eyes, they will put *it* in their hands and take *it*.' "

⁷So the king of Israel called all the elders of the land, and said, "Notice, please, and see how this *man* seeks trouble, for he sent to me for my wives, my children, my silver, and my gold; and I did not deny him."

⁸And all the elders and all the people said to him, "Do not listen or consent."

⁹Therefore he said to the messengers of Ben-Hadad, "Tell my lord the king, 'All that you sent for to your servant the first time I will do, but this thing I cannot do.' "

And the messengers departed and brought back word to him.

¹⁰Then Ben-Hadad sent to him and said, "The gods do so to me, and more also, if enough dust is left of Samaria for a handful for each of the people who follow me."

¹¹So the king of Israel answered and said, "Tell *him*, 'Let not the one who puts on *his armor* boast like the one who takes *it off*.' "

¹²And it happened when *Ben-Hadad* heard this message, as he and the kings *were* drinking at the command post, that he said to his servants, "Get ready." And they got ready to attack the city.

¹³Suddenly a prophet approached Ahab king of Israel, saying, "Thus says the LORD: 'Have you seen all this great multitude? Behold, I will deliver it into your hand today, and you shall know that I *am* the LORD.' "

¹⁴So Ahab said, "By whom?"

And he said, "Thus says the LORD: 'By the young leaders of the provinces.' "

Then he said, "Who will set the battle in order?"

And he answered, "You."

¹⁵Then he mustered the young leaders of the provinces, and there were two hundred and thirty-two; and after them he mustered all the people, all the children of Israel—seven thousand.

¹⁶So they went out at noon. Meanwhile Ben-Hadad and the thirty-two kings helping him were getting drunk at the command post. ¹⁷The young leaders of the provinces went out first. And Ben-Hadad sent out *a patrol*, and they told him, saying, "Men are coming out of Sa-

maria!" ¹⁸So he said, "If they have come out for peace, take them alive; and if they have come out for war, take them alive."

¹⁹Then these young leaders of the provinces went out of the city with the army which followed them. ²⁰And each one killed his man; so the Syrians fled, and Israel pursued them; and Ben-Hadad the king of Syria escaped on a horse with the cavalry. ²¹Then the king of Israel went out and attacked the horses and chariots, and killed the Syrians with a great slaughter.

²²And the prophet came to the king of Israel and said to him, "Go, strengthen yourself; take note, and see what you should do, for in the spring of the year the king of Syria will come up against you."

THE SYRIANS AGAIN DEFEATED

²³Then the servants of the king of Syria said to him, "Their gods *are* gods of the hills. Therefore they were stronger than we; but if we fight against them in the plain, surely we will be stronger than they. ²⁴So do this thing: Dismiss the kings, each from his position, and put captains in their places; ²⁵and you shall muster an army like the army that you have lost, horse for horse and chariot for chariot. Then we will fight against them in the plain; surely we will be stronger than they."

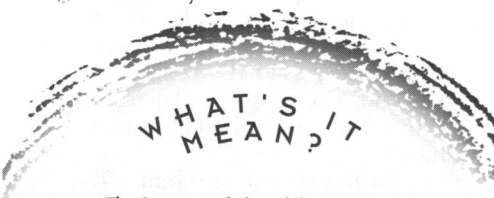

WHAT'S IT MEAN?

The Canaanites believed that each god controlled one specific area of the physical world. Ben-Hadad's officials believed Israel's God controlled the hills, so they figured if they moved the fight to flat land the Israelites would be helpless. Would it surprise you to learn that their plan failed miserably?

1 Kings 20:23

And he listened to their voice and did so.

²⁶So it was, in the spring of the year, that Ben-Hadad mustered the Syrians and went up to Aphek to fight against Israel. ²⁷And the children of Israel were mustered and given provisions, and they went against them. Now the children of Israel encamped before them like two little flocks of goats, while the Syrians filled the countryside.

²⁸Then a man of God came and spoke to the

king of Israel, and said, "Thus says the LORD: 'Because the Syrians have said, "The LORD *is* God of the hills, but He *is* not God of the valleys," therefore I will deliver all this great multitude into your hand, and you shall know that I *am* the LORD'." ²⁹And they encamped opposite each other for seven days. So it was that on the seventh day the battle was joined; and the children of Israel killed one hundred thousand foot soldiers *of* the Syrians in one day. ³⁰But the rest fled to Aphek, into the city; then a wall fell on twenty-seven thousand of the men *who were* left.

And Ben-Hadad fled and went into the city, into an inner chamber.

AHAB'S TREATY WITH BEN-HADAD

³¹Then his servants said to him, "Look now, we have heard that the kings of the house of Israel *are* merciful kings. Please, let us put sackcloth around our waists and ropes around our heads, and go out to the king of Israel; perhaps he will spare your life." ³²So they wore sackcloth around their waists and *put* ropes around their heads, and came to the king of Israel and said, "Your servant Ben-Hadad says, 'Please let me live'."

And he said, "*Is* he still alive? He *is* my brother."

³³Now the men were watching closely to see whether *any sign of mercy would come* from him; and they quickly grasped *at this word* and said, "Your brother Ben-Hadad."

So he said, "Go, bring him." Then Ben-Hadad came out to him; and he had him come up into the chariot.

³⁴So *Ben-Hadad* said to him, "The cities which my father took from your father I will restore; and you may set up marketplaces for yourself in Damascus, as my father did in Samaria."

Then *Ahab said*, "I will send you away with this treaty." So he made a treaty with him and sent him away.

AHAB CONDEMNED

³⁵Now a certain man of the sons of the prophets said to his neighbor by the word of the LORD, "Strike me, please." And the man refused to strike him. ³⁶Then he said to him, "Because you have not obeyed the voice of the LORD, surely, as soon as you depart from me, a lion shall kill you." And as soon as he left him, a lion found him and killed him.

³⁷And he found another man, and said, "Strike me, please." So the man struck him, inflicting a wound. ³⁸Then the prophet departed and waited for the king by the road, and disguised himself with a bandage over his eyes. ³⁹Now as the king passed by, he cried out to the king and said, "Your servant went out into the midst of the battle; and there, a man came over and brought a man to me, and said, 'Guard this man; if by any means he is missing, your life shall be for his life, or else you shall pay a talent of silver.' ⁴⁰While your servant was busy here and there, he was gone."

Then the king of Israel said to him, "So *shall* your judgment *be*; you yourself have decided *it*."

⁴¹And he hastened to take the bandage away from his eyes; and the king of Israel recognized him as one of the prophets. ⁴²Then he said to him, "Thus says the LORD: 'Because you have let slip out of *your* hand a man whom I appointed to utter destruction, therefore your life shall go for his life, and your people for his people'. "

⁴³So the king of Israel went to his house sullen and displeased, and came to Samaria.

NABOTH IS MURDERED FOR HIS VINEYARD

¹And it came to pass after these things *that* Naboth the Jezreelite had a vineyard which *was* in Jezreel, next to the palace of Ahab king of Samaria. ²So Ahab spoke to Naboth, saying, "Give me your vineyard, that I may have it for a vegetable garden, because it *is* near, next to my house; and for it I will give you a vineyard better than it. *Or*, if it seems good to you, I will give you its worth in money."

³But Naboth said to Ahab, "The LORD forbid that I should give the inheritance of my fathers to you!"

⁴So Ahab went into his house sullen and displeased because of the word which Naboth the Jezreelite had spoken to him; for he had said, "I will not give you the inheritance of my fathers." And he lay down on his bed, and turned away his face, and would eat no food. ⁵But Jezebel his wife came to him, and said to him, "Why is your spirit so sullen that you eat no food?"

⁶He said to her, "Because I spoke to Naboth the Jezreelite, and said to him, 'Give me your vineyard for money; or else, if it pleases you, I will give you *another* vineyard for it'. And he answered, 'I will not give you my vineyard.' "

⁷Then Jezebel his wife said to him, "You now exercise authority over Israel! Arise, eat food, and let your heart be cheerful; I will give you the vineyard of Naboth the Jezreelite."

⁸And she wrote letters in Ahab's name, sealed *them* with his seal, and sent the letters to the elders and the nobles who *were* dwelling in the city with Naboth. ⁹She wrote in the letters, saying,

Proclaim a fast, and seat Naboth with high honor among the people; ¹⁰and seat two men, scoundrels, before him to bear witness against him, saying, You have blasphemed God and the king. *Then* take him out, and stone him, that he may die.

¹¹So the men of his city, the elders and nobles who were inhabitants of his city, did as Jezebel had sent to them, as it *was* written in the letters which she had sent to them. ¹²They proclaimed a fast, and seated Naboth with high honor among the people. ¹³And two men, scoundrels, came in and sat before him; and the scoundrels witnessed against him, against Naboth, in the presence of the people, saying, "Naboth has blasphemed God and the king!" Then they took him outside the city and stoned him with stones, so that he died. ¹⁴Then they sent to Jezebel, saying, "Naboth has been stoned and is dead."

¹⁵And it came to pass, when Jezebel heard that Naboth had been stoned and was dead, that Jezebel said to Ahab, "Arise, take possession of the vineyard of Naboth the Jezreelite, which he refused to give you for money; for Naboth is not alive, but dead." ¹⁶So it was, when Ahab heard that Naboth was dead, that Ahab got up and went down to take possession of the vineyard of Naboth the Jezreelite.

THE LORD CONDEMNS AHAB

¹⁷Then the word of the LORD came to Elijah the Tishbite, saying, ¹⁸"Arise, go down to meet Ahab king of Israel, who *lives* in Samaria. There *he is*, in the vineyard of Naboth, where he has gone down to take possession of it. ¹⁹You shall speak to him, saying, 'Thus says the LORD: "Have you murdered and also taken possession?" ' And you shall speak to him, saying, 'Thus says the LORD: "In the place where dogs licked the blood of Naboth, dogs shall lick your blood, even yours." ' "

²⁰So Ahab said to Elijah, "Have you found me, O my enemy?"

And he answered, "I have found *you,* because you have sold yourself to do evil in the sight of the LORD: ²¹'Behold, I will bring calamity on you. I will take away your posterity, and will cut off from Ahab every male in Israel, both bond and free. ²²I will make your house like the house of Jeroboam the son of Nebat, and like the house of Baasha the son of Ahijah, because of the provocation with which you

have provoked *Me* to anger, and made Israel sin.' ²³And concerning Jezebel the LORD also spoke, saying, 'The dogs shall eat Jezebel by the wall*ᵃ* of Jezreel.' ²⁴The dogs shall eat whoever belongs to Ahab and dies in the city, and the birds of the air shall eat whoever dies in the field."

²⁵But there was no one like Ahab who sold himself to do wickedness in the sight of the LORD, because Jezebel his wife stirred him up. ²⁶And he behaved very abominably in following idols, according to all *that* the Amorites had done, whom the LORD had cast out before the children of Israel.

²⁷So it was, when Ahab heard those words, that he tore his clothes and put sackcloth on his body, and fasted and lay in sackcloth, and went about mourning.

²⁸And the word of the LORD came to Elijah the Tishbite, saying, ²⁹"See how Ahab has humbled himself before Me? Because he has humbled himself before Me, I will not bring the calamity in his days. In the days of his son I will bring the calamity on his house."

MICAIAH WARNS AHAB

¹Now three years passed without war between Syria and Israel. ²Then it came to pass, in the third year, that Jehoshaphat the king of Judah went down to *visit* the king of Israel.

³And the king of Israel said to his servants, "Do you know that Ramoth in Gilead *is* ours, but we hesitate to take it out of the hand of the king of Syria?" ⁴So he said to Jehoshaphat, "Will you go with me to fight at Ramoth Gilead?"

Jehoshaphat said to the king of Israel, "I *am* as you *are,* my people as your people, my horses as your horses." ⁵Also Jehoshaphat said to the king of Israel, "Please inquire for the word of the LORD today."

⁶Then the king of Israel gathered the prophets together, about four hundred men, and said to them, "Shall I go against Ramoth Gilead to fight, or shall I refrain?"

So they said, "Go up, for the Lord will deliver *it* into the hand of the king."

⁷And Jehoshaphat said, *"Is there* not still a prophet of the LORD here, that we may inquire of Him?"*ᵃ*

⁸So the king of Israel said to Jehoshaphat, *"There is* still one man, Micaiah the son of Imlah, by whom we may inquire of the LORD; but I hate him, because he does not prophesy good concerning me, but evil."

And Jehoshaphat said, "Let not the king say such things!"

⁹Then the king of Israel called an officer and said, "Bring Micaiah the son of Imlah quickly!"

¹⁰The king of Israel and Jehoshaphat the king of Judah, having put on *their* robes, sat each on his throne, at a threshing floor at the entrance of the gate of Samaria; and all the prophets prophesied before them. ¹¹Now Zedekiah the son of Chenaanah had made horns of iron for himself; and he said, "Thus says the LORD: 'With these you shall gore the Syrians until they are destroyed.'" ¹²And all the prophets prophesied so, saying, "Go up to Ramoth Gilead and prosper, for the LORD will deliver *it* into the king's hand."

¹³Then the messenger who had gone to call Micaiah spoke to him, saying, "Now listen, the words of the prophets with one accord encourage the king. Please, let your word be like the word of one of them, and speak encouragement."

¹⁴And Micaiah said, "*As* the LORD lives, whatever the LORD says to me, that I will speak."

¹⁵Then he came to the king; and the king said to him, "Micaiah, shall we go to war against Ramoth Gilead, or shall we refrain?"

And he answered him, "Go and prosper, for the LORD will deliver *it* into the hand of the king!"

¹⁶So the king said to him, "How many times shall I make you swear that you tell me nothing but the truth in the name of the LORD?"

¹⁷Then he said, "I saw all Israel scattered on the mountains, as sheep that have no shepherd. And the LORD said, 'These have no master. Let each return to his house in peace.'"

¹⁸And the king of Israel said to Jehoshaphat, "Did I not tell you he would not prophesy good concerning me, but evil?"

¹⁹Then *Micaiah* said, "Therefore hear the word of the LORD: I saw the LORD sitting on His throne, and all the host of heaven standing by, on His right hand and on His left. ²⁰And the LORD said, 'Who will persuade Ahab to go up, that he may fall at Ramoth Gilead?' So one spoke in this manner, and another spoke in that manner. ²¹Then a spirit came forward and stood before the LORD, and said, 'I will persuade him.' ²²The LORD said to him, 'In what way?' So he said, 'I will go out and be a lying spirit in the mouth of all his prophets.' And the LORD said, 'You shall persuade *him*, and also prevail. Go

out and do so.' ²³Therefore look! The LORD has put a lying spirit in the mouth of all these prophets of yours, and the LORD has declared disaster against you."

²⁴Now Zedekiah the son of Chenaanah went near and struck Micaiah on the cheek, and said, "Which way did the spirit from the LORD go from me to speak to you?"

²⁵And Micaiah said, "Indeed, you shall see on that day when you go into an inner chamber to hide!"

²⁶So the king of Israel said, "Take Micaiah, and return him to Amon the governor of the city and to Joash the king's son; ²⁷and say, 'Thus says the king: "Put this *fellow* in prison, and feed him with bread of affliction and water of affliction, until I come in peace."'"

²⁸But Micaiah said, "If you ever return in peace, the LORD has not spoken by me." And he said, "Take heed, all you people!"

AHAB DIES IN BATTLE

²⁹So the king of Israel and Jehoshaphat the king of Judah went up to Ramoth Gilead. ³⁰And the king of Israel said to Jehoshaphat, "I will disguise myself and go into battle; but you put on your robes." So the king of Israel disguised himself and went into battle.

³¹Now the king of Syria had commanded the thirty-two captains of his chariots, saying, "Fight with no one small or great, but only with the king of Israel." ³²So it was, when the captains of the chariots saw Jehoshaphat, that they said, "Surely it *is* the king of Israel!" Therefore they turned aside to fight against him, and Jehoshaphat cried out. ³³And it happened, when the captains of the chariots saw that it *was* not the king of Israel, that they turned back from pursuing him. ³⁴Now a *certain* man drew a bow at random, and struck the king of Israel between the joints of his armor. So he said to the driver of his chariot, "Turn around and take me out of the battle, for I am wounded."

³⁵The battle increased that day; and the king was propped up in his chariot, facing the Syrians, and died at evening. The blood ran out from the wound onto the floor of the chariot. ³⁶Then, as the sun was going down, a shout went throughout the army, saying, "Every man to his city, and every man to his own country!"

³⁷So the king died, and was brought to Samaria. And they buried the king in Samaria. ³⁸Then *someone* washed the chariot at a pool in

> "And Micaiah said, 'As the LORD lives, whatever the LORD says to me, that I will speak.'" (1 Kings 22:14)

Samaria, and the dogs licked up his blood while the harlots bathed,*a* according to the word of the LORD which He had spoken. ³⁹Now the rest of the acts of Ahab, and all that he did, the ivory house which he built and all the cities that he built, *are* they not written in the book of the chronicles of the kings of Israel? ⁴⁰So Ahab rested with his fathers. Then Ahaziah his son reigned in his place.

W H A T ' S   I T   M E A N ?

Ahab's palace was the original "White House." Not only were the walls decorated with ivory, but they were also made of white marble that looked like ivory.

1 Kings 22:39

JEHOSHAPHAT REIGNS IN JUDAH

⁴¹Jehoshaphat the son of Asa had become king over Judah in the fourth year of Ahab king of Israel. ⁴²Jehoshaphat *was* thirty-five years old when he became king, and he reigned twenty-five years in Jerusalem. His mother's name *was* Azubah the daughter of Shilhi. ⁴³And he walked in all the ways of his father Asa. He did not turn aside from them, doing *what was* right in the eyes of the LORD. Nevertheless the high places were not taken away, *for* the people offered sacrifices and burned incense on the high places. ⁴⁴Also Jehoshaphat made peace with the king of Israel.

⁴⁵Now the rest of the acts of Jehoshaphat, the might that he showed, and how he made war, *are* they not written in the book of the chronicles of the kings of Judah? ⁴⁶And the rest of the perverted persons,*a* who remained in the days of his father Asa, he banished from the land. ⁴⁷*There was* then no king in Edom, only a deputy of the king.

⁴⁸Jehoshaphat made merchant ships*a* to go to Ophir for gold; but they never sailed, for the ships were wrecked at Ezion Geber. ⁴⁹Then Ahaziah the son of Ahab said to Jehoshaphat, "Let my servants go with your servants in the ships." But Jehoshaphat would not.

⁵⁰And Jehoshaphat rested with his fathers, and was buried with his fathers in the City of David his father. Then Jehoram his son reigned in his place.

AHAZIAH REIGNS IN ISRAEL

⁵¹Ahaziah the son of Ahab became king over Israel in Samaria in the seventeenth year of Jehoshaphat king of Judah, and reigned two years over Israel. ⁵²He did evil in the sight of the LORD, and walked in the way of his father and in the way of his mother and in the way of Jeroboam the son of Nebat, who had made Israel sin; ⁵³for he served Baal and worshiped him, and provoked the LORD God of Israel to anger, according to all that his father had done.

22:38 *a*Syriac and Targum read *they washed his armor.*   **22:46** *a*Hebrew *qadesh,* that is, one practicing sodomy and prostitution in religious rituals   **22:48** *a*Or *ships of Tarshish*

2 kings

CONTENT

Second Kings is the story of the divided kingdoms of the Hebrews: Israel and Judah. Each kingdom had its own kings and its own priests and its own prophets. But one thing they had in common: their governments went from bad to worse with only a few exceptions. The people continued to disregard God even though He sent prophets again and again to set them straight.

Through the years, each kingdom became a weakling spiritually and morally. After years of disobedience and struggle, they became sitting ducks for the larger nations around them. Assyria, a nation known for its cruelty in warfare, eventually attacked Israel. Babylon, a rich and strong nation to the south, attacked Judah. The Hebrew people were carried away from their countries to be slaves and prisoners in a foreign place.

The Hebrew people continued to lose their land because they wouldn't listen to God. They wouldn't listen to Him about how to govern their land or how to treat each other. They wouldn't listen to Him about *how* to worship and *who* to worship. This is their story so that we can learn from their mistakes.

Outline

Purpose

No nation marked by moral and spiritual decay can survive.

Theme

Lessons from the Ruin of Israel and Judah

Date of writing

590–550 B.C.

> "And the LORD said, 'I will also remove Judah from My sight, as I have removed Israel, and will cast off this city Jerusalem which I have chosen, and the house of which I said, "My name shall be there" ' " (23:27).

Bible Talk

The Divided Kingdom

Readers of, particularly, Second Kings have been known to get a little confused about the different kingdoms that Israel split into. You know how some movies skip back and forth between two story lines? Well, that's what Second Kings does between kingdoms. So here's the scoop.

Israel divided into two kingdoms (get ready; this is gonna' be tough): the northern kingdom and the southern kingdom. (Okay, not sooo tough.) What makes it confusing is that the northern kingdom is still called Israel. The southern kingdom is called Judah. Israel was bigger than Judah.

So when you're reading along and a new king is introduced, just remember to notice which kingdom he was in so you don't get mixed up.

WASN'T IT OBVIOUS?

Wasn't it obvious that the Hebrews needed to take God seriously? Don't you wonder sometimes what got in their way when they should have been listening to God and obeying Him?

It's easy to wonder and even laugh at these people who seemed to avoid the obvious: Do what God says and things will go better for you! But the truth is, we do the same thing today. God told these people, "Worship only Me; I am the true God." He tells us, "Worship only Me. Don't trust anything else to get you through this life."

Yet they, and we, go our own way and worship and trust in other things to guide us and to rescue us from the difficult parts of life. Our world is not that far from theirs, is it?

GOD JUDGES AHAZIAH

[1]Moab rebelled against Israel after the death of Ahab.

[2]Now Ahaziah fell through the lattice of his upper room in Samaria, and was injured; so he sent messengers and said to them, "Go, inquire of Baal-Zebub, the god of Ekron, whether I shall recover from this injury." [3]But the angel[a] of the LORD said to Elijah the Tishbite, "Arise, go up to meet the messengers of the king of Samaria, and say to them, 'Is it because there is no God in Israel that you are going to inquire of Baal-Zebub, the god of Ekron?' [4]Now therefore, thus says the LORD: 'You shall not come down from the bed to which you have gone up, but you shall surely die.'" So Elijah departed.

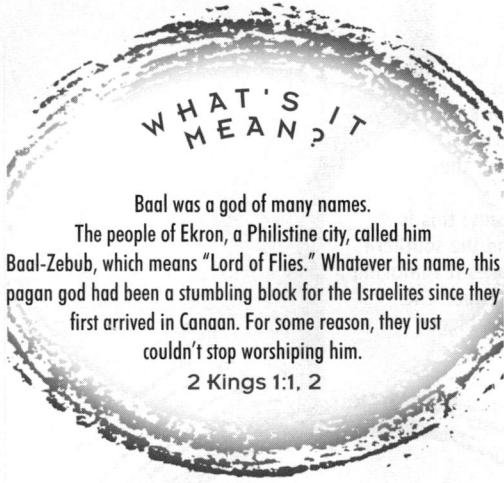

WHAT'S IT MEAN?

Baal was a god of many names. The people of Ekron, a Philistine city, called him Baal-Zebub, which means "Lord of Flies." Whatever his name, this pagan god had been a stumbling block for the Israelites since they first arrived in Canaan. For some reason, they just couldn't stop worshiping him.

2 Kings 1:1, 2

[5]And when the messengers returned to him, he said to them, "Why have you come back?"

[6]So they said to him, "A man came up to meet us, and said to us, 'Go, return to the king who sent you, and say to him, "Thus says the LORD: 'Is it because there is no God in Israel that you are sending to inquire of Baal-Zebub, the god of Ekron? Therefore you shall not come down from the bed to which you have gone up, but you shall surely die.'"'"

[7]Then he said to them, "What kind of man was it who came up to meet you and told you these words?"

[8]So they answered him, "A hairy man wearing a leather belt around his waist."

And he said, "It is Elijah the Tishbite."

[9]Then the king sent to him a captain of fifty with his fifty men. So he went up to him; and there he was, sitting on the top of a hill. And he spoke to him: "Man of God, the king has said, 'Come down!'"

[10]So Elijah answered and said to the captain of fifty, "If I am a man of God, then let fire come down from heaven and consume you and your fifty men." And fire came down from heaven and consumed him and his fifty. [11]Then he sent to him another captain of fifty with his fifty men.

And he answered and said to him: "Man of God, thus has the king said, 'Come down quickly!'"

[12]So Elijah answered and said to them, "If I am a man of God, let fire come down from heaven and consume you and your fifty men." And the fire of God came down from heaven and consumed him and his fifty.

[13]Again, he sent a third captain of fifty with his fifty men. And the third captain of fifty went up, and came and fell on his knees before Elijah, and pleaded with him, and said to him: "Man of God, please let my life and the life of these fifty servants of yours be precious in your sight. [14]Look, fire has come down from heaven and burned up the first two captains of fifties with their fifties. But let my life now be precious in your sight."

[15]And the angel[a] of the LORD said to Elijah, "Go down with him; do not be afraid of him." So he arose and went down with him to the king. [16]Then he said to him, "Thus says the LORD: 'Because you have sent messengers to inquire of Baal-Zebub, the god of Ekron, is it because there is no God in Israel to inquire of His word? Therefore you shall not come down from the bed to which you have gone up, but you shall surely die.'"

[17]So Ahaziah died according to the word of the LORD which Elijah had spoken. Because he had no son, Jehoram[a] became king in his place, in the second year of Jehoram the son of Jehoshaphat, king of Judah.

[18]Now the rest of the acts of Ahaziah which he did, are they not written in the book of the chronicles of the kings of Israel?

ELIJAH ASCENDS TO HEAVEN

[1]And it came to pass, when the LORD was about to take up Elijah into heaven by a whirlwind, that Elijah went with Elisha from Gilgal. [2]Then Elijah said to Elisha, "Stay here, please, for the LORD has sent me on to Bethel."

But Elisha said, "As the LORD lives, and as your soul lives, I will not leave you!" So they went down to Bethel.

[3]Now the sons of the prophets who were at Bethel came out to Elisha, and said to him, "Do

1:3 [a]Or Angel   1:15 [a]Or Angel   1:17 [a]The son of Ahab king of Israel (compare 3:1)

you know that the LORD will take away your master from over you today?"

And he said, "Yes, I know; keep silent!"

⁴Then Elijah said to him, "Elisha, stay here, please, for the LORD has sent me on to Jericho."

But he said, "*As* the LORD lives, and *as* your soul lives, I will not leave you!" So they came to Jericho.

⁵Now the sons of the prophets who *were* at Jericho came to Elisha and said to him, "Do you know that the LORD will take away your master from over you today?"

So he answered, "Yes, I know; keep silent!"

⁶Then Elijah said to him, "Stay here, please, for the LORD has sent me on to the Jordan."

But he said, "*As* the LORD lives, and *as* your soul lives, I will not leave you!" So the two of them went on. ⁷And fifty men of the sons of the prophets went and stood facing *them* at a distance, while the two of them stood by the Jordan. ⁸Now Elijah took his mantle, rolled *it* up, and struck the water; and it was divided this way and that, so that the two of them crossed over on dry ground.

⁹And so it was, when they had crossed over, that Elijah said to Elisha, "Ask! What may I do for you, before I am taken away from you?"

Elisha said, "Please let a double portion of your spirit be upon me."

¹⁰So he said, "You have asked a hard thing. *Nevertheless,* if you see me *when I am* taken from you, it shall be so for you; but if not, it shall not be *so.*" ¹¹Then it happened, as they continued on and talked, that suddenly a chariot of fire *appeared* with horses of fire, and separated the two of them; and Elijah went up by a whirlwind into heaven.

¹²And Elisha saw *it,* and he cried out, "My father, my father, the chariot of Israel and its horsemen!" So he saw him no more. And he took hold of his own clothes and tore them into two pieces. ¹³He also took up the mantle of Elijah that had fallen from him, and went back and stood by the bank of the Jordan. ¹⁴Then he took the mantle of Elijah that had fallen from him, and struck the water, and said, "Where *is* the LORD God of Elijah?" And when he also had struck the water, it was divided this way and that; and Elisha crossed over.

¹⁵Now when the sons of the prophets who *were* from Jericho saw him, they said, "The spirit of Elijah rests on Elisha." And they came to meet him, and bowed to the ground before him. ¹⁶Then they said to him, "Look now, there are fifty strong men with your servants. Please let them go and search for your master, lest perhaps the Spirit of the LORD has taken him up

and cast him upon some mountain or into some valley."

And he said, "You shall not send anyone."

¹⁷But when they urged him till he was ashamed, he said, "Send *them!*" Therefore they sent fifty men, and they searched for three days but did not find him. ¹⁸And when they came back to him, for he had stayed in Jericho, he said to them, "Did I not say to you, 'Do not go'?"

ELISHA PERFORMS MIRACLES

¹⁹Then the men of the city said to Elisha, "Please notice, the situation of this city *is* pleasant, as my lord sees; but the water *is* bad, and the ground barren."

²⁰And he said, "Bring me a new bowl, and put salt in it." So they brought *it* to him. ²¹Then he went out to the source of the water, and cast in the salt there, and said, "Thus says the LORD: 'I have healed this water; from it there shall be no more death or barrenness.'" ²²So the water remains healed to this day, according to the word of Elisha which he spoke.

²³Then he went up from there to Bethel; and as he was going up the road, some youths came from the city and mocked him, and said to him, "Go up, you baldhead! Go up, you baldhead!"

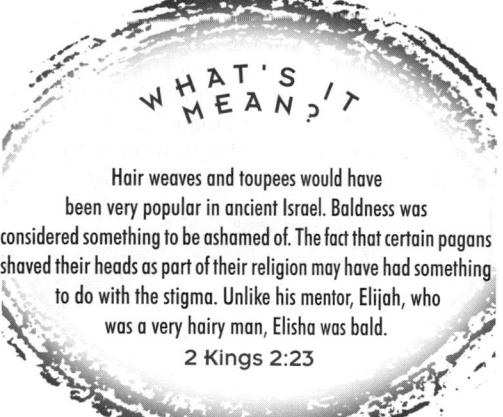

WHAT'S IT MEAN?

Hair weaves and toupees would have been very popular in ancient Israel. Baldness was considered something to be ashamed of. The fact that certain pagans shaved their heads as part of their religion may have had something to do with the stigma. Unlike his mentor, Elijah, who was a very hairy man, Elisha was bald.

2 Kings 2:23

²⁴So he turned around and looked at them, and pronounced a curse on them in the name of the LORD. And two female bears came out of the woods and mauled forty-two of the youths. ²⁵Then he went from there to Mount Carmel, and from there he returned to Samaria.

MOAB REBELS AGAINST ISRAEL

¹Now Jehoram the son of Ahab became king over Israel at Samaria in the eighteenth year of Jehoshaphat king of Judah, and reigned twelve years. ²And he did evil in the sight of the LORD,

but not like his father and mother; for he put away the *sacred* pillar of Baal that his father had made. ³Nevertheless he persisted in the sins of Jeroboam the son of Nebat, who had made Israel sin; he did not depart from them.

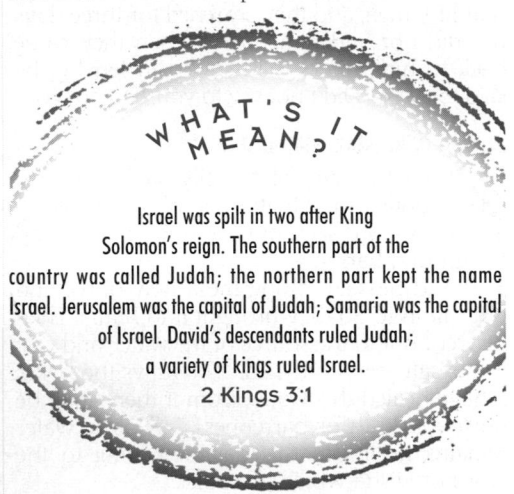

WHAT'S IT MEAN?

Israel was spilt in two after King Solomon's reign. The southern part of the country was called Judah; the northern part kept the name Israel. Jerusalem was the capital of Judah; Samaria was the capital of Israel. David's descendants ruled Judah; a variety of kings ruled Israel.

2 Kings 3:1

⁴Now Mesha king of Moab was a sheepbreeder, and he regularly paid the king of Israel one hundred thousand lambs and the wool of one hundred thousand rams. ⁵But it happened, when Ahab died, that the king of Moab rebelled against the king of Israel.

⁶So King Jehoram went out of Samaria at that time and mustered all Israel. ⁷Then he went and sent to Jehoshaphat king of Judah, saying, "The king of Moab has rebelled against me. Will you go with me to fight against Moab?"

WHAT'S IT MEAN?

Moab and Jerusalem were on opposite sides of the Dead Sea. By marching south through the Wilderness of Edom, the Israelites probably surprised the Moabites, who were expecting an attack from the north.

2 Kings 3:8

And he said, "I will go up; I *am* as you *are*, my people as your people, my horses as your horses." ⁸Then he said, "Which way shall we go up?"

And he answered, "By way of the Wilderness of Edom."

⁹So the king of Israel went with the king of Judah and the king of Edom, and they marched on that roundabout route seven days; and there was no water for the army, nor for the animals that followed them. ¹⁰And the king of Israel said, "Alas! For the LORD has called these three kings together to deliver them into the hand of Moab."

¹¹But Jehoshaphat said, "*Is there* no prophet of the LORD here, that we may inquire of the LORD by him?"

So one of the servants of the king of Israel answered and said, "Elisha the son of Shaphat *is* here, who poured water on the hands of Elijah."

¹²And Jehoshaphat said, "The word of the LORD is with him." So the king of Israel and Jehoshaphat and the king of Edom went down to him.

¹³Then Elisha said to the king of Israel, "What have I to do with you? Go to the prophets of your father and the prophets of your mother."

But the king of Israel said to him, "No, for the LORD has called these three kings *together* to deliver them into the hand of Moab."

¹⁴And Elisha said, "*As* the LORD of hosts lives, before whom I stand, surely were it not that I regard the presence of Jehoshaphat king of Judah, I would not look at you, nor see you. ¹⁵But now bring me a musician."

Then it happened, when the musician played, that the hand of the LORD came upon him. ¹⁶And he said, "Thus says the LORD: 'Make this valley full of ditches.' ¹⁷For thus says the LORD: 'You shall not see wind, nor shall you see rain; yet that valley shall be filled with water, so that you, your cattle, and your animals may drink.' ¹⁸And this is a simple matter in the sight of the LORD; He will also deliver the Moabites into your hand. ¹⁹Also you shall attack every fortified city and every choice city, and shall cut down every good tree, and stop up every spring of water, and ruin every good piece of land with stones."

²⁰Now it happened in the morning, when the grain offering was offered, that suddenly water came by way of Edom, and the land was filled with water.

²¹And when all the Moabites heard that the kings had come up to fight against them, all who were able to bear arms and older were gathered; and they stood at the border. ²²Then they rose up early in the morning, and the sun was shining on the water; and the Moabites

ELISHA made a difference

As far as Elisha knew, his job that day was to take his father's twelve yoke of oxen and plow the family fields. He was busy. Then the old prophet Elijah walked by and tossed his mantle over Elisha's shoulders. Life was never the same again.

Elijah was following God's direction. God called Elisha through Elijah. But Elisha had to respond. He struggled. He ran after Elijah and asked for time to say a proper good-bye to his parents. Elijah's answer made it clear that this wasn't about following an old prophet but about following God's call. So Elisha sacrificed his oxen, used the yoke for firewood, shared the barbecue with the plowing crew, and placed the invisible yoke of service to God on his own shoulders.

Cutting Edge

As Elijah's helper, Elisha watched a man of God in action. He learned. Just before God took Elijah, Elisha had the opportunity to make a request. He asked for a double helping of the Spirit of God, which had been in Elijah. He didn't just want to be like his mentor; he wanted to be as available to God as his mentor had been. For more than fifty years, Elisha demonstrated in various ways what a difference a person can make when motivated and filled by the Spirit of God.

YOU can, too!

There's a lot we don't know about Elisha's story. Did he walk away from important responsibilities? He was one—twelfth of the workforce that day. His parents had a lot of help in the field. Perhaps they heard all the commotion and joined the party. The point is that when God's call required Elisha to walk away from all that was familiar to him, he did.

God's call in **your Life** may not require you to move somewhere else. But it will change the focus of your life. It may not change what you do, but it will definitely affect why you do it. Use Elisha's experience to visualize a prayer: Lord, help me know Your call when the mantle falls on my shoulders. Help me follow You.

Want to know more? Read about Elisha's life in 1 Kings 19:16—2 Kings 13:20.

saw the water on the other side *as* red as blood. ²³And they said, "This is blood; the kings have surely struck swords and have killed one another; now therefore, Moab, to the spoil!"

²⁴So when they came to the camp of Israel, Israel rose up and attacked the Moabites, so that they fled before them; and they entered *their* land, killing the Moabites. ²⁵Then they destroyed the cities, and each man threw a stone on every good piece of land and filled it; and they stopped up all the springs of water and cut down all the good trees. But they left the stones of Kir Haraseth *intact*. However the slingers surrounded and attacked it.

²⁶And when the king of Moab saw that the battle was too fierce for him, he took with him seven hundred men who drew swords, to break through to the king of Edom, but they could not. ²⁷Then he took his eldest son who would have reigned in his place, and offered him *as* a burnt offering upon the wall; and there was great indignation against Israel. So they departed from him and returned to *their own* land.

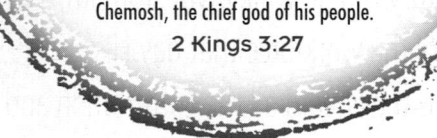

WHAT'S IT MEAN?

Somewhere in ancient history someone came up with the idea that sacrificing children was the way to win favor with gods. Mesha obviously believed in that idea. The Moabite king was so desperate to prevent his troops from being defeated that he killed his own son as an offering to Chemosh, the chief god of his people.

2 Kings 3:27

ELISHA AND THE WIDOW'S OIL

¹A certain woman of the wives of the sons of the prophets cried out to Elisha, saying, "Your servant my husband is dead, and you know that your servant feared the LORD. And the creditor is coming to take my two sons to be his slaves."

²So Elisha said to her, "What shall I do for you? Tell me, what do you have in the house?" And she said, "Your maidservant has nothing in the house but a jar of oil."

³Then he said, "Go, borrow vessels from everywhere, from all your neighbors—empty vessels; do not gather just a few. ⁴And when you have come in, you shall shut the door be-

hind you and your sons; then pour it into all those vessels, and set aside the full ones."

⁵So she went from him and shut the door behind her and her sons, who brought *the vessels* to her; and she poured *it* out. ⁶Now it came to pass, when the vessels were full, that she said to her son, "Bring me another vessel."

And he said to her, "*There is* not another vessel." So the oil ceased. ⁷Then she came and told the man of God. And he said, "Go, sell the oil and pay your debt; and you *and* your sons live on the rest."

FAITH

What's a good example of faith? (4:1–7)

ELISHA RAISES THE SHUNAMMITE'S SON

⁸Now it happened one day that Elisha went to Shunem, where there *was* a notable woman, and she persuaded him to eat some food. So it was, as often as he passed by, he would turn in there to eat some food. ⁹And she said to her husband, "Look now, I know that this *is* a holy man of God, who passes by us regularly. ¹⁰Please, let us make a small upper room on the wall; and let us put a bed for him there, and a table and a chair and a lampstand; so it will be, whenever he comes to us, he can turn in there."

¹¹And it happened one day that he came there, and he turned in to the upper room and lay down there. ¹²Then he said to Gehazi his servant, "Call this Shunammite woman." When he had called her, she stood before him. ¹³And he said to him, "Say now to her, 'Look, you have been concerned for us with all this care. What *can* I do for you? Do you want me to speak on your behalf to the king or to the commander of the army?' "

She answered, "I dwell among my own people."

¹⁴So he said, "What then *is* to be done for her?"

And Gehazi answered, "Actually, she has no son, and her husband is old."

¹⁵So he said, "Call her." When he had called her, she stood in the doorway. ¹⁶Then he said, "About this time next year you shall embrace a son."

And she said, "No, my lord. Man of God, do not lie to your maidservant!"

¹⁷But the woman conceived, and bore a son when the appointed time had come, of which Elisha had told her.

¹⁸And the child grew. Now it happened one day that he went out to his father, to the reapers. ¹⁹And he said to his father, "My head, my head!"

So he said to a servant, "Carry him to his mother." [20]When he had taken him and brought him to his mother, he sat on her knees till noon, and *then* died. [21]And she went up and laid him on the bed of the man of God, shut *the door* upon him, and went out. [22]Then she called to her husband, and said, "Please send me one of the young men and one of the donkeys, that I may run to the man of God and come back."

[23]So he said, "Why are you going to him today? *It is* neither the New Moon nor the Sabbath."

And she said, "*It is* well." [24]Then she saddled a donkey, and said to her servant, "Drive, and go forward; do not slacken the pace for me unless I tell you." [25]And so she departed, and went to the man of God at Mount Carmel.

So it was, when the man of God saw her afar off, that he said to his servant Gehazi, "Look, the Shunammite woman! [26]Please run now to meet her, and say to her, '*Is it* well with you? *Is it* well with your husband? *Is it* well with the child?' "

And she answered, "*It is* well." [27]Now when she came to the man of God at the hill, she caught him by the feet, but Gehazi came near to push her away. But the man of God said, "Let her alone; for her soul *is* in deep distress, and the LORD has hidden *it* from me, and has not told me."

[28]So she said, "Did I ask a son of my lord? Did I not say, 'Do not deceive me'?"

[29]Then he said to Gehazi, "Get yourself ready, and take my staff in your hand, and be on your way. If you meet anyone, do not greet him; and if anyone greets you, do not answer him; but lay my staff on the face of the child."

[30]And the mother of the child said, "*As the* LORD lives, and *as* your soul lives, I will not leave you." So he arose and followed her. [31]Now Gehazi went on ahead of them, and laid the staff on the face of the child; but *there was* neither voice nor hearing. Therefore he went back to meet him, and told him, saying, "The child has not awakened."

[32]When Elisha came into the house, there was the child, lying dead on his bed. [33]He went in therefore, shut the door behind the two of them, and prayed to the LORD. [34]And he went up and lay on the child, and put his mouth on his mouth, his eyes on his eyes, and his hands on his hands; and he stretched himself out on the child, and the flesh of the child became warm. [35]He returned and walked back and forth in the house, and again went up and stretched himself out on him; then the child sneezed seven times, and the child opened his eyes. [36]And he called Gehazi and said, "Call this Shunammite woman." So he called her. And when she came in to him, he said, "Pick up your son." [37]So she went in, fell at his feet, and bowed to the ground; then she picked up her son and went out.

ELISHA PURIFIES THE POT OF STEW

[38]And Elisha returned to Gilgal, and *there was* a famine in the land. Now the sons of the prophets *were* sitting before him; and he said to his servant, "Put on the large pot, and boil stew for the sons of the prophets." [39]So one went out into the field to gather herbs, and found a wild vine, and gathered from it a lapful of wild gourds, and came and sliced *them* into the pot of stew, though they did not know *what they were*. [40]Then they served it to the men to eat. Now it happened, as they were eating the stew, that they cried out and said, "Man of God, *there is* death in the pot!" And they could not eat *it.*

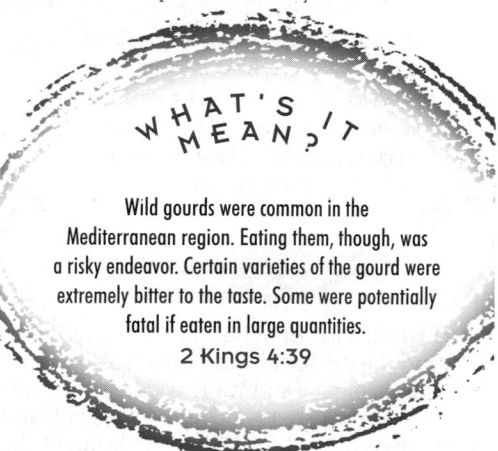

WHAT'S IT MEAN?

Wild gourds were common in the Mediterranean region. Eating them, though, was a risky endeavor. Certain varieties of the gourd were extremely bitter to the taste. Some were potentially fatal if eaten in large quantities.

2 Kings 4:39

[41]So he said, "Then bring some flour." And he put *it* into the pot, and said, "Serve *it* to the people, that they may eat." And there was nothing harmful in the pot.

ELISHA FEEDS ONE HUNDRED MEN

[42]Then a man came from Baal Shalisha, and brought the man of God bread of the firstfruits, twenty loaves of barley bread, and newly ripened grain in his knapsack. And he said, "Give *it* to the people, that they may eat."

[43]But his servant said, "What? Shall I set this before one hundred men?"

He said again, "Give it to the people, that they may eat; for thus says the LORD: 'They shall eat and have *some* left over.' " [44]So he set *it* before them; and they ate and had *some* left over, according to the word of the LORD.

NAAMAN'S LEPROSY HEALED

[1]Now Naaman, commander of the army of the king of Syria, was a great and honorable man in the eyes of his master, because by him the LORD had given victory to Syria. He was also a mighty man of valor, *but* a leper. [2]And the Syrians had gone out on raids, and had brought back captive a young girl from the land of Israel. She waited on Naaman's wife. [3]Then she said to her mistress, "If only my master *were* with the prophet who *is* in Samaria! For he would heal him of his leprosy." [4]And *Naaman* went in and told his master, saying, "Thus and thus said the girl who *is* from the land of Israel."

WHAT'S IT MEAN?

Samaria was a logical choice for the capital of the northern kingdom of Israel. It was located about halfway between the Sea of Galilee and the Dead Sea, and about halfway between the Jordan River and the Mediterranean Sea—right smack in the middle of the territory.

2 Kings 5:3

[5]Then the king of Syria said, "Go now, and I will send a letter to the king of Israel."

So he departed and took with him ten talents of silver, six thousand *shekels* of gold, and ten changes of clothing. [6]Then he brought the letter to the king of Israel, which said,

Now be advised, when this letter comes to you, that I have sent Naaman my servant to you, that you may heal him of his leprosy.

[7]And it happened, when the king of Israel read the letter, that he tore his clothes and said, "*Am I* God, to kill and make alive, that this man sends a man to me to heal him of his leprosy? Therefore please consider, and see how he seeks a quarrel with me."

[8]So it was, when Elisha the man of God heard that the king of Israel had torn his clothes, that he sent to the king, saying, "Why have you torn your clothes? Please let him

come to me, and he shall know that there is a prophet in Israel."

[9]Then Naaman went with his horses and chariot, and he stood at the door of Elisha's house. [10]And Elisha sent a messenger to him, saying, "Go and wash in the Jordan seven times, and your flesh shall be restored to you, and *you shall* be clean." [11]But Naaman became furious, and went away and said, "Indeed, I said to myself, 'He will surely come out *to me*, and stand and call on the name of the LORD his God, and wave his hand over the place, and heal the leprosy.' [12]*Are* not the Abanah[a] and the Pharpar, the rivers of Damascus, better than all the waters of Israel? Could I not wash in them and be clean?" So he turned and went away in a rage. [13]And his servants came near and spoke to him, and said, "My father, *if* the prophet had told you *to do* something great, would you not have done *it?* How much more then, when he says to you, 'Wash, and be clean'?" [14]So he went down and dipped seven times in the Jordan, according to the saying of the man of God; and his flesh was restored like the flesh of a little child, and he was clean.

[15]And he returned to the man of God, he and all his aides, and came and stood before him; and he said, "Indeed, now I know that *there is* no God in all the earth, except in Israel; now therefore, please take a gift from your servant."

GOD

Who else is like God? (5:15)

[16]But he said, "*As* the LORD lives, before whom I stand, I will receive nothing." And he urged him to take *it,* but he refused.

[17]So Naaman said, "Then, if not, please let your servant be given two mule-loads of earth; for your servant will no longer offer either burnt offering or sacrifice to other gods, but to the LORD. [18]Yet in this thing may the LORD pardon your servant: when my master goes into the temple of Rimmon to worship there, and he leans on my hand, and I bow down in the temple of Rimmon—when I bow down in the temple of Rimmon, may the LORD please pardon your servant in this thing."

[19]Then he said to him, "Go in peace." So he departed from him a short distance.

GEHAZI'S GREED

[20]But Gehazi, the servant of Elisha the man of God, said, "Look, my master has spared Naaman this Syrian, while not receiving from his hands what he brought; but *as* the LORD lives, I

5:12 [a]Following Kethib, Septuagint, and Vulgate; Qere, Syriac, and Targum read *Amanah.*

will run after him and take something from him." ²¹So Gehazi pursued Naaman. When Naaman saw *him* running after him, he got down from the chariot to meet him, and said, "Is all well?"

²²And he said, "All *is* well. My master has sent me, saying, 'Indeed, just now two young men of the sons of the prophets have come to me from the mountains of Ephraim. Please give them a talent of silver and two changes of garments.'"

²³So Naaman said, "Please, take two talents." And he urged him, and bound two talents of silver in two bags, with two changes of garments, and handed *them* to two of his servants; and they carried *them* on ahead of him. ²⁴When he came to the citadel, he took *them* from their hand, and stored *them* away in the house; then he let the men go, and they departed. ²⁵Now he went in and stood before his master. Elisha said to him, "Where *did you go*, Gehazi?"

And he said, "Your servant did not go anywhere."

²⁶Then he said to him, "Did not my heart go *with you* when the man turned back from his chariot to meet you? *Is it* time to receive money and to receive clothing, olive groves and vineyards, sheep and oxen, male and female servants? ²⁷Therefore the leprosy of Naaman shall cling to you and your descendants forever." And he went out from his presence leprous, *as white* as snow.

THE FLOATING AX HEAD

¹And the sons of the prophets said to Elisha, "See now, the place where we dwell with you is too small for us. ²Please, let us go to the Jordan, and let every man take a beam from there, and let us make there a place where we may dwell."

So he answered, "Go."

³Then one said, "Please consent to go with your servants."

And he answered, "I will go." ⁴So he went with them. And when they came to the Jordan, they cut down trees. ⁵But as one was cutting down a tree, the iron *ax head* fell into the water; and he cried out and said, "Alas, master! For it was borrowed."

⁶So the man of God said, "Where did it fall?" And he showed him the place. So he cut off a stick, and threw *it* in there; and he made the iron float. ⁷Therefore he said, "Pick *it* up for yourself." So he reached out his hand and took it.

THE BLINDED SYRIANS CAPTURED

⁸Now the king of Syria was making war against Israel; and he consulted with his servants, saying, "My camp *will be* in such and such a place." ⁹And the man of God sent to the king of Israel, saying, "Beware that you do not pass this place, for the Syrians are coming down there." ¹⁰Then the king of Israel sent *someone* to the place of which the man of God had told him. Thus he warned him, and he was watchful there, not just once or twice.

¹¹Therefore the heart of the king of Syria was greatly troubled by this thing; and he called his servants and said to them, "Will you not show me which of us *is* for the king of Israel?"

¹²And one of his servants said, "None, my lord, O king; but Elisha, the prophet who *is* in Israel, tells the king of Israel the words that you speak in your bedroom."

¹³So he said, "Go and see where he *is*, that I may send and get him."

And it was told him, saying, "Surely *he is* in Dothan."

¹⁴Therefore he sent horses and chariots and a great army there, and they came by night and surrounded the city. ¹⁵And when the servant of the man of God arose early and went out, there was an army, surrounding the city with horses and chariots. And his servant said to him, "Alas, my master! What shall we do?"

¹⁶So he answered, "Do not fear, for those who *are* with us *are* more than those who *are* with them." ¹⁷And Elisha prayed, and said, "LORD, I pray, open his eyes that he may see." Then the LORD opened the eyes of the young man, and he saw. And behold, the mountain *was* full of horses and chariots of fire all around Elisha. ¹⁸So when *the Syrians* came down to him, Elisha prayed to the LORD, and said, "Strike this people, I pray, with blindness." And He struck them with blindness according to the word of Elisha.

¹⁹Now Elisha said to them, "This *is* not the way, nor *is* this the city. Follow me, and I will

"So he answered, 'Do not fear, for those who are with us are more than those who are with them.' And Elisha prayed, and said, 'LORD, I pray, open his eyes that he may see.'"
(2 Kings 6:16, 17a)

bring you to the man whom you seek." But he led them to Samaria.

20So it was, when they had come to Samaria, that Elisha said, "LORD, open the eyes of these *men*, that they may see." And the LORD opened their eyes, and they saw; and there *they were*, inside Samaria!

21Now when the king of Israel saw them, he said to Elisha, "My father, shall I kill *them*? Shall I kill *them*?"

22But he answered, "You shall not kill *them*. Would you kill those whom you have taken captive with your sword and your bow? Set food and water before them, that they may eat and drink and go to their master." 23Then he prepared a great feast for them; and after they ate and drank, he sent them away and they went to their master. So the bands of Syrian *raiders* came no more into the land of Israel.

SYRIA BESIEGES SAMARIA IN FAMINE

24And it happened after this that Ben-Hadad king of Syria gathered all his army, and went up and besieged Samaria. 25And there was a great famine in Samaria; and indeed they besieged it until a donkey's head was *sold* for eighty *shekels* of silver, and one-fourth of a kab of dove droppings for five *shekels* of silver.

26Then, as the king of Israel was passing by on the wall, a woman cried out to him, saying, "Help, my lord, O king!"

27And he said, "If the LORD does not help you, where can I find help for you? From the threshing floor or from the winepress?" 28Then the king said to her, "What is troubling you?"

And she answered, "This woman said to me, 'Give your son, that we may eat him today, and we will eat my son tomorrow.' 29So we boiled my son, and ate him. And I said to her on the next day, 'Give your son, that we may eat him'; but she has hidden her son."

30Now it happened, when the king heard the words of the woman, that he tore his clothes; and as he passed by on the wall, the people looked, and there underneath *he had* sackcloth on his body. 31Then he said, "God do so to me and more also, if the head of Elisha the son of Shaphat remains on him today!"

32But Elisha was sitting in his house, and the elders were sitting with him. And *the king* sent a man ahead of him, but before the messenger came to him, he said to the elders, "Do you see how this son of a murderer has sent someone to take away my head? Look, when the messenger comes, shut the door, and hold him fast at the door. *Is* not the sound of his master's feet behind him?" 33And while he was still talking

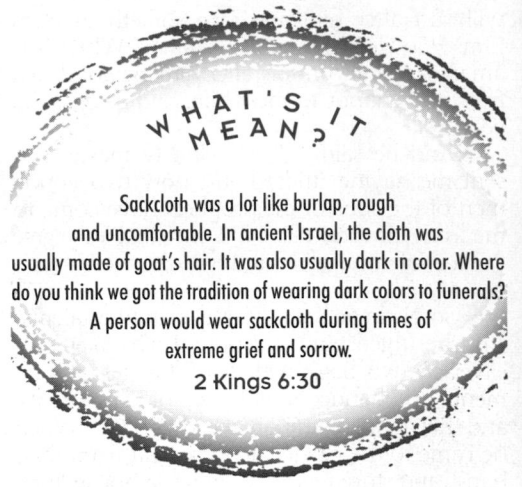

with them, there was the messenger, coming down to him; and then *the king* said, "Surely this calamity *is* from the LORD; why should I wait for the LORD any longer?"

1Then Elisha said, "Hear the word of the LORD. Thus says the LORD: 'Tomorrow about this time a seah of fine flour *shall be sold* for a shekel, and two seahs of barley for a shekel, at the gate of Samaria.' "

2So an officer on whose hand the king leaned answered the man of God and said, "Look, *if* the LORD would make windows in heaven, could this thing be?"

And he said, "In fact, you shall see *it* with your eyes, but you shall not eat of it."

THE SYRIANS FLEE

3Now there were four leprous men at the entrance of the gate; and they said to one another, "Why are we sitting here until we die? 4If we say, 'We will enter the city,' the famine *is* in the city, and we shall die there. And if we sit here, we die also. Now therefore, come, let us surrender to the army of the Syrians. If they keep us alive, we shall live; and if they kill us, we shall only die." 5And they rose at twilight to go to the camp of the Syrians; and when they had come to the outskirts of the Syrian camp, to their surprise no one *was* there. 6For the LORD had caused the army of the Syrians to hear the noise of chariots and the noise of horses—the noise of a great army; so they said to one another, "Look, the king of Israel has hired against us the kings of the Hittites and the kings of the Egyptians to attack us!" 7Therefore they arose and fled at twilight, and left the camp intact—their tents, their horses, and their donkeys—and they fled for their lives. 8And when these lepers came to the outskirts of the camp, they went into one tent and ate and drank, and carried from it silver and gold and clothing, and went and hid *them*; then they came back and entered another tent, and carried *some* from there *also*, and went and hid *it*.

⁹Then they said to one another, "We are not doing right. This day *is* a day of good news, and we remain silent. If we wait until morning light, some punishment will come upon us. Now therefore, come, let us go and tell the king's household." ¹⁰So they went and called to the gatekeepers of the city, and told them, saying, "We went to the Syrian camp, and surprisingly no one *was* there, not a human sound—only horses and donkeys tied, and the tents intact." ¹¹And the gatekeepers called out, and they told *it* to the king's household inside.

¹²So the king arose in the night and said to his servants, "Let me now tell you what the Syrians have done to us. They know that we *are* hungry; therefore they have gone out of the camp to hide themselves in the field, saying, 'When they come out of the city, we shall catch them alive, and get into the city.' "

¹³And one of his servants answered and said, "Please, let several *men* take five of the remaining horses which are left in the city. Look, they *may either become* like all the multitude of Israel that are left in it; or indeed, *I say*, they *may become* like all the multitude of Israel left from those who are consumed; so let us send them and see." ¹⁴Therefore they took two chariots with horses; and the king sent them in the direction of the Syrian army, saying, "Go and see." ¹⁵And they went after them to the Jordan; and indeed all the road *was* full of garments and weapons which the Syrians had thrown away in their haste. So the messengers returned and told the king. ¹⁶Then the people went out and plundered the tents of the Syrians. So a seah of fine flour was *sold* for a shekel, and two seahs of barley for a shekel, according to the word of the LORD.

¹⁷Now the king had appointed the officer on whose hand he leaned to have charge of the gate. But the people trampled him in the gate, and he died, just as the man of God had said, who spoke when the king came down to him. ¹⁸So it happened just as the man of God had spoken to the king, saying, "Two seahs of barley for a shekel, and a seah of fine flour for a shekel, shall be *sold* tomorrow about this time in the gate of Samaria."

¹⁹Then that officer had answered the man of God, and said, "Now look, *if* the LORD would make windows in heaven, could such a thing be?"

And he had said, "In fact, you shall see *it* with your eyes, but you shall not eat of it." ²⁰And so it happened to him, for the people trampled him in the gate, and he died.

THE KING RESTORES THE SHUNAMMITE'S LAND

¹Then Elisha spoke to the woman whose son he had restored to life, saying, "Arise and go, you and your household, and stay wherever you can; for the LORD has called for a famine, and furthermore, it will come upon the land for seven years." ²So the woman arose and did according to the saying of the man of God, and she went with her household and dwelt in the land of the Philistines seven years.

³It came to pass, at the end of seven years, that the woman returned from the land of the Philistines; and she went to make an appeal to the king for her house and for her land. ⁴Then the king talked with Gehazi, the servant of the man of God, saying, "Tell me, please, all the great things Elisha has done." ⁵Now it happened, as he was telling the king how he had restored the dead to life, that there was the woman whose son he had restored to life, appealing to the king for her house and for her land. And Gehazi said, "My lord, O king, this *is* the woman, and this *is* her son whom Elisha restored to life." ⁶And when the king asked the woman, she told him.

So the king appointed a certain officer for her, saying, "Restore all that *was* hers, and all the proceeds of the field from the day that she left the land until now."

DEATH OF BEN-HADAD

⁷Then Elisha went to Damascus, and Ben-Hadad king of Syria was sick; and it was told him, saying, "The man of God has come here." ⁸And the king said to Hazael, "Take a present in your hand, and go to meet the man of God, and inquire of the LORD by him, saying, 'Shall I recover from this disease?' " ⁹So Hazael went to meet him and took a present with him, of every good thing of Damascus, forty camel-loads; and he came and stood before him, and said, "Your son Ben-Hadad king of Syria has sent me to you, saying, 'Shall I recover from this disease?' "

¹⁰And Elisha said to him, "Go, say to him, 'You shall certainly recover.' However the LORD has shown me that he will really die." ¹¹Then he set his countenance in a stare until he was ashamed; and the man of God wept. ¹²And Hazael said, "Why is my lord weeping?"

He answered, "Because I know the evil that you will do to the children of Israel: Their strongholds you will set on fire, and their young men you will kill with the sword; and you will dash their children, and rip open their women with child."

[13]So Hazael said, "But what *is* your servant—a dog, that he should do this gross thing?"

And Elisha answered, "The LORD has shown me that you *will become* king over Syria."

[14]Then he departed from Elisha, and came to his master, who said to him, "What did Elisha say to you?" And he answered, "He told me you would surely recover." [15]But it happened on the next day that he took a thick cloth and dipped *it* in water, and spread *it* over his face so that he died; and Hazael reigned in his place.

JEHORAM REIGNS IN JUDAH

[16]Now in the fifth year of Joram the son of Ahab, king of Israel, Jehoshaphat *having been* king of Judah, Jehoram the son of Jehoshaphat began to reign as king of Judah. [17]He was thirty-two years old when he became king, and he reigned eight years in Jerusalem. [18]And he walked in the way of the kings of Israel, just as the house of Ahab had done, for the daughter of Ahab was his wife; and he did evil in the sight of the LORD. [19]Yet the LORD would not destroy Judah, for the sake of his servant David, as He promised him to give a lamp to him *and* his sons forever.

WHAT'S IT MEAN?

The rebellion against Joram stretched from Edom, which was south of the Dead Sea, to Libnah, which was only about twenty-five miles from Jerusalem.
2 Kings 8:20

[20]In his days Edom revolted against Judah's authority, and made a king over themselves. [21]So Joram[a] went to Zair, and all his chariots with him. Then he rose by night and attacked the Edomites who had surrounded him and the captains of the chariots; and the troops fled to their tents. [22]Thus Edom has been in revolt against Judah's authority to this day. And Libnah revolted at that time.

[23]Now the rest of the acts of Joram, and all that he did, *are* they not written in the book of the chronicles of the kings of Judah? [24]So Joram rested with his fathers, and was buried with his fathers in the City of David. Then Ahaziah his son reigned in his place.

AHAZIAH REIGNS IN JUDAH

[25]In the twelfth year of Joram the son of Ahab, king of Israel, Ahaziah the son of Jehoram, king of Judah, began to reign. [26]Ahaziah *was* twenty-two years old when he became king, and he reigned one year in Jerusalem. His mother's name *was* Athaliah the granddaughter of Omri, king of Israel. [27]And he walked in the way of the house of Ahab, and did evil in the sight of the LORD, like the house of Ahab, for he *was* the son-in-law of the house of Ahab.

WHAT'S IT MEAN?

Because it was located on the border of Israel and Syria, Ramoth Gilead was the site of many bloody battles between the two countries. While Joram was recuperating from his injuries in Jezreel, his army officers were fighting in Ramoth Gilead.
2 Kings 8:28, 29

[28]Now he went with Joram the son of Ahab to war against Hazael king of Syria at Ramoth Gilead; and the Syrians wounded Joram. [29]Then King Joram went back to Jezreel to recover from the wounds which the Syrians had inflicted on him at Ramah, when he fought against Hazael king of Syria. And Ahaziah the son of Jehoram, king of Judah, went down to see Joram the son of Ahab in Jezreel, because he was sick.

JEHU ANOINTED KING OF ISRAEL

[1]And Elisha the prophet called one of the sons of the prophets, and said to him, "Get yourself ready, take this flask of oil in your hand, and go to Ramoth Gilead. [2]Now when you arrive at that place, look there for Jehu the

son of Jehoshaphat, the son of Nimshi, and go in and make him rise up from among his associates, and take him to an inner room. ³Then take the flask of oil, and pour *it* on his head, and say, 'Thus says the LORD: "I have anointed you king over Israel." ' Then open the door and flee, and do not delay."

⁴So the young man, the servant of the prophet, went to Ramoth Gilead. ⁵And when he arrived, there *were* the captains of the army sitting; and he said, "I have a message for you, Commander."

Jehu said, "For which *one* of us?"

And he said, "For you, Commander." ⁶Then he arose and went into the house. And he poured the oil on his head, and said to him, "Thus says the LORD God of Israel: 'I have anointed you king over the people of the LORD, over Israel. ⁷You shall strike down the house of Ahab your master, that I may avenge the blood of My servants the prophets, and the blood of all the servants of the LORD, at the hand of Jezebel. ⁸For the whole house of Ahab shall perish; and I will cut off from Ahab all the males in Israel, both bond and free. ⁹So I will make the house of Ahab like the house of Jeroboam the son of Nebat, and like the house of Baasha the son of Ahijah. ¹⁰The dogs shall eat Jezebel on the plot *of ground* at Jezreel, and *there shall be* none to bury *her*.' " And he opened the door and fled.

¹¹Then Jehu came out to the servants of his master, and *one* said to him, "Is all well? Why did this madman come to you?"

And he said to them, "You know the man and his babble."

¹²And they said, "A lie! Tell us now." So he said, "Thus and thus he spoke to me, saying, 'Thus says the LORD: "I have anointed you king over Israel." ' "

¹³Then each man hastened to take his garment and put *it* under him on the top of the steps; and they blew trumpets, saying, "Jehu is king!"

JORAM OF ISRAEL KILLED

¹⁴So Jehu the son of Jehoshaphat, the son of Nimshi, conspired against Joram. (Now Joram had been defending Ramoth Gilead, he and all Israel, against Hazael king of Syria. ¹⁵But King Joram had returned to Jezreel to recover from the wounds which the Syrians had inflicted on him when he fought with Hazael king of Syria.) And Jehu said, "If you are so minded, let no one leave *or* escape from the city to go and tell *it* in Jezreel." ¹⁶So Jehu rode in a chariot and went to Jezreel, for Joram was laid up there; and Ahaziah king of Judah had come down to see Joram.

¹⁷Now a watchman stood on the tower in Jezreel, and he saw the company of Jehu as he came, and said, "I see a company of men."

And Joram said, "Get a horseman and send him to meet them, and let him say, 'Is it peace?' "

¹⁸So the horseman went to meet him, and said, "Thus says the king: 'Is it peace?' "

And Jehu said, "What have you to do with peace? Turn around and follow me."

So the watchman reported, saying, "The messenger went to them, but is not coming back."

¹⁹Then he sent out a second horseman who came to them, and said, "Thus says the king: 'Is it peace?' "

And Jehu answered, "What have you to do with peace? Turn around and follow me."

²⁰So the watchman reported, saying, "He went up to them and is not coming back; and the driving *is* like the driving of Jehu the son of Nimshi, for he drives furiously!"

²¹Then Joram said, "Make ready." And his chariot was made ready. Then Joram king of Israel and Ahaziah king of Judah went out, each in his chariot; and they went out to meet Jehu, and met him on the property of Naboth the Jezreelite. ²²Now it happened, when Joram saw Jehu, that he said, "Is *it* peace, Jehu?"

So he answered, "What peace, as long as the harlotries of your mother Jezebel and her witchcraft *are so* many?"

²³Then Joram turned around and fled, and said to Ahaziah, "Treachery, Ahaziah!" ²⁴Now Jehu drew his bow with full strength and shot Jehoram between his arms; and the arrow came out at his heart, and he sank down in his chariot. ²⁵Then *Jehu* said to Bidkar his captain, "Pick *him* up, *and* throw him into the tract of the field of Naboth the Jezreelite; for remember, when you and I were riding together behind Ahab his father, that the LORD laid this burden upon him: ²⁶'Surely I saw yesterday the blood of Naboth and the blood of his sons,' says the LORD, 'and I will repay you in this plot,' says the LORD. Now therefore, take *and* throw him on the plot *of ground*, according to the word of the LORD."

AHAZIAH OF JUDAH KILLED

²⁷But when Ahaziah king of Judah saw *this*, he fled by the road to Beth Haggan.*ᵃ* So Jehu pursued him, and said, "Shoot him also in the

---

9:27 ᵃLiterally *The Garden House*

chariot." *And they shot him* at the Ascent of Gur, which is by Ibleam. Then he fled to Megiddo, and died there. [28]And his servants carried him in the chariot to Jerusalem, and buried him in his tomb with his fathers in the City of David. [29]In the eleventh year of Joram the son of Ahab, Ahaziah had become king over Judah.

JEZEBEL'S VIOLENT DEATH

[30]Now when Jehu had come to Jezreel, Jezebel heard *of it;* and she put paint on her eyes and adorned her head, and looked through a window. [31]Then, as Jehu entered at the gate, she said, "*Is it* peace, Zimri, murderer of your master?"

WHAT'S IT MEAN?

As far as the Israelites were concerned, Jezebel's death was one of the most gruesome endings imaginable. For one thing, the Israelites considered it a tragedy not to be buried properly. Jehu didn't want to insult a member of the royal family—even someone as wicked as Jezebel—by not burying her body. Before he could prepare a grave, though, Jezebel's body was eaten by dogs. This only added to the gruesomeness of the story. You see, the Israelites considered dogs to be filthy scavengers.

2 Kings 9:34–37

[32]And he looked up at the window, and said, "Who *is* on my side? Who?" So two *or* three eunuchs looked out at him. [33]Then he said, "Throw her down." So they threw her down, and *some* of her blood spattered on the wall and on the horses; and he trampled her underfoot. [34]And when he had gone in, he ate and drank. Then he said, "Go now, see to this accursed *woman,* and bury her, for she was a king's daughter." [35]So they went to bury her, but they found no more of her than the skull and the feet and the palms of *her* hands. [36]Therefore they came back and told him. And he said, "This *is* the word of the LORD, which He spoke by His servant Elijah the Tishbite, saying, 'On the plot *of ground* at Jezreel dogs shall eat the flesh of Jezebel;[a] [37]and the corpse of Jezebel shall be as refuse on the surface of the field, in

the plot at Jezreel, so that they shall not say, "Here *lies* Jezebel." ' "

AHAB'S SEVENTY SONS KILLED

[1]Now Ahab had seventy sons in Samaria. And Jehu wrote and sent letters to Samaria, to the rulers of Jezreel,[a] to the elders, and to those who reared Ahab's *sons,* saying:

2   Now as soon as this letter comes to you, since your master's sons *are* with you, and you have chariots and horses, a fortified city also, and weapons, [3]choose the best qualified of your master's sons, set *him* on his father's throne, and fight for your master's house.

[4]But they were exceedingly afraid, and said, "Look, two kings could not stand up to him; how then can we stand?" [5]And he who *was* in charge of the house, and he who *was* in charge of the city, the elders also, and those who reared *the sons,* sent to Jehu, saying, "We *are* your servants, we will do all you tell us; but we will not make anyone king. Do *what is* good in your sight." [6]Then he wrote a second letter to them, saying:

If you *are* for me and will obey my voice, take the heads of the men, your master's sons, and come to me at Jezreel by this time tomorrow.

Now the king's sons, seventy persons, *were* with the great men of the city, *who* were rearing them. [7]So it was, when the letter came to them, that they took the king's sons and slaughtered seventy persons, put their heads in baskets and sent *them* to him at Jezreel.

[8]Then a messenger came and told him, saying, "They have brought the heads of the king's sons."

And he said, "Lay them in two heaps at the entrance of the gate until morning."

[9]So it was, in the morning, that he went out and stood, and said to all the people, "You *are* righteous. Indeed I conspired against my master and killed him; but who killed all these? [10]Know now that nothing shall fall to the earth of the word of the LORD which the LORD spoke concerning the house of Ahab; for the LORD has done what He spoke by His servant Elijah." [11]So Jehu killed all who remained of the house of Ahab in Jezreel, and all his great men and his

---

9:36 [a]1 Kings 21:23   **10:1** [a]Following Masoretic Text, Syriac, and Targum; Septuagint reads *Samaria;* Vulgate reads *city.*

close acquaintances and his priests, until he left him none remaining.

AHAZIAH'S FORTY-TWO BROTHERS KILLED

¹²And he arose and departed and went to Samaria. On the way, at Beth Eked[a] of the Shepherds, ¹³Jehu met with the brothers of Ahaziah king of Judah, and said, "Who *are* you?"

So they answered, "We *are* the brothers of Ahaziah; we have come down to greet the sons of the king and the sons of the queen mother."

¹⁴And he said, "Take them alive!" So they took them alive, and killed them at the well of Beth Eked, forty-two men; and he left none of them.

THE REST OF AHAB'S FAMILY KILLED

¹⁵Now when he departed from there, he met Jehonadab the son of Rechab, *coming* to meet him; and he greeted him and said to him, "Is your heart right, as my heart *is* toward your heart?"

And Jehonadab answered, "It is."

Jehu said, "If it is, give *me* your hand." So he gave *him* his hand, and he took him up to him into the chariot. ¹⁶Then he said, "Come with me, and see my zeal for the LORD." So they had him ride in his chariot. ¹⁷And when he came to Samaria, he killed all who remained to Ahab in Samaria, till he had destroyed them, according to the word of the LORD which He spoke to Elijah.

WORSHIPERS OF BAAL KILLED

¹⁸Then Jehu gathered all the people together, and said to them, "Ahab served Baal a little, Jehu will serve him much. ¹⁹Now therefore, call to me all the prophets of Baal, all his servants, and all his priests. Let no one be missing, for I have a great sacrifice for Baal. Whoever is missing shall not live." But Jehu acted deceptively, with the intent of destroying the worshipers of Baal. ²⁰And Jehu said, "Proclaim a solemn assembly for Baal." So they proclaimed *it.* ²¹Then Jehu sent throughout all Israel; and all the worshipers of Baal came, so that there was not a man left who did not come. So they came into the temple[a] of Baal, and the temple of Baal was full from one end to the other. ²²And he said to the one in charge of the wardrobe, "Bring out vestments for all the worshipers of Baal." So he brought out vestments for them. ²³Then Jehu and Jehonadab the son of Rechab went into the temple of Baal, and said to the worshipers of Baal, "Search and see that no servants of the LORD are here with you, but only the worshipers of Baal." ²⁴So they went in to offer sacrifices and burnt offerings. Now Jehu had appointed for himself eighty men on the outside, and had said, "If any of the men whom I have brought into your hands escapes, *whoever lets him escape, it shall be* his life for the life of the other."

²⁵Now it happened, as soon as he had made an end of offering the burnt offering, that Jehu said to the guard and to the captains, "Go in *and* kill them; let no one come out!" And they killed them with the edge of the sword; then the guards and the officers threw *them* out, and went into the inner room of the temple of Baal. ²⁶And they brought the *sacred* pillars out of the temple of Baal and burned them. ²⁷Then they broke down the *sacred* pillar of Baal, and tore down the temple of Baal and made it a refuse dump to this day. ²⁸Thus Jehu destroyed Baal from Israel.

²⁹However Jehu did not turn away from the sins of Jeroboam the son of Nebat, who had made Israel sin, *that is,* from the golden calves that *were* at Bethel and Dan. ³⁰And the LORD said to Jehu, "Because you have done well in doing *what is* right in My sight, *and* have done to the house of Ahab all that *was* in My heart, your sons shall sit on the throne of Israel to the fourth *generation.*" ³¹But Jehu took no heed to walk in the law of the LORD God of Israel with all his heart; for he did not depart from the sins of Jeroboam, who had made Israel sin.

DEATH OF JEHU

³²In those days the LORD began to cut off *parts* of Israel; and Hazael conquered them in all the territory of Israel ³³from the Jordan eastward: all the land of Gilead—Gad, Reuben, and Manasseh—from Aroer, which *is* by the River Arnon, including Gilead and Bashan.

³⁴Now the rest of the acts of Jehu, all that he did, and all his might, *are* they not written in the book of the chronicles of the kings of Israel? ³⁵So Jehu rested with his fathers, and they buried him in Samaria. Then Jehoahaz his son reigned in his place. ³⁶And the period that Jehu reigned over Israel in Samaria *was* twenty-eight years.

ATHALIAH REIGNS IN JUDAH

¹When Athaliah the mother of Ahaziah saw that her son was dead, she arose and destroyed all the royal heirs. ²But Jehosheba, the daughter of King Joram, sister of Ahaziah, took Joash the

10:12 [a]Or *The Shearing House*   **10:21** [a]Literally *house,* and so elsewhere in this chapter son of Ahaziah, and stole him away from among the king's sons *who were* being murdered; and they hid him and his nurse in the bedroom, from Athaliah, so that he was not killed. ³So he was hidden with her in the house of the LORD for six years, while Athaliah reigned over the land.

JOASH CROWNED KING OF JUDAH

⁴In the seventh year Jehoiada sent and brought the captains of hundreds—of the bodyguards and the escorts—and brought them into the house of the LORD to him. And he made a covenant with them and took an oath from them in the house of the LORD, and showed them the king's son. ⁵Then he commanded them, saying, "This *is* what you shall do: One-third of you who come on duty on the Sabbath shall be keeping watch over the king's house, ⁶one-third *shall be* at the gate of Sur, and one-third at the gate behind the escorts. You shall keep the watch of the house, lest it be broken down. ⁷The two contingents of you who go off duty on the Sabbath shall keep the watch of the house of the LORD for the king. ⁸But you shall surround the king on all sides, every man with his weapons in his hand; and whoever comes within range, let him be put to death. You are to be with the king as he goes out and as he comes in."

⁹So the captains of the hundreds did according to all that Jehoiada the priest commanded. Each of them took his men who were to be on duty on the Sabbath, with those who were going off duty on the Sabbath, and came to Jehoiada the priest. ¹⁰And the priest gave the captains of hundreds the spears and shields which *had belonged* to King David, that were in the temple of the LORD. ¹¹Then the escorts stood, every man with his weapons in his hand, all around the king, from the right side of the temple to the left side of the temple, by the altar and the house. ¹²And he brought out the king's son, put the crown on him, and *gave him* the Testimony;*ᵃ* they made him king and anointed him, and they clapped their hands and said, "Long live the king!"

WHAT'S IT MEAN?

Pouring olive oil on a person's head—also known as anointing—was a way of indicating that the person had been chosen by God for a special task, such as being a prophet, priest, or king. The traditional response after witnessing an anointment was a raucous ovation, just like the one Joash received.

2 Kings 11:12

DEATH OF ATHALIAH

¹³Now when Athaliah heard the noise of the escorts *and* the people, she came to the people *in* the temple of the LORD. ¹⁴When she looked, there was the king standing by a pillar according to custom; and the leaders and the trumpeters were by the king. All the people of the land were rejoicing and blowing trumpets. So Athaliah tore her clothes and cried out, "Treason! Treason!"

¹⁵And Jehoiada the priest commanded the captains of the hundreds, the officers of the army, and said to them, "Take her outside under guard, and slay with the sword whoever follows her." For the priest had said, "Do not let her be killed in the house of the LORD." ¹⁶So they seized her; and she went by way of the horses' entrance *into* the king's house, and there she was killed.

¹⁷Then Jehoiada made a covenant between the LORD, the king, and the people, that they should be the LORD's people, and *also* between the king and the people. ¹⁸And all the people of the land went to the temple of Baal, and tore it down. They thoroughly broke in pieces its altars and images, and killed Mattan the priest of Baal before the altars. And the priest appointed officers over the house of the LORD. ¹⁹Then he took the captains of hundreds, the bodyguards, the escorts, and all the people of the land; and they brought the king

> **"Then Jehoiada made a covenant between the LORD, the king, and the people, that they should be the LORD's people, and also between the king and the people." (2 Kings 11:17)**

11:12 *ᵃ*That is, the Law (compare Exodus 25:16, 21 and Deuteronomy 31:9) down from the house of the LORD, and went by way of the gate of the escorts to the king's house. Then he sat on the throne of the kings. [20]So all the people of the land rejoiced; and the city was quiet, for they had slain Athaliah with the sword *in* the king's house. [21]Jehoash *was* seven years old when he became king.

JEHOASH REPAIRS THE TEMPLE

[1]In the seventh year of Jehu, Jehoash[a] became king, and he reigned forty years in Jerusalem. His mother's name *was* Zibiah of Beersheba. [2]Jehoash did *what was* right in the sight of the LORD all the days in which Jehoiada the priest instructed him. [3]But the high places were not taken away; the people still sacrificed and burned incense on the high places.

[4]And Jehoash said to the priests, "All the money of the dedicated gifts that are brought into the house of the LORD—each man's census money, each man's assessment money[a]— and all the money that a man purposes in his heart to bring into the house of the LORD, [5]let the priests take *it* themselves, each from his constituency; and let them repair the damages of the temple, wherever any dilapidation is found."

GIVING

Is the amount you give to God a personal decision? (12:4, 5)

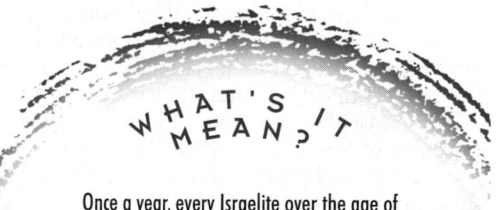

WHAT'S IT MEAN?

Once a year, every Israelite over the age of twenty donated a certain amount of money to be used for the temple. Other people gave gold and silver as gifts to show how much they appreciated what the Lord had done for them. Since there was no such thing as the First National Bank of Israel, the money and other valuables were stored in the temple.

2 Kings 12:4

[6]Now it was so, by the twenty-third year of King Jehoash, *that* the priests had not repaired the damages of the temple. [7]So King Jehoash called Jehoiada the priest and the *other* priests, and said to them, "Why have you not repaired the damages of the temple? Now therefore, do not take *more* money from your constituency, but deliver it for repairing the damages of the temple." [8]And the priests agreed that they would neither receive *more* money from the people, nor repair the damages of the temple.

[9]Then Jehoiada the priest took a chest, bored a hole in its lid, and set it beside the altar, on the right side as one comes into the house of the LORD; and the priests who kept the door put there all the money brought into the house of the LORD. [10]So it was, whenever they saw that *there was* much money in the chest, that the king's scribe and the high priest came up and put it in bags, and counted the money that was found in the house of the LORD. [11]Then they gave the money, which had been apportioned, into the hands of those who did the work, who had the oversight of the house of the LORD; and they paid it out to the carpenters and builders who worked on the house of the LORD, [12]and to masons and stonecutters, and for buying timber and hewn stone, to repair the damage of the house of the LORD, and for all that was paid out to repair the temple. [13]However there were not made for the house of the LORD basins of silver, trimmers, sprinkling-bowls, trumpets, any articles of gold or articles of silver, from the money brought into the house of the LORD. [14]But they gave that to the workmen, and they repaired the house of the LORD with it. [15]Moreover they did not require an account from the men into whose hand they delivered the money to be paid to workmen, for they dealt faithfully. [16]The money from the trespass offerings and the money from the sin offerings was not brought into the house of the LORD. It belonged to the priests.

HAZAEL THREATENS JERUSALEM

[17]Hazael king of Syria went up and fought against Gath, and took it; then Hazael set his face to go up to Jerusalem. [18]And Jehoash king of Judah took all the sacred things that his fathers, Jehoshaphat and Jehoram and Ahaziah, kings of Judah, had dedicated, and his own sacred things, and all the gold found in the treasuries of the house of the LORD and in the king's house, and sent *them* to Hazael king of Syria. Then he went away from Jerusalem.

DEATH OF JOASH

[19]Now the rest of the acts of Joash,[a] and all that he did, *are* they not written in the book of the chronicles of the kings of Judah? [20]And his servants arose and formed a

---

12:1 [a]Spelled *Joash* in 11:2ff   **12:4** [a]Compare Leviticus 27:2ff   **12:19** [a]Spelled *Jehoash* in 12:1ff conspiracy, and killed Joash in the house of the Millo,[a] which goes down to Silla. [21]For Jozachar[a] the son of Shimeath and Jehozabad the son of Shomer,[b] his servants, struck him. So he died, and they buried him with his fathers in the City of David. Then Amaziah his son reigned in his place.

JEHOAHAZ REIGNS IN ISRAEL

[1]In the twenty-third year of Joash[a] the son of Ahaziah, king of Judah, Jehoahaz the son of Jehu became king over Israel in Samaria, *and reigned* seventeen years. [2]And he did evil in the sight of the LORD, and followed the sins of Jeroboam the son of Nebat, who had made Israel sin. He did not depart from them.

[3]Then the anger of the LORD was aroused against Israel, and He delivered them into the hand of Hazael king of Syria, and into the hand of Ben-Hadad the son of Hazael, all *their* days. [4]So Jehoahaz pleaded with the LORD, and the LORD listened to him; for He saw the oppression of Israel, because the king of Syria oppressed them. [5]Then the LORD gave Israel a deliverer, so that they escaped from under the hand of the Syrians; and the children of Israel dwelt in their tents as before. [6]Nevertheless they did not depart from the sins of the house of Jeroboam, who had made Israel sin, *but* walked in them; and the wooden image[a] also remained in Samaria. [7]For He left of the army of Jehoahaz only fifty horsemen, ten chariots, and ten thousand foot soldiers; for the king of Syria had destroyed them and made them like the dust at threshing.

[8]Now the rest of the acts of Jehoahaz, all that he did, and his might, *are* they not written in the book of the chronicles of the kings of Israel? [9]So Jehoahaz rested with his fathers, and they buried him in Samaria. Then Joash his son reigned in his place.

JEHOASH REIGNS IN ISRAEL

[10]In the thirty-seventh year of Joash king of Judah, Jehoash[a] the son of Jehoahaz became king over Israel in Samaria, *and reigned* sixteen years. [11]And he did evil in the sight of the LORD. He did not depart from all the sins of Jeroboam the son of Nebat, who made Israel sin, *but* walked in them.

[12]Now the rest of the acts of Joash, all that he did, and his might with which he fought against Amaziah king of Judah, *are* they not written in the book of the chronicles of the kings of Israel? [13]So Joash rested with his fathers. Then Jeroboam sat on his throne. And Joash was buried in Samaria with the kings of Israel.

DEATH OF ELISHA

[14]Elisha had become sick with the illness of which he would die. Then Joash the king of Israel came down to him, and wept over his face, and said, "O my father, my father, the chariots of Israel and their horsemen!"

[15]And Elisha said to him, "Take a bow and some arrows." So he took himself a bow and some arrows. [16]Then he said to the king of Israel, "Put your hand on the bow." So he put his hand *on it,* and Elisha put his hands on the king's hands. [17]And he said, "Open the east window"; and he opened *it.* Then Elisha said, "Shoot"; and he shot. And he said, "The arrow of the LORD's deliverance and the arrow of deliverance from Syria; for you must strike the Syrians at Aphek till you have destroyed *them.*" [18]Then he said, "Take the arrows"; so he took *them.* And he said to the king of Israel, "Strike the ground"; so he struck three times, and stopped. [19]And the man of God was angry with him, and said, "You should have struck five or six times; then you would have struck Syria till you had destroyed *it!* But now you will strike Syria *only* three times."

[20]Then Elisha died, and they buried him. And the *raiding* bands from Moab invaded the land in the spring of the year. [21]So it was, as they were burying a man, that suddenly they spied a band *of raiders;* and they put the man in the tomb of Elisha; and when the man was let down and touched the bones of Elisha, he revived and stood on his feet.

ISRAEL RECAPTURES CITIES FROM SYRIA

[22]And Hazael king of Syria oppressed Israel all the days of Jehoahaz. [23]But the LORD was gracious to them, had compassion on them, and regarded them, because of His covenant with Abraham, Isaac, and Jacob, and would not yet destroy them or cast them from His presence.

[24]Now Hazael king of Syria died. Then Ben-Hadad his son reigned in his place. [25]And Jehoash[a] the son of Jehoahaz recaptured from the hand of Ben-Hadad, the son of Hazael, the cities which he had taken out of the hand of Jehoahaz his father by war. Three times

---

12:20 [a]Literally *The Landfill*　　**12:21** [a]Called *Zabad* in 2 Chronicles 24:26　[b]Called *Shimrith* in 2 Chronicles 24:26　**13:1** [a]Spelled *Jehoash* in 12:1ff　**13:6** [a]Hebrew *Asherah,* a Canaanite goddess　**13:10** [a]Spelled *Joash* in verse 9　**13:25** [a]Spelled *Joash* in verses 12–14, 25

Joash defeated him and recaptured the cities of Israel.

AMAZIAH REIGNS IN JUDAH

[1]In the second year of Joash the son of Jehoahaz, king of Israel, Amaziah the son of Joash, king of Judah, became king. [2]He was twenty-five years old when he became king, and he reigned twenty-nine years in Jerusalem. His mother's name was Jehoaddan of Jerusalem. [3]And he did *what was* right in the sight of the LORD, yet not like his father David; he did everything as his father Joash had done. [4]However the high places were not taken away, and the people still sacrificed and burned incense on the high places.

[5]Now it happened, as soon as the kingdom was established in his hand, that he executed his servants who had murdered his father the king. [6]But the children of the murderers he did not execute, according to what is written in the Book of the Law of Moses, in which the LORD commanded, saying, "Fathers shall not be put to death for their children, nor shall children be put to death for their fathers; but a person shall be put to death for his own sin."[a]

[7]He killed ten thousand Edomites in the Valley of Salt, and took Sela by war, and called its name Joktheel to this day.

WHAT'S IT MEAN?

The cedar trees of Lebanon might be compared to the redwood trees of California. Some cedars grow up to one hundred feet tall, with trunks forty-five feet in diameter. Jehoash insulted Amaziah by comparing the king of Judah's power and influence to a thistle and comparing his own power and influence to a cedar tree.

2 Kings 14:9

[8]Then Amaziah sent messengers to Jehoash[a] the son of Jehoahaz, the son of Jehu, king of Israel, saying, "Come, let us face one another *in battle*." [9]And Jehoash king of Israel sent to Amaziah king of Judah, saying, "The thistle that *was* in Lebanon sent to the cedar that *was* in Lebanon, saying, 'Give your daughter to my son as wife'; and a wild beast that *was* in Lebanon passed by and trampled the thistle. [10]You have indeed defeated Edom, and your heart has lifted you up. Glory *in that*, and stay at home; for why should you meddle with trouble so that you fall—you and Judah with you?"

[11]But Amaziah would not heed. Therefore Jehoash king of Israel went out; so he and Amaziah king of Judah faced one another at Beth Shemesh, which *belongs* to Judah. [12]And Judah was defeated by Israel, and every man fled to his tent. [13]Then Jehoash king of Israel captured Amaziah king of Judah, the son of Jehoash, the son of Ahaziah, at Beth Shemesh; and he went to Jerusalem, and broke down the wall of Jerusalem from the Gate of Ephraim to the Corner Gate—four hundred cubits. [14]And he took all the gold and silver, all the articles that were found in the house of the LORD and in the treasuries of the king's house, and hostages, and returned to Samaria.

[15]Now the rest of the acts of Jehoash which he did—his might, and how he fought with Amaziah king of Judah—*are* they not written in the book of the chronicles of the kings of Israel? [16]So Jehoash rested with his fathers, and was buried in Samaria with the kings of Israel. Then Jeroboam his son reigned in his place.

[17]Amaziah the son of Joash, king of Judah, lived fifteen years after the death of Jehoash the son of Jehoahaz, king of Israel. [18]Now the rest of the acts of Amaziah, *are* they not written in the book of the chronicles of the kings of Judah? [19]And they formed a conspiracy against him in Jerusalem, and he fled to Lachish; but they sent after him to Lachish and killed him there. [20]Then they brought him on horses, and he was buried at Jerusalem with his fathers in the City of David.

[21]And all the people of Judah took Azariah,[a] who *was* sixteen years old, and made him king instead of his father Amaziah. [22]He built Elath and restored it to Judah, after the king rested with his fathers.

JEROBOAM II REIGNS IN ISRAEL

[23]In the fifteenth year of Amaziah the son of Joash, king of Judah, Jeroboam the son of Joash, king of Israel, became king in Samaria, *and reigned* forty-one years. [24]And he did evil in the sight of the LORD; he did not depart from all the sins of Jeroboam the son of Nebat, who had made Israel sin. [25]He restored the territory of

14:6 [a]Deuteronomy 24:16   **14:8** [a]Spelled *Joash* in 13:12ff and 2 Chronicles 25:17ff   **14:21** [a]Called *Uzziah* in 2 Chronicles 26:1ff, Isaiah 6:1, and elsewhere

Israel from the entrance of Hamath to the Sea of the Arabah, according to the word of the LORD God of Israel, which He had spoken through His servant Jonah the son of Amittai, the prophet who *was* from Gath Hepher. [26]For the LORD saw *that* the affliction of Israel *was* very bitter; and whether bond or free, there was no helper for Israel. [27]And the LORD did not say that He would blot out the name of Israel from under heaven; but He saved them by the hand of Jeroboam the son of Joash.

[28]Now the rest of the acts of Jeroboam, and all that he did—his might, how he made war, and how he recaptured for Israel, from Damascus and Hamath, *what had belonged* to Judah— *are* they not written in the book of the chronicles of the kings of Israel? [29]So Jeroboam rested with his fathers, the kings of Israel. Then Zechariah his son reigned in his place.

AZARIAH REIGNS IN JUDAH

[1]In the twenty-seventh year of Jeroboam king of Israel, Azariah the son of Amaziah, king of Judah, became king. [2]He was sixteen years old when he became king, and he reigned fifty-two years in Jerusalem. His mother's name *was* Jecholiah of Jerusalem. [3]And he did *what was* right in the sight of the LORD, according to all that his father Amaziah had done, [4]except that the high places were not removed; the people still sacrificed and burned incense on the high places. [5]Then the LORD struck the king, so that he was a leper until the day of his death; so he dwelt in an iso-

LEADERSHIP

Does God hold leaders accountable for how they lead? (15:3–5)

WHAT'S IT MEAN?

Azariah's leprosy may not have been the serious disease we call leprosy today. Whatever the ailment was, though, it was contagious; and it kept Azariah from taking part in religious and social events.

2 Kings 15:5

lated house. And Jotham the king's son *was* over the *royal* house, judging the people of the land.

[6]Now the rest of the acts of Azariah, and all that he did, *are* they not written in the book of the chronicles of the kings of Judah? [7]So Azariah rested with his fathers, and they buried him with his fathers in the City of David. Then Jotham his son reigned in his place.

ZECHARIAH REIGNS IN ISRAEL

[8]In the thirty-eighth year of Azariah king of Judah, Zechariah the son of Jeroboam reigned over Israel in Samaria six months. [9]And he did evil in the sight of the LORD, as his fathers had done; he did not depart from the sins of Jeroboam the son of Nebat, who had made Israel sin. [10]Then Shallum the son of Jabesh conspired against him, and struck and killed him in front of the people; and he reigned in his place.

[11]Now the rest of the acts of Zechariah, indeed they *are* written in the book of the chronicles of the kings of Israel.

[12]This *was* the word of the LORD which He spoke to Jehu, saying, "Your sons shall sit on the throne of Israel to the fourth *generation*."[a] And so it was.

SHALLUM REIGNS IN ISRAEL

[13]Shallum the son of Jabesh became king in the thirty-ninth year of Uzziah[a] king of Judah; and he reigned a full month in Samaria. [14]For Menahem the son of Gadi went up from Tirzah, came to Samaria, and struck Shallum the son of Jabesh in Samaria and killed him; and he reigned in his place.

[15]Now the rest of the acts of Shallum, and the conspiracy which he led, indeed they *are* written in the book of the chronicles of the kings of Israel. [16]Then from Tirzah, Menahem attacked Tiphsah, all who *were* there, and its territory. Because they did not surrender, therefore he attacked *it*. All the women there who were with child he ripped open.

MENAHEM REIGNS IN ISRAEL

[17]In the thirty-ninth year of Azariah king of Judah, Menahem the son of Gadi became king over Israel, *and reigned* ten years in Samaria. [18]And he did evil in the sight of the LORD; he did not depart all his days from the sins of Jeroboam the son of Nebat, who had made Israel sin. [19]Pul[a] king of Assyria came against the land; and Menahem gave Pul a thousand talents of

---

15:12 [a]2 Kings 10:30   **15:13** [a]Called *Azariah* in 14:21ff and 15:1ff   **15:19** [a]That is, Tiglath-Pileser III (compare verse 29)

silver, that his hand might be with him to strengthen the kingdom under his control. [20]And Menahem exacted the money from Israel, from all the very wealthy, from each man fifty shekels of silver, to give to the king of Assyria. So the king of Assyria turned back, and did not stay there in the land.

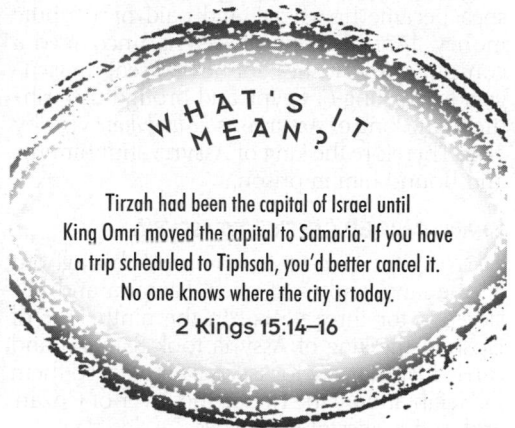

WHAT'S IT MEAN?

Tirzah had been the capital of Israel until King Omri moved the capital to Samaria. If you have a trip scheduled to Tiphsah, you'd better cancel it. No one knows where the city is today.

2 Kings 15:14–16

[21]Now the rest of the acts of Menahem, and all that he did, *are* they not written in the book of the chronicles of the kings of Israel? [22]So Menahem rested with his fathers. Then Pekahiah his son reigned in his place.

PEKAHIAH REIGNS IN ISRAEL

[23]In the fiftieth year of Azariah king of Judah, Pekahiah the son of Menahem became king over Israel in Samaria, *and reigned* two years. [24]And he did evil in the sight of the LORD; he did not depart from the sins of Jeroboam the son of Nebat, who had made Israel sin. [25]Then Pekah the son of Remaliah, an officer of his, conspired against him and killed him in Samaria, in the citadel of the king's house, along with Argob and Arieh; and with him were fifty men of Gilead. He killed him and reigned in his place.

[26]Now the rest of the acts of Pekahiah, and all that he did, indeed they *are* written in the book of the chronicles of the kings of Israel.

PEKAH REIGNS IN ISRAEL

[27]In the fifty-second year of Azariah king of Judah, Pekah the son of Remaliah became king over Israel in Samaria, *and reigned* twenty years. [28]And he did evil in the sight of the LORD; he did not depart from the sins of Jeroboam the son of Nebat, who had made Israel sin. [29]In the days of Pekah king of Israel, Tiglath-Pileser king of Assyria came and took Ijon, Abel Beth Maachah, Janoah, Kedesh, Hazor, Gilead, and Gali-

lee, all the land of Naphtali; and he carried them captive to Assyria. [30]Then Hoshea the son of Elah led a conspiracy against Pekah the son of Remaliah, and struck and killed him; so he reigned in his place in the twentieth year of Jotham the son of Uzziah.

[31]Now the rest of the acts of Pekah, and all that he did, indeed they *are* written in the book of the chronicles of the kings of Israel.

JOTHAM REIGNS IN JUDAH

[32]In the second year of Pekah the son of Remaliah, king of Israel, Jotham the son of Uzziah, king of Judah, began to reign. [33]He was twenty-five years old when he became king, and he reigned sixteen years in Jerusalem. His mother's name *was* Jerusha[a] the daughter of Zadok. [34]And he did *what was* right in the sight of the LORD; he did according to all that his father Uzziah had done. [35]However the high places were not removed; the people still sacrificed and burned incense on the high places. He built the Upper Gate of the house of the LORD.

[36]Now the rest of the acts of Jotham, and all that he did, *are* they not written in the book of the chronicles of the kings of Judah? [37]In those days the LORD began to send Rezin king of Syria and Pekah the son of Remaliah against Judah. [38]So Jotham rested with his fathers, and was buried with his fathers in the City of David his father. Then Ahaz his son reigned in his place.

AHAZ REIGNS IN JUDAH

[1]In the seventeenth year of Pekah the son of Remaliah, Ahaz the son of Jotham, king of Judah, began to reign. [2]Ahaz *was* twenty years old when he became king, and he reigned sixteen years in Jerusalem; and he did not do *what was* right in the sight of the LORD his God, as his father David *had done.* [3]But he walked in the way of the kings of Israel; indeed he made his son pass through the fire, according to the abominations of the nations whom the LORD had cast out from before the children of Israel. [4]And he sacrificed and burned incense on the high places, on the hills, and under every green tree.

[5]Then Rezin king of Syria and Pekah the son of Remaliah, king of Israel, came up to Jerusalem to *make* war; and they besieged Ahaz but could not overcome *him.* [6]At that time Rezin king of Syria captured Elath for Syria, and drove the men of Judah from Elath. Then the Edomites[a] went to Elath, and dwell there to this day.

[7]So Ahaz sent messengers to Tiglath-Pileser

15:33 [a]Spelled *Jerushah* in 2 Chronicles 27:1   **16:6** [a]Some ancient authorities read *Syrians.*

king of Assyria, saying, "I *am* your servant and your son. Come up and save me from the hand of the king of Syria and from the hand of the king of Israel, who rise up against me." [8]And Ahaz took the silver and gold that was found in the house of the LORD, and in the treasuries of the king's house, and sent *it as* a present to the king of Assyria. [9]So the king of Assyria heeded him; for the king of Assyria went up against Damascus and took it, carried *its people* captive to Kir, and killed Rezin.

[10]Now King Ahaz went to Damascus to meet Tiglath-Pileser king of Assyria, and saw an altar that *was* at Damascus; and King Ahaz sent to Urijah the priest the design of the altar and its pattern, according to all its workmanship. [11]Then Urijah the priest built an altar according to all that King Ahaz had sent from Damascus. So Urijah the priest made *it* before King Ahaz came back from Damascus. [12]And when the king came back from Damascus, the king saw the altar; and the king approached the altar and made offerings on it. [13]So he burned his burnt offering and his grain offering; and he poured his drink offering and sprinkled the blood of his peace offerings on the altar. [14]He also brought the bronze altar which *was* before the LORD, from the front of the temple—from between the *new* altar and the house of the LORD—and put it on the north side of the *new* altar. [15]Then King Ahaz commanded Urijah the priest, saying, "On the great *new* altar burn the morning burnt offering, the evening grain offering, the king's burnt sacrifice, and his grain offering, with the burnt offering of all the people of the land, their grain offering, and their drink offerings; and sprinkle on it all the blood of the burnt offering and all the blood of the sacrifice. And the bronze altar shall be for me to inquire *by*." [16]Thus did Urijah the priest, according to all that King Ahaz commanded.

[17]And King Ahaz cut off the panels of the carts, and removed the lavers from them; and he took down the Sea from the bronze oxen that *were* under it, and put it on a pavement of stones. [18]Also he removed the Sabbath pavilion which they had built in the temple, and he removed the king's outer entrance from the house of the LORD, on account of the king of Assyria.

[19]Now the rest of the acts of Ahaz which he did, *are* they not written in the book of the chronicles of the kings of Judah? [20]So Ahaz rested with his fathers, and was buried with his fathers in the City of David. Then Hezekiah his son reigned in his place.

17:10 [a]Hebrew *Asherim,* Canaanite deities

HOSHEA REIGNS IN ISRAEL

[1]In the twelfth year of Ahaz king of Judah, Hoshea the son of Elah became king of Israel in Samaria, *and he reigned* nine years. [2]And he did evil in the sight of the LORD, but not as the kings of Israel who were before him. [3]Shalmaneser king of Assyria came up against him; and Hoshea became his vassal, and paid him tribute money. [4]And the king of Assyria uncovered a conspiracy by Hoshea; for he had sent messengers to So, king of Egypt, and brought no tribute to the king of Assyria, as *he had done* year by year. Therefore the king of Assyria shut him up, and bound him in prison.

ISRAEL CARRIED CAPTIVE TO ASSYRIA

[5]Now the king of Assyria went throughout all the land, and went up to Samaria and besieged it for three years. [6]In the ninth year of Hoshea, the king of Assyria took Samaria and carried Israel away to Assyria, and placed them in Halah and by the Habor, the River of Gozan, and in the cities of the Medes.

WHAT'S IT MEAN?

The defeat at the hands of the Assyrians was the beginning of the end for the northern kingdom of Israel. Having twenty-seven thousand members of your community kidnapped and held as prisoners is bound to have a negative effect on any country. The Assyrians conquered Israel in 722 B.C., a full 135 years before Judah was destroyed by the Babylonians.
2 Kings 17:6

[7]For so it was that the children of Israel had sinned against the LORD their God, who had brought them up out of the land of Egypt, from under the hand of Pharaoh king of Egypt; and they had feared other gods, [8]and had walked in the statutes of the nations whom the LORD had cast out from before the children of Israel, and of the kings of Israel, which they had made. [9]Also the children of Israel secretly did against the LORD their God things that *were* not right, and they built for themselves high places in all their cities, from watchtower to fortified city. [10]They set up for themselves *sacred* pillars and wooden images[a]

on every high hill and under every green tree. [11]There they burned incense on all the high places, like the nations whom the LORD had carried away before them; and they did wicked things to provoke the LORD to anger, [12]for they served idols, of which the LORD had said to them, "You shall not do this thing."

[13]Yet the LORD testified against Israel and against Judah, by all of His prophets, every seer, saying, "Turn from your evil ways, and keep My commandments *and* My statutes, according to all the law which I commanded your fathers, and which I sent to you by My servants the prophets." [14]Nevertheless they would not hear, but stiffened their necks, like the necks of their fathers, who did not believe in the LORD their God. [15]And they rejected His statutes and His covenant that He had made with their fathers, and His testimonies which He had testified against them; they followed idols, became idolaters, and *went* after the nations who *were* all around them, *concerning* whom the LORD had charged them that they should not do like them. [16]So they left all the commandments of the LORD their God, made for themselves a molded image *and* two calves, made a wooden image and worshiped all the host of heaven, and served Baal. [17]And they caused their sons and daughters to pass through the fire, practiced witchcraft and soothsaying, and sold themselves to do evil in the sight of the LORD, to provoke Him to anger. [18]Therefore the LORD was very angry with Israel, and removed them from His sight; there was none left but the tribe of Judah alone.

CULT

How does God feel about cultic practices? (17:17)

[19]Also Judah did not keep the commandments of the LORD their God, but walked in the statutes of Israel which they made. [20]And the LORD rejected all the descendants of Israel, af-

WHAT'S IT MEAN?

Why bring in foreigners to replace the Israelites? To keep the Israelites from uniting and rebelling against Assyria.
2 Kings 17:24

flicted them, and delivered them into the hand of plunderers, until He had cast them from His sight. [21]For He tore Israel from the house of David, and they made Jeroboam the son of Nebat king. Then Jeroboam drove Israel from following the LORD, and made them commit a great sin. [22]For the children of Israel walked in all the sins of Jeroboam which he did; they did not depart from them, [23]until the LORD removed Israel out of His sight, as He had said by all His servants the prophets. So Israel was carried away from their own land to Assyria, *as it is* to this day.

ASSYRIA RESETTLES SAMARIA

[24]Then the king of Assyria brought *people* from Babylon, Cuthah, Ava, Hamath, and from Sepharvaim, and placed *them* in the cities of Samaria instead of the children of Israel; and they took possession of Samaria and dwelt in its cities. [25]And it was so, at the beginning of their dwelling there, *that* they did not fear the LORD; therefore the LORD sent lions among them, which killed *some* of them. [26]So they spoke to the king of Assyria, saying, "The nations whom you have removed and placed in the cities of Samaria do not know the rituals of the God of the land; therefore He has sent lions among them, and indeed, they are killing them because they do not know the rituals of the God of the land." [27]Then the king of Assyria commanded, saying, "Send there one of the priests whom you brought from there; let him go and dwell there, and let him teach them the rituals of the God of the land." [28]Then one of the priests whom they had carried away from Samaria came and dwelt in Bethel, and taught them how they should fear the LORD.

[29]However every nation continued to make gods of its own, and put *them* in the shrines on the high places which the Samaritans had made, *every* nation in the cities where they dwelt. [30]The men of Babylon made Succoth Benoth, the men of Cuth made Nergal, the men of Hamath made Ashima, [31]and the Avites made Nibhaz and Tartak; and the Sepharvites burned their children in fire to Adrammelech and Anammelech, the gods of Sepharvaim. [32]So they feared the LORD, and from every class they appointed for themselves priests of the high places, who sacrificed for them in the shrines of the high places. [33]They feared the LORD, yet served their own gods—according to the rituals of the nations from among whom they were carried away.

[34]To this day they continue practicing the former rituals; they do not fear the LORD, nor

On the Edge

You shall not fear other gods, nor bow down to them nor serve them nor sacrifice to them; but the LORD, who brought you up from the land of Egypt with great power and an outstretched arm, Him you shall fear, Him you shall worship, and to Him you shall offer sacrifice. And the statutes, the ordinances, the law, and the commandment which He wrote for you, you shall be careful to observe forever; you shall not fear other gods. And the covenant that I have made with you, you shall not forget, nor shall you fear other gods (2 Kin. 17:35–38).

God has revealed Himself in mighty ways because He wants us to worship only Him. He wants us to know that He is all-powerful and supremely wise. There is no one else who can even compare to God. No one else deserves our prayer or our praise. As the One who made us and saved us, only God is worthy of a life completely devoted to Him. He is worshiped when we live our daily lives for His glory. How you spoke to your parents at breakfast, the way you acted at school, what you watch on TV—it all matters when you decide to live a life that worships God. Don't let your friends trick you into believing that what they think counts—what God thinks matters most. Has your life been an act of worship today?

SEE FOR YOURSELF:
Ex. 20:5; Josh. 4:24;
Ps. 115:12, 13;
Joel 2:32

do they follow their statutes or their ordinances, or the law and commandment which the LORD had commanded the children of Jacob, whom He named Israel, ³⁵with whom the LORD had made a covenant and charged them, saying: "You shall not fear other gods, nor bow down to them nor serve them nor sacrifice to them; ³⁶but the LORD, who brought you up from the land of Egypt with great power and an outstretched arm, Him you shall fear, Him you shall worship, and to Him you shall offer sacrifice. ³⁷And the statutes, the ordinances, the law, and the commandment which He wrote for you, you shall be careful to observe forever; you shall not fear other gods. ³⁸And the covenant that I have made with you, you shall not forget, nor shall you fear other gods. ³⁹But the LORD your God you shall fear; and He will deliver you from the hand of all your enemies." ⁴⁰However they did not obey, but they followed their former rituals. ⁴¹So these nations feared the LORD, yet served their carved images; also their children and their children's children have continued doing as their fathers did, even to this day.

HEZEKIAH REIGNS IN JUDAH

¹Now it came to pass in the third year of Hoshea the son of Elah, king of Israel, *that* Hezekiah the son of Ahaz, king of Judah, began to reign. ²He was twenty-five years old when he became king, and he reigned twenty-nine years in Jerusalem. His mother's name *was* Abi*ᵃ* the daughter of Zechariah. ³And he did *what was* right in the sight of the LORD, according to all that his father David had done.

⁴He removed the high places and broke the *sacred* pillars, cut down the wooden image*ᵃ* and broke in pieces the bronze serpent that Moses had made; for until those days the children of Israel burned incense to it, and called it Nehushtan.*ᵇ* ⁵He trusted in the LORD God of Israel, so that after him was none like him among all the kings of Judah, nor who were before him. ⁶For he held fast to the LORD; he did not depart from following Him, but kept His commandments, which the LORD had commanded Moses. ⁷The LORD was with him; he prospered wherever he went. And he rebelled against the king of Assyria and did not serve him. ⁸He subdued the Philistines, as far as Gaza and its territory, from watchtower to fortified city.

⁹Now it came to pass in the fourth year of King Hezekiah, which *was* the seventh year of Hoshea the son of Elah, king of Israel, *that* Shalmaneser king of Assyria came up against Samaria and besieged it. ¹⁰And at the end of three years they took it. In the sixth year of Hezekiah, that *is*, the ninth year of Hoshea king of Israel, Samaria was taken. ¹¹Then the king of Assyria carried Israel away captive to Assyria, and put them in Halah and by the Habor, the River of Gozan, and in the cities of the Medes, ¹²because they did not obey the voice of the LORD their God, but transgressed His covenant *and* all that Moses the servant of the LORD had commanded; and they would neither hear nor do *them*.

18:2 *ᵃCalled Abijah in 2 Chronicles 29:1ff* **18:4** *ᵃHebrew Asherah, a Canaanite goddess* *ᵇLiterally Bronze Thing*

¹³And in the fourteenth year of King Hezekiah, Sennacherib king of Assyria came up against all the fortified cities of Judah and took them. ¹⁴Then Hezekiah king of Judah sent to the king of Assyria at Lachish, saying, "I have done wrong; turn away from me; whatever you impose on me I will pay." And the king of Assyria assessed Hezekiah king of Judah three hundred talents of silver and thirty talents of gold. ¹⁵So Hezekiah gave *him* all the silver that was found in the house of the LORD and in the treasuries of the king's house. ¹⁶At that time Hezekiah stripped *the gold from* the doors of the temple of the LORD, and *from* the pillars which Hezekiah king of Judah had overlaid, and gave it to the king of Assyria.

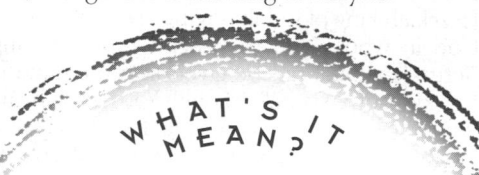

"You shall not fear other gods, nor bow down to them nor serve them nor sacrifice to them." (2 Kings 17:35b)

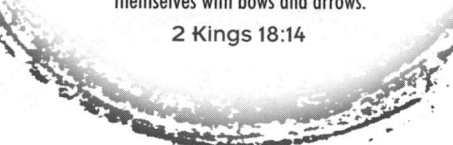

WHAT'S IT MEAN?

Sennacherib, the king of Assyria, was so proud of his victory in Lachish that he had a scene of the battle recreated on one of the walls of his palace in Nineveh. The scene showed his Assyrian soldiers attacking with battering rams and other weapons while the inhabitants of Lachish tried to defend themselves with bows and arrows.

2 Kings 18:14

SENNACHERIB BOASTS AGAINST THE LORD

¹⁷Then the king of Assyria sent *the* Tartan,^a *the* Rabsaris,^b *and the* Rabshakeh^c from Lachish, with a great army against Jerusalem, to King Hezekiah. And they went up and came to Jerusalem. When they had come up, they went and stood by the aqueduct from the upper pool, which *was* on the highway to the Fuller's Field. ¹⁸And when they had called to the king, Eliakim the son of Hilkiah, who *was* over the household, Shebna the scribe, and Joah the son of Asaph, the recorder, came out to them. ¹⁹Then *the* Rabshakeh said to them, "Say now to Hezekiah, 'Thus says the great king, the king of Assyria: "What confidence *is* this in which you trust? ²⁰You speak of *having* plans and power for war; but *they are* mere words. And in whom do you trust, that you rebel against me? ²¹Now look! You are trusting in the staff of this broken reed, Egypt, on which if a man leans, it will go into his hand and pierce it. So *is* Pharaoh king of Egypt to all who trust in him. ²²But if you say to me, 'We trust in the LORD our God,' *is* it not He whose high places and whose altars Hezekiah has taken away, and said to Judah and Jerusalem, 'You shall worship before this altar in Jerusalem'?" ' ²³Now therefore, I urge you, give a pledge to my master the king of Assyria, and I will give you two thousand horses—if you are able on your part to put riders on them! ²⁴How then will you repel one captain of the least of my master's servants, and put your trust in Egypt for chariots and horsemen? ²⁵Have I now come up without the LORD against this place to destroy it? The LORD said to me, 'Go up against this land, and destroy it.' "

²⁶Then Eliakim the son of Hilkiah, Shebna, and Joah said to *the* Rabshakeh, "Please speak to your servants in Aramaic, for we understand *it;* and do not speak to us in Hebrew^a in the hearing of the people who *are* on the wall."

WHAT'S IT MEAN?

Aramaic was the language of choice for the ancient Babylonians, Assyrians, and eventually almost everyone in the Palestine region. Those who didn't know Aramaic were at a serious disadvantage when it came to conducting business or diplomacy in a foreign city.

2 Kings 18:26

²⁷But *the* Rabshakeh said to them, "Has my master sent me to your master and to you to speak these words, and not to the men who sit on the wall, who will eat and drink their own waste with you?"

18:17 ^aA title, probably *Commander in Chief* ^bA title, probably *Chief Officer* ^cA title, probably *Chief of Staff* or *Governor* **18:26** ^aLiterally *Judean*

28Then *the* Rabshakeh stood and called out with a loud voice in Hebrew, and spoke, saying, "Hear the word of the great king, the king of Assyria! 29Thus says the king: 'Do not let Hezekiah deceive you, for he shall not be able to deliver you from his hand; 30nor let Hezekiah make you trust in the LORD, saying, "The LORD will surely deliver us; this city shall not be given into the hand of the king of Assyria." ' 31Do not listen to Hezekiah; for thus says the king of Assyria: 'Make *peace* with me by a present and come out to me; and every one of you eat from his own vine and every one from his own fig tree, and every one of you drink the waters of his own cistern; 32until I come and take you away to a land like your own land, a land of grain and new wine, a land of bread and vineyards, a land of olive groves and honey, that you may live and not die. But do not listen to Hezekiah, lest he persuade you, saying, "The LORD will deliver us." 33Has any of the gods of the nations at all delivered its land from the hand of the king of Assyria? 34Where *are* the gods of Hamath and Arpad? Where *are* the gods of Sepharvaim and Hena and Ivah? Indeed, have they delivered Samaria from my hand? 35Who among all the gods of the lands have delivered their countries from my hand, that the LORD should deliver Jerusalem from my hand?' "

36But the people held their peace and answered him not a word; for the king's commandment was, "Do not answer him." 37Then Eliakim the son of Hilkiah, who *was* over the household, Shebna the scribe, and Joah the son of Asaph, the recorder, came to Hezekiah with *their* clothes torn, and told him the words of *the* Rabshakeh.

ISAIAH ASSURES DELIVERANCE

1And so it was, when King Hezekiah heard *it*, that he tore his clothes, covered himself with sackcloth, and went into the house of the LORD. 2Then he sent Eliakim, who *was* over the household, Shebna the scribe, and the elders of the priests, covered with sackcloth, to Isaiah the prophet, the son of Amoz. 3And they said to him, "Thus says Hezekiah: 'This day *is* a day of trouble, and rebuke, and blasphemy; for the children have come to birth, but *there is* no strength to bring them forth. 4It may be that the LORD your God will hear all the words of *the* Rabshakeh, whom his master the king of Assyria has sent to reproach the living God, and will rebuke the words which the LORD your God has heard. Therefore lift up *your* prayer for the remnant that is left.' "

5So the servants of King Hezekiah came to Isaiah. 6And Isaiah said to them, "Thus you shall say to your master, 'Thus says the LORD: "Do not be afraid of the words which you have heard, with which the servants of the king of Assyria have blasphemed Me. 7Surely I will send a spirit upon him, and he shall hear a rumor and return to his own land; and I will cause him to fall by the sword in his own land." ' "

SENNACHERIB'S THREAT AND HEZEKIAH'S PRAYER

8Then *the* Rabshakeh returned and found the king of Assyria warring against Libnah, for he heard that he had departed from Lachish. 9And the king heard concerning Tirhakah king of Ethiopia, "Look, he has come out to make war with you." So he again sent messengers to Hezekiah, saying, 10"Thus you shall speak to Hezekiah king of Judah, saying: 'Do not let your God in whom you trust deceive you, saying, "Jerusalem shall not be given into the hand of the king of Assyria." 11Look! You have heard what the kings of Assyria have done to all lands by utterly destroying them; and shall you be delivered? 12Have the gods of the nations delivered those whom my fathers have destroyed, Gozan and Haran and Rezeph, and the people of Eden who *were* in Telassar? 13Where *is* the king of Hamath, the king of Arpad, and the king of the city of Sepharvaim, Hena, and Ivah?' "

WHAT'S IT MEAN?

The Assyrians were on a roll, conquering cities left and right. When they got to Israel, they obviously weren't very worried about the Israelites' God. After all, the cities they had defeated earlier had their gods, too—and none of those gods had bothered to help their people. The Assyrians expected the same thing from the Israelites.

2 Kings 19:12

14And Hezekiah received the letter from the hand of the messengers, and read it; and Hezekiah went up to the house of the LORD, and spread it before the LORD. 15Then Hezekiah prayed before the LORD, and said: "O LORD God of Israel, *the One* who dwells *between* the cherubim, You are God, You alone, of all the kingdoms of the earth. You have made heaven and earth. [16]Incline Your ear, O LORD, and hear; open Your eyes, O LORD, and see; and hear the words of Sennacherib, which he has sent to reproach the living God. [17]Truly, LORD, the kings of Assyria have laid waste the nations and their lands, [18]and have cast their gods into the fire; for they *were* not gods, but the work of men's hands— wood and stone. Therefore they destroyed them. [19]Now therefore, O LORD our God, I pray, save us from his hand, that all the kingdoms of the earth may know that You *are* the LORD God, You alone."

HOPE

What should you do when the situation is hopeless? (19:14–19)

THE WORD OF THE LORD CONCERNING SENNACHERIB

[20]Then Isaiah the son of Amoz sent to Hezekiah, saying, "Thus says the LORD God of Israel: 'Because you have prayed to Me against Sennacherib king of Assyria, I have heard.' [21]This *is* the word which the LORD has spoken concerning him:

'The virgin, the daughter of Zion,
Has despised you, laughed you to scorn;
The daughter of Jerusalem
Has shaken *her* head behind your back!

[22] 'Whom have you reproached and
    blasphemed?
Against whom have you raised *your*
    voice,
And lifted up your eyes on high?
Against the Holy *One* of Israel.
[23] By your messengers you have reproached
    the Lord,
And said: "By the multitude of my
    chariots
I have come up to the height of the
    mountains,
To the limits of Lebanon;
I will cut down its tall cedars
And its choice cypress trees;
I will enter the extremity of its borders,
To its fruitful forest.
[24] I have dug and drunk strange water,
And with the soles of my feet I have
    dried up
All the brooks of defense."

[25] 'Did you not hear long ago
How I made it,
From ancient times that I formed it?
Now I have brought it to pass,
That you should be
For crushing fortified cities *into* heaps of
    ruins.
[26] Therefore their inhabitants had little
    power;
They were dismayed and confounded;
They were *as* the grass of the field
And the green herb,
As the grass on the housetops
And *grain* blighted before it is grown.

[27] 'But I know your dwelling place,
Your going out and your coming in,
And your rage against Me.
[28] Because your rage against
    Me and your tumult
Have come up to My
    ears,
Therefore I will put My
    hook in your nose
And My bridle in your
    lips,
And I will turn you back
By the way which you came.

PRIDE

What does God think of our pride? (19:27, 28)

[29]"This *shall be* a sign to you:

You shall eat this year such as grows of
    itself,
And in the second year what springs
    from the same;
Also in the third year sow and reap,
Plant vineyards and eat the fruit of them.
[30] And the remnant who have escaped of
    the house of Judah
Shall again take root downward,
And bear fruit upward.
[31] For out of Jerusalem shall go a remnant,
And those who escape from Mount Zion.
The zeal of the LORD of hosts[a] will do
    this.'

[32]"Therefore thus says the LORD concerning the king of Assyria:

'He shall not come into this city,
Nor shoot an arrow there,
Nor come before it with shield,
Nor build a siege mound against it.

19:31 [a]Following many Hebrew manuscripts and ancient versions (compare Isaiah 37:32); Masoretic Text omits *of hosts*.

33 By the way that he came,
By the same shall he return;
And he shall not come into this city,
Says the LORD.
34 'For I will defend this city, to save it
For My own sake and for My servant
David's sake.' "

SENNACHERIB'S DEFEAT AND DEATH

35 And it came to pass on a certain night that the angel[a] of the LORD went out, and killed in the camp of the Assyrians one hundred and eighty-five thousand; and when *people* arose early in the morning, there were the corpses—all dead. 36 So Sennacherib king of Assyria departed and went away, returned *home*, and remained at Nineveh. 37 Now it came to pass, as he was worshiping in the temple of Nisroch his god, that his sons Adrammelech and Sharezer struck him down with the sword; and they escaped into the land of Ararat. Then Esarhaddon his son reigned in his place.

HEZEKIAH'S LIFE EXTENDED

1 In those days Hezekiah was sick and near death. And Isaiah the prophet, the son of Amoz, went to him and said to him, "Thus says the LORD: 'Set your house in order, for you shall die, and not live.' "

2 Then he turned his face toward the wall, and prayed to the LORD, saying, 3 "Remember now, O LORD, I pray, how I have walked before You in truth and with a loyal heart, and have done *what was* good in Your sight." And Hezekiah wept bitterly.

4 And it happened, before Isaiah had gone out into the middle court, that the word of the LORD came to him, saying, 5 "Return and tell Hezekiah the leader of My people, 'Thus says the LORD, the God of David your father: "I have heard your prayer, I have seen your tears; surely I will heal you. On the third day you shall go up to the house of the LORD. 6 And I will add to your days fifteen years. I will deliver you and this city from the hand of the king of Assyria; and I will defend this city for My own sake, and for the sake of My servant David." ' "

> GOD
>
> How does God fight for His people? (20:6)

7 Then Isaiah said, "Take a lump of figs." So they took and laid *it* on the boil, and he recovered.

8 And Hezekiah said to Isaiah, "What *is* the sign that the LORD will heal me, and that I shall go up to the house of the LORD the third day?"

9 Then Isaiah said, "This is the sign to you from the LORD, that the LORD will do the thing which He has spoken: *shall* the shadow go forward ten degrees or go backward ten degrees?"

10 And Hezekiah answered, "It is an easy thing for the shadow to go down ten degrees; no, but let the shadow go backward ten degrees."

11 So Isaiah the prophet cried out to the LORD, and He brought the shadow ten degrees backward, by which it had gone down on the sundial of Ahaz.

THE BABYLONIAN ENVOYS

12 At that time Berodach-Baladan[a] the son of Baladan, king of Babylon, sent letters and a present to Hezekiah, for he heard that Hezekiah had been sick. 13 And Hezekiah was attentive to them, and showed them all the house of his treasures—the silver and gold, the spices and precious ointment, and all[a] his armory—all that was found among his treasures. There was nothing in his house or in all his dominion that Hezekiah did not show them.

14 Then Isaiah the prophet went to King Hezekiah, and said to him, "What did these men say, and from where did they come to you?"

So Hezekiah said, "They came from a far country, from Babylon."

15 And he said, "What have they seen in your house?"

So Hezekiah answered, "They have seen all that *is* in my house; there is nothing among my treasures that I have not shown them."

16 Then Isaiah said to Hezekiah, "Hear the word of the LORD: 17 'Behold, the days are coming when all that *is* in your house, and what your fathers have accumulated until this day, shall be carried to Babylon; nothing shall be left,' says the LORD. 18 'And they shall take away some of your sons who will descend from you, whom you will beget; and they shall be eunuchs in the palace of the king of Babylon.' "

19 So Hezekiah said to Isaiah, "The word of the LORD which you have spoken *is* good!" For he said, "Will there not be peace and truth at least in my days?"

DEATH OF HEZEKIAH

20 Now the rest of the acts of Hezekiah—all his might, and how he made a pool and a tunnel

---

19:35 [a]Or *Angel*   **20:12** [a]Spelled *Merodach-Baladan* in Isaiah 39:1   **20:13** [a]Following many Hebrew manuscripts, Syriac, and Targum; Masoretic Text omits *all*.

and brought water into the city—are they not written in the book of the chronicles of the kings of Judah? 21So Hezekiah rested with his fathers. Then Manasseh his son reigned in his place.

MANASSEH REIGNS IN JUDAH

1Manasseh was twelve years old when he became king, and he reigned fifty-five years in Jerusalem. His mother's name was Hephzibah. 2And he did evil in the sight of the LORD, according to the abominations of the nations whom the LORD had cast out before the children of Israel. 3For he rebuilt the high places which Hezekiah his father had destroyed; he raised up altars for Baal, and made a wooden image,a as Ahab king of Israel had done; and he worshiped all the host of heavenb and served them. 4He also built altars in the house of the LORD, of which the LORD had said, "In Jerusalem I will put My name." 5And he built altars for all the host of heaven in the two courts of the house of the LORD. 6Also he made his son pass through the fire, practiced soothsaying, used witchcraft, and consulted spiritists and mediums. He did much evil in the sight of the LORD, to provoke Him to anger. 7He even set a carved image of Asheraha that he had made, in the house of which the LORD had said to David and to Solomon his son, "In this house and in Jerusalem, which I have chosen out of all the tribes of Israel, I will put My name forever; 8and I will not make the feet of Israel wander anymore from the land which I gave their fathers—only if they are careful to do according to all that I have commanded them, and according to all the law that My servant Moses commanded them." 9But they paid no attention, and Manasseh seduced them to do more evil than the nations whom the LORD had destroyed before the children of Israel.

> **TEMPTATION**
> What can you do to avoid temptation? (21:8, 9)

10And the LORD spoke by His servants the prophets, saying, 11"Because Manasseh king of Judah has done these abominations (he has acted more wickedly than all the Amorites who were before him, and has also made Judah sin with his idols), 12therefore thus says the LORD God of Israel: 'Behold, I am bringing such calamity upon Jerusalem and Judah, that whoever hears of it, both his ears will tingle. 13And I will stretch over Jerusalem the measuring line of Samaria and the plummet of the house of Ahab; I will wipe Jerusalem as one wipes a dish,

wiping it and turning it upside down. 14So I will forsake the remnant of My inheritance and deliver them into the hand of their enemies; and they shall become victims of plunder to all their enemies, 15because they have done evil in My sight, and have provoked Me to anger since the day their fathers came out of Egypt, even to this day.'"

On the Edge

[Manasseh] practiced soothsaying, used witchcraft, and consulted spiritists and mediums. He did much evil in the sight of the LORD, to provoke Him to anger (2 Kin. 21:6, 7).

Asking soothsayers (fortune-tellers) for advice is listed here as a sinful thing that makes the Lord very angry. It is an insult to God to believe that a human being can look into the future and know the plans of the Lord. His ways and thoughts are so far above our thoughts. (See Isaiah 55:8, 9.) Why pay money to speak to someone who will just give you his or her best guess?

Instead, get in touch with the Maker, the Master Designer, the One who *really* knows everything. Ask Him for advice. He's been waiting to help you make sense of it all. His guidance will not be confusing or misleading. He will not stutter or fumble—He will clearly lead your steps. So go ahead, stop any time, any place, and ask God for His advice. Listen when He answers you through His Word or in your heart. Then follow through—do what He says, walk where He leads. You can count on Him to know exactly what will happen in your future. He's never wrong.

SEE FOR YOURSELF:
Lev. 20:6; Deut. 18:10;
Is. 40:13, 14;
Rom. 11:33

16Moreover Manasseh shed very much innocent blood, till he had filled Jerusalem from one end to another, besides his sin by which he made Judah sin, in doing evil in the sight of the LORD.

17Now the rest of the acts of Manasseh—all that he did, and the sin that he committed—are

---

21:3 aHebrew *Asherah*, a Canaanite goddess bThe gods of the Assryians **21:7** aA Canaanite goddess

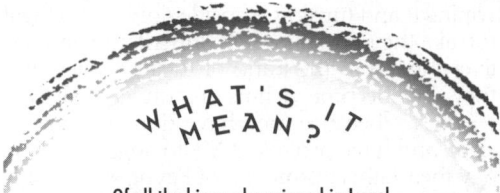

WHAT'S IT MEAN?

Of all the kings who reigned in Israel and Judah, Manasseh held the throne longest. That's unfortunate, because Manasseh truly was an evil person. He built altars to pagan gods, reintroduced astrology to the Israelites, and personally practiced witchcraft. Along the way, he also put many innocent people to death. As if that weren't enough, Jewish tradition says Manasseh put Isaiah to death by ordering that the prophet be sawed in half.

2 Kings 21:16

they not written in the book of the chronicles of the kings of Judah? [18]So Manasseh rested with his fathers, and was buried in the garden of his own house, in the garden of Uzza. Then his son Amon reigned in his place.

AMON'S REIGN AND DEATH

[19]Amon *was* twenty-two years old when he became king, and he reigned two years in Jerusalem. His mother's name *was* Meshullemeth the daughter of Haruz of Jotbah. [20]And he did evil in the sight of the LORD, as his father Manasseh had done. [21]So he walked in all the ways that his father had walked; and he served the idols that his father had served, and worshiped them. [22]He forsook the LORD God of his fathers, and did not walk in the way of the LORD.

[23]Then the servants of Amon conspired against him, and killed the king in his own house. [24]But the people of the land executed all those who had conspired against King Amon. Then the people of the land made his son Josiah king in his place.

[25]Now the rest of the acts of Amon which he did, *are* they not written in the book of the chronicles of the kings of Judah? [26]And he was buried in his tomb in the garden of Uzza. Then Josiah his son reigned in his place.

JOSIAH REIGNS IN JUDAH

[1]Josiah *was* eight years old when he became king, and he reigned thirty-one years in Jerusalem. His mother's name *was* Jedidah the daughter of Adaiah of Bozkath. [2]And he did *what was* right in the sight of the LORD, and walked in all

the ways of his father David; he did not turn aside to the right hand or to the left.

HILKIAH FINDS THE BOOK OF THE LAW

[3]Now it came to pass, in the eighteenth year of King Josiah, *that* the king sent Shaphan the scribe, the son of Azaliah, the son of Meshullam, to the house of the LORD, saying: [4]"Go up to Hilkiah the high priest, that he may count the money which has been brought into the house of the LORD, which the doorkeepers have gathered from the people. [5]And let them deliver it into the hand of those doing the work, who are the overseers in the house of the LORD; let them give it to those who *are* in the house of the LORD doing the work, to repair the damages of the house—[6]to carpenters and builders and masons—and to buy timber and hewn stone to repair the house. [7]However there need be no accounting made with them of the money delivered into their hand, because they deal faithfully."

WHAT'S IT MEAN?

No one knows for sure which book Hilkiah found in the temple that day. Probably the best guess is Deuteronomy, which contains many specific laws condemning idolatry and other things the Israelites were practicing when Josiah became king.

2 Kings 22:8

[8]Then Hilkiah the high priest said to Shaphan the scribe, "I have found the Book of the Law in the house of the LORD." And Hilkiah gave the book to Shaphan, and he read it. [9]So Shaphan the scribe went to the king, bringing the king word, saying, "Your servants have gathered the money that was found in the house, and have delivered it into the hand of those who do the work, who oversee the house of the LORD." [10]Then Shaphan the scribe showed the king, saying, "Hilkiah the priest has given me a book." And Shaphan read it before the king.

[11]Now it happened, when the king heard the words of the Book of the Law, that he tore his clothes. [12]Then the king commanded Hilkiah the priest, Ahikam the son of Shaphan, Achbor[a]

22:12 [a]*Abdon the son of Micah* in 2 Chronicles 34:20

the son of Michaiah, Shaphan the scribe, and Asaiah a servant of the king, saying, ¹³"Go, inquire of the LORD for me, for the people and for all Judah, concerning the words of this book that has been found; for great *is* the wrath of the LORD that is aroused against us, because our fathers have not obeyed the words of this book, to do according to all that is written concerning us."

¹⁴So Hilkiah the priest, Ahikam, Achbor, Shaphan, and Asaiah went to Huldah the prophetess, the wife of Shallum the son of Tikvah, the son of Harhas, keeper of the wardrobe. (She dwelt in Jerusalem in the Second Quarter.) And they spoke with her. ¹⁵Then she said to them, "Thus says the LORD God of Israel, 'Tell the man who sent you to Me, ¹⁶"Thus says the LORD: 'Behold, I will bring calamity on this place and on its inhabitants—all the words of the book which the king of Judah has read— ¹⁷because they have forsaken Me and burned incense to other gods, that they might provoke Me to anger with all the works of their hands. Therefore My wrath shall be aroused against this place and shall not be quenched.' " ' ¹⁸But as for the king of Judah, who sent you to inquire of the LORD, in this manner you shall speak to him, 'Thus says the LORD God of Israel: "*Concerning* the words which you have heard— ¹⁹because your heart was tender, and you humbled yourself before the LORD when you heard what I spoke against this place and against its inhabitants, that they would become a desolation and a curse, and you tore your clothes and wept before Me, I also have heard *you*," says the LORD. ²⁰Surely, therefore, I will gather you to your fathers, and you shall be gathered to your grave in peace; and your eyes shall not see all the calamity which I will bring on this place." ' " So they brought back word to the king.

JOSIAH RESTORES TRUE WORSHIP

¹Now the king sent them to gather all the elders of Judah and Jerusalem to him. ²The king went up to the house of the LORD with all the men of Judah, and with him all the inhabitants of Jerusalem—the priests and the prophets and all the people, both small and great. And he read in their hearing all the words of the Book of the Covenant which had been found in the house of the LORD.

³Then the king stood by a pillar and made a covenant before the LORD, to follow the LORD and to keep His commandments and His testimonies and His statutes, with all *his* heart and all *his* soul, to perform the words of this covenant that were written in this book. And all the people took a stand for the covenant. ⁴And the king commanded Hilkiah the high priest, the priests of the second order, and the doorkeepers, to bring out of the temple of the LORD all the articles that were made for Baal, for Asherah,ᵃ and for all the host of heaven;ᵇ and he burned them outside Jerusalem in the fields of Kidron, and carried their ashes to Bethel. ⁵Then he removed the idolatrous priests whom the kings of Judah had ordained to burn incense on the high places in the cities of Judah and in the places all around Jerusalem, and those who burned incense to Baal, to the sun, to the moon, to the constellations, and to all the host of heaven. ⁶And he brought out the wooden imageᵃ from the house of the LORD, to the Brook Kidron outside Jerusalem, burned it at the Brook Kidron and ground *it* to ashes, and threw its ashes on the graves of the common people. ⁷Then he tore down the *ritual* booths of the perverted personsᵃ that *were* in the house of the LORD, where the women wove hangings for the wooden image. ⁸And he brought all the priests from the cities of Judah, and defiled the high places where the priests had burned incense, from Geba to Beersheba; also he broke down the high places at the gates which *were* at the entrance of the Gate of Joshua the governor of the city, which *were* to the left of the city gate. ⁹Nevertheless the priests of the high places did not come up to the altar of the LORD in Jerusalem, but they ate unleavened bread among their brethren.

¹⁰And he defiled Topheth, which *is* in the Valley of the Sonᵃ of Hinnom, that no man might make his son or his daughter pass

LEADERSHIP

How can leaders influence their people for good? (23:3)

"Then the king stood by a pillar and made a covenant before the LORD, to follow the LORD and to keep His commandments."
(2 Kings 23:3a)

23:4 ᵃA Canaanite goddess ᵇThe gods of the Assyrians   **23:6** ᵃHebrew *Asherah*, a Canaanite goddess
23:7 ᵃHebrew *qedeshim*, that is, those practicing sodomy and prostitution in religious rituals   **23:10** ᵃKethib reads *Sons*.

through the fire to Molech. [11]Then he removed the horses that the kings of Judah had dedicated to the sun, at the entrance to the house of the LORD, by the chamber of Nathan-Melech, the officer who *was* in the court; and he burned the chariots of the sun with fire. [12]The altars that *were* on the roof, the upper chamber of Ahaz, which the kings of Judah had made, and the altars which Manasseh had made in the two courts of the house of the LORD, the king broke down and pulverized there, and threw their dust into the Brook Kidron. [13]Then the king defiled the high places that *were* east of Jerusalem, which *were* on the south of the Mount of Corruption, which Solomon king of Israel had built for Ashtoreth the abomination of the Sidonians, for Chemosh the abomination of the Moabites, and for Milcom the abomination of the people of Ammon. [14]And he broke in pieces the *sacred* pillars and cut down the wooden images, and filled their places with the bones of men.

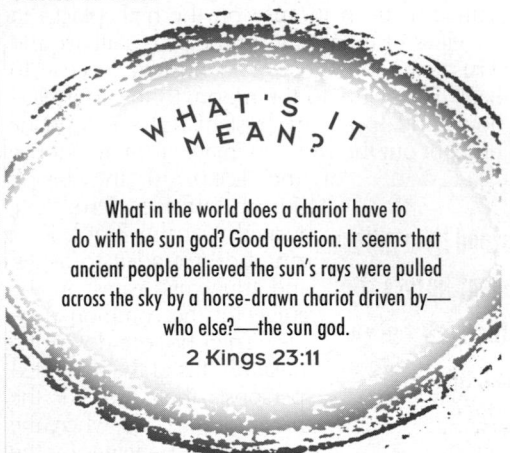

WHAT'S IT MEAN?

What in the world does a chariot have to do with the sun god? Good question. It seems that ancient people believed the sun's rays were pulled across the sky by a horse-drawn chariot driven by—who else?—the sun god.

2 Kings 23:11

[15]Moreover the altar that *was* at Bethel, *and* the high place which Jeroboam the son of Nebat, who made Israel sin, had made, both that altar and the high place he broke down; and he burned the high place *and* crushed *it* to powder, and burned the wooden image. [16]As Josiah turned, he saw the tombs that *were* there on the mountain. And he sent and took the bones out of the tombs and burned *them* on the altar, and defiled it according to the word of the LORD which the man of God proclaimed, who proclaimed these words. [17]Then he said, "What gravestone *is* this that I see?"

So the men of the city told him, "*It is* the tomb of the man of God who came from Judah and proclaimed these things which you have done against the altar of Bethel."

[18]And he said, "Let him alone; let no one move his bones." So they let his bones alone, with the bones of the prophet who came from Samaria.

[19]Now Josiah also took away all the shrines of the high places that *were* in the cities of Samaria, which the kings of Israel had made to provoke the LORD[a] to anger; and he did to them according to all the deeds he had done in Bethel. [20]He executed all the priests of the high places who *were* there, on the altars, and burned men's bones on them; and he returned to Jerusalem.

[21]Then the king commanded all the people, saying, "Keep the Passover to the LORD your God, as *it is* written in this Book of the Covenant." [22]Such a Passover surely had never been held since the days of the judges who judged Israel, nor in all the days of the kings of Israel and the kings of Judah. [23]But in the eighteenth year of King Josiah this Passover was held before the LORD in Jerusalem. [24]Moreover Josiah put away those who consulted mediums and spiritists, the household gods and idols, all the abominations that were seen in the land of Judah and in Jerusalem, that he might perform the words of the law which were written in the book that Hilkiah the priest found in the house of the LORD. [25]Now before him there was no king like him, who turned to the LORD with all his heart, with all his soul, and with all his might, according to all the Law of Moses; nor after him did *any* arise like him.

IMPENDING JUDGMENT ON JUDAH

[26]Nevertheless the LORD did not turn from the fierceness of His great wrath, with which His anger was aroused against Judah, because of all the provocations with which Manasseh had provoked Him. [27]And the LORD said, "I will also remove Judah from My sight, as I have removed Israel, and will cast off this city Jerusalem which I have chosen, and the house of which I said, 'My name shall be there.' "[a]

JOSIAH DIES IN BATTLE

[28]Now the rest of the acts of Josiah, and all that he did, *are* they not written in the book of the chronicles of the kings of Judah? [29]In his days Pharaoh Necho king of Egypt went to the aid of the king of Assyria, to the River Euphra-

23:19 [a]Following Septuagint, Syriac, and Vulgate; Masoretic Text and Targum omit *the* LORD.
23:27 [a]1 Kings 8:29

tes; and King Josiah went against him. And *Pharaoh Necho* killed him at Megiddo when he confronted him. ³⁰Then his servants moved his body in a chariot from Megiddo, brought him to Jerusalem, and buried him in his own tomb. And the people of the land took Jehoahaz the son of Josiah, anointed him, and made him king in his father's place.

WHAT'S IT MEAN?

Megiddo was located in a "high traffic" area on the road between Egypt and Syria. Its location made Megiddo an ideal military base. The battle mentioned in this verse was fought in 609 B.C.

2 Kings 23:29

THE REIGN AND CAPTIVITY OF JEHOAHAZ

³¹Jehoahaz *was* twenty-three years old when he became king, and he reigned three months in Jerusalem. His mother's name *was* Hamutal the daughter of Jeremiah of Libnah. ³²And he did evil in the sight of the LORD, according to all that his fathers had done. ³³Now Pharaoh Necho put him in prison at Riblah in the land of Hamath, that he might not reign in Jerusalem; and he imposed on the land a tribute of one hundred talents of silver and a talent of gold. ³⁴Then Pharaoh Necho made Eliakim the son of Josiah king in place of his father Josiah, and changed his name to Jehoiakim. And *Pharaoh* took Jehoahaz and went to Egypt, and heᵃ died there.

JEHOIAKIM REIGNS IN JUDAH

³⁵So Jehoiakim gave the silver and gold to Pharaoh; but he taxed the land to give money according to the command of Pharaoh; he exacted the silver and gold from the people of the land, from every one according to his assessment, to give *it* to Pharaoh Necho. ³⁶Jehoiakim *was* twenty-five years old when he became king, and he reigned eleven years in Jerusalem. His mother's name *was* Zebudah the daughter of Pedaiah of Rumah. ³⁷And he did evil in the sight of the LORD, according to all that his fathers had done.

23:34 ᵃThat is, Jehoahaz

JUDAH OVERRUN BY ENEMIES

¹In his days Nebuchadnezzar king of Babylon came up, and Jehoiakim became his vassal for three years. Then he turned and rebelled against him. ²And the LORD sent against him *raiding* bands of Chaldeans, bands of Syrians, bands of Moabites, and bands of the people of Ammon; He sent them against Judah to destroy it, according to the word of the LORD which He had spoken by His servants the prophets. ³Surely at the commandment of the LORD *this* came upon Judah, to remove *them* from His sight because of the sins of Manasseh, according to all that he had done, ⁴and also because of the innocent blood that he had shed; for he had filled Jerusalem with innocent blood, which the LORD would not pardon.

⁵Now the rest of the acts of Jehoiakim, and all that he did, *are* they not written in the book of the chronicles of the kings of Judah? ⁶So Jehoiakim rested with his fathers. Then Jehoiachin his son reigned in his place.

⁷And the king of Egypt did not come out of his land anymore, for the king of Babylon had taken all that belonged to the king of Egypt from the Brook of Egypt to the River Euphrates.

THE REIGN AND CAPTIVITY OF JEHOIACHIN

⁸Jehoiachin *was* eighteen years old when he became king, and he reigned in Jerusalem three months. His mother's name *was* Nehushta the daughter of Elnathan of Jerusalem. ⁹And he did evil in the sight of the LORD, according to all that his father had done.

¹⁰At that time the servants of Nebuchadnezzar king of Babylon came up against Jerusalem, and the city was besieged. ¹¹And Nebuchadnezzar king of Babylon came against the city, as his servants were besieging it. ¹²Then Jehoiachin king of Judah, his mother, his servants, his princes, and his officers went out to the king of Babylon; and the king of Babylon, in the eighth year of his reign, took him prisoner.

THE CAPTIVITY OF JERUSALEM

¹³And he carried out from there all the treasures of the house of the LORD and the treasures of the king's house, and he cut in pieces all the articles of gold which Solomon king of Israel had made in the temple of the LORD, as the LORD had said. ¹⁴Also he carried into captivity all Jerusalem: all the captains and all the mighty men of valor, ten thousand captives, and all the craftsmen and smiths. None remained except the poorest people of the land. ¹⁵And he carried

Jehoiachin captive to Babylon. The king's mother, the king's wives, his officers, and the mighty of the land he carried into captivity from Jerusalem to Babylon. ¹⁶All the valiant men, seven thousand, and craftsmen and smiths, one thousand, all *who were* strong *and* fit for war, these the king of Babylon brought captive to Babylon.

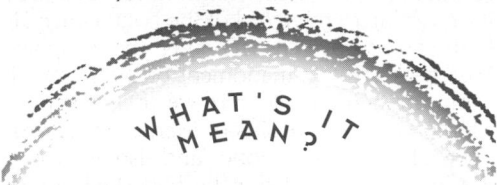

Welcome to the Babylonian Exile. In 597 B.C., Babylon attacked and defeated Jerusalem and carried off thousands of people, including King Jehoiachin himself. These people were held captive for seventy years, until after the Persians conquered Babylon. It was the Persian king, Cyrus, who eventually allowed the Jewish people to return to their homeland and rebuild the temple.

2 Kings 24:11

ZEDEKIAH REIGNS IN JUDAH

¹⁷Then the king of Babylon made Mattaniah, *Jehoiachin's*ᵃ uncle, king in his place, and changed his name to Zedekiah.

¹⁸Zedekiah *was* twenty-one years old when he became king, and he reigned eleven years in Jerusalem. His mother's name *was* Hamutal the daughter of Jeremiah of Libnah. ¹⁹He also did evil in the sight of the LORD, according to all that Jehoiakim had done. ²⁰For because of the anger of the LORD *this* happened in Jerusalem and Judah, that He finally cast them out from His presence. Then Zedekiah rebelled against the king of Babylon.

THE FALL AND CAPTIVITY OF JUDAH

¹Now it came to pass in the ninth year of his reign, in the tenth month, on the tenth *day* of the month, *that* Nebuchadnezzar king of Babylon and all his army came against Jerusalem and encamped against it; and they built a siege wall against it all around. ²So the city was besieged until the eleventh year of King Zedekiah. ³By the ninth *day* of the *fourth* month the famine had become so severe in the city that there was no food for the people of the land.

⁴Then the city wall was broken through, and all the men of war *fled* at night by way of the gate between two walls, which was by the king's garden, even though the Chaldeans *were* still encamped all around against the city. And *the king*ᵃ went by way of the plain.ᵇ ⁵But the army of the Chaldeans pursued the king, and they overtook him in the plains of Jericho. All his army was scattered from him. ⁶So they took the king and brought him up to the king of Babylon at Riblah, and they pronounced judgment on him. ⁷Then they killed the sons of Zedekiah before his eyes, put out the eyes of Zedekiah, bound him with bronze fetters, and took him to Babylon.

⁸And in the fifth month, on the seventh *day* of the month (which *was* the nineteenth year of King Nebuchadnezzar king of Babylon), Nebuzaradan the captain of the guard, a servant of the king of Babylon, came to Jerusalem. ⁹He burned the house of the LORD and the king's house; all the houses of Jerusalem, that is, all the houses of the great, he burned with fire. ¹⁰And all the army of the Chaldeans who *were with* the captain of the guard broke down the walls of Jerusalem all around.

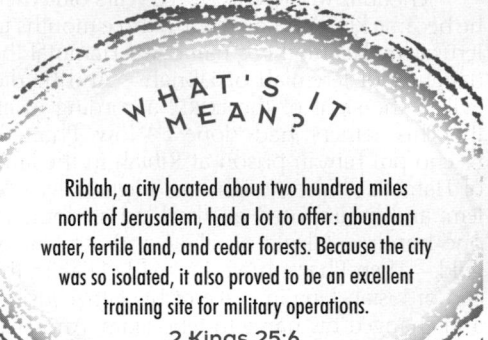

Riblah, a city located about two hundred miles north of Jerusalem, had a lot to offer: abundant water, fertile land, and cedar forests. Because the city was so isolated, it also proved to be an excellent training site for military operations.

2 Kings 25:6

¹¹Then Nebuzaradan the captain of the guard carried away captive the rest of the people *who* remained in the city and the defectors who had deserted to the king of Babylon, with the rest of the multitude. ¹²But the captain of the guard left *some* of the poor of the land as vinedressers and farmers. ¹³The bronze pillars that *were* in the house of the LORD, and the carts and the bronze Sea that *were* in the house of the LORD, the Chaldeans broke in pieces, and carried their bronze to Babylon. ¹⁴They also took away the pots, the shovels, the trimmers, the

spoons, and all the bronze utensils with which the priests ministered. [15]The firepans and the basins, the things of solid gold and solid silver, the captain of the guard took away. [16]The two pillars, one Sea, and the carts, which Solomon had made for the house of the LORD, the bronze of all these articles was beyond measure. [17]The height of one pillar *was* eighteen cubits, and the capital on it *was* of bronze. The height of the capital was three cubits, and the network and pomegranates all around the capital were all of bronze. The second pillar was the same, with a network.

WHAT'S IT MEAN?

This was a serious moving project. The bronze Sea alone was almost fifteen feet in diameter, more than seven feet deep, and three inches thick. It weighed more than ten tons and could hold about ten thousand gallons of water.

2 Kings 25:13

[18]And the captain of the guard took Seraiah the chief priest, Zephaniah the second priest, and the three doorkeepers. [19]He also took out of the city an officer who had charge of the men of war, five men of the king's close associates who were found in the city, the chief recruiting officer of the army, who mustered the people of the land, and sixty men of the people of the land *who were* found in the city. [20]So Nebuzaradan, captain of the guard, took these and brought them to the king of Babylon at Riblah. [21]Then the king of Babylon struck them and put them to death at Riblah in the land of Hamath. Thus Judah was carried away captive from its own land.

GEDALIAH MADE GOVERNOR OF JUDAH

[22]Then he made Gedaliah the son of Ahikam, the son of Shaphan, governor over the people who remained in the land of Judah, whom Nebuchadnezzar king of Babylon had left. [23]Now when all the captains of the armies, they and *their* men, heard that the king of Babylon had made Gedaliah governor, they came to Gedaliah at Mizpah—Ishmael the son of Nethaniah, Johanan the son of Careah, Seraiah the son of Tanhumeth the Netophathite, and Jaazaniah[a] the son of a Maachathite, they and their men. [24]And Gedaliah took an oath before them and their men, and said to them, "Do not be afraid of the servants of the Chaldeans. Dwell in the land and serve the king of Babylon, and it shall be well with you."

[25]But it happened in the seventh month that Ishmael the son of Nethaniah, the son of Elishama, of the royal family, came with ten men and struck and killed Gedaliah, the Jews, as well as the Chaldeans who were with him at Mizpah. [26]And all the people, small and great, and the captains of the armies, arose and went to Egypt; for they were afraid of the Chaldeans.

JEHOIACHIN RELEASED FROM PRISON

[27]Now it came to pass in the thirty-seventh year of the captivity of Jehoiachin king of Judah, in the twelfth month, on the twenty-seventh *day* of the month, *that* Evil-Merodach[a] king of Babylon, in the year that he began to reign, released Jehoiachin king of Judah from prison. [28]He spoke kindly to him, and gave him a more prominent seat than those of the kings who *were* with him in Babylon. [29]So Jehoiachin changed from his prison garments, and he ate bread regularly before the king all the days of his life. [30]And as for his provisions, *there was* a regular ration given him by the king, a portion for each day, all the days of his life.

25:23 [a]Spelled *Jezaniah* in Jeremiah 40:8   **25:27** [a]Literally *Man of Marduk*

1 Chronicles

CONTENT You might remember that First and Second Kings were the sequel to First and Second Samuel. You might assume that First Chronicles would then be another sequel, but you would be wrong. First and Second Chronicles present the same story line as First and Second Kings but from a different perspective and by a different storyteller.

The books of the Kings tell the *facts* of the stories. "This king was good and the people followed God. That king was bad and the people fell away *again*." But the Chronicles tell the "whys." The people fell away because they were not wholehearted about obeying God. God did not bless them unless they became wholehearted again.

Having the benefit of another perspective is a good thing. Knowing the facts teaches us lessons, but knowing *why* the facts happened teaches us how to keep from making the same mistakes. When you read the First Chronicles, remember to look for the "whys." Remember to ask yourself how wholehearted you are. Remember that a kingdom falls for the same reason a person does—letting go of God's hand.

Purpose God blesses those whose desire is to worship and to serve Him.

Theme Encouragement and Exhortation from Judah's Spiritual Heritage

Date of writing 430–425 B.C.

> "Yours, O LORD, is the greatness, the power and the glory, the victory and the majesty; for all that is in heaven and in earth is Yours; Yours is the kingdom, O LORD, and You are exalted as head over all" (29:11).

Bible Talk

Genealogies

First of all, let's get this out of the way right here at the beginning: yes, there are a lot of lists of genealogies in the Chronicles. They aren't fun to read. You are allowed to skip some verses. But don't give up on both books because they have some lists in them.

Genealogies don't seem so important to us today. A lot of us don't know much about our great-great-great-grandfather. But to the Hebrews, family history was everything. One reason for this was that the Hebrews were looking forward to the Messiah (Jesus) being born. They knew He would be a descendant of Abraham and then of David. If they kept those families straight, they would have a better chance of spotting the Messiah when He made His appearance.

WHAT'S THE BIG DEAL WITH THE TEMPLE?

You'll read a lot in First Chronicles about David making preparations for the temple. The important part of that is not how much gold David gathered or how many cedars of Lebanon (really nice lumber) he had brought in. The important part of that part of this story is that it was important for the Hebrews to honor God's presence in their lives. The temple was their way of doing that.

Remember that Jesus hadn't come on the scene yet to help them understand that God resides *in* us. So they still felt like they had to go to a place to honor God. If you remember their history, then you remember that they needed all the reminders of God's presence that they could get. The temple was a *very* big deal.

THE FAMILY OF ADAM—SETH TO ABRAHAM

¹Adam, Seth, Enosh, ²Cainan,*a* Mahalalel, Jared, ³Enoch, Methuselah, Lamech, ⁴Noah,*a* Shem, Ham, and Japheth.

⁵The sons of Japheth *were* Gomer, Magog, Madai, Javan, Tubal, Meshech, and Tiras. ⁶The sons of Gomer *were* Ashkenaz, Diphath,*a* and Togarmah. ⁷The sons of Javan *were* Elishah, Tarshishah,*a* Kittim, and Rodanim.*b*

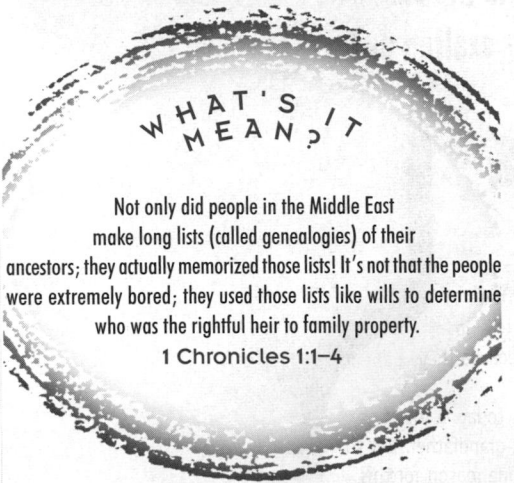

Not only did people in the Middle East make long lists (called genealogies) of their ancestors; they actually memorized those lists! It's not that the people were extremely bored; they used those lists like wills to determine who was the rightful heir to family property.

1 Chronicles 1:1–4

⁸The sons of Ham *were* Cush, Mizraim, Put, and Canaan. ⁹The sons of Cush *were* Seba, Havilah, Sabta,*a* Raama,*b* and Sabtecha. The sons of Raama *were* Sheba and Dedan. ¹⁰Cush begot Nimrod; he began to be a mighty one on the earth. ¹¹Mizraim begot Ludim, Anamim, Lehabim, Naphtuhim, ¹²Pathrusim, Casluhim (from whom came the Philistines and the Caphtorim). ¹³Canaan begot Sidon, his firstborn, and Heth; ¹⁴the Jebusite, the Amorite, and the Girgashite; ¹⁵the Hivite, the Arkite, and the Sinite; ¹⁶the Arvadite, the Zemarite, and the Hamathite.

¹⁷The sons of Shem *were* Elam, Asshur, Arphaxad, Lud, Aram, Uz, Hul, Gether, and Meshech.*a* ¹⁸Arphaxad begot Shelah, and Shelah begot Eber. ¹⁹To Eber were born two sons: the name of one *was* Peleg,*a* for in his days the earth was divided; and his brother's name *was* Joktan. ²⁰Joktan begot Almodad, Sheleph, Hazarmaveth, Jerah, ²¹Hadoram, Uzal, Diklah, ²²Ebal,*a* Abimael, Sheba, ²³Ophir, Havilah, and Jobab. All these *were* the sons of Joktan.

²⁴Shem, Arphaxad, Shelah, ²⁵Eber, Peleg, Reu, ²⁶Serug, Nahor, Terah, ²⁷and Abram, who *is* Abraham. ²⁸The sons of Abraham *were* Isaac and Ishmael.

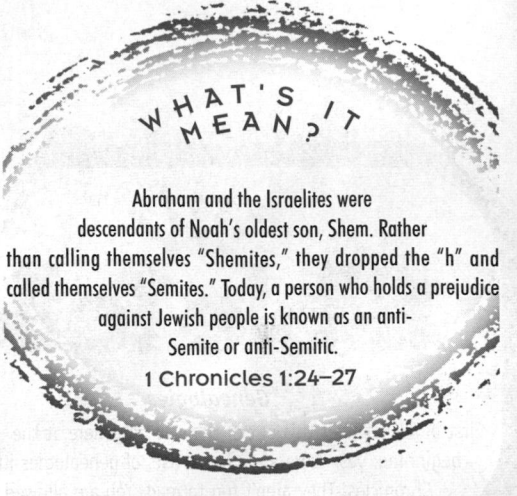

Abraham and the Israelites were descendants of Noah's oldest son, Shem. Rather than calling themselves "Shemites," they dropped the "h" and called themselves "Semites." Today, a person who holds a prejudice against Jewish people is known as an anti-Semite or anti-Semitic.

1 Chronicles 1:24–27

THE FAMILY OF ISHMAEL

²⁹These *are* their genealogies: The firstborn of Ishmael *was* Nebajoth; then Kedar, Adbeel, Mibsam, ³⁰Mishma, Dumah, Massa, Hadad,*a* Tema, ³¹Jetur, Naphish, and Kedemah. These *were* the sons of Ishmael.

THE FAMILY OF KETURAH

³²Now the sons born to Keturah, Abraham's concubine, *were* Zimran, Jokshan, Medan, Midian, Ishbak, and Shuah. The sons of Jokshan *were* Sheba and Dedan. ³³The sons of Midian *were* Ephah, Epher, Hanoch, Abida, and Eldaah. All these were the children of Keturah.

THE FAMILY OF ISAAC

³⁴And Abraham begot Isaac. The sons of Isaac *were* Esau and Israel. ³⁵The sons of Esau *were* Eliphaz, Reuel, Jeush, Jaalam, and Korah. ³⁶And the sons of Eliphaz *were* Teman, Omar, Zephi,*a* Gatam, *and* Kenaz; and *by* Timna,*b* Amalek. ³⁷The sons of Reuel *were* Nahath, Zerah, Shammah, and Mizzah.

THE FAMILY OF SEIR

³⁸The sons of Seir *were* Lotan, Shobal, Zibeon, Anah, Dishon, Ezer, and Dishan. ³⁹And the sons of Lotan *were* Hori and Homam; Lotan's sister *was* Timna. ⁴⁰The sons of Shobal *were*

1:2 *a*Hebrew *Qenan*   **1:4** *a*Following Masoretic Text and Vulgate; Septuagint adds *the sons of Noah.*
1:6 *a*Spelled *Riphath* in Genesis 10:3   **1:7** *a*Spelled *Tarshish* in Genesis 10:4   *b*Spelled *Dodanim* in Genesis 10:4
1:9 *a*Spelled *Sabtah* in Genesis 10:7   *b*Spelled *Raamah* in Genesis 10:7   **1:17** *a*Spelled *Mash* in Genesis 10:23
1:19 *a*Literally *Division*   **1:22** *a*Spelled *Obal* in Genesis 10:28   **1:30** *a*Spelled *Hadar* in Genesis 25:15
1:36 *a*Spelled *Zepho* in Genesis 36:11   *b*Compare Genesis 36:12

Alian,*a* Manahath, Ebal, Shephi,*b* and Onam. The sons of Zibeon *were* Ajah and Anah. ⁴¹The son of Anah *was* Dishon. The sons of Dishon *were* Hamran,*a* Eshban, Ithran, and Cheran. ⁴²The sons of Ezer *were* Bilhan, Zaavan, *and* Jaakan.*a* The sons of Dishan *were* Uz and Aran.

THE KINGS OF EDOM

⁴³Now these *were* the kings who reigned in the land of Edom before a king reigned over the children of Israel: Bela the son of Beor, and the name of his city was Dinhabah. ⁴⁴And when Bela died, Jobab the son of Zerah of Bozrah reigned in his place. ⁴⁵When Jobab died, Husham of the land of the Temanites reigned in his place. ⁴⁶And when Husham died, Hadad the son of Bedad, who attacked Midian in the field of Moab, reigned in his place. The name of his city *was* Avith. ⁴⁷When Hadad died, Samlah of Masrekah reigned in his place. ⁴⁸And when Samlah died, Saul of Rehoboth-by-the-River reigned in his place. ⁴⁹When Saul died, Baal-Hanan the son of Achbor reigned in his place. ⁵⁰And when Baal-Hanan died, Hadad*a* reigned in his place; and the name of his city was Pai.*b* His wife's name was Mehetabel the daughter of Matred, the daughter of Mezahab. ⁵¹Hadad died also. And the chiefs of Edom were Chief Timnah, Chief Aliah,*a* Chief Jetheth, ⁵²Chief Aholibamah, Chief Elah, Chief Pinon, ⁵³Chief Kenaz, Chief Teman, Chief Mibzar, ⁵⁴Chief Magdiel, and Chief Iram. These *were* the chiefs of Edom.

THE FAMILY OF ISRAEL

¹These *were* the sons of Israel: Reuben, Simeon, Levi, Judah, Issachar, Zebulun, ²Dan, Joseph, Benjamin, Naphtali, Gad, and Asher.

FROM JUDAH TO DAVID

³The sons of Judah *were* Er, Onan, and Shelah. *These* three were born to him by the daughter of Shua, the Canaanitess. Er, the firstborn of Judah, was wicked in the sight of the LORD; so He killed him. ⁴And Tamar, his daughter-in-law, bore him Perez and Zerah. All the sons of Judah *were* five.

SIN
How might God severely judge sin? (2:3)

⁵The sons of Perez *were* Hezron and Hamul. ⁶The sons of Zerah *were* Zimri, Ethan, Heman, Calcol, and Dara—five of them in all.

⁷The son of Carmi *was* Achar,*a* the troubler of Israel, who transgressed in the accursed thing.

⁸The son of Ethan *was* Azariah.

⁹Also the sons of Hezron who were born to him *were* Jerahmeel, Ram, and Chelubai.*a* ¹⁰Ram begot Amminadab, and Amminadab begot Nahshon, leader of the children of Judah; ¹¹Nahshon begot Salma,*a* and Salma begot Boaz; ¹²Boaz begot Obed, and Obed begot Jesse; ¹³Jesse begot Eliab his firstborn, Abinadab the second, Shimea*a* the third, ¹⁴Nethanel the fourth, Raddai the fifth, ¹⁵Ozem the sixth, *and* David the seventh.

Read 1:1—2:15 carefully and you'll discover that David, who was of the tribe of Judah, was a direct descendant of Adam, Noah, and Abraham. As the genealogies of the Gospels of Matthew and Luke show, David was also a direct ancestor of Jesus.

1 Chronicles 2:13–15

¹⁶Now their sisters *were* Zeruiah and Abigail. And the sons of Zeruiah *were* Abishai, Joab, and Asahel—three. ¹⁷Abigail bore Amasa; and the father of Amasa *was* Jether the Ishmaelite.*a*

THE FAMILY OF HEZRON

¹⁸Caleb the son of Hezron had children by Azubah, *his* wife, and by Jerioth. Now these were her sons: Jesher, Shobab, and Ardon. ¹⁹When Azubah died, Caleb took Ephrath*a* as his wife, who bore him Hur. ²⁰And Hur begot Uri, and Uri begot Bezalel.

²¹Now afterward Hezron went in to the daughter of Machir the father of Gilead, whom he married when he *was* sixty years old; and she bore him Segub. ²²Segub begot Jair, who had twenty-three cities in the land of Gilead.

1:40 *a*Spelled *Alvan* in Genesis 36:23 *b*Spelled *Shepho* in Genesis 36:23 **1:41** *a*Spelled *Hemdan* in Genesis 36:26 **1:42** *a*Spelled *Akan* in Genesis 36:27 **1:50** *a*Spelled *Hadar* in Genesis 36:39 *b*Spelled *Pau* in Genesis 36:39 **1:51** *a*Spelled *Alvah* in Genesis 36:40 **2:7** *a*Spelled *Achan* in Joshua 7:1 and elsewhere **2:9** *a*Spelled *Caleb* in 2:18, 42 **2:11** *a*Spelled *Salmon* in Ruth 4:21 and Luke 3:32 **2:13** *a*Spelled *Shammah* in 1 Samuel 16:9 and elsewhere **2:17** *a*Compare 2 Samuel 17:25 **2:19** *a*Spelled *Ephrathah* elsewhere

²³(Geshur and Syria took from them the towns of Jair, with Kenath and its towns—sixty towns.) All these *belonged to* the sons of Machir the father of Gilead. ²⁴After Hezron died in Caleb Ephrathah, Hezron's wife Abijah bore him Ashhur the father of Tekoa.

THE FAMILY OF JERAHMEEL

²⁵The sons of Jerahmeel, the firstborn of Hezron, *were* Ram, the firstborn, and Bunah, Oren, Ozem, *and* Ahijah. ²⁶Jerahmeel had another wife, whose name was Atarah; she was the mother of Onam. ²⁷The sons of Ram, the firstborn of Jerahmeel, were Maaz, Jamin, and Eker. ²⁸The sons of Onam were Shammai and Jada. The sons of Shammai *were* Nadab and Abishur.

²⁹And the name of the wife of Abishur *was* Abihail, and she bore him Ahban and Molid. ³⁰The sons of Nadab *were* Seled and Appaim; Seled died without children. ³¹The son of Appaim *was* Ishi, the son of Ishi *was* Sheshan, and Sheshan's son *was* Ahlai. ³²The sons of Jada, the brother of Shammai, *were* Jether and Jonathan; Jether died without children. ³³The sons of Jonathan *were* Peleth and Zaza. These were the sons of Jerahmeel.

³⁴Now Sheshan had no sons, only daughters. And Sheshan had an Egyptian servant whose name *was* Jarha. ³⁵Sheshan gave his daughter to Jarha his servant as wife, and she bore him Attai. ³⁶Attai begot Nathan, and Nathan begot Zabad; ³⁷Zabad begot Ephlal, and Ephlal begot Obed; ³⁸Obed begot Jehu, and Jehu begot Azariah; ³⁹Azariah begot Helez, and Helez begot Eleasah; ⁴⁰Eleasah begot Sismai, and Sismai begot Shallum; ⁴¹Shallum begot Jekamiah, and Jekamiah begot Elishama.

THE FAMILY OF CALEB

⁴²The descendants of Caleb the brother of Jerahmeel *were* Mesha, his firstborn, who was the father of Ziph, and the sons of Mareshah the father of Hebron. ⁴³The sons of Hebron *were* Korah, Tappuah, Rekem, and Shema. ⁴⁴Shema begot Raham the father of Jorkoam, and Rekem begot Shammai. ⁴⁵And the son of Shammai *was* Maon, and Maon *was* the father of Beth Zur.

⁴⁶Ephah, Caleb's concubine, bore Haran, Moza, and Gazez; and Haran begot Gazez. ⁴⁷And the sons of Jahdai *were* Regem, Jotham, Geshan, Pelet, Ephah, and Shaaph.

⁴⁸Maachah, Caleb's concubine, bore Sheber and Tirhanah. ⁴⁹She also bore Shaaph the father of Madmannah, Sheva the father of Machbenah and the father of Gibea. And the daughter of Caleb *was* Achsah.

⁵⁰These were the descendants of Caleb: The sons of Hur, the firstborn of Ephrathah, *were* Shobal the father of Kirjath Jearim, ⁵¹Salma the father of Bethlehem, *and* Hareph the father of Beth Gader.

⁵²And Shobal the father of Kirjath Jearim had descendants: Haroeh, *and* half of the *families of* Manuhoth.^a ⁵³The families of Kirjath Jearim *were* the Ithrites, the Puthites, the Shumathites, and the Mishraites. From these came the Zorathites and the Eshtaolites.

⁵⁴The sons of Salma *were* Bethlehem, the Netophathites, Atroth Beth Joab, half of the Manahethites, and the Zorites.

⁵⁵And the families of the scribes who dwelt at Jabez *were* the Tirathites, the Shimeathites, *and* the Suchathites. These *were* the Kenites who came from Hammath, the father of the house of Rechab.

THE FAMILY OF DAVID

¹Now these were the sons of David who were born to him in Hebron: The firstborn *was* Amnon, by Ahinoam the Jezreelitess; the second, Daniel,^a by Abigail the Carmelitess; ²the third, Absalom the son of Maacah, the daughter of Talmai, king of Geshur; the fourth, Adonijah the son of Haggith; ³the fifth, Shephatiah, by Abital; the sixth, Ithream, by his wife Eglah.

⁴*These* six were born to him in Hebron. There he reigned seven years and six months, and in Jerusalem he reigned thirty-three years. ⁵And these were born to him in Jerusalem: Shimea,^a Shobab, Nathan, and Solomon—four by Bathshua^b the daughter of Ammiel.^c ⁶Also *there* were Ibhar, Elishama,^a Eliphelet,^b ⁷Nogah, Nepheg, Japhia, ⁸Elishama, Eliada,^a and Eliphelet—nine *in all.* ⁹*These were* all the sons of David, besides the sons of the concubines, and Tamar their sister.

THE FAMILY OF SOLOMON

¹⁰Solomon's son *was* Rehoboam; Abijah^a *was* his son, Asa his son, Jehoshaphat his son, ¹¹Joram^a his son, Ahaziah his son, Joash^b his

---

2:52 ^aSame as *the Manahethites,* verse 54 **3:1** ^aCalled *Chileab* in 2 Samuel 3:3 **3:5** ^aSpelled *Shammua* in 14:4 and 2 Samuel 5:14 ^bSpelled *Bathsheba* in 2 Samuel 11:3 ^cCalled *Eliam* in 2 Samuel 11:3 **3:6** ^aSpelled *Elishua* in 14:5 and 2 Samuel 5:15 ^bSpelled *Elpelet* in 14:5 **3:8** ^aSpelled *Beeliada* in 14:7 **3:10** ^aSpelled *Abijam* in 1 Kings 15:1 **3:11** ^aSpelled *Jehoram* in 2 Kings 1:17 and 8:16 ^bSpelled *Jehoash* in 2 Kings 12:1

son, ¹²Amaziah his son, Azariah^a his son, Jotham his son, ¹³Ahaz his son, Hezekiah his son, Manasseh his son, ¹⁴Amon his son, *and* Josiah his son. ¹⁵The sons of Josiah *were* Johanan the firstborn, the second Jehoiakim, the third Zedekiah, and the fourth Shallum.^a ¹⁶The sons of Jehoiakim *were* Jeconiah his son *and* Zedekiah^a his son.

The southern kingdom of Judah outlasted the northern kingdom of Israel by about 125 years. Samaria, the capital of the northern kingdom, was defeated by the Assyrians in 722 B.C. Jerusalem, the capital of the southern kingdom, was conquered by the Babylonians in 597 B.C. Jeconiah, the king of Judah at the time of its defeat, was among the captives taken to Babylon.

1 Chronicles 3:17

THE FAMILY OF JECONIAH

¹⁷And the sons of Jeconiah^a *were* Assir,^b Shealtiel his son, ¹⁸and Malchiram, Pedaiah, Shenazzar, Jecamiah, Hoshama, and Nedabiah. ¹⁹The sons of Pedaiah *were* Zerubbabel and Shimei. The sons of Zerubbabel *were* Meshullam, Hananiah, Shelomith their sister, ²⁰and Hashubah, Ohel, Berechiah, Hasadiah, and Jushab-Hesed—five *in all*.

²¹The sons of Hananiah *were* Pelatiah and Jeshaiah, the sons of Rephaiah, the sons of Arnan, the sons of Obadiah, and the sons of Shechaniah. ²²The son of Shechaniah was Shemaiah. The sons of Shemaiah *were* Hattush, Igal, Bariah, Neariah, and Shaphat—six *in all*. ²³The sons of Neariah *were* Elioenai, Hezekiah, and Azrikam—three *in all*. ²⁴The sons of Elioenai *were* Hodaviah, Eliashib, Pelaiah, Akkub, Johanan, Delaiah, and Anani—seven *in all*.

THE FAMILY OF JUDAH

¹The sons of Judah *were* Perez, Hezron, Carmi, Hur, and Shobal. ²And Reaiah the son of Shobal begot Jahath, and Jahath begot Ahumai and Lahad. These *were* the families of the Zorathites. ³These *were* the sons *of the father* of Etam: Jezreel, Ishma, and Idbash; and the name of their sister *was* Hazelelponi; ⁴and Penuel *was* the father of Gedor, and Ezer *was the* father of Hushah.

These *were* the sons of Hur, the firstborn of Ephrathah the father of Bethlehem.

⁵And Ashhur the father of Tekoa had two wives, Helah and Naarah. ⁶Naarah bore him Ahuzzam, Hepher, Temeni, and Haahashtari. These *were* the sons of Naarah. ⁷The sons of Helah *were* Zereth, Zohar, and Ethnan; ⁸and Koz begot Anub, Zobebah, and the families of Aharhel the son of Harum.

⁹Now Jabez was more honorable than his brothers, and his mother called his name Jabez,^a saying, "Because I bore *him* in pain." ¹⁰And Jabez called on the God of Israel saying, "Oh, that You would bless me indeed, and enlarge my territory, that Your hand would be with me, and that You would keep *me* from evil, that I may not cause pain!" So God granted him what he requested.

Zerubbabel led the first group of Jewish exiles back to Jerusalem after they had spent seventy years as captives in Babylon. (By the way, an exile is a person who has been separated from his country.) He became the governor of Judah and started the long, slow process of rebuilding the temple, which had been completely destroyed. Haggai and Zechariah, two prophets of God, encouraged Zerubbabel in his work.

1 Chronicles 3:19

¹¹Chelub the brother of Shuhah begot Mehir, who *was* the father of Eshton. ¹²And Eshton begot Beth-Rapha, Paseah, and Tehinnah the father of Ir-Nahash. These *were* the men of Rechah.

¹³The sons of Kenaz *were* Othniel and Seraiah. The sons of Othniel *were* Hathath,^a ¹⁴and Meonothai *who* begot Ophrah. Seraiah begot Joab the father of Ge Harashim,^a for they were

---

3:12 ^aCalled *Uzziah* in Isaiah 6:1   **3:15** ^aCalled *Jehoahaz* in 2 Kings 23:31   **3:16** ^aCompare 2 Kings 24:17
3:17 ^aAlso called *Coniah* in Jeremiah 22:24 and *Jehoiachin* in 2 Kings 24:8   ^bOr *Jeconiah the captive were*
4:9 ^aLiterally *He Will Cause Pain*   **4:13** ^aSeptuagint and Vulgate add *and Meonothai*.   **4:14** ^aLiterally *Valley of Craftsmen*

craftsmen. ¹⁵The sons of Caleb the son of Jephunneh *were* Iru, Elah, and Naam. The son of Elah *was* Kenaz. ¹⁶The sons of Jehallelel *were* Ziph, Ziphah, Tiria, and Asarel. ¹⁷The sons of Ezrah *were* Jether, Mered, Epher, and Jalon. And *Mered's wife*ᵃ bore Miriam, Shammai, and Ishbah the father of Eshtemoa. ¹⁸(His wife Jehudijahᵃ bore Jered the father of Gedor, Heber the father of Sochoh, and Jekuthiel the father of Zanoah.) And these were the sons of Bithiah the daughter of Pharaoh, whom Mered took.

¹⁹The sons of Hodiah's wife, the sister of Naham, *were* the fathers of Keilah the Garmite and of Eshtemoa the Maachathite. ²⁰And the sons of Shimon *were* Amnon, Rinnah, Ben-Hanan, and Tilon. And the sons of Ishi *were* Zoheth and Ben-Zoheth.

²¹The sons of Shelah the son of Judah *were* Er the father of Lecah, Laadah the father of Mareshah, and the families of the house of the linen workers of the house of Ashbea; ²²also Jokim, the men of Chozeba, and Joash; Saraph, who ruled in Moab, and Jashubi-Lehem. Now the records are ancient. ²³These *were* the potters and those who dwell at Netaimᵃ and Gederah;ᵇ there they dwelt with the king for his work.

THE FAMILY OF SIMEON

²⁴The sons of Simeon *were* Nemuel, Jamin, Jarib,ᵃ Zerah,ᵇ *and* Shaul, ²⁵Shallum his son, Mibsam his son, and Mishma his son. ²⁶And the sons of Mishma *were* Hamuel his son, Zacchur his son, and Shimei his son. ²⁷Shimei had sixteen sons and six daughters; but his brothers did not have many children, nor did any of their families multiply as much as the children of Judah.

²⁸They dwelt at Beersheba, Moladah, Hazar Shual, ²⁹Bilhah, Ezem, Tolad, ³⁰Bethuel, Hormah, Ziklag, ³¹Beth Marcaboth, Hazar Susim, Beth Biri, and at Shaaraim. These *were* their cities until the reign of David. ³²And their villages *were* Etam, Ain, Rimmon, Tochen, and Ashan—five cities— ³³and all the villages that *were* around these cities as far as Baal.ᵃ These *were* their dwelling places, and they maintained their genealogy: ³⁴Meshobab, Jamlech, and Joshah the son of Amaziah; ³⁵Joel, and Jehu the son of Joshibiah, the son of Seraiah, the son of Asiel; ³⁶Elioenai, Jaakobah, Jeshohaiah, Asaiah, Adiel, Jesimiel, and Benaiah; ³⁷Ziza the son of Shiphi, the son of Allon, the son of Jedaiah, the son of Shimri, the son of Shemaiah— ³⁸these mentioned by name *were* leaders in their families, and their father's house increased greatly.

WHAT'S IT MEAN?

When the land of Canaan was divided among the twelve tribes of Israel, Simeon received territory in the south, near the Edom border and the desert that led to Egypt. Despite the fact that Simeon's entire piece of land was located inside Judah's much larger territory, the Simeonites managed to maintain their own identity.

1 Chronicles 4:28–31

³⁹So they went to the entrance of Gedor, as far as the east side of the valley, to seek pasture for their flocks. ⁴⁰And they found rich, good pasture, and the land *was* broad, quiet, and peaceful; for some Hamites formerly lived there. ⁴¹These recorded by name came in the days of Hezekiah king of Judah; and they attacked their tents and the Meunites who were found there, and utterly destroyed them, as it is to this day. So they dwelt in their place, because *there was* pasture for their flocks there. ⁴²Now *some* of them, five hundred men of the sons of Simeon, went to Mount Seir, having as their captains Pelatiah, Neariah, Rephaiah, and Uzziel, the sons of Ishi. ⁴³And they defeated the rest of the Amalekites who had escaped. They have dwelt there to this day.

THE FAMILY OF REUBEN

¹Now the sons of Reuben the firstborn of Israel—he *was* indeed the firstborn, but because he defiled his father's bed, his birthright was given to the sons of Joseph, the son of Israel, so that the genealogy is not listed according to the birthright; ²yet Judah prevailed over his brothers, and from him *came* a ruler, although the birthright was Joseph's—³the sons of Reuben the firstborn of Israel were Hanoch, Pallu, Hezron, and Carmi.

⁴The sons of Joel *were* Shemaiah his son, Gog his son, Shimei his son, ⁵Micah his son, Reaiah his son, Baal his son, ⁶and Beerah his son, whom Tiglath-Pileserᵃ king of Assyria carried into cap-

---

4:17 ᵃLiterally *she*   **4:18** ᵃOr *His Judean wife*   **4:23** ᵃLiterally *Plants* ᵇLiterally *Hedges*   **4:24** ᵃCalled *Jachin* in Genesis 46:10 ᵇCalled *Zohar* in Genesis 46:10   **4:33** ᵃOr *Baalath Beer* (compare Joshua 19:8)   **5:6** ᵃHebrew *Tilgath-Pileser* tivity. He *was* leader of the Reubenites. [7]And his brethren by their families, when the genealogy of their generations was registered: the chief, Jeiel, and Zechariah, [8]and Bela the son of Azaz, the son of Shema, the son of Joel, who dwelt in Aroer, as far as Nebo and Baal Meon. [9]Eastward they settled as far as the entrance of the wilderness this side of the River Euphrates, because their cattle had multiplied in the land of Gilead.

[10]Now in the days of Saul they made war with the Hagrites, who fell by their hand; and they dwelt in their tents throughout the entire *area* east of Gilead.

THE FAMILY OF GAD

[11]And the children of Gad dwelt next to them in the land of Bashan as far as Salcah: [12]Joel *was* the chief, Shapham the next, then Jaanai and Shaphat in Bashan, [13]and their brethren of their father's house: Michael, Meshullam, Sheba, Jorai, Jachan, Zia, and Eber—seven *in all.* [14]These *were* the children of Abihail the son of Huri, the son of Jaroah, the son of Gilead, the son of Michael, the son of Jeshishai, the son of Jahdo, the son of Buz; [15]Ahi the son of Abdiel, the son of Guni, *was* chief of their father's house. [16]And *the Gadites* dwelt in Gilead, in Bashan and in its villages, and in all the common-lands of Sharon within their borders. [17]All these were registered by genealogies in the days of Jotham king of Judah, and in the days of Jeroboam king of Israel.

[18]The sons of Reuben, the Gadites, and half the tribe of Manasseh *had* forty-four thousand seven hundred and sixty valiant men, men able to bear shield and sword, to shoot with the bow, and skillful in war, who went to war. [19]They made war with the Hagrites, Jetur, Naphish, and Nodab. [20]And they were helped against them, and the Hagrites were delivered into their hand, and all who *were* with them, for they cried out to God in the battle. He heeded their prayer, because they put their trust in Him. [21]Then they took away their livestock—fifty thousand of their camels, two hundred and fifty thousand of their sheep, and two thousand of their donkeys—also one hundred thousand of their men; [22]for many fell dead, because the war *was* God's. And they dwelt in their place until the captivity.

THE FAMILY OF MANASSEH (EAST)

[23]So the children of the half-tribe of Manasseh dwelt in the land. Their *numbers* increased from Bashan to Baal Hermon, that is, to Senir, or Mount Hermon. [24]These *were* the heads of their fathers' houses: Epher, Ishi, Eliel, Azriel, Jeremiah, Hodaviah, and Jahdiel. They were mighty men of valor, famous men, *and* heads of their fathers' houses.

[25]And they were unfaithful to the God of their fathers, and played the harlot after the gods of the peoples of the land, whom God had destroyed before them. [26]So the God of Israel stirred up the spirit of Pul king of Assyria, that is, Tiglath-Pileser[a] king of Assyria. He carried the Reubenites, the Gadites, and the half-tribe of Manasseh into captivity. He took them to Halah, Habor, Hara, and the river of Gozan to this day.

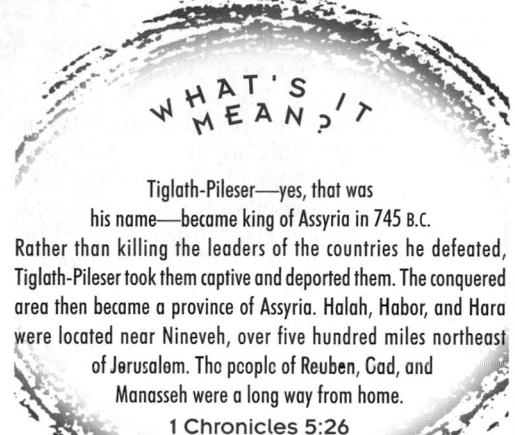

WHAT'S IT MEAN?

Tiglath-Pileser—yes, that was his name—became king of Assyria in 745 B.C. Rather than killing the leaders of the countries he defeated, Tiglath-Pileser took them captive and deported them. The conquered area then became a province of Assyria. Halah, Habor, and Hara were located near Nineveh, over five hundred miles northeast of Jerusalem. The people of Reuben, Gad, and Manasseh were a long way from home.

1 Chronicles 5:26

THE FAMILY OF LEVI

[1]The sons of Levi *were* Gershon, Kohath, and Merari. [2]The sons of Kohath *were* Amram, Izhar, Hebron, and Uzziel. [3]The children of Amram *were* Aaron, Moses, and Miriam. And the sons of Aaron *were* Nadab, Abihu, Eleazar, and Ithamar. [4]Eleazar begot Phinehas, *and* Phinehas begot Abishua; [5]Abishua begot Bukki, and Bukki begot Uzzi; [6]Uzzi begot Zerahiah, and Zerahiah begot Meraioth; [7]Meraioth begot Amariah, and Amariah begot Ahitub; [8]Ahitub begot Zadok, and Zadok begot Ahimaaz; [9]Ahimaaz begot Azariah, and Azariah begot Johanan; [10]Johanan begot Azariah (it was he who ministered as priest in the temple that Solomon built in Jerusalem); [11]Azariah begot Amariah, and Amariah begot Ahitub; [12]Ahitub begot Zadok, and Zadok begot Shallum; [13]Shallum begot Hilkiah, and Hilkiah begot Azariah; [14]Azariah begot Seraiah,

5:26 [a]Hebrew *Tilgath-Pilneser*

and Seraiah begot Jehozadak. ¹⁵Jehozadak went *into captivity* when the LORD carried Judah and Jerusalem into captivity by the hand of Nebuchadnezzar.

¹⁶The sons of Levi *were* Gershon,ᵃ Kohath, and Merari. ¹⁷These are the names of the sons of Gershon: Libni and Shimei. ¹⁸The sons of Kohath *were* Amram, Izhar, Hebron, and Uzziel. ¹⁹The sons of Merari *were* Mahli and Mushi. Now these *are* the families of the Levites according to their fathers: ²⁰Of Gershon *were* Libni his son, Jahath his son, Zimmah his son, ²¹Joah his son, Iddo his son, Zerah his son, *and* Jeatherai his son. ²²The sons of Kohath *were* Amminadab his son, Korah his son, Assir his son, ²³Elkanah his son, Ebiasaph his son, Assir his son, ²⁴Tahath his son, Uriel his son, Uzziah his son, and Shaul his son. ²⁵The sons of Elkanah *were* Amasai and Ahimoth. ²⁶*As for* Elkanah,ᵃ the sons of Elkanah *were* Zophaiᵇ his son, Nahathᶜ his son, ²⁷Eliabᵃ his son, Jeroham his son, *and* Elkanah his son. ²⁸The sons of Samuel *were* Joelᵃ the firstborn, and Abijah the second.ᵇ ²⁹The sons of Merari *were* Mahli, Libni his son, Shimei his son, Uzzah his son, ³⁰Shimea his son, Haggiah his son, *and* Asaiah his son.

MUSICIANS IN THE HOUSE OF THE LORD

³¹Now these are the men whom David appointed over the service of song in the house of the LORD, after the ark came to rest. ³²They were ministering with music before the dwelling place of the tabernacle of meeting, until Solomon had built the house of the LORD in Jerusalem, and they served in their office according to their order.

³³And these *are* the ones who ministered with their sons: Of the sons of the Kohathites *were* Heman the singer, the son of Joel, the son of Samuel, ³⁴the son of Elkanah, the son of Jeroham, the son of Eliel,ᵃ the son of Toah,ᵇ ³⁵the son of Zuph, the son of Elkanah, the son of Mahath, the son of Amasai, ³⁶the son of Elkanah, the son of Joel, the son of Azariah, the son of Zephaniah, ³⁷the son of Tahath, the son of Assir, the son of Ebiasaph, the son of Korah, ³⁸the son of Izhar, the son of Kohath, the son of

Levi, the son of Israel. ³⁹And his brother Asaph, who stood at his right hand, *was* Asaph the son of Berachiah, the son of Shimea, ⁴⁰the son of Michael, the son of Baaseiah, the son of Malchijah, ⁴¹the son of Ethni, the son of Zerah, the son of Adaiah, ⁴²the son of Ethan, the son of Zimmah, the son of Shimei, ⁴³the son of Jahath, the son of Gershon, the son of Levi.

⁴⁴Their brethren, the sons of Merari, on the left hand, *were* Ethan the son of Kishi, the son of Abdi, the son of Malluch, ⁴⁵the son of Hashabiah, the son of Amaziah, the son of Hilkiah, ⁴⁶the son of Amzi, the son of Bani, the son of Shamer, ⁴⁷the son of Mahli, the son of Mushi, the son of Merari, the son of Levi.

⁴⁸And their brethren, the Levites, *were* appointed to every kind of service of the tabernacle of the house of God.

> "Now these are the men whom David appointed over the service of song in the house of the LORD, after the ark came to rest."
> (1 Chronicles 6:31)

WHAT'S IT MEAN?

The rules and procedures for entering the Most Holy Place were extremely strict and extremely important to follow. Only the high priest was allowed to enter the inner room of the tabernacle (tent) of meeting. Even he was allowed to enter only once a year, to ask God's forgiveness for Israel's sins. The only piece of furniture allowed in the Most Holy Place was the ark of the covenant, which the Israelites considered to be God's earthly throne. The ark, which was made of acacia wood and covered with gold, contained the two flat stones on which the Law of Moses was written.

1 Chronicles 6:48

THE FAMILY OF AARON

⁴⁹But Aaron and his sons offered sacrifices on the altar of burnt offering and on the altar of incense, for all the work of the Most Holy *Place*, and to make atonement for Israel, according to all that Moses the servant of God had com-

---

6:16 ᵃHebrew *Gershom* (alternate spelling of *Gershon*, as in verses 1, 17, 20, 43, 62, and 71) **6:26** ᵃCompare verse 35 ᵇSpelled *Zuph* in verse 35 and 1 Samuel 1:1 ᶜCompare verse 34 **6:27** ᵃCompare verse 34 **6:28** ᵃFollowing Septuagint, Syriac, and Arabic (compare verse 33 and 1 Samuel 8:2) ᵇHebrew *Vasheni* **6:34** ᵃSpelled *Elihu* in 1 Samuel 1:1 ᵇSpelled *Tohu* in 1 Samuel 1:1

manded. ⁵⁰Now these *are* the sons of Aaron: Eleazar his son, Phinehas his son, Abishua his son, ⁵¹Bukki his son, Uzzi his son, Zerahiah his son, ⁵²Meraioth his son, Amariah his son, Ahitub his son, ⁵³Zadok his son, *and* Ahimaaz his son.

OBEDIENCE

What's a good example of obeying God? (6:49)

DWELLING PLACES OF THE LEVITES

⁵⁴Now these *are* their dwelling places throughout their settlements in their territory, for they were *given* by lot to the sons of Aaron, of the family of the Kohathites: ⁵⁵They gave them Hebron in the land of Judah, with its surrounding common-lands. ⁵⁶But the fields of the city and its villages they gave to Caleb the son of Jephunneh. ⁵⁷And to the sons of Aaron they gave *one of* the cities of refuge, Hebron; also Libnah with its common-lands, Jattir, Eshtemoa with its common-lands, ⁵⁸Hilen*ᵃ* with its common-lands, Debir with its common-lands, ⁵⁹Ashan*ᵃ* with its common-lands, and Beth Shemesh with its common-lands. ⁶⁰And from the tribe of Benjamin: Geba with its common-lands, Alemeth*ᵃ* with its common-lands, and Anathoth with its common-lands. All their cities among their families *were* thirteen.

WHAT'S IT MEAN?

The Levites were the designated priests of Israel. They were responsible for taking care of the tabernacle of meeting, the altar, and the people's sacrifices. They were also responsible for meeting the spiritual needs of their fellow Israelites. Because their job was to take care of the various tribes, the Levites did not receive a specific area of land when they moved to Canaan. Instead, they were given forty-eight cities scattered throughout Israel.

1 Chronicles 6:64

⁶¹To the rest of the family of the tribe of the Kohathites *they gave* by lot ten cities from half the tribe of Manasseh. ⁶²And to the sons of Gershon, throughout their families, *they gave* thirteen cities from the tribe of Issachar, from the tribe of Asher, from the tribe of Naphtali, and from the tribe of Manasseh in Bashan. ⁶³To the sons of Merari, throughout their families, *they gave* twelve cities from the tribe of Reuben, from the tribe of Gad, and from the tribe of Zebulun. ⁶⁴So the children of Israel gave *these* cities with their common-lands to the Levites. ⁶⁵And they gave by lot from the tribe of the children of Judah, from the tribe of the children of Simeon, and from the tribe of the children of Benjamin these cities which are called by *their* names.

⁶⁶Now some of the families of the sons of Kohath *were given* cities as their territory from the tribe of Ephraim. ⁶⁷And they gave them *one of* the cities of refuge, Shechem with its common-lands, in the mountains of Ephraim, also Gezer with its common-lands, ⁶⁸Jokmeam with its common-lands, Beth Horon with its common-lands, ⁶⁹Aijalon with its common-lands, and Gath Rimmon with its common-lands. ⁷⁰And from the half-tribe of Manasseh: Aner with its common-lands and Bileam with its common-lands, for the rest of the family of the sons of Kohath.

⁷¹From the family of the half-tribe of Manasseh the sons of Gershon *were given* Golan in Bashan with its common-lands and Ashtaroth with its common-lands. ⁷²And from the tribe of Issachar: Kedesh with its common-lands, Daberath with its common-lands, ⁷³Ramoth with its common-lands, and Anem with its common-lands. ⁷⁴And from the tribe of Asher: Mashal with its common-lands, Abdon with its common-lands, ⁷⁵Hukok with its common-lands, and Rehob with its common-lands. ⁷⁶And from the tribe of Naphtali: Kedesh in Galilee with its common-lands, Hammon with its common-lands, and Kirjathaim with its common-lands.

⁷⁷From the tribe of Zebulun the rest of the children of Merari *were given* Rimmon*ᵃ* with its common-lands and Tabor with its common-lands. ⁷⁸And on the other side of the Jordan, across from Jericho, on the east side of the Jordan, *they were given* from the tribe of Reuben: Bezer in the wilderness with its common-lands, Jahzah with its common-lands, ⁷⁹Kedemoth with its common-lands, and Mephaath with its common-lands. ⁸⁰And from the tribe of Gad: Ramoth in Gilead with its common-lands, Mahanaim with its common-lands, ⁸¹Heshbon with its common-lands, and Jazer with its common-lands.

6:58 *ᵃ*Spelled *Holon* in Joshua 21:15   **6:59** *ᵃ*Spelled *Ain* in Joshua 21:16   **6:60** *ᵃ*Spelled *Almon* in Joshua 21:18   **6:77** *ᵃ*Hebrew *Rimmono*, alternate spelling of *Rimmon*; see 4:32

THE FAMILY OF ISSACHAR

¹The sons of Issachar *were* Tola, Puah,*ᵃ* Jashub, and Shimron—four *in all.* ²The sons of Tola *were* Uzzi, Rephaiah, Jeriel, Jahmai, Jibsam, and Shemuel, heads of their father's house. *The sons* of Tola *were* mighty men of valor in their generations; their number in the days of David *was* twenty-two thousand six hundred. ³The son of Uzzi *was* Izrahiah, and the sons of Izrahiah *were* Michael, Obadiah, Joel, and Ishiah. All five of them *were* chief men. ⁴And with them, by their generations, according to their fathers' houses, *were* thirty-six thousand troops ready for war; for they had many wives and sons.

⁵Now their brethren among all the families of Issachar *were* mighty men of valor, listed by their genealogies, eighty-seven thousand in all.

THE FAMILY OF BENJAMIN

⁶*The sons* of Benjamin *were* Bela, Becher, and Jediael—three *in all.* ⁷The sons of Bela were Ezbon, Uzzi, Uzziel, Jerimoth, and Iri—five *in all.* They *were* heads of *their* fathers' houses, and they were listed by their genealogies, twenty-two thousand and thirty-four mighty men of valor.

⁸The sons of Becher *were* Zemirah, Joash, Eliezer, Elioenai, Omri, Jerimoth, Abijah, Anathoth, and Alemeth. All these *are* the sons of Becher. ⁹And they were recorded by genealogy according to their generations, heads of their fathers' houses, twenty thousand two hundred mighty men of valor. ¹⁰The son of Jediael *was* Bilhan, and the sons of Bilhan *were* Jeush, Benjamin, Ehud, Chenaanah, Zethan, Tharshish, and Ahishahar.

¹¹All these sons of Jediael *were* heads of their fathers' houses; *there were* seventeen thousand two hundred mighty men of valor fit to go out for war *and* battle. ¹²Shuppim and Huppim*ᵃ* were the sons of Ir, *and* Hushim *was* the son of Aher.

THE FAMILY OF NAPHTALI

¹³The sons of Naphtali *were* Jahziel,*ᵃ* Guni, Jezer, and Shallum,*ᵇ* the sons of Bilhah.

THE FAMILY OF MANASSEH (WEST)

¹⁴The descendants of Manasseh: his Syrian concubine bore him Machir the father of Gilead, the father of Asriel.*ᵃ* ¹⁵Machir took as his wife *the sister* of Huppim and Shuppim,*ᵃ* whose name *was* Maachah. The name of *Gilead's* grandson*ᵇ* was Zelophehad,*ᶜ* but Zelophehad begot only daughters. ¹⁶(Maachah the wife of Machir bore a son, and she called his name Peresh. The name of his brother *was* Sheresh, and his sons *were* Ulam and Rakem. ¹⁷The son of Ulam *was* Bedan.) These *were* the descendants of Gilead the son of Machir, the son of Manasseh.

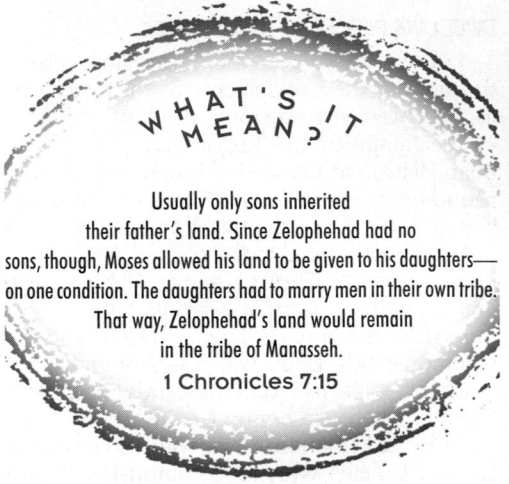

WHAT'S IT MEAN?

Usually only sons inherited their father's land. Since Zelophehad had no sons, though, Moses allowed his land to be given to his daughters—on one condition. The daughters had to marry men in their own tribe. That way, Zelophehad's land would remain in the tribe of Manasseh.

1 Chronicles 7:15

¹⁸His sister Hammoleketh bore Ishhod, Abiezer, and Mahlah.

¹⁹And the sons of Shemida were Ahian, Shechem, Likhi, and Aniam.

THE FAMILY OF EPHRAIM

²⁰The sons of Ephraim *were* Shuthelah, Bered his son, Tahath his son, Eladah his son, Tahath his son, ²¹Zabad his son, Shuthelah his son, and Ezer and Elead. The men of Gath who were born in *that* land killed *them* because they came down to take away their cattle. ²²Then Ephraim their father mourned many days, and his brethren came to comfort him.

²³And when he went in to his wife, she conceived and bore a son; and he called his name Beriah,*ᵃ* because tragedy had come upon his house. ²⁴Now his daughter *was* Sheerah, who built Lower and Upper Beth Horon and Uzzen Sheerah; ²⁵and Rephah *was* his son, *as well as* Resheph, and Telah his son, Tahan his son, ²⁶Laadan his son, Ammihud his son, Elishama his son, ²⁷Nun*ᵃ* his son, and Joshua his son.

²⁸Now their possessions and dwelling places *were* Bethel and its towns: to the east Naaran, to the west Gezer and its towns, and Shechem and

---

7:1 *ᵃ*Spelled *Puvah* in Genesis 46:13   **7:12** *ᵃ*Called *Hupham* in Numbers 26:39   **7:13** *ᵃ*Spelled *Jahzeel* in Genesis 46:24 *ᵇ*Spelled *Shillem* in Genesis 46:24   **7:14** *ᵃ*The son of Gilead (compare Numbers 26:30, 31)
7:15 *ᵃ*Compare verse 12 *ᵇ*Literally *the second* *ᶜ*Compare Numbers 26:30–33   **7:23** *ᵃ*Literally *In Tragedy*
7:27 *ᵃ*Hebrew *Non*

its towns, as far as Ayyah*a* and its towns; [29]and by the borders of the children of Manasseh *were* Beth Shean and its towns, Taanach and its towns, Megiddo and its towns, Dor and its towns. In these dwelt the children of Joseph, the son of Israel.

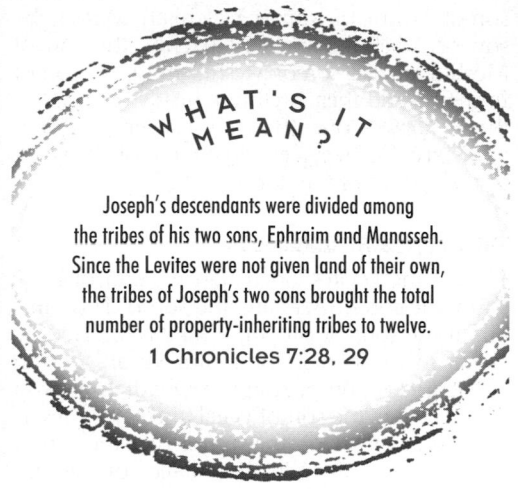

WHAT'S IT MEAN?

Joseph's descendants were divided among the tribes of his two sons, Ephraim and Manasseh. Since the Levites were not given land of their own, the tribes of Joseph's two sons brought the total number of property-inheriting tribes to twelve.

1 Chronicles 7:28, 29

THE FAMILY OF ASHER

[30]The sons of Asher *were* Imnah, Ishvah, Ishvi, Beriah, and their sister Serah. [31]The sons of Beriah *were* Heber and Malchiel, who was the father of Birzaith.*a* [32]And Heber begot Japhlet, Shomer,*a* Hotham,*b* and their sister Shua. [33]The sons of Japhlet *were* Pasach, Bimhal, and Ashvath. These *were* the children of Japhlet. [34]The sons of Shemer *were* Ahi, Rohgah, Jehubbah, and Aram. [35]And the sons of his brother Helem *were* Zophah, Imna, Shelesh, and Amal. [36]The sons of Zophah *were* Suah, Harnepher, Shual, Beri, Imrah, [37]Bezer, Hod, Shamma, Shilshah, Jithran,*a* and Beera. [38]The sons of Jether *were* Jephunneh, Pispah, and Ara. [39]The sons of Ulla *were* Arah, Haniel, and Rizia.

[40]All these *were* the children of Asher, heads of *their* fathers' houses, choice men, mighty men of valor, chief leaders. And they were recorded by genealogies among the army fit for battle; their number *was* twenty-six thousand.

THE FAMILY TREE OF KING SAUL OF BENJAMIN

[1]Now Benjamin begot Bela his firstborn, Ashbel the second, Aharah*a* the third, [2]Nohah the fourth, and Rapha the fifth. [3]The sons of Bela *were* Addar,*a* Gera, Abihud, [4]Abishua, Naaman, Ahoah, [5]Gera, Shephuphan, and Huram.

[6]These *are* the sons of Ehud, who were the heads of the fathers' *houses* of the inhabitants of Geba, and who forced them to move to Manahath: [7]Naaman, Ahijah, and Gera who forced them to move. He begot Uzza and Ahihud.

[8]Also Shaharaim had children in the country of Moab, after he had sent away Hushim and Baara his wives. [9]By Hodesh his wife he begot Jobab, Zibia, Mesha, Malcam, [10]Jeuz, Sachiah, and Mirmah. These *were* his sons, heads of their fathers' *houses*.

[11]And by Hushim he begot Abitub and Elpaal. [12]The sons of Elpaal *were* Eber, Misham, and Shemed, who built Ono and Lod with its towns; [13]and Beriah and Shema, who *were* heads of their fathers' *houses* of the inhabitants of Aijalon, who drove out the inhabitants of Gath. [14]Ahio, Shashak, Jeremoth, [15]Zebadiah, Arad, Eder, [16]Michael, Ispah, and Joha *were* the sons of Beriah. [17]Zebadiah, Meshullam, Hizki, Heber, [18]Ishmerai, Jizliah, and Jobab *were* the sons of Elpaal. [19]Jakim, Zichri, Zabdi, [20]Elienai, Zillethai, Eliel, [21]Adaiah, Beraiah, and Shimrath *were* the sons of Shimei. [22]Ishpan, Eber, Eliel, [23]Abdon, Zichri, Hanan, [24]Hananiah, Elam, Antothijah, [25]Iphdeiah, and Penuel *were* the sons of Shashak. [26]Shamsherai, Shehariah, Athaliah, [27]Jaareshiah, Elijah, and Zichri *were* the sons of Jeroham.

[28]These *were* heads of the fathers' *houses* by their generations, chief men. These dwelt in Jerusalem.

[29]Now the father of Gibeon, whose wife's name *was* Maacah, dwelt at Gibeon. [30]And his firstborn son *was* Abdon, then Zur, Kish, Baal, Nadab, [31]Gedor, Ahio, Zecher, [32]and Mikloth, who begot Shimeah.*a* They also dwelt alongside their relatives in Jerusalem, with their brethren. [33]Ner*a* begot Kish, Kish begot Saul, and Saul begot Jonathan, Malchishua, Abinadab,*b* and Esh-Baal.*c* [34]The son of Jonathan *was* Merib-Baal,*a* and Merib-Baal begot Micah. [35]The sons of Micah *were* Pithon, Melech, Tarea, and Ahaz. [36]And Ahaz begot Jehoaddah;*a* Jehoaddah begot Alemeth, Azmaveth, and Zimri; and Zimri begot Moza. [37]Moza begot Binea, Raphah*a* his son, Eleasah his son, *and* Azel his son.

[38]Azel had six sons whose names *were* these:

7:28 *a*Many Hebrew manuscripts, Bomberg, Septuagint, Targum, and Vulgate read *Gazza.* **7:31** *a*Or *Birzavith* or *Birzoth* **7:32** *a*Spelled *Shemer* in verse 34 *b*Spelled *Helem* in verse 35 **7:37** *a*Spelled *Jether* in verse 38 **8:1** *a*Spelled *Ahiram* in Numbers 26:38 **8:3** *a*Called *Ard* in Numbers 26:40 **8:32** *a*Spelled *Shimeam* in 9:38 **8:33** *a*Also the son of Gibeon (compare 9:36, 39) *b*Called *Jishui* in 1 Samuel 14:49 *c*Called *Ishbosheth* in 2 Samuel 2:8 and elsewhere **8:34** *a*Called *Mephibosheth* in 2 Samuel 4:4 **8:36** *a*Spelled *Jarah* in 9:42 **8:37** *a*Spelled *Rephaiah* in 9:43

Azrikam, Bocheru, Ishmael, Sheariah, Obadiah, and Hanan. All these *were* the sons of Azel. [39]And the sons of Eshek his brother *were* Ulam his firstborn, Jeush the second, and Eliphelet the third.

[40]The sons of Ulam were mighty men of valor—archers. *They* had many sons and grandsons, one hundred and fifty *in all*. These *were* all sons of Benjamin.

[1]So all Israel was recorded by genealogies, and indeed, they *were* inscribed in the book of the kings of Israel. But Judah was carried away captive to Babylon because of their unfaithfulness. [2]And the first inhabitants who *dwelt* in their possessions in their cities *were* Israelites, priests, Levites, and the Nethinim.

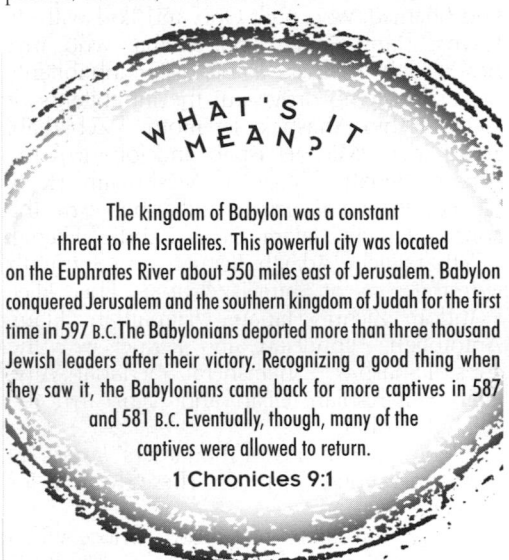

WHAT'S IT MEAN?

The kingdom of Babylon was a constant threat to the Israelites. This powerful city was located on the Euphrates River about 550 miles east of Jerusalem. Babylon conquered Jerusalem and the southern kingdom of Judah for the first time in 597 B.C. The Babylonians deported more than three thousand Jewish leaders after their victory. Recognizing a good thing when they saw it, the Babylonians came back for more captives in 587 and 581 B.C. Eventually, though, many of the captives were allowed to return.

1 Chronicles 9:1

Dwellers in Jerusalem
[3]Now in Jerusalem the children of Judah dwelt, and some of the children of Benjamin, and of the children of Ephraim and Manasseh: [4]Uthai the son of Ammihud, the son of Omri, the son of Imri, the son of Bani, of the descendants of Perez, the son of Judah. [5]Of the Shilonites: Asaiah the firstborn and his sons. [6]Of the sons of Zerah: Jeuel, and their brethren— six hundred and ninety. [7]Of the sons of Benjamin: Sallu the son of Meshullam, the son of Hodaviah, the son of Hassenuah; [8]Ibneiah the son of Jeroham; Elah the son of Uzzi, the son of Michri; Meshullam the son of Shephatiah, the son of Reuel, the son of Ibnijah; [9]and their brethren, according to their generations— nine hundred and fifty-six. All these men *were* heads of a father's *house* in their fathers' houses.

THE PRIESTS AT JERUSALEM

[10]Of the priests: Jedaiah, Jehoiarib, and Jachin; [11]Azariah the son of Hilkiah, the son of Meshullam, the son of Zadok, the son of Meraioth, the son of Ahitub, the officer over the house of God; [12]Adaiah the son of Jeroham, the son of Pashur, the son of Malchijah; Maasai the son of Adiel, the son of Jahzerah, the son of Meshullam, the son of Meshillemith, the son of Immer; [13]and their brethren, heads of their fathers' *houses*—one thousand seven hundred and sixty. *They were* very able men for the work of the service of the house of God.

THE LEVITES AT JERUSALEM

[14]Of the Levites: Shemaiah the son of Hasshub, the son of Azrikam, the son of Hashabiah, of the sons of Merari; [15]Bakbakkar, Heresh, Galal, and Mattaniah the son of Micah, the son of Zichri, the son of Asaph; [16]Obadiah the son of Shemaiah, the son of Galal, the son of Jeduthun; and Berechiah the son of Asa, the son of Elkanah, who lived in the villages of the Netophathites.

THE LEVITE GATEKEEPERS

[17]And the gatekeepers *were* Shallum, Akkub, Talmon, Ahiman, and their brethren. Shallum *was* the chief. [18]Until then *they had been* gatekeepers for the camps of the children of Levi at the King's Gate on the east.

[19]Shallum the son of Kore, the son of Ebiasaph, the son of Korah, and his brethren, from his father's house, the Korahites, *were* in charge of the work of the service, gatekeepers of the tabernacle. Their fathers had been keepers of the entrance to the camp of the LORD. [20]And Phinehas the son of Eleazar had been the officer over them in time past; the LORD *was* with him. [21]Zechariah the son of Meshelemiah *was* keeper of the door of the tabernacle of meeting.

[22]All those chosen as gatekeepers *were* two hundred and twelve. They were recorded by their genealogy, in their villages. David and Samuel the seer had appointed them to their trusted office. [23]So they and their children *were* in charge of the gates of the house of the LORD, the house of the tabernacle, by assignment. [24]The gatekeepers were assigned to the four directions: the east, west, north, and south. [25]And their brethren in their villages *had* to come with them from time to time for seven days. [26]For in this trusted office *were* four chief gatekeepers; they were Levites. And they had charge over the chambers and treasuries of the house of God. [27]And they lodged *all* around the house of

God because they *had* the responsibility, and they *were* in charge of opening *it* every morning.

OTHER LEVITE RESPONSIBILITIES

[28]Now *some* of them were in charge of the serving vessels, for they brought them in and took them out by count. [29]*Some* of them *were* appointed over the furnishings and over all the implements of the sanctuary, and over the fine flour and the wine and the oil and the incense and the spices. [30]And *some* of the sons of the priests made the ointment of the spices.

[31]Mattithiah of the Levites, the firstborn of Shallum the Korahite, had the trusted office over the things that were baked in the pans. [32]And some of their brethren of the sons of the Kohathites *were* in charge of preparing the showbread for every Sabbath.

[33]These are the singers, heads of the fathers' *houses* of the Levites, *who lodged* in the chambers, *and were* free *from other duties;* for they were employed in *that* work day and night. [34]These heads of the fathers' *houses* of the Levites *were* heads throughout their generations. They dwelt at Jerusalem.

THE FAMILY OF KING SAUL

[35]Jeiel the father of Gibeon, whose wife's name *was* Maacah, dwelt at Gibeon. [36]His firstborn son *was* Abdon, then Zur, Kish, Baal, Ner, Nadab, [37]Gedor, Ahio, Zechariah,*a* and Mikloth. [38]And Mikloth begot Shimeam.*a* They also dwelt alongside their relatives in Jerusalem, with their brethren. [39]Ner begot Kish, Kish begot Saul, and Saul begot Jonathan, Malchishua, Abinadab, and Esh-Baal. [40]The son of Jonathan *was* Merib-Baal, and Merib-Baal begot Micah. [41]The sons of Micah *were* Pithon, Melech, Tahrea,*a and Ahaz.*b* [42]And Ahaz begot Jarah;*a* Jarah begot Alemeth, Azmaveth, and Zimri; and Zimri begot Moza; [43]Moza begot Binea, Rephaiah*a* his son, Eleasah his son, and Azel his son.

[44]And Azel had six sons whose names *were* these: Azrikam, Bocheru, Ishmael, Sheariah, Obadiah, and Hanan; these *were* the sons of Azel.

TRAGIC END OF SAUL AND HIS SONS

[1]Now the Philistines fought against Israel; and the men of Israel fled from before the Philistines, and fell slain on Mount Gilboa. [2]Then the Philistines followed hard after Saul and his sons. And the Philistines killed Jonathan, Abinadab, and Malchishua, Saul's sons. [3]The battle became fierce against Saul. The archers hit him, and he was wounded by the archers. [4]Then Saul said to his armorbearer, "Draw your sword, and thrust me through with it, lest these uncircumcised men come and abuse me." But his armorbearer would not, for he was greatly afraid. Therefore Saul took a sword and fell on it. [5]And when his armorbearer saw that Saul was dead, he also fell on his sword and died. [6]So Saul and his three sons died, and all his house died together. [7]And when all the men of Israel who *were* in the valley saw that they had fled and that Saul and his sons were dead, they forsook their cities and fled; then the Philistines came and dwelt in them.

[8]So it happened the next day, when the Philistines came to strip the slain, that they found Saul and his sons fallen on Mount Gilboa. [9]And they stripped him and took his head and his armor, and sent word *throughout* the land of the Philistines to proclaim the news *in the temple* of their idols and among the people. [10]Then they put his armor in the temple of their gods, and fastened his head in the temple of Dagon.

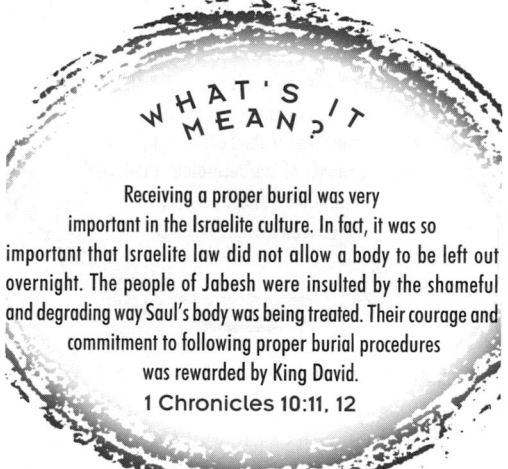

WHAT'S IT MEAN?

Receiving a proper burial was very important in the Israelite culture. In fact, it was so important that Israelite law did not allow a body to be left out overnight. The people of Jabesh were insulted by the shameful and degrading way Saul's body was being treated. Their courage and commitment to following proper burial procedures was rewarded by King David.
1 Chronicles 10:11, 12

[11]And when all Jabesh Gilead heard all that the Philistines had done to Saul, [12]all the valiant men arose and took the body of Saul and the bodies of his sons; and they brought them to Jabesh, and buried their bones under the tamarisk tree at Jabesh, and fasted seven days.

[13]So Saul died for his unfaithfulness which he had committed against the LORD, because he

did not keep the word of the LORD, and also because he consulted a medium for guidance. [14]But *he* did not inquire of the LORD; therefore He killed him, and turned the kingdom over to David the son of Jesse.

CULT

Does God judge cultic practices? (10:13, 14)

DAVID MADE KING OVER ALL ISRAEL

[1]Then all Israel came together to David at Hebron, saying, "Indeed we *are* your bone and your flesh. [2]Also, in time past, even when Saul was king, you *were* the one who led Israel out and brought them in; and the LORD your God said to you, 'You shall shepherd My people Israel, and be ruler over My people Israel.'" [3]Therefore all the elders of Israel came to the king at Hebron, and David made a covenant with them at Hebron before the LORD. And they anointed David king over Israel, according to the word of the LORD by Samuel.

WHAT'S IT MEAN?

David's challenge to his men was simple: The first person to attack Jerusalem would be named commander-in-chief of the army. Interestingly, the winner of the "Jerusalem challenge" was David's nephew Joab.

1 Chronicles 11:5–8

THE CITY OF DAVID

[4]And David and all Israel went to Jerusalem, which is Jebus, where the Jebusites *were*, the inhabitants of the land. [5]But the inhabitants of Jebus said to David, "You shall not come in here!" Nevertheless David took the stronghold of Zion (that is, the City of David). [6]Now David said, "Whoever attacks the Jebusites first shall be chief and captain." And Joab the son of Zeruiah went up first, and became chief. [7]Then David dwelt in the stronghold; therefore they called it the City of David. [8]And he built the city around it, from the Millo[a] to the surrounding area. Joab repaired the rest of the city. [9]So David went on

and became great, and the LORD of hosts *was* with him.

THE MIGHTY MEN OF DAVID

[10]Now these *were* the heads of the mighty men whom David had, who strengthened themselves with him in his kingdom, with all Israel, to make him king, according to the word of the LORD concerning Israel.

[11]And this *is* the number of the mighty men whom David had: Jashobeam the son of a Hachmonite, chief of the captains;[a] he had lifted up his spear against three hundred, killed *by* him at one time.

[12]After him *was* Eleazar the son of Dodo, the Ahohite, who *was one* of the three mighty men. [13]He was with David at Pasdammim. Now there the Philistines were gathered for battle, and there was a piece of ground full of barley. So the people fled from the Philistines. [14]But they stationed themselves in the middle of *that* field, defended it, and killed the Philistines. So the LORD brought about a great victory.

SUCCESS

Can we trust God for our success? (11:14)

[15]Now three of the thirty chief men went down to the rock to David, into the cave of Adullam; and the army of the Philistines encamped in the Valley of Rephaim. [16]David *was* then in the stronghold, and the garrison of the Philistines *was* then in Bethlehem. [17]And David said with longing, "Oh, that someone would give me a drink of water from the well of Bethlehem, which is by the gate!" [18]So the three broke through the camp of the Philistines, drew water from the well of Bethlehem that *was* by the gate, and took *it* and brought *it* to David. Nevertheless David would not drink it, but poured it out to the LORD. [19]And he said, "Far be it from me, O my God, that I should do this! Shall I drink the blood of these men *who have put* their lives *in jeopardy*? For at the risk of their lives they brought it." Therefore he would not drink it. These things were done by the three mighty men.

[20]Abishai the brother of Joab was chief of *another* three.[a] He had lifted up his spear against three hundred *men*, killed *them*, and won a name among *these* three. [21]Of the three he was more honored than the other two men. Therefore he became their captain. However he did not attain to the *first* three.

[22]Benaiah was the son of Jehoiada, the son

11:8 [a]Literally *The Landfill* **11:11** [a]Following Qere; Kethib, Septuagint, and Vulgate read *the thirty* (compare 2 Samuel 23:8). **11:20** [a]Following Masoretic Text, Septuagint, and Vulgate; Syriac reads *thirty*.

of a valiant man from Kabzeel, who had done many deeds. He had killed two lion-like heroes of Moab. He also had gone down and killed a lion in the midst of a pit on a snowy day. ²³And he killed an Egyptian, a man of *great* height, five cubits tall. In the Egyptian's hand *there was* a spear like a weaver's beam; and he went down to him with a staff, wrested the spear out of the Egyptian's hand, and killed him with his own spear. ²⁴These *things* Benaiah the son of Jehoiada did, and won a name among three mighty men. ²⁵Indeed he was more honored than the thirty, but he did not attain to the *first* three. And David appointed him over his guard.

²⁶Also the mighty warriors *were* Asahel the brother of Joab, Elhanan the son of Dodo of Bethlehem, ²⁷Shammoth the Harorite,ᵃ Helez the Pelonite,ᵇ ²⁸Ira the son of Ikkesh the Tekoite, Abiezer the Anathothite, ²⁹Sibbechai the Hushathite, Ilai the Ahohite, ³⁰Maharai the Netophathite, Heledᵃ the son of Baanah the Netophathite, ³¹Ithaiᵃ the son of Ribai of Gibeah, of the sons of Benjamin, Benaiah the Pirathonite, ³²Huraiᵃ of the brooks of Gaash, Abielᵇ the Arbathite, ³³Azmaveth the Baharumite,ᵃ Eliahba the Shaalbonite, ³⁴the sons of Hashem the Gizonite, Jonathan the son of Shageh the Hararite, ³⁵Ahiam the son of Sacar the Hararite, Eliphal the son of Ur, ³⁶Hepher the Mecherathite, Ahijah the Pelonite, ³⁷Hezro the Carmelite, Naarai the son of Ezbai, ³⁸Joel the brother of Nathan, Mibhar the son of Hagri, ³⁹Zelek the Ammonite, Naharai the Berothiteᵃ (the armorbearer of Joab the son of Zeruiah), ⁴⁰Ira the Ithrite, Gareb the Ithrite, ⁴¹Uriah the Hittite, Zabad the son of Ahlai, ⁴²Adina the son of Shiza the Reubenite (a chief of the Reubenites) and thirty with him, ⁴³Hanan the son of Maachah, Joshaphat the Mithnite, ⁴⁴Uzzia the Ashterathite, Shama and Jeiel the sons of Hotham the Aroerite, ⁴⁵Jediael the son of Shimri, and Joha his brother, the Tizite, ⁴⁶Eliel the Mahavite, Jeribai and Joshaviah the sons of Elnaam, Ithmah the Moabite, ⁴⁷Eliel, Obed, and Jaasiel the Mezobaite.

THE GROWTH OF DAVID'S ARMY

¹Now these *were* the men who came to David at Ziklag while he was still a fugitive from Saul the son of Kish; and they *were* among the mighty men, helpers in the war, ²armed with bows, using both the right hand and the left in *hurling* stones and *shooting* arrows with the bow. *They were* of Benjamin, Saul's brethren.

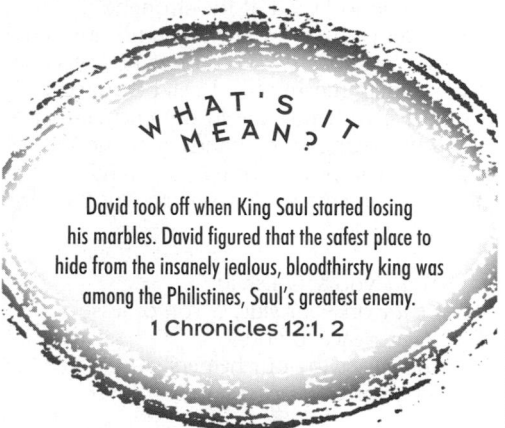

WHAT'S IT MEAN?

David took off when King Saul started losing his marbles. David figured that the safest place to hide from the insanely jealous, bloodthirsty king was among the Philistines, Saul's greatest enemy.
1 Chronicles 12:1, 2

³The chief *was* Ahiezer, then Joash, the sons of Shemaah the Gibeathite; Jeziel and Pelet the sons of Azmaveth; Berachah, and Jehu the Anathothite; ⁴Ishmaiah the Gibeonite, a mighty man among the thirty, and over the thirty; Jeremiah, Jahaziel, Johanan, and Jozabad the Gederathite; ⁵Eluzai, Jerimoth, Bealiah, Shemariah, and Shephatiah the Haruphite; ⁶Elkanah, Jisshiah, Azarel, Joezer, and Jashobeam, the Korahites; ⁷and Joelah and Zebadiah the sons of Jeroham of Gedor.

⁸*Some* Gadites joined David at the stronghold in the wilderness, mighty men of valor, men trained for battle, who could handle shield and spear, whose faces *were* like the faces of lions, and *were* as swift as gazelles on the mountains: ⁹Ezer the first, Obadiah the second, Eliab the third, ¹⁰Mishmannah the fourth, Jeremiah the fifth, ¹¹Attai the sixth, Eliel the seventh, ¹²Johanan the eighth, Elzabad the ninth, ¹³Jeremiah the tenth, and Machbanai the

> "Now these were the heads of the mighty men whom David had, who strengthened themselves with him in his kingdom, with all Israel, to make him king, according to the word of the LORD concerning Israel."
> **(1 Chronicles 11:10)**

11:27 ᵃSpelled *Harodite* in 2 Samuel 23:25 ᵇCalled *Paltite* in 2 Samuel 23:26 **11:30** ᵃSpelled *Heleb* in 2 Samuel 23:29 and *Heldai* in 1 Chronicles 27:15 **11:31** ᵃSpelled *Ittai* in 2 Samuel 23:29 **11:32** ᵃSpelled *Hiddai* in 2 Samuel 23:30 ᵇSpelled *Abi-Albon* in 2 Samuel 23:31 **11:33** ᵃSpelled *Barhumite* in 2 Samuel 23:31 **11:39** ᵃSpelled *Beerothite* in 2 Samuel 23:37

eleventh. ¹⁴These *were* from the sons of Gad, captains of the army; the least was over a hundred, and the greatest was over a thousand. ¹⁵These *are* the ones who crossed the Jordan in the first month, when it had overflowed all its banks; and they put to flight all *those* in the valleys, to the east and to the west.

¹⁶Then some of the sons of Benjamin and Judah came to David at the stronghold. ¹⁷And David went out to meet them, and answered and said to them, "If you have come peaceably to me to help me, my heart will be united with you; but if to betray me to my enemies, since *there is* no wrong in my hands, may the God of our fathers look and bring judgment." ¹⁸Then the Spirit came upon Amasai, chief of the captains, *and he said:*

> "*We are* yours, O David;
> We *are* on your side, O son of Jesse!
> Peace, peace to you,
> And peace to your helpers!
> For your God helps you."

So David received them, and made them captains of the troop.

¹⁹And *some* from Manasseh defected to David when he was going with the Philistines to battle against Saul; but they did not help them, for the lords of the Philistines sent him away by agreement, saying, "He may defect to his master Saul *and endanger* our heads." ²⁰When he went to Ziklag, those of Manasseh who defected to him were Adnah, Jozabad, Jediael, Michael, Jozabad, Elihu, and Zillethai, captains of the thousands who *were* from Manasseh. ²¹And they helped David against the bands *of raiders,* for they *were* all mighty men of valor, and they were captains in the army. ²²For at *that* time they came to David day by day to help him, until *it was* a great army, like the army of God.

DAVID'S ARMY AT HEBRON

²³Now these *were* the numbers of the divisions *that were* equipped for war, *and* came to David at Hebron to turn *over* the kingdom of Saul to him, according to the word of the LORD: ²⁴of the sons of Judah bearing shield and spear, six thousand eight hundred armed for war; ²⁵of the sons of Simeon, mighty men of valor fit for war, seven thousand one hundred; ²⁶of the sons of Levi four thousand six hundred; ²⁷Jehoiada, the leader of the Aaronites, and with him three thousand seven hundred; ²⁸Zadok, a young man, a valiant warrior, and from his father's house twenty-two captains; ²⁹of the sons of

Benjamin, relatives of Saul, three thousand (until then the greatest part of them had remained loyal to the house of Saul); ³⁰of the sons of Ephraim twenty thousand eight hundred, mighty men of valor, famous men throughout their father's house; ³¹of the half-tribe of Manasseh eighteen thousand, who were designated by name to come and make David king; ³²of the sons of Issachar who had understanding of the times, to know what Israel ought to do, their chiefs were two hundred; and all their brethren were at their command; ³³of Zebulun there were fifty thousand who went out to battle, expert in war with all weapons of war, stouthearted men who could keep ranks; ³⁴of Naphtali one thousand captains, and with them thirty-seven thousand with shield and spear; ³⁵of the Danites who could keep battle formation, twenty-eight thousand six hundred; ³⁶of Asher, those who could go out to war, able to keep battle formation, forty thousand; ³⁷of the Reubenites and the Gadites and the half-tribe of Manasseh, from the other side of the Jordan, one hundred and twenty thousand armed for battle with every *kind* of weapon of war.

³⁸All these men of war, who could keep ranks, came to Hebron with a loyal heart, to make David king over all Israel; and all the rest of Israel *were* of one mind to make David king. ³⁹And they were there with David three days, eating and drinking, for their brethren had prepared for them. ⁴⁰Moreover those who were near to them, from as far away as Issachar and Zebulun and Naphtali, were bringing food on donkeys and camels, on mules and oxen—provisions of flour and cakes of figs and cakes of raisins, wine and oil and oxen and sheep abundantly, for *there was* joy in Israel.

THE ARK BROUGHT FROM KIRJATH JEARIM

¹Then David consulted with the captains of thousands and hundreds, *and* with every leader. ²And David said to all the assembly of Israel, "If *it seems* good to you, and if it is of the LORD our God, let us send out to our brethren everywhere *who are* left in all the land of Israel, and with them to the priests and Levites *who are* in their cities *and* their common-lands, that they may gather together to us; ³and let us bring the ark of our God back to us, for we have not inquired at it since the days of Saul." ⁴Then all the assembly said that they would do so, for the thing was right in the eyes of all the people.

⁵So David gathered all Israel together, from Shihor in Egypt to as far as the entrance of Hamath, to bring the ark of God from Kirjath Jearim. ⁶And David and all Israel went up to

Baalah,*a* to Kirjath Jearim, which belonged to Judah, to bring up from there the ark of God the LORD, who dwells *between* the cherubim, where *His* name is proclaimed. ⁷So they carried the ark of God on a new cart from the house of Abinadab, and Uzza and Ahio drove the cart. ⁸Then David and all Israel played *music* before God with all *their* might, with singing, on harps, on stringed instruments, on tambourines, on cymbals, and with trumpets.

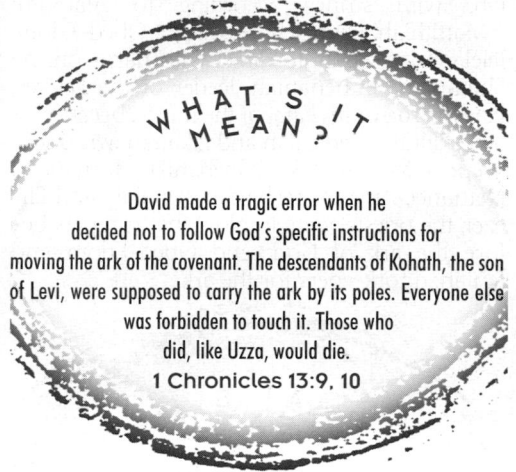

WHAT'S IT MEAN?

David made a tragic error when he decided not to follow God's specific instructions for moving the ark of the covenant. The descendants of Kohath, the son of Levi, were supposed to carry the ark by its poles. Everyone else was forbidden to touch it. Those who did, like Uzza, would die.
1 Chronicles 13:9, 10

⁹And when they came to Chidon's*a* threshing floor, Uzza put out his hand to hold the ark, for the oxen stumbled. ¹⁰Then the anger of the LORD was aroused against Uzza, and He struck him because he put his hand to the ark; and he died there before God. ¹¹And David became angry because of the LORD's outbreak against Uzza; therefore that place is called Perez Uzza*a* to this day. ¹²David was afraid of God that day, saying, "How can I bring the ark of God to me?"

¹³So David would not move the ark with him into the City of David, but took it aside into the house of Obed-Edom the Gittite. ¹⁴The ark of God remained with the family of Obed-Edom in his house three months. And the LORD blessed the house of Obed-Edom and all that he had.

DAVID ESTABLISHED AT JERUSALEM

¹Now Hiram king of Tyre sent messengers to David, and cedar trees, with masons and carpenters, to build him a house. ²So David knew that the LORD had established him as king over Israel, for his kingdom was highly exalted for the sake of His people Israel.

³Then David took more wives in Jerusalem, and David begot more sons and daughters. ⁴And these are the names of his children whom he had in Jerusalem: Shammua,*a* Shobab, Nathan, Solomon, ⁵Ibhar, Elishua,*a* Elpelet,*b* ⁶Nogah, Nepheg, Japhia, ⁷Elishama, Beeliada,*a* and Eliphelet.

THE PHILISTINES DEFEATED

⁸Now when the Philistines heard that David had been anointed king over all Israel, all the Philistines went up to search for David. And David heard *of it* and went out against them. ⁹Then the Philistines went and made a raid on the Valley of Rephaim. ¹⁰And David inquired of God, saying, "Shall I go up against the Philistines? Will You deliver them into my hand?"

The LORD said to him, "Go up, for I will deliver them into your hand."

¹¹So they went up to Baal Perazim, and David defeated them there. Then David said, "God has broken through my enemies by my hand like a breakthrough of water." Therefore they called the name of that place Baal Perazim.*a* ¹²And when they left their gods there, David gave a commandment, and they were burned with fire.

¹³Then the Philistines once again made a raid on the valley. ¹⁴Therefore David inquired again of God, and God said to him, "You shall not go up after them; circle around them, and come upon them in front of the mulberry trees. ¹⁵And it shall be, when you hear a sound of marching in the tops of the mulberry trees, then you shall go out to battle, for God has gone out before you to strike the camp of the Philistines." ¹⁶So David did as God commanded him, and they drove back the army of the Philistines from Gibeon as far as Gezer. ¹⁷Then the fame of David went out into all lands, and the LORD brought the fear of him upon all nations.

THE ARK BROUGHT TO JERUSALEM

¹*David* built houses for himself in the City of David; and he prepared a place for the ark of God, and pitched a tent for it. ²Then David said, "No one may carry the ark of God but the Levites, for the LORD has chosen them to carry the ark of God and to minister before Him forever." ³And David gathered all Israel together at

GUIDANCE

Can we trust God to lead us? (14:10)

13:6 *a*Called *Baale Judah* in 2 Samuel 6:2   13:9 *a*Called *Nachon* in 2 Samuel 6:6   13:11 *a*Literally *Outburst Against Uzza*   14:4 *a*Spelled *Shimea* in 3:5   14:5 *a*Spelled *Elishama* in 3:6   *b*Spelled *Eliphelet* in 3:6   14:7 *a*Spelled *Eliada* in 3:8   14:11 *a*Literally *Master of Breakthroughs*

Jerusalem, to bring up the ark of the LORD to its place, which he had prepared for it. ⁴Then David assembled the children of Aaron and the Levites: ⁵of the sons of Kohath, Uriel the chief, and one hundred and twenty of his brethren; ⁶of the sons of Merari, Asaiah the chief, and two hundred and twenty of his brethren; ⁷of the sons of Gershom, Joel the chief, and one hundred and thirty of his brethren; ⁸of the sons of Elizaphan, Shemaiah the chief, and two hundred of his brethren; ⁹of the sons of Hebron, Eliel the chief, and eighty of his brethren; ¹⁰of the sons of Uzziel, Amminadab the chief, and one hundred and twelve of his brethren.

¹¹And David called for Zadok and Abiathar the priests, and for the Levites: for Uriel, Asaiah, Joel, Shemaiah, Eliel, and Amminadab. ¹²He said to them, "You *are* the heads of the fathers' *houses* of the Levites; sanctify yourselves, you and your brethren, that you may bring up the ark of the LORD God of Israel to *the place* I have prepared for it. ¹³For because you *did* not *do it* the first *time*, the LORD our God broke out against us, because we did not consult Him about the proper order."

¹⁴So the priests and the Levites sanctified themselves to bring up the ark of the LORD God of Israel. ¹⁵And the children of the Levites bore the ark of God on their shoulders, by its poles, as Moses had commanded according to the word of the LORD.

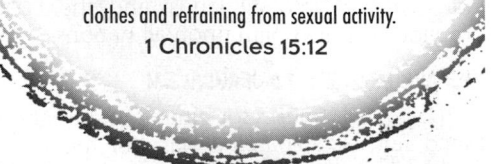

The priests couldn't just walk in off the street and start performing sacrifices and leading religious services. They were required to follow special procedures to prepare themselves. These procedures included washing themselves and their clothes and refraining from sexual activity.
1 Chronicles 15:12

¹⁶Then David spoke to the leaders of the Levites to appoint their brethren *to be* the singers accompanied by instruments of music, stringed instruments, harps, and cymbals, by raising the voice with resounding joy. ¹⁷So the Levites appointed Heman the son of Joel; and of his brethren, Asaph the son of Berechiah; and of their brethren, the sons of Merari, Ethan the son of Kushaiah; ¹⁸and with them their brethren of the second *rank*: Zechariah, Ben,ᵃ Jaaziel, Shemiramoth, Jehiel, Unni, Eliab, Benaiah, Maaseiah, Mattithiah, Elipheleh, Mikneiah, Obed-Edom, and Jeiel, the gatekeepers; ¹⁹the singers, Heman, Asaph, and Ethan, *were* to sound the cymbals of bronze; ²⁰Zechariah, Aziel, Shemiramoth, Jehiel, Unni, Eliab, Maaseiah, and Benaiah, with strings according to Alamoth; ²¹Mattithiah, Elipheleh, Mikneiah, Obed-Edom, Jeiel, and Azaziah, to direct with harps on the Sheminith; ²²Chenaniah, leader of the Levites, was instructor *in charge of* the music, because he *was* skillful; ²³Berechiah and Elkanah *were* doorkeepers for the ark; ²⁴Shebaniah, Joshaphat, Nethanel, Amasai, Zechariah, Benaiah, and Eliezer, the priests, were to blow the trumpets before the ark of God; and Obed-Edom and Jehiah, doorkeepers for the ark.

Linen cloth was handwoven from the fibers of the hemp plant. For the most part, only people of great wealth or power wore linen in ancient times. Priests and those who served in the temple were the exception. They were required by God's law to wear white linen uniforms.
1 Chronicles 15:27

²⁵So David, the elders of Israel, and the captains over thousands went to bring up the ark of the covenant of the LORD from the house of Obed-Edom with joy. ²⁶And so it was, when God helped the Levites who bore the ark of the covenant of the LORD, that they offered seven bulls and seven rams. ²⁷David was clothed with a robe of fine linen, as were all the Levites who bore the ark, the singers, and Chenaniah the music master *with* the singers. David also wore a linen ephod. ²⁸Thus all Israel brought up the ark of the covenant of the LORD with shouting and with the sound of the horn, with trumpets and with cymbals, making music with stringed instruments and harps.

²⁹And it happened, *as* the ark of the cov-

15:18 ᵃFollowing Masoretic Text and Vulgate; Septuagint omits *Ben*.

enant of the LORD came to the City of David, that Michal, Saul's daughter, looked through a window and saw King David whirling and playing music; and she despised him in her heart.

THE ARK PLACED IN THE TABERNACLE

¹So they brought the ark of God, and set it in the midst of the tabernacle that David had erected for it. Then they offered burnt offerings and peace offerings before God. ²And when David had finished offering the burnt offerings and the peace offerings, he blessed the people in the name of the LORD. ³Then he distributed to everyone of Israel, both man and woman, to everyone a loaf of bread, a piece *of meat*, and a cake of raisins.

⁴And he appointed some of the Levites to minister before the ark of the LORD, to commemorate, to thank, and to praise the LORD God of Israel: ⁵Asaph the chief, and next to him Zechariah, *then* Jeiel, Shemiramoth, Jehiel, Mattithiah, Eliab, Benaiah, and Obed-Edom: Jeiel with stringed instruments and harps, but Asaph made music with cymbals; ⁶Benaiah and Jahaziel the priests regularly *blew* the trumpets before the ark of the covenant of God.

THANKFULNESS

What should we do when we are thankful? (16:4–36)

DAVID'S SONG OF THANKSGIVING

⁷On that day David first delivered *this psalm* into the hand of Asaph and his brethren, to thank the LORD:

8   Oh, give thanks to the LORD!
     Call upon His name;
     Make known His deeds among the peoples!
9   Sing to Him, sing psalms to Him;
     Talk of all His wondrous works!
10   Glory in His holy name;
     Let the hearts of those rejoice who seek the LORD!
11   Seek the LORD and His strength;
     Seek His face evermore!
12   Remember His marvelous works which He has done,
     His wonders, and the judgments of His mouth,
13   O seed of Israel His servant,
     You children of Jacob, His chosen ones!

14   He *is* the LORD our God;
     His judgments *are* in all the earth.

15   Remember His covenant forever,
     The word which He commanded, for a thousand generations,

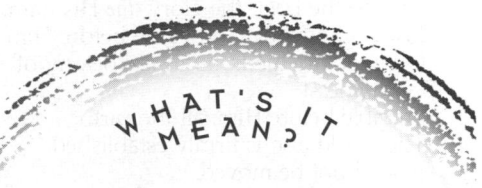

WHAT'S IT MEAN?

Don't get confused here. Jacob and Israel were the same person. *Israel* was the name given to Jacob after he wrestled with a mysterious stranger who turned out to be an angel of God—or perhaps even God Himself. Later, the name *Israel* was given to the nation that was made up of Jacob's twelve sons and their descendants.

1 Chronicles 16:13

16   *The covenant which* He made with Abraham,
     And His oath to Isaac,
17   And confirmed it to Jacob for a statute,
     To Israel *for* an everlasting covenant,
18   Saying, "To you I will give the land of Canaan
     As the allotment of your inheritance,"
19   When you were few in number,
     Indeed very few, and strangers in it.

20   When they went from one nation to another,
     And from *one* kingdom to another people,
21   He permitted no man to do them wrong;
     Yes, He rebuked kings for their sakes,
22   *Saying,* "Do not touch My anointed ones,
     And do My prophets no harm."ᵃ

23   Sing to the LORD, all the earth;
     Proclaim the good news of His salvation from day to day.
24   Declare His glory among the nations,
     His wonders among all peoples.

WITNESSING

What should we tell others about God? (16:24)

25   For the LORD *is* great and greatly to be praised;
     He *is* also to be feared above all gods.
26   For all the gods of the peoples *are* idols,
     But the LORD made the heavens.
27   Honor and majesty *are* before Him;
     Strength and gladness are in His place.

16:22 ᵃCompare verses 8–22 with Psalm 105:1–15

28 Give to the LORD, O families of the
    peoples,
   Give to the LORD glory and strength.
29 Give to the LORD the glory *due* His name;
   Bring an offering, and come before Him.
   Oh, worship the LORD in the beauty of
    holiness!
30 Tremble before Him, all the earth.
   The world also is firmly established,
   It shall not be moved.

31 Let the heavens rejoice, and let the earth
    be glad;
   And let them say among the nations, "The
    LORD reigns."
32 Let the sea roar, and all its fullness;
   Let the field rejoice, and all that *is* in it.
33 Then the trees of the woods shall rejoice
    before the LORD,
   For He is coming to judge the earth.*a*

34 Oh, give thanks to the LORD, for *He is*
    good!
   For His mercy *endures* forever.*a*
35 And say, "Save us, O God of our
    salvation;
   Gather us together, and deliver us from
    the Gentiles,
   To give thanks to Your holy name,
   To triumph in Your praise."

36 Blessed *be* the LORD God of Israel
   From everlasting to everlasting!*a*

And all the people said, "Amen!" and praised the
LORD.

REGULAR WORSHIP MAINTAINED

37 So he left Asaph and his brothers there before the ark of the covenant of the LORD to minister before the ark regularly, as every
day's work required; 38and
Obed-Edom with his sixty-
eight brethren, including
Obed-Edom the son of Jeduthun, and Hosah, *to be* gatekeepers; 39and Zadok the priest
and his brethren the priests, be-
fore the tabernacle of the LORD at the high place
that *was* at Gibeon, 40to offer burnt offerings to
the LORD on the altar of burnt offering regularly,
morning and evening, and *to do* according to all
that is written in the Law of the LORD which He
commanded Israel; 41and with them Heman

WORSHIP

Why should
we worship
God?
(16:34)

and Jeduthun and the rest who were chosen,
who were designated by name, to give thanks
to the LORD, because His mercy *endures* forever;
42and with them Heman and Jeduthun, to
sound aloud with trumpets and cymbals and
the musical instruments of God. Now the sons
of Jeduthun *were* gatekeepers.

WHAT'S IT MEAN?

The ark of the covenant was in Jerusalem
in a tent David had built. The tent and the altar that
had been built under Moses' direction were kept in Gibeon, about
six miles away. When Solomon built his temple years later,
he set up the tabernacle (tent) of meeting as a
permanent display inside the building.
1 Chronicles 16:39

43Then all the people departed, every man to
his house; and David returned to bless his
house.

GOD'S COVENANT WITH DAVID

1Now it came to pass, when David was
dwelling in his house, that David said to Nathan the prophet, "See now, I dwell in a house
of cedar, but the ark of the covenant of the
LORD *is* under tent curtains."
2Then Nathan said to David, "Do all that *is*
in your heart, for God *is* with you."
3But it happened that night that the word of
God came to Nathan, saying, 4"Go and tell My
servant David, 'Thus says the LORD: "You shall
not build Me a house to dwell in. 5For I have
not dwelt in a house since the time that I
brought up Israel, even to this day, but have
gone from tent to tent, and from *one* tabernacle
to another. 6Wherever I have moved about with
all Israel, have I ever spoken a word to any of
the judges of Israel, whom I commanded to
shepherd My people, saying, 'Why have you
not built Me a house of cedar?' " ' 7Now therefore, thus shall you say to My servant David,
'Thus says the LORD of hosts: "I took you from
the sheepfold, from following the sheep, to be
ruler over My people Israel. 8And I have been
with you wherever you have gone, and have

16:33 *a*Compare verses 23–33 with Psalm 96:1–13   **16:34** *a*Compare verse 34 with Psalm 106:1
16:36 *a*Compare verses 35, 36 with Psalm 106:47, 48

cut off all your enemies from before you, and have made you a name like the name of the great men who *are* on the earth. [9]Moreover I will appoint a place for My people Israel, and will plant them, that they may dwell in a place of their own and move no more; nor shall the sons of wickedness oppress them anymore, as previously, [10]since the time that I commanded judges *to be* over My people Israel. Also I will subdue all your enemies. Furthermore I tell you that the LORD will build you a house.[a] [11]And it shall be, when your days are fulfilled, when you must go *to be* with your fathers, that I will set up your seed after you, who will be of your sons; and I will establish his kingdom. [12]He shall build Me a house, and I will establish his throne forever. [13]I will be his Father, and he shall be My son; and I will not take My mercy away from him, as I took *it* from *him* who was before you. [14]And I will establish him in My house and in My kingdom forever; and his throne shall be established forever." ' "

[15]According to all these words and according to all this vision, so Nathan spoke to David.

[16]Then King David went in and sat before the LORD; and he said: "Who *am* I, O LORD God?

And what is my house, that You have brought me this far? [17]And *yet* this was a small thing in Your sight, O God; and You have *also* spoken of Your servant's house for a great while to come, and have regarded me according to the rank of a man of high degree, O LORD God. [18]What more can David *say* to You for the honor of Your servant? For You know Your servant. [19]O LORD, for Your servant's sake, and according to Your own heart, You have done all this greatness, in making known all these great things. [20]O LORD, *there is* none like You, nor *is there any* God besides You, according to all that we have heard with our ears. [21]And who *is* like Your people Israel, the one nation on the earth whom God went to redeem for Himself *as* a people—to make for Yourself a name by great and awesome deeds, by driving out nations from before Your people whom You redeemed from Egypt? [22]For You have made Your people Israel Your very own people forever; and You, LORD, have become their God.

[23]"And now, O LORD, the word which You have spoken concerning Your servant and concerning his house, *let it* be established forever, and do as You have said. [24]So let it be

> "For You have made Your people Israel Your very own people forever; and You, LORD, have become their God."
> (1 Chronicles 17:22)

17:10 [a]That is, a royal dynasty

✦ Promise

HE PROMISES THAT ISRAEL WILL BE HIS PEOPLE FOREVER.

For You have made Your people Israel Your very own people forever; and You, LORD, have become their God (1 Chr. 17:22).

Can you imagine belonging to someone forever—even way after you're dead? God has chosen Israel to belong to Him forever. As a Christian, you are a part of Israel. One of the most awesome things about becoming a Christian is that "forever" becomes a real part of your life. Even though your body will eventually die, your spirit will live forever. When your life on earth is over, you will enter into a new kind of life in heaven. It's mind-blowing to think about, but you really will live forever with God. Just because you are a Christian, you won't always be perfect. You'll make mistakes, have regrets, and wish you'd made different choices. Through all those times, you still belong to God. When He says you belong to Him forever, He means forever—even when you do stuff He wouldn't be pleased with. He's chosen you to be a part of Israel. And you'll belong to Him from now on. Forever *never* ends.

SEE FOR YOURSELF:

Ex. 2:23–25; 1 Chr. 16:11–13; Is. 43:20, 21; 1 Pet. 2:9, 10

established, that Your name may be magnified forever, saying, 'The LORD of hosts, the God of Israel, *is* Israel's God.' And let the house of Your servant David be established before You. ²⁵For You, O my God, have revealed to Your servant that You will build him a house. Therefore Your servant has found it *in his heart* to pray before You. ²⁶And now, LORD, You are God, and have promised this goodness to Your servant. ²⁷Now You have been pleased to bless the house of Your servant, that it may continue before You forever; for You have blessed it, O LORD, and *it shall be* blessed forever."

TRUST

Whose promises always come true?
(17:26, 27)

DAVID'S FURTHER CONQUESTS

¹After this it came to pass that David attacked the Philistines, subdued them, and took Gath and its towns from the hand of the Philistines. ²Then he defeated Moab, and the Moabites became David's servants, *and* brought tribute.

³And David defeated Hadadezer*ᵃ* king of Zobah *as far as* Hamath, as he went to establish his power by the River Euphrates. ⁴David took from him one thousand chariots, seven thousand*ᵃ* horsemen, and twenty thousand foot soldiers. Also David hamstrung all the chariot *horses,* except that he spared enough of them for one hundred chariots.

⁵When the Syrians of Damascus came to help Hadadezer king of Zobah, David killed twenty-two thousand of the Syrians. ⁶Then David put *garrisons* in Syria of Damascus; and the Syrians became David's servants, *and* brought tribute. So the LORD preserved David wherever he went. ⁷And David took the shields of gold that were on the servants of Hadadezer, and brought them to Jerusalem. ⁸Also from Tibhath*ᵃ* and from Chun, cities of Hadadezer, David brought a large amount of bronze, with which Solomon made the bronze Sea, the pillars, and the articles of bronze.

⁹Now when Tou*ᵃ* king of Hamath heard that David had defeated all the army of Hadadezer king of Zobah, ¹⁰he sent Hadoram*ᵃ* his son to King David, to greet him and bless him, because he had fought against Hadadezer and defeated him (for Hadadezer had been at war with Tou); and *Hadoram brought with him* all kinds of articles of gold, silver, and bronze. ¹¹King David

also dedicated these to the LORD, along with the silver and gold that he had brought from all *these* nations—from Edom, from Moab, from the people of Ammon, from the Philistines, and from Amalek.

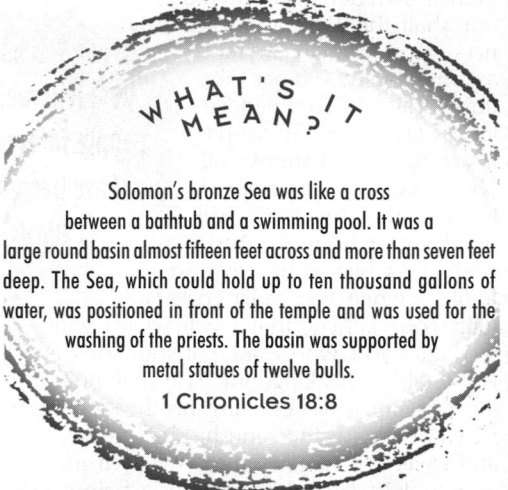

WHAT'S IT MEAN?

Solomon's bronze Sea was like a cross between a bathtub and a swimming pool. It was a large round basin almost fifteen feet across and more than seven feet deep. The Sea, which could hold up to ten thousand gallons of water, was positioned in front of the temple and was used for the washing of the priests. The basin was supported by metal statues of twelve bulls.

1 Chronicles 18:8

¹²Moreover Abishai the son of Zeruiah killed eighteen thousand Edomites*ᵃ* in the Valley of Salt. ¹³He also put garrisons in Edom, and all the Edomites became David's servants. And the LORD preserved David wherever he went.

DAVID'S ADMINISTRATION

¹⁴So David reigned over all Israel, and administered judgment and justice to all his people. ¹⁵Joab the son of Zeruiah *was* over the army; Jehoshaphat the son of Ahilud *was* recorder; ¹⁶Zadok the son of Ahitub and Abimelech the son of Abiathar *were* the priests; Shavsha*ᵃ* *was* the scribe; ¹⁷Benaiah the son of Jehoiada *was* over the Cherethites and the Pelethites; and David's sons *were* chief ministers at the king's side.

THE AMMONITES AND SYRIANS DEFEATED

¹It happened after this that Nahash the king of the people of Ammon died, and his son reigned in his place. ²Then David said, "I will show kindness to Hanun the son of Nahash, because his father showed kindness to me." So David sent messengers to comfort him concerning his father. And David's servants came to Hanun in the land of the people of Ammon to comfort him.

18:3 *ᵃ*Hebrew *Hadarezer,* and so throughout chapters 18 and 19   **18:4** *ᵃ*Or *seven hundred* (compare 2 Samuel 8:4)   **18:8** *ᵃ*Spelled *Betah* in 2 Samuel 8:8   **18:9** *ᵃ*Spelled *Toi* in 2 Samuel 8:9, 10   **18:10** *ᵃ*Spelled *Joram* in 2 Samuel 8:10   **18:12** *ᵃ*Or *Syrians* (compare 2 Samuel 8:13)   **18:16** *ᵃ*Spelled *Seraiah* in 2 Samuel 8:17

³And the princes of the people of Ammon said to Hanun, "Do you think that David really honors your father because he has sent comforters to you? Did his servants not come to you to search and to overthrow and to spy out the land?"

⁴Therefore Hanun took David's servants, shaved them, and cut off their garments in the middle, at their buttocks, and sent them away. ⁵Then *some* went and told David about the men; and he sent to meet them, because the men were greatly ashamed. And the king said, "Wait at Jericho until your beards have grown, and *then* return."

⁶When the people of Ammon saw that they had made themselves repulsive to David, Hanun and the people of Ammon sent a thousand talents of silver to hire for themselves chariots and horsemen from Mesopotamia,ᵃ from Syrian Maacah, and from Zobah.ᵇ ⁷So they hired for themselves thirty-two thousand chariots, with the king of Maacah and his people, who came and encamped before Medeba. Also the people of Ammon gathered together from their cities, and came to battle.

WHAT'S IT MEAN?

The Ammonites were longtime enemies of the Israelites who lived across the Jordan River from Israel. Rabbah, the capital city of the Ammonites, is better known today as Amman, Jordan.

1 Chronicles 19:6

⁸Now when David heard *of it*, he sent Joab and all the army of the mighty men. ⁹Then the people of Ammon came out and put themselves in battle array before the gate of the city, and the kings who had come *were* by themselves in the field. ¹⁰When Joab saw that the battle line was against him before and behind, he chose some of Israel's best, and put *them* in battle array against the Syrians. ¹¹And the rest of the people he put under the command of Abishai his brother, and they set *themselves* in battle array

against the people of Ammon. ¹²Then he said, "If the Syrians are too strong for me, then you shall help me; but if the people of Ammon are too strong for you, then I will help you. ¹³Be of good courage, and let us be strong for our people and for the cities of our God. And may the LORD do *what is* good in His sight."

¹⁴So Joab and the people who *were* with him drew near for the battle against the Syrians, and they fled before him. ¹⁵When the people of Ammon saw that the Syrians were fleeing, they also fled before Abishai his brother, and entered the city. So Joab went to Jerusalem.

¹⁶Now when the Syrians saw that they had been defeated by Israel, they sent messengers and brought the Syrians who were beyond the River,ᵃ and Shophachᵇ the commander of Hadadezer's army *went* before them. ¹⁷When it was told David, he gathered all Israel, crossed over the Jordan and came upon them, and set up in battle array against them. So when David had set up in *battle* array against the Syrians, they fought with him. ¹⁸Then the Syrians fled before Israel; and David killed seven thousandᵃ charioteers and forty thousand foot soldiersᵇ of the Syrians, and killed Shophach the commander of the army. ¹⁹And when the servants of Hadadezer saw that they were defeated by Israel, they made peace with David and became his servants. So the Syrians were not willing to help the people of Ammon anymore.

RABBAH IS CONQUERED

¹It happened in the spring of the year, at the time kings go out *to battle,* that Joab led out the armed forces and ravaged the country of the people of Ammon, and came and besieged Rabbah. But David stayed at Jerusalem. And Joab defeated Rabbah and overthrew it. ²Then David took their king's crown from his head, and found it to weigh a talent of gold, and *there were* precious stones in it. And it was set on David's head. Also he brought out the spoil of the city in great abundance. ³And he brought out the people who *were* in it, and put *them* to workᵃ with saws, with iron picks, and with axes. So David did to all the cities of the people of Ammon. Then David and all the people returned *to* Jerusalem.

PHILISTINE GIANTS DESTROYED

⁴Now it happened afterward that war broke out at Gezer with the Philistines, at which time

---

19:6 ᵃHebrew *Aram Naharaim* ᵇSpelled *Zoba* in 2 Samuel 10:6   **19:16** ᵃThat is, the Euphrates ᵇSpelled *Shobach* in 2 Samuel 10:16   **19:18** ᵃOr *seven hundred* (compare 2 Samuel 10:18) ᵇOr *horsemen* (compare 2 Samuel 10:18)   **20:3** ᵃSeptuagint reads *cut them.*

Sibbechai the Hushathite killed Sippai,*a who was one* of the sons of the giant. And they were subdued.

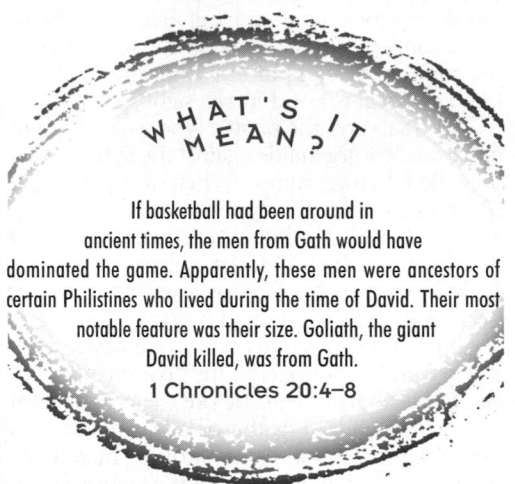

WHAT'S IT MEAN?

If basketball had been around in ancient times, the men from Gath would have dominated the game. Apparently, these men were ancestors of certain Philistines who lived during the time of David. Their most notable feature was their size. Goliath, the giant David killed, was from Gath.

1 Chronicles 20:4–8

⁵Again there was war with the Philistines, and Elhanan the son of Jair*a* killed Lahmi the brother of Goliath the Gittite, the shaft of whose spear *was* like a weaver's beam.

⁶Yet again there was war at Gath, where there was a man of *great* stature, with twenty-four fingers and toes, six *on each hand* and six *on each foot;* and he also was born to the giant. ⁷So when he defied Israel, Jonathan the son of Shimea,*a* David's brother, killed him.

⁸These were born to the giant in Gath, and they fell by the hand of David and by the hand of his servants.

THE CENSUS OF ISRAEL AND JUDAH

¹Now Satan stood up against Israel, and moved David to number Israel. ²So David said to Joab and to the leaders of the people, "Go, number Israel from Beersheba to Dan, and bring the number of them to me that I may know *it.*"

³And Joab answered, "May the LORD make His people a hundred times more than they are. But, my lord the king, *are* they not all my lord's servants? Why then does my lord require this thing? Why should he be a cause of guilt in Israel?"

⁴Nevertheless the king's word prevailed against Joab. Therefore Joab departed and went throughout all Israel and came to Jerusalem. ⁵Then Joab gave the sum of the number of the people to David. All Israel *had* one million one hundred thousand men who drew the sword, and Judah *had* four hundred and seventy thousand men who drew the sword. ⁶But he did not count Levi and Benjamin among them, for the king's word was abominable to Joab.

⁷And God was displeased with this thing; therefore He struck Israel.

⁸So David said to God, "I have sinned greatly, because I have done this thing; but now, I pray, take away the iniquity of Your servant, for I have done very foolishly."

SIN

How should we feel about our own sin? (21:7, 8)

⁹Then the LORD spoke to Gad, David's seer, saying, ¹⁰"Go and tell David, saying, 'Thus says the LORD: "I offer you three *things;* choose one of them for yourself, that I may do *it* to you." ' "

¹¹So Gad came to David and said to him, "Thus says the LORD: 'Choose for yourself, ¹²either three*a* years of famine, or three months to be defeated by your foes with the sword of your enemies overtaking *you,* or else for three days the sword of the LORD—the plague in the land, with the angel*b* of the LORD destroying throughout all the territory of Israel.' Now consider what answer I should take back to Him who sent me."

¹³And David said to Gad, "I am in great distress. Please let me fall into the hand of the LORD, for His mercies *are* very great; but do not let me fall into the hand of man."

¹⁴So the LORD sent a plague upon Israel, and seventy thousand men of Israel fell. ¹⁵And God sent an angel to Jerusalem to destroy it. As he*a* was destroying, the LORD looked and relented of the disaster, and said to the angel who was destroying, "It is enough; now restrain your*b* hand." And the angel of the LORD stood by the threshing floor of Ornan*c* the Jebusite.

¹⁶Then David lifted his eyes and saw the angel of the LORD standing between earth and heaven, having in his hand a drawn sword stretched out over Jerusalem. So David and the elders, clothed in sackcloth, fell on their faces. ¹⁷And David said to God, "Was it not I who commanded the people to be numbered? I am the one who has sinned and done evil indeed; but these sheep, what have they done? Let Your hand, I pray, O LORD my God, be against me and my father's house, but not against Your people that they should be plagued."

¹⁸Therefore, the angel of the LORD commanded Gad to say to David that David should

---

20:4 *a*Spelled *Saph* in 2 Samuel 21:18　**20:5** *a*Spelled *Jaare-Oregim* in 2 Samuel 21:19　**20:7** *a*Spelled *Shimeah* in 2 Samuel 21:21 and *Shammah* in 1 Samuel 16:9　**21:12** *a*Or *seven* (compare 2 Samuel 24:13)　*b*Or *Angel,* and so elsewhere in this chapter　**21:15** *a*Or *He* *b*Or *Your* *c*Spelled *Araunah* in 2 Samuel 24:16

go and erect an altar to the LORD on the threshing floor of Ornan the Jebusite. ¹⁹So David went up at the word of Gad, which he had spoken in the name of the LORD. ²⁰Now Ornan turned and saw the angel; and his four sons *who were* with him hid themselves, but Ornan continued threshing wheat. ²¹So David came to Ornan, and Ornan looked and saw David. And he went out from the threshing floor, and bowed before David with *his* face to the ground. ²²Then David said to Ornan, "Grant me the place of *this* threshing floor, that I may build an altar on it to the LORD. You shall grant it to me at the full price, that the plague may be withdrawn from the people."

²³But Ornan said to David, "Take *it* to yourself, and let my lord the king do *what is* good in his eyes. Look, I *also* give *you* the oxen for burnt offerings, the threshing implements for wood, and the wheat for the grain offering; I give *it* all."

²⁴Then King David said to Ornan, "No, but I will surely buy *it* for the full price, for I will not take what is yours for the LORD, nor offer burnt offerings with *that which* costs *me* nothing." ²⁵So David gave Ornan six hundred shekels of gold by weight for the place. ²⁶And David built there an altar to the LORD, and offered burnt offerings and peace offerings, and called on the LORD; and He answered him from heaven by fire on the altar of burnt offering.

²⁷So the LORD commanded the angel, and he returned his sword to its sheath.

²⁸At that time, when David saw that the LORD had answered him on the threshing floor of Ornan the Jebusite, he sacrificed there. ²⁹For the tabernacle of the LORD and the altar of the burnt offering, which Moses had made in the wilderness, *were* at that time at the high place in Gibeon. ³⁰But David could not go before it to inquire of God, for he was afraid of the sword of the angel of the LORD.

DAVID PREPARES TO BUILD THE TEMPLE

¹Then David said, "This *is* the house of the LORD God, and this *is* the altar of burnt offering for Israel." ²So David commanded to gather the aliens who *were* in the land of Israel; and he appointed masons to cut hewn stones to build the house of God. ³And David prepared iron in abundance for the nails of the doors of the gates and for the joints, and bronze in abundance beyond measure, ⁴and cedar trees in abundance; for the Sidonians and those from Tyre brought much cedar wood to David.

⁵Now David said, "Solomon my son *is* young and inexperienced, and the house to be built for the LORD *must be* exceedingly magnificent, famous and glorious throughout all countries. I will now make preparation for it." So David made abundant preparations before his death.

⁶Then he called for his son Solomon, and charged him to build a house for the LORD God of Israel. ⁷And David said to Solomon: "My son, as for me, it was in my mind to build a house to the name of the LORD my God; ⁸but the word of the LORD came to me, saying, 'You have shed much blood and have made great wars; you shall not build a house for My name, because you have shed much blood on the earth in My sight. ⁹Behold, a son shall be born to you, who shall be a man of rest; and I will give him rest from all his enemies all around. His name shall be Solomon,ᵃ for I will give peace and quietness to Israel in his days. ¹⁰He shall build a house for My name, and he shall be My son, and I *will be* his Father; and I will establish the throne of his kingdom over Israel forever.' ¹¹Now, my son, may the LORD be with you; and may you prosper, and build the house of the LORD your God, as He has said to you. ¹²Only may the LORD give you wisdom and understanding, and give you charge concerning Israel, that you may keep the law of the LORD your God. ¹³Then you will prosper, if you take care to fulfill the statutes and judgments with which the LORD charged Moses concerning Israel. Be strong and of good courage; do not fear nor be dismayed. ¹⁴Indeed I have taken much trouble to prepare for the house of the LORD one hundred thousand talents of gold and one million talents of silver, and bronze and iron beyond measure, for it is so abundant. I have prepared timber and stone also, and you may add to them. ¹⁵Moreover *there are* workmen with you in abundance: woodsmen and stonecutters, and all types of skillful men for every kind of work. ¹⁶Of gold and silver and bronze and iron *there is* no limit. Arise and begin working, and the LORD be with you."

¹⁷David also commanded all the leaders of Israel to help Solomon his son, *saying,* ¹⁸"Is not the LORD your God with you? And has He *not* given you rest on every side? For He has given the inhabitants of the land into my hand, and the land is subdued before the LORD and before His people. ¹⁹Now set your heart and your soul to seek the LORD your God. Therefore arise and build the sanctuary of the LORD God, to bring the ark of the covenant of the LORD and the

holy articles of God into the house that is to be built for the name of the LORD."

THE DIVISIONS OF THE LEVITES

¹So when David was old and full of days, he made his son Solomon king over Israel.

²And he gathered together all the leaders of Israel, with the priests and the Levites. ³Now the Levites were numbered from the age of thirty years and above; and the number of individual males was thirty-eight thousand. ⁴Of these, twenty-four thousand were to look after the work of the house of the LORD, six thousand were officers and judges, ⁵four thousand were gatekeepers, and four thousand praised the LORD with musical instruments, "which I made," said David, "for giving praise."

⁶Also David separated them into divisions among the sons of Levi: Gershon, Kohath, and Merari.

⁷Of the Gershonites: Laadan[a] and Shimei. ⁸The sons of Laadan: the first Jehiel, then Zetham and Joel—three in all. ⁹The sons of Shimei: Shelomith, Haziel, and Haran—three in all. These were the heads of the fathers' houses of Laadan. ¹⁰And the sons of Shimei: Jahath, Zina,[a] Jeush, and Beriah. These were the four sons of Shimei. ¹¹Jahath was the first and Zizah the second. But Jeush and Beriah did not have many sons; therefore they were assigned as one father's house.

¹²The sons of Kohath: Amram, Izhar, Hebron, and Uzziel—four in all. ¹³The sons of Amram: Aaron and Moses; and Aaron was set apart, he and his sons forever, that he should sanctify the most holy things, to burn incense before the LORD, to minister to Him, and to give the blessing in His name forever. ¹⁴Now the sons of Moses the man of God were reckoned to the tribe of Levi. ¹⁵The sons of Moses were Gershon[a] and Eliezer. ¹⁶Of the sons of Gershon, Shebuel[a] was the first. ¹⁷Of the descendants of Eliezer, Rehabiah was the first. And Eliezer had no other sons, but the sons of Rehabiah were very many. ¹⁸Of the sons of Izhar, Shelomith was the first. ¹⁹Of the sons of Hebron, Jeriah was the first, Amariah the second, Jahaziel the third, and Jekameam the fourth. ²⁰Of the sons of Uzziel, Michah was the first and Jesshiah the second.

²¹The sons of Merari were Mahli and Mushi. The sons of Mahli were Eleazar and Kish. ²²And Eleazar died, and had no sons, but only daughters; and their brethren, the sons of Kish, took them as wives. ²³The sons of Mushi were Mahli, Eder, and Jeremoth—three in all.

²⁴These were the sons of Levi by their fathers' houses—the heads of the fathers' houses as they were counted individually by the number of their names, who did the work for the service of the house of the LORD, from the age of twenty years and above.

WHAT'S IT MEAN?

Only the direct descendants of Aaron were allowed to serve as priests. The other Levites assisted the priests in their work. The instructions for making sacrifices, worshiping God, and caring for the tabernacle of meeting and everything in it were spelled out by Moses in the Book of Leviticus. Once the temple was built, the Levites would carry out their duties there, instead of in the tabernacle of meeting.

1 Chronicles 23:27–32

²⁵For David said, "The LORD God of Israel has given rest to His people, that they may dwell in Jerusalem forever"; ²⁶and also to the Levites, "They shall no longer carry the tabernacle, or any of the articles for its service." ²⁷For by the last words of David the Levites were numbered from twenty years old and above; ²⁸because their duty was to help the sons of Aaron in the service of the house of the LORD, in the courts and in the chambers, in the purifying of all holy things and the work of the service of the house of God, ²⁹both with the showbread and the fine flour for the grain offering, with the unleavened cakes and what is baked in the pan, with what is mixed and with all kinds of measures and sizes; ³⁰to stand every morning to thank and praise the LORD, and likewise at evening; ³¹and at every presentation of a burnt offering to the LORD on the Sabbaths and on the New Moons and on the set feasts, by number according to the ordinance governing them, regularly before the LORD; ³²and that they should attend to the needs of the tabernacle of meeting, the needs of the holy place, and the needs of the sons of Aaron their brethren in the work of the house of the LORD.

23:7 [a]Spelled Libni in Exodus 6:17   **23:10** [a]Septuagint and Vulgate read Zizah (compare verse 11).
23:15 [a]Hebrew Gershom (compare 6:16)   **23:16** [a]Spelled Shubael in 24:20

THE DIVISIONS OF THE PRIESTS

¹Now *these are* the divisions of the sons of Aaron. The sons of Aaron *were* Nadab, Abihu, Eleazar, and Ithamar. ²And Nadab and Abihu died before their father, and had no children; therefore Eleazar and Ithamar ministered as priests. ³Then David with Zadok of the sons of Eleazar, and Ahimelech of the sons of Ithamar, divided them according to the schedule of their service.

⁴There were more leaders found of the sons of Eleazar than of the sons of Ithamar, and *thus* they were divided. Among the sons of Eleazar *were* sixteen heads of *their* fathers' houses, and eight heads of their fathers' houses among the sons of Ithamar. ⁵Thus they were divided by lot, one group as another, for there were officials of the sanctuary and officials *of the house* of God, from the sons of Eleazar and from the sons of Ithamar. ⁶And the scribe, Shemaiah the son of Nethanel, *one of* the Levites, wrote them down before the king, the leaders, Zadok the priest, Ahimelech the son of Abiathar, and the heads of the fathers' *houses* of the priests and Levites, one father's house taken for Eleazar and *one* for Ithamar.

⁷Now the first lot fell to Jehoiarib, the second to Jedaiah, ⁸the third to Harim, the fourth to Seorim, ⁹the fifth to Malchijah, the sixth to Mijamin, ¹⁰the seventh to Hakkoz, the eighth to Abijah, ¹¹the ninth to Jeshua, the tenth to Shecaniah, ¹²the eleventh to Eliashib, the twelfth to Jakim, ¹³the thirteenth to Huppah, the fourteenth to Jeshebeab, ¹⁴the fifteenth to Bilgah, the sixteenth to Immer, ¹⁵the seventeenth to Hezir, the eighteenth to Happizzez,ᵃ ¹⁶the nineteenth to Pethahiah, the twentieth to Jehezekel,ᵃ ¹⁷the twenty-first to Jachin, the twenty-second to Gamul, ¹⁸the twenty-third to Delaiah, the twenty-fourth to Maaziah.

¹⁹This *was* the schedule of their service for coming into the house of the LORD according to their ordinance by the hand of Aaron their father, as the LORD God of Israel had commanded him.

OTHER LEVITES

²⁰And the rest of the sons of Levi: of the sons of Amram, Shubael;ᵃ of the sons of Shubael, Jehdeiah. ²¹Concerning Rehabiah, of the sons of Rehabiah, the first *was* Isshiah. ²²Of the Izhar-

ites, Shelomoth;ᵃ of the sons of Shelomoth, Jahath. ²³Of the sons *of Hebron,*ᵃ Jeriah *was the first,*ᵇ Amariah the second, Jahaziel the third, *and* Jekameam the fourth. ²⁴Of the sons of Uzziel, Michah; of the sons of Michah, Shamir. ²⁵The brother of Michah, Isshiah; of the sons of Isshiah, Zechariah. ²⁶The sons of Merari *were* Mahli and Mushi; the son of Jaaziah, Beno. ²⁷The sons of Merari by Jaaziah *were* Beno, Shoham, Zaccur, and Ibri. ²⁸Of Mahli: Eleazar, who had no sons. ²⁹Of Kish: the son of Kish, Jerahmeel.

³⁰Also the sons of Mushi *were* Mahli, Eder, and Jerimoth. These *were* the sons of the Levites according to their fathers' houses.

³¹These also cast lots just as their brothers the sons of Aaron did, in the presence of King David, Zadok, Ahimelech, and the heads of the fathers' *houses* of the priests and Levites. The chief fathers *did* just as their younger brethren.

WHAT'S MEAN₂IT

Ever wonder who introduced music as part of a worship service? It was King David. David's son, Solomon, carried on the tradition in grand style after the temple was built. Nearly three hundred "master musicians" led the four thousand members of the choir and orchestra in carrying out their duties.

1 Chronicles 25:1

THE MUSICIANS

¹Moreover David and the captains of the army separated for the service *some* of the sons of Asaph, of Heman, and of Jeduthun, who *should* prophesy with harps, stringed instruments, and cymbals. And the number of the skilled men performing their service was: ²Of the sons of Asaph: Zaccur, Joseph, Nethaniah, and Asharelah;ᵃ the sons of Asaph *were* under the direction of Asaph, who prophesied according to the order of the king. ³Of Jeduthun, the sons of Jeduthun: Gedaliah, Zeri,ᵃ Jeshaiah, Shimei, Hashabiah, and Mattithiah, six,ᵇ under

---

24:15 ᵃSeptuagint and Vulgate read *Aphses.*   **24:16** ᵃMasoretic Text reads *Jehezkel.*   **24:20** ᵃSpelled *Shebuel* in 23:16   **24:22** ᵃSpelled *Shelomith* in 23:18   **24:23** ᵃSupplied from 23:19 (following some Hebrew manuscripts and Septuagint manuscripts)   ᵇSupplied from 23:19 (following some Hebrew manuscripts and Septuagint manuscripts)   **25:2** ᵃSpelled *Jesharelah* in verse 14   **25:3** ᵃSpelled *Jizri* in verse 11   ᵇ*Shimei,* appearing in one Hebrew and several Septuagint manuscripts, completes the total of six sons (compare verse 17).

the direction of their father Jeduthun, who prophesied with a harp to give thanks and to praise the LORD. [4]Of Heman, the sons of Heman: Bukkiah, Mattaniah, Uzziel,[a] Shebuel,[b] Jerimoth,[c] Hananiah, Hanani, Eliathah, Giddalti, Romamti-Ezer, Joshbekashah, Mallothi, Hothir, and Mahazioth. [5]All these were the sons of Heman the king's seer in the words of God, to exalt his horn.[a] For God gave Heman fourteen sons and three daughters.

[6]All these were under the direction of their father for the music in the house of the LORD, with cymbals, stringed instruments, and harps, for the service of the house of God. Asaph, Jeduthun, and Heman were under the authority of the king. [7]So the number of them, with their brethren who were instructed in the songs of the LORD, all who were skillful, was two hundred and eighty-eight.

[8]And they cast lots for their duty, the small as well as the great, the teacher with the student. [9]Now the first lot for Asaph came out for Joseph; the second for Gedaliah, him with his brethren and sons, twelve; [10]the third for Zaccur, his sons and his brethren, twelve; [11]the fourth for Jizri,[a] his sons and his brethren, twelve; [12]the fifth for Nethaniah, his sons and his brethren, twelve; [13]the sixth for Bukkiah, his sons and his brethren, twelve; [14]the seventh for Jesharelah,[a] his sons and his brethren, twelve; [15]the eighth for Jeshaiah, his sons and his brethren, twelve; [16]the ninth for Mattaniah, his sons and his brethren, twelve; [17]the tenth for Shimei, his sons and his brethren, twelve; [18]the eleventh for Azarel,[a] his sons and his brethren, twelve; [19]the twelfth for Hashabiah, his sons and his brethren, twelve; [20]the thirteenth for Shubael,[a] his sons and his brethren, twelve; [21]the fourteenth for Mattithiah, his sons and his brethren, twelve; [22]the fifteenth for Jeremoth,[a] his sons and his brethren, twelve; [23]the sixteenth for Hananiah, his sons and his brethren, twelve; [24]the seventeenth for Joshbekashah, his sons and his brethren, twelve; [25]the eighteenth for Hanani, his sons and his brethren, twelve; [26]the nineteenth for Mallothi, his sons and his brethren, twelve; [27]the twentieth for Eliathah, his sons and his brethren, twelve; [28]the twenty-first for Hothir, his sons and his brethren, twelve; [29]the twenty-second for Giddalti, his sons and his brethren, twelve; [30]the twenty-

third for Mahazioth, his sons and his brethren, twelve; [31]the twenty-fourth for Romamti-Ezer, his sons and his brethren, twelve.

THE GATEKEEPERS

[1]Concerning the divisions of the gatekeepers: of the Korahites, Meshelemiah the son of Kore, of the sons of Asaph. [2]And the sons of Meshelemiah were Zechariah the firstborn, Jediael the second, Zebadiah the third, Jathniel the fourth, [3]Elam the fifth, Jehohanan the sixth, Eliehoenai the seventh.

[4]Moreover the sons of Obed-Edom were Shemaiah the firstborn, Jehozabad the second, Joah the third, Sacar the fourth, Nethanel the fifth, [5]Ammiel the sixth, Issachar the seventh, Peulthai the eighth; for God blessed him.

[6]Also to Shemaiah his son were sons born who governed their fathers' houses, because they were men of great ability. [7]The sons of Shemaiah were Othni, Rephael, Obed, and Elzabad, whose brothers Elihu and Semachiah were able men. [8]All these were of the sons of Obed-Edom, they and their sons and their brethren, able men with strength for the work: sixty-two of Obed-Edom.

[9]And Meshelemiah had sons and brethren, eighteen able men.

[10]Also Hosah, of the children of Merari, had sons: Shimri the first (for though he was not the firstborn, his father made him the first), [11]Hilkiah the second, Tebaliah the third, Zechariah the fourth; all the sons and brethren of Hosah were thirteen.

[12]Among these were the divisions of the gatekeepers, among the chief men, having duties just like their brethren, to serve in the house of the LORD. [13]And they cast lots for each gate, the small as well as the great, according to their father's house. [14]The lot for the East Gate fell to Shelemiah. Then they cast lots for his son Zechariah, a wise counselor, and his lot came out for the North Gate; [15]to Obed-Edom the South Gate, and to his sons the storehouse.[a] [16]To Shuppim and Hosah the lot came out for the West Gate, with the Shallecheth Gate on the ascending highway—watchman opposite watchman. [17]On the east were six Levites, on the north four each day, on the south four each day, and for the storehouse[a] two by two. [18]As for the Parbar[a] on the west, there were four on

25:4 [a]Spelled *Azarel* in verse 18 [b]Spelled *Shubael* in verse 20 [c]Spelled *Jeremoth* in verse 22 **25:5** [a]That is, to increase his power or influence **25:11** [a]Spelled *Zeri* in verse 3 **25:14** [a]Spelled *Asharelah* in verse 2 **25:18** [a]Spelled *Uzziel* in verse 4 **25:20** [a]Spelled *Shebuel* in verse 4 **25:22** [a]Spelled *Jerimoth* in verse 4 **26:15** [a]Hebrew *asuppim* **26:17** [a]Hebrew *asuppim* **26:18** [a]Probably a court or colonnade extending west of the temple the highway *and* two at the Parbar. [19]These were the divisions of the gatekeepers among the sons of Korah and among the sons of Merari.

All money and treasures that were taken in battle or dedicated to the Lord by grateful Israelites were kept in the temple for safekeeping. (The only banks in Israel at that time were the banks of the Jordan River.) The money was used to maintain the temple and keep it properly furnished. For extra security, Solomon's temple had a courtyard with a wall and gates around it.

1 Chronicles 26:20

THE TREASURIES AND OTHER DUTIES

[20]Of the Levites, Ahijah *was* over the treasuries of the house of God and over the treasuries of the dedicated things. [21]The sons of Laadan, the descendants of the Gershonites of Laadan, heads of their fathers' *houses*, of Laadan the Gershonite: Jehieli. [22]The sons of Jehieli, Zetham and Joel his brother, *were* over the treasuries of the house of the LORD. [23]Of the Amramites, the Izharites, the Hebronites, and the Uzzielites: [24]Shebuel the son of Gershom, the son of Moses, *was* overseer of the treasuries. [25]And his brethren by Eliezer *were* Rehabiah his son, Jeshaiah his son, Joram his son, Zichri his son, and Shelomith his son.

[26]This Shelomith and his brethren *were* over all the treasuries of the dedicated things which King David and the heads of fathers' *houses*, the captains over thousands and hundreds, and the captains of the army, had dedicated. [27]Some of the spoils won in battles they dedicated to maintain the house of the LORD. [28]And all that Samuel the seer, Saul the son of Kish, Abner the son of Ner, and Joab the son of Zeruiah had dedicated, every dedicated *thing*, was under the hand of Shelomith and his brethren.

MONEY
What's a good way to spend some of the money we earn? (26:27)

[29]Of the Izharites, Chenaniah and his sons *performed* duties as officials and judges over Israel outside Jerusalem.

[30]Of the Hebronites, Hashabiah and his brethren, one thousand seven hundred able men, had the oversight of Israel on the west side of the Jordan for all the business of the LORD, and in the service of the king. [31]Among the Hebronites, Jerijah *was* head of the Hebronites according to his genealogy of the fathers. In the fortieth year of the reign of David they were sought, and there were found among them capable men at Jazer of Gilead. [32]And his brethren *were* two thousand seven hundred able men, heads of fathers' *houses*, whom King David made officials over the Reubenites, the Gadites, and the half-tribe of Manasseh, for every matter pertaining to God and the affairs of the king.

Even though the Hebrew calendar had twelve months, it was much different from the one we use today. The Hebrew year began in spring—what would be our late March or early April. The months followed the cycle of the moon, from crescent to full. Later, the Israelites adopted the calendar of the Babylonians, which also began in the spring.

1 Chronicles 27:1

THE MILITARY DIVISIONS

[1]And the children of Israel, according to their number, the heads of fathers' *houses*, the captains of thousands and hundreds and their officers, served the king in every matter of the *military* divisions. *These divisions* came in and went out month by month throughout all the months of the year, each division *having* twenty-four thousand.

[2]Over the first division for the first month *was* Jashobeam the son of Zabdiel, and in his division *were* twenty-four thousand; [3]he *was* of the children of Perez, and the chief of all the captains of the army for the first month. [4]Over the division of the second month *was* Dodai[a] an Ahohite, and of his division Mikloth also *was* the leader; in his division *were* twenty-four thousand. [5]The third captain of the army for

---

27:4 [a]Hebrew *Dodai*, usually spelled *Dodo* (compare 2 Samuel 23:9)

the third month *was* Benaiah, the son of Jehoiada the priest, who was chief; in his division *were* twenty-four thousand. [6]This was the Benaiah *who was* mighty *among* the thirty, and was over the thirty; in his division *was* Ammizabad his son. [7]The fourth *captain* for the fourth month *was* Asahel the brother of Joab, and Zebadiah his son after him; in his division *were* twenty-four thousand. [8]The fifth *captain* for the fifth month *was* Shamhuth[a] the Izrahite; in his division were twenty-four thousand. [9]The sixth *captain* for the sixth month *was* Ira the son of Ikkesh the Tekoite; in his division *were* twenty-four thousand. [10]The seventh *captain* for the seventh month *was* Helez the Pelonite, of the children of Ephraim; in his division *were* twenty-four thousand. [11]The eighth *captain* for the eighth month *was* Sibbechai the Hushathite, of the Zarhites; in his division *were* twenty-four thousand. [12]The ninth *captain* for the ninth month *was* Abiezer the Anathothite, of the Benjamites; in his division *were* twenty-four thousand. [13]The tenth *captain* for the tenth month *was* Maharai the Netophathite, of the Zarhites; in his division *were* twenty-four thousand. [14]The eleventh *captain* for the eleventh month *was* Benaiah the Pirathonite, of the children of Ephraim; in his division *were* twenty-four thousand. [15]The twelfth *captain* for the twelfth month *was* Heldai[a] the Netophathite, of Othniel; in his division *were* twenty-four thousand.

LEADERS OF TRIBES

[16]Furthermore, over the tribes of Israel: the officer over the Reubenites *was* Eliezer the son of Zichri; over the Simeonites, Shephatiah the son of Maachah; [17]*over* the Levites, Hashabiah the son of Kemuel; over the Aaronites, Zadok; [18]*over* Judah, Elihu, *one* of David's brothers; *over* Issachar, Omri the son of Michael; [19]*over* Zebulun, Ishmaiah the son of Obadiah; *over* Naphtali, Jerimoth the son of Azriel; [20]*over* the children of Ephraim, Hoshea the son of Azaziah; *over* the half-tribe of Manasseh, Joel the son of Pedaiah; [21]*over* the half-*tribe* of Manasseh in Gilead, Iddo the son of Zechariah; *over* Benjamin, Jaasiel the son of Abner; [22]*over* Dan, Azarel the son of Jeroham. These *were* the leaders of the tribes of Israel.

[23]But David did not take the number of those twenty years old and under, because the LORD had said He would multiply Israel like the stars of the heavens. [24]Joab the son of Zeruiah began a census, but he did not finish, for wrath came upon Israel because of this census; nor was the number recorded in the account of the chronicles of King David.

OTHER STATE OFFICIALS

[25]And Azmaveth the son of Adiel *was* over the king's treasuries; and Jehonathan the son of Uzziah was over the storehouses in the field, in the cities, in the villages, and in the fortresses. [26]Ezri the son of Chelub was over those who did the work of the field for tilling the ground. [27]And Shimei the Ramathite *was* over the vineyards, and Zabdi the Shiphmite was over the produce of the vineyards for the supply of wine. [28]Baal-Hanan the Gederite was over the olive trees and the sycamore trees that *were* in the lowlands, and Joash *was* over the store of oil. [29]And Shitrai the Sharonite *was* over the herds that fed in Sharon, and Shaphat the son of Adlai was over the herds *that were* in the valleys. [30]Obil the Ishmaelite *was* over the camels, Jehdeiah the Meronothite *was* over the donkeys, [31]and Jaziz the Hagrite *was* over the flocks. All these *were* the officials over King David's property.

[32]Also Jehonathan, David's uncle, *was* a counselor, a wise man, and a scribe; and Jehiel the son of Hachmoni *was* with the king's sons. [33]Ahithophel *was* the king's counselor, and Hushai the Archite *was* the king's companion. [34]After Ahithophel *was* Jehoiada the son of Benaiah, then Abiathar. And the general of the king's army *was* Joab.

SOLOMON INSTRUCTED TO BUILD THE TEMPLE

[1]Now David assembled at Jerusalem all the leaders of Israel: the officers of the tribes and the captains of the divisions who served the king, the captains over thousands and captains over hundreds, and the stewards over all the substance and possessions of the king and of his sons, with the officials, the valiant men, and all the mighty men of valor.

[2]Then King David rose to his feet and said, "Hear me, my brethren and my people: I *had* it in my heart to build a house of rest for the ark of the covenant of the LORD, and for the footstool of our God, and had made preparations to build it. [3]But God said to me, 'You shall not build a house for My name, because you *have been* a man of war and have shed blood.' [4]However the LORD God of Israel chose me above all the house of my father to be king over Israel forever, for He has chosen Judah *to be* the ruler.

27:8 [a]Spelled *Shammoth* in 11:27 and *Shammah* in 2 Samuel 23:11   **27:15** [a]Spelled *Heled* in 11:30 and *Heleb* in 2 Samuel 23:29

And of the house of Judah, the house of my father, and among the sons of my father, He was pleased with me to make *me* king over all Israel. [5]And of all my sons (for the LORD has given me many sons) He has chosen my son Solomon to sit on the throne of the kingdom of the LORD over Israel. [6]Now He said to me, 'It is your son Solomon *who* shall build My house and My courts; for I have chosen him *to be* My son, and I will be his Father. [7]Moreover I will establish his kingdom forever, if he is steadfast to observe My commandments and My judgments, as it is this day.' [8]Now therefore, in the sight of all Israel, the assembly of the LORD, and in the hearing of our God, be careful to seek out all the commandments of the LORD your God, that you may possess this good land, and leave *it* as an inheritance for your children after you forever.

"Now He said to me, 'It is your son Solomon who shall build My house and My courts; for I have chosen him to be My son, and I will be his Father.' "
(i Chronicles 28:6)

FAMILY

What's a good legacy parents can leave their children? (28:8)

[9]"As for you, my son Solomon, know the God of your father, and serve Him with a loyal heart and with a willing mind; for the LORD searches all hearts and understands all the intent of the thoughts. If you seek Him, He will be found by you; but if you forsake Him, He will cast you off forever. [10]Consider now, for the LORD has chosen you to build a house for the sanctuary; be strong, and do it."

[11]Then David gave his son Solomon the plans for the vestibule, its houses, its treasuries, its upper chambers, its inner chambers, and the place of the mercy seat; [12]and the plans for all that he had by the Spirit, of the courts of the house of the LORD, of all the chambers all around, of the treasuries of the house of God, and of the treasuries for the dedicated things; [13]also for the division of the priests and the Levites, for all the work of the service of the house of the LORD, and for all the articles of service in the house of the LORD. [14]*He gave* gold by weight for *things* of gold, for all articles used in every kind of service; also *silver* for all articles of silver by weight, for all articles used in every kind of service; [15]the weight for the lampstands of gold, and their lamps of gold, by weight for each lampstand and its lamps; for the lampstands of silver by weight, for the lampstand and its lamps, according to the use of each lampstand. [16]And by weight *he gave* gold for the tables of the showbread, for each table, and silver for the tables of silver; [17]also pure gold for the forks, the basins, the pitchers of pure gold, and the golden bowls—*he gave* gold by weight for every bowl; and for the silver bowls, *silver* by weight for every bowl; [18]and refined gold by weight for the altar of incense, and for the construction of the chariot, that is, the gold cherubim that spread *their wings* and overshadowed the ark of the covenant of the LORD. [19]"All *this*," said David, "the LORD made me understand in writing, by His hand upon me, all the works of these plans."

[20]And David said to his son Solomon, "Be strong and of good courage, and do *it*; do not fear nor be dismayed, for the LORD God—my God—*will be* with you. He will not leave you nor forsake you, until you have finished all the work for the service of the house of the LORD. [21]*Here are* the divisions of the priests and the Levites for all the service of the house of God; and every willing craftsman *will be* with you for all manner of workmanship, for every kind of service; also the leaders and all the people *will be* completely at your command."

OFFERINGS FOR BUILDING THE TEMPLE

[1]Furthermore King David said to all the assembly: "My son Solomon, whom alone God has chosen, *is* young and inexperienced; and the work *is* great, because the temple[a] *is* not for man but for the LORD God. [2]Now for the house of my God I have prepared with all my might: gold for *things to be made of* gold, silver for *things of* silver, bronze for *things of* bronze, iron for *things of* iron, wood for *things of* wood, onyx stones, *stones* to be set, glistening stones of various colors, all kinds of precious stones, and marble slabs in abundance. [3]Moreover, because I have set my affection on the house of my God, I have given to the house of my God, over and above all that I have prepared for the holy house, my own special treasure of gold and silver: [4]three thousand talents of gold, of the gold of Ophir, and seven thousand talents of refined silver, to overlay the walls of the houses; [5]the

gold for *things of* gold and the silver for *things of* silver, and for all kinds of work *to be done* by the hands of craftsmen. Who *then* is willing to consecrate himself this day to the LORD?"

⁶Then the leaders of the fathers' *houses,* leaders of the tribes of Israel, the captains of thousands and of hundreds, with the officers over the king's work, offered willingly. ⁷They gave for the work of the house of God five thousand talents and ten thousand darics of gold, ten thousand talents of silver, eighteen thousand talents of bronze, and one hundred thousand talents of iron. ⁸And whoever had *precious* stones gave *them* to the treasury of the house of the LORD, into the hand of Jehiel*ᵃ* the Gershonite. ⁹Then the people rejoiced, for they had offered willingly, because with a loyal heart they had offered willingly to the LORD; and King David also rejoiced greatly.

DAVID'S PRAISE TO GOD

¹⁰Therefore David blessed the LORD before all the assembly; and David said:

"Blessed are You, LORD God of Israel, our
    Father, forever and ever.
¹¹ Yours, O LORD, *is* the greatness,
    The power and the glory,
    The victory and the majesty;
    For all *that is* in heaven and in earth *is*
        Yours;
    Yours *is* the kingdom, O LORD,
    And You are exalted as head over all.
¹² Both riches and honor *come* from You,
    And You reign over all.
    In Your hand *is* power
        and might;
    In Your hand *it is* to
        make great
    And to give strength to
        all.

¹³ "Now therefore, our God,
    We thank You
    And praise Your glorious name.
¹⁴ But who *am* I, and who *are* my people,
    That we should be able to offer so
        willingly as this?
    For all things *come* from You,
    And of Your own we have given You.
¹⁵ For we *are* aliens and pilgrims before
        You,
    As *were* all our fathers;
    Our days on earth *are* as a shadow,
    And without hope.

¹⁶"O LORD our God, all this abundance that we have prepared to build You a house for Your holy name is from Your hand, and *is* all Your own. ¹⁷I know also, my God, that You test the heart and have pleasure in uprightness. As for me, in the uprightness of my heart I have willingly offered all these *things;* and now with joy I have seen Your people, who are present here to offer willingly to You. ¹⁸O LORD God of Abraham, Isaac, and Israel, our fathers, keep this forever in the intent of the thoughts of the heart of Your people, and fix their heart toward You. ¹⁹And give my son Solomon a loyal heart to keep Your commandments and Your testimonies and Your statutes, to do all *these things,* and to build the temple*ᵃ* for which I have made provision."

²⁰Then David said to all the assembly, "Now bless the LORD your God." So all the assembly blessed the LORD God of their fathers, and bowed their heads and prostrated themselves before the LORD and the king.

SOLOMON ANOINTED KING

²¹And they made sacrifices to the LORD and offered burnt offerings to the LORD on the next day: a thousand bulls, a thousand rams, a thousand lambs, with their drink offerings, and sacrifices in abundance for all Israel. ²²So they ate and drank before the LORD with great gladness on that day. And they made Solomon the son of David king the second time, and anointed *him* before the LORD *to be* the leader, and Zadok *to be* priest. ²³Then Solomon sat on the throne of the LORD as king instead of David his father, and prospered; and all Israel obeyed him. ²⁴All the leaders and the mighty men, and

> **WORRY**
> Where should we find the confidence we need to survive? (29:12)

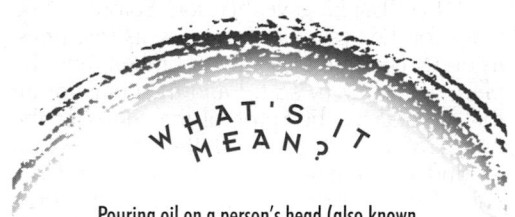

WHAT'S IT MEAN?

Pouring oil on a person's head (also known as anointing) was a way of indicating that God had chosen that person for a certain job or position. Zadok had been faithful to Solomon when another high priest, Abiathar, had helped Solomon's brother, Adonijah, in his unsuccessful attempt to overthrow Solomon.

1 Chronicles 29:22

29:8 *ᵃ*Possibly the same as Jehieli (compare 26:21, 22)   **29:19** *ᵃ*Literally *palace* also all the sons of King David, submitted themselves to King Solomon. [25]So the LORD exalted Solomon exceedingly in the sight of all Israel, and bestowed on him *such* royal majesty as had not been on any king before him in Israel.

THE CLOSE OF DAVID'S REIGN

[26]Thus David the son of Jesse reigned over all Israel. [27]And the period that he reigned over Israel *was* forty years; seven years he reigned in Hebron, and thirty-three *years* he reigned in Jerusalem. [28]So he died in a good old age, full of days and riches and honor; and Solomon his son reigned in his place. [29]Now the acts of King David, first and last, indeed they *are* written in the book of Samuel the seer, in the book of Nathan the prophet, and in the book of Gad the seer, [30]with all his reign and his might, and the events that happened to him, to Israel, and to all the kingdoms of the lands.

2 chronicles

CONTENT   When you read some of the previous books of the Bible, like First and Second Kings and First Chronicles, you sometimes feel like you might hurt your neck! It can feel like you're watching a Ping-Pong tournament the way the Hebrews fall away from God, then return to God, then fall away from God, then return to God. Unfortunately they fall away a few more times than they return.

But the Book of Second Chronicles doesn't tell the story of all the kings and all the people. This book concentrates on the southern kingdom of Judah, and it concentrates on the stand-up kind of guys that rule. It tells the stories of kings like Josiah and Joash who became kings when they were young, but really made a difference.

Second Chronicles reminds us that when we take a chance and stand up for God, He meets us every time. He doesn't hang us out to dry alone. He just wants us to have the faith to stand up and do the right thing.

Purpose   God is always faithful to those who put Him first.

Theme   Encouragement and Exhortation from Judah's Spiritual Heritage

Date of writing   430–425 B.C.

> "If My people who are called by My name will humble themselves, and pray and seek My face, and turn from their wicked ways, then I will hear from heaven, and will forgive their sin and heal their land" (7:14).

Bible Talk

Why?

Second Chronicles is that kind of book that prompts us to ask a lot of "why" questions. Why did the people keep falling away even though they saw God take care of them over and over? Why did they worship false gods, even though they should have known they were false? Why did they disobey God even after He clearly told them what to do? Why did they ignore the obvious and fall away again and again?

We have to ask ourselves the same questions. Why do we do what is wrong when we know what is right? Why do we get afraid even though God promises to take care of us? Why do we make friends with people who will push us farther away from God? Why do we ignore the obvious and fall away again and again?

WHAT'S WITH THE BLOOD AND GORE?

As you read through these historical books of the Old Testament, you might wonder after a while if all they did was fight. It really was a barbaric time in history. Remember that Judah had become unbelievably wealthy during Solomon's rule. They weren't just wealthy; they were famous for being wealthy. So as the kingdom split and as the government weakened, the country became more of a target for invaders.

Keep in mind, too, that at this time, boundaries for land ownership were up for grabs to the strongest bully. There weren't any maps with black lines that showed who owned what. That was all being formed. It was definitely a different world.

SOLOMON REQUESTS WISDOM

[1]Now Solomon the son of David was strengthened in his kingdom, and the LORD his God *was* with him and exalted him exceedingly. [2]And Solomon spoke to all Israel, to the captains of thousands and of hundreds, to the judges, and to every leader in all Israel, the heads of the fathers' *houses.* [3]Then Solomon, and all the assembly with him, went to the high place that *was* at Gibeon; for the tabernacle of meeting with God was there, which Moses the servant of the LORD had made in the wilderness. [4]But David had brought up the ark of God from Kirjath Jearim to *the place* David had prepared for it, for he had pitched a tent for it at Jerusalem. [5]Now the bronze altar that Bezalel the son of Uri, the son of Hur, had made, he put[a] before the tabernacle of the LORD; Solomon and the assembly sought Him *there.* [6]And Solomon went up there to the bronze altar before the LORD, which *was* at the tabernacle of meeting, and offered a thousand burnt offerings on it.

[7]On that night God appeared to Solomon, and said to him, "Ask! What shall I give you?"

[8]And Solomon said to God: "You have shown great mercy to David my father, and have made me king in his place. [9]Now, O LORD God, let Your promise to David my father be established, for You have made me king over a people like the dust of the earth in multitude. [10]Now give me wisdom and knowledge, that I may go out and come in before this people; for who can judge this great people of Yours?"

> **PRAYER**
>
> What can we pray for?
> (1:9, 10)

[11]Then God said to Solomon: "Because this was in your heart, and you have not asked riches or wealth or honor or the life of your enemies, nor have you asked long life—but have asked wisdom and knowledge for yourself, that you may judge My people over whom I have made you king—[12]wisdom and knowledge *are* granted to you; and I will give you riches and wealth and honor, such as none of the kings have had who *were* before you, nor shall any after you have the like."

SOLOMON'S MILITARY AND ECONOMIC POWER

[13]So Solomon came to Jerusalem from the high place that *was* at Gibeon, from before the tabernacle of meeting, and reigned over Israel. [14]And Solomon gathered chariots and horse-men; he had one thousand four hundred chariots and twelve thousand horsemen, whom he stationed in the chariot cities and with the king in Jerusalem. [15]Also the king made silver and gold as common in Jerusalem as stones, and he made cedars as abundant as the sycamores which *are* in the lowland. [16]And Solomon had horses imported from Egypt and Keveh; the king's merchants bought them in Keveh at the *current* price. [17]They also acquired and imported from Egypt a chariot for six hundred *shekels* of silver, and a horse for one hundred and fifty; thus, through their agents,[a] they exported them to all the kings of the Hittites and the kings of Syria.

WHAT'S IT MEAN?

Solomon recognized that the best way to strengthen Israel's military force was to invest in chariots, the most important piece of battle machinery available at that time. Ancient chariots came in all styles and sizes. Some were pulled by two horses, others by four. Some carried two riders; others carried four. The problem with chariots was the expense. Building, buying, and maintaining a fleet of chariots required more than a few shekels. Only the wealthiest nations could afford to keep a strong chariot force. Later in Israel's history, as the kingdom declined in wealth and power, the use of chariots declined drastically. By the time King Jehoahaz came to power, Israel was down to ten measly chariots in their military. The rest had been destroyed in battle.

2 Chronicles 1:16, 17

SOLOMON PREPARES TO BUILD THE TEMPLE

[1]Then Solomon determined to build a temple for the name of the LORD, and a royal house for himself. [2]Solomon selected seventy thousand men to bear burdens, eighty thousand to quarry *stone* in the mountains, and three thousand six hundred to oversee them.

[3]Then Solomon sent to Hiram[a] king of Tyre saying:

As you have dealt with David my father, and sent him cedars to build himself a house to dwell in, *so deal with me.* [4]Behold,

---

1:5 [a]Some authorities read *it was there.*   **1:17** [a]Literally *by their hands*   **2:3** [a]Hebrew *Huram* (compare 1 Kings 5:1)

I am building a temple for the name of the LORD my God, to dedicate it to Him, to burn before Him sweet incense, for the continual showbread, for the burnt offerings morning and evening, on the Sabbaths, on the New Moons, and on the set feasts of the LORD our God. This is an ordinance forever to Israel.

5 And the temple which I build will be great, for our God is greater than all gods. 6But who is able to build Him a temple, since heaven and the heaven of heavens cannot contain Him? Who am I then, that I should build Him a temple, except to burn sacrifice before Him?

7 Therefore send me at once a man skillful to work in gold and silver, in bronze and iron, in purple and crimson and blue, who has skill to engrave with the skillful men who are with me in Judah and Jerusalem, whom David my father provided. 8Also send me cedar and cypress and algum logs from Lebanon, for I know that your servants have skill to cut timber in Lebanon; and indeed my servants will be with your servants, 9to prepare timber for me in abundance, for the temple which I am about to build shall be great and wonderful.

10 And indeed I will give to your servants, the woodsmen who cut timber, twenty thousand kors of ground wheat, twenty thousand kors of barley, twenty thousand baths of wine, and twenty thousand baths of oil.

11Then Hiram king of Tyre answered in writing, which he sent to Solomon:

Because the LORD loves His people, He has made you king over them.

12Hiram*a* also said:

Blessed be the LORD God of Israel, who made heaven and earth, for He has given King David a wise son, endowed with prudence and understanding, who will build a temple for the LORD and a royal house for himself!

13 And now I have sent a skillful man, endowed with understanding, Huram*a* my master*b* craftsman 14(the son of a woman of the daughters of Dan, and his father was a man of Tyre), skilled to work in gold and silver, bronze and iron, stone and wood, purple and blue, fine linen and crimson, and to make any engraving and to accomplish any plan which may be given to him, with your skillful men and with the skillful men of my lord David your father.

15 Now therefore, the wheat, the barley, the oil, and the wine which my lord has spoken of, let him send to his servants. 16And we will cut wood from Lebanon, as much as you need; we will bring it to you in rafts by sea to Joppa, and you will carry it up to Jerusalem.

17Then Solomon numbered all the aliens who were in the land of Israel, after the census in which David his father had numbered them; and there were found to be one hundred and fifty-three thousand six hundred. 18And he made seventy thousand of them bearers of burdens, eighty thousand stonecutters in the mountain, and three thousand six hundred overseers to make the people work.

WHAT'S IT MEAN?

Call it what you want, but the non-Israelite workers were little more than slaves who were owned by the state. Solomon assigned 250 Israelites to supervise these workers and keep them under control.
2 Chronicles 2:18

SOLOMON BUILDS THE TEMPLE

1Now Solomon began to build the house of the LORD at Jerusalem on Mount Moriah, where the LORD*a* had appeared to his father David, at the place that David had prepared on the threshing floor of Ornan*b* the Jebusite. 2And he

---

2:12 *a*Hebrew Huram (compare 1 Kings 5:1) **2:13** *a*Spelled Hiram in 1 Kings 7:13 *b*Literally father (compare 1 Kings 7:13, 14) **3:1** *a*Literally He, following Masoretic Text and Vulgate; Septuagint reads the LORD; Targum reads the Angel of the LORD. *b*Spelled Araunah in 2 Samuel 24:16ff began to build on the second *day* of the second month in the fourth year of his reign.

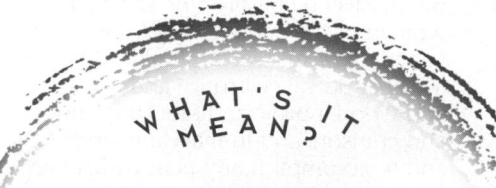

WHAT'S IT MEAN?

How did Solomon know where to build his temple? Years earlier, God had shown Solomon's father, David, the spot by lighting David's sacrifice with fire from heaven. The temple Solomon had built was later destroyed by the Babylonians. In Jesus' day, another temple—this one built by Herod the Great—sat on the site. If you were to go to Israel today, you would find a building known as the Dome of the Rock there.

2 Chronicles 3:1, 2

[3]This is the foundation which Solomon laid for building the house of God: The length *was* sixty cubits (by cubits according to the former measure) and the width twenty cubits. [4]And the vestibule that *was* in front *of the sanctuary*[a] was twenty cubits long across the width of the house, and the height *was* one hundred and[b] twenty. He overlaid the inside with pure gold. [5]The larger room[a] he paneled with cypress which he overlaid with fine gold, and he carved palm trees and chainwork on it. [6]And he decorated the house with precious stones for beauty, and the gold *was* gold from Parvaim. [7]He also overlaid the house—the beams and doorposts, its walls and doors—with gold; and he carved cherubim on the walls.

[8]And he made the Most Holy Place. Its length was according to the width of the house, twenty cubits, and its width twenty cubits. He overlaid it with six hundred talents of fine gold. [9]The weight of the nails *was* fifty shekels of gold; and he overlaid the upper area with gold. [10]In the Most Holy Place he made two cherubim, fashioned by carving, and overlaid them with gold. [11]The wings of the cherubim *were* twenty cubits in *overall* length: one wing *of the one cherub was* five cubits, touching the wall of the room, and the other wing *was* five cubits, touching the wing of the other cherub; [12]one wing of the other cherub *was* five cubits, touch-

ing the wall of the room, and the other wing *also was* five cubits, touching the wing of the other cherub. [13]The wings of these cherubim spanned twenty cubits overall. They stood on their feet, and they faced inward. [14]And he made the veil of blue, purple, crimson, and fine linen, and wove cherubim into it.

[15]Also he made in front of the temple[a] two pillars thirty-five[b] cubits high, and the capital that *was* on the top of each of *them* was five cubits. [16]He made wreaths of chainwork, as in the inner sanctuary, and put *them* on top of the pillars; and he made one hundred pomegranates, and put *them* on the wreaths of chainwork. [17]Then he set up the pillars before the temple, one on the right hand and the other on the left; he called the name of the one on the right hand Jachin, and the name of the one on the left Boaz.

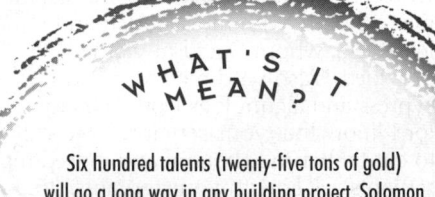

WHAT'S IT MEAN?

Six hundred talents (twenty-five tons of gold) will go a long way in any building project. Solomon used it to coat the walls of the Most Holy Place in his temple about one-fifth of an inch thick.

2 Chronicles 3:8

FURNISHINGS OF THE TEMPLE

[1]Moreover he made a bronze altar: twenty cubits was its length, twenty cubits its width, and ten cubits its height.

[2]Then he made the Sea of cast *bronze*, ten cubits from one brim to the other; *it was* completely round. Its height *was* five cubits, and a line of thirty cubits measured its circumference. [3]And under it *was* the likeness of oxen encircling it all around, ten to a cubit, all the way around the Sea. The oxen *were* cast in two rows, when it was cast. [4]It stood on twelve oxen: three looking toward the north, three looking toward the west, three looking toward the south, and three looking toward the east; the Sea *was set* upon them, and all their back parts *pointed* inward. [5]It *was* a handbreadth thick; and

3:4 [a]The main room of the temple; elsewhere called the holy place (compare 1 Kings 6:3) [b]Following Masoretic Text, Septuagint, and Vulgate; Arabic, some manuscripts of the Septuagint, and Syriac omit *one hundred and*. **3:5** [a]Literally *house* **3:15** [a]Literally *house* [b]Or *eighteen* (compare 1 Kings 7:15; 2 Kings 25:17; and Jeremiah 52:21) its brim was shaped like the brim of a cup, *like a lily blossom.* It contained three thousand*ᵃ* baths.

⁶He also made ten lavers, and put five on the right side and five on the left, to wash in them; such things as they offered for the burnt offering they would wash in them, but the Sea *was* for the priests to wash in. ⁷And he made ten lampstands of gold according to their design, and set *them* in the temple, five on the right side and five on the left. ⁸He also made ten tables, and placed *them* in the temple, five on the right side and five on the left. And he made one hundred bowls of gold.

⁹Furthermore he made the court of the priests, and the great court and doors for the court; and he overlaid these doors with bronze. ¹⁰He set the Sea on the right side, toward the southeast.

¹¹Then Huram made the pots and the shovels and the bowls. So Huram finished doing the work that he was to do for King Solomon for the house of God: ¹²the two pillars and the bowl-shaped capitals *that were* on top of the two pillars; the two networks covering the two bowl-shaped capitals which *were* on top of the pillars; ¹³four hundred pomegranates for the two networks (two rows of pomegranates for each network, to cover the two bowl-shaped capitals that *were* on the pillars); ¹⁴he also made carts and the lavers on the carts; ¹⁵one Sea and twelve oxen under it; ¹⁶also the pots, the shovels, the forks—and all their articles Huram his master*ᵃ* craftsman made of burnished bronze for King Solomon for the house of the LORD.

¹⁷In the plain of Jordan the king had them cast in clay molds, between Succoth and Zeredah.*ᵃ* ¹⁸And Solomon had all these articles made in such great abundance that the weight of the bronze was not determined.

¹⁹Thus Solomon had all the furnishings made for the house of God: the altar of gold and the tables on which *was* the showbread; ²⁰the lampstands with their lamps of pure gold, to burn in the prescribed manner in front of the inner sanctuary, ²¹with the flowers and the lamps and the wick-trimmers of gold, of purest gold; ²²the trimmers, the bowls, the ladles, and the censers of pure gold. As for the entry of the sanctuary, its inner doors to the Most Holy *Place,* and the doors of the main hall of the temple, *were* gold.

¹So all the work that Solomon had done for the house of the LORD was finished; and Sol-

omon brought in the things which his father David had dedicated: the silver and the gold and all the furnishings. And he put *them* in the treasuries of the house of God.

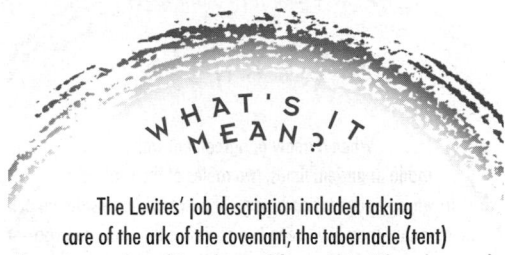

WHAT'S IT MEAN?

The Levites' job description included taking care of the ark of the covenant, the tabernacle (tent) of meeting, and anything else used for worship. When the temple was finished, the ark of the covenant was moved into the Most Holy Place. The tabernacle of meeting may have been set up as a permanent display inside the temple as well.

2 Chronicles 5:4, 5

THE ARK BROUGHT INTO THE TEMPLE

²Now Solomon assembled the elders of Israel and all the heads of the tribes, the chief fathers of the children of Israel, in Jerusalem, that they might bring the ark of the covenant of the LORD up from the City of David, which *is* Zion. ³Therefore all the men of Israel assembled with the king at the feast, which *was* in the seventh month. ⁴So all the elders of Israel came, and the Levites took up the ark. ⁵Then they brought up the ark, the tabernacle of meeting, and all the holy furnishings that *were* in the tabernacle. The priests and the Levites brought them up. ⁶Also King Solomon, and all the congregation of Israel who were assembled with him before the ark, were sacrificing sheep and oxen that could not be counted or numbered for multitude. ⁷Then the priests brought in the ark of the covenant of the LORD to its place, into the inner sanctuary of the temple,*ᵃ* to the Most Holy *Place,* under the wings of the cherubim. ⁸For the cherubim spread *their* wings over the place of the ark, and the cherubim overshadowed the ark and its poles. ⁹The poles extended so that the ends of the poles of the ark could be seen from *the holy place,* in front of the inner sanctuary; but they could not be seen from outside. And they are there to this day. ¹⁰Nothing was in the ark except the two tablets which Moses put *there* at Horeb, when the LORD made *a covenant*

4:5 *ᵃOr two thousand* (compare 1 Kings 7:26) **4:16** *ᵃLiterally father* **4:17** *ᵃSpelled Zaretan in 1 Kings 7:46*
5:7 *ᵃLiterally house*

with the children of Israel, when they had come out of Egypt.

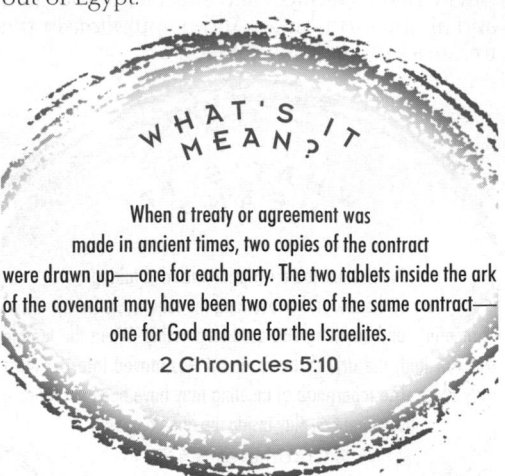

WHAT'S IT MEAN?

When a treaty or agreement was made in ancient times, two copies of the contract were drawn up—one for each party. The two tablets inside the ark of the covenant may have been two copies of the same contract—one for God and one for the Israelites.

2 Chronicles 5:10

[11]And it came to pass when the priests came out of the *Most* Holy *Place* (for all the priests who *were* present had sanctified themselves, without keeping to their divisions), [12]and the Levites *who were* the singers, all those of Asaph and Heman and Jeduthun, with their sons and their brethren, stood at the east end of the altar, clothed in white linen, having cymbals, stringed instruments and harps, and with them one hundred and twenty priests sounding with trumpets—[13]indeed it came to pass, when the trumpeters and singers *were* as one, to make one sound to be heard in praising and thanking the LORD, and when they lifted up their voice with the trumpets and cymbals and instruments of music, and praised the LORD, *saying:*

" *For He is* good,
For His mercy *endures* forever,"[a]

that the house, the house of the LORD, was filled with a cloud, [14]so that the priests could not continue ministering because of the cloud; for the glory of the LORD filled the house of God. [1]Then Solomon spoke:

"The LORD said
He would dwell in the dark cloud.
[2]   I have surely built You an exalted house,
And a place for You to dwell in forever."

SOLOMON'S SPEECH UPON COMPLETION OF THE WORK

[3]Then the king turned around and blessed the whole assembly of Israel, while all the as-

sembly of Israel was standing. [4]And he said: "Blessed *be* the LORD God of Israel, who has fulfilled with His hands *what* He spoke with His mouth to my father David, saying, [5]'Since the day that I brought My people out of the land of Egypt, I have chosen no city from any tribe of Israel *in which* to build a house, that My name might be there, nor did I choose any man to be a ruler over My people Israel. [6]Yet I have chosen Jerusalem, that My name may be there, and I have chosen David to be over My people Israel.' [7]Now it was in the heart of my father David to build a temple[a] for the name of the LORD God of Israel. [8]But the LORD said to my father David, 'Whereas it was in your heart to build a temple for My name, you did well in that it was in your heart. [9]Nevertheless you shall not build the temple, but your son who will come from your body, he shall build the temple for My name.' [10]So the LORD has fulfilled His word which He spoke, and I have filled the position of my father David, and sit on the throne of Is-

On the Edge

They lifted up their voice with the trumpets and cymbals and instruments of music, and praised the LORD, saying: "For He is good, for His mercy endures forever" (2 Chr. 5:13).

It's hard to imagine mercy (compassionate, loving concern) that never ends. Your boyfriend loved you yesterday, but he loves someone else today. Your parents seem to love you more when your grades are good and your chores are done. You know someone whose dad just left because he doesn't love the mom anymore. Love seems to come and go very easily down here on earth. But there is Someone who is truly in love with you. He can't keep His eyes off of you. He is so proud that you belong to Him. The love of God will never disappoint you. His commitment is forever. There will be no trial separations, no grounds for divorce. He is good, and you are the one He loves without end.

SEE FOR YOURSELF:
Rom. 5:8–11;
Eph. 2:4–7;
1 John 4:7–11

5:13 [a]Compare Psalm 106:1   **6:7** [a]Literally *house*, and so in verses 8–10 rael, as the LORD promised; and I have built the temple for the name of the LORD God of Israel. [11]And there I have put the ark, in which *is* the covenant of the LORD which He made with the children of Israel."

SOLOMON'S PRAYER OF DEDICATION

[12]Then *Solomon*[a] stood before the altar of the LORD in the presence of all the assembly of Israel, and spread out his hands [13](for Solomon had made a bronze platform five cubits long, five cubits wide, and three cubits high, and had set it in the midst of the court; and he stood on it, knelt down on his knees before all the assembly of Israel, and spread out his hands toward heaven); [14]and he said: "LORD God of Israel, *there is* no God in heaven or on earth like You, who keep *Your* covenant and mercy with Your servants who walk before You with all their hearts. [15]You have kept what You promised Your servant David my father; You have both spoken with Your mouth and fulfilled *it* with Your hand, as *it is* this day. [16]Therefore, LORD God of Israel, now keep what You promised Your servant David my father, saying, 'You shall not fail to have a man sit before Me on the throne of Israel, only if your sons take heed to their way, that they walk in My law as you have walked before Me.' [17]And now, O LORD God of Israel, let Your word come true, which You have spoken to Your servant David.

[18]"But will God indeed dwell with men on the earth? Behold, heaven and the heaven of heavens cannot contain You. How much less this temple[a] which I have built! [19]Yet regard the prayer of Your servant and his supplication, O LORD my God, and listen to the cry and the prayer which Your servant is praying before You: [20]that Your eyes may be open toward this temple day and night, toward the place where *You* said *You would* put Your name, that You may hear the prayer which Your servant makes toward this place. [21]And may You hear the supplications of Your servant and of Your people Israel, when they pray toward this place. Hear from heaven Your dwelling place, and when You hear, forgive.

[22]"If anyone sins against his neighbor, and is forced to take an oath, and comes *and* takes an oath before Your altar in this temple, [23]then hear from heaven, and act, and judge Your servants, bringing retribution on the wicked by bringing his way on his own head, and justifying the righteous by giving him according to his righteousness.

[24]"Or if Your people Israel are defeated before an enemy because they have sinned against You, and return and confess Your name, and pray and make supplication before You in this temple, [25]then hear from heaven and forgive the sin of Your people Israel, and bring them back to the land which You gave to them and their fathers.

> **SIN**
> Do we really need to confess sin to God? (6:24)

[26]"When the heavens are shut up and there is no rain because they have sinned against You, when they pray toward this place and confess Your name, and turn from their sin because You afflict them, [27]then hear *in* heaven, and forgive the sin of Your servants, Your people Israel, that You may teach them the good way in which they should walk; and send rain on Your land which You have given to Your people as an inheritance.

[28]"When there is famine in the land, pestilence or blight or mildew, locusts or grasshoppers; when their enemies besiege them in the land of their cities; whatever plague or whatever sickness *there is;* [29]whatever prayer, whatever supplication is *made* by anyone, or by all Your people Israel, when each one knows his own burden and his own grief, and spreads out his hands to this temple: [30]then hear from heaven Your dwelling place, and forgive, and give to everyone according to all his ways, whose heart You know (for You alone know the hearts of the sons of men), [31]that they may fear You, to walk in Your ways as long as they live in the land which You gave to our fathers.

[32]"Moreover, concerning a foreigner, who is not of Your people Israel, but has come from a far country for the sake of Your great name and Your mighty hand and Your outstretched arm, when they come and pray in this temple; [33]then hear from heaven Your dwelling place, and do according to all for which the foreigner calls to

> "May You hear the supplications of Your servant and of Your people Israel, when they pray toward this place. . . . and when You hear, forgive."
> (2 Chronicles 6:21)

6:12 [a]Literally *he* (compare 1 Kings 8:22)   **6:18** [a]Literally *house*

You, that all peoples of the earth may know Your name and fear You, as *do* Your people Israel, and that they may know that this temple which I have built is called by Your name.

[34]"When Your people go out to battle against their enemies, wherever You send them, and when they pray to You toward this city which You have chosen and the temple which I have built for Your name, [35]then hear from heaven their prayer and their supplication, and maintain their cause.

WHAT'S IT MEAN?

Here's the story of two kingdoms. See if you can identify the reason for their radically different endings. In 722 B.C., the Assyrians captured the city of Samaria and took the ten tribes of the northern kingdom of Israel into captivity. There is no indication that any of those tribes ever returned to Israel. In 586 B.C., the Babylonians captured the city of Jerusalem and took the two tribes of the southern kingdom of Judah into captivity. While they were captives in Babylon, the people of Judah asked God to forgive their sins. Years later, they were allowed to return to Jerusalem and rebuild their temple.

2 Chronicles 6:36–39

[36]"When they sin against You (for *there is* no one who does not sin), and You become angry with them and deliver them to the enemy, and they take them captive to a land far or near; [37]yet when they come to themselves in the land where they were carried captive, and repent, and make supplication to You in the land of their captivity, saying, 'We have sinned, we have done wrong, and have committed wickedness'; [38]and *when* they return to You with all their heart and with all their soul in the land of their captivity, where they have been carried captive, and pray toward their land which You gave to their fathers, the city which You have chosen, and toward the temple which I have built for Your name: [39]then hear from heaven Your dwelling place their prayer and their supplications, and maintain their cause, and forgive Your people who have sinned against You.

[40]Now, my God, I pray, let Your eyes be open and *let* Your ears *be* attentive to the prayer *made* in this place.

[41] "Now therefore,
      Arise, O LORD God, to Your resting place,
      You and the ark of Your strength.
      Let Your priests, O LORD God, be clothed
         with salvation,
      And let Your saints rejoice in goodness.

[42] "O LORD God, do not turn away the face
         of Your Anointed;
      Remember the mercies of Your servant
         David."[a]

SOLOMON DEDICATES THE TEMPLE

[1]When Solomon had finished praying, fire came down from heaven and consumed the burnt offering and the sacrifices; and the glory of the LORD filled the temple.[a] [2]And the priests could not enter the house of the LORD, because the glory of the LORD had filled the LORD's house. [3]When all the children of Israel saw how the fire came down, and the glory of the LORD on the temple, they bowed their faces to the ground on the pavement, and worshiped and praised the LORD, *saying:*

   "For *He is* good,
   For His mercy *endures* forever."[a]

[4]Then the king and all the people offered sacrifices before the LORD. [5]King Solomon offered a sacrifice of twenty-two thousand bulls and one hundred and twenty thousand sheep. So the king and all the people dedicated the house of God. [6]And the priests attended to their services; the Levites also with instruments of the music of the LORD, which King David had made to praise the LORD, saying, "For His mercy *endures* forever,"[a] whenever David offered praise by their ministry. The priests sounded trumpets opposite them, while all Israel stood.

[7]Furthermore Solomon consecrated the middle of the court that *was* in front of the house of the LORD; for there he offered burnt offerings and the fat of the peace offerings, because the bronze altar which Solomon had made was not able to receive the burnt offerings, the grain offerings, and the fat.

[8]At that time Solomon kept the feast seven days, and all Israel with him, a very great assembly from the entrance of Hamath to the

6:42 [a]Compare Psalm 132:8–10   **7:1** [a]Literally *house*   **7:3** [a]Compare Psalm 106:1   **7:6** [a]Compare Psalm 106:1

Brook of Egypt.*[a]* [9]And on the eighth day they held a sacred assembly, for they observed the dedication of the altar seven days, and the feast seven days. [10]On the twenty-third day of the seventh month he sent the people away to their tents, joyful and glad of heart for the good that the LORD had done for David, for Solomon, and for His people Israel. [11]Thus Solomon finished the house of the LORD and the king's house; and Solomon successfully accomplished all that came into his heart to make in the house of the LORD and in his own house.

WHAT'S IT MEAN?

Where were all of these people coming from? The Brook of Egypt was the southern and western border of Israel and Egypt. Hamath was the northern border of Israel—what we call Lebanon today. People poured in from all directions to celebrate the completion of the temple in Jerusalem and, most importantly, to worship God in the new facility.

2 Chronicles 7:8

GOD'S SECOND APPEARANCE TO SOLOMON

[12]Then the LORD appeared to Solomon by night, and said to him: "I have heard your prayer, and have chosen this place for Myself as a house of sacrifice. [13]When I shut up heaven and there is no rain, or command the locusts to devour the land, or send pestilence among My people, [14]if My people who are called by My name will humble themselves, and pray and seek My face, and turn from their wicked ways, then I will hear from heaven, and will forgive their sin and heal their land. [15]Now My eyes will be open and My ears attentive to prayer *made* in this place. [16]For now I have chosen and sanctified this house, that My name may be there forever; and My eyes and My heart will be there perpetually. [17]As for you, if you walk before Me as your father David walked, and do according to all that I have commanded you, and if you keep My statutes

SUCCESS

How should we pray to obtain success? (7:14)

and My judgments, [18]then I will establish the throne of your kingdom, as I covenanted with David your father, saying, 'You shall not fail *to have* a man as ruler in Israel.'

[19]"But if you turn away and forsake My statutes and My commandments which I have set before you, and go and serve other gods, and worship them, [20]then I will uproot them from My land which I have given them; and this house which I have sanctified for My name I will cast out of My sight, and will make it a proverb and a byword among all peoples.

[21]"And *as for* this house, which is exalted, everyone who passes by it will be astonished and say, 'Why has the LORD done thus to this land and this house?' [22]Then they will answer, 'Because they forsook the LORD God of their fathers, who brought them out of the land of Egypt, and embraced other gods, and worshiped them and served them; therefore He has brought all this calamity on them.'"

FOLLOWING GOD

Does God put conditions on our obedience? (7:17)

SOLOMON'S ADDITIONAL ACHIEVEMENTS

[1]It came to pass at the end of twenty years, when Solomon had built the house of the LORD and his own house, [2]that the cities which Hiram*[a]* had given to Solomon, Solomon built them; and he settled the children of Israel there. [3]And Solomon went to Hamath Zobah and seized it. [4]He also built Tadmor in the wilderness, and all the storage cities which he built in Hamath. [5]He built Upper Beth Horon and Lower Beth Horon, fortified cities *with* walls, gates, and bars, [6]also Baalath and all the storage cities that Solomon had, and all the chariot cities and the cities of the cavalry, and all that Solomon desired to build in Jerusalem, in Lebanon, and in all the land of his dominion.

[7]All the people *who were* left of the Hittites, Amorites, Perizzites, Hivites, and Jebusites, who *were* not of Israel—[8]that is, their descendants who were left in the land after them, whom the children of Israel did not destroy—from these Solomon raised forced labor, as it is to this day. [9]But Solomon did not make the children of Israel servants for his work. Some *were* men of war, captains of his officers, captains of his chariots, and his cavalry. [10]And others *were* chiefs of the officials of King Solomon: two hundred and fifty, who ruled over the people. [11]Now Solomon brought the daughter of

7:8 *[a]*That is, the Shihor (compare 1 Chronicles 13:5) **8:2** *[a]*Hebrew *Huram* (compare 2 Chronicles 2:3)

Pharaoh up from the City of David to the house he had built for her, for he said, "My wife shall not dwell in the house of David king of Israel, because *the places* to which the ark of the LORD has come are holy."

Here we see the two sides of Solomon's personality. For whatever reason, he wanted to marry the Pharaoh's daughter, so he did—not caring that the Lord had forbidden Israelites from marrying foreigners. At the same time, though, he cared so much about the holiness of God's temple that he moved his new wife to another house so that her idol worship wouldn't cause problems.

2 Chronicles 8:11

¹²Then Solomon offered burnt offerings to the LORD on the altar of the LORD which he had built before the vestibule, ¹³according to the daily rate, offering according to the commandment of Moses, for the Sabbaths, the New Moons, and the three appointed yearly feasts—the Feast of Unleavened Bread, the Feast of Weeks, and the Feast of Tabernacles. ¹⁴And, according to the order of David his father, he appointed the divisions of the priests for their service, the Levites for their duties (to praise and serve before the priests) as the duty of each day required, and the gatekeepers by their divisions at each gate; for so David the man of God had commanded. ¹⁵They did not depart from the command of the king to the priests and Levites concerning any matter or concerning the treasuries.

¹⁶Now all the work of Solomon was well-ordered from[a] the day of the foundation of the house of the LORD until it was finished. So the house of the LORD was completed.

¹⁷Then Solomon went to Ezion Geber and Elath[a] on the seacoast, in the land of Edom. ¹⁸And Hiram sent him ships by the hand of his servants, and servants who knew the sea. They went with the servants of Solomon to Ophir, and acquired four hundred and fifty talents of gold from there, and brought it to King Solomon.

THE QUEEN OF SHEBA'S PRAISE OF SOLOMON

¹Now when the queen of Sheba heard of the fame of Solomon, she came to Jerusalem to test Solomon with hard questions, *having* a very great retinue, camels that bore spices, gold in abundance, and precious stones; and when she came to Solomon, she spoke with him about all that was in her heart. ²So Solomon answered all her questions; there was nothing so difficult for Solomon that he could not explain it to her. ³And when the queen of Sheba had seen the wisdom of Solomon, the house that he had built, ⁴the food on his table, the seating of his servants, the service of his waiters and their apparel, his cupbearers and their apparel, and his entryway by which he went up to the house of the LORD, there was no more spirit in her.

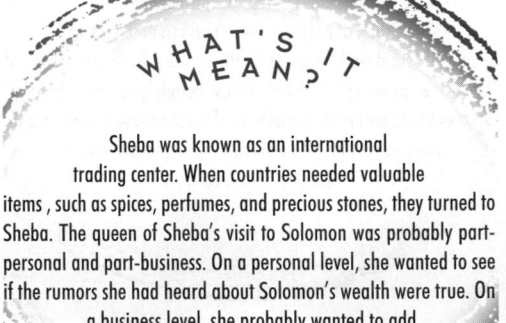

Sheba was known as an international trading center. When countries needed valuable items, such as spices, perfumes, and precious stones, they turned to Sheba. The queen of Sheba's visit to Solomon was probably part-personal and part-business. On a personal level, she wanted to see if the rumors she had heard about Solomon's wealth were true. On a business level, she probably wanted to add Solomon and Israel to her list of clients.

2 Chronicles 9:1

⁵Then she said to the king: "*It was* a true report which I heard in my own land about your words and your wisdom. ⁶However I did not believe their words until I came and saw with my own eyes; and indeed the half of the greatness of your wisdom was not told me. You exceed the fame of which I heard. ⁷Happy *are* your men and happy *are* these your servants, who stand continually before you and hear your wisdom! ⁸Blessed be the LORD your God, who delighted in you, setting you on His throne *to be* king for the LORD your God! Because your God has loved Israel, to establish them forever, therefore He made you king over them, to do justice and righteousness."

⁹And she gave the king one hundred and twenty talents of gold, spices in great abun-

8:16 [a]Following Septuagint, Syriac, and Vulgate; Masoretic Text reads *as far as.*   **8:17** [a]Hebrew *Eloth* (compare 2 Kings 14:22) dance, and precious stones; there never were any spices such as those the queen of Sheba gave to King Solomon.

[10]Also, the servants of Hiram and the servants of Solomon, who brought gold from Ophir, brought algum[a] wood and precious stones. [11]And the king made walkways *of the* algum[a] wood for the house of the LORD and for the king's house, also harps and stringed instruments for singers; and there were none such *as these* seen before in the land of Judah.

[12]Now King Solomon gave to the queen of Sheba all she desired, whatever she asked, *much more* than she had brought to the king. So she turned and went to her own country, she and her servants.

SOLOMON'S GREAT WEALTH

[13]The weight of gold that came to Solomon yearly was six hundred and sixty-six talents of gold, [14]besides *what* the traveling merchants and traders brought. And all the kings of Arabia and governors of the country brought gold and silver to Solomon. [15]And King Solomon made two hundred large shields of hammered gold; six hundred *shekels* of hammered gold went into each shield. [16]*He also made* three hundred shields of hammered gold; three hundred *shekels*[a] of gold went into each shield. The king put them in the House of the Forest of Lebanon.

[17]Moreover the king made a great throne of ivory, and overlaid it with pure gold. [18]The throne *had* six steps, with a footstool of gold, *which were* fastened to the throne; there were armrests on either side of the place of the seat, and two lions stood beside the armrests. [19]Twelve lions stood there, one on each side of the six steps; nothing like *this* had been made for any *other* kingdom.

[20]All King Solomon's drinking vessels *were* gold, and all the vessels of the House of the Forest of Lebanon *were* pure gold. Not *one was* silver, for this was accounted as nothing in the days of Solomon. [21]For the king's ships went to Tarshish with the servants of Hiram.[a] Once every three years the merchant ships[b] came, bringing gold, silver, ivory, apes, and monkeys.[c]

[22]So King Solomon surpassed all the kings of the earth in riches and wisdom. [23]And all the kings of the earth sought the presence of Solomon to hear his wisdom, which God had put in his heart. [24]Each man brought his present: articles of silver and gold, garments, armor,

spices, horses, and mules, at a set rate year by year.

[25]Solomon had four thousand stalls for horses and chariots, and twelve thousand horsemen whom he stationed in the chariot cities and with the king at Jerusalem.

[26]So he reigned over all the kings from the River[a] to the land of the Philistines, as far as the border of Egypt. [27]The king made silver *as common* in Jerusalem as stones, and he made cedar trees as abundant as the sycamores which *are* in the lowland. [28]And they brought horses to Solomon from Egypt and from all lands.

DEATH OF SOLOMON

[29]Now the rest of the acts of Solomon, first and last, *are* they not written in the book of Nathan the prophet, in the prophecy of Ahijah the Shilonite, and in the visions of Iddo the seer concerning Jeroboam the son of Nebat? [30]Solomon reigned in Jerusalem over all Israel forty years. [31]Then Solomon rested with his fathers, and was buried in the City of David his father. And Rehoboam his son reigned in his place.

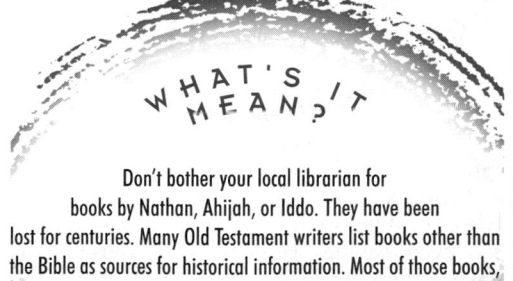

WHAT'S IT MEAN?

Don't bother your local librarian for books by Nathan, Ahijah, or Iddo. They have been lost for centuries. Many Old Testament writers list books other than the Bible as sources for historical information. Most of those books, however, have been lost to history.

2 Chronicles 9:29

THE REVOLT AGAINST REHOBOAM

[1]And Rehoboam went to Shechem, for all Israel had gone to Shechem to make him king. [2]So it happened, when Jeroboam the son of Nebat heard *it* (he was in Egypt, where he had fled from the presence of King Solomon), that Jeroboam returned from Egypt. [3]Then they sent for him

FRIENDSHIP

How can friends pull you down? (10:1–14)

and called him. And Jeroboam and all Israel came and spoke to Rehoboam, saying, [4]"Your father made our yoke heavy; now therefore, lighten the burdensome service of your father and his heavy yoke which he put on us, and we will serve you."

WHAT'S IT MEAN?

Talk about being put in an awkward position! While Jeroboam was serving as a chief advisor to King Solomon, the prophet Ahijah told him that God was angry with Solomon for worshiping foreign gods. As a result, Solomon's kingdom was going to be torn apart. To demonstrate what was going to happen, Ahijah tore his coat into twelve pieces and gave ten of them to Jeroboam. He explained that Jeroboam would be given ten of the tribes of Israel to rule over. As you might imagine, Solomon was furious when he heard that his own advisor was going to replace him as king. Solomon was so furious, in fact, that he tried to kill Jeroboam. Jeroboam escaped and did not return to the kingdom until after Solomon's death.

2 Chronicles 10:2

[5]So he said to them, "Come back to me after three days." And the people departed.

[6]Then King Rehoboam consulted the elders who stood before his father Solomon while he still lived, saying, "How do you advise *me* to answer these people?"

[7]And they spoke to him, saying, "If you are kind to these people, and please them, and speak good words to them, they will be your servants forever."

[8]But he rejected the advice which the elders had given him, and consulted the young men who had grown up with him, who stood before him. [9]And he said to them, "What advice do you give? How should we answer this people who have spoken to me, saying, 'Lighten the yoke which your father put on us'?"

[10]Then the young men who had grown up with him spoke to him, saying, "Thus you should speak to the people who have spoken to you, saying, 'Your father made our yoke heavy, but you make *it* lighter on us'—thus you shall say to them: 'My little *finger* shall be thicker than my father's waist! [11]And now, whereas my father put a heavy yoke on you, I will add to your yoke; my father chastised you with whips, but I *will chastise you* with scourges!' "[a]

[12]So Jeroboam and all the people came to Rehoboam on the third day, as the king had directed, saying, "Come back to me the third day." [13]Then the king answered them roughly. King Rehoboam rejected the advice of the elders, [14]and he spoke to them according to the advice of the young men, saying, "My father[a] made your yoke heavy, but I will add to it; my father chastised you with whips, but I *will chastise you* with scourges!"[b] [15]So the king did not listen to the people; for the turn *of events* was from God, that the LORD might fulfill His word, which He had spoken by the hand of Ahijah the Shilonite to Jeroboam the son of Nebat.

[16]Now when all Israel *saw* that the king did not listen to them, the people answered the king, saying:

"What share have we in David?
  We have no inheritance in the son of Jesse.
  Every man to your tents, O Israel!
  Now see to your own house, O David!"

So all Israel departed to their tents. [17]But Rehoboam reigned over the children of Israel who dwelt in the cities of Judah.

[18]Then King Rehoboam sent Hadoram, who *was* in charge of revenue; but the children of Israel stoned him with stones, and he died. Therefore King Rehoboam mounted *his* chariot in haste to flee to Jerusalem. [19]So Israel has been in rebellion against the house of David to this day.

[1]Now when Rehoboam came to Jerusalem, he assembled from the house of Judah and Benjamin one hundred and eighty thousand chosen *men* who were warriors, to fight against Israel, that he might restore the kingdom to Rehoboam.

[2]But the word of the LORD came to Shemaiah the man of God, saying, [3]"Speak to Rehoboam the son of Solomon, king of Judah, and to all Israel in Judah and Benjamin, saying, [4]Thus says the LORD: 'You shall not go up or fight against your brethren! Let every man return to his house, for this thing is from Me.' ' " Therefore they obeyed the words of the LORD, and turned back from attacking Jeroboam.

REHOBOAM FORTIFIES THE CITIES

[5]So Rehoboam dwelt in Jerusalem, and built cities for defense in Judah. [6]And he built Bethle-

---

10:11 [a]Literally *scorpions*   **10:14** [a]Following many Hebrew manuscripts, Septuagint, Syriac, and Vulgate (compare verse 10 and 1 Kings 12:14); Masoretic Text reads I. [b]Literally *scorpions* hem, Etam, Tekoa, [7]Beth Zur, Sochoh, Adullam, [8]Gath, Mareshah, Ziph, [9]Adoraim, Lachish, Azekah, [10]Zorah, Aijalon, and Hebron, which are in Judah and Benjamin, fortified cities. [11]And he fortified the strongholds, and put captains in them, and stores of food, oil, and wine. [12]Also in every city *he put* shields and spears, and made them very strong, having Judah and Benjamin on his side.

Jeroboam was afraid that if the people returned to Jerusalem to worship God, he would lose his control over them. To keep them away from Jerusalem, Jeroboam made two golden idols in the shape of calves for the people to worship in Bethel and Dan. As if that weren't enough, Jeroboam appointed priests who were not from the tribe of Levi—another no-no, as far as God was concerned.

2 Chronicles 11:15

PRIESTS AND LEVITES MOVE TO JUDAH

[13]And from all their territories the priests and the Levites who *were* in all Israel took their stand with him. [14]For the Levites left their commonlands and their possessions and came to Judah and Jerusalem, for Jeroboam and his sons had rejected them from serving as priests to the LORD. [15]Then he appointed for himself priests for the high places, for the demons, and the calf idols which he had made. [16]And after *the Levites left,[a]* those from all the tribes of Israel, such as set their heart to seek the LORD God of Israel, came to Jerusalem to sacrifice to the LORD God of their fathers. [17]So they strengthened the kingdom of Judah, and made Rehoboam the son of Solomon strong for three years, because they

walked in the way of David and Solomon for three years.

THE FAMILY OF REHOBOAM

[18]Then Rehoboam took for himself as wife Mahalath the daughter of Jerimoth the son of David, *and of* Abihail the daughter of Eliah the son of Jesse. [19]And she bore him children: Jeush, Shamariah, and Zaham. [20]After her he took Maachah the granddaughter[a] of Absalom; and she bore him Abijah, Attai, Ziza, and Shelomith. [21]Now Rehoboam loved Maachah the granddaughter of Absalom more than all his wives and his concubines; for he took eighteen wives and sixty concubines, and begot twenty-eight sons and sixty daughters. [22]And Rehoboam appointed Abijah the son of Maachah as chief, *to be* leader among his brothers; for he *intended* to make him king. [23]He dealt wisely, and dispersed some of his sons throughout all the territories of Judah and Benjamin, to every fortified city; and he gave them provisions in abundance. He also sought many wives *for them.*

EGYPT ATTACKS JUDAH

[1]Now it came to pass, when Rehoboam had established the kingdom and had strengthened himself, that he forsook the law of the LORD, and all Israel along with him. [2]And it happened in the fifth year of King Rehoboam *that* Shishak king of Egypt came up against Jerusalem, because they had transgressed against the LORD, [3]with twelve hundred chariots, sixty thousand horsemen, and people without number who came with him out of Egypt—the Lubim and the Sukkiim and the Ethiopians. [4]And he took the fortified cities of Judah and came to Jerusalem.

[5]Then Shemaiah the prophet came to Rehoboam and the leaders of Judah, who were gathered together in Jerusalem because of Shishak, and said to them, "Thus says the LORD: 'You have forsaken Me, and therefore I also have left you in the hand of Shishak.' "

SUCCESS

When can success be bad for us? (12:1)

"So they strengthened the kingdom of Judah, and made Rehoboam the son of Solomon strong for three years, because they walked in the way of David and Solomon for three years." (2 Chronicles 11:17)

11:16 [a]Literally *after them*   **11:20** [a]Literally *daughter,* but in the broader sense of granddaughter (compare 2 Chronicles 13:2)

⁶So the leaders of Israel and the king humbled themselves; and they said, "The LORD *is* righteous."

⁷Now when the LORD saw that they humbled themselves, the word of the LORD came to Shemaiah, saying, "They have humbled themselves; *therefore* I will not destroy them, but I will grant them some deliverance. My wrath shall not be poured out on Jerusalem by the hand of Shishak. ⁸Nevertheless they will be his servants, that they may distinguish My service from the service of the kingdoms of the nations."

⁹So Shishak king of Egypt came up against Jerusalem, and took away the treasures of the house of the LORD and the treasures of the king's house; he took everything. He also carried away the gold shields which Solomon had made. ¹⁰Then King Rehoboam made bronze shields in their place, and committed *them* to the hands of the captains of the guard, who guarded the doorway of the king's house. ¹¹And whenever the king entered the house of the LORD, the guard would go and bring them out; then they would take them back into the guardroom. ¹²When he humbled himself, the wrath of the LORD turned from him, so as not to destroy *him* completely; and things also went well in Judah.

THE END OF REHOBOAM'S REIGN

¹³Thus King Rehoboam strengthened himself in Jerusalem and reigned. Now Rehoboam *was* forty-one years old when he became king; and he reigned seventeen years in Jerusalem, the city which the LORD had chosen out of all the tribes of Israel, to put His name there. His mother's name *was* Naamah, an Ammonitess. ¹⁴And he did evil, because he did not prepare his heart to seek the LORD.

¹⁵The acts of Rehoboam, first and last, *are* they not written in the book of Shemaiah the prophet, and of Iddo the seer concerning genealogies? And *there were* wars between Rehoboam and Jeroboam all their days. ¹⁶So Rehoboam rested with his fathers, and was buried in the City of David. Then Abijah*ᵃ* his son reigned in his place.

ABIJAH REIGNS IN JUDAH

¹In the eighteenth year of King Jeroboam, Abijah became king over Judah. ²He reigned three years in Jerusalem. His mother's name *was* Michaiah*ᵃ* the daughter of Uriel of Gibeah.

And there was war between Abijah and Jeroboam. ³Abijah set the battle in order with an army of valiant warriors, four hundred thousand choice men. Jeroboam also drew up in battle formation against him with eight hundred thousand choice men, mighty men of valor.

⁴Then Abijah stood on Mount Zemaraim, which *is* in the mountains of Ephraim, and said, "Hear me, Jeroboam and all Israel: ⁵Should you not know that the LORD God of Israel gave the dominion over Israel to David forever, to him and his sons, by a covenant of salt? ⁶Yet Jeroboam the son of Nebat, the servant of Solomon the son of David, rose up and rebelled against his lord. ⁷Then worthless rogues gathered to him, and strengthened themselves against Rehoboam the son of Solomon, when Rehoboam was young and inexperienced and could not withstand them. ⁸And now you think to withstand the kingdom of the LORD, which is in the hand of the sons of David; and you *are* a great multitude, and with you are the gold calves which Jeroboam made for you as gods. ⁹Have you not cast out the priests of the LORD, the sons of Aaron, and the Levites, and made for yourselves priests, like the peoples of *other* lands, so that whoever comes to consecrate himself with a young bull and seven rams may be a priest of *things that are* not gods? ¹⁰But as for us, the LORD *is* our God, and we have not forsaken Him; and the priests who minister to the LORD *are* the sons of Aaron, and the Levites *attend* to *their* duties. ¹¹And they burn to the LORD every morning and every evening burnt sacrifices and sweet incense; *they* also *set* the showbread *in order on* the pure *gold* table, and the lampstand of gold with its lamps to burn every evening; for we keep the command of the LORD our God, but you have forsaken Him. ¹²Now look, God Himself is with us as *our* head, and His priests with sounding trumpets to sound the alarm against you. O children of Israel, do not fight against the LORD God of your fathers, for you shall not prosper!"

¹³But Jeroboam caused an ambush to go around behind them; so they were in front of Judah, and the ambush *was* behind them. ¹⁴And when Judah looked around, to their surprise the battle line *was* at both front and rear; and they cried out to the LORD, and the priests sounded the trumpets. ¹⁵Then the men of Judah gave a shout; and as the men of Judah shouted, it happened that God struck Jeroboam and all Israel before Abijah and Judah. ¹⁶And the children of Israel fled before Judah, and God delivered them into their hand. ¹⁷Then Abijah and his people struck them with a great slaughter;

12:16 *ᵃ*Spelled *Abijam* in 1 Kings 14:31　　**13:2** *ᵃ*Spelled *Maachah* in 11:20, 21 and 1 Kings 15:2

so five hundred thousand choice men of Israel fell slain. [18]Thus the children of Israel were subdued at that time; and the children of Judah prevailed, because they relied on the LORD God of their fathers.

On the Edge

We keep the command of the LORD our God, but you have forsaken Him. Now look, God Himself is with us as our head, and His priests with sounding trumpets to sound the alarm against you (2 Chr. 13:11, 12).

Remember choosing sides for kickball in the third grade? Whether you were the captain of the team or the last one chosen, it was always a huge relief to be on the team with the best kicker. Victory was sure. You could breathe easy—the best players were on your team. A win was in sight.

Well, you can take another deep breath and relax—God is with you, on your side, for life. He wants you to show up for the games, bring your best attitude, be committed to the coach, and play your heart out. The rest is up to Him. He will carry the whole team. Your victory has already been decided. It's a sure thing. You've been warming up long enough; it's time to get in the game. Go for it!

SEE FOR YOURSELF:
2 Chr. 32:8;
Ps. 118:5–9; Zech. 10:5

[19]And Abijah pursued Jeroboam and took cities from him: Bethel with its villages, Jeshanah with its villages, and Ephrain[a] with its villages. [20]So Jeroboam did not recover strength again in the days of Abijah; and the LORD struck him, and he died. [21]But Abijah grew mighty, married fourteen wives, and begot twenty-two sons and sixteen daughters. [22]Now the rest of the acts of Abijah, his ways, and his sayings *are* written in the annals of the prophet Iddo.

[1]So Abijah rested with his fathers, and they buried him in the City of David. Then Asa his son reigned in his place. In his days the land was quiet for ten years.

ASA REIGNS IN JUDAH

[2]Asa did *what was* good and right in the eyes of the LORD his God, [3]for he removed the altars of the foreign *gods* and the high places, and broke down the *sacred* pillars and cut down the wooden images. [4]He commanded Judah to seek the LORD God of their fathers, and to observe the law and the commandment. [5]He also removed the high places and the incense altars from all the cities of Judah, and the kingdom was quiet under him. [6]And he built fortified cities in Judah, for the land had rest; he had no war in those years, because the LORD had given him rest. [7]Therefore he said to Judah, "Let us build these cities and make walls around *them,* and towers, gates, and bars, *while* the land *is* yet before us, because we have sought the LORD our God; we have sought *Him,* and He has given us rest on every side." So they built and prospered. [8]And Asa had an army of three hundred thousand from Judah who carried shields and spears, and from Benjamin two hundred and eighty thousand men who carried shields and drew bows; all these *were* mighty men of valor.

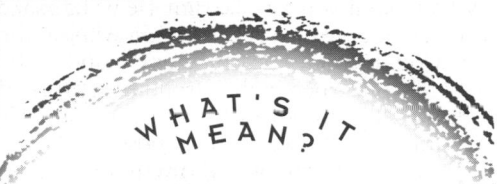

WHAT'S IT MEAN?

In ancient times, Ethiopia was the area beyond the southern part of Egypt. The country was controlled by Egypt until after David's death. The Egyptians often hired Ethiopians to fight on their side in times of war. Very little is known about the battle between Zerah's Ethiopian army and Judah's army, except that Judah was quite the underdog.

2 Chronicles 14:9

[9]Then Zerah the Ethiopian came out against them with an army of a million men and three hundred chariots, and he came to Mareshah. [10]So Asa went out against him, and they set the troops in battle array in the Valley of Zephathah at Mareshah. [11]And Asa cried out to the LORD his God, and said, "LORD, *it is* nothing for You to help, whether with many or with those who have

TRIALS

Where can we find rest? (14:11)

13:19 [a]Or *Ephron*

no power; help us, O LORD our God, for we rest on You, and in Your name we go against this multitude. O LORD, You *are* our God; do not let man prevail against You!"

[12]So the LORD struck the Ethiopians before Asa and Judah, and the Ethiopians fled. [13]And Asa and the people who *were* with him pursued them to Gerar. So the Ethiopians were overthrown, and they could not recover, for they were broken before the LORD and His army. And they carried away very much spoil. [14]Then they defeated all the cities around Gerar, for the fear of the LORD came upon them; and they plundered all the cities, for there was exceedingly much spoil in them. [15]They also attacked the livestock enclosures, and carried off sheep and camels in abundance, and returned to Jerusalem.

THE REFORMS OF ASA

[1]Now the Spirit of God came upon Azariah the son of Oded. [2]And he went out to meet Asa, and said to him: "Hear me, Asa, and all Judah and Benjamin. The LORD *is* with you while you are with Him. If you seek Him, He will be found by you; but if you forsake Him, He will forsake you. [3]For a long time Israel *has been* without the true God, without a teaching priest, and without law; [4]but when in their trouble they turned to the LORD God of Israel, and sought Him, He was found by them. [5]And in those times *there was* no peace to the one who went out, nor to the one who came in, but great turmoil *was* on all the inhabitants of the lands. [6]So nation was destroyed by nation, and city by city, for God troubled them with every adversity. [7]But you, be strong and do not let your hands be weak, for your work shall be rewarded!"

[8]And when Asa heard these words and the prophecy of Oded[a] the prophet, he took courage, and removed the abominable idols from all the land of Judah and Benjamin and from the cities which he had taken in the mountains of Ephraim; and he restored the altar of the LORD that *was* before the vestibule of the LORD. [9]Then he gathered all Judah and Benjamin, and those who dwelt with them from Ephraim, Manasseh, and Simeon, for they came over to him in great numbers from Israel when they saw that the LORD his God was with him.

[10]So they gathered together at Jerusalem in the third month, in the fifteenth year of the reign of Asa. [11]And they offered to the LORD at that time seven hundred bulls and seven thousand sheep from the spoil they had brought. [12]Then they entered into a covenant to seek the LORD God of their fathers with all their heart and with all their soul; [13]and whoever would not seek the LORD God of Israel was to be put to death, whether small or great, whether man or woman. [14]Then they took an oath before the LORD with a loud voice, with shouting and trumpets and rams' horns. [15]And all Judah rejoiced at the oath, for they had sworn with all their heart and sought Him with all their soul; and He was found by them, and the LORD gave them rest all around.

[16]Also he removed Maachah, the mother of Asa the king, from *being* queen mother, because she had made an obscene image of Asherah;[a] and Asa cut down her obscene image, then crushed and burned *it* by the Brook Kidron. [17]But the high places were not removed from Israel. Nevertheless the heart of Asa was loyal all his days.

FOLLOWING GOD
How should we follow God? (15:15)

WHAT'S IT MEAN?
The Israelites had adopted several different Canaanite gods and goddesses as their own. Asherah, though, was one of their favorites. Shrines to Asherah were scattered throughout the land, especially on hilltops and in groves of trees. The shrines were easy to spot because they were marked by carved wooden poles.
2 Chronicles 15:16, 17

[18]He also brought into the house of God the things that his father had dedicated and that he himself had dedicated: silver and gold and utensils. [19]And there was no war until the thirty-fifth year of the reign of Asa.

ASA'S TREATY WITH SYRIA

[1]In the thirty-sixth year of the reign of Asa, Baasha king of Israel came up against Judah and built Ramah, that he might let none go out or come in to Asa king of Judah. [2]Then Asa brought silver and gold from the treasuries of

---

15:8 [a]Following Masoretic Text and Septuagint; Syriac and Vulgate read *Azariah the son of Oded* (compare verse 1).   **15:16** [a]A Canaanite deity the house of the LORD and of the king's house, and sent to Ben-Hadad king of Syria, who dwelt in Damascus, saying, ³"Let there be a treaty between you and me, as there was between my father and your father. See, I have sent you silver and gold; come, break your treaty with Baasha king of Israel, so that he will withdraw from me."

⁴So Ben-Hadad heeded King Asa, and sent the captains of his armies against the cities of Israel. They attacked Ijon, Dan, Abel Maim, and all the storage cities of Naphtali. ⁵Now it happened, when Baasha heard it, that he stopped building Ramah and ceased his work. ⁶Then King Asa took all Judah, and they carried away the stones and timber of Ramah, which Baasha had used for building; and with them he built Geba and Mizpah.

HANANI'S MESSAGE TO ASA

⁷And at that time Hanani the seer came to Asa king of Judah, and said to him: "Because you have relied on the king of Syria, and have not relied on the LORD your God, therefore the army of the king of Syria has escaped from your hand. ⁸Were the Ethiopians and the Lubim not a huge army with very many chariots and horsemen? Yet, because you relied on the LORD, He delivered them into your hand. ⁹For the eyes of the LORD run to and fro throughout the whole earth, to show Himself strong on behalf of those whose heart is loyal to Him. In this you have done foolishly; therefore from now on you shall have wars." ¹⁰Then Asa was angry

with the seer, and put him in prison, for he was enraged at him because of this. And Asa oppressed some of the people at that time.

ILLNESS AND DEATH OF ASA

¹¹Note that the acts of Asa, first and last, are indeed written in the book of the kings of Judah and Israel. ¹²And in the thirty-ninth year of his reign, Asa became diseased in his feet, and his malady was severe; yet in his disease he did not seek the LORD, but the physicians.

¹³So Asa rested with his fathers; he died in the forty-first year of his reign. ¹⁴They buried him in his own tomb, which he had made for himself in the City of David; and they laid him in the bed which was filled with spices and various ingredients prepared in a mixture of ointments. They made a very great burning for him.

JEHOSHAPHAT REIGNS IN JUDAH

¹Then Jehoshaphat his son reigned in his place, and strengthened himself against Israel. ²And he placed troops in all the fortified cities of Judah, and set garrisons in the land of Judah and in the cities of Ephraim which Asa his father had taken. ³Now the LORD was with Jehoshaphat, because he walked in the former ways of his father David; he did not seek the Baals, ⁴but sought the God[a] of his father, and walked in His commandments and not according to the acts of Israel. ⁵Therefore the LORD established the kingdom in his hand; and all Judah gave presents to Jehoshaphat, and he had riches and honor in abundance. ⁶And his

17:4 ªSeptuagint reads LORD God.

⁖ Promise   HE PROMISES TO KEEP AN EYE ON YOU CONSTANTLY.

For the eyes of the LORD run to and fro throughout the whole earth, to show Himself strong on behalf of those whose heart is loyal to Him (2 Chr. 16:9).

God watches you constantly. He's not peering down from heaven so He can whack you on the head when you blow it, but to give an extra measure of strength to people who are being faithful. He gives strength and support to those who are obedient—to those whose hearts belong to Him. If you've ever tried to be obedient, you know that most of the time it takes more courage to do the right thing than to follow the crowd. He promises to see you and your efforts. He will make your weak knees strong. He will give your voice power and authority. He will sense your fear and cast it out. Your job is to be faithful. God promises to never miss a thing.

SEE FOR YOURSELF:
Ps. 34:15; 139:1–6; 1 Pet. 3:12

heart took delight in the ways of the LORD; moreover he removed the high places and wooden images from Judah.

⁷Also in the third year of his reign he sent his leaders, Ben-Hail, Obadiah, Zechariah, Nethanel, and Michaiah, to teach in the cities of Judah. ⁸And with them *he sent* Levites: Shemaiah, Nethaniah, Zebadiah, Asahel, Shemiramoth, Jehonathan, Adonijah, Tobijah, and Tobadonijah—the Levites; and with them Elishama and Jehoram, the priests. ⁹So they taught in Judah, and *had* the Book of the Law of the LORD with them; they went throughout all the cities of Judah and taught the people.

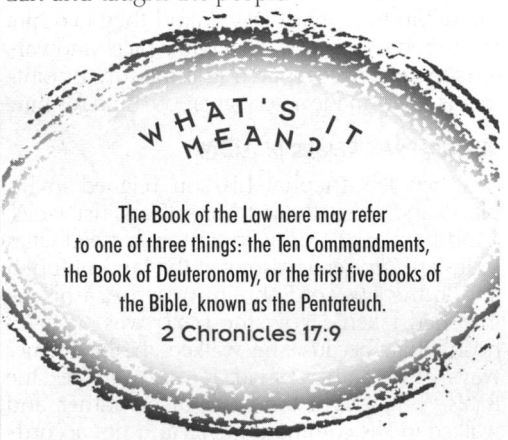

The Book of the Law here may refer
to one of three things: the Ten Commandments,
the Book of Deuteronomy, or the first five books of
the Bible, known as the Pentateuch.
2 Chronicles 17:9

¹⁰And the fear of the LORD fell on all the kingdoms of the lands that *were* around Judah, so that they did not make war against Jehoshaphat. ¹¹Also *some* of the Philistines brought Jehoshaphat presents and silver as tribute; and the Arabians brought him flocks, seven thousand seven hundred rams and seven thousand seven hundred male goats.

¹²So Jehoshaphat became increasingly powerful, and he built fortresses and storage cities in Judah. ¹³He had much property in the cities of Judah; and the men of war, mighty men of valor, *were* in Jerusalem.

¹⁴These *are* their numbers, according to their fathers' houses. Of Judah, the captains of thousands: Adnah the captain, and with him three hundred thousand mighty men of valor; ¹⁵and next to him *was* Jehohanan the captain, and with him two hundred and eighty thousand; ¹⁶and next to him *was* Amasiah the son of Zichri, who willingly offered himself to the LORD, and with him two hundred thousand mighty men of valor. ¹⁷Of Benjamin: Eliada a mighty man of valor, and with him two hundred thousand men armed with bow and

shield; ¹⁸and next to him *was* Jehozabad, and with him one hundred and eighty thousand prepared for war. ¹⁹These served the king, besides those the king put in the fortified cities throughout all Judah.

Ramoth Gilead was located
near the border of Israel and Syria, about fifty to
sixty miles from Samaria. Being that close to the border meant that
Ramoth Gilead had seen its share of battles between the two nations.
When the Israelites first arrived in Canaan, the city of Ramoth
Gilead was given to the tribe of Gad and was
declared a city of safety.
2 Chronicles 18:2

MICAIAH WARNS AHAB

¹Jehoshaphat had riches and honor in abundance; and by marriage he allied himself with Ahab. ²After some years he went down to *visit* Ahab in Samaria; and Ahab killed sheep and oxen in abundance for him and the people who were with him, and persuaded him to go up *with him* to Ramoth Gilead. ³So Ahab king of Israel said to Jehoshaphat king of Judah, "Will you go with me *against* Ramoth Gilead?"

And he answered him, "I *am* as you *are*, and my people as your people; *we will be* with you in the war."

⁴Also Jehoshaphat said to the king of Israel, "Please inquire for the word of the LORD today."

⁵Then the king of Israel gathered the prophets together, four hundred men, and said to them, "Shall we go to war against Ramoth Gilead, or shall I refrain?"

So they said, "Go up, for God will deliver it into the king's hand."

⁶But Jehoshaphat said, "*Is there* not still a prophet of the LORD here, that we may inquire of Him?"ᵃ

⁷So the king of Israel said to Jehoshaphat, "*There is* still one man by whom we may inquire of the LORD; but I hate him, because he never prophesies good concerning me, but always evil. He *is* Micaiah the son of Imla."

18:6 ᵃOr *him*

And Jehoshaphat said, "Let not the king say such things!"

⁸Then the king of Israel called one *of his* officers and said, "Bring Micaiah the son of Imla quickly!"

⁹The king of Israel and Jehoshaphat king of Judah, clothed in *their* robes, sat each on his throne; and they sat at a threshing floor at the entrance of the gate of Samaria; and all the prophets prophesied before them. ¹⁰Now Zedekiah the son of Chenaanah had made horns of iron for himself; and he said, "Thus says the LORD: 'With these you shall gore the Syrians until they are destroyed.' "

¹¹And all the prophets prophesied so, saying, "Go up to Ramoth Gilead and prosper, for the LORD will deliver *it* into the king's hand."

¹²Then the messenger who had gone to call Micaiah spoke to him, saying, "Now listen, the words of the prophets with one accord encourage the king. Therefore please let your word be like *the word of* one of them, and speak encouragement."

¹³And Micaiah said, "*As* the LORD lives, whatever my God says, that I will speak."

¹⁴Then he came to the king; and the king said to him, "Micaiah, shall we go to war against Ramoth Gilead, or shall I refrain?"

And he said, "Go and prosper, and they shall be delivered into your hand!"

¹⁵So the king said to him, "How many times shall I make you swear that you tell me nothing but the truth in the name of the LORD?"

¹⁶Then he said, "I saw all Israel scattered on the mountains, as sheep that have no shepherd. And the LORD said, 'These have no master. Let each return to his house in peace.' "

¹⁷And the king of Israel said to Jehoshaphat, "Did I not tell you he would not prophesy good concerning me, but evil?"

¹⁸Then *Micaiah* said, "Therefore hear the word of the LORD: I saw the LORD sitting on His throne, and all the host of heaven standing on His right hand and His left. ¹⁹And the LORD said, 'Who will persuade Ahab king of Israel to go up, that he may fall at Ramoth Gilead?' So one spoke in this manner, and another spoke in that manner. ²⁰Then a spirit came forward and stood before the LORD, and said, 'I will persuade him.' The LORD said to him, 'In what way?' ²¹So he said, 'I will go out and be a lying spirit in the mouth of all his prophets.' And *the* LORD said, 'You shall persuade *him* and also prevail; go out and do so.' ²²Therefore look! The LORD has put a lying spirit in the mouth of these prophets of yours, and the LORD has declared disaster against you."

²³Then Zedekiah the son of Chenaanah went near and struck Micaiah on the cheek, and said, "Which way did the spirit from the LORD go from me to speak to you?"

²⁴And Micaiah said, "Indeed you shall see on that day when you go into an inner chamber to hide!"

²⁵Then the king of Israel said, "Take Micaiah, and return him to Amon the governor of the city and to Joash the king's son; ²⁶and say, 'Thus says the king: "Put this *fellow* in prison, and feed him with bread of affliction and water of affliction, until I return in peace." ' "

²⁷But Micaiah said, "If you ever return in peace, the LORD has not spoken by me." And he said, "Take heed, all you people!"

AHAB DIES IN BATTLE

²⁸So the king of Israel and Jehoshaphat the king of Judah went up to Ramoth Gilead. ²⁹And the king of Israel said to Jehoshaphat, "I will disguise myself and go into battle; but you put on your robes." So the king of Israel disguised himself, and they went into battle.

³⁰Now the king of Syria had commanded the captains of the chariots who *were* with him, saying, "Fight with no one small or great, but only with the king of Israel."

³¹So it was, when the captains of the chariots saw Jehoshaphat, that they said, "It *is* the king of Israel!" Therefore they surrounded him to attack; but Jehoshaphat cried out, and the LORD helped him, and God diverted them from him. ³²For so it was, when the captains of the chariots saw that it was not the king of Israel, that they turned back from pursuing him. ³³Now a certain man drew a bow at random, and struck the king of Israel between the joints of his armor. So he said to the driver of his chariot, "Turn around and take me out of the battle, for I am wounded." ³⁴The battle increased that day, and the king of Israel propped *himself* up in *his* chariot facing the Syrians until evening; and about the time of sunset he died.

¹Then Jehoshaphat the king of Judah returned safely to his house in Jerusalem. ²And Jehu the son of Hanani the seer went out to meet him, and said to King Jehoshaphat, "Should you help the wicked and love those who hate the LORD? Therefore the wrath of the LORD *is* upon you. ³Nevertheless good things are found in you, in that you have removed the wooden images from the land, and have prepared your heart to seek God."

THE REFORMS OF JEHOSHAPHAT

⁴So Jehoshaphat dwelt at Jerusalem; and he went out again among the people from

Beersheba to the mountains of Ephraim, and brought them back to the LORD God of their fathers. ⁵Then he set judges in the land throughout all the fortified cities of Judah, city by city, ⁶and said to the judges, "Take heed to what you are doing, for you do not judge for man but for the LORD, who is with you in the judgment. ⁷Now therefore, let the fear of the LORD be upon you; take care and do it, for there is no iniquity with the LORD our God, no partiality, nor taking of bribes."

LEADERSHIP

How should leaders make decisions? (19:5–7)

WHAT'S IT MEAN?

Jehoshaphat wasn't satisfied with changing the religious life of Judah. He wanted to change the judicial system as well. He succeeded—so well, in fact, that his system became a model for Jewish society throughout the years.

2 Chronicles 19:5–11

⁸Moreover in Jerusalem, for the judgment of the LORD and for controversies, Jehoshaphat appointed some of the Levites and priests, and some of the chief fathers of Israel, when they returned to Jerusalem.ᵃ ⁹And he commanded them, saying, "Thus you shall act in the fear of the LORD, faithfully and with a loyal heart: ¹⁰Whatever case comes to you from your brethren who dwell in their cities, whether of bloodshed or offenses against law or commandment, against statutes or ordinances, you shall warn them, lest they trespass against the LORD and wrath come upon you and your brethren. Do this, and you will not be guilty. ¹¹And take notice: Amariah the chief priest is over you in all matters of the LORD; and Zebadiah the son of Ishmael, the ruler of the house of Judah, for all the king's matters; also the Levites will be officials before you. Behave courageously, and the LORD will be with the good."

WHAT'S IT MEAN?

Fasting—that is, going without food for a certain period of time—was a common practice in ancient Israel. Usually it was done as part of a religious ceremony or as a way to show grief or repentance. Officially, the Israelites were only required to fast on the Day of Atonement. Sometimes, though, the leaders of the country would call for a voluntary fast during times of war.

2 Chronicles 20:3

AMMON, MOAB, AND MOUNT SEIR DEFEATED

¹It happened after this that the people of Moab with the people of Ammon, and others with them besides the Ammonites,ᵃ came to battle against Jehoshaphat. ²Then some came and told Jehoshaphat, saying, "A great multitude is coming against you from beyond the sea, from Syria;ᵃ and they are in Hazazon Tamar" (which is En Gedi). ³And Jehoshaphat feared, and set himself to seek the LORD, and proclaimed a fast throughout all Judah. ⁴So Judah gathered together to ask help from the LORD; and from all the cities of Judah they came to seek the LORD.

⁵Then Jehoshaphat stood in the assembly of Judah and Jerusalem, in the house of the LORD, before the new court, ⁶and said: "O LORD God of our fathers, are You not God in heaven, and do You not rule over all the kingdoms of the nations, and in Your hand is there not power and might, so that no one is able to withstand You? ⁷Are You not our God, who drove out the inhabitants of this land before Your people Israel, and gave it to the descendants of Abraham Your friend forever? ⁸And they dwell in it, and have built You a sanctuary in it for Your name, saying, ⁹'If disaster comes upon us—

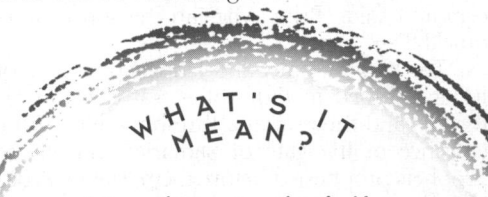

"Behave courageously, and the LORD will be with the good."
(2 Chronicles 19:11b)

19:8 ᵃSeptuagint and Vulgate read for the inhabitants of Jerusalem. **20:1** ᵃFollowing Masoretic Text and Vulgate; Septuagint reads Meunites (compare 26:7). **20:2** ᵃFollowing Masoretic Text, Septuagint, and Vulgate; some Hebrew manuscripts and Old Latin read Edom.

sword, judgment, pestilence, or famine—we will stand before this temple and in Your presence (for Your name *is* in this temple), and cry out to You in our affliction, and You will hear and save." ¹⁰And now, here are the people of Ammon, Moab, and Mount Seir—whom You would not let Israel invade when they came out of the land of Egypt, but they turned from them and did not destroy them— ¹¹here they are, rewarding us by coming to throw us out of Your possession which You have given us to inherit. ¹²O our God, will You not judge them? For we have no power against this great multitude that is coming against us; nor do we know what to do, but our eyes *are* upon You."

¹³Now all Judah, with their little ones, their wives, and their children, stood before the LORD.

¹⁴Then the Spirit of the LORD came upon Jahaziel the son of Zechariah, the son of Benaiah, the son of Jeiel, the son of Mattaniah, a Levite of the sons of Asaph, in the midst of the assembly. ¹⁵And he said, "Listen, all you of Judah and you inhabitants of Jerusalem, and you, King Jehoshaphat! Thus says the LORD to you: 'Do not be afraid nor dismayed because of this great multitude, for the battle *is* not yours, but God's. ¹⁶Tomorrow go down against them. They will surely come up by the Ascent of Ziz, and you will find them at the end of the brook before the Wilderness of Jeruel. ¹⁷You will not *need* to fight in this *battle.* Position yourselves, stand still and see the salvation of the LORD, who is with you, O Judah and Jerusalem!' Do not fear or be dismayed; tomorrow go out against them, for the LORD *is* with you."

¹⁸And Jehoshaphat bowed his head with *his* face to the ground, and all Judah and the inhabitants of Jerusalem bowed before the LORD, worshiping the LORD. ¹⁹Then the Levites of the children of the Kohathites and of the children of the Korahites stood up to praise the LORD God of Israel with voices loud and high.

²⁰So they rose early in the morning and went out into the Wilderness of Tekoa; and as they went out, Jehoshaphat stood and said, "Hear me, O Judah and you inhabitants of Jerusalem: Believe in the LORD your God, and you shall be established; believe His prophets, and you shall prosper." ²¹And when he had consulted with the people, he appointed those who

FEAR

Why should we not be afraid? (20:15)

should sing to the LORD, and who should praise the beauty of holiness, as they went out before the army and were saying:

"Praise the LORD,
For His mercy *endures* forever."*ᵃ*

²²Now when they began to sing and to praise, the LORD set ambushes against the people of Ammon, Moab, and Mount Seir, who had come against Judah; and they were defeated. ²³For the people of Ammon and Moab stood up against the inhabitants of Mount Seir to utterly kill and destroy *them.* And when they had made an end of the inhabitants of Seir, they helped to destroy one another.

²⁴So when Judah came to a place overlooking the wilderness, they looked toward the multitude; and there *were* their dead bodies, fallen on the earth. No one had escaped.

²⁵When Jehoshaphat and his people came to take away their spoil, they found among them an abundance of valuables on the dead bodies,*ᵃ* and precious jewelry, which they stripped off for themselves, more than they could carry away; and they were three days gathering the spoil because there was so much. ²⁶And on the fourth day they assembled in the Valley of Berachah, for there they blessed the LORD; therefore the name of that place was called The Valley of Berachah*ᵃ* until this day. ²⁷Then they returned, every man of Judah and Jerusalem, with Jehoshaphat in front of them, to go back to Jerusalem with joy, for the LORD had made them rejoice over their enemies. ²⁸So they came to Jerusalem, with stringed instruments and harps and trumpets, to the house of the LORD. ²⁹And the fear of God was on all the kingdoms of *those* countries when they heard that the LORD had fought against the enemies of Israel. ³⁰Then the realm of Jehoshaphat was quiet, for his God gave him rest all around.

THE END OF JEHOSHAPHAT'S REIGN

³¹So Jehoshaphat was king over Judah. *He was* thirty-five years old when he became king, and he reigned twenty-five years in Jerusalem. His mother's name *was* Azubah the daughter of Shilhi. ³²And he walked in the way of his father Asa, and did not turn aside from it, doing *what was* right in the sight of the LORD. ³³Nevertheless the high places were not taken away, for as yet the people had not directed their hearts to the God of their fathers.

20:21 *ᵃ*Compare Psalm 106:1   **20:25** *ᵃ*A few Hebrew manuscripts, Old Latin, and Vulgate read *garments;* Septuagint reads *armor.*   **20:26** *ᵃ*Literally *Blessing*

³⁴Now the rest of the acts of Jehoshaphat, first and last, indeed they *are* written in the book of Jehu the son of Hanani, which *is* mentioned in the book of the kings of Israel.

³⁵After this Jehoshaphat king of Judah allied himself with Ahaziah king of Israel, who acted very wickedly. ³⁶And he allied himself with him to make ships to go to Tarshish, and they made the ships in Ezion Geber. ³⁷But Eliezer the son of Dodavah of Mareshah prophesied against Jehoshaphat, saying, "Because you have allied yourself with Ahaziah, the LORD has destroyed your works." Then the ships were wrecked, so that they were not able to go to Tarshish.

JEHORAM REIGNS IN JUDAH

¹And Jehoshaphat rested with his fathers, and was buried with his fathers in the City of David. Then Jehoram his son reigned in his place. ²He had brothers, the sons of Jehoshaphat: Azariah, Jehiel, Zechariah, Azaryahu, Michael, and Shephatiah; all these *were* the sons of Jehoshaphat king of Israel. ³Their father gave them great gifts of silver and gold and precious things, with fortified cities in Judah; but he gave the kingdom to Jehoram, because he *was* the firstborn.

⁴Now when Jehoram was established over the kingdom of his father, he strengthened himself and killed all his brothers with the sword, and also *others* of the princes of Israel.

WHAT'S IT MEAN?

During David's reign, Israel had conquered the land of Edom and stationed military troops there. Later, Solomon built a port city on the Red Sea in Edom, which he still considered to be part of his kingdom. When Jehoshaphat was king, the Edomites started a rebellion, but couldn't finish it. They tried once more when Jehoram was king and finally succeeded in regaining control of their land.

2 Chronicles 21:10

⁵Jehoram *was* thirty-two years old when he became king, and he reigned eight years in Jerusalem. ⁶And he walked in the way of the kings of Israel, just as the house of Ahab had done, for he had the daughter of Ahab as a wife; and he did evil in the sight of the LORD. ⁷Yet the LORD would not destroy the house of David, because of the covenant that He had made with David, and since He had promised to give a lamp to him and to his sons forever.

⁸In his days Edom revolted against Judah's authority, and made a king over themselves. ⁹So Jehoram went out with his officers, and all his chariots with him. And he rose by night and attacked the Edomites who had surrounded him and the captains of the chariots. ¹⁰Thus Edom has been in revolt against Judah's authority to this day. At that time Libnah revolted against his rule, because he had forsaken the LORD God of his fathers. ¹¹Moreover he made high places in the mountains of Judah, and caused the inhabitants of Jerusalem to commit harlotry, and led Judah astray.

¹²And a letter came to him from Elijah the prophet, saying,

Thus says the LORD God of your father David:
Because you have not walked in the ways of Jehoshaphat your father, or in the ways of Asa king of Judah, ¹³but have walked in the way of the kings of Israel, and have made Judah and the inhabitants of Jerusalem to play the harlot like the harlotry of the house of Ahab, and also have killed your brothers, those of your father's household, *who were* better than yourself, ¹⁴behold, the LORD will strike your people with a serious affliction—your children, your wives, and all your possessions; ¹⁵and you *will become* very sick with a disease of your intestines, until your intestines come out by reason of the sickness, day by day.

¹⁶Moreover the LORD stirred up against Jehoram the spirit of the Philistines and the Arabians who *were* near the Ethiopians. ¹⁷And they came up into Judah and invaded it, and carried away all the possessions that were found in the king's house, and also his sons and his wives, so that there was not a son left to him except Jehoahaz,ᵃ the youngest of his sons.

¹⁸After all this the LORD struck him in his intestines with an incurable disease. ¹⁹Then it happened in the course of time, after the end of two years, that his intestines came out because of his sickness; so he died in severe pain. And his people made no burning for him, like the burning for his fathers.

²⁰He was thirty-two years old when he be-

21:17 ᵃElsewhere called *Ahaziah* (compare 2 Chronicles 22:1) came king. He reigned in Jerusalem eight years and, to no one's sorrow, departed. However they buried him in the City of David, but not in the tombs of the kings.

AHAZIAH REIGNS IN JUDAH

¹Then the inhabitants of Jerusalem made Ahaziah his youngest son king in his place, for the raiders who came with the Arabians into the camp had killed all the older *sons*. So Ahaziah the son of Jehoram, king of Judah, reigned. ²Ahaziah *was* forty-two*ᵃ* years old when he became king, and he reigned one year in Jerusalem. His mother's name *was* Athaliah the granddaughter of Omri. ³He also walked in the ways of the house of Ahab, for his mother advised him to do wickedly. ⁴Therefore he did evil in the sight of the LORD, like the house of Ahab; for they were his counselors after the death of his father, to his destruction. ⁵He also followed their advice, and went with Jehoram*ᵃ* the son of Ahab king of Israel to war against Hazael king of Syria at Ramoth Gilead; and the Syrians wounded Joram. ⁶Then he returned to Jezreel to recover from the wounds which he had received at Ramah, when he fought against Hazael king of Syria. And Azariah*ᵃ* the son of Jehoram, king of Judah, went down to see Jehoram the son of Ahab in Jezreel, because he was sick.

The prophet Elisha had anointed Jehu as the eleventh king of Israel and had given him instructions to wipe out the family of Ahab. Ahab knew about his death sentence. Years before, the prophet Elijah had warned Ahab that his family would be destroyed because of the evil things he had done.

2 Chronicles 22:7

⁷His going to Joram was God's occasion for Ahaziah's downfall; for when he arrived, he went out with Jehoram against Jehu the son of Nimshi, whom the LORD had anointed to cut off the house of Ahab. ⁸And it happened, when Jehu was executing judgment on the house of Ahab, and found the princes of Judah and the sons of Ahaziah's brothers who served Ahaziah, that he killed them. ⁹Then he searched for Ahaziah; and they caught him (he was hiding in Samaria), and brought him to Jehu. When they had killed him, they buried him, "because," they said, "he is the son of Jehoshaphat, who sought the LORD with all his heart."

So the house of Ahaziah had no one to assume power over the kingdom.

ATHALIAH REIGNS IN JUDAH

¹⁰Now when Athaliah the mother of Ahaziah saw that her son was dead, she arose and destroyed all the royal heirs of the house of Judah. ¹¹But Jehoshabeath,*ᵃ* the daughter of the king, took Joash the son of Ahaziah, and stole him away from among the king's sons who were being murdered, and put him and his nurse in a bedroom. So Jehoshabeath, the daughter of King Jehoram, the wife of Jehoiada the priest (for she was the sister of Ahaziah), hid him from Athaliah so that she did not kill him. ¹²And he was hidden with them in the house of God for six years, while Athaliah reigned over the land.

JOASH CROWNED KING OF JUDAH

¹In the seventh year Jehoiada strengthened himself, *and made a* covenant with the captains of hundreds: Azariah the son of Jeroham, Ishmael the son of Jehohanan, Azariah the son of Obed, Maaseiah the son of Adaiah, and Elishaphat the son of Zichri. ²And they went throughout Judah and gathered the Levites from all the cities of Judah, and the chief fathers of Israel, and they came to Jerusalem. ³Then all the assembly made a covenant with the king in the house of God. And he said to them, "Behold, the king's son shall reign, as the LORD has said of the sons of David. ⁴This *is* what you shall do: One-third of you entering on the Sabbath, of the priests and the Levites, *shall be* keeping watch over the doors; ⁵one-third *shall be* at the king's house; and one-third at the Gate of the Foundation. All the people *shall be* in the courts of the house of the LORD. ⁶But let no one come into the house of the LORD except the priests and those of the Levites who serve. They may go in, for they *are* holy; but all the people shall keep the watch of the LORD. ⁷And the Levites shall surround the king on all sides, every man with his weapons in his hand;

22:2 *ᵃ*Or *twenty-two* (compare 2 Kings 8:26)   **22:5** *ᵃ*Also spelled *Joram* (compare verses 5 and 7; 2 Kings 8:28; and elsewhere)   **22:6** *ᵃ*Some Hebrew manuscripts, Septuagint, Syriac, Vulgate, and 2 Kings 8:29 read *Ahaziah.*
22:11 *ᵃ*Spelled *Jehosheba* in 2 Kings 11:2

and whoever comes into the house, let him be put to death. You are to be with the king when he comes in and when he goes out."

⁸So the Levites and all Judah did according to all that Jehoiada the priest commanded. And each man took his men who were to be on duty on the Sabbath, with those who were going *off duty* on the Sabbath; for Jehoiada the priest had not dismissed the divisions. ⁹And Jehoiada the priest gave to the captains of hundreds the spears and the large and small shields which *had belonged* to King David, that *were* in the temple of God. ¹⁰Then he set all the people, every man with his weapon in his hand, from the right side of the temple to the left side of the temple, along by the altar and by the temple, all around the king. ¹¹And they brought out the king's son, put the crown on him, *gave him* the Testimony,ᵃ and made him king. Then Jehoiada and his sons anointed him, and said, "*Long* live the king!"

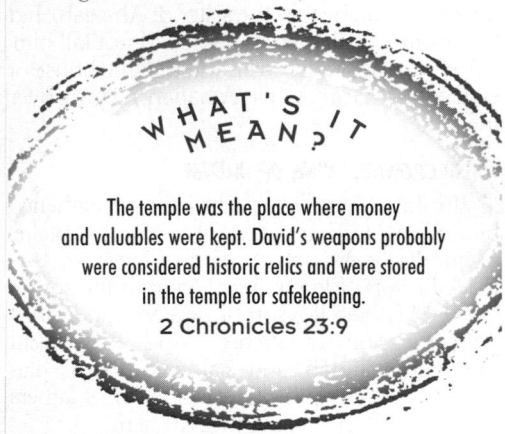

WHAT'S IT MEAN?

The temple was the place where money and valuables were kept. David's weapons probably were considered historic relics and were stored in the temple for safekeeping.
2 Chronicles 23:9

DEATH OF ATHALIAH

¹²Now when Athaliah heard the noise of the people running and praising the king, she came to the people *in* the temple of the LORD. ¹³When she looked, there was the king standing by his pillar at the entrance; and the leaders and the trumpeters *were* by the king. All the people of the land were rejoicing and blowing trumpets, also the singers with musical instruments, and those who led in praise. So Athaliah tore her clothes and said, "Treason! Treason!"

¹⁴And Jehoiada the priest brought out the captains of hundreds who were set over the army, and said to them, "Take her outside under guard, and slay with the sword whoever follows her." For the priest had said, "Do not kill her in the house of the LORD."

¹⁵So they seized her; and she went by way of the entrance of the Horse Gate *into* the king's house, and they killed her there.

¹⁶Then Jehoiada made a covenant between himself, the people, and the king, that they should be the LORD's people. ¹⁷And all the people went to the templeᵃ of Baal, and tore it down. They broke in pieces its altars and images, and killed Mattan the priest of Baal before the altars. ¹⁸Also Jehoiada appointed the oversight of the house of the LORD to the hand of the priests, the Levites, whom David had assigned in the house of the LORD, to offer the burnt offerings of the LORD, as *it is* written in the Law of Moses, with rejoicing and with singing, *as it was established* by David. ¹⁹And he set the gatekeepers at the gates of the house of the LORD, so that no one *who was* in any way unclean should enter.

²⁰Then he took the captains of hundreds, the nobles, the governors of the people, and all the people of the land, and brought the king down from the house of the LORD; and they went through the Upper Gate to the king's house, and set the king on the throne of the kingdom. ²¹So all the people of the land rejoiced; and the city was quiet, for they had slain Athaliah with the sword.

JOASH REPAIRS THE TEMPLE

¹Joash *was* seven years old when he became king, and he reigned forty years in Jerusalem. His mother's name *was* Zibiah of Beersheba. ²Joash did *what was* right in the sight of the LORD all the days of Jehoiada the priest. ³And Jehoiada took two wives for him, and he had sons and daughters.

⁴Now it happened after this *that* Joash set his heart on repairing the house of the LORD. ⁵Then he gathered the priests and the Levites, and said to them, "Go out to the cities of Judah, and gather from all Israel money to repair the house of your God from year to year, and see that you do it quickly."

However the Levites did not do it quickly. ⁶So the king called Jehoiada the chief *priest*, and said to him, "Why have you not required the Levites to bring in from Judah and from Jerusalem the collection, *according to the commandment* of Moses the servant of the LORD and of the assembly of Israel, for the tabernacle of witness?" ⁷For the sons of Athaliah, that wicked woman, had broken into the house of God, and had also presented all the dedicated things of the house of the LORD to the Baals.

23:11 ᵃThat is, the Law (compare Exodus 25:16, 21; 31:18)   **23:17** ᵃLiterally *house*

⁸Then at the king's command they made a chest, and set it outside at the gate of the house of the LORD. ⁹And they made a proclamation throughout Judah and Jerusalem to bring to the LORD the collection *that* Moses the servant of God *had imposed* on Israel in the wilderness. ¹⁰Then all the leaders and all the people rejoiced, brought their contributions, and put *them* into the chest until all had given. ¹¹So it was, at that time, when the chest was brought to the king's official by the hand of the Levites, and when they saw that *there was* much money, that the king's scribe and the high priest's officer came and emptied the chest, and took it and returned it to its place. Thus they did day by day, and gathered money in abundance.

¹²The king and Jehoiada gave it to those who did the work of the service of the house of the LORD; and they hired masons and carpenters to repair the house of the LORD, and also those who worked in iron and bronze to restore the house of the LORD. ¹³So the workmen labored, and the work was completed by them; they restored the house of God to its original condition and reinforced it. ¹⁴When they had finished, they brought the rest of the money before the king and Jehoiada; they made from it articles for the house of the LORD, articles for serving and offering, spoons and vessels of gold and silver. And they offered burnt offerings in the house of the LORD continually all the days of Jehoiada.

APOSTASY OF JOASH

¹⁵But Jehoiada grew old and was full of days, and he died; *he was* one hundred and thirty years old when he died. ¹⁶And they buried him in the City of David among the kings, because he had done good in Israel, both toward God and His house.

¹⁷Now after the death of Jehoiada the leaders of Judah came and bowed down to the king. And the king listened to them. ¹⁸Therefore they left the house of the LORD God of their fathers, and served wooden images and idols; and wrath came upon Judah and Jerusalem because of their trespass. ¹⁹Yet He sent prophets to them, to bring them back to the LORD; and they testified against them, but they would not listen.

²⁰Then the Spirit of God came upon Zechariah the son of Jehoiada the priest, who stood above the people, and said to them, "Thus says God: 'Why do you transgress the commandments of the LORD, so that you cannot prosper? Because you have forsaken the LORD, He also has forsaken you.'" ²¹So they conspired against him, and at the command of the king they stoned him with stones in the court of the house of the LORD. ²²Thus Joash the king did not remember the kindness which Jehoiada his father had done to him, but killed his son; and as he died, he said, "The LORD look on *it,* and repay!"

DEATH OF JOASH

²³So it happened in the spring of the year *that* the army of Syria came up against him; and they came to Judah and Jerusalem, and destroyed all the leaders of the people from among the people, and sent all their spoil to the king of Damascus. ²⁴For the army of the Syrians came with a small company of men; but the LORD delivered a very great army into their hand, because they had forsaken the LORD God of their fathers. So they executed judgment against Joash. ²⁵And when they had withdrawn from him (for they left him severely wounded), his own servants conspired against him because of the blood of the sons*ᵃ* of Jehoiada the priest, and killed him on his bed. So he died. And they buried him in the City of David, but they did not bury him in the tombs of the kings.

²⁶These are the ones who conspired against him: Zabad*ᵃ* the son of Shimeath the Ammonitess, and Jehozabad the son of Shimrith*ᵇ* the Moabitess. ²⁷Now *concerning* his sons, and the many oracles about him, and the repairing of the house of God, indeed they *are* written in the annals of the book of the kings. Then Amaziah his son reigned in his place.

AMAZIAH REIGNS IN JUDAH

¹Amaziah *was* twenty-five years old *when* he became king, and he reigned twenty-nine years in Jerusalem. His mother's name *was* Jehoaddan of Jerusalem. ²And he did *what was* right in the sight of the LORD, but not with a loyal heart.

³Now it happened, as soon as the kingdom was established for him, that he executed his servants who had murdered his father the king. ⁴However he did not execute their children, but

> "And he did what was right in the sight of the LORD, but not with a loyal heart."
> (2 Chronicles 25:2)

24:25 *ᵃ*Septuagint and Vulgate read *son* (compare verses 20–22). 24:26 *ᵃ*Or *Jozachar* (compare 2 Kings 12:21) *ᵇ*Or *Shomer* (compare 2 Kings 12:21) *did* as *it is* written in the Law in the Book of Moses, where the LORD commanded, saying, "The fathers shall not be put to death for their children, nor shall the children be put to death for their fathers; but a person shall die for his own sin."*a*

THE WAR AGAINST EDOM

⁵Moreover Amaziah gathered Judah together and set over them captains of thousands and captains of hundreds, according to *their* fathers' houses, throughout all Judah and Benjamin; and he numbered them from twenty years old and above, and found them to be three hundred thousand choice *men, able* to go to war, who could handle spear and shield. ⁶He also hired one hundred thousand mighty men of valor from Israel for one hundred talents of silver. ⁷But a man of God came to him, saying, "O king, do not let the army of Israel go with you, for the LORD *is* not with Israel—*not with* any of the children of Ephraim. ⁸But if you go, be gone! Be strong in battle! *Even so,* God shall make you fall before the enemy; for God has power to help and to overthrow."

⁹Then Amaziah said to the man of God, "But what *shall we* do about the hundred talents which I have given to the troops of Israel?"

And the man of God answered, "The LORD is able to give you much more than this." ¹⁰So Amaziah discharged the troops that had come to him from Ephraim, to go back home. Therefore their anger was greatly aroused against Judah, and they returned home in great anger.

¹¹Then Amaziah strengthened himself, and leading his people, he went to the Valley of Salt and killed ten thousand of the people of Seir. ¹²Also the children of Judah took captive ten thousand alive, brought them to the top of the rock, and cast them down from the top of the rock, so that they all were dashed in pieces.

¹³But as for the soldiers of the army which Amaziah had discharged, so that they would not go with him to battle, they raided the cities of Judah from Samaria to Beth Horon, killed three thousand in them, and took much spoil.

¹⁴Now it was so, after Amaziah came from the slaughter of the Edomites, that he brought the gods of the people of Seir, set them up *to be* his gods, and bowed down before them and burned incense to them. ¹⁵Therefore the anger of the LORD was aroused against Amaziah, and He sent him a prophet who said to him, "Why have you sought the gods of the people, which

could not rescue their own people from your hand?"

¹⁶So it was, as he talked with him, that *the king* said to him, "Have we made you the king's counselor? Cease! Why should you be killed?"

Then the prophet ceased, and said, "I know that God has determined to destroy you, because you have done this and have not heeded my advice."

ISRAEL DEFEATS JUDAH

¹⁷Now Amaziah king of Judah asked advice and sent to Joash*a* the son of Jehoahaz, the son of Jehu, king of Israel, saying, "Come, let us face one another *in battle.*"

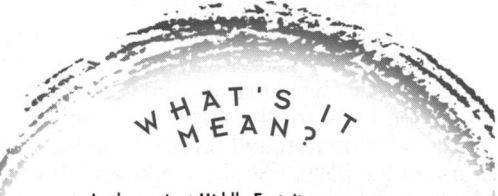

WHAT'S IT MEAN?

In the ancient Middle East, it was common for people to tell stories or to make odd comparisons to get their point across. These stories were known as parables. Jesus later used parables to illustrate heavenly truths. Joash compared himself to a strong, valuable cedar and Amaziah to a useless little thistle. Joash was warning that Amaziah's pride was going to get him into trouble.

2 Chronicles 25:18

¹⁸And Joash king of Israel sent to Amaziah king of Judah, saying, "The thistle that *was* in Lebanon sent to the cedar that was in Lebanon, saying, 'Give your daughter to my son as wife'; and a wild beast that *was* in Lebanon passed by and trampled the thistle. ¹⁹Indeed you say that you have defeated the Edomites, and your heart is lifted up to boast. Stay at home now; why should you meddle with trouble, that you should fall—you and Judah with you?"

²⁰But Amaziah would not heed, for it *came* from God, that He might give them into the hand *of their enemies,* because they sought the gods of Edom. ²¹So Joash king of Israel went out; and he and Amaziah king of Judah faced one another at Beth Shemesh, which *belongs* to Judah. ²²And Judah was defeated by Israel, and every man fled to his tent. ²³Then Joash the king of Israel captured Amaziah king of Judah, the son of Joash, the son of Jehoahaz, at Beth Shemesh; and he brought him to Jerusalem, and

broke down the wall of Jerusalem from the Gate of Ephraim to the Corner Gate—four hundred cubits. [24]And *he took* all the gold and silver, all the articles that were found in the house of God with Obed-Edom, the treasures of the king's house, and hostages, and returned to Samaria.

DEATH OF AMAZIAH

[25]Amaziah the son of Joash, king of Judah, lived fifteen years after the death of Joash the son of Jehoahaz, king of Israel. [26]Now the rest of the acts of Amaziah, from first to last, indeed *are* they not written in the book of the kings of Judah and Israel? [27]After the time that Amaziah turned away from following the LORD, they made a conspiracy against him in Jerusalem, and he fled to Lachish; but they sent after him to Lachish and killed him there. [28]Then they brought him on horses and buried him with his fathers in the City of Judah.

UZZIAH REIGNS IN JUDAH

[1]Now all the people of Judah took Uzziah,[a] who *was* sixteen years old, and made him king instead of his father Amaziah. [2]He built Elath[a] and restored it to Judah, after the king rested with his fathers.

[3]Uzziah *was* sixteen years old when he became king, and he reigned fifty-two years in Jerusalem. His mother's name was Jecholiah of Jerusalem. [4]And he did *what was* right in the sight of the LORD, according to all that his father Amaziah had done. [5]He sought God in the days of Zechariah, who had understanding in the visions[a] of God; and as long as he sought the LORD, God made him prosper.

> **INTEGRITY**
>
> What's someone look like who has integrity? (26:4)

[6]Now he went out and made war against the Philistines, and broke down the wall of Gath, the wall of Jabneh, and the wall of Ashdod; and he built cities *around* Ashdod and among the Philistines. [7]God helped him against the Philistines, against the Arabians who lived in Gur Baal, and against the Meunites. [8]Also the Ammonites brought tribute to Uzziah. His fame spread as far as the entrance of Egypt, for he became exceedingly strong.

[9]And Uzziah built towers in Jerusalem at the Corner Gate, at the Valley Gate, and at the corner buttress of the wall; then he fortified them. [10]Also he built towers in the desert. He dug many wells, for he had much livestock, both in the lowlands and in the plains; *he also had* farmers and vinedressers in the mountains and in Carmel, for he loved the soil.

WHAT'S IT MEAN?

Judah's opponents here were of Arabian descent. Gur Baal, a desert city, was home to a group of Arabs. The Meunites were likely members of an Arabian tribe from Maon, a city south of the Dead Sea.
2 Chronicles 26:7

[11]Moreover Uzziah had an army of fighting men who went out to war by companies, according to the number on their roll as prepared by Jeiel the scribe and Maaseiah the officer, under the hand of Hananiah, *one* of the king's captains. [12]The total number of chief officers[a] of the mighty men of valor *was* two thousand six hundred. [13]And under their authority *was* an army of three hundred and seven thousand five hundred, that made war with mighty power, to help the king against the enemy. [14]Then

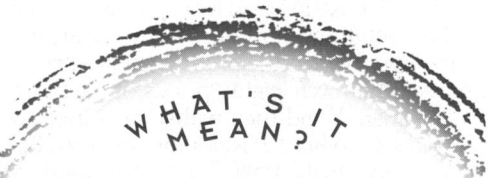

WHAT'S IT MEAN?

It wasn't easy being a farmer in ancient Israel. If you weren't dealing with drought, you were probably trying to protect your crops from certain wandering tribes who made their living raiding farms. Some farmers built towers to provide defense against such raids. As for the drought, wells were the best solution to water shortage. Wells were large holes farmers dug—sometimes in solid rock—to hold rainwater. The water collected in the wells was used for the farmer's flocks of animals as well as his crops. A good rain could fill a very large well, if the collection system was properly designed.
2 Chronicles 26:10

26:1 [a]Called *Azariah* in 2 Kings 14:21ff   **26:2** [a]Hebrew *Eloth*   **26:5** [a]Several Hebrew manuscripts, Septuagint, Syriac, Targum, and Arabic read *fear*.   **26:12** [a]Literally *chief fathers*

Uzziah prepared for them, for the entire army, shields, spears, helmets, body armor, bows, and slings *to cast* stones. ¹⁵And he made devices in Jerusalem, invented by skillful men, to be on the towers and the corners, to shoot arrows and large stones. So his fame spread far and wide, for he was marvelously helped till he became strong.

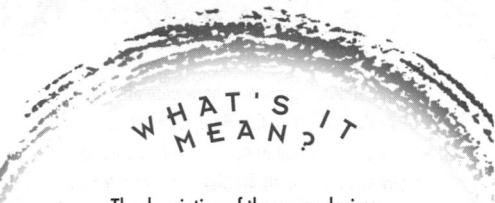

The description of these war devices seems to suggest that they were like catapults. From about 800 B.C. to A.D. 1500, catapults were among the most feared weapons of war. They were capable of firing objects between 350 and 500 yards. (Imagine being hit with something that was fired almost five football fields away!) Of course, bows and arrows weren't exactly kids' toys. An arrow fired from a bow could travel up to 300 yards.

2 Chronicles 26:15

THE PENALTY FOR UZZIAH'S PRIDE

¹⁶But when he was strong his heart was lifted up, to *his* destruction, for he transgressed against the LORD his God by entering the temple of the LORD to burn incense on the altar of incense. ¹⁷So Azariah the priest went in after him, and with him were eighty priests of the LORD—valiant men. ¹⁸And they withstood King Uzziah, and said to him, "*It is* not for you, Uzziah, to burn incense to the LORD, but for the priests, the sons of Aaron, who are consecrated to burn incense. Get out of the sanctuary, for you have trespassed! You *shall have* no honor from the LORD God."

¹⁹Then Uzziah became furious; and he *had* a censer in his hand to burn incense. And while he was angry with the priests, leprosy broke out on his forehead, before the priests in the house of the LORD, beside the incense altar. ²⁰And Azariah the chief priest and all the priests looked at him, and there, on his forehead, he *was* leprous; so they thrust him out of that place. Indeed he also hurried to get out, because the LORD had struck him.

²¹King Uzziah was a leper until the day of his death. He dwelt in an isolated house, be-cause he was a leper; for he was cut off from the house of the LORD. Then Jotham his son *was* over the king's house, judging the people of the land.

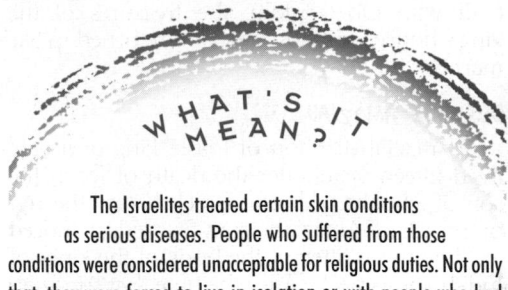

The Israelites treated certain skin conditions as serious diseases. People who suffered from those conditions were considered unacceptable for religious duties. Not only that, they were forced to live in isolation or with people who had similar afflictions until the disease cleared up.

2 Chronicles 26:21

²²Now the rest of the acts of Uzziah, from first to last, the prophet Isaiah the son of Amoz wrote. ²³So Uzziah rested with his fathers, and they buried him with his fathers in the field of burial which *belonged* to the kings, for they said, "He is a leper." Then Jotham his son reigned in his place.

JOTHAM REIGNS IN JUDAH

¹Jotham *was* twenty-five years old when he became king, and he reigned sixteen years in Jerusalem. His mother's name *was* Jerushah[a] the daughter of Zadok. ²And he did *what was* right in the sight of the LORD, according to all that his father Uzziah had done (although he did not enter the temple of the LORD). But still the people acted corruptly.

³He built the Upper Gate of the house of the LORD, and he built extensively on the wall of Ophel. ⁴Moreover he built cities in the mountains of Judah, and in the forests he built fortresses and towers. ⁵He also fought with the king of the Ammonites and defeated them. And the people of Ammon gave him in that year one hundred talents of silver, ten thousand kors of wheat, and ten thousand of barley. The people of Ammon paid this to him in the second and third years also. ⁶So Jotham became mighty, because he prepared his ways before the LORD his God.

⁷Now the rest of the acts of Jotham, and all his wars and his ways, indeed they *are* written in the book of the kings of Israel and Judah. ⁸He

27:1 *a*Spelled *Jerusha* in 2 Kings 15:33

was twenty-five years old when he became king, and he reigned sixteen years in Jerusalem. ⁹So Jotham rested with his fathers, and they buried him in the City of David. Then Ahaz his son reigned in his place.

AHAZ REIGNS IN JUDAH

¹Ahaz *was* twenty years old when he became king, and he reigned sixteen years in Jerusalem; and he did not do *what was* right in the sight of the LORD, as his father David *had done.* ²For he walked in the ways of the kings of Israel, and made molded images for the Baals. ³He burned incense in the Valley of the Son of Hinnom, and burned his children in the fire, according to the abominations of the nations whom the LORD had cast out before the children of Israel. ⁴And he sacrificed and burned incense on the high places, on the hills, and under every green tree.

WHAT'S IT MEAN?

The Canaanites figured that the best way to get on the good side of their gods was to kill a human being as an offering to them. God wanted His people to have nothing to do with the disgusting practice of human sacrifice.

2 Chronicles 28:3

SYRIA AND ISRAEL DEFEAT JUDAH

⁵Therefore the LORD his God delivered him into the hand of the king of Syria. They defeated him, and carried away a great multitude of them as captives, and brought *them* to Damascus. Then he was also delivered into the hand of the king of Israel, who defeated him with a great slaughter. ⁶For Pekah the son of Remaliah killed one hundred and twenty thousand in Judah in one day, all valiant men, because they had forsaken the LORD God of their fathers. ⁷Zichri, a mighty man of Ephraim, killed Maaseiah the king's son, Azrikam the officer over the house, and Elkanah *who was* second to the king. ⁸And the children of Israel carried away captive of their brethren two hundred thousand women, sons, and daughters; and they

also took away much spoil from them, and brought the spoil to Samaria.

ISRAEL RETURNS THE CAPTIVES

⁹But a prophet of the LORD was there, whose name *was* Oded; and he went out before the army that came to Samaria, and said to them: "Look, because the LORD God of your fathers was angry with Judah, He has delivered them into your hand; but you have killed them in a rage *that* reaches up to heaven. ¹⁰And now you propose to force the children of Judah and Jerusalem to be your male and female slaves; *but are* you not also guilty before the LORD your God? ¹¹Now hear me, therefore, and return the captives, whom you have taken captive from your brethren, for the fierce wrath of the LORD is upon you."

¹²Then some of the heads of the children of Ephraim, Azariah the son of Johanan, Berechiah the son of Meshillemoth, Jehizkiah the son of Shallum, and Amasa the son of Hadlai, stood up against those who came from the war, ¹³and said to them, "You shall not bring the captives here, for we *already* have offended the LORD. You intend to add to our sins and to our guilt; for our guilt is great, and *there is* fierce wrath against Israel." ¹⁴So the armed men left the captives and the spoil before the leaders and all the assembly. ¹⁵Then the men who were designated by name rose up and took the captives, and from the spoil they clothed all who were naked among them, dressed them and gave them sandals, gave them food and drink, and anointed them; and they let all the feeble ones ride on donkeys. So they brought them to their brethren at Jericho, the city of palm trees. Then they returned to Samaria.

ASSYRIA REFUSES TO HELP JUDAH

¹⁶At the same time King Ahaz sent to the kings*ᵃ* of Assyria to help him. ¹⁷For again the Edomites had come, attacked Judah, and carried away captives. ¹⁸The Philistines also had invaded the cities of the lowland and of the South of Judah, and had taken Beth Shemesh, Aijalon, Gederoth, Sochoh with its villages, Timnah with its villages, and Gimzo with its villages; and they dwelt there. ¹⁹For the LORD brought Judah low because of Ahaz king of Israel, for he had encouraged moral decline in Judah and had been continually unfaithful to the LORD. ²⁰Also Tiglath-Pileser*ᵃ* king of Assyria came to him and distressed him, and did not assist him. ²¹For Ahaz took part *of the treasures*

28:16 *ᵃ*Septuagint, Syriac, and Vulgate read *king* (compare verse 20).   **28:20** *ᵃ*Hebrew *Tilgath-Pilneser* from the house of the LORD, from the house of the king, and from the leaders, and he gave *it* to the king of Assyria; but he did not help him.

APOSTASY AND DEATH OF AHAZ

²²Now in the time of his distress King Ahaz became increasingly unfaithful to the LORD. This *is that* King Ahaz. ²³For he sacrificed to the gods of Damascus which had defeated him, saying, "Because the gods of the kings of Syria help them, I will sacrifice to them that they may help me." But they were the ruin of him and of all Israel. ²⁴So Ahaz gathered the articles of the house of God, cut in pieces the articles of the house of God, shut up the doors of the house of the LORD, and made for himself altars in every corner of Jerusalem. ²⁵And in every single city of Judah he made high places to burn incense to other gods, and provoked to anger the LORD God of his fathers.

²⁶Now the rest of his acts and all his ways, from first to last, indeed they *are* written in the book of the kings of Judah and Israel. ²⁷So Ahaz rested with his fathers, and they buried him in the city, in Jerusalem; but they did not bring him into the tombs of the kings of Israel. Then Hezekiah his son reigned in his place.

HEZEKIAH REIGNS IN JUDAH

¹Hezekiah became king *when he was* twenty-five years old, and he reigned twenty-nine years in Jerusalem. His mother's name *was* Abijah*ᵃ* the daughter of Zechariah. ²And he did *what was* right in the sight of the LORD, according to all that his father David had done.

HEZEKIAH CLEANSES THE TEMPLE

³In the first year of his reign, in the first month, he opened the doors of the house of the LORD and repaired them. ⁴Then he brought in the priests and the Levites, and gathered them in the East Square, ⁵and said to them: "Hear me, Levites! Now sanctify yourselves, sanctify the house of the LORD God of your fathers, and carry out the rubbish from the holy *place.* ⁶For our fathers have trespassed and done evil in the eyes of the LORD our God; they have forsaken Him, have turned their faces away from the dwelling place of the LORD, and turned *their* backs *on Him.* ⁷They have also shut up the doors of the vestibule, put out the lamps, and have not burned incense or offered burnt offerings in the holy *place* to the God of Israel. ⁸Therefore the wrath of the LORD fell upon Judah and Jerusalem, and He has given them up

to trouble, to desolation, and to jeering, as you see with your eyes. ⁹For indeed, because of this our fathers have fallen by the sword; and our sons, our daughters, and our wives *are* in captivity.

¹⁰"Now *it is* in my heart to make a covenant with the LORD God of Israel, that His fierce wrath may turn away from us. ¹¹My sons, do not be negligent now, for the LORD has chosen you to stand before Him, to serve Him, and that you should minister to Him and burn incense."

¹²Then these Levites arose: Mahath the son of Amasai and Joel the son of Azariah, of the sons of the Kohathites; of the sons of Merari, Kish the son of Abdi and Azariah the son of Jehallelel; of the Gershonites, Joah the son of Zimmah and Eden the son of Joah; ¹³of the sons of Elizaphan, Shimri and Jeiel; of the sons of Asaph, Zechariah and Mattaniah; ¹⁴of the sons of Heman, Jehiel and Shimei; and of the sons of Jeduthun, Shemaiah and Uzziel.

¹⁵And they gathered their brethren, sanctified themselves, and went according to the commandment of the king, at the words of the LORD, to cleanse the house of the LORD. ¹⁶Then the priests went into the inner part of the house of the LORD to cleanse *it,* and brought out all the debris that they found in the temple of the LORD to the court of the house of the LORD. And the Levites took *it* out and carried *it* to the Brook Kidron.

¹⁷Now they began to sanctify on the first *day* of the first month, and on the eighth day of the month they came to the vestibule of the LORD. So they sanctified the house of the LORD in eight days, and on the sixteenth day of the first month they finished.

¹⁸Then they went in to King Hezekiah and said, "We have cleansed all the house of the LORD, the altar of burnt offerings with all its articles, and the table of the showbread with all its articles. ¹⁹Moreover all the articles which King Ahaz in his reign had cast aside in his transgression we have prepared and sanctified; and there they *are,* before the altar of the LORD."

HEZEKIAH RESTORES TEMPLE WORSHIP

²⁰Then King Hezekiah rose early, gathered the rulers of the city, and went up to the house of the LORD. ²¹And they brought seven bulls, seven rams, seven lambs, and seven male goats for a sin offering for the kingdom, for the sanctuary, and for Judah. Then he commanded the priests, the sons of Aaron, to offer *them* on the altar of the LORD. ²²So they killed the bulls, and

29:1 *ᵃ*Spelled *Abi* in 2 Kings 18:2

the priests received the blood and sprinkled *it* on the altar. Likewise they killed the rams and sprinkled the blood on the altar. They also killed the lambs and sprinkled the blood on the altar. [23]Then they brought out the male goats *for the* sin offering before the king and the assembly, and they laid their hands on them. [24]And the priests killed them; and they presented their blood on the altar as a sin offering to make an atonement for all Israel, for the king commanded *that* the burnt offering and the sin offering *be made* for all Israel.

WHAT'S IT MEAN?

Each part of the sacrifice ritual had an important meaning. Touching the sacrificial animal symbolized that the sins of the priest and the people were being transferred to the animal. The animal carrying the people's sin was then either killed or taken away. Splattering the blood on the altar represented the forgiveness of sins.
2 Chronicles 29:23, 24

[25]And he stationed the Levites in the house of the LORD with cymbals, with stringed instruments, and with harps, according to the commandment of David, of Gad the king's seer, and of Nathan the prophet; for thus *was* the commandment of the LORD by his prophets. [26]The Levites stood with the instruments of David, and the priests with the trumpets. [27]Then Hezekiah commanded *them* to offer the burnt offering on the altar. And when the burnt offering began, the song of the LORD *also* began, with the trumpets and with the instruments of David king of Israel. [28]So all the assembly worshiped, the singers sang, and the trumpeters sounded; all *this continued* until the burnt offering was finished. [29]And when they had finished offering, the king and all who were present with him bowed and worshiped. [30]Moreover King Hezekiah and the leaders commanded the Levites to sing praise to the LORD with the words of David and of Asaph the seer. So they sang praises with gladness, and they bowed their heads and worshiped.

[31]Then Hezekiah answered and said, "Now *that* you have consecrated yourselves to the LORD, come near, and bring sacrifices and thank offerings into the house of the LORD." So the assembly brought in sacrifices and thank offerings, and as many as were of a willing heart *brought* burnt offerings. [32]And the number of the burnt offerings which the assembly brought was seventy bulls, one hundred rams, *and* two hundred lambs; all these *were* for a burnt offering to the LORD. [33]The consecrated things *were* six hundred bulls and three thousand sheep. [34]But the priests were too few, so that they could not skin all the burnt offerings; therefore their brethren the Levites helped them until the work was ended and until the *other* priests had sanctified themselves, for the Levites were more diligent in sanctifying themselves than the priests. [35]Also the burnt offerings *were* in abundance, with the fat of the peace offerings and *with* the drink offerings for *every* burnt offering.

So the service of the house of the LORD was set in order. [36]Then Hezekiah and all the people rejoiced that God had prepared the people, since the events took place so suddenly.

HEZEKIAH KEEPS THE PASSOVER

[1]And Hezekiah sent to all Israel and Judah, and also wrote letters to Ephraim and Manasseh, that they should come to the house of the LORD at Jerusalem, to keep the Passover to the LORD God of Israel. [2]For the king and his leaders and all the assembly in Jerusalem had agreed to keep the Passover in the second month. [3]For they could not keep it at the regular time,[a] because a sufficient number of priests had not consecrated themselves, nor had the people gathered together at Jerusalem. [4]And the matter pleased the king and all the assembly. [5]So they resolved to make a proclamation throughout all Israel, from Beersheba to Dan, that they should come to keep the Passover to the LORD God of Israel at Jerusalem, since they had not done *it* for a long *time* in the *prescribed* manner.

[6]Then the runners went throughout all Israel and Judah with the letters from the king and his leaders, and spoke according to the command of the king: "Children of Israel, return to the LORD God of Abraham, Isaac, and Israel; then He will return to the remnant of you who have escaped from the hand of the kings of Assyria. [7]And do not be like your fathers and your brethren, who trespassed against the LORD God of their fathers, so that He gave them up to desolation, as you see. [8]Now do not be stiffnecked, as your fathers *were,* but yield yourselves to the LORD; and enter His sanctuary,

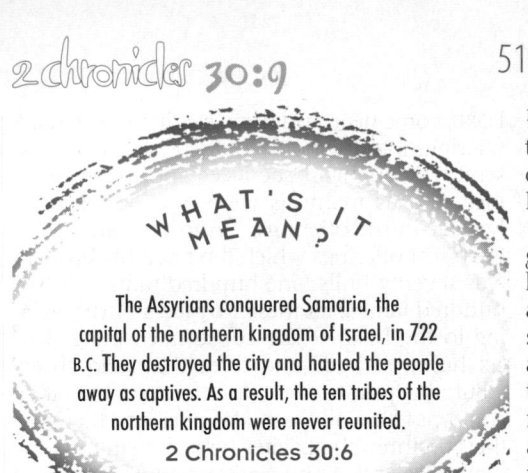

WHAT'S IT MEAN?

The Assyrians conquered Samaria, the capital of the northern kingdom of Israel, in 722 B.C. They destroyed the city and hauled the people away as captives. As a result, the ten tribes of the northern kingdom were never reunited.

2 Chronicles 30:6

which He has sanctified forever, and serve the LORD your God, that the fierceness of His wrath may turn away from you. ⁹For if you return to the LORD, your brethren and your children *will be treated* with compassion by those who lead them captive, so that they may come back to this land; for the LORD your God *is* gracious and merciful, and will not turn *His* face from you if you return to Him."

¹⁰So the runners passed from city to city through the country of Ephraim and Manasseh, as far as Zebulun; but they laughed at them and mocked them. ¹¹Nevertheless some from Asher, Manasseh, and Zebulun humbled themselves and came to Jerusalem.

> **"For the LORD your God is gracious and merciful, and will not turn His face from you if you return to Him."**
> (2 Chronicles 30:9b)

¹²Also the hand of God was on Judah to give them singleness of heart to obey the command of the king and the leaders, at the word of the LORD.

¹³Now many people, a very great assembly, gathered at Jerusalem to keep the Feast of Unleavened Bread in the second month. ¹⁴They arose and took away the altars that *were* in Jerusalem, and they took away all the incense altars and cast *them* into the Brook Kidron. ¹⁵Then they slaughtered the Passover *lambs* on the fourteenth *day* of the second month. The priests and the Levites were ashamed, and sanctified themselves, and brought the burnt offerings to the house of the LORD. ¹⁶They stood in their place according to their custom, according to the Law of Moses the man of God; the priests sprinkled the blood *received* from the hand of the Levites. ¹⁷For *there were* many in the assembly who had not sanctified themselves; therefore the Levites had charge of the slaughter of the Passover *lambs* for everyone *who was* not clean, to sanctify *them* to the LORD. ¹⁸For a multitude of the people, many from Ephraim, Manasseh, Issachar, and Zebulun, had not cleansed themselves, yet they ate the Passover contrary to what was written. But Hezekiah prayed for them, saying, "May the good LORD provide atonement for everyone ¹⁹*who* prepares his heart to seek God, the LORD God of his fathers, though *he is* not *cleansed* according to the purification of the

---

Promise HE PROMISES TO BE GRACIOUS AND MERCIFUL.

For the LORD your God is gracious and merciful, and will not turn His face from you if you return to Him (2 Chr. 30:9).

Kindhearted people sometimes make us suspicious. We wonder, *Is she for real? Is he like this all the time? What does she want from me?* Unfortunately, some people have learned how to use kindness to manipulate and charm others for selfish purposes. You don't have to wonder about God's kindness. He *is* for real. There are no strings attached. He is truly gracious, generous, sympathetic, and tolerant toward you. He cannot be unkind. There's nothing manipulative about God. He owns the whole world, so He won't charm you into giving Him something. He's always got your best interest at heart. He's genuinely gracious, kind, and merciful. You can trust Him because He loves you so purely and so much.

SEE FOR YOURSELF:

Ps. 111:4; 145:8; Gal. 5:22, 23; 2 Tim. 2:1

sanctuary." [20]And the LORD listened to Hezekiah and healed the people.

[21]So the children of Israel who were present at Jerusalem kept the Feast of Unleavened Bread seven days with great gladness; and the Levites and the priests praised the LORD day by day, *singing* to the LORD, accompanied by loud instruments. [22]And Hezekiah gave encouragement to all the Levites who taught the good knowledge of the LORD; and they ate throughout the feast seven days, offering peace offerings and making confession to the LORD God of their fathers.

[23]Then the whole assembly agreed to keep *the feast* another seven days, and they kept it *another* seven days with gladness. [24]For Hezekiah king of Judah gave to the assembly a thousand bulls and seven thousand sheep, and the leaders gave to the assembly a thousand bulls and ten thousand sheep; and a great number of priests sanctified themselves. [25]The whole assembly of Judah rejoiced, also the priests and Levites, all the assembly that came from Israel, the sojourners who came from the land of Israel, and those who dwelt in Judah. [26]So there was great joy in Jerusalem, for since the time of Solomon the son of David, king of Israel, *there had* been nothing like this in Jerusalem. [27]Then the priests, the Levites, arose and blessed the people, and their voice was heard; and their prayer came up to His holy dwelling place, to heaven.

WHAT'S IT MEAN?

Shrines to Asherah and other Canaanite gods were scattered throughout the land, especially on hilltops and in groves of trees. The shrines were easy to spot because they were marked by carved wooden poles.

2 Chronicles 31:1

THE REFORMS OF HEZEKIAH

[1]Now when all this was finished, all Israel who were present went out to the cities of Judah and broke the sacred pillars in pieces, cut down the wooden images, and threw down the high places and the altars—from all Judah, Benjamin, Ephraim, and Manasseh— until they had utterly destroyed them all. Then all the children of Israel returned to their own cities, every man to his possession.

[2]And Hezekiah appointed the divisions of the priests and the Levites according to their divisions, each man according to his service, the priests and Levites for burnt offerings and peace offerings, to serve, to give thanks, and to praise in the gates of the camp[a] of the LORD. [3]The king also *appointed* a portion of his possessions for the burnt offerings: for the morning and evening burnt offerings, the burnt offerings for the Sabbaths and the New Moons and the set feasts, as *it is* written in the Law of the LORD.

[4]Moreover he commanded the people who dwelt in Jerusalem to contribute support for the priests and the Levites, that they might devote themselves to the Law of the LORD.

[5]As soon as the commandment was circulated, the children of Israel brought in abundance the firstfruits of grain and wine, oil and honey, and of all the produce of the field; and they brought in abundantly the tithe of everything. [6]And the children of Israel and Judah, who dwelt in the cities of Judah, brought the tithe of oxen and sheep; also the tithe of holy things which were consecrated to the LORD their God they laid in heaps.

[7]In the third month they began laying them in heaps, and they finished in the seventh month. [8]And when Hezekiah and the leaders came and saw the heaps, they blessed the LORD and His people Israel. [9]Then Hezekiah questioned the priests and the Levites concerning the heaps. [10]And Azariah the chief priest, from the house of Zadok, answered him and said, "Since *the people* began to bring the offerings into the house of the LORD, we have had enough to eat and have plenty left, for the LORD has blessed His people; and what is left *is* this great abundance."

[11]Now Hezekiah commanded *them* to prepare rooms in the house of the LORD, and they prepared them. [12]Then they faithfully brought in the offerings, the tithes, and the dedicated things; Cononiah the Levite had charge of them, and Shimei his brother *was* the next. [13]Jehiel, Azaziah, Nahath, Asahel, Jerimoth, Jozabad, Eliel, Ismachiah, Mahath, and Benaiah *were* overseers under the hand of Cononiah and

GIVING

Who benefits when we give to the church? (31:4)

31:2 [a]That is, the temple

Shimei his brother, at the commandment of Hezekiah the king and Azariah the ruler of the house of God. [14]Kore the son of Imnah the Levite, the keeper of the East Gate, *was* over the freewill offerings to God, to distribute the offerings of the LORD and the most holy things. [15]And under him *were* Eden, Miniamin, Jeshua, Shemaiah, Amariah, and Shecaniah, *his* faithful assistants in the cities of the priests, to distribute allotments to their brethren by divisions, to the great as well as the small.

[16]Besides those males from three years old and up who were written in the genealogy, they distributed to everyone who entered the house of the LORD his daily portion for the work of his service, by his division, [17]and to the priests who were written in the genealogy according to their father's house, and to the Levites from twenty years old and up according to their work, by their divisions, [18]and to all who were written in the genealogy—their little ones and their wives, their sons and daughters, the whole company of them—for in their faithfulness they sanctified themselves in holiness.

[19]Also for the sons of Aaron the priests, *who were* in the fields of the common-lands of their cities, in every single city, *there were* men who were designated by name to distribute portions to all the males among the priests and to all who were listed by genealogies among the Levites.

[20]Thus Hezekiah did throughout all Judah, and he did what *was* good and right and true before the LORD his God. [21]And in every work that he began in the service of the house of God, in the law and in the commandment, to seek his God, he did *it* with all his heart. So he prospered.

SENNACHERIB BOASTS AGAINST THE LORD

[1]After these deeds of faithfulness, Sennacherib king of Assyria came and entered Judah; he encamped against the fortified cities, thinking to win them over to himself. [2]And when Hezekiah saw that Sennacherib had come, and that his purpose was to make war against Jerusalem, [3]he consulted with his leaders and commanders[a] to stop the water from the springs which *were* outside the city; and they helped him. [4]Thus many people gathered together who stopped all the springs and the brook that ran through the land, saying, "Why should the kings[a] of Assyria come and find much water?" [5]And he strengthened himself, built up all the

wall that was broken, raised *it* up to the towers, and *built* another wall outside; also he repaired the Millo[a] *in* the City of David, and made weapons and shields in abundance. [6]Then he set military captains over the people, gathered them together to him in the open square of the city gate, and gave them encouragement, saying, [7]"Be strong and courageous; do not be afraid nor dismayed before the king of Assyria, nor before all the multitude that *is* with him; for *there are* more with us than with him. [8]With him is an arm of flesh; but with us *is* the LORD our God, to help us and to fight our battles." And the people were strengthened by the words of Hezekiah king of Judah.

WHAT'S IT MEAN?

Sennacherib's biggest claims to fame as king of Assyria were his conquering of Babylon in 689 B.C., his work on his capital in Nineveh, and his cruel attacks on Judah in which he destroyed forty-six towns and villages and took many captives.
2 Chronicles 32:1

[9]After this Sennacherib king of Assyria sent his servants to Jerusalem (but he and all the forces with him *laid siege* against Lachish), to Hezekiah king of Judah, and to all Judah who *were* in Jerusalem, saying, [10]"Thus says Sennacherib king of Assyria: 'In what do you trust, that you remain under siege in Jerusalem? [11]Does not Hezekiah persuade you to give yourselves over to die by famine and by thirst, saying, "The LORD our God will deliver us from the hand of the king of Assyria"? [12]Has not the same Hezekiah taken away His high places and His altars, and commanded Judah and Jerusalem, saying, "You shall worship before one altar and burn incense on it"? [13]Do you not know what I and my fathers have done to all the peoples of *other* lands? Were the gods of the nations of those lands in any way able to deliver their lands out of my hand? [14]Who *was there* among all the gods of those nations that my fathers utterly destroyed that could deliver his people

32:3 [a]Literally *mighty men*   **32:4** [a]Following Masoretic Text and Vulgate; Arabic, Septuagint, and Syriac read *king*.   **32:5** [a]Literally *The Landfill*

from my hand, that your God should be able to deliver you from my hand? [15]Now therefore, do not let Hezekiah deceive you or persuade you like this, and do not believe him; for no god of any nation or kingdom was able to deliver his people from my hand or the hand of my fathers. How much less will your God deliver you from my hand?' "

[16]Furthermore, his servants spoke against the LORD God and against His servant Hezekiah.

[17]He also wrote letters to revile the LORD God of Israel, and to speak against Him, saying, "As the gods of the nations of *other* lands have not delivered their people from my hand, so the God of Hezekiah will not deliver His people from my hand." [18]Then they called out with a loud voice in Hebrew[a] to the people of Jerusalem who *were* on the wall, to frighten them and trouble them, that they might take the city. [19]And they spoke against the God of Jerusalem, as against the gods of the people of the earth—the work of men's hands.

SENNACHERIB'S DEFEAT AND DEATH

[20]Now because of this King Hezekiah and the prophet Isaiah, the son of Amoz, prayed and cried out to heaven. [21]Then the LORD sent an angel who cut down every mighty man of valor, leader, and captain in the camp of the king of Assyria. So he returned shamefaced to his own land. And when he had gone into the temple of his god, some of his own offspring struck him down with the sword there.

[22]Thus the LORD saved Hezekiah and the inhabitants of Jerusalem from the hand of Sennacherib the king of Assyria, and from the hand of all *others*, and guided them[a] on every side. [23]And many brought gifts to the LORD at Jerusalem, and presents to Hezekiah king of Judah, so that he was exalted in the sight of all nations thereafter.

HEZEKIAH HUMBLES HIMSELF

[24]In those days Hezekiah was sick and near death, and he prayed to the LORD; and He spoke to him and gave him a sign. [25]But Hezekiah did not repay according to the favor *shown* him, for his heart was lifted up; therefore wrath was looming over him and over Judah and Jerusalem. [26]Then Hezekiah humbled himself for the pride of his heart, he and the inhabitants of Jerusalem, so that the wrath of the LORD did not come upon them in the days of Hezekiah.

HEZEKIAH'S WEALTH AND HONOR

[27]Hezekiah had very great riches and honor. And he made himself treasuries for silver, for gold, for precious stones, for spices, for shields, and for all kinds of desirable items; [28]storehouses for the harvest of grain, wine, and oil; and stalls for all kinds of livestock, and folds for

32:18 [a]Literally *Judean*   **32:22** [a]Septuagint reads *gave them rest*; Vulgate reads *gave them treasures*.

Promise   HE PROMISES TO FIGHT WITH YOU ON YOUR SIDE.

Be strong and courageous; do not be afraid nor dismayed before the king of Assyria, nor before all the multitude that is with him; for there are more with us than with him. With him is an arm of flesh; but with us is the LORD our God, to help us and to fight our battles (2 Chr. 32:7, 8).

Ever had someone stick up for you? They walked right into the middle of your conflict and took your side? Awesome. Did you ever have someone decide to do more than watch? They cared enough to get involved, to actually stick their neck out and speak up for you. It's an incredible feeling to have someone help you fight your fight. All of a sudden you feel stronger, the enemy seems weaker, and your confidence gets a boost. God is ready to fight for you. He is on your side, ready to intervene and do battle. You are not fighting alone. All the power of the supernatural is right beside you. So look ahead with hope and assurance that the strongest Warrior fights for you.

SEE FOR YOURSELF:
2 Chr. 13:10–12; Zeph. 2:7; Zech. 10:5

flocks.[a] 29Moreover he provided cities for himself, and possessions of flocks and herds in abundance; for God had given him very much property. 30This same Hezekiah also stopped the water outlet of Upper Gihon, and brought the water by tunnel[a] to the west side of the City of David. Hezekiah prospered in all his works.

31However, *regarding* the ambassadors of the princes of Babylon, whom they sent to him to inquire about the wonder that was *done* in the land, God withdrew from him, in order to test him, that He might know all *that was* in his heart.

DEATH OF HEZEKIAH

32Now the rest of the acts of Hezekiah, and his goodness, indeed they *are* written in the vision of Isaiah the prophet, the son of Amoz, *and* in the book of the kings of Judah and Israel. 33So Hezekiah rested with his fathers, and they buried him in the upper tombs of the sons of David; and all Judah and the inhabitants of Jerusalem honored him at his death. Then Manasseh his son reigned in his place.

Manasseh apparently was determined to disobey as many of God's laws as he possibly could. Sorcery and witchcraft—attempting to do things outside the realm of nature—had been banned since the Law of Moses was handed down. Human sacrifice was detested by God. Putting an idol in the temple was like a slap in the face to the Lord. As if all of that weren't enough, according to Jewish tradition, Manasseh was responsible for the murder of the prophet Isaiah. He was the one who gave the command to saw God's prophet in half.
2 Chronicles 33:6, 7

MANASSEH REIGNS IN JUDAH

1Manasseh *was* twelve years old when he became king, and he reigned fifty-five years in Jerusalem. 2But he did evil in the sight of the LORD, according to the abominations of the nations whom the LORD had cast out before the

children of Israel. 3For he rebuilt the high places which Hezekiah his father had broken down; he raised up altars for the Baals, and made wooden images; and he worshiped all the host of heaven[a] and served them. 4He also built altars in the house of the LORD, of which the LORD had said, "In Jerusalem shall My name be forever." 5And he built altars for all the host of heaven in the two courts of the house of the LORD. 6Also he caused his sons to pass through the fire in the Valley of the Son of Hinnom; he practiced sooth-saying, used witchcraft and sorcery, and consulted mediums and spiritists. He did much evil in the sight of the LORD, to provoke Him to anger. 7He even set a carved image, the idol which he had

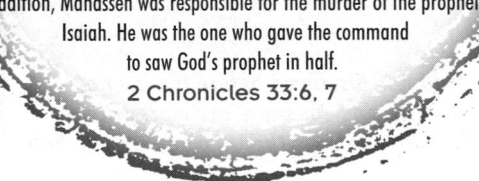

ABORTION
What does God think about killing children? (33:6)

made, in the house of God, of which God had said to David and to Solomon his son, "In this house and in Jerusalem, which I have chosen out of all the tribes of Israel, I will put My name forever; 8and I will not again remove the foot of Israel from the land which I have appointed for your fathers—only if they are careful to do all that I have commanded them, according to the whole law and the statutes and the ordinances by the hand of Moses." 9So Manasseh seduced Judah and the inhabitants of Jerusalem to do more evil than the nations whom the LORD had destroyed before the children of Israel.

MANASSEH RESTORED AFTER REPENTANCE

10And the LORD spoke to Manasseh and his people, but they would not listen. 11Therefore the LORD brought upon them the captains of the army of the king of Assyria, who took Manasseh with hooks,[a] bound him with bronze *fetters*, and carried him off to Babylon. 12Now when he was in affliction, he implored the LORD his God, and humbled himself greatly before the God of his fathers, 13and prayed to Him; and He received his entreaty, heard his supplication, and brought him back to Jerusalem into his kingdom. Then Manasseh knew that the LORD *was* God.

14After this he built a wall outside the City of David on the west side of Gihon, in the valley, as far as the entrance of the Fish Gate; and *it* enclosed Ophel, and he raised it to a very great height. Then he put military captains in all the fortified cities of Judah. 15He took away the for-

---

32:28 [a]Following Septuagint and Vulgate; Arabic and Syriac omit *folds for flocks*; Masoretic Text reads *flocks for sheepfolds*. **32:30** [a]Literally *brought it straight* (compare 2 Kings 20:20) **33:3** [a]The gods of the Assyrians **33:11** [a]That is, nose hooks (compare 2 Kings 19:28) eign gods and the idol from the house of the LORD, and all the altars that he had built in the mount of the house of the LORD and in Jerusalem; and he cast *them* out of the city. [16]He also repaired the altar of the LORD, sacrificed peace offerings and thank offerings on it, and commanded Judah to serve the LORD God of Israel. [17]Nevertheless the people still sacrificed on the high places, *but* only to the LORD their God.

DEATH OF MANASSEH

[18]Now the rest of the acts of Manasseh, his prayer to his God, and the words of the seers who spoke to him in the name of the LORD God of Israel, indeed they *are written* in the book[a] of the kings of Israel. [19]Also his prayer and *how* God received his entreaty, and all his sin and trespass, and the sites where he built high places and set up wooden images and carved images, before he was humbled, indeed they *are* written among the sayings of Hozai.[a] [20]So Manasseh rested with his fathers, and they buried him in his own house. Then his son Amon reigned in his place.

AMON'S REIGN AND DEATH

[21]Amon *was* twenty-two years old when he became king, and he reigned two years in Jerusalem. [22]But he did evil in the sight of the LORD, as his father Manasseh had done; for Amon sacrificed to all the carved images which his father Manasseh had made, and served them. [23]And he did not humble himself before the LORD, as his father Manasseh had humbled himself; but Amon trespassed more and more.

[24]Then his servants conspired against him, and killed him in his own house. [25]But the people of the land executed all those who had conspired against King Amon. Then the people of the land made his son Josiah king in his place.

JOSIAH REIGNS IN JUDAH

[1]Josiah *was* eight years old when he became king, and he reigned thirty-one years in Jerusalem. [2]And he did *what was* right in the sight of the LORD, and walked in the ways of his father David; *he* did *not* turn aside to the right hand or to the left.

[3]For in the eighth year of his reign, while he was still young, he began to seek the God of his father David; and in the twelfth year he began to purge Judah and Jerusalem of the high places, the wooden images, the carved images, and the molded images. [4]They broke down the altars of the Baals in his presence, and the in-

cense altars which *were* above them he cut down; and the wooden images, the carved images, and the molded images he broke in pieces, and made dust of them and scattered *it* on the graves of those who had sacrificed to them. [5]He also burned the bones of the priests on their altars, and cleansed Judah and Jerusalem. [6]And *so he did* in the cities of Manasseh, Ephraim, and Simeon, as far as Naphtali and all around, with axes.[a] [7]When he had broken down the altars and the wooden images, had beaten the carved images into powder, and cut down all the incense altars throughout all the land of Israel, he returned to Jerusalem.

HILKIAH FINDS THE BOOK OF THE LAW

[8]In the eighteenth year of his reign, when he had purged the land and the temple,[a] he sent Shaphan the son of Azaliah, Maaseiah the governor of the city, and Joah the son of Joahaz the recorder, to repair the house of the LORD his God. [9]When they came to Hilkiah the high priest, they delivered the money that was brought into the house of God, which the Levites who kept the doors had gathered from the hand of Manasseh and Ephraim, from all the remnant of Israel, from all Judah and Benjamin, and *which* they had brought back to Jerusalem. [10]Then they put *it* in the hand of the foremen who had the oversight of the house of the LORD; and they gave it to the workmen who worked in the house of the LORD, to repair and restore the house. [11]They gave *it* to the craftsmen and builders to buy hewn stone and timber for beams, and to floor the houses which the kings of Judah had destroyed. [12]And the men did the work faithfully. Their overseers *were* Jahath and Obadiah the Levites, of the sons of Merari, and Zechariah and Meshullam, of the sons of the Kohathites, to supervise. *Others of* the Levites, all of whom were skillful with instruments of music, [13]*were* over the burden bearers and *were* overseers of all who did work in any kind of service. And *some* of the Levites *were* scribes, officers, and gatekeepers.

[14]Now when they brought out the money that was brought into the house of the LORD, Hilkiah the priest found the Book of the Law of the LORD *given* by Moses. [15]Then Hilkiah answered and said to Shaphan the scribe, "I have found the Book of the Law in the house of the LORD." And Hilkiah gave the book to Shaphan. [16]So Shaphan carried the book to the king, bringing the king word, saying, "All that was committed to your servants they are doing.

33:18 [a]Literally *words*   **33:19** [a]Septuagint reads *the seers.*   **34:6** [a]Literally *swords*   **34:8** [a]Literally *house*

[17]And they have gathered the money that was found in the house of the LORD, and have delivered it into the hand of the overseers and the workmen." [18]Then Shaphan the scribe told the king, saying, "Hilkiah the priest has given me a book." And Shaphan read it before the king.

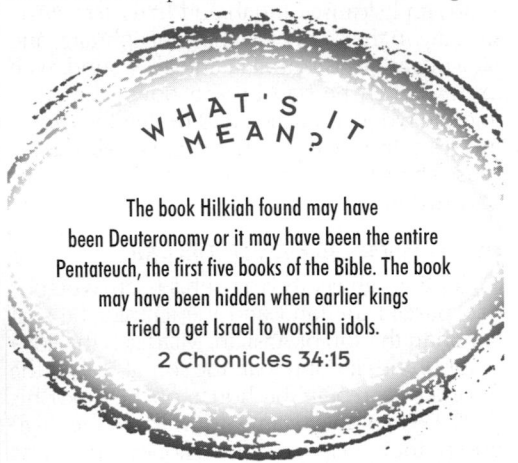

WHAT'S IT MEAN?

The book Hilkiah found may have been Deuteronomy or it may have been the entire Pentateuch, the first five books of the Bible. The book may have been hidden when earlier kings tried to get Israel to worship idols.

2 Chronicles 34:15

[19]Thus it happened, when the king heard the words of the Law, that he tore his clothes. [20]Then the king commanded Hilkiah, Ahikam the son of Shaphan, Abdon[a] the son of Micah, Shaphan the scribe, and Asaiah a servant of the king, saying, [21]"Go, inquire of the LORD for me, and for those who are left in Israel and Judah, concerning the words of the book that is found; for great is the wrath of the LORD that is poured out on us, because our fathers have not kept the word of the LORD, to do according to all that is written in this book."

[22]So Hilkiah and those the king had appointed went to Huldah the prophetess, the wife of Shallum the son of Tokhath,[a] the son of Hasrah,[b] keeper of the wardrobe. (She dwelt in Jerusalem in the Second Quarter.) And they spoke to her to that effect.

[23]Then she answered them, "Thus says the LORD God of Israel, 'Tell the man who sent you to Me, [24]"Thus says the LORD: 'Behold, I will bring calamity on this place and on its inhabitants, all the curses that are written in the book which they have read before the king of Judah, [25]because they have forsaken Me and burned incense to other gods, that they might provoke Me to anger with all the works of their hands. Therefore My wrath will be poured out on this place, and not be quenched.' " ' [26]But as for the king of Judah, who sent you to inquire of the LORD, in this manner you shall speak to him,

'Thus says the LORD God of Israel: "Concerning the words which you have heard— [27]because your heart was tender, and you humbled yourself before God when you heard His words against this place and against its inhabitants, and you humbled yourself before Me, and you tore your clothes and wept before Me, I also have heard you," says the LORD. [28]"Surely I will gather you to your fathers, and you shall be gathered to your grave in peace; and your eyes shall not see all the calamity which I will bring on this place and its inhabitants." ' " So they brought back word to the king.

JOSIAH RESTORES TRUE WORSHIP

[29]Then the king sent and gathered all the elders of Judah and Jerusalem. [30]The king went up to the house of the LORD, with all the men of Judah and the inhabitants of Jerusalem—the priests and the Levites, and all the people, great and small. And he read in their hearing all the words of the Book of the Covenant which had been found in the house of the LORD. [31]Then the king stood in his place and made a covenant before the LORD, to follow the LORD, and to keep His commandments and His testimonies and His statutes with all his heart and all his soul, to perform the words of the covenant that were written in this book. [32]And he made all who were present in Jerusalem and Benjamin take a stand. So the inhabitants of Jerusalem did according to the covenant of God, the God of their fathers. [33]Thus Josiah removed all the abominations from all the country that belonged to the children of Israel, and made all who were present in Israel diligently serve the LORD their God. All his days they did not depart from following the LORD God of their fathers.

> **BIBLE**
>
> How hard should we try to obey the Bible? (34:31)

JOSIAH KEEPS THE PASSOVER

[1]Now Josiah kept a Passover to the LORD in Jerusalem, and they slaughtered the Passover lambs on the fourteenth day of the first month. [2]And he set the priests in their duties and encouraged them for the service of the house of the LORD. [3]Then he said to the Levites who taught all Israel, who were holy to the LORD: "Put the holy ark in the house which Solomon the son of David, king of Israel, built. It shall no longer be a burden on your shoulders. Now serve the LORD your God and His people Israel.

34:20 [a]Achbor the son of Michaiah in 2 Kings 22:12   **34:22** [a]Spelled Tikvah in 2 Kings 22:14   [b]Spelled Harhas in 2 Kings 22:14

⁴Prepare *yourselves* according to your fathers' houses, according to your divisions, following the written instruction of David king of Israel and the written instruction of Solomon his son. ⁵And stand in the holy *place* according to the divisions of the fathers' houses of your brethren the *lay* people, and *according to* the division of the father's house of the Levites. ⁶So slaughter the Passover *offerings*, consecrate yourselves, and prepare *them* for your brethren, that *they* may do according to the word of the LORD by the hand of Moses."

WHAT'S IT MEAN?

The ark of the covenant was a wooden box covered with gold. The ark had been built according to plans that God had given to Moses. It had rings on its sides so that priests could run poles through them and lift the box without actually touching it. Because the Israelites believed the ark contained God's power, occasionally they carried it with them into battle.

2 Chronicles 35:3

⁷Then Josiah gave the *lay* people lambs and young goats from the flock, all for Passover *offerings* for all who were present, to the number of thirty thousand, as well as three thousand cattle; these *were* from the king's possessions. ⁸And his leaders gave willingly to the people, to the priests, and to the Levites. Hilkiah, Zechariah, and Jehiel, rulers of the house of God, gave to the priests for the Passover *offerings* two thousand six hundred *from the flock*, and three hundred cattle. ⁹Also Conaniah, his brothers Shemaiah and Nethanel, and Hashabiah and Jeiel and Jozabad, chief of the Levites, gave to the Levites for Passover *offerings* five thousand *from the flock* and five hundred cattle.

¹⁰So the service was prepared, and the priests stood in their places, and the Levites in their divisions, according to the king's command. ¹¹And they slaughtered the Passover *offerings*; and the priests sprinkled *the blood* with their hands, while the Levites skinned *the animals*. ¹²Then they removed the burnt offerings that *they* might give them to the divisions of the fathers' houses of the *lay* people, to offer to the LORD, as *it is* written in the Book of Moses. And so *they* did with the cattle. ¹³Also they roasted

the Passover *offerings* with fire according to the ordinance; but the *other* holy *offerings* they boiled in pots, in caldrons, and in pans, and divided *them* quickly among all the *lay* people. ¹⁴Then afterward they prepared portions for themselves and for the priests, because the priests, the sons of Aaron, *were busy* in offering burnt offerings and fat until night; therefore the Levites prepared portions for themselves and for the priests, the sons of Aaron. ¹⁵And the singers, the sons of Asaph, *were* in their places, according to the command of David, Asaph, Heman, and Jeduthun the king's seer. Also the gatekeepers were at each gate; they did not have to leave their position, because their brethren the Levites prepared portions for them.

¹⁶So all the service of the LORD was prepared the same day, to keep the Passover and to offer burnt offerings on the altar of the LORD, according to the command of King Josiah. ¹⁷And the children of Israel who were present kept the Passover at that time, and the Feast of Unleavened Bread for seven days. ¹⁸There had been no Passover kept in Israel like that since the days of Samuel the prophet; and none of the kings of Israel had kept such a Passover as Josiah kept, with the priests and the Levites, all Judah and Israel who were present, and the inhabitants of Jerusalem. ¹⁹In the eighteenth year of the reign of Josiah this Passover was kept.

JOSIAH DIES IN BATTLE

²⁰After all this, when Josiah had prepared the temple, Necho king of Egypt came up to fight against Carchemish by the Euphrates; and Josiah went out against him. ²¹But he sent messengers to him, saying, "What have I to do with you, king of Judah? *I have* not *come* against you this day, but against the house with which I have war; for God commanded me to make haste. Refrain *from meddling with* God, who *is* with me, lest He destroy you." ²²Nevertheless Josiah would not turn his face from him, but disguised himself so that he might fight with him, and did not heed the words of Necho from the mouth of God. So he came to fight in the Valley of Megiddo.

²³And the archers shot King Josiah; and the king said to his servants, "Take me away, for I am severely wounded." ²⁴His servants therefore took him out of that chariot and put him in the second chariot that he had, and they brought him to Jerusalem. So he died, and was buried in *one of* the tombs of his fathers. And all Judah and Jerusalem mourned for Josiah.

²⁵Jeremiah also lamented for Josiah. And to this day all the singing men and the singing

women speak of Josiah in their lamentations. They made it a custom in Israel; and indeed they *are* written in the Laments. ²⁶Now the rest of the acts of Josiah and his goodness, according to *what was* written in the Law of the LORD, ²⁷and his deeds from first to last, indeed they *are* written in the book of the kings of Israel and Judah.

THE REIGN AND CAPTIVITY OF JEHOAHAZ

¹Then the people of the land took Jehoahaz the son of Josiah, and made him king in his father's place in Jerusalem. ²Jehoahaz*ᵃ was* twenty-three years old when he became king, and he reigned three months in Jerusalem. ³Now the king of Egypt deposed him at Jerusalem; and he imposed on the land a tribute of one hundred talents of silver and a talent of gold. ⁴Then the king of Egypt made *Jehoahaz'sᵃ* brother Eliakim king over Judah and Jerusalem, and changed his name to Jehoiakim. And Necho took Jehoahazᵇ his brother and carried him off to Egypt.

WHAT'S IT MEAN?

The attack described here was the first of three by Nebuchadnezzar's forces that eventually resulted in the destruction of the temple, the city of Jerusalem, and the kingdom of Judah. Nebuchadnezzar deported scores of Israelites to other regions of his empire, using them as slave labor for various construction projects.

2 Chronicles 36:6

THE REIGN AND CAPTIVITY OF JEHOIAKIM

⁵Jehoiakim *was* twenty-five years old when he became king, and he reigned eleven years in Jerusalem. And he did evil in the sight of the LORD his God. ⁶Nebuchadnezzar king of Babylon came up against him, and bound him in bronze *fetters* to carry him off to Babylon. ⁷Nebuchadnezzar also carried off *some* of the articles from the house of the LORD to Babylon, and put them in his temple at Babylon. ⁸Now the rest of the acts of Jehoiakim, the abominations which he did, and what was found against him, indeed they *are* written in the book of the kings of

Israel and Judah. Then Jehoiachin his son reigned in his place.

THE REIGN AND CAPTIVITY OF JEHOIACHIN

⁹Jehoiachin *was* eightᵃ years old when he became king, and he reigned in Jerusalem three months and ten days. And he did evil in the sight of the LORD. ¹⁰At the turn of the year King Nebuchadnezzar summoned *him* and took him to Babylon, with the costly articles from the house of the LORD, and made Zedekiah, *Jehoiakim'sᵃ* brother, king over Judah and Jerusalem.

ZEDEKIAH REIGNS IN JUDAH

¹¹Zedekiah *was* twenty-one years old when he became king, and he reigned eleven years in Jerusalem. ¹²He did evil in the sight of the LORD his God, *and* did not humble himself before Jeremiah the prophet, *who spoke* from the mouth of the LORD. ¹³And he also rebelled against King Nebuchadnezzar, who had made him swear *an oath* by God; but he stiffened his neck and hardened his heart against turning to the LORD God of Israel. ¹⁴Moreover all the leaders of the priests and the people transgressed more and more, *according* to all the abominations of the nations, and defiled the house of the LORD which He had consecrated in Jerusalem.

WHAT'S IT MEAN?

After Cyrus's Persian army defeated the Babylonians in 539 B.C., his nation became the most powerful empire in the ancient world. Surprisingly, Cyrus didn't let that power go to his head. He maintained his reputation as a wise and tolerant ruler. In fact, he even allowed the Jewish captives to return to Jerusalem and rebuild their temple. Though Cyrus may not have believed in Israel's God, he is praised in the Bible for his role in God's plan.

2 Chronicles 36:22

THE FALL OF JERUSALEM

¹⁵And the LORD God of their fathers sent *warnings* to them by His messengers, rising up early and sending *them*, because He had com-

---

36:2 ᵃMasoretic Text reads *Joahaz*. **36:4** ᵃLiterally *his* ᵇMasoretic Text reads *Joahaz*. **36:9** ᵃSome Hebrew manuscripts, Septuagint, Syriac, and 2 Kings 24:8 read *eighteen*. **36:10** ᵃLiterally *his* (compare 2 Kings 24:17)

passion on His people and on His dwelling place. ¹⁶But they mocked the messengers of God, despised His words, and scoffed at His prophets, until the wrath of the LORD arose against His people, till *there was* no remedy.

¹⁷Therefore He brought against them the king of the Chaldeans, who killed their young men with the sword in the house of their sanctuary, and had no compassion on young man or virgin, on the aged or the weak; He gave *them* all into his hand. ¹⁸And all the articles from the house of God, great and small, the treasures of the house of the LORD, and the treasures of the king and of his leaders, all *these* he took to Babylon. ¹⁹Then they burned the house of God, broke down the wall of Jerusalem, burned all its palaces with fire, and destroyed all its precious possessions. ²⁰And those who escaped from the sword he carried away to Babylon, where they became servants to him and his sons until the rule of the kingdom of Persia, ²¹to fulfill the word of the LORD by the mouth of Jeremiah, until the land had enjoyed her Sabbaths. As long as she lay desolate she kept Sabbath, to fulfill seventy years.

> "And He has commanded me to build Him a house at Jerusalem which is in Judah."
> (2 Chronicles 36:23b)

THE PROCLAMATION OF CYRUS

²²Now in the first year of Cyrus king of Persia, that the word of the LORD by the mouth of Jeremiah might be fulfilled, the LORD stirred up the spirit of Cyrus king of Persia, so that he made a proclamation throughout all his kingdom, and also *put it* in writing, saying,

²³ Thus says Cyrus king of Persia:

All the kingdoms of the earth the LORD God of heaven has given me. And He has commanded me to build Him a house at Jerusalem which is in Judah. Who *is* among you of all His people? May the LORD his God *be* with him, and let him go up!

CONTENT Imagine . . . seventy years ago your parents and grandparents got dragged away from their homeland and resettled into a new country. You were born there, grew up and raised your kids there. Now your kids are grown and you've got grand-children there. One day, you get the news that a new king has taken over and he has offered you the opportunity to move back to the land your parents left behind. You can move back home.

Home?

That was the dilemma that Ezra and his people faced in Babylon. Only a few of them made the choice to actually return to their hometown, Jerusalem. When they did, they found their city in ruins. All they could do was start over. They started rebuilding the temple. They started rebuilding their homes. They started figuring out their cultural heritage.

Ezra returned to Jerusalem after the temple was rebuilt, but before the people had renewed their relationship with God. He helped them see that the condition of the place of worship is important, but not as important as the condition of the hearts of the worshipers.

Outline

Purpose God keeps the promises He makes to Israel, and He keeps His promises to us.

Theme Exiles' Return to Jerusalem and Temple Reconstruction

Date of writing 457–444 B.C.

"For Ezra had prepared his heart to seek the Law of the LORD, and to do it, and to teach statutes and ordinances in Israel" (7:10).

Bible Talk

Intermarriage

One of the issues that Ezra addressed with the Jewish people was intermarriage, or marrying someone from another culture. Intermarriage wasn't a moral problem. People are people no matter what culture they are from. But intermarriage *was* a spiritual problem. All the surrounding cultures worshiped idols.

Marrying someone doesn't mean you will take on all their beliefs and practices, but it does mean that you will be influenced by them. The Hebrews already had a reputation for giving in to peer pressure, particularly where false gods were concerned. If the Hebrews married into one of the cultures that worshiped idols, it was almost a sure thing that they would embrace the worship of idols as well.

You really can't exaggerate how big a deal this idol worship stuff was to God. The first *and* second of the Ten Commandments (see Exodus 20) had to do with it.

THE TEMPLE

Restoring the temple was one of the biggest tasks facing the exiles who had returned to Jerusalem. If you look back through the history of the Hebrews, you'll see that the way they treated the temple almost *always* ran parallel with the respect they had for God. In the days before their exile to Babylon, getting the temple back in shape after one of their irreligious "benders" wasn't as big of a deal. But by the time Ezra returned to Jerusalem, the temple wasn't just in disrepair. It had been destroyed! This mirrored the faith of Ezra's people, and it broke his heart.

So when the people of Israel set about to rebuild the temple they were also setting about to restore their faith in and their relationship with God.

END OF THE BABYLONIAN CAPTIVITY

¹Now in the first year of Cyrus king of Persia, that the word of the LORD by the mouth of Jeremiah might be fulfilled, the LORD stirred up the spirit of Cyrus king of Persia, so that he made a proclamation throughout all his kingdom, and also *put it* in writing, saying,

2   Thus says Cyrus king of Persia:
All the kingdoms of the earth the LORD God of heaven has given me. And He has commanded me to build Him a house at Jerusalem which *is* in Judah. ³Who *is* among you of all His people? May his God be with him, and let him go up to Jerusalem which *is* in Judah, and build the house of the LORD God of Israel (He *is* God), which *is* in Jerusalem. ⁴And whoever is left in any place where he dwells, let the men of his place help him with silver and gold, with goods and livestock, besides the freewill offerings for the house of God which *is* in Jerusalem.

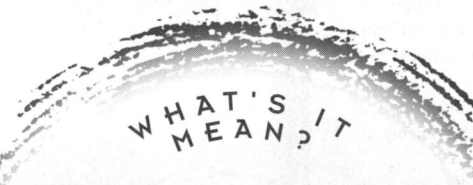

King Cyrus was killed in battle around 530 B.C. after a pretty successful career as ruler of Persia. Among the accomplishments that might have been included in his obituary was his conquering of the Medes, the Lydians, and the Babylonians. Unlike other ancient kings, Cyrus allowed the people he defeated to worship their own gods.

Ezra 1:2, 3

⁵Then the heads of the fathers' *houses* of Judah and Benjamin, and the priests and the Levites, with all whose spirits God had moved, arose to go up and build the house of the LORD which *is* in Jerusalem. ⁶And all those who *were* around them encouraged them with articles of silver and gold, with goods and livestock, and with precious things, besides all *that* was willingly offered.

⁷King Cyrus also brought out the articles of the house of the LORD, which Nebuchadnezzar had taken from Jerusalem and put in the temple of his gods; ⁸and Cyrus king of Persia brought them out by the hand of Mithredath the treasurer, and counted them out to Sheshbazzar the prince of Judah. ⁹This *is* the number of them: thirty gold platters, one thousand silver platters, twenty-nine knives, ¹⁰thirty gold basins, four hundred and ten silver basins of a similar *kind*, *and* one thousand other articles. ¹¹All the articles of gold and silver *were* five thousand four hundred. All *these* Sheshbazzar took with the captives who were brought from Babylon to Jerusalem.

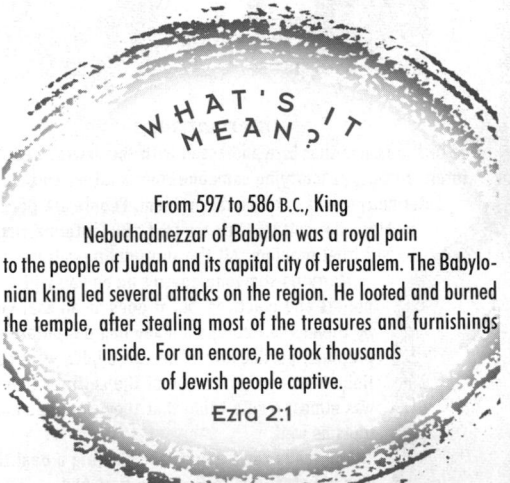

From 597 to 586 B.C., King Nebuchadnezzar of Babylon was a royal pain to the people of Judah and its capital city of Jerusalem. The Babylonian king led several attacks on the region. He looted and burned the temple, after stealing most of the treasures and furnishings inside. For an encore, he took thousands of Jewish people captive.

Ezra 2:1

THE CAPTIVES WHO RETURNED TO JERUSALEM

¹Now*ᵃ* these *are* the people of the province who came back from the captivity, of those who had been carried away, whom Nebuchadnezzar the king of Babylon had carried away to Babylon, and who returned to Jerusalem and Judah, everyone to his *own* city.

²*Those* who came with Zerubbabel *were* Jeshua, Nehemiah, Seraiah, Reelaiah, Mordecai, Bilshan, Mispar,*ᵃ* Bigvai, Rehum,*ᵇ* *and* Baanah. The number of the men of the people of Israel: ³the people of Parosh, two thousand one hundred and seventy-two; ⁴the people of Shephatiah, three hundred and seventy-two; ⁵the people of Arah, seven hundred and seventy-five; ⁶the people of Pahath-Moab, of the people of Jeshua *and* Joab, two thousand eight hundred and twelve; ⁷the people of Elam, one thousand two hundred and fifty-four; ⁸the people of Zattu, nine hundred and forty-five; ⁹the people of Zaccai, seven hundred and sixty; ¹⁰the people of

---

2:1 *ᵃ*Compare this chapter with Nehemiah 7:6–73.   **2:2** *ᵃ*Spelled *Mispereth* in Nehemiah 7:7 *ᵇ*Spelled *Nehum* in Nehemiah 7:7

Bani,[a] six hundred and forty-two; [11]the people of Bebai, six hundred and twenty-three; [12]the people of Azgad, one thousand two hundred and twenty-two; [13]the people of Adonikam, six hundred and sixty-six; [14]the people of Bigvai, two thousand and fifty-six; [15]the people of Adin, four hundred and fifty-four; [16]the people of Ater of Hezekiah, ninety-eight; [17]the people of Bezai, three hundred and twenty-three; [18]the people of Jorah,[a] one hundred and twelve; [19]the people of Hashum, two hundred and twenty-three; [20]the people of Gibbar,[a] ninety-five; [21]the people of Bethlehem, one hundred and twenty-three; [22]the men of Netophah, fifty-six; [23]the men of Anathoth, one hundred and twenty-eight; [24]the people of Azmaveth,[a] forty-two; [25]the people of Kirjath Arim,[a] Chephirah, and Beeroth, seven hundred and forty-three; [26]the people of Ramah and Geba, six hundred and twenty-one; [27]the men of Michmas, one hundred and twenty-two; [28]the men of Bethel and Ai, two hundred and twenty-three; [29]the people of Nebo, fifty-two; [30]the people of Magbish, one hundred and fifty-six; [31]the people of the other Elam, one thousand two hundred and fifty-four; [32]the people of Harim, three hundred and twenty; [33]the people of Lod, Hadid, and Ono, seven hundred and twenty-five; [34]the people of Jericho, three hundred and forty-five; [35]the people of Senaah, three thousand six hundred and thirty.

[36]The priests: the sons of Jedaiah, of the house of Jeshua, nine hundred and seventy-three; [37]the sons of Immer, one thousand and fifty-two; [38]the sons of Pashhur, one thousand two hundred and forty-seven; [39]the sons of Harim, one thousand and seventeen.

[40]The Levites: the sons of Jeshua and Kadmiel, of the sons of Hodaviah,[a] seventy-four.

[41]The singers: the sons of Asaph, one hundred and twenty-eight.

[42]The sons of the gatekeepers: the sons of Shallum, the sons of Ater, the sons of Talmon, the sons of Akkub, the sons of Hatita, and the sons of Shobai, one hundred and thirty-nine in all.

[43]The Nethinim: the sons of Ziha, the sons of Hasupha, the sons of Tabbaoth, [44]the sons of Keros, the sons of Siaha,[a] the sons of Padon, [45]the sons of Lebanah, the sons of Hagabah, the sons of Akkub, [46]the sons of Hagab, the sons of

Shalmai, the sons of Hanan, [47]the sons of Giddel, the sons of Gahar, the sons of Reaiah, [48]the sons of Rezin, the sons of Nekoda, the sons of Gazzam, [49]the sons of Uzza, the sons of Paseah, the sons of Besai, [50]the sons of Asnah, the sons of Meunim, the sons of Nephusim,[a] [51]the sons of Bakbuk, the sons of Hakupha, the sons of Harhur, [52]the sons of Bazluth,[a] the sons of Mehida, the sons of Harsha, [53]the sons of Barkos, the sons of Sisera, the sons of Tamah, [54]the sons of Neziah, and the sons of Hatipha.

[55]The sons of Solomon's servants: the sons of Sotai, the sons of Sophereth, the sons of Peruda,[a] [56]the sons of Jaala, the sons of Darkon, the sons of Giddel, [57]the sons of Shephatiah, the sons of Hattil, the sons of Pochereth of Zebaim, and the sons of Ami.[a] [58]All the Nethinim and the children of Solomon's servants were three hundred and ninety-two.

[59]And these *were* the ones who came up from Tel Melah, Tel Harsha, Cherub, Addan,[a] and Immer; but they could not identify their father's house or their genealogy,[b] whether they *were* of Israel: [60]the sons of Delaiah, the sons of Tobiah, and the sons of Nekoda, six hundred and fifty-two; [61]and of the sons of the priests: the sons of Habaiah, the sons of Koz,[a] and the sons of Barzillai, who took a wife of the daughters of Barzillai the Gileadite, and was called by their name. [62]These sought their listing *among* those who were registered by genealogy, but they were not found; therefore they *were excluded* from the priesthood as defiled. [63]And the

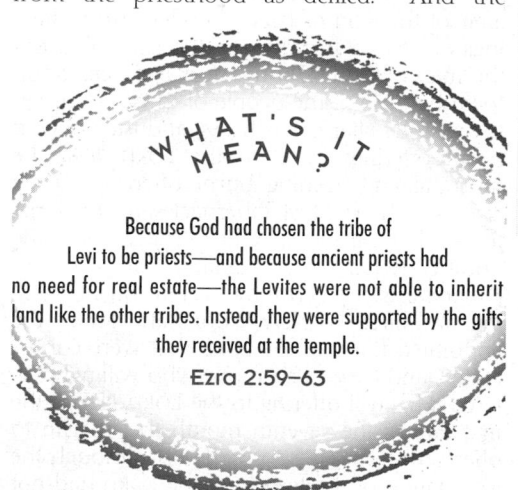

WHAT'S IT MEAN?

Because God had chosen the tribe of Levi to be priests—and because ancient priests had no need for real estate—the Levites were not able to inherit land like the other tribes. Instead, they were supported by the gifts they received at the temple.

Ezra 2:59–63

2:10 [a]Spelled *Binnui* in Nehemiah 7:15 **2:18** [a]Called *Hariph* in Nehemiah 7:24 **2:20** [a]Called *Gibeon* in Nehemiah 7:25 **2:24** [a]Called *Beth Azmaveth* in Nehemiah 7:28 **2:25** [a]Called *Kirjath Jearim* in Nehemiah 7:29 **2:40** [a]Spelled *Hodevah* in Nehemiah 7:43 **2:44** [a]Spelled *Sia* in Nehemiah 7:47 **2:50** [a]Spelled *Nephishesim* in Nehemiah 7:52 **2:52** [a]Spelled *Bazlith* in Nehemiah 7:54 **2:55** [a]Spelled *Perida* in Nehemiah 7:57 **2:57** [a]Spelled *Amon* in Nehemiah 7:59 **2:59** [a]Spelled *Addon* in Nehemiah 7:61 [b]Literally *seed* **2:61** [a]Or *Hakkoz* governor[a] said to them that they should not eat of the most holy things till a priest could consult with the Urim and Thummim.

[64]The whole assembly together *was* forty-two thousand three hundred *and* sixty, [65]besides their male and female servants, of whom *there were* seven thousand three hundred and thirty-seven; and they had two hundred men and women singers. [66]Their horses *were* seven hundred and thirty-six, their mules two hundred and forty-five, [67]their camels four hundred and thirty-five, and *their* donkeys six thousand seven hundred and twenty.

[68]*Some* of the heads of the fathers' *houses,* when they came to the house of the LORD which *is* in Jerusalem, offered freely for the house of God, to erect it in its place: [69]According to their ability, they gave to the treasury for the work sixty-one thousand gold drachmas, five thousand minas of silver, and one hundred priestly garments.

[70]So the priests and the Levites, *some* of the people, the singers, the gatekeepers, and the Nethinim, dwelt in their cities, and all Israel in their cities.

WORSHIP RESTORED AT JERUSALEM

[1]And when the seventh month had come, and the children of Israel *were* in the cities, the people gathered together as one man to Jerusalem. [2]Then Jeshua the son of Jozadak[a] and his brethren the priests, and Zerubbabel the son of Shealtiel and his brethren, arose and built the altar of the God of Israel, to offer burnt offerings on it, as *it is* written in the Law of Moses the man of God. [3]Though fear *had come* upon them because of the people of those countries, they set the altar on its bases; and they offered burnt offerings on it to the LORD, *both* the morning and evening burnt offerings. [4]They also kept the Feast of Tabernacles, as *it is* written, and *offered* the daily burnt offerings in the number required by ordinance for each day. [5]Afterwards *they offered* the regular burnt offering, and *those* for New Moons and for all the appointed feasts of the LORD that were consecrated, and *those* of everyone who willingly offered a freewill offering to the LORD. [6]From the first day of the seventh month they began to offer burnt offerings to the LORD, although the foundation of the temple of the LORD had not been laid. [7]They also gave money to the masons and the carpenters, and food, drink, and oil to the people of Sidon and Tyre to bring cedar logs from Lebanon to the sea, to Joppa, according to the permission which they had from Cyrus king of Persia.

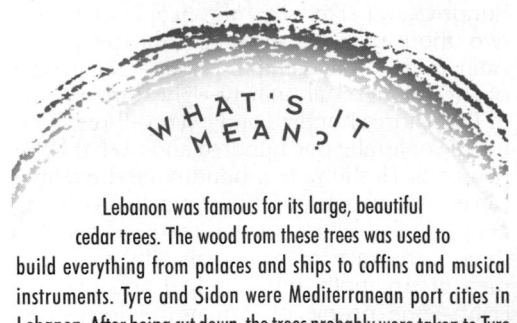

WHAT'S IT MEAN?

Lebanon was famous for its large, beautiful cedar trees. The wood from these trees was used to build everything from palaces and ships to coffins and musical instruments. Tyre and Sidon were Mediterranean port cities in Lebanon. After being cut down, the trees probably were taken to Tyre and Sidon, loaded onto rafts, and floated to Joppa. From there, they probably were hauled across land for the remaining thirty-five miles to Jerusalem.

Ezra 3:7

RESTORATION OF THE TEMPLE BEGINS

[8]Now in the second month of the second year of their coming to the house of God at Jerusalem, Zerubbabel the son of Shealtiel, Jeshua the son of Jozadak,[a] and the rest of their brethren the priests and the Levites, and all those who had come out of the captivity to Jerusalem, began *work* and appointed the Levites from twenty years old and above to oversee the work of the house of the LORD. [9]Then Jeshua *with* his sons and brothers, Kadmiel *with* his sons, and the sons of Judah,[a] arose as one to oversee those working on the house of God: the sons of Henadad *with* their sons and their brethren the Levites.

[10]When the builders laid the foundation of the temple of the LORD, the priests stood[a] in their apparel with trumpets, and the Levites, the sons of Asaph, with cymbals, to praise the LORD, according to the ordinance of David king of Israel. [11]And they sang responsively, praising and giving thanks to the LORD:

"For *He is* good,
For His mercy *endures*
forever toward Israel."[a]

LOVE
Does God love me forever? (3:11)

Then all the people shouted with a great shout, when they praised the LORD, because the foundation of the house of the LORD was laid.

On the Edge

For He is good, for His mercy endures forever toward Israel (Ezra 3:11).

"Good" can be a fleeting thing for us. Some days we think we have it, and sometimes it's hard to hold on to. A misunderstanding can turn really good friends into enemies overnight. We can have a good attitude toward one person and be totally rude to the next. Your favorite ice cream may taste really good, but after six scoops, it's gross. People can even get so confused that they believe that wrong and sinful things are good—like drugs, premarital sex, and pornography.

But God is nothing like we are. He is all good. He cannot change His mind because He misunderstood; He is not fickle with people. You can't get too much of His goodness. He is good on every level, all the time. Let those words about God's goodness remind you that everything He does is for your good. You may struggle with good, but God never will.

SEE FOR YOURSELF:
Ex. 33:19; 2 Sam. 7:28;
Ps. 31:19; 100:5;
Rom. 8:28

"Let us build with you, for we seek your God as you *do*; and we have sacrificed to Him since the days of Esarhaddon king of Assyria, who brought us here." ³But Zerubbabel and Jeshua and the rest of the heads of the fathers' *houses* of Israel said to them, "You may do nothing with us to build a house for our God; but we alone will build to the LORD God of Israel, as King Cyrus the king of Persia has commanded us." ⁴Then the people of the land tried to discourage the people of Judah. They troubled them in building, ⁵and hired counselors against them to frustrate their purpose all the days of Cyrus king of Persia, even until the reign of Darius king of Persia.

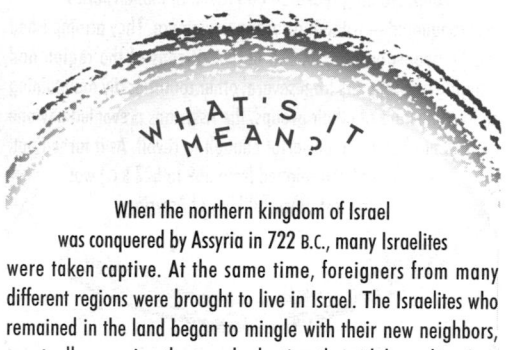

WHAT'S IT MEAN?

When the northern kingdom of Israel was conquered by Assyria in 722 B.C., many Israelites were taken captive. At the same time, foreigners from many different regions were brought to live in Israel. The Israelites who remained in the land began to mingle with their new neighbors, eventually marrying them and adopting their idol worship. As a result, they were no longer a distinct people—either physically or spiritually.

Ezra 4:2

¹²But many of the priests and Levites and heads of the fathers' *houses,* old men who had seen the first temple, wept with a loud voice when the foundation of this temple was laid before their eyes. Yet many shouted aloud for joy, ¹³so that the people could not discern the noise of the shout of joy from the noise of the weeping of the people, for the people shouted with a loud shout, and the sound was heard afar off.

RESISTANCE TO REBUILDING THE TEMPLE

¹Now when the adversaries of Judah and Benjamin heard that the descendants of the captivity were building the temple of the LORD God of Israel, ²they came to Zerubbabel and the heads of the fathers' *houses,* and said to them,

REBUILDING OF JERUSALEM OPPOSED

⁶In the reign of Ahasuerus, in the beginning of his reign, they wrote an accusation against the inhabitants of Judah and Jerusalem.

⁷In the days of Artaxerxes also, Bishlam, Mithredath, Tabel, and the rest of their companions wrote to Artaxerxes king of Persia; and the letter *was* written in Aramaic script, and translated into the Aramaic language. ⁸Rehum[a] the commander and Shimshai the scribe wrote a letter against Jerusalem to King Artaxerxes in this fashion:

⁹ From[a] Rehum the commander, Shimshai the scribe, and the rest of their companions —*representatives* of the Dinaites, the Apharsathchites, the

4:8 ªThe original language of Ezra 4:8 through 6:18 is Aramaic.   4:9 ªLiterally *Then*

Tarpelites, the people of Persia and Erech and Babylon and Shushan,[b] the Dehavites, the Elamites, [10]and the rest of the nations whom the great and noble Osnapper took captive and settled in the cities of Samaria and the remainder beyond the River[a]—and so forth.[b]

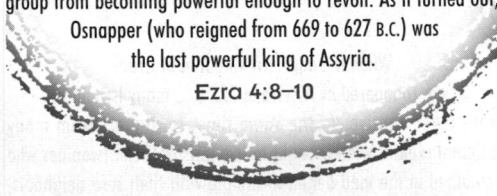

WHAT'S IT MEAN?

The Assyrians were particularly good at preventing rebellion and revolt in the territories they conquered—without resorting to violence. They accomplished this by deporting most of the native citizens of the region and bringing in foreigners from several other countries. By maintaining an even mixture of ethnic groups, the Assyrians prevented any one group from becoming powerful enough to revolt. As it turned out, Osnapper (who reigned from 669 to 627 B.C.) was the last powerful king of Assyria.

Ezra 4:8–10

[11](This *is* a copy of the letter that they sent him)

To King Artaxerxes from your servants, the men *of the region* beyond the River, and so forth:[a]

[12] Let it be known to the king that the Jews who came up from you have come to us at Jerusalem, and are building the rebellious and evil city, and are finishing *its* walls and repairing the foundations. [13]Let it now be known to the king that, if this city is built and the walls completed, they will not pay tax, tribute, or custom, and the king's treasury will be diminished. [14]Now because we receive support from the palace, it was not proper for us to see the king's dishonor; therefore we have sent and informed the king, [15]that search may be made in the book of the records of your fathers. And you will find in the book of the records and know that this city *is* a rebellious city, harmful to kings and provinces, and

that they have incited sedition within the city in former times, for which cause this city was destroyed.

[16] We inform the king that if this city is rebuilt and its walls are completed, the result will be that you will have no dominion beyond the River.

[17]The king sent an answer:

To Rehum the commander, *to* Shimshai the scribe, *to* the rest of their companions who dwell in Samaria, and *to* the remainder beyond the River:

Peace, and so forth.[a]

[18] The letter which you sent to us has been clearly read before me. [19]And I gave the command, and a search has been made, and it was found that this city in former times has revolted against kings, and rebellion and sedition have been fostered in it. [20]There have also been mighty kings over Jerusalem, who have ruled over all *the region* beyond the River; and tax, tribute, and custom were paid to them. [21]Now give the command to make these men cease, that this city may not be built until the command is given by me. [22] Take heed now that you do not fail to do this. Why should damage increase to the hurt of the kings?

[23]Now when the copy of King Artaxerxes' letter *was* read before Rehum, Shimshai the scribe, and their companions, they went up in haste to Jerusalem against the Jews, and by force of arms made them cease. [24]Thus the work of the house of God which *is* at Jerusalem ceased, and it was discontinued until the second year of the reign of Darius king of Persia.

RESTORATION OF THE TEMPLE RESUMED

[1]Then the prophet Haggai and Zechariah the son of Iddo, prophets, prophesied to the Jews who *were* in Judah and Jerusalem, in the name of the God of Israel, *who was* over them. [2]So Zerubbabel the son of Shealtiel and Jeshua the son of Jozadak[a] rose up and began to build the house of God which *is* in Jerusalem; and the prophets of God *were* with them, helping them.

4:9 [b]Or *Susa*   **4:10** [a]That is, the Euphrates   [b]Literally *and now*   **4:11** [a]Literally *and now*   **4:17** [a]Literally *and now*   **5:2** [a]Spelled *Jehozadak* in 1 Chronicles 6:14

³At the same time Tattenai the governor of *the region* beyond the River[a] and Shethar-Boznai and their companions came to them and spoke thus to them: "Who has commanded you to build this temple and finish this wall?" ⁴Then, accordingly, we told them the names of the men who were constructing this building. ⁵But the eye of their God was upon the elders of the Jews, so that they could not make them cease till a report could go to Darius. Then a written answer was returned concerning this *matter.* ⁶This is a copy of the letter that Tattenai sent:

The governor of *the region* beyond the River, and Shethar-Boznai, and his companions, the Persians who *were in the region* beyond the River, to Darius the king.

⁷(They sent a letter to him, in which was written thus)

To Darius the king:

All peace.

⁸ Let it be known to the king that we went into the province of Judea, to the temple of the great God, which is being built with heavy stones, and timber is being laid in the walls; and this work goes on diligently and prospers in their hands.

⁹ Then we asked those elders, *and* spoke thus to them: "Who commanded you to build this temple and to finish these walls?" ¹⁰We also asked them their names to inform you, that we might write the names of the men who *were* chief among them.

¹¹ And thus they returned us an answer, saying: "We are the servants of the God of heaven and earth, and we are rebuilding the temple that was built many years ago, which a great king of Israel built and completed. ¹²But because our fathers provoked the God of heaven to wrath, He gave them into the hand of Nebuchadnezzar king of Babylon, the Chaldean, *who* destroyed this temple and carried the people away to Babylon. ¹³However, in the first year of Cyrus king of Babylon, King Cyrus issued a decree to build this house of God. ¹⁴Also, the gold and silver articles of the house of God, which Nebuchadnezzar had taken from the temple that *was* in Jerusalem and carried into the temple of Babylon—those King Cyrus took from the temple of Babylon, and they were given to one named Sheshbazzar, whom he had made governor. ¹⁵And he said to him, 'Take these articles; go, carry them to the temple *site* that *is* in Jerusalem, and let the house of God be rebuilt on its former site.' ¹⁶Then the same Sheshbazzar came *and* laid the foundation of the house of God which *is* in Jerusalem; but from that time even until now it has been under construction, and it is not finished."

17 Now therefore, if *it seems* good to the king, let a search be made in the king's treasure house, which *is* there in Babylon, whether it is *so* that a decree was issued by King Cyrus to build this house of God at Jerusalem, and let the king send us his pleasure concerning this *matter.*

THE DECREE OF DARIUS

¹Then King Darius issued a decree, and a search was made in the archives,[a] where the treasures were stored in Babylon. ²And at Achmetha,[a] in the palace that *is* in the province of Media, a scroll was found, and in it a record *was* written thus:

3 In the first year of King Cyrus, King Cyrus issued a decree *concerning* the house of God at Jerusalem: "Let the house be rebuilt, the place where they offered sacrifices; and let the foundations of it be firmly laid, its height sixty cubits *and* its width sixty cubits, ⁴with three rows of heavy stones and one row of new timber. Let the expenses be paid from the king's treasury. ⁵Also let the gold and silver articles of the house of God, which Nebuchadnezzar took from the temple which *is* in Jerusalem and brought to Babylon, be restored and taken back to the temple which *is* in Jerusalem, *each* to its place; and deposit *them* in the house of God"—

6 Now *therefore*, Tattenai, governor of *the region* beyond the River, and Shethar-

Boznai, and your companions the Persians who *are* beyond the River, keep yourselves far from there. [7]Let the work of this house of God alone; let the governor of the Jews and the elders of the Jews build this house of God on its site.

[8] Moreover I issue a decree *as to* what you shall do for the elders of these Jews, for the building of this house of God: Let the cost be paid at the king's expense from taxes *on the region* beyond the River; this is to be given immediately to these men, so that they are not hindered. [9]And whatever they need—young bulls, rams, and lambs for the burnt offerings of the God of heaven, wheat, salt, wine, and oil, according to the request of the priests who *are* in Jerusalem—let it be given them day by day without fail, [10]that they may offer sacrifices of sweet aroma to the God of heaven, and pray for the life of the king and his sons.

[11] Also I issue a decree that whoever alters this edict, let a timber be pulled from his house and erected, and let him be hanged on it; and let his house be made a refuse heap because of this. [12]And may the God who causes His name to dwell there destroy any king or people who put their hand to alter it, or to destroy this house of God which is in Jerusalem. I Darius issue a decree; let it be done diligently.

THE TEMPLE COMPLETED AND DEDICATED

[13]Then Tattenai, governor of *the region* beyond the River, Shethar-Boznai, and their companions diligently did according to what King Darius had sent. [14]So the elders of the Jews built, and they prospered through the prophesying of Haggai the prophet and Zechariah the son of Iddo. And they built and finished *it*, according to the commandment of the God of Israel, and according to the command of Cyrus, Darius, and Artaxerxes king of Persia. [15]Now the temple was finished on the third day of the month of Adar, which was in the sixth year of the reign of King Darius. [16]Then the children of Israel, the priests and the Levites and the rest of the descendants of the captivity, celebrated the dedication of this house of God with joy. [17]And they offered sacrifices at the dedication of this house of God, one hundred bulls, two hundred rams, four hundred lambs, and as a sin offering for all Israel twelve male goats, according to the

number of the tribes of Israel. [18]They assigned the priests to their divisions and the Levites to their divisions, over the service of God in Jerusalem, as it is written in the Book of Moses.

WHAT'S IT MEAN?

The new temple was completed in 516 B.C., seventy years after Nebuchadnezzar had destroyed the original. Cyrus had given the okay to rebuild the temple in 539 B.C., but the construction was delayed for fifteen years by the Samaritans, who opposed the rebuilding project. The new temple was much smaller and less impressive than the original. What's more, many of the original furnishings, including the ark of the covenant, were never found.

Ezra 6:15

THE PASSOVER CELEBRATED

[19]And the descendants of the captivity kept the Passover on the fourteenth *day* of the first month. [20]For the priests and the Levites had purified themselves; all of them *were ritually* clean. And they slaughtered the Passover *lambs* for all the descendants of the captivity, for their brethren the priests, and for themselves. [21]Then the children of Israel who had returned from the captivity ate together with all who had separated themselves from the filth of the nations of the land in order to seek the LORD God of Israel. [22]And they kept the Feast of Unleavened Bread seven days with joy; for the LORD made them joyful, and turned the heart of the king of Assyria toward them, to strengthen their hands in the work of the house of God, the God of Israel.

THE ARRIVAL OF EZRA

[1]Now after these things, in the reign of Artaxerxes king of Persia, Ezra the son of Seraiah, the son of Azariah, the son of Hilkiah, [2]the son of Shallum, the son of Zadok, the son of Ahitub, [3]the son of Amariah, the son of Azariah, the son of Meraioth, [4]the son of Zerahiah, the son of Uzzi, the son of Bukki, [5]the son of Abishua, the son of Phinehas, the son of Eleazar, the son of Aaron the chief priest—[6]this Ezra came up from Babylon; and he *was* a skilled scribe in the Law of Moses, which the LORD God of Israel had given. The king granted him all his request,

according to the hand of the LORD his God upon him. [7]*Some* of the children of Israel, the priests, the Levites, the singers, the gatekeepers, and the Nethinim came up to Jerusalem in the seventh year of King Artaxerxes. [8]And Ezra came to Jerusalem in the fifth month, which *was* in the seventh year of the king. [9]On the first *day* of the first month he began *his* journey from Babylon, and on the first *day* of the fifth month he came to Jerusalem, according to the good hand of his God upon him. [10]For Ezra had prepared his heart to seek the Law of the LORD, and to do *it*, and to teach statutes and ordinances in Israel.

WHAT'S IT MEAN?

The fact that Ezra was able to trace his family tree back to Aaron, the brother of Moses and the first high priest, gave him authority in the eyes of the Israelites. Genealogies were extremely important in ancient Israel. As far as the Israelites were concerned, Ezra's family background gave him the right to teach and preach the Law of Moses.

Ezra 7:1–6

THE LETTER OF ARTAXERXES TO EZRA

[11]This *is* a copy of the letter that King Artaxerxes gave Ezra the priest, the scribe, expert in the words of the commandments of the LORD, and of His statutes to Israel:

[12] Artaxerxes,[a] king of kings,

To Ezra the priest, a scribe of the Law of the God of heaven:

Perfect *peace*, and so forth.[b]

[13] I issue a decree that all those of the people of Israel and the priests and Levites in my realm, who volunteer to go up to Jerusalem, may go with you. [14]And whereas you are being sent by the king and his seven counselors to inquire concerning Judah and Jerusalem, with regard to the Law of your God which *is* in your hand; [15]and *whereas you are* to carry the silver and gold which the king and his counselors have freely offered to the God of Israel, whose dwelling *is* in Jerusalem; [16]and *whereas* all the silver and gold that you may find in all the province of Babylon, along with the freewill offering of the people and the priests, *are to be* freely offered for the house of their God in Jerusalem—[17]now therefore, be careful to buy with this money bulls, rams, and lambs, with their grain offerings and their drink offerings, and offer them on the altar of the house of your God in Jerusalem.

[18] And whatever seems good to you and your brethren to do with the rest of the silver and the gold, do it according to the will of your God. [19]Also the articles that are given to you for the service of the house of your God, deliver in full before the God of Jerusalem. [20]And whatever more may be needed for the house of your God, which you may have occasion to provide, pay *for it* from the king's treasury.

[21] And I, *even* I, Artaxerxes the king, issue a decree to all the treasurers who *are in the region* beyond the River, that whatever Ezra the priest, the scribe of the Law of the God of heaven, may require of you, let it be done diligently, [22]up to one hundred talents of silver, one hundred kors of wheat, one hundred baths of wine, one hundred baths of oil, and salt without prescribed limit. [23]Whatever is commanded by the God of heaven, let it diligently be done for the house of the God of heaven. For why should there be wrath against the realm of the king and his sons?

[24] Also we inform you that it shall not be lawful to impose tax, tribute, or custom *on* any of the priests, Levites, singers,

"For Ezra had prepared his heart to seek the Law of the LORD, and to do it, and to teach statutes and ordinances in Israel." (Ezra 7:10)

gatekeepers, Nethinim, or servants of this house of God. [25]And you, Ezra, according to your God–given wisdom, set magistrates and judges who may judge all the people who *are in the region* beyond the River, all such as know the laws of your God; and teach those who do not know *them*. [26]Whoever will not observe the law of your God and the law of the king, let judgment be executed speedily on him, whether *it be* death, or banishment, or confiscation of goods, or imprisonment.

[27]Blessed *be* the LORD God of our fathers, who has put *such a thing* as this in the king's heart, to beautify the house of the LORD which *is* in Jerusalem, [28]and has extended mercy to me before the king and his counselors, and before all the king's mighty princes.

So I was encouraged, as the hand of the LORD my God *was* upon me; and I gathered leading men of Israel to go up with me.

HEADS OF FAMILIES WHO RETURNED WITH EZRA

[1]These *are* the heads of their fathers' *houses*, and *this is* the genealogy of those who went up with me from Babylon, in the reign of King Artaxerxes: [2]of the sons of Phinehas, Gershom; of the sons of Ithamar, Daniel; of the sons of David, Hattush; [3]of the sons of Shecaniah, of the sons of Parosh, Zechariah; and registered with him *were* one hundred and fifty males; [4]of the sons of Pahath-Moab, Eliehoenai the son of Zerahiah, and with him two hundred males; [5]of the sons of Shechaniah,[a] Ben-Jahaziel, and with him three hundred males; [6]of the sons of Adin, Ebed the son of Jonathan, and with him fifty males; [7]of the sons of Elam, Jeshaiah the son of Athaliah, and with him seventy males; [8]of the sons of Shephatiah, Zebadiah the son of Michael, and with him eighty males; [9]of the sons of Joab, Obadiah the son of Jehiel, and with him two hundred and eighteen males; [10]of the sons of Shelomith,[a] Ben-Josiphiah, and with him one hundred and sixty males; [11]of the sons of Bebai, Zechariah the son of Bebai, and with him twenty-eight males; [12]of the sons of Azgad, Johanan the son of Hakkatan, and with him one hundred and ten males; [13]of the last sons of Adonikam, whose names *are* these—Eliphelet, Jeiel, and Shemaiah—and with them sixty males; [14]also of the sons of Bigvai, Uthai and Zabbud, and with them seventy males.

SERVANTS FOR THE TEMPLE

[15]Now I gathered them by the river that flows to Ahava, and we camped there three days. And I looked among the people and the priests, and found none of the sons of Levi there. [16]Then I sent for Eliezer, Ariel, Shemaiah, Elnathan, Jarib, Elnathan, Nathan, Zechariah, and Meshullam, leaders; also for Joiarib and Elnathan, men of understanding. [17]And I gave them a command for Iddo the chief man at the place Casiphia, and I told them what they should say to Iddo *and* his brethren[a] the Nethinim at the place Casiphia—that they should bring us servants for the house of our God. [18]Then, by the good hand of our God upon us, they brought us a man of understanding, of the sons of Mahli the son of Levi, the son of Israel, namely Sherebiah, with his sons and brothers, eighteen men; [19]and Hashabiah, and with him Jeshaiah of the sons of Merari, his brothers and their sons, twenty men; [20]also of the Nethinim, whom David and the leaders had appointed for the service of the Levites, two hundred and twenty Nethinim. All of them were designated by name.

FASTING AND PRAYER FOR PROTECTION

[21]Then I proclaimed a fast there at the river of Ahava, that we might humble ourselves before our God, to seek from Him the right way for us and our little ones and all our possessions. [22]For I was ashamed to request of the king an escort of soldiers and horsemen to help us against the enemy on the road, because we had spoken to the king, saying, "The hand of our God *is* upon all those for good who seek Him, but His power and His wrath *are* against all those who forsake Him." [23]So we fasted and entreated our God for this, and He answered our prayer.

GIFTS FOR THE TEMPLE

[24]And I separated twelve of the leaders of the priests—Sherebiah, Hashabiah, and ten of their brethren with them—[25]and weighed out to them the silver, the gold, and the articles, the offering for the house of our God which the king and his counselors and his princes, and all Israel *who were* present, had offered. [26]I weighed into their hand six hundred and fifty talents of silver, silver articles *weighing* one hundred talents, one hundred talents of gold, [27]twenty gold basins *worth* a thousand drachmas, and two

---

8:5 [a]Following Masoretic Text and Vulgate; Septuagint reads *the sons of Zatho, Shechaniah.* **8:10** [a]Following Masoretic Text and Vulgate; Septuagint reads *the sons of Banni, Shelomith.* **8:17** [a]Following Vulgate; Masoretic Text reads *to Iddo his brother;* Septuagint reads *to their brethren.*

vessels of fine polished bronze, precious as gold. ²⁸And I said to them, "You *are* holy to the LORD; the articles *are* holy also; and the silver and the gold *are* a freewill offering to the LORD God of your fathers. ²⁹Watch and keep *them* until you weigh *them* before the leaders of the priests and the Levites and heads of the fathers' *houses* of Israel in Jerusalem, *in* the chambers of the house of the LORD." ³⁰So the priests and the Levites received the silver and the gold and the articles by weight, to bring *them* to Jerusalem to the house of our God.

THE RETURN TO JERUSALEM

³¹Then we departed from the river of Ahava on the twelfth *day* of the first month, to go to Jerusalem. And the hand of our God was upon us, and He delivered us from the hand of the enemy and from ambush along the road. ³²So we came to Jerusalem, and stayed there three days.

³³Now on the fourth day the silver and the gold and the articles were weighed in the house of our God by the hand of Meremoth the son of Uriah the priest, and with him *was* Eleazar the son of Phinehas; with them *were* the Levites, Jozabad the son of Jeshua and Noadiah the son of Binnui, ³⁴with the number *and* weight of everything. All the weight was written down at that time.

³⁵The children of those who had been carried away captive, who had come from the captivity, offered burnt offerings to the God of Israel: twelve bulls for all Israel, ninety-six rams, seventy-seven lambs, and twelve male goats *as* a sin offering. All *this was* a burnt offering to the LORD.

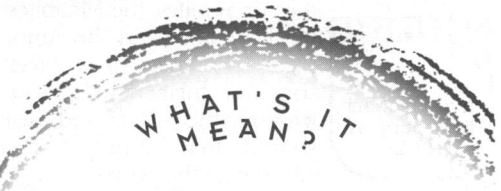

Most of the tribes of Israel were not able to return to Jerusalem after the northern kingdom was conquered in 722 B.C. The two tribes that were able to make the trip back were Judah and Benjamin, who offered sacrifices on behalf of the missing tribes.

Ezra 8:31–35

³⁶And they delivered the king's orders to the king's satraps and the governors *in the region* beyond the River. So they gave support to the people and the house of God.

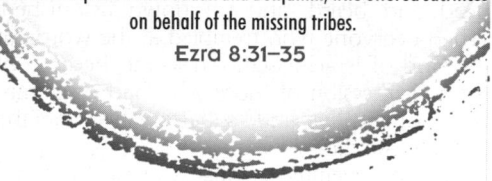

Promise

HE PROMISES TO TAKE CARE OF THOSE WHO TRULY SEEK HIM.

The hand of our God is upon all those for good who seek Him, but His power and His wrath are against all those who forsake Him (Ezra 8:22).

Are you a genuine seeker? When you're with other people who are worshiping the Lord, where is your heart? In other words, do you *worship* when you worship? Is your mind participating in the things that are being said? Or are you just pretending? Eyes closed, mind wandering. Bible open, words blurry. Singing songs because you know them, not because you mean them. Don't answer these questions out loud, and don't start feeling guilty if you know that all the answers are "yes" in your life. God already knows the condition of your heart.

The point is that God takes care of everyone who truly worships Him. Do you long to be cared for by God? Then worship Him from your heart. Even if you don't feel super-spiritual, tell Him what you think and how you feel. Think about how awesome He is, and then tell Him about it. When you sing a song, really pay attention to the words and sing them like you believe them. Pray a lot. Read the Bible so you can get to know God better. The more real He is to you, the more true your worship will be. Don't be lazy or distracted. No one can take care of you the way God can. Just be a genuine seeker.

SEE FOR YOURSELF:

Is. 29:13; John 4:23, 24

INTERMARRIAGE WITH PAGANS

[1]When these things were done, the leaders came to me, saying, "The people of Israel and the priests and the Levites have not separated themselves from the peoples of the lands, with respect to the abominations of the Canaanites, the Hittites, the Perizzites, the Jebusites, the Ammonites, the Moabites, the Egyptians, and the Amorites. [2]For they have taken some of their daughters *as wives* for themselves and their sons, so that the holy seed is mixed with the peoples of *those* lands. Indeed, the hand of the leaders and rulers has been foremost in this trespass." [3]So when I heard this thing, I tore my garment and my robe, and plucked out some of the hair of my head and beard, and sat down astonished. [4]Then everyone who trembled at the words of the God of Israel assembled to me, because of the transgression of those who had been carried away captive, and I sat astonished until the evening sacrifice.

[5]At the evening sacrifice I arose from my fasting; and having torn my garment and my robe, I fell on my knees and spread out my hands to the LORD my God. [6]And I said: "O my God, I am too ashamed and humiliated to lift up my face to You, my God; for our iniquities have risen higher than *our* heads, and our guilt has grown up to the heavens. [7]Since the days of our fathers to this day we *have been* very guilty, and for our iniquities we, our kings, *and* our priests have been delivered into the hand of the kings of the lands, to the sword, to captivity, to plunder, and to humiliation, as *it is* this day. [8]And now for a little while grace has been *shown* from the LORD our God, to leave us a remnant to escape, and to give us a peg in His holy place, that our God may enlighten our eyes and give us a measure of revival in our bondage. [9]For we *were* slaves. Yet our God did not forsake us in our bondage; but He extended mercy to us in the sight of the kings of Persia, to revive us, to repair the house of our God, to rebuild its ruins, and to give us a wall in Judah and Jerusalem. [10]And now, O our God, what shall we say after this? For we have forsaken Your commandments, [11]which You commanded by Your servants the prophets, saying, 'The land which you are entering to possess is an unclean land, with the uncleanness of the peoples of the lands, with their abominations which have filled it from one end to another with their impurity. [12]Now therefore, do not give your daughters as wives for their sons, nor take their daughters to your sons; and never seek their peace or prosperity, that you may be strong and eat the good of the land, and leave *it* as an inheritance to your children forever.' [13]And after all that has come upon us for our evil deeds and for our great guilt, since You our God have punished us less than our iniquities *deserve*, and have given us *such* deliverance as this, [14]should we again break Your commandments, and join in marriage with the people *committing* these abominations? Would You not be angry with us until You had consumed *us*, so that *there would be* no remnant or survivor? [15]O LORD God of Israel, You *are* righteous, for we are left as a remnant, as *it is* this day. Here we *are* before You, in our guilt, though no one can stand before You because of this!"

CONFESSION OF IMPROPER MARRIAGES

[1]Now while Ezra was praying, and while he was confessing, weeping, and bowing down before the house of God, a very large assembly of men, women, and children gathered to him from Israel; for the people wept very bitterly. [2]And Shechaniah the son of Jehiel, *one* of the sons of Elam, spoke up and said to Ezra, "We have trespassed against our God, and have taken pagan wives from the peoples of the land; yet now there is hope in Israel in spite of this. [3]Now therefore, let us make a covenant with our God to put away all these wives and those who have been born to them, according to the advice of my master and of those who tremble at the commandment of our God; and let it be done according to the law. [4]Arise, for *this* matter *is* your *responsibility*. We also *are* with you. Be of good courage, and do *it*."

[5]Then Ezra arose, and made the leaders of the priests, the Levites, and all Israel swear an oath that they would do according to this word. So they swore an oath. [6]Then Ezra rose up from before the house of God, and went into the chamber of Jehohanan the son of Eliashib; and *when* he came there, he ate no bread and drank no water, for he mourned because of the guilt of those from the captivity.

[7]And they issued a proclamation throughout Judah and Jerusalem to all the descendants of the captivity, that they must gather at Jerusalem, [8]and that whoever would not come within

LEADERSHIP

Can leaders' morals affect their people? (9:2)

SIN

What should we do when we realize that we've sinned? (9:6)

HOPE

Will God still love us even if we sin? (10:2)

three days, according to the instructions of the leaders and elders, all his property would be confiscated, and he himself would be separated from the assembly of those from the captivity.

WHAT'S IT MEAN?

"Peoples of the land" were not necessarily those of another race, but were any who worshiped "foreign" gods—that is, any persons who worshiped a deity or deities other than the Lord God of Israel.

Ezra 10:2

⁹So all the men of Judah and Benjamin gathered at Jerusalem within three days. It *was* the ninth month, on the twentieth of the month; and all the people sat in the open square of the house of God, trembling because of *this* matter and because of heavy rain. ¹⁰Then Ezra the priest stood up and said to them, "You have transgressed and have taken pagan wives, adding to the guilt of Israel. ¹¹Now therefore, make confession to the LORD God of your fathers, and do His will; separate yourselves from the peoples of the land, and from the pagan wives."

¹²Then all the assembly answered and said with a loud voice, "Yes! As you have said, so we must do. ¹³But *there are* many people; *it is* the season for heavy rain, and we are not able to stand outside. Nor *is this* the work of one or two days, for *there are* many of us who have transgressed in this matter. ¹⁴Please, let the leaders of our entire assembly stand; and let all those in our cities who have taken pagan wives come at appointed times, together with the elders and judges of their cities, until the fierce wrath of our God is turned away from us in this matter." ¹⁵Only Jonathan the son of Asahel and Jahaziah the son of Tikvah opposed this, and Meshullam and Shabbethai the Levite gave them support.

¹⁶Then the descendants of the captivity did so. And Ezra the priest, *with* certain heads of the fathers' *households,* were set apart by the fathers' *households,* each of them by name; and they sat down on the first day of the tenth month to examine the matter. ¹⁷By the first day of the first month they finished *questioning* all the men who had taken pagan wives.

PAGAN WIVES PUT AWAY

¹⁸And among the sons of the priests who had taken pagan wives *the following* were found of the sons of Jeshua the son of Jozadak,ᵃ and his brothers: Maaseiah, Eliezer, Jarib, and Gedaliah. ¹⁹And they gave their promise that they would put away their wives; and *being* guilty, *they presented* a ram of the flock as their trespass offering.

²⁰Also of the sons of Immer: Hanani and Zebadiah; ²¹of the sons of Harim: Maaseiah, Elijah, Shemaiah, Jehiel, and Uzziah; ²²of the sons of Pashhur: Elioenai, Maaseiah, Ishmael, Nethanel, Jozabad, and Elasah.

²³Also of the Levites: Jozabad, Shimei, Kelaiah (the same *is* Kelita), Pethahiah, Judah, and Eliezer.

²⁴Also of the singers: Eliashib; and of the gatekeepers: Shallum, Telem, and Uri.

²⁵And others of Israel: of the sons of Parosh: Ramiah, Jeziah, Malchiah, Mijamin, Eleazar, Malchijah, and Benaiah; ²⁶of the sons of Elam: Mattaniah, Zechariah, Jehiel, Abdi, Jeremoth, and Eliah; ²⁷of the sons of Zattu: Elioenai, Eliashib, Mattaniah, Jeremoth, Zabad, and Aziza; ²⁸of the sons of Bebai: Jehohanan, Hananiah, Zabbai, *and* Athlai; ²⁹of the sons of Bani: Meshullam, Malluch, Adaiah, Jashub, Sheal, *and* Ramoth;ᵃ ³⁰of the sons of Pahath-Moab: Adna, Chelal, Benaiah, Maaseiah, Mattaniah, Bezalel, Binnui, and Manasseh; ³¹*of* the sons of Harim: Eliezer, Ishijah, Malchijah, Shemaiah, Shimeon, ³²Benjamin, Malluch, *and* Shemariah; ³³of the sons of Hashum: Mattenai, Mattattah, Zabad, Eliphelet, Jeremai, Manasseh, *and* Shimei; ³⁴of the sons of Bani: Maadai, Amram, Uel, ³⁵Benaiah, Bedeiah, Cheluh,ᵃ ³⁶Vaniah, Meremoth, Eliashib, ³⁷Mattaniah, Mattenai, Jaasai,ᵃ ³⁸Bani, Binnui, Shimei, ³⁹Shelemiah, Nathan, Adaiah, ⁴⁰Machnadebai, Shashai, Sharai, ⁴¹Azarel, Shelemiah, Shemariah, ⁴²Shallum, Amariah, *and* Joseph; ⁴³of the sons of Nebo: Jeiel, Mattithiah, Zabad, Zebina, Jaddai,ᵃ Joel, *and* Benaiah.

⁴⁴All these had taken pagan wives, and *some* of them had wives *by whom* they had children.

nehemiah

CONTENT

Nehemiah was the administrative assistant and *wine taster* for the king. That means one of his job responsibilities was to taste the king's wine to make sure it wasn't poisoned. If Nehemiah drank the wine and fell down dead, that was a big clue to the king that something might be amiss. Now that's a good job to highlight on career awareness day, huh?

Short of the possible poisoning scenario, Nehemiah really did have a lot of authority and prestige in his position as a government official. He asked for a leave of absence, though. Many Jews had traveled back to Jerusalem to rebuild the city. The temple was rebuilt, but the city wall was still in ruins. Nehemiah wanted to help. Amazingly enough, the king let him go.

The Book of Nehemiah is famous for its down-to-earth story about organization. Nehemiah and his workers finished the wall in fifty-two days. That was a feat considering the wall was wide enough for the workmen to walk all the way around the city on top of it. It was even more of a feat considering they had to do a lot of the work with a tool in one hand and a weapon in the other.

Outline

Purpose

Leaders with vision and courage can set the direction of a society.

Themes

Godly Leadership, Cooperation, Opposition to Success

Date of writing

457–444 B.C.

Bible Talk

God Uses People in All Professions

Sometimes we think that God will only use people whose job is in the church or in the pulpit. That is not true at all. God uses people who have faith in Him wherever they are. Nehemiah is a great example of this.

Nehemiah was a government official. God did change Nehemiah's place of work in the course of using him, but He didn't change him into a prophet or a priest. He just changed his place of operation from a palace to a city. Nehemiah's gift was still the gift of organization. God used that gift for His glory whether Nehemiah was serving a king or serving His people.

FEAST OF TABERNACLES

If you've read much of the Old Testament, you know that the Jews had a lot of traditions. They had feasts. They had holy days. It could seem like they were always celebrating *something*.

God established most of those traditions. He established them as a kind of 3-D history book. Each of the Jewish feasts commemorated a big event in their history where God really pulled them through. Passover, for instance, was a feast that reminded the people how God brought them out of Egypt. The Feast of Tabernacles, or Booths, which Nehemiah re-instated, reminded them of God's provision when they camped out in the wilderness for forty years.

In a world where books were scarce and video cameras were nonexistent, traditions helped the Hebrews remember their history and God's goodness.

NEHEMIAH PRAYS FOR HIS PEOPLE

[1]The words of Nehemiah the son of Hachaliah.

It came to pass in the month of Chislev, *in* the twentieth year, as I was in Shushan[a] the citadel, [2]that Hanani one of my brethren came with men from Judah; and I asked them concerning the Jews who had escaped, who had survived the captivity, and concerning Jerusalem. [3]And they said to me, "The survivors who are left from the captivity in the province *are* there in great distress and reproach. The wall of Jerusalem *is* also broken down, and its gates *are* burned with fire."

[4]So it was, when I heard these words, that I sat down and wept, and mourned *for many* days; I was fasting and praying before the God of heaven.

[5]And I said: "I pray, LORD God of heaven, O great and awesome God, *You* who keep *Your* covenant and mercy with those who love You[a] and observe Your[b] commandments, [6]please let Your ear be attentive and Your eyes open, that You may hear the prayer of Your servant which I pray before You now, day and night, for the children of Israel Your servants, and confess the sins of the children of

WHAT'S IT MEAN?

A quick word about the author: Nehemiah was a servant of the king of Persia. At the beginning of the story, he was in Shushan (in what is now Iran), where Persian kings went for the winter. More importantly, Nehemiah was almost a thousand miles away from his homeland.

Nehemiah 1:1

FEELINGS

What should we do when we're sad? (1:4)

Israel which we have sinned against You. Both my father's house and I have sinned. [7]We have acted very corruptly against You, and have not kept the commandments, the statutes, nor the ordinances which You commanded Your servant Moses. [8]Remember, I pray, the word that You commanded Your servant Moses, saying, 'If you are unfaithful, I will scatter you among the nations;[a] [9]but if you return to Me, and keep My commandments and do them, though some of you were cast out to the farthest part of the

1:1 [a]Or *Susa*   **1:5** [a]Literally *Him* [b]Literally *His*   **1:8** [a]Leviticus 26:33

Promise   HE PROMISES YOU CAN ALWAYS RETURN TO HIM.

Remember, I pray, the word that You commanded Your servant Moses, saying, "If you are unfaithful, I will scatter you among the nations; but if you return to Me, and keep My commandments and do them, though some of you were cast out to the farthest part of the heavens, yet I will gather them from there, and bring them to the place which I have chosen as a dwelling for My name" (Neh. 1:8, 9).

So you haven't spoken to God in a long time. Okay, a really long time. You made this big commitment, told all your family and friends, started going to church, went on a few retreats, sang around a campfire, bought a Bible with your name on it—the whole deal. Then you never followed through. You put the Bible in a drawer, slept in on Sundays, stopped talking to God, and eventually you just turned your back and walked away.

It's been a long time—years. The yearning that drew you to God is back, but even bigger, and now there's guilt—the guilt that comes from meeting the Maker of the universe and then trying to live like He doesn't exist. Is God disappointed? Probably. Has He given up on you? Nope. What's next? Return to God. He is kind and compassionate. He will welcome you home. Don't delay—every day lived apart from God is a totally wasted day.

SEE FOR YOURSELF:
Joel 2:12, 13; Rom. 3:23, 24

heavens, *yet* I will gather them from there, and bring them to the place which I have chosen as a dwelling for My name."*a* ¹⁰Now these *are* Your servants and Your people, whom You have redeemed by Your great power, and by Your strong hand. ¹¹O Lord, I pray, please let Your ear be attentive to the prayer of Your servant, and to the prayer of Your servants who desire to fear Your name; and let Your servant prosper this day, I pray, and grant him mercy in the sight of this man."

For I was the king's cupbearer.

> "O Lord, I pray, please let Your ear be attentive to the prayer of Your servant."
> (Nehemiah 1:11a)

NEHEMIAH SENT TO JUDAH

¹And it came to pass in the month of Nisan, in the twentieth year of King Artaxerxes, *when* wine *was* before him, that I took the wine and gave it to the king. Now I had never been sad in his presence before. ²Therefore the king said to me, "Why *is* your face sad, since you *are* not sick? This *is* nothing but sorrow of heart."

So I became dreadfully afraid, ³and said to the king, "May the king live forever! Why should my face not be sad, when the city, the place of my fathers' tombs, *lies* waste, and its gates are burned with fire?"

⁴Then the king said to me, "What do you request?"

So I prayed to the God of heaven. ⁵And I said to the king, "If it pleases the king, and if your servant has found favor in your sight, I ask that you send me to Judah, to the city of my fathers' tombs, that I may rebuild it."

PRAYER
Do you need to kneel to pray?
(2:4)

⁶Then the king said to me (the queen also sitting beside him), "How long will your journey be? And when will you return?" So it pleased the king to send me; and I set him a time.

⁷Furthermore I said to the king, "If it pleases the king, let letters be given to me for the governors *of the region* beyond the River,*a* that they must permit me to pass through till I come to Judah, ⁸and a letter to Asaph the keeper of the king's forest, that he must give me timber to make beams for the gates of the citadel which *pertains* to the temple,*a* for the city wall, and for the house that I will occupy." And the king

granted *them* to me according to the good hand of my God upon me.

⁹Then I went to the governors *in the region* beyond the River, and gave them the king's letters. Now the king had sent captains of the army and horsemen with me. ¹⁰When Sanballat the Horonite and Tobiah the Ammonite official*a* heard *of it*, they were deeply disturbed that a man had come to seek the well-being of the children of Israel.

NEHEMIAH VIEWS THE WALL OF JERUSALEM

¹¹So I came to Jerusalem and was there three days. ¹²Then I arose in the night, I and a few men with me; I told no one what my God had put in my heart to do at Jerusalem; nor was there any animal with me, except the one on which I rode. ¹³And I went out by night through the Valley Gate to the Serpent Well and the Refuse Gate, and viewed the walls of Jerusalem which were broken down and its gates which were burned with fire. ¹⁴Then I went on to the Fountain Gate and to the King's Pool, but *there was* no room for the animal under me to pass. ¹⁵So I went up in the night by the valley,

WHAT'S IT MEAN?

Historical documents indicate that a man named Sanballat served as the governor of Samaria, the land to the north of Jerusalem—a region that had once been part of the Israelite kingdom. A devastating Assyrian attack in 722 B.C. led to the fall of Samaria. As was their custom with the territories they conquered, the Assyrians took many Israelites away as captives and brought in many foreigners to live in Canaan. It wasn't long before the Israelites who were left behind started getting involved with the new kids in town. Not only did the Israelites begin marrying and having kids with the foreigners, they also adopted their idol worship. This mingling continued generation after generation until the distinction between the Israelites and the foreigners disappeared altogether. The descendants of these mixed marriages were known as Samaritans.
Nehemiah 2:10

1:9 *a*Deuteronomy 30:2–5   **2:7** *a*That is, the Euphrates, and so elsewhere in this book
2:8 *a*Literally *house*   **2:10** *a*Literally *servant*, and so elsewhere in this book

and viewed the wall; then I turned back and entered by the Valley Gate, and so returned. ¹⁶And the officials did not know where I had gone or what I had done; I had not yet told the Jews, the priests, the nobles, the officials, or the others who did the work.

¹⁷Then I said to them, "You see the distress that we *are* in, how Jerusalem *lies* waste, and its gates are burned with fire. Come and let us build the wall of Jerusalem, that we may no longer be a reproach." ¹⁸And I told them of the hand of my God which had been good upon me, and also of the king's words that he had spoken to me.

So they said, "Let us rise up and build." Then they set their hands to *this* good *work*.

¹⁹But when Sanballat the Horonite, Tobiah the Ammonite official, and Geshem the Arab heard *of it*, they laughed at us and despised us, and said, "What *is* this thing that you are doing? Will you rebel against the king?"

²⁰So I answered them, and said to them, "The God of heaven Himself will prosper us; therefore we His servants will arise and build, but you have no heritage or right or memorial in Jerusalem."

REBUILDING THE WALL

¹Then Eliashib the high priest rose up with his brethren the priests and built the Sheep Gate; they consecrated it and hung its doors. They built as far as the Tower of the Hundred,*ᵃ and* consecrated it, then as far as the Tower of Hananel. ²Next to *Eliashibᵃ* the men of Jericho built. And next to them Zaccur the son of Imri built.

³Also the sons of Hassenaah built the Fish Gate; they laid its beams and hung its doors with its bolts and bars. ⁴And next to them Meremoth the son of Urijah, the son of Koz,ᵃ made repairs. Next to them Meshullam the son of Berechiah, the son of Meshezabel, made repairs. Next to them Zadok the son of Baana made repairs. ⁵Next to them the Tekoites made repairs; but their nobles did not put their shouldersᵃ to the work of their Lord.

⁶Moreover Jehoiada the son of Paseah and Meshullam the son of Besodeiah repaired the Old Gate; they laid its beams and hung its doors, with its bolts and bars. ⁷And next to them Melatiah the Gibeonite, Jadon the Meronothite, the men of Gibeon and Mizpah, repaired the residenceᵃ of the governor *of the region* beyond the River. ⁸Next to him Uzziel the son of

Harhaiah, one of the goldsmiths, made repairs. Also next to him Hananiah, oneᵃ of the perfumers, made repairs; and they fortified Jerusalem as far as the Broad Wall. ⁹And next to them Rephaiah the son of Hur, leader of half the district of Jerusalem, made repairs. ¹⁰Next to them Jedaiah the son of Harumaph made repairs in front of his house. And next to him Hattush the son of Hashabniah made repairs.

WHAT'S IT MEAN?

If you're having a hard time getting your bearings, just remember that the description of the gates in the wall starts at the northeast corner and goes around to the left. The total distance around the wall was about a mile and a half.

Nehemiah 3:1

¹¹Malchijah the son of Harim and Hashub the son of Pahath-Moab repaired another section, as well as the Tower of the Ovens. ¹²And next to him was Shallum the son of Hallohesh, leader of half the district of Jerusalem; he and his daughters made repairs.

¹³Hanun and the inhabitants of Zanoah repaired the Valley Gate. They built it, hung its doors with its bolts and bars, and *repaired* a thousand cubits of the wall as far as the Refuse Gate.

¹⁴Malchijah the son of Rechab, leader of the district of Beth Haccerem, repaired the Refuse Gate; he built it and hung its doors with its bolts and bars.

¹⁵Shallun the son of Col-Hozeh, leader of the district of Mizpah, repaired the Fountain Gate; he built it, covered it, hung its doors with its bolts and bars, and repaired the wall of the Pool of Shelah by the King's Garden, as far as the stairs that go down from the City of David. ¹⁶After him Nehemiah the son of Azbuk, leader of half the district of Beth Zur, made repairs as far as *the place* in front of the tombsᵃ of David, to the man-made pool, and as far as the House of the Mighty.

¹⁷After him the Levites, *under* Rehum the son of Bani, made repairs. Next to him Hashabiah,

---

3:1 ᵃHebrew *Hammeah*, also at 12:39   **3:2** ᵃLiterally *On his hand*   **3:4** ᵃOr *Hakkoz*   **3:5** ᵃLiterally *necks*
3:7 ᵃLiterally *throne*   **3:8** ᵃLiterally *the son*   **3:16** ᵃSeptuagint, Syriac, and Vulgate read *tomb*.

leader of half the district of Keilah, made repairs for his district. ¹⁸After him their brethren, *under Bavai*ᵃ the son of Henadad, leader of the *other* half of the district of Keilah, made repairs. ¹⁹And next to him Ezer the son of Jeshua, the leader of Mizpah, repaired another section in front of the Ascent to the Armory at the buttress. ²⁰After him Baruch the son of Zabbaiᵃ carefully repaired the other section, from the buttress to the door of the house of Eliashib the high priest. ²¹After him Meremoth the son of Urijah, the son of Koz,ᵃ repaired another section, from the door of the house of Eliashib to the end of the house of Eliashib.

²²And after him the priests, the men of the plain, made repairs. ²³After him Benjamin and Hasshub made repairs opposite their house. After them Azariah the son of Maaseiah, the son of Ananiah, made repairs by his house. ²⁴After him Binnui the son of Henadad repaired another section, from the house of Azariah to the buttress, even as far as the corner. ²⁵Palal the son of Uzai *made repairs* opposite the buttress, and on the tower which projects from the king's upper house that *was* by the court of the prison. After him Pedaiah the son of Parosh *made repairs.*

²⁶Moreover the Nethinim who dwelt in Ophel *made repairs* as far as *the place* in front of the Water Gate toward the east, and on the projecting tower. ²⁷After them the Tekoites repaired another section, next to the great projecting tower, and as far as the wall of Ophel.

²⁸Beyond the Horse Gate the priests made repairs, each in front of his *own* house. ²⁹After them Zadok the son of Immer made repairs in front of his *own* house. After him Shemaiah the son of Shechaniah, the keeper of the East Gate, made repairs. ³⁰After him Hananiah the son of Shelemiah, and Hanun, the sixth son of Zalaph, repaired another section. After him Meshullam the son of Berechiah made repairs in front of his dwelling. ³¹After him Malchijah, one of the goldsmiths, made repairs as far as the house of the Nethinim and of the merchants, in front of the Miphkadᵃ Gate, and as far as the upper room at the corner. ³²And between the upper room at the corner, as far as the Sheep Gate, the goldsmiths and the merchants made repairs.

THE WALL DEFENDED AGAINST ENEMIES

4 ¹But it so happened, when Sanballat heard that we were rebuilding the wall, that he was furious and very indignant, and mocked the Jews. ²And he spoke before his brethren and the army of Samaria, and said, "What are these feeble Jews doing? Will they fortify themselves? Will they offer sacrifices? Will they complete it in a day? Will they revive the stones from the heaps of rubbish—*stones* that are burned?"

³Now Tobiah the Ammonite *was* beside him, and he said, "Whatever they build, if even a fox goes up *on it,* he will break down their stone wall."

⁴Hear, O our God, for we are despised; turn their reproach on their own heads, and give them as plunder to a land of captivity! ⁵Do not cover their iniquity, and do not let their sin be blotted out from before You; for they have provoked *You* to anger before the builders.

⁶So we built the wall, and the entire wall was joined together up to half its *height,* for the people had a mind to work.

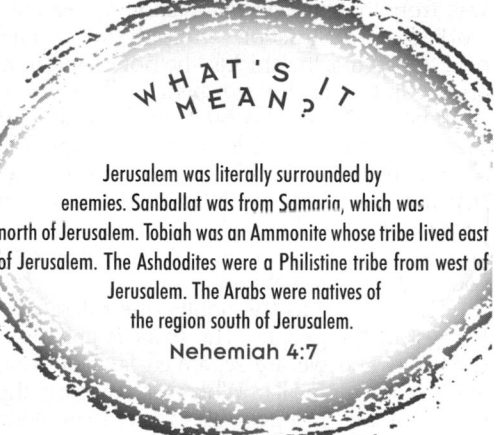

WHAT'S IT MEAN?

Jerusalem was literally surrounded by enemies. Sanballat was from Samaria, which was north of Jerusalem. Tobiah was an Ammonite whose tribe lived east of Jerusalem. The Ashdodites were a Philistine tribe from west of Jerusalem. The Arabs were natives of the region south of Jerusalem.

Nehemiah 4:7

⁷Now it happened, when Sanballat, Tobiah, the Arabs, the Ammonites, and the Ashdodites heard that the walls of Jerusalem were being restored and the gaps were beginning to be closed, that they became very angry, ⁸and all of them conspired together to come *and* attack Jerusalem and create confusion. ⁹Nevertheless we made our prayer to our God, and because of them we set a watch against them day and night.

¹⁰Then Judah said, "The strength of the laborers is failing, and *there is* so much rubbish that we are not able to build the wall."

¹¹And our adversaries said, "They will neither know nor see anything, till we come into

3:18 ᵃFollowing Masoretic Text and Vulgate; some Hebrew manuscripts, Septuagint, and Syriac read *Binnui* (compare verse 24). **3:20** ᵃA few Hebrew manuscripts, Syriac, and Vulgate read *Zaccai.* **3:21** ᵃOr *Hakkoz* **3:31** ᵃLiterally *Inspection* or *Recruiting*

their midst and kill them and cause the work to cease."

¹²So it was, when the Jews who dwelt near them came, that they told us ten times, "From whatever place you turn, *they will be* upon us."

¹³Therefore I positioned *men* behind the lower parts of the wall, at the openings; and I set the people according to their families, with their swords, their spears, and their bows. ¹⁴And I looked, and arose and said to the nobles, to the leaders, and to the rest of the people, "Do not be afraid of them. Remember the Lord, great and awesome, and fight for your brethren, your sons, your daughters, your wives, and your houses."

ENEMIES

Should we be afraid of our enemies? (4:14)

¹⁵And it happened, when our enemies heard that it was known to us, and *that* God had brought their plot to nothing, that all of us returned to the wall, everyone to his work. ¹⁶So it was, from that time on, *that* half of my servants worked at construction, while the other half held the spears, the shields, the bows, and *wore* armor; and the leaders *were* behind all the house of Judah. ¹⁷Those who built on the wall, and those who carried burdens, loaded themselves so that with one hand they worked at construction, and with the other held a weapon. ¹⁸Every one of the builders had his sword girded at his side as he built. And the one who sounded the trumpet *was* beside me.

¹⁹Then I said to the nobles, the rulers, and the rest of the people, "The work *is* great and extensive, and we are separated far from one another on the wall. ²⁰Wherever you hear the sound of the trumpet, rally to us there. Our God will fight for us."

²¹So we labored in the work, and half of *the* men*ᵃ* held the spears from daybreak until the stars appeared. ²²At the same time I also said to the people, "Let each man and his servant stay at night in Jerusalem, that they may be our guard by night and a working party by day." ²³So neither I, my brethren, my servants, nor the men of the guard who followed me took off our clothes, *except* that everyone took them off for washing.

NEHEMIAH DEALS WITH OPPRESSION

¹And there was a great outcry of the people and their wives against their Jewish brethren. ²For there were those who said, "We, our sons, and our daughters *are* many; therefore let us get grain, that we may eat and live."

³There were also *some* who said, "We have mortgaged our lands and vineyards and houses, that we might buy grain because of the famine."

⁴There were also those who said, "We have borrowed money for the king's tax *on* our lands and vineyards. ⁵Yet now our flesh *is* as the flesh of our brethren, our children as their children; and indeed we are forcing our sons and our daughters to be slaves, and *some* of our daughters have been brought into slavery. *It is* not in our power *to redeem them*, for other men have our lands and vineyards."

⁶And I became very angry when I heard their outcry and these words. ⁷After serious thought, I rebuked the nobles and rulers, and said to them, "Each of you is exacting usury from his brother." So I called a great assembly against them. ⁸And I said to them, "According to our ability we have redeemed our Jewish brethren who were sold to the nations. Now indeed, will you even sell your brethren? Or should they be sold to us?"

ENCOURAGEMENT

How should we stand up for those who need help? (5:7–11)

Then they were silenced and found nothing *to say.* ⁹Then I said, "What you are doing *is* not good. Should you not walk in the fear of our God because of the reproach of the nations, our enemies? ¹⁰I also, *with* my brethren and my servants, am lending them money and grain. Please, let us stop this usury! ¹¹Restore now to them, even this day, their lands, their vineyards, their olive groves, and their houses, also a hundredth of the money and the grain, the new wine and the oil, that you have charged them."

¹²So they said, "We will restore *it,* and will require nothing from them; we will do as you say."

Then I called the priests, and required an oath from them that they would do according to this promise. ¹³Then I shook out the fold of my garment*ᵃ* and said, "So may God shake out each man from his house, and from his property, who does not perform this promise. Even thus may he be shaken out and emptied."

And all the assembly said, "Amen!" and praised the LORD. Then the people did according to this promise.

THE GENEROSITY OF NEHEMIAH

¹⁴Moreover, from the time that I was appointed to be their governor in the land of

4:21 *ᵃ*Literally *them*   **5:13** *ᵃ*Literally *my lap*

Judah, from the twentieth year until the thirty-second year of King Artaxerxes, twelve years, neither I nor my brothers ate the governor's provisions. ¹⁵But the former governors who *were* before me laid burdens on the people, and took from them bread and wine, besides forty shekels of silver. Yes, even their servants bore rule over the people, but I did not do so, because of the fear of God. ¹⁶Indeed, I also continued the work on this wall, and we*ᵃ* did not buy any land. All my servants *were* gathered there for the work.

¹⁷And at my table *were* one hundred and fifty Jews and rulers, besides those who came to us from the nations around us. ¹⁸Now *that* which was prepared daily *was* one ox *and* six choice sheep. Also fowl were prepared for me, and once every ten days an abundance of all kinds of wine. Yet in spite of this I did not demand the governor's provisions, because the bondage was heavy on this people.

¹⁹Remember me, my God, for good, *according to* all that I have done for this people.

CONSPIRACY AGAINST NEHEMIAH

¹Now it happened when Sanballat, Tobiah, Geshem the Arab, and the rest of our enemies heard that I had rebuilt the wall, and *that* there were no breaks left in it (though at that time I had not hung the doors in the gates), ²that Sanballat and Geshem sent to me, saying, "Come, let us meet together among the villages in the plain of Ono." But they thought to do me harm.

³So I sent messengers to them, saying, "I *am* doing a great work, so that I cannot come down. Why should the work cease while I leave it and go down to you?"

⁴But they sent me this message four times, and I answered them in the same manner.

⁵Then Sanballat sent his servant to me as before, the fifth time, with an open letter in his hand. ⁶In it *was* written:

It is reported among the nations, and Geshem*ᵃ* says, *that* you and the Jews plan to rebel; therefore, according to these rumors, you are rebuilding the wall, that you may be their king. ⁷And you have also appointed prophets to proclaim concerning you at Jerusalem, saying, "*There is* a king in Judah!" Now these matters will be reported to the king. So come, therefore, and let us consult together.

⁸Then I sent to him, saying, "No such things as you say are being done, but you invent them in your own heart."

⁹For they all *were trying to* make us afraid, saying, "Their hands will be weakened in the work, and it will not be done."

Now therefore, *O God*, strengthen my hands.

¹⁰Afterward I came to the house of Shemaiah the son of Delaiah, the son of Mehetabel, who *was* a secret informer; and he said, "Let us meet together in the house of God, within the temple, and let us close the doors of the temple, for they are coming to kill you; indeed, at night they will come to kill you."

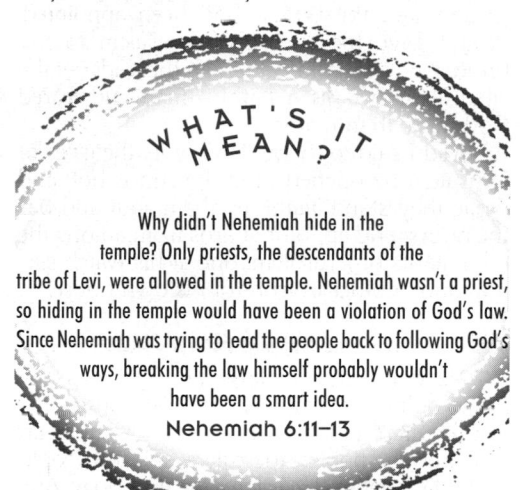

WHAT'S IT MEAN?

Why didn't Nehemiah hide in the temple? Only priests, the descendants of the tribe of Levi, were allowed in the temple. Nehemiah wasn't a priest, so hiding in the temple would have been a violation of God's law. Since Nehemiah was trying to lead the people back to following God's ways, breaking the law himself probably wouldn't have been a smart idea.
Nehemiah 6:11–13

¹¹And I said, "Should such a man as I flee? And who *is there* such as I who would go into the temple to save his life? I will not go in!" ¹²Then I perceived that God had not sent him at all, but that he pronounced *this* prophecy against me because Tobiah and Sanballat had hired him. ¹³For this reason he *was* hired, that I should be afraid and act that way and sin, so *that* they might have *cause* for an evil report, that they might reproach me.

¹⁴My God, remember Tobiah and Sanballat, according to these their works, and the prophetess Noadiah and the rest of the prophets who would have made me afraid.

THE WALL COMPLETED

¹⁵So the wall was finished on the twenty-fifth *day* of Elul, in fifty-two days. ¹⁶And it happened, when all our enemies heard *of it*, and all the nations around us saw *these things*, that they were very disheartened in their own eyes; for

---

5:16 *ᵃ*Following Masoretic Text; Septuagint, Syriac, and Vulgate read *I*.　**6:6** *ᵃ*Hebrew *Gashmu*

they perceived that this work was done by our God.

¹⁷Also in those days the nobles of Judah sent many letters to Tobiah, and *the letters of* Tobiah came to them. ¹⁸For many in Judah were pledged to him, because he was the son-in-law of Shechaniah the son of Arah, and his son Jehohanan had married the daughter of Meshullam the son of Berechiah. ¹⁹Also they reported his good deeds before me, and reported my words to him. Tobiah sent letters to frighten me.

¹Then it was, when the wall was built and I had hung the doors, when the gatekeepers, the singers, and the Levites had been appointed, ²that I gave the charge of Jerusalem to my brother Hanani, and Hananiah the leader of the citadel, for he *was* a faithful man and feared God more than many. ³And I said to them, "Do not let the gates of Jerusalem be opened until the sun is hot; and while they stand *guard,* let them shut and bar the doors; and appoint guards from among the inhabitants of Jerusalem, one at his watch station and another in front of his own house."

THE CAPTIVES WHO RETURNED TO JERUSALEM

⁴Now the city *was* large and spacious, but the people in it *were* few, and the houses *were* not rebuilt. ⁵Then my God put it into my heart to gather the nobles, the rulers, and the people, that they might be registered by genealogy. And I found a register of the genealogy of those who had come up in the first *return,* and found written in it:

⁶   These^a *are* the people of the province who came back from the captivity, of those who had been carried away, whom Nebuchadnezzar the king of Babylon had carried away, and who returned to Jerusalem and Judah, everyone to his city.

⁷   Those who came with Zerubbabel *were* Jeshua, Nehemiah, Azariah, Raamiah, Nahamani, Mordecai, Bilshan, Mispereth,^a Bigvai, Nehum, and Baanah.

      The number of the men of the people of Israel: ⁸the sons of Parosh, two thousand one hundred and seventy-two;
⁹the sons of Shephatiah, three hundred and seventy-two;

¹⁰the sons of Arah, six hundred and fifty-two;
¹¹the sons of Pahath-Moab, of the sons of Jeshua and Joab, two thousand eight hundred and eighteen;
¹²the sons of Elam, one thousand two hundred and fifty-four;
¹³the sons of Zattu, eight hundred and forty-five;
¹⁴the sons of Zaccai, seven hundred and sixty;
¹⁵the sons of Binnui,^a six hundred and forty-eight;
¹⁶the sons of Bebai, six hundred and twenty-eight;
¹⁷the sons of Azgad, two thousand three hundred and twenty-two;
¹⁸the sons of Adonikam, six hundred and sixty-seven;
¹⁹the sons of Bigvai, two thousand and sixty-seven;
²⁰the sons of Adin, six hundred and fifty-five;
²¹the sons of Ater of Hezekiah, ninety-eight;
²²the sons of Hashum, three hundred and twenty-eight;
²³the sons of Bezai, three hundred and twenty-four;
²⁴the sons of Hariph,^a one hundred and twelve;
²⁵the sons of Gibeon,^a ninety-five;
²⁶the men of Bethlehem and Netophah, one hundred and eighty-eight;
²⁷the men of Anathoth, one hundred and twenty-eight;
²⁸the men of Beth Azmaveth,^a forty-two;
²⁹the men of Kirjath Jearim, Chephirah, and Beeroth, seven hundred and forty-three;
³⁰the men of Ramah and Geba, six hundred and twenty-one;
³¹the men of Michmas, one hundred and twenty-two;
³²the men of Bethel and Ai, one hundred and twenty-three;
³³the men of the other Nebo, fifty-two;
³⁴the sons of the other Elam, one thousand two hundred and fifty-four;
³⁵the sons of Harim, three hundred and twenty;
³⁶the sons of Jericho, three hundred and forty-five;
³⁷the sons of Lod, Hadid, and Ono, seven hundred and twenty-one;

7:6 ^aCompare verses 6–72 with Ezra 2:1–70   **7:7** ^aSpelled *Mispar* in Ezra 2:2   **7:15** ^aSpelled *Bani* in Ezra 2:10   **7:24** ^aCalled *Jorah* in Ezra 2:18   **7:25** ^aCalled *Gibbar* in Ezra 2:20   **7:28** ^aCalled *Azmaveth* in Ezra 2:24

[38]the sons of Senaah, three thousand nine hundred and thirty.

[39] The priests: the sons of Jedaiah, of the house of Jeshua, nine hundred and seventy-three;
[40]the sons of Immer, one thousand and fifty-two;
[41]the sons of Pashhur, one thousand two hundred and forty-seven;
[42]the sons of Harim, one thousand and seventeen.

[43] The Levites: the sons of Jeshua, of Kadmiel, *and* of the sons of Hodevah,[a] seventy-four.

[44] The singers: the sons of Asaph, one hundred and forty-eight.

[45] The gatekeepers: the sons of Shallum, the sons of Ater, the sons of Talmon, the sons of Akkub, the sons of Hatita, the sons of Shobai, one hundred and thirty-eight.

[46] The Nethinim: the sons of Ziha, the sons of Hasupha, the sons of Tabbaoth, [47]the sons of Keros, the sons of Sia,[a] the sons of Padon, [48]the sons of Lebana,[a] the sons of Hagaba,[b] the sons of Salmai,[c] [49]the sons of Hanan, the sons of Giddel, the sons of Gahar, [50]the sons of Reaiah, the sons of Rezin, the sons of Nekoda, [51]the sons of Gazzam, the sons of Uzza, the sons of Paseah, [52]the sons of Besai, the sons of Meunim, the sons of Nephishesim,[a] [53]the sons of Bakbuk, the sons of Hakupha, the sons of Harhur,

[54]the sons of Bazlith,[a] the sons of Mehida, the sons of Harsha, [55]the sons of Barkos, the sons of Sisera, the sons of Tamah, [56]the sons of Neziah, and the sons of Hatipha.

[57] The sons of Solomon's servants: the sons of Sotai, the sons of Sophereth, the sons of Perida,[a] [58]the sons of Jaala, the sons of Darkon, the sons of Giddel, [59]the sons of Shephatiah, the sons of Hattil, the sons of Pochereth of Zebaim, and the children of Amon.[a] [60]All the Nethinim, and the sons of Solomon's servants, *were* three hundred and ninety-two.

[61] And these *were* the ones who came up from Tel Melah, Tel Harsha, Cherub, Addon,[a] and Immer, but they could not identify their father's house nor their lineage, whether they *were* of Israel: [62]the sons of Delaiah, the sons of Tobiah, the sons of Nekoda, six hundred and forty-two; [63]and of the priests: the sons of Habaiah, the sons of Koz,[a] the sons of Barzillai, who took a wife of the daughters of Barzillai the Gileadite, and was called by their name. [64]These sought their listing *among* those who were registered by genealogy, but it was not found; therefore they were excluded from the priesthood as defiled. [65]And the governor[a] said to them that they should not eat of the most holy things till a priest could consult with the Urim and Thummim.

[66] Altogether the whole assembly *was* forty-two thousand three hundred and sixty, [67]besides their male and female servants, of whom *there were* seven thousand three hundred and thirty-seven; and they had

---

7:43 [a]Spelled *Hodaviah* in Ezra 2:40 **7:47** [a]Spelled *Siaha* in Ezra 2:44 **7:48** [a]Masoretic Text reads *Lebanah.*
[b]Masoretic Text reads *Hogabah.* [c]Or *Shalmai,* or *Shamlai* **7:52** [a]Spelled *Nephusim* in Ezra 2:50
7:54 [a]Spelled *Bazluth* in Ezra 2:52 **7:57** [a]Spelled *Peruda* in Ezra 2:55 **7:59** [a]Spelled *Ami* in Ezra 2:57
7:61 [a]Spelled *Addan* in Ezra 2:59 **7:63** [a]Or *Hakkoz* **7:65** [a]Hebrew *Tirshatha*

two hundred and forty-five men and women singers. [68]Their horses were seven hundred and thirty-six, their mules two hundred and forty-five, [69]*their* camels four hundred and thirty-five, *and* donkeys six thousand seven hundred and twenty.

[70] And some of the heads of the fathers' houses gave to the work. The governor[a] gave to the treasury one thousand gold drachmas, fifty basins, and five hundred and thirty priestly garments. [71]Some of the heads of the fathers' *houses* gave to the treasury of the work twenty thousand gold drachmas, and two thousand two hundred silver minas. [72]And that which the rest of the people gave *was* twenty thousand gold drachmas, two thousand silver minas, and sixty-seven priestly garments.

[73]So the priests, the Levites, the gatekeepers, the singers, *some* of the people, the Nethinim, and all Israel dwelt in their cities.

EZRA READS THE LAW

When the seventh month came, the children of Israel *were* in their cities.

[1]Now all the people gathered together as one man in the open square that *was* in front of the Water Gate; and they told Ezra the scribe to bring the Book of the Law of Moses, which the LORD had commanded Israel. [2]So Ezra the priest brought the Law before the assembly of men and women and all who *could* hear with understanding on the first day of the seventh month. [3]Then he read from it in the open square that *was* in front of the Water Gate from morning until midday, before the men and women and those who could understand; and the ears of all the people *were attentive* to the Book of the Law.

[4]So Ezra the scribe stood on a platform of wood which they had made for the purpose; and beside him, at his right hand, stood Mattithiah, Shema, Anaiah, Urijah, Hilkiah, and Maaseiah; and at his left hand Pedaiah, Mishael, Malchijah, Hashum, Hashbadana, Zechariah, *and* Meshullam. [5]And Ezra opened the book in the sight of all the people, for he was *standing* above all the people; and when he opened it, all the people stood up. [6]And Ezra blessed the LORD, the great God.

> "And Ezra blessed the Lord, the great God."
> (Nehemiah 8:6)

Then all the people answered, "Amen, Amen!" while lifting up their hands. And they bowed their heads and worshiped the LORD with *their* faces to the ground.

[7]Also Jeshua, Bani, Sherebiah, Jamin, Akkub, Shabbethai, Hodijah, Maaseiah, Kelita, Azariah, Jozabad, Hanan, Pelaiah, and the Levites, helped the people to understand the Law; and the people *stood* in their place. [8]So they read distinctly from the book, in the Law of God; and they gave the sense, and helped *them* to understand the reading.

BIBLE
Is it important to understand the Bible? (8:8)

[9]And Nehemiah, who *was* the governor,[a] Ezra the priest *and* scribe, and the Levites who taught the people said to all the people, "This day *is* holy to the LORD your God; do not mourn nor weep." For all the people wept, when they heard the words of the Law.

[10]Then he said to them, "Go your way, eat the fat, drink the sweet, and send portions to those for whom nothing is prepared; for *this* day *is* holy to our Lord. Do not sorrow, for the joy of the LORD is your strength."

[11]So the Levites quieted all the people, saying, "Be still, for the day *is* holy; do not be grieved." [12]And all the people went their way to eat and drink, to send portions and rejoice greatly, because they understood the words that were declared to them.

THE FEAST OF TABERNACLES

[13]Now on the second day the heads of the fathers' *houses* of all the people, with the priests and Levites, were gathered to Ezra the scribe, in order to understand the words of the Law. [14]And they found written in the Law, which the LORD had commanded by Moses, that the children of Israel should dwell in booths during the feast of the seventh month, [15]and that they should announce and proclaim in all their cities and in Jerusalem, saying, "Go out to the mountain, and bring olive branches, branches of oil trees, myrtle branches, palm branches, and branches of leafy trees, to make booths, as *it is* written."

[16]Then the people went out and brought *them* and made themselves booths, each one on the roof of his house, or in their courtyards or the courts of the house of God, and in the open square of the Water Gate and in the open square of the Gate of Ephraim. [17]So the whole

assembly of those who had returned from the captivity made booths and sat under the booths; for since the days of Joshua the son of Nun until that day the children of Israel had not done so. And there was very great gladness. [18]Also day by day, from the first day until the last day, he read from the Book of the Law of God. And they kept the feast seven days; and on the eighth day *there was* a sacred assembly, according to the *prescribed* manner.

WHAT'S IT MEAN?

The Feast of Booths was like a yearly campout for the Israelites. During this harvest celebration, the people made temporary shelters out of leafy tree branches and then lived in those shelters for a short time. The Feast was intended to remind the Israelites of the time their ancestors wandered in the desert, with no homes of their own, after Moses led them out of Egypt.

Nehemiah 8:14

THE PEOPLE CONFESS THEIR SINS

[1]Now on the twenty-fourth day of this month the children of Israel were assembled with fasting, in sackcloth, and with dust on their heads.[a] [2]Then those of Israelite lineage separated themselves from all foreigners; and they stood and confessed their sins and the iniquities of their fathers. [3]And they stood up in their place and read from the Book of the Law of the LORD their God *for one*-fourth of the day; and *for another* fourth they confessed and worshiped the LORD their God.

[4]Then Jeshua, Bani, Kadmiel, Shebaniah, Bunni, Sherebiah, Bani, *and* Chenani stood on the stairs of the Levites and cried out with a loud voice to the LORD their God. [5]And the Levites, Jeshua, Kadmiel, Bani, Hashabniah, Sherebiah, Hodijah, Shebaniah, *and* Pethahiah, said:

"Stand up *and* bless the LORD your God
Forever and ever!

"Blessed be Your glorious name,
Which is exalted above all blessing and
praise!

[6] You alone *are* the LORD;
You have made heaven,
The heaven of heavens, with all their host,
The earth and everything on it,
The seas and all that is in them,
And You preserve them all.
The host of heaven worships You.

[7] "You *are* the LORD God,
Who chose Abram,
And brought him out of Ur of the
Chaldeans,
And gave him the name Abraham;
[8] You found his heart faithful before You,
And made a covenant with him
To give the land of the Canaanites,
The Hittites, the Amorites,

9:1 [a]Literally *earth on them*

The Perizzites, the Jebusites,
And the Girgashites—
To give *it* to his descendants.
You have performed Your words,
For You *are* righteous.

9 "You saw the affliction of our fathers in
     Egypt,
   And heard their cry by the Red Sea.
10 You showed signs and wonders against
     Pharaoh,
   Against all his servants,
   And against all the people of his land.
   For You knew that they acted proudly
     against them.
   So You made a name for Yourself, as *it is*
     this day.
11 And You divided the sea before them,
   So that they went through the midst of
     the sea on the dry land;
   And their persecutors You threw into the
     deep,
   As a stone into the mighty waters.
12 Moreover You led them by day with a
     cloudy pillar,
   And by night with a pillar of fire,
   To give them light on the road
   Which they should travel.

13 "You came down also on Mount Sinai,
   And spoke with them from heaven,
   And gave them just ordinances and true
     laws,
   Good statutes and commandments.
14 You made known to them Your
     holy Sabbath,
   And commanded them
     precepts, statutes and
     laws,
   By the hand of Moses
     Your servant.
15 You gave them bread from
     heaven for their hunger,
   And brought them water out of the rock
     for their thirst,
   And told them to go in to possess the
     land
   Which You had sworn to give them.

16 "But they and our fathers acted proudly,
   Hardened their necks,
   And did not heed Your commandments.
17 They refused to obey,
   And they were not mindful of Your
     wonders

That You did among them.
But they hardened their necks,
And in their rebellion[a]
They appointed a leader
To return to their bondage.
But You *are* God,
Ready to pardon,
Gracious and merciful,
Slow to anger,
Abundant in kindness,
And did not forsake
     them.

18 "Even when they made a molded calf for
     themselves,
   And said, 'This *is* your god
   That brought you up out of Egypt,'

FORGIVENESS

What is God
known for?
(9:17)

BIBLE

Where did
the Bible
come from?
(9:14)

On the Edge

But You are God, ready to pardon, gracious and merciful, slow to anger, abundant in kindness (Neh. 9:17).

Patience should be put on the "endangered character trait" list. You rarely see patience anymore. Maybe everyone has already used up all their patience. No one wants to wait for anything—ever. Overnight mail moved too slowly, so someone invented the fax machine. But sometimes it takes a while for the fax to get through; so, thank goodness, someone invented e-mail. One push of a button, and your friend immediately has your message or very important document. Who knows what's next? Maybe think-mail, where you just have to think and your thoughts are instantly processed around the world.

So to say that God is "slow to anger" means He's patient with us—and we do try His patience! This is not to say that God is outdated in our fast-paced, we-need-to-know-now society. He's not. It's just that in our rush to know more and do more we have forgotten how to wait. God models the virtue for us. He is very patient, especially about important things, like waiting for the people He loves.

SEE FOR YOURSELF:
Neh. 9:30; Ps. 145:8;
     2 Pet. 3:9

9:17 [a]Following Masoretic Text and Vulgate; Septuagint reads *in Egypt.*

And worked great provocations,
19 Yet in Your manifold mercies
You did not forsake them in the
wilderness.
The pillar of the cloud did not depart
from them by day,
To lead them on the road;
Nor the pillar of fire by night,
To show them light,
And the way they should go.
20 You also gave Your
good Spirit to
instruct them,
And did not withhold
Your manna from
their mouth,
And gave them water for
their thirst.
21 Forty years You sustained them in the
wilderness;
They lacked nothing;
Their clothes did not wear out[a]
And their feet did not swell.

22 "Moreover You gave them kingdoms and
nations,
And divided them into districts.[a]
So they took possession of the land of
Sihon,
The land of[b] the king of Heshbon,
And the land of Og king of Bashan.

FOLLOWING GOD

Who will
teach us to
follow God?
(9:20)

WHAT'S IT MEAN?

Sihon and Og were Amorite
kings who ruled areas east of the Jordan
River. In one of Israel's proudest victories, both kings
were defeated by Moses and the Israelites, who were
heading for the Promised Land.
Nehemiah 9:22

23 You also multiplied their children as the
stars of heaven,
And brought them into the land
Which You had told their fathers
To go in and possess.

24 So the people went in
And possessed the land;
You subdued before them the inhabitants
of the land,
The Canaanites,
And gave them into their hands,
With their kings
And the people of the land,
That they might do with them as they
wished.
25 And they took strong cities and a rich
land,
And possessed houses full of all goods,
Cisterns *already* dug, vineyards, olive
groves,
And fruit trees in abundance.
So they ate and were filled and grew fat,
And delighted themselves in Your great
goodness.

26 "Nevertheless they were disobedient
And rebelled against You,
Cast Your law behind their backs
And killed Your prophets, who testified
against them
To turn them to Yourself;
And they worked great provocations.
27 Therefore You delivered them into the
hand of their enemies,
Who oppressed them;
And in the time of their
trouble,
When they cried to You,
You heard from heaven;
And according to Your
abundant mercies
You gave them deliverers
who saved them
From the hand of their enemies.

28 "But after they had rest,
They again did evil before You.
Therefore You left them in the hand of
their enemies,
So that they had dominion over them;
Yet when they returned and cried out to
You,
You heard from heaven;
And many times You delivered them
according to Your mercies,
29 And testified against them,
That You might bring them back to Your
law.
Yet they acted proudly,

FEELINGS

Does God
care when we
hurt?
(9:27)

9:21 [a]Compare Deuteronomy 29:5   **9:22** [a]Literally *corners*   [b]Following Masoretic Text and Vulgate; Septuagint
omits *The land of.*

And did not heed Your commandments,
But sinned against Your judgments,
'Which if a man does, he shall live by
them.'[a]
And they shrugged their shoulders,
Stiffened their necks,
And would not hear.
30 Yet for many years You had patience with
them,
And testified against them by Your Spirit
in Your prophets.
Yet they would not listen;
Therefore You gave them into the hand of
the peoples of the lands.
31 Nevertheless in Your great mercy
You did not utterly consume them nor
forsake them;
For You *are* God, gracious and merciful.

32 "Now therefore, our God,
The great, the mighty, and awesome God,
Who keeps covenant and mercy:
Do not let all the trouble seem small
before You
That has come upon us,
Our kings and our princes,
Our priests and our prophets,
Our fathers and on all Your people,
From the days of the kings of Assyria
until this day.
33 However You *are* just in all that has
befallen us;
For You have dealt faithfully,
But we have done wickedly.
34 Neither our kings nor our princes,
Our priests nor our fathers,
Have kept Your law,
Nor heeded Your commandments and
Your testimonies,
With which You testified against them.
35 For they have not served You in their
kingdom,
Or in the many good *things* that You gave
them,
Or in the large and rich land which You
set before them;
Nor did they turn from their wicked
works.

36 "Here we *are*, servants today!
And the land that You gave to our
fathers,
To eat its fruit and its bounty,
Here we *are*, servants in it!
37 And it yields much increase to the kings

You have set over us,
Because of our sins;
Also they have dominion over our bodies
and our cattle
At their pleasure;
And we *are* in great distress.

38 "And because of all this,
We make a sure *covenant* and write *it*;
Our leaders, our Levites, *and* our priests
seal *it*."

THE PEOPLE WHO SEALED THE COVENANT

1Now those who placed *their* seal on *the doc-ument were:*

Nehemiah the governor, the son of
Hacaliah, and Zedekiah, 2Seraiah, Azariah,
Jeremiah, 3Pashhur, Amariah, Malchijah,
4Hattush, Shebaniah, Malluch, 5Harim,
Meremoth, Obadiah, 6Daniel, Ginnethon,
Baruch, 7Meshullam, Abijah, Mijamin,
8Maaziah, Bilgai, *and* Shemaiah. These *were*
the priests.
9The Levites: Jeshua the son of
Azaniah, Binnui of the sons of Henadad,
and Kadmiel.
10Their brethren: Shebaniah, Hodijah,
Kelita, Pelaiah, Hanan, 11Micha, Rehob,
Hashabiah, 12Zaccur, Sherebiah,
Shebaniah, 13Hodijah, Bani, *and* Beninu.
14The leaders of the people: Parosh,
Pahath-Moab, Elam, Zattu, Bani, 15Bunni,
Azgad, Bebai, 16Adonijah, Bigvai, Adin,
17Ater, Hezekiah, Azzur, 18Hodijah,
Hashum, Bezai, 19Hariph, Anathoth,
Nebai, 20Magpiash, Meshullam, Hezir,
21Meshezabel, Zadok, Jaddua, 22Pelatiah,
Hanan, Anaiah, 23Hoshea, Hananiah,
Hasshub, 24Hallohesh, Pilha, Shobek,
25Rehum, Hashabnah, Maaseiah, 26Ahijah,
Hanan, Anan, 27Malluch, Harim, *and*
Baanah.

THE COVENANT THAT WAS SEALED

28Now the rest of the people—the priests, the
Levites, the gatekeepers, the singers, the Nethinim, and all those who had separated themselves from the peoples of the lands to the Law
of God, their wives, their sons, and their daughters, everyone who had knowledge and understanding—29these joined with their brethren,
their nobles, and entered into a curse and an
oath to walk in God's Law, which was given by
Moses the servant of God, and to observe and

9:29 [a]Leviticus 18:5

do all the commandments of the LORD our Lord, and His ordinances and His statutes: ³⁰We would not give our daughters as wives to the peoples of the land, nor take their daughters for our sons; ³¹*if* the peoples of the land brought wares or any grain to sell on the Sabbath day, we would not buy it from them on the Sabbath, or on a holy day; and we would forego the seventh year's *produce* and the exacting of every debt.

³²Also we made ordinances for ourselves, to exact from ourselves yearly one-third of a shekel for the service of the house of our God: ³³for the showbread, for the regular grain offering, for the regular burnt offering of the Sabbaths, the New Moons, and the set feasts; for the holy things, for the sin offerings to make atonement for Israel, and all the work of the house of our God. ³⁴We cast lots among the priests, the Levites, and the people, for *bringing* the wood offering into the house of our God, according to our fathers' houses, at the appointed times year by year, to burn on the altar of the LORD our God as *it is* written in the Law.

The Levites didn't have their own land or means of income. The rest of the Israelites supported them by giving them one-tenth of every harvest. The Levites, in turn, supported the priests by giving them one-tenth of everything they received. If this one-tenth stuff sounds familiar, it should. This system, called tithing, was established in the Law of Moses.
Nehemiah 10:38

³⁵And *we made ordinances* to bring the firstfruits of our ground and the firstfruits of all fruit of all trees, year by year, to the house of the LORD; ³⁶to bring the firstborn of our sons and our cattle, as *it is* written in the Law, and the firstborn of our herds and our flocks, to the house of our God, to the priests who minister in the house of our God; ³⁷to bring the firstfruits of our dough, our offerings, the fruit from all kinds of trees, *the* new wine and oil, to the priests, to the storerooms of the house of our God; and to bring the tithes of our land to the Levites, for the Levites should receive the tithes in all our farming communities. ³⁸And the

priest, the descendant of Aaron, shall be with the Levites when the Levites receive tithes; and the Levites shall bring up a tenth of the tithes to the house of our God, to the rooms of the storehouse.

³⁹For the children of Israel and the children of Levi shall bring the offering of the grain, of the new wine and the oil, to the storerooms where the articles of the sanctuary *are, where* the priests who minister and the gatekeepers and the singers *are;* and we will not neglect the house of our God.

THE PEOPLE DWELLING IN JERUSALEM

¹Now the leaders of the people dwelt at Jerusalem; the rest of the people cast lots to bring one out of ten to dwell in Jerusalem, the holy city, and nine-tenths *were to dwell* in *other* cities. ²And the people blessed all the men who willingly offered themselves to dwell at Jerusalem.

³These *are* the heads of the province who dwelt in Jerusalem. (But in the cities of Judah everyone dwelt in his own possession in their cities—Israelites, priests, Levites, Nethinim, and descendants of Solomon's servants.) ⁴Also in Jerusalem dwelt *some* of the children of Judah and of the children of Benjamin.

The children of Judah: Athaiah the son of Uzziah, the son of Zechariah, the son of Amariah, the son of Shephatiah, the son of Mahalalel, of the children of Perez; ⁵and Maaseiah the son of Baruch, the son of Col-Hozeh, the son of Hazaiah, the son of Adaiah, the son of Joiarib, the son of Zechariah, the son of Shiloni. ⁶All the sons of Perez who dwelt at Jerusalem *were* four hundred and sixty-eight valiant men.

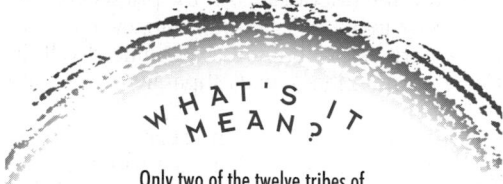

Only two of the twelve tribes of Israel—Judah and Benjamin—made it back to their homeland intact following the Babylonian captivity. The Levites were not counted as a tribe, even though they were descendants of one of Jacob's (or Israel's) sons. To replace Levi in the count, Joseph was divided into two tribes, Manasseh and Ephraim.
Nehemiah 11:4–6

⁷And these are the sons of Benjamin: Sallu the son of Meshullam, the son of Joed, the son of Pedaiah, the son of Kolaiah, the son of

Maaseiah, the son of Ithiel, the son of Jeshaiah; [8]and after him Gabbai *and* Sallai, nine hundred and twenty-eight. [9]Joel the son of Zichri *was* their overseer, and Judah the son of Senuah*a was* second over the city.

[10]Of the priests: Jedaiah the son of Joiarib, and Jachin; [11]Seraiah the son of Hilkiah, the son of Meshullam, the son of Zadok, the son of Meraioth, the son of Ahitub, *was* the leader of the house of God. [12]Their brethren who did the work of the house *were* eight hundred and twenty-two; and Adaiah the son of Jeroham, the son of Pelaliah, the son of Amzi, the son of Zechariah, the son of Pashhur, the son of Malchijah, [13]and his brethren, heads of the fathers' *houses, were* two hundred and forty-two; and Amashai the son of Azarel, the son of Ahzai, the son of Meshillemoth, the son of Immer, [14]and their brethren, mighty men of valor, *were* one hundred and twenty-eight. Their overseer *was* Zabdiel the son of *one of* the great men.*a*

[15]Also of the Levites: Shemaiah the son of Hasshub, the son of Azrikam, the son of Hashabiah, the son of Bunni; [16]Shabbethai and Jozabad, of the heads of the Levites, *had* the oversight of the business outside of the house of God; [17]Mattaniah the son of Micha,*a* the son of Zabdi, the son of Asaph, the leader *who* began the thanksgiving with prayer; Bakbukiah, the second among his brethren; and Abda the son of Shammua, the son of Galal, the son of Jeduthun. [18]All the Levites in the holy city *were* two hundred and eighty-four.

[19]Moreover the gatekeepers, Akkub, Talmon, and their brethren who kept the gates, *were* one hundred and seventy-two.

[20]And the rest of Israel, of the priests *and* Levites, *were* in all the cities of Judah, everyone in his inheritance. [21]But the Nethinim dwelt in Ophel. And Ziha and Gishpa *were* over the Nethinim.

[22]Also the overseer of the Levites at Jerusalem *was* Uzzi the son of Bani, the son of Hashabiah, the son of Mattaniah, the son of Micha, of the sons of Asaph, the singers in charge of the service of the house of God. [23]For *it was* the king's command concerning them that a certain portion should be for the singers, a quota day by day. [24]Pethahiah the son of Meshezabel, of the children of Zerah the son of Judah, *was* the king's deputy*a* in all matters concerning the people.

THE PEOPLE DWELLING OUTSIDE JERUSALEM

[25]And as for the villages with their fields, *some* of the children of Judah dwelt in Kirjath Arba and its villages, Dibon and its villages, Jekabzeel and its villages; [26]in Jeshua, Moladah, Beth Pelet, [27]Hazar Shual, and Beersheba and its villages; [28]in Ziklag and Meconah and its villages; [29]in En Rimmon, Zorah, Jarmuth, [30]Zanoah, Adullam, and their villages; in Lachish and its fields; in Azekah and its villages. They dwelt from Beersheba to the Valley of Hinnom.

[31]Also the children of Benjamin from Geba *dwelt* in Michmash, Aija, and Bethel, and their villages; [32]in Anathoth, Nob, Ananiah; [33]in Hazor, Ramah, Gittaim; [34]in Hadid, Zeboim, Neballat; [35]in Lod, Ono, *and* the Valley of Craftsmen. [36]Some of the Judean divisions of Levites *were* in Benjamin.

THE PRIESTS AND LEVITES

[1]Now these *are* the priests and the Levites who came up with Zerubbabel the son of Shealtiel, and Jeshua: Seraiah, Jeremiah, Ezra, [2]Amariah, Malluch, Hattush, [3]Shechaniah, Rehum, Meremoth, [4]Iddo, Ginnethoi,*a* Abijah, [5]Mijamin, Maadiah, Bilgah, [6]Shemaiah, Joiarib, Jedaiah, [7]Sallu, Amok, Hilkiah, *and* Jedaiah.

These *were* the heads of the priests and their brethren in the days of Jeshua.

[8]Moreover the Levites *were* Jeshua, Binnui, Kadmiel, Sherebiah, Judah, *and* Mattaniah *who* led the thanksgiving *psalms,* he and his brethren. [9]Also Bakbukiah and Unni, their brethren, *stood* across from them in *their* duties.

[10]Jeshua begot Joiakim, Joiakim begot Eliashib, Eliashib begot Joiada, [11]Joiada begot Jonathan, and Jonathan begot Jaddua.

[12]Now in the days of Joiakim, the priests, the heads of the fathers' *houses were:* of Seraiah, Meraiah; of Jeremiah, Hananiah; [13]of Ezra, Meshullam; of Amariah, Jehohanan; [14]of Melichu,*a* Jonathan; of Shebaniah,*b* Joseph; [15]of Harim,*a* Adna; of Meraioth,*b* Helkai; [16]of Iddo, Zechariah; of Ginnethon, Meshullam; [17]of Abijah, Zichri; *the son of* Minjamin;*a* of Moadiah,*b* Piltai; [18]of Bilgah, Shammua; of Shemaiah, Jehonathan; [19]of Joiarib, Mattenai; of Jedaiah, Uzzi; [20]of Sallai,*a* Kallai; of Amok, Eber; [21]of Hilkiah, Hashabiah; *and* of Jedaiah, Nethanel.

[22]During the reign of Darius the Persian, a record *was also kept* of the Levites and priests *who had been* heads of their fathers' *houses* in the

---

11:9 *a*Or *Hassenuah*   **11:14** *a*Or *the son of Haggedolim*   **11:17** *a*Or *Michah*   **11:24** *a*Literally *at the king's hand*
12:4 *a*Or *Ginnethon* (compare verse 16)   **12:14** *a*Or *Malluch* (compare verse 2)   *b*Or *Shechaniah* (compare verse 3)   **12:15** *a*Or *Rehum* (compare verse 3)   *b*Or *Meremoth* (compare verse 3)   **12:17** *a*Or *Mijamin* (compare verse 5)   *b*Or *Maadiah* (compare verse 5)   **12:20** *a*Or *Sallu* (compare verse 7)

days of Eliashib, Joiada, Johanan, and Jaddua. [23]The sons of Levi, the heads of the fathers' *houses* until the days of Johanan the son of Eliashib, *were* written in the book of the chronicles.

[24]And the heads of the Levites *were* Hashabiah, Sherebiah, and Jeshua the son of Kadmiel, with their brothers across from them, to praise *and* give thanks, group alternating with group, according to the command of David the man of God. [25]Mattaniah, Bakbukiah, Obadiah, Meshullam, Talmon, and Akkub *were* gatekeepers keeping the watch at the storerooms of the gates. [26]These *lived* in the days of Joiakim the son of Jeshua, the son of Jozadak,[a] and in the days of Nehemiah the governor, and of Ezra the priest, the scribe.

> "They sought out the Levites in all their places, to bring them to Jerusalem to celebrate the dedication with gladness."
> (Nehemiah 12:27b)

NEHEMIAH DEDICATES THE WALL

[27]Now at the dedication of the wall of Jerusalem they sought out the Levites in all their places, to bring them to Jerusalem to celebrate the dedication with gladness, both with thanksgivings and singing, *with* cymbals and stringed instruments and harps. [28]And the sons of the singers gathered together from the countryside around Jerusalem, from the villages of the Netophathites, [29]from the house of Gilgal, and from the fields of Geba and Azmaveth; for the singers had built themselves villages all around Jerusalem. [30]Then the priests and Levites purified themselves, and purified the people, the gates, and the wall.

VICTORY

Who should we dedicate our victory to? (12:27, 43)

[31]So I brought the leaders of Judah up on the wall, and appointed two large thanksgiving choirs. *One* went to the right hand on the wall toward the Refuse Gate. [32]After them went Hoshaiah and half of the leaders of Judah, [33]and Azariah, Ezra, Meshullam, [34]Judah, Benjamin, Shemaiah, Jeremiah, [35]and some of the priests' sons with trumpets—Zechariah the son of Jonathan, the son of Shemaiah, the son of Mattaniah, the son of Michaiah, the son of Zaccur, the son of Asaph, [36]and his brethren, Shemaiah, Azarel, Milalai, Gilalai, Maai, Nethanel, Judah, *and* Hanani, with the musical instruments of David the man of God. And Ezra the scribe *went* before them. [37]By the Fountain Gate, in front of them, they went up the stairs of the City of David, on the stairway of the wall, beyond the house of David, as far as the Water Gate eastward.

[38]The other thanksgiving choir went the opposite *way*, and I *was* behind them with half of the people on the wall, going past the Tower of the Ovens as far as the Broad Wall, [39]and above the Gate of Ephraim, above the Old Gate, above the Fish Gate, the Tower of Hananel, the Tower of the Hundred, as far as the Sheep Gate; and they stopped by the Gate of the Prison.

[40]So the two thanksgiving choirs stood in the house of God, likewise I and the half of the rulers with me; [41]and the priests, Eliakim, Maaseiah, Minjamin,[a] Michaiah, Elioenai, Zechariah, *and* Hananiah, with trumpets; [42]also Maaseiah, Shemaiah, Eleazar, Uzzi, Jehohanan, Malchijah, Elam, and Ezer. The singers sang loudly with Jezrahiah the director.

WHAT'S IT MEAN?

The Israelites loved their music. They found reasons to sing for any occasion, whether it was a battle victory, a religious ceremony, or a death. Most of the time, though, they sang to worship the Lord. About the only time the Israelites didn't feel like singing was during their captivity in Babylon. According to Psalm 137, the Babylonians had commanded the Israelites to perform, but the Jewish captives were too heartbroken about the destruction of their temple and their capital city.
Nehemiah 12:27

[43]Also that day they offered great sacrifices, and rejoiced, for God had made them rejoice with great joy; the women and the children also rejoiced, so that the joy of Jerusalem was heard afar off.

TEMPLE RESPONSIBILITIES

[44]And at the same time some were appointed over the rooms of the storehouse for

---

12:26 [a]Spelled *Jehozadak* in 1 Chronicles 6:14   **12:41** [a]Or *Mijamin* (compare verse 5)

the offerings, the firstfruits, and the tithes, to gather into them from the fields of the cities the portions specified by the Law for the priests and Levites; for Judah rejoiced over the priests and Levites who ministered. ⁴⁵Both the singers and the gatekeepers kept the charge of their God and the charge of the purification, according to the command of David *and* Solomon his son. ⁴⁶For in the days of David and Asaph of old *there were* chiefs of the singers, and songs of praise and thanksgiving to God. ⁴⁷In the days of Zerubbabel and in the days of Nehemiah all Israel gave the portions for the singers and the gatekeepers, a portion for each day. They also consecrated *holy things* for the Levites, and the Levites consecrated *them* for the children of Aaron.

PRINCIPLES OF SEPARATION

¹On that day they read from the Book of Moses in the hearing of the people, and in it was found written that no Ammonite or Moabite should ever come into the assembly of God, ²because they had not met the children of Israel with bread and water, but hired Balaam against them to curse them. However, our God turned the curse into a blessing. ³So it was, when they had heard the Law, that they separated all the mixed multitude from Israel.

THE REFORMS OF NEHEMIAH

⁴Now before this, Eliashib the priest, having authority over the storerooms of the house of our God, *was* allied with Tobiah. ⁵And he had prepared for him a large room, where previously they had stored the grain offerings, the frankincense, the articles, the tithes of grain, the new wine and oil, which were commanded *to be given* to the Levites and singers and gatekeepers, and the offerings for the priests. ⁶But during all this I was not in Jerusalem, for in the thirty-second year of Artaxerxes king of Babylon I had returned to the king. Then after certain days I obtained leave from the king, ⁷and I came to Jerusalem and discovered the evil that Eliashib had done for Tobiah, in preparing a room for him in the courts of the house of God. ⁸And it grieved me bitterly; therefore I threw all the household goods of Tobiah out of the room. ⁹Then I commanded them to cleanse the rooms; and I brought back into them the articles of the house of God, with the grain offering and the frankincense.

¹⁰I also realized that the portions for the Levites had not been given *them;* for each of the Levites and the singers who did the work had gone back to his field. ¹¹So I contended with the rulers, and said, "Why is the house of God forsaken?" And I gathered them together and set them in their place. ¹²Then all Judah brought the tithe of the grain and the new wine and the oil to the storehouse. ¹³And I appointed as treasurers over the storehouse Shelemiah the priest and Zadok the scribe, and of the Levites, Pedaiah; and next to them *was* Hanan the son of Zaccur, the son of Mattaniah; for they were considered faithful, and their task *was* to distribute to their brethren.

¹⁴Remember me, O my God, concerning this, and do not wipe out my good deeds that I have done for the house of my God, and for its services!

WHAT'S IT MEAN?

According to the Law of Moses, the last day of the week—the Sabbath day—was to be set aside for rest and worship. The pattern of working six days and resting one was based on God's schedule at creation. For six days He created the universe, and on the seventh day He rested. Setting aside the Sabbath for rest was a way of showing that God ruled over the nation of Israel.

Nehemiah 13:15

¹⁵In those days I saw *people* in Judah treading wine presses on the Sabbath, and bringing in sheaves, and loading donkeys with wine, grapes, figs, and all *kinds of* burdens, which they brought into Jerusalem on the Sabbath day. And I warned *them* about the day on which they were selling provisions. ¹⁶Men of Tyre dwelt there also, who brought in fish and all kinds of goods, and sold *them* on the Sabbath to the children of Judah, and in Jerusalem.

¹⁷Then I contended with the nobles of Judah, and said to them, "What evil thing *is* this that you do, by which you profane the Sabbath day? ¹⁸Did not your fathers do thus, and did not our God bring all this disaster on us and on this city? Yet you bring added wrath on Israel by profaning the Sabbath."

¹⁹So it was, at the gates of Jerusalem, as it began to be dark before the Sabbath, that I commanded the gates to be shut, and charged that they must not be opened till after the Sabbath. Then I posted *some* of my servants at the gates, *so that* no burdens would be brought in

on the Sabbath day. [20]Now the merchants and sellers of all kinds of wares lodged outside Jerusalem once or twice.

[21]Then I warned them, and said to them, "Why do you spend the night around the wall? If you do *so* again, I will lay hands on you!" From that time on they came no *more* on the Sabbath. [22]And I commanded the Levites that they should cleanse themselves, and that they should go and guard the gates, to sanctify the Sabbath day.

Remember me, O my God, *concerning* this also, and spare me according to the greatness of Your mercy!

[23]In those days I also saw Jews *who* had married women of Ashdod, Ammon, *and* Moab. [24]And half of their children spoke the language of Ashdod, and could not speak the language of Judah, but spoke according to the language of one or the other people.

[25]So I contended with them and cursed them, struck some of them and pulled out their hair, and made them swear by God, *saying*, "You shall not give your daughters as wives to their sons, nor take their daughters for your sons or yourselves. [26]Did not Solomon king of Israel sin by these things? Yet among many nations there was no king like him, who was beloved of his God; and God made him king over all Israel. Nevertheless pagan women caused even him to sin. [27]Should we then hear of your doing all this great evil, transgressing against our God by marrying pagan women?"

[28]And *one* of the sons of Joiada, the son of Eliashib the high priest, *was* a son-in-law of Sanballat the Horonite; therefore I drove him from me.

[29]Remember them, O my God, because they have defiled the priesthood and the covenant of the priesthood and the Levites.

[30]Thus I cleansed them of everything pagan. I also assigned duties to the priests and the Levites, each to his service, [31]and *to bringing* the wood offering and the firstfruits at appointed times.

Remember me, O my God, for good!

BLESSING

Is it wrong to ask God for blessings? (13:31)

esther

CONTENT

The story of Esther is a spy/thriller if ever there was one. Think about it. A young woman changes her name. She then hides the fact that she is a part of a minority group treated with extreme prejudice in her culture. She enters a yearlong beauty contest in which the winner will become queen of the nation. She actually wins the contest and becomes the king's favorite. Then just when things are looking really good, she faces a situation where she has to reveal her identity to the king (risking her life) in order to catch the villain and save her people from destruction.

If you add in a walkie-talkie watch, you've got a movie script! But the important thing about Esther's story isn't the intrigue. The important thing is that God used Esther because she was willing to trust Him and take some risks. Esther knew that God put her where she was for a reason, so when she saw the opportunity to make a difference she took it.

As it turned out, Esther did save her people. She also saved the life of a family member and saw that the bad guy was punished. There's nothing like a story with a happy ending, is there?

Outline

1:1—2:23 .... Esther Becomes Queen
3:1–15 .... Haman's Plot to Destroy the Jews
4:1–17 .... Mordecai Asks for Esther's Help
5:1—6:14 .... Mordecai Is Honored, Not Killed
7:1–10 .... Haman Is Put to Death
8:1—9:19 .... The Jews Defend Themselves and Kill Their Enemies
9:20–32 .... The Feast of Purim
10:1–3 .... The Greatness of Ahasuerus and Mordecai

Purpose

God works quietly through cause and effect to achieve His purposes in history and in our lives.

Theme

Teamwork That Shaped a Nation

Date of writing

464–435 B.C.

> "For if you remain completely silent at this time, relief and deliverance will arise for the Jews from another place, but you and your father's house will perish. Yet who knows whether you have come to the kingdom for such a time as this?" (4:14).

Bible Talk

God Builds Our Platforms

Esther's role as queen gave her a platform. It gave her a place where her voice could be heard and she could make a difference. She didn't know it, though, until God asked her to speak up.

Has God given you a platform? Are you a leader in a group? Do you have younger brothers and sisters that listen to you? Do you help with younger kids at church or at school? Wherever you are, God can say something through your life. That is the platform that God has built for you.

Sometimes we don't know that we can do something that matters until God asks us to speak up. Then He uses us. Don't underestimate your opportunities to make a difference.

HAMAN

Haman was a bigot. He hated a group of people because of their race. He hated the Jews. Haman was also power-hungry and deceitful. He used people to make himself look good.

There was one Jew that Haman really had it in for: Mordecai, Esther's cousin. Haman couldn't stand Mordecai because Mordecai had the one thing Haman didn't, people's respect.

If you like a story where the bad guy gets it in the end, read about Haman. He built gallows on which to hang his enemy Mordecai, but in the end the gallows were used on Haman and justice was done.

THE KING DETHRONES QUEEN VASHTI

¹Now it came to pass in the days of Ahasuerus*ᵃ* (this *was* the Ahasuerus who reigned over one hundred and twenty-seven provinces, from India to Ethiopia), ²in those days when King Ahasuerus sat on the throne of his kingdom, which *was* in Shushan*ᵃ* the citadel, ³that in the third year of his reign he made a feast for all his officials and servants—the powers of Persia and Media, the nobles, and the princes of the provinces *being* before him—⁴when he showed the riches of his glorious kingdom and the splendor of his excellent majesty for many days, one hundred and eighty days *in all*.

WHAT'S IT MEAN?

Ahasuerus (you may know him better as Xerxes) became king of Persia after the death of his father, Darius. Under Darius's reign, the Jewish people, who had been held captive for over a century, were allowed to return to their homeland. Surprisingly, not all of the Jews wanted to return to Jerusalem. Some of the ones who had been born in captivity wanted to stay in Persia, the only home they had ever known. As a result, there were thousands of Jewish people living in Persia during the reign of Ahasuerus.

Esther 1:1

⁵And when these days were completed, the king made a feast lasting seven days for all the people who were present in Shushan the citadel, from great to small, in the court of the garden of the king's palace. ⁶*There were* white and blue linen *curtains* fastened with cords of fine linen and purple on silver rods and marble pillars; *and the* couches *were* of gold and silver on a *mosaic* pavement of alabaster, turquoise, and white and black marble. ⁷And they served drinks in golden vessels, each vessel being different from the other, with royal wine in abundance, according to the generosity of the king. ⁸In accordance with the law, the drinking was not compulsory; for so the king had ordered all the officers of his household, that they should do according to each man's pleasure.

⁹Queen Vashti also made a feast for the women *in* the royal palace which *belonged* to King Ahasuerus.

¹⁰On the seventh day, when the heart of the king was merry with wine, he commanded Mehuman, Biztha, Harbona, Bigtha, Abagtha, Zethar, and Carcas, seven eunuchs who served in the presence of King Ahasuerus, ¹¹to bring Queen Vashti before the king, *wearing* her royal crown, in order to show her beauty to the people and the officials, for she *was* beautiful to behold. ¹²But Queen Vashti refused to come at the king's command *brought* by *his* eunuchs; therefore the king was furious, and his anger burned within him.

¹³Then the king said to the wise men who understood the times (for this *was* the king's manner toward all who knew law and justice, ¹⁴those closest to him *being* Carshena, Shethar, Admatha, Tarshish, Meres, Marsena, and Memucan, the seven princes of Persia and Media, who had access to the king's presence, *and* who ranked highest in the kingdom): ¹⁵"What *shall we* do to Queen Vashti, according to law, because she did not obey the command of King Ahasuerus *brought to her* by the eunuchs?"

¹⁶And Memucan answered before the king and the princes: "Queen Vashti has not only wronged the king, but also all the princes, and all the people who *are* in all the provinces of King Ahasuerus. ¹⁷For the queen's behavior will become known to all women, so that they will despise their husbands in their eyes, when they report, 'King Ahasuerus commanded Queen Vashti to be brought in before him, but she did not come.' ¹⁸This very day the *noble* ladies of Persia and Media will say to all the king's officials that they have heard of the behavior of the queen. Thus *there will be* excessive contempt and wrath. ¹⁹If it pleases the king, let a royal decree go out from him, and let it be recorded in the laws of the Persians and the Medes, so that it will not be altered, that Vashti shall come no more before King Ahasuerus; and let the king give her royal position to another who is better than she. ²⁰When the king's decree which he will make is proclaimed throughout all his empire (for it is great), all wives will honor their husbands, both great and small."

²¹And the reply pleased the king and the princes, and the king did according to the word of Memucan. ²²Then he sent letters to all the king's provinces, to each province in its own script, and to every people in their own language, that each man should be master in his own house, and speak in the language of his own people.

1:1 *ᵃ*Generally identified with Xerxes I (485–464 B.C.)   **1:2** *ᵃ*Or *Susa*, and so throughout this book

ESTHER BECOMES QUEEN

[1]After these things, when the wrath of King Ahasuerus subsided, he remembered Vashti, what she had done, and what had been decreed against her. [2]Then the king's servants who attended him said: "Let beautiful young virgins be sought for the king; [3]and let the king appoint officers in all the provinces of his kingdom, that they may gather all the beautiful young virgins to Shushan the citadel, into the women's quarters, under the custody of Hegai[a] the king's eunuch, custodian of the women. And let beauty preparations be given *them*. [4]Then let the young woman who pleases the king be queen instead of Vashti."

This thing pleased the king, and he did so.

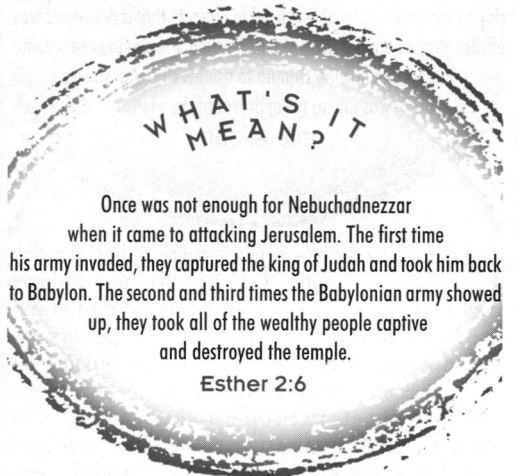

Once was not enough for Nebuchadnezzar when it came to attacking Jerusalem. The first time his army invaded, they captured the king of Judah and took him back to Babylon. The second and third times the Babylonian army showed up, they took all of the wealthy people captive and destroyed the temple.

Esther 2:6

[5]In Shushan the citadel there was a certain Jew whose name *was* Mordecai the son of Jair, the son of Shimei, the son of Kish, a Benjamite. [6]*Kish*[a] had been carried away from Jerusalem with the captives who had been captured with Jeconiah[b] king of Judah, whom Nebuchadnezzar the king of Babylon had carried away. [7]And *Mordecai* had brought up Hadassah, that *is*, Esther, his uncle's daughter, for she had neither father nor mother. The young woman *was* lovely and beautiful. When her father and mother died, Mordecai took her as his own daughter.

[8]So it was, when the king's command and decree were heard, and when many young women were gathered at Shushan the citadel, *under* the custody of Hegai, that Esther also was taken to the king's palace, into the care of Hegai the custodian of the women. [9]Now the young woman pleased him, and she obtained his favor; so he readily gave beauty preparations to her, besides her allowance. Then seven choice maidservants were provided for her from the king's palace, and he moved her and her maidservants to the best *place* in the house of the women.

[10]Esther had not revealed her people or family, for Mordecai had charged her not to reveal it. [11]And every day Mordecai paced in front of the court of the women's quarters, to learn of Esther's welfare and what was happening to her.

FAMILY
What's a good example of love for family? (2:11)

[12]Each young woman's turn came to go in to King Ahasuerus after she had completed twelve months' preparation, according to the regulations for the women, for thus were the days of their preparation apportioned: six months with oil of myrrh, and six months with perfumes and preparations for beautifying women. [13]Thus *prepared*, *each* young woman went to the king, and she was given whatever she desired to take with her from the women's quarters to the king's palace. [14]In the evening she went, and in the morning she returned to the second house of the women, to the custody of Shaashgaz, the king's eunuch who kept the concubines. She would not go in to the king again unless the king delighted in her and called for her by name.

[15]Now when the turn came for Esther the daughter of Abihail the uncle of Mordecai, who had taken her as his daughter, to go in to the king, she requested nothing but what Hegai the king's eunuch, the custodian of the women, advised. And Esther obtained favor in the sight of all who saw her. [16]So Esther was taken to King Ahasuerus, into his royal palace, in the tenth month, which *is* the month of Tebeth, in the seventh year of his reign. [17]The king loved Esther more than all the *other* women, and she obtained grace and favor in his sight more than all the virgins; so he set the royal crown upon her head and made her queen instead of Vashti. [18]Then the king made a great feast, the Feast of Esther, for all his officials and servants; and he proclaimed a holiday in the provinces and gave gifts according to the generosity of a king.

MORDECAI DISCOVERS A PLOT

[19]When virgins were gathered together a second time, Mordecai sat within the king's gate. [20]Now Esther had not revealed her family and her people, just as Mordecai had charged her, for Esther obeyed the command of Mordecai as when she was brought up by him.

2:3 [a]Hebrew *Hege*   **2:6** [a]Literally *Who*   [b]Same as *Jehoiachin*, 2 Kings 24:6 and elsewhere

²¹In those days, while Mordecai sat within the king's gate, two of the king's eunuchs, Bigthan and Teresh, doorkeepers, became furious and sought to lay hands on King Ahasuerus. ²²So the matter became known to Mordecai, who told Queen Esther, and Esther informed the king in Mordecai's name. ²³And when an inquiry was made into the matter, it was confirmed, and both were hanged on a gallows; and it was written in the book of the chronicles in the presence of the king.

HAMAN'S CONSPIRACY AGAINST THE JEWS

¹After these things King Ahasuerus promoted Haman, the son of Hammedatha the Agagite, and advanced him and set his seat above all the princes who *were* with him. ²And all the king's servants who *were* within the king's gate bowed and paid homage to Haman, for so the king had commanded concerning him. But Mordecai would not bow or pay homage. ³Then the king's servants who *were* within the king's gate said to Mordecai, "Why do you transgress the king's command?" ⁴Now it happened, when they spoke to him daily and he would not listen to them, that they told *it* to Haman, to see whether Mordecai's words would stand; for *Mordecai* had told them that he *was* a Jew. ⁵When Haman saw that Mordecai did not bow or pay him homage, Haman was filled with wrath. ⁶But he disdained to lay hands on Mordecai alone, for they had told him of the people of Mordecai. Instead, Haman sought to destroy all the Jews who *were* throughout the whole kingdom of Ahasuerus—the people of Mordecai.

⁷In the first month, which is the month of Nisan, in the twelfth year of King Ahasuerus, they cast Pur (that *is*, the lot), before Haman to determine the day and the month,ᵃ until *it fell on the* twelfth *month,ᵇ* which *is* the month of Adar.

⁸Then Haman said to King Ahasuerus, "There is a certain people scattered and dispersed among the people in all the provinces of your kingdom; their laws *are* different from all *other* people's, and they do not keep the king's laws. Therefore it *is* not fitting for the king to let them remain. ⁹If it pleases the king, let *a decree* be written that they be destroyed, and I will pay ten thousand talents of silver into the hands of those who do the work, to bring *it* into the king's treasuries."

¹⁰So the king took his signet ring from his hand and gave it to Haman, the son of Hammedatha the Agagite, the enemy of the Jews. ¹¹And the king said to Haman, "The money and the people *are* given to you, to do with them as seems good to you."

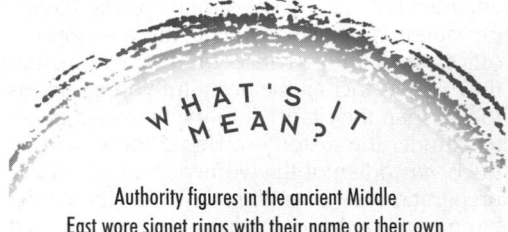

WHAT'S IT MEAN?

Authority figures in the ancient Middle East wore signet rings with their name or their own personal symbol on them. The rings were designed so that the raised name or symbol would make an impression on a seal made of moist clay or wet wax. The seal was used to indicate that a document was official. Putting one's ring on a seal was similar to signing one's name today. By allowing Haman to use his ring, Ahasuerus was giving his approval of the plan.

Esther 3:10

¹²Then the king's scribes were called on the thirteenth day of the first month, and *a decree* was written according to all that Haman commanded—to the king's satraps, to the governors who *were* over each province, to the officials of all people, to every province according to its script, and to every people in their language. In the name of King Ahasuerus it was written, and sealed with the king's signet ring. ¹³And the letters were sent by couriers into all the king's provinces, to destroy, to kill, and to annihilate all the Jews, both young and old, little children and women, in one day, on the thirteenth *day* of the twelfth *month*, which *is* the month of Adar, and to plunder their possessions.ᵃ ¹⁴A copy of the document was to be issued as law in every province, being published for all people, that they should be ready for that day. ¹⁵The couriers went out, hastened by the king's command; and the decree was proclaimed in Shushan the citadel. So the king and Haman sat down to drink, but the city of Shushan was perplexed.

ESTHER AGREES TO HELP THE JEWS

¹When Mordecai learned all that had happened, he tore his clothes and put on sackcloth and ashes, and went out into the midst of the city. He cried out with a loud and bitter cry. ²He

---

3:7 ᵃSeptuagint adds *to destroy the people of Mordecai in one day;* Vulgate adds *the nation of the Jews should be destroyed.* ᵇFollowing Masoretic Text and Vulgate; Septuagint reads *and the lot fell on the fourteenth of the month.* **3:13** ᵃSeptuagint adds the text of the letter here.

went as far as the front of the king's gate, for no one *might* enter the king's gate clothed with sackcloth. ³And in every province where the king's command and decree arrived, *there was* great mourning among the Jews, with fasting, weeping, and wailing; and many lay in sackcloth and ashes.

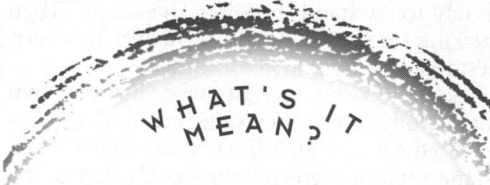

WHAT'S IT MEAN?

People in ancient times wore sackcloth only in times of great sorrow or distress. If you've ever felt sackcloth, you know why they didn't wear it more often. The cloth was a dark, scratchy material made of goat's hair. The sackcloth outfit was usually topped off by ashes on the person's head. This odd combination symbolized the person's sadness about a specific situation and the sin that caused it. The tradition of wearing dark clothing to funerals came from the custom of wearing sackcloth in times of sorrow.

Esther 4:1

⁴So Esther's maids and eunuchs came and told her, and the queen was deeply distressed. Then she sent garments to clothe Mordecai and take his sackcloth away from him, but he would not accept *them*. ⁵Then Esther called Hathach, *one* of the king's eunuchs whom he had appointed to attend her, and she gave him a command concerning Mordecai, to learn what and why this *was*. ⁶So Hathach went out to Mordecai in the city square that *was* in front of the king's gate. ⁷And Mordecai told him all that had happened to him, and the sum of money that Haman had promised to pay into the king's treasuries to destroy the Jews. ⁸He also gave him a copy of the written decree for their destruction, which was given at Shushan, that he might show it to Esther and explain it to her, and that he might command her to go in to the king to make supplication to him and plead before him for her people. ⁹So Hathach returned and told Esther the words of Mordecai.

¹⁰Then Esther spoke to Hathach, and gave him a command for Mordecai: ¹¹"All the king's servants and the people of the king's provinces know that any man or woman who goes into the inner court to the king, who has not been called, *he has* but one law: put *all* to death, except the one to whom the king holds out the golden scepter, that he may live. Yet I myself have not been called to go in to the king these thirty days." ¹²So they told Mordecai Esther's words.

¹³And Mordecai told *them* to answer Esther: "Do not think in your heart that you will escape in the king's palace any more than all the other Jews. ¹⁴For if you remain completely silent at this time, relief and deliverance will arise for the Jews from another place, but you and your father's house will perish. Yet who knows whether you have come to the kingdom for *such* a time as this?"

> **FUTURE**
> Does God put us in situations to make a difference? (4:14)

¹⁵Then Esther told *them* to reply to Mordecai: ¹⁶"Go, gather all the Jews who are present in Shushan, and fast for me; neither eat nor drink for three days, night or day. My maids and I will fast likewise. And so I will go to the king, which *is* against the law; and if I perish, I perish!"

¹⁷So Mordecai went his way and did according to all that Esther commanded him.ᵃ

ESTHER'S BANQUET

¹Now it happened on the third day that Esther put on *her* royal *robes* and stood in the inner court of the king's palace, across from the king's house, while the king sat on his royal throne in the royal house, facing the entrance of the house.ᵃ ²So it was, when the king saw Queen Esther standing in the court, *that* she found favor in his sight, and the king held out to Esther the golden scepter that *was* in his hand. Then Esther went near and touched the top of the scepter.

"Go, gather all the Jews who are present in Shushan, and fast for me." (Esther 4:16a)

³And the king said to her, "What do you wish, Queen Esther? What *is* your request? It shall be given to you—up to half the kingdom!"

⁴So Esther answered, "If it pleases the king, let the king and Haman come today to the banquet that I have prepared for him."

⁵Then the king said, "Bring Haman quickly, that he may do as Esther has said." So the king

---

4:17 ᵃSeptuagint adds a prayer of Mordecai here. **5:1** ᵃSeptuagint adds many extra details in verses 1 and 2.

and Haman went to the banquet that Esther had prepared.

⁶At the banquet of wine the king said to Esther, "What *is* your petition? It shall be granted you. What *is* your request, up to half the kingdom? It shall be done!"

⁷Then Esther answered and said, "My petition and request *is this:* ⁸If I have found favor in the sight of the king, and if it pleases the king to grant my petition and fulfill my request, then let the king and Haman come to the banquet which I will prepare for them, and tomorrow I will do as the king has said."

HAMAN'S PLOT AGAINST MORDECAI

⁹So Haman went out that day joyful and with a glad heart; but when Haman saw Mordecai in the king's gate, and that he did not stand or tremble before him, he was filled with indignation against Mordecai. ¹⁰Nevertheless Haman restrained himself and went home, and he sent and called for his friends and his wife Zeresh. ¹¹Then Haman told them of his great riches, the multitude of his children, everything in which the king had promoted him, and how he had advanced him above the officials and servants of the king.

¹²Moreover Haman said, "Besides, Queen Esther invited no one but me to come in with the king to the banquet that she prepared; and tomorrow I am again invited by her, along with the king. ¹³Yet all this avails me nothing, so long as I see Mordecai the Jew sitting at the king's gate."

WHAT'S IT MEAN?

There were no ropes involved in a Persian hanging. Instead, the person was nailed to a stake; later, his corpse was "hung" in a public place where everyone could see it.

Esther 5:14

¹⁴Then his wife Zeresh and all his friends said to him, "Let a gallows be made, fifty cubits high, and in the morning suggest to the king that Mordecai be hanged on it; then go merrily with the king to the banquet."

And the thing pleased Haman; so he had the gallows made.

THE KING HONORS MORDECAI

¹That night the king could not sleep. So one was commanded to bring the book of the records of the chronicles; and they were read before the king. ²And it was found written that Mordecai had told of Bigthana and Teresh, two of the king's eunuchs, the doorkeepers who had sought to lay hands on King Ahasuerus. ³Then the king said, "What honor or dignity has been bestowed on Mordecai for this?"

And the king's servants who attended him said, "Nothing has been done for him."

⁴So the king said, "Who *is* in the court?" Now Haman had *just* entered the outer court of the king's palace to suggest that the king hang Mordecai on the gallows that he had prepared for him.

⁵The king's servants said to him, "Haman is there, standing in the court."

And the king said, "Let him come in."

⁶So Haman came in, and the king asked him, "What shall be done for the man whom the king delights to honor?"

Now Haman thought in his heart, "Whom would the king delight to honor more than me?" ⁷And Haman answered the king, "*For* the man whom the king delights to honor, ⁸let a royal robe be brought which the king has worn, and a horse on which the king has ridden, which has a royal crest placed on its head. ⁹Then let this robe and horse be delivered to the hand of one of the king's most noble princes, that he may array the man whom the king delights to honor. Then parade him on horseback through the city square, and proclaim before him: 'Thus shall it be done to the man whom the king delights to honor!' "

¹⁰Then the king said to Haman, "Hurry, take the robe and the horse, as you have suggested, and do so for Mordecai the Jew who sits within the king's gate! Leave nothing undone of all that you have spoken."

¹¹So Haman took the robe and the horse, arrayed Mordecai and led him on horseback through the city square, and proclaimed before him, "Thus shall it be done to the man whom the king delights to honor!"

¹²Afterward Mordecai went back to the king's gate. But Haman hurried to his house, mourning and with his head covered. ¹³When Haman told his wife Zeresh and all his friends everything that had happened to him, his wise men and his wife Zeresh said to him, "If Mordecai, before whom you have begun to fall, is of Jewish descent, you will not prevail against him but will surely fall before him."

¹⁴While they *were* still talking with him, the

king's eunuchs came, and hastened to bring Haman to the banquet which Esther had prepared.

HAMAN HANGED INSTEAD OF MORDECAI

[1]So the king and Haman went to dine with Queen Esther. [2]And on the second day, at the banquet of wine, the king again said to Esther, "What *is* your petition, Queen Esther? It shall be granted you. And what *is* your request, up to half the kingdom? It shall be done!"

[3]Then Queen Esther answered and said, "If I have found favor in your sight, O king, and if it pleases the king, let my life be given me at my petition, and my people at my request. [4]For we have been sold, my people and I, to be destroyed, to be killed, and to be annihilated. Had we been sold as male and female slaves, I would have held my tongue, although the enemy could never compensate for the king's loss."

[5]So King Ahasuerus answered and said to Queen Esther, "Who is he, and where is he, who would dare presume in his heart to do such a thing?"

[6]And Esther said, "The adversary and enemy *is* this wicked Haman!"

So Haman was terrified before the king and queen.

[7]Then the king arose in his wrath from the banquet of wine *and went* into the palace garden; but Haman stood before Queen Esther, pleading for his life, for he saw that evil was determined against him by the king. [8]When the king returned from the palace garden to the place of the banquet of wine, Haman had fallen across the couch where Esther *was*. Then the king said, "Will he also assault the queen while I *am* in the house?"

As the word left the king's mouth, they covered Haman's face. [9]Now Harbonah, one of the eunuchs, said to the king, "Look! The gallows, fifty cubits high, which Haman made for Mordecai, who spoke good on the king's behalf, is standing at the house of Haman." Then the king said, "Hang him on it!"

[10]So they hanged Haman on the gallows that he had prepared for Mordecai. Then the king's wrath subsided.

ESTHER SAVES THE JEWS

[1]On that day King Ahasuerus gave Queen Esther the house of Haman, the enemy of the Jews. And Mordecai came before the king, for Esther had told how he *was related* to her. [2]So the king took off his signet ring, which he had taken from Haman, and gave it to Mordecai;

and Esther appointed Mordecai over the house of Haman.

[3]Now Esther spoke again to the king, fell down at his feet, and implored him with tears to counteract the evil of Haman the Agagite, and the scheme which he had devised against the Jews. [4]And the king held out the golden scepter toward Esther. So Esther arose and stood before the king, [5]and said, "If it pleases the king, and if I have found favor in his sight and the thing *seems* right to the king and I am pleasing in his eyes, let it be written to revoke the letters devised by Haman, the son of Hammedatha the Agagite, which he wrote to annihilate the Jews who *are* in all the king's provinces. [6]For how can I endure to see the evil that will come to my people? Or how can I endure to see the destruction of my countrymen?"

WHAT'S IT MEAN?

Thanks to Persian law, a king could not legally revoke or change a law once it was established. Knowing that he couldn't undo the law that called for the slaughter of the Jewish people, the quick-thinking king passed a new law that allowed Jews to defend themselves and even take revenge on their enemies.

Esther 8:8–12

[7]Then King Ahasuerus said to Queen Esther and Mordecai the Jew, "Indeed, I have given Esther the house of Haman, and they have hanged him on the gallows because he *tried to* lay his hand on the Jews. [8]You yourselves write a *decree* concerning the Jews, as you please, in the king's name, and seal *it* with the king's signet ring; for whatever is written in the king's name and sealed with the king's signet ring no one can revoke."

[9]So the king's scribes were called at that time, in the third month, which *is* the month of Sivan, on the twenty-third *day*; and it was written, according to all that Mordecai commanded, to the Jews, the satraps, the governors, and the princes of the provinces from India to Ethiopia, one hundred and twenty-seven provinces *in all*, to every province in its own script, to every people in their own language, and to the Jews in their own script and language. [10]And he wrote in the name of King Ahasuerus, sealed *it*

with the king's signet ring, and sent letters by couriers on horseback, riding on royal horses bred from swift steeds.[a]

[11]By these letters the king permitted the Jews who *were* in every city to gather together and protect their lives—to destroy, kill, and annihilate all the forces of any people or province that would assault them, *both* little children and women, and to plunder their possessions, [12]on one day in all the provinces of King Ahasuerus, on the thirteenth *day* of the twelfth month, which *is* the month of Adar.[a] [13]A copy of the document was to be issued as a decree in every province and published for all people, so that the Jews would be ready on that day to avenge themselves on their enemies. [14]The couriers who rode on royal horses went out, hastened and pressed on by the king's command. And the decree was issued in Shushan the citadel.

[15]So Mordecai went out from the presence of the king in royal apparel of blue and white, with a great crown of gold and a garment of fine linen and purple; and the city of Shushan rejoiced and was glad. [16]The Jews had light and gladness, joy and honor. [17]And in every province and city, wherever the king's command and decree came, the Jews had joy and gladness, a feast and a holiday. Then many of the people of the land became Jews, because fear of the Jews fell upon them.

THE JEWS DESTROY THEIR TORMENTORS

[1]Now in the twelfth month, that *is*, the month of Adar, on the thirteenth day, *the time* came for the king's command and his decree to be executed. On the day that the enemies of the Jews had hoped to overpower them, the opposite occurred, in that the Jews themselves overpowered those who hated them. [2]The Jews gathered together in their cities throughout all the provinces of King Ahasuerus to lay hands on those who sought their harm. And no one could withstand them, because fear of them fell upon all people. [3]And all the officials of the provinces, the satraps, the governors, and all those doing the king's work, helped the Jews, because the fear of Mordecai fell upon them. [4]For Mordecai *was* great in the king's palace, and his fame spread throughout all the provinces; for this man Mordecai became increasingly prominent. [5]Thus the Jews defeated all their enemies with the stroke of the sword, with slaughter and destruction, and did what they pleased with those who hated them.

[6]And in Shushan the citadel the Jews killed and destroyed five hundred men. [7]Also Parshandatha, Dalphon, Aspatha, [8]Poratha, Adalia, Aridatha, [9]Parmashta, Arisai, Aridai, and Vajezatha—[10]the ten sons of Haman the son of Hammedatha, the enemy of the Jews—they killed; but they did not lay a hand on the plunder.

[11]On that day the number of those who were killed in Shushan the citadel was brought to the king. [12]And the king said to Queen Esther, "The Jews have killed and destroyed five hundred men in Shushan the citadel, and the ten sons of Haman. What have they done in the rest of the king's provinces? Now what *is* your petition? It shall be granted to you. Or what *is* your further request? It shall be done."

[13]Then Esther said, "If it pleases the king, let it be granted to the Jews who *are* in Shushan to do again tomorrow according to today's decree, and let Haman's ten sons be hanged on the gallows."

[14]So the king commanded this to be done; the decree was issued in Shushan, and they hanged Haman's ten sons.

[15]And the Jews who *were* in Shushan gathered together again on the fourteenth day of the month of Adar and killed three hundred men at Shushan; but they did not lay a hand on the plunder.

[16]The remainder of the Jews in the king's provinces gathered together and protected their lives, had rest from their enemies, and killed seventy-five thousand of their enemies; but they did not lay a hand on the plunder. [17]*This was* on the thirteenth day of the month of Adar. And on the fourteenth of *the month*[a] they rested and made it a day of feasting and gladness.

THE FEAST OF PURIM

[18]But the Jews who *were* at Shushan assembled together on the thirteenth *day*, as well as on the fourteenth; and on the fifteenth of *the month*[a] they rested, and made it a day of feasting and gladness. [19]Therefore the Jews of the villages who dwelt in the unwalled towns celebrated the fourteenth day of the month of Adar *with* gladness and feasting, as a holiday, and for sending presents to one another.

[20]And Mordecai wrote these things and sent letters to all the Jews, near and far, who *were* in all the provinces of King Ahasuerus, [21]to establish among them that they should celebrate yearly the fourteenth and fifteenth days of the

---

8:10 [a]Literally *sons of the swift horses*　　**8:12** [a]Septuagint adds the text of the letter here.　　**9:17** [a]Literally *it*
9:18 [a]Literally *it*

month of Adar, 22as the days on which the Jews had rest from their enemies, as the month which was turned from sorrow to joy for them, and from mourning to a holiday; that they should make them days of feasting and joy, of sending presents to one another and gifts to the poor. 23So the Jews accepted the custom which they had begun, as Mordecai had written to them, 24because Haman, the son of Hammedatha the Agagite, the enemy of all the Jews, had plotted against the Jews to annihilate them, and had cast Pur (that *is*, the lot), to consume them and destroy them; 25but when *Esther*[a] came before the king, he commanded by letter that this[b] wicked plot which *Haman* had devised against the Jews should return on his own head, and that he and his sons should be hanged on the gallows.

26So they called these days Purim, after the name Pur. Therefore, because of all the words of this letter, what they had seen concerning this matter, and what had happened to them, 27the Jews established and imposed it upon themselves and their descendants and all who would join them, that without fail they should celebrate these two days every year, according to the written *instructions* and according to the *prescribed* time, 28that these days *should be* remembered and kept throughout every generation, every family, every province, and every city, that these days of Purim should not fail *to be observed* among the Jews, and *that* the memory of them should not perish among their descendants.

29Then Queen Esther, the daughter of Abihail, with Mordecai the Jew, wrote with full authority to confirm this second letter about Purim. 30And *Mordecai* sent letters to all the Jews, to the one hundred and twenty-seven provinces of the kingdom of Ahasuerus, *with* words of peace and truth, 31to confirm these days of Purim at their *appointed* time, as Morde-

cai the Jew and Queen Esther had prescribed for them, and as they had decreed for themselves and their descendants concerning matters of their fasting and lamenting. 32So the decree of Esther confirmed these matters of Purim, and it was written in the book.

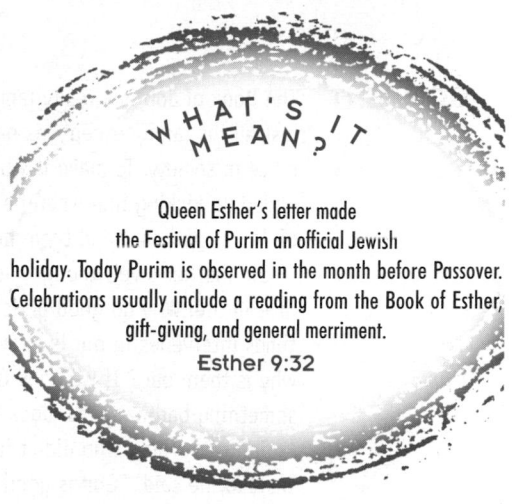

WHAT'S IT MEAN?

Queen Esther's letter made the Festival of Purim an official Jewish holiday. Today Purim is observed in the month before Passover. Celebrations usually include a reading from the Book of Esther, gift-giving, and general merriment.

Esther 9:32

MORDECAI'S ADVANCEMENT

1And King Ahasuerus imposed tribute on the land and *on* the islands of the sea. 2Now all the acts of his power and his might, and the account of the greatness of Mordecai, to which the king advanced him, *are* they not written in the book of the chronicles of the kings of Media and Persia? 3For Mordecai the Jew *was* second to King Ahasuerus, and was great among the Jews and well received by the multitude of his brethren, seeking the good of his people and speaking peace to all his countrymen.[a]

LEADERSHIP

What's a good way to get your followers to like you? (10:3)

9:25 [a]Literally *she* or *it* [b]Literally *his*　10:3 [a]Literally *seed*. Septuagint and Vulgate add a dream of Mordecai here; Vulgate adds six more chapters.

CONTENT   The Book of Job is a really famous story about a man who suffered . . . *a lot*. He lost all his family except his nagging wife. He lost his wealth, his health, and his place in society. To make it worse, his three friends came to "console" him and ended up kicking him when he was down. Those are the obvious facts of the Book of Job as you can read them here.

On another level, though, Job is a story about the most difficult questions we face in life. Why do good people have bad things happen to them? If God sometimes intervenes in our lives, why doesn't He *always* intervene? If God is good, then why is there bad? If we obey God, why aren't we always rewarded for it? If something bad happens, does that mean we are being punished?

Job was a man who didn't just say "God is good" when good things happened. Instead, he said, "God is good and life is hard, but God is still good." That's pretty amazing isn't it? The Book of Job reminds us that just because we can't always figure life out doesn't mean God is not who He says He is.

Purpose   We are to trust God's wisdom and His love when troubles come.

Theme   The Suffering of the Godly and the Sovereignty of God

Date of writing   Uncertain

> "Though He slay me, yet will I trust Him. Even so, I will defend my own ways before Him" (13:15).

Bible Talk

The Advice of Friends

Job was in a bad way. His wife knew it, and his friends knew it.

Job's friends heard about his troubles and did what friends do. They came to help. At first they did a pretty good job; but then, they started trying to fix the situation. They were convinced that Job had brought his troubles on himself. In the end they made him feel worse about it all because they tried to tell him it was all his fault.

Job listened to their long-winded speeches, but he just didn't believe that they were right. So even though he was miserable and worn out, he stood his ground. Sometimes friends are the hardest people to stand up to. Job gives us a good example of how to do this.

SATAN'S PLACE IN THE SCENARIO

The Book of Job gives us a major insight into the role of Satan in our world. Yes, he's real. No, he doesn't wear a red suit. Yes, he used to be an angel, a servant of God. Yes, he still has conversations with God. That's an amazing fact, isn't it?

When the Book of Job opens, Satan is having a conversation with God. God mentions Job and his faithfulness. Satan says something like, "Sure, he's a good man because he only knows good times. Give him some hard times and he'll turn his back on You."

Satan was wrong about Job. Doesn't that whole scenario make you wonder, though, what kind of conversation God and Satan would have about you?

JOB AND HIS FAMILY IN UZ

[1]There was a man in the land of Uz, whose name *was* Job; and that man was blameless and upright, and one who feared God and shunned evil. [2]And seven sons and three daughters were born to him. [3]Also, his possessions were seven thousand sheep, three thousand camels, five hundred yoke of oxen, five hundred female donkeys, and a very large household, so that this man was the greatest of all the people of the East.

> **CHARACTER**
> Who is a good model of integrity? (1:1)

[4]And his sons would go and feast *in their* houses, each on his *appointed* day, and would send and invite their three sisters to eat and drink with them. [5]So it was, when the days of feasting had run their course, that Job would send and sanctify them, and he would rise early in the morning and offer burnt offerings *according to* the number of them all. For Job said, "It may be that my sons have sinned and cursed[a] God in their hearts." Thus Job did regularly.

SATAN ATTACKS JOB'S CHARACTER

[6]Now there was a day when the sons of God came to present themselves before the LORD, and Satan[a] also came among them. [7]And the LORD said to Satan, "From where do you come?"

So Satan answered the LORD and said, "From going to and fro on the earth, and from walking back and forth on it."

[8]Then the LORD said to Satan, "Have you considered My servant Job, that *there is* none like him on the earth, a blameless and upright man, one who fears God and shuns evil?"

[9]So Satan answered the LORD and said, "Does Job fear God for nothing? [10]Have You not made a hedge around him, around his household, and around all that he has on every side? You have blessed the work of his hands, and his possessions have increased in the land. [11]But now, stretch out Your hand and touch all that he has, and he will surely curse You to Your face!"

[12]And the LORD said to Satan, "Behold, all that he has *is* in your power; only do not lay a hand on his *person*."

So Satan went out from the presence of the LORD.

JOB LOSES HIS PROPERTY AND CHILDREN

[13]Now there was a day when his sons and daughters *were* eating and drinking wine in their oldest brother's house; [14]and a messenger came to Job and said, "The oxen were plowing and the donkeys feeding beside them, [15]when the Sabeans[a] raided *them* and took them away—indeed they have killed the servants with the edge of the sword; and I alone have escaped to tell you!"

WHAT'S IT MEAN?

The Sabeans and Chaldeans weren't the kind of people you would want as neighbors. They made their living by raiding villages and farms, feeding themselves on crops and livestock that were raised by other people. Centuries later, the Chaldeans dominated the land of Babylonia.

Job 1:15–17

[16]While he *was* still speaking, another also came and said, "The fire of God fell from heaven and burned up the sheep and the servants, and consumed them; and I alone have escaped to tell you!"

[17]While he *was* still speaking, another also came and said, "The Chaldeans formed three bands, raided the camels and took them away, yes, and killed the servants with the edge of the sword; and I alone have escaped to tell you!"

[18]While he *was* still speaking, another also came and said, "Your sons and daughters *were* eating and drinking wine in their oldest brother's house, [19]and suddenly a great wind came from across[a] the wilderness and struck the four corners of the house, and it fell on the young people, and they are dead; and I alone have escaped to tell you!"

[20]Then Job arose, tore his robe, and shaved his head; and he fell to the ground and worshiped. [21]And he said:

> "Naked I came from my
> mother's womb,
> And naked shall I return
> there.
> The LORD gave, and the
> LORD has taken away;
> Blessed be the name of
> the LORD."

> **MONEY**
> What's more valuable than possessions? (1:21, 22)

1:5 [a]Literally *blessed*, but used here in the evil sense, and so in verse 11 and 2:5, 9   **1:6** [a]Literally *the Adversary*, and so throughout this book   **1:15** [a]Literally *Sheba* (compare 6:19)   **1:19** [a]Septuagint omits *across*.

²²In all this Job did not sin nor charge God with wrong.

SATAN ATTACKS JOB'S HEALTH

¹Again there was a day when the sons of God came to present themselves before the LORD, and Satan came also among them to present himself before the LORD. ²And the LORD said to Satan, "From where do you come?"

Satan answered the LORD and said, "From going to and fro on the earth, and from walking back and forth on it."

³Then the LORD said to Satan, "Have you considered My servant Job, that *there is* none like him on the earth, a blameless and upright man, one who fears God and shuns evil? And still he holds fast to his integrity, although you incited Me against him, to destroy him without cause."

⁴So Satan answered the LORD and said, "Skin for skin! Yes, all that a man has he will give for his life. ⁵But stretch out Your hand now, and touch his bone and his flesh, and he will surely curse You to Your face!"

⁶And the LORD said to Satan, "Behold, he *is* in your hand, but spare his life."

⁷So Satan went out from the presence of the LORD, and struck Job with painful boils from the sole of his foot to the crown of his head. ⁸And he took for himself a potsherd with which to scrape himself while he sat in the midst of the ashes.

WHAT'S IT MEAN?

The conversation that follows seems to suggest that Eliphaz was the oldest and most respected of Job's friends. That's not surprising. Teman, Eliphaz's hometown, was known for its wise men.

Job 2:11

⁹Then his wife said to him, "Do you still hold fast to your integrity? Curse God and die!"

¹⁰But he said to her, "You speak as one of the foolish women speaks. Shall we indeed accept good from God, and shall we not accept adversity?" In all this Job did not sin with his lips.

JOB'S THREE FRIENDS

¹¹Now when Job's three friends heard of all this adversity that had come upon him, each one came from his own place—Eliphaz the Temanite, Bildad the Shuhite, and Zophar the Naamathite. For they had made an appointment together to come and mourn with him, and to comfort him. ¹²And when they raised their eyes from afar, and did not recognize him, they lifted their voices and wept; and each one tore his robe and sprinkled dust on his head toward heaven. ¹³So they sat down with him on the ground seven days and seven nights, and no one spoke a word to him, for they saw that *his* grief was very great.

FRIENDSHIP

What should we do to help hurting friends? (2:11)

> "Shall we indeed accept good from God, and shall we not accept adversity?"
> (Job 2:10b)

JOB DEPLORES HIS BIRTH

¹After this Job opened his mouth and cursed the day of his *birth.* ²And Job spoke, and said:

3 "May the day perish on which I was born,
And the night *in which* it was said,
'A male child is conceived.'

4 May that day be darkness;
May God above not seek it,
Nor the light shine upon it.

5 May darkness and the shadow of death claim it;
May a cloud settle on it;
May the blackness of the day terrify it.

6 *As for* that night, may darkness seize it;
May it not rejoice*ᵃ* among the days of the year,
May it not come into the number of the months.

7 Oh, may that night be barren!
May no joyful shout come into it!

8 May those curse it who curse the day,
Those who are ready to arouse Leviathan.

9 May the stars of its morning be dark;
May it look for light, but *have* none,
And not see the dawning of the day;

10 Because it did not shut up the doors of my *mother's* womb,
Nor hide sorrow from my eyes.

3:6 *ᵃ*Septuagint, Syriac, Targum, and Vulgate read *be joined.*

11 "Why did I not die at birth?
   Why did I *not* perish when I came from the womb?
12 Why did the knees receive me?
   Or why the breasts, that I should nurse?
13 For now I would have lain still and been quiet,
   I would have been asleep;
   Then I would have been at rest
14 With kings and counselors of the earth,
   Who built ruins for themselves,
15 Or with princes who had gold,
   Who filled their houses *with* silver;
16 Or *why* was I not hidden like a stillborn child,
   Like infants who never saw light?
17 There the wicked cease *from* troubling,
   And there the weary are at rest.
18 *There* the prisoners rest together;
   They do not hear the voice of the oppressor.
19 The small and great are there,
   And the servant *is* free from his master.

20 "Why is light given to him who is in misery,
   And life to the bitter of soul,
21 Who long for death, but it does not *come*,
   And search for it more than hidden treasures;
22 Who rejoice exceedingly,
   And are glad when they can find the grave?
23 *Why is light given* to a man whose way is hidden,
   And whom God has hedged in?
24 For my sighing comes before I eat,[a]
   And my groanings pour out like water.
25 For the thing I greatly feared has come upon me,
   And what I dreaded has happened to me.
26 I am not at ease, nor am I quiet;
   I have no rest, for trouble comes."

ELIPHAZ: JOB HAS SINNED

1 Then Eliphaz the Temanite answered and said:

2 "If one attempts a word with you, will you become weary?
   But who can withhold himself from speaking?
3 Surely you have instructed many,
   And you have strengthened weak hands.

4 Your words have upheld him who was stumbling,
   And you have strengthened the feeble knees;
5 But now it comes upon you, and you are weary;
   It touches you, and you are troubled.
6 *Is* not your reverence your confidence?
   And the integrity of your ways your hope?

ENCOURAGEMENT

How can we encourage others? (4:4)

WHAT'S IT MEAN?

Job's "conversation" with his friends was probably a lot different from the talks you have with your friends. Job's friends spoke in what are called "cycles" of debate. Eliphaz, Bildad, and Zophar took turns talking to Job in three different cycles. (Though, for some reason, Zophar chose not to say anything in the third cycle.) After each of their speeches, Job was given a chance to reply.

Job 4:1

7 "Remember now, who *ever* perished being innocent?
   Or where were the upright *ever* cut off?
8 Even as I have seen,
   Those who plow iniquity
   And sow trouble reap the same.
9 By the blast of God they perish,
   And by the breath of His anger they are consumed.
10 The roaring of the lion,
   The voice of the fierce lion,
   And the teeth of the young lions are broken.
11 The old lion perishes for lack of prey,
   And the cubs of the lioness are scattered.

12 "Now a word was secretly brought to me,
   And my ear received a whisper of it.
13 In disquieting thoughts from the visions of the night,
   When deep sleep falls on men,
14 Fear came upon me, and trembling,

3:24 [a]Literally *my bread*

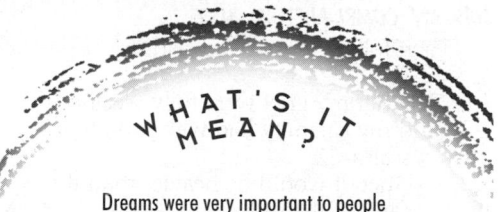

WHAT'S IT MEAN?

Dreams were very important to people in ancient times. Nighttime visions like the one Eliphaz experienced were thought to be messages from God. Sometimes those visions predicted the future; other times, they explained important truths to people like Eliphaz.

Job 4:13

Which made all my bones shake.
15 Then a spirit passed before my face;
The hair on my body stood up.
16 It stood still,
But I could not discern its appearance.
A form *was* before my eyes;
There was silence;
Then I heard a voice *saying:*
17 'Can a mortal be more righteous than
God?
Can a man be more pure than his Maker?
18 If He puts no trust in His servants,
If He charges His angels with error,
19 How much more those who dwell in
houses of clay,
Whose foundation is in the dust,
Who are crushed before a moth?
20 They are broken in pieces from morning
till evening;
They perish forever, with no one
regarding.
21 Does not their own excellence go away?
They die, even without wisdom.'

ELIPHAZ: JOB IS CHASTENED BY GOD

1 "Call out now;
Is there anyone who will answer you?
And to which of the holy ones will you
turn?
2 For wrath kills a foolish man,
And envy slays a simple one.
3 I have seen the foolish taking root,
But suddenly I cursed his dwelling place.
4 His sons are far from safety,
They are crushed in the gate,
And *there is* no deliverer.

5 Because the hungry eat up his harvest,
Taking it even from the thorns,[a]
And a snare snatches their substance.[b]
6 For affliction does not come from the
dust,
Nor does trouble spring from the ground;
7 Yet man is born to trouble,
As the sparks fly upward.

8 "But as for me, I would seek God,
And to God I would commit my cause—
9 Who does great things, and unsearchable,
Marvelous things without number.
10 He gives rain on the earth,
And sends waters on the fields.
11 He sets on high those who are lowly,
And those who mourn are lifted to safety.
12 He frustrates the devices of the crafty,
So that their hands cannot carry out their
plans.
13 He catches the wise in their own
craftiness,
And the counsel of the cunning comes
quickly upon them.
14 They meet with darkness in the daytime,
And grope at noontime as in the night.
15 But He saves the needy from the sword,
From the mouth of the mighty,
And from their hand.
16 So the poor have hope,
And injustice shuts her mouth.

17 "Behold, happy *is* the
man whom God
corrects;
Therefore do not despise
the chastening of the
Almighty.
18 For He bruises, but He binds up;
He wounds, but His hands make whole.
19 He shall deliver you in six troubles,
Yes, in seven no evil shall touch you.
20 In famine He shall redeem you from
death,
And in war from the power of the sword.
21 You shall be hidden from the scourge of
the tongue,
And you shall not be afraid of
destruction when it comes.
22 You shall laugh at destruction and famine,
And you shall not be afraid of the beasts
of the earth.
23 For you shall have a covenant with the
stones of the field,

DISCIPLINE

Is God's discipline good? (5:17)

5:5 [a]Septuagint reads *They shall not be taken from evil men;* Vulgate reads *And the armed man shall take him by violence.* [b]Septuagint reads *The might shall draw them off;* Vulgate reads *And the thirsty shall drink up their riches.*

A large family and a long,
healthy life were considered to be rewards
from God for living in a way that pleased Him. You can imagine
the kind of things that were said about people who lost their
families and their health.

Job 5:25, 26

And the beasts of the field shall be at peace with you.

24 You shall know that your tent *is* in peace;
You shall visit your dwelling and find nothing amiss.

25 You shall also know that your descendants *shall be* many,
And your offspring like the grass of the earth.

26 You shall come to the grave at a full age,
As a sheaf of grain ripens in its season.

27 Behold, this we have searched out;
It *is* true.
Hear it, and know for yourself."

JOB: MY COMPLAINT IS JUST

1 Then Job answered and said:

2 "Oh, that my grief were fully weighed,
And my calamity laid with it on the scales!

3 For then it would be heavier than the sand of the sea—
Therefore my words have been rash.

4 For the arrows of the Almighty *are* within me;
My spirit drinks in their poison;
The terrors of God are arrayed against me.

5 Does the wild donkey bray when it has grass,
Or does the ox low over its fodder?

6 Can flavorless food be eaten without salt?
Or is there *any* taste in the white of an egg?

7 My soul refuses to touch them;
They *are* as loathsome food to me.

8 "Oh, that I might have my request,
That God would grant *me* the thing that I long for!

9 That it would please God to crush me,
That He would loose His hand and cut me off!

10 Then I would still have comfort;
Though in anguish I would exult,
He will not spare;
For I have not concealed the words of the Holy One.

Promise HE PROMISES TO DELIVER YOU FROM HARM TIME AFTER TIME.

He shall deliver you in six troubles, yes, in seven no evil shall touch you (Job 5:19).

Only in heaven will we know how many times God has rescued us from harm. The list probably fills books: family car delayed in traffic to avoid three-car pile-up; grounded from the big sophomore party and kept from the lure of drugs and a police raid; army of angels sent to protect unsuspecting students from attempted mugging on campus. Sometimes we can look back and know that God put His hand on us, directed our steps, and protected us. But most of the time we walk around totally unaware of His divine intervention on our behalf. Time after time He keeps us safe from things we can see, and even the things we can't. Take a minute to thank Him for keeping watch over the big and the little things in your life and for guarding every move you make.

SEE FOR YOURSELF:
Ps. 7:10; Nah. 1:7; 2 Thess. 3:3

11 "What strength do I have, that I should
  hope?
  And what *is* my end, that I should
  prolong my life?
12 *Is* my strength the strength of stones?
  Or is my flesh bronze?
13 *Is* my help not within me?
  And is success driven from me?

14 "To him who is afflicted, kindness *should be
  shown* by his friend,
  Even though he forsakes the fear of the
  Almighty.
15 My brothers have dealt deceitfully like a
  brook,
  Like the streams of the brooks that pass
  away,
16 Which are dark because of the ice,
  And into which the snow vanishes.
17 When it is warm, they cease to flow;
  When it is hot, they vanish from their
  place.
18 The paths of their way turn aside,
  They go nowhere and perish.
19 The caravans of Tema look,
  The travelers of Sheba hope for them.
20 They are disappointed because they were
  confident;
  They come there and are confused.
21 For now you are nothing,
  You see terror and are afraid.
22 Did I ever say, 'Bring *something* to me'?
  Or, 'Offer a bribe for me from your
  wealth'?
23 Or, 'Deliver me from the enemy's hand'?
  Or, 'Redeem me from the hand of
  oppressors'?

24 "Teach me, and I will hold my tongue;
  Cause me to understand wherein I have
  erred.
25 How forceful are right words!
  But what does your arguing prove?
26 Do you intend to rebuke *my* words,
  And the speeches of a desperate one,
  which are as wind?
27 Yes, you overwhelm the fatherless,
  And you undermine your friend.
28 Now therefore, be pleased to look
  at me;
  For I would never lie to your face.
29 Yield now, let there be no injustice!
  Yes, concede, my righteousness still
  stands!
30 Is there injustice on my tongue?
  Cannot my taste discern the unsavory?

JOB: MY SUFFERING IS COMFORTLESS

1 "*Is there* not a time of hard service for man
  on earth?
  Are not his days also like the days of a
  hired man?
2 Like a servant who earnestly desires the
  shade,
  And like a hired man who eagerly looks
  for his wages,
3 So I have been allotted months of futility,
  And wearisome nights have been
  appointed to me.
4 When I lie down, I say, 'When shall I arise,
  And the night be ended?'
  For I have had my fill of tossing till dawn.
5 My flesh is caked with worms and dust,
  My skin is cracked and breaks out afresh.

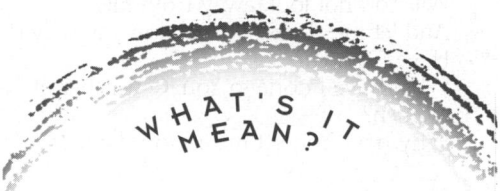

WHAT'S IT MEAN?

Weaving involved a large
frame (called a loom) with thread stretched
across it. Using a shuttle, the weaver would then pull another piece
of thread crosswise through the frame—in a quick back-and-forth
rhythm—to create fabric.

Job 7:6

6 "My days are swifter than a weaver's
  shuttle,
  And are spent without hope.
7 Oh, remember that my life *is* a breath!
  My eye will never again see good.
8 The eye of him who sees me will see me
  no *more*;
  While your *eyes* are upon me, I shall no
  longer *be*.
9 *As* the cloud disappears and vanishes
  away,
  So he who goes down to the grave does
  not come up.
10 He shall never return to his house,
  Nor shall his place know him anymore.

11 "Therefore I will not restrain my mouth;
  I will speak in the anguish of my spirit;
  I will complain in the bitterness of my
  soul.
12 *Am* I a sea, or a sea serpent,

That You set a guard over me?

13 When I say, 'My bed will comfort me,
My couch will ease my complaint,'

14 Then You scare me with dreams
And terrify me with visions,

15 So that my soul chooses strangling
And death rather than my body.[a]

16 I loathe my life;
I would not live forever.
Let me alone,
For my days are but a breath.

17 "What is man, that You should exalt him,
That You should set Your heart on him,

18 That You should visit him every morning,
And test him every moment?

19 How long?
Will You not look away from me,
And let me alone till I swallow my saliva?

20 Have I sinned?
What have I done to You, O watcher of
men?
Why have You set me as Your target,

So that I am a burden to myself?[a]

21 Why then do You not pardon my
transgression,
And take away my iniquity?
For now I will lie down in the dust,
And You will seek me diligently,
But I will no longer be."

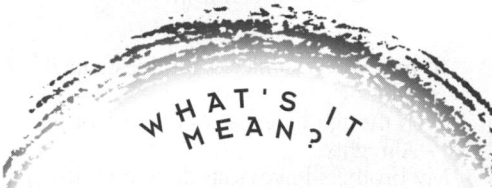

WHAT'S IT MEAN?

If anyone asks you the same papyrus
question that Bildad asked Job, the answer is no.
The papyrus plant grows in the water of swamps and marshes.
Papyrus stalks are about the thickness of a person's wrist and can
reach as high as twelve feet. More than anything else, papyrus
resembles an oversize piece of grass. The Egyptians used papyrus to
make paper, blankets, sandals, and rafts.

Job 8:11

On the Edge

*For we were born yesterday,
and know nothing, because our
days on earth are a shadow
(Job 8:9).*

Ever had anyone say, "You think you
know everything"? They were being sarcas-
tic, taking a jab at you. They were reminding you that your knowledge is limited. The
Book of Job says the same thing—
that you are only on this earth a
short time and you know very
little. Job says that you would be
wise to learn from your parents
and grandparents, and all the years they
have already lived. Because of their age, we
assume they couldn't possibly contribute
anything to our generation. Not so. You'd be
foolish to believe they haven't felt the
emotions you deal with or struggled to
make hard decisions. So lay down your
stereotypes, listen to your ancestors, and
learn from their understanding. The more
you listen, the more you learn.

SEE FOR YOURSELF:
Prov. 4:1–5; 23:12

BILDAD: JOB SHOULD REPENT

1 Then Bildad the Shuhite answered and said:

2 "How long will you speak these things,
And the words of your mouth be like a
strong wind?

3 Does God subvert judgment?
Or does the Almighty pervert justice?

4 If your sons have sinned against Him,
He has cast them away for their
transgression.

5 If you would earnestly seek God
And make your supplication to the
Almighty,

6 If you were pure and upright,
Surely now He would awake for you,
And prosper your rightful dwelling place.

7 Though your beginning was small,
Yet your latter end would increase
abundantly.

8 "For inquire, please, of the former age,
And consider the things discovered by
their fathers;

9 For we were born yesterday, and know
nothing,

7:15 [a]Literally my bones   **7:20** [a]Following Masoretic Text, Targum, and Vulgate; Septuagint and Jewish
tradition read to You.

Because our days on earth *are* a shadow.

10 Will they not teach you and tell you,
And utter words from their heart?

11 "Can the papyrus grow up without a
marsh?
Can the reeds flourish without water?

12 While it *is* yet green *and* not cut down,
It withers before any *other* plant.

13 So *are* the paths of all who forget God;
And the hope of the hypocrite shall
perish,

14 Whose confidence shall be cut off,
And whose trust *is* a spider's web.

15 He leans on his house, but it does not
stand.
He holds it fast, but it does not endure.

16 He grows green in the sun,
And his branches spread
out in his garden.

17 His roots wrap around
the rock heap,
And look for a place in
the stones.

18 If he is destroyed from
his place,
Then *it* will deny him,
saying, 'I have not seen you.'

19 "Behold, this is the joy of His way,
And out of the earth others will grow.

20 Behold, God will not cast away the
blameless,
Nor will He uphold the evildoers.

21 He will yet fill your mouth with laughing,
And your lips with rejoicing.

22 Those who hate you will be clothed with
shame,
And the dwelling place of the wicked will
come to nothing."[a]

JOB: THERE IS NO MEDIATOR

1 Then Job answered and said:

2 "Truly I know *it is* so,
But how can a man be righteous before
God?

3 If one wished to contend
with Him,
He could not answer
Him one time out of
a thousand.

4 *God is* wise in heart and
mighty in strength.
Who has hardened
himself against Him
and prospered?

5 He removes the
mountains, and they
do not know
When He overturns them in His anger;

6 He shakes the earth out of its place,

"Behold, God will not cast
away the blameless,
nor will He uphold
the evildoers."
(Job 8:20)

8:22 [a]Literally *will not be*

Promise HE PROMISES TO GIVE YOU SOMETHING TO LAUGH ABOUT.

Behold, God will not cast away the blameless, nor will He uphold the evildoers. He will yet fill your mouth with laughing, and your lips with rejoicing (Job 8:20, 21).

Are you a smiler or a frowner? Do you naturally notice happy things, or are you a walking vessel of gloom and doom? How about laughing? Do you remember the last time you laughed until your sides hurt, and your eyes watered, and you begged for mercy—you just couldn't laugh anymore? However long it's been, whatever your natural disposition, God promises to give you something to laugh about. He promises to walk right into your most depressing day and turn things around. God didn't put you here to see how awful He could make you feel. He put you here to glorify Him and to enjoy life. So invite Him into your day and tell Him you really need something to laugh about. Watch Him do a miracle on your behalf. No heart is too hard, no day is too far gone, when the Maker of laughter keeps His promise.

SEE FOR YOURSELF:
1 Sam. 2:1; Ps. 126:1–3

And the chambers of the south;
10 He does great things past finding out,
Yes, wonders without number.
11 If He goes by me, I do not see *Him*;
If He moves past, I do not perceive Him;
12 If He takes away, who can hinder Him?
Who can say to Him, 'What are You doing?'
13 God will not withdraw His anger,
The allies of the proud[a] lie prostrate beneath Him.

On the Edge

Truly I know it is so, but how can a man be righteous before God? (Job 9:2).

Most of us get into trouble by convincing ourselves that we're okay. Basically good people. No major sin happening. No blatant disrespect. Decent grades in school. Things at home are calm. So we're sailing along just fine.

But Job says that no human is righteous (innocent) in the sight of God—and that's true—before you get saved. When you become a Christian, God gives you a new heart. What you're dealing with is a sinful *nature,* not a sinful heart. In spite of the fact that you do (and will) sin, the great news is that God is more gracious than you could ever imagine, and you can be more accepted and loved than you ever hoped.

SEE FOR YOURSELF:
Rom. 3:23, 24;
Gal. 3:22; 1 John 1:8

On the Edge

He does great things past finding out, yes, wonders without number. If He goes by me, I do not see Him; if He moves past, I do not perceive Him (Job 9:10, 11).

In this passage, Job ponders the hugeness of God. His miracles are beyond our understanding. His creativity is awesome, and we are part of it. His justice is supreme and fair. He is so amazing that He moves right past us, and we don't even know it. He is closer than we could imagine, so why do we doubt His wisdom and His power? We have mistakenly believed that God is up there somewhere, far away, looking down. He seems remote and out of touch. Distant. But God is here. Intimate. So close. He moves right past you. Are you willing to trust the One who is beside you to care for you and to love you? His presence is real. His patience is incredible. Since He has already been with you all this time, why keep ignoring Him?

SEE FOR YOURSELF:
Ps. 119:151; 145:18

And its pillars tremble;
7 He commands the sun, and it does not rise;
He seals off the stars;
8 He alone spreads out the heavens,
And treads on the waves of the sea;
9 He made the Bear, Orion, and the Pleiades,

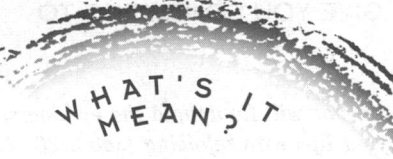

WHAT'S IT MEAN?

If you know anything about astronomy, you know that the Bear and Orion are bright clusters of stars. You may even be able to find them on starry nights. Pleiades is a bit more difficult to spot. In fact, of the hundreds of stars that make up the constellation Pleiades, only six or seven are visible to the naked eye.

Job 9:9

14 "How then can I answer Him,
And choose my words *to reason* with Him?
15 For though I were righteous, I could not answer Him;
I would beg mercy of my Judge.
16 If I called and He answered me,
I would not believe that He was listening to my voice.
17 For He crushes me with a tempest,

9:13 [a]Hebrew *rahab*

And multiplies my wounds without
    cause.

18 He will not allow me to catch my breath,
    But fills me with bitterness.

19 If *it is a matter* of strength, indeed *He is*
    strong;
    And if of justice, who will appoint my
    day *in court?*

20 Though I were righteous, my own mouth
    would condemn me;
    Though I *were* blameless, it would prove
    me perverse.

21 "I am blameless, yet I do not know myself;
    I despise my life.

22 It *is* all one *thing*;
    Therefore I say, 'He destroys the blameless
    and the wicked.'

23 If the scourge slays suddenly,
    He laughs at the plight of the innocent.

24 The earth is given into the hand of the
    wicked.
    He covers the faces of its judges.
    If it is not *He*, who else could it be?

25 "Now my days are swifter than a runner;
    They flee away, they see no good.

26 They pass by like swift ships,
    Like an eagle swooping on its prey.

27 If I say, 'I will forget my complaint,
    I will put off my sad face and wear a
    smile,'

28 I am afraid of all my sufferings;
    I know that You will not hold me
    innocent.

29 *If* I am condemned,
    Why then do I labor in vain?

30 If I wash myself with snow water,
    And cleanse my hands with soap,

31 Yet You will plunge me into the pit,
    And my own clothes will abhor me.

32 "For *He is* not a man, as I *am,*
    That I may answer Him,
    And that we should go to court together.

33 Nor is there any mediator between us,
    Who may lay his hand on us both.

34 Let Him take His rod away from me,
    And do not let dread of Him terrify me.

35 *Then* I would speak and not fear Him,
    But it is not so with me.

JOB: I WOULD PLEAD WITH GOD

1 "My soul loathes my life;
    I will give free course to my complaint,
    I will speak in the bitterness of my soul.

2 I will say to God, 'Do not condemn me;

    Show me why You contend with me.

3 *Does it* seem good to You that You should
    oppress,
    That You should despise the work of Your
    hands,
    And smile on the counsel of the wicked?

4 Do You have eyes of flesh?
    Or do You see as man sees?

5 *Are* Your days like the days of a mortal
    man?
    Are Your years like the days of a mighty
    man,

6 That You should seek for my iniquity
    And search out my sin,

7 Although You know that I am not
    wicked,
    And *there is* no one who can deliver from
    Your hand?

8 'Your hands have made me and fashioned
    me,
    An intricate unity;
    Yet You would destroy me.

9 Remember, I pray, that You have made
    me like clay.
    And will You turn me into dust again?

10 Did You not pour me out like milk,
    And curdle me like cheese,

11 Clothe me with skin and flesh,
    And knit me together with bones and
    sinews?

12 You have granted me life and favor,
    And Your care has preserved my spirit.

13 'And these *things* You have hidden in Your
    heart;
    I know that this *was* with You:

14 If I sin, then You mark me,
    And will not acquit me of my iniquity.

15 If I am wicked, woe to me;
    Even *if* I am righteous, I cannot lift up my
    head.
    I am full of disgrace;
    See my misery!

16 If *my head* is exalted,
    You hunt me like a fierce lion,
    And again You show Yourself awesome
    against me.

17 You renew Your witnesses against me,
    And increase Your indignation toward
    me;
    Changes and war are *ever* with me.

18 'Why then have You brought me out of
    the womb?
    Oh, that I had perished and no eye had
    seen me!

19 I would have been as though I had not
    been.
    I would have been carried from the
       womb to the grave.
20 Are not my days few?
    Cease! Leave me alone, that I may take a
       little comfort,
21 Before I go *to the place from which* I shall
    not return,
    To the land of darkness and the shadow
       of death,
22 A land as dark as darkness *itself,*
    As the shadow of death, without any
       order,
    Where even the light *is* like darkness.' "

WHAT'S IT MEAN?

"The land of darkness and the shadow
of death" refers to Sheol, the place of the dead,
according to ancient Hebrew beliefs. Sheol was pictured as a dark
and gloomy underground world where the souls of both good and
bad people lived after death. Sheol was also the place where people
were thought to receive their eternal punishment or
reward, according to how they lived.

Job 10:21, 22

ZOPHAR URGES JOB TO REPENT

1 Then Zophar the Naamathite answered and
said:

2 "Should not the multitude of words be
      answered?
    And should a man full of talk be
       vindicated?
3 Should your empty talk make men hold
      their peace?
    And when you mock, should no one
       rebuke you?
4 For you have said,
    'My doctrine *is* pure,
    And I am clean in your eyes.'
5 But oh, that God would speak,
    And open His lips against you,
6 That He would show you the secrets of
      wisdom!
    For *they would* double *your* prudence.
    Know therefore that God exacts from you
    Less than your iniquity *deserves.*

7 "Can you search out the deep things of
      God?
    Can you find out the limits of the
       Almighty?
8 *They are* higher than heaven—what can
      you do?
    Deeper than Sheol—what can you
       know?
9 Their measure *is* longer than the earth
    And broader than the sea.

On the Edge

*Can you search out the deep
things of God? Can you find out the
limits of the Almighty? They are
higher than heaven—what can you do?
Deeper than Sheol—what can you
know? (Job 11:7, 8).*

To say that God is mysterious is to say
that we don't fully understand Him. We
don't understand how He creates or how He
makes decisions. His timing seems slow to
us. Heaven is a big mystery; and all those
miracles, well, we just don't get it. There are
so many aspects of God that we can't totally
grasp. That's where Colossians 2:2, 3 comes
in. Paul writes that Christ is the key to
God's mystery. Jesus physically came to this
earth and through His ministry began to
unveil the mysteries of God. Paul
also writes in 1 Corinthians
13:12 that "now we see in a
mirror, dimly, but then face to
face." As you grow stronger in your relationship with the Lord, you'll begin to know
Him more and more. But even when you're
90 years old and have walked with Him
every day, there will still be magnificent
mysteries about Him. He's that big. Do you
have faith, even in the mystery of God?

SEE FOR YOURSELF:
Deut. 29:29; 1 Cor. 2:7;
13:12; Col. 2:2, 3

10 "If He passes by, imprisons, and gathers *to*
      judgment,
    Then who can hinder Him?
11 For He knows deceitful
      men;
    He sees wickedness also.
    Will He not then
      consider *it?*

GOD

Does God
see people
sin?
(11:11)

12 For an empty-headed man will be wise,
When a wild donkey's colt is born a man.

13 "If you would prepare your heart,
And stretch out your hands toward Him;
14 If iniquity *were* in your hand, *and you* put
it far away,
And would not let wickedness dwell in
your tents;
15 Then surely you could lift up your face
without spot;
Yes, you could be steadfast, and not fear;
16 Because you would forget *your* misery,
And remember *it* as waters *that have*
passed away,
17 And *your* life would be brighter than
noonday.
Though you were dark, you would be like
the morning.
18 And you would be secure, because there
is hope;
Yes, you would dig *around you, and* take
your rest in safety.
19 You would also lie down, and no one
would make *you* afraid;
Yes, many would court your favor.
20 But the eyes of the wicked will fail,
And they shall not escape,
And their hope—loss of life!"

JOB ANSWERS HIS CRITICS

¹Then Job answered and said:

2 "No doubt you *are* the people,
And wisdom will die with you!
3 But I have understanding as well as you;
I *am* not inferior to you.
Indeed, who does not *know* such things
as these?

4 "I am one mocked by his friends,
Who called on God, and He answered
him,
The just and blameless *who is* ridiculed.
5 A lamp[a] is despised in the thought of one
who is at ease;
It is made ready for those whose feet slip.
6 The tents of robbers prosper,
And those who provoke God are secure—
In what God provides by His hand.

7 "But now ask the beasts, and they will
teach you;
And the birds of the air, and they will tell
you;

8 Or speak to the earth, and it will teach
you;
And the fish of the sea will explain to
you.
9 Who among all these does not know
That the hand of the LORD has done this,
10 In whose hand *is* the life of every living
thing,
And the breath of all mankind?
11 Does not the ear test words
And the mouth taste its food?
12 Wisdom *is* with aged men,
And with length of days, understanding.

On the Edge

*Does not the ear test words
and the mouth taste its food?
Wisdom is with aged men, and with
length of days, understanding (Job
12:11, 12).*

All those years your grandparents have
lived have brought them much wisdom.
They have watched several generations go
through all the stuff of life, they've seen a
lot of people grow up, they've seen people
succeed, and they've seen people fail. They
may or may not have made wise choices
with their lives, but by now they've had lots
of time to process the path they chose.
They'd be happy to tell you about their
successes and the things they would
do over again. They'd be so
honored that you cared enough
to ask. By the time it's too late,
and your grandparents are long
gone, you'll realize how much they had to
offer you. So take some time to get to know
them. Ask them lots of questions. Ask about
their childhood, their dreams, their dis-
appointments. The smartest people are the
ones who can learn from others—you could
really learn a lot from your grandparents.

SEE FOR YOURSELF:
Prov. 17:6; 20:29

13 "With Him *are* wisdom and strength,
He has counsel and understanding.
14 If He breaks *a thing* down, it cannot be
rebuilt;
If He imprisons a man, there can be no
release.

12:5 [a]Or *disaster*

15 If He withholds the waters, they dry up;
   If He sends them out, they overwhelm the
      earth.
16 With Him *are* strength and prudence.
   The deceived and the deceiver *are* His.
17 He leads counselors away plundered,
   And makes fools of the judges.
18 He loosens the bonds of kings,
   And binds their waist with a belt.
19 He leads princes*ª* away plundered,
   And overthrows the mighty.
20 He deprives the trusted ones of speech,
   And takes away the discernment of the
      elders.
21 He pours contempt on princes,
   And disarms the mighty.
22 He uncovers deep things out of darkness,
   And brings the shadow of death to light.
23 He makes nations great, and destroys
      them;
   He enlarges nations, and guides them.
24 He takes away the understanding*ª* of the
      chiefs of the people of the earth,
   And makes them wander in a pathless
      wilderness.
25 They grope in the dark without light,
   And He makes them stagger like a
      drunken *man.*

1 "Behold, my eye has seen all *this*,
   My ear has heard and understood it.
2 What you know, I also know;
   I *am* not inferior to you.
3 But I would speak to the Almighty,
   And I desire to reason with God.
4 But you forgers of lies,
   You *are* all worthless physicians.
5 Oh, that you would be silent,
   And it would be your wisdom!
6 Now hear my reasoning,
   And heed the pleadings of my lips.
7 Will you speak wickedly for God,
   And talk deceitfully for Him?
8 Will you show partiality for Him?
   Will you contend for God?
9 Will it be well when He searches you out?
   Or can you mock Him as one mocks a
      man?
10 He will surely rebuke you
   If you secretly show partiality.
11 Will not His excellence make you afraid,
   And the dread of Him fall upon you?
12 Your platitudes *are* proverbs of ashes,
   Your defenses are defenses of clay.

13 "Hold your peace with me, and let me
      speak,
   Then let come on me what *may!*
14 Why do I take my flesh in my teeth,
   And put my life in my hands?
15 Though He slay me, yet will I trust Him.
   Even so, I will defend my own ways
      before Him.
16 He also *shall* be my salvation,
   For a hypocrite could not come before
      Him.
17 Listen carefully to my speech,
   And to my declaration with your ears.
18 See now, I have prepared *my* case,
   I know that I shall be vindicated.
19 Who *is* he *who* will contend with me?
   If now I hold my tongue, I perish.

JOB'S DESPONDENT PRAYER

20 "Only two *things* do not do to me,
   Then I will not hide myself from You:
21 Withdraw Your hand far from me,
   And let not the dread of You make me
      afraid.
22 Then call, and I will answer;
   Or let me speak, then You respond to me.
23 How many *are* my iniquities and sins?
   Make me know my transgression and my
      sin.
24 Why do You hide Your face,
   And regard me as Your enemy?
25 Will You frighten a leaf driven to and fro?
   And will You pursue dry stubble?
26 For You write bitter things against me,
   And make me inherit the iniquities of my
      youth.
27 You put my feet in the stocks,
   And watch closely all my paths.
   You set a limit*ª* for the soles of my feet.

28 "Man*ª* decays like a rotten thing,
   Like a garment that is moth-eaten.

1 "Man *who is* born of woman
   Is of few days and full of trouble.
2 He comes forth like a flower and
      fades away;
   He flees like a shadow
      and does not
      continue.
3 And do You open Your
      eyes on such a one,
   And bring me*ª* to
      judgment with Yourself?

TRIALS

Will we have
problems
in life?
(14:1)

12:19 *ª*Literally *priests*, but not in a technical sense   **12:24** *ª*Literally *heart*   **13:27** *ª*Literally *inscribe a
print*   **13:28** *ª*Literally *He*   **14:3** *ª*Septuagint, Syriac, and Vulgate read *him.*

4 Who can bring a clean *thing* out of an
unclean?
No one!
5 Since his days *are* determined,
The number of his months *is* with You;
You have appointed his limits, so that he
cannot pass.
6 Look away from him that he may rest,
Till like a hired man he finishes his day.

7 "For there is hope for a tree,
If it is cut down, that it will sprout again,
And that its tender shoots will not cease.
8 Though its root may grow old in the
earth,
And its stump may die in the ground,
9 *Yet* at the scent of water it will bud
And bring forth branches like a plant.
10 But man dies and is laid away;
Indeed he breathes his last
And where *is* he?
11 *As* water disappears from the sea,
And a river becomes parched and dries up,
12 So man lies down and does not rise.
Till the heavens *are* no more,
They will not awake
Nor be roused from their sleep.

13 "Oh, that You would hide me in the grave,
That You would conceal me until Your
wrath is past,
That You would appoint me a set time,
and remember me!
14 If a man dies, shall he live *again*?
All the days of my hard service I will
wait,
Till my change comes.
15 You shall call, and I will answer You;
You shall desire the work of Your hands.
16 For now You number my steps,
But do not watch over my sin.
17 My transgression *is* sealed up in a bag,
And You cover[a] my iniquity.

18 "But *as* a mountain falls *and* crumbles
away,
And *as* a rock is moved from its place;
19 *As* water wears away stones,
And as torrents wash away the soil of the
earth;
So You destroy the hope of man.
20 You prevail forever against him, and he
passes on;
You change his countenance and send
him away.

21 His sons come to honor, and he does not
know *it;*
They are brought low, and he does not
perceive *it.*
22 But his flesh will be in pain over it,
And his soul will mourn over it."

ELIPHAZ ACCUSES JOB OF FOLLY

1 Then Eliphaz the Temanite answered and
said:

2 "Should a wise man answer with empty
knowledge,
And fill himself with the east wind?
3 Should he reason with unprofitable talk,
Or by speeches with which he can do no
good?
4 Yes, you cast off fear,
And restrain prayer before God.
5 For your iniquity teaches your mouth,
And you choose the tongue of the
crafty.
6 Your own mouth condemns you, and
not I;
Yes, your own lips testify against you.

7 "*Are* you the first man *who* was born?
Or were you made before the hills?
8 Have you heard the counsel of God?
Do you limit wisdom to yourself?
9 What do you know that we do not
know?
What do you understand that *is* not in
us?
10 Both the gray-haired and the aged *are*
among us,
Much older than your father.
11 *Are* the consolations of God too small for
you,
And the word *spoken* gently[a] with you?
12 Why does your heart carry you away,
And what do your eyes wink at,
13 That you turn your spirit against God,
And let *such* words go out of your
mouth?

14 "What *is* man, that he could be pure?
And *he who is* born of a woman, that he
could be righteous?
15 If *God* puts no trust in His saints,
And the heavens are not pure in His
sight,
16 How much less man, *who is* abominable
and filthy,
Who drinks iniquity like water!

14:17 [a]Literally *plaster over*   **15:11** [a]Septuagint reads *a secret thing.*

17 "I will tell you, hear me;
What I have seen I will declare,
18 What wise men have told,
Not hiding *anything received* from their fathers,
19 To whom alone the land was given,
And no alien passed among them:
20 The wicked man writhes with pain all *his* days,
And the number of years is hidden from the oppressor.
21 Dreadful sounds *are* in his ears;
In prosperity the destroyer comes upon him.
22 He does not believe that he will return from darkness,
For a sword is waiting for him.
23 He wanders about for bread, *saying*, 'Where *is* it?'
He knows that a day of darkness is ready at his hand.
24 Trouble and anguish make him afraid;
They overpower him, like a king ready for battle.
25 For he stretches out his hand against God,
And acts defiantly against the Almighty,
26 Running stubbornly against Him
With his strong, embossed shield.

27 "Though he has covered his face with his fatness,
And made *his* waist heavy with fat,
28 He dwells in desolate cities,
In houses which no one inhabits,
Which are destined to become ruins.
29 He will not be rich,
Nor will his wealth continue,
Nor will his possessions overspread the earth.
30 He will not depart from darkness;
The flame will dry out his branches,
And by the breath of His mouth he will go away.
31 Let him not trust in futile *things*, deceiving himself,
For futility will be his reward.
32 It will be accomplished before his time,
And his branch will not be green.
33 He will shake off his unripe grape like a vine,

And cast off his blossom like an olive tree.
34 For the company of hypocrites *will be* barren,
And fire will consume the tents of bribery.
35 They conceive trouble and bring forth futility;
Their womb prepares deceit."

JOB REPROACHES HIS PITILESS FRIENDS

1 Then Job answered and said:

2 "I have heard many such things;
Miserable comforters *are* you all!
3 Shall words of wind have an end?
Or what provokes you that you answer?
4 I also could speak as you *do*,
If your soul were in my soul's place.
I could heap up words against you,
And shake my head at you;
5 *But* I would strengthen you with my mouth,
And the comfort of my lips would relieve *your grief.*

6 "Though I speak, my grief is not relieved;
And *if* I remain silent, how am I eased?
7 But now He has worn me out;
You have made desolate all my company.
8 You have shriveled me up,
And it is a witness *against me;*
My leanness rises up against me
And bears witness to my face.
9 He tears *me* in His wrath, and hates me;
He gnashes at me with His teeth;
My adversary sharpens His gaze on me.
10 They gape at me with their mouth,
They strike me reproachfully on the cheek,
They gather together against me.
11 God has delivered me to the ungodly,
And turned me over to the hands of the wicked.
12 I was at ease, but He has shattered me;
He also has taken *me* by my neck, and shaken me to pieces;
He has set me up for His target,
13 His archers surround me.
He pierces my heart[a] and does not pity;

"I have heard many such things; miserable comforters are you all!" (Job 16:2)

16:13 [a]Literally *kidneys*

He pours out my gall on the ground.
14 He breaks me with wound upon wound;
He runs at me like a warrior.[a]

15 "I have sewn sackcloth over my skin,
And laid my head[a] in the dust.
16 My face is flushed from weeping,
And on my eyelids is the shadow of
death;
17 Although no violence is in my hands,
And my prayer is pure.

WHAT'S IT MEAN?

People in ancient times wore sackcloth
to express their great sorrow or distress. Sackcloth
was a dark, scratchy material made of goat's hair. People who
wore it often put ashes on their head as an additional symbol of
their sorrowful state. The tradition of wearing dark clothing to
funerals came from the custom of wearing
sackcloth in times of sorrow.

Job 16:15, 16

18 "O earth, do not cover my blood,
And let my cry have no resting place!
19 Surely even now my witness is in
heaven,
And my evidence is on high.
20 My friends scorn me;
My eyes pour out tears to God.
21 Oh, that one might plead for a man with
God,
As a man pleads for his neighbor!
22 For when a few years are finished,
I shall go the way of no return.

JOB PRAYS FOR RELIEF

1 "My spirit is broken,
My days are extinguished,
The grave is ready for me.
2 Are not mockers with me?
And does not my eye dwell on their
provocation?

3 "Now put down a pledge for me with
Yourself.

Who is he who will shake hands with me?
4 For You have hidden their heart from
understanding;
Therefore You will not exalt them.
5 He who speaks flattery to his friends,
Even the eyes of his children will fail.

6 "But He has made me a byword of the
people,
And I have become one in whose face
men spit.
7 My eye has also grown dim because of
sorrow,
And all my members are like shadows.
8 Upright men are astonished at this,
And the innocent stirs himself up against
the hypocrite.
9 Yet the righteous will hold to his way,
And he who has clean hands will be
stronger and stronger.

10 "But please, come back again, all of you,[a]
For I shall not find one wise man among
you.
11 My days are past,
My purposes are broken off,
Even the thoughts of my heart.
12 They change the night into day;
'The light is near,' they say, in the face of
darkness.
13 If I wait for the grave as my house,
If I make my bed in the darkness,
14 If I say to corruption, 'You are my father,'
And to the worm, 'You are my mother
and my sister,'
15 Where then is my hope?
As for my hope, who can see it?
16 Will they go down to the gates of
Sheol?
Shall we have rest together in the dust?"

BILDAD: THE WICKED ARE PUNISHED

1 Then Bildad the Shuhite answered and said:

2 "How long till you put an end to words?
Gain understanding, and afterward we
will speak.
3 Why are we counted as beasts,
And regarded as stupid in your sight?
4 You who tear yourself in anger,
Shall the earth be forsaken for you?
Or shall the rock be removed from its
place?

16:14 [a]Vulgate reads giant.   **16:15** [a]Literally horn   **17:10** [a]Following some Hebrew manuscripts, Septuagint,
Syriac, and Vulgate; Masoretic Text and Targum read all of them.

5 "The light of the wicked indeed goes out,
And the flame of his fire does not shine.
6 The light is dark in his tent,
And his lamp beside him is put out.
7 The steps of his strength are shortened,
And his own counsel casts him down.
8 For he is cast into a net by his own feet,
And he walks into a snare.
9 The net takes *him* by the heel,
And a snare lays hold of him.
10 A noose *is* hidden for him on the ground,
And a trap for him in the road.
11 Terrors frighten him on every side,
And drive him to his feet.
12 His strength is starved,
And destruction *is* ready at his side.
13 It devours patches of his skin;
The firstborn of death devours his limbs.
14 He is uprooted from the shelter of his
tent,
And they parade him before the king of
terrors.
15 They dwell in his tent *who are* none of his;
Brimstone is scattered on his dwelling.
16 His roots are dried out below,
And his branch withers above.
17 The memory of him perishes from the
earth,
And he has no name among the
renowned.*a*
18 He is driven from light into darkness,
And chased out of the world.
19 He has neither son nor posterity among
his people,
Nor any remaining in his dwellings.
20 Those in the west are astonished at his
day,
As those in the east are frightened.
21 Surely such *are* the dwellings of the
wicked,
And this *is* the place *of him who* does not
know God."

JOB TRUSTS IN HIS REDEEMER

19 ¹Then Job answered and said:

2 "How long will you torment my soul,
And break me in pieces with words?
3 These ten times you have reproached me;
You are not ashamed *that* you have
wronged me.*a*
4 And if indeed I have erred,
My error remains with me.
5 If indeed you exalt *yourselves* against me,

And plead my disgrace against me,
6 Know then that God has wronged me,
And has surrounded me with His net.

WHAT'S IT MEAN?

Job wasn't actually counting the number
of times his friends made him feel bad. "Ten times"
was an expression meaning "often."
Job 19:3

7 "If I cry out concerning wrong, I am not
heard.
If I cry aloud, *there is* no justice.
8 He has fenced up my way, so that I
cannot pass;
And He has set darkness in my paths.
9 He has stripped me of my glory,
And taken the crown *from* my head.
10 He breaks me down on every side,
And I am gone;
My hope He has uprooted like a tree.
11 He has also kindled His wrath against
me,
And He counts me as *one of* His enemies.
12 His troops come together
And build up their road against me;
They encamp all around my tent.

13 "He has removed my brothers far from
me,
And my acquaintances are completely
estranged from me.
14 My relatives have failed,
And my close friends have forgotten me.
15 Those who dwell in my house, and my
maidservants,
Count me as a stranger;
I am an alien in their sight.
16 I call my servant, but he gives no
answer;
I beg him with my mouth.
17 My breath is offensive to my wife,
And I am repulsive to the children of my
own body.

18:17 *a*Literally *before the outside,* meaning distinguished, famous **19:3** *a*A Jewish tradition reads *make yourselves
strange to me.*

18 Even young children despise me;
I arise, and they speak against me.
19 All my close friends abhor me,
And those whom I love have turned
against me.
20 My bone clings to my skin and to my
flesh,
And I have escaped by the skin of my
teeth.

21 "Have pity on me, have pity on me, O you
my friends,
For the hand of God has struck me!
22 Why do you persecute me as God *does*,
And are not satisfied with my flesh?

23 "Oh, that my words were written!
Oh, that they were inscribed in a book!
24 That they were engraved on a rock
With an iron pen and lead, forever!
25 For I know *that* my Redeemer lives,
And He shall stand at last on the earth;
26 And after my skin is destroyed, this *I
know*,
That in my flesh I shall see God,
27 Whom I shall see for myself,
And my eyes shall behold, and not
another.
How my heart yearns within me!
28 If you should say, 'How shall we
persecute him?'—
Since the root of the matter is found in
me,
29 Be afraid of the sword for yourselves;
For wrath *brings* the punishment of the
sword,
That you may know *there is* a
judgment."

WHAT'S IT MEAN?

Apparently Job believed that his body would be resurrected at some point after his death. Like many others in his culture, Job probably believed that God would one day rescue the souls of righteous people in Sheol, the place of the dead. They believed that God would then pair up those souls with their bodies and whisk them away to heaven.

Job 19:26

ZOPHAR'S SERMON ON THE WICKED MAN

20
1Then Zophar the Naamathite answered and
said:

2 "Therefore my anxious thoughts make me
answer,
Because of the turmoil within me.
3 I have heard the rebuke that reproaches
me,
And the spirit of my understanding
causes me to answer.

4 "Do you *not* know this of old,
Since man was placed on earth,
5 That the triumphing of the wicked is
short,
And the joy of the hypocrite is *but* for a
moment?
6 Though his haughtiness mounts up to the
heavens,
And his head reaches to the clouds,
7 *Yet* he will perish forever like his own
refuse;
Those who have seen him will say,
'Where is he?'
8 He will fly away like a dream, and not be
found;
Yes, he will be chased away like a vision
of the night.
9 The eye *that* saw him will *see him* no
more,
Nor will his place behold him anymore.
10 His children will seek the favor of the
poor,
And his hands will restore his wealth.
11 His bones are full of his youthful vigor,
But it will lie down with him in the dust.

12 "Though evil is sweet in his mouth,
And he hides it under his tongue,
13 *Though* he spares it and does not forsake
it,
But still keeps it in his mouth,
14 *Yet* his food in his stomach turns sour;
It becomes cobra venom within him.
15 He swallows down riches
And vomits them up again;
God casts them out of his belly.
16 He will suck the poison of cobras;
The viper's tongue will slay him.
17 He will not see the streams,
The rivers flowing with honey and
cream.
18 He will restore that for which he labored,
And will not swallow *it* down;
From the proceeds of business
He will get no enjoyment.

¹⁹ For he has oppressed *and* forsaken the poor,
He has violently seized a house which he did not build.

WHAT'S IT MEAN?

Though it may sound like a disgusting drink, the biblical phrase "honey and cream" actually symbolized wealth. Cream was a staple of everyday Hebrew life, a major food source for the Israelites. Honey, on the other hand, was considered a delicacy or a rare treat.

Job 20:17

²⁰ "Because he knows no quietness in his heart,ᵃ
He will not save anything he desires.
²¹ Nothing is left for him to eat;
Therefore his well-being will not last.
²² In his self-sufficiency he will be in distress;
Every hand of misery will come against him.
²³ *When* he is about to fill his stomach,
God will cast on him the fury of His wrath,
And will rain *it* on him while he is eating.
²⁴ He will flee from the iron weapon;
A bronze bow will pierce him through.
²⁵ It is drawn, and comes out of the body;
Yes, the glittering *point comes* out of his gall.
Terrors *come* upon him;
²⁶ Total darkness *is* reserved for his treasures.
An unfanned fire will consume him;
It shall go ill with him who is left in his tent.
²⁷ The heavens will reveal his iniquity,
And the earth will rise up against him.
²⁸ The increase of his house will depart,
And his goods will flow away in the day of His wrath.
²⁹ This *is* the portion from God for a wicked man,
The heritage appointed to him by God."

JOB'S DISCOURSE ON THE WICKED

¹Then Job answered and said:

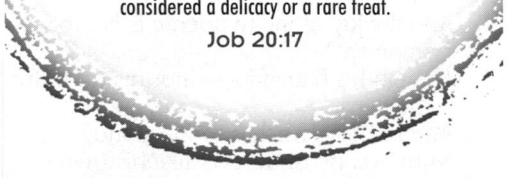

² "Listen carefully to my speech,
And let this be your consolation.
³ Bear with me that I may speak,
And after I have spoken, keep mocking.

⁴ "As for me, *is* my complaint against man?
And if *it were,* why should I not be impatient?
⁵ Look at me and be astonished;
Put *your* hand over *your* mouth.
⁶ Even when I remember I am terrified,
And trembling takes hold of my flesh.
⁷ Why do the wicked live *and* become old,
Yes, become mighty in power?
⁸ Their descendants are established with them in their sight,
And their offspring before their eyes.
⁹ Their houses *are* safe from fear,
Neither *is* the rod of God upon them.
¹⁰ Their bull breeds without failure;
Their cow calves without miscarriage.
¹¹ They send forth their little ones like a flock,
And their children dance.
¹² They sing to the tambourine and harp,
And rejoice to the sound of the flute.
¹³ They spend their days in wealth,
And in a moment go down to the grave.ᵃ
¹⁴ Yet they say to God, 'Depart from us,
For we do not desire the knowledge of Your ways.
¹⁵ Who *is* the Almighty, that we should serve Him?
And what profit do we have if we pray to Him?'
¹⁶ Indeed their prosperity *is* not in their hand;
The counsel of the wicked is far from me.

¹⁷ "How often is the lamp of the wicked put out?
How often does their destruction come upon them,
The sorrows *God* distributes in His anger?
¹⁸ They are like straw before the wind,
And like chaff that a storm carries away.
¹⁹ *They say,* 'God lays up one'sᵃ iniquity for his children';
Let Him recompense him, that he may know *it.*
²⁰ Let his eyes see his destruction,

20:20 ᵃLiterally *belly*   **21:13** ᵃOr *Sheol*   **21:19** ᵃLiterally *his*

And let him drink of the wrath of the
Almighty.
21 For what does he care about his
household after him,
When the number of his months is cut in
half?

22 "Can *anyone* teach God
knowledge,
Since He judges those on
high?
23 One dies in his full
strength,
Being wholly at ease and
secure;
24 His pails*a* are full of milk,
And the marrow of his bones is moist.
25 Another man dies in the bitterness of his
soul,
Never having eaten with pleasure.
26 They lie down alike in the dust,
And worms cover them.

27 "Look, I know your thoughts,
And the schemes *with which* you would
wrong me.
28 For you say,
'Where *is* the house of the prince?
And where *is* the tent,*a*
The dwelling place of the wicked?'
29 Have you not asked those who travel the
road?
And do you not know their signs?
30 For the wicked are reserved for the day of
doom;
They shall be brought out on the day of
wrath.
31 Who condemns his way to his face?
And who repays him *for what* he has
done?
32 Yet he shall be brought to the grave,
And a vigil kept over the tomb.
33 The clods of the valley shall be sweet to
him;
Everyone shall follow him,
As countless *have gone* before him.
34 How then can you comfort me with
empty words,
Since falsehood remains in your
answers?"

ELIPHAZ ACCUSES JOB OF WICKEDNESS

1Then Eliphaz the Temanite answered and
said:

GOD
Is God
perfect?
(21:22)

2 "Can a man be profitable to God,
Though he who is wise may be profitable
to himself?
3 *Is it* any pleasure to the Almighty that
you are righteous?
Or *is it* gain *to Him* that you make your
ways blameless?

4 "Is it because of your fear of Him that He
corrects you,
And enters into judgment with you?
5 *Is* not your wickedness great,
And your iniquity without end?
6 For you have taken pledges from your
brother for no reason,
And stripped the naked of their clothing.
7 You have not given the weary water to
drink,
And you have withheld bread from the
hungry.
8 But the mighty man possessed the land,
And the honorable man dwelt in it.
9 You have sent widows away empty,
And the strength of the fatherless was
crushed.
10 Therefore snares *are* all around you,
And sudden fear troubles you,
11 Or darkness *so that* you cannot see;
And an abundance of water covers you.

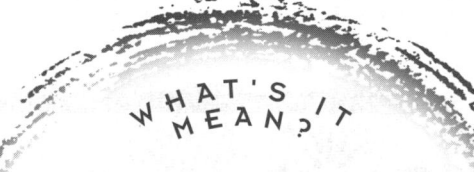

WHAT'S IT MEAN?

The sins Eliphaz mentioned may not seem
terrible today, but in ancient times they were pretty
serious. The wealthy were expected to take care of poor people,
orphans, and widows, without demanding or expecting anything in
return. Home owners were expected to welcome traveling guests and
strangers alike, inviting them into their homes and
treating them like family.
Job 22:6–9

12 "Is not God in the height of heaven?
And see the highest stars, how lofty they
are!
13 And you say, 'What does God know?
Can He judge through the deep darkness?

21:24 *a*Septuagint and Vulgate read *bowels;* Syriac reads *sides;* Targum reads *breasts.* **21:28** *a*Vulgate omits
the tent.

14 Thick clouds cover Him, so that He
cannot see,
And He walks above the circle of
heaven.'
15 Will you keep to the old way
Which wicked men have trod,
16 Who were cut down before their time,
Whose foundations were swept away by
a flood?
17 They said to God, 'Depart
from us!
What can the Almighty
do to them?'[a]
18 Yet He filled their
houses with good
things;
But the counsel of the
wicked is far from
me.

19 "The righteous see *it* and are
glad,
And the innocent laugh at them:
20 'Surely our adversaries[a] are cut down,
And the fire consumes their remnant.'
21 "Now acquaint yourself with Him, and be
at peace;

> "Now acquaint yourself
> with Him, and be at peace;
> thereby good will come
> to you."
> (Job 22:21)

Thereby good will come to you.
22 Receive, please, instruction from His
mouth,
And lay up His words in your heart.
23 If you return to the Almighty, you will be
built up;
You will remove iniquity far from your
tents.
24 Then you will lay your
gold in the dust,
And the *gold* of Ophir
among the stones of
the brooks.
25 Yes, the Almighty will
be your gold[a]
And your precious
silver;
26 For then you will have
your delight in the
Almighty,
And lift up your face to
God.
27 You will make your prayer to Him,
He will hear you,
And you will pay your vows.
28 You will also declare a thing,
And it will be established for you;
So light will shine on your ways.

22:17 [a]Septuagint and Syriac read *us*.   **22:20** [a]Septuagint reads *substance*.   **22:25** [a]The ancient versions suggest *defense*; Hebrew reads *gold* as in verse 24.

Promise
HE PROMISES TO HEAR AND ANSWER YOUR PRAYERS.

You will make your prayer to Him, He will hear you, and you will pay your vows (Job 22:27).

Some high school kids meet once a week before school to pray. Last week they prayed for a job for one of their dads, for a grandmother to be healed of cancer, and for a friend who had a hard exam coming up. This week they met and as soon as they got together, the reports began: "My dad got a job the very morning we prayed!" "My grandmother's doctor can't find any trace of the cancer." "Our friend thinks he did well on his exam and thanks you for praying." They all were looking at each other in amazement. "Wow," someone said, "God really answered our prayers!" Sure, God answers your prayers, but we sometimes pray with so much doubt that we're totally shocked when He does.

Pray with assurance that God promises to answer. Expect Him to work and watch for His action. Remember that God will answer in one of three ways—yes, no, or wait. Praying is not holy manipulation. God will choose in His wisdom how to respond.

SEE FOR YOURSELF:
Deut. 4:5–8; Ps. 28:6; 40:1–17

29 When they cast *you* down, and you say,
'Exaltation *will come!'*
Then He will save the humble *person.*
30 He will *even* deliver one who is not
innocent;
Yes, he will be delivered by the purity of
your hands."

JOB PROCLAIMS GOD'S RIGHTEOUS JUDGMENTS

¹Then Job answered and said:

2 "Even today my complaint is bitter;
My[a] hand is listless because of my
groaning.
3 Oh, that I knew where I might find Him,
That I might come to His seat!
4 I would present *my* case before Him,
And fill my mouth with arguments.
5 I would know the words *which* He would
answer me,
And understand what He would say to
me.
6 Would He contend with me in His great
power?
No! But He would take *note* of me.
7 There the upright could reason with Him,
And I would be delivered forever from
my Judge.

8 "Look, I go forward, but He is not *there,*
And backward, but I cannot perceive
Him;
9 When He works on the left hand, I
cannot behold *Him;*
When He turns to the right hand, I
cannot see *Him.*
10 But He knows the way that I take;
When He has tested me, I shall come forth
as gold.
11 My foot has held fast to His steps;
I have kept His way and not
turned aside.
12 I have not departed
from the
commandment of His
lips;
I have treasured the
words of His mouth
More than my necessary
food.

FOLLOWING GOD

How should
we follow
God?
(23:11, 12)

13 "But He *is* unique, and who can make Him
change?
And *whatever* His soul desires, *that* He
does.

On the Edge

*When He works on the left
hand, I cannot behold Him; when
He turns to the right hand, I cannot
see Him (Job 23:9).*

Who blew the wind through your hair
this morning? Who brought the sun over the
horizon once again? Who changed the
seasons while you weren't even
looking? It was God! The One
who is always at work. While you
slept, He was preparing your day.
While you haven't noticed, He is ordering
your life. He is strengthening your gifts and
giving you ideas about what you really have
to do. We have downtime, unproductive
days, and mental blocks. We take vacations,
and naps, and study hall. We can go for days
and not accomplish one thing. Not God. He
is always at work. Always creating, always
protecting, always loving.

SEE FOR YOURSELF:
Ps. 121:3, 4; John 5:17

14 For He performs *what is* appointed for
me,
And many such *things are* with Him.
15 Therefore I am terrified at His presence;
When I consider *this,* I am afraid of
Him.

WHAT'S IT MEAN?

Here's a Bible lesson that might come in handy
if you're planning to buy gold nuggets in the near
future. After gold is mined, it must be refined. That means the ore
must be heated to the point that the metal separates from the rock.
People who bought gold in Job's day would test it first to see if the
metal had been mixed with less valuable materials. They would have
an expert metalsmith or smelter scrape, cut, and
heat the gold as part of the testing process.
Job 23:10

23:2 ªFollowing Masoretic Text, Targum, and Vulgate; Septuagint and Syriac read *His.*

16 For God made my heart weak,
And the Almighty terrifies me;
17 Because I was not cut off from the
presence of darkness,
And He did *not* hide deep darkness from
my face.

JOB COMPLAINS OF VIOLENCE ON THE EARTH

1 "*Since* times are not hidden from the
Almighty,
Why do those who know Him see not
His days?

2 "*Some* remove landmarks;
They seize flocks violently and feed *on*
them;
3 They drive away the donkey of the
fatherless;
They take the widow's ox as a pledge.
4 They push the needy off the road;
All the poor of the land are forced to
hide.
5 Indeed, *like* wild donkeys in the desert,
They go out to their work, searching for
food.
The wilderness *yields* food for them *and*
for *their* children.
6 They gather their fodder in the field
And glean in the vineyard of the
wicked.
7 They spend the night naked, without
clothing,
And have no covering in the cold.
8 They are wet with the showers of the
mountains,
And huddle around the rock for want of
shelter.

WHAT'S IT MEAN?

In ancient times, stones were used
to mark the boundaries of people's property.
Moving those stones in order to extend one's
property was a big-time no-no.
Job 24:2

9 "*Some* snatch the fatherless from the
breast,
And take a pledge from the poor.

10 They cause *the poor* to go naked, without
clothing;
And they take away the sheaves from the
hungry.
11 They press out oil within their walls,
And tread winepresses, yet suffer
thirst.
12 The dying groan in the city,
And the souls of the wounded cry out;
Yet God does not charge *them* with
wrong.

WHAT'S IT MEAN?

If light and daytime represented goodness
and truth, what do you suppose darkness and night
represented? If you said they symbolized sin, evil,
and death, give yourself a pat on the back.
Job 24:13–17

13 "There are those who rebel against the
light;
They do not know its ways
Nor abide in its paths.
14 The murderer rises with the light;
He kills the poor and needy;
And in the night he is like a thief.
15 The eye of the adulterer waits for the
twilight,
Saying, 'No eye will see me';
And he disguises *his* face.
16 In the dark they break into houses
Which they marked for themselves in the
daytime;
They do not know the light.
17 For the morning is the same to them as
the shadow of death;
If *someone* recognizes *them,*
They are in the terrors of the shadow of
death.

18 "They *should be* swift on the face of the
waters,
Their portion *should be* cursed in the
earth,
So that no *one would* turn into the way of
their vineyards.
19 As drought and heat consume the snow
waters,

So the grave[a] *consumes those who* have sinned.

20 The womb *should* forget him,
The worm *should* feed sweetly on him;
He *should* be remembered no more,
And wickedness *should* be broken like a tree.

21 For he preys on the barren *who* do not bear,
And does no good for the widow.

22 "But *God* draws the mighty away with His power;
He rises up, but no *man* is sure of life.

23 He gives them security, and they rely *on it*;
Yet His eyes *are* on their ways.

24 They are exalted for a little while,
Then they are gone.
They are brought low;
They are taken out of the way like all *others*;
They dry out like the heads of grain.

25 "Now if *it is* not *so*, who will prove me a liar,
And make my speech worth nothing?"

BILDAD: HOW CAN MAN BE RIGHTEOUS?

1 Then Bildad the Shuhite answered and said:

2 "Dominion and fear *belong* to Him;
He makes peace in His high places.

3 Is there any number to His armies?
Upon whom does His light not rise?

4 How then can man be righteous before God?
Or how can he be pure *who is* born of a woman?

5 If even the moon does not shine,
And the stars are not pure in His sight,

6 How much less man, *who is* a maggot,
And a son of man, *who is* a worm?"

JOB: MAN'S FRAILTY AND GOD'S MAJESTY

1 But Job answered and said:

2 "How have you helped *him who is* without power?
How have you saved the arm *that has* no strength?

3 How have you counseled *one who has* no wisdom?
And *how* have you declared sound advice to many?

4 To whom have you uttered words?
And whose spirit came from you?

5 "The dead tremble,
Those under the waters and those inhabiting them.

6 Sheol *is* naked before Him,
And Destruction has no covering.

7 He stretches out the north over empty space;
He hangs the earth on nothing.

8 He binds up the water in His thick clouds,
Yet the clouds are not broken under it.

9 He covers the face of *His* throne,
And spreads His cloud over it.

10 He drew a circular horizon on the face of the waters,
At the boundary of light and darkness.

11 The pillars of heaven tremble,
And are astonished at His rebuke.

12 He stirs up the sea with His power,
And by His understanding He breaks up the storm.

13 By His Spirit He adorned the heavens;
His hand pierced the fleeing serpent.

14 Indeed these *are* the mere edges of His ways,
And how small a whisper we hear of Him!
But the thunder of His power who can understand?"

JOB MAINTAINS HIS INTEGRITY

1 Moreover Job continued his discourse, and said:

2 "*As* God lives, *who* has taken away my justice,
And the Almighty, *who* has made my soul bitter,

3 As long as my breath *is* in me,
And the breath of God in my nostrils,

4 My lips will not speak wickedness,
Nor my tongue utter deceit.

5 Far be it from me
That I should say you are right;
Till I die I will not put away my integrity from me.

6 My righteousness I hold fast, and will not let it go;
My heart shall not reproach *me* as long as I live.

HUMILITY

How do people compare to God? (25:6)

7 "May my enemy be like the wicked,
And he who rises up against me like the
unrighteous.
8 For what is the hope of the hypocrite,
Though he may gain *much*,
If God takes away his life?
9 Will God hear his cry
When trouble comes upon him?
10 Will he delight himself in the Almighty?
Will he always call on God?

11 "I will teach you about the hand of God;
What *is* with the Almighty I will not
conceal.
12 Surely all of you have seen *it*;
Why then do you behave with complete
nonsense?

13 "This is the portion of a wicked man with
God,
And the heritage of oppressors, received
from the Almighty:
14 If his children are multiplied, *it is* for the
sword;
And his offspring shall not be satisfied
with bread.
15 Those who survive him shall be buried in
death,
And their[a] widows shall not weep,
16 Though he heaps up silver like dust,
And piles up clothing like clay—
17 He may pile *it* up, but the just will wear *it*,
And the innocent will divide the silver.
18 He builds his house like a moth,[a]
Like a booth *which* a watchman makes.
19 The rich man will lie down,
But not be gathered *up*;[a]
He opens his eyes,
And he *is* no more.
20 Terrors overtake him like a flood;
A tempest steals him away in the night.
21 The east wind carries him away, and he is
gone;
It sweeps him out of his place.
22 It hurls against him and does not spare;
He flees desperately from its power.
23 *Men* shall clap their hands at him,
And shall hiss him out of his place.

JOB'S DISCOURSE ON WISDOM

1 "Surely there is a mine for silver,
And a place *where* gold is refined.

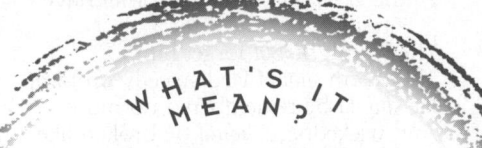

WHAT'S IT MEAN?

The people of the ancient Middle East were
expert miners. Archaeologists have found that the
Egyptians dug mining tunnels more than one hundred feet deep. They
carried the ore they discovered to the surface in baskets. In addition
to precious metals like gold, copper, and silver, the miners brought
up valuable resources like gemstones.
Job 28:1, 2

2 Iron is taken from the earth,
And copper *is* smelted *from* ore.
3 *Man* puts an end to darkness,
And searches every recess
For ore in the darkness and the shadow
of death.
4 He breaks open a shaft away from
people;
In places forgotten by feet
They hang far away from men;
They swing to and fro.
5 *As for* the earth, from it comes bread,
But underneath it is turned up as by fire;
6 Its stones *are* the source of sapphires,
And it contains gold dust.
7 *That* path no bird knows,
Nor has the falcon's eye seen it.
8 The proud lions[a] have not trodden it,
Nor has the fierce lion passed over it.
9 He puts his hand on the flint;
He overturns the mountains at the roots.
10 He cuts out channels in the rocks,
And his eye sees every precious thing.
11 He dams up the streams from trickling;
What is hidden he brings forth to light.

12 "But where can wisdom be found?
And where *is* the place of understanding?
13 Man does not know its value,
Nor is it found in the land of the living.
14 The deep says, '*It is* not in me';
And the sea says, '*It is* not with me.'
15 It cannot be purchased for gold,

27:15 [a]Literally *his* **27:18** [a]Following Masoretic Text and Vulgate; Septuagint and Syriac read *spider* (compare
8:14); Targum reads *decay*. **27:19** [a]Following Masoretic Text and Targum; Septuagint and Syriac read *But shall
not add* (that is, do it again); Vulgate reads *But take away nothing*. **28:8** [a]Literally *sons of pride*, figurative of the
great lions

Nor can silver be weighed *for* its price.
16 It cannot be valued in the gold of Ophir,
In precious onyx or sapphire.
17 Neither gold nor crystal can equal it,
Nor can it be exchanged for jewelry of
fine gold.
18 No mention shall be made of coral or
quartz,
For the price of wisdom *is* above rubies.
19 The topaz of Ethiopia cannot equal it,
Nor can it be valued in pure gold.

20 "From where then does wisdom come?
And where *is* the place of understanding?
21 It is hidden from the eyes of all living,
And concealed from the birds of the air.
22 Destruction and Death say,
'We have heard a report about it with our
ears.'
23 God understands its way,
And He knows its place.
24 For He looks to the ends of the earth,
And sees under the whole heavens,
25 To establish a weight for the wind,
And apportion the waters by measure.
26 When He made a law for the rain,
And a path for the thunderbolt,
27 Then He saw *wisdom*ᵃ and declared it;
He prepared it, indeed, He searched it
out.
28 And to man He said,
'Behold, the fear of the Lord, that *is*
wisdom,
And to depart from evil *is*
understanding.' "

JOB'S SUMMARY DEFENSE

29 ¹Job further continued his discourse, and
said:

2 "Oh, that I were as *in* months past,
As *in* the days when God watched over
me;
3 When His lamp shone upon my head,
And when by His light I walked *through*
darkness;
4 Just as I was in the days of my prime,
When the friendly counsel of God *was*
over my tent;
5 When the Almighty *was* yet with me,
When my children *were* around me;
6 When my steps were bathed with cream,ᵃ
And the rock poured out rivers of oil for
me!

7 "When I went out to the gate by the city,
When I took my seat in the open square,
8 The young men saw me and hid,
And the aged arose *and* stood;
9 The princes refrained from talking,
And put *their* hand on their mouth;
10 The voice of nobles was hushed,
And their tongue stuck to the roof of
their mouth.
11 When the ear heard, then it blessed me,
And when the eye saw, then it approved
me;
12 Because I delivered the poor who cried out,
The fatherless and *the one who* had no
helper.
13 The blessing of a perishing *man* came
upon me,
And I caused the widow's heart to sing
for joy.
14 I put on righteousness, and it clothed me;
My justice *was* like a robe and a turban.
15 I *was* eyes to the blind,
And I *was* feet to the lame.
16 I *was* a father to the poor,
And I searched out the case *that* I did not
know.
17 I broke the fangs of the wicked,
And plucked the victim from his teeth.

18 "Then I said, 'I shall die in my nest,
And multiply *my* days as the sand.
19 My root *is* spread out to the waters,
And the dew lies all night on my branch.
20 My glory *is* fresh within me,
And my bow is renewed in my hand.'

21 "*Men* listened to me and waited,
And kept silence for my counsel.
22 After my words they did not speak again,
And my speech settled on them *as dew.*
23 They waited for me *as* for the rain,
And they opened their mouth wide *as* for
the spring rain.
24 *If* I mocked at them, they did not believe *it,*
And the light of my countenance they did
not cast down.
25 I chose the way for them, and sat as chief;
So I dwelt as a king in the army,
As one *who* comforts mourners.

30 ¹ "But now they mock at me, *men* younger
than I,
Whose fathers I disdained to put with the
dogs of my flock.

28:27 ᵃLiterally *it*   **29:6** ᵃMasoretic Text reads *wrath;* ancient versions and some Hebrew manuscripts read
cream (compare 20:17).

2 Indeed, what *profit* is the strength of their
  hands to me?
  Their vigor has perished.
3 *They are* gaunt from want and famine,
  Fleeing late to the wilderness, desolate
  and waste,
4 Who pluck mallow by the bushes,
  And broom tree roots *for* their food.
5 They were driven out from among *men,*
  They shouted at them as *at* a thief.
6 *They had* to live in the clefts of the
  valleys,
  In caves of the earth and the rocks.
7 Among the bushes they brayed,
  Under the nettles they nestled.
8 *They were* sons of fools,
  Yes, sons of vile men;
  They were scourged from the land.

9 "And now I am their taunting song;
  Yes, I am their byword.
10 They abhor me, they keep far from me;
  They do not hesitate to spit in my face.
11 Because He has loosed my[a] bowstring
  and afflicted me,
  They have cast off restraint before me.
12 At *my* right *hand* the rabble arises;
  They push away my feet,
  And they raise against me their ways of
  destruction.
13 They break up my path,
  They promote my calamity;
  They have no helper.
14 They come as broad breakers;
  Under the ruinous storm they roll along.
15 Terrors are turned upon me;
  They pursue my honor as the wind,
  And my prosperity has passed like a
  cloud.

16 "And now my soul is poured out because
  of my *plight;*
  The days of affliction take hold of me.
17 My bones are pierced in me at night,
  And my gnawing pains take no rest.
18 By great force my garment is disfigured;
  It binds me about as the collar of my
  coat.
19 He has cast me into the mire,
  And I have become like dust and ashes.

20 "I cry out to You, but You do not answer
  me;
  I stand up, and You regard me.
21 *But* You have become cruel to me;

With the strength of Your hand You
  oppose me.
22 You lift me up to the wind and cause me
  to ride *on it;*
  You spoil my success.
23 For I know *that* You will bring me *to*
  death,
  And *to* the house appointed for all living.

WHAT'S IT MEAN?

What's wrong with jackals and
ostriches? Most likely, Job was referring to the
lonesome, disturbing sounds they make. Jackals and ostriches were
considered unclean animals by the Israelites and were associated
with desolation and despair.
Job 30:29

24 "Surely He would not stretch out *His* hand
  against a heap of ruins,
  If they cry out when He destroys *it.*
25 Have I not wept for him who was in
  trouble?
  Has *not* my soul grieved for the poor?
26 But when I looked for good, evil came *to*
  me;
  And when I waited for light, then came
  darkness.
27 My heart is in turmoil and cannot rest;
  Days of affliction confront me.
28 I go about mourning, but not in the sun;
  I stand up in the assembly *and* cry out
  for help.
29 I am a brother of jackals,
  And a companion of ostriches.
30 My skin grows black and falls from me;
  My bones burn with fever.
31 My harp is *turned* to mourning,
  And my flute to the voice of those who
  weep.

1 "I have made a covenant
  with my eyes;
  Why then should I look
  upon a young
  woman?

LUST

How should
we maintain
purity?
(31:1)

30:11 [a]Following Masoretic Text, Syriac, and Targum; Septuagint and Vulgate read *His.*

2   For what *is* the allotment of God from
        above,
    And the inheritance of the Almighty from
        on high?
3   *Is* it not destruction for the wicked,
    And disaster for the workers of iniquity?
4   Does He not see my ways,
    And count all my steps?

5   "If I have walked with
        falsehood,
    Or if my foot has
        hastened to
        deceit,
6   Let me be weighed
        on honest scales,
    That God may
        know my
        integrity.
7   If my step has turned
        from the way,
    Or my heart walked after
        my eyes,
    Or if any spot adheres to my hands,
8   *Then* let me sow, and another eat;
    Yes, let my harvest be rooted out.

> "If I have walked with falsehood,
> or if my foot has hastened to deceit,
> let me be weighed on honest scales,
> that God may know my integrity."
> (Job 31:5, 6)

WHAT'S IT MEAN?

In the ancient Middle East, a person
accused of a crime was required to take an oath of
innocence. Job went one step further and submitted himself to the
toughest polygraph test imaginable. He swore that he was innocent
of all the accusations and called on God to
punish him if he was lying.
Job 31:5–8

9   "If my heart has been enticed by a
        woman,
    Or *if* I have lurked at my neighbor's
        door,
10 *Then* let my wife grind for another,
    And let others bow down over her.
11 For that *would be* wickedness;
    Yes, it *would be* iniquity *deserving of*
        judgment.

12 For that *would be* a fire *that* consumes to
        destruction,
    And would root out all my increase.

13 "If I have despised the cause of my male
        or female servant
            When they
                complained
                against me,
14   What then shall I do
                when God rises
                up?
            When He punishes,
                how shall I
                answer Him?
15   Did not He who
                made me in the
                womb make
                them?
            Did not the same
                One fashion us in
                the womb?

16 "If I have kept the poor from *their* desire,
    Or caused the eyes of the widow to fail,
17 Or eaten my morsel by myself,
    So that the fatherless could not eat of it
18 (But from my youth I reared him as a
        father,
    And from my mother's womb I guided
        the widow[a]);
19 If I have seen anyone perish for lack of
        clothing,
    Or any poor *man* without covering;
20 If his heart[a] has not blessed me,
    And *if* he was *not* warmed with the fleece
        of my sheep;
21 If I have raised my hand against the
        fatherless,
    When I saw I had help in the gate;
22 *Then* let my arm fall from my shoulder,
    Let my arm be torn from the socket.
23 For destruction *from* God *is* a terror to
        me,
    And because of His magnificence I cannot
        endure.

24 "If I have made gold my hope,
    Or said to fine gold, '*You are* my
        confidence';
25 If I have rejoiced because my wealth *was*
        great,
    And because my hand had gained much;
26 If I have observed the sun[a] when it
        shines,

31:18 [a]Literally *her* (compare verse 16)   **31:20** [a]Literally *loins*   **31:26** [a]Literally *light*

27 Or the moon moving *in* brightness,
So that my heart has been secretly
enticed,
And my mouth has kissed my hand;
28 This also *would be* an iniquity *deserving of*
judgment,
For I would have denied God *who is*
above.

29 "If I have rejoiced at the destruction of him
who hated me,
Or lifted myself up when evil found him
30 (Indeed I have not allowed my mouth to
sin
By asking for a curse on his soul);
31 If the men of my tent have not said,
'Who is there that has not been satisfied
with his meat?'
32 (*But* no sojourner had to lodge in the
street,
For I have opened my doors to the
traveler[a]);
33 If I have covered my transgressions as
Adam,
By hiding my iniquity in my bosom,
34 Because I feared the great multitude,
And dreaded the contempt of families,
So that I kept silence
And did not go out of the door—
35 Oh, that I had one to hear me!
Here is my mark.
Oh, that the Almighty would answer me,
That my Prosecutor had written a book!
36 Surely I would carry it on my shoulder,
And bind it on me *like* a crown;
37 I would declare to Him the number of
my steps;
Like a prince I would approach Him.

38 "If my land cries out against me,
And its furrows weep together;
39 If I have eaten its fruit[a] without money,
Or caused its owners to lose their lives;
40 *Then* let thistles grow instead of wheat,
And weeds instead of barley."

The words of Job are ended.

ELIHU CONTRADICTS JOB'S FRIENDS

1 So these three men ceased answering Job,
because he *was* righteous in his own eyes.
2 Then the wrath of Elihu, the son of Barachel
the Buzite, of the family of Ram, was aroused

against Job; his wrath was aroused because he
justified himself rather than God. 3 Also against
his three friends his wrath was aroused, because they had found no answer, and *yet* had
condemned Job.

4 Now because they *were* years older than he,
Elihu had waited to speak to Job.[a] 5 When Elihu
saw that *there was* no answer in the mouth of
these three men, his wrath was aroused.

6 So Elihu, the son of Barachel the Buzite, answered and said:

"I *am* young in years, and you *are* very
old;
Therefore I was afraid,
And dared not declare my opinion to
you.
7 I said, 'Age[a] should speak,
And multitude of years should teach
wisdom.'
8 But *there is* a spirit in man,
And the breath of the Almighty gives him
understanding.
9 Great men[a] are not *always* wise,
Nor do the aged *always* understand
justice.

10 "Therefore I say, 'Listen to me,
I also will declare my opinion.'
11 Indeed I waited for your words,
I listened to your reasonings, while you
searched out what to say.
12 I paid close attention to you;
And surely not one of you convinced Job,
Or answered his words—
13 Lest you say,
'We have found wisdom';
God will vanquish him, not man.
14 Now he has not directed *his* words
against me;
So I will not answer him with your
words.

15 "They are dismayed and answer no more;
Words escape them.
16 And I have waited, because they did not
speak,
Because they stood still *and* answered no
more.
17 I also will answer my part,
I too will declare my opinion.
18 For I am full of words;
The spirit within me compels me.

31:32 [a]Following Septuagint, Syriac, Targum, and Vulgate; Masoretic Text reads *road.*   **31:39** [a]Literally *its*
strength   **32:4** [a]Vulgate reads *till Job had spoken.*   **32:7** [a]Literally *Days,* that is, years   **32:9** [a]Or *Men of many*
years

19 Indeed my belly *is* like wine *that* has no
    vent;
    It is ready to burst like new wineskins.
20 I will speak, that I may find relief;
    I must open my lips and answer.
21 Let me not, I pray, show partiality to
    anyone;
    Nor let me flatter any man.
22 For I do not know how to flatter,
    Else my Maker would soon take me away.

ELIHU CONTRADICTS JOB

1 "But please, Job, hear my speech,
    And listen to all my words.
2 Now, I open my mouth;
    My tongue speaks in my mouth.
3 My words *come* from my upright heart;
    My lips utter pure knowledge.
4 The Spirit of God has made me,
    And the breath of the Almighty gives me
    life.
5 If you can answer me,
    Set *your words* in order before me;
    Take your stand.
6 Truly I *am* as your spokesman[a] before
    God;
    I also have been formed out of clay.
7 Surely no fear of me will terrify you,
    Nor will my hand be heavy on you.

8 "Surely you have spoken in my hearing,
    And I have heard the sound of *your*
    words, *saying,*
9 'I *am* pure, without transgression;
    I *am* innocent, and *there is* no iniquity in
    me.
10 Yet He finds occasions against me,
    He counts me as His enemy;
11 He puts my feet in the stocks,
    He watches all my paths.'

12 "Look, *in* this you are not righteous.
    I will answer you,
    For God is greater than man.
13 Why do you contend with Him?
    For He does not give an accounting of
    any of His words.
14 For God may speak in one way, or in
    another,
    Yet man does not perceive it.
15 In a dream, in a vision of the night,
    When deep sleep falls upon men,
    While slumbering on their beds,
16 Then He opens the ears of men,
    And seals their instruction.

17 In order to turn man *from his* deed,
    And conceal pride from man,
18 He keeps back his soul from the Pit,
    And his life from perishing by the
    sword.

19 "*Man* is also chastened with pain on his
    bed,
    And with strong *pain* in many of his
    bones,
20 So that his life abhors bread,
    And his soul succulent food.
21 His flesh wastes away from sight,
    And his bones stick out *which once* were
    not seen.
22 Yes, his soul draws near the Pit,
    And his life to the executioners.

23 "If there is a messenger for him,
    A mediator, one among a thousand,
    To show man His uprightness,
24 Then He is gracious to him, and says,
    'Deliver him from going down to the Pit;
    I have found a ransom';
25 His flesh shall be young like a child's,
    He shall return to the days of his youth.

On the Edge

*For God may speak in one way,
or in another, yet man does not
perceive it (Job 33:14).*

God can speak to us in as many ways as
He can imagine. He is very creative when it
comes to getting our attention. He can
whisper to us while we are still, or shout to
us in our busyness. We can read
the Bible and know that He has
just spoken directly to our situation. A teacher may teach from
the Scripture and God speaks through him
or her. He uses billboards, phone calls, hugs
from friends, successes, failures, and ordinary humdrum experiences. He will do
whatever it takes, intervene whenever
necessary to get you to look up and know
that He is God. Do you have eyes to see? Do
you have ears to hear God speaking to you?

SEE FOR YOURSELF:
1 Cor. 2:13; 2 Pet. 1:21;
Rev. 2:7

33:6 ᵃLiterally *as your mouth*

26 He shall pray to God, and He will delight
in him,
He shall see His face with joy,
For He restores to man His righteousness.
27 Then he looks at men and says,
'I have sinned, and perverted *what was*
right,
And it did not profit me.'
28 He will redeem his[a] soul from going
down to the Pit,
And his[b] life shall see the light.

On the Edge

Behold, God works all these things, twice, in fact, three times with a man (Job 33:29).

"Just one more chance, please, please. I promise to get it right this time." Ever said that to your parents, or to your teacher, or to God? While your parents or teacher may tire of saying, "Okay, one more time, give it a shot," God never will. Even when you are tired of trying, God will lift you up, give you a pep talk, and tell you to try again. When you don't deserve a second chance, God will let you have one. He loves you so much that He will never give up on you. He longs for you, and He delights in welcoming you back when you've blown it. So if you've given up on God, feel like you've used up all your chances, messed up really big this time—there is great news: You belong to the God who gives you chance after chance. Run to Him.

SEE FOR YOURSELF:
Ps. 130:4; Hos. 14:4;
Luke 7:48; 1 John 1:9

29 "Behold, God works all these *things*,
Twice, *in fact*, three *times* with a man,
30 To bring back his soul from the Pit,
That he may be enlightened with the light
of life.

31 "Give ear, Job, listen to me;
Hold your peace, and I will speak.
32 If you have anything to say, answer me;
Speak, for I desire to justify you.
33 If not, listen to me;

Hold your peace, and I will teach you
wisdom."

ELIHU PROCLAIMS GOD'S JUSTICE

1 Elihu further answered and said:

2 "Hear my words, you wise *men*;
Give ear to me, you who have
knowledge.
3 For the ear tests words
As the palate tastes food.
4 Let us choose justice for ourselves;
Let us know among ourselves what *is*
good.

5 "For Job has said, 'I am righteous,
But God has taken away my justice;
6 Should I lie concerning my right?
My wound *is* incurable, *though I am*
without transgression.'
7 What man *is* like Job,
Who drinks scorn like water,
8 Who goes in company with the workers
of iniquity,
And walks with wicked men?
9 For he has said, 'It profits a man nothing
That he should delight in God.'

10 "Therefore listen to me, you men of
understanding:
Far be it from God *to do* wickedness,
And *from* the Almighty to *commit*
iniquity.
11 For He repays man *according to* his work,
And makes man to find a reward
according to *his* way.
12 Surely God will never do wickedly,
Nor will the Almighty pervert justice.
13 Who gave Him charge over the earth?
Or who appointed *Him over* the whole
world?
14 If He should set His heart on it,
If He should gather to Himself His Spirit
and His breath,
15 All flesh would perish together,
And man would return to dust.

16 "If *you have* understanding, hear this;
Listen to the sound of my words:
17 Should one who hates justice govern?
Will you condemn *Him who is* most just?
18 *Is it fitting* to say to a king, 'You *are*
worthless,'
And to nobles, 'You *are* wicked'?
19 Yet He is not partial to princes,

33:28 [a]Or *my* (Kethib) [b]Or *my* (Kethib)

Nor does He regard the rich more than the poor;
For they *are* all the work of His hands.
20 In a moment they die, in the middle of the night;
The people are shaken and pass away;
The mighty are taken away without a hand.

---

21 "For His eyes *are* on the ways of man,
And He sees all his steps.
22 There is no darkness nor shadow of death
Where the workers of iniquity may hide themselves.
23 For He need not further consider a man,
That he should go before God in judgment.
24 He breaks in pieces mighty men without inquiry,
And sets others in their place.
25 Therefore He knows their works;
He overthrows *them* in the night,
And they are crushed.
26 He strikes them as wicked *men*
In the open sight of others,

27 Because they turned back from Him,
And would not consider any of His ways,
28 So that they caused the cry of the poor to come to Him;
For He hears the cry of the afflicted.
29 When He gives quietness, who then can make trouble?
And when He hides *His* face, who then can see Him,
Whether *it is* against a nation or a man alone?—
30 That the hypocrite should not reign,
Lest the people be ensnared.

31 "For has *anyone* said to God,
'I have borne *chastening*;
I will offend no more;
32 Teach me *what* I do not see;
If I have done iniquity, I will do no more'?
33 Should He repay *it* according to your *terms*,
Just because you disavow it?
You must choose, and not I;
Therefore speak what you know.

34 "Men of understanding say to me,
Wise men who listen to me:
35 'Job speaks without knowledge,
His words *are* without wisdom.'
36 Oh, that Job were tried to the utmost,
Because *his* answers *are like* those of wicked men!
37 For he adds rebellion to his sin;
He claps *his hands* among us,
And multiplies his words against God."

ELIHU CONDEMNS SELF-RIGHTEOUSNESS

1 Moreover Elihu answered and said:

2 "Do you think this is right?
Do you say,
'My righteousness is more than God's'?
3 For you say,
'What advantage will it be to You?
What profit shall I have, more than *if* I had sinned?'

4 "I will answer you,
And your companions with you.
5 Look to the heavens and see;
And behold the clouds—
They are higher than you.
6 If you sin, what do you accomplish against Him?
Or, *if* your transgressions are multiplied, what do you do to Him?

7 If you are righteous, what do you give Him?
  Or what does He receive from your hand?
8 Your wickedness affects a man such as you,
  And your righteousness a son of man.

9 "Because of the multitude of oppressions they cry out;
  They cry out for help because of the arm of the mighty.
10 But no one says, 'Where *is* God my Maker,
  Who gives songs in the night,
11 Who teaches us more than the beasts of the earth,
  And makes us wiser than the birds of heaven?'
12 There they cry out, but He does not answer,
  Because of the pride of evil men.
13 Surely God will not listen to empty *talk*,
  Nor will the Almighty regard it.
14 Although you say you do not see Him,
  Yet justice *is* before Him, and you must wait for Him.
15 And now, because He has not punished in His anger,
  Nor taken much notice of folly,
16 Therefore Job opens his mouth in vain;
  He multiplies words without knowledge."

ELIHU PROCLAIMS GOD'S GOODNESS

1 Elihu also proceeded and said:

2 "Bear with me a little, and I will show you
  That *there are* yet words to speak on God's behalf.
3 I will fetch my knowledge from afar;
  I will ascribe righteousness to my Maker.
4 For truly my words *are* not false;
  One who is perfect in knowledge *is* with you.

5 "Behold, God *is* mighty, but despises *no one*;
  He is mighty in strength of understanding.
6 He does not preserve the life of the wicked,
  But gives justice to the oppressed.
7 He does not withdraw His eyes from the righteous;
  But *they are* on the throne with kings,

For He has seated them forever,
And they are exalted.
8 And if *they are* bound in fetters,
  Held in the cords of affliction,
9 Then He tells them their work and their transgressions—
  That they have acted defiantly.
10 He also opens their ear to instruction,
  And commands that they turn from iniquity.
11 If they obey and serve *Him*,
  They shall spend their days in prosperity,
  And their years in pleasures.
12 But if they do not obey,
  They shall perish by the sword,
  And they shall die without knowledge.[a]

13 "But the hypocrites in heart store up wrath;
  They do not cry for help when He binds them.
14 They die in youth,
  And their life *ends* among the perverted persons.[a]

On the Edge

Behold, God is mighty, but despises no one; He is mighty in strength of understanding (Job 36:5).

Why does God care about everyone? Because each one of us is His creation, fashioned by Him, and completely loved. How does God care? He provides all that we need. He waits patiently for us to seek Him. He is faithful to guide our steps and order our days. He pours grace all over us. What can we do to get God to care about us more? Nothing. We are already cared for completely just because we belong to Him. When will His caring end? Never. He promises to be with us always. How can you be like God? Care about other people even more than you care about yourself.

SEE FOR YOURSELF:
  John 13:34, 35;
    Gal. 2:20;
    1 John 4:7–11

36:12 [a]Masoretic Text reads *as one without knowledge.* **36:14** [a]Hebrew *qedeshim*, that is, those practicing sodomy and prostitution in religious rituals

JONATHAN made a difference

Perhaps the most powerful way in which people make a difference in one another's lives has to do with friendship. Jonathan's friendship wasn't cheap. It cost him his father's trust, though he never betrayed his father. Jonathan made a difference in David's life because he recognized God's hand on David. Jonathan was an able and courageous leader in his own right. If his father hadn't turned from God, Jonathan would have made a good king. Instead, he accepted the role of David's loyal friend.

Jonathan made a difference because he understood the difference between blind and open-eyed loyalty. He had his priorities straight. He knew that loyalty doesn't justify helping someone do wrong. Jonathan's father, King Saul, wanted to kill David. Jonathan neither helped nor prevented his father's plans, but he warned his friend David. Jonathan remained with his father. He died with his father. Jonathan was able to be a loyal son and a loyal friend—to death. How did Jonathan keep his loyalties straight? He had an ultimate loyalty to God and His ways. His human loyalties were always controlled by his loyalty to his heavenly Father. That made the difference. That ultimate loyalty allowed Jonathan to make a difference.

Cutting Edge

YOU can, too!

You have probably found that loyalties at the human level compete for attention. How do you decide between family and friends? The choices can be heartbreaking. They will be practically impossible until you establish a higher, single loyalty. No one deserves your ultimate loyalty but God. Have you established that ultimate loyalty?

Want to know more? Read about Jonathan in (1 Samuel 13—31.)
Note also (2 Samuel 1 and 9.)

DAVID made a difference

Like little brothers often do, David got the jobs no one else wanted. His big brothers got to play soldier while David played shepherd with real sheep. But he turned what others didn't want into an adventure. He did so well tending his father's flock that his heavenly Father entrusted him with a kingdom. What David learned from the sheep made a difference in many people's lives.

The youthful David made good use of his time. He developed his abilities to sing and sling. He practiced singing and playing the harp to the sheep and was later a powerful comfort to King Saul when he played. He became a marksman with his sling as he protected the flock. Later, he made quite an impression on Goliath the giant with that same sling. Goliath didn't see the truth of what God can do with a committed young person until it hit him right between the eyes.

Cutting Edge

We don't know when David actually wrote Psalm 23, the Shepherd's Psalm. But everything in that psalm David learned when he was young. Those early experiences made him. Growing up is not just the passing of a certain number of years; it is the construction of a character. People and places had a big part in creating David's character. But David was also open to God's work in his life. As long has David lived the truth of his words, "The LORD is my shepherd; I shall not want," he made the right kind of difference with his life.

YOU can, too!

The difference you can make may not be apparent right now, but you can be sure it is being constructed. What you are doing these days at home and school may not seem any greater a project than watching a bunch of sheep. You can imagine defeating a giant like Goliath, but what you face is a geometry quiz tomorrow. You want to sing for the multitudes, but you're struggling with piano lessons. When you're having days that aren't so great, it's hard to feel you're on your way to greatness.

Here's the point: Until you can discover God's part in the little, boring things in your life, you will not understand God's part in the big things of life. The more you allow God to make a difference each day in your life, the more your life will make a difference in other's lives.

Want to know more? David's life is recounted in (1 Samuel 16—1 Kings 2.) Read Psalm 23 and identify "places" in your life right now that are like the "places" in that psalm (that is, green pastures, still waters, valley of the shadow of death, and so on).

SOLOMON made a difference

Solomon turned out to be an example of almost everything he preached for and against! He should have listened better to himself. His wisest act was to humbly ask God for wisdom; his most foolish act was to live as if he were exempt from the very truths he taught others. So, for example, he published many proverbs on marriage, but violated every one of them himself.

In his unusual autobiography Ecclesiastes, Solomon gives indication that he realized what a mess he had made out of his life. The book reveals a man who had the unusual circumstance of having the resources and opportunity to have and to try anything. So he did. His life answers the question Jesus asked years later, "What profit is it to a man if he gains the whole world, and loses his own soul?" (Matt. 16:26). Solomon reported that such a man ends up chasing wind.

Solomon certainly made a difference in history. He built a great temple for God in Jerusalem. He enlarged the borders of the kingdom of Israel. He applied wisdom to a system of public works and foreign diplomacy. The treasury of his kingdom overflowed with riches. From a worldly point of view, Solomon was an outstanding success. But his internal life decayed away as he failed to faithfully follow his own advice: "Trust in the LORD with all your heart, and lean not on your own understanding; in all your ways acknowledge Him, and He shall direct your paths" (Prov. 3:5, 6).

YOU can, too! The Bible includes many examples of people who started out well but finished poorly. You can probably think of some examples in our own times. Those who make the best kind of difference are those who don't give up once they begin to live for God.

We don't know how long the race called life will be, but we will fail and fall if we expect it to be a short sprint. The account of the difference you make in your life for God will not be over until God puts the final touches on your story.

Want to know more? In order to get a perspective on Solomon, you should read not only the history of his life and the times he grew up in 2 Sam. 12:24—1 Kin. 11:43 but also his own writings in Proverbs, Ecclesiastes, and Song of Solomon.

NAAMAN'S WIFE'S SERVANT GIRL made a difference

Some heroes in God's great story make a difference while remaining anonymous. Their nameless role highlights God's work. And God always knows who they are. Naaman was a Syrian soldier during the ministry of Elisha the prophet. He contracted leprosy. His wife's servant was a young Jewish girl who had been kidnapped during a Syrian raid on Israel.

The only things we know about this young woman are that both her faith and her compassion were genuine. Instead of resenting her situation, she offered hope of healing to Naaman by suggesting he consult with God's prophet. Her timing was perfect. Naaman was desperate enough to try almost anything. His pride still had to be crushed, but his decision to seek help from God eventually led to his healing.

Cutting Edge

That young girl represents the most numerous category of God's servants. They are in this life unnamed and often overlooked. Their all-too-brief stories hint that God always has a lot more going on in this world that any one of us can keep under observation. But God sees it all. No act of kindness or gesture of faith goes unnoticed. The God who keeps track of sparrows won't miss the brief suggestions, the words of wisdom, and those moments when a true believer gives another person a reason to consider God. In the end, we will find out that many more made a bigger difference than we ever expected.

YOU can, too!

When you live to serve God, you will often find yourself an anonymous participant in His plans. If you insist on recognition, you will probably experience frustration. If you settle for service, with your attention fixed on your divine Master, you can anticipate hearing the word, "Well done, good servant" (Luke 19:17). You will be surprised by what a difference that will make!

Want to know more? This young girl's story is told in 2 Kings 5:1–27.

15 He delivers the poor in their affliction,
And opens their ears in oppression.

16 "Indeed He would have brought you out
of dire distress,
Into a broad place where *there is* no
restraint;
And what is set on your table *would be*
full of richness.
17 But you are filled with the judgment due
the wicked;
Judgment and justice take hold *of you.*
18 Because *there is* wrath, *beware* lest He take
you away with *one* blow;
For a large ransom would not help you
avoid *it.*
19 Will your riches,
Or all the mighty forces,
Keep you from distress?
20 Do not desire the night,
When people are cut off in their place.
21 Take heed, do not turn to iniquity,
For you have chosen this rather than
affliction.

22 "Behold, God is exalted by His power;
Who teaches like Him?
23 Who has assigned Him His way,
Or who has said, 'You have done
wrong'?

ELIHU PROCLAIMS GOD'S MAJESTY

24 "Remember to magnify His work,
Of which men have sung.
25 Everyone has seen it;
Man looks on *it* from afar.

26 "Behold, God *is* great, and we do not
know *Him;*
Nor can the number of His years *be*
discovered.
27 For He draws up drops of water,
Which distill as rain from the mist,
28 Which the clouds drop down
And pour abundantly on man.
29 Indeed, can *anyone* understand the
spreading of clouds,
The thunder from His canopy?
30 Look, He scatters His light upon it,
And covers the depths of the sea.
31 For by these He judges the peoples;
He gives food in abundance.
32 He covers *His* hands with lightning,
And commands it to strike.
33 His thunder declares it,
The cattle also, concerning the rising
storm.

WHAT'S IT MEAN?

Electrical storms are pretty common in Palestine during the spring and fall. Not only do these storms bring lightning and thunder; they bring strong winds, dust clouds, heavy rains, and damaging hail. You can understand why the writers of the Bible used these storms to illustrate the power of God.

Job 36:32, 33

1 "At this also my heart trembles,
And leaps from its place.
2 Hear attentively the thunder of His voice,
And the rumbling *that* comes from His
mouth.
3 He sends it forth under the whole
heaven,
His lightning to the ends of the earth.
4 After it a voice roars;
He thunders with His majestic voice,
And He does not restrain them when His
voice is heard.
5 God thunders marvelously with His
voice;
He does great things which we cannot
comprehend.
6 For He says to the snow, 'Fall on the
earth';
Likewise to the gentle rain and the heavy
rain of His strength.
7 He seals the hand of every man,
That all men may know His work.
8 The beasts go into dens,
And remain in their lairs.
9 From the chamber *of the south* comes the
whirlwind,
And cold from the scattering winds *of the
north.*
10 By the breath of God ice is given,
And the broad waters are frozen.
11 Also with moisture He saturates the thick
clouds;
He scatters His bright clouds.
12 And they swirl about, being turned by
His guidance,
That they may do whatever He
commands them

On the face of the whole earth.[a]

13 He causes it to come,
Whether for correction,
Or for His land,
Or for mercy.

14 "Listen to this, O Job;
Stand still and consider the
wondrous works of
God.

15 Do you know when
God dispatches them,
And causes the light of
His cloud to shine?

16 Do you know how the
clouds are balanced,
Those wondrous works of
Him who is perfect in knowledge?

17 Why *are* your garments hot,
When He quiets the earth by the south
wind?

> "Listen to this, O Job;
> stand still and consider the
> wondrous works of God."
> (Job 37:14)

18 With Him, have you spread out the skies,
Strong as a cast metal mirror?

19 "Teach us what we should say to Him,
For we can prepare nothing because of
the darkness.

20 Should He be told that I
wish to speak?
If a man were to speak,
surely he would be
swallowed up.

21 Even now *men* cannot
look at the light *when
it is* bright in the skies,
When the wind has
passed and cleared
them.

22 He comes from the north
as golden *splendor;*
With God *is* awesome majesty.

23 *As for* the Almighty, we cannot find Him;
He is excellent in power,
In judgment and abundant justice;
He does not oppress.

24 Therefore men fear Him;
He shows no partiality to any *who are*
wise of heart."

THE LORD REVEALS HIS OMNIPOTENCE TO JOB

1 Then the LORD answered Job out of the
whirlwind, and said:

2 "Who *is* this who darkens counsel
By words without knowledge?

3 Now prepare yourself like a man;

On the Edge

*Even now men cannot look at
the light when it is bright in the
skies, when the wind has passed and
cleared them. He comes from the north
as golden splendor; with God is
awesome majesty (Job 37:21, 22).*

Ever tried to look at the midday sun?
You can't—and you're not even supposed to
try. It will damage your eyes. The sun is
thousands of miles away from the earth,
and yet you can't look at its brightness. If
we were to travel to the sun, we would burn
up long before we got there because of the
intensity of the heat. There is nothing on
this earth to compare with the
power of the sun. Job says that
the power of God is even brighter
than the sun. Imagine that. To
God the sun is probably like a nice
campfire. It's a fire that God built Himself
and hung in the heavens. We sometimes
forget how awesome God is. The next time
you watch a sunset, think about God and
remember that His power is even stronger.

SEE FOR YOURSELF:
Deut. 10:17;
1 Chr. 29:11, 12;
Ps. 47:2

WHAT'S IT MEAN?

Here's a word you can throw around the next
time you want to show someone how much you know
about biblical things: *theophany*. It means a visible appearance of
God. Job witnessed a theophany when the Lord came to him in the
whirlwind. As was true when Moses carried on a conversation with
the burning bush, Job didn't actually see God; he
saw the effects of God's presence.

Job 38:1

I will question you, and you shall answer Me.

4 "Where were you when I laid the
     foundations of the earth?
     Tell *Me,* if you have understanding.
5 Who determined its measurements?
     Surely you know!
     Or who stretched the line upon it?
6 To what were its foundations fastened?
     Or who laid its cornerstone,
7 When the morning stars sang together,
     And all the sons of God shouted for joy?

8 "Or *who* shut in the sea with doors,
     When it burst forth *and* issued from the
      womb;
9 When I made the clouds its garment,
     And thick darkness its swaddling band;
10 When I fixed My limit for it,
     And set bars and doors;
11 When I said,
     'This far you may come, but no farther,
     And here your proud waves must stop!'

12 "Have you commanded the morning since
     your days *began,*
     And caused the dawn to know its place,
13 That it might take hold of the ends of the
     earth,
     And the wicked be shaken out of it?
14 It takes on form like clay *under* a seal,
     And stands out like a garment.
15 From the wicked their light is withheld,
     And the upraised arm is broken.

16 "Have you entered the springs of the sea?
     Or have you walked in search of the
      depths?
17 Have the gates of death been revealed to
     you?
     Or have you seen the doors of the
      shadow of death?
18 Have you comprehended the breadth of
     the earth?
     Tell *Me,* if you know all this.

19 "Where *is* the way *to* the dwelling of light?
     And darkness, where *is* its place,
20 That you may take it to its territory,
     That you may know the paths *to* its home?
21 Do you know *it,* because you were born
     then,
     Or *because* the number of your days *is*
     great?

22 "Have you entered the treasury of snow,
     Or have you seen the treasury of hail,
23 Which I have reserved for the time of
     trouble,
     For the day of battle and war?
24 By what way is light diffused,
     Or the east wind scattered over the earth?

25 "Who has divided a channel for the
     overflowing *water,*
     Or a path for the thunderbolt,
26 To cause it to rain on a land *where there is*
     no one,
     A wilderness in which *there is* no man;
27 To satisfy the desolate waste,
     And cause to spring forth the growth of
     tender grass?
28 Has the rain a father?
     Or who has begotten the drops of dew?
29 From whose womb comes the ice?
     And the frost of heaven, who gives it
     birth?
30 The waters harden like stone,
     And the surface of the deep is frozen.

31 "Can you bind the cluster of the Pleiades,
     Or loose the belt of Orion?
32 Can you bring out Mazzaroth[a] in its
     season?
     Or can you guide the Great Bear with its
     cubs?
33 Do you know the ordinances of the
     heavens?
     Can you set their dominion over the
     earth?

34 "Can you lift up your voice to the clouds,
     That an abundance of water may cover
     you?
35 Can you send out lightnings, that they
     may go,
     And say to you, 'Here we *are!'?
36 Who has put wisdom in the mind?[a]
     Or who has given understanding to the
     heart?
37 Who can number the clouds by wisdom?
     Or who can pour out the bottles of
     heaven,
38 When the dust hardens in clumps,
     And the clods cling together?

39 "Can you hunt the prey for the lion,
     Or satisfy the appetite of the young lions,
40 When they crouch in *their* dens,
     Or lurk in their lairs to lie in wait?

38:32 [a]Literally *Constellations*   **38:36** [a]Literally *inward parts*

41 Who provides food for the raven,
When its young ones cry to God,
And wander about for lack of food?

1 "Do you know the time when the wild
mountain goats bear young?
Or can you mark when the deer gives
birth?
2 Can you number the months *that* they
fulfill?
Or do you know the time when they bear
young?
3 They bow down,
They bring forth their young,
They deliver their offspring.*a*
4 Their young ones are healthy,
They grow strong with grain;
They depart and do not return to them.

5 "Who set the wild donkey free?
Who loosed the bonds of the onager,
6 Whose home I have made the wilderness,
And the barren land his dwelling?
7 He scorns the tumult of the city;
He does not heed the shouts of the driver.
8 The range of the mountains *is* his pasture,
And he searches after every green thing.

9 "Will the wild ox be willing to serve you?
Will he bed by your manger?
10 Can you bind the wild ox in the furrow
with ropes?
Or will he plow the valleys behind you?
11 Will you trust him because his strength *is*
great?
Or will you leave your labor to him?
12 Will you trust him to bring home your
grain,
And gather it to your threshing floor?

13 "The wings of the ostrich wave proudly,
But are her wings and pinions *like the*
kindly stork's?
14 For she leaves her eggs on the ground,
And warms them in the dust;
15 She forgets that a foot may crush them,
Or that a wild beast may break them.
16 She treats her young harshly, as though
they were not hers;
Her labor is in vain, without concern,
17 Because God deprived her of wisdom,
And did not endow her with
understanding.
18 When she lifts herself on high,
She scorns the horse and its rider.

W H A T' S
IT
M E A N ?

Ostriches have a reputation
for being dumb animals because of the way they
treat their eggs. Rather than protect their young like most birds
do, ostriches leave their eggs unattended, covered over with
sand, throughout the day.
Job 39:13–17

19 "Have you given the horse strength?
Have you clothed his neck with thunder?*a*
20 Can you frighten him like a locust?
His majestic snorting strikes terror.
21 He paws in the valley, and rejoices in *his*
strength;
He gallops into the clash of arms.
22 He mocks at fear, and is not frightened;
Nor does he turn back from the sword.
23 The quiver rattles against him,
The glittering spear and javelin.
24 He devours the distance with fierceness
and rage;
Nor does he come to a halt because the
trumpet *has* sounded.
25 At *the blast of* the trumpet he says, 'Aha!'
He smells the battle from afar,
The thunder of captains and shouting.

26 "Does the hawk fly by your wisdom,
And spread its wings toward the south?
27 Does the eagle mount up at your
command,
And make its nest on high?
28 On the rock it dwells and resides,
On the crag of the rock and the stronghold.
29 From there it spies out the prey;
Its eyes observe from afar.
30 Its young ones suck up blood;
And where the slain *are*, there it *is*."

1Moreover the LORD answered
Job, and said:

2 "Shall the one who
contends with the
Almighty correct *Him*?

GOD

Do we have
a right to
correct God?
(40:2)

39:3 *a*Literally *pangs*, figurative of offspring   39:19 *a*Or *a mane*

He who rebukes God, let him answer it."

JOB'S RESPONSE TO GOD

³Then Job answered the LORD and said:

4 "Behold, I am vile;
What shall I answer You?
I lay my hand over my mouth.

5 Once I have spoken, but I will not answer;
Yes, twice, but I will proceed no further."

GOD'S CHALLENGE TO JOB

⁶Then the LORD answered Job out of the whirlwind, and said:

7 "Now prepare yourself like a man;
I will question you, and you shall answer Me:

8 "Would you indeed annul My judgment?
Would you condemn Me that you may be justified?

9 Have you an arm like God?
Or can you thunder with a voice like His?

10 Then adorn yourself *with* majesty and splendor,
And array yourself with glory and beauty.

11 Disperse the rage of your wrath;
Look on everyone *who is* proud, and humble him.

12 Look on everyone *who is* proud, *and* bring him low;
Tread down the wicked in their place.

13 Hide them in the dust together,
Bind their faces in hidden *darkness*.

14 Then I will also confess to you
That your own right hand can save you.

15 "Look now at the behemoth,ᵃ which I made *along* with you;
He eats grass like an ox.

16 See now, his strength *is* in his hips,
And his power *is* in his stomach muscles.

17 He moves his tail like a cedar;
The sinews of his thighs are tightly knit.

18 His bones *are like* beams of bronze,
His ribs like bars of iron.

19 He *is* the first of the ways of God;
Only He who made him can bring near His sword.

20 Surely the mountains yield food for him,
And all the beasts of the field play there.

21 He lies under the lotus trees,
In a covert of reeds and marsh.

22 The lotus trees cover him *with* their shade;
The willows by the brook surround him.

23 Indeed the river may rage,
Yet he is not disturbed;
He is confident, though the Jordan gushes into his mouth,

24 *Though* he takes it in his eyes,
Or one pierces *his* nose with a snare.

1 "Can you draw out Leviathanᵃ with a hook,
Or *snare* his tongue with a line *which* you lower?

2 Can you put a reed through his nose,
Or pierce his jaw with a hook?

3 Will he make many supplications to you?
Will he speak softly to you?

4 Will he make a covenant with you?
Will you take him as a servant forever?

5 Will you play with him as *with* a bird,
Or will you leash him for your maidens?

6 Will *your* companions make a banquetᵃ of him?
Will they apportion him among the merchants?

7 Can you fill his skin with harpoons,
Or his head with fishing spears?

8 Lay your hand on him;
Remember the battle—
Never do it again!

9 Indeed, *any* hope of *overcoming* him is false;
Shall *one not* be overwhelmed at the sight of him?

10 No one *is so* fierce that he would dare stir him up.
Who then is able to stand against Me?

11 Who has preceded Me, that I should pay *him*?
Everything under heaven is Mine.

12 "I will not concealᵃ his limbs,
His mighty power, or his graceful proportions.

13 Who can remove his outer coat?
Who can approach *him* with a double bridle?

14 Who can open the doors of his face,
With his terrible teeth all around?

15 *His* rows of scales are *his* pride,
Shut up tightly *as with* a seal;

16 One is so near another
That no air can come between them;

40:15 ᵃA large animal, exact identity unknown **41:1** ᵃA large sea creature, exact identity unknown
41:6 ᵃOr *bargain over him* **41:12** ᵃLiterally *keep silent about*

On the Edge

Who has preceded Me, that I should pay him? Everything under heaven is Mine (Job 41:11).

Ever feel like the world is out of control? People are doing the craziest things with the place God has given them. Abusing their bodies with any substance imaginable. Treating one another with total disrespect. Violent attitudes and behavior are rampant. It would be easy to think that God has turned His back and left. He has gotten fed up with the whole mess and just quit. Who would blame Him? We would have quit a long time ago. But not God.

He is still in command of the world. His power has not been weakened. His plans have not been changed. He isn't even surprised at how badly we've messed up. He knows that when we choose not to follow Him, we wander around, trying to fix everything ourselves, and finally make things worse. The Commander is still leading. The world still belongs to Him. Will you follow, or will you join the chaos?

SEE FOR YOURSELF:
2 Sam. 23:5; Is. 9:7;
Mark 1:27

17 They are joined one to another,
They stick together and cannot be parted.
18 His sneezings flash forth light,
And his eyes *are* like the eyelids of the morning.
19 Out of his mouth go burning lights;
Sparks of fire shoot out.
20 Smoke goes out of his nostrils,
As *from* a boiling pot and burning rushes.
21 His breath kindles coals,
And a flame goes out of his mouth.
22 Strength dwells in his neck,
And sorrow dances before him.
23 The folds of his flesh are joined together;
They are firm on him and cannot be moved.
24 His heart is as hard as stone,
Even as hard as the lower *millstone.*
25 When he raises himself up, the mighty are afraid;
Because of his crashings they are beside[a] themselves.

41:25 [a]Or *purify themselves*

26 *Though* the sword reaches him, it cannot avail;
Nor does spear, dart, or javelin.
27 He regards iron as straw,
And bronze as rotten wood.
28 The arrow cannot make him flee;
Slingstones become like stubble to him.
29 Darts are regarded as straw;
He laughs at the threat of javelins.
30 His undersides *are* like sharp potsherds;
He spreads pointed *marks* in the mire.
31 He makes the deep boil like a pot;
He makes the sea like a pot of ointment.
32 He leaves a shining wake behind him;
One would think the deep had white hair.
33 On earth there is nothing like him,
Which is made without fear.
34 He beholds every high *thing;*
He *is* king over all the children of pride."

JOB'S REPENTANCE AND RESTORATION

1 Then Job answered the LORD and said:

2 "I know that You can do everything,
And that no purpose *of Yours* can be withheld from You.
3 *You asked,* 'Who *is* this who hides counsel without knowledge?'
Therefore I have uttered what I did not understand,
Things too wonderful for me, which I did not know.

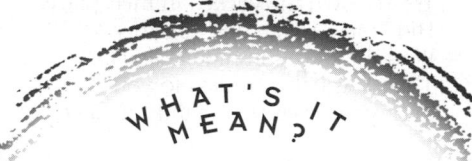

WHAT'S IT MEAN?

Do you know what your name means? If you had lived in Bible times, you would have. In the ancient world, a person's name was important because it revealed something about the person. The names of Job's daughters all reflect their beauty. *Jemimah* means "Turtledove." (Don't laugh—doves are used in the Bible as symbols of beauty, innocence, and gentleness.) *Keziah* means "Cinnamon," which was a plant that produced oil for perfumes. *Keren-Happuch* means "Horn, or Container, of Antimony." Antimony was a metal-gray mineral that was ground to powder and worn as eye makeup.
Job 42:13, 14

4   Listen, please, and let me speak;
     You *said*, 'I will question you, and you
          shall answer Me'.

5   "I have heard of You by the hearing of the
          ear,
     But now my eye sees You.
6   Therefore I abhor *myself*,
     And repent in dust and ashes."

⁷And so it was, after the LORD had spoken these words to Job, that the LORD said to Eliphaz the Temanite, "My wrath is aroused against you and your two friends, for you have not spoken of Me *what is* right, as My servant Job *has*. ⁸Now therefore, take for yourselves seven bulls and seven rams, go to My servant Job, and offer up for yourselves a burnt offering; and My servant Job shall pray for you. For I will accept him, lest I deal with you *according to your* folly; because you have not spoken of Me *what is* right, as My servant Job *has*."

⁹So Eliphaz the Temanite and Bildad the Shuhite *and* Zophar the Naamathite went and did as the LORD commanded them; for the LORD had accepted Job. ¹⁰And the LORD restored Job's losses*ᵃ* when he prayed for his friends. Indeed the LORD gave Job twice as much as he had before. ¹¹Then all his brothers, all his sisters, and all those who had been his acquaintances before, came to him and ate food with him in his house; and they consoled him and comforted him for all the adversity that the LORD had brought upon him. Each one gave him a piece of silver and each a ring of gold.

¹²Now the LORD blessed the latter *days* of Job more than his beginning; for he had fourteen thousand sheep, six thousand camels, one thousand yoke of oxen, and one thousand female donkeys. ¹³He also had seven sons and three daughters. ¹⁴And he called the name of the first Jemimah, the name of the second Keziah, and the name of the third Keren-Happuch. ¹⁵In all the land were found no women *so* beautiful as the daughters of Job; and their father gave them an inheritance among their brothers.

¹⁶After this Job lived one hundred and forty years, and saw his children and grandchildren *for* four generations. ¹⁷So Job died, old and full of days.

42:10 *ᵃ*Literally *Job's captivity*, that is, what was captured from Job

CONTENT

Music is a gift, but it is also a tool and a talent. Our society uses music to do everything from selling to inspiring to dancing to teaching. God uses music, too. The official roles in the early worship of the Jews included official musicians and song leaders. While their music was different from the music you hear today, it was just as important in worship.

Psalms is basically a book of lyric sheets. Some of the lyrics tell who wrote them. Some tell why the songs were written. They are a lot like a CD cover in that way. Some of the Psalms have musical notations like "Selah."

The topics of the psalms were like a mixture of hits from a contemporary Christian radio station. Worship was a hot topic, but it wasn't the only topic. Some psalms were about regret; some were about joy; some were about anger. Music did the same thing for those ancient songwriters that it does for songwriters today: it helped them process life. Some of the psalms were honest to the point of being raw, but all of them related to living a life of faith in a world that is sometimes faithless.

Outline

1—41 .... Book I
42—72 .... Book II
73—89 .... Book III
90—106 .... Book IV
107—150 .... Book V

Purpose

We can come to God freely, whether our hearts are broken or filled with praise.

Theme

Communion with God in Prayer and Praise

Date of writing

1410–c. 430 B.C.

Bible Talk

The Ancient Hebrew Worship Band

If you play in an acoustic band at church, you probably have drums, guitar, and a keyboard as your main instruments. If you play in an orchestra, you have a string section and some brass and woodwinds.

If you had played in an ancient Hebrew worship band of any kind, you would also have had instruments that you could blow into, or strum, or beat, but they would have looked a little different.

Your drums would have been called tambourines. The cymbals would have been small enough to fit on your fingers. The strings might have been laid down on your lap to play. The horns might have been made from animal horns rather than from metal.

HEBREW MUSIC AND POETRY

While the psalms are like lyric sheets, they don't rhyme like lyrics we learn today. Hebrew poetry was built on a concept instead of a rhyming scheme. The first line stated the concept. The second line built on it.

Hebrew poetry also used alphabetical structures. In its original language, one of the psalms is written so that each line starts with a letter of the alphabet . . . *in order* no less. So, when you read a psalm, it won't be sing-songy. And if you heard a psalm sung with its original tune, it wouldn't be catchy to your ear. But the truth of the psalm would fit today as surely as when it was written.

Book One: Psalms 1—41

PSALM 1

THE WAY OF THE RIGHTEOUS AND THE END OF THE UNGODLY

1 Blessed *is* the man
Who walks not in the
counsel of the
ungodly,
Nor stands in the
path of sinners,
Nor sits in the seat of
the scornful;

2 But his delight *is* in the law of
the LORD,

> "But his delight is in the law of the LORD, and in His law he meditates day and night."
> (Psalm 1:2)

And in His law he meditates day and
night.

3 He shall be like a tree
Planted by the rivers of water,
That brings forth its
fruit in its season,
Whose leaf also shall
not wither;
And whatever he does
shall prosper.

4 The ungodly *are* not so,
But *are* like the chaff
which the wind
drives away.

5 Therefore the ungodly
shall not stand in
the judgment,
Nor sinners in the congregation of the
righteous.

6 For the LORD knows the way of the
righteous,
But the way of the ungodly shall perish.

PSALM 2

THE MESSIAH'S TRIUMPH AND KINGDOM

1 Why do the nations rage,
And the people plot a vain thing?
2 The kings of the earth set themselves,
And the rulers take counsel together,
Against the LORD and against His
Anointed, *saying,*
3 "Let us break Their bonds in pieces
And cast away Their cords from us."

On the Edge

He shall be like a tree planted by the rivers of water, that brings forth its fruit in its season, whose leaf also shall not wither; and whatever he does shall prosper (Ps. 1:3).

Think about a tree growing beside a river. Would it be a dry, ugly tree with brown, cracking leaves? No, that tree would always be alive and full with lush, green leaves. Even in the middle of a drought, that tree would thrive because the river would give it all the water it needed.

"He shall be like a tree planted by the rivers of water." The word *he* refers to the godly man described in verses 1 and 2. This individual doesn't listen to friends or other people who tell him to go against what God wants. He doesn't make fun of God, even if it seems like everyone else does. This man is delighted when he thinks about what God says, so the man does what pleases Him.

If you've made up your mind to follow Jesus, ask yourself if you fit that description. *You* are like that tree growing beside a river. God's Spirit is the river that flows by you and offers you all the life and strength you need. When you get your life from His Spirit, you're always able to succeed in God's eyes, even if everything around you seems out of control.

SEE FOR YOURSELF:
Num. 24:6, 7;
Ps. 52:8; Jer. 17:7, 8;
Zech. 14:8

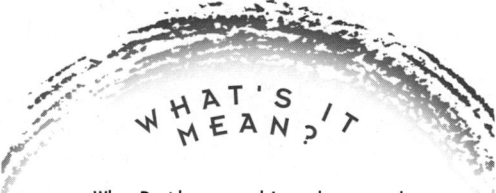

WHAT'S IT MEAN?

When David conquered Jerusalem around 1000 B.C., he got something extra in the process—an ancient Jebusite fortress known as Zion. The fortress itself, which was located in the highest part of the city, didn't amount to much. Its name, for some reason, did. Years later, when Solomon built the temple on Mount Moriah, the entire area in and around Jerusalem came to be known as Zion. Eventually, Zion was used to refer to the entire nation of Israel.

Psalm 2:6

4 He who sits in the heavens shall laugh;
   The LORD shall hold them in derision.
5 Then He shall speak to them in His
       wrath,
   And distress them in His deep displeasure:
6 "Yet I have set My King
   On My holy hill of Zion."

7 "I will declare the decree:
   The LORD has said to Me,
   'You *are* My Son,
   Today I have begotten You.
8 Ask of Me, and I will give *You*
   The nations *for* Your inheritance,
   And the ends of the earth *for* Your
       possession.
9 You shall break[a] them with a rod of iron;
   You shall dash them to pieces like a
       potter's vessel.'"

10 Now therefore, be wise, O kings;
   Be instructed, you judges of the earth.
11 Serve the LORD with fear,
   And rejoice with trembling.
12 Kiss the Son,[a] lest He[b] be angry,
   And you perish *in* the way,
   When His wrath is kindled but a little.
   Blessed *are* all those who put their trust in
       Him.

PSALM 3

THE LORD HELPS HIS TROUBLED PEOPLE

A Psalm of David when he fled
from Absalom his son.

1 LORD, how they have increased who
       trouble me!
   Many *are* they who rise up against me.
2 Many *are* they who say of me,
   "*There is* no help for him in God." Selah

3 But You, O LORD, *are* a shield for me,
   My glory and the One who lifts up my
       head.
4 I cried to the LORD with my voice,
   And He heard me from His holy hill. Selah

5 I lay down and slept;
   I awoke, for the LORD sustained me.
6 I will not be afraid of ten thousands of
       people

Who have set *themselves* against me all
       around.

7 Arise, O LORD;
   Save me, O my God!
   For You have struck all my enemies on
       the cheekbone;
   You have broken the teeth of the ungodly.
8 Salvation *belongs* to the LORD.
   Your blessing *is* upon Your people.   Selah

PSALM 4

THE SAFETY OF THE FAITHFUL

To the Chief Musician. With stringed
instruments. A Psalm of David.

1 Hear me when I call, O God of my
       righteousness!
   You have relieved me in *my* distress;
   Have mercy on me, and hear my prayer.

2 How long, O you sons of men,
   Will you turn my glory to shame?
   How long will you love worthlessness
   And seek falsehood?   Selah
3 But know that the LORD has set apart[a] for
       Himself him who is godly;
   The LORD will hear when I call to Him.

WHAT'S IT MEAN?

The heart's not simply a hollow,
muscular organ, as far as Bible writers were
concerned. They believed the heart is the center of a person's character. They believed it's the source not only of emotions, but also of
thoughts and decision making. They believed that both good and
evil actions get their start in the heart.
Psalm 4:4

4 Be angry, and do not sin.
   Meditate within your heart on your bed,
       and be still.   Selah

2:9 [a]Following Masoretic Text and Targum; Septuagint, Syriac, and Vulgate read *rule* (compare Revelation 2:27).   **2:12** [a]Septuagint and Vulgate read *Embrace discipline;* Targum reads *Receive instruction.* [b]Septuagint reads *the LORD.*   **4:3** [a]Many Hebrew manuscripts, Septuagint, Targum, and Vulgate read *made wonderful.*

5 Offer the sacrifices of righteousness,
And put your trust in the LORD.

6 *There are* many who say,
"Who will show us *any* good?"
LORD, lift up the light of Your
countenance upon us.
7 You have put gladness in my heart,
More than in the season that their grain
and wine increased.
8 I will both lie down in peace, and sleep;
For You alone, O LORD, make me dwell in
safety.

PSALM 5

A PRAYER FOR GUIDANCE

To the Chief Musician. With flutes.[a]
A Psalm of David.

1 Give ear to my words, O LORD,
Consider my meditation.
2 Give heed to the voice of my cry,
My King and my God,
For to You I will pray.
3 My voice You shall hear in the morning,
O LORD;
In the morning I will direct *it* to You,
And I will look up.

4 For You *are* not a God who takes pleasure
in wickedness,
Nor shall evil dwell with You.
5 The boastful shall not stand in Your sight;
You hate all workers of iniquity.
6 You shall destroy those who speak
falsehood;
The LORD abhors the bloodthirsty and
deceitful man.

7 But as for me, I will come into Your
house in the multitude of Your mercy;
In fear of You I will worship toward Your
holy temple.
8 Lead me, O LORD, in Your righteousness
because of my enemies;
Make Your way straight before my face.

9 For *there is* no faithfulness in their
mouth;
Their inward part *is* destruction;
Their throat *is* an open tomb;
They flatter with their tongue.
10 Pronounce them guilty, O God!
Let them fall by their own counsels;

Cast them out in the multitude of their
transgressions,
For they have rebelled against You.

11 But let all those rejoice who put their trust
in You;
Let them ever shout for joy, because You
defend them;
Let those also who love Your
name
Be joyful in You.
12 For You, O LORD, will
bless the righteous;
With favor You will
surround him as *with*
a shield.

BLESSING
Does
God bless
ungodly
people?
(5:12)

PSALM 6

A PRAYER OF FAITH IN TIME OF DISTRESS

To the Chief Musician. With stringed
instruments. On an eight-stringed harp.[a]
A Psalm of David.

1 O LORD, do not rebuke me in Your anger,
Nor chasten me in Your hot displeasure.
2 Have mercy on me, O LORD, for I *am*
weak;
O LORD, heal me, for my bones are
troubled.
3 My soul also is greatly troubled;
But You, O LORD—how long?

4 Return, O LORD, deliver me!
Oh, save me for Your mercies' sake!
5 For in death *there is* no remembrance of
You;
In the grave who will give You thanks?

6 I am weary with my groaning;
All night I make my bed swim;
I drench my couch with my tears.
7 My eye wastes away because of grief;
It grows old because of all my enemies.

8 Depart from me, all you workers of
iniquity;
For the LORD has heard the voice of my
weeping.
9 The LORD has heard my supplication;
The LORD will receive my prayer.
10 Let all my enemies be ashamed and
greatly troubled;
Let them turn back *and* be ashamed
suddenly.

5:title [a]Hebrew *nehiloth*   **6:title** [a]Hebrew *sheminith*

PSALM 7

PRAYER AND PRAISE FOR DELIVERANCE FROM ENEMIES

A Meditation[a] of David, which he sang
to the LORD concerning the words
of Cush, a Benjamite.

1 O LORD my God, in You I put my trust;
Save me from all those who persecute
me;
And deliver me,
2 Lest they tear me like a lion,
Rending *me* in pieces, while *there is* none
to deliver.

3 O LORD my God, if I have done this:
If there is iniquity in my hands,
4 If I have repaid evil to him who was at
peace with me,
Or have plundered my enemy without
cause,
5 Let the enemy pursue me and overtake
me;
Yes, let him trample my life to the earth,
And lay my honor in the dust.   Selah

6 Arise, O LORD, in Your anger;
Lift Yourself up because of the rage of my
enemies,
Rise up for me[a] *to* the judgment You have
commanded!
7 So the congregation of the peoples shall
surround You;

On the Edge

*My defense is of God, who saves
the upright in heart (Ps. 7:10).*
God protects the person whose heart
is right toward Him. Having your heart
right toward Him doesn't have anything to
do with being perfect or knocking yourself
out trying to do the right thing all the time.
A person who has an upright heart knows
that he or she isn't perfect. That person
realizes that his only hope comes from the
fact that Jesus died to make things right
for him.
Admitting those things takes humility.
That's a word that most people don't talk
about very often, maybe because their
picture of humility is a mealy-mouthed
person who looks at the floor all
the time. But for a real picture of
humility, look at Jesus. It's one
of the most outstanding parts of
His personality.
A heart that's humble is the kind of
heart God is looking for. That's the kind of
person He can use to get the job done. He
protects that person in a special way because He knows that person is ready to do
what He wants.

SEE FOR YOURSELF:
Job 5:19; Ps. 121:7, 8;
2 Thess. 3:3

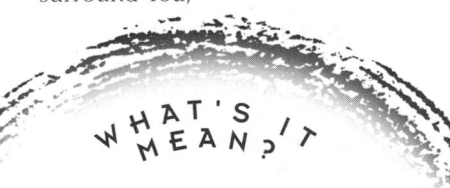

WHAT'S IT MEAN?

No one knows for sure who Cush the
Benjamite was, but he may have been a buddy of
Saul's since they both came from the tribe of Benjamin. Saul's
jealous rages, which were fueled by his mental problems, prompted
him to try to kill David on several occasions. Anyone wanting to get
in good with the king, then, simply had to tell a lie about David to
reinforce Saul's delusions. Some of Saul's supporters
even tried to kill David themselves.

Psalm 7:1 and psalm title

For their sakes, therefore, return on high.
8 The LORD shall judge the peoples;
Judge me, O LORD, according to my
righteousness,
And according to my integrity within me.

9 Oh, let the wickedness of the wicked
come to an end,
But establish the just;
For the righteous God tests the hearts and
minds.
10 My defense *is* of God,
Who saves the upright in heart.

11 God *is* a just judge,
And God is angry *with the wicked* every
day.
12 If he does not turn back,
He will sharpen His sword;

7:title [a]Hebrew *Shiggaion*   **7:6** [a]Following Masoretic Text, Targum, and Vulgate; Septuagint reads *O LORD
my God.*

He bends His bow and makes it ready.
13 He also prepares for Himself instruments
of death;
He makes His arrows into fiery shafts.

14 Behold, *the wicked* brings forth iniquity;
Yes, he conceives trouble and brings forth
falsehood.
15 He made a pit and dug it out,
And has fallen into the ditch *which* he
made.
16 His trouble shall return upon his own
head,
And his violent dealing shall come down
on his own crown.

17 I will praise the LORD according to His
righteousness,
And will sing praise to the name of the
LORD Most High.

PSALM 8

THE GLORY OF THE LORD IN CREATION

To the Chief Musician. On the instrument
of Gath.[a] A Psalm of David.

1 O LORD, our Lord,
How excellent *is* Your name in all the
earth,
Who have set Your glory above the
heavens!

2 Out of the mouth of babes and nursing
infants
You have ordained strength,
Because of Your enemies,
That You may silence the enemy and the
avenger.

3 When I consider Your heavens, the work
of Your fingers,
The moon and the stars, which You have
ordained,
4 What is man that You are mindful of him,
And the son of man that You visit him?
5 For You have made him a little lower
than the angels,[a]
And You have crowned him with glory
and honor.

6 You have made him to have dominion
over the works of Your hands;
You have put all *things* under his feet,

On the Edge

*For You have made him a little
lower than the angels, and You
have crowned him with glory and
honor (Ps. 8:5).*

In this psalm, David is amazed that the
awesome God of heaven would use people to
rule the earth. David says that we seem like
weaklings, not worthy of such a place of
honor. Has anyone told you lately that you
are worth a crown of glory? worth a place of
honor? Well, you are. And David says that's
the way God thinks of you. Sometimes it
may seem like your worth comes from your
report card or your batting average, but it
doesn't. Accomplishments are
great, but they don't make you
more acceptable to God. You
couldn't get God to love you more,
even if you tried. He has loved you completely from the first time He thought of
you. He's your biggest fan. He adores you.
You hold a place of honor in His heart. He's
so proud of you and so in love with you that
He's put a crown of glory and honor on you.

SEE FOR YOURSELF:
Luke 2:32; Rom. 2:10;
2 Tim. 2:10

7 All sheep and oxen—
Even the beasts of the field,
8 The birds of the air,
And the fish of the sea
That pass through the paths of the seas.

9 O LORD, our Lord,
How excellent *is* Your name in all the
earth!

PSALM 9

PRAYER AND THANKSGIVING FOR THE LORD'S RIGHTEOUS JUDGMENTS

To the Chief Musician. To *the tune of* "Death
of the Son."[a] A Psalm of David.

1 I will praise *You*, O LORD, with my whole
heart;
I will tell of all Your marvelous works.
2 I will be glad and rejoice in You;

8:title [a]Hebrew *Al Gittith*   **8:5** [a]Hebrew *Elohim, God*; Septuagint, Syriac, Targum, and Jewish tradition
translate as *angels*.   **9:title** [a]Hebrew *Muth Labben*

I will sing praise to Your name, O Most
High.

3 When my enemies turn back,
They shall fall and perish at Your
presence.
4 For You have maintained my right and
my cause;
You sat on the throne judging in
righteousness.
5 You have rebuked the nations,
You have destroyed the wicked;
You have blotted out their name forever
and ever.

6 O enemy, destructions are
finished forever!
And you have destroyed
cities;
Even their memory has
perished.
7 But the LORD shall
endure forever;
He has prepared His throne for judgment.
8 He shall judge the world in righteousness,
And He shall administer judgment for the
peoples in uprightness.

9 The LORD also will be a refuge for the
oppressed,
A refuge in times of trouble.
10 And those who know Your name will put
their trust in You;
For You, LORD, have not forsaken those
who seek You.

JUDGMENT

**Who is the
ultimate
authority?
(9:7, 8)**

11 Sing praises to the LORD, who dwells in
Zion!
Declare His deeds among the people.
12 When He avenges blood, He remembers
them;
He does not forget the cry of the humble.

13 Have mercy on me, O LORD!
Consider my trouble from those who
hate me,
You who lift me up from the gates of
death,
14 That I may tell of all Your praise
In the gates of the daughter of Zion.
I will rejoice in Your salvation.

15 The nations have sunk down in the pit
which they made;
In the net which they hid, their own foot
is caught.
16 The LORD is known *by* the judgment He
executes;
The wicked is snared in the work of his
own hands.
Meditation.*a* Selah

17 The wicked shall be turned into hell,
And all the nations that forget God.
18 For the needy shall not always
be forgotten;
The expectation of the
poor shall *not* perish
forever.

19 Arise, O LORD,
Do not let man prevail;
Let the nations be judged in Your sight.
20 Put them in fear, O LORD,
That the nations may know themselves *to
be but* men. Selah

HOPE

**Who does
God give
hope?
(9:18)**

WHAT'S IT MEAN?

For the most part, the people who lived
in the nations surrounding Israel were sinful
and corrupt, enemies of God. That didn't mean they were hopeless,
though. The miracles that God performed for the Israelites often
caught the attention of other nations. Those who recognized
the power of Israel's God were given an
opportunity to serve Him.
Psalm 9:11

PSALM 10

A SONG OF CONFIDENCE IN GOD'S TRIUMPH OVER EVIL

1 Why do You stand afar off, O LORD?
Why do You hide in times of trouble?
2 The wicked in *his* pride persecutes the
poor;
Let them be caught in the plots which
they have devised.

3 For the wicked boasts of his heart's desire;
He blesses the greedy *and* renounces the
LORD.

9:16 *a*Hebrew *Higgaion*

⁴ The wicked in his proud countenance
  does not seek *God*;
God *is* in none of his thoughts.

⁵ His ways are always prospering;
Your judgments *are* far above, out of his
  sight;
As for all his enemies, he sneers at them.

⁶ He has said in his heart, "I shall not be
  moved;
I shall never be in adversity."

⁷ His mouth is full of cursing and deceit
  and oppression;
Under his tongue *is* trouble and iniquity.

⁸ He sits in the lurking places of the
  villages;
In the secret places he murders the
  innocent;
His eyes are secretly fixed on the helpless.

⁹ He lies in wait secretly, as a lion in his
  den;
He lies in wait to catch the poor;
He catches the poor when he draws him
  into his net.

¹⁰ So he crouches, he lies low,
That the helpless may fall by his strength.

¹¹ He has said in his heart,
"God has forgotten;
He hides His face;
He will never see."

WHAT'S IT MEAN?

Can you imagine having to worry
about lion attacks while you traveled? People in
ancient Palestine faced that danger every day. Apparently the king
of the jungle was a very real problem in Israel's territory. The animals were known to spring from their hiding places among the thickets near the Jordan River to pounce on people passing by. If
you're planning a trip to the Holy Land,
relax—the lions are long gone.

Psalm 10:9

¹² Arise, O LORD!
O God, lift up Your hand!
Do not forget the humble.

¹³ Why do the wicked renounce God?

He has said in his heart,
"You will not require *an account*."

¹⁴ But You have seen, for You observe
  trouble and grief,
To repay *it* by Your hand.
The helpless commits himself to You;
You are the helper of the fatherless.

¹⁵ Break the arm of the wicked and the evil
  man;
Seek out his wickedness *until* You find
  none.

¹⁶ The LORD *is* King forever and ever;
The nations have perished out of His
  land.

¹⁷ LORD, You have heard the desire of the
  humble;
You will prepare their heart;
You will cause Your ear to hear,

¹⁸ To do justice to the fatherless and the
  oppressed,
That the man of the earth may oppress
  no more.

WHAT'S IT MEAN?

Just as a metalsmith working with gold or
silver uses fire to purify the good and get rid of the
bad, God uses the fire of His judgment to purify us and get rid of the
bad. Do the fiery coals and flaming brimstone in this passage remind
you of any other Bible stories? The cities of Sodom and Gomorrah
were destroyed by fireballs from heaven after
God judged their wickedness.

Psalm 11:5, 6

PSALM 11

FAITH IN THE LORD'S RIGHTEOUSNESS

To the Chief Musician. A Psalm of David.

¹ In the LORD I put my trust;
How can you say to my soul,
"Flee *as* a bird to your mountain"?

² For look! The wicked bend *their* bow,
They make ready their arrow on the
  string,

That they may shoot secretly at the
upright in heart.
3 If the foundations are destroyed,
What can the righteous do?

4 The LORD *is* in His holy temple,
The LORD's throne *is* in heaven;
His eyes behold,
His eyelids test the sons of men.
5 The LORD tests the righteous,
But the wicked and the one who loves
violence His soul hates.
6 Upon the wicked He will rain coals;
Fire and brimstone and a burning wind
Shall be the portion of their cup.

7 For the LORD *is* righteous,
He loves righteousness;
His countenance beholds the upright.[a]

PSALM 12

MAN'S TREACHERY AND GOD'S CONSTANCY

To the Chief Musician. On an eight-stringed
harp.[a]
A Psalm of David.

1 Help, LORD, for the godly man ceases!
For the faithful disappear from among the
sons of men.
2 They speak idly everyone with his
neighbor;
With flattering lips *and* a double heart
they speak.

3 May the LORD cut off all flattering lips,
And the tongue that speaks proud things,

WHAT'S IT MEAN?

If you want to find silver, you've got to look in
rocks made of lead ore. If you want to get silver from
the rock, you've got to heat the rock to extreme temperatures. If you
want to purify the silver and make it more valuable, you've got to
repeat the heating process over and over again.
Psalm 12:6

4 Who have said,
"With our tongue we will prevail;
Our lips *are* our own;
Who *is* lord over us?"

5 "For the oppression of the
poor, for the sighing
of the needy,
Now I will arise," says the
LORD;
"I will set *him* in the safety
for which he yearns."

> **PAIN**
> Who
> does God
> watch over?
> (12:5)

6 The words of the LORD *are* pure words,
Like silver tried in a furnace of earth,
Purified seven times.
7 You shall keep them, O LORD,
You shall preserve them from this
generation forever.

8 The wicked prowl on every side,
When vileness is exalted among the sons
of men.

PSALM 13

TRUST IN THE SALVATION OF THE LORD

To the Chief Musician. A Psalm of David.

1 How long, O LORD? Will You forget me
forever?
How long will You hide Your face from
me?
2 How long shall I take counsel in my soul,
Having sorrow in my heart daily?
How long will my enemy be exalted over
me?

3 Consider *and* hear me, O LORD
my God;
Enlighten my eyes,
Lest I sleep the *sleep of*
death;
4 Lest my enemy say,
"I have prevailed against
him";
Lest those who trouble me rejoice when I
am moved.

> **LIGHT**
> Who
> enlightens
> our path?
> (13:3)

5 But I have trusted in Your mercy;
My heart shall rejoice in Your salvation.
6 I will sing to the LORD,
Because He has dealt bountifully with
me.

11:7 [a]*Or The upright beholds His countenance* **12:title** [a]*Hebrew sheminith*

PSALM 14

FOLLY OF THE GODLESS, AND GOD'S FINAL TRIUMPH

To the Chief Musician. A Psalm of David.

1 The fool has said in his heart,
"*There is* no God."
They are corrupt,
They have done abominable works,
There is none who does good.

WHAT'S IT MEAN?

A lack of respect for God and His laws was the worst kind of ignorance, as far as David was concerned. The person who rejected God was considered the biggest fool of them all.

Psalm 14:1

2 The LORD looks down from heaven upon
the children of men,
To see if there are any who understand,
who seek God.
3 They have all turned aside,
They have together become corrupt;
There is none who does good,
No, not one.

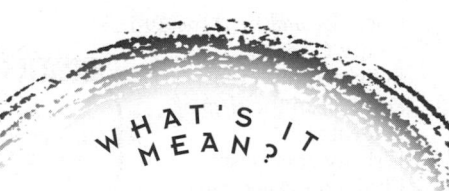

WHAT'S IT MEAN?

What made Zion such a holy hill?
David had brought the ark of the Testimony there for safekeeping. What made the ark of the Testimony so special? It contained the actual tablets of the Ten Commandments, which God Himself had given to Moses.

Psalm 15:1

4 Have all the workers of iniquity no
knowledge,
Who eat up my people *as* they eat bread,
And do not call on the LORD?
5 There they are in great fear,
For God *is* with the generation of the
righteous.
6 You shame the counsel of the poor,
But the LORD *is* his refuge.

7 Oh, that the salvation of Israel *would come*
out of Zion!
When the LORD brings back the captivity
of His people,
Let Jacob rejoice *and* Israel be glad.

PSALM 15

THE CHARACTER OF THOSE WHO MAY DWELL WITH THE LORD

A Psalm of David.

1 LORD, who may abide in Your tabernacle?
Who may dwell in Your holy hill?

2 He who walks uprightly,
And works righteousness,
And speaks the truth in his heart;
3 He *who* does not backbite with his
tongue,
Nor does evil to his neighbor,
Nor does he take up a reproach
against his friend;
4 In whose eyes a vile person is despised,
But he honors those who fear the
LORD;
He *who* swears to his own hurt and does
not change;
5 He *who* does not put out his money at
usury,
Nor does he take a bribe against the
innocent.

He who does these *things* shall never be
moved.

PSALM 16

THE HOPE OF THE FAITHFUL, AND THE MESSIAH'S VICTORY

A Michtam of David.

1 Preserve me, O God, for in You I put my
trust.

2   *O my soul*, you have said to the LORD,
"You *are* my Lord,
My goodness is nothing apart from You."

3   As for the saints who *are* on the earth,
"They are the excellent ones, in whom is
all my delight."

4   Their sorrows shall be multiplied who
hasten *after* another *god;*
Their drink offerings of blood I will not
offer,
Nor take up their names on my lips.

5   O LORD, *You are* the portion of my
inheritance and my cup,
You maintain my lot.

6   The lines have fallen to me in pleasant
places;
Yes, I have a good inheritance.

7   I will bless the LORD who has
given me counsel;
My heart also instructs
me in the night
seasons.

8   I have set the LORD
always before me;
Because *He is* at my right
hand I shall not be
moved.

9   Therefore my heart is glad, and my glory
rejoices;
My flesh also will rest in hope.

10   For You will not leave my soul in Sheol,
Nor will You allow Your Holy One to see
corruption.

11   You will show me the path of life;
In Your presence *is* fullness of joy;
At Your right hand *are* pleasures
forevermore.

PSALM 17

PRAYER WITH CONFIDENCE IN FINAL SALVATION

A Prayer of David.

1   Hear a just cause, O LORD,
Attend to my cry;
Give ear to my prayer *which is*
not from deceitful lips.

2   Let my vindication come
from Your presence;
Let Your eyes look on the
things that are
upright.

3   You have tested my heart;
You have visited *me* in the night;
You have tried me and have found
nothing;
I have purposed that my mouth shall not
transgress.

4   Concerning the works of men,
By the word of Your lips,
I have kept away from the paths of the
destroyer.

5   Uphold my steps in Your paths,
That my footsteps may not slip.

6   I have called upon You, for You will hear
me, O God;
Incline Your ear to me, *and* hear my
speech.

7   Show Your marvelous lovingkindness by
Your right hand,
O You who save those who trust *in You*
From those who rise up *against them.*

8 Keep me as the apple of Your eye;
Hide me under the shadow of Your
    wings,
9 From the wicked who oppress me,
From my deadly enemies who surround
    me.

10 They have closed up their fat *hearts;*
With their mouths they speak proudly.
11 They have now surrounded us in our
    steps;
They have set their eyes, crouching down
    to the earth,
12 As a lion is eager to tear his prey,
And like a young lion lurking in secret
    places.

13 Arise, O LORD,
Confront him, cast him
    down;
Deliver my life from the
    wicked with Your sword,
14 With Your hand from men,
    O LORD,
From men of the world *who have*
    their portion in *this* life,
And whose belly You fill with Your
    hidden treasure.
They are satisfied with children,
And leave the rest of their *possession* for
    their babes.

15 As for me, I will see Your face in
    righteousness;
I shall be satisfied when I awake in Your
    likeness.

PSALM 18

GOD THE SOVEREIGN SAVIOR

To the Chief Musician. A Psalm of David
    the servant of the LORD, who spoke
to the LORD the words of this song on the
    day that the LORD delivered him from
    the hand of all his enemies and from
    the hand of Saul. And he said:

1 I will love You, O LORD, my strength.
2 The LORD is my rock and my fortress and
    my deliverer;
My God, my strength, in whom I will
    trust;
My shield and the horn of my salvation,
    my stronghold.

3 I will call upon the LORD, *who is worthy* to
    be praised;
So shall I be saved from my enemies.

4 The pangs of death surrounded me,
And the floods of ungodliness made me
    afraid.
5 The sorrows of Sheol surrounded me;
The snares of death confronted me.
6 In my distress I called upon the LORD,
And cried out to my God;
He heard my voice from His temple,
And my cry came before Him, *even* to His
    ears.

7 Then the earth shook and
    trembled;
The foundations of the hills
    also quaked and were
    shaken,
Because He was angry.
8 Smoke went up from His
    nostrils,
And devouring fire from
    His mouth;
Coals were kindled by it.
9 He bowed the heavens also, and came
    down
With darkness under His feet.
10 And He rode upon a cherub, and flew;
He flew upon the wings of the wind.
11 He made darkness His secret place;
His canopy around Him *was* dark waters
And thick clouds of the skies.
12 From the brightness before Him,
His thick clouds passed with hailstones
    and coals of fire.

13 The LORD thundered from heaven,
And the Most High uttered His voice,
Hailstones and coals of fire.*a*
14 He sent out His arrows and scattered the
    foe,
Lightnings in abundance, and He
    vanquished them.
15 Then the channels of the sea were seen,
The foundations of the world were
    uncovered
At Your rebuke, O LORD,
At the blast of the breath of Your nostrils.

16 He sent from above, He took me;
He drew me out of many waters.
17 He delivered me from my strong enemy,

"I will love You,
O LORD,
my strength."
(Psalm 18:1)

18:13 *a*Following Masoretic Text, Targum, and Vulgate; a few Hebrew manuscripts and Septuagint omit
Hailstones and coals of fire.

From those who hated me,
For they were too strong for me.
18 They confronted me in the day of my calamity,
But the LORD was my support.
19 He also brought me out into a broad place;
He delivered me because He delighted in me.

WHAT'S IT MEAN?

Forget about muscles and killer instinct!
As far as the Israelites were concerned, the
best warriors were the ones who
were fast and agile.
Psalm 18:33

20 The LORD rewarded me according to my righteousness;
According to the cleanness of my hands He has recompensed me.
21 For I have kept the ways of the LORD,
And have not wickedly departed from my God.
22 For all His judgments *were* before me,
And I did not put away His statutes from me.
23 I was also blameless before Him,
And I kept myself from my iniquity.
24 Therefore the LORD has recompensed me according to my righteousness,
According to the cleanness of my hands in His sight.

25 With the merciful You will show Yourself merciful;
With a blameless man You will show Yourself blameless;
26 With the pure You will show Yourself pure;
And with the devious You will show Yourself shrewd.
27 For You will save the humble people,
But will bring down haughty looks.

28 For You will light my lamp;
The LORD my God will enlighten my darkness.

29 For by You I can run against a troop,
By my God I can leap over a wall.
30 *As for* God, His way *is* perfect;
The word of the LORD is proven;
He *is* a shield to all who trust in Him.

31 For who *is* God, except the LORD?
And who *is* a rock, except our God?
32 *It is* God who arms me with strength,
And makes my way perfect.
33 He makes my feet like the *feet of* deer,
And sets me on my high places.
34 He teaches my hands to make war,
So that my arms can bend a bow of bronze.

35 You have also given me the shield of Your salvation;
Your right hand has held me up,
Your gentleness has made me great.
36 You enlarged my path under me,
So my feet did not slip.

37 I have pursued my enemies and overtaken them;
Neither did I turn back again till they were destroyed.
38 I have wounded them,
So that they could not rise;
They have fallen under my feet.
39 For You have armed me with strength for the battle;
You have subdued under me those who rose up against me.
40 You have also given me the necks of my enemies,
So that I destroyed those who hated me.
41 They cried out, but *there was* none to save;

WHAT'S IT MEAN?

David knew what he was talking about
when it came to being armed for battle. His life
was filled with struggles and fights. He battled Goliath, he battled
Saul, he battled Saul's family, he battled the Ammonites, he battled
the Syrians, he battled the Philistines—he even battled his own son
for control of Israel!
Psalm 18:39

Even to the LORD, but He did not answer them.

42 Then I beat them as fine as the dust before the wind;
I cast them out like dirt in the streets.

43 You have delivered me from the strivings of the people;
You have made me the head of the nations;
A people I have not known shall serve me.

44 As soon as they hear of me they obey me;
The foreigners submit to me.

45 The foreigners fade away,
And come frightened from their hideouts.

46 The LORD lives!
Blessed *be* my Rock!
Let the God of my salvation be exalted.

47 *It is* God who avenges me,
And subdues the peoples under me;

48 He delivers me from my enemies.
You also lift me up above those who rise against me;
You have delivered me from the violent man.

49 Therefore I will give thanks to You,
O LORD, among the Gentiles,
And sing praises to Your name.

50 Great deliverance He gives to His king,
And shows mercy to His anointed,
To David and his descendants forevermore.

PSALM 19

THE PERFECT REVELATION OF THE LORD

To the Chief Musician. A Psalm of David.

1 The heavens declare the glory of God;
And the firmament shows His handiwork.

2 Day unto day utters speech,
And night unto night reveals knowledge.

3 *There is* no speech nor language
Where their voice is not heard.

4 Their line[a] has gone out through all the earth,
And their words to the end of the world.

In them He has set a tabernacle for the sun,

19:4 [a]Septuagint, Syriac, and Vulgate read *sound*; Targum reads *business*.

Promise   HE PROMISES HE WILL BE WORSHIPED FOREVER.

The fear of the LORD is clean, enduring forever (Ps. 19:9).

Think about it. Some people worship their money. Some people worship their cars. Some people worship their careers. Maybe you don't see them bow down to these things, and maybe they don't call them "god"; but they think about them constantly, and all their effort and energy go into making them bigger or better or both. That's worship, or "fear," indicating what they hold to be most important in life. But the car eventually ends up in the junkyard. The money gets spent. The career ends in retirement.

Other people worship things that they think are God. They honor the forces of nature or the stars. Or they pray to a statue or a city. Their rituals make them feel better, but they're still worshiping *things*.

God is totally different. He is a Person. He will live forever. He doesn't rust, wear out, or run out. When everything on earth has decayed or burned up or blown away, He will still be running the show. And the people who chose to worship Him (instead of their cars) will still be singing His praises.

Even when the earth has passed away, there will be worship in heaven for all of eternity. Awesome.

SEE FOR YOURSELF:
Ps. 22:27; Zeph. 2:11; Rev. 15:4

5 Which *is* like a bridegroom coming out of
   his chamber,
   And rejoices like a strong man to run its
   race.
6 Its rising *is* from one end of heaven,
   And its circuit to the other end;
   And there is nothing hidden from its heat.

7 The law of the LORD *is* perfect, converting
   the soul;
   The testimony of the LORD *is* sure, making
   wise the simple;
8 The statutes of the LORD *are* right,
   rejoicing the heart;
   The commandment of the LORD *is* pure,
   enlightening the eyes;
9 The fear of the LORD *is* clean, enduring
   forever;
   The judgments of the LORD *are* true *and*
   righteous altogether.
10 More to be desired *are they* than gold,
   Yea, than much fine gold;
   Sweeter also than honey and the
   honeycomb.
11 Moreover by them Your servant is
   warned,
   And in keeping them *there is*
   great reward.

12 Who can understand *his*
   errors?
   Cleanse me from secret
   faults.
13 Keep back Your servant
   also from presumptuous
   sins;
   Let them not have dominion over me.
   Then I shall be blameless,
   And I shall be innocent of great
   transgression.

14 Let the words of my mouth and the
   meditation of my heart
   Be acceptable in Your sight,
   O LORD, my strength and my Redeemer.

GUILT
Can
we hide sins
from God?
(19:12, 13)

PSALM 20

THE ASSURANCE OF GOD'S SAVING WORK

To the Chief Musician. A Psalm of David.

1 May the LORD answer you in the day of
   trouble;
   May the name of the God of Jacob
   defend you;

2 May He send you help from the
   sanctuary,
   And strengthen you out of Zion;
3 May He remember all your offerings,
   And accept your burnt sacrifice.   Selah

WHAT'S IT MEAN?

Banners were large flags that were used as
"scoreboards" during battles. You could always tell
which side was winning a skirmish by the banner that was raised.
You can probably imagine how much those banners meant to the
soldiers. Seeing their banner raised must have been a tremendous
encouragement to the warriors. Seeing an opponent's banner raised,
on the other hand, may have been an
incentive to fight harder.
Psalm 20:5

4 May He grant you according to your
   heart's *desire,*
   And fulfill all your purpose.
5 We will rejoice in your salvation,
   And in the name of our God we will set
   up *our* banners!
   May the LORD fulfill all your petitions.

6 Now I know that the LORD saves His
   anointed;
   He will answer him from His holy heaven
   With the saving strength of His right hand.

7 Some *trust* in chariots, and some in
   horses;
   But we will remember the name of the
   LORD our God.
8 They have bowed down and fallen;
   But we have risen and stand upright.

9 Save, LORD!
   May the King answer us when we call.

PSALM 21

JOY IN THE SALVATION OF THE LORD

To the Chief Musician. A Psalm of David.

1 The king shall have joy in Your strength,
   O LORD;

And in Your salvation how greatly shall he rejoice!
2 You have given him his heart's desire,
And have not withheld the request of his lips.   Selah

3 For You meet him with the blessings of goodness;
You set a crown of pure gold upon his head.
4 He asked life from You, *and* You gave *it* to him—
Length of days forever and ever.
5 His glory *is* great in Your salvation;
Honor and majesty You have placed upon him.
6 For You have made him most blessed forever;
You have made him exceedingly glad with Your presence.
7 For the king trusts in the LORD,
And through the mercy of the Most High he shall not be moved.

8 Your hand will find all Your enemies;
Your right hand will find those who hate You.
9 You shall make them as a fiery oven in the time of Your anger;
The LORD shall swallow them up in His wrath,
And the fire shall devour them.
10 Their offspring You shall destroy from the earth,
And their descendants from among the sons of men.

"Eli, eli, lama sabachthani?" is the Hebrew translation of David's first question in this psalm. Those foreign words may seem familiar to you even if you've never studied Hebrew in your life. Jesus quoted them on the cross, after He had taken the responsibility of paying the price of death for the sins of the world.

Psalm 22:1

11 For they intended evil against You;
They devised a plot *which* they are not able *to perform.*
12 Therefore You will make them turn their back;
You will make ready *Your arrows* on Your string toward their faces.

13 Be exalted, O LORD, in Your own strength!
We will sing and praise Your power.

PSALM 22

THE SUFFERING, PRAISE, AND POSTERITY OF THE MESSIAH

To the Chief Musician. Set to "The Deer of the Dawn."[a] A Psalm of David.

1 My God, My God, why have You forsaken Me?
Why are You so far from helping Me,
And from the words of My groaning?
2 O My God, I cry in the daytime, but You do not hear;
And in the night season, and am not silent.

3 But You *are* holy,
Enthroned in the praises of Israel.
4 Our fathers trusted in You;
They trusted, and You delivered them.
5 They cried to You, and were delivered;
They trusted in You, and were not ashamed.

6 But I *am* a worm, and no man;
A reproach of men, and despised by the people.
7 All those who see Me ridicule Me;
They shoot out the lip, they shake the head, *saying,*
8 "He trusted[a] in the LORD, let Him rescue Him;
Let Him deliver Him, since He delights in Him!"

9 But You *are* He who took Me out of the womb;
You made Me trust *while* on My mother's breasts.
10 I was cast upon You from birth.
From My mother's womb
You *have been* My God.

22:title [a]Hebrew *Aijeleth Hashahar*   22:8 [a]Septuagint, Syriac, and Vulgate read *hoped;* Targum reads *praised.*

11 Be not far from Me,
For trouble *is* near;
For *there is* none to help.

12 Many bulls have surrounded Me;
Strong *bulls* of Bashan have encircled Me.
13 They gape at Me *with* their mouths,
Like a raging and roaring lion.

14 I am poured out like water,
And all My bones are out of joint;
My heart is like wax;
It has melted within Me.
15 My strength is dried up like a potsherd,
And My tongue clings to My jaws;
You have brought Me to the dust of
death.

16 For dogs have surrounded Me;
The congregation of the wicked has
enclosed Me.
They pierced[a] My hands and My feet;
17 I can count all My bones.
They look *and* stare at Me.
18 They divide My garments among them,
And for My clothing they cast lots.

19 But You, O LORD, do not be far from Me;
O My Strength, hasten to help Me!
20 Deliver Me from the sword,

My precious *life* from the power of the
dog.
21 Save Me from the lion's mouth
And from the horns of the wild oxen!

You have answered Me.

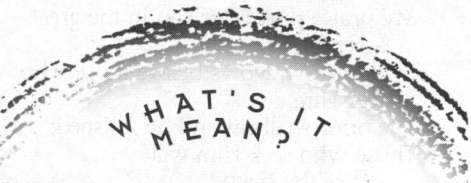

WHAT'S IT MEAN?

The dogs of ancient Israel certainly
weren't man's best friend. In fact, they were more
like scavengers than house pets. Traveling in packs, these wild
creatures were known for attacking and killing the weak and the
helpless. They ate discarded food and anything
else they could find to stay alive.
Psalm 22:16

22 I will declare Your name to My brethren;
In the midst of the assembly I will praise
You.
23 You who fear the LORD, praise Him!

22:16 [a]Following some Hebrew manuscripts, Septuagint, Syriac, Vulgate; Masoretic Text reads *Like a lion.*

Promise HE PROMISES TO FILL YOU WITH HIS PRAISES.

My praise shall be of You in the great assembly; I will pay My vows before those who fear Him (Ps. 22:25).

When God's people come together, they usually praise Him. That's what He expects. Because of that, people spend a lot of time trying hard to praise the Lord—with the right music, the right words, the right posture. You may even be sitting or standing in the pew trying to work up the frame of mind that will please God and make you feel good, too.

If that's the case, there's nothing wrong with your motives or the motives of the people who plan the songs and the prayers and the standing and sitting. But David had a different idea about how he was going to praise God. He was determined to praise God—no matter what. He knew that when he did his part by *choosing* to praise that God would fill him with praise. The happiness that David had in God's presence came straight from God.

So when you get together with other people who love God, make up your mind that you're going to praise God. Think about His goodness, His power, His awesome love. Ask Him to fill your heart with praise like He did for David. And He will.

SEE FOR YOURSELF:
Ps. 4:7; Is. 61:11; Rom. 15:13

All you descendants of Jacob, glorify Him,
And fear Him, all you offspring of Israel!
24 For He has not despised nor abhorred the
affliction of the afflicted;
Nor has He hidden His face from Him;
But when He cried to Him, He heard.

25 My praise *shall be* of You in the great
assembly;
I will pay My vows before those who
fear Him.
26 The poor shall eat and be satisfied;
Those who seek Him will
praise the LORD.
Let your heart live
forever!

27 All the ends of the
world
Shall remember and
turn to the LORD,
And all the families of
the nations
Shall worship before You.*a*
28 For the kingdom *is* the LORD's,
And He rules over the nations.

29 All the prosperous of the earth
Shall eat and worship;

All those who go down to the dust
Shall bow before Him,
Even he who cannot keep himself
alive.

30 A posterity shall serve Him.
It will be recounted of the Lord to the *next*
generation,
31 They will come and declare His
righteousness to a people who will be
born,
That He has done *this.*

"The LORD is my shepherd;
I shall not want.
He makes me to lie down
in green pastures."
(Psalm 23:1, 2a)

PSALM 23

THE LORD THE SHEPHERD OF HIS PEOPLE

A Psalm of David.

1 The LORD *is* my
shepherd;
I shall not want.
2 He makes me to lie
down in green
pastures;
He leads me beside the still waters.
3 He restores my soul;

22:27 *a*Following Masoretic Text, Septuagint, and Targum; Arabic, Syriac, and Vulgate read *Him.*

Promise   HE PROMISES YOU WILL NEVER WANT FOR ANYTHING.

The LORD is my shepherd; I shall not want (Ps. 23:1).

David had a rock-solid confidence in God. He didn't wonder whether God was going to give him food to eat, clothes to wear, or a place to live. Part of that confidence came out of David's experiences. In spite of all the scrapes and tight places he found himself in, God had never let him be hurt or go hungry. And part of that confidence came from the fact that David knew God very well. He knew Him like a best friend. He knew that God was—and is—kind, loving, and powerful.

There was another reason that David could say, "I shall not want." All of David's hopes and dreams were caught up in the Lord. Even if he had been forced to go without some of the things that people consider necessities, he wouldn't have missed them much. David's relationship with God meant everything to him. As long as he knew that God was leading him and that their friendship was where it was supposed to be, David had the thing he wanted most. All the rest was extra.

As you grow toward having the same attitude that David did, you'll see—like David did—that God never lets you go without the things you really need. He is the one thing you need most.

SEE FOR YOURSELF:

Is. 49:10; Luke 12:29–31; John 6:35

He leads me in the paths of righteousness
For His name's sake.

4 Yea, though I walk through the valley of
the shadow of death,
I will fear no evil;
For You *are* with me;
Your rod and Your staff, they comfort me.

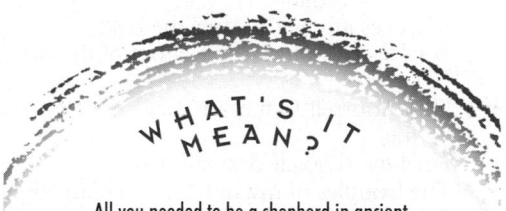

What's It Mean?

All you needed to be a shepherd in ancient
times were sheep (obviously) and a rod. A shepherd's
rod was a stick with a hook at the end of it. With it, a shepherd could
gently nudge a stray sheep back into line or, using the hook, pull a
sheep from a dangerous spot. The rod was also used as a weapon to
defend the flock against wolves and other invaders.
Psalm 23:4

5 You prepare a table before me in the
presence of my enemies;
You anoint my head with oil;
My cup runs over.
6 Surely goodness and mercy shall follow
me
All the days of my life;
And I will dwell[a] in the house of the
LORD
Forever.

PSALM 24

THE KING OF GLORY AND HIS KINGDOM

A Psalm of David.

1 The earth *is* the LORD's, and all its fullness,
The world and those who dwell therein.
2 For He has founded it upon the seas,
And established it upon the waters.

3 Who may ascend into the hill of the
LORD?
Or who may stand in His holy place?

4 He who has clean hands and a pure
heart,
Who has not lifted up his
soul to an idol,
Nor sworn deceitfully.
5 He shall receive blessing
from the LORD,
And righteousness from
the God of his salvation.
6 This *is* Jacob, the generation of those who
seek Him,
Who seek Your face.   Selah

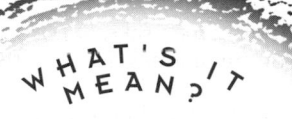

BLESSING
When
are we
blessed?
(24:3–6)

7 Lift up your heads, O you gates!
And be lifted up, you everlasting doors!
And the King of glory shall come in.
8 Who *is* this King of glory?
The LORD strong and mighty,
The LORD mighty in battle.
9 Lift up your heads, O you gates!
Lift up, you everlasting doors!
And the King of glory shall come in.
10 Who is this King of glory?
The LORD of hosts,
He *is* the King of glory.   Selah

What's It Mean?

Many Bible experts believe David wrote this
psalm as part of the celebration for when he brought
the ark of the Lord to Jerusalem. Years before, the ark had been
captured during a battle with the Philistines. When David became
king, he made Jerusalem his capital and had the recovered ark moved
there. Because the ark contained the tablets on which God had
written the Ten Commandments, it was a major part
of the Israelites' worship.
Psalm 24:1

PSALM 25

A PLEA FOR DELIVERANCE AND FORGIVENESS

A Psalm of David.

1 To You, O LORD, I lift up my soul.
2 O my God, I trust in You;
Let me not be ashamed;

23:6 [a]Following Septuagint, Syriac, Targum, and Vulgate; Masoretic Text reads *return*.

Let not my enemies triumph over me.
3 Indeed, let no one who waits on You be
ashamed;
Let those be ashamed who deal
treacherously without cause.

4 Show me Your ways, O LORD;
Teach me Your paths.
5 Lead me in Your truth and teach me,
For You *are* the God of my salvation;
On You I wait all the day.

6 Remember, O LORD, Your tender mercies
and Your lovingkindnesses,
For they *are* from of old.
7 Do not remember the sins of my youth,
nor my transgressions;
According to Your mercy remember me,
For Your goodness' sake, O LORD.

8 Good and upright *is* the LORD;
Therefore He teaches sinners in the way.
9 The humble He guides in justice,
And the humble He teaches His way.
10 All the paths of the LORD *are* mercy and
truth,
To such as keep His covenant and His
testimonies.
11 For Your name's sake, O LORD,
Pardon my iniquity, for it *is* great.

12 Who *is* the man that fears the LORD?
Him shall He[a] teach in the way He[b]
chooses.

WHAT'S IT MEAN?

The covenant (or agreement) between God
and the Israelites was first made with Abraham,
Isaac, and Jacob. After God led the Israelites out of Egypt, He confirmed the covenant with Moses and the people. The deal went like
this: God would make Israel into a great nation and bless its people.
In return, the Israelites would serve God faithfully, obeying and
worshiping Him as the only true God. The Israelites violated the
covenant many times, but each time they renewed it,
God held up His side of the agreement.
Psalm 25:10

13 He himself shall dwell in
prosperity,
And his descendants
shall inherit the earth.
14 The secret of the LORD *is*
with those who fear
Him,
And He will show them
His covenant.

FEAR

Should
Christians
ever be afraid
of God?
(25:12–15)

15 My eyes *are* ever toward the LORD,
For He shall pluck my feet out of the net.

16 Turn Yourself to me, and have mercy on
me,
For I *am* desolate and afflicted.
17 The troubles of my heart have enlarged;
Bring me out of my distresses!
18 Look on my affliction and my pain,
And forgive all my sins.
19 Consider my enemies, for they are many;
And they hate me with cruel hatred.
20 Keep my soul, and deliver me;
Let me not be ashamed, for I put my trust
in You.
21 Let integrity and uprightness preserve me,
For I wait for You.

22 Redeem Israel, O God,
Out of all their troubles!

PSALM 26

A PRAYER FOR DIVINE SCRUTINY AND REDEMPTION

A Psalm of David.

1 Vindicate me, O LORD,
For I have walked in my integrity.
I have also trusted in the LORD;
I shall not slip.
2 Examine me, O LORD, and prove me;
Try my mind and my heart.
3 For Your lovingkindness *is* before my
eyes,
And I have walked in Your truth.
4 I have not sat with idolatrous mortals,
Nor will I go in with hypocrites.
5 I have hated the assembly of evildoers,
And will not sit with the wicked.

6 I will wash my hands in innocence;
So I will go about Your altar, O LORD,
7 That I may proclaim with the voice of
thanksgiving,
And tell of all Your wondrous works.

25:12 [a]Or *he* [b]Or *he*

WHAT'S IT MEAN?

In Old Testament times, God occasionally showed His "glory," a visible symbol of His presence, to human beings. The best way to describe this glory is as a burning fire or a bright light. God's glory appeared in the tabernacle over the lid of the ark of the covenant.

Psalm 26:8

8   LORD, I have loved the habitation of Your house,
And the place where Your glory dwells.

9   Do not gather my soul with sinners,
Nor my life with bloodthirsty men,

10   In whose hands *is* a sinister scheme,
And whose right hand is full of bribes.

11   But as for me, I will walk in my integrity;
Redeem me and be merciful to me.

12   My foot stands in an even place;
In the congregations I will bless the LORD.

PSALM 27

AN EXUBERANT DECLARATION OF FAITH

A Psalm of David.

1   The LORD *is* my light and
my salvation;
Whom shall I fear?
The LORD *is* the strength
of my life;
Of whom shall I be afraid?

2   When the wicked came against me
To eat up my flesh,
My enemies and foes,
They stumbled and fell.

3   Though an army may encamp against
me,
My heart shall not fear;
Though war may rise against me,
In this I *will be* confident.

4   One *thing* I have desired of the LORD,
That will I seek:

LIGHT
Is God ever called light? (27:1)

On the Edge

Hear, O LORD, when I cry with my voice! Have mercy also upon me, and answer me. When You said, "Seek My face," my heart said to You, "Your face, LORD, I will seek." Do not hide Your face from me; do not turn Your servant away in anger; You have been my help; do not leave me nor forsake me, O God of my salvation. When my father and my mother forsake me, then the LORD will take care of me (Ps. 27:7–10).

If you've just found out that you're pregnant, you are probably feeling a multitude of emotions—disbelief, fear, confusion, loneliness, regret, and maybe anger, and others. Your life has changed forever. During the next months, you're going to have to make some very responsible decisions, so an important first step is to gather a support team. Hopefully your family and friends will be your team; but, if not, there are other options like a crisis pregnancy center, or other Christian agencies that assist pregnant women. As you begin to process everything and make decisions, the most important place you can look for guidance is to the Lord. You can cry out to God and ask Him to take care of you. Keep reminding yourself of Psalm 27:14.

Do not be afraid to do the right thing. God has not abandoned you. He already has a plan and purpose for your baby's life. Take care of your body so that the baby will be healthy. And make sure that your child will be raised by godly parents in a safe and loving home. God will honor your faithfulness to Him. He answers people when they cry out to Him. He promises that He will take care of you.

SEE FOR YOURSELF:
Ps. 27:14; Is. 1:18, 19;
Jer. 29:11, 12;
Hos. 6:1, 2; 14:1–9;
Mark 3:28

That I may dwell in the house of the LORD
All the days of my life,
To behold the beauty of the LORD,
And to inquire in His temple.

5   For in the time of trouble

He shall hide me in His pavilion;
In the secret place of His tabernacle
He shall hide me;
He shall set me high upon a rock.

WHAT'S IT MEAN?

Before Solomon built the temple,
the tabernacle was the place the Israelites went to
worship God. The tabernacle was considered the house of God because His "glory," a symbol of His presence, appeared over the ark of
the Testimony, which was kept in the tabernacle.

Psalm 27:4

6 And now my head shall be lifted up
above my enemies all around me;
Therefore I will offer sacrifices of joy in
His tabernacle;
I will sing, yes, I will sing praises to the
LORD.

7 Hear, O LORD, *when* I cry with my voice!
Have mercy also upon me, and answer
me.
8 *When You said*, "Seek My face,"
My heart said to You, "Your face, LORD, I
will seek."
9 Do not hide Your face from me;
Do not turn Your servant away in anger;
You have been my help;
Do not leave me nor forsake me,
O God of my salvation.
10 When my father and my mother forsake
me,
Then the LORD will take care of me.

11 Teach me Your way, O LORD,
And lead me in a smooth path, because
of my enemies.
12 Do not deliver me to the will of my
adversaries;
For false witnesses have risen against me,
And such as breathe out violence.
13 *I would have lost heart,* unless I had
believed
That I would see the goodness of the
LORD
In the land of the living.

14 Wait on the LORD;
Be of good courage,
And He shall strengthen your heart;
Wait, I say, on the LORD!

PSALM 28

REJOICING IN ANSWERED PRAYER

A Psalm of David.

1 To You I will cry, O LORD my Rock:
Do not be silent to me,
Lest, if You *are* silent to me,
I become like those who go down to the
pit.
2 Hear the voice of my supplications
When I cry to You,
When I lift up my hands toward Your
holy sanctuary.

3 Do not take me away with the wicked
And with the workers of iniquity,
Who speak peace to their neighbors,
But evil *is* in their hearts.
4 Give them according to their deeds,
And according to the wickedness of their
endeavors;
Give them according to the work of their
hands;
Render to them what they deserve.
5 Because they do not regard the works of
the LORD,
Nor the operation of His hands,
He shall destroy them
And not build them up.

6 Blessed *be* the LORD,

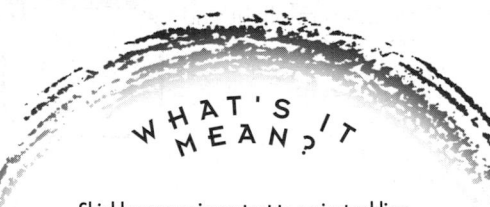

WHAT'S IT MEAN?

Shields were as important to ancient soldiers
as swords and spears were. Since few ancient armies
wore body armor, shields were the only defense soldiers had against
enemy arrows and swords. These shields came in all shapes and sizes,
and could be made of leather, wood, or metal.

Psalm 28:7

Because He has heard the voice of my
    supplications!

7 The LORD *is* my strength and my shield;
My heart trusted in Him, and I am
    helped;
Therefore my heart greatly rejoices,
And with my song I will praise Him.

8 The LORD *is* their strength,[a]
And He *is* the saving refuge of His
    anointed.
9 Save Your people,
And bless Your inheritance;
Shepherd them also,
And bear them up forever.

PSALM 29

PRAISE TO GOD IN HIS HOLINESS AND MAJESTY

A Psalm of David.

1 Give unto the LORD, O you
    mighty ones,
Give unto the LORD glory
    and strength.
2 Give unto the LORD the
    glory due to His
    name;
Worship the LORD in the
    beauty of holiness.

WORSHIP

What should we give to the Lord during worship? (29:1, 2)

3 The voice of the LORD *is* over the waters;
The God of glory thunders;
The LORD *is* over many waters.
4 The voice of the LORD *is* powerful;
The voice of the LORD *is* full of majesty.

5 The voice of the LORD breaks the cedars,
Yes, the LORD splinters the cedars of
    Lebanon.
6 He makes them also skip like a calf,
Lebanon and Sirion like a young wild ox.
7 The voice of the LORD divides the flames
    of fire.

8 The voice of the LORD shakes the
    wilderness;
The LORD shakes the Wilderness of
    Kadesh.
9 The voice of the LORD makes the deer give
    birth,
And strips the forests bare;

And in His temple everyone says,
    "Glory!"

10 The LORD sat *enthroned* at the Flood,
And the LORD sits as King forever.
11 The LORD will give strength to His people;
The LORD will bless His people with
    peace.

PSALM 30

THE BLESSEDNESS OF ANSWERED PRAYER

A Psalm. A Song at the dedication
of the house of David.

1 I will extol You, O LORD, for You have
    lifted me up,
And have not let my foes rejoice over me.
2 O LORD my God, I cried out to You,
And You healed me.
3 O LORD, You brought my soul up from
    the grave;
You have kept me alive, that I should not
    go down to the pit.[a]

4 Sing praise to the LORD, you saints of His,
And give thanks at the remembrance of
    His holy name.[a]
5 For His anger *is but for* a moment,
His favor *is for* life;
Weeping may endure for a night,
But joy *comes* in the morning.

6 Now in my prosperity I said,
"I shall never be moved."
7 LORD, by Your favor You have made my
    mountain stand strong;
You hid Your face, *and* I was troubled.

8 I cried out to You, O LORD;
And to the LORD I made supplication:
9 "What profit *is there* in my blood,
When I go down to the pit?
Will the dust praise You?
Will it declare Your truth?
10 Hear, O LORD, and have mercy on me;
LORD, be my helper!"

11 You have turned for me my mourning
    into dancing;
You have put off my sackcloth and
    clothed me with gladness,

28:8 [a]Following Masoretic Text and Targum; Septuagint, Syriac, and Vulgate read *the strength of His people.*
30:3 [a]Following Qere and Targum; Kethib, Septuagint, Syriac, and Vulgate read *from those who descend to the pit.* **30:4** [a]Or *His holiness*

12 To the end that *my* glory may sing praise
   to You and not be silent.
   O LORD my God, I will give thanks to You
   forever.

PSALM 31

THE LORD A FORTRESS IN ADVERSITY

To the Chief Musician. A Psalm of David.

1 In You, O LORD, I put my trust;
   Let me never be ashamed;
   Deliver me in Your righteousness.
2 Bow down Your ear to me,
   Deliver me speedily;
   Be my rock of refuge,
   A fortress of defense to save me.

3 For You *are* my rock and my fortress;
   Therefore, for Your name's sake,
   Lead me and guide me.
4 Pull me out of the net which they have
   secretly laid for me,
   For You *are* my strength.
5 Into Your hand I commit my spirit;
   You have redeemed me, O LORD God of
   truth.

6 I have hated those who regard useless
   idols;
   But I trust in the LORD.
7 I will be glad and rejoice in Your mercy,
   For You have considered my trouble;
   You have known my soul in adversities,
8 And have not shut me up into the hand
   of the enemy;
   You have set my feet in a wide place.

9 Have mercy on me, O LORD, for I am in
   trouble;
   My eye wastes away with grief,
   Yes, my soul and my body!
10 For my life is spent with grief,
   And my years with sighing;
   My strength fails because of my iniquity,
   And my bones waste away.
11 I am a reproach among all my enemies,
   But especially among my neighbors,
   And *am* repulsive to my acquaintances;
   Those who see me outside flee from me.
12 I am forgotten like a dead man, out of
   mind;
   I am like a broken vessel.
13 For I hear the slander of many;
   Fear *is* on every side;

While they take counsel together against
   me,
   They scheme to take away my life.

14 But as for me, I trust in You, O LORD;
   I say, "You *are* my God."
15 My times *are* in Your hand;
   Deliver me from the hand of my enemies,
   And from those who persecute me.
16 Make Your face shine upon Your servant;
   Save me for Your mercies' sake.
17 Do not let me be ashamed, O LORD, for I
   have called upon You;
   Let the wicked be ashamed;
   Let them be silent in the grave.
18 Let the lying lips be put to silence,
   Which speak insolent things proudly and
   contemptuously against the righteous.

19 Oh, how great *is* Your goodness,
   Which You have laid up for those who
   fear You,
   Which You have prepared for those who
   trust in You
   In the presence of the sons of men!
20 You shall hide them in the secret place of
   Your presence
   From the plots of man;
   You shall keep them secretly in a pavilion
   From the strife of tongues.

21 Blessed *be* the LORD,
   For He has shown me His marvelous
   kindness in a strong city!
22 For I said in my haste,
   "I am cut off from before Your eyes";
   Nevertheless You heard the voice of my
   supplications
   When I cried out to You.

23 Oh, love the LORD, all you His saints!
   For the LORD preserves the faithful,
   And fully repays the proud person.
24 Be of good courage,
   And He shall strengthen your heart,
   All you who hope in the LORD.

PSALM 32

THE JOY OF FORGIVENESS

A Psalm of David. A Contemplation.[a]

1 Blessed *is he whose* transgression *is*
   forgiven,
   Whose sin *is* covered.

32:title [a]Hebrew *Maschil*

2 Blessed *is* the man to whom the LORD
  does not impute iniquity,
And in whose spirit *there is* no deceit.

3 When I kept silent, my bones grew old
Through my groaning all the day long.

4 For day and night Your hand was heavy
  upon me;
My vitality was turned into the drought
  of summer. Selah

5 I acknowledged my sin to
  You,
And my iniquity I have
  not hidden.
I said, "I will confess my
  transgressions to the
  LORD,"
And You forgave the
  iniquity of my sin.
Selah

GUILT

What happens to our guilt when our sins are forgiven? (32:5)

6 For this cause everyone who is godly
  shall pray to You
In a time when You may be found;
Surely in a flood of great waters
They shall not come near him.

7 You *are* my hiding place;
You shall preserve me from trouble;
You shall surround me with songs of
  deliverance. Selah

8 I will instruct you and teach you in the
  way you should go;
I will guide you with My eye.

9 Do not be like the horse *or* like the
  mule,
Which have no understanding,
Which must be harnessed with bit and
  bridle,
Else they will not come near you.

10 Many sorrows *shall be* to the wicked;
But he who trusts in the LORD, mercy
  shall surround him.

11 Be glad in the LORD and rejoice, you
  righteous;
And shout for joy, all *you* upright in
  heart!

PSALM 33

THE SOVEREIGNTY OF THE LORD IN CREATION AND HISTORY

1 Rejoice in the LORD, O you righteous!
For praise from the upright is
  beautiful.

2 Praise the LORD with the harp;
Make melody to Him with an instrument
  of ten strings.

3 Sing to Him a new song;
Play skillfully with a shout of joy.

4 For the word of the LORD *is* right,
And all His work *is done* in truth.

5 He loves righteousness and justice;
The earth is full of the goodness of the
  LORD.

Promise — HE PROMISES TO TEACH YOU.

I will instruct you and teach you in the way you should go; I will guide you with My eye (Ps. 32:8).

Who was your favorite teacher? Do you remember that person well? You probably do. Maybe he or she took a special interest in you; didn't let you get away with anything; believed in you more than you believed in yourself; made you want to learn; had high expectations of what you could do; actually made school fun. Whatever the reason, you remember that teacher well, and you're so glad he or she was a part of your growing up.

God promises to be your teacher—Life 101. He says that He will point out the road you should follow and that He will watch over you. He has the answers to all of your questions. By His Holy Spirit, He'll even guide you to what is true (see John 16:13). So if you were thinking about skipping God's class, don't. Listen to Him and His wise instruction. He's the last guidance counselor you'll ever need.

SEE FOR YOURSELF:
Prov. 2:6; Is. 2:3; John 14:26; 16:13

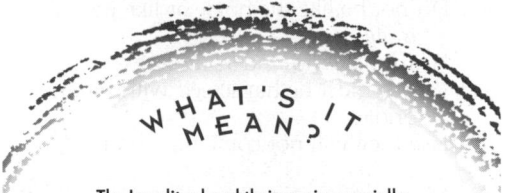

WHAT'S IT MEAN?

The Israelites loved their music, especially when it came time to worship the Lord. Specific groups of Levites were assigned to sing in the choir or play in the orchestra that performed in or near the tabernacle. The orchestra was made up of stringed instruments, such as guitars and harps, as well as percussion instruments, such as tambourines and cymbals.

Psalm 33:2

6 By the word of the LORD the heavens
    were made,
   And all the host of them by the breath of
    His mouth.
7 He gathers the waters of the sea together
    as a heap;*a*
   He lays up the deep in storehouses.

8 Let all the earth fear the LORD;
   Let all the inhabitants of the world stand
    in awe of Him.
9 For He spoke, and it was *done;*
   He commanded, and it stood fast.

10 The LORD brings the counsel of the
     nations to nothing;
    He makes the plans of the peoples of no
     effect.
11 The counsel of the LORD stands forever,
    The plans of His heart to all generations.
12 Blessed *is* the nation whose God *is* the
     LORD,
    The people He has chosen as His own
     inheritance.

13 The LORD looks from heaven;
    He sees all the sons of men.
14 From the place of His dwelling He looks
    On all the inhabitants of the earth;
15 He fashions their hearts individually;
    He considers all their works.

16 No king *is* saved by the multitude of an
     army;

A mighty man is not delivered by great
    strength.
17 A horse *is* a vain hope for safety;
    Neither shall it deliver *any* by its great
     strength.

18 Behold, the eye of the LORD *is* on those
     who fear Him,
    On those who hope in His mercy,
19 To deliver their soul from death,
    And to keep them alive in famine.

20 Our soul waits for the LORD;
    He *is* our help and our shield.
21 For our heart shall rejoice in Him,
    Because we have trusted in His holy
     name.
22 Let Your mercy, O LORD, be upon us,
    Just as we hope in You.

On the Edge

For the word of the LORD is right, and all His work is done in truth (Ps. 33:4).

Who do you trust? Most people have a few friends who they think are trustworthy. Most people trust their parents and their brothers and sisters, at least to some extent. Maybe you have a favorite teacher or a coach you feel you can trust.

Has someone you trusted ever hurt you? That seems to happen to just about everybody at some point during their lives. Maybe you misjudged your friend and found out that person couldn't be trusted after all. More often, someone you've trusted for a long time makes a mistake that ends up hurting you. That doesn't mean you should stop trusting that person. It just means you need to accept the fact that person isn't perfect—and forgive.

But trusting God isn't like that. He *is* perfect. He never lies, never misses the smallest details of any situation, never makes a mistake. You can count on every word He says. Everything He does is meant for something good in your life.

SEE FOR YOURSELF:
Is. 49:7; 1 Cor. 1:9;
2 Thess. 3:3

33:7 *a*Septuagint, Targum, and Vulgate read *in a vessel.*

PSALM 34

THE HAPPINESS OF THOSE WHO TRUST IN GOD

A Psalm of David when he pretended madness before Abimelech, who drove him away, and he departed.

1 I will bless the LORD at all times;
His praise *shall* continually *be* in my mouth.

2 My soul shall make its boast in the LORD;
The humble shall hear *of it* and be glad.

3 Oh, magnify the LORD with me,
And let us exalt His name together.

4 I sought the LORD, and He heard me,
And delivered me from all my fears.

5 They looked to Him and were radiant,
And their faces were not ashamed.

6 This poor man cried out, and the LORD heard *him*,
And saved him out of all his troubles.

7 The angel[a] of the LORD encamps all around those who fear Him,
And delivers them.

8 Oh, taste and see that the LORD *is* good;
Blessed *is* the man *who* trusts in Him!

9 Oh, fear the LORD, you His saints!
There is no want to those who fear Him.

10 The young lions lack and suffer hunger;
But those who seek the LORD shall not lack any good *thing.*

11 Come, you children, listen to me;
I will teach you the fear of the LORD.

12 Who *is* the man *who* desires life,
And loves *many* days, that he may see good?

13 Keep your tongue from evil,
And your lips from speaking deceit.

14 Depart from evil and do good;
Seek peace and pursue it.

15 The eyes of the LORD *are* on the righteous,
And His ears *are open* to their cry.

16 The face of the LORD *is* against those who do evil,
To cut off the remembrance of them from the earth.

17 *The righteous* cry out, and the LORD hears,
And delivers them out of all their troubles.

18 The LORD *is* near to those who have a broken heart,
And saves such as have a contrite spirit.

EMOTIONS

Where can we find healing for a broken heart? (34:18)

19 Many *are* the afflictions of the righteous,
But the LORD delivers him out of them all.

20 He guards all his bones;
Not one of them is broken.

21 Evil shall slay the wicked,
And those who hate the righteous shall be condemned.

34:7 [a]Or *Angel*

Promise   HE PROMISES THAT HIS ADVICE AND PLANS WILL NEVER CHANGE.

The counsel of the LORD stands forever, the plans of His heart to all generations (Ps. 33:11).

Do you know what God thinks of you? He thinks you're the best. You belong to Him and are like His prize. He has compassion toward you because He knows your weak places. He created you out of pure love. He *wanted* you to be alive. He has made plans for all of eternity—plans that will never change, because God's thoughts will never change. He's got a plan for you. Your heart, your mind, and your body were designed with His plan in mind. You can run from God's plan for the rest of your life, but you will never change His mind or mess with His plan. He knows what you would be great at and He built you to do it. Ask Him to show you what He made you for. Invite Him to remind you when you forget. Then go for it.

SEE FOR YOURSELF:
Jer. 29:11; Dan. 6:26; Mal. 3:6

22 The LORD redeems the soul of His
    servants,
  And none of those who trust in Him
    shall be condemned.

On the Edge

*Oh, fear the LORD, you His saints!
There is no want to those who fear
Him (Ps. 34:9).*

Ever feel like just one of the guys (or
one of the girls)? You know, you go to the
same school as all of your friends, hang out
at the same places, like the same bands,
wear the same style of clothing, watch the
same movies, play the same sports, have the
same tennis shoes . . . Maybe you have red
hair and your friends have brown, but
mostly you're all just about alike—regular
kids.

The Lord doesn't see you as one of the
guys. He says you are special—not in a
cheesy way, but in the way that a treasure is
special. You are rare, one-of-a-kind. When
He looks at you, He goes, "Wow."

He feels that way about you all the time,
not just when you pray or worship.
That's one of the ways He honors
you. Psalm 34:9 says that you are
to honor (fear) Him, too. You
don't have to be all stuffy or
religious to honor the Lord. You just have to
think about Him, consider what He wants,
follow His direction, spend time with Him.
Thank Him for making you His special
treasure and feel the same about Him—that
He is your treasure. One of the best ways to
honor Him is to look at Him and go, "Wow."

SEE FOR YOURSELF:
Deut. 26:18;
1 Cor. 1:30, 31;
Heb. 2:11

PSALM 35

THE LORD THE AVENGER OF HIS PEOPLE

A Psalm of David.

1 Plead *my cause*, O LORD, with those who
    strive with me;
  Fight against those who fight against me.
2 Take hold of shield and buckler,

  And stand up for my help.
3 Also draw out the spear,
  And stop those who pursue me.
  Say to my soul,
  "I *am* your salvation."

4 Let those be put to shame and brought to
    dishonor
  Who seek after my life;
  Let those be turned back and brought to
    confusion
  Who plot my hurt.
5 Let them be like chaff before the wind,
  And let the angel[a] of the LORD chase *them.*
6 Let their way be dark and slippery,
  And let the angel of the LORD pursue
    them.
7 For without cause they have hidden their
    net for me *in* a pit,
  Which they have dug without cause for
    my life.
8 Let destruction come upon him
    unexpectedly,
  And let his net that he has hidden catch
    himself;
  Into that very destruction let him fall.

9 And my soul shall be joyful in the LORD;
  It shall rejoice in His salvation.
10 All my bones shall say,
  "LORD, who *is* like You,
  Delivering the poor from him who is too
    strong for him,
  Yes, the poor and the needy from him
    who plunders him?"

11 Fierce witnesses rise up;
  They ask me *things* that I do not know.
12 They reward me evil for good,
  To the sorrow of my soul.
13 But as for me, when they were sick,
  My clothing *was* sackcloth;
  I humbled myself with fasting;
  And my prayer would return to my own
    heart.
14 I paced about as though *he were* my friend
    or brother;
  I bowed down heavily, as one who
    mourns *for his* mother.

15 But in my adversity they rejoiced
  And gathered together;
  Attackers gathered against me,
  And I did not know *it;*
  They tore *at me* and did not cease;

16 With ungodly mockers at feasts
They gnashed at me with their teeth.

17 Lord, how long will You look on?
Rescue me from their destructions,
My precious *life* from the lions.

18 I will give You thanks in the great
assembly;
I will praise You among many people.

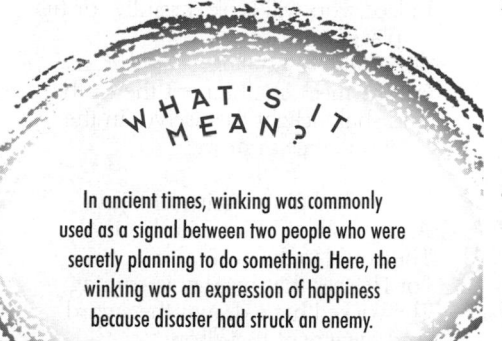

WHAT'S IT MEAN?

In ancient times, winking was commonly used as a signal between two people who were secretly planning to do something. Here, the winking was an expression of happiness because disaster had struck an enemy.

Psalm 35:19

19 Let them not rejoice over me who are
wrongfully my enemies;
Nor let them wink with the eye who hate
me without a cause.

20 For they do not speak peace,
But they devise deceitful matters
Against *the* quiet ones in the land.

21 They also opened their mouth wide
against me,
And said, "Aha, aha!
Our eyes have seen *it.*"

22 *This* You have seen, O Lord;
Do not keep silence.
O Lord, do not be far from me.

23 Stir up Yourself, and awake to my
vindication,
To my cause, my God and my Lord.

24 Vindicate me, O Lord my God, according
to Your righteousness;
And let them not rejoice over me.

25 Let them not say in their hearts, "Ah, so
we would have it!"
Let them not say, "We have swallowed
him up."

26 Let them be ashamed and brought to
mutual confusion
Who rejoice at my hurt;

Let them be clothed with shame and
dishonor
Who exalt themselves against me.

27 Let them shout for joy and be glad,
Who favor my righteous cause;
And let them say continually,
"Let the Lord be magnified,
Who has pleasure in the prosperity of His
servant."

28 And my tongue shall speak of Your
righteousness
And of Your praise all the day long.

PSALM 36

MAN'S WICKEDNESS AND GOD'S PERFECTIONS

To the Chief Musician. A Psalm of David
the servant of the Lord.

1 An oracle within my heart concerning the
transgression of the wicked:
There is no fear of God before his eyes.

2 For he flatters himself in his own eyes,
When he finds out his iniquity *and* when
he hates.

3 The words of his mouth *are* wickedness
and deceit;
He has ceased to be wise *and* to do good.

4 He devises wickedness on his bed;
He sets himself in a way *that is* not good;
He does not abhor evil.

5 Your mercy, O Lord, *is* in the heavens;
Your faithfulness *reaches* to the clouds.

6 Your righteousness *is* like the great
mountains;
Your judgments *are* a great deep;
O Lord, You preserve man and beast.

7 How precious *is* Your lovingkindness,
O God!
Therefore the children of men put their
trust under the shadow of Your wings.

8 They are abundantly satisfied with the
fullness of Your house,
And You give them drink from the river
of Your pleasures.

9 For with You *is* the fountain of life;
In Your light we see light.

10 Oh, continue Your lovingkindness to
those who know You,
And Your righteousness to the upright in
heart.

11 Let not the foot of pride come against me,

And let not the hand of the wicked drive me away.

12 There the workers of iniquity have fallen;
They have been cast down and are not able to rise.

WHAT'S IT MEAN?

Not much rain falls in Israel between May and September, which means that water is precious. Old Testament writers often used rain (here called "the fountain of life") as a symbol of God's blessing and drought as a symbol of God's punishment.
Psalm 36:9

PSALM 37

THE HERITAGE OF THE RIGHTEOUS AND THE CALAMITY OF THE WICKED

A Psalm of David.

1 Do not fret because of evildoers,
Nor be envious of the workers of iniquity.

JEALOUSY
Can we ever envy evil people? (37:1)

2 For they shall soon be cut down like the grass,
And wither as the green herb.

3 Trust in the LORD, and do good;
Dwell in the land, and feed on His faithfulness.

4 Delight yourself also in the LORD,
And He shall give you the desires of your heart.

5 Commit your way to the LORD,
Trust also in Him,
And He shall bring it to pass.

6 He shall bring forth your righteousness as the light,
And your justice as the noonday.

7 Rest in the LORD, and wait patiently for Him;
Do not fret because of him who prospers in his way,

Because of the man who brings wicked schemes to pass.

8 Cease from anger, and forsake wrath;
Do not fret—it only causes harm.

9 For evildoers shall be cut off;
But those who wait on the LORD,
They shall inherit the earth.

10 For yet a little while and the wicked shall be no more;
Indeed, you will look carefully for his place,
But it shall be no more.

11 But the meek shall inherit the earth,
And shall delight themselves in the abundance of peace.

12 The wicked plots against the just,
And gnashes at him with his teeth.

13 The Lord laughs at him,
For He sees that his day is coming.

14 The wicked have drawn the sword
And have bent their bow,
To cast down the poor and needy,
To slay those who are of upright conduct.

15 Their sword shall enter their own heart,
And their bows shall be broken.

16 A little that a righteous man has
Is better than the riches of many wicked.

17 For the arms of the wicked shall be broken,
But the LORD upholds the righteous.

18 The LORD knows the days of the upright,
And their inheritance shall be forever.

19 They shall not be ashamed in the evil time,
And in the days of famine they shall be satisfied.

20 But the wicked shall perish;
And the enemies of the LORD,
Like the splendor of the meadows, shall vanish.
Into smoke they shall vanish away.

21 The wicked borrows and does not repay,
But the righteous shows mercy and gives.

22 For those blessed by Him shall inherit the earth,
But those cursed by Him shall be cut off.

ASSURANCE
Does God always care for His children? (37:23, 24)

23 The steps of a good man are ordered by the LORD,

And He delights in his way.

24 Though he fall, he shall not be utterly
cast down;
For the LORD upholds *him with* His hand.

25 I have been young, and *now* am old;
Yet I have not seen the righteous forsaken,
Nor his descendants begging bread.

26 *He is* ever merciful, and lends;
And his descendants *are* blessed.

27 Depart from evil, and do good;
And dwell forevermore.

28 For the LORD loves justice,
And does not forsake His saints;
They are preserved forever,
But the descendants of the wicked shall
be cut off.

29 The righteous shall inherit the land,
And dwell in it forever.

30 The mouth of the righteous speaks
wisdom,
And his tongue talks of justice.

31 The law of his God *is* in his heart;
None of his steps shall slide.

32 The wicked watches the righteous,
And seeks to slay him.

33 The LORD will not leave him in his hand,
Nor condemn him when he is judged.

34 Wait on the LORD,
And keep His way,
And He shall exalt you to inherit the
land;
When the wicked are cut off, you shall
see *it.*

35 I have seen the wicked in great power,
And spreading himself like a native green
tree.

36 Yet he passed away,[a] and behold, he *was*
no *more;*
Indeed I sought him, but he could not be
found.

37 Mark the blameless *man,* and observe the
upright;
For the future of *that* man *is* peace.

38 But the transgressors shall be destroyed
together;
The future of the wicked shall be cut off.

39 But the salvation of the righteous *is* from
the LORD;
He is their strength in the time of trouble.

40 And the LORD shall help them and deliver
them;

37:36 [a]Following Masoretic Text, Septuagint, and Targum; Syriac and Vulgate read *I passed by.*

Promise   HE PROMISES TO NEVER FORSAKE YOU.

*For the LORD loves justice, and does not forsake His saints; they are preserved
forever, but the descendants of the wicked shall be cut off (Ps. 37:28).*

Do you ever think the people who don't give a rip about God have really good lives? You
probably know some people who don't give God a second thought, but they have nice clothes,
good grades, lots of friends. There are definitely a lot of famous musicians, actors, athletes, and
politicians who don't do a lot of good things, but they're living the "good life" all the same. It's
easy to want what they have and to wonder why God let them have things He doesn't give to you.
Sometimes when you compare your life to theirs, you think, *Man, where is God, anyway?*

Psalm 37 reminds you that the situation isn't always what it looks like. The people who don't
care about God have what Jesus called a "house on the sand" (Matt. 7:26). It may be a really
nice house, but it can't stand up for long. The people who refuse to obey God have nothing to
show for their lives in the end. When it looks like God is blessing them and leaving you to
fend for yourself, you need to know that He is still on your side. He will *never* forsake you. He
won't collapse when a storm blows in or run away when things are rough. He's here to stay.

SEE FOR YOURSELF:
Deut. 31:6; Matt. 7:26; 18:12–14; 28:20

He shall deliver them from the wicked,
And save them,
Because they trust in Him.

PSALM 38

PRAYER IN TIME OF CHASTENING

A Psalm of David.
To bring to remembrance.

1 O LORD, do not rebuke me in Your
       wrath,
    Nor chasten me in Your hot displeasure!
2 For Your arrows pierce me deeply,
    And Your hand presses me down.

3 *There is* no soundness in my flesh
    Because of Your anger,
    Nor *any* health in my bones
    Because of my sin.
4 For my iniquities have gone over my
       head;
    Like a heavy burden they are too heavy
       for me.
5 My wounds are foul *and* festering
    Because of my foolishness.

6 I am troubled, I am bowed down greatly;
    I go mourning all the day long.
7 For my loins are full of inflammation,
    And *there is* no soundness in my flesh.
8 I am feeble and severely broken;
    I groan because of the turmoil of my
       heart.

9 Lord, all my desire *is* before You;
    And my sighing is not hidden from You.
10 My heart pants, my strength fails me;
    As for the light of my eyes, it also has
       gone from me.

11 My loved ones and my friends stand
       aloof from my plague,
    And my relatives stand afar off.
12 Those also who seek my life lay snares *for
       me;*
    Those who seek my hurt speak of
       destruction,
    And plan deception all the day long.

13 But I, like a deaf *man,* do not hear;
    And *I am* like a mute *who* does not open
       his mouth.

14 Thus I am like a man who does not hear,
    And in whose mouth *is* no response.

15 For in You, O LORD, I hope;
    You will hear, O Lord my God.
16 For I said, "*Hear me,* lest they rejoice over
       me,
    Lest, when my foot slips, they exalt
       themselves against me."

17 For I *am* ready to fall,
    And my sorrow *is* continually before
       me.
18 For I will declare my iniquity;
    I will be in anguish over my sin.
19 But my enemies *are* vigorous, *and* they are
       strong;
    And those who hate me wrongfully have
       multiplied.
20 Those also who render evil for good,
    They are my adversaries, because I follow
       what is good.

21 Do not forsake me, O LORD;
    O my God, be not far from me!
22 Make haste to help me,
    O Lord, my salvation!

On the Edge

Lord, all my desire is before You; and my sighing is not hidden from You (Ps. 38:9).

What do you secretly want to do with your life? Want to be an undertaker, but think all your friends would laugh? Want to be a chemist, but can't imagine how it could possibly happen? What does your heart long to do? God knows every one of your deepest desires. He put them there. He knows what makes you feel like time just flew by. He knows what fills you up and gives you a purpose. He knows what makes you so angry that you just have to do something. So trust Him with your dreams and passions. He will not laugh. He is not surprised. He knows exactly how to make it all happen. His timing will be perfect.

SEE FOR YOURSELF:
Is. 66:18; Heb. 4:12

PSALM 39

PRAYER FOR WISDOM AND FORGIVENESS

To the Chief Musician. To Jeduthun.
A Psalm of David.

1 I said, "I will guard my ways,
Lest I sin with my tongue;
I will restrain my mouth with a muzzle,
While the wicked are before me."
2 I was mute with silence,
I held my peace *even* from good;
And my sorrow was stirred up.
3 My heart was hot within me;
While I was musing, the fire burned.
Then I spoke with my tongue:

4 "LORD, make me to know my end,
And what *is* the measure of my days,
That I may know how frail I *am.*
5 Indeed, You have made my days *as*
handbreadths,
And my age *is* as nothing before You;
Certainly every man at his best state *is*
but vapor. Selah
6 Surely every man walks about like a
shadow;
Surely they busy themselves in vain;
He heaps up *riches,*
And does not know who will gather
them.

WHAT'S IT MEAN?

Jeduthun, the guy who gets credit at the beginning of this psalm, was appointed by David to serve as one of the three chief musicians in the tabernacle. Jeduthun was also known as Ethan.
Psalm 39 title

7 "And now, Lord, what do I wait for?
My hope *is* in You.
8 Deliver me from all my transgressions;
Do not make me the reproach of the
foolish.
9 I was mute, I did not open my mouth,
Because it was You who did *it.*
10 Remove Your plague from me;

I am consumed by the blow of Your
hand.
11 When with rebukes You correct man for
iniquity,
You make his beauty melt away like a
moth;
Surely every man *is* vapor. Selah

WHAT'S IT MEAN?

Moths are mentioned several times in the Bible as symbols of destruction. Here's how the little critters are able to do so much damage. Female moths often lay their eggs in clothing. When the eggs hatch, the newborn larvae eat the fibers of the clothing. Because the larvae chew quietly, the owner of the clothing may not know that damage is being done until it's too late.
Psalm 39:11

12 "Hear my prayer, O LORD,
And give ear to my cry;
Do not be silent at my tears;
For I *am* a stranger with You,
A sojourner, as all my fathers *were.*
13 Remove Your gaze from me, that I may
regain strength,
Before I go away and am no more."

PSALM 40

FAITH PERSEVERING IN TRIAL

To the Chief Musician.
A Psalm of David.

1 I waited patiently for the LORD;
And He inclined to me,
And heard my cry.
2 He also brought me up out of a horrible
pit,
Out of the miry clay,
And set my feet upon a rock,
And established my steps.
3 He has put a new song in my mouth—
Praise to our God;
Many will see *it* and fear,
And will trust in the LORD.

4 Blessed *is* that man who makes the LORD
his trust,
And does not respect the proud, nor such
as turn aside to lies.
5 Many, O LORD my God, *are* Your
wonderful works
Which You have done;
And Your thoughts toward us
Cannot be recounted to You in order;
If I would declare and speak *of them,*
They are more than can be numbered.

6 Sacrifice and offering You did not desire;
My ears You have opened.
Burnt offering and sin offering You did
not require.
7 Then I said, "Behold, I come;
In the scroll of the book *it is* written of
me.
8 I delight to do Your will, O my God,
And Your law *is* within my heart."

9 I have proclaimed the good news of
righteousness
In the great assembly;
Indeed, I do not restrain my lips,
O LORD, You Yourself know.
10 I have not hidden Your righteousness
within my heart;
I have declared Your faithfulness and
Your salvation;
I have not concealed Your lovingkindness
and Your truth
From the great assembly.

11 Do not withhold Your tender mercies
from me, O LORD;
Let Your lovingkindness and Your truth
continually preserve me.
12 For innumerable evils have surrounded
me;
My iniquities have overtaken me, so that
I am not able to look up;
They are more than the hairs of my head;
Therefore my heart fails me.

13 Be pleased, O LORD, to
deliver me;
O LORD, make haste to
help me!
14 Let them be ashamed
and brought to mutual
confusion
Who seek to destroy my life;
Let them be driven backward and
brought to dishonor
Who wish me evil.

PRAYER
Who
should
we go to for
help?
(40:13)

15 Let them be confounded because of their
shame,
Who say to me, "Aha, aha!"
16 Let all those who seek You rejoice and be
glad in You;
Let such as love Your salvation say
continually,
"The LORD be magnified!"
17 But I *am* poor and needy;
Yet the LORD thinks upon me.
You *are* my help and my deliverer;
Do not delay, O my God.

PSALM 41

THE BLESSING AND SUFFERING OF THE GODLY

To the Chief Musician. A Psalm of David.

1 Blessed *is* he who considers the poor;
The LORD will deliver him in time of
trouble.
2 The LORD will preserve him and keep him
alive,
And he will be blessed on the earth;
You will not deliver him to the will of his
enemies.
3 The LORD will strengthen
him on his bed of
illness;
You will sustain him on
his sickbed.
4 I said, "LORD, be merciful to
me;
Heal my soul, for I have sinned against
You."
5 My enemies speak evil of me:
"When will he die, and his name perish?"
6 And if he comes to see *me,* he speaks lies;
His heart gathers iniquity to itself;
When he goes out, he tells *it.*

7 All who hate me whisper together against
me;
Against me they devise my hurt.
8 "An evil disease," *they say,* "clings to him.
And *now* that he lies down, he will rise
up no more."
9 Even my own familiar friend in whom I
trusted,
Who ate my bread,
Has lifted up *his* heel against me.

10 But You, O LORD, be merciful to me, and
raise me up,

SICKNESS
Does God
care for the
sick?
(41:1–13)

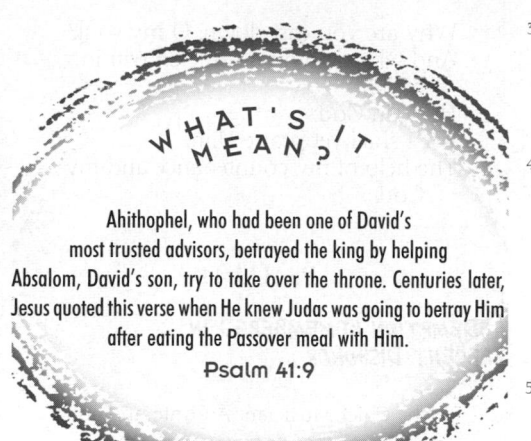

WHAT'S IT MEAN?

Ahithophel, who had been one of David's most trusted advisors, betrayed the king by helping Absalom, David's son, try to take over the throne. Centuries later, Jesus quoted this verse when He knew Judas was going to betray Him after eating the Passover meal with Him.

Psalm 41:9

3 My tears have been my food day and
        night,
    While they continually say to me,
    "Where *is* your God?"

4 When I remember these *things*,
    I pour out my soul within me.
    For I used to go with the multitude;
    I went with them to the house of God,
    With the voice of joy and praise,
    With a multitude that kept a pilgrim
        feast.

5 Why are you cast down, O my soul?
    And *why* are you disquieted
        within me?
    Hope in God, for I shall
        yet praise Him
    For the help of His
        countenance.[a]

DOUBT

Can our doubts be overcome?
(42:5, 6)

    That I may repay them.
11 By this I know that You are well pleased
        with me,
    Because my enemy does not triumph
        over me.
12 As for me, You uphold me in my
        integrity,
    And set me before Your face forever.

13 Blessed *be* the LORD God of Israel
    From everlasting to everlasting!
    Amen and Amen.

6 O my God,[a] my soul is cast
        down within me;
    Therefore I will remember You from the
        land of the Jordan,
    And from the heights of Hermon,
    From the Hill Mizar.
7 Deep calls unto deep at the noise of Your
        waterfalls;
    All Your waves and billows have gone
        over me.

8   The LORD will
            command His
            lovingkindness
            in the daytime,
        And in the night
            His song *shall
            be* with me—
        A prayer to the
            God of my life.

Book Two:
Psalms 42—72

PSALM 42

**YEARNING FOR GOD
IN THE MIDST
OF DISTRESSES**

"The LORD will command His lovingkindness in the daytime, and in the night His song shall be with me— a prayer to the God of my life."
(Psalm 42:8)

9   I will say to God
            my Rock,
        "Why have You
            forgotten me?
    Why do I go mourning because of the
        oppression of the enemy?"

To the Chief Musician.
    A Contemplation[a]
    of the sons of Korah.

1 As the deer pants for the
        water brooks,
    So pants my soul for You, O God.
2 My soul thirsts for God, for the living
        God.
    When shall I come and appear before
        God?[a]

10 *As* with a breaking of my bones,
    My enemies reproach me,
    While they say to me all day long,
    "Where *is* your God?"

42:title [a]Hebrew *Maschil*   **42:2** [a]Following Masoretic Text and Vulgate; some Hebrew manuscripts, Septuagint, Syriac, and Targum read *I see the face of God*.   **42:5** [a]Following Masoretic Text and Targum; a few Hebrew manuscripts, Septuagint, Syriac, and Vulgate read *The help of my countenance, my God.*
42:6 [a]Following Masoretic Text and Targum; a few Hebrew manuscripts, Septuagint, Syriac, and Vulgate put *my God* at the end of verse 5.

11　Why are you cast down, O my soul?
　　And why are you disquieted within
　　　me?
　　Hope in God;
　　For I shall yet praise Him,
　　The help of my countenance and my
　　　God.

PSALM 43

PRAYER TO GOD IN TIME OF TROUBLE

　　Vindicate me, O God,
1　And plead my cause against an ungodly
　　　nation;
　　Oh, deliver me from the deceitful and
　　　unjust man!
2　For You *are* the God of my strength;
　　Why do You cast me off?
　　Why do I go mourning because of the
　　　oppression of the enemy?

3　Oh, send out Your light and Your
　　　truth!
　　Let them lead me;
　　Let them bring me to Your holy hill
　　And to Your tabernacle.
4　Then I will go to the altar of God,
　　To God my exceeding joy;
　　And on the harp I will praise You,
　　O God, my God.

5　Why are you cast down, O my soul?
　　And why are you disquieted within
　　　me?
　　Hope in God;
　　For I shall yet praise Him,
　　The help of my countenance and my
　　　God.

PSALM 44

REDEMPTION REMEMBERED IN PRESENT DISHONOR

　　To the Chief Musician. A Contemplation[a]
　　　of the sons of Korah.

1　We have heard with our ears, O God,
　　Our fathers have told us,
　　The deeds You did in their days,
　　In days of old:
2　You drove out the nations with Your
　　　hand,
　　But them You planted;
　　You afflicted the peoples, and cast them
　　　out.
3　For they did not gain possession of the
　　　land by their own sword,
　　Nor did their own arm save them;
　　But it was Your right hand, Your arm, and
　　　the light of Your countenance,
　　Because You favored them.

44:title [a]Hebrew *Maschil*

Promise   HE PROMISES TO BE YOUR GOD.

Why are you cast down, O my soul? And why are you disquieted within me? Hope in God; for I shall yet praise Him, the help of my countenance and my God (Ps. 43:5).

Have you ever thought, *There are millions of people in the world. How can God keep up with all of us? How can He pay any attention to me? How can He hear my prayers when everybody else is talking to Him, too?* Thoughts like that will blow your mind, but God is so much bigger than your mind. Psalm 43:5 has two words that will help put your mind at ease: "my God." In order to have a close and growing relationship with God, you have to make Him personal. You have to know that He is *your* God. Here's a suggestion: When you pray, just say to the Lord, "You are *my* God." Put the emphasis on the word *my*. Even though there are lots of Christians in the world, your relationship with God is not like anybody else's. He made you to stand out from everybody else. Those things that set you apart from other people are the things that give you a unique place with Him. When you feel like a dot in the middle of a swarm of Christians who need God's love and attention, just remember that He is *your* God.

SEE FOR YOURSELF:
Ps. 63:1; 118:28; Is. 25:1; Jer. 31:20

WHAT'S IT MEAN?

God wanted every generation of Israelites
to know what He had done for their ancestors.
Though written records of past events were kept, few people had
access to them. That's why it was important for the Israelites to tell
their children and grandchildren about their history.

Psalm 44:1

4   You are my King, O God;[a]
    Command[b] victories for Jacob.
5   Through You we will push down our
        enemies;
    Through Your name we will trample
        those who rise up against us.
6   For I will not trust in my bow,
    Nor shall my sword save me.
7   But You have saved us from our enemies,
    And have put to shame those who hated
        us.
8   In God we boast all day long,
    And praise Your name forever.   Selah

9   But You have cast *us* off and put us to
        shame,
    And You do not go out with our armies.
10 You make us turn back from the enemy,
    And those who hate us have taken spoil
        for themselves.
11 You have given us up like sheep *intended*
        for food,
    And have scattered us among the
        nations.
12 You sell Your people for *next to* nothing,
    And are not enriched by selling them.

13 You make us a reproach to our neighbors,
    A scorn and a derision to those all
        around us.
14 You make us a byword among the
        nations,
    A shaking of the head among the peoples.
15 My dishonor *is* continually before me,
    And the shame of my face has covered me,

16 Because of the voice of him who
        reproaches and reviles,
    Because of the enemy and the avenger.

17 All this has come upon us;
    But we have not forgotten You,
    Nor have we dealt falsely with Your
        covenant.
18 Our heart has not turned back,
    Nor have our steps departed from Your
        way;
19 But You have severely broken us in the
        place of jackals,
    And covered us with the shadow of
        death.

20 If we had forgotten the name of our God,
    Or stretched out our hands to a foreign
        god,
21 Would not God search this out?
    For He knows the secrets of the heart.
22 Yet for Your sake we are killed all day
        long;
    We are accounted as sheep for the
        slaughter.

23 Awake! Why do You sleep, O Lord?
    Arise! Do not cast *us* off forever.
24 Why do You hide Your face,
    And forget our affliction and our
        oppression?
25 For our soul is bowed down to the dust;
    Our body clings to the ground.
26 Arise for our help,
    And redeem us for Your mercies' sake.

PSALM 45

THE GLORIES OF THE MESSIAH AND HIS BRIDE

To the Chief Musician. Set to "The Lilies."[a]
A Contemplation[b] of the sons of Korah.
A Song of Love.

1   My heart is overflowing with a good
        theme;
    I recite my composition concerning the
        King;
    My tongue *is* the pen of a ready writer.

2   You are fairer than the sons of men;
    Grace is poured upon Your lips;

44:4 [a]Following Masoretic Text and Targum; Septuagint and Vulgate read *and my God.* [b]Following Masoretic Text and Targum; Septuagint, Syriac, and Vulgate read *Who commands.* **45:title** [a]Hebrew *Shoshannim* [b]Hebrew *Maschil*

Therefore God has blessed You forever.
3 Gird Your sword upon *Your* thigh,
    O Mighty One,
  With Your glory and Your majesty.
4 And in Your majesty ride prosperously
    because of truth, humility, *and*
    righteousness;
  And Your right hand shall teach You
    awesome things.
5 Your arrows *are* sharp in the heart of the
    King's enemies;
  The peoples fall under You.

WHAT'S IT MEAN?

The royal household must have shelled
out quite a bit of money for the rare and expensive
spices mentioned here. Myrrh was a plant used to make perfumes,
among other things. It was also one of the presents the wise men
brought to the baby Jesus. The aloes were not the plants we know
today, but were actually trees whose fragrant wood was used for
perfume and incense. Cassia plants smelled a lot like cinnamon. All
three spices were associated with
the oil used to anoint kings.
Psalm 45:8

6 Your throne, O God, *is* forever and ever;
  A scepter of righteousness *is* the scepter
    of Your kingdom.
7 You love righteousness and hate
    wickedness;
  Therefore God, Your God, has anointed
    You
  With the oil of gladness more than Your
    companions.
8 All Your garments are scented with myrrh
    and aloes *and* cassia,
  Out of the ivory palaces, by which they
    have made You glad.
9 Kings' daughters *are* among Your
    honorable women;
  At Your right hand stands the queen in
    gold from Ophir.

10 Listen, O daughter,
   Consider and incline your ear;
   Forget your own people also, and your
     father's house;

11 So the King will greatly desire your
     beauty;
   Because He *is* your Lord, worship Him.
12 And the daughter of Tyre *will come* with a
     gift;
   The rich among the people will seek your
     favor.

13 The royal daughter *is* all glorious within
     the palace;
   Her clothing *is* woven with gold.
14 She shall be brought to the King in robes
     of many colors;
   The virgins, her companions who follow
     her, shall be brought to You.
15 With gladness and rejoicing they shall be
     brought;
   They shall enter the King's palace.

16 Instead of Your fathers shall be Your sons,
   Whom You shall make princes in all the
     earth.
17 I will make Your name to be remembered
     in all generations;
   Therefore the people shall praise You
     forever and ever.

PSALM 46

GOD THE REFUGE OF HIS PEOPLE AND CONQUEROR OF THE NATIONS

*To the Chief Musician. A Psalm of the sons
of Korah. A Song for Alamoth.*

1 God *is* our refuge and strength,
  A very present help in trouble.
2 Therefore we will not fear,
  Even though the earth be removed,

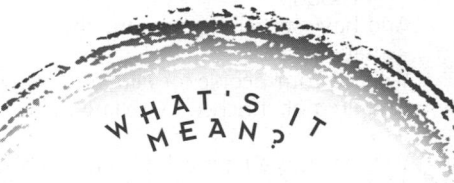

WHAT'S IT MEAN?

In ancient times, oceans and seas
were thought of as things to be feared. Bible writers
occasionally used the sea as a symbol of trouble. Rivers, on the other
hand, were considered good and helpful. In this passage, the sea
represents destruction and the river represents
the blessings of God.
Psalm 46:2–4

And though the mountains be carried into the midst of the sea;
3 *Though* its waters roar *and* be troubled,
Though the mountains shake with its swelling. Selah

4 *There is* a river whose streams shall make glad the city of God,
The holy *place* of the tabernacle of the Most High.
5 God *is* in the midst of her, she shall not be moved;
God shall help her, just at the break of dawn.
6 The nations raged, the kingdoms were moved;
He uttered His voice, the earth melted.

7 The LORD of hosts *is* with us;
The God of Jacob *is* our refuge. Selah

8 Come, behold the works of the LORD,
Who has made desolations in the earth.
9 He makes wars cease to the end of the earth;
He breaks the bow and cuts the spear in two;
He burns the chariot in the fire.

10 Be still, and know that I *am* God;
I will be exalted among the nations,
I will be exalted in the earth!

11 The LORD of hosts *is* with us;
The God of Jacob *is* our refuge. Selah

PSALM 47

PRAISE TO GOD, THE RULER OF THE EARTH

To the Chief Musician. A Psalm of the sons of Korah.

1 Oh, clap your hands, all you peoples!
Shout to God with the voice of triumph!
2 For the LORD Most High *is* awesome;
He is a great King over all the earth.
3 He will subdue the peoples under us,
And the nations under our feet.
4 He will choose our inheritance for us,
The excellence of Jacob whom He loves. Selah

5 God has gone up with a shout,
The LORD with the sound of a trumpet.
6 Sing praises to God, sing praises!
Sing praises to our King, sing praises!
7 For God *is* the King of all the earth;
Sing praises with understanding.

8 God reigns over the nations;
God sits on His holy throne.
9 The princes of the people have gathered together,
The people of the God of Abraham.
For the shields of the earth *belong* to God;
He is greatly exalted.

Promise   HE PROMISES TO BE READY TO HELP.

God is our refuge and strength, a very present help in trouble (Ps. 46:1).

God is "a very present help" always ready to aid His children. When the nation of Israel found itself face-to-face with an enemy, God didn't have to go recruit an army and buy some weapons. He already had an army of angels—and enough power in His little finger to wipe out the enemy. Sometimes God used the men of Israel's army; sometimes He used a bunch of trumpets; but whatever He did, Israel came out on top—as long as they obeyed Him.

Well, that same power, the "refuge and strength," is for you, too. God is always ready to help you. When you ask for His help with a tough decision, He doesn't have to go research the problem. He's got more knowledge and wisdom than even Albert Einstein could get a handle on. If money is what you need, He doesn't have to go to the bank and get a loan. Everything on earth belongs to Him anyway. Everything you need is wrapped up in God. He doesn't have to get it together before He can help. All He needs is for you to ask.

SEE FOR YOURSELF:
Josh. 1:9; Prov. 2:4–7; Is. 35:3, 4

PSALM 48

THE GLORY OF GOD IN ZION

A Song. A Psalm of the sons of Korah.

1 Great *is* the LORD, and greatly to be
 praised
 In the city of our God,
 In His holy mountain.
2 Beautiful in elevation,
 The joy of the whole earth,
 Is Mount Zion *on* the sides of the north,
 The city of the great King.
3 God *is* in her palaces;
 He is known as her refuge.

4 For behold, the kings assembled,
 They passed by together.
5 They saw *it, and* so they marveled;
 They were troubled, they hastened away.
6 Fear took hold of them there,
 And pain, as of a woman in birth pangs,
7 *As when* You break the ships of Tarshish
 With an east wind.

8 As we have heard,
 So we have seen
 In the city of the LORD of hosts,
 In the city of our God:
 God will establish it forever.   Selah

9 We have thought, O God, on Your
 lovingkindness,
 In the midst of Your temple.
10 According to Your name, O God,
 So *is* Your praise to the ends of the earth;

11 Your right hand is full of righteousness.
 Let Mount Zion rejoice,
 Let the daughters of Judah be glad,
 Because of Your judgments.

12 Walk about Zion,
 And go all around her.
 Count her towers;
13 Mark well her bulwarks;
 Consider her palaces;
 That you may tell *it* to the
 generation following.
14 For this *is* God,
 Our God forever and
 ever;
 He will be our guide
 Even to death.[a]

GOD'S WILL

Can Christians be hopeful about the future? (48:14)

PSALM 49

THE CONFIDENCE OF THE FOOLISH

To the Chief Musician. A Psalm
 of the sons of Korah.

1 Hear this, all peoples;
 Give ear, all inhabitants of the world,
2 Both low and high,
 Rich and poor together.
3 My mouth shall speak wisdom,
 And the meditation of my heart *shall give*
 understanding.
4 I will incline my ear to a proverb;
 I will disclose my dark saying on the
 harp.

5 Why should I fear in the days of evil,
 When the iniquity at my heels surrounds
 me?
6 Those who trust in their wealth
 And boast in the multitude of their riches,
7 None *of them* can by any means redeem
 his brother,
 Nor give to God a ransom for him—
8 For the redemption of their souls *is* costly,
 And it shall cease forever—
9 That he should continue to live eternally,
 And not see the Pit.

10 For he sees wise men die;
 Likewise the fool and the senseless person
 perish,
 And leave their wealth to others.
11 Their inner thought *is that* their houses
 will last forever,[a]

WHAT'S IT MEAN?

The city of Jerusalem, located on top of Mount Zion, was surrounded by a wall to protect its citizens from their enemies. Towers were built at various points on the wall so that lookouts could spot coming attacks.
Psalm 48:12

48:14 [a]Following Masoretic Text and Syriac; Septuagint and Vulgate read *Forever.* **49:11** [a]Septuagint, Syriac, Targum, and Vulgate read *Their graves shall be their houses forever.*

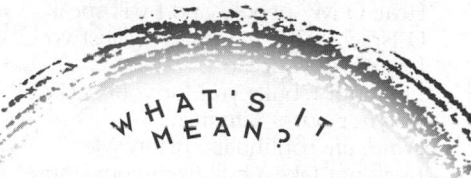

WHAT'S IT MEAN?

Israelite poets were like folk singers. They often read their poems with musical accompaniment, usually from a stringed instrument. Greek poets, among others, also presented their work with a musical background.

Psalm 49:4

Their dwelling places to all generations;
They call *their* lands after their own
   names.
12 Nevertheless man, *though* in honor, does
   not remain;[a]
He is like the beasts *that* perish.

13 This is the way of those who *are*
   foolish,
And of their posterity who approve their
   sayings.   Selah
14 Like sheep they are laid in the grave;
Death shall feed on them;

The upright shall have dominion over
   them in the morning;
And their beauty shall be consumed in
   the grave, far from their dwelling.
15 But God will redeem my soul from the
   power of the grave,
For He shall receive me.   Selah

16 Do not be afraid when one becomes rich,
When the glory of his house is increased;
17 For when he dies he shall carry nothing
   away;
His glory shall not descend after him.
18 Though while he lives he blesses himself
(For *men* will praise you when you do
   well for yourself),
19 He shall go to the generation of his
   fathers;
They shall never see light.
20 A man *who is* in honor, yet does not
   understand,
Is like the beasts *that* perish.

PSALM 50

GOD THE RIGHTEOUS JUDGE

A Psalm of Asaph.

1 The Mighty One, God the LORD,
Has spoken and called the earth

49:12 [a]Following Masoretic Text and Targum; Septuagint, Syriac, and Vulgate read *understand* (compare verse 20).

Promise   HE PROMISES TO REDEEM YOU FROM THE POWER OF DEATH.

But God will redeem my soul from the power of the grave, for He shall receive me (Ps. 49:15).

For the person who doesn't believe in Jesus, death has a lot of power. Death for them is the end of life on earth and the beginning of hell—forever. But Jesus promises to rescue His believers "from the power of the grave." He is the One who drove death into the ground. He is more powerful than death. He has beaten death for you. All He asks is that you believe that He died just for you and that you let Him redeem you. Then follow Him. What that means is that you have to give up trying to save yourself. You will never be good enough, do enough good deeds, or accomplish enough great things to overcome death. You don't even have to try anymore.

Right now, right where you are, tell Jesus that you can't do it yourself; you are drowning in your own sin. Ask Him to reach in and rescue you. Hold on tightly as He pulls you to shore and breathes new life into you. Then stand up and follow the One who has rescued you for eternity.

SEE FOR YOURSELF:
Is. 25:8; 1 Cor. 15:55; Rev. 21:4

On the Edge

Nevertheless man, though in honor, does not remain; he is like the beasts that perish (Ps. 49:12).

Justin was sixteen years old and a really awesome kid—the kind of guy everyone wanted to be around. He had such a great attitude—he even made work fun. One Tuesday night after supper, he hopped in his car to go to a Bible study. His mom kissed him and reminded him to buckle up and drive safely. Two miles from his house, Justin crossed the yellow line and hit another car. Justin died and so did the lady in the other car. No one could believe that Justin was gone. He had so much life ahead of him—he was really going to make a difference. A part of God's design is that we all die sometime. And even when we don't understand, we cling to the truth that God's timing is perfect. The coolest thing about Justin is that he really loved God and lived a life that proved it. When Justin left this earth and entered the presence of his Lord, the angels sang and the Savior surely said, "Well done, My son. I am so pleased with you."

SEE FOR YOURSELF:
Eccl. 2:15, 16; 3:19, 20;
Matt. 25:23;
1 Cor. 15:21, 22

From the rising of the sun to its going
down.
2 Out of Zion, the perfection of beauty,
God will shine forth.
3 Our God shall come, and shall not keep
silent;
A fire shall devour before Him,
And it shall be very tempestuous all
around Him.

4 He shall call to the heavens from above,
And to the earth, that He may judge His
people:
5 "Gather My saints together to Me,
Those who have made a covenant with
Me by sacrifice."
6 Let the heavens declare His righteousness,
For God Himself *is* Judge.   Selah

7 "Hear, O My people, and I will speak,
O Israel, and I will testify against you;
I *am* God, your God!
8 I will not rebuke you for your sacrifices
Or your burnt offerings,
Which are continually before Me.
9 I will not take a bull from your house,
Nor goats out of your folds.
10 For every beast of the forest *is* Mine,
And the cattle on a thousand hills.
11 I know all the birds of the mountains,
And the wild beasts of the field *are* Mine.

12 "If I were hungry, I would not tell you;
For the world *is* Mine, and all its fullness.
13 Will I eat the flesh of bulls,
Or drink the blood of goats?
14 Offer to God thanksgiving,
And pay your vows to the Most High.
15 Call upon Me in the day of trouble;
I will deliver you, and you shall glorify
Me."

16 But to the wicked God says:
"What *right* have you to declare My
statutes,
Or take My covenant in your mouth,
17 Seeing you hate instruction
And cast My words behind you?
18 When you saw a thief, you consented[a]
with him,
And have been a partaker with
adulterers.
19 You give your mouth to evil,
And your tongue frames deceit.
20 You sit *and* speak against your brother;
You slander your own mother's son.
21 These *things* you have done, and I kept
silent;

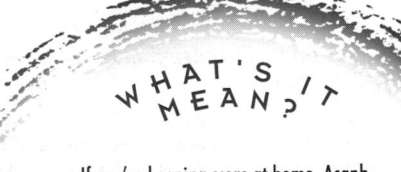

WHAT'S IT MEAN?

If you're keeping score at home, Asaph, who served as a chief musician in the tabernacle, is credited with writing twelve of the one hundred fifty psalms that appear in the Bible.
Psalm 50 title

50:18 [a]Septuagint, Syriac, Targum, and Vulgate read *ran.*

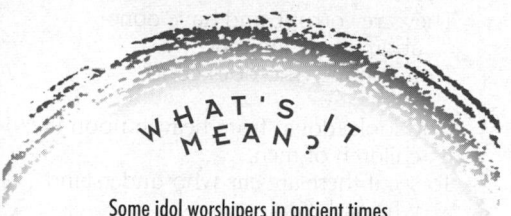

WHAT'S IT MEAN?

Some idol worshipers in ancient times believed that their gods got hungry and actually ate the animals that were sacrificed to them. They believed their gods needed the food to live. The God of Israel, on the other hand, did not need the sacrifices offered by His people; He found pleasure in the obedience of those who followed Him.

Psalm 50:13

You thought that I was altogether like you;
But I will rebuke you,
And set *them* in order before your eyes.

22 "Now consider this, you who forget God,
Lest I tear *you* in pieces,
And *there be* none to deliver:
23 Whoever offers praise glorifies Me;
And to him who orders *his* conduct *aright*
I will show the salvation of God."

PSALM 51

A PRAYER OF REPENTANCE

To the Chief Musician. A Psalm of David when Nathan the prophet went to him, after he had gone in to Bathsheba.

1 Have mercy upon me, O God,
According to Your lovingkindness;
According to the multitude of Your tender mercies,
Blot out my transgressions.
2 Wash me thoroughly from my iniquity,
And cleanse me from my sin.

3 For I acknowledge my transgressions,
And my sin *is* always before me.
4 Against You, You only, have I sinned,

And done *this* evil in Your sight—
That You may be found just when You speak,[a]
And blameless when You judge.

5 Behold, I was brought forth in iniquity,
And in sin my mother conceived me.
6 Behold, You desire truth in the inward parts,
And in the hidden *part* You will make me to know wisdom.

7 Purge me with hyssop, and I shall be clean;
Wash me, and I shall be whiter than snow.
8 Make me hear joy and gladness,
That the bones You have broken may rejoice.
9 Hide Your face from my sins,
And blot out all my iniquities.

10 Create in me a clean heart, O God,
And renew a steadfast spirit within me.
11 Do not cast me away from Your presence,
And do not take Your Holy Spirit from me.

12 Restore to me the joy of Your salvation,
And uphold me *by Your* generous Spirit.
13 *Then* I will teach transgressors Your ways,
And sinners shall be converted to You.

14 Deliver me from the guilt of bloodshed, O God,
The God of my salvation,
And my tongue shall sing aloud of Your righteousness.
15 O Lord, open my lips,
And my mouth shall show forth Your praise.
16 For You do not desire sacrifice, or else I would give *it;*
You do not delight in burnt offering.
17 The sacrifices of God *are* a broken spirit,
A broken and a contrite heart—
These, O God, You will not despise.

18 Do good in Your good pleasure to Zion;
Build the walls of Jerusalem.
19 Then You shall be pleased with the sacrifices of righteousness,
With burnt offering and whole burnt offering;
Then they shall offer bulls on Your altar.

TRUTH
How does God want us to live?
(51:1–6)

PSALM 52

THE END OF THE WICKED AND THE PEACE OF THE GODLY

To the Chief Musician. A Contemplation[a] of David when Doeg the Edomite went and told Saul, and said to him, "David has gone to the house of Ahimelech."

1 Why do you boast in evil, O mighty
    man?
  The goodness of God *endures* continually.
2 Your tongue devises destruction,
  Like a sharp razor, working deceitfully.
3 You love evil more than good,
  Lying rather than speaking righteousness.
                                    Selah
4 You love all devouring words,
  You deceitful tongue.

5 God shall likewise destroy you forever;
  He shall take you away, and pluck you
    out of *your* dwelling place,
  And uproot you from the land of the
    living.   Selah
6 The righteous also shall see and fear,
  And shall laugh at him, *saying,*
7 "Here is the man *who* did not make God
    his strength,
  But trusted in the abundance of his
    riches,
  And strengthened himself in his
    wickedness."

8 But I *am* like a green olive tree in the
    house of God;
  I trust in the mercy of God forever and
    ever.
9 I will praise You forever,
  Because You have done *it;*
  And in the presence of Your saints
  I will wait on Your name, for *it is*
    good.

PSALM 53

FOLLY OF THE GODLESS, AND THE RESTORATION OF ISRAEL

To the Chief Musician. Set to "Mahalath." A Contemplation[a] of David.

1 The fool has said in his heart,
  "*There is* no God."

They are corrupt, and have done
    abominable iniquity;
  There is none who does good.

2 God looks down from heaven upon the
    children of men,
  To see if there are *any* who understand,
    who seek God.
3 Every one of them has turned aside;
  They have together become corrupt;
  There is none who does good,
  No, not one.

4 Have the workers of iniquity no
    knowledge,
  Who eat up my people *as* they eat bread,
  And do not call upon God?
5 There they are in great fear
  Where no fear was,
  For God has scattered the bones of him
    who encamps against you;
  You have put *them* to shame,
  Because God has despised them.

6 Oh, that the salvation of Israel would
    come out of Zion!
  When God brings back the captivity of
    His people,
  Let Jacob rejoice *and* Israel be glad.

PSALM 54

ANSWERED PRAYER FOR DELIVERANCE FROM ADVERSARIES

To the Chief Musician. With stringed instruments.[a] A Contemplation[b] of David when the Ziphites went and said to Saul, "Is David not hiding with us?"

1 Save me, O God, by Your name,
  And vindicate me by Your strength.
2 Hear my prayer, O God;
  Give ear to the words of my mouth.
3 For strangers have risen up against me,
  And oppressors have sought after my life;
  They have not set God before them. Selah

4 Behold, God *is* my helper;
  The Lord *is* with those who uphold my
    life.
5 He will repay my enemies for their evil.
  Cut them off in Your truth.

6 I will freely sacrifice to You;

52:title [a]Hebrew *Maschil*   **53:title** [a]Hebrew *Maschil*   **54:title** [a]Hebrew *neginoth* [b]Hebrew *Maschil*

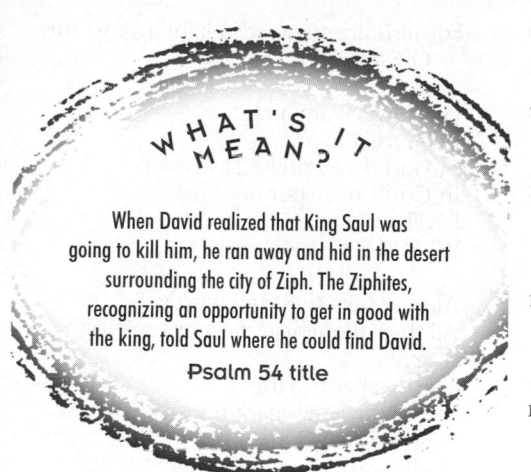

I will praise Your name, O LORD, for *it is* good.

7 For He has delivered me out of all trouble;
And my eye has seen *its desire* upon my enemies.

PSALM 55

TRUST IN GOD CONCERNING THE TREACHERY OF FRIENDS

To the Chief Musician. With stringed instruments.[a] A Contemplation[b] of David.

1 Give ear to my prayer, O God,
And do not hide Yourself from my supplication.

2 Attend to me, and hear me;
I am restless in my complaint, and moan noisily,

3 Because of the voice of the enemy,
Because of the oppression of the wicked;
For they bring down trouble upon me,
And in wrath they hate me.

4 My heart is severely pained within me,
And the terrors of death have fallen upon me.

5 Fearfulness and trembling have come upon me,
And horror has overwhelmed me.

6 So I said, "Oh, that I had wings like a dove!
I would fly away and be at rest.

7 Indeed, I would wander far off,
And remain in the wilderness.   Selah

8 I would hasten my escape
From the windy storm *and* tempest."

9 Destroy, O Lord, *and* divide their tongues,
For I have seen violence and strife in the city.

10 Day and night they go around it on its walls;
Iniquity and trouble *are* also in the midst of it.

11 Destruction *is* in its midst;
Oppression and deceit do not depart from its streets.

12 For *it is* not an enemy *who* reproaches me;
Then I could bear *it.*
Nor *is it* one *who* hates me who has exalted *himself* against me;
Then I could hide from him.

13 But *it was* you, a man my equal,
My companion and my acquaintance.

14 We took sweet counsel together,
And walked to the house of God in the throng.

FRIENDSHIP Can friends cause us pain? (55:12–14)

15 Let death seize them;
Let them go down alive into hell,
For wickedness *is* in their dwellings *and* among them.

16 As for me, I will call upon God,
And the LORD shall save me.

17 Evening and morning and at noon
I will pray, and cry aloud,
And He shall hear my voice.

18 He has redeemed my soul in peace from the battle *that was* against me,
For there were many against me.

19 God will hear, and afflict them,
Even He who abides from of old.   Selah
Because they do not change,
Therefore they do not fear God.

20 He has put forth his hands against those who were at peace with him;
He has broken his covenant.

21 *The words* of his mouth were smoother than butter,
But war *was* in his heart;
His words were softer than oil,
Yet they *were* drawn swords.

22 Cast your burden on the LORD,
And He shall sustain you;
He shall never permit the righteous to be
moved.

23 But You, O God, shall bring them down
to the pit of destruction;
Bloodthirsty and deceitful men shall not
live out half their days;
But I will trust in You.

On the Edge

You number my wanderings; put my tears into Your bottle; are they not in Your book? (Ps. 56:8).

Ever been through a time when it seemed like your heartache would never go away? The tears keep pouring out. The suffering seems endless. You're convinced you'll never be happy again. After a while you wonder if God even notices your broken heart. If He did, then surely He would do something—quick. God says that He has stored each one of your tears in a bottle. God knows you intimately, and He has not turned His back on your suffering. Even when you feel completely alone, God has not abandoned you. He sees your tear-stained pillow. He hears you cry yourself to sleep. It breaks His heart to see you hurt. Do not be afraid. He is there—close enough to catch each one of your tears.

SEE FOR YOURSELF:
Is. 38:5

For *there are* many who fight against me,
O Most High.

3 Whenever I am afraid,
I will trust in You.
4 In God (I will praise His word),
In God I have put my trust;
I will not fear.
What can flesh do to me?

5 All day they twist my words;
All their thoughts *are* against me for
evil.
6 They gather together,
They hide, they mark my steps,
When they lie in wait for my life.
7 Shall they escape by iniquity?
In anger cast down the peoples, O God!

8 You number my wanderings;
Put my tears into Your bottle;
Are they not in Your book?
9 When I cry out *to You,*
Then my enemies will turn back;
This I know, because God *is* for me.
10 In God (I will praise *His* word),
In the LORD (I will praise *His* word),
11 In God I have put my trust;
I will not be afraid.
What can man do to me?

12 Vows *made* to You *are binding* upon me,
O God;
I will render praises to You,
13 For You have delivered my soul from
death.
Have You not *kept* my feet from falling,
That I may walk before God
In the light of the living?

PSALM 56

PRAYER FOR RELIEF FROM TORMENTORS

To the Chief Musician. Set to
"The Silent Dove in Distant Lands."*a*
A Michtam of David when the Philistines
captured him in Gath.

1 Be merciful to me, O God, for man would
swallow me up;
Fighting all day he oppresses me.
2 My enemies would hound *me* all day,

PSALM 57

PRAYER FOR SAFETY FROM ENEMIES

To the Chief Musician. Set to
"Do Not Destroy."*a* A Michtam of David
when he fled from Saul into the cave.

1 Be merciful to me, O God, be merciful to
me!
For my soul trusts in You;
And in the shadow of Your wings I will
make my refuge,
Until *these* calamities have passed by.

56:title *a*Hebrew *Jonath Elem Rechokim*　　**57:title** *a*Hebrew *Al Tashcheth*

WHAT'S IT MEAN?

Throughout the Bible, wings are used as symbols of protection and safety. If that seems odd to you, consider the way a mother hen covers her babies with her wings. In the same way, God shelters His children from danger.

Psalm 57:1

2 I will cry out to God Most High,
To God who performs *all things* for me.
3 He shall send from heaven and save me;
He reproaches the one who would
swallow me up.   Selah
God shall send forth His mercy and His
truth.

4 My soul *is* among lions;
I lie *among* the sons of men
Who are set on fire,
Whose teeth *are* spears and arrows,
And their tongue a sharp sword.
5 Be exalted, O God, above the heavens;
Let Your glory *be* above all the earth.

WHAT'S IT MEAN?

Have you ever seen the trail of slime a snail leaves behind when it crawls? In ancient times, people believed that the slime was actually part of the snail itself. They believed that as the snail traveled, it left behind more and more of itself, growing smaller and smaller, until it disappeared completely.

Psalm 58:8

6 They have prepared a net for my steps;
My soul is bowed down;
They have dug a pit before me;

Into the midst of it they *themselves* have
fallen.   Selah

7 My heart is steadfast, O God, my heart is
steadfast;
I will sing and give praise.
8 Awake, my glory!
Awake, lute and harp!
I will awaken the dawn.

9 I will praise You, O Lord, among the
peoples;
I will sing to You among the nations.
10 For Your mercy reaches unto the heavens,
And Your truth unto the clouds.

11 Be exalted, O God, above the heavens;
Let Your glory *be* above all the earth.

PSALM 58

THE JUST JUDGMENT OF THE WICKED

To the Chief Musician. Set to
"Do Not Destroy." [a] A Michtam of David.

1 Do you indeed speak righteousness, you
silent ones?
Do you judge uprightly, you sons of
men?
2 No, in heart you work wickedness;
You weigh out the violence of your hands
in the earth.

3 The wicked are estranged from the
womb;
They go astray as soon as they are born,
speaking lies.
4 Their poison *is* like the poison of a
serpent;
They are like the deaf cobra *that* stops its
ear,
5 Which will not heed the voice of
charmers,
Charming ever so skillfully.

6 Break their teeth in their mouth, O God!
Break out the fangs of the young lions,
O LORD!
7 Let them flow away as waters *which* run
continually;
When he bends *his* bow,
Let his arrows be as if cut in pieces.
8 *Let them be* like a snail which melts away
as it goes,

58:title [a]Hebrew *Al Tashcheth*

Like a stillborn child of a woman, that
    they may not see the sun.

9 Before your pots can feel *the burning*
    thorns,
    He shall take them away as with a
    whirlwind,
    As in His living and burning wrath.
10 The righteous shall rejoice when he sees
    the vengeance;
    He shall wash his feet in the blood of the
    wicked,
11 So that men will say,
    "Surely *there is* a reward for the righteous;
    Surely He is God who judges in the
    earth."

PSALM 59

THE ASSURED JUDGMENT OF THE WICKED

To the Chief Musician. Set to
"Do Not Destroy."[a] A Michtam of David
when Saul sent men, and they watched
the house in order to kill him.

1 Deliver me from my enemies, O my God;
    Defend me from those who rise up
    against me.
2 Deliver me from the workers of iniquity,
    And save me from bloodthirsty men.

3 For look, they lie in wait for my life;
    The mighty gather against me,
    Not *for* my transgression nor *for* my sin,
    O LORD.
4 They run and prepare themselves
    through no fault *of mine.*

    Awake to help me, and behold!
5 You therefore, O LORD God of hosts, the
    God of Israel,
    Awake to punish all the nations;
    Do not be merciful to any wicked
    transgressors.   Selah

6 At evening they return,
    They growl like a dog,
    And go all around the city.
7 Indeed, they belch with their mouth;
    Swords *are* in their lips;
    For *they say,* "Who hears?"

8 But You, O LORD, shall laugh at them;
    You shall have all the nations in derision.
9 I will wait for You, O You his Strength;[a]
    For God *is* my defense.
10 My God of mercy[a] shall come to meet
    me;
    God shall let me see *my desire* on my
    enemies.

11 Do not slay them, lest my people forget;
    Scatter them by Your power,
    And bring them down,
    O Lord our shield.
12 *For* the sin of their mouth *and* the words
    of their lips,
    Let them even be taken in their pride,
    And for the cursing and lying *which* they
    speak.
13 Consume *them* in wrath, consume *them,*
    That they *may* not *be;*
    And let them know that God rules in
    Jacob
    To the ends of the earth.   Selah

WHAT'S IT MEAN?

Stray dogs in ancient Israel kept out of
sight during the daytime. At night, however,
they could be heard throughout the land, barking
and scrounging for food. Dogs were extremely
unpopular creatures with the Israelites.

Psalm 59:14

14 And at evening they return,
    They growl like a dog,
    And go all around the city.
15 They wander up and down for food,
    And howl[a] if they are not satisfied.

16 But I will sing of Your power;
    Yes, I will sing aloud of Your mercy in the
    morning;

59:title [a]Hebrew *Al Tashcheth*   **59:9** [a]Following Masoretic Text and Syriac; some Hebrew manuscripts,
Septuagint, Targum, and Vulgate read *my Strength.*   **59:10** [a]Following Qere; some Hebrew manuscripts,
Septuagint, and Vulgate read *My God, His mercy*; Kethib, some Hebrew manuscripts and Targum read *O God,
my mercy*; Syriac reads *O God, Your mercy.*   **59:15** [a]Following Septuagint and Vulgate; Masoretic Text, Syriac,
and Targum read *spend the night.*

For You have been my defense
And refuge in the day of my trouble.

17 To You, O my Strength, I will sing praises;
For God *is* my defense,
My God of mercy.

PSALM 60

URGENT PRAYER FOR THE RESTORED FAVOR OF GOD

To the Chief Musician. Set to "Lily of the
Testimony."[a] A Michtam of David.
For teaching. When he fought against
Mesopotamia and Syria of Zobah, and Joab
returned and killed twelve thousand Edomites
in the Valley of Salt.

1 O God, You have cast us off;
You have broken us down;
You have been displeased;
Oh, restore us again!

2 You have made the earth tremble;
You have broken it;
Heal its breaches, for it is shaking.

3 You have shown Your people hard things;
You have made us drink the wine of
confusion.

4 You have given a banner to those who
fear You,
That it may be displayed because of the
truth.   Selah

5 That Your beloved may be delivered,
Save *with* Your right hand, and hear me.

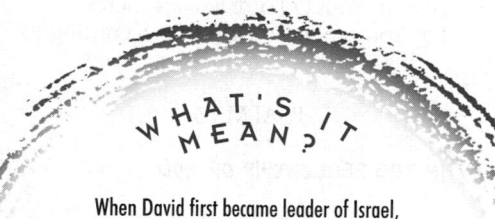

WHAT'S IT MEAN?

When David first became leader of Israel,
he had to deal not only with the nation's enemies,
but also with people in his own country who refused to accept him as
king. Eventually, the territories mentioned in this passage recognized
that God had chosen David as leader of Israel and submitted to his
rule. What's more, the Lord gave David and his troops military
victories over such long-time enemies as the Moabites,
the Edomites, and the Philistines.

Psalm 60:6–8

6 God has spoken in His holiness:
"I will rejoice;
I will divide Shechem
And measure out the Valley of Succoth.

7 Gilead *is* Mine, and Manasseh *is* Mine;
Ephraim also *is* the helmet for My head;
Judah *is* My lawgiver.

8 Moab *is* My washpot;
Over Edom I will cast My shoe;
Philistia, shout in triumph because of
Me."

9 Who will bring me *to* the strong city?
Who will lead me to Edom?

10 *Is it* not You, O God, *who* cast us off?
And You, O God, *who* did not go out
with our armies?

11 Give us help from trouble,
For the help of man *is* useless.

12 Through God we will do valiantly,
For *it is* He *who* shall tread down our
enemies.[a]

PSALM 61

ASSURANCE OF GOD'S ETERNAL PROTECTION

To the Chief Musician. On a stringed
instrument.[a] A Psalm of David.

1 Hear my cry, O God;
Attend to my prayer.

2 From the end of the earth I will cry to
You,
When my heart is overwhelmed;
Lead me to the rock that is higher than I.

3 For You have been a shelter for me,
A strong tower from the enemy.

4 I will abide in Your tabernacle forever;
I will trust in the shelter of Your wings.
Selah

5 For You, O God, have heard my vows;
You have given *me* the heritage of those
who fear Your name.

6 You will prolong the king's life,
His years as many generations.

7 He shall abide before God forever.
Oh, prepare mercy and truth, *which* may
preserve him!

8 So I will sing praise to Your name
forever,
That I may daily perform my vows.

PSALM 62

A CALM RESOLVE TO WAIT FOR THE SALVATION OF GOD

To the Chief Musician. To Jeduthun.
A Psalm of David.

1 Truly my soul silently *waits* for God;
From Him *comes* my salvation.
2 He only *is* my rock and my salvation;
He is my defense;
I shall not be greatly moved.

3 How long will you attack a man?
You shall be slain, all of you,
Like a leaning wall and a tottering fence.

4 They only consult to cast *him* down from
his high position;
They delight in lies;
They bless with their mouth,
But they curse inwardly.   Selah

5 My soul, wait silently for God
alone,
For my expectation *is*
from Him.
6 He only *is* my rock and
my salvation;
He is my defense;
I shall not be moved.
7 In God *is* my salvation and
my glory;
The rock of my strength,
And my refuge, *is* in God.

DOUBT
Can
we find
refuge in
God?
(62:6)

8 Trust in Him at all times, you people;
Pour out your heart before Him;
God *is* a refuge for us.   Selah

9 Surely men of low degree *are* a vapor,
Men of high degree *are* a lie;
If they are weighed on the scales,
They *are* altogether *lighter* than vapor.
10 Do not trust in oppression,
Nor vainly hope in robbery;
If riches increase,
Do not set *your* heart *on them.*

11 God has spoken once,
Twice I have heard this:
That power *belongs* to God.
12 Also to You, O Lord, *belongs* mercy;
For You render to each one according to
his work.

On the Edge

Surely men of low degree are a vapor, men of high degree are a lie; if they are weighed on the scales, they are altogether lighter than vapor (Ps. 62:9).

It seems weird for David to say that we humans are only a vapor, that, like a puff of air, none of us is truly great. After all, when he was a teenager, he killed the giant Goliath with a *slingshot!* Then he led Israel's army to defeat the mighty Philistines in battle after battle. He became the greatest warrior and king in Israel's history.

But David knew that everything he did was nothing compared to God. He had a grip on just how huge God is. Look at Psalm 62:11, 12. David tells us that power and mercy belong to God. When a person begins to really understand (in his or her heart) how powerful and how kind the Lord is, it's impossible to be cocky. When you begin to see yourself as you really are before the Lord, you're amazed at how awesome He is and how little you are.

God uses little people. He uses humble people—people who are seeing how small they are compared to Him. He doesn't want us to go around thinking we're dirt. He wants us to go around thinking about how enormous He is.

SEE FOR YOURSELF:
Job 14:2; Eccl. 6:12;
Is. 40:6–8;
James 4:14

PSALM 63

JOY IN THE FELLOWSHIP OF GOD

A Psalm of David when he was
in the wilderness of Judah.

1 O God, You *are* my God;
Early will I seek You;
My soul thirsts for You;
My flesh longs for You
In a dry and thirsty land
Where there is no water.
2 So I have looked for You in the sanctuary,
To see Your power and Your glory.

3 Because Your lovingkindness *is* better
than life,

My lips shall praise You.
4 Thus I will bless You while I live;
I will lift up my hands in Your name.
5 My soul shall be satisfied as with marrow
and fatness,
And my mouth shall praise You with
joyful lips.

6 When I remember You on my bed,
I meditate on You in the *night* watches.
7 Because You have been my help,
Therefore in the shadow of Your wings I
will rejoice.
8 My soul follows close behind You;
Your right hand upholds me.

9 But those *who* seek my life, to destroy *it,*
Shall go into the lower parts of the earth.
10 They shall fall by the sword;
They shall be a portion for jackals.

11 But the king shall rejoice in God;
Everyone who swears by Him shall
glory;
But the mouth of those who speak lies
shall be stopped.

PSALM 64

OPPRESSED BY THE WICKED BUT REJOICING IN THE LORD

To the Chief Musician. A Psalm of David.

1 Hear my voice, O God, in my
meditation;
Preserve my life from fear of the enemy.
2 Hide me from the secret plots of the
wicked,
From the rebellion of the workers of
iniquity,
3 Who sharpen their tongue like a sword,
And bend *their bows to shoot* their
arrows—bitter words,
4 That they may shoot in secret at the
blameless;
Suddenly they shoot at him and do not
fear.

5 They encourage themselves *in* an evil
matter;
They talk of laying snares secretly;
They say, "Who will see them?"
6 They devise iniquities:
"We have perfected a shrewd scheme."
Both the inward thought and the heart of
man are deep.

7 But God shall shoot at them *with* an
arrow;
Suddenly they shall be wounded.
8 So He will make them stumble over their
own tongue;
All who see them shall flee away.
9 All men shall fear,
And shall declare the work of God;
For they shall wisely consider His doing.

10 The righteous shall be glad in the LORD,
and trust in Him.
And all the upright in heart shall glory.

PSALM 65

PRAISE TO GOD FOR HIS SALVATION AND PROVIDENCE

To the Chief Musician. A Psalm
of David. A Song.

1 Praise is awaiting You, O God, in Zion;
And to You the vow shall be performed.
2 O You who hear prayer,
To You all flesh will come.
3 Iniquities prevail against me;
As for our transgressions,
You will provide atonement for them.

4 Blessed *is the man* You choose,
And cause to approach *You,*
That he may dwell in Your courts.
We shall be satisfied with the goodness of
Your house,
Of Your holy temple.

5 *By* awesome deeds in righteousness You
will answer us,
O God of our salvation,
You who are the confidence of all the ends
of the earth,
And of the far-off seas;
6 Who established the mountains by His
strength,
Being clothed with power;
7 You who still the noise of the seas,
The noise of their waves,
And the tumult of the peoples.
8 They also who dwell in the farthest parts
are afraid of Your signs;
You make the outgoings of the morning
and evening rejoice.

9 You visit the earth and water it,
You greatly enrich it;
The river of God is full of water;

You provide their grain,
For so You have prepared it.

10 You water its ridges abundantly,
You settle its furrows;
You make it soft with showers,
You bless its growth.

11 You crown the year with Your goodness,
And Your paths drip *with* abundance.

12 They drop *on* the pastures of the
wilderness,
And the little hills rejoice on every side.

13 The pastures are clothed with flocks;
The valleys also are covered with grain;
They shout for joy, they also sing.

PSALM 66

PRAISE TO GOD FOR HIS AWESOME WORKS

To the Chief Musician. A
Song. A Psalm.

1 Make a joyful shout
to God, all the
earth!

2 Sing out the honor of
His name;
Make His praise glorious.

3 Say to God,
"How awesome are Your works!
Through the greatness of Your power
Your enemies shall submit themselves to
You.

4 All the earth shall worship You
And sing praises to You;
They shall sing praises *to* Your name."
Selah

5 Come and see the works of God;
He is awesome *in His* doing toward the
sons of men.

6 He turned the sea into dry *land;*
They went through the river on foot.
There we will rejoice in Him.

7 He rules by His power forever;
His eyes observe the nations;
Do not let the rebellious exalt themselves.
Selah

8 Oh, bless our God,
you peoples!
And make the voice
of His praise to be
heard,

9 Who keeps our soul
among the living,
And does not allow
our feet to be
moved.

10 For You, O God,
have tested us;
You have refined us
as silver is refined.

11 You brought us into
the net;
You laid affliction on our backs.

12 You have caused men to ride over our
heads;
We went through fire and through water;
But You brought us out to rich *fulfillment.*

13 I will go into Your house with burnt
offerings;
I will pay You my vows,

14 Which my lips have uttered
And my mouth has spoken when I was
in trouble.

15 I will offer You burnt sacrifices of fat
animals,
With the sweet aroma of rams;
I will offer bulls with goats.   Selah

16 Come *and* hear, all you who fear God,
And I will declare what He has done for
my soul.

17 I cried to Him with my mouth,
And He was extolled with my tongue.

18 If I regard iniquity in my heart,
The Lord will not hear.

19 *But* certainly God has heard *me;*

"Make a joyful shout to God,
all the earth!
Sing out the honor of His name;
make His praise glorious."
(Psalm 66:1, 2)

WHAT'S IT MEAN?

If you've ever seen the movie *The Ten Commandments,* you know the scene this verse is describing. The king of Egypt, after letting the Israelites leave his country, changed his mind and sent his army to bring them back. His plan was to trap the Israelites at the Red Sea, and it almost worked—almost. Just when things looked hopeless for the Israelites, God parted the waters of the sea, making a path of dry land through the middle of it. The Israelites were able to walk across to the other side. When the Egyptians tried to follow, the water collapsed on top of them, and they drowned.

Psalm 66:6

He has attended to the voice of my
   prayer.

20 Blessed *be* God,
   Who has not turned away my prayer,
   Nor His mercy from me!

PSALM 67

AN INVOCATION AND A DOXOLOGY

To the Chief Musician. On stringed
   instruments.[a] A Psalm. A Song.

1 God be merciful to us and bless us,
   And cause His face to shine upon us,
                                           Selah
2 That Your way may be known on earth,
   Your salvation among all nations.

3 Let the peoples praise You, O God;
   Let all the peoples praise You.
4 Oh, let the nations be glad and sing for
      joy!
   For You shall judge the people
      righteously,
   And govern the nations on earth.   Selah

5 Let the peoples praise You, O God;
   Let all the peoples praise You.
6 *Then* the earth shall yield her increase;
   God, our own God, shall bless us.
7 God shall bless us,
   And all the ends of the earth shall fear Him.

PSALM 68

THE GLORY OF GOD IN HIS GOODNESS TO ISRAEL

To the Chief Musician. A Psalm
   of David. A Song.

1 Let God arise,
   Let His enemies be scattered;
   Let those also who hate Him flee before
      Him.
2 As smoke is driven away,
   So drive *them* away;
   As wax melts before the fire,
   So let the wicked perish at the presence of
      God.
3 But let the righteous be glad;
   Let them rejoice before God;
   Yes, let them rejoice exceedingly.

4 Sing to God, sing praises to His name;
   Extol Him who rides on the clouds,[a]
   By His name YAH,
   And rejoice before Him.

WHAT'S IT MEAN?

The Israelites' neighbors worshiped
many different gods and goddesses. They believed
that each deity controlled one area of nature. For example, they
believed one god controlled the sun, another controlled the rain, and
so on. David wanted to make it clear that God not only ruled over all
areas of nature, but He had actually created them.
Psalm 68:4

5 A father of the fatherless,
      a defender of widows,
   Is God in His holy
      habitation.
6 God sets the solitary in
      families;
   He brings out those who
      are bound into prosperity;
   But the rebellious dwell in a dry *land.*

CARING
Does
God care
for needy
people?
(68:5)

7 O God, when You went out before Your
      people,
   When You marched through the
      wilderness,   Selah
8 The earth shook;
   The heavens also dropped *rain* at the
      presence of God;
   Sinai itself *was moved* at the presence of
      God, the God of Israel.
9 You, O God, sent a plentiful rain,
   Whereby You confirmed Your inheritance,
   When it was weary.
10 Your congregation dwelt in it;
   You, O God, provided from Your
      goodness for the poor.

11 The Lord gave the word;
   Great *was* the company of those who
      proclaimed *it:*

67:title [a]Hebrew *neginoth*   **68:4** [a]Masoretic Text reads *deserts*; Targum reads *heavens* (compare verse 34 and
Isaiah 19:1).

12 "Kings of armies flee, they flee,
   And she who remains at home divides
      the spoil.
13 Though you lie down among the
      sheepfolds,
   You will be like the wings of a dove
      covered with silver,
   And her feathers with yellow gold."
14 When the Almighty scattered kings in it,
   It was *white* as snow in Zalmon.

15 A mountain of God *is* the mountain of
      Bashan;
   A mountain *of many* peaks *is* the
      mountain of Bashan.
16 Why do you fume with envy, you
      mountains of *many* peaks?
   This is the mountain *which* God desires to
      dwell in;
   Yes, the LORD will dwell *in it* forever.

17 The chariots of God *are* twenty thousand,
   Even thousands of thousands;
   The Lord is among them *as in* Sinai, in
      the Holy *Place.*
18 You have ascended on high,
   You have led captivity captive;
   You have received gifts among men,
   Even *from* the rebellious,
   That the LORD God might dwell *there.*

WHAT'S IT MEAN?

Mount Sinai, which is also known as Mount
Horeb, is located in the desert area between Israel
and Egypt. Its biggest claim to fame is that it was the place where
God gave Moses the Ten Commandments. As for the thousands of
chariots mentioned in this verse, they may refer to
the angels that surround the Lord.
Psalm 68:17

19 Blessed *be* the Lord,
   Who daily loads us *with benefits,*
   The God of our salvation!
20 Our God *is* the God of salvation;

And to GOD the Lord *belong* escapes from
   death.
21 But God will wound the head of His
      enemies,
   The hairy scalp of the one who still goes
      on in his trespasses.
22 The Lord said, "I will bring back from
      Bashan,
   I will bring *them* back from the depths of
      the sea,
23 That your foot may crush *them[a]* in blood,
   And the tongues of your dogs *may have*
      their portion from *your* enemies."

WHAT'S IT MEAN?

Bashan, which was located east of the
Jordan River, was a fertile area of land that belonged
to the tribe of Manasseh. Later in Israel's history, the area became
known as much for its selfish and arrogant inhabitants as for its
plentiful harvests and choice livestock.
Psalm 68:22

24 They have seen Your procession, O God,
   The procession of my God, my King, into
      the sanctuary.
25 The singers went before, the players on
      instruments *followed* after;
   Among *them were* the maidens playing
      timbrels.
26 Bless God in the congregations,
   The Lord, from the fountain of Israel.
27 There *is* little Benjamin, their leader,
   The princes of Judah *and* their company,
   The princes of Zebulun *and* the princes of
      Naphtali.

28 Your God has commanded[a] your
      strength;
   Strengthen, O God, what You have done
      for us.

Selah 29 Because of Your temple at Jerusalem,
   Kings will bring presents to You.

68:23 [a]Septuagint, Syriac, Targum, and Vulgate read *you may dip your foot.* **68:28** [a]Septuagint, Syriac,
Targum, and Vulgate read *Command, O God.*

30 Rebuke the beasts of the reeds,
The herd of bulls with the calves of the
  peoples,
Till everyone submits himself with pieces of
  silver.
Scatter the peoples *who* delight in war.
31 Envoys will come out of Egypt;
Ethiopia will quickly stretch out her
  hands to God.

32 Sing to God, you kingdoms of the earth;
Oh, sing praises to the Lord,   Selah
33 To Him who rides on the heaven of
  heavens, *which were* of old!
Indeed, He sends out His voice, a mighty
  voice.
34 Ascribe strength to God;
His excellence *is* over Israel,
And His strength *is* in the clouds.
35 O God, *You are* more awesome than Your
  holy places.
The God of Israel *is* He who gives
  strength and power to *His* people.

Blessed *be* God!

PSALM 69

AN URGENT PLEA FOR HELP IN TROUBLE

To the Chief Musician. Set to "The Lilies."[a]
  A Psalm of David.

1 Save me, O God!
For the waters have
  come up to *my* neck.
2 I sink in deep mire,
Where *there is* no
  standing;
I have come into deep
  waters,
Where the floods overflow me.
3 I am weary with my crying;
My throat is dry;
My eyes fail while I wait for my God.

4 Those who hate me without a cause
Are more than the hairs of my head;
They are mighty who would destroy me,
Being my enemies wrongfully;
Though I have stolen nothing,
I *still* must restore *it*.

5 O God, You know my foolishness;
And my sins are not hidden from You.

6 Let not those who wait for You, O Lord
  GOD of hosts, be ashamed because of
  me;
Let not those who seek You be
  confounded because of me, O God of
  Israel.
7 Because for Your sake I have borne
  reproach;
Shame has covered my face.
8 I have become a stranger to my brothers,
And an alien to my mother's children;
9 Because zeal for Your house has eaten me
  up,
And the reproaches of those who
  reproach You have fallen on me.
10 When I wept *and chastened* my soul with
  fasting,
That became my reproach.
11 I also made sackcloth my garment;
I became a byword to them.
12 Those who sit in the gate speak against
  me,
And I *am* the song of the drunkards.

13 But as for me, my prayer *is* to You,
O LORD, *in* the acceptable time;
O God, in the multitude of Your mercy,
Hear me in the truth of Your salvation.
14 Deliver me out of the mire,
And let me not sink;
Let me be delivered from those who hate
  me,
And out of the deep waters.
15 Let not the floodwater overflow me,
Nor let the deep swallow me up;
And let not the pit shut its mouth on me.

16 Hear me, O LORD, for Your
  lovingkindness *is* good;
Turn to me according to the multitude of
  Your tender mercies.
17 And do not hide Your face from Your
  servant,
For I am in trouble;
Hear me speedily.
18 Draw near to my soul, *and* redeem it;
Deliver me because of my enemies.

19 You know my reproach, my shame, and
  my dishonor;
My adversaries *are* all before You.
20 Reproach has broken my heart,
And I am full of heaviness;
I looked *for someone* to take pity, but *there
  was* none;

WORRY
What should our response be in times of stress? (69)

69:title [a]Hebrew *Shoshannim*

And for comforters, but I found none.
21 They also gave me gall for my food,
And for my thirst they gave me vinegar
to drink.

22 Let their table become a snare before
them,
And their well-being a trap.
23 Let their eyes be darkened, so that they
do not see;
And make their loins shake continually.
24 Pour out Your indignation upon them,
And let Your wrathful anger take hold of
them.
25 Let their dwelling place be desolate;
Let no one live in their tents.
26 For they persecute the *ones* You have
struck,
And talk of the grief of those You have
wounded.
27 Add iniquity to their iniquity,
And let them not come into Your
righteousness.
28 Let them be blotted out of the book of
the living,
And not be written with the righteous.

WHAT'S IT MEAN?

Forget the *Guinness Book of World
Records*. This is the book you want your name
mentioned in. Anyone whose name is erased from this book will
not be able to spend eternity in heaven with the Lord. Obviously,
the Lord doesn't need a book to remind Him who His followers
are—He is God, after all. The idea of a book of names may have
come from the ancient practice of relying on written genealogies
to determine who was supposed to receive an
inheritance or serve as a priest or Levite.
Psalm 69:28

29 But I *am* poor and sorrowful;
Let Your salvation, O God, set me up on
high.
30 I will praise the name of God with a
song,
And will magnify Him with thanksgiving.

31 *This* also shall please the LORD better than
an ox *or* bull,
Which has horns and hooves.
32 The humble shall see *this and* be glad;
And you who seek God, your hearts shall
live.
33 For the LORD hears the poor,
And does not despise His prisoners.

34 Let heaven and earth praise Him,
The seas and everything that moves in
them.
35 For God will save Zion
And build the cities of Judah,
That they may dwell there and possess it.
36 Also, the descendants of His servants
shall inherit it,
And those who love His name shall dwell
in it.

PSALM 70

PRAYER FOR RELIEF FROM ADVERSARIES

To the Chief Musician. *A Psalm* of David.
To bring to remembrance.

1 *Make haste,* O God, to deliver me!
Make haste to help me, O LORD!

2 Let them be ashamed and confounded
Who seek my life;
Let them be turned back[a] and confused
Who desire my hurt.
3 Let them be turned back because of their
shame,
Who say, "Aha, aha!"

4 Let all those who seek You rejoice and be
glad in You;
And let those who love Your salvation
say continually,
"Let God be magnified!"

5 But I *am* poor and needy;
Make haste to me, O God!
You *are* my help and my deliverer;
O LORD, do not delay.

PSALM 71

GOD THE ROCK OF SALVATION

1 In You, O LORD, I put my trust;
Let me never be put to shame.

70:2 [a]Following Masoretic Text, Septuagint, Targum, and Vulgate; some Hebrew manuscripts and Syriac read
be appalled (compare 40:15).

2 Deliver me in Your righteousness, and
cause me to escape;
Incline Your ear to me, and save me.
3 Be my strong refuge,
To which I may resort continually;
You have given the commandment to
save me,
For You *are* my rock and my fortress.

4 Deliver me, O my God, out of the hand
of the wicked,
Out of the hand of the unrighteous and
cruel man.
5 For You are my hope, O Lord GOD;
You are my trust from my youth.
6 By You I have been upheld from birth,
You are He who took me out of my
mother's womb.
My praise *shall be* continually of You.

7 I have become as a wonder to many,
But You *are* my strong refuge.
8 Let my mouth be filled *with* Your praise
And with Your glory all the day.

9 Do not cast me off in the time of old age;
Do not forsake me when my strength
fails.
10 For my enemies speak against me;
And those who lie in wait for my life take
counsel together,
11 Saying, "God has forsaken him;

Pursue and take him, for *there is* none to
deliver *him.*"

12 O God, do not be far from me;
O my God, make haste to help me!
13 Let them be confounded *and* consumed
Who are adversaries of my life;
Let them be covered *with* reproach and
dishonor
Who seek my hurt.

14 But I will hope continually,
And will praise You yet more and more.
15 My mouth shall tell of Your righteousness
And Your salvation all the day,
For I do not know *their* limits.
16 I will go in the strength of the Lord GOD;
I will make mention of Your
righteousness, of Yours only.

17 O God, You have taught me from my
youth;
And to this *day* I declare Your wondrous
works.
18 Now also when *I am* old and grayheaded,
O God, do not forsake me,
Until I declare Your strength to *this*
generation,
Your power to everyone *who* is to come.

19 Also Your righteousness, O God, *is* very
high,

Promise HE PROMISES TO BE FAITHFUL.

Also with the lute I will praise You—and Your faithfulness, O my God! (Ps. 71:22).

A mom and dad lose their only daughter two days before her fifteenth birthday. She was riding
in a car that was hit by a drunk driver. Devastated, they start the long process of grieving for a
child who wasn't supposed to die before they did. Several months later they come to your school
and tell you how difficult the last few months have been. The pain has been incredible for them.
Then they say something that grabs you. "All we have left is God. We couldn't have made it
without Him. He has been so faithful."

You begin to understand what His faithfulness is. He is helping those parents just make it from
day to day. He is giving them hope that they won't hurt forever. He is sending them people to
give them compassion. On days when they hurt so much they can hardly breathe, He stays
right beside them. He carries them when they cannot walk and gives them smiles when they
thought smiles were gone forever.

Don't wait for an emergency to find out how faithful He is. He's faithful in your good times,
too. Be on the lookout for your faithful Father.

SEE FOR YOURSELF:
Neh. 1:5; Ps. 36:5

You who have done great things;
O God, who *is* like You?

20 *You,* who have shown me great and
   severe troubles,
Shall revive me again,
And bring me up again from the depths
   of the earth.

21 You shall increase my greatness,
And comfort me on every side.

22 Also with the lute I will praise You—
And Your faithfulness, O my God!
To You I will sing with the harp,
O Holy One of Israel.

23 My lips shall greatly rejoice when I sing
   to You,
And my soul, which You have redeemed.

24 My tongue also shall talk of Your
   righteousness all the day long;
For they are confounded,
For they are brought to shame
Who seek my hurt.

PSALM 72

GLORY AND UNIVERSALITY OF THE MESSIAH'S REIGN

A Psalm of Solomon.

1 Give the king Your judgments, O God,
And Your righteousness to the king's
   Son.

2 He will judge Your people with
   righteousness,
And Your poor with justice.

3 The mountains will bring peace to the
   people,
And the little hills, by righteousness.

4 He will bring justice to the poor of the
   people;
He will save the children of the needy,
And will break in pieces the oppressor.

5 They shall fear You[a]
As long as the sun and moon endure,
Throughout all generations.

6 He shall come down like rain upon the
   grass before mowing,
Like showers *that* water the earth.

7 In His days the righteous shall flourish,
And abundance of peace,
Until the moon is no more.

8 He shall have dominion also from sea to
   sea,
And from the River to the ends of the
   earth.

9 Those who dwell in the wilderness will
   bow before Him,
And His enemies will lick the dust.

10 The kings of Tarshish and of the isles
Will bring presents;
The kings of Sheba and Seba
Will offer gifts.

11 Yes, all kings shall fall down before
   Him;
All nations shall serve Him.

12 For He will deliver the needy when he
   cries,
The poor also, and *him* who has no
   helper.

13 He will spare the poor and needy,
And will save the souls of the needy.

·ː· On the Edge

Blessed be the LORD God, the God of Israel, who only does wondrous things! (Ps. 72:18).

A miracle is an event that happens in a way that nature doesn't normally work. A car is crushed from every angle, but the driver comes away unharmed. A kid walks in healed after doctors declare that there's no hope. The wildest troublemaker in town gets saved and starts telling everybody what God has done in his life. A Man dead three days in a grave gets up and appears to over 500 people.

If you've ever seen a miracle, you can be sure that you were witnessing the hand of God working. You experienced a supernatural event. Only God can do miracles. Sometimes He uses people in the process, but no man can work a miracle by his own power. You've got to have God for a miracle. The purpose of a miracle is to bring glory to God and to remind us of His amazing love toward us. Miracles force us to stop looking at ourselves and our limitations. We have to look up at God and His mighty power. A miracle is meant to get our attention and cause us to be amazed at our God.

SEE FOR YOURSELF:
Ex. 34:10; Mic. 7:15

72:5 [a]Following Masoretic Text and Targum; Septuagint and Vulgate read *They shall continue.*

14 He will redeem their life from oppression
and violence;
And precious shall be their blood in His
sight.

15 And He shall live;
And the gold of Sheba will be given to
Him;
Prayer also will be made for Him
continually,
And daily He shall be praised.

16 There will be an abundance of grain in
the earth,
On the top of the mountains;
Its fruit shall wave like Lebanon;
And *those* of the city shall flourish like
grass of the earth.

17 His name shall endure forever;
His name shall continue as long as the
sun.
And *men* shall be blessed in Him;
All nations shall call Him blessed.

18 Blessed *be* the LORD God, the God of
Israel,
Who only does wondrous things!

19 And blessed *be* His glorious name forever!
And let the whole earth be filled *with* His
glory.
Amen and Amen.

20 The prayers of David the son of Jesse are
ended.

Book Three: Psalms 73—89

PSALM 73

THE TRAGEDY OF THE WICKED, AND THE BLESSEDNESS OF TRUST IN GOD

A Psalm of Asaph.

1 Truly God *is* good to Israel,
To such as are pure in
heart.

2 But as for me, my feet
had almost stumbled;
My steps had nearly
slipped.

3 For I *was* envious of the
boastful,

JEALOUSY

Is it right
to envy the
prosperity of
the wicked?
(73:2, 3)

When I saw the prosperity of the
wicked.

4 For *there are* no pangs in their death,
But their strength *is* firm.

5 They *are* not in trouble *as other* men,
Nor are they plagued like *other* men.

6 Therefore pride serves as their necklace;
Violence covers them *like* a garment.

7 Their eyes bulge[a] with abundance;
They have more than heart could wish.

8 They scoff and speak wickedly *concerning*
oppression;
They speak loftily.

9 They set their mouth against the heavens,
And their tongue walks through the
earth.

10 Therefore his people return here,
And waters of a full *cup* are drained by
them.

11 And they say, "How does God know?
And is there knowledge in the Most
High?"

12 Behold, these *are* the ungodly,
Who are always at ease;
They increase *in* riches.

13 Surely I have cleansed my heart *in* vain,
And washed my hands in innocence.

14 For all day long I have been plagued,
And chastened every morning.

15 If I had said, "I will speak thus,"
Behold, I would have been untrue to the
generation of Your children.

16 When I thought *how* to understand this,
It *was* too painful for me—

17 Until I went into the sanctuary of God;
Then I understood their end.

18 Surely You set them in slippery places;
You cast them down to destruction.

19 Oh, how they are *brought* to desolation,
as in a moment!
They are utterly consumed with terrors.

20 As a dream when *one* awakes,
So, Lord, when You awake,
You shall despise their image.

21 Thus my heart was grieved,
And I was vexed in my mind.

22 I *was* so foolish and ignorant;
I was *like* a beast before You.

23 Nevertheless I *am* continually with You;
You hold *me* by my right hand.

73:7 [a]Targum reads *face bulges;* Septuagint, Syriac, and Vulgate read *iniquity bulges.*

24 You will guide me with Your counsel,
And afterward receive me *to* glory.

25 Whom have I in heaven *but You?*
And *there is* none upon earth *that* I desire
besides You.
26 My flesh and my heart fail;
But God *is* the strength of my heart and
my portion forever.

27 For indeed, those who are far from You
shall perish;
You have destroyed all those who desert
You for harlotry.
28 But *it is* good for me to draw near to
God;
I have put my trust in the Lord GOD,
That I may declare all Your works.

PSALM 74

A PLEA FOR RELIEF FROM OPPRESSORS

A Contemplation*ᵃ* of Asaph.

1 O God, why have You cast *us* off forever?
Why does Your anger smoke against the
sheep of Your pasture?
2 Remember Your congregation, *which* You
have purchased of old,
The tribe of Your inheritance, *which* You
have redeemed—
This Mount Zion where You have dwelt.
3 Lift up Your feet to the perpetual
desolations.
The enemy has damaged everything in
the sanctuary.
4 Your enemies roar in the midst of Your
meeting place;
They set up their banners *for* signs.
5 They seem like men who lift up
Axes among the thick trees.
6 And now they break down its carved
work, all at once,
With axes and hammers.
7 They have set fire to Your sanctuary;
They have defiled the dwelling place of
Your name to the ground.
8 They said in their hearts,
"Let us destroy them altogether."
They have burned up all the meeting
places of God in the land.

9 We do not see our signs;
There is no longer any prophet;

Nor *is there* any among us who knows
how long.
10 O God, how long will the adversary
reproach?
Will the enemy blaspheme Your name
forever?
11 Why do You withdraw Your hand, even
Your right hand?
Take it out of Your bosom and destroy
them.
12 For God *is* my King from of old,
Working salvation in the midst of the
earth.
13 You divided the sea by Your
strength;
You broke the heads of the sea serpents in
the waters.
14 You broke the heads of Leviathan in
pieces,
And gave him *as* food to the people
inhabiting the wilderness.
15 You broke open the fountain and the
flood;
You dried up mighty rivers.
16 The day *is* Yours, the night also *is*
Yours;
You have prepared the light and the
sun.
17 You have set all the borders of the
earth;
You have made summer and winter.

18 Remember this, *that* the enemy has
reproached, O LORD,
And *that* a foolish people has blasphemed
Your name.
19 Oh, do not deliver the life of Your
turtledove to the wild beast!
Do not forget the life of Your poor
forever.
20 Have respect to the covenant;
For the dark places of the earth are full of
the haunts of cruelty.
21 Oh, do not let the oppressed return
ashamed!
Let the poor and needy praise Your
name.

22 Arise, O God, plead Your own cause;
Remember how the foolish man
reproaches You daily.
23 Do not forget the voice of Your
enemies;
The tumult of those who rise up against
You increases continually.

74:title *ᵃ*Hebrew *Maschil*

675

PSALM 75

THANKSGIVING FOR GOD'S RIGHTEOUS JUDGMENT

To the Chief Musician. Set to "Do Not Destroy."ᵃ A Psalm of Asaph. A Song.

1 We give thanks to You, O God, we give thanks!
For Your wondrous works declare *that* Your name is near.

2 "When I choose the proper time,
I will judge uprightly.
3 The earth and all its inhabitants are dissolved;
I set up its pillars firmly.   Selah

4 "I said to the boastful, 'Do not deal boastfully,'
And to the wicked, 'Do not lift up the horn.
5 Do not lift up your horn on high;
Do *not* speak with a stiff neck.' "

6 For exaltation *comes* neither from the east
Nor from the west nor from the south.
7 But God *is* the Judge:
He puts down one,
And exalts another.
8 For in the hand of the LORD *there is* a cup,
And the wine is red;
It is fully mixed, and He pours it out;
Surely its dregs shall all the wicked of the earth
Drain *and* drink down.

9 But I will declare forever,
I will sing praises to the God of Jacob.

10 "All the horns of the wicked I will also cut off,
But the horns of the righteous shall be exalted."

PSALM 76

THE MAJESTY OF GOD IN JUDGMENT

To the Chief Musician. On stringed instruments.ᵃ A Psalm of Asaph. A Song.

1 In Judah God *is* known;
His name *is* great in Israel.

2 In Salemᵃ also is His tabernacle,
And His dwelling place in Zion.
3 There He broke the arrows of the bow,
The shield and sword of battle.   Selah

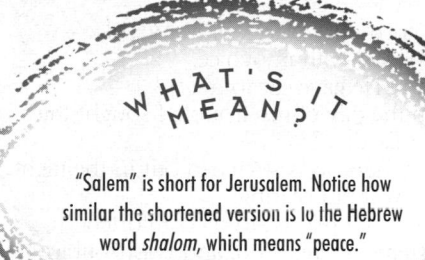

"Salem" is short for Jerusalem. Notice how similar the shortened version is to the Hebrew word *shalom*, which means "peace."
Psalm 76:2

4 You *are* more glorious and excellent
Than the mountains of prey.
5 The stouthearted were plundered;
They have sunk into their sleep;
And none of the mighty men have found the use of their hands.
6 At Your rebuke, O God of Jacob,
Both the chariot and horse were cast into a dead sleep.

7 You, Yourself, *are* to be feared;
And who may stand in Your presence
When once You are angry?
8 You caused judgment to be heard from heaven;
The earth feared and was still,
9 When God arose to judgment,
To deliver all the oppressed of the earth.   Selah

10 Surely the wrath of man shall praise You;
With the remainder of wrath You shall gird Yourself.

11 Make vows to the LORD your God, and pay *them*;
Let all who are around Him bring presents to Him who ought to be feared.
12 He shall cut off the spirit of princes;
He is awesome to the kings of the earth.

PSALM 77

THE CONSOLING MEMORY OF GOD'S REDEMPTIVE WORKS

To the Chief Musician. To Jeduthun.
A Psalm of Asaph.

1 I cried out to God with my voice—
To God with my voice;
And He gave ear to me.

2 In the day of my trouble I sought the Lord;
My hand was stretched out in the night without ceasing;
My soul refused to be comforted.

3 I remembered God, and was troubled;
I complained, and my spirit was overwhelmed. Selah

4 You hold my eyelids *open;*
I am so troubled that I cannot speak.

5 I have considered the days of old,
The years of ancient times.

6 I call to remembrance my song in the night;
I meditate within my heart,
And my spirit makes diligent search.

7 Will the Lord cast off forever?
And will He be favorable no more?

8 Has His mercy ceased forever?
Has *His* promise failed forevermore?

9 Has God forgotten to be gracious?
Has He in anger shut up His tender mercies? Selah

10 And I said, "This *is* my anguish;
But I will *remember* the years of the right hand of the Most High."

11 I will remember the works of the LORD;
Surely I will remember Your wonders of old.

12 I will also meditate on all Your work,
And talk of Your deeds.

13 Your way, O God, *is* in the sanctuary;
Who *is* so great a God as *our* God?

14 You *are* the God who does wonders;
You have declared Your strength among the peoples.

15 You have with *Your* arm redeemed Your people,
The sons of Jacob and Joseph. Selah

16 The waters saw You, O God;
The waters saw You, they were afraid;
The depths also trembled.

17 The clouds poured out water;
The skies sent out a sound;
Your arrows also flashed about.

18 The voice of Your thunder *was* in the whirlwind;
The lightnings lit up the world;
The earth trembled and shook.

19 Your way *was* in the sea,
Your path in the great waters,
And Your footsteps were not known.

20 You led Your people like a flock
By the hand of Moses and Aaron.

PSALM 78

GOD'S KINDNESS TO REBELLIOUS ISRAEL

A Contemplation[a] of Asaph.

1 Give ear, O my people, *to* my law;
Incline your ears to the words of my mouth.

2 I will open my mouth in a parable;
I will utter dark sayings of old,

3 Which we have heard and known,
And our fathers have told us.

4 We will not hide *them* from their children,
Telling to the generation to come the praises of the LORD,
And His strength and His wonderful works that He has done.

5 For He established a testimony in Jacob,
And appointed a law in Israel,
Which He commanded our fathers,

WHAT'S IT MEAN?

The phrase "right hand" is a way of describing God's strength. Specifically, the phrase is used to describe God's highly visible actions, such as the miracles He performed around the time of the Israelites' Exodus from Egypt.
Psalm 77:10

78:title [a]Hebrew *Maschil*

That they should make them known to
    their children;
6 That the generation to come might know
    them,
The children *who* would be born,
That they may arise and declare *them* to
    their children,
7 That they may set their hope in God,
And not forget the works of God,
But keep His commandments;
8 And may not be like their fathers,
A stubborn and rebellious generation,
A generation *that* did not set its heart
    aright,
And whose spirit was not faithful to
    God.

WHAT'S IT MEAN?

Ephraim had been the most important of the
twelve tribes of Israel from the time of Joshua to the
time Saul became king. Unfortunately, though, the Ephraimites
eventually turned to idol worship and began to disobey God. Their
descendants forgot about everything God had done for them.
Interestingly, the specific incident referred to in this
verse is not described anywhere else in Scripture.
Psalm 78:9

9 The children of Ephraim, *being* armed *and*
    carrying bows,
Turned back in the day of battle.
10 They did not keep the covenant of God;
They refused to walk in His law,
11 And forgot His works
And His wonders that He had shown
    them.
12 Marvelous things He did in the sight of
    their fathers,
In the land of Egypt, *in* the field of Zoan.
13 He divided the sea and caused them to
    pass through;
And He made the waters stand up like a
    heap.
14 In the daytime also He led them with the
    cloud,
And all the night with a light of fire.
15 He split the rocks in the wilderness,

And gave *them* drink in abundance like
    the depths.
16 He also brought streams out of the rock,
And caused waters to run down like
    rivers.

17 But they sinned even more against Him
By rebelling against the Most High in the
    wilderness.
18 And they tested God in their heart
By asking for the food of their fancy.
19 Yes, they spoke against God:
They said, "Can God prepare a table in
    the wilderness?
20 Behold, He struck the rock,
So that the waters gushed out,
And the streams overflowed.
Can He give bread also?
Can He provide meat for His people?"

21 Therefore the LORD heard *this* and was
    furious;
So a fire was kindled against Jacob,
And anger also came up against Israel,
22 Because they did not believe in God,
And did not trust in His salvation.
23 Yet He had commanded the clouds
    above,
And opened the doors of heaven,
24 Had rained down manna on them to eat,
And given them of the bread of heaven.
25 Men ate angels' food;
He sent them food to the full.

WHAT'S IT MEAN?

Zoan, a city in Egypt, may have been
the starting point for the Israelites' escape
from captivity under Moses' leadership.
Psalm 78:12

26 He caused an east wind to blow in the
    heavens;
And by His power He brought in the
    south wind.
27 He also rained meat on them like the
    dust,
Feathered fowl like the sand of the seas;

28 And He let *them* fall in the midst of their
　　camp,
　　All around their dwellings.
29 So they ate and were well filled,
　　For He gave them their own desire.
30 They were not deprived of their craving;
　　But while their food *was* still in their
　　　mouths,
31 The wrath of God came against them,
　　And slew the stoutest of them,
　　And struck down the choice *men* of
　　　Israel.

32 In spite of this they still sinned,
　　And did not believe in His wondrous
　　　works.
33 Therefore their days He consumed in
　　　futility,
　　And their years in fear.

34 When He slew them, then they sought
　　　Him;
　　And they returned and sought earnestly
　　　for God.
35 Then they remembered that God *was*
　　　their rock,
　　And the Most High God their Redeemer.
36 Nevertheless they flattered Him with their
　　　mouth,
　　And they lied to Him with their tongue;
37 For their heart was not steadfast with
　　　Him,
　　Nor were they faithful in His covenant.
38 But He, *being* full of compassion, forgave
　　　their iniquity,
　　And did not destroy *them.*
　　Yes, many a time He turned His anger
　　　away,
　　And did not stir up all His wrath;
39 For He remembered that they *were but*
　　　flesh,
　　A breath that passes away and does not
　　　come again.

40 How often they provoked Him in the
　　　wilderness,
　　And grieved Him in the desert!
41 Yes, again and again they tempted God,
　　And limited the Holy One of Israel.
42 They did not remember His power:
　　The day when He redeemed them from
　　　the enemy,
43 When He worked His signs in Egypt,
　　And His wonders in the field of Zoan;
44 Turned their rivers into blood,
　　And their streams, that they could not
　　　drink.

45 He sent swarms of flies among them,
　　which devoured them,
　　And frogs, which destroyed them.
46 He also gave their crops to the caterpillar,
　　And their labor to the locust.
47 He destroyed their vines with hail,
　　And their sycamore trees with frost.
48 He also gave up their cattle to the hail,
　　And their flocks to fiery lightning.
49 He cast on them the fierceness of His
　　　anger,
　　Wrath, indignation, and trouble,
　　By sending angels of destruction *among*
　　　them.
50 He made a path for His anger;
　　He did not spare their soul from death,
　　But gave their life over to the plague,
51 And destroyed all the firstborn in Egypt,
　　The first of *their* strength in the tents of
　　　Ham.
52 But He made His own people go forth
　　　like sheep,
　　And guided them in the wilderness like a
　　　flock;
53 And He led them on safely, so that they
　　　did not fear;
　　But the sea overwhelmed their enemies.
54 And He brought them to His holy border,
　　This mountain *which* His right hand had
　　　acquired.
55 He also drove out the nations before them,
　　Allotted them an inheritance by survey,
　　And made the tribes of Israel dwell in
　　　their tents.

56 Yet they tested and provoked the Most
　　　High God,
　　And did not keep His testimonies,
57 But turned back and acted unfaithfully
　　　like their fathers;
　　They were turned aside like a deceitful
　　　bow.
58 For they provoked Him to anger with
　　　their high places,
　　And moved Him to jealousy with their
　　　carved images.
59 When God heard *this,* He was furious,
　　And greatly abhorred Israel,
60 So that He forsook the tabernacle of
　　　Shiloh,
　　The tent He had placed among men,
61 And delivered His strength into captivity,
　　And His glory into the enemy's hand.
62 He also gave His people over to the
　　　sword,
　　And was furious with His inheritance.
63 The fire consumed their young men,

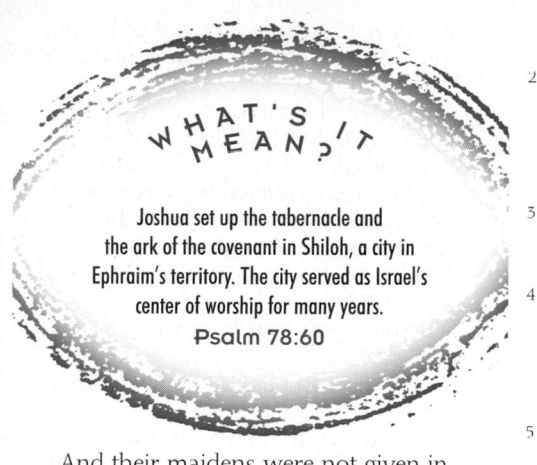

WHAT'S IT MEAN?

Joshua set up the tabernacle and the ark of the covenant in Shiloh, a city in Ephraim's territory. The city served as Israel's center of worship for many years.

Psalm 78:60

And their maidens were not given in
marriage.
64 Their priests fell by the sword,
And their widows made no lamentation.

65 Then the Lord awoke as *from* sleep,
Like a mighty man who shouts because
of wine.
66 And He beat back His enemies;
He put them to a perpetual reproach.

67 Moreover He rejected the tent of Joseph,
And did not choose the tribe of Ephraim,
68 But chose the tribe of Judah,
Mount Zion which He loved.
69 And He built His sanctuary like the
heights,
Like the earth which He has established
forever.
70 He also chose David His servant,
And took him from the sheepfolds;
71 From following the ewes that had young
He brought him,
To shepherd Jacob His people,
And Israel His inheritance.
72 So he shepherded them
according to the
integrity of his heart,
And guided them by the
skillfulness of his
hands.

INTEGRITY
Is it important
for leaders to
have
integrity?
(78:72)

PSALM 79

A DIRGE AND A PRAYER FOR ISRAEL, DESTROYED BY ENEMIES

A Psalm of Asaph.

1 O God, the nations have come into Your
inheritance;

Your holy temple they have defiled;
They have laid Jerusalem in heaps.
2 The dead bodies of Your servants
They have given *as* food for the birds of
the heavens,
The flesh of Your saints to the beasts of
the earth.
3 Their blood they have shed like water all
around Jerusalem,
And *there was* no one to bury *them.*
4 We have become a reproach to our
neighbors,
A scorn and derision to those who are
around us.

5 How long, LORD?
Will You be angry forever?
Will Your jealousy burn like fire?
6 Pour out Your wrath on the nations that
do not know You,
And on the kingdoms that do not call on
Your name.
7 For they have devoured Jacob,
And laid waste his dwelling place.

WHAT'S IT MEAN?

The events described in this verse took place in 597 B.C., when King Nebuchadnezzar and his Babylonian army conquered Jerusalem. Many Israelites were captured and taken to Babylonia as prisoners. Others were simply killed, their bodies left to rot.

Psalm 79:1

8 Oh, do not remember former iniquities
against us!
Let Your tender mercies come speedily to
meet us,
For we have been brought very low.
9 Help us, O God of our salvation,
For the glory of Your name;
And deliver us, and provide atonement
for our sins,
For Your name's sake!
10 Why should the nations say,
"Where *is* their God?"
Let there be known among the nations in
our sight

The avenging of the blood of Your
servants *which has been* shed.

11 Let the groaning of the prisoner come
before You;
According to the greatness of Your power
Preserve those who are appointed to die;

12 And return to our neighbors sevenfold
into their bosom
Their reproach with which they have
reproached You, O Lord.

13 So we, Your people and sheep of Your
pasture,
Will give You thanks forever;
We will show forth Your praise to all
generations.

PSALM 80

PRAYER FOR ISRAEL'S RESTORATION

To the Chief Musician. Set to "The Lilies." *a*
A Testimony *b* of Asaph. A Psalm.

1 Give ear, O Shepherd of Israel,
You who lead Joseph like a flock;
You who dwell *between* the cherubim,
shine forth!

2 Before Ephraim, Benjamin, and Manasseh,
Stir up Your strength,
And come *and* save us!

3 Restore us, O God;
Cause Your face to shine,
And we shall be saved!

4 O LORD God of hosts,
How long will You be angry
Against the prayer of Your people?

5 You have fed them with the
bread of tears,
And given them tears to
drink in great
measure.

6 You have made us a
strife to our
neighbors,
And our enemies laugh
among themselves.

7 Restore us, O God of hosts;
Cause Your face to shine,
And we shall be saved!

8 You have brought a vine out of Egypt;
You have cast out the nations, and
planted it.

9 You prepared *room* for it,
And caused it to take deep root,
And it filled the land.

10 The hills were covered with its shadow,
And the mighty cedars with its boughs.

11 She sent out her boughs to the Sea, *a*
And her branches to the River. *b*

12 Why have You broken down her
hedges,
So that all who pass by the way pluck
her *fruit*?

13 The boar out of the woods uproots it,
And the wild beast of the field devours it.

14 Return, we beseech You, O God of hosts;
Look down from heaven and see,
And visit this vine

15 And the vineyard which Your right hand
has planted,
And the branch *that* You made strong for
Yourself.

16 *It is* burned with fire, *it is* cut down;
They perish at the rebuke of Your
countenance.

17 Let Your hand be upon the man of Your
right hand,
Upon the son of man *whom* You made
strong for Yourself.

18 Then we will not turn back from You;
Revive us, and we will call upon Your
name.

19 Restore us, O LORD God of hosts;
Cause Your face to shine,
And we shall be saved!

PSALM 81

AN APPEAL FOR ISRAEL'S REPENTANCE

To the Chief Musician.
On an instrument of Gath. *a*
A Psalm of Asaph.

1 Sing aloud to God our
strength;
Make a joyful shout to
the God of Jacob.

2 Raise a song and strike the timbrel,

> "Sing aloud to God
> our strength;
> make a joyful shout to
> the God of Jacob."
> (Psalm 81:1)

80:title *a*Hebrew *Shoshannim* *b*Hebrew *Eduth* **80:11** *a*That is, the Mediterranean *b*That is, the Euphrates
81:title *a*Hebrew *Al Gittith*

The pleasant harp with
the lute.

3 Blow the trumpet at the
time of the New
Moon,
At the full moon, on our
solemn feast day.
4 For this *is* a statute for Israel,
A law of the God of Jacob.
5 This He established in Joseph *as a*
testimony,
When He went throughout the land of
Egypt,
Where I heard a language I did not
understand.

6 "I removed his shoulder from the burden;
His hands were freed from the baskets.
7 You called in trouble, and I delivered you;
I answered you in the secret place of
thunder;
I tested you at the waters of Meribah.
Selah

MUSIC
How is music
useful?
(81:1–5)

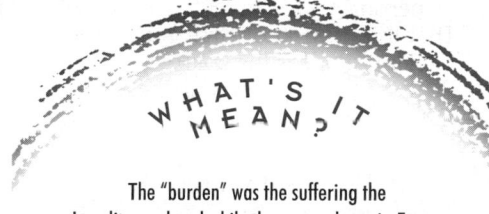

WHAT'S IT MEAN?

The "burden" was the suffering the
Israelites endured while they were slaves in Egypt.
The "baskets" were the containers workers carried while making
bricks for the Egyptians. Brick workers were often forced to carry
wooden beams with a basket hanging from each end
to hold materials or finished bricks.
Psalm 81:6

8 "Hear, O My people, and I will admonish
you!
O Israel, if you will listen to Me!
9 There shall be no foreign god among
you;
Nor shall you worship any foreign god.
10 I *am* the LORD your God,
Who brought you out of the land of
Egypt;
Open your mouth wide, and I will fill it.

11 "But My people would not heed My
voice,
And Israel would *have* none of Me.
12 So I gave them over to their own
stubborn heart,
To walk in their own counsels.

13 "Oh, that My people would listen to Me,
That Israel would walk in My ways!
14 I would soon subdue their enemies,
And turn My hand against their
adversaries.
15 The haters of the LORD would pretend
submission to Him,
But their fate would endure forever.
16 He would have fed them also with the
finest of wheat;
And with honey from the rock I would
have satisfied you."

PSALM 82

A PLEA FOR JUSTICE

A Psalm of Asaph.

1 God stands in the congregation of the
mighty;
He judges among the gods.[a]
2 How long will you judge unjustly,
And show partiality to the wicked?   Selah
3 Defend the poor and
fatherless;
Do justice to the afflicted
and needy.
4 Deliver the poor and
needy;
Free *them* from the hand
of the wicked.

PROTECTION
Who
should
protect the
helpless?
(82:3, 4)

5 They do not know, nor do they
understand;
They walk about in darkness;
All the foundations of the earth are
unstable.

6 I said, "You *are* gods,[a]
And all of you *are* children of the Most
High.
7 But you shall die like men,
And fall like one of the princes."

8 Arise, O God, judge the earth;
For You shall inherit all nations.

82:1 [a]Hebrew *elohim, mighty ones*; that is, the judges   **82:6** [a]Hebrew *elohim, mighty ones*; that is, the judges

PSALM 83

PRAYER TO FRUSTRATE CONSPIRACY AGAINST ISRAEL

A Song. A Psalm of Asaph.

1 Do not keep silent, O God!
Do not hold Your peace,
And do not be still, O God!
2 For behold, Your enemies make a tumult;
And those who hate You have lifted up
their head.
3 They have taken crafty counsel against
Your people,
And consulted together against Your
sheltered ones.
4 They have said, "Come, and let us cut
them off from *being* a nation,
That the name of Israel may be
remembered no more."

5 For they have consulted together with
one consent;
They form a confederacy against You:
6 The tents of Edom and the Ishmaelites;
Moab and the Hagrites;
7 Gebal, Ammon, and Amalek;
Philistia with the inhabitants of Tyre;
8 Assyria also has joined with them;
They have helped the children of Lot.
Selah

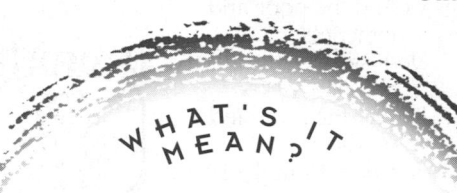

WHAT'S IT MEAN?

The one thing these enemies had in common
was that they all had been defeated by the Israelites
in an unlikely manner. The Midianites, who were led by Oreb and
Zeeb and later by Zebah and Zalmunna (obviously "Z" names were
popular with Midianite parents), put together an enormous army to
fight the Israelites, yet were defeated by Gideon and his tiny band of
soldiers. The army of Jabin, under the command of Sisera, lost to an
Israelite army led by a woman, Deborah. Sisera escaped, but was
later killed by another woman, Jael, who hammered a tent peg into
his head while he slept. (Yes, you read that right.)
Psalm 83:9–11

9 Deal with them as *with* Midian,
As *with* Sisera,
As *with* Jabin at the Brook Kishon,
10 Who perished at En Dor,
Who became *as* refuse on the earth.
11 Make their nobles like Oreb and like
Zeeb,
Yes, all their princes like Zebah and
Zalmunna,
12 Who said, "Let us take for ourselves
The pastures of God for a possession."

13 O my God, make them like the whirling
dust,
Like the chaff before the wind!
14 As the fire burns the woods,
And as the flame sets the mountains on
fire,
15 So pursue them with Your tempest,
And frighten them with Your storm.
16 Fill their faces with shame,
That they may seek Your name, O LORD.
17 Let them be confounded and dismayed
forever;
Yes, let them be put to shame and
perish,
18 That they may know that You, whose
name alone *is* the LORD,
Are the Most High over all the earth.

PSALM 84

THE BLESSEDNESS OF DWELLING IN THE HOUSE OF GOD

*To the Chief Musician. On an instrument
of Gath.*[a] *A Psalm of the sons
of Korah.*

1 How lovely *is* Your tabernacle,
O LORD of hosts!
2 My soul longs, yes, even faints
For the courts of the LORD;
My heart and my flesh cry out for the
living God.

3 Even the sparrow has found a home,
And the swallow a nest for herself,
Where she may lay her young—
Even Your altars, O LORD of hosts,
My King and my God.
4 Blessed *are* those who dwell in Your
house;
They will still be praising You. *Selah*

84:title [a]Hebrew *Al Gittith*

5 Blessed *is* the man whose strength *is* in
You,
Whose heart *is* set on pilgrimage.
6 *As they* pass through the Valley of Baca,
They make it a spring;
The rain also covers it with pools.
7 They go from strength to strength;
Each one appears before God in Zion.ᵃ

8 O LORD God of hosts, hear my prayer;
Give ear, O God of Jacob!   Selah
9 O God, behold our shield,
And look upon the face of Your
anointed.

10 For a day in Your courts *is* better than a
thousand.
I would rather be a doorkeeper in the
house of my God
Than dwell in the tents of wickedness.
11 For the LORD God *is* a sun and shield;
The LORD will give grace and glory;
No good *thing* will He withhold
From those who walk uprightly.

12 O LORD of hosts,
Blessed *is* the man who trusts in You!

PSALM 85

PRAYER THAT THE LORD WILL RESTORE FAVOR TO THE LAND

To the Chief Musician. A Psalm
of the sons of Korah.

1 LORD, You have been favorable to Your
land;
You have brought back the captivity of
Jacob.
2 You have forgiven the iniquity of Your
people;
You have covered all their sin.   Selah
3 You have taken away all Your wrath;
You have turned from the fierceness of
Your anger.

4 Restore us, O God of our salvation,
And cause Your anger toward us to
cease.
5 Will You be angry with us forever?
Will You prolong Your anger to all
generations?
6 Will You not revive us again,
That Your people may rejoice in You?
7 Show us Your mercy, LORD,
And grant us Your salvation.

84:7 ᵃSeptuagint, Syriac, and Vulgate read *The God of gods shall be seen.*

Promise   HE PROMISES PEACE TO HIS FAITHFUL PEOPLE.

I will hear what God the LORD will speak, for He will speak peace to His people and to His saints; but let them not turn back to folly (Ps. 85:8).

Faithfulness, the way God defines it, is not a stuck-like-glue observance of a bunch of rules you learn in Sunday school. What's going on inside you is more important to God than what you do. So the faithful person obeys, not because he has incredible willpower, but because his heart is turned toward God all the time. When a faithful person fails, she is quick to admit it, talk to Jesus about it, and accept His forgiveness. The faithful person is humble, meaning he doesn't think he can live his life—any part of it—without God.

This is the kind of person God promises peace to. Now, having peace doesn't mean everything that happens in your life will be wonderful and you won't ever be sad or get upset. The peace that God gives is a way-down-in-your-gut confidence that everything that happens to you, good or bad, is something He will use to bring you closer to Him and make you more like Him. As your friendship with Jesus grows, this peace will take root in your heart. He promises it will!

SEE FOR YOURSELF:
Mic. 5:4, 5; John 14:27

8 I will hear what God the LORD will speak,
For He will speak peace
To His people and to His saints;
But let them not turn back to folly.

9 Surely His salvation *is* near to those who
fear Him,
That glory may dwell in our land.

10 Mercy and truth have met together;
Righteousness and peace have kissed.

11 Truth shall spring out of the earth,
And righteousness shall look down from
heaven.

12 Yes, the LORD will give *what is* good;
And our land will yield its increase.

13 Righteousness will go before Him,
And shall make His footsteps *our*
pathway.

PSALM 86

PRAYER FOR MERCY, WITH MEDITATION ON THE EXCELLENCIES OF THE LORD

A Prayer of David.

1 Bow down Your ear, O LORD, hear me;
For I *am* poor and needy.

2 Preserve my life, for I *am* holy;
You are my God;
Save Your servant who trusts in You!

3 Be merciful to me, O Lord,

4 For I cry to You all day long.
Rejoice the soul of Your servant,
For to You, O Lord, I lift up my
soul.

5 For You, Lord, *are* good, and ready to forgive,
And abundant in mercy
to all those who call
upon You.

FORGIVENESS
Why does
God forgive
us?
(86:5)

6 Give ear, O LORD, to my
prayer;
And attend to the voice of my
supplications.

7 In the day of my trouble I will call upon
You,
For You will answer me.

8 Among the gods *there is* none like You,
O Lord;
Nor *are there any works* like Your works.

9 All nations whom You have made
Shall come and worship before You,
O Lord,
And shall glorify Your name.

10 For You *are* great, and do wondrous
things;
You alone *are* God.

11 Teach me Your way, O LORD;
I will walk in Your truth;
Unite my heart to fear Your name.

Promise   HE PROMISES TO READILY FORGIVE YOU.

For You, Lord, are good, and ready to forgive, and abundant in mercy to all those who call upon You (Ps. 86:5).

In Luke 15, Jesus tells the story of a guy who wanted to live his own life. So he asked his dad for the money he was supposed to inherit later and left home. Of course, his money eventually ran out, and he had to get the worst job he could think of—feeding pigs. He was so hungry he wished he could eat some of what they were having. Finally, he got tired of living that way and decided to go home. He didn't expect things to be exactly like they were before he left, but he thought his dad might give him a job as a servant.

His dad surprised him. He saw him coming and ran down the road to meet him. His father was so excited to see him that he threw a big party.

Jesus told this story to give you a picture of just how ready God is to forgive you. He's like that dad, standing on the porch, looking down the road for you—*running* toward you when He sees you coming. He doesn't forgive you because He has to. He forgives you because, like that dad, He loves you; and what He wants more than anything else is to have you home with Him.

SEE FOR YOURSELF:

Ps. 145:8; Mark 11:25, 26; Luke 15:11–32; 1 John 1:9

12 I will praise You, O Lord my God, with all
    my heart,
And I will glorify Your name
    forevermore.
13 For great *is* Your mercy
    toward me,
And You have delivered
    my soul from the
    depths of Sheol.

HELL

Who will be
saved from
hell?
(86:13)

14 O God, the proud have risen against me,
And a mob of violent *men* have sought
    my life,
And have not set You before them.
15 But You, O Lord, *are* a God full of
    compassion, and gracious,
Longsuffering and abundant in mercy
    and truth.

16 Oh, turn to me, and have mercy on me!
Give Your strength to Your servant,
And save the son of Your maidservant.
17 Show me a sign for good,
That those who hate me may see *it* and
    be ashamed,
Because You, LORD, have helped me and
    comforted me.

PSALM 87

THE GLORIES OF THE CITY OF GOD

A Psalm of the sons of Korah. A Song.

1 His foundation *is* in the holy mountains.
2 The LORD loves the gates of Zion
More than all the dwellings of Jacob.
3 Glorious things are spoken of you,
O city of God!   **Selah**

WHAT'S IT MEAN?

Zion, the hill where Solomon built his
temple, was the center for all worship in Israel. It
was also the place the Lord promised to meet
the Israelites when they gathered there.
Psalm 87:1, 2

4 "I will make mention of Rahab and
    Babylon to those who know Me;
Behold, O Philistia and Tyre, with
    Ethiopia:
'This *one* was born there.' "

5 And of Zion it will be said,
"This *one* and that *one* were born in her;
And the Most High Himself shall
    establish her."
6 The LORD will record,
When He registers the peoples:
"This *one* was born there."   **Selah**

7 Both the singers and the players on
    instruments *say*,
"All my springs *are* in you."

PSALM 88

A PRAYER FOR HELP IN DESPONDENCY

*A Song. A Psalm of the sons of Korah.
To the Chief Musician. Set to
"Mahalath Leannoth." A Contemplation[a]
of Heman the Ezrahite.*

1 O LORD, God of my salvation,
I have cried out day and night before
    You.
2 Let my prayer come before You;
Incline Your ear to my cry.

3 For my soul is full of troubles,
And my life draws near to the grave.
4 I am counted with those who go down to
    the pit;
I am like a man *who has* no strength,
5 Adrift among the dead,
Like the slain who lie in the grave,
Whom You remember no more,
And who are cut off from Your hand.

6 You have laid me in the lowest pit,
In darkness, in the depths.
7 Your wrath lies heavy upon me,
And You have afflicted *me* with all Your
    waves.   **Selah**
8 You have put away my acquaintances far
    from me;
You have made me an abomination to
    them;
I am shut up, and I cannot get out;
9 My eye wastes away because of
    affliction.

88:title [a]Hebrew *Maschil*

LORD, I have called daily upon You;
I have stretched out my hands to You.

10 Will You work wonders for the dead?
Shall the dead arise *and* praise You?

                               Selah

11 Shall Your lovingkindness be declared in
the grave?
Or Your faithfulness in the place of
destruction?

12 Shall Your wonders be known in the
dark?
And Your righteousness in the land of
forgetfulness?

13 But to You I have cried out, O LORD,
And in the morning my prayer comes
before You.

14 LORD, why do You cast off my soul?
Why do You hide Your face from me?

15 I *have been* afflicted and ready to die from
my youth;
I suffer Your terrors;
I am distraught.

16 Your fierce wrath has gone over me;
Your terrors have cut me off.

17 They came around me all day long like
water;
They engulfed me altogether.

18 Loved one and friend You have put far
from me,
And my acquaintances into darkness.

PSALM 89

REMEMBERING THE COVENANT WITH DAVID, AND SORROW FOR LOST BLESSINGS

A Contemplation[a] of Ethan the Ezrahite.

1 I will sing of the mercies of the LORD
forever;
With my mouth will I make known Your
faithfulness to all generations.

2 For I have said, "Mercy shall be built up
forever;
Your faithfulness You shall establish in the
very heavens."

3 "I have made a covenant with My
chosen,
I have sworn to My servant David:

4 'Your seed I will establish forever,
And build up your throne to all
generations.'"

                            Selah

5 And the heavens will praise Your
wonders, O LORD;
Your faithfulness also in the assembly of
the saints.

6 For who in the heavens can be compared
to the LORD?
Who among the sons of the mighty can
be likened to the LORD?

7 God is greatly to be feared in the
assembly of the saints,
And to be held in reverence by all *those*
around Him.

8 O LORD God of hosts,
Who *is* mighty like You, O LORD?
Your faithfulness also surrounds You.

9 You rule the raging of the sea;
When its waves rise, You still them.

10 You have broken Rahab in pieces, as one
who is slain;
You have scattered Your enemies with
Your mighty arm.

11 The heavens *are* Yours, the earth also *is*
Yours;
The world and all its fullness, You have
founded them.

12 The north and the south, You have
created them;
Tabor and Hermon rejoice in Your name.

13 You have a mighty arm;
Strong is Your hand, *and* high is Your
right hand.

14 Righteousness and justice *are* the
foundation of Your throne;
Mercy and truth go before Your face.

15 Blessed *are* the people who know the
joyful sound!
They walk, O LORD, in the light of Your
countenance.

16 In Your name they rejoice all day long,
And in Your righteousness they are
exalted.

17 For You *are* the glory of their strength,
And in Your favor our horn is exalted.

18 For our shield *belongs* to the LORD,
And our king to the Holy One of Israel.

19 Then You spoke in a vision to Your holy
one,[a]
And said: "I have given help to *one who is*
mighty;
I have exalted one chosen from the
people.

20 I have found My servant David;

89:title [a]Hebrew *Maschil*   **89:19** [a]Following many Hebrew manuscripts; Masoretic Text, Septuagint, Targum, and Vulgate read *holy ones.*

With My holy oil I have anointed him,
21 With whom My hand shall be
    established;
Also My arm shall strengthen him.
22 The enemy shall not outwit him,
Nor the son of wickedness afflict him.
23 I will beat down his foes before his face,
And plague those who hate him.

24 "But My faithfulness and My mercy *shall
    be* with him,
And in My name his horn shall be
    exalted.
25 Also I will set his hand over the sea,
And his right hand over the rivers.
26 He shall cry to Me, 'You *are* my Father,
My God, and the rock of my salvation.'
27 Also I will make him *My* firstborn,
The highest of the kings of the earth.
28 My mercy I will keep for him forever,
And My covenant shall stand firm with
    him.
29 His seed also I will make *to endure* forever,
And his throne as the days of heaven.

30 "If his sons forsake My law
And do not walk in My judgments,
31 If they break My statutes
And do not keep My commandments,
32 Then I will punish their transgression
    with the rod,
And their iniquity with stripes.
33 Nevertheless My lovingkindness I will not
    utterly take from him,
Nor allow My faithfulness to fail.
34 My covenant I will not break,
Nor alter the word that has gone out of
    My lips.
35 Once I have sworn by My holiness;
I will not lie to David:
36 His seed shall endure forever,
And his throne as the sun before Me;
37 It shall be established forever like the
    moon,
Even *like* the faithful witness in the sky."
                                        Selah

38 But You have cast off and abhorred,
You have been furious with Your
    anointed.
39 You have renounced the covenant of
    Your servant;
You have profaned his crown *by casting it*
    to the ground.
40 You have broken down all his hedges;

You have brought his strongholds to ruin.
41 All who pass by the way plunder him;
He is a reproach to his neighbors.
42 You have exalted the right hand of his
    adversaries;
You have made all his enemies rejoice.
43 You have also turned back the edge of his
    sword,
And have not sustained him in the battle.
44 You have made his glory cease,
And cast his throne down to the ground.
45 The days of his youth You have
    shortened;
You have covered him with shame. Selah

46 How long, LORD?
Will You hide Yourself
    forever?
Will Your wrath burn like
    fire?
47 Remember how short
    my time is;
For what futility have You created all the
    children of men?
48 What man can live and not see death?
Can he deliver his life from the power of
    the grave?   Selah

49 Lord, where *are* Your former
    lovingkindnesses,
Which You swore to David in Your truth?
50 Remember, Lord, the reproach of Your
    servants—
How I bear in my bosom *the reproach of* all
    the many peoples,
51 With which Your enemies have
    reproached, O LORD,
With which they have reproached the
    footsteps of Your anointed.

52 Blessed *be* the LORD forevermore!
Amen and Amen.

DEATH

Who will face
death?
(89:46–48)

Book Four: Psalms 90—106

PSALM 90

THE ETERNITY OF GOD, AND MAN'S FRAILTY

A Prayer of Moses the man of God.

1 Lord, You have been our dwelling place[a]
    in all generations.
2 Before the mountains were brought forth,

90:1 [a]Septuagint, Targum, and Vulgate read *refuge.*

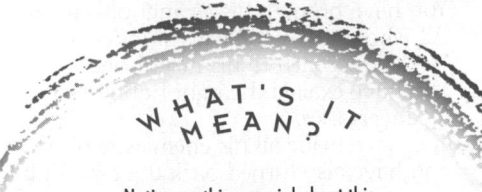

WHAT'S IT MEAN?

Notice anything special about this psalm? It's the only one written by Moses. Not only that, but it's probably the oldest one in the entire collection. Written near the end of the Israelites' forty years of wandering in the wilderness, the psalm offers a prayer for the new generation of Israelites who were about to enter and conquer the land God had promised to them.

Psalm 90:1 and psalm title

Or ever You had formed the earth and
    the world,
Even from everlasting to everlasting, You
    are God.

3 You turn man to destruction,
And say, "Return, O children of men."
4 For a thousand years in Your sight
Are like yesterday when it is past,
And *like* a watch in the night.
5 You carry them away *like* a flood;
They are like a sleep.
In the morning they are like grass *which*
    grows up:
6 In the morning it flourishes and grows
    up;
In the evening it is cut down and
    withers.

7 For we have been consumed by Your
    anger,
And by Your wrath we are terrified.
8 You have set our iniquities before You,
Our secret *sins* in the light of Your
    countenance.
9 For all our days have passed away in
    Your wrath;
We finish our years like a sigh.
10 The days of our lives *are* seventy years;
And if by reason of strength *they are*
    eighty years,
Yet their boast *is* only labor and sorrow;
For it is soon cut off, and we fly away.
11 Who knows the power of Your anger?
For as the fear of You, *so is* Your wrath.
12 So teach *us* to number our days,
That we may gain a heart of wisdom.

13 Return, O LORD!
How long?
And have compassion on Your
    servants.
14 Oh, satisfy us early with Your mercy,
That we may rejoice and be glad all our
    days!
15 Make us glad according to the days *in
    which* You have afflicted us,
The years *in which* we have seen
    evil.
16 Let Your work appear to Your
    servants,
And Your glory to their children.
17 And let the beauty of the LORD our God
    be upon us,
And establish the work of our hands for
    us;
Yes, establish the work of our hands.

On the Edge

You carry them away like a flood; they are like a sleep. In the morning they are like grass which grows up: In the morning it flourishes and grows up; in the evening it is cut down and withers (Ps. 90:5, 6).

Compared to God, who was never born and will never die, your life is like a blade of grass that grows up at dawn and withers by sunset. Our time on earth is short, so the really important question is, "How are you going to spend your life?" Are you going to waste most of it, hoping to make the last few years count, or will you max out your days to the glory of God?

Don't waste any more time. It's time to lock on to the things that you really love to do and pursue them with all your heart. It's time to get serious about your relationship with God. Before you know it, you'll be standing in His presence, giving an account of what you did on earth. It's time to love the people you need to forgive. It's time to plug in to your family. It's time to stop whining and look for the good in your life. The matter is urgent. A blink of the eye and you'll be gone.

SEE FOR YOURSELF:
Job 14:2; Eccl. 6:12;
Is. 40:6–8

PSALM 91

SAFETY OF ABIDING IN THE PRESENCE OF GOD

1 He who dwells in the secret place of the
Most High
Shall abide under the shadow of the
Almighty.
2 I will say of the LORD, "He is my refuge
and my fortress;
My God, in Him I will trust."

3 Surely He shall deliver you from the
snare of the fowler[a]
And from the perilous
pestilence.
4 He shall cover you with
His feathers,
And under His wings
you shall take refuge;
His truth shall be your
shield and buckler.
5 You shall not be afraid of
the terror by night,
Nor of the arrow that flies by day,
6 Nor of the pestilence that walks in
darkness,
Nor of the destruction that lays waste at
noonday.

7 A thousand may fall at your side,
And ten thousand at your right hand;
But it shall not come near you.

FEAR
What two things does God tell us that we do not need to fear? (91:5)

WHAT'S IT MEAN?

The Hebrew day was divided into four
sections: midnight or night, which was 12 a.m. to
6 a.m.; morning, which was 6 a.m. to 12 p.m.; midday or noonday,
which was 12 p.m. to 6 p.m.; and evening, which was 6 p.m. to
12 a.m. The point of these verses is that the Lord
offers round-the-clock protection.
Psalm 91:5, 6

8 Only with your eyes shall you look,
And see the reward of the wicked.

9 Because you have made the LORD, who is
my refuge,
Even the Most High, your dwelling place,
10 No evil shall befall you,
Nor shall any plague come near your
dwelling;
11 For He shall give His angels charge over
you,
To keep you in all your ways.
12 In their hands they shall bear you up,
Lest you dash your foot against a stone.

91:3 [a]That is, one who catches birds in a trap or snare

Promise HE PROMISES TO COMMAND HIS ANGELS TO DEFEND AND PROTECT YOU.

*For He shall give His angels charge over you, to keep you in all your ways.
In their hands they shall bear you up, lest you dash your foot against a stone
(Ps. 91:11, 12).*

A lot of people seem to be confused about angels. They like the idea of angels, their protection and presence, but they haven't paid much attention to the Commander of angels. We wear angel pins, read angel books, and hang little angels on everything. Maybe it's just easier to believe in them than in God. They don't ask you for a commitment. They don't convict you of sin. But here's the kicker—angels can't save you either. Angels belong to God. And God uses angels to protect His believers. He can deploy them at any time to defend His followers. They do as they are commanded by Him. So rest secure, knowing that angels hover around those who love God— but loving God is the key.

SEE FOR YOURSELF:
Ps. 34:7; Matt. 4:6; Luke 4:10, 11

13 You shall tread upon the lion and the
cobra,
The young lion and the serpent you shall
trample underfoot.

14 "Because he has set his love upon Me,
therefore I will deliver him;
I will set him on high, because he has
known My name.
15 He shall call upon Me, and I will answer
him;
I *will be* with him in trouble;
I will deliver him and honor him.
16 With long life I will satisfy him,
And show him My salvation."

PSALM 92

PRAISE TO THE LORD FOR HIS LOVE AND FAITHFULNESS

A Psalm. A Song for the Sabbath day.

1 *It is* good to give thanks to the LORD,
And to sing praises to Your name,
O Most High;
2 To declare Your lovingkindness in the
morning,
And Your faithfulness every night,
3 On an instrument of ten strings,
On the lute,
And on the harp,
With harmonious sound.
4 For You, LORD, have made me glad
through Your work;
I will triumph in the works of Your
hands.

5 O LORD, how great are Your works!
Your thoughts are very deep.
6 A senseless man does not know,

Nor does a fool understand this.
7 When the wicked spring up like grass,
And when all the workers of iniquity
flourish,
It is that they may be destroyed forever.

8 But You, LORD, *are* on high forevermore.
9 For behold, Your enemies, O LORD,
For behold, Your enemies shall perish;
All the workers of iniquity shall be
scattered.

10 But my horn You have exalted like a wild
ox;
I have been anointed with fresh oil.
11 My eye also has seen *my desire* on my
enemies;
My ears hear *my desire* on the wicked
Who rise up against me.

12 The righteous shall flourish like a palm
tree,
He shall grow like a cedar in Lebanon.
13 Those who are planted in the house of
the LORD
Shall flourish in the courts of our God.
14 They shall still bear fruit in old age;
They shall be fresh and flourishing,
15 To declare that the LORD is upright;
He is my rock, and *there is* no
unrighteousness in Him.

PSALM 93

THE ETERNAL REIGN OF THE LORD

1 The LORD reigns, He is clothed with
majesty;
The LORD is clothed,
He has girded Himself with strength.
Surely the world is established, so that it
cannot be moved.
2 Your throne *is* established from of old;
You *are* from everlasting.

3 The floods have lifted up, O LORD,
The floods have lifted up their voice;
The floods lift up their waves.
4 The LORD on high *is* mightier
Than the noise of many waters,
Than the mighty waves of the sea.

5 Your testimonies are very sure;
Holiness adorns Your house,
O LORD, forever.

WHAT'S IT MEAN?

The wild ox was considered untamable. The
animal, which used its horn as a weapon, was a
symbol of strength to the Israelites.
Psalm 92:10

PSALM 94

GOD THE REFUGE OF THE RIGHTEOUS

1 O LORD God, to whom vengeance
    belongs—
O God, to whom vengeance belongs,
    shine forth!
2 Rise up, O Judge of the earth;
Render punishment to the proud.
3 LORD, how long will the wicked,
How long will the wicked triumph?

4 They utter speech, *and* speak insolent
    things;
All the workers of iniquity boast in
    themselves.
5 They break in pieces Your people,
    O LORD,
And afflict Your heritage.
6 They slay the widow and the stranger,
And murder the fatherless.
7 Yet they say, "The LORD does not see,
Nor does the God of Jacob understand."

8 Understand, you senseless among the
    people;
And *you* fools, when will you be wise?
9 He who planted the ear, shall He not
    hear?
He who formed the eye, shall He not see?
10 He who instructs the nations, shall He
    not correct,
He who teaches man knowledge?
11 The LORD knows the thoughts of man,
That they *are* futile.

12 Blessed *is* the man whom You instruct,
    O LORD,
And teach out of Your law,
13 That You may give him rest from the
    days of adversity,
Until the pit is dug for the wicked.
14 For the LORD will not cast off His people,
Nor will He forsake His inheritance.
15 But judgment will return to righteousness,
And all the upright in heart will follow it.

16 Who will rise up for me against the
    evildoers?
Who will stand up for me against the
    workers of iniquity?
17 Unless the LORD *had been* my help,
My soul would soon have settled in
    silence.
18 If I say, "My foot slips,"

19 Your mercy, O LORD, will hold me up.
In the multitude of my anxieties within
    me,
Your comforts delight my soul.

20 Shall the throne of iniquity, which devises
    evil by law,
Have fellowship with You?
21 They gather together against the life of the
    righteous,
And condemn innocent blood.
22 But the LORD has been my defense,
And my God the rock of my refuge.
23 He has brought on them their own
    iniquity,
And shall cut them off in their own
    wickedness;
The LORD our God shall cut them off.

PSALM 95

A CALL TO WORSHIP AND OBEDIENCE

1 Oh come, let us sing to the LORD!
Let us shout joyfully to the Rock of our
    salvation.
2 Let us come before His presence with
    thanksgiving;
Let us shout joyfully to Him with psalms.
3 For the LORD *is* the great God,
And the great King above all gods.
4 In His hand *are* the deep places of the
    earth;
The heights of the hills *are* His also.
5 The sea *is* His, for He made it;
And His hands formed the dry *land.*

6 Oh come, let us worship and bow
    down;
Let us kneel before the LORD our Maker.
7 For He *is* our God,
And we *are* the people of His pasture,
And the sheep of His hand.

Today, if you will hear His voice:
8 "Do not harden your hearts, as in the
    rebellion,[a]
As *in* the day of trial[b] in the wilderness,
9 When your fathers tested Me;
They tried Me, though they saw My
    work.
10 For forty years I was grieved with *that*
    generation,
And said, 'It *is* a people who go astray in
    their hearts,
And they do not know My ways.'

95:8 [a]Or *Meribah* [b]Or *Massah*

On the Edge

For He is our God, and we are the people of His pasture, and the sheep of His hand (Ps. 95:7).

Sheep are the only animals that need a shepherd for outside care. They would wander off, starve to death, or fall off a cliff if it weren't for the shepherd. The Lord calls us His sheep because, in the same way, we need Him to guide us, to protect us, and to provide for our needs. Sometimes a shepherd will carry a helpless lamb in his arms, and a wonderful thing happens during that bonding process—the lamb finds security and learns to trust his shepherd. When the lamb begins to walk, he will never stray from the shepherd's side again. Are you a wandering sheep? God as your shepherd will coax you back into the flock time and again, and He will hold you close to encourage you to stay with Him.

SEE FOR YOURSELF:
Ps. 100:3; Is. 53:6;
John 10:1–16

11 So I swore in My wrath,
'They shall not enter My rest.' "

PSALM 96

A SONG OF PRAISE TO GOD COMING IN JUDGMENT

1 Oh, sing to the LORD a new song!
Sing to the LORD, all the earth.
2 Sing to the LORD, bless His name;
Proclaim the good news of His salvation
from day to day.
3 Declare His glory among the nations,
His wonders among all peoples.

4 For the LORD *is* great and greatly to be
praised;
He *is* to be feared above all gods.
5 For all the gods of the peoples *are* idols,
But the LORD made the heavens.
6 Honor and majesty *are* before Him;
Strength and beauty *are* in His sanctuary.

7 Give to the LORD, O families of the
peoples,
Give to the LORD glory and strength.
8 Give to the LORD the glory *due* His name;
Bring an offering, and come into His
courts.
9 Oh, worship the LORD in the beauty of
holiness!
Tremble before Him, all the earth.

10 Say among the nations, "The LORD reigns;
The world also is firmly established,
It shall not be moved;
He shall judge the peoples righteously."

11 Let the heavens rejoice, and let the earth
be glad;
Let the sea roar, and all its fullness;
12 Let the field be joyful, and all that *is* in it.
Then all the trees of the woods will
rejoice before the LORD.
13 For He is coming, for He is coming to
judge the earth.
He shall judge the world with
righteousness,
And the peoples with His truth.

PSALM 97

A SONG OF PRAISE TO THE SOVEREIGN LORD

1 The LORD reigns;
Let the earth rejoice;
Let the multitude of isles be glad!

2 Clouds and darkness surround Him;
Righteousness and justice *are* the
foundation of His throne.
3 A fire goes before Him,
And burns up His enemies round about.
4 His lightnings light the world;
The earth sees and trembles.
5 The mountains melt like wax at the
presence of the LORD,
At the presence of the Lord of the whole
earth.
6 The heavens declare His righteousness,
And all the peoples see His glory.

7 Let all be put to shame who serve carved
images,
Who boast of idols.
Worship Him, all *you* gods.
8 Zion hears and is glad,
And the daughters of Judah rejoice
Because of Your judgments, O LORD.
9 For You, LORD, *are* most high above all
the earth;
You are exalted far above all gods.

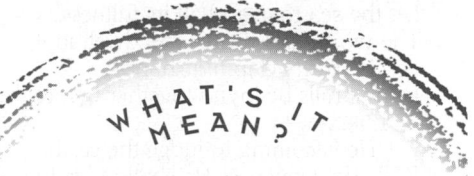

10 You who love the LORD, hate evil!
He preserves the souls of His saints;
He delivers them out of the hand of the
wicked.
11 Light is sown for the righteous,
And gladness for the upright in heart.
12 Rejoice in the LORD, you righteous,
And give thanks at the remembrance of
His holy name.ᵃ

PSALM 98

A SONG OF PRAISE TO THE LORD FOR HIS SALVATION AND JUDGMENT

A Psalm.

1 Oh, sing to the LORD a new song!
For He has done marvelous things;
His right hand and His holy arm have
gained Him the victory.
2 The LORD has made known His
salvation;
His righteousness He has revealed in the
sight of the nations.
3 He has remembered His mercy and His
faithfulness to the house of Israel;
All the ends of the earth have seen the
salvation of our God.

97:12 ᵃOr His holiness

WHAT'S IT MEAN?

The horns used by musicians in ancient Israel were quite different from the horns used today. Whereas today's horns are made of highly polished brass, the horns of ancient Israel were made of . . . well, horns—animal horns, that is. After removing the horn from an animal such as a wild ox or ram, the musician would cut off the end of it, and blow through it. These horns, which were also known as shofars, were used by priests and Levites for religious events. They were also used to sound an attack during wartime.

Psalm 98:6

4 Shout joyfully to the LORD, all the earth;
Break forth in song, rejoice, and sing
praises.
5 Sing to the LORD with the harp,
With the harp and the sound of a psalm,
6 With trumpets and the sound of a horn;
Shout joyfully before the LORD, the King.

Promise   HE PROMISES TO BE A FAIR AND EQUAL JUDGE.

For He is coming to judge the earth. With righteousness He shall judge the world, and the peoples with equity (Ps. 98:9).

How many times have you complained to someone, "Hey, that's not fair?" When someone who didn't study half as long as you did for a history test gets a better grade. When you have to be home at eleven but all your friends get to stay out till midnight. When your little sister gets to wear makeup a couple of years before you did.

Life doesn't seem fair, especially when you look at the world around you—murderers who don't go to jail because of legal technicalities, innocent little kids who are hurt by people they trust, people killed by drunk drivers. Sometimes you can think that God doesn't care about justice.

But, of course, He does. It's just that when He looks at these things, He sees a much bigger picture than you do. He sees from the beginning of time to the end of time in one glance. He knows what's in store for people who choose to hurt others and for the innocent people who suffer because of them. And He isn't going to play favorites, either. The only thing that will prevent people from getting exactly what they deserve will be the mercy that Jesus gives. That mercy will only be available to those who have trusted in Him.

SEE FOR YOURSELF:
Ps. 7:9; 119:137; Is. 30:18; Zeph. 3:5

7 Let the sea roar, and all its fullness,
The world and those who dwell in it;
8 Let the rivers clap *their* hands;
Let the hills be joyful together before the
LORD,
9 For He is coming to judge the earth.
With righteousness He shall judge the
world,
And the peoples with equity.

PSALM 99

PRAISE TO THE LORD FOR HIS HOLINESS

1 The LORD reigns;
Let the peoples tremble!
He dwells *between* the cherubim;
Let the earth be moved!
2 The LORD *is* great in Zion,
And He *is* high above all the peoples.
3 Let them praise Your great and awesome
name—
He *is* holy.

4 The King's strength also loves justice;
You have established equity;
You have executed justice and
righteousness in Jacob.
5 Exalt the LORD our God,
And worship at His footstool—
He *is* holy.

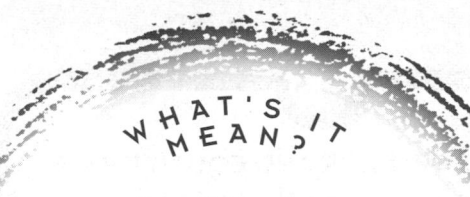

WHAT'S IT MEAN?

Moses and Aaron, who led
the Israelites out of Egypt, were leaders
when Israel became a nation. Samuel was a leader when Israel
became a kingdom. He appointed Saul as the first king and David
as the second king of Israel.

Psalm 99:6

6 Moses and Aaron were among His
priests,
And Samuel was among those who called
upon His name;
They called upon the LORD, and He
answered them.
7 He spoke to them in the cloudy pillar;

On the Edge

*For the LORD is good; His mercy
is everlasting, and His truth endures to all generations (Ps. 100:5).*

Goodness is not a product of God. It is
an attribute of God. In other words, it is not
something God does; it is something God is.
It will never change. Think about it this
way. If you were born Hispanic, that's what
you are. No matter what you do, you will
always be Hispanic. God will always be good.
Because He is eternally good, everything
that comes from Him is good, too. His will is
goodness. He shows us goodness, and He
expects it from us.

What's good about you? There's nothing
geeky about being good. In fact, it takes a
really strong and disciplined person to be
good. Do other people see goodness in
you? Do you give goodness
freely? If you do, keep it up.
If you don't, it's never too late
to start. What's the worst that
could happen? Someone could throw it
back in your face, but at least you gave
some goodness. Maybe it'll have its impact
months or years from now. Someone could
return your goodness . . . and the world
would be better for a moment. Give it a
shot.

SEE FOR YOURSELF:
Ezra 3:11; Ps. 145:9;
Jer. 33:11; Mark 10:18

They kept His testimonies and the
ordinance He gave them.

8 You answered them, O LORD our God;
You were to them God-Who-Forgives,
Though You took vengeance on their
deeds.
9 Exalt the LORD our God,
And worship at His holy hill;
For the LORD our God *is* holy.

PSALM 100

A SONG OF PRAISE FOR THE LORD'S FAITHFULNESS TO HIS PEOPLE

A Psalm of Thanksgiving.

1 Make a joyful shout to the LORD, all you
lands!

2   Serve the LORD with gladness;
    Come before His presence with singing.
3   Know that the LORD, He *is* God;
    It is He *who* has made us, and not we
        ourselves;[a]
    We are His people and the sheep of His
        pasture.

4   Enter into His gates with thanksgiving,
    And into His courts with praise.
    Be thankful to Him, *and* bless His name.
5   For the LORD *is* good;
    His mercy *is* everlasting,
    And His truth *endures* to all generations.

PSALM 101

PROMISED FAITHFULNESS TO THE LORD

A Psalm of David.

1   I will sing of mercy and justice;
    To You, O LORD, I will sing praises.

2   I will behave wisely in a perfect way.
    Oh, when will You come to me?
    I will walk within my house with a
        perfect heart.

3   I will set nothing wicked before my eyes;
    I hate the work of those who fall away;
    It shall not cling to me.
4   A perverse heart shall depart from me;
    I will not know wickedness.

5   Whoever secretly slanders his
        neighbor,
    Him I will destroy;
    The one who has a
        haughty look and a
        proud heart,
    Him I will not endure.

INTEGRITY

Does
integrity take
effort?
(101:3–8)

6   My eyes *shall be* on the
        faithful of the land,
    That they may dwell with me;
    He who walks in a perfect way,
    He shall serve me.
7   He who works deceit shall not dwell
        within my house;
    He who tells lies shall not continue in my
        presence.
8   Early I will destroy all the wicked of the
        land,

On the Edge

I will set nothing wicked before my eyes; I hate the work of those who fall away; it shall not cling to me (Ps. 101:3).

A club's initiation is like a test to see if you are worthy of the club. The greater test in this case is the test of your character. At many times in your walk as a believer, you will be tested, most of the time in your weakest places. A character test puts all your talk on the line. You may have been talking "Jesus talk" for a long time, but it's time to walk the talk. If your club asks you to do something illegal, or immoral, or offensive—don't. Don't even try to rationalize it. Just walk away. If they won't allow you to join—their loss. Why associate yourself with people who look cool on the outside but encourage evil on the inside? Doing the right thing may cost you. It may cost you the club, or some friends, or some status thing. But God promises to honor your right decisions. He will bless you for choosing well.

SEE FOR YOURSELF:
Ps. 1:1; Rom.12:9;
1 Cor. 15:33, 34;
Phil. 4:8

That I may cut off all the evildoers from
    the city of the LORD.

PSALM 102

THE LORD'S ETERNAL LOVE

A Prayer of the afflicted, when he is
overwhelmed and pours out his complaint
before the LORD.

1   Hear my prayer, O LORD,
    And let my cry come to You.
2   Do not hide Your face from me in the day
        of my trouble;
    Incline Your ear to me;
    In the day that I call, answer me speedily.

3   For my days are consumed like smoke,
    And my bones are burned like a hearth.

100:3 [a]Following Kethib, Septuagint, and Vulgate; Qere, many Hebrew manuscripts, and Targum read *we are His.*

4 My heart is stricken and withered like
grass,
So that I forget to eat my bread.
5 Because of the sound of my groaning
My bones cling to my skin.
6 I am like a pelican of the wilderness;
I am like an owl of the desert.
7 I lie awake,
And am like a sparrow alone on the
housetop.

8 My enemies reproach me all
day long;
Those who deride me
swear an oath against
me.
9 For I have eaten ashes
like bread,
And mingled my drink
with weeping,
10 Because of Your indignation
and Your wrath;
For You have lifted me up and cast me
away.
11 My days *are* like a shadow that lengthens,
And I wither away like grass.

**"Hear my prayer,
O LORD, and let
my cry come to You."
(Psalm 102:1)**

WHAT'S IT MEAN?

The Babylonians weren't content with
attacking Jerusalem once. In 586 B.C., they returned
to finish the job. Led by Nebuchadnezzar, the Babylonian forces looted
and destroyed Solomon's temple. For fifty years the temple lay in
ruins, until a group of Jews returned home from captivity to rebuild
the structure. The job was finished around 515 B.C. Like the temple,
the walls of Jerusalem lay in shambles until Nehemiah
led a reconstruction project in 445 B.C.
Psalm 102:13, 14

12 But You, O LORD, shall endure forever,
And the remembrance of Your name to
all generations.
13 You will arise *and* have mercy on Zion;
For the time to favor her,
Yes, the set time, has come.
14 For Your servants take pleasure in her
stones,
And show favor to her dust.

15 So the nations shall fear the name of the
LORD,
And all the kings of the earth Your glory.
16 For the LORD shall build up Zion;
He shall appear in His glory.
17 He shall regard the prayer of the destitute,
And shall not despise their prayer.

18 This will be written for the generation to
come,
That a people yet to be created may
praise the LORD.
19 For He looked down
from the height of His
sanctuary;
From heaven the LORD
viewed the earth,
20 To hear the groaning of
the prisoner,
To release those
appointed to death,
21 To declare the name of
the LORD in Zion,
And His praise in Jerusalem,
22 When the peoples are gathered together,
And the kingdoms, to serve the LORD.

23 He weakened my strength in the way;
He shortened my days.
24 I said, "O my God,
Do not take me away in the midst of my
days;
Your years *are* throughout all generations.
25 Of old You laid the foundation of the
earth,
And the heavens *are* the work of Your
hands.
26 They will perish, but You will endure;
Yes, they will all grow old like a garment;
Like a cloak You will change them,
And they will be changed.
27 But You *are* the same,
And Your years will have no end.
28 The children of Your servants will
continue,
And their descendants will be established
before You."

PSALM 103

PRAISE FOR THE LORD'S MERCIES

A Psalm of David.

1 Bless the LORD, O my soul;
And all that is within me, *bless* His holy
name!

2 Bless the LORD, O my soul,
And forget not all His benefits:
3 Who forgives all your iniquities,
Who heals all your diseases,
4 Who redeems your life from
destruction,
Who crowns you with lovingkindness
and tender mercies,
5 Who satisfies your mouth with good
things,
So that your youth is renewed like the
eagle's.

WHAT'S IT MEAN?

Here are three things you
may not have known about eagles.
One, they can stay in the air for hours at a time. Two, they use their
powerful claws to grab and kill their prey. Three, they can live
for thirty years in the wild.
Psalm 103:5

6 The LORD executes righteousness
And justice for all who are oppressed.
7 He made known His ways to Moses,
His acts to the children of Israel.
8 The LORD is merciful and gracious,
Slow to anger, and abounding in
mercy.
9 He will not always strive with us,
Nor will He keep His anger forever.
10 He has not dealt with us according to our
sins,
Nor punished us according to our
iniquities.

11 For as the heavens are high above the
earth,
So great is His mercy toward those who
fear Him;
12 As far as the east is from the west,
So far has He removed our transgressions
from us.
13 As a father pities his children,
So the LORD pities those who fear Him.
14 For He knows our frame;
He remembers that we are dust.

15 As for man, his days are like grass;
As a flower of the field, so he flourishes.
16 For the wind passes over it, and it is
gone,
And its place remembers it no more.[a]
17 But the mercy of the LORD is from
everlasting to everlasting
On those who fear Him,
And His righteousness to children's
children,
18 To such as keep His covenant,
And to those who remember His
commandments to do them.

19 The LORD has established His throne in
heaven,
And His kingdom rules over all.

20 Bless the LORD, you His angels,
Who excel in strength, who do His word,
Heeding the voice of His
word.
21 Bless the LORD, all you
His hosts,
You ministers of His, who
do His pleasure.
22 Bless the LORD, all His
works,
In all places of His dominion.

Bless the LORD, O my soul!

ANGELS
Who
do angels
serve?
(103:21)

PSALM 104

PRAISE TO THE SOVEREIGN LORD FOR HIS CREATION AND PROVIDENCE

1 Bless the LORD, O my soul!

O LORD my God, You are very great:
You are clothed with honor and majesty,
2 Who cover Yourself with light as with a
garment,
Who stretch out the heavens like a
curtain.

3 He lays the beams of His upper chambers
in the waters,
Who makes the clouds His chariot,
Who walks on the wings of the wind,
4 Who makes His angels spirits,
His ministers a flame of fire.

5 You who laid the foundations of the earth,
So that it should not be moved forever,

103:16 [a]Compare Job 7:10

6 You covered it with the deep as *with* a
    garment;
    The waters stood above the mountains.
7 At Your rebuke they fled;
    At the voice of Your thunder they
    hastened away.
8 They went up over the mountains;
    They went down into the valleys,
    To the place which You founded for
    them.
9 You have set a boundary that they may
    not pass over,
    That they may not return to cover the
    earth.

10 He sends the springs into the valleys;
    They flow among the hills.
11 They give drink to every beast of the
    field;
    The wild donkeys quench their thirst.
12 By them the birds of the heavens have
    their home;
    They sing among the branches.
13 He waters the hills from His upper
    chambers;
    The earth is satisfied with the fruit of
    Your works.

14 He causes the grass to grow for the cattle,
    And vegetation for the service of man,
    That he may bring forth food from the
    earth,
15 And wine *that* makes glad the heart of
    man,
    Oil to make *his* face shine,
    And bread *which* strengthens man's heart.
16 The trees of the LORD are full *of sap*,
    The cedars of Lebanon which He planted,
17 Where the birds make their nests;
    The stork has her home in the fir trees.
18 The high hills *are* for the wild goats;
    The cliffs are a refuge for the rock
    badgers.*a*

19 He appointed the moon for seasons;
    The sun knows its going down.
20 You make darkness, and it is night,
    In which all the beasts of the forest creep
    about.
21 The young lions roar after their prey,
    And seek their food from God.
22 *When* the sun rises, they gather together
    And lie down in their dens.
23 Man goes out to his work
    And to his labor until the evening.

24 O LORD, how manifold are Your works!
    In wisdom You have made them all.
    The earth is full of Your possessions—
25 This great and wide sea,
    In which *are* innumerable teeming
    things,
    Living things both small and great.
26 There the ships sail about;
    There is that Leviathan
    Which You have made to play there.

27 These all wait for You,
    That You may give *them* their food in due
    season.
28 *What* You give them they gather in;
    You open Your hand, they are filled with
    good.
29 You hide Your face, they are troubled;
    You take away their breath, they die and
    return to their dust.
30 You send forth Your Spirit, they are
    created;
    And You renew the face of the earth.

31 May the glory of the LORD endure
    forever;
    May the LORD rejoice in His works.
32 He looks on the earth, and it trembles;
    He touches the hills, and they smoke.

33 I will sing to the LORD as long as I live;
    I will sing praise to my God while I have
    my being.
34 May my meditation be sweet to Him;
    I will be glad in the LORD.
35 May sinners be consumed from the
    earth,
    And the wicked be no more.

    Bless the LORD, O my soul!
    Praise the LORD!

PSALM 105

THE ETERNAL FAITHFULNESS OF THE LORD

1 Oh, give thanks to the LORD!
    Call upon His name;
    Make known His deeds among the
    peoples!
2 Sing to Him, sing psalms to Him;
    Talk of all His wondrous works!
3 Glory in His holy name;
    Let the hearts of those rejoice who seek
    the LORD!

104:18 *a*Or *rock hyrax* (compare Leviticus 11:5)

4 Seek the LORD and His strength;
Seek His face evermore!
5 Remember His marvelous works which
He has done,
His wonders, and the judgments of His
mouth,
6 O seed of Abraham His servant,
You children of Jacob, His chosen ones!

7 He *is* the LORD our God;
His judgments *are* in all the earth.
8 He remembers His covenant forever,
The word *which* He commanded, for a
thousand generations,
9 *The covenant* which He made with
Abraham,
And His oath to Isaac,
10 And confirmed it to Jacob for a statute,
To Israel *as* an everlasting covenant,
11 Saying, "To you I will give the land of
Canaan
As the allotment of your inheritance,"
12 When they were few in number,
Indeed very few, and strangers in it.

13 When they went from one nation to
another,
From *one* kingdom to another people,
14 He permitted no one to do them wrong;
Yes, He rebuked kings for their sakes,
15 *Saying,* "Do not touch My anointed
ones,
And do My prophets no harm."

16 Moreover He called for a famine in the
land;
He destroyed all the provision of bread.
17 He sent a man before them—
Joseph—*who* was sold as a slave.
18 They hurt his feet with fetters,
He was laid in irons.
19 Until the time that his word came to
pass,
The word of the LORD tested him.
20 The king sent and released him,
The ruler of the people let him go free.
21 He made him lord of his house,
And ruler of all his possessions,
22 To bind his princes at his pleasure,
And teach his elders wisdom.

23 Israel also came into Egypt,
And Jacob dwelt in the land of Ham.
24 He increased His people greatly,
And made them stronger than their
enemies.

25 He turned their heart to hate His people,
To deal craftily with His servants.

26 He sent Moses His servant,
And Aaron whom He had chosen.
27 They performed His signs among them,
And wonders in the land of Ham.
28 He sent darkness, and made *it* dark;
And they did not rebel against His
word.
29 He turned their waters into blood,
And killed their fish.
30 Their land abounded with frogs,
Even in the chambers of their kings.
31 He spoke, and there came swarms of flies,
And lice in all their territory.
32 He gave them hail for rain,
And flaming fire in their land.
33 He struck their vines also, and their fig
trees,
And splintered the trees of their territory.
34 He spoke, and locusts came,
Young locusts without number,
35 And ate up all the vegetation in their
land,
And devoured the fruit of their ground.
36 He also destroyed all the firstborn in their
land,
The first of all their strength.

37 He also brought them out with silver and
gold,
And *there was* none feeble among His
tribes.
38 Egypt was glad when they departed,
For the fear of them had fallen upon
them.
39 He spread a cloud for a covering,
And fire to give light in the night.
40 *The people* asked, and He brought quail,
And satisfied them with the bread of
heaven.
41 He opened the rock, and water gushed
out;
It ran in the dry places *like* a river.

42 For He remembered His holy promise,
And Abraham His servant.
43 He brought out His people with joy,
His chosen ones with gladness.
44 He gave them the lands of the Gentiles,
And they inherited the labor of the
nations,
45 That they might observe His statutes
And keep His laws.

Praise the LORD!

PSALM 106

JOY IN FORGIVENESS OF ISRAEL'S SINS

1 Praise the LORD!

Oh, give thanks to the LORD, for *He is*
good!
For His mercy *endures* forever.

2 Who can utter the mighty acts of the
LORD?
Who can declare all His praise?
3 Blessed *are* those who keep justice,
And he who does[a] righteousness at all
times!

4 Remember me, O LORD, with the favor
You have toward Your people.
Oh, visit me with Your salvation,
5 That I may see the benefit of Your chosen
ones,
That I may rejoice in the gladness of Your
nation,
That I may glory with Your inheritance.

6 We have sinned with our fathers,
We have committed iniquity,
We have done wickedly.
7 Our fathers in Egypt did not understand
Your wonders;
They did not remember the multitude of
Your mercies,
But rebelled by the sea—the Red Sea.

8 Nevertheless He saved them for His
name's sake,
That He might make His mighty power
known.
9 He rebuked the Red Sea also, and it dried
up;
So He led them through the depths,
As through the wilderness.
10 He saved them from the hand of him
who hated *them,*
And redeemed them from the hand of the
enemy.
11 The waters covered their enemies;
There was not one of them left.
12 Then they believed His words;
They sang His praise.

13 They soon forgot His works;
They did not wait for His counsel,
14 But lusted exceedingly in the wilderness,

15 And tested God in the desert.
And He gave them their request,
But sent leanness into their soul.

16 When they envied Moses in the camp,
And Aaron the saint of the LORD,
17 The earth opened up and swallowed
Dathan,
And covered the faction of Abiram.
18 A fire was kindled in their company;
The flame burned up the wicked.

WHAT'S IT MEAN?

As descendants of Reuben, Jacob's firstborn son, Dathan and Abiram believed that they and their tribe—and not Moses—should have been the political leaders of Israel. Their punishment for challenging Moses' authority was as unusual and severe as it was unexpected. The earth beneath the rebels' feet opened up, and Dathan and Abiram, along with all of their belongings, disappeared into the earth. God took care of the other people who joined in the rebellion with a fireball from heaven.
Psalm 106:17, 18

19 They made a calf in Horeb,
And worshiped the molded image.
20 Thus they changed their glory
Into the image of an ox that eats grass.
21 They forgot God their Savior,
Who had done great things in Egypt,
22 Wondrous works in the land of Ham,
Awesome things by the Red Sea.
23 Therefore He said that He would destroy
them,
Had not Moses His chosen one stood
before Him in the breach,
To turn away His wrath, lest He destroy
them.

IDOLATRY
In what circumstances are we prone to give in to idolatry? (106:19)

24 Then they despised the pleasant land;

106:3 [a]Septuagint, Syriac, Targum, and Vulgate read *those who do.*

25 They did not believe His word,
But complained in their tents,
And did not heed the voice of the LORD.
26 Therefore He raised His hand *in an oath*
against them,
To overthrow them in the wilderness,
27 To overthrow their descendants among
the nations,
And to scatter them in the lands.

28 They joined themselves also
to Baal of Peor,
And ate sacrifices made
to the dead.
29 Thus they provoked
Him to anger with
their deeds,
And the plague broke
out among them.
30 Then Phinehas stood up
and intervened,
And the plague was stopped.
31 And that was accounted to him for
righteousness
To all generations forevermore.

32 They angered *Him* also at the waters of
strife,[a]
So that it went ill with Moses on account
of them;
33 Because they rebelled against His Spirit,
So that he spoke rashly with his lips.

34 They did not destroy the peoples,
Concerning whom the LORD had
commanded them,
35 But they mingled with the
Gentiles
And learned their works;
36 They served their idols,
Which became a snare to
them.
37 They even sacrificed their
sons
And their daughters to
demons,
38 And shed innocent blood,
The blood of their sons and daughters,
Whom they sacrificed to the idols of
Canaan;
And the land was polluted with blood.
39 Thus they were defiled by their own
works,
And played the harlot by their own
deeds.

DEMONS
Are demons happy when people worship false gods? (106:37)

40 Therefore the wrath of the LORD was
kindled against His people,
So that He abhorred His own inheritance.
41 And He gave them into the hand of the
Gentiles,
And those who hated them ruled over
them.
42 Their enemies also oppressed them,
And they were brought into subjection
under their hand.
43 Many times He delivered
them;
But they rebelled in their
counsel,
And were brought low
for their iniquity.

44 Nevertheless He regarded
their affliction,
When He heard their cry;
45 And for their sake He
remembered His
covenant,
And relented according to the multitude
of His mercies.
46 He also made them to be pitied
By all those who carried them away captive.

47 Save us, O LORD our God,
And gather us from among the Gentiles,
To give thanks to Your holy name,
To triumph in Your praise.

48 Blessed *be* the LORD God of Israel
From everlasting to everlasting!
And let all the people say, "Amen!"

Praise the LORD!

Book Five: Psalms 107—150

PSALM 107

THANKSGIVING TO THE LORD FOR HIS GREAT WORKS OF DELIVERANCE

1 Oh, give thanks to the LORD, for *He is*
good!
For His mercy *endures*
forever.
2 Let the redeemed of
the LORD say *so,*
Whom He has
redeemed from the
hand of the enemy,

"Oh, give thanks to the LORD, for He is good! For His mercy endures forever." (Psalm 107:1)

THANKFULNESS
Why should we thank the Lord? (107:1–3)

3 And gathered out of the lands,
From the east and from the west,
From the north and from the south.

4 They wandered in the wilderness in a
desolate way;
They found no city to dwell in.
5 Hungry and thirsty,
Their soul fainted in them.
6 Then they cried out to the LORD in their
trouble,
And He delivered them out of their
distresses.
7 And He led them forth by the right way,
That they might go to a city for a
dwelling place.
8 Oh, that *men* would give thanks to the
LORD *for* His goodness,
And *for* His wonderful works to the
children of men!
9 For He satisfies the longing soul,
And fills the hungry soul with goodness.

10 Those who sat in darkness and in the
shadow of death,
Bound in affliction and irons—
11 Because they rebelled against the words
of God,
And despised the counsel of the Most
High,
12 Therefore He brought down their heart
with labor;
They fell down, and *there was* none to
help.
13 Then they cried out to the LORD in their
trouble,
And He saved them out of their distresses.
14 He brought them out of darkness and the
shadow of death,
And broke their chains in pieces.
15 Oh, that *men* would give thanks to the
LORD *for* His goodness,
And *for* His wonderful works to the
children of men!
16 For He has broken the gates of bronze,
And cut the bars of iron in two.

17 Fools, because of their transgression,
And because of their iniquities, were
afflicted.
18 Their soul abhorred all manner of food,
And they drew near to the gates of
death.
19 Then they cried out to the LORD in their
trouble,
And He saved them out of their distresses.
20 He sent His word and healed them,

On the Edge

*He brought them out of darkness
and the shadow of death, and
broke their chains in pieces
(Ps. 107:14).*

In the Bible, the word *darkness* refers to
ignorance, hiding, and sin. *Light* indicates
truth, openness, and the presence of God.
Jesus told Nicodemus, "And this is the
condemnation, that the light has come into
the world, and men loved darkness rather
than light, because their deeds were evil.
For everyone practicing evil hates the light
and does not come to the light, lest his
deeds should be exposed" (John 3:19, 20).
Because people loved the darkness—their
evil way of life—they rejected the light,
Jesus.

When you made Jesus your Lord, He
rescued you from darkness. You are no
longer ignorant of the wrong things you do
or of God's love for you in spite
of them. You don't have to be
ashamed of anything. Even sin
doesn't have to hold you back
from God's love.

Instead, Jesus has revealed His truth to
you. He's given you the peace and confidence you need to share yourself with
others. Most of all, He's become your Friend.

Look back to the time before you were a
Christian. Look how far you've come. You've
come out of the darkness of sin into the
light and love of Jesus.

SEE FOR YOURSELF:
Is. 9:2; Eph. 5:8;
1 Pet. 2:9; 1 John 1:5

And delivered *them* from their
destructions.
21 Oh, that *men* would give thanks to the
LORD *for* His goodness,
And *for* His wonderful works to the
children of men!
22 Let them sacrifice the sacrifices of
thanksgiving,
And declare His works with rejoicing.

23 Those who go down to the sea in ships,
Who do business on great waters,
24 They see the works of the LORD,
And His wonders in the deep.
25 For He commands and raises the stormy
wind,

Which lifts up the waves of the sea.

26 They mount up to the heavens,
They go down again to the depths;
Their soul melts because of trouble.

27 They reel to and fro, and stagger like a
drunken man,
And are at their wits' end.

28 Then they cry out to the LORD in their
trouble,
And He brings them out of their distresses.

29 He calms the storm,
So that its waves are still.

30 Then they are glad because they are quiet;
So He guides them to their desired haven.

31 Oh, that *men* would give thanks to the
LORD *for* His goodness,
And *for* His wonderful works to the
children of men!

32 Let them exalt Him also in the assembly
of the people,
And praise Him in the company of the
elders.

33 He turns rivers into a wilderness,
And the watersprings into dry ground;

34 A fruitful land into barrenness,
For the wickedness of those who dwell in
it.

35 He turns a wilderness into pools of water,
And dry land into watersprings.

36 There He makes the hungry dwell,
That they may establish a city for a
dwelling place,

37 And sow fields and plant vineyards,
That they may yield a fruitful harvest.

38 He also blesses them, and they multiply
greatly;
And He does not let their cattle decrease.

39 When they are diminished and brought
low
Through oppression, affliction and
sorrow,

40 He pours contempt on princes,
And causes them to wander in the
wilderness *where there is* no way;

41 Yet He sets the poor on high, far from
affliction,
And makes *their* families like a flock.

42 The righteous see *it* and rejoice,
And all iniquity stops its mouth.

43 Whoever *is* wise will observe these *things,*
And they will understand the
lovingkindness of the LORD.

PSALM 108

ASSURANCE OF GOD'S VICTORY OVER ENEMIES

A Song. A Psalm of David.

1 O God, my heart is steadfast;
I will sing and give praise, even with my
glory.

2 Awake, lute and harp!
I will awaken the dawn.

3 I will praise You, O LORD, among the
peoples,
And I will sing praises to You among the
nations.

4 For Your mercy *is* great above the
heavens,
And Your truth *reaches* to the clouds.

5 Be exalted, O God, above the heavens,
And Your glory above all the earth;

6 That Your beloved may be delivered,
Save *with* Your right hand, and hear me.

7 God has spoken in His holiness:
"I will rejoice;
I will divide Shechem
And measure out the Valley of Succoth.

8 Gilead *is* Mine; Manasseh *is* Mine;
Ephraim also *is* the helmet for My head;
Judah *is* My lawgiver.

9 Moab *is* My washpot;
Over Edom I will cast My shoe;
Over Philistia I will triumph."

10 Who will bring me *into* the strong city?
Who will lead me to Edom?

11 *Is it* not *You,* O God, *who* cast us off?
And *You,* O God, *who* did not go out with
our armies?

12 Give us help from trouble,
For the help of man is useless.

13 Through God we will do valiantly,
For *it is* He *who* shall tread down our
enemies.[a]

PSALM 109

PLEA FOR JUDGMENT OF FALSE ACCUSERS

To the Chief Musician. A Psalm of David.

1 Do not keep silent,
O God of my praise!

2 For the mouth of the wicked and the
mouth of the deceitful

108:13 [a]Compare verses 6–13 with 60:5–12

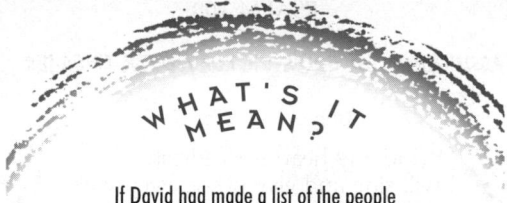

WHAT'S IT MEAN?

If David had made a list of the people
who lied about him or spread false rumors to make
him look bad, here are three names that would have topped the list:
King Saul, his one-time friend and predecessor to the throne; Shimei,
a member of Saul's family; and Absalom,
David's overly ambitious son.
Psalm 109:2

Have opened against me;
They have spoken against me with a
lying tongue.
3 They have also surrounded me with
words of hatred,
And fought against me without a cause.
4 In return for my love they are my
accusers,
But I *give myself to* prayer.
5 Thus they have rewarded me evil for
good,
And hatred for my love.

6 Set a wicked man over him,
And let an accuser[a] stand at his right
hand.
7 When he is judged, let him be found
guilty,
And let his prayer become sin.
8 Let his days be few,
And let another take his office.
9 Let his children be fatherless,
And his wife a widow.
10 Let his children continually be
vagabonds, and beg;
Let them seek *their bread*[a] also from their
desolate places.
11 Let the creditor seize all that he has,
And let strangers plunder his labor.
12 Let there be none to extend mercy to
him,
Nor let there be any to favor his
fatherless children.
13 Let his posterity be cut off,
And in the generation following let their
name be blotted out.

14 Let the iniquity of his fathers be
remembered before the LORD,
And let not the sin of his mother be
blotted out.
15 Let them be continually before the LORD,
That He may cut off the memory of them
from the earth;
16 Because he did not remember to show
mercy,
But persecuted the poor and needy man,
That he might even slay the broken in
heart.
17 As he loved cursing, so let it come to him;
As he did not delight in blessing, so let it
be far from him.
18 As he clothed himself with cursing as
with his garment,
So let it enter his body like water,
And like oil into his bones.
19 Let it be to him like the garment which
covers him,
And for a belt with which he girds
himself continually.
20 *Let* this *be* the LORD's reward to my
accusers,
And to those who speak evil against my
person.

21 But You, O GOD the Lord,
Deal with me for Your name's sake;
Because Your mercy *is* good, deliver me.
22 For I *am* poor and needy,
And my heart is wounded within me.
23 I am gone like a shadow when it
lengthens;
I am shaken off like a locust.
24 My knees are weak through fasting,
And my flesh is feeble from lack of
fatness.
25 I also have become a reproach to them;
When they look at me, they shake their
heads.

26 Help me, O LORD my God!
Oh, save me according to Your mercy,
27 That they may know that this *is* Your
hand—
That You, LORD, have done it!
28 Let them curse, but You bless;
When they arise, let them be ashamed,
But let Your servant rejoice.
29 Let my accusers be clothed with shame,
And let them cover themselves with their
own disgrace as with a mantle.

109:6 [a]Hebrew *satan*   **109:10** [a]Following Masoretic Text and Targum; Septuagint and Vulgate read *be cast out.*

30 I will greatly praise the LORD with my
   mouth;
   Yes, I will praise Him among the
   multitude.
31 For He shall stand at the right hand of
   the poor,
   To save *him* from those who condemn
   him.

PSALM 110

ANNOUNCEMENT OF THE MESSIAH'S REIGN

A Psalm of David.

1 The LORD said to my Lord,
  "Sit at My right hand,
  Till I make Your enemies Your footstool."
2 The LORD shall send the rod of Your
  strength out of Zion.
  Rule in the midst of Your enemies!

This is what Bible experts call a "messianic
psalm," meaning that it predicts something about
Jesus Christ, the Messiah. You might be interested to know that this
psalm holds the record for being quoted more often in the New
Testament than any other psalm in the Bible.
Psalm 110:1

3 Your people *shall be* volunteers
  In the day of Your power;
  In the beauties of holiness, from the
   womb of the morning,
  You have the dew of Your youth.
4 The LORD has sworn
  And will not relent,
  "You *are* a priest forever
  According to the order of Melchizedek."

5 The Lord *is* at Your right hand;
  He shall execute kings in the day of His
   wrath.
6 He shall judge among the nations,
  He shall fill *the places* with dead bodies,
  He shall execute the heads of many
   countries.

Melchizedek is one of the most mysterious
figures in the Bible. Here's what we know about him.
During the time of Abraham, Melchizedek reigned as the king
of Salem, a city whose name was later expanded to Jerusalem.
When Abraham met Melchizedek, he gave the king ten percent
of what he had just won in battle. That would seem to indicate
that Abraham viewed Melchizedek as having the authority of a
priest. Many Bible experts believe that Melchizedek was an Old
Testament preview of Christ, who is also described in
the Bible as both a king and a priest.
Psalm 110:4

7 He shall drink of the brook by the
   wayside;
  Therefore He shall lift up the head.

PSALM 111

PRAISE TO GOD FOR HIS FAITHFULNESS AND JUSTICE

1 Praise the LORD!

  I will praise the LORD with *my* whole
   heart,
  In the assembly of the upright and *in* the
   congregation.

2 The works of the LORD *are* great,
  Studied by all who have pleasure in them.
3 His work *is* honorable and glorious,
  And His righteousness endures forever.
4 He has made His wonderful works to be
   remembered;
  The LORD *is* gracious and full of
   compassion.
5 He has given food to those who fear
   Him;
  He will ever be mindful of His covenant.
6 He has declared to His people the power
   of His works,
  In giving them the heritage of the nations.

7 The works of His hands *are* verity and
   justice;
  All His precepts *are* sure.

8   They stand fast forever and ever,
     And are done in truth and uprightness.
9   He has sent redemption to His people;
     He has commanded His covenant
       forever:
     Holy and awesome *is* His name.

10   The fear of the L ORD *is* the beginning of
       wisdom;
     A good understanding have all those
       who do *His commandments.*
     His praise endures forever.

PSALM 112

THE BLESSED STATE OF THE RIGHTEOUS

1   Praise the L ORD!

     Blessed *is* the man *who* fears the L ORD,
     Who delights greatly in His
       commandments.

2   His descendants will be mighty on
       earth;
     The generation of the upright will be
       blessed.
3   Wealth and riches *will be*
       in his house,
     And his righteousness
       endures forever.
4   Unto the upright there
       arises light in the
       darkness;
     He is gracious, and full of compassion,
       and righteous.

BLESSING
Who does
God bless?
(112:1–3)

5   A good man deals graciously and lends;
     He will guide his affairs with discretion.
6   Surely he will never be shaken;
     The righteous will be in
       everlasting
       remembrance.
7   He will not be afraid of
       evil tidings;
     His heart is steadfast,
       trusting in the L ORD.
8   His heart *is* established;
     He will not be afraid,
     Until he sees *his desire* upon his enemies.

FEAR
Should we
fear bad
news?
(112:7)

9   He has dispersed abroad,
     He has given to the poor;
     His righteousness endures forever;
     His horn will be exalted with honor.
10   The wicked will see *it* and be grieved;
     He will gnash his teeth and melt away;
     The desire of the wicked shall perish.

PSALM 113

THE MAJESTY AND CONDESCENSION OF GOD

1   Praise the L ORD!

     Praise, O servants of the L ORD,
     Praise the name of the L ORD!
2   Blessed be the name of the L ORD
     From this time forth and forevermore!
3   From the rising of the sun to its going
       down
     The L ORD's name *is* to be praised.

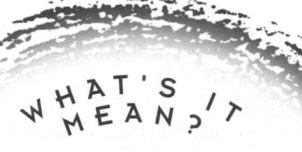

WHAT'S IT MEAN?

Psalms 113 through 118, a group of songs
also known as the *Hallel* (short for "hallelujah"),
play an important role in the traditional Jewish Passover celebration. Psalms 113 and 114 are read or sung before the seder, or meal.
Psalms 115 through 118 are read
or sung after their meal.
Psalm 113:1

4   The L ORD *is* high above all nations,
     His glory above the heavens.
5   Who *is* like the L ORD our God,
     Who dwells on high,
6   Who humbles Himself to behold
     The things that are in the heavens and in
       the earth?

7   He raises the poor out of the dust,
     And lifts the needy out of the ash heap,
8   That He may seat *him* with princes—
     With the princes of His people.
9   He grants the barren woman a home,
     Like a joyful mother of children.

     Praise the L ORD!

PSALM 114

THE POWER OF GOD IN HIS DELIVERANCE
OF ISRAEL

1   When Israel went out of Egypt,
     The house of Jacob from a people of
       strange language,

2   Judah became His sanctuary,
    And Israel His dominion.

3   The sea saw *it* and fled;
    Jordan turned back.
4   The mountains skipped like rams,
    The little hills like lambs.
5   What ails you, O sea, that you fled?
    O Jordan, *that* you turned back?
6   O mountains, *that* you skipped like rams?
    O little hills, like lambs?

7   Tremble, O earth, at the presence of the
        Lord,
    At the presence of the God of Jacob,
8   Who turned the rock *into* a pool of
        water,
    The flint into a fountain of waters.

PSALM 115

THE FUTILITY OF IDOLS AND THE TRUSTWORTHINESS OF GOD

1   Not unto us, O LORD, not unto us,
    But to Your name give glory,
    Because of Your mercy,
    Because of Your truth.
2   Why should the Gentiles say,
    "So where *is* their God?"

3   But our God *is* in heaven;
    He does whatever He pleases.
4   Their idols *are* silver and gold,
    The work of men's hands.

5   They have mouths, but they do not
        speak;
    Eyes they have, but they do not see;
6   They have ears, but they do not hear;
    Noses they have, but they do not smell;
7   They have hands, but they do not handle;
    Feet they have, but they do not walk;
    Nor do they mutter through their throat.
8   Those who make them are like them;
    So is everyone who trusts in them.

9   O Israel, trust in the LORD;
    He *is* their help and their shield.
10 O house of Aaron, trust in the LORD;
    He *is* their help and their shield.
11 You who fear the LORD, trust in the LORD;
    He *is* their help and their shield.

12 The LORD has been mindful of *us*;
    He will bless us;
    He will bless the house of Israel;
    He will bless the house of Aaron.
13 He will bless those who fear the LORD,
    Both small and great.

14 May the LORD give you increase more
        and more,
    You and your children.
15 *May* you *be* blessed by the LORD,
    Who made heaven and earth.

16 The heaven, *even* the heavens, *are* the
        LORD's;
    But the earth He has given to the children
        of men.

Promise   HE PROMISES TO BLESS HIS WORSHIPERS.

He will bless those who fear the LORD, both small and great (Ps. 115:13).

Worshiping the Lord involves being in His presence, looking with the eyes of your heart at His awesome greatness. Although you can't possibly understand everything about God, piece by piece He'll reveal Himself to you as you keep looking at Him, worshiping Him with your whole heart, living your life in His presence.

There is a power in His presence, in continually looking at Him, that changes you way down deep. Paul described it this way: "But we all, with unveiled face," meaning there's no veil blocking our view of Him. "We . . . are being transformed into the same image from glory to glory, just as by the Spirit of the Lord" (2 Cor. 3:18).

This is the blessing that He promises to His worshipers—change from the inside out. This blessing allows you to accomplish what God had in mind when He made you—to have a growing friendship with Him and to become like His Son.

SEE FOR YOURSELF:
Ezra 8:22, 23; Ps. 103:13; 115:12

17 The dead do not praise the LORD,
  Nor any who go down into silence.
18 But we will bless the LORD
  From this time forth and forevermore.

  Praise the LORD!

PSALM 116

THANKSGIVING FOR DELIVERANCE FROM DEATH

1 I love the LORD, because He has heard
  My voice *and* my supplications.
2 Because He has inclined His ear to me,
  Therefore I will call *upon Him* as long as I live.

3 The pains of death surrounded me,
  And the pangs of Sheol laid hold of me;
  I found trouble and sorrow.
4 Then I called upon the name of the LORD:
  "O LORD, I implore You,
  deliver my soul!"

5 Gracious *is* the LORD,
  and righteous;
  Yes, our God *is* merciful.
6 The LORD preserves the simple;
  I was brought low, and He saved me.
7 Return to your rest, O my soul,
  For the LORD has dealt bountifully with you.

8 For You have delivered my soul from death,
  My eyes from tears,
  And my feet from falling.
9 I will walk before the LORD
  In the land of the living.
10 I believed, therefore I spoke,
  "I am greatly afflicted."
11 I said in my haste,
  "All men *are* liars."

12 What shall I render to the LORD
  For all His benefits toward me?
13 I will take up the cup of salvation,
  And call upon the name of the LORD.
14 I will pay my vows to the LORD
  Now in the presence of all His people.

15 Precious in the sight of the LORD
  Is the death of His saints.

16 O LORD, truly I *am* Your servant;
  I *am* Your servant, the son of Your maidservant;
  You have loosed my bonds.
17 I will offer to You the sacrifice of thanksgiving,
  And will call upon the name of the LORD.

18 I will pay my vows to the LORD
  Now in the presence of all His people,
19 In the courts of the LORD's house,
  In the midst of you, O Jerusalem.

  Praise the LORD!

PSALM 117

LET ALL PEOPLES PRAISE THE LORD

1 Praise the LORD, all you Gentiles!
  Laud Him, all you peoples!
2 For His merciful kindness is great toward us,
  And the truth of the LORD *endures* forever.

  Praise the LORD!

PSALM 118

PRAISE TO GOD FOR HIS EVERLASTING MERCY

1 Oh, give thanks to the LORD, for *He is* good!
  For His mercy *endures* forever.

2 Let Israel now say,
  "His mercy *endures* forever."
3 Let the house of Aaron now say,
  "His mercy *endures* forever."
4 Let those who fear the LORD now say,
  "His mercy *endures* forever."

5 I called on the LORD in distress;
  The LORD answered me *and set me* in a broad place.
6 The LORD *is* on my side;
  I will not fear.
  What can man do to me?
7 The LORD is for me among those who help me;

> "The LORD is on my side;
> I will not fear.
> What can man do to me?"
> (Psalm 118:6)

DEATH

Should Christians be afraid of death?
(116:1–15)

Therefore I shall see *my desire* on those
who hate me.

8 *It is* better to trust in the LORD
Than to put confidence in man.

9 *It is* better to trust in the LORD
Than to put confidence in princes.

10 All nations surrounded me,
But in the name of the LORD I will
destroy them.

11 They surrounded me,
Yes, they surrounded me;
But in the name of the LORD I will
destroy them.

12 They surrounded me like bees;
They were quenched like a fire of
thorns;
For in the name of the LORD I will destroy
them.

13 You pushed me violently, that I might fall,
But the LORD helped me.

14 The LORD *is* my strength and song,
And He has become my salvation.*ᵃ*

15 The voice of rejoicing and salvation
Is in the tents of the righteous;
The right hand of the LORD does valiantly.

16 The right hand of the LORD is exalted;
The right hand of the LORD does valiantly.

17 I shall not die, but live,
And declare the works of the LORD.

18 The LORD has chastened me severely,
But He has not given me over to death.

19 Open to me the gates of righteousness;
I will go through them,
And I will praise the LORD.

20 This is the gate of the LORD,
Through which the righteous shall enter.

21 I will praise You,
For You have answered me,
And have become my salvation.

22 The stone *which* the builders rejected
Has become the chief cornerstone.

23 This was the LORD's doing;
It *is* marvelous in our eyes.

24 This *is* the day the LORD has made;
We will rejoice and be glad in it.

25 Save now, I pray, O LORD;
O LORD, I pray, send now prosperity.

26 Blessed *is* he who comes in the name of
the LORD!

We have blessed you from the house of
the LORD.

27 God *is* the LORD,
And He has given us light;
Bind the sacrifice with cords to the horns
of the altar.

28 You *are* my God, and I will praise You;
You are my God, I will exalt You.

29 Oh, give thanks to the LORD, for *He is*
good!
For His mercy *endures* forever.

This psalm, which also happens to be the
longest chapter in the Bible, is an acrostic. What that
means is, in the original Hebrew, each of the psalm's twenty-two
sections begins with a corresponding letter of the Hebrew alphabet—
from *aleph* to *tau*. (If it were written in English, the first line of the
first section would begin with *A*, the second section would begin with
B, and so on.) Each section is made up of eight verses. To make matters
more interesting, the eight verses of each section are formed by
couplets. The first letter of each couplet
matches the first letter of the section.

Psalm 119:1

PSALM 119

MEDITATIONS ON THE EXCELLENCIES OF THE WORD OF GOD

א ALEPH

1 Blessed *are* the undefiled in the way,
Who walk in the law of the LORD!

2 Blessed *are* those who keep
His testimonies,
Who seek Him with the
whole heart!

3 They also do no iniquity;
They walk in His ways.

4 You have commanded *us*
To keep Your precepts
diligently.

5 Oh, that my ways were directed
To keep Your statutes!

PURITY

How can we
remain
pure?
(119:1–20)

6 Then I would not be ashamed,
When I look into all Your
commandments.
7 I will praise You with uprightness of
heart,
When I learn Your righteous judgments.
8 I will keep Your statutes;
Oh, do not forsake me utterly!

ב BETH
9 How can a young man cleanse his way?
By taking heed according to Your word.
10 With my whole heart I have sought You;
Oh, let me not wander from Your
commandments!
11 Your word I have hidden in my heart,
That I might not sin against You.
12 Blessed *are* You, O LORD!
Teach me Your statutes.
13 With my lips I have declared
All the judgments of Your mouth.
14 I have rejoiced in the way of Your
testimonies,
As *much as* in all riches.
15 I will meditate on Your precepts,
And contemplate Your ways.
16 I will delight myself in Your statutes;
I will not forget Your word.

ג GIMEL
17 Deal bountifully with Your servant,
That I may live and keep Your word.
18 Open my eyes, that I may see
Wondrous things from Your law.
19 I *am* a stranger in the earth;

Do not hide Your commandments from
me.
20 My soul breaks with longing
For Your judgments at all times.
21 You rebuke the proud—the cursed,
Who stray from Your commandments.
22 Remove from me reproach and contempt,
For I have kept Your testimonies.
23 Princes also sit *and* speak against me,
But Your servant meditates on Your
statutes.
24 Your testimonies also *are* my delight
And my counselors.

ד DALETH
25 My soul clings to the dust;
Revive me according to Your word.
26 I have declared my ways, and You
answered me;
Teach me Your statutes.
27 Make me understand the way of Your
precepts;
So shall I meditate on Your wonderful
works.
28 My soul melts from heaviness;
Strengthen me according to Your word.
29 Remove from me the way of lying,
And grant me Your law graciously.
30 I have chosen the way of truth;
Your judgments I have laid *before me.*
31 I cling to Your testimonies;
O LORD, do not put me to shame!
32 I will run the course of Your
commandments,
For You shall enlarge my heart.

Promise   HE PROMISES TO STRENGTHEN YOU.

My soul melts from heaviness; strengthen me according to Your word
(Ps. 119:28).

Having one of those blacker than black days? Just make the world stop—you want to get off? No one is making sense. Nothing helps. You keep fighting back tears. You are overcome with sorrow and pain. No one could possibly understand. Maybe no one can understand—no one but God.

God promises to encourage you in your darkest hour. If you will seek Him with all of your heart, He will come to you. He will show you the path that leads out of your situation. He will conduct a holy pep rally just for you. He will wipe away your tears. He will carry your heavy load. He is much better at all this than you are, so let Him take it from here. Climb up into His strong arms. Lay your head down. And rest.

SEE FOR YOURSELF:
Matt. 11:28–30; Rom. 15:4

ה HE
33 Teach me, O LORD, the way of Your
   statutes,
   And I shall keep it *to* the end.
34 Give me understanding, and I shall keep
   Your law;
   Indeed, I shall observe it with *my* whole
   heart.
35 Make me walk in the path of Your
   commandments,
   For I delight in it.
36 Incline my heart to Your testimonies,
   And not to covetousness.
37 Turn away my eyes from looking at
   worthless things,
   And revive me in Your way.[a]
38 Establish Your word to Your servant,
   Who *is devoted* to fearing You.
39 Turn away my reproach which I dread,
   For Your judgments *are* good.
40 Behold, I long for Your precepts;
   Revive me in Your righteousness.

ו WAW
41 Let Your mercies come also to me,
   O LORD—
   Your salvation according to Your word.
42 So shall I have an answer for him who
   reproaches me,
   For I trust in Your word.
43 And take not the word of truth utterly
   out of my mouth,
   For I have hoped in Your ordinances.
44 So shall I keep Your law continually,
   Forever and ever.
45 And I will walk at liberty,
   For I seek Your precepts.
46 I will speak of Your testimonies also
   before kings,
   And will not be ashamed.
47 And I will delight myself in Your
   commandments,
   Which I love.
48 My hands also I will lift up to Your
   commandments,
   Which I love,
   And I will meditate on Your statutes.

ז ZAYIN
49 Remember the word to Your servant,
   Upon which You have caused me to
   hope.
50 This *is* my comfort in my affliction,
   For Your word has given me life.

51 The proud have me in great derision,
   Yet I do not turn aside from Your law.
52 I remembered Your judgments of old,
   O LORD,
   And have comforted myself.
53 Indignation has taken hold of me
   Because of the wicked, who forsake Your
   law.
54 Your statutes have been my songs
   In the house of my pilgrimage.
55 I remember Your name in the night,
   O LORD,
   And I keep Your law.
56 This has become mine,
   Because I kept Your precepts.

ח HETH
57 *You are* my portion, O LORD;
   I have said that I would keep Your words.
58 I entreated Your favor with *my* whole
   heart;
   Be merciful to me according to Your
   word.
59 I thought about my ways,
   And turned my feet to Your testimonies.
60 I made haste, and did not delay
   To keep Your commandments.
61 The cords of the wicked have bound me,
   But I have not forgotten Your law.
62 At midnight I will rise to give thanks to
   You,
   Because of Your righteous judgments.
63 I *am* a companion of all who fear You,
   And of those who keep Your precepts.
64 The earth, O LORD, is full of Your mercy;
   Teach me Your statutes.

ט TETH
65 You have dealt well with Your servant,
   O LORD, according to Your word.
66 Teach me good judgment and
   knowledge,
   For I believe Your commandments.
67 Before I was afflicted I went astray,
   But now I keep Your word.
68 You *are* good, and do good;
   Teach me Your statutes.
69 The proud have forged a lie against me,
   But I will keep Your precepts with *my*
   whole heart.
70 Their heart is as fat as grease,
   But I delight in Your law.
71 *It is* good for me that I have been
   afflicted,

119:37 [a]Following Masoretic Text, Septuagint, and Vulgate; Targum reads *Your words*.

That I may learn Your statutes.
72 The law of Your mouth *is* better to me
Than thousands of *coins of* gold and
silver.

ʾ YOD
73 Your hands have made me and fashioned
me;
Give me understanding, that I may learn
Your commandments.
74 Those who fear You will be glad when
they see me,
Because I have hoped in Your word.
75 I know, O LORD, that Your judgments *are*
right,
And *that* in faithfulness You have afflicted
me.
76 Let, I pray, Your merciful kindness be for
my comfort,
According to Your word to Your
servant.
77 Let Your tender mercies come to me, that
I may live;
For Your law *is* my delight.
78 Let the proud be ashamed,
For they treated me wrongfully with
falsehood;
But I will meditate on Your precepts.
79 Let those who fear You turn to me,
Those who know Your testimonies.

80 Let my heart be blameless regarding Your
statutes,
That I may not be ashamed.

** כ KAPH**
81 My soul faints for Your salvation,
But I hope in Your word.
82 My eyes fail *from searching* Your word,
Saying, "When will You comfort me?"
83 For I have become like a wineskin in
smoke,
Yet I do not forget Your statutes.
84 How many *are* the days of Your servant?
When will You execute judgment on
those who persecute me?
85 The proud have dug pits for me,
Which *is* not according to Your law.
86 All Your commandments *are* faithful;
They persecute me wrongfully;
Help me!
87 They almost made an end of me on earth,
But I did not forsake Your precepts.
88 Revive me according to Your
lovingkindness,
So that I may keep the testimony of Your
mouth.

ל LAMED
89 Forever, O LORD,
Your word is settled in heaven.

Promise HE PROMISES TO COMFORT YOU WITH HIS KINDNESS.

Let, I pray, Your merciful kindness be for my comfort, according to Your word to Your servant (Ps. 119:76).

You studied your brains out for the chemistry exam. The teacher handed it back to you with a big fat "D" on it. All your friends and their parents went camping last weekend, but your family wasn't invited. You were laughed out of the locker room for refusing to take some pills that were supposed to help you train better. The coolest guy in school asked you out and then only wanted you to write his research paper.

Disappointment. Rejection. Failure. Sometimes it seems unbearable. You need someone to hear your story and say they understand. You need someone to let you cry and give you a big hug. You need someone to comfort you. Where do you go?

There are lots of places to run to, but most of them will leave you empty. God promises to be there and to really comfort you. His love brings faith for the moment and hope for the future. He gives you strength when you don't have any. He looks into your heart and sees how you're feeling and what you need. Then He pours out comfort by His Holy Spirit. No wonder they call Him the Comforter.

SEE FOR YOURSELF:
Is. 49:13; John 14:15–18; 2 Cor. 1:3

90 Your faithfulness *endures* to all
      generations;
    You established the earth, and it abides.
91 They continue this day according to Your
      ordinances,
    For all *are* Your servants.
92 Unless Your law *had been* my delight,
    I would then have perished in my
      affliction.
93 I will never forget Your precepts,
    For by them You have given me life.
94 I *am* Yours, save me;
    For I have sought Your precepts.
95 The wicked wait for me to destroy me,
    But I will consider Your testimonies.
96 I have seen the consummation of all
      perfection,
    But Your commandment *is* exceedingly
      broad.

מ MEM
97 Oh, how I love Your law!
    It *is* my meditation all the
      day.
98 You, through Your
      commandments, make
      me wiser than my
      enemies;
    For they *are* ever with me.
99 I have more understanding
      than all my teachers,
    For Your testimonies *are* my meditation.
100 I understand more than the ancients,
    Because I keep Your precepts.
101 I have restrained my feet from every evil
      way,
    That I may keep Your word.
102 I have not departed from Your judgments,
    For You Yourself have taught me.
103 How sweet are Your words to my taste,
    Sweeter than honey to my mouth!
104 Through Your precepts I get
      understanding;
    Therefore I hate every false
      way.

נ NUN
105 Your word *is* a lamp to
      my feet
    And a light to my path.
106 I have sworn and
      confirmed
    That I will keep Your righteous
      judgments.
107 I am afflicted very much;
    Revive me, O LORD, according to Your
      word.

108 Accept, I pray, the freewill offerings of my
      mouth, O LORD,
    And teach me Your judgments.
109 My life *is* continually in my hand,
    Yet I do not forget Your law.
110 The wicked have laid a snare for me,
    Yet I have not strayed from Your precepts.
111 Your testimonies I have taken as a
      heritage forever,
    For they *are* the rejoicing of my heart.
112 I have inclined my heart to perform Your
      statutes
    Forever, to the very end.

ס SAMEK
113 I hate the double-minded,
    But I love Your law.
114 You *are* my hiding place and my shield;
    I hope in Your word.
115 Depart from me, you evildoers,
    For I will keep the commandments of my
      God!
116 Uphold me according to Your word, that
      I may live;
    And do not let me be ashamed of my
      hope.
117 Hold me up, and I shall be safe,
    And I shall observe Your statutes
      continually.
118 You reject all those who stray from Your
      statutes,
    For their deceit *is* falsehood.
119 You put away all the wicked of the earth
      like dross;
    Therefore I love Your testimonies.
120 My flesh trembles for fear of You,
    And I am afraid of Your judgments.

ע AYIN
121 I have done justice and righteousness;
    Do not leave me to my oppressors.
122 Be surety for Your servant for good;
    Do not let the proud oppress me.
123 My eyes fail *from seeking* Your salvation
    And Your righteous word.
124 Deal with Your servant according to Your
      mercy,
    And teach me Your statutes.
125 I *am* Your servant;
    Give me understanding,
    That I may know Your testimonies.
126 *It is* time for *You* to act, O LORD,
    For they have regarded Your law as void.
127 Therefore I love Your commandments
    More than gold, yes, than fine gold!
128 Therefore all *Your* precepts *concerning* all
      things

BIBLE
What does
the Bible
give us?
(119:99)

DECISIONS
What helps
us make
decisions?
(119:105)

I consider *to be* right;
I hate every false way.

ב PE

129 Your testimonies are wonderful;
Therefore my soul keeps them.
130 The entrance of Your words gives light;
It gives understanding to the simple.
131 I opened my mouth and panted,
For I longed for Your commandments.
132 Look upon me and be merciful to me,
As Your custom *is* toward those who love
Your name.
133 Direct my steps by Your word,
And let no iniquity have dominion over
me.
134 Redeem me from the oppression of man,
That I may keep Your
precepts.
135 Make Your face shine
upon Your servant,
And teach me Your
statutes.
136 Rivers of water run
down from my eyes,
Because *men* do not keep
Your law.

צ TSADDE

137 Righteous *are* You, O LORD,
And upright *are* Your judgments.
138 Your testimonies, *which* You have
commanded,
Are righteous and very faithful.
139 My zeal has consumed me,
Because my enemies have forgotten Your
words.
140 Your word *is* very pure;
Therefore Your servant loves it.
141 I *am* small and despised,
Yet I do not forget Your precepts.
142 Your righteousness *is* an everlasting
righteousness,
And Your law *is* truth.
143 Trouble and anguish have overtaken me,
Yet Your commandments *are* my delights.
144 The righteousness of Your testimonies *is*
everlasting;
Give me understanding, and I shall live.

ק QOPH

145 I cry out with *my* whole heart;
Hear me, O LORD!
I will keep Your statutes.
146 I cry out to You;
Save me, and I will keep Your testimonies.
147 I rise before the dawning of the morning,

And cry for help;
I hope in Your word.
148 My eyes are awake through the *night*
watches,
That I may meditate on Your word.
149 Hear my voice according to Your
lovingkindness;
O LORD, revive me according to Your
justice.
150 They draw near who follow after
wickedness;
They are far from Your law.
151 You *are* near, O LORD,
And all Your commandments *are* truth.
152 Concerning Your testimonies,
I have known of old that You have
founded them forever.

ר RESH

153 Consider my affliction
and deliver me,
For I do not forget Your
law.
154 Plead my cause and
redeem me;
Revive me according to
Your word.
155 Salvation *is* far from the
wicked,
For they do not seek Your statutes.
156 Great *are* Your tender mercies, O LORD;
Revive me according to Your judgments.
157 Many *are* my persecutors and my
enemies,
Yet I do not turn from Your testimonies.
158 I see the treacherous, and am disgusted,
Because they do not keep Your word.
159 Consider how I love Your precepts;
Revive me, O LORD, according to Your
lovingkindness.
160 The entirety of Your word *is* truth,
And every one of Your righteous
judgments *endures* forever.

ש SHIN

161 Princes persecute me without a cause,
But my heart stands in awe of Your word.
162 I rejoice at Your word
As one who finds great treasure.
163 I hate and abhor lying,
But I love Your law.
164 Seven times a day I praise You,
Because of Your righteous judgments.
165 Great peace have those who love Your
law,
And nothing causes them to stumble.
166 LORD, I hope for Your salvation,

> "I cry out with my whole heart; hear me, O LORD! I will keep Your statutes."
> (Psalm 119:145)

And I do Your commandments.
167 My soul keeps Your testimonies,
And I love them exceedingly.
168 I keep Your precepts and Your
testimonies,
For all my ways *are* before You.

ת TAU
169 Let my cry come before You, O LORD;
Give me understanding according to Your
word.
170 Let my supplication come before You;
Deliver me according to Your word.
171 My lips shall utter praise,
For You teach me Your statutes.
172 My tongue shall speak of Your word,
For all Your commandments *are*
righteousness.
173 Let Your hand become my help,
For I have chosen Your precepts.
174 I long for Your salvation, O LORD,
And Your law *is* my delight.
175 Let my soul live, and it shall praise You;
And let Your judgments help me.
176 I have gone astray like a lost sheep;
Seek Your servant,
For I do not forget Your commandments.

PSALM 120

PLEA FOR RELIEF FROM BITTER FOES

A Song of Ascents.

1 In my distress I cried to the LORD,
And He heard me.

2 Deliver my soul, O LORD, from lying
lips
And from a deceitful tongue.

3 What shall be given to you,
Or what shall be done to you,
You false tongue?
4 Sharp arrows of the warrior,
With coals of the broom tree!

WHAT'S IT MEAN?

Other nations were free to mistreat slaves
and foreigners, but Israel was expected—by God
Himself, no less—to respect the foreigners who came to their land.
Apparently, Meshech and Kedar were cities on the edge of the desert
whose citizens were known for their violence.

Psalm 120:5

5 Woe is me, that I dwell in Meshech,
That I dwell among the tents of Kedar!
6 My soul has dwelt too long
With one who hates peace.
7 I *am for* peace;
But when I speak, they *are* for war.

Promise — HE PROMISES NOT TO FALL ASLEEP ON YOU.

Behold, He who keeps Israel shall neither slumber nor sleep (Ps. 121:4).

The Lord is the protector of Israel—and of everyone who puts his or her trust in Him. He
protects you from the enemy of His people, Satan. Satan hates the fact that you want to live for
God. He will throw whatever he can at you to get you off track. But as long as you stand under
God's protection—trusting Him and obeying Him—Satan's plans don't have a lot of effect.
And God doesn't ever let His guard down. He doesn't get bored or tired. Unlike humans, He
doesn't need rest to renew His mind and body. That means you can call on Him anytime you
feel the enemy's attack. If Satan needles you with doubt at midnight, if he attacks you with
fear at three A.M., if he throws you a temptation at high noon—whatever and whenever—the
Lord can hear you call Him and will rescue you.

SEE FOR YOURSELF:
Deut. 11:12; Ps. 11:4; Is. 40:28

PSALM 121

GOD THE HELP OF THOSE WHO SEEK HIM

A Song of Ascents.

1 I will lift up my eyes to the hills—
From whence comes my help?
2 My help *comes* from the LORD,
Who made heaven and earth.

3 He will not allow your foot to be moved;
He who keeps you will not slumber.
4 Behold, He who keeps Israel
Shall neither slumber nor sleep.

5 The LORD *is* your keeper;
The LORD *is* your shade at your right
hand.
6 The sun shall not strike you by day,
Nor the moon by night.

7 The LORD shall preserve you from all evil;
He shall preserve your soul.
8 The LORD shall preserve your going out
and your coming in
From this time forth, and even
forevermore.

On the Edge

I was glad when they said to me, "Let us go into the house of the LORD" (Ps. 122:1).

Going to church is important for several reasons. First, the church is something God wanted and established on earth. It's the place He's made for His people to come together and learn about Him and serve Him and worship Him. Second, it's a place for you to find Christian friends and people you can look up to. Third, it's a place for you to get to know God and His Word and a place where you can be encouraged.

You may be thinking, *Yeah, but those things don't really happen. The church is full of hypocrites.* You're right. It is. It's full of humans—imperfect people who blow it, just like you. Jesus came to help imperfect people. What's important is that there are also some incredible people in church, people whose hearts are really longing to be like Jesus. These people can be awesome friends and role models for you.

You may be thinking, *Okay, but church is stuffy and boring.* But there are so many kinds of churches today—some with forms of music (even electric guitars and drums!) and worship that may really appeal to you. Or that are led by young, energetic pastors who really know how to relate to you.

Give church a chance. Look around at different ones; just make sure you find one that confesses Jesus Christ as the only Lord and Savior. Pray about your decision and ask Him to help you find your place. Get involved and grow with other Christians. You'll be glad you did.

SEE FOR YOURSELF:
Ps. 26:8; John 2:17;
Acts 2:46, 47;
Heb. 10:25

PSALM 122

THE JOY OF GOING TO THE HOUSE OF THE LORD

A Song of Ascents. Of David.

1 I was glad when they said to me,
"Let us go into the house of the LORD."
2 Our feet have been standing
Within your gates, O Jerusalem!

3 Jerusalem is built
As a city that is compact together,
4 Where the tribes go up,
The tribes of the LORD,
To the Testimony of Israel,
To give thanks to the name of the LORD.
5 For thrones are set there for judgment,
The thrones of the house of David.

6 Pray for the peace of Jerusalem:
"May they prosper who love you.
7 Peace be within your walls,
Prosperity within your palaces."
8 For the sake of my brethren and
companions,
I will now say, "Peace *be* within you."
9 Because of the house of the LORD our
God
I will seek your good.

PSALM 123

PRAYER FOR RELIEF FROM CONTEMPT

A Song of Ascents.

1 Unto You I lift up my eyes,
O You who dwell in the heavens.

2 Behold, as the eyes of servants *look* to the hand of their masters,
As the eyes of a maid to the hand of her mistress,
So our eyes *look* to the LORD our God,
Until He has mercy on us.

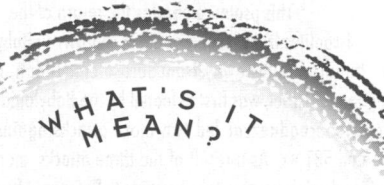

WHAT'S IT MEAN?

Being a servant in ancient times was hard work. Servants were expected to sit quietly in a corner, watching carefully for even the slightest indication that their master needed something.
Psalm 123:2

3 Have mercy on us, O LORD, have mercy on us!
For we are exceedingly filled with contempt.
4 Our soul is exceedingly filled
With the scorn of those who are at ease,
With the contempt of the proud.

PSALM 124

THE LORD THE DEFENSE OF HIS PEOPLE

A Song of Ascents. Of David.

1 "If it had not been the LORD who was on our side,"
Let Israel now say—
2 "If it had not been the LORD who was on our side,
When men rose up against us,
3 Then they would have swallowed us alive,
When their wrath was kindled against us;
4 Then the waters would have overwhelmed us,
The stream would have gone over our soul;
5 Then the swollen waters
Would have gone over our soul."

6 Blessed *be* the LORD,

Who has not given us *as* prey to their teeth.
7 Our soul has escaped as a bird from the snare of the fowlers;[a]
The snare is broken, and we have escaped.
8 Our help *is* in the name of the LORD,
Who made heaven and earth.

PSALM 125

THE LORD THE STRENGTH OF HIS PEOPLE

A Song of Ascents.

1 Those who trust in the LORD
Are like Mount Zion,
Which cannot be moved, *but* abides forever.
2 As the mountains surround Jerusalem,

On the Edge

Those who trust in the LORD are like Mount Zion, which cannot be moved, but abides forever (Ps. 125:1).

Real trust goes a lot deeper than being able to say, "Yeah, sure, I believe in God." James said, "You believe that there is one God. You do well. Even the demons believe—and tremble!" (James 2:19). Real trust means letting go of your life and your heart and giving God control of them. It means obeying Him. James used Abraham as an example: "Do you see that faith was working together with [Abraham's] works, and by works faith was made perfect?" (James 2:22).

People who trust God in this way are like Mount Zion. They're immovable, unshakable. The way a mountain stands up against the forces of nature, they are able, by God's Spirit, to stand against all the stuff that life throws at them.

But Mount Zion isn't just any mountain. This is the spot in Jerusalem God chose for His temple, the place where He would live among His people. Now that you've put your trust in Him, He makes His home in you.

SEE FOR YOURSELF:
Heb. 12:22–29

124:7 [a]That is, persons who catch birds in a trap or snare

So the LORD surrounds His people
From this time forth and forever.

3 For the scepter of wickedness shall not
rest
On the land allotted to the righteous,
Lest the righteous reach out their hands
to iniquity.

4 Do good, O LORD, to *those who are* good,
And to *those who are* upright in their
hearts.

5 As for such as turn aside to their crooked
ways,
The LORD shall lead them away
With the workers of iniquity.

Peace *be* upon Israel!

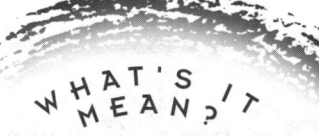

WHAT'S IT MEAN?

Jerusalem was a fairly well-protected city.
The mountains that surrounded Jerusalem sloped
into valleys on the eastern and western sides of the city, making it
difficult for opposing armies to attack from those directions. The
ravines that lay south of the city made it difficult for an
enemy to approach from that direction as well.

Psalm 125:2

PSALM 126

A JOYFUL RETURN TO ZION

A Song of Ascents.

1 When the LORD brought back the
captivity of Zion,
We were like those who dream.
2 Then our mouth was filled with laughter,
And our tongue with singing.
Then they said among the nations,
"The LORD has done great things for
them."
3 The LORD has done great things for us,
And we are glad.

4 Bring back our captivity, O LORD,
As the streams in the South.

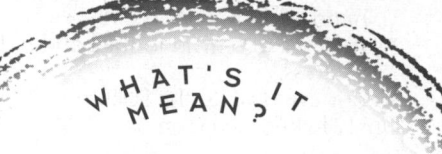

WHAT'S IT MEAN?

This psalm celebrates the return of the
Israelites from seventy years of captivity in Babylonia,
five hundred miles away from Jerusalem. Judah, the southern
kingdom of Israel, was first defeated by the Babylonians in 597 B.C.
King Nebuchadnezzar led two more attacks against the city in
586 and 581 B.C. As a result of the three attacks, more than forty-
five hundred Jews were taken captive to Babylon. After the Persians
conquered Babylonia, the Jews were allowed to return to Jerusalem
and rebuild their temple.

Psalm 126:1

5 Those who sow in tears
Shall reap in joy.
6 He who continually goes forth weeping,
Bearing seed for sowing,
Shall doubtless come again with rejoicing,
Bringing his sheaves *with him*.

PSALM 127

LABORING AND PROSPERING WITH THE LORD

A Song of Ascents. Of Solomon.

1 Unless the LORD builds the house,
They labor in vain who build it;
Unless the LORD guards the city,
The watchman stays awake in vain.
2 *It is* vain for you to rise up early,
To sit up late,
To eat the bread of sorrows;
For so He gives His beloved sleep.

3 Behold, children *are* a heritage
from the LORD,
The fruit of the womb *is*
a reward.
4 Like arrows in the hand
of a warrior,
So *are* the children of
one's youth.
5 Happy *is* the man who has
his quiver full of them;
They shall not be ashamed,
But shall speak with their enemies in the
gate.

ABORTION
Where are
children
from?
(127:3)

PSALM 128

BLESSINGS OF THOSE WHO FEAR THE LORD

A Song of Ascents.

1 Blessed *is* every one who fears the LORD,
Who walks in His ways.

2 When you eat the labor of your hands,
You *shall be* happy, and *it shall be* well
with you.

3 Your wife *shall be* like a fruitful vine
In the very heart of your house,
Your children like olive plants
All around your table.

4 Behold, thus shall the man be blessed
Who fears the LORD.

5 The LORD bless you out of Zion,
And may you see the good of Jerusalem
All the days of your life.

6 Yes, may you see your children's
children.

Peace *be* upon Israel!

PSALM 129

SONG OF VICTORY OVER ZION'S ENEMIES

A Song of Ascents.

1 "Many a time they have afflicted me from
my youth,"
Let Israel now say—

2 "Many a time they have afflicted me from
my youth;
Yet they have not prevailed against me.

3 The plowers plowed on my back;
They made their furrows long."

4 The LORD *is* righteous;
He has cut in pieces the cords of the
wicked.

5 Let all those who hate Zion
Be put to shame and turned back.

6 Let them be as the grass *on* the
housetops,
Which withers before it grows up,

7 With which the reaper does not fill his
hand,
Nor he who binds sheaves, his arms.

8 Neither let those who pass by them say,
"The blessing of the LORD *be* upon you;
We bless you in the name of the
LORD!"

On the Edge

The LORD is righteous; He has cut in pieces the cords of the wicked (Ps. 129:4).

God always is righteous. That doesn't just mean that He follows the rules. Of course He does—they're His rules. But He goes beyond that. He does what is right for *you*. He knows you inside and out, and everything that comes into your life from His hand is the very best thing that could happen in your life. He gives you what you need to become the person He wants you to be—someone who's more and more like His Son. But don't think that everything that happens to you is something God does. When you or someone close to you sins, that has an effect on your life—but sin is *never* God's will. Or sometimes Satan hurts you. God allowed that with Job—the bad things that happened to Job did not come from Him, but He knew what Job was going through.

Here's what's cool—God can even take people's mistakes and Satan's wicked plans and turn them into something good. Romans 8:28 says, "And we know that all things work together for good to those who love God, to those who are the called according to His purpose." He is so good at doing right, He takes even the crummy stuff in your life and turns it into something great—something that makes you stronger and brings you closer to Him.

SEE FOR YOURSELF:
Ps. 7:9; 119:137;
Is. 30:18

PSALM 130

WAITING FOR THE REDEMPTION OF THE LORD

A Song of Ascents.

1 Out of the depths I have cried to You,
O LORD;

2 Lord, hear my voice!
Let Your ears be attentive
To the voice of my supplications.

3 If You, LORD, should mark iniquities,
O Lord, who could stand?

4 But *there is* forgiveness with You,
That You may be feared.

5 I wait for the LORD, my soul waits,
And in His word I do hope.
6 My soul *waits* for the Lord
More than those who watch for the
morning—
Yes, more than those who watch for the
morning.

7 O Israel, hope in the LORD;
For with the LORD *there is* mercy,
And with Him *is* abundant redemption.
8 And He shall redeem Israel
From all his iniquities.

PSALM 131

SIMPLE TRUST IN THE LORD

A Song of Ascents. Of David.

1 LORD, my heart is not haughty,
Nor my eyes lofty.
Neither do I concern myself with great
matters,
Nor with things too profound for me.

2 Surely I have calmed and quieted my
soul,
Like a weaned child with his mother;
Like a weaned child *is* my soul within me.

3 O Israel, hope in the LORD
From this time forth and forever.

PSALM 132

THE ETERNAL DWELLING OF GOD IN ZION

A Song of Ascents.

1 LORD, remember David
And all his afflictions;
2 How he swore to the LORD,
And vowed to the Mighty One of Jacob:
3 "Surely I will not go into the chamber of
my house,
Or go up to the comfort of my bed;
4 I will not give sleep to my eyes
Or slumber to my eyelids,
5 Until I find a place for the LORD,
A dwelling place for the Mighty One of
Jacob."

6 Behold, we heard of it in Ephrathah;
We found it in the fields of the woods.[a]
7 Let us go into His tabernacle;

Let us worship at His footstool.
8 Arise, O LORD, to Your resting place,
You and the ark of Your strength.
9 Let Your priests be clothed with
righteousness,
And let Your saints shout for joy.

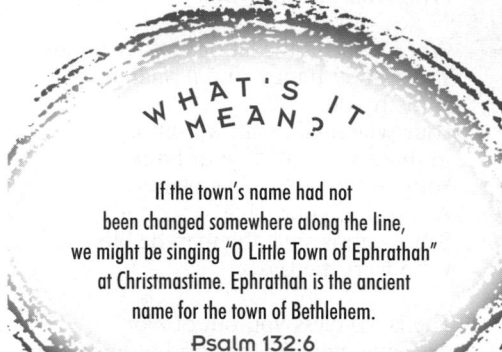

WHAT'S IT MEAN?

If the town's name had not
been changed somewhere along the line,
we might be singing "O Little Town of Ephrathah"
at Christmastime. Ephrathah is the ancient
name for the town of Bethlehem.
Psalm 132:6

10 For Your servant David's sake,
Do not turn away the face of Your
Anointed.

11 The LORD has sworn *in* truth to David;
He will not turn from it:
"I will set upon your throne the fruit of
your body.
12 If your sons will keep My covenant
And My testimony which I shall teach
them,
Their sons also shall sit upon your throne
forevermore."

13 For the LORD has chosen Zion;
He has desired *it* for His dwelling
place:
14 "This *is* My resting place forever;
Here I will dwell, for I have desired it.
15 I will abundantly bless her provision;
I will satisfy her poor with bread.
16 I will also clothe her priests with
salvation,
And her saints shall shout aloud for joy.
17 There I will make the horn of David
grow;
I will prepare a lamp for My Anointed.
18 His enemies I will clothe with shame,
But upon Himself His crown shall
flourish."

132:6 [a]Hebrew *Jaar*

PSALM 133

BLESSED UNITY OF THE PEOPLE OF GOD

A Song of Ascents. Of David.

1 Behold, how good and how pleasant *it is*
For brethren to dwell together in unity!

2 *It is* like the precious oil upon the head,
Running down on the beard,
The beard of Aaron,
Running down on the edge of his
garments.

3 *It is* like the dew of Hermon,
Descending upon the mountains of Zion;
For there the LORD commanded the
blessing—
Life forevermore.

PSALM 134

PRAISING THE LORD IN HIS HOUSE AT NIGHT

A Song of Ascents.

1 Behold, bless the LORD,
All *you* servants of the LORD,
Who by night stand in the house of the
LORD!

2 Lift up your hands *in* the sanctuary,
And bless the LORD.

3 The LORD who made heaven and earth
Bless you from Zion!

PSALM 135

PRAISE TO GOD IN CREATION AND REDEMPTION

1 Praise the LORD!

Praise the name of the LORD;
Praise *Him*, O you servants of the LORD!

2 You who stand in the house of the LORD,
In the courts of the house of our God,

3 Praise the LORD, for the LORD *is* good;
Sing praises to His name, for *it is* pleasant.

4 For the LORD has chosen Jacob for
Himself,
Israel for His special treasure.

5 For I know that the LORD *is* great,
And our Lord *is* above all gods.

6 Whatever the LORD pleases He does,
In heaven and in earth,
In the seas and in all deep places.

On the Edge

Whatever the LORD pleases He does, in heaven and in earth, in the seas and in all deep places (Ps. 135:6).

The most reassuring thing you could know about God is that He is in control. Totally in charge. Doing as He pleases. Our sin has not thrown a wrench in His plans. He is not stressed out by our foolishness. He is not confused about which way to go. He still sits on the throne of heaven. If you think that the world is spinning out of control and that all hope is long gone, then you don't know about the sovereignty of God. He is working in and through what seems like craziness to accomplish His divine purposes. His plans will not be changed. You do not have to be nervous or wonder. God is in charge, both in the world, and in the lives of His believers.

SEE FOR YOURSELF:
Ps. 115:3; Jer. 10:13;
Rom. 8:28

7 He causes the vapors to ascend from the
ends of the earth;
He makes lightning for the rain;
He brings the wind out of His treasuries.

8 He destroyed the firstborn of Egypt,
Both of man and beast.

9 He sent signs and wonders into the midst
of you, O Egypt,
Upon Pharaoh and all his servants.

10 He defeated many nations
And slew mighty kings—

11 Sihon king of the Amorites,
Og king of Bashan,
And all the kingdoms of Canaan—

12 And gave their land *as* a heritage,
A heritage to Israel His people.

13 Your name, O LORD, *endures* forever,
Your fame, O LORD, throughout all
generations.

14 For the LORD will judge His people,
And He will have compassion on His
servants.

15 The idols of the nations *are* silver and
gold,

The work of men's hands.
16 They have mouths, but they do not
        speak;
    Eyes they have, but they do not see;
17 They have ears, but they do not hear;
    Nor is there *any* breath in their mouths.
18 Those who make them are like them;
    So is everyone who trusts in them.

19 Bless the LORD, O house of Israel!
    Bless the LORD, O house of Aaron!
20 Bless the LORD, O house of Levi!
    You who fear the LORD, bless the LORD!
21 Blessed be the LORD out of Zion,
    Who dwells in Jerusalem!

    Praise the LORD!

PSALM 136

THANKSGIVING TO GOD FOR HIS ENDURING MERCY

1   Oh, give thanks to the LORD, for *He is*
        good!
    For His mercy *endures* forever.
2   Oh, give thanks to the God of gods!
    For His mercy *endures* forever.
3   Oh, give thanks to the Lord of lords!
    For His mercy *endures* forever:

4   To Him who alone does great wonders,
    For His mercy *endures* forever;
5   To Him who by wisdom made the
        heavens,
    For His mercy *endures* forever;
6   To Him who laid out the earth above the
        waters,
    For His mercy *endures* forever;
7   To Him who made great lights,
    For His mercy *endures* forever—
8   The sun to rule by day,
    For His mercy *endures* forever;
9   The moon and stars to rule by night,
    For His mercy *endures* forever.

10 To Him who struck Egypt in their
        firstborn,
    For His mercy *endures* forever;
11 And brought out Israel from among
        them,
    For His mercy *endures* forever;
12 With a strong hand, and with an
        outstretched arm,
    For His mercy *endures* forever;
13 To Him who divided the Red Sea in two,
    For His mercy *endures* forever;

On the Edge

Oh, give thanks to the LORD, for He is good! For His mercy endures forever (Ps. 136:1).

This whole chapter in Psalm 136 tells about God's enduring mercy. He loves us with an unconditional love. It doesn't matter what you look like, what your breath smells like, how much money you have, or what your past is like. God loves you anyway! Regardless of anything, God loves you just the same. That's the kind of love we need to have for each other. We need to look at the world through Jesus' eyes.

There's a story in Mark 2 about four men who brought a man, crippled with disease, to Jesus. There was not enough room for them, so they ripped a hole in the roof where Jesus was teaching and lowered the man down through the hole. Now that's compassion. When Jesus saw their faith, He healed the man.

These four men loved their friend with an unconditional love. They were willing to rip off a roof to get him healed. He was sick with disease, and so he probably didn't look or smell that good. They probably had needs themselves, but the only thing they were concerned about was getting their friend to Jesus! Unconditional love.

Next time you've failed and feel like nobody cares, remember that God loves you unconditionally. Like those friends, He's willing to rip a roof off in order to show you the love and mercy you need.

SEE FOR YOURSELF:
John 14:21; Rom. 5:5;
    1 John 4:10, 16

14 And made Israel pass through the midst
        of it,
    For His mercy *endures* forever;
15 But overthrew Pharaoh and his army in
        the Red Sea,
    For His mercy *endures* forever;
16 To Him who led His people through the
        wilderness,
    For His mercy *endures* forever;
17 To Him who struck down great kings,
    For His mercy *endures* forever;
18 And slew famous kings,
    For His mercy *endures* forever—

19 Sihon king of the Amorites,
  For His mercy *endures* forever;
20 And Og king of Bashan,
  For His mercy *endures* forever—
21 And gave their land as a heritage,
  For His mercy *endures* forever;
22 A heritage to Israel His servant,
  For His mercy *endures* forever.

23 Who remembered us in our lowly
    state,
  For His mercy *endures* forever;
24 And rescued us from our enemies,
  For His mercy *endures* forever;
25 Who gives food to all flesh,
  For His mercy *endures* forever.

26 Oh, give thanks to the God of heaven!
  For His mercy *endures* forever.

PSALM 137

LONGING FOR ZION IN A FOREIGN LAND

1 By the rivers of Babylon,
  There we sat down, yea, we wept
  When we remembered Zion.
2 We hung our harps
  Upon the willows in the midst of it.

3 For there those who carried us away
    captive asked of us a song,
  And those who plundered us *requested*
    mirth,
  Saying, "Sing us *one* of the songs of
    Zion!"

4 How shall we sing the LORD's song
  In a foreign land?
5 If I forget you, O Jerusalem,
  Let my right hand forget *its skill!*
6 If I do not remember you,
  Let my tongue cling to the roof of my
    mouth—
  If I do not exalt Jerusalem
  Above my chief joy.

7 Remember, O LORD, against the sons of
    Edom
  The day of Jerusalem,
  Who said, "Raze *it*, raze *it*,
  To its very foundation!"

8 O daughter of Babylon, who are to be
    destroyed,
  Happy the one who repays you as you
    have served us!
9 Happy the one who takes and dashes
  Your little ones against the rock!

Promise   HE PROMISES ALWAYS TO BE MERCIFUL TO YOU.

The LORD will perfect that which concerns me; Your mercy, O LORD, endures forever; do not forsake the works of Your hands (Ps. 138:8).

Some people have this idea of God as the "Big Guy" sitting up in heaven with a giant paddle just waiting for someone to step out of line so He can use it. Well, it's obvious that God isn't pleased when you do something you know you shouldn't. But He's not the guy with the paddle. His discipline comes out of His love. Everything He does, even if it's not so pleasant to you at the time, has your best interest at heart.

Look at how Jesus talked to Martha when she complained to Him about her sister: "Martha, Martha, you are worried and troubled about many things. But one thing is needed, and Mary has chosen that good part, which will not be taken away from her" (Luke 10:41, 42). He didn't scream at her; He just gently pointed her in the right way. He treated Thomas the same way. When Thomas wouldn't believe that Jesus had risen from the dead until he saw and touched Jesus' wounded hands, Jesus didn't refuse to show him what he needed to see. He did say, "Thomas, because you have seen Me, you have believed. Blessed are those who have not seen and yet have believed" (John 20:29).

You can count on God to treat you gently and mercifully, even when He's letting you know you're out of line.

SEE FOR YOURSELF:
2 Chr. 30:9; Lam. 3:22

PSALM 138

THE LORD'S GOODNESS TO THE FAITHFUL

A Psalm of David.

1 I will praise You with my whole heart;
   Before the gods I will sing praises to
   You.
2 I will worship toward
      Your holy temple,
   And praise Your name
   For Your lovingkindness
      and Your truth;
   For You have magnified
      Your word above all
      Your name.

THANKFULNESS

What should
we be
thankful for?
(138:1–8)

3 In the day when I cried out, You
      answered me,
   And made me bold *with* strength in my
      soul.

4 All the kings of the earth shall praise You,
      O LORD,
   When they hear the words of Your
      mouth.
5 Yes, they shall sing of the ways of the
      LORD,
   For great *is* the glory of the LORD.
6 Though the LORD *is* on high,
   Yet He regards the lowly;
   But the proud He knows from afar.

7 Though I walk in the midst of trouble,
      You will revive me;
   You will stretch out Your hand
   Against the wrath of my enemies,
   And Your right hand will save me.
8 The LORD will perfect *that which* concerns
      me;
   Your mercy, O LORD, *endures* forever;
   Do not forsake the works of Your
      hands.

PSALM 139

GOD'S PERFECT KNOWLEDGE OF MAN

For the Chief Musician. A Psalm of David.

1 O LORD, You have searched me and
      known *me.*
2 You know my sitting down and my rising
      up;
   You understand my thought afar off.
3 You comprehend my path and my lying
      down,

4 And are acquainted with all my ways.
   For *there is* not a word on my tongue,
   But behold, O LORD, You know it
      altogether.
5 You have hedged me behind and before,
   And laid Your hand upon me.
6 *Such* knowledge *is* too wonderful for me;
   It is high, I cannot *attain* it.

7 Where can I go from Your Spirit?
   Or where can I flee from Your presence?
8 If I ascend into heaven, You *are* there;
   If I make my bed in hell, behold, You *are*
      there.
9 *If* I take the wings of the morning,
   And dwell in the uttermost parts of the
      sea,

On the Edge

*If I ascend into heaven, You are
there; if I make my bed in hell,
behold, You are there (Ps. 139:8).*

Do you ever wish you could hide from
God? Maybe you really want to do something you know He wouldn't approve of. Is
it easier to go against your conscience if
you pretend that God doesn't know what
you're up to?

But the truth is, you can't hide from
God. When you run a red light, He's there.
He's there when you sneak a look at someone else's paper during a test. If you stick
out your tongue (or worse) behind the back
of someone who made you mad, He sees it.
If you talk bad about someone when they're
not around, He hears you.

You can't even hide from God
what's going on inside you. He's
spirit, and He's everywhere—
even inside your head and heart.
He knows what you think and feel. He sees
it when you're jealous or angry. He knows
when you're lonely or sad. You can't get
away from Him. And once you realize what
He's all about, how much He loves you, why
would you want to? It's okay for Him to see
all about you. He knows you're not perfect,
and He's working on you.

SEE FOR YOURSELF:
   Jer. 23:23

10 Even there Your hand shall lead me,
   And Your right hand shall hold me.

11 If I say, "Surely the darkness shall fall[a] on
    me,"
Even the night shall be light about me;
12 Indeed, the darkness shall not hide from
    You,
But the night shines as the day;
The darkness and the light *are* both alike
    to You.

13 For You formed my
    inward parts;
You covered me in my
    mother's womb.
14 I will praise You, for I am
    fearfully *and*
    wonderfully made;[a]
Marvelous are Your works,
And *that* my soul knows very well.
15 My frame was not hidden from You,
When I was made in secret,
And skillfully wrought in
    the lowest parts of the
    earth.
16 Your eyes saw my
    substance, being yet
    unformed.
And in Your book they
    all were written,
The days fashioned for me,
When *as yet there were* none of them.

17 How precious also are Your thoughts to
    me, O God!
How great is the sum of them!
18 *If* I should count them, they would be
    more in number than the sand;
When I awake, I am still with You.

19 Oh, that You would slay the wicked,
    O God!
Depart from me, therefore, you
    bloodthirsty men.
20 For they speak against You wickedly;
Your enemies take *Your name* in vain.[a]
21 Do I not hate them, O LORD, who hate
    You?
And do I not loathe those who rise up
    against You?
22 I hate them with perfect hatred;
I count them my enemies.

23 Search me, O God, and know my heart;
Try me, and know my anxieties;

LIFE

Does God
create each
person care-
fully?
(139:13, 14)

ABORTION

Are children
formed by
chance?
(139:13–16)

On the Edge

*My frame was not hidden from
You, when I was made in secret,
and skillfully wrought in the lowest
parts of the earth. Your eyes saw my
substance, being yet unformed. And
in Your book they all were written,
the days fashioned for me, when as
yet there were none of them*
(Ps. 139:15, 16).

Read all of Psalm 139 to find out how
God knows you. Totally. There's nothing you
can ever think or do that God doesn't know
about. He even knows what you're going to
do before you do it. That could be scary if
you think of God as the "Man Upstairs"
who's just sitting around waiting to catch
you doing something wrong.

Relax. God isn't like that. Because you're
one of His children, you can be glad that
God knows you inside and out. He knows
and appreciates what you're good at. He
knows exactly what He's got planned for
your life. He understands the things that
are hard for you. He won't let you face a
temptation that you can't stand up to. Since
God knows you so completely,
you don't ever have to be afraid
to share your whole heart with
Him. He won't laugh at you or
reject you. The fact that God knows you says
a lot about His enormous mind and His
limitless love. But it also says something
about you. It says that you are so important
that *God* spends His time thinking about
you. He's in love with you!

SEE FOR YOURSELF:
1 Chr. 28:9; Job 23:9, 10;
Acts 15:8; Rom. 8:27

24 And see if *there is any* wicked way in me,
And lead me in the way everlasting.

PSALM 140

PRAYER FOR DELIVERANCE FROM EVIL MEN

To the Chief Musician. A Psalm of David.

1 Deliver me, O LORD, from evil men;
Preserve me from violent men,

139:11 [a]Vulgate and Symmachus read *cover.*   **139:14** [a]Following Masoretic Text and Targum; Septuagint, Syriac,
and Vulgate read *You are fearfully wonderful.*   **139:20** [a]Septuagint and Vulgate read *They take your cities in
vain.*

2 Who plan evil things in *their* hearts;
They continually gather together *for* war.
3 They sharpen their tongues like a
serpent;
The poison of asps *is* under their lips.
Selah

4 Keep me, O LORD, from the hands of the
wicked;
Preserve me from violent men,
Who have purposed to make my steps
stumble.
5 The proud have hidden a snare for me,
and cords;
They have spread a net by the wayside;
They have set traps for me. Selah

6 I said to the LORD: "You *are* my God;
Hear the voice of my supplications,
O LORD.
7 O GOD the Lord, the strength of my
salvation,
You have covered my head in the day of
battle.
8 Do not grant, O LORD, the desires of the
wicked;
Do not further his *wicked* scheme,
Lest they be exalted. Selah

9 "*As for* the head of those who surround
me,
Let the evil of their lips cover them;
10 Let burning coals fall upon them;
Let them be cast into the fire,
Into deep pits, that they rise not up again.
11 Let not a slanderer be established in the
earth;
Let evil hunt the violent man to
overthrow *him.*"

12 I know that the LORD will maintain
The cause of the afflicted,
And justice for the poor.
13 Surely the righteous shall give thanks to
Your name;
The upright shall dwell in Your presence.

PSALM 141

PRAYER FOR SAFEKEEPING FROM WICKEDNESS

A Psalm of David.

1 LORD, I cry out to You;
Make haste to me!

Give ear to my voice when I cry out to
You.
2 Let my prayer be set before You *as*
incense,
The lifting up of my hands *as* the evening
sacrifice.

3 Set a guard, O LORD, over my mouth;
Keep watch over the door of my lips.
4 Do not incline my heart to any evil
thing,
To practice wicked works
With men who work iniquity;
And do not let me eat of their delicacies.

5 Let the righteous strike me;
It shall be a kindness.
And let him rebuke me;
It shall be as excellent oil;
Let my head not refuse it.

For still my prayer *is* against the deeds of
the wicked.
6 Their judges are overthrown by the sides
of the cliff,
And they hear my words, for they are
sweet.
7 Our bones are scattered at the mouth of
the grave,
As when one plows and breaks up the
earth.

8 But my eyes *are* upon You, O GOD the
Lord;
In You I take refuge;
Do not leave my soul destitute.
9 Keep me from the snares they have laid
for me,
And from the traps of the workers of
iniquity.
10 Let the wicked fall into their own nets,
While I escape safely.

PSALM 142

A PLEA FOR RELIEF FROM PERSECUTORS

A Contemplation[a] of David. A Prayer
when he was in the cave.

1 I cry out to the LORD with my voice;
With my voice to the LORD I make my
supplication.
2 I pour out my complaint before Him;
I declare before Him my trouble.

142:title [a]Hebrew *Maschil*

WHAT'S IT MEAN?

Apparently David wrote this psalm while he was on the run from the murderous King Saul. To escape Saul's jealous rage and mental instability, David spent some time hiding out in the cave of Adullam (or En Gedi). That may be the place where this psalm was written.

Psalm 142 title

3   When my spirit was
       overwhelmed
       within me,
    Then You knew my
       path.
    In the way in which I
       walk
    They have secretly set a
       snare for me.
4   Look on *my* right hand and see,
    For *there is* no one who acknowledges me;
    Refuge has failed me;
    No one cares for my soul.

5   I cried out to You, O LORD:
    I said, "You *are* my refuge,
    My portion in the land of the living.
6   Attend to my cry,
    For I am brought very low;
    Deliver me from my persecutors,
    For they are stronger than I.
7   Bring my soul out of prison,
    That I may praise Your name;
    The righteous shall surround me,
    For You shall deal bountifully with me."

DISCOURAGEMENT

Who should we bring our complaints to? (142:1–7)

PSALM 143

AN EARNEST APPEAL FOR GUIDANCE AND DELIVERANCE

A Psalm of David.

1   Hear my prayer, O LORD,
    Give ear to my supplications!
    In Your faithfulness answer me,
    And in Your righteousness.

2   Do not enter into judgment with Your
       servant,
    For in Your sight no one living is
       righteous.

3   For the enemy has persecuted my soul;
    He has crushed my life to the ground;
    He has made me dwell in darkness,
    Like those who have long been dead.
4   Therefore my spirit is overwhelmed
       within me;
    My heart within me is distressed.

5   I remember the days of old;
    I meditate on all Your works;
    I muse on the work of Your hands.
6   I spread out my hands to You;
    My soul *longs* for You like a thirsty land.
                                        Selah

7   Answer me speedily, O LORD;
    My spirit fails!
    Do not hide Your face from me,
    Lest I be like those who go down into the
       pit.
8   Cause me to hear Your lovingkindness in
       the morning,
    For in You do I trust;
    Cause me to know the way in which I
       should walk,
    For I lift up my soul to You.

9   Deliver me, O LORD, from my enemies;
    In You I take shelter.[a]
10 Teach me to do Your will,
    For You *are* my God;
    Your Spirit *is* good.
    Lead me in the land of uprightness.

11 Revive me, O LORD, for Your name's sake!
    For Your righteousness' sake bring my
       soul out of trouble.
12 In Your mercy cut off my enemies,
    And destroy all those who afflict my soul;
    For I *am* Your servant.

PSALM 144

A SONG TO THE LORD WHO PRESERVES AND PROSPERS HIS PEOPLE

A Psalm of David.

1   Blessed *be* the LORD my Rock,
    Who trains my hands for war,

143:9 *ᵃSeptuagint and Vulgate read To You I flee.*

And my fingers for battle—
2 My lovingkindness and my fortress,
My high tower and my deliverer,
My shield and *the One* in whom I take refuge,
Who subdues my people[a] under me.

3 LORD, what *is* man, that You take knowledge of him?
Or the son of man, that You are mindful of him?
4 Man is like a breath;
His days *are* like a passing shadow.

7 Stretch out Your hand from above;
Rescue me and deliver me out of great waters,
From the hand of foreigners,
8 Whose mouth speaks lying words,
And whose right hand *is* a right hand of falsehood.

9 I will sing a new song to You, O God;
On a harp of ten strings I will sing praises to You,
10 *The One* who gives salvation to kings,
Who delivers David His servant
From the deadly sword.

11 Rescue me and deliver me from the hand of foreigners,
Whose mouth speaks lying words,
And whose right hand *is* a right hand of falsehood—
12 That our sons *may be* as plants grown up in their youth;
That our daughters *may be* as pillars,
Sculptured in palace style;
13 *That* our barns *may be* full,
Supplying all kinds of produce;
That our sheep may bring forth thousands
And ten thousands in our fields;
14 *That* our oxen *may be* well laden;
That there be no breaking in or going out;
That there be no outcry in our streets.
15 Happy *are* the people who are in such a state;
Happy *are* the people whose God *is* the LORD!

On the Edge

Man is like a breath; his days are like a passing shadow (Ps. 144:4).

Sometimes on a cloudy day, there's a tiny break in the clouds that the sun tries to shine through. Just for a second you can see your shadow—just barely—on the sidewalk. When the clouds shift, your shadow disappears.

David said your life is like that shadow—it shows up for just a short moment, and then it's gone. It sure doesn't seem that way right now. Right now, it seems like your life stretches out forever in front of you. In a lot of ways, your life is just beginning. The important thing to do is to make the things you're doing count. The old saying "Time flies when you're having fun" is true. One day you'll wake up and wonder how you got so old. God gives you life one day at a time. When a day or a moment is gone, it's history. Pay attention to your life every day. Don't waste it by wanting to be older or smarter or better-looking. Make it count.

SEE FOR YOURSELF:
Job 14:12; Ps. 62:9; Eccl. 6:12

PSALM 145

A SONG OF GOD'S MAJESTY AND LOVE

A Praise of David.

1 I will extol You, my God, O King;
And I will bless Your name forever and ever.
2 Every day I will bless You,
And I will praise Your name forever and ever.
3 Great *is* the LORD, and greatly to be praised;
And His greatness *is* unsearchable.
4 One generation shall praise Your works to another,

5 Bow down Your heavens, O LORD, and come down;
Touch the mountains, and they shall smoke.
6 Flash forth lightning and scatter them;
Shoot out Your arrows and destroy them.

10 All Your works shall praise You, O LORD,
And Your saints shall bless You.
11 They shall speak of the glory of Your
kingdom,
And talk of Your power,
12 To make known to the sons of men His
mighty acts,
And the glorious majesty of His kingdom.
13 Your kingdom *is* an everlasting kingdom,
And Your dominion *endures* throughout
all generations.*a*

14 The LORD upholds all who fall,
And raises up all *who are* bowed down.
15 The eyes of all look expectantly to You,
And You give them their food in due
season.
16 You open Your hand
And satisfy the desire of every living
thing.

17 The LORD *is* righteous in all His ways,
Gracious in all His works.
18 The LORD *is* near to all who call upon
Him,
To all who call upon Him in truth.
19 He will fulfill the desire of those who fear
Him;
He also will hear their cry and save them.
20 The LORD preserves all who love Him,
But all the wicked He will destroy.
21 My mouth shall speak the praise of the
LORD,
And all flesh shall bless His holy name
Forever and ever.

On the Edge

Great is the LORD, and greatly to be praised; and His greatness is unsearchable (Ps. 145:3).

It seems the apostle Paul knew God better than anyone. But even he found God too awesome to imagine. "Oh, the depth of the riches both of the wisdom and knowledge of God! How unsearchable are His judgments and His ways past finding out!" he wrote to the Romans (Rom. 11:33). In another letter he wrote, "For now we see in a mirror, dimly, but then face to face. Now I know in part, but then I shall know just as I also am known" (1 Cor. 13:12).

Trying to understand God all at once is like trying to count the stars in the sky. It's just too big of a job. The more you learn of His power to create, to save, to change; the more you see of His forgiveness, His grace, His love; the more you understand of His incredible intelligence (after all, the principles of math and physics were all His ideas)—the more you realize that you have a long way to go. Knowing Him is a journey that takes a lifetime. It's worth it.

SEE FOR YOURSELF:
2 Chr. 2:5; Job 33:12;
John 14:28;
1 John 3:20

And shall declare Your mighty acts.
5 I*a* will meditate on the glorious splendor
of Your majesty,
And on Your wondrous works.*b*
6 *Men* shall speak of the might of Your
awesome acts,
And I will declare Your greatness.
7 They shall utter the memory of Your great
goodness,
And shall sing of Your righteousness.

8 The LORD *is* gracious and full of
compassion,
Slow to anger and great in mercy.
9 The LORD *is* good to all,
And His tender mercies *are* over all His
works.

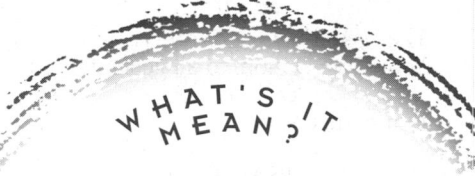

WHAT'S IT MEAN?

This psalm was written as an acrostic. In its original Hebrew form, each of the psalm's twenty-two sections begins with a corresponding letter of the Hebrew alphabet—from *aleph* to *tau*. (If it were written in English, the first line of the first section would begin with *A*, the second section would begin with *B*, and so on.)
Psalm 145:1

145:5 *a*Following Masoretic Text and Targum; Dead Sea Scrolls, Septuagint, Syriac, and Vulgate read *They*. *b*Literally *on the words of Your wondrous works* **145:13** *a*Following Masoretic Text and Targum; Dead Sea Scrolls, Septuagint, Syriac, and Vulgate add *The LORD is faithful in all His words, And holy in all His works.*

PSALM 146

THE HAPPINESS OF THOSE WHOSE HELP IS THE LORD

1   Praise the LORD!

    Praise the LORD, O my soul!
2   While I live I will praise the LORD;
    I will sing praises to my God while I have
        my being.

3   Do not put your trust in princes,
    Nor in a son of man, in whom *there is* no
        help.
4   His spirit departs, he returns to his earth;
    In that very day his plans perish.

5   Happy *is he* who *has* the God of Jacob for
        his help,
    Whose hope *is* in the LORD his God,
6   Who made heaven and earth,
    The sea, and all that *is* in them;
    Who keeps truth forever,
7   Who executes justice for the oppressed,
    Who gives food to the hungry.
    The LORD gives freedom to the prisoners.

8   The LORD opens *the eyes of* the blind;
    The LORD raises those who are bowed
        down;
    The LORD loves the righteous.
9   The LORD watches over the strangers;
    He relieves the fatherless and widow;
    But the way of the wicked He turns
        upside down.

10 The LORD shall reign forever—
    Your God, O Zion, to all generations.

    Praise the LORD!

PSALM 147

PRAISE TO GOD FOR HIS WORD AND PROVIDENCE

1   Praise the LORD!
    For *it is* good to sing praises to our God;
    For *it is* pleasant, *and* praise is beautiful.

2   The LORD builds up Jerusalem;
    He gathers together the outcasts of Israel.
3   He heals the brokenhearted
    And binds up their wounds.
4   He counts the number of the stars;
    He calls them all by name.
5   Great *is* our Lord, and mighty in power;

On the Edge

Great is our Lord, and mighty in power; His understanding is infinite (Ps. 147:5).

What tests your limits of understanding? Advanced calculus? Some basketball star's gravity-defying slam dunks? Italian opera? The creation of the world in six days? At some point, we just don't get it. It's beyond us. We can't get our arms around it. Our brain won't process anymore. Our capacity to understand is limited, but God understands everything. Sometimes we don't even understand why we do things. But God does. He has infinite understanding. He sees into our souls very clearly. So when you're feeling confused and the way seems fuzzy, turn to the One who understands everything infinitely. He gives flawless directions, and His advice is perfect.

SEE FOR YOURSELF:
Ps. 139; Heb. 4:13;
1 John 3:20

    His understanding *is* infinite.
6   The LORD lifts up the humble;
    He casts the wicked down to the ground.

7   Sing to the LORD with thanksgiving;
    Sing praises on the harp to our God,
8   Who covers the heavens with clouds,
    Who prepares rain for the earth,
    Who makes grass to grow on the
        mountains.
9   He gives to the beast its food,
    And to the young ravens that cry.

10 He does not delight in the strength of the
        horse;
    He takes no pleasure in the legs of a man.
11 The LORD takes pleasure in those who
        fear Him,
    In those who hope in His mercy.

12 Praise the LORD, O Jerusalem!
    Praise your God, O Zion!
13 For He has strengthened the bars of your
        gates;
    He has blessed your children within you.
14 He makes peace *in* your borders,
    And fills you with the finest wheat.

15 He sends out His command *to the* earth;
His word runs very swiftly.
16 He gives snow like wool;
He scatters the frost like ashes;
17 He casts out His hail like morsels;
Who can stand before His cold?
18 He sends out His word and melts them;
He causes His wind to blow, *and the*
waters flow.

19 He declares His word to Jacob,
His statutes and His judgments to Israel.
20 He has not dealt thus with any nation;
And *as for His* judgments, they have not
known them.

Praise the LORD!

PSALM 148

PRAISE TO THE LORD FROM CREATION

1 Praise the LORD!

Praise the LORD from the
heavens;
Praise Him in the heights!
2 Praise Him, all His
angels;
Praise Him, all His hosts!
3 Praise Him, sun and
moon;
Praise Him, all you stars of light!
4 Praise Him, you heavens of heavens,
And you waters above the heavens!

5 Let them praise the name of the LORD,
For He commanded and they were
created.
6 He also established them forever and
ever;
He made a decree which shall not pass
away.

7 Praise the LORD from the earth,
You great sea creatures and all the depths;
8 Fire and hail, snow and clouds;
Stormy wind, fulfilling His word;
9 Mountains and all hills;
Fruitful trees and all cedars;
10 Beasts and all cattle;
Creeping things and flying fowl;
11 Kings of the earth and all peoples;
Princes and all judges of the earth;
12 Both young men and maidens;
Old men and children.

ANGELS
Who do
angels
praise?
(148:2)

13 Let them praise the name of the LORD,
For His name alone is exalted;
His glory *is* above the earth and heaven.
14 And He has exalted the horn of His
people,
The praise of all His saints—
Of the children of Israel,
A people near to Him.

Praise the LORD!

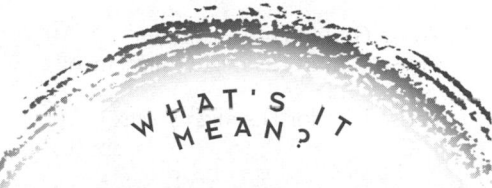

WHAT'S IT MEAN?

In ancient Israel, dancing was considered a
form of celebration and worship. As an expression of
joy, both men and women danced to the music of
tambourines and stringed instruments.
Psalm 149:3

PSALM 149

PRAISE TO GOD FOR HIS SALVATION AND JUDGMENT

1 Praise the LORD!

Sing to the LORD a new song,
And His praise in the assembly of saints.

2 Let Israel rejoice in their Maker;
Let the children of Zion be joyful in their
King.
3 Let them praise His name with the dance;
Let them sing praises to Him with the
timbrel and harp.
4 For the LORD takes pleasure in His people;
He will beautify the humble with
salvation.

5 Let the saints be joyful in glory;
Let them sing aloud on their beds.
6 *Let* the high praises of God *be* in their
mouth,
And a two-edged sword in their hand,
7 To execute vengeance on the nations,
And punishments on the peoples;
8 To bind their kings with chains,
And their nobles with fetters of iron;

9 To execute on them the written
  judgment—
This honor have all His saints.

Praise the LORD!

PSALM 150

LET ALL THINGS PRAISE THE LORD

1 Praise the LORD!

Praise God in His sanctuary;
Praise Him in His mighty firmament!

2 Praise Him for His mighty acts;

Praise Him according to His excellent
  greatness!

3 Praise Him with the sound of the
  trumpet;
Praise Him with the lute and harp!
4 Praise Him with the timbrel and dance;
Praise Him with stringed instruments and
  flutes!
5 Praise Him with loud cymbals;
Praise Him with clashing cymbals!

6 Let everything that has breath praise the
  LORD.

Praise the LORD!

proverbs

CONTENT

It seems like everyone speaks a proverb at some time in their lives: "Don't count your chickens before they're hatched." "Look before you leap." "Give him an inch and he'll take a mile." Proverbs are colorful ways to say something wise. They are little pieces of truth wrapped up in something sweet so we can swallow them more easily.

The problem with human proverbs is that they often contradict:

"Look before you leap" (be cautious), but "he who hesitates is lost" (don't be too cautious).

"Absence makes the heart grow fonder" (your sweetie will like you *more* after summer break), but "Out of sight, out of mind" (your sweetie won't like you at all after summer break).

The Book of Proverbs is different in that it is *God's* wisdom. Some of Proverbs is lighthearted. Some is even downright funny. Don't be fooled, though. It is God's truth.

Reading Proverbs is like sitting on the porch of heaven and listening to the wisest, most famous of the saints telling us what they have learned about life. Better than that, though, the proverbs are like God Himself giving us everyday advice about everyday situations.

Outline

Purpose

The wise person makes choices that are both godly and practical.

Theme

Universal Principles for Living

Date of writing

950–700 B.C.

Bible Talk

A Proverb a Day Keeps the What Away?

Here's a thought. There are thirty-one chapters in Proverbs. There are thirty or thirty-one days in most months. If you want a new Bible reading plan, just read a chapter of Proverbs every day. You don't have to worry about losing your place or remembering where you are. Just look at the date!

The great thing about reading in Proverbs is the variety. Each time you read a chapter, something different can jump right off the page and tap you on the shoulder.

A chapter in Proverbs every day may not keep the doctor away, or be worth two chapters in the bush, but it will remind you that God calls us to choose wisdom over foolishness and it takes His help to do it.

PRACTICAL DIRECTION FROM GOD

Sometimes the Bible gets the reputation for not being practical . . . particularly by people who never read it. For so long, the only Bible we had to read in English was a Bible that used really old English and so was hard to understand.

But whether the Bible is written in modern English, old English, or not English at all, the truth is that the Bible was written by God. He wrote it through the minds and experiences of real people who faced life just like we do—by faith.

Proverbs is a great example of how practical the Bible is. A whole book on making good choices—not being lazy, loving your parents, being a good friend. This is real life stuff. This is the stuff we care about. This is the stuff that God helps us with.

THE BEGINNING OF KNOWLEDGE

¹The proverbs of Solomon the son of David, king of Israel:

2 To know wisdom and instruction,
To perceive the words of understanding,
3 To receive the instruction of wisdom,
Justice, judgment, and equity;
4 To give prudence to the simple,
To the young man knowledge and
discretion—
5 A wise *man* will hear and
increase learning,
And a man of
understanding will
attain wise counsel,
6 To understand a proverb
and an enigma,
The words of the wise and
their riddles.

7 The fear of the LORD *is* the beginning of
knowledge,
But fools despise wisdom and instruction.

EDUCATION
How can
wise people
increase their
education?
(1:5)

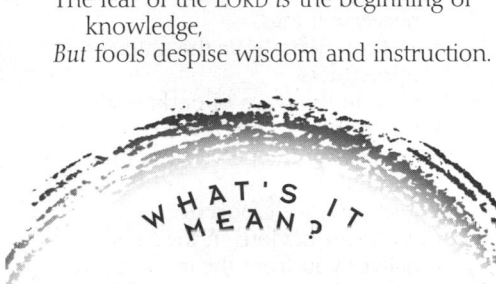

WHAT'S IT MEAN?

Solomon was a young guy, perhaps no
more than twenty years old, when he became the
third king of Israel. During his forty-year reign, from about 970
to 930 B.C., Solomon became so famous for his wisdom that people
from other nations traveled to Jerusalem
just to hear him speak.
Proverbs 1:1

SHUN EVIL COUNSEL

8 My son, hear the instruction of your
father,
And do not forsake the law of your
mother;
9 For they *will be* a graceful ornament on
your head,
And chains about your neck.

10 My son, if sinners entice you,
Do not consent.

11 If they say, "Come with us,
Let us lie in wait to *shed* blood;
Let us lurk secretly for the innocent
without cause;
12 Let us swallow them alive like Sheol,ᵃ
And whole, like those who go down to
the Pit;
13 We shall find all *kinds* of precious
possessions,
We shall fill our houses with spoil;
14 Cast in your lot among us,
Let us all have one purse"—
15 My son, do not walk in the way with
them,
Keep your foot from their path;
16 For their feet run to evil,
And they make haste to shed blood.
17 Surely, in vain the net is spread
In the sight of any bird;
18 But they lie in wait for their *own* blood,
They lurk secretly for their *own* lives.
19 So *are* the ways of everyone who is
greedy for gain;
It takes away the life of its owners.

THE CALL OF WISDOM

20 Wisdom calls aloud outside;
She raises her voice in the open
squares.
21 She cries out in the chief concourses,ᵃ
At the openings of the gates in the city
She speaks her words:
22 "How long, you simple ones, will you love
simplicity?
For scorners delight in their scorning,
And fools hate knowledge.
23 Turn at my rebuke;
Surely I will pour out my spirit on you;
I will make my words known to you.
24 Because I have called and you refused,
I have stretched out my hand and no one
regarded,
25 Because you disdained all my counsel,
And would have none of my rebuke,
26 I also will laugh at your calamity;
I will mock when your terror comes,
27 When your terror comes like a storm,
And your destruction comes like a
whirlwind,
When distress and anguish come upon
you.

28 "Then they will call on me, but I will not
answer;

1:12 ᵃOr *the grave* **1:21** ᵃSeptuagint, Syriac, and Targum read *top of the walls*; Vulgate reads *the head of multitudes.*

They will seek me diligently, but they will not find me.

29 Because they hated knowledge
And did not choose the fear of the LORD,

30 They would have none of my counsel
And despised my every rebuke.

31 Therefore they shall eat the fruit of their own way,
And be filled to the full with their own fancies.

32 For the turning away of the simple will slay them,
And the complacency of fools will destroy them;

33 But whoever listens to me will dwell safely,
And will be secure, without fear of evil."

THE VALUE OF WISDOM

1 My son, if you receive my words,
And treasure my commands within you,

2 So that you incline your ear to wisdom,
And apply your heart to understanding;

3 Yes, if you cry out for discernment,
And lift up your voice for understanding,

4 If you seek her as silver,
And search for her as *for* hidden treasures;

5 Then you will understand the fear of the LORD,
And find the knowledge of God.

6 For the LORD gives wisdom;

7 From His mouth *come* knowledge and understanding;
He stores up sound wisdom for the upright;
He is a shield to those who walk uprightly;

8 He guards the paths of justice,
And preserves the way of His saints.

9 Then you will understand righteousness and justice,
Equity *and* every good path.

10 When wisdom enters your heart,
And knowledge is pleasant to your soul,

11 Discretion will preserve you;
Understanding will keep you,

12 To deliver you from the way of evil,
From the man who speaks perverse things,

13 From those who leave the paths of uprightness
To walk in the ways of darkness;

14 Who rejoice in doing evil,
And delight in the perversity of the wicked;

15 Whose ways *are* crooked,
And *who are* devious in their paths;

16 To deliver you from the immoral woman,

TEMPTATION

How do we guard against temptation? (2:10–14)

Promise HE PROMISES TO GIVE YOU HELPFUL WISDOM AND UNDERSTANDING.

For the LORD gives wisdom; from His mouth come knowledge and understanding; He stores up sound wisdom for the upright; He is a shield to those who walk uprightly (Prov. 2:6, 7).

Has anyone ever given you bad advice? Maybe they told you to take psychology because it was a breeze and then the year you take it, a new teacher makes it the hardest class in school. Maybe someone gave you some bad directions that told you to turn left instead of right. Forty miles later when you run out of civilization, you realize that you've probably gone the wrong way. Bad advice—when you lack the wisdom to know the advice is bad—can ruin a day, a year, or an entire life.

God promises to give you wisdom and common sense. He says that you just have to search for Him, take time to ask Him, obey Him, and He will be faithful to give you the help you need. He is the Source of all that is wise and helpful. He waits patiently for you to stop fumbling around and ask Him for His helpful advice.

SEE FOR YOURSELF:
Mic. 7:7; Luke 11:10; 2 Thess. 3:3; James 1:5

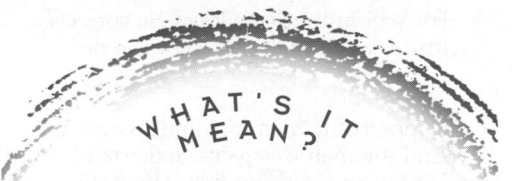

From the seductress *who* flatters with her
words,

17 Who forsakes the companion of her
youth,
And forgets the covenant of her God.

18 For her house leads down to death,
And her paths to the dead;

19 None who go to her return,
Nor do they regain the paths of life—

20 So you may walk in the way of goodness,
And keep *to* the paths of righteousness.

21 For the upright will dwell in the land,
And the blameless will remain in it;

22 But the wicked will be cut off from the
earth,
And the unfaithful will be uprooted
from it.

GUIDANCE FOR THE YOUNG

1 My son, do not forget my law,
But let your heart keep my commands;

2 For length of days and long life
And peace they will add to you.

3 Let not mercy and truth forsake you;
Bind them around your neck,
Write them on the tablet of your heart,

4 *And* so find favor and high esteem
In the sight of God and
man.

MERCY

Why is mercy
important?
(3:3, 4)

5 Trust in the LORD with all
your heart,
And lean not on your
own understanding;

6 In all your ways
acknowledge Him,
And He shall direct*a* your
paths.

7 Do not be wise in your
own eyes;
Fear the LORD and depart
from evil.

8 It will be health to your flesh,*a*
And strength*b* to your bones.

TRUST

How are we
to trust God?
(3:5, 6)

3:6 *a*Or *make smooth* or *straight*   **3:8** *a*Literally *navel,* figurative of the body   *b*Literally *drink* or *refreshment*

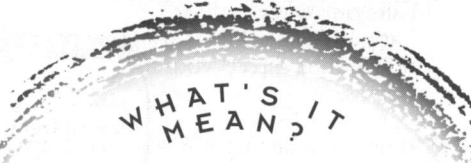

WHAT'S IT MEAN?

Here's how tithing worked in ancient times: The Israelites were commanded to give ten percent of everything they had—including crops, livestock, and money—to God. The Israelites gave their tithes to the Levites, the people who worked in the temple. The Levites, in turn, gave ten percent of everything they received to the priests. The priests offered a sacrifice to the Lord for their tithe. Tithing is a way for people to acknowledge that everything they receive comes from and belongs to God.

Proverbs 3:9

12 For whom the LORD loves He corrects,
Just as a father the son *in whom* he delights.

13 Happy *is* the man *who* finds wisdom,
And the man *who* gains understanding;

14 For her proceeds *are* better than the profits of silver,
And her gain than fine gold.

15 She *is* more precious than rubies,
And all the things you may desire cannot compare with her.

16 Length of days *is* in her right hand,
In her left hand riches and honor.

17 Her ways *are* ways of pleasantness,
And all her paths *are* peace.

18 She *is* a tree of life to those who take hold of her,
And happy *are all* who retain her.

19 The LORD by wisdom founded the earth;
By understanding He established the heavens;

20 By His knowledge the depths were broken up,
And clouds drop down the dew.

9 Honor the LORD with your possessions,
And with the firstfruits of all your increase;

10 So your barns will be filled with plenty,
And your vats will overflow with new wine.

11 My son, do not despise the chastening of the LORD,
Nor detest His correction;

"The LORD by wisdom founded the earth; by understanding He established the heavens."
(Proverbs 3:19)

21 My son, let them not depart from your eyes—
Keep sound wisdom and discretion;

Promise   HE PROMISES TO DIRECT YOUR PATHS.

Trust in the LORD with all your heart, and lean not on your own understanding; in all your ways acknowledge Him, and He shall direct your paths (Prov. 3:5, 6).

If you trust in the Lord with all your heart—not just saying you believe in Him, but really living a godly life—then He promises to do two things. First, He will lead you to the right path. In other words, He will show you what you are supposed to do with your life, what turns to make, when to stop, when to go. He promises to give clear directions to people who are seeking and trusting Him. Second, He will clear the path of obstacles, making it smooth for you. So, not only will He show you the way to walk, but He also promises to go before you and clear away the things that could trip you up. He will fill up the holes you could fall into. He will straighten the road so the walk is easier. He will make the journey more enjoyable for those who trust in Him.

SEE FOR YOURSELF:
John 16:13; 2 Cor. 2:14; Rev. 7:17

22 So they will be life to your soul
And grace to your neck.
23 Then you will walk safely in your way,
And your foot will not stumble.
24 When you lie down, you will not be
afraid;
Yes, you will lie down and your sleep will
be sweet.
25 Do not be afraid of sudden terror,
Nor of trouble from the wicked when it
comes;
26 For the LORD will be your confidence,
And will keep your foot from being
caught.

27 Do not withhold good from those to
whom it is due,
When it is in the power of your hand to
do so.
28 Do not say to your neighbor,
"Go, and come back,
And tomorrow I will give it,"
When you have it with you.
29 Do not devise evil against your neighbor,
For he dwells by you for safety's sake.
30 Do not strive with a man without cause,
If he has done you no harm.

31 Do not envy the oppressor,
And choose none of his ways;
32 For the perverse person is an abomination
to the LORD,
But His secret counsel is with the upright.
33 The curse of the LORD is on the house of
the wicked,
But He blesses the home of the just.
34 Surely He scorns the scornful,
But gives grace to the humble.
35 The wise shall inherit glory,
But shame shall be the legacy of fools.

SECURITY IN WISDOM

1 Hear, my children, the instruction of a
father,
And give attention to know
understanding;
2 For I give you good doctrine:
Do not forsake my law.
3 When I was my father's son,
Tender and the only one in the sight of
my mother,
4 He also taught me, and said to me:
"Let your heart retain my words;
Keep my commands, and live.
5 Get wisdom! Get understanding!

Do not forget, nor turn away from the
words of my mouth.
6 Do not forsake her, and she will preserve
you;
Love her, and she will keep you.
7 Wisdom is the principal thing;
Therefore get wisdom.
And in all your getting, get understanding.
8 Exalt her, and she will promote you;
She will bring you honor, when you
embrace her.
9 She will place on your head an ornament
of grace;
A crown of glory she will deliver to you."

10 Hear, my son, and receive my sayings,
And the years of your life will be many.
11 I have taught you in the way of wisdom;
I have led you in right paths.
12 When you walk, your steps will not be
hindered,
And when you run, you
will not stumble.
13 Take firm hold of
instruction, do not let
go;
Keep her, for she is your
life.

DISCIPLINE

Why is
instruction or
discipline
important to
me?
(4:13)

14 Do not enter the path of
the wicked,
And do not walk in the way of evil.
15 Avoid it, do not travel on it;
Turn away from it and pass on.
16 For they do not sleep unless they have
done evil;
And their sleep is taken away unless they
make someone fall.
17 For they eat the bread of wickedness,
And drink the wine of violence.

18 But the path of the just is like the shining
sun,a
That shines ever brighter unto the perfect
day.
19 The way of the wicked is like darkness;
They do not know what makes them
stumble.

20 My son, give attention to my words;
Incline your ear to my sayings.
21 Do not let them depart from your eyes;
Keep them in the midst of your heart;
22 For they are life to those who find them,
And health to all their flesh.

4:18 aLiterally light

On the Edge

But the path of the just is like the shining sun, that shines ever brighter unto the perfect day (Prov. 4:18).

A match is struck inside the heart of each believer at the very moment he or she decides to trust in Jesus Christ as the One who delivers him or her from sin. For some, the flame burns dimly for a while. And for others, it's the match that sets the forest on fire. As you begin to learn more about the Lord—His forgiveness and grace—the flame begins to burn brighter. At some point you decide to begin living what you believe—giving forgiveness and grace to others. The flame burns brighter still. You grow in knowledge and in truth. You begin to understand they call grace amazing. Then one day you realize that you look more like Jesus today than you did this time last year. You decide that that's a great goal—each year looking more like Jesus than you ever have before. The fire has become a blaze, and your lifestyle keeps getting brighter and brighter.

SEE FOR YOURSELF:
Judg. 5:31; Dan. 12:3;
Luke 11:36

23 Keep your heart with all diligence,
For out of it *spring* the issues of life.
24 Put away from you a deceitful mouth,
And put perverse lips far from you.
25 Let your eyes look straight ahead,
And your eyelids look right before you.
26 Ponder the path of your feet,
And let all your ways be established.
27 Do not turn to the right or the left;
Remove your foot from evil.

THE PERIL OF ADULTERY

1 My son, pay attention to my wisdom;
Lend your ear to my understanding,
2 That you may preserve discretion,

GOSSIP
How should we treat gossip? (4:24)

3 And your lips may keep knowledge.
For the lips of an immoral woman drip honey,
And her mouth *is* smoother than oil;
4 But in the end she is bitter as wormwood,
Sharp as a two-edged sword.
5 Her feet go down to death,
Her steps lay hold of hell.[a]
6 Lest you ponder *her* path of life—
Her ways are unstable;
You do not know *them.*

7 Therefore hear me now, *my* children,
And do not depart from the words of my mouth.
8 Remove your way far from her,
And do not go near the door of her house,
9 Lest you give your honor to others,
And your years to the cruel *one*;
10 Lest aliens be filled with your wealth,
And your labors *go* to the house of a foreigner;
11 And you mourn at last,
When your flesh and your body are consumed,
12 And say:
"How I have hated instruction,
And my heart despised correction!
13 I have not obeyed the voice of my teachers,
Nor inclined my ear to those who instructed me!
14 I was on the verge of total ruin,
In the midst of the assembly and congregation."

15 Drink water from your own cistern,
And running water from your own well.
16 Should your fountains be dispersed abroad,
Streams of water in the streets?
17 Let them be only your own,
And not for strangers with you.
18 Let your fountain be blessed,
And rejoice with the wife of your youth.
19 *As a* loving deer and a graceful doe,
Let her breasts satisfy you at all times;
And always be enraptured with her love.
20 For why should you, my son, be enraptured by an immoral woman,
And be embraced in the arms of a seductress?

5:5 [a]Or *Sheol*

21 For the ways of man *are* before the eyes
    of the LORD,
    And He ponders all his paths.
22 His own iniquities entrap the wicked *man,*
    And he is caught in the cords of his sin.
23 He shall die for lack of instruction,
    And in the greatness of his folly he shall
    go astray.

DANGEROUS PROMISES

1 My son, if you become surety for your
    friend,
    If you have shaken hands in pledge for a
    stranger,
2 You are snared by the words of your
    mouth;
    You are taken by the words of your
    mouth.
3 So do this, my son, and deliver yourself;
    For you have come into the hand of your
    friend:
    Go and humble yourself;
    Plead with your friend.
4 Give no sleep to your eyes,
    Nor slumber to your eyelids.
5 Deliver yourself like a gazelle from the
    hand *of the hunter,*
    And like a bird from the hand of the
    fowler.*a*

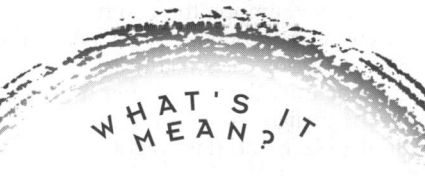

WHAT'S IT MEAN?

Here's something you probably didn't
know: There are more than one hundred types of
ants in Palestine. The type the author singles out in this passage
is the harvester ant. Harvester ants build their nests near fields
or places where grain is separated from chaff. The ants collect fallen
grain one seed at a time, carrying it back to their
nest and storing it for cold weather.
Proverbs 6:6

THE FOLLY OF INDOLENCE

6 Go to the ant, you sluggard!
    Consider her ways and be wise,
7 Which, having no captain,
    Overseer or ruler,
8 Provides her supplies in the summer,
    And gathers her food in the harvest.
9 How long will you slumber, O sluggard?
    When will you rise from your sleep?
10 A little sleep, a little slumber,
    A little folding of the hands to sleep—
11 So shall your poverty come on you like a
    prowler,
    And your need like an armed man.

THE WICKED MAN

12 A worthless person, a wicked man,
    Walks with a perverse mouth;
13 He winks with his eyes,
    He shuffles his feet,
    He points with his fingers;
14 Perversity *is* in his heart,
    He devises evil continually,
    He sows discord.
15 Therefore his calamity shall come
    suddenly;
    Suddenly he shall be broken without
    remedy.

16 These six *things* the LORD
    hates,
    Yes, seven *are* an
    abomination to Him:
17 A proud look,
    A lying tongue,
    Hands that shed
    innocent blood,
18 A heart that devises wicked plans,
    Feet that are swift in running to evil,
19 A false witness *who* speaks lies,
    And one who sows discord among
    brethren.

MURDER
How does the
Lord feel
about
murder?
(6:16, 17)

BEWARE OF ADULTERY

20 My son, keep your father's command,
    And do not forsake the law of your
    mother.
21 Bind them continually upon
    your heart;
    Tie them around your
    neck.
22 When you roam, they*a*
    will lead you;
    When you sleep, they
    will keep you;
    And *when* you awake, they
    will speak with you.
23 For the commandment *is* a lamp,
    And the law a light;
    Reproofs of instruction *are* the way of life,
24 To keep you from the evil woman,

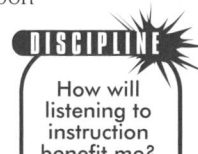

DISCIPLINE
How will
listening to
instruction
benefit me?
(6:20–23)

6:5 *a*That is, one who catches birds in a trap or snare   **6:22** *a*Literally *it*

On the Edge

My son, keep your father's command, and do not forsake the law of your mother (Prov. 6:20).

    In the military, new recruits are taught that above everything else they must respect their commanders. They may disagree with their decisions or their lifestyles, but they are required to respect their positions of leadership. In much the same way, God requires that you respect your parents. He chose them to lead your family and to train you. In His wisdom, He made a perfect decision. Even when you disagree with your parents, you are called to respect them just because they are your mom and dad. Respect means that you obey their instruction—let it guide you and protect you. God influences your life directly through the leadership of your parents. It's the way He set things in order. It's the design that works best. It glorifies God when you respect your parents.

SEE FOR YOURSELF:
Matt. 15:4; Eph. 6:1–3

From the flattering tongue of a seductress.

25   Do not lust after her beauty in your heart,
    Nor let her allure you with her eyelids.

26   For by means of a harlot
    A man is reduced to a crust of bread;
    And an adulteress[a] will prey upon his precious life.

27   Can a man take fire to his bosom,
    And his clothes not be burned?

28   Can one walk on hot coals,
    And his feet not be seared?

29   So *is* he who goes in to his neighbor's wife;
    Whoever touches her shall not be innocent.

30   *People* do not despise a thief
    If he steals to satisfy himself when he is starving.

31   Yet *when* he is found, he must restore sevenfold;
    He may have to give up all the substance of his house.

32   Whoever commits adultery with a woman lacks understanding;
    He *who* does so destroys his own soul.

33   Wounds and dishonor he will get,
    And his reproach will not be wiped away.

34   For jealousy *is* a husband's fury;
    Therefore he will not spare in the day of vengeance.

35   He will accept no recompense,
    Nor will he be appeased though you give many gifts.

1   My son, keep my words,
    And treasure my commands within you.

2   Keep my commands and live,
    And my law as the apple of your eye.

3   Bind them on your fingers;
    Write them on the tablet of your heart.

4   Say to wisdom, "You *are* my sister,"
    And call understanding *your* nearest kin,

5   That they may keep you from the immoral woman,
    From the seductress *who* flatters with her words.

THE CRAFTY HARLOT

6   For at the window of my house
    I looked through my lattice,

7   And saw among the simple,
    I perceived among the youths,
    A young man devoid of understanding,

8   Passing along the street near her corner;
    And he took the path to her house

9   In the twilight, in the evening,
    In the black and dark night.

10   And there a woman met him,
    With the attire of a harlot, and a crafty heart.

11   She *was* loud and rebellious,
    Her feet would not stay at home.

12   At times *she was* outside, at times in the open square,
    Lurking at every corner.

13   So she caught him and kissed him;
    With an impudent face she said to him:

14   "*I have* peace offerings with me;
    Today I have paid my vows.

15   So I came out to meet you,
    Diligently to seek your face,
    And I have found you.

16   I have spread my bed with tapestry,
    Colored coverings of Egyptian linen.

17   I have perfumed my bed
    With myrrh, aloes, and cinnamon.

6:26 [a]Literally *a man's wife*, that is, of another

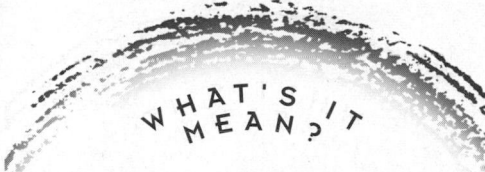

WHAT'S IT MEAN?

According to God's Law, after the priest had taken his portion of a peace offering, the person who offered the sacrifice was given the rest of the meat to take home. The only stipulation was that it all had to be eaten within two days. That meant the person usually ended up inviting his friends and neighbors over to help him finish the sacrificial food. Since meat wasn't served very often in ancient times, these post-sacrifice meals usually turned into festive events—celebrations of God's forgiveness.

Proverbs 7:14

18 Come, let us take our fill of love until morning;
  Let us delight ourselves with love.
19 For my husband *is* not at home;
  He has gone on a long journey;
20 He has taken a bag of money with him,
  And will come home on the appointed day."

21 With her enticing speech she caused him to yield,
  With her flattering lips she seduced him.
22 Immediately he went after her, as an ox goes to the slaughter,
  Or as a fool to the correction of the stocks,[a]
23 Till an arrow struck his liver.
  As a bird hastens to the snare,
  He did not know it *would cost* his life.

24 Now therefore, listen to me, *my* children;
  Pay attention to the words of my mouth:
25 Do not let your heart turn aside to her ways,
  Do not stray into her paths;
26 For she has cast down many wounded,
  And all who were slain by her were strong *men.*
27 Her house *is* the way to hell,[a]
  Descending to the chambers of death.

THE EXCELLENCE OF WISDOM

1 Does not wisdom cry out,
  And understanding lift up her voice?
2 She takes her stand on the top of the high hill,
  Beside the way, where the paths meet.
3 She cries out by the gates, at the entry of the city,
  At the entrance of the doors:
4 "To you, O men, I call,
  And my voice *is* to the sons of men.
5 O you simple ones, understand prudence,
  And you fools, be of an understanding heart.
6 Listen, for I will speak of excellent things,
  And from the opening of my lips *will come* right things;
7 For my mouth will speak truth;
  Wickedness *is* an abomination to my lips.
8 All the words of my mouth *are* with righteousness;
  Nothing crooked or perverse *is* in them.
9 They *are* all plain to him who understands,
  And right to those who find knowledge.
10 Receive my instruction, and not silver,
  And knowledge rather than choice gold;
11 For wisdom *is* better than rubies,
  And all the things one may desire cannot be compared with her.

12 "I, wisdom, dwell with prudence,
  And find out knowledge *and* discretion.
13 The fear of the LORD *is* to hate evil;
  Pride and arrogance and the evil way
  And the perverse mouth I hate.
14 Counsel *is* mine, and sound wisdom;
  I *am* understanding, I have strength.
15 By me kings reign,
  And rulers decree justice.
16 By me princes rule, and nobles,
  All the judges of the earth.[a]
17 I love those who love me,
  And those who seek me diligently will find me.
18 Riches and honor *are* with me,
  Enduring riches and righteousness.
19 My fruit *is* better than gold, yes, than fine gold,
  And my revenue than choice silver.

WISDOM
What comes with wisdom? (8:12–14)

7:22 [a]Septuagint, Syriac, and Targum read *as a dog to bonds;* Vulgate reads *as a lamb . . . to bonds.*
7:27 [a]Or *Sheol*   **8:16** [a]Masoretic Text, Syriac, Targum, and Vulgate read *righteousness;* Septuagint, Bomberg, and some manuscripts and editions read *earth.*

20 I traverse the way of righteousness,
In the midst of the paths of justice,
21 That I may cause those who love me to
inherit wealth,
That I may fill their treasuries.

22 "The LORD possessed me at the beginning
of His way,
Before His works of old.
23 I have been established from everlasting,
From the beginning, before there was ever
an earth.
24 When *there were* no depths I was brought
forth,
When *there were* no fountains abounding
with water.
25 Before the mountains were settled,
Before the hills, I was brought forth;
26 While as yet He had not made the earth
or the fields,
Or the primal dust of the world.
27 When He prepared the heavens, I *was*
there,
When He drew a circle on the face of the
deep,
28 When He established the clouds above,
When He strengthened the fountains of
the deep,
29 When He assigned to the sea its limit,
So that the waters would not transgress
His command,
When He marked out the foundations of
the earth,
30 Then I was beside Him *as* a master
craftsman;[a]
And I was daily *His* delight,
Rejoicing always before Him,
31 Rejoicing in His inhabited
world,
And my delight *was*
with the sons of
men.

32 "Now therefore, listen
to me, *my*
children,
For blessed *are those*
who keep my ways.
33 Hear instruction and be
wise,
And do not disdain *it.*
34 Blessed is the man who listens to me,
Watching daily at my gates,
Waiting at the posts of my doors.
35 For whoever finds me finds life,

WHAT'S IT MEAN?

Seven was a very important number
to the ancient Israelites, who believed the
numeral represented holiness or perfection. The number's history
can be traced all the way back to Creation, when God worked six days
and rested on the seventh. The number seven pops up throughout
the Bible in dreams, visions, and rituals.

Proverbs 9:1

And obtains favor from the LORD;
36 But he who sins against me wrongs his
own soul;
All those who hate me love death."

THE WAY OF WISDOM

1 Wisdom has built her house,
She has hewn out her seven pillars;
2 She has slaughtered her meat,
She has mixed her wine,
She has also furnished her table.
3 She has sent out her maidens,
She cries out from the highest places of
the city,
4 "Whoever *is* simple, let him turn in here!"
As for him who lacks understanding, she
says to him,
5 "Come, eat of my bread
And drink of the wine
I have mixed.
6 Forsake foolishness
and live,
And go in the way of
understanding.

7 "He who corrects a
scoffer gets shame
for himself,
And he who rebukes a
wicked *man only*
harms himself.
8 Do not correct a
scoffer, lest he hate
you;
Rebuke a wise *man,* and he will love
you.

"The fear of the LORD is the
beginning of wisdom,
and the knowledge of the Holy
One is understanding."
(Proverbs 9:10)

8:30 [a]A Jewish tradition reads *one brought up.*

9 Give *instruction* to a wise *man*, and he will
be still wiser;
Teach a just *man*, and he will increase in
learning.

On the Edge

*"The fear of the LORD is the
beginning of wisdom, and the
knowledge of the Holy One is understanding" (Prov. 9:10).*

Ever get in a situation where your back's
against the wall and you have no clue what
to do? Ever need to make an important
decision about your circumstances, but the
problem is bigger than you are? Those are
the times you need wisdom. You need to
look at things from God's perspective and
know what to do—that's wisdom. You know
you need it, but how do you get it?

Proverbs 9:10 says that the beginning of
wisdom is "the fear of the LORD." In other
words, wisdom starts with respect for God.
The more you learn to respect and obey the
Lord, the more wisdom you'll gain. Remember that respect and obedience are two
separate actions. To respect the Lord is to
know that He knows best and to care about
what He thinks. It is to consult Him when
you're in a tough spot. Obedience is a step
beyond respect. To obey the Lord is to act on
what He's told you.

The verse goes on to say that to have
understanding, you need "knowledge of the Holy One." Knowing
God is much deeper than knowing *about* God. Knowing Him
won't happen overnight, and no
one will ever know Him completely; but as
you spend time with Him, you'll eventually
begin to know Him more and more. He will
give you wisdom. Just respect Him, obey
Him, and know Him.

SEE FOR YOURSELF:
Dan. 2:21; Eph. 1:17;
James 3:17

10 "The fear of the LORD *is* the beginning of
wisdom,
And the knowledge of the Holy One *is*
understanding.
11 For by me your days will be multiplied,
And years of life will be added to you.

12 If you are wise, you are wise for yourself,
And *if* you scoff, you will bear *it* alone."

THE WAY OF FOLLY

13 A foolish woman is clamorous;
She is simple, and knows nothing.
14 For she sits at the door of her house,
On a seat *by* the highest places of the city,
15 To call to those who pass by,
Who go straight on their way:
16 "Whoever *is* simple, let him turn in here";
And *as for* him who lacks understanding,
she says to him,
17 "Stolen water is sweet,
And bread *eaten* in secret is pleasant."
18 But he does not know that the dead *are*
there,
That her guests *are* in the depths of hell.[a]

WISE SAYINGS OF SOLOMON

1 The proverbs of Solomon:

A wise son makes a glad father,
But a foolish son *is* the grief of his mother.

2 Treasures of wickedness profit nothing,
But righteousness delivers from death.
3 The LORD will not allow the righteous
soul to famish,
But He casts away the desire of the
wicked.

4 He who has a slack hand becomes poor,
But the hand of the diligent makes rich.
5 He who gathers in summer *is* a wise son;
He who sleeps in harvest *is* a son who
causes shame.

6 Blessings *are* on the head of the righteous,
But violence covers the mouth of the
wicked.
7 The memory of the righteous *is* blessed,
But the name of the wicked will rot.

8 The wise in heart will receive commands,
But a prating fool will fall.

9 He who walks with integrity walks
securely,
But he who perverts his ways will
become known.

10 He who winks with the eye causes
trouble,
But a prating fool will fall.

9:18 [a]Or *Sheol*

11 The mouth of the righteous *is* a well of life,
But violence covers the mouth of the wicked.

12 Hatred stirs up strife,
But love covers all sins.

On the Edge

Hatred stirs up strife, but love covers all sins (Prov. 10:12).

It's going to happen just by virtue of being sisters. Maybe the next time it'll be you. You're running late for school. Nothing is ironed. You look over at her closet, and there's the perfect shirt to throw on. You put it on and think, *I'll explain later. I'm sure she wouldn't mind.* Some things in life are worth getting upset about. And some things are best overlooked. Borrowed clothes between sisters is not a big deal—even when she didn't ask, even when you don't ask.

You could do the mature thing next time and say, "It's okay if you wear my clothes. But when it's not an emergency, I'd really appreciate it if you would ask me." Give your sister the same respect. Build bridges toward her. A sister is an awesome gift from God, even when she gets on your nerves. Love her and try to overlook the little stuff.

SEE FOR YOURSELF:
Rom. 12:9, 10;
1 Cor. 13:4; Eph 4:1–3;
1 John 4:7

---

13 Wisdom is found on the lips of him who has understanding,
But a rod *is* for the back of him who is devoid of understanding.

14 Wise *people* store up knowledge,
But the mouth of the foolish *is* near destruction.

15 The rich man's wealth *is* his strong city;
The destruction of the poor *is* their poverty.

16 The labor of the righteous *leads* to life,
The wages of the wicked to sin.

17 He who keeps instruction *is in* the way of life,
But he who refuses correction goes astray.

18 Whoever hides hatred *has* lying lips,
And whoever spreads slander *is* a fool.

19 In the multitude of words sin is not lacking,
But he who restrains his lips *is* wise.

20 The tongue of the righteous *is* choice silver;
The heart of the wicked *is worth* little.

21 The lips of the righteous feed many,
But fools die for lack of wisdom.[a]

22 The blessing of the LORD makes *one* rich,
And He adds no sorrow with it.

23 To do evil *is* like sport to a fool,
But a man of understanding has wisdom.

24 The fear of the wicked will come upon him,
And the desire of the righteous will be granted.

25 When the whirlwind passes by, the wicked *is* no *more,*
But the righteous *has* an everlasting foundation.

FOLLOWING GOD

What's the hope of a righteous person? (10:24, 25)

26 As vinegar to the teeth and smoke to the eyes,
So *is* the lazy *man* to those who send him.

27 The fear of the LORD prolongs days,
But the years of the wicked will be shortened.

28 The hope of the righteous *will be* gladness,
But the expectation of the wicked will perish.

29 The way of the LORD *is* strength for the upright,
But destruction *will come* to the workers of iniquity.

30 The righteous will never be removed,
But the wicked will not inhabit the earth.

31 The mouth of the righteous brings forth wisdom,
But the perverse tongue will be cut out.

10:21 [a]Literally *heart*

32 The lips of the righteous know what is
acceptable,
But the mouth of the wicked *what is*
perverse.

1 Dishonest scales *are* an abomination to
the LORD,
But a just weight *is* His delight.

2 When pride comes, then comes shame;
But with the humble *is* wisdom.

On the Edge

Dishonest scales are an abomination to the LORD, but a just weight is His delight (Prov. 11:1).

Cheating has to do with integrity. A great way to define integrity is to think of it as "what you do when no one's looking." What do you do when no one is looking? The Lord says that He hates cheating (dishonest scales). That covers the answers you saw and used from the test next to you, all the homework you copied from your friend before school, the money you secretly "borrowed" from your mom's purse, and the gum you accidentally forgot to pay for but kept anyway. Cheating only brings some small momentary rewards. In the long run, it all catches up to you. God sees the whole thing. Even worse, He sees inside your heart and knows all about your selfish motives. The next time you are tempted to look and think, *It would be only one time* or *It might even help my grade,* listen to the siren that goes off in your head. It's the Holy Spirit saying, "Don't!" You may forfeit some correct answers, but the God who sees everything will not overlook your integrity. His rewards are more valuable than a test grade and they last for eternity.

SEE FOR YOURSELF:
1 Cor. 13:6;
Eph. 4:15, 28

3 The integrity of the upright will guide
them,
But the perversity of the unfaithful will
destroy them.
4 Riches do not profit in the day of wrath,
But righteousness delivers from death.

5 The righteousness of the blameless will
direct[a] his way aright,
But the wicked will fall by his own
wickedness.
6 The righteousness of the upright will
deliver them,
But the unfaithful will be caught by *their*
lust.

7 When a wicked man dies, *his* expectation
will perish,
And the hope of the unjust perishes.
8 The righteous is delivered from trouble,
And it comes to the wicked
instead.
9 The hypocrite with *his*
mouth destroys his
neighbor,
But through knowledge
the righteous will be
delivered.
10 When it goes well with
the righteous, the city
rejoices;
And when the wicked perish, *there is*
jubilation.
11 By the blessing of the upright the city is
exalted,
But it is overthrown by the mouth of the
wicked.

HYPOCRISY
What effect does the hypocrite have on those around him? (11:9)

12 He who is devoid of wisdom despises his
neighbor,
But a man of understanding holds his
peace.
13 A talebearer reveals secrets,
But he who is of a faithful spirit conceals
a matter.

14 Where *there is* no counsel, the people fall;
But in the multitude of counselors *there is*
safety.

15 He who is surety for a stranger will suffer,
But one who hates being surety is secure.

16 A gracious woman retains honor,
But ruthless *men* retain riches.
17 The merciful man does good for his own
soul,
But *he who is* cruel troubles his own flesh.
18 The wicked *man* does deceptive work,
But he who sows righteousness *will have*
a sure reward.

11:5 *a*Or *make smooth* or *straight*

19 As righteousness *leads* to life,
   So he who pursues evil *pursues it* to his
   own death.
20 Those who are of a perverse heart *are* an
   abomination to the LORD,
   But *the* blameless in their ways *are* His
   delight.
21 *Though they* join forces,[a] the wicked will
   not go unpunished;
   But the posterity of the righteous will be
   delivered.

22 *As* a ring of gold in a swine's snout,
   So is a lovely woman who lacks
   discretion.

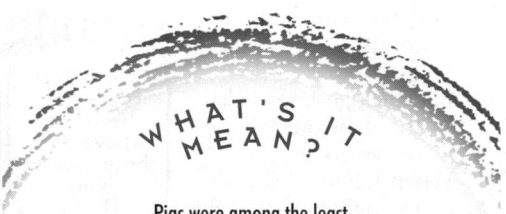

WHAT'S IT MEAN?

Pigs were among the least
popular animals in ancient Israel. They were
considered "unclean" and were unsuitable for food, according
to God's Law. Throughout the Bible, pigs are used to symbolize
greed, filth, or shame.
Proverbs 11:22

23 The desire of the righteous *is* only good,
   But the expectation of the wicked *is*
   wrath.

24 There is *one* who scatters, yet increases
   more;
   And there is *one* who withholds more
   than is right,
   But it *leads* to poverty.
25 The generous soul will be made rich,
   And he who waters will also be watered
   himself.
26 The people will curse him who withholds
   grain,
   But blessing *will be* on the head of him
   who sells *it*.

27 He who earnestly seeks good finds
   favor,
   But trouble will come to him who seeks
   evil.

28 He who trusts in his riches will fall,
   But the righteous will flourish like
   foliage.

29 He who troubles his own house will
   inherit the wind,
   And the fool *will be* servant to the wise of
   heart.

30 The fruit of the righteous *is a* tree of life,
   And he who wins souls *is* wise.

31 If the righteous will be recompensed on
   the earth,
   How much more the ungodly and the
   sinner.

1 Whoever loves instruction loves knowledge,
   But he who hates correction *is* stupid.

2 A good *man* obtains favor from the
   LORD,
   But a man of wicked intentions He will
   condemn.

3 A man is not established by wickedness,
   But the root of the righteous cannot be
   moved.

4 An excellent[a] wife *is* the crown of her
   husband,
   But she who causes shame *is* like
   rottenness in his bones.

5 The thoughts of the righteous *are* right,
   But the counsels of the wicked *are*
   deceitful.
6 The words of the wicked *are*, "Lie in wait
   for blood,"
   But the mouth of the upright will deliver
   them.

7 The wicked are overthrown and *are* no
   more,
   But the house of the righteous will stand.

8 A man will be commended according to
   his wisdom,
   But he who is of a perverse heart will be
   despised.

9 Better *is the one* who is slighted but has a
   servant,
   Than he who honors himself but lacks
   bread.

11:21 [a]Literally *hand to hand*   **12:4** [a]Literally *A wife of valor*

10 A righteous *man* regards the life of his
       animal,
    But the tender mercies of the wicked *are*
       cruel.

11 He who tills his land will be satisfied with
       bread,
    But he who follows frivolity *is* devoid of
       understanding.*ᵃ*

12 The wicked covet the catch of evil *men*,
    But the root of the righteous yields *fruit*.

13 The wicked is ensnared by the
       transgression of *his* lips,
    But the righteous will come through
       trouble.

14 A man will be satisfied with good by the
       fruit of *his* mouth,
    And the recompense of a man's hands
       will be rendered to him.

15 The way of a fool *is* right in his own
       eyes,
    But he who heeds counsel *is* wise.

16 A fool's wrath is known at once,
    But a prudent *man* covers shame.

17 He *who* speaks truth declares
       righteousness,
    But a false witness, deceit.

18 There is one who speaks like the piercings
       of a sword,
    But the tongue of the wise *promotes*
       health.

19 The truthful lip shall be established
       forever,
    But a lying tongue *is* but for a moment.

20 Deceit is in the heart of those who devise
       evil,
    But counselors of peace have joy.

21 No grave trouble will overtake the
       righteous,
    But the wicked shall be filled with evil.

22 Lying lips *are* an abomination to the
       LORD,
    But those who deal truthfully *are* His
       delight.

23 A prudent man conceals knowledge,
    But the heart of fools proclaims
       foolishness.

24 The hand of the diligent will rule,
    But the lazy *man* will be put to forced
       labor.

On the Edge

The hand of the diligent will rule, but the lazy man will be put to forced labor (Prov. 12:24).

Forty algebra problems, a paper on the people of Zaire, Spanish vocabulary words—every night another pile of homework. Even though you may get tired of having work to do at home, the sacrifice will be worth it in the end. Verse 24 says that the diligent—those who work hard—become leaders, and the lazy are put on forced labor—become slaves. You may not become a slave in the full sense of the word, but you will *become* a slave to your lack of knowledge. Without hard work, there won't be success in a career. It will be hard to progress past low-paying jobs, and the lack of discipline will make it hard to hold on to good jobs. If you have goals and if you want to make a difference with your life, then you really need to do your homework. Even when you can't imagine how you will ever use the information, just press on. Know that each little accomplishment is building your character. You will be stronger, wiser, and more disciplined—all because you were faithful to do your homework.

SEE FOR YOURSELF:
   Prov. 24:33, 34;
   Eccl. 9:10; Gal. 6:4

25 Anxiety in the heart of man
       causes depression,
    But a good word
       makes it glad.

26 The righteous should
       choose his friends
       carefully,
    For the way of the
       wicked leads them
       astray.

DISCOURAGEMENT

How are we
to respond to
discourage-
ment?
(12:25)

27 The lazy *man* does not roast what he
       took in hunting,
    But diligence *is* man's precious
       possession.

28 In the way of righteousness *is* life,
    And in *its* pathway *there is* no death.

12:11 *ᵃ*Literally *heart*

1 A wise son *heeds* his father's instruction,
But a scoffer does not listen to rebuke.

2 A man shall eat well by the fruit of *his*
mouth,
But the soul of the unfaithful feeds on
violence.

3 He who guards his mouth preserves his
life,
But he who opens wide his lips shall have
destruction.

4 The soul of a lazy *man*
desires, and *has*
nothing;
But the soul of the
diligent shall be made
rich.

LAZINESS

If diligence
brings
wealth, what
does laziness
bring?
(13:4)

5 A righteous *man* hates
lying,
But a wicked *man* is loathsome and
comes to shame.

6 Righteousness guards *him whose* way is
blameless,
But wickedness overthrows the sinner.

7 There is one who makes himself rich, yet
has nothing;
And one who makes himself poor, yet *has*
great riches.

8 The ransom of a man's life *is* his riches,
But the poor does not hear rebuke.

9 The light of the righteous rejoices,
But the lamp of the wicked will be put
out.

10 By pride comes nothing but strife,
But with the well-advised *is* wisdom.

11 Wealth *gained by* dishonesty will be
diminished,
But he who gathers by labor will
increase.

12 Hope deferred makes the heart sick,
But *when* the desire comes, *it is* a tree of
life.

13 He who despises the word will be
destroyed,
But he who fears the commandment will
be rewarded.

14 The law of the wise *is* a fountain of
life,

On the Edge

*A wise son heeds his father's
instruction, but a scoffer does not
listen to rebuke (Prov. 13:1).*

The difference between what you want
and what your parents want is all about
perspective. You see what everyone else is
doing and long to be a part of the fun. Your
parents see a much bigger picture—the part
that you don't want to think about—the
stuff you know will never happen to you.
When you say, "Why can't my curfew be one
hour later; what's the big deal?" they see
the reality—the later it gets, the more
drunk drivers on the road, violent crimes
increase, fatigue causes people to make
poor decisions, and the list goes on.

Your parents' years have brought them
wisdom. And God has given them
you to be responsible for. Proverbs says that wise sons and
daughters heed their parents'
instructions. Your parents are the instruments through which God builds your life
and gives you direction. Even if you have a
hard time accepting their judgment, learn
to respect their authority. Do not be the
stubborn child who ignores his parents and
grows up to be a fool.

SEE FOR YOURSELF:
Prov. 12:1, 15; 13:10;
20:20

To turn *one* away from the snares of
death.

15 Good understanding gains favor,
But the way of the unfaithful *is* hard.

16 Every prudent *man* acts with
knowledge,
But a fool lays open *his* folly.

17 A wicked messenger falls into trouble,
But a faithful ambassador *brings* health.

18 Poverty and shame *will come* to him who
disdains correction,
But he who regards a rebuke will be
honored.

19 A desire accomplished is sweet to the
soul,
But *it is* an abomination to fools to
depart from evil.

20 He who walks with wise *men* will be wise,
But the companion of fools will be destroyed.

21 Evil pursues sinners,
But to the righteous, good shall be repaid.

22 A good *man* leaves an inheritance to his children's children,
But the wealth of the sinner is stored up for the righteous.

23 Much food *is in* the fallow *ground* of the poor,
And for lack of justice there is waste.*a*

24 He who spares his rod hates his son,
But he who loves him disciplines him promptly.

25 The righteous eats to the satisfying of his soul,
But the stomach of the wicked shall be in want.

1 The wise woman builds her house,
But the foolish pulls it down with her hands.

2 He who walks in his uprightness fears the LORD,
But *he who is* perverse in his ways despises Him.

3 In the mouth of a fool *is* a rod of pride,
But the lips of the wise will preserve them.

4 Where no oxen *are,* the trough *is* clean;
But much increase *comes* by the strength of an ox.

5 A faithful witness does not lie,
But a false witness will utter lies.

6 A scoffer seeks wisdom and does not *find* it,
But knowledge *is* easy to him who understands.

7 Go from the presence of a foolish man,
When you do not perceive *in him* the lips of knowledge.

8 The wisdom of the prudent *is* to understand his way,
But the folly of fools *is* deceit.

9 Fools mock at sin,
But among the upright *there is* favor.

10 The heart knows its own bitterness,
And a stranger does not share its joy.

11 The house of the wicked will be overthrown,
But the tent of the upright will flourish.

12 There is a way *that seems* right to a man,
But its end *is* the way of death.

13 Even in laughter the heart may sorrow,
And the end of mirth *may be* grief.

14 The backslider in heart will be filled with his own ways,
But a good man *will be satisfied* from above.*a*

15 The simple believes every word,
But the prudent considers well his steps.

16 A wise *man* fears and departs from evil,
But a fool rages and is self-confident.

17 A quick-tempered *man* acts foolishly,
And a man of wicked intentions is hated.

18 The simple inherit folly,
But the prudent are crowned with knowledge.

19 The evil will bow before the good,
And the wicked at the gates of the righteous.

20 The poor *man* is hated even by his own neighbor,
But the rich *has* many friends.

21 He who despises his neighbor sins;
But he who has mercy on the poor, happy *is* he.

22 Do they not go astray who devise evil?
But mercy and truth *belong* to those who devise good.

23 In all labor there is profit,
But idle chatter*a* *leads* only to poverty.

24 The crown of the wise is their riches,
But the foolishness of fools *is* folly.

25 A true witness delivers souls,
But a deceitful *witness* speaks lies.

13:23 *a*Literally *what is swept away*   **14:14** *a*Literally *from above himself*   **14:23** *a*Literally *talk of the lips*

26 In the fear of the LORD *there is* strong
confidence,
And His children will have a place of
refuge.
27 The fear of the LORD *is* a fountain of life,
To turn *one* away from the snares of
death.

28 In a multitude of people *is* a king's honor,
But in the lack of people *is* the downfall
of a prince.

29 *He who is* slow to wrath has great
understanding,
But *he who is* impulsive[a] exalts folly.

30 A sound heart *is* life to the body,
But envy *is* rottenness to
the bones.

31 He who oppresses the
poor reproaches his
Maker,
But he who honors Him
has mercy on the
needy.

MERCY

Who do we
honor by
being
merciful to
the needy?
(14:31)

32 The wicked is banished in his
wickedness,
But the righteous has a refuge in his
death.

33 Wisdom rests in the heart of him who
has understanding,
But *what is* in the heart of fools is made
known.

34 Righteousness exalts a nation,
But sin *is* a reproach to *any* people.

35 The king's favor *is*
toward a wise
servant,
But his wrath *is against*
him who causes
shame.

1 A soft answer turns
away wrath,
But a harsh word stirs up
anger.
2 The tongue of the wise uses knowledge
rightly,
But the mouth of fools pours forth
foolishness.

3 The eyes of the LORD *are* in every place,
Keeping watch on the evil and the good.

4 A wholesome tongue *is* a tree of life,
But perverseness in it breaks the spirit.

WHAT'S IT
MEAN?

A fool is not necessarily an unintelligent
person. The biggest fools are people who
don't care about God and who can't tell the difference
between right and wrong.
Proverbs 15:2

5 A fool despises his father's instruction,
But he who receives correction is
prudent.

6 *In* the house of the righteous *there is*
much treasure,
But in the revenue of the wicked is
trouble.

7 The lips of the wise disperse knowledge,
But the heart of the fool *does* not *do* so.

8 The sacrifice of the wicked *is* an
abomination to the LORD,
But the prayer of the upright *is* His
delight.

9 The way of the wicked
is an abomination
to the LORD,
But He loves him who
follows
righteousness.

10 Harsh discipline *is* for
him who forsakes
the way,
And he who hates
correction will die.

11 Hell[a] and Destruction[b]
are before the LORD;
So how much more the hearts of the
sons of men.

"In the fear of the LORD
there is strong confidence,
and His children will have a
place of refuge."
(Proverbs 14:26)

14:29 [a]Literally *short of spirit*   15:11 [a]Or *Sheol* [b]Hebrew *Abaddon*

12 A scoffer does not love one who
    corrects him,
Nor will he go to the
    wise.

13 A merry heart makes a
    cheerful countenance,
But by sorrow of the
    heart the spirit is
    broken.

14 The heart of him who has understanding
    seeks knowledge,
But the mouth of fools feeds on
    foolishness.

15 All the days of the afflicted *are* evil,
But he who is of a merry heart *has* a
    continual feast.

16 Better *is* a little with the fear of the
    LORD,
Than great treasure with trouble.
17 Better *is* a dinner of herbs[a] where love is,
Than a fatted calf with hatred.

DISCIPLINE
What
happens to
the one who
ignores
discipline?
(15:10)

WHAT'S IT MEAN?

In most ancient Israelite families, meat was
served only on special occasions, such as when they
were entertaining guests or celebrating a religious festival. Only the
wealthiest people in the land could afford to eat meat regularly. The
rest ate mostly fruits, vegetables, and grains.
Proverbs 15:17

18 A wrathful man stirs up strife,
But *he who is* slow to anger allays
    contention.

19 The way of the lazy *man is* like a hedge of
    thorns,
But the way of the upright *is* a highway.

20 A wise son makes a father glad,
But a foolish man despises his mother.

21 Folly *is* joy *to him who is* destitute of
    discernment,
But a man of understanding walks
    uprightly.

22 Without counsel, plans go awry,
But in the multitude of counselors they
    are established.

On the Edge

*Without counsel, plans go awry,
but in the multitude of counselors
they are established (Prov. 15:22).*
When it comes to making decisions, it
doesn't matter how old you are. The smartest thing to do is to consult with wise people and think about their counsel when you
make your plans. It's just that when you are
younger, you live with your wise
counsel—your parents. As long
as you are in your parents' home,
God has made them the guardians of your decisions. They are
responsible to Him for the freedoms they
give to you and for the decisions they let
you make on your own. Little by little, as
you get older, more things will be left up to
you. As you choose wisely, you will be given
even more freedom. Your day is coming—all
the decisions will be yours. In all your
independence, don't be surprised if you find
yourself calling home just to ask, "What do
you think about this?"
SEE FOR YOURSELF:
Eph. 6:1–3; Col. 3:20;
1 Pet. 5:5

23 A man has joy by the answer of his
    mouth,
And a word *spoken* in due season, how
    good *it is!*

24 The way of life *winds* upward for the
    wise,
That he may turn away from hell[a] below.

25 The LORD will destroy the house of the
    proud,
But He will establish the boundary of the
    widow.

15:17 [a]Or *vegetables* **15:24** [a]Or *Sheol*

26 The thoughts of the wicked *are* an
    abomination to the LORD,
    But *the words* of the pure *are* pleasant.

27 He who is greedy for gain troubles his
    own house,
    But he who hates bribes will live.

28 The heart of the righteous studies how to
    answer,
    But the mouth of the wicked pours forth
    evil.

29 The LORD *is* far from the wicked,
    But He hears the prayer of the righteous.

30 The light of the eyes rejoices the heart,
    And a good report makes the bones
    healthy.*[a]*

31 The ear that hears the rebukes of life
    Will abide among the wise.
32 He who disdains instruction despises his
    own soul,
    But he who heeds rebuke gets
    understanding.
33 The fear of the LORD *is* the instruction of
    wisdom,
    And before honor *is* humility.

1 The preparations of the heart *belong* to
    man,
    But the answer of the tongue *is* from the
    LORD.

2 All the ways of a man *are* pure in his
    own eyes,
    But the LORD weighs the spirits.

3 Commit your works to
    the LORD,
    And your thoughts will
    be established.

4 The LORD has made all
    for Himself,
    Yes, even the wicked for the day of doom.

5 Everyone proud in heart *is* an
    abomination to the LORD;
    Though they join forces,*[a]* none will go
    unpunished.

6 In mercy and truth
    Atonement is provided for iniquity;

On the Edge

The preparations of the heart belong to man, but the answer of the tongue is from the LORD. All the ways of a man are pure in his own eyes, but the LORD weighs the spirits. Commit your works to the LORD, and your thoughts will be established (Prov. 16:1–3).

Choosing a college is a big decision, but not too big for God. As you and your parents begin to narrow the field, make sure you are continually covering the whole process in prayer. If God directs your steps, Proverbs 16:3 says you'll succeed ("your thoughts will be established"). Your plans have no strength if they're not from God. Begin by choosing the schools that interest you and have a curriculum in your field of study. Then "commit your works to the LORD" by taking time to pray. Visit some campuses. Take time to pray. Apply for scholarships and grants. Take time to pray. Talk over finances with your parents. Take time to pray. Go through the acceptance letters and ask yourself, "Can I honor God and live a life that glorifies Him at any of these schools?" If the answer is yes, then pick the one you like. If the answer is no, then throw out the losers, and choose from the remainder. Between you and God and your parents, you are sure to make a wise decision and have a great life in college.

SEE FOR YOURSELF:
Ps. 37:5; Prov. 3:6;
Matt. 6:33

TRUST

What is a
result of
trusting God?
(16:3)

And by the fear of the LORD *one* departs
    from evil.

7 When a man's ways please the LORD,
    He makes even his enemies to be at peace
    with him.

8 Better *is* a little with righteousness,
    Than vast revenues without justice.

9 A man's heart plans his way,
    But the LORD directs his steps.

15:30 *[a]*Literally *fat*   **16:5** *[a]*Literally *hand to hand*

10 Divination *is* on the lips of the king;
His mouth must not transgress in
judgment.

11 Honest weights and scales *are* the
LORD'S;
All the weights in the bag *are* His work.

12 *It is* an abomination for kings to commit
wickedness,
For a throne is established by
righteousness.

13 Righteous lips *are* the delight of kings,
And they love him who speaks *what is*
right.

14 As messengers of death *is* the king's
wrath,
But a wise man will appease it.

15 In the light of the king's face *is* life,
And his favor *is* like a cloud of the
latter rain.

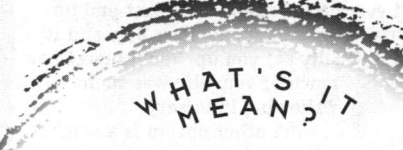

WHAT'S IT MEAN?

Because it's located in a desert region, the land
of Israel experiences frequent droughts. Because the
ancient Israelites relied on farming for so many of their basic needs,
they considered rain a precious gift from God. Long droughts were
thought by many people to be God's judgment
on the sins of the people.
Proverbs 16:15

16 How much better to get wisdom than
gold!
And to get understanding is to be chosen
rather than silver.

17 The highway of the upright *is* to depart
from evil;
He who keeps his way preserves his
soul.

18 Pride *goes* before destruction,
And a haughty spirit before a fall.

19 Better *to be* of a humble spirit with the
lowly,
Than to divide the spoil with the proud.

20 He who heeds the word wisely will find
good,

And whoever trusts in the LORD, happy
is he.

21 The wise in heart will be called
prudent,
And sweetness of the lips increases
learning.

22 Understanding *is* a wellspring of life to
him who has it.
But the correction of fools *is* folly.

23 The heart of the wise teaches his
mouth,
And adds learning to his lips.

24 Pleasant words *are like* a honeycomb,
Sweetness to the soul and health to the
bones.

25 There is a way *that seems* right to a man,
But its end *is* the way of death.

26 The person who labors, labors for
himself,
For his *hungry* mouth drives him *on*.

27 An ungodly man digs up
evil,
And *it is* on his lips like a
burning fire.

28 A perverse man sows
strife,
And a whisperer
separates the best of
friends.

GOSSIP

What are
some of the
negative
results of
gossip?
(16:28)

29 A violent man entices his
neighbor,
And leads him in a way *that is* not
good.

30 He winks his eye to devise perverse
things;
He purses his lips *and* brings about
evil.

31 The silver-haired head *is* a crown of
glory,
If it is found in the way of
righteousness.

32 *He who is* slow to anger *is* better than the
mighty,
And he who rules his spirit than he who
takes a city.

33 The lot is cast into the lap,
But its every decision *is* from the LORD.

1   Better *is* a dry morsel with quietness,
Than a house full of feasting[a] *with* strife.

2   A wise servant will rule over a son who
causes shame,
And will share an inheritance among the
brothers.

3   The refining pot *is* for silver and the
furnace for gold,
But the LORD tests the hearts.

4   An evildoer gives heed to false lips;
A liar listens eagerly to a spiteful tongue.

5   He who mocks the poor reproaches his
Maker;
He who is glad at calamity will not go
unpunished.

6   Children's children *are* the crown of old
men,
And the glory of children *is* their father.

7   Excellent speech is not becoming to a
fool,
Much less lying lips to a prince.

8   A present *is* a precious stone in the eyes
of its possessor;
Wherever he turns, he prospers.

9   He who covers a transgression
seeks love,
But he who repeats a
matter separates
friends.

ENEMIES

How can we
avoid making
enemies?
(17:9)

10   Rebuke is more effective
for a wise *man*
Than a hundred blows on
a fool.

11   An evil *man* seeks only rebellion;
Therefore a cruel messenger will be sent
against him.

12   Let a man meet a bear robbed of her cubs,
Rather than a fool in his folly.

13   Whoever rewards evil for good,
Evil will not depart from his house.

14   The beginning of strife *is like* releasing
water;

On the Edge

*He who covers a transgression
seeks love, but he who repeats a
matter separates friends (Prov.
17:9).*

If you've been hurt by a friend, you've
probably got some big scars. The truth is,
you've only got a couple of options about
how to handle your pain. You can look at
your scars every day and let them remind
you how hurt you've been. You can think
about them all the time. You can spend
hours plotting revenge or deciding what
kind of snide remark to make the next time
you see your friend. You can tell everybody
else how badly you were treated. You can
hold a grudge. Eventually that grudge will
turn to hatred and bitterness. And you
won't ever be satisfied. You'll just end up
rehearsing your pain day after day, and it
will finally eat you up. You'll regret how
much of your life was spent
wallowing in misery.

The other option is a combination of two powerful expressions: grace and forgiveness. Grace means
forgiving a friend even when he or she
doesn't deserve it. After that, live your
forgiveness. Your words and your actions
will show that you have truly forgiven.

The first option keeps you in chains. The
second one sets you free. Forgiveness frees
your heart to love your friend the way God
loves you.

SEE FOR YOURSELF:
Eph. 4:32; Col. 3:13;
1 John 4:7

Therefore stop contention before a
quarrel starts.

15   He who justifies the wicked, and he who
condemns the just,
Both of them alike *are* an abomination to
the LORD.

16   Why *is there* in the hand of a fool the
purchase price of wisdom,
Since *he has* no heart *for it?*

17   A friend loves at all times,
And a brother is born for adversity.

17:1 [a]Or *sacrificial meals*

18 A man devoid of understanding shakes
hands in a pledge,
And becomes surety for his friend.

19 He who loves transgression loves strife,
And he who exalts his gate seeks destruction.

20 He who has a deceitful heart finds no
good,
And he who has a perverse tongue falls
into evil.

21 He who begets a scoffer *does so* to his
sorrow,
And the father of a fool has no joy.

22 A merry heart does good, *like* medicine,*a*
But a broken spirit dries the bones.

23 A wicked *man* accepts a bribe behind the
back*a*
To pervert the ways of justice.

24 Wisdom *is* in the sight of him who has
understanding,
But the eyes of a fool *are* on the ends of
the earth.

25 A foolish son *is* a grief to his father,
And bitterness to her who bore him.

26 Also, to punish the righteous *is* not good,
Nor to strike princes for *their* uprightness.

27 He who has knowledge spares his words,
And a man of understanding is of a calm
spirit.

28 Even a fool is counted wise when he
holds his peace;
When he shuts his lips, *he is considered*
perceptive.

1 A man who isolates himself
seeks his own desire;
He rages against all wise
judgment.

2 A fool has no delight in
understanding,
But in expressing his own
heart.

EDUCATION

Is education
for every-
body?
(18:2)

3 When the wicked comes, contempt comes
also;
And with dishonor *comes* reproach.

4 The words of a man's mouth *are* deep
waters;
The wellspring of wisdom *is* a flowing
brook.

5 *It is* not good to show partiality to the
wicked,
Or to overthrow the righteous in
judgment.

6 A fool's lips enter into contention,
And his mouth calls for blows.

7 A fool's mouth *is* his destruction,
And his lips *are* the snare of his soul.

8 The words of a talebearer *are* like tasty
trifles,*a*
And they go down into the inmost body.

9 He who is slothful in his work
Is a brother to him who is a great
destroyer.

10 The name of the LORD *is* a strong tower;
The righteous run to it and are safe.

11 The rich man's wealth *is* his strong city,
And like a high wall in his own esteem.

12 Before destruction the heart of a man is
haughty,
And before honor *is* humility.

13 He who answers a matter before he
hears *it*,
It *is* folly and shame to him.

14 The spirit of a man will sustain him in
sickness,
But who can bear a broken spirit?

15 The heart of the prudent acquires
knowledge,
And the ear of the wise seeks knowledge.

16 A man's gift makes room for him,
And brings him before great men.

17 The first *one* to plead his cause *seems* right,
Until his neighbor comes and examines
him.

18 Casting lots causes contentions to cease,
And keeps the mighty apart.

19 A brother offended *is harder to win* than a
strong city,

17:22 *aOr makes medicine even better*   17:23 *aLiterally from the bosom*   18:8 *aA Jewish tradition reads wounds.*

And contentions *are* like the bars of a castle.

WHAT'S IT MEAN?

"Casting lots" was a lot like flipping a coin or drawing straws to determine who's going to do something. The only difference is that many Israelites believed God influenced the outcome when lots were cast. Therefore, it was His will, and not blind luck, that determined the results.

Proverbs 18:18

20 A man's stomach shall be satisfied from the fruit of his mouth;
From the produce of his lips he shall be filled.

21 Death and life *are* in the power of the tongue,
And those who love it will eat its fruit.

22 *He who* finds a wife finds a good *thing,*
And obtains favor from the LORD.

23 The poor *man* uses entreaties,
But the rich answers roughly.

24 A man *who has* friends must himself be friendly,[a]
But there is a friend *who* sticks closer than a brother.

19

1 Better *is* the poor who walks in his integrity
Than *one who is* perverse in his lips, and is a fool.

2 Also it is not good *for* a soul *to be* without knowledge,
And he sins who hastens with *his* feet.

3 The foolishness of a man twists his way,
And his heart frets against the LORD.

4 Wealth makes many friends,
But the poor is separated from his friend.

5 A false witness will not go unpunished,
And *he who* speaks lies will not escape.

6 Many entreat the favor of the nobility,
And every man *is* a friend to one who gives gifts.

7 All the brothers of the poor hate him;
How much more do his friends go far from him!
He may pursue *them with* words, *yet* they abandon *him*.

8 He who gets wisdom loves his own soul;
He who keeps understanding will find good.

On the Edge

He who gets wisdom loves his own soul; he who keeps understanding will find good (Prov. 19:8).

Josh was fourteen years old. After he died, people talked about his football ability, his great personality, his good looks, and his love for God. One night he was at home and accidentally killed himself by "huffing" fluorocarbons. His friends said he was just experimenting and wasn't a habitual user. He didn't mean to do it. He was just "messing around." Josh didn't use good sense. Getting a "buzz" from huffing seemed pretty harmless. He probably didn't even think it was dangerous. But it was a tragically unwise choice that ended his life after fourteen short years.

Whether it's huffing, or drag racing, you have to separate yourself from the potential "thrill" and ask, "Is this wise? What could the consequences be? What is the absolute worst thing that could happen? Could I hurt myself or someone else?" Make sure you know how much damage could be done to yourself or other people. The Holy Spirit will give you direction. But you have to follow through and do the right thing. It takes guts not to follow the crowd. God will provide the guts—all you have to do is ask Him.

SEE FOR YOURSELF:
1 Cor. 6:19, 20; Col. 3:5;
1 Pet. 1:13–16

18:24 [a]Following Greek manuscripts, Syriac, Targum, and Vulgate; Masoretic Text reads *may come to ruin.*

9 A false witness will not go unpunished,
And *he who* speaks lies shall perish.

10 Luxury is not fitting for a fool,
Much less for a servant to rule over
princes.

11 The discretion of a man
makes him slow to
anger,
And his glory *is* to
overlook a
transgression.

12 The king's wrath *is* like the
roaring of a lion,
But his favor *is* like dew on the grass.

13 A foolish son *is* the ruin of his father,
And the contentions of a wife *are* a
continual dripping.

14 Houses and riches *are* an inheritance from
fathers,
But a prudent wife *is* from the LORD.

15 Laziness casts *one* into a
deep sleep,
And an idle person will
suffer hunger.

16 He who keeps the
commandment keeps his soul,
But he who is careless[a] of his ways will die.

17 He who has pity on the poor lends to the
LORD,
And He will pay back what he has given.

18 Chasten your son while there is hope,
And do not set your heart on his
destruction.[a]

19 *A man of* great wrath will suffer
punishment;
For if you rescue *him,* you will have to do
it again.

20 Listen to counsel and receive instruction,
That you may be wise in your latter
days.

21 There are many plans in a man's
heart,

> "The discretion of a man
> makes him slow to anger,
> and his glory is to overlook
> a transgression."
> (Proverbs 19:11)

Nevertheless the LORD's counsel—that will
stand.

22 What is desired in a man is kindness,
And a poor man is better than a liar.

23 The fear of the LORD
leads to life,
And *he who has it*
will abide in
satisfaction;
He will not be visited
with evil.

24 A lazy *man* buries his
hand in the bowl,[a]
And will not so much as bring it to his
mouth again.

25 Strike a scoffer, and the simple will
become wary;
Rebuke one who has understanding, *and*
he will discern knowledge.

26 He who mistreats *his* father *and* chases
away *his* mother
Is a son who causes shame and brings
reproach.

27 Cease listening to instruction, my son,
And you will stray from the words of
knowledge.

28 A disreputable witness scorns justice,
And the mouth of the wicked devours
iniquity.

29 Judgments are prepared for scoffers,
And beatings for the backs of fools.

1 Wine *is* a mocker,
Strong drink *is* a brawler,
And whoever is led astray by it is not wise.

2 The wrath[a] of a king *is* like the roaring of
a lion;
Whoever provokes him to anger sins
against his own life.

3 *It is* honorable for a man to stop striving,
Since any fool can start a quarrel.

4 The lazy *man* will not plow because of
winter;

LAZINESS

If you are lazy,
what can you
expect?
(19:15)

19:16 [a]Literally *despises,* figurative of recklessness or carelessness   19:18 [a]Literally *to put him to death;* a Jewish
tradition reads *on his crying.*   19:24 [a]Septuagint and Syriac read *bosom;* Targum and Vulgate read *armpit.*
20:2 [a]Literally *fear* or *terror* which is produced by the king's wrath

He will beg during harvest and *have* nothing.

5 Counsel in the heart of man *is like* deep water,
But a man of understanding will draw it out.

6 Most men will proclaim each his own goodness,
But who can find a faithful man?

7 The righteous *man* walks in his integrity;
His children *are* blessed after him.

8 A king who sits on the throne of judgment
Scatters all evil with his eyes.

9 Who can say, "I have made my heart clean,
I am pure from my sin"?

10 Diverse weights *and* diverse measures,
They *are* both alike, an abomination to the LORD.

HYPOCRISY

What does God think of a person with double standards? (20:10)

11 Even a child is known by his deeds,
Whether what he does *is* pure and right.

12 The hearing ear and the seeing eye,
The LORD has made them both.

13 Do not love sleep, lest you come to poverty;
Open your eyes, *and* you will be satisfied with bread.

14 "*It is* good for nothing,"[a] cries the buyer;
But when he has gone his way, then he boasts.

15 There is gold and a multitude of rubies,
But the lips of knowledge *are* a precious jewel.

16 Take the garment of one who is surety *for* a stranger,
And hold it as a pledge *when it* is for a seductress.

17 Bread gained by deceit *is* sweet to a man,
But afterward his mouth will be filled with gravel.

18 Plans are established by counsel;
By wise counsel wage war.

19 He who goes about *as* a talebearer reveals secrets;
Therefore do not associate with one who flatters with his lips.

20 Whoever curses his father or his mother,
His lamp will be put out in deep darkness.

On the Edge

Whoever curses his father or his mother, his lamp will be put out in deep darkness . . . Do not say, "I will recompense evil"; wait for the LORD, and He will save you (Prov. 20:20, 22).

Ashley's mom got this new device that you put on your car. It plays forty different songs through your horn. One day in the junior high carpool line, Ashley's mom decide to play "parking lot DJ" and started playing songs through the horn. They were old songs, geeky songs—"Oh Susanna" and "Tea for Two." Really hip stuff *cannot* be played through a car horn. Mom thought it was a riot. Ashley thought it was the most humiliating thing that could possibly happen. Ashley tried to figure out what she could do that would be equally embarrassing to her mother, but nothing came close to that musical horn.

Finally, Ashley decided to take the high road. She sat down and told her mom how mortified she was, that it was not funny, and that she wanted her to stop. Mom apologized for being so goofy. She really had thought it was funny. Now she just entertains construction workers as she drives by and the school parking lot is quiet.

Parents can be really embarrassing, intentionally or without even knowing it. When it gets to you, work through it. Talk it out. Tell them how you feel. Be honest and don't try to get even. Your parents will appreciate your maturity.

SEE FOR YOURSELF:
Matt. 5:9; 1 Cor. 13:4–7

20:14 [a]Literally *evil, evil*

21 An inheritance gained hastily at the
beginning
Will not be blessed at the end.

22 Do not say, "I will recompense evil";
Wait for the LORD, and He will save you.

23 Diverse weights *are* an abomination to the
LORD,
And dishonest scales *are* not good.

24 A man's steps *are* of the LORD;
How then can a man understand his own
way?

25 *It is* a snare for a man to devote rashly
something as holy,
And afterward to reconsider *his* vows.

26 A wise king sifts out the wicked,
And brings the threshing wheel over them.

27 The spirit of a man *is* the lamp of the
LORD,
Searching all the inner depths of his
heart.*a*

28 Mercy and truth preserve the king,
And by lovingkindness he upholds his
throne.

29 The glory of young men *is* their
strength,
And the splendor of old men *is* their gray
head.

30 Blows that hurt cleanse away evil,
As *do* stripes the inner depths of the
heart.*a*

21 1 The king's heart *is* in the hand of the
LORD,
Like the rivers of water; He turns it
wherever He wishes.

2 Every way of a man *is* right in his own
eyes,
But the LORD weighs the hearts.

3 To do righteousness and justice
Is more acceptable to the LORD than
sacrifice.

4 A haughty look, a proud heart,
And the plowing*a* of the wicked *are* sin.

5 The plans of the diligent *lead* surely to
plenty,
But *those of* everyone *who is* hasty, surely
to poverty.

6 Getting treasures by a lying tongue
Is the fleeting fantasy of those who seek
death.*a*

7 The violence of the wicked will destroy
them,*a*
Because they refuse to do justice.

8 The way of a guilty man *is* perverse;*a*
But *as for* the pure, his work *is* right.

WHAT'S IT MEAN?

The roof was one of the main features
of ancient Israelite houses. Some people used their
roof as a deck or terrace. Others covered it with a layer of grass
to keep rain from soaking through into the house. Still others
used it to dry foods such as figs and corn in the sun. Usually people
reached the roof via an outside staircase. A railing or low wall
usually ran around the perimeter of the roof to keep
people from falling off.
Proverbs 21:9

9 Better to dwell in a corner of a housetop,
Than in a house shared with a
contentious woman.

10 The soul of the wicked desires evil;
His neighbor finds no favor in his eyes.

11 When the scoffer is punished, the simple
is made wise;
But when the wise is instructed, he
receives knowledge.

12 The righteous *God* wisely considers the
house of the wicked,

20:27 *a*Literally *the rooms of the belly*   **20:30** *a*Literally *the rooms of the belly*   **21:4** *a*Or *lamp*
21:6 *a*Septuagint reads *Pursue vanity on the snares of death;* Vulgate reads *Is vain and foolish, and shall stumble on
the snares of death;* Targum reads *They shall be destroyed, and they shall fall who seek death.*   **21:7** *a*Literally *drag
them away*   **21:8** *a*Or *The way of a man is perverse and strange*

On the Edge

The righteous God wisely considers the house of the wicked, overthrowing the wicked for their wickedness (Prov. 21:12).

As children, we continually watch our brothers and sisters, making sure they never get more than we do. A bigger scoop of ice cream could launch a full-fledged attack of whining. We grow up and hang onto that attitude. In our eyes, no one is entitled to more. No one should be able to get away with anything. The teams should always be equal—the best players evenly distributed. The problem is that we don't always have the whole story. That's where God comes in. He shows up and levels the playing field. He is always fair. He always does what is right. He always rewards those who deserve it. It's just that His ways are different from ours. His timing is perfect. Sometimes you'll get rewarded on earth, and sometimes you won't see the reward until you're in heaven. Next time you think you're being shortchanged, take it up with the Lord. Allow Him to calm your heart and give you eyes to see His fairness.

SEE FOR YOURSELF:
Ezek. 18:20;
Amos 5:24;
Matt. 25:26

Overthrowing the wicked for *their* wickedness.

13 Whoever shuts his ears to the cry of the poor
Will also cry himself and not be heard.

14 A gift in secret pacifies anger,
And a bribe behind the back,[a] strong wrath.

15 *It is* a joy for the just to do justice,
But destruction *will come* to the workers of iniquity.

16 A man who wanders from the way of understanding
Will rest in the assembly of the dead.

17 He who loves pleasure *will be* a poor man;
He who loves wine and oil will not be rich.

18 The wicked *shall be* a ransom for the righteous,
And the unfaithful for the upright.

19 Better to dwell in the wilderness,
Than with a contentious and angry woman.

20 *There is* desirable treasure,
And oil in the dwelling of the wise,
But a foolish man squanders it.

21 He who follows righteousness and mercy
Finds life, righteousness and honor.

22 A wise *man* scales the city of the mighty,
And brings down the trusted stronghold.

23 Whoever guards his mouth and tongue
Keeps his soul from troubles.

24 A proud *and* haughty *man*—"Scoffer" *is* his name;
He acts with arrogant pride.

25 The desire of the lazy *man* kills him,
For his hands refuse to labor.

26 He covets greedily all day long,
But the righteous gives and does not spare.

27 The sacrifice of the wicked *is* an abomination;
How much more *when* he brings it with wicked intent!

28 A false witness shall perish,
But the man who hears *him* will speak endlessly.

29 A wicked man hardens his face,
But *as for* the upright, he establishes[a] his way.

30 *There is* no wisdom or understanding
Or counsel against the LORD.

31 The horse *is* prepared for the day of battle,
But deliverance *is* of the LORD.

21:14 [a]Literally *in the bosom*   **21:29** [a]Qere and Septuagint read *understands.*

1 A *good* name is to be chosen rather than
    great riches,
Loving favor rather than silver and gold.

2 The rich and the poor have this in
    common,
The LORD *is* the maker of them all.

On the Edge

A good name is to be chosen
rather than great riches, loving
favor rather than silver and gold
(Prov. 22:1).

Don't ever let anyone else make decisions about your reputation or your character. So, someone wants you to do something
you don't want to do—they plead with you,
they promise you the moon, they charm
you, they tell you they love you. Your mind
is screaming "No!" Your heart is racing.
Your gut tells you to run. That's the Holy
Spirit speaking to you. Don't miss Him. Do
not be deceived! Do not fall into Satan's
trap. Protect your integrity. Muster up all
your courage and say, "No." Then remove
yourself from temptation. Go
home. Send (or take) your date
home. Get a ride home. Just get
away from the pressure to make
a bad decision. To have a good
name and and to be respected is more
valuable than silver and gold. You are building your character when you make hard
decisions that are right and strong. God
sees your faithfulness, and He will bless
your name.

SEE FOR YOURSELF:
   Prov. 12:3; 15:21;
   Eph. 6:10–17

3 A prudent *man* foresees evil and hides
    himself,
But the simple pass on and are
    punished.

4 By humility *and* the fear
    of the LORD
Are riches and honor and
    life.

5 Thorns *and* snares *are* in
    the way of the
    perverse;

HUMILITY

Does God
bless a
humble
person?
(22:4)

He who guards his soul will be far from
    them.

6 Train up a child in the way he should go,
And when he is old he will not depart
    from it.

7 The rich rules over the poor,
And the borrower *is* servant to the lender.

8 He who sows iniquity will reap sorrow,
And the rod of his anger will fail.

9 He who has a generous eye will be
    blessed,
For he gives of his bread to the poor.

10 Cast out the scoffer, and contention will
    leave;
Yes, strife and reproach will cease.

11 He who loves purity of heart
And has grace on his lips,
The king *will be* his friend.

12 The eyes of the LORD preserve knowledge,
But He overthrows the words of the
    faithless.

13 The lazy *man* says, "*There is* a lion
    outside!
I shall be slain in the streets!"

14 The mouth of an immoral woman *is* a
    deep pit;
He who is abhorred by the LORD will fall
    there.

15 Foolishness *is* bound up in the heart of a
    child;
The rod of correction will drive it far
    from him.

16 He who oppresses the poor to increase
    his *riches,*
And he who gives to the rich, *will* surely
    come to poverty.

SAYINGS OF THE WISE

17 Incline your ear and hear the words of
    the wise,
And apply your heart to my knowledge;

18 For *it is* a pleasant thing if you keep them
    within you;
Let them all be fixed upon your lips,

19 So that your trust may be in the LORD;
I have instructed you today, even you.

20 Have I not written to you excellent
     things
   Of counsels and knowledge,
21 That I may make you know the certainty
     of the words of truth,
   That you may answer words of truth
   To those who send to you?

22 Do not rob the poor because he *is*
     poor,
   Nor oppress the afflicted at the gate;
23 For the LORD will plead their cause,
   And plunder the soul of those who
     plunder them.

24 Make no friendship with an angry man,
   And with a furious man do not go,
25 Lest you learn his ways
   And set a snare for your soul.

26 Do not be one of those who shakes
     hands in a pledge,
   One of those who is surety for debts;
27 If you have nothing *with which* to pay,
   Why should he take away your bed from
     under you?

28 Do not remove the ancient landmark
   Which your fathers have set.

29 Do you see a man *who* excels in his
     work?
   He will stand before kings;
   He will not stand before unknown *men.*

1 When you sit down to eat with a ruler,
   Consider carefully what *is* before you;
2 And put a knife to your throat
   If you *are* a man given to appetite.
3 Do not desire his delicacies,
   For they *are* deceptive food.

4 Do not overwork to be rich;
   Because of your own understanding,
     cease!
5 Will you set your eyes on that which is
     not?
   For *riches* certainly make themselves
     wings;
   They fly away like an eagle *toward*
     heaven.

6 Do not eat the bread of a miser,[a]
   Nor desire his delicacies;
7 For as he thinks in his heart, so *is* he.

On the Edge

Consider carefully what is before you; and put a knife to your throat if you are a man given to appetite. Do not desire his delicacies, for they are deceptive food (Prov. 23:1b–3).

To binge for any reason is to abuse the intended use of food. A variety of emotions could trigger the desire to binge—a great report card, an awful report card, someone really cool asks you out, or everyone leaves you out. Depression, celebration, loneliness, frustration, and anger are some of the feelings that can trigger a massive pig-out. So if any emotion can be a potential reason to eat, then bingeing has to do with self-control.

You can't live your life running from one binge to the next for comfort. Self-control comes from the Holy Spirit. And the Holy Spirit resides in the heart of every believer. You may have already established some really deep patterns in regard to bingeing. If so, a medical professional or counselor may be the best route to understanding how you got to this place, and how the Holy Spirit can restore control.

You shouldn't binge because it's harmful to the temple God gave you and because you are using food to insulate yourself from reality. When you eat instead of dealing with the issues in your life, you stick your head in the sand and hope it'll all go away. When you look up again, the issues are still there, and you still haven't learned to deal with life. Food is a poor substitute for the love and power of God, which are what you really need in order to deal with your life. Learning to run to the Father instead of to food may take a lot of work. But the effort will be worth it. Your life will be changed and God will be pleased.

SEE FOR YOURSELF:
Prov. 13:25; 23:20;
1 Cor. 6:19, 20

"Eat and drink!" he says to you,
   But his heart is not with you.
8 The morsel you have eaten, you will
     vomit up,
   And waste your pleasant words.

23:6 [a]Literally *one who has an evil eye*

9　Do not speak in the hearing of a fool,
For he will despise the wisdom of your
words.

WHAT'S IT MEAN?

In ancient times, property lines were
marked by stones. Since wealth was measured
in part by how much land a person owned, moving those stone
markers was like stealing land from someone else. Such land grab-
bing was forbidden by God's Law.

Proverbs 23:10

10　Do not remove the ancient landmark,
Nor enter the fields of the fatherless;
11　For their Redeemer *is* mighty;
He will plead their cause against you.

12　Apply your heart to instruction,
And your ears to words of knowledge.

13　Do not withhold correction from a child,
For *if* you beat him with a rod, he will
not die.
14　You shall beat him with a rod,
And deliver his soul from hell.*a*

15　My son, if your heart is wise,
My heart will rejoice—indeed, I myself;
16　Yes, my inmost being will rejoice
When your lips speak right things.

17　Do not let your heart envy sinners,
But *be zealous* for the fear of the LORD all
the day;
18　For surely there is a hereafter,
And your hope will not be cut off.

19　Hear, my son, and be wise;
And guide your heart in the way.
20　Do not mix with winebibbers,
Or with gluttonous eaters of meat;
21　For the drunkard and the glutton will
come to poverty,
And drowsiness will clothe *a man* with
rags.

23:14 *a*Or *Sheol*

22　Listen to your father who begot you,
And do not despise your mother when
she is old.

23　Buy the truth, and do not sell *it,*
Also wisdom and instruction and
understanding.

On the Edge

*Who has woe? . . . Who has
redness of eyes? Those who linger
long at the wine, those who go in
search of mixed wine. Do not look on
the wine when it is red, when it
sparkles in the cup, when it swirls
around smoothly; at the last it bites
like a serpent, and stings like a viper.
Your eyes will see strange things, and
your heart will utter perverse things.
Yes, you will be like one who lies down
in the midst of the sea, or like one who
lies at the top of the mast, saying: ". . .
When shall I awake, that I may seek
another drink?" (Prov. 23:29–35)*

The problem with drinking is that it's so
easily abused. Most people don't stop with a
glass of wine at dinner; they continue to
drink until they are either lightheaded and
confused, or drunk and totally disoriented.
Either way, their judgment is impaired.
They can harm themselves or anyone else in
their path.

A lot of believers have decided to just
stay clear of alcohol. Proverbs says it seems
attractive, but eventually it is as devastating
and as painful as a snakebite.

Drinking may cause you to
make decisions that seem fun at
the time, but stupid the next
morning. In fact, it's entirely
possible that you could do something that you have to pay for the rest of
your life. People tell you not to drink because they care that you make wise decisions and that you live a long and healthy
life. You'd be smart to take their advice.
Don't let a chemical control you.

SEE FOR YOURSELF:
Prov. 13:15; 14:18;
20:1; 31:4, 5

24 The father of the righteous will greatly
   rejoice,
   And he who begets a wise *child* will
   delight in him.
25 Let your father and your mother be glad,
   And let her who bore you rejoice.

26 My son, give me your heart,
   And let your eyes observe my ways.
27 For a harlot *is* a deep pit,
   And a seductress *is* a narrow well.
28 She also lies in wait as *for* a victim,
   And increases the unfaithful among men.

29 Who has woe?
   Who has sorrow?
   Who has contentions?
   Who has complaints?
   Who has wounds without cause?
   Who has redness of eyes?
30 Those who linger long at the wine,
   Those who go in search of mixed wine.
31 Do not look on the wine when it is red,
   When it sparkles in the cup,
   When it swirls around smoothly;
32 At the last it bites like a serpent,
   And stings like a viper.
33 Your eyes will see strange things,
   And your heart will utter perverse things.
34 Yes, you will be like one who lies down
   in the midst of the sea,
   Or like one who lies at the top of the
   mast, *saying:*
35 "They have struck me, *but* I was not hurt;
   They have beaten me, but I did not feel *it.*
   When shall I awake, that I may seek
   another *drink?*"

1 Do not be envious of evil men,
   Nor desire to be with them;
2 For their heart devises violence,
   And their lips talk of troublemaking.

3 Through wisdom a
   house is built,
   And by understanding it
   is established;
4 By knowledge the rooms
   are filled
   With all precious and
   pleasant riches.

5 A wise man *is* strong,
   Yes, a man of knowledge increases
   strength;
6 For by wise counsel you will wage your
   own war,

And in a multitude of counselors *there is*
   safety.

7 Wisdom *is* too lofty for a fool;
   He does not open his mouth in the gate.

8 He who plots to do evil
   Will be called a schemer.
9 The devising of foolishness *is* sin,
   And the scoffer *is* an abomination to men.

10 *If* you faint in the day of adversity,
   Your strength *is* small.

11 Deliver *those who* are drawn toward
   death,
   And hold back *those* stumbling to the
   slaughter.
12 If you say, "Surely we did not know this,"
   Does not He who weighs the hearts
   consider *it?*
   He who keeps your soul, does He *not*
   know *it?*
   And will He *not* render to *each* man
   according to his deeds?

13 My son, eat honey because *it is* good,
   And the honeycomb *which is* sweet to
   your taste;
14 So *shall* the knowledge of wisdom *be* to
   your soul;
   If you have found *it,* there is a prospect,
   And your hope will not be cut off.

15 Do not lie in wait, O wicked *man,* against
   the dwelling of the righteous;
   Do not plunder his resting place;
16 For a righteous *man* may fall seven times
   And rise again,
   But the wicked shall fall by calamity.

17 Do not rejoice when your enemy falls,
   And do not let your heart be glad when
   he stumbles;
18 Lest the Lᴏʀᴅ see *it,* and it displease Him,
   And He turn away His wrath from him.

19 Do not fret because of evildoers,
   Nor be envious of the wicked;
20 For there will be no prospect for the evil
   man;
   The lamp of the wicked will be put out.

21 My son, fear the Lᴏʀᴅ and the king;
   Do not associate with those given to
   change;
22 For their calamity will rise suddenly,

WISDOM

Why is
wisdom
important?
(24:3, 4)

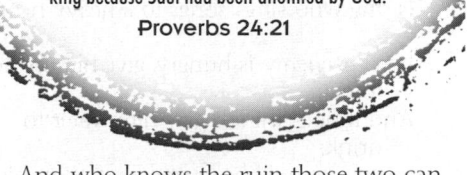

WHAT'S IT MEAN?

The first three kings of Israel were all anointed by a prophet before they were officially crowned. Anointing involved pouring olive oil on the head of the king-to-be. The ritual was important, because it indicated that the king had been chosen by God Himself. Questioning the king's authority was like questioning God's authority. David recognized that when King Saul was trying to kill him. He refused to retaliate against the king because Saul had been anointed by God.

Proverbs 24:21

And who knows the ruin those two can
bring?

FURTHER SAYINGS OF THE WISE

²³These *things* also *belong* to the wise:

It is not good to show partiality in
judgment.
²⁴ He who says to the wicked, "You *are*
righteous,"
Him the people will curse;
Nations will abhor him.
²⁵ But those who rebuke *the wicked* will have
delight,
And a good blessing will come upon them.

²⁶ He who gives a right answer kisses the
lips.

²⁷ Prepare your outside work,
Make it fit for yourself in the field;
And afterward build your house.

²⁸ Do not be a witness against your
neighbor without cause,
For would you deceive*ᵃ* with your lips?
²⁹ Do not say, "I will do to him just as he
has done to me;
I will render to the man according to his
work."

³⁰ I went by the field of the lazy *man*,
And by the vineyard of the man devoid
of understanding;

³¹ And there it was, all overgrown with
thorns;
Its surface was covered with nettles;
Its stone wall was broken down.
³² When I saw *it*, I considered *it* well;
I looked on *it and* received instruction:
³³ A little sleep, a little slumber,
A little folding of the hands to rest;
³⁴ So shall your poverty come *like* a prowler,
And your need like an armed man.

FURTHER WISE SAYINGS OF SOLOMON

¹These also *are* proverbs of Solomon which
the men of Hezekiah king of Judah copied:

² *It is* the glory of God to conceal a matter,
But the glory of kings *is* to search out a
matter.

³ *As* the heavens for height and the earth
for depth,
So the heart of kings *is* unsearchable.

⁴ Take away the dross from silver,
And it will go to the silversmith *for*
jewelry.
⁵ Take away the wicked from before the
king,
And his throne will be established in
righteousness.

⁶ Do not exalt yourself in the presence of
the king,
And do not stand in the place of the great;
⁷ For *it is* better that he say to you,
"Come up here,"
Than that you should be put lower in the
presence of the prince,
Whom your eyes have seen.

⁸ Do not go hastily to court;
For what will you do in the end,
When your neighbor has put you to
shame?
⁹ Debate your case with your neighbor,
And do not disclose the secret to
another;
¹⁰ Lest he who hears *it* expose your shame,
And your reputation be ruined.

¹¹ A word fitly spoken *is like* apples of gold
In settings of silver.
¹² *Like* an earring of gold and an ornament
of fine gold
Is a wise rebuker to an obedient ear.

24:28 *ᵃ*Septuagint and Vulgate read *Do not deceive.*

13 Like the cold of snow in time of harvest
Is a faithful messenger to those who send
him,
For he refreshes the soul of his masters.

14 Whoever falsely boasts of giving
Is like clouds and wind without rain.

15 By long forbearance a ruler is
persuaded,
And a gentle tongue breaks a bone.

16 Have you found honey?
Eat only as much as you need,
Lest you be filled with it and vomit.

17 Seldom set foot in your neighbor's house,
Lest he become weary of you and hate
you.

18 A man who bears false witness against
his neighbor
Is like a club, a sword, and a sharp arrow.

19 Confidence in an unfaithful *man* in time
of trouble
Is like a bad tooth and a foot out of joint.

20 *Like* one who takes away a garment in
cold weather,
And like vinegar on soda,
Is one who sings songs to a heavy heart.

21 If your enemy is hungry, give him bread
to eat;
And if he is thirsty, give him water to
drink;

22 For *so* you will heap coals of fire on his
head,
And the LORD will reward you.

23 The north wind brings forth rain,
And a backbiting tongue an angry
countenance.

24 *It is* better to dwell in a corner of a
housetop,
Than in a house shared with a
contentious woman.

25 *As* cold water to a weary soul,
So *is* good news from a far country.

26 A righteous *man* who falters before the
wicked
Is like a murky spring and a polluted well.

27 *It is* not good to eat much honey;
So to seek one's own glory *is not* glory.

28 Whoever *has* no rule over his own spirit
Is like a city broken down, without walls.

1 As snow in summer and rain in harvest,
So honor is not fitting for a fool.

2 Like a flitting sparrow, like a flying
swallow,
So a curse without cause shall not alight.

3 A whip for the horse,
A bridle for the donkey,
And a rod for the fool's back.

On the Edge

A man who bears false witness against his neighbor is like a club, a sword, and a sharp arrow. Confidence in an unfaithful man in time of trouble is like a bad tooth and a foot out of joint. . . . If your enemy is hungry, give him bread to eat; and if he is thirsty, give him water to drink; for so you will heap coals of fire on his head, and the LORD will reward you (Prov. 25:18, 19, 21, 22).

Here in Proverbs and later in the New Testament, the writers give us some wisdom about friends who tell lies or treat us badly. The advice is to do exactly the opposite of what your friends do. Even in your disappointment and anger, you are supposed to be Christlike. Luke 6:28 says to "bless those who curse you, and pray for those who spitefully use you." By loving those who hurt you, "you will heap coals of fire on his head." Wow, that's pretty hard advice. Your reputation has been shattered. Your pride has been wounded. Your tender heart is broken. And God wants you to do what? Yep, He says to love them anyway—even give food to them if they are hungry. Oh yeah, and pray for them, too. By doing so, you prove the strength of your character. That's God's way.

SEE FOR YOURSELF:
Matt. 18:21, 22;
Luke 6:28; 17:3, 4;
Col. 3:13

4 Do not answer a fool according to his
folly,
Lest you also be like him.
5 Answer a fool according to his folly,
Lest he be wise in his own eyes.
6 He who sends a message by the hand of
a fool
Cuts off *his own* feet *and* drinks violence.
7 *Like* the legs of the lame that hang limp
Is a proverb in the mouth of fools.
8 Like one who binds a stone in a sling
Is he who gives honor to a fool.
9 *Like* a thorn *that* goes into the hand of a
drunkard
Is a proverb in the mouth of fools.
10 The great *God* who formed everything
Gives the fool *his* hire and the
transgressor *his* wages.[a]
11 As a dog returns to his own vomit,
So a fool repeats his folly.
12 Do you see a man wise in his own eyes?
There is more hope for a fool than for
him.

13 The lazy *man* says, "*There is* a lion in the
road!
A fierce lion *is* in the streets!"
14 *As* a door turns on its hinges,
So *does* the lazy *man* on his bed.
15 The lazy *man* buries his hand in the
bowl;[a]
It wearies him to bring it back to his
mouth.
16 The lazy *man is* wiser in his own eyes
Than seven men who can answer
sensibly.

17 He who passes by *and* meddles in a
quarrel not his own
Is like one who takes a dog by the ears.

18 Like a madman who throws firebrands,
arrows, and death,
19 *Is* the man *who* deceives his neighbor,
And says, "I was only joking!"

20 Where *there is* no wood, the
fire goes out;
And where *there is* no
talebearer, strife ceases.
21 *As* charcoal *is* to burning
coals, and wood to
fire,
So *is* a contentious man
to kindle strife.

GOSSIP

What is one
benefit found
when gossip
is stopped?
(26:20)

On the Edge

*He who passes by and meddles in
a quarrel not his own is like one
who takes a dog by the ears (Prov.
26:17).*

Your friends are arguing? Get out. Hurry.
Proverbs 26:17 says it would be better to
grab a dog by the ears than to take part in
your friends' argument. The middle of your
friends' argument is a lose-lose situation.
The best that could happen is that
they will make up, and only one
of them will be mad at you.
Politely tell them that you love
them both too much to be pulled
into their disagreement. No matter what
you think, it's best to keep your mouth
shut. They have to resolve things themselves. You can't relay information. Refuse
to take sides. Let them both know that you
want to spend time with them, but until
this whole thing blows over, you have to
step aside. Let them work it out. You will be
spared lots of time and heartache if you
quickly get out of the picture.

SEE FOR YOURSELF:
Prov. 11:12; 13:3;
17:27; 27:12

22 The words of a talebearer *are* like tasty
trifles,
And they go down into the inmost
body.

23 Fervent lips with a wicked heart
Are like earthenware covered with silver
dross.

24 He who hates, disguises *it* with his lips,
And lays up deceit within himself;
25 When he speaks kindly, do not believe
him,
For *there are* seven abominations in his
heart;
26 *Though his* hatred is covered by deceit,
His wickedness will be revealed before the
assembly.

27 Whoever digs a pit will fall into it,
And he who rolls a stone will have it roll
back on him.

26:10 [a]The Hebrew is difficult; ancient and modern translators differ greatly.   **26:15** [a]Compare 19:24

28 A lying tongue hates *those who are*
      crushed by it,
   And a flattering mouth works ruin.

1 Do not boast about tomorrow,
   For you do not know what a day may
      bring forth.

2 Let another man praise you, and not your
      own mouth;
   A stranger, and not your own lips.

3 A stone *is* heavy and sand *is* weighty,
   But a fool's wrath *is* heavier than both of
      them.

4 Wrath *is* cruel and anger a torrent,
   But who *is* able to stand before jealousy?

5 Open rebuke *is* better
   Than love carefully concealed.

6 Faithful *are* the wounds of a friend,
   But the kisses of an enemy *are* deceitful.

7 A satisfied soul loathes the honeycomb,
   But to a hungry soul every bitter thing *is*
      sweet.

8 Like a bird that wanders from its nest
   Is a man who wanders from his place.

9 Ointment and perfume delight the heart,
   And the sweetness of a man's friend *gives*
      delight by hearty counsel.

10 Do not forsake your own friend or your
      father's friend,
   Nor go to your brother's house in the
      day of your calamity;
   Better *is* a neighbor nearby than a brother
      far away.

11 My son, be wise, and make my heart glad,
   That I may answer him who reproaches
      me.

12 A prudent *man* foresees evil *and* hides
      himself;
   The simple pass on *and* are punished.

13 Take the garment of him who is surety
      for a stranger,
   And hold it in pledge *when* he is surety
      for a seductress.

14 He who blesses his friend with a loud
      voice, rising early in the morning,
   It will be counted a curse to him.

15 A continual dripping on a very rainy day
   And a contentious woman are alike;
16 Whoever restrains her restrains the wind,
   And grasps oil with his right hand.

17 *As* iron sharpens iron,
   So a man sharpens the countenance of
      his friend.

18 Whoever keeps the fig tree will eat its
      fruit;
   So he who waits on his master will be
      honored.

19 As in water face *reflects* face,
   So a man's heart *reveals* the man.

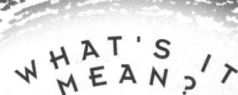

WHAT'S IT
MEAN?

The ancient Hebrews pictured death as a
monster with an enormous mouth and an appetite
that was never satisfied. No matter how many people
it "ate," there was always room for more.
Proverbs 27:20

20 Hell*a* and Destruction*b* are never full;
   So the eyes of man are never satisfied.

21 The refining pot *is* for silver and the
      furnace for gold,
   And a man *is valued* by what others say
      of him.

22 Though you grind a fool in a mortar with
      a pestle along with crushed grain,
   Yet his foolishness will not depart from
      him.

23 Be diligent to know the state of your
      flocks,
   And attend to your herds;
24 For riches *are* not forever,

27:20 *a*Or *Sheol* *b*Hebrew *Abaddon*

Nor does a crown *endure* to all generations.

25 *When* the hay is removed, and the tender grass shows itself,
And the herbs of the mountains are gathered in,

26 The lambs *will provide* your clothing,
And the goats the price of a field;

27 *You shall have* enough goats' milk for your food,
For the food of your household,
And the nourishment of your maidservants.

1 The wicked flee when no one pursues,
But the righteous are bold as a lion.

2 Because of the transgression of a land,
many *are* its princes;
But by a man of understanding *and* knowledge
Right will be prolonged.

3 A poor man who oppresses the poor
Is like a driving rain which leaves no food.

4 Those who forsake the law praise the wicked,
But such as keep the law contend with them.

5 Evil men do not understand justice,
But those who seek the LORD understand all.

6 Better *is* the poor who walks in his integrity
Than one perverse *in his* ways, though he *be* rich.

7 Whoever keeps the law *is* a discerning son,
But a companion of gluttons shames his father.

8 One who increases his possessions by usury and extortion
Gathers it for him who will pity the poor.

9 One who turns away his ear from hearing the law,
Even his prayer *is* an abomination.

10 Whoever causes the upright to go astray in an evil way,
He himself will fall into his own pit;
But the blameless will inherit good.

WHAT'S IT MEAN?

Banking rules in ancient Israel were pretty strict. God's Law prohibited people from charging interest on loans made to poor people. Borrowers could not be forced to give up their coats as collateral for loans. Lenders were not allowed to use force to collect payment. The way God saw it, every person in the community was responsible for taking care of the poor, the widowed, the orphaned, and the disabled members of society.

Proverbs 28:8

11 The rich man *is* wise in his own eyes,
But the poor who has understanding searches him out.

12 When the righteous rejoice, *there is* great glory;
But when the wicked arise, men hide themselves.

13 He who covers his sins will not prosper,
But whoever confesses and forsakes *them* will have mercy.

14 Happy *is* the man who is always reverent,
But he who hardens his heart will fall into calamity.

15 *Like* a roaring lion and a charging bear
Is a wicked ruler over poor people.

WHAT'S IT MEAN?

Believe it or not, lions and bears were serious problems in ancient Israel. Lions often hid in the tall grass beside the Jordan River or in the surrounding forests and attacked unsuspecting people. The Asian black bears in the area were a threat not only to humans, but also to livestock and even crops.

Proverbs 28:15

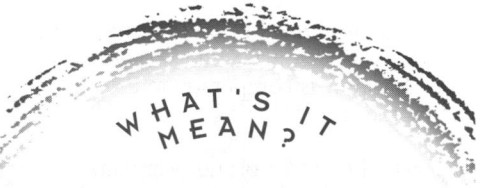

16 A ruler who lacks understanding *is* a
great oppressor,
But he who hates covetousness will
prolong *his* days.

17 A man burdened with bloodshed will flee
into a pit;
Let no one help him.

18 Whoever walks blamelessly will be
saved,
But *he who is* perverse *in his* ways will
suddenly fall.

19 He who tills his land will
have plenty of bread,
But he who follows
frivolity will have
poverty enough!

20 A faithful man will
abound with
blessings,
But he who hastens to
be rich will not go
unpunished.

21 To show partiality *is* not good,
Because for a piece of bread a man will
transgress.

22 A man with an evil eye hastens after
riches,
And does not consider that poverty will
come upon him.

23 He who rebukes a man will find more
favor afterward
Than he who flatters with the tongue.

24 Whoever robs his father or his mother,
And says, "*It is* no transgression,"
The same *is* companion to a
destroyer.

25 He who is of a proud heart stirs
up strife,
But he who trusts in the
LORD will be
prospered.

26 He who trusts in his
own heart is a fool,
But whoever walks
wisely will be delivered.

27 He who gives to the poor will not lack,
But he who hides his eyes will have
many curses.

28 When the wicked arise, men hide
themselves;
But when they perish, the righteous
increase.

1 He who is often rebuked, *and* hardens *his*
neck,
Will suddenly be destroyed, and that
without remedy.

2 When the righteous are
in authority, the
people rejoice;
But when a wicked
man rules, the
people groan.

3 Whoever loves
wisdom makes his
father rejoice,
But a companion of
harlots wastes *his*
wealth.

4 The king establishes the land by justice,
But he who receives bribes overthrows it.

5 A man who flatters his neighbor
Spreads a net for his feet.

6 By transgression an evil man is snared,
But the righteous sings and rejoices.

7 The righteous considers the cause of the
poor,
But the wicked does not understand *such*
knowledge.

8 Scoffers set a city aflame,
But wise *men* turn away wrath.

9 *If* a wise man contends with a foolish
man,
Whether *the fool* rages or laughs, *there is*
no peace.

10 The bloodthirsty hate the blameless,
But the upright seek his well-being.[a]

11 A fool vents all his feelings,[a]
But a wise *man* holds them back.

"Whoever walks blamelessly
will be saved,
but he who is perverse in his
ways will suddenly fall."
(Proverbs 28:18)

TRUST

How does the
Lord bless
those who
trust Him?
(28:25, 26)

29:10 [a]Literally *soul*   **29:11** [a]Literally *spirit*

12 If a ruler pays attention to lies,
All his servants *become* wicked.

13 The poor *man* and the oppressor have
this in common:
The LORD gives light to the eyes of both.

14 The king who judges the poor with truth,
His throne will be established forever.

15 The rod and rebuke give wisdom,
But a child left *to himself* brings shame to
his mother.

16 When the wicked are multiplied,
transgression increases;
But the righteous will see their fall.

17 Correct your son, and he will give you rest;
Yes, he will give delight to your soul.

18 Where *there is* no revelation,*a* the people
cast off restraint;
But happy *is* he who keeps the law.

19 A servant will not be corrected by mere
words;
For though he understands, he will not
respond.

20 Do you see a man hasty in his words?
There is more hope for a fool than for him.

21 He who pampers his servant from
childhood
Will have him as a son in the end.

22 An angry man stirs up strife,
And a furious man abounds in
transgression.

23 A man's pride will bring him low,
But the humble in
spirit will retain
honor.

24 Whoever is a partner
with a thief hates his
own life;
He swears to tell the truth,*a*
but reveals nothing.

25 The fear of man brings a snare,
But whoever trusts in the LORD shall be
safe.

EMBARRASSMENT

What causes
embarrass-
ment?
(29:23)

26 Many seek the ruler's favor,
But justice for man *comes* from the LORD.

27 An unjust man *is* an abomination to the
righteous,
And *he who is* upright in the way *is* an
abomination to the wicked.

THE WISDOM OF AGUR

1 The words of Agur the son of Jakeh, *his* utterance. This man declared to Ithiel—to Ithiel
and Ucal:

2 Surely I *am* more stupid than *any* man,
And do not have the understanding of a
man.

3 I neither learned wisdom
Nor have knowledge of the Holy One.

4 Who has ascended into heaven, or
descended?
Who has gathered the wind in His fists?
Who has bound the waters in a garment?
Who has established all the ends of the
earth?
What *is* His name, and what *is* His Son's
name,
If you know?

5 Every word of God *is* pure;
He *is* a shield to those who put their trust
in Him.

6 Do not add to His words,
Lest He rebuke you, and you be found a
liar.

7 Two *things* I request of You
(Deprive me not before I die):

8 Remove falsehood and lies far from me;
Give me neither poverty nor riches—
Feed me with the food allotted to me;

9 Lest I be full and deny *You,*
And say, "Who *is* the LORD?"
Or lest I be poor and steal,
And profane the name of my God.

10 Do not malign a servant to his master,
Lest he curse you, and you be found
guilty.

11 *There is* a generation *that* curses its father,
And does not bless its mother.

12 *There is* a generation *that is* pure in its
own eyes,
Yet is not washed from its filthiness.

29:18 *a*Or *prophetic vision*   **29:24** *a*Literally *hears the adjuration*

13 There is a generation—oh, how lofty are
   their eyes!
   And their eyelids are lifted up.
14 There is a generation whose teeth *are like*
   swords,
   And whose fangs *are like* knives,
   To devour the poor from off the earth,
   And the needy from *among* men.

15 The leech has two daughters—
   Give *and* Give!

   There are three *things that* are never
   satisfied,
   Four never say, "Enough!":
16 The grave,*a*
   The barren womb,
   The earth *that* is not satisfied with water—
   And the fire never says, "Enough!"

17 The eye *that* mocks *his* father,
   And scorns obedience to *his* mother,
   The ravens of the valley will pick it out,
   And the young eagles will eat it.

18 There are three *things which* are too
   wonderful for me,
   Yes, four *which* I do not understand:
19 The way of an eagle in the air,

The way of a serpent on a rock,
The way of a ship in the midst of the sea,
And the way of a man with a virgin.

20 This *is* the way of an adulterous woman:
   She eats and wipes her mouth,
   And says, "I have done no wickedness."

21 For three *things* the earth is perturbed,
   Yes, for four it cannot bear up:
22 For a servant when he reigns,
   A fool when he is filled with food,
23 A hateful *woman* when she is married,
   And a maidservant who succeeds her
   mistress.

24 There are four *things which* are little on
   the earth,
   But they *are* exceedingly wise:
25 The ants *are* a people not strong,
   Yet they prepare their food in the
   summer;
26 The rock badgers*a* are a feeble folk,
   Yet they make their homes in the crags;
27 The locusts have no king,
   Yet they all advance in ranks;
28 The spider*a* skillfully grasps with its
   hands,
   And it is in kings' palaces.

30:16 *a*Or *Sheol*   **30:26** *a*Or *hyraxes*   **30:28** *a*Or *lizard*

Promise
HE PROMISES THAT EVERYTHING HE SAYS IS TRUE.

Every word of God is pure; He is a shield to those who put their trust in Him (Prov. 30:5).

Have you ever told "a little white lie"? You know, what you said was not quite true, but it didn't hurt anybody and it got you out of a tight spot. Or maybe your skill is telling your mom something that is *technically* true. When you've finished explaining, what she thinks happened and what really happened are two different things. That's the way human beings are—they shade the truth this way and that, turning what's black and white into shades of gray.

But God isn't like that. Everything He says is pure and true, not barely sliding by on a variation of the truth. His honesty doesn't depend on technicalities. And God isn't just honest. He's also right. You might make a statement that you thought was true, only to find out later that you were wrong. But God doesn't make mistakes.

His word is so reliable that you can use it for a shield. That's what Jesus did when Satan tempted Him (see Matt. 4:1–11). He used God's words to protect His heart. It's good to know that there are no cracks in the shield: Everything He says is true.

SEE FOR YOURSELF:
Prov. 12:19; Matt. 4:1–11

29 There are three *things which* are majestic
   in pace,
   Yes, four *which* are stately in walk:
30 A lion, *which is* mighty among beasts
   And does not turn away from any;
31 A greyhound,[a]
   A male goat also,
   And a king *whose* troops *are* with him.[b]

32 If you have been foolish in exalting
   yourself,
   Or if you have devised evil, *put your* hand
   on *your* mouth.
33 For *as* the churning of milk produces
   butter,
   And wringing the nose produces blood,
   So the forcing of wrath produces strife.

THE WORDS OF KING LEMUEL'S MOTHER

1 The words of King Lemuel, the utterance
which his mother taught him:

2 What, my son?
   And what, son of my womb?
   And what, son of my vows?
3 Do not give your strength to women,
   Nor your ways to that which destroys
   kings.

4 *It is* not for kings, O Lemuel,
   It is not for kings to drink wine,
   Nor for princes intoxicating drink;
5 Lest they drink and forget the law,
   And pervert the justice of all the afflicted.
6 Give strong drink to him who is
   perishing,
   And wine to those who are bitter of
   heart.
7 Let him drink and forget his poverty,
   And remember his misery no more.

8 Open your mouth for the speechless,
   In the cause of all *who are* appointed to
   die.[a]
9 Open your mouth, judge righteously,
   And plead the cause of the poor and
   needy.

THE VIRTUOUS WIFE

10 Who[a] can find a virtuous[b] wife?
   For her worth *is* far above rubies.
11 The heart of her husband safely trusts
   her;

So he will have no lack of gain.
12 She does him good and not evil
   All the days of her life.
13 She seeks wool and flax,
   And willingly works with her hands.
14 She is like the merchant ships,
   She brings her food from afar.
15 She also rises while it is yet night,
   And provides food for her household,
   And a portion for her maidservants.
16 She considers a field and buys it;
   From her profits she plants a vineyard.
17 She girds herself with strength,
   And strengthens her arms.
18 She perceives that her
   merchandise *is* good,
   And her lamp does not
   go out by night.
19 She stretches out her
   hands to the distaff,
   And her hand holds the
   spindle.
20 She extends her hand to the
   poor,
   Yes, she reaches out her hands to the
   needy.
21 She is not afraid of snow for her
   household,
   For all her household *is* clothed with
   scarlet.
22 She makes tapestry for herself;
   Her clothing *is* fine linen and purple.
23 Her husband is known in the gates,
   When he sits among the elders of the land.
24 She makes linen garments and sells *them*,
   And supplies sashes for the merchants.
25 Strength and honor *are* her clothing;
   She shall rejoice in time to come.
26 She opens her mouth with wisdom,
   And on her tongue *is* the law of kindness.
27 She watches over the ways of her
   household,
   And does not eat the bread of idleness.
28 Her children rise up and call her blessed;
   Her husband *also*, and he praises her:
29 "Many daughters have done well,
   But you excel them all."
30 Charm *is* deceitful and beauty *is* passing,
   But a woman *who* fears the LORD, she
   shall be praised.
31 Give her of the fruit of her hands,
   And let her own works praise her in the
   gates.

RESPECT

Is respect
easily
gained?
(31:10, 11,
18–23)

30:31 [a]Exact identity unknown [b]A Jewish tradition reads *a king against whom there is no uprising.*
31:8 [a]Literally *sons of passing away* **31:10** [a]Verses 10 through 31 are an alphabetic acrostic in Hebrew
(compare Psalm 119). [b]Literally *a wife of valor,* in the sense of all forms of excellence

ecclesiastes

CONTENT

Ecclesiastes was written by a man who had it all and found out it wasn't enough.

You've got to understand that he *literally* had it all. He had all the money you could imagine. He had the possessions of the richest man on earth. He had wives and wannabe-wives at every turn. He had unlimited power. He had prestige. He had superstardom and fame. Everything his society could make available was his.

He also did everything. He tried every kind of recreation. Every form of entertainment and amusement was his for the bidding. What a life!

After he had it all and did it all, he wrote this book to leave a legacy of what he thought about having it all. He said, "Without God, none of it matters."

Some people think Ecclesiastes is a little depressing. After all, we spend our lives wanting the things this man, King Solomon, had. It's not much fun to think that everything we dream about won't really bring us happiness. On the other hand, though, putting our lives in perspective with God out in front should mean we'll enjoy our lives more because everything we do means something.

Outline

1:1—2:26 .... The Search for Meaning in Life
3:1–8 .... Everything Has Its Time
3:9—6:12 .... Life Isn't Always Fair, So Live Wisely
7:1—8:17 .... Practical Wisdom
9:1—11:6 .... No One Knows What the Future Will Bring
11:7—12:14 .... Respect and Obey God

Purpose

Apart from God, life can have no meaning.

Theme

A Quest for Something of True Value in This Life

Date of writing

935 B.C.

> "Let us hear the conclusion of the whole matter: Fear God and keep His commandments, for this is man's all. For God will bring every work into judgment, including every secret thing, whether good or evil" (12:13, 14).

Bible Talk

Solomon's Wealth

It is true that in Solomon's day he didn't have all the conveniences that we have today. He didn't have electricity or computers or automobiles. But don't let that fool you. Solomon had stuff that would turn the heads of people in any age. The Bible says that he made silver as common as stones. He was surrounded by gold. He had hundreds of wives. He lived in an extravagant, beautiful palace. There was nothing that he might want that he couldn't have.

He had all this because, when God came to him in a dream and said He would give Solomon anything he asked for, Solomon asked for wisdom. He didn't ask for riches or wives or horses. God honored Solomon's wisdom by giving it all to him.

CELEBRITIES

We look at a lot of celebrities today like Solomon's people would have looked at him. We assume that because they *have* a lot of things and money to buy more things that they must be happy. We assume that if we had everything a celebrity has then we would be happy. Ecclesiastes tells us otherwise. We don't often get to sit down and have a heart-to-heart with superstars. But that's exactly what Ecclesiastes is. It seems like he would be saying, "Come on over to money, fame, and fortune! The water's nice and warm!" Instead he's saying, "If you are not connected to God, if He's not the source of your joy, you won't find it here any more than you find it right where you are."

THE VANITY OF LIFE

¹The words of the Preacher, the son of David, king in Jerusalem.

² "Vanity*a* of vanities", says the Preacher;
"Vanity of vanities, all *is* vanity."

³ What profit has a man from all his labor
In which he toils under the sun?
⁴ *One* generation passes away, and *another*
generation comes;
But the earth abides forever.
⁵ The sun also rises, and the sun goes
down,
And hastens to the place where it arose.
⁶ The wind goes toward the south,
And turns around to the north;
The wind whirls about continually,
And comes again on its circuit.
⁷ All the rivers run into the sea,
Yet the sea *is* not full;
To the place from which the rivers come,
There they return again.
⁸ All things *are* full of labor;
Man cannot express *it.*
The eye is not satisfied with seeing,
Nor the ear filled with hearing.

⁹ That which has been *is* what will be,
That which *is* done is what will be done,
And *there is* nothing new under the sun.
¹⁰ Is there anything of which it may be said,
"See, this *is* new"?
It has already been in ancient times
before us.
¹¹ *There is* no remembrance of former *things,*
Nor will there be any remembrance of
things that are to come
By *those* who will come after.

THE GRIEF OF WISDOM

¹²I, the Preacher, was king over Israel in Jerusalem. ¹³And I set my heart to seek and search out by wisdom concerning all that is done under heaven; this burdensome task God has given to the sons of man, by which they may be exercised. ¹⁴I have seen all the works that are done under the sun; and indeed, all *is* vanity and grasping for the wind.

On the Edge

All things are full of labor; man cannot express it. The eye is not satisfied with seeing, nor the ear filled with hearing (Eccl. 1:8).

A lot of people spend all their lives trying to get satisfied. Cars, clothes, tattoos, body piercing, drugs—whatever the latest thing is to make you feel like somebody. Solomon says in Ecclesiastes that nothing will ever do it. Nothing will ever make you feel satisfied. New clothes may fill you up for a few days. And then you're empty again. The high doesn't last long enough. Without Jesus, nothing matters. There is no purpose in life, and even the coolest stuff only brings momentary pleasure. Solomon says that apart from Jesus you will never enjoy your time on earth or the things you've been given. It's all meaningless without the Savior. Without Jesus, this is all there is—no future, no eternity to look forward to. So when your heart is aching, your life seems empty, and you feel lost, go to Jesus to be filled up and satisfied. He will not disappoint you.

SEE FOR YOURSELF:
1 Cor 15:58; Gal. 6:8;
Phil. 3:7, 12–14

WHAT'S IT MEAN?

Solomon was something of a celebrity during his lifetime. During his forty-year reign as king, people would come to Jerusalem from faraway countries just to hear Solomon say something wise. Not only did Solomon know a lot about human nature and the scientific world, he is also considered to be the most important and influential philosopher of the ancient Near East.
Ecclesiastes 1:16

¹⁵ *What is* crooked cannot be made straight,
And what is lacking cannot be numbered.

¹⁶I communed with my heart, saying, "Look, I have attained greatness, and have gained more wisdom than all who were before me in Jerusa-

lem. My heart has understood great wisdom and knowledge." [17]And I set my heart to know wisdom and to know madness and folly. I perceived that this also is grasping for the wind.

[18] For in much wisdom *is* much grief,
And he who increases knowledge
increases sorrow.

THE VANITY OF PLEASURE

[1]I said in my heart, "Come now, I will test you with mirth; therefore enjoy pleasure"; but surely, this also *was* vanity. [2]I said of laughter— "Madness!"; and of mirth, "What does it accomplish?" [3]I searched in my heart *how* to gratify my flesh with wine, while guiding my heart with wisdom, and how to lay hold on folly, till I might see what *was* good for the sons of men to do under heaven all the days of their lives.

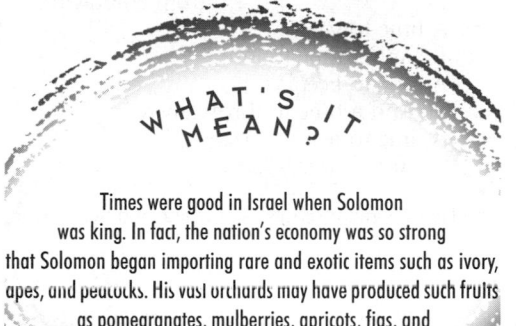

Times were good in Israel when Solomon was king. In fact, the nation's economy was so strong that Solomon began importing rare and exotic items such as ivory, apes, and peacocks. His vast orchards may have produced such fruits as pomegranates, mulberries, apricots, figs, and apples, as well as almonds and sycamores.
Ecclesiastes 2:4, 5

[4]I made my works great, I built myself houses, and planted myself vineyards. [5]I made myself gardens and orchards, and I planted all *kinds* of fruit trees in them. [6]I made myself water pools from which to water the growing trees of the grove. [7]I acquired male and female servants, and had servants born in my house. Yes, I had greater possessions of herds and flocks than all who were in Jerusalem before me. [8]I also gathered for myself silver and gold and the special treasures of kings and of the provinces. I acquired male and female singers, the delights of the sons of men, *and* musical instruments[a] of all kinds.

[9]So I became great and excelled more than all who were before me in Jerusalem. Also my wisdom remained with me.

[10] Whatever my eyes desired I did not keep from them.
I did not withhold my heart from any pleasure,
For my heart rejoiced in all my labor;
And this was my reward from all my labor.
[11] Then I looked on all the works that my hands had done
And on the labor in which I had toiled;
And indeed all *was* vanity and grasping for the wind.
There was no profit under the sun.

THE END OF THE WISE AND THE FOOL

[12] Then I turned myself to consider wisdom and madness and folly;
For what *can* the man *do* who succeeds the king?—
Only what he has already done.
[13] Then I saw that wisdom excels folly
As light excels darkness.
[14] The wise man's eyes *are* in his head,
But the fool walks in darkness.
Yet I myself perceived
That the same event happens to them all.

[15] So I said in my heart,
"As it happens to the fool,
It also happens to me,
And why was I then more wise?"
Then I said in my heart,
"This also *is* vanity."
[16] For *there is* no more remembrance of the wise than of the fool forever,
Since all that now *is* will be forgotten in the days to come.
And how does a wise *man* die?
As the fool!

[17]Therefore I hated life because the work that was done under the sun *was* distressing to me, for all *is* vanity and grasping for the wind. [18]Then I hated all my labor in which I had toiled under the sun, because I must leave it to the man who will come after me. [19]And who knows whether he will be wise or a fool? Yet he will rule over all my labor in which I toiled and in which I have shown myself wise under the sun. This also *is* vanity. [20]Therefore I turned my heart and despaired of all the labor in which I had toiled under the sun. [21]For there is a man whose labor *is* with wisdom, knowledge, and skill; yet he must leave his heritage to a man

2:8 [a]Exact meaning unknown

who has not labored for it. This also *is* vanity and a great evil. ²²For what has man for all his labor, and for the striving of his heart with which he has toiled under the sun? ²³For all his days *are* sorrowful, and his work burdensome; even in the night his heart takes no rest. This also is vanity.

²⁴Nothing *is* better for a man *than* that he should eat and drink, and *that* his soul should enjoy good in his labor. This also, I saw, was from the hand of God. ²⁵For who can eat, or who can have enjoyment, more than I?ᵃ ²⁶For *God* gives wisdom and knowledge and joy to a man who *is* good in His sight; but to the sinner He gives the work of gathering and collecting, that he may give to *him who is* good before God. This also *is* vanity and grasping for the wind.

EVERYTHING HAS ITS TIME

1 To everything *there is* a season,
A time for every purpose under heaven:

"To everything there is a season, a time for every purpose under heaven."
(Ecclesiastes 3:1)

2 A time to be born,
And a time to die;
A time to plant,
And a time to pluck *what is* planted;
3 A time to kill,
And a time to heal;
A time to break down,
And a time to build up;
4 A time to weep,
And a time to laugh;
A time to mourn,
And a time to dance;
5 A time to cast away stones,
And a time to gather stones;
A time to embrace,
And a time to refrain from embracing;
6 A time to gain,
And a time to lose;
A time to keep,
And a time to throw away;
7 A time to tear,
And a time to sew;

2:25 ᵃFollowing Masoretic Text, Targum, and Vulgate; some Hebrew manuscripts, Septuagint, and Syriac read *without Him.*

Promise   HE PROMISES TO MAKE EVERYTHING HAPPEN IN ITS TIME.

[God] has made everything beautiful in its time. Also He has put eternity in their hearts, except that no one can find out the work that God does from beginning to end (Eccl. 3:11).

You're walking down the hall thinking about the two brand-new five-dollar bills in your wallet, and a guy you owe three bucks to comes around the corner. You're really tempted to cheat on a test, but the smart girl who sits next to you is absent that day. You're thinking about sending a card to a girl who looks like she needs cheering up, and when you find your student directory in the bottom of your locker, it's opened to the page that has her address on it.

Coincidences? If you've been hanging out with God for very long, you probably don't think so. He has a way of bringing even these little things together at the right time. It's one of the ways He reminds us that He's got everything under control.

That's His way with the big things in life, too. The list that Solomon put together in Ecclesiastes 3:1–8 includes some things that don't sound too good. But everything God allows in your life—even sadness—has a purpose, and He has worked out the timing perfectly. He can do that because He knows you better than you do. And He knows what's coming next, too. If the timing seems lousy to you, trust that God knows something you don't know.

SEE FOR YOURSELF:
Acts 4:28; Rom. 8:28; 2 Tim. 1:9

A time to keep silence,
And a time to speak;
8   A time to love,
And a time to hate;
A time of war,
And a time of peace.

THE GOD-GIVEN TASK

[9]What profit has the worker from that in which he labors? [10]I have seen the God-given task with which the sons of men are to be occupied. [11]He has made everything beautiful in its time. Also He has put eternity in their hearts, except that no one can find out the work that God does from beginning to end.

[12]I know that nothing *is* better for them than to rejoice, and to do good in their lives, [13]and also that every man should eat and drink and enjoy the good of all his labor—it *is* the gift of God.

14   I know that whatever God does,
It shall be forever.
Nothing can be added to it,
And nothing taken from it.
God does *it*, that men should fear before Him.
15   That which is has already been,
And what is to be has already been;
And God requires an account of what is past.

INJUSTICE SEEMS TO PREVAIL

[16]Moreover I saw under the sun:

In the place of judgment,
Wickedness *was* there;
And *in* the place of righteousness,
Iniquity *was* there.

[17]I said in my heart,

"God shall judge the righteous and the wicked,
For *there is* a time there for every purpose and for every work."

[18]I said in my heart, "Concerning the condition of the sons of men, God tests them, that they may see that they themselves are *like* animals." [19]For what happens to the sons of men also happens to animals; one thing befalls them: as one dies, so dies the other. Surely, they all have one breath; man has no advantage over ani-

mals, for all *is* vanity. [20]All go to one place: all are from the dust, and all return to dust. [21]Who knows the spirit of the sons of men, which goes upward, and the spirit of the animal, which goes down to the earth?[a] [22]So I perceived that nothing *is* better than that a man should rejoice in his own works, for that *is* his heritage. For who can bring him to see what will happen after him?

[1]Then I returned and considered all the oppression that is done under the sun:

And look! The tears of the oppressed,
But they have no comforter—
On the side of their oppressors *there is* power,
But they have no comforter.
2   Therefore I praised the dead who were already dead,
More than the living who are still alive.
3   Yet, better than both *is he* who has never existed,
Who has not seen the evil work that is done under the sun.

THE VANITY OF SELFISH TOIL

[4]Again, I saw that for all toil and every skillful work a man is envied by his neighbor. This also *is* vanity and grasping for the wind.

5   The fool folds his hands
And consumes his own flesh.
6   Better a handful *with* quietness
Than both hands full, *together with* toil and grasping for the wind.

WHAT'S IT MEAN?

In ancient times, true success was measured by the size of a person's family. The more kids a person had, the more successful—and favored by God—he was thought to be. Women who were unable to bear children were thought to be cursed by God. Since parents were expected to provide for their kids' needs, it made sense that they would work hard.

Ecclesiastes 4:8

3:21 [a]Septuagint, Syriac, Targum, and Vulgate read *Who knows whether the spirit . . . goes upward, and whether . . . goes downward to the earth?*

7Then I returned, and I saw vanity under the sun:

8   There is one alone, without companion:
He has neither son nor brother.
Yet *there is* no end to all his labors,
Nor is his eye satisfied with riches.
But he never asks,
"For whom do I toil and deprive myself of good?"
This also *is* vanity and a grave misfortune.

THE VALUE OF A FRIEND

9   Two *are* better than one,
Because they have a good reward for their labor.

10   For if they fall, one will lift up his companion.

But woe to him *who is* alone when he falls,
For *he has* no one to help him up.

11   Again, if two lie down together, they will keep warm;
But how can one be warm *alone*?

12   Though one may be overpowered by another, two can withstand him.
And a threefold cord is not quickly broken.

POPULARITY PASSES AWAY

13   Better a poor and wise youth
Than an old and foolish king who will be admonished no more.

14   For he comes out of prison to be king,
Although he was born poor in his kingdom.

15   I saw all the living who walk under the sun;
They were with the second youth who stands in his place.

16   *There was* no end of all the people over whom he was made king;
Yet those who come afterward will not rejoice in him.
Surely this also *is* vanity and grasping for the wind.

FEAR GOD, KEEP YOUR VOWS

1Walk prudently when you go to the house of God; and draw near to hear rather than to give the sacrifice of fools, for they do not know that they do evil.

2   Do not be rash with your mouth,
And let not your heart utter anything hastily before God.
For God *is* in heaven, and you on earth;
Therefore let your words be few.

3   For a dream comes through much activity,
And a fool's voice *is known* by his many words.

4   When you make a vow to God, do not delay to pay it;
For *He has* no pleasure in fools.
Pay what you have vowed—

5   Better not to vow than to vow and not pay.

6Do not let your mouth cause your flesh to sin, nor say before the messenger *of God* that it *was* an error. Why should God be angry at your

On the Edge

Two are better than one, because they have a good reward for their labor. For if they fall, one will lift up his companion. But woe to him who is alone when he falls, for he has no one to help him up (Eccl. 4:9, 10).

Chances are, your parents are more concerned that you get hooked up with a good group of friends than about your passionate commitment to the Latin Club. It's important for you to do things you enjoy with people you enjoy. Activities at school or church offer opportunities for you to develop the ability to get along with other people and to build your leadership skills. They give you a place to focus your energy and increase your talents and abilities. They're great practice for life later on.

Life is all about living and working with other people. Some of the most successful people in the workforce are those who were very involved in high school. On the other hand, kids who isolate themselves or spend a lot of time alone often get into trouble. Get involved. Learn to be a part of a group. Learn to work with other people. You'll be glad you did.

SEE FOR YOURSELF:
Prov. 22:24;
1 Cor. 15:33

excuse[a] and destroy the work of your hands? [7]For in the multitude of dreams and many words *there is* also vanity. But fear God.

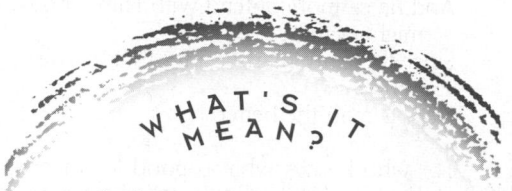

WHAT'S IT MEAN?

"Lord, if you just get me out of this mess, I promise I will . . ." Sound familiar? Like us, people in ancient times made all kinds of promises to God about what they would do if He helped them. For example, a person might have promised to make a certain kind of sacrifice if God heard his prayer. This verse serves as a reminder that God doesn't take such promises lightly.

Ecclesiastes 5:4

THE VANITY OF GAIN AND HONOR

[8]If you see the oppression of the poor, and the violent perversion of justice and righteousness in a province, do not marvel at the matter; for high official watches over high official, and higher officials are over them. [9]Moreover the profit of the land is for all; *even* the king is served from the field.

[10] He who loves silver will not be satisfied
    with silver;
Nor he who loves abundance, with
    increase.
This also *is* vanity.

[11] When goods increase,
They increase who eat them;
So what profit have the owners
Except to see *them* with their eyes?

[12] The sleep of a laboring man *is* sweet,
Whether he eats little or much;
But the abundance of the rich will not
    permit him to sleep.

[13] There is a severe evil *which* I have seen
    under the sun:
Riches kept for their owner to his hurt.
[14] But those riches perish through
    misfortune;
When he begets a son, *there is* nothing in
    his hand.

[15] As he came from his mother's womb,
    naked shall he return,
To go as he came;
And he shall take nothing from his labor
Which he may carry away in his hand.

On the Edge

Do not let your mouth cause your flesh to sin, nor say before the messenger of God that it was an error. Why should God be angry at your excuse and destroy the work of your hands? (Eccl. 5:6).

How many times have you heard it? "Do not let your mouth cause your flesh to sin," or, "Don't let your mouth get you in trouble." How many times have you let it? You were sassy to your mom, and she washed your mouth out with soap. You called your brother a name, and he punched you in the nose. You said something unkind about someone, and it got back to them.

Solomon, the writer of Ecclesiastes, is considered one of the wisest men ever. You'd be wise to take his advice. He knew that once you say something to somebody, you can never take it back. If you get angry and scream something you don't really mean, it could still hurt someone. You could say something innocent that gets twisted around and makes you look really bad. Proverbs 18:21 says that "death and life are in the power of the tongue." It's true. Your words are powerful. They can encourage, inspire, comfort, or explain; or they can hurt, bite, sting, or devastate. Choose your words carefully and make them good. Count to ten before you spout off a bunch of insults you'll later regret. Your words can be death or life!

SEE FOR YOURSELF:
Prov. 10:14; 18:6, 7, 21;
Luke 6:45; Eph. 4:29

[16] And this also *is* a severe evil—
Just exactly as he came, so shall he go.
And what profit has he who has labored
    for the wind?
[17] All his days he also eats in darkness,
And *he has* much sorrow and sickness
    and anger.

5:6 [a]Literally *voice*

¹⁸Here is what I have seen: *It is* good and fitting *for one* to eat and drink, and to enjoy the good of all his labor in which he toils under the sun all the days of his life which God gives him; for it *is* his heritage. ¹⁹As for every man to whom God has given riches and wealth, and given him power to eat of it, to receive his heritage and rejoice in his labor—this *is* the gift of God. ²⁰For he will not dwell unduly on the days of his life, because God keeps *him* busy with the joy of his heart.

¹There is an evil which I have seen under the sun, and it *is* common among men: ²A man to whom God has given riches and wealth and honor, so that he lacks nothing for himself of all he desires; yet God does not give him power to eat of it, but a foreigner consumes it. This *is* vanity, and it *is* an evil affliction.

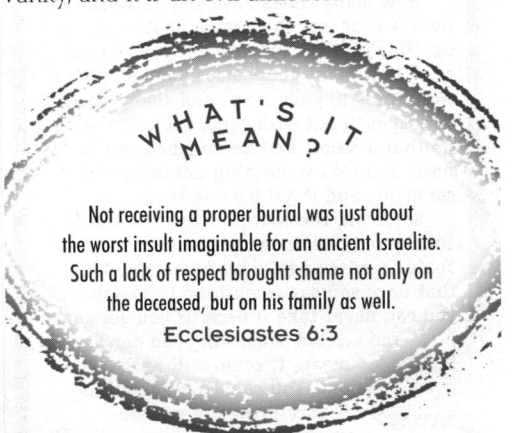

WHAT'S IT MEAN?

Not receiving a proper burial was just about the worst insult imaginable for an ancient Israelite. Such a lack of respect brought shame not only on the deceased, but on his family as well.

Ecclesiastes 6:3

³If a man begets a hundred *children* and lives many years, so that the days of his years are many, but his soul is not satisfied with goodness, or indeed he has no burial, I say *that* a stillborn child *is* better than he—⁴for it comes in vanity and departs in darkness, and its name is covered with darkness. ⁵Though it has not seen the sun or known *anything*, this has more rest than that man, ⁶even if he lives a thousand years twice—but has not seen goodness. Do not all go to one place?

⁷ All the labor of man *is* for his mouth,
And yet the soul is not satisfied.
⁸ For what more has the wise *man* than the fool?
What does the poor man have,
Who knows *how* to walk before the living?
⁹ Better *is* the sight of the eyes than the wandering of desire.
This also *is* vanity and grasping for the wind.

¹⁰ Whatever one is, he has been named already,
For it is known that he *is* man;
And he cannot contend with Him who is mightier than he.
¹¹ Since there are many things that increase vanity,
How *is* man the better?

¹²For who knows what *is* good for man in life, all the days of his vain life which he passes like a shadow? Who can tell a man what will happen after him under the sun?

THE VALUE OF PRACTICAL WISDOM

¹ A good name *is* better than precious ointment,
And the day of death than the day of one's birth;
² Better to go to the house of mourning
Than to go to the house of feasting,
For that *is* the end of all men;
And the living will take *it* to heart.
³ Sorrow *is* better than laughter,
For by a sad countenance the heart is made better.
⁴ The heart of the wise *is* in the house of mourning,
But the heart of fools *is* in the house of mirth.

⁵ *It is* better to hear the rebuke of the wise
Than for a man to hear the song of fools.
⁶ For like the crackling of thorns under a pot,
So *is* the laughter of the fool.
This also is vanity.
⁷ Surely oppression destroys a wise *man's* reason,
And a bribe debases the heart.

⁸ The end of a thing *is* better than its beginning;
The patient in spirit *is* better than the proud in spirit.
⁹ Do not hasten in your spirit to be angry,
For anger rests in the bosom of fools.
¹⁰ Do not say,
"Why were the former days better than these?"
For you do not inquire wisely concerning this.

¹¹ Wisdom *is* good with an inheritance,
And profitable to those who see the sun.
¹² For wisdom *is* a defense *as* money *is* a defense,

But the excellence of knowledge *is that*
   wisdom gives life to those who have it.

13 Consider the work of God;
   For who can make straight what He has
      made crooked?
14 In the day of prosperity be joyful,
   But in the day of adversity consider:
   Surely God has appointed the one as well
      as the other,
   So that man can find out nothing *that will*
      come after him.

15 I have seen everything in my days of
vanity:

   There is a just *man* who perishes in his
      righteousness,
   And there is a wicked *man* who prolongs
      life in his wickedness.

16 Do not be overly righteous,
   Nor be overly wise:
   Why should you destroy yourself?
17 Do not be overly wicked,
   Nor be foolish:
   Why should you die before your time?
18 *It is* good that you grasp this,
   And also not remove your hand from the
      other;
   For he who fears God will escape them
      all.

19 Wisdom strengthens the wise
   More than ten rulers of the city.

20 For *there is* not a just man on earth who
      does good
   And does not sin.

21 Also do not take to heart everything
      people say,
   Lest you hear your servant cursing
      you.
22 For many times, also, your own heart has
      known
   That even you have cursed others.

23 All this I have proved by wisdom.
   I said, "I will be wise";
   But it *was* far from me.
24 As for that which is far off and
      exceedingly deep,
   Who can find it out?
25 I applied my heart to know,
   To search and seek out wisdom and the
      reason *of things,*

On the Edge

For there is not a just man on earth who does good and does not sin (Eccl. 7:20).

A woman was being harassed because of the bad things she had done. People yelled and jeered at her because her sin was so ugly. They were going to stone her to death. But Jesus said, "He who is without sin among you, let him throw a stone at her first" (John 8:7). The angry crowd, one by one, dropped their stones and walked away. When each person had looked at his own life, he realized that his sin was just as ugly as hers.

As hard as you may try, you aren't sinless. You don't always do the right thing. You're human and you're not perfect. In the pit of sin is where Jesus comes and gently shows you that you can't do it by yourself. You desperately need a Savior. There is no one alive who doesn't. Don't beat yourself up about your sin. Turn to the One who can save you from it.

SEE FOR YOURSELF:
Ps. 51; John 8:7;
Rom. 3:23; Heb. 12:1

   To know the wickedness of folly,
   Even of foolishness *and* madness.
26 And I find more bitter than death
   The woman whose heart *is* snares and
      nets,
   Whose hands *are* fetters.
   He who pleases God shall escape from
      her,
   But the sinner shall be trapped by her.

27 "Here is what I have found," says the
      Preacher,
   "*Adding* one thing to the other to find out
      the reason,
28 Which my soul still seeks but I cannot
      find:
   One man among a thousand I have
      found,
   But a woman among all these I have not
      found.
29 Truly, this only I have found:
   That God made man upright,
   But they have sought out many
      schemes."

Most women received very little respect in ancient times. In fact, they were often treated more like possessions than people. Some women were even given as gifts! For example, when two countries signed a treaty, it was customary for the less powerful nation to present women to the leader of the more powerful nation. That's how Solomon, the leader of the very powerful Israelite nation, came to have hundreds of wives and concubines, women who were little more than possessions to him. Many of Solomon's wives came from foreign countries and worshiped foreign gods.

Ecclesiastes 7:28

1 Who *is* like a wise *man*?
    And who knows the interpretation of a
       thing?
    A man's wisdom makes his face shine,
    And the sternness of his face is changed.

OBEY AUTHORITIES FOR GOD'S SAKE

2 I *say*, "Keep the king's commandment for the sake of your oath to God. 3 Do not be hasty to go from his presence. Do not take your stand for an evil thing, for he does whatever pleases him."

4 Where the word of a king *is*, *there is*
       power;
    And who may say to him, "What are you
       doing?"
5 He who keeps his command will
       experience nothing harmful;
    And a wise man's heart discerns both
       time and judgment,
6 Because for every matter there is a time
       and judgment,
    Though the misery of man increases
       greatly.
7 For he does not know what will happen;
    So who can tell him when it will occur?
8 No one has power over the spirit to
       retain the spirit,
    And no one has power in the day of
       death.

    There is no release from that war,
    And wickedness will not deliver those
       who are given to it.

9 All this I have seen, and applied my heart to every work that is done under the sun: *There is* a time in which one man rules over another to his own hurt.

On the Edge

No one has power over the spirit to retain the spirit, and no one has power in the day of death. There is no release from that war, and wickedness will not deliver those who are given to it (Eccl. 8:8).

You control your own destiny. You've heard that before, right? It's true to a certain extent. What you put into your life now will impact what you get out of it later. That's true of how hard you work at school or in your job. It's true of how you treat your parents. It's true of the kind of people you pick to be your friends.

But there's a whole lot in life that you can't control. You can't decide whether there's going to be a flood or a drought this year. You can't control how many people get hired for a summer job. You can't control the price of a soda. You can't control what other people do. But all these things can have an effect on you.

Does that mean you should get really scared worrying about all the things that *could* happen without your being able to stop them? That wasn't Jesus' advice. He said don't sweat it. Let God take care of all that stuff that's out of your hands. You just concentrate on doing the things He wants you to do. You'll be a lot less frustrated if you quit worrying about things you can't control.

SEE FOR YOURSELF:
   Matt. 6:34;
   Luke 12:29–31;
   1 Pet. 5:7

DEATH COMES TO ALL

10 Then I saw the wicked buried, who had come and gone from the place of holiness, and they were forgotten[a] in the city where they had so done. This also *is* vanity. 11 Because the sen-

---

8:10 [a]Some Hebrew manuscripts, Septuagint, and Vulgate read *praised*.

tence against an evil work is not executed speedily, therefore the heart of the sons of men is fully set in them to do evil. ¹²Though a sinner does evil a hundred *times*, and his *days* are prolonged, yet I surely know that it will be well with those who fear God, who fear before Him. ¹³But it will not be well with the wicked; nor will he prolong *his* days, *which are* as a shadow, because he does not fear before God.

¹⁴There is a vanity which occurs on earth, that there are just *men* to whom it happens according to the work of the wicked; again, there are wicked *men* to whom it happens according to the work of the righteous. I said that this also *is* vanity.

¹⁵So I commended enjoyment, because a man has nothing better under the sun than to eat, drink, and be merry; for this will remain with him in his labor *all* the days of his life which God gives him under the sun.

¹⁶When I applied my heart to know wisdom and to see the business that is done on earth, even though one sees no sleep day or night, ¹⁷then I saw all the work of God, that a man cannot find out the work that is done under the sun. For though a man labors to discover *it*, yet he will not find *it*; moreover, though a wise *man* attempts to know *it*, he will not be able to find *it*.

¹For I considered all this in my heart, so that I could declare it all: that the righteous and the wise and their works *are* in the hand of God. People know neither love nor hatred *by* anything *they see* before them. ²All things *come* alike to all:

> One event *happens* to the righteous and
>   the wicked;
> To the good,*ᵃ* the clean, and the unclean;
> To him who sacrifices and him who does
>   not sacrifice.
> As is the good, so *is* the sinner;
> He who takes an oath as *he* who fears an
>   oath.

³This *is* an evil in all that is done under the sun: that one thing *happens* to all. Truly the hearts of the sons of men are full of evil; madness *is* in their hearts while they live, and after that *they go* to the dead. ⁴But for him who is joined to all the living there is hope, for a living dog is better than a dead lion.

⁵ For the living know that they will die;
    But the dead know nothing,
    And they have no more reward,

⁶ For the memory of them is forgotten.
    Also their love, their hatred, and their
      envy have now perished;
    Nevermore will they have a share
    In anything done under the sun.

WHAT'S IT MEAN?

In ancient Israel, the dog and the lion were on opposite ends of the popularity spectrum. The dogs of that era were wild creatures that traveled in packs, preyed on the weak, ate garbage, and stole food from the villages. You can imagine how popular they were with the Israelites. Lions, on the other hand, were respected for their size and strength. Although they were a very real danger to the Israelites, they also served as symbols of majesty and courage. Calling someone a dog in ancient Israel was an extremely offensive insult. Calling someone a lion was an extremely high compliment.

Ecclesiastes 9:4

⁷ Go, eat your bread with joy,
    And drink your wine with a merry heart;
    For God has already accepted your
      works.
⁸ Let your garments always be white,
    And let your head lack no oil.

⁹Live joyfully with the wife whom you love all the days of your vain life which He has given you under the sun, all your days of vanity; for that *is* your portion in life, and in the labor which you perform under the sun. ¹⁰Whatever your hand finds to do, do *it* with your might; for *there is* no work or device or knowledge or wisdom in the grave where you are going.

¹¹I returned and saw under the sun that—

> The race *is* not to the swift,
> Nor the battle to the strong,
> Nor bread to the wise,
> Nor riches to men of understanding,
> Nor favor to men of skill;
> But time and chance happen to them all.

¹² For man also does not know his time:
    Like fish taken in a cruel net,
    Like birds caught in a snare,

9:2 *ᵃ*Septuagint, Syriac, and Vulgate read *good and bad.*

17 Words of the wise, *spoken* quietly, *should be* heard
Rather than the shout of a ruler of fools.

18 Wisdom *is* better than weapons of war;
But one sinner destroys much good."

1 Dead flies putrefy[a] the perfumer's ointment,
And cause it to give off a foul odor;
So does a little folly to one respected for wisdom *and* honor.

2 A wise man's heart *is* at his right hand,
But a fool's heart at his left.

3 Even when a fool walks along the way,
He lacks wisdom,
And he shows everyone *that* he *is* a fool.

4 If the spirit of the ruler rises against you,
Do not leave your post;
For conciliation pacifies great offenses.

On the Edge

Let your garments always be white, and let your head lack no oil (Eccl. 9:8).

Why not? Solomon says that life is too short to not enjoy it. He says, "Let your garments always be white, and let your head lack no oil." In other words, always be clean and look your best. Too soon you'll be at the end of your life, and you won't want to have looked like a bum all the way through it. God has given you a gift in your body. Even if you're not the most handsome or most beautiful, everybody appreciates your efforts to do the best with what you've got.

Neat and clean doesn't mean "hippest and most expensive." It means clean clothes, combed hair, brushed teeth. All of those things will show the world that you have dignity and self-respect. Think of it as a "thank you" to God for making you as you are. After all, if you look like you care about yourself and take yourself seriously, other people will, too.

SEE FOR YOURSELF:
Num. 8:6; Zech. 3;
Rev. 19:7, 8

WHAT'S IT MEAN?

Perfumes and ointments were very expensive in Solomon's day, many of them because they had to be imported from other countries. These fragrances were used not only for religious ceremonies, but also to cover up body odor. Add together a warm climate and an infrequent bathing schedule, and you'll come up with some nasty smells.

Ecclesiastes 10:1

So the sons of men *are* snared in an evil time,
When it falls suddenly upon them.

WISDOM SUPERIOR TO FOLLY

13This wisdom I have also seen under the sun, and it *seemed* great to me: 14*There was* a little city with few men in it; and a great king came against it, besieged it, and built great snares[a] around it. 15Now there was found in it a poor wise man, and he by his wisdom delivered the city. Yet no one remembered that same poor man. 16Then I said:

"Wisdom *is* better than strength.
Nevertheless the poor man's wisdom *is* despised,
And his words are not heard.

"Words of the wise, spoken quietly, should be heard rather than the shout of a ruler of fools."
(Ecclesiastes 9:17)

5 There is an evil I have seen under the sun,
As an error proceeding from the ruler:

6 Folly is set in great dignity,
While the rich sit in a lowly place.

7 I have seen servants on horses,
While princes walk on the ground like servants.

8 He who digs a pit will fall into it,
And whoever breaks through a wall will be bitten by a serpent.

9:14 [a]Septuagint, Syriac, and Vulgate read *bulwarks.* **10:1** [a]Targum and Vulgate omit *putrefy.*

9 He who quarries stones may be hurt by
    them,
    And he who splits wood may be
      endangered by it.
10 If the ax is dull,
    And one does not sharpen the edge,
    Then he must use more strength;
    But wisdom brings success.

11 A serpent may bite when *it is* not
    charmed;
    The babbler is no different.
12 The words of a wise man's mouth *are*
    gracious,
    But the lips of a fool shall swallow him
      up;
13 The words of his mouth begin with
    foolishness,
    And the end of his talk *is* raving madness.
14 A fool also multiplies words.
    No man knows what is to be;
    Who can tell him what will be after him?
15 The labor of fools wearies them,
    For they do not even know how to go to
      the city!

16 Woe to you, O land, when your king *is* a
    child,
    And your princes feast in the morning!
17 Blessed *are* you, O land, when your king
    is the son of nobles,
    And your princes feast at the proper
      time—
    For strength and not for drunkenness!
18 Because of laziness the building decays,
    And through idleness of hands the house
      leaks.
19 A feast is made for laughter,
    And wine makes merry;
    But money answers everything.

20 Do not curse the king, even in your
    thought;
    Do not curse the rich, even in your
      bedroom;
    For a bird of the air may carry your
      voice,
    And a bird in flight may tell the matter.

THE VALUE OF DILIGENCE

1 Cast your bread upon the waters,
    For you will find it after many days.
2 Give a serving to seven, and also to eight,
    For you do not know what evil will be
      on the earth.

3 If the clouds are full of rain,
    They empty *themselves* upon the earth;
    And if a tree falls to the south or the
      north,
    In the place where the tree falls, there it
      shall lie.
4 He who observes the wind will not sow,
    And he who regards the clouds will not
      reap.

5 As you do not know what *is* the way of
    the wind,[a]
    Or how the bones *grow* in the womb of
      her who is with child,
    So you do not know the works of God
      who makes everything.
6 In the morning sow your seed,
    And in the evening do not withhold your
      hand;
    For you do not know which will prosper,

On the Edge

But if a man lives many years and rejoices in them all, yet let him remember the days of darkness, for they will be many. All that is coming is vanity (Eccl. 11:8).

The past is long gone. Tomorrow is a dream, and right now is the only moment you have to enjoy. Are you wishing your life away, hoping that the next thing will make you happy? When I get my driver's license. When I graduate. When I get to college. When I get married. The wish list could go on forever. One day you'll be old and realize you missed the whole thing. God has given you every moment of your life as a gift. How are you living this gift? Are you hoping someone will come into your life and give it meaning? Are you wanting your teenage years to be over so you can be an adult? Are you wishing it would just all go away? Are you just numb to the passage of time? If so, ask the Lord to restore your joy, to give you eyes to see your purpose, and to help you make the most of these once-in-a-lifetime days.

SEE FOR YOURSELF:
Prov. 27:1; Eccl. 3:11–13;
1 Pet. 4:7

11:5 [a]Or *spirit*

Either this or that,
Or whether both alike *will be* good.

7 Truly the light is sweet,
And *it is* pleasant for the eyes to behold
the sun;
8 But if a man lives many years
And rejoices in them all,
Yet let him remember the days of
darkness,
For they will be many.
All that is coming *is* vanity.

SEEK GOD IN EARLY LIFE

9 Rejoice, O young man, in your youth,
And let your heart cheer you in the days
of your youth;
Walk in the ways of your heart,
And in the sight of your eyes;
But know that for all these
God will bring you into judgment.
10 Therefore remove sorrow from your
heart,
And put away evil from your flesh,
For childhood and youth *are* vanity.

1 Remember now your Creator in the days
of your youth,
Before the difficult days come,
And the years draw near when you say,
"I have no pleasure in them":
2 While the sun and the light,
The moon and the stars,
Are not darkened,

And the clouds do not return after the
rain;
3 In the day when the keepers of the house
tremble,
And the strong men bow down;
When the grinders cease because they are
few,
And those that look through the
windows grow dim;
4 When the doors are shut in the streets,
And the sound of grinding is low;
When one rises up at the sound of a bird,
And all the daughters of music are
brought low.
5 Also they are afraid of height,
And of terrors in the way;
When the almond tree blossoms,
The grasshopper is a burden,
And desire fails.
For man goes to his eternal home,
And the mourners go about the streets.

6 *Remember your Creator* before the silver
cord is loosed,[a]
Or the golden bowl is broken,
Or the pitcher shattered at the fountain,
Or the wheel broken at the well.
7 Then the dust will return to the earth as it
was,
And the spirit will return to God who
gave it.

8 "Vanity of vanities," says the Preacher,
"All *is* vanity."

12:6 [a]Following Qere and Targum; Kethib reads *removed*; Septuagint and Vulgate read *broken*.

·::· Promise   HE PROMISES TO JUDGE ALL THE WORK WE DO.

For God will bring every work into judgment, including every secret thing,
whether good or evil (Eccl. 12:14).

Your mom asks you to take out the trash. You get an attitude, moan and complain, and finally take it out after you're both upset. You casually take some cash from your brother's dresser. You need it; he's got it. You're family. So what? Each situation seems kind of harmless—a bad attitude and "borrowing" some money. But God promises to judge all we do. He saw a kid who dishonored his mom and hasn't caught onto the idea of doing "all things without complaining" (Phil. 2:14). He saw stealing instead of "borrowing." You may choose to whitewash your life and pretend you're an okay guy—not a lot of sin to deal with, no major infractions. But God sees things as they really are. Ask Him to give you His perspective, so that you can begin to clean up the stuff you've been pretending isn't so bad. Then you can walk clean before Him.

SEE FOR YOURSELF:
1 Sam. 2:10; Ps. 9:8; 50:6; 2 Tim. 4:8

THE WHOLE DUTY OF MAN

⁹And moreover, because the Preacher was wise, he still taught the people knowledge; yes, he pondered and sought out *and* set in order many proverbs. ¹⁰The Preacher sought to find acceptable words; and *what was* written *was* upright—words of truth. ¹¹The words of the wise are like goads, and the words of scholars*ᵃ* are like well-driven nails, given by one Shepherd. ¹²And further, my son, be admonished by these. Of making many books *there is* no end, and much study *is* wearisome to the flesh.

¹³Let us hear the conclusion of the whole matter:

Fear God and keep His commandments,
For this is man's all.
14 For God will bring every work into
    judgment,
Including every secret thing,
Whether good or evil.

12:11 *ᵃ*Literally *masters of the assemblies*

Song of Solomon

CONTENT   A good word to describe Song of Solomon might be . . . *mushy*. Basically, this book of the Bible is a love poem. It's a poetic story about a young man (Solomon) and a young woman (his bride). They are infatuated. They are in love. They are caught up in romance. They are *crazy* about each other!

Their story tells us something important about God. He created us to need each other. He created romance. He created sex. All of that is good in its place.

You know how it is: Sometimes adults get very cautious with you about getting too serious too early and making mistakes. Sometimes they get so cautious that it can seem like anything that has to do with "the birds and bees" is a bad thing. Those adults have every reason to be cautious. Sexuality is a powerful force, one that requires a lot of maturity and self-control (even for the over-30 crowd!). But it's also true that the chemistry between men and women and all that it leads to was created by God. In the right place it is exciting and wonderful—and important enough for God to dedicate a whole book to it in His Word.

Purpose   The true meaning and joy of sex is found only in marriage.

Theme   The Quest for Authentic Love

Date of writing   965 B.C.

Bible Talk

The Lure of the Human Body

People talk a lot these days about private zones and inappropriate touch. In our culture we are having to redefine the boundaries. At what point does physical attraction toward someone overstep proper bounds and become sexual harassment? Can we be too attentive to another person—physically?

The characters in the poem we know as the Song of Solomon talk a lot about different parts of the body. They admire each other. This book of the Bible reminds us that God made the human body to be beautiful to our eyes. He made us to want to touch and be touched.

God also gives us the responsibility to give ourselves only to the person that we commit to for life before God, like Solomon and his bride.

WHY POETRY?

Why would God include a love poem in the very Book that He uses to call us to faith? Why not just say "sex is good in the right context" and leave it at that. Why not just point out the right and wrong and be done with it?

Because that's not what God is about. He doesn't just want our obedience; He wants our faith and love. He doesn't just communicate to us in do's and don'ts; He communicates to us within the context of our humanity. Whether that means a love poem, or putting on actual human flesh, that is what God does to connect with us, His creations.

¹The song of songs, which *is* Solomon's.

THE BANQUET

THE SHULAMITE[a]
2 Let him kiss me with the kisses of his
mouth—
For your[b] love *is* better than wine.
3 Because of the fragrance of your good
ointments,
Your name *is* ointment poured forth;
Therefore the virgins love you.
4 Draw me away!

THE DAUGHTERS OF JERUSALEM
We will run after you.[a]

THE SHULAMITE
The king has brought me into his
chambers.

THE DAUGHTERS OF JERUSALEM
We will be glad and rejoice in you.[b]

We will remember your[c] love more than
wine.

THE SHULAMITE
Rightly do they love you.[d]

5 I *am* dark, but lovely,
O daughters of Jerusalem,
Like the tents of Kedar,
Like the curtains of Solomon.
6 Do not look upon me, because I *am* dark,
Because the sun has tanned me.
My mother's sons were angry with me;
They made me the keeper of the vineyards,
But my own vineyard I have not kept.

(TO HER BELOVED)
7 Tell me, O you whom I love,
Where you feed *your flock*,
Where you make *it* rest at noon.
For why should I be as one who veils
herself[a]
By the flocks of your companions?

THE BELOVED
8 If you do not know, O fairest among
women,

Follow in the footsteps of the flock,
And feed your little goats
Beside the shepherds' tents.
9 I have compared you, my love,
To my filly among Pharaoh's chariots.
10 Your cheeks are lovely with ornaments,
Your neck with chains *of gold*.

THE DAUGHTERS OF JERUSALEM
11 We will make you[a] ornaments of gold
With studs of silver.

THE SHULAMITE
12 While the king *is* at his table,
My spikenard sends forth its fragrance.
13 A bundle of myrrh *is* my beloved to me,
That lies all night between my breasts.
14 My beloved *is* to me a cluster of henna
blooms
In the vineyards of En Gedi.

WHAT'S IT MEAN?

You may be wondering why the author would
compare his beloved to a dove, of all things. The
ancient Israelites appreciated the faithfulness, the beauty, and
especially the gentleness of the bird. A dove is one of the few
creatures that will not attempt to defend itself when it's attacked.
Instead, it will simply call out in distress.
Song of Solomon 1:15

THE BELOVED
15 Behold, you *are* fair, my love!
Behold, you *are* fair!
You *have* dove's eyes.

THE SHULAMITE
16 Behold, you *are* handsome, my beloved!
Yes, pleasant!
Also our bed *is* green.
17 The beams of our houses *are* cedar,
And our rafters of fir.

1:2 [a]A Palestinian young woman (compare 6:13). The speaker and audience are identified according to the
number, gender, and person of the Hebrew words. Occasionally the identity is not certain. [b]Masculine
singular, that is, the Beloved **1:4** [a]Masculine singular, that is, the Beloved [b]Feminine singular, that is, the
Shulamite [c]Masculine singular, that is, the Beloved [d]Masculine singular, that is, the Beloved
1:7 [a]Septuagint, Syriac, and Vulgate read *wanders*. **1:11** [a]Feminine singular, that is, the Shulamite

1 I *am* the rose of Sharon,
  And the lily of the valleys.

THE BELOVED

2 Like a lily among thorns,
  So is my love among the daughters.

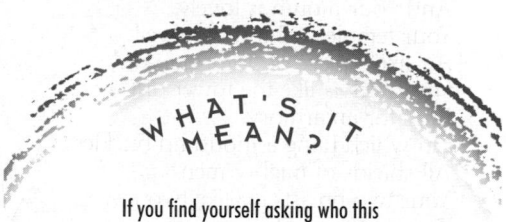

WHAT'S IT MEAN?

If you find yourself asking who this Sharon person was, you may be surprised to learn that it's a place—specifically, it's a fertile coastal region in Israel known for its beautiful flowers. The rose mentioned in this verse probably wasn't what we know as a rose. Instead, it may have been a mountain tulip, an anemone, or a saffron. Since those flowers grew in abundance in Sharon, the woman was implying that she is nothing special.

Song of Solomon 2:1

THE SHULAMITE

3 Like an apple tree among the trees of the
    woods,
  So is my beloved among the sons.
  I sat down in his shade with great
    delight,
  And his fruit *was* sweet to my taste.

THE SHULAMITE TO THE DAUGHTERS OF JERUSALEM

4 He brought me to the banqueting house,
  And his banner over me *was* love.
5 Sustain me with cakes of raisins,
  Refresh me with apples,
  For I *am* lovesick.

6 His left hand *is* under my head,
  And his right hand embraces me.
7 I charge you, O daughters of Jerusalem,
  By the gazelles or by the does of the field,
  Do not stir up nor awaken love
  Until it pleases.

THE BELOVED'S REQUEST

THE SHULAMITE

8 The voice of my beloved!
  Behold, he comes

Leaping upon the mountains,
Skipping upon the hills.
9 My beloved is like a gazelle or a young
    stag.
  Behold, he stands behind our wall;
  He is looking through the windows,
  Gazing through the lattice.

10 My beloved spoke, and said to me:
  "Rise up, my love, my fair one,
  And come away.
11 For lo, the winter is past,
  The rain is over *and* gone.
12 The flowers appear on the earth;
  The time of singing has come,
  And the voice of the turtledove
  Is heard in our land.
13 The fig tree puts forth her green figs,
  And the vines *with* the tender grapes
  Give a good smell.
  Rise up, my love, my fair one,
  And come away!

14 "O my dove, in the clefts of the rock,
  In the secret *places* of the cliff,
  Let me see your face,
  Let me hear your voice;
  For your voice *is* sweet,
  And your face *is* lovely."

HER BROTHERS

15 Catch us the foxes,
  The little foxes that spoil the vines,
  For our vines *have* tender grapes.

THE SHULAMITE

16 My beloved *is* mine, and I *am* his.
  He feeds *his flock* among the lilies.

(TO HER BELOVED)

17 Until the day breaks
  And the shadows flee away,
  Turn, my beloved,
  And be like a gazelle
  Or a young stag
  Upon the mountains of Bether.*a*

A TROUBLED NIGHT

THE SHULAMITE

1 By night on my bed I sought the one I
    love;
  I sought him, but I did not find him.
2 "I will rise now," *I said,*
  "And go about the city;

2:17 *a*Literally *Separation*

In the streets and in the squares
I will seek the one I love."
I sought him, but I did not find him.
3 The watchmen who go about the city
   found me;
   I said,
   "Have you seen the one I love?"

4 Scarcely had I passed by them,
  When I found the one I love.
  I held him and would not let him go,
  Until I had brought him to the house of
     my mother,
  And into the chamber of her who
     conceived me.

5 I charge you, O daughters of Jerusalem,
  By the gazelles or by the does of the field,
  Do not stir up nor awaken love
  Until it pleases.

THE COMING OF SOLOMON

THE SHULAMITE
6 Who *is* this coming out of the wilderness
  Like pillars of smoke,
  Perfumed with myrrh and frankincense,
  With all the merchant's fragrant powders?
7 Behold, it *is* Solomon's couch,
  With sixty valiant men around it,
  Of the valiant of Israel.
8 They all hold swords,
  Being expert in war.
  Every man *has* his sword on his thigh
  Because of fear in the night.

9 Of the wood of Lebanon
  Solomon the King
  Made himself a palanquin:ᵃ
10 He made its pillars *of* silver,
   Its support *of* gold,
   Its seat *of* purple,
   Its interior paved *with* love
   By the daughters of Jerusalem.
11 Go forth, O daughters of Zion,
   And see King Solomon with the crown
   With which his mother crowned him
   On the day of his wedding,
   The day of the gladness of his heart.

THE BELOVED
1 Behold, you *are* fair, my love!
  Behold, you *are* fair!
  You *have* dove's eyes behind your veil.
  Your hair *is* like a flock of goats,

Going down from Mount Gilead.
2 Your teeth *are* like a flock of shorn *sheep*
  Which have come up from the washing,
  Every one of which bears twins,
  And none *is* barren among them.
3 Your lips *are* like a strand of scarlet,
  And your mouth is lovely.
  Your temples behind your veil
  Are like a piece of pomegranate.
4 Your neck *is* like the tower of David,
  Built for an armory,
  On which hang a thousand bucklers,
  All shields of mighty men.
5 Your two breasts *are* like two fawns,
  Twins of a gazelle,
  Which feed among the lilies.

6 Until the day breaks
  And the shadows flee away,
  I will go my way to the mountain of
     myrrh
  And to the hill of frankincense.

7 You *are* all fair, my love,
  And *there is* no spot in you.
8 Come with me from Lebanon, *my* spouse,
  With me from Lebanon.
  Look from the top of Amana,
  From the top of Senir and Hermon,
  From the lions' dens,
  From the mountains of the leopards.

9 You have ravished my heart,
  My sister, *my* spouse;
  You have ravished my heart
  With one *look* of your eyes,
  With one link of your necklace.
10 How fair is your love,
   My sister, *my* spouse!
   How much better than wine is your love,
   And the scent of your perfumes
   Than all spices!
11 Your lips, O *my* spouse,
   Drip as the honeycomb;
   Honey and milk *are* under your tongue;
   And the fragrance of your garments
   Is like the fragrance of Lebanon.

12 A garden enclosed
   Is my sister, *my* spouse,
   A spring shut up,
   A fountain sealed.
13 Your plants *are* an orchard of
      pomegranates
   With pleasant fruits,

3:9 ᵃA portable enclosed chair

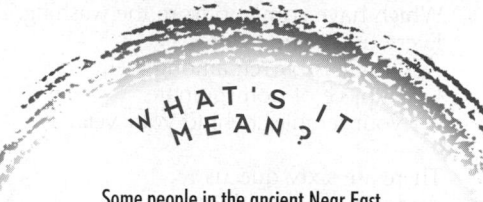

WHAT'S IT MEAN?

Some people in the ancient Near East closed their gardens to visitors in order to protect their privacy and preserve their water supply. Because of the frequent droughts in the area, water in Israel was tough to come by.

Song of Solomon 4:12

For my head is covered with dew,
My locks with the drops of the night."

3 I have taken off my robe;
How can I put it on *again*?
I have washed my feet;
How can I defile them?

4 My beloved put his hand
By the latch *of the door*,
And my heart yearned for him.

5 I arose to open for my beloved,
And my hands dripped *with* myrrh,
My fingers with liquid myrrh,
On the handles of the lock.

6 I opened for my beloved,
But my beloved had turned away *and* was gone.
My heart leaped up when he spoke.
I sought him, but I could not find him;
I called him, but he gave me no answer.

7 The watchmen who went about the city found me.
They struck me, they wounded me;
The keepers of the walls
Took my veil away from me.

8 I charge you, O daughters of Jerusalem,
If you find my beloved,
That you tell him I *am* lovesick!

14 Fragrant henna with spikenard,
Spikenard and saffron,
Calamus and cinnamon,
With all trees of frankincense,
Myrrh and aloes,
With all the chief spices—

15 A fountain of gardens,
A well of living waters,
And streams from Lebanon.

THE SHULAMITE

16 Awake, O north *wind*,
And come, O south!
Blow upon my garden,
That its spices may flow out.
Let my beloved come to his garden
And eat its pleasant fruits.

THE BELOVED

1 I have come to my garden, my sister, *my* spouse;
I have gathered my myrrh with my spice;
I have eaten my honeycomb with my honey;
I have drunk my wine with my milk.

(TO HIS FRIENDS)

Eat, O friends!
Drink, yes, drink deeply,
O beloved ones!

THE SHULAMITE'S TROUBLED EVENING

THE SHULAMITE

2 I sleep, but my heart is awake;
It is the voice of my beloved!
He knocks, *saying*,
"Open for me, my sister, my love,
My dove, my perfect one;

THE DAUGHTERS OF JERUSALEM

9 What *is* your beloved
More than *another* beloved,
O fairest among women?
What *is* your beloved
More than *another* beloved,
That you so charge us?

THE SHULAMITE

10 My beloved *is* white and ruddy,
Chief among ten thousand.

11 His head *is like* the finest gold;
His locks *are* wavy,
And black as a raven.

12 His eyes *are* like doves
By the rivers of waters,
Washed with milk,
And fitly set.

13 His cheeks *are* like a bed of spices,
Banks of scented herbs.
His lips *are* lilies,
Dripping liquid myrrh.

14 His hands *are* rods of gold
Set with beryl.
His body *is* carved ivory
Inlaid *with* sapphires.

15 His legs *are* pillars of marble
Set on bases of fine gold.
His countenance *is* like Lebanon,
Excellent as the cedars.
16 His mouth *is* most sweet,
Yes, he *is* altogether lovely.
This *is* my beloved,
And this *is* my friend,
O daughters of Jerusalem!

At one time, Lebanon was covered with
cedar trees, which were known for their size and
beauty. The Phoenicians, who inhabited the land, cut down the trees
and sold the wood to other nations for use in constructing ships,
buildings, and other things.
Song of Solomon 5:15

THE DAUGHTERS OF JERUSALEM

1 Where has your beloved gone,
O fairest among women?
Where has your beloved turned aside,
That we may seek him with you?

THE SHULAMITE

2 My beloved has gone to his garden,
To the beds of spices,
To feed *his flock* in the gardens,
And to gather lilies.
3 I *am* my beloved's,
And my beloved *is* mine.
He feeds *his flock* among the lilies.

PRAISE OF THE SHULAMITE'S BEAUTY

THE BELOVED

4 O my love, you *are as* beautiful as
Tirzah,
Lovely as Jerusalem,
Awesome as *an army* with banners!
5 Turn your eyes away from me,
For they have overcome me.
Your hair *is* like a flock of goats
Going down from Gilead.
6 Your teeth *are* like a flock of sheep

Which have come up from the washing;
Every one bears twins,
And none *is* barren among them.
7 Like a piece of pomegranate
Are your temples behind your veil.

8 There are sixty queens
And eighty concubines,
And virgins without number.
9 My dove, my perfect one,
Is the only one,
The only one of her mother,
The favorite of the one who bore her.
The daughters saw her
And called her blessed,
The queens and the concubines,
And they praised her.

Gilead, located east of the Jordan River,
was known for its lush plant life. The land was an
ideal grazing place for sheep, goats, and other
livestock. Speaking of actual goats, did you know
that the ones raised in the ancient Near
East had long, silky black hair?
Song of Solomon 6:5

10 Who is she who looks forth as the
morning,
Fair as the moon,
Clear as the sun,
Awesome as *an army* with banners?

THE SHULAMITE

11 I went down to the garden of nuts
To see the verdure of the valley,
To see whether the vine had budded
And the pomegranates had bloomed.
12 Before I was even aware,
My soul had made me
As the chariots of my noble people.[a]

THE BELOVED AND HIS FRIENDS

13 Return, return, O Shulamite;
Return, return, that we may look upon
you!

6:12 [a]Hebrew *Ammi Nadib*

THE SHULAMITE

What would you see in the Shulamite—
As it were, the dance of the two camps?[a]

EXPRESSIONS OF PRAISE

THE BELOVED

1 How beautiful are your feet in sandals,
O prince's daughter!
The curves of your thighs *are* like jewels,
The work of the hands of a skillful
workman.

2 Your navel *is* a rounded goblet;
It lacks no blended beverage.
Your waist *is* a heap of wheat
Set about with lilies.

3 Your two breasts *are* like two fawns,
Twins of a gazelle.

4 Your neck *is* like an
ivory tower,
Your eyes *like* the
pools in Heshbon
By the gate of Bath
Rabbim.
Your nose *is* like the
tower of Lebanon
Which looks toward
Damascus.

5 Your head *crowns* you like
Mount Carmel,
And the hair of your head *is* like purple;
A king *is* held captive by *your* tresses.

6 How fair and how pleasant you are,
O love, with your delights!

7 This stature of yours is like a palm tree,
And your breasts *like* its clusters.

8 I said, "I will go up to the palm tree,
I will take hold of its branches."
Let now your breasts be like clusters of
the vine,
The fragrance of your breath like apples,

9 And the roof of your mouth like the best
wine.

THE SHULAMITE

The wine goes *down* smoothly for my
beloved,
Moving gently the lips of sleepers.[a]

10 I *am* my beloved's,
And his desire *is* toward me.

11 Come, my beloved,
Let us go forth to the field;
Let us lodge in the villages.

12 Let us get up early to the vineyards;
Let us see if the vine has budded,
Whether the grape blossoms are open,
And the pomegranates are in bloom.
There I will give you my love.

13 The mandrakes give off a fragrance,
And at our gates *are* pleasant *fruits*,
All manner, new and old,
Which I have laid up for you, my
beloved.

1 Oh, that you were like my brother,
Who nursed at my mother's breasts!
If I should find you outside,
I would kiss you;
I would not be despised.

2 I would lead you *and* bring you
Into the house of my
mother,
She *who* used to
instruct me.
I would cause you
to drink of spiced
wine,
Of the juice of my
pomegranate.

(TO THE DAUGHTERS
OF JERUSALEM)

3 His left hand *is* under
my head,
And his right hand
embraces me.

4 I charge you, O daughters of Jerusalem,
Do not stir up nor awaken love
Until it pleases.

LOVE RENEWED IN LEBANON

A RELATIVE

5 Who *is* this coming up from the
wilderness,
Leaning upon her beloved?

I awakened you under the apple tree.
There your mother brought you forth;
There she *who* bore you
brought *you* forth.

THE SHULAMITE TO HER
BELOVED

6 Set me as a seal upon
your heart,
As a seal upon your
arm;

> "For love is as strong as death,
> jealousy as cruel as the grave;
> its flames are flames of fire,
> a most vehement flame."
> (Song of Solomon 8:6b)"

MARRIAGE
Where does
romantic
love come
from?
(8:6)

6:13 [a]Hebrew *Mahanaim*   **7:9** [a]Septuagint, Syriac, and Vulgate read *lips and teeth*.

For love *is as* strong as death,
Jealousy *as* cruel as the grave;[a]
Its flames *are* flames of fire,
A most vehement[b] flame.

7   Many waters cannot quench love,
Nor can the floods drown it.
If a man would give for love
All the wealth of his house,
It would be utterly despised.

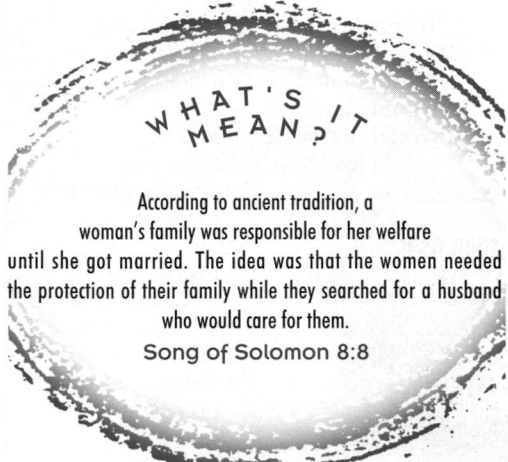

WHAT'S IT MEAN?

According to ancient tradition, a woman's family was responsible for her welfare until she got married. The idea was that the women needed the protection of their family while they searched for a husband who would care for them.

Song of Solomon 8:8

THE SHULAMITE'S BROTHERS
8   We have a little sister,
And she has no breasts.
What shall we do for our sister

In the day when she is spoken for?
9   If she *is* a wall,
We will build upon her
A battlement of silver;
And if she *is* a door,
We will enclose her
With boards of cedar.

THE SHULAMITE
10   I *am* a wall,
And my breasts like towers;
Then I became in his eyes
As one who found peace.
11   Solomon had a vineyard at Baal Hamon;
He leased the vineyard to keepers;
Everyone was to bring for its fruit
A thousand silver coins.

(TO SOLOMON)
12   My own vineyard *is* before me.
You, O Solomon, *may have* a thousand,
And those who tend its fruit two
        hundred.

THE BELOVED
13   You who dwell in the gardens,
The companions listen for your voice—
Let me hear it!

THE SHULAMITE
14   Make haste, my beloved,
And be like a gazelle
Or a young stag
On the mountains of spices.

8:6 [a]Or *Sheol* [b]Literally *A flame of Yah* (a poetic form of *YHWH, the* LORD)

isaiah

CONTENT Isaiah was a big fish in the prophet pond. He was well educated and a good communicator. He was known for being the most evangelistic of the prophets. That means instead of preaching only to God's people, he invited people to know God. He was also respected by government officials of his day and was able to influence Israel's government from the top on down.

Imagine Isaiah as a street preacher walking around town wearing a big sandwich sign. (You know those signs that hang from your shoulders with a message hanging down in front of you and behind you.) If that had been the case, Isaiah's sign on the front would have said, "STOP SINNING!" That wouldn't be unusual for a prophet to say. All the prophets said that. But Isaiah's prophetic sign had a flip side. On the back side it would have said, "GOD WILL SAVE YOU." Isaiah talked about salvation more than any other prophet.

Isaiah was convinced that salvation was possible if only people would repent of their sins and put their faith in God's goodness instead of their own. This truth was his passion. Sharing it was his life's mission.

Outline

Purpose God firmly intends to bless humanity.

Theme Salvation

Date of writing 740–680 B.C.

Bible Talk

Isaiah's Vision

What do you think heaven would look like if you could peel back the layers of reality-as-we-know-it and see right in? Isaiah got a glimpse of heaven. He saw a throne and a temple. He saw six-winged creatures worshiping God. These creatures sang a song you might recognize. It starts out, "Holy, Holy, Holy." If you go to church a lot, you probably have heard some songs that are based on this vision of Isaiah's.

When Isaiah was faced with God's holiness, he became so painfully aware of his own unholiness. It's like if you go to a party and stand by somebody who is dressed fancier than you've ever seen before, you suddenly evaluate how you are dressed. When Isaiah compared himself to God, he realized that he needed to be forgiven and cleaned up.

GOD AND SIN

Have you ever seen those shock collars for dogs that are used to teach them not to bark or not to cross over an invisible fence (made of electrical currents)? Sometimes it seems like it would be easier to learn not to sin if God used those electronic collars on us. How easy would it be to stop lying if every time you lied you felt an electric current run through your body?

God doesn't give us collars, though. He just gives us a conscience. He also gives us people, like Isaiah, who understand that God is holy and we are not. These people remind us that understanding God's holiness should affect how we live our lives.

¹The vision of Isaiah the son of Amoz, which he saw concerning Judah and Jerusalem in the days of Uzziah, Jotham, Ahaz, *and* Hezekiah, kings of Judah.

THE WICKEDNESS OF JUDAH

2 Hear, O heavens, and give ear, O earth!
For the LORD has spoken:
"I have nourished and brought up children,
And they have rebelled against Me;
3 The ox knows its owner
And the donkey its master's crib;
But Israel does not know,
My people do not consider."

WHAT'S IT MEAN?

Solomon's reign marked the end of Israel as a united country. After Solomon died, the nation split into two kingdoms, Israel and Judah. The prophet Isaiah was alive when Israel, the northern kingdom, was conquered by the Assyrians in 722 B.C.

Isaiah 1:1

4 Alas, sinful nation,
A people laden with iniquity,
A brood of evildoers,
Children who are corrupters!
They have forsaken the LORD,
They have provoked to anger
The Holy One of Israel,
They have turned away backward.

5 Why should you be stricken again?
You will revolt more and more.
The whole head is sick,
And the whole heart faints.
6 From the sole of the foot even to the head,
There is no soundness in it,
But wounds and bruises and putrefying sores;
They have not been closed or bound up,
Or soothed with ointment.

7 Your country *is* desolate,
Your cities *are* burned with fire;

Strangers devour your land in your presence;
And *it is* desolate, as overthrown by strangers.
8 So the daughter of Zion is left as a booth in a vineyard,
As a hut in a garden of cucumbers,
As a besieged city.
9 Unless the LORD of hosts
Had left to us a very small remnant,
We would have become like Sodom,
We would have been made like Gomorrah.

10 Hear the word of the LORD,
You rulers of Sodom;
Give ear to the law of our God,
You people of Gomorrah:
11 "To what purpose *is* the multitude of your sacrifices to Me?"
Says the LORD.
"I have had enough of burnt offerings of rams
And the fat of fed cattle.
I do not delight in the blood of bulls,
Or of lambs or goats.

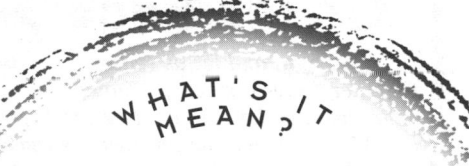

WHAT'S IT MEAN?

The last thing a city wanted to be compared to was Sodom and Gomorrah. These two towns, which may have been located near the southern end of the Dead Sea, were destroyed by fire and sulfur from heaven. God handed down the "death penalty" for Sodom and Gomorrah because of their extreme wickedness.

Isaiah 1:9

12 "When you come to appear before Me,
Who has required this from your hand,
To trample My courts?
13 Bring no more futile sacrifices;
Incense is an abomination to Me.
The New Moons, the Sabbaths, and the calling of assemblies—
I cannot endure iniquity and the sacred meeting.
14 Your New Moons and your appointed feasts
My soul hates;

They are a trouble to Me,
I am weary of bearing *them*.
15 When you spread out your hands,
I will hide My eyes from you;
Even though you make many prayers,
I will not hear.
Your hands are full of blood.

16 "Wash yourselves, make yourselves clean;
Put away the evil of your doings from
before My eyes.
Cease to do evil,
17 Learn to do good;
Seek justice,
Rebuke the oppressor;*a*
Defend the fatherless,
Plead for the widow.

18 "Come now, and let us reason
together,"
Says the LORD,

SIN
What should we do about sin in our lives?
(1:16–18)

On the Edge

"Come now, and let us reason together," says the LORD, "Though your sins are like scarlet, they shall be as white as snow; though they are red like crimson, they shall be as wool" (Is. 1:18).

You've got a personal invitation to a private dinner with a king. What? Sure you do. It's right here in Isaiah 1:18. God invites you to come and reason things out. He's letting you know that He really wants you to talk over your life with Him. It's not that He doesn't already know exactly what's going on—He just wants the pleasure of knowing you care enough about Him to share it. Specifically, this verse is referring to sin. The Lord invites people to confess their sin to Him and turn their lives around. With God, it's that simple. All you've got to do to get your life headed in the right direction is talk it over with Him. He'll take it from there.

SEE FOR YOURSELF:
Ps. 51:9; 62:8;
Is. 43:25

"Though your sins are like scarlet,
They shall be as white as snow;
Though they are red like crimson,
They shall be as wool.
19 If you are willing and obedient,
You shall eat the good of the land;
20 But if you refuse and rebel,
You shall be devoured by the sword";
For the mouth of the LORD has spoken.

THE DEGENERATE CITY

21 How the faithful city has become a
harlot!
It was full of justice;
Righteousness lodged in it,
But now murderers.
22 Your silver has become dross,
Your wine mixed with water.
23 Your princes *are* rebellious,
And companions of thieves;
Everyone loves bribes,
And follows after rewards.
They do not defend the fatherless,
Nor does the cause of the widow come
before them.

24 Therefore the Lord says,
The LORD of hosts, the Mighty One of
Israel,
"Ah, I will rid Myself of My adversaries,
And take vengeance on My enemies.
25 I will turn My hand against you,
And thoroughly purge away your dross,
And take away all your alloy.
26 I will restore your judges as at the first,
And your counselors as at the beginning.
Afterward you shall be called the city of
righteousness, the faithful city."

27 Zion shall be redeemed with justice,
And her penitents with righteousness.
28 The destruction of transgressors and of
sinners *shall be* together,
And those who forsake the LORD shall be
consumed.
29 For they*a* shall be ashamed of the
terebinth trees
Which you have desired;
And you shall be embarrassed because of
the gardens
Which you have chosen.
30 For you shall be as a terebinth whose leaf
fades,
And as a garden that has no water.

1:17 *a*Some ancient versions read *the oppressed.* **1:29** *a*Following Masoretic Text, Septuagint, and Vulgate; some Hebrew manuscripts and Targum read *you.*

31 The strong shall be as tinder,
And the work of it as a spark;
Both will burn together,
And no one shall quench *them*.

THE FUTURE HOUSE OF GOD

1The word that Isaiah the son of Amoz saw concerning Judah and Jerusalem.

2 Now it shall come to pass in the latter days
That the mountain of the LORD's house
Shall be established on the top of the mountains,
And shall be exalted above the hills;
And all nations shall flow to it.
3 Many people shall come and say,
"Come, and let us go up to the mountain of the LORD,
To the house of the God of Jacob;
He will teach us His ways,
And we shall walk in His paths."
For out of Zion shall go forth the law,
And the word of the LORD from Jerusalem.
4 He shall judge between the nations,
And rebuke many people;
They shall beat their swords into plowshares,
And their spears into pruning hooks;
Nation shall not lift up sword against nation,
Neither shall they learn war anymore.

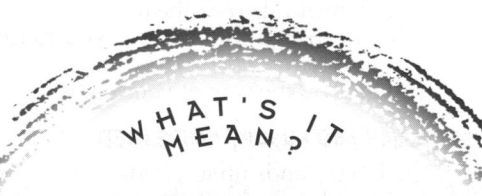

WHAT'S IT MEAN?

Here's a quick review of Israel's early history: Jacob, who was also called Israel, had twelve sons. From those sons came the twelve tribes of Israel. During Isaiah's time, the temple where the Israelites worshiped God was located on Moriah in Jerusalem, in the territory that belonged to the tribe of Judah.

Isaiah 2:3

THE DAY OF THE LORD

5 O house of Jacob, come and let us walk
In the light of the LORD.

6 For You have forsaken Your people, the house of Jacob,

WHAT'S IT MEAN?

The Philistines, who lived along the coast of the Mediterranean Sea, had been among the Israelites' most notorious enemies. Over the years, though, the hatred between the two nations cooled and old grudges were forgotten. The Israelites even began to allow their children to marry Philistines, despite the fact that such marriages went against God's Law.

Isaiah 2:6

Because they are filled with eastern ways;
They *are* soothsayers like the Philistines,
And they are pleased with the children of foreigners.
7 Their land is also full of silver and gold,
And there is no end to their treasures;
Their land is also full of horses,
And there is no end to their chariots.
8 Their land is also full of idols;
They worship the work of their own hands,
That which their own fingers have made.
9 People bow down,
And each man humbles himself;
Therefore do not forgive them.

10 Enter into the rock, and hide in the dust,
From the terror of the LORD
And the glory of His majesty.
11 The lofty looks of man shall be humbled,
The haughtiness of men shall be bowed down,
And the LORD alone shall be exalted in that day.

12 For the day of the LORD of hosts
Shall come upon everything proud and lofty,
Upon everything lifted up—
And it shall be brought low—
13 Upon all the cedars of Lebanon *that are* high and lifted up,
And upon all the oaks of Bashan;
14 Upon all the high mountains,
And upon all the hills *that are* lifted up;
15 Upon every high tower,
And upon every fortified wall;
16 Upon all the ships of Tarshish,

And upon all the beautiful sloops.

17 The loftiness of man shall be bowed
down,
And the haughtiness of men shall be
brought low;
The LORD alone will be exalted in that day,

18 But the idols He shall utterly abolish.

19 They shall go into the holes of the rocks,
And into the caves of the earth,
From the terror of the LORD
And the glory of His majesty,
When He arises to shake the earth
mightily.

20 In that day a man will cast away his idols
of silver
And his idols of gold,
Which they made, each for himself to
worship,
To the moles and bats,

21 To go into the clefts of the rocks,
And into the crags of the rugged rocks,
From the terror of the LORD
And the glory of His majesty,
When He arises to shake the earth
mightily.

22 Sever yourselves from such a man,
Whose breath is in his nostrils;
For of what account is he?

JUDGMENT ON JUDAH AND JERUSALEM

1 For behold, the Lord, the LORD of hosts,
Takes away from Jerusalem and from
Judah
The stock and the store,
The whole supply of bread and the whole
supply of water;

2 The mighty man and the man of war,
The judge and the prophet,
And the diviner and the elder;

3 The captain of fifty and the honorable
man,
The counselor and the skillful artisan,
And the expert enchanter.

4 "I will give children to be their princes,
And babes shall rule over them.

5 The people will be oppressed,
Every one by another and every one by
his neighbor;
The child will be insolent toward the
elder,
And the base toward the honorable."

6 When a man takes hold of his brother
In the house of his father, saying,
"You have clothing;
You be our ruler,
And let these ruins be under your power,"ᵃ

7 In that day he will protest, saying,
"I cannot cure your ills,
For in my house is neither food nor
clothing;
Do not make me a ruler of the people."

8 For Jerusalem stumbled,
And Judah is fallen,
Because their tongue and their doings
Are against the LORD,
To provoke the eyes of His glory.

9 The look on their countenance witnesses
against them,
And they declare their sin as Sodom;
They do not hide it.
Woe to their soul!
For they have brought evil upon
themselves.

10 "Say to the righteous that it shall be well
with them,
For they shall eat the fruit of their doings.

11 Woe to the wicked! It shall be ill with him,
For the reward of his hands shall be
given him.

12 As for My people, children are their
oppressors,
And women rule over them.
O My people! Those who lead you cause
you to err,
And destroy the way of your paths."

OPPRESSION AND LUXURY CONDEMNED

13 The LORD stands up to plead,
And stands to judge the people.

14 The LORD will enter into judgment
With the elders of His people
And His princes:
"For you have eaten up the vineyard;
The plunder of the poor is in your
houses.

15 What do you mean by crushing My
people
And grinding the faces of the poor?"
Says the Lord GOD of hosts.

16 Moreover the LORD says:

"Because the daughters of Zion are
haughty,

3:6 ᵃLiterally hand

And walk with outstretched necks
And wanton eyes,
Walking and mincing *as* they go,
Making a jingling with
  their feet,

17 Therefore the Lord will
  strike with a scab
The crown of the head of
  the daughters of Zion,
And the LORD will
  uncover their secret
  parts."

VANITY

What does
God think
about
vanity?
(3:16–18)

18 In that day the Lord will take away the
    finery:
    The jingling anklets, the scarves, and the
      crescents;
19 The pendants, the bracelets, and the veils;
20 The headdresses, the leg ornaments, and
      the headbands;
    The perfume boxes, the charms,
21   and the rings;
    The nose jewels,
22   the festal apparel, and the mantles;
    The outer garments, the purses,
23   and the mirrors;
    The fine linen, the turbans, and the robes.

24And so it shall be:

    Instead of a sweet smell there will be a
      stench;
    Instead of a sash, a rope;
    Instead of well-set hair, baldness;
    Instead of a rich robe, a girding of
      sackcloth;
    And branding instead of beauty.
25 Your men shall fall by the sword,
    And your mighty in the war.

26 Her gates shall lament and mourn,
    And she *being* desolate shall sit on the
      ground.

1   And in that day seven women shall take
      hold of one man, saying,
    "We will eat our own food and wear our
      own apparel;
    Only let us be called by your name,
    To take away our reproach."

THE RENEWAL OF ZION

2   In that day the Branch of the LORD shall
      be beautiful and glorious;
    And the fruit of the earth *shall be* excellent
      and appealing
    For those of Israel who have escaped.

3And it shall come to pass that *he who is* left
in Zion and remains in Jerusalem will be called
holy—everyone who is recorded among the
living in Jerusalem. 4When the Lord has washed
away the filth of the daughters of Zion, and
purged the blood of Jerusalem from her midst,
by the spirit of judgment and by the spirit of
burning, 5then the LORD will create above every
dwelling place of Mount Zion, and above her
assemblies, a cloud and smoke by day and the
shining of a flaming fire by night. For over all
the glory there *will be* a covering. 6And there
will be a tabernacle for shade in the daytime
from the heat, for a place of refuge, and for a
shelter from storm and rain.

GOD'S DISAPPOINTING VINEYARD

1   Now let me sing to my Well-beloved
    A song of my Beloved regarding His
      vineyard:

    My Well-beloved has a vineyard
    On a very fruitful hill.
2   He dug it up and cleared out its stones,
    And planted it with the choicest vine.
    He built a tower in its midst,
    And also made a winepress in it;
    So He expected *it* to bring forth *good*
      grapes,
    But it brought forth wild grapes.

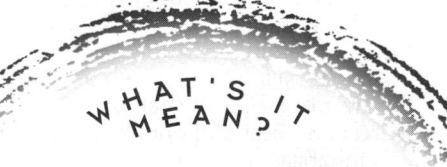

WHAT'S IT MEAN?

Why would someone build a tower in the
middle of a vineyard? To prevent people from
stealing grapes. From the tower, a guard could spot thieves
attempting a fruit heist. He could also defend the vineyard from that
vantage point with a bow and arrow or a slingshot. The more the
grapes ripened, the more the vineyard
owner would step up his security.
Isaiah 5:2

3   "And now, O inhabitants of Jerusalem and
      men of Judah,
    Judge, please, between Me and My
      vineyard.
4   What more could have been done to My
      vineyard
    That I have not done in it?

Why then, when I expected *it* to bring
   forth *good* grapes,
Did it bring forth wild grapes?

5 And now, please let Me tell you what I
   will do to My vineyard:
I will take away its hedge, and it shall be
   burned;
And break down its wall, and it shall be
   trampled down.

6 I will lay it waste;
It shall not be pruned or dug,
But there shall come up briers and thorns.
I will also command the clouds
That they rain no rain on it."

7 For the vineyard of the LORD of hosts *is*
   the house of Israel,
And the men of Judah are His pleasant
   plant.
He looked for justice, but behold,
   oppression;
For righteousness, but behold, a cry *for*
   help.

IMPENDING JUDGMENT ON EXCESSES

8 Woe to those who join house to
   house;
They add field to field,
Till *there is* no place
Where they may dwell
   alone in the midst of
   the land!

9 In my hearing the LORD of
   hosts *said,*
"Truly, many houses shall be desolate,
Great and beautiful ones, without
   inhabitant.

10 For ten acres of vineyard shall yield one
   bath,
And a homer of seed shall yield one
   ephah."

11 Woe to those who rise early in the
   morning,
That they may follow intoxicating drink;
Who continue until night, *till* wine
   inflames them!

12 The harp and the strings,
The tambourine and flute,
And wine are in their feasts;
But they do not regard the work of the
   LORD,
Nor consider the operation of His hands.

13 Therefore my people have gone into
   captivity,
Because *they have* no knowledge;

Their honorable men *are* famished,
And their multitude dried up with thirst.

14 Therefore Sheol has enlarged itself
And opened its mouth beyond measure;
Their glory and their multitude and their
   pomp,
And he who is jubilant, shall descend
   into it.

15 People shall be brought down,
Each man shall be humbled,
And the eyes of the lofty shall be
   humbled.

16 But the LORD of hosts shall be exalted in
   judgment,
And God who is holy shall be hallowed
   in righteousness.

17 Then the lambs shall feed in their pasture,
And in the waste places of the fat ones
   strangers shall eat.

18 Woe to those who draw iniquity with
   cords of vanity,
And sin as if with a cart rope;

19 That say, "Let Him make speed *and* hasten
   His work,
That we may see *it;*
And let the counsel of the Holy One of
   Israel draw near and come,
That we may know *it.*"

20 Woe to those who call evil good, and
   good evil;
Who put darkness for light, and light for
   darkness;
Who put bitter for sweet, and sweet for
   bitter!

21 Woe to *those who are* wise in their own
   eyes,
And prudent in their own sight!

22 Woe to men mighty at
   drinking wine,
Woe to men valiant for
   mixing intoxicating
   drink,

23 Who justify the wicked
   for a bribe,
And take away justice from
   the righteous man!

24 Therefore, as the fire devours the stubble,
And the flame consumes the chaff,
So their root will be as rottenness,
And their blossom will ascend like dust;
Because they have rejected the law of the
   LORD of hosts,

GREED

What's wrong with greed? (5:8)

DRINKING

Is obsessive drinking bad for us? (5:22)

And despised the word of the Holy One
   of Israel.
25 Therefore the anger of the LORD is
   aroused against His people;
He has stretched out His
   hand against them
And stricken them,
And the hills trembled.
Their carcasses *were* as
   refuse in the midst
   of the streets.

For all this His anger is
   not turned away,
But His hand *is* stretched
   out still.

26 He will lift up a banner to the nations
   from afar,
And will whistle to them from the end of
   the earth;
Surely they shall come with speed, swiftly.
27 No one will be weary or stumble among
   them,
No one will slumber or sleep;
Nor will the belt on their loins be loosed,
Nor the strap of their sandals be broken;
28 Whose arrows *are* sharp,
And all their bows bent;
Their horses' hooves will seem like flint,
And their wheels like a whirlwind.
29 Their roaring *will be* like a lion,
They will roar like young lions;
Yes, they will roar
And lay hold of the prey;
They will carry *it* away safely,
And no one will deliver.
30 In that day they will roar against them
Like the roaring of the sea.
And if *one* looks to the land,
Behold, darkness *and* sorrow;
And the light is darkened by the clouds.

ISAIAH CALLED TO BE A PROPHET

1 In the year that King Uzziah died, I saw the Lord sitting on a throne, high and lifted up, and the train of His *robe* filled the temple. 2 Above it stood seraphim; each one had six wings: with two he covered his face, with two he covered his feet, and with two he flew. 3 And one cried to another and said:

"Holy, holy, holy *is* the LORD of hosts;
The whole earth *is* full of His glory!"

ANGELS
What do some angels look like? (6:2)

4 And the posts of the door were shaken by the voice of him who cried out, and the house was filled with smoke.
5 So I said:

"Woe *is* me, for I am
   undone!
Because I *am* a man of
   unclean lips,
And I dwell in the midst
   of a people of
   unclean lips;
For my eyes have seen
   the King,
The LORD of hosts."

"Holy, holy, holy is the LORD of hosts; the whole earth is full of His glory!" (Isaiah 6:3)

6 Then one of the seraphim flew to me, having in his hand a live coal *which* he had taken with the tongs from the altar. 7 And he touched my mouth *with it*, and said:

"Behold, this has touched your lips;
Your iniquity is taken away,
And your sin purged."

8 Also I heard the voice of the Lord, saying:

"Whom shall I send,
And who will go for Us?"

Then I said, "Here *am* I! Send me."
9 And He said, "Go, and tell this people:

'Keep on hearing, but do not understand;
Keep on seeing, but do not perceive.'

10 "Make the heart of this people dull,
And their ears heavy,
And shut their eyes;
Lest they see with their eyes,
And hear with their ears,
And understand with their heart,
And return and be healed."

11 Then I said, "Lord, how long?"
And He answered:

"Until the cities are laid waste and without
   inhabitant,
The houses are without a man,
The land is utterly desolate,
12 The LORD has removed men far away,
And the forsaken places *are* many in the
   midst of the land.
13 But yet a tenth *will be* in it,
And will return and be for consuming,
As a terebinth tree or as an oak,

Whose stump *remains* when it is cut
   down.
So the holy seed *shall be* its stump."

ISAIAH SENT TO KING AHAZ

[1]Now it came to pass in the days of Ahaz the son of Jotham, the son of Uzziah, king of Judah, *that* Rezin king of Syria and Pekah the son of Remaliah, king of Israel, went up to Jerusalem to *make* war against it, but could not prevail against it. [2]And it was told to the house of David, saying, "Syria's forces are deployed in Ephraim." So his heart and the heart of his people were moved as the trees of the woods are moved with the wind.

[3]Then the LORD said to Isaiah, "Go out now to meet Ahaz, you and Shear-Jashub[a] your son, at the end of the aqueduct from the upper pool, on the highway to the Fuller's Field, [4]and say to him: 'Take heed, and be quiet; do not fear or be fainthearted for these two stubs of smoking firebrands, for the fierce anger of Rezin and Syria, and the son of Remaliah. [5]Because Syria, Ephraim, and the son of Remaliah have plotted evil against you, saying, [6]"Let us go up against Judah and trouble it, and let us make a gap in its wall for ourselves, and set a king over them, the son of Tabel"—[7]thus says the Lord GOD:

   "It shall not stand,
      Nor shall it come to pass.
[8]   For the head of Syria *is* Damascus,
      And the head of Damascus *is* Rezin.
      Within sixty-five years Ephraim will be
         broken,
      So that it will not *be* a people.
[9]   The head of Ephraim *is* Samaria,
      And the head of Samaria *is* Remaliah's
         son.
      If you will not believe,
      Surely you shall not be established." ' "

THE IMMANUEL PROPHECY

[10]Moreover the LORD spoke again to Ahaz, saying, [11]"Ask a sign for yourself from the LORD your God; ask it either in the depth or in the height above."

[12]But Ahaz said, "I will not ask, nor will I test the LORD!"

[13]Then he said, "Hear now, O house of David! *Is it* a small thing for you to weary men, but will you weary my God also? [14]Therefore the Lord Himself will give you a sign: Behold, the virgin shall conceive and bear a Son, and

shall call His name Immanuel.[a] [15]Curds and honey He shall eat, that He may know to refuse the evil and choose the good. [16]For before the Child shall know to refuse the evil and choose the good, the land that you dread will be forsaken by both her kings. [17]The LORD will bring the king of Assyria upon you and your people and your father's house—days that have not come since the day that Ephraim departed from Judah."

JESUS

Was Jesus born of a virgin? (7:14)

[18]   And it shall come to pass in that day
      That the LORD will whistle for the fly
      That *is* in the farthest part of the rivers of
         Egypt,
      And for the bee that *is* in the land of
         Assyria.
[19]   They will come, and all of them will rest
      In the desolate valleys and in the clefts of
         the rocks,
      And on all thorns and in all pastures.

[20]   In the same day the Lord will shave with
         a hired razor,
      With those from beyond the River,[a] with
         the king of Assyria,
      The head and the hair of the legs,
      And will also remove the beard.

WHAT'S IT MEAN?

A hair weaving business would have been a hit with men in ancient Israel, because they took great pride in their hair. Baldness was considered an embarrassment. For the most part, the only people who shaved were Levites, victims of skin disease, and people in mourning. To be shaved (involuntarily) by someone else was a tremendous insult.
Isaiah 7:20

[21]   It shall be in that day
      That a man will keep alive a young cow
         and two sheep;
[22]   So it shall be, from the abundance of milk
         they give,

7:3 [a]Literally *A Remnant Shall Return*   **7:14** [a]Literally *God-With-Us*   **7:20** [a]That is, the Euphrates

That he will eat curds;
For curds and honey everyone will eat
  who is left in the land.

23 It shall happen in that day,
That wherever there could be a thousand
  vines
Worth a thousand *shekels* of silver,
It will be for briers and thorns.
24 With arrows and bows men will come
  there,
Because all the land will become briers
  and thorns.

25 And to any hill which could be dug with
  the hoe,
You will not go there for fear of briers
  and thorns;
But it will become a range for oxen
And a place for sheep to roam.

ASSYRIA WILL INVADE THE LAND

¹Moreover the LORD said to me, "Take a large scroll, and write on it with a man's pen concerning Maher-Shalal-Hash-Baz.ª ²And I will take for Myself faithful witnesses to record, Uriah the priest and Zechariah the son of Jeberechiah."

³Then I went to the prophetess, and she conceived and bore a son. Then the LORD said to me, "Call his name Maher-Shalal-Hash-Baz; ⁴for before the child shall have knowledge to cry 'My father' and 'My mother', the riches of Damascus and the spoil of Samaria will be taken away before the king of Assyria."

⁵The LORD also spoke to me again, saying:

6 "Inasmuch as these people refused
The waters of Shiloah that flow softly,
And rejoice in Rezin and in Remaliah's
  son;
7 Now therefore, behold, the Lord brings
  up over them
The waters of the River,ª strong and
  mighty—
The king of Assyria and all his glory;
He will go up over all his channels
And go over all his banks.
8 He will pass through Judah,
He will overflow and pass over,
He will reach up to the neck;
And the stretching out of his wings
Will fill the breadth of Your land,
  O Immanuel.ª

9 "Be shattered, O you peoples, and be
  broken in pieces!
Give ear, all you from far countries.
Gird yourselves, but be broken in pieces;
Gird yourselves, but be broken in pieces.
10 Take counsel together, but it will come to
  nothing;
Speak the word, but it will not stand,
For God *is* with us."ª

FEAR GOD, HEED HIS WORD

¹¹For the LORD spoke thus to me with a strong hand, and instructed me that I should not walk in the way of this people, saying:

12 "Do not say, 'A conspiracy,'
Concerning all that this people call a
  conspiracy,
Nor be afraid of their threats, nor be
  troubled.
13 The LORD of hosts, Him you shall hallow;
Let Him *be* your fear,
And *let* Him *be* your dread.
14 He will be as a sanctuary,
But a stone of stumbling and a rock of
  offense
To both the houses of Israel,
As a trap and a snare to the inhabitants
  of Jerusalem.
15 And many among them shall stumble;
They shall fall and be broken,
Be snared and taken."

16 Bind up the testimony,
Seal the law among my disciples.
17 And I will wait on the LORD,
Who hides His face from the house of
  Jacob;
And I will hope in Him.
18 Here am I and the children whom the
  LORD has given me!
We are for signs and wonders in Israel
From the LORD of hosts,
Who dwells in Mount Zion.

¹⁹And when they say to you, "Seek those who are mediums and wizards, who whisper and mutter," should not a people seek their God? *Should they seek* the dead on behalf of the living? ²⁰To the law and to the testimony! If they do not speak according to this word, *it is* because *there is* no light in them.

²¹They will pass through it hard-pressed and hungry; and it shall happen, when they are

---

8:1 ªLiterally *Speed the Spoil, Hasten the Booty* **8:7** ªThat is, the Euphrates **8:8** ªLiterally *God-With-Us*
8:10 ªHebrew *Immanuel*

hungry, that they will be enraged and curse their king and their God, and look upward. [22]Then they will look to the earth, and see trouble and darkness, gloom of anguish; and *they will be* driven into darkness.

THE GOVERNMENT OF THE PROMISED SON

1   Nevertheless the gloom *will* not *be* upon
       her who *is* distressed,
    As when at first He lightly esteemed
    The land of Zebulun and the land of
       Naphtali,
    And afterward more heavily oppressed
       her,
    By the way of the sea, beyond the Jordan,
    In Galilee of the Gentiles.
2   The people who walked in darkness
    Have seen a great light;
    Those who dwelt in the land of the
       shadow of death,
    Upon them a light has shined.

3   You have multiplied the nation
    And increased its joy;[a]
    They rejoice before You
    According to the joy of harvest,
    As *men* rejoice when they divide the spoil.
4   For You have broken the yoke of his
       burden
    And the staff of his shoulder,
    The rod of his oppressor,
    As in the day of Midian.
5   For every warrior's sandal from the noisy
       battle,
    And garments rolled in blood,
    Will be used for burning *and* fuel of fire.

6   For unto us a Child is born,
    Unto us a Son is given;
    And the government will
       be upon His shoulder.
    And His name will be
       called
    Wonderful, Counselor,
       Mighty God,
    Everlasting Father, Prince of
       Peace.
7   Of the increase of *His* government and
       peace
    There will be no end,
    Upon the throne of David and over His
       kingdom,
    To order it and establish it with judgment
       and justice

JESUS

What is
Jesus
known for?
(9:6)

On the Edge

For unto us a Child is born, unto us a Son is given; and the government will be upon His shoulder. And His name will be called Wonderful, Counselor, Mighty God, Everlasting Father, Prince of Peace (Is. 9:6).

Seems like everybody is looking for a little peace and quiet these days. There's so much happening so fast in your life and in the world. There's so much to be confused about and you've got a really busy life—school, sports, church, friends, family. Whatever is going on in your life, it can get pretty hectic trying to figure it all out. But stop. It's time for some peace in your life. Jesus is the One who gives you peace. He whispers calm into your crazy situation. He gives you a break from the frantic worry that sometimes overwhelms you. When you get into His presence, there is peace. When you take your eyes off of your circumstances long enough to turn them toward Him, you immediately find relief. Remember, Jesus refuses to panic. No matter how hurried or confused your life may be, take a second to put the Prince of Peace on the throne of your life. Then you won't panic either.

SEE FOR YOURSELF:
John 14:27; Acts 10:36;
Col. 3:15

From that time forward, even forever.
    The zeal of the Lord of hosts will perform
       this.

THE PUNISHMENT OF SAMARIA

8   The Lord sent a word against Jacob,
    And it has fallen on Israel.
9   All the people will know—
    Ephraim and the inhabitant of Samaria—
    Who say in pride and arrogance of heart:
10   "The bricks have fallen down,
    But we will rebuild with hewn stones;
    The sycamores are cut down,
    But we will replace *them* with cedars."
11   Therefore the LORD shall set up
    The adversaries of Rezin against him,

9:3 [a]Following Qere and Targum; Kethib and Vulgate read *not increased joy;* Septuagint reads *Most of the people You brought down in Your joy.*

And spur his enemies on,
12 The Syrians before and the Philistines
      behind;
And they shall devour Israel with an
      open mouth.

For all this His anger is not turned away,
But His hand *is* stretched out still.

13 For the people do not turn to Him who
      strikes them,
Nor do they seek the LORD of hosts.
14 Therefore the LORD will cut off head and
      tail from Israel,
Palm branch and bulrush in one day.
15 The elder and honorable, he *is* the head;
The prophet who teaches lies, he *is* the
      tail.
16 For the leaders of this people cause *them*
      to err,
And *those who are* led by them are
      destroyed.
17 Therefore the Lord will have no joy in
      their young men,
Nor have mercy on their fatherless and
      widows;
For everyone *is* a hypocrite and an
      evildoer,
And every mouth speaks folly.

For all this His anger is not turned away,
But His hand *is* stretched out still.

18 For wickedness burns as the fire;
It shall devour the briers and thorns,
And kindle in the thickets of the forest;
They shall mount up *like* rising smoke.
19 Through the wrath of the LORD of hosts
The land is burned up,
And the people shall be as fuel for the fire;
No man shall spare his brother.
20 And he shall snatch on the right hand
And be hungry;
He shall devour on the left hand
And not be satisfied;
Every man shall eat the flesh of his own
      arm.
21 Manasseh *shall devour* Ephraim, and
      Ephraim Manasseh;
Together they *shall be* against Judah.

For all this His anger is not turned away,
But His hand *is* stretched out still.

1 "Woe to those who decree unrighteous
      decrees,
Who write misfortune,

2 *Which* they have prescribed
To rob the needy of justice,
And to take what is right from the poor
      of My people,
That widows may be their prey,
And *that* they may rob the fatherless.
3 What will you do in the day of
      punishment,
And in the desolation *which* will come
      from afar?
To whom will you flee for help?
And where will you leave your glory?
4 Without Me they shall bow down among
      the prisoners,
And they shall fall among the slain."

For all this His anger is not turned away,
But His hand *is* stretched out still.

ARROGANT ASSYRIA ALSO JUDGED

5 "Woe to Assyria, the rod of My anger
And the staff in whose hand is My
      indignation.
6 I will send him against an ungodly
      nation,
And against the people of My wrath
I will give him charge,
To seize the spoil, to take the prey,
And to tread them down like the mire of
      the streets.
7 Yet he does not mean so,
Nor does his heart think so;
But *it is* in his heart to destroy,
And cut off not a few nations.
8 For he says,
'*Are* not my princes altogether kings?
9 *Is* not Calno like Carchemish?
Is not Hamath like Arpad?
Is not Samaria like Damascus?
10 As my hand has found the kingdoms of
      the idols,
Whose carved images excelled those of
      Jerusalem and Samaria,
11 As I have done to Samaria and her idols,
Shall I not do also to Jerusalem and her
      idols?' "

12Therefore it shall come to pass, when the
Lord has performed all His work on Mount
Zion and on Jerusalem, *that He will say,* "I will
punish the fruit of the arrogant heart of the king
of Assyria, and the glory of his haughty looks."
13For he says:

"By the strength of my hand I have
      done *it,*
And by my wisdom, for I am prudent;

Also I have removed the boundaries of
   the people,
And have robbed their treasuries;
So I have put down the inhabitants like a
   valiant *man.*
14 My hand has found like a nest the riches
   of the people,
And as one gathers eggs *that are* left,
I have gathered all the earth;
And there was no one who moved *his*
   wing,
Nor opened *his* mouth with even a
   peep."

15 Shall the ax boast itself against him who
   chops with it?
Or shall the saw exalt itself against him
   who saws with it?
As if a rod could wield *itself* against those
   who lift it up,
Or as if a staff could lift up, *as if it were*
   not wood!
16 Therefore the Lord, the Lord[a] of hosts,
Will send leanness among his fat ones;
And under his glory
He will kindle a burning
Like the burning of a fire.
17 So the Light of Israel will be for a fire,
And his Holy One for a flame;
It will burn and devour
His thorns and his briers in one day.
18 And it will consume the glory of his
   forest and of his fruitful field,
Both soul and body;
And they will be as when a sick man
   wastes away.
19 Then the rest of the trees of his forest
Will be so few in number
That a child may write them.

THE RETURNING REMNANT OF ISRAEL
20 And it shall come to pass in that day
That the remnant of Israel,
And such as have escaped of the house
   of Jacob,
Will never again depend on him who
   defeated them,
But will depend on the LORD, the Holy
   One of Israel, in truth.
21 The remnant will return, the remnant of
   Jacob,
To the Mighty God.
22 For though your people, O Israel, be as
   the sand of the sea,
A remnant of them will return;

The destruction decreed shall overflow
   with righteousness.
23 For the Lord GOD of hosts
Will make a determined end
In the midst of all the land.

24Therefore thus says the Lord GOD of hosts:
"O My people, who dwell in Zion, do not be
afraid of the Assyrian. He shall strike you with a
rod and lift up his staff against you, in the manner of Egypt. 25For yet a very little while and the
indignation will cease, as will My anger in their
destruction." 26And the LORD of hosts will stir up
a scourge for him like the slaughter of Midian
at the rock of Oreb; *as* His rod was on the sea,
so will He lift it up in the manner of Egypt.

WHAT'S IT MEAN?

The Midianites were longtime enemies of the
Israelites. Gideon, who had been appointed by God
as a "judge" or leader of the Israelites (long before the nation had a
king), led a small band of soldiers in battle against an enormous army
of Midianites. God fought on the side of the Israelites. Guess who
won the battle? Two Midianite leaders were captured during the fight.
One was put to death on the rock of Horeb,
the other at a nearby winepress.
Isaiah 10:26

27 It shall come to pass in that day
That his burden will be taken away from
   your shoulder,
And his yoke from your neck,
And the yoke will be destroyed because
   of the anointing oil.

28 He has come to Aiath,
He has passed Migron;
At Michmash he has attended to his
   equipment.
29 They have gone along the ridge,
They have taken up lodging at Geba.
Ramah is afraid,
Gibeah of Saul has fled.
30 Lift up your voice,
O daughter of Gallim!
Cause it to be heard as far as Laish—

10:16 [a]Following Bomberg; Masoretic Text and Dead Sea Scrolls read *YHWH* (*the* LORD).

O poor Anathoth![a]

31 Madmenah has fled,
The inhabitants of Gebim seek refuge.

32 As yet he will remain at Nob that day;
He will shake his fist at the mount of the
daughter of Zion,
The hill of Jerusalem.

33 Behold, the Lord,
The LORD of hosts,
Will lop off the
bough with
terror;
Those of high
stature *will be*
hewn down,
And the haughty
will be humbled.

34 He will cut down the
thickets of the forest
with iron,
And Lebanon will fall by the Mighty
One.

THE REIGN OF JESSE'S OFFSPRING

1 There shall come forth a Rod from the
stem of Jesse,
And a Branch shall grow out of his roots.

2 The Spirit of the LORD shall rest upon
Him,
The Spirit of wisdom and understanding,
The Spirit of counsel and might,

The Spirit of knowledge and of the fear of
the LORD.

3 His delight *is* in the fear of the LORD,
And He shall not judge by the sight of
His eyes,
Nor decide by the
hearing of His
ears;

4 But with
righteousness
He shall judge
the poor,
And decide with
equity for the
meek of the
earth;
He shall strike the
earth with the
rod of His
mouth,
And with the breath of His lips He shall
slay the wicked.

5 Righteousness shall be the belt of His
loins,
And faithfulness the belt of His waist.

6 "The wolf also shall dwell with the lamb,
The leopard shall lie down with the
young goat,
The calf and the young lion and the
fatling together;

> "The Spirit of the LORD shall rest upon Him, the Spirit of wisdom and understanding, the Spirit of counsel and might, the Spirit of knowledge and of the fear of the LORD."
> (Isaiah 11:2)

10:30 [a]Following Masoretic Text, Targum, and Vulgate; Septuagint and Syriac read *Listen to her, O Anathoth.*

Promise HE PROMISES TO GIVE YOU UNDERSTANDING, WISDOM, AND KNOWLEDGE.

The Spirit of the LORD shall rest upon Him, the Spirit of wisdom and understanding, the Spirit of counsel and might, the Spirit of knowledge and of the fear of the LORD (Is. 11:2).

This verse is talking specifically about a king who will arise from David's family. This king would be Jesus and He would receive understanding, wisdom, knowledge, and might from the Spirit of the Lord. But does that mean the Spirit won't give those gifts to anyone else? No, of course not. The Spirit of God gives understanding, wisdom, and knowledge to anyone who asks. He is the Source of those things. Read John 14—16 to see what the Holy Spirit's jobs are. You'll see some things that remind you of this verse. When you get in a situation where you need understanding, wisdom, or knowledge beyond your own, ask the Spirit for His help. He'll always be there for you.

SEE FOR YOURSELF:
Prov. 2:6; Luke 24:45; John 14—16; Col. 1:9; James 3:17

And a little child shall lead them.
7 The cow and the bear shall graze;
Their young ones shall lie down together;
And the lion shall eat straw like the ox.
8 The nursing child shall play by the
cobra's hole,
And the weaned child shall put his hand
in the viper's den.
9 They shall not hurt nor destroy in all My
holy mountain,
For the earth shall be full of the
knowledge of the LORD
As the waters cover the sea.

10 "And in that day there shall be a Root of
Jesse,
Who shall stand as a banner to the
people;
For the Gentiles shall seek Him,
And His resting place shall be glorious."

11 It shall come to pass in that day
That the Lord shall set His hand again the
second time
To recover the remnant of His people
who are left,
From Assyria and Egypt,
From Pathros and Cush,
From Elam and Shinar,
From Hamath and the islands of the sea.

12 He will set up a banner for the nations,
And will assemble the outcasts of Israel,
And gather together the dispersed of
Judah
From the four corners of the earth.
13 Also the envy of Ephraim shall depart,
And the adversaries of Judah shall be cut
off;
Ephraim shall not envy Judah,
And Judah shall not harass Ephraim.
14 But they shall fly down upon the shoulder
of the Philistines toward the west;
Together they shall plunder the people of
the East;
They shall lay their hand on Edom and
Moab;
And the people of Ammon shall obey
them.
15 The LORD will utterly destroy*a* the tongue
of the Sea of Egypt;
With His mighty wind He will shake His
fist over the River,*b*
And strike it in the seven streams,

And make *men* cross over dryshod.
16 There will be a highway for the remnant
of His people
Who will be left from Assyria,
As it was for Israel
In the day that he came up from the land
of Egypt.

A HYMN OF PRAISE

1 And in that day you will say:

"O LORD, I will praise You;
Though You were angry with me,
Your anger is turned away, and You
comfort me.
2 Behold, God *is* my salvation,
I will trust and not be afraid;
'For YAH, the LORD, *is* my strength
and song;
He also has become my
salvation.' "*a*

3 Therefore with joy you
will draw water
From the wells of salvation.

4 And in that day you will say:

"Praise the LORD, call upon His name;
Declare His deeds among the peoples,
Make mention that His name is exalted.
5 Sing to the LORD,
For He has done excellent things;
This *is* known in all the earth.
6 Cry out and shout, O inhabitant of Zion,
For great *is* the Holy One of Israel in your
midst!"

PROCLAMATION AGAINST BABYLON

1 The burden against Babylon which Isaiah
the son of Amoz saw.

2 "Lift up a banner on the high mountain,
Raise your voice to them;
Wave your hand, that they may enter the
gates of the nobles.
3 I have commanded My sanctified ones;
I have also called My mighty ones for My
anger—
Those who rejoice in My exaltation."

4 The noise of a multitude in the
mountains,
Like that of many people!

COURAGE
Where can
we get
courage?
(12:2)

11:15 *a*Following Masoretic Text and Vulgate; Septuagint, Syriac, and Targum read *dry up.* *b*That is, the
Euphrates   **12:2** *a*Exodus 15:2

9 Behold, the day of the LORD comes,
Cruel, with both wrath and fierce anger,
To lay the land desolate;
And He will destroy its sinners from it.
10 For the stars of heaven and their constellations
Will not give their light;
The sun will be darkened in its going forth,
And the moon will not cause its light to shine.

11 "I will punish the world for *its* evil,
And the wicked for their iniquity;
I will halt the arrogance of the proud,
And will lay low the haughtiness of the terrible.
12 I will make a mortal more rare than fine gold,
A man more than the golden wedge of Ophir.
13 Therefore I will shake the heavens,
And the earth will move out of her place,
In the wrath of the LORD of hosts
And in the day of His fierce anger.
14 It shall be as the hunted gazelle,
And as a sheep that no man takes up;
Every man will turn to his own people,
And everyone will flee to his own land.
15 Everyone who is found will be thrust through,
And everyone who is captured will fall by the sword.
16 Their children also will be dashed to pieces before their eyes;
Their houses will be plundered
And their wives ravished.

17 "Behold, I will stir up the Medes against them,
Who will not regard silver;
And *as for* gold, they will not delight in it.
18 Also *their* bows will dash the young men to pieces,
And they will have no pity on the fruit of the womb;
Their eye will not spare children.
19 And Babylon, the glory of kingdoms,
The beauty of the Chaldeans' pride,
Will be as when God overthrew Sodom and Gomorrah.
20 It will never be inhabited,
Nor will it be settled from generation to generation;
Nor will the Arabian pitch tents there,
Nor will the shepherds make their sheepfolds there.

A tumultuous noise of the kingdoms of nations gathered together!
The LORD of hosts musters
The army for battle.
5 They come from a far country,
From the end of heaven—
The LORD and His weapons of indignation,
To destroy the whole land.

6 Wail, for the day of the LORD *is* at hand!
It will come as destruction from the Almighty.
7 Therefore all hands will be limp,
Every man's heart will melt,
8 And they will be afraid.
Pangs and sorrows will take hold of *them;*
They will be in pain as a woman in childbirth;
They will be amazed at one another;
Their faces *will be like* flames.

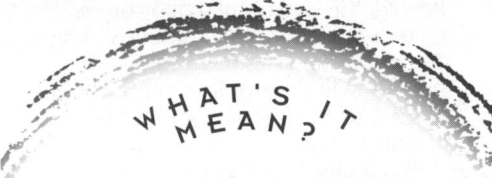

WHAT'S IT MEAN?

The city of Babylon, located between the Tigris and Euphrates Rivers, was a site to behold. For starters, the city, which was spread over six square miles, was protected by walls eighty-five feet thick. Eight major gates led to the city, each one named for a Babylonian god. The main temple, which was dedicated to Marduk, the god of war, featured a seven-story tower built with nearly sixty million bricks. To top it all off, the royal palace contained the hanging gardens of Babylon—one of the seven wonders of the ancient world.

Isaiah 13:19

21 But wild beasts of the desert will lie there,
And their houses will be full of owls;
Ostriches will dwell there,
And wild goats will caper there.
22 The hyenas will howl in their citadels,
And jackals in their pleasant palaces.
Her time *is* near to come,
And her days will not be prolonged."

MERCY ON JACOB

1 For the LORD will have mercy on Jacob, and will still choose Israel, and settle them in their own land. The strangers will be joined with them, and they will cling to the house of Jacob. 2 Then people will take them and bring them to their place, and the house of Israel will possess them for servants and maids in the land of the LORD; they will take them captive whose captives they were, and rule over their oppressors.

FALL OF THE KING OF BABYLON

3 It shall come to pass in the day the LORD gives you rest from your sorrow, and from your fear and the hard bondage in which you were made to serve, 4 that you will take up this proverb against the king of Babylon, and say:

"How the oppressor has ceased,
The golden*a* city ceased!
5 The LORD has broken the staff of the wicked,
The scepter of the rulers;
6 He who struck the people in wrath with a continual stroke,

He who ruled the nations in anger,
Is persecuted *and* no one hinders.
7 The whole earth is at rest and quiet;
They break forth into singing.
8 Indeed the cypress trees rejoice over you,
And the cedars of Lebanon,
Saying, 'Since you were cut down,
No woodsman has come up against us.'

9 "Hell from beneath is excited about you,
To meet *you* at your coming;
It stirs up the dead for you,
All the chief ones of the earth;
It has raised up from their thrones
All the kings of the nations.
10 They all shall speak and say to you:
'Have you also become as weak as we?
Have you become like us?
11 Your pomp is brought down to Sheol,
And the sound of your stringed instruments;
The maggot is spread under you,
And worms cover you.'

THE FALL OF LUCIFER

12 "How you are fallen from heaven,
O Lucifer,*a* son of the morning!
How you are cut down to the ground,
You who weakened the nations!
13 For you have said in your heart:
'I will ascend into heaven,
I will exalt my throne above the stars of God;
I will also sit on the mount of the congregation
On the farthest sides of the north;
14 I will ascend above the heights of the clouds,
I will be like the Most High.'
15 Yet you shall be brought down to Sheol,
To the lowest depths of the Pit.

16 "Those who see you will gaze at you,
And consider you, *saying:*
'*Is* this the man who made the earth tremble,
Who shook kingdoms,
17 Who made the world as a wilderness
And destroyed its cities,
Who did not open the house of his prisoners?'

ANGER

Will anger be punished? (14:5, 6)

14:4 *a*Or insolent   14:12 *a*Literally *Day Star*

18 "All the kings of the nations,
    All of them, sleep in glory,
    Everyone in his own house;
19 But you are cast out of your grave
    Like an abominable branch,
    Like the garment of those who are slain,
    Thrust through with a sword,
    Who go down to the stones of the pit,
    Like a corpse trodden underfoot.
20 You will not be joined with them in
        burial,
    Because you have destroyed your land
    And slain your people.
    The brood of evildoers shall never be
        named.
21 Prepare slaughter for his children
    Because of the iniquity of their fathers,
    Lest they rise up and possess the land,
    And fill the face of the world with cities."

BABYLON DESTROYED

22 "For I will rise up against them," says the
        LORD of hosts,
    "And cut off from Babylon the name and
        remnant,
    And offspring and posterity," says the LORD.
23 "I will also make it a possession for the
        porcupine,
    And marshes of muddy water;
    I will sweep it with the broom of
        destruction," says the LORD of hosts.

WHAT'S IT MEAN?

At the height of its power (around 1100 B.C.), the Assyrian Empire stretched from Babylon in the east to the Mediterranean Sea in the west. Check it out on a map—that's a big chunk of land. The capital of the empire was Nineveh, located about three hundred miles north of Babylon on the Tigris River. The Assyrian Empire eventually fell when Babylon rebelled against it.

Isaiah 14:25

ASSYRIA DESTROYED

24 The LORD of hosts has sworn, saying,
    "Surely, as I have thought, so it shall come
        to pass,
    And as I have purposed, *so* it shall stand:
25 That I will break the Assyrian in My
        land,
    And on My mountains tread him
        underfoot.
    Then his yoke shall be removed from
        them,

Promise HE PROMISES THAT EVERYTHING WILL HAPPEN AS HE HAS PLANNED.

The LORD of hosts has sworn, saying, "Surely, as I have thought, so it shall come to pass, and as I have purposed, so it shall stand" (Is. 14:24).

Isaiah gave the nation of Israel a message from God. Much of his message had to do with a Person called "the Messiah," who would bring the nation back to God and restore peace. Isaiah's prophecy came true when Jesus came to live on the earth—even though it didn't happen the way most of the Israelites thought it would. Still, God's plan had been written out, through Isaiah and others, so that they could see it.

In fact, all through the Bible, God tells you about His plans. Many of His plans have to do with you. You have a God-planned purpose in life, which is to know Him and to love Him like a best friend. He plans for you to become like His perfect Son. He plans for you to win out over that part of you that really likes to be selfish. He plans for you to be part of a group of people who love Him and want to see things go His way on planet Earth. He plans for you to change the world, at least your little corner of it.

What He plans is going to happen. Let Him use you to get the job done.

SEE FOR YOURSELF:
Is. 42:9; 46:10, 11; Ezek. 12:25; Dan. 4:35

And his burden removed from their
   shoulders.
26 This *is* the purpose that is purposed
   against the whole earth,
   And this *is* the hand that is stretched out
   over all the nations.
27 For the LORD of hosts has purposed,
   And who will annul *it?*
   His hand *is* stretched out,
   And who will turn it back?"

PHILISTIA DESTROYED

28 This is the burden which came in the year
that King Ahaz died.

29 "Do not rejoice, all you of Philistia,
   Because the rod that struck you is
   broken;
   For out of the serpent's roots will come
   forth a viper,
   And its offspring *will be* a fiery flying
   serpent.
30 The firstborn of the poor will feed,
   And the needy will lie down in safety;
   I will kill your roots with famine,
   And it will slay your remnant.
31 Wail, O gate! Cry, O city!
   All you of Philistia *are* dissolved;
   For smoke will come from the north,
   And no one *will be* alone in his appointed
   times."

32 What will they answer the messengers of
   the nation?
   That the LORD has founded Zion,
   And the poor of His people shall take
   refuge in it.

PROCLAMATION AGAINST MOAB

1 The burden against Moab.

Because in the night Ar of Moab is laid
   waste
And destroyed,
Because in the night Kir of Moab is laid
   waste
And destroyed,
2 He has gone up to the temple[a] and
   Dibon,
To the high places to weep.
Moab will wail over Nebo and over
   Medeba;

On all their heads *will be* baldness,
And every beard cut off.
3 In their streets they will clothe themselves
   with sackcloth;
On the tops of their houses
And in their streets
Everyone will wail, weeping bitterly.
4 Heshbon and Elealeh will cry out,
   Their voice shall be heard as far as Jahaz;
   Therefore the armed soldiers[a] of Moab
   will cry out;
   His life will be burdensome to him.

5 "My heart will cry out for Moab;
   His fugitives *shall flee* to Zoar,
   Like a three-year-old heifer.[a]
   For by the Ascent of Luhith
   They will go up with weeping;
   For in the way of Horonaim
   They will raise up a cry of destruction,
6 For the waters of Nimrim will be
   desolate,
   For the green grass has withered away;
   The grass fails, there is nothing green.
7 Therefore the abundance they have
   gained,
   And what they have laid up,
   They will carry away to the Brook of the
   Willows.
8 For the cry has gone all around the
   borders of Moab,
   Its wailing to Eglaim
   And its wailing to Beer Elim.
9 For the waters of Dimon[a] will be full of
   blood;
   Because I will bring more upon Dimon,[b]
   Lions upon him who escapes from Moab,
   And on the remnant of the land."

MOAB DESTROYED

1 Send the lamb to the ruler of the land,
   From Sela to the wilderness,
   To the mount of the daughter of Zion.
2 For it shall be as a wandering bird
   thrown out of the nest;
   So shall be the daughters of Moab at the
   fords of the Arnon.

3 "Take counsel, execute judgment;
   Make your shadow like the night in the
   middle of the day;
   Hide the outcasts,

15:2 [a]Hebrew *bayith,* literally *house*   15:4 [a]Following Masoretic Text, Targum, and Vulgate; Septuagint and
Syriac read *loins.*   15:5 [a]Or *The Third Eglath,* an unknown city (compare Jeremiah 48:34)   15:9 [a]Following
Masoretic Text and Targum; Dead Sea Scrolls and Vulgate read *Dibon;* Septuagint reads *Rimon.*   [b]Following
Masoretic Text and Targum; Dead Sea Scrolls and Vulgate read *Dibon;* Septuagint reads *Rimon.*

4 Do not betray him who escapes.
Let My outcasts dwell with you, O Moab;
Be a shelter to them from the face of the
spoiler.
For the extortioner is at an end,
Devastation ceases,
The oppressors are consumed out of the
land.

5 In mercy the throne will be established;
And One will sit on it in truth, in the
tabernacle of David,
Judging and seeking justice and hastening
righteousness."

6 We have heard of the pride of Moab—
He is very proud—
Of his haughtiness and his pride and his
wrath;
But his lies *shall* not *be* so.

7 Therefore Moab shall wail for Moab;
Everyone shall wail.
For the foundations of Kir Haraseth you
shall mourn;
Surely *they are* stricken.

8 For the fields of Heshbon languish,
And the vine of Sibmah;
The lords of the nations have broken
down its choice plants,
Which have reached to Jazer
And wandered through the wilderness.
Her branches are stretched out,
They are gone over the sea.

9 Therefore I will bewail the vine of Sibmah,
With the weeping of Jazer;
I will drench you with my tears,
O Heshbon and Elealeh;
For battle cries have fallen
Over your summer fruits and
your harvest.

10 Gladness is taken away,
And joy from the
plentiful field;
In the vineyards there
will be no singing,
Nor will there be
shouting;
No treaders will tread out
wine in the presses;
I have made their shouting cease.

11 Therefore my heart shall resound like a
harp for Moab,
And my inner being for Kir Heres.

12 And it shall come to pass,
When it is seen that Moab is weary on
the high place,
That he will come to his sanctuary to
pray;
But he will not prevail.

13 This *is* the word which the LORD has spoken concerning Moab since that time. 14But now the LORD has spoken, saying, "Within three years, as the years of a hired man, the glory of Moab will be despised with all that great multitude, and the remnant *will be* very small *and* feeble."

PROCLAMATION AGAINST SYRIA AND ISRAEL

1 The burden against Damascus.

"Behold, Damascus will cease from *being* a
city,
And it will be a ruinous heap.

2 The cities of Aroer *are* forsaken;*a*
They will be for flocks
Which lie down, and no one will make
them afraid.

3 The fortress also will cease from
Ephraim,
The kingdom from Damascus,
And the remnant of Syria;
They will be as the glory of the children
of Israel,"
Says the LORD of hosts.

4 "In that day it shall come to pass
That the glory of Jacob will wane,
And the fatness of his flesh grow
lean.

5 It shall be as when the
harvester gathers the
grain,
And reaps the heads
with his arm;
It shall be as he who
gathers heads of
grain
In the Valley of
Rephaim.

6 Yet gleaning grapes will
be left in it,
Like the shaking of an
olive tree,
Two *or* three olives at the top of the
uppermost bough,

"In that day a man will look to his Maker, and his eyes will have respect for the Holy One of Israel."
(Isaiah 17:7)

17:2 *a*Following Masoretic Text and Vulgate; Septuagint reads *It shall be forsaken forever;* Targum reads *Its cities shall be forsaken and desolate.*

Four *or* five in its most fruitful branches,"
Says the LORD God of Israel.

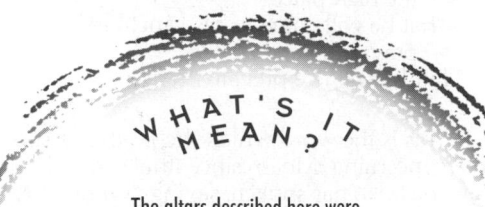

7 In that day a man will look to his Maker,
And his eyes will have respect for the
Holy One of Israel.
8 He will not look to the altars,
The work of his hands;
He will not respect what his fingers have
made,
Nor the wooden images*a* nor the incense
altars.

9 In that day his strong cities will be as a
forsaken bough*a*
And an uppermost branch,*b*
Which they left because of the children of
Israel;
And there will be desolation.

10 Because you have
forgotten the God of
your salvation,
And have not been
mindful of the Rock
of your stronghold,
Therefore you will plant
pleasant plants
And set out foreign seedlings;
11 In the day you will make your plant to
grow,
And in the morning you will make your
seed to flourish;
But the harvest *will be* a heap of ruins
In the day of grief and desperate sorrow.

12 Woe to the multitude of many people
Who make a noise like the roar of the
seas,
And to the rushing of nations
That make a rushing like the rushing of
mighty waters!
13 The nations will rush like the rushing of
many waters;
But *God* will rebuke them and they will
flee far away,
And be chased like the chaff of the
mountains before the wind,
Like a rolling thing before the
whirlwind.
14 Then behold, at eventide, trouble!
And before the morning, he *is* no more.
This *is* the portion of those who plunder
us,
And the lot of those who rob us.

PROCLAMATION AGAINST ETHIOPIA

1 Woe to the land shadowed with buzzing
wings,
Which *is* beyond the rivers of Ethiopia,
2 Which sends ambassadors by sea,
Even in vessels of reed on the waters,
saying,
"Go, swift messengers, to a nation tall and
smooth *of skin,*
To a people terrible from their beginning
onward,
A nation powerful and treading down,
Whose land the rivers divide."

3 All inhabitants of the world and dwellers
on the earth:
When he lifts up a banner on the
mountains, you see *it;*

17:8 *a*Hebrew *Asherim*, Canaanite deities   **17:9** *a*Septuagint reads *Hivites;* Targum reads *laid waste;* Vulgate
reads *as the plows.* *b*Septuagint reads *Amorites;* Targum reads *in ruins;* Vulgate reads *corn.*

And when he blows a trumpet, you
hear *it*.
4 For so the LORD said to me,
"I will take My rest,
And I will look from My dwelling place
Like clear heat in sunshine,
Like a cloud of dew in the heat of
harvest."
5 For before the harvest, when the bud is
perfect
And the sour grape is ripening in the
flower,
He will both cut off the sprigs with
pruning hooks
And take away *and* cut down the
branches.
6 They will be left together for the
mountain birds of prey
And for the beasts of the earth;
The birds of prey will summer on them,
And all the beasts of the earth will winter
on them.

7 In that time a present will be brought to
the LORD of hosts
From[a] a people tall and smooth *of skin,*
And from a people terrible from their
beginning onward,
A nation powerful and treading down,
Whose land the rivers divide—
To the place of the name of the LORD of
hosts,
To Mount Zion.

PROCLAMATION AGAINST EGYPT

19 ¹The burden against Egypt.

Behold, the LORD rides on a swift cloud,
And will come into Egypt;
The idols of Egypt will totter at His
presence,
And the heart of Egypt will melt in its
midst.

2 "I will set Egyptians against Egyptians;
Everyone will fight against his brother,
And everyone against his neighbor,
City against city, kingdom against
kingdom.
3 The spirit of Egypt will fail in its midst;
I will destroy their counsel,
And they will consult the idols and the
charmers,
The mediums and the sorcerers.

4 And the Egyptians I will give
Into the hand of a cruel master,
And a fierce king will rule over them,"
Says the Lord, the LORD of hosts.

WHAT'S IT MEAN?

Because Egypt receives very little rainfall, its
people rely on the Nile for their water. The Nile
floods its banks nearly every year, watering the soil and creating a
fertile farmland in the midst of a desert region. In those years when
the Nile did not flood, the Egyptians experienced drought and
famine. Today the Aswan Dam and the High Dam allow Egyptian
officials to control the flooding and preserve water.
Isaiah 19:5

5 The waters will fail from the sea,
And the river will be wasted and dried
up.
6 The rivers will turn foul;
The brooks of defense will be emptied
and dried up;
The reeds and rushes will wither.
7 The papyrus reeds by the River,[a] by the
mouth of the River,
And everything sown by the River,
Will wither, be driven away, and be no
more.
8 The fishermen also will mourn;
All those will lament who cast hooks into
the River,
And they will languish who spread nets
on the waters.
9 Moreover those who work in fine flax
And those who weave fine fabric will be
ashamed;
10 And its foundations will be broken.
All who make wages *will be* troubled of
soul.

11 Surely the princes of Zoan *are* fools;
Pharaoh's wise counselors give foolish
counsel.
How do you say to Pharaoh, "I *am* the
son of the wise,

18:7 [a]Following Dead Sea Scrolls, Septuagint, and Vulgate; Masoretic Text omits *From;* Targum reads *To.*
19:7 [a]That is, the Nile

The son of ancient kings?"

12 Where *are* they?
Where are your wise men?
Let them tell you now,
And let them know what the LORD of
    hosts has purposed against Egypt.

13 The princes of Zoan have become fools;
The princes of Noph[a] are deceived;
They have also deluded Egypt,
Those who are the mainstay of its tribes.

14 The LORD has mingled a perverse spirit in
    her midst;
And they have caused Egypt to err in all
    her work,
As a drunken man staggers in his vomit.

15 Neither will there be *any* work for Egypt,
Which the head or tail,
Palm branch or bulrush, may do.[a]

16In that day Egypt will be like women, and will be afraid and fear because of the waving of the hand of the LORD of hosts, which He waves over it. 17And the land of Judah will be a terror to Egypt; everyone who makes mention of it will be afraid in himself, because of the counsel of the LORD of hosts which He has determined against it.

EGYPT, ASSYRIA, AND ISRAEL BLESSED

18In that day five cities in the land of Egypt will speak the language of Canaan and swear by the LORD of hosts; one will be called the City of Destruction.[a]

19In that day there will be an altar to the LORD in the midst of the land of Egypt, and a pillar to the LORD at its border. 20And it will be for a sign and for a witness to the LORD of hosts in the land of Egypt; for they will cry to the LORD because of the oppressors, and He will send them a Savior and a Mighty One, and He will deliver them. 21Then the LORD will be known to Egypt, and the Egyptians will know the LORD in that day, and will make sacrifice and offering; yes, they will make a vow to the LORD and perform *it.* 22And the LORD will strike Egypt, He will strike and heal *it;* they will return to the LORD, and He will be entreated by them and heal them.

23In that day there will be a highway from Egypt to Assyria, and the Assyrian will come into Egypt and the Egyptian into Assyria, and the Egyptians will serve with the Assyrians. 24In that day Israel will be one of three with

Egypt and Assyria—a blessing in the midst of the land, 25whom the LORD of hosts shall bless, saying, "Blessed *is* Egypt My people, and Assyria the work of My hands, and Israel My inheritance."

THE SIGN AGAINST EGYPT AND ETHIOPIA

1In the year that Tartan[a] came to Ashdod, when Sargon the king of Assyria sent him, and he fought against Ashdod and took it, 2at the same time the LORD spoke by Isaiah the son of Amoz, saying, "Go, and remove the sackcloth from your body, and take your sandals off your feet." And he did so, walking naked and barefoot.

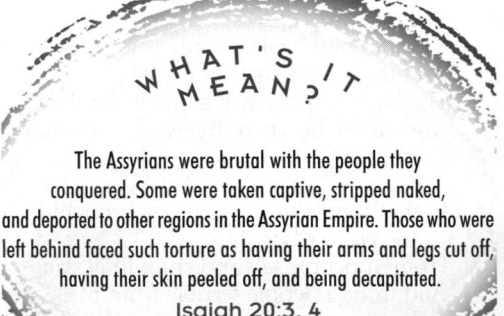

WHAT'S IT MEAN?

The Assyrians were brutal with the people they conquered. Some were taken captive, stripped naked, and deported to other regions in the Assyrian Empire. Those who were left behind faced such torture as having their arms and legs cut off, having their skin peeled off, and being decapitated.

Isaiah 20:3, 4

3Then the LORD said, "Just as My servant Isaiah has walked naked and barefoot three years *for* a sign and a wonder against Egypt and Ethiopia, 4so shall the king of Assyria lead away the Egyptians as prisoners and the Ethiopians as captives, young and old, naked and barefoot, with their buttocks uncovered, to the shame of Egypt. 5Then they shall be afraid and ashamed of Ethiopia their expectation and Egypt their glory. 6And the inhabitant of this territory will say in that day, 'Surely such *is* our expectation, wherever we flee for help to be delivered from the king of Assyria; and how shall we escape?' "

THE FALL OF BABYLON PROCLAIMED

1The burden against the Wilderness of the Sea.

As whirlwinds in the South pass through,
So it comes from the desert, from a
    terrible land.

19:13 [a]That is, ancient Memphis   **19:15** [a]Compare Isaiah 9:14–16   **19:18** [a]Some Hebrew manuscripts, Arabic, Dead Sea Scrolls, Targum, and Vulgate read *Sun;* Septuagint reads *Asedek* (literally *Righteousness*).
20:1 [a]Or *the Commander in Chief*

2   A distressing vision is declared to me;
The treacherous dealer deals
    treacherously,
And the plunderer plunders.
Go up, O Elam!
Besiege, O Media!
All its sighing I have made to cease.

3   Therefore my loins are filled with pain;
Pangs have taken hold of me, like the
    pangs of a woman in labor.
I was distressed when *I* heard *it*;
I was dismayed when *I* saw *it*.
4   My heart wavered, fearfulness frightened
    me;
The night for which I longed He turned
    into fear for me.
5   Prepare the table,
Set a watchman in the tower,
Eat and drink.
Arise, you princes,
Anoint the shield!

6   For thus has the Lord said to me:
"Go, set a watchman,
Let him declare what he sees."
7   And he saw a chariot *with* a pair of
    horsemen,
A chariot of donkeys, *and* a chariot of
    camels,
And he listened earnestly with great care.
8   Then he cried, "A lion,[a] my Lord!
I stand continually on the watchtower in
    the daytime;
I have sat at my post every night.
9   And look, here comes a chariot of men
    with a pair of horsemen!"
Then he answered and said,
"Babylon is fallen, is fallen!
And all the carved images of her gods
He has broken to the ground."

10   Oh, my threshing and the grain of my
    floor!
That which I have heard from the LORD
    of hosts,
The God of Israel,
I have declared to you.

PROCLAMATION AGAINST EDOM

11 The burden against Dumah.

He calls to me out of Seir,
"Watchman, what of the night?
Watchman, what of the night?"

12   The watchman said,
"The morning comes, and also the night.
If you will inquire, inquire;
Return! Come back!"

PROCLAMATION AGAINST ARABIA

13 The burden against Arabia.

In the forest in Arabia you will lodge,
O you traveling companies of Dedanites.
14   O inhabitants of the land of Tema,
Bring water to him who is thirsty;
With their bread they met him who fled.
15   For they fled from the swords, from the
    drawn sword,
From the bent bow, and from the distress
    of war.

16 For thus the LORD has said to me: "Within
a year, according to the year of a hired man, all
the glory of Kedar will fail; 17 and the remainder
of the number of archers, the mighty men of
the people of Kedar, will be diminished; for the
LORD God of Israel has spoken *it.*"

PROCLAMATION AGAINST JERUSALEM

1 The burden against the Valley of Vision.

What ails you now, that you have all
    gone up to the housetops,
2   You who are full of noise,
A tumultuous city, a joyous city?
Your slain *men are* not slain with the
    sword,
Nor dead in battle.
3   All your rulers have fled together;
They are captured by the archers.
All who are found in you are bound
    together;
They have fled from afar.
4   Therefore I said, "Look away from me,
I will weep bitterly;
Do not labor to comfort me
Because of the plundering of the daughter
    of my people."

5   For *it is* a day of trouble and treading
    down and perplexity
By the Lord GOD of hosts
In the Valley of Vision—
Breaking down the walls
And of crying to the mountain.
6   Elam bore the quiver
With chariots of men *and* horsemen,
And Kir uncovered the shield.

21:8 [a]Dead Sea Scrolls read *Then the observer cried.*

7 It shall come to pass *that* your choicest
    valleys
Shall be full of chariots,
And the horsemen shall set themselves in
    array at the gate.

8 He removed the protection of Judah.
You looked in that day to the armor of
    the House of the Forest;
9 You also saw the damage to the city of
    David,
That it was great;
And you gathered together the waters of
    the lower pool.
10 You numbered the houses of Jerusalem,
And the houses you broke down
To fortify the wall.
11 You also made a reservoir between the
    two walls
For the water of the old pool.
But you did not look to its Maker,
Nor did you have respect for Him who
    fashioned it long ago.

12 And in that day the Lord GOD of hosts
Called for weeping and for mourning,
For baldness and for girding with
    sackcloth.
13 But instead, joy and gladness,
Slaying oxen and killing sheep,
Eating meat and drinking wine:
"Let us eat and drink, for tomorrow we
    die!"

14 Then it was revealed in my hearing by
    the LORD of hosts,
"Surely for this iniquity there will be no
    atonement for you,
Even to your death," says the Lord GOD of
    hosts.

THE JUDGMENT ON SHEBNA

15 Thus says the Lord GOD of hosts:

"Go, proceed to this steward,
To Shebna, who *is* over the house, *and*
    say:
16 'What have you here, and whom have
    you here,
That you have hewn a sepulcher here,
As he who hews himself a sepulcher on
    high,
Who carves a tomb for himself in a rock?
17 Indeed, the LORD will throw you away
    violently,

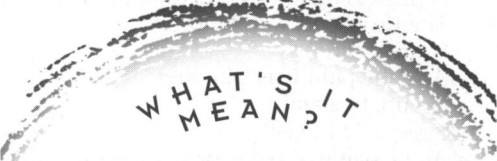

WHAT'S IT MEAN?

When ordinary people died in ancient times,
they were buried in shallow graves covered with
stone slabs. The wealthy and powerful, on the other hand, often built
elaborate tombs for themselves. These tombs were either created
from natural caves or carved out of stone. The person's possessions
were usually buried along with his body, in case he "needed" them
in the afterlife. Shebna was an official in the government of Judah
who tried to make himself like the king by building
a custom sepulcher for himself.
Isaiah 22:15–19

O mighty man,
And will surely seize you.
18 He will surely turn violently and toss you
    like a ball
Into a large country;
There you shall die, and there your
    glorious chariots
Shall be the shame of your master's
    house.
19 So I will drive you out of your office,
And from your position he will pull you
    down.*ᵃ*

20 'Then it shall be in that day,
That I will call My servant Eliakim the
    son of Hilkiah;
21 I will clothe him with your robe
And strengthen him with your belt;
I will commit your responsibility into his
    hand.
He shall be a father to the inhabitants of
    Jerusalem
And to the house of Judah.
22 The key of the house of David
I will lay on his shoulder;
So he shall open, and no one shall shut;
And he shall shut, and no one shall open.
23 I will fasten him *as* a peg in a secure
    place,
And he will become a glorious throne to
    his father's house.

24 'They will hang on him all the glory of his
father's house, the offspring and the posterity,

22:19 *ᵃ*Septuagint omits *he will pull you down;* Syriac, Targum, and Vulgate read *I will pull you down.*

all vessels of small quantity, from the cups to all the pitchers. ²⁵In that day,' says the LORD of hosts, 'the peg that is fastened in the secure place will be removed and be cut down and fall, and the burden that *was* on it will be cut off; for the LORD has spoken.'"

PROCLAMATION AGAINST TYRE

¹The burden against Tyre.

Wail, you ships of Tarshish!
For it is laid waste,
So that there is no house, no harbor;
From the land of Cyprus*a* it is revealed to
them.

2   Be still, you inhabitants of the coastland,
You merchants of Sidon,
Whom those who cross the sea have
filled.*a*
3   And on great waters the grain of Shihor,
The harvest of the River,*a* *is* her revenue;
And she is a marketplace for the nations.

4   Be ashamed, O Sidon;
For the sea has spoken,
The strength of the sea, saying,
"I do not labor, nor bring forth children;
Neither do I rear young men,
Nor bring up virgins."
5   When the report *reaches* Egypt,
They also will be in agony at the report
of Tyre.

6   Cross over to Tarshish;
Wail, you inhabitants of the coastland!
7   *Is* this your joyous *city,*
Whose antiquity *is* from ancient days,
Whose feet carried her far off to dwell?
8   Who has taken this counsel against Tyre,
the crowning *city,*
Whose merchants *are* princes,
Whose traders *are* the honorable of the
earth?
9   The LORD of hosts has purposed it,
To bring to dishonor the pride of all glory,
To bring into contempt all the honorable
of the earth.

10   Overflow through your land like the
River,*a*
O daughter of Tarshish;
There is no more strength.

11   He stretched out His hand over the sea,
He shook the kingdoms;
The LORD has given a commandment
against Canaan
To destroy its strongholds.
12   And He said, "You will rejoice no more,
O you oppressed virgin daughter of
Sidon.
Arise, cross over to Cyprus;
There also you will have no rest."

13   Behold, the land of the Chaldeans,
This people *which* was not;
Assyria founded it for wild beasts of the
desert.
They set up its towers,
They raised up its palaces,
And brought it to ruin.

14   Wail, you ships of Tarshish!
For your strength is laid waste.

¹⁵Now it shall come to pass in that day that Tyre will be forgotten seventy years, according to the days of one king. At the end of seventy years it will happen to Tyre as *in* the song of the harlot:

16   "Take a harp, go about the city,
You forgotten harlot;
Make sweet melody, sing many songs,
That you may be remembered."

¹⁷And it shall be, at the end of seventy years, that the LORD will deal with Tyre. She will return to her hire, and commit fornication with all the kingdoms of the world on the face of the earth. ¹⁸Her gain and her pay will be set apart for the LORD; it will not be treasured nor laid up, for her gain will be for those who dwell before the LORD, to eat sufficiently, and for fine clothing.

IMPENDING JUDGMENT ON THE EARTH

1   Behold, the LORD makes the earth empty
and makes it waste,
Distorts its surface
And scatters abroad its inhabitants.
2   And it shall be:
As with the people, so with the priest;
As with the servant, so with his master;
As with the maid, so with her mistress;
As with the buyer, so with the seller;

23:1 *a*Hebrew *Kittim,* western lands, especially Cyprus **23:2** *a*Following Masoretic Text and Vulgate; Septuagint and Targum read *Passing over the water;* Dead Sea Scrolls read *Your messengers passing over the sea.* **23:3** *a*That is, the Nile **23:10** *a*That is, the Nile

As with the lender, so with the borrower;
As with the creditor, so with the debtor.
3 The land shall be entirely emptied and
utterly plundered,
For the LORD has spoken this word.

4 The earth mourns *and* fades away,
The world languishes *and* fades away;
The haughty people of the earth languish.
5 The earth is also defiled under its
inhabitants,
Because they have transgressed the laws,
Changed the ordinance,
Broken the everlasting covenant.
6 Therefore the curse has devoured the
earth,
And those who dwell in it are desolate.
Therefore the inhabitants of the earth are
burned,
And few men *are* left.

7 The new wine fails, the vine languishes,
All the merry-hearted sigh.
8 The mirth of the tambourine ceases,
The noise of the jubilant ends,
The joy of the harp ceases.
9 They shall not drink wine with a song;
Strong drink is bitter to those who
drink it.
10 The city of confusion is broken down;
Every house is shut up, so that none may
go in.
11 *There is* a cry for wine in the streets,
All joy is darkened,
The mirth of the land is gone.
12 In the city desolation is left,
And the gate is stricken
with destruction.
13 When it shall be thus
in the midst of the
land among the
people,
It shall be like the
shaking of an
olive tree,
Like the gleaning of
grapes when the
vintage is done.

14 They shall lift up their voice, they
shall sing;
For the majesty of the LORD
They shall cry aloud from the sea.
15 Therefore glorify the LORD in the dawning
light,
The name of the LORD God of Israel in
the coastlands of the sea.

16 From the ends of the earth we have heard
songs:
"Glory to the righteous!"
But I said, "I am ruined, ruined!
Woe to me!
The treacherous dealers have dealt
treacherously,
Indeed, the treacherous dealers have dealt
very treacherously."

17 Fear and the pit and the snare
Are upon you, O inhabitant of the
earth.
18 And it shall be
That he who flees from the noise of the
fear
Shall fall into the pit,
And he who comes up from the midst of
the pit
Shall be caught in the snare;
For the windows from on high are
open,
And the foundations of the earth are
shaken.

19 The earth is violently broken,
The earth is split open,
The earth is shaken exceedingly.
20 The earth shall reel to and fro like a
drunkard,
And shall totter like a hut;
Its transgression shall be heavy
upon it,
And it will fall, and not rise again.

21 It shall come to pass
in that day
That the LORD will
punish on high the
host of exalted
ones,
And on the earth the
kings of the earth.
22 They will be gathered
together,
As prisoners are
gathered in the pit,
And will be shut up
in the prison;
After many days
they will be
punished.
23 Then the moon will be disgraced
And the sun ashamed;
For the LORD of hosts will reign
On Mount Zion and in Jerusalem
And before His elders, gloriously.

"They shall lift up their voice, they shall sing; for the majesty of the LORD they shall cry aloud from the sea."
(Isaiah 24:14)

PRAISE TO GOD

1   O LORD, You *are* my God.
    I will exalt You,
    I will praise Your name,
    For You have done wonderful *things;*
    Your counsels of old *are* faithfulness *and*
      truth.

2   For You have made a city a ruin,
    A fortified city a ruin,
    A palace of foreigners to be a city no
      more;
    It will never be rebuilt.

3   Therefore the strong people will glorify
      You;
    The city of the terrible nations will fear
      You.

4   For You have been a strength to the poor,
    A strength to the needy in his distress,
    A refuge from the storm,
    A shade from the heat;
    For the blast of the terrible ones *is* as a
      storm *against* the wall.

5   You will reduce the noise of aliens,
    As heat in a dry place;
    As heat in the shadow of a cloud,
    The song of the terrible ones will be
      diminished.

6   And in this mountain
    The LORD of hosts will make for all
      people
    A feast of choice pieces,
    A feast of wines on the lees,
    Of fat things full of marrow,
    Of well-refined wines on the lees.

7   And He will destroy on this mountain
    The surface of the covering cast over all
      people,
    And the veil that is spread over all
      nations.

8   He will swallow up death forever,
    And the Lord GOD will
      wipe away tears from
      all faces;
    The rebuke of His people
    He will take away from
      all the earth;
    For the LORD has spoken.

HEAVEN

What will
be missing
in heaven?
(25:8)

9   And it will be said in that day:
    "Behold, this *is* our God;
    We have waited for Him, and He will save
      us.
    This *is* the LORD;
    We have waited for Him;
    We will be glad and rejoice in His
      salvation."

10   For on this mountain the hand of the
      LORD will rest,
    And Moab shall be trampled down under
      Him,

Promise   HE PROMISES TO DESTROY DEATH AND TEARS.

He will swallow up death forever, and the Lord GOD will wipe away tears from all faces; the rebuke of His people He will take away from all the earth; for the LORD has spoken (Is. 25:8).

When Jesus died and came back to life, He dealt death a mortal blow. He gave notice to anyone who would believe in Him that there was a power greater than death. His friends don't have to be afraid of death because they know that their physical death is not the end. And there will come a day when no one dies anymore.

Something else happened when Jesus died on the cross. He did battle with the spiritual death that had cast a shadow over planet Earth since Adam and Eve had left the Garden of Eden. If you put your confidence in Jesus' goodness rather than your own, the seemingly irresistible urge to go your own way (instead of God's way) doesn't have to run your life.

And Jesus promises that your tears will come to an end, too. That's because all the things that make you sad—someone's parents getting a divorce, people getting sick, even natural disasters—are part of a world that's not perfect because of sin. Jesus has already beat sin; and just like death, sin's days of having any say in our lives are coming to an end. Then we'll see what Revelation 21:4 reports: "The former things have passed away."

SEE FOR YOURSELF:
Rom. 8:2; 2 Tim. 1:10; Rev. 21:4

11 As straw is trampled down for the refuse
heap.
And He will spread out His hands in their
midst
As a swimmer reaches out to swim,
And He will bring down their pride
Together with the trickery of their hands.

12 The fortress of the high fort of your
walls
He will bring down, lay low,
And bring to the ground, down to the
dust.

A SONG OF SALVATION

1 In that day this song will be sung in the
land of Judah:

"We have a strong city;
God will appoint salvation *for* walls and
bulwarks.
2 Open the gates,
That the righteous nation which keeps the
truth may enter in.
3 You will keep *him* in perfect peace,
Whose mind *is* stayed *on* You,
Because he trusts in You.
4 Trust in the LORD forever,
For in YAH, the LORD, *is* everlasting
strength.*a*
5 For He brings down those who dwell on
high,
The lofty city;
He lays it low,
He lays it low to the ground,
He brings it down to the dust.
6 The foot shall tread it down—
The feet of the poor
And the steps of the needy."

7 The way of the just *is* uprightness;
O Most Upright,
You weigh the path of the just.
8 Yes, in the way of Your judgments,
O LORD, we have waited for You;
The desire of *our* soul *is* for Your name
And for the remembrance of You.
9 With my soul I have desired You in the
night,
Yes, by my spirit within me I will seek
You early;
For when Your judgments *are* in the
earth,
The inhabitants of the world will learn
righteousness.

10 Let grace be shown to the wicked,
Yet he will not learn righteousness;
In the land of uprightness he will deal
unjustly,
And will not behold the majesty of the
LORD.
11 LORD, *when* Your hand is lifted up, they
will not see.
But they will see and be ashamed
For *their* envy of people;
Yes, the fire of Your enemies shall devour
them.

12 LORD, You will establish peace for us,
For You have also done all our works
in us.
13 O LORD our God, masters besides You
Have had dominion over us;
But by You only we make mention of
Your name.
14 *They are* dead, they will not live;
They are deceased, they will not rise.
Therefore You have punished and
destroyed them,
And made all their memory to perish.
15 You have increased the nation, O LORD,
You have increased the nation;
You are glorified;
You have expanded all the borders of the
land.

16 LORD, in trouble they have visited You,
They poured out a prayer *when* Your
chastening *was* upon them.
17 As a woman with child
Is in pain and cries out in her pangs,
When she draws near the time of her
delivery,
So have we been in Your sight,
O LORD.
18 We have been with child, we have been
in pain;
We have, as it were, brought forth wind;
We have not accomplished any
deliverance in the earth,
Nor have the inhabitants of the world
fallen.

19 Your dead shall live;
Together with my dead body*a* they shall
arise.
Awake and sing, you who dwell in dust;
For your dew *is like* the dew of herbs,
And the earth shall cast out the dead.

26:4 *a*Or *Rock of Ages* **26:19** *a*Following Masoretic Text and Vulgate; Syriac and Targum read *their dead bodies;* Septuagint reads *those in the tombs.*

TAKE REFUGE FROM THE COMING JUDGMENT

20 Come, my people, enter your chambers,
And shut your doors behind you;
Hide yourself, as it were, for a little moment,
Until the indignation is past.

21 For behold, the LORD comes out of His place
To punish the inhabitants of the earth for their iniquity;
The earth will also disclose her blood,
And will no more cover her slain.

1 In that day the LORD with His severe sword, great and strong,
Will punish Leviathan the fleeing serpent,
Leviathan that twisted serpent;
And He will slay the reptile that *is* in the sea.

THE RESTORATION OF ISRAEL

2 In that day sing to her,
"A vineyard of red wine!ᵃ
3 I, the LORD, keep it,
I water it every moment;
Lest any hurt it,
I keep it night and day.
4 Fury *is* not in Me.
Who would set briers *and* thorns
Against Me in battle?
I would go through them,
I would burn them together.
5 Or let him take hold of My strength,
That he may make peace with Me;
And he shall make peace with Me."

6 Those who come He shall cause to take root in Jacob;
Israel shall blossom and bud,
And fill the face of the world with fruit.

7 Has He struck Israel as He struck those who struck him?
Or has He been slain according to the slaughter of those who were slain by Him?
8 In measure, by sending it away,
You contended with it.
He removes *it* by His rough wind
In the day of the east wind.
9 Therefore by this the iniquity of Jacob will be covered;
And this *is* all the fruit of taking away his sin:

When he makes all the stones of the altar
Like chalkstones that are beaten to dust,
Wooden imagesᵃ and incense altars shall not stand.

10 Yet the fortified city *will be* desolate,
The habitation forsaken and left like a wilderness;
There the calf will feed, and there it will lie down
And consume its branches.
11 When its boughs are withered, they will be broken off;
The women come *and* set them on fire.
For it *is* a people of no understanding;
Therefore He who made them will not have mercy on them,
And He who formed them will show them no favor.

God's intended boundaries for Israel were Egypt on the west and the Euphrates River on the east. The Lord had promised to give all of the land in between to the descendants of Abraham, Isaac, and Jacob. The Israelites, though, never claimed all of what was rightfully theirs. They allowed other nations to live in the land that God had given to them.
Isaiah 27:12

12 And it shall come to pass in that day
That the LORD will thresh,
From the channel of the Riverᵃ to the Brook of Egypt;
And you will be gathered one by one,
O you children of Israel.

13 So it shall be in that day:
The great trumpet will be blown;
They will come, who are about to perish in the land of Assyria,
And they who are outcasts in the land of Egypt,

27:2 ᵃFollowing Masoretic Text (Kittel's *Biblia Hebraica*), Bomberg, and Vulgate; Masoretic Text (*Biblia Hebraica Stuttgartensia*), some Hebrew manuscripts, and Septuagint read *delight*; Targum reads *choice vineyard*.
27:9 ᵃHebrew *Asherim*, Canaanite deities   **27:12** ᵃThat is, the Euphrates

And shall worship the LORD in the holy
   mount at Jerusalem.

WOE TO EPHRAIM AND JERUSALEM

1 Woe to the crown of pride, to the
   drunkards of Ephraim,
Whose glorious beauty *is* a fading flower
Which *is* at the head of the verdant
   valleys,
To those who are overcome with wine!
2 Behold, the Lord has a mighty and strong
   one,
Like a tempest of hail and a destroying
   storm,
Like a flood of mighty waters
   overflowing,
Who will bring *them* down to the earth
   with *His* hand.
3 The crown of pride, the drunkards of
   Ephraim,
Will be trampled underfoot;
4 And the glorious beauty is a fading
   flower
Which *is* at the head of the verdant valley,
Like the first fruit before the summer,
Which an observer sees;
He eats it up while it is still in his hand.

5 In that day the LORD of hosts will be
For a crown of glory and a diadem of
   beauty
To the remnant of His people,
6 For a spirit of justice to him who sits in
   judgment,
And for strength to those who turn back
   the battle at the gate.

7 But they also have erred through wine,
And through intoxicating drink are out of
   the way;
The priest and the prophet have erred
   through intoxicating drink,
They are swallowed up by wine,
They are out of the way through
   intoxicating drink;
They err in vision, they stumble *in*
   judgment.
8 For all tables are full of vomit *and* filth;
No place *is clean.*

9 "Whom will he teach knowledge?
And whom will he make to understand
   the message?
Those *just* weaned from milk?
Those *just* drawn from the breasts?
10 For precept *must be* upon precept, precept
   upon precept,

Line upon line, line upon line,
Here a little, there a little."

11 For with stammering lips and another
   tongue
He will speak to this people,
12 To whom He said, "This *is* the rest *with*
   which
You may cause the weary to rest,"
And, "This *is* the refreshing";
Yet they would not hear.
13 But the word of the LORD was to them,
"Precept upon precept, precept upon
   precept,
Line upon line, line upon line,
Here a little, there a little,"
That they might go and fall backward,
   and be broken
And snared and caught.

14 Therefore hear the word of the LORD, you
   scornful men,
Who rule this people who *are* in
   Jerusalem,
15 Because you have said, "We have made a
   covenant with death,
And with Sheol we are in agreement.
When the overflowing scourge passes
   through,
It will not come to us,
For we have made lies our refuge,
And under falsehood we have hidden
   ourselves."

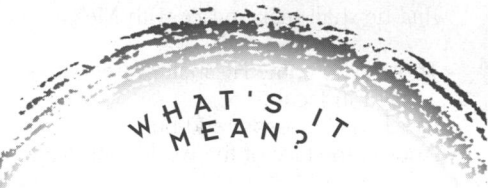

WHAT'S IT MEAN?

When David conquered Jerusalem around
1000 B.C., he set up his capital in an ancient fortress
known as Zion. Years later, when Solomon built the temple on Mount
Moriah, the entire area in and around Jerusalem came to be known
as Zion. Eventually, Zion was used to refer
to the entire nation of Israel.
Isaiah 28:16

A CORNERSTONE IN ZION

16 Therefore thus says the Lord GOD:

"Behold, I lay in Zion a stone for a
   foundation,

A tried stone, a precious
    cornerstone, a sure
    foundation;
Whoever believes will
    not act hastily.
17 Also I will make justice
    the measuring line,
And righteousness the
    plummet;
The hail will sweep away the refuge of
    lies,
And the waters will overflow the hiding
    place.
18 Your covenant with death will be
    annulled,
And your agreement with Sheol will not
    stand;
When the overflowing scourge passes
    through,
Then you will be trampled down by it.
19 As often as it goes out it will take you;
For morning by morning it will pass over,
And by day and by night;
It will be a terror just to understand the
    report."

20 For the bed is too short to stretch out *on,*
And the covering so narrow that one
    cannot wrap himself *in it.*
21 For the LORD will rise up as *at* Mount
    Perazim,
He will be angry as in the Valley of
    Gibeon—
That He may do His work, His awesome
    work,
And bring to pass His act, His unusual
    act.
22 Now therefore, do not be
    mockers,
Lest your bonds be made
    strong;
For I have heard from the
    Lord GOD of hosts,
A destruction determined
    even upon the whole
    earth.

COMFORT
Where can
we find
stress-
relief?
(28:16)

**"Give ear and hear
my voice, listen and
hear my speech."
(Isaiah 28:23)**

LISTEN TO THE TEACHING OF GOD
23 Give ear and hear my voice,
Listen and hear my speech.
24 Does the plowman keep plowing all day
    to sow?
Does he keep turning his soil and
    breaking the clods?
25 When he has leveled its surface,

Does he not sow the black cummin
And scatter the cummin,
Plant the wheat in rows,
The barley in the appointed place,
And the spelt in its place?
26 For He instructs him in right judgment,
His God teaches him.

27 For the black cummin is not threshed
    with a threshing sledge,
Nor is a cartwheel rolled over the
    cummin;
But the black cummin is beaten out with
    a stick,
And the cummin with a rod.
28 Bread *flour* must be ground;
Therefore he does not thresh it forever,
Break *it with* his cartwheel,
Or crush *it with* his horsemen.
29 This also comes from the LORD of hosts,
Who is wonderful in counsel *and* excellent
    in guidance.

WOE TO JERUSALEM
1 "Woe to Ariel,[a] to Ariel, the city *where*
    David dwelt!
Add year to year;
Let feasts come around.
2 Yet I will distress Ariel;
There shall be heaviness and sorrow,
And it shall be to Me as Ariel.
3 I will encamp against you all around,
I will lay siege against you with a mound,
And I will raise siegeworks against you.
4 You shall be brought down,
You shall speak out of the ground;
        Your speech shall be low,
          out of the dust;
        Your voice shall be like a
          medium's, out of the
          ground;
        And your speech shall
          whisper out of the dust.

5 "Moreover the multitude of
        your foes
        Shall be like fine dust,
And the multitude of the terrible ones
Like chaff that passes away;
Yes, it shall be in an instant, suddenly.
6 You will be punished by the LORD of
    hosts
With thunder and earthquake and great
    noise,
With storm and tempest

29:1 [a]That is, Jerusalem

And the flame of devouring fire.
7 The multitude of all the nations who fight
against Ariel,
Even all who fight against her and her
fortress,
And distress her,
Shall be as a dream of a night vision.
8 It shall even be as when a hungry man
dreams,
And look—he eats;
But he awakes, and his soul is still empty;
Or as when a thirsty man dreams,
And look—he drinks;
But he awakes, and indeed *he is* faint,
And his soul still craves:
So the multitude of all the nations shall
be,
Who fight against Mount Zion."

THE BLINDNESS OF DISOBEDIENCE

9 Pause and wonder!
Blind yourselves and be blind!
They are drunk, but not with wine;
They stagger, but not with intoxicating
drink.
10 For the LORD has poured out on you
The spirit of deep sleep,
And has closed your eyes, namely, the
prophets;
And He has covered your heads, *namely,*
the seers.

11 The whole vision has become to you like
the words of a book that is sealed, which *men*
deliver to one who is literate, saying, "Read this,
please."
And he says, "I cannot, for it *is* sealed."
12 Then the book is delivered to one who is
illiterate, saying, "Read this, please."
And he says, "I am not literate."
13 Therefore the Lord said:

"Inasmuch as these people
draw near with their
mouths
And honor Me with
their lips,
But have removed their hearts far from
Me,
And their fear toward Me is taught by the
commandment of men,
14 Therefore, behold, I will again do a
marvelous work
Among this people,
A marvelous work and a wonder;
For the wisdom of their wise *men* shall
perish,

And the understanding of their prudent
men shall be hidden."

15 Woe to those who seek deep to hide their
counsel far from the LORD,
And their works are in the dark;
They say, "Who sees us?" and, "Who
knows us?"
16 Surely you have things turned around!
Shall the potter be esteemed as the
clay;
For shall the thing made say of him who
made it,
"He did not make me"?
Or shall the thing formed say of him who
formed it,
"He has no understanding"?

FUTURE RECOVERY OF WISDOM

17 *Is* it not yet a very little while
Till Lebanon shall be turned into a fruitful
field,
And the fruitful field be esteemed as a
forest?
18 In that day the deaf shall hear the words
of the book,
And the eyes of the blind shall see out of
obscurity and out of darkness.
19 The humble also shall increase *their* joy in
the LORD,
And the poor among men shall rejoice
In the Holy One of Israel.
20 For the terrible one is brought to
nothing,
The scornful one is consumed,
And all who watch for iniquity are cut
off—
21 Who make a man an offender by a word,
And lay a snare for him who reproves in
the gate,
And turn aside the just by empty words.

22 Therefore thus says the LORD, who
redeemed Abraham, concerning the house of
Jacob:

"Jacob shall not now be ashamed,
Nor shall his face now grow pale;
23 But when he sees his children,
The work of My hands, in his midst,
They will hallow My name,
And hallow the Holy One of Jacob,
And fear the God of Israel.
24 These also who erred in spirit will come
to understanding,
And those who complained will learn
doctrine."

HYPOCRISY

What is
hypocrisy?
(29:13)

FUTILE CONFIDENCE IN EGYPT

1 "Woe to the rebellious children," says the
LORD,
"Who take counsel, but not of Me,
And who devise plans, but not of My
Spirit,
That they may add sin to sin;
2 Who walk to go down to Egypt,
And have not asked My advice,
To strengthen themselves in the strength
of Pharaoh,
And to trust in the shadow of Egypt!
3 Therefore the strength of Pharaoh
Shall be your shame,
And trust in the shadow of Egypt
Shall be *your* humiliation.
4 For his princes were at Zoan,
And his ambassadors came to Hanes.
5 They were all ashamed of a people *who*
could not benefit them,
Or be help or benefit,
But a shame and also a reproach."

6 The burden against the beasts of the South.

Through a land of trouble and anguish,
From which *came* the lioness and lion,
The viper and fiery flying serpent,
They will carry their riches on the backs
of young donkeys,
And their treasures on the humps of
camels,
To a people *who* shall not profit;
7 For the Egyptians shall help in vain and
to no purpose.
Therefore I have called her
Rahab-Hem-Shebeth.[a]

A REBELLIOUS PEOPLE

8 Now go, write it before them on a
tablet,
And note it on a scroll,
That it may be for time to come,
Forever and ever:
9 That this *is* a rebellious people,
Lying children,
Children *who* will not hear the law of the
LORD;
10 Who say to the seers, "Do not see,"
And to the prophets, "Do not prophesy to
us right things;
Speak to us smooth things, prophesy
deceits.
11 Get out of the way,
Turn aside from the path,

Cause the Holy One of Israel
To cease from before us."

12 Therefore thus says the Holy One of Israel:

"Because you despise this word,
And trust in oppression and perversity,
And rely on them,
13 Therefore this iniquity shall be to you
Like a breach ready to fall,
A bulge in a high wall,
Whose breaking comes suddenly, in an
instant.
14 And He shall break it like the breaking of
the potter's vessel,
Which is broken in pieces;
He shall not spare.
So there shall not be found among its
fragments
A shard to take fire from the hearth,
Or to take water from the cistern."

15 For thus says the Lord GOD, the Holy One
of Israel:

"In returning and rest you
shall be saved;
In quietness and
confidence shall be
your strength."
But you would not,
16 And you said, "No, for
we will flee on
horses"—
Therefore you shall flee!
And, "We will ride on *swift horses*"—
Therefore those who pursue you shall be
swift!

17 One thousand *shall flee* at the threat of one,
At the threat of five you shall flee,
Till you are left as a pole on top of a
mountain
And as a banner on a hill.

GOD WILL BE GRACIOUS

18 Therefore the LORD will wait, that He may
be gracious to you;
And therefore He will be exalted, that He
may have mercy on you.
For the LORD *is* a God of justice;
Blessed *are* all those who wait for Him.

19 For the people shall dwell in Zion at
Jerusalem;

COURAGE

Where
should we
go to find
courage?
(30:15)

30:7 [a] Literally *Rahab Sits Idle*

You shall weep no more.
He will be very gracious to you at the
sound of your cry;
When He hears it, He will answer you.
20 And *though* the Lord gives you
The bread of adversity and the water of
affliction,
Yet your teachers will not be moved into
a corner anymore,
But your eyes shall see your teachers.
21 Your ears shall hear a word behind you,
saying,
"This *is* the way, walk in it,"
Whenever you turn to the right hand
Or whenever you turn to the left.
22 You will also defile the covering of your
images of silver,
And the ornament of your molded
images of gold.
You will throw them away as an unclean
thing;
You will say to them, "Get away!"

WHAT'S IT
MEAN?

A season of drought was devastating to
the Israelites, who relied on agriculture for
their living. A season of rain, on the other
hand, was a powerful symbol of hope.
Isaiah 30:23

23 Then He will give the rain for your seed
With which you sow the ground,
And bread of the increase of the earth;
It will be fat and plentiful.
In that day your cattle will feed
In large pastures.
24 Likewise the oxen and the young donkeys
that work the ground
Will eat cured fodder,
Which has been winnowed with the
shovel and fan.
25 There will be on every high mountain
And on every high hill
Rivers *and* streams of waters,
In the day of the great slaughter,
When the towers fall.
26 Moreover the light of the moon will be as
the light of the sun,

And the light of the sun will be sevenfold,
As the light of seven days,
In the day that the LORD binds up the
bruise of His people
And heals the stroke of their wound.

JUDGMENT ON ASSYRIA

27 Behold, the name of the LORD comes from
afar,
Burning *with* His anger,
And *His* burden *is* heavy;
His lips are full of indignation,
And His tongue like a devouring fire.
28 His breath is like an overflowing stream,
Which reaches up to the neck,
To sift the nations with the sieve of
futility;
And *there shall be* a bridle in the jaws of
the people,
Causing *them* to err.

29 You shall have a song
As in the night *when* a holy festival is
kept,
And gladness of heart as when one goes
with a flute,
To come into the mountain of the LORD,
To the Mighty One of Israel.
30 The LORD will cause His glorious voice to
be heard,
And show the descent of His arm,
With the indignation of *His* anger
And the flame of a devouring fire,
With scattering, tempest, and hailstones.
31 For through the voice of the LORD
Assyria will be beaten down,
As He strikes with the rod.
32 And *in* every place where the staff of
punishment passes,
Which the LORD lays on him,
It will be with tambourines and harps;
And in battles of brandishing He will
fight with it.
33 For Tophet *was* established of old,
Yes, for the king it is prepared.
He has made *it* deep and large;
Its pyre *is* fire with much wood;
The breath of the LORD, like a stream of
brimstone,
Kindles it.

THE FOLLY OF NOT TRUSTING GOD

1 Woe to those who go down to Egypt for
help,
And rely on horses,
Who trust in chariots because *they are*
many,

And in horsemen because they are very
strong,
But who do not look to the Holy One of
Israel,
Nor seek the LORD!
2 Yet He also *is* wise and will bring disaster,
And will not call back His words,
But will arise against the house of
evildoers,
And against the help of those who work
iniquity.
3 Now the Egyptians *are* men, and not
God;
And their horses are flesh, and not spirit.
When the LORD stretches out His hand,
Both he who helps will fall,
And he who is helped will fall down;
They all will perish together.

GOD WILL DELIVER JERUSALEM

4For thus the LORD has spoken to me:

"As a lion roars,
And a young lion over his prey
(When a multitude of shepherds is
summoned against him,
He will not be afraid of their voice
Nor be disturbed by their noise),
So the LORD of hosts will come down
To fight for Mount Zion and for its hill.
5 Like birds flying about,
So will the LORD of hosts defend
Jerusalem.
Defending, He will also deliver *it*;
Passing over, He will preserve *it.*"

6Return *to Him* against whom
the children of Israel have
deeply revolted. 7For in that
day every man shall throw
away his idols of silver and his
idols of gold—sin, which your
own hands have made for
yourselves.

MONEY

What is
more
lasting
than our
things?
(31:6, 7)

8 "Then Assyria shall fall by a sword not of
man,
And a sword not of mankind shall
devour him.
But he shall flee from the sword,
And his young men shall become forced
labor.
9 He shall cross over to his stronghold for
fear,
And his princes shall be afraid of the
banner,"
Says the LORD,

Whose fire *is* in Zion
And whose furnace *is* in Jerusalem.

A REIGN OF RIGHTEOUSNESS

1 Behold, a king will reign in righteousness,
And princes will rule with justice.
2 A man will be as a hiding place from the
wind,
And a cover from the tempest,
As rivers of water in a dry place,
As the shadow of a great rock in a weary
land.
3 The eyes of those who see will not be dim,
And the ears of those who hear will
listen.
4 Also the heart of the rash will understand
knowledge,
And the tongue of the stammerers will be
ready to speak plainly.

5 The foolish person will no longer be
called generous,
Nor the miser said *to be* bountiful;
6 For the foolish person will speak
foolishness,
And his heart will work iniquity:
To practice ungodliness,
To utter error against the LORD,
To keep the hungry unsatisfied,
And he will cause the drink of the thirsty
to fail.
7 Also the schemes of the schemer *are* evil;
He devises wicked plans
To destroy the poor with lying words,
Even when the needy speaks justice.
8 But a generous man devises generous
things,
And by generosity he shall stand.

CONSEQUENCES OF COMPLACENCY

9 Rise up, you women who are at ease,
Hear my voice;
You complacent daughters,
Give ear to my speech.
10 In a year and *some* days
You will be troubled, you complacent
women;
For the vintage will fail,
The gathering will not come.
11 Tremble, you *women* who are at ease;
Be troubled, you complacent ones;
Strip yourselves, make yourselves bare,
And gird *sackcloth* on *your* waists.

12 People shall mourn upon their breasts
For the pleasant fields, for the fruitful
vine.

13 On the land of my people will come up
      thorns *and* briers,
    Yes, on all the happy homes *in* the joyous
      city;
14 Because the palaces will be forsaken,
    The bustling city will be deserted.
    The forts and towers will become lairs
      forever,
    A joy of wild donkeys, a pasture of
      flocks—
15 Until the Spirit is poured upon us from
      on high,
    And the wilderness becomes a fruitful
      field,
    And the fruitful field is counted as a forest.

THE PEACE OF GOD'S REIGN

16 Then justice will dwell in
      the wilderness,
    And righteousness
      remain in the
      fruitful field.
17 The work of
      righteousness will
      be peace,
    And the effect of
      righteousness,
      quietness and
      assurance forever.
18 My people will dwell in a
      peaceful habitation,
    In secure dwellings, and in quiet resting
      places,
19 Though hail comes down on the forest,
    And the city is brought low in
      humiliation.

20 Blessed *are* you who sow beside all
      waters,
    Who send out freely the feet of the ox
      and the donkey.

A PRAYER IN DEEP DISTRESS

1 Woe to you who plunder, though you
      have not *been* plundered;
    And you who deal treacherously, though
      they have not dealt treacherously with
      you!
    When you cease plundering,
    You will be plundered;
    When you make an end of dealing
      treacherously,
    They will deal treacherously with you.

2 O LORD, be gracious to us;
    We have waited for You.
    Be their[a] arm every morning,
    Our salvation also in the time of
      trouble.
3 At the noise of the tumult the people shall
      flee;
    When You lift Yourself up, the nations
      shall be scattered;
4 And Your plunder shall be gathered
    Like the gathering of the caterpillar;
    As the running to and fro of locusts,
    He shall run upon them.

5 The LORD is exalted, for He dwells on
      high;
    He has filled Zion
      with justice and
      righteousness.
6 Wisdom and
      knowledge will be
      the stability of your
      times,
    And the strength of
      salvation;
    The fear of the LORD *is*
      His treasure.

7 Surely their valiant
      ones shall cry
      outside,
    The ambassadors of peace shall weep
      bitterly.
8 The highways lie waste,
    The traveling man ceases.
    He has broken the covenant,
    He has despised the cities,[a]
    He regards no man.
9 The earth mourns *and* languishes,
    Lebanon is shamed *and* shriveled;
    Sharon is like a wilderness,
    And Bashan and Carmel shake off *their*
      fruits.

IMPENDING JUDGMENT ON ZION

10 "Now I will rise," says the LORD;
    "Now I will be exalted,
    Now I will lift Myself up.
11 You shall conceive chaff,
    You shall bring forth stubble;
    Your breath, *as* fire, shall devour you.
12 And the people shall be *like* the burnings
      of lime;

> "The work of righteousness
> will be peace, and the effect
> of righteousness, quietness
> and assurance forever."
> (Isaiah 32:17)

33:2 [a]Septuagint omits *their*; Syriac, Targum, and Vulgate read *our*.   **33:8** [a]Following Masoretic Text and Vulgate; Dead Sea Scrolls read *witnesses*; Septuagint omits *cities*; Targum reads *They have been removed from their cities.*

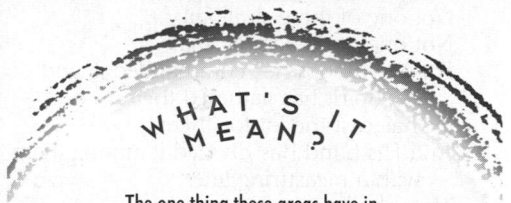

WHAT'S IT MEAN?

The one thing these areas have in common is natural beauty. Mount Lebanon towers over the region and produces majestic cedar trees. The fertile Sharon Valley was known for its breathtaking variety of flowers and plant life. Bashan was famous for its abundant wheat fields and vast herds of livestock. Mount Carmel is a beautiful, wooded mountain overlooking the Mediterranean Sea.

Isaiah 33:9

Like thorns cut up they shall be burned in the fire.

13 Hear, you *who are* afar off, what I have done;
And you *who are* near, acknowledge My might."

14 The sinners in Zion are afraid;
Fearfulness has seized the hypocrites:
"Who among us shall dwell with the devouring fire?
Who among us shall dwell with everlasting burnings?"

15 He who walks righteously and speaks uprightly,
He who despises the gain of oppressions,
Who gestures with his hands, refusing bribes,
Who stops his ears from hearing of bloodshed,
And shuts his eyes from seeing evil:

16 He will dwell on high;
His place of defense *will be* the fortress of rocks;
Bread will be given him,
His water *will be* sure.

THE LAND OF THE MAJESTIC KING

17 Your eyes will see the King in His beauty;
They will see the land that is very far off.

18 Your heart will meditate on terror:
"Where *is* the scribe?
Where *is* he who weighs?
Where *is* he who counts the towers?"

19 You will not see a fierce people,
A people of obscure speech, beyond perception,

Of a stammering tongue *that you* cannot understand.

20 Look upon Zion, the city of our appointed feasts;
Your eyes will see Jerusalem, a quiet home,
A tabernacle *that* will not be taken down;
Not one of its stakes will ever be removed,
Nor will any of its cords be broken.

21 But there the majestic LORD *will be* for us
A place of broad rivers *and* streams,
In which no galley with oars will sail,
Nor majestic ships pass by

22 (For the LORD *is* our Judge,
The LORD *is* our Lawgiver,
The LORD *is* our King;
He will save us);

23 Your tackle is loosed,
They could not strengthen their mast,
They could not spread the sail.

Then the prey of great plunder is divided;
The lame take the prey.

24 And the inhabitant will not say, "I am sick";
The people who dwell in it *will be* forgiven *their* iniquity.

JUDGMENT ON THE NATIONS

1 Come near, you nations, to hear;
And heed, you people!
Let the earth hear, and all that is in it,
The world and all things that come forth from it.

2 For the indignation of the LORD *is* against all nations,
And *His* fury against all their armies;
He has utterly destroyed them,
He has given them over to the slaughter.

3 Also their slain shall be thrown out;
Their stench shall rise from their corpses,
And the mountains shall be melted with their blood.

4 All the host of heaven shall be dissolved,
And the heavens shall be rolled up like a scroll;
All their host shall fall down
As the leaf falls from the vine,
And as *fruit* falling from a fig tree.

5 "For My sword shall be bathed in heaven;
Indeed it shall come down on Edom,
And on the people of My curse, for judgment.

6 The sword of the LORD is filled with
blood,
It is made overflowing with fatness,
With the blood of lambs and goats,
With the fat of the kidneys of rams.
For the LORD has a sacrifice in Bozrah,
And a great slaughter in the land of
Edom.

7 The wild oxen shall come down with
them,
And the young bulls with the mighty
bulls;
Their land shall be soaked with blood,
And their dust saturated with fatness."

8 For *it is* the day of the LORD's vengeance,
The year of recompense for the cause of
Zion.

9 Its streams shall be turned into pitch,
And its dust into brimstone;
Its land shall become burning pitch.

10 It shall not be quenched night or day;
Its smoke shall ascend forever.
From generation to generation it shall lie
waste;
No one shall pass through it forever and
ever.

11 But the pelican and the porcupine shall
possess it,
Also the owl and the raven shall dwell
in it.
And He shall stretch out over it
The line of confusion and the stones of
emptiness.

12 They shall call its nobles to the kingdom,
But none *shall be* there, and all its princes
shall be nothing.

13 And thorns shall come up in its palaces,
Nettles and brambles in its fortresses;
It shall be a habitation of jackals,
A courtyard for ostriches.

14 The wild beasts of the desert shall also
meet with the jackals,
And the wild goat shall bleat to its
companion;
Also the night creature shall rest there,
And find for herself a place of rest.

15 There the arrow snake shall make her
nest and lay *eggs*
And hatch, and gather *them* under her
shadow;
There also shall the hawks be gathered,
Every one with her mate.

16 "Search from the book of the LORD, and
read:

Not one of these shall fail;
Not one shall lack her mate.
For My mouth has commanded it, and
His Spirit has gathered them.

17 He has cast the lot for them,
And His hand has divided it among them
with a measuring line.
They shall possess it forever;
From generation to generation they shall
dwell in it."

THE FUTURE GLORY OF ZION

1 The wilderness and the wasteland shall
be glad for them,
And the desert shall rejoice and blossom
as the rose;

2 It shall blossom abundantly and rejoice,
Even with joy and singing.
The glory of Lebanon shall be given to it,
The excellence of Carmel and Sharon.
They shall see the glory of the LORD,
The excellency of our God.

3 Strengthen the weak hands,
And make firm the feeble knees.

4 Say to those *who are* fearful-hearted,
"Be strong, do not fear!
Behold, your God will come *with*
vengeance,
With the recompense of God;
He will come and save you."

5 Then the eyes of the blind shall be
opened,
And the ears of the deaf shall be
unstopped.

6 Then the lame shall leap like a deer,
And the tongue of the dumb sing.
For waters shall burst forth in the
wilderness,
And streams in the desert.

7 The parched ground shall become a pool,
And the thirsty land springs of water;
In the habitation of jackals, where each
lay,
There shall be grass with reeds and rushes.

8 A highway shall be there, and a road,
And it shall be called the Highway of
Holiness.
The unclean shall not pass over it,
But it *shall be* for others.
Whoever walks the road, although a fool,
Shall not go astray.

9 No lion shall be there,
Nor shall *any* ravenous beast go up on it;
It shall not be found there.

10 But the redeemed shall walk *there*,
And the ransomed of the
LORD shall return,
And come to Zion
with singing,
With everlasting joy on
their heads.
They shall obtain joy and
gladness,
And sorrow and sighing
shall flee away.

FOLLOWING GOD

Where will
following
God lead
us?
(35:10)

SENNACHERIB BOASTS AGAINST THE LORD

[1]Now it came to pass in the fourteenth year of King Hezekiah *that* Sennacherib king of Assyria came up against all the fortified cities of Judah and took them. [2]Then the king of Assyria sent *the* Rabshakeh[a] with a great army from Lachish to King Hezekiah at Jerusalem. And he stood by the aqueduct from the upper pool, on the highway to the Fuller's Field. [3]And Eliakim the son of Hilkiah, who was over the household, Shebna the scribe, and Joah the son of Asaph, the recorder, came out to him.

[4]Then *the* Rabshakeh said to them, "Say now to Hezekiah, 'Thus says the great king, the king of Assyria: "What confidence is this in which you trust? [5]I say you speak of having plans and power for war; but *they are* mere words. Now in whom do you trust, that you rebel against me? [6]Look! You are trusting in the staff of this broken reed, Egypt, on which if a man leans, it will go into his hand and pierce it. So *is* Pharaoh king of Egypt to all who trust in him.

[7]"But if you say to me, 'We trust in the LORD our God,' *is it* not He whose high places and whose altars Hezekiah has taken away, and said to Judah and Jerusalem, 'You shall worship before this altar'?" ' [8]Now therefore, I urge you, give a pledge to my master the king of Assyria, and I will give you two thousand horses—if you are able on your part to put riders on them! [9]How then will you repel one captain of the least of my master's servants, and put your trust in Egypt for chariots and horsemen? [10]Have I now come up without the LORD against this land to destroy it? The LORD said to me, 'Go up against this land, and destroy it.' "

[11]Then Eliakim, Shebna, and Joah said to *the* Rabshakeh, "Please speak to your servants in Aramaic, for we understand *it*; and do not speak to us in Hebrew[a] in the hearing of the people who *are* on the wall."

[12]But *the* Rabshakeh said, "Has my master sent me to your master and to you to speak these words, and not to the men who sit on the wall, who will eat and drink their own waste with you?"

WHAT'S IT MEAN?

The average Israelite of Isaiah's day spoke and understood only Hebrew. Some, especially those who did business with people from other countries, also spoke Aramaic, the language of the Persians, Syrians, and Babylonians.

Isaiah 36:11

[13]Then *the* Rabshakeh stood and called out with a loud voice in Hebrew, and said, "Hear the words of the great king, the king of Assyria! [14]Thus says the king: 'Do not let Hezekiah deceive you, for he will not be able to deliver you; [15]nor let Hezekiah make you trust in the LORD, saying, "The LORD will surely deliver us; this city will not be given into the hand of the king of Assyria." ' [16]Do not listen to Hezekiah; for thus says the king of Assyria: 'Make *peace* with me *by a* present and come out to me; and every one of you eat from his own vine and every one from his own fig tree, and every one of you drink the waters of his own cistern; [17]until I come and take you away to a land like your own land, a land of grain and new wine, a land of bread and vineyards. [18]*Beware* lest Hezekiah persuade you, saying, "The LORD will deliver us." Has any one of the gods of the nations delivered its land from the hand of the king of Assyria? [19]Where *are* the gods of Hamath and Arpad? Where *are* the gods of Sepharvaim? Indeed, have they delivered Samaria from my hand? [20]Who among all the gods of these lands have delivered their countries from my hand, that the LORD should deliver Jerusalem from my hand?' "

[21]But they held their peace and answered him not a word; for the king's commandment was, "Do not answer him." [22]Then Eliakim the son of Hilkiah, who *was* over the household, Shebna the scribe, and Joah the son of Asaph, the recorder, came to Hezekiah with *their* clothes torn, and told him the words of *the* Rabshakeh.

36:2 [a]A title, probably *Chief of Staff* or *Governor*   **36:11** [a]Literally *Judean*

ISAIAH ASSURES DELIVERANCE

¹And so it was, when King Hezekiah heard *it*, that he tore his clothes, covered himself with sackcloth, and went into the house of the LORD. ²Then he sent Eliakim, who *was* over the household, Shebna the scribe, and the elders of the priests, covered with sackcloth, to Isaiah the prophet, the son of Amoz. ³And they said to him, "Thus says Hezekiah: 'This day *is* a day of trouble and rebuke and blasphemy; for the children have come to birth, but *there is* no strength to bring them forth. ⁴It may be that the LORD your God will hear the words of *the* Rabshakeh, whom his master the king of Assyria has sent to reproach the living God, and will rebuke the words which the LORD your God has heard. Therefore lift up *your* prayer for the remnant that is left.' "

⁵So the servants of King Hezekiah came to Isaiah. ⁶And Isaiah said to them, "Thus you shall say to your master, 'Thus says the LORD: "Do not be afraid of the words which you have heard, with which the servants of the king of Assyria have blasphemed Me. ⁷Surely I will send a spirit upon him, and he shall hear a rumor and return to his own land; and I will cause him to fall by the sword in his own land." ' "

SENNACHERIB'S THREAT AND HEZEKIAH'S PRAYER

⁸Then *the* Rabshakeh returned, and found the king of Assyria warring against Libnah, for he heard that he had departed from Lachish. ⁹And the king heard concerning Tirhakah king of Ethiopia, "He has come out to make war with you." So when he heard *it*, he sent messengers to Hezekiah, saying, ¹⁰"Thus you shall speak to Hezekiah king of Judah, saying: 'Do not let your God in whom you trust deceive you, saying, "Jerusalem shall not be given into the hand of the king of Assyria." ¹¹Look! You have heard

what the kings of Assyria have done to all lands by utterly destroying them; and shall you be delivered? ¹²Have the gods of the nations delivered those whom my fathers have destroyed, Gozan and Haran and Rezeph, and the people of Eden who *were* in Telassar? ¹³Where *is* the king of Hamath, the king of Arpad, and the king of the city of Sepharvaim, Hena, and Ivah?' "

¹⁴And Hezekiah received the letter from the hand of the messengers, and read it; and Hezekiah went up to the house of the LORD, and spread it before the LORD. ¹⁵Then Hezekiah prayed to the LORD, saying: ¹⁶"O LORD of hosts, God of Israel, *the One* who dwells *between* the cherubim, You *are* God, You alone, of all the kingdoms of the earth. You have made heaven and earth. ¹⁷Incline Your ear, O LORD, and hear; open Your eyes, O LORD, and see; and hear all the words of Sennacherib, which he has sent to reproach the living God. ¹⁸Truly, LORD, the kings of Assyria have laid waste all the nations and their lands, ¹⁹and have cast their gods into the fire; for they *were* not gods, but the work of men's hands—wood and stone. Therefore they destroyed them. ²⁰Now therefore, O LORD our God, save us from his hand, that all the kingdoms of the earth may know that You *are* the LORD, You alone."

TRIALS

Who will help us overcome our problems? (37:20)

THE WORD OF THE LORD CONCERNING SENNACHERIB

²¹Then Isaiah the son of Amoz sent to Hezekiah, saying, "Thus says the LORD God of Israel, 'Because you have prayed to Me against Sennacherib king of Assyria, ²²this *is* the word which the LORD has spoken concerning him:

"The virgin, the daughter of Zion,
Has despised you, laughed you to scorn;
The daughter of Jerusalem
Has shaken *her* head behind your back!

23 "Whom have you reproached and blasphemed?
Against whom have you raised *your* voice,
And lifted up your eyes on high?
Against the Holy One of Israel.

24 By your servants you have reproached the Lord,
And said, 'By the multitude of my chariots

I have come up to the height of the
    mountains,
To the limits of Lebanon;
I will cut down its tall cedars
And its choice cypress trees;
I will enter its farthest height,
To its fruitful forest.
25   I have dug and drunk water,
And with the soles of my feet I have
    dried up
All the brooks of defense.'

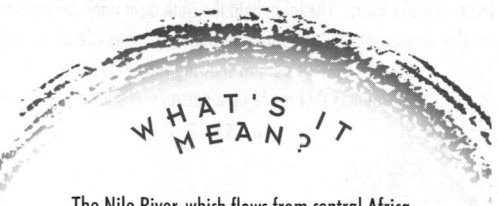

The Nile River, which flows from central Africa
to the Mediterranean region, is over 3,500 miles
long. The Nile is big enough to provide water for the entire nation
of Egypt. Do you suppose Sennacherib really believed that he was
more powerful than the Nile?

Isaiah 37:25

26   "Did you not hear long ago
How I made it,
From ancient times that I formed it?
Now I have brought it to pass,
That you should be
For crushing fortified cities *into* heaps of
    ruins.
27   Therefore their inhabitants *had* little
    power;
They were dismayed and confounded;
They were *as* the grass of the field
And the green herb,
As the grass on the
    housetops
And grain blighted
    before it is grown.

28   "But I know your
    dwelling place,
Your going out and your
    coming in,
And your rage against Me.
29   Because your rage against Me
    and your tumult
Have come up to My ears,

Therefore I will put My hook in your
    nose
And My bridle in your lips,
And I will turn you back
By the way which you came." '

30"This *shall be* a sign to you:

You shall eat this year such as grows of
    itself,
And the second year what springs from
    the same;
Also in the third year sow and reap,
Plant vineyards and eat the fruit of them.
31   And the remnant who have escaped of
    the house of Judah
Shall again take root downward,
And bear fruit upward.
32   For out of Jerusalem shall go a remnant,
And those who escape from Mount Zion.
The zeal of the LORD of hosts will do this.

33"Therefore thus says the LORD concerning
the king of Assyria:

'He shall not come into this city,
Nor shoot an arrow there,
Nor come before it with shield,
Nor build a siege mound against it.
34   By the way that he came,
By the same shall he return;
And he shall not come into this city,'
Says the LORD.
35   'For I will defend this city, to save it
For My own sake and for My servant
    David's sake.' "

SENNACHERIB'S DEFEAT AND DEATH

36Then the angel[a] of the LORD went out, and
killed in the camp of the Assyrians one hundred and eighty-five thousand; and when *people*
arose early in the morning, there
were the corpses—all dead.
37So Sennacherib king of Assyria departed and went
away, returned *home,* and remained at Nineveh. 38Now it
came to pass, as he was worshiping in the house of Nisroch his god, that his sons
Adrammelech and Sharezer
struck him down with the
sword; and they escaped into the
land of Ararat. Then Esarhaddon his son
reigned in his place.

"For I will defend this
city, to save it for My own
sake and for My servant
David's sake."
(Isaiah 37:35)

37:36 [a]Or *Angel*

HEZEKIAH'S LIFE EXTENDED

¹In those days Hezekiah was sick and near death. And Isaiah the prophet, the son of Amoz, went to him and said to him, "Thus says the LORD: 'Set your house in order, for you shall die and not live.' "

²Then Hezekiah turned his face toward the wall, and prayed to the LORD, ³and said, "Remember now, O LORD, I pray, how I have walked before You in truth and with a loyal heart, and have done *what is* good in Your sight." And Hezekiah wept bitterly.

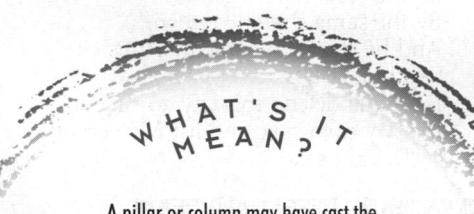

PRAYER

What's an example of answered prayer? (38:1–6)

⁴And the word of the LORD came to Isaiah, saying, ⁵"Go and tell Hezekiah, 'Thus says the LORD, the God of David your father: "I have heard your prayer, I have seen your tears; surely I will add to your days fifteen years. ⁶I will deliver you and this city from the hand of the king of Assyria, and I will defend this city." ' ⁷And this *is* the sign to you from the LORD, that the LORD will do this thing which He has spoken: ⁸Behold, I will bring the shadow on the sundial, which has gone down with the sun on the sundial of Ahaz, ten degrees backward." So the sun returned ten degrees on the dial by which it had gone down.

WHAT'S IT MEAN?

A pillar or column may have cast the shadow that served as a sundial. As the shadow moved up or down, it indicated the passing of time. Unfortunately, because the exact design of the sundial is unknown, it's impossible to tell how much time was lost.

Isaiah 38:8

⁹This is the writing of Hezekiah king of Judah, when he had been sick and had recovered from his sickness:

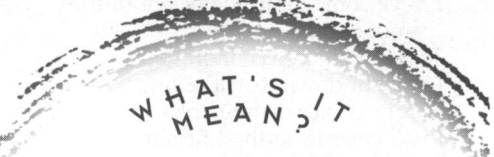

WHAT'S IT MEAN?

Ever wonder how people in ancient times made clothes? The only things they needed were thread and a loom. What's a loom, you ask? It's a large frame with threads stretched across it. Weavers threaded yarn back and forth across the loom to make fabric. The loom held the cloth tight until the weaver cut the threads of the material. The Bible describes life as a cloth woven by God, its pattern showing the events and experiences that made up a person's existence.

Isaiah 38:12

10   I said,
     "In the prime of my life
      I shall go to the gates of Sheol;
      I am deprived of the remainder of my
           years."
11   I said,
     "I shall not see YAH,
      The LORD*ᵃ* in the land of the living;
      I shall observe man no more among the
           inhabitants of the world.*ᵇ*
12   My life span is gone,
      Taken from me like a shepherd's tent;
      I have cut off my life like a weaver.
      He cuts me off from the loom;
      From day until night You make an end of
           me.
13   I have considered until morning—
      Like a lion,
      So He breaks all my bones;
      From day until night You make an end of
           me.
14   Like a crane *or* a swallow, so I chattered;
      I mourned like a dove;
      My eyes fail *from looking* upward.
      O LORD,*ᵃ* I am oppressed;
      Undertake for me!

15   "What shall I say?
      He has both spoken to me,*ᵃ*
      And He Himself has done *it.*
      I shall walk carefully all my years
      In the bitterness of my soul.

38:11 *ᵃ*Hebrew *YAH, YAH* *ᵇ*Following some Hebrew manuscripts; Masoretic Text and Vulgate read *rest;* Septuagint omits *among the inhabitants of the world;* Targum reads *land.* **38:14** *ᵃ*Following Bomberg; Masoretic Text and Dead Sea Scrolls read *Lord.* **38:15** *ᵃ*Following Masoretic Text and Vulgate; Dead Sea Scrolls and Targum read *And shall I say to Him;* Septuagint omits first half of this verse.

16 O Lord, by these *things men* live;
And in all these *things is* the life of my
   spirit;
So You will restore me and make me live.
17 Indeed *it was* for *my own* peace
That I had great bitterness;
But You have lovingly *delivered* my soul
   from the pit of corruption,
For You have cast all my sins behind
   Your back.
18 For Sheol cannot thank You,
Death cannot praise You;
Those who go down to the pit cannot
   hope for Your truth.
19 The living, the living man, he shall praise
   You,
As I *do* this day;
The father shall make known Your truth
   to the children.

20 "The LORD *was ready* to save me;
Therefore we will sing my songs with
   stringed instruments
All the days of our life, in the house of
   the LORD."

21Now Isaiah had said, "Let them take a lump of figs, and apply *it* as a poultice on the boil, and he shall recover."
22And Hezekiah had said, "What *is* the sign that I shall go up to the house of the LORD?"

THE BABYLONIAN ENVOYS

1At that time Merodach-Baladan[a] the son of Baladan, king of Babylon, sent letters and a present to Hezekiah, for he heard that he had been sick and had recovered. 2And Hezekiah was pleased with them, and showed them the house of his treasures—the silver and gold, the spices and precious ointment, and all his armory—all that was found among his treasures. There was nothing in his house or in all his dominion that Hezekiah did not show them.
3Then Isaiah the prophet went to King Hezekiah, and said to him, "What did these men say, and from where did they come to you?"
So Hezekiah said, "They came to me from a far country, from Babylon."
4And he said, "What have they seen in your house?"
So Hezekiah answered, "They have seen all that *is* in my house; there is nothing among my treasures that I have not shown them."
5Then Isaiah said to Hezekiah, "Hear the word of the LORD of hosts: 6"Behold, the days are coming when all that *is* in your house, and what your fathers have accumulated until this day, shall be carried to Babylon; nothing shall be left,' says the LORD. 7'And they shall take away *some* of your sons who will descend from you, whom you will beget; and they shall be eunuchs in the palace of the king of Babylon.' "

WHAT'S IT MEAN?

In 586 B.C., Jerusalem was destroyed by King Nebuchadnezzar and his Babylonian forces. Rather than killing everyone in sight, the king took as many as 4,500 Jews back to Babylon as captives. The healthiest and brightest of these captives were chosen to serve in the royal palace.
Isaiah 39:7

8So Hezekiah said to Isaiah, "The word of the LORD which you have spoken *is* good!" For he said, "At least there will be peace and truth in my days."

GOD'S PEOPLE ARE COMFORTED

1 "Comfort, yes, comfort My people!"
Says your God.
2 "Speak comfort to Jerusalem, and cry out
   to her,
That her warfare is ended,
That her iniquity is pardoned;
For she has received from the LORD's
   hand
Double for all her sins."

3 The voice of one crying in the wilderness:
"Prepare the way of the LORD;
Make straight in the desert[a]
A highway for our God.
4 Every valley shall be exalted
And every mountain and hill brought
   low;
The crooked places shall be made straight
And the rough places smooth;
5 The glory of the LORD shall be revealed,
And all flesh shall see *it* together;
For the mouth of the LORD has spoken."

39:1 [a]Spelled *Berodach-Baladan* in 2 Kings 20:12   **40:3** [a]Following Masoretic Text, Targum, and Vulgate; Septuagint omits *in the desert*.

6   The voice said, "Cry out!"
And he[a] said, "What shall I cry?"

" All flesh *is* grass,
And all its loveliness *is* like the flower of
the field.
7   The grass withers, the flower fades,
Because the breath of the LORD blows
upon it;
Surely the people *are* grass.
8   The grass withers, the flower fades,
But the word of our God stands forever."

9   O Zion,
You who bring good tidings,
Get up into the high mountain;
O Jerusalem,
You who bring good tidings,
Lift up your voice with strength,
Lift *it* up, be not afraid;
Say to the cities of Judah, "Behold your
God!"

10   Behold, the Lord GOD shall come with a
strong *hand,*
And His arm shall rule for Him;
Behold, His reward *is* with Him,
And His work before Him.
11   He will feed His flock like a shepherd;
He will gather the lambs with His arm,
And carry *them* in His bosom,
And gently lead those who are with young.

12   Who has measured the waters[a] in the
hollow of His hand,
Measured heaven with a span
And calculated the dust of the earth in a
measure?
Weighed the mountains in scales
And the hills in a balance?
13   Who has directed the Spirit of the LORD,
Or *as* His counselor has taught Him?
14   With whom did He take counsel, and *who*
instructed Him,
And taught Him in the path of justice?
Who taught Him knowledge,
And showed Him the way of
understanding?

15   Behold, the nations *are* as a drop in a
bucket,
And are counted as the small dust on the
scales;

Look, He lifts up the isles as a very little
thing.
16   And Lebanon *is* not sufficient to burn,
Nor its beasts sufficient for a burnt
offering.
17   All nations before Him *are* as nothing,
And they are counted by Him less than
nothing and worthless.

18   To whom then will you liken God?
Or what likeness will you compare to
Him?
19   The workman molds an image,
The goldsmith overspreads it with gold,
And the silversmith casts silver chains.
20   Whoever *is* too impoverished for *such* a
contribution
Chooses a tree *that* will not rot;
He seeks for himself a skillful workman
To prepare a carved image *that* will not
totter.

21   Have you not known?
Have you not heard?
Has it not been told you from the
beginning?
Have you not understood from the
foundations of the earth?
22   *It is* He who sits above the circle of the
earth,
And its inhabitants *are* like grasshoppers,
Who stretches out the heavens like a
curtain,
And spreads them out like a tent to dwell
in.
23   He brings the princes to nothing;
He makes the judges of the earth useless.

24   Scarcely shall they be planted,
Scarcely shall they be sown,
Scarcely shall their stock take root in the
earth,
When He will also blow on them,
And they will wither,
And the whirlwind will take them away
like stubble.

25   "To whom then will you liken Me,
Or *to whom* shall I be equal?" says the
Holy One.
26   Lift up your eyes on high,
And see who has created these *things,*
Who brings out their host by number;

40:6 [a]Following Masoretic Text and Targum; Dead Sea Scrolls, Septuagint, and Vulgate read *I.*
40:12 [a]Following Masoretic Text, Septuagint, and Vulgate; Dead Sea Scrolls read *waters of the sea;* Targum reads
waters of the world.

He calls them all by name,
By the greatness of His might
And the strength of *His* power;
Not one is missing.

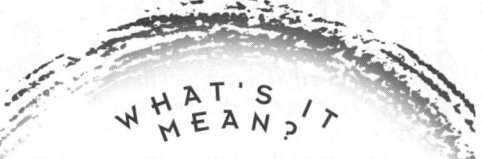

WHAT'S IT MEAN?

Many people in ancient times believed that
the destiny of their nation was controlled by heavenly
bodies—stars, planets, the sun, the moon, and so forth. Professional
astrologers were in constant demand to help kings and their officials
keep track of what was going on in the sky and to interpret what it
meant. These astrologers claimed to be able to predict the future
based on the movement of the planets and stars.

Isaiah 40:26

27 Why do you say, O Jacob,
And speak, O Israel:
"My way is hidden from the
LORD,
And my just claim is
passed over by my
God"?
28 Have you not known?
Have you not heard?
The everlasting God, the
LORD,
The Creator of the ends of the earth,
Neither faints nor is weary.
His understanding is unsearchable.
29 He gives power to the weak,
And to *those who have* no might
He increases strength.
30 Even the youths shall
faint and be weary,
And the young men shall
utterly fall,
31 But those who wait on
the LORD
Shall renew *their* strength;
They shall mount up with
wings like eagles,
They shall run and not be weary,
They shall walk and not faint.

TRUST
Why can
we trust
God?
(40:25–28)

STRENGTH
Will God
help us
soar to
new
heights?
(40:29–31)

ISRAEL ASSURED OF GOD'S HELP

1 "Keep silence before Me, O coastlands,
And let the people renew *their* strength!

On the Edge

*Have you not known? Have you
not heard? The everlasting God, the
LORD, the Creator of the ends of the
earth, neither faints nor is weary. His
understanding is unsearchable. He gives
power to the weak, and to those who
have no might He increases strength.
Even the youths shall faint and be
weary, and the young men shall utterly
fall, but those who wait on the LORD
shall renew their strength; they shall
mount up with wings like eagles, they
shall run and not be weary, they shall
walk and not faint (Is. 40:28–31).*

Everyone goes through times in life
when they feel like nothing is happening.
Working hard with very few accomplishments. Nothing's new on the horizon. Each
day looks the same and feels the same.
Goals are just as far away as they've always
been. It gets tiring to work so hard, be so
committed, and see no fruit.

Isaiah says that even young people get
tired and weary, so tired that they can
stumble and fall. But hope for tired people
comes from the Lord. He says that if you
trust in Him, He will give you a new
strength—not just the ability to
survive another day, but new
strength that lifts you up and
makes you soar. It's the difference between just surviving tomorrow and soaring above the day with the
strength and presence of an eagle. You don't
have to figure out how to be the eagle.
That's God's gift to those who trust in Him
and who call on Him on the days when life
seems to be going nowhere.

SEE FOR YOURSELF:
Ps. 65:3, 5; Jer. 15:20;
Hab. 3:19

Let them come near, then let them speak;
Let us come near together for judgment.

2 "Who raised up one from the east?
Who in righteousness called him to His
feet?
Who gave the nations before him,
And made *him* rule over kings?
Who gave *them* as the dust *to* his sword,
As driven stubble to his bow?

3 Who pursued them, *and* passed safely
  By the way *that* he had not gone with his
      feet?
4 Who has performed and
      done *it*,
  Calling the generations
      from the beginning?
  'I, the LORD, am the first;
  And with the last I *am*
      He.' "

Is God
eternal?
(41:4)

5 The coastlands saw *it* and feared,
  The ends of the earth were afraid;
  They drew near and came.
6 Everyone helped his neighbor,
  And said to his brother,
  "Be of good courage!"
7 So the craftsman encouraged the
      goldsmith;
  He who smooths *with* the hammer
      inspired him who strikes the anvil,
  Saying, "It *is* ready for the soldering";
  Then he fastened it with pegs,
  That it might not totter.

8 "But you, Israel, *are* My servant,
  Jacob whom I have chosen,
  The descendants of Abraham My friend.
9 *You* whom I have taken from the ends of
      the earth,
  And called from its farthest regions,
  And said to you,
  'You *are* My servant,
  I have chosen you and have not cast you
      away:
10 Fear not, for I *am* with you;
   Be not dismayed, for I *am* your God.
   I will strengthen you,
   Yes, I will help you,
   I will uphold you with My righteous right
       hand.'

11 "Behold, all those who were incensed
       against you
   Shall be ashamed and disgraced;
   They shall be as nothing,
   And those who strive with you shall
       perish.
12 You shall seek them and not find
       them—
   Those who contended with you.
   Those who war against you
   Shall be as nothing,
   As a nonexistent thing.
13 For I, the LORD your God, will hold your
       right hand,
   Saying to you, 'Fear not, I will help you.'

On the Edge

*For I, the LORD your God, will
hold your right hand, saying to
you, "Fear not, I will help you"
(Is. 41:13).*

Remember the story of Shadrach, Meshach, and Abed-Nego (Dan. 3)? The king
had them thrown into the fire because they
wouldn't bow to him. But the fire didn't
burn them up; and when people looked into
the flames, they saw *four* men. Well, the
fourth person was Jesus. Because He was
with those guys, they didn't burn. In fact,
they didn't even smell like smoke when
they came out!

Well, Jesus is with you in the same way.
In Isaiah, He says He is holding your hand.
He goes with you through the fire
of hard times in your life, preventing the flames from injuring
you but letting the heat melt
away some of the things about you
that are not godly. With your hand in His,
He can calm you down when things aren't
going so well. If you won't let go of Him, He
can lead you to the place He wants you to
be.

SEE FOR YOURSELF:
Ps. 37:24; Prov. 2:7;
Hab. 3:19; Rom. 8:26;
Heb. 13:6

14 "Fear not, you worm Jacob,
   You men of Israel!
   I will help you," says the LORD
   And your Redeemer, the Holy One of
       Israel.
15 "Behold, I will make you into a new
       threshing sledge with sharp teeth;
   You shall thresh the mountains and beat
       them small,
   And make the hills like chaff.
16 You shall winnow them, the wind shall
       carry them away,
   And the whirlwind shall scatter them;
   You shall rejoice in the LORD,
   And glory in the Holy One of Israel.

17 "The poor and needy seek water, but *there*
       is none,
   Their tongues fail for thirst.
   I, the LORD, will hear them;
   I, the God of Israel, will not forsake them.

WHAT'S IT MEAN?

The next time you need to thresh grain, but
don't have any modern equipment for the job, do
what the ancient Israelites did. Embed some sharp stones or metal
spikes in a log, then drag that log over the grain to crush it and tear
the kernels from the stalks. Once that's finished, throw the entire mess
in the air and let wind blow away the useless husks.

Isaiah 41:15, 16

18 I will open rivers in desolate heights,
And fountains in the midst of the valleys;
I will make the wilderness a pool of
water,
And the dry land springs of water.
19 I will plant in the wilderness the cedar
and the acacia tree,
The myrtle and the oil tree;
I will set in the desert the cypress tree *and*
the pine
And the box tree together,
20 That they may see and know,
And consider and understand together,
That the hand of the LORD has done this,
And the Holy One of Israel has created it.

THE FUTILITY OF IDOLS

21 "Present your case," says the LORD.
"Bring forth your strong *reasons*," says the
King of Jacob.
22 "Let them bring forth and show us what
will happen;
Let them show the former things, what
they *were*,
That we may consider them,
And know the latter end of them;
Or declare to us things to come.
23 Show the things that are to come
hereafter,
That we may know that you *are* gods;
Yes, do good or do evil,
That we may be dismayed and see *it*
together.
24 Indeed you *are* nothing,
And your work *is* nothing;
He who chooses you *is* an abomination.

25 "I have raised up one from the north,
And he shall come;
From the rising of the sun he shall call on
My name;
And he shall come against princes as
though mortar,
As the potter treads clay.
26 Who has declared from the beginning,
that we may know?
And former times, that we may say, '*He is*
righteous'?
Surely *there is* no one who shows,
Surely *there is* no one who declares,
Surely *there is* no one who hears your
words.
27 The first time *I said* to Zion,
'Look, there they are!'
And I will give to Jerusalem one who
brings good tidings.
28 For I looked, and *there was* no man;
I looked among them, but *there was* no
counselor,
Who, when I asked of them, could
answer a word.
29 Indeed they *are* all worthless;[a]
Their works *are* nothing;
Their molded images *are* wind and
confusion.

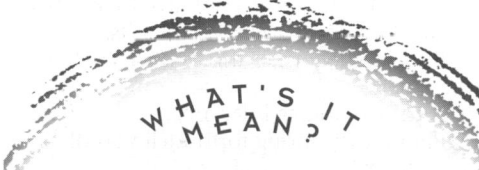

WHAT'S IT MEAN?

Who was this mysterious ruler from the
north? Why, none other than Cyrus, the king of
Persia! After Cyrus conquered Babylon in 538 B.C., he allowed the
Jewish people to return to their homeland of Judah. Unlike the kings
of Babylon, Cyrus encouraged people to worship whatever gods they
wished and in whatever way they wanted. When the Jews wanted to
rebuild their destroyed temple in Jerusalem, Cyrus
even provided the supplies.

Isaiah 41:25

THE SERVANT OF THE LORD

1 "Behold! My Servant whom I uphold,
My Elect One *in whom* My soul delights!
I have put My Spirit upon Him;
He will bring forth justice to the Gentiles.

41:29 [a]Following Masoretic Text and Vulgate; Dead Sea Scrolls, Syriac, and Targum read *nothing;* Septuagint
omits the first line.

2 He will not cry out, nor raise *His* voice,
Nor cause His voice to be heard in the street.

3 A bruised reed He will not break,
And smoking flax He will not quench;
He will bring forth justice for truth.

4 He will not fail nor be discouraged,
Till He has established justice in the earth;
And the coastlands shall wait for His law."

5 Thus says God the LORD,
Who created the heavens and stretched them out,
Who spread forth the earth and that which comes from it,
Who gives breath to the people on it,
And spirit to those who walk on it:

6 "I, the LORD, have called You in righteousness,
And will hold Your hand;
I will keep You and give You as a covenant to the people,
As a light to the Gentiles,

7 To open blind eyes,
To bring out prisoners from the prison,
Those who sit in darkness from the prison house.

8 I *am* the LORD, that *is* My name;
And My glory I will not give to another,
Nor My praise to carved images.

9 Behold, the former things have come to pass,
And new things I declare;
Before they spring forth I tell you of them."

PRAISE TO THE LORD

10 Sing to the LORD a new song,
And His praise from the ends of the earth,
You who go down to the sea, and all that is in it,
You coastlands and you inhabitants of them!

11 Let the wilderness and its cities lift up *their voice,*
The villages *that* Kedar inhabits.
Let the inhabitants of Sela sing,
Let them shout from the top of the mountains.

12 Let them give glory to the LORD,
And declare His praise in the coastlands.

13 The LORD shall go forth like a mighty man;
He shall stir up *His* zeal like a man of war.

He shall cry out, yes, shout aloud;
He shall prevail against His enemies.

PROMISE OF THE LORD'S HELP

14 "I have held My peace a long time,
I have been still and restrained Myself.
Now I will cry like a woman in labor,
I will pant and gasp at once.

15 I will lay waste the mountains and hills,
And dry up all their vegetation;
I will make the rivers coastlands,
And I will dry up the pools.

16 I will bring the blind by a way they did not know;
I will lead them in paths they have not known.
I will make darkness light before them,
And crooked places straight.
These things I will do for them,
And not forsake them.

17 They shall be turned back,
They shall be greatly ashamed,
Who trust in carved images,
Who say to the molded images,
'You *are* our gods.'

18 "Hear, you deaf;
And look, you blind, that you may see.

19 Who *is* blind but My servant,
Or deaf as My messenger *whom* I send?
Who *is* blind as *he who is* perfect,
And blind as the LORD's servant?

20 Seeing many things, but you do not observe;
Opening the ears, but he does not hear."

ISRAEL'S OBSTINATE DISOBEDIENCE

21 The LORD is well pleased for His righteousness' sake;
He will exalt the law and make *it* honorable.

22 But this *is* a people robbed and plundered;
All of them are snared in holes,
And they are hidden in prison houses;
They are for prey, and no one delivers;
For plunder, and no one says, "Restore!"

23 Who among you will give ear to this?
Who will listen and hear for the time to come?

24 Who gave Jacob for plunder, and Israel to the robbers?

"Sing to the LORD a new song, and His praise from the ends of the earth."
(Isaiah 42:10a)

Was it not the LORD,
He against whom we have sinned?
For they would not walk in His ways,
Nor were they obedient to His law.
25 Therefore He has poured on him the fury
of His anger
And the strength of battle;
It has set him on fire all around,
Yet he did not know;
And it burned him,
Yet he did not take *it* to heart.

THE REDEEMER OF ISRAEL

1 But now, thus says the LORD, who created
you, O Jacob,
And He who formed you, O Israel:
"Fear not, for I have redeemed you;
I have called *you* by your name;
You *are* Mine.
2 When you pass through the waters, I *will*
be with you;
And through the rivers, they shall not
overflow you.
When you walk through the fire, you
shall not be burned,
Nor shall the flame scorch you.
3 For I *am* the LORD your God,
The Holy One of Israel, your Savior;
I gave Egypt for your ransom,
Ethiopia and Seba in your place.
4 Since you were precious in My sight,
You have been honored,
And I have loved you;
Therefore I will give men for you,
And people for your life.
5 Fear not, for I *am* with you;
I will bring your descendants from the
east,
And gather you from the west;
6 I will say to the north, 'Give them up!'
And to the south, 'Do not keep them
back!'
Bring My sons from afar,
And My daughters from the ends of the
earth—
7 Everyone who is called by My name,
Whom I have created for My glory;
I have formed him, yes, I have made
him."

8 Bring out the blind people who have
eyes,
And the deaf who have ears.
9 Let all the nations be gathered together,
And let the people be assembled.
Who among them can declare this,
And show us former things?

Let them bring out their witnesses, that
they may be justified;
Or let them hear and say, "*It is* truth."
10 "You *are* My witnesses," says the LORD,
"And My servant whom I have chosen,
That you may know and believe Me,
And understand that I *am* He.
Before Me there was no God formed,
Nor shall there be after Me.
11 I, *even* I, *am* the LORD,
And besides Me *there is* no savior.
12 I have declared and saved,
I have proclaimed,
And *there was* no foreign *god* among you;
Therefore you *are* My witnesses,"
Says the LORD, "that I *am* God.
13 Indeed before the day *was*, I *am* He;
And *there is* no one who can deliver out
of My hand;
I work, and who will reverse it?"

14 Thus says the LORD, your Redeemer,
The Holy One of Israel:
"For your sake I will send to Babylon,
And bring them all down as fugitives—
The Chaldeans, who rejoice in their
ships.
15 I *am* the LORD, your Holy One,
The Creator of Israel, your King."

WHAT'S IT MEAN?

The king of Egypt, after letting the Israelites
leave his country, changed his mind and sent his
army to bring them back. His plan was to trap the Israelites at the
Red Sea. Just when things looked hopeless for the Israelites, God
parted the waters of the sea to make a path of dry land through the
middle of it. The Israelites were able to walk across to the other
side. When the Egyptians tried to follow, the water
collapsed on top of them, and they drowned.
Isaiah 43:16

16 Thus says the LORD, who makes a way in
the sea
And a path through the mighty waters,
17 Who brings forth the chariot and horse,
The army and the power
(They shall lie down together, they shall
not rise;

PLEADING WITH UNFAITHFUL ISRAEL

22 "But you have not called upon Me,
    O Jacob;
And you have been weary of Me,
    O Israel.
23 You have not brought Me the sheep for
    your burnt offerings,
Nor have you honored Me with your
    sacrifices.
I have not caused you to serve with grain
    offerings,
Nor wearied you with incense.
24 You have bought Me no sweet cane with
    money,
Nor have you satisfied Me with the fat of
    your sacrifices;

On the Edge

Do not remember the former things, nor consider the things of old. Behold, I will do a new thing, now it shall spring forth; shall you not know it? I will even make a road in the wilderness and rivers in the desert (Is. 43:18, 19).

One of the few things that you can count on in this lifetime is change. Just when you have everything kind of figured out, boom—it's time to go in a different direction. So many things happen that throw us off balance—new schools every few years, best friends move away, divorce, new teachers with new expectations, Dad gets transferred and the whole family has to move, new stepparents with stepsiblings, the death of someone you love. Life is continually changing.

Isaiah says not to look back and long for what used to be, that God is creating something new—new roads in the wilderness and new rivers in the desert. You may be a creature of habit, and change may make you uncomfortable. But one measure of your success will be how easily you adapt to change—to the new things God is doing in your life. You will miss all the blessing He has for you in this day if you continue to long for the past. Set your eyes toward the future and welcome the new paths that God is making for you.

SEE FOR YOURSELF:
Is. 42:16; Jer. 29:11;
2 Cor. 5:17

On the Edge

Yet hear me now, O Jacob My servant, and Israel whom I have chosen. Thus says the LORD who made you and formed you from the womb, who will help you: "Fear not, O Jacob My servant; and you, Jeshurun, whom I have chosen" (Is. 44:1, 2).

Does your teacher have a favorite student—someone she has chosen to be teacher's pet? Does your coach have an athlete who's obviously his choice for MVP? Do you see favoritism in choices made in your church or in your family? Sometimes, the same person will be the favorite everywhere they go. If you're the favored person, you can get to feeling pretty special. If you're not, it can be the pits.

God says *you* are His favorite—His chosen one. There's nobody else on earth He loves more than He loves you. When He sees you coming to pray or to worship Him, He's so glad you want to be with Him. He wants to be with you, too. You aren't just His favorite when you're down or left out and nobody else will give you a second glance. You're His favorite even when your ego doesn't need that kind of boost. No matter where you go or what you go through, you're always God's chosen one.

SEE FOR YOURSELF:
Job 34:19; Jer. 9:24;
John 3:16; Acts 10:34

They are extinguished, they are quenched
    like a wick):
18 "Do not remember the former things,
    Nor consider the things of old.
19 Behold, I will do a new thing,
    Now it shall spring forth;
    Shall you not know it?
    I will even make a road in the wilderness
    And rivers in the desert.
20 The beast of the field will honor Me,
    The jackals and the ostriches,
    Because I give waters in the wilderness
    And rivers in the desert,
    To give drink to My people, My chosen.
21 This people I have formed for Myself;
    They shall declare My praise.

But you have burdened Me with your sins,
You have wearied Me with your iniquities.

25 "I, *even* I, *am* He who blots out your transgressions for My own sake;
And I will not remember your sins.
26 Put Me in remembrance;
Let us contend together;
State your *case,* that you may be acquitted.
27 Your first father sinned,
And your mediators have transgressed against Me.
28 Therefore I will profane the princes of the sanctuary;
I will give Jacob to the curse,
And Israel to reproaches.

GOD'S BLESSING ON ISRAEL

1 "Yet hear me now, O Jacob My servant,
And Israel whom I have chosen.
2 Thus says the LORD who made you
And formed you from the womb, *who* will help you:
'Fear not, O Jacob My servant;
And you, Jeshurun, whom I have chosen.
3 For I will pour water on him who is thirsty,
And floods on the dry ground;
I will pour My Spirit on your descendants,

And My blessing on your offspring;
4 They will spring up among the grass
Like willows by the watercourses.'
5 One will say, 'I *am* the LORD's';
Another will call *himself* by the name of Jacob;
Another will write *with* his hand, 'The LORD's',
And name *himself* by the name of Israel.

THERE IS NO OTHER GOD

6 "Thus says the LORD, the King of Israel,
And his Redeemer, the LORD of hosts:
'I *am* the First and I *am* the Last;
Besides Me *there is* no God.
7 And who can proclaim as I do?
Then let him declare it and set it in order for Me,
Since I appointed the ancient people.
And the things that are coming and shall come,
Let them show these to them.
8 Do not fear, nor be afraid;
Have I not told you from that time, and declared *it*?
You *are* My witnesses.
Is there a God besides Me?
Indeed *there is* no other Rock;
I know not *one*.' "

IDOLATRY IS FOOLISHNESS

9 Those who make an image, all of them *are* useless,

Promise HE PROMISES TO FORGET YOUR PAST SINS.

I, even I, am He who blots out your transgressions for My own sake; and I will not remember your sins (Is. 43:25).

What kind of past do you have? Decent? Wild? Funny? Tragic? Wonderful? Boring? Whatever the case, everybody has a past. No one just sprouts up on earth at forty years old. Everyone you know either has grown up or will grow up.

Sometimes people have a hard time with the Lord because of things they've done or said or thought (or things they haven't) in the past. Guess what? It doesn't matter.

When you confess your sins to God and ask Him to forgive you, He does. Forever. He doesn't hide them in a book under His mattress. He totally forgets what you've done. When you pray to Him, He thinks of you as totally innocent. It's as if you never did anything wrong. Never be afraid to go to the Lord because of your past. He's in the business of making bad things turn out good, ugly things turn out beautiful, and of making hurts heal. Start fresh with Him.

SEE FOR YOURSELF:
Is. 54:4; 65:17; 2 Cor. 5:17; Heb. 10:17; 1 John 1:9; Rev. 21:5

And their precious things shall not
      profit;
They *are* their own witnesses;
They neither see nor know, that they may
      be ashamed.
10 Who would form a god or mold an
      image
      That profits him nothing?
11 Surely all his companions would be
      ashamed;
      And the workmen, they *are* mere men.
      Let them all be gathered together,
      Let them stand up;
      Yet they shall fear,
      They shall be ashamed together.

12 The blacksmith with the tongs works one
      in the coals,
      Fashions it with hammers,
      And works it with the strength of his
      arms.
      Even so, he is hungry, and his strength
      fails;
      He drinks no water and is faint.

13 The craftsman stretches out *his* rule,
      He marks one out with chalk;
      He fashions it with a plane,
      He marks it out with the compass,
      And makes it like the figure of a man,
      According to the beauty of a man, that it
      may remain in the house.
14 He cuts down cedars for himself,
      And takes the cypress and the oak;
      He secures *it* for himself among the trees
      of the forest.
      He plants a pine, and the rain
      nourishes *it*.

15 Then it shall be for a man to burn,
      For he will take some of it and warm
      himself;
      Yes, he kindles *it* and bakes bread;
      Indeed he makes a god and worships *it*;
      He makes it a carved image, and falls
      down to it.
16 He burns half of it in the fire;
      With this half he eats meat;
      He roasts a roast, and is satisfied.
      He even warms *himself* and says,
      "Ah! I am warm,
      I have seen the fire."
17 And the rest of it he makes into a god,
      His carved image.
      He falls down before it and worships *it*,
      Prays to it and says,
      "Deliver me, for you *are* my god!"

18 They do not know nor understand;
      For He has shut their eyes, so that they
      cannot see,
      And their hearts, so that they cannot
      understand.
19 And no one considers in his heart,
      Nor *is there* knowledge nor understanding
      to say,
      "I have burned half of it in the fire,
      Yes, I have also baked bread on its coals;
      I have roasted meat and eaten *it*;
      And shall I make the rest of it an
      abomination?
      Shall I fall down before a block of
      wood?"
20 He feeds on ashes;
      A deceived heart has turned him aside;
      And he cannot deliver his soul,
      Nor say, "*Is there* not a lie in my right
      hand?"

ISRAEL IS NOT FORGOTTEN

21 "Remember these, O Jacob,
      And Israel, for you *are* My servant;
      I have formed you, you *are* My servant;
      O Israel, you will not be forgotten by Me!
22 I have blotted out, like a thick cloud, your
      transgressions,
      And like a cloud, your sins.
      Return to Me, for I have redeemed you."

23 Sing, O heavens, for the LORD has done *it*!
      Shout, you lower parts of the earth;
      Break forth into singing, you mountains,
      O forest, and every tree in it!
      For the LORD has redeemed Jacob,
      And glorified Himself in Israel.

JUDAH WILL BE RESTORED

24 Thus says the LORD, your Redeemer,
      And He who formed you from the
      womb:
      "I *am* the LORD, who makes all *things*,
      Who stretches out the heavens all alone,
      Who spreads abroad the earth by Myself;
25 Who frustrates the signs of the babblers,
      And drives diviners mad;
      Who turns wise men backward,
      And makes their knowledge foolishness;
26 Who confirms the word of His servant,
      And performs the counsel of His
      messengers;
      Who says to Jerusalem, 'You shall be
      inhabited,'
      To the cities of Judah, 'You shall be built,'
      And I will raise up her waste places;
27 Who says to the deep, 'Be dry!

And I will dry up your rivers';

28 Who says of Cyrus, '*He is* My shepherd,
And he shall perform all My pleasure,
Saying to Jerusalem, "You shall be built,"
And to the temple, "Your foundation shall
be laid." '

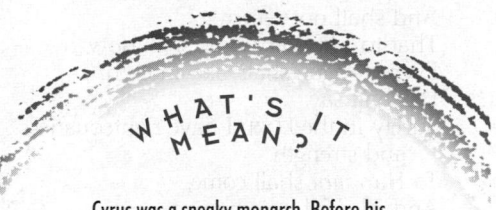

WHAT'S IT MEAN?

Cyrus was a sneaky monarch. Before his
Persian forces attacked Babylon, Cyrus and his men
built dams and redirected the water that flowed into the city. While
the Babylonian king, Belshazzar, was throwing a wild party, Cyrus
led his men through the empty water tunnels. Caught by surprise,
the Babylonian forces surrendered immediately
and Belshazzar was put to death.

Isaiah 45:1

CYRUS, GOD'S INSTRUMENT

1 'Thus says the LORD to His anointed,
To Cyrus, whose right hand I have
held—
To subdue nations before him
And loose the armor of kings,
To open before him the double doors,
So that the gates will not be shut:

2 'I will go before you
And make the crooked places*a* straight;
I will break in pieces the gates of bronze
And cut the bars of iron.

3 I will give you the treasures
of darkness
And hidden riches of
secret places,
That you may know
that I, the LORD,
Who call *you* by your
name,
Am the God of Israel.

4 For Jacob My servant's
sake,
And Israel My elect,
I have even called you by your name;
I have named you, though you have not
known Me.

5 I *am* the LORD, and *there is* no other;

There *is* no God besides Me.
I will gird you, though you have not
known Me,

6 That they may know from the rising of
the sun to its setting
That *there is* none besides Me.
I *am* the LORD, and *there is* no other;

7 I form the light and create darkness,
I make peace and create calamity;
I, the LORD, do all these *things.*'

8 "Rain down, you heavens, from above,
And let the skies pour down
righteousness;
Let the earth open, let them bring forth
salvation,
And let righteousness spring up
together.
I, the LORD, have created it.

9 "Woe to him who strives with his
Maker!
Let the potsherd *strive* with the potsherds
of the earth!
Shall the clay say to him who forms it,
'What are you making?'
Or shall your handiwork *say,* 'He has no
hands'?

10 Woe to him who says to *his* father, 'What
arc you begetting?'
Or to the woman, 'What have you
brought forth?' "

11 Thus says the LORD,
The Holy One of Israel, and his Maker:
"Ask Me of things to come concerning My
sons;
And concerning the
work of My hands,
you command Me.

12 I have made the earth,
And created man on it.
I—My hands—stretched
out the heavens,
And all their host I have
commanded.

13 I have raised him up in
righteousness,
And I will direct all his
ways;
He shall build My city
And let My exiles go free,
Not for price nor reward,"
Says the LORD of hosts.

"I am the LORD, and there is no other; there is no God besides Me."
(Isaiah 45:5)

45:2 *a*Dead Sea Scrolls and Septuagint read *mountains;* Targum reads *I will trample down the walls;* Vulgate
reads *I will humble the great ones of the earth.*

THE LORD, THE ONLY SAVIOR

¹⁴Thus says the LORD:

"The labor of Egypt and merchandise of
    Cush
And of the Sabeans, men of stature,
Shall come over to you, and they shall be
    yours;
They shall walk behind you,
They shall come over in chains;
And they shall bow down to you.
They will make supplication to you,
    saying, 'Surely God *is* in you,
And *there is* no other;
There is no other God.' "

¹⁵ Truly You *are* God, who hide Yourself,
    O God of Israel, the Savior!
¹⁶ They shall be ashamed
    And also disgraced, all of them;
    They shall go in confusion together,
    Who are makers of idols.
¹⁷ *But* Israel shall be saved by the LORD
    With an everlasting salvation;
    You shall not be ashamed or disgraced
    Forever and ever.

¹⁸ For thus says the LORD,
    Who created the heavens,
    Who is God,
    Who formed the earth and made it,
    Who has established it,
    Who did not create it in vain,
    Who formed it to be inhabited:
    "I *am* the LORD, and *there is* no other.
¹⁹ I have not spoken in secret,
    In a dark place of the earth;
    I did not say to the seed of Jacob,
    'Seek Me in vain';
    I, the LORD, speak righteousness,
    I declare things that are right.

²⁰ "Assemble yourselves and come;
    Draw near together,
    You *who have* escaped from the nations.
    They have no knowledge,
    Who carry the wood of their carved
        image,
    And pray to a god *that* cannot save.
²¹ Tell and bring forth *your case;*
    Yes, let them take counsel together.
    Who has declared this from ancient time?
    Who has told it from that time?
    Have not I, the LORD?
    And *there is* no other God besides Me,
    A just God and a Savior;
    There is none besides Me.

²² "Look to Me, and be saved,
    All you ends of the earth!
    For I *am* God, and *there is* no other.
²³ I have sworn by Myself;
    The word has gone out of My mouth *in*
        righteousness,
    And shall not return,
    That to Me every knee shall bow,
    Every tongue shall take an oath.
²⁴ He shall say,
    'Surely in the LORD I have righteousness
        and strength.
    To Him *men* shall come,
    And all shall be ashamed
    Who are incensed against Him.
²⁵ In the LORD all the descendants of Israel
    Shall be justified, and shall glory.' "

DEAD IDOLS AND THE LIVING GOD

¹ Bel bows down, Nebo stoops;
    Their idols were on the beasts and on the
        cattle.
    Your carriages *were* heavily loaded,
    A burden to the weary *beast.*
² They stoop, they bow down together;
    They could not deliver the burden,
    But have themselves gone into captivity.

WHAT'S IT MEAN?

Bel (who was also known as Marduk) and
Nebo were two of the Babylonians' favorite gods. Bel,
the god of war, was the main deity of Babylon. Nebo, the god of
education and wisdom, was thought to be Bel's son. Remember King
Nebuchadnezzar, the guy who destroyed Jerusalem and took the
Israelites captive? It's no coincidence that the first part of his name
sounds an awful lot like the name of Nebo.

Isaiah 46:1

³ "Listen to Me, O house of Jacob,
    And all the remnant of the house of
        Israel,
    Who have been upheld *by Me* from birth,
    Who have been carried from the womb:
⁴ Even to *your* old age, I *am* He,
    And *even* to gray hairs I will carry *you!*
    I have made, and I will bear;
    Even I will carry, and will deliver *you.*

5 "To whom will you liken Me, and make
     Me equal
   And compare Me, that we should be
     alike?
6 They lavish gold out of the bag,
   And weigh silver on the scales;
   They hire a goldsmith, and he makes it a
     god;
   They prostrate themselves, yes, they
     worship.
7 They bear it on the shoulder, they
     carry it
   And set it in its place, and it stands;
   From its place it shall not move.
   Though *one* cries out to it, yet it cannot
     answer
   Nor save him out of his trouble.

8 "Remember this, and show yourselves
     men;
   Recall to mind, O you transgressors.
9 Remember the former things of old,
   For I *am* God, and *there is* no other;
   I *am* God, and *there is* none like Me,
10 Declaring the end from the beginning,
   And from ancient times *things* that are
     not *yet* done,
   Saying, 'My counsel shall stand,
   And I will do all My pleasure,'
11 Calling a bird of prey from the east,
   The man who executes My counsel, from
     a far country.
   Indeed I have spoken *it;*

I will also bring it to pass.
I have purposed *it;*
I will also do it.

12 "Listen to Me, you stubborn-hearted,
   Who *are* far from righteousness:
13 I bring My righteousness near, it shall not
     be far off;
   My salvation shall not linger.
   And I will place salvation in Zion,
   For Israel My glory.

THE HUMILIATION OF BABYLON

1 "Come down and sit in the dust,
   O virgin daughter of Babylon;
   Sit on the ground without a throne,
   O daughter of the Chaldeans!
   For you shall no more be called
   Tender and delicate.
2 Take the millstones and grind meal.
   Remove your veil,
   Take off the skirt,
   Uncover the thigh,
   Pass through the rivers.
3 Your nakedness shall be uncovered,
   Yes, your shame will be seen;
   I will take vengeance,
   And I will not arbitrate with a man."

4 *As for* our Redeemer, the LORD of hosts *is*
     His name,
   The Holy One of Israel.

Promise   HE PROMISES TO BE THERE WHEN YOU'RE OLD.

Even to your old age, I am He, and even to gray hairs I will carry you! I have made, and I will bear; even I will carry, and will deliver you (Is. 46:4).

It can be a little scary to think about getting old. To you, getting old may mean losing some of the things that are very important to you right now: your good looks, your sharp mind, your athletic ability. You may picture yourself struggling to survive on a monthly Social Security check or wandering through the halls of a nursing home.

It's true that, as you get older, your body, your income, and even your address will probably go through a lot of changes. Some of these changes will be your idea; some won't.

So where's your security? Is it in these things that change from year to year? Or is it in the person who is "the same yesterday, today, and forever" (Heb. 13:8)? Jesus says that He will take care of you and keep you safe when you're old. He will be just as strong, just as trustworthy, just as loving then as He is now. And when you've been His friend for sixty years, you'll still be discovering how awesome He is.

SEE FOR YOURSELF:
Rom. 8:38; Heb. 1:12; 13:8; 1 Pet. 1:5

5 "Sit in silence, and go into darkness,
O daughter of the Chaldeans;
For you shall no longer be called
The Lady of Kingdoms.
6 I was angry with My people;
I have profaned My inheritance,
And given them into your hand.
You showed them no mercy;
On the elderly you laid your yoke very
heavily.
7 And you said, 'I shall be a lady forever,'
So that you did not take these *things* to
heart,
Nor remember the latter end of them.

8 "Therefore hear this now, *you who are*
given to pleasures,
Who dwell securely,
Who say in your heart, 'I *am,* and *there is*
no one else besides me;
I shall not sit *as* a widow,
Nor shall I know the loss of children';
9 But these two *things* shall come to you
In a moment, in one day:
The loss of children, and widowhood.
They shall come upon you in their
fullness
Because of the multitude of your
sorceries,
For the great abundance of your
enchantments.

10 "For you have trusted in your wickedness;
You have said, 'No one sees me';
Your wisdom and your knowledge have
warped you;
And you have said in your heart,
'I *am,* and *there is* no one else besides me.'
11 Therefore evil shall come upon you;
You shall not know from where it arises.
And trouble shall fall upon you;
You will not be able to put it off.
And desolation shall come upon you
suddenly,
Which you shall not know.

12 "Stand now with your enchantments
And the multitude of your sorceries,
In which you have labored from your
youth—
Perhaps you will be able to profit,
Perhaps you will prevail.
13 You are wearied in the multitude of your
counsels;
Let now the astrologers, the stargazers,
And the monthly prognosticators
Stand up and save you

From what shall come upon you.
14 Behold, they shall be as stubble,
The fire shall burn them;
They shall not deliver themselves
From the power of the flame;
It shall not *be* a coal to be warmed by,
Nor a fire to sit before!
15 Thus shall they be to you
With whom you have labored,
Your merchants from your youth;
They shall wander each one to his quarter.
No one shall save you.

On the Edge

You are wearied in the multitude of your counsels; let now the astrologers, the stargazers, and the monthly prognosticators stand up and save you from what shall come upon you. Behold, they shall be as stubble, the fire shall burn them; they shall not deliver themselves from the power of the flame; it shall not be a coal to be warmed by, nor a fire to sit before! (Is. 47:13, 14).

"You will be lucky in love toward the end of the month." "Be careful when you choose new friends." "What's your sign?" Sound familiar? You can find phrases like these in almost every popular fashion magazine and daily newspaper. There are people who trust astrology so much that they actually make decisions based on their horoscopes. Whoa. If you're a Christian, you can use the astrology pages to line your garbage can. You've got something so much greater—and someone you can totally depend on—the Holy Spirit. His job is to guide you, to help you make good decisions, and to give you insight about your future (see John 16:13).

Isaiah 47:14 says that people who consult the stars are helpless. John 14:16 says that the Holy Spirit is sent from God to help you. Always put your trust in God, who knows everything. Never put your trust in a psychic or an astrologer. God says, "They shall not deliver themselves from the power of the flame." In other words, they can't save themselves, so they certainly can't save you. Only He can.

SEE FOR YOURSELF:
2 Kin. 21:6; Jer. 33:3

ISRAEL REFINED FOR GOD'S GLORY

1 "Hear this, O house of Jacob,
    Who are called by the name of Israel,
    And have come forth from the
        wellsprings of Judah;
    Who swear by the name of the LORD,
    And make mention of the God of
        Israel,
    But not in truth or in righteousness;

2 For they call themselves after the holy
        city,
    And lean on the God of Israel;
    The LORD of hosts *is* His name:

3 "I have declared the former things from
        the beginning;
    They went forth from My mouth, and I
        caused them to hear *it.*
    Suddenly I did *them,* and they came to
        pass.

4 Because I knew that you *were*
        obstinate,
    And your neck *was* an iron sinew,
    And your brow bronze,

5 Even from the beginning I have declared
        it to you;
    Before it came to pass I proclaimed *it* to
        you,
    Lest you should say, 'My idol has done
        them,
    And my carved image and my molded
        image
    Have commanded them.'

6 "You have heard;
    See all this.
    And will you not declare *it?*
    I have made you hear new things from
        this time,
    Even hidden things, and you did not
        know them.

7 They are created now and not from the
        beginning;
    And before this day you have not heard
        them,
    Lest you should say, 'Of course I knew
        them.'

8 Surely you did not hear,
    Surely you did not know;
    Surely from long ago your ear was not
        opened.
    For I knew that you would deal very
        treacherously,
    And were called a transgressor from the
        womb.

9 "For My name's sake I will defer My
        anger,
    And *for* My praise I will restrain it from
        you,
    So that I do not cut you off.

10 Behold, I have refined you, but not as
        silver;
    I have tested you in the furnace of
        affliction.

11 For My own sake, for My own sake, I
        will do *it;*
    For how should *My name* be profaned?
    And I will not give My glory to another.

GOD'S ANCIENT PLAN TO REDEEM ISRAEL

12 "Listen to Me, O Jacob,
    And Israel, My called:
    I *am* He, I *am* the First,
    I *am* also the Last.

13 Indeed My hand has laid the foundation
        of the earth,
    And My right hand has stretched out the
        heavens;
    When I call to them,
    They stand up together.

14 "All of you, assemble yourselves, and hear!
    Who among them has declared these
        things?
    The LORD loves him;
    He shall do His pleasure on Babylon,
    And His arm *shall be against* the
        Chaldeans.

15 I, *even* I, have spoken;
    Yes, I have called him,
    I have brought him, and his way will
        prosper.

16 "Come near to Me, hear this:
    I have not spoken in secret from the
        beginning;
    From the time that it was, I *was* there.
    And now the Lord GOD and His Spirit
    Have[a] sent Me."

17 Thus says the LORD, your Redeemer,
    The Holy One of Israel:
    "I *am* the LORD your God,
    Who teaches you to profit,
    Who leads you by the way you
        should go.

18 Oh, that you had heeded My
        commandments!
    Then your peace would have been like a
        river,

48:16 [a]The Hebrew verb is singular.

And your righteousness like the waves of
the sea.

19 Your descendants also would have been
like the sand,
And the offspring of your body like the
grains of sand;
His name would not have been cut off
Nor destroyed from before Me."

20 Go forth from Babylon!
Flee from the Chaldeans!
With a voice of singing,
Declare, proclaim this,
Utter it to the end of the earth;
Say, "The LORD has redeemed
His servant Jacob!"

21 And they did not thirst
When He led them through the deserts;
He caused the waters to flow from the
rock for them;
He also split the rock, and the waters
gushed out.

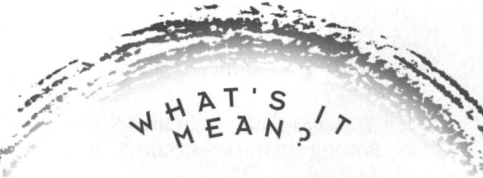

WHAT'S IT MEAN?

God took care of the thirsty
Israelites in the desert by giving them water
to drink from an ordinary rock. The Israelites remembered that
period—just after their ancestors' escape from Egypt—as a time
when God was especially close to them.

Isaiah 48:21

22 "*There is* no peace," says the LORD, "for the
wicked."

THE SERVANT, THE LIGHT TO THE GENTILES

1 "Listen, O coastlands, to Me,
And take heed, you
peoples from afar!
The LORD has called Me
from the womb;
From the matrix of My
mother He has made
mention of My name.

2 And He has made My
mouth like a sharp sword;
In the shadow of His hand He has
hidden Me,

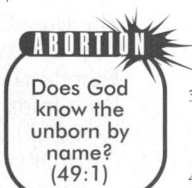

ABORTION

Does God
know the
unborn by
name?
(49:1)

And made Me a polished shaft;
In His quiver He has hidden Me."

3 "And He said to me,
'You *are* My servant, O Israel,
In whom I will be glorified.'

4 Then I said, 'I have labored in vain,
I have spent my strength for nothing and
in vain;
Yet surely my just reward *is* with the LORD,
And my work with my God.'"

On the Edge

*Listen, O coastlands, to Me, and
take heed, you peoples from afar!
The LORD has called Me from the womb;
from the matrix of My mother He has
made mention of My name. And He has
made My mouth like a sharp sword; in
the shadow of His hand He has hidden
Me, and made Me a polished shaft;
in His quiver He has hidden Me (Is.
49:1, 2).*

Remember when you were in kindergarten and you made plaster imprints of your
hands or a sculpture out of pipe cleaners?
Remember how excited you were? When you
made something you were proud of, you
couldn't wait to show it off. You were so
careful until you got it home and put it in a
safe place. And every once in awhile you'd
take a look at it and grin. You loved it.

God made you and that's why He loves
you. You were His idea. You have His eyes,
His hands, because you are made in His
likeness. Even though you may not always
act like your Father, the truth is that you
are His child and His love for you will never
end. Just as you carefully created your
kindergarten masterpiece, God crafted each
part of your being just exactly
the way He wanted it. He made
you a certain way so that you
could be everything wonderful
that He wants you to be. You're a part of His
heart because He thought of you and then
gave those thoughts life and created you.
He's in love with you. He thinks you're
awesome. And you are, because you're His.

SEE FOR YOURSELF:
Gen. 1:27;
Is. 43:7; 44:2;
1 John 3:1

5   "And now the LORD says,
Who formed Me from the womb *to be*
    His Servant,
To bring Jacob back to Him,
So that Israel is gathered to Him[a]
(For I shall be glorious in the eyes of the
    LORD,
And My God shall be My
    strength),
6   Indeed He says,
'It is too small a thing
    that You should be
    My Servant
To raise up the tribes of
    Jacob,
And to restore the
    preserved ones of Israel;
I will also give You as a light
    to the Gentiles,
That You should be My salvation to the
    ends of the earth.' "

7   Thus says the LORD,
The Redeemer of Israel, their
    Holy One,
To Him whom man despises,
To Him whom the nation abhors,
To the Servant of rulers:
"Kings shall see and arise,
Princes also shall worship,
Because of the LORD who is faithful,
The Holy One of Israel;
And He has chosen You."

8Thus says the LORD:

"In an acceptable time I have heard You,
And in the day of salvation I have helped
    You;
I will preserve You and give You
As a covenant to the people,
To restore the earth,
To cause them to inherit the desolate
    heritages;
9   That You may say to the prisoners, 'Go
    forth,'
To those who *are* in darkness, 'Show
    yourselves.'

"They shall feed along the roads,
And their pastures *shall be* on all desolate
    heights.
10   They shall neither hunger nor thirst,
Neither heat nor sun shall strike them;

For He who has mercy on them will lead
    them,
Even by the springs of water He will
    guide them.
11   I will make each of My mountains a
    road,
       And My highways shall
       be elevated.
12   Surely these shall come
       from afar;
Look! Those from the
       north and the west,
And these from the land
       of Sinim."

13   Sing, O heavens!
Be joyful, O earth!
And break out in
       singing, O mountains!
For the LORD has comforted His
    people,
And will have mercy on His afflicted.

GOD WILL REMEMBER ZION
14   But Zion said, "The LORD has forsaken
    me,
And my Lord has forgotten me."

15   "Can a woman forget her nursing child,
And not have compassion on the son of
    her womb?
Surely they may forget,
Yet I will not forget you.
16   See, I have inscribed you on the palms *of*
    My hands;
Your walls *are* continually before Me.
17   Your sons[a] shall make haste;
Your destroyers and those who laid you
    waste
Shall go away from you.
18   Lift up your eyes, look around and see;
All these gather together *and* come to
    you.
As I live," says the LORD,
"You shall surely clothe yourselves with
    them all as an ornament,
And bind them *on you* as a bride *does*.

19   "For your waste and desolate places,
And the land of your destruction,
Will even now be too small for the
    inhabitants;
And those who swallowed you up will be
    far away.

> "For the LORD has comforted His people, and will have mercy on His afflicted."
> (Isaiah 49:13b)

49:5 [a]Qere, Dead Sea Scrolls, and Septuagint read *is gathered to Him*; Kethib reads *is not gathered*.
49:17 [a]Dead Sea Scrolls, Septuagint, Targum, and Vulgate read *builders*.

20 The children you will have,
After you have lost the others,
Will say again in your ears,
'The place *is* too small for me;
Give me a place where I may dwell'.

21 Then you will say in your heart,
'Who has begotten these for me,
Since I have lost my children and am
desolate,
A captive, and wandering to and fro?
And who has brought these up?
There I was, left alone;
But these, where *were* they?' "

22 Thus says the Lord GOD:

"Behold, I will lift My hand in an oath to
the nations,
And set up My standard for the
peoples;
They shall bring your sons in *their* arms,
And your daughters shall be carried on
their shoulders;

23 Kings shall be your foster fathers,
And their queens your nursing
mothers;
They shall bow down to you with *their*
faces to the earth,
And lick up the dust of your feet.
Then you will know that I *am* the LORD,
For they shall not be ashamed who wait
for Me."

24 Shall the prey be taken from the mighty,
Or the captives of the righteous*ᵃ* be
delivered?

25 But thus says the LORD:

"Even the captives of the mighty shall be
taken away,
And the prey of the terrible be
delivered;
For I will contend with him who
contends with you,
And I will save your children.

26 I will feed those who oppress you with
their own flesh,
And they shall be drunk with their own
blood as with sweet wine.
All flesh shall know
That I, the LORD, *am* your Savior,
And your Redeemer, the Mighty One of
Jacob."

THE SERVANT, ISRAEL'S HOPE

1 Thus says the LORD:

"Where *is* the certificate of your mother's
divorce,
Whom I have put away?
Or which of My creditors *is it* to whom I
have sold you?
For your iniquities you have sold
yourselves,
And for your transgressions your mother
has been put away.

2 Why, when I came, *was there* no man?
Why, when I called, *was there* none to
answer?
Is My hand shortened at all that it cannot
redeem?
Or have I no power to deliver?
Indeed with My rebuke I dry up the sea,
I make the rivers a wilderness;
Their fish stink because *there is* no water,
And die of thirst.

3 I clothe the heavens with blackness,
And I make sackcloth their covering."

WHAT'S IT MEAN?

People in ancient times wore sackcloth
only in times of great sorrow or distress. If you've
ever felt sackcloth, you know why they didn't wear it more often. The
cloth was a dark, scratchy material made of goat's hair. The modern
tradition of wearing dark clothing to funerals and memorial services
is based on the ancient custom of wearing
sackcloth in times of sorrow.
Isaiah 50:3

4 "The Lord GOD has given Me
The tongue of the learned,
That I should know how to speak
A word in season to *him who is* weary.
He awakens Me morning by morning,
He awakens My ear
To hear as the learned.

5 The Lord GOD has opened My ear;
And I was not rebellious,
Nor did I turn away.

49:24 *ᵃ*Following Masoretic Text and Targum; Dead Sea Scrolls, Syriac, and Vulgate read *the mighty*;
Septuagint reads *unjustly*.

6 I gave My back to those who struck *Me,*
   And My cheeks to those who plucked out
      the beard;
   I did not hide My face from shame and
      spitting.

7 "For the Lord GOD will help Me;
   Therefore I will not be disgraced;
   Therefore I have set My face like a flint,
   And I know that I will not be ashamed.
8 *He is* near who justifies Me;
   Who will contend with Me?
   Let us stand together.
   Who *is* My adversary?
   Let him come near Me.
9 Surely the Lord GOD will help Me;
   Who *is* he *who* will condemn Me?
   Indeed they will all grow old like a
      garment;
   The moth will eat them up.

10 "Who among you fears the LORD?
   Who obeys the voice of His Servant?
   Who walks in darkness
   And has no light?
   Let him trust in the name of the LORD
   And rely upon his God.
11 Look, all you who kindle a fire,
   Who encircle *yourselves* with sparks:
   Walk in the light of your fire and in the
      sparks you have kindled—
   This you shall have from My hand:
   You shall lie down in torment.

THE LORD COMFORTS ZION

1 "Listen to Me, you who follow after
      righteousness,
   You who seek the LORD:
   Look to the rock *from which* you were
      hewn,
   And to the hole of the pit *from which* you
      were dug.
2 Look to Abraham your father,
   And to Sarah *who* bore you;
   For I called him alone,
   And blessed him and increased him."

3 For the LORD will comfort Zion,
   He will comfort all her waste places;
   He will make her wilderness like Eden,
   And her desert like the garden of the
      LORD;
   Joy and gladness will be found in it,
   Thanksgiving and the voice of melody.

4 "Listen to Me, My people;
   And give ear to Me, O My nation:

   For law will proceed from Me,
   And I will make My justice rest
   As a light of the peoples.
5 My righteousness *is* near,
   My salvation has gone forth,
   And My arms will judge the peoples;
   The coastlands will wait upon Me,
   And on My arm they will trust.
6 Lift up your eyes to the heavens,
   And look on the earth beneath.
   For the heavens will vanish away like
      smoke,
   The earth will grow old like a garment,
   And those who dwell in it will die in like
      manner;
   But My salvation will be forever,
   And My righteousness will not be
      abolished.

7 "Listen to Me, you who know
      righteousness,
   You people in whose heart *is* My law:
   Do not fear the reproach of men,
   Nor be afraid of their insults.
8 For the moth will eat them up like a
      garment,
   And the worm will eat them like wool;
   But My righteousness will be forever,
   And My salvation from generation to
      generation"

WHAT'S IT MEAN?

"Rahab" in this passage is not a woman,
but a sea monster. (Yes, you read that right.)
According to a popular ancient myth, a dragonlike creature named
Rahab tried to prevent God from creating the world. Needless to say,
God defeated Rahab and her followers. Later, the name *Rahab* came
to symbolize Egypt and the years the
Israelites spent there.
Isaiah 51:9

9 Awake, awake, put on strength,
   O arm of the LORD!
   Awake as in the ancient days,
   In the generations of old.
   Are You not *the arm* that cut Rahab
      apart,
   And wounded the serpent?

10   *Are* You not *the One* who dried up the sea,
    The waters of the great deep;
    That made the depths of the sea a road
    For the redeemed to cross over?
11   So the ransomed of the LORD shall
      return,
    And come to Zion with singing,
    With everlasting joy on their heads.
    They shall obtain joy and gladness;
    Sorrow and sighing shall flee away.

12   "I, *even* I, *am* He who comforts
      you.
    Who *are* you that you
      should be afraid
    Of a man *who* will die,
    And of the son of a man
      who will be made like
      grass?
13   And you forget the LORD
      your Maker,
    Who stretched out the heavens
    And laid the foundations of the earth;
    You have feared continually every day
    Because of the fury of the oppressor,
    When *he has* prepared to destroy.
    And where *is* the fury of the oppressor?
14   The captive exile hastens, that he may be
      loosed,
    That he should not die in the pit,
    And that his bread should not fail.
15   But I *am* the LORD your God,
    Who divided the sea whose waves
      roared—
    The LORD of hosts *is* His name.
16   And I have put My words in your
      mouth;
    I have covered you with the shadow of
      My hand,
    That I may plant the heavens,
    Lay the foundations of the earth,
    And say to Zion, 'You *are* My people.' "

GOD'S FURY REMOVED

17   Awake, awake!
    Stand up, O Jerusalem,
    You who have drunk at the hand of the
      LORD
    The cup of His fury;
    You have drunk the dregs of the cup of
      trembling,
    And drained *it* out.
18   *There is* no one to guide her
    Among all the sons she has brought
      forth;

DEVOTION

Is it possible to forget about God? (51:12, 13)

WHAT'S IT MEAN?

A cup that came from God's hand was a common symbol in ancient times for a person's (or a nation's) destiny. A cup of His fury symbolized punishment for a sin. A cup of His blessing symbolized a bright future.

Isaiah 51:17

    Nor *is there any* who takes her by the
      hand
    Among all the sons she has brought up.
19   These two *things* have come to you;
    Who will be sorry for you?—
    Desolation and destruction, famine and
      sword—
    By whom will I comfort you?
20   Your sons have fainted,
    They lie at the head of all the streets,
    Like an antelope in a net;
    They are full of the fury of the LORD,
    The rebuke of your God.

21   Therefore please hear this, you afflicted,
    And drunk but not with wine.
22   Thus says your Lord,
    The LORD and your God,
    Who pleads the cause of His people:
    "See, I have taken out of your hand
    The cup of trembling,
    The dregs of the cup of My fury;
    You shall no longer drink it.
23   But I will put it into the hand of those
      who afflict you,
    Who have said to you,[a]
    'Lie down, that we may walk over you.'
    And you have laid your body like the
      ground,
    And as the street, for those who walk
      over."

GOD REDEEMS JERUSALEM

1   Awake, awake!
    Put on your strength, O Zion;
    Put on your beautiful garments,
    O Jerusalem, the holy city!
    For the uncircumcised and the unclean

51:23 [a]Literally *your soul*

Shall no longer come to you.
2   Shake yourself from the dust, arise;
    Sit down, O Jerusalem!
    Loose yourself from the bonds of your
        neck,
    O captive daughter of Zion!

3 For thus says the LORD:

"You have sold yourselves for nothing,
    And you shall be redeemed without
        money."

4 For thus says the Lord GOD:

"My people went down at first
    Into Egypt to dwell there;
    Then the Assyrian oppressed them
        without cause.
5   Now therefore, what have I here," says the
        LORD,
"That My people are taken away for
        nothing?
    Those who rule over them
    Make them wail,"*a* says the LORD,
"And My name *is* blasphemed continually
        every day.
6   Therefore My people shall know My
        name;
    Therefore *they shall know* in that day
    That I *am* He who speaks:
    'Behold, *it is* I.' "

7   How beautiful upon the mountains
    Are the feet of him who brings good
        news,
    Who proclaims peace,
    Who brings glad tidings of good *things*,
    Who proclaims salvation,
    Who says to Zion,
"Your God reigns!"
8   Your watchmen shall lift up *their* voices,
    With their voices they shall sing
        together;
    For they shall see eye to eye
    When the LORD brings back Zion.
9   Break forth into joy, sing together,
    You waste places of Jerusalem!
    For the LORD has comforted His people,
    He has redeemed Jerusalem.
10 The LORD has made bare His holy arm
    In the eyes of all the nations;
    And all the ends of the earth shall see
    The salvation of our God.

11 Depart! Depart! Go out from there,
    Touch no unclean *thing;*
    Go out from the midst of her,
    Be clean,
    You who bear the vessels of the LORD.
12 For you shall not go out with haste,
    Nor go by flight;
    For the LORD will go before you,
    And the God of Israel *will be* your rear
        guard.

THE SIN-BEARING SERVANT

13 Behold, My Servant shall deal prudently;
    He shall be exalted and extolled and be
        very high.
14 Just as many were astonished at you,
    So His visage was marred more than any
        man,
    And His form more than the sons of men;
15 So shall He sprinkle*a* many nations.
    Kings shall shut their mouths at Him;
    For what had not been told them they
        shall see,
    And what they had not heard they shall
        consider.

1   Who has believed our report?
    And to whom has the arm of the LORD
        been revealed?
2   For He shall grow up before Him as a
        tender plant,
    And as a root out of dry ground.
    He has no form or comeliness;
    And when we see Him,
    There is no beauty that we should desire
        Him.
3   He is despised and rejected by men,
    A Man of sorrows and acquainted with
        grief.
    And we hid, as it were, *our* faces from
        Him;
    He was despised, and we did not esteem
        Him.

4   Surely He has borne our griefs
    And carried our sorrows;
    Yet we esteemed Him stricken,
    Smitten by God, and afflicted.
5   But He *was* wounded for our
        transgressions,
    He was bruised for our iniquities;
    The chastisement for our peace *was* upon
        Him,
    And by His stripes we are healed.

52:5 *a*Dead Sea Scrolls read *Mock;* Septuagint reads *Marvel and wail;* Targum reads *Boast themselves;* Vulgate
reads *Treat them unjustly.*   **52:15** *a*Or *startle*

6 All we like sheep have gone
astray;
We have turned, every
one, to his own way;
And the LORD has laid
on Him the iniquity of
us all.

SIN

What
happens to
the sin of
Christians?
(53:6)

7 He was oppressed and
He was afflicted,
Yet He opened not His mouth;
He was led as a lamb to the slaughter,
And as a sheep before its shearers is
silent,

8 So He opened not His mouth.
He was taken from prison and from
judgment,
And who will declare His generation?
For He was cut off from the land of the
living;
For the transgressions of My people He
was stricken.

9 And they[a] made His grave with the
wicked—
But with the rich at His death,
Because He had done no violence,
Nor *was any* deceit in His mouth.

10 Yet it pleased the LORD to bruise Him;
He has put *Him* to grief.
When You make His soul an offering for
sin,
He shall see *His* seed, He shall prolong
His days,
And the pleasure of the LORD shall
prosper in His hand.

11 He shall see the labor of His soul,[a] *and* be
satisfied.
By His knowledge My righteous Servant
shall justify many,
For He shall bear their iniquities.

12 Therefore I will divide Him a portion
with the great,
And He shall divide the spoil with the
strong,
Because He poured out His soul unto
death,
And He was numbered with the
transgressors,
And He bore the sin of many,
And made intercession for the
transgressors.

On the Edge

All we like sheep have gone astray; we have turned, every one, to his own way; and the LORD has laid on Him the iniquity of us all (Is. 53:6).

God had a purpose in mind when He made you. His idea was that you would be His friend, love Him, and do things His way. Somehow, though, it seemed better to you to do things your way. Eventually you found yourself a long way from God.

A sheep who wanders astray from the shepherd is in big trouble because the shepherd is the one who keeps him safe and makes sure he has all the things he needs. God is your Shepherd; and when you decided to go your way instead of His, you put some distance between you and the Person who has everything you need.

It seemed important to God for you to understand that you have wandered away from Him: "*All we* like sheep have gone astray." That could be a downer. But this verse is actually part of a very hopeful passage telling what Jesus is like and what He did for the "sheep" who had walked away from God. "He bore the sin of many, and made intercession for the transgressors" (53:12). Now you can find your way back to the Shepherd.

SEE FOR YOURSELF:
Ps. 95:7; Is. 53:12;
Jer. 50:6; Ezek. 34:12

A PERPETUAL COVENANT OF PEACE

1 "Sing, O barren,
You *who* have not borne!
Break forth into singing, and cry aloud,
You *who* have not labored with child!
For more *are* the children of the
desolate
Than the children of the married woman,"
says the LORD.

2 "Enlarge the place of your tent,
And let them stretch out the curtains of
your dwellings;
Do not spare;
Lengthen your cords,
And strengthen your stakes.

53:9 [a]Literally *he* or *He*   **53:11** [a]Following Masoretic Text, Targum, and Vulgate; Dead Sea Scrolls and Septuagint read *From the labor of His soul He shall see light.*

3 For you shall expand to the right and to
the left,
And your descendants will inherit the
nations,
And make the desolate cities inhabited.

4 "Do not fear, for you will not be ashamed;
Neither be disgraced, for you will not be
put to shame;
For you will forget the shame of your
youth,
And will not remember the reproach of
your widowhood
anymore.

5 For your Maker *is* your
husband,
The LORD of hosts *is* His
name;
And your Redeemer *is*
the Holy One of
Israel;
He is called the God of the
whole earth.

> "And your Redeemer is the Holy One of Israel; He is called the God of the whole earth."
> (Isaiah 54:5b)

6 For the LORD has called you
Like a woman forsaken and grieved in
spirit,
Like a youthful wife when you were
refused,"
Says your God.

7 "For a mere moment I have forsaken you,
But with great mercies I will gather you.

8 With a little wrath I hid My face from
you for a moment;
But with everlasting kindness I will have
mercy on you,"
Says the LORD, your Redeemer.

9 "For this *is* like the waters of Noah to Me;
For as I have sworn
That the waters of Noah would no longer
cover the earth,
So have I sworn
That I would not be angry with you, nor
rebuke you.

10 For the mountains shall depart
And the hills be removed,
But My kindness shall not depart from
you,
Nor shall My covenant of peace be
removed,"
Says the LORD, who has mercy on you.

11 "O you afflicted one,
Tossed with tempest, *and* not comforted,
Behold, I will lay your stones with
colorful gems,
And lay your foundations with sapphires.

12 I will make your pinnacles of rubies,
Your gates of crystal,
And all your walls of precious stones.

13 All your children *shall be* taught by the
LORD,
And great *shall be* the peace of your
children.

14 In righteousness you shall be established;
You shall be far from oppression, for you
shall not fear;
And from terror, for it shall not come
near you.

15 Indeed they shall surely
assemble, *but* not
because of Me.
Whoever assembles
against you shall fall
for your sake.

16 "Behold, I have created
the blacksmith
Who blows the coals in
the fire,
Who brings forth an
instrument for his
work;
And I have created the spoiler to destroy.

17 No weapon formed against you shall
prosper,
And every tongue *which* rises against you
in judgment
You shall condemn.
This *is* the heritage of the servants of the
LORD,
And their righteousness *is* from Me,"
Says the LORD.

AN INVITATION TO ABUNDANT LIFE

1 "Ho! Everyone who thirsts,
Come to the waters;
And you who have no money,
Come, buy and eat.
Yes, come, buy wine and milk
Without money and without price.

2 Why do you spend money for *what is*
not bread,
And your wages for *what* does not
satisfy?
Listen carefully to Me, and eat *what is*
good,
And let your soul delight itself in
abundance.

3 Incline your ear, and come to Me.
Hear, and your soul shall live;
And I will make an everlasting covenant
with you—
The sure mercies of David.

4 Indeed I have given him *as* a witness to
   　the people,
   A leader and commander for the people.
5 Surely you shall call a nation you do not
   　know,
   And nations *who* do not know you shall
   　run to you,
   Because of the LORD your God,
   And the Holy One of Israel;
   For He has glorified you."

6 Seek the LORD while He may be found,
   Call upon Him while He is near.
7 Let the wicked forsake his way,
   And the unrighteous man his thoughts;
   Let him return to the LORD,
   And He will have mercy on him;
   And to our God,
   For He will abundantly pardon.

8 "For My thoughts *are* not your thoughts,
   Nor *are* your ways My ways," says the
   　LORD.
9 "For *as* the heavens are higher than the
   　earth,
   So are My ways higher than your ways,
   And My thoughts than your thoughts.

10 "For as the rain comes down, and the
   　snow from heaven,
   And do not return there,
   But water the earth,
   And make it bring forth and bud,
   That it may give seed to the sower
   And bread to the eater,

11 So shall My word be that goes forth from
   　My mouth;
   It shall not return to Me void,
   But it shall accomplish what I please,
   And it shall prosper *in the thing* for which
   　I sent it.

12 "For you shall go out with joy,
   And be led out with peace;
   The mountains and the hills
   Shall break forth into singing before you,
   And all the trees of the field shall clap
   　their hands.
13 Instead of the thorn shall come up the
   　cypress tree,
   And instead of the brier shall come up
   　the myrtle tree;
   And it shall be to the LORD for a name,
   For an everlasting sign *that* shall not be
   　cut off."

SALVATION FOR THE GENTILES

1 Thus says the LORD:

"Keep justice, and do righteousness,
   For My salvation *is* about to come,
   And My righteousness to be revealed.
2 Blessed *is* the man *who* does this,
   And the son of man *who* lays hold on it;
   Who keeps from defiling the Sabbath,
   And keeps his hand from doing any evil."

3 Do not let the son of the foreigner
   Who has joined himself to the LORD
   Speak, saying,

Promise   HE PROMISES TO LOVE YOU FOREVER.

Incline your ear, and come to Me. Hear, and your soul shall live; and I will make an
everlasting covenant with you—the sure mercies of David (Is. 55:3).

Can you imagine having someone be eternally loyal to you, someone who loves you forever?
For most of us, even the thought that there is an eternity just blows our mind. We can't imagine
being eighty years old—much less living forever and ever and ever. God loves you so much that
He promises not only to let you live with Him forever, but also to love you and be loyal to you.
That's the ultimate friendship!

God has so much confidence in who you are, who He made you to be, that He wants to spend
forever with you. Even if every friend you ever had were to desert you, He would still be there
loving you. If you did something and hacked off everyone you know, He would be loyal to you.
God hasn't committed Himself to you for the length of your life, but for the length of *His* life—
for all eternity.

SEE FOR YOURSELF:
Jer. 31:3, 4; Hos. 14:4; Rom. 8:35–39

"The LORD has utterly separated me from
   His people";
  Nor let the eunuch say,
"Here I am, a dry tree."
4   For thus says the LORD:
"To the eunuchs who keep My Sabbaths,
And choose what pleases Me,
And hold fast My covenant,
5   Even to them I will give in My house
And within My walls a place and a
   name
Better than that of sons and daughters;
I will give them[a] an everlasting name
That shall not be cut off.

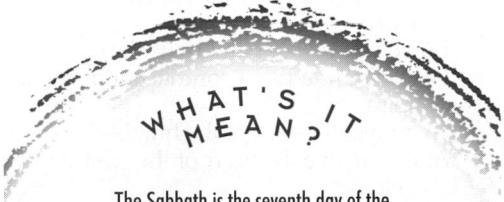

WHAT'S IT MEAN?

The Sabbath is the seventh day of the
week—Saturday, not Sunday. God instructed His
people to set aside the seventh day of each week for Him. All forms
of normal work were forbidden on the Sabbath. Only acts of kindness, worship, and emergency were allowed. Keeping one's Saturday schedule free from work was a way of
showing submission to God.
Isaiah 56:4

6   "Also the sons of the foreigner
Who join themselves to the LORD, to serve
   Him,
And to love the name of the LORD, to be
   His servants—
Everyone who keeps from defiling the
   Sabbath,
And holds fast My covenant—
7   Even them I will bring to My holy
   mountain,
And make them joyful in My house of
   prayer.
Their burnt offerings and their sacrifices
Will be accepted on My altar;
For My house shall be called a house of
   prayer for all nations."
8   The Lord GOD, who gathers the outcasts
   of Israel, says,
"Yet I will gather to him
Others besides those who are gathered to
   him."

ISRAEL'S IRRESPONSIBLE LEADERS

9   All you beasts of the field, come to
   devour,
All you beasts in the forest.
10 His watchmen *are* blind,
They are all ignorant;
They *are* all dumb dogs,
They cannot bark;
Sleeping, lying down, loving to
   slumber.
11 Yes, *they are* greedy dogs
Which never have enough.
And they *are* shepherds
Who cannot understand;
They all look to their own way,
Every one for his own gain,
From his *own* territory.
12 "Come," *one says,* "I will bring wine,
And we will fill ourselves with
   intoxicating drink;
Tomorrow will be as today,
And much more abundant."

ISRAEL'S FUTILE IDOLATRY

1   The righteous perishes,
And no man takes *it* to heart;
Merciful men *are* taken away,
While no one considers
That the righteous is taken away from
   evil.
2   He shall enter into peace;
They shall rest in their beds,
Each one walking *in* his uprightness.

3   "But come here,
You sons of the sorceress,
You offspring of the adulterer and the
   harlot!
4   Whom do you ridicule?
Against whom do you make a wide
   mouth
And stick out the tongue?
Are you not children of transgression,
Offspring of falsehood,
5   Inflaming yourselves with gods under
   every green tree,
Slaying the children in the valleys,
Under the clefts of the rocks?
6   Among the smooth *stones* of the stream
Is your portion;
They, they, *are* your lot!
Even to them you have poured a drink
   offering,
You have offered a grain offering.
Should I receive comfort in these?

56:5 [a]Literally *him*

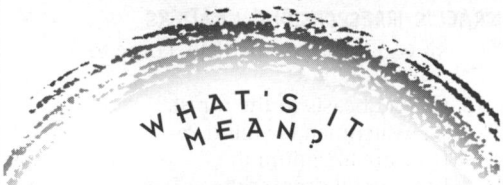

WHAT'S IT MEAN?

For some reason, the pagans in and around Israel preferred to worship their idols on hilltops or in groves of trees. Many of their so-called worship ceremonies were actually little more than sexual orgies. Some ceremonies called for children to be sacrificed. God despised such pagan rituals and specifically told the Israelites not to get involved in them.

Isaiah 57:5

7   "On a lofty and high mountain
    You have set your bed;
    Even there you went up
    To offer sacrifice.
8   Also behind the doors and their posts
    You have set up your remembrance;
    For you have uncovered yourself *to those
    other* than Me,
    And have gone up to them;
    You have enlarged your bed
    And made *a covenant* with them;
    You have loved their bed,
    Where you saw *their* nudity.*a*
9   You went to the king with ointment,
    And increased your perfumes;
    You sent your messengers far off,
    And *even* descended to Sheol.
10 You are wearied in the length of your
    way;
    Yet you did not say, 'There is no hope.'
    You have found the life of your hand;
    Therefore you were not grieved.

11 "And of whom have you been afraid, or
    feared,
    That you have lied
    And not remembered Me,
    Nor taken *it* to your heart?
    Is it not because I have held My peace
    from of old
    That you do not fear Me?
12 I will declare your righteousness
    And your works,
    For they will not profit you.
13 When you cry out,
    Let your collection *of idols* deliver you.

    But the wind will carry them all away,
    A breath will take *them*.
    But he who puts his trust in Me shall
    possess the land,
    And shall inherit My holy mountain."

HEALING FOR THE BACKSLIDER

14 And one shall say,
    "Heap it up! Heap it up!
    Prepare the way,
    Take the stumbling block out of the way
    of My people."

15 For thus says the High and Lofty One
    Who inhabits eternity, whose name *is*
    Holy:
    "I dwell in the high and holy *place*,
    With him *who* has a contrite and humble
    spirit,
    To revive the spirit of the humble,
    And to revive the heart of the contrite
    ones.
16 For I will not contend forever,
    Nor will I always be angry;
    For the spirit would fail before Me,
    And the souls *which* I have made.
17 For the iniquity of his covetousness
    I was angry and struck him;
    I hid and was angry,
    And he went on backsliding in the way
    of his heart.
18 I have seen his ways, and will heal him;
    I will also lead him,
    And restore comforts to him
    And to his mourners.

19 "I create the fruit of the lips:
    Peace, peace to *him who is* far off and to
    him who is near,"
    Says the LORD,
    "And I will heal him."
20 But the wicked *are* like the troubled sea,
    When it cannot rest,
    Whose waters cast up mire and dirt.

21 "*There is* no peace,"
    Says my God, "for the wicked."

FASTING THAT PLEASES GOD

1   "Cry aloud, spare not;
    Lift up your voice like a trumpet;
    Tell My people their transgression,
    And the house of Jacob their sins.
2   Yet they seek Me daily,
    And delight to know My ways,

57:8 *a*Literally *hand*, a euphemism

As a nation that did righteousness,
And did not forsake the ordinance of
their God.
They ask of Me the ordinances of justice;
They take delight in approaching God.
3 'Why have we fasted,' *they say,* 'and You
have not seen?
Why have we afflicted our souls, and You
take no notice?'

"In fact, in the day of your fast you find
pleasure,
And exploit all your laborers.
4 Indeed you fast for strife and debate,
And to strike with the fist of wickedness.
You will not fast as *you do* this day,
To make your voice heard on high.
5 Is it a fast that I have chosen,
A day for a man to afflict his soul?
Is it to bow down his head like a
bulrush,
And to spread out
sackcloth and ashes?
Would you call this a
fast,
And an acceptable day to
the LORD?

HYPOCRISY
How is
religion
more than
occasional
actions?
(58:5–7)

6 "*Is* this not the fast that I
have chosen:
To loose the bonds of wickedness,
To undo the heavy burdens,
To let the oppressed go free,
And that you break every yoke?
7 *Is it* not to share your bread with the
hungry,
And that you bring to your house the
poor who are cast out;
When you see the naked, that you cover
him,
And not hide yourself from your own
flesh?
8 Then your light shall break forth like the
morning,
Your healing shall spring forth speedily,
And your righteousness shall go before
you;
The glory of the LORD shall be your rear
guard.
9 Then you shall call, and the LORD will
answer;
You shall cry, and He will say, 'Here I *am.*'

"If you take away the yoke from your
midst,
The pointing of the finger, and speaking
wickedness,

10 *If* you extend your soul to the hungry
And satisfy the afflicted soul,
Then your light shall dawn in the
darkness,
And your darkness shall *be* as the
noonday.
11 The LORD will guide you continually,
And satisfy your soul in drought,
And strengthen your bones;
You shall be like a watered garden,
And like a spring of water, whose waters
do not fail.
12 Those from among you
Shall build the old waste places;
You shall raise up the foundations of
many generations;
And you shall be called the Repairer of
the Breach,
The Restorer of Streets to Dwell In.

13 "If you turn away your foot from the
Sabbath,
From doing your pleasure on My holy
day,
And call the Sabbath a delight,
The holy *day* of the LORD honorable,
And shall honor Him, not doing your
own ways,
Nor finding your own pleasure,
Nor speaking *your own* words,
14 Then you shall delight yourself in the
LORD;
And I will cause you to ride on the high
hills of the earth,
And feed you with the heritage of Jacob
your father.
The mouth of the LORD has spoken."

SEPARATED FROM GOD

1 Behold, the LORD's hand is not
shortened,
That it cannot save;
Nor His ear heavy,
That it cannot hear.
2 But your iniquities have separated you
from your God;
And your sins have hidden *His* face from
you,
So that He will not hear.
3 For your hands are defiled with blood,
And your fingers with iniquity;
Your lips have spoken lies,
Your tongue has muttered perversity.

4 No one calls for justice,
Nor does *any* plead for truth.
They trust in empty words and speak lies;

They conceive evil and bring forth iniquity.

5 They hatch vipers' eggs and weave the spider's web;
He who eats of their eggs dies,
And *from* that which is crushed a viper breaks out.

6 Their webs will not become garments,
Nor will they cover themselves with their works;
Their works *are* works of iniquity,
And the act of violence *is* in their hands.

7 Their feet run to evil,
And they make haste to shed innocent blood;
Their thoughts *are* thoughts of iniquity;
Wasting and destruction *are* in their paths.

8 The way of peace they have not known,
And *there is* no justice in their ways;
They have made themselves crooked paths;
Whoever takes that way shall not know peace.

SIN CONFESSED

9 Therefore justice is far from us,
Nor does righteousness overtake us;
We look for light, but there is darkness!
For brightness, *but* we walk in blackness!

10 We grope for the wall like the blind,
And we grope as if *we* had no eyes;
We stumble at noonday as at twilight;
We are as dead *men* in desolate places.

11 We all growl like bears,
And moan sadly like doves;
We look for justice, but *there is* none;
For salvation, *but* it is far from us.

12 For our transgressions are multiplied before You,
And our sins testify against us;
For our transgressions *are* with us,
And *as for* our iniquities, we know them:

13 In transgressing and lying against the LORD,
And departing from our God,
Speaking oppression and revolt,
Conceiving and uttering from the heart words of falsehood.

14 Justice is turned back,
And righteousness stands afar off;

For truth is fallen in the street,
And equity cannot enter.

15 So truth fails,
And he *who* departs from evil makes himself a prey.

THE REDEEMER OF ZION

Then the LORD saw *it*, and it displeased Him
That *there was* no justice.

16 He saw that *there was* no man,
And wondered that *there was* no intercessor;
Therefore His own arm brought salvation for Him;
And His own righteousness, it sustained Him.

17 For He put on righteousness as a breastplate,
And a helmet of salvation on His head;
He put on the garments of vengeance for clothing,
And was clad with zeal as a cloak.

18 According to *their* deeds, accordingly He will repay,
Fury to His adversaries,
Recompense to His enemies;
The coastlands He will fully repay.

19 So shall they fear
The name of the LORD from the west,
And His glory from the rising of the sun;
When the enemy comes in like a flood,
The Spirit of the LORD will lift up a standard against him.

20 "The Redeemer will come to Zion,
And to those who turn from transgression in Jacob,"
Says the LORD.

> "The Redeemer will come to Zion, and to those who turn from transgression in Jacob."
> (Isaiah 59:20)

21 "As for Me," says the LORD, "this *is* My covenant with them: My Spirit who *is* upon you, and My words which I have put in your mouth, shall not depart from your mouth, nor from the mouth of your descendants, nor from the mouth of your descendants' descendants," says the LORD, "from this time and forevermore."

THE GENTILES BLESS ZION

1 Arise, shine;
For your light has come!
And the glory of the LORD is risen upon you.

2 For behold, the darkness shall cover the
      earth,
   And deep darkness the people;
   But the LORD will arise over you,
   And His glory will be seen upon you.
3 The Gentiles shall come to your light,
   And kings to the brightness of your
      rising.

4 "Lift up your eyes all around, and see:
   They all gather together, they come to
      you;
   Your sons shall come from afar,
   And your daughters shall be nursed at
      your side.
5 Then you shall see and become radiant,
   And your heart shall swell with joy;
   Because the abundance of the sea shall be
      turned to you,
   The wealth of the Gentiles shall come to
      you.
6 The multitude of camels shall cover your
      land,
   The dromedaries of Midian and Ephah;
   All those from Sheba shall come;
   They shall bring gold and incense,
   And they shall proclaim the praises of the
      LORD.
7 All the flocks of Kedar shall be gathered
      together to you,
   The rams of Nebaioth shall minister to
      you;
   They shall ascend with acceptance on My
      altar,
   And I will glorify the house of My glory.

8 "Who *are* these *who* fly like a cloud,
   And like doves to their roosts?
9 Surely the coastlands shall wait for Me;
   And the ships of Tarshish *will come* first,
   To bring your sons from afar,
   Their silver and their gold with them,
   To the name of the LORD your God,
   And to the Holy One of Israel,
   Because He has glorified you.

10 "The sons of foreigners shall build up your
      walls,
   And their kings shall minister to you;
   For in My wrath I struck you,
   But in My favor I have had mercy on
      you.
11 Therefore your gates shall be open
      continually;
   They shall not be shut day or night,
   That *men* may bring to you the wealth of
      the Gentiles,

WHAT'S IT MEAN?

Many ancient cities were protected on
all sides by enormous walls. The gates in
those walls were always closed at night to
keep out thieves and enemy armies.

Isaiah 60:11

   And their kings in procession.
12 For the nation and kingdom which will
      not serve you shall perish,
   And *those* nations shall be utterly ruined.

13 "The glory of Lebanon shall come to you,
   The cypress, the pine, and the box tree
      together,
   To beautify the place of My sanctuary;
   And I will make the place of My feet
      glorious.
14 Also the sons of those who afflicted you
   Shall come bowing to you,
   And all those who despised you shall fall
      prostrate at the soles of your feet;
   And they shall call you The City of the
      LORD,
   Zion of the Holy One of Israel.

15 "Whereas you have been forsaken and
      hated,
   So that no one went through *you*,
   I will make you an eternal excellence,
   A joy of many generations.
16 You shall drink the milk of the Gentiles,
   And milk the breast of kings;
   You shall know that I, the LORD, *am* your
      Savior
   And your Redeemer, the Mighty One of
      Jacob.

17 "Instead of bronze I will bring gold,
   Instead of iron I will bring silver,
   Instead of wood, bronze,
   And instead of stones, iron.
   I will also make your officers peace,
   And your magistrates righteousness.
18 Violence shall no longer be heard in your
      land,
   Neither wasting nor destruction within
      your borders;

But you shall call your walls Salvation,
And your gates Praise.

GOD THE GLORY OF HIS PEOPLE

19 "The sun shall no longer be your light by
   day,
   Nor for brightness shall the moon give
   light to you;
   But the LORD will be to you an everlasting
   light,
   And your God your glory.
20 Your sun shall no longer go down,
   Nor shall your moon withdraw itself;
   For the LORD will be your everlasting
   light,
   And the days of your mourning shall be
   ended.
21 Also your people *shall* all *be* righteous;
   They shall inherit the land forever,
   The branch of My planting,
   The work of My hands,
   That I may be glorified.
22 A little one shall become a thousand,
   And a small one a strong nation.
   I, the LORD, will hasten it in its time."

THE GOOD NEWS OF SALVATION

1 "The Spirit of the Lord GOD *is* upon Me,
   Because the LORD has anointed Me
   To preach good tidings to the poor;
   He has sent Me to heal the
      brokenhearted,
   To proclaim liberty to the captives,
   And the opening of the prison to *those
      who are* bound;
2 To proclaim the acceptable year of the
      LORD,
   And the day of vengeance of our God;
   To comfort all who mourn,
3 To console those who mourn in Zion,
   To give them beauty for ashes,
   The oil of joy for mourning,
   The garment of praise for the spirit of
      heaviness;
   That they may be called trees of
      righteousness,
   The planting of the LORD, that He may be
      glorified."

4 And they shall rebuild the old ruins,
   They shall raise up the former
      desolations,
   And they shall repair the ruined cities,
   The desolations of many generations.
5 Strangers shall stand and feed your
      flocks,
   And the sons of the foreigner

   Shall be your plowmen and your
      vinedressers.
6 But you shall be named the priests of the
      LORD,
   They shall call you the servants of our
      God.
   You shall eat the riches of the Gentiles,
   And in their glory you shall boast.
7 Instead of your shame *you shall have*
      double *honor,*
   And *instead of* confusion they shall rejoice
      in their portion.
   Therefore in their land they shall possess
      double;
   Everlasting joy shall be theirs.

8 "For I, the LORD, love justice;
   I hate robbery for burnt offering;

On the Edge

[The Spirit of the Lord GOD has sent Me] to console those who mourn in Zion, to give them beauty for ashes, the oil of joy for mourning, the garment of praise for the spirit of heaviness; that they may be called trees of righteousness, the planting of the LORD, that He may be glorified (Is. 61:1–3).

Throughout the Bible, trees symbolize people. So it makes sense that you would be planted by the Lord. Think of a farmer. Why does he plant a crop? He plants so that the seeds will grow strong and eventually produce a harvest for him. But he doesn't just throw the seeds in a hole and hope they produce. He takes care of them and does all he can to help them grow.

The Lord does the same thing with you. He plants you and gives you life. Then as you grow, He helps you and does all He can to make you strong. He helps your roots go deep, so you won't be easily destroyed. He gives you living water—the life of Jesus. He gives you His Word—almost like a fertilizer—to help you be more than you would be without it. Then, one day you are part of His harvest. You are one of the people who has produced well for Him and honored His name.

SEE FOR YOURSELF:
Ps. 1:1–3; Jer. 17:7, 8; 24:6; Amos 9:15

I will direct their work in truth,
And will make with them an everlasting
covenant.

9 Their descendants shall be known among
the Gentiles,
And their offspring among the people.
All who see them shall acknowledge
them,
That they *are* the posterity *whom* the LORD
has blessed."

10 I will greatly rejoice in the LORD,
My soul shall be joyful in my God;
For He has clothed me with the garments
of salvation,
He has covered me with the robe of
righteousness,
As a bridegroom decks *himself* with
ornaments,
And as a bride adorns *herself* with her
jewels.

11 For as the earth brings forth its bud,
As the garden causes the things that are
sown in it to spring forth,
So the Lord GOD will cause righteousness
and praise to spring forth before all
the nations.

ASSURANCE OF ZION'S SALVATION

1 For Zion's sake I will not hold My peace,
And for Jerusalem's sake I will not rest,
Until her righteousness goes forth as
brightness,
And her salvation as a lamp *that* burns.

2 The Gentiles shall see your
righteousness,
And all kings your glory.
You shall be called by a new name,
Which the mouth of the LORD will name.

3 You shall also be a crown of glory
In the hand of the LORD,
And a royal diadem
In the hand of your God.

4 You shall no longer be termed Forsaken,
Nor shall your land any more be termed
Desolate;
But you shall be called Hephzibah,[a] and
your land Beulah;[b]
For the LORD delights in you,
And your land shall
be married.

5 For *as* a young man
marries a virgin,
So shall your sons marry
you;

THANKFULNESS

Is God
thankful for
you?
(62:5)

And *as* the bridegroom rejoices over the
bride,
So shall your God rejoice over you.

6 I have set watchmen on your walls,
O Jerusalem;
They shall never hold their peace day or
night.
You who make mention of the LORD, do
not keep silent,

7 And give Him no rest till He establishes
And till He makes Jerusalem a praise in
the earth.

8 The LORD has sworn by His right hand
And by the arm of His strength:
"Surely I will no longer give your grain
As food for your enemies;
And the sons of the foreigner shall not
drink your new wine,
For which you have labored.

On the Edge

*You shall also be a crown of
glory in the hand of the LORD, and a
royal diadem in the hand of your God
(Is. 62:3).*

Christians talk a lot about the things
God gives them—faith, peace, forgiveness—
everything they need, really. That's okay.
It's good to think about all the good stuff
God has given you and to say thanks.

But have you ever wondered what's in it
for Jesus? He left the greatest place you
can imagine (heaven) to spend years on
planet Earth. It was definitely not a step up
for Him. And He didn't exactly get the royal
treatment while He was here,
either. So what's His reward—
what does He get out of the
deal?

You are His reward. You are what He
wants for His trouble. You are His crown—
which means your relationship with Him
brings Him glory. After everything He gave
up to make that happen, He deserves His
crown. He deserves you. Let Him have more
of your life every day.

SEE FOR YOURSELF:
2 Tim. 4:8; Rev. 14:14

62:4 [a]Literally *My Delight Is in Her* [b]Literally *Married*

⁹ But those who have gathered it shall
eat it,
And praise the LORD;
Those who have brought it together shall
drink it in My holy courts."

¹⁰ Go through,
Go through the gates!
Prepare the way for the people;
Build up,
Build up the highway!
Take out the stones,
Lift up a banner for the peoples!

¹¹ Indeed the LORD has proclaimed
To the end of the world:
"Say to the daughter of Zion,
'Surely your salvation is coming;
Behold, His reward *is* with Him,
And His work before Him.' "

¹² And they shall call them The Holy
People,
The Redeemed of the LORD;
And you shall be called Sought Out,
A City Not Forsaken.

THE LORD IN JUDGMENT AND SALVATION

¹ Who *is* this who comes from Edom,
With dyed garments from Bozrah,
This *One who is* glorious in His apparel,
Traveling in the greatness of His
strength?—

"I who speak in righteousness, mighty to
save."

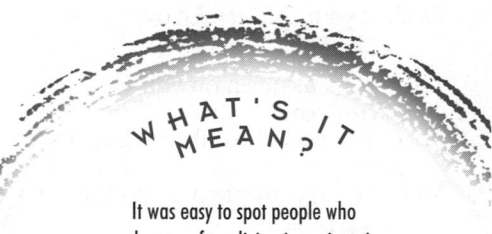

WHAT'S IT MEAN?

It was easy to spot people who
pressed grapes for a living in ancient times.
Because they literally had to stomp on the grapes with their bare feet
to make juice, these vineyard workers developed stains on their legs
and clothes that would not go away.

Isaiah 63:2

² Why *is* Your apparel red,
And Your garments like one who treads
in the winepress?

³ "I have trodden the winepress alone,
And from the peoples no one *was* with
Me.
For I have trodden them in My anger,
And trampled them in My fury;
Their blood is sprinkled upon My
garments,
And I have stained all My robes.

⁴ For the day of vengeance *is* in My heart,
And the year of My redeemed has come.

⁵ I looked, but *there was* no one to help,
And I wondered
That *there was* no one to uphold;
Therefore My own arm brought salvation
for Me;
And My own fury, it sustained Me.

⁶ I have trodden down the peoples in My
anger,
Made them drunk in My fury,
And brought down their strength to the
earth."

GOD'S MERCY REMEMBERED

⁷ I will mention the lovingkindnesses of the
LORD
And the praises of the LORD,
According to all that the LORD has
bestowed on us,
And the great goodness
toward the house of
Israel,
Which He has bestowed
on them according to
His mercies,
According to the
multitude of His
lovingkindnesses.

MERCY

What kind
of limits are
on God's
mercy?
(63:7)

⁸ For He said, "Surely they *are* My people,
Children *who* will not lie."
So He became their Savior.

⁹ In all their affliction He was afflicted,
And the Angel of His Presence saved
them;
In His love and in His pity He redeemed
them;
And He bore them and carried them
All the days of old.

¹⁰ But they rebelled and grieved His Holy
Spirit;
So He turned Himself against them as an
enemy,
And He fought against them.

¹¹ Then he remembered the days of old,
Moses *and* his people, *saying:*
"Where *is* He who brought them up out of
the sea

On the Edge

But they rebelled and grieved His Holy Spirit; so He turned Himself against them as an enemy, and He fought against them (Is. 63:10).

God is always ready and willing to forgive you when you admit to Him that you've done something wrong. He's so quick to do that for you that it's easy sometimes to take His forgiveness for granted, to treat it as automatic. After all, He promised He would forgive you, and He does what He promises.

But what you need to understand—to feel way down deep in your heart—is how it makes God feel when you decide not to do the right thing. When you sin, it hurts God—just like it hurts you when one of your friends does something that makes you think they don't care about your friendship anymore. It's important for you to realize that when you choose the wrong way, it hurts the Person who gave you everything good that's in your life. That doesn't mean that you should spend a week or two feeling guilty. But being aware of what you've done can help you to truly repent instead of quickly saying "I'm sorry" and then almost as quickly doing it again.

Know that your sin hurts God. Be quick to repent. After all, He's the best Friend you've got.

SEE FOR YOURSELF:
    Eph. 4:30;
    1 Thess. 5:19

With the shepherd of His flock?
Where *is* He who put His Holy Spirit
    within them,
12 Who led *them* by the right hand of
    Moses,
With His glorious arm,
Dividing the water before them
To make for Himself an everlasting
    name,
13 Who led them through the deep,
As a horse in the wilderness,
That they might not stumble?"

14 As a beast goes down into the valley,
And the Spirit of the LORD causes him to
    rest,
So You lead Your people,
To make Yourself a glorious name.

A PRAYER OF PENITENCE
15 Look down from heaven,
And see from Your habitation, holy and
    glorious.
Where *are* Your zeal and Your
    strength,
The yearning of Your heart and Your
    mercies toward me?
Are they restrained?
16 Doubtless You *are* our Father,
Though Abraham was ignorant of us,
And Israel does not acknowledge us.
You, O LORD, *are* our Father;
Our Redeemer from Everlasting *is* Your
    name.
17 O LORD, why have You made us stray
    from Your ways,
And hardened our heart from Your fear?
Return for Your servants' sake,
The tribes of Your inheritance.
18 Your holy people have possessed *it* but a
    little while;
Our adversaries have trodden down Your
    sanctuary.
19 We have become *like* those of old, over
    whom You never ruled,
Those who were never called by Your
    name.

1 Oh, that You would rend the heavens!
That You would come down!
That the mountains might shake at Your
    presence—
2 As fire burns brushwood,
As fire causes water to boil—
To make Your name known to Your
    adversaries,
That the nations may tremble at Your
    presence!
3 When You did awesome things *for which*
    we did not look,
You came down,
The mountains shook at Your presence.
4 For since the beginning of the world
Men have not heard nor perceived by the
    ear,
Nor has the eye seen any God besides
    You,
Who acts for the one who waits for
    Him.
5 You meet him who rejoices and does
    righteousness,
Who remembers You in Your ways.
You are indeed angry, for we have
    sinned—
In these ways we continue;
And we need to be saved.

6 But we are all like an unclean *thing,*
And all our righteousnesses *are* like filthy
    rags;
We all fade as a leaf,
And our iniquities, like the
    wind,
Have taken us away.
7 And *there is* no one
    who calls on Your
    name,
Who stirs himself up
    to take hold of
    You;
For You have hidden
    Your face from us,
And have consumed us
    because of our
    iniquities.

> "But now, O LORD, You are our Father; we are the clay, and You our potter; and all we are the work of Your hand."
> (Isaiah 64:8)

8 But now, O LORD,
You *are* our Father;
We *are* the clay, and You our potter;
And all we *are* the work of Your hand.
9 Do not be furious,
    O LORD,
Nor remember
    iniquity forever;
Indeed, please look—
    we all *are* Your
    people!
10 Your holy cities are a
    wilderness,
Zion is a wilderness,
Jerusalem a
    desolation.
11 Our holy and
    beautiful temple,
Where our fathers praised You,
Is burned up with fire;
And all our pleasant things are laid waste.
12 Will You restrain Yourself because of these
    things, O LORD?
Will You hold Your peace, and afflict us
    very severely?

THE RIGHTEOUSNESS OF GOD'S JUDGMENT

1 "I was sought by *those who* did not ask *for*
    Me;
I was found by *those who* did not seek Me.
I said, 'Here I am, here I am,'
To a nation *that* was not called by My
    name.
2 I have stretched out My hands all day
    long to a rebellious people,
Who walk in a way *that is* not good,
According to their own thoughts;
3 A people who provoke Me to anger
    continually to My face;
Who sacrifice in gardens,
And burn incense on altars of brick;
4 Who sit among the graves,
And spend the night in the tombs;
Who eat swine's flesh,
And the broth of abominable things is in
    their vessels;
5 Who say, 'Keep to yourself,
Do not come near me,
For I am holier than you!'
These *are* smoke in My nostrils,
A fire that burns all the day.

6 "Behold, *it is* written before Me:
I will not keep silence, but will repay—
Even repay into their bosom—
7 Your iniquities and the iniquities of your
    fathers together,"

On the Edge

But now, O LORD, You are our Father; we are the clay, and You our potter; and all we are the work of Your hand (Is. 64:8).

God makes you who you are. He gave you the talents you were born with. Your personality came from Him, too. All the things that happen to you He uses to help you become the person He wants you to be. He also gives you some discipline and a lot of gentle leading.

But God needs your cooperation. If you won't listen to Him or if you're always complaining every time your life isn't going the way you planned, then it's going to take a long time for you to change. But if you let Him do what He needs to do, the change will come quicker.

That's the key—let *Him* do it. You can make yourself more patient, more loving, or more thoughtful only by letting God change the way you think (see Rom. 12:2). You can decide to change your actions ("I will not yell, I will not yell, I will not yell"), but unless you change on the inside, it'll fall apart after awhile. Changing your actions is not a bad idea. But ask Him to make the *real* change. That's His job.

SEE FOR YOURSELF:
Rom. 12:2; 1 Cor. 7:7;
1 Pet. 4:10

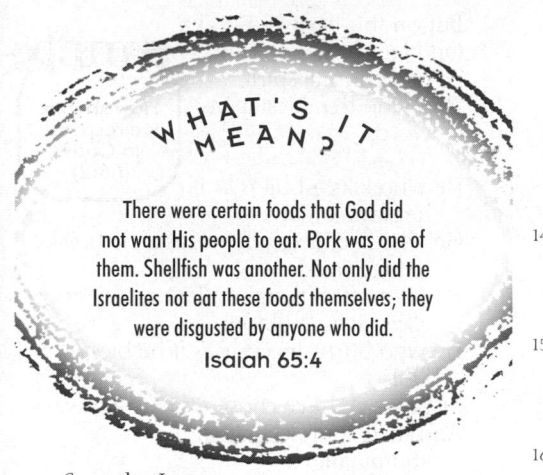

WHAT'S IT MEAN?

There were certain foods that God did not want His people to eat. Pork was one of them. Shellfish was another. Not only did the Israelites not eat these foods themselves; they were disgusted by anyone who did.

Isaiah 65:4

Says the LORD,
"Who have burned incense on the
mountains
And blasphemed Me on the hills;
Therefore I will measure their former
work into their bosom."

8Thus says the LORD:

"As the new wine is found in the cluster,
And *one* says, 'Do not destroy it,
For a blessing *is* in it,'
So will I do for My servants' sake,
That I may not destroy them all.
9 I will bring forth descendants from Jacob,
And from Judah an heir of My
mountains;
My elect shall inherit it,
And My servants shall dwell there.
10 Sharon shall be a fold of flocks,
And the Valley of Achor a place for herds
to lie down,
For My people who have sought Me.

11 "But you *are* those who forsake the LORD,
Who forget My holy mountain,
Who prepare a table for Gad,*a*
And who furnish a drink offering for
Meni.*b*
12 Therefore I will number you for the
sword,
And you shall all bow down to the
slaughter;
Because, when I called, you did not
answer;
When I spoke, you did not hear,
But did evil before My eyes,
And chose *that* in which I do not delight."

13Therefore thus says the Lord GOD:

"Behold, My servants shall eat,
But you shall be hungry;
Behold, My servants shall drink,
But you shall be thirsty;
Behold, My servants shall rejoice,
But you shall be ashamed;
14 Behold, My servants shall sing for joy of
heart,
But you shall cry for sorrow of heart,
And wail for grief of spirit.
15 You shall leave your name as a curse to
My chosen;
For the Lord GOD will slay you,
And call His servants by another name;
16 So that he who blesses himself in the
earth
Shall bless himself in the God of truth;
And he who swears in the earth
Shall swear by the God of truth;
Because the former troubles are forgotten,
And because they are hidden from My
eyes.

THE GLORIOUS NEW CREATION

17 "For behold, I create new heavens and a
new earth;
And the former shall not be remembered
or come to mind.
18 But be glad and rejoice forever in what I
create;
For behold, I create Jerusalem *as* a
rejoicing,
And her people a joy.
19 I will rejoice in Jerusalem,
And joy in My people;
The voice of weeping shall no longer be
heard in her,
Nor the voice of crying.

20 "No more shall an infant from there *live
but a few* days,
Nor an old man who has not fulfilled his
days;
For the child shall die one hundred years
old,
But the sinner *being* one hundred years
old shall be accursed.
21 They shall build houses and inhabit *them;*
They shall plant vineyards and eat their
fruit.
22 They shall not build and another
inhabit;
They shall not plant and another eat;

65:11 *a*Literally *Troop* or *Fortune*, a pagan deity   *b*Literally *Number* or *Destiny*, a pagan deity

For as the days of a tree, *so shall be* the
    days of My people,
And My elect shall long enjoy the work
    of their hands.
23 They shall not labor in vain,
    Nor bring forth children for trouble;
For they *shall be* the descendants of the
    blessed of the LORD,
And their offspring with them.

24 "It shall come to pass
    That before they call, I will answer;
And while they are still speaking, I will
    hear.
25 The wolf and the lamb shall feed together,
    The lion shall eat straw like the ox,
And dust *shall be* the serpent's food.
They shall not hurt nor destroy in all My
    holy mountain,"
Says the LORD.

TRUE WORSHIP AND FALSE

¹Thus says the LORD:

"Heaven *is* My throne,
And earth *is* My footstool.
Where *is* the house that you will build
    Me?
And where *is* the place of My rest?
2 For all those *things* My hand has made,
And all those *things* exist,"
Says the LORD.

"But on this *one* will I look:
    On *him who is* poor and
      of a contrite spirit,
And who trembles at My
    word.

WORSHIP
How should
we respond
to God?
(66:2)

3 "He who kills a bull *is as if*
    he slays a man;
He who sacrifices a lamb, *as if* he breaks
    a dog's neck;
He who offers a grain offering, *as if he*
    offers swine's blood;
He who burns incense, *as if* he blesses an
    idol.
Just as they have chosen their own ways,
And their soul delights in their
    abominations,
4 So will I choose their delusions,
    And bring their fears on them;
Because, when I called, no one answered,
When I spoke they did not hear;
But they did evil before My eyes,
And chose *that* in which I do not
    delight."

THE LORD VINDICATES ZION

5 Hear the word of the LORD,
    You who tremble at His word:
"Your brethren who hated you,
Who cast you out for My name's sake,
    said,
'Let the LORD be glorified,

Promise   HE PROMISES TO ANSWER YOUR PRAYERS.

It shall come to pass that before they call, I will answer; and while they are still speaking, I will hear (Is. 65:24).

Your best friend is lying in a hospital bed. She was in a car wreck over the weekend and the doctors have said she probably won't live through the night. You remember when your parents used to make you go to Sunday school. You remember God. You pray, for the first time in years, and beg God to let your friend live. He does.

Do you believe God answers your prayers? Not "Do you believe because you think you're supposed to?" but do you really believe it? When you pray, do you just hope your prayer makes it all the way up to heaven, or do you know in your heart that God is listening to you? God says He will answer your prayers before you even get through praying. Now that is awesome! He knows you so well that He gets to work on your request before it even gets out of your mouth. Remember, not all prayers have the same "yes" answer. God is totally wise, and He knows exactly what's best for you. It's important for you to pray according to God's will, and you can find that in His Word. Sometimes He says, "Not yet." Whether your answer is yes, no, or not yet, He hears you and goes to work before you finish praying.

SEE FOR YOURSELF:
Deut. 4:5–8; Job 22:27; Ps. 28:6; 91:15

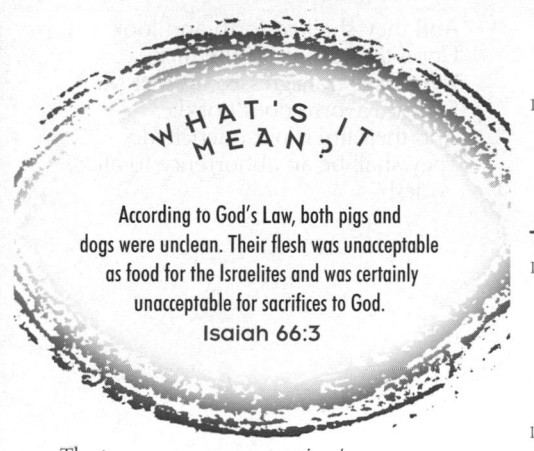

WHAT'S IT MEAN?

According to God's Law, both pigs and dogs were unclean. Their flesh was unacceptable as food for the Israelites and was certainly unacceptable for sacrifices to God.

Isaiah 66:3

That we may see your joy.'
But they shall be ashamed."

6   The sound of noise from the city!
A voice from the temple!
The voice of the LORD,
Who fully repays His enemies!

7   "Before she was in labor, she gave birth;
Before her pain came,
She delivered a male child.
8   Who has heard such a thing?
Who has seen such things?
Shall the earth be made to give birth in one day?
Or shall a nation be born at once?
For as soon as Zion was in labor,
She gave birth to her children.
9   Shall I bring to the time of birth, and not cause delivery?" says the LORD.
"Shall I who cause delivery shut up *the womb?*" says your God.
10   "Rejoice with Jerusalem,
And be glad with her, all you who love her;
Rejoice for joy with her, all you who mourn for her;
11   That you may feed and be satisfied
With the consolation of her bosom,
That you may drink deeply and be delighted
With the abundance of her glory."

12For thus says the LORD:

"Behold, I will extend peace to her like a river,
And the glory of the Gentiles like a flowing stream.

Then you shall feed;
On *her* sides shall you be carried,
And be dandled on *her* knees.
13   As one whom his mother comforts,
So I will comfort you;
And you shall be comforted in Jerusalem."

THE REIGN AND INDIGNATION OF GOD

14   When you see *this*, your heart shall rejoice,
And your bones shall flourish like grass;
The hand of the LORD shall be known to His servants,
And *His* indignation to His enemies.
15   For behold, the LORD will come with fire
And with His chariots, like a whirlwind,
To render His anger with fury,
And His rebuke with flames of fire.
16   For by fire and by His sword
The LORD will judge all flesh;
And the slain of the LORD shall be many.

17   "Those who sanctify themselves and purify themselves,
To go to the gardens
After an *idol* in the midst,
Eating swine's flesh and the abomination and the mouse,
Shall be consumed together," says the LORD.

18"For I *know* their works and their thoughts. It shall be that I will gather all nations and tongues; and they shall come and see My glory. 19I will set a sign among them; and those among them who escape I will send to the nations: *to* Tarshish and Pul[a] and Lud, who draw the bow, and Tubal and Javan, *to* the coastlands afar off who have not heard My fame nor seen My glory. And they shall declare My glory among the Gentiles. 20Then they shall bring all your brethren for an offering to the LORD out of all nations, on horses and in chariots and in litters, on mules and on camels, to My holy mountain Jerusalem," says the LORD, "as the children of Israel bring an offering in a clean vessel into the house of the LORD. 21And I will also take some of them for priests *and* Levites," says the LORD.

22   "For as the new heavens and the new earth
Which I will make shall remain before Me," says the LORD,

"So shall your descendants and your
name remain.
23 And it shall come to pass
That from one New Moon to another,
And from one Sabbath to another,
All flesh shall come to worship before
Me," says the LORD.

24 "And they shall go forth and look
Upon the corpses of the men
Who have transgressed against Me.
For their worm does not die,
And their fire is not quenched.
They shall be an abhorrence to all
flesh."

jeremiah

CONTENT

Jeremiah was not what you would call a diplomat. He didn't spend a lot of energy trying to find the softest way to say something. He just blurted out the truth and let his listeners deal with it in whatever way they wanted to. Because of this he wasn't a particularly loved prophet.

He wasn't a particularly happy prophet either. Jeremiah's heart was broken over the sin of his people. He knew that, if they didn't stay strong spiritually, they would eventually lose everything. He kept telling them, but they didn't listen.

Jeremiah is called the weeping prophet. What a reputation! But when you think about it, people cry because they are sad. People are sad because they have lost something whether it's a possession or a friend. Jeremiah knew that his people were going to be destroyed eventually because of their sin. That was something to be sad about. His tears showed his people a picture of how God felt about their lifestyle.

Outline

Purpose

It is wise to heed God's warnings and honor His messengers.

Theme

Failure to Repent Will Lead to Destruction

Date of writing

626–586 B.C.

"But this is what I commanded them, saying, 'Obey My voice, and I will be your God, and you shall be My people. And walk in all the ways that I have commanded you, that it may be well with you.' Yet they did not obey or incline their ear, but followed the counsels and the dictates of their evil hearts, and went backward and not forward" (7:23, 24).

Bible Talk

This Is Your Brain...

Have you seen those commercials where someone takes an egg and says, "This is your brain"? Then they break the egg into a hot frying pan and say, "This is your brain on drugs."

Jeremiah actually did an ancient version of that commercial. He got a clay pot and stood in front of his people. He basically told them, "This is your life." Then he threw the pot to the ground and it broke, of course, into little pieces. Then he told them, "This is your life without obeying God's law."

Whether it's a frying egg or a broken clay pot, the truth is still the same. God teaches us how to live. When we don't live the way He has designed, destruction is going to come one way or another, sooner or later.

CONSEQUENCES

The Book of Jeremiah is really about consequences. Jeremiah's people were living their lives as if God didn't matter at all. The consequences for that was that when they needed God's protection they didn't get it. Eventually they were taken away like prisoners to a foreign country. They lost everything. How's that for consequences?

We deal with consequences, too. When we live our lives the way God wants us to, it's easier to find His guidance and direction. But if we live our lives as if God doesn't matter, then we don't even recognize His voice when He gives us direction. If we disregard God long enough, we don't recognize His help at all. We might not become exiles, but we'll be alone just the same.

¹The words of Jeremiah the son of Hilkiah, of the priests who *were* in Anathoth in the land of Benjamin, ²to whom the word of the LORD came in the days of Josiah the son of Amon, king of Judah, in the thirteenth year of his reign. ³It came also in the days of Jehoiakim the son of Josiah, king of Judah, until the end of the eleventh year of Zedekiah the son of Josiah, king of Judah, until the carrying away of Jerusalem captive in the fifth month.

WHAT'S IT MEAN?

Judah was invaded by King Nebuchadnezzar and his Babylonian forces in 597 B.C. The Babylonians took King Jehoiachin and more than three thousand other Jewish people as prisoners. As if that weren't enough, the Babylonians came back for more in 586 B.C. This time they destroyed the temple, along with the city itself. They also took about eight hundred more people as prisoners.
Jeremiah 1:3

THE PROPHET IS CALLED

⁴Then the word of the LORD came to me, saying:

5 "Before I formed you in the womb
    I knew you;
Before you were born I
    sanctified you;
I ordained you a prophet
    to the nations."

ABORTION
What does God know about us before we're born? (1:5)

⁶Then said I:

"Ah, Lord GOD!
Behold, I cannot speak, for I *am* a
    youth."

⁷But the LORD said to me:

"Do not say, 'I *am* a youth,'
For you shall go to all to whom I send
    you,
And whatever I command you, you shall
    speak.
8 Do not be afraid of their faces,
For I *am* with you to deliver you," says
    the LORD.

⁹Then the LORD put forth His hand and touched my mouth, and the LORD said to me:

"Behold, I have put My words in your
    mouth.
10 See, I have this day set you over the
    nations and over the kingdoms,
To root out and to pull down,
To destroy and to throw down,
To build and to plant."

¹¹Moreover the word of the LORD came to me, saying, "Jeremiah, what do you see?"
And I said, "I see a branch of an almond tree."
¹²Then the LORD said to me, "You have seen well, for I am ready to perform My word."
¹³And the word of the LORD came to me the second time, saying, "What do you see?"
And I said, "I see a boiling pot, and it is facing away from the north."
¹⁴Then the LORD said to me:

"Out of the north calamity shall break
    forth
On all the inhabitants of the land.
15 For behold, I am calling
All the families of the kingdoms of the
    north," says the LORD;
"They shall come and each one set his
    throne
At the entrance of the gates of Jerusalem,
Against all its walls all around,
And against all the cities of Judah.
16 I will utter My judgments
Against them concerning all their
    wickedness,
Because they have forsaken Me,
Burned incense to other gods,
And worshiped the works of their own
    hands.

17 "Therefore prepare yourself and arise,
And speak to them all that I command
    you.
Do not be dismayed before their faces,
Lest I dismay you before them.
18 For behold, I have made you this day
A fortified city and an iron pillar,
And bronze walls against the whole
    land—
Against the kings of Judah,
Against its princes,
Against its priests,
And against the people of the land.
19 They will fight against you,
But they shall not prevail against you.

For I *am* with you," says the LORD, "to deliver you."

GOD'S CASE AGAINST ISRAEL

[1]Moreover the word of the LORD came to me, saying, [2]"Go and cry in the hearing of Jerusalem, saying, 'Thus says the LORD:

"I remember you,
The kindness of your youth,
The love of your betrothal,
When you went after Me in the wilderness,
In a land not sown.
[3] Israel *was* holiness to the LORD,
The firstfruits of His increase.
All that devour him will offend;
Disaster will come upon them," says the LORD.' "

[4]Hear the word of the LORD, O house of Jacob and all the families of the house of Israel. [5]Thus says the LORD:

"What injustice have your fathers found in Me,
That they have gone far from Me,
Have followed idols,
And have become idolaters?
[6] Neither did they say,
'Where *is* the LORD,
Who brought us up out of the land of Egypt,
Who led us through the wilderness,
Through a land of deserts and pits,
Through a land of drought and the shadow of death,
Through a land that no one crossed
And where no one dwelt?'
[7] I brought you into a bountiful country,
To eat its fruit and its goodness.
But when you entered, you defiled My land
And made My heritage an abomination.
[8] The priests did not say, 'Where *is* the LORD?'
And those who handle the law did not know Me;
The rulers also transgressed against Me;

The prophets prophesied by Baal,
And walked after *things that* do not profit.

[9] "Therefore I will yet bring charges against you," says the LORD,
"And against your children's children I will bring charges.
[10] For pass beyond the coasts of Cyprus[a] and see,
Send to Kedar[b] and consider diligently,
And see if there has been such *a thing*.
[11] Has a nation changed *its* gods,
Which *are* not gods?
But My people have changed their Glory
For *what* does not profit.
[12] Be astonished, O heavens, at this,
And be horribly afraid;
Be very desolate," says the LORD.
[13] "For My people have committed two evils:
They have forsaken Me, the fountain of living waters,
And hewn themselves cisterns—broken cisterns that can hold no water.

[14] "*Is* Israel a servant?
Is he a homeborn *slave*?
Why is he plundered?
[15] The young lions roared at him, *and* growled;

They made his land waste;
His cities are burned, without inhabitant.
[16] Also the people of Noph[a] and Tahpanhes
Have broken the crown of your head.
[17] Have you not brought this on yourself,
In that you have forsaken the LORD your God
When He led you in the way?
[18] And now why take the road to Egypt,
To drink the waters of Sihor?
Or why take the road to Assyria,
To drink the waters of the River?[a]
[19] Your own wickedness will correct you,
And your backslidings will rebuke you.
Know therefore and see that *it is* an evil and bitter *thing*

> " 'Therefore I will yet bring charges against you,' says the LORD, 'and against your children's children I will bring charges.' "
> (Jeremiah 2:9)

2:10 [a]Hebrew *Kittim*, western lands, especially Cyprus   [b]In the northern Arabian desert, representative of the eastern cultures   **2:16** [a]That is, Memphis in ancient Egypt   **2:18** [a]That is, the Euphrates

That you have forsaken the LORD your
God,
And the fear of Me *is* not in you,"
Says the Lord GOD of hosts.

20 "For of old I have broken your yoke *and*
burst your bonds;
And you said, 'I will not transgress,'
When on every high hill and under every
green tree
You lay down, playing the harlot.
21 Yet I had planted you a noble vine, a seed
of highest quality.
How then have you turned before Me
Into the degenerate plant of an alien
vine?
22 For though you wash yourself with lye,
and use much soap,
Yet your iniquity is marked before Me,"
says the Lord GOD.

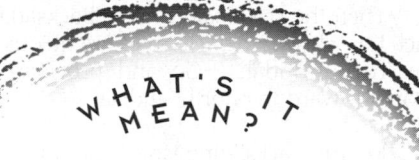

WHAT'S IT MEAN?

Baal worship is a little hard to explain, so pay
attention. The Canaanites, the people who lived in
the land God had promised to the Israelites, worshiped Baal as their
chief god. Apparently, though, Baal assumed many different forms.
The one that was most important to the Canaanites and their
neighbors was the god of crops and livestock. Many people seemed
to "customize" Baal to fit their specific needs. He was
known by different names in different places.
Jeremiah 2:23

23 "How can you say, 'I am not polluted,
I have not gone after the Baals'?
See your way in the valley;
Know what you have done:
You are a swift dromedary breaking loose
in her ways,
24 A wild donkey used to the wilderness,
That sniffs at the wind in her desire;
In her time of mating, who can turn her
away?
All those who seek her will not weary
themselves;
In her month they will find her.
25 Withhold your foot from being unshod,
and your throat from thirst.
But you said, 'There is no hope.

No! For I have loved aliens, and after
them I will go.'

26 "As the thief is ashamed when he is found
out,
So is the house of Israel ashamed;
They and their kings and their princes,
and their priests and their prophets,
27 Saying to a tree, 'You *are* my father,'
And to a stone, 'You gave birth to me.'
For they have turned *their* back to Me,
and not *their* face.
But in the time of their trouble
They will say, 'Arise and save us.'
28 But where *are* your gods that you have
made for yourselves?
Let them arise,
If they can save you in the time of your
trouble;
For *according to* the number of your cities
Are your gods, O Judah.

29 "Why will you plead with Me?
You all have transgressed against Me,"
says the LORD.
30 "In vain I have chastened your children;
They received no correction.
Your sword has devoured your prophets
Like a destroying lion.

31 "O generation, see the word of the LORD!
Have I been a wilderness to Israel,
Or a land of darkness?
Why do My people say, 'We are lords;
We will come no more to You'?
32 Can a virgin forget her ornaments,
Or a bride her attire?
Yet My people have forgotten Me days
without number.

33 "Why do you beautify your way to seek
love?
Therefore you have also taught
The wicked women your ways.
34 Also on your skirts is found
The blood of the lives of the poor
innocents.
I have not found it by secret search,
But plainly on all these things.
35 Yet you say, 'Because I am innocent,
Surely His anger shall turn from me.'
Behold, I will plead My case against you,
Because you say, 'I have not sinned.'
36 Why do you gad about so much to
change your way?
Also you shall be ashamed of Egypt as
you were ashamed of Assyria.

37   Indeed you will go forth from him
     With your hands on your head;
     For the LORD has rejected your trusted
       allies,
     And you will not prosper by them.

ISRAEL IS SHAMELESS

1   "They say, 'If a man divorces his wife,
     And she goes from him
     And becomes another man's,
     May he return to her again?'
     Would not that land be greatly polluted?
     But you have played the harlot with
       many lovers;
     Yet return to Me," says the LORD.

2   "Lift up your eyes to the desolate heights
       and see:
     Where have you not lain *with men?*
     By the road you have sat for them
     Like an Arabian in the wilderness;
     And you have polluted the land
     With your harlotries and your
       wickedness.
3   Therefore the showers have been
       withheld,
     And there has been no latter rain.
     You have had a harlot's forehead;
     You refuse to be ashamed.
4   Will you not from this time cry to Me,
     'My Father, You *are* the guide of my
       youth?
5   Will He remain angry forever?
     Will He keep it to the end?'
     Behold, you have spoken and done evil
       things,
     As you were able."

A CALL TO REPENTANCE

6The LORD said also to me in the days of Josiah the king: "Have you seen what backsliding Israel has done? She has gone up on every high mountain and under every green tree, and there played the harlot? 7And I said, after she had done all these *things,* 'Return to Me'. But she did not return. And her treacherous sister Judah saw it. 8Then I saw that for all the causes for which backsliding Israel had committed adultery, I had put her away and given her a certificate of divorce; yet her treacherous sister Judah did not fear, but went and played the harlot also. 9So it came to pass, through her casual harlotry, that she defiled the land and committed adultery with stones and trees. 10And yet for all this her treacherous sister Judah has not turned to Me with her whole heart, but in pretense," says the LORD.

11Then the LORD said to me, "Backsliding Israel has shown herself more righteous than treacherous Judah. 12Go and proclaim these words toward the north, and say:

     'Return, backsliding Israel', says the LORD;
     'I will not cause My anger to fall on you.
     For I *am* merciful', says the LORD;
     'I will not remain angry forever.
13   Only acknowledge your iniquity,
     That you have transgressed against the
       LORD your God,
     And have scattered your charms
     To alien deities under every green tree,
     And you have not obeyed My voice', says
       the LORD.

14"Return, O backsliding children," says the LORD; "for I am married to you. I will take you, one from a city and two from a family, and I will bring you to Zion. 15And I will give you shepherds according to My heart, who will feed you with knowledge and understanding.

16"Then it shall come to pass, when you are multiplied and increased in the land in those days," says the LORD, "that they will say no more, 'The ark of the covenant of the LORD'. It shall not come to mind, nor shall they remember it, nor shall they visit *it,* nor shall it be made anymore.

17"At that time Jerusalem shall be called The Throne of the LORD, and all the nations shall be gathered to it, to the name of the LORD, to Jerusalem. No more shall they follow the dictates of their evil hearts.

18"In those days the house of Judah shall

walk with the house of Israel, and they shall come together out of the land of the north to the land that I have given as an inheritance to your fathers.

On the Edge

And I said:

"You shall call Me, 'My Father,' and not turn away from Me" (Jer. 3:19b).

Though it might be easy to skip over this verse and just keep going, God is trying to show us a powerful truth. Notice here that God wants to be your Father. What does that really mean? You are His child. Just think about that for a moment. You are a child of God! The God who created the heavens and earth, and every living, breathing thing, is your Dad!

Your natural father may not be a good role model; in fact, many people don't even know who their natural father is. Whatever the case, God wants to fill that empty spot. He has promised not to turn away from anyone fatherless! Remember, your earthly parents aren't perfect. They may let you down, but God never will. He's never going to hurt you. He's never going to break a promise. He's never going to be a bad example. God will never leave you nor turn His back on you. In other words, He's with you for the long haul, all the way to the end. Now that's a *great* Dad!

SEE FOR YOURSELF:
Ps. 2:7; 68:5; Is. 64:8;
Matt. 5:48; 2 Cor. 6:18;
Eph. 5:1

19"But I said:

'How can I put you among the children
And give you a pleasant land,
A beautiful heritage of the hosts of
   nations?'

"And I said:

'You shall call Me, "My Father,"
And not turn away from Me.'
20 Surely, *as* a wife treacherously departs
   from her husband,
So have you dealt treacherously with Me,
O house of Israel," says the LORD.

21 A voice was heard on the desolate heights,
Weeping *and* supplications of the children
   of Israel.
For they have perverted their way;
They have forgotten the LORD their God

22 "Return, you backsliding children,
And I will heal your backslidings."

"Indeed we do come to You,
For You are the LORD our God.
23 Truly, in vain *is salvation hoped for* from
   the hills,
And from the multitude of mountains;
Truly, in the LORD our God
Is the salvation of Israel.
24 For shame has devoured
The labor of our fathers from our youth—
Their flocks and their herds,
Their sons and their daughters.
25 We lie down in our shame,
And our reproach covers us.
For we have sinned against the LORD our
   God,
We and our fathers,
From our youth even to this day,
And have not obeyed the voice of the
   LORD our God."

1 "If you will return, O Israel," says the LORD,
"Return to Me;
And if you will put away your
   abominations out of My sight,
Then you shall not be moved.
2 And you shall swear, 'The LORD lives,'
In truth, in judgment, and in
   righteousness;
The nations shall bless themselves in Him,
And in Him they shall glory."

3For thus says the LORD to the men of Judah and Jerusalem:

"Break up your fallow ground,
And do not sow among thorns.
4 Circumcise yourselves to the LORD,
And take away the foreskins of your
   hearts,
You men of Judah and inhabitants of
   Jerusalem,
Lest My fury come forth like fire,
And burn so that no one can quench *it*,
Because of the evil of your doings."

AN IMMINENT INVASION

5Declare in Judah and proclaim in Jerusalem, and say:

"Blow the trumpet in the land;
Cry, 'Gather together,'
And say, 'Assemble yourselves,
And let us go into the fortified cities'.
6 Set up the standard toward Zion.
Take refuge! Do not delay!
For I will bring disaster from the north,
And great destruction."

7 The lion has come up from his thicket,
And the destroyer of nations is on his
way.
He has gone forth from his place
To make your land desolate.
Your cities will be laid waste,
Without inhabitant.
8 For this, clothe yourself with sackcloth,
Lament and wail.
For the fierce anger of the LORD
Has not turned back from us.

WHAT'S IT MEAN?

People in ancient times wore sackcloth
only in times of great distress or grief. If you've ever
felt sackcloth, you know why it wasn't a popular clothing choice. The
cloth was a dark, scratchy material made of goat's hair. The modern
tradition of wearing dark clothing to funerals and memorial services
is based on the ancient custom of wearing
sackcloth in times of sorrow.
Jeremiah 4:8

9 "And it shall come to pass in that day,"
says the LORD,
"That the heart of the king shall perish,
And the heart of the princes;
The priests shall be astonished,
And the prophets shall wonder."

10 Then I said, "Ah, Lord GOD!
Surely You have greatly deceived this
people and Jerusalem,
Saying, 'You shall have peace,'
Whereas the sword reaches to the heart."

11 At that time it will be said
To this people and to Jerusalem,
"A dry wind of the desolate heights blows
in the wilderness

Toward the daughter of My people—
Not to fan or to cleanse—
12 A wind too strong for these will come for
Me;
Now I will also speak judgment against
them."

13 "Behold, he shall come up like clouds,
And his chariots like a whirlwind.
His horses are swifter than eagles.
Woe to us, for we are plundered!"

14 O Jerusalem, wash your heart from
wickedness,
That you may be saved.
How long shall your evil thoughts lodge
within you?
15 For a voice declares from Dan
And proclaims affliction from Mount
Ephraim:
16 "Make mention to the nations,
Yes, proclaim against Jerusalem,
That watchers come from a far country
And raise their voice against the cities of
Judah.
17 Like keepers of a field they are against her
all around,
Because she has been rebellious against
Me," says the LORD.
18 "Your ways and your doings
Have procured these things for you.
This is your wickedness,
Because it is bitter,
Because it reaches to your heart."

SORROW FOR THE DOOMED NATION
19 O my soul, my soul!
I am pained in my very heart!
My heart makes a noise in me;
I cannot hold my peace,
Because you have heard, O my soul,
The sound of the trumpet,
The alarm of war.
20 Destruction upon destruction is cried,
For the whole land is plundered.
Suddenly my tents are plundered,
And my curtains in a moment.
21 How long will I see the standard,
And hear the sound of the trumpet?

22 "For My people are foolish,
They have not known Me.
They are silly children,
And they have no understanding.
They are wise to do evil,
But to do good they have no
knowledge."

23 I beheld the earth, and indeed *it was*
    without form, and void;
And the heavens, they *had* no light.
24 I beheld the mountains, and indeed they
    trembled,
And all the hills moved back and forth.
25 I beheld, and indeed *there was* no man,
And all the birds of the heavens had fled.
26 I beheld, and indeed the fruitful land *was*
    a wilderness,
And all its cities were broken down
At the presence of the LORD,
By His fierce anger.

27 For thus says the LORD:

"The whole land shall be desolate;
Yet I will not make a full end.
28 For this shall the earth mourn,
And the heavens above be black,
Because I have spoken.
I have purposed and will not relent,
Nor will I turn back from it.
29 The whole city shall flee from the noise of
    the horsemen and bowmen.
They shall go into thickets and climb up
    on the rocks.
Every city *shall be* forsaken,
And not a man shall dwell in it.

30 "And *when* you *are* plundered,
What will you do?
Though you clothe yourself with crimson,
Though you adorn *yourself* with
    ornaments of gold,
Though you enlarge your eyes with paint,
In vain you will make yourself fair;
Your lovers will despise you;
They will seek your life.

31 "For I have heard a voice as of a woman
    in labor,
The anguish as of her who brings forth
    her first child,
The voice of the daughter of Zion
    bewailing herself;
She spreads her hands, *saying,*
'Woe *is* me now, for my soul is weary
Because of murderers!'

THE JUSTICE OF GOD'S JUDGMENT

1 "Run to and fro through the streets of
    Jerusalem;
See now and know;
And seek in her open places
If you can find a man,
If there is *anyone* who executes judgment,

Who seeks the truth,
And I will pardon her.
2 Though they say, '*As* the LORD lives,'
Surely they swear falsely."

3 O LORD, *are* not Your eyes on the truth?
You have stricken them,
But they have not grieved;
You have consumed them,
But they have refused to receive
    correction.
They have made their faces harder than
    rock;
They have refused to return.

4 Therefore I said, "Surely these *are* poor.
They are foolish;
For they do not know the way of the
    LORD,
The judgment of their God.
5 I will go to the great men and speak to
    them,
For they have known the way of the
    LORD,
The judgment of their God."

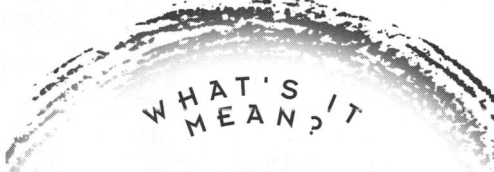

WHAT'S IT MEAN?

Lions and leopards and wolves—oh my!
Believe it or not, lions were a common danger for
people in ancient Israel. Travelers who passed by the tall, grassy
areas near the Jordan River were wise to keep their eyes open for
lions. Leopards and wolves weren't necessarily threats to human life,
but they did attack livestock, threatening people's livelihood. All three
animals are used throughout the Bible
as symbols of God's judgment.
Jeremiah 5:6

But these have altogether broken the yoke
And burst the bonds.
6 Therefore a lion from the forest shall slay
    them,
A wolf of the deserts shall destroy
    them;
A leopard will watch over their cities.
Everyone who goes out from there shall
    be torn in pieces,
Because their transgressions are many;
Their backslidings have increased.

7 "How shall I pardon you for this?
  Your children have forsaken Me
  And sworn by *those that are* not gods.
  When I had fed them to the full,
  Then they committed adultery
  And assembled themselves by troops in
      the harlots' houses.
8 They were *like* well-fed lusty
      stallions;
  Every one neighed after his neighbor's
      wife.
9 Shall I not punish *them* for these *things*?"
      says the LORD.
  "And shall I not avenge Myself on such a
      nation as this?

10 "Go up on her walls and destroy,
  But do not make a complete end.
  Take away her branches,
  For they *are* not the LORD's.
11 For the house of Israel and the house of
      Judah
  Have dealt very treacherously with Me,"
      says the LORD.

12 They have lied about the
      LORD,
  And said, "*It is* not He.
  Neither will evil come
      upon us,
  Nor shall we see
      sword or famine.
13 And the prophets
      become wind,
  For the word *is* not in
      them.
  Thus shall it be done to them."

14 Therefore thus says the LORD God of hosts:

  "Because you speak this word,
  Behold, I will make My words in your
      mouth fire,
  And this people wood,
  And it shall devour them.
15 Behold, I will bring a nation against you
      from afar,
  O house of Israel," says the LORD.
  "It *is* a mighty nation,
  It *is* an ancient nation,
  A nation whose language you do not
      know,
  Nor can you understand what they say.
16 Their quiver *is* like an open tomb;
  They *are* all mighty men.
17 And they shall eat up your harvest and
      your bread,

Which your sons and daughters should
      eat.
  They shall eat up your flocks and your
      herds;
  They shall eat up your vines and your fig
      trees;
  They shall destroy your fortified cities,
  In which you trust, with the sword.

18 "Nevertheless in those days," says the LORD,
"I will not make a complete end of you. 19 And it
will be when you say, 'Why does the LORD our
God do all these *things* to us?' then you shall
answer them, 'Just as you have forsaken Me
and served foreign gods in your land, so you
shall serve aliens in a land *that is* not yours.'

20 "Declare this in the house of Jacob
  And proclaim it in Judah, saying,
21 'Hear this now, O foolish people,
  Without understanding,
  Who have eyes and see not,
  And who have ears and hear not:
22   Do you not fear Me?'
           says the LORD.
       'Will you not tremble at
           My presence,
       Who have placed the
           sand as the bound
           of the sea,
       By a perpetual decree,
           that it cannot pass
           beyond it?
       And though its waves
           toss to and fro,
       Yet they cannot
           prevail;
  Though they roar, yet they cannot pass
      over it.
23   But this people has a defiant and
           rebellious heart;
       They have revolted and departed.
24   They do not say in their heart,
  "Let us now fear the LORD our God,
  Who gives rain, both the former and the
      latter, in its season.
  He reserves for us the appointed weeks of
      the harvest."
25   Your iniquities have turned these *things*
           away,
       And your sins have withheld good from
           you.

26 'For among My people are found wicked
      men;
  They lie in wait as one who sets snares;
  They set a trap;

> " 'Do you not fear Me?'
>   says the LORD.
>   'Will you not tremble at
>   My presence?' "
>   (Jeremiah 5:22a)

They catch men.

27 As a cage is full of birds,
So their houses *are* full of deceit.
Therefore they have become great and
grown rich.

28 They have grown fat, they are sleek;
Yes, they surpass the deeds of the wicked;
They do not plead the cause,
The cause of the fatherless;
Yet they prosper,
And the right of the needy they do not
defend.

29 Shall I not punish *them* for these *things?'*
says the LORD.
'Shall I not avenge Myself on such a
nation as this?'

30 "An astonishing and horrible thing
Has been committed in the land:

31 The prophets prophesy falsely,
And the priests rule by their *own* power;
And My people love *to have it* so.
But what will you do in the end?

IMPENDING DESTRUCTION FROM THE NORTH

1 "O you children of Benjamin,
Gather yourselves to flee from the midst
of Jerusalem!
Blow the trumpet in Tekoa,
And set up a signal-fire in Beth
Haccerem;
For disaster appears out of the north,
And great destruction.

2 I have likened the daughter of Zion
To a lovely and delicate woman.

3 The shepherds with their flocks shall
come to her.
They shall pitch *their* tents against her all
around.
Each one shall pasture in his own place."

4 "Prepare war against her;
Arise, and let us go up at noon.
Woe to us, for the day goes away,
For the shadows of the evening are
lengthening.

5 Arise, and let us go by night,
And let us destroy her palaces."

6 For thus has the LORD of hosts said:

"Cut down trees,
And build a mound against Jerusalem.
This *is* the city to be punished.
She *is* full of oppression in her midst.

7 As a fountain wells up with water,
So she wells up with her wickedness.

Violence and plundering are heard in her.
Before Me continually *are* grief and
wounds.

8 Be instructed, O Jerusalem,
Lest My soul depart from you;
Lest I make you desolate,
A land not inhabited."

9 Thus says the LORD of hosts:

"They shall thoroughly glean as a vine the
remnant of Israel;
As a grape-gatherer, put your hand back
into the branches."

10 To whom shall I speak and give warning,
That they may hear?
Indeed their ear *is* uncircumcised,
And they cannot give heed.
Behold, the word of the LORD is a
reproach to them;
They have no delight in it.

11 Therefore I am full of the fury of the
LORD.
I am weary of holding *it* in.
"I will pour it out on the children outside,
And on the assembly of young men
together;
For even the husband shall be taken with
the wife,
The aged with *him who is* full of days.

12 And their houses shall be turned over to
others,
Fields and wives together;
For I will stretch out My hand
Against the inhabitants of the land," says
the LORD.

13 "Because from the least of them even to
the greatest of them,
Everyone *is* given to covetousness;
And from the prophet even to the priest,
Everyone deals falsely.

14 They have also healed the hurt of My
people slightly,
Saying, 'Peace, peace!'
When *there is* no peace.

15 Were they ashamed when
they had committed
abomination?
No! They were not at all
ashamed;
Nor did they know how
to blush.
Therefore they shall fall
among those who fall;
At the time I punish them,
They shall be cast down," says the LORD.

GUILT

Are conse-
quences to
sin severe
even if we
don't realize
our guilt?
(6:15)

¹⁶Thus says the LORD:

"Stand in the ways and see,
And ask for the old paths, where the
  good way *is*,
And walk in it;
Then you will find rest for your souls.
But they said, 'We will not walk *in it*.'
¹⁷ Also, I set watchmen over you, *saying*,
'Listen to the sound of the trumpet!'
But they said, 'We will not listen.'
¹⁸ Therefore hear, you nations,
And know, O congregation, what *is*
  among them.
¹⁹ Hear, O earth!
Behold, I will certainly bring calamity on
  this people—
The fruit of their thoughts,
Because they have not heeded My words
Nor My law, but rejected it.
²⁰ For what purpose to Me
Comes frankincense from Sheba,
And sweet cane from a far country?
Your burnt offerings *are* not acceptable,
Nor your sacrifices sweet to Me."

²¹Therefore thus says the LORD:

"Behold, I will lay stumbling blocks before
  this people,
And the fathers and the sons together
  shall fall on them.
The neighbor and his friend shall perish."

²²Thus says the LORD:

"Behold, a people comes from the north
  country,
And a great nation will be raised from the
  farthest parts of the earth.
²³ They will lay hold on bow and spear;
They *are* cruel and have no mercy;
Their voice roars like the sea;
And they ride on horses,
As men of war set in array against you,
  O daughter of Zion."

²⁴ We have heard the report of it;
Our hands grow feeble.
Anguish has taken hold of us,
Pain as of a woman in labor.
²⁵ Do not go out into the field,
Nor walk by the way.
Because of the sword of the enemy,
Fear *is* on every side.
²⁶ O daughter of my people,
Dress in sackcloth

And roll about in ashes!
Make mourning *as for* an only son, most
  bitter lamentation;
For the plunderer will suddenly come
  upon us.

²⁷ "I have set you *as* an assayer *and* a fortress
  among My people,
That you may know and test their way.
²⁸ They *are* all stubborn rebels, walking as
  slanderers.
They are bronze and iron,
They *are* all corrupters;
²⁹ The bellows blow fiercely,
The lead is consumed by the fire;
The smelter refines in vain,
For the wicked are not drawn off.
³⁰ *People* will call them rejected silver,
Because the LORD has rejected them."

TRUSTING IN LYING WORDS

¹The word that came to Jeremiah from the LORD, saying, ²"Stand in the gate of the LORD's house, and proclaim there this word, and say, 'Hear the word of the LORD, all *you of* Judah who enter in at these gates to worship the LORD!' " ³Thus says the LORD of hosts, the God of Israel: "Amend your ways and your doings, and I will cause you to dwell in this place. ⁴Do not trust in these lying words, saying, 'The temple of the LORD, the temple of the LORD, the temple of the LORD *are* these.'

⁵"For if you thoroughly amend your ways and your doings, if you thoroughly execute judgment between a man and his neighbor, ⁶*if* you do not oppress the stranger, the fatherless, and the widow, and do not shed innocent blood in this place, or walk after other gods to your hurt, ⁷then I will cause you to dwell in this place, in the land that I gave to your fathers forever and ever.

⁸"Behold, you trust in lying words that cannot profit. ⁹Will you steal, murder, commit adultery, swear falsely, burn incense to Baal, and walk after other gods whom you do not know, ¹⁰and *then* come and stand before Me in this house which is called by My name, and say, 'We are delivered to do all these abominations'? ¹¹Has this house, which is called by My name, become a den of thieves in your eyes? Behold, I, even I, have seen *it*," says the LORD.

¹²"But go now to My place which *was* in Shiloh, where I set My name at the first, and see what I did to it because of the wickedness of

CHARACTER

How should
we treat
others?
(7:8–11)

My people Israel. ¹³And now, because you have done all these works," says the LORD, "and I spoke to you, rising up early and speaking, but you did not hear, and I called you, but you did not answer, ¹⁴therefore I will do to the house which is called by My name, in which you trust, and to this place which I gave to you and your fathers, as I have done to Shiloh. ¹⁵And I will cast you out of My sight, as I have cast out all your brethren—the whole posterity of Ephraim.

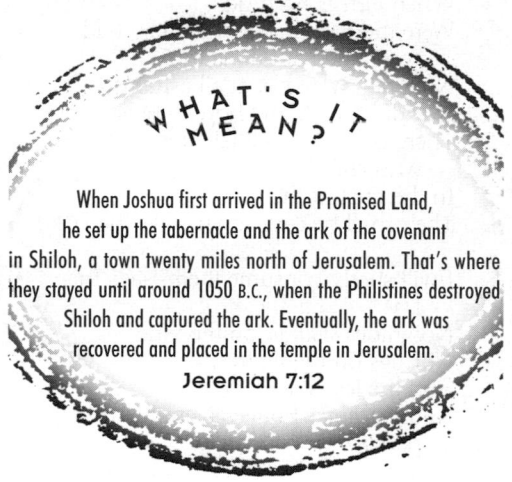

WHAT'S IT MEAN?

When Joshua first arrived in the Promised Land, he set up the tabernacle and the ark of the covenant in Shiloh, a town twenty miles north of Jerusalem. That's where they stayed until around 1050 B.C., when the Philistines destroyed Shiloh and captured the ark. Eventually, the ark was recovered and placed in the temple in Jerusalem.

Jeremiah 7:12

¹⁶"Therefore do not pray for this people, nor lift up a cry or prayer for them, nor make intercession to Me; for I will not hear you. ¹⁷Do you not see what they do in the cities of Judah and in the streets of Jerusalem? ¹⁸The children gather wood, the fathers kindle the fire, and the women knead dough, to make cakes for the queen of heaven; and *they* pour out drink offerings to other gods, that they may provoke Me to anger. ¹⁹Do they provoke Me to anger?" says the LORD. "*Do they* not *provoke* themselves, to the shame of their own faces?"

²⁰Therefore thus says the Lord GOD: "Behold, My anger and My fury will be poured out on this place—on man and on beast, on the trees of the field and on the fruit of the ground. And it will burn and not be quenched."

²¹Thus says the LORD of hosts, the God of Israel: "Add your burnt offerings to your sacrifices and eat meat. ²²For I did not speak to your fathers, or command them in the day that I brought them out of the land of Egypt, concerning burnt offerings or sacrifices. ²³But this is what I commanded them, saying, 'Obey My voice, and I will be your God, and you shall be My people. And walk in all the ways that I have commanded you, that it may be well with you.' ²⁴Yet they did not obey or incline their ear, but

followed the counsels *and* the dictates of their evil hearts, and went backward and not forward. ²⁵Since the day that your fathers came out of the land of Egypt until this day, I have even sent to you all My servants the prophets, daily rising up early and sending *them*. ²⁶Yet they did not obey Me or incline their ear, but stiffened their neck. They did worse than their fathers.

²⁷"Therefore you shall speak all these words to them, but they will not obey you. You shall also call to them, but they will not answer you.

JUDGMENT ON OBSCENE RELIGION

²⁸"So you shall say to them, 'This *is* a nation that does not obey the voice of the LORD their God nor receive correction. Truth has perished and has been cut off from their mouth. ²⁹Cut off your hair and cast *it* away, and take up a lamentation on the desolate heights; for the LORD has rejected and forsaken the generation of His wrath.' ³⁰For the children of Judah have done evil in My sight," says the LORD. "They have set their abominations in the house which is called by My name, to pollute it. ³¹And they have built the high places of Tophet, which *is* in the Valley of the Son of Hinnom, to burn their sons and their daughters in the fire, which I did not command, nor did it come into My heart.

WHAT'S IT MEAN?

Normally, it would have been easy to tell who was an Egyptian and who was an Israelite, based on appearance alone. The Egyptians preferred a clean-cut look, while the Israelites wore their hair and beards long. For the Israelites, shaving one's hair was a sign of deep distress or mourning.

Jeremiah 7:29

³²"Therefore behold, the days are coming," says the LORD, "when it will no more be called Tophet, or the Valley of the Son of Hinnom, but the Valley of Slaughter; for they will bury in Tophet until there is no room. ³³The corpses of this people will be food for the birds of the heaven and for the beasts of the earth. And no one will frighten *them away*. ³⁴Then I will cause to cease from the cities of Judah and from the streets of Jerusalem the voice of mirth and the

voice of gladness, the voice of the bridegroom and the voice of the bride. For the land shall be desolate.

1"At that time," says the LORD, "they shall bring out the bones of the kings of Judah, and the bones of its princes, and the bones of the priests, and the bones of the prophets, and the bones of the inhabitants of Jerusalem, out of their graves. 2They shall spread them before the sun and the moon and all the host of heaven, which they have loved and which they have served and after which they have walked, which they have sought and which they have worshiped. They shall not be gathered nor buried; they shall be like refuse on the face of the earth. 3Then death shall be chosen rather than life by all the residue of those who remain of this evil family, who remain in all the places where I have driven them," says the LORD of hosts.

THE PERIL OF FALSE TEACHING

4"Moreover you shall say to them, 'Thus says the LORD:

"Will they fall and not rise?
Will one turn away and not return?
5 Why has this people slidden back,
Jerusalem, in a perpetual backsliding?
They hold fast to deceit,
They refuse to return.
6 I listened and heard,
But they do not speak aright.
No man repented of his wickedness,
Saying, 'What have I done?'
Everyone turned to his own course,
As the horse rushes into the battle.

7 "Even the stork in the heavens
Knows her appointed times;
And the turtledove, the swift, and the swallow
Observe the time of their coming.
But My people do not know the judgment of the LORD.

8 "How can you say, 'We *are* wise,
And the law of the LORD *is* with us'?
Look, the false pen of the scribe certainly works falsehood.
9 The wise men are ashamed,
They are dismayed and taken.
Behold, they have rejected the word of the LORD;
So what wisdom do they have?
10 Therefore I will give their wives to others,
And their fields to those who will inherit *them*;

Because from the least even
to the greatest
Everyone is given to covetousness;
From the prophet even
to the priest
Everyone deals falsely.
11 For they have healed the
hurt of the daughter of My people slightly,
Saying, 'Peace, peace!'
When *there is* no peace.
12 Were they ashamed when they had committed abomination?
No! They were not at all ashamed,
Nor did they know how to blush.
Therefore they shall fall among those who fall;
In the time of their punishment
They shall be cast down," says the LORD.

13 "I will surely consume them," says the LORD.
"No grapes *shall be* on the vine,
Nor figs on the fig tree,
And the leaf shall fade;
And *the things* I have given them shall pass away from them." ' "

14 "Why do we sit still?
Assemble yourselves,
And let us enter the fortified cities,
And let us be silent there.
For the LORD our God has put us to silence
And given us water of gall to drink,
Because we have sinned against the LORD.

15 "*We* looked for peace, but no good *came*;
And for a time of health, and there was trouble!
16 The snorting of His horses was heard from Dan.
The whole land trembled at the sound of the neighing of His strong ones;
For they have come and devoured the land and all that is in it,
The city and those who dwell in it."

17 "For behold, I will send serpents among you,
Vipers which cannot be charmed,
And they shall bite you," says the LORD.

THE PROPHET MOURNS FOR THE PEOPLE

18 I would comfort myself in sorrow;
My heart *is* faint in me.

GREED

What does God think of greed? (8:10)

19 Listen! The voice,
   The cry of the daughter of my people
   From a far country:
   "Is not the LORD in Zion?
   Is not her King in her?"

   "Why have they provoked Me to anger
   With their carved images—
   With foreign idols?"

20 "The harvest is past,
   The summer is ended,
   And we are not saved!"

21 For the hurt of the daughter of my people
       I am hurt.
   I am mourning;
   Astonishment has taken hold of me.
22 Is there no balm in Gilead,
   Is there no physician there?
   Why then is there no recovery
   For the health of the daughter of my
       people?

1 Oh, that my head were waters,
   And my eyes a fountain of tears,
   That I might weep day and night
   For the slain of the daughter of my people!
2 Oh, that I had in the wilderness
   A lodging place for travelers;
   That I might leave my people,
   And go from them!
   For they are all adulterers,
   An assembly of treacherous men.

3 "And like their bow they have bent their
       tongues for lies.
   They are not valiant for the truth on the
       earth.
   For they proceed from evil to evil,
   And they do not know Me," says the
       LORD.
4 "Everyone take heed to his neighbor,
   And do not trust any brother;
   For every brother will utterly supplant,
   And every neighbor will walk with
       slanderers.
5 Everyone will deceive his neighbor,
   And will not speak the truth;
   They have taught their tongue to speak
       lies;
   They weary themselves to commit
       iniquity.
6 Your dwelling place is in the midst of
       deceit;
   Through deceit they refuse to know Me,"
       says the LORD.

7 Therefore thus says the LORD of hosts:

   "Behold, I will refine them and try them;
   For how shall I deal with the
       daughter of My
       people?
8 Their tongue is an arrow
       shot out;
   It speaks deceit;
   One speaks peaceably to
       his neighbor with his
       mouth,

VALUES

Are our
values
important?
(9:7–9)

Promise   HE PROMISES TO PURIFY YOUR HEART.

*Therefore thus says the LORD of hosts: "Behold, I will refine them and try them;
for how shall I deal with the daughter of My people?" (Jer. 9:7).*

Sometimes we get paralyzed in our daily walk with God. We wake up one morning, take a look
in the mirror, see our sin and its ugliness, and push God away. We might spend the next weeks or
months trying to figure out how to make ourselves more presentable. But you can't refine and
purify your own heart. What you can do is stay hooked up to God through prayer, and you can
constantly renew your mind by memorizing and meditating on Scripture. God can make the
unclean holy and restore beauty to the unlovely. No matter how ugly your heart or how sinful
your life has been, God can clean and restore. Ask Him daily to purify your heart. If you're
continually allowing God in to remove your sin, your walk with Him stays fresh, and you stay
acceptable to Him.

SEE FOR YOURSELF:
Zech. 13:9; Acts 15:9; Titus 2:14

But in his heart he lies in wait.
9 Shall I not punish them for these *things?*"
    says the LORD.
"Shall I not avenge Myself on such a
    nation as this?"

10 I will take up a weeping and wailing for
    the mountains,
And for the dwelling places of the
    wilderness a lamentation,
Because they are burned up,
So that no one can pass through;
Nor can *men* hear the voice of the cattle.
Both the birds of the heavens and the
    beasts have fled;
They are gone.

11 "I will make Jerusalem a heap of ruins, a
    den of jackals.
I will make the cities of Judah desolate,
    without an inhabitant."

12Who *is* the wise man who may understand this? And *who is he* to whom the mouth
of the LORD has spoken, that he may declare it?
Why does the land perish *and* burn up like a
wilderness, so that no one can pass through?
13And the LORD said, "Because they have forsaken My law which I set before them, and
have not obeyed My voice, nor walked according to it, 14but they have walked according to
the dictates of their own hearts and after the
Baals, which their fathers taught them," 15there-
fore thus says the LORD of hosts, the God of Israel: "Behold, I will feed them, this people, with
wormwood, and give them water of gall to
drink. 16I will scatter them also among the Gentiles, whom neither they nor their fathers have
known. And I will send a sword after them until I have consumed them."

THE PEOPLE MOURN IN JUDGMENT

17Thus says the LORD of hosts:

"Consider and call for the mourning
    women,
That they may come;
And send for skillful wailing women,
That they may come.
18 Let them make haste
And take up a wailing for us,
That our eyes may run with tears,
And our eyelids gush with water.
19 For a voice of wailing is heard from Zion:
'How we are plundered!
We are greatly ashamed,
Because we have forsaken the land,

Because we have been cast out of our
    dwellings.' "

20 Yet hear the word of the LORD, O women,
And let your ear receive the word of His
    mouth;
Teach your daughters wailing,
And everyone her neighbor a
    lamentation.
21 For death has come through our
    windows,
Has entered our palaces,
To kill off the children—*no longer to be*
    outside!
And the young men—*no longer* on the
    streets!

22 Speak, "Thus says the LORD:

'Even the carcasses of men shall fall as
    refuse on the open field,
Like cuttings after the harvester,
And no one shall gather *them*.' "

23Thus says the LORD:

"Let not the wise *man* glory in his wisdom,
Let not the mighty *man* glory in his
    might,
Nor let the rich *man* glory in his riches;
24 But let him who glories glory in this,
That he understands and knows Me,
That I *am* the LORD, exercising
    lovingkindness, judgment, and
    righteousness in the earth.
For in these I delight," says the LORD.

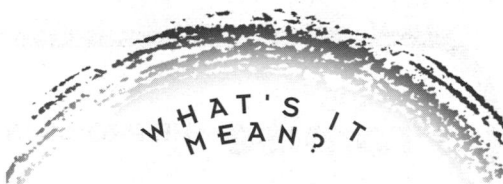

WHAT'S IT MEAN?

Circumcision is a minor operation performed on
the sex organ of male babies, usually within a few
days after birth. For the Israelites, circumcision was an outward sign
of their agreement with God. Other nations in the Near East also
practiced circumcision, but waited until the young
man was entering adulthood.
Jeremiah 9:25, 26

25"Behold, the days are coming," says the
LORD, "that I will punish all *who are* circumcised

with the uncircumcised—²⁶Egypt, Judah, Edom, the people of Ammon, Moab, and all *who are in* the farthest corners, who dwell in the wilderness. For all *these* nations *are* uncircumcised, and all the house of Israel *are* uncircumcised in the heart."

IDOLS AND THE TRUE GOD

¹Hear the word which the LORD speaks to you, O house of Israel.
²Thus says the LORD:

"Do not learn the way of the Gentiles;
Do not be dismayed at the signs of heaven,
For the Gentiles are dismayed at them.
³ For the customs of the peoples *are* futile;
For *one* cuts a tree from the forest,
The work of the hands of the workman, with the ax.
⁴ They decorate it with silver and gold;
They fasten it with nails and hammers
So that it will not topple.
⁵ They *are* upright, like a palm tree,
And they cannot speak;
They must be carried,
Because they cannot go *by themselves.*
Do not be afraid of them,
For they cannot do evil,
Nor can they do any good."

⁶ Inasmuch as *there is* none like You, O LORD
(You *are* great, and
Your name *is* great in might),
⁷ Who would not fear You, O King of the nations?
For this is Your rightful due.
For among all the wise *men* of the nations,
And in all their kingdoms,
There is none like You.
⁸ But they are altogether dull-hearted and foolish;
A wooden idol *is* a worthless doctrine.
⁹ Silver is beaten into plates;
It is brought from Tarshish,
And gold from Uphaz,
The work of the craftsman
And of the hands of the metalsmith;
Blue and purple *are* their clothing;
They *are* all the work of skillful *men.*

¹⁰ But the LORD *is* the true God;
He *is* the living God and the everlasting King.
At His wrath the earth will tremble,
And the nations will not be able to endure His indignation.

¹¹Thus you shall say to them: "The gods that have not made the heavens and the earth shall perish from the earth and from under these heavens."

¹² He has made the earth by His power,
He has established the world by His wisdom,
And has stretched out the heavens at His discretion.
¹³ When He utters His voice,
There is a multitude of waters in the heavens:
"And He causes the vapors to ascend from the ends of the earth.
He makes lightning for the rain,
He brings the wind out of His treasuries."*ᵃ*

¹⁴ Everyone is dull-hearted, without knowledge;
Every metalsmith is put to shame by an image;
For his molded image *is* falsehood,
And *there is* no breath in them.
¹⁵ They *are* futile, a work of errors;
In the time of their punishment they shall perish.
¹⁶ The Portion of Jacob *is* not like them,
For He *is* the Maker of all *things,*
And Israel *is* the tribe of His inheritance;
The LORD of hosts *is* His name.

THE COMING CAPTIVITY OF JUDAH

¹⁷ Gather up your wares from the land,
O inhabitant of the fortress!

¹⁸For thus says the LORD:

"Behold, I will throw out at this time
The inhabitants of the land,

"Inasmuch as there is none like You, O LORD . . . who would not fear You, O King of the nations?" (Jeremiah 10:6, 7a)

10:13 ᵃPsalm 135:7

JEREMIAH made a difference

Our superficial impression of prophets makes it difficult to imagine what they were like as kids. Did they thunder judgment as five-year-olds? Were they prematurely bearded? The Bible (as usual) has a way of correcting our impressions. Prophets came in all shapes and sizes. Usually, they were normal. Often, the idea of being called as God's prophet came as just as much a shock to them as it would to us. Jeremiah was probably typical.

When God called Jeremiah to be a prophet, Jeremiah's immediate answer admitted insecurity and inexperience. He felt he couldn't speak, and he claimed he was too young. God didn't tell Jeremiah he was wrong. In fact, God agreed with Jeremiah. The newly appointed prophet was a tongue-tied beginner. God told him to stop thinking of himself that way and to start thinking about how God was going to make up for those obvious weaknesses. God gave Jeremiah three unforgettable promises as part of his commission: (1) God's guidance (1:7); (2) God's words (v. 7); (3) God's companionship (v. 8). God also gave Jeremiah three commands: (1) Don't use your youth as an excuse (v. 7); (2) Go where I send you (v. 7); (3) Don't be afraid (v. 8). Jeremiah didn't have a easy life. He may have been the least popular prophet. He spent time in prison. Some of his writings were burned. He was even dropped in the bottom of a well. God kept His promise.

Cutting Edge

We know Jeremiah always knew God was with him, because he complained to God constantly! They had a continual conversation, no matter what Jeremiah was doing or where he was.

One of the ways Jeremiah made a difference was by demonstrating a faith that expressed genuine feelings to God. Jeremiah didn't edit his prayers. He didn't tell God what he thought God wanted to hear. He told God what God already knew. Honest prayer changes the person who prays.

YOU can, too! God knows you inside out. God designed you. Like Jeremiah, you will discover that the more you are open to God's direction, the more you will find God using both your abilities and your inabilities to accomplish His purposes. God will make a difference with you as you are and in spite of the way you are. He will make a difference in you as He is making a difference through you. As God told Jeremiah, "I am with you to deliver you" (Jer. 1:8).

Want to know more? You can read Jeremiah's writings and about his life in Jeremiah and Lamentations.

And will distress them,
That they may find *it so.*"

19 Woe is me for my hurt!
My wound is severe.
But I say, "Truly this *is* an infirmity,
And I must bear it."
20 My tent is plundered,
And all my cords are broken;
My children have gone from me,
And they *are* no more.
There is no one to pitch my tent anymore,
Or set up my curtains.

21 For the shepherds have become dull-hearted,
And have not sought the LORD;
Therefore they shall not prosper,
And all their flocks shall be scattered.
22 Behold, the noise of the report has come,
And a great commotion out of the north country,
To make the cities of Judah desolate, a den of jackals.

WHAT'S IT MEAN?

Jackals were desert creatures, similar to dogs, that fed on garbage. They were especially unpopular with the Israelites not only because they destroyed crops, but also because they smelled bad.

Jeremiah 10:22

23 O LORD, I know the way of man *is* not in himself;
It is not in man who walks to direct his own steps.
24 O LORD, correct me, but with justice;
Not in Your anger, lest You bring me to nothing.
25 Pour out Your fury on the Gentiles, who do not know You,
And on the families who do not call on Your name;
For they have eaten up Jacob,
Devoured him and consumed him,
And made his dwelling place desolate.

THE BROKEN COVENANT

1 The word that came to Jeremiah from the LORD, saying, 2 "Hear the words of this covenant, and speak to the men of Judah and to the inhabitants of Jerusalem; 3 and say to them, 'Thus says the LORD God of Israel: "Cursed *is* the man who does not obey the words of this covenant 4 which I commanded your fathers in the day I brought them out of the land of Egypt, from the iron furnace, saying, 'Obey My voice, and do according to all that I command you; so shall you be My people, and I will be your God,' 5 that I may establish the oath which I have sworn to your fathers, to give them 'a land flowing with milk and honey,'*a* as *it is* this day.' ' "

And I answered and said, "So be it, LORD."

6 Then the LORD said to me, "Proclaim all these words in the cities of Judah and in the streets of Jerusalem, saying: 'Hear the words of this covenant and do them. 7 For I earnestly exhorted your fathers in the day I brought them up out of the land of Egypt, until this day, rising early and exhorting, saying, "Obey My voice." 8 Yet they did not obey or incline their ear, but everyone followed the dictates of his evil heart; therefore I will bring upon them all the words of this covenant, which I commanded *them* to do, but *which* they have not done.' "

OBEDIENCE

How important is it to obey God? (11:7)

9 And the LORD said to me, "A conspiracy has been found among the men of Judah and among the inhabitants of Jerusalem. 10 They have turned back to the iniquities of their forefathers who refused to hear My words, and they have gone after other gods to serve them; the house of Israel and the house of Judah have broken My covenant which I made with their fathers."

11 Therefore thus says the LORD: "Behold, I will surely bring calamity on them which they will not be able to escape; and though they cry out to Me, I will not listen to them. 12 Then the cities of Judah and the inhabitants of Jerusalem will go and cry out to the gods to whom they offer incense, but they will not save them at all in the time of their trouble. 13 For *according to* the number of your cities were your gods, O Judah; and *according to* the number of the streets of Jerusalem you have set up altars to *that* shameful thing, altars to burn incense to Baal.

14 "So do not pray for this people, or lift up a

cry or prayer for them; for I will not hear *them* in the time that they cry out to Me because of their trouble.

15 "What has My beloved to do in My house,
Having done lewd deeds with many?
And the holy flesh has passed from you.
When you do evil, then you rejoice.
16 The LORD called your name,
Green Olive Tree, Lovely *and* of Good Fruit.
With the noise of a great tumult
He has kindled fire on it,
And its branches are broken.

17"For the LORD of hosts, who planted you, has pronounced doom against you for the evil of the house of Israel and of the house of Judah, which they have done against themselves to provoke Me to anger in offering incense to Baal."

JEREMIAH'S LIFE THREATENED

18Now the LORD gave me knowledge *of it,* and I know *it;* for You showed me their doings. 19But I *was* like a docile lamb brought to the slaughter; and I did not know that they had devised schemes against me, *saying,* "Let us destroy the tree with its fruit, and let us cut him off from the land of the living, that his name may be remembered no more."

20 But, O LORD of hosts,
You who judge righteously,
Testing the mind and the heart,
Let me see Your vengeance on them,
For to You I have revealed my cause.

21"Therefore thus says the LORD concerning the men of Anathoth who seek your life, saying, 'Do not prophesy in the name of the LORD, lest you die by our hand'— 22therefore thus says the LORD of hosts: 'Behold, I will punish them. The young men shall die by the sword, their sons and their daughters shall die by famine; 23and there shall be no remnant of them, for I will bring catastrophe on the men of Anathoth, *even* the year of their punishment.'"

JEREMIAH'S QUESTION

1 Righteous *are* You, O LORD, when I plead with You;
Yet let me talk with You about *Your* judgments.

Why does the way of the wicked prosper?
Why are those happy who deal so treacherously?
2 You have planted them, yes, they have taken root;
They grow, yes, they bear fruit.
You *are* near in their mouth
But far from their mind.

3 But You, O LORD, know me;
You have seen me,
And You have tested my heart toward You.
Pull them out like sheep for the slaughter,
And prepare them for the day of slaughter.
4 How long will the land mourn,
And the herbs of every field wither?
The beasts and birds are consumed,
For the wickedness of those who dwell there,
Because they said, "He will not see our final end."

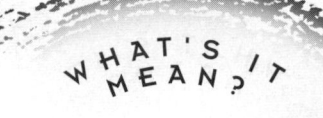

WHAT'S IT MEAN?

Traveling the floodplain of the Jordan River would have been extremely difficult. Not only was it overgrown with shrubs, brush, trees, and vines, it was also crawling with dangerous wild animals that were known to attack passersby.
Jeremiah 12:5

THE LORD ANSWERS JEREMIAH

5 "If you have run with the footmen, and they have wearied you,
Then how can you contend with horses?
And *if* in the land of peace,
In which you trusted, *they wearied you,*
Then how will you do in the floodplain*ᵃ* of the Jordan?
6 For even your brothers, the house of your father,
Even they have dealt treacherously with you;

12:5 *ᵃOr thicket*

Yes, they have called a multitude after you.
Do not believe them,
Even though they speak smooth words to you.

7 "I have forsaken My house, I have left My heritage;
I have given the dearly beloved of My soul into the hand of her enemies.
8 My heritage is to Me like a lion in the forest;
It cries out against Me;
Therefore I have hated it.
9 My heritage *is* to Me *like* a speckled vulture;
The vultures all around *are* against her.
Come, assemble all the beasts of the field,
Bring them to devour!

10 "Many rulers[a] have destroyed My vineyard,
They have trodden My portion underfoot;
They have made My pleasant portion a desolate wilderness.
11 They have made it desolate;
Desolate, it mourns to Me;
The whole land is made desolate,
Because no one takes *it* to heart.
12 The plunderers have come
On all the desolate heights in the wilderness,
For the sword of the LORD shall devour
From *one* end of the land to the *other* end of the land;
No flesh shall have peace.
13 They have sown wheat but reaped thorns;
They have put themselves to pain *but do* not profit.
But be ashamed of your harvest
Because of the fierce anger of the LORD."

14Thus says the LORD: "Against all My evil neighbors who touch the inheritance which I have caused My people Israel to inherit—behold, I will pluck them out of their land and pluck out the house of Judah from among them. 15Then it shall be, after I have plucked them out, that I will return and have compassion on them and bring them back, everyone to his heritage and everyone to his land. 16And it shall be, if they will learn carefully the ways of My people, to swear by My name, 'As the LORD lives,' as they taught My people to swear by Baal, then they shall be established in the midst of My people. 17But if they do not obey, I will utterly pluck up and destroy that nation," says the LORD.

SYMBOL OF THE LINEN SASH

1Thus the LORD said to me: "Go and get yourself a linen sash, and put it around your waist, but do not put it in water." 2So I got a sash according to the word of the LORD, and put *it* around my waist.

3And the word of the LORD came to me the second time, saying, 4"Take the sash that you acquired, which *is* around your waist, and arise, go to the Euphrates,[a] and hide it there in a hole in the rock." 5So I went and hid it by the Euphrates, as the LORD commanded me.

6Now it came to pass after many days that the LORD said to me, "Arise, go to the Euphrates, and take from there the sash which I commanded you to hide there." 7Then I went to the Euphrates and dug, and I took the sash from the place where I had hidden it; and there was the sash, ruined. It was profitable for nothing.

8Then the word of the LORD came to me, saying, 9"Thus says the LORD: 'In this manner I will ruin the pride of Judah and the great pride of Jerusalem. 10This evil people, who refuse to hear My words, who follow the dictates of their hearts, and walk after other gods to serve them and worship them, shall be just like this sash which is profitable for nothing. 11For as the sash clings to the waist of a man, so I have caused the whole house of Israel and the whole house of Judah to cling to Me,' says the LORD, 'that they may become My people, for renown, for praise, and for glory; but they would not hear.'

SYMBOL OF THE WINE BOTTLES

12"Therefore you shall speak to them this word: 'Thus says the LORD God of Israel: "Every bottle shall be filled with wine." '

"And they will say to you, 'Do we not certainly know that every bottle will be filled with wine?'

13"Then you shall say to them, 'Thus says the LORD: "Behold, I will fill all the inhabitants of this land—even the kings who sit on David's throne, the priests, the prophets, and all the inhabitants of Jerusalem—with drunkenness! 14And I will dash them one against another, even the fathers and the sons together," says the LORD. "I will not pity nor spare nor have mercy, but will destroy them." ' "

12:10 [a]Literally *shepherds* or *pastors*   **13:4** [a]Hebrew *Perath*

PRIDE PRECEDES CAPTIVITY

15 Hear and give ear:
Do not be proud,
For the LORD has spoken.
16 Give glory to the LORD your
God
Before He causes
darkness,
And before your feet
stumble
On the dark mountains,
And while you are
looking for light,
He turns it into the
shadow of death
And makes *it* dense darkness.
17 But if you will not hear it,
My soul will weep in secret for *your*
pride;
My eyes will weep bitterly
And run down with tears,
Because the LORD's flock has been taken
captive.

18 Say to the king and to the queen mother,
"Humble yourselves;
Sit down,
For your rule shall collapse, the crown of
your glory."
19 The cities of the South shall be shut up,
And no one shall open *them;*
Judah shall be carried away captive, all of
it;
It shall be wholly carried away captive.

20 Lift up your eyes and see
Those who come from the north.
Where *is* the flock *that* was given to you,
Your beautiful sheep?
21 What will you say when He punishes
you?
For you have taught them
To be chieftains, to be head over you.
Will not pangs seize you,
Like a woman in labor?
22 And if you say in your heart,
"Why have these things come upon me?"
For the greatness of your iniquity
Your skirts have been
uncovered,
Your heels made bare.
23 Can the Ethiopian
change his skin or the
leopard its spots?
Then may you also do
good who are
accustomed to do evil.

24 "Therefore I will scatter them like stubble
That passes away by the wind of the
wilderness.
25 This is your lot,
The portion of your
measures from Me,"
says the LORD,
"Because you have
forgotten Me
And trusted in
falsehood.
26 Therefore I will uncover
your skirts over your
face,
That your shame may
appear.
27 I have seen your
adulteries
And your *lustful* neighings,
The lewdness of your harlotry,
Your abominations on the hills in the
fields.
Woe to you, O Jerusalem!
Will you still not be made clean?"

SWORD, FAMINE, AND PESTILENCE

1 The word of the LORD that came to Jeremiah concerning the droughts.

2 "Judah mourns,
And her gates languish;
They mourn for the land,
And the cry of Jerusalem has gone up.
3 Their nobles have sent their lads for
water;
They went to the cisterns *and* found no
water.
They returned with their vessels empty;
They were ashamed and confounded
And covered their heads.
4 Because the ground is parched,
For there was no rain in the land,
The plowmen were ashamed;
They covered their heads.
5 Yes, the deer also gave birth in the field,
But left because there was no grass.
6 And the wild donkeys stood in the
desolate heights;
They sniffed at the wind like jackals;
Their eyes failed because *there was* no
grass."

7 O LORD, though our iniquities testify
against us,
Do it for Your name's sake;
For our backslidings are many,
We have sinned against You.

> "Give glory to the LORD
> your God before He causes
> darkness, and before your
> feet stumble."
> (Jeremiah 13:16a)

VALUES

How do our
values affect
our decisions?
(13:23)

8 O the Hope of Israel, his Savior in time of
   trouble,
   Why should You be like a stranger in the
   land,
   And like a traveler *who* turns aside to
   tarry for a night?
9 Why should You be like a man
   astonished,
   Like a mighty one *who* cannot save?
   Yet You, O LORD, *are* in our midst,
   And we are called by Your name;
   Do not leave us!

¹⁰Thus says the LORD to this people:

"Thus they have loved to wander;
They have not restrained their feet.
Therefore the LORD does not accept them;
He will remember their iniquity now,
And punish their sins."

¹¹Then the LORD said to me, "Do not pray for
this people, for *their* good. ¹²When they fast, I
will not hear their cry; and when they offer
burnt offering and grain offering, I will not accept them. But I will consume them by the
sword, by the famine, and by the pestilence."
¹³Then I said, "Ah, Lord GOD! Behold, the
prophets say to them, 'You shall not see the
sword, nor shall you have famine, but I will
give you assured peace in this place.'"
¹⁴And the LORD said to me, "The prophets
prophesy lies in My name. I have not sent
them, commanded them, nor spoken to them;
they prophesy to you a false vision, divination,
a worthless thing, and the deceit of their heart.
¹⁵Therefore thus says the LORD concerning the
prophets who prophesy in My name, whom I
did not send, and who say, 'Sword and famine
shall not be in this land'—'By sword and famine those prophets shall be consumed! ¹⁶And
the people to whom they prophesy shall be
cast out in the streets of Jerusalem because of
the famine and the sword; they will have no
one to bury them—them nor their wives, their
sons nor their daughters—for I will pour their
wickedness on them.'
¹⁷"Therefore you shall say this word to them:

'Let my eyes flow with tears night and
day,
And let them not cease;
For the virgin daughter of my people
Has been broken with a mighty stroke,
with a very severe blow.
18 If I go out to the field,
Then behold, those slain with the sword!

And if I enter the city,
Then behold, those sick from famine!
Yes, both prophet and priest go about in
a land they do not know.'"

THE PEOPLE PLEAD FOR MERCY

19 Have You utterly rejected Judah?
Has Your soul loathed Zion?
Why have You stricken us so that *there is*
no healing for us?
We looked for peace, but *there was* no
good;
And for the time of healing, and there
was trouble.
20 We acknowledge, O LORD, our wickedness
And the iniquity of our fathers,
For we have sinned against You.
21 Do not abhor *us*, for Your name's sake;
Do not disgrace the throne of Your glory.
Remember, do not break Your covenant
with us.
22 Are there any among the idols of the
nations that can cause rain?
Or can the heavens give showers?
Are You not He, O LORD our God?
Therefore we will wait for You,
Since You have made all these.

THE LORD WILL NOT RELENT

¹Then the LORD said to me, "*Even* if Moses
and Samuel stood before Me, My mind *would*
not *be* favorable toward this people. Cast *them*
out of My sight, and let them go forth. ²And it
shall be, if they say to you, 'Where should we
go?' then you shall tell them, 'Thus says the
LORD:

"Such as *are* for death, to death;
And such as *are* for the sword, to the
sword;
And such as *are* for the famine, to the
famine;
And such as *are* for the captivity, to the
captivity." '

³"And I will appoint over them four forms *of*
destruction," says the LORD: "the sword to slay,
the dogs to drag, the birds of the heavens and
the beasts of the earth to devour and destroy. ⁴I
will hand them over to trouble, to all kingdoms
of the earth, because of Manasseh the son of
Hezekiah, king of Judah, for what he did in Jerusalem.

5 "For who will have pity on you,
O Jerusalem?
Or who will bemoan you?

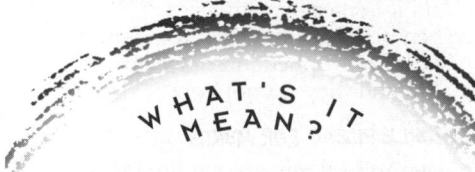

WHAT'S IT MEAN?

Of all the kings of Judah, Manasseh, was the worst. We're talking about an unbelievably wicked guy, one who sacrificed his own son to the pagan god Molech. To seal his reputation as an enemy of God, it's likely that Manasseh executed the prophet Isaiah by having him sawn in half.

Jeremiah 15:4

Or who will turn aside to ask how you
are doing?
6 You have forsaken Me," says the LORD,
"You have gone backward.
Therefore I will stretch out My hand
against you and destroy you;
I am weary of relenting!
7 And I will winnow them with a
winnowing fan in the gates of the
land;
I will bereave *them* of children;
I will destroy My people,
Since they do not return from their ways.
8 Their widows will be increased to Me
more than the sand of the seas;
I will bring against them,
Against the mother of the young men,
A plunderer at noonday;
I will cause anguish and terror to fall on
them suddenly.

9 "She languishes who has borne seven;
She has breathed her last;
Her sun has gone down
While *it was* yet day;
She has been ashamed and confounded.
And the remnant of them I will deliver to
the sword
Before their enemies," says the LORD.

JEREMIAH'S DEJECTION
10 Woe is me, my mother,
That you have borne me,
A man of strife and a man of contention
to the whole earth!
I have neither lent for interest,

Nor have men lent to me for interest.
Every one of them curses me.

11The LORD said:

"Surely it will be well with your remnant;
Surely I will cause the enemy to intercede
with you
In the time of adversity and in the time of
affliction.
12 Can anyone break iron,
The northern iron and the bronze?
13 Your wealth and your treasures
I will give as plunder without price,
Because of all your sins,
Throughout your territories.
14 And I will make *you* cross over with[a]
your enemies
Into a land *which* you do not know;
For a fire is kindled in My anger,
Which shall burn upon you."

15 O LORD, You know;
Remember me and visit me,
And take vengeance for me on my
persecutors.
In Your enduring patience, do not take
me away.
Know that for Your sake I have suffered
rebuke.
16 Your words were found, and I ate them,
And Your word was to me the joy and
rejoicing of my heart;
For I am called by Your name,
O LORD God of hosts.
17 I did not sit in the assembly of the
mockers,
Nor did I rejoice;
I sat alone because of Your hand,
For You have filled me with indignation.
18 Why is my pain perpetual
And my wound incurable,
Which refuses to be healed?
Will You surely be to me like an
unreliable stream,
As waters *that* fail?

THE LORD REASSURES JEREMIAH
19Therefore thus says the LORD:

"If you return,
Then I will bring you back;
You shall stand before Me;
If you take out the precious from the vile,

15:14 [a]Following Masoretic Text and Vulgate; Septuagint, Syriac, and Targum read *cause you to serve* (compare 17:4).

You shall be as My mouth.
Let them return to you,
But you must not return to them.

20 And I will make you to this people a
   fortified bronze wall;
   And they will fight against you,
   But they shall not prevail against you;
   For I *am* with you to save you
   And deliver you," says the LORD.

21 "I will deliver you from the hand of the
   wicked,
   And I will redeem you from the grip of
   the terrible."

JEREMIAH'S LIFESTYLE AND MESSAGE

¹The word of the LORD also came to me, saying, ²"You shall not take a wife, nor shall you
have sons or daughters in this place." ³For thus
says the LORD concerning the sons and daughters who are born in this place, and concerning
their mothers who bore them and their fathers
who begot them in this land: ⁴"They shall die
gruesome deaths; they shall not be lamented
nor shall they be buried, *but* they shall be like
refuse on the face of the earth. They shall be
consumed by the sword and by famine, and
their corpses shall be meat for the birds of
heaven and for the beasts of the earth."

WHAT'S IT MEAN?

Receiving a proper burial was very
important in the culture of the ancient Near
East. It was considered especially shameful and
degrading for a corpse to be left exposed to the
ravages of weather and wild animals.
Jeremiah 16:5, 6

⁵For thus says the LORD: "Do not enter the
house of mourning, nor go to lament or bemoan them; for I have taken away My peace
from this people," says the LORD, "lovingkindness and mercies. ⁶Both the great and the
small shall die in this land. They shall not be
buried; neither shall men lament for them, cut
themselves, nor make themselves bald for them.
⁷Nor shall *men* break *bread* in mourning for
them, to comfort them for the dead; nor shall
men give them the cup of consolation to drink
for their father or their mother. ⁸Also you shall

not go into the house of feasting to sit with
them, to eat and drink."

⁹For thus says the LORD of hosts, the God of
Israel: "Behold, I will cause to cease from this
place, before your eyes and in your days, the
voice of mirth and the voice of gladness, the
voice of the bridegroom and the voice of the
bride.

WHAT'S IT MEAN?

When Jerusalem was conquered by
Babylon in 586 B.C., the Jewish people who
were taken captive had to learn a whole new way of life, including
new religions and new customs. The Jews were held captive in
Babylon for seventy years.
Jeremiah 16:13

¹⁰"And it shall be, when you show this people all these words, and they say to you, 'Why
has the LORD pronounced all this great disaster
against us? Or what *is* our iniquity? Or what *is*
our sin that we have committed against the
LORD our God?' ¹¹then you shall say to them,
'Because your fathers have forsaken Me', says
the LORD; 'they have walked after other gods
and have served them and worshiped them,
and have forsaken Me and not kept My law.
¹²And you have done worse than your fathers,
for behold, each one follows the dictates of his
own evil heart, so that no one listens to Me.
¹³Therefore I will cast you out of this land into a
land that you do not know, neither you nor
your fathers; and there you shall serve other
gods day and night, where I will not show you
favor.'

GOD WILL RESTORE ISRAEL

¹⁴"Therefore behold, the days are coming,"
says the LORD, "that it shall no more be said,
'The LORD lives who brought up the children of
Israel from the land of Egypt,' ¹⁵but, 'The LORD
lives who brought up the children of Israel
from the land of the north and from all the
lands where He had driven them.' For I will
bring them back into their land which I gave to
their fathers.

¹⁶"Behold, I will send for many fishermen,"
says the LORD, "and they shall fish them; and

afterward I will send for many hunters, and they shall hunt them from every mountain and every hill, and out of the holes of the rocks. ¹⁷For My eyes *are* on all their ways; they are not hidden from My face, nor is their iniquity hidden from My eyes. ¹⁸And first I will repay double for their iniquity and their sin, because they have defiled My land; they have filled My inheritance with the carcasses of their detestable and abominable idols."

SIN
Can we hide sin from God? (16:17)

19   O LORD, my strength and my fortress,
   My refuge in the day of affliction,
   The Gentiles shall come to You
   From the ends of the earth and say,
   "Surely our fathers have inherited lies,
   Worthlessness and unprofitable *things*."
20   Will a man make gods for himself,
   Which *are* not gods?

21   "Therefore behold, I will this once cause
     them to know,
   I will cause them to know
   My hand and My might;
   And they shall know that My name *is* the
   LORD.

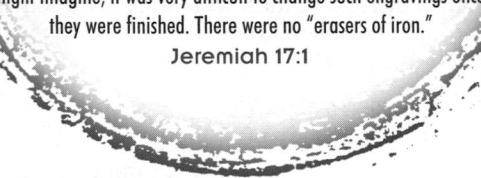

WHAT'S IT MEAN?

"Pens of iron" were used to carve public records, announcements, and calendars in stone. The stones were then displayed in places where people could see them. Often the same announcement was posted in more than one place. As you might imagine, it was very difficult to change such engravings once they were finished. There were no "erasers of iron."

Jeremiah 17:1

JUDAH'S SIN AND PUNISHMENT

1   "The sin of Judah *is* written with a pen of
     iron;
   With the point of a diamond *it is*
     engraved
   On the tablet of their heart,

2   And on the horns of your altars,
   While their children remember
   Their altars and their wooden images^a
   By the green trees on the high hills.
3   O My mountain in the field,
   I will give as plunder your wealth, all
     your treasures,
   And your high places of sin within all
     your borders.
4   And you, even yourself,
   Shall let go of your heritage which I gave
     you;
   And I will cause you to serve your
     enemies
   In the land which you do not know;
   For you have kindled a fire in My anger
   which shall burn forever."

⁵Thus says the LORD:

   "Cursed *is* the man who trusts in man
   And makes flesh his strength,
   Whose heart departs from the LORD.
6   For he shall be like a shrub in the desert,
   And shall not see when good comes,
   But shall inhabit the parched places in the
     wilderness,
   In a salt land *which is* not inhabited.

7   "Blessed *is* the man who trusts in the
     LORD,
   And whose hope is the LORD.
8   For he shall be like a tree planted by the
     waters,
   Which spreads out its roots by the river,
   And will not fear^a when heat comes;
   But its leaf will be green,
   And will not be anxious in the year of
     drought,
   Nor will cease from yielding fruit.

9   "The heart *is* deceitful above all *things,*
   And desperately wicked;
   Who can know it?
10   I, the LORD, search the heart,
   I test the mind,
   Even to give every man according to his
     ways,
   According to the fruit of his doings.

11   "*As* a partridge that broods but does not
     hatch,
   So is he who gets riches, but not by right;
   It will leave him in the midst of his days,
   And at his end he will be a fool."

17:2 ^aHebrew *Asherim,* Canaanite deities   **17:8** ^aQere and Targum read *see.*

12 A glorious high throne from the
    beginning
    Is the place of our sanctuary.
13 O LORD, the hope of Israel,
    All who forsake You shall be ashamed.

  "Those who depart from Me
    Shall be written in the earth,
    Because they have forsaken the LORD,
    The fountain of living waters."

On the Edge

Heal me, O LORD, and I shall be healed; save me, and I shall be saved, for You are my praise" (Jer. 17:14).

Sexual abuse is such a tragedy. The victims who are left behind may suffer for years with the hurt and pain they've endured. One's most powerful healing comes when God's is invited to be part of the process. First, He can help you forgive the person who violated you. He can restore feelings that had become numb, replace anger with love, and He can even return a commitment to virginity. Your body may have been violated, but the commitment of your heart must endure—to wait on marriage before choosing sex. The Lord will prepare a spouse who is loving and understanding. And He will honor the marriage of one who didn't let the evil of this world get the final victory. What a gift to your future spouse to be able to say, "I may have been sexually abused, and I was powerless against it, but in every choice I've made, I have chosen to wait for you."

SEE FOR YOURSELF:
Ps. 40:1–3; 116:5–7;
Is. 41:13; 57:18, 19;
Hos. 14:4

JEREMIAH PRAYS FOR DELIVERANCE

14 Heal me, O LORD, and I shall be healed;
    Save me, and I shall be saved,
    For You *are* my praise.
15 Indeed they say to me,
    "Where *is* the word of the LORD?
    Let it come now!"
16 As for me, I have not hurried away from
    being a shepherd *who* follows You,
    Nor have I desired the woeful day;

You know what came out of my lips;
    It was right there before You.
17 Do not be a terror to me;
    You *are* my hope in the day of doom.
18 Let them be ashamed who persecute me,
    But do not let me be put to shame;
    Let them be dismayed,
    But do not let me be dismayed.
    Bring on them the day of doom,
    And destroy them with double
      destruction!

HALLOW THE SABBATH DAY

19Thus the LORD said to me: "Go and stand in the gate of the children of the people, by which the kings of Judah come in and by which they go out, and in all the gates of Jerusalem; 20and say to them, 'Hear the word of the LORD, you kings of Judah, and all Judah, and all the inhabitants of Jerusalem, who enter by these gates. 21Thus says the LORD: "Take heed to yourselves, and bear no burden on the Sabbath day, nor bring *it* in by the gates of Jerusalem; 22nor carry a burden out of your houses on the Sabbath day, nor do any work, but hallow the Sabbath day, as I commanded your fathers. 23But they did not obey nor incline their ear, but made their neck stiff, that they might not hear nor receive instruction.

WHAT'S IT MEAN?

The Sabbath is the seventh day of the week, Saturday. God instructed His people to set aside the seventh day of each week for Him. All forms of normal work were forbidden on the Sabbath. Only acts of kindness, worship, and emergency were allowed. Keeping one's Saturday schedule free from work was a way of showing submission to God. Refusing to observe the Sabbath was a way of showing rebellion against God.
Jeremiah 17:21–24

24"And it shall be, if you heed Me carefully," says the LORD, "to bring no burden through the gates of this city on the Sabbath day, but hallow the Sabbath day, to do no work in it, 25then shall enter the gates of this city kings and princes sitting on the throne of David, riding in chariots and on horses, they and their princes, accompanied by the men of Judah and the inhabitants of Jerusalem; and this city shall remain forever. ²⁶And they shall come from the cities of Judah and from the places around Jerusalem, from the land of Benjamin and from the lowland, from the mountains and from the South, bringing burnt offerings and sacrifices, grain offerings and incense, bringing sacrifices of praise to the house of the LORD.

²⁷"But if you will not heed Me to hallow the Sabbath day, such as not carrying a burden when entering the gates of Jerusalem on the Sabbath day, then I will kindle a fire in its gates, and it shall devour the palaces of Jerusalem, and it shall not be quenched." ' "

THE POTTER AND THE CLAY

¹The word which came to Jeremiah from the LORD, saying: ²"Arise and go down to the potter's house, and there I will cause you to hear My words." ³Then I went down to the potter's house, and there he was, making something at the wheel. ⁴And the vessel that he made of clay was marred in the hand of the potter; so he made it again into another vessel, as it seemed good to the potter to make.

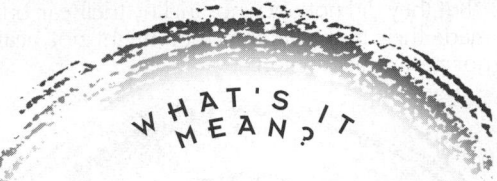

WHAT'S IT MEAN?

A pottery wheel is a small round disk that the potter moves by turning a connected disk with his foot. While the wheel spins, the potter shapes a piece of clay sitting on the disk. Even the best potters find it hard to shape the clay precisely. Sometimes they have to start over again if the clay won't cooperate.

Jeremiah 18:3

⁵Then the word of the LORD came to me, saying: ⁶"O house of Israel, can I not do with you as this potter?" says the LORD. "Look, as the clay is in the potter's hand, so are you in My hand, O house of Israel! ⁷The instant I speak concerning a nation and concerning a kingdom, to pluck up, to pull down, and to destroy it, ⁸if that nation against whom I have spoken turns from its evil, I will relent of the disaster that I thought to bring upon it. ⁹And the instant I speak concerning a nation and concerning a kingdom, to build and to plant it, ¹⁰if it does evil in My sight so that it does not obey My voice,

On the Edge

"O house of Israel, can I not do with you as this potter?" says the LORD. "Look, as the clay is in the potter's hand, so are you in My hand, O house of Israel!" (Jer. 18:6).

You are like clay in the hands of the potter. The potter decides what shape he wants the clay to become, and then he molds and forms the clay into that shape. If he finds a flaw in the bowl he's making—he starts over. God, in His wisdom, has decided what shape our lives will take. He will mold us until we have become what He has envisioned. Did you know that you are just clay? Think about the job of clay—to rest in the potter's hands and to hold the shape he forms. If you sense that God is molding your life into one that pleases Him, then do the job of clay—rest in His hands and trust Him. The clay cannot argue with the potter. The potter's wisdom is greater and he ultimately decides on the shapes that please him. Trust God; He will lovingly mold you like a lump of clay. He will work out the flaws, and He may even start over, but the result will be pleasing to His eyes.

SEE FOR YOURSELF:
Is. 64:8; Rom. 9:20, 21

then I will relent concerning the good with which I said I would benefit it.

¹¹"Now therefore, speak to the men of Judah and to the inhabitants of Jerusalem, saying, 'Thus says the LORD: "Behold, I am fashioning a disaster and devising a plan against you. Return now every one from his evil way, and make your ways and your doings good." ' "

FUTURE
What's the future of someone who doesn't turn from sin? (18:11)

GOD'S WARNING REJECTED

¹²And they said, "That is hopeless! So we will walk according to our own plans, and we will every one obey the dictates of his evil heart."

¹³Therefore thus says the LORD:

" Ask now among the Gentiles,
   Who has heard such things?
   The virgin of Israel has done a very
      horrible thing.

14   Will *a man* leave the snow water of
          Lebanon,
     Which comes from the rock of the field?
     Will the cold flowing waters be forsaken
          for strange waters?

15   "Because My people have forgotten Me,
     They have burned incense to worthless
          idols.
     And they have caused themselves to
          stumble in their ways,
     From the ancient paths,
     To walk in pathways and not on a
          highway,
16   To make their land desolate *and* a
          perpetual hissing;
     Everyone who passes by it will be
          astonished
     And shake his head.
17   I will scatter them as with an east wind
          before the enemy;
     I will show them*ᵃ* the back and not the
          face
     In the day of their calamity."

JEREMIAH PERSECUTED

18Then they said, "Come and let us devise
plans against Jeremiah; for the law shall not
perish from the priest, nor counsel from the
wise, nor the word from the prophet. Come and
let us attack him with the tongue, and let us not
give heed to any of his words."

19   Give heed to me, O LORD,
     And listen to the voice of those who
          contend with me!
20   Shall evil be repaid for good?
     For they have dug a pit for my life.
     Remember that I stood before You
     To speak good for them,
     To turn away Your wrath from them.
21   Therefore deliver up their children to the
          famine,
     And pour out their *blood*
     By the force of the sword;
     Let their wives *become* widows
     And bereaved of their children.
     Let their men be put to death,
     Their young men *be* slain
     By the sword in battle.
22   Let a cry be heard from their houses,
     When You bring a troop suddenly upon
          them;
     For they have dug a pit to take me,
     And hidden snares for my feet.

23   Yet, LORD, You know all their counsel
     Which is against me, to slay *me*.
     Provide no atonement for their iniquity,
     Nor blot out their sin from Your sight;
     But let them be overthrown before You.
     Deal *thus* with them
     In the time of Your anger.

THE SIGN OF THE BROKEN FLASK

1Thus says the LORD: "Go and get a potter's
earthen flask, and *take* some of the elders of the
people and some of the elders of the priests.
2And go out to the Valley of the Son of Hinnom, which *is* by the entry of the Potsherd
Gate; and proclaim there the words that I will
tell you, 3and say, 'Hear the word of the LORD, O
kings of Judah and inhabitants of Jerusalem.
Thus says the LORD of hosts, the God of Israel:
"Behold, I will bring such a catastrophe on this
place, that whoever hears of it, his ears will tingle.

4"Because they have forsaken Me and made
this an alien place, because they have burned
incense in it to other gods whom neither they,
their fathers, nor the kings of Judah have
known, and have filled this place with the
blood of the innocents 5(they have also built
the high places of Baal, to burn their sons with
fire *for* burnt offerings to Baal, which I did not
command or speak, nor did it come into My
mind), 6therefore behold, the days are coming,"
says the LORD, "that this place shall no more be
called Tophet or the Valley of the Son of Hinnom, but the Valley of Slaughter. 7And I will
make void the counsel of Judah and Jerusalem
in this place, and I will cause them to fall by the
sword before their enemies and by the hands of
those who seek their lives; their corpses I will
give as meat for the birds of the heaven and for
the beasts of the earth. 8I will make this city desolate and a hissing; everyone who passes by it
will be astonished and hiss because of all its
plagues. 9And I will cause them to eat the flesh
of their sons and the flesh of their daughters,
and everyone shall eat the flesh of his friend in
the siege and in the desperation with which
their enemies and those who seek their lives
shall drive them to despair." '

10"Then you shall break the flask in the sight
of the men who go with you, 11and say to them,
'Thus says the LORD of hosts: "Even so I will
break this people and this city, as *one* breaks a
potter's vessel, which cannot be made whole
again; and they shall bury *them* in Tophet till
there is no place to bury. 12Thus I will do to this

18:17 *ᵃ*Following Septuagint, Syriac, Targum, and Vulgate; Masoretic Text reads *look them in.*

place," says the LORD, "and to its inhabitants, and make this city like Tophet. ¹³And the houses of Jerusalem and the houses of the kings of Judah shall be defiled like the place of Tophet, because of all the houses on whose roofs they have burned incense to all the host of heaven, and poured out drink offerings to other gods.' ' "

¹⁴Then Jeremiah came from Tophet, where the LORD had sent him to prophesy; and he stood in the court of the Lord's house and said to all the people, ¹⁵"Thus says the LORD of hosts, the God of Israel: 'Behold, I will bring on this city and on all her towns all the doom that I have pronounced against it, because they have stiffened their necks that they might not hear My words.' "

THE WORD OF GOD TO PASHHUR

¹Now Pashhur the son of Immer, the priest who *was* also chief governor in the house of the LORD, heard that Jeremiah prophesied these things. ²Then Pashhur struck Jeremiah the prophet, and put him in the stocks that *were* in the high gate of Benjamin, which *was* by the house of the LORD.

³And it happened on the next day that Pashhur brought Jeremiah out of the stocks. Then Jeremiah said to him, "The LORD has not called your name Pashhur, but Magor-Missabib.*ᵃ* ⁴For thus says the LORD: 'Behold, I will make you a terror to yourself and to all your friends; and they shall fall by the sword of their enemies, and your eyes shall see *it*. I will give all Judah into the hand of the king of Babylon, and he shall carry them captive to Babylon and slay them with the sword. ⁵Moreover I will deliver all the wealth of this city, all its produce, and all its precious things; all the treasures of the kings of Judah I will give into the hand of their enemies, who will plunder them, seize them, and carry them to Babylon. ⁶And you, Pashhur, and all who dwell in your house, shall go into captivity. You shall go to Babylon, and there you shall die, and be buried there, you and all your friends, to whom you have prophesied lies.' "

JEREMIAH'S UNPOPULAR MINISTRY

7   O LORD, You induced me, and I was
        persuaded;
    You are stronger than I, and have
        prevailed.
    I am in derision daily;
    Everyone mocks me.

8   For when I spoke, I cried out;
    I shouted, "Violence and plunder!"
    Because the word of the LORD was made
        to me
    A reproach and a derision daily.
9   Then I said, "I will not make mention of
        Him,
    Nor speak anymore in His name."
    But *His word* was in my heart like a
        burning fire
    Shut up in my bones;
    I was weary of holding *it* back,
    And I could not.
10 For I heard many mocking:
    "Fear on every side!"
    "Report," *they say,* "and we will report it!"
    All my acquaintances watched for my
        stumbling, *saying,*
    "Perhaps he can be induced;
    Then we will prevail against him,
    And we will take our revenge on him."

11 But the LORD *is* with me as a mighty,
        awesome One.
    Therefore my persecutors will stumble,
        and will not prevail.
    They will be greatly ashamed, for they
        will not prosper.
    Their everlasting confusion will never be
        forgotten.
12 But, O LORD of hosts,
    You who test the
        righteous,
    And see the mind and
        heart,
    Let me see Your
        vengeance on them;
    For I have pleaded my
        cause before You.

JUDGMENT

Does God judge motives? (20:12)

13 Sing to the LORD! Praise the LORD!
    For He has delivered the life of the poor
    From the hand of evildoers.

14 Cursed *be* the day in which I was born!
    Let the day not be blessed in which my
        mother bore me!
15 Let the man *be* cursed
    Who brought news to my father, saying,
    "A male child has been born to you!"
    Making him very glad.
16 And let that man be like the cities
    Which the LORD overthrew, and did not
        relent;
    Let him hear the cry in the morning

20:3 *ᵃ*Literally *Fear on Every Side*

¹⁸ Why did I come forth from the womb to
    see labor and sorrow,
    That my days should be consumed with
    shame?

On the Edge

*But, O Lord of hosts, You who
test the righteous, and see the
mind and heart (Jer. 20:12a).*

There is a huge difference between a
test and a temptation! God will never *tempt*
you with evil (James 1:13). However, you
will encounter testings from God. It works
sort of like school. Just like a teacher, God
will test you to help you see if you've truly
learned what He's been teaching you.

You are sitting in class, and you find out
your former best friend is going through a
tough time. His dad has run off with his
secretary, leaving your friend and his mom
to fend for themselves. Now, the reason he
is your former best friend is because you
found out he was spreading some false
rumors about you. What are you going to
do?

(a) Rejoice under your breath, thinking
he got what he deserved, while spreading
the news about what his dad has done all
around the school.

(b) Feel bad for him, but let him work
through this all on his own.

(c) Look past your own hurts and see a
friend who really needs somebody to encourage him through this situation with the
Word of God, as well as with plenty of love
and understanding.

If you answered "c," you passed the test!
If your answer was "a" or "b,"
you are probably going to have
to take the same test, or one just
like it, over again before long.
Pass the test the first time, and you
won't have to keep taking it. There's a big
difference between knowing what to do and
doing what you know! The difference is
between passing or failing. Get in God's
Word, find out what to do, and do the right
thing. Pass the test!

SEE FOR YOURSELF:
Ps. 7:9; 26:2; Jer. 17:10;
    James 1:12–15

JERUSALEM'S DOOM IS SEALED

¹The word which came to Jeremiah from the
LORD when King Zedekiah sent to him Pashhur
the son of Melchiah, and Zephaniah the son of
Maaseiah, the priest, saying, ²"Please inquire of
the LORD for us, for Nebuchadnezzar[a] king of
Babylon makes war against us. Perhaps the
LORD will deal with us according to all His
wonderful works, that *the king* may go away
from us."

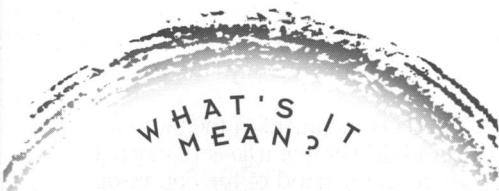

WHAT'S IT MEAN?

Nebuchadnezzar was a hero to the Babylonians
and an enemy to the Israelites. During his forty-year
reign as king of Babylon, Nebuchadnezzar extended the borders of
his country and collected heavy taxes from the people of Judah. When
King Hezekiah of Judah started refusing to pay taxes, Nebuchadnezzar and his forces attacked Jerusalem and held the city in siege until
586 B.C., when the people of Judah finally surrendered. Nebuchadnezzar then destroyed the temple and took many
Jews back to Babylon as prisoners.
Jeremiah 21:2

³Then Jeremiah said to them, "Thus you
shall say to Zedekiah, ⁴Thus says the LORD God
of Israel: "Behold, I will turn back the weapons
of war that *are* in your hands, with which you
fight against the king of Babylon and the
Chaldeans[a] who besiege you outside the walls;
and I will assemble them in the midst of this
city. ⁵I Myself will fight against you with an
outstretched hand and with a strong arm, even
in anger and fury and great wrath. ⁶I will strike
the inhabitants of this city, both man and beast;
they shall die of a great pestilence. ⁷And afterward," says the LORD, "I will deliver Zedekiah
king of Judah, his servants and the people, and
such as are left in this city from the pestilence
and the sword and the famine, into the hand of
Nebuchadnezzar king of Babylon, into the
hand of their enemies, and into the hand of
those who seek their life; and he shall strike

And the shouting at noon,
¹⁷ Because he did not kill me from the
    womb,
    That my mother might have been my
    grave,
    And her womb always enlarged *with me*.

21:2 [a]Hebrew *Nebuchadrezzar*, and so elsewhere   **21:4** [a]Or *Babylonians* them with the edge of the sword. He shall not spare them, or have pity or mercy." '

⁸"Now you shall say to this people, 'Thus says the LORD: "Behold, I set before you the way of life and the way of death. ⁹He who remains in this city shall die by the sword, by famine, and by pestilence; but he who goes out and defects to the Chaldeans who besiege you, he shall live, and his life shall be as a prize to him. ¹⁰For I have set My face against this city for adversity and not for good," says the LORD. "It shall be given into the hand of the king of Babylon, and he shall burn it with fire." '

MESSAGE TO THE HOUSE OF DAVID

¹¹"And concerning the house of the king of Judah, *say*, 'Hear the word of the LORD, ¹²O house of David! Thus says the LORD:

"Execute judgment in the morning;
And deliver *him who is* plundered
Out of the hand of the oppressor,
Lest My fury go forth like fire
And burn so that no one can quench *it*,
Because of the evil of your doings.

¹³ "Behold, I *am* against you, O inhabitant of
    the valley,
  And rock of the plain," says the LORD,
  "Who say, 'Who shall come down against us?
  Or who shall enter our dwellings?'
¹⁴ But I will punish you according to the
    fruit of your doings," says the LORD;
  "I will kindle a fire in its forest,
  And it shall devour all things around it." ' "

¹Thus says the LORD: "Go down to the house of the king of Judah, and there speak this word, ²and say, 'Hear the word of the LORD, O king of Judah, you who sit on the throne of David, you and your servants and your people who enter these gates! ³Thus says the LORD: "Execute judgment and righteousness, and deliver the plundered out of the hand of the oppressor. Do no wrong and do no violence to the stranger, the fatherless, or the widow, nor shed innocent blood in this place. ⁴For if you indeed do this thing, then shall enter the gates of this house, riding on horses and in chariots, accompanied by servants and people, kings who sit on the throne of David. ⁵But if you will not hear these words, I swear by Myself," says the LORD, "that this house shall become a desolation." ' "

⁶For thus says the LORD to the house of the king of Judah:

"You *are* Gilead to Me,
  The head of Lebanon;
  Yet I surely will make you a wilderness,
  Cities *which* are not inhabited.
⁷ I will prepare destroyers against you,
  Everyone with his weapons;
  They shall cut down your choice cedars
  And cast *them* into the fire.

⁸And many nations will pass by this city; and everyone will say to his neighbor, 'Why has the LORD done so to this great city?' ⁹Then they will answer, 'Because they have forsaken the covenant of the LORD their God, and worshiped other gods and served them.' "

¹⁰ Weep not for the dead, nor bemoan him;
  Weep bitterly for him who goes away,
  For he shall return no more,
  Nor see his native country.

MESSAGE TO THE SONS OF JOSIAH

¹¹For thus says the LORD concerning Shallum[a] the son of Josiah, king of Judah, who reigned instead of Josiah his father, who went from this place: "He shall not return here anymore, ¹²but he shall die in the place where they have led him captive, and shall see this land no more.

¹³ "Woe to him who builds his house by
    unrighteousness
  And his chambers by injustice,
  Who uses his neighbor's service without
    wages
  And gives him nothing for his work,
¹⁴ Who says, 'I will build myself a wide
    house with spacious chambers,
  And cut out windows for it,
  Paneling *it* with cedar
  And painting *it* with vermilion.'

¹⁵ "Shall you reign because you enclose
    yourself in cedar?
  Did not your father eat and drink,
  And do justice and righteousness?
  Then *it was* well with him.
¹⁶ He judged the cause of the poor and
    needy;
  Then *it was* well.
  Was not this knowing Me?" says the LORD.
¹⁷ "Yet your eyes and your heart *are* for
    nothing but your covetousness,
  For shedding innocent blood,
  And practicing oppression and violence."

22:11 *ᵃ*Also called *Jehoahaz*

[18]Therefore thus says the LORD concerning Jehoiakim the son of Josiah, king of Judah:

> "They shall not lament for him,
> *Saying,* 'Alas, my brother!' or 'Alas, my sister!'
> They shall not lament for him,
> *Saying,* 'Alas, master!' or 'Alas, his glory!'
> [19] He shall be buried with the burial of a donkey,
> Dragged and cast out beyond the gates of Jerusalem.

> [20] "Go up to Lebanon, and cry out,
> And lift up your voice in Bashan;
> Cry from Abarim,
> For all your lovers are destroyed.
> [21] I spoke to you in your prosperity,
> *But* you said, 'I will not hear.'
> This *has been* your manner from your youth,
> That you did not obey My voice.
> [22] The wind shall eat up all your rulers,
> And your lovers shall go into captivity;
> Surely then you will be ashamed and humiliated
> For all your wickedness.
> [23] O inhabitant of Lebanon,
> Making your nest in the cedars,
> How gracious will you be when pangs come upon you,
> Like the pain of a woman in labor?

MESSAGE TO CONIAH

[24]"*As I live,*" says the LORD, "though Coniah[a] the son of Jehoiakim, king of Judah, were the signet on My right hand, yet I would pluck you off; [25]and I will give you into the hand of those who seek your life, and into the hand *of those* whose face you fear—the hand of Nebuchadnezzar king of Babylon and the hand of the Chaldeans. [26]So I will cast you out, and your mother who bore you, into another country where you were not born; and there you shall die. [27]But to the land to which they desire to return, there they shall not return.

> [28] "Is this man Coniah a despised, broken idol—
> A vessel in which *is* no pleasure?
> Why are they cast out, he and his descendants,

> And cast into a land which they do not know?
> [29] O earth, earth, earth,
> Hear the word of the LORD!
> [30] Thus says the LORD:
> 'Write this man down as childless,
> A man *who* shall not prosper in his days;
> For none of his descendants shall prosper,
> Sitting on the throne of David,
> And ruling anymore in Judah.' "

THE BRANCH OF RIGHTEOUSNESS

[1]"Woe to the shepherds who destroy and scatter the sheep of My pasture!" says the LORD. [2]Therefore thus says the LORD God of Israel against the shepherds who feed My people: "You have scattered My flock, driven them away, and not attended to them. Behold, I will attend to you for the evil of your doings," says the LORD. [3]"But I will gather the remnant of My flock out of all countries where I have driven them, and bring them back to their folds; and they shall be fruitful and increase. [4]I will set up shepherds over them who will feed them; and they shall fear no more, nor be dismayed, nor shall they be lacking," says the LORD.

"A King shall reign and prosper, and execute judgment and righteousness in the earth."
(Jeremiah 23:5b)

> [5] "Behold, *the* days are coming," says the LORD,

"That I will raise to David a Branch of
    righteousness;
A King shall reign and prosper,
And execute judgment and righteousness
    in the earth.
6 In His days Judah will be saved,
    And Israel will dwell safely;
Now this *is* His name by which He will
    be called:

THE LORD OUR RIGHTEOUSNESS.*a*

7"Therefore, behold, *the* days are coming,"
says the LORD, "that they shall no longer say, 'As
the LORD lives who brought up the children of
Israel from the land of Egypt,' 8but, 'As the LORD
lives who brought up and led the descendants
of the house of Israel from the north country
and from all the countries where I had driven
them.' And they shall dwell in their own land."

FALSE PROPHETS AND EMPTY ORACLES

9 My heart within me is broken
    Because of the prophets;
    All my bones shake.
I am like a drunken man,
And like a man whom wine has
    overcome,
Because of the LORD,
And because of His holy words.
10 For the land is full of adulterers;
For because of a curse the land
    mourns.
The pleasant places of the wilderness are
    dried up.
Their course of life is evil,
And their might *is* not right.

11 "For both prophet and priest are profane;
Yes, in My house I have found their
    wickedness," says the LORD.
12 "Therefore their way shall be to them
Like slippery *ways;*
In the darkness they shall be driven on
And fall in them;
For I will bring disaster on them,
The year of their punishment," says the
    LORD.
13 "And I have seen folly in the prophets of
    Samaria:
They prophesied by Baal
And caused My people Israel to err.
14 Also I have seen a horrible thing in the
    prophets of Jerusalem:
They commit adultery and walk in lies;

They also strengthen the hands of
    evildoers,
So that no one turns back from his
    wickedness.
All of them are like Sodom to Me,
And her inhabitants like Gomorrah.

15"Therefore thus says the LORD of hosts
concerning the prophets:

'Behold, I will feed them with wormwood,
And make them drink the water of gall;
For from the prophets of Jerusalem
Profaneness has gone out into all the
    land.' "

16Thus says the LORD of hosts:

"Do not listen to the words
    of the prophets who
    prophesy to you.
They make you
    worthless;
They speak a vision of
    their own heart,
Not from the mouth of the
    LORD.

HOPE
When is our hope misplaced? (23:16)

17 They continually say to those who
    despise Me,
'The LORD has said, "You shall have
    peace" ';
And *to* everyone who walks according to
    the dictates of his own heart, they say,
'No evil shall come upon you.' "

18 For who has stood in the counsel of the
    LORD,
And has perceived and heard His word?
Who has marked His word and heard *it?*
19 Behold, a whirlwind of the LORD has gone
    forth in fury—
A violent whirlwind!
It will fall violently on the head of the
    wicked.
20 The anger of the LORD will not turn back
Until He has executed and performed the
    thoughts of His heart.
In the latter days you will understand it
    perfectly.

21 "I have not sent these prophets, yet they
    ran.
I have not spoken to them, yet they
    prophesied.
22 But if they had stood in My counsel,

And had caused My people to hear My
    words,
Then they would have turned them from
    their evil way
And from the evil of their doings.

23   "*Am* I a God near at hand," says the LORD,
    "And not a God afar off?
24   Can anyone hide himself in secret places,
    So I shall not see him?" says the LORD;
    "Do I not fill heaven and earth?" says the
    LORD.

25"I have heard what the prophets have said
who prophesy lies in My name, saying, 'I have
dreamed, I have dreamed!' 26How long will *this*
be in the heart of the prophets who prophesy
lies? Indeed *they are* prophets of the deceit of
their own heart, 27who try to make My people
forget My name by their dreams which everyone tells his neighbor, as their fathers forgot My
name for Baal.

28   "The prophet who has a dream, let him tell
    a dream;
    And he who has My word, let him speak
    My word faithfully.
    What *is* the chaff to the wheat?" says the
    LORD.
29   "*Is* not My word like a fire?" says the
    LORD,
    "And like a hammer *that* breaks the rock
    in pieces?

30"Therefore behold, I *am* against the prophets," says the LORD, "who steal My words every
one from his neighbor. 31Behold, I *am* against
the prophets," says the LORD, "who use their
tongues and say, 'He says.' 32Behold, I *am* against
those who prophesy false dreams," says the
LORD, "and tell them, and cause My people to
err by their lies and by their recklessness. Yet I
did not send them or command them; therefore
they shall not profit this people at all," says the
LORD.

33"So when these people or the prophet or
the priest ask you, saying, 'What is the oracle of
the LORD?' you shall then say to them, 'What
oracle?'*a* I will even forsake you," says the LORD.
34"And *as for* the prophet and the priest and the
people who say, 'The oracle of the LORD!' I will
even punish that man and his house. 35Thus
every one of you shall say to his neighbor, and
every one to his brother, 'What has the LORD
answered?' and, 'What has the LORD spoken?'

36And the oracle of the LORD you shall mention
no more. For every man's word will be his oracle, for you have perverted the words of the living God, the LORD of hosts, our God. 37Thus
you shall say to the prophet, 'What has the
LORD answered you?' and, 'What has the LORD
spoken?' 38But since you say, 'The oracle of the
LORD!' therefore thus says the LORD: 'Because
you say this word, "The oracle of the LORD!"
and I have sent to you, saying, "Do not say, 'The
oracle of the LORD!' " 39therefore behold, I, even
I, will utterly forget you and forsake you, and
the city that I gave you and your fathers, and
will cast you out of My presence. 40And I will
bring an everlasting reproach upon you, and a
perpetual shame, which shall not be forgotten.' "

THE SIGN OF TWO BASKETS OF FIGS

1The LORD showed me, and there were two
baskets of figs set before the temple of the LORD,
after Nebuchadnezzar king of Babylon had carried away captive Jeconiah the son of Jehoiakim, king of Judah, and the princes of Judah
with the craftsmen and smiths, from Jerusalem,
and had brought them to Babylon. 2One basket
had very good figs, like the figs *that are* first ripe;
and the other basket *had* very bad figs which
could not be eaten, they were so bad. 3Then the
LORD said to me, "What do you see, Jeremiah?"

And I said, "Figs, the good figs, very good;
and the bad, very bad, which cannot be eaten,
they are so bad."

4Again the word of the LORD came to me,
saying, 5"Thus says the LORD, the God of Israel:
'Like these good figs, so will I acknowledge
those who are carried away captive from Judah,
whom I have sent out of this place for *their own*
good, into the land of the Chaldeans. 6For I will
set My eyes on them for good, and I will bring
them back to this land; I will build them and
not pull *them* down, and I will plant them and
not pluck *them* up. 7Then I will give them a
heart to know Me, that I *am* the LORD; and they
shall be My people, and I will be their God, for
they shall return to Me with their whole heart.

8'And as the bad figs which cannot be eaten,
they are so bad'—surely thus says the LORD—
'so will I give up Zedekiah the king of Judah, his
princes, the residue of Jerusalem who remain in
this land, and those who dwell in the land of
Egypt. 9I will deliver them to trouble into all the
kingdoms of the earth, for *their harm, to be* a reproach and a byword, a taunt and a curse, in all
places where I shall drive them. 10And I will
send the sword, the famine, and the pestilence

23:33 *a*Septuagint, Targum, and Vulgate read *'You are the burden'.*

among them, till they are consumed from the land that I gave to them and their fathers.'"

SEVENTY YEARS OF DESOLATION

[1]The word that came to Jeremiah concerning all the people of Judah, in the fourth year of Jehoiakim the son of Josiah, king of Judah (which *was* the first year of Nebuchadnezzar king of Babylon), [2]which Jeremiah the prophet spoke to all the people of Judah and to all the inhabitants of Jerusalem, saying: [3]"From the thirteenth year of Josiah the son of Amon, king of Judah, even to this day, this *is* the twenty-third year in which the word of the LORD has come to me; and I have spoken to you, rising early and speaking, but you have not listened. [4]And the LORD has sent to you all His servants the prophets, rising early and sending *them*, but you have not listened nor inclined your ear to hear. [5]They said, 'Repent now everyone of his evil way and his evil doings, and dwell in the land that the LORD has given to you and your fathers forever and ever. [6]Do not go after other gods to serve them and worship them, and do not provoke Me to anger with the works of your hands; and I will not harm you.' [7]Yet you have not listened to Me," says the LORD, "that you might provoke Me to anger with the works of your hands to your own hurt.

[8]"Therefore thus says the LORD of hosts: 'Because you have not heard My words, [9]behold, I will send and take all the families of the north,' says the LORD, 'and Nebuchadnezzar the king of Babylon, My servant, and will bring them against this land, against its inhabitants, and against these nations all around, and will utterly destroy them, and make them an astonishment, a hissing, and perpetual desolations. [10]Moreover I will take from them the voice of mirth and the voice of gladness, the voice of the bridegroom and the voice of the bride, the sound of the millstones and the light of the lamp. [11]And this whole land shall be a desolation *and* an astonishment, and these nations shall serve the king of Babylon seventy years.

[12]'Then it will come to pass, when seventy years are completed, *that* I will punish the king of Babylon and that nation, the land of the Chaldeans, for their iniquity,' says the LORD; 'and I will make it a perpetual desolation. [13]So I will bring on that land all My words which I have pronounced against it, all that is written in this book, which Jeremiah has prophesied concerning all the nations. [14](For many nations and great kings shall be served by them also; and I

will repay them according to their deeds and according to the works of their own hands.)'"

JUDGMENT ON THE NATIONS

[15]For thus says the LORD God of Israel to me: "Take this wine cup of fury from My hand, and cause all the nations, to whom I send you, to drink it. [16]And they will drink and stagger and go mad because of the sword that I will send among them."

[17]Then I took the cup from the LORD's hand, and made all the nations drink, to whom the LORD had sent me: [18]Jerusalem and the cities of Judah, its kings and its princes, to make them a desolation, an astonishment, a hissing, and a curse, as *it is* this day; [19]Pharaoh king of Egypt, his servants, his princes, and all his people; [20]all the mixed multitude, all the kings of the land of Uz, all the kings of the land of the Philistines (namely, Ashkelon, Gaza, Ekron, and the remnant of Ashdod); [21]Edom, Moab, and the people of Ammon; [22]all the kings of Tyre, all the kings of Sidon, and the kings of the coastlands which *are* across the sea; [23]Dedan, Tema, Buz, and all *who are* in the farthest corners; [24]all the kings of Arabia and all the kings of the mixed multitude who dwell in the desert; [25]all the kings of Zimri, all the kings of Elam, and all the kings of the Medes; [26]all the kings of the north, far and near, one with another; and all the kingdoms of the world which *are* on the face of the earth. Also the king of Sheshach[a] shall drink after them.

[27]"Therefore you shall say to them, 'Thus says the LORD of hosts, the God of Israel: "Drink, be drunk, and vomit! Fall and rise no more, because of the sword which I will send among you." ' [28]And it shall be, if they refuse to take the cup from your hand to drink, then you shall say to them, 'Thus says the LORD of hosts: "You shall certainly drink! [29]For behold, I begin to bring calamity on the city which is called by My name, and should you be utterly unpunished? You shall not be unpunished, for I will call for a sword on all the inhabitants of the earth," says the LORD of hosts.'

[30]"Therefore prophesy against them all these words, and say to them:

'The LORD will roar from on high,
And utter His voice from His holy
   habitation;
He will roar mightily against His fold.
He will give a shout, as those who tread
   the grapes,

25:26 [a]A code word for Babylon (compare 51:41)

Against all the inhabitants of the earth.
31 A noise will come to the ends of the
earth—
For the LORD has a controversy with the
nations;
He will plead His case with all flesh.
He will give those *who are* wicked to the
sword,' says the LORD."

³²Thus says the LORD of hosts:

"Behold, disaster shall go forth
From nation to nation,
And a great whirlwind shall be raised up
From the farthest parts of the earth.

³³"And at that day the slain of the LORD shall be
from *one* end of the earth even to the *other* end
of the earth. They shall not be lamented, or
gathered, or buried; they shall become refuse
on the ground.

34 "Wail, shepherds, and cry!
Roll about *in the ashes,*
You leaders of the flock!
For the days of your slaughter and your
dispersions are fulfilled;
You shall fall like a precious vessel.
35 And the shepherds will have no way to
flee,
Nor the leaders of the flock to escape.
36 A voice of the cry of the shepherds,
And a wailing of the leaders to the flock
will be heard.
For the LORD has plundered their pasture,
37 And the peaceful dwellings are cut down
Because of the fierce anger of the LORD.
38 He has left His lair like the lion;
For their land is desolate
Because of the fierceness of the Oppressor,
And because of His fierce anger."

JEREMIAH SAVED FROM DEATH

¹In the beginning of the reign of Jehoiakim
the son of Josiah, king of Judah, this word came
from the LORD, saying, ²"Thus says the LORD:
'Stand in the court of the LORD's house, and
speak to all the cities of Judah, which come to
worship *in* the LORD's house, all the words that
I command you to speak to them. Do not diminish a word. ³Perhaps everyone will listen
and turn from his evil way, that I may relent
concerning the calamity which I purpose to
bring on them because of the evil of their doings.' ⁴And you shall say to them, 'Thus says the
LORD: "If you will not listen to Me, to walk in
My law which I have set before you, ⁵to heed

the words of My servants the prophets whom I
sent to you, both rising up early and sending
them (but you have not heeded), ⁶then I will
make this house like Shiloh, and will make this
city a curse to all the nations of the earth." ' "

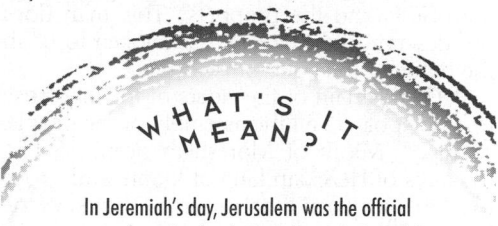

WHAT'S IT MEAN?

In Jeremiah's day, Jerusalem was the official
center of worship for the Jewish people. It hadn't
always been, though. When Joshua first led the Israelites into the
Promised Land, he set up the ark of the covenant and the tabernacle
in the city of Shiloh. Years later, the Philistines destroyed Shiloh and
left with the ark of the covenant. The ark was later recovered and
moved to Jerusalem, where King David established
the new center of Jewish worship.
Jeremiah 26:6

⁷So the priests and the prophets and all the
people heard Jeremiah speaking these words in
the house of the LORD. ⁸Now it happened,
when Jeremiah had made an end of speaking
all that the LORD had commanded *him* to speak
to all the people, that the priests and the prophets and all the people seized him, saying, "You
will surely die! ⁹Why have you prophesied in
the name of the LORD, saying, 'This house shall
be like Shiloh, and this city shall be desolate,
without an inhabitant'?" And all the people
were gathered against Jeremiah in the house of
the LORD.
¹⁰When the princes of Judah heard these
things, they came up from the king's house to
the house of the LORD and sat down in the entry of the New Gate of the LORD's *house.* ¹¹And
the priests and the prophets spoke to the
princes and all the people, saying, "This man
deserves to die! For he has prophesied against
this city, as you have heard with your ears."
¹²Then Jeremiah spoke to all the princes and
all the people, saying: "The LORD sent me to
prophesy against this house and against this
city with all the words that you have heard.
¹³Now therefore, amend your ways and your
doings, and obey the voice of the LORD your
God; then the LORD will relent concerning the
doom that He has pronounced against you.
¹⁴As for me, here I am, in your hand; do with
me as seems good and proper to you. ¹⁵But
know for certain that if you put me to death,

you will surely bring innocent blood on yourselves, on this city, and on its inhabitants; for truly the LORD has sent me to you to speak all these words in your hearing."

¹⁶So the princes and all the people said to the priests and the prophets, "This man does not deserve to die. For he has spoken to us in the name of the LORD our God."

¹⁷Then certain of the elders of the land rose up and spoke to all the assembly of the people, saying: ¹⁸"Micah of Moresheth prophesied in the days of Hezekiah king of Judah, and spoke to all the people of Judah, saying, 'Thus says the LORD of hosts:

"Zion shall be plowed *like* a field,
 Jerusalem shall become heaps of ruins,
 And the mountain of the temple^a
 Like the bare hills of the forest." '^b

¹⁹Did Hezekiah king of Judah and all Judah ever put him to death? Did he not fear the LORD and seek the LORD's favor? And the LORD relented concerning the doom which He had pronounced against them. But we are doing great evil against ourselves."

²⁰Now there was also a man who prophesied in the name of the LORD, Urijah the son of Shemaiah of Kirjath Jearim, who prophesied against this city and against this land according to all the words of Jeremiah. ²¹And when Jehoiakim the king, with all his mighty men and all the princes, heard his words, the king sought to put him to death; but when Urijah heard *it*, he was afraid and fled, and went to Egypt. ²²Then Jehoiakim the king sent men to Egypt: Elnathan the son of Achbor, and *other* men *who went* with him to Egypt. ²³And they brought Urijah from Egypt and brought him to Jehoiakim the king, who killed him with the sword and cast his dead body into the graves of the common people. ²⁴Nevertheless the hand of Ahikam the son of Shaphan was with Jeremiah, so that they should not give him into the hand of the people to put him to death.

FRIENDSHIP

Can standing up for a friend make a difference? (26:24)

SYMBOL OF THE BONDS AND YOKES

¹In the beginning of the reign of Jehoiakim^a the son of Josiah, king of Judah, this word came to Jeremiah from the LORD, saying,^b ²"Thus says the LORD to me: 'Make for yourselves bonds and yokes, and put them on your neck, ³and send them to the king of Edom, the king of Moab, the king of the Ammonites, the king of Tyre, and the king of Sidon, by the hand of the messengers who come to Jerusalem to Zedekiah king of Judah. ⁴And command them to say to their masters, "Thus says the LORD of hosts, the God of Israel—thus you shall say to your masters: ⁵'I have made the earth, the man and the beast that *are* on the ground, by My great power and by My outstretched arm, and have given it to whom it seemed proper to Me. ⁶And now I have given all these lands into the hand of Nebuchadnezzar the king of Babylon, My servant; and the beasts of the field I have also given him to serve him. ⁷So all nations shall serve him and his son and his son's son, until the time of his land comes; and then many nations and great kings shall make him serve them. ⁸And it shall be, *that* the nation and kingdom which will not serve Nebuchadnezzar the king of Babylon, and which will not put its neck under the yoke of the king of Babylon, that nation I will punish,' says the LORD, 'with the sword, the famine, and the pestilence, until I have consumed them by his hand. ⁹Therefore do not listen to your prophets, your diviners, your dreamers, your soothsayers, or your sorcerers, who speak to you, saying, "You shall not serve the king of Babylon." ¹⁰For they prophesy a lie to you, to remove you far from your land; and I will drive you out, and you will perish. ¹¹But the nations that bring their necks under the yoke of the king of Babylon and serve him, I will let them remain in their own land,' says the LORD, 'and they shall till it and dwell in it.' " '"

¹²I also spoke to Zedekiah king of Judah according to all these words, saying, "Bring your necks under the yoke of the king of Babylon, and serve him and his people, and live! ¹³Why will you die, you and your people, by the sword, by the famine, and by the pestilence, as the LORD has spoken against the nation that will not serve the king of Babylon? ¹⁴Therefore do not listen to the words of the prophets who speak to you, saying, 'You shall not serve the king of Babylon,' for they prophesy a lie to you; ¹⁵for I have not sent them," says the LORD, "yet they prophesy a lie in My name, that I may drive you out, and that you may perish, you and the prophets who prophesy to you."

¹⁶Also I spoke to the priests and to all this people, saying, "Thus says the LORD: 'Do not lis-

---

26:18 ^aLiterally *house* ^bCompare Micah 3:12   **27:1** ^aFollowing Masoretic Text, Targum, and Vulgate; some Hebrew manuscripts, Arabic, and Syriac read *Zedekiah* (compare 27:3, 12; 28:1). ^bSeptuagint omits verse 1.

ten to the words of your prophets who prophesy to you, saying, "Behold, the vessels of the LORD's house will now shortly be brought back from Babylon"; for they prophesy a lie to you. ¹⁷Do not listen to them; serve the king of Babylon, and live! Why should this city be laid waste? ¹⁸But if they *are* prophets, and if the word of the LORD is with them, let them now make intercession to the LORD of hosts, that the vessels which are left in the house of the LORD, *in* the house of the king of Judah, and at Jerusalem, do not go to Babylon.'

WHAT'S IT MEAN?

The Sea was an enormous bronze bowl created by Solomon. Fifteen feet in diameter and weighing more than ten tons, the bowl was used by priests for their cleansing rituals. Nebuchadnezzar's forces broke the bowl when they destroyed the temple in 586 B.C.
Jeremiah 27:19–21

¹⁹"For thus says the LORD of hosts concerning the pillars, concerning the Sea, concerning the carts, and concerning the remainder of the vessels that remain in this city, ²⁰which Nebuchadnezzar king of Babylon did not take, when he carried away captive Jeconiah the son of Jehoiakim, king of Judah, from Jerusalem to Babylon, and all the nobles of Judah and Jerusalem—²¹yes, thus says the LORD of hosts, the God of Israel, concerning the vessels that remain in the house of the LORD, and in the house of the king of Judah and of Jerusalem: ²²'They shall be carried to Babylon, and there they shall be until the day that I visit them,' says the LORD. 'Then I will bring them up and restore them to this place.'"

HANANIAH'S FALSEHOOD AND DOOM

¹And it happened in the same year, at the beginning of the reign of Zedekiah king of Judah, in the fourth year *and* in the fifth month, *that* Hananiah the son of Azur the prophet, who *was* from Gibeon, spoke to me in the house of the LORD in the presence of the priests and of all the people, saying, ²"Thus speaks the LORD of hosts, the God of Israel, saying: 'I have broken the yoke of the king of Babylon. ³Within

two full years I will bring back to this place all the vessels of the LORD's house, that Nebuchadnezzar king of Babylon took away from this place and carried to Babylon. ⁴And I will bring back to this place Jeconiah the son of Jehoiakim, king of Judah, with all the captives of Judah who went to Babylon,' says the LORD, 'for I will break the yoke of the king of Babylon.'"

⁵Then the prophet Jeremiah spoke to the prophet Hananiah in the presence of the priests and in the presence of all the people who stood in the house of the LORD, ⁶and the prophet Jeremiah said, "Amen! The LORD do so; the LORD perform your words which you have prophesied, to bring back the vessels of the LORD's house and all who were carried away captive, from Babylon to this place. ⁷Nevertheless hear now this word that I speak in your hearing and in the hearing of all the people: ⁸The prophets who have been before me and before you of old prophesied against many countries and great kingdoms—of war and disaster and pestilence. ⁹As for the prophet who prophesies of peace, when the word of the prophet comes to pass, the prophet will be known *as* one whom the LORD has truly sent."

¹⁰Then Hananiah the prophet took the yoke off the prophet Jeremiah's neck and broke it. ¹¹And Hananiah spoke in the presence of all the people, saying, "Thus says the LORD: 'Even so I will break the yoke of Nebuchadnezzar king of Babylon from the neck of all nations within the space of two full years.'" And the prophet Jeremiah went his way.

WHAT'S IT MEAN?

A yoke was a bar that rested on the neck of a work animal, such as an ox, a horse, or a cow. The wagon or plow that the animal was supposed to pull was then attached to the yoke. Most yokes were made of wood. An iron yoke obviously would be much heavier and harder to bear. Throughout the Bible, a yoke is used as a symbol of oppression or punishment.
Jeremiah 28:13, 14

¹²Now the word of the LORD came to Jeremiah, after Hananiah the prophet had broken the yoke from the neck of the prophet Jeremiah, saying, ¹³"Go and tell Hananiah, saying, 'Thus

says the LORD: "You have broken the yokes of wood, but you have made in their place yokes of iron." ¹⁴For thus says the LORD of hosts, the God of Israel: "I have put a yoke of iron on the neck of all these nations, that they may serve Nebuchadnezzar king of Babylon; and they shall serve him. I have given him the beasts of the field also." ' "

¹⁵Then the prophet Jeremiah said to Hananiah the prophet, "Hear now, Hananiah, the LORD has not sent you, but you make this people trust in a lie. ¹⁶Therefore thus says the LORD: 'Behold, I will cast you from the face of the earth. This year you shall die, because you have taught rebellion against the LORD.' "

¹⁷So Hananiah the prophet died the same year in the seventh month.

JEREMIAH'S LETTER TO THE CAPTIVES

¹Now these *are* the words of the letter that Jeremiah the prophet sent from Jerusalem to the remainder of the elders who were carried away captive—to the priests, the prophets, and all the people whom Nebuchadnezzar had carried away captive from Jerusalem to Babylon. ²(This happened after Jeconiah the king, the queen mother, the eunuchs, the princes of Judah and Jerusalem, the craftsmen, and the smiths had departed from Jerusalem.) ³*The letter was sent* by the hand of Elasah the son of Shaphan, and Gemariah the son of Hilkiah, whom Zedekiah king of Judah sent to Babylon, to Nebuchadnezzar king of Babylon, saying,

⁴ Thus says the LORD of hosts, the God of Israel, to all who were carried away captive, whom I have caused to be carried away from Jerusalem to Babylon:

⁵ Build houses and dwell *in them*; plant gardens and eat their fruit. ⁶Take wives and beget sons and daughters; and take wives for your sons and give your daughters to husbands, so that they may bear sons and daughters—that you may be increased there, and not diminished. ⁷And seek the peace of the city where I have caused you to be carried away captive, and pray to the LORD for it; for in its peace you will have peace. ⁸For thus says the LORD of hosts, the God of Israel: Do not let your prophets and your diviners who are

PRAYER

Why should I pray for people or places I don't like? (29:7)

in your midst deceive you, nor listen to your dreams which you cause to be dreamed. ⁹For they prophesy falsely to you in My name; I have not sent them, says the LORD.

¹⁰ For thus says the LORD: After seventy years are completed at Babylon, I will visit you and perform My good word toward you, and cause you to return to this place. ¹¹For I know the thoughts that I think toward you, says the LORD, thoughts of peace and not of evil, to give you a future and a hope. ¹²Then you will call upon Me and go and pray to Me, and I will listen to you. ¹³And you will seek Me and find *Me*, when you search for Me with all your heart. ¹⁴I will be found by you, says the LORD, and I will bring you back from your captivity; I will gather you from all the nations and from all the places where I have driven you, says the LORD, and I will bring you to the place from which I cause you to be carried away captive.

¹⁵ Because you have said, "The LORD has raised up prophets for us in Babylon"— ¹⁶therefore thus says the LORD concerning the king who sits on the throne of David, concerning all the people who dwell in this city, and concerning your brethren who have not gone out with you into captivity— ¹⁷thus says the LORD of hosts: Behold, I will send on them the sword, the famine, and the pestilence, and will make them like rotten figs that cannot be eaten, they are so bad. ¹⁸And I will pursue them with the sword, with famine, and with pestilence; and I will deliver them to trouble among all the kingdoms of the earth—to be a curse, an astonishment, a hissing, and a reproach among all the nations where I have driven them, ¹⁹because they have not heeded My words, says the LORD, which I sent to them by My servants the prophets, rising up early and sending *them*; neither would you heed, says the LORD. ²⁰Therefore hear the word of the LORD, all you of the captivity, whom I have sent from Jerusalem to Babylon.

²¹ Thus says the LORD of hosts, the God of Israel, concerning Ahab the son of Kolaiah, and Zedekiah the son of Maaseiah, who prophesy a lie to you in

My name: Behold, I will deliver them into the hand of Nebuchadnezzar king of Babylon, and he shall slay them before your eyes. ²²And because of them a curse shall be taken up by all the captivity of Judah who *are* in Babylon, saying, "The Lord make you like Zedekiah and Ahab, whom the king of Babylon roasted in the fire"; ²³because they have done disgraceful things in Israel, have committed adultery with their neighbors' wives, and have spoken lying words in My name, which I have not commanded them. Indeed I know, and *am* a witness, says the Lord.

24 You shall also speak to Shemaiah the Nehelamite, saying, ²⁵Thus speaks the Lord of hosts, the God of Israel, saying: You have sent letters in your name to all the people who *are* at Jerusalem, to Zephaniah the son of Maaseiah the priest, and to all the priests, saying, ²⁶"The Lord has made you priest instead of Jehoiada the priest, so that there should be officers *in* the house of the Lord over every man *who* is demented and considers himself a prophet, that you should put him in prison and in the stocks. ²⁷Now therefore, why have you not rebuked Jeremiah of Anathoth who makes himself a prophet to you? ²⁸For he has sent to us *in*

Babylon, saying, 'This *captivity is* long; build houses and dwell *in them*, and plant gardens and eat their fruit.' "

29 Now Zephaniah the priest read this letter in the hearing of Jeremiah the prophet. ³⁰Then the word of the Lord came to Jeremiah, saying: ³¹Send to all those in captivity, saying, Thus says the Lord concerning Shemaiah the Nehelamite: Because Shemaiah has prophesied to you, and I have not sent him, and he has caused you to trust in a lie—³²therefore thus says the Lord: Behold, I will punish Shemaiah the Nehelamite and his family: he shall not have anyone to dwell among this people, nor shall he see the good that I will do for My people, says the Lord, because he has taught rebellion against the Lord.

RESTORATION OF ISRAEL AND JUDAH

¹The word that came to Jeremiah from the Lord, saying, ²"Thus speaks the Lord God of Israel, saying: 'Write in a book for yourself all the words that I have spoken to you. ³For behold, the days are coming,' says the Lord, 'that I will bring back from captivity My people Israel and Judah,' says the Lord. 'And I will cause them to return to the land that I gave to their fathers, and they shall possess it.' "

Promise   HE PROMISES YOU A FUTURE OF HOPE.

For I know the thoughts that I think toward you, says the Lord, thoughts of peace and not of evil, to give you a future and a hope (Jer. 29:11).

A student's life can feel like a roller coaster ride—lots of ups and downs. Sometimes you're upside down in a tunnel, wondering which way is out. If you can hang on, the ride is incredible and is a time you'll look back on and smile at. But some students get stuck on the ride during a power failure. They're sitting in the tunnel wondering when they'll get out. Does anyone even know they're there? When will this ride be over? Life can get kind of dark sometimes. The downs seem to hang around too long, and the power is taking forever to come back on. Some students lose their hope in these scary places. Maybe they've never heard about God's promise to fill their future with hope. He promises to ride with you, restore power where there is none, and return order when things seem upside down and confusing. He promises that more good is ahead of you. There is everything to live for. Your future is bright and blessed because you belong to Him. Stand on His promise and look toward the future—dream great dreams, and hope against the odds. You have everything to look forward to.

SEE FOR YOURSELF:
Prov. 23:17, 18; 2 Thess. 2:16; 1 Tim. 1:1; 1 Pet. 1:3

WHAT'S IT MEAN?

Before books were created in the second
or third century A.D., documents were written on
an early form of paper called papyrus or on pieces of smooth, thin
leather. The pieces were then glued or sewn together to make a scroll.
Most ancient scrolls were about eight inches wide and about fifteen
to twenty feet long. Some were as long as thirty-five feet. To read a
scroll, a person held it with one hand and
unrolled it with the other.

Jeremiah 30:1, 2

⁴Now these *are* the words that the LORD
spoke concerning Israel and Judah.
⁵"For thus says the LORD:

'We have heard a voice of trembling,
Of fear, and not of peace.
6 Ask now, and see,
Whether a man is ever in labor with
child?
So why do I see every man *with* his
hands on his loins
Like a woman in labor,
And all faces turned pale?
7 Alas! For that day *is* great,
So that none *is* like it;
And it *is* the time of Jacob's trouble,
But he shall be saved out of it.

8 'For it shall come to pass in
that day,'
Says the LORD of hosts,
'*That* I will break his
yoke from your
neck,
And will burst your
bonds;
Foreigners shall no
more enslave them.
9 But they shall serve the
LORD their God,
And David their king,
Whom I will raise up for them.

10 "Therefore do not fear, O My servant
Jacob,' says the LORD,
'Nor be dismayed, O Israel;
For behold, I will save you from afar,

And your seed from the land of their
captivity.
Jacob shall return, have rest and be quiet,
And no one shall make *him* afraid.
11 For I *am* with you,' says the LORD, 'to save
you;
Though I make a full end of all nations
where I have scattered you,
Yet I will not make a complete end of
you.
But I will correct you in justice,
And will not let you go altogether
unpunished.'

12"For thus says the LORD:

'Your affliction *is* incurable,
Your wound *is* severe.
13 *There is* no one to plead your cause,
That you may be bound up;
You have no healing medicines.
14 All your lovers have forgotten you;
They do not seek you;
For I have wounded you with the wound
of an enemy,
With the chastisement of a cruel one,
For the multitude of your iniquities,
Because your sins have increased.
15 Why do you cry about your affliction?
Your sorrow *is* incurable.
Because of the multitude of your
iniquities,
Because your sins have increased,
I have done these things to you.

16 'Therefore all those who devour you shall
be devoured;
And all your
adversaries, every
one of them, shall
go into captivity;
Those who plunder
you shall become
plunder,
And all who prey
upon you I will
make a prey.
17 For I will restore health
to you
And heal you of your
wounds,' says the
LORD,
'Because they called you an outcast *saying*:
"This *is* Zion;
No one seeks her." '

18"Thus says the LORD:

> "But they shall serve
> the LORD their God, and
> David their king, whom I
> will raise up for them."
> (Jeremiah 30:9)

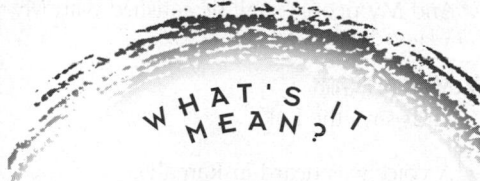

WHAT'S IT MEAN?

The people of Judah were held captive by the Babylonians for seventy years. Their captivity ended when Babylon was conquered by Persia. Cyrus, the king of Persia, allowed the Jewish people to return to their homeland and rebuild their temple.

Jeremiah 30:18

'Behold, I will bring back the captivity of
Jacob's tents,
And have mercy on his dwelling places;
The city shall be built upon its own
mound,
And the palace shall remain according to
its own plan.
19 Then out of them shall proceed
thanksgiving
And the voice of those who make merry;
I will multiply them, and they shall not
diminish;
I will also glorify them, and they shall not
be small.
20 Their children also shall be as before,
And their congregation shall be
established before Me;
And I will punish all who oppress them.
21 Their nobles shall be from among them,
And their governor shall come from their
midst;
Then I will cause him to draw near,
And he shall approach Me;
For who is this who pledged his heart to
approach Me?' says the LORD.
22 'You shall be My people,
And I will be your God.' "

23 Behold, the whirlwind of the LORD
Goes forth with fury,
A continuing whirlwind;
It will fall violently on the head of the
wicked.
24 The fierce anger of the LORD will not
return until He has done it,
And until He has performed the intents of
His heart.

In the latter days you will consider it.

THE REMNANT OF ISRAEL SAVED

1 "At the same time," says the LORD, "I will be the God of all the families of Israel, and they shall be My people."
2 Thus says the LORD:

"The people who survived the sword
Found grace in the wilderness—
Israel, when I went to give him rest."

3 The LORD has appeared of old to me,
saying:
"Yes, I have loved you with an everlasting
love;
Therefore with lovingkindness I have
drawn you.
4 Again I will build you, and you shall be
rebuilt,
O virgin of Israel!
You shall again be adorned with your
tambourines,
And shall go forth in the dances of those
who rejoice.
5 You shall yet plant vines on the
mountains of Samaria;
The planters shall plant and eat them as
ordinary food.
6 For there shall be a day
When the watchmen will cry on
Mount Ephraim,
'Arise, and let us go up to
Zion,
To the LORD our God.' "

FUTURE Is the future of Christians bright? (31:6)

7 For thus says the LORD:

"Sing with gladness for Jacob,
And shout among the chief of the
nations;
Proclaim, give praise, and say,
'O LORD, save Your people,
The remnant of Israel!'
8 Behold, I will bring them from the north
country,
And gather them from the ends of the
earth,
Among them the blind and the lame,
The woman with child
And the one who labors with child,
together;
A great throng shall return there.
9 They shall come with weeping,
And with supplications I will lead them.
I will cause them to walk by the rivers of
waters,
In a straight way in which they shall not
stumble;

For I am a Father to Israel,
And Ephraim *is* My firstborn.

10 "Hear the word of the LORD, O nations,
And declare *it* in the isles afar off, and
say,
'He who scattered Israel will gather him,
And keep him as a shepherd *does* his
flock.'
11 For the LORD has redeemed Jacob,
And ransomed him from the hand of one
stronger than he.
12 Therefore they shall come and sing in the
height of Zion,
Streaming to the goodness of the LORD—
For wheat and new wine and oil,
For the young of the flock and the herd;
Their souls shall be like a well-watered
garden,
And they shall sorrow no more at all.

13 "Then shall the virgin rejoice in the dance,
And the young men and the old, together;
For I will turn their mourning to joy,
Will comfort them,
And make them rejoice rather than
sorrow.
14 I will satiate the soul of the priests with
abundance,

And My people shall be satisfied with My
goodness, says the LORD."

MERCY ON EPHRAIM

15 Thus says the LORD:

"A voice was heard in Ramah,
Lamentation *and* bitter weeping,
Rachel weeping for her children,
Refusing to be comforted for her children,
Because they *are* no more."

16 Thus says the LORD:

"Refrain your voice from weeping,
And your eyes from tears;
For your work shall be rewarded, says
the LORD,
And they shall come back from the land
of the enemy.
17 There is hope in your future, says the
LORD,
That *your* children shall come back to
their own border.

18 "I have surely heard Ephraim bemoaning
himself:
'You have chastised me, and I was
chastised,

⋰ Promise   HE PROMISES TO TURN YOUR SORROW INTO JOY.

*Then shall the virgin rejoice in the dance, and the young men and the old, together;
for I will turn their mourning to joy, will comfort them, and make them rejoice rather
than sorrow (Jer. 31:13).*

God can use things that seem bad to make you glad. You may think you're doomed, but later
find out that God had a good purpose in the situation. Think about how you feel when you and
your dad have a disagreement and then you finally straighten things out. Or when you're about
to fail algebra, but you work really hard and pull your grade up to a B. You feel relieved and
happy when a bad situation comes to an end.

Sometimes there are habits or friendships you have to let go of because you know that God
doesn't approve. That can be tough. But there's satisfaction you get from obedience that replaces
that sad feeling after a while. God is on your side! He's for you! He wants to see you joyful,
healthy, and strong. He cares about you even more than you do! He is God, and He can do
anything. He's especially good at turning your hardest times into your greatest blessings.

Look at what He did for Joseph (see Gen. 37—50). Joseph's brothers sold him into slavery
and thought he'd probably live a miserably hard life. Instead, God made him a strong and
successful leader. His brothers even bowed down to him! What they had meant for bad, God
meant for good. Hard times will come. Hang in there with God and watch what He will do!

SEE FOR YOURSELF:
Gen. 50:20; Ps. 30:11, 12; Is. 61:3

JOSIAH made a difference

Among all the kings of Judah and Israel, including David and Solomon, God's Word gives a unique place to Josiah. "Now before him there was no king like him, who turned to the LORD with all his heart, with all his soul, and with all his might, according to all the Law of Moses; nor after him did any arise like him" (2 Kin. 23:25).

Josiah became king of Judah when he was eight years old. His wicked father had been assassinated. Scripture tells us little of Josiah's adolescence. If he had a royal hero, it was probably his godly great-grandfather Hezekiah. By the time Josiah reached his mid-twenties, he was anxious to make a difference in his nation for God. He organized the renovation of the temple in Jerusalem, which had been neglected. In the process, an even greater neglect was discovered. A scroll containing God's Law was delivered to the king. Confronted with the promises and warnings of God's Word, Josiah humbled himself before God. That attitude of responsiveness to God—of wanting to act wholeheartedly on any truthful information discovered about God—made Josiah stand out.

Cutting Edge

Under Josiah's leadership, there was a national revival of true worship. The king aggressively removed the evidences of paganism from the land. And he reinstituted the joyful celebration of Passover, remembering the faithfulness of God. Josiah made a difference because he demonstrated that even a king can live by the great commandment! (see Mark 12:28-34).

YOU can, too! What is your immediate response when you gain a new insight about God? Most of what we learn will change our view of God or our view of ourselves. Too often, young people will acknowledge that what they have learned about God is true, but they probably won't act on that truth until later in life. Can you hear yourself saying, "Sure, I know God wants my undivided commitment, and someday I plan to give Him that. But for now, I've got other plans . . ." Postponing or rejecting God's guidance will insure that your life will make the wrong kind of difference. Josiah didn't wait to turn his life over to God.

Want to know more? Josiah's reign is told twice in Scripture:
2 Kings 21:24—23:30; 2 Chronicles 33:25—35:27.
Jeremiah also mentions him in Jeremiah 1:1–3; 22:11, 18.

ESTHER made a difference

Young people often get frustrated over decisions made by others, which affect their lives. Esther would have understood. Most of the important decisions in her life—where to live, who would raise her, whom she would marry, how she would be treated—were all made by others. She grew up in a foreign land. Her parents died and she was raised by an uncle. She was picked for a beauty contest and found herself a queen. Even that position, surrounded by countless beautiful women, had little job security. That left her the most important decision of all: how she would respond to the situations in her life.

Esther didn't have to look for an opportunity to make a difference—it came looking for her. A man named Haman who hated Jewish people decided to wipe them out. He managed to convince the king that Jews were different and should be destroyed. Suddenly, Esther became the central figure in a life-and-death struggle. Her uncle reminded her, "Who knows whether you have come to the kingdom for such a time as this?"

Esther's courage and wisdom in making the most of her situation offer an inspiring example. She turned the tables on Haman and gave her people a fighting chance. She risked her life, but Haman paid for his hatred with his life. Esther did not choose the size or the shape of the biggest challenge in her life, but she did choose her response well. Her choice made a difference for her people.

Cutting Edge

YOU can, too! You very well may feel surrounded and crushed by the decisions others have made. You may be in a good place or a bad place where you don't want to be. Trouble may be knocking at your door. You can still make a difference! In fact, you will. How you respond and the choices you make will determine a lot of the future.

You may not know exactly what the future holds, but make your choices today deliberate ones. Choose to ask God for help. God does know what the future holds. Make decisions relying on Him. God can sort out what's happened and give you a way to go on. He will make a difference so you can make the right kind of difference with your life.

Want to know more? Esther's story carries her name in the Bible.

SHADRACH, MESHACH, AND ABED-NEGO made a difference

You can tell who your real friends are when the heat is on! Standing together with a couple of friends against a death threat takes both courage and confidence in one another. These three backed each other up and made a difference. Their boldness provided an opportunity for God to confront a king.

Shadrach, Meshach, and Abed-Nego spoke and lived as one. They were wise men in the service of king Nebuchadnezzar, but their higher allegiance was to God. Their work did not usually conflict with their faith. But those who hated them maneuvered the king into a prideful act— creating a huge statue, which everyone was required to worship. As expected, Shadrach, Meshach, and Abed-Nego refused. No insult to the king was intended. They simply refused to go along with the idea that Nebuchadnezzar was any kind of god.

Cutting Edge

Whenever individuals take a stand on principle, they can expect resistance. For our three heroes, it came in the form of a roaring furnace. The heat got turned up. Shadrach, Meshach, and Abed-Nego came up with one of the finest and boldest statements of faith recorded in Scripture: "Our God whom we serve is able to deliver us from the burning fiery furnace, and He will deliver us from your hand, O king. But if not, let it be known to you, O king, that we do not serve your gods, nor will we worship the gold image which you have set up" (Dan. 3:17, 18). They entrusted their lives to God and left the results in God's hands. They stood together—with God. God stood together with them in the furnace. Their faith made a difference. YOU can, too!

Furnaces come in many shapes and sizes. Often they are nothing more than the heat of public ridicule or rejection. We are tempted every day to avoid the elevated heat of conflict by compromising our faith as well as God's truth. When we learn God's truth and make it a point to practice faithfulness when the heat goes up, we will see that God can do amazing things in our lives, too. You won't always be able to pick your furnaces; be sure to pick some good friends who can stand with you and with God.

Want to know more? You can read about Shadrach, Meshach, and Abed-Nego's friendship and service to God in Daniel.

MARY THE MOTHER OF JESUS made a difference

We can learn a lot about ourselves and other people by the way we act when we're surprised. The unexpected doesn't give us time to pretend or to slip into our disguises. Fear, confidence, courage, and cowardice are frequently revealed by the sudden. We know little about the character of Mary the mother of Jesus other than what we see through her responses. It was through her responses that she made a difference.

An angel's visit ranks high on the list of the unexpected. Mary was startled. She listened to Gabriel. Her initial response was a single question of amazement, "How can this be, since I do not know a man?" (Luke 1:34). Mary knew how things worked. She was a child of a culture whose history was filled with women who gave birth with God's help. But husbands had always been involved. She didn't have one yet. So, how was this to come about?

Cutting Edge

Gabriel's instructions were very specific. Mary was not to do anything. God's Spirit would do it all. Again, we are not told what Mary thought or how she felt. We only know her servantlike response: "Let it be to me according to your word" (Luke 1:38). As soon as God let her know she didn't have to worry about the details, Mary left things in God's hands. That's how she made a difference. She participated and cooperated in God's wonderful plan. She didn't try to take control.

YOU can, too! One lesson you can take from Mary involves thinking about how you react to surprises. You may have to ask other people to help you see yourself. If you are responding well to the unexpected, congratulations! You are on track. You will probably find, though, that sometimes your responses will indicate an area in which you need to grow. Do you get angry, discouraged, doubtful, or completely confused by the unexpected? What do these responses tell you about your life?

Assume that God wants to make a difference in and through your life. Expect God to guide you. Consider that His guidance may come in surprising or unexpected ways. Are you training your responses?

Want to know more? Mary was part of the scene in all four Gospels. She takes center stage in Luke 1:26—2:52.

Like an untrained bull;
Restore me, and I will return,
For You *are* the LORD my God.
19 Surely, after my turning, I repented;
And after I was instructed, I struck myself
on the thigh;
I was ashamed, yes, even humiliated,
Because I bore the reproach of my youth.'
20 *Is* Ephraim My dear son?
Is he a pleasant child?
For though I spoke against him,
I earnestly remember him still;
Therefore My heart yearns for him;
I will surely have mercy on him, says the
LORD.

21 "Set up signposts,
Make landmarks;
Set your heart toward the highway,
The way in *which* you went.
Turn back, O virgin of Israel,
Turn back to these your cities.
22 How long will you gad about,
O you backsliding daughter?
For the LORD has created a new thing in
the earth—
A woman shall encompass a man."

FUTURE PROSPERITY OF JUDAH

23Thus says the LORD of hosts, the God of Israel: "They shall again use this speech in the land of Judah and in its cities, when I bring back their captivity: 'The LORD bless you, O home of justice, *and* mountain of holiness!' 24And there shall dwell in Judah itself, and in all its cities together, farmers and those going out with flocks. 25For I have satiated the weary soul, and I have replenished every sorrowful soul."

26After this I awoke and looked around, and my sleep was sweet to me.

27"Behold, the days are coming, says the LORD, that I will sow the house of Israel and the house of Judah with the seed of man and the seed of beast. 28And it shall come to pass, *that* as I have watched over them to pluck up, to break down, to throw down, to destroy, and to afflict, so I will watch over them to build and to plant, says the LORD. 29In those days they shall say no more:

'The fathers have eaten sour grapes,
And the children's teeth are set on edge.'

30But every one shall die for his own iniquity; every man who eats the sour grapes, his teeth shall be set on edge.

On the Edge

But this is the covenant that I will make with the house of Israel after those days, says the LORD: I will put My law in their minds, and write it on their hearts; and I will be their God, and they shall be My people (Jer. 31:33).

God made a covenant, or agreement, with the people of Israel after He miraculously rescued them from slavery in Egypt. Under the covenant, they had to perform a lot of rituals and make sacrifices in order to please Him. God said that He would bless them as long as they obeyed the laws He had given them. But they couldn't do it. They were constantly breaking their agreement with God.

God spoke to Jeremiah and asked him to tell the Jewish people that He (God) was going to make a new covenant with them. That new agreement was put in place when Jesus died on the cross as a one-time perfect sacrifice for everybody's sins. But this time the covenant wasn't just for Jews. Jesus specifically gave the apostle Paul the job of telling Gentiles, or non-Jews, about Him (see Acts 9:15). So whether you're Jewish or not, God's new agreement with His people is for you, too.

"I will put My law in their minds, and write it on their hearts." That's part of God's new covenant. This time, it has nothing to do with sacrifices or rituals. Instead, you just have to get your heart right with Jesus. Trust Jesus and obey Him with all of your heart.

SEE FOR YOURSELF:
Matt. 26:26–28;
Heb. 8:10; 12:24

A NEW COVENANT

31"Behold, the days are coming, says the LORD, when I will make a new covenant with the house of Israel and with the house of Judah—32not according to the covenant that I made with their fathers in the day *that* I took them by the hand to lead them out of the land of Egypt, My covenant which they broke, though I was a husband to them,[a] says the LORD. 33But this *is* the covenant that I will make

31:32 [a]Following Masoretic Text, Targum, and Vulgate; Septuagint and Syriac read *and I turned away from them.*

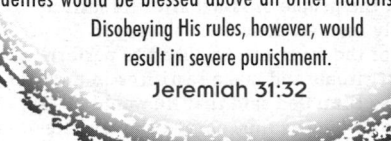

God made His agreement with the people of Israel shortly after He led them out of captivity in Egypt. On Mount Sinai, he gave Moses two pieces of stone. These stones contained specific instructions on Israel's part of the agreement. God spelled out in detail how the Israelites were supposed to live. In return for obeying God's rules for living, the Israelites would be blessed above all other nations on earth. Disobeying His rules, however, would result in severe punishment.

Jeremiah 31:32

with the house of Israel after those days, says the LORD: I will put My law in their minds, and write it on their hearts; and I will be their God, and they shall be My people. ³⁴No more shall every man teach his neighbor, and every man his brother, saying, 'Know the LORD,' for they all shall know Me, from the least of them to the greatest of them, says the LORD. For I will forgive their iniquity, and their sin I will remember no more."

³⁵ Thus says the LORD,
  Who gives the sun for a light by day,
  The ordinances of the moon and the stars
    for a light by night,
  Who disturbs the sea,
  And its waves roar
  (The LORD of hosts *is* His name):

³⁶ "If those ordinances depart
  From before Me, says the LORD,
  Then the seed of Israel shall also cease
  From being a nation before Me forever."

³⁷Thus says the LORD:

  "If heaven above can be measured,
  And the foundations of the earth
    searched out beneath,
  I will also cast off all the seed of Israel
  For all that they have done, says the LORD.

³⁸"Behold, the days are coming, says the LORD, that the city shall be built for the LORD from the Tower of Hananel to the Corner Gate. ³⁹The surveyor's line shall again extend straight forward over the hill Gareb; then it shall turn toward Goath. ⁴⁰And the whole valley of the dead bodies and of the ashes, and all the fields as far as the Brook Kidron, to the corner of the Horse Gate toward the east, *shall be* holy to the LORD. It shall not be plucked up or thrown down anymore forever."

JEREMIAH BUYS A FIELD

¹The word that came to Jeremiah from the LORD in the tenth year of Zedekiah king of Judah, which was the eighteenth year of Nebuchadnezzar. ²For then the king of Babylon's army besieged Jerusalem, and Jeremiah the prophet was shut up in the court of the prison, which *was in* the king of Judah's house. ³For Zedekiah king of Judah had shut him up, saying, "Why do you prophesy and say, 'Thus says the LORD: "Behold, I will give this city into the hand of the king of Babylon, and he shall take it; ⁴and Zedekiah king of Judah shall not escape from the hand of the Chaldeans, but shall surely be delivered into the hand of the king of Babylon, and shall speak with him face to face,ᵃ and see him eye to eye; ⁵then he shall lead Zedekiah to Babylon, and there he shall be until I visit him," says the LORD; "though you fight with the Chaldeans, you shall not succeed" '?"

⁶And Jeremiah said, "The word of the LORD came to me, saying, ⁷'Behold, Hanamel the son of Shallum your uncle will come to you, saying, "Buy my field which *is* in Anathoth, for the right of redemption *is* yours to buy *it.*" ' ⁸Then Hanamel my uncle's son came to me in the court of the prison according to the word of the LORD, and said to me, 'Please buy my field that *is* in Anathoth, which *is* in the country of Benjamin; for the right of inheritance *is* yours, and the redemption yours; buy *it* for yourself.' Then I knew that this was the word of the LORD. ⁹I bought the field from Hanamel, the son of my uncle who *was* in Anathoth, and weighed *out to* him the money—seventeen shekels of silver. ¹⁰And I signed the deed and sealed *it,* took witnesses, and weighed the money on the scales. ¹¹So I took the purchase deed, *both* that which was sealed *according* to the law and custom, and that which was open; ¹²and I gave the purchase deed to Baruch the son of Neriah, son of Mahseiah, in the presence of Hanamel my uncle's *son,* and in the presence of the witnesses who signed the purchase deed, before all the Jews who sat in the court of the prison.

32:4 ᵃLiterally *mouth to mouth*

¹³"Then I charged Baruch before them, saying, ¹⁴Thus says the LORD of hosts, the God of Israel: "Take these deeds, both this purchase deed which is sealed and this deed which is open, and put them in an earthen vessel, that they may last many days." ¹⁵For thus says the LORD of hosts, the God of Israel: "Houses and fields and vineyards shall be possessed again in this land." '

JEREMIAH PRAYS FOR UNDERSTANDING

¹⁶"Now when I had delivered the purchase deed to Baruch the son of Neriah, I prayed to the LORD, saying: ¹⁷Ah, Lord GOD! Behold, You have made the heavens and the earth by Your great power and outstretched arm. There is nothing too hard for You. ¹⁸*You* show lovingkindness to thousands, and repay the iniquity of the fathers into the bosom of their children after them—the Great, the Mighty God, whose name *is* the LORD of hosts. ¹⁹*You are* great in counsel and mighty in work, for Your eyes *are* open to all the ways of the sons of men, to give everyone according to his ways and according to the fruit of his doings. ²⁰You have set signs and wonders in the land of Egypt, to this day, and in Israel and among *other* men; and You have made Yourself a name, as it is this day. ²¹You have brought Your people Israel out of the land of Egypt with signs and wonders, with a strong hand and an outstretched arm, and with great terror; ²²You have given them this land, of which You swore to their fathers to give them—"a land flowing with milk and honey."*a* ²³And they came in and took possession of it, but they have not obeyed Your voice or walked in Your law. They have done nothing of all that You commanded them to do; therefore You have caused all this calamity to come upon them.

²⁴"Look, the siege mounds! They have come to the city to take it; and the city has been given into the hand of the Chaldeans who fight against it, because of the sword and famine and pestilence. What You have spoken has happened; there You see *it!* ²⁵And You have said to me, O Lord GOD, "Buy the field for money, and take witnesses"!—yet the city has been given into the hand of the Chaldeans.' "

GOD'S ASSURANCE OF THE PEOPLE'S RETURN

²⁶Then the word of the LORD came to Jeremiah, saying, ²⁷"Behold, I *am* the LORD, the God of all flesh. Is there anything too hard for Me? ²⁸Therefore thus says the LORD: 'Behold, I will give this city into the hand of the Chaldeans, into the hand of Nebuchadnezzar king of Babylon, and he shall take it. ²⁹And the Chaldeans who fight against this city shall come and set fire to this city and burn it, with the houses on whose roofs they have offered incense to Baal and poured out drink offerings to other gods, to provoke Me to anger; ³⁰because the children of Israel and the children of Judah have done only evil before Me from their youth. For the children of Israel have provoked Me only to anger with the work of their hands,' says the LORD. ³¹'For this city has been to Me *a provocation of* My anger and My fury from the day that they built it, even to this day; so I will remove it from before My face ³²because of all the evil of the children of Israel and the children of Judah, which they have done to provoke Me to anger—they, their kings, their princes, their priests, their prophets, the men of Judah, and the inhabitants of Jerusalem. ³³And they have turned to Me the back, and not the face; though I taught them, rising up early and teaching *them,* yet they have not listened to receive instruction. ³⁴But they set their abominations in the house which is called by My name, to defile it. ³⁵And they built the high places of Baal which *are* in the Valley of the Son of Hinnom, to cause their sons and their daughters to pass through *the fire* to Molech, which I did not command them, nor did it come into My mind that they should do this abomination, to cause Judah to sin.'

³⁶"Now therefore, thus says the LORD, the God of Israel, concerning this city of which you say, 'It shall be delivered into the hand of the king of Babylon by the sword, by the famine, and by the pestilence: ³⁷Behold, I will gather them out of all countries where I have driven them in My anger, in My fury, and in great wrath; I will bring them back to this place, and I will cause them to dwell safely. ³⁸They shall be My people, and I will be their God; ³⁹then I will give them one heart and one way, that they may fear Me forever, for the good of them and their children after them. ⁴⁰And I will make an everlasting covenant with them, that I will not turn away from doing them good; but I will put My fear in their hearts so that they will not depart from Me. ⁴¹Yes, I will rejoice over them to do them good, and I will assuredly plant them in this land, with all My heart and with all My soul.'

ASSURANCE

How long do God's promises last? (32:40, 41)

42"For thus says the LORD: 'Just as I have brought all this great calamity on this people, so I will bring on them all the good that I have promised them. 43And fields will be bought in this land of which you say, "It is desolate, without man or beast; it has been given into the hand of the Chaldeans." 44Men will buy fields for money, sign deeds and seal *them*, and take witnesses, in the land of Benjamin, in the places around Jerusalem, in the cities of Judah, in the cities of the mountains, in the cities of the lowland, and in the cities of the South; for I will cause their captives to return,' says the LORD."

EXCELLENCE OF THE RESTORED NATION

1Moreover the word of the LORD came to Jeremiah a second time, while he was still shut up in the court of the prison, saying, 2"Thus says the LORD who made it, the LORD who formed it to establish it (the LORD *is* His name): 3'Call to Me, and I will answer you, and show you great and mighty things, which you do not know.'

4"For thus says the LORD, the God of Israel, concerning the houses of this city and the houses of the kings of Judah, which have been pulled down *to fortify*a against the siege mounds and the sword: 5'They come to fight with the Chaldeans, but *only* to fill their places a with the dead bodies of men whom I will slay in My anger and My fury, all for whose wickedness I have hidden My face from this city. 6Behold, I will bring it health and healing; I will heal them and reveal to them the abundance of peace and truth. 7And I will cause the captives of Judah and the captives of Israel to return, and will rebuild those places as at the first. 8I will cleanse them from all their iniquity by which they have sinned against Me, and I will pardon all their iniquities by which they have sinned and by which they have transgressed against Me. 9Then it shall be to Me a name of joy, a praise, and an honor before all nations of the earth, who shall hear all the good that I do to them; they shall fear and tremble for all the goodness and all the prosperity that I provide for it.'

10"Thus says the LORD: 'Again there shall be heard in this place—of which you say, "It *is* desolate, without man and without beast"—in the cities of Judah, in the streets of Jerusalem that are desolate, without man and without inhabitant and without beast, 11the voice of joy

33:4 aCompare Isaiah 22:10　　**33:5** aCompare 2 Kings 23:14

Promise　HE PROMISES TO DO GOOD THINGS FOR YOU FOREVER.

They shall be My people, and I will be their God; then I will give them one heart and one way, that they may fear Me forever, for the good of them and their children after them. And I will make an everlasting covenant with them, that I will not turn away from doing them good; but I will put My fear in their hearts so that they will not depart from Me. Yes, I will rejoice over them to do them good, and I will assuredly plant them in this land, with all My heart and with all My soul (Jer. 32:38–41).

On this earth, the good stuff always runs out. Things we look forward to finally arrive and then they're over. You open your last birthday present. You have to go home from vacation. The lights have to come off of the Christmas tree. All the anticipation is over, the event has taken place, you've got memories and some snapshots.

Have you ever heard anyone say, "I can't help anymore. I'm worn out. I've done all I can do. I just don't have anything left to give"? Maybe they've run out of time or money or energy or enthusiasm. That's just life as a human. Our resources are limited. Our passions change.

But the Lord never gets to the end of His goodness or His ability to help. He promises to always do good things for you. He won't whine when you ask for His help or get worn out and need a break. He is at work in your most awesome days, doing what is best for you. He will be excited about you *forever*. And He'll be doing good things for you all the while.

SEE FOR YOURSELF:
Rom. 8:28

and the voice of gladness, the voice of the bridegroom and the voice of the bride, the voice of those who will say:

"Praise the LORD of hosts,
For the LORD *is* good,
For His mercy *endures* forever"—

and of those *who will* bring the sacrifice of praise into the house of the LORD. For I will cause the captives of the land to return as at the first', says the LORD.

¹²"Thus says the LORD of hosts: 'In this place which is desolate, without man and without beast, and in all its cities, there shall again be a dwelling place of shepherds causing *their* flocks to lie down. ¹³In the cities of the mountains, in the cities of the lowland, in the cities of the South, in the land of Benjamin, in the places around Jerusalem, and in the cities of Judah, the flocks shall again pass under the hands of him who counts *them*,' says the LORD.

> "Praise the LORD of hosts, for the LORD is good, for His mercy endures forever." (Jeremiah 33:11b)

¹⁴"Behold, the days are coming', says the LORD, 'that I will perform that good thing which I have promised to the house of Israel and to the house of Judah:

¹⁵ 'In those days and at that time
I will cause to grow up to David
A Branch of
    righteousness;
He shall execute
    judgment and
    righteousness in the
    earth.
¹⁶ In those days Judah
    will be saved,
And Jerusalem will
    dwell safely.
And this *is the name* by
    which she will be
    called:

THE LORD OUR RIGHTEOUSNESS.'ᵃ

¹⁷"For thus says the LORD: 'David shall never lack a man to sit on the throne of the house of Israel; ¹⁸nor shall the priests, the Levites, lack a

33:16 ᵃCompare 23:5, 6

Promise
HE PROMISES TO CLEANSE YOU FROM YOUR GUILT (INIQUITY).

I will cleanse them from all their iniquity by which they have sinned against Me, and I will pardon all their iniquities by which they have sinned and by which they have transgressed against Me (Jer. 33:8).

When Jeremiah gave God's message to the people of Israel, the whole country was seriously messed up. The people were doing some things that you would be shocked to hear about even in these days, and God was pretty mad about it. Jeremiah warned them that God was going to punish them, but they didn't change their ways. Jeremiah began to think they were pretty hopeless.

But God knew better. He knew that the people were not going to turn things around soon and that He would have to follow through with His punishment. But He also knew that after the people lived through all the terrible things that were going to happen, a lot of them would come to their senses. Then, in spite of all the awful things they had done, God said He would take their iniquities away.

That's God's promise to everyone who will come to his senses and turn to God. That's His promise to you—even if you think that what you've done is too horrible to mention. Jesus has declared you "not guilty." He's already taken your punishment. Turn around, face Him, repent, ask forgiveness, and He will take your guilt away.

SEE FOR YOURSELF:
Is. 43:25; Jer. 31:34; 1 John 1:9

man to offer burnt offerings before Me, to kindle grain offerings, and to sacrifice continually.' "

THE PERMANENCE OF GOD'S COVENANT

¹⁹And the word of the LORD came to Jeremiah, saying, ²⁰"Thus says the LORD: 'If you can break My covenant with the day and My covenant with the night, so that there will not be day and night in their season, ²¹then My covenant may also be broken with David My servant, so that he shall not have a son to reign on his throne, and with the Levites, the priests, My ministers. ²²As the host of heaven cannot be numbered, nor the sand of the sea measured, so will I multiply the descendants of David My servant and the Levites who minister to Me.' "

²³Moreover the word of the LORD came to Jeremiah, saying, ²⁴"Have you not considered what these people have spoken, saying, 'The two families which the LORD has chosen, He has also cast them off'? Thus they have despised My people, as if they should no more be a nation before them.

²⁵"Thus says the LORD: 'If My covenant *is* not with day and night, *and if* I have not appointed the ordinances of heaven and earth, ²⁶then I will cast away the descendants of Jacob and David My servant, *so* that I will not take *any* of his descendants *to be* rulers over the descendants of Abraham, Isaac, and Jacob. For I will cause their captives to return, and will have mercy on them.' "

ZEDEKIAH WARNED BY GOD

¹The word which came to Jeremiah from the LORD, when Nebuchadnezzar king of Babylon and all his army, all the kingdoms of the earth under his dominion, and all the people, fought against Jerusalem and all its cities, saying, ²"Thus says the LORD, the God of Israel: 'Go and speak to Zedekiah king of Judah and tell him, "Thus says the LORD: 'Behold, I will give this city into the hand of the king of Babylon, and he shall burn it with fire. ³And you shall not escape from his hand, but shall surely be taken and delivered into his hand; your eyes shall see the eyes of the king of Babylon, he shall speak with you face to face,ᵃ and you shall go to Babylon.' " ' ⁴Yet hear the word of the LORD, O Zedekiah king of Judah! Thus says the LORD concerning you: 'You shall not die by the sword. ⁵You shall die in peace; as in the ceremonies of your fathers, the former kings who were before you, so they shall burn incense for you and lament for you, *saying,* "Alas, lord!"

For I have pronounced the word, says the LORD.' "

⁶Then Jeremiah the prophet spoke all these words to Zedekiah king of Judah in Jerusalem, ⁷when the king of Babylon's army fought against Jerusalem and all the cities of Judah that were left, against Lachish and Azekah; for *only* these fortified cities remained of the cities of Judah.

TREACHEROUS TREATMENT OF SLAVES

⁸*This is* the word that came to Jeremiah from the LORD, after King Zedekiah had made a covenant with all the people who *were* at Jerusalem to proclaim liberty to them: ⁹that every man should set free his male and female slave—a Hebrew man or woman—that no one should keep a Jewish brother in bondage. ¹⁰Now when all the princes and all the people, who had entered into the covenant, heard that everyone should set free his male and female slaves, that no one should keep them in bondage anymore, they obeyed and let *them* go. ¹¹But afterward they changed their minds and made the male and female slaves return, whom they had set free, and brought them into subjection as male and female slaves.

¹²Therefore the word of the LORD came to Jeremiah from the LORD, saying, ¹³"Thus says the LORD, the God of Israel: 'I made a covenant with your fathers in the day that I brought them out of the land of Egypt, out of the house of bondage, saying, ¹⁴"At the end of seven years let every man set free his Hebrew brother, who has been sold to him; and when he has served you six years, you shall let him go free from you." But your fathers did not obey Me nor incline their ear. ¹⁵Then you recently turned and did what was right in My sight—every man proclaiming liberty to his neighbor; and you made a covenant before Me in the house which is called by My name. ¹⁶Then you turned around and profaned My name, and every one of you brought back his male and female slaves, whom he had set at liberty, at their pleasure, and brought them back into subjection, to be your male and female slaves.'

¹⁷"Therefore thus says the LORD: 'You have not obeyed Me in proclaiming liberty, every one to his brother and every one to his neighbor. Behold, I proclaim liberty to you,' says the LORD—'to the sword, to pestilence, and to famine! And I will deliver you to trouble among all the kingdoms of the earth. ¹⁸And I will give the men who have transgressed My covenant, who

---

34:3 ᵃLiterally *mouth to mouth*

have not performed the words of the covenant which they made before Me, when they cut the calf in two and passed between the parts of it— [19]the princes of Judah, the princes of Jerusalem, the eunuchs, the priests, and all the people of the land who passed between the parts of the calf— [20]I will give them into the hand of their enemies and into the hand of those who seek their life. Their dead bodies shall be for meat for the birds of the heaven and the beasts of the earth. [21]And I will give Zedekiah king of Judah and his princes into the hand of their enemies, into the hand of those who seek their life, and into the hand of the king of Babylon's army which has gone back from you. [22]Behold, I will command,' says the LORD, 'and cause them to return to this city. They will fight against it and take it and burn it with fire; and I will make the cities of Judah a desolation without inhabitant.' "

WHAT'S IT MEAN?

You may be wondering why the two parties of the covenant cut the animal in half. It was to demonstrate what would happen to the party that broke the covenant.
Jeremiah 34:18

THE OBEDIENT RECHABITES

[1]The word which came to Jeremiah from the LORD in the days of Jehoiakim the son of Josiah, king of Judah, saying, [2]"Go to the house of the Rechabites, speak to them, and bring them into the house of the LORD, into one of the chambers, and give them wine to drink."

[3]Then I took Jaazaniah the son of Jeremiah, the son of Habazziniah, his brothers and all his sons, and the whole house of the Rechabites, [4]and I brought them into the house of the LORD, into the chamber of the sons of Hanan the son of Igdaliah, a man of God, which *was* by the chamber of the princes, above the chamber of Maaseiah the son of Shallum, the keeper of the door. [5]Then I set before the sons of the house of the Rechabites bowls full of wine, and cups; and I said to them, "Drink wine."

[6]But they said, "We will drink no wine, for Jonadab the son of Rechab, our father, com-

WHAT'S IT MEAN?

The people of the ancient Near East liked their wine—a lot. More specifically, they liked a lot of wine. The Rechabites were the exception. These nomads refused to drink wine or participate in the corrupt lifestyle of the people around them.
Jeremiah 35:2

manded us, saying, 'You shall drink no wine, you nor your sons, forever. [7]You shall not build a house, sow seed, plant a vineyard, nor have *any of these;* but all your days you shall dwell in tents, that you may live many days in the land where you are sojourners.' [8]Thus we have obeyed the voice of Jonadab the son of Rechab, our father, in all that he charged us, to drink no wine all our days, we, our wives, our sons, or our daughters, [9]nor to build ourselves houses to dwell in; nor do we have vineyard, field, or seed. [10]But we have dwelt in tents, and have obeyed and done according to all that Jonadab our father commanded us. [11]But it came to pass, when Nebuchadnezzar king of Babylon came up into the land, that we said, 'Come, let us go to Jerusalem for fear of the army of the Chaldeans and for fear of the army of the Syrians.' So we dwell at Jerusalem."

[12]Then came the word of the LORD to Jeremiah, saying, [13]"Thus says the LORD of hosts, the God of Israel: 'Go and tell the men of Judah and the inhabitants of Jerusalem, "Will you not receive instruction to obey My words?" says the LORD. [14]"The words of Jonadab the son of Rechab, which he commanded his sons, not to drink wine, are performed; for to this day they drink none, and obey their father's commandment. But although I have spoken to you, rising early and speaking, you did not obey Me. [15]I have also sent to you all My servants the prophets, rising up early and sending *them,* saying, 'Turn now everyone from his evil way, amend your doings, and do not go after other gods to serve them; then you will dwell in the land which I have given you and your fathers.' But you have not inclined your ear, nor obeyed Me. [16]Surely the sons of Jonadab the son of Rechab have performed the commandment of

their father, which he commanded them, but this people has not obeyed Me.' '

[17]"Therefore thus says the LORD God of hosts, the God of Israel: 'Behold, I will bring on Judah and on all the inhabitants of Jerusalem all the doom that I have pronounced against them; because I have spoken to them but they have not heard, and I have called to them but they have not answered.' "

[18]And Jeremiah said to the house of the Rechabites, "Thus says the LORD of hosts, the God of Israel: 'Because you have obeyed the commandment of Jonadab your father, and kept all his precepts and done according to all that he commanded you, [19]therefore thus says the LORD of hosts, the God of Israel: "Jonadab the son of Rechab shall not lack a man to stand before Me forever." ' "

THE SCROLL READ IN THE TEMPLE

[1]Now it came to pass in the fourth year of Jehoiakim the son of Josiah, king of Judah, *that* this word came to Jeremiah from the LORD, saying: [2]"Take a scroll of a book and write on it all the words that I have spoken to you against Israel, against Judah, and against all the nations, from the day I spoke to you, from the days of Josiah even to this day. [3]It may be that the house of Judah will hear all the adversities which I purpose to bring upon them, that everyone may turn from his evil way, that I may forgive their iniquity and their sin."

[4]Then Jeremiah called Baruch the son of Neriah; and Baruch wrote on a scroll of a book, at the instruction of Jeremiah,[a] all the words of the LORD which He had spoken to him. [5]And Jeremiah commanded Baruch, saying, "I *am* confined, I cannot go into the house of the LORD. [6]You go, therefore, and read from the scroll which you have written at my instruction,[a] the words of the LORD, in the hearing of the people in the LORD's house on the day of fasting. And you shall also read them in the hearing of all Judah who come from their cities. [7]It may be that they will present their supplication before the LORD, and everyone will turn from his evil way. For great *is* the anger and the fury that the LORD has pronounced against this people." [8]And Baruch the son of Neriah did according to all that Jeremiah the prophet commanded him, reading from the book the words of the LORD in the LORD's house.

[9]Now it came to pass in the fifth year of Jehoiakim the son of Josiah, king of Judah, in the ninth month, *that* they proclaimed a fast before the LORD to all the people in Jerusalem, and to all the people who came from the cities of Judah to Jerusalem. [10]Then Baruch read from the book the words of Jeremiah in the house of the LORD, in the chamber of Gemariah the son of Shaphan the scribe, in the upper court at the entry of the New Gate of the LORD's house, in the hearing of all the people.

THE SCROLL READ IN THE PALACE

[11]When Michaiah the son of Gemariah, the son of Shaphan, heard all the words of the LORD from the book, [12]he then went down to the king's house, into the scribe's chamber; and there all the princes were sitting—Elishama the scribe, Delaiah the son of Shemaiah, Elnathan the son of Achbor, Gemariah the son of Shaphan, Zedekiah the son of Hananiah, and all the princes. [13]Then Michaiah declared to them all the words that he had heard when Baruch read the book in the hearing of the people. [14]Therefore all the princes sent Jehudi the son of Nethaniah, the son of Shelemiah, the son of Cushi, to Baruch, saying, "Take in your hand the scroll from which you have read in the hearing of the people, and come." So Baruch the son of Neriah took the scroll in his hand and came to them. [15]And they said to him, "Sit down now, and read it in our hearing." So Baruch read *it* in their hearing.

[16]Now it happened, when they had heard all the words, that they looked in fear from one to another, and said to Baruch, "We will surely tell the king of all these words." [17]And they asked Baruch, saying, "Tell us now, how did you write all these words—at his instruction?"[a]

[18]So Baruch answered them, "He proclaimed with his mouth all these words to me, and I wrote *them* with ink in the book."

[19]Then the princes said to Baruch, "Go and hide, you and Jeremiah; and let no one know where you are."

THE KING DESTROYS JEREMIAH'S SCROLL

[20]And they went to the king, into the court; but they stored the scroll in the chamber of Elishama the scribe, and told all the words in the hearing of the king. [21]So the king sent Jehudi to bring the scroll, and he took it from Elishama the scribe's chamber. And Jehudi read it in the hearing of the king and in the hearing of all the princes who stood beside the king. [22]Now the king was sitting in the winter house in the ninth month, with *a fire* burning on the hearth before him. [23]And it happened, when Jehudi had read

---

36:4 [a]Literally *from Jeremiah's mouth*   **36:6** [a]Literally *from my mouth*   **36:17** [a]Literally *with his mouth*

three or four columns, *that the king* cut it with the scribe's knife and cast *it* into the fire that *was* on the hearth, until all the scroll was consumed in the fire that *was* on the hearth. ²⁴Yet they were not afraid, nor did they tear their garments, the king nor any of his servants who heard all these words. ²⁵Nevertheless Elnathan, Delaiah, and Gemariah implored the king not to burn the scroll; but he would not listen to them. ²⁶And the king commanded Jerahmeel the king's*ᵃ* son, Seraiah the son of Azriel, and Shelemiah the son of Abdeel, to seize Baruch the scribe and Jeremiah the prophet, but the LORD hid them.

WHAT'S IT MEAN?

You may be surprised to learn that Jerusalem has its share of cold spells in the winter—and even receives occasional snow. In ancient Judah, people who lived in two-story homes usually stayed on the first floor in the winter, then moved to the better-ventilated second floor in the summer.

Jeremiah 36:20–22

JEREMIAH REWRITES THE SCROLL

²⁷Now after the king had burned the scroll with the words which Baruch had written at the instruction of Jeremiah,*ᵃ* the word of the LORD came to Jeremiah, saying: ²⁸Take yet another scroll, and write on it all the former words that were in the first scroll which Jehoiakim the king of Judah has burned. ²⁹And you shall say to Jehoiakim king of Judah, 'Thus says the LORD: "You have burned this scroll, saying, 'Why have you written in it that the king of Babylon will certainly come and destroy this land, and cause man and beast to cease from here?' " ³⁰Therefore thus says the LORD concerning Jehoiakim king of Judah: "He shall have no one to sit on the throne of David, and his dead body shall be cast out to the heat of the day and the frost of the night. ³¹I will punish him, his family, and his servants for their iniquity; and I will bring on them, on the inhabitants of Jerusalem, and on the men of Judah all

the doom that I have pronounced against them; but they did not heed." ' "

³²Then Jeremiah took another scroll and gave it to Baruch the scribe, the son of Neriah, who wrote on it at the instruction of Jeremiah*ᵃ* all the words of the book which Jehoiakim king of Judah had burned in the fire. And besides, there were added to them many similar words.

ZEDEKIAH'S VAIN HOPE

¹Now King Zedekiah the son of Josiah reigned instead of Coniah the son of Jehoiakim, whom Nebuchadnezzar king of Babylon made king in the land of Judah. ²But neither he nor his servants nor the people of the land gave heed to the words of the LORD which He spoke by the prophet Jeremiah.

³And Zedekiah the king sent Jehucal the son of Shelemiah, and Zephaniah the son of Maaseiah, the priest, to the prophet Jeremiah, saying, "Pray now to the LORD our God for us." ⁴Now Jeremiah was coming and going among the people, for they had not *yet* put him in prison. ⁵Then Pharaoh's army came up from Egypt; and when the Chaldeans who were besieging Jerusalem heard news of them, they departed from Jerusalem.

⁶Then the word of the LORD came to the prophet Jeremiah, saying, ⁷"Thus says the LORD, the God of Israel, 'Thus you shall say to the king of Judah, who sent you to Me to inquire of Me: "Behold, Pharaoh's army which has come up to help you will return to Egypt, to their own land. ⁸And the Chaldeans shall come back and fight against this city, and take it and burn it with fire." ' ⁹Thus says the LORD: 'Do not deceive yourselves, saying, "The Chaldeans will surely depart from us," for they will not depart. ¹⁰For though you had defeated the whole army of the Chaldeans who fight against you, and there remained *only* wounded men among them, they would rise up, every man in his tent, and burn the city with fire.' "

JEREMIAH IMPRISONED

¹¹And it happened, when the army of the Chaldeans left *the siege* of Jerusalem for fear of Pharaoh's army, ¹²that Jeremiah went out of Jerusalem to go into the land of Benjamin to claim his property there among the people. ¹³And when he was in the Gate of Benjamin, a captain of the guard *was* there whose name *was* Irijah the son of Shelemiah, the son of Hananiah;

36:26 *ᵃ*Hebrew *Hammelech*   **36:27** *ᵃ*Literally *from Jeremiah's mouth*   **36:32** *ᵃ*Literally *from Jeremiah's mouth* and he seized Jeremiah the prophet, saying, "You are defecting to the Chaldeans!"

[14]Then Jeremiah said, "False! I am not defecting to the Chaldeans." But he did not listen to him.

So Irijah seized Jeremiah and brought him to the princes. [15]Therefore the princes were angry with Jeremiah, and they struck him and put him in prison in the house of Jonathan the scribe. For they had made that the prison.

[16]When Jeremiah entered the dungeon and the cells, and Jeremiah had remained there many days, [17]then Zedekiah the king sent and took him out. The king asked him secretly in his house, and said, "Is there any word from the LORD?"

And Jeremiah said, "There is." Then he said, "You shall be delivered into the hand of the king of Babylon!"

[18]Moreover Jeremiah said to King Zedekiah, "What offense have I committed against you, against your servants, or against this people, that you have put me in prison? [19]Where now are your prophets who prophesied to you, saying, 'The king of Babylon will not come against you or against this land?' [20]Therefore please hear now, O my lord the king. Please, let my petition be accepted before you, and do not make me return to the house of Jonathan the scribe, lest I die there."

[21]Then Zedekiah the king commanded that they should commit Jeremiah to the court of the prison, and that they should give him daily a piece of bread from the bakers' street, until all the bread in the city was gone. Thus Jeremiah remained in the court of the prison.

JEREMIAH IN THE DUNGEON

[1]Now Shephatiah the son of Mattan, Gedaliah the son of Pashhur, Jucal[a] the son of Shelemiah, and Pashhur the son of Malchiah heard the words that Jeremiah had spoken to all the people, saying, [2]"Thus says the LORD: 'He who remains in this city shall die by the sword, by famine, and by pestilence; but he who goes over to the Chaldeans shall live; his life shall be as a prize to him, and he shall live.'[a] [3]Thus says the LORD: 'This city shall surely be given into the hand of the king of Babylon's army, which shall take it.' "

[4]Therefore the princes said to the king, "Please, let this man be put to death, for thus he weakens the hands of the men of war who remain in this city, and the hands of all the people, by speaking such words to them. For this man does not seek the welfare of this people, but their harm."

[5]Then Zedekiah the king said, "Look, he is in your hand. For the king can do nothing against you." [6]So they took Jeremiah and cast him into the dungeon of Malchiah the king's[a] son, which was in the court of the prison, and they let Jeremiah down with ropes. And in the dungeon there was no water, but mire. So Jeremiah sank in the mire.

WHAT'S IT MEAN?

Malchiah's dungeon was actually a cistern. Palestine doesn't get much rain in the summer months. That's why wells and cisterns were so valuable to the people. Cisterns collected water during the rainy winter season and stored it for use in summer. Wells, on the other hand, got their water from underground sources. Many ancient wells were extremely deep. Jacob's Well, which still exists today, is seventy-five feet deep.
Jeremiah 38:6

[7]Now Ebed-Melech the Ethiopian, one of the eunuchs, who was in the king's house, heard that they had put Jeremiah in the dungeon. When the king was sitting at the Gate of Benjamin, [8]Ebed-Melech went out of the king's house and spoke to the king, saying: [9]"My lord the king, these men have done evil in all that they have done to Jeremiah the prophet, whom they have cast into the dungeon, and he is likely to die from hunger in the place where he is. For there is no more bread in the city." [10]Then the king commanded Ebed-Melech the Ethiopian, saying, "Take from here thirty men with you, and lift Jeremiah the prophet out of the dungeon before he dies." [11]So Ebed-Melech took the men with him and went into the house of the king under the treasury, and took from there old clothes and old rags, and let them down by ropes into the dungeon to Jeremiah. [12]Then Ebed-Melech the Ethiopian said to Jeremiah, "Please put these old clothes and rags under your armpits, under the ropes." And Jeremiah did so. [13]So they pulled Jeremiah up with ropes and lifted him out of the dungeon. And Jeremiah remained in the court of the prison.

38:1 [a]Same as Jehucal (compare 37:3)   **38:2** [a]Compare 21:9   **38:6** [a]Hebrew Hammelech

ZEDEKIAH'S FEARS AND JEREMIAH'S ADVICE

[14]Then Zedekiah the king sent and had Jeremiah the prophet brought to him at the third entrance of the house of the LORD. And the king said to Jeremiah, "I will ask you something. Hide nothing from me."

[15]Jeremiah said to Zedekiah, "If I declare *it* to you, will you not surely put me to death? And if I give you advice, you will not listen to me."

[16]So Zedekiah the king swore secretly to Jeremiah, saying, "*As* the LORD lives, who made our very souls, I will not put you to death, nor will I give you into the hand of these men who seek your life."

[17]Then Jeremiah said to Zedekiah, "Thus says the LORD, the God of hosts, the God of Israel: 'If you surely surrender to the king of Babylon's princes, then your soul shall live; this city shall not be burned with fire, and you and your house shall live. [18]But if you do not surrender to the king of Babylon's princes, then this city shall be given into the hand of the Chaldeans; they shall burn it with fire, and you shall not escape from their hand.' "

[19]And Zedekiah the king said to Jeremiah, "I am afraid of the Jews who have defected to the Chaldeans, lest they deliver me into their hand, and they abuse me."

[20]But Jeremiah said, "They shall not deliver *you*. Please, obey the voice of the LORD which I speak to you. So it shall be well with you, and your soul shall live. [21]But if you refuse to surrender, this *is* the word that the LORD has shown me: [22]Now behold, all the women who are left in the king of Judah's house *shall be* surrendered to the king of Babylon's princes, and those *women* shall say:

"Your close friends have set upon you
And prevailed against you;
Your feet have sunk in the mire,
And they have turned away again."

[23]'So they shall surrender all your wives and children to the Chaldeans. You shall not escape from their hand, but shall be taken by the hand of the king of Babylon. And you shall cause this city to be burned with fire.' "

[24]Then Zedekiah said to Jeremiah, "Let no one know of these words, and you shall not die.

[25]But if the princes hear that I have talked with you, and they come to you and say to you, 'Declare to us now what you have said to the king, and also what the king said to you; do not hide *it* from us, and we will not put you to death,' [26]then you shall say to them, 'I presented my request before the king, that he would not make me return to Jonathan's house to die there.' "

[27]Then all the princes came to Jeremiah and asked him. And he told them according to all these words that the king had commanded. So they stopped speaking with him, for the conversation had not been heard. [28]Now Jeremiah remained in the court of the prison until the day that Jerusalem was taken. And he was *there* when Jerusalem was taken.

THE FALL OF JERUSALEM

[1]In the ninth year of Zedekiah king of Judah, in the tenth month, Nebuchadnezzar king of Babylon and all his army came against Jerusalem, and besieged it. [2]In the eleventh year of Zedekiah, in the fourth month, on the ninth *day* of the month, the city was penetrated.

[3]Then all the princes of the king of Babylon came in and sat in the Middle Gate: Nergal-Sharezer, Samgar-Nebo, Sarsechim, Rabsaris,[a] Nergal-Sarezer, Rabmag,[b] with the rest of the princes of the king of Babylon.

[4]So it was, when Zedekiah the king of Judah and all the men of war saw them, that they fled and went out of the city by night, by way of the king's garden, by the gate between the two walls. And he went out by way of the plain.[a] [5]But the Chaldean army pursued them and overtook Zedekiah in the plains of Jericho. And when they had captured him, they brought him up to Nebuchadnezzar king of Babylon, to Riblah in the land of Hamath, where he pronounced judgment on him. [6]Then the king of Babylon killed the sons of Zedekiah before his eyes in Riblah; the king of Babylon also killed all the nobles of Judah. [7]Moreover he put out Zedekiah's eyes, and bound him with bronze fetters to carry him off to Babylon. [8]And the Chaldeans burned the king's house and the houses of the people with fire, and broke down the walls of Jerusalem. [9]Then Nebuzaradan the captain of the guard carried away captive to

> "Please, obey the voice of the LORD which I speak to you. So it shall be well with you, and your soul shall live."
> (Jeremiah 38:20b)

39:3 [a]A title, probably *Chief Officer;* also verse 13 [b]A title, probably *Troop Commander;* also verse 13
39:4 [a]Or *the Arabah,* that is, the Jordan Valley

Babylon the remnant of the people who remained in the city and those who defected to him, with the rest of the people who remained. [10]But Nebuzaradan the captain of the guard left in the land of Judah the poor people, who had nothing, and gave them vineyards and fields at the same time.

JEREMIAH GOES FREE

[11]Now Nebuchadnezzar king of Babylon gave charge concerning Jeremiah to Nebuzaradan the captain of the guard, saying, [12]"Take him and look after him, and do him no harm; but do to him just as he says to you." [13]So Nebuzaradan the captain of the guard sent Nebushasban, Rabsaris, Nergal-Sharezer, Rabmag, and all the king of Babylon's chief officers; [14]then they sent someone to take Jeremiah from the court of the prison, and committed him to Gedaliah the son of Ahikam, the son of Shaphan, that he should take him home. So he dwelt among the people.

[15]Meanwhile the word of the LORD had come to Jeremiah while he was shut up in the court of the prison, saying, [16]"Go and speak to Ebed-Melech the Ethiopian, saying, 'Thus says the LORD of hosts, the God of Israel: "Behold, I will bring My words upon this city for adversity and not for good, and they shall be performed in that day before you. [17]But I will deliver you in that day," says the LORD, "and you shall not be given into the hand of the men of whom you are afraid. [18]For I will surely deliver you, and you shall not fall by the sword; but your life shall be as a prize to you, because you have put your trust in Me," says the LORD.' "

JEREMIAH WITH GEDALIAH THE GOVERNOR

[1]The word that came to Jeremiah from the LORD after Nebuzaradan the captain of the guard had let him go from Ramah, when he had taken him bound in chains among all who were carried away captive from Jerusalem and Judah, who were carried away captive to Babylon.

[2]And the captain of the guard took Jeremiah and said to him: "The LORD your God has pronounced this doom on this place. [3]Now the LORD has brought it, and has done just as He said. Because you people have sinned against the LORD, and not obeyed His voice, therefore this thing has come upon you. [4]And now look, I free you this day from the chains that were on your hand. If it seems good to you to come with me to Babylon, come, and I will look after you. But if it seems wrong for you to come with me to Babylon, remain here. See, all the land is before you; wherever it seems good and convenient for you to go, go there."

[5]Now while Jeremiah had not yet gone back, Nebuzaradan said, "Go back to Gedaliah the son of Ahikam, the son of Shaphan, whom the king of Babylon has made governor over the cities of Judah, and dwell with him among the people. Or go wherever it seems convenient for you to go." So the captain of the guard gave him rations and a gift and let him go. [6]Then Jeremiah went to Gedaliah the son of Ahikam, to Mizpah, and dwelt with him among the people who were left in the land.

[7]And when all the captains of the armies who were in the fields, they and their men, heard that the king of Babylon had made Gedaliah the son of Ahikam governor in the land, and had committed to him men, women, children, and the poorest of the land who had not been carried away captive to Babylon, [8]then they came to Gedaliah at Mizpah—Ishmael the son of Nethaniah, Johanan and Jonathan the sons of Kareah, Seraiah the son of Tanhumeth, the sons of Ephai the Netophathite, and Jezaniah[a] the son of a Maachathite, they and their men. [9]And Gedaliah the son of Ahikam, the son of Shaphan, took an oath before them and their men, saying, "Do not be afraid to serve the Chaldeans. Dwell in the land and serve the king of Babylon, and it shall be well with you. [10]As for me, I will indeed dwell at Mizpah and serve the Chaldeans who come to us. But you, gather wine and summer fruit and oil, put them in your vessels, and dwell in your cities that you have taken." [11]Likewise, when all the Jews who were in Moab, among the Ammonites, in Edom, and who were in all the countries, heard that the king of Babylon had left a remnant of Judah, and that he had set over them Gedaliah the son of Ahikam, the son of Shaphan, [12]then all the Jews returned out of all places where they had been driven, and came to the land of Judah, to Gedaliah at Mizpah, and gathered wine and summer fruit in abundance.

[13]Moreover Johanan the son of Kareah and all the captains of the forces that were in the fields came to Gedaliah at Mizpah, [14]and said to him, "Do you certainly know that Baalis the king of the Ammonites has sent Ishmael the son of Nethaniah to murder you?" But Gedaliah the son of Ahikam did not believe them.

[15]Then Johanan the son of Kareah spoke secretly to Gedaliah in Mizpah, saying, "Let me

40:8 [a]Spelled Jaazaniah in 2 Kings 25:23

go, please, and I will kill Ishmael the son of Nethaniah, and no one will know *it*. Why should he murder you, so that all the Jews who are gathered to you would be scattered, and the remnant in Judah perish?"

¹⁶But Gedaliah the son of Ahikam said to Johanan the son of Kareah, "You shall not do this thing, for you speak falsely concerning Ishmael."

INSURRECTION AGAINST GEDALIAH

¹Now it came to pass in the seventh month *that* Ishmael the son of Nethaniah, the son of Elishama, of the royal family and of the officers of the king, came with ten men to Gedaliah the son of Ahikam, at Mizpah. And there they ate bread together in Mizpah. ²Then Ishmael the son of Nethaniah, and the ten men who were with him, arose and struck Gedaliah the son of Ahikam, the son of Shaphan, with the sword, and killed him whom the king of Babylon had made governor over the land. ³Ishmael also struck down all the Jews who were with him, *that is*, with Gedaliah at Mizpah, and the Chaldeans who were found there, the men of war.

⁴And it happened, on the second day after he had killed Gedaliah, when as yet no one knew *it*, ⁵that certain men came from Shechem, from Shiloh, and from Samaria, eighty men with their beards shaved and their clothes torn, having cut themselves, with offerings and incense in their hand, to bring *them* to the house of the LORD. ⁶Now Ishmael the son of Nethaniah went out from Mizpah to meet them, weeping as he went along; and it happened as he met them that he said to them, "Come to Gedaliah the son of Ahikam!" ⁷So it was, when they came into the midst of the city, that Ishmael the son of Nethaniah killed them *and cast them* into the midst of a pit, he and the men who were with him. ⁸But ten men were found among them who said to Ishmael, "Do not kill us, for we have treasures of wheat, barley, oil, and honey in the field." So he desisted and did not kill them among their brethren. ⁹Now the pit into which Ishmael had cast all the dead bodies of the men whom he had slain, because of Gedaliah, *was* the same one Asa the king had made for fear of Baasha king of Israel. Ishmael the son of Nethaniah filled it with *the* slain. ¹⁰Then Ishmael carried away captive all the rest of the people who *were* in Mizpah, the king's daughters and all the people who remained in Mizpah, whom Nebuzaradan the captain of the guard had committed to Gedaliah the son of Ahikam. And Ishmael the son of Nethaniah carried them away captive and departed to go over to the Ammonites.

¹¹But when Johanan the son of Kareah and all the captains of the forces that *were* with him heard of all the evil that Ishmael the son of Nethaniah had done, ¹²they took all the men and went to fight with Ishmael the son of Nethaniah; and they found him by the great pool that *is* in Gibeon. ¹³So it was, when all the people who *were* with Ishmael saw Johanan the son of Kareah, and all the captains of the forces who *were* with him, that they were glad. ¹⁴Then all the people whom Ishmael had carried away captive from Mizpah turned around and came back, and went to Johanan the son of Kareah. ¹⁵But Ishmael the son of Nethaniah escaped from Johanan with eight men and went to the Ammonites.

¹⁶Then Johanan the son of Kareah, and all the captains of the forces that were with him, took from Mizpah all the rest of the people whom he had recovered from Ishmael the son of Nethaniah after he had murdered Gedaliah the son of Ahikam—the mighty men of war and the women and the children and the eunuchs, whom he had brought back from Gibeon. ¹⁷And they departed and dwelt in the habitation of Chimham, which is near Bethlehem, as they went on their way to Egypt, ¹⁸because of the Chaldeans; for they were afraid of them, because Ishmael the son of Nethaniah had murdered Gedaliah the son of Ahikam, whom the king of Babylon had made governor in the land.

THE FLIGHT TO EGYPT FORBIDDEN

¹Now all the captains of the forces, Johanan the son of Kareah, Jezaniah the son of Hoshaiah, and all the people, from the least to the greatest, came near ²and said to Jeremiah the prophet, "Please, let our petition be acceptable to you, and pray for us to the LORD your God, for all this remnant (since we are left *but* a few of many, as you can see), ³that the LORD your God may show us the way in which we should walk and the thing we should do."

⁴Then Jeremiah the prophet said to them, "I have heard. Indeed, I will pray to the LORD your God according to your words, and it shall be, *that* whatever the LORD answers you, I will declare *it* to you. I will keep nothing back from you."

⁵So they said to Jeremiah, "Let the LORD be a true and faithful witness between us, if we do not do according to everything which the LORD your God sends us by you. ⁶Whether *it is* pleasing or displeasing, we will obey the voice of the

LORD our God to whom we send you, that it may be well with us when we obey the voice of the LORD our God."

OBEDIENCE

What will obeying God get us? (42:6)

[7]And it happened after ten days that the word of the LORD came to Jeremiah. [8]Then he called Johanan the son of Kareah, all the captains of the forces which *were* with him, and all the people from the least even to the greatest, [9]and said to them, "Thus says the LORD, the God of Israel, to whom you sent me to present your petition before Him: [10]'If you will still remain in this land, then I will build you and not pull *you* down, and I will plant you and not pluck *you* up. For I relent concerning the disaster that I have brought upon you. [11]Do not be afraid of the king of Babylon, of whom you are afraid; do not be afraid of him,' says the LORD, 'for I *am* with you, to save you and deliver you from his hand. [12]And I will show you mercy, that he may have mercy on you and cause you to return to your own land.'

[13]"But if you say, 'We will not dwell in this land,' disobeying the voice of the LORD your God, [14]saying, 'No, but we will go to the land of Egypt where we shall see no war, nor hear the sound of the trumpet, nor be hungry for bread, and there we will dwell'— [15]Then hear now the word of the LORD, O remnant of Judah! Thus says the LORD of hosts, the God of Israel: 'If you wholly set your faces to enter Egypt, and go to dwell there, [16]then it shall be *that* the sword which you feared shall overtake you there in the land of Egypt; the famine of which you were afraid shall follow close after you there *in* Egypt; and there you shall die. [17]So shall it be with all the men who set their faces to go to Egypt to dwell there. They shall die by the sword, by famine, and by pestilence. And none of them shall remain or escape from the disaster that I will bring upon them.'

[18]"For thus says the LORD of hosts, the God of Israel: 'As My anger and My fury have been poured out on the inhabitants of Jerusalem, so will My fury be poured out on you when you enter Egypt. And you shall be an oath, an astonishment, a curse, and a reproach; and you shall see this place no more.'

[19]"The LORD has said concerning you, O remnant of Judah, 'Do not go to Egypt!' Know certainly that I have admonished you this day. [20]For you were hypocrites in your hearts when you sent me to the LORD your God, saying, 'Pray for us to the LORD our God, and according to all that the LORD your God says, so declare to us and we will do *it*.' [21]And I have this day declared *it* to you, but you have not obeyed the voice of the LORD your God, or anything which He has sent you by me. [22]Now therefore, know certainly that you shall die by the sword, by famine, and by pestilence in the place where you desire to go to dwell."

JEREMIAH TAKEN TO EGYPT

[1]Now it happened, when Jeremiah had stopped speaking to all the people all the words of the LORD their God, for which the LORD their God had sent him to them, all these words, [2]that Azariah the son of Hoshaiah, Johanan the son of Kareah, and all the proud men spoke, saying to Jeremiah, "You speak falsely! The LORD our God has not sent you to say, 'Do not go to Egypt to dwell there.' [3]But Baruch the son of Neriah has set you against us, to deliver us into the hand of the Chaldeans, that they may put us to death or carry us away captive to Babylon." [4]So Johanan the son of Kareah, all the captains of the forces, and all the people would not obey the voice of the LORD, to remain in the land of Judah. [5]But Johanan the son of Kareah and all the captains of the forces took all the remnant of Judah who had returned to dwell in the land of Judah, from all nations where they had been driven—[6]men, women, children, the king's daughters, and every person whom Nebuzaradan the captain of the guard had left with Gedaliah the son of Ahikam, the son of Shaphan, and Jeremiah the prophet and Baruch the son of Neriah. [7]So they went to the land of Egypt, for they did not obey the voice of the LORD. And they went as far as Tahpanhes.

[8]Then the word of the LORD came to Jeremiah in Tahpanhes, saying, [9]"Take large stones in your hand, and hide them in the sight of the men of Judah, in the clay in the brick courtyard which *is* at the entrance to Pharaoh's house in Tahpanhes; [10]and say to them, 'Thus says the LORD of hosts, the God of Israel: "Behold, I will send and bring Nebuchadnezzar the king of Babylon, My servant, and will set his throne above these stones that I have hidden. And he will spread his royal pavilion over them. [11]When he comes, he shall strike the land of Egypt *and deliver* to death *those appointed* for death, and to captivity *those appointed* for captivity, and to the sword *those appointed* for the sword. [12]I[a] will kindle a fire in the houses of the gods of Egypt, and he shall burn them and carry them away captive. And he shall array

---

43:12 [a]Following Masoretic Text and Targum; Septuagint, Syriac, and Vulgate read *He.*

himself with the land of Egypt, as a shepherd puts on his garment, and he shall go out from there in peace. ¹³He shall also break the *sacred* pillars of Beth Shemesh*ᵃ* that *are* in the land of Egypt; and the houses of the gods of the Egyptians he shall burn with fire." ' "

ISRAELITES WILL BE PUNISHED IN EGYPT

¹The word that came to Jeremiah concerning all the Jews who dwell in the land of Egypt, who dwell at Migdol, at Tahpanhes, at Noph,*ᵃ* and in the country of Pathros, saying, ²"Thus says the LORD of hosts, the God of Israel: 'You have seen all the calamity that I have brought on Jerusalem and on all the cities of Judah; and behold, this day they *are* a desolation, and no one dwells in them, ³because of their wickedness which they have committed to provoke Me to anger, in that they went to burn incense *and* to serve other gods whom they did not know, they nor you nor your fathers. ⁴However I have sent to you all My servants the prophets, rising early and sending *them,* saying, "Oh, do not do this abominable thing that I hate!" ⁵But they did not listen or incline their ear to turn from their wickedness, to burn no incense to other gods. ⁶So My fury and My anger were poured out and kindled in the cities of Judah and in the streets of Jerusalem; and they are wasted *and* desolate, as it is this day.'

⁷"Now therefore, thus says the LORD, the God of hosts, the God of Israel: 'Why do you commit *this* great evil against yourselves, to cut off from you man and woman, child and infant, out of Judah, leaving none to remain, ⁸in that you provoke Me to wrath with the works of your hands, burning incense to other gods in the land of Egypt where you have gone to dwell, that you may cut yourselves off and be a curse and a reproach among all the nations of the earth? ⁹Have you forgotten the wickedness of your fathers, the wickedness of the kings of Judah, the wickedness of their wives, your own wickedness, and the wickedness of your wives, which they committed in the land of Judah and in the streets of Jerusalem? ¹⁰They have not been humbled, to this day, nor have they feared; they have not walked in My law or in My statutes that I set before you and your fathers.'

¹¹"Therefore thus says the LORD of hosts, the God of Israel: 'Behold, I will set My face against you for catastrophe and for cutting off all Judah. ¹²And I will take the remnant of Judah who have set their faces to go into the land of Egypt to dwell there, and they shall all be consumed *and* fall in the land of Egypt. They shall be consumed by the sword *and* by famine. They shall die, from the least to the greatest, by the sword and by famine; and they shall be an oath, an astonishment, a curse and a reproach! ¹³For I will punish those who dwell in the land of Egypt, as I have punished Jerusalem, by the sword, by famine, and by pestilence, ¹⁴so that none of the remnant of Judah who have gone into the land of Egypt to dwell there shall escape or survive, lest they return to the land of Judah, to which they desire to return and dwell. For none shall return except those who escape.' "

¹⁵Then all the men who knew that their wives had burned incense to other gods, with all the women who stood by, a great multitude, and all the people who dwelt in the land of Egypt, in Pathros, answered Jeremiah, saying: ¹⁶"*As for* the word that you have spoken to us in the name of the LORD, we will not listen to you! ¹⁷But we will certainly do whatever has gone out of our own mouth, to burn incense to the queen of heaven and pour out drink offerings to her, as we have done, we and our fathers, our kings and our princes, in the cities of Judah and in the streets of Jerusalem. For *then* we had plenty of food, were well-off, and saw no trouble. ¹⁸But since we stopped burning incense to the queen of heaven and pouring out drink offerings to her, we have lacked everything and have been consumed by the sword and by famine."

WHAT'S IT MEAN?

"Queen of heaven" refers to the goddess Astarte, the companion of the popular Canaanite god, Baal. Also known as Ishtar or Ashtoreth, Astarte was similar to Venus, the Roman goddess of love.
Jeremiah 44:17

¹⁹*The women also said,* "And when we burned incense to the queen of heaven and poured out drink offerings to her, did we make cakes for her, to worship her, and pour out drink offerings to her without our husbands' *permission?*"

²⁰Then Jeremiah spoke to all the people—the men, the women, and all the people who had given him *that* answer—saying: ²¹"The incense that you burned in the cities of Judah and in the streets of Jerusalem, you and your fathers, your kings and your princes, and the people of the land, did not the LORD remember them, and did it *not* come into His mind? ²²So the LORD could no longer bear *it*, because of the evil of your doings *and* because of the abominations which you committed. Therefore your land is a desolation, an astonishment, a curse, and without an inhabitant, as *it is* this day. ²³Because you have burned incense and because you have sinned against the LORD, and have not obeyed the voice of the LORD or walked in His law, in His statutes or in His testimonies, therefore this calamity has happened to you, as *at* this day."

²⁴Moreover Jeremiah said to all the people and to all the women, "Hear the word of the LORD, all Judah who *are* in the land of Egypt! ²⁵Thus says the LORD of hosts, the God of Israel, saying: 'You and your wives have spoken with your mouths and fulfilled with your hands, saying, "We will surely keep our vows that we have made, to burn incense to the queen of heaven and pour out drink offerings to her." You will surely keep your vows and perform your vows!' ²⁶Therefore hear the word of the LORD, all Judah who dwell in the land of Egypt: 'Behold, I have sworn by My great name,' says the LORD, 'that My name shall no more be named in the mouth of any man of Judah in all the land of Egypt, saying, "The Lord GOD lives." ²⁷Behold, I will watch over them for adversity and not for good. And all the men of Judah who *are* in the land of Egypt shall be consumed by the sword and by famine, until there is an end to them. ²⁸Yet a small number who escape the sword shall return from the land of Egypt to the land of Judah; and all the remnant of Judah, who have gone to the land of Egypt to dwell there, shall know whose words will stand, Mine or theirs. ²⁹And this *shall be* a sign to you,' says the LORD, 'that I will punish you in this place, that you may know that My words will surely stand against you for adversity.'

³⁰"Thus says the LORD: 'Behold, I will give Pharaoh Hophra king of Egypt into the hand of his enemies and into the hand of those who seek his life, as I gave Zedekiah king of Judah into the hand of Nebuchadnezzar king of Babylon, his enemy who sought his life.' "

ASSURANCE TO BARUCH

¹The word that Jeremiah the prophet spoke to Baruch the son of Neriah, when he had written these words in a book at the instruction of Jeremiah,ᵃ in the fourth year of Jehoiakim the son of Josiah, king of Judah, saying, ²"Thus says the LORD, the God of Israel, to you, O Baruch: ³'You said, "Woe is me now! For the LORD has added grief to my sorrow. I fainted in my sighing, and I find no rest." '

⁴"Thus you shall say to him, 'Thus says the LORD: "Behold, what I have built I will break down, and what I have planted I will pluck up, that is, this whole land. ⁵And do you seek great things for yourself? Do not seek *them*; for behold, I will bring adversity on all flesh," says the LORD. "But I will give your life to you as a prize in all places, wherever you go." ' "

> "Moreover Jeremiah said to all the people and to all the women, 'Hear the word of the LORD, all Judah who are in the land of Egypt!' "
> (Jeremiah 45:24)

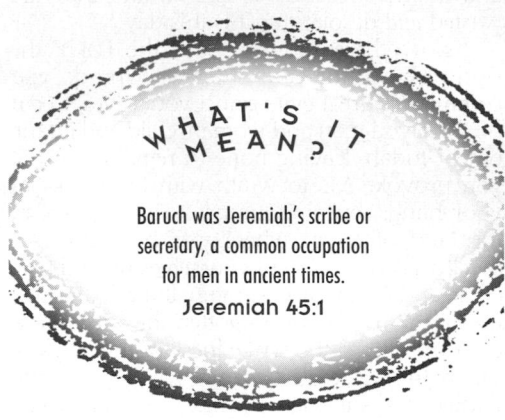

WHAT'S IT MEAN?

Baruch was Jeremiah's scribe or secretary, a common occupation for men in ancient times.
Jeremiah 45:1

JUDGMENT ON EGYPT

¹The word of the LORD which came to Jeremiah the prophet against the nations. ²Against Egypt.

Concerning the army of Pharaoh Necho, king of Egypt, which was by the River Euphrates in Carchemish, and which Nebuchadnezzar king of Babylon defeated in the fourth year of Jehoiakim the son of Josiah, king of Judah:

45:1 ᵃLiterally *from Jeremiah's mouth*

³ "Order the buckler and shield,
   And draw near to battle!
⁴ Harness the horses,
   And mount up, you horsemen!
   Stand forth with *your* helmets,
   Polish the spears,
   Put on the armor!
⁵ Why have I seen them dismayed *and*
     turned back?
   Their mighty ones are beaten down;
   They have speedily fled,
   And did not look back,
   For fear *was* all around," says the LORD.
⁶ "Do not let the swift flee away,
   Nor the mighty man escape;
   They will stumble and fall
   Toward the north, by the River Euphrates.

WHAT'S IT MEAN?

Before modern dams were constructed, the Nile River flooded its banks nearly every year, covering the farmland of Egypt.
Jeremiah 46:7

⁷ "Who *is* this coming up like a flood,
   Whose waters move like the rivers?
⁸ Egypt rises up like a flood,
   And *its* waters move like the rivers;
   And he says, 'I will go up *and* cover the
     earth,
   I will destroy the city and its inhabitants.'
⁹ Come up, O horses, and rage, O chariots!
   And let the mighty men come forth:
   The Ethiopians and the Libyans who
     handle the shield,
   And the Lydians who handle *and* bend
     the bow.
¹⁰ For this *is* the day of the Lord GOD of
     hosts,
   A day of vengeance,
   That He may avenge Himself on His
     adversaries.
   The sword shall devour;
   It shall be satiated and made drunk with
     their blood;
   For the Lord GOD of hosts has a sacrifice

WHAT'S IT MEAN?

In case anyone asks, Ethiopians came from the land south of Egypt, Libyans came from the land west of Egypt, and Lydians came from what is now Turkey.
Jeremiah 46:9

In the north country by the River
   Euphrates.

¹¹ "Go up to Gilead and take balm,
   O virgin, the daughter of Egypt;
   In vain you will use many medicines;
   You shall not be cured.
¹² The nations have heard of your shame,
   And your cry has filled the land;
   For the mighty man has stumbled against
     the mighty;
   They both have fallen together."

BABYLONIA WILL STRIKE EGYPT

¹³The word that the LORD spoke to Jeremiah the prophet, how Nebuchadnezzar king of Babylon would come *and* strike the land of Egypt.

¹⁴ "Declare in Egypt, and proclaim in
     Migdol;
   Proclaim in Noph*ᵃ* and in Tahpanhes;
   Say, 'Stand fast and prepare yourselves,
   For the sword devours all around you.'
¹⁵ Why are your valiant *men* swept away?
   They did not stand
   Because the LORD drove them away.
¹⁶ He made many fall;
   Yes, one fell upon another.
   And they said, 'Arise!
   Let us go back to our own people
   And to the land of our nativity
   From the oppressing sword.'
¹⁷ They cried there,
   'Pharaoh, king of Egypt, *is but* a noise.
   He has passed by the appointed time!'

¹⁸ "*As* I live," says the King,
   Whose name *is* the LORD of hosts,
   "Surely as Tabor *is* among the mountains

46:14 *ᵃ*That is, ancient Memphis

And as Carmel by the sea, *so* he shall
  come.
19 O you daughter dwelling in Egypt,
  Prepare yourself to go into captivity!
  For Noph[a] shall be waste and desolate,
    without inhabitant.

20 "Egypt *is* a very pretty heifer,
  But destruction comes, it comes from the
    north.
21 Also her mercenaries are in her midst like
    fat bulls,
  For they also are turned back,
  They have fled away together.
  They did not stand,
  For the day of their calamity had come
    upon them,
  The time of their punishment.
22 Her noise shall go like a serpent,
  For they shall march with an army
  And come against her with axes,
  Like those who chop wood.

23 "They shall cut down her forest," says the
    LORD,
  "Though it cannot be searched,
  Because they *are* innumerable,
  And more numerous than grasshoppers.
24 The daughter of Egypt shall be
    ashamed;
  She shall be delivered into the hand
  Of the people of the north."

25The LORD of hosts, the God of Israel, says:
"Behold, I will bring punishment on Amon[a] of
No,[b] and Pharaoh and Egypt, with their gods
and their kings—Pharaoh and those who trust
in him. 26And I will deliver them into the hand
of those who seek their lives, into the hand of
Nebuchadnezzar king of Babylon and the hand
of his servants. Afterward it shall be inhabited
as in the days of old," says the LORD.

GOD WILL PRESERVE ISRAEL
27 "But do not fear, O My servant Jacob,
  And do not be dismayed,
    O Israel!
  For behold, I will save
    you from afar,
  And your offspring from
    the land of their
    captivity;
  Jacob shall return, have
    rest and be at ease;
  No one shall make *him* afraid.

28 Do not fear, O Jacob My servant," says the
    LORD,
  "For I *am* with you;
  For I will make a complete end of all the
    nations
  To which I have driven you,
  But I will not make a complete end of
    you.
  I will rightly correct you,
  For I will not leave you wholly
    unpunished."

JUDGMENT ON PHILISTIA
1The word of the LORD that came to Jeremiah the prophet against the Philistines, before
Pharaoh attacked Gaza.
  2Thus says the LORD:

  "Behold, waters rise out of the north,
  And shall be an overflowing flood;
  They shall overflow the land and all that
    is in it,
  The city and those who dwell within;
  Then the men shall cry,
  And all the inhabitants of the land shall
    wail.
3 At the noise of the stamping hooves of
    his strong horses,
  At the rushing of his chariots,
  At the rumbling of his wheels,
  The fathers will not look back for *their*
    children,
  Lacking courage,
4 Because of the day that comes to plunder
    all the Philistines,
  To cut off from Tyre and Sidon every
    helper who remains;
  For the LORD shall plunder the
    Philistines,
  The remnant of the country of
    Caphtor.
5 Baldness has come upon Gaza,
  Ashkelon is cut off
  With the remnant of their valley.
  How long will you cut yourself?

6 "O you sword of the LORD,
  How long until you are quiet?
  Put yourself up into your scabbard,
  Rest and be still!
7 How can it be quiet,
  Seeing the LORD has given it a charge
  Against Ashkelon and against the
    seashore?
  There He has appointed it."

FEAR

Who can
conquer our
fears?
(46:27)

JUDGMENT ON MOAB

48

[1]Against Moab.

Thus says the LORD of hosts, the God of Israel:

"Woe to Nebo!
For it is plundered,
Kirjathaim is shamed *and* taken;
The high stronghold[a] is shamed and dismayed—
2   No more praise of Moab.
In Heshbon they have devised evil against her:
'Come, and let us cut her off as a nation.'
You also shall be cut down,
O Madmen![a]
The sword shall pursue you;
3   A voice of crying *shall be* from Horonaim:
'Plundering and great destruction!'

4   "Moab is destroyed;
Her little ones have caused a cry to be heard;[a]
5   For in the Ascent of Luhith they ascend with continual weeping;
For in the descent of Horonaim the enemies have heard a cry of destruction.

6   "Flee, save your lives!
And be like the juniper[a] in the wilderness.
7   For because you have trusted in your works and your treasures,
You also shall be taken.
And Chemosh shall go forth into captivity,
His priests and his princes together.
8   And the plunderer shall come against every city;
No one shall escape.
The valley also shall perish,
And the plain shall be destroyed,
As the LORD has spoken.

9   "Give wings to Moab,
That she may flee and get away;
For her cities shall be desolate,
Without any to dwell in them.
10   Cursed *is* he who does the work of the LORD deceitfully,
And cursed *is* he who keeps back his sword from blood.

11   "Moab has been at ease from his[a] youth;
He has settled on his dregs,
And has not been emptied from vessel to vessel,
Nor has he gone into captivity.
Therefore his taste remained in him,
And his scent has not changed.

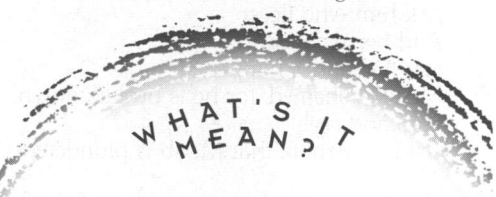

WHAT'S IT MEAN?

To understand Jeremiah's description of Moab, you have to know that when wine was made in ancient times, the bottles were left in places where they would not be touched. The winemakers wanted the grape juice to ferment and the sediment to settle at the bottom of the bottle. The wine was not considered fit for drinking until it had been poured through a strainer to remove the sediment.

Jeremiah 48:11

12   "Therefore behold, the days are coming," says the LORD,
"That I shall send him wine-workers
Who will tip him over
And empty his vessels
And break the bottles.
13   Moab shall be ashamed of Chemosh,
As the house of Israel was ashamed of Bethel, their confidence.

14   "How can you say, 'We *are* mighty
And strong men for the war'?
15   Moab is plundered and gone up *from* her cities;
Her chosen young men have gone down to the slaughter," says the King,
Whose name *is* the LORD of hosts.

16   "The calamity of Moab *is* near at hand,
And his affliction comes quickly.
17   Bemoan him, all you who are around him;
And all you who know his name,
Say, 'How the strong staff is broken,
The beautiful rod!'

48:1 [a]Hebrew *Misgab*   **48:2** [a]A city of Moab   **48:4** [a]Following Masoretic Text, Targum, and Vulgate; Septuagint reads *Proclaim it in Zoar.*   **48:6** [a]Or *Aroer,* a city of Moab   **48:11** [a]The Hebrew uses masculine and feminine pronouns interchangeably in this chapter.

18 "O daughter inhabiting Dibon,
   Come down from *your* glory,
   And sit in thirst;
   For the plunderer of Moab has come
      against you,
   He has destroyed your strongholds.
19 O inhabitant of Aroer,
   Stand by the way and watch;
   Ask him who flees
   And her who escapes;
   Say, 'What has happened?'
20 Moab is shamed, for he is broken down.
   Wail and cry!
   Tell it in Arnon, that Moab is plundered.

21 "And judgment has come on the plain
      country:
   On Holon and Jahzah and Mephaath,
22 On Dibon and Nebo and Beth
      Diblathaim,
23 On Kirjathaim and Beth Gamul and Beth
      Meon,
24 On Kerioth and Bozrah,
   On all the cities of the land of Moab,
   Far or near.
25 The horn of Moab is cut off,
   And his arm is broken," says the LORD.

26 "Make him drunk,
   Because he exalted *himself* against the
      LORD.
   Moab shall wallow in his vomit,
   And he shall also be in derision.
27 For was not Israel a derision to you?
   Was he found among thieves?
   For whenever you speak of him,
   You shake *your head in scorn.*
28 You who dwell in Moab,
   Leave the cities and dwell in the rock,
   And be like the dove *which* makes her
      nest
   In the sides of the cave's mouth.

29 "We have heard the pride of Moab
   (He *is* exceedingly proud),
   Of his loftiness and arrogance and pride,
   And of the haughtiness of his heart."
30 "I know his wrath," says the LORD,
   "But it *is* not right;
   His lies have made nothing right.
31 Therefore I will wail for Moab,
   And I will cry out for all Moab;
   I[a] will mourn for the men of Kir Heres.

32 O vine of Sibmah! I will weep for you
      with the weeping of Jazer.
   Your plants have gone over the sea,
   They reach to the sea of Jazer.
   The plunderer has fallen on your summer
      fruit and your vintage.
33 Joy and gladness are taken
   From the plentiful field
   And from the land of Moab;
   I have caused wine to fail from the
      winepresses;
   No one will tread with joyous shouting—
   Not joyous shouting!

34 "From the cry of Heshbon to Elealeh and
      to Jahaz
   They have uttered their voice,
   From Zoar to Horonaim,
   Like a three-year-old heifer;[a]
   For the waters of Nimrim also shall be
      desolate.

35 "Moreover," says the LORD,
   "I will cause to cease in Moab
   The one who offers *sacrifices* in the high
      places
   And burns incense to his gods.
36 Therefore My heart shall wail like flutes
      for Moab,
   And like flutes My heart shall wail
   For the men of Kir Heres.
   Therefore the riches they have acquired
      have perished.

37 "For every head *shall be* bald, and every
      beard clipped;
   On all the hands *shall be* cuts, and on the
      loins sackcloth—
38 A general lamentation
   On all the housetops of Moab,
   And in its streets;
   For I have broken Moab like a vessel in
      which *is* no pleasure," says the LORD.
39 "They shall wail:
   'How she is broken down!
   How Moab has turned her back with
      shame!'
   So Moab shall be a derision
   And a dismay to all those about her."

40 For thus says the LORD:

   "Behold, one shall fly like an eagle,
   And spread his wings over Moab.

48:31 [a]Following Dead Sea Scrolls, Septuagint, and Vulgate; Masoretic Text reads *He.*   **48:34** [a]Or *The Third Eglath,* an unknown city (compare Isaiah 15:5)

41   Kerioth is taken,
And the strongholds are surprised;
The mighty men's hearts in Moab on that
     day shall be
Like the heart of a woman in birth pangs.
42   And Moab shall be destroyed as a people,
Because he exalted *himself* against the
     LORD.
43   Fear and the pit and the snare *shall be*
     upon you,
O inhabitant of Moab," says the LORD.
44   "He who flees from the fear shall fall into
     the pit,
And he who gets out of the pit shall be
     caught in the snare.
For upon Moab, upon it I will bring
The year of their punishment," says the
     LORD.

WHAT'S IT MEAN?

Sihon blew his big chance to help the Israelites
when he refused Moses' request to let God's people
pass through the land of the Amorites. He then made matters worse
by attacking the Israelites. Needless to say, he was killed and his army
was defeated. The Israelite tribes of Gad and Reuben took control of
the land that had belonged to the Amorites.
Jeremiah 48:45

45   "Those who fled stood under the shadow
     of Heshbon
Because of exhaustion.
But a fire shall come out of Heshbon,
A flame from the midst of Sihon,
And shall devour the brow of Moab,
The crown of the head of the sons of
     tumult.
46   Woe to you, O Moab!
The people of Chemosh perish;
For your sons have been taken captive,
And your daughters captive.

47   "Yet I will bring back the captives of Moab
In the latter days," says the LORD.

Thus far *is* the judgment of Moab.

JUDGMENT ON AMMON

1 Against the Ammonites.
Thus says the LORD:

"Has Israel no sons?
  Has he no heir?
  Why *then* does Milcom[a] inherit Gad,
  And his people dwell in its cities?
2   Therefore behold, the days are coming,"
     says the LORD,
"That I will cause to be heard an alarm of
     war
  In Rabbah of the Ammonites;
  It shall be a desolate mound,
  And her villages shall be burned with fire.
  Then Israel shall take possession of his
     inheritance," says the LORD.

3   "Wail, O Heshbon, for Ai is plundered!
  Cry, you daughters of Rabbah,
  Gird yourselves with sackcloth!
  Lament and run to and fro by the walls;
  For Milcom shall go into captivity
  With his priests and his princes together.
4   Why do you boast in the valleys,
  Your flowing valley, O backsliding
     daughter?
  Who trusted in her treasures, *saying,*
  'Who will come against me?'
5   Behold, I will bring fear upon you,"
  Says the Lord GOD of hosts,
"From all those who are around you;
  You shall be driven out, everyone
     headlong,
  And no one will gather those who
     wander off.
6   But afterward I will bring back
  The captives of the people of Ammon,"
     says the LORD.

JUDGMENT ON EDOM

7 Against Edom.
Thus says the LORD of hosts:

"*Is* wisdom no more in Teman?
  Has counsel perished from the prudent?
  Has their wisdom vanished?
8   Flee, turn back, dwell in the depths,
     O inhabitants of Dedan!
  For I will bring the calamity of Esau upon
     him,
  The time *that* I will punish him.
9   If grape-gatherers came to you,
  Would they not leave *some* gleaning
     grapes?

49:1 [a]Hebrew *Malcam*, literally *their king*, a god of the Ammonites; also called *Molech* (compare verse 3)

If thieves by night,
Would they not destroy until they have enough?
10 But I have made Esau bare;
I have uncovered his secret places,*a*
And he shall not be able to hide himself.
His descendants are plundered,
His brethren and his neighbors,
And he *is* no more.
11 Leave your fatherless children,
I will preserve *them* alive;
And let your widows trust in Me."

12For thus says the LORD: "Behold, those whose judgment *was* not to drink of the cup have assuredly drunk. And *are* you the one who will altogether go unpunished? You shall not go unpunished, but you shall surely drink *of it.* 13For I have sworn by Myself," says the LORD, "that Bozrah shall become a desolation, a reproach, a waste, and a curse. And all its cities shall be perpetual wastes."

14 I have heard a message from the LORD,
And an ambassador has been sent to the nations:
"Gather together, come against her,
And rise up to battle!

15 "For indeed, I will make you small among nations,
Despised among men.

16 Your fierceness has deceived you,
The pride of your heart,
O you who dwell in the clefts of the rock,
Who hold the height of the hill!
Though you make your nest as high as the eagle,
I will bring you down from there," says the LORD.*a*

17 "Edom also shall be an astonishment;
Everyone who goes by it will be astonished
And will hiss at all its plagues.
18 As in the overthrow of Sodom and Gomorrah
And their neighbors," says the LORD,
"No one shall remain there,
Nor shall a son of man dwell in it.

19 "Behold, he shall come up like a lion from the floodplain*a* of the Jordan
Against the dwelling place of the strong;
But I will suddenly make him run away from her.
And who *is* a chosen *man that* I may appoint over her?
For who *is* like Me?
Who will arraign Me?
And who *is* that shepherd
Who will withstand Me?"

> "Therefore hear the counsel of the LORD that He has taken against Edom, and His purposes that He has proposed against the inhabitants of Teman." (Jeremiah 49:20a)

20 Therefore hear the counsel of the LORD that He has taken against Edom,
And His purposes that He has proposed against the inhabitants of Teman:
Surely the least of the flock shall draw them out;
Surely He shall make their dwelling places desolate with them.
21 The earth shakes at the noise of their fall;
At the cry its noise is heard at the Red Sea.
22 Behold, He shall come up and fly like the eagle,
And spread His wings over Bozrah;
The heart of the mighty men of Edom in that day shall be
Like the heart of a woman in birth pangs.

49:10 *a*Compare Obadiah 5, 6   **49:16** *a*Compare Obadiah 3, 4   **49:19** *a*Or *thicket*

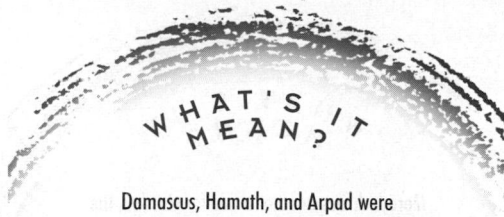

WHAT'S IT MEAN?

Damascus, Hamath, and Arpad were all important cities in Syria. Damascus, the capital, is located about 140 miles northeast of the Dead Sea. Not only is Damascus one of the oldest cities in the world; it is still an important part of the region today.

Jeremiah 49:23

And they shall cry out to them,
'Fear *is* on every side!'

30 "Flee, get far away! Dwell in the depths,
O inhabitants of Hazor!" says the LORD.
"For Nebuchadnezzar king of Babylon has
taken counsel against you,
And has conceived a plan against you.

31 "Arise, go up to the wealthy nation that
dwells securely," says the LORD,
"Which has neither gates nor bars,
Dwelling alone.

32 Their camels shall be for booty,
And the multitude of their cattle for
plunder.
I will scatter to all winds those in the
farthest corners,
And I will bring their calamity from all its
sides," says the LORD.

33 "Hazor shall be a dwelling for jackals, a
desolation forever;
No one shall reside there,
Nor son of man dwell in it."

JUDGMENT ON DAMASCUS

23 Against Damascus.

"Hamath and Arpad are shamed,
For they have heard bad news.
They are fainthearted;
There is trouble on the sea;
It cannot be quiet.

24 Damascus has grown feeble;
She turns to flee,
And fear has seized *her.*
Anguish and sorrows have taken her like
a woman in labor.

25 Why is the city of praise not deserted, the
city of My joy?

26 Therefore her young men shall fall in her
streets,
And all the men of war shall be cut off in
that day," says the LORD of hosts.

27 "I will kindle a fire in the wall of
Damascus,
And it shall consume the palaces of Ben-
Hadad."[a]

JUDGMENT ON KEDAR AND HAZOR

28 Against Kedar and against the kingdoms of
Hazor, which Nebuchadnezzar king of Babylon
shall strike.

Thus says the LORD:

"Arise, go up to Kedar,
And devastate the men of the East!

29 Their tents and their flocks they shall take
away.
They shall take for themselves their
curtains,
All their vessels and their camels;

JUDGMENT ON ELAM

34 The word of the LORD that came to Jeremiah the prophet against Elam, in the beginning
of the reign of Zedekiah king of Judah, saying,
35 "Thus says the LORD of hosts:

'Behold, I will break the bow of Elam,
The foremost of their might.

36 Against Elam I will bring the four winds
From the four quarters of heaven,
And scatter them toward all those winds;
There shall be no nations where the
outcasts of Elam will not go.

37 For I will cause Elam to be dismayed
before their enemies

WHAT'S IT MEAN?

Elam was located east of Israel, in the mountains and plains north of the Persian Gulf. Today that area is part of Iran.

Jeremiah 49:34, 35

49:27 [a]Compare Amos 1:4

And before those who seek their life.
I will bring disaster upon them,
My fierce anger,' says the LORD;
'And I will send the sword after them
Until I have consumed them.
38 I will set My throne in Elam,
And will destroy from there the king and
the princes,' says the LORD.

39 "But it shall come to pass in the latter
days:
I will bring back the captives of Elam,'
says the LORD."

JUDGMENT ON BABYLON AND BABYLONIA

¹The word that the LORD spoke against Babylon *and* against the land of the Chaldeans by
Jeremiah the prophet.

2   "Declare among the nations,
Proclaim, and set up a standard;
Proclaim—do not conceal *it*—
Say, 'Babylon is taken, Bel is shamed.
Merodach[a] is broken in pieces;
Her idols are humiliated,
Her images are broken in pieces.'
3   For out of the north a nation comes up
against her,
Which shall make her land desolate,
And no one shall dwell therein.
They shall move, they shall depart,
Both man and beast.

50:2 [a]A Babylonian god; sometimes spelled *Marduk*

WHAT'S IT MEAN?

Merodach was another name for Marduk, the
chief god of the Babylonians. The people of Babylon
believed that Marduk created the world, and they
looked to him to protect their kingdom.

Jeremiah 50:2

4   "In those days and in that time," says the
LORD,
"The children of Israel shall come,
They and the children of Judah
together;
With continual weeping they shall come,
And seek the LORD their God.
5   They shall ask the way to Zion,
With their faces toward it, *saying*,
'Come and let us join ourselves to the
LORD
In a perpetual covenant
That will not be forgotten.'

6   "My people have been lost sheep.
Their shepherds have led them astray;

Promise   HE PROMISES TO BE YOUR DWELLING PLACE.

*Because they have sinned against the LORD, the habitation of justice, the LORD,
the hope of their fathers (Jer. 50:7b).*

You're thinking, *Dwelling place, what's so great about a dwelling place?* Back in Bible days,
people's wealth was wrapped up in their land—the place where they dwelled. It was a place
where their sheep could graze on plenty and in complete protection from the wild animals.
God has promised that He will be our "habitation of justice"—*our true home.* He is the One who is
our Protector and our Provider. He is our safe place in the middle of the jungle! He is the One
who gives hope. When we learn to stop worrying and put our hope in God, our hearts are surrounded by an intense peace, which can't be penetrated by anything the enemy throws our
way (see Phil. 4:6, 7). It's easy to put our hope in other people and other things, but remember that people and things will never provide a good place to "dwell." God is our true dwelling
place, and He won't fail us!

SEE FOR YOURSELF:
Ps. 16:1; 64:1; John 10:10; 17:11; Heb. 11:1

They have turned them away *on the* mountains.
They have gone from mountain to hill;
They have forgotten their resting place.

7 All who found them have devoured them;
And their adversaries said, 'We have not offended,
Because they have sinned against the LORD, the habitation of justice,
The LORD, the hope of their fathers.'

8 "Move from the midst of Babylon,
Go out of the land of the Chaldeans;
And be like the rams before the flocks.
9 For behold, I will raise and cause to come up against Babylon
An assembly of great nations from the north country,
And they shall array themselves against her;
From there she shall be captured.
Their arrows *shall be* like *those* of an expert warrior;[a]
None shall return in vain.
10 And Chaldea shall become plunder;
All who plunder her shall be satisfied,"
says the LORD.

11 "Because you were glad, because you rejoiced,
You destroyers of My heritage,
Because you have grown fat like a heifer threshing grain,
And you bellow like bulls,
12 Your mother shall be deeply ashamed;
She who bore you shall be ashamed.
Behold, the least of the nations *shall be* a wilderness,
A dry land and a desert.
13 Because of the wrath of the LORD
She shall not be inhabited,
But she shall be wholly desolate.
Everyone who goes by Babylon shall be horrified
And hiss at all her plagues.

14 "Put yourselves in array against Babylon all around,
All you who bend the bow;
Shoot at her, spare no arrows,
For she has sinned against the LORD.
15 Shout against her all around;
She has given her hand,

Her foundations have fallen,
Her walls are thrown down;
For it *is* the vengeance of the LORD.
Take vengeance on her.
As she has done, so do to her.
16 Cut off the sower from Babylon,
And him who handles the sickle at harvest time.
For fear of the oppressing sword
Everyone shall turn to his own people,
And everyone shall flee to his own land.

17 "Israel *is* like scattered sheep;
The lions have driven *him* away.
First the king of Assyria devoured him;
Now at last this Nebuchadnezzar king of Babylon has broken his bones."

18 Therefore thus says the LORD of hosts, the God of Israel:

"Behold, I will punish the king of Babylon and his land,
As I have punished the king of Assyria.
19 But I will bring back Israel to his home,
And he shall feed on Carmel and Bashan;
His soul shall be satisfied on Mount Ephraim and Gilead.
20 In those days and in that time," says the LORD,
"The iniquity of Israel shall be sought, but *there shall be* none;
And the sins of Judah, but they shall not be found;
For I will pardon those whom I preserve.

21 "Go up against the land of Merathaim, against it,
And against the inhabitants of Pekod.
Waste and utterly destroy them," says the LORD,
"And do according to all that I have commanded you.
22 A sound of battle *is* in the land,
And of great destruction.
23 How the hammer of the whole earth has been cut apart and broken!
How Babylon has become a desolation among the nations!
I have laid a snare for you;
24 You have indeed been trapped,
O Babylon,
And you were not aware;
You have been found and also caught,

50:9 [a]Following some Hebrew manuscripts, Septuagint, and Syriac; Masoretic Text, Targum, and Vulgate read *a warrior who makes childless.*

Because you have contended against the
LORD.

25 The LORD has opened His armory,
And has brought out the weapons of His
indignation;
For this *is* the work of the Lord GOD of
hosts
In the land of the Chaldeans.

26 Come against her from the farthest
border;
Open her storehouses;
Cast her up as heaps of ruins,
And destroy her utterly;
Let nothing of her be left.

27 Slay all her bulls,
Let them go down to the slaughter.
Woe to them!
For their day has come, the time of their
punishment.

28 The voice of those who flee and escape
from the land of Babylon
Declares in Zion the vengeance of the
LORD our God,
The vengeance of His temple.

29 "Call together the archers against Babylon.
All you who bend the bow, encamp
against it all around;
Let none of them escape.*a*
Repay her according to her work;
According to all she has done, do to her;
For she has been proud against the LORD,
Against the Holy One of Israel.

30 Therefore her young men shall fall in the
streets,
And all her men of war shall be cut off in
that day," says the LORD.

31 "Behold, I *am* against you,
O most haughty one!" says the Lord GOD
of hosts;
"For your day has come,
The time *that* I will punish
you.*a*

32 The most proud shall
stumble and fall,
And no one will raise
him up;
I will kindle a fire in his
cities,
And it will devour all
around him."

33Thus says the LORD of hosts:

PRIDE

What is the
reward of
arrogant
people?
(50:32)

"The children of Israel *were* oppressed,
Along with the children of Judah;
All who took them captive have held
them fast;
They have refused to let them go.

34 Their Redeemer *is* strong;
The LORD of hosts *is* His name.
He will thoroughly plead their case,
That He may give rest to the land,
And disquiet the inhabitants of Babylon.

35 "A sword *is* against the Chaldeans," says
the LORD,
"Against the inhabitants of Babylon,
And against her princes and her wise
men.

36 A sword *is* against the soothsayers, and
they will be fools.
A sword *is* against her mighty men, and
they will be dismayed.

37 A sword *is* against their horses,
Against their chariots,
And against all the mixed peoples who
are in her midst;
And they will become like women.
A sword *is* against her treasures, and they
will be robbed.

38 A drought*a* *is* against her waters, and they
will be dried up.
For it *is* the land of carved images,
And they are insane with *their* idols.

39 "Therefore the wild desert beasts shall
dwell *there* with the jackals,
And the ostriches shall dwell in it.
It shall be inhabited no more forever,
Nor shall it be dwelt in from generation
to generation.

40 As God overthrew Sodom and
Gomorrah
And their neighbors," says the LORD,
"*So* no one shall reside there,
Nor son of man dwell in it.

41 "Behold, a people shall come from the
north,
And a great nation and many kings
Shall be raised up from the ends of the
earth.

42 They shall hold the bow and the lance;
They *are* cruel and shall not show mercy.
Their voice shall roar like the sea;
They shall ride on horses,

50:29 *a*Qere, some Hebrew manuscripts, Septuagint, and Targum add *to her*.   **50:31** *a*Following Masoretic
Text and Targum; Septuagint and Vulgate read *The time of your punishment*.   **50:38** *a*Following Masoretic Text,
Targum, and Vulgate; Syriac reads *sword*; Septuagint omits *A drought is*.

Set in array, like a man for the battle,
Against you, O daughter of Babylon.

43 "The king of Babylon has heard the report
　　about them,
And his hands grow feeble;
Anguish has taken hold of him,
Pangs as of a woman in childbirth.

44 "Behold, he shall come up like a lion from
　　the floodplain[a] of the Jordan
Against the dwelling place of the strong;
But I will make them suddenly run away
　　from her.
And who *is* a chosen *man that* I may
　　appoint over her?
For who *is* like Me?
Who will arraign Me?
And who *is* that shepherd
Who will withstand Me?"

45 Therefore hear the counsel of the LORD
　　that He has taken against Babylon,
And His purposes that He has proposed
　　against the land of the Chaldeans:
Surely the least of the flock shall draw
　　them out;
Surely He will make their dwelling place
　　desolate with them.

46 At the noise of the taking of Babylon
The earth trembles,
And the cry is heard among the nations.

THE UTTER DESTRUCTION OF BABYLON

¹Thus says the LORD:

"Behold, I will raise up against Babylon,
Against those who dwell in Leb Kamai,[a]
A destroying wind.

2 And I will send winnowers to Babylon,
Who shall winnow her
　　and empty her land.
For in the day of doom
They shall be against
　　her all around.

3 Against *her* let the
　　archer bend his
　　bow,
And lift himself up
　　against *her* in his
　　armor.
Do not spare her young
　　men;
Utterly destroy all her army.

4 Thus the slain shall fall in the land of the
　　Chaldeans,
And *those* thrust through in her streets.

5 For Israel is not forsaken, nor Judah,
By his God, the LORD of hosts,
Though their land was filled with sin
　　against the Holy One of Israel."

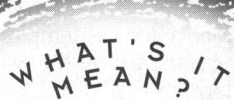

WHAT'S IT MEAN?

The Bible often compares God's judgment to a cup filled with suffering. Babylon was described as a "golden cup in the LORD's hand," because the Babylonians conquered the countries God wanted to punish.
Jeremiah 51:7

6 Flee from the midst of Babylon,
And every one save his life!
Do not be cut off in her iniquity,
For this *is* the time of the LORD's
　　vengeance;
He shall recompense her.

7 Babylon *was* a golden cup in the LORD's
　　hand,
That made all the earth drunk.
The nations drank her wine;
Therefore the nations are deranged.

8 Babylon has suddenly fallen and been
　　destroyed.
Wail for her!
Take balm for her pain;
　　　　Perhaps she may be
　　　　　healed.

9 We would have healed
　　Babylon,
But she is not healed.
Forsake her, and let us
　　go everyone to his
　　own country;
For her judgment
　　reaches to heaven
　　and is lifted up to
　　the skies.

10 The LORD has revealed
　　our righteousness.

"The LORD has revealed our righteousness. Come and let us declare in Zion the work of the LORD our God."
(Jeremiah 51:10)

50:44 [a]Or *thicket*　　**51:1** [a]A code word for Chaldea (Babylonia); may be translated *The Midst of Those Who Rise Up Against Me*

Come and let us declare in Zion the work
of the LORD our God.

11 Make the arrows bright!
Gather the shields!
The LORD has raised up the spirit of the
kings of the Medes.
For His plan is against Babylon to destroy
it,
Because it is the vengeance of the LORD,
The vengeance for His temple.

12 Set up the standard on the walls of
Babylon;
Make the guard strong,
Set up the watchmen,
Prepare the ambushes.
For the LORD has both devised and done
What He spoke against the inhabitants of
Babylon.

13 O you who dwell by many waters,
Abundant in treasures,
Your end has come,
The measure of your covetousness.

14 The LORD of hosts has sworn by Himself:
"Surely I will fill you with men, as with
locusts,
And they shall lift up a shout against
you."

15 He has made the earth by His power;
He has established the world by His
wisdom,
And stretched out the heaven by His
understanding.

16 When He utters His voice—
There is a multitude of waters in the
heavens:
"He causes the vapors to ascend from the
ends of the earth;
He makes lightnings for the rain;
He brings the wind out of His treasuries."[a]

17 Everyone is dull-hearted, without
knowledge;
Every metalsmith is put to shame by the
carved image;
For his molded image is falsehood,
And there is no breath in them.

18 They are futile, a work of errors;
In the time of their punishment they shall
perish.

19 The Portion of Jacob is not like them,
For He is the Maker of all things;
And Israel is the tribe of His inheritance.
The LORD of hosts is His name.

20 "You are My battle-ax and weapons of
war:
For with you I will break the nation in
pieces;
With you I will destroy kingdoms;

21 With you I will break in pieces the horse
and its rider;
With you I will break in pieces the chariot
and its rider;

22 With you also I will break in pieces man
and woman;
With you I will break in pieces old and
young;
With you I will break in pieces the young
man and the maiden;

23 With you also I will break in pieces the
shepherd and his flock;
With you I will break in pieces the farmer
and his yoke of oxen;
And with you I will break in pieces
governors and rulers.

24 "And I will repay Babylon
And all the inhabitants of Chaldea
For all the evil they have done
In Zion in your sight," says the LORD.

25 "Behold, I am against you, O destroying
mountain,
Who destroys all the earth," says the
LORD.
"And I will stretch out My hand against
you,
Roll you down from the rocks,
And make you a burnt mountain.

26 They shall not take from you a stone for
a corner
Nor a stone for a foundation,
But you shall be desolate forever," says the
LORD.

27 Set up a banner in the land,
Blow the trumpet among the nations!
Prepare the nations against her,
Call the kingdoms together against her:
Ararat, Minni, and Ashkenaz.
Appoint a general against her;
Cause the horses to come up like the
bristling locusts.

28 Prepare against her the nations,
With the kings of the Medes,
Its governors and all its rulers,
All the land of his dominion.

29 And the land will tremble and
sorrow;

51:16 ªPsalm 135:7

For every purpose of the LORD shall be
   performed against Babylon,
To make the land of Babylon a desolation
   without inhabitant.
30 The mighty men of Babylon have ceased
   fighting,
They have remained in their
   strongholds;
Their might has failed,
They became *like* women;
They have burned her dwelling places,
The bars of her *gate* are broken.
31 One runner will run to meet another,
And one messenger to meet another,
To show the king of Babylon that his city
   is taken on *all* sides;
32 The passages are blocked,
The reeds they have burned with fire,
And the men of war are terrified.

33 For thus says the LORD of hosts, the God of
Israel:

   "The daughter of Babylon *is* like a
      threshing floor
   When it is time to thresh her;
   Yet a little while
   And the time of her harvest will come."

34 "Nebuchadnezzar the king of Babylon
   Has devoured me, he has crushed me;
He has made me an empty vessel,
He has swallowed me up like a monster;
He has filled his stomach with my
   delicacies,
He has spit me out.
35 Let the violence *done* to me and my flesh
   be upon Babylon,"
The inhabitant of Zion will say;
"And my blood be upon the inhabitants
   of Chaldea!"
Jerusalem will say.

36 Therefore thus says the LORD:

   "Behold, I will plead your case and take
      vengeance for you.
   I will dry up her sea and make her
      springs dry.
37 Babylon shall become a heap,
A dwelling place for jackals,
An astonishment and a hissing,
Without an inhabitant.
38 They shall roar together like lions,
They shall growl like lions' whelps.

39 In their excitement I will prepare their
   feasts;
I will make them drunk,
That they may rejoice,
And sleep a perpetual sleep
And not awake," says the LORD.
40 "I will bring them down
Like lambs to the slaughter,
Like rams with male goats.

41 "Oh, how Sheshach[a] is taken!
Oh, how the praise of the whole earth is
   seized!
How Babylon has become desolate
   among the nations!
42 The sea has come up over Babylon;
She is covered with the multitude of its
   waves.
43 Her cities are a desolation,
A dry land and a wilderness,
A land where no one dwells,
Through which no son of man passes.
44 I will punish Bel in Babylon,
And I will bring out of his mouth what
   he has swallowed;
And the nations shall not stream to him
   anymore.
Yes, the wall of Babylon shall fall.

45 "My people, go out of the midst of her!
And let everyone deliver himself from the
   fierce anger of the LORD.
46 And lest your heart faint,
And you fear for the rumor that *will be*
   heard in the land
(A rumor will come *one* year,
And after that, in *another* year
A rumor *will come,*
And violence in the land,
Ruler against ruler),
47 Therefore behold, the days are coming
That I will bring judgment on the carved
   images of Babylon;
Her whole land shall be ashamed,
And all her slain shall fall in her midst.
48 Then the heavens and the earth and all
   that *is* in them
Shall sing joyously over Babylon;
For the plunderers shall come to her from
   the north," says the LORD.

49 As Babylon *has caused* the slain of Israel
   to fall,
So at Babylon the slain of all the earth
   shall fall.

51:41 [a] A code word for Babylon (compare Jeremiah 25:26)

50 You who have escaped the sword,
Get away! Do not stand still!
Remember the LORD afar off,
And let Jerusalem come to your mind.

51 We are ashamed because we have heard
reproach.
Shame has covered our faces,
For strangers have come into the
sanctuaries of the LORD's house.

52 "Therefore behold, the days are coming,"
says the LORD,
"That I will bring judgment on her carved
images,
And throughout all her land the
wounded shall groan.
53 Though Babylon were to mount up to
heaven,
And though she were to fortify the height
of her strength,
Yet from Me plunderers would come to
her," says the LORD.

54 The sound of a cry comes from Babylon,
And great destruction from the land of
the Chaldeans,
55 Because the LORD is plundering
Babylon
And silencing her loud voice,
Though her waves roar like great
waters,
And the noise of their voice is uttered,
56 Because the plunderer comes against her,
against Babylon,
And her mighty men are taken.
Every one of their bows is broken;
For the LORD is the God of recompense,
He will surely repay.

57 "And I will make drunk
Her princes and wise men,
Her governors, her deputies, and her
mighty men.
And they shall sleep a perpetual sleep
And not awake," says the King,
Whose name is the LORD of hosts.

58Thus says the LORD of hosts:

"The broad walls of Babylon shall be
utterly broken,
And her high gates shall be burned with
fire;
The people will labor in vain,
And the nations, because of the fire;
And they shall be weary."

JEREMIAH'S COMMAND TO SERAIAH

59The word which Jeremiah the prophet commanded Seraiah the son of Neriah, the son of Mahseiah, when he went with Zedekiah the king of Judah to Babylon in the fourth year of his reign. And Seraiah was the quartermaster. 60So Jeremiah wrote in a book all the evil that would come upon Babylon, all these words that are written against Babylon. 61And Jeremiah said to Seraiah, "When you arrive in Babylon and see it, and read all these words, 62then you shall say, 'O LORD, You have spoken against this place to cut it off, so that none shall remain in it, neither man nor beast, but it shall be desolate forever.' 63Now it shall be, when you have finished reading this book, that you shall tie a stone to it and throw it out into the Euphrates. 64Then you shall say, 'Thus Babylon shall sink and not rise from the catastrophe that I will bring upon her. And they shall be weary.' "

Thus far are the words of Jeremiah.

THE FALL OF JERUSALEM REVIEWED

1Zedekiah was twenty-one years old when he became king, and he reigned eleven years in Jerusalem. His mother's name was Hamutal the daughter of Jeremiah of Libnah. 2He also did evil in the sight of the LORD, according to all that Jehoiakim had done. 3For because of the anger of the LORD this happened in Jerusalem and Judah, till He finally cast them out from His presence. Then Zedekiah rebelled against the king of Babylon.

WHAT'S IT MEAN?

Instead of fighting, ancient armies would "besiege" a city by surrounding it to prevent anyone from going in or out. During such a siege, the attacking army would keep food and water from entering the city, causing the people inside to die of hunger and thirst, if they did not surrender. Some sieges lasted months—even years. Jerusalem fell after a siege in 586 B.C.
Jeremiah 52:5, 6

4Now it came to pass in the ninth year of his reign, in the tenth month, on the tenth day of the month, that Nebuchadnezzar king of Babylon and all his army came against Jerusalem and encamped against it; and *they* built a siege wall against it all around. ⁵So the city was besieged until the eleventh year of King Zedekiah. ⁶By the fourth month, on the ninth day of the month, the famine had become so severe in the city that there was no food for the people of the land. ⁷Then the city wall was broken through, and all the men of war fled and went out of the city at night by way of the gate between the two walls, which *was* by the king's garden, even though the Chaldeans *were* near the city all around. And they went by way of the plain.ᵃ

⁸But the army of the Chaldeans pursued the king, and they overtook Zedekiah in the plains of Jericho. All his army was scattered from him. ⁹So they took the king and brought him up to the king of Babylon at Riblah in the land of Hamath, and he pronounced judgment on him. ¹⁰Then the king of Babylon killed the sons of Zedekiah before his eyes. And he killed all the princes of Judah in Riblah. ¹¹He also put out the eyes of Zedekiah; and the king of Babylon bound him in bronze fetters, took him to Babylon, and put him in prison till the day of his death.

THE TEMPLE AND CITY PLUNDERED AND BURNED

¹²Now in the fifth month, on the tenth *day* of the month (which *was* the nineteenth year of King Nebuchadnezzar king of Babylon), Nebuzaradan, the captain of the guard, *who* served the king of Babylon, came to Jerusalem. ¹³He burned the house of the LORD and the king's house; all the houses of Jerusalem, that is, all the houses of the great, he burned with fire. ¹⁴And all the army of the Chaldeans who *were* with the captain of the guard broke down all the walls of Jerusalem all around. ¹⁵Then Nebuzaradan the captain of the guard carried away captive *some* of the poor people, the rest of the people who remained in the city, the defectors who had deserted to the king of Babylon, and the rest of the craftsmen. ¹⁶But Nebuzaradan the captain of the guard left *some* of the poor of the land as vinedressers and farmers.

¹⁷The bronze pillars that *were* in the house of the LORD, and the carts and the bronze Sea that *were* in the house of the LORD, the Chaldeans broke in pieces, and carried all their bronze to Babylon. ¹⁸They also took away the pots, the shovels, the trimmers, the bowls, the spoons, and all the bronze utensils with which the priests ministered. ¹⁹The basins, the firepans, the bowls, the pots, the lampstands, the spoons, and the cups, whatever *was* solid gold and whatever *was* solid silver, the captain of the guard took away. ²⁰The two pillars, one Sea, the twelve bronze bulls which *were* under *it, and* the carts, which King Solomon had made for the house of the LORD—the bronze of all these articles was beyond measure. ²¹Now *concerning* the pillars: the height of one pillar *was* eighteen cubits, a measuring line of twelve cubits could measure its circumference, and its thickness *was* four fingers; *it was* hollow. ²²A capital of bronze *was* on it; and the height of one capital *was* five cubits, with a network and pomegranates all around the capital, all of bronze. The second pillar, with pomegranates was the same. ²³There were ninety-six pomegranates on the sides; all the pomegranates, all around on the network, *were* one hundred.

THE PEOPLE TAKEN CAPTIVE TO BABYLONIA

²⁴The captain of the guard took Seraiah the chief priest, Zephaniah the second priest, and the three doorkeepers. ²⁵He also took out of the city an officer who had charge of the men of war, seven men of the king's close associates who were found in the city, the principal scribe of the army who mustered the people of the land, and sixty men of the people of the land who were found in the midst of the city. ²⁶And Nebuzaradan the captain of the guard took these and brought them to the king of Babylon at Riblah. ²⁷Then the king of Babylon struck them and put them to death at Riblah in the land of Hamath. Thus Judah was carried away captive from its own land.

²⁸These *are* the people whom Nebuchadnezzar carried away captive: in the seventh year, three thousand and twenty-three Jews; ²⁹in the eighteenth year of Nebuchadnezzar he carried away captive from Jerusalem eight hundred and thirty-two persons; ³⁰in the twenty-third year of Nebuchadnezzar, Nebuzaradan the captain of the guard carried away captive of the Jews seven hundred and forty-five persons. All the persons *were* four thousand six hundred.

JEHOIACHIN RELEASED FROM PRISON

³¹Now it came to pass in the thirty-seventh year of the captivity of Jehoiachin king of Judah, in the twelfth month, on the twenty-fifth *day* of the month, *that* Evil-Merodachᵃ king of Babylon, in the first *year* of his reign, lifted up the head of Jehoiachin king of Judah and

---

52:7 ᵃOr *the Arabah,* that is, the Jordan Valley   **52:31** ᵃOr *Awil-Marduk*

brought him out of prison. ³²And he spoke kindly to him and gave him a more prominent seat than those of the kings who *were* with him in Babylon. ³³So Jehoiachin changed from his prison garments, and he ate bread regularly be-fore the king all the days of his life. ³⁴And as for his provisions, there was a regular ration given him by the king of Babylon, a portion for each day until the day of his death, all the days of his life.

Lamentations

CONTENT You might remember the prophet, Jeremiah, who wrote the book named after him. He talked and preached and cried and warned his people that if they didn't straighten up something bad was going to happen. Something bad *did* happen. The people were taken away from their land and held captive in Babylon. It was during this time that Jeremiah wrote Lamentations.

You can think of Lamentations as being like somebody singing the blues. The music we call "the blues" is music about the most difficult parts of life. It originated from a people and in a time that was hopeless and hard. When these people put music to their sorrow, it gave them a way to express their feelings. That's what the Lamentations did for the Hebrews.

Lamentations is actually a book of five songs. In that day they were sung as funeral dirges, which would be an appropriate thing to sing if the life of your whole nation was falling apart.

The name *Lamentations* comes from the word *lament*. A lament is a mournful cry. The whole Book of Lamentations is a mournful cry about the horrible situation the Hebrews got into because they didn't pay attention to the way God wanted them to live their lives.

Outline
1:1–22 .... First Lament: The Sorrows of Captive Jerusalem
2:1–22 .... Second Lament: The Lord's Anger with Jerusalem
3:1–66 .... Third Lament: Hope Through God's Mercy
4:1–22 .... Fourth Lament: Jerusalem Punished
5:1–22 .... Fifth Lament: A Prayer for Restoration

Purpose Persistent sin brings judgment that crushes the spirit.

Theme Suffering as Punishment for Sin

Date of writing 586–584 B.C.

JERUSALEM IN AFFLICTION

1   How lonely sits the city
That was full of people!
How like a widow is she,
Who *was* great among the nations!
The princess among the provinces
Has become a slave!

2   She weeps bitterly in the night,
Her tears *are* on her
cheeks;
Among all her lovers
She has none to
comfort *her.*
All her friends
have dealt
treacherously
with her;
They have become
her enemies.

3   Judah has gone into
captivity,
Under affliction and hard
servitude;
She dwells among the nations,
She finds no rest;
All her persecutors overtake her in dire
straits.

WHAT'S IT MEAN?

Abandoned city gates in ancient times
would have seemed as unusual as empty freeways
during rush hour today. Usually the gates of ancient cities were
crowded with people and bustling with activity. The city gates were
where most business and legal transactions took place. In addition,
there was the constant flow of caravan
traffic in and out of the city.
Lamentations 1:4

4   The roads to Zion mourn
Because no one comes to the set feasts.
All her gates are desolate;
Her priests sigh,
Her virgins are afflicted,
And she *is* in bitterness.

5   Her adversaries have become the master,
Her enemies prosper;
For the LORD has afflicted her
Because of the multitude of her
transgressions.
Her children have gone into captivity
before the enemy.

6   And from the daughter of Zion
All her splendor
has departed.
Her princes have
become like deer
That find no
pasture,
That flee without
strength
Before the pursuer.

7   In the days of her
affliction and
roaming,
Jerusalem
remembers all
her pleasant
things
That she had in the days of old.
When her people fell into the hand of the
enemy,
With no one to help her,
The adversaries saw her
And mocked at her downfall.[a]

8   Jerusalem has sinned gravely,
Therefore she has become vile.[a]
All who honored her despise her
Because they have seen her nakedness;
Yes, she sighs and turns away.

9   Her uncleanness *is* in her skirts;
She did not consider her destiny;
Therefore her collapse was awesome;
She had no comforter.
"O LORD, behold my affliction,
For *the* enemy is exalted!"

10   The adversary has spread his hand
Over all her pleasant things;
For she has seen the nations enter her
sanctuary,
Those whom You commanded
Not to enter Your assembly.

11   All her people sigh,
They seek bread;

> **"How lonely sits the city that was full of people! How like a widow is she, who was great among the nations! The princess among the provinces has become a slave!"**
> **(Lamentations 1:1)**

1:7 [a]Vulgate reads *her Sabbaths.*   **1:8** [a]Septuagint and Vulgate read *moved* or *removed.*

They have given their valuables for food
   to restore life.
"See, O LORD, and consider,
   For I am scorned."

12 "Is it nothing to you, all you who pass by?
   Behold and see
   If there is any sorrow like my sorrow,
   Which has been brought on me,
   Which the LORD has inflicted
   In the day of His fierce anger.

13 "From above He has sent fire into my
      bones,
   And it overpowered them;
   He has spread a net for my feet
   And turned me back;
   He has made me desolate
   And faint all the day.

14 "The yoke of my transgressions was
      bound;a
   They were woven together by His hands,
   And thrust upon my neck.
   He made my strength fail;
   The Lord delivered me into the hands of
      those whom I am not able to withstand.

15 "The Lord has trampled underfoot all my
      mighty men in my midst;
   He has called an assembly against me
   To crush my young men;
   The Lord trampled as in a winepress
   The virgin daughter of Judah.

16 "For these things I weep;
   My eye, my eye overflows with water;
   Because the comforter, who should
      restore my life,
   Is far from me.
   My children are desolate
   Because the enemy prevailed."

17 Zion spreads out her hands,
   But no one comforts her;
   The LORD has commanded concerning
      Jacob
   That those around him become his
      adversaries;
   Jerusalem has become an unclean thing
      among them.

18 "The LORD is righteous,
   For I rebelled against His commandment.
   Hear now, all peoples,

And behold my sorrow;
My virgins and my
   young men
Have gone into
   captivity.

DISOBEDIENCE

Is God
right to
punish the
disobedient?
(1:18)

19 "I called for my lovers,
   But they deceived me;
   My priests and my elders
   Breathed their last in the city,
   While they sought food
   To restore their life.

20 "See, O LORD, that I am in distress;
   My soul is troubled;
   My heart is overturned within me,
   For I have been very rebellious.
   Outside the sword bereaves,
   At home it is like death.

21 "They have heard that I sigh,
   But no one comforts me.
   All my enemies have heard of my
      trouble;
   They are glad that You have done it.
   Bring on the day You have announced,
   That they may become like me.

22 "Let all their wickedness come before You,
   And do to them as You have done to me
   For all my transgressions;
   For my sighs are many,
   And my heart is faint."

GOD'S ANGER WITH JERUSALEM

1   How the Lord has covered the daughter
      of Zion
   With a cloud in His anger!
   He cast down from heaven to the earth
   The beauty of Israel,
   And did not remember His footstool
   In the day of His anger.

2   The Lord has swallowed up and has not
      pitied
   All the dwelling places of Jacob.
   He has thrown down in His wrath
   The strongholds of the daughter of Judah;
   He has brought them down to the
      ground;
   He has profaned the kingdom and its
      princes.

3   He has cut off in fierce anger
   Every horn of Israel;

1:14 aFollowing Masoretic Text and Targum; Septuagint, Syriac, and Vulgate read watched over.

He has drawn back His right hand
From before the enemy.
He has blazed against Jacob like a flaming
   fire
Devouring all around.

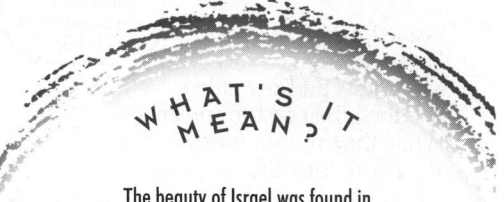

WHAT'S IT MEAN?

The beauty of Israel was found in
the temple that Solomon had built on Zion,
and in the ark of the covenant, which contained the Ten Commandments, God's instructions for living. That beauty was marred when
King Nebuchadnezzar and his Babylonian forces captured Jerusalem and burned the temple.

Lamentations 2:1

4   Standing like an enemy, He has bent His
       bow;
    With His right hand, like an adversary,
    He has slain all *who were* pleasing to His
       eye;
    On the tent of the daughter of Zion,
    He has poured out His fury like fire.

5   The Lord was like an enemy.
    He has swallowed up Israel,
    He has swallowed up all her palaces;
    He has destroyed her strongholds,
    And has increased mourning and
       lamentation
    In the daughter of Judah.

6   He has done violence to His tabernacle,
    As if it were a garden;
    He has destroyed His place of assembly;
    The LORD has caused
    The appointed feasts and Sabbaths to be
       forgotten in Zion.
    In His burning indignation He has
       spurned the king and the priest.

7   The Lord has spurned His altar,
    He has abandoned His sanctuary;
    He has given up the walls of her palaces
    Into the hand of the enemy.
    They have made a noise in the house of
       the LORD
    As on the day of a set feast.

8   The LORD has purposed to destroy
    The wall of the daughter of Zion.
    He has stretched out a line;
    He has not withdrawn His hand from
       destroying;
    Therefore He has caused the rampart and
       wall to lament;
    They languished together.

9   Her gates have sunk into the ground;
    He has destroyed and broken her bars.
    Her king and her princes *are* among the
       nations;
    The Law *is* no *more*,
    And her prophets find no vision from the
       LORD.

10 The elders of the daughter of Zion
    Sit on the ground *and* keep silence;
    They throw dust on their heads
    And gird themselves with sackcloth.
    The virgins of Jerusalem
    Bow their heads to the ground.

11 My eyes fail with tears,
    My heart is troubled;
    My bile is poured on the ground
    Because of the destruction of the daughter
       of my people,
    Because the children and the infants
    Faint in the streets of the city.

WHAT'S IT MEAN?

Honoring the Sabbath was one of the
Ten Commandments God gave to the Israelites
through Moses. The Israelites honored it by resting every seventh day
of the week. In addition to the Sabbaths, the Israelites celebrated
many other festivals and holidays, including
Passover and the New Moon festival.

Lamentations 2:6

12 They say to their mothers,
    "Where *is* grain and wine?"
    As they swoon like the wounded
    In the streets of the city,
    As their life is poured out
    In their mothers' bosom.

13 How shall I console you?
To what shall I liken you,
O daughter of Jerusalem?
What shall I compare with you, that I
may comfort you,
O virgin daughter of Zion?
For your ruin *is* spread wide as the sea;
Who can heal you?

14 Your prophets have seen for you
False and deceptive visions;
They have not uncovered your iniquity,
To bring back your captives,
But have envisioned for you false
prophecies and delusions.

15 All who pass by clap *their* hands at you;
They hiss and shake their heads
At the daughter of Jerusalem:
"*Is* this the city that is called
'The perfection of beauty,
The joy of the whole earth'?"

16 All your enemies have opened their
mouth against you;
They hiss and gnash *their* teeth.
They say, "We have swallowed *her* up!
Surely this *is* the day we have waited for;
We have found *it,* we have seen *it!*"

17 The LORD has done what He
purposed;
He has fulfilled His word
Which He commanded
in days of old.
He has thrown down
and has not pitied,
And He has caused an
enemy to rejoice over
you;
He has exalted the horn of your
adversaries.

Does God accomplish His plans? (2:17)

18 Their heart cried out to the Lord,
"O wall of the daughter of Zion,
Let tears run down like a river day and
night;
Give yourself no relief;
Give your eyes no rest.

19 "Arise, cry out in the night,
At the beginning of the watches;
Pour out your heart like water before the
face of the Lord.
Lift your hands toward Him

For the life of your young children,
Who faint from hunger at the head of
every street."

20 "See, O LORD, and consider!
To whom have You done this?
Should the women eat their offspring,
The children they have cuddled?[a]
Should the priest and prophet be slain
In the sanctuary of the Lord?

21 "Young and old lie
On the ground in the streets;
My virgins and my young men
Have fallen by the sword;
You have slain *them* in the day of Your
anger,
You have slaughtered *and* not pitied.

22 "You have invited as to a feast day
The terrors that surround me.
In the day of the LORD's anger
There was no refugee or survivor.
Those whom I have borne and
brought up
My enemies have destroyed."

THE PROPHET'S ANGUISH AND HOPE

1 I *am* the man *who* has seen affliction by
the rod of His wrath.
2 He has led me and made *me* walk
In darkness and not *in* light.
3 Surely He has turned His hand against
me
Time and time again throughout the day.

4 He has aged my flesh and my skin,
And broken my bones.
5 He has besieged me
And surrounded *me* with bitterness and
woe.
6 He has set me in dark places
Like the dead of long ago.

7 He has hedged me in so that I cannot get
out;
He has made my chain heavy.
8 Even when I cry and shout,
He shuts out my prayer.
9 He has blocked my ways with hewn
stone;
He has made my paths crooked.

10 He *has been* to me a bear lying in wait,
Like a lion in ambush.

2:20 ᵃVulgate reads *a span long.*

11 He has turned aside my ways and torn
    me in pieces;
   He has made me desolate.
12 He has bent His bow
   And set me up as a target for the arrow.

13 He has caused the arrows of His quiver
   To pierce my loins.[a]
14 I have become the ridicule of all my
    people—
   Their taunting song all the day.
15 He has filled me with bitterness,
   He has made me drink wormwood.

16 He has also broken my teeth with gravel,
   And covered me with ashes.
17 You have moved my soul far from peace;
   I have forgotten prosperity.
18 And I said, "My strength and my hope
   Have perished from the LORD."

19 Remember my affliction and roaming,
   The wormwood and the gall.
20 My soul still remembers
   And sinks within me.
21 This I recall to my mind,
   Therefore I have hope.

22 *Through* the LORD's
    mercies we are not
    consumed,
   Because His compassions
    fail not.
23 *They are* new every morning;
   Great *is* Your faithfulness.

24 "The LORD *is* my portion," says my soul,
   "Therefore I hope in Him!"

WHAT'S IT MEAN?

And they say junk food is bad for you. . . .
Some tribes in the ancient Near East used to mix
sand, gravel, and other solid substances in the food they gave
to their prisoners. You can imagine the digestive problems that
resulted from this diet, but don't forget about the dental nightmares
it caused as well. The hard objects wore down and broke the teeth of
the prisoners, causing them tremendous pain.

Lamentations 3:16

25 The LORD *is* good to those who wait for
    Him,
   To the soul *who* seeks Him.
26 *It is* good that *one* should hope and wait
    quietly
   For the salvation of the LORD.
27 *It is* good for a man to bear
   The yoke in his youth.

28 Let him sit alone and keep silent,
   Because *God* has laid *it* on him;
29 Let him put his mouth in the dust—

HOPE
Can
we have
hope in bad
situations?
(3:21, 22)

Promise   HE PROMISES TO SHOW YOU COMPASSION EACH MORNING.

[God's] compassions fail not. They are new every morning; great is Your faithfulness (Lam. 3:22b, 23).

You lay your head on your pillow tonight and know it's been a terrible day. Your sin got the best of you all day long. Where did your self-control go? Guilt and shame begin to swallow you. You feel so far away from God. *He must really be disappointed,* you think. All you want to do is hide—hide from your friends and yourself, but mostly from God. But the right thing to do is to run to Him. He is tender and loving. His forgiveness is pure and cleansing. His compassion brings comfort. His mercy grants freedom, His lovingkindness lets you open your eyes in the morning and be glad for the new day. It's a start-over day. It's a clean-slate day. It's a new day, with new compassion from the God of new beginnings.

SEE FOR YOURSELF:
Ps. 90:14; 118:1–4; 2 Cor. 1:3

Looks down and sees.

30 Let him give *his* cheek to the one who
strikes him,
And be full of reproach.

51 My eyes bring suffering to my soul
Because of all the daughters of my city.

31 For the Lord will not cast off forever.
32 Though He causes grief,
Yet He will show compassion
According to the multitude of His mercies.
33 For He does not afflict willingly,
Nor grieve the children of men.

52 My enemies without cause
Hunted me down like a bird.
53 They silenced*a* my life in the pit
And threw stones at me.
54 The waters flowed over my head;
I said, "I am cut off!"

34 To crush under one's feet
All the prisoners of the earth,
35 To turn aside the justice *due* a man
Before the face of the Most High,
36 Or subvert a man in his cause—
The Lord does not approve.

55 I called on Your name, O LORD,
From the lowest pit.
56 You have heard my voice:
"Do not hide Your ear
From my sighing, from my cry for help."
57 You drew near on the day I called on
You,
And said, "Do not fear!"

37 Who *is* he *who* speaks and it comes to
pass,
When the Lord has not commanded *it?*
38 *Is it* not from the mouth of the Most
High
That woe and well-being proceed?
39 Why should a living man complain,
A man for the punishment of his sins?

58 O Lord, You have pleaded the case for my
soul;
You have redeemed my life.
59 O LORD, You have seen *how* I am
wronged;
Judge my case.
60 You have seen all their vengeance,
All their schemes against me.

40 Let us search out and examine our ways,
And turn back to the LORD;
41 Let us lift our hearts and hands
To God in heaven.
42 We have transgressed and rebelled;
You have not pardoned.

61 You have heard their reproach, O LORD,
All their schemes against me,
62 The lips of my enemies
And their whispering against me all the
day.
63 Look at their sitting down and their rising
up;
I *am* their taunting song.

43 You have covered *Yourself* with anger
And pursued us;
You have slain *and* not pitied.
44 You have covered Yourself with a cloud,
That prayer should not pass through.
45 You have made us an offscouring and
refuse
In the midst of the peoples.

64 Repay them, O LORD,
According to the work of their hands.
65 Give them a veiled*a* heart;
Your curse *be* upon them!
66 In Your anger,
Pursue and destroy them
From under the heavens of the LORD.

46 All our enemies
Have opened their mouths against us.
47 Fear and a snare have come upon us,
Desolation and destruction.
48 My eyes overflow with rivers of water
For the destruction of the daughter of my
people.

THE DEGRADATION OF ZION

1 How the gold has become dim!
How changed the fine gold!
The stones of the sanctuary are scattered
At the head of every street.

49 My eyes flow and do not cease,
Without interruption,
50 Till the LORD from heaven

2 The precious sons of Zion,
Valuable as fine gold,

3:53 *a*Septuagint reads *put to death.*   3:65 *a*A Jewish tradition reads *sorrow of.*

How they are regarded as clay pots,
The work of the hands of the potter!

3 Even the jackals present their breasts
To nurse their young;
But the daughter of my people *is* cruel,
Like ostriches in the wilderness.

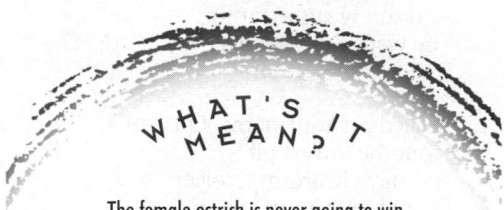

WHAT'S IT MEAN?

The female ostrich is never going to win
any "mother of the year" awards in the animal
kingdom. Most birds build nests to protect their young ones. The
ostrich simply drops her eggs in the sand and takes off, letting
the heat of the sun warm them. Things don't improve much after
the eggs have hatched, either. If the mother ostrich feels threatened,
she won't hesitate to abandon her young ones to save her own skin.
The Israelites considered the ostrich's
"parenting" style to be cruel.
Lamentations 4:3

4 The tongue of the infant clings
To the roof of its mouth for thirst;
The young children ask for bread,
But no one breaks *it* for them.

5 Those who ate delicacies
Are desolate in the streets;
Those who were brought up in scarlet
Embrace ash heaps.

6 The punishment of the iniquity of the
    daughter of my people
Is greater than the punishment of the sin
    of Sodom,
Which was overthrown in a moment,
With no hand to help her!

7 Her Nazirites[a] were brighter than snow
And whiter than milk;
They were more ruddy in body than
    rubies,
Like sapphire in their appearance.

8 *Now* their appearance is blacker than
    soot;
They go unrecognized in the streets;

Their skin clings to their bones,
It has become as dry as wood.

9 *Those* slain by the sword are better off
Than *those* who die of hunger;
For these pine away,
Stricken *for lack* of the fruits of the field.

10 The hands of the compassionate women
Have cooked their own children;
They became food for them
In the destruction of the daughter of my
    people.

11 The LORD has fulfilled His fury,
He has poured out His fierce anger.
He kindled a fire in Zion,
And it has devoured its foundations.

12 The kings of the earth,
And all inhabitants of the world,
Would not have believed
That the adversary and the enemy
Could enter the gates of Jerusalem—

13 Because of the sins of her prophets
And the iniquities of her priests,
Who shed in her midst
The blood of the just.

14 They wandered blind in the streets;
They have defiled themselves with blood,
So that no one would touch their
    garments.

15 They cried out to them,
"Go away, unclean!
Go away, go away,
Do not touch us!"
When they fled and wandered,
Those among the nations said,
"They shall no longer dwell *here*."

16 The face[a] of the LORD scattered them;
He no longer regards them.
The people do not respect the priests
Nor show favor to the elders.

17 Still our eyes failed us,
Watching vainly for our help;
In our watching we watched
For a nation *that* could not save *us*.

18 They tracked our steps
So that we could not walk in our streets.

4:7 [a]Or *nobles*   **4:16** [a]Targum reads *anger*.

Our end was near;
Our days were over,
For our end had come.

19 Our pursuers were swifter
Than the eagles of the heavens.
They pursued us on the mountains
And lay in wait for us in the wilderness.

20 The breath of our nostrils, the anointed of
the LORD,
Was caught in their pits,
Of whom we said, "Under his shadow
We shall live among the nations."

21 Rejoice and be glad, O daughter of Edom,
You who dwell in the land of Uz!
The cup shall also pass over to you
And you shall become drunk and make
yourself naked.

22 The punishment of your iniquity is
accomplished,
O daughter of Zion;
He will no longer send you into captivity.
He will punish your iniquity,
O daughter of Edom;
He will uncover your sins!

A PRAYER FOR RESTORATION

1 Remember, O LORD, what has come upon
us;
Look, and behold our
reproach!
2 Our inheritance has been
turned over to aliens,
And our houses to
foreigners.
3 We have become
orphans and waifs,
Our mothers are like
widows.

4 We pay for the water we
drink,
And our wood comes at a price.
5 They pursue at our heels;[a]
We labor and have no rest.
6 We have given our hand to the Egyptians
And the Assyrians, to be satisfied with
bread.

7 Our fathers sinned and are no more,
But we bear their iniquities.
8 Servants rule over us;
There is none to deliver us from their
hand.
9 We get our bread at the risk of our lives,
Because of the sword in the wilderness.

10 Our skin is hot as an oven,
Because of the fever of famine.
11 They ravished the women in Zion,
The maidens in the cities of Judah.
12 Princes were hung up by their hands,
And elders were not respected.
13 Young men ground at the millstones;
Boys staggered under loads of wood.
14 The elders have ceased gathering at the
gate,
And the young men from their music.

15 The joy of our heart has ceased;
Our dance has turned into
mourning.
16 The crown has fallen
from our head.
Woe to us, for we have
sinned!
17 Because of this our heart
is faint;
Because of these things our eyes grow
dim,

18 Because of Mount
Zion which is
desolate,
With foxes walking
about on it.

19 You, O LORD, remain
forever;
Your throne from
generation to
generation.
20 Why do You forget us
forever,
And forsake us for so
long a time?
21 Turn us back to You, O LORD, and we will
be restored;
Renew our days as of old,
22 Unless You have utterly rejected us,
And are very angry with us!

TRIALS

What causes
some trials?
(5:16)

"Turn us back to You,
O LORD, and we will be
restored . . . unless You
have utterly rejected us."
(Lamentations 5:21a, 22a)

5:5 [a]Literally necks

CONTENT   Imagine trying to explain something that you have never seen before, that is made out of substances that don't exist and that functions in dimensions that are not a part of your world. Your explanation might turn out a bit confusing, don't you think? And don't you think that you would end up making a lot of comparisons? "It was like this, except . . ." "It was sort of like that, only it didn't . . ." If you can imagine that kind of explanation, then you are ready to read the Book of Ezekiel.

Ezekiel preached his message while his people were being held captive in Babylon. The other prophets, for years, had told these people that if they didn't change their ways they would self-destruct as a culture. Now they were facing that very destruction and they were *still* disregarding God. It was at this point that God called Ezekiel to give them one more chance to repent.

Ezekiel was preaching to people who were in a mess. He encouraged them by reminding them that there was a brighter future waiting. He also confronted their sin, which was the reason for the mess in the first place.

Purpose   Count on God to judge sin as well as to bless.

Theme   Destruction of Jerusalem and Its Restoration

Date of writing   593–571 B.C.

Bible Talk

The Dry Bones

One of the most famous visions of Ezekiel is the vision of a whole valley of skeletons. An old spiritual calls them "dry bones." It must have looked like something out of an Indiana Jones-kind of story. But if it was amazing to see that valley of skeletons, imagine how amazing it must have been to see them reconnect and be brought back to life: a whole valley of old bones suddenly rattling together, gathering some skin on them, and becoming an army.

God's point in giving Ezekiel this vision was that we are never so far gone that God can't give us new life if we'll just turn to Him and repent. That's good news, isn't it? No matter where we are or what a mess we've made, we are never too far gone.

WHY DIDN'T PEOPLE LISTEN?

When you review the history of the Hebrew people, it's sort of exasperating that by the time of Ezekiel they still hadn't learned to trust God and obey Him. God had been working miracles among these people since their very first forefather, Abraham. God had saved this nation from death time after time. God had proved Himself. What made these people keep missing the point?

We can't really and truly answer that question. But if we look at our own lives, we can get a big clue to the answer. It seems to be our human nature to choose our own way rather than God's way. We still do it today, even after God has proven Himself. When we look at ourselves, the Hebrews aren't so hard to understand.

EZEKIEL'S VISION OF GOD

¹Now it came to pass in the thirtieth year, in the fourth *month*, on the fifth *day* of the month, as I *was* among the captives by the River Chebar, *that* the heavens were opened and I saw visions*ᵃ* of God. ²On the fifth *day* of the month, which *was* in the fifth year of King Jehoiachin's captivity, ³the word of the LORD came expressly to Ezekiel the priest, the son of Buzi, in the land of the Chaldeans*ᵃ* by the River Chebar; and the hand of the LORD was upon him there.

⁴Then I looked, and behold, a whirlwind was coming out of the north, a great cloud with raging fire engulfing itself; and brightness *was* all around it and radiating out of its midst like the color of amber, out of the midst of the fire. ⁵Also from within it *came* the likeness of four living creatures. And this *was* their appearance: they had the likeness of a man. ⁶Each one had four faces, and each one had four wings. ⁷Their legs *were* straight, and the soles of their feet *were* like the soles of calves' feet. They sparkled like the color of burnished bronze. ⁸The hands of a man *were* under their wings on their four sides; and each of the four had faces and wings. ⁹Their wings touched one another. *The creatures* did not turn when they went, but each one went straight forward.

The bizarre appearance of these angels show us just how powerful they are. You see, each of their four faces looks like one of the most powerful creatures on earth—a man, a lion, an ox (a bull), and an eagle. Think about it. Human beings rule over every creature on earth. The lion is the king of the jungle. Bulls are the strongest tame animals. Eagles are the fastest, strongest birds. If the angels that surround God are so powerful, imagine how mighty He is!

Ezekiel 1:10

¹⁰As for the likeness of their faces, *each* had the face of a man; each of the four had the face of a lion on the right side, each of the four had the face of an ox on the left side, and each of the four had the face of an eagle. ¹¹Thus *were* their faces. Their wings stretched upward; two *wings* of each one touched one another, and two covered their bodies. ¹²And each one went straight forward; they went wherever the spirit wanted to go, and they did not turn when they went.

¹³As for the likeness of the living creatures, their appearance *was* like burning coals of fire, like the appearance of torches going back and forth among the living creatures. The fire was bright, and out of the fire went lightning. ¹⁴And the living creatures ran back and forth, in appearance like a flash of lightning.

¹⁵Now as I looked at the living creatures, behold, a wheel *was* on the earth beside each living creature with its four faces. ¹⁶The appearance of the wheels and their workings *was* like the color of beryl, and all four had the same likeness. The appearance of their workings *was*, as it were, a wheel in the middle of a wheel. ¹⁷When they moved, they went toward any one of four directions; they did not turn aside when they went. ¹⁸As for their rims, they were so high they were awesome; and their rims *were* full of eyes, all around the four of them. ¹⁹When the living creatures went, the wheels went beside them; and when the living creatures were lifted up from the earth, the wheels were lifted up. ²⁰Wherever the spirit wanted to go, they went, *because* there the spirit went; and the wheels were lifted together with them, for the spirit of the living creatures*ᵃ* *was* in the wheels. ²¹When those went, *these* went; when those stood, *these* stood; and when those were lifted up from the earth, the wheels were lifted up together with them, for the spirit of the living creatures*ᵃ* *was* in the wheels.

²²The likeness of the firmament above the heads of the living creatures*ᵃ* *was* like the color of an awesome crystal, stretched out over their heads. ²³And under the firmament their wings *spread out* straight, one toward another. Each one had two which covered one side, and each one had two which covered the other side of the body. ²⁴When they went, I heard the noise of their wings, like the noise of many waters, like the voice of the Almighty, a tumult like the noise of an army; and when they stood still, they let down their wings. ²⁵A voice came from above the firmament that *was* over their heads;

1:1 *ᵃ*Following Masoretic Text, Septuagint, and Vulgate; Syriac and Targum read *a vision.*   **1:3** *ᵃ*Or *Babylonians,* and so elsewhere in this book   **1:20** *ᵃ*Literally *living creature;* Septuagint and Vulgate read *spirit of life;* Targum reads *creatures.*   **1:21** *ᵃ*Literally *living creature;* Septuagint and Vulgate read *spirit of life;* Targum reads *creatures.*   **1:22** *ᵃ*Following Septuagint, Targum, and Vulgate; Masoretic Text reads *living creature.*

whenever they stood, they let down their wings.

²⁶And above the firmament over their heads *was* the likeness of a throne, in appearance like a sapphire stone; on the likeness of the throne *was* a likeness with the appearance of a man high above it. ²⁷Also from the appearance of His waist and upward I saw, as it were, the color of amber with the appearance of fire all around within it; and from the appearance of His waist and downward I saw, as it were, the appearance of fire with brightness all around. ²⁸Like the appearance of a rainbow in a cloud on a rainy day, so *was* the appearance of the brightness all around it. This *was* the appearance of the likeness of the glory of the LORD.

ANGELS
Is the appearance of angels frightening? (1:27, 28)

EZEKIEL SENT TO REBELLIOUS ISRAEL

So when I saw *it*, I fell on my face, and I heard a voice of One speaking.

¹And He said to me, "Son of man, stand on your feet, and I will speak to you." ²Then the Spirit entered me when He spoke to me, and set me on my feet; and I heard Him who spoke to me. ³And He said to me: "Son of man, I am sending you to the children of Israel, to a rebellious nation that has rebelled against Me; they and their fathers have transgressed against Me to this very day. ⁴For *they are* impudent and stubborn children. I am sending you to them, and you shall say to them, 'Thus says the Lord GOD.' ⁵As for them, whether they hear or whether they refuse—for they *are* a rebellious house—yet they will know that a prophet has been among them.

⁶"And you, son of man, do not be afraid of them nor be afraid of their words, though briers and thorns *are* with you and you dwell among scorpions; do not be afraid of their words or dismayed by their looks, though they *are* a rebellious house. ⁷You shall speak My words to them, whether they hear or whether they refuse, for they *are* rebellious. ⁸But you, son of man, hear what I say to you. Do not be rebellious like that rebellious house; open your mouth and eat what I give you."

⁹Now when I looked, there was a hand stretched out to me; and behold, a scroll of a book *was* in it. ¹⁰Then He spread it before me; and *there was* writing on the inside and on the outside, and written on it *were* lamentations and mourning and woe.

¹Moreover He said to me, "Son of man, eat what you find; eat this scroll, and go, speak to

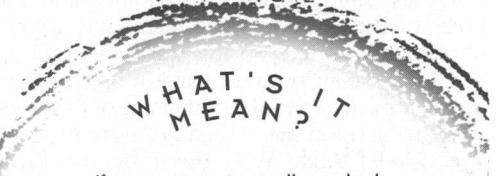

WHAT'S IT MEAN?

If someone ever tries to sell you a book from Old Testament times, don't buy it—it's a fake. Ancient documents were not written in book form, they were written on long pieces of paper or leather called scrolls. Since most scrolls were usually thirty-five pages or longer, ancient librarians discovered that the best way to store them was to roll them up on a stick (like toilet paper). A tag with the title written on it was attached to the scroll.

Ezekiel 2:9

the house of Israel." ²So I opened my mouth, and He caused me to eat that scroll.

³And He said to me, "Son of man, feed your belly, and fill your stomach with this scroll that I give you." So I ate, and it was in my mouth like honey in sweetness.

⁴Then He said to me: "Son of man, go to the house of Israel and speak with My words to them. ⁵For you *are* not sent to a people of unfamiliar speech and of hard language, *but* to the house of Israel, ⁶not to many people of unfamiliar speech and of hard language, whose words you cannot understand. Surely, had I sent you to them, they would have listened to you. ⁷But the house of Israel will not listen to you, because they will not listen to Me; for all the house of Israel *are* impudent and hard-hearted. ⁸Behold, I have made your face strong against their faces, and your forehead strong against their foreheads. ⁹Like adamant stone, harder than flint, I have made your forehead; do not be afraid of them, nor be dismayed at their looks, though they *are* a rebellious house."

¹⁰Moreover He said to me: "Son of man, receive into your heart all My words that I speak to you, and hear with your ears. ¹¹And go, get to the captives, to the children of your people, and speak to them and tell them, 'Thus says the Lord GOD,' whether they hear, or whether they refuse."

¹²Then the Spirit lifted me up, and I heard behind me a great thunderous voice: "Blessed *is* the glory of the LORD from His place!" ¹³*I also heard* the noise of the wings of the living

CHARACTER
Where can we get strength of character? (3:8)

creatures that touched one another, and the noise of the wheels beside them, and a great thunderous noise. [14]So the Spirit lifted me up and took me away, and I went in bitterness, in the heat of my spirit; but the hand of the LORD was strong upon me. [15]Then I came to the captives at Tel Abib, who dwelt by the River Chebar; and I sat where they sat, and remained there astonished among them seven days.

EZEKIEL IS A WATCHMAN

[16]Now it came to pass at the end of seven days that the word of the LORD came to me, saying, [17]"Son of man, I have made you a watchman for the house of Israel; therefore hear a word from My mouth, and give them warning from Me: [18]When I say to the wicked, 'You shall surely die', and you give him no warning, nor speak to warn the wicked from his wicked way, to save his life, that same wicked *man* shall die in his iniquity; but his blood I will require at your hand. [19]Yet, if you warn the wicked, and he does not turn from his wickedness, nor from his wicked way, he shall die in his iniquity; but you have delivered your soul.

WHAT'S IT MEAN?

City watchmen in ancient times were responsible for the safety of their citizens. These early security guards kept a lookout on the city walls for enemy attacks or any other possible dangers. If they failed to do their job properly, they were held personally responsible for any lost lives or damaged property.
Ezekiel 3:17

[20]"Again, when a righteous *man* turns from his righteousness and commits iniquity, and I lay a stumbling block before him, he shall die; because you did not give him warning, he shall die in his sin, and his righteousness which he has done shall not be remembered; but his blood I will require at your hand. [21]Nevertheless if you warn the righteous *man* that the righteous should not sin, and he does not sin, he shall surely live because he took warning; also you will have delivered your soul."

[22]Then the hand of the LORD was upon me there, and He said to me, "Arise, go out into the plain, and there I shall talk with you."

[23]So I arose and went out into the plain, and behold, the glory of the LORD stood there, like the glory which I saw by the River Chebar; and I fell on my face. [24]Then the Spirit entered me and set me on my feet, and spoke with me and said to me: "Go, shut yourself inside your house. [25]And you, O son of man, surely they will put ropes on you and bind you with them, so that you cannot go out among them. [26]I will make your tongue cling to the roof of your mouth, so that you shall be mute and not be one to rebuke them, for they *are* a rebellious house. [27]But when I speak with you, I will open your mouth, and you shall say to them, 'Thus says the Lord GOD'. He who hears, let him hear; and he who refuses, let him refuse; for they *are* a rebellious house.

THE SIEGE OF JERUSALEM PORTRAYED

[1]"You also, son of man, take a clay tablet and lay it before you, and portray on it a city, Jerusalem. [2]Lay siege against it, build a siege wall against it, and heap up a mound against it; set camps against it also, and place battering rams against it all around. [3]Moreover take for yourself an iron plate, and set it *as* an iron wall between you and the city. Set your face against it, and it shall be besieged, and you shall lay siege against it. This *will be* a sign to the house of Israel.

[4]"Lie also on your left side, and lay the iniquity of the house of Israel upon it. *According* to the number of the days that you lie on it, you shall bear their iniquity. [5]For I have laid on you the years of their iniquity, according to the number of the days, three hundred and ninety days; so you shall bear the iniquity of the house of Israel. [6]And when you have completed them, lie again on your right side; then you shall bear the iniquity of the house of Judah forty days. I have laid on you a day for each year.

[7]"Therefore you shall set your face toward the siege of Jerusalem; your arm *shall be* uncovered, and you shall prophesy against it. [8]And surely I will restrain you so that you cannot turn from one side to another till you have ended the days of your siege.

[9]"Also take for yourself wheat, barley, beans, lentils, millet, and spelt; put them into one vessel, and make bread of them for yourself. *During* the number of days that you lie on your side, three hundred and ninety days, you shall eat it. [10]And your food which you eat *shall be* by weight, twenty shekels a day; from time to time you shall eat it. [11]You shall also drink water by measure, one-sixth of a hin; from time to time

you shall drink. ¹²And you shall eat it *as* barley cakes; and bake it using fuel of human waste in their sight."

¹³Then the LORD said, "So shall the children of Israel eat their defiled bread among the Gentiles, where I will drive them."

¹⁴So I said, "Ah, Lord GOD! Indeed I have never defiled myself from my youth till now; I have never eaten what died of itself or was torn by beasts, nor has abominable flesh ever come into my mouth."

¹⁵Then He said to me, "See, I am giving you cow dung instead of human waste, and you shall prepare your bread over it."

¹⁶Moreover He said to me, "Son of man, surely I will cut off the supply of bread in Jerusalem; they shall eat bread by weight and with anxiety, and shall drink water by measure and with dread, ¹⁷that they may lack bread and water, and be dismayed with one another, and waste away because of their iniquity.

A SWORD AGAINST JERUSALEM

¹"And you, son of man, take a sharp sword, take it as a barber's razor, and pass *it* over your head and your beard; then take scales to weigh and divide the hair. ²You shall burn with fire one-third in the midst of the city, when the days of the siege are finished; then you shall take one-third and strike around *it* with the sword, and one-third you shall scatter in the wind: I will draw out a sword after them. ³You shall also take a small number of them and bind them in the edge of your *garment.* ⁴Then take some of them again and throw them into the midst of the fire, and burn them in the fire. From there a fire will go out into all the house of Israel.

⁵"Thus says the Lord GOD: 'This *is* Jerusalem; I have set her in the midst of the nations and the countries all around her. ⁶She has rebelled against My judgments by doing wickedness more than the nations, and against My statutes more than the countries that *are* all around her; for they have refused My judgments, and they have not walked in My statutes.' ⁷Therefore thus says the Lord GOD: 'Because you have multiplied *disobedience* more than the nations that *are* all around you, have not walked in My statutes nor kept My judgments, nor even done*ᵃ* according to the judgments of the nations that *are* all around you'—⁸therefore thus says the Lord GOD: 'Indeed I, even I, *am* against you and will execute judgments in your midst in the sight of

the nations. ⁹And I will do among you what I have never done, and the like of which I will never do again, because of all your abominations. ¹⁰Therefore fathers shall eat *their* sons in your midst, and sons shall eat their fathers; and I will execute judgments among you, and all of you who remain I will scatter to all the winds.

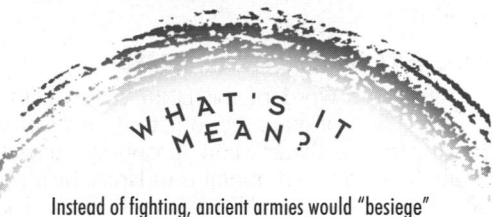

WHAT'S IT MEAN?

Instead of fighting, ancient armies would "besiege" a city by surrounding it to prevent anyone from going in or out. During such a siege, the attacking army would keep food and water from entering the city, causing the people inside to die of hunger and thirst. Some sieges lasted months—even years. You can imagine how desperate and horrible conditions became inside the city after such a long period of time. Jerusalem fell after Nebuchadnezzar besieged it in 586 B.C.

Ezekiel 5:10

¹¹"Therefore, *as* I live,' says the Lord GOD, 'surely, because you have defiled My sanctuary with all your detestable things and with all your abominations, therefore I will also diminish *you;* My eye will not spare, nor will I have any pity. ¹²One-third of you shall die of the pestilence, and be consumed with famine in your midst; and one-third shall fall by the sword all around you; and I will scatter another third to all the winds, and I will draw out a sword after them.

WORSHIP

Why is pure worship important? (5:11)

¹³"Thus shall My anger be spent, and I will cause My fury to rest upon them, and I will be avenged; and they shall know that I, the LORD, have spoken *it* in My zeal, when I have spent My fury upon them. ¹⁴Moreover I will make you a waste and a reproach among the nations that *are* all around you, in the sight of all who pass by.

¹⁵"So it*ᵃ* shall be a reproach, a taunt, a lesson, and an astonishment to the nations that *are* all around you, when I execute judgments among you in anger and in fury and in furious rebukes. I, the LORD, have spoken. ¹⁶When I send against them the terrible arrows of famine

5:7 *ᵃ*Following Masoretic Text, Septuagint, Targum, and Vulgate; many Hebrew manuscripts and Syriac read *but have done* (compare 11:12). **5:15** *ᵃ*Septuagint, Syriac, Targum, and Vulgate read *you.*

which shall be for destruction, which I will send to destroy you, I will increase the famine upon you and cut off your supply of bread. [17]So I will send against you famine and wild beasts, and they will bereave you. Pestilence and blood shall pass through you, and I will bring the sword against you. I, the LORD, have spoken.' "

JUDGMENT ON IDOLATROUS ISRAEL

[1]Now the word of the LORD came to me, saying: [2]"Son of man, set your face toward the mountains of Israel, and prophesy against them, [3]and say, 'O mountains of Israel, hear the word of the Lord GOD! Thus says the Lord GOD to the mountains, to the hills, to the ravines, and to the valleys: "Indeed I, *even* I, will bring a sword against you, and I will destroy your high places. [4]Then your altars shall be desolate, your incense altars shall be broken, and I will cast down your slain *men* before your idols. [5]And I will lay the corpses of the children of Israel before their idols, and I will scatter your bones all around your altars. [6]In all your dwelling places the cities shall be laid waste, and the high places shall be desolate, so that your altars may be laid waste and made desolate, your idols may be broken and made to cease, your incense altars may be cut down, and your works may be abolished. [7]The slain shall fall in your midst, and you shall know that I *am* the LORD.

WHAT'S IT MEAN?

Even touching a dead body was enough to disqualify a person from worshiping the Lord or taking part in a religious ceremony. Because dead bodies were considered extremely unclean, a ritual or sacrifice was required before the person who touched a corpse was considered clean again.

Ezekiel 6:5

[8]"Yet I will leave a remnant, so that you may have *some* who escape the sword among the nations, when you are scattered through the countries. [9]Then those of you who escape will remember Me among the nations where they are carried captive, because I was crushed by their adulterous heart which has departed from Me, and by their eyes which play the harlot af-

ter their idols; they will loathe themselves for the evils which they committed in all their abominations. [10]And they shall know that I *am* the LORD; I have not said in vain that I would bring this calamity upon them."

[11]Thus says the Lord GOD: "Pound your fists and stamp your feet, and say, 'Alas, for all the evil abominations of the house of Israel! For they shall fall by the sword, by famine, and by pestilence. [12]He who is far off shall die by the pestilence, he who is near shall fall by the sword, and he who remains and is besieged shall die by the famine. Thus will I spend My fury upon them. [13]Then you shall know that I *am* the LORD, when their slain are among their idols all around their altars, on every high hill, on all the mountaintops, under every green tree, and under every thick oak, wherever they offered sweet incense to all their idols. [14]So I will stretch out My hand against them and make the land desolate, yes, more desolate than the wilderness toward Diblah, in all their dwelling places. Then they shall know that I *am* the LORD.' ' "

JUDGMENT ON ISRAEL IS NEAR

[1]Moreover the word of the LORD came to me, saying, [2]"And you, son of man, thus says the Lord GOD to the land of Israel:

'An end! The end has come upon the four corners of the land.
3   Now the end *has come* upon you,
     And I will send My anger against you;
     I will judge you according to
          your ways,
     And I will repay you for
          all your
          abominations.
4   My eye will not spare
          you,
     Nor will I have pity;
     But I will repay your ways,
     And your abominations will be in your
          midst;
     Then you shall know that I *am* the LORD!'

JUDGMENT
Who will judge us?
(7:3, 4)

[5]"Thus says the Lord GOD:

'A disaster, a singular disaster;
     Behold, it has come!
6   An end has come,
     The end has come;
     It has dawned for you;
     Behold, it has come!
7   Doom has come to you, you who dwell
          in the land;

The time has come,
A day of trouble *is* near,
And not of rejoicing in the mountains.

8 Now upon you I will soon pour out My
fury,
And spend My anger upon you;
I will judge you according to your ways,
And I will repay you for all your
abominations.

9 'My eye will not spare,
Nor will I have pity;
I will repay you according to your ways,
And your abominations will be in your
midst.
Then you shall know that I *am* the LORD
who strikes.

10 'Behold, the day!
Behold, it has come!
Doom has gone out;
The rod has blossomed,
Pride has budded.
11 Violence has risen up into a rod of
wickedness;
None of them *shall remain,*
None of their multitude,
None of them;
Nor *shall there be* wailing for them.
12 The time has come,
The day draws near.

'Let not the buyer rejoice,
Nor the seller mourn,
For wrath *is* on their whole multitude.
13 For the seller shall not return to what has
been sold,
Though he may still be alive;
For the vision concerns the whole
multitude,
And it shall not turn back;
No one will strengthen himself
Who lives in iniquity.

14 'They have blown the trumpet and made
everyone ready,
But no one goes to battle;
For My wrath *is* on all their multitude.
15 The sword *is* outside,
And the pestilence and famine within.
Whoever *is* in the field
Will die by the sword;
And whoever *is* in the city,
Famine and pestilence will devour him.

16 'Those who survive will escape and be on
the mountains

Like doves of the valleys,
All of them mourning,
Each for his iniquity.
17 Every hand will be feeble,
And every knee will be *as* weak *as* water.
18 They will also be girded with sackcloth;
Horror will cover them;
Shame *will be* on every face,
Baldness on all their heads.

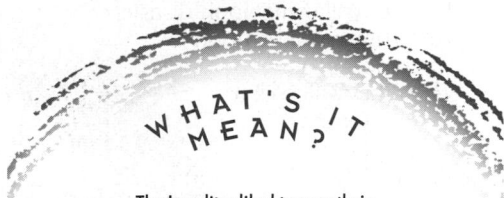

WHAT'S IT MEAN?

The Israelites liked to wear their
hair and beards long. They thought it made
them look attractive and manly. To them, a clean-shaven head was
something to be ashamed of. The only time an Israelite man would
have considered shaving his head was in
severe distress or sorrow.
Ezekiel 7:18

19 'They will throw their silver into the
streets,
And their gold will be like refuse;
Their silver and their gold will not be able
to deliver them
In the day of the wrath of the LORD;
They will not satisfy their souls,
Nor fill their stomachs,
Because it became their stumbling block
of iniquity.

20 'As for the beauty of his ornaments,
He set it in majesty;
But they made from it
The images of their abominations—
Their detestable things;
Therefore I have made it
Like refuse to them.
21 I will give it as plunder
Into the hands of strangers,
And to the wicked of the earth as spoil;
And they shall defile it.
22 I will turn My face from them,
And they will defile My secret place;
For robbers shall enter it and defile it.

23 'Make a chain,
For the land is filled with crimes of blood,
And the city is full of violence.

24 Therefore I will bring the worst of the
    Gentiles,
  And they will possess their houses;
  I will cause the pomp of the strong to
    cease,
  And their holy places shall be defiled.
25 Destruction comes;
  They will seek peace, but *there shall be*
    none.
26 Disaster will come upon disaster,
  And rumor will be upon
    rumor.
  Then they will seek a
    vision from a
    prophet;
  But the law will
    perish from the
    priest,
  And counsel from
    the elders.

27 'The king will mourn,
  The prince will be clothed
    with desolation,
  And the hands of the common people
    will tremble.
  I will do to them according to their way,
  And according to what they deserve I will
    judge them;
  Then they shall know that I *am* the
    LORD!' "

> "I will do to them according to their way, and according to what they deserve I will judge them; then they shall know that I am the LORD!"
> (Ezekiel 7:27b)

ABOMINATIONS IN THE TEMPLE

1 And it came to pass in the sixth year, in the sixth *month*, on the fifth *day* of the month, as I sat in my house with the elders of Judah sitting before me, that the hand of the Lord GOD fell upon me there. 2 Then I looked, and there was a likeness, like the appearance of fire—from the appearance of His waist and downward, fire; and from His waist and upward, like the appearance of brightness, like the color of amber. 3 He stretched out the form of a hand, and took me by a lock of my hair; and the Spirit lifted me up between earth and heaven, and brought me in visions of God to Jerusalem, to the door of the north gate of the inner *court,* where the seat of the image of jealousy *was,* which provokes to jealousy. 4 And behold, the glory of the God of Israel *was* there, like the vision that I saw in the plain.
  5 Then He said to me, "Son of man, lift your eyes now toward the north." So I lifted my eyes toward the north, and there, north of the altar gate, was this image of jealousy in the entrance.
  6 Furthermore He said to me, "Son of man, do you see what they are doing, the great abominations that the house of Israel commits here, to make Me go far away from My sanctuary? Now turn again, you will see greater abominations." 7 So He brought me to the door of the court; and when I looked, there was a hole in the wall. 8 Then He said to me, "Son of man, dig into the wall"; and when I dug into the wall, there was a door.
  9 And He said to me, "Go in, and see the wicked abominations which they are doing there." 10 So I went in and saw, and there—every sort of creeping thing, abominable beasts, and all the idols of the house of Israel, portrayed all around on the walls. 11 And there stood before them seventy men of the elders of the house of Israel, and in their midst stood Jaazaniah the son of Shaphan. Each man had a censer in his hand, and a thick cloud of incense went up.
  12 Then He said to me, "Son of man, have you seen what the elders of the house of Israel do in the dark, every man in the room of his idols? For they say, 'The LORD does not see us, the LORD has forsaken the land.' "

WHAT'S IT MEAN?

The Lord had the Israelites on a very strict diet.
He identified certain animals as clean and others as unclean. The Israelites were free to eat all of the clean animals they could get their hands on, but unclean animals were off-limits. Here are just some of the animals that were on the "clean" menu: cattle, goats, sheep, fish with scales, and many kinds of birds. Animals considered unclean included snails, pigs, vultures, shellfish, and dogs.
Ezekiel 8:10

13 And He said to me, "Turn again, *and* you will see greater abominations that they are doing." 14 So He brought me to the door of the north gate of the LORD's house; and to my dismay, women were sitting there weeping for Tammuz.
  15 Then He said to me, "Have you seen *this,* O son of man? Turn again, you will see greater

abominations than these." ¹⁶So He brought me into the inner court of the LORD's house; and there, at the door of the temple of the LORD, between the porch and the altar, *were* about twenty-five men with their backs toward the temple of the LORD and their faces toward the east, and they were worshiping the sun toward the east.

¹⁷And He said to me, "Have you seen *this,* O son of man? Is it a trivial thing to the house of Judah to commit the abominations which they commit here? For they have filled the land with violence; then they have returned to provoke Me to anger. Indeed they put the branch to their nose. ¹⁸Therefore I also will act in fury. My eye will not spare nor will I have pity; and though they cry in My ears with a loud voice, I will not hear them."

THE WICKED ARE SLAIN

¹Then He called out in my hearing with a loud voice, saying, "Let those who have charge over the city draw near, each *with* a deadly weapon in his hand." ²And suddenly six men came from the direction of the upper gate, which faces north, each with his battle-ax in his hand. One man among them *was* clothed with linen and had a writer's inkhorn at his side. They went in and stood beside the bronze altar.

³Now the glory of the God of Israel had gone up from the cherub, where it had been, to the threshold of the temple.*ᵃ* And He called to the man clothed with linen, who *had* the writer's inkhorn at his side; ⁴and the LORD said to him, "Go through the midst of the city,

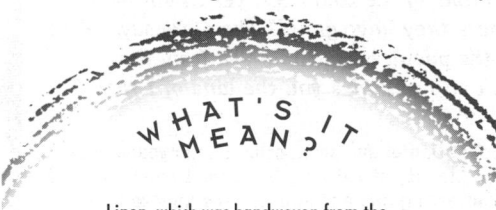

WHAT'S IT MEAN?

Linen, which was handwoven from the fibers of the hemp plant, was considered to be the highest-quality fabric in the ancient world. For the most part, only people of great wealth or power wore linen. Priests and those who served in the temple were the exception. They, too, wore linen. The white linen uniforms that the priests wore were designed according to the instructions in the Law of Moses.

Ezekiel 9:2

through the midst of Jerusalem, and put a mark on the foreheads of the men who sigh and cry over all the abominations that are done within it."

⁵To the others He said in my hearing, "Go after him through the city and kill; do not let your eye spare, nor have any pity. ⁶Utterly slay old *and* young men, maidens and little children and women; but do not come near anyone on whom *is* the mark; and begin at My sanctuary." So they began with the elders who *were* before the temple. ⁷Then He said to them, "Defile the temple, and fill the courts with the slain. Go out!" And they went out and killed in the city.

⁸So it was, that while they were killing them, I was left *alone;* and I fell on my face and cried out, and said, "Ah, Lord GOD! Will You destroy all the remnant of Israel in pouring out Your fury on Jerusalem?"

⁹Then He said to me, 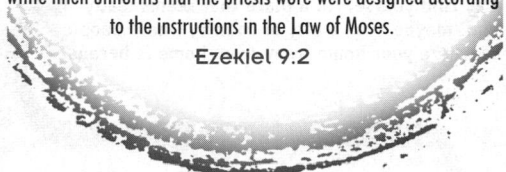 "The iniquity of the house of Israel and Judah *is* exceedingly great, and the land is full of bloodshed, and the city full of perversity; for they say, 'The LORD has forsaken the land, and the LORD does not see!' ¹⁰And as for Me also, My eye will neither spare, nor will I have pity, *but* I will recompense their deeds on their own head."

¹¹Just then, the man clothed with linen, who *had* the inkhorn at his side, reported back and said, "I have done as You commanded me."

THE GLORY DEPARTS FROM THE TEMPLE

¹And I looked, and there in the firmament that was above the head of the cherubim, there appeared something like a sapphire stone, having the appearance of the likeness of a throne. ²Then He spoke to the man clothed with linen, and said, "Go in among the wheels, under the cherub, fill your hands with coals of fire from among the cherubim, and scatter *them* over the city." And he went in as I watched.

³Now the cherubim were standing on the south side of the temple*ᵃ* when the man went in, and the cloud filled the inner court. ⁴Then the glory of the LORD went up from the cherub, *and paused* over the threshold of the temple; and the house was filled with the cloud, and the court was full of the brightness of the LORD's glory. ⁵And the sound of the wings of the cherubim was heard *even* in the outer court, like the voice of Almighty God when He speaks.

⁶Then it happened, when He commanded the man clothed in linen, saying, "Take fire from

RESPONSIBILITY What are we responsible for? (9:9, 10)

among the wheels, from among the cherubim," that he went in and stood beside the wheels. [7]And the cherub stretched out his hand from among the cherubim to the fire that *was* among the cherubim, and took *some of it* and put *it* into the hands of the *man* clothed with linen, who took *it* and went out. [8]The cherubim appeared to have the form of a man's hand under their wings.

[9]And when I looked, there were four wheels by the cherubim, one wheel by one cherub and another wheel by each other cherub; the wheels appeared *to have* the color of a beryl stone. [10]*As for* their appearance, all four looked alike—as it were, a wheel in the middle of a wheel. [11]When they went, they went toward *any of* their four directions; they did not turn aside when they went, but followed in the direction the head was facing. They did not turn aside when they went. [12]And their whole body, with their back, their hands, their wings, and the wheels that the four had, *were* full of eyes all around. [13]As for the wheels, they were called in my hearing, "Wheel."

[14]Each one had four faces: the first face *was* the face of a cherub, the second face the face of a man, the third the face of a lion, and the fourth the face of an eagle. [15]And the cherubim were lifted up. This *was* the living creature I saw by the River Chebar. [16]When the cherubim went, the wheels went beside them; and when the cherubim lifted their wings to mount up from the earth, the same wheels also did not turn from beside them. [17]When *the cherubim*[a] stood still, *the wheels* stood still, and when *one*[b] was lifted up, *the other*[c] lifted itself up, for the spirit of the living creature *was* in them.

[18]Then the glory of the LORD departed from the threshold of the temple and stood over the cherubim. [19]And the cherubim lifted their wings and mounted up from the earth in my sight. When they went out, the wheels *were* beside them; and they stood at the door of the east gate of the LORD's house, and the glory of the God of Israel *was* above them.

[20]This *is* the living creature I saw under the God of Israel by the River Chebar, and I knew

10:17 [a]Literally *they* [b]Literally *they* [c]Literally *they*

∴ Promise   HE PROMISES TO BE YOUR HOME-AWAY-FROM-HOME.

Therefore say, "Thus says the Lord GOD: 'Although I have cast them far off among the Gentiles, and although I have scattered them among the countries, yet I shall be a little sanctuary for them in the countries where they have gone.'" Therefore say, "Thus says the Lord GOD: 'I will gather you from the peoples, assemble you from the countries where you have been scattered, and I will give you the land of Israel'" (Ezek. 11:16, 17).

Around 600 B.C., an enemy king took the prophet Daniel and some other strong young men away from Jerusalem, where God's temple was, to the city of Babylon. But Daniel was faithful to God, and God showed that He was with Daniel by protecting him and allowing the king to notice him and give him lots of authority.

Ezekiel was one of the men taken to Babylon with Daniel. The people who were left in Jerusalem were saying that God had not gone to Babylon with them. But the things that happened to them there told a different story. And Ezekiel had God's word on it: "I shall be a little sanctuary for them in the countries where they have gone." In other words, "I am your home-away-from-home."

As you try to do what God wants you to do, you may find yourself in a place that seems really far from Him—a state university, a job you can't stand, maybe even a city or country where people don't seem to care about God. But He promises to be where your home-away-from-home is because His Spirit lives inside of you.

SEE FOR YOURSELF:
Ex. 33:14; Lev. 26:12; Deut. 31:8; Ps. 37:28; Matt. 28:19, 20

they *were* cherubim. [21]Each one had four faces and each one four wings, and the likeness of the hands of a man *was* under their wings. [22]And the likeness of their faces *was* the same *as* the faces which I had seen by the River Chebar, their appearance and their persons. They each went straight forward.

JUDGMENT ON WICKED COUNSELORS

[1]Then the Spirit lifted me up and brought me to the East Gate of the LORD's house, which faces eastward; and there at the door of the gate were twenty-five men, among whom I saw Jaazaniah the son of Azzur, and Pelatiah the son of Benaiah, princes of the people. [2]And He said to me: "Son of man, these *are* the men who devise iniquity and give wicked counsel in this city, [3]who say, '*The time is* not near to build houses; this *city is* the caldron, and we *are* the meat.' [4]Therefore prophesy against them, prophesy, O son of man!"

[5]Then the Spirit of the LORD fell upon me, and said to me, "Speak! 'Thus says the LORD: "Thus you have said, O house of Israel; for I know the things that come into your mind. [6]You have multiplied your slain in this city, and you have filled its streets with the slain." [7]Therefore thus says the Lord GOD: "Your slain whom you have laid in its midst, they *are* the meat, and this *city is* the caldron; but I shall bring you out of the midst of it. [8]You have feared the sword; and I will bring a sword upon you," says the Lord GOD. [9]"And I will bring you out of its midst, and deliver you into the hands of strangers, and execute judgments on you. [10]You shall fall by the sword. I will judge you at the border of Israel. Then you shall know that I *am* the LORD. [11]This *city* shall not be your caldron, nor shall you be the meat in its midst. I will judge you at the border of Israel. [12]And you shall know that I *am* the LORD; for you have not walked in My statutes nor executed My judgments, but have done according to the customs of the Gentiles which *are* all around you.'"'"

DECISIONS

When is peer pressure bad? (11:12)

[13]Now it happened, while I was prophesying, that Pelatiah the son of Benaiah died. Then I fell on my face and cried with a loud voice, and said, "Ah, Lord GOD! Will You make a complete end of the remnant of Israel?"

GOD WILL RESTORE ISRAEL

[14]Again the word of the LORD came to me, saying, [15]"Son of man, your brethren, your relatives, your countrymen, and all the house of Israel in its entirety, *are* those about whom the inhabitants of Jerusalem have said, 'Get far away from the LORD; this land has been given to us as a possession.' [16]Therefore say, 'Thus says the Lord GOD: "Although I have cast them far off among the Gentiles, and although I have scattered them among the countries, yet I shall be a little sanctuary for them in the countries where they have gone."' [17]Therefore say, 'Thus says the Lord GOD: "I will gather you from the

On the Edge

Then I will give them one heart, and I will put a new spirit within them, and take the stony heart out of their flesh, and give them a heart of flesh (Ezek. 11:19).

You may have a heart to obey God down deep inside, but He still requires you to make a choice. You can choose to obey Him or to disobey Him. The rewards are great if you choose to obey. In fact, the Holy Spirit will give you warning signs. Has there ever been a time where you were about to sin, and WHAM! There was this still, small voice that was saying, "Don't do it!" Well, that was the voice of the Holy Spirit. At that moment you had to make a choice to listen to that voice and obey, or to block out that voice and sin.

Your heart starts out as a heart of flesh. The more you continue to disobey the Holy Spirit, your heart of flesh turns hard into stone, and that can and will lead to problems. Once your heart is hard, you won't be able to hear the still, small voice. Then what? You will walk blindly into all sorts of trouble that could have otherwise been avoided by obeying the promptings of the Holy Spirit.

God is a loving God. Never forget it. He wants to take away any stubbornness or hardness and give you a heart of flesh. If your heart has become hard, ask God to forgive you and take away your stubbornness. But even after you ask Him to give you a heart to obey Him, the actual choice is up to you. Choose obedience, and tap into God's blessings today!

SEE FOR YOURSELF:
Ezek. 36:26;
Matt. 5:8; Luke 8:15;
Heb. 10:22

peoples, assemble you from the countries where you have been scattered, and I will give you the land of Israel." ' ¹⁸And they will go there, and they will take away all its detestable things and all its abominations from there. ¹⁹Then I will give them one heart, and I will put a new spirit within them,ᵃ and take the stony heart out of their flesh, and give them a heart of flesh, ²⁰that they may walk in My statutes and keep My judgments and do them; and they shall be My people, and I will be their God. ²¹But as for those whose hearts follow the desire for their detestable things and their abominations, I will recompense their deeds on their own heads," says the Lord GOD.

FOLLOWING GOD

How can we have a changed life? (11:19)

²²So the cherubim lifted up their wings, with the wheels beside them, and the glory of the God of Israel was high above them. ²³And the glory of the LORD went up from the midst of the city and stood on the mountain, which is on the east side of the city.

²⁴Then the Spirit took me up and brought me in a vision by the Spirit of God into Chaldea,ᵃ to those in captivity. And the vision that I had seen went up from me. ²⁵So I spoke to those in captivity of all the things the LORD had shown me.

JUDAH'S CAPTIVITY PORTRAYED

¹Now the word of the LORD came to me, saying: ²"Son of man, you dwell in the midst of a rebellious house, which has eyes to see but does not see, and ears to hear but does not hear; for they are a rebellious house.

³"Therefore, son of man, prepare your belongings for captivity, and go into captivity by day in their sight. You shall go from your place into captivity to another place in their sight. It may be that they will consider, though they are a rebellious house. ⁴By day you shall bring out your belongings in their sight, as though going into captivity; and at evening you shall go in their sight, like those who go into captivity. ⁵Dig through the wall in their sight, and carry your belongings out through it. ⁶In their sight you shall bear them on your shoulders and carry them out at twilight; you shall cover your face, so that you cannot see the ground, for I have made you a sign to the house of Israel."

⁷So I did as I was commanded. I brought out my belongings by day, as though going into captivity, and at evening I dug through the wall with my hand. I brought them out at twilight, and I bore them on my shoulder in their sight.

⁸And in the morning the word of the LORD came to me, saying, ⁹"Son of man, has not the house of Israel, the rebellious house, said to you, 'What are you doing?' ¹⁰Say to them, 'Thus says the Lord GOD: "This burden concerns the prince in Jerusalem and all the house of Israel who are among them." ' ¹¹Say, 'I am a sign to you. As I have done, so shall it be done to them; they shall be carried away into captivity.' ¹²And the prince who is among them shall bear his belongings on his shoulder at twilight and go out. They shall dig through the wall to carry them out through it. He shall cover his face, so that he cannot see the ground with his eyes. ¹³I will also spread My net over him, and he shall be caught in My snare. I will bring him to Babylon, to the land of the Chaldeans; yet he shall not see it, though he shall die there. ¹⁴I will scatter to every wind all who are around him to help him, and all his troops; and I will draw out the sword after them.

WHAT'S IT MEAN?

Zedekiah's story definitely does not have a happy ending. When he and his army tried to sneak out of the city during the siege, the Babylonians caught them. Zedekiah was forced to watch while his sons were put to death. It would be the last thing he ever saw. His eyes were then poked out, and he was led away to Babylon as a blind captive.
Ezekiel 12:14

¹⁵"Then they shall know that I am the LORD, when I scatter them among the nations and disperse them throughout the countries. ¹⁶But I will spare a few of their men from the sword, from famine, and from pestilence, that they may declare all their abominations among the Gentiles wherever they go. Then they shall know that I am the LORD."

JUDGMENT NOT POSTPONED

¹⁷Moreover the word of the LORD came to me, saying, ¹⁸"Son of man, eat your bread with quaking, and drink your water with trembling and anxiety. ¹⁹And say to the people of the

land, 'Thus says the Lord GOD to the inhabitants of Jerusalem *and* to the land of Israel: "They shall eat their bread with anxiety, and drink their water with dread, so that her land may be emptied of all who are in it, because of the violence of all those who dwell in it. ²⁰Then the cities that are inhabited shall be laid waste, and the land shall become desolate; and you shall know that I *am* the LORD." ' "

²¹And the word of the LORD came to me, saying, ²²"Son of man, what *is* this proverb *that* you *people* have about the land of Israel, which says, 'The days are prolonged, and every vision fails'? ²³Tell them therefore, 'Thus says the Lord GOD: "I will lay this proverb to rest, and they shall no more use it as a proverb in Israel." But say to them, "The days are at hand, and the fulfillment of every vision. ²⁴For no more shall there be any false vision or flattering divination within the house of Israel. ²⁵For I *am* the LORD. I speak, and the word which I speak will come to pass; it will no more be postponed; for in your days, O rebellious house, I will say the word and perform it," says the Lord GOD.' "

²⁶Again the word of the LORD came to me, saying, ²⁷"Son of man, look, the house of Israel is saying, 'The vision that he sees *is* for many days *from now*, and he prophesies of times far off.' ²⁸Therefore say to them, 'Thus says the Lord GOD: "None of My words will be postponed any more, but the word which I speak will be done," says the Lord GOD.' "

WOE TO FOOLISH PROPHETS

¹And the word of the LORD came to me, saying, ²"Son of man, prophesy against the prophets of Israel who prophesy, and say to those who prophesy out of their own heart, 'Hear the word of the LORD!' ³Thus says the Lord GOD: "Woe to the foolish prophets, who follow their own spirit and have seen nothing! ⁴O Israel, your prophets are like foxes in the deserts. ⁵You have not gone up into the gaps to build a wall for the house of Israel to stand in battle on the day of the LORD. ⁶They have envisioned futility and false divination, saying, 'Thus says the LORD!' But the LORD has not sent them; yet they hope that the word may be confirmed. ⁷Have you not seen a futile vision, and have you not spoken false divination? You say, 'The LORD says,' but I have not spoken."

IDOLATRY
What does God condemn? (12:24)

CULT
Why are cults dangerous? (13:7)

⁸Therefore thus says the Lord GOD: "Because you have spoken nonsense and envisioned lies, therefore I *am* indeed against you," says the Lord GOD. ⁹"My hand will be against the prophets who envision futility and who divine lies; they shall not be in the assembly of My people, nor be written in the record of the house of Israel, nor shall they enter into the land of Israel. Then you shall know that I *am* the Lord GOD.

¹⁰"Because, indeed, because they have seduced My people, saying, 'Peace!' when *there is* no peace—and one builds a wall, and they plaster it with untempered *mortar*—¹¹say to those who plaster *it* with untempered *mortar*, that it will fall. There will be flooding rain, and you, O great hailstones, shall fall; and a stormy wind shall tear *it* down. ¹²Surely, when the wall has fallen, will it not be said to you, 'Where *is* the mortar with which you plastered *it?*' "

¹³Therefore thus says the Lord GOD: "I will cause a stormy wind to break forth in My fury; and there shall be a flooding rain in My anger, and great hailstones in fury to consume *it.* ¹⁴So I will break down the wall you have plastered with untempered *mortar*, and bring it down to the ground, so that its foundation will be uncovered; it will fall, and you shall be consumed in the midst of it. Then you shall know that I *am* the LORD.

WHAT'S IT MEAN?

These so-called "magic charms" were pieces of jewelry that had spells and chants written on them. Some people believed these charms protected them from sickness, evil spirits, and other dangers. Today, such charms, often called amulets, are still very popular in some parts of the world.
Ezekiel 13:18

¹⁵"Thus will I accomplish My wrath on the wall and on those who have plastered it with untempered *mortar*; and I will say to you, 'The wall *is* no *more*, nor those who plastered it, ¹⁶*that is,* the prophets of Israel who prophesy concerning Jerusalem, and who see visions of peace for her when *there is* no peace,' " says the Lord GOD.

¹⁷"Likewise, son of man, set your face against

the daughters of your people, who prophesy out of their own heart; prophesy against them, [18]and say, 'Thus says the Lord GOD: "Woe to the *women* who sew *magic* charms on their sleeves[a] and make veils for the heads of people of every height to hunt souls! Will you hunt the souls of My people, and keep yourselves alive? [19]And will you profane Me among My people for handfuls of barley and for pieces of bread, killing people who should not die, and keeping people alive who should not live, by your lying to My people who listen to lies?"

[20]"Therefore thus says the Lord GOD: "Behold, I *am* against your *magic* charms by which you hunt souls there like birds. I will tear them from your arms, and let the souls go, the souls you hunt like birds. [21]I will also tear off your veils and deliver My people out of your hand, and they shall no longer be as prey in your hand. Then you shall know that I *am* the LORD.

[22]"Because with lies you have made the heart of the righteous sad, whom I have not made sad; and you have strengthened the hands of the wicked, so that he does not turn from his wicked way to save his life. [23]Therefore you shall no longer envision futility nor practice divination; for I will deliver My people out of your hand, and you shall know that I *am* the LORD." ' "

IDOLATRY WILL BE PUNISHED

[1]Now some of the elders of Israel came to me and sat before me. [2]And the word of the LORD came to me, saying, [3]"Son of man, these men have set up their idols in their hearts, and put before them that which causes them to stumble into iniquity. Should I let Myself be inquired of at all by them?

[4]"Therefore speak to them, and say to them, 'Thus says the Lord GOD: "Everyone of the house of Israel who sets up his idols in his heart, and puts before him what causes him to stumble into iniquity, and then comes to the prophet, I the LORD will answer him who comes, according to the multitude of his idols, [5]that I may seize the house of Israel by their heart, because they are all estranged from Me by their idols." '

[6]"Therefore say to the house of Israel, 'Thus says the Lord GOD: "Repent, turn away from your idols, and turn your faces away from all your abominations. [7]For anyone of the house of Israel, or of the strangers who dwell in Israel, who separates himself from Me and sets up his idols in his heart and puts before him what causes him to stumble into iniquity, then comes to a prophet to inquire of him concerning Me, I the LORD will answer him by Myself. [8]I will set My face against that man and make him a sign and a proverb, and I will cut him off from the midst of My people. Then you shall know that I *am* the LORD.

[9]"And if the prophet is induced to speak anything, I the LORD have induced that prophet, and I will stretch out My hand against him and destroy him from among My people Israel. [10]And they shall bear their iniquity; the punishment of the prophet shall be the same as the punishment of the one who inquired, [11]that the house of Israel may no longer stray from Me, nor be profaned anymore with all their transgressions, but that they may be My people and I may be their God," says the Lord GOD.' "

JUDGMENT ON PERSISTENT UNFAITHFULNESS

[12]The word of the LORD came again to me, saying: [13]"Son of man, when a land sins against Me by persistent unfaithfulness, I will stretch out My hand against it; I will cut off its supply of bread, send famine on it, and cut off man and beast from it. [14]Even *if* these three men, Noah, Daniel, and Job, were in it, they would deliver *only* themselves by their righteousness," says the Lord GOD.

[15]"If I cause wild beasts to pass through the land, and they empty it, and make it so desolate that no man may pass through because of the beasts, [16]*even though* these three men *were* in it, *as* I live," says the Lord GOD, "they would deliver neither sons nor daughters; only they would be delivered, and the land would be desolate.

[17]"Or if I bring a sword on that land, and say, 'Sword, go through the land', and I cut off man and beast from it, [18]even *though* these three men *were* in it, *as* I live," says the Lord GOD, "they would deliver neither sons nor daughters, but only they themselves would be delivered.

> "Therefore say to the house of Israel, 'Thus says the Lord GOD: "Repent, turn away from your idols, and turn your faces away from all your abominations." ' "
> (Ezekiel 14:6)

13:18 [a]Literally *over all the joints of My hands*; Vulgate reads *under every elbow*; Septuagint and Targum read *on all elbows of the hands.*

¹⁹"Or *if* I send a pestilence into that land and pour out My fury on it in blood, and cut off from it man and beast, ²⁰even *though* Noah, Daniel, and Job *were* in it, *as* I live," says the Lord GOD, "they would deliver neither son nor daughter; they would deliver *only* themselves by their righteousness."

²¹For thus says the Lord GOD: "How much more it shall be when I send My four severe judgments on Jerusalem—the sword and famine and wild beasts and pestilence—to cut off man and beast from it? ²²Yet behold, there shall be left in it a remnant who will be brought out, *both* sons and daughters; surely they will come out to you, and you will see their ways and their doings. Then you will be comforted concerning the disaster that I have brought upon Jerusalem, all that I have brought upon it. ²³And they will comfort you, when you see their ways and their doings; and you shall know that I have done nothing without cause that I have done in it," says the Lord GOD.

THE OUTCAST VINE

¹Then the word of the LORD came to me, saying: ²"Son of man, how is the wood of the vine *better* than any other wood, the vine branch which is among the trees of the forest? ³Is wood taken from it to make any object? Or can *men* make a peg from it to hang any vessel on? ⁴Instead, it is thrown into the fire for fuel; the fire devours both ends of it, and its middle is burned. Is it useful for *any* work? ⁵Indeed, when it was whole, no object could be made from it. How much less will it be useful for *any* work when the fire has devoured it, and it is burned?

⁶"Therefore thus says the Lord GOD: 'Like the wood of the vine among the trees of the forest, which I have given to the fire for fuel, so I will give up the inhabitants of Jerusalem; ⁷and I will set My face against them. They will go out from *one* fire, but *another* fire shall devour them. Then you shall know that I *am* the LORD, when I set My face against them. ⁸Thus I will make the land desolate, because they have persisted in unfaithfulness', says the Lord GOD."

GOD'S LOVE FOR JERUSALEM

¹Again the word of the LORD came to me, saying, ²"Son of man, cause Jerusalem to know her abominations, ³and say, 'Thus says the Lord GOD to Jerusalem: "Your birth and your nativity *are* from the land of Canaan; your father *was* an Amorite and your mother a Hittite. ⁴*As for* your nativity, on the day you were born your navel

cord was not cut, nor were you washed in water to cleanse *you;* you were not rubbed with salt nor wrapped in swaddling cloths. ⁵No eye pitied you, to do any of these things for you, to have compassion on you; but you were thrown out into the open field, when you yourself were loathed on the day you were born.

WHAT'S IT MEAN?

There was nothing special about the city of Jerusalem before Solomon chose it as the site of God's temple. The Hittites and Amorites had built the city long before the Israelites arrived in Canaan. When construction of the temple was finished, however, the city became the center of Israel's religious life.
Ezekiel 16:3

⁶"And when I passed by you and saw you struggling in your own blood, I said to you in your blood, 'Live!' Yes, I said to you in your blood, 'Live!' ⁷I made you thrive like a plant in the field; and you grew, matured, and became very beautiful. *Your* breasts were formed, your hair grew, but you *were* naked and bare.

⁸"When I passed by you again and looked upon you, indeed your time *was* the time of love; so I spread My wing over you and covered your nakedness. Yes, I swore an oath to you and entered into a covenant with you, and you became Mine," says the Lord GOD.

⁹"Then I washed you in water; yes, I thoroughly washed off your blood, and I anointed you with oil. ¹⁰I clothed you in embroidered cloth and gave you sandals of badger skin; I clothed you with fine linen and covered you with silk. ¹¹I adorned you with ornaments, put bracelets on your wrists, and a chain on your neck. ¹²And I put a jewel in your nose, earrings in your ears, and a beautiful crown on your head. ¹³Thus you were adorned with gold and silver, and your clothing *was of* fine linen, silk, and embroidered cloth. You ate *pastry of* fine flour, honey, and oil. You were exceedingly beautiful, and succeeded to royalty. ¹⁴Your fame went out among the nations because of your beauty, for it *was* perfect through My splendor which I had bestowed on you," says the Lord GOD.

JERUSALEM'S HARLOTRY

15"But you trusted in your own beauty, played the harlot because of your fame, and poured out your harlotry on everyone passing by who *would have* it. 16You took some of your garments and adorned multicolored high places for yourself, and played the harlot on them. *Such* things should not happen, nor be. 17You have also taken your beautiful jewelry from My gold and My silver, which I had given you, and made for yourself male images and played the harlot with them. 18You took your embroidered garments and covered them, and you set My oil and My incense before them. 19Also My food which I gave you—the pastry of fine flour, oil, and honey *which* I fed you—you set it before them as sweet incense; and *so* it was," says the Lord GOD.

20"Moreover you took your sons and your daughters, whom you bore to Me, and these you sacrificed to them to be devoured. *Were* your *acts* of harlotry a small matter, 21that you have slain My children and offered them up to them by causing them to pass through *the fire?* 22And in all your abominations and acts of harlotry you did not remember the days of your youth, when you were naked and bare, struggling in your blood.

23"Then it was so, after all your wickedness—'Woe, woe to you!' says the Lord GOD—24*that* you also built for yourself a shrine, and made a high place for yourself in every street. 25You built your high places at the head of every road, and made your beauty to be abhorred. You offered yourself to everyone who passed by, and multiplied your acts of harlotry. 26You also committed harlotry with the Egyptians, your very fleshly neighbors, and increased your acts of harlotry to provoke Me to anger.

> **LUST**
> What will unchecked lust get us? (16:26)

27"Behold, therefore, I stretched out My hand against you, diminished your allotment, and gave you up to the will of those who hate you, the daughters of the Philistines, who were ashamed of your lewd behavior. 28You also played the harlot with the Assyrians, because you were insatiable; indeed you played the harlot with them and still were not satisfied. 29Moreover you multiplied your acts of harlotry as far as the land of the trader, Chaldea; and even then you were not satisfied.

30"How degenerate is your heart!" says the Lord GOD, "seeing you do all these *things,* the deeds of a brazen harlot.

JERUSALEM'S ADULTERY

31"You erected your shrine at the head of every road, and built your high place in every street. Yet you were not like a harlot, because you scorned payment. 32*You are* an adulterous wife, *who* takes strangers instead of her husband. 33Men make payment to all harlots, but you made your payments to all your lovers, and hired them to come to you from all around for your harlotry. 34You are the opposite of *other* women in your harlotry, because no one solicited you to be a harlot. In that you gave payment but no payment was given you, therefore you are the opposite."

JERUSALEM'S LOVERS WILL ABUSE HER

35'Now then, O harlot, hear the word of the LORD! 36Thus says the Lord GOD: "Because your filthiness was poured out and your nakedness uncovered in your harlotry with your lovers, and with all your abominable idols, and because of the blood of your children which you gave to them, 37surely, therefore, I will gather all your lovers with whom you took pleasure, all those you loved, *and* all those you hated; I will gather them from all around against you and will uncover your nakedness to them, that they may see all your nakedness. 38And I will judge you as women who break wedlock or shed blood are judged; I will bring blood upon you in fury and jealousy. 39I will also give you into their hand, and they shall throw down your shrines and break down your high places. They shall also strip you of your clothes, take your beautiful jewelry, and leave you naked and bare.

40"They shall also bring up an assembly against you, and they shall stone you with stones and thrust you through with their swords. 41They shall burn your houses with fire, and execute judgments on you in the sight of many women; and I will make you cease playing the harlot, and you shall no longer hire lovers. 42So I will lay to rest My fury toward you, and My jealousy shall depart from you. I will be quiet, and be angry no more. 43Because you did not remember the days of your youth, but agitated Me*a* with all these *things,* surely I will also recompense your deeds on *your own* head," says the Lord GOD. "And you shall not commit lewdness in addition to all your abominations.

16:43 *a*Following Septuagint, Syriac, Targum, and Vulgate; Masoretic Text reads *were agitated with Me.*

MORE WICKED THAN SAMARIA AND SODOM

⁴⁴"Indeed everyone who quotes proverbs will use *this* proverb against you: 'Like mother, like daughter!' ⁴⁵You *are* your mother's daughter, loathing husband and children; and you *are* the sister of your sisters, who loathed their husbands and children; your mother *was* a Hittite and your father an Amorite.

⁴⁶"Your elder sister *is* Samaria, who dwells with her daughters to the north of you; and your younger sister, who dwells to the south of you, *is* Sodom and her daughters. ⁴⁷You did not walk in their ways nor act according to their abominations; but, as *if that were* too little, you became more corrupt than they in all your ways.

⁴⁸"*As* I live," says the Lord GOD, "neither your sister Sodom nor her daughters have done as you and your daughters have done. ⁴⁹Look, this was the iniquity of your sister Sodom: She and her daughter had pride, fullness of food, and abundance of idleness; neither did she strengthen the hand of the poor and needy. ⁵⁰And they were haughty and committed abomination before Me; therefore I took them away as I saw *fit*.ᵃ

⁵¹"Samaria did not commit half of your sins; but you have multiplied your abominations more than they, and have justified your sisters by all the abominations which you have done. ⁵²You who judged your sisters, bear your own shame also, because the sins which you committed were more abominable than theirs; they are more righteous than you. Yes, be disgraced also, and bear your own shame, because you justified your sisters.

⁵³"When I bring back their captives, the captives of Sodom and her daughters, and the captives of Samaria and her daughters, then *I will also bring back* the captives of your captivity among them, ⁵⁴that you may bear your own shame and be disgraced by all that you did when you comforted them. ⁵⁵When your sisters, Sodom and her daughters, return to their former state, and Samaria and her daughters return to their former state, then you and your daughters will return to your former state. ⁵⁶For your sister Sodom was not a byword in your mouth in the days of your pride, ⁵⁷before your wickedness was uncovered. It was like the time of the reproach of the daughters of Syriaᵃ and

PRIDE

Does God condemn arrogance? (16:49)

all *those* around her, and of the daughters of the Philistines, who despise you everywhere. ⁵⁸You have paid for your lewdness and your abominations," says the LORD. ⁵⁹For thus says the Lord GOD: "I will deal with you as you have done, who despised the oath by breaking the covenant.

AN EVERLASTING COVENANT

⁶⁰"Nevertheless I will remember My covenant with you in the days of your youth, and I will establish an everlasting covenant with you. ⁶¹Then you will remember your ways and be ashamed, when you receive your older and your younger sisters; for I will give them to you for daughters, but not because of My covenant with you. ⁶²And I will establish My covenant with you. Then you shall know that I *am* the LORD, ⁶³that you may remember and be ashamed, and never open your mouth anymore because of your shame, when I provide you an atonement for all you have done," says the Lord GOD.' "

THE EAGLES AND THE VINE

¹And the word of the LORD came to me, saying, ²"Son of man, pose a riddle, and speak a parable to the house of Israel, ³and say, 'Thus says the Lord GOD:

"A great eagle with large wings and long
    pinions,
Full of feathers of various colors,
Came to Lebanon
And took from the cedar the highest
    branch.
4 He cropped off its topmost young twig
And carried it to a land of trade;
He set it in a city of merchants.
5 Then he took some of the seed of the land
And planted it in a fertile field;
He placed *it* by abundant waters
And set it like a willow tree.
6 And it grew and became a spreading vine
    of low stature;
Its branches turned toward him,
But its roots were under it.
So it became a vine,
Brought forth branches,
And put forth shoots.

7 "But there was anotherᵃ great eagle with
    large wings and many feathers;

16:50 ᵃVulgate reads *you saw;* Septuagint reads *he saw;* Targum reads *as was revealed to Me.* **16:57** ᵃFollowing Masoretic Text, Septuagint, Targum, and Vulgate; many Hebrew manuscripts and Syriac read *Edom.* **17:7** ᵃFollowing Septuagint, Syriac, and Vulgate; Masoretic Text and Targum read *one.*

And behold, this vine bent its roots
   toward him,
And stretched its branches toward him,
From the garden terrace where it had
   been planted,
That he might water it.
8 It was planted in good soil by many
   waters,
To bring forth branches, bear fruit,
And become a majestic vine." '

⁹"Say, 'Thus says the Lord God:

"Will it thrive?
Will he not pull up its roots,
Cut off its fruit,
And leave it to wither?
All of its spring leaves will wither,
And no great power or many people
Will be needed to pluck it up by its roots.
10 Behold, *it is* planted,
Will it thrive?
Will it not utterly wither when the east
   wind touches it?
It will wither in the garden terrace where
   it grew." ' "

¹¹Moreover the word of the Lord came to
me, saying, ¹²"Say now to the rebellious house:
'Do you not know what these *things mean?*' Tell
them, 'Indeed the king of Babylon went to Jerusalem and took its king and princes, and led
them with him to Babylon. ¹³And he took the
king's offspring, made a covenant with him,
and put him under oath. He also took away the
mighty of the land, ¹⁴that the kingdom might be
brought low and not lift itself up, *but* that by
keeping his covenant it might stand. ¹⁵But he
rebelled against him by sending his ambassadors to Egypt, that they might give him horses
and many people. Will he prosper? Will he who
does such *things* escape? Can he break a covenant and still be delivered?

¹⁶'*As* I live,' says the Lord God, 'surely in the
place *where* the king *dwells* who made him king,
whose oath he despised and whose covenant
he broke—with him in the midst of Babylon he
shall die. ¹⁷Nor will Pharaoh with *his* mighty
army and great company do anything in the
war, when they heap up a siege mound and
build a wall to cut off many persons. ¹⁸Since he
despised the oath by breaking the covenant,
and in fact gave his hand and still did all these
things, he shall not escape.' "

¹⁹Therefore thus says the Lord God: "*As* I
live, surely My oath which he despised, and My
covenant which he broke, I will recompense on
his own head. ²⁰I will spread My net over him,
and he shall be taken in My snare. I will bring
him to Babylon and try him there for the treason which he committed against Me. ²¹All his
fugitives*ᵃ* with all his troops shall fall by the
sword, and those who remain shall be scattered
to every wind; and you shall know that I, the
Lord, have spoken."

ISRAEL EXALTED AT LAST

²²Thus says the Lord God: "I will take also
one of the highest branches of the high cedar
and set *it* out. I will crop off from the topmost
of its young twigs a tender one, and will plant *it*
on a high and prominent mountain. ²³On the
mountain height of Israel I will plant it; and it
will bring forth boughs, and bear fruit, and be a
majestic cedar. Under it will dwell birds of every
sort; in the shadow of its branches they will
dwell. ²⁴And all the trees of the field shall know
that I, the Lord, have brought down the high
tree and exalted the low tree, dried up the green
tree and made the dry tree flourish; I, the Lord,
have spoken and have done *it.*"

WHAT'S IT MEAN?

If you were a Bible writer, what would you use
to symbolize the strength of David's royal family
line? The cedar tree would be a good choice, since it can grow as high
as one hundred feet and as wide as fifty feet. What would you use to
symbolize Jesus, a descendant of David? How about a cedar twig that
grows strong and provides shelter and shade?
Ezekiel 17:22

A FALSE PROVERB REFUTED

¹The word of the Lord came to me again,
saying, ²"What do you mean when you use this
proverb concerning the land of Israel, saying:

'The fathers have eaten sour grapes,
   And the children's teeth are set on edge'?

17:21 *ᵃ*Following Masoretic Text and Vulgate; many Hebrew manuscripts and Syriac read *choice men;* Targum
reads *mighty men;* Septuagint omits *All his fugitives.*

3"As I live," says the Lord GOD, "you shall no longer use this proverb in Israel.

4 "Behold, all souls are Mine;
The soul of the father
As well as the soul of the son is Mine;
The soul who sins shall die.
5 But if a man is just
And does what is lawful
and right,
6 If he has not eaten on
the mountains,
Nor lifted up his
eyes to the idols
of the house of
Israel,
Nor defiled his
neighbor's wife,
Nor approached a
woman during her
impurity;
7 If he has not oppressed
anyone,
But has restored to the debtor his pledge;
Has robbed no one by violence,
But has given his bread to the hungry
And covered the naked with clothing;
8 If he has not exacted usury
Nor taken any increase,
But has withdrawn his hand from
iniquity
And executed true judgment between man
and man;
9 If he has walked in My statutes
And kept My judgments faithfully—
He is just;
He shall surely live!"
Says the Lord GOD.

10 "If he begets a son who is a robber
Or a shedder of blood,
Who does any of these things,
11 And does none of those duties,
But has eaten on the mountains
Or defiled his neighbor's wife;
12 If he has oppressed the poor and needy,
Robbed by violence,
Not restored the pledge,
Lifted his eyes to the idols,
Or committed abomination;
13 If he has exacted usury
Or taken increase—
Shall he then live?
He shall not live!
If he has done any of these abominations,

He shall surely die;
His blood shall be upon him.

14 "If, however, he begets a son
Who sees all the sins which his father has
done,
And considers but does not do likewise;
15 Who has not eaten on the mountains,
Nor lifted his eyes
to the idols of the
house of Israel,
Nor defiled his
neighbor's wife;
16 Has not oppressed
anyone,
Nor withheld a
pledge,
Nor robbed by
violence,
But has given his
bread to the
hungry
And covered the
naked with
clothing;
17 Who has withdrawn his hand from the
poor[a]
And not received usury or increase,
But has executed My judgments
And walked in My statutes—
He shall not die for the iniquity of his
father;
He shall surely live!

18 "As for his father,
Because he cruelly
oppressed,
Robbed his brother by
violence,
And did what is not good
among his people,
Behold, he shall die for his iniquity.

TURN AND LIVE

19"Yet you say, 'Why should the son not bear the guilt of the father?' Because the son has done what is lawful and right, and has kept all My statutes and observed them, he shall surely live. 20The soul who sins shall die. The son shall not bear the guilt of the father, nor the father bear the guilt of the son. The righteousness of the righteous shall be upon himself, and the wickedness of the wicked shall be upon himself. 21"But if a wicked man turns from all his sins which he has committed, keeps all My statutes,

> ' 'If he has walked in My statutes and kept My judgments faithfully—he is just; he shall surely live!' says the Lord GOD." (Ezekiel 18:9)

FAMILY Can children break the chain of sin and disobedience in a family? (18:14–19)

and does what is lawful and right, he shall surely live; he shall not die. ²²None of the transgressions which he has committed shall be remembered against him; because of the righteousness which he has done, he shall live. ²³Do I have any pleasure at all that the wicked should die?" says the Lord GOD, "*and* not that he should turn from his ways and live?

²⁴"But when a righteous man turns away from his righteousness and commits iniquity, and does according to all the abominations that the wicked *man* does, shall he live? All the righteousness which he has done shall not be remembered; because of the unfaithfulness of which he is guilty and the sin which he has committed, because of them he shall die.

²⁵"Yet you say, 'The way of the Lord is not fair.' Hear now, O house of Israel, is it not My way which is fair, and your ways which are not fair? ²⁶When a righteous *man* turns away from his righteousness, commits iniquity, and dies in it, it is because of the iniquity which he has done that he dies. ²⁷Again, when a wicked *man* turns away from the wickedness which he committed, and does what is lawful and right, he preserves himself alive. ²⁸Because he considers and turns away from all the transgressions which he committed, he shall surely live; he shall not die. ²⁹Yet the house of Israel says, 'The way of the Lord is not fair.' O house of Israel, is it not My ways which are fair, and your ways which are not fair?

³⁰"Therefore I will judge you, O house of Israel, every one according to his ways," says the Lord GOD. "Repent, and turn from all your transgressions, so that iniquity will not be your ruin. ³¹Cast away from you all the transgressions which you have committed, and get yourselves a new heart and a new spirit. For why should you die, O house of Israel? ³²For I have no pleasure in the death of one who dies," says the Lord GOD. "Therefore turn and live!"

ISRAEL DEGRADED

¹"Moreover take up a lamentation for the princes of Israel, ²and say:

'What *is* your mother? A lioness:
  She lay down among the lions;
    Among the young lions she nourished her cubs.
³ She brought up one of her cubs,
    And he became a young lion;

He learned to catch prey,
And he devoured men.
4 The nations also heard of him;
  He was trapped in their pit,
  And they brought him with chains to the land of Egypt.

WHAT'S IT MEAN?

If someone were to write a song in your memory after your death, how would you want to be described or portrayed? In this funeral song (or lamentation), the nation of Israel is portrayed as a female lion. Two kings of Israel, Jehoahaz and Jehoiachin, are portrayed as lion cubs. Jehoahaz reigned for only three months before he was taken as a prisoner to Egypt in 609 B.C. Jehoiachin's story is practically the same. He reigned for only three months before being captured and taken to Babylon in 597 B.C.

Ezekiel 19:1–9

5 'When she saw that she waited, *that* her hope was lost,
  She took another of her cubs *and* made him a young lion.
6 He roved among the lions,
  And became a young lion;
  He learned to catch prey;
  He devoured men.
7 He knew their desolate places,ᵃ
  And laid waste their cities;
  The land with its fullness was desolated
  By the noise of his roaring.
8 Then the nations set against him from the provinces on every side,
  And spread their net over him;
  He was trapped in their pit.
9 They put him in a cage with chains,
  And brought him to the king of Babylon;
  They brought him in nets,
  That his voice should no longer be heard on the mountains of Israel.

10 'Your mother *was* like a vine in your bloodline,ᵃ

19:7 ᵃSeptuagint reads *He stood in insolence*; Targum reads *He destroyed its palaces*; Vulgate reads *He learned to make widows*.   **19:10** ᵃLiterally *blood*, following Masoretic Text, Syriac, and Vulgate; Septuagint reads *like a flower on a pomegranate tree*; Targum reads *in your likeness*.

WHAT'S IT MEAN?

If you read a description in the Bible of a fruitful tree growing near water, it usually symbolizes a nation that is experiencing peace and prosperity.

Ezekiel 19:10

Planted by the waters,
Fruitful and full of branches
Because of many waters.
11 She had strong branches for scepters of rulers.
She towered in stature above the thick branches,
And was seen in her height amid the dense foliage.
12 But she was plucked up in fury,
She was cast down to the ground,
And the east wind dried her fruit.
Her strong branches were broken and withered;
The fire consumed them.
13 And now she *is* planted in the wilderness,
In a dry and thirsty land.
14 Fire has come out from a rod of her branches
And devoured her fruit,
So that she has no strong branch—a scepter for ruling.' "

This *is* a lamentation, and has become a lamentation.

THE REBELLIONS OF ISRAEL

1 It came to pass in the seventh year, in the fifth *month,* on the tenth *day* of the month, *that* certain of the elders of Israel came to inquire of the LORD, and sat before me. 2 Then the word of the LORD came to me, saying, 3 "Son of man, speak to the elders of Israel, and say to them, 'Thus says the Lord GOD: "Have you come to inquire of Me? *As* I live," says the Lord GOD, "I will not be inquired of by you." ' 4 Will you judge them, son of man, will you judge *them?* Then make known to them the abominations of their fathers.

5 "Say to them, 'Thus says the Lord GOD: "On the day when I chose Israel and raised My hand in an oath to the descendants of the house of Jacob, and made Myself known to them in the land of Egypt, I raised My hand in an oath to them, saying, 'I *am* the LORD your God.' 6 On that day I raised My hand in an oath to them, to bring them out of the land of Egypt into a land that I had searched out for them, 'flowing with milk and honey,'[a] the glory of all lands. 7 Then I said to them, 'Each of you, throw away the abominations which are before his eyes, and do not defile yourselves with the idols of Egypt. I *am* the LORD your God.' 8 But they rebelled against Me and would not obey Me. They did not all cast away the abominations which were before their eyes, nor did they forsake the idols of Egypt. Then I said, 'I will pour out My fury on them and fulfill My anger against them in the midst of the land of Egypt.' 9 But I acted for My name's sake, that it should not be profaned before the Gentiles among whom they *were,* in whose sight I had made Myself known to them, to bring them out of the land of Egypt.

10 "Therefore I made them go out of the land of Egypt and brought them into the wilderness. 11 And I gave them My statutes and showed them My judgments, 'which, *if* a man does, he shall live by them.'[a] 12 Moreover I also gave them My Sabbaths, to be a sign between them and Me, that they might know that I *am* the LORD who sanctifies them. 13 Yet the house of Israel rebelled against Me in the wilderness; they did not walk in My statutes; they despised My judgments, 'which, *if* a man does, he shall live by them';[a] and they greatly defiled My Sabbaths. Then I said I would pour out My fury on them in the wilderness, to consume them. 14 But I acted for My name's sake, that it should not be profaned before the Gentiles, in whose sight I had brought them out. 15 So I also raised My hand in an oath to them in the wilderness, that I would not bring them into the land which I had given *them,* 'flowing with milk and honey,'[a] the glory of all lands, 16 because they despised My judgments and did not walk in My statutes, but profaned My Sabbaths; for their heart went after their idols. 17 Nevertheless My eye spared them from destruction. I did not make an end of them in the wilderness.

18 "But I said to their children in the wilderness, 'Do not walk in the statutes of your fathers, nor observe their judgments, nor defile yourselves with their idols. 19 I *am* the LORD your

20:6 [a]Exodus 3:8   **20:11** [a]Leviticus 18:5   **20:13** [a]Leviticus 18:5   **20:15** [a]Exodus 3:8

God: Walk in My statutes, keep My judgments, and do them; [20]hallow My Sabbaths, and they will be a sign between Me and you, that you may know that I *am* the LORD your God.'

[21]"Notwithstanding, the children rebelled against Me; they did not walk in My statutes, and were not careful to observe My judgments, 'which, *if* a man does, he shall live by them';[a] but they profaned My Sabbaths. Then I said I would pour out My fury on them and fulfill My anger against them in the wilderness. [22]Nevertheless I withdrew My hand and acted for My name's sake, that it should not be profaned in the sight of the Gentiles, in whose sight I had brought them out. [23]Also I raised My hand in an oath to those in the wilderness, that I would scatter them among the Gentiles and disperse them throughout the countries, [24]because they had not executed My judgments, but had despised My statutes, profaned My Sabbaths, and their eyes were fixed on their fathers' idols.

[25]"Therefore I also gave them up to statutes *that were* not good, and judgments by which they could not live; [26]and I pronounced them unclean because of their ritual gifts, in that they caused all their firstborn to pass through *the fire*, that I might make them desolate and that they might know that I am the LORD." '

[27]"Therefore, son of man, speak to the house of Israel, and say to them, 'Thus says the Lord GOD: "In this too your fathers have blasphemed Me, by being unfaithful to Me. [28]When I brought them into the land *concerning* which I had raised My hand in an oath to give them, and they saw all the high hills and all the thick trees, there they offered their sacrifices and provoked Me with their offerings. There they also sent up their sweet aroma and poured out their drink offerings. [29]Then I said to them, 'What *is* this high place to which you go?' So its name is called Bamah[a] to this day." ' [30]Therefore say to the house of Israel, 'Thus says the Lord GOD: "Are you defiling yourselves in the manner of your fathers, and committing harlotry according to their abominations? [31]For when you offer your gifts and make your sons pass through the fire, you defile yourselves with all your idols, even to this day. So shall I be inquired of by you, O house of Israel? *As* I live," says the Lord GOD, "I will not be inquired of by you. [32]What you have in your mind shall never be, when you say, 'We will be like the Gentiles, like the families in other countries, serving wood and stone.'

GOD WILL RESTORE ISRAEL

[33]"*As* I live," says the Lord GOD, "surely with a mighty hand, with an outstretched arm, and with fury poured out, I will rule over you. [34]I will bring you out from the peoples and gather you out of the countries where you are scattered, with a mighty hand, with an outstretched arm, and with fury poured out. [35]And I will bring you into the wilderness of the peoples, and there I will plead My case with you face to face. [36]Just as I pleaded My case with your fathers in the wilderness of the land of Egypt, so I will plead My case with you," says the Lord GOD.

[37]"I will make you pass under the rod, and I will bring you into the bond of the covenant; [38]I will purge the rebels from among you, and those who transgress against Me; I will bring them out of the country where they dwell, but they shall not enter the land of Israel. Then you will know that I *am* the LORD.

[39]"As for you, O house of Israel," thus says the Lord GOD: "Go, serve every one of you his idols—and hereafter—if you will not obey Me; but profane My holy name no more with your gifts and your idols. [40]For on My holy mountain, on the mountain height of Israel," says the Lord GOD, "there all the house of Israel, all of them in the land, shall serve Me; there I will accept them, and there I will require your offerings and the firstfruits of your sacrifices, together with all your holy things. [41]I will accept you as a sweet aroma when I bring you out from the peoples and gather you out of the countries where you have been scattered; and I will be hallowed in you before the Gentiles. [42]Then you shall know that I *am* the LORD, when I bring you into the land of Israel, into the country *for* which I raised My hand in an oath to give to your fathers. [43]And there you shall remember your ways and all your doings with which you were defiled; and you shall loathe yourselves in your own sight because of all the evils that you have committed. [44]Then you shall know that I *am* the LORD, when I have dealt with you for My name's sake, not according to your wicked ways nor according to your corrupt doings, O house of Israel," says the Lord GOD.' "

FIRE IN THE FOREST

[45]Furthermore the word of the LORD came to me, saying, [46]"Son of man, set your face toward the south; preach against the south and prophesy against the forest land, the South,[a] [47]and say

---

20:21 [a]Leviticus 18:5   **20:29** [a]Literally *High Place*   **20:46** [a]Hebrew *Negev*

to the forest of the South, 'Hear the word of the LORD! Thus says the Lord GOD: "Behold, I will kindle a fire in you, and it shall devour every green tree and every dry tree in you; the blazing flame shall not be quenched, and all faces from the south to the north shall be scorched by it. ⁴⁸All flesh shall see that I, the LORD, have kindled it; it shall not be quenched." ' "

⁴⁹Then I said, "Ah, Lord GOD! They say of me, 'Does he not speak parables?' "

BABYLON, THE SWORD OF GOD

¹And the word of the LORD came to me, saying, ²"Son of man, set your face toward Jerusalem, preach against the holy places, and prophesy against the land of Israel; ³and say to the land of Israel, 'Thus says the LORD: "Behold, I *am* against you, and I will draw My sword out of its sheath and cut off both righteous and wicked from you. ⁴Because I will cut off both righteous and wicked from you, therefore My sword shall go out of its sheath against all flesh from south *to* north, ⁵that all flesh may know that I, the LORD, have drawn My sword out of its sheath; it shall not return anymore." ' ⁶Sigh therefore, son of man, with a breaking heart, and sigh with bitterness before their eyes. ⁷And it shall be when they say to you, 'Why are you sighing?' that you shall answer, 'Because of the news; when it comes, every heart will melt, all hands will be feeble, every spirit will faint, and all knees will be weak *as* water. Behold, it is coming and shall be brought to pass', says the Lord GOD."

⁸Again the word of the LORD came to me, saying, ⁹"Son of man, prophesy and say, 'Thus says the LORD!' Say:

'A sword, a sword is sharpened
And also polished!
¹⁰ Sharpened to make a dreadful slaughter,
Polished to flash like lightning!
Should we then make mirth?
It despises the scepter of My son,
As it does all wood.
¹¹ And He has given it to be polished,
That it may be handled;
This sword is sharpened, and it is
   polished
To be given into the hand of the slayer.

¹² "Cry and wail, son of man;
For it will be against My people,
Against all the princes of Israel.
Terrors including the sword will be
   against My people;
Therefore strike *your* thigh.

¹³ "Because *it is* a testing,
And what if *the sword* despises even the
   scepter?
The scepter shall be no *more*,"

says the Lord GOD.

¹⁴ "You therefore, son of man, prophesy,
And strike *your* hands together.
The third time let the sword do double
   damage.
It *is* the sword *that* slays,
The sword that slays the great *men,*
That enters their private chambers.
¹⁵ I have set the point of the sword against
   all their gates,
That the heart may melt and many may
   stumble.
Ah! *It is* made bright;
It is grasped for slaughter:

¹⁶ "Swords at the ready!
Thrust right!
Set your blade!
Thrust left—
Wherever your edge is ordered!

¹⁷ "I also will beat My fists together,
And I will cause My fury to rest;
I, the LORD, have spoken."

¹⁸The word of the LORD came to me again, saying: ¹⁹"And son of man, appoint for yourself two ways for the sword of the king of Babylon to go; both of them shall go from the same land. Make a sign; put *it* at the head of the road to the city. ²⁰Appoint a road for the sword to go to Rabbah of the Ammonites, and to Judah, into fortified Jerusalem. ²¹For the king of Babylon stands at the parting of the road, at the fork of the two roads, to use divination: he shakes the arrows, he consults the images, he looks at the liver. ²²In his right hand is the divination for Jerusalem: to set up battering rams, to call for a slaughter, to lift the voice with shouting, to set battering rams against the gates, to heap up a *siege* mound, and to build a wall. ²³And it will be to them like a false divination in the eyes of those who have sworn oaths with them; but he will bring their iniquity to remembrance, that they may be taken.

²⁴"Therefore thus says the Lord GOD: 'Because you have made your iniquity to be remembered, in that your transgressions are uncovered, so that in all your doings your sins appear—because you have come to remembrance, you shall be taken in hand.

25'Now to you, O profane, wicked prince of Israel, whose day has come, whose iniquity *shall* end, 26thus says the Lord GOD:

"Remove the turban, and take off the
  crown;
Nothing *shall remain* the
  same.
Exalt the humble, and
  humble the exalted.
27 Overthrown, overthrown,
I will make it overthrown!
It shall be no *longer*,
Until He comes whose right
  it is,
And I will give it *to Him*." '

> "Exalt the humble, and humble the exalted."
> (Ezekiel 21:26b)

A SWORD AGAINST THE AMMONITES

28"And you, son of man, prophesy and say, 'Thus says the Lord GOD concerning the Ammonites and concerning their reproach,' and say:

'A sword, a sword *is* drawn,
Polished for slaughter,
For consuming, for flashing—
29 While they see false visions for you,
While they divine a lie to you,
To bring you on the necks of the wicked,
  the slain
Whose day has come,
Whose iniquity *shall* end.

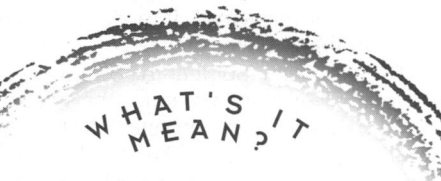

WHAT'S IT MEAN?

If the Magic Eight Ball had been around in ancient times, the Babylonians probably would have used it to try to predict their future. After all, they used practically every other method you can imagine (and some you couldn't imagine in a million years) to find out what lay ahead for them. For example, when they were trying to decide which city to attack, Babylonian officials would drop arrows with names written on them. The officials would then plan their military strategy based on the way the arrows landed. Some Babylonians tried to consult the dead using idols. Others cut open sheep livers—yes, sheep livers—and predicted the future based on the shape and condition of the animals' internal organs.

Ezekiel 21:21

30 'Return *it* to its sheath.
I will judge you
In the place where you were created,
In the land of your nativity.
31 I will pour out My indignation on you;
  I will blow against you
    with the fire of My
    wrath,
  And deliver you into the
    hands of brutal men
    who are skillful to
    destroy.
32 You shall be fuel for the
  fire;
  Your blood shall be in the
    midst of the land.
You shall not be remembered,
For I the LORD have spoken.' "

SINS OF JERUSALEM

1Moreover the word of the LORD came to me, saying, 2"Now, son of man, will you judge, will you judge the bloody city? Yes, show her all her abominations! 3Then say, 'Thus says the Lord GOD: "The city sheds blood in her own midst, that her time may come; and she makes idols within herself to defile herself. 4You have become guilty by the blood which you have shed, and have defiled yourself with the idols which you have made. You have caused your days to draw near, and have come to *the end of* your years; therefore I have made you a reproach to the nations, and a mockery to all countries. 5Those near and *those* far from you will mock you as infamous *and* full of tumult.

6"Look, the princes of Israel: each one has used his power to shed blood in you. 7In you they have made light of father and mother; in your midst they have oppressed the stranger; in you they have mistreated the fatherless and the widow. 8You have despised My holy things and profaned My Sabbaths. 9In you are men who slander to cause bloodshed; in you are those who eat on the mountains; in your midst they commit lewdness. 10In you men uncover their fathers' nakedness; in you they violate women who are set apart during their impurity. 11One commits abomination with his neighbor's wife; another lewdly defiles his daughter-in-law; and another in you violates his sister, his father's daughter. 12In you they take bribes to shed blood; you take usury and increase; you have made profit from your neighbors by extortion, and have forgotten Me," says the Lord GOD.

> **SEX**
> Does God care about sex? (22:10–12)

¹³"Behold, therefore, I beat My fists at the dishonest profit which you have made, and at the bloodshed which has been in your midst. ¹⁴Can your heart endure, or can your hands remain strong, in the days when I shall deal with you? I, the LORD, have spoken, and will do *it.* ¹⁵I will scatter you among the nations, disperse you throughout the countries, and remove your filthiness completely from you. ¹⁶You shall defile yourself in the sight of the nations; then you shall know that I *am* the LORD." ' "

ISRAEL IN THE FURNACE

¹⁷The word of the LORD came to me, saying, ¹⁸"Son of man, the house of Israel has become dross to Me; they *are* all bronze, tin, iron, and lead, in the midst of a furnace; they have become dross from silver. ¹⁹Therefore thus says the Lord GOD: 'Because you have all become dross, therefore behold, I will gather you into the midst of Jerusalem. ²⁰*As men* gather silver, bronze, iron, lead, and tin into the midst of a furnace, to blow fire on it, to melt *it;* so I will gather *you* in My anger and in My fury, and I will leave *you there* and melt you. ²¹Yes, I will gather you and blow on you with the fire of My wrath, and you shall be melted in its midst. ²²As silver is melted in the midst of a furnace, so shall you be melted in its midst; then you shall know that I, the LORD, have poured out My fury on you.' "

ISRAEL'S WICKED LEADERS

²³And the word of the LORD came to me, saying, ²⁴"Son of man, say to her: 'You *are* a land that is not cleansed[a] or rained on in the day of indignation.' ²⁵The conspiracy of her prophets[a] in her midst is like a roaring lion tearing the prey; they have devoured people; they have taken treasure and precious things; they have made many widows in her midst. ²⁶Her priests have violated My law and profaned My holy things; they have not distinguished between the holy and unholy, nor have they made known *the difference* between the unclean and the clean; and they have hidden their eyes from My Sabbaths, so that I am profaned among them. ²⁷Her princes in her midst *are* like wolves tearing the prey, to shed blood, to destroy people, and to get dishonest gain. ²⁸Her prophets plastered them with untempered *mortar,* seeing false visions, and divining lies for them, saying, 'Thus says the Lord GOD', when the LORD had not spoken. ²⁹The people of the land have used oppressions, committed robbery, and mistreated the poor and needy; and they wrongfully oppress the stranger. ³⁰So I sought for a man among them who would make a wall, and stand in the gap before Me on behalf of the land, that I should not destroy it; but I found no one. ³¹Therefore I have poured out My indignation on them; I have consumed them with the fire of My wrath; and I have recompensed their deeds on their own heads," says the Lord GOD.

WHAT'S IT MEAN?

If you're looking to separate precious silver from useless ore, you'll need heat—a lot of intense, extreme heat. The heat melts the impurities in the rock and causes them to rise to the surface, where they can be skimmed away. If you want to purify the silver and make it more valuable, you've got to repeat the heating process over and over again.

Ezekiel 22:18

TWO HARLOT SISTERS

¹The word of the LORD came again to me, saying:

2   "Son of man, there were two women,
    The daughters of one mother.
3   They committed harlotry in Egypt,
    They committed harlotry in their youth;
    Their breasts were there embraced,
    Their virgin bosom was there pressed.
4   Their names: Oholah[a] the elder and
      Oholibah[b] her sister;
    They were Mine,
    And they bore sons and daughters.
    As for their names,
    Samaria *is* Oholah, and Jerusalem *is*
      Oholibah.

THE OLDER SISTER, SAMARIA

5   "Oholah played the harlot even though
      she was Mine;

22:24 [a]Following Masoretic Text, Syriac, and Vulgate; Septuagint reads *showered upon.*   **22:25** [a]Following Masoretic Text and Vulgate; Septuagint reads *princes;* Targum reads *scribes.*   **23:4** [a]Literally *Her Own Tabernacle* [b]Literally *My Tabernacle Is in Her*

And she lusted for her lovers, the
neighboring Assyrians,

6 *Who were* clothed in purple,
Captains and rulers,
All of them desirable young men,
Horsemen riding on horses.

7 Thus she committed her harlotry with
them,
All of them choice men of Assyria;
And with all for whom she lusted,
With all their idols, she defiled herself.

8 She has never given up her harlotry
brought from Egypt,
For in her youth they had lain with her,
Pressed her virgin bosom,
And poured out their immorality upon
her.

9 "Therefore I have delivered her
Into the hand of her lovers,
Into the hand of the Assyrians,
For whom she lusted.

10 They uncovered her nakedness,
Took away her sons and daughters,
And slew her with the sword;
She became a byword among women,
For they had executed judgment on her.

THE YOUNGER SISTER, JERUSALEM

11"Now although her sister Oholibah saw
this, she became more corrupt in her lust than
she, and in her harlotry more corrupt than her
sister's harlotry.

12 "She lusted for the neighboring Assyrians,
Captains and rulers,
Clothed most gorgeously,
Horsemen riding on horses,
All of them desirable young men.

13 Then I saw that she was defiled;
Both *took* the same way.

14 But she increased her harlotry;
She looked at men portrayed on the wall,
Images of Chaldeans portrayed in
vermilion,

15 Girded with belts around their waists,
Flowing turbans on their heads,
All of them looking like captains,
In the manner of the Babylonians of
Chaldea,
The land of their nativity.

16 As soon as her eyes saw them,
She lusted for them
And sent messengers to them in Chaldea.

17 "Then the Babylonians came to her, into
the bed of love,

And they defiled her with their
immorality;
So she was defiled by them, and alienated
herself from them.

18 She revealed her harlotry and uncovered
her nakedness.
Then I alienated Myself from her,
As I had alienated Myself from her sister.

19 "Yet she multiplied her harlotry
In calling to remembrance the days of her
youth,
When she had played the harlot in the
land of Egypt.

20 For she lusted for her paramours,
Whose flesh *is like* the flesh of donkeys,
And whose issue *is like* the issue of
horses.

21 Thus you called to remembrance the
lewdness of your youth,
When the Egyptians pressed your bosom
Because of your youthful breasts.

JUDGMENT ON JERUSALEM

22"Therefore, Oholibah, thus says the Lord
GOD:

'Behold, I will stir up your lovers against
you,
From whom you have alienated yourself,
And I will bring them against you from
every side:

23 The Babylonians,
All the Chaldeans,
Pekod, Shoa, Koa,
All the Assyrians with them,
All of them desirable young men,
Governors and rulers,
Captains and men of renown,
All of them riding on horses.

24 And they shall come against you
With chariots, wagons, and war-horses,
With a horde of people.
They shall array against you
Buckler, shield, and helmet all around.

'I will delegate judgment to them,
And they shall judge you according to
their judgments.

25 I will set My jealousy against you,
And they shall deal furiously with you;
They shall remove your nose and your
ears,
And your remnant shall fall by the
sword;
They shall take your sons and your
daughters,

And your remnant shall be devoured by
    fire.
26 They shall also strip you of your clothes
    And take away your beautiful jewelry.

27 'Thus I will make you cease your
    lewdness and your harlotry
    Brought from the land of Egypt,
    So that you will not lift your eyes to
    them,
    Nor remember Egypt anymore'.

28"For thus says the Lord GOD: 'Surely I will deliver you into the hand of those you hate, into the hand *of those* from whom you alienated yourself. 29They will deal hatefully with you, take away all you have worked for, and leave you naked and bare. The nakedness of your harlotry shall be uncovered, both your lewdness and your harlotry. 30I will do these *things* to you because you have gone as a harlot after the Gentiles, because you have become defiled by their idols. 31You have walked in the way of your sister; therefore I will put her cup in your hand'.

32"Thus says the Lord GOD:

'You shall drink of your sister's cup,
    The deep and wide one;
    You shall be laughed to scorn
    And held in derision;
    It contains much.
33 You will be filled with drunkenness and
    sorrow,
    The cup of horror and desolation,
    The cup of your sister Samaria.
34 You shall drink and drain it,
    You shall break its shards,
    And tear at your own breasts;
    For I have spoken',
    Says the Lord GOD.

35"Therefore thus says the Lord GOD:

'Because you have forgotten Me and cast
    Me behind your back,
    Therefore you shall bear the *penalty*
    Of your lewdness and your harlotry.' "

BOTH SISTERS JUDGED

36The LORD also said to me: "Son of man, will you judge Oholah and Oholibah? Then declare to them their abominations. 37For they have committed adultery, and blood *is* on their hands. They have committed adultery with their idols, and even sacrificed their sons whom they bore to Me, passing them through *the fire,*

to devour *them.* 38Moreover they have done this to Me: They have defiled My sanctuary on the same day and profaned My Sabbaths. 39For after they had slain their children for their idols, on the same day they came into My sanctuary to profane it; and indeed thus they have done in the midst of My house.

40"Furthermore you sent for men to come from afar, to whom a messenger *was* sent; and there they came. And you washed yourself for them, painted your eyes, and adorned yourself with ornaments. 41You sat on a stately couch, with a table prepared before it, on which you had set My incense and My oil. 42The sound of a carefree multitude *was* with her, and Sabeans *were* brought from the wilderness with men of the common sort, who put bracelets on their wrists and beautiful crowns on their heads. 43Then I said concerning *her who had grown* old in adulteries, 'Will they commit harlotry with her now, and she *with them?*' 44Yet they went in to her, as men go in to a woman who plays the harlot; thus they went in to Oholah and Oholibah, the lewd women. 45But righteous men will judge them after the manner of adulteresses, and after the manner of women who shed blood, because they *are* adulteresses, and blood *is* on their hands.

46"For thus says the Lord GOD: 'Bring up an assembly against them, give them up to trouble and plunder. 47The assembly shall stone them with stones and execute them with their swords; they shall slay their sons and their daughters, and burn their houses with fire. 48Thus I will cause lewdness to cease from the land, that all women may be taught not to practice your lewdness. 49They shall repay you for your lewdness, and you shall pay for your idolatrous sins. Then you shall know that I *am* the Lord GOD.' "

SYMBOL OF THE COOKING POT

1Again, in the ninth year, in the tenth month, on the tenth *day* of the month, the word of the LORD came to me, saying, 2"Son of man, write down the name of the day, this very day—the king of Babylon started his siege against Jerusalem this very day. 3And utter a parable to the rebellious house, and say to them, 'Thus says the Lord GOD:

"Put on a pot, set *it* on,
    And also pour water into it.
4 Gather pieces *of meat* in it,
    Every good piece,
    The thigh and the shoulder.
    Fill *it* with choice cuts;

5   Take the choice of the flock.
      Also pile *fuel* bones under it,
      Make it boil well,
      And let the cuts simmer in it."

6 Therefore thus says the Lord GOD:

    "Woe to the bloody city,
      To the pot whose scum *is* in it,
      And whose scum is not gone from it!
      Bring it out piece by piece,
      On which no lot has fallen.
7   For her blood is in her midst;
      She set it on top of a rock;
      She did not pour it on the ground,
      To cover it with dust.
8   That it may raise up fury and take
         vengeance,
      I have set her blood on top of a rock,
      That it may not be covered."

9 Therefore thus says the Lord GOD:

    "Woe to the bloody city!
      I too will make the pyre great.
10   Heap on the wood,
      Kindle the fire;
      Cook the meat well,
      Mix in the spices,
      And let the cuts be burned up.

11   "Then set the pot empty on the coals,
      That it may become hot and its bronze
         may burn,
      That its filthiness may be melted in it,
      That its scum may be consumed.
12   She has grown weary with lies,
      And her great scum has not gone from
         her.
      Let her scum *be* in the fire!
13   In your filthiness *is* lewdness.
      Because I have cleansed you, and you
         were not cleansed,
      You will not be cleansed of your filthiness
         anymore,
      Till I have caused My fury to rest upon
         you.
14   I, the LORD, have spoken *it;*
      It shall come to pass, and I will do *it;*
      I will not hold back,
      Nor will I spare,
      Nor will I relent;
      According to your ways
      And according to your deeds

      They[a] will judge you,"
      Says the Lord GOD.' "

THE PROPHET'S WIFE DIES

15 Also the word of the LORD came to me, saying, 16 "Son of man, behold, I take away from you the desire of your eyes with one stroke; yet you shall neither mourn nor weep, nor shall your tears run down. 17 Sigh in silence, make no mourning for the dead; bind your turban on your head, and put your sandals on your feet; do not cover *your* lips, and do not eat man's bread *of sorrow.*"

18 So I spoke to the people in the morning, and at evening my wife died; and the next morning I did as I was commanded.

19 And the people said to me, "Will you not tell us what these *things signify* to us, that you behave so?"

20 Then I answered them, "The word of the LORD came to me, saying, 21 'Speak to the house of Israel, "Thus says the Lord GOD: 'Behold, I will profane My sanctuary, your arrogant boast, the desire of your eyes, the delight of your soul; and your sons and daughters whom you left behind shall fall by the sword. 22 And you shall do as I have done; you shall not cover *your* lips nor eat man's bread *of sorrow.* 23 Your turbans shall be on your heads and your sandals on your feet; you shall neither mourn nor weep, but you shall pine away in your iniquities and mourn with one another. 24 Thus Ezekiel is a sign to you; according to all that he has done you shall do; and when this comes, you shall know that I *am* the Lord GOD.' "

25 'And you, son of man—*will it* not *be* in the day when I take from them their stronghold, their joy and their glory, the desire of their eyes, and that on which they set their minds, their sons and their daughters: 26 on that day one who escapes will come to you to let *you* hear *it* with *your* ears; 27 on that day your mouth will be opened to him who has escaped; you shall speak and no longer be mute. Thus you will be a sign to them, and they shall know that I *am* the LORD.' "

PROCLAMATION AGAINST AMMON

1 The word of the LORD came to me, saying, 2 "Son of man, set your face against the Ammonites, and prophesy against them. 3 Say to the Ammonites, 'Hear the word of the Lord GOD! Thus says the Lord GOD: "Because you said, 'Aha!' against My sanctuary when it was profaned, and against the land of Israel when it

---

24:14 [a]Septuagint, Syriac, Targum, and Vulgate read *I.*

was desolate, and against the house of Judah when they went into captivity, [4]indeed, therefore, I will deliver you as a possession to the men of the East, and they shall set their encampments among you and make their dwellings among you; they shall eat your fruit, and they shall drink your milk. [5]And I will make Rabbah a stable for camels and Ammon a resting place for flocks. Then you shall know that I *am* the LORD."

[6]"For thus says the Lord GOD: "Because you clapped *your* hands, stamped your feet, and rejoiced in heart with all your disdain for the land of Israel, [7]indeed, therefore, I will stretch out My hand against you, and give you as plunder to the nations; I will cut you off from the peoples, and I will cause you to perish from the countries; I will destroy you, and you shall know that I *am* the LORD."

PROCLAMATION AGAINST MOAB

[8]"Thus says the Lord GOD: "Because Moab and Seir say, 'Look! The house of Judah *is* like all the nations,' [9]therefore, behold, I will clear the territory of Moab of cities, of the cities on its frontier, the glory of the country, Beth Jeshimoth, Baal Meon, and Kirjathaim. [10]To the men of the East I will give it as a possession, together with the Ammonites, that the Ammonites may not be remembered among the nations. [11]And I will execute judgments upon Moab, and they shall know that I *am* the LORD."

PROCLAMATION AGAINST EDOM

[12]"Thus says the Lord GOD: "Because of what Edom did against the house of Judah by taking vengeance, and has greatly offended by avenging itself on them," [13]therefore thus says the Lord GOD: "I will also stretch out My hand against Edom, cut off man and beast from it, and make it desolate from Teman; Dedan shall fall by the sword. [14]I will lay My vengeance on Edom by the hand of My people Israel, that they may do in Edom according to My anger and according to My fury; and they shall know My vengeance," says the Lord GOD.

PROCLAMATION AGAINST PHILISTIA

[15]"Thus says the Lord GOD: "Because the Philistines dealt vengefully and took vengeance with a spiteful heart, to destroy because of the old hatred," [16]therefore thus says the Lord GOD: "I will stretch out My hand against the Philistines, and I will cut off the Cherethites and destroy the remnant of the seacoast. [17]I will execute great vengeance on them with furious rebukes; and they shall know that I *am* the LORD, when I lay My vengeance upon them." ' "

WHAT'S IT MEAN?

The citizens of Tyre weren't exactly heartbroken when Jerusalem was destroyed. They recognized a business opportunity when they saw it. With Israel out of the way, Tyre was free to expand its control over the caravans that passed through the area and boost its already successful trade business.

Ezekiel 26:2

PROCLAMATION AGAINST TYRE

[1]And it came to pass in the eleventh year, on the first *day* of the month, *that* the word of the LORD came to me, saying, [2]"Son of man, because Tyre has said against Jerusalem, 'Aha! She is broken who *was* the gateway of the peoples; now she is turned over to me; I shall be filled; she is laid waste.'

[3]"Therefore thus says the Lord GOD: 'Behold, I *am* against you, O Tyre, and will cause many nations to come up against you, as the sea causes its waves to come up. [4]And they shall destroy the walls of Tyre and break down her towers; I will also scrape her dust from her, and make her like the top of a rock. [5]It shall be *a place for* spreading nets in the midst of the sea, for I have spoken,' says the Lord GOD; 'it shall become plunder for the nations. [6]Also her daughter *villages* which

"For thus says the Lord GOD: 'Because you clapped your hands, stamped your feet, and rejoiced in heart with all your disdain for the land of Israel, indeed, therefore, I will stretch out My hand against you, and give you as plunder to the nations.' "
(Ezekiel 25:6, 7a)

are in the fields shall be slain by the sword. Then they shall know that I am the LORD.'

7"For thus says the Lord GOD: 'Behold, I will bring against Tyre from the north Nebuchadnezzar*a* king of Babylon, king of kings, with horses, with chariots, and with horsemen, and an army with many people. 8He will slay with the sword your daughter *villages* in the fields; he will heap up a siege mound against you, build a wall against you, and raise a defense against you. 9He will direct his battering rams against your walls, and with his axes he will break down your towers. 10Because of the abundance of his horses, their dust will cover you; your walls will shake at the noise of the horsemen, the wagons, and the chariots, when he enters your gates, as men enter a city that has been breached. 11With the hooves of his horses he will trample all your streets; he will slay your people by the sword, and your strong pillars will fall to the ground. 12They will plunder your riches and pillage your merchandise; they will break down your walls and destroy your pleasant houses; they will lay your stones, your timber, and your soil in the midst of the water. 13I will put an end to the sound of your songs, and the sound of your harps shall be heard no more. 14I will make you like the top of a rock; you shall be *a place for* spreading nets, and you shall never be rebuilt, for I the LORD have spoken,' says the Lord GOD.

15"Thus says the Lord GOD to Tyre: 'Will the coastlands not shake at the sound of your fall, when the wounded cry, when slaughter is made in the midst of you? 16Then all the princes of the sea will come down from their thrones, lay aside their robes, and take off their embroidered garments; they will clothe themselves with trembling; they will sit on the ground, tremble *every* moment, and be astonished at you. 17And they will take up a lamentation for you, and say to you:

"How you have perished,
O one inhabited by seafaring men,
O renowned city,
Who was strong at sea,
She and her inhabitants,
Who caused their terror *to be* on all her
    inhabitants!
18 Now the coastlands tremble on the day
        of your fall;
    Yes, the coastlands by the sea are troubled
        at your departure."'

19"For thus says the Lord GOD: 'When I make you a desolate city, like cities that are not inhabited, when I bring the deep upon you, and great waters cover you, 20then I will bring you down with those who descend into the Pit, to the people of old, and I will make you dwell in the lowest part of the earth, in places desolate from antiquity, with those who go down to the Pit, so that you may never be inhabited; and I shall establish glory in the land of the living. 21I will make you a terror, and you *shall be* no *more;* though you are sought for, you will never be found again,' says the Lord GOD."

LAMENTATION FOR TYRE

1The word of the LORD came again to me, saying, 2"Now, son of man, take up a lamentation for Tyre, 3and say to Tyre, 'You who are situated at the entrance of the sea, merchant of the peoples on many coastlands, thus says the Lord GOD:

"O Tyre, you have said,
'I *am* perfect in beauty.'
4   Your borders *are* in the midst of the seas.
    Your builders have perfected your beauty.
5   They made all *your* planks of fir trees
        from Senir;
    They took a cedar from Lebanon to make
        you a mast.
6   *Of* oaks from Bashan they made your
        oars;
    The company of Ashurites have inlaid
        your planks
    With ivory from the coasts of Cyprus.*a*
7   Fine embroidered linen from Egypt was
        what you spread for your sail;
    Blue and purple from the coasts of
        Elishah was what covered you.

8 "Inhabitants of Sidon and Arvad were
        your oarsmen;
    Your wise men, O Tyre, were in you;
    They became your pilots.
9   Elders of Gebal and its wise men
    Were in you to caulk your seams;
    All the ships of the sea
    And their oarsmen were in you
    To market your merchandise.

10 "Those from Persia, Lydia,*a* and Libya*b*
    Were in your army as men of war;
    They hung shield and helmet in you;
    They gave splendor to you.

<hr>

26:7 *a*Hebrew *Nebuchadrezzar,* and so elsewhere in this book   **27:6** *a*Hebrew *Kittim,* western lands, especially Cyprus   **27:10** *a*Hebrew *Lud*   *b*Hebrew *Put*

11 Men of Arvad with your army *were* on
     your walls *all* around,
    And the men of Gammad were in your
     towers;
    They hung their shields on your walls *all*
     around;
    They made your beauty perfect.

12"Tarshish *was* your merchant because of your many luxury goods. They gave you silver, iron, tin, and lead for your goods. 13Javan, Tubal, and Meshech *were* your traders. They bartered human lives and vessels of bronze for your merchandise. 14Those from the house of Togarmah traded for your wares with horses, steeds, and mules. 15The men of Dedan *were* your traders; many isles *were* the market of your hand. They brought you ivory tusks and ebony as payment. 16Syria *was* your merchant because of the abundance of goods you made. They gave you for your wares emeralds, purple, embroidery, fine linen, corals, and rubies. 17Judah and the land of Israel *were* your traders. They traded for your merchandise wheat of Minnith, millet, honey, oil, and balm. 18Damascus *was* your merchant because of the abundance of goods you made, because of your many luxury items, with the wine of Helbon and with white wool. 19Dan and Javan paid for your wares, traversing back and forth. Wrought iron, cassia, and cane were among your merchandise. 20Dedan *was* your merchant in saddlecloths for riding. 21Arabia and all the princes of Kedar *were* your regular merchants. They traded with you in lambs, rams, and goats. 22The merchants of Sheba and Raamah *were* your merchants. They traded for your wares the choicest spices, all kinds of precious stones, and gold. 23Haran, Canneh, Eden, the merchants of Sheba, Assyria, *and* Chilmad *were* your merchants. 24These *were* your merchants in choice items—in purple clothes, in embroidered garments, in chests of multicolored apparel, in sturdy woven cords, which were in your marketplace.

25 "The ships of Tarshish were carriers of
     your merchandise.
    You were filled and very glorious in the
     midst of the seas.
26 Your oarsmen brought you into many
     waters,
    But the east wind broke you in the midst
     of the seas.

27 "Your riches, wares, and merchandise,
    Your mariners and pilots,
    Your caulkers and merchandisers,
    All your men of war who *are* in you,
    And the entire company which *is* in your
     midst,
    Will fall into the midst of the seas on the
     day of your ruin.
28 The common-land will shake at the
     sound of the cry of your pilots.

29 "All who handle the oar,
    The mariners,
    All the pilots of the sea
    Will come down from their ships *and*
     stand on the shore.
30 They will make their voice heard because
     of you;
    They will cry bitterly and cast dust on
     their heads;
    They will roll about in ashes;
31 They will shave themselves completely
     bald because of you,
    Gird themselves with sackcloth,
    And weep for you
    With bitterness of heart *and* bitter wailing.
32 In their wailing for you
    They will take up a lamentation,
    And lament for you:
    'What *city is* like Tyre,
    Destroyed in the midst of the sea?

33 'When your wares went out by sea,
    You satisfied many people;
    You enriched the kings of the earth
    With your many luxury goods and your
     merchandise.
34 But you are broken by the seas in the
     depths of the waters;
    Your merchandise and the entire
     company will fall in your midst.
35 All the inhabitants of the isles will be
     astonished at you;
    Their kings will be greatly afraid,
    And *their* countenance will be troubled.
36 The merchants among the peoples will
     hiss at you;
    You will become a horror, and *be* no
     more forever.' " ' "

PROCLAMATION AGAINST THE KING OF TYRE

1The word of the LORD came to me again, saying, 2"Son of man, say to the prince of Tyre, 'Thus says the Lord GOD:

    "Because your heart *is* lifted up,
    And you say, 'I *am* a god,
    I sit *in* the seat of gods,
    In the midst of the seas,'
    Yet you *are* a man, and not a god,

Though you set your heart as the heart of
a god
3 (Behold, you *are* wiser than Daniel!
There is no secret that can be hidden
from you!
4 With your wisdom and your
understanding
You have gained riches for yourself,
And gathered gold and silver
into your
treasuries;
5 By your great wisdom
in trade you have
increased your riches,
And your heart is lifted
up because of your
riches)",

TALENTS

How can our
gifts work
against us?
(28:5)

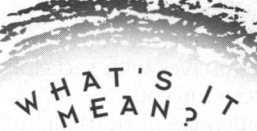

WHAT'S IT MEAN?

Daniel, a captive Jew in Babylon, had
been blessed with some talents that made him
an extremely useful young man. You probably know that people
took dreams very seriously in ancient times. Daniel had the ability
to explain dreams (often without even hearing them described first)
and, in some cases, to predict the future based on those dreams.
Because of his ability, he landed a job as an
advisor to the king of Babylon.
Ezekiel 28:3

6'Therefore thus says the Lord GOD:

"Because you have set your heart as the
heart of a god,
7 Behold, therefore, I will bring strangers
against you,
The most terrible of the nations;
And they shall draw their swords against
the beauty of your wisdom,
And defile your splendor.
8 They shall throw you down into the Pit,
And you shall die the death of the slain
In the midst of the seas.

9 "Will you still say before him who slays
you,
'I *am* a god'?
But you *shall be* a man, and not a god,
In the hand of him who slays you.

10 You shall die the death of the
uncircumcised
By the hand of aliens;
For I have spoken," says the Lord GOD.' "

LAMENTATION FOR THE KING OF TYRE

11Moreover the word of the LORD came to
me, saying, 12"Son of man, take up a lamentation for the king of Tyre, and say to him, 'Thus
says the Lord GOD:

"You *were* the seal of perfection,
Full of wisdom and perfect in beauty.
13 You were in Eden, the garden of God;
Every precious stone *was* your covering:
The sardius, topaz, and diamond,
Beryl, onyx, and jasper,
Sapphire, turquoise, and emerald with
gold.
The workmanship of your timbrels and
pipes
Was prepared for you on the day you
were created.

14 "You *were* the anointed cherub who
covers;
I established you;
You were on the holy mountain of God;
You walked back and forth in the midst
of fiery stones.
15 You *were* perfect in your ways from the
day you were created,
Till iniquity was found in you.

16 "By the abundance of your trading
You became filled with violence within,
And you sinned;
Therefore I cast you as a profane thing
Out of the mountain of God;
And I destroyed you, O covering cherub,
From the midst of the fiery stones.

17 "Your heart was lifted up because of your
beauty;
You corrupted your wisdom for the sake
of your splendor;
I cast you to the ground,
I laid you before kings,
That they might gaze at you.

18 "You defiled your sanctuaries
By the multitude of your iniquities,
By the iniquity of your trading;
Therefore I brought fire from your midst;
It devoured you,
And I turned you to ashes upon the earth
In the sight of all who saw you.

19 All who knew you among the peoples are
    astonished at you;
You have become a horror,
And *shall be* no more forever." ' "

PROCLAMATION AGAINST SIDON

20Then the word of the LORD came to me, saying, 21"Son of man, set your face toward Sidon, and prophesy against her, 22and say, 'Thus says the Lord GOD:

"Behold, I *am* against you, O Sidon;
I will be glorified in your midst;
And they shall know that I *am* the LORD,
When I execute judgments in her and am
    hallowed in her.
23 For I will send pestilence upon her,
And blood in her streets;
The wounded shall be judged in her
    midst
By the sword against her on every side;
Then they shall know that I *am* the LORD.

24"And there shall no longer be a pricking brier or a painful thorn for the house of Israel from among all *who are* around them, who despise them. Then they shall know that I *am* the Lord GOD."

ISRAEL'S FUTURE BLESSING

25'Thus says the Lord GOD: "When I have gathered the house of Israel from the peoples among whom they are scattered, and am hallowed in them in the sight of the Gentiles, then they will dwell in their own land which I gave to My servant Jacob. 26And they will dwell safely there, build houses, and plant vineyards; yes, they will dwell securely, when I execute judgments on all those around them who despise them. Then they shall know that I *am* the LORD their God." ' "

PROCLAMATION AGAINST EGYPT

1In the tenth year, in the tenth *month,* on the twelfth *day* of the month, the word of the LORD came to me, saying, 2"Son of man, set your face against Pharaoh king of Egypt, and prophesy against him, and against all Egypt. 3Speak, and say, 'Thus says the Lord GOD:

"Behold, I *am* against you,
O Pharaoh king of Egypt,

O great monster who lies in the midst of
    his rivers,
Who has said, 'My River*ᵃ is* my own;
I have made *it* for myself.'
4 But I will put hooks in your jaws,
And cause the fish of your rivers to stick
    to your scales;
I will bring you up out of the midst of
    your rivers,
And all the fish in your rivers will stick to
    your scales.
5 I will leave you in the wilderness,
You and all the fish of your rivers;
You shall fall on the open field;
You shall not be picked up or gathered.*ᵃ*
I have given you as food
To the beasts of the field
And to the birds of the heavens.

6 "Then all the inhabitants of Egypt
Shall know that I *am* the LORD,
Because they have been a staff of reed to
    the house of Israel.
7 When they took hold of you with the
    hand,
You broke and tore all their shoulders;*ᵃ*
When they leaned on you,
You broke and made all their backs
    quiver."

8Therefore thus says the Lord GOD: "Surely I will bring a sword upon you and cut off from you man and beast. 9And the land of Egypt shall become desolate and waste; then they will know that I *am* the LORD, because he said, 'The River *is* mine, and I have made *it.*' 10Indeed, therefore, I *am* against you and against your rivers, and I will make the land of Egypt utterly waste and desolate, from Migdol*ᵃ to* Syene, as far as the border of Ethiopia. 11Neither foot of man shall pass through it nor foot of beast pass through it, and it shall be uninhabited forty years. 12I will make the land of Egypt desolate in the midst of the countries *that are* desolate; and among the cities *that are* laid waste, her cities shall be desolate forty years; and I will scatter the Egyptians among the nations and disperse them throughout the countries."

13'Yet, thus says the Lord GOD: "At the end of forty years I will gather the Egyptians from the peoples among whom they were scattered. 14I will bring back the captives of Egypt and cause them to return to the land of Pathros, to the

---

29:3 *ᵃ*That is, the Nile   **29:5** *ᵃ*Following Masoretic Text, Septuagint, and Vulgate; some Hebrew manuscripts and Targum read *buried.*   **29:7** *ᵃ*Following Masoretic Text and Vulgate; Septuagint and Syriac read *hand.* **29:10** *ᵃ*Or *tower*

land of their origin, and there they shall be a lowly kingdom. [15]It shall be the lowliest of kingdoms; it shall never again exalt itself above the nations, for I will diminish them so that they will not rule over the nations anymore. [16]No longer shall it be the confidence of the house of Israel, but will remind them of *their* iniquity when they turned to follow them. Then they shall know that I *am* the Lord GOD." ' "

BABYLONIA WILL PLUNDER EGYPT

[17]And it came to pass in the twenty-seventh year, in the first *month*, on the first *day* of the month, *that* the word of the LORD came to me, saying, [18]"Son of man, Nebuchadnezzar king of Babylon caused his army to labor strenuously against Tyre; every head *was* made bald, and every shoulder rubbed raw; yet neither he nor his army received wages from Tyre, for the labor which they expended on it. [19]Therefore thus says the Lord GOD: 'Surely I will give the land of Egypt to Nebuchadnezzar king of Babylon; he shall take away her wealth, carry off her spoil, and remove her pillage; and that will be the wages for his army. [20]I have given him the land of Egypt *for* his labor, because they worked for Me,' says the Lord GOD. [21]'In that day I will cause the horn of the house of Israel to spring forth, and I will open your mouth to speak in their midst. Then they shall know that I *am* the LORD.' "

EGYPT AND HER ALLIES WILL FALL

[1]The word of the LORD came to me again, saying, [2]"Son of man, prophesy and say, 'Thus says the Lord GOD:

"Wail, 'Woe to the day!'
[3] For the day *is* near,
Even the day of the
LORD *is* near;
It will be a day of clouds,
the time of the Gentiles.
[4] The sword shall come upon Egypt,
And great anguish shall be in Ethiopia,
When the slain fall in Egypt,
And they take away her wealth,
And her foundations are broken down.

[5]"Ethiopia, Libya,[a] Lydia,[b] all the mingled people, Chub, and the men of the lands who are allied, shall fall with them by the sword."
[6]'Thus says the LORD:

"Those who uphold Egypt shall fall,
And the pride of her power shall come down.
From Migdol *to* Syene
Those within her shall fall by the sword,"
Says the Lord GOD.

[7] "They shall be desolate in the midst of the desolate countries,
And her cities shall be in the midst of the cities *that are* laid waste.
[8] Then they will know that I *am* the LORD,
When I have set a fire in Egypt
And all her helpers are destroyed.
[9] On that day messengers shall go forth from Me in ships
To make the careless Ethiopians afraid,
And great anguish shall come upon them,
As on the day of Egypt;
For indeed it is coming!"

[10]'Thus says the Lord GOD:

"I will also make a multitude of Egypt to cease
By the hand of Nebuchadnezzar king of Babylon.
[11] He and his people with him, the most terrible of the nations,
Shall be brought to destroy the land;
They shall draw their swords against Egypt,
And fill the land with the slain.
[12] I will make the rivers dry,
And sell the land into the hand of the wicked;
I will make the land waste, and all that is in it,
By the hand of aliens.
I, the LORD, have spoken."

[13]'Thus says the Lord GOD:

"I will also destroy the idols,
And cause the images to cease from Noph;[a]
There shall no longer be princes from the land of Egypt;
I will put fear in the land of Egypt.
[14] I will make Pathros desolate,
Set fire to Zoan,
And execute judgments in No.[a]
[15] I will pour My fury on Sin,[a] the strength of Egypt;

> "Those who uphold Egypt shall fall, and the pride of her power shall come down."
> (Ezekiel 30:6a)

30:5 [a]Hebrew *Put* [b]Hebrew *Lud*   **30:13** [a]That is, ancient Memphis   **30:14** [a]That is, ancient Thebes
30:15 [a]That is, ancient Pelusium

I will cut off the multitude of No,
16 And set a fire in Egypt;
Sin shall have great pain,
No shall be split open,
And Noph *shall be in* distress daily.
17 The young men of Aven*ᵃ* and Pi Beseth
    shall fall by the sword,
And these *cities* shall go into captivity.
18 At Tehaphnehes*ᵃ* the day shall also be
    darkened,*ᵇ*
When I break the yokes of Egypt there.
And her arrogant strength shall cease in
    her;
As for her, a cloud shall cover her,
And her daughters shall go into captivity.
19 Thus I will execute judgments on Egypt,
Then they shall know that I *am* the
LORD." ' "

PROCLAMATION AGAINST PHARAOH

²⁰And it came to pass in the eleventh year, in the first *month*, on the seventh *day* of the month, *that* the word of the LORD came to me, saying, ²¹"Son of man, I have broken the arm of Pharaoh king of Egypt; and see, it has not been bandaged for healing, nor a splint put on to bind it, to make it strong enough to hold a sword. ²²Therefore thus says the Lord GOD: 'Surely I *am* against Pharaoh king of Egypt, and will break his arms, both the strong one and the one that was broken; and I will make the sword fall out of his hand. ²³I will scatter the Egyptians among the nations, and disperse them throughout the countries. ²⁴I will strengthen the arms of the king of Babylon and put My sword in his hand; but I will break Pharaoh's arms, and he will groan before him with the groanings of a mortally wounded *man*. ²⁵Thus I will strengthen the arms of the king of Babylon, but the arms of Pharaoh shall fall down; they shall know that I *am* the LORD, when I put My sword into the hand of the king of Babylon and he stretches it out against the land of Egypt. ²⁶I will scatter the Egyptians among the nations and disperse them throughout the countries. Then they shall know that I *am* the LORD.' "

EGYPT CUT DOWN LIKE A GREAT TREE

¹Now it came to pass in the eleventh year, in the third *month*, on the first *day* of the month, *that* the word of the LORD came to me, saying, ²"Son of man, say to Pharaoh king of Egypt and to his multitude:

'Whom are you like in your greatness?
3 Indeed Assyria *was* a cedar in Lebanon,
With fine branches that shaded the forest,
And of high stature;
And its top was among the thick boughs.
4 The waters made it grow,
Underground waters gave it height,
With their rivers running around the
    place where it was planted,
And sent out rivulets to all the trees of
    the field.

5 'Therefore its height was exalted above all
    the trees of the field;
Its boughs were multiplied,
And its branches became long because of
    the abundance of water,
As it sent them out.
6 All the birds of the heavens made their
    nests in its boughs;
Under its branches all the beasts of the
    field brought forth their young;
And in its shadow all great nations made
    their home.

7 'Thus it was beautiful in greatness and in
    the length of its branches,
Because its roots reached to abundant
    waters.
8 The cedars in the garden of God could
    not hide it;
The fir trees were not like its boughs,
And the chestnut*ᵃ* trees were not like its
    branches;
No tree in the garden of God was like it
    in beauty.
9 I made it beautiful with a multitude of
    branches,
So that all the trees of Eden envied it,
That *were* in the garden of God.'

¹⁰"Therefore thus says the Lord GOD: 'Because you have increased in height, and it set its top among the thick boughs, and its heart was lifted up in its height, ¹¹therefore I will deliver it into the hand of the mighty one of the nations, and he shall surely deal with it; I have driven it out for its wickedness. ¹²And aliens, the most terrible of the nations, have cut it down and left it; its branches have fallen on the mountains and in all the valleys; its boughs lie broken by all the rivers of the land; and all the peoples of

---

30:17 *ᵃ*That is, ancient On (Heliopolis)   **30:18** *ᵃ*Spelled *Tahpanhes* in Jeremiah 43:7 and elsewhere
*ᵇ*Following many Hebrew manuscripts, Bomberg, Septuagint, Syriac, Targum, and Vulgate; Masoretic Text reads *refrained.*   **31:8** *ᵃ*Hebrew *armon*

the earth have gone from under its shadow and left it.

13 'On its ruin will remain all the birds of the heavens,
And all the beasts of the field will come to its branches—

14So that no trees by the waters may ever again exalt themselves for their height, nor set their tops among the thick boughs, that no tree which drinks water may ever be high enough to reach up to them.

'For they have all been delivered to death,
To the depths of the earth,
Among the children of men who go down to the Pit.'

15"Thus says the Lord GOD: 'In the day when it went down to hell, I caused mourning. I covered the deep because of it. I restrained its rivers, and the great waters were held back. I caused Lebanon to mourn for it, and all the trees of the field wilted because of it. 16I made the nations shake at the sound of its fall, when I cast it down to hell together with those who descend into the Pit; and all the trees of Eden, the choice and best of Lebanon, all that drink water, were comforted in the depths of the earth. 17They also went down to hell with it, with those *slain* by the sword; and *those who were* its *strong* arm dwelt in its shadows among the nations.
18'To which of the trees in Eden will you then be likened in glory and greatness? Yet you shall be brought down with the trees of Eden to the depths of the earth; you shall lie in the midst of the uncircumcised, with *those* slain by the sword. This *is* Pharaoh and all his multitude,' says the Lord GOD."

LAMENTATION FOR PHARAOH AND EGYPT

1And it came to pass in the twelfth year, in the twelfth *month*, on the first *day* of the month, *that* the word of the LORD came to me, saying, 2"Son of man, take up a lamentation for Pharaoh king of Egypt, and say to him:

'You are like a young lion among the nations,
And you *are* like a monster in the seas,
Bursting forth in your rivers,
Troubling the waters with your feet,
And fouling their rivers.'

3"Thus says the Lord GOD:

'I will therefore spread My net over you with a company of many people,
And they will draw you up in My net.
4 Then I will leave you on the land;
I will cast you out on the open fields,
And cause to settle on you all the birds of the heavens.
And with you I will fill the beasts of the whole earth.
5 I will lay your flesh on the mountains,
And fill the valleys with your carcass.

WHAT'S IT MEAN?

Not having a proper burial may not seem like a big deal to you, but it was the ultimate insult for people in the ancient Near East. Egyptian kings were especially concerned about their afterlife accommodations. Not only did they build elaborate tombs for themselves, they also stocked those tombs with their favorite treasures and anything else they thought they needed for the hereafter.
Ezekiel 32:4

6 'I will also water the land with the flow of your blood,
Even to the mountains;
And the riverbeds will be full of you.
7 When *I* put out your light,
I will cover the heavens, and make its stars dark;
I will cover the sun with a cloud,
And the moon shall not give her light.
8 All the bright lights of the heavens I will make dark over you,
And bring darkness upon your land,'
Says the Lord GOD.

9'I will also trouble the hearts of many peoples, when I bring your destruction among the nations, into the countries which you have not known. 10Yes, I will make many peoples astonished at you, and their kings shall be horribly afraid of you when I brandish My sword before them; and they shall tremble *every* moment, every man for his own life, in the day of your fall.'
11"For thus says the Lord GOD: 'The sword of the king of Babylon shall come upon you. 12By the swords of the mighty warriors, all of them

the most terrible of the nations, I will cause your multitude to fall.

'They shall plunder the pomp of Egypt,
And all its multitude shall be destroyed.
13 Also I will destroy all its animals
From beside its great waters;
The foot of man shall muddy them no
more,
Nor shall the hooves of animals muddy
them.
14 Then I will make their waters clear,
And make their rivers run like oil,'
Says the Lord GOD.

15 'When I make the land of Egypt desolate,
And the country is destitute of all that
once filled it,
When I strike all who dwell in it,
Then they shall know that I am the LORD.

16 'This is the lamentation
With which they shall lament her;
The daughters of the nations shall lament
her;
They shall lament for her, for Egypt,
And for all her multitude,'
Says the Lord GOD."

EGYPT AND OTHERS CONSIGNED TO THE PIT

17It came to pass also in the twelfth year, on the fifteenth day of the month, that the word of the LORD came to me, saying:

18 "Son of man, wail over the multitude of
Egypt,
And cast them down to the depths of the
earth,
Her and the daughters of the famous
nations,
With those who go down to the Pit:
19 'Whom do you surpass in beauty?
Go down, be placed with the
uncircumcised.'

20 "They shall fall in the midst of those slain
by the sword;
She is delivered to the sword,
Drawing her and all her multitudes.
21 The strong among the mighty
Shall speak to him out of the midst of
hell
With those who help him:
'They have gone down,
They lie with the uncircumcised, slain by
the sword.'

22 "Assyria is there, and all her company,
With their graves all around her,
All of them slain, fallen by the sword.
23 Her graves are set in the recesses of the
Pit,
And her company is all around her
grave,
All of them slain, fallen by the sword,
Who caused terror in the land of the
living.

24 "There is Elam and all her multitude,
All around her grave,
All of them slain, fallen by the sword,
Who have gone down uncircumcised to
the lower parts of the earth,
Who caused their terror in the land of the
living;
Now they bear their shame with those
who go down to the Pit.
25 They have set her bed in the midst of the
slain,
With all her multitude,
With her graves all around it,
All of them uncircumcised, slain by the
sword;
Though their terror was caused
In the land of the living,
Yet they bear their shame
With those who go down to the Pit;
It was put in the midst of the slain.

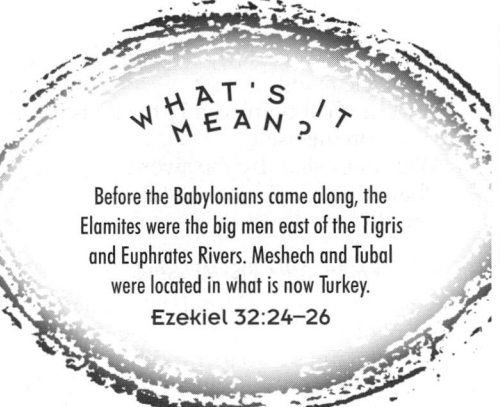

WHAT'S IT MEAN?

Before the Babylonians came along, the
Elamites were the big men east of the Tigris
and Euphrates Rivers. Meshech and Tubal
were located in what is now Turkey.
Ezekiel 32:24–26

26 "There are Meshech and Tubal and all their
multitudes,
With all their graves around it,
All of them uncircumcised, slain by the
sword,
Though they caused their terror in the
land of the living.
27 They do not lie with the mighty
Who are fallen of the uncircumcised,

Who have gone down to hell with their
weapons of war;
They have laid their swords under their
heads,
But their iniquities will be on their bones,
Because of the terror of the mighty in the
land of the living.
28 Yes, you shall be broken in the midst of
the uncircumcised,
And lie with *those* slain by the sword.

29 "There *is* Edom,
Her kings and all her princes,
Who despite their might
Are laid beside *those* slain by the sword;
They shall lie with the uncircumcised,
And with those who go down to the Pit.
30 There *are* the princes of the north,
All of them, and all the Sidonians,
Who have gone down with the slain
In shame at the terror which they caused
by their might;
They lie uncircumcised with *those* slain by
the sword,
And bear their shame with those who go
down to the Pit.

31 "Pharaoh will see them
And be comforted over all his multitude,
Pharaoh and all his army,
Slain by the sword,"
Says the Lord GOD.

32 "For I have caused My terror in the land
of the living;
And he shall be placed in the midst of the
uncircumcised
With *those* slain by the sword,
Pharaoh and all his multitude,"
Says the Lord GOD.

THE WATCHMAN AND HIS MESSAGE

¹Again the word of the LORD came to me,
saying, ²"Son of man, speak to the children of
your people, and say to them: 'When I bring the
sword upon a land, and the people of the land
take a man from their territory and make him
their watchman, ³when he sees the sword coming upon the land, if he blows the trumpet and
warns the people, ⁴then whoever hears the
sound of the trumpet and does not take warning, if the sword comes and takes him away, his
blood shall be on his *own* head. ⁵He heard the
sound of the trumpet, but did not take warning;
his blood shall be upon himself. But he who
takes warning will save his life. ⁶But if the
watchman sees the sword coming and does not

blow the trumpet, and the
people are not warned,
and the sword comes and
takes *any* person from among
them, he is taken away in his
iniquity; but his blood I will
require at the watchman's
hand.'

⁷"So you, son of man: I have made you a
watchman for the house of Israel; therefore you
shall hear a word from My mouth and warn
them for Me. ⁸When I say to the wicked, 'O
wicked *man*, you shall surely die!' and you do
not speak to warn the wicked from his way,
that wicked *man* shall die in his iniquity; but his
blood I will require at your hand. ⁹Nevertheless
if you warn the wicked to turn from his way,
and he does not turn from his way, he shall die
in his iniquity; but you have delivered your
soul.

¹⁰"Therefore you, O son of man, say to the
house of Israel: 'Thus you say, "If our transgressions and our sins *lie* upon us, and we pine
away in them, how can we then live?" ' ¹¹Say to
them: '*As* I live,' says the Lord GOD, 'I have no
pleasure in the death of the wicked, but that the
wicked turn from his way and live. Turn, turn
from your evil ways! For why should you die,
O house of Israel?'

THE FAIRNESS OF GOD'S JUDGMENT

¹²"Therefore you, O son of man, say to the
children of your people: 'The righteousness of
the righteous man shall not deliver him in the
day of his transgression; as for the wickedness
of the wicked, he shall not fall because of it in
the day that he turns from his wickedness; nor
shall the righteous be able to live because of *his
righteousness* in the day that he sins.' ¹³When I
say to the righteous *that* he shall surely live, but
he trusts in his own righteousness and commits
iniquity, none of his righteous works shall be
remembered; but because of the iniquity that
he has committed, he shall die. ¹⁴Again, when I
say to the wicked, 'You shall surely die,' if he
turns from his sin and does what is lawful and
right, ¹⁵if the wicked restores the pledge, gives
back what he has stolen, and walks in the statutes of life without committing iniquity, he shall
surely live; he shall not die. ¹⁶None of his sins
which he has committed shall be remembered
against him; he has done what is lawful and
right; he shall surely live.

¹⁷"Yet the children of your people say, 'The
way of the LORD is not fair.' But it is their way
which is not fair! ¹⁸When the righteous turns
from his righteousness and commits iniquity,

RESPONSIBILITY

Are we
responsible
to help
others?
(33:1–6)

he shall die because of it. [19]But when the wicked turns from his wickedness and does what is lawful and right, he shall live because of it. [20]Yet you say, 'The way of the LORD is not fair.' O house of Israel, I will judge every one of you according to his own ways."

THE FALL OF JERUSALEM

[21]And it came to pass in the twelfth year of our captivity, in the tenth *month,* on the fifth *day* of the month, *that* one who had escaped from Jerusalem came to me and said, "The city has been captured!"

[22]Now the hand of the LORD had been upon me the evening before the man came who had escaped. And He had opened my mouth; so when he came to me in the morning, my mouth was opened, and I was no longer mute.

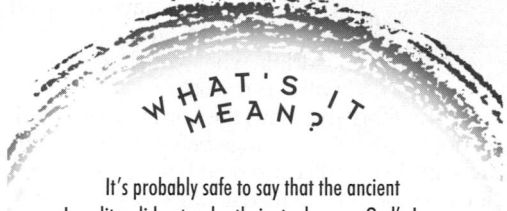

WHAT'S IT MEAN?

It's probably safe to say that the ancient Israelites did not order their steaks rare. God's Law specifically prohibited them from eating or drinking blood in any form. That meant all meat had to be drained and thoroughly cooked before it was served. Why such a ban on blood? The idol-worshiping neighbors of Israel all included blood-drinking rituals in their "religious" ceremonies. By avoiding blood all together, the Israelites found a way to stand out.
Ezekiel 33:25

THE CAUSE OF JUDAH'S RUIN

[23]Then the word of the LORD came to me, saying: [24]"Son of man, they who inhabit those ruins in the land of Israel are saying, 'Abraham was only one, and he inherited the land. But we *are* many; the land has been given to us as a possession.'

[25]"Therefore say to them, 'Thus says the Lord GOD: "You eat *meat* with blood, you lift up your eyes toward your idols, and shed blood. Should you then possess the land? [26]You rely on your sword, you commit abominations, and you defile one another's wives. Should you then possess the land?" '

[27]"Say thus to them, 'Thus says the Lord GOD: "*As* I live, surely those who *are* in the ruins shall fall by the sword, and the one who *is* in the open field I will give to the beasts to be de-

voured, and those who *are* in the strongholds and caves shall die of the pestilence. [28]For I will make the land most desolate, her arrogant strength shall cease, and the mountains of Israel shall be so desolate that no one will pass through. [29]Then they shall know that I *am* the LORD, when I have made the land most desolate because of all their abominations which they have committed." '

HEARING AND NOT DOING

[30]"As for you, son of man, the children of your people are talking about you beside the walls and in the doors of the houses; and they speak to one another, everyone saying to his brother, 'Please come and hear what the word is that comes from the LORD.' [31]So they come to you as people do, they sit before you *as* My people, and they hear your words, but they do not do them; for with their mouth they show much love, *but* their hearts pursue their *own* gain. [32]Indeed you *are* to them as a very lovely song of one who has a pleasant voice and can play well on an instrument; for they hear your words, but they do not do them. [33]And when this comes to pass—surely it will come—then they will know that a prophet has been among them."

IRRESPONSIBLE SHEPHERDS

[1]And the word of the LORD came to me, saying, [2]"Son of man, prophesy against the shepherds of Israel, prophesy and say to them, 'Thus says the Lord GOD to the shepherds: "Woe to the shepherds of Israel who feed themselves! Should not the shepherds feed the flocks? [3]You

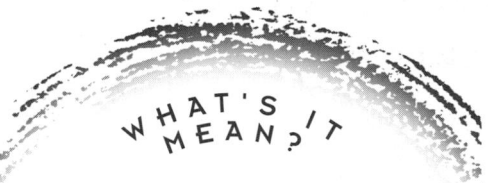

WHAT'S IT MEAN?

Quick, name the animal that is mentioned in the Bible more often than any other animal. If you guessed "sheep," you're correct! Sheep have been an especially important part of Israel's history, providing the Israelites with wool for clothes and meat for food and sacrifices. Because sheep are nearly helpless by themselves, they depend on a shepherd to guide and protect them. A good shepherd knows when and where to lead his flock to water and is willing to risk his life for the animals.
Ezekiel 34:2

eat the fat and clothe yourselves with the wool; you slaughter the fatlings, *but* you do not feed the flock. [4]The weak you have not strengthened, nor have you healed those who were sick, nor bound up the broken, nor brought back what was driven away, nor sought what was lost; but with force and cruelty you have ruled them. [5]So they were scattered because *there was* no shepherd; and they became food for all the beasts of the field when they were scattered. [6]My sheep wandered through all the mountains, and on every high hill; yes, My flock was scattered over the whole face of the earth, and no one was seeking or searching *for them*."

[7]Therefore, you shepherds, hear the word of the LORD: [8]"*As* I live," says the Lord GOD, "surely because My flock became a prey, and My flock became food for every beast of the field, because *there was* no shepherd, nor did My shepherds search for My flock, but the shepherds fed themselves and did not feed My flock"— [9]therefore, O shepherds, hear the word of the LORD! [10]Thus says the Lord GOD: "Behold, I *am* against the shepherds, and I will require My flock at their hand; I will cause them to cease feeding the sheep, and the shepherds shall feed themselves no more; for I will deliver My flock from their mouths, that they may no longer be food for them."

GOD, THE TRUE SHEPHERD

[11]'For thus says the Lord GOD: "Indeed I Myself will search for My sheep and seek them out. [12]As a shepherd seeks out his flock on the day he is among his scattered sheep, so will I seek out My sheep and deliver them from all the places where they were scattered on a cloudy and dark day. [13]And I will bring them out from the peoples and gather them from the countries, and will bring them to their own land; I will feed them on the mountains of Israel, in the valleys and in all the inhabited places of the country. [14]I will feed them in good pasture, and their fold shall be on the high mountains of Israel. There they shall lie down in a good fold and feed in rich pasture on the mountains of Israel. [15]I will feed My flock, and I will make them lie down," says the Lord GOD. [16]"I will seek what was lost and bring back

what was driven away, bind up the broken and strengthen what was sick; but I will destroy the fat and the strong, and feed them in judgment."

[17]'And *as for* you, O My flock, thus says the Lord GOD: "Behold, I shall judge between sheep and sheep, between rams and goats. [18]*Is it* too little for you to have eaten up the good pasture, that you must tread down with your feet the residue of your pasture—and to have drunk of the clear waters, that you must foul the residue with your feet? [19]And *as for* My flock, they eat what you have trampled with your feet, and they drink what you have fouled with your feet."

[20]'Therefore thus says the Lord GOD to them: "Behold, I Myself will judge between the fat and the lean sheep. [21]Because you have pushed with side and shoulder, butted all the weak ones with your horns, and scattered them abroad, [22]therefore I will save My flock, and they shall no longer be a prey; and I will judge between sheep and sheep. [23]I will establish one shepherd over them, and he shall feed them—My servant David. He shall feed them and be their shepherd. [24]And I, the LORD, will be their God, and My servant David a prince among them; I, the LORD, have spoken.

[25]"I will make a covenant of peace with them, and cause wild beasts to cease from the land; and they will dwell safely in the wilderness and sleep in the woods. [26]I will make them and the places all around My hill a blessing; and I will cause showers to come down in their season; there shall be showers of blessing. [27]Then the trees of the field shall yield their fruit, and the earth shall yield her increase. They shall be safe in their land; and they shall know that I *am* the LORD, when I have broken the bands of their yoke and delivered them from the hand of those who enslaved them. [28]And they shall no longer be a prey for the nations, nor shall beasts of the land devour them; but they shall dwell safely, and no one shall make *them* afraid. [29]I will raise up for them a garden of renown, and they shall no longer be consumed with hunger in the land, nor bear the shame of the Gentiles anymore. [30]Thus they shall know that I, the LORD their God, *am* with them, and they,

> "As a shepherd seeks out his flock on the day he is among his scattered sheep, so will I seek out My sheep and deliver them from all the places where they were scattered on a cloudy and dark day."
> (Ezekiel 34:12)

the house of Israel, *are* My people," says the Lord GOD.' "

³¹"You are My flock, the flock of My pasture; you *are* men, *and* I *am* your God," says the Lord GOD.

JUDGMENT ON MOUNT SEIR

¹Moreover the word of the LORD came to me, saying, ²"Son of man, set your face against Mount Seir and prophesy against it, ³and say to it, 'Thus says the Lord GOD:

"Behold, O Mount Seir, I *am* against you;
I will stretch out My hand against you,
And make you most desolate;
4   I shall lay your cities waste,
And you shall be desolate.
Then you shall know that I *am* the LORD.

⁵"Because you have had an ancient hatred, and have shed *the blood of* the children of Israel by the power of the sword at the time of their calamity, *when* their iniquity *came to an* end, ⁶therefore, *as* I live," says the Lord GOD, "I will prepare you for blood, and blood shall pursue you; since you have not hated blood, therefore blood shall pursue you. ⁷Thus I will make Mount Seir most desolate, and cut off from it the one who leaves and the one who returns. ⁸And I will fill its mountains with the slain; on your hills and in your valleys and in all your ravines those who are slain by the sword shall fall. ⁹I will make you perpetually desolate, and your cities shall be uninhabited; then you shall know that I *am* the LORD.

¹⁰"Because you have said, 'These two nations and these two countries shall be mine, and we will possess them,' although the LORD was there, ¹¹therefore, *as* I live," says the Lord GOD, "I will

Promise   HE PROMISES TO BE YOUR SHEPHERD.

"I will make a covenant of peace with them, and cause wild beasts to cease from the land; and they will dwell safely in the wilderness and sleep in the woods. I will make them and the places all around My hill a blessing; and I will cause showers to come down in their season; there shall be showers of blessing. Then the trees of the field shall yield their fruit, and the earth shall yield her increase. They shall be safe in their land; and they shall know that I am the LORD, when I have broken the bands of their yoke and delivered them from the hand of those who enslaved them. And they shall no longer be a prey for the nations, nor shall beasts of the land devour them; but they shall dwell safely, and no one shall make them afraid. I will raise up for them a garden of renown, and they shall no longer be consumed with hunger in the land, nor bear the shame of the Gentiles anymore. Thus they shall know that I, the LORD their God, am with them, and they, the house of Israel, are My people," says the Lord GOD. "You are My flock, the flock of My pasture; you are men, and I am your God," says the Lord GOD (Ezek. 34:25–31).

Can you remember being two or three years old? Were you expected to buy your own groceries, pay your own bills, and build your own house at that age? Of course not! A two-year-old is a helpless child, unable to do much without proper help or guidance. Even when you grow up, God says you will still be helpless. He calls us His flock because sheep are the most helpless of all animals. They don't know how to find new fields to graze. They can't protect themselves from wild animals. They are so fearful that they would just huddle together and die if they didn't have a shepherd. The shepherd is the one who keeps them fed and watered and safe.

The Lord promises to be your Shepherd. He will rescue lost people. He will bandage and heal us when we're wounded. He will make sure that we have all we need. He will calm our fears and protect us from our enemies. When you feel like a little lost sheep, wandering around aimlessly, remember that the Shepherd is waiting for you. He's calling your name. Run to Him.

SEE FOR YOURSELF:
Ps. 23; Is. 53:6; Ezek. 34:11–15

WHAT'S IT MEAN?

The descendants of Esau were rugged mountain folk, living in Mount Seir. Their problems with the Israelites began when Jacob (or Israel) tricked his brother, Esau, out of his inheritance.

Ezekiel 35:2

do according to your anger and according to the envy which you showed in your hatred against them; and I will make Myself known among them when I judge you. ¹²Then you shall know that I *am* the LORD. I have heard all your blasphemies which you have spoken against the mountains of Israel, saying, 'They are desolate; they are given to us to consume.' ¹³Thus with your mouth you have boasted against Me and multiplied your words against Me; I have heard *them.*"

¹⁴'Thus says the Lord GOD: "The whole earth will rejoice when I make you desolate. ¹⁵As you rejoiced because the inheritance of the house of Israel was desolate, so I will do to you; you shall be desolate, O Mount Seir, as well as all of Edom—all of it! Then they shall know that I *am* the LORD." '

HATRED
What will God hold us accountable to? (35:11, 12)

PRIDE
Should we avoid boasting? (35:13)

BLESSING ON ISRAEL

¹"And you, son of man, prophesy to the mountains of Israel, and say, 'O mountains of Israel, hear the word of the LORD! ²Thus says the Lord GOD: "Because the enemy has said of you, 'Aha! The ancient heights have become our possession,' " ' ³therefore prophesy, and say, 'Thus says the Lord GOD: "Because they made *you* desolate and swallowed you up on every side, so that you became the possession of the rest of the nations, and you are taken up by the lips of talkers and slandered by the people"— ⁴therefore, O mountains of Israel, hear the word of the Lord GOD! Thus says the Lord GOD to the mountains, the hills, the rivers, the valleys, the desolate wastes, and the cities that have been forsaken, which became plunder and mockery to the rest of the nations all around—⁵therefore thus says the Lord GOD: "Surely I have spoken in My burning jealousy against the rest of the nations and against all Edom, who gave My land to themselves as a possession, with whole-hearted joy *and* spiteful minds, in order to plunder its open country." '

⁶"Therefore prophesy concerning the land of Israel, and say to the mountains, the hills, the rivers, and the valleys, 'Thus says the Lord GOD: "Behold, I have spoken in My jealousy and My fury, because you have borne the shame of the nations." ⁷Therefore thus says the Lord GOD: "I have raised My hand in an oath that surely the nations that *are* around you shall bear their own shame. ⁸But you, O mountains of Israel, you shall shoot forth your branches and yield your fruit to My people Israel, for they are about to come. ⁹For indeed I *am* for you, and I will turn to you, and you shall be tilled and sown. ¹⁰I will multiply men upon you, all the house of Israel, all of it; and the cities shall be inhabited and the ruins rebuilt. ¹¹I will multiply upon you man and beast; and they shall increase and bear young; I will make you inhabited as in former times, and do better *for you* than at your beginnings. Then you shall know that I *am* the LORD. ¹²Yes, I will cause men to walk on you, My people Israel; they shall take possession of you, and you shall be their inheritance; no more shall you bereave them *of children.*"

¹³'Thus says the Lord GOD: "Because they say to you, 'You devour men and bereave your nation *of children,*' ¹⁴therefore you shall devour men no more, nor bereave your nation anymore," says the Lord GOD. ¹⁵Nor will I let you hear the taunts of the nations anymore, nor bear the reproach of the peoples anymore, nor shall you cause your nation to stumble anymore," says the Lord GOD.' "

THE RENEWAL OF ISRAEL

¹⁶Moreover the word of the LORD came to me, saying: ¹⁷"Son of man, when the house of Israel dwelt in their own land, they defiled it by their own ways and deeds; to Me their way was like the uncleanness of a woman in her customary impurity. ¹⁸Therefore I poured out My fury on them for the blood they had shed on the land, and for their idols *with which* they had defiled it. ¹⁹So I scattered them among the nations, and they were dispersed throughout the

countries; I judged them according to their ways and their deeds. ²⁰When they came to the nations, wherever they went, they profaned My holy name—when they said of them, 'These *are* the people of the LORD, *and* yet they have gone out of His land'. ²¹But I had concern for My holy name, which the house of Israel had profaned among the nations wherever they went.

DISOBEDIENCE
Is it wrong to misuse God's name?
(36:20)

²²"Therefore say to the house of Israel, 'Thus says the Lord GOD: "I do not do *this* for your sake, O house of Israel, but for My holy name's sake, which you have profaned among the nations wherever you went. ²³And I will sanctify My great name, which has been profaned among the nations, which you have profaned in their midst; and the nations shall know that I *am* the LORD," says the Lord GOD, "when I am hallowed in you before their eyes. ²⁴For I will take you from among the nations, gather you out of all countries, and bring you into your own land. ²⁵Then I will sprinkle clean water on you, and you shall be clean; I will cleanse you from all your filthiness and from all your idols. ²⁶I will give you a new heart and put a new spirit within you; I will take the heart of stone out of your flesh and give you a heart of flesh. ²⁷I will put My Spirit within you and cause you to walk in My statutes, and you will keep My judgments and do *them*. ²⁸Then you shall dwell in the land that I gave to your fathers; you shall be My people, and I will be your God. ²⁹I will deliver you from all your uncleannesses. I will call for the grain and multiply it, and bring no famine upon you. ³⁰And I will multiply the fruit of your trees and the increase of your fields, so that you need never again bear the reproach of famine among the nations. ³¹Then you will remember your evil ways and your deeds that *were* not good; and you will loathe yourselves in your own sight, for your iniquities and your abominations. ³²Not for your sake do I do *this*," says the Lord GOD, "let it be known to you. Be ashamed and confounded for your own ways, O house of Israel!"

³³'Thus says the Lord GOD: "On the day that I cleanse you from all your iniquities, I will also enable *you* to dwell in the cities, and the ruins shall be rebuilt. ³⁴The desolate land shall be tilled instead of lying desolate in the sight of all who pass by. ³⁵So they will say, 'This land that was desolate has become like the garden of Eden; and the wasted, desolate, and ruined cities *are now* fortified *and* inhabited'. ³⁶Then the nations which are left all around you shall know that I, the LORD, have rebuilt the ruined places *and* planted what was desolate. I, the LORD, have spoken *it*, and I will do *it*."

BELIEF
Is God's word reliable?
(36:36)

³⁷'Thus says the Lord GOD: "I will also let the house of Israel inquire of Me to do this for them: I will increase their men like a flock. ³⁸Like a flock *offered as* holy *sacrifices*, like the flock at Jerusalem on its feast days, so shall the ruined cities be filled with flocks of men. Then they shall know that I *am* the LORD."' "

Promise   HE PROMISES TO GIVE YOU A NEW HEART.

I will give you a new heart and put a new spirit within you; I will take the heart of stone out of your flesh and give you a heart of flesh (Ezek. 36:26).

God didn't say He would just repair your old, dirty heart. He says He is going to perform a complete transplant, taking the old stubborn heart away and giving you a brand-new one. Doctors have come to the conclusion that some people's hearts are beyond repair, and the only way for them to survive is for them to receive a heart transplant. The same is true spiritually; the only way for us to live life the way God wants us to is to get a fresh start. He exchanges the old for the new. When God gives us this transplant, things don't look the same to us. It's not just a different attitude, but a brand-new life! We don't need to settle for a repair job when God has a whole new, wonderful life for each one of us.

SEE FOR YOURSELF:
Ps. 51:10; Jer. 32:39; Ezek. 11:19; John 3:3;
2 Cor. 5:17; Rev. 21:5

THE DRY BONES LIVE

¹The hand of the LORD came upon me and brought me out in the Spirit of the LORD, and set me down in the midst of the valley; and it *was* full of bones. ²Then He caused me to pass by them all around, and behold, *there were* very many in the open valley; and indeed *they were* very dry. ³And He said to me, "Son of man, can these bones live?"

So I answered, "O Lord GOD, You know."

⁴Again He said to me, "Prophesy to these bones, and say to them, 'O dry bones, hear the word of the LORD! ⁵Thus says the Lord GOD to these bones: "Surely I will cause breath to enter into you, and you shall live. ⁶I will put sinews on you and bring flesh upon you, cover you with skin and put breath in you; and you shall live. Then you shall know that I *am* the LORD." ' "

⁷So I prophesied as I was commanded; and as I prophesied, there was a noise, and suddenly a rattling; and the bones came together, bone to bone. ⁸Indeed, as I looked, the sinews and the flesh came upon them, and the skin covered them over; but *there was* no breath in them.

⁹Also He said to me, "Prophesy to the breath, prophesy, son of man, and say to the breath, 'Thus says the Lord GOD: "Come from the four winds, O breath, and breathe on these slain, that they may live." ' " ¹⁰So I prophesied as He commanded me, and breath came into them, and they lived, and stood upon their feet, an exceedingly great army.

¹¹Then He said to me, "Son of man, these bones are the whole house of Israel. They indeed say, 'Our bones are dry, our hope is lost, and we ourselves are cut off!' ¹²Therefore prophesy and say to them, 'Thus says the Lord GOD: "Behold, O My people, I will open your graves and cause you to come up from your graves, and bring you into the land of Israel. ¹³Then you shall know that I *am* the LORD, when I have opened your graves, O My people, and brought you up from your graves. ¹⁴I will put My Spirit in you, and you shall live, and I will place you in your own land. Then you shall know that I, the LORD, have spoken *it* and performed *it*," says the LORD.' "

ONE KINGDOM, ONE KING

¹⁵Again the word of the LORD came to me, saying, ¹⁶"As for you, son of man, take a stick for yourself and write on it: 'For Judah and for the children of Israel, his companions.' Then take another stick and write on it, 'For Joseph, the stick of Ephraim, and *for* all the house of Israel, his companions.' ¹⁷Then join them one to another for yourself into one stick, and they will become one in your hand.

¹⁸"And when the children of your people speak to you, saying, 'Will you not show us what you *mean* by these?'—¹⁹say to them, 'Thus says the Lord GOD: "Surely I will take the stick of Joseph, which *is* in the hand of Ephraim, and the tribes of Israel, his companions; and I will

---

Promise   HE PROMISES THAT YOU WILL LIVE.

"I will put My Spirit in you, and you shall live, and I will place you in your own land. Then you shall know that I, the LORD, have spoken it and performed it," says the LORD (Ezek. 37:14).

How many times have you said, "This is killin' me!"? Maybe it was a term paper, a hard soccer practice in the beating sun, your little brother's trumpet practice, or being grounded when all the best parties are going on. All kinds of things can make you feel "like you're gonna die."

Sometimes there are serious situations that really do "kill" you emotionally, or that can make you feel like your heart really is dead. You may really feel like your life is over. Your parents divorce. Someone you love dies. A friend stabs you in the back. You're diagnosed with a chronic disease. You suffer a major disappointment.

God says, "I will put My Spirit in you, and you shall live." Hang on to that verse. You *will* live. The Spirit of God breathes new life into you. When you can't go on, He puts fresh life into you. He knows when something is "killin' " you. He knows when you need a boost. The Spirit of God is more powerful than you know. Ask Him, and He'll help you live again.

SEE FOR YOURSELF:
Jer. 49:6; Zeph. 3:20; Zech. 10:6

join them with it, with the stick of Judah, and make them one stick, and they will be one in My hand." ' ²⁰And the sticks on which you write will be in your hand before their eyes.

²¹"Then say to them, 'Thus says the Lord GOD: "Surely I will take the children of Israel from among the nations, wherever they have gone, and will gather them from every side and bring them into their own land; ²²and I will make them one nation in the land, on the mountains of Israel; and one king shall be king over them all; they shall no longer be two nations, nor shall they ever be divided into two kingdoms again. ²³They shall not defile themselves anymore with their idols, nor with their detestable things, nor with any of their transgressions; but I will deliver them from all their dwelling places in which they have sinned, and will cleanse them. Then they shall be My people, and I will be their God.

²⁴"David My servant *shall be* king over them, and they shall all have one shepherd; they shall also walk in My judgments and observe My statutes, and do them. ²⁵Then they shall dwell in the land that I have given to Jacob My servant, where your fathers dwelt; and they shall dwell there, they, their children, and their children's children, forever; and My servant David *shall be* their prince forever. ²⁶Moreover I will make a covenant of peace with them, and it shall be an everlasting covenant with them; I will establish them and multiply them, and I will set My sanctuary in their midst forevermore. ²⁷My tabernacle also shall be with them; indeed I will be their God, and they shall be My people. ²⁸The nations also will know that I, the LORD, sanctify Israel, when My sanctuary is in their midst forevermore." ' "

GOG AND ALLIES ATTACK ISRAEL

¹Now the word of the LORD came to me, saying, ²"Son of man, set your face against Gog, of the land of Magog, the prince of Rosh,ᵃ Meshech, and Tubal, and prophesy against him, ³and say, 'Thus says the Lord GOD: "Behold, I *am* against you, O Gog, the prince of Rosh, Meshech, and Tubal. ⁴I will turn you around, put hooks into your jaws, and lead you out, with all your army, horses, and horsemen, all splendidly clothed, a great company *with* bucklers and shields, all of them handling swords. ⁵Persia, Ethiopia,ᵃ and Libyaᵇ are with them, all

of them *with* shield and helmet; ⁶Gomer and all its troops; the house of Togarmah *from* the far north and all its troops—many people *are* with you.

⁷"Prepare yourself and be ready, you and all your companies that are gathered about you; and be a guard for them. ⁸After many days you will be visited. In the latter years you will come into the land of those brought back from the sword *and* gathered from many people on the mountains of Israel, which had long been desolate; they were brought out of the nations, and now all of them dwell safely. ⁹You will ascend, coming like a storm, covering the land like a cloud, you and all your troops and many peoples with you."

¹⁰'Thus says the Lord GOD: "On that day it shall come to pass *that* thoughts will arise in your mind, and you will make an evil plan: ¹¹You will say, 'I will go up against a land of unwalled villages; I will go to a peaceful people, who dwell safely, all of them dwelling without walls, and having neither bars nor gates'—¹²to take plunder and to take booty, to stretch out your hand against the waste places *that are* again inhabited, and against a people gathered from the nations, who have acquired livestock and goods, who dwell in the midst of the land. ¹³Sheba, Dedan, the merchants of Tarshish, and all their young lions will say to you, 'Have you come to take plunder? Have you gathered your army to take booty, to carry away silver and gold, to take away livestock and goods, to take great plunder?' " '

¹⁴"Therefore, son of man, prophesy and say to Gog, 'Thus says the Lord GOD: "On that day when My people Israel dwell safely, will you not know *it*? ¹⁵Then you will come from your place out of the far north, you and many peoples with you, all of them riding on horses, a great company and a mighty army. ¹⁶You will come up against My people Israel like a cloud, to cover the land. It will be in the latter days that I will bring you against My land, so that the nations may know Me, when I am hallowed in you, O Gog, before their eyes." ¹⁷Thus says the Lord GOD: "Are *you* he of whom I have spoken in former days by My servants the prophets of Israel, who prophesied for years in those days that I would bring you against them?

JUDGMENT ON GOG

¹⁸"And it will come to pass at the same time, when Gog comes against the land of Israel," says

---

FORGIVENESS

Is God's forgiveness possible? (37:23)

---

the Lord GOD, "*that* My fury will show in My face. ¹⁹For in My jealousy *and* in the fire of My wrath I have spoken: 'Surely in that day there shall be a great earthquake in the land of Israel, ²⁰so that the fish of the sea, the birds of the heavens, the beasts of the field, all creeping things that creep on the earth, and all men who *are* on the face of the earth shall shake at My presence. The mountains shall be thrown down, the steep places shall fall, and every wall shall fall to the ground.' ²¹I will call for a sword against Gog throughout all My mountains," says the Lord GOD. "Every man's sword will be against his brother. ²²And I will bring him to judgment with pestilence and bloodshed; I will rain down on him, on his troops, and on the many peoples who *are* with him, flooding rain, great hailstones, fire, and brimstone. ²³Thus I will magnify Myself and sanctify Myself, and I will be known in the eyes of many nations. Then they shall know that I *am* the LORD." '

GOD

Will the world ever see God's greatness? (38:23)

GOG'S ARMIES DESTROYED

¹"And you, son of man, prophesy against Gog, and say, 'Thus says the Lord GOD: "Behold, I *am* against you, O Gog, the prince of Rosh,*ᵃ* Meshech, and Tubal; ²and I will turn you around and lead you on, bringing you up from the far north, and bring you against the mountains of Israel. ³Then I will knock the bow out of your left hand, and cause the arrows to fall out of your right hand. ⁴You shall fall upon the mountains of Israel, you and all your troops and the peoples who *are* with you; I will give you to birds of prey of every sort and *to* the beasts of the field to be devoured. ⁵You shall fall on the open field; for I have spoken," says the Lord GOD. ⁶"And I will send fire on Magog and on those who live in security in the coastlands. Then they shall know that I *am* the LORD. ⁷So I will make My holy name known in the midst of My people Israel, and I will not *let them* profane My holy name anymore. Then the nations shall know that *I am* the LORD, the Holy One in Israel. ⁸Surely it is coming, and it shall be done," says the Lord GOD. "This *is* the day of which I have spoken.

⁹"Then those who dwell in the cities of Israel will go out and set on fire and burn the weapons, both the shields and bucklers, the bows and arrows, the javelins and spears; and they will make fires with them for seven years. ¹⁰They will not take wood from the field nor cut down *any* from the forests, because they will make fires with the weapons; and they will plunder those who plundered them, and pillage those who pillaged them," says the Lord GOD.

THE BURIAL OF GOG

¹¹"It will come to pass in that day *that* I will give Gog a burial place there in Israel, the valley of those who pass by east of the sea; and it will obstruct travelers, because there they will bury Gog and all his multitude. Therefore they will call *it* the Valley of Hamon Gog.*ᵃ* ¹²For seven months the house of Israel will be burying them, in order to cleanse the land. ¹³Indeed all the people of the land will be burying, and they will gain renown for it on the day that I am glorified," says the Lord GOD. ¹⁴"They will set apart men regularly employed, with the help of a search party,*ᵃ* to pass through the land and bury those bodies remaining on the ground, in order to cleanse it. At the end of seven months they will make a search. ¹⁵The search party will pass through the land; and when *anyone* sees a man's bone, he shall set up a marker by it, till the buriers have buried it in the Valley of Hamon Gog. ¹⁶*The* name of *the* city *will* also *be* Hamonah. Thus they shall cleanse the land." '

A TRIUMPHANT FESTIVAL

¹⁷"And as for you, son of man, thus says the Lord GOD, 'Speak to every sort of bird and to every beast of the field:

> " Assemble yourselves and come;
> Gather together from all sides to My
>   sacrificial meal
> Which I am sacrificing for you,
> A great sacrificial meal on the mountains
>   of Israel,
> That you may eat flesh and drink blood.
> 18 You shall eat the flesh of the mighty,
> Drink the blood of the princes of the
>   earth,
> Of rams and lambs,
> Of goats and bulls,
> All of them fatlings of Bashan.
> 19 You shall eat fat till you are full,
> And drink blood till you are drunk,
> At My sacrificial meal
> Which I am sacrificing for you.
> 20 You shall be filled at My table
> With horses and riders,

39:1 *ᵃ*Targum, Vulgate and Aquila read *chief prince of.*   **39:11** *ᵃ*Literally *The Multitude of Gog*   **39:14** *ᵃ*Literally *those who pass through*

With mighty men
And with all the men of war," says the
Lord GOD.

ISRAEL RESTORED TO THE LAND

21"I will set My glory among the nations; all the nations shall see My judgment which I have executed, and My hand which I have laid on them. 22So the house of Israel shall know that I *am* the LORD their God from that day forward. 23The Gentiles shall know that the house of Israel went into captivity for their iniquity; because they were unfaithful to Me, therefore I hid My face from them. I gave them into the hand of their enemies, and they all fell by the sword. 24According to their uncleanness and according to their transgressions I have dealt with them, and hidden My face from them." '

25"Therefore thus says the Lord GOD: 'Now I will bring back the captives of Jacob, and have mercy on the whole house of Israel; and I will be jealous for My holy name—26after they have borne their shame, and all their unfaithfulness in which they were unfaithful to Me, when they dwelt
safely in their *own* land
and no one made *them*
afraid. 27When I have
brought them back
from the peoples and
gathered them out of
their enemies' lands,
and I am hallowed in
them in the sight of
many nations, 28then
they shall know that I
am the LORD their God,
who sent them into cap-
tivity among the nations,
but also brought them back
to their land, and left none of them cap-
tive any longer. 29And I will not hide My face from them anymore; for I shall have poured out My Spirit on the house of Israel," says the Lord GOD."

A NEW CITY, A NEW TEMPLE

1In the twenty-fifth year of our captivity, at the beginning of the year, on the tenth *day* of the month, in the fourteenth year after the city was captured, on the very same day the hand of the LORD was upon me; and He took me there. 2In the visions of God He took me into the land of Israel and set me on a very high mountain; on it toward the south *was* some-

thing like the structure of a city. 3He took me there, and behold, *there was* a man whose appearance *was* like the appearance of bronze. He had a line of flax and a measuring rod in his hand, and he stood in the gateway.

4And the man said to me, "Son of man, look with your eyes and hear with your ears, and fix your mind on everything I show you; for you *were* brought here so that I might show *them* to you. Declare to the house of Israel everything you see." 5Now there was a wall all around the outside of the temple.*a* In the man's hand was a measuring rod six cubits long, *each being a* cubit and a handbreadth; and he measured the width of the wall structure, one rod; and the height, one rod.

THE EASTERN GATEWAY OF THE TEMPLE

6Then he went to the gateway which faced east; and he went up its stairs and measured the threshold of the gateway, *which was* one rod wide, and the other threshold *was* one rod wide. 7Each gate chamber *was* one rod long and one rod wide; between the
gate chambers *was a space*
of five cubits; and the
threshold of the gate-
way by the vestibule
of the inside gate *was*
one rod. 8He also
measured the vesti-
bule of the inside gate,
one rod. 9Then he
measured the vesti-
bule of the gateway,
eight cubits; and the
gateposts, two cubits.
The vestibule of the
gate *was* on the inside.
10In the eastern gateway *were*
three gate chambers on one side and three on the other; the three *were* all the same size; also the gateposts were of the same size on this side and that side.

11He measured the width of the entrance to the gateway, ten cubits; *and* the length of the gate, thirteen cubits. 12*There was* a space in front of the gate chambers, one cubit *on this side* and one cubit on that side; the gate chambers *were* six cubits on this side and six cubits on that side. 13Then he measured the gateway from the roof of *one* gate chamber to the roof of the other; the width *was* twenty-five cubits, as door faces door. 14He measured the gateposts, sixty cubits high, and the court all around the

> "I will set My glory among the nations; all the nations shall see My judgment which I have executed, and My hand which I have laid on them. So the house of Israel shall know that I am the LORD their God from that day forward."
>
> (Ezekiel 39:21, 22)

gateway *extended* to the gatepost. ¹⁵*From the* front of the entrance gate to the front of the vestibule of the inner gate *was* fifty cubits. ¹⁶*There were* beveled window *frames* in the gate chambers and in their intervening archways on the inside of the gateway all around, and likewise in the vestibules. *There were* windows all around on the inside. And on each gatepost *were* palm trees.

THE OUTER COURT

¹⁷Then he brought me into the outer court; and *there were* chambers and a pavement made all around the court; thirty chambers faced the pavement. ¹⁸The pavement was by the side of the gateways, corresponding to the length of the gateways; *this was* the lower pavement. ¹⁹Then he measured the width from the front of the lower gateway to the front of the inner court exterior, one hundred cubits toward the east and the north.

THE NORTHERN GATEWAY

²⁰On the outer court was also a gateway facing north, and he measured its length and its width. ²¹Its gate chambers, three on this side and three on that side, its gateposts and its archways, had the same measurements as the first gate; its length *was* fifty cubits and its width twenty-five cubits. ²²Its windows and those of its archways, and also its palm trees, *had* the same measurements as the gateway facing east; it was ascended by seven steps, and its archway *was* in front of it. ²³A gate of the inner court was opposite the northern gateway, just as the eastern *gateway;* and he measured from gateway to gateway, one hundred cubits.

THE SOUTHERN GATEWAY

²⁴After that he brought me toward the south, and there a gateway was facing south; and he measured its gateposts and archways according to these same measurements. ²⁵*There were* windows in it and in its archways all around like those windows; its length *was* fifty cubits and its width twenty-five cubits. ²⁶Seven steps led up to it, and its archway *was* in front of them; and it had palm trees on its gateposts, one on this side and one on that side. ²⁷*There was* also a gateway on the inner court, facing south; and he measured from gateway to gateway toward the south, one hundred cubits.

GATEWAYS OF THE INNER COURT

²⁸Then he brought me to the inner court through the southern gateway; he measured the southern gateway according to these same measurements. ²⁹Also its gate chambers, its gateposts, and its archways *were* according to these same measurements; *there were* windows in it and in its archways all around; *it was* fifty cubits long and twenty-five cubits wide. ³⁰*There were* archways all around, twenty-five cubits long and five cubits wide. ³¹Its archways faced the outer court, palm trees *were* on its gateposts, and going up to it *were* eight steps.

³²And he brought me into the inner court facing east; he measured the gateway according to these same measurements. ³³Also its gate chambers, its gateposts, and its archways *were* according to these same measurements; and *there were* windows in it and in its archways all around; *it was* fifty cubits long and twenty-five cubits wide. ³⁴Its archways faced the outer court, and palm trees *were* on its gateposts on this side and on that side; and going up to it *were* eight steps.

³⁵Then he brought me to the north gateway and measured *it* according to these same measurements—³⁶also its gate chambers, its gateposts, and its archways. It had windows all around; its length *was* fifty cubits and its width twenty-five cubits. ³⁷Its gateposts faced the outer court, palm trees *were* on its gateposts on this side and on that side, and going up to it *were* eight steps.

WHERE SACRIFICES WERE PREPARED

³⁸*There was* a chamber and its entrance by the gateposts of the gateway, where they washed the burnt offering. ³⁹In the vestibule of the gateway *were* two tables on this side and two tables on that side, on which to slay the burnt offering, the sin offering, and the trespass offering. ⁴⁰At the outer side of the vestibule, as one goes up to the entrance of the northern gateway, *were* two tables; and on the other side of the vestibule of the gateway *were* two tables. ⁴¹Four tables *were* on this side and four tables on that side, by the side of the gateway, eight tables on which they slaughtered *the sacrifices.* ⁴²*There were* also four tables of hewn stone for the burnt offering, one cubit and a half long, one cubit and a half wide, and one cubit high; on these they laid the instruments with which they slaughtered the burnt offering and the sacrifice. ⁴³Inside *were* hooks, a handbreadth wide, fastened all around; and the flesh of the sacrifices *was* on the tables.

CHAMBERS FOR SINGERS AND PRIESTS

⁴⁴Outside the inner gate *were* the chambers for the singers in the inner court, one facing south at the side of the northern gateway, and

the other facing north at the side of the southern gateway. ⁴⁵Then he said to me, "This chamber which faces south *is* for the priests who have charge of the temple. ⁴⁶The chamber which faces north *is* for the priests who have charge of the altar; these *are* the sons of Zadok, from the sons of Levi, who come near the LORD to minister to Him."

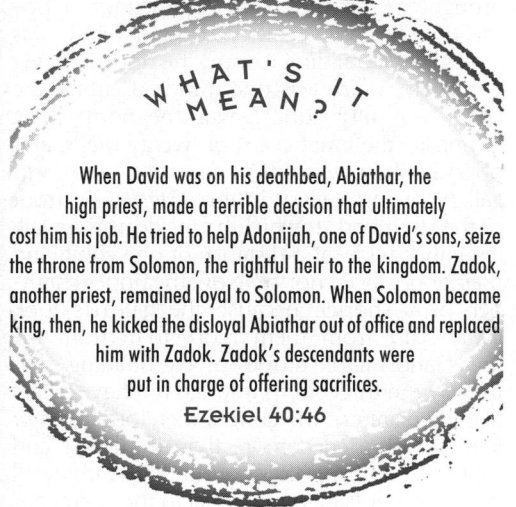

WHAT'S IT MEAN?

When David was on his deathbed, Abiathar, the high priest, made a terrible decision that ultimately cost him his job. He tried to help Adonijah, one of David's sons, seize the throne from Solomon, the rightful heir to the kingdom. Zadok, another priest, remained loyal to Solomon. When Solomon became king, then, he kicked the disloyal Abiathar out of office and replaced him with Zadok. Zadok's descendants were put in charge of offering sacrifices.

Ezekiel 40:46

DIMENSIONS OF THE INNER COURT AND VESTIBULE

⁴⁷And he measured the court, one hundred cubits long and one hundred cubits wide, foursquare. The altar *was* in front of the temple. ⁴⁸Then he brought me to the vestibule of the temple and measured the doorposts of the vestibule, five cubits on this side and five cubits on that side; and the width of the gateway was three cubits on this side and three cubits on that side. ⁴⁹The length of the vestibule *was* twenty cubits, and the width eleven cubits; and by the steps which led up to it *there were* pillars by the doorposts, one on this side and another on that side.

DIMENSIONS OF THE SANCTUARY

¹Then he brought me into the sanctuary[a] and measured the doorposts, six cubits wide on one side and six cubits wide on the other side— the width of the tabernacle. ²The width of the entryway *was* ten cubits, and the side walls of the entrance *were* five cubits on this side and five cubits on the other side; and he measured

its length, forty cubits, and its width, twenty cubits.

³Also he went inside and measured the doorposts, two cubits; and the entrance, six cubits *high;* and the width of the entrance, seven cubits. ⁴He measured the length, twenty cubits; and the width, twenty cubits, beyond the sanctuary; and he said to me, "This *is* the Most Holy Place."

THE SIDE CHAMBERS ON THE WALL

⁵Next, he measured the wall of the temple, six cubits. The width of each side chamber all around the temple *was* four cubits on every side. ⁶The side chambers *were* in three stories, one above the other, thirty chambers in each story; they rested on ledges which *were* for the side chambers all around, that they might be supported, but not fastened to the wall of the temple. ⁷As one went up from story to story, the side chambers became wider all around, because their supporting ledges in the wall of the temple ascended like steps; therefore the width of the structure increased as one went up *from* the lowest *story* to the highest by way of the middle one. ⁸I also saw an elevation all around the temple; it was the foundation of the side chambers, a full rod, *that is,* six cubits high. ⁹The thickness of the outer wall of the side chambers *was* five cubits, and so also the remaining terrace by the place of the side chambers of the temple. ¹⁰And between *it and* the *wall* chambers was a width of twenty cubits all around the

WHAT'S IT MEAN?

If this floor plan seems familiar, it's because it's similar to the one Solomon used when he built the original temple—as well as the one Moses used when he constructed the original tabernacle. The Most Holy Place, where the ark of the covenant and the tablets that contained the Ten Commandments were located, was a perfect cube, equal in length, width, and height. If you're wondering where to go to see such a magnificent structure, don't bother. The temple whose plans Ezekiel saw has not yet been built.

Ezekiel 41:3, 4

41:1 [a]Hebrew *heykal,* here the main room of the temple, sometimes called the *holy place* (compare Exodus 26:33)

temple on every side. ¹¹The doors of the side chambers opened on the terrace, one door toward the north and another toward the south; and the width of the terrace *was* five cubits all around.

THE BUILDING AT THE WESTERN END

¹²The building that faced the separating courtyard at its western end *was* seventy cubits wide; the wall of the building *was* five cubits thick all around, and its length ninety cubits.

DIMENSIONS AND DESIGN OF THE TEMPLE AREA

¹³So he measured the temple, one hundred cubits long; and the separating courtyard with the building and its walls *was* one hundred cubits long; ¹⁴also the width of the eastern face of the temple, including the separating courtyard, *was* one hundred cubits. ¹⁵He measured the length of the building behind it, facing the separating courtyard, with its galleries on the one side and on the other side, one hundred cubits, as well as the inner temple and the porches of the court, ¹⁶their doorposts and the beveled window frames. And the galleries all around their three stories opposite the threshold were paneled with wood from the ground to the windows—the windows were covered—¹⁷from the space above the door, even to the inner room,ᵃ as well as outside, and on every wall all around, inside and outside, by measure.

¹⁸And *it was* made with cherubim and palm trees, a palm tree between cherub and cherub. *Each* cherub had two faces, ¹⁹so that the face of a man *was* toward a palm tree on one side, and the face of a young lion toward a palm tree on the other side; thus *it was* made throughout the temple all around. ²⁰From the floor to the space above the door, and on the wall of the sanctuary, cherubim and palm trees *were* carved.

²¹The doorposts of the temple *were* square, *as was* the front of the sanctuary; their appearance was similar. ²²The altar *was* of wood, three cubits high, and its length two cubits. Its corners, its length, and its sides *were* of wood; and he said to me, "This *is* the table that *is* before the LORD."

²³The temple and the sanctuary had two doors. ²⁴The doors had two panels *apiece,* two folding panels: two *panels* for one door and two panels for the other *door.* ²⁵Cherubim and palm trees *were* carved on the doors of the temple just as they *were* carved on the walls. A wooden canopy *was* on the front of the vesti-

bule outside. ²⁶*There were* beveled window *frames* and palm trees on one side and on the other, on the sides of the vestibule—also on the side chambers of the temple and on the canopies.

THE CHAMBERS FOR THE PRIESTS

¹Then he brought me out into the outer court, by the way toward the north; and he brought me into the chamber which *was* opposite the separating courtyard, and which *was* opposite the building toward the north. ²Facing the length, *which was* one hundred cubits (the width was fifty cubits), was the north door. ³Opposite the inner court of twenty *cubits,* and opposite the pavement of the outer court, *was* gallery against gallery in three *stories.* ⁴In front of the chambers, toward the inside, *was* a walk ten cubits wide, at a distance of one cubit; and their doors faced north. ⁵Now the upper chambers *were* shorter, because the galleries took away *space* from them more than from the lower and middle stories of the building. ⁶For they *were* in three *stories* and did not have pillars like the pillars of the courts; therefore *the upper level* was shortened more than the lower and middle levels from the ground up. ⁷And a wall which *was* outside ran parallel to the chambers, at the front of the chambers, toward the outer court; its length *was* fifty cubits. ⁸The length of the chambers toward the outer court *was* fifty cubits, whereas that facing the temple *was* one hundred cubits. ⁹At the lower chambers *was* the entrance on the east side, as one goes into them from the outer court.

¹⁰Also *there were* chambers in the thickness of the wall of the court toward the east, opposite the separating courtyard and opposite the building. ¹¹*There was* a walk in front of them also, and their appearance *was* like the chambers which *were* toward the north; they *were* as long and as wide as the others, and all their exits and entrances *were* according to plan. ¹²And corresponding to the doors of the chambers that *were* facing south, as one enters them, *there was* a door in front of the walk, the way directly in front of the wall toward the east.

¹³Then he said to me, "The north chambers *and* the south chambers, which *are* opposite the separating courtyard, *are* the holy chambers where the priests who approach the LORD shall eat the most holy offerings. There they shall lay the most holy offerings—the grain offering, the sin offering, and the trespass offering—for the place *is* holy. ¹⁴When the priests enter them,

---

41:17 ᵃLiterally *house,* here *the Most Holy Place*

they shall not go out of the holy *chamber* into the outer court; but there they shall leave their garments in which they minister, for they *are* holy. They shall put on other garments; then they may approach *that* which *is* for the people."

OUTER DIMENSIONS OF THE TEMPLE

¹⁵Now when he had finished measuring the inner temple, he brought me out through the gateway that faces toward the east, and measured it all around. ¹⁶He measured the east side with the measuring rod,ᵃ five hundred rods by the measuring rod all around. ¹⁷He measured the north side, five hundred rods by the measuring rod all around. ¹⁸He measured the south side, five hundred rods by the measuring rod. ¹⁹He came around to the west side *and* measured five hundred rods by the measuring rod. ²⁰He measured it on the four sides; it had a wall all around, five hundred *cubits* long and five hundred wide, to separate the holy areas from the common.

THE TEMPLE, THE LORD'S DWELLING PLACE

¹Afterward he brought me to the gate, the gate that faces toward the east. ²And behold, the glory of the God of Israel came from the way of the east. His voice *was* like the sound of many waters; and the earth shone with His glory. ³*It was* like the appearance of the vision which I saw—like the vision which I saw when Iᵃ came to destroy the city. The visions *were* like the vision which I saw by the River Chebar; and I fell on my face. ⁴And the glory of the LORD came into the temple by way of the gate which faces toward the east. ⁵The Spirit lifted me up and brought me into the inner court; and behold, the glory of the LORD filled the temple.

⁶Then I heard *Him* speaking to me from the temple, while a man stood beside me. ⁷And He said to me, "Son of man, *this is* the place of My throne and the place of the soles of My feet, where I will dwell in the midst of the children of Israel forever. No more shall the house of Israel defile My holy name, they nor their kings, by their harlotry or with the carcasses of their kings on their high places. ⁸When they set their threshold by My threshold, and their doorpost by My doorpost, with a wall between them and Me, they defiled My holy name by the abominations which they committed; therefore I have consumed them in My anger. ⁹Now let them put their harlotry and the carcasses of their

kings far away from Me, and I will dwell in their midst forever.

¹⁰"Son of man, describe the temple to the house of Israel, that they may be ashamed of their iniquities; and let them measure the pattern. ¹¹And if they are ashamed of all that they have done, make known to them the design of the temple and its arrangement, its exits and its entrances, its entire design and all its ordinances, all its forms and all its laws. Write *it* down in their sight, so that they may keep its whole design and all its ordinances, and perform them. ¹²This *is* the law of the temple: The whole area surrounding the mountaintop *is* most holy. Behold, this *is* the law of the temple.

DIMENSIONS OF THE ALTAR

¹³"These are the measurements of the altar in cubits (the *cubit is* one cubit and a handbreadth): the base one cubit high and one cubit wide, with a rim all around its edge of one span. This *is* the height of the altar: ¹⁴from the base on the ground to the lower ledge, two cubits; the width of the ledge, one cubit; from the smaller ledge to the larger ledge, four cubits; and the width of the ledge, *one* cubit. ¹⁵The altar hearth *is* four cubits high, with four horns extending upward from the hearth. ¹⁶The altar hearth *is* twelve cubits long, twelve wide, square at its four corners; ¹⁷the ledge, fourteen *cubits* long and fourteen wide on its four sides, with a rim of half a cubit around it; its base, one cubit all around; and its steps face toward the east."

CONSECRATING THE ALTAR

¹⁸And He said to me, "Son of man, thus says the Lord GOD: 'These *are* the ordinances for the altar on the day when it is made, for sacrificing burnt offerings on it, and for sprinkling blood on it. ¹⁹You shall give a young bull for a sin offering to the priests, the Levites, who are of the seed of Zadok, who approach Me to minister to Me,' says the Lord GOD. ²⁰'You shall take some of its blood and put *it* on the four horns of the altar, on the four corners of the ledge, and on the rim around it; thus you shall cleanse it and make atonement for it. ²¹Then you shall also take the bull of the sin offering, and burn it in the appointed place of the temple, outside the sanctuary. ²²On the second day you shall offer a kid of the goats without blemish for a sin offering; and they shall cleanse the altar, as they cleansed *it* with the bull. ²³When you have finished cleansing *it*, you shall offer a young bull

---

42:16 ᵃCompare 40:5   **43:3** ᵃSome Hebrew manuscripts and Vulgate read *He*.

without blemish, and a ram from the flock without blemish. [24]When you offer them before the LORD, the priests shall throw salt on them, and they will offer them up *as* a burnt offering to the LORD. [25]Every day for seven days you shall prepare a goat *for* a sin offering; they shall also prepare a young bull and a ram from the flock, both without blemish. [26]Seven days they shall make atonement for the altar and purify it, and so consecrate *it.* [27]When these days are over it shall be, on the eighth day and thereafter, that the priests shall offer your burnt offerings and your peace offerings on the altar; and I will accept you', says the Lord GOD."

THE EAST GATE AND THE PRINCE

[1]Then He brought me back to the outer gate of the sanctuary which faces toward the east, but it *was* shut. [2]And the LORD said to me, "This gate shall be shut; it shall not be opened, and no man shall enter by it, because the LORD God of Israel has entered by it; therefore it shall be shut. [3]*As for* the prince, *because* he *is* the prince, he may sit in it to eat bread before the LORD; he shall enter by way of the vestibule of the gateway, and go out the same way."

THOSE ADMITTED TO THE TEMPLE

[4]Also He brought me by way of the north gate to the front of the temple; so I looked, and behold, the glory of the LORD filled the house of the LORD; and I fell on my face. [5]And the LORD said to me, "Son of man, mark well, see with your eyes and hear with your ears, all that I say to you concerning all the ordinances of the house of the LORD and all its laws. Mark well who may enter the house and all who go out from the sanctuary.

[6]"Now say to the rebellious, to the house of Israel, 'Thus says the Lord GOD: "O house of Israel, let Us have no more of all your abominations. [7]When you brought in foreigners, uncircumcised in heart and uncircumcised in flesh, to be in My sanctuary to defile it—My house—and when you offered My food, the fat and the blood, then they broke My covenant because of all your abominations. [8]And you have not kept charge of My holy things, but you have set *others* to keep charge of

My sanctuary for you." [9]Thus says the Lord GOD: "No foreigner, uncircumcised in heart or uncircumcised in flesh, shall enter My sanctuary, including any foreigner who *is* among the children of Israel.

LAWS GOVERNING PRIESTS

[10]"And the Levites who went far from Me, when Israel went astray, who strayed away from Me after their idols, they shall bear their iniquity. [11]Yet they shall be ministers in My sanctuary, *as* gatekeepers of the house and ministers of the house; they shall slay the burnt offering and the sacrifice for the people, and they shall stand before them to minister to them. [12]Because they ministered to them before their idols and caused the house of Israel to fall into iniquity, therefore I have raised My hand in an oath against them," says the Lord GOD, "that they shall bear their iniquity. [13]And they shall not come near Me to minister to Me as priest, nor come near any of My holy things, nor into the Most Holy *Place;* but they shall bear their shame and their abominations which they have committed. [14]Nevertheless I will make them keep charge of the temple, for all its work, and for all that has to be done in it.

[15]"But the priests, the Levites, the sons of Zadok, who kept charge of My sanctuary when the children of Israel went astray from Me, they shall come near Me to minister to Me; and they shall stand before Me to offer to Me the fat and the blood," says the Lord GOD. [16]"They shall enter My sanctuary, and they shall come near My table to minister to Me, and they shall keep My charge. [17]And it shall be, whenever they enter the gates of the inner court, that they shall put on linen garments; no wool shall come upon them while they minister within the gates of the inner court or within the house. [18]They shall have linen turbans on their heads and linen trousers on their bodies; they shall not clothe themselves with *anything that causes* sweat. [19]When they go out to the outer court, to the *outer* court to the people, they shall take off their garments in which they have ministered, leave them in the holy chambers, and put on other garments; and

> "Son of man, mark well, see with your eyes and hear with your ears, all that I say to you concerning all the ordinances of the house of the LORD and all its laws. Mark well who may enter the house and all who go out from the sanctuary."
> (Ezekiel 44:5)

WHAT'S IT MEAN?

Linen cloth was handwoven from the fibers of the flax plant and bleached snow-white to symbolize innocence and purity. Every part of the priest's uniform, from his headwear to his underwear, was made of white linen.

Ezekiel 44:17

in their holy garments they shall not sanctify the people.

20"They shall neither shave their heads, nor let their hair grow long, but they shall keep their hair well trimmed. 21No priest shall drink wine when he enters the inner court. 22They shall not take as wife a widow or a divorced woman, but take virgins of the descendants of the house of Israel, or widows of priests.

23"And they shall teach My people *the difference* between the holy and the unholy, and cause them to discern between the unclean and the clean. 24In controversy they shall stand as judges, *and* judge it according to My judgments. They shall keep My laws and My statutes in all My appointed meetings, and they shall hallow My Sabbaths.

25"They shall not defile *themselves* by coming near a dead person. Only for father or mother, for son or daughter, for brother or unmarried sister may they defile themselves. 26After he is cleansed, they shall count seven days for him. 27And on the day that he goes to the sanctuary to minister in the sanctuary, he must offer his sin offering in the inner court," says the Lord GOD.

28"It shall be, in regard to their inheritance, *that* I *am* their inheritance. You shall give them no possession in Israel, for I *am* their possession. 29They shall eat the grain offering, the sin offering, and the trespass offering; every dedicated thing in Israel shall be theirs. 30The best of all firstfruits of any kind, and every sacrifice of any kind from all your sacrifices, shall be the priest's; also you shall give to the priest the first of your ground meal, to cause a blessing to rest on your house. 31The priests shall not eat anything, bird or beast, that died naturally or was torn *by wild beasts.*

THE HOLY DISTRICT

1"Moreover, when you divide the land by lot into inheritance, you shall set apart a district for the LORD, a holy section of the land; its length *shall be* twenty-five thousand *cubits,* and the width ten thousand. It *shall be* holy throughout its territory all around. 2Of this there shall be a square plot for the sanctuary, five hundred by five hundred *rods,* with fifty cubits around it for an open space. 3So this is the district you shall measure: twenty-five thousand *cubits* long and ten thousand wide; in it shall be the sanctuary, the Most Holy *Place.* 4It shall be a holy *section* of the land, belonging to the priests, the ministers of the sanctuary, who come near to minister to the LORD; it shall be a place for their houses and a holy place for the sanctuary. 5*An area* twenty-five thousand *cubits* long and ten thousand wide shall belong to the Levites, the ministers of the temple; they shall have twenty chambers as a possession.*a*

PROPERTIES OF THE CITY AND THE PRINCE

6"You shall appoint as the property of the city *an area* five thousand *cubits* wide and twenty-five thousand long, adjacent to the district of the holy *section;* it shall belong to the whole house of Israel.

7"The prince shall have *a section* on one side and the other of the holy district and the city's property; and bordering on the holy district and the city's property, extending westward on the west side and eastward on the east side, the length *shall be* side by side with one of the *tribal* portions, from the west border to the east border. 8The land shall be his possession in Israel; and My princes shall no more oppress My people, but they shall give *the rest of* the land to the house of Israel, according to their tribes."

LAWS GOVERNING THE PRINCE

9"Thus says the Lord GOD: "Enough, O princes of Israel! Remove violence and plundering, execute justice and righteousness, and stop dispossessing My people," says the Lord GOD. 10"You shall have honest scales, an honest ephah, and an honest bath. 11The ephah and the bath shall be of the same measure, so that the bath contains one-tenth of a homer, and the ephah one-tenth of a homer; their measure shall be according to the homer. 12The shekel *shall be* twenty gerahs; twenty shekels, twenty-five

HONESTY
What does God require of us? (45:9–11)

shekels, *and* fifteen shekels shall be your mina. ¹³"This *is* the offering which you shall offer: you shall give one–sixth of an ephah from a homer of wheat, and one–sixth of an ephah from a homer of barley. ¹⁴The ordinance concerning oil, the bath of oil, *is* one-tenth of a bath from a kor. A kor *is* a homer or ten baths, for ten baths *are* a homer. ¹⁵And one lamb shall be given from a flock of two hundred, from the rich pastures of Israel. These shall be for grain offerings, burnt offerings, and peace offerings, to make atonement for them," says the Lord GOD. ¹⁶"All the people of the land shall give this offering for the prince in Israel. ¹⁷Then it shall be the prince's part *to give* burnt offerings, grain offerings, and drink offerings, at the feasts, the New Moons, the Sabbaths, and at all the appointed seasons of the house of Israel. He shall prepare the sin offering, the grain offering, the burnt offering, and the peace offerings to make atonement for the house of Israel."

KEEPING THE FEASTS

¹⁸Thus says the Lord GOD: "In the first *month*, on the first *day* of the month, you shall take a young bull without blemish and cleanse the sanctuary. ¹⁹The priest shall take some of the blood of the sin offering and put *it* on the doorposts of the temple, on the four corners of the ledge of the altar, and on the gateposts of the gate of the inner court. ²⁰And so you shall do on the seventh *day* of the month for everyone who has sinned unintentionally or in ignorance. Thus you shall make atonement for the temple.

WHAT'S IT MEAN?

What exactly are the people of Israel recalling when they observe Passover? Why, only one of the most important events in the nation's history—the escape from slavery in Egypt! On the day of the first Passover, the angel of death passed through the streets of Egypt, killing the firstborn son in every house that was not marked with blood. Because the Israelites had smeared blood on their doorposts, the death angel "passed over" their homes and their sons were spared.

Ezekiel 45:21

²¹"In the first *month*, on the fourteenth day of the month, you shall observe the Passover, a feast of seven days; unleavened bread shall be eaten. ²²And on that day the prince shall prepare for himself and for all the people of the land a bull *for* a sin offering. ²³On the seven days of the feast he shall prepare a burnt offering to the LORD, seven bulls and seven rams without blemish, daily for seven days, and a kid of the goats daily *for* a sin offering. ²⁴And he shall prepare a grain offering of one ephah for each bull and one ephah for each ram, together with a hin of oil for each ephah.

²⁵"In the seventh *month*, on the fifteenth day of the month, at the feast, he shall do likewise for seven days, according to the sin offering, the burnt offering, the grain offering, and the oil."

THE MANNER OF WORSHIP

¹Thus says the Lord GOD: "The gateway of the inner court that faces toward the east shall be shut the six working days; but on the Sabbath it shall be opened, and on the day of the New Moon it shall be opened. ²The prince shall enter by way of the vestibule of the gateway from the outside, and stand by the gatepost. The priests shall prepare his burnt offering and his peace offerings. He shall worship at the threshold of the gate. Then he shall go out, but the gate shall not be shut until evening. ³Likewise the people of the land shall worship at the entrance to this gateway before the LORD on the Sabbaths and the New Moons. ⁴The burnt offering that the prince offers to the LORD on the Sabbath day *shall be* six lambs without blemish, and a ram without blemish; ⁵and the grain offering *shall be one* ephah for a ram, and the grain offering for the lambs, as much as he wants to give, as well as a hin of oil with every ephah. ⁶On the day of the New Moon *it shall be* a young bull without blemish, six lambs, and a ram; they shall be without blemish. ⁷He shall prepare a grain offering of an ephah for a bull, an ephah for a ram, as much as he wants to give for the lambs, and a hin of oil with every ephah. ⁸When the prince enters, he shall go in by way of the vestibule of the gateway, and go out the same way.

⁹"But when the people of the land come before the LORD on the appointed feast days, whoever enters by way of the north gate to worship shall go out by way of the south gate; and whoever enters by way of the south gate shall go out by way of the north gate. He shall not return by way of the gate through which he came, but shall go out through the opposite gate. ¹⁰The prince shall then be in their midst. When they go in, he shall go in; and when they go out, he shall go out. ¹¹At the festivals and the

appointed feast days the grain offering shall be an ephah for a bull, an ephah for a ram, as much as he wants to give for the lambs, and a hin of oil with every ephah.

12"Now when the prince makes a voluntary burnt offering or voluntary peace offering to the LORD, the gate that faces toward the east shall then be opened for him; and he shall prepare his burnt offering and his peace offerings as he did on the Sabbath day. Then he shall go out, and after he goes out the gate shall be shut. 13"You shall daily make a burnt offering to the LORD *of* a lamb of the first year without blemish; you shall prepare it every morning. 14And you shall prepare a grain offering with it every morning, a sixth of an ephah, and a third of a hin of oil to moisten the fine flour. This grain offering is a perpetual ordinance, to be made regularly to the LORD. 15Thus they shall prepare the lamb, the grain offering, and the oil, *as* a regular burnt offering every morning."

THE PRINCE AND INHERITANCE LAWS

16'Thus says the Lord GOD: "If the prince gives a gift *of some* of his inheritance to any of his sons, it shall belong to his sons; it is their possession by inheritance. 17But if he gives a gift of some of his inheritance to one of his servants, it shall be his until the year of liberty, after which it shall return to the prince. But his inheritance shall belong to his sons; it shall become theirs. 18Moreover the prince shall not take any of the people's inheritance by evicting them from their property; he shall provide an inheritance for his sons from his own property, so that none of My people may be scattered from his property.' '"

HOW THE OFFERINGS WERE PREPARED

19Now he brought me through the entrance, which *was* at the side of the gate, into the holy chambers of the priests which face toward the north; and there a place *was* situated at their extreme western end. 20And he said to me, "This *is* the place where the priests shall boil the trespass offering and the sin offering, *and* where they shall bake the grain offering, so that they do not bring *them* out into the outer court to sanctify the people."

21Then he brought me out into the outer court and caused me to pass by the four corners of the court; and in fact, in every corner of the court *there was another* court. 22In the four corners of the court *were* enclosed courts, forty *cubits* long and thirty wide; all four corners *were* the same size. 23*There was* a row *of building stones* all around in them, all around the four of them;

and cooking hearths were made under the rows of stones all around. 24And he said to me, "These *are* the kitchens where the ministers of the temple shall boil the sacrifices of the people."

THE HEALING WATERS AND TREES

1Then he brought me back to the door of the temple; and there was water, flowing from under the threshold of the temple toward the east, for the front of the temple faced east; the water was flowing from under the right side of the temple, south of the altar. 2He brought me out by way of the north gate, and led me around on the outside to the outer gateway that faces east; and there was water, running out on the right side.

3And when the man went out to the east with the line in his hand, he measured one thousand cubits, and he brought me through the waters; the water *came up to my* ankles. 4Again he measured one thousand and brought me through the waters; the water *came up to my* knees. Again he measured one thousand and brought me through; the water *came up to my* waist. 5Again he measured one thousand, *and it was* a river that I could not cross; for the water was too deep, water in which one must swim, a river that could not be crossed. 6He said to me, "Son of man, have you seen *this*?" Then he brought me and returned me to the bank of the river.

WHAT'S IT MEAN?

The Dead Sea was given its name for a reason. It's unable to support fish or plant life. The Jordan River and other fresh water sources flow into it, but nothing flows out of it. Everything just sits and stagnates. You're probably familiar with the salty taste of ocean water; water from the Dead Sea is ten times as salty! The idea of the Dead Sea one day supporting life is an incredible notion.

Ezekiel 47:8

7When I returned, there, along the bank of the river, *were* very many trees on one side and the other. 8Then he said to me: "This water flows toward the eastern region, goes down into the valley, and enters the sea. When *it* reaches the sea, *its* waters are healed. 9And it shall be *that* every living thing that moves, wherever the rivers go, will live. There will be a very great multitude of fish, because these waters go there; for they will be healed, and everything will live wherever the river goes. ¹⁰It shall be *that* fishermen will stand by it from En Gedi to En Eglaim; they will be *places* for spreading their nets. Their fish will be of the same kinds as the fish of the Great Sea, exceedingly many. ¹¹But its swamps and marshes will not be healed; they will be given over to salt. ¹²Along the bank of the river, on this side and that, will grow all *kinds of* trees used for food; their leaves will not wither, and their fruit will not fail. They will bear fruit every month, because their water flows from the sanctuary. Their fruit will be for food, and their leaves for medicine."

BORDERS OF THE LAND

¹³Thus says the Lord GOD: "These *are* the borders by which you shall divide the land as an inheritance among the twelve tribes of Israel. Joseph *shall have two* portions. ¹⁴You shall inherit it equally with one another; for I raised My hand in an oath to give it to your fathers, and this land shall fall to you as your inheritance.

¹⁵"This *shall be* the border of the land on the north: from the Great Sea, *by* the road to Hethlon, as one goes to Zedad, ¹⁶Hamath, Berothah, Sibraim (which *is* between the border of Damascus and the border of Hamath), to Hazar Hatticon (which *is* on the border of Hauran). ¹⁷Thus the boundary shall be from the Sea to Hazar Enan, the border of Damascus; and as for the north, northward, it is the border of Hamath. *This is* the north side.

¹⁸"On the east side you shall mark out the border from between Hauran and Damascus, and between Gilead and the land of Israel, along the Jordan, and along the eastern side of the sea. *This is* the east side.

¹⁹"The south side, toward the South,ᵃ *shall be* from Tamar to the waters of Meribah by Kadesh, along the brook to the Great Sea. *This is* the south side, toward the South.

²⁰"The west side *shall be* the Great Sea, from the *southern* boundary until one comes to a point opposite Hamath. This *is* the west side.

²¹"Thus you shall divide this land among yourselves according to the tribes of Israel. ²²It shall be that you will divide it by lot as an inheritance for yourselves, and for the strangers who dwell among you and who bear children among you. They shall be to you as native-born among the children of Israel; they shall

have an inheritance with you among the tribes of Israel. ²³And it shall be *that* in whatever tribe the stranger dwells, there you shall give *him* his inheritance," says the Lord GOD.

DIVISION OF THE LAND

¹"Now these *are* the names of the tribes: From the northern border along the road to Hethlon at the entrance of Hamath, to Hazar Enan, the border of Damascus northward, in the direction of Hamath, *there shall be* one *section for* Dan from its east to its west side; ²by the border of Dan, from the east side to the west, one *section for* Asher; ³by the border of Asher, from the east side to the west, one *section for* Naphtali; ⁴by the border of Naphtali, from the east side to the west, one *section for* Manasseh; ⁵by the border of Manasseh, from the east side to the west, one *section for* Ephraim; ⁶by the border of Ephraim, from the east side to the west, one *section for* Reuben; ⁷by the border of Reuben, from the east side to the west, one *section for* Judah; ⁸by the border of Judah, from the east side to the west, shall be the district which you shall set apart, twenty-five thousand *cubits* in width, and *in* length the same as one of the *other* portions, from the east side to the west, with the sanctuary in the center.

⁹"The district that you shall set apart for the LORD *shall be* twenty-five thousand *cubits* in length and ten thousand in width. ¹⁰To these— to the priests—the holy district shall belong: on the north twenty-five thousand *cubits in length,* on the west ten thousand in width, on the east ten thousand in width, and on the south twenty-five thousand in length. The sanctuary of the LORD shall be in the center. ¹¹*It shall be* for the priests of the sons of Zadok, who are sanctified, who have kept My charge, who did not go astray when the children of Israel went astray, as the Levites went astray. ¹²And *this* district of land that is set apart shall be to them a thing most holy by the border of the Levites.

¹³"Opposite the border of the priests, the Levites *shall have an area* twenty-five thousand *cubits* in length and ten thousand in width; its entire length *shall be* twenty-five thousand and its width ten thousand. ¹⁴And they shall not sell or exchange any of it; they may not alienate this best *part* of the land, for *it is* holy to the LORD.

¹⁵"The five thousand *cubits* in width that remain, along the edge of the twenty-five thousand, shall be for general use by the city, for dwellings and common-land; and the city shall

be in the center. ¹⁶These *shall be* its measurements: the north side four thousand five hundred *cubits*, the south side four thousand five hundred, the east side four thousand five hundred, and the west side four thousand five hundred. ¹⁷The common-land of the city shall be: to the north two hundred and fifty *cubits*, to the south two hundred and fifty, to the east two hundred and fifty, and to the west two hundred and fifty. ¹⁸The rest of the length, alongside the district of the holy *section, shall be* ten thousand *cubits* to the east and ten thousand to the west. It shall be adjacent to the district of the holy *section*, and its produce shall be food for the workers of the city. ¹⁹The workers of the city, from all the tribes of Israel, shall cultivate it. ²⁰The entire district *shall be* twenty-five thousand *cubits* by twenty-five thousand *cubits*, foursquare. You shall set apart the holy district with the property of the city.

²¹"The rest *shall belong* to the prince, on one side and on the other of the holy district and of the city's property, next to the twenty-five thousand *cubits* of the *holy* district as far as the eastern border, and westward next to the twenty-five thousand as far as the western border, adjacent to the *tribal* portions; *it shall belong* to the prince. It shall be the holy district, and the sanctuary of the temple *shall be* in the center. ²²Moreover, apart from the possession of the Levites and the possession of the city *which are* in the midst of what *belongs* to the prince, *the area* between the border of Judah and the border of Benjamin shall belong to the prince.

²³"As for the rest of the tribes, from the east side to the west, Benjamin *shall have* one *section;* ²⁴by the border of Benjamin, from the east side to the west, Simeon *shall have* one *section;* ²⁵by the border of Simeon, from the east side to the west, Issachar *shall have* one *section;* ²⁶by the border of Issachar, from the east side to the west, Zebulun *shall have* one *section;* ²⁷by the border of Zebulun, from the east side to the west, Gad *shall have* one *section;* ²⁸by the border of Gad, on the south side, toward the South,^a the border shall be from Tamar *to* the waters of Meribah *by* Kadesh, along the brook to the Great Sea. ²⁹This *is* the land which you shall divide by lot as an inheritance among the tribes of Israel, and these *are* their portions," says the Lord GOD.

THE GATES OF THE CITY AND ITS NAME

³⁰"These *are* the exits of the city. On the north side, measuring four thousand five hundred *cubits* ³¹(the gates of the city *shall be* named after the tribes of Israel), the three gates northward: one gate for Reuben, one gate for Judah, and one gate for Levi; ³²on the east side, four thousand five hundred *cubits*, three gates: one gate for Joseph, one gate for Benjamin, and one gate for Dan; ³³on the south side, measuring four thousand five hundred *cubits*, three gates: one gate for Simeon, one gate for Issachar, and one gate for Zebulun; ³⁴on the west side, four thousand five hundred *cubits* with their three gates: one gate for Gad, one gate for Asher, and one gate for Naphtali. ³⁵All the way around *shall be* eighteen thousand *cubits;* and the name of the city from *that* day *shall be:* THE LORD *IS* THERE."^a

48:28 ^aHebrew *Negev*   **48:35** ^aHebrew *YHWH Shammah*

CONTENT   Daniel's name means, "God Is My Judge." As you read this book that includes Daniel's life and prophecies, you can see why his name fits him. Daniel was committed to doing what was right, no matter whom it displeased as long as it pleased God. He wasn't worried about being judged by anyone else.

    The Book of Daniel is a book written in a variety of styles. It has stories about stand-up kinds of guys who refused to be bullied into disrespecting God. Remember Daniel in the lions' den? Remember the fiery furnace? Those famous stories come from this book.

    But the Book of Daniel isn't just a listing of true accounts. It is also a book of prophecies. Daniel was an interpreter of dreams. He could see past the reality of this world and sometimes see into the next world, the new heaven and earth.

    To this very day, people read Daniel to get clues about how the end of the world as we know it will happen. The hows and whens are not always clear, but we know the event is getting closer every day.

Purpose   God controls the flow of history and the circumstances of believers in pagan lands.

Theme   God Controls the Destiny of All Nations

Date of writing   605–530 B.C.

Bible Talk

A Politician, Not a Prophet

We usually think of someone who writes a book of the Bible as somebody like a pastor or a prophet. The truth is that Daniel was a politician. He grew up with a great sense of discernment and a conscience that wouldn't quit. With the opportunities afforded him because of his gifts of interpretation, he got to see his legal system work from inside the king's castle and that is where he became an influence.

Knowing that about Daniel's life reminds us that God uses people in whatever line of work they pursue. Whether it's a courtroom, a pulpit, or a governor's mansion, God works through us when we are faithful to His call.

HOW TO STAND TALL

Daniel was a prime example of a creative problem solver. When his story opens, Daniel is faced with a difficult choice. He is being offered the best food in the kingdom, but the food is off of Daniel's diet (which was prescribed by God in Leviticus). Daniel could have refused to eat, but instead he worked through the channels of authority that were already in place. He proposed a solution and it worked out.

On other occasions, though, like when Daniel was supposed to stop praying, he didn't negotiate. He simply refused.

Daniel is a good example for us. It's good to work within the current system, but when the current system won't budge, a person's got to do what a person's got to do.

DANIEL AND HIS FRIENDS OBEY GOD

¹In the third year of the reign of Jehoiakim king of Judah, Nebuchadnezzar king of Babylon came to Jerusalem and besieged it. ²And the Lord gave Jehoiakim king of Judah into his hand, with some of the articles of the house of God, which he carried into the land of Shinar to the house of his god; and he brought the articles into the treasure house of his god.

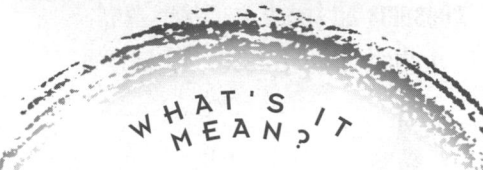

WHAT'S IT MEAN?

Let's introduce the major characters of the book. Nebuchadnezzar, the king of Babylon, led three attacks on the nation of Judah and the city of Jerusalem, capturing thousands of Jewish people in the process. Daniel was captured during the first attack, along with three of his friends— Hananiah, Mishael, and Azariah. (You may know them better as Shadrach, Meshach, and Abed-Nego.)

Daniel 1:1

³Then the king instructed Ashpenaz, the master of his eunuchs, to bring some of the children of Israel and some of the king's descendants and some of the nobles, ⁴young men in whom *there was* no blemish, but good-looking, gifted in all wisdom, possessing knowledge and quick to understand, who *had* ability to serve in the king's palace, and whom they might teach the language and literature of the Chaldeans. ⁵And the king appointed for them a daily provision of the king's delicacies and of the wine which he drank, and three years of training for them, so that at the end of *that time* they might serve before the king. ⁶Now from among those of the sons of Judah were Daniel, Hananiah, Mishael, and Azariah. ⁷To them the chief of the eunuchs gave names: he gave Daniel *the name* Belteshazzar; to Hananiah, Shadrach; to Mishael, Meshach; and to Azariah, Abed-Nego.

⁸But Daniel purposed in his heart that he would not defile himself with the portion of the king's delicacies, nor with the wine which he drank; therefore he requested of the chief of the eunuchs that he might not defile himself. ⁹Now God had brought Daniel into the favor and goodwill of the chief of the eunuchs. ¹⁰And the chief of the eunuchs said to Daniel, "I fear my lord the king, who has appointed your food and drink. For why should he see your faces looking worse than the young men who *are* your age? Then you would endanger my head before the king."

¹¹So Daniel said to the steward[a] whom the chief of the eunuchs had set over Daniel, Hananiah, Mishael, and Azariah, ¹²"Please test your servants for ten days, and let them give us vegetables to eat and water to drink. ¹³Then let our appearance be examined before you, and the appearance of the young men who eat the portion of the king's delicacies; and as you see fit, *so* deal with your servants." ¹⁴So he consented with them in this matter, and tested them ten days.

¹⁵And at the end of ten days their features appeared better and fatter in flesh than all the young men who ate the portion of the king's delicacies. ¹⁶Thus the steward took away their portion of delicacies and the wine that they were to drink, and gave them vegetables.

¹⁷As for these four young men, God gave them knowledge and skill in all literature and wisdom; and Daniel had understanding in all visions and dreams.

TALENTS

Who gives us our gifts? (1:17)

¹⁸Now at the end of the days, when the king had said that they should be brought in, the chief of the eunuchs brought them in before Nebuchadnezzar. ¹⁹Then the king interviewed[a] them, and among them all none was found like Daniel, Hananiah, Mishael, and Azariah; therefore they served before the king. ²⁰And in all matters of wisdom *and* understanding about which the king examined them, he found them ten times better than all the magicians *and* astrologers who *were* in all his realm. ²¹Thus

> "To them the chief of the eunuchs gave names: he gave Daniel the name Belteshazzar; to Hananiah, Shadrach; to Mishael, Meshach; and to Azariah, Abed-Nego."
> (Daniel 1:7)

1:11 [a]Hebrew *Melzar,* also in verse 16　**1:19** [a]Literally *talked with them*

Daniel continued until the first year of King Cyrus.

NEBUCHADNEZZAR'S DREAM

¹Now in the second year of Nebuchadnezzar's reign, Nebuchadnezzar had dreams; and his spirit was *so* troubled that his sleep left him. ²Then the king gave the command to call the magicians, the astrologers, the sorcerers, and the Chaldeans to tell the king his dreams. So they came and stood before the king. ³And the king said to them, "I have had a dream, and my spirit is anxious to know the dream."

⁴Then the Chaldeans spoke to the king in Aramaic,ᵃ "O king, live forever! Tell your servants the dream, and we will give the interpretation."

⁵The king answered and said to the Chaldeans, "My decision is firm: if you do not make known the dream to me, and its interpretation, you shall be cut in pieces, and your houses shall be made an ash heap. ⁶However, if you tell the dream and its interpretation, you shall receive from me gifts, rewards, and great honor. Therefore tell me the dream and its interpretation."

⁷They answered again and said, "Let the king tell his servants the dream, and we will give its interpretation."

WHAT'S IT MEAN?

Because there were so many countries in the ancient Near East trying to do business with each other, they needed a common language they could use to make their lives easier. Aramaic was the language they chose. By the time Jesus was born, Aramaic had replaced Hebrew as the language spoken by most Jews. Daniel 2:4b—7:28 is written in Aramaic.
Daniel 2:4

⁸The king answered and said, "I know for certain that you would gain time, because you see that my decision is firm: ⁹if you do not make known the dream to me, *there is only* one

2:4 ᵃThe original language of Daniel 2:4b through 7:28 is Aramaic.

Promise HE PROMISES TO CONTROL HUMAN EVENTS.

[God] changes the times and the seasons; He removes kings and raises up kings; He gives wisdom to the wise and knowledge to those who have understanding. He reveals deep and secret things (Dan. 2:21, 22a).

Daniel praised God for being the One who both gives rulers their power and takes their power away. It's almost surprising to hear Daniel say that—when you realize the situation he was in. King Nebuchadnezzar had attacked Jerusalem. He had captured the king and taken many valuable things from God's temple. He also captured a lot of able-bodied young men, including Daniel and some of his friends, to serve him in Babylon.

Nebuchadnezzar certainly wasn't a godly man, and Daniel could have resented all the things Nebuchadnezzar did. But he realized that the king's power came from God and that God let Nebuchadnezzar defeat Jerusalem for a reason. God had a plan that, for the time being, revolved around Nebuchadnezzar's success.

When you look at the world today, it may be hard for you to believe that God's in control. He is the One who puts leaders in their places, and He is able to change their hearts. He has all of the wisdom and knowledge they need to be good leaders. Unfortunately, not all leaders seek Him. Be a person who prays for leaders. Ask God to turn their hearts toward Him. Ask for His wisdom and knowledge on their behalf. God has put them in their positions because He has a plan that's invisible. He *is* in control.

SEE FOR YOURSELF:
Job 41:11; Eccl. 9:1; Is. 54:5;
Jer. 10:23; 23:24; Dan. 4:35

decree for you! For you have agreed to speak lying and corrupt words before me till the time has changed. Therefore tell me the dream, and I shall know that you can give me its interpretation."

[10]The Chaldeans answered the king, and said, "There is not a man on earth who can tell the king's matter; therefore no king, lord, or ruler has *ever* asked such things of any magician, astrologer, or Chaldean. [11]*It is* a difficult thing that the king requests, and there is no other who can tell it to the king except the gods, whose dwelling is not with flesh."

[12]For this reason the king was angry and very furious, and gave the command to destroy all the wise *men* of Babylon. [13]So the decree went out, and they began killing the wise *men;* and they sought Daniel and his companions, to kill *them.*

GOD REVEALS NEBUCHADNEZZAR'S DREAM

[14]Then with counsel and wisdom Daniel answered Arioch, the captain of the king's guard, who had gone out to kill the wise *men* of Babylon; [15]he answered and said to Arioch the king's captain, "Why is the decree from the king so urgent?" Then Arioch made the decision known to Daniel.

[16]So Daniel went in and asked the king to give him time, that he might tell the king the interpretation. [17]Then Daniel went to his house, and made the decision known to Hananiah, Mishael, and Azariah, his companions, [18]that they might seek mercies from the God of heaven concerning this secret, so that Daniel and his companions might not perish with the rest of the wise *men* of Babylon. [19]Then the secret was revealed to Daniel in a night vision. So Daniel blessed the God of heaven.

[20]Daniel answered and said:

"Blessed be the name of God forever and ever,
  For wisdom and might are His.
21 And He changes the times and the seasons;
  He removes kings and raises up kings;
  He gives wisdom to the wise
  And knowledge to those who have understanding.
22 He reveals deep and secret things;
  He knows what *is* in the darkness,
  And light dwells with Him.

23 "I thank You and praise You,
  O God of my fathers;
  You have given me wisdom and might,
  And have now made known to me what we asked of You,
  For You have made known to us the king's demand."

DANIEL EXPLAINS THE DREAM

[24]Therefore Daniel went to Arioch, whom the king had appointed to destroy the wise *men* of Babylon. He went and said thus to him: "Do not destroy the wise *men* of Babylon; take me before the king, and I will tell the king the interpretation."

[25]Then Arioch quickly brought Daniel before the king, and said thus to him, "I have found a man of the captives[a] of Judah, who will make known to the king the interpretation."

[26]The king answered and said to Daniel, whose name *was* Belteshazzar, "Are you able to make known to me the dream which I have seen, and its interpretation?"

[27]Daniel answered in the presence of the king, and said, "The secret which the king has demanded, the wise *men,* the astrologers, the magicians, and the soothsayers cannot declare to the king. [28]But there is a God in heaven who reveals secrets, and He has made known to King Nebuchadnezzar what will be in the latter days. Your dream, and the visions of your head upon your bed, were these: [29]As for you, O king, thoughts came *to* your *mind while* on your bed, *about* what would come to pass after this; and He who reveals secrets has made known to you what will be. [30]But as for me, this secret has not been revealed to me because I have more wisdom than anyone living, but for *our* sakes who make known the interpretation to the king, and that you may know the thoughts of your heart.

[31]"You, O king, were watching; and behold, a great image! This great image, whose splendor *was* excellent, stood before you; and its form *was* awesome. [32]This image's head *was* of fine gold, its chest and arms of silver, its belly and thighs[a] of bronze, [33]its legs of iron, its feet partly of iron and partly of clay.[a] [34]You watched while a stone was cut out without hands, which struck the image on its feet of iron and clay, and broke them in pieces. [35]Then the iron, the clay, the bronze, the silver, and the gold were crushed together, and became like chaff from the summer threshing floors; the wind carried

---

2:25 [a]Literally *of the sons of the captivity*   **2:32** [a]Or *sides*   **2:33** [a]Or *baked clay,* and so in verses 34, 35, and 42

them away so that no trace of them was found. And the stone that struck the image became a great mountain and filled the whole earth. ³⁶"This *is* the dream. Now we will tell the interpretation of it before the king. ³⁷You, O king, *are* a king of kings. For the God of heaven has given you a kingdom, power, strength, and glory; ³⁸and wherever the children of men dwell, or the beasts of the field and the birds of the heaven, He has given *them* into your hand, and has made you ruler over them all—you *are* this head of gold. ³⁹But after you shall arise another kingdom inferior to yours; then another, a third kingdom of bronze, which shall rule over all the earth. ⁴⁰And the fourth kingdom shall be as strong as iron, inasmuch as iron breaks in pieces and shatters everything; and like iron that crushes, *that kingdom* will break in pieces and crush all the others. ⁴¹Whereas you saw the feet and toes, partly of potter's clay and partly of iron, the kingdom shall be divided; yet the strength of the iron shall be in it, just as you saw the iron mixed with ceramic clay. ⁴²And *as* the toes of the feet *were* partly of iron and partly of clay, *so* the kingdom shall be partly strong and partly fragile. ⁴³As you saw iron mixed with ceramic clay, they will mingle with the seed of men; but they will not adhere to one another, just as iron does not mix with clay. ⁴⁴And in the days of these kings the God of heaven will set up a kingdom which shall never be destroyed; and the kingdom shall not be left to other people; it shall break in pieces and consume all these kingdoms, and it shall stand forever. ⁴⁵Inasmuch as you saw that the stone was cut out of the mountain without hands, and that it broke in pieces the iron, the bronze, the clay, the silver, and the gold—the great God has made known to the king what will come to pass after this. The dream is certain, and its interpretation is sure."

DANIEL AND HIS FRIENDS PROMOTED

⁴⁶Then King Nebuchadnezzar fell on his face, prostrate before Daniel, and commanded that they should present an offering and incense to him. ⁴⁷The king answered Daniel, and said, "Truly your God *is* the God of gods, the Lord of kings, and a revealer of secrets, since you could reveal this secret." ⁴⁸Then the king promoted Daniel and gave him many great gifts; and he made him ruler over the whole province of Babylon, and chief administrator over all the wise *men* of Babylon. ⁴⁹Also Daniel petitioned the king, and he set Shadrach, Me-

shach, and Abed-Nego over the affairs of the province of Babylon; but Daniel *sat* in the gate*ᵃ* of the king.

THE IMAGE OF GOLD

¹Nebuchadnezzar the king made an image of gold, whose height *was* sixty cubits *and* its width six cubits. He set it up in the plain of Dura, in the province of Babylon. ²And King Nebuchadnezzar sent *word* to gather together the satraps, the administrators, the governors, the counselors, the treasurers, the judges, the magistrates, and all the officials of the provinces, to come to the dedication of the image which King Nebuchadnezzar had set up. ³So the satraps, the administrators, the governors, the counselors, the treasurers, the judges, the magistrates, and all the officials of the provinces gathered together for the dedication of the image that King Nebuchadnezzar had set up; and they stood before the image that Nebuchadnezzar had set up. ⁴Then a herald cried aloud: "To you it is commanded, O peoples, nations, and languages, ⁵*that* at the time you hear the sound of the horn, flute, harp, lyre, *and* psaltery, in symphony with all kinds of music, you shall fall down and worship the gold image that King Nebuchadnezzar has set up; ⁶and whoever does not fall down and worship shall be cast immediately into the midst of a burning fiery furnace."

⁷So at that time, when all the people heard the sound of the horn, flute, harp, *and* lyre, in symphony with all kinds of music, all the people, nations, and languages fell down *and* worshiped the gold image which King Nebuchadnezzar had set up.

DANIEL'S FRIENDS DISOBEY THE KING

⁸Therefore at that time certain Chaldeans came forward and accused the Jews. ⁹They spoke and said to King Nebuchadnezzar, "O king, live forever! ¹⁰You, O king, have made a decree that everyone who hears the sound of the horn, flute, harp, lyre, *and* psaltery, in symphony with all kinds of music, shall fall down and worship the gold image; ¹¹and whoever does not fall down and worship shall be cast into the midst of a burning fiery furnace. ¹²There are certain Jews whom you have set over the affairs of the province of Babylon: Shadrach, Meshach, and Abed-Nego; these men, O king, have not paid due regard to you. They do not serve your gods or worship the gold image which you have set up."

2:49 *ᵃ*That is, the king's court

¹³Then Nebuchadnezzar, in rage and fury, gave the command to bring Shadrach, Meshach, and Abed-Nego. So they brought these men before the king. ¹⁴Nebuchadnezzar spoke, saying to them, "Is it true, Shadrach, Meshach, and Abed-Nego, that you do not serve my gods or worship the gold image which I have set up? ¹⁵Now if you are ready at the time you hear the sound of the horn, flute, harp, lyre, and psaltery, in symphony with all kinds of music, and you fall down and worship the image which I have made, good! But if you do not worship, you shall be cast immediately into the midst of a burning fiery furnace. And who is the god who will deliver you from my hands?"

¹⁶Shadrach, Meshach, and Abed-Nego answered and said to the king, "O Nebuchadnezzar, we have no need to answer you in this matter. ¹⁷If that is the case, our God whom we serve is able to deliver us from the burning fiery furnace, and He will deliver us from your hand, O king. ¹⁸But if not, let it be known to you, O king, that we do not serve your gods, nor will we worship the gold image which you have set up."

SAVED IN FIERY TRIAL

¹⁹Then Nebuchadnezzar was full of fury, and the expression on his face changed toward Shadrach, Meshach, and Abed-Nego. He spoke and commanded that they heat the furnace seven times more than it was usually heated. ²⁰And he commanded certain mighty men of valor who were in his army to bind Shadrach, Meshach, and Abed-Nego, and cast them into the burning fiery furnace. ²¹Then these men were bound in their coats, their trousers, their turbans, and their other garments, and were cast into the midst of the burning fiery furnace. ²²Therefore, because the king's command was urgent, and the furnace exceedingly hot, the flame of the fire killed those men who took up Shadrach, Meshach, and Abed-Nego. ²³And these three men, Shadrach, Meshach, and Abed-Nego, fell down bound into the midst of the burning fiery furnace.

²⁴Then King Nebuchadnezzar was astonished; and he rose in haste and spoke, saying to his counselors, "Did we not cast three men bound into the midst of the fire?"

They answered and said to the king, "True, O king."

²⁵"Look!" he answered, "I see four men loose, walking in the midst of the fire; and they are not hurt, and the form of the fourth is like the Son of God."ᵃ

NEBUCHADNEZZAR PRAISES GOD

²⁶Then Nebuchadnezzar went near the mouth of the burning fiery furnace and spoke, saying, "Shadrach, Meshach, and Abed-Nego, servants of the Most High God, come out, and come here." Then Shadrach, Meshach, and Abed-Nego came from the midst of the fire. ²⁷And the satraps, administrators, governors, and the king's counselors gathered together, and they saw these men on whose bodies the fire had no power; the hair of their head was not singed nor were their garments affected, and the smell of fire was not on them.

²⁸Nebuchadnezzar spoke, saying, "Blessed be the God of Shadrach, Meshach, and Abed-Nego, who sent His Angelᵃ and delivered His servants who trusted in Him, and they have frustrated the king's word, and yielded their bodies, that they should not serve nor worship any god except their own God! ²⁹Therefore I make a decree that any people, nation, or language which speaks anything amiss against the God of Shadrach, Meshach, and Abed-Nego shall be cut in pieces, and their houses shall be made an ash heap; because there is no other God who can deliver like this."

³⁰Then the king promoted Shadrach, Meshach, and Abed-Nego in the province of Babylon.

NEBUCHADNEZZAR'S SECOND DREAM

4 ¹ Nebuchadnezzar the king,

To all peoples, nations, and languages that dwell in all the earth:

Peace be multiplied to you.

² I thought it good to declare the signs and wonders that the Most High God has worked for me.

³ How great are His signs,
And how mighty His wonders!
His kingdom is an everlasting kingdom,
And His dominion is from generation to generation.

⁴ I, Nebuchadnezzar, was at rest in my house, and flourishing in my palace. ⁵I saw a dream which made me afraid, and the thoughts on my bed and the visions

of my head troubled me. ⁶Therefore I issued a decree to bring in all the wise *men* of Babylon before me, that they might make known to me the interpretation of the dream. ⁷Then the magicians, the astrologers, the Chaldeans, and the soothsayers came in, and I told them the dream; but they did not make known to me its interpretation. ⁸But at last Daniel came before me (his name *is* Belteshazzar, according to the name of my god; in him *is* the Spirit of the Holy God), and I told the dream before him, *saying:* ⁹"Belteshazzar, chief of the magicians, because I know that the Spirit of the Holy God *is* in you, and no secret troubles you, explain to me the visions of my dream that I have seen, and its interpretation.

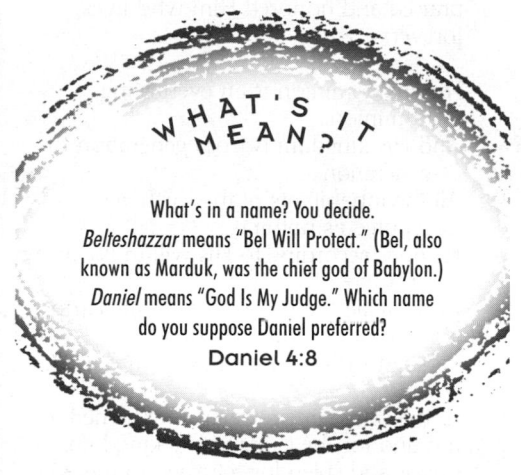

WHAT'S IT MEAN?

What's in a name? You decide. *Belteshazzar* means "Bel Will Protect." (Bel, also known as Marduk, was the chief god of Babylon.) *Daniel* means "God Is My Judge." Which name do you suppose Daniel preferred?
Daniel 4:8

¹⁰ "These *were* the visions of my head *while* on my bed:

I was looking, and behold,
A tree in the midst of the earth,
And its height was great.
¹¹ The tree grew and became strong;
Its height reached to the heavens,
And it could be seen to the ends of all the
　earth.
¹² Its leaves *were* lovely,
Its fruit abundant,
And in it *was* food for all.
The beasts of the field found shade
　under it,
The birds of the heavens dwelt in its
　branches,
And all flesh was fed from it.

¹³ "I saw in the visions of my head *while* on my bed, and there was a watcher, a holy one, coming down from heaven. ¹⁴He cried aloud and said thus:

'Chop down the tree and cut off its
　branches,
Strip off its leaves and scatter its fruit.
Let the beasts get out from under it,
And the birds from its branches.
¹⁵ Nevertheless leave the stump and roots in
　the earth,
Bound with a band of iron and bronze,
In the tender grass of the field.
Let it be wet with the dew of heaven,
And let him graze with the beasts
On the grass of the earth.
¹⁶ Let his heart be changed from *that of* a
　man,
Let him be given the heart of a beast,
And let seven times*ᵃ* pass over him.

¹⁷ 'This decision *is* by the decree of the
　watchers,
And the sentence by the word of the holy
　ones,
In order that the living may know
That the Most High rules in the kingdom
　of men,
Gives it to whomever He will,
And sets over it the lowest of men.'

¹⁸ "This dream I, King Nebuchadnezzar, have seen. Now you, Belteshazzar, declare its interpretation, since all the wise *men* of my kingdom are not able to make known to me the interpretation; but you *are* able, for the Spirit of the Holy God *is* in you."

DANIEL EXPLAINS THE SECOND DREAM

¹⁹ Then Daniel, whose name was Belteshazzar, was astonished for a time, and his thoughts troubled him. *So* the king spoke, and said, "Belteshazzar, do not let the dream or its interpretation trouble you."

Belteshazzar answered and said, "My lord, *may* the dream concern those who hate you, and its interpretation concern your enemies!

²⁰ "The tree that you saw, which grew and became strong, whose height reached to the heavens and which *could be seen* by all the earth, ²¹whose leaves *were* lovely and

its fruit abundant, in which *was* food for all, under which the beasts of the field dwelt, and in whose branches the birds of the heaven had their home—²²it *is* you, O king, who have grown and become strong; for your greatness has grown and reaches to the heavens, and your dominion to the end of the earth.

23 "And inasmuch as the king saw a watcher, a holy one, coming down from heaven and saying, 'Chop down the tree and destroy it, but leave its stump and roots in the earth, *bound* with a band of iron and bronze in the tender grass of the field; let it be wet with the dew of heaven, and let him graze with the beasts of the field, till seven times pass over him'; ²⁴this is the interpretation, O king, and this is the decree of the Most High, which has come upon my lord the king: ²⁵They shall drive you from men, your dwelling shall be with the beasts of the field, and they shall make you eat grass like oxen. They shall wet you with the dew of heaven, and seven times shall pass over you, till you know that the Most High rules in the kingdom of men, and gives it to whomever He chooses.

26 "And inasmuch as they gave the command to leave the stump *and* roots of the tree, your kingdom shall be assured to you, after you come to know that Heaven rules. ²⁷Therefore, O king, let my advice be acceptable to you; break off your sins by *being* righteous, and your iniquities by showing mercy to *the* poor. Perhaps there may be a lengthening of your prosperity."

NEBUCHADNEZZAR'S HUMILIATION

28 All *this* came upon King Nebuchadnezzar. ²⁹At the end of the twelve months he was walking about the royal palace of Babylon. ³⁰The king spoke, saying, "Is not this great Babylon, that I have built for a royal dwelling by my mighty power and for the honor of my majesty?"

31 While the word *was still* in the king's mouth, a voice fell from heaven: "King Nebuchadnezzar, to you it is spoken: the kingdom has departed from you! ³²And they shall drive you from men, and your dwelling *shall be* with the beasts of the

field. They shall make you eat grass like oxen; and seven times shall pass over you, until you know that the Most High rules in the kingdom of men, and gives it to whomever He chooses."

33 That very hour the word was fulfilled concerning Nebuchadnezzar; he was driven from men and ate grass like oxen; his body was wet with the dew of heaven till his hair had grown like eagles' *feathers* and his nails like birds' *claws*.

NEBUCHADNEZZAR PRAISES GOD

34 And at the end of the time*ᵃ* I, Nebuchadnezzar, lifted my eyes to heaven, and my understanding returned to me; and I blessed the Most High and praised and honored Him who lives forever:

For His dominion *is* an everlasting
   dominion,
And His kingdom *is* from generation to
   generation.
35 All the inhabitants of the earth *are*
   reputed as nothing;
He does according to His will in the army
   of heaven
And *among* the inhabitants of the earth.
No one can restrain His hand
Or say to Him, "What have You done?"

36 At the same time my reason returned to me, and for the glory of my kingdom, my honor and splendor returned to me. My counselors and nobles resorted to me, I was restored to my kingdom, and excellent majesty was added to me. ³⁷Now I, Nebuchadnezzar, praise and extol and honor the King of heaven, all of whose works *are* truth, and His ways justice. And those who walk in pride He is able to put down.

BELSHAZZAR'S FEAST

¹Belshazzar the king made a great feast for a thousand of his lords, and drank wine in the presence of the thousand. ²While he tasted the wine, Belshazzar gave the command to bring the gold and silver vessels which his father Nebuchadnezzar had taken from the temple which *had been* in Jerusalem, that the king and his lords, his wives, and his concubines might drink from them. ³Then they brought the gold

4:34 *ᵃ*Literally *days*

vessels that had been taken from the temple of the house of God which *had been* in Jerusalem; and the king and his lords, his wives, and his concubines drank from them. ⁴They drank wine, and praised the gods of gold and silver, bronze and iron, wood and stone.

⁵In the same hour the fingers of a man's hand appeared and wrote opposite the lampstand on the plaster of the wall of the king's palace; and the king saw the part of the hand that wrote. ⁶Then the king's countenance changed, and his thoughts troubled him, so that the joints of his hips were loosened and his knees knocked against each other. ⁷The king cried aloud to bring in the astrologers, the Chaldeans, and the soothsayers. The king spoke, saying to the wise *men* of Babylon, "Whoever reads this writing, and tells me its interpretation, shall be clothed with purple and *have* a chain of gold around his neck; and he shall be the third ruler in the kingdom." ⁸Now all the king's wise *men* came, but they could not read the writing, or make known to the king its interpretation. ⁹Then King Belshazzar was greatly troubled, his countenance was changed, and his lords were astonished.

> "Now I, Nebuchadnezzar, praise and extol and honor the King of heaven, all of whose works are truth, and His ways justice. And those who walk in pride He is able to put down."
> (Daniel 4:37)

¹⁰The queen, because of the words of the king and his lords, came to the banquet hall. The queen spoke, saying, "O king, live forever! Do not let your thoughts trouble you, nor let your countenance change. ¹¹There is a man in your kingdom in whom *is* the Spirit of the Holy God. And in the days of your father, light and understanding and wisdom, like the wisdom of the gods, were found in him; and King Nebuchadnezzar your father—your father the king—made him chief of the magicians, astrologers, Chaldeans, *and* soothsayers. ¹²Inasmuch as an excellent spirit, knowledge, understanding, interpreting dreams, solving riddles, and explaining enigmas*ᵃ* were found in this Daniel, whom the king named Belteshazzar, now let Daniel be called, and he will give the interpretation."

THE WRITING ON THE WALL EXPLAINED

¹³Then Daniel was brought in before the king. The king spoke, and said to Daniel, "*Are* you that Daniel who is one of the captives*ᵃ* from Judah, whom my father the king brought from Judah? ¹⁴I have heard of you, that the Spirit of God *is* in you, and *that* light and understanding and excellent wisdom are found in you. ¹⁵Now the wise *men*, the astrologers, have been brought in before me, that they should read this writing and make known to me its interpretation, but they could not give the interpretation of the thing. ¹⁶And I have heard of you, that you can give interpretations and explain enigmas. Now if you can read the writing and make known to me its interpretation, you shall be clothed with purple and *have* a chain of gold around your neck, and shall be the third ruler in the kingdom."

¹⁷Then Daniel answered, and said before the king, "Let your gifts be for yourself, and give your rewards to another; yet I will read the writing to the king, and make known to him the interpretation. ¹⁸O king, the Most High God

WHAT'S IT MEAN?

Who is this guy Belshazzar, and what's he doing ruling Babylon? The story is a little complicated, so hang on. After Nebuchadnezzar died, his son Evil-Merodach became king. Evil-Merodach ruled for two years before being assassinated by his brother-in-law, Nergal-Sarezer. (Got that?) Nergal-Sarezer ruled for less than three years before he died and was succeeded by his son, Labashi-Marduk. Labashi-Marduk reigned for all of two months before he was assassinated. (Still with us?) Next came Nabonidus, who may have been Nebuchadnezzar's son-in-law. In the third year of his reign, Nabonidus appointed his son as coruler of the nation. The Bible doesn't mention Nabonidus, but we know from other historical documents that he suffered from a terrible disease. As a result, he left the kingdom of Babylon in the hands of his son . . . Belshazzar. (Any questions?)

Daniel 5:1

gave Nebuchadnezzar your father a kingdom and majesty, glory and honor. [19]And because of the majesty that He gave him, all peoples, nations, and languages trembled and feared before him. Whomever he wished, he executed; whomever he wished, he kept alive; whomever he wished, he set up; and whomever he wished, he put down. [20]But when his heart was lifted up, and his spirit was hardened in pride, he was deposed from his kingly throne, and they took his glory from him. [21]Then he was driven from the sons of men, his heart was made like the beasts, and his dwelling *was* with the wild donkeys. They fed him with grass like oxen, and his body was wet with the dew of heaven, till he knew that the Most High God rules in the kingdom of men, and appoints over it whomever He chooses.

[22]"But you his son, Belshazzar, have not humbled your heart, although you knew all this. [23]And you have lifted yourself up against the Lord of heaven. They have brought the vessels of His house before you, and you and your lords, your wives and your concubines, have drunk wine from them. And you have praised the gods of silver and gold, bronze and iron, wood and stone, which do not see or hear or know; and the God who *holds* your breath in His hand and owns all your ways, you have not glorified. [24]Then the fingers[a] of the hand were sent from Him, and this writing was written.

[25]"And this is the inscription that was written:

MENE,[a] MENE, TEKEL,[b] UPHARSIN.[c]

[26]This *is* the interpretation of *each* word. MENE: God has numbered your kingdom, and finished it; [27]TEKEL: You have been weighed in the balances, and found wanting; [28]PERES: Your kingdom has been divided, and given to the Medes and Persians."[a] [29]Then Belshazzar gave the command, and they clothed Daniel with purple and *put* a chain of gold around his neck, and made a proclamation concerning him that he should be the third ruler in the kingdom.

BELSHAZZAR'S FALL

[30]That very night Belshazzar, king of the Chaldeans, was slain. [31]And Darius the Mede received the kingdom, *being* about sixty-two years old.

THE PLOT AGAINST DANIEL

6
[1]It pleased Darius to set over the kingdom one hundred and twenty satraps, to be over the whole kingdom; [2]and over these, three governors, of whom Daniel *was* one, that the satraps might give account to them, so that the king would suffer no loss. [3]Then this Daniel distinguished himself above the governors and satraps, because an excellent spirit *was* in him; and the king gave thought to setting him over the whole realm. [4]So the governors and satraps sought to find *some* charge against Daniel concerning the kingdom; but they could find no charge or fault, because he *was* faithful; nor was there any error or fault found in him. [5]Then these men

INTEGRITY

How does integrity help us? (6:4, 5)

said, "We shall not find any charge against this Daniel unless we find *it* against him concerning the law of his God."

[6]So these governors and satraps thronged before the king, and said thus to him: "King Darius, live forever! [7]All the governors of the kingdom, the administrators and satraps, the counselors and advisors, have consulted together to establish a royal statute and to make a firm decree, that whoever petitions any god or man for thirty days, except you, O king, shall be cast into the den of lions. [8]Now, O king, establish the decree and sign the writing, so that it cannot be changed, according to the law of the Medes and Persians, which does not alter." [9]Therefore King Darius signed the written decree.

DANIEL IN THE LIONS' DEN

[10]Now when Daniel knew that the writing was signed, he went home. And in his upper room, with his windows open toward Jerusalem, he knelt down on his knees three times that day, and prayed and gave thanks before his God, as was his custom since early days.

[11]Then these men assembled and found Daniel praying and making supplication before his God. [12]And they went before the king, and spoke concerning the king's decree: "Have you not signed a decree that every man who petitions any god or man within thirty days, except you, O king, shall be cast into the den of lions?"

The king answered and said, "The thing *is* true, according to the law of the Medes and Persians, which does not alter."

5:24 [a]Literally *palm*   **5:25** [a]Literally *a mina* (50 shekels) from the verb "to number"   [b]Literally *a shekel* from the verb "to weigh"   [c]Literally *and half-shekels* from the verb "to divide"   **5:28** [a]Aramaic *Paras,* consonant with *Peres*

¹³So they answered and said before the king, "That Daniel, who is one of the captives*a* from Judah, docs not show duc rcgard for you, O king, or for the decree that you have signed, but makes his petition three times a day."

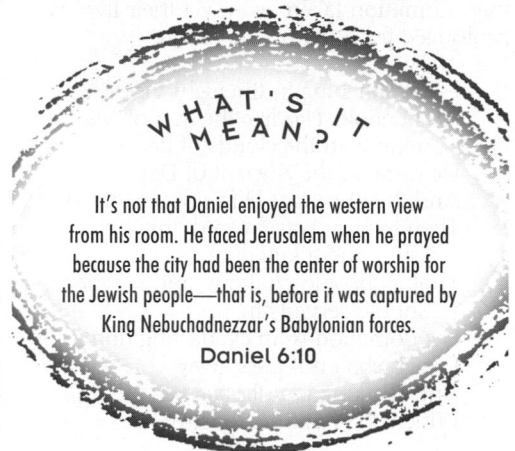

WHAT'S IT MEAN?

It's not that Daniel enjoyed the western view from his room. He faced Jerusalem when he prayed because the city had been the center of worship for the Jewish people—that is, before it was captured by King Nebuchadnezzar's Babylonian forces.

Daniel 6:10

¹⁴And the king, when he heard *these* words, was greatly displeased with himself, and set *his* heart on Daniel to deliver him; and he labored till the going down of the sun to deliver him. ¹⁵Then these men approached the king, and said to the king, "Know, O king, that *it is* the law of the Medes and Persians that no decree or statute which the king establishes may be changed." ¹⁶So the king gave the command, and they brought Daniel and cast *him* into the den of lions. *But* the king spoke, saying to Daniel, "Your God, whom you serve continually, He will deliver you." ¹⁷Then a stone was brought and laid on the mouth of the den, and the king sealed it with his own signet ring and with the signets of his lords, that the purpose concerning Daniel might not be changed.

DANIEL SAVED FROM THE LIONS

¹⁸Now the king went to his palace and spent the night fasting; and no musicians*a* were brought before him. Also his sleep went from him. ¹⁹Then the king arose very early in the morning and went in haste to the den of lions. ²⁰And when he came to the den, he cried out with a lamenting voice to Daniel. The king spoke, saying to Daniel, "Daniel, servant of the living God, has your God, whom you serve continually, been able to deliver you from the lions?"

²¹Then Daniel said to the king, "O king, live forever! ²²My God sent His angel and shut the lions' mouths, so that they have not hurt me, because I was found innocent before Him; and also, O king, I have done no wrong before you."

²³Now the king was exceedingly glad for him, and commanded that they should take Daniel up out of the den. So Daniel was taken up out of the den, and no injury whatever was found on him, because he believed in his God.

DARIUS HONORS GOD

²⁴And the king gave the command, and they brought those men who had accused Daniel, and they cast *them* into the den of lions—them, their children, and their wives; and the lions overpowered them, and broke all their bones in pieces before they ever came to the bottom of the den.

²⁵Then King Darius wrote:

To all peoples, nations, and languages that dwell in all the earth:

Peace be multiplied to you.

²⁶ I make a decree that in every dominion of my kingdom *men must* tremble and fear before the God of Daniel.

For He *is* the living God,
And steadfast forever;
His kingdom *is the one* which shall not be destroyed,
And His dominion *shall endure* to the end.
²⁷ He delivers and rescues,
And He works signs and wonders
In heaven and on earth,
Who has delivered Daniel from the power of the lions.

²⁸So this Daniel prospered in the reign of Darius and in the reign of Cyrus the Persian.

VISION OF THE FOUR BEASTS

¹In the first year of Belshazzar king of Babylon, Daniel had a dream and visions of his head *while* on his bed. Then he wrote down the dream, telling the main facts.*a*

²Daniel spoke, saying, "I saw in my vision by night, and behold, the four winds of heaven were stirring up the Great Sea. ³And four great beasts came up from the sea, each different from the other. ⁴The first *was* like a lion, and had eagle's wings. I watched till its wings were

6:13 *a*Literally *of the sons of the captivity*   **6:18** *a*Exact meaning unknown   **7:1** *a*Literally *the head* (or *chief*) *of the words*

plucked off; and it was lifted up from the earth and made to stand on two feet like a man, and a man's heart was given to it.

⁵"And suddenly another beast, a second, like a bear. It was raised up on one side, and *had* three ribs in its mouth between its teeth. And they said thus to it: 'Arise, devour much flesh!'

⁶"After this I looked, and there was another, like a leopard, which had on its back four wings of a bird. The beast also had four heads, and dominion was given to it.

⁷"After this I saw in the night visions, and behold, a fourth beast, dreadful and terrible, exceedingly strong. It had huge iron teeth; it was devouring, breaking in pieces, and trampling the residue with its feet. It *was* different from all the beasts that *were* before it, and it had ten horns. ⁸I was considering the horns, and there was another horn, a little one, coming up among them, before whom three of the first horns were plucked out by the roots. And there, in this horn, *were* eyes like the eyes of a man, and a mouth speaking pompous words.

WHAT'S IT MEAN?

If you've ever seen an ox or bull use its horn as a weapon, you know why Bible writers used "horn" to symbolize power and influence.

Daniel 7:8

VISION OF THE ANCIENT OF DAYS

9   "I watched till thrones were put in place,
         And the Ancient of Days was seated;
         His garment *was* white as snow,
         And the hair of His head *was* like pure
            wool.
         His throne *was* a fiery flame,
         Its wheels a burning fire;
10   A fiery stream issued
         And came forth from before Him.
         A thousand thousands ministered to
            Him;
         Ten thousand times ten thousand stood
            before Him.
         The court*ᵃ* was seated,
         And the books were opened.

¹¹"I watched then because of the sound of the pompous words which the horn was speaking; I watched till the beast was slain, and its body destroyed and given to the burning flame. ¹²As for the rest of the beasts, they had their dominion taken away, yet their lives were prolonged for a season and a time.

13   "I was watching in the night visions,
         And behold, *One* like the Son of Man,
         Coming with the clouds of heaven!
         He came to the Ancient of Days,
         And they brought Him near before Him.
14   Then to Him was given dominion and
            glory and a kingdom,
         That all peoples, nations, and languages
            should serve Him.
         His dominion *is* an everlasting dominion,
         Which shall not pass away,
         And His kingdom *the one*
         Which shall not be destroyed.

DANIEL'S VISIONS INTERPRETED

¹⁵"I, Daniel, was grieved in my spirit within *my* body, and the visions of my head troubled me. ¹⁶I came near to one of those who stood by, and asked him the truth of all this. So he told me and made known to me the interpretation of these things: ¹⁷'Those great beasts, which are four, *are* four kings*ᵃ* *which* arise out of the earth. ¹⁸But the saints of the Most High shall receive the kingdom, and possess the kingdom forever, even forever and ever.'

¹⁹"Then I wished to know the truth about the fourth beast, which was different from all the others, exceedingly dreadful, *with* its teeth of iron and its nails of bronze, *which* devoured, broke in pieces, and trampled the residue with its feet; ²⁰and the ten horns that *were* on its head, and the other *horn* which came up, before which three fell, namely, that horn which had eyes and a mouth which spoke pompous words, whose appearance *was* greater than his fellows. ²¹"I was watching; and the same horn was making war against the saints, and prevailing against them, ²²until the Ancient of Days came, and a judgment was made in *favor* of the saints of the Most High, and the time came for the saints to possess the kingdom.

²³"Thus he said:

         'The fourth beast shall be
         A fourth kingdom on earth,

7:10 *ᵃOr judgment*   **7:17** *ᵃRepresenting their kingdoms (compare verse 23)*

Which shall be different from all *other*
   kingdoms,
And shall devour the whole earth,
Trample it and break it in pieces.
24 The ten horns *are* ten kings
Who shall arise from this kingdom.
And another shall rise after them;
He shall be different from the first *ones*,
And shall subdue three kings.
25 He shall speak *pompous* words against the
   Most High,
Shall persecute[a] the saints of the Most
   High,
And shall intend to change times and law.
Then *the saints* shall be given into his
   hand
For a time and times and half a time.

26 'But the court shall be seated,
And they shall take away his dominion,
To consume and destroy *it* forever.
27 Then the kingdom and dominion,
And the greatness of the kingdoms under
   the whole heaven,
Shall be given to the people, the saints of
   the Most High.
His kingdom *is* an everlasting kingdom,
And all dominions shall serve and obey
   Him.'

28"This *is* the end of the account.[a] As for me,
Daniel, my thoughts greatly troubled me, and
my countenance changed; but I kept the matter
in my heart."

VISION OF A RAM AND A GOAT

1 In the third year of the reign of King Belshazzar a vision appeared *to* me—to me, Daniel—after the one that appeared to me the first
time. 2 I saw in the vision, and it so happened
while I was looking, that I *was* in Shushan, the
citadel, which *is* in the province of Elam; and I
saw in the vision that I was by the River Ulai.
3 Then I lifted my eyes and saw, and there,
standing beside the river, was a ram which had
two horns, and the two horns *were* high; but
one *was* higher than the other, and the higher
one came up last. 4 I saw the ram pushing westward, northward, and southward, so that no
animal could withstand him; nor *was there any*
that could deliver from his hand, but he did
according to his will and became great.

5 And as I was considering, suddenly a male
goat came from the west, across the surface of
the whole earth, without touching the ground;

and the goat *had* a notable horn between his
eyes. 6 Then he came to the ram that had two
horns, which I had seen standing beside the
river, and ran at him with furious power. 7 And I
saw him confronting the ram; he was moved
with rage against him, attacked the ram, and
broke his two horns. There was no power in
the ram to withstand him, but he cast him
down to the ground and trampled him; and
there was no one that could deliver the ram
from his hand.

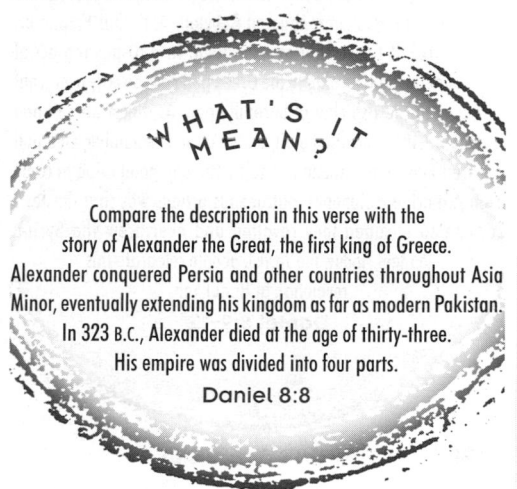

WHAT'S IT MEAN?

Compare the description in this verse with the
story of Alexander the Great, the first king of Greece.
Alexander conquered Persia and other countries throughout Asia
Minor, eventually extending his kingdom as far as modern Pakistan.
In 323 B.C., Alexander died at the age of thirty-three.
His empire was divided into four parts.
Daniel 8:8

8 Therefore the male goat grew very great;
but when he became strong, the large horn was
broken, and in place of it four notable ones
came up toward the four winds of heaven.
9 And out of one of them came a little horn
which grew exceedingly great toward the south,
toward the east, and toward the Glorious *Land*.
10 And it grew up to the host of heaven; and it
cast down *some* of the host and *some* of the stars
to the ground, and trampled them. 11 He even
exalted *himself* as high as the Prince of the host;
and by him the daily *sacrifices* were taken away,
and the place of His sanctuary was cast down.
12 Because of transgression, an army was given
over *to the horn* to oppose the daily *sacrifices*;
and he cast truth down to the ground. He did
all this and prospered.

13 Then I heard a holy one speaking; and an-
other holy one said to that certain *one* who was
speaking, "How long *will* the vision *be, concerning* the daily *sacrifices* and the transgression of
desolation, the giving of both the sanctuary and
the host to be trampled underfoot?"

14 And he said to me, "For two thousand
three hundred days;[a] then the sanctuary shall
be cleansed."

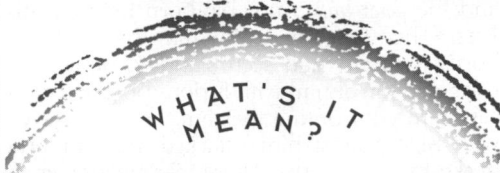

WHAT'S IT MEAN?

The nasty little horn described in these verses may refer to a Syrian king named Antiochus Epiphanes. If you were consciously trying to make yourself an enemy of God, you probably couldn't do any better than Antiochus Epiphanes did. After the Medes and Persians conquered Babylon, Antiochus Epiphanes took control of the temple in Jerusalem. In a disgusting act of blasphemy, he built an altar to the Greek god Zeus directly over what had been the Jewish altar of burnt offering. As if that weren't bad enough, he then sacrificed a pig on the altar. (Remember, God had declared pigs to be unclean animals.) The one good thing to come from Antiochus Epiphanes' outrageous actions was that the Jews became so enraged they revolted and overthrew the Syrian leaders. Today, the Jewish people celebrate this revolution at Hanukkah.

Daniel 8:9–12

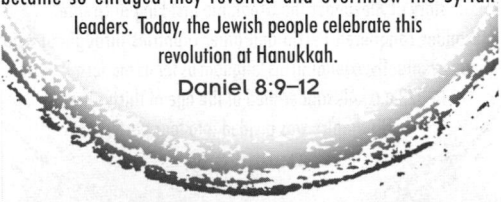

GABRIEL INTERPRETS THE VISION

¹⁵Then it happened, when I, Daniel, had seen the vision and was seeking the meaning, that suddenly there stood before me one having the appearance of a man. ¹⁶And I heard a man's voice between *the banks of* the Ulai, who called, and said, "Gabriel, make this *man* understand the vision." ¹⁷So he came near where I stood, and when he came I was afraid and fell on my face; but he said to me, "Understand, son of man, that the vision *refers* to the time of the end." ¹⁸Now, as he was speaking with me, I was in a deep sleep with my face to the ground; but he touched me, and stood me upright. ¹⁹And he said, "Look, I am making known to you what shall happen in the latter time of the indignation; for at the appointed time the end *shall be.* ²⁰The ram which you saw, having the two horns—*they are* the kings of Media and Persia. ²¹And the male goat *is* the kingdom*ᵃ* of Greece. The large horn that *is* between its eyes *is* the first king. ²²As for the broken *horn* and the four that stood up in its place, four kingdoms shall arise out of that nation, but not with its power.

²³ "And in the latter time of their kingdom,
When the transgressors have reached
their fullness,

A king shall arise,
Having fierce features,
Who understands sinister schemes.
²⁴ His power shall be mighty, but not by his
own power;
He shall destroy fearfully,
And shall prosper and thrive;
He shall destroy the mighty, and *also* the
holy people.

²⁵ "Through his cunning
He shall cause deceit to prosper under his
rule;*ᵃ*
And he shall exalt *himself* in his heart.
He shall destroy many in *their* prosperity.
He shall even rise against the Prince of
princes;
But he shall be broken without *human*
means.*ᵇ*

²⁶ "And the vision of the evenings and
mornings
Which was told is true;
Therefore seal up the vision,
For *it refers* to many days *in the future.*"

²⁷And I, Daniel, fainted and was sick for days; afterward I arose and went about the king's business. I was astonished by the vision, but no one understood it.

DANIEL'S PRAYER FOR THE PEOPLE

¹In the first year of Darius the son of Ahasuerus, of the lineage of the Medes, who was made king over the realm of the Chaldeans— ²in the first year of his reign I, Daniel, understood by the books the number of the years *specified* by the word of the LORD through Jeremiah the prophet, that He would accomplish seventy years in the desolations of Jerusalem. ³Then I set my face toward the Lord God to make request by prayer and supplications, with fasting, sackcloth, and ashes. ⁴And I prayed to the LORD my God, and made confession, and said, "O Lord, great and awesome God, who keeps His covenant and mercy with those who love Him, and with those who keep His commandments, ⁵we have sinned and committed iniquity, we have done wickedly and rebelled, even by departing from Your precepts and Your judgments. ⁶Neither have we heeded Your servants the prophets, who spoke in Your name to our kings and our princes, to our fathers and all the people of the land. ⁷O Lord, righteousness

---

8:21 *ᵃ*Literally *king,* representing his kingdom (compare 7:17, 23)   **8:25** *ᵃ*Literally *hand* *ᵇ*Literally *hand*

belongs to You, but to us shame of face, as *it is* this day—to the men of Judah, to the inhabitants of Jerusalem and all Israel, those near and those far off in all the countries to which You have driven them, because of the unfaithfulness which they have committed against You.

8"O Lord, to us *belongs* shame of face, to our kings, our princes, and our fathers, because we have sinned against You. 9To the Lord our God *belong* mercy and forgiveness, though we have rebelled against Him. 10We have not obeyed the voice of the LORD our God, to walk in His laws, which He set before us by His servants the prophets. 11Yes, all Israel has transgressed Your law, and has departed so as not to obey Your voice; therefore the curse and the oath written in the Law of Moses the servant of God have been poured out on us, because we have sinned against Him. 12And He has confirmed His words, which He spoke against us and against our judges who judged us, by bringing upon us a great disaster; for under the whole heaven such has never been done as what has been done to Jerusalem.

13"As *it is* written in the Law of Moses, all this disaster has come upon us; yet we have not made our prayer before the LORD our God, that we might turn from our iniquities and understand Your truth. 14Therefore the LORD has kept the disaster in mind, and brought it upon us; for the LORD our God *is* righteous in all the works which He does, though we have not obeyed His voice. 15And now, O Lord our God, who brought Your people out of the land of Egypt with a mighty hand, and made Yourself a name, as *it is* this day—we have sinned, we have done wickedly!

16"O Lord, according to all Your righteousness, I pray, let Your anger and Your fury be turned away from Your city Jerusalem, Your holy mountain; because for our sins, and for the iniquities of our fathers, Jerusalem and Your people *are* a reproach to all *those* around us. 17Now therefore, our God, hear the prayer of Your servant, and his supplications, and for the Lord's sake cause Your face to shine on Your sanctuary, which is desolate. 18O my God, incline Your ear and hear; open Your eyes and see our desolations, and the city which is called by Your name; for we do not present our supplications before You because of our righteous deeds, but because of Your great mercies. 19O Lord, hear! O Lord, forgive! O Lord, listen and act! Do not delay for Your own sake, my God, for Your city and Your people are called by Your name."

THE SEVENTY-WEEKS PROPHECY

20Now while I *was* speaking, praying, and confessing my sin and the sin of my people Israel, and presenting my supplication before the LORD my God for the holy mountain of my God, 21yes, while I *was* speaking in prayer, the man Gabriel, whom I had seen in the vision at the beginning, being caused to fly swiftly, reached me about the time of the evening offering. 22And he informed *me*, and talked with me, and said, "O Daniel, I have now come forth to give you skill to understand. 23At the beginning of your supplications the command went out, and I have come to tell *you*, for you *are* greatly beloved; therefore consider the matter, and understand the vision:

24   "Seventy weeks*a* are determined
    For your people and for your holy city,
    To finish the transgression,
    To make an end of*b* sins,
    To make reconciliation for iniquity,
    To bring in everlasting righteousness,
    To seal up vision and prophecy,
    And to anoint the Most Holy.

25   "Know therefore and understand,
    That from the going forth of the command
    To restore and build Jerusalem
    Until Messiah the Prince,
    There shall be seven weeks and sixty-two weeks;
    The street*a* shall be built again, and the wall,*b*
    Even in troublesome times.

> "And I prayed to the LORD my God, and made confession, and said, 'O Lord, great and awesome God, who keeps His covenant and mercy with those who love Him, and with those who keep His commandments.' "
> (Daniel 9:4)

9:24 *a*Literally *sevens*, and so throughout the chapter *b*Following Qere, Septuagint, Syriac, and Vulgate; Kethib and Theodotion read *To seal up.* **9:25** *a*Or *open square* *b*Or *moat*

26 "And after the sixty-two weeks
    Messiah shall be cut off, but not for
        Himself;
    And the people of the prince who is to
        come
    Shall destroy the city and the sanctuary.
    The end of it *shall be* with a flood,
    And till the end of the war desolations
        are determined.
27 Then he shall confirm a covenant with
        many for one week;
    But in the middle of the week
    He shall bring an end to sacrifice and
        offering.
    And on the wing of abominations shall
        be one who makes desolate,
    Even until the consummation, which is
        determined,
    Is poured out on the desolate."

VISION OF THE GLORIOUS MAN

¹In the third year of Cyrus king of Persia a message was revealed to Daniel, whose name was called Belteshazzar. The message *was* true, but the appointed time *was* long;*ᵃ* and he understood the message, and had understanding of the vision. ²In those days I, Daniel, was mourning three full weeks. ³I ate no pleasant food, no meat or wine came into my mouth, nor did I anoint myself at all, till three whole weeks were fulfilled.

⁴Now on the twenty-fourth day of the first month, as I was by the side of the great river, that *is,* the Tigris,*ᵃ* ⁵I lifted my eyes and looked, and behold, a certain man clothed in linen, whose waist *was* girded with gold of Uphaz!

⁶His body *was* like beryl, his face like the appearance of lightning, his eyes like torches of fire, his arms and feet like burnished bronze in color, and the sound of his words like the voice of a multitude.

⁷And I, Daniel, alone saw the vision, for the men who were with me did not see the vision; but a great terror fell upon them, so that they fled to hide themselves. ⁸Therefore I was left alone when I saw this great vision, and no strength remained in me; for my vigor was turned to frailty in me, and I retained no strength. ⁹Yet I heard the sound of his words; and while I heard the sound of his words I was in a deep sleep on my face, with my face to the ground.

PROPHECIES CONCERNING PERSIA AND GREECE

¹⁰Suddenly, a hand touched me, which made me tremble on my knees and *on* the palms of my hands. ¹¹And he said to me, "O Daniel, man greatly beloved, understand the words that I speak to you, and stand upright, for I have now been sent to you." While he was speaking this word to me, I stood trembling.

¹²Then he said to me, "Do not fear, Daniel, for from the first day that you set your heart to understand, and to humble yourself before your God, your words were heard; and I have come because of your words. ¹³But the prince of the kingdom of Persia withstood me twenty-one days; and behold, Michael, one of the chief princes, came to help me, for I had been left alone there with the kings of Persia. ¹⁴Now I have come to make you understand what will happen to your people in the latter days, for the vision *refers* to *many* days yet *to come.*"

¹⁵When he had spoken such words to me, I turned my face toward the ground and became speechless. ¹⁶And suddenly, *one* having the likeness of the sons*ᵃ* of men touched my lips; then I opened my mouth and spoke, saying to him who stood before me, "My lord, because of the vision my sorrows have overwhelmed me, and I have retained no strength. ¹⁷For how can this servant of my lord talk with you, my lord? As for me, no strength remains in me now, nor is any breath left in me."

¹⁸Then again, *the one* having the likeness of a man touched me and strengthened me. ¹⁹And he said, "O man greatly beloved, fear not! Peace *be* to you; be strong, yes, be strong!"

10:1 *ᵃ*Or *and of great conflict*   **10:4** *ᵃ*Hebrew *Hiddekel*   **10:16** *ᵃ*Theodotion and Vulgate read *the son;* Septuagint reads *a hand.*

On the Edge

Suddenly a hand touched me, which made me tremble on my knees and on the palms of my hands. And he said to me, "O Daniel, man greatly beloved, understand the words that I speak to you, and stand upright, for I have now been sent to you" (Dan. 10:10, 11a).

What a powerful story! Here we have Daniel entranced in a vision from God. When it was over, he fell down on his face and went to sleep. All of a sudden, an angel of the Lord lifted him up and told him that he was loved by God. Then several verses later, the angel said it again: "O man greatly beloved, fear not! Peace be to you; be strong, yes, be strong!" (v. 19). And you know what? Daniel was brave and strong. You may be thinking: *If an angel of the Lord woke me up to tell me that, I'd be brave and strong, too.* Well, he already has. It's in this book. God thinks highly of *you!* He wants only the best for you. You're His child. You're His project. He wants to pour out blessings on you. God doesn't need an angel to tell you, because it's in His Word.

It doesn't matter how difficult things seem to your natural mind. You have a supernatural God! You can be brave and strong. In fact, Daniel 11:32 says that "the people who know their God shall be *strong,* and carry out great exploits" (italics added). You must realize right now that you are strong. So get out there and start doing great things for God! After all, you are loved by God. Remember, it doesn't matter what anyone else thinks of you. You're special to God. Don't forget it!

SEE FOR YOURSELF:
Deut. 31:6; Dan. 9:23; 10:18, 19; 2 Tim. 1:7

So when he spoke to me I was strengthened, and said, "Let my lord speak, for you have strengthened me."

²⁰Then he said, "Do you know why I have come to you? And now I must return to fight with the prince of Persia; and when I have gone forth, indeed the prince of Greece will come.

²¹But I will tell you what is noted in the Scripture of Truth. (No one upholds me against these, except Michael your prince.

¹"Also in the first year of Darius the Mede, I, *even* I, stood up to confirm and strengthen him.) ²And now I will tell you the truth: Behold, three more kings will arise in Persia, and the fourth shall be far richer than *them* all; by his strength, through his riches, he shall stir up all against the realm of Greece. ³Then a mighty king shall arise, who shall rule with great dominion, and do according to his will. ⁴And when he has arisen, his kingdom shall be broken up and divided toward the four winds of heaven, but not among his posterity nor according to his dominion with which he ruled; for his kingdom shall be uprooted, even for others besides these.

WARRING KINGS OF NORTH AND SOUTH

⁵"Also the king of the South shall become strong, as well as *one* of his princes; and he shall gain power over him and have dominion. His dominion *shall be* a great dominion. ⁶And at the end of *some* years they shall join forces, for the daughter of the king of the South shall go to the king of the North to make an agreement; but she shall not retain the power of her authority,ᵃ and neither he nor his authorityᵇ shall stand; but she shall be given up, with those who brought her, and with him who begot her, and with him who strengthened her in *those* times. ⁷But from a branch of her roots *one* shall arise in his place, who shall come with an army, enter the fortress of the king of the North, and deal with them and prevail. ⁸And he shall also carry their gods captive to Egypt, with their princesᵃ *and* their precious articles of silver and gold; and he shall continue *more* years than the king of the North.

⁹"Also *the king of the North* shall come to the kingdom of the king of the South, but shall return to his own land. ¹⁰However his sons shall stir up strife, and assemble a multitude of great forces; and *one* shall certainly come and overwhelm and pass through; then he shall return to his fortress and stir up strife.

¹¹"And the king of the South shall be moved with rage, and go out and fight with him, with the king of the North, who shall muster a great multitude; but the multitude shall be given into the hand of his *enemy.* ¹²When he has taken away the multitude, his heart will be lifted up; and he will cast down tens of thousands, but he will not prevail. ¹³For the king of the North will return and muster a multitude greater than the

11:6 ᵃLiterally *arm* ᵇLiterally *arm*   **11:8** ᵃOr *molded images*

former, and shall certainly come at the end of some years with a great army and much equipment.

¹⁴"Now in those times many shall rise up against the king of the South. Also, violent men*ᵃ* of your people shall exalt themselves in fulfillment of the vision, but they shall fall. ¹⁵So the king of the North shall come and build a siege mound, and take a fortified city; and the forces*ᵃ* of the South shall not withstand *him*. Even his choice troops *shall have* no strength to resist. ¹⁶But he who comes against him shall do according to his own will, and no one shall stand against him. He shall stand in the Glorious Land with destruction in his power.*ᵃ*

¹⁷"He shall also set his face to enter with the strength of his whole kingdom, and upright ones*ᵃ* with him; thus shall he do. And he shall give him the daughter of women to destroy it; but she shall not stand *with him*, or be for him. ¹⁸After this he shall turn his face to the coastlands, and shall take many. But a ruler shall bring the reproach against them to an end; and with the reproach removed, he shall turn back on him. ¹⁹Then he shall turn his face toward the fortress of his own land; but he shall stumble and fall, and not be found.

²⁰"There shall arise in his place one who imposes taxes *on* the glorious kingdom; but within a few days he shall be destroyed, but not in anger or in battle. ²¹And in his place shall arise a vile person, to whom they will not give the honor of royalty; but he shall come in peaceably, and seize the kingdom by intrigue. ²²With the force*ᵃ* of a flood they shall be swept away from before him and be broken, and also the prince of the covenant. ²³And after the league *is made* with him he shall act deceitfully, for he shall come up and become strong with a small *number of* people. ²⁴He shall enter peaceably, even into the richest places of the province; and he shall do *what* his fathers have not done, nor his forefathers: he shall disperse among them the plunder, spoil, and riches; and he shall devise his plans against the strongholds, but *only* for a time.

²⁵"He shall stir up his power and his courage against the king of the South with a great army. And the king of the South shall be stirred up to battle with a very great and mighty army; but he shall not stand, for they shall devise plans against him. ²⁶Yes, those who eat of the portion of his delicacies shall destroy him; his army

shall be swept away, and many shall fall down slain. ²⁷Both these kings' hearts *shall be* bent on evil, and they shall speak lies at the same table; but it shall not prosper, for the end *will* still *be* at the appointed time. ²⁸While returning to his land with great riches, his heart shall be *moved* against the holy covenant; so he shall do *damage* and return to his own land.

THE NORTHERN KING'S BLASPHEMIES

²⁹"At the appointed time he shall return and go toward the south; but it shall not be like the former or the latter. ³⁰For ships from Cyprus*ᵃ* shall come against him; therefore he shall be grieved, and return in rage against the holy covenant, and do *damage*.

"So he shall return and show regard for those who forsake the holy covenant. ³¹And forces*ᵃ* shall be mustered by him, and they shall defile the sanctuary fortress; then they shall take away the daily *sacrifices*, and place *there* the abomination of desolation. ³²Those who do wickedly against the covenant he shall corrupt with flattery; but the people who know their God shall be strong, and carry out *great exploits*. ³³And those of the people who understand shall instruct many; yet *for many* days they shall fall by sword and flame, by captivity and plundering. ³⁴Now when they fall, they shall be aided with a little help; but many shall join with them by intrigue. ³⁵And *some* of those of understanding shall fall, to refine them, purify *them*, and make *them* white, *until* the time of the end; because *it is* still for the appointed time.

³⁶"Then the king shall do according to his own will: he shall exalt and magnify himself above every god, shall speak blasphemies against the God of gods, and shall prosper till the wrath has been accomplished; for what has been determined shall be done. ³⁷He shall regard neither the God*ᵃ* of his fathers nor the desire of women, nor regard any god; for he shall exalt himself above *them* all. ³⁸But in their place he shall honor a god of fortresses; and a god which his fathers did not know he shall honor with gold and silver, with precious stones and pleasant things. ³⁹Thus he shall act against the strongest fortresses with a foreign god, which he shall acknowledge, *and* advance *its* glory; and he shall cause them to rule over many, and divide the land for gain.

THE NORTHERN KING'S CONQUESTS

40"At the time of the end the king of the South shall attack him; and the king of the North shall come against him like a whirlwind, with chariots, horsemen, and with many ships; and he shall enter the countries, overwhelm *them*, and pass through. 41He shall also enter the Glorious Land, and many *countries* shall be overthrown; but these shall escape from his hand: Edom, Moab, and the prominent people of Ammon. 42He shall stretch out his hand against the countries, and the land of Egypt shall not escape. 43He shall have power over the treasures of gold and silver, and over all the precious things of Egypt; also the Libyans and Ethiopians *shall follow* at his heels. 44But news from the east and the north shall trouble him; therefore he shall go out with great fury to destroy and annihilate many. 45And he shall plant the tents of his palace between the seas and the glorious holy mountain; yet he shall come to his end, and no one will help him.

PROPHECY OF THE END TIME

1   "At that time Michael shall stand up,
The great prince who stands *watch* over
    the sons of your people;
And there shall be a time of trouble,
Such as never was since there was a
    nation,
Even to that time.
And at that time your people shall be
    delivered,
Every one who is found written in the
    book.
2   And many of those who sleep in the dust
    of the earth shall awake,
Some to everlasting life,
Some to shame *and* everlasting contempt.
3   Those who are wise shall shine

Like the brightness of the firmament,
And those who turn many to
    righteousness
Like the stars forever and ever.

4"But you, Daniel, shut up the words, and seal the book until the time of the end; many shall run to and fro, and knowledge shall increase."

5Then I, Daniel, looked; and there stood two others, one on this riverbank and the other on that riverbank. 6And *one* said to the man clothed in linen, who *was* above the waters of the river, "How long shall the fulfillment of these wonders *be*?"

7Then I heard the man clothed in linen, who *was* above the waters of the river, when he held up his right hand and his left hand to heaven, and swore by Him who lives forever, that *it shall be* for a time, times, and half *a time*; and when the power of the holy people has been completely shattered, all these *things* shall be finished.

8Although I heard, I did not understand. Then I said, "My lord, what *shall be* the end of these *things*?"

9And he said, "Go *your way*, Daniel, for the words *are* closed up and sealed till the time of the end. 10Many shall be purified, made white, and refined, but the wicked shall do wickedly; and none of the wicked shall understand, but the wise shall understand.

11"And from the time *that* the daily *sacrifice* is taken away, and the abomination of desolation is set up, *there shall be* one thousand two hundred and ninety days. 12Blessed *is* he who waits, and comes to the one thousand three hundred and thirty-five days.

13"But you, go *your way* till the end; for you shall rest, and will arise to your inheritance at the end of the days."

DANIEL made a difference

Adults don't usually expect kids to be wise. That's why a young person with wisdom makes such an impression. Daniel proved young people can be wise. And he did it in a very difficult situation.

Daniel was taken hostage when his nation (Judah) was defeated in war. Young men were taken to Babylon to serve as slaves. But Daniel and his friends made an impression on their captors by their behavior and qualifications. They were assigned to training in the palace.

Because Daniel had already dedicated his life to God, he was faced with some tough choices. He had to decide how he was going to take care of himself. For example, he chose not to eat the rich foods from the king's table. He believed that compromising his diet would lead to other compromises. But he also showed wisdom in the way he acted. His decision wasn't rude or selfish. He found a way to accomplish his goal while honoring those to whom he was responsible.

Cutting Edge

YOU can, too!

Like Daniel, refuse to do anything based on the claim that "everybody" is doing it. Those who are not willing to stand alone and be different if necessary won't make a difference with their lives, either. Even decisions about what we eat and how we work with those around us say a lot about how much we really want to honor God in the way we live. Anyone who tells you it doesn't matter how you live doesn't care about what God thinks. It's best to model your life after people who do care about His plans for them. That will help you be a better model, too, for everyone around you.

Want to know more? Read more of Daniel's early years in Daniel 1:1–21.

CONTENT The Hebrew people struggled with idolatry throughout their whole existence. Whether they were wandering a desert, exiled in Babylon, or happy at home, they had a real problem being faithful to God. God warned them through leaders and prophets and kings, but it never failed—along would come a false god to worship and off they would go.

God used the prophet Hosea to give the people an object lesson. He asked Hosea to do something outlandish—even crazy—so the people would know how God felt about idolatry. God told Hosea to marry a prostitute, a hooker, a woman who stays with men for money. Believe it or not, Hosea did it. Her name was Gomer.

As you can guess, Gomer was not faithful to Hosea. She left him. He brought her back. She wandered away. He loved her still.

God commanded Hosea to do this because He wanted to show Hosea's people that they had treated God like Gomer treated Hosea. They wandered away, but God brought them back. They worshiped other gods, but God loved them still. God wanted them to see His love and learn to have faithful hearts.

Purpose   God remains committed to us even when we are unfaithful to Him.

Theme   Return to God

Date of writing   750–720 B.C.

¹The word of the LORD that came to Hosea the son of Beeri, in the days of Uzziah, Jotham, Ahaz, *and* Hezekiah, kings of Judah, and in the days of Jeroboam the son of Joash, king of Israel.

THE FAMILY OF HOSEA

²When the LORD began to speak by Hosea, the LORD said to Hosea:

"Go, take yourself a
   wife of harlotry
And children of
   harlotry,
For the land has
   committed great
   harlotry
By departing from
   the LORD."

³So he went and took Gomer the daughter of Diblaim, and she conceived and bore him a son. ⁴Then the LORD said to him:

"Call his name Jezreel,
   For in a little *while*
I will avenge the bloodshed of Jezreel on
   the house of Jehu,
And bring an end to the kingdom of the
   house of Israel.
5   It shall come to pass in that day
   That I will break the bow of Israel in the
   Valley of Jezreel."

"Go, take yourself a wife of harlotry and children of harlotry, for the land has committed great harlotry by departing from the LORD."
(Hosea 1:2b)

⁶And she conceived again and bore a daughter. Then *God* said to him:

"Call her name Lo-Ruhamah,*ᵃ*
   For I will no longer have mercy on the
      house of Israel,
   But I will utterly take them away.*ᵇ*
7   Yet I will have mercy on the house of
      Judah,
         Will save them by the
            LORD their God,
         And will not save
            them by bow,
         Nor by sword or
            battle,
         By horses or
            horsemen."

⁸Now when she had weaned Lo-Ruhamah, she conceived and bore a son. ⁹Then *God* said:

"Call his name Lo-Ammi,*ᵃ*
   For you *are* not My people,
   And I will not be your *God.*

THE RESTORATION OF ISRAEL

10   "Yet the number of the children of Israel
   Shall be as the sand of the sea,
   Which cannot be measured or numbered.
   And it shall come to pass
   In the place where it was said to them,
   'You *are* not My people,'*ᵃ*
   There it shall be said to them,
   '*You are* sons of the living God.'
11   Then the children of Judah and the
      children of Israel
   Shall be gathered together,
   And appoint for themselves one head;
   And they shall come up out of the land,
   For great *will be* the day of Jezreel!
1   Say to your brethren, 'My people,'*ᵃ*
   And to your sisters, 'Mercy*ᵇ* *is* shown.'

GOD'S UNFAITHFUL PEOPLE

2   "Bring charges against your mother, bring
      charges;
   For she *is* not My wife, nor *am* I her
      Husband!
   Let her put away her harlotries from her
      sight,
   And her adulteries from between her
      breasts;

WHAT'S IT MEAN?

The Israel that existed during Hosea's time was actually two separate nations. The northern kingdom, which was called Israel, had Samaria as its capital. The southern kingdom, which was called Judah, had Jerusalem as its capital. The descendants of David ruled Judah from Jerusalem, which also served as the nation's religious center.

Hosea 1:1

1:6 *ᵃ*Literally *No-Mercy* *ᵇ*Or *That I may forgive them at all* 1:9 *ᵃ*Literally *Not-My-People* 1:10 *ᵃ*Hebrew *lo-ammi* (compare verse 9) 2:1 *ᵃ*Hebrew *Ammi* (compare 1:9, 10) *ᵇ*Hebrew *Ruhamah* (compare 1:6)

3 Lest I strip her naked
And expose her, as in the day she was
born,
And make her like a wilderness,
And set her like a dry land,
And slay her with thirst.

WHAT'S IT MEAN?

Baal was the favorite god of the people who lived in Canaan before the Israelites. The Canaanites believed that Baal was responsible for making things fertile and productive, including crops, livestock, and humans. When the Israelites got to Canaan, they, too, started worshiping Baal, as well as several other Canaanite gods. Shrines to Baal were usually located on hilltops or in groves of trees. Statues of Baal were often made of gold and silver.

Hosea 2:8

4 "I will not have mercy on her children,
For they *are* the children of harlotry.
5 For their mother has played the harlot;
She who conceived them has behaved
shamefully.

For she said, 'I will go after my lovers,
Who give *me* my bread and my water,
My wool and my linen,
My oil and my drink.'

6 "Therefore, behold,
I will hedge up your way with thorns,
And wall her in,
So that she cannot find her paths.
7 She will chase her lovers,
But not overtake them;
Yes, she will seek them, but not find *them*.
Then she will say,
'I will go and return to my first husband,
For then *it was* better for me than now.'
8 For she did not know
That I gave her grain, new wine, and oil,
And multiplied her silver and gold—
Which they prepared for Baal.

9 "Therefore I will return and take away
My grain in its time
And My new wine in its season,
And will take back My wool and My
linen,
Given to cover her nakedness.
10 Now I will uncover her lewdness in the
sight of her lovers,
And no one shall deliver her from My
hand.
11 I will also cause all her mirth to cease,
Her feast days,
Her New Moons,

Promise   HE PROMISES YOU WILL KNOW HIM.

"And it shall be, in that day," says the LORD, *"that you will call Me 'My Husband,' and no longer call Me 'My Master,'. . . I will betroth you to Me forever; yes, I will betroth you to Me in righteousness and justice, in lovingkindness and mercy; I will betroth you to Me in faithfulness, and you shall know the LORD"* (Hos. 2:16, 19, 20).

How do you know who God is? He says that you will know because He will give you justice, righteousness, mercy, lovingkindness, and faithfulness. He says that He will be as a husband and not as a master. In other words, He will treat you with love and tenderness and not with arrogance or harshness. He is not there to boss you around and make you work like a dog. He is there to be in love with you, to give you kindness when you don't deserve it, to be faithful to you when you aren't faithful to Him, to help you live the way He wants you to, to help you reach your full potential, to know the true goodness of your heart when you do something you shouldn't, to encourage you, to understand when no one else can. It's this *unconditional love* that helps you know Him.

SEE FOR YOURSELF:
2 Chr. 5:13; Ps. 91:14; Jer. 31:3; Hos. 14:4; 1 John 3:1

Her Sabbaths—
All her appointed feasts.

12 "And I will destroy her vines and her fig
trees,
Of which she has said,
'These *are* my wages that my lovers have
given me.'
So I will make them a forest,
And the beasts of the field shall eat them.

13 I will punish her
For the days of the Baals to which she
burned incense.
She decked herself with her earrings and
jewelry,
And went after her lovers;
But Me she forgot," says the LORD.

GOD'S MERCY ON HIS PEOPLE

14 "Therefore, behold, I will allure her,
Will bring her into the wilderness,
And speak comfort to her.

15 I will give her her vineyards from there,
And the Valley of Achor as a door of
hope;
She shall sing there,
As in the days of her youth,
As in the day when she came up from
the land of Egypt.

16 "And it shall be, in that day,"
Says the LORD,
"*That* you will call Me 'My Husband,'*a*
And no longer call Me 'My Master,'*b*

17 For I will take from her mouth the names
of the Baals,
And they shall be remembered by their
name no more.

18 In that day I will make a covenant for
them
With the beasts of the field,
With the birds of the air,
And *with* the creeping things of the
ground.
Bow and sword of battle I will shatter
from the earth,
To make them lie down safely.

19 "I will betroth you to Me forever;
Yes, I will betroth you to Me
In righteousness and justice,
In lovingkindness and mercy;

20 I will betroth you to Me in faithfulness,
And you shall know the LORD.

21 "It shall come to pass in that day
That I will answer," says the LORD;
"I will answer the heavens,
And they shall answer the earth.

22 The earth shall answer
With grain,
With new wine,
And with oil;
They shall answer Jezreel.*a*

23 Then I will sow her for Myself in the
earth,
And I will have mercy on *her who had* not
obtained mercy;*a*
Then I will say to *those who were* not My
people,*b*
'You *are* My people!'
And they shall say, '*You are* my God!' "

ISRAEL WILL RETURN TO GOD

1Then the LORD said to me, "Go again, love a
woman *who is* loved by a lover*a* and is committing adultery, just like the love of the LORD for
the children of Israel, who look to other gods
and love *the* raisin cakes *of the pagans*."
2So I bought her for myself for fifteen *shekels*
of silver, and one and one-half homers of barley. 3And I said to her, "You shall stay with me
many days; you shall not play the harlot, nor
shall you have a man—so, too, *will I be* toward
you."

WHAT'S IT MEAN?

Ever had a raisin cake? If so, did you like it? In
ancient times, cakes made of dried raisins were very
popular. In fact, some Israelites used raisin cakes in
their pagan rituals as they worshiped a goddess
known as the "queen of heaven."
Hosea 3:1

4For the children of Israel shall abide many
days without king or prince, without sacrifice
or *sacred* pillar, without ephod or teraphim. 5Af-
terward the children of Israel shall return and
seek the LORD their God and David their king.
They shall fear the LORD and His goodness in
the latter days.

2:16 *a*Hebrew *Ishi* *b*Hebrew *Baali* **2:22** *a*Literally *God Will Sow* **2:23** *a*Hebrew *lo-ruhamah* *b*Hebrew
lo-ammi **3:1** *a*Literally *friend* or *husband*

GOD'S CHARGE AGAINST ISRAEL

1 Hear the word of the LORD,
You children of Israel,
For the LORD *brings* a charge against the
inhabitants of the land:

"There is no truth or mercy
Or knowledge of God in the land.
2 *By* swearing and lying,
Killing and stealing and committing
adultery,
They break all restraint,
With bloodshed upon bloodshed.
3 Therefore the land will mourn;
And everyone who dwells there will
waste away
With the beasts of the field
And the birds of the air;
Even the fish of the sea will be taken
away.

4 "Now let no man contend, or rebuke
another;
For your people *are* like those who
contend with the priest.
5 Therefore you shall stumble in the day;
The prophet also shall stumble with you
in the night;
And I will destroy your mother.
6 My people are destroyed for lack of
knowledge.
Because you have rejected knowledge,
I also will reject you from being priest
for Me;
Because you have
forgotten the law of
your God,
I also will forget your
children.

7 "The more they increased,
The more they sinned
against Me;
I will change[a] their glory[b] into shame.
8 They eat up the sin of My people;
They set their heart on their iniquity.
9 And it shall be: like people, like priest.
So I will punish them for their ways,
And reward them for their deeds.
10 For they shall eat, but not have enough;
They shall commit harlotry, but not
increase;

Because they have ceased obeying the
LORD.

THE IDOLATRY OF ISRAEL

11 "Harlotry, wine, and new wine enslave the
heart.
12 My people ask counsel from their
wooden *idols,*
And their staff informs them.
For the spirit of harlotry has caused *them*
to stray,
And they have played the harlot against
their God.
13 They offer sacrifices on the mountaintops,
And burn incense on the hills,
Under oaks, poplars, and terebinths,
Because their shade *is* good.
Therefore your daughters commit
harlotry,
And your brides commit adultery.

14 "I will not punish your daughters when
they commit harlotry,
Nor your brides when they commit
adultery;
For *the men* themselves go apart with
harlots,
And offer sacrifices with a ritual harlot.[a]
Therefore people *who* do not understand
will be trampled.

15 "Though you, Israel, play the harlot,
Let not Judah offend.
Do not come up to Gilgal,
Nor go up to Beth Aven,
Nor swear an oath, *saying,* 'As the LORD
lives'—

16 "For Israel is stubborn
Like a stubborn calf;
Now the LORD will let them forage
Like a lamb in open country.

17 "Ephraim *is* joined to idols,
Let him alone.
18 Their drink is rebellion,
They commit harlotry continually.
Her rulers dearly love dishonor.[a]
19 The wind has wrapped her up in its
wings,
And they shall be ashamed because of
their sacrifices.

DISOBEDIENCE
What if we neglect God's word? (4:6)

4:7 [a]Following Masoretic Text, Septuagint, and Vulgate; scribal tradition, Syriac, and Targum read *They will change.* [b]Following Masoretic Text, Septuagint, Syriac, Targum, and Vulgate; scribal tradition reads *My glory.* **4:14** [a]Compare Deuteronomy 23:18 **4:18** [a]Hebrew is difficult; a Jewish tradition reads *Her rulers shamefully love, 'Give!'*

IMPENDING JUDGMENT ON ISRAEL AND JUDAH

1 "Hear this, O priests!
Take heed, O house of Israel!
Give ear, O house of the king!
For yours *is* the judgment,
Because you have been a snare to
Mizpah
And a net spread on Tabor.
2 The revolters are deeply involved in
slaughter,
Though I rebuke them all.
3 I know Ephraim,
And Israel is not hidden from Me;
For now, O Ephraim, you commit
harlotry;
Israel is defiled.

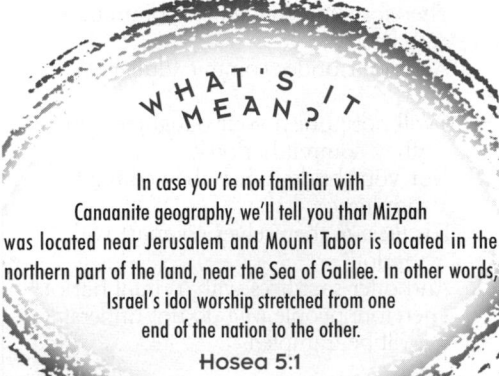

WHAT'S IT MEAN?

In case you're not familiar with
Canaanite geography, we'll tell you that Mizpah
was located near Jerusalem and Mount Tabor is located in the
northern part of the land, near the Sea of Galilee. In other words,
Israel's idol worship stretched from one
end of the nation to the other.

Hosea 5:1

4 "They do not direct their deeds
Toward turning to their God,
For the spirit of harlotry is in their midst,
And they do not know the LORD.
5 The pride of Israel testifies to his face;
Therefore Israel and Ephraim stumble in
their iniquity;
Judah also stumbles with them.

6 "With their flocks and herds
They shall go to seek the LORD,
But they will not find *Him*;
He has withdrawn Himself from them.
7 They have dealt treacherously with the
LORD,
For they have begotten pagan children.
Now a New Moon shall devour them
and their heritage.

8 "Blow the ram's horn in Gibeah,
The trumpet in Ramah!
Cry aloud *at* Beth Aven,

'*Look* behind you, O Benjamin!'
9 Ephraim shall be desolate in the day of
rebuke;
Among the tribes of Israel I make known
what is sure.

10 "The princes of Judah are like those who
remove a landmark;
I will pour out my wrath on them like
water.
11 Ephraim is oppressed *and* broken in
judgment,
Because he willingly walked by *human*
precept.
12 Therefore I *will be* to Ephraim like a
moth,
And to the house of Judah like rottenness.

13 "When Ephraim saw his sickness,
And Judah *saw* his wound,
Then Ephraim went to Assyria
And sent to King Jareb;
Yet he cannot cure you,
Nor heal you of your wound.
14 For I *will be* like a lion to Ephraim,
And like a young lion to the house of
Judah.
I, *even* I, will tear *them* and go away;
I will take *them* away, and no one shall
rescue.
15 I will return again to My place
Till they acknowledge their offense.
Then they will seek My face;
In their affliction they will earnestly seek
Me."

A CALL TO REPENTANCE

1 Come, and let us return to the LORD;
For He has torn, but He will heal us;
He has stricken, but He will bind us up.
2 After two days He will revive us;
On the third day He will raise us up,
That we may live in His sight.
3 Let us know,
Let us pursue the knowledge of the LORD.
His going forth is established as the
morning;
He will come to us like the rain,
Like the latter *and* former rain to the
earth.

IMPENITENCE OF ISRAEL AND JUDAH

4 "O Ephraim, what shall I do to you?
O Judah, what shall I do to you?
For your faithfulness is like a morning
cloud,
And like the early dew it goes away.

5   Therefore I have hewn *them* by the
        prophets,
    I have slain them by the words of My
        mouth;
    And your judgments *are like* light *that*
        goes forth.
6   For I desire mercy and not sacrifice,
    And the knowledge of God more than
        burnt offerings.

7   "But like men[a] they transgressed the
        covenant;
    There they dealt treacherously with Me.
8   Gilead *is* a city of evildoers
    And defiled with blood.
9   As bands of robbers lie in wait for a man,
    So the company of priests murder on the
        way to Shechem;
    Surely they commit lewdness.
10 I have seen a horrible thing in the house
        of Israel:
    There *is* the harlotry of Ephraim;
    Israel is defiled.
11 Also, O Judah, a harvest is appointed for
        you,
    When I return the captives of My people.

1   "When I would have healed Israel,
    Then the iniquity of Ephraim was
        uncovered,
    And the wickedness of Samaria.
    For they have committed fraud;
    A thief comes in;
    A band of robbers takes spoil outside.
2   They do not consider in their hearts
    That I remember all their wickedness;
    Now their own deeds have surrounded
        them;
    They are before My face.
3   They make a king glad with their
        wickedness,
    And princes with their lies.

4   "They *are* all adulterers.
    Like an oven heated by a baker—
    He ceases stirring *the fire* after kneading
        the dough,
    Until it is leavened.
5   In the day of our king
    Princes have made *him* sick, inflamed
        with wine;
    He stretched out his hand with scoffers.
6   They prepare their heart like an oven,
    While they lie in wait;

    Their baker[a] sleeps all night;
    In the morning it burns like a flaming fire.
7   They are all hot, like an oven,
    And have devoured their judges;
    All their kings have fallen.
    None among them calls upon Me.

8   "Ephraim has mixed himself among the
        peoples;
    Ephraim is a cake unturned.
9   Aliens have devoured his strength,
    But he does not know *it;*
    Yes, gray hairs are here and there on him,
    Yet he does not know *it.*
10 And the pride of Israel testifies to his face,
    But they do not return to the LORD their
        God,
    Nor seek Him for all this.

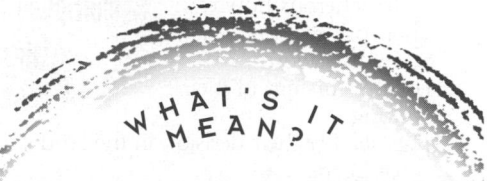

WHAT'S IT MEAN?

For a while, Israel paid "protection money"—in the
form of taxes—to Assyria to keep them from attacking.
When the Israelites got tired of giving their hard earned money to
a foreign king, they decided to team up with the Egyptians and
fight Assyria. In 722 B.C., the Assyrians responded by attacking
Samaria, the capital of the northern kingdom, and taking the
people of Israel captive. The northern kingdom
never recovered from the devastation.
Hosea 7:11

FUTILE RELIANCE ON THE NATIONS

11 "Ephraim also is like a silly dove, without
        sense—
    They call to Egypt,
    They go to Assyria.
12 Wherever they go, I will spread My net
        on them;
    I will bring them down
        like birds of the air;
    I will chastise them
    According to what their
        congregation has
        heard.

SIN

What does
God think of
our sin?
(7:13)

13 "Woe to them, for they have fled from Me!

6:7 [a]Or *like Adam*   **7:6** [a]Following Masoretic Text and Vulgate; Syriac and Targum read *Their anger;*
Septuagint reads *Ephraim.*

Destruction to them,
Because they have transgressed against Me!
Though I redeemed them,
Yet they have spoken lies against Me.

14 They did not cry out to Me with their
    heart
    When they wailed upon their beds.

"They assemble together for*a* grain and
    new wine,
They rebel against Me;*b*
15 Though I disciplined *and*
    strengthened their arms,
Yet they devise evil
    against Me;
16 They return, *but* not to
    the Most High;*a*
They are like a
    treacherous bow.
Their princes shall fall
    by the sword
For the cursings of their
    tongue.
This *shall be* their derision in the land
    of Egypt.

THE APOSTASY OF ISRAEL

1 "*Set* the trumpet*a* to your mouth!
    He shall come like an eagle against the
    house of the LORD,
    Because they have transgressed My
    covenant
    And rebelled against My law.
2 Israel will cry to Me,

> "For Israel has forgotten his Maker, and has built temples; Judah also has multiplied fortified cities."
> (Hosea 8:14a)

WHAT'S IT MEAN?

The "calf" in this verse was probably an idol that people worshiped in Samaria. The capital city of the northern kingdom had the dubious distinction of being the center of the nation's pagan worship. Calves and bulls were especially popular idols in ancient times. People believed the animals symbolized fertility.

Hosea 8:5

'My God, we know You!'
Israel has rejected the good;
The enemy will pursue him.

4 "They set up kings, but not by Me;
    They made princes, but I did not
    acknowledge *them*.
    From their silver and gold
    They made idols for themselves—
    That they might be cut off.
5   Your calf is rejected,
        O Samaria!
    My anger is aroused
        against them—
    How long until they
        attain to innocence?
6 For from Israel *is* even
        this:
    A workman made it,
        and it *is* not God;
    But the calf of Samaria
        shall be broken to
        pieces.

7 "They sow the wind,
    And reap the whirlwind.
    The stalk has no bud;
    It shall never produce meal.
    If it should produce,
    Aliens would swallow it up.
8 Israel is swallowed up;
    Now they are among the Gentiles
    Like a vessel in which *is* no pleasure.
9 For they have gone up to Assyria,
    Like a wild donkey alone by itself;
    Ephraim has hired lovers.
10 Yes, though they have hired among the
        nations,
    Now I will gather them;
    And they shall sorrow a little,*a*
    Because of the burden*b* of the king of
        princes.

11 "Because Ephraim has made many altars
        for sin,
    They have become for him altars for
        sinning.
12 I have written for him the great things of
        My law,
    But they were considered a strange thing.
13 *For* the sacrifices of My offerings they
        sacrifice flesh and eat *it*,

7:14 *a*Following Masoretic Text and Targum; Vulgate reads *thought upon*; Septuagint reads *slashed themselves for* (compare 1 Kings 18:28). *b*Following Masoretic Text, Syriac, and Targum; Septuagint omits *They rebel against Me*; Vulgate reads *They departed from Me.*   **7:16** *a*Or *upward*   **8:1** *a*Hebrew *shophar*, ram's horn   **8:10** *a*Or *begin to diminish* *b*Or *oracle*

But the LORD does not accept them.
Now He will remember their iniquity and
  punish their sins.
They shall return to Egypt.

14 "For Israel has forgotten his Maker,
  And has built temples;[a]
  Judah also has multiplied fortified cities;
  But I will send fire upon his cities,
  And it shall devour his palaces."

JUDGMENT OF ISRAEL'S SIN

1   Do not rejoice, O Israel, with joy like *other*
      peoples,
    For you have played the harlot against
      your God.
    You have made love *for* hire on every
      threshing floor.
2   The threshing floor and the winepress
    Shall not feed them,
    And the new wine shall fail in her.

WHAT'S IT MEAN?

The harvest season in Israel was a time of celebration. Unfortunately for them, the Israelites chose to honor Baal at their celebrations instead of the Lord God, who had provided for the people's needs. The threshing floors of Israel, the places where edible kernels of grain were separated from the rest of the plant, were usually located on high ground, as were shrines to Baal. As you might imagine, the practices at the two sites were often combined.
Hosea 9:1

3   They shall not dwell in the LORD's land,
    But Ephraim shall return to Egypt,
    And shall eat unclean *things* in Assyria.
4   They shall not offer wine *offerings* to the
      LORD,
    Nor shall their sacrifices be pleasing to
      Him.
    It shall be like bread of mourners to them;
    All who eat it shall be defiled.
    For their bread *shall be* for their *own* life;
    It shall not come into the house of the
      LORD.

5   What will you do in the appointed day,
    And in the day of the feast of the LORD?
6   For indeed they are gone because of
      destruction.
    Egypt shall gather them up;
    Memphis shall bury them.
    Nettles shall possess their valuables of
      silver;
    Thorns *shall be* in their tents.

WHAT'S IT MEAN?

Memphis—the city in Egypt, not Tennessee—was known for its pyramids and tombs, not to mention the Sphinx. Located on the west bank of the Nile River, about thirteen miles from Cairo, the city was destroyed in the Middle Ages.
Hosea 9:6

7   The days of punishment have come;
    The days of recompense have come.
    Israel knows!
    The prophet *is* a fool,
    The spiritual man *is* insane,
    Because of the greatness of your iniquity
      and great enmity.
8   The watchman of Ephraim *is* with my
      God;
    But the prophet *is* a fowler's[a] snare in all
      his ways—
    Enmity in the house of his God.
9   They are deeply corrupted,
    As in the days of Gibeah.
    He will remember their iniquity;
    He will punish their sins.

10 "I found Israel
    Like grapes in the wilderness;
    I saw your fathers
    As the firstfruits on the fig tree in its first
      season.
    But they went to Baal Peor,
    And separated themselves *to that*
      shame;
    They became an abomination like the
      thing they loved.

8:14 [a]Or *palaces*   9:8 [a]That is, one who catches birds in a trap or snare

11 As for Ephraim, their glory shall fly away
   like a bird—
   No birth, no pregnancy, and no
     conception!
12 Though they bring up their children,
   Yet I will bereave them to the last man.
   Yes, woe to them when I depart from
     them!
13 Just as I saw Ephraim like Tyre, planted in
   a pleasant place,
   So Ephraim will bring out his children to
     the murderer."

14 Give them, O LORD—
   What will You give?
   Give them a miscarrying womb
   And dry breasts!

15 "All their wickedness is in Gilgal,
   For there I hated them.
   Because of the evil of their deeds
   I will drive them from My house;
   I will love them no more.
   All their princes are rebellious.
16 Ephraim is stricken,
   Their root is dried up;
   They shall bear no fruit.
   Yes, were they to bear children,
   I would kill the darlings of their womb."

17 My God will cast them away,
   Because they did not obey Him;
   And they shall be wanderers among the
     nations.

ISRAEL'S SIN AND CAPTIVITY

1 Israel empties his vine;
   He brings forth fruit for himself.
   According to the multitude of his fruit
   He has increased the altars;
   According to the bounty of his land
   They have embellished his sacred pillars.
2 Their heart is divided;
   Now they are held guilty.
   He will break down their altars;
   He will ruin their sacred pillars.

3 For now they say,
  "We have no king,
   Because we did not fear the LORD.
   And as for a king, what would he do for
     us?"
4 They have spoken words,
   Swearing falsely in making a covenant.

Thus judgment springs up like hemlock in
   the furrows of the field.

5 The inhabitants of Samaria fear
   Because of the calf[a] of Beth Aven.
   For its people mourn for it,
   And its priests shriek for it—
   Because its glory has departed from it.
6 The idol also shall be carried to Assyria
   As a present for King Jareb.
   Ephraim shall receive shame,
   And Israel shall be ashamed of his own
     counsel.

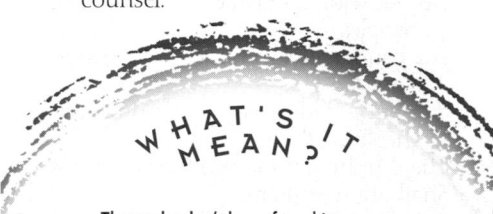

WHAT'S IT MEAN?

Those who don't learn from history are
destined to repeat it. To prove the point, we offer the
example of Jeroboam, Solomon's son. This shortsighted king decided
to have two golden calves made. These idols were then placed in
Bethel and Dan to make them convenient for worshipers in the
northern kingdom. If the whole golden calf thing sounds familiar,
it's because Aaron made the same mistake—committed the same
sin—centuries earlier while Moses was on Mount Sinai talking to
God. Would it surprise you to learn that God was every bit as angry
at Jeroboam and his followers as He was
at Aaron and his followers?
Hosea 10:5

7 As for Samaria, her king is cut off
   Like a twig on the water.
8 Also the high places of Aven, the sin of
     Israel,
   Shall be destroyed.
   The thorn and thistle shall grow on their
     altars;
   They shall say to the mountains, "Cover
     us!"
   And to the hills, "Fall on us!"

9 "O Israel, you have sinned from the days
     of Gibeah;
   There they stood.
   The battle in Gibeah against the children
     of iniquity[a]

10:5 [a]Literally calves   10:9 [a]So read many Hebrew manuscripts, Septuagint, and Vulgate; Masoretic Text reads unruliness.

10   Did not overtake them.
When *it is* My desire, I will chasten them.
Peoples shall be gathered against them
When I bind them for their two
     transgressions.*a*

11   Ephraim *is* a trained heifer
That loves to thresh *grain;*
But I harnessed her fair neck,
I will make Ephraim pull *a plow.*
Judah shall plow;
Jacob shall break his clods."

On the Edge

Sow for yourselves righteousness; reap in mercy; break up your fallow ground, for it is time to seek the LORD, till He comes and rains righteousness on you (Hos. 10:12).

Have you ever been out in a field on a hot summer day when suddenly it started to pour rain? You got soaking wet, and felt totally refreshed! Think about this verse for a moment. It says that God will send His righteousness like rain when we worship Him. Are you ready for some of that rain? Do you want it to drench your friends and family? Don't you just want everybody you meet to get soaked with God's saving rain? Did you know you can be a rainmaker? When we worship the Lord, He pours out His refreshing rain! God's thunderstorms are rolling into your circumstances, ready to rain down His saving power! So the next time it starts raining outside, let that be a reminder of what God wants to do in your life.

SEE FOR YOURSELF:
Ps. 20:6; 33:20; 37:40;
109:26; Acts 3:19

---

12   Sow for yourselves righteousness;
Reap in mercy;
Break up your fallow ground,
For *it is* time to seek the LORD,
Till He comes and rains righteousness on
     you.

13   You have plowed wickedness;
You have reaped iniquity.
You have eaten the fruit of lies,
Because you trusted in your own way,
In the multitude of your mighty men.

14   Therefore tumult shall arise among your
     people,
And all your fortresses shall be plundered
As Shalman plundered Beth Arbel in the
     day of battle—
A mother dashed in pieces upon *her*
     children.

15   Thus it shall be done to you, O Bethel,
Because of your great wickedness.
At dawn the king of Israel
Shall be cut off utterly.

GOD'S CONTINUING LOVE FOR ISRAEL

1   "When Israel *was* a child, I loved
     him,
And out of Egypt I called
     My son.

2   *As* they called them,*a*
So they went from
     them;*b*
They sacrificed to the
     Baals,
And burned incense to carved images.

GOD

Does
God love
His people?
(11:1)

3   "I taught Ephraim to walk,
Taking them by their arms;*a*
But they did not know that I healed them.

4   I drew them with gentle cords,*b*
With bands of love,
And I was to them as those who take the
     yoke from their neck.*a*
I stooped *and* fed them.

5   "He shall not return to the land of Egypt;
But the Assyrian shall be his king,
Because they refused to repent.

6   And the sword shall slash in his cities,
Devour his districts,
And consume *them,*
Because of their own counsels.

7   My people are bent on backsliding from Me.
Though they call to the Most High,*a*
None at all exalt *Him.*

8   "How can I give you up, Ephraim?
How can I hand you over, Israel?
How can I make you like Admah?

10:10 *a*Or *in their two habitations*   **11:2** *a*Following Masoretic Text and Vulgate; Septuagint reads *Just as I called them;* Targum interprets as *I sent prophets to a thousand of them.*   *b*Following Masoretic Text, Targum, and Vulgate; Septuagint reads *from My face.*   **11:3** *a*Some Hebrew manuscripts, Septuagint, Syriac, and Vulgate read *My arms.*   **11:4** *a*Literally *cords of a man*   *b*Literally *jaws*   **11:7** *a*Or *upward*

How can I set you like Zeboiim?
My heart churns within Me;
My sympathy is stirred.
9 I will not execute the fierceness of My
anger;
I will not again destroy Ephraim.
For I *am* God, and not man,
The Holy One in your midst;
And I will not come with terror.[a]

10 "They shall walk after the LORD.
He will roar like a lion.
When He roars,
Then *His* sons shall come trembling from
the west;
11 They shall come trembling like a bird
from Egypt,
Like a dove from the land of Assyria.
And I will let them dwell in their houses,"
Says the LORD.

GOD'S CHARGE AGAINST EPHRAIM

12 "Ephraim has encircled Me with lies,
And the house of Israel with deceit;
But Judah still walks with God,
Even with the Holy One[a] *who is* faithful.

1 "Ephraim feeds on the wind,
And pursues the east wind;
He daily increases lies and desolation.
Also they make a covenant with the
Assyrians,
And oil is carried to Egypt.

2 "The LORD also *brings* a charge against
Judah,
And will punish Jacob according to his
ways;
According to his deeds He will
recompense him.
3 He took his brother by the heel in the
womb,
And in his strength he struggled with
God.[a]
4 Yes, he struggled with the Angel and
prevailed;
He wept, and sought favor from Him.
He found Him *in* Bethel,
And there He spoke to us—
5 That is, the LORD God of hosts.
The LORD *is* His memorable name.
6 So you, by *the help of* your God, return;
Observe mercy and justice,
And wait on your God continually.

7 "A cunning Canaanite!
Deceitful scales *are* in his hand;
He loves to oppress.
8 And Ephraim said,
'Surely I have become rich,
I have found wealth for myself;
In all my labors
They shall find in me no iniquity that *is*
sin.'

9 "But I *am* the LORD your God,
Ever since the land of Egypt;
I will again make you dwell in tents,
As in the days of the appointed feast.
10 I have also spoken by the prophets,
And have multiplied visions;
I have given symbols through the witness
of the prophets."

11 Though Gilead *has* idols—
Surely they are vanity—
Though they sacrifice bulls in Gilgal,
Indeed their altars *shall be* heaps in the
furrows of the field.

12 Jacob fled to the country of Syria;
Israel served for a spouse,
And for a wife he tended *sheep.*
13 By a prophet the LORD brought Israel out
of Egypt,
And by a prophet he was preserved.
14 Ephraim provoked *Him* to anger most
bitterly;
Therefore his Lord will leave the guilt of
his bloodshed upon him,
And return his reproach upon him.

RELENTLESS JUDGMENT ON ISRAEL

1 When Ephraim spoke, trembling,
He exalted *himself* in Israel;
But when he offended through Baal
worship, he died.
2 Now they sin more and more,
And have made for themselves molded
images,
Idols of their silver, according to their
skill;
All of it *is* the work of craftsmen.
They say of them,
"Let the men who sacrifice[a] kiss the
calves!"
3 Therefore they shall be like the morning
cloud
And like the early dew that passes away,

11:9 [a]*Or I will not enter a city*   **11:12** [a]*Or holy ones*   **12:3** [a]*Compare Genesis 32:28*   **13:2** [a]*Or those who offer human sacrifice*

They were filled and their heart was
   exalted;
Therefore they forgot Me.

7 "So I will be to them like a lion;
   Like a leopard by the road I will lurk;
8 I will meet them like a bear deprived *of*
   her cubs;
   I will tear open their rib cage,
   And there I will devour them like a lion.
   The wild beast shall tear them.

9 "O Israel, you are destroyed,[a]
   But your help[b] *is* from Me.
10 I will be your King;[a]
   Where *is any other,*
   That he may save you in all your cities?
   And your judges to whom you said,
   'Give me a king and princes'?
11 I gave you a king in My anger,
   And took *him* away in My wrath.

12 "The iniquity of Ephraim *is* bound up;
   His sin *is* stored up.
13 The sorrows of a woman in childbirth
     shall come upon him.
   He *is* an unwise son,
   For he should not stay long where
     children are born.

14 "I will ransom them from the power of the
     grave;[a]
   I will redeem them from death.
   O Death, I will be your plagues![b]
   O Grave,[c] I will be your destruction![d]
   Pity is hidden from My eyes."

15 Though he is fruitful among *his*
     brethren,
   An east wind shall come;
   The wind of the LORD shall come up from
     the wilderness.
   Then his spring shall become dry,
   And his fountain shall be dried up.
   He shall plunder the treasury of every
     desirable prize.
16 Samaria is held guilty,[a]
   For she has rebelled against her God.
   They shall fall by the sword,
   Their infants shall be dashed in pieces,
   And their women with child ripped
     open.

On the Edge

Yet I am the LORD your God ever since the land of Egypt, and you shall know no God but Me; for there is no savior besides Me (Hos. 13:4).

Check out the last part of this verse. Did you know that in the Hebrew, the word for "Savior" means "Victor," "Deliverer," "Rescuer"? That means that Jesus is your rescuer from darkness to light. You have been delivered, and you are victorious! The only way this can happen is with Jesus in your life. Jesus is the only way to God, and God is the only One who can save. In fact, Romans 10:13 says that "whoever calls on the name of the LORD shall be saved." This word *saved,* in the Greek, is translated in several ways: "to be rescued from danger"; "to save from suffering and disease"; "to make well"; "to heal and restore to health"; "to make whole." This should get you excited!

Not only is God the only One who can save you from sin, but He is the only One who can rescue you from evil. He is the only One who can save you from suffering and disease. He is the only One who can truly make you well, the only One who can heal and restore your health.

There are so many people that you rub shoulders with every day who are searching for a remedy in their lives. You have that cure, and His name is Jesus! Let them know you have the answer they've been looking for. He is the only One who saves!

SEE FOR YOURSELF:
John 6:44; Rom. 10:13;
Col. 1:13

Like chaff blown off from a threshing
   floor
And like smoke from a chimney.

4 "Yet I *am* the LORD your God
   Ever since the land of Egypt,
   And you shall know no God but Me;
   For *there is* no savior besides Me.
5 I knew you in the wilderness,
   In the land of great drought.
6 When they had pasture, they were filled;

13:9 [a]Literally *it* or *he destroyed you* [b]Literally *in your help*   **13:10** [a]Septuagint, Syriac, Targum, and Vulgate read *Where is your king?*   **13:14** [a]Or *Sheol* [b]Septuagint reads *where is your punishment?* [c]Or *Sheol* [d]Septuagint reads *where is your sting?*   **13:16** [a]Septuagint reads *shall be disfigured*

ISRAEL RESTORED AT LAST

1 O Israel, return to the LORD your God,
For you have stumbled because of your
iniquity;
2 Take words with you,
And return to the LORD.
Say to Him,
"Take away all iniquity;
Receive *us* graciously,
For we will offer the sacrifices[a] of our
lips.
3 Assyria shall not save us,
We will not ride on horses,
Nor will we say anymore to the work of
our hands, '*You are* our gods.'
For in You the fatherless finds mercy."

4 "I will heal their backsliding,
I will love them freely,
For My anger has turned away from him.
5 I will be like the dew to Israel;
He shall grow like the lily,
And lengthen his roots like Lebanon.

6 His branches shall spread;
His beauty shall be like an olive tree,
And his fragrance like Lebanon.
7 Those who dwell under his shadow shall
return;
They shall be revived *like* grain,
And grow like a vine.
Their scent[a] *shall be* like the wine of
Lebanon.

8 "Ephraim *shall say,* 'What have I to do
anymore with idols?'
I have heard and observed him.
I *am* like a green cypress tree;
Your fruit is found in Me."

9 Who *is* wise?
Let him understand these things.
Who is prudent?
Let him know them.
For the ways of the LORD *are* right;
The righteous walk in them,
But transgressors stumble in them.

14:2 [a]Literally *bull calves;* Septuagint reads *fruit.*   **14:7** [a]Literally *remembrance*

Promise   HE PROMISES TO LOVE YOU FREELY.

I will heal their backsliding, I will love them freely, for My anger has turned away from him (Hos. 14:4).

A father says to his son, "I've loved you for years. I've done my best. But this is it. You've gone too far this time. I want you out of my house. I don't even love you anymore. You are no longer my son." A boyfriend says to his girlfriend, "I really did love you, but now that we've had sex, it's different. I just don't feel the same. I guess it's over." A coach says to his team, "You guys better pull yourselves together. If we don't win tonight I don't ever want to see your faces again!"

Limits. Conditions. Terms. Humans have a hard time loving without limits, so it can be hard to imagine a God who does. But that's His promise—to freely love you beyond anything you've ever experienced here on earth. He sees your scars. He's even been hurt by your sin and by the times you've rejected Him. And He still loves you. He will never kick you out, never love-you-and-leave-you, never throw you off the team. We humans just can't grasp a limitless love. So you'll have to trust Him. He'll prove it.

SEE FOR YOURSELF:
Ps. 36:10; Jer. 31:3; Lam. 3:22; 1 John 3:1; 4:7–11

joel

CONTENT Life pretty much seems in our control, doesn't it? If we work hard in school, we get good grades. If we get good grades, we'll get a good job one day. If we plant crops, they will grow. If we feed our dog, he will stick around. Sometimes life seems so certain and so sure that we forget how fragile it is.

That's how it was for the people of Joel's day. Things were going pretty well. There hadn't been a disaster in awhile. Tragedy seemed far away. There was only one problem: The people were still not being faithful to God and, even if circumstances felt good, judgment was on its way.

Joel's message was about those consequences, and they came in the form of flying grasshopper-type insects that could strip a farmer's land in almost the time it took them to fly across it. These grasshoppers were called locusts. Joel's warning about locusts reminded his people that life is *not* in our control. We need God's help to face the future as well as the present. We can't just live as if God is unnecessary when any minute the locusts will be on their way.

Outline 1:1—2:17 .... Locusts and an Enemy Army
2:18–32 .... The Lord Will Bless His People
3:1–21 .... The Lord Will Punish the Nations

Purpose Repent and avoid judgment by God.

Theme The Judgment and Grace of God

Date of writing 830 or 600 B.C.

¹The word of the LORD that came to Joel the son of Pethuel.

THE LAND LAID WASTE

2 Hear this, you elders,
   And give ear, all you inhabitants of the
      land!
   Has *anything like* this happened in your
      days,
   Or even in the days of your fathers?
3 Tell your children about it,
   Let your children *tell* their children,
   And their children another generation.

4 What the chewing locust[a] left, the
      swarming locust has eaten;
   What the swarming locust left, the
      crawling locust has eaten;
   And what the crawling locust left, the
      consuming locust has eaten.

WHAT'S IT MEAN?

At first glance, the locust seems like a pretty unlikely creature of destruction. It looks like a large grasshopper with two sets of wings and a brown-colored body two to three inches long. Nothing to be worried about, right? Did we mention that locusts travel in swarms large enough to blot out the sun in the sky? An average-size swarm of locusts, numbering in the millions, can strip a field completely bare—down to its last leaf—within minutes.

Joel 1:4

5 Awake, you drunkards, and weep;
   And wail, all you drinkers of wine,
   Because of the new wine,
   For it has been cut off from your mouth.
6 For a nation has come up against My
      land,
   Strong, and without number;
   His teeth *are* the teeth of a lion,
   And he has the fangs of a fierce lion.
7 He has laid waste My vine,
   And ruined My fig tree;
   He has stripped it bare and thrown *it*
      away;
   Its branches are made white.

8 Lament like a virgin girded with sackcloth
   For the husband of her youth.
9 The grain offering and the drink offering
   Have been cut off from the house of the
      LORD;
   The priests mourn, who minister to the
      LORD.
10 The field is wasted,
   The land mourns;
   For the grain is ruined,
   The new wine is dried up,
   The oil fails.

11 Be ashamed, you farmers,
   Wail, you vinedressers,
   For the wheat and the barley;
   Because the harvest of the field has
      perished.
12 The vine has dried up,
   And the fig tree has withered;
   The pomegranate tree,
   The palm tree also,
   And the apple tree—
   All the trees of the field are withered;
   Surely joy has withered away from the
      sons of men.

MOURNING FOR THE LAND

13 Gird yourselves and lament, you priests;
   Wail, you who minister before the altar;
   Come, lie all night in sackcloth,
   You who minister to my God;
   For the grain offering and the drink
      offering
   Are withheld from the house of your
      God.
14 Consecrate a fast,
   Call a sacred assembly;
   Gather the elders
   And all the inhabitants of the land
   Into the house of the LORD your God,
   And cry out to the LORD.

15 Alas for the day!
   For the day of the LORD *is* at hand;
   It shall come as destruction from the
      Almighty.
16 Is not the food cut off before our eyes,
   Joy and gladness from the house of our
      God?
17 The seed shrivels under the clods,
   Storehouses are in shambles;
   Barns are broken down,
   For the grain has withered.
18 How the animals groan!

1:4 [a]Exact identity of these locusts is unknown.

The herds of cattle are restless,
Because they have no pasture;
Even the flocks of sheep suffer
 punishment.[a]

19 O LORD, to You I cry out;
For fire has devoured the
 open pastures,
And a flame has burned
 all the trees of the field.
20 The beasts of the field also
 cry out to You,
For the water brooks are
 dried up,
And fire has devoured the open
 pastures.

THE DAY OF THE LORD

1 Blow the trumpet in Zion,
And sound an alarm in My holy
 mountain!
Let all the inhabitants of the land tremble;
For the day of the LORD is coming,
For it is at hand:
2 A day of darkness and gloominess,
A day of clouds and thick darkness,
Like the morning *clouds* spread over the
 mountains.
A people *come*, great and strong,
The like of whom has never been;
Nor will there ever be any *such* after
 them,
Even for many successive generations.

WHAT'S IT MEAN?

Two questions need to be answered here:
(1) Where is Zion? (2) What's with the trumpet?
Mount Zion is the hill in Jerusalem where Solomon built the first
temple. The trumpet was an ancestor of the modern church bell. It
was used to call people together for religious ceremonies and
special festivals. Occasionally it was used to sound an
alarm or to call troops to battle.
Joel 2:1

3 A fire devours before them,
And behind them a flame burns;

The land *is* like the Garden of Eden
 before them,
And behind them a desolate wilderness;
Surely nothing shall escape them.
4 Their appearance is like the
 appearance of horses;
And like swift steeds, so
 they run.
5 With a noise like chariots
Over mountaintops they
 leap,
Like the noise of a flaming
 fire that devours the
 stubble,
Like a strong people set in
 battle array.

6 Before them the people writhe in pain;
All faces are drained of color.[a]
7 They run like mighty men,
They climb the wall like men of war;
Every one marches in formation,
And they do not break ranks.
8 They do not push one another;
Every one marches in his own column.[a]
Though they lunge between the weapons,
They are not cut down.[b]
9 They run to and fro in the city,
They run on the wall;
They climb into the houses,
They enter at the windows like a thief.

10 The earth quakes before them,
The heavens tremble;
The sun and moon grow dark,
And the stars diminish their brightness.
11 The LORD gives voice before His army,
For His camp is very great;
For strong *is the One* who executes His
 word.
For the day of the LORD *is* great and very
 terrible;
Who can endure it?

A CALL TO REPENTANCE

12 "Now, therefore," says the LORD,
"Turn to Me with all your heart,
With fasting, with weeping, and with
 mourning."
13 So rend your heart, and not your
 garments;
Return to the LORD your God,
For He *is* gracious and merciful,
Slow to anger, and of great kindness;
And He relents from doing harm.

> "Alas for the day!
> For the day of the LORD
> is at hand."
> (Joel 1:15a)

1:18 [a]Septuagint and Vulgate read *are made desolate.* **2:6** [a]Septuagint, Targum, and Vulgate read *gather blackness.* **2:8** [a]Literally *his own highway* [b]That is, they are not halted by losses

14 Who knows *if* He will turn and relent,
And leave a blessing behind Him—
A grain offering and a drink offering
For the LORD your God?

15 Blow the trumpet in Zion,
Consecrate a fast,
Call a sacred assembly;
16 Gather the people,
Sanctify the congregation,
Assemble the elders,
Gather the children and nursing babes;
Let the bridegroom go out from his
chamber,
And the bride from her dressing room.
17 Let the priests, who minister to the LORD,
Weep between the porch and the altar;
Let them say, "Spare Your people, O LORD,
And do not give Your heritage to
reproach,
That the nations should rule over them.
Why should they say among the peoples,
'Where *is* their God?' "

THE LAND REFRESHED

18 Then the LORD will be zealous for His
land,
And pity His people.

19 The LORD will answer and say to His
people,
"Behold, I will send you grain and new
wine and oil,
And you will be satisfied by them;
I will no longer make you a reproach
among the nations.

20 "But I will remove far from you the
northern *army*,
And will drive him away into a barren
and desolate land,
With his face toward the eastern sea
And his back toward the western sea;
His stench will come up,
And his foul odor will rise,
Because he has done monstrous things."

21 Fear not, O land;
Be glad and rejoice,
For the LORD has done marvelous
things!
22 Do not be afraid, you beasts of the field;
For the open pastures are springing up,
And the tree bears its fruit;
The fig tree and the vine yield their
strength.
23 Be glad then, you children of Zion,
And rejoice in the LORD your God;

Promise   HE PROMISES HIS SPIRIT TO EVERYONE.

And it shall come to pass afterward that I will pour out My Spirit on all flesh; your sons and your daughters shall prophesy, your old men shall dream dreams, your young men shall see visions (Joel 2:28).

As you know, the Book of Joel is a book of prophecy—a book that tells what would happen in the future. Joel prophesied that a time would come on earth when God would give His Spirit to everyone. God would even use young people, Joel said, to prophesy from visions—to speak God's words and proclaim the good news.

Joel's prophecy came true in the second chapter of Acts. The Holy Spirit fell on a group of believers and changed the world forever. The Holy Spirit lives inside of you if you are a Christian. He is not some mysterious "it." He is the third Person of the Trinity, right there beside the Father and the Son. Before Jesus died, He told His disciples that He would send them Someone even better than He was—the Holy Spirit (see John 16:5–15). The Holy Spirit is available to you today. He is the One who helps you, who teaches you, who guides you into full truth, and who gives Jesus' message to you. The Holy Spirit is here—in your heart. He lives in you. Get to know Him. He's the best friend you'll ever have!

SEE FOR YOURSELF:
Ezek. 39:29; Hag. 2:4, 5; John 16:4–15;
2 Tim. 1:14; 1 John 4:13

For He has given you the former rain
   faithfully,[a]
And He will cause the rain to come down
   for you—
The former rain,
And the latter rain in the first *month*.
24 The threshing floors shall be full of
   wheat,
And the vats shall overflow with new
   wine and oil.

25 "So I will restore to you the years that the
   swarming locust has eaten,
The crawling locust,
The consuming locust,
And the chewing locust,[a]
My great army which I sent among you.
26 You shall eat in plenty and be satisfied,
And praise the name of the LORD your
   God,
Who has dealt wondrously with you;
And My people shall never be put to
   shame.
27 Then you shall know that I *am* in the
   midst of Israel:
I *am* the LORD your God
And there is no other.
My people shall never be put to shame.

GOD'S SPIRIT POURED OUT
28 "And it shall come to pass afterward
That I will pour out My Spirit on all
   flesh;
Your sons and your daughters shall
   prophesy,
Your old men shall dream dreams,
Your young men shall see visions.
29 And also on *My* menservants and on *My*
   maidservants
I will pour out My Spirit in those days.

30 "And I will show wonders in the heavens
   and in the earth:
Blood and fire and pillars of smoke.
31 The sun shall be turned into darkness,
And the moon into blood,
Before the coming of the
   great and awesome
   day of the LORD.
32 And it shall come to
   pass
That whoever calls on
   the name of the LORD
Shall be saved.

SALVATION
Who can
be saved?
(2:32)

For in Mount Zion and in Jerusalem there
   shall be deliverance,
As the LORD has said,
Among the remnant whom the LORD
   calls.

GOD JUDGES THE NATIONS
1 "For behold, in those days and at that
   time,
When I bring back the captives of Judah
   and Jerusalem,
2 I will also gather all nations,
And bring them down to the Valley of
   Jehoshaphat;
And I will enter into judgment with them
   there
On account of My people, My heritage
   Israel,
Whom they have scattered among the
   nations;
They have also divided up My land.
3 They have cast lots for My people,
Have given a boy *as payment* for a harlot,
And sold a girl for wine, that they may
   drink.

WHAT'S IT MEAN?

Tyre and Sidon were Mediterranean
coastal cities famous for their trading business.
They weren't necessarily enemies of the Israelites, but they were
anxious for Jerusalem to fall so that they could take over the
trade routes controlled by Judah.
Joel 3:4

4 "Indeed, what have you to do with Me,
O Tyre and Sidon, and all the coasts of
   Philistia?
Will you retaliate against Me?
But if you retaliate against Me,
Swiftly and speedily I will return your
   retaliation upon your own head;
5 Because you have taken My silver and
   My gold,

2:23 [a]Or *the teacher of righteousness*   **2:25** [a]Compare 1:4

And have carried into your temples My
    prized possessions.
6 Also the people of Judah and the people
    of Jerusalem
You have sold to the Greeks,
That you may remove them far from
    their borders.

7 "Behold, I will raise them
Out of the place to which you have sold
    them,
And will return your retaliation upon
    your own head.
8 I will sell your sons and your daughters
Into the hand of the people of Judah,
And they will sell them to the Sabeans,[a]
To a people far off;
For the LORD has spoken."

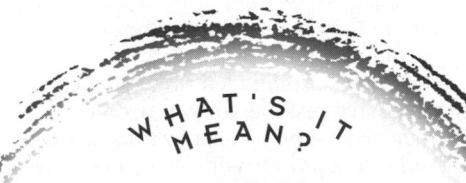

WHAT'S IT MEAN?

How about a quick lesson in ancient
wine making? At harvesttime, grapes were gathered
in baskets and carried to the winepress. (This is where things get a
little disgusting.) Barefoot workers would then stomp on the grapes,
squeezing out the juice. The juice that squirted out flowed down a
slope into another container. There it was collected in clay jars or
wineskins and stored until it fermented and became wine. The days
of harvesting and squashing the grapes were times of celebration
and joy for the people of Judah and Israel.

Joel 3:13

9 Proclaim this among the nations:
"Prepare for war!
Wake up the mighty men,
Let all the men of war draw near,
Let them come up.
10 Beat your plowshares into swords
And your pruning hooks into spears;
Let the weak say, 'I am strong.' "
11 Assemble and come, all you nations,
And gather together all around.
Cause Your mighty ones to go down
    there, O LORD.

12 "Let the nations be wakened, and come up
    to the Valley of Jehoshaphat;
For there I will sit to judge all the
    surrounding nations.
13 Put in the sickle, for the harvest is ripe.
Come, go down;
For the winepress is full,
The vats overflow—
For their wickedness is great."

14 Multitudes, multitudes in the valley of
    decision!
For the day of the LORD is near in the
    valley of decision.
15 The sun and moon will grow dark,
And the stars will diminish their
    brightness.
16 The LORD also will roar from Zion,
And utter His voice from Jerusalem;
The heavens and earth will shake;
But the LORD will be a shelter for His
    people,
And the strength of the children of Israel.

17 "So you shall know that I am the LORD
    your God,
Dwelling in Zion My holy mountain.
Then Jerusalem shall be holy,
And no aliens shall ever pass through her
    again."

GOD BLESSES HIS PEOPLE

18 And it will come to pass in that day
That the mountains shall drip with new
    wine,
The hills shall flow with milk,
And all the brooks of Judah shall be
    flooded with water;
A fountain shall flow from the house of
    the LORD
And water the Valley of Acacias.

19 "Egypt shall be a desolation,
And Edom a desolate wilderness,
Because of violence against the people of
    Judah,
For they have shed innocent blood in
    their land.
20 But Judah shall abide forever,
And Jerusalem from generation to
    generation.
21 For I will acquit them of the guilt of
    bloodshed, whom I had not acquitted;
For the LORD dwells in Zion."

3:8 [a]Literally *Shebaites* (compare Isaiah 60:6 and Ezekiel 27:22)

Amos

CONTENT

Amos was a prophet at a time when life was good for Israel. The economy was stable. Business was booming. War was at a minimum. It was a great time to be alive for the Hebrews.

It was also a great time to be comfortable, to be complacent, and to be self-centered. Life was going so well, in general, that people really didn't want to be bothered with unpleasantness. They didn't want to think about the poor and the struggling elements of their society. They didn't want to think about obedience to God. They didn't want to have to think too much at all.

That's when Amos stepped in to say, "Do you know what God thinks of your selfish, comfortable existence? He thinks it has nothing to do with Him at all. You are living apart from God and apart from people who need you. Wake up and start living a better life."

While Amos's message wasn't welcomed, it was necessary. Many poor people in his land were receiving no help from those that were better off. These same wealthy people would show up at religious services and put on a show that they were living according to God's law, but their lives were empty of compassion.

Outline

1:1—3:2 .... Crimes of the Nations Will Be Punished
3:3—6:14 .... Israel and Samaria Will Be Destroyed
7:1—9:10 .... Five Visions of Israel's Punishment
9:11–15 .... Israel's Bright Future

Purpose

Immorality and injustice show a society that has lost contact with God.

Theme

The Judgment of God Is About to Fall on Israel

Date of writing

760 B.C.

¹The words of Amos, who was among the sheepbreeders*ᵃ* of Tekoa, which he saw concerning Israel in the days of Uzziah king of Judah, and in the days of Jeroboam the son of Joash, king of Israel, two years before the earthquake.

²And he said:

> "The LORD roars from Zion,
> And utters His voice from Jerusalem;
> The pastures of the shepherds mourn,
> And the top of Carmel withers."

Syria, the area northeast of the Sea of Galilee, had been under Israel's control during the reign of David. Things changed when David's son, Solomon, became king. Syria, with its capital city of Damascus, united with other nations in the area against Israel. From that point on, the Syrians and the Israelites battled each other frequently in war.

Amos 1:3

JUDGMENT ON THE NATIONS

³Thus says the LORD:

> "For three transgressions of Damascus, and for four,
> I will not turn away its *punishment*,
> Because they have threshed Gilead with implements of iron.
> 4 But I will send a fire into the house of Hazael,
> Which shall devour the palaces of Ben-Hadad.
> 5 I will also break the *gate* bar of Damascus,
> And cut off the inhabitant from the Valley of Aven,
> And the one who holds the scepter from Beth Eden.
> The people of Syria shall go captive to Kir,"
> Says the LORD.

⁶Thus says the LORD:

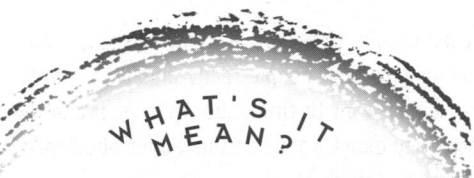

The Philistines lived in coastal cities along the Mediterranean Sea. Not content with merely one capital city, the Philistines boasted five: Gaza, Ashdod, Ashkelon, Gath, and Ekron. The Israelites and Philistines were long-time enemies, but their battles were especially nasty during David's lifetime.

Amos 1:6

> "For three transgressions of Gaza, and for four,
> I will not turn away its *punishment*,
> Because they took captive the whole captivity
> To deliver *them* up to Edom.
> 7 But I will send a fire upon the wall of Gaza,
> Which shall devour its palaces.
> 8 I will cut off the inhabitant from Ashdod,
> And the one who holds the scepter from Ashkelon;
> I will turn My hand against Ekron,
> And the remnant of the Philistines shall perish,"
> Says the Lord GOD.

⁹Thus says the LORD:

> "For three transgressions of Tyre, and for four,
> I will not turn away its *punishment*,
> Because they delivered up the whole captivity to Edom,
> And did not remember the covenant of brotherhood.
> 10 But I will send a fire upon the wall of Tyre,
> Which shall devour its palaces."

¹¹Thus says the LORD:

> "For three transgressions of Edom, and for four,
> I will not turn away its *punishment*,
> Because he pursued his brother with the sword,

1:1 *ᵃ*Compare 2 Kings 3:4

And cast off all pity;
His anger tore perpetually,
And he kept his wrath forever.
12 But I will send a fire upon Teman,
Which shall devour the palaces of Bozrah."

13Thus says the LORD:

"For three transgressions of the people of
   Ammon, and for four,
I will not turn away its *punishment*,
Because they ripped open the women
   with child in Gilead,
That they might enlarge their territory.
14 But I will kindle a fire in the wall of
   Rabbah,
And it shall devour its palaces,
Amid shouting in the day of battle,
And a tempest in the day of the
   whirlwind.
15 Their king shall go into captivity,
He and his princes together,"
Says the LORD.

WHAT'S IT MEAN?

The people of Ammon were actually distant relatives of the Israelites. They were descendants of Lot, the nephew of Abraham (the father of the Jews). Rabbah, the capital of ancient Ammon, is today known as Amman, the capital of Jordan.

Amos 1:13

1Thus says the LORD:

"For three transgressions of Moab, and for
   four,
I will not turn away its *punishment*,
Because he burned the bones of the king
   of Edom to lime.
2 But I will send a fire upon Moab,
And it shall devour the palaces of Kerioth;
Moab shall die with tumult,
With shouting *and* trumpet sound.
3 And I will cut off the judge from its midst,
And slay all its princes with him,"
Says the LORD.

JUDGMENT ON JUDAH

4Thus says the LORD:

"For three transgressions of Judah, and for
   four,
I will not turn away its *punishment*,
Because they have despised the law of the
   LORD,
And have not kept His commandments.
Their lies lead them astray,
Lies which their fathers followed.
5 But I will send a fire upon Judah,
And it shall devour the palaces of
   Jerusalem."

JUDGMENT ON ISRAEL

6Thus says the LORD:

"For three transgressions of Israel, and for
   four,
I will not turn away its *punishment*,
Because they sell the righteous for silver,
And the poor for a pair of sandals.
7 They pant after[a] the dust of the earth
   which is on the head of the poor,
And pervert the way of the humble.
A man and his father go in to the *same*
   girl,
To defile My holy name.
8 They lie down by every altar on clothes
   taken in pledge,
And drink the wine of the condemned *in*
   the house of their god.

9 "Yet *it was* I *who* destroyed the Amorite
   before them,
Whose height *was* like the height of the
   cedars,
And he *was as* strong as the oaks;
Yet I destroyed his fruit above
And his roots beneath.
10 Also *it was* I *who* brought you up from
   the land of Egypt,
And led you forty years through the
   wilderness,
To possess the land of the Amorite.
11 I raised up some of your sons as
   prophets,
And some of your young men as
   Nazirites.
Is it not so, O you children of Israel?"
Says the LORD.
12 "But you gave the Nazirites wine to drink,
And commanded the prophets saying,
'Do not prophesy!'

2:7 [a]Or *trample on*

¹³ "Behold, I am weighed down by you,
As a cart full of sheaves is weighed
down.
¹⁴ Therefore flight shall perish from the
swift,
The strong shall not strengthen his
power,
Nor shall the mighty deliver
himself;
¹⁵ He shall not stand who
handles the bow,
The swift of foot shall
not escape,
Nor shall he who rides a
horse deliver himself.
¹⁶ The most courageous
men of might
Shall flee naked in that day,"
Says the LORD.

AUTHORITY OF THE PROPHET'S MESSAGE

¹Hear this word that the LORD has spoken
against you, O children of Israel, against the
whole family which I brought up from the land
of Egypt, saying:

² "You only have I known of all the families
of the earth;
Therefore I will punish you for all your
iniquities."

³ Can two walk together, unless they are
agreed?
⁴ Will a lion roar in the forest, when he has
no prey?
Will a young lion cry out of his den, if he
has caught nothing?
⁵ Will a bird fall into a snare on the earth,
where there is no trap for it?
Will a snare spring up from the earth, if it
has caught nothing at all?
⁶ If a trumpet is blown in a city, will not
the people be afraid?
If there is calamity in a city, will not the
LORD have done *it?*

⁷ Surely the Lord GOD does nothing,
Unless He reveals His secret to His
servants the prophets.
⁸ A lion has roared!
Who will not fear?
The Lord GOD has spoken!
Who can but prophesy?

> "A lion has roared!
> Who will not fear?
> The Lord GOD has spoken!
> Who can but prophesy?"
> (Amos 3:8)

PUNISHMENT OF ISRAEL'S SINS

⁹ "Proclaim in the palaces at Ashdod,^a
And in the palaces in the land of Egypt,
and say:
'Assemble on the mountains of Samaria;
See great tumults in her
midst,
And the oppressed
within her.
¹⁰ For they do not know
to do right,'
Says the LORD,
'Who store up violence
and robbery in their
palaces.' "

¹¹Therefore thus says the
Lord GOD:

"An adversary *shall be* all around the land;
He shall sap your strength from you,
And your palaces shall be plundered."

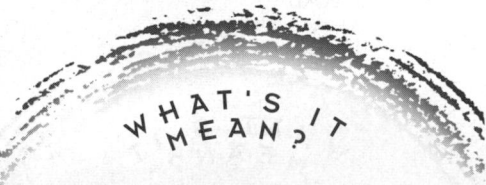

WHAT'S IT MEAN?

A devastating Assyrian attack in 722 B.C. led
to the fall of Samaria, the capital of the northern
kingdom of Israel. As was their custom with the territories they
conquered, the Assyrians took many Israelites away as captives and
brought in many foreigners to live in Canaan. It wasn't long before
the Israelites who were left behind started getting involved with the
new kids in town. Not only did the Israelites begin marrying and
having kids with the foreigners, but they also adopted their idol worship. This mingling continued generation after generation until the
distinction between the Israelites and the foreigners disappeared
altogether. The descendants of these mixed
marriages were known as Samaritans.
Amos 3:12

¹²Thus says the LORD:

"As a shepherd takes from the mouth of a
lion
Two legs or a piece of an ear,
So shall the children of Israel be taken
out

3:9 ^aFollowing Masoretic Text; Septuagint reads *Assyria.*

Who dwell in Samaria—
In the corner of a bed and on the edge*a*
of a couch!
13 Hear and testify against the house of
Jacob,"
Says the Lord GOD, the God of hosts,
14 "That in the day I punish Israel for their
transgressions,
I will also visit *destruction* on the altars of
Bethel;
And the horns of the altar shall be cut off
And fall to the ground.
15 I will destroy the winter house along with
the summer house;
The houses of ivory shall perish,
And the great houses shall have an end,"
Says the LORD.

1 Hear this word, you cows of Bashan,
who *are* on the mountain of Samaria,
Who oppress the poor,
Who crush the needy,
Who say to your husbands,*a* "Bring *wine*,
let us drink!"
2 The Lord GOD has sworn by His holiness:
"Behold, the days shall come upon you
When He will take you away with
fishhooks,
And your posterity with fishhooks.
3 You will go out *through* broken *walls*,
Each one straight ahead of *her*,
And you will be cast into Harmon,"
Says the LORD.

4 "Come to Bethel and transgress,
At Gilgal multiply transgression;

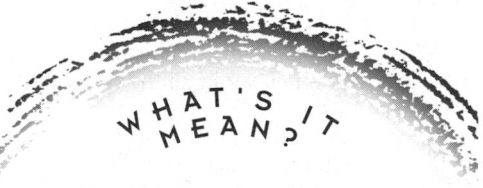

WHAT'S IT MEAN?

Bethel and Gilgal were both important cities in
Israel's history. Bethel was the place where Jacob had
his life-changing dream of a stairway to heaven. Gilgal was the site
of a memorial to God for His protection of the Israelites when they
crossed the Jordan River. The people of Israel proved their lack of
respect for their history by making both places
centers for pagan worship.

Amos 4:4

Bring your sacrifices every morning,
Your tithes every three days.*a*
5 Offer a sacrifice of thanksgiving with
leaven,
Proclaim *and* announce the freewill
offerings;
For this you love,
You children of Israel!"
Says the Lord GOD.

ISRAEL DID NOT ACCEPT CORRECTION

6 "Also I gave you cleanness of teeth in all
your cities.
And lack of bread in all your places;
Yet you have not returned to Me,"
Says the LORD.

7 "I also withheld rain from you,
When *there were* still three months to the
harvest.
I made it rain on one city,
I withheld rain from another city.
One part was rained upon,
And where it did not rain the part
withered.
8 So two *or* three cities wandered to
another city to drink water,
But they were not satisfied;
Yet you have not returned to Me,"
Says the LORD.

9 "I blasted you with blight and mildew.
When your gardens increased,
Your vineyards,
Your fig trees,
And your olive trees,
The locust devoured *them*;
Yet you have not returned to Me,"
Says the LORD.

10 "I sent among you a plague after the
manner of Egypt;
Your young men I killed with a sword,
Along with your captive horses;
I made the stench of your camps come
up into your nostrils;
Yet you have not returned to Me,"
Says the LORD.

11 "I overthrew *some* of you,
As God overthrew Sodom and Gomorrah,
And you were like a firebrand plucked
from the burning;
Yet you have not returned to Me,"
Says the LORD.

3:12 *a*The Hebrew is uncertain.   **4:1** *a*Literally *their lords* or *their masters*   **4:4** *a*Or *years* (compare
Deuteronomy 14:28)

12 "Therefore thus will I do to you, O Israel;
Because I will do this to you,
Prepare to meet your God, O Israel!"

13 For behold,
He who forms mountains,
And creates the wind,
Who declares to man what his[a]
     thought *is,*
And makes the morning darkness,
Who treads the high places of the earth—
The LORD God of hosts *is* His name.

A LAMENT FOR ISRAEL

1 Hear this word which I take up against you,
a lamentation, O house of Israel:

2   The virgin of Israel has fallen;
She will rise no more.
She lies forsaken on her land;
There is no one to raise her up.

3 For thus says the Lord GOD:

"The city that goes out by a thousand
Shall have a hundred left,
And that which goes out by a hundred
Shall have ten left to the house of Israel."

A CALL TO REPENTANCE

4 For thus says the LORD to the house of Israel:

"Seek Me and live;
5   But do not seek Bethel,
Nor enter Gilgal,
Nor pass over to Beersheba;
For Gilgal shall surely go into captivity,
And Bethel shall come to nothing.
6   Seek the LORD and live,
Lest He break out like fire *in* the house of
    Joseph,
And devour *it,*
With no one to quench *it* in Bethel—
7   You who turn justice to wormwood,
And lay righteousness to rest in the
    earth!"

8   He made the Pleiades and Orion;
He turns the shadow of death into
    morning
And makes the day dark as night;
He calls for the waters of the sea
And pours them out on the face of the
    earth;

The LORD *is* His name.
9   He rains ruin upon the strong,
So that fury comes upon the fortress.

10 They hate the one who rebukes in the
    gate,
And they abhor the one who speaks
    uprightly.
11 Therefore, because you tread down the
    poor
And take grain taxes from him,
Though you have built houses of hewn
    stone,
Yet you shall not dwell in them;
You have planted pleasant vineyards,
But you shall not drink wine from them.
12 For I know your manifold transgressions
And your mighty sins:
Afflicting the just *and* taking bribes;
Diverting the poor *from justice* at the gate.
13 Therefore the prudent keep silent at that
    time,
For it *is* an evil time.

14 Seek good and not evil,
That you may live;
So the LORD God of hosts will be with
    you,
As you have spoken.
15 Hate evil, love good;
Establish justice in the gate.
It may be that the LORD God of hosts
Will be gracious to the remnant of Joseph.

THE DAY OF THE LORD

16 Therefore the LORD God of hosts, the Lord,
says this:

"*There shall be* wailing in all streets,
And they shall say in all the highways,
'Alas! Alas!'
They shall call the farmer to mourning,
And skillful lamenters to wailing.
17 In all vineyards *there shall be* wailing,
For I will pass through you,"
Says the LORD.

18 Woe to you who desire the day of the
    LORD!
For what good *is* the day of the LORD to
    you?
It *will be* darkness, and not light.
19 It *will be* as though a man fled from a
    lion,
And a bear met him!

4:13 [a]Or *His*

Or *as though* he went into the house,
Leaned his hand on the wall,
And a serpent bit him!

20 Is not the day of the LORD darkness, and
not light?
Is it not very dark, with no brightness
in it?

21 "I hate, I despise your feast days,
And I do not savor your sacred
assemblies.

22 Though you offer Me burnt offerings and
your grain offerings,
I will not accept *them*,
Nor will I regard your fattened peace
offerings.

23 Take away from Me the noise of your
songs,
For I will not hear the
melody of your
stringed instruments.

24 But let justice run down
like water,
And righteousness like a
mighty stream.

CHARACTER

Does God
care about
righteousness?
(5:24)

25 "Did you offer Me sacrifices and offerings
In the wilderness forty years, O house of
Israel?

26 You also carried Sikkuth*a* your king*b*
And Chiun,*c* your idols,
The star of your gods,
Which you made for yourselves.

27 Therefore I will send you into captivity
beyond Damascus,"
Says the LORD, whose name *is* the God of
hosts.

WARNINGS TO ZION AND SAMARIA

1 Woe to you *who are* at ease in Zion,
And trust in Mount Samaria,
Notable persons in the chief nation,
To whom the house of Israel comes!

2 Go over to Calneh and see;
And from there go to Hamath the great;
Then go down to Gath of the Philistines.
Are you better than these kingdoms?
Or is their territory greater than your
territory?

3 *Woe to* you who put far off the day of
doom,
Who cause the seat of violence to come
near;

4 Who lie on beds of ivory,
Stretch out on your couches,
Eat lambs from the flock
And calves from the midst of the stall;

5:26 *a*A pagan deity *h*Septuagint and Vulgate read *tabernacle of Moloch.* *c*A pagan deity

---

Promise   HE PROMISES TO BE WITH YOU.

*Seek good and not evil, that you may live; so the LORD God of hosts will be with you,
as you have spoken (Amos 5:14).*

A lot of groups and nations claim to have God on their side. Sometimes even the opposing
sides in a war both say their cause is the one God favors. But God said that this promise is
conditional: He's with you *if* you stop doing the wrong thing and start doing the right thing.

Easier said than done? In fact, relying on your own ability, you'll think it's impossible. Even
David failed to obey God at times. But David was quick to turn back to God when he messed up.
David understood what God really wanted. "You do not delight in burnt offering," he told God. "The
sacrifices of God are a broken spirit, a broken and a contrite heart—these, O God, You will not
despise" (Ps. 51:16, 17). God wants a perfect heart, one that you constantly wash with
repentance and forgiveness.

When God says you must start doing right, He's not looking for exact perfection. He's
looking for someone who really wants to obey Him, who will pray like David did: "Create in me
a clean heart, O God, and renew a steadfast spirit within me" (Ps. 51:10). If that's what you
want, He is definitely on your side.

SEE FOR YOURSELF:
2 Chr. 13:10–12; Ps. 118:5–9; Zech. 10:5

WHAT'S IT MEAN?

The one thing the cities listed in this verse had in common was that they were all losers in war. Calneh and Hamath were cities in Syria that had been conquered by the Assyrians. Gath had experienced its share of defeat as well.

Amos 6:2

5 Who sing idly to the sound of stringed
   instruments,
   And invent for yourselves musical
   instruments like David;
6 Who drink wine from bowls,
   And anoint yourselves with the best
   ointments,
   But are not grieved for the affliction of
   Joseph.
7 Therefore they shall now go captive as
   the first of the captives,
   And those who recline at banquets shall
   be removed.

8 The Lord GOD has sworn by Himself,
   The LORD God of hosts says:
   "I abhor the pride of Jacob,
   And hate his palaces;
   Therefore I will deliver up *the* city
   And all that is in it."

9 Then it shall come to pass, that if ten men remain in one house, they shall die. 10 And when a relative *of the dead,* with one who will burn *the bodies,* picks up the bodies[a] to take them out of the house, he will say to one inside the house, "*Are there* any more with you?"
   Then someone will say, "None."
   And he will say, "Hold your tongue! For we dare not mention the name of the LORD."

11 For behold, the LORD gives a command:
   He will break the great house into bits,
   And the little house into pieces.

12 Do horses run on rocks?
   Does *one* plow *there* with oxen?
   Yet you have turned justice into gall,
   And the fruit of righteousness into
   wormwood,
13 You who rejoice over Lo Debar,[a]
   Who say, "Have we not taken Karnaim[b]
   for ourselves
   By our own strength?"

14 "But, behold, I will raise up a nation
   against you,
   O house of Israel,"
   Says the LORD God of hosts;
   "And they will afflict you from the
   entrance of Hamath
   To the Valley of the Arabah."

VISION OF THE LOCUSTS

1 Thus the Lord GOD showed me: Behold, He formed locust swarms at the beginning of the late crop; indeed *it was* the late crop after the king's mowings. 2 And so it was, when they had finished eating the grass of the land, that I said:

"O Lord GOD, forgive, I pray!
Oh, that Jacob may stand,
For he *is* small!"
3 *So* the LORD relented concerning this.
"It shall not be," said the LORD.

VISION OF THE FIRE

4 Thus the Lord GOD showed me: Behold, the Lord GOD called for conflict by fire, and it consumed the great deep and devoured the territory. 5 Then I said:

"O Lord GOD, cease, I pray!
Oh, that Jacob may stand,
For he *is* small!"
6 *So* the LORD relented concerning this.
"This also shall not be," said the Lord GOD.

VISION OF THE PLUMB LINE

7 Thus He showed me: Behold, the Lord stood on a wall *made* with a plumb line, with a plumb line in His hand. 8 And the LORD said to me, "Amos, what do you see?"
   And I said, "A plumb line."
   Then the Lord said:

"Behold, I am setting a plumb line
In the midst of My people Israel;
I will not pass by them anymore.
9 The high places of Isaac shall be desolate,
And the sanctuaries of Israel shall be laid
waste.

6:10 [a]Literally *bones* **6:13** [a]Literally *Nothing* [b]Literally *Horns,* symbol of strength

I will rise with the sword against the house of Jeroboam."

AMAZIAH'S COMPLAINT

¹⁰Then Amaziah the priest of Bethel sent to Jeroboam king of Israel, saying, "Amos has conspired against you in the midst of the house of Israel. The land is not able to bear all his words. ¹¹For thus Amos has said:

'Jeroboam shall die by the sword,
And Israel shall surely be led away
    captive
From their own land.' "

¹²Then Amaziah said to Amos:

"Go, you seer!
Flee to the land of Judah.
There eat bread,
And there prophesy.
13 But never again prophesy at Bethel,
For it *is* the king's sanctuary,
And it *is* the royal residence."

¹⁴Then Amos answered, and said to Amaziah:

"I *was* no prophet,
Nor *was* I a son of a prophet,
But I *was* a sheepbreeder*ᵃ*
And a tender of sycamore fruit.
15 Then the LORD took me as I followed the
    flock,
And the LORD said to me,
'Go, prophesy to My people Israel.'
16 Now therefore, hear the word of the
    LORD:
You say, 'Do not prophesy against
    Israel,
And do not spout against the house of
    Isaac.'

¹⁷"Therefore thus says the LORD:

'Your wife shall be a harlot in the city;
Your sons and daughters shall fall by the
    sword;
Your land shall be divided by *survey*
    line;
You shall die in a defiled land;
And Israel shall surely be led away
    captive
From his own land.' "

VISION OF THE SUMMER FRUIT

¹Thus the Lord GOD showed me: Behold, a basket of summer fruit. ²And He said, "Amos, what do you see?"

So I said, "A basket of summer fruit."

Then the LORD said to me:

"The end has come upon My people
    Israel;
I will not pass by them anymore.
3   And the songs of the temple
Shall be wailing in that day,"
Says the Lord GOD—
"Many dead bodies everywhere,
They shall be thrown out in silence."

4   Hear this, you who swallow up*ᵃ* the
    needy,
And make the poor of the land fail,

⁵Saying:

"When will the New Moon be past,
That we may sell grain?
And the Sabbath,
That we may trade wheat?
Making the ephah small and the shekel
    large,
Falsifying the scales by deceit,
6   That we may buy the poor for silver,
And the needy for a pair of
    sandals—
Even sell the bad wheat?"

7   The LORD has sworn by the pride of
    Jacob:
"Surely I will never forget any of their
    works.
8   Shall the land not tremble for this,
And everyone mourn who dwells in it?

WHAT'S IT MEAN?

Keep in mind that Jacob was also called
Israel. The descendants of his twelve sons
became the twelve tribes of Israel.
Amos 8:7

7:14 *ᵃ*Compare 2 Kings 3:4   **8:4** *ᵃ*Or *trample on* (compare 2:7)

All of it shall swell like the River,[a]
Heave and subside
Like the River of Egypt.

9 "And it shall come to pass in that day,"
   says the Lord GOD,
"That I will make the sun go down at
   noon,
And I will darken the earth in broad
   daylight;
10 I will turn your feasts into mourning,
And all your songs into lamentation;
I will bring sackcloth on every waist,
And baldness on every head;
I will make it like mourning for an only
   son,
And its end like a bitter day.

11 "Behold, the days are coming," says the
   Lord GOD,
"That I will send a famine on the land,
Not a famine of bread,
Nor a thirst for water,
But of hearing the words of the LORD.
12 They shall wander from sea to sea,
And from north to east;
They shall run to and fro, seeking the
   word of the LORD,
But shall not find *it*.

13 "In that day the fair virgins
And strong young men
Shall faint from thirst.
14 Those who swear by the sin[a] of
   Samaria,
Who say,
'As your god lives, O Dan!'

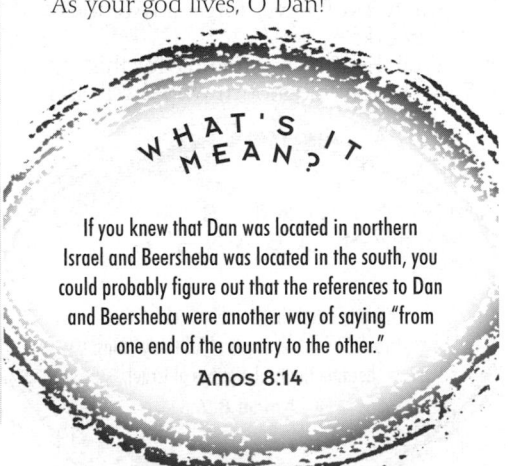

WHAT'S IT MEAN?

If you knew that Dan was located in northern
Israel and Beersheba was located in the south, you
could probably figure out that the references to Dan
and Beersheba were another way of saying "from
one end of the country to the other."

Amos 8:14

And, 'As the way of Beersheba lives!'
They shall fall and never rise again."

THE DESTRUCTION OF ISRAEL

9 [1]I saw the Lord standing by the altar, and He
said:

"Strike the doorposts, that the thresholds
   may shake,
And break them on the heads of them all.
I will slay the last of them with the
   sword.
He who flees from them shall not get
   away,
And he who escapes from them shall not
   be delivered.

2 "Though they dig into hell,[a]
From there My hand shall take them;
Though they climb up to heaven,
From there I will bring them down;
3 And though they hide themselves on top
   of Carmel,
From there I will search and take them;
Though they hide from My sight at the
   bottom of the sea,
From there I will command the serpent,
   and it shall bite them;
4 Though they go into captivity before their
   enemies,
From there I will command the sword,
And it shall slay them.
I will set My eyes on them for harm and
   not for good."

5 The Lord GOD of hosts,
He who touches the earth and it melts,
And all who dwell there mourn;
All of it shall swell like the River,[a]
And subside like the River of Egypt.
6 He who builds His layers in the sky,
And has founded His strata in the earth;
Who calls for the waters of the sea,
And pours them out on the face of the
   earth—
The LORD *is* His name.

7 "*Are* you not like the people of Ethiopia to
   Me,
O children of Israel?" says the LORD.
"Did I not bring up Israel from the land of
   Egypt,
The Philistines from Caphtor,
And the Syrians from Kir?

8:8 [a]That is, the Nile; some Hebrew manuscripts, Septuagint, Syriac, Targum, and Vulgate read *River*;
Masoretic Text reads *the light*.   **8:14** [a]Or *Ashima*, a Syrian goddess   **9:2** [a]Or *Sheol*   **9:5** [a]That is, the Nile

8 "Behold, the eyes of the Lord GOD *are* on
the sinful kingdom,
And I will destroy it from the face of the
earth;
Yet I will not utterly destroy the house of
Jacob,"
Says the LORD.

9 "For surely I will command,
And will sift the house of Israel among all
nations,
As *grain* is sifted in a sieve;
Yet not the smallest grain shall fall to the
ground.
10 All the sinners of My people shall
die by the sword,
Who say, 'The calamity
shall not overtake
nor confront us.'

ISRAEL WILL BE RESTORED

11 "On that day I will
raise up
The tabernacle^a of
David, which
has fallen down,
And repair its damages;
I will raise up its ruins,
And rebuild it as in the days of old;
12 That they may possess the remnant of
Edom,^a

And all the Gentiles who are called by
My name,"
Says the LORD who does this thing.

13 "Behold, the days are coming," says the
LORD,
"When the plowman shall overtake the
reaper,
And the treader of grapes him who sows
seed;
The mountains shall drip with sweet wine,
And all the hills shall flow *with it.*
14 I will bring back the captives of My
people Israel;
They shall build the
waste cities and
inhabit *them;*
They shall plant
vineyards and
drink wine from
them;
They shall also
make gardens
and eat fruit
from them.
15 I will plant them in
their land,
And no longer
shall they be
pulled up
From the land I have given them,"
Says the LORD your God.

> "On that day I will raise up
> the tabernacle of David,
> which has fallen down, and
> repair its damages; I will
> raise up its ruins, and rebuild
> it as in the days of old."
> (Amos 9:11)

9:11 ^aLiterally *booth*, figure of a deposed dynasty   9:12 ^aSeptuagint reads *mankind.*

obadiah

CONTENT Obadiah's prophecy pertained to a neighboring nation. There had been a rift between Edom and Israel for many generations. It actually was more of a family feud than a rift. A few hundred years before, Israel's ancestor and Edom's ancestor were brothers. Israel cheated Edom out of the family fortune, so to speak. This created some bad vibes. As it works with bad vibes, they were passed down from generation to generation and got bigger and fiercer along the way. If Israel received blessings, then Edom booed. If Israel fell into hard times, then Edom cheered.

Finally, Obadiah, a prophet of God, stood up to say, "ENOUGH!"

While Israel was, by no means, a perfect nation, they were God's chosen people. To stand against Israel was like taking sides against God! For Edom to continue to bully and harass God's people would *not* do. Obadiah sent the message loud and clear that Edom would face the consequences for being a bully.

What were those consequences to be? Edom would die out completely as a nation. Wow!—that was pretty harsh. Was God serious?

Have you seen Edom on a map lately?

Outline
1–9 .... God's Judgment on Edom
10–14 .... Edom's Cruelty Toward Israel
15–21 .... Israel's Victory

Purpose God will judge those who harass His people.

Theme God's Judgment on Edom

Date of writing 586 B.C.

THE COMING JUDGMENT ON EDOM

¹The vision of Obadiah.

Thus says the Lord GOD concerning
    Edom
(We have heard a report from the LORD,
And a messenger has been sent among
    the nations, *saying,*
"Arise, and let us rise up against her for
    battle"):

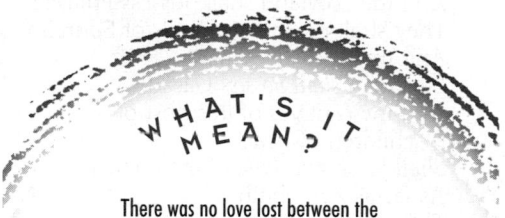

WHAT'S IT MEAN?

There was no love lost between the
Edomites, the descendants of Esau, and the
Israelites, the descendants of Jacob. Apparently the sibling rivalry that
existed between the two brothers was passed on to their descendants.
When the Israelites were on their way to the Promised Land for the
first time, the king of Edom refused to let them cross through his land.
As a result, the Israelites were forced to travel through the desert.
The bad feelings between the two countries
continued for centuries.

Obadiah 1

² "Behold, I will make you small among the
    nations;
You shall be greatly despised.
³ The pride of your heart has deceived
    you,
You who dwell in the clefts of the rock,
Whose habitation is high;
You who say in your heart, 'Who will
    bring me down to the ground?'
⁴ Though you ascend *as* high as the eagle,
And though you set your nest among the
    stars,
From there I will bring you down," says
    the LORD.

⁵ "If thieves had come to you,
If robbers by night—
Oh, how you will be cut off!—
Would they not have stolen till they had
    enough?
If grape-gatherers had come to you,
Would they not have left *some* gleanings?

⁶ "Oh, how Esau shall be searched out!
How his hidden treasures shall be sought
    after!
⁷ All the men in your confederacy
Shall force you to the border;
The men at peace with you
Shall deceive you *and* prevail against
    you.
Those who eat your bread shall lay a trap[a]
    for you.
No one is aware of it.

⁸ "Will I not in that day," says the LORD,
"Even destroy the wise *men* from Edom,
And understanding from the mountains
    of Esau?
⁹ Then your mighty men, O Teman, shall
    be dismayed,
To the end that everyone from the
    mountains of Esau
May be cut off by slaughter.

EDOM MISTREATED HIS BROTHER

¹⁰ "For violence against your brother
    Jacob,
Shame shall cover you,
And you shall be cut off forever.
¹¹ In the day that you stood on the other
    side—
In the day that strangers carried captive
    his forces,
When foreigners entered his gates
And cast lots for Jerusalem—
Even you *were* as one of them.

¹² "But you should not have gazed on the
    day of your brother
In the day of his captivity;[a]
Nor should you have rejoiced over the
    children of Judah
In the day of their destruction;
Nor should you have spoken proudly
In the day of distress.
¹³ You should not have entered the gate of
    My people
In the day of their calamity.
Indeed, you should not have gazed on
    their affliction
In the day of their calamity,
Nor laid *hands* on their substance
In the day of their calamity.
¹⁴ You should not have stood at the
    crossroads
To cut off those among them who
    escaped;

7 [a]Or *wound,* or *plot*   **12** [a]Literally *on the day he became a foreigner*

Nor should you have delivered up those
　　among them who remained
In the day of distress.

15 "For the day of the LORD
　　upon all the nations *is*
　　near;
　　As you have done, it
　　shall be done to you;
　　Your reprisal shall return
　　upon your own head.

JUDGMENT
Will we reap
what we
sow?
(15)

16 For as you drank on My holy mountain,
　　So shall all the nations drink continually;
　　Yes, they shall drink, and swallow,
　　And they shall be as though they had
　　never been.

ISRAEL'S FINAL TRIUMPH

17 "But on Mount Zion there shall be
　　deliverance,
　　And there shall be holiness;
　　The house of Jacob shall possess their
　　possessions.

18 The house of Jacob shall be a fire,

And the house of Joseph a flame;
But the house of Esau *shall be* stubble;
They shall kindle them and devour
　　them,
And no survivor shall *remain* of the
　　house of Esau,"
For the LORD has spoken.

19 The South*ᵃ* shall possess the mountains
　　of Esau,
And the Lowland shall possess Philistia.
They shall possess the fields of Ephraim
And the fields of Samaria.
Benjamin *shall possess* Gilead.

20 And the captives of this host of the
　　children of Israel
Shall possess the land of the Canaanites
As far as Zarephath.
The captives of Jerusalem who are in
　　Sepharad
Shall possess the cities of the South.*ᵃ*

21 Then saviors*ᵃ* shall come to Mount Zion
To judge the mountains of Esau,
And the kingdom shall be the LORD's.

19 *ᵃ*Hebrew *Negev*　20 *ᵃ*Hebrew *Negev*　21 *ᵃ*Or *deliverers*

CONTENT Jonah is a story about the stubbornness of human nature versus the stubborn grace of God.

In one corner, you have a prophet who is so caught up in his own hate and prejudice against Nineveh that he would rather run from God than preach there. In the other corner, you have a God who loves both the delinquent prophet and the evil city and would rather give them both a hard time than let them stay the way they are.

The prophet throws the first punch by hopping a ship that's headed the opposite way from Nineveh. God counters the blow by sending a storm and big fish which, working together, give the prophet three days to evaluate his choices.

At the end of round one, Jonah does go to Nineveh.

That's the most famous part of the story, but in round two is the real knockout. Once Jonah preaches to Nineveh, the people respond beautifully. They repent of their sin and God puts off their destruction. A happy ending?

Not yet. Jonah is still so full of hate for these people that he is disappointed that they repented. Did you get that? The *prophet* is *disappointed* that the people *repented*.

You decide who won after you've read the rest.

Outline

Purpose We are to adopt God's gracious attitude toward all.

Theme God's Compassion for All People

Date of writing 750 B.C.

> "Those who regard worthless idols forsake their own Mercy. But I will sacrifice to You with the voice of thanksgiving; I will pay what I have vowed. Salvation is of the LORD" (2:8, 9).

Bible Talk

God's Call

Sometimes we look at God's call as a scary thing. Sometimes we think that God will call us to do the one thing we just think we can't bear to do. In the case of Jonah, this was true; but, because Jonah's hate was a sin, it needed to be faced rather than run away from.

In your life, discovering God's call, or task, for you will be a process that might have scary parts and will certainly have fun parts. But you can feel certain that God does not rule our hearts just waiting with glee until He can make us do the thing we most dread. In fact, God most often calls us to do what He has already put a passion and a dream in our hearts to do.

GOD'S GRACE FOR THE GREEDY?

If you had lived in Jonah's country in Jonah's day, his hatred for the people of Nineveh would not have seemed so unusual. Nineveh was the capital of Assyria, a cruel and warlike nation that had threatened Israel for years. Jonah had reason to be angry, fearful, and hesitant to offer himself, much less God's grace, to this city. This brings us to the same issue that Jonah struggled with: why should God be gracious to those who are not gracious to others? Most often, we would rather see the bad guys get beaten up in the end. If they get away with their evil, we feel disappointed. But God's grace is God's business. Jonah's story reminds us to leave judgment to God and trust Him to do what is just in the end.

JONAH'S DISOBEDIENCE

¹Now the word of the LORD came to Jonah the son of Amittai, saying, ²"Arise, go to Nineveh, that great city, and cry out against it; for their wickedness has come up before Me." ³But Jonah arose to flee to Tarshish from the presence of the LORD. He went down to Joppa, and found a ship going to Tarshish; so he paid the fare, and went down into it, to go with them to Tarshish from the presence of the LORD.

THE STORM AT SEA

⁴But the LORD sent out a great wind on the sea, and there was a mighty tempest on the sea, so that the ship was about to be broken up. ⁵Then the mariners were afraid; and every man cried out to his god, and threw the cargo that *was* in the ship into the sea, to lighten the load.ᵃ But Jonah had gone down into the lowest parts of the ship, had lain down, and was fast asleep.

The city of Nineveh was about five hundred miles away from Jonah's home. After King Sennacherib made Nineveh the capital of the Assyrian Empire, he really improved the city. In addition to many beautiful temples, Sennacherib built a seventy-one-room palace, a botanical garden, a zoo, and several parks.

Jonah 1:1, 2

⁶So the captain came to him, and said to him, "What do you mean, sleeper? Arise, call on your God; perhaps your God will consider us, so that we may not perish."

⁷And they said to one another, "Come, let us cast lots, that we may know for whose cause this trouble *has come* upon us." So they cast lots, and the lot fell on Jonah. ⁸Then they said to him, "Please tell us! For whose cause *is* this trouble upon us? What is your occupation? And where do you come from? What is your country? And of what people are you?"

⁹So he said to them, "I *am* a Hebrew; and I fear the LORD, the God of heaven, who made the sea and the dry *land*."

JONAH THROWN INTO THE SEA

¹⁰Then the men were exceedingly afraid, and said to him, "Why have you done this?" For the men knew that he fled from the presence of the LORD, because he had told them. ¹¹Then they said to him, "What shall we do to you that the sea may be calm for us?"—for the sea was growing more tempestuous.

On the Edge

Now the word of the LORD came to Jonah the son of Amittai, saying, "Arise, go to Nineveh, that great city, and cry out against it; for their wickedness has come up before Me." But Jonah arose to flee to Tarshish from the presence of the LORD. He went down to Joppa, and found a ship going to Tarshish; so he paid the fare, and went down into it, to go with them to Tarshish from the presence of the LORD (Jon. 1:1–3).

God called Jonah to go to Nineveh. Jonah was so afraid to go that he got on a ship going in the opposite direction—toward Spain. You know the rest of the story. Jonah was thrown overboard and swallowed by a big fish. Inside the fish he decided to do what God wanted. The fish spit him up and Jonah went to Nineveh. Why do we always think that what God wants us to do will be awful? We hear Him call and we sense His leading, and then we run off to Spain trying to get away from Him. Where do you think God is calling you? Are you ready? Or are you buying a ticket to Spain? Will He have to send a big fish to get your attention? God is a loving God; and while there may be hard days, He would not call you to do something you hate. You may be afraid because something is new and different, but you don't have to be afraid that God is wrong. He knows you, and He knows when you're ready for the task. So when God calls you to Nineveh—go quickly. The belly of a fish is not a cool place to start trusting God.

SEE FOR YOURSELF:
Ps. 37:4, 23, 24; 40:6–8; John 4:34; Phil. 2:13

1:5 ᵃLiterally *from upon them*

¹²And he said to them, "Pick me up and throw me into the sea; then the sea will become calm for you. For I know that this great tempest *is* because of me."

¹³Nevertheless the men rowed hard to return to land, but they could not, for the sea continued to grow more tempestuous against them. ¹⁴Therefore they cried out to the LORD and said, "We pray, O LORD, please do not let us perish for this man's life, and do not charge us with innocent blood; for You, O LORD, have done as it pleased You." ¹⁵So they picked up Jonah and threw him into the sea, and the sea ceased from its raging. ¹⁶Then the men feared the LORD exceedingly, and offered a sacrifice to the LORD and took vows.

JONAH'S PRAYER AND DELIVERANCE

¹⁷Now the LORD had prepared a great fish to swallow Jonah. And Jonah was in the belly of the fish three days and three nights.

2 ¹Then Jonah prayed to the LORD his God from the fish's belly. ²And he said:

"I cried out to the LORD because of my affliction,
And He answered me.

"Out of the belly of Sheol I cried,
And You heard my voice.
3 For You cast me into the deep,
Into the heart of the seas,
And the floods surrounded me;
All Your billows and Your waves passed over me.
4 Then I said, 'I have been cast out of Your sight;

Yet I will look again toward Your holy temple.'
5 The waters surrounded me, *even* to my soul;
The deep closed around me;
Weeds were wrapped around my head.
6 I went down to the moorings of the mountains;
The earth with its bars *closed* behind me forever;
Yet You have brought up my life from the pit,
O LORD, my God.

7 "When my soul fainted within me,
I remembered the LORD;
And my prayer went *up* to You,
Into Your holy temple.

8 "Those who regard worthless idols
Forsake their own Mercy.
9 But I will sacrifice to You
With the voice of thanksgiving;
I will pay what I have vowed.
Salvation *is* of the LORD."

¹⁰So the LORD spoke to the fish, and it vomited Jonah onto dry *land*.

JONAH PREACHES AT NINEVEH

3 ¹Now the word of the LORD came to Jonah the second time, saying, ²"Arise, go to Nineveh, that great city, and preach to it the message that I tell you." ³So Jonah arose and went to Nineveh, according to the word of the LORD. Now Nineveh was an exceedingly great city, a three-day journey*ᵃ in extent*. ⁴And Jonah began to

3:3 *ᵃ*Exact meaning unknown

enter the city on the first day's walk. Then he cried out and said, "Yet forty days, and Nineveh shall be overthrown!"

THE PEOPLE OF NINEVEH BELIEVE

5So the people of Nineveh believed God, proclaimed a fast, and put on sackcloth, from the greatest to the least of them. 6Then word came to the king of Nineveh; and he arose from his throne and laid aside his robe, covered *himself* with sackcloth and sat in ashes. 7And he caused *it* to be proclaimed and published throughout Nineveh by the decree of the king and his nobles, saying,

> Let neither man nor beast, herd nor flock, taste anything; do not let them eat, or drink water. 8But let man and beast be covered with sackcloth, and cry mightily to God; yes, let every one turn from his evil way and from the violence that is in his hands. 9Who can tell *if* God will turn and relent, and turn away from His fierce anger, so that we may not perish?

10Then God saw their works, that they turned from their evil way; and God relented from the disaster that He had said He would bring upon them, and He did not do it.

JONAH'S ANGER AND GOD'S KINDNESS

1But it displeased Jonah exceedingly, and he became angry. 2So he prayed to the LORD, and said, "Ah, LORD, was not this what I said when I was still in my country? Therefore I fled previously to Tarshish; for I know that You *are* a gracious and merciful God, slow to anger and abundant in lovingkindness, One who relents from doing harm. 3Therefore now, O LORD, please take my life from me, for *it is* better for me to die than to live!"

4Then the LORD said, "*Is it* right for you to be angry?"

5So Jonah went out of the city and sat on the east side of the city. There he made himself a shelter and sat under it in the shade, till he might see what would become of the city. 6And the LORD God prepared a plant*ᵃ* and made it come up over Jonah, that it might be shade for his head to deliver him from his misery. So Jonah was very grateful for the plant. 7But as morning dawned the next day God prepared a worm, and it *so* damaged the plant that it withered. 8And it happened, when the sun arose, that God prepared a vehement east wind; and the sun beat on Jonah's head, so that he grew faint. Then he wished death for himself, and said, "*It is* better for me to die than to live."

9Then God said to Jonah, "*Is it* right for you to be angry about the plant?"

And he said, "*It is* right for me to be angry, even to death!"

10But the LORD said, "You have had pity on the plant for which you have not labored, nor made it grow, which came up in a night and perished in a night. 11And should I not pity Nineveh, that great city, in which are more than one hundred and twenty thousand persons who cannot discern between their right hand and their left—and much livestock?"

4:6 *ᵃ*Hebrew *kikayon,* exact identity unknown

CONTENT Several things set Micah apart as a prophet. First, a lot of the prophets preached to either the northern kingdom, Samaria, or the southern kingdom, Judah. Micah preached to both. This is significant since there was a longtime feud between the kingdoms. It shows that Micah knew how to rise above petty human conflicts.

Second, Micah actually prophesied that Bethlehem would be the town that Jesus would be born in (psychic circuit, eat your heart out!). This is an amazing feat, since prophets of the Old Testament weren't known as people who told the future in specifics.

Third, Micah was known for being practical, down-to-earth. He talked about faith in a way that let his listeners and readers know what God expects on a day-to-day basis rather than on a Sunday-to-Sunday basis. One of the most famous passages in Micah describes the godly walk as doing justice, loving mercy, and walking humbly with God (6:8).

The message of the Book of Micah is one that calls us to repent of our sins and to live our lives honorably. It calls us to be good people and to live out our faith, not only in how we worship God but also in how we treat other people.

Outline

Purpose We are to be as concerned as God is with personal and social morality.

Theme Incomparability of the Compassionate Lord

Date of writing 730 B.C.

¹The word of the LORD that came to Micah of Moresheth in the days of Jotham, Ahaz, *and* Hezekiah, kings of Judah, which he saw concerning Samaria and Jerusalem.

THE COMING JUDGMENT ON ISRAEL

2 Hear, all you peoples!
Listen, O earth, and all that is in it!
Let the Lord GOD be a
    witness against you,
The Lord from His holy
    temple.

3 For behold, the LORD is
    coming out of His
    place;
He will come down
And tread on the high
    places of the earth.

4 The mountains will melt
    under Him,
And the valleys will split
Like wax before the fire,
Like waters poured down a steep place.

5 All this is for the transgression of Jacob
And for the sins of the house of Israel.
What *is* the transgression of Jacob?
Is it not Samaria?
And what *are* the high places of Judah?
Are they not Jerusalem?

> "For behold, the LORD is
> coming out of His place;
> He will come down
> and tread on the high
> places of the earth."
> (Micah 1:3)

6 "Therefore I will make Samaria a heap of
    ruins in the field,

Places for planting a vineyard;
I will pour down her stones into the
    valley,
And I will uncover her foundations.

7 All her carved images shall be beaten to
    pieces,
And all her pay as a harlot shall be
    burned with the fire;
All her idols I will lay
    desolate,
For she gathered *it*
    from the pay of a
    harlot,
And they shall return
    to the pay of a
    harlot."

MOURNING FOR ISRAEL AND JUDAH

8 Therefore I will wail
    and howl,
I will go stripped and naked;
I will make a wailing like the jackals
And a mourning like the ostriches,

9 For her wounds *are* incurable.
For it has come to Judah;
It has come to the gate of My people—
To Jerusalem.

10 Tell *it* not in Gath,
Weep not at all;
In Beth Aphrah[a]
Roll yourself in the dust.

11 Pass by in naked shame, you inhabitant
    of Shaphir;
The inhabitant of Zaanan[a] does not go
    out.
Beth Ezel mourns;
Its place to stand is taken away from
    you.

12 For the inhabitant of Maroth pined[a] for
    good,
But disaster came down from the LORD
To the gate of Jerusalem.

13 O inhabitant of Lachish,
Harness the chariot to the swift steeds
(She *was* the beginning of sin to the
    daughter of Zion),
For the transgressions of Israel were
    found in you.

14 Therefore you shall give presents to
    Moresheth Gath;[a]

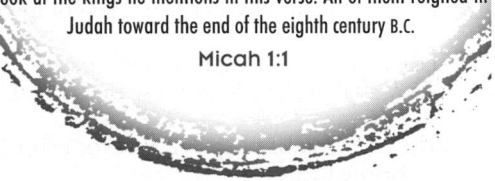

WHAT'S IT MEAN?

During Micah's lifetime, Israel was actually split into two different nations. The northern kingdom, which was called Israel, had Samaria as its capital. The southern kingdom, which was called Judah, had Jerusalem as its capital. Both capital cities also served as the main worship centers for their nation. If you'd like to know when Micah lived, all you need to do is look at the kings he mentions in this verse. All of them reigned in Judah toward the end of the eighth century B.C.

Micah 1:1

1:10 [a]Literally *House of Dust*   **1:11** [a]Literally *Going Out*   **1:12** [a]Literally *was sick*   **1:14** [a]Literally *Possession of Gath*

The houses of Achzib[b] *shall be* a lie to the
  kings of Israel.
15 I will yet bring an heir to you,
   O inhabitant of Mareshah;[a]
The glory of Israel shall come to
  Adullam.
16 Make yourself bald and cut off your hair,
Because of your precious children;
Enlarge your baldness like an eagle,
For they shall go from you into captivity.

WHAT'S IT MEAN?

The Israelites liked to wear their hair and beards
long. They thought it made them look attractive and
manly (or womanly, depending on the sex). To them, a clean-shaven
head was something to be ashamed of. Aside from priests and Levites,
the only Israelite man who would have considered shaving his head was
one who was going through a time of extreme
sadness or mourning.

Micah 1:16

WOE TO EVILDOERS

1 Woe to those who devise iniquity,
  And work out evil on their beds!
At morning light they practice it,
Because it is in the power of their hand.
2 They covet fields and take *them* by
  violence,
Also houses, and seize *them*.
So they oppress a man and his house,
A man and his inheritance.

3 Therefore thus says the LORD:

"Behold, against this family I am devising
  disaster,
From which you cannot remove your
  necks;
Nor shall you walk haughtily,
For this *is* an evil time.
4 In that day *one* shall take up a proverb
  against you,
And lament with a bitter lamentation,
  saying:
'We are utterly destroyed!

He has changed the heritage of my
  people;
How He has removed *it* from me!
To a turncoat He has divided our fields.' "

5 Therefore you will have no one to
  determine boundaries[a] by lot
In the assembly of the LORD.

LYING PROPHETS

6 "Do not prattle," *you say to those* who
  prophesy.
So they shall not prophesy to you;[a]
They shall not return insult for insult.[b]
7 *You who are* named the house of Jacob:
"Is the Spirit of the LORD restricted?
Are these His doings?
Do not My words do good
To him who walks uprightly?

8 "Lately My people have risen up as an
  enemy—
You pull off the robe with the garment
From those who trust *you*, as they
  pass by,
Like men returned from war.
9 The women of My people you cast out
From their pleasant houses;
From their children
You have taken away My glory forever.

10 "Arise and depart,
For this *is* not *your* rest;
Because it is defiled, it shall destroy,
Yes, with utter destruction.
11 If a man should walk in a false spirit
And speak a lie, *saying*,
'I will prophesy to you of wine and drink,'
Even he would be the prattler of this
  people.

ISRAEL RESTORED

12 "I will surely assemble all of you, O Jacob,
I will surely gather the remnant of Israel;
I will put them together like sheep of the
  fold,[a]
Like a flock in the midst of their pasture;
They shall make a loud noise because of
  so many people.
13 The one who breaks open will come up
  before them;
They will break out,
Pass through the gate,
And go out by it;

1:14 [b]Literally *Lie* **1:15** [a]Literally *Inheritance* **2:5** [a]Literally *one casting a surveyor's line* **2:6** [a]Literally *to these* [b]Vulgate reads *He shall not take shame.* **2:12** [a]Hebrew *Bozrah*

Their king will pass before them,
With the LORD at their head."

WICKED RULERS AND PROPHETS

¹And I said:

"Hear now, O heads of Jacob,
And you rulers of the house of Israel:
Is it not for you to know justice?
2 You who hate good and love evil;
Who strip the skin from My people,ᵃ
And the flesh from their bones;
3 Who also eat the flesh of My people,
Flay their skin from them,
Break their bones,
And chop *them* in pieces
Like *meat* for the pot,
Like flesh in the caldron."

4 Then they will cry to the LORD,
But He will not hear them;
He will even hide His face from them at
that time,
Because they have been evil in their
deeds.

5 Thus says the LORD concerning the
prophets
Who make my people stray;
Who chant "Peace"
While they chew with their teeth,
But who prepare war against him
Who puts nothing into their mouths:

6 "Therefore you shall have night without
vision,
And you shall have darkness without
divination;
The sun shall go down on the prophets,
And the day shall be dark for them.
7 So the seers shall be ashamed,
And the diviners abashed;
Indeed they shall all cover their lips;
For *there is* no answer from God."

8 But truly I am full of power by the Spirit
of the LORD,
And of justice and might,
To declare to Jacob his transgression
And to Israel his sin.
9 Now hear this,
You heads of the house of Jacob
And rulers of the house of Israel,
Who abhor justice
And pervert all equity,
10 Who build up Zion with bloodshed
And Jerusalem with iniquity:
11 Her heads judge for a bribe,
Her priests teach for pay,
And her prophets divine for money.
Yet they lean on the LORD, and say,
"Is not the LORD among us?
No harm can come upon us."
12 Therefore because of you
Zion shall be plowed *like* a field,
Jerusalem shall become heaps of ruins,
And the mountain of the templeᵃ
Like the bare hills of the forest.

3:2 ᵃLiterally *them*   **3:12** ᵃLiterally *house*

Promise   HE PROMISES TO BE YOUR KING.

The one who breaks open will come up before them; they will break out, pass through the gate, and go out by it; their king will pass before them, with the LORD at their head (Mic. 2:13).

Sometimes, for a moment, people wonder what it would be like to be a part of a royal family—wealth, privilege, honor, and a strong heritage. You are a member of the family of God, and He promises to be your king. That makes you the son or daughter of the King. You will be honored because you belong to Him. You take part in the wealth of your Father. He doesn't rule with an iron fist, but with a loving heart. It may be difficult to understand it all now, but you are truly a child of the King. Your title can never be removed, and the Lord will never be dethroned. He will reign forever.

SEE FOR YOURSELF:
Is. 33:22; Zech. 14:9; Matt. 27:37; 1 Tim. 6:15;
Rev. 19:16

THE LORD'S REIGN IN ZION

1 Now it shall come to pass in the latter
  days
  That the mountain of the LORD's house
  Shall be established on the top of the
  mountains,
  And shall be exalted above the hills;
  And peoples shall flow to it.
2 Many nations shall come and say,
  "Come, and let us go up to the mountain
  of the LORD,
  To the house of the God of Jacob;
  He will teach us His ways,
  And we shall walk in His paths."
  For out of Zion the law shall go forth,
  And the word of the LORD from
  Jerusalem.
3 He shall judge between many peoples,
  And rebuke strong nations afar off;
  They shall beat their swords into
  plowshares,
  And their spears into pruning hooks;
  Nation shall not lift up sword against
  nation,
  Neither shall they learn war anymore.[a]

4 But everyone shall sit under his vine and
  under his fig tree,
  And no one shall make *them* afraid;
  For the mouth of the LORD of hosts has
  spoken.
5 For all people walk each in the name of
  his god,

4:3 [a]Compare Isaiah 2:2–4

WHAT'S IT MEAN?

"The mountain of the LORD's house" was Mount
Moriah in Jerusalem. When David was king, God
selected the spot where He wanted His temple built and even
supplied the blueprints. David's son, Solomon, was the one who
actually oversaw the construction of the temple.

Micah 4:1

But we will walk in the name of the LORD
  our God
Forever and ever.

ZION'S FUTURE TRIUMPH

6 "In that day," says the LORD,
  "I will assemble the lame,
  I will gather the outcast
  And those whom I have afflicted;
7 I will make the lame a remnant,
  And the outcast a strong nation;
  So the LORD will reign over them in
  Mount Zion
  From now on, even forever.

Promise   HE PROMISES REST AND FREEDOM FROM FEAR.

But everyone shall sit under his vine and under his fig tree, and no one shall
make them afraid; for the mouth of the LORD of hosts has spoken (Mic. 4:4).

"Your kingdom come. Your will be done on earth as it is in heaven" (Matt. 6:10). This is one of
the things Jesus told His followers to pray for whenever they talked to God. Can you imagine
what the world would be like if people on earth obeyed Him as faithfully as the angels do now?
There'd be no divorce, no drunk drivers, no drug deals, no car jackings. There wouldn't even be any
war. It's hard to believe that could ever happen.
  But Jesus wasn't telling you to pray for something impossible. That time is coming, and
Micah describes it in this passage. He gives you a picture of a rest and security, not behind
locked windows and doors but out in the peaceful shade. And note Micah's words of assurance:
"For the mouth of the LORD of hosts has spoken." Someday God will give rest to all of His
people. Be encouraged; you're included.

SEE FOR YOURSELF:
Ps. 16:8, 9; Matt. 11:28; Heb. 4:9

8 And you, O tower of the flock,
The stronghold of the daughter of Zion,
To you shall it come,
Even the former dominion shall come,
The kingdom of the daughter of
  Jerusalem."

9 Now why do you cry aloud?
Is there no king in your midst?
Has your counselor perished?
For pangs have seized you like a woman
  in labor.
10 Be in pain, and labor to bring forth,
O daughter of Zion,
Like a woman in birth pangs.
For now you shall go forth from the city,
You shall dwell in the field,
And to Babylon you shall go.
There you shall be delivered;
There the LORD will redeem you
From the hand of your enemies.

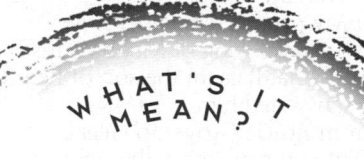

WHAT'S IT MEAN?

Nebuchadnezzar, the king of Babylon, was a real
pain in the neck to the Jewish people. He led three
different attacks against Judah, over the years taking
thousands of Jews back to Babylon as prisoners. In
586 B.C., Nebuchadnezzar and his army burned
down the temple in Jerusalem.

Micah 4:10

11 Now also many nations have gathered
  against you,
Who say, "Let her be defiled,
And let our eye look upon Zion."
12 But they do not know the thoughts of the
  LORD,
Nor do they understand His counsel;
For He will gather them like sheaves to
  the threshing floor.

13 "Arise and thresh, O daughter of Zion;
For I will make your horn iron,
And I will make your hooves bronze;
You shall beat in pieces many peoples;
I will consecrate their gain to the LORD,
And their substance to the Lord of the
  whole earth."

1 Now gather yourself in troops,
O daughter of troops;
He has laid siege against us;
They will strike the judge of Israel with a
  rod on the cheek.

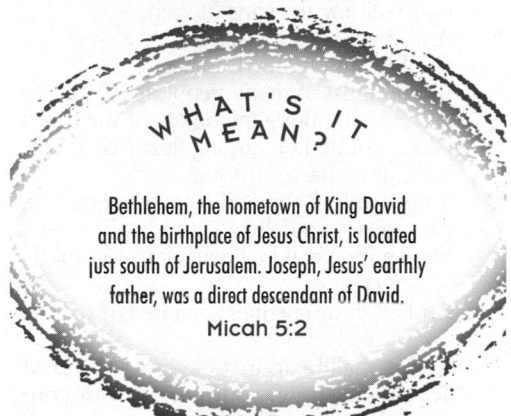

WHAT'S IT MEAN?

Bethlehem, the hometown of King David
and the birthplace of Jesus Christ, is located
just south of Jerusalem. Joseph, Jesus' earthly
father, was a direct descendant of David.

Micah 5:2

THE COMING MESSIAH
2 "But you, Bethlehem Ephrathah,
Though you are little among the
  thousands of Judah,
Yet out of you shall come forth to Me
The One to be Ruler in Israel,
Whose goings forth *are* from of old,
From everlasting."

3 Therefore He shall give them up,
Until the time *that* she who is in labor
  has given birth;
Then the remnant of His brethren
Shall return to the children of Israel.
4 And He shall stand and feed *His flock*
In the strength of the LORD,
In the majesty of the name of the LORD
  His God;
And they shall abide,
For now He shall be great
To the ends of the earth;
5 And this *One* shall be peace.

JUDGMENT ON ISRAEL'S ENEMIES
When the Assyrian comes into our land,
And when he treads in our palaces,
Then we will raise against him
Seven shepherds and eight princely men.
6 They shall waste with the sword the land
  of Assyria,
And the land of Nimrod at its entrances;
Thus He shall deliver *us* from the
  Assyrian,
When he comes into our land
And when he treads within our borders.

7 Then the remnant of Jacob
Shall be in the midst of many peoples,
Like dew from the LORD,
Like showers on the grass,
That tarry for no man
Nor wait for the sons of men.
8 And the remnant of Jacob
Shall be among the Gentiles,
In the midst of many peoples,
Like a lion among the beasts of the forest,
Like a young lion among flocks of sheep,
Who, if he passes through,
Both treads down and tears in pieces,
And none can deliver.
9 Your hand shall be lifted against your
adversaries,
And all your enemies shall be cut off.

10 "And it shall be in that day," says the LORD,
"That I will cut off your horses from your
midst
And destroy your chariots.
11 I will cut off the cities of your land
And throw down all your strongholds.
12 I will cut off sorceries from your hand,
And you shall have no soothsayers.
13 Your carved images I will also cut off,
And your *sacred* pillars from your midst;
You shall no more worship the work of
your hands;
14 I will pluck your wooden images*a* from
your midst;
Thus I will destroy your cities.
15 And I will execute vengeance in anger
and fury
On the nations that have not heard."*a*

WHAT'S IT MEAN?

According to the ancient Canaanites, Asherah,
the goddess of fertility, was the wife of Baal, the
number one god in the land. When the Israelites got to Canaan, they
started worshiping Baal, Asherah, and many other pagan gods. The
places where people worshiped Asherah were
marked by carved wooden poles.

Micah 5:14

GOD PLEADS WITH ISRAEL

1 Hear now what the LORD says:

"Arise, plead your case before the
mountains,
And let the hills hear your voice.
2 Hear, O you mountains, the LORD's
complaint,
And you strong foundations of the earth;
For the LORD has a complaint against His
people,
And He will contend with Israel.

3 "O My people, what have I done to you?
And how have I wearied you?
Testify against Me.
4 For I brought you up from the land of
Egypt,
I redeemed you from the house of
bondage;
And I sent before you Moses, Aaron, and
Miriam.
5 O My people, remember now
What Balak king of Moab counseled,
And what Balaam the son of Beor
answered him,
From Acacia Grove*a* to Gilgal,
That you may know the righteousness of
the LORD."

6 With what shall I come before the LORD,
And bow myself before the High God?
Shall I come before Him with burnt
offerings,
With calves a year old?
7 Will the LORD be pleased with thousands
of rams,
Ten thousand rivers of oil?
Shall I give my firstborn *for* my
transgression,
The fruit of my body *for* the sin of my
soul?

8 He has shown you,
O man, what *is* good;
And what does the LORD
require of you
But to do justly,
To love mercy,
And to walk humbly with your God?

DEVOTION

What does
God require
of us?
(6:8)

PUNISHMENT OF ISRAEL'S INJUSTICE

9 The LORD's voice cries to the city—
Wisdom shall see Your name:

5:14 *a*Hebrew *Asherim*, Canaanite deities　**5:15** *a*Or *obeyed*　**6:5** *a*Hebrew *Shittim* (compare Numbers 25:1;
Joshua 2:1; 3:1)

"Hear the rod!
Who has appointed it?

10 Are there yet the treasures of wickedness
In the house of the wicked,
And the short measure *that is* an
abomination?

11 Shall I count pure *those* with the wicked
scales,
And with the bag of deceitful weights?

12 For her rich men are full of violence,
Her inhabitants have spoken lies,
And their tongue is deceitful in their
mouth.

13 "Therefore I will also make *you* sick by
striking you,
By making *you* desolate because of your
sins.

14 You shall eat, but not be satisfied;
Hunger[a] *shall be* in your midst.
You may carry *some* away,[b] but shall not
save *them*;
And what you do rescue I will give over
to the sword.

15 "You shall sow, but not reap;
You shall tread the olives, but not anoint
yourselves with oil;
And *make* sweet wine, but not drink wine.

16 For the statutes of Omri are kept;
All the works of Ahab's house *are done*;
And you walk in their counsels,
That I may make you a desolation,
And your inhabitants a hissing.
Therefore you shall bear the reproach of
My people."[a]

SORROW FOR ISRAEL'S SINS

1 Woe is me!
For I am like those who gather summer
fruits,
Like those who glean vintage grapes;
There is no cluster to eat
Of the first-ripe fruit *which* my soul
desires.

2 The faithful *man* has perished from the
earth,
And *there is* no one upright among men.
They all lie in wait for blood;
Every man hunts his brother with a net.

3 That they may successfully do evil with
both hands—
The prince asks *for gifts*,

The judge *seeks* a bribe,
And the great *man* utters his evil desire;
So they scheme together.

4 The best of them *is* like a brier;
The most upright *is sharper* than a thorn
hedge;
The day of your watchman and your
punishment comes;
Now shall be their perplexity.

5 Do not trust in a friend;
Do not put your confidence in a
companion;

∵∴ On the Edge

The faithful man has perished from the earth, and there is no one upright among men. They all lie in wait for blood; every man hunts his brother with a net (Mic. 7:2).

You weren't born with the desire to faithfully please God and do the things He wants. No one was. Instead, you were born with the natural tendency to try to get the best for yourself and let others take the leftovers. It's not a pretty fact, but it's the truth and everybody has to come to grips with it.

Thankfully God didn't leave you at the mercy of your natural tendencies. He gave you parents and other adults—friends, teachers, grandparents, etc.—to teach you about right and wrong. There are also rules in your school and laws in your state to keep your selfish desires—and everybody else's—from wreaking havoc. You may not realize it, but these outside forces have a lot to do with the worst of your human nature not getting the best of you.

There's good news, though. The outside forces were meant to be temporary. Because you don't have a lot of faith in your own goodness—because you trust Jesus instead—God's Spirit lives inside you. Now your actions can be determined by an inside force that is constantly changing you into a different person.

SEE FOR YOURSELF:
Ps. 14:2, 3; Is. 53:6;
Jer. 50:6; Hos. 4:1

6:14 [a]Or *Emptiness* or *Humiliation* [b]Targum and Vulgate read *You shall take hold.* **6:16** [a]Following Masoretic Text, Targum, and Vulgate; Septuagint reads *of nations.*

Guard the doors of your mouth
From her who lies in your bosom.
6 For son dishonors father,
Daughter rises against her mother,
Daughter-in-law against her mother-in-
law;
A man's enemies *are* the men of his own
household.
7 Therefore I will look to the LORD;
I will wait for the God of
my salvation;
My God will hear me.

ISRAEL'S CONFESSION AND COMFORT

8 Do not rejoice over me,
my enemy;
When I fall, I will arise;
When I sit in darkness,
The LORD *will be* a light
to me.
9 I will bear the indignation of the LORD,
Because I have sinned against Him,
Until He pleads my case
And executes justice for me.
He will bring me forth to the light;
I will see His righteousness.
10 Then *she who is* my enemy will see,
And shame will cover her who said
to me,

> "Therefore I will look
> to the LORD;
> I will wait for the God
> of my salvation;
> my God will hear me."
> (Micah 7:7)

"Where is the LORD your God?"
My eyes will see her;
Now she will be trampled down
Like mud in the streets.

11 *In* the day when your walls are to be
built,
In that day the decree
shall go far and
wide.[a]
12 *In* that day they[a] shall
come to you
From Assyria and the
fortified cities,[b]
From the fortress[c] to
the River,[d]
From sea to sea,
And mountain *to*
mountain.
13 Yet the land shall be
desolate
Because of those who
dwell in it,
And for the fruit of their deeds.

GOD WILL FORGIVE ISRAEL

14 Shepherd Your people with Your staff,
The flock of Your heritage,
Who dwell solitarily *in* a woodland,
In the midst of Carmel;

7:11 [a]Or *the boundary shall be extended*   **7:12** [a]Literally *he*, collective of the captives   [b]Hebrew *arey mazor*, possibly *cities of Egypt*   [c]Hebrew *mazor*, possibly *Egypt*   [d]That is, the Euphrates

Promise   HE PROMISES TO SUBDUE OUR SINS AND CAST THEM INTO THE SEA.

He will again have compassion on us, and will subdue our iniquities. You will cast all our sins into the depths of the sea (Mic. 7:19).

Sin can haunt you for years. Out of the blue, you may have a flashback of something you did long ago and flinch. You may wonder if God does the same thing. Does He keep a video of your sins—the oldies plus the new releases? At His leisure, He pops in your tape and reviews it? Look at Micah 7:19. It says that God subdues, or conquers, our sins and casts them "into the depths of the sea." No videos. The tapes are erased on purpose. He hurls them into the sea. He can't replay your stuff because He doesn't have it anymore. He's done what only He can do—erased your sin forever. It's totally amazing. It's totally grace. To God, forgiven means forgotten. Someone once said that God throws our sin into the sea and puts up a "No Fishing" sign. No one is allowed to go and fish them out. In your attempt to be more like God, stop playing back your sin tapes. Don't bring them up to yourself or to Him. Accept His forgiveness and don't look back.

SEE FOR YOURSELF:
Is. 43:25; Jer. 31:34; Heb. 10:15–17; 1 John 1:9

Let them feed *in* Bashan and Gilead,
As in days of old.

15 "As in the days when you came out of the
    land of Egypt,
  I will show them[a] wonders."

16 The nations shall see and be ashamed of
    all their might;
  They shall put *their* hand over *their*
    mouth;
  Their ears shall be deaf.
17 They shall lick the dust like a serpent;
  They shall crawl from their holes like
    snakes of the earth.
  They shall be afraid of the LORD our God,
  And shall fear because of You.
18 Who *is* a God like You,
  Pardoning iniquity
  And passing over the transgression of the
    remnant of His heritage?

  He does not retain His anger forever,
  Because He delights *in* mercy.
19 He will again have compassion on us,
  And will subdue our iniquities.

  You will cast all our[a] sins
  Into the depths of the sea.

20 You will give truth to Jacob
  And mercy to Abraham,
  Which You have sworn to our fathers
  From days of old.

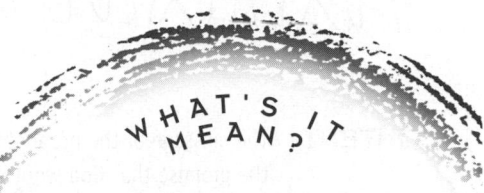

WHAT'S IT MEAN?

Egypt was the first great oppressor of Israel.
The Egyptians held the Israelites in slavery for
several generations before the Lord used Moses to set the people free.
Assyria and Babylon were the second and third great oppressors.
The Assyrians destroyed Samaria, the capital of the northern kingdom of Israel, in 722 B.C. The Babylonians destroyed Jerusalem in
586 B.C. That was hardly the end of the story, though. Seventy years
after Jerusalem was destroyed, a group of Jewish people were
released from captivity in Babylon and allowed to return to the city
to rebuild the temple. Roughly seventy years after that, another group
of Jews, this one led by Nehemiah, was allowed to
return to Jerusalem to rebuild the city's walls.
Micah 7:12

7:15 [a]Literally *him*, collective for the captives   **7:19** [a]Literally *their*

CONTENT

The message of the prophet Nahum is a final showdown between good and evil. It's the promise that God would deal with the nation of Assyria, specifically with its capital city, Nineveh, once and for all.

When you think of Nineveh, think of an old western town without a sheriff. The bandits had taken over, and there was no justice to be found. It was not a place where you'd like to raise your kids or even have to ride a stagecoach through. Decency had been ridden out of this savage town before sunset a long time ago.

Nineveh had given Israel grief for hundreds of years. After Nahum's message, Assyria actually did ravage Israel, tearing the people from their homes and keeping them in exile for a time.

Nahum's prophecy was a word of good news even if Nineveh had a few more years to give Israel grief. The good news was that God's cavalry was on its way, dressed in white and ready to win. Judgment would eventually, but definitely, fall on Nineveh.

Outline

Purpose

Godless nations like Assyria will surely fall.

Theme

God's Judgment on the City of Nineveh

Date of writing

620 B.C.

[1]The burden[a] against Nineveh. The book of the vision of Nahum the Elkoshite.

GOD'S WRATH ON HIS ENEMIES

2   God *is* jealous, and the LORD avenges;
    The LORD avenges and *is* furious.
    The LORD will take vengeance on His adversaries,
    And He reserves *wrath* for His enemies;
3   The LORD *is* slow to anger and great in power,
    And will not at all acquit *the wicked.*

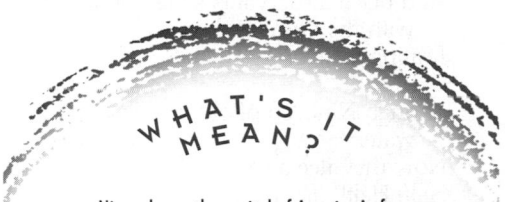

WHAT'S IT MEAN?

Nineveh was the capital of Assyria. As far
as the Jewish people were concerned, the Assyrians
were the biggest troublemakers on the block. The Assyrians
destroyed Samaria, the capital of the northern kingdom of Israel, in
722 B.C. They also tried to conquer Judah, the southern kingdom, by
surrounding Jerusalem and not allowing any food, water, or
supplies to enter the city. Ultimately, they failed in their attempt,
but not before causing the people of
Jerusalem to suffer terribly.

Nahum 1:1

    The LORD has His way
    In the whirlwind and in the storm,
    And the clouds *are* the dust of His feet.
4   He rebukes the sea and makes it dry,
    And dries up all the rivers.
    Bashan and Carmel wither,
    And the flower of Lebanon wilts.
5   The mountains quake before Him,
    The hills melt,
    And the earth heaves[a] at His presence,
    Yes, the world and all who dwell in it.

6   Who can stand before His indignation?
    And who can endure the fierceness of His anger?
    His fury is poured out like fire,
    And the rocks are thrown down by Him.

7   The LORD *is* good,
    A stronghold in the day of trouble;
    And He knows those who trust in Him.
8   But with an overflowing flood
    He will make an utter end of its place,
    And darkness will pursue His enemies.

TRIALS

Where can
we find
protection?
(1:7)

9   What do you conspire against the LORD?
    He will make an utter end *of it.*
    Affliction will not rise up a second time.
10   For while tangled *like* thorns,
    And while drunken *like* drunkards,
    They shall be devoured like stubble fully dried.
11   From you comes forth *one*
    Who plots evil against the LORD,
    A wicked counselor.

[12]Thus says the LORD:

    "Though *they are* safe, and likewise many,
    Yet in this manner they will be cut down
    When he passes through.
    Though I have afflicted you,
    I will afflict you no more;
13   For now I will break off his yoke from you,
    And burst your bonds apart."

14   The LORD has given a command concerning you:
    "Your name shall be perpetuated no longer.
    Out of the house of your gods
    I will cut off the carved image and the molded image.

WHAT'S IT MEAN?

Is your city or town famous for anything?
Bashan was known for its oak trees. Carmel was
known for its breathtaking view of the Mediterranean
Sea. Lebanon, a forest north of Israel, was
known for its towering cedar trees.

Nahum 1:4

1:1 [a]Or *oracle*   **1:5** [a]Targum reads *burns.*

I will dig your grave,
For you are vile."

15 Behold, on the mountains
The feet of him who brings good tidings,
Who proclaims peace!
O Judah, keep your appointed feasts,
Perform your vows.
For the wicked one shall no more pass
     through you;
He is utterly cut off.

THE DESTRUCTION OF NINEVEH

1 He who scatters[a] has come up before
     your face.
Man the fort!
Watch the road!
Strengthen *your* flanks!
Fortify *your* power mightily.

2 For the LORD will restore the excellence of
     Jacob
Like the excellence of Israel,
For the emptiers have emptied them out
And ruined their vine branches.

WHAT'S IT MEAN?

Chariots were a pretty scary sight to an
army heading into battle. These intimidating war
machines were powered by two or more horses, and usually held two
or three soldiers. One person drove, while the other(s) fired arrows
at the enemy. Sometimes one soldier served
as a shield bearer.
Nahum 2:3, 4

3 The shields of his mighty men *are* made
     red,
The valiant men *are* in scarlet.
The chariots *come* with flaming torches
In the day of his preparation,
And the spears are brandished.[a]
4 The chariots rage in the streets,
They jostle one another in the broad
     roads;

They seem like torches,
They run like lightning.

5 He remembers his nobles;
They stumble in their walk;
They make haste to her walls,
And the defense is prepared.
6 The gates of the rivers are opened,
And the palace is dissolved.
7 It is decreed:[a]
She shall be led away captive,
She shall be brought up;
And her maidservants shall lead *her* as
     with the voice of doves,
Beating their breasts.

8 Though Nineveh of old *was* like a pool of
     water,
Now they flee away.
"Halt! Halt!" *they cry;*
But no one turns back.
9 Take spoil of silver!
Take spoil of gold!
There is no end of treasure,
Or wealth of every desirable prize.
10 She is empty, desolate, and waste!
The heart melts, and the knees shake;
Much pain *is* in every side,
And all their faces are drained of color.[a]

11 Where *is* the dwelling of the lions,
And the feeding place of the young
     lions,
Where the lion walked, the lioness *and*
     lion's cub,
And no one made *them* afraid?
12 The lion tore in pieces enough for his
     cubs,
Killed for his lionesses,
Filled his caves with prey,
And his dens with flesh.

13"Behold, I *am* against you," says the LORD of
hosts, "I will burn your[a] chariots in smoke, and
the sword shall devour your young lions; I will
cut off your prey from the earth, and the voice
of your messengers shall be heard no more."

THE WOE OF NINEVEH

1 Woe to the bloody city!
It *is* all full of lies *and* robbery.
Its victim never departs.
2 The noise of a whip

2:1 [a]Vulgate reads *He who destroys.*   **2:3** [a]Literally *the cypresses are shaken;* Septuagint and Syriac read *the horses rush about;* Vulgate reads *the drivers are stupefied.*   **2:7** [a]Hebrew *Huzzab*   **2:10** [a]Compare Joel 2:6 **2:13** [a]Literally *her*

And the noise of rattling wheels,
Of galloping horses,
Of clattering chariots!
3   Horsemen charge with bright sword and
        glittering spear.
    There is a multitude of slain,
    A great number of bodies,
    Countless corpses—
    They stumble over the corpses—
4   Because of the multitude of harlotries of
        the seductive harlot,
    The mistress of sorceries,
    Who sells nations through her harlotries,
    And families through her sorceries.

5   "Behold, I *am* against you," says the LORD
        of hosts;
    "I will lift your skirts over your face,
    I will show the nations your nakedness,
    And the kingdoms your shame.
6   I will cast abominable filth upon you,
    Make you vile,
    And make you a spectacle.
7   It shall come to pass *that* all who look
        upon you
    Will flee from you, and say,
    'Nineveh is laid waste!
    Who will bemoan her?'
    Where shall I seek comforters for you?"

8   Are you better than No Amon[a]
    That was situated by the River,[b]
    That had the waters around her,
    Whose rampart *was* the sea,
    Whose wall *was* the sea?

9   Ethiopia and Egypt *were* her strength,
    And *it was* boundless;
    Put and Lubim were your[a] helpers.
10 Yet she *was* carried away,
    She went into captivity;
    Her young children also were dashed to
        pieces
    At the head of every street;
    They cast lots for her honorable men,
    And all her great men were bound in
        chains.
11 You also will be drunk;
    You will be hidden;
    You also will seek refuge from the enemy.

12 All your strongholds *are* fig trees with
        ripened figs:
    If they are shaken,
    They fall into the mouth of the eater.
13 Surely, your people in your midst *are*
        women!
    The gates of your land are wide open for
        your enemies;
    Fire shall devour the bars of your *gates*.

14 Draw your water for the siege!
    Fortify your strongholds!
    Go into the clay and tread the mortar!
    Make strong the brick kiln!
15 There the fire will devour you,
    The sword will cut you off;
    It will eat you up like a locust.

    Make yourself many—like the locust!
    Make yourself many— like the *swarming*
        locusts!
16 You have multiplied your merchants
        more than the stars of heaven.
    The locust plunders and flies away.
17 Your commanders *are* like *swarming*
        locusts,
    And your generals like great
        grasshoppers,
    Which camp in the hedges on a cold day;
    When the sun rises they flee away,
    And the place where they *are* is not
        known.

18 Your shepherds slumber, O king of
        Assyria;
    Your nobles rest *in the dust*.
    Your people are scattered on the
        mountains,
    And no one gathers them.

3:8 [a]That is, ancient Thebes; Targum and Vulgate read *populous Alexandria*. [b]Literally *rivers*, that is, the Nile
and the surrounding canals   **3:9** [a]Septuagint reads *her*.

19 Your injury *has* no healing,
Your wound is severe.
All who hear news of you
Will clap *their* hands over you,
For upon whom has not your wickedness
passed continually?

habakkuk

CONTENT

The Book of Habakkuk addresses some of the same issues as the Book of Job. Remember Job? He was a good man, but he suffered. His friends tried to tell him it was his fault. All of them tried to figure out exactly why bad things happen to people who try to be good.

It's like a math equation that just doesn't compute. It seems like life should work like this:

Living a good life + being a good person = having good things happen to you.

But even if we live a good life and are good people, we can never be sure what is on the other side of the equal sign. That is what Job and his friends struggled with. That is what Habakkuk struggled with. That is what we sometimes struggle with.

In the first two chapters, Habakkuk asks God those hard questions, and God gives him some good answers. Life isn't fair, but God is just. Sometimes it takes a while to find the final equal sign. Sometimes it takes all your life. Life on earth is about learning to live a life of faith and becoming what God wants us to be in the process. Those things don't make life any more fair; they just make it worth living.

Outline

1:1—2:20 .... Habakkuk Questions God's Judgments, and the Lord Answers
3:1–19 .... Habakkuk Gives Praise to the Lord

Purpose

There is no real "success" for the wicked.

Theme

The Just Shall Live By Faith

Date of writing

612 B.C.

¹The burden*ᵃ* which the prophet Habakkuk saw.

THE PROPHET'S QUESTION

2   O Lᴏʀᴅ, how long shall I cry,
    And You will not hear?
    Even cry out to You, "Violence!"
    And You will not save.
3   Why do You show me iniquity,
    And cause *me* to see trouble?
    For plundering and violence *are* before
        me;
    There is strife, and contention arises.
4   Therefore the law is powerless,
    And justice never goes forth.
    For the wicked surround the righteous;
    Therefore perverse judgment proceeds.

THE LORD'S REPLY

5   "Look among the nations and watch—
    Be utterly astounded!
    For *I will* work a work in your days
    Which you would not believe, though it
        were told *you.*
6   For indeed I am raising up the Chaldeans,
    A bitter and hasty nation
    Which marches through the breadth of
        the earth,
    To possess dwelling places *that are* not
        theirs.
7   They are terrible and dreadful;
    Their judgment and their dignity proceed
        from themselves.
8   Their horses also are swifter than
        leopards,

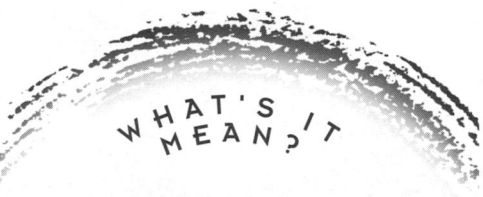

Let's set the time frame for this conversation between Habakkuk and God. The Babylonians (or Chaldeans, as they were also known) were on a roll, having defeated both Egypt and Assyria in battle. In 612 B.C., they destroyed the city of Nineveh, the capital of Assyria. Less than thirty years later, the Babylonians, led by King Nebuchadnezzar, would conquer the city of Jerusalem and burn down the temple built by Solomon.

Habakkuk 1:6

On the Edge

Are You not from everlasting,
O Lᴏʀᴅ my God, my Holy One?
(Hab. 1:12a).

Have you ever sat around thinking about how God created everything, and then wondered, *Yeah, but where did God come from?* Well, the answer is that He has always existed. He's everlasting—no beginning, no end. Compare Habakkuk 1:12 with Genesis 1:1. Notice that the Genesis verse says, "In the beginning God . . ." He has always been. He was never born; He will never die. That can blow your mind. It's just too big to grasp. We are so used to a start and a finish for everything. God has no birthday, no expiration date. He always was, even before the earth was created. He is now, right where you are. He will always be, long after you and the earth have passed away (see Rev. 1:8).

SEE FOR YOURSELF:
   Gen. 1:1; Is. 57:15;
        John 1:1;
   1 Tim. 1:17; Rev. 1:8

    And more fierce than evening wolves.
    Their chargers charge ahead;
    Their cavalry comes from afar;
    They fly as the eagle *that* hastens to eat.

9   "They all come for violence;
    Their faces are set *like* the east wind.
    They gather captives like sand.
10 They scoff at kings,
    And princes are scorned by them.
    They deride every stronghold,
    For they heap up earthen *mounds* and
        seize it.
11 Then *his* mind*ᵃ* changes, and he
        transgresses;
    He commits offense,
    Ascribing this power to his god."

THE PROPHET'S SECOND QUESTION

12 Are You not from everlasting,
    O Lᴏʀᴅ my God, my Holy One?
    We shall not die.
    O Lᴏʀᴅ, You have appointed them for
        judgment;

1:1 *ᵃ*Or *oracle*   **1:11** *ᵃ*Literally *spirit* or *wind*

O Rock, You have marked them for
    correction.

13 *You are* of purer eyes than to behold evil,
    And cannot look on wickedness.
    Why do You look on those who deal
        treacherously,
    And hold Your tongue when the wicked
        devours
    A *person* more righteous than he?

14 *Why* do You make men like fish of the
        sea,
    Like creeping things *that have* no ruler
        over them?

15 They take up all of them with a hook,
    They catch them in their net,
    And gather them in their dragnet.
    Therefore they rejoice and are glad.

16 Therefore they sacrifice to their net,
    And burn incense to their dragnet;
    Because by them their share *is* sumptuous
    And their food plentiful.

17 Shall they therefore empty their net,
    And continue to slay nations without pity?

1 I will stand my watch
    And set myself on the rampart,
    And watch to see what He will say to me,
    And what I will answer when I am
        corrected.

2:5 *a*Or *Sheol*

THE JUST LIVE BY FAITH

2 Then the LORD answered me and said:

    "Write the vision
    And make *it* plain on tablets,
    That he may run who reads it.

3 For the vision *is* yet for an appointed
        time;
    But at the end it will speak, and it will not
        lie.
    Though it tarries, wait for it;
    Because it will surely come,
    It will not tarry.

4 "Behold the proud,
    His soul is not upright in him;
    But the just shall live by his faith.

WOE TO THE WICKED

5 "Indeed, because he transgresses by wine,
    He is a proud man,
    And he does not stay at home.
    Because he enlarges his desire as hell,*a*
    And he *is* like death, and cannot be
        satisfied,
    He gathers to himself all nations
    And heaps up for himself all peoples.

6 "Will not all these take up a proverb
        against him,

Promise HE PROMISES TO BE TRUTHFUL ABOUT THE FUTURE.

For the vision is yet for an appointed time; but at the end it will speak, and it will not lie. Though it tarries, wait for it; because it will surely come, it will not tarry (Hab. 2:3).

Everyone wants you to believe what they have to say about the future. Grocery store magazines report new predictions about the future every month or so. Late-night psychics want you to call so they can tell you about your future. And newspaper horoscopes want you to read every day to find out how this day will go. The whole business of "future-telling" is one big scam. Millions spend money because they want someone—anyone—to give them encouragement and hope. Their empty words have no value. You can only trust what God says about the future. Only His truth can guide your life. Everything else will fall short. So if you need to consult someone about a decision or life even, turn to the One who has been to the future and knows the whole story. You can trust what He says. You can build your life on His truth.

SEE FOR YOURSELF:
Josh. 21:45; Ps. 18:30; Prov. 30:5;
Jer. 29:11; John 17:17

And a taunting riddle against him, and
 say,
'Woe to him who increases
What is not his—how long?
And to him who loads himself with
 many pledges'?[a]

7 Will not your creditors[a] rise up suddenly?
Will they not awaken who oppress you?
And you will become their booty.

8 Because you have plundered many
 nations,
All the remnant of the people shall
 plunder you,
Because of men's blood
And the violence of the land *and* the city,
And of all who dwell in it.

9 "Woe to him who covets evil gain for his
 house,
That he may set his nest on high,
That he may be delivered from the power
 of disaster!

10 You give shameful counsel to your house,
Cutting off many peoples,
And sin *against* your soul.

11 For the stone will cry out from the wall,
And the beam from the timbers will
 answer it.

12 "Woe to him who builds a town with
 bloodshed,
Who establishes a city by iniquity!

13 Behold, *is it* not of the LORD of hosts
That the peoples labor to feed the fire,[a]
And nations weary themselves in vain?

14 For the earth will be filled
With the knowledge of the glory of the
 LORD,
As the waters cover the sea.

15 "Woe to him who gives drink to his
 neighbor,
Pressing[a] him *to* your bottle,
Even to make *him* drunk,
That you may look on his nakedness!

16 You are filled with shame instead of glory.
You also—drink!
And be exposed as uncircumcised![a]
The cup of the LORD's right hand *will be*
 turned against you,
And utter shame will be on your glory.

17 For the violence *done to* Lebanon will
 cover you,
And the plunder of beasts *which* made
 them afraid,
Because of men's blood
And the violence of the land *and* the city,
And of all who dwell in it.

18 "What profit is the image, that its maker
 should carve it,
The molded image, a teacher of lies,
That the maker of its mold should trust
 in it,
To make mute idols?

19 Woe to him who says to wood, 'Awake!'
To silent stone, 'Arise! It shall teach!'
Behold, it is overlaid with gold and silver,
Yet in it there is no breath at all.

20 "But the LORD is in His holy temple.
Let all the earth keep silence before Him."

THE PROPHET'S PRAYER

1 A prayer of Habakkuk the prophet, on
Shigionoth.[a]

2 O LORD, I have heard Your speech *and*
 was afraid;
O LORD, revive Your work in the midst of
 the years!
In the midst of the years make *it* known;
In wrath remember mercy.

3 God came from Teman,
The Holy One from Mount Paran.　　Selah

His glory covered the heavens,
And the earth was full of His praise.

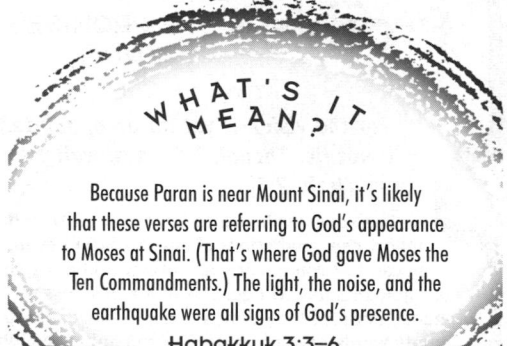

WHAT'S IT MEAN?

Because Paran is near Mount Sinai, it's likely
that these verses are referring to God's appearance
to Moses at Sinai. (That's where God gave Moses the
Ten Commandments.) The light, the noise, and the
earthquake were all signs of God's presence.
Habakkuk 3:3–6

2:6 [a]Syriac and Vulgate read *thick clay.*　**2:7** [a]Literally *those who bite you*　**2:13** [a]Literally *for what satisfies fire,*
that is, for what is of no lasting value　**2:15** [a]Literally *Attaching* or *Joining*　**2:16** [a]Dead Sea Scrolls and
Septuagint read *And reel!*; Syriac and Vulgate read *And fall fast asleep!*　**3:1** [a]Exact meaning unknown

4 *His* brightness was like the light;
He had rays *flashing* from His hand,
And there His power *was* hidden.
5 Before Him went pestilence,
And fever followed at His feet.

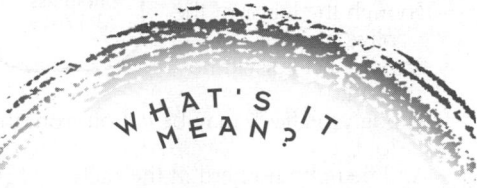

The people of Cushan are usually referred
to as Ethiopians in the Bible. The people of Cushan
and Midian were nomads, wandering tribesmen who lived in tents.
When God parted the Red Sea for the Israelites, they passed from
the land of Cush to the land of Midian.

Habakkuk 3:7

6 He stood and measured the earth;
He looked and startled the nations.
And the everlasting mountains were
scattered,
The perpetual hills bowed.
His ways *are* everlasting.

3:9 *a*Literally *rods* or *tribes* (compare verse 14)

7 I saw the tents of Cushan in affliction;
The curtains of the land of Midian
trembled.

8 O Lord, were *You* displeased with the
rivers,
Was Your anger against the rivers,
Was Your wrath against the sea,
That You rode on Your horses,
Your chariots of salvation?
9 Your bow was made quite ready;
Oaths were sworn over *Your* arrows.*a*
Selah

You divided the earth with rivers.
10 The mountains saw You *and* trembled;
The overflowing of the water passed by.
The deep uttered its voice,
And lifted its hands on high.
11 The sun and moon stood still in their
habitation;
At the light of Your arrows they went,
At the shining of Your glittering spear.

12 You marched through the land in
indignation;
You trampled the nations in anger.
13 You went forth for the salvation of Your
people,
For salvation with Your Anointed.

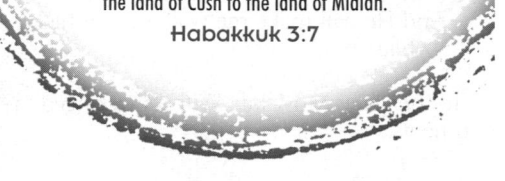

Promise HE PROMISES TO PREPARE YOU FOR LIFE'S
JOURNEY.

*The Lord God is my strength; He will make my feet like deer's feet, and He will
make me walk on my high hills (Hab. 3:19).*

Did you know that God gives you feet like a deer? Habakkuk shows us that picture—feet that
are able to climb steep mountains, steady even when the path is slippery. God prepares you for
the steep, slippery places in your life—when you have to cope with the tough stuff, when you
face a strong temptation, when life is just hard. God gives you the strength to stand strong and
bold when things get rough.

But God may not give you those deer feet automatically, like an instant miracle. You may have
to feel what it's like to slip and almost fall, especially if you start up the mountain by yourself. Even Habakkuk said: "When I heard, my body trembled; my lips quivered at the voice"
(v. 16).

You can look at your stumbling steps as a gift from God. He's showing you that you can't
make it without Him. If you start to fall, it's a little reminder that deer feet aren't a product of
your own inner strength. They come from your faith in Him and in His Spirit living inside you.

SEE FOR YOURSELF:
Ps. 61:1–3; Is. 35:6; 42:16

You struck the head from the house of
the wicked,
By laying bare from foundation to neck.
Selah

14 You thrust through with his own arrows
The head of his villages.
They came out like a whirlwind to scatter
me;
Their rejoicing was like feasting on the
poor in secret.
15 You walked through the sea with Your
horses,
Through the heap of great waters.

16 When I heard, my body trembled;
My lips quivered at *the* voice;
Rottenness entered my bones;
And I trembled in myself,
That I might rest in the day of trouble.
When he comes up to the people,
He will invade them with his troops.

3:19 [a]Hebrew *YHWH Adonai*

A HYMN OF FAITH

17 Though the fig tree
may not blossom,
Nor fruit be on the
vines;
Though the labor of the
olive may fail,
And the fields yield no
food;
Though the flock may be cut off from the
fold,
And there be no herd in the stalls—
18 Yet I will rejoice in the LORD,
I will joy in the God of my salvation.

19 The LORD God[a] is my strength;
He will make my feet like deer's *feet*,
And He will make me walk on my high
hills.

To the Chief Musician. With my stringed instruments.

ENCOURAGEMENT

Are we ever
helpless?
(3:17–19)

Zephaniah

CONTENT

Have you ever seen a natural disaster film? Whether it's a volcano or an earthquake or a nuclear power plant gone wrong, there is always someone running around right before the explosion making one last effort to make the people understand what is about to happen. The person usually looks frazzled and wide-eyed and full of passion about his or her message.

That might have been what Zephaniah looked like. He was the last prophet to preach to Judah before judgment fell and they were taken away into captivity.

The problems Zephaniah's people faced were national problems. They had become an evil people who sacrificed their own children to false gods and spit in the face of the true God. They disrespected and disregarded everything God had done for them. As a nation, they were going to face some consequences that would change their lives forever.

The heart of Zephaniah's message, though, is personal responsibility. The problem may have been nationwide, but the solution was only as big as each person's own heart. They needed to make a choice, each of them, to obey what God told them to do.

Outline

Purpose

God's discipline purges evil and motivates us to return to Him.

Theme

The Wrath of a Loving God

Date of writing

607 B.C.

¹The word of the LORD which came to Zephaniah the son of Cushi, the son of Gedaliah, the son of Amariah, the son of Hezekiah, in the days of Josiah the son of Amon, king of Judah.

THE GREAT DAY OF THE LORD

2   "I will utterly consume everything
    From the face of the land,"
    Says the LORD;
3   "I will consume man and beast;
    I will consume the birds of the heavens,
    The fish of the sea,
    And the stumbling blocks*a* along with the
      wicked.
    I will cut off man from the face of the
      land,"
    Says the LORD.

4   "I will stretch out My hand against Judah,
    And against all the inhabitants of
      Jerusalem.
    I will cut off every trace of Baal from this
      place,
    The names of the idolatrous priests*a* with
      the *pagan* priests—
5   Those who worship the host of heaven
    on the housetops;
    Those who worship and swear *oaths* by
    the LORD,

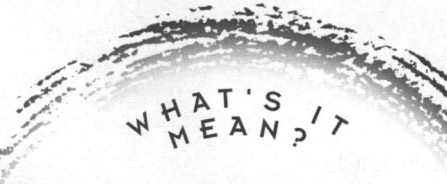

WHAT'S IT MEAN?

When it came to pagan gods, the Israelites weren't choosy. They worshiped just about anything. Baal was the chief god of the Canaanites, but the Israelites adopted him as their own. The followers of Milcom (or Molech, as he was also known) sacrificed children as part of their worship rituals. That didn't bother the Israelites, who were eager to join in the disgusting proceedings, despite the fact that God had specifically forbidden human sacrifice. Not satisfied with merely worshiping idols, the Israelites also got involved in astrology and started worshiping the sun, the moon, and the stars. As part of their worship, they poured out drink offerings and burnt incense on their rooftops.

Zephaniah 1:4, 5

    But who *also* swear by Milcom;*a*
6   Those who have turned back from
    following the LORD,
    And have not sought the LORD, nor
      inquired of Him."

7   Be silent in the presence of the Lord GOD;
    For the day of the LORD *is* at hand,
    For the LORD has prepared a sacrifice;
    He has invited*a* His guests.

8   "And it shall be,
    In the day of the LORD's sacrifice,
    That I will punish the princes and the
      king's children,
    And all such as are clothed with foreign
      apparel.
9   In the same day I will punish
    All those who leap over the threshold,*a*
    Who fill their masters' houses with
      violence and deceit.

10   "And there shall be on that day," says the
    LORD,
  "The sound of a mournful cry from the
    Fish Gate,
    A wailing from the Second Quarter,
    And a loud crashing from the hills.
11   Wail, you inhabitants of Maktesh!*a*
    For all the merchant people are cut down;
    All those who handle money are cut off.

12   "And it shall come to pass at that time
    That I will search Jerusalem with lamps,
    And punish the men
    Who are settled in complacency,*a*
    Who say in their heart,
    'The LORD will not do good,
    Nor will He do evil.'
13   Therefore their goods shall become booty,
    And their houses a desolation;
    They shall build houses, but not inhabit
      them;
    They shall plant vineyards, but not drink
      their wine."

14   The great day of the LORD *is* near;
    It is near and hastens quickly.
    The noise of the day of the LORD is bitter;
    There the mighty men shall cry out.
15   That day *is* a day of wrath,
    A day of trouble and distress,
    A day of devastation and desolation,

1:3 *a*Figurative of idols   **1:4** *a*Hebrew *chemarim*   **1:5** *a*Or *Malcam*, an Ammonite god, also called *Molech* compare Leviticus 18:21)   **1:7** *a*Literally *set apart, consecrated*   **1:9** *a*Compare 1 Samuel 5:5   **1:11** *a*Literally *Mortar*, a market district of Jerusalem   **1:12** *a*Literally *on their lees*, that is, settled like the dregs of wine

A day of darkness and gloominess,
A day of clouds and thick darkness,
16 A day of trumpet and alarm
Against the fortified cities
And against the high towers.

17 "I will bring distress upon men,
And they shall walk like blind men,
Because they have sinned against the
  LORD;
Their blood shall be poured out like dust,
And their flesh like refuse."

18 Neither their silver nor their gold
Shall be able to deliver them
In the day of the LORD's wrath;
But the whole land shall be devoured
By the fire of His jealousy,
For He will make speedy riddance
Of all those who dwell in the land.

The Philistines lived west of Israel, along the
coast of the Mediterranean Sea. For some reason,
the Philistines decided they needed more than one capital city in
their nation. Gaza, Ashdod, Ashkelon, and Ekron were all capitals
of Philistia. Actually, there had been a fifth capital, Gath, but it was
under Judah's control during Zephaniah's day.
Zephaniah 2:4, 5

A CALL TO REPENTANCE

1 Gather yourselves together, yes, gather
    together,
  O undesirable*a* nation,
2 Before the decree is issued,
  Or the day passes like chaff,
  Before the LORD's fierce anger comes
    upon you,
  Before the day of the
    LORD's anger comes
    upon you!
3 Seek the LORD, all you
    meek of the earth,
  Who have upheld His
    justice.

HUMILITY

Is humility
important?
(2:3)

Seek righteousness, seek humility.
It may be that you will be hidden
In the day of the LORD's anger.

JUDGMENT ON NATIONS

4 For Gaza shall be forsaken,
  And Ashkelon desolate;
  They shall drive out Ashdod at noonday,
  And Ekron shall be uprooted.
5 Woe to the inhabitants of the seacoast,
  The nation of the Cherethites!
  The word of the LORD *is* against you,
  O Canaan, land of the Philistines:
  "I will destroy you;
  So there shall be no inhabitant."

6 The seacoast shall be pastures,
  With shelters*a* for shepherds and folds for
    flocks.
7 The coast shall be for the remnant of the
    house of Judah;
  They shall feed *their* flocks there;
  In the houses of Ashkelon they shall lie
    down at evening.
  For the LORD their God will intervene for
    them,
  And return their captives.

8 "I have heard the reproach of Moab,
  And the insults of the people of Ammon,
  With which they have reproached My
    people,
  And made arrogant threats against their
    borders.

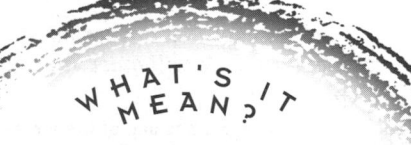

The people of Moab and Ammon were actually
distant relatives of the Israelites. The Moabites and
Ammonites were descendants of Lot, Abraham's nephew. (The
Israelites, of course, were descendants of Abraham.) Despite the fact
that they were "kin," the people of Moab and Ammon were enemies
of Israel. The comparisons to Sodom and Gomorrah probably would
have gotten people's attention. Both of those cities were destroyed
by God in an awesome display of fire from heaven.
Zephaniah 2:8, 9

2:1 *a*Or *shameless*   **2:6** *a*Literally *excavations*, either underground huts or cisterns

9 Therefore, as I live,"
Says the LORD of hosts, the God of Israel,
"Surely Moab shall be like Sodom,
And the people of Ammon like
　　Gomorrah—
Overrun with weeds and saltpits,
And a perpetual desolation.
The residue of My people shall plunder
　　them,
And the remnant of My people shall
　　possess them."

10 This they shall have for their pride,
Because they have reproached and made
　　arrogant threats
Against the people of the LORD of hosts.
11 The LORD *will be* awesome to them,
For He will reduce to nothing all the gods
　　of the earth;
People shall worship Him,
Each one from his place,
Indeed all the shores of the nations.

12 "You Ethiopians also,
You shall be slain by My sword."

13 And He will stretch out His hand against
　　the north,

Destroy Assyria,
And make Nineveh a desolation,
As dry as the wilderness.
14 The herds shall lie down in her midst,
Every beast of the nation.
Both the pelican and the bittern
Shall lodge on the capitals *of her pillars;*
Their voice shall sing in the windows;
Desolation *shall be* at the threshold;
For He will lay bare the cedar work.
15 This is the rejoicing city
That dwelt securely,
That said in her heart,
"I *am it,* and *there is* none besides me."
How has she become a desolation,
A place for beasts to lie down!
Everyone who passes by her
Shall hiss and shake his fist.

THE WICKEDNESS OF JERUSALEM

1 Woe to her who is rebellious and
　　polluted,
To the oppressing city!
2 She has not obeyed *His* voice,
She has not received correction;
She has not trusted in the LORD,
She has not drawn near to her God.

Promise   HE PROMISES TO RESTORE YOU WITH HIS LOVE.

The LORD your God in your midst, the Mighty One, will save; He will rejoice over you with gladness, He will quiet you with His love, He will rejoice over you with singing (Zeph. 3:17).

Zephaniah 3:17 is one of the most awesome verses in all the minor prophets. It shows you incredible truths about God and about yourself. It reveals such a tender and delightful side of the Lord in the middle of some hard prophecies. He rejoices and sings! People don't usually think of God rejoicing and singing, but He does! He's excited because of *you.* When *you* don't feel like you're worth much, remember that God is singing because of you. And on top of His rejoicing and singing, you get a blessing. He restores your life with His love. Everybody needs restoration. Life sometimes gets pretty routine and you find yourself feeling stale and soggy on the inside. You find that you can't spruce up your own heart, because God is the One who changes hearts. He promises to meet you in those stale times. He promises "to quiet you with His love." There's nothing that adds zest to life more than the breath wind of the Spirit of God blowing through your heart. It does more for you on the inside than a squirt from the garden hose on a steamy afternoon. It brings you back to life. It gives you passion again. It refuels your energy. And it stokes the fire of God that's inside of you. He does it all without thunder and lightning. He does it with such tenderness—just by His love, which touches all your deepest places. Never, ever forget that you are the one who makes God sing. And He is the One who "will quiet you with His love."

SEE FOR YOURSELF:
Ps. 23:1–3; 80:18; 147:3; Acts 3:19–21

4   Her prophets are insolent, treacherous
      people;
    Her priests have polluted the sanctuary,
    They have done violence to the law.
5   The LORD *is* righteous in her midst,
    He will do no unrighteousness.
    Every morning He brings His justice to
      light;
    He never fails,
    But the unjust knows no shame.

6   "I have cut off nations,
    Their fortresses are devastated;
    I have made their streets desolate,
    With none passing by.
    Their cities are destroyed;
    There is no one, no inhabitant.
7   I said, 'Surely you will fear Me,
    You will receive instruction'—
    So that her dwelling would not be cut
      off,
    Despite everything for which I punished
      her.
    But they rose early and corrupted all their
      deeds.

A FAITHFUL REMNANT

8   "Therefore wait for Me," says the LORD,
    "Until the day I rise up for plunder;[a]
    My determination *is* to gather the nations
    To My assembly of kingdoms,
    To pour on them My indignation,
    All My fierce anger;
    All the earth shall be devoured
    With the fire of My jealousy.

9   "For then I will restore to the peoples a
      pure language,
    That they all may call on the name of the
      LORD,
    To serve Him with one accord.
10 From beyond the rivers of Ethiopia
    My worshipers,
    The daughter of My dispersed ones,
    Shall bring My offering.
11 In that day you shall not be shamed for
      any of your deeds
    In which you transgress against Me;
    For then I will take away from your midst
    Those who rejoice in your pride,
    And you shall no longer be haughty
    In My holy mountain.
12 I will leave in your midst
    A meek and humble people,

On the Edge

"I will gather those who sorrow over the appointed assembly, who are among you, to whom its reproach is a burden. Behold, at that time I will deal with all who afflict you; I will save the lame, and gather those who were driven out; I will appoint them for praise and fame in every land where they were put to shame. At that time I will bring you back, even at the time I gather you; for I will give you fame and praise among all the peoples of the earth, when I return your captives before your eyes," says the LORD (Zeph. 3:18–20).

There are all kinds of reasons for feeling like a misfit. Maybe you're a lot taller than everybody else you know and you stand out physically. Maybe you live in a part of town different from where most of the people you know live. Maybe you have a whole different set of values and you're labeled a "goody-goody."

For whatever reason, feeling like you don't fit in can be a painful, lonely place. For some people, the situation changes when they go to a new school or move to a new neighborhood or when they get older. Some people go all the way through their lives feeling like they don't belong. But the truth is, you do belong. You belong to the Lord. He is in love with you. You always have a place with Him. He is always glad to see you. He has such a heart for you. Seek His direction for your life. He's got a plan for you, and no one else will fit it as perfectly as you will. Ask Him to bring people you can love and be loved by into your life. He is faithful. He wants you to be happy. He's there to help you.

SEE FOR YOURSELF:
Ps. 31:5; Is. 56:8;
Mic. 4:7; Zeph. 3:17

---

3   Her princes in her midst *are* roaring
      lions;
    Her judges *are* evening wolves
    That leave not a bone till morning.

3:8 [a]Septuagint and Syriac read *for witness*; Targum reads *for the day of My revelation for judgment*; Vulgate reads *for the day of My resurrection that is to come.*

And they shall trust in the name of the
LORD.

13 The remnant of Israel shall do no
unrighteousness
And speak no lies,
Nor shall a deceitful tongue be found in
their mouth;
For they shall feed *their* flocks and lie
down,
And no one shall make *them* afraid."

JOY IN GOD'S FAITHFULNESS

14 Sing, O daughter of Zion!
Shout, O Israel!
Be glad and rejoice with all *your* heart,
O daughter of Jerusalem!
15 The LORD has taken away your
judgments,
He has cast out your enemy.
The King of Israel, the LORD, *is* in your
midst;
You shall see[a] disaster no more.

16 In that day it shall be said to Jerusalem:
"Do not fear;
Zion, let not your hands be weak.
17 The LORD your God in your midst,
The Mighty One, will save;
He will rejoice over you with gladness,
He will quiet *you* with His love,
He will rejoice over you with singing."

18 "I will gather those who sorrow over the
appointed assembly,

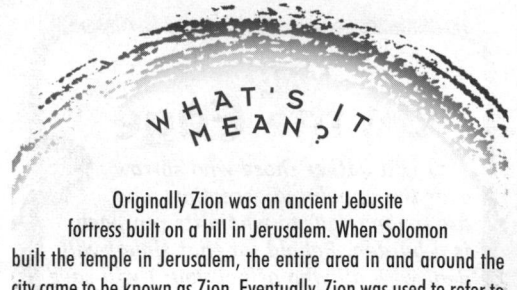

WHAT'S IT MEAN?

Originally Zion was an ancient Jebusite
fortress built on a hill in Jerusalem. When Solomon
built the temple in Jerusalem, the entire area in and around the
city came to be known as Zion. Eventually, Zion was used to refer to
the entire nation of Israel.

Zephaniah 3:16

Who are among you,
To whom its reproach *is* a burden.
19 Behold, at that time
I will deal with all who afflict you;
I will save the lame,
And gather those who were driven out;
I will appoint them for praise and fame
In every land where they were put to
shame.
20 At that time I will bring you back,
Even at the time I gather you;
For I will give you fame and praise
Among all the peoples of the earth,
When I return your captives before your
eyes,"
Says the LORD.

3:15 [a]Some Hebrew manuscripts, Septuagint, and Bomberg read *see*; Masoretic Text and Vulgate read *fear*.

CONTENT
If you've been reading through the Bible, you are very familiar by now with the history of the Hebrews. They continued to go through these cycles of obeying God, then not obeying God, then being beaten up by other countries, then finally returning to God and regaining their natural strength. When Haggai preached his message, the Hebrews were in one of those recovery times.

They had returned home after being held captive in Babylon for seventy years. They had spent ten years rebuilding their homes, rebuilding their businesses, and starting on the temple. Just *starting* on the temple? They had been putting off one of the most important parts of their cultural and religious heritage!

You see, the temple was a special place to the Hebrews, because it represented God's presence with them. If it wasn't important enough to them to rebuild the temple (after ten years!), then their priorities were definitely out of whack.

So Haggai told them that. He told them to think about what they were doing. He told them that putting God first is the real key to getting back on track and being strong enough to face life. Those lessons would be good ones for today as well, huh?

Outline

Purpose
Obedience to God's word brings blessings.

Theme
Rebuilding the Temple

Date of writing
520 B.C.

THE COMMAND TO BUILD GOD'S HOUSE

[1]In the second year of King Darius, in the sixth month, on the first day of the month, the word of the LORD came by Haggai the prophet to Zerubbabel the son of Shealtiel, governor of Judah, and to Joshua the son of Jehozadak, the high priest, saying, [2]"Thus speaks the LORD of hosts, saying: 'This people says, "The time has not come, the time that the LORD's house should be built." ' "

WHAT'S IT MEAN?

If you had to be held prisoner by a foreign king, Darius was the kind of king you'd want on the throne. Like Cyrus before him, Darius allowed his captives to practice their own religion. Not only did he let the Jews who had returned to Jerusalem continue rebuilding the temple, he also sent money to help with the construction and livestock to be used as sacrifices.

Haggai 1:1

[3]Then the word of the LORD came by Haggai the prophet, saying, [4]"Is it time for you yourselves to dwell in your paneled houses, and this temple[a] to lie in ruins?" [5]Now therefore, thus says the LORD of hosts: "Consider your ways!

[6] "You have sown much, and bring in little;
You eat, but do not have enough;
You drink, but you are not filled with drink;
You clothe yourselves, but no one is warm;
And he who earns wages,
Earns wages to put into a bag with holes."

[7]Thus says the LORD of hosts: "Consider your ways! [8]Go up to the mountains and bring wood and build the temple, that I may take pleasure in it and be glorified," says the LORD. [9]"You looked for much, but indeed it came to little; and when you brought it home, I blew it away. Why?" says the LORD of hosts. "Because of My house

that is in ruins, while every one of you runs to his own house. [10]Therefore the heavens above you withhold the dew, and the earth withholds its fruit. [11]For I called for a drought on the land and the mountains, on the grain and the new wine and the oil, on whatever the ground brings forth, on men and livestock, and on all the labor of your hands."

THE PEOPLE'S OBEDIENCE

[12]Then Zerubbabel the son of Shealtiel, and Joshua the son of Jehozadak, the high priest, with all the remnant of the people, obeyed the voice of the LORD their God, and the words of Haggai the prophet, as the LORD their God had sent him; and the people feared the presence of the LORD. [13]Then Haggai, the LORD's messenger, spoke the LORD's message to the people, saying, "I am with you, says the LORD." [14]So the LORD stirred up the spirit of Zerubbabel the son of Shealtiel, governor of Judah, and the spirit of Joshua the son of Jehozadak, the high priest, and the spirit of all the remnant of the people; and they came and worked on the house of the LORD of hosts, their God, [15]on the twenty-fourth day of the sixth month, in the second year of King Darius.

THE COMING GLORY OF GOD'S HOUSE

[1]In the seventh month, on the twenty-first of the month, the word of the LORD came by Haggai the prophet, saying: [2]"Speak now to Zerubbabel the son of Shealtiel, governor of Judah, and to Joshua the son of Jehozadak, the high priest, and to the remnant of the people, saying: [3]'Who is left among you who saw this temple[a] in its former glory? And how do you see it now? In comparison with it, is this not in your eyes as nothing? [4]Yet now be strong, Zerubbabel,' says the LORD; 'and be strong, Joshua, son of Jehozadak, the high priest; and be strong, all you people of the land,' says the LORD, 'and work; for I am with you,' says the LORD of hosts. [5]'According to the word that I covenanted with you when you came out of Egypt, so My Spirit remains among you; do not fear!'

[6]"For thus says the LORD of hosts: 'Once

COURAGE

Why should we be confident? (2:4)

"Then Haggai, the LORD's messenger, spoke the LORD's message to the people, saying, 'I am with you, says the LORD.' "
(Haggai 1:13)

1:4 [a]Literally *house*, and so in verse 8   **2:3** [a]Literally *house*, and so in verses 7 and 9 more (it *is* a little while) I will shake heaven and earth, the sea and dry land; [7]and I will shake all nations, and they shall come to the Desire of All Nations,[a] and I will fill this temple with glory', says the LORD of hosts. [8]'The silver *is* Mine, and the gold *is* Mine', says the LORD of hosts. [9]'The glory of this latter temple shall be greater than the former', says the LORD of hosts. 'And in this place I will give peace', says the LORD of hosts."

WHAT'S IT MEAN?

When the Jewish people returned to Jerusalem, they found some familiar faces in charge. Zerubbabel was the grandson of Jehoiakim, one of the last kings to reign in Judah before the Babylonian invasion. King Cyrus of Persia allowed Zerubbabel to lead a group of Jews back to Jerusalem to begin rebuilding the temple. Cyrus also appointed Zerubbabel governor of Judah. Joshua was the son of Jehozadak, who was high priest when the Jewish people were deported to Babylon. Zerubbabel served as the political leader of the returning Jews; Joshua served as the spiritual leader.

Haggai 1:12

THE PEOPLE ARE DEFILED

[10]On the twenty-fourth *day* of the ninth *month*, in the second year of Darius, the word of the LORD came by Haggai the prophet, saying, [11]"Thus says the LORD of hosts: 'Now, ask the priests *concerning the* law, saying, [12]'If one carries holy meat in the fold of his garment, and with the edge he touches bread or stew, wine or oil, or any food, will it become holy?'' "

Then the priests answered and said, "No."

[13]And Haggai said, "If *one who is* unclean *because* of a dead body touches any of these, will it be unclean?"

So the priests answered and said, "It shall be unclean."

[14]Then Haggai answered and said, " 'So is this people, and so is this nation before Me', says the LORD, 'and so is every work of their hands; and what they offer there is unclean.

PROMISED BLESSING

[15]'And now, carefully consider from this day forward: from before stone was laid upon stone in the temple of the LORD—[16]since those *days*, when *one* came to a heap of twenty ephahs, there were *but* ten; when *one* came to the wine vat to draw out fifty baths from the press, there were *but* twenty. [17]I struck you with blight and mildew and hail in all the labors of your hands; yet you did not *turn* to Me', says the LORD. [18]'Consider now from this day forward, from the twenty-fourth day of the ninth month, from the day that the foundation of the LORD's temple was laid—consider it: [19]Is the seed still in the barn? As yet the vine, the fig tree, the pomegranate, and the olive tree have not yielded *fruit*. But from this day I will bless *you*.' "

ZERUBBABEL CHOSEN AS A SIGNET

[20]And again the word of the LORD came to Haggai on the twenty-fourth day of the month, saying, [21]"Speak to Zerubbabel, governor of Judah, saying:

'I will shake heaven and earth.
[22] I will overthrow the throne of kingdoms;
I will destroy the strength of the Gentile kingdoms.
I will overthrow the chariots
And those who ride in them;
The horses and their riders shall come down,
Every one by the sword of his brother.

[23]'In that day', says the LORD of hosts, 'I will take you, Zerubbabel My servant, the son of Shealtiel', says the LORD, 'and will make you like a signet *ring*; for I have chosen you', says the LORD of hosts."

2:7 [a]Or *the desire of all nations*

CONTENT Zechariah's message came to the group of Hebrews who had returned to Jerusalem and found it in ruins and inhabited by foreigners. These people wanted to reestablish their homes and rebuild the temple, but it was really hard and discouraging.

Zechariah's message did two things. First, it was a rah-rah kind of cheer to remind the people that what they were doing was worth the effort. (You know how hard it is to work on something when you feel like you're wasting your time.)

Within Zechariah's pep rally, though, were some amazing prophecies about the coming of Christ. Part of his reasoning for rebuilding the temple and the city was to get Jerusalem ready for the Messiah, the promise that he believed would make all this better.

Zechariah's message is a good one for us today as well. Sometimes a life of faith can feel like a losing season. Sometimes it seems like our team will never win again. Zechariah reminds us that the season isn't over until God says it is. Until then, we've got to stay in the game and get ready for Jesus' arrival on the scene.

Outline

Purpose God remains in control of history and will triumph.

Theme The Lord Remembers Zion

Date of writing 515 B.C.

Bible Talk

What's Everybody Waiting For?

In one way or another, all the prophets were looking toward the coming of Jesus Christ. It seems like if you talked to any of them long enough, the subject would certainly come up.

Understand that the whole identity of the Jewish people was wrapped up in the coming of the Messiah. God made the first promise about the Messiah to Adam and Eve, and the main reason for establishing the Jewish nation through Abraham was that Jesus would come through his family.

Every comfort that was given to the Hebrews as they struggled had somewhere as its message that Jesus would come and He would fix things. As we look *back* at history, Jesus' arrival seems right on time. If we had lived in 400 B.C., we might have felt differently.

PROPHECIES OF THE MESSIAH

If prophecy were a sport, like baseball, Zechariah would have been a home run hitter.

He prophesied that Jesus would ride into Jerusalem on a donkey (9:9), which He did.

He prophesied that Judas would betray Jesus for thirty pieces of silver (11:12), which he did.

He prophesied that Jesus' side would be pierced (12:10) and that His blood would cleanse our sin (13:1), which it was and it does.

He prophesied that Jesus would have scars in His hands and side (13:6) and that He would be arrested and deserted by His disciples (13:7), which He did and He was and they did.

Zechariah also prophesied that Jesus would return a second time to reign on earth (14:4), which He will.

A CALL TO REPENTANCE

[1]In the eighth month of the second year of Darius, the word of the LORD came to Zechariah the son of Berechiah, the son of Iddo the prophet, saying, [2]"The LORD has been very angry with your fathers. [3]Therefore say to them, 'Thus says the LORD of hosts: "Return to Me", says the LORD of hosts, "and I will return to you", says the LORD of hosts. [4]"Do not be like your fathers, to whom the former prophets preached, saying, 'Thus says the LORD of hosts: "Turn now from your evil ways and your evil deeds." ' But they did not hear nor heed Me," says the LORD.

[5] "Your fathers, where *are* they?
 And the prophets, do they live forever?
[6] Yet surely My words and My statutes,
 Which I commanded My servants the
  prophets,
 Did they not overtake your fathers?

"So they returned and said:

'Just as the LORD of hosts determined to
  do to us,
 According to our ways and according to
  our deeds,
 So He has dealt with us.' " ' "

WHAT'S IT MEAN?

Since Darius was the king of Persia, and since Persia controlled the land of Judah and the city of Jerusalem, Darius had the final say in the things that went on in Jerusalem. Not only had he allowed the Jews to continue rebuilding the temple, he also had kicked in some money for the project himself.
Zechariah 1:1

VISION OF THE HORSES

[7]On the twenty-fourth day of the eleventh month, which is the month Shebat, in the second year of Darius, the word of the LORD came to Zechariah the son of Berechiah, the son of Iddo the prophet: [8]I saw by night, and behold, a man riding on a red horse, and it stood among the myrtle trees in the hollow; and behind him *were* horses: red, sorrel, and white. [9]Then I said,

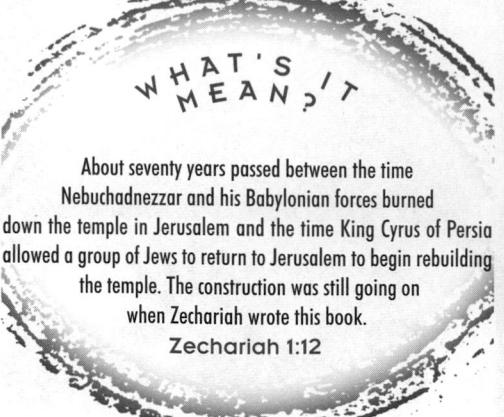

WHAT'S IT MEAN?

About seventy years passed between the time Nebuchadnezzar and his Babylonian forces burned down the temple in Jerusalem and the time King Cyrus of Persia allowed a group of Jews to return to Jerusalem to begin rebuilding the temple. The construction was still going on when Zechariah wrote this book.
Zechariah 1:12

"My lord, what *are* these?" So the angel who talked with me said to me, "I will show you what they *are*."

[10]And the man who stood among the myrtle trees answered and said, "These *are the ones* whom the LORD has sent to walk to and fro throughout the earth."

[11]So they answered the Angel of the LORD, who stood among the myrtle trees, and said, "We have walked to and fro throughout the earth, and behold, all the earth is resting quietly."

THE LORD WILL COMFORT ZION

[12]Then the Angel of the LORD answered and said, "O LORD of hosts, how long will You not have mercy on Jerusalem and on the cities of Judah, against which You were angry these seventy years?"

[13]And the LORD answered the angel who talked to me, *with* good *and* comforting words. [14]So the angel who spoke with me said to me, "Proclaim, saying, 'Thus says the LORD of hosts:

"I am zealous for Jerusalem
 And for Zion with great zeal.
[15] I am exceedingly angry with the nations
   at ease;
 For I was a little angry,
 And they helped—*but* with evil *intent*."

[16]'Therefore thus says the LORD:

"I am returning to Jerusalem with mercy;
 My house shall be built in it", says the
   LORD of hosts,
"And a *surveyor's* line shall be stretched out
   over Jerusalem." '

[17]"Again proclaim, saying, 'Thus says the LORD of hosts:

"My cities shall again spread out through prosperity;
The LORD will again comfort Zion,
And will again choose Jerusalem.'" '"

VISION OF THE HORNS

[18]Then I raised my eyes and looked, and there *were* four horns. [19]And I said to the angel who talked with me, "What *are* these?"

So he answered me, "These *are* the horns that have scattered Judah, Israel, and Jerusalem."

[20]Then the LORD showed me four craftsmen. [21]And I said, "What are these coming to do?"

So he said, "These *are* the horns that scattered Judah, so that no one could lift up his head; but the craftsmen[a] are coming to terrify them, to cast out the horns of the nations that lifted up *their* horn against the land of Judah to scatter it."

VISION OF THE MEASURING LINE

[1]Then I raised my eyes and looked, and behold, a man with a measuring line in his hand. [2]So I said, "Where are you going?"

And he said to me, "To measure Jerusalem, to see what *is* its width and what *is* its length."

[3]And there *was* the angel who talked with me, going out; and another angel was coming out to meet him, [4]who said to him, "Run, speak to this young man, saying: 'Jerusalem shall be inhabited *as* towns without walls, because of the multitude of men and livestock in it. [5]For I,' says the LORD, 'will be a wall of fire all around her, and I will be the glory in her midst.'"

FUTURE JOY OF ZION AND MANY NATIONS

[6]"Up, up! Flee from the land of the north," says the LORD; "for I have spread you abroad like the four winds of heaven," says the LORD. [7]Up, Zion! Escape, you who dwell with the daughter of Babylon."

[8]For thus says the LORD of hosts: "He sent Me after glory, to the nations which plunder you; for he who touches you touches the apple of His eye. [9]For surely I will shake My hand against them, and they shall become spoil for their servants. Then you will know that the LORD of hosts has sent Me.

[10]"Sing and rejoice, O daughter of Zion! For

ENCOURAGEMENT

Is God close to us? (2:10)

behold, I am coming and I will dwell in your midst," says the LORD. [11]"Many nations shall be joined to the LORD in that day, and they shall become My people. And I will dwell in your midst. Then you will know that the LORD of hosts has sent Me to you. [12]And the LORD will take possession of Judah as His inheritance in the Holy Land, and will again choose Jerusalem. [13]Be silent, all flesh, before the LORD, for He is aroused from His holy habitation!"

VISION OF THE HIGH PRIEST

[1]Then he showed me Joshua the high priest standing before the Angel of the LORD, and Satan standing at his right hand to oppose him. [2]And the LORD said to Satan, "The LORD rebuke you, Satan! The LORD who has chosen Jerusalem rebuke you! *Is* this not a brand plucked from the fire?"

[3]Now Joshua was clothed with filthy garments, and was standing before the Angel.

[4]Then He answered and spoke to those who

On the Edge

Be silent, all flesh, before the LORD, for He is aroused from His holy habitation! (Zech. 2:13).

Somebody started this rumor about God that a lot of people seem to believe. They said, "He's up there somewhere." Some even call Him "the Man upstairs." They seem to think that He's far away, beyond our reach, looking down from His comfortable throne. They must not have heard that God is here! He is "aroused from His holy habitation." That means He is involved. He is not shouting orders from some mountaintop. He is beside you—interacting in your life. Those who believe that God is out there somewhere must not know Him very well. It's hard to love from a distance. Relationships get built through closeness and intimacy, not across a galaxy. The Lord longs to be with you, not rule you from afar. So next time you hear the rumor, don't believe it—God is here!

SEE FOR YOURSELF:
Is. 12:6; Ezek. 37:27;
Joel 2:27; Hab. 2:20;
Zeph. 3:17; Matt. 18:20

stood before Him, saying, "Take away the filthy garments from him." And to him He said, "See, I have removed your iniquity from you, and I will clothe you with rich robes."

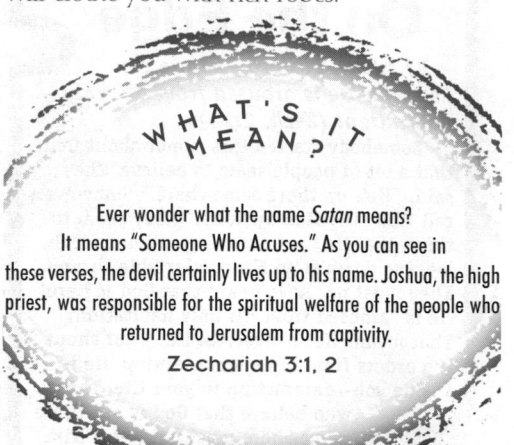

Ever wonder what the name *Satan* means? It means "Someone Who Accuses." As you can see in these verses, the devil certainly lives up to his name. Joshua, the high priest, was responsible for the spiritual welfare of the people who returned to Jerusalem from captivity.
Zechariah 3:1, 2

⁵And I said, "Let them put a clean turban on his head."

So they put a clean turban on his head, and they put the clothes on him. And the Angel of the LORD stood by.

The headgear worn by the high priests of Israel was unusual, to say the least. The turban was a long piece of white linen cloth that was wrapped around the head and fastened in the back. Attached to the front of the turban was a gold sign engraved with the words "Holiness to the Lord."
Zechariah 3:5

THE COMING BRANCH

⁶Then the Angel of the LORD admonished Joshua, saying, ⁷"Thus says the LORD of hosts:

'If you will walk in My ways,
And if you will keep My command,
Then you shall also judge My house,
And likewise have charge of My courts;
I will give you places to walk
Among these who stand here.

⁸ 'Hear, O Joshua, the high priest,
You and your companions who sit before you,
For they are a wondrous sign;
For behold, I am bringing forth My Servant the BRANCH.
⁹ For behold, the stone
That I have laid before Joshua:
Upon the stone *are* seven eyes.
Behold, I will engrave its inscription,'
Says the LORD of hosts,
'And I will remove the iniquity of that land in one day.
¹⁰ In that day,' says the LORD of hosts,
'Everyone will invite his neighbor
Under his vine and under his fig tree.' "

VISION OF THE LAMPSTAND AND OLIVE TREES

¹Now the angel who talked with me came back and wakened me, as a man who is wakened out of his sleep. ²And he said to me, "What do you see?"

So I said, "I am looking, and there is a lampstand of solid gold with a bowl on top of it, and on the *stand* seven lamps with seven pipes to the seven lamps. ³Two olive trees *are* by it, one at the right of the bowl and the other at its left." ⁴So I answered and spoke to the angel who talked with me, saying, "What *are* these, my lord?"

⁵Then the angel who talked with me answered and said to me, "Do you not know what these are?"

And I said, "No, my lord."

⁶So he answered and said to me:

"This *is* the word of the LORD to Zerubbabel:
'Not by might nor by power, but by My Spirit,'
Says the LORD of hosts.
⁷ 'Who *are* you, O great mountain?
Before Zerubbabel *you shall become* a plain!
And he shall bring forth the capstone
With shouts of "Grace, grace to it!" ' "

⁸Moreover the word of the LORD came to me, saying:

⁹ "The hands of Zerubbabel
Have laid the foundation of this temple;ᵃ
His hands shall also finish *it*.
Then you will know
That the LORD of hosts has sent Me to you.

4:9 ᵃLiterally *house*

¹⁰ For who has despised the day of small
    things?
For these seven rejoice to see
The plumb line in the hand of
    Zerubbabel.
They are the eyes of the LORD,
Which scan to and fro throughout the
    whole earth."

¹¹Then I answered and said to him, "What *are* these two olive trees—at the right of the lampstand and at its left?" ¹²And I further answered and said to him, "What *are these* two olive branches that *drip* into the receptacles^a of the two gold pipes from which the golden *oil* drains?"

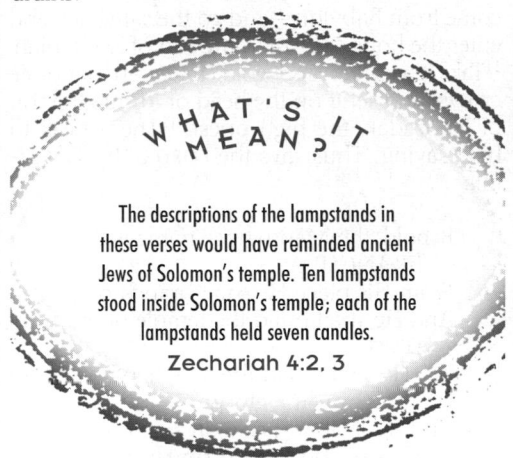

WHAT'S IT MEAN?

The descriptions of the lampstands in these verses would have reminded ancient Jews of Solomon's temple. Ten lampstands stood inside Solomon's temple; each of the lampstands held seven candles.

Zechariah 4:2, 3

¹³Then he answered me and said, "Do you not know what these *are*?"
And I said, "No, my lord."
¹⁴So he said, "These *are* the two anointed ones, who stand beside the Lord of the whole earth."

VISION OF THE FLYING SCROLL

¹Then I turned and raised my eyes, and saw there a flying scroll.
²And he said to me, "What do you see?"
So I answered, "I see a flying scroll. Its length *is* twenty cubits and its width ten cubits."
³Then he said to me, "This *is* the curse that goes out over the face of the whole earth: 'Every thief shall be expelled,' according *to* this side of *the scroll*; and, 'Every perjurer shall be expelled,' according *to* that side of it."

⁴ "I will send out *the curse*," says the LORD of
    hosts;
"It shall enter the house of the thief

On the Edge

So [the angel] answered and said to me: "This is the word of the LORD to Zerubbabel: 'Not by might nor by power, but by My Spirit,' says the LORD of hosts" (Zech. 4:6).

You are growing up in a time when people think they can do almost anything. Sports records are being broken every day. Scientists are discovering cures for diseases that were once considered incurable. Virtual reality can take us places we never thought we could go. It's true, technology and information have enabled humans to do a lot with their minds and bodies and abilities. But humans are still people. No matter how advanced we get, we will never even come close to being as awesome and powerful and advanced as God is.

God says that we are to depend on His Spirit. He wants us to learn to trust His Spirit instead of our own power. There are certain things that His Spirit can do that you could never do in your own strength—such as touch and change and heal a person way down deep inside. God's ways may be different from yours. When you follow His Spirit, you may need to keep your mouth shut instead of telling someone off. He may lead you to make a decision that doesn't seem to make sense; then later you realize that *not* doing it would have been devastating for you.

He leads in lots of different ways. No matter how strong or how smart you are, you can't outdo the Spirit of God. He's the One you can totally depend on.

SEE FOR YOURSELF:
Prov. 3:5, 6; Is. 55:8, 9;
Matt. 19:26; 1 Cor. 2:10–12;
Gal. 5:16, 17

And the house of the one who swears
    falsely by My name.
It shall remain in the midst of his house
And consume it, with its timber and
    stones."

VISION OF THE WOMAN IN A BASKET

⁵Then the angel who talked with me came out and said to me, "Lift your eyes now, and see what this *is* that goes forth."

4:12 ^aLiterally *into the hands of*

⁶So I asked, "What *is* it?" And he said, "It *is* a basket*a* that is going forth."

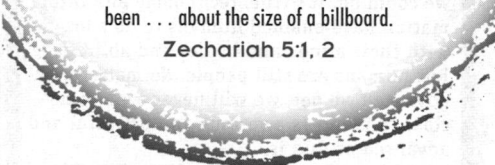

WHAT'S IT MEAN?

Ancient documents were not written in book form; they were written on long pieces of paper or leather called scrolls. Since most scrolls were usually thirty-five pages or longer, ancient librarians discovered that the best way to store them was to roll them up on a stick (like toilet paper). You may not be familiar with ancient measuring units such as cubits, so we'll do the calculations for you. A scroll twenty cubits by ten cubits would have been . . . about the size of a billboard.

Zechariah 5:1, 2

He also said, "This *is* their resemblance throughout the earth: ⁷Here *is* a lead disc lifted up, and this *is* a woman sitting inside the basket"; ⁸then he said, "This *is* Wickedness!" And he thrust her down into the basket, and threw the lead cover*a* over its mouth. ⁹Then I raised my eyes and looked, and there *were* two women, coming with the wind in their wings; for they had wings like the wings of a stork, and they lifted up the basket between earth and heaven.

¹⁰So I said to the angel who talked with me, "Where are they carrying the basket?"

¹¹And he said to me, "To build a house for it in the land of Shinar;*a* when it is ready, *the bas-ket* will be set there on its base."

VISION OF THE FOUR CHARIOTS

¹Then I turned and raised my eyes and looked, and behold, four chariots *were* coming from between two mountains, and the mountains *were* mountains of bronze. ²With the first chariot *were* red horses, with the second chariot black horses, ³with the third chariot white horses, and with the fourth chariot dappled horses—strong *steeds*. ⁴Then I answered and said to the angel who talked with me, "What *are* these, my lord?"

⁵And the angel answered and said to me, "These *are* four spirits of heaven, who go out from *their* station before the Lord of all the earth. ⁶The one with the black horses is going to the north country, the white are going after them, and the dappled are going toward the south country." ⁷Then the strong *steeds* went out, eager to go, that they might walk to and fro throughout the earth. And He said, "Go, walk to and fro throughout the earth." So they walked to and fro throughout the earth. ⁸And He called to me, and spoke to me, saying, "See, those who go toward the north country have given rest to My Spirit in the north country."

THE COMMAND TO CROWN JOSHUA

⁹Then the word of the Lord came to me, saying: ¹⁰"Receive *the gift* from the captives—from Heldai, Tobijah, and Jedaiah, who have come from Babylon—and go the same day and enter the house of Josiah the son of Zephaniah. ¹¹Take the silver and gold, make an elaborate crown, and set *it* on the head of Joshua the son of Jehozadak, the high priest. ¹²Then speak to him, saying, 'Thus says the Lord of hosts, say-ing:

"Behold, the Man whose name *is* the
  BRANCH!
From His place He shall branch out,
And He shall build the temple of the
  Lord;
¹³   Yes, He shall build the temple of the Lord.
He shall bear the glory,
And shall sit and rule on His throne;
So He shall be a priest on His throne,
And the counsel of peace shall be
  between them both." '

¹⁴"Now the elaborate crown shall be for a memorial in the temple of the Lord for Helem,*a* Tobijah, Jedaiah, and Hen the son of Zephaniah. ¹⁵Even those from afar shall come and build the temple of the Lord. Then you shall know that the Lord of hosts has sent Me to you. And *this* shall come to pass if you diligently obey the voice of the Lord your God."

OBEDIENCE BETTER THAN FASTING

¹Now in the fourth year of King Darius it came to pass *that* the word of the Lord came to Zechariah, on the fourth day of the ninth month, Chislev, ²when *the people*a* sent Sherezer,*b* with Regem-Melech and his men, *to* the house of God,*c* to pray before the Lord, ³*and* to ask the priests who *were* in the house of the Lord of

---

5:6 *a*Hebrew *ephah*, a measuring container, and so elsewhere   **5:8** *a*Literally *stone*   **5:11** *a*That is, Babylon
6:14 *a*Following Masoretic Text, Targum, and Vulgate; Syriac reads *for Heldai* (compare verse 10); Septuagint reads *for the patient ones*.   **7:2** *a*Literally *they* (compare verse 5) *b*Or *Sar-Ezer* *c*Hebrew *Bethel*

hosts, and the prophets, saying, "Should I weep in the fifth month and fast as I have done for so many years?"

[4]Then the word of the LORD of hosts came to me, saying, [5]"Say to all the people of the land, and to the priests: 'When you fasted and mourned in the fifth and seventh *months* during those seventy years, did you really fast for Me—for Me? [6]When you eat and when you drink, do you not eat and drink *for yourselves?* [7]*Should you* not *have obeyed* the words which the LORD proclaimed through the former prophets when Jerusalem and the cities around it were inhabited and prosperous, and the South[a] and the Lowland were inhabited?' "

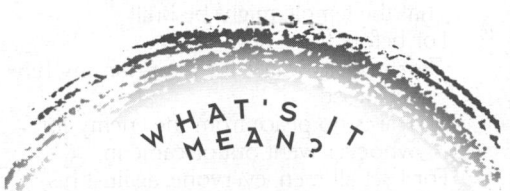

WHAT'S IT MEAN?

The Jewish people never forgot the day their beloved temple was destroyed by the Babylonians. In fact, while they were in captivity, the Jews fasted—they didn't eat food—during the fifth month of each year to commemorate the event. They also fasted during the seventh month of every year in remembrance of Gedaliah, the Jewish governor appointed by King Nebuchadnezzar who was murdered two months into his term.

Zechariah 7:4, 5

DISOBEDIENCE RESULTED IN CAPTIVITY

[8]Then the word of the LORD came to Zechariah, saying, [9]"Thus says the LORD of hosts:

'Execute true justice,
Show mercy and
     compassion
Everyone to his brother.
[10] Do not oppress the
     widow or the
     fatherless,
The alien or the poor.
Let none of you plan evil
     in his heart
Against his brother.'

CARING

How should we treat others? (7:9)

[11]But they refused to heed, shrugged their shoulders, and stopped their ears so that they could not hear. [12]Yes, they made their hearts like

7:7 [a]Hebrew *Negev*

flint, refusing to hear the law and the words which the LORD of hosts had sent by His Spirit through the former prophets. Thus great wrath came from the LORD of hosts. [13]Therefore it happened, *that* just as He proclaimed and they would not hear, so they called out and I would not listen," says the LORD of hosts. [14]"But I scattered them with a whirlwind among all the nations which they had not known. Thus the land became desolate after them, so that no one passed through or returned; for they made the pleasant land desolate."

JERUSALEM, HOLY CITY OF THE FUTURE

[1]Again the word of the LORD of hosts came, saying, [2]"Thus says the LORD of hosts:

'I am zealous for Zion with great zeal;
  With great fervor I am zealous for her.'

[3]"Thus says the LORD:

'I will return to Zion,
  And dwell in the midst of
    Jerusalem.
  Jerusalem shall be called
    the City of Truth,
  The Mountain of the
    LORD of hosts,
  The Holy Mountain.'

[4]"Thus says the LORD of hosts:

'Old men and old women
    shall again sit
  In the streets of Jerusalem,
  Each one with his staff in his hand
  Because of great age.
[5] The streets of the city
  Shall be full of boys and girls
  Playing in its streets.'

[6]"Thus says the LORD of hosts:

'If it is marvelous in the eyes of the
    remnant of this people in these days,
  Will it also be marvelous in My eyes?'
  Says the LORD of hosts.

[7]"Thus says the LORD of hosts:

'Behold, I will save My people from the
    land of the east
  And from the land of the west;
[8] I will bring them *back*,

And they shall dwell in the midst of
    Jerusalem.
  They shall be My people
  And I will be their God,
  In truth and righteousness.'

[9]"Thus says the LORD of hosts:

'Let your hands be strong,
  You who have been hearing in these days
  These words by the mouth of the
    prophets,
  Who *spoke* in the day the foundation was
    laid
  For the house of the LORD of hosts,
  That the temple might be built.
[10] For before these days
  There were no wages for man nor any hire
    for beast;
  There was no peace from the enemy for
    whoever went out or came in;
  For I set all men, everyone, against his
    neighbor.

[11]But now I *will* not *treat* the remnant of this people as in the former days,' says the LORD of hosts.

[12] 'For the seed *shall be*
    prosperous,
  The vine shall give its
    fruit,
  The ground shall give
    her increase,
  And the heavens shall
    give their dew—
I will cause the remnant of this people
  To possess all these.
[13] And it shall come to pass
  That just as you were a curse among the
    nations,
  O house of Judah and house of Israel,
  So I will save you, and you shall be a
    blessing.
  Do not fear,
  Let your hands be strong.'

[14]"For thus says the LORD of hosts:

'Just as I determined to punish you
  When your fathers provoked Me to
    wrath,'
  Says the LORD of hosts,
  'And I would not relent,
[15] So again in these days
  I am determined to do good

"So again in these days I am determined to do good to Jerusalem and to the house of Judah. Do not fear."
(Zechariah 8:15)

17 Let none of you think evil in your[a] heart
    against your neighbor;
And do not love a false oath.
For all these *are things* that I hate,'
Says the LORD."

18 Then the word of the LORD of hosts came to me, saying, 19 "Thus says the LORD of hosts:

'The fast of the fourth *month,*
The fast of the fifth,
The fast of the seventh,
And the fast of the tenth,
Shall be joy and gladness and cheerful
    feasts
For the house of Judah.
Therefore love truth and peace.'

20 "Thus says the LORD of hosts:

'Peoples shall yet come,
Inhabitants of many cities;
21 The inhabitants of one *city* shall go to
    another, saying,
"Let us continue to go and pray before the
    LORD,
And seek the LORD of hosts.
I myself will go also."
22 Yes, many peoples and strong nations
Shall come to seek the LORD of hosts in
    Jerusalem,
And to pray before the LORD.'

23 "Thus says the LORD of hosts: 'In those days ten men from every language of the nations shall grasp the sleeve of a Jewish man, saying, "Let us go with you, for we have heard *that* God *is* with you." ' "

ISRAEL DEFENDED AGAINST ENEMIES

1 The burden[a] of the word of the LORD
Against the land of Hadrach,
And Damascus its resting place
(For the eyes of men
And all the tribes of Israel
Are on the LORD);
2 Also *against* Hamath, *which* borders on it,
And *against* Tyre and Sidon, though they
    are very wise.

3 For Tyre built herself a tower,
Heaped up silver like the dust,
And gold like the mire of the streets.
4 Behold, the LORD will cast her out;

On the Edge

These are the things you shall do: Speak each man the truth to his neighbor; give judgment in your gates for truth, justice, and peace (Zech. 8:16).

Have you ever blown it with another person? When you have, the first thing you've got to do is to be truthful with yourself. Cut yourself a big slice of humble pie, put down your pride, don't try to justify yourself—just admit it. You messed up. Whether you meant to or not, it happened. All friendships have their ups and downs. The key to great relationships is being able to work out the stuff that comes between you.

Next you've got to be honest with God. Confess your sin. Let Him see that you know you've done wrong and that you're sorry. Ask Him to forgive you. He'll forgive you before you finish asking. Then ask Him to help you deal with your friend—to help you know what to say and how to make things right.

The hardest part may be facing your friend and admitting that you aren't perfect, that you blew it and you're sorry. Ask for your friend's forgiveness. A good Christian friend may surprise you and say "I've already forgiven you."

There are other things that will help you patch up a relationship, too. Walking in true forgiveness and grace, learning to overlook the little stuff, doing your best to love with the love that Jesus has, encouraging, supporting, having good times together—all of these things build good relationships and make it easier to work through the rough spots.

SEE FOR YOURSELF:
    2 Cor. 2:7, 8;
    Eph. 4:25–32;
    1 John 4:7

To Jerusalem and to the house of Judah.
Do not fear.
16 These *are* the things you shall do:
Speak each man the truth to his
    neighbor;
Give judgment in your gates for truth,
    justice, and peace;

8:17 [a]Literally *his*   **9:1** [a]Or *oracle*

He will destroy her power in the sea,
And she will be devoured by fire.

5　Ashkelon shall see *it* and fear;
Gaza also shall be very sorrowful;
And Ekron, for He dried up her
　expectation.
The king shall perish from Gaza,
And Ashkelon shall not be inhabited.

6　"A mixed race shall settle in Ashdod,
And I will cut off the pride of the
　Philistines.
7　I will take away the blood from his
　mouth,
And the abominations from between his
　teeth.
But he who remains, even he *shall be* for
　our God,
And shall be like a leader in Judah,
And Ekron like a Jebusite.
8　I will camp around My house
Because of the army,
Because of him who passes by and him
　who returns.
No more shall an oppressor pass through
　them,
For now I have seen with My eyes.

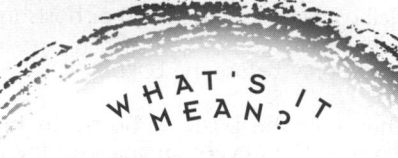

WHAT'S IT MEAN?

You've probably never seen a picture of a
donkey being ridden into battle. Unlike horses, which
were used primarily for war, donkeys were animals of peace. They
were ridden by princes and kings (Judg. 5:10; 10:14; 12:14; 2 Sam.
16:1, 2). When Jesus rode into Jerusalem for the last week of His
earthly ministry, He was sitting on a young donkey.

Zechariah 9:9

THE COMING KING

9　"Rejoice greatly, O daughter of Zion!
Shout, O daughter of Jerusalem!
Behold, your King is coming to you;
He *is* just and having salvation,
Lowly and riding on a donkey,
A colt, the foal of a donkey.
10　I will cut off the chariot from Ephraim

And the horse from Jerusalem;
The battle bow shall be cut off.
He shall speak peace to the nations;
His dominion *shall be* 'from sea to sea,
And from the River to the ends of the
　earth.'*a*

GOD WILL SAVE HIS PEOPLE

11　"As for you also,
Because of the blood of your covenant,
I will set your prisoners free from the
　waterless pit.
12　Return to the stronghold,
You prisoners of hope.
Even today I declare
That I will restore double to you.
13　For I have bent Judah, My *bow*,
Fitted the bow with Ephraim,
And raised up your sons, O Zion,
Against your sons, O Greece,
And made you like the sword of a mighty
　man."

14　Then the LORD will be seen over them,
And His arrow will go forth like lightning.
The Lord GOD will blow the trumpet,
And go with whirlwinds from the south.
15　The LORD of hosts will defend them;
They shall devour and subdue with
　slingstones.
They shall drink *and* roar as if with wine;
They shall be filled *with blood* like basins,
Like the corners of the altar.
16　The LORD their God will save them in that
　day,
As the flock of His people.
For they *shall be like* the jewels of a
　crown,
Lifted like a banner over His land—
17　For how great is its*a* goodness
And how great its*b* beauty!
Grain shall make the young men thrive,
And new wine the young women.

RESTORATION OF JUDAH AND ISRAEL

1　Ask the LORD for rain
In the time of the latter rain.*a*
The LORD will make flashing clouds;
He will give them showers of rain,
Grass in the field for everyone.

2　For the idols*a* speak delusion;
The diviners envision lies,
And tell false dreams;
They comfort in vain.

9:10 *a*Psalm 72:8　**9:17** *a*Or *His* *b*Or *His*　**10:1** *a*That is, spring rain　**10:2** *a*Hebrew *teraphim*

Therefore *the people* wend their way like sheep;
They are in trouble because *there is* no shepherd.

3 "My anger is kindled against the shepherds,
And I will punish the goatherds.
For the LORD of hosts will visit His flock,
The house of Judah,
And will make them as His royal horse in the battle.

4 From him comes the cornerstone,
From him the tent peg,
From him the battle bow,
From him every ruler[a] together.

5 They shall be like mighty men,
Who tread down *their enemies*
In the mire of the streets in the battle.
They shall fight because the LORD is with them,
And the riders on horses shall be put to shame.

6 "I will strengthen the house of Judah,
And I will save the house of Joseph.
I will bring them back,
Because I have mercy on them.
They shall be as though I had not cast them aside;
For I *am* the LORD their God,

And I will hear them.

7 *Those of* Ephraim shall be like a mighty man,
And their heart shall rejoice as if with wine.
Yes, their children shall see *it* and be glad;
Their heart shall rejoice in the LORD.

8 I will whistle for them and gather them,
For I will redeem them;
And they shall increase as they once increased.

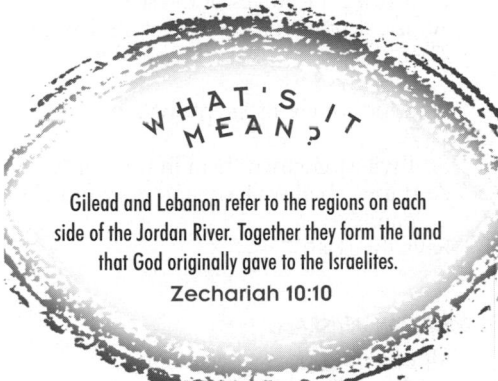

WHAT'S IT MEAN?

Gilead and Lebanon refer to the regions on each side of the Jordan River. Together they form the land that God originally gave to the Israelites.
Zechariah 10:10

9 "I will sow them among the peoples,
And they shall remember Me in far countries;

10:4 [a]Or *despot*

Promise   HE PROMISES TO STRENGTHEN YOU.

"So I will strengthen them in the LORD, and they shall walk up and down in His name," says the LORD (Zech. 10:12).

The Lord says that He will strengthen His people because He is their Lord. He has chosen to show His power and His personality in the lives of the people who live for Him. The problems you face are just opportunities for God to show His stuff. It's a chance for Him to show what He can do (His awesome power) and what He will do (His incredible kindness and mercy).

In his second letter to the Christians who lived Corinth, Paul gave a long list of the difficulties he had faced. One thing in particular seemed to bother him though he didn't say what it was. He just said that he had asked the Lord three times to change things. But God answered, "My grace is sufficient for you, for My strength is made perfect in weakness" (2 Cor. 12:9). When you feel weak or overwhelmed in your life, be disciplined enough to get out your Bible and soak yourself in God's Word. Pray to Him. There's strength for you in His presence.

SEE FOR YOURSELF:
Ps. 68:35; Is. 30:15; Hab. 3:19; 2 Cor. 12:9, 10; Phil. 4:13

They shall live, together with their
children,
And they shall return.
10 I will also bring them back from the land
of Egypt,
And gather them from Assyria.
I will bring them into the land of Gilead
and Lebanon,
Until no *more room* is found for them.
11 He shall pass through the sea with
affliction,
And strike the waves of the sea:
All the depths of the River*a* shall dry up.
Then the pride of Assyria shall be
brought down,
And the scepter of Egypt shall depart.

12 "So I will strengthen them in the LORD,
And they shall walk up and down in His
name,"
Says the LORD.

DESOLATION OF ISRAEL

1 Open your doors, O Lebanon,
That fire may devour your cedars.
2 Wail, O cypress, for the cedar has fallen,
Because the mighty *trees* are ruined.
Wail, O oaks of Bashan,
For the thick forest has come down.
3 *There is* the sound of wailing shepherds!
For their glory is in ruins.
There is the sound of roaring lions!
For the pride*a* of the Jordan is in ruins.

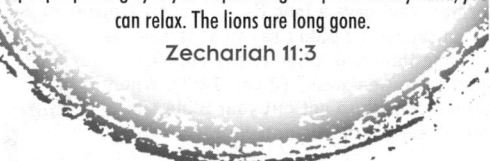

WHAT'S IT MEAN?

Can you imagine having to worry about lion
attacks while you traveled? People in ancient Israel
faced that danger every day. Lions were known to spring from their
hiding places among the thickets near the Jordan River to pounce
on people passing by. If you're planning a trip to the Holy Land, you
can relax. The lions are long gone.

Zechariah 11:3

PROPHECY OF THE SHEPHERDS

4Thus says the LORD my God, "Feed the flock
for slaughter, 5whose owners slaughter them
and feel no guilt; those who sell them say,
'Blessed be the LORD, for I am rich'; and their
shepherds do not pity them. 6For I will no longer pity the inhabitants of the land," says the
LORD. "But indeed I will give everyone into his
neighbor's hand and into the hand of his king.
They shall attack the land, and I will not deliver
them from their hand."

7So I fed the flock for slaughter, in particular
the poor of the flock.*a* I took for myself two
staffs: the one I called Beauty,*b* and the other I
called Bonds;*c* and I fed the flock. 8I dismissed
the three shepherds in one month. My soul
loathed them, and their soul also abhorred me.
9Then I said, "I will not feed you. Let what is
dying die, and what is perishing perish. Let
those that are left eat each other's flesh." 10And I
took my staff, Beauty, and cut it in two, that I
might break the covenant which I had made
with all the peoples. 11So it was broken on that
day. Thus the poor*a* of the flock, who were
watching me, knew that it *was* the word of the
LORD. 12Then I said to them, "If it is agreeable to
you, give *me* my wages; and if not, refrain." So
they weighed out for my wages thirty *pieces* of
silver.

13And the LORD said to me, "Throw it to the
potter"—that princely price they set on me. So I
took the thirty *pieces* of silver and threw them
into the house of the LORD for the potter. 14Then
I cut in two my other staff, Bonds, that I might
break the brotherhood between Judah and Israel.

15And the LORD said to me, "Next, take for
yourself the implements of a foolish shepherd.
16For indeed I will raise up a shepherd in the
land *who* will not care for those who are cut off,
nor seek the young, nor heal those that are broken, nor feed those that still stand. But he will
eat the flesh of the fat and tear their hooves in
pieces.

17 "Woe to the worthless shepherd,
Who leaves the flock!
A sword *shall be* against his arm
And against his right eye;
His arm shall completely wither,
And his right eye shall be totally
blinded."

10:11 *a*That is, the Nile   **11:3** *a*Or *floodplain, thicket*   **11:7** *a*Following Masoretic Text, Targum, and Vulgate;
Septuagint reads *for the Canaanites.* *b*Or *Grace,* and so in verse 10 *c*Or *Unity,* and so in verse 14
11:11 *a*Following Masoretic Text, Targum, and Vulgate; Septuagint reads *the Canaanites.*

THE COMING DELIVERANCE OF JUDAH

¹The burden*a* of the word of the LORD against Israel. Thus says the LORD, who stretches out the heavens, lays the foundation of the earth, and forms the spirit of man within him: ²"Behold, I will make Jerusalem a cup of drunkenness to all the surrounding peoples, when they lay siege against Judah and Jerusalem. ³And it shall happen in that day that I will make Jerusalem a very heavy stone for all peoples; all who would heave it away will surely be cut in pieces, though all nations of the earth are gathered against it. ⁴In that day," says the LORD, "I will strike every horse with confusion, and its rider with madness; I will open My eyes on the house of Judah, and will strike every horse of the peoples with blindness. ⁵And the governors of Judah shall say in their heart, 'The inhabitants of Jerusalem *are* my strength in the LORD of hosts, their God.' ⁶In that day I will make the governors of Judah like a firepan in the woodpile, and like a fiery torch in the sheaves; they shall devour all the surrounding peoples on the right hand and on the left, but Jerusalem shall be inhabited again in her own place—Jerusalem.

W H A T ' S
M E A N ? ' T

A cup that came from God's hand was a common symbol in ancient times for a person's (or a nation's) destiny. A cup of His anger symbolized punishment for a sin. A cup of His blessing symbolized a bright future.

Zechariah 12:2

⁷"The LORD will save the tents of Judah first, so that the glory of the house of David and the glory of the inhabitants of Jerusalem shall not become greater than that of Judah. ⁸In that day the LORD will defend the inhabitants of Jerusalem; the one who is feeble among them in that day shall be like David, and the house of David *shall be* like God, like the Angel of the LORD before them. ⁹It shall be in that day *that* I will seek to destroy all the nations that come against Jerusalem.

MOURNING FOR THE PIERCED ONE

¹⁰"And I will pour on the house of David and on the inhabitants of Jerusalem the Spirit of grace and supplication; then they will look on Me whom they pierced. Yes, they will mourn for Him as one mourns for *his* only *son*, and grieve for Him as one grieves for a firstborn. ¹¹In that day there shall be a great mourning in Jerusalem, like the mourning at Hadad Rimmon in the plain of Megiddo.*a* ¹²And the land shall mourn, every family by itself: the family of the house of David by itself, and their wives by themselves; the family of the house of Nathan by itself, and their wives by themselves; ¹³the family of the house of Levi by itself, and their wives by themselves; the family of Shimei by itself, and their wives by themselves; ¹⁴all the families that remain, every family by itself, and their wives by themselves.

IDOLATRY CUT OFF

¹"In that day a fountain shall be opened for the house of David and for the inhabitants of Jerusalem, for sin and for uncleanness.

²"It shall be in that day," says the LORD of hosts, "*that* I will cut off the names of the idols from the land, and they shall no longer be remembered. I will also cause the prophets and the unclean spirit to depart from the land.

GUILT

How can we be made guilt-free? (13:1)

³It shall come to pass *that* if anyone still prophesies, then his father and mother who begot him will say to him, 'You shall not live, because you have spoken lies in the name of the LORD.' And his father and mother who begot him shall thrust him through when he prophesies.

⁴"And it shall be in that day *that* every prophet will be ashamed of his vision when he prophesies; they will not wear a robe of coarse hair to deceive. ⁵But he will say, 'I *am* no prophet, I *am* a farmer; for a man taught me to keep cattle from my youth.' ⁶And *one* will say to him, 'What *are* these wounds between your arms?'*a* Then he will answer, '*Those* with which I was wounded in the house of my friends.'

THE SHEPHERD SAVIOR

⁷   "Awake, O sword, against My Shepherd,
    Against the Man who is My
        Companion,"
    Says the LORD of hosts.
    "Strike the Shepherd,
    And the sheep will be scattered;

12:1 *a*Or *oracle*   **12:11** *a*Hebrew *Megiddon*   **13:6** *a*Or *hands*

WHAT'S IT MEAN?

Just as a metalsmith working with gold or silver uses fire to purify the good and get rid of the bad, God uses the fire of His judgment to purify people and get rid of the bad.

Zechariah 13:9

Then I will turn My hand against the little ones.

8 And it shall come to pass in all the land,"
Says the LORD,
"*That* two-thirds in it shall be cut off *and* die,
But *one*-third shall be left in it:
9 I will bring the *one*-third through the fire,
Will refine them as silver is refined,
And test them as gold is tested.

They will call on My name,
And I will answer them.
I will say, 'This *is* My people';
And each one will say, 'The LORD *is* my God.' "

THE DAY OF THE LORD

1 Behold, the day of the LORD is coming,
And your spoil will be divided in your midst.
2 For I will gather all the nations to battle against Jerusalem;
The city shall be taken,
The houses rifled,
And the women ravished.
Half of the city shall go into captivity,
But the remnant of the people shall not be cut off from the city.

3 Then the LORD will go forth
And fight against those nations,
As He fights in the day of battle.
4 And in that day His feet will stand on the Mount of Olives,
Which faces Jerusalem on the east.
And the Mount of Olives shall be split in two,

Promise   HE PROMISES TO REFINE AND TEST YOU.

I will bring the one-third through the fire, will refine them as silver is refined, and test them as gold is tested. They will call on My name, and I will answer them. I will say, "This is My people"; and each one will say, "The LORD is my God" (Zech. 13:9).

Have you ever gotten a ring that was supposed to be high quality, but made your finger turn green? You think, *This thing is cheap. It's fake.* Why? Because it isn't pure gold. It hasn't been through the refining process necessary to remove all the impurities from the metal. Maybe the ring was beautiful in the case, but it looks awful on your hand because now your finger's green. You've got a cheap ring, full of junk. It could have been beautiful, but the goldsmith didn't take the time or energy to purify the gold.

God wants you to be pure—in every way. He wants your thoughts to be pure. He wants your actions to be pure. He wants you physically, morally, spiritually, and sexually pure. He doesn't want you to just look good. He wants you to be beautiful through and through. It's a two-step process. *You* make the decision to allow the Lord to work in your life; then *He* does the purifying. He does it by renewing your mind with His Word and by speaking to you by His Spirit. The process may not always be pleasant for you, but God will not leave you in the fire to burn up. He will bring you out at the perfect time and finish the process.

When a ring is put on a finger, it's put to the test. If it's pure, it's beautiful. If it isn't, almost everything it touches turns green. When you've been purified by the Lord, you will be as beautiful as pure gold.

SEE FOR YOURSELF:
Jer. 9:7; Dan. 11:35; 12:10

From east to west,
Making a very large valley;
Half of the mountain shall move toward
    the north
And half of it toward the south.

5   Then you shall flee *through* My mountain
        valley,
    For the mountain valley shall reach to
        Azal.
    Yes, you shall flee
    As you fled from the earthquake
    In the days of Uzziah king of Judah.

    Thus the LORD my God will come,
    And all the saints with You.[a]

6   It shall come to pass in that day
    That there will be no light;
    The lights will diminish.
7   It shall be one day
    Which is known to the LORD—
    Neither day nor night.
    But at evening time it shall happen
    That it will be light.

8   And in that day it shall be
    That living waters shall flow from
        Jerusalem,
    Half of them toward the eastern sea
    And half of them toward the western sea;
    In both summer and winter it shall occur.
9   And the LORD shall be King over all the
        earth.
    In that day it shall be—
    "The LORD *is* one,"[a]
    And His name one.

¹⁰All the land shall be turned into a plain from Geba to Rimmon south of Jerusalem. *Jerusalem*[a] shall be raised up and inhabited in her place from Benjamin's Gate to the place of the First Gate and the Corner Gate, and *from* the Tower of Hananel to the king's winepresses.

11   *The people* shall dwell in it;
     And no longer shall there be utter
        destruction,
     But Jerusalem shall be safely inhabited.

¹²And this shall be the plague with which the LORD will strike all the people who fought against Jerusalem:

Their flesh shall dissolve while they stand
    on their feet,
Their eyes shall dissolve in their sockets,
And their tongues shall dissolve in their
    mouths.

13   It shall come to pass in that day
     That a great panic from the LORD will be
        among them.
     Everyone will seize the hand of his
        neighbor,
     And raise his hand against his neighbor's
        hand;
14   Judah also will fight at Jerusalem.
     And the wealth of all the surrounding
        nations
     Shall be gathered together:
     Gold, silver, and apparel in great
        abundance.

15   Such also shall be the plague
     On the horse *and* the mule,
     On the camel and the donkey,
     And on all the cattle that will be in those
        camps.
     So *shall* this plague *be*.

THE NATIONS WORSHIP THE KING

¹⁶And it shall come to pass *that* everyone who is left of all the nations which came against Jerusalem shall go up from year to year to worship the King, the LORD of hosts, and to keep the Feast of Tabernacles. ¹⁷And it shall be *that* whichever of the families of the earth do not come up to Jerusalem to worship the King, the LORD of hosts, on them there will be no rain. ¹⁸If the family of Egypt will not come up and enter in, they *shall have* no *rain;* they shall receive the plague with which the LORD strikes the nations who do not come up to keep the Feast of Tabernacles. ¹⁹This shall be the punishment of Egypt and the punishment of all the nations that do not come up to keep the Feast of Tabernacles.

²⁰In that day "HOLINESS TO THE LORD" shall be *engraved* on the bells of the horses. The pots in the LORD's house shall be like the bowls before the altar. ²¹Yes, every pot in Jerusalem and Judah shall be holiness to the LORD of hosts.[a] Everyone who sacrifices shall come and take them and cook in them. In that day there shall no longer be a Canaanite in the house of the LORD of hosts.

14:5 [a]Or *you;* Septuagint, Targum, and Vulgate read *Him.*   **14:9** [a]Compare Deuteronomy 6:4
14:10 [a]Literally *She*   **14:21** [a]Or *on every pot . . . shall be* (engraved) *"HOLINESS TO THE LORD OF HOSTS"*

malachi

CONTENT

Have you ever been excited about something, like a family trip or a party with friends, and it turns out to be nothing like you had thought? Maybe you'd been looking forward to the trip for a long time. Maybe you had imagined how fun it was going to be and how everyone would enjoy it. But, then when reality happened, it just wasn't as bright and shiny as it was in your head.

That's how the Hebrews felt at the time when Malachi preached and wrote his message. They had struggled through some *extremely* hard times. After being exiled from their country, they returned, resettled, and rebuilt the temple and the city walls. All of that involved years of work.

When it was done, they expected that God would bless them and their lives would be like the "good old days"—when they were happy and rich and in God's favor.

The problem was that they were still missing the point about obedience to God. They were sitting back expecting God to fix everything. They halfheartedly did what they needed to do, but they weren't *being* the people they needed to be.

Malachi addressed this with them through a series of questions and answers. See what you think.

Outline

Purpose

We need to check and make sure God has first place in our lives.

Theme

Reassurance of God's Love and Justice

Date of writing

430 B.C.

Bible Talk

Second Best Is Not Enough

When God originally established the customs of the Hebrews (this was back in the days of Moses), He taught them to bring their best to offer to Him. This established His priority in their lives. It taught them not to put their trust in their crops or their riches, but in God.

During the days of Malachi, the people were still going through the motions of bringing sacrifices; but instead of bringing their best offerings, they were bringing their damaged goods. It was just a shadow of obedience, not the real thing.

They weren't establishing their lives around God's truth; they were fitting Him in where it worked for them. This was their error. If we look, we can see that same error in our world today.

ALMOST ANONYMOUS PROPHET

We don't know much about the prophet Malachi. In fact, we don't know anything more than what is revealed in this book: He was a man who spoke out for God and who called people to serve God wholeheartedly.

It would be great, wouldn't it, to only be known for what we said for God? It would be great to be remembered for the times we spread God's word.

Malachi spoke God's truth. We don't know anything else about him, but his life can inspire us to do the same thing.

¹The burden*a* of the word of the LORD to Israel by Malachi.

ISRAEL BELOVED OF GOD

2 "I have loved you," says the LORD.
"Yet you say, 'In what way have You loved
us?'
Was not Esau Jacob's brother?"
Says the LORD.
"Yet Jacob I have loved;
3 But Esau I have hated,
And laid waste his mountains and his
heritage
For the jackals of the wilderness."

WHAT'S IT MEAN?

Jacob and Esau were the two sons of Isaac. As
the older brother, Esau was legally entitled to the
larger inheritance from his father. Yet God chose to bless Jacob, and
he became Isaac's number one heir. You may also know Jacob by his
God-given name, Israel. You may know his twelve
sons as the twelve tribes of Israel.

Malachi 1:2

4 Even though Edom has said,
"We have been impoverished,
But we will return and build the desolate
places,"

Thus says the LORD of hosts:

"They may build, but I will throw down;
They shall be called the Territory of
Wickedness,
And the people against whom the LORD
will have indignation forever.
5 Your eyes shall see,
And you shall say,
'The LORD is magnified beyond the border
of Israel.'

POLLUTED OFFERINGS

6 "A son honors *his* father,
And a servant *his* master.
If then I am the Father,

Where *is* My honor?
And if I *am* a Master,
Where *is* My reverence?
Says the LORD of hosts
To you priests who despise My name.
Yet you say, 'In what way have we
despised Your name?'

7 "You offer defiled food on My altar,
But say,
'In what way have we defiled You?'
By saying,
'The table of the LORD is contemptible.'
8 And when you offer the blind as a
sacrifice,
Is it not evil?
And when you offer the lame and sick,
Is it not evil?
Offer it then to your governor!
Would he be pleased with you?
Would he accept you favorably?"
Says the LORD of hosts.

9 "But now entreat God's favor,
That He may be gracious to us.
While this is being *done* by your hands,
Will He accept you favorably?"
Says the LORD of hosts.
10 "Who *is there* even among you who would
shut the doors,
So that you would not kindle fire *on* My
altar in vain?
I have no pleasure in you,"
Says the LORD of hosts,
"Nor will I accept an offering from your
hands.
11 For from the rising of the sun, even to its
going down,
My name *shall be* great
among the Gentiles;
In every place incense
shall be offered to My
name,
And a pure offering;
For My name shall be
great among the
nations,"
Says the LORD of hosts.

REPUTATION
How great
is God's
reputation?
(1:11)

12 "But you profane it,
In that you say,
'The table of the LORD*a* is defiled;
And its fruit, its food, *is* contemptible.'
13 You also say,
'Oh, what a weariness!'

1:1 *a*Or *oracle* **1:12** *a*Following Bomberg; Masoretic Text reads *Lord.*

And you sneer at it,"
Says the LORD of hosts.
"And you bring the stolen, the lame, and
    the sick;
Thus you bring an offering!
Should I accept this from your hand?"
Says the LORD.
14 "But cursed *be* the deceiver
Who has in his flock a male,
And takes a vow,
But sacrifices to the Lord what is
    blemished—
For I *am* a great King,"
Says the LORD of hosts,
"And My name *is to be* feared among the
    nations.

CORRUPT PRIESTS

1 "And now, O priests, this commandment is
    for you.
2 If you will not hear,
And if you will not take *it* to heart,
To give glory to My name,"
Says the LORD of hosts,
"I will send a curse upon you,
And I will curse your blessings.
Yes, I have cursed them already,
Because you do not take *it* to heart.

3 "Behold, I will rebuke your descendants
And spread refuse on your faces,
The refuse of your solemn feasts;
And *one* will take you away with it.
4 Then you shall know that I have sent this
    commandment to you,
That My covenant with Levi may
    continue,"
Says the LORD of hosts.
5 "My covenant was with him, *one* of life
    and peace,
And I gave them to him *that he might* fear
    Me;
So he feared Me
And was reverent before My name.
6 The law of truth[a] was in his mouth,
And injustice was not found on his lips.
He walked with Me in peace and equity,
And turned many away from iniquity.

7 "For the lips of a priest should keep
    knowledge,
And *people* should seek the law from his
    mouth;
For he is the messenger of the LORD of
    hosts.

8 But you have departed from the way;
You have caused many to stumble at the
    law.
You have corrupted the covenant of Levi,"
Says the LORD of hosts.
9 "Therefore I also have made you
    contemptible and base
Before all the people,
Because you have not kept My ways
But have shown partiality in the law."

TREACHERY OF INFIDELITY

10 Have we not all one Father?
Has not one God created us?
Why do we deal treacherously with one
    another
By profaning the covenant of the fathers?
11 Judah has dealt treacherously,
And an abomination has been committed
    in Israel and in Jerusalem,
For Judah has profaned
The LORD's holy *institution* which He
    loves:
He has married the daughter of a foreign
    god.
12 May the LORD cut off from the tents of
    Jacob
The man who does this, being awake and
    aware,[a]
Yet who brings an offering to the LORD of
    hosts!

13 And this is the second thing you do:
You cover the altar of the LORD with tears,
With weeping and crying;
So He does not regard the offering
    anymore,
Nor receive *it* with goodwill from your
    hands.
14 Yet you say, "For what reason?"
Because the LORD has been witness
Between you and the wife of your youth,
With whom you have dealt treacherously;
Yet she is your companion
And your wife by covenant.
15 But did He not make *them* one,
Having a remnant of the Spirit?
And why one?
He seeks godly offspring.
Therefore take heed to your spirit,
And let none deal treacherously with the
    wife of his youth.

16 "For the LORD God of Israel says
That He hates divorce,

2:6 [a]Or *true instruction*   **2:12** [a]Talmud and Vulgate read *teacher and student.*

For it covers one's garment with violence,"
Says the LORD of hosts.
"Therefore take heed to
your spirit,
That you do not deal
treacherously."

MARRIAGE
What does
God think of
divorce?
(2:16)

17 You have wearied the
LORD with your words;
Yet you say,
"In what way have we wearied *Him?*"
In that you say,
"Everyone who does evil
Is good in the sight of the LORD,
And He delights in them,"
Or, "Where *is* the God of justice?"

THE COMING MESSENGER

1 "Behold, I send My messenger,
And he will prepare the way before Me.
And the Lord, whom you seek,
Will suddenly come to His temple,
Even the Messenger of the covenant,
In whom you delight.
Behold, He is coming,"
Says the LORD of hosts.

2 "But who can endure the day of His
coming?
And who can stand when He appears?
For He *is* like a refiner's fire
And like launderers' soap.

3 He will sit as a refiner and a purifier of
silver;
He will purify the sons of Levi,
And purge them as gold and silver,
That they may offer to the LORD
An offering in righteousness.

4 "Then the offering of Judah and Jerusalem
Will be pleasant to the LORD,
As in the days of old,
As in former years.

5 And I will come near you
for judgment;
I will be a swift witness
Against sorcerers,
Against adulterers,
Against perjurers,
Against those who
exploit wage earners
and widows and orphans,
And against those who turn away an
alien—
Because they do not fear Me,"
Says the LORD of hosts.

JUDGMENT
What does
God
condemn?
(3:5)

6 "For I *am* the LORD, I do not change;
Therefore you are not consumed, O sons
of Jacob.

7 Yet from the days of your fathers
You have gone away from My ordinances
And have not kept *them.*
Return to Me, and I will return to you,"

Promise HE PROMISES NOT TO CHANGE.

"For I am the LORD, I do not change; therefore you are not consumed, O sons of Jacob. Yet from the days of your fathers you have gone away from My ordinances and have not kept them. Return to Me, and I will return to you," says the LORD of hosts (Mal. 3:6, 7a).

Athletes, even great ones, have their "off" days, days when the star basketball player can't rise above the other team and score enough points to win the game, when the best running back in the league fumbles inside the ten-yard line, when the sprinter who hasn't lost a race in seventy-six starts suddenly finds himself in second place.

You have your "off" days, too. There are days when you feel like being nice to everybody and days when you want everybody to just get out of your face. Some days it seems easy to do what God wants you to do; other days it seems hard to even care what He thinks. This mood-iness is part of human nature. But God doesn't change. He is totally consistent. He's not kind one day and selfish the next. He is always faithful. He never does wrong. You can count on His power, His love, and His goodness, day in and day out.

SEE FOR YOURSELF:
Ps. 102:27; Heb. 1:12; 13:8

Says the LORD of hosts.
"But you said,
'In what way shall we return?'

DO NOT ROB GOD

8 "Will a man rob God?
Yet you have robbed Me!
But you say,
'In what way have we robbed You?'
In tithes and offerings.
9 You are cursed with a curse,
For you have robbed Me,
Even this whole nation.
10 Bring all the tithes into the storehouse,
That there may be food in My house,
And try Me now in this,"
Says the LORD of hosts,
"If I will not open for you the windows of
heaven
And pour out for you *such* blessing
That *there will* not *be room* enough *to
receive it.*

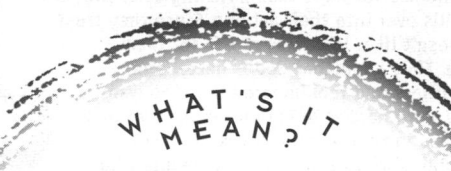

WHAT'S IT MEAN?

Here's how tithing worked in ancient times:
The Israelites were commanded to give ten percent of
everything they had—including crops, livestock, and money—to
God. The Israelites gave their tithes to the Levites, the people who
worked in the temple. The Levites, in turn, gave ten percent of
everything they received to the priests. The priests offered a sacrifice
to the Lord for their tithe. The third-year tithe was given to help
support the poor and needy.
Malachi 3:10

11 "And I will rebuke the devourer for your
sakes,
So that he will not destroy the fruit of
your ground,
Nor shall the vine fail to bear fruit for
you in the field,"
Says the LORD of hosts;
12 And all nations will call you blessed,
For you will be a delightful land,"
Says the LORD of hosts.

THE PEOPLE COMPLAIN HARSHLY

13 "Your words have been harsh against Me,"
Says the LORD,
"Yet you say,
'What have we spoken against
You?'
14 You have said,
'It is useless to serve God;
What profit *is it* that we
have kept His
ordinance,
And that we have walked
as mourners
Before the LORD of hosts?
15 So now we call the proud blessed,
For those who do wickedness are raised
up;
They even tempt God and go free.' "

A BOOK OF REMEMBRANCE

16 Then those who feared the LORD spoke to
one another,
And the LORD listened and heard *them*;
So a book of remembrance was written
before Him
For those who fear the LORD
And who meditate on His name.
17 "They shall be Mine," says the LORD of
hosts,
"On the day that I make them My jewels.[a]
And I will spare them
As a man spares his own son who serves
him."
18 Then you shall again discern
Between the righteous and the wicked,
Between one who serves God
And one who does not serve Him.

THE GREAT DAY OF GOD

1 "For behold, the day is coming,
Burning like an oven,
And all the proud, yes, all who do
wickedly will be stubble.
And the day which is coming shall burn
them up,"
Says the LORD of hosts,
"That will leave them neither root nor
branch.
2 But to you who fear My name
The Sun of Righteousness shall arise
With healing in His wings;
And you shall go out
And grow fat like stall-fed calves.
3 You shall trample the wicked,

3:17 [a]Literally *special treasure*

For they shall be ashes under the soles of
your feet
On the day that I do *this*,"
Says the LORD of hosts.

4 "Remember the Law of Moses, My servant,
Which I commanded him in Horeb for all
Israel,
With the statutes and judgments.

5 Behold, I will send you Elijah the prophet
Before the coming of the great and
dreadful day of the LORD.

6 And he will turn
The hearts of the fathers to the children,
And the hearts of the children to their
fathers,
Lest I come and strike the earth with a
curse."

∵ Promise

HE PROMISES VICTORY FOR THOSE WHO HONOR HIS NAME.

But to you who fear My name the Sun of Righteousness shall arise with healing in His wings; and you shall go out and grow fat like stall-fed calves (Mal. 4:2).

Read Malachi 4:1 and look at the contrast between the people mentioned there and the ones described in verse 2. The difference between these two groups of people begins in their hearts. The people in verse 1 are proud. They believe in themselves more than anything else. They think they deserve the best. Of course, their attitude spills over into their actions. Since they trust themselves and not God, they do some things God doesn't like. It's a way of life for them.

But the people in verse 2 have a different attitude. They know that God is better and stronger than they could ever be. They praise His greatness and feel honored that God wants to be their friend. They want to please Him, and they work hard at doing the things that make Him happy. Their record isn't perfect, but what God sees in their hearts makes Him smile.

The day of judgment will not be a good day for proud, sinful people. But the people who honor the Lord "shall go out and grow fat like stall-fed calves." In other words, peace and security await.

SEE FOR YOURSELF:
Ps. 31:19; 34:9; Eccl. 8:12

THE NEW TESTAMENT

CONTENT Eventually in school you'll study "If-Then" statements. It might be in a math class or a logic class or a philosophy class, but they'll come up. *If* a=b and b=c, *then* a=c. Or *if* Maggie is a four-legged animal that barks, *then* Maggie is probably a dog. If-then statements are the way we put together information and come to a conclusion.

The Book, or Gospel, of Matthew is an if-then kind of book. It is a great book to start the New Testament, because Matthew opens by referring to the Old Testament. He uses the prophecies of the Old Testament to convince his readers of one thing: Jesus is the Messiah we've been waiting for.

Matthew's point in writing his biography of Jesus' ministry is to show the connection between the promises and prophecies of the Old Testament and the life and ministry of Jesus Christ in the New Testament. Basically Matthew's message is, "*If* all these prophecies that we have studied and believed are fulfilled in this one Man, *then* Jesus of Nazareth is the Messiah!

Because of this, Matthew's Gospel is full of Old Testament prophecy. He logically and painstakingly writes Jesus' story in an effort to say, "Jesus is the One we've been waiting for! Put your trust in Him."

Outline

Purpose King Jesus teaches us how to live as good citizens in His kingdom.

Themes Jesus Is the Fulfillment of Old Testament Prophecies Concerning the Messiah; His Disciples Are Called to a New Covenant, to Live at a Higher Dimension Than the Old Ever Realized

Date of writing 50s or 60s A.D.

Bible Talk

Jesus in the Face of the Pharisees

Some of the religious leaders of Jesus' day were the Pharisees. The problem with the Pharisees was that they were hypocrites. They had their religious ideas all backwards. Instead of glorifying God, they glorified themselves. Instead of leading out of humility, they led out of pride. Instead of expecting to serve people, they expected to be served. Jesus said they looked good on the outside, but inside they were dirty (23:25). He called them whitewashed graves (23:27) and poisonous snakes (23:33). (Okay, now tell us how you *really* feel.)

Even though the Pharisees were religious leaders, they were Jesus' biggest enemies. They didn't want to admit Jesus was the Son of God because they would lose their control over the Hebrews. They missed the point entirely.

THE REVOLUTION OF JESUS CHRIST

A lot of the passages in the Book of Matthew are famous words that we hear many times if we grow up in the church. In fact, we can hear them so often that we forget what mind-blowers these words were when Jesus first said them.

Take the Sermon on the Mount for instance (chapters 5—7). In one simple talk, Jesus changed the whole definition of spirituality. To the people of that day, being spiritual meant obeying rules. The more rules you obeyed, the more spiritual you were. Jesus taught that the rules won't save you; your faith will save you. The rules just show you that you need God.

Jesus made a lot of people mad by saying these things. In the process, He started a revolution called Christianity.

THE GENEALOGY OF JESUS CHRIST

¹The book of the genealogy of Jesus Christ, the Son of David, the Son of Abraham:

²Abraham begot Isaac, Isaac begot Jacob, and Jacob begot Judah and his brothers. ³Judah begot Perez and Zerah by Tamar, Perez begot Hezron, and Hezron begot Ram. ⁴Ram begot Amminadab, Amminadab begot Nahshon, and Nahshon begot Salmon. ⁵Salmon begot Boaz by Rahab, Boaz begot Obed by Ruth, Obed begot Jesse, ⁶and Jesse begot David the king.

David the king begot Solomon by her *who had been the wife*ᵃ of Uriah. ⁷Solomon begot Rehoboam, Rehoboam begot Abijah, and Abijah begot Asa.ᵃ ⁸Asa begot Jehoshaphat, Jehoshaphat begot Joram, and Joram begot Uzziah. ⁹Uzziah begot Jotham, Jotham begot Ahaz, and Ahaz begot Hezekiah. ¹⁰Hezekiah begot Manasseh, Manasseh begot Amon,ᵃ and Amon begot Josiah. ¹¹Josiah begot Jeconiah and his brothers about the time they were carried away to Babylon.

WHAT'S IT MEAN?

More than six hundred years before Jesus was born, King Nebuchadnezzar and his Babylonian army destroyed the city of Jerusalem and carried away most of its inhabitants, forcing them to live as prisoners hundreds of miles from home in Babylonia. Their captivity lasted seventy years.

Matthew 1:11

¹²And after they were brought to Babylon, Jeconiah begot Shealtiel, and Shealtiel begot Zerubbabel. ¹³Zerubbabel begot Abiud, Abiud begot Eliakim, and Eliakim begot Azor. ¹⁴Azor begot Zadok, Zadok begot Achim, and Achim begot Eliud. ¹⁵Eliud begot Eleazar, Eleazar begot Matthan, and Matthan begot Jacob. ¹⁶And Jacob begot Joseph the husband of Mary, of whom was born Jesus who is called Christ.

¹⁷So all the generations from Abraham to David *are* fourteen generations, from David until the captivity in Babylon *are* fourteen genera-

On the Edge

Now the birth of Jesus Christ was as follows: After His mother Mary was betrothed to Joseph, before they came together, she was found with child of the Holy Spirit. Then Joseph her husband, being a just man, and not wanting to make her a public example, was minded to put her away secretly. But while he thought about these things, behold, an angel of the Lord appeared to him in a dream, saying, "Joseph, son of David, do not be afraid to take to you Mary your wife, for that which is conceived in her is of the Holy Spirit" (Matt. 1:18–20).

In this passage, Joseph and Mary were engaged. In those days, engagements lasted one year for the purpose of proving sexual purity. During the engagement, Mary discovered that she was pregnant by God's Holy Spirit. Matthew says that Joseph was "a just [good] man," which is why he called off the wedding. He knew that Mary could have been stoned if people found out that she was pregnant during the engagement. An angel came to Joseph and told him to go ahead and marry before the engagement time was over. Joseph did what was honorable and right for Mary, and for the child, Jesus.

If your girlfriend is pregnant, it is up to you to do the honorable thing. No matter how young you are, or how afraid, you can make wise decisions with the help of the Lord, parents, and pastors. A wise decision may mean adoption. It may mean marriage. The most important thing now is that this child deserves a mother and a father who love him, and are willing to care for him. Being a "just man" may mean that for a time, you have to sacrifice your reputation, your plans, or your interests. Just keep asking yourself, "What is best for the child?" Trust the Lord to guide you. Be brave enough to do what is right.

SEE FOR YOURSELF:
Luke 1:26–28; 6:31;
2 John 5, 6

1:6 ᵃWords in italic type have been added for clarity. They are not found in the original Greek.
1:7 ᵃNU-Text reads *Asaph*. **1:10** ᵃNU-Text reads *Amos*.

tions, and from the captivity in Babylon until the Christ *are* fourteen generations.

CHRIST BORN OF MARY

[18]Now the birth of Jesus Christ was as follows: After His mother Mary was betrothed to Joseph, before they came together, she was found with child of the Holy Spirit. [19]Then Joseph her husband, being a just *man*, and not wanting to make her a public example, was minded to put her away secretly. [20]But while he thought about these things, behold, an angel of the Lord appeared to him in a dream, saying, "Joseph, son of David, do not be afraid to take to you Mary your wife, for that which is conceived in her is of the Holy Spirit. [21]And she will bring forth a Son, and you shall call His name JESUS, for He will save His people from their sins."

[22]So all this was done that it might be fulfilled which was spoken by the Lord through the prophet, saying: [23]"*Behold, the virgin shall be with child, and bear a Son, and they shall call His name Immanuel*,"[a] which is translated, "God with us."

> "Now after Jesus was born in Bethlehem of Judea in the days of Herod the king, behold, wise men from the East came to Jerusalem."
> (Matthew 2:1)

WISE MEN FROM THE EAST

[1]Now after Jesus was born in Bethlehem of Judea in the days of Herod the king, behold, wise men from the East came to Jerusalem, [2]saying, "Where is He who has been born King of the Jews? For we have seen His star in the East and have come to worship Him."

[3]When Herod the king heard *this*, he was troubled, and all Jerusalem with him. [4]And when he had gathered all the chief priests and scribes of the people together, he inquired of them where the Christ was to be born.

[5]So they said to him, "In Bethlehem of Judea, for thus it is written by the prophet:

6 '*But you, Bethlehem, in the land of Judah,*
   Are not the least among the rulers of
     Judah;
   For out of you shall come a Ruler
   Who will shepherd My people Israel.' "[a]

[7]Then Herod, when he had secretly called the wise men, determined from them what time the star appeared. [8]And he sent them to Bethlehem and said, "Go and search carefully for the young Child, and when you have found *Him*, bring back word to me, that I may come and worship Him also."

[9]When they heard the king, they departed; and behold, the star which they had seen in the East went before them, till it came and stood over where the young Child was. [10]When they saw the star, they rejoiced with exceedingly great joy. [11]And when they had come into the house, they saw the young Child with Mary His mother, and fell down and worshiped Him. And when they had opened their treasures, they presented gifts to Him: gold, frankincense, and myrrh.

[12]Then, being divinely warned in a dream that they should not return to Herod, they departed for their own country another way.

WHAT'S IT MEAN?

At the time of Jesus' birth, the Roman Empire included pretty much the entire known world. Obviously, that's a lot of area to rule. To maintain control, the Roman senate selected governors to rule over various regions in the empire. Herod was selected to rule Judea in 37 B.C. Look up the word *paranoid* in the dictionary and you may find a picture of Herod next to it. This guy was so desperate to hang on to the throne that he killed anyone he suspected of even wanting to become king. That included three of his own sons.

Matthew 2:1

THE FLIGHT INTO EGYPT

[13]Now when they had departed, behold, an angel of the Lord appeared to Joseph in a

[24]Then Joseph, being aroused from sleep, did as the angel of the Lord commanded him and took to him his wife, [25]and did not know her till she had brought forth her firstborn Son.[a] And he called His name JESUS.

1:23 [a]Isaiah 7:14. Words in oblique type in the New Testament are quoted from the Old Testament.
1:25 [a]NU-Text reads *a Son*.   **2:6** [a]Micah 5:2

dream, saying, "Arise, take the young Child and His mother, flee to Egypt, and stay there until I bring you word; for Herod will seek the young Child to destroy Him."

[14]When he arose, he took the young Child and His mother by night and departed for Egypt, [15]and was there until the death of Herod, that it might be fulfilled which was spoken by the Lord through the prophet, saying, *"Out of Egypt I called My Son."* [a]

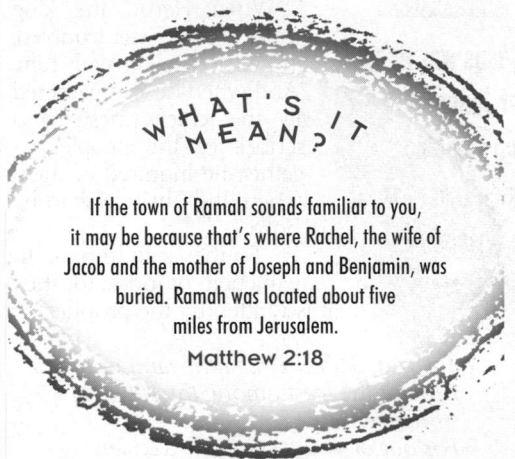

If the town of Ramah sounds familiar to you, it may be because that's where Rachel, the wife of Jacob and the mother of Joseph and Benjamin, was buried. Ramah was located about five miles from Jerusalem.

Matthew 2:18

MASSACRE OF THE INNOCENTS

[16]Then Herod, when he saw that he was deceived by the wise men, was exceedingly angry; and he sent forth and put to death all the male children who were in Bethlehem and in all its districts, from two years old and under, according to the time which he had determined from the wise men. [17]Then was fulfilled what was spoken by Jeremiah the prophet, saying:

[18] *"A voice was heard in Ramah,*
Lamentation, weeping, and great
mourning,
Rachel weeping for her children,
Refusing to be comforted,
Because they are no more." [a]

THE HOME IN NAZARETH

[19]Now when Herod was dead, behold, an angel of the Lord appeared in a dream to Joseph in Egypt, [20]saying, "Arise, take the young Child and His mother, and go to the land of Israel, for those who sought the young Child's life are dead." [21]Then he arose, took the young Child and His mother, and came into the land of Israel.

[22]But when he heard that Archelaus was reigning over Judea instead of his father Herod, he was afraid to go there. And being warned by God in a dream, he turned aside into the region of Galilee. [23]And he came and dwelt in a city called Nazareth, that it might be fulfilled which was spoken by the prophets, "He shall be called a Nazarene."

JOHN THE BAPTIST PREPARES THE WAY

[1]In those days John the Baptist came preaching in the wilderness of Judea, [2]and saying, "Repent, for the kingdom of heaven is at hand!" [3]For this is he who was spoken of by the prophet Isaiah, saying:

"The voice of one crying in the wilderness:
'Prepare the way of the LORD;
Make His paths straight.'" [a]

[4]Now John himself was clothed in camel's hair, with a leather belt around his waist; and his food was locusts and wild honey. [5]Then Jerusalem, all Judea, and all the region around the Jordan went out to him [6]and were baptized by him in the Jordan, confessing their sins.

Think of the Pharisees and Sadducees as rival gangs. Instead of fighting with guns and knives, though, these rivals fought with words and ideas. The Pharisees were ordinary, middle-class people who emphasized the importance of obeying the Law God had given Moses. The Sadducees were wealthy and powerful individuals, many of whom served as priests. These two groups of Jewish scholars interpreted Scripture differently and argued over issues, such as the resurrection of the dead and the existence of angels. Because they knew so much about Scripture, members of both groups tended to take pride in themselves and to criticize others.

Matthew 3:7

[7]But when he saw many of the Pharisees and Sadducees coming to his baptism, he said to them, "Brood of vipers! Who warned you to flee from the wrath to come? [8]Therefore bear fruits worthy of repentance, [9]and do not think to say to yourselves, 'We have Abraham as *our*

2:15 [a]Hosea 11:1   **2:18** [a]Jeremiah 31:15   **3:3** [a]Isaiah 40:3

father.' For I say to you that God is able to raise up children to Abraham from these stones. [10]And even now the ax is laid to the root of the trees. Therefore every tree which does not bear good fruit is cut down and thrown into the fire. [11]I indeed baptize you with water unto repentance, but He who is coming after me is mightier than I, whose sandals I am not worthy to carry. He will baptize you with the Holy Spirit and fire.[a] [12]His winnowing fan *is* in His hand, and He will thoroughly clean out His threshing floor, and gather His wheat into the barn; but He will burn up the chaff with unquenchable fire."

JOHN BAPTIZES JESUS

[13]Then Jesus came from Galilee to John at the Jordan to be baptized by him. [14]And John *tried to* prevent Him, saying, "I need to be baptized by You, and are You coming to me?"

[15]But Jesus answered and said to him, "Permit *it to be so* now, for thus it is fitting for us to fulfill all righteousness." Then he allowed Him.

[16]When He had been baptized, Jesus came up immediately from the water; and behold, the heavens were opened to Him, and He[a] saw the Spirit of God descending like a dove and alighting upon Him. [17]And suddenly a voice came from heaven, saying, "This is My beloved Son, in whom I am well pleased."

SATAN TEMPTS JESUS

[1]Then Jesus was led up by the Spirit into the wilderness to be tempted by the devil. [2]And when He had fasted forty days and forty nights, afterward He was hungry. [3]Now when the tempter came to Him, he said, "If You are the Son of God, command that these stones become bread."

[4]But He answered and said, "It is written, '*Man shall not live by bread alone, but by every word that proceeds from the mouth of God.*' "[a]

[5]Then the devil took Him up into the holy city, set Him on the pinnacle of the temple, [6]and said to Him, "If You are the Son of God, throw Yourself down. For it is written:

> '*He shall give His angels charge over you,*'

and,

> '*In their hands they shall bear you up,*
> *Lest you dash your foot against a*
> *stone.*' "[a]

[7]Jesus said to him, "It is written again, '*You shall not tempt the LORD your God.*' "[a]

[8]Again, the devil took Him up on an exceedingly high mountain, and showed Him all the kingdoms of the world and their glory. [9]And he said to Him, "All these things I will give You if You will fall down and worship me."

[10]Then Jesus said to him, "Away with you,[a] Satan! For it is written, '*You shall worship the LORD your God, and Him only you shall serve.*' "[b]

[11]Then the devil left Him, and behold, angels came and ministered to Him.

On the Edge

When He had been baptized, Jesus came up immediately from the water; and behold, the heavens were opened to Him, and He saw the Spirit of God descending like a dove and alighting upon Him (Matt. 3:16).

There are two ceremonies Jesus gave for every believer to observe—communion and baptism. Why should we get baptized? Because Jesus did, and He did it publicly. Getting baptized tells the world about your faith in Jesus as your Savior. This lets people know that you mean business with God, and that you're going to live for Him, with courage and excitement! Not only does God want you to profess Him by being baptized in water, but He also wants you to be a witness for Him by being filled daily with His Holy Spirit. Why be baptized in the Holy Spirit? Because we need the power we receive from it. Acts 1:8 says, "But you shall receive power when the Holy Spirit has come upon you." We don't need to depend on our own strength and ability. God makes unlimited strength and power available to us through His Holy Spirit. As a teenager, you need that power to make a difference for Him. Everyone does. Jesus is the baptizer. Let Him baptize you with His power today!

SEE FOR YOURSELF:
    Matt. 28:19;
    Acts 2:38; 8:12;
    Rom. 6:3–5

3:11 [a]M-Text omits *and fire.*   **3:16** [a]Or *he*   **4:4** [a]Deuteronomy 8:3   **4:6** [a]Psalm 91:11, 12
4:7 [a]Deuteronomy 6:16   **4:10** [a]M-Text reads *Get behind Me.*   [b]Deuteronomy 6:13

JESUS BEGINS HIS GALILEAN MINISTRY

¹²Now when Jesus heard that John had been put in prison, He departed to Galilee. ¹³And leaving Nazareth, He came and dwelt in Capernaum, which is by the sea, in the regions of Zebulun and Naphtali, ¹⁴that it might be fulfilled which was spoken by Isaiah the prophet, saying:

¹⁵ "The land of Zebulun and the land of
       Naphtali,
    By the way of the sea, beyond the Jordan,
    Galilee of the Gentiles:
¹⁶ The people who sat in darkness have seen
       a great light,
    And upon those who sat in the region
       and shadow of death
    Light has dawned." ª

¹⁷From that time Jesus began to preach and to say, "Repent, for the kingdom of heaven is at hand."

Galilee, a Roman province in northern Palestine, was the setting of most of Jesus' ministry of teaching and miracles on earth. Jesus' hometown of Nazareth was located in Galilee, and most of His disciples came from the region. The city of Capernaum, which became the headquarters of Jesus' ministry, was located on the shores of the Sea of Galilee.

Matthew 4:12, 13

FOUR FISHERMEN CALLED AS DISCIPLES

¹⁸And Jesus, walking by the Sea of Galilee, saw two brothers, Simon called Peter, and Andrew his brother, casting a net into the sea; for they were fishermen. ¹⁹Then He said to them, "Follow Me, and I will make you fishers of men." ²⁰They immediately left *their* nets and followed Him.

²¹Going on from there, He saw two other brothers, James *the son* of Zebedee, and John his brother, in the boat with Zebedee their father, mending their nets. He called them, ²²and immediately they left the boat and their father, and followed Him.

JESUS HEALS A GREAT MULTITUDE

²³And Jesus went about all Galilee, teaching in their synagogues, preaching the gospel of the kingdom, and healing all kinds of sickness and all kinds of disease among the people. ²⁴Then His fame went throughout all Syria; and they brought to Him all sick people who were afflicted with various diseases and torments, and those who were demon-possessed, epileptics, and paralytics; and He healed them. ²⁵Great multitudes followed Him—from Galilee, and *from* Decapolis, Jerusalem, Judea, and beyond the Jordan.

THE BEATITUDES

¹And seeing the multitudes, He went up on a mountain, and when He was seated His disciples came to Him. ²Then He opened His mouth and taught them, saying:

³ "Blessed *are* the poor in spirit,
       For theirs is the kingdom of heaven.
⁴ Blessed *are* those who mourn,
       For they shall be comforted.
⁵ Blessed *are* the meek,
       For they shall inherit the earth.
⁶ Blessed *are* those who hunger and thirst
          for righteousness,
       For they shall be filled.
⁷ Blessed *are* the merciful,
       For they shall obtain mercy.
⁸ Blessed *are* the pure in heart,
       For they shall see God.
⁹ Blessed *are* the peacemakers,
       For they shall be called sons of God.
¹⁰ Blessed *are* those who are persecuted for
          righteousness' sake,
       For theirs is the kingdom of heaven.

¹¹"Blessed are you when they revile and persecute you, and say all kinds of evil against you falsely for My sake. ¹²Rejoice and be exceedingly glad, for great *is* your reward in heaven, for so they persecuted the prophets who were before you.

BELIEVERS ARE SALT AND LIGHT

¹³"You are the salt of the earth; but if the salt loses its flavor, how shall it be seasoned? It is then good for nothing but to be thrown out and trampled underfoot by men.

¹⁴"You are the light of the world. A city that is set on a hill cannot be hidden. ¹⁵Nor do they light a lamp and put it under a basket, but on a lampstand, and it gives light to all *who are* in the

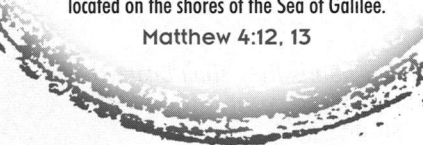

4:16 ªIsaiah 9:1, 2

On the Edge

You are the salt of the earth; but if the salt loses its flavor, how shall it be seasoned? It is then good for nothing but to be thrown out and trampled underfoot by men. You are the light of the world. A city that is set on a hill cannot be hidden (Matt. 5:13, 14).

Jesus teaches in Matthew 5:13, 14 that part of being a Christian is being salt and light to this world. Being salt means that a follower of Jesus creates a thirst for greater information. When you meet someone who is different and has superior qualities, you want to know why that person is different. Have you ever met someone who was really cool, had a great attitude even when life was hard, did nice things for no obvious reason, and later found out that he was a Christian? That explained it. That person was being salt. He made people want to know what made him different. How about light? A light shines and gives direction. It points people toward the right path. Do you know Christians who radiate Jesus? Others are drawn to them. Their lives are examples that many want to follow. People see their goodness and know it is Jesus who lives in them. Jesus says don't hide who you are. Don't put your light under a basket where others can't see it. Go boldly into the world and give 'em Jesus. You are bound to change the place where you are when others see Jesus in you.

SEE FOR YOURSELF:
Mark 9:50; Luke 14:34; Phil. 2:15

the least of these commandments, and teaches men so, shall be called least in the kingdom of heaven; but whoever does and teaches *them*, he shall be called great in the kingdom of heaven. [20]For I say to you, that unless your righteousness exceeds *the righteousness* of the scribes and Pharisees, you will by no means enter the kingdom of heaven.

MURDER BEGINS IN THE HEART

[21]"You have heard that it was said to those of old, *'You shall not murder,*[a] and whoever murders will be in danger of the judgment.' [22]But I say to you that whoever is angry with his brother without a cause[a] shall be in danger of the judgment. And whoever says to his brother, 'Raca!' shall be in danger of the council. But whoever says, 'You fool!' shall be in danger of hell fire. [23]Therefore if you bring your gift to the altar, and there remember that your brother has something against you, [24]leave your gift there before the altar, and go your way. First be reconciled to your brother, and then come and offer your gift. [25]Agree with your adversary quickly, while you are on the way with him, lest your adversary deliver you to the judge, the judge hand you over to the officer, and you be thrown into prison. [26]Assuredly, I say to you, you will by no means get out of there till you have paid the last penny.

MURDER
What is the same as murder in God's eyes? (5:21, 22)

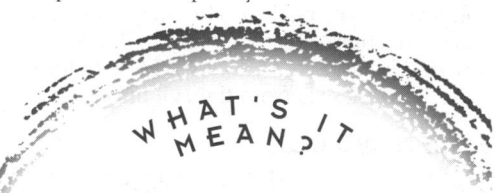

WHAT'S IT MEAN?

An altar was a platform used to hold things that people offered to God. Offerings of fruit and vegetables were made by people who wanted to show their appreciation to God for a healthy herd or a good crop. Animal offerings were made as substitute payments for sin.

Matthew 5:23

house. [16]Let your light so shine before men, that they may see your good works and glorify your Father in heaven.

CHRIST FULFILLS THE LAW

[17]"Do not think that I came to destroy the Law or the Prophets. I did not come to destroy but to fulfill. [18]For assuredly, I say to you, till heaven and earth pass away, one jot or one tittle will by no means pass from the law till all is fulfilled. [19]Whoever therefore breaks one of

ADULTERY IN THE HEART

[27]"You have heard that it was said to those of old,[a] *'You shall not commit adultery.'*[b] [28]But I

5:21 [a]Exodus 20:13; Deuteronomy 5:17　　**5:22** [a]NU-Text omits *without a cause.*　　**5:27** [a]NU-Text and M-Text omit *to those of old.* [b]Exodus 20:14; Deuteronomy 5:18

say to you that whoever looks at a woman to lust for her has already committed adultery with her in his heart. ²⁹If your right eye causes you to sin, pluck it out and cast *it* from you; for it is more profitable for you that one of your members perish, than for your whole body to be cast into hell. ³⁰And if your right hand causes you to sin, cut it off and cast *it* from you; for it is more profitable for you that one of your members perish, than for your whole body to be cast into hell.

SEX

Where do sexual sins begin? (5:27–30)

MARRIAGE IS SACRED AND BINDING

³¹"Furthermore it has been said, 'Whoever divorces his wife, let him give her a certificate of divorce.' ³²But I say to you that whoever divorces his wife for any reason except sexual immorality*a* causes her to commit adultery; and whoever marries a woman who is divorced commits adultery.

JESUS FORBIDS OATHS

³³"Again you have heard that it was said to those of old, 'You shall not swear falsely, but shall perform your oaths to the Lord.' ³⁴But I say to you, do not swear at all: neither by heaven, for it is God's throne; ³⁵nor by the earth, for it is His footstool; nor by Jerusalem, for it is the city of the great King. ³⁶Nor shall you swear by your head, because you cannot make one hair white or black. ³⁷But let your 'Yes' be 'Yes,' and your 'No,' 'No.' For whatever is more than these is from the evil one.

GO THE SECOND MILE

³⁸"You have heard that it was said, '*An eye for an eye and a tooth for a tooth.*'*a* ³⁹But I tell you not to resist an evil person. But whoever slaps you on your right cheek, turn the other to him also. ⁴⁰If anyone wants to sue you and take away your tunic, let him have *your* cloak also. ⁴¹And whoever compels you to go one mile, go with him two. ⁴²Give to him who asks you, and from him who wants to borrow from you do not turn away.

LOVE

Do we have to love our enemies? (5:43, 44)

LOVE YOUR ENEMIES

⁴³"You have heard that it was said, '*You shall love your*

On the Edge

He makes His sun rise on the evil and on the good, and sends rain on the just and on the unjust (Matt. 5:45).

It's a fact. You *will* eventually reap what you sow. Matthew 5:45 is talking about a "rain" of blessing or cursing—good things or bad things. You've got a choice (see Deut. 30:19). Most people are ready for God to rain down His blessings upon them. But how do you get it to happen?

Simple. One way is to love your enemies. Worldly wisdom tells you to love your neighbor and hate your enemy. Jesus says we have to love our neighbor *and* our enemy. That's right, love your enemy! When you love an enemy, you are actually piling burning coals upon his or her head. In other words, God will take care of enemies with the kind of rain you don't want!

What exactly are you supposed to do for your enemies? Pray for them, feed them, give them something to drink, clothe them, and love them. By doing this, you will never be defeated by evil, but you will defeat evil with good (see Rom. 12:21). Then God can and will reward you. Remember, it's the goodness of God that leads people to ask forgiveness and turn from their sin. Start praying for your enemies right now, and let God shower you with His blessings!

SEE FOR YOURSELF:
Matt. 5:9; Luke 6:35; Rom. 12:20

---

neighbora and hate your enemy.' ⁴⁴But I say to you, love your enemies, bless those who curse you, do good to those who hate you, and pray for those who spitefully use you and persecute you,*a* ⁴⁵that you may be sons of your Father in heaven; for He makes His sun rise on the evil and on the good, and sends rain on the just and on the unjust. ⁴⁶For if you love those who love you, what reward have you? Do not even the tax collectors do the same? ⁴⁷And if you greet your brethren*a* only, what do you do more *than* others? Do not even the tax collectors*b* do so?

5:32 *a*Or *fornication*   **5:38** *a*Exodus 21:24; Leviticus 24:20; Deuteronomy 19:21   **5:43** *a*Compare Leviticus 19:18   **5:44** *a*NU-Text omits three clauses from this verse, leaving, *"But I say to you, love your enemies and pray for those who persecute you."*   **5:47** *a*M-Text reads *friends.*   *b*NU-Text reads *Gentiles.*

[48]Therefore you shall be perfect, just as your Father in heaven is perfect.

DO GOOD TO PLEASE GOD

[1]"Take heed that you do not do your charitable deeds before men, to be seen by them. Otherwise you have no reward from your Father in heaven. [2]Therefore, when you do a charitable deed, do not sound a trumpet before you as the hypocrites do in the synagogues and in the streets, that they may have glory from men. Assuredly, I say to you, they have their reward. [3]But when you do a charitable deed, do not let your left hand know what your right hand is doing, [4]that your charitable deed may be in secret; and your Father who sees in secret will Himself reward you openly.[a]

THE MODEL PRAYER

[5]"And when you pray, you shall not be like the hypocrites. For they love to pray standing in the synagogues and on the corners of the streets, that they may be seen by men. Assuredly, I say to you, they have their reward. [6]But you, when you pray, go into your room, and when you have shut your door, pray to your Father who *is* in the secret *place;* and your Father who sees in secret will reward you openly.[a] [7]And when you pray, do not use vain repetitions as the heathen *do.* For they think that they will be heard for their many words.

PRAYER

Who taught the disciples how to pray? (6:9–13)

[8]"Therefore do not be like them. For your Father knows the things you have need of before you ask Him. [9]In this manner, therefore, pray:

Our Father in heaven,
Hallowed be Your name.
[10] Your kingdom come.
Your will be done
On earth as *it is* in heaven.
[11] Give us this day our daily bread.
[12] And forgive us our debts,
As we forgive our debtors.
[13] And do not lead us into temptation,

> "But you, when you pray, go into your room, and when you have shut your door, pray to your Father who is in the secret place; and your Father who sees in secret will reward you openly."
> (Matthew 6:6)

But deliver us from the evil one.
For Yours is the kingdom and the power and the glory forever. Amen.[a]

[14]"For if you forgive men their trespasses, your heavenly Father will also forgive you. [15]But if you do not forgive men their trespasses, neither will your Father forgive your trespasses.

FASTING TO BE SEEN ONLY BY GOD

[16]"Moreover, when you fast, do not be like the hypocrites, with a sad countenance. For they disfigure their faces that they may appear to men to be fasting. Assuredly, I say to you, they have their reward. [17]But you, when you fast, anoint your head and wash your face, [18]so that you do not appear to men to be fasting, but to your Father who *is* in the secret *place;* and your Father who sees in secret will reward you openly.[a]

WHAT'S IT MEAN?

The Jewish people were required by God to set aside one day a year for fasting, or going without food. This day, called the Day of Atonement, gave people an opportunity to think about the sins they had committed and to ask for forgiveness.
Matthew 6:16

LAY UP TREASURES IN HEAVEN

[19]"Do not lay up for yourselves treasures on earth, where moth and rust destroy and where thieves break in and steal; [20]but lay up for yourselves treasures in heaven, where neither moth nor rust

MONEY

What's most important? (6:19, 20)

6:4 [a]NU-Text omits *openly.* **6:6** [a]NU-Text omits *openly.* **6:13** [a]NU-Text omits *For Yours* through *Amen.*
6:18 [a]NU-Text and M-Text omit *openly.*

destroys and where thieves do not break in and steal. ²¹For where your treasure is, there your heart will be also.

THE LAMP OF THE BODY

²²"The lamp of the body is the eye. If therefore your eye is good, your whole body will be full of light. ²³But if your eye is bad, your whole body will be full of darkness. If therefore the light that is in you is darkness, how great *is* that darkness!

On the Edge

But seek first the kingdom of God and His righteousness, and all these things shall be added to you (Matt. 6:33).

No matter what the decision, you can take your advice from Matthew 6:33 and do what Jesus said: "Seek first the kingdom of God and His righteousness." When trying to decide which option is best or what path to choose, ask yourself, "Which way would bring God glory?" If God would be honored in any decision, then choose the one you like the most. God hasn't put you on earth to make you miserable. A lot of Christians mistakenly think that the most miserable option must surely be God's will. That's not true. God has given you preferences and passions on purpose. He knows you will accomplish more for the kingdom when you are working in an area you love. If bringing God glory is your first priority, then you will always make wise decisions. They may sometimes be tough, but in the end, you will have made the right choice.

SEE FOR YOURSELF:
Josh. 6:27; Prov. 22:1;
Is. 11:2; 12:6;
Luke 12:31

YOU CANNOT SERVE GOD AND RICHES

²⁴"No one can serve two masters; for either he will hate the one and love the other, or else he will be loyal to the one and despise the other. You cannot serve God and mammon.

DO NOT WORRY

²⁵"Therefore I say to you, do not worry about your life, what you will eat or what you will drink; nor about your body, what you will put on. Is not life more than food and the body more than clothing? ²⁶Look at the birds of the air, for they neither sow nor reap nor gather into barns; yet your heavenly Father feeds them. Are you not of more value than they? ²⁷Which of you by worrying can add one cubit to his stature?

²⁸"So why do you worry about clothing? Consider the lilies of the field, how they grow: they neither toil nor spin; ²⁹and yet I say to you that even Solomon in all his glory was not arrayed like one of these. ³⁰Now if God so clothes the grass of the field, which today is, and tomorrow is thrown into the oven, *will He* not much more *clothe* you, O you of little faith?

³¹"Therefore do not worry, saying, 'What shall we eat?' or 'What shall we drink?' or 'What shall we wear?' ³²For after all these things the Gentiles seek. For your heavenly Father knows that you need all these things. ³³But seek first the kingdom of God and His righteousness, and all these things shall be added to you. ³⁴Therefore do not worry about tomorrow, for tomorrow will worry about its own things. Sufficient for the day *is* its own trouble.

DO NOT JUDGE

¹"Judge not, that you be not judged. ²For with what judgment you judge, you will be judged; and with the measure you use, it will be measured back to you. ³And why do you look at the speck in your brother's eye, but do not consider the plank in your own eye? ⁴Or how can you say to your brother, 'Let me remove the speck from your eye'; and look, a plank *is* in your own eye? ⁵Hypocrite! First remove the plank from your own eye, and then you will see clearly to remove the speck from your brother's eye.

DECISIONS

What do we need to do before we criticize others? (7:3–5)

⁶"Do not give what is holy to the dogs; nor cast your pearls before swine, lest they trample them under their feet, and turn and tear you in pieces.

KEEP ASKING, SEEKING, KNOCKING

⁷"Ask, and it will be given to you; seek, and you will find; knock, and it will be opened to you. ⁸For everyone who asks receives, and he who seeks finds, and to him who knocks it will be opened. ⁹Or what man is there among you who, if his son asks for bread, will give him a stone? ¹⁰Or if he asks for a fish, will he give him a serpent? ¹¹If you then, being evil, know how

to give good gifts to your children, how much more will your Father who is in heaven give good things to those who ask Him! [12]Therefore, whatever you want men to do to you, do also to them, for this is the Law and the Prophets.

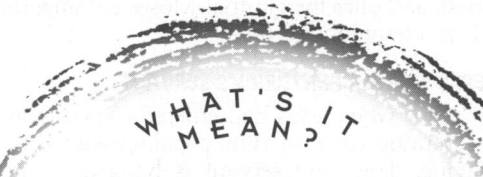

WHAT'S IT MEAN?

Dogs weren't considered "man's best friend" in ancient times. In fact, they probably rated pretty high on the "man's worst enemy" list. Dogs of Jesus' day were wild, vicious animals that traveled in packs, eating garbage and occasionally attacking people. Members of the swine family were even more unpopular, believe it or not. Pigs were considered unclean, so the Jewish people wanted nothing to do with them. Bible writers often used the pig as a symbol of greed and filth.

Matthew 7:6

THE NARROW WAY

[13]"Enter by the narrow gate; for wide *is* the gate and broad *is* the way that leads to destruction, and there are many who go in by it. [14]Because[a] narrow *is* the gate and difficult *is* the way which leads to life, and there are few who find it.

HEAVEN

Will many people be allowed to enter heaven? (7:13, 14)

YOU WILL KNOW THEM BY THEIR FRUITS

[15]"Beware of false prophets, who come to you in sheep's clothing, but inwardly they are ravenous wolves. [16]You will know them by their fruits. Do men gather grapes from thornbushes or figs from thistles? [17]Even so, every good tree bears good fruit, but a bad tree bears bad fruit. [18]A good tree cannot bear bad fruit, nor *can* a bad tree bear good fruit. [19]Every tree that does not bear good fruit is cut down and thrown into the fire. [20]Therefore by their fruits you will know them.

ETERNAL LIFE

Who is eternal life reserved for? (7:21)

I NEVER KNEW YOU

[21]"Not everyone who says to Me, 'Lord, Lord,' shall enter the kingdom of heaven, but he who does the will of My Father in heaven. [22]Many will say to Me in that day, 'Lord, Lord, have we not prophesied in Your name, cast out demons in Your name, and done many wonders in Your name?' [23]And then I will declare to them, 'I never knew you; depart from Me, you who practice lawlessness!'

BUILD ON THE ROCK

[24]"Therefore whoever hears these sayings of Mine, and does them, I will liken him to a wise man who built his house on the rock: [25]and the rain descended, the floods came, and the winds blew and beat on that house; and it did not fall, for it was founded on the rock.

[26]"But everyone who hears these sayings of Mine, and does not do them, will be like a foolish man who built his house on the sand: [27]and

On the Edge

Whatever you want men to do to you, do also to them, for this is the Law and the Prophets (Matt. 7:12).

This verse has been called the "Golden Rule." It's as valuable as gold and it'll work every time you use it. It's been quoted and misquoted for years. It isn't just about being nice; it's a lot more than that. Look at what Jesus says leading up to this. Love people who are against you; pray for the person who's mean to you; if someone wants to borrow something, give him more than what he asks for and don't ask him to give it back. You wouldn't dare *ask* anyone to treat you that well—you'd feel like you were using her—but you'd like it if she did, right?

Jesus isn't telling you to be a doormat. He's showing you how to follow His example. His whole life was about two things: pleasing God and helping other people. He wants you to be more concerned about others than you are about yourself. Look out for others and trust God to look out for you. Always think about how you'd want someone to treat you. That's the heart of the Golden Rule.

SEE FOR YOURSELF:
Zech. 8:16; Luke 6:31; 2 John 5, 6

7:14 [a]NU-Text and M-Text read *How . . . !*

the rain descended, the floods came, and the winds blew and beat on that house; and it fell. And great was its fall."

²⁸And so it was, when Jesus had ended these sayings, that the people were astonished at His teaching, ²⁹for He taught them as one having authority, and not as the scribes.

On the Edge

He taught them as one having authority, and not as the scribes (Matt. 7:29).

This passage of Scripture tells us that the crowds were surprised because Jesus taught with authority. We're not talking about your basic authority; we're talking about power! There is power in the words of Jesus. Look at what Hebrews 4:12 says: "For the word of God is living and powerful, and sharper than any two-edged sword, piercing even to the division of soul and spirit, and of joints and marrow, and is a discerner of the thoughts and intents of the heart." Start putting the Word of God in your mind and heart today, so that when troubles come against you, you can use it like a sword.

When the devil tempted Jesus in the wilderness, what did Jesus do? He spoke the Word of God. He said, "It is written . . ." (see Matt. 4:4, 6, 10). And you know what? The devil split. We need to do the same. John 1:1 tells us, "In the beginning was the Word, and the Word was with God, and the Word was God." Jesus is the Word, and He wants to teach you today. As you begin to study the Scriptures, you will begin to gain understanding of what the verses mean. This will help you live every day of the week and cause you to walk in victory! Remember, the Bible isn't meant to be difficult. You'll never know until you dive in. Let Jesus be *your* Teacher!

SEE FOR YOURSELF:
Matt. 4:1, 2; 2 Tim. 2:15; Heb. 4:12

JESUS CLEANSES A LEPER

¹When He had come down from the mountain, great multitudes followed Him. ²And behold, a leper came and worshiped Him, saying, "Lord, if You are willing, You can make me clean."

³Then Jesus put out *His* hand and touched him, saying, "I am willing; be cleansed." Immediately his leprosy was cleansed.

⁴And Jesus said to him, "See that you tell no one; but go your way, show yourself to the priest, and offer the gift that Moses commanded, as a testimony to them."

JESUS HEALS A CENTURION'S SERVANT

⁵Now when Jesus had entered Capernaum, a centurion came to Him, pleading with Him, ⁶saying, "Lord, my servant is lying at home paralyzed, dreadfully tormented."

⁷And Jesus said to him, "I will come and heal him."

⁸The centurion answered and said, "Lord, I am not worthy that You should come under my roof. But only speak a word, and my servant will be healed. ⁹For I also am a man under authority, having soldiers under me. And I say to this *one*, 'Go,' and he goes; and to another, 'Come,' and he comes; and to my servant, 'Do this,' and he does *it*."

¹⁰When Jesus heard *it*, He marveled, and said to those who followed, "Assuredly, I say to you, I have not found such great faith, not even in Israel! ¹¹And I say to you that many will come from east and west, and sit down with Abraham, Isaac, and Jacob in the kingdom of heaven. ¹²But the sons of the kingdom will be cast out into outer darkness. There will be weeping and gnashing of teeth." ¹³Then Jesus said to the centurion, "Go your way; and as you have believed, *so* let it be done for you." And his servant was healed that same hour.

HELL — What will the people in hell be doing? (8:12)

PETER'S MOTHER-IN-LAW HEALED

¹⁴Now when Jesus had come into Peter's house, He saw his wife's mother lying sick with a fever. ¹⁵So He touched her hand, and the fever left her. And she arose and served them.ᵃ

MANY HEALED AFTER SABBATH SUNSET

¹⁶When evening had come, they brought to Him many who were demon-possessed. And He cast out the spirits with a word, and healed all who were sick, ¹⁷that it might be fulfilled which was spoken by Isaiah the prophet, saying:

"*He Himself took our infirmities
And bore our sicknesses.*"ᵃ

8:15 ᵃNU-Text and M-Text read *Him*.   **8:17** ᵃIsaiah 53:4

THE COST OF DISCIPLESHIP

¹⁸And when Jesus saw great multitudes about Him, He gave a command to depart to the other side. ¹⁹Then a certain scribe came and said to Him, "Teacher, I will follow You wherever You go."

²⁰And Jesus said to him, "Foxes have holes and birds of the air *have* nests, but the Son of Man has nowhere to lay *His* head."

²¹Then another of His disciples said to Him, "Lord, let me first go and bury my father."

²²But Jesus said to him, "Follow Me, and let the dead bury their own dead."

WIND AND WAVE OBEY JESUS

²³Now when He got into a boat, His disciples followed Him. ²⁴And suddenly a great tempest arose on the sea, so that the boat was covered with the waves. But He was asleep. ²⁵Then His disciples came to *Him* and awoke Him, saying, "Lord, save us! We are perishing!"

²⁶But He said to them, "Why are you fearful, O you of little faith?" Then He arose and rebuked the winds and the sea, and there was a great calm. ²⁷So the men marveled, saying, "Who can this be, that even the winds and the sea obey Him?"

TWO DEMON-POSSESSED MEN HEALED

²⁸When He had come to the other side, to the country of the Gergesenes,^a there met Him two demon-possessed *men*, coming out of the tombs, exceedingly fierce, so that no one could pass that way. ²⁹And suddenly they cried out, saying, "What have we to do with You, Jesus, You Son of God? Have You come here to torment us before the time?"

³⁰Now a good way off from them there was a herd of many swine feeding. ³¹So the demons begged Him, saying, "If You cast us out, permit us to go away^a into the herd of swine."

³²And He said to them, "Go." So when they had come out, they went into the herd of swine. And suddenly the whole herd of swine ran violently down the steep place into the sea, and perished in the water.

³³Then those who kept *them* fled; and they went away into the city and told everything, including what *had happened* to the demon-possessed *men*. ³⁴And behold, the whole city came out to meet Jesus. And when they saw Him, they begged *Him* to depart from their region.

JESUS FORGIVES AND HEALS A PARALYTIC

¹So He got into a boat, crossed over, and came to His own city. ²Then behold, they brought to Him a paralytic lying on a bed. When Jesus saw their faith, He said to the paralytic, "Son, be of good cheer; your sins are forgiven you."

³And at once some of the scribes said within themselves, "This Man blasphemes!"

⁴But Jesus, knowing their thoughts, said, "Why do you think evil in your hearts? ⁵For which is easier, to say, '*Your* sins are forgiven you,' or to say, 'Arise and walk'? ⁶But that you may know that the Son of Man has power on earth to forgive sins"—then He said to the paralytic, "Arise, take up your bed, and go to your house." ⁷And he arose and departed to his house.

⁸Now when the multitudes saw *it*, they marveled^a and glorified God, who had given such power to men.

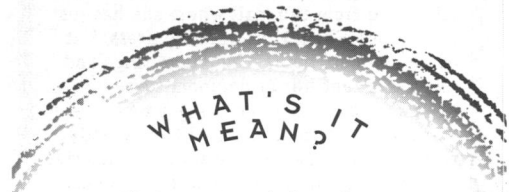

The Roman Empire had a tax-happy government. The Romans taxed everything from property to imported goods to fishing rights. They even collected taxes from the Jews for worshiping at the temple! The Romans claimed that the money was used to pay for the upkeep of the building. Some Bible experts have estimated that the average Jewish household lost as much as forty percent of their income to taxes.

Matthew 9:9

MATTHEW THE TAX COLLECTOR

⁹As Jesus passed on from there, He saw a man named Matthew sitting at the tax office. And He said to him, "Follow Me." So he arose and followed Him.

¹⁰Now it happened, as Jesus sat at the table in the house, *that* behold, many tax collectors and sinners came and sat down with Him and His disciples. ¹¹And when the Pharisees saw *it*, they said to His disciples, "Why does your Teacher eat with tax collectors and sinners?"

¹²When Jesus heard *that*, He said to them, "Those who are well have no need of a

On the Edge

And Jesus said to them, "Can the friends of the bridegroom mourn as long as the bridegroom is with them? But the days will come when the bridegroom will be taken away from them, and then they will fast" (Matt. 9:15).

In this passage of Scripture, Jesus was foretelling that He would be taken away from His disciples. In other words, the Bridegroom was getting ready to be taken out of the picture and put on a cross. Can you imagine how devastated the disciples must have been?

Picture a young bride-to-be who is out getting ready for her big wedding day. One of the happiest moments of her life. She is returning from the mall where she has just picked out a beautiful wedding dress; but when she gets home, the phone rings and she hears that her bridegroom-to-be has been shot and killed on his way home from work while trying to stop a little old lady from being robbed on the subway. She cries until she has no more strength; she doesn't want anything to eat; she can't sleep that night. Suddenly at midnight she gets another phone call that tells her that her fiancé is fine and there was a mix-up in the communication. He has been at the police station giving a statement and he couldn't get away. She is thrilled because the groom is alive and *the wedding is on!*

The disciples thought they had lost Jesus forever when He was put on the cross. But they were misinformed. Jesus is not dead—He is alive! He has defeated death, hell, and the grave! He is coming back for a pure bride—one without spot or wrinkle. What a wedding day that will be when we see Jesus face-to-face! Don't be misinformed. The wedding is on! Begin preparing yourself now, for He is the Bridegroom! Get ready!

SEE FOR YOURSELF:
Matt. 25:1–13;
Mark 2:20; Luke 5:34

sacrifice.'[a] For I did not come to call the righteous, but sinners, to repentance."[b]

JESUS IS QUESTIONED ABOUT FASTING

[14]Then the disciples of John came to Him, saying, "Why do we and the Pharisees fast often,[a] but Your disciples do not fast?"

[15]And Jesus said to them, "Can the friends of the bridegroom mourn as long as the bridegroom is with them? But the days will come when the bridegroom will be taken away from them, and then they will fast. [16]No one puts a piece of unshrunk cloth on an old garment; for the patch pulls away from the garment, and the tear is made worse. [17]Nor do they put new wine into old wineskins, or else the wineskins break, the wine is spilled, and the wineskins are ruined. But they put new wine into new wineskins, and both are preserved."

WHAT'S IT MEAN?

What's a wineskin? Good question. A wineskin was a bag used for storing liquids. Did we mention that the bag was made of the hide (or skin) of a goat or another animal? When grape juice was stored in a new wineskin, the fermentation process (the chemical changes that cause grape juice to become wine) made the wineskin stretch and swell. The older a wineskin got, the more stiff and brittle it became. When grape juice was poured into an old wineskin, often the container would break.
Matthew 9:17

A GIRL RESTORED TO LIFE AND A WOMAN HEALED

[18]While He spoke these things to them, behold, a ruler came and worshiped Him, saying, "My daughter has just died, but come and lay Your hand on her and she will live." [19]So Jesus arose and followed him, and so *did* His disciples.

[20]And suddenly, a woman who had a flow of blood for twelve years came from behind and touched the hem of His garment. [21]For she said to herself, "If only I may touch His garment, I shall be made well." [22]But Jesus turned around, and when He saw her He said, "Be of

physician, but those who are sick. [13]But go and learn what *this* means: '*I desire mercy and not*

9:13 [a]Hosea 6:6 [b]NU-Text omits *to repentance.*   **9:14** [a]NU-Text brackets *often* as disputed.

good cheer, daughter; your faith has made you well." And the woman was made well from that hour.

²³When Jesus came into the ruler's house, and saw the flute players and the noisy crowd wailing, ²⁴He said to them, "Make room, for the girl is not dead, but sleeping." And they ridiculed Him. ²⁵But when the crowd was put outside, He went in and took her by the hand, and the girl arose. ²⁶And the report of this went out into all that land.

TWO BLIND MEN HEALED

²⁷When Jesus departed from there, two blind men followed Him, crying out and saying, "Son of David, have mercy on us!"

²⁸And when He had come into the house, the blind men came to Him. And Jesus said to them, "Do you believe that I am able to do this?"

They said to Him, "Yes, Lord."

²⁹Then He touched their eyes, saying, "According to your faith let it be to you." ³⁰And their eyes were opened. And Jesus sternly warned them, saying, "See *that* no one knows *it*." ³¹But when they had departed, they spread the news about Him in all that country.

A MUTE MAN SPEAKS

³²As they went out, behold, they brought to Him a man, mute and demon-possessed. ³³And when the demon was cast out, the mute spoke. And the multitudes marveled, saying, "It was never seen like this in Israel!"

³⁴But the Pharisees said, "He casts out demons by the ruler of the demons."

THE COMPASSION OF JESUS

³⁵Then Jesus went about all the cities and villages, teaching in their synagogues, preaching the gospel of the kingdom, and healing every sickness and every disease among the people.*a* ³⁶But when He saw the multitudes, He was moved with compassion for them, because they were weary*a* and scattered, like sheep having no shepherd. ³⁷Then He said to His disciples, "The harvest truly *is* plentiful, but the laborers *are* few. ³⁸Therefore pray the Lord of the harvest to send out laborers into His harvest."

THE TWELVE APOSTLES

¹And when He had called His twelve disciples to *Him*, He gave them power *over* unclean spirits, to cast them out, and to heal all kinds of sickness and all kinds of disease. ²Now the names of the twelve apostles are these: first, Simon, who is called Peter, and Andrew his brother; James the *son* of Zebedee, and John his brother; ³Philip and Bartholomew; Thomas and Matthew the tax collector; James the *son* of Alphaeus, and Lebbaeus, whose surname was*a* Thaddaeus; ⁴Simon the Cananite,*a* and Judas Iscariot, who also betrayed Him.

SENDING OUT THE TWELVE

⁵These twelve Jesus sent out and commanded them, saying: "Do not go into the way of the Gentiles, and do not enter a city of the Samaritans. ⁶But go rather to the lost sheep of the house of Israel. ⁷And as you go, preach, saying, 'The kingdom of heaven is at hand.' ⁸Heal the sick, cleanse the lepers, raise the dead,*a* cast out demons. Freely you have received, freely give. ⁹Provide neither gold nor silver nor copper in

> "But Jesus turned around, and when He saw her He said, 'Be of good cheer, daughter; your faith has made you well.' And the woman was made well from that hour."
> (Matthew 9:22)

WHAT'S IT MEAN?

As far as the Israelites were concerned, there were only three types of people in the world: Jews, Gentiles, and Samaritans. The Jews were the descendants of Abraham. The Gentiles were the people who weren't Jews. The Samaritans were a mixture of the two, the result of mixed marriages between Jews and Gentiles.

Matthew 10:5

your money belts, ¹⁰nor bag for *your* journey, nor two tunics, nor sandals, nor staffs; for a worker is worthy of his food.

¹¹"Now whatever city or town you enter, inquire who in it is worthy, and stay there till you go out. ¹²And when you go into a household, greet it. ¹³If the household is worthy, let your peace come upon it. But if it is not worthy, let your peace return to you. ¹⁴And whoever will not receive you nor hear your words, when you depart from that house or city, shake off the dust from your feet. ¹⁵Assuredly, I say to you, it will be more tolerable for the land of Sodom and Gomorrah in the day of judgment than for that city!

PERSECUTIONS ARE COMING

¹⁶"Behold, I send you out as sheep in the midst of wolves. Therefore be wise as serpents and harmless as doves. ¹⁷But beware of men, for they will deliver you up to councils and scourge you in their synagogues. ¹⁸You will be brought before governors and kings for My sake, as a testimony to them and to the Gentiles. ¹⁹But when they deliver you up, do not worry about how or what you should speak. For it will be given to you in that hour what you should speak; ²⁰for it is not you who speak, but the Spirit of your Father who speaks in you.

²¹"Now brother will deliver up brother to death, and a father *his* child; and children will rise up against parents and cause them to be put to death. ²²And you will be hated by all for My name's sake. But he who endures to the end will be saved. ²³When they persecute you in this city, flee to another. For assuredly, I say to you, you will not have gone through the cities of Israel before the Son of Man comes.

²⁴"A disciple is not above *his* teacher, nor a servant above his master. ²⁵It is enough for a disciple that he be like his teacher, and a servant like his master. If they have called the master of the house Beelzebub,ᵃ how much more *will they call* those of his household! ²⁶Therefore do not fear them. For there is nothing covered that will not be revealed, and hidden that will not be known.

HATRED

Will people ever hate me because I love Jesus? (10:22)

JESUS TEACHES THE FEAR OF GOD

²⁷"Whatever I tell you in the dark, speak in the light; and what you hear in the ear, preach on the housetops. ²⁸And do not fear those who kill the body but cannot kill the soul. But rather fear Him who is able to destroy both soul and body in hell. ²⁹Are not two sparrows sold for a copper coin? And not one of them falls to the ground apart from your Father's will. ³⁰But the very hairs of your head are all numbered. ³¹Do not fear therefore; you are of more value than many sparrows.

CONFESS CHRIST BEFORE MEN

³²"Therefore whoever confesses Me before men, him I will also confess before My Father

10:25 ᵃNU-Text and M-Text read *Beelzebul.*

Promise   HE PROMISES TO TELL YOU WHAT TO SAY.

For it is not you who speak, but the Spirit of your Father who speaks in you (Matt. 10:20).

Have you ever been in a situation where you just didn't know what to say? Maybe you were "smack-dab" in the middle of witnessing to someone, and suddenly you didn't know what to do? This has happened to everybody. In this verse, Jesus was telling His disciples that He was sending them out to be witnesses, and He assured them they should not be worried about what to say or how to say it. Why? Because the Holy Spirit was going to give them the words to say. One of the cool parts of being a Christian is that you don't have to live on your own. Jesus is right there with you. He's never going to leave you or stand you up. He's always ready to speak to you and through you. So the next time you're sharing Jesus with a friend, or someone at school is drilling you about Christianity, remember *He* is the One who speaks. The Holy Spirit will give you the words to say. Just calm down, and let Him do it. He always will, because His Word never fails!

SEE FOR YOURSELF:
2 Sam. 23:2; Acts 1:16; Rom. 8:26

who is in heaven. ³³But whoever denies Me before men, him I will also deny before My Father who is in heaven.

WHAT'S IT MEAN?

Sparrows were what people offered to God when they couldn't afford a goat or sheep. They were considered a "poor man's sacrifice."

Matthew 10:29

CHRIST BRINGS DIVISION

³⁴"Do not think that I came to bring peace on earth. I did not come to bring peace but a sword. ³⁵For I have come to '*set a man against his father, a daughter against her mother, and a daughter-in-law against her mother-in-law*'; ³⁶and '*a man's enemies will be those of his own household.*'ᵃ ³⁷He who loves father or mother more than Me is not worthy of Me. And he who loves son or daughter more than Me is not worthy of Me. ³⁸And he who does not take his cross and follow after Me is not worthy of Me. ³⁹He who finds his life will lose it, and he who loses his life for My sake will find it.

A CUP OF COLD WATER

⁴⁰"He who receives you receives Me, and he who receives Me receives Him who sent Me. ⁴¹He who receives a prophet in the name of a prophet shall receive a prophet's reward. And he who receives a righteous man in the name of a righteous man shall receive a righteous man's reward. ⁴²And whoever gives one of these little ones only a cup of cold *water* in the name of a disciple, assuredly, I say to you, he shall by no means lose his reward."

JOHN THE BAPTIST SENDS MESSENGERS TO JESUS

¹Now it came to pass, when Jesus finished commanding His twelve disciples, that He departed from there to teach and to preach in their cities.

²And when John had heard in prison about the works of Christ, he sent two ofᵃ his disciples ³and said to Him, "Are You the Coming One, or do we look for another?"

⁴Jesus answered and said to them, "Go and tell John the things which you hear and see: ⁵*The* blind see and *the* lame walk; *the* lepers are cleansed and *the* deaf hear; *the* dead are raised up and *the* poor have the gospel preached to them. ⁶And blessed is he who is not offended because of Me."

⁷As they departed, Jesus began to say to the multitudes concerning John: "What did you go out into the wilderness to see? A reed shaken by the wind? ⁸But what did you go out to see? A man clothed in soft garments? Indeed, those who wear soft *clothing* are in kings' houses. ⁹But what did you go out to see? A prophet? Yes, I say to you, and more than a prophet. ¹⁰For this is *he* of whom it is written:

'*Behold, I send My messenger before Your face,*
Who will prepare Your way before You.'ᵃ

¹¹"Assuredly, I say to you, among those born of women there has not risen one greater than John the Baptist; but he who is least in the kingdom of heaven is greater than he. ¹²And from the days of John the Baptist until now the kingdom of heaven suffers violence, and the violent take it by force. ¹³For all the prophets and the law prophesied until John. ¹⁴And if you are willing to receive *it*, he is Elijah who is to come. ¹⁵He who has ears to hear, let him hear!

¹⁶"But to what shall I liken this generation? It is like children sitting in the marketplaces and calling to their companions, ¹⁷and saying:

'We played the flute for you,
And you did not dance;
We mourned to you,
And you did not lament.'

¹⁸For John came neither eating nor drinking, and they say, 'He has a demon.' ¹⁹The Son of Man came eating and drinking, and they say, 'Look, a glutton and a winebibber, a friend of tax collectors and sinners!' But wisdom is justified by her children."ᵃ

WOE TO THE IMPENITENT CITIES

²⁰Then He began to rebuke the cities in which most of His mighty works had been done, because they did not repent: ²¹"Woe to you, Chorazin! Woe to you, Bethsaida! For if the mighty works which were done in you had

---

10:36 ᵃMicah 7:6 **11:2** ᵃNU-Text reads *by* for *two of.* **11:10** ᵃMalachi 3:1 **11:19** ᵃNU-Text reads *works.*

been done in Tyre and Sidon, they would have repented long ago in sackcloth and ashes. [22]But I say to you, it will be more tolerable for Tyre and Sidon in the day of judgment than for you. [23]And you, Capernaum, who are exalted to heaven, will be[a] brought down to Hades; for if the mighty works which were done in you had been done in Sodom, it would have remained until this day. [24]But I say to you that it shall be more tolerable for the land of Sodom in the day of judgment than for you."

> "Come to Me, all you who labor and are heavy laden, and I will give you rest. Take My yoke upon you and learn from Me, for I am gentle and lowly in heart, and you will find rest for your souls."
> (Matthew 11:28, 29)

JESUS GIVES TRUE REST

[25]At that time Jesus answered and said, "I thank You, Father, Lord of heaven and earth, that You have hidden these things from *the* wise and prudent and have revealed them to babes. [26]Even so, Father, for so it seemed good in Your sight. [27]All things have been delivered to Me by My Father,

TRIALS
What does Christ promise us when we're dealing with trials? (11:25–30)

and no one knows the Son except the Father. Nor does anyone know the Father except the Son, and *the one* to whom the Son wills to reveal Him. [28]Come to Me, all *you* who labor and are heavy laden, and I will give you rest. [29]Take My yoke upon you and learn from Me, for I am gentle and lowly in heart, and you will find rest for your souls. [30]For My yoke *is* easy and My burden is light."

JESUS IS LORD OF THE SABBATH

[1]At that time Jesus went through the grainfields on the Sabbath. And His disciples were hungry, and began to pluck heads of grain and to eat. [2]And when the Pharisees saw *it*, they said to Him, "Look, Your disciples are doing what is not lawful to do on the Sabbath!"

[3]But He said to them, "Have you not read what David did when he was hungry, he and those who were with him: [4]how he entered the house of God and ate the showbread which was not lawful for him to eat, nor for those

11:23 [a]NU-Text reads *will you be exalted to heaven? No, you will be.*

Promise   HE PROMISES YOU REST.

Come to Me, all you who labor and are heavy laden, and I will give you rest (Matt. 11:28).

Have you ever been hiking in the mountains with a huge backpack strapped to your back all day long? What's the first thing you did when you finally reached your destination—the top? You unstrapped that pack, stretched out on the ground, and rested, right? Oh, what a feeling! At that very moment, there was nothing better than removing that weight, lying down, and resting.

A lot of people carry around heavy backpacks every day of their lives. Now they don't carry a literal pack, but a backpack of sin, a suitcase full of guilt, or a huge load of worry. Jesus wants to give us rest. He wants to help us. It's not worth carrying around a bunch of heavy junk when all we have to do is come to Jesus and let Him take the weight off our shoulders. He paid the price to carry it so we don't have to!

When He says that He will give you rest, He means it. If you can learn to rest in Jesus as a teenager, you'll be a step ahead of a lot of adults. The key is to really learn what Jesus has done for you—what burdens He bears for you—and then to let Him have them. When you do what you're supposed to do and let Him do what He's supposed to do, then you can rest in Him.

SEE FOR YOURSELF:
Ps. 55:22; 94:13; Eccl. 10:15; Is. 14:3

who were with him, but only for the priests? ⁵Or have you not read in the law that on the Sabbath the priests in the temple profane the Sabbath, and are blameless? ⁶Yet I say to you that in this place there is *One* greater than the temple. ⁷But if you had known what *this* means, '*I desire mercy and not sacrifice*,'ᵃ you would not have condemned the guiltless. ⁸For the Son of Man is Lord evenᵃ of the Sabbath."

WHAT'S IT MEAN?

Know your New Testament geography!
Chorazin and Bethsaida were towns on the shore of the Sea of Galilee, just a few miles from Capernaum. Tyre and Sidon were coastal cities on the Mediterranean Sea, in what is now Lebanon. Tyre especially had a long history of being condemned by God's prophets in the Old Testament.

Matthew 11:21

HEALING ON THE SABBATH

⁹Now when He had departed from there, He went into their synagogue. ¹⁰And behold, there was a man who had a withered hand. And they asked Him, saying, "Is it lawful to heal on the Sabbath?"—that they might accuse Him.

WHAT'S IT MEAN?

God felt so strongly about honoring the Sabbath that He included it as one of the Ten Commandments. The logical question, then, is how to honor it. The Jews set aside the last day of each week for worshiping God. During the Sabbath, people were allowed to work only in cases of emergency.

Matthew 12:9–14

¹¹Then He said to them, "What man is there among you who has one sheep, and if it falls

On the Edge

Behold! My Servant whom I have chosen, My Beloved in whom My soul is well pleased! I will put My Spirit upon Him, and He will declare justice to the Gentiles (Matt. 12:18).

A survey was recently taken to find out the priorities of the generation before World War II and of the generation after World War II. The generation before World War II listed their priorities in this order: God, family, country, etc. . . . This group listed themselves third or fourth on their priority lists.

Of the people born after World War II, around ninety-eight percent listed themselves as first on the list. In other words, more people are self-centered now than ever before. They want to serve themselves more than they want to serve others.

God has something better for us. Jesus, our Lord and example, came to serve. He was the ultimate Servant. We need to strive to be like Jesus and to work on becoming servants. What is a servant? One who will do anything for anybody with a good attitude and a willing heart. So, the next time you get asked to do something that's not so glorious or fun, smile real big (as you remember what Jesus would do), and say, "Sure, I'd be happy to!" Watch what God will do in your life. He's going to exalt you!

SEE FOR YOURSELF:
Prov. 11:2; Matt. 20:28; 23:12; Mark 9:35; 10:44; John 13:4–9; Phil. 2:3–8

into a pit on the Sabbath, will not lay hold of it and lift *it* out? ¹²Of how much more value then is a man than a sheep? Therefore it is lawful to do good on the Sabbath." ¹³Then He said to the man, "Stretch out your hand." And he stretched *it* out, and it was restored as whole as the other. ¹⁴Then the Pharisees went out and plotted against Him, how they might destroy Him.

BEHOLD, MY SERVANT

¹⁵But when Jesus knew *it,* He withdrew from there. And great multitudesᵃ followed Him, and

12:7 ᵃHosea 6:6 **12:8** ᵃNU-Text and M-Text omit *even.* **12:15** ᵃNU-Text brackets *multitudes* as disputed.

He healed them all. ¹⁶Yet He warned them not to make Him known, ¹⁷that it might be fulfilled which was spoken by Isaiah the prophet, saying:

¹⁸ *"Behold! My Servant whom I have chosen,*
My Beloved in whom My soul is well
*   pleased!*
I will put My Spirit upon Him,
And He will declare justice to the Gentiles.
¹⁹ *He will not quarrel nor cry out,*
Nor will anyone hear His voice in the
*   streets.*
²⁰ *A bruised reed He will not break,*
And smoking flax He will not quench,
Till He sends forth justice to victory;
²¹ *And in His name Gentiles will trust."* ᵃ

A HOUSE DIVIDED CANNOT STAND

²²Then one was brought to Him who was demon-possessed, blind and mute; and He healed him, so that the blind andᵃ mute man both spoke and saw. ²³And all the multitudes were amazed and said, "Could this be the Son of David?"

²⁴Now when the Pharisees heard *it* they said, "This *fellow* does not cast out demons except by Beelzebub,ᵃ the ruler of the demons."

WHAT'S IT MEAN?

Beelzebub was the name of a pagan god of the Canaanites that the Jewish people believed ruled over all evil spirits. Elsewhere in the Bible he is called Satan, or the devil.
Matthew 12:24

²⁵But Jesus knew their thoughts, and said to them: "Every kingdom divided against itself is brought to desolation, and every city or house divided against itself will not stand. ²⁶If Satan casts out Satan, he is divided against himself. How then will his kingdom stand? ²⁷And if I cast out demons by Beelzebub, by whom do your sons cast *them* out? Therefore they shall be your judges. ²⁸But if I cast out demons by the Spirit of God, surely the kingdom of God has

come upon you. ²⁹Or how can one enter a strong man's house and plunder his goods, unless he first binds the strong man? And then he will plunder his house. ³⁰He who is not with Me is against Me, and he who does not gather with Me scatters abroad.

THE UNPARDONABLE SIN

³¹"Therefore I say to you, every sin and blasphemy will be forgiven men, but the blasphemy *against* the Spirit will not be forgiven men. ³²Anyone who speaks a word against the Son of Man, it will be forgiven him; but whoever speaks against the Holy Spirit, it will not be forgiven him, either in this age or in the *age* to come.

A TREE KNOWN BY ITS FRUIT

³³"Either make the tree good and its fruit good, or else make the tree bad and its fruit bad; for a tree is known by *its* fruit. ³⁴Brood of vipers! How can you, being evil, speak good things? For out of the abundance of the heart the mouth speaks. ³⁵A good man out of the good treasure of his heartᵃ brings forth good things, and an evil man out of the evil treasure brings forth evil things. ³⁶But I say to you that for every idle word men may speak, they will give account of it in the day of judgment. ³⁷For by your words you will be justified, and by your words you will be condemned."

JUDGMENT

Will God judge the words we speak? (12:36)

THE SCRIBES AND PHARISEES ASK FOR A SIGN

³⁸Then some of the scribes and Pharisees answered, saying, "Teacher, we want to see a sign from You."

³⁹But He answered and said to them, "An evil and adulterous generation seeks after a sign, and no sign will be given to it except the sign of the prophet Jonah. ⁴⁰For as Jonah was three days and three nights in the belly of the great fish, so will the Son of Man be three days and three nights in the heart of the earth. ⁴¹The men of Nineveh will rise up in the judgment with this generation and condemn it, because they repented at the preaching of Jonah; and indeed a greater than Jonah *is* here. ⁴²The queen of the South will rise up in the judgment with this generation and condemn it, for she came from the ends of the earth to hear the wisdom of Solomon; and indeed a greater than Solomon *is* here.

12:21 ᵃIsaiah 42:1-4   **12:22** ᵃNU-Text omits *blind and.*
12:35 ᵃNU-Text and M-Text omit *of his heart.*

12:24 ᵃNU-Text and M-Text read *Beelzebul.*

AN UNCLEAN SPIRIT RETURNS

⁴³"When an unclean spirit goes out of a man, he goes through dry places, seeking rest, and finds none. ⁴⁴Then he says, 'I will return to my house from which I came.' And when he comes, he finds *it* empty, swept, and put in order. ⁴⁵Then he goes and takes with him seven other spirits more wicked than himself, and they enter and dwell there; and the last *state* of that man is worse than the first. So shall it also be with this wicked generation."

JESUS' MOTHER AND BROTHERS SEND FOR HIM

⁴⁶While He was still talking to the multitudes, behold, His mother and brothers stood outside, seeking to speak with Him. ⁴⁷Then one said to Him, "Look, Your mother and Your brothers are standing outside, seeking to speak with You."

⁴⁸But He answered and said to the one who told Him, "Who is My mother and who are My brothers?" ⁴⁹And He stretched out His hand toward His disciples and said, "Here are My mother and My brothers! ⁵⁰For whoever does the will of My Father in heaven is My brother and sister and mother."

THE PARABLE OF THE SOWER

¹On the same day Jesus went out of the house and sat by the sea. ²And great multitudes were gathered together to Him, so that He got into a boat and sat; and the whole multitude stood on the shore.

³Then He spoke many things to them in parables, saying: "Behold, a sower went out to sow. ⁴And as he sowed, some *seed* fell by the wayside; and the birds came and devoured them. ⁵Some fell on stony places, where they did not have much earth; and they immediately sprang up because they had no depth of earth. ⁶But when the sun was up they were scorched, and because they had no root they withered away. ⁷And some fell among thorns, and the thorns sprang up and choked them. ⁸But others fell on good ground and yielded a crop: some a hundredfold, some sixty, some thirty. ⁹He who has ears to hear, let him hear!"

THE PURPOSE OF PARABLES

¹⁰And the disciples came and said to Him, "Why do You speak to them in parables?"

¹¹He answered and said to them, "Because it has been given to you to know the mysteries of the kingdom of heaven, but to them it has not been given. ¹²For whoever has, to him more will be given, and he will have abundance; but

whoever does not have, even what he has will be taken away from him. ¹³Therefore I speak to them in parables, because seeing they do not see, and hearing they do not hear, nor do they understand. ¹⁴And in them the prophecy of Isaiah is fulfilled, which says:

'Hearing you will hear and shall not
      understand,
   And seeing you will see and not perceive;
¹⁵ For the hearts of this people have grown
      dull.
   Their ears are hard of hearing,
   And their eyes they have closed,
   Lest they should see with their eyes and
      hear with their ears,
   Lest they should understand with their
      hearts and turn,
   So that I should*ᵃ* heal them.'*ᵇ*

¹⁶But blessed *are* your eyes for they see, and your ears for they hear; ¹⁷for assuredly, I say to you that many prophets and righteous *men* desired to see what you see, and did not see *it*, and to hear what you hear, and did not hear *it*.

THE PARABLE OF THE SOWER EXPLAINED

¹⁸"Therefore hear the parable of the sower: ¹⁹When anyone hears the word of the kingdom, and does not understand *it*, then the wicked *one* comes and snatches away what was sown in his heart. This is he who received seed by the wayside. ²⁰But he who received the seed on stony places, this is he who hears the word and immediately receives it with joy; ²¹yet he has no root in himself, but endures only for a while. For when tribulation or persecution arises because of the word, immediately he stumbles. ²²Now he who received seed among the thorns is he who hears the word, and the cares of this world and the deceitfulness of riches choke the word, and he becomes unfruitful. ²³But he who received seed on the good ground is he who hears the word and understands *it*, who indeed bears fruit and produces: some a hundredfold, some sixty, some thirty."

THE PARABLE OF THE WHEAT AND THE TARES

²⁴Another parable He put forth to them, saying: "The kingdom of heaven is like a man who sowed good seed in his field; ²⁵but while men slept, his enemy came and sowed tares among the wheat and went his way. ²⁶But when the grain had sprouted and produced a crop, then the tares also appeared. ²⁷So the servants of the

13:15 *ᵃ*NU-Text and M-Text read *would.* *ᵇ*Isaiah 6:9, 10

owner came and said to him, 'Sir, did you not sow good seed in your field? How then does it have tares?' [28]He said to them, 'An enemy has done this.' The servants said to him, 'Do you want us then to go and gather them up?' [29]But he said, 'No, lest while you gather up the tares you also uproot the wheat with them. [30]Let both grow together until the harvest, and at the time of harvest I will say to the reapers, "First gather together the tares and bind them in bundles to burn them, but gather the wheat into my barn." ' "

> "Then the righteous will shine forth as the sun in the kingdom of their Father. He who has ears to hear, let him hear!"
> (Matthew 13:43)

THE PARABLE OF THE MUSTARD SEED

[31]Another parable He put forth to them, saying: "The kingdom of heaven is like a mustard seed, which a man took and sowed in his field, [32]which indeed is the least of all the seeds; but when it is grown it is greater than the herbs and becomes a tree, so that the birds of the air come and nest in its branches."

THE PARABLE OF THE LEAVEN

[33]Another parable He spoke to them: "The kingdom of heaven is like leaven, which a woman took and hid in three measures[a] of meal till it was all leavened."

PROPHECY AND THE PARABLES

[34]All these things Jesus spoke to the multitude in parables; and without a parable He did not speak to them, [35]that it might be fulfilled which was spoken by the prophet, saying:

> "I will open My mouth in parables;
> I will utter things kept secret from the
> foundation of the world."[a]

THE PARABLE OF THE TARES EXPLAINED

[36]Then Jesus sent the multitude away and went into the house. And His disciples came to Him, saying, "Explain to us the parable of the tares of the field."

[37]He answered and said to them: "He who sows the good seed is the Son of Man. [38]The field is the world, the good seeds are the sons of the kingdom, but the tares are the sons of the wicked one. [39]The enemy who sowed them is the devil, the harvest is the end of the age, and

the reapers are the angels. [40]Therefore as the tares are gathered and burned in the fire, so it will be at the end of this age. [41]The Son of Man will send out His angels, and they will gather out of His kingdom all things that offend, and those who practice lawlessness, [42]and will cast them into the furnace of fire. There will be wailing and gnashing of teeth. [43]Then the righteous will shine forth as the sun in the kingdom of their Father. He who has ears to hear, let him hear!

THE PARABLE OF THE HIDDEN TREASURE

[44]"Again, the kingdom of heaven is like treasure hidden in a field, which a man found and hid; and for joy over it he goes and sells all that he has and buys that field.

THE PARABLE OF THE PEARL OF GREAT PRICE

[45]"Again, the kingdom of heaven is like a merchant seeking beautiful pearls, [46]who, when he had found one pearl of great price, went and sold all that he had and bought it.

THE PARABLE OF THE DRAGNET

[47]"Again, the kingdom of heaven is like a dragnet that was cast into the sea and gathered some of every kind, [48]which, when it was full, they drew to shore; and they sat down and gathered the good into vessels, but threw the bad away. [49]So it will be at the end of the age. The angels will come forth, separate the wicked from among the just, [50]and cast them into the furnace of fire. There will be wailing and gnashing of teeth."

[51]Jesus said to them,[a] "Have you understood all these things?"

They said to Him, "Yes, Lord."[b]

[52]Then He said to them, "Therefore every scribe instructed concerning[a] the kingdom of heaven is like a householder who brings out of his treasure things new and old."

JESUS REJECTED AT NAZARETH

[53]Now it came to pass, when Jesus had finished these parables, that He departed from there. [54]When He had come to His own country, He taught them in their synagogue, so that they were astonished and said, "Where did this

---

13:33 [a]Greek sata, approximately two pecks in all   **13:35** [a]Psalm 78:2   **13:51** [a]NU-Text omits Jesus said to them.   [b]NU-Text omits Lord.   **13:52** [a]Or for

Man get this wisdom and *these* mighty works? [55]Is this not the carpenter's son? Is not His mother called Mary? And His brothers James, Joses,[a] Simon, and Judas? [56]And His sisters, are they not all with us? Where then did this *Man* get all these things?" [57]So they were offended at Him.

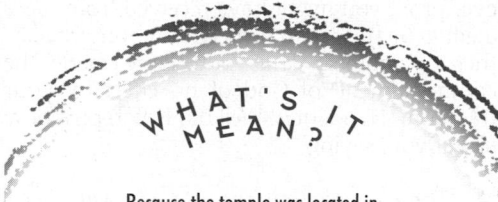

WHAT'S IT MEAN?

Because the temple was located in Jerusalem, many Jews had to travel a long way to "officially" worship God. As a result, many of them could not visit the temple on a regular basis. Instead, they formed small, local meeting places called synagogues. At first, the synagogues were simply places people met to read God's Law and pray together. Eventually, though, they became centers of community life.

Matthew 13:54

But Jesus said to them, "A prophet is not without honor except in his own country and in his own house." [58]Now He did not do many mighty works there because of their unbelief.

JOHN THE BAPTIST BEHEADED

[1]At that time Herod the tetrarch heard the report about Jesus [2]and said to his servants, "This is John the Baptist; he is risen from the dead, and therefore these powers are at work in him." [3]For Herod had laid hold of John and bound him, and put *him* in prison for the sake of Herodias, his brother Philip's wife. [4]Because John had said to him, "It is not lawful for you to have her." [5]And although he wanted to put him to death, he feared the multitude, because they counted him as a prophet.

EMBARRASSMENT
What can embarrassment lead to? (14:1–12)

[6]But when Herod's birthday was celebrated, the daughter of Herodias danced before them and pleased Herod. [7]Therefore he promised with an oath to give her whatever she might ask.

[8]So she, having been prompted by her mother, said, "Give me John the Baptist's head here on a platter."

[9]And the king was sorry; nevertheless, because of the oaths and because of those who sat with him, he commanded *it* to be given to *her.* [10]So he sent and had John beheaded in prison. [11]And his head was brought on a platter and given to the girl, and she brought *it* to her mother. [12]Then his disciples came and took away the body and buried it, and went and told Jesus.

FEEDING THE FIVE THOUSAND

[13]When Jesus heard *it,* He departed from there by boat to a deserted place by Himself. But when the multitudes heard it, they followed Him on foot from the cities. [14]And when Jesus went out He saw a great multitude; and He was moved with compassion for them, and healed their sick. [15]When it was evening, His disciples came to Him, saying, "This is a deserted place, and the hour is already late. Send the multitudes away, that they may go into the villages and buy themselves food."

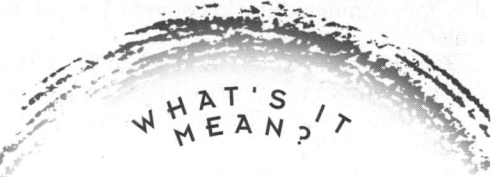

WHAT'S IT MEAN?

Herod the Great, the ruler of Judea, died when Jesus was very young. His kingdom was divided among his three sons. Antipas was the name of the son who inherited the region of Galilee, the place where both Jesus and John the Baptist lived most of their adult lives. Whenever "Herod" is mentioned in the Bible, it usually refers to Antipas. Not only was Antipas the one who had John the Baptist murdered, he also played a part in Jesus' trial and death.

Matthew 14:1

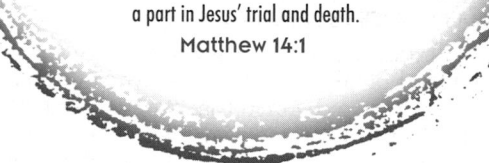

[16]But Jesus said to them, "They do not need to go away. You give them something to eat."

[17]And they said to Him, "We have here only five loaves and two fish."

[18]He said, "Bring them here to Me." [19]Then He commanded the multitudes to sit down on the grass. And He took the five loaves and the two fish, and looking up to heaven, He blessed and broke and gave the loaves to the disciples; and the disciples gave to the multitudes. [20]So they all ate and were filled, and they took up twelve baskets full of the fragments that

13:55 [a]NU-Text reads *Joseph.*

remained. ²¹Now those who had eaten were about five thousand men, besides women and children.

JESUS WALKS ON THE SEA

²²Immediately Jesus made His disciples get into the boat and go before Him to the other side, while He sent the multitudes away. ²³And when He had sent the multitudes away, He went up on the mountain by Himself to pray. Now when evening came, He was alone there. ²⁴But the boat was now in the middle of the sea,ᵃ tossed by the waves, for the wind was contrary.

²⁵Now in the fourth watch of the night Jesus went to them, walking on the sea. ²⁶And when the disciples saw Him walking on the sea, they were troubled, saying, "It is a ghost!" And they cried out for fear.

²⁷But immediately Jesus spoke to them, saying, "Be of good cheer! It is I; do not be afraid."

²⁸And Peter answered Him and said, "Lord, if it is You, command me to come to You on the water."

²⁹So He said, "Come." And when Peter had come down out of the boat, he walked on the water to go to Jesus. ³⁰But when he saw that the wind *was* boisterous,ᵃ he was afraid; and beginning to sink he cried out, saying, "Lord, save me!"

³¹And immediately Jesus stretched out *His* hand and caught him, and said to him, "O you of little faith, why did you doubt?" ³²And when they got into the boat, the wind ceased.

³³Then those who were in the boat came andᵃ worshiped Him, saying, "Truly You are the Son of God."

MANY TOUCH HIM AND ARE MADE WELL

³⁴When they had crossed over, they came to the land ofᵃ Gennesaret. ³⁵And when the men of that place recognized Him, they sent out into all that surrounding region, brought to Him all who were sick, ³⁶and begged Him that they might only touch the hem of His garment. And as many as touched *it* were made perfectly well.

DEFILEMENT COMES FROM WITHIN

¹Then the scribes and Pharisees who were from Jerusalem came to Jesus, saying, ²"Why do Your disciples transgress the tradition of the elders? For they do not wash their hands when they eat bread."

³He answered and said to them, "Why do you also transgress the commandment of God because of your tradition? ⁴For God commanded, saying, *'Honor your father and your mother';*ᵃ and, *'He who curses father or mother, let him be put to death.'*ᵇ ⁵But you say, 'Whoever says to his father or mother, "Whatever profit you might have received from me *is* a gift *to God*"—* ⁶then he need not honor his father or mother.'ᵃ Thus you have made the commandmentᵇ of God of no effect by your tradition. ⁷Hypocrites! Well did Isaiah prophesy about you, saying:

8   *'These people draw near to Me with their*
   mouth,
   Andᵃ honor Me with their lips,
   But their heart is far from Me.
9   *And in vain they worship Me,*
   Teaching as doctrines the commandments
   of men.' "ᵃ

¹⁰When He had called the multitude to *Himself*, He said to them, "Hear and understand: ¹¹Not what goes into the mouth defiles a man; but what comes out of the mouth, this defiles a man."

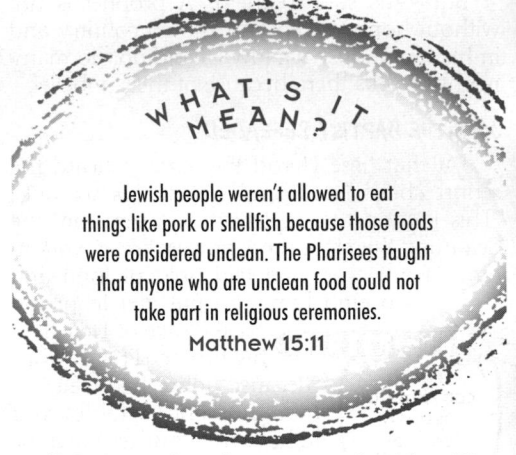

WHAT'S IT MEAN?

Jewish people weren't allowed to eat things like pork or shellfish because those foods were considered unclean. The Pharisees taught that anyone who ate unclean food could not take part in religious ceremonies.
Matthew 15:11

¹²Then His disciples came and said to Him, "Do You know that the Pharisees were offended when they heard this saying?"

¹³But He answered and said, "Every plant which My heavenly Father has not planted will be uprooted. ¹⁴Let them alone. They are blind leaders of the blind. And if the blind leads the blind, both will fall into a ditch."

---

[15]Then Peter answered and said to Him, "Explain this parable to us."

[16]So Jesus said, "Are you also still without understanding? [17]Do you not yet understand that whatever enters the mouth goes into the stomach and is eliminated? [18]But those things which proceed out of the mouth come from the heart, and they defile a man. [19]For out of the heart proceed evil thoughts, murders, adulteries, fornications, thefts, false witness, blasphemies. [20]These are *the things* which defile a man, but to eat with unwashed hands does not defile a man."

HONESTY

What do lies do to our position before God? (15:18–20)

A GENTILE SHOWS HER FAITH

[21]Then Jesus went out from there and departed to the region of Tyre and Sidon. [22]And behold, a woman of Canaan came from that region and cried out to Him, saying, "Have mercy on me, O Lord, Son of David! My daughter is severely demon-possessed."

[23]But He answered her not a word.

And His disciples came and urged Him, saying, "Send her away, for she cries out after us."

[24]But He answered and said, "I was not sent except to the lost sheep of the house of Israel."

[25]Then she came and worshiped Him, saying, "Lord, help me!"

[26]But He answered and said, "It is not good to take the children's bread and throw *it* to the little dogs."

[27]And she said, "Yes, Lord, yet even the little dogs eat the crumbs which fall from their masters' table."

[28]Then Jesus answered and said to her, "O woman, great *is* your faith! Let it be to you as you desire." And her daughter was healed from that very hour.

JESUS HEALS GREAT MULTITUDES

[29]Jesus departed from there, skirted the Sea of Galilee, and went up on the mountain and sat down there. [30]Then great multitudes came to Him, having with them *the* lame, blind, mute, maimed, and many others; and they laid them down at Jesus' feet, and He healed them. [31]So the multitude marveled when they saw *the* mute speaking, *the* maimed made whole, *the* lame walking, and *the* blind seeing; and they glorified the God of Israel.

FEEDING THE FOUR THOUSAND

[32]Now Jesus called His disciples to *Himself* and said, "I have compassion on the multitude, because they have now continued with Me three days and have nothing to eat. And I do not want to send them away hungry, lest they faint on the way."

[33]Then His disciples said to Him, "Where could we get enough bread in the wilderness to fill such a great multitude?"

[34]Jesus said to them, "How many loaves do you have?"

And they said, "Seven, and a few little fish."

[35]So He commanded the multitude to sit down on the ground. [36]And He took the seven loaves and the fish and gave thanks, broke *them* and gave *them* to His disciples; and the disciples *gave* to the multitude. [37]So they all ate and were filled, and they took up seven large baskets full of the fragments that were left. [38]Now those who ate were four thousand men, besides women and children. [39]And He sent away the multitude, got into the boat, and came to the region of Magdala.[a]

THE PHARISEES AND SADDUCEES SEEK A SIGN

[1]Then the Pharisees and Sadducees came, and testing Him asked that He would show them a sign from heaven. [2]He answered and said to them, "When it is evening you say, '*It will be* fair weather, for the sky is red'; [3]and in the morning, '*It will be* foul weather today, for the sky is red and threatening.' Hypocrites![a] You know how to discern the face of the sky, but you cannot *discern* the signs of the times. [4]A wicked and adulterous generation seeks after a sign, and no sign shall be given to it except the sign of the prophet[a] Jonah." And He left them and departed.

THE LEAVEN OF THE PHARISEES AND SADDUCEES

[5]Now when His disciples had come to the other side, they had forgotten to take bread. [6]Then Jesus said to them, "Take heed and beware of the leaven of the Pharisees and the Sadducees."

[7]And they reasoned among themselves, saying, "*It is* because we have taken no bread."

[8]But Jesus, being aware of *it*, said to them, "O you of little faith, why do you reason among yourselves because you have brought no bread?[a] [9]Do you not yet understand, or remember the five loaves of the five thousand and

how many baskets you took up? [10]Nor the seven loaves of the four thousand and how many large baskets you took up? [11]How is it you do not understand that I did not speak to you concerning bread?—*but* to beware of the leaven of the Pharisees and Sadducees." [12]Then they understood that He did not tell *them* to beware of the leaven of bread, but of the doctrine of the Pharisees and Sadducees.

PETER CONFESSES JESUS AS THE CHRIST

[13]When Jesus came into the region of Caesarea Philippi, He asked His disciples, saying, "Who do men say that I, the Son of Man, am?"

[14]So they said, "Some *say* John the Baptist, some Elijah, and others Jeremiah or one of the prophets."

[15]He said to them, "But who do you say that I am?"

[16]Simon Peter answered and said, "You are the Christ, the Son of the living God."

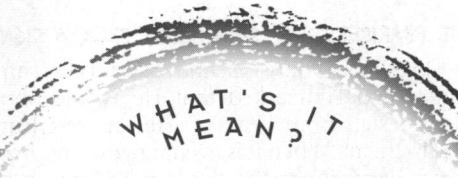

"Simon Peter answered and said, 'You are the Christ, the Son of the living God.' "
(Matthew 16:16)

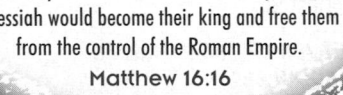

WHAT'S IT MEAN?

Many Jews were waiting for God to send them a special person they called the "Messiah," from a Hebrew word meaning "anointed one." (In case you're wondering, *Christ* is from the Greek for the word *Messiah*.) In Old Testament times, kings, priests, and prophets were all anointed, which means they had oil poured on their heads to show that they were specially chosen by God. The Jews of Jesus' day believed that the Messiah would become their king and free them from the control of the Roman Empire.

Matthew 16:16

[17]Jesus answered and said to him, "Blessed are you, Simon Bar-Jonah, for flesh and blood has not revealed *this* to you, but My Father who is in heaven. [18]And I also say to you that you are Peter, and on this rock I will build My church, and the gates of Hades shall not prevail against it. [19]And I will give you the keys of the kingdom of heaven, and whatever you bind on earth will be bound in heaven, and whatever you loose on earth will be loosed[a] in heaven."

[20]Then He commanded His disciples that they should tell no one that He was Jesus the Christ.

JESUS PREDICTS HIS DEATH AND RESURRECTION

[21]From that time Jesus began to show to His disciples that He must go to Jerusalem, and suffer many things from the elders and chief priests and scribes, and be killed, and be raised the third day.

[22]Then Peter took Him aside and began to rebuke Him, saying, "Far be it from You, Lord; this shall not happen to You!"

[23]But He turned and said to Peter, "Get behind Me, Satan! You are an offense to Me, for you are not mindful of the things of God, but the things of men."

TAKE UP THE CROSS AND FOLLOW HIM

[24]Then Jesus said to His disciples, "If anyone desires to come after Me, let him deny himself, and take up his cross, and follow Me. [25]For whoever desires to save his life will lose it, but whoever loses his life for My sake will find it. [26]For what profit is it to a man if he gains the whole world, and loses his own soul? Or what will a man give in exchange for his soul? [27]For the Son of Man will come in the glory of His Father with His angels, and then He will reward each according to his works.

JESUS TRANSFIGURED ON THE MOUNT

[28]Assuredly, I say to you, there are some standing here who shall not taste death till they see the Son of Man coming in His kingdom."

[1]Now after six days Jesus took Peter, James, and John his brother, led them up on a high mountain by themselves; [2]and He was transfigured before them. His face shone like the sun, and His clothes became as white as the light. [3]And behold, Moses and Elijah appeared to them, talking with Him. [4]Then Peter answered and said to Jesus, "Lord, it is good for us to be here; if You wish, let us[a] make here three tabernacles: one for You, one for Moses, and one for Elijah."

[5]While he was still speaking, behold, a bright cloud overshadowed them; and suddenly a voice came out of the cloud, saying, "This is My

16:19 [a]*Or will have been bound . . . will have been loosed*　**17:4** [a]NU-Text reads *I will.*

beloved Son, in whom I am well pleased. Hear Him!" 6And when the disciples heard *it*, they fell on their faces and were greatly afraid. 7But Jesus came and touched them and said, "Arise, and do not be afraid." 8When they had lifted up their eyes, they saw no one but Jesus only.

9Now as they came down from the mountain, Jesus commanded them, saying, "Tell the vision to no one until the Son of Man is risen from the dead."

10And His disciples asked Him, saying, "Why then do the scribes say that Elijah must come first?"

11Jesus answered and said to them, "Indeed, Elijah is coming first*a* and will restore all things. 12But I say to you that Elijah has come already, and they did not know him but did to him whatever they wished. Likewise the Son of Man is also about to suffer at their hands." 13Then the disciples understood that He spoke to them of John the Baptist.

A BOY IS HEALED

14And when they had come to the multitude, a man came to Him, kneeling down to Him and saying, 15"Lord, have mercy on my son, for he is an epileptic*a* and suffers severely; for he often falls into the fire and often into the water. 16So I brought him to Your disciples, but they could not cure him."

17Then Jesus answered and said, "O faithless and perverse generation, how long shall I be with you? How long shall I bear with you? Bring him here to Me." 18And Jesus rebuked the demon, and it came out of him; and the child was cured from that very hour.

19Then the disciples came to Jesus privately and said, "Why could we not cast it out?"

20So Jesus said to them, "Because of your unbelief;*a* for assuredly, I say to you, if you have faith as a mustard seed, you will say to this mountain, 'Move from here to there', and it will move; and nothing will be impossible for you. 21However, this kind does not go out except by prayer and fasting."*a*

JESUS AGAIN PREDICTS HIS DEATH AND RESURRECTION

22Now while they were staying*a* in Galilee, Jesus said to them, "The Son of Man is about to be betrayed into the hands of men, 23and they will kill Him, and the third day He will be raised up." And they were exceedingly sorrowful.

PETER AND HIS MASTER PAY THEIR TAXES

24When they had come to Capernaum,*a* those who received the *temple* tax came to Peter and said, "Does your Teacher not pay the *temple* tax?" 25He said, "Yes."

WHAT'S IT MEAN?

Every Jew over the age of twenty was expected to kick in some money every year to help take care of the temple in Jerusalem, which had been built by Herod the Great. The temple tax of a half-shekel was nothing to sneeze at. A half-shekel was about two days' wages for most Jews.

Matthew 17:24

And when he had come into the house, Jesus anticipated him, saying, "What do you think, Simon? From whom do the kings of the earth take customs or taxes, from their sons or from strangers?"

26Peter said to Him, "From strangers."

Jesus said to him, "Then the sons are free. 27Nevertheless, lest we offend them, go to the sea, cast in a hook, and take the fish that comes up first. And when you have opened its mouth, you will find a piece of money;*a* take that and give it to them for Me and you."

WHO IS THE GREATEST?

1At that time the disciples came to Jesus, saying, "Who then is greatest in the kingdom of heaven?"

2Then Jesus called a little child to Him, set him in the midst of them, 3and said, "Assuredly, I say to you, unless you are converted and become as little children, you will by no means enter the kingdom of heaven. 4Therefore whoever humbles himself as this little child is the greatest in the kingdom of heaven. 5Whoever receives one little child like this in My name receives Me.

JESUS WARNS OF OFFENSES

6"Whoever causes one of these little ones who believe in Me to sin, it would be better for

---

17:11 *a*NU-Text omits *first*.   **17:15** *a*Literally *moonstruck*   **17:20** *a*NU-Text reads *little faith*.   **17:21** *a*NU-Text omits this verse.   **17:22** *a*NU-Text reads *gathering together*.   **17:24** *a*NU-Text reads *Capharnaum* (here and elsewhere).   **17:27** *a*Greek *stater*, the exact amount to pay the temple tax (didrachma) for two him if a millstone were hung around his neck, and he were drowned in the depth of the sea. ⁷Woe to the world because of offenses! For offenses must come, but woe to that man by whom the offense comes!

⁸"If your hand or foot causes you to sin, cut it off and cast *it* from you. It is better for you to enter into life lame or maimed, rather than having two hands or two feet, to be cast into the everlasting fire. ⁹And if your eye causes you to sin, pluck it out and cast *it* from you. It is better for you to enter into life with one eye, rather than having two eyes, to be cast into hell fire.

THE PARABLE OF THE LOST SHEEP

¹⁰"Take heed that you do not despise one of these little ones, for I say to you that in heaven their angels always see the face of My Father who is in heaven. ¹¹For the Son of Man has come to save that which was lost.*a*

¹²"What do you think? If a man has a hundred sheep, and one of them goes astray, does he not leave the ninety-nine and go to the mountains to seek the one that is straying? ¹³And if he should find it, assuredly, I say to you, he rejoices more over that *sheep* than over the ninety-nine that did not go astray. ¹⁴Even so it is not the will of your Father who is in heaven that one of these little ones should perish.

WHAT'S IT MEAN?

The Romans hired local Jewish citizens to do their dirty work when it came to collecting taxes. Honesty was certainly not a requirement for the job of tax collector. Most collectors charged their fellow Jews more than they really owed and kept the extra cash for themselves. That, and the fact that they worked for the hated Romans, made Jewish tax collectors about the most unpopular people around.

Matthew 18:17

DEALING WITH A SINNING BROTHER

¹⁵"Moreover if your brother sins against you, go and tell him his fault between you and him alone. If he hears you, you have gained your brother. ¹⁶But if he will not hear, take with you one or two more, that *'by the mouth of two or three witnesses every word may be established.'*a* ¹⁷ And if he refuses to hear them, tell *it* to the church. But if he refuses even to hear the church, let him be to you like a heathen and a tax collector.

¹⁸"Assuredly, I say to you, whatever you bind on earth will be bound in heaven, and whatever you loose on earth will be loosed in heaven.

¹⁹"Again I say*a* to you that if two of you agree on earth concerning anything that they ask, it will be done for them by My Father in heaven. ²⁰For where two or three are gathered together in My name, I am there in the midst of them."

THE PARABLE OF THE UNFORGIVING SERVANT

²¹Then Peter came to Him and said, "Lord, how often shall my brother sin against me, and I forgive him? Up to seven times?"

²²Jesus said to him, "I do not say to you, up to seven times, but up to seventy times seven. ²³Therefore the kingdom of heaven is like a certain king who wanted to settle accounts with his servants. ²⁴And when he had begun to settle accounts, one

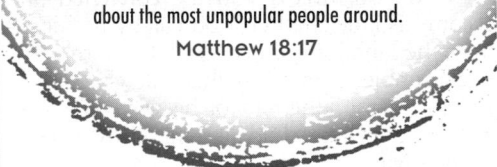

FORGIVENESS

How many times should I forgive someone before I stop? (18:21–35)

was brought to him who owed him ten thousand talents. ²⁵But as he was not able to pay, his master commanded that he be sold, with his wife and children and all that he had, and that payment be made. ²⁶The servant therefore fell down before him, saying, 'Master, have patience with me, and I will pay you all.' ²⁷Then the master of that servant was moved with compassion, released him, and forgave him the debt.

²⁸"But that servant went out and found one of his fellow servants who owed him a hundred denarii; and he laid hands on him and took *him* by the throat, saying, 'Pay me what you owe!' ²⁹So his fellow servant fell down at his feet*a* and begged him, saying, 'Have patience with me, and I will pay you all.'*b* ³⁰And he would not, but went and threw him into prison till he should pay the debt. ³¹So when his fellow servants saw what had been done, they were very grieved, and came and told their master all that had been done. ³²Then his master, after he had called him, said to him, 'You wicked servant! I forgave you all that debt because you

begged me. ³³Should you not also have had compassion on your fellow servant, just as I had pity on you?' ³⁴And his master was angry, and delivered him to the torturers until he should pay all that was due to him.

³⁵"So My heavenly Father also will do to you if each of you, from his heart, does not forgive his brother his trespasses."ᵃ

MARRIAGE AND DIVORCE

¹Now it came to pass, when Jesus had finished these sayings, *that* He departed from Galilee and came to the region of Judea beyond the Jordan. ²And great multitudes followed Him, and He healed them there.

³The Pharisees also came to Him, testing Him, and saying to Him, "Is it lawful for a man to divorce his wife for *just* any reason?"

⁴And He answered and said to them, "Have you not read that He who madeᵃ *them* at the beginning 'made them male and female,'ᵇ ⁵and said, 'For this reason a man shall leave his father and mother and be joined to his wife, and the two shall become one flesh'?ᵃ ⁶So then, they are no longer two but one flesh. Therefore what God has joined together, let not man separate."

⁷They said to Him, "Why then did Moses command to give a certificate of divorce, and to put her away?"

⁸He said to them, "Moses, because of the hardness of your hearts, permitted you to divorce your wives, but from the beginning it was not so. ⁹And I say to you, whoever divorces his wife, except for sexual immorality,ᵃ and marries another, commits adultery; and whoever marries her who is divorced commits adultery."

¹⁰His disciples said to Him, "If such is the case of the man with *his* wife, it is better not to marry."

JESUS TEACHES ON CELIBACY

¹¹But He said to them, "All cannot accept this saying, but only *those* to whom it has been given: ¹²For there are eunuchs who were born thus from *their* mother's womb, and there are eunuchs who were made eunuchs by men, and there are eunuchs who have made themselves eunuchs for the kingdom of heaven's sake. He who is able to accept *it*, let him accept *it*."

JESUS BLESSES LITTLE CHILDREN

¹³Then little children were brought to Him that He might put *His* hands on them and pray, but the disciples rebuked them. ¹⁴But Jesus said, "Let the little children come to Me, and do not forbid them; for of such is the kingdom of heaven." ¹⁵And He laid *His* hands on them and departed from there.

JESUS COUNSELS THE RICH YOUNG RULER

¹⁶Now behold, one came and said to Him, "Goodᵃ Teacher, what good thing shall I do that I may have eternal life?"

¹⁷So He said to him, "Why do you call Me good?ᵃ No one is good but One, *that is*, God.ᵇ But if you want to enter into life, keep the commandments."

¹⁸He said to Him, "Which ones?"

Jesus said, " 'You shall not murder,' 'You shall not commit adultery,' 'You shall not steal,' 'You shall not bear false witness,' ¹⁹'Honor your father and your mother,'ᵃ and, 'You shall love your neighbor as yourself.' "ᵇ

²⁰The young man said to Him, "All these things I have kept from my youth.ᵃ What do I still lack?"

²¹Jesus said to him, "If you want to be perfect, go, sell what you have and give to the poor, and you will have treasure in heaven; and come, follow Me."

²²But when the young man heard that saying, he went away sorrowful, for he had great possessions.

WITH GOD ALL THINGS ARE POSSIBLE

²³Then Jesus said to His disciples, "Assuredly, I say to you that it is hard for a rich man to enter the kingdom of heaven. ²⁴And again I say to you, it is easier for a camel to go through the eye of a needle than for a rich man to enter the kingdom of God."

²⁵When His disciples heard *it*, they were

> "But Jesus said, 'Let the little children come to Me, and do not forbid them; for of such is the kingdom of heaven.' "
> (Matthew 19:14)

18:35 ᵃNU-Text omits *his trespasses*. **19:4** ᵃNU-Text reads *created*. ᵇGenesis 1:27; 5:2 **19:5** ᵃGenesis 2:24 **19:9** ᵃOr *fornication* **19:16** ᵃNU-Text omits *Good*. **19:17** ᵃNU-Text reads *Why do you ask Me about what is good?* ᵇNU-Text reads *There is One who is good*. **19:19** ᵃExodus 20:12–16; Deuteronomy 5:16–20 ᵇLeviticus 19:18 **19:20** ᵃNU-Text omits *from my youth*.

greatly astonished, saying, "Who then can be saved?"

²⁶But Jesus looked at *them* and said to them, "With men this is impossible, but with God all things are possible."

²⁷Then Peter answered and said to Him, "See, we have left all and followed You. Therefore what shall we have?"

²⁸So Jesus said to them, "Assuredly I say to you, that in the regeneration, when the Son of Man sits on the throne of His glory, you who have followed Me will also sit on twelve thrones, judging the twelve tribes of Israel. ²⁹And everyone who has left houses or brothers or sisters or father or mother or wife*ᵃ* or children or lands, for My name's sake, shall receive a hundredfold, and inherit eternal life. ³⁰But many *who are* first will be last, and the last first.

THE PARABLE OF THE WORKERS IN THE VINEYARD

¹"For the kingdom of heaven is like a landowner who went out early in the morning to hire laborers for his vineyard. ²Now when he had agreed with the laborers for a denarius a day, he sent them into his vineyard. ³And he went out about the third hour and saw others standing idle in the marketplace, ⁴and said to them, 'You also go into the vineyard, and whatever is right I will give you.' So they went. ⁵Again he went out about the sixth and the ninth hour, and did likewise. ⁶And about the eleventh hour he went out and found others standing idle,*ᵃ* and said to them, 'Why have you been standing here idle all day?' ⁷They said to him, 'Because no one hired us.' He said to them, 'You also go into the vineyard, and whatever is right you will receive.'*ᵃ*

⁸"So when evening had come, the owner of the vineyard said to his steward, 'Call the laborers and give them *their* wages, beginning with the last to the first.' ⁹And when those came who *were hired* about the eleventh hour, they each received a denarius. ¹⁰But when the first came, they supposed that they would receive more; and they likewise received each a denarius. ¹¹And when they had received *it*, they complained against the landowner, ¹²saying, 'These last *men* have worked *only* one hour, and you made them equal to us who have borne the burden and the heat of the day.' ¹³But he an-

swered one of them and said, 'Friend, I am doing you no wrong. Did you not agree with me for a denarius? ¹⁴Take *what is* yours and go your way. I wish to give to this last man *the same* as to you. ¹⁵Is it not lawful for me to do what I wish with my own things? Or is your eye evil because I am good?' ¹⁶So the last will be first, and the first last. For many are called, but few chosen."*ᵃ*

JESUS A THIRD TIME PREDICTS HIS DEATH AND RESURRECTION

¹⁷Now Jesus, going up to Jerusalem, took the twelve disciples aside on the road and said to them, ¹⁸"Behold, we are going up to Jerusalem, and the Son of Man will be betrayed to the chief priests and to the scribes; and they will condemn Him to death, ¹⁹and deliver Him to the Gentiles to mock and to scourge and to crucify. And the third day He will rise again."

GREATNESS IS SERVING

²⁰Then the mother of Zebedee's sons came to Him with her sons, kneeling down and asking something from Him.

²¹And He said to her, "What do you wish?"

She said to Him, "Grant that these two sons of mine may sit, one on Your right hand and the other on the left, in Your kingdom."

²²But Jesus answered and said, "You do not know what you ask. Are you able to drink the cup that I am about to drink, and be baptized with the baptism that I am baptized with?"*ᵃ*

They said to Him, "We are able."

²³So He said to them, "You will indeed drink My cup, and be baptized with the baptism that I am baptized with;*ᵃ* but to sit on My right hand and on My left is not Mine to give, but *it is for those* for whom it is prepared by My Father."

²⁴And when the ten heard *it*, they were greatly displeased with the two brothers. ²⁵But Jesus called them to *Himself* and said, "You know that the rulers of the Gentiles lord it over them, and those who are great exercise authority over them. ²⁶Yet it shall not be so among you; but whoever desires to become great among you, let him be your servant. ²⁷And whoever desires to be first among you, let him

LEADERSHIP
Do leaders have to serve others? (20:26–28)

19:29 *ᵃ*NU-Text omits *or wife.*   **20:6** *ᵃ*NU-Text omits *idle.*   **20:7** *ᵃ*NU-Text omits the last clause of this verse.   **20:16** *ᵃ*NU-Text omits the last sentence of this verse.   **20:22** *ᵃ*NU-Text omits *and be baptized with the baptism that I am baptized with.*   **20:23** *ᵃ*NU-Text omits *and be baptized with the baptism that I am baptized with.*

be your slave— [28]just as the Son of Man did not come to be served, but to serve, and to give His life a ransom for many."

TWO BLIND MEN RECEIVE THEIR SIGHT

[29]Now as they went out of Jericho, a great multitude followed Him. [30]And behold, two blind men sitting by the road, when they heard that Jesus was passing by, cried out, saying, "Have mercy on us, O Lord, Son of David!"

[31]Then the multitude warned them that they should be quiet; but they cried out all the more, saying, "Have mercy on us, O Lord, Son of David!"

[32]So Jesus stood still and called them, and said, "What do you want Me to do for you?"

[33]They said to Him, "Lord, that our eyes may be opened." [34]So Jesus had compassion and touched their eyes. And immediately their eyes received sight, and they followed Him.

THE TRIUMPHAL ENTRY

[1]Now when they drew near Jerusalem, and came to Bethphage,[a] at the Mount of Olives, then Jesus sent two disciples, [2]saying to them, "Go into the village opposite you, and immediately you will find a donkey tied, and a colt with her. Loose *them* and bring *them* to Me. [3]And if anyone says anything to you, you shall say, 'The Lord has need of them,' and immediately he will send them."

[4]All[a] this was done that it might be fulfilled which was spoken by the prophet, saying:

[5]　"*Tell the daughter of Zion,*
　　'*Behold, your King is coming to you,*
　　Lowly, and sitting on a donkey,
　　A colt, the foal of a donkey.' "[a]

[6]So the disciples went and did as Jesus commanded them. [7]They brought the donkey and the colt, laid their clothes on them, and set Him[a] on them. [8]And a very great multitude spread their clothes on the road; others cut down branches from the trees and spread *them* on the road. [9]Then the multitudes who went before and those who followed cried out, saying:

"Hosanna to the Son of David!
'*Blessed is He who comes in the name of
　the* LORD!'[a]
Hosanna in the highest!"

[10]And when He had come into Jerusalem, all the city was moved, saying, "Who is this?"

[11]So the multitudes said, "This is Jesus, the prophet from Nazareth of Galilee."

JESUS CLEANSES THE TEMPLE

[12]Then Jesus went into the temple of God[a] and drove out all those who bought and sold in the temple, and overturned the tables of the money changers and the seats of those who sold doves. [13]And He said to them, "It is written, '*My house shall be called a house of prayer,*'[a] but you have made it a '*den of thieves.*' "[b]

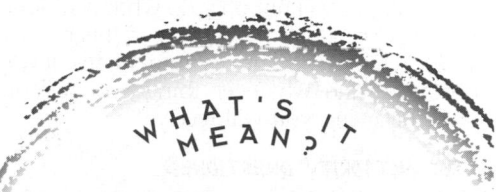

WHAT'S IT MEAN?

Coins with pagan symbols on them could not be used in the temple. They had to be exchanged for acceptable coins. Likewise, only certain animals could be offered as sacrifices. People who could not afford a goat or a sheep could offer a dove as a sacrifice. Local businessmen saw these restrictions as an opportunity to make money. They set up tables in the temple courtyard and sold approved coins and doves for outrageous prices. Believe it or not, the family of the high priest, who controlled the temple business, were the ones raking in the profit.

Matthew 21:12

[14]Then *the* blind and *the* lame came to Him in the temple, and He healed them. [15]But when the chief priests and scribes saw the wonderful things that He did, and the children crying out in the temple and saying, "Hosanna to the Son of David!" they were indignant [16]and said to Him, "Do You hear what these are saying?"

And Jesus said to them, "Yes. Have you never read,

'*Out of the mouth of babes and nursing
　infants
You have perfected praise*'?"[a]

[17]Then He left them and went out of the city to Bethany, and He lodged there.

21:1 [a]M-Text reads *Bethsphage.*　**21:4** [a]NU-Text omits *All.*　**21:5** [a]Zechariah 9:9　**21:7** [a]NU-Text reads *and He sat.*　**21:9** [a]Psalm 118:26　**21:12** [a]NU-Text omits *of God.*　**21:13** [a]Isaiah 56:7　[b]Jeremiah 7:11　**21:16** [a]Psalm 8:2

THE FIG TREE WITHERED

[18]Now in the morning, as He returned to the city, He was hungry. [19]And seeing a fig tree by the road, He came to it and found nothing on it but leaves, and said to it, "Let no fruit grow on you ever again." Immediately the fig tree withered away.

THE LESSON OF THE WITHERED FIG TREE

[20]And when the disciples saw *it*, they marveled, saying, "How did the fig tree wither away so soon?"

[21]So Jesus answered and said to them, "Assuredly, I say to you, if you have faith and do not doubt, you will not only do what was done to the fig tree, but also if you say to this mountain, 'Be removed and be cast into the sea,' it will be done. [22]And whatever things you ask in prayer, believing, you will receive."

JESUS' AUTHORITY QUESTIONED

[23]Now when He came into the temple, the chief priests and the elders of the people confronted Him as He was teaching, and said, "By what authority are You doing these things? And who gave You this authority?"

[24]But Jesus answered and said to them, "I also will ask you one thing, which if you tell Me, I likewise will tell you by what authority I do these things: [25]The baptism of John—where was it from? From heaven or from men?"

And they reasoned among themselves, saying, "If we say, 'From heaven,' He will say to us, 'Why then did you not believe him?' [26]But if we say, 'From men,' we fear the multitude, for all count John as a prophet." [27]So they answered Jesus and said, "We do not know."

And He said to them, "Neither will I tell you by what authority I do these things.

THE PARABLE OF THE TWO SONS

[28]"But what do you think? A man had two sons, and he came to the first and said, 'Son, go, work today in my vineyard.' [29]He answered and said, 'I will not,' but afterward he regretted it and went. [30]Then he came to the second and said likewise. And he answered and said, 'I *go*, sir,' but he did not go. [31]Which of the two did the will of *his* father?"

They said to Him, "The first."

Jesus said to them, "Assuredly, I say to you that tax collectors and harlots enter the kingdom of God before you. [32]For John came to you in the way of righteousness, and you did not believe him; but tax collectors and harlots believed him; and when you saw *it*, you did not afterward relent and believe him.

THE PARABLE OF THE WICKED VINEDRESSERS

[33]"Hear another parable: There was a certain landowner who planted a vineyard and set a hedge around it, dug a winepress in it and built a tower. And he leased it to vinedressers and went into a far country. [34]Now when vintage-time drew near, he sent his servants to the vinedressers, that they might receive its fruit. [35]And the vinedressers took his servants, beat one, killed one, and stoned another. [36]Again he sent other servants, more than the first, and they did likewise to them. [37]Then last of all he sent his son to them, saying, 'They will respect my son.' [38]But when the vinedressers saw the son, they said among themselves, 'This is the heir. Come, let us kill him and seize his inheritance.' [39]So they took him and cast *him* out of the vineyard and killed *him*.

[40]"Therefore, when the owner of the vineyard comes, what will he do to those vinedressers?"

[41]They said to Him, "He will destroy those wicked men miserably, and lease *his* vineyard to other vinedressers who will render to him the fruits in their seasons."

[42]Jesus said to them, "Have you never read in the Scriptures:

'The stone which the builders rejected
Has become the chief cornerstone.
This was the LORD's doing,
And it is marvelous in our eyes'?[a]

[43]"Therefore I say to you, the kingdom of God will be taken from you and given to a nation bearing the fruits of it. [44]And whoever falls on this stone will be broken; but on whomever it falls, it will grind him to powder."

[45]Now when the chief priests and Pharisees heard His parables, they perceived that He was speaking of them. [46]But when they sought to lay hands on Him, they feared the multitudes, because they took Him for a prophet.

THE PARABLE OF THE WEDDING FEAST

[1]And Jesus answered and spoke to them again by parables and said: [2]"The kingdom of heaven is like a certain king who arranged a marriage for his son, [3]and sent out his servants to call those who were invited to the wedding; and they were not willing to come. [4]Again, he sent out other servants, saying, 'Tell those who

are invited, "See, I have prepared my dinner; my oxen and fatted cattle *are* killed, and all things *are* ready. Come to the wedding." ' ⁵But they made light of it and went their ways, one to his own farm, another to his business. ⁶And the rest seized his servants, treated *them* spitefully, and killed *them*. ⁷But when the king heard *about it*, he was furious. And he sent out his armies, destroyed those murderers, and burned up their city. ⁸Then he said to his servants, 'The wedding is ready, but those who were invited were not worthy. ⁹Therefore go into the highways, and as many as you find, invite to the wedding.' ¹⁰So those servants went out into the highways and gathered together all whom they found, both bad and good. And the wedding *hall* was filled with guests.

¹¹"But when the king came in to see the guests, he saw a man there who did not have on a wedding garment. ¹²So he said to him, 'Friend, how did you come in here without a wedding garment?' And he was speechless. ¹³Then the king said to the servants, 'Bind him hand and foot, take him away, and*ᵃ* cast *him* into outer darkness; there will be weeping and gnashing of teeth.'

¹⁴"For many are called, but few *are* chosen."

WHAT'S IT MEAN?

If you lived in the Roman Empire and you ever needed to know who the current emperor was, all you had to do was look at a coin. His image was stamped on one side of it. The other side usually had some religious or pagan symbol on it. During Jesus' day, the face on the coin was that of Emperor Tiberius.

Matthew 22:17–21

THE PHARISEES: IS IT LAWFUL TO PAY TAXES TO CAESAR?

¹⁵Then the Pharisees went and plotted how they might entangle Him in *His* talk. ¹⁶And they sent to Him their disciples with the Herodians, saying, "Teacher, we know that You are true, and teach the way of God in truth; nor do You care about anyone, for You do not regard the person of men. ¹⁷Tell us, therefore, what do You think? Is it lawful to pay taxes to Caesar, or not?"

¹⁸But Jesus perceived their wickedness, and said, "Why do you test Me, *you* hypocrites? ¹⁹Show Me the tax money."

So they brought Him a denarius.

²⁰And He said to them, "Whose image and inscription *is* this?"

²¹They said to Him, "Caesar's."

And He said to them, "Render therefore to Caesar the things that are Caesar's, and to God the things that are God's." ²²When they had heard *these words*, they marveled, and left Him and went their way.

THE SADDUCEES: WHAT ABOUT THE RESURRECTION?

²³The same day the Sadducees, who say there is no resurrection, came to Him and asked Him, ²⁴saying: "Teacher, Moses said that if a man dies, having no children, his brother shall marry his wife and raise up offspring for his brother. ²⁵Now there were with us seven brothers. The first died after he had married, and having no offspring, left his wife to his brother. ²⁶Likewise the second also, and the third, even to the seventh. ²⁷Last of all the woman died also. ²⁸Therefore, in the resurrection, whose wife of the seven will she be? For they all had her."

²⁹Jesus answered and said to them, "You are mistaken, not knowing the Scriptures nor the power of God. ³⁰For in the resurrection they neither marry nor are given in marriage, but are like angels of God*ᵃ* in heaven. ³¹But concerning the

ANGELS

Do angels get married? (22:30)

resurrection of the dead, have you not read what was spoken to you by God, saying, ³²'*I am the God of Abraham, the God of Isaac, and the God of Jacob*'?*ᵃ* God is not the God of the dead, but of the living." ³³And when the multitudes heard *this*, they were astonished at His teaching.

THE SCRIBES: WHICH IS THE FIRST COMMANDMENT OF ALL?

³⁴But when the Pharisees heard that He had silenced the Sadducees, they gathered together. ³⁵Then one of them, a lawyer, asked *Him* a question, testing Him, and saying, ³⁶"Teacher, which is the great commandment in the law?"

³⁷Jesus said to him, " '*You shall love the* LORD *your God with all your heart, with all*

22:13 *ᵃ*NU-Text omits *take him away, and.* **22:30** *ᵃ*NU-Text omits *of God.* **22:32** *ᵃ*Exodus 3:6, 15 your soul, and with all your mind.'*a* ³⁸This is *the* first and great commandment. ³⁹And *the* second is like it: *'You shall love your neighbor as yourself.'*a* ⁴⁰On these two commandments hang all the Law and the Prophets."

On the Edge

"Teacher, which is the great commandment in the law?" Jesus said to him, " 'You shall love the LORD *your God with all your heart, with all your soul, and with all your mind.' " (Matt. 22:36, 37).*

Well, this is it. This is *the* most important commandment. If you've decided to get serious about God, then this commandment is the place to start. Every element of being Christlike is built on this principle. Learning to love the Lord with your heart, soul, and mind will be a continual process that lasts your whole life. But you've got to start. So what does it look like to love the Lord with every part of you? It means that you begin to love the way God loves, think the way God thinks, act the way God acts, and hate the things God hates. If you have begun to get serious about God, don't hold back. His love for you has no limits or hesitations. You have absolutely nothing to lose and everything to gain by going for it.

Don't be disappointed if you're not an overnight sensation. Remember, this is a process—learning to spend time with Him; giving and receiving grace; working on areas that don't look anything like God; forgiving and being forgiven; trusting; slowly, ever so wonderfully, looking more and more like the One you love. Imitation is the highest form of adoration. Be an imitator of God.

SEE FOR YOURSELF:
  Deut. 6:5;
  Mark 12:32, 33;
  Eph. 5:1, 2

JESUS: HOW CAN DAVID CALL HIS DESCENDANT LORD?

⁴¹While the Pharisees were gathered together, Jesus asked them, ⁴²saying, "What do you think about the Christ? Whose Son is He?"

They said to Him, "*The Son* of David."

⁴³He said to them, "How then does David in the Spirit call Him '*Lord*,' saying:

⁴⁴ '*The* LORD *said to my Lord,*
  "*Sit at My right hand,*
    Till I make Your enemies Your
      footstool" '?*a*

⁴⁵If David then calls Him '*Lord*,' how is He his Son?" ⁴⁶And no one was able to answer Him a word, nor from that day on did anyone dare question Him anymore.

WOE TO THE SCRIBES AND PHARISEES

¹Then Jesus spoke to the multitudes and to His disciples, ²saying: "The scribes and the Pharisees sit in Moses' seat. ³Therefore whatever they tell you to observe,*a* *that* observe and do, but do not do according to their works; for they say, and do not do. ⁴For they bind heavy burdens, hard to bear, and lay *them* on men's shoulders; but they *themselves* will not move them with one of their fingers. ⁵But all their works they do to be seen by men. They make their phylacteries broad and enlarge the borders of their garments. ⁶They love the best places at feasts, the best seats in the synagogues, ⁷greetings in the marketplaces, and to be called by men, 'Rabbi, Rabbi.' ⁸But you, do not be called 'Rabbi'; for One is your Teacher, the Christ,*a* and you are all brethren. ⁹Do not call anyone on earth your father; for One is your Father, He who is in heaven. ¹⁰And do not be called teachers; for One is your Teacher, the Christ. ¹¹But he who is greatest among you shall be your servant. ¹²And whoever exalts himself will be humbled, and he who humbles himself will be exalted.

¹³"But woe to you, scribes and Pharisees, hypocrites! For you shut up the kingdom of heaven against men; for you neither go in *yourselves*, nor do you allow those who are entering to go in. ¹⁴Woe to you, scribes and Pharisees, hypocrites! For you devour widows' houses, and for a pretense make long prayers. Therefore you will receive greater condemnation.*a*

¹⁵"Woe to you, scribes and Pharisees, hypocrites! For you travel land and sea to win one proselyte, and when he is won, you make him twice as much a son of hell as yourselves.

¹⁶"Woe to you, blind guides, who say, 'Whoever swears by the temple, it is nothing; but whoever swears by the gold of the temple, he is

---

22:37 *a*Deuteronomy 6:5 **22:39** *a*Leviticus 19:18 **22:44** *a*Psalm 110:1 **23:3** *a*NU-Text omits *to observe.*
23:8 *a*NU-Text omits *the Christ.* **23:14** *a*NU-Text omits this verse.

all things on it. [21]He who swears by the temple, swears by it and by Him who dwells[a] in it. [22]And he who swears by heaven, swears by the throne of God and by Him who sits on it.

WHAT'S IT MEAN?

The Pharisees were sticklers for detail. The Law that God gave to Moses commanded the Israelites to give ten percent of their income—including livestock, crops, and money—to the priests and Levites who served in the temple. The Pharisees carried things one step further and gave ten percent of their herbs and spices.

Matthew 23:23

[23]"Woe to you, scribes and Pharisees, hypocrites! For you pay tithe of mint and anise and cummin, and have neglected the weightier *matters* of the law: justice and mercy and faith. These you ought to have done, without leaving the others undone. [24]Blind guides, who strain out a gnat and swallow a camel!

[25]"Woe to you, scribes and Pharisees, hypocrites! For you cleanse the outside of the cup and dish, but inside they are full of extortion and self-indulgence.[a] [26]Blind Pharisee, first cleanse the inside of the cup and dish, that the outside of them may be clean also.

PURITY
Can outward purity substitute for inner purity? (23:25–28)

[27]"Woe to you, scribes and Pharisees, hypocrites! For you are like whitewashed tombs which indeed appear beautiful outwardly, but inside are full of dead *men's* bones and all uncleanness. [28]Even so you also outwardly appear righteous to men, but inside you are full of hypocrisy and lawlessness.

[29]"Woe to you, scribes and Pharisees, hypocrites! Because you build the tombs of the prophets and adorn the monuments of the righteous, [30]and say, 'If we had lived in the days of our fathers, we would not have been partakers with them in the blood of the prophets.' [31]"Therefore you are witnesses against yourselves that you are sons of those who murdered the prophets. [32]Fill up, then, the measure of your fathers' *guilt*. [33]Serpents, brood of vipers!

On the Edge

But you, do not be called "Rabbi"; for One is your Teacher, the Christ, and you are all brethren. Do not call anyone on earth your father; for One is your Father, He who is in heaven (Matt. 23:8, 9).

As you learn about Jesus' life on earth, one thing you notice is that He seemed to enjoy hanging around notorious sinners more than He did the Jewish religious leaders. To thieves and prostitutes He said, "Your sins are forgiven" (see Luke 7:48), but He warned the Pharisees and teachers, "Woe to you" (Matt. 23:16).

The Pharisees were snobs. These religious leaders actually thought they were better than the rest of the Jewish people. Because they knew a lot about Scripture and religious customs, they figured that God liked them more than He liked everybody else. Jesus could see their conceited attitude and hated it.

Jesus told His disciples that God's kingdom is not made up of special people and regular people. The people who follow Jesus are all equal, and He loves each one exactly the same. If you've struggled with feelings of inferiority or insecurity, know that God never sees you as inferior to anyone. If you've gotten an attitude about how cool you are, God isn't impressed. God can peer into a high school classroom and see the most popular student in school sitting beside the biggest outcast; yet He loves them both the same. No matter how you feel, God thinks you're awesome—just as awesome as the next person. Everybody's equal with Him. No one has a better chance than you do!

SEE FOR YOURSELF:
Job 34:19; 36:5;
Matt. 7:8; Acts 13:39

obliged *to perform it.* [17]Fools and blind! For which is greater, the gold or the temple that sanctifies[a] the gold? [18]And, 'Whoever swears by the altar, it is nothing; but whoever swears by the gift that is on it, he is obliged *to perform it.* [19]Fools and blind! For which is greater, the gift or the altar that sanctifies the gift? [20]Therefore he who swears by the altar, swears by it and by

How can you escape the condemnation of hell? ³⁴Therefore, indeed, I send you prophets, wise men, and scribes: *some* of them you will kill and crucify, and *some* of them you will scourge in your synagogues and persecute from city to city, ³⁵that on you may come all the righteous blood shed on the earth, from the blood of righteous Abel to the blood of Zechariah, son of Berechiah, whom you murdered between the temple and the altar. ³⁶Assuredly, I say to you, all these things will come upon this generation.

"How often I wanted to gather your children together, as a hen gathers her chicks under her wings, but you were not willing!" (Matthew 23:37)

JESUS LAMENTS OVER JERUSALEM

³⁷"O Jerusalem, Jerusalem, the one who kills the prophets and stones those who are sent to her! How often I wanted to gather your children together, as a hen gathers her chicks under *her* wings, but you were not willing! ³⁸See! Your house is left to you desolate; ³⁹for I say to you, you shall see Me no more till you say, 'Blessed *is* He who comes in the name of the LORD!' "ᵃ

JESUS PREDICTS THE DESTRUCTION OF THE TEMPLE

¹Then Jesus went out and departed from the temple, and His disciples came up to show Him the buildings of the temple. ²And Jesus said to them, "Do you not see all these things? Assuredly, I say to you, not *one* stone shall be left here upon another, that shall not be thrown down."

THE SIGNS OF THE TIMES AND THE END OF THE AGE

³Now as He sat on the Mount of Olives, the disciples came to Him privately, saying, "Tell us, when will these things be? And what *will be* the sign of Your coming, and of the end of the age?"

⁴And Jesus answered and said to them: "Take heed that no one deceives you. ⁵For many will come in My name, saying, 'I am the Christ,' and will deceive many. ⁶And you will hear of wars and rumors of wars. See that you are not troubled; for allᵃ *these things* must come to pass, but the end is not yet. ⁷For nation will rise against nation, and kingdom against kingdom. And there will be famines, pestilences,ᵃ and earth-

quakes in various places. ⁸All these *are* the beginning of sorrows.

⁹"Then they will deliver you up to tribulation and kill you, and you will be hated by all nations for My name's sake. ¹⁰And then many will be offended, will betray one another, and will hate one another. ¹¹Then many false prophets will rise up and deceive many. ¹²And because lawlessness will abound, the love of many will grow cold. ¹³But he who endures to the end shall be saved. ¹⁴And this gospel of the kingdom will be preached in all the world as a witness to all the nations, and then the end will come.

WHAT'S IT MEAN?

To make his Jewish subjects happy, Herod the Great completely renovated the temple in Jerusalem. Work on the temple itself was completed in 9 B.C. The renovation of the rest of the enormous temple complex was not completed until A.D. 64. In fact, the temple was finished just in time for the Romans to destroy it six years later after a Jewish revolt.

Matthew 24:1

THE GREAT TRIBULATION

¹⁵"Therefore when you see the '*abomination of desolation*,'ᵃ spoken of by Daniel the prophet, standing in the holy place" (whoever reads, let him understand), ¹⁶"then let those who are in Judea flee to the mountains. ¹⁷Let him who is on the housetop not go down to take anything out of his house. ¹⁸And let him who is in the field not go back to get his clothes. ¹⁹But woe to those who are pregnant and to those who are nursing babies in those days! ²⁰And pray that your flight may not be in winter or on the Sabbath. ²¹For then there will be great tribulation, such as has not been since the beginning of the world until this time, no, nor ever shall be. ²²And unless those days were shortened, no

23:39 ᵃPsalm 118:26 **24:6** ᵃNU-Text omits *all*. **24:7** ᵃNU-Text omits *pestilences*. **24:15** ᵃDaniel 11:31; 12:11

flesh would be saved; but for the elect's sake those days will be shortened.

On the Edge

Jesus answered, "Take heed that no one deceives you" (Matt. 24:4). This is a great chapter in the Bible. Jesus is foretelling some of the things that are going to happen before He comes back to the earth—wars, rumors of wars, famines, earthquakes, etc. He goes on to tell us not to worry or be afraid because these things must happen before He comes back. But before He goes into all of this, He says that there will be many people who claim to be Jesus and then warns us not to be fooled by them. You've seen this already.

Remember the suicide by the cult group called "Heaven's Gate"? All of the people in that compound died because they allowed themselves to be fooled. Adam and Eve were cast out of the garden because they allowed themselves to be fooled. Esau lost his inheritance to Jacob because he allowed himself to be fooled. Samson lost his strength and his life because he allowed himself to be fooled.

You don't have to allow yourself to be fooled by some false prophet who claims to be Jesus or claims to be from God. If something doesn't line up with the Word of God, then don't believe it. There are more fruitcakes around today than ever before. This is what we call a *sign of the times.*

Jesus is coming back. No one knows exactly when, so stay tight with God and don't be fooled!

SEE FOR YOURSELF:
Matt. 7:15; 24:11, 24;
Luke 21:8; 2 Pet.
2:1; 1 John 4:1

23"Then if anyone says to you, 'Look, here *is* the Christ!' or 'There!' do not believe *it.* 24For false christs and false prophets will rise and show great signs and wonders to deceive, if possible, even the elect. 25See, I have told you beforehand.

26"Therefore if they say to you, 'Look, He is in the desert!' do not go out; *or* 'Look, *He is* in the inner rooms!' do not believe *it.* 27For as the lightning comes from the east and flashes to the west, so also will the coming of the Son of Man be. 28For wherever the carcass is, there the eagles will be gathered together.

THE COMING OF THE SON OF MAN

29"Immediately after the tribulation of those days the sun will be darkened, and the moon will not give its light; the stars will fall from heaven, and the powers of the heavens will be shaken. 30Then the sign of the Son of Man will appear in heaven, and then all the tribes of the earth will mourn, and they will see the Son of Man coming on the clouds of heaven with power and great glory. 31And He will send His angels with a great sound of a trumpet, and they will gather together His elect from the four winds, from one end of heaven to the other.

THE PARABLE OF THE FIG TREE

32"Now learn this parable from the fig tree: When its branch has already become tender and puts forth leaves, you know that summer *is* near. 33So you also, when you see all these things, know that it[a] is near—at the doors! 34Assuredly, I say to you, this generation will by no means pass away till all these things take place. 35Heaven and earth will pass away, but My words will by no means pass away.

NO ONE KNOWS THE DAY OR HOUR

36"But of that day and hour no one knows, not even the angels of heaven,[a] but My Father only. 37But as the days of Noah *were,* so also will the coming of the Son of Man be. 38For as in the days before the flood, they were eating and drinking, marrying and giving in marriage, until the day that Noah entered the ark, 39and did not know until the flood came and took them all away, so also will the coming of the Son of Man be. 40Then two *men* will be in the field: one will be taken and the other left. 41Two *women will be* grinding at the mill: one will be taken and the other left. 42Watch therefore, for you do not know what hour[a] your Lord is coming. 43But know this, that if the master of the house had known what hour the thief would come, he would have watched and not allowed his house to be broken into. 44Therefore you also be ready, for the Son of Man is coming at an hour you do not expect.

THE FAITHFUL SERVANT AND THE EVIL SERVANT

45"Who then is a faithful and wise servant, whom his master made ruler over his household, to give them food in due season? 46Blessed

24:33 [a]Or He   24:36 [a]NU-Text adds *nor the Son.*   24:42 [a]NU-Text reads *day.*

is that servant whom his master, when he comes, will find so doing. [47]Assuredly, I say to you that he will make him ruler over all his goods. [48]But if that evil servant says in his heart, 'My master is delaying his coming,'[a] [49]and begins to beat *his* fellow servants, and to eat and drink with the drunkards, [50]the master of that servant will come on a day when he is not looking for *him* and at an hour that he is not aware of, [51]and will cut him in two and appoint *him* his portion with the hypocrites. There shall be weeping and gnashing of teeth.

THE PARABLE OF THE WISE AND FOOLISH VIRGINS

[1]"Then the kingdom of heaven shall be likened to ten virgins who took their lamps and went out to meet the bridegroom. [2]Now five of them were wise, and five *were* foolish. [3]Those who *were* foolish took their lamps and took no oil with them, [4]but the wise took oil in their vessels with their lamps. [5]But while the bridegroom was delayed, they all slumbered and slept.

WHAT'S IT MEAN?

The lamps of New Testament times looked like miniature teapots. A wick was placed in the spout and olive oil was poured through a hole in the top. A lamp with one wick and a full load of oil could burn for about four hours.

Matthew 25:1

[6]"And at midnight a cry was *heard:* 'Behold, the bridegroom is coming;[a] go out to meet him!' [7]Then all those virgins arose and trimmed their lamps. [8]And the foolish said to the wise, 'Give us *some* of your oil, for our lamps are going out.' [9]But the wise answered, saying, 'No, lest there should not be enough for us and you; but go rather to those who sell, and buy for yourselves.' [10]And while they went to buy, the bridegroom came, and those who were ready went in with him to the wedding; and the door was shut.

[11]"Afterward the other virgins came also, saying, 'Lord, Lord, open to us!' [12]But he answered and said, 'Assuredly, I say to you, I do not know you.'

[13]"Watch therefore, for you know neither the day nor the hour[a] in which the Son of Man is coming.

> "Watch therefore, for you know neither the day nor the hour in which the Son of Man is coming."
> (Matthew 25:13)

THE PARABLE OF THE TALENTS

[14]"For *the kingdom of heaven is* like a man traveling to a far country, *who* called his own servants and delivered his goods to them. [15]And to one he gave five talents, to another two, and to another one, to each according to his own ability; and immediately he went on a journey. [16]Then he who had received the five talents went and traded with them, and made another five talents. [17]And likewise he who *had received* two gained two more also. [18]But he who had received one went and dug in the ground, and hid his lord's money. [19]After a long time the lord of those servants came and settled accounts with them.

[20]"So he who had received five talents came and brought five other talents, saying, 'Lord, you delivered to me five talents; look, I have gained five more talents besides them.' [21]His lord said to him, 'Well *done*, good and faithful servant; you were faithful over a few things, I will make you ruler over many things. Enter into the joy of your lord.' [22]He also who had received two talents came and said, 'Lord, you delivered to me two talents; look, I have gained two more talents besides them.' [23]His lord said to him, 'Well *done*, good and faithful servant; you have been faithful over a few things, I will make you ruler over many things. Enter into the joy of your lord.'

[24]"Then he who had received the one talent came and said, 'Lord, I knew you to be a hard man, reaping where you have not sown, and gathering where you have not scattered seed. [25]And I was afraid, and went and hid your talent in the ground. Look, *there* you have *what is* yours.'

[26]"But his lord answered and said to him, 'You wicked and lazy servant, you knew that I reap where I have not sown, and gather where

---

24:48 [a]NU-Text omits *his coming.* **25:6** [a]NU-Text omits *is coming.* **25:13** [a]NU-Text omits the rest of this verse.

I have not scattered seed. ²⁷So you ought to have deposited my money with the bankers, and at my coming I would have received back my own with interest. ²⁸So take the talent from him, and give *it* to him who has ten talents.

²⁹"For to everyone who has, more will be given, and he will have abundance; but from him who does not have, even what he has will be taken away. ³⁰And cast the unprofitable servant into the outer darkness. There will be weeping and gnashing of teeth."

THE SON OF MAN WILL JUDGE THE NATIONS

³¹"When the Son of Man comes in His glory, and all the holy*ᵃ* angels with Him, then He will sit on the throne of His glory. ³²All the nations will be gathered before Him, and He will separate them one from another, as a shepherd divides *his* sheep from the goats. ³³And He will set the sheep on His right hand, but the goats on the left. ³⁴Then the King will say to those on His right hand, 'Come, you blessed of My Father, inherit the kingdom prepared for you from the foundation of the world: ³⁵for I was hungry and you gave Me food; I was thirsty and you gave Me drink; I was a stranger and you took Me in; ³⁶I *was* naked and you clothed Me; I was sick and you visited Me; I was in prison and you came to Me.'

³⁷"Then the righteous will answer Him, saying, 'Lord, when did we see You hungry and feed *You*, or thirsty and give *You* drink? ³⁸When did we see You a stranger and take *You* in, or naked and clothe *You*? ³⁹Or when did we see You sick, or in prison, and come to You?' ⁴⁰And the King will answer and say to them, 'Assuredly, I say to you, inasmuch as you did *it* to one of the least of these My brethren, you did *it* to Me.'

SICKNESS

Who should believers show compassion? (25:34–40)

⁴¹"Then He will also say to those on the left hand, 'Depart from Me, you cursed, into the everlasting fire prepared for the devil and his angels: ⁴²for I was hungry and you gave Me no food; I was thirsty and you gave Me no drink; ⁴³I was a stranger and you did not take Me in, naked and you did not clothe Me, sick and in prison and you did not visit Me.'

⁴⁴"Then they also will answer Him,*ᵃ* saying, 'Lord, when did we see You hungry or thirsty or a stranger or naked or sick or in prison, and did not minister to You?' ⁴⁵Then He will answer them, saying, 'Assuredly, I say to you, inasmuch as you did not do *it* to one of the least of these, you did not do *it* to Me.' ⁴⁶And these will go away into everlasting punishment, but the righteous into eternal life."

THE PLOT TO KILL JESUS

¹Now it came to pass, when Jesus had finished all these sayings, *that* He said to His disciples, ²"You know that after two days is the Passover, and the Son of Man will be delivered up to be crucified."

³Then the chief priests, the scribes,*ᵃ* and the elders of the people assembled at the palace of the high priest, who was called Caiaphas, ⁴and plotted to take Jesus by trickery and kill *Him*. ⁵But they said, "Not during the feast, lest there be an uproar among the people."

THE ANOINTING AT BETHANY

⁶And when Jesus was in Bethany at the house of Simon the leper, ⁷a woman came to Him having an alabaster flask of very costly fragrant oil, and she poured *it* on His head as He sat *at the table*. ⁸But when His disciples saw *it*, they were indignant, saying, "Why this waste? ⁹For this fragrant oil might have been sold for much and given to *the* poor."

¹⁰But when Jesus was aware of *it*, He said to them, "Why do you trouble the woman? For she has done a good work for Me. ¹¹For you have the poor with you always, but Me you do not have always. ¹²For in pouring this fragrant oil on My body, she did *it* for My burial. ¹³Assuredly, I say to you, wherever this gospel is preached in the whole world, what this woman has done will also be told as a memorial to her."

JUDAS AGREES TO BETRAY JESUS

¹⁴Then one of the twelve, called Judas Iscariot, went to the chief priests ¹⁵and said, "What are you willing to give me if I deliver Him to you?" And they counted out to him thirty pieces of silver. ¹⁶So from that time he sought opportunity to betray Him.

JESUS CELEBRATES PASSOVER WITH HIS DISCIPLES

¹⁷Now on the first *day of the Feast* of Unleavened Bread the disciples came to Jesus, saying to Him, "Where do You want us to prepare for You to eat the Passover?"

¹⁸And He said, "Go into the city to a certain man, and say to him, 'The Teacher says, "My time is at hand; I will keep the Passover at your house with My disciples." ' "

25:31 *ᵃ*NU-Text omits *holy*. **25:44** *ᵃ*NU-Text and M-Text omit *Him*. **26:3** *ᵃ*NU-Text omits *the scribes*.

¹⁹So the disciples did as Jesus had directed them; and they prepared the Passover.

²⁰When evening had come, He sat down with the twelve. ²¹Now as they were eating, He said, "Assuredly, I say to you, one of you will betray Me."

²²And they were exceedingly sorrowful, and each of them began to say to Him, "Lord, is it I?"

²³He answered and said, "He who dipped *his* hand with Me in the dish will betray Me. ²⁴The Son of Man indeed goes just as it is written of Him, but woe to that man by whom the Son of Man is betrayed! It would have been good for that man if he had not been born."

²⁵Then Judas, who was betraying Him, answered and said, "Rabbi, is it I?"

He said to him, "You have said it."

JESUS INSTITUTES THE LORD'S SUPPER

²⁶And as they were eating, Jesus took bread, blessed*ᵃ* and broke *it*, and gave *it* to the disciples and said, "Take, eat; this is My body."

²⁷Then He took the cup, and gave thanks, and gave *it* to them, saying, "Drink from it, all of you. ²⁸For this is My blood of the new*ᵃ* covenant, which is shed for many for the remission of sins. ²⁹But I say to you, I will not drink of this fruit of the vine from now on until that day when I drink it new with you in My Father's kingdom."

WHAT'S IT MEAN?

Bread was a major part of the Jewish diet in New Testament times. Often it was served with a stew or sauce. Several people would share one bowl of sauce, taking turns dipping their bread into it before each bite.

Matthew 26:26

³⁰And when they had sung a hymn, they went out to the Mount of Olives.

JESUS PREDICTS PETER'S DENIAL

³¹Then Jesus said to them, "All of you will be made to stumble because of Me this night, for it is written:

'I will strike the Shepherd,
And the sheep of the flock will be
scattered.'*ᵃ*

³²But after I have been raised, I will go before you to Galilee."

³³Peter answered and said to Him, "Even if all are made to stumble because of You, I will never be made to stumble."

³⁴Jesus said to him, "Assuredly, I say to you that this night, before the rooster crows, you will deny Me three times."

³⁵Peter said to Him, "Even if I have to die with You, I will not deny You!"

And so said all the disciples.

THE PRAYER IN THE GARDEN

³⁶Then Jesus came with them to a place called Gethsemane, and said to the disciples, "Sit here while I go and pray over there." ³⁷And He took with Him Peter and the two sons of Zebedee, and He began to be sorrowful and deeply distressed. ³⁸Then He said to them, "My soul is exceedingly sorrowful, even to death. Stay here and watch with Me."

³⁹He went a little farther and fell on His face, and prayed, saying, "O My Father, if it is possible, let this cup pass from Me; nevertheless, not as I will, but as You *will*."

⁴⁰Then He came to the disciples and found them sleeping, and said to Peter, "What! Could you not watch with Me one hour? ⁴¹Watch and pray, lest you enter into temptation. The spirit indeed *is* willing, but the flesh *is* weak."

⁴²Again, a second time, He went away and prayed, saying, "O My Father, if this cup cannot pass away from Me unless*ᵃ* I drink it, Your will be done." ⁴³And He came and found them asleep again, for their eyes were heavy.

⁴⁴So He left them, went away again, and prayed the third time, saying the same words. ⁴⁵Then He came to His disciples and said to them, "Are *you* still sleeping and resting? Behold, the hour is at hand, and the Son of Man is being betrayed into the hands of sinners. ⁴⁶Rise, let us be going. See, My betrayer is at hand."

BETRAYAL AND ARREST IN GETHSEMANE

⁴⁷And while He was still speaking, behold, Judas, one of the twelve, with a great multitude with swords and clubs, came from the chief priests and elders of the people.

⁴⁸Now His betrayer had given them a sign, saying, "Whomever I kiss, He is the One; seize

26:26 *ᵃ*M-Text reads *gave thanks for.* **26:28** *ᵃ*NU-Text omits *new.* **26:31** *ᵃ*Zechariah 13:7 **26:42** *ᵃ*NU-Text reads *if this may not pass away unless.*

Him." ⁴⁹Immediately he went up to Jesus and said, "Greetings, Rabbi!" and kissed Him.

⁵⁰But Jesus said to him, "Friend, why have you come?"

Then they came and laid hands on Jesus and took Him. ⁵¹And suddenly, one of those *who were* with Jesus stretched out *his* hand and drew his sword, struck the servant of the high priest, and cut off his ear.

⁵²But Jesus said to him, "Put your sword in its place, for all who take the sword will perishᵃ by the sword. ⁵³Or do you think that I cannot now pray to My Father, and He will provide Me with more than twelve legions of angels? ⁵⁴How then could the Scriptures be fulfilled, that it must happen thus?"

⁵⁵In that hour Jesus said to the multitudes, "Have you come out, as against a robber, with swords and clubs to take Me? I sat daily with you, teaching in the temple, and you did not seize Me. ⁵⁶But all this was done that the Scriptures of the prophets might be fulfilled."

Then all the disciples forsook Him and fled.

JESUS FACES THE SANHEDRIN

⁵⁷And those who had laid hold of Jesus led *Him* away to Caiaphas the high priest, where the scribes and the elders were assembled. ⁵⁸But Peter followed Him at a distance to the high priest's courtyard. And he went in and sat with the servants to see the end.

⁵⁹Now the chief priests, the elders,ᵃ and all the council sought false testimony against Jesus to put Him to death, ⁶⁰but found none. Even though many false witnesses came forward, they found none.ᵃ But at last two false witnessesᵇ came forward ⁶¹and said, "This *fellow* said, 'I am able to destroy the temple of God and to build it in three days.' "

⁶²And the high priest arose and said to Him, "Do You answer nothing? What *is it* these men testify against You?" ⁶³But Jesus kept silent. And the high priest answered and said to Him, "I put You under oath by the living God: Tell us if You are the Christ, the Son of God!"

⁶⁴Jesus said to him, "*It is as* you said. Nevertheless, I say to you, hereafter you will see the Son of Man sitting at the right hand of the Power, and coming on the clouds of heaven."

⁶⁵Then the high priest tore his clothes, saying, "He has spoken blasphemy! What further need do we have of witnesses? Look, now you have heard His blasphemy! ⁶⁶What do you think?"

They answered and said, "He is deserving of death."

⁶⁷Then they spat in His face and beat Him; and others struck *Him* with the palms of their hands, ⁶⁸saying, "Prophesy to us, Christ! Who is the one who struck You?"

> "Now the chief priests, the elders, and all the council sought false testimony against Jesus to put Him to death, but found none."
> (Matthew 26:59, 60a)

PETER DENIES JESUS, AND WEEPS BITTERLY

⁶⁹Now Peter sat outside in the courtyard. And a servant girl came to him, saying, "You also were with Jesus of Galilee."

⁷⁰But he denied it before *them* all, saying, "I do not know what you are saying."

⁷¹And when he had gone out to the gateway, another *girl* saw him and said to those *who were* there, "This *fellow* also was with Jesus of Nazareth."

⁷²But again he denied with an oath, "I do not know the Man!"

⁷³And a little later those who stood by came up and said to Peter, "Surely you also are *one* of them, for your speech betrays you."

⁷⁴Then he began to curse and swear, *saying,* "I do not know the Man!"

Immediately a rooster crowed. ⁷⁵And Peter remembered the word of Jesus who had said to him, "Before the rooster crows, you will deny Me three times." So he went out and wept bitterly.

JESUS HANDED OVER TO PONTIUS PILATE

¹When morning came, all the chief priests and elders of the people plotted against Jesus to put Him to death. ²And when they had bound Him, they led Him away and delivered Him to Pontiusᵃ Pilate the governor.

JUDAS HANGS HIMSELF

³Then Judas, His betrayer, seeing that He had been condemned, was remorseful and brought back the thirty pieces of silver to the chief

---

26:52 ᵃM-Text reads *die.*   **26:59** ᵃNU-Text omits *the elders.*   **26:60** ᵃNU-Text puts a comma after *but found none,* does not capitalize *Even,* and omits *they found none.* ᵇNU-Text omits *false witnesses.*   **27:2** ᵃNU-Text omits *Pontius.*

priests and elders, ⁴saying, "I have sinned by betraying innocent blood."

And they said, "What *is that* to us? You see *to it!*"

⁵Then he threw down the pieces of silver in the temple and departed, and went and hanged himself.

⁶But the chief priests took the silver pieces and said, "It is not lawful to put them into the treasury, because they are the price of blood." ⁷And they consulted together and bought with them the potter's field, to bury strangers in. ⁸Therefore that field has been called the Field of Blood to this day.

⁹Then was fulfilled what was spoken by Jeremiah the prophet, saying, *"And they took the thirty pieces of silver, the value of Him who was priced,* whom they of the children of Israel priced, ¹⁰*and gave them for the potter's field, as the* LORD *directed me."* ᵃ

JESUS FACES PILATE

¹¹Now Jesus stood before the governor. And the governor asked Him, saying, "Are You the King of the Jews?"

Jesus said to him, *"It is as* you say." ¹²And while He was being accused by the chief priests and elders, He answered nothing.

¹³Then Pilate said to Him, "Do You not hear how many things they testify against You?" ¹⁴But He answered him not one word, so that the governor marveled greatly.

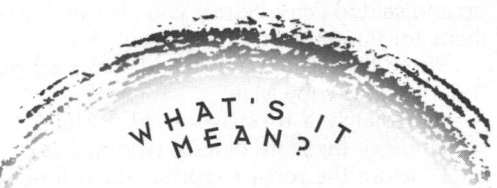

Pontius Pilate was the Roman governor of Judea and Samaria from A.D. 26 to 36. Pilate lived in Samaria, so you may be wondering what he was doing in Jerusalem. He and his troops were in town for the Passover feast to prevent rioting among the thousands of Jews who had traveled to the city for the annual holiday.
Matthew 27:11–14

TAKING THE PLACE OF BARABBAS

¹⁵Now at the feast the governor was accustomed to releasing to the multitude one pris-

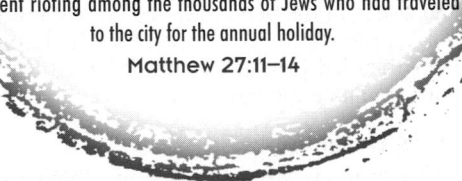

On the Edge

I have sinned by betraying innocent blood (Matt. 27:4).

When Judas found out that the Jewish leaders intended to have Jesus executed, it was like a lightbulb came on in his head. He suddenly realized what he had done—the simple kiss that had earned him thirty silver coins was going to cost Jesus His life. Judas knew that Jesus was innocent of all the charges the Jews brought against Him, and they were going to kill Him anyway.

But Jesus wasn't just innocent under the man-made law of the land; He was also innocent in God's eyes. He *literally* never did anything wrong. And His innocence wasn't just a natural thing because He was God's Son. He still had to make choices. Meanwhile Satan did all he could to convince Jesus not to choose God's way. Hebrews 4:15 says, "For we do not have a High Priest who cannot sympathize with our weaknesses, but was in all points tempted as we are, yet without sin."

Because Jesus is innocent, His blood is an acceptable sacrifice to God for your sins. And because He didn't give in to temptation, He paved the way for you to stand up to Satan's tricks, because His Spirit lives in you. When you do sin, confess, repent, and ask His forgiveness and Jesus will declare you innocent, too.

SEE FOR YOURSELF:
Luke 23:14, 15;
2 Cor. 5:21; Heb. 4:15

oner whom they wished. ¹⁶And at that time they had a notorious prisoner called Barabbas.ᵃ ¹⁷Therefore, when they had gathered together, Pilate said to them, "Whom do you want me to release to you? Barabbas, or Jesus who is called Christ?" ¹⁸For he knew that they had handed Him over because of envy.

¹⁹While he was sitting on the judgment seat, his wife sent to him, saying, "Have nothing to do with that just Man, for I have suffered many things today in a dream because of Him."

²⁰But the chief priests and elders persuaded the multitudes that they should ask for Barabbas and destroy Jesus. ²¹The governor answered

27:10 ᵃJeremiah 32:6–9   **27:16** ᵃNU-Text reads *Jesus Barabbas.*

and said to them, "Which of the two do you want me to release to you?"

They said, "Barabbas!"

²²Pilate said to them, "What then shall I do with Jesus who is called Christ?"

They all said to him, "Let Him be crucified!"

²³Then the governor said, "Why, what evil has He done?"

But they cried out all the more, saying, "Let Him be crucified!"

²⁴When Pilate saw that he could not prevail at all, but rather *that* a tumult was rising, he took water and washed *his* hands before the multitude, saying, "I am innocent of the blood of this just Person.ᵃ You see *to it.*"

²⁵And all the people answered and said, "His blood *be* on us and on our children."

²⁶Then he released Barabbas to them; and when he had scourged Jesus, he delivered *Him* to be crucified.

THE SOLDIERS MOCK JESUS

²⁷Then the soldiers of the governor took Jesus into the Praetorium and gathered the whole garrison around Him. ²⁸And they stripped Him and put a scarlet robe on Him. ²⁹When they had twisted a crown of thorns, they put *it* on His head, and a reed in His right hand. And they bowed the knee before Him and mocked Him, saying, "Hail, King of the Jews!" ³⁰Then they spat on Him, and took the reed and struck Him on the head. ³¹And when they had mocked Him, they took the robe off Him, put His *own* clothes on Him, and led Him away to be crucified.

THE KING ON A CROSS

³²Now as they came out, they found a man of Cyrene, Simon by name. Him they compelled to bear His cross. ³³And when they had come to a place called Golgotha, that is to say, Place of a Skull, ³⁴they gave Him sourᵃ wine mingled with gall to drink. But when He had tasted *it,* He would not drink.

³⁵Then they crucified Him, and divided His garments, casting lots,ᵃ that it might be fulfilled which was spoken by the prophet:

" *They divided My garments among them,*
And for My clothing they cast lots." ᵇ

³⁶Sitting down, they kept watch over Him there. ³⁷And they put up over His head the accusation written against Him:

THIS IS JESUS THE KING OF THE JEWS.

³⁸Then two robbers were crucified with Him, one on the right and another on the left.

³⁹And those who passed by blasphemed Him, wagging their heads ⁴⁰and saying, "You who destroy the temple and build *it* in three days, save Yourself! If You are the Son of God, come down from the cross."

⁴¹Likewise the chief priests also, mocking with the scribes and elders,ᵃ said, ⁴²"He saved others; Himself He cannot save. If He is the King of Israel,ᵃ let Him now come down from the cross, and we will believe Him.ᵇ ⁴³He trusted in God; let Him deliver Him now if He will have Him; for He said, 'I am the Son of God.' "

⁴⁴Even the robbers who were crucified with Him reviled Him with the same thing.

JESUS DIES ON THE CROSS

⁴⁵Now from the sixth hour until the ninth hour there was darkness over all the land. ⁴⁶And about the ninth hour Jesus cried out with a loud voice, saying, "Eli, Eli, lama sabachthani?" that is, *"My God, My God, why have You forsaken Me?"* ᵃ

⁴⁷Some of those who stood there, when they heard *that,* said, "This Man is calling for Elijah!" ⁴⁸Immediately one of them ran and took a sponge, filled *it* with sour wine and put *it* on a reed, and offered it to Him to drink.

⁴⁹The rest said, "Let Him alone; let us see if Elijah will come to save Him."

⁵⁰And Jesus cried out again with a loud voice, and yielded up His spirit.

⁵¹Then, behold, the veil of the temple was torn in two from top to bottom; and the earth quaked, and the rocks were split, ⁵²and the graves were opened; and many bodies of the saints who had fallen asleep were raised; ⁵³and coming out of the graves after His resurrection, they went into the holy city and appeared to many.

⁵⁴So when the centurion and those with him, who were guarding Jesus, saw the earthquake and the things that had happened, they feared greatly, saying, "Truly this was the Son of God!"

⁵⁵And many women who followed Jesus

27:24 ᵃNU-Text omits *just.*   **27:34** ᵃNU-Text omits *sour.*   **27:35** ᵃNU-Text and M-Text omit the rest of this verse.   ᵇPsalm 22:18   **27:41** ᵃM-Text reads *with the scribes, the Pharisees, and the elders.*   **27:42** ᵃNU-Text reads *He is the King of Israel!*   ᵇNU-Text and M-Text read *we will believe in Him.*   **27:46** ᵃPsalm 22:1

from Galilee, ministering to Him, were there looking on from afar, ⁵⁶among whom were Mary Magdalene, Mary the mother of James and Joses,ᵃ and the mother of Zebedee's sons.

JESUS BURIED IN JOSEPH'S TOMB

⁵⁷Now when evening had come, there came a rich man from Arimathea, named Joseph, who himself had also become a disciple of Jesus. ⁵⁸This man went to Pilate and asked for the body of Jesus. Then Pilate commanded the body to be given to him. ⁵⁹When Joseph had taken the body, he wrapped it in a clean linen cloth, ⁶⁰and laid it in his new tomb which he had hewn out of the rock; and he rolled a large stone against the door of the tomb, and departed. ⁶¹And Mary Magdalene was there, and the other Mary, sitting opposite the tomb.

PILATE SETS A GUARD

⁶²On the next day, which followed the Day of Preparation, the chief priests and Pharisees gathered together to Pilate, ⁶³saying, "Sir, we remember, while He was still alive, how that deceiver said, 'After three days I will rise.' ⁶⁴Therefore command that the tomb be made secure until the third day, lest His disciples come by nightᵃ and steal Him *away*, and say to the people, 'He has risen from the dead.' So the last deception will be worse than the first."

⁶⁵Pilate said to them, "You have a guard; go your way, make *it* as secure as you know how." ⁶⁶So they went and made the tomb secure, sealing the stone and setting the guard.

HE IS RISEN

¹Now after the Sabbath, as the first *day* of the week began to dawn, Mary Magdalene and the other Mary came to see the tomb. ²And behold, there was a great earthquake; for an angel of the Lord descended from heaven, and came and rolled back the stone from the door,ᵃ and sat on it. ³His countenance was like lightning, and his clothing as white as snow. ⁴And the guards shook for fear of him, and became like dead *men*.

⁵But the angel answered and said to the women, "Do not be afraid, for I know that you seek Jesus who was crucified. ⁶He is not here; for He is risen, as He said. Come, see the place where the Lord lay. ⁷And go quickly and tell His

disciples that He is risen from the dead, and indeed He is going before you into Galilee; there you will see Him. Behold, I have told you."

⁸So they went out quickly from the tomb with fear and great joy, and ran to bring His disciples word.

THE WOMEN WORSHIP THE RISEN LORD

⁹And as they went to tell His disciples,ᵃ behold, Jesus met them, saying, "Rejoice!" So they came and held Him by the feet and worshiped Him. ¹⁰Then Jesus said to them, "Do not be afraid. Go *and* tell My brethren to go to Galilee, and there they will see Me."

On the Edge

Go therefore and make disciples of all the nations, baptizing them in the name of the Father and of the Son and of the Holy Spirit (Matt. 28:19).

Notice what this verse is saying. It instructs us to go and make disciples—not just converts, but disciples. We want to do more than just see people give their hearts to the Lord. We want to help them mature and grow in Him. Aren't you glad that someone helped you? When you gave your heart to Jesus, God just didn't throw you out and say, "Okay, you're on your own now."

If people are going to be developed, they have to be discipled. What is a disciple? A disciple is more than a follower of Christ. A disciple (according to the *American Heritage Dictionary*) is "one who assists in spreading the teachings of another." So what's our job? To assist in spreading the gospel, to be totally devoted to God, and to stick to Him like glue. We want to see people get saved and stick with it. Let's help our friends develop and grow so they can help others!

SEE FOR YOURSELF:
Mark 16:15, 16;
Luke 24:46, 47;
John 20:21;
Acts 5:42

27:56 ᵃNU-Text reads *Joseph*.   **27:64** ᵃNU-Text omits *by night*.   **28:2** ᵃNU-Text omits *from the door*.
28:9 ᵃNU-Text omits the first clause of this verse.

THE SOLDIERS ARE BRIBED

¹¹Now while they were going, behold, some of the guard came into the city and reported to the chief priests all the things that had happened. ¹²When they had assembled with the elders and consulted together, they gave a large sum of money to the soldiers, ¹³saying, "Tell them, 'His disciples came at night and stole Him *away* while we slept.' ¹⁴And if this comes to the governor's ears, we will appease him and make you secure." ¹⁵So they took the money and did as they were instructed; and this saying is commonly reported among the Jews until this day.

WITNESSING

Is witnessing a command? (28:16–20)

THE GREAT COMMISSION

¹⁶Then the eleven disciples went away into Galilee, to the mountain which Jesus had appointed for them. ¹⁷When they saw Him, they worshiped Him; but some doubted.

¹⁸And Jesus came and spoke to them, saying, "All authority has been given to Me in heaven and on earth. ¹⁹Go therefore[a] and make disciples of all the nations, baptizing them in the name of the Father and of the Son and of the Holy Spirit, ²⁰teaching them to observe all things that I have commanded you; and lo, I am with you always, *even* to the end of the age." Amen.[a]

LONELINESS

Are we ever alone? (28:20)

28:19 [a]M-Text omits *therefore*. **28:20** [a]NU-Text omits *Amen.*

CONTENT
If Mark were making a movie of Jesus' life (rather than a Gospel), there would have been *no* good time to go to the lobby to get popcorn. It would have been an action movie all the way. In fact, Mark is famous for using the word *immediately*. Each time a "scene" ended, Jesus *immediately* headed for the next place.

Mark was writing his version of the Gospel for a particular audience, the Romans. The Romans didn't grow up reading the Old Testament, so they wouldn't care that Jesus fulfilled prophecy. The Romans were conquerors and soldiers. They would care about the miracles Jesus performed and the people He helped. Mark didn't write so much about what Jesus *said* as about what Jesus *did*.

But even though Mark's movie would have been an action movie, Jesus (as the hero) was very different from our heroes today. Jesus made a difference by helping people one-on-one. Jesus didn't wreck cars (or chariots) and beat up people. He made a difference with the power of His love.

Most of the Romans in Mark's town were probably in some kind of military service. Seeing Jesus in this light would have shown them a whole new way to live and lead, which is what Jesus came to do.

Outline
1:1–8 .... The Message of John the Baptist
1:9–13 .... The Baptism and Temptation of Jesus
1:14—9:50 .... Jesus in Galilee
10:1–52 .... Jesus Goes from Galilee to Jerusalem
11:1—15:47 .... Jesus' Last Week: His Trial and Death
16:1–8 .... Jesus Is Alive
16:9–20 .... Jesus Appears to His Followers

Purpose
A relationship with God calls for complete commitment to doing His will.

Theme
The Suffering Son of Man Who Is, in Fact, the Son of God

Date of writing
60s A.D.

> "When He had called the people to Himself, with His disciples also, He said to them, 'Whoever desires to come after Me, let him deny himself, and take up his cross, and follow Me'" (8:34).

Bible Talk

Why Were There Romans in Israel?

Good question. Have you ever heard of the Roman Empire? Have you heard that phrase "All roads lead to Rome"? Mark was writing his Gospel at a time when Rome controlled most of the world. That included Israel.

When one country controls another country, they often send soldiers there to keep an eye on everything. When they do, you call that country "occupied." Israel was an "occupied" country, and it was "occupied" by the Romans. So, in terms of government, there was a lot of Roman input.

Many of the Hebrews resented the Romans. They wanted the Romans to go back to Rome and leave them alone. It says something about Mark that he would care enough about the Romans that he would write an account of Jesus' life so they could understand the significance of it.

JESUS THE SERVANT

Mark is famous for portraying Jesus as a servant. He highlights the fact that Jesus did not come into the world to change it through power and strength, but through gentleness and love. Mark tells stories of Jesus reaching out to the outcasts of society, the people that no one would even touch or go near. Mark tells stories of Jesus spending time with people who were considered lower class. Mark wanted his readers to know that they could count on Jesus to reach out to them rather than hitting them over the head in some power-hungry frenzy.

JOHN THE BAPTIST PREPARES THE WAY

[1]The beginning of the gospel of Jesus Christ, the Son of God. [2]As it is written in the Prophets:[a]

"Behold, I send My messenger before Your face,
Who will prepare Your way before You."[b]
[3] "The voice of one crying in the wilderness:
'Prepare the way of the LORD;
Make His paths straight.' "[a]

[4]John came baptizing in the wilderness and preaching a baptism of repentance for the remission of sins. [5]Then all the land of Judea, and those from Jerusalem, went out to him and were all baptized by him in the Jordan River, confessing their sins.

[6]Now John was clothed with camel's hair and with a leather belt around his waist, and he ate locusts and wild honey. [7]And he preached, saying, "There comes One after me who is mightier than I, whose sandal strap I am not worthy to stoop down and loose. [8]I indeed baptized you with water, but He will baptize you with the Holy Spirit."

JOHN BAPTIZES JESUS

[9]It came to pass in those days that Jesus came from Nazareth of Galilee, and was baptized by John in the Jordan. [10]And immediately, coming up from[a] the water, He saw the heavens parting and the Spirit descending upon Him like a dove. [11]Then a voice came from heaven, "You are My beloved Son, in whom I am well pleased."

SATAN TEMPTS JESUS

[12]Immediately the Spirit drove Him into the wilderness. [13]And He was there in the wilderness forty days, tempted by Satan, and was with the wild beasts; and the angels ministered to Him.

JESUS BEGINS HIS GALILEAN MINISTRY

[14]Now after John was put in prison, Jesus came to Galilee, preaching the gospel of the kingdom[a] of God, [15]and saying, "The time is fulfilled, and the kingdom of God is at hand. Repent, and believe in the gospel."

FOUR FISHERMEN CALLED AS DISCIPLES

[16]And as He walked by the Sea of Galilee, He saw Simon and Andrew his brother casting a net into the sea; for they were fishermen. [17]Then Jesus said to them, "Follow Me, and I will make you become fishers of men." [18]They immediately left their nets and followed Him.

[19]When He had gone a little farther from there, He saw James the son of Zebedee, and John his brother, who also were in the boat mending their nets. [20]And immediately He called them, and they left their father Zebedee

⋮⋮⋮ On the Edge

Immediately, coming up from the water, He saw the heavens parting and the Spirit descending upon Him like a dove. Then a voice came from heaven, "You are My beloved Son, in whom I am well pleased" (Mark 1:10, 11).

Where are you from? In what part of the world were you raised? One of the first things we ask a stranger is, "Where are you from?" Knowing where someone is from tells us a lot about him or her—why he/she has an accent, what kind of climate he/she's used to, which sports teams he/she might like the most. We can ask questions about favorite foods and whether he or she knows the one person we know from his/her city.

The Son of God is from heaven and there is so much we can know about Him because we know where He's from. He comes from the place reserved for the King of kings. He has been there with God the Father and God the Holy Spirit from the very beginning. Heaven is God's home and the place He created for those who know Him. To live in heaven is an honor—a gift to those who accept Jesus here on earth.

In heaven, the Lord is continually being praised by the angels. There is no sickness or sadness there. We know that Jesus is royal, perfect, and worthy of our praise because He has come from the perfect place of heaven. He has walked among us, but He is not from around here. His righteousness and holiness give Him away. He is from heaven.

SEE FOR YOURSELF:
Matt. 3:16; John 1:1;
Acts 10:38; Rev. 21:4

1:2 [a]NU-Text reads *Isaiah the prophet.* [b]Malachi 3:1   **1:3** [a]Isaiah 40:3   **1:10** [a]NU-Text reads *out of.*
1:14 [a]NU-Text omits *of the kingdom.*

in the boat with the hired servants, and went after Him.

The temple, the main worship center for the Jewish people, was located in Jerusalem. The problem was that many people lived too far from Jerusalem to go to the temple regularly. What were these people supposed to do when they wanted to worship God and hear His Word read? Many of them built synagogues, local places of worship. Jesus and His followers were no strangers to the synagogue in Capernaum. Four of the disciples—Simon Peter, Andrew, James, and John—were hometown boys.

Mark 1:21

JESUS CASTS OUT AN UNCLEAN SPIRIT

²¹Then they went into Capernaum, and immediately on the Sabbath He entered the synagogue and taught. ²²And they were astonished at His teaching, for He taught them as one having authority, and not as the scribes.

²³Now there was a man in their synagogue with an unclean spirit. And he cried out, ²⁴saying, "Let us alone! What have we to do with You, Jesus of Nazareth? Did You come to destroy us? I know who You are—the Holy One of God!"

²⁵But Jesus rebuked him, saying, "Be quiet, and come out of him!" ²⁶And when the unclean spirit had convulsed him and cried out with a loud voice, he came out of him. ²⁷Then they were all amazed, so that they questioned among themselves, saying, "What is this? What new doctrine is this? For with authority[a] He commands even the unclean spirits, and they obey Him." ²⁸And immediately His fame spread throughout all the region around Galilee.

PETER'S MOTHER-IN-LAW HEALED

²⁹Now as soon as they had come out of the synagogue, they entered the house of Simon and Andrew, with James and John. ³⁰But Simon's wife's mother lay sick with a fever, and they told Him about her at once. ³¹So He came and took her by the hand and lifted her up, and immediately the fever left her. And she served them.

1:27 ᵃNU-Text reads *What is this? A new doctrine with authority.*

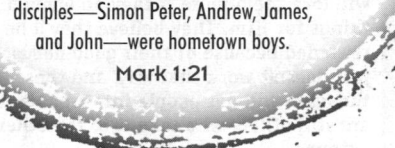

Promise   HE PROMISES TO BRING GOOD NEWS.

He said to them, "Let us go into the next towns, that I may preach there also, because for this purpose I have come forth" (Mark 1:38).

Not too long after Jesus started traveling around telling people about God's kingdom, He visited His hometown. On the Sabbath, He went to the local synagogue, where someone asked Him to read from the Scriptures. He read from the Book of Isaiah: "The Spirit of the LORD is upon Me, because He has anointed Me to preach the gospel to the poor; He has sent Me to heal the brokenhearted, to proclaim liberty to the captives and recovery of sight to the blind, to set at liberty those who are oppressed; to proclaim the acceptable year of the LORD." When Jesus finished reading, He said, "Today this Scripture is fulfilled in your hearing" (Luke 4:16–21).

Jesus wanted the people to know that what seemed impossible was possible with God. When matters seemed hopeless, God was able to turn things around.

Jesus knew why He was on earth and put His whole heart into fulfilling the purpose God had given Him. That's still His purpose today. What He came to earth to do then in the flesh, His Word and His Spirit continue to do today. Be serious about reading His Word. If you want to know what Jesus said when He lived on earth, read Matthew, Mark, Luke, and John. See what good news He has for you!

SEE FOR YOURSELF:
Matt. 4:23; 9:35; Luke 4:18, 19; 20:1

MANY HEALED AFTER SABBATH SUNSET

[32]At evening, when the sun had set, they brought to Him all who were sick and those who were demon-possessed. [33]And the whole city was gathered together at the door. [34]Then He healed many who were sick with various diseases, and cast out many demons; and He did not allow the demons to speak, because they knew Him.

DEMONS

Can demons hurt Jesus? (1:34)

PREACHING IN GALILEE

[35]Now in the morning, having risen a long while before daylight, He went out and departed to a solitary place; and there He prayed. [36]And Simon and those *who were* with Him searched for Him. [37]When they found Him, they said to Him, "Everyone is looking for You."

[38]But He said to them, "Let us go into the next towns, that I may preach there also, because for this purpose I have come forth."

[39]And He was preaching in their synagogues throughout all Galilee, and casting out demons.

JESUS CLEANSES A LEPER

[40]Now a leper came to Him, imploring Him, kneeling down to Him and saying to Him, "If You are willing, You can make me clean."

[41]Then Jesus, moved with compassion, stretched out *His* hand and touched him, and said to him, "I am willing; be cleansed." [42]As soon as He had spoken, immediately the leprosy left him, and he was cleansed. [43]And He strictly warned him and sent him away at once, [44]and said to him, "See that you say nothing to anyone; but go your way, show yourself to the priest, and offer for your cleansing those things which Moses commanded, as a testimony to them."

[45]However, he went out and began to proclaim *it* freely, and to spread the matter, so that Jesus could no longer openly enter the city, but was outside in deserted places; and they came to Him from every direction.

JESUS FORGIVES AND HEALS A PARALYTIC

[1]And again He entered Capernaum after *some* days, and it was heard that He was in the house. [2]Immediately[a] many gathered together, so that there was no longer room to receive *them*, not even near the door. And He preached the word to them. [3]Then they came to Him, bringing a paralytic who was carried by four men. [4]And when they could not come near Him because of the crowd, they uncovered the roof where He was. So when they had broken through, they let down the bed on which the paralytic was lying.

[5]When Jesus saw their faith, He said to the paralytic, "Son, your sins are forgiven you." [6]And some of the scribes were sitting there

On the Edge

Why does this Man speak blasphemies like this? Who can forgive sins but God alone? (Mark 2:7).

Has anyone ever done something wrong to you, and instead of apologizing and making it right, he or she tried to correct his/her wrong by doing something nice for you? How did that make you feel? Really, you just wanted an apology, right?

Well, sometimes we do that to God. There are a lot of people who believe they can work their way to heaven or that God will love them more if they do enough things for Him. They believe they'll be rewarded because of their good deeds. It just doesn't work that way, and these thoughts will get people into trouble. There are still others who take it to the other extreme.

These are the kind of people who believe they have to suffer just like Jesus did, so they beat themselves with whips, crawl across glass, and even hang on crosses for hours at a time in order to receive forgiveness. Both of these ways are false.

God, and God alone, is the only Person who can forgive. You can't get His forgiveness from your parents or from the people you hang out with. Sure, they can (and should) forgive your shortcomings by not holding them against you, but only God can erase them from your record permanently. All you have to do is confess your sins to Him and repent and—instantly—they're gone forever.

Confess your sins to the Lord today. He's the only One who can get rid of them for you!

SEE FOR YOURSELF:
Matt. 9:6; Mark 2:10; Luke 5:20, 24; Eph. 2:9

and reasoning in their hearts, [7]"Why does this *Man* speak blasphemies like this? Who can forgive sins but God alone?"

[8]But immediately, when Jesus perceived in His spirit that they reasoned thus within themselves, He said to them, "Why do you reason about these things in your hearts? [9]Which is easier, to say to the paralytic, '*Your* sins are forgiven you,' or to say, 'Arise, take up your bed and walk'? [10]But that you may know that the Son of Man has power on earth to forgive sins"—He said to the paralytic, [11]"I say to you, arise, take up your bed, and go to your house." [12]Immediately he arose, took up the bed, and went out in the presence of them all, so that all were amazed and glorified God, saying, "We never saw *anything* like this!"

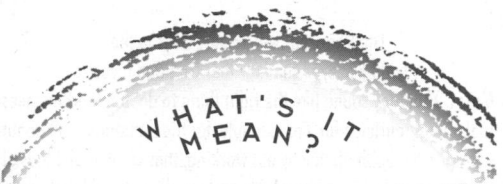

WHAT'S IT MEAN?

You name it, and the Roman Empire probably charged a tax for it. The Jews expected to be taxed for everything they did, whether it was buying property or worshiping at the temple. To collect these outrageous taxes, the Romans hired local Jewish citizens. These collectors were known for charging their fellow Jews more money than they really owed and keeping the extra cash for themselves. Because of this, and because the collectors worked for the hated Roman government, taxmen were usually seen as traitors to their people.

Mark 2:16

MATTHEW THE TAX COLLECTOR

[13]Then He went out again by the sea; and all the multitude came to Him, and He taught them. [14]As He passed by, He saw Levi the *son of* Alphaeus sitting at the tax office. And He said to him, "Follow Me." So he arose and followed Him.

[15]Now it happened, as He was dining in *Levi's* house, that many tax collectors and sinners also sat together with Jesus and His disciples; for there were many, and they followed Him. [16]And when the scribes and[a] Pharisees saw Him eating with the tax collectors and sinners, they said to His disciples, "How *is it* that He eats and drinks with tax collectors and sinners?"

[17]When Jesus heard it, He said to them, "Those who are well have no need of a physician, but those who are sick. I did not come to call *the* righteous, but sinners, to repentance."[a]

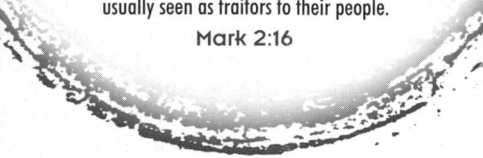

On the Edge

When Jesus heard it, He said to them, "Those who are well have no need of a physician, but those who are sick. I did not come to call the righteous, but sinners, to repentance" (Mark 2:17).

The Pharisees didn't understand what Jesus was all about. For one thing, He hung out with people they would have crossed the street to avoid. The Pharisees thought they were way too holy to rub elbows with those people.

What Jesus said to them is like music to your ears if you think you've done such horrible things that God could never love you. He lets you know right off the bat that He's more interested in changing sinners than in recruiting good, religious people to His cause.

But does that mean that Jesus isn't interested in you if you haven't gotten messed up in sex or drugs or haven't broken the law? Not at all. When He said He wasn't inviting "the righteous," He was talking about the attitude in people's hearts. People who consider themselves "righteous" (good), like the Pharisees, don't think they need Jesus. People who know they are sinners—whether their sins are obvious to everyone or the invisible sins of the heart—know they need Jesus. He welcomes them with open arms.

SEE FOR YOURSELF:
Matt. 9:12, 13;
Luke 5:31, 32; 19:10

JESUS IS QUESTIONED ABOUT FASTING

[18]The disciples of John and of the Pharisees were fasting. Then they came and said to Him, "Why do the disciples of John and of the Pharisees fast, but Your disciples do not fast?"

[19]And Jesus said to them, "Can the friends of the bridegroom fast while the bridegroom is with them? As long as they have the bridegroom

2:16 [a]NU-Text reads *of the.* **2:17** [a]NU-Text omits *to repentance.*

with them they cannot fast. ²⁰But the days will come when the bridegroom will be taken away from them, and then they will fast in those days. ²¹No one sews a piece of unshrunk cloth on an old garment; or else the new piece pulls away from the old, and the tear is made worse. ²²And no one puts new wine into old wineskins; or else the new wine bursts the wineskins, the wine is spilled, and the wineskins are ruined. But new wine must be put into new wineskins."

JESUS IS LORD OF THE SABBATH

²³Now it happened that He went through the grainfields on the Sabbath; and as they went His disciples began to pluck the heads of grain. ²⁴And the Pharisees said to Him, "Look, why do they do what is not lawful on the Sabbath?"

²⁵But He said to them, "Have you never read what David did when he was in need and hungry, he and those with him: ²⁶how he went into the house of God *in the days* of Abiathar the high priest, and ate the showbread, which is not lawful to eat except for the priests, and also gave some to those who were with him?"

²⁷And He said to them, "The Sabbath was made for man, and not man for the Sabbath. ²⁸Therefore the Son of Man is also Lord of the Sabbath."

HEALING ON THE SABBATH

¹And He entered the synagogue again, and a man was there who had a withered hand. ²So they watched Him closely, whether He would heal him on the Sabbath, so that they might accuse Him. ³And He said to the man who had the withered hand, "Step forward." ⁴Then He said to them, "Is it lawful on the Sabbath to do good or to do evil, to save life or to kill?" But they kept silent. ⁵And when He had looked around at them with anger, being grieved by the hardness of their hearts, He said to the man, "Stretch out your hand." And he stretched *it* out, and his hand was restored as whole as the other.ᵃ ⁶Then the Pharisees went out and immediately plotted with the Herodians against Him, how they might destroy Him.

A GREAT MULTITUDE FOLLOWS JESUS

⁷But Jesus withdrew with His disciples to the sea. And a great multitude from Galilee followed Him, and from Judea ⁸and Jerusalem and Idumea and beyond the Jordan; and those from Tyre and Sidon, a great multitude, when they heard how many things He was doing, came to Him. ⁹So He told His disciples that a small boat should be kept ready for Him because of the multitude, lest they should crush Him. ¹⁰For He healed many, so that as many as had afflictions pressed about Him to touch Him. ¹¹And the unclean spirits, whenever they saw Him, fell down before Him and cried out, saying, "You are the Son of God." ¹²But He sternly warned them that they should not make Him known.

WHAT'S IT MEAN?

The Pharisees were really strict in the way they obeyed the Law that God had given to Moses. That may sound like the right thing to do, but the Pharisees took things much too far. For example, for the commandment about honoring the Sabbath day by not working, they created all kinds of rules and regulations about what people could and couldn't do, how far they were allowed to walk, and so on.

Mark 3:2

THE TWELVE APOSTLES

¹³And He went up on the mountain and called to *Him* those He Himself wanted. And they came to Him. ¹⁴Then He appointed twelve,ᵃ that they might be with Him and that He might send them out to preach, ¹⁵and to have power to heal sicknesses andᵃ to cast out demons: ¹⁶Simon,ᵃ to whom He gave the name Peter; ¹⁷James the *son* of Zebedee and John the brother of James, to whom He gave the name Boanerges, that is, "Sons of Thunder"; ¹⁸Andrew, Philip, Bartholomew, Matthew, Thomas, James the *son* of Alphaeus, Thaddaeus, Simon the Cananite; ¹⁹and Judas Iscariot, who also betrayed Him. And they went into a house.

A HOUSE DIVIDED CANNOT STAND

²⁰Then the multitude came together again, so that they could not so much as eat bread. ²¹But when His own people heard *about this*, they went out to lay hold of Him, for they said, "He is out of His mind."

3:5 ᵃNU-Text omits *as whole as the other.*   **3:14** ᵃNU-Text adds *whom He also named apostles.*   **3:15** ᵃNU-Text omits *to heal sicknesses and.*   **3:16** ᵃNU-Text reads *and He appointed the twelve: Simon. . . .*

²²And the scribes who came down from Jerusalem said, "He has Beelzebub," and, "By the ruler of the demons He casts out demons."

WHAT'S IT MEAN?

The Jewish people believed that Beelzebub was king of the demons, the being in charge of all evil spirits. You might know him better as Satan, or the devil.

Mark 3:22

²³So He called them to *Himself* and said to them in parables: "How can Satan cast out Satan? ²⁴If a kingdom is divided against itself, that kingdom cannot stand. ²⁵And if a house is divided against itself, that house cannot stand. ²⁶And if Satan has risen up against himself, and is divided, he cannot stand, but has an end. ²⁷No one can enter a strong man's house and plunder his goods, unless he first binds the strong man. And then he will plunder his house.

3:32 ᵃNU-Text and M-Text add *and Your sisters.*

THE UNPARDONABLE SIN

²⁸"Assuredly, I say to you, all sins will be forgiven the sons of men, and whatever blasphemies they may utter; ²⁹but he who blasphemes against the Holy Spirit never has forgiveness, but is subject to eternal condemnation"—³⁰because they said, "He has an unclean spirit."

JESUS' MOTHER AND BROTHERS SEND FOR HIM

³¹Then His brothers and His mother came, and standing outside they sent to Him, calling Him. ³²And a multitude was sitting around Him; and they said to Him, "Look, Your mother and Your brothersᵃ are outside seeking You."

³³But He answered them, saying, "Who is My mother, or My brothers?" ³⁴And He looked around in a circle at those who sat about Him, and said, "Here are My mother and My brothers! ³⁵For whoever does the will of God is My brother and My sister and mother."

THE PARABLE OF THE SOWER

¹And again He began to teach by the sea. And a great multitude was gathered to Him, so that He got into a boat and sat *in it* on the sea; and the whole multitude was on the land facing the sea. ²Then He taught them many things by parables, and said to them in His teaching:

Promise   HE PROMISES ANYTHING CAN BE FORGIVEN.

Assuredly I say to you, all sins will be forgiven the sons of men, and whatever blasphemies they may utter (Mark 3:28).

Be encouraged! It doesn't matter what you've done in the past, where you've done it, or who you've done it with. God loves you and wants to forgive you. In fact, God has more grace than you can imagine. You may *feel* like you've blown it, and then again, you may *have* blown it. It doesn't matter. Jesus is more than ready to give you a fresh start. He wants you to run to Him, not away from Him!

Remember when David blew it with Bathsheba? Then he blew it again by having her husband killed. David kept messing up trying to cover his sin. God sent the prophet Nathan to confront him. David's eyes were finally opened, and he repented. God forgave David, and in the Book of Acts he was known as "a man after [God's] own heart" (Acts 13:22). If David can be forgiven, so can you. But the key is this: David repented. He didn't just apologize. He was truly sorry in his heart. To repent means to turn from sin and go the other direction. Whatever it is that you need to be forgiven from, give it to God right now. Ask for forgiveness: tell Him you're sorry, repent, and move on.

Even good people may fall many times, but they will get back up! God is the One who will always forgive, no matter what you've done. He loves you!

SEE FOR YOURSELF:

Ps. 51; Prov. 24:16; Jer. 33:8; Ezek. 36:25–27; Titus 2:14; 1 John 1:7, 9

On the Edge

Whoever does the will of God is My brother and My sister and mother (Mark 3:35).

Did you know that you belong to the family of Christ? You are a brother or sister of the Lord Himself; and, as a member of His family, you are royal and privileged. Because you are a brother or sister of Christ, you are perfectly cared for and protected. Your earthly family may fall short, but this family will never let you down. Some students don't know who they belong to. They aren't living like brothers and sisters of Christ, because His true brothers and sisters don't abuse their bodies, don't abuse people, and don't abuse privileges. They don't need an alternative lifestyle, because they have been promised an eternal lifestyle. Maybe you've been living like the rest of the world because you didn't know about your family—a family of grace, but a family of conviction and strong character. You are called to carry on the heritage of the family of Christ.

SEE FOR YOURSELF:
Matt. 12:48; 23:8

given to know the mystery of the kingdom of God; but to those who are outside, all things come in parables, ¹²so that

> 'Seeing they may see and not perceive,
> And hearing they may hear and not
>   understand;
> Lest they should turn,
> And their sins be forgiven them.' "ᵃ

THE PARABLE OF THE SOWER EXPLAINED

¹³And He said to them, "Do you not understand this parable? How then will you understand all the parables? ¹⁴The sower sows the word. ¹⁵And these are the ones by the wayside where the word is sown. When they hear, Satan comes immediately and takes away the word that was sown in their hearts. ¹⁶These likewise are the ones sown on stony ground who, when they hear the word, immediately receive it with gladness; ¹⁷and they have no root in themselves, and so endure only for a time. Afterward, when tribulation or persecution arises for the word's sake, immediately they stumble. ¹⁸Now these are the ones sown among thorns; *they are* the ones who hear the word, ¹⁹and the cares of this world, the deceitfulness of riches, and the desires for other things entering in choke the word, and it becomes unfruitful. ²⁰But these are the ones sown on good ground, those who hear the word, accept *it*, and bear fruit: some thirtyfold, some sixty, and some a hundred."

LIGHT UNDER A BASKET

²¹Also He said to them, "Is a lamp brought to be put under a basket or under a bed? Is it not to be set on a lampstand? ²²For there is nothing hidden which will not be revealed, nor has anything been kept secret but that it should come to light. ²³If anyone has ears to hear, let him hear."

²⁴Then He said to them, "Take heed what you hear. With the same measure you use, it will be measured to you; and to you who hear, more will be given. ²⁵For whoever has, to him more will be given; but whoever does not have, even what he has will be taken away from him."

THE PARABLE OF THE GROWING SEED

²⁶And He said, "The kingdom of God is as if a man should scatter seed on the ground, ²⁷and should sleep by night and rise by day, and the

³"Listen! Behold, a sower went out to sow. ⁴And it happened, as he sowed, *that* some *seed* fell by the wayside; and the birds of the airᵃ came and devoured it. ⁵Some fell on stony ground, where it did not have much earth; and immediately it sprang up because it had no depth of earth. ⁶But when the sun was up it was scorched, and because it had no root it withered away. ⁷And some *seed* fell among thorns; and the thorns grew up and choked it, and it yielded no crop. ⁸But other *seed* fell on good ground and yielded a crop that sprang up, increased and produced: some thirtyfold, some sixty, and some a hundred."

⁹And He said to them,ᵃ "He who has ears to hear, let him hear!"

THE PURPOSE OF PARABLES

¹⁰But when He was alone, those around Him with the twelve asked Him about the parable. ¹¹And He said to them, "To you it has been

---

4:4 ᵃNU-Text and M-Text omit *of the air.*   **4:9** ᵃNU-Text and M-Text omit *to them.*
4:12 ᵃIsaiah 6:9, 10

seed should sprout and grow, he himself does not know how. [28]For the earth yields crops by itself: first the blade, then the head, after that the full grain in the head. [29]But when the grain ripens, immediately he puts in the sickle, because the harvest has come."

THE PARABLE OF THE MUSTARD SEED

[30]Then He said, "To what shall we liken the kingdom of God? Or with what parable shall we picture it? [31]*It is* like a mustard seed which, when it is sown on the ground, is smaller than all the seeds on earth; [32]but when it is sown, it grows up and becomes greater than all herbs, and shoots out large branches, so that the birds of the air may nest under its shade."

WHAT'S IT MEAN?

The mustard seed is proof of the old saying, "Big things come in small packages." One tiny mustard seed—a seed much smaller than a kernel of corn—is capable of producing a plant up to fifteen feet high.

Mark 4:31

JESUS' USE OF PARABLES

[33]And with many such parables He spoke the word to them as they were able to hear *it.* [34]But without a parable He did not speak to them. And when they were alone, He explained all things to His disciples.

WIND AND WAVE OBEY JESUS

[35]On the same day, when evening had come, He said to them, "Let us cross over to the other side." [36]Now when they had left the multitude, they took Him along in the boat as He was. And other little boats were also with Him. [37]And a great windstorm arose, and the waves beat into the boat, so that it was already filling. [38]But He was in the stern, asleep on a pillow. And they awoke Him and said to Him, "Teacher, do You not care that we are perishing?"

[39]Then He arose and rebuked the wind, and said to the sea, "Peace, be still!" And the wind ceased and there was a great calm. [40]But He said to them, "Why are you so fearful? How *is it* that you have no faith?"[a] [41]And they feared exceedingly, and said to one another, "Who can this be, that even the wind and the sea obey Him!"

On the Edge

And with many such parables He spoke the word to them as they were able to hear it. But without a parable He did not speak to them (Mark 4:33, 34).

Think back to last week's sermon at church. Maybe your mind wandered for part of the time, but what made you look up and really listen? The story. Maybe it was funny, maybe tragic, but you were definitely listening. The pastor had your attention. Jesus was a great communicator. He knew that people love to listen to stories. He told the deep and incredible truths of His kingdom in the form of stories so that the people could understand what He was really saying. People listened to His parables and then retold them to their friends. Read the stories of Jesus and hear the truth He is speaking to you.

SEE FOR YOURSELF:
Matt. 13:13, 34, 35

A DEMON-POSSESSED MAN HEALED

[1]Then they came to the other side of the sea, to the country of the Gadarenes.[a] [2]And when He had come out of the boat, immediately there met Him out of the tombs a man with an unclean spirit, [3]who had *his* dwelling among the tombs; and no one could bind him,[a] not even with chains, [4]because he had often been bound with shackles and chains. And the chains had been pulled apart by him, and the shackles broken in pieces; neither could anyone tame him. [5]And always, night and day, he was in the mountains and in the tombs, crying out and cutting himself with stones.

DEMONS
What do demons want to do to people? (5:5)

[6]When he saw Jesus from afar, he ran and worshiped Him. [7]And he cried out with a loud

---

4:40 [a]NU-Text reads *Have you still no faith?*   **5:1** [a]NU-Text reads *Gerasenes.*   **5:3** [a]NU-Text adds *anymore.*

voice and said, "What have I to do with You, Jesus, Son of the Most High God? I implore You by God that You do not torment me."

⁸For He said to him, "Come out of the man, unclean spirit!" ⁹Then He asked him, "What *is* your name?"

And he answered, saying, "My name *is* Legion; for we are many." ¹⁰Also he begged Him earnestly that He would not send them out of the country.

¹¹Now a large herd of swine was feeding there near the mountains. ¹²So all the demons begged Him, saying, "Send us to the swine, that we may enter them." ¹³And at once Jesusᵃ gave them permission. Then the unclean spirits went out and entered the swine (there were about two thousand); and the herd ran violently down the steep place into the sea, and drowned in the sea.

¹⁴So those who fed the swine fled, and they told *it* in the city and in the country. And they went out to see what it was that had happened. ¹⁵Then they came to Jesus, and saw the one *who had been* demon-possessed and had the legion, sitting and clothed and in his right mind. And they were afraid. ¹⁶And those who saw it told them how it happened to him *who had been* demon-possessed, and about the swine. ¹⁷Then they began to plead with Him to depart from their region.

¹⁸And when He got into the boat, he who had been demon-possessed begged Him that he might be with Him. ¹⁹However, Jesus did not permit him, but said to him, "Go home to your friends, and tell them what great things the Lord has done for you, and how He has had compassion on you." ²⁰And he departed and began to proclaim in Decapolis all that Jesus had done for him; and all marveled.

A GIRL RESTORED TO LIFE AND A WOMAN HEALED

²¹Now when Jesus had crossed over again by boat to the other side, a great multitude gathered to Him; and He was by the sea. ²²And behold, one of the rulers of the synagogue came, Jairus by name. And when he saw Him, he fell at His feet ²³and begged Him earnestly, saying, "My little daughter lies at the point of death. Come and lay Your hands on her, that she may be healed, and she will live." ²⁴So *Jesus*

went with him, and a great multitude followed Him and thronged Him.

²⁵Now a certain woman had a flow of blood for twelve years, ²⁶and had suffered many things from many physicians. She had spent all that she had and was no better, but rather grew worse. ²⁷When she heard about Jesus, she came behind *Him* in the crowd and touched His garment. ²⁸For she said, "If only I may touch His clothes, I shall be made well."

²⁹Immediately the fountain of her blood was dried up, and she felt in *her* body that she was healed of the affliction. ³⁰And Jesus, immediately knowing in Himself that power had gone out of Him, turned around in the crowd and said, "Who touched My clothes?"

³¹But His disciples said to Him, "You see the multitude thronging You, and You say, 'Who touched Me?'"

³²And He looked around to see her who had done this thing. ³³But the woman, fearing and trembling, knowing what had happened to her, came and fell down before Him and told Him the whole truth. ³⁴And He said to her, "Daughter, your faith has made you well. Go in peace, and be healed of your affliction."

³⁵While He was still speaking, *some* came from the ruler of the synagogue's *house* who said, "Your daughter is dead. Why trouble the Teacher any further?"

³⁶As soon as Jesus heard the word that was spoken, He said to the ruler of the synagogue, "Do not be afraid; only believe." ³⁷And He permitted no one to follow Him except Peter, James, and John the brother of James. ³⁸Then He came to the house of the ruler of the synagogue, and saw a tumult and those who wept and wailed loudly. ³⁹When He came in, He said to them, "Why make this commotion and weep? The child is not dead, but sleeping."

⁴⁰And they ridiculed Him. But when He had put them all outside, He took the father and the mother of the child, and those *who were* with Him, and entered where the child was lying. ⁴¹Then He took the child by the hand, and said to her, "Talitha, cumi," which is translated, "Little girl, I say to you, arise." ⁴²Immediately the girl arose and walked, for she was twelve years *of age*. And they were overcome with great amazement. ⁴³But He commanded them strictly

> "Go home to your friends, and tell them what great things the Lord has done for you, and how He has had compassion on you."
> (Mark 5:19)

5:13 ᵃNU-Text reads *And He gave.*

that no one should know it, and said that *something* should be given her to eat.

JESUS REJECTED AT NAZARETH

[1]Then He went out from there and came to His own country, and His disciples followed Him. [2]And when the Sabbath had come, He began to teach in the synagogue. And many hearing *Him* were astonished, saying, "Where *did* this Man *get* these things? And what wisdom *is* this which is given to Him, that such mighty works are performed by His hands! [3]Is this not the carpenter, the Son of Mary, and brother of James, Joses, Judas, and Simon? And are not His sisters here with us?" So they were offended at Him.

[4]But Jesus said to them, "A prophet is not without honor except in his own country, among his own relatives, and in his own house." [5]Now He could do no mighty work there, except that He laid His hands on a few sick people and healed *them*. [6]And He marveled because of their unbelief. Then He went about the villages in a circuit, teaching.

SENDING OUT THE TWELVE

[7]And He called the twelve to *Himself*, and began to send them out two *by* two, and gave them power over unclean spirits. [8]He commanded them to take nothing for the journey except a staff—no bag, no bread, no copper in *their* money belts—[9]but to wear sandals, and not to put on two tunics.

[10]Also He said to them, "In whatever place you enter a house, stay there till you depart from that place. [11]And whoever[a] will not receive you nor hear you, when you depart from there, shake off the dust under your feet as a testimony against them.[b] Assuredly, I say to you, it will be more tolerable for Sodom and Gomorrah in the day of judgment than for that city!"

[12]So they went out and preached that *people* should repent. [13]And they cast out many demons, and anointed with oil many who were sick, and healed *them*.

JOHN THE BAPTIST BEHEADED

[14]Now King Herod heard *of Him*, for His name had become well known. And he said, "John the Baptist is risen from the dead, and therefore these powers are at work in him."

[15]Others said, "It is Elijah."

And others said, "It is the Prophet, or[a] like one of the prophets."

[16]But when Herod heard, he said, "This is John, whom I beheaded; he has been raised from the dead!" [17]For Herod himself had sent and laid hold of John, and bound him in prison for the sake of Herodias, his brother Philip's wife; for he had married her. [18]Because John had said to Herod, "It is not lawful for you to have your brother's wife."

WHAT'S IT MEAN?

The prophet Elijah prophesied more than 850 years before Jesus. Why would anyone confuse the two? Perhaps it was because of the way Elijah's time on earth ended. You see, Elijah didn't die; he was taken directly to heaven. Some Old Testament writers predicted that the living, breathing Elijah would return to earth one day. The Jewish people expected him to return just before the Messiah came to set them free from Rome's control.

Mark 6:15

[19]Therefore Herodias held it against him and wanted to kill him, but she could not; [20]for Herod feared John, knowing that he *was* a just and holy man, and he protected him. And when he heard him, he did many things, and heard him gladly.

[21]Then an opportune day came when Herod on his birthday gave a feast for his nobles, the high officers, and the chief *men* of Galilee. [22]And when Herodias' daughter herself came in and danced, and pleased Herod and those who sat with him, the king said to the girl, "Ask me whatever you want, and I will give *it* to you." [23]He also swore to her, "Whatever you ask me, I will give you, up to half my kingdom."

[24]So she went out and said to her mother, "What shall I ask?"

And she said, "The head of John the Baptist!"

[25]Immediately she came in with haste to the king and asked, saying, "I want you to give me at once the head of John the Baptist on a platter."

[26]And the king was exceedingly sorry; *yet*, because of the oaths and because of those who sat with him, he did not want to refuse her. [27]Immediately the king sent an executioner and commanded his head to be brought. And he

---

6:11 [a]NU-Text reads *whatever place*. [b]NU-Text omits the rest of this verse. **6:15** [a]NU-Text and M-Text omit *or*.

went and beheaded him in prison, ²⁸brought his head on a platter, and gave it to the girl; and the girl gave it to her mother. ²⁹When his disciples heard *of it*, they came and took away his corpse and laid it in a tomb.

FEEDING THE FIVE THOUSAND

³⁰Then the apostles gathered to Jesus and told Him all things, both what they had done and what they had taught. ³¹And He said to them, "Come aside by yourselves to a deserted place and rest a while." For there were many coming and going, and they did not even have time to eat. ³²So they departed to a deserted place in the boat by themselves.

³³But the multitudes*ᵃ* saw them departing, and many knew Him and ran there on foot from all the cities. They arrived before them and came together to Him. ³⁴And Jesus, when He came out, saw a great multitude and was moved with compassion for them, because they were like sheep not having a shepherd. So He began to teach them many things. ³⁵When the day was now far spent, His disciples came to Him and said, "This is a deserted place, and already the hour *is* late. ³⁶Send them away, that they may go into the surrounding country and villages and buy themselves bread;*ᵃ* for they have nothing to eat."

³⁷But He answered and said to them, "You give them something to eat."

And they said to Him, "Shall we go and buy two hundred denarii worth of bread and give them *something* to eat?"

³⁸But He said to them, "How many loaves do you have? Go and see."

And when they found out they said, "Five, and two fish."

³⁹Then He commanded them to make them all sit down in groups on the green grass. ⁴⁰So they sat down in ranks, in hundreds and in fifties. ⁴¹And when He had taken the five loaves and the two fish, He looked up to heaven, blessed and broke the loaves, and gave *them* to His disciples to set before them; and the two fish He divided among *them* all. ⁴²So they all ate and were filled. ⁴³And they took up twelve baskets full of fragments and of the fish. ⁴⁴Now those who had eaten the loaves were about*ᵃ* five thousand men.

JESUS WALKS ON THE SEA

⁴⁵Immediately He made His disciples get into the boat and go before Him to the other side, to

On the Edge

They all saw Him and were troubled. But immediately He talked with them and said to them, "Be of good cheer! It is I; do not be afraid" (Mark 6:50).

Here we have one of the greatest stories of all time. Can you imagine sitting in a boat with the wind and the waves beating against it? You are trying to get to the other side of the lake and not going anywhere; all of a sudden . . . "Hey, there's Jesus walking on the water!" What happened? The disciples flipped out, but Jesus said, "Be of good cheer! It is I; do not be afraid."

When you're trying to get somewhere and it seems like you're stuck in the middle of all sorts of problems and that nothing is going your way, you don't need to flip out and get terrified. Jesus is saying, "I'm right here with you, because I'm Jesus!"

He will always show us a way out of our storms. For Peter, it was to leap out of the security of the boat and walk on the water to go to Jesus. Even when Peter began to sink Jesus was right there to help him up. Someone once said, "I'd rather be a wet water-walker than a dry boat-sitter any day!" Good advice.

You or someone you know may be sitting in the boat in the middle of a storm. Jesus is telling us not to worry because He is there with us. He is right there with you now.

SEE FOR YOURSELF:
Deut. 31:6; Josh. 1:5;
Ps. 37:25, 28;
Heb. 13:5

Bethsaida, while He sent the multitude away. ⁴⁶And when He had sent them away, He departed to the mountain to pray. ⁴⁷Now when evening came, the boat was in the middle of the sea; and He *was* alone on the land. ⁴⁸Then He saw them straining at rowing, for the wind was against them. Now about the fourth watch of the night He came to them, walking on the sea, and would have passed them by. ⁴⁹And when they saw Him walking on the sea, they supposed it was a ghost, and cried out; ⁵⁰for they

6:33 *ᵃ*NU-Text and M-Text read *they.* **6:36** *ᵃ*NU-Text reads *something to eat* and omits the rest of this verse. **6:44** *ᵃ*NU-Text and M-Text omit *about.*

all saw Him and were troubled. But immediately He talked with them and said to them, "Be of good cheer! It is I; do not be afraid." [51]Then He went up into the boat to them, and the wind ceased. And they were greatly amazed in themselves beyond measure, and marveled. [52]For they had not understood about the loaves, because their heart was hardened.

MANY TOUCH HIM AND ARE MADE WELL

[53]When they had crossed over, they came to the land of Gennesaret and anchored there. [54]And when they came out of the boat, immediately the people recognized Him, [55]ran through that whole surrounding region, and began to carry about on beds those who were sick to wherever they heard He was. [56]Wherever He entered, into villages, cities, or the country, they laid the sick in the marketplaces, and begged Him that they might just touch the hem of His garment. And as many as touched Him were made well.

DEFILEMENT COMES FROM WITHIN

[1]Then the Pharisees and some of the scribes came together to Him, having come from Jerusalem. [2]Now when[a] they saw some of His disciples eat bread with defiled, that is, with unwashed hands, they found fault. [3]For the Pharisees and all the Jews do not eat unless they wash *their* hands in a special way, holding the tradition of the elders. [4]*When they come* from the marketplace, they do not eat unless they wash. And there are many other things which they have received and hold, *like* the washing of cups, pitchers, copper vessels, and couches. [5]Then the Pharisees and scribes asked Him, "Why do Your disciples not walk according to the tradition of the elders, but eat bread with unwashed hands?"

[6]He answered and said to them, "Well did Isaiah prophesy of you hypocrites, as it is written:

'This people honors Me with their lips,
But their heart is far from Me.
[7] And in vain they worship Me,
Teaching as doctrines the commandments
of men.'[a]

[8]For laying aside the commandment of God, you hold the tradition of men[a]—the washing of pitchers and cups, and many other such things you do."

[9]He said to them, "*All too* well you reject the commandment of God, that you may keep your tradition. [10]For Moses said, '*Honor your father and your mother*';[a] and, '*He who curses father or mother, let him be put to death.*'[b] [11]But you say, 'If a man says to his father or mother, "Whatever profit you might have received from me *is* Corban"—' (that is, a gift *to* God), [12]then you no longer let him do anything for his father or his mother, [13]making the word of God of no effect through your tradition which you have handed down. And many such things you do."

[14]When He had called all the multitude to *Himself*, He said to them, "Hear Me, everyone, and understand: [15]There is nothing that enters a man from outside which can defile him; but the things which come out of him, those are the things that defile a man. [16]If anyone has ears to hear, let him hear!"[a]

[17]When He had entered a house away from the crowd, His disciples asked Him concerning the parable. [18]So He said to them, "Are you thus without understanding also? Do you not perceive that whatever enters a man from outside cannot defile him, [19]because it does not enter his heart but his stomach, and is eliminated, *thus* purifying all foods?"[a] [20]And He said, "What comes out of a man, that defiles a man. [21]For from within, out of the heart of men, proceed evil thoughts, adulteries, fornications, murders, [22]thefts, covetousness, wickedness, deceit, lewdness, an evil eye, blasphemy, pride, foolishness. [23]All these evil things come from within and defile a man."

A GENTILE SHOWS HER FAITH

[24]From there He arose and went to the region of Tyre and Sidon.[a] And He entered a house and wanted no one to know *it*, but He could not be hidden. [25]For a woman whose young daughter had an unclean spirit heard about Him, and she came and fell at His feet. [26]The woman was a Greek, a Syro-Phoenician by birth, and she kept asking Him to cast the demon out of her daughter. [27]But Jesus said to her, "Let the children be filled first, for it is not good to take the children's bread and throw *it* to the little dogs."

[28]And she answered and said to Him, "Yes,

7:2 [a]NU-Text omits *when* and *they found fault*.   **7:7** [a]Isaiah 29:13   **7:8** [a]NU-Text omits the rest of this verse.
7:10 [a]Exodus 20:12; Deuteronomy 5:16 [b]Exodus 21:17   **7:16** [a]NU-Text omits this verse.   **7:19** [a]NU Text
ends quotation with *eliminated*, setting off the final clause as Mark's comment that Jesus has declared all
foods clean.   **7:24** [a]NU-Text omits *and Sidon*.

Lord, yet even the little dogs under the table eat from the children's crumbs."

²⁹Then He said to her, "For this saying go your way; the demon has gone out of your daughter."

³⁰And when she had come to her house, she found the demon gone out, and her daughter lying on the bed.

WHAT'S IT MEAN?

Were most of the dogs of Jesus' time wild scavengers that ate garbage and caused all kinds of problems for people? (Yes.) Did Jews of that era insult Gentiles by calling them "dogs"? (Yes.) Did Jesus brutally insult the Gentile woman who came to Him for help? (No.) In this verse, "dogs" refers to the household pets that would sit under the table at mealtime and eat any crumbs that fell.

Mark 7:27

JESUS HEALS A DEAF-MUTE

³¹Again, departing from the region of Tyre and Sidon, He came through the midst of the region of Decapolis to the Sea of Galilee. ³²Then they brought to Him one who was deaf and had an impediment in his speech, and they begged Him to put His hand on him. ³³And He took him aside from the multitude, and put His fingers in his ears, and He spat and touched his tongue. ³⁴Then, looking up to heaven, He sighed, and said to him, "Ephphatha," that is, "Be opened."

³⁵Immediately his ears were opened, and the impediment of his tongue was loosed, and he spoke plainly. ³⁶Then He commanded them that they should tell no one; but the more He commanded them, the more widely they proclaimed it. ³⁷And they were astonished beyond measure, saying, "He has done all things well. He makes both the deaf to hear and the mute to speak."

FEEDING THE FOUR THOUSAND

¹In those days, the multitude being very great and having nothing to eat, Jesus called His disciples to Him and said to them, ²"I have compassion on the multitude, because they have now continued with Me three days and have nothing to eat. ³And if I send them away hungry to their own houses, they will faint on the way; for some of them have come from afar."

⁴Then His disciples answered Him, "How can one satisfy these people with bread here in the wilderness?"

⁵He asked them, "How many loaves do you have?"

And they said, "Seven."

⁶So He commanded the multitude to sit down on the ground. And He took the seven loaves and gave thanks, broke *them* and gave *them* to His disciples to set before *them*; and they set *them* before the multitude. ⁷They also had a few small fish; and having blessed them, He said to set them also before *them*. ⁸So they ate and were filled, and they took up seven large baskets of leftover fragments. ⁹Now those who had eaten were about four thousand. And He sent them away, ¹⁰immediately got into the boat with His disciples, and came to the region of Dalmanutha.

THE PHARISEES SEEK A SIGN

¹¹Then the Pharisees came out and began to dispute with Him, seeking from Him a sign from heaven, testing Him. ¹²But He sighed deeply in His spirit, and said, "Why does this generation seek a sign? Assuredly, I say to you, no sign shall be given to this generation."

BEWARE OF THE LEAVEN OF THE PHARISEES AND HEROD

¹³And He left them, and getting into the boat again, departed to the other side. ¹⁴Now the disciples[a] had forgotten to take bread, and they did not have more than one loaf with them in the boat. ¹⁵Then He charged them, saying, "Take heed, beware of the leaven of the Pharisees and the leaven of Herod."

¹⁶And they reasoned among themselves, saying, "It is because we have no bread."

¹⁷But Jesus, being aware of *it*, said to them, "Why do you reason because you have no bread? Do you not yet perceive nor understand? Is your heart still[a] hardened? ¹⁸Having eyes, do you not see? And having ears, do you not hear? And do you not remember? ¹⁹When I broke the five loaves for the five thousand, how many baskets full of fragments did you take up?"

They said to Him, "Twelve."

²⁰"Also, when I broke the seven for the four thousand, how many large baskets full of fragments did you take up?"

And they said, "Seven."

²¹So He said to them, "How *is it* you do not understand?"

WHAT'S IT MEAN?

Have you ever seen yeast (leaven) in action? Just a tiny bit of yeast added to a loaf of bread will work wonders. As the yeast ferments, it makes the dough bubble and then rise. Before long, the entire loaf is affected. The fast-acting and wide-reaching effects of yeast may explain why the Bible uses it to symbolize sin or evil.

Mark 8:15

A BLIND MAN HEALED AT BETHSAIDA

²²Then He came to Bethsaida; and they brought a blind man to Him, and begged Him to touch him. ²³So He took the blind man by the hand and led him out of the town. And when He had spit on his eyes and put His hands on him, He asked him if he saw anything.

²⁴And he looked up and said, "I see men like trees, walking."

²⁵Then He put *His* hands on his eyes again and made him look up. And he was restored and saw everyone clearly. ²⁶Then He sent him away to his house, saying, "Neither go into the town, nor tell anyone in the town."ᵃ

PETER CONFESSES JESUS AS THE CHRIST

²⁷Now Jesus and His disciples went out to the towns of Caesarea Philippi; and on the road He asked His disciples, saying to them, "Who do men say that I am?"

²⁸So they answered, "John the Baptist; but some *say*, Elijah; and others, one of the prophets."

²⁹He said to them, "But who do you say that I am?"

Peter answered and said to Him, "You are the Christ."

³⁰Then He strictly warned them that they should tell no one about Him.

8:26 ᵃNU-Text reads *"Do not even go into the town."*

On the Edge

He said to them, "But who do you say that I am?"

Peter answered and said to Him, "You are the Christ" (Mark 8:29).

When Jesus was born, the Jews were living under the Roman government. They hated it. They had to pay ridiculously high taxes. They had no rights because they weren't Roman citizens.

Israel's prophets had said that a Messiah, God's Chosen One, would come to set the people free. Most of the Jews believed that the Messiah would appear in power and glory, maybe even raise a large army, and overthrow the Roman government that had Israel under its thumb. The Messiah would establish God's kingdom—an independent Jewish nation—on earth.

Jesus didn't exactly fit the bill. He came to set them free—from their sins, their sicknesses, and the oppression of their real enemy (Satan) rather than from the Romans. He never spoke against the Roman government and even suggested that God wanted them to pay taxes to Caesar.

But Peter recognized that Jesus was the Chosen One, even though he may not have understood (yet) that the kingdom Jesus had come to establish was not a political regime, but a kingdom of the heart and of the spirit.

Jesus is the Messiah. Let Him be the ruler of your heart right now—not just in the easy places, but also in the places that may be hard for you to submit to Him. Let Him be the King of your whole life.

SEE FOR YOURSELF:
John 1:41; 6:69; 11:27

JESUS PREDICTS HIS DEATH AND RESURRECTION

³¹And He began to teach them that the Son of Man must suffer many things, and be rejected by the elders and chief priests and scribes, and be killed, and after three days rise again. ³²He spoke this word openly. Then Peter took Him aside and began to rebuke Him. ³³But when He had turned around and looked at His disciples, He rebuked Peter, saying, "Get behind Me, Satan! For you are not mindful of the things of God, but the things of men."

own soul? [37]Or what will a man give in exchange for his soul? [38]For whoever is ashamed of Me and My words in this adulterous and sinful generation, of him the Son of Man also will be ashamed when He comes in the glory of His Father with the holy angels."

JESUS TRANSFIGURED ON THE MOUNT

[1]And He said to them, "Assuredly, I say to you that there are some standing here who will not taste death till they see the kingdom of God present with power."

[2]Now after six days Jesus took Peter, James, and John, and led them up on a high mountain apart by themselves; and He was transfigured before them. [3]His clothes became shining, exceedingly white, like snow, such as no launderer on earth can whiten them. [4]And Elijah appeared to them with Moses, and they were talking with Jesus. [5]Then Peter answered and said to Jesus, "Rabbi, it is good for us to be here; and let us make three tabernacles: one for You, one for Moses, and one for Elijah"—[6]because he did not know what to say, for they were greatly afraid.

[7]And a cloud came and overshadowed them; and a voice came out of the cloud, saying, "This is My beloved Son. Hear Him!" [8]Suddenly, when they had looked around, they saw no one anymore, but only Jesus with themselves.

[9]Now as they came down from the mountain, He commanded them that they should tell no one the things they had seen, till the Son of Man had risen from the dead. [10]So they kept this word to themselves, questioning what the rising from the dead meant.

[11]And they asked Him, saying, "Why do the scribes say that Elijah must come first?"

[12]Then He answered and told them, "Indeed, Elijah is coming first and restores all things. And how is it written concerning the Son of Man, that He must suffer many things and be treated with contempt? [13]But I say to you that Elijah has also come, and they did to him whatever they wished, as it is written of him."

A BOY IS HEALED

[14]And when He came to the disciples, He saw a great multitude around them, and scribes disputing with them. [15]Immediately, when they saw Him, all the people were greatly amazed, and running to *Him*, greeted Him. [16]And He asked the scribes, "What are you discussing with them?"

[17]Then one of the crowd answered and said, "Teacher, I brought You my son, who has a mute spirit. [18]And wherever it seizes him, it

TAKE UP THE CROSS AND FOLLOW HIM

[34]When He had called the people to *Himself*, with His disciples also, He said to them, "Whoever desires to come after Me, let him deny himself, and take up his cross, and follow Me. [35]For whoever desires to save his life will lose it, but whoever loses his life for My sake and the gospel's will save it. [36]For what will it profit a man if he gains the whole world, and loses his

throws him down; he foams at the mouth, gnashes his teeth, and becomes rigid. So I spoke to Your disciples, that they should cast it out, but they could not."

¹⁹He answered him and said, "O faithless generation, how long shall I be with you? How long shall I bear with you? Bring him to Me." ²⁰Then they brought him to Him. And when he saw Him, immediately the spirit convulsed him, and he fell on the ground and wallowed, foaming at the mouth.

²¹So He asked his father, "How long has this been happening to him?"

And he said, "From childhood. ²²And often he has thrown him both into the fire and into the water to destroy him. But if You can do anything, have compassion on us and help us."

²³Jesus said to him, "If you can believe,ᵃ all things *are* possible to him who believes."

²⁴Immediately the father of the child cried out and said with tears, "Lord, I believe; help my unbelief!"

> "If anyone desires to be first, he shall be last of all and servant of all."
> (Mark 9:35b)

W H A T ' S I T M E A N ?

Galilee, a Mediterranean coastal region, was the center of Jesus' ministry of teaching and miracles on earth. Jesus' hometown of Nazareth was located in Galilee. All of the disciples except Judas Iscariot came from the area.
Mark 9:30

²⁵When Jesus saw that the people came running together, He rebuked the unclean spirit, saying to it, "Deaf and dumb spirit, I command you, come out of him and enter him no more!" ²⁶Then *the spirit* cried out, convulsed him greatly, and came out of him. And he became as one dead, so that many said, "He is dead." ²⁷But Jesus took him by the hand and lifted him up, and he arose.

²⁸And when He had come into the house, His disciples asked Him privately, "Why could we not cast it out?"

²⁹So He said to them, "This kind can come out by nothing but prayer and fasting."ᵃ

JESUS AGAIN PREDICTS HIS DEATH AND RESURRECTION

³⁰Then they departed from there and passed through Galilee, and He did not want anyone to know *it*. ³¹For He taught His disciples and said to them, "The Son of Man is being betrayed into the hands of men, and they will kill Him. And after He is killed, He will rise the third day." ³²But they did not understand this saying, and were afraid to ask Him.

WHO IS THE GREATEST?

³³Then He came to Capernaum. And when He was in the house He asked them, "What was it you disputed among yourselves on the road?" ³⁴But they kept silent, for on the road they had disputed among themselves who *would be the* greatest. ³⁵And He sat down, called the twelve, and said to them, "If anyone desires to be first, he shall be last of all and servant of all." ³⁶Then He took a little child and set him in the midst of them. And when He had taken him in His arms, He said to them, ³⁷"Whoever receives one of these little children in My name receives Me; and whoever receives Me, receives not Me but Him who sent Me."

JESUS FORBIDS SECTARIANISM

³⁸Now John answered Him, saying, "Teacher, we saw someone who does not follow us casting out demons in Your name, and we forbade him because he does not follow us."

³⁹But Jesus said, "Do not forbid him, for no one who works a miracle in My name can soon afterward speak evil of Me. ⁴⁰For he who is not against us is on ourᵃ side. ⁴¹For whoever gives you a cup of water to drink in My name, because you belong to Christ, assuredly, I say to you, he will by no means lose his reward.

GIVING
What is the result of giving to others? (9:41)

JESUS WARNS OF OFFENSES

⁴²"But whoever causes one of these little ones who believe in Me to stumble, it would be better for him if a millstone were hung around

---

9:23 ᵃNU-Text reads " 'If You can!' All things. . . .' **9:29** ᵃNU-Text omits *and fasting.* **9:40** ᵃM-Text reads *against you is on your side.*

his neck, and he were thrown into the sea. ⁴³If your hand causes you to sin, cut it off. It is better for you to enter into life maimed, rather than having two hands, to go to hell, into the fire that shall never be quenched— ⁴⁴where

> 'Their worm does not die
> And the fire is not quenched.'ᵃ

⁴⁵And if your foot causes you to sin, cut it off. It is better for you to enter life lame, rather than having two feet, to be cast into hell, into the fire that shall never be quenched— ⁴⁶where

> 'Their worm does not die
> And the fire is not quenched.'ᵃ

⁴⁷And if your eye causes you to sin, pluck it out. It is better for you to enter the kingdom of God with one eye, rather than having two eyes, to be cast into hell fire— ⁴⁸where

> 'Their worm does not die
> And the fire is not quenched.'ᵃ

TASTELESS SALT IS WORTHLESS

⁴⁹"For everyone will be seasoned with fire,ᵃ and every sacrifice will be seasoned with salt. ⁵⁰Salt *is* good, but if the salt loses its flavor, how will you season it? Have salt in yourselves, and have peace with one another."

WHAT'S IT MEAN?

Salt wasn't just used for flavoring in Jesus' day. It was also used in sacrifices and as a preservative. Most salt in Galilee came from the Dead Sea, which is nine times saltier than ocean water. It wasn't like the salt we use today, though. Because it contained many impurities, salt in New Testament times became stale pretty quickly.

Mark 9:49, 50

MARRIAGE AND DIVORCE

¹Then He arose from there and came to the region of Judea by the other side of the Jordan. And multitudes gathered to Him again, and as He was accustomed, He taught them again.

²The Pharisees came and asked Him, "Is it lawful for a man to divorce *his* wife?" testing Him.

³And He answered and said to them, "What did Moses command you?"

⁴They said, "Moses permitted *a man* to write a certificate of divorce, and to dismiss *her.*"

⁵And Jesus answered and said to them, "Because of the hardness of your heart he wrote you this precept. ⁶But from the beginning of the creation, God *'made them male and female.'ᵃ* ⁷*For this reason a man shall leave his father and mother and be joined to his wife,* ⁸*and the two shall become one flesh';ᵃ* so then they are no longer two, but one flesh. ⁹Therefore what God has joined together, let not man separate."

¹⁰In the house His disciples also asked Him again about the same *matter.* ¹¹So He said to them, "Whoever divorces his wife and marries another commits adultery against her. ¹²And if a woman divorces her husband and marries another, she commits adultery."

JESUS BLESSES LITTLE CHILDREN

¹³Then they brought little children to Him, that He might touch them; but the disciples rebuked those who brought *them.* ¹⁴But when Jesus saw *it,* He was greatly displeased and said to them, "Let the little children come to Me, and do not forbid them; for of such is the kingdom of God. ¹⁵Assuredly, I say to you, whoever does not receive the kingdom of God as a little child will by no means enter it." ¹⁶And He took them up in His arms, laid *His* hands on them, and blessed them.

JESUS COUNSELS THE RICH YOUNG RULER

¹⁷Now as He was going out on the road, one came running, knelt before Him, and asked Him, "Good Teacher, what shall I do that I may inherit eternal life?"

¹⁸So Jesus said to him, "Why do you call Me good? No one *is* good but One, *that is,* God. ¹⁹You know the commandments: *'Do not commit adultery,' 'Do not murder,' 'Do not steal,' 'Do not bear false witness,' 'Do not defraud,' 'Honor your father and your mother.' "ᵃ

9:44 ᵃNU-Text omits this verse. **9:46** ᵃNU-Text omits the last clause of verse 45 and all of verse 46.
9:48 ᵃIsaiah 66:24 **9:49** ᵃNU-Text omits the rest of this verse. **10:6** ᵃGenesis 1:27; 5:2 **10:8** ᵃGenesis 2:24
10:19 ᵃExodus 20:12–16; Deuteronomy 5:16–20

²⁰And he answered and said to Him, "Teacher, all these things I have kept from my youth."

²¹Then Jesus, looking at him, loved him, and said to him, "One thing you lack: Go your way, sell whatever you have and give to the poor, and you will have treasure in heaven; and come, take up the cross, and follow Me."

MONEY

What can money do to our relationship with God? (10:17–24)

²²But he was sad at this word, and went away sorrowful, for he had great possessions.

WITH GOD ALL THINGS ARE POSSIBLE

²³Then Jesus looked around and said to His disciples, "How hard it is for those who have riches to enter the kingdom of God!" ²⁴And the disciples were astonished at His words. But Jesus answered again and said to them, "Children, how hard it is for those who trust in riches^a to enter the kingdom of God! ²⁵It is easier for a camel to go through the eye of a needle than for a rich man to enter the kingdom of God."

²⁶And they were greatly astonished, saying among themselves, "Who then can be saved?"

²⁷But Jesus looked at them and said, "With men *it is* impossible, but not with God; for with God all things are possible."

²⁸Then Peter began to say to Him, "See, we have left all and followed You."

²⁹So Jesus answered and said, "Assuredly, I say to you, there is no one who has left house or brothers or sisters or father or mother or wife^a or children or lands, for My sake and the gospel's, ³⁰who shall not receive a hundredfold now in this time—houses and brothers and sisters and mothers and children and lands, with persecutions—and in the age to come, eternal life. ³¹But many *who are* first will be last, and the last first."

JESUS A THIRD TIME PREDICTS HIS DEATH AND RESURRECTION

³²Now they were on the road, going up to Jerusalem, and Jesus was going before them; and they were amazed. And as they followed they were afraid. Then He took the twelve aside again and began to tell them the things that would happen to Him: ³³"Behold, we are going up to Jerusalem, and the Son of Man will be betrayed to the chief priests and to the scribes; and they will condemn Him to death and deliver Him to the Gentiles; ³⁴and they will mock Him,

On the Edge

Jesus looked at them and said, "With men it is impossible, but not with God; for with God all things are possible" (Mark 10:27).

Wow! What a promise! *God can do anything!* This Scripture should kick the limits right out of your dreams! There are plenty of things that you cannot do on your own, but with Christ *all* things are possible. Too many times we let our circumstances swallow us. We wear out, give up, and throw in the towel. We need to grab hold of this verse and realize that Jesus is the One who can do anything! You might need healing, money, help on a big test, a job, insight on how to witness to a stubborn, unsaved friend, or just a spot on the basketball team. It doesn't matter what your need is. With Christ, all things are possible. In fact, we have a promise that says that the same Spirit which raised Christ from the dead lives in you! Now that's power!

The Bible teaches us not to give up when things get tough. Hold on to God. There's a story in Mark 10:46–52 about a blind man named Bartimaeus. Bartimaeus needed a miracle, and he heard that Jesus was passing by. He began to cry out to Jesus, and the crowd told him to shut up. So he cried out even louder. Jesus stopped, turned around, and asked the man nine words that changed Bartimaeus's life forever: "What do you want Me to do for you?" You know what? Bartimaeus got his miracle.

So the next time people are telling you that such-and-such will never happen, just smile with steadfast confidence in God's Word, knowing that, with Him, nothing is impossible!

SEE FOR YOURSELF:
Matt. 17:20;
Mark 10:46–52;
Luke 1:37

and scourge Him, and spit on Him, and kill Him. And the third day He will rise again."

GREATNESS IS SERVING

³⁵Then James and John, the sons of Zebedee, came to Him, saying, "Teacher, we want You to do for us whatever we ask."

10:24 ^aNU-Text omits *for those who trust in riches.*   **10:29** ^aNU-Text omits *or wife.*

³⁶And He said to them, "What do you want Me to do for you?"

³⁷They said to Him, "Grant us that we may sit, one on Your right hand and the other on Your left, in Your glory."

³⁸But Jesus said to them, "You do not know what you ask. Are you able to drink the cup that I drink, and be baptized with the baptism that I am baptized with?"

³⁹They said to Him, "We are able."

So Jesus said to them, "You will indeed drink the cup that I drink, and with the baptism I am baptized with you will be baptized; ⁴⁰but to sit on My right hand and on My left is not Mine to give, but *it is for those* for whom it is prepared."

⁴¹And when the ten heard *it*, they began to be greatly displeased with James and John. ⁴²But Jesus called them to *Himself* and said to them, "You know that those who are considered rulers over the Gentiles lord it over them, and their great ones exercise authority over them. ⁴³Yet it shall not be so among you; but whoever desires to become great among you shall be your servant. ⁴⁴And whoever of you desires to be first shall be slave of all. ⁴⁵For even the Son of Man did not come to be served, but to serve, and to give His life a ransom for many."

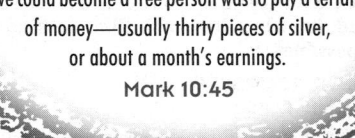

The secret to Rome's success was slave labor. It's been estimated that one out of every five people in the Roman Empire was a slave. Slaves in New Testament times had very few rights. Some were treated worse than animals. The only way a slave could become a free person was to pay a certain amount of money—usually thirty pieces of silver, or about a month's earnings.

Mark 10:45

JESUS HEALS BLIND BARTIMAEUS

⁴⁶Now they came to Jericho. As He went out of Jericho with His disciples and a great multitude, blind Bartimaeus, the son of Timaeus, sat by the road begging. ⁴⁷And when he heard that it was Jesus of Nazareth, he began to cry out and say, "Jesus, Son of David, have mercy on me!"

⁴⁸Then many warned him to be quiet; but he cried out all the more, "Son of David, have mercy on me!"

⁴⁹So Jesus stood still and commanded him to be called.

Then they called the blind man, saying to him, "Be of good cheer. Rise, He is calling you."

⁵⁰And throwing aside his garment, he rose and came to Jesus.

⁵¹So Jesus answered and said to him, "What do you want Me to do for you?"

The blind man said to Him, "Rabboni, that I may receive my sight."

⁵²Then Jesus said to him, "Go your way; your faith has made you well." And immediately he received his sight and followed Jesus on the road.

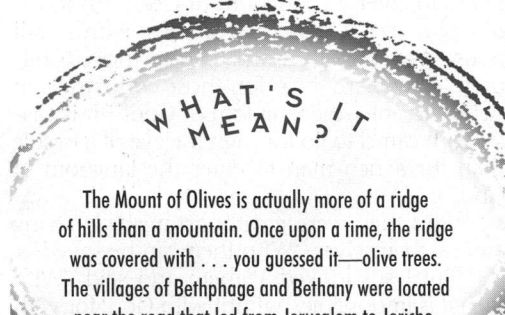

The Mount of Olives is actually more of a ridge of hills than a mountain. Once upon a time, the ridge was covered with . . . you guessed it—olive trees. The villages of Bethphage and Bethany were located near the road that led from Jerusalem to Jericho.

Mark 11:1

THE TRIUMPHAL ENTRY

¹Now when they drew near Jerusalem, to Bethphage*ᵃ* and Bethany, at the Mount of Olives, He sent two of His disciples; ²and He said to them, "Go into the village opposite you; and as soon as you have entered it you will find a colt tied, on which no one has sat. Loose it and bring *it*. ³And if anyone says to you, 'Why are you doing this?' say, 'The Lord has need of it,' and immediately he will send it here."

⁴So they went their way, and found the*ᵃ* colt tied by the door outside on the street, and they loosed it. ⁵But some of those who stood there said to them, "What are you doing, loosing the colt?"

⁶And they spoke to them just as Jesus had commanded. So they let them go. ⁷Then they brought the colt to Jesus and threw their clothes on it, and He sat on it. ⁸And many spread their clothes on the road, and others cut down leafy

11:1 *ᵃ*M-Text reads *Bethsphage*.　**11:4** *ᵃ*NU-Text and M-Text read *a*.

branches from the trees and spread *them* on the road. ⁹Then those who went before and those who followed cried out, saying:

> "Hosanna!
> *'Blessed is He who comes in the name of the* LORD*!'*ᵃ

¹⁰   Blessed *is* the kingdom of our father David
> That comes in the name of the Lord!ᵃ
> Hosanna in the highest!"

¹¹And Jesus went into Jerusalem and into the temple. So when He had looked around at all things, as the hour was already late, He went out to Bethany with the twelve.

THE FIG TREE WITHERED

¹²Now the next day, when they had come out from Bethany, He was hungry. ¹³And seeing from afar a fig tree having leaves, He went to see if perhaps He would find something on it. When He came to it, He found nothing but leaves, for it was not the season for figs. ¹⁴In response Jesus said to it, "Let no one eat fruit from you ever again."

And His disciples heard *it.*

JESUS CLEANSES THE TEMPLE

¹⁵So they came to Jerusalem. Then Jesus went into the temple and began to drive out those who bought and sold in the temple, and overturned the tables of the money changers and the seats of those who sold doves. ¹⁶And He would not allow anyone to carry wares through the temple. ¹⁷Then He taught, saying to them, "Is it not written, *'My house shall be called a house of prayer for all nations'?*ᵃ But you have made it a *'den of thieves.' "*ᵇ

¹⁸And the scribes and chief priests heard it and sought how they might destroy Him; for they feared Him, because all the people were astonished at His teaching. ¹⁹When evening had come, He went out of the city.

THE LESSON OF THE WITHERED FIG TREE

²⁰Now in the morning, as they passed by, they saw the fig tree dried up from the roots. ²¹And Peter, remembering, said to Him, "Rabbi, look! The fig tree which You cursed has withered away."

²²So Jesus answered and said to them, "Have faith in God. ²³For assuredly, I say to you, whoever says to this mountain, 'Be removed and be cast into the sea,' and does not doubt in his heart, but believes that those things he says will be done, he will have whatever he says. ²⁴Therefore I say to you, whatever things you ask when you pray, believe that you receive *them,* and you will have *them.*

FORGIVENESS AND PRAYER

²⁵"And whenever you stand praying, if you have anything against anyone, forgive him, that your Father in heaven may also forgive you your trespasses. ²⁶But if you do not forgive, neither will your Father in heaven forgive your trespasses."ᵃ

JESUS' AUTHORITY QUESTIONED

²⁷Then they came again to Jerusalem. And as He was walking in the temple, the chief priests, the scribes, and the elders came to Him. ²⁸And they said to Him, "By what authority are You doing these things? And who gave You this authority to do these things?"

²⁹But Jesus answered and said to them, "I also will ask you one question; then answer Me, and I will tell you by what authority I do these things: ³⁰The baptism of John—was it from heaven or from men? Answer Me."

³¹And they reasoned among themselves, saying, "If we say, 'From heaven,' He will say, 'Why then did you not believe him?' ³²But if we say, 'From men' "—they feared the people, for all counted John to have been a prophet indeed. ³³So they answered and said to Jesus, "We do not know."

WHAT'S IT MEAN?

Coins with pagan symbols on them could not be used in the temple. They had to be exchanged for acceptable coins. Likewise, only certain animals could be offered as sacrifices. Local businessmen saw dollar signs in these restrictions. They set up tables in the temple courtyard and sold approved coins and animals at marked-up prices. You won't believe who else benefited from this price gouging—the family of the high priest, who controlled the temple business.

Mark 11:15

11:9 ᵃPsalm 118:26   **11:10** ᵃNU-Text omits *in the name of the Lord.*   **11:17** ᵃIsaiah 56:7 ᵇJeremiah 7:11
11:26 ᵃNU-Text omits this verse.

And Jesus answered and said to them, "Neither will I tell you by what authority I do these things."

On the Edge

Whenever you stand praying, if you have anything against anyone, forgive him, that your Father in heaven may also forgive you your trespasses. But if you do not forgive, neither will your Father in heaven forgive your trespasses (Mark 11:25, 26).

Jesus makes it pretty clear that Christians are to never quit forgiving. But why? Mark says that we've got to forgive other people if we want God to forgive us. Like it or not, it's the truth. If you forgive others of their wrongs, your Father will forgive you. If not, then your sins will not be forgiven. As in many other places in the Bible, God is calling us to be like Him. He is a forgiving God who wants to restore relationships. He wants you to be forgiving, too. A heart that's willing to forgive is exactly like the heart of God. No matter what our sin, His forgiveness comes freely and wipes out whatever we've done. That doesn't mean you may not have to endure the consequences; it just means that God doesn't hold your sin against you. God knows, too, that unforgiveness will eat you up on the inside. It can paralyze you emotionally. Forgiving sets you free. So when a friend comes to apologize for hurting you—quickly forgive her and welcome her back into your life. God always does the same for you.

SEE FOR YOURSELF:
Matt. 6:14, 15; 18:21, 22;
Luke 6:37; 2 Cor. 2:7

THE PARABLE OF THE WICKED VINEDRESSERS

¹Then He began to speak to them in parables: "A man planted a vineyard and set a hedge around *it*, dug *a place for* the wine vat and built a tower. And he leased it to vinedressers and went into a far country. ²Now at vintage-time he sent a servant to the vinedressers, that he might receive some of the fruit of the vineyard from the vinedressers. ³And they took *him* and beat him and sent *him* away empty-handed.

⁴Again he sent them another servant, and at him they threw stones,ᵃ wounded *him* in the head, and sent *him* away shamefully treated. ⁵And again he sent another, and him they killed; and many others, beating some and killing some. ⁶Therefore still having one son, his beloved, he also sent him to them last, saying, 'They will respect my son.' ⁷But those vinedressers said among themselves, 'This is the heir. Come, let us kill him, and the inheritance will be ours.' ⁸So they took him and killed *him* and cast *him* out of the vineyard.

⁹"Therefore what will the owner of the vineyard do? He will come and destroy the vinedressers, and give the vineyard to others. ¹⁰Have you not even read this Scripture:

'The stone which the builders rejected
Has become the chief cornerstone.
¹¹ This was the LORD's doing,
And it is marvelous in our eyes'? "ᵃ

¹²And they sought to lay hands on Him, but feared the multitude, for they knew He had spoken the parable against them. So they left Him and went away.

THE PHARISEES: IS IT LAWFUL TO PAY TAXES TO CAESAR?

¹³Then they sent to Him some of the Pharisees and the Herodians, to catch Him in *His* words. ¹⁴When they had come, they said to Him, "Teacher, we know that You are true, and care about no one; for You do not regard the person of men, but teach the way of God in truth. Is it lawful to pay taxes to Caesar, or not? ¹⁵Shall we pay, or shall we not pay?"

But He, knowing their hypocrisy, said to them, "Why do you test Me? Bring Me a denarius that I may see *it*." ¹⁶So they brought *it*.

And He said to them, "Whose image and inscription *is* this?" They said to Him, "Caesar's."

¹⁷And Jesus answered and said to them, "Render to Caesar the things that are Caesar's, and to God the things that are God's."

And they marveled at Him.

THE SADDUCEES: WHAT ABOUT THE RESURRECTION?

¹⁸Then *some* Sadducees, who say there is no resurrection, came to Him; and they asked Him, saying: ¹⁹"Teacher, Moses wrote to us that if a man's brother dies, and leaves *his* wife behind, and leaves no children, his brother should take his wife and raise up offspring for his brother.

12:4 ᵃNU-Text omits *and at him they threw stones.*   **12:11** ᵃPsalm 118:22, 23

[20]Now there were seven brothers. The first took a wife; and dying, he left no offspring. [21]And the second took her, and he died; nor did he leave any offspring. And the third likewise. [22]So the seven had her and left no offspring. Last of all the woman died also. [23]Therefore, in the resurrection, when they rise, whose wife will she be? For all seven had her as wife."

[24]Jesus answered and said to them, "Are you not therefore mistaken, because you do not know the Scriptures nor the power of God? [25]For when they rise from the dead, they neither marry nor are given in marriage, but are like angels in heaven. [26]But concerning the dead, that they rise, have you not read in the book of Moses, in the *burning* bush *passage*, how God spoke to him, saying, '*I am the God of Abraham, the God of Isaac, and the God of Jacob*'?[a] [27]He is not the God of the dead, but the God of the living. You are therefore greatly mistaken."

" 'And you shall love the LORD your God with all your heart, with all your soul, with all your mind, and with all your strength.' This is the first commandment."
(Mark 12:30)

our God, the LORD is one. [30]And you shall love the LORD your God with all your heart, with all your soul, with all your mind, and with all your strength.'[a] This *is* the first commandment.[b] [31]And the second, like *it, is* this: '*You shall love your neighbor as yourself.*'[a] There is no other commandment greater than these."

[32]So the scribe said to Him, "Well *said,* Teacher. You have spoken the truth, for there is one God, and there is no other but He. [33]And to love Him with all the heart, with all the understanding, with all the soul,[a] and with all the strength, and to love one's neighbor as oneself, is more than all the whole burnt offerings and sacrifices."

[34]Now when Jesus saw that he answered wisely, He said to him, "You are not far from the kingdom of God."

But after that no one dared question Him.

LOVE

What is the most important command that God has given us?
(12:29, 30)

JESUS: HOW CAN DAVID CALL HIS DESCENDANT LORD?

[35]Then Jesus answered and said, while He taught in the temple, "How *is it* that the scribes say that the Christ is the Son of David? [36]For David himself said by the Holy Spirit:

'The LORD said to my Lord,
"Sit at My right hand,
Till I make Your enemies Your
footstool." '[a]

[37]Therefore David himself calls Him '*LORD*'; how is He *then* his Son?"

And the common people heard Him gladly.

WHAT'S IT MEAN?

If Jesus' words seem familiar, it's because they come from the Old Testament Book of Deuteronomy. Jesus was quoting what's known as the Shema, which was a summary (of sorts) of the main points of the Jewish faith. The Shema is still used today to call Jewish people to worship.
Mark 12:29, 30

BEWARE OF THE SCRIBES

[38]Then He said to them in His teaching, "Beware of the scribes, who desire to go around in long robes, *love* greetings in the marketplaces, [39]the best seats in the synagogues, and the best places at feasts, [40]who devour widows' houses, and for a pretense make long prayers. These will receive greater condemnation."

THE SCRIBES: WHICH IS THE FIRST COMMANDMENT OF ALL?

[28]Then one of the scribes came, and having heard them reasoning together, perceiving[a] that He had answered them well, asked Him, "Which is the first commandment of all?"

[29]Jesus answered him, "The first of all the commandments *is:* 'Hear, O Israel, the LORD

12:26 [a]Exodus 3:6, 15   **12:28** [a]NU-Text reads *seeing.*   **12:30** [a]Deuteronomy 6:4, 5   [b]NU-Text omits this sentence.   **12:31** [a]Leviticus 19:18   **12:33** [a]NU-Text omits *with all the soul.*   **12:36** [a]Psalm 110:1

THE WIDOW'S TWO MITES

41Now Jesus sat opposite the treasury and saw how the people put money into the treasury. And many *who were* rich put in much. 42Then one poor widow came and threw in two mites,ª which make a quadrans. 43So He called His disciples to *Himself* and said to them, "Assuredly, I say to you that this poor widow has put in more than all those who have given to the treasury; 44for they all put in out of their abundance, but she out of her poverty put in all that she had, her whole livelihood."

JESUS PREDICTS THE DESTRUCTION OF THE TEMPLE

1Then as He went out of the temple, one of His disciples said to Him, "Teacher, see what manner of stones and what buildings *are here!*"

2And Jesus answered and said to him, "Do you see these great buildings? Not *one* stone shall be left upon another, that shall not be thrown down."

THE SIGNS OF THE TIMES AND THE END OF THE AGE

3Now as He sat on the Mount of Olives opposite the temple, Peter, James, John, and Andrew asked Him privately, 4"Tell us, when will these things be? And what *will be* the sign when all these things will be fulfilled?"

WHAT'S IT MEAN?

It's no wonder the disciple was in awe of the temple. The building itself was a work of art, constructed over a thirty-year period on the orders of Herod the Great. The front columns stood forty feet high. Some of the marble stones used for the walls of the building were almost forty feet long! (Can you imagine how much they must have weighed?)

Mark 13:1

5And Jesus, answering them, began to say: "Take heed that no one deceives you. 6For many will come in My name, saying, 'I am *He*', and will deceive many. 7But when you hear of wars and rumors of wars, do not be troubled; for *such things* must happen, but the end *is* not yet. 8For nation will rise against nation, and kingdom against kingdom. And there will be earthquakes in various places, and there will be famines and troubles.ª These *are* the beginnings of sorrows.

12:42 ªGreek *lepta*, very small copper coins worth a fraction of a penny   **13:8** ªNU-Text omits *and troubles*.

Promise

HE PROMISES THAT THE GOOD NEWS WILL BE PREACHED TO ALL NATIONS.

And the gospel must first be preached to all the nations. (Mark 13:10).

One of these days, the world as you know it won't even exist. One glorious day, everyone on earth will hear the explosive blast of a trumpet and that will be the end. Whoa! Can you imagine what it's going to be like when Jesus Christ comes back to earth and sets up His kingdom?

There won't be any more violence on the streets. There won't be any more cancer to kill the people you love. Even the deepest, most private pain in your own heart will be gone. The devil won't be able to torment you and cause devastation anywhere, because he'll be burning in a lake of fire.

But some things have to happen before Jesus returns to rule with perfect peace and justice. He says that "the gospel must first be preached to all the nations." Now that's something you can help with! You can go on a mission trip while you're a teen. That's the best time to go! Start to pray about it now. Ask God where He wants to send you and how you are to get the money to go. One of the conditions for Jesus' return is for the good news to be preached in all nations. You can go and do it!

SEE FOR YOURSELF:

Matt. 24:30, 31; Rev. 22:20

⁹"But watch out for yourselves, for they will deliver you up to councils, and you will be beaten in the synagogues. You will be brought[a] before rulers and kings for My sake, for a testimony to them. ¹⁰And the gospel must first be preached to all the nations. ¹¹But when they arrest *you* and deliver you up, do not worry beforehand, or premeditate[a] what you will speak. But whatever is given you in that hour, speak that; for it is not you who speak, but the Holy Spirit. ¹²Now brother will betray brother to death, and a father *his* child; and children will rise up against parents and cause them to be put to death. ¹³And you will be hated by all for My name's sake. But he who endures to the end shall be saved.

THE GREAT TRIBULATION

¹⁴"So when you see the *'abomination of desolation,'*[a] spoken of by Daniel the prophet,[b] standing where it ought not" (let the reader understand), "then let those who are in Judea flee to the mountains. ¹⁵Let him who is on the housetop not go down into the house, nor enter to take anything out of his house. ¹⁶And let him who is in the field not go back to get his clothes. ¹⁷But woe to those who are pregnant and to those who are nursing babies in those days! ¹⁸And pray that your flight may not be in winter. ¹⁹For *in* those days there will be tribulation, such as has not been since the beginning of the creation which God created until this time, nor ever shall be. ²⁰And unless the Lord had shortened those days, no flesh would be saved; but for the elect's sake, whom He chose, He shortened the days.

²¹"Then if anyone says to you, 'Look, here *is* the Christ!' or, 'Look, *He is* there!' do not believe it. ²²For false christs and false prophets will rise and show signs and wonders to deceive, if possible, even the elect. ²³But take heed, see, I have told you all things beforehand.

THE COMING OF THE SON OF MAN

²⁴"But in those days, after that tribulation, the sun will be darkened, and the moon will not give its light; ²⁵the stars of heaven will fall, and the powers in the heavens will be shaken. ²⁶Then they will see the Son of Man coming in the clouds with great power and glory. ²⁷And then He will send His angels, and gather together His elect from the four winds, from the farthest part of earth to the farthest part of heaven.

13:9 [a]NU-Text and M-Text read *will stand.*   **13:11** [a]NU-Text omits *or premeditate.*   **13:14** [a]Daniel 11:31; 12:11   [b]NU-Text omits *spoken of by Daniel the prophet.*

Promise   HE PROMISES HIS WORDS WILL LAST FOREVER.

Heaven and earth will pass away, but My words will by no means pass away (Mark 13:31).

The earth and the sky look like the strongest, most permanent things around. In fact, if there's one thing that most people will bet on, it's that—cloudy or clear—the sun will come out tomorrow. It's a lot easier to bank on the things you can see rather than on the things you can't see.

But Jesus looked at the huge blue sky above Him and the solid, dusty earth under His feet and told His disciples that the things He was saying would outlast the earth and sky. He wanted them to know that even though it might not look like it, it would be better for them to invest in things they couldn't see—the kingdom of God that He was telling them about—rather than in things they could see.

It will be tempting for you to spend your time and your energy going after things that you can see—an education, a good job, a nice place to live, neat stuff to make your life comfortable, a family of your own eventually. There's certainly nothing wrong with those things. But Jesus is encouraging you, even warning you, to give the best and the most of your time and energy to the things that will last forever—His Word, His kingdom, and your relationship with Him.

SEE FOR YOURSELF:
Is. 40:8

THE PARABLE OF THE FIG TREE

28"Now learn this parable from the fig tree: When its branch has already become tender, and puts forth leaves, you know that summer is near. 29So you also, when you see these things happening, know that it[a] is near—at the doors! 30Assuredly, I say to you, this generation will by no means pass away till all these things take place. 31Heaven and earth will pass away, but My words will by no means pass away.

NO ONE KNOWS THE DAY OR HOUR

32"But of that day and hour no one knows, not even the angels in heaven, nor the Son, but only the Father. 33Take heed, watch and pray; for you do not know when the time is. 34It is like a man going to a far country, who left his house and gave authority to his servants, and to each his work, and commanded the door-keeper to watch. 35Watch therefore, for you do not know when the master of the house is coming—in the evening, at midnight, at the crowing of the rooster, or in the morning— 36lest, coming suddenly, he find you sleeping. 37And what I say to you, I say to all: Watch!"

THE PLOT TO KILL JESUS

1After two days it was the Passover and the Feast of Unleavened Bread. And the chief priests and the scribes sought how they might take Him by trickery and put Him to death. 2But they said, "Not during the feast, lest there be an uproar of the people."

THE ANOINTING AT BETHANY

3And being in Bethany at the house of Simon the leper, as He sat at the table, a woman came having an alabaster flask of very costly oil of spikenard. Then she broke the flask and poured it on His head. 4But there were some who were indignant among themselves, and said, "Why was this fragrant oil wasted? 5For it might have been sold for more than three hundred denarii and given to the poor." And they criticized her sharply.

6But Jesus said, "Let her alone. Why do you trouble her? She has done a good work for Me. 7For you have the poor with you always, and whenever you wish you may do them good; but Me you do not have always. 8She has done what she could. She has come beforehand to anoint My body for burial. 9Assuredly, I say to you, wherever this gospel is preached in the whole world, what this woman has done will also be told as a memorial to her."

JUDAS AGREES TO BETRAY JESUS

10Then Judas Iscariot, one of the twelve, went to the chief priests to betray Him to them. 11And when they heard it, they were glad, and promised to give him money. So he sought how he might conveniently betray Him.

JESUS CELEBRATES THE PASSOVER WITH HIS DISCIPLES

12Now on the first day of Unleavened Bread, when they killed the Passover lamb, His disciples said to Him, "Where do You want us to go and prepare, that You may eat the Passover?"

13And He sent out two of His disciples and said to them, "Go into the city, and a man will meet you carrying a pitcher of water; follow him. 14Wherever he goes in, say to the master of the house, 'The Teacher says, "Where is the guest room in which I may eat the Passover with My disciples?" ' 15Then he will show you a large upper room, furnished and prepared; there make ready for us."

16So His disciples went out, and came into the city, and found it just as He had said to them; and they prepared the Passover.

17In the evening He came with the twelve. 18Now as they sat and ate, Jesus said, "Assuredly, I say to you, one of you who eats with Me will betray Me."

19And they began to be sorrowful, and to say to Him one by one, "Is it I?" And another said, "Is it I?"[a]

20He answered and said to them, "It is one of the twelve, who dips with Me in the dish. 21The Son of Man indeed goes just as it is written of Him, but woe to that man by whom the Son of Man is betrayed! It would have been good for that man if he had never been born."

JESUS INSTITUTES THE LORD'S SUPPER

22And as they were eating, Jesus took bread, blessed and broke it, and gave it to them and said, "Take, eat;[a] this is My body."

23Then He took the cup, and when He had given thanks He gave it to them, and they all drank from it. 24And He said to them, "This is My blood of the new[a] covenant, which is shed for many. 25Assuredly, I say to you, I will no longer drink of the fruit of the vine until that day when I drink it new in the kingdom of God."

26And when they had sung a hymn, they went out to the Mount of Olives.

13:29 [a]Or He   14:19 [a]NU-Text omits this sentence.   14:22 [a]NU-Text omits eat.   14:24 [a]NU-Text omits new.

JESUS PREDICTS PETER'S DENIAL

27Then Jesus said to them, "All of you will be made to stumble because of Me this night,ᵃ for it is written:

'I will strike the Shepherd,
And the sheep will be scattered.'ᵇ

28"But after I have been raised, I will go before you to Galilee."

29Peter said to Him, "Even if all are made to stumble, yet I *will* not *be*."

30Jesus said to him, "Assuredly, I say to you that today, *even* this night, before the rooster crows twice, you will deny Me three times."

31But he spoke more vehemently, "If I have to die with You, I will not deny You!"

And they all said likewise.

THE PRAYER IN THE GARDEN

32Then they came to a place which was named Gethsemane; and He said to His disciples, "Sit here while I pray." 33And He took Peter, James, and John with Him, and He began to be troubled and deeply distressed. 34Then He said to them, "My soul is exceedingly sorrowful, *even* to death. Stay here and watch."

35He went a little farther, and fell on the ground, and prayed that if it were possible, the hour might pass from Him. 36And He said, "Abba, Father, all things *are* possible for You. Take this cup away from Me; nevertheless, not what I will, but what You *will*."

37Then He came and found them sleeping, and said to Peter, "Simon, are you sleeping? Could you not watch one hour? 38Watch and pray, lest you enter into temptation. The spirit indeed *is* willing, but the flesh *is* weak."

39Again He went away and prayed, and spoke the same words. 40And when He returned, He found them asleep again, for their eyes were heavy; and they did not know what to answer Him.

41Then He came the third time and said to them, "Are you still sleeping and resting? It is enough! The hour has come; behold, the Son of Man is being betrayed into the hands of sinners. 42Rise, let us be going. See, My betrayer is at hand."

BETRAYAL AND ARREST IN GETHSEMANE

43And immediately, while He was still speaking, Judas, one of the twelve, with a great multitude with swords and clubs, came from the chief priests and the scribes and the elders.

44Now His betrayer had given them a signal, saying, "Whomever I kiss, He is the One; seize Him and lead *Him* away safely."

45As soon as he had come, immediately he went up to Him and said to Him, "Rabbi, Rabbi!" and kissed Him.

46Then they laid their hands on Him and took Him. 47And one of those who stood by drew his sword and struck the servant of the high priest, and cut off his ear. 48Then Jesus answered and said to them, "Have you come out, as against a robber, with swords and clubs to take Me? 49I was daily with you in the temple teaching, and you did not seize Me. But the Scriptures must be fulfilled."

50Then they all forsook Him and fled.

A YOUNG MAN FLEES NAKED

51Now a certain young man followed Him, having a linen cloth thrown around *his* naked *body*. And the young men laid hold of him, 52and he left the linen cloth and fled from them naked.

JESUS FACES THE SANHEDRIN

53And they led Jesus away to the high priest; and with him were assembled all the chief priests, the elders, and the scribes. 54But Peter followed Him at a distance, right into the courtyard of the high priest. And he sat with the servants and warmed himself at the fire.

55Now the chief priests and all the council sought testimony against Jesus to put Him to death, but found none. 56For many bore false witness against Him, but their testimonies did not agree.

57Then some rose up and bore false witness against Him, saying, 58"We heard Him say, 'I will destroy this temple made with hands, and within three days I will build another made without hands.' " 59But not even then did their testimony agree.

60And the high priest stood up in the midst and asked Jesus, saying, "Do You answer nothing? What *is it* these men testify against You?" 61But He kept silent and answered nothing.

Again the high priest asked Him, saying to Him, "Are You the Christ, the Son of the Blessed?"

62Jesus said, "I am. And you will see the Son of Man sitting at the right hand of the Power, and coming with the clouds of heaven."

JESUS
Will the Messiah come again?
(14:61, 62)

14:27 ᵃNU-Text omits *because of Me this night.* ᵇZechariah 13:7

⁶³Then the high priest tore his clothes and said, "What further need do we have of witnesses? ⁶⁴You have heard the blasphemy! What do you think?"

And they all condemned Him to be deserving of death.

⁶⁵Then some began to spit on Him, and to blindfold Him, and to beat Him, and to say to Him, "Prophesy!" And the officers struck Him with the palms of their hands.ᵃ

PETER DENIES JESUS, AND WEEPS

⁶⁶Now as Peter was below in the courtyard, one of the servant girls of the high priest came. ⁶⁷And when she saw Peter warming himself, she looked at him and said, "You also were with Jesus of Nazareth."

⁶⁸But he denied it, saying, "I neither know nor understand what you are saying." And he went out on the porch, and a rooster crowed.

⁶⁹And the servant girl saw him again, and began to say to those who stood by, "This is one of them." ⁷⁰But he denied it again.

And a little later those who stood by said to Peter again, "Surely you are one of them; for you are a Galilean, and your speech shows it."ᵃ

⁷¹Then he began to curse and swear, "I do not know this Man of whom you speak!"

⁷²A second time the rooster crowed. Then Peter called to mind the word that Jesus had said to him, "Before the rooster crows twice, you will deny Me three times." And when he thought about it, he wept.

JESUS FACES PILATE

¹Immediately, in the morning, the chief priests held a consultation with the elders and scribes and the whole council; and they bound Jesus, led Him away, and delivered Him to Pilate. ²Then Pilate asked Him, "Are You the King of the Jews?"

He answered and said to him, "It is as you say."

³And the chief priests accused Him of many things, but He answered nothing. ⁴Then Pilate asked Him again, saying, "Do You answer nothing? See how many things they testify against You!"ᵃ ⁵But Jesus still answered nothing, so that Pilate marveled.

TAKING THE PLACE OF BARABBAS

⁶Now at the feast he was accustomed to releasing one prisoner to them, whomever they requested. ⁷And there was one named Barab-bas, who was chained with his fellow rebels; they had committed murder in the rebellion. ⁸Then the multitude, crying aloud,ᵃ began to ask him to do just as he had always done for them. ⁹But Pilate answered them, saying, "Do you want me to release to you the King of the Jews?" ¹⁰For he knew that the chief priests had handed Him over because of envy.

¹¹But the chief priests stirred up the crowd, so that he should rather release Barabbas to them. ¹²Pilate answered and said to them again, "What then do you want me to do with Him whom you call the King of the Jews?"

¹³So they cried out again, "Crucify Him!"

¹⁴Then Pilate said to them, "Why, what evil has He done?"

But they cried out all the more, "Crucify Him!"

¹⁵So Pilate, wanting to gratify the crowd, released Barabbas to them; and he delivered Jesus, after he had scourged Him, to be crucified.

THE SOLDIERS MOCK JESUS

¹⁶Then the soldiers led Him away into the hall called Praetorium, and they called together the whole garrison. ¹⁷And they clothed Him with purple; and they twisted a crown of thorns, put it on His head, ¹⁸and began to salute Him, "Hail, King of the Jews!" ¹⁹Then they struck Him on the head with a reed and spat on Him; and bowing the knee, they worshiped Him. ²⁰And when they had mocked Him, they took the purple off Him, put His own clothes on Him, and led Him out to crucify Him.

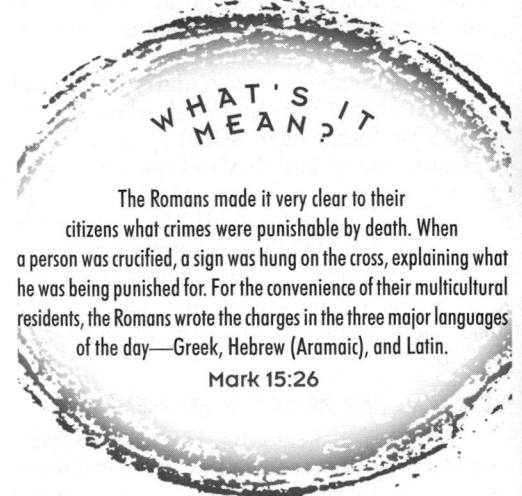

WHAT'S IT MEAN?

The Romans made it very clear to their citizens what crimes were punishable by death. When a person was crucified, a sign was hung on the cross, explaining what he was being punished for. For the convenience of their multicultural residents, the Romans wrote the charges in the three major languages of the day—Greek, Hebrew (Aramaic), and Latin.
Mark 15:26

14:65 ᵃNU-Text reads received Him with slaps. **14:70** ᵃNU-Text omits and your speech shows it.
15:4 ᵃNU-Text reads of which they accuse You. **15:8** ᵃNU-Text reads going up.

THE KING ON A CROSS

²¹Then they compelled a certain man, Simon a Cyrenian, the father of Alexander and Rufus, as he was coming out of the country and passing by, to bear His cross. ²²And they brought Him to the place Golgotha, which is translated, Place of a Skull. ²³Then they gave Him wine mingled with myrrh to drink, but He did not take *it.* ²⁴And when they crucified Him, they divided His garments, casting lots for them to determine what every man should take.

²⁵Now it was the third hour, and they crucified Him. ²⁶And the inscription of His accusation was written above:

THE KING OF THE JEWS.

²⁷With Him they also crucified two robbers, one on His right and the other on His left. ²⁸So the Scripture was fulfilled*ᵃ* which says, *"And He was numbered with the transgressors."ᵇ*

²⁹And those who passed by blasphemed Him, wagging their heads and saying, "Aha! *You* who destroy the temple and build *it* in three days, ³⁰save Yourself, and come down from the cross!"

³¹Likewise the chief priests also, mocking among themselves with the scribes, said, "He saved others; Himself He cannot save. ³²Let the Christ, the King of Israel, descend now from the cross, that we may see and believe."*ᵃ*

Even those who were crucified with Him reviled Him.

JESUS DIES ON THE CROSS

³³Now when the sixth hour had come, there was darkness over the whole land until the ninth hour. ³⁴And at the ninth hour Jesus cried out with a loud voice, saying, "Eloi, Eloi, lama sabachthani?" which is translated, *"My God, My God, why have You forsaken Me?"ᵃ*

³⁵Some of those who stood by, when they heard *that,* said, "Look, He is calling for Elijah!" ³⁶Then someone ran and filled a sponge full of sour wine, put *it* on a reed, and offered *it* to Him to drink, saying, "Let Him alone; let us see if Elijah will come to take Him down."

³⁷And Jesus cried out with a loud voice, and breathed His last.

³⁸Then the veil of the temple was torn in two from top to bottom. ³⁹So when the centurion, who stood opposite Him, saw that He cried out like this and breathed His last,*ᵃ* he said, "Truly this Man was the Son of God!"

On the Edge

Jesus cried out with a loud voice, and breathed His last (Mark 15:37).

We hear a lot about Jesus dying for the whole world, and we know that we're included in the whole world part. But did you know that Jesus died just for *you?* Before Jesus came to earth, He knew about you. He knew what you would look like. He knew what your name and your personality would be. He even knew you would sin. Even more than knowing about you, He loved you. He loved you so much, that if you had been the *only* person to ever live on earth, He would have come to die for you. You aren't just one of many or a face in the crowd. When He hung on the cross, you were in His mind. He sacrificed His life so that you could live for eternity with Him. You are the reason Jesus came, lived, died, and rose from the grave. He paid for your sin through His own death. He knows you intimately and wants you to know Him—the One who died so you could live forever with Him.

SEE FOR YOURSELF:
Matt. 27:20;
Rom. 5:6, 8, 18; 8:32

---

⁴⁰There were also women looking on from afar, among whom were Mary Magdalene, Mary the mother of James the Less and of Joses, and Salome, ⁴¹who also followed Him and ministered to Him when He was in Galilee, and many other women who came up with Him to Jerusalem.

JESUS BURIED IN JOSEPH'S TOMB

⁴²Now when evening had come, because it was the Preparation Day, that is, the day before the Sabbath, ⁴³Joseph of Arimathea, a prominent council member, who was himself waiting for the kingdom of God, coming and taking courage, went in to Pilate and asked for the body of Jesus. ⁴⁴Pilate marveled that He was already dead; and summoning the centurion, he asked him if He had been dead for some time. ⁴⁵So when he found out from the centurion, he granted the body to Joseph. ⁴⁶Then he bought

---

15:28 *ᵃ*Isaiah 53:12 *ᵇ*NU-Text omits this verse.   **15:32** *ᵃ*M-Text reads *believe Him.*   **15:34** *ᵃ*Psalm 22:1
15:39 *ᵃ*NU-Text reads *that He thus breathed His last.*

fine linen, took Him down, and wrapped Him in the linen. And he laid Him in a tomb which had been hewn out of the rock, and rolled a stone against the door of the tomb. ⁴⁷And Mary Magdalene and Mary *the mother* of Joses observed where He was laid.

WHAT'S IT MEAN?

Crucifixion usually was not a quick way to die. Unless the person had been severely beaten before being crucified, he could actually survive several days on the cross! One of the most common causes of death among those who were crucified was suffocation. Because of the outstretched position, when the person became too exhausted to raise himself up to breathe, he simply suffocated.

Mark 15:44

HE IS RISEN

¹Now when the Sabbath was past, Mary Magdalene, Mary *the mother* of James, and Salome bought spices, that they might come and anoint Him. ²Very early in the morning, on the first *day* of the week, they came to the tomb when the sun had risen. ³And they said among themselves, "Who will roll away the stone from the door of the tomb for us?" ⁴But when they looked up, they saw that the stone had been rolled away—for it was very large. ⁵And entering the tomb, they saw a young man clothed in a long white robe sitting on the right side; and they were alarmed.

⁶But he said to them, "Do not be alarmed. You seek Jesus of Nazareth, who was crucified. He is risen! He is not here. See the place where they laid Him. ⁷But go, tell His disciples—and Peter—that He is going before you into Galilee; there you will see Him, as He said to you."

⁸So they went out quickly*ᵃ* and fled from the tomb, for they trembled and were amazed. And they said nothing to anyone, for they were afraid.

MARY MAGDALENE SEES THE RISEN LORD

⁹Now when *He* rose early on the first *day* of the week, He appeared first to Mary Magdalene, out of whom He had cast seven demons. ¹⁰She

On the Edge

He who believes and is baptized will be saved; but he who does not believe will be condemned (Mark 16:16).

God designed the world so that there would be consequences for sin. He also required that a payment be made for sin. He knew we could never pay for all our sins. Without payment, the eternal consequence is condemnation and separation from God in hell—forever. His heart was broken by that thought. The only way to save us was to send someone to be perfect, and to die the death that *we* deserved. To give us a way out of eternal damnation, He sent His perfect Son, Jesus.

Jesus lived a sinless life and then died as a sacrifice for our sins. God said that Jesus' death was enough to pay for everyone's sin. Nothing else needed to be done. Nothing else could be done. The payment has been made for all of your sin.

To receive the benefit of Jesus' death, you have to believe in Him. Deciding to believe that Jesus Christ died for you is called "being saved." Believing in Him saves you from being condemned and separated from God forever. Your friends may want you to be saved because they can't imagine heaven without you. Your family wants you to be saved because they don't ever want to leave you. But the Lord, more than anything, wants you to be saved because He created you, and He loves you more than you can understand. He doesn't want you to be judged and spend eternity apart from Him in hell.

There are all kinds of great reasons to be saved, but the best one has to do with being with God forever. Heaven is reserved for those who decide to believe that Jesus Christ is who He said He was. You are free to choose. God will not force you to love Him. Forced love is not true love. But today, if you hear His voice and know these things are true, do not harden your heart. Run to Him and be saved!

SEE FOR YOURSELF:
Matt. 3:16;
John 3:16, 17; 10:8, 9;
Acts 3:19, 20;
Rom. 6:22, 23

16:8 ᵃNU-Text and M-Text omit *quickly.*

went and told those who had been with Him, as they mourned and wept. [11]And when they heard that He was alive and had been seen by her, they did not believe.

JESUS APPEARS TO TWO DISCIPLES

[12]After that, He appeared in another form to two of them as they walked and went into the country. [13]And they went and told *it* to the rest, *but* they did not believe them either.

THE GREAT COMMISSION

[14]Later He appeared to the eleven as they sat at the table; and He rebuked their unbelief and hardness of heart, because they did not believe those who had seen Him after He had risen. [15]And He said to them, "Go into all the world and preach the gospel to every creature. [16]He who believes and is baptized will be saved; but he who does not believe will be condemned. [17]And these signs will follow those who believe: In My name they will cast out demons; they will speak with new tongues; [18]they[a] will take up serpents; and if they drink anything deadly, it will by no means hurt them; they will lay hands on the sick, and they will recover."

CHRIST ASCENDS TO GOD'S RIGHT HAND

[19]So then, after the Lord had spoken to them, He was received up into heaven, and sat down at the right hand of God. [20]And they went out and preached everywhere, the Lord working with *them* and confirming the word through the accompanying signs. Amen.[a]

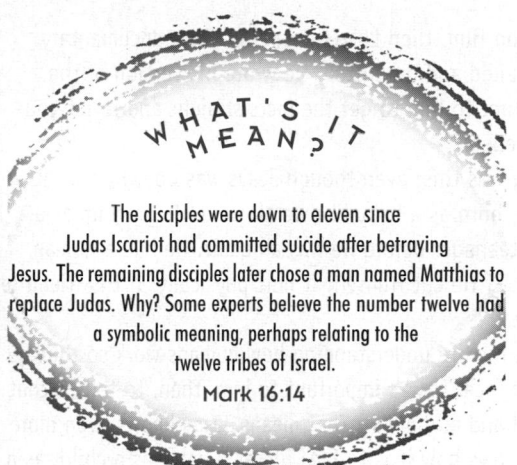

WHAT'S IT MEAN?

The disciples were down to eleven since Judas Iscariot had committed suicide after betraying Jesus. The remaining disciples later chose a man named Matthias to replace Judas. Why? Some experts believe the number twelve had a symbolic meaning, perhaps relating to the twelve tribes of Israel.

Mark 16:14

16:18 [a]NU-Text reads *and in their hands they will.*   **16:20** Verses 9–20 are bracketed in NU-Text as not original. They are lacking in Codex Sinaiticus and Codex Vaticanus, although nearly all other manuscripts of Mark contain them.

CONTENT If Mark's Gospel is like an action film, then Luke's Gospel is like a documentary.

Luke was a doctor: very detailed and organized. He wrote his version of the Gospel that way. It was important to him to get the facts straight and to let you know exactly how things happened.

Luke's main point in writing was this: even though Jesus was God, He was also really and truly human. He was born as a baby like we all were. He grew up as a child like we all do. He was a teenager before He was an adult. He had a human body. He had human emotions. If He cut Himself, it hurt physically. If His friend let Him down, it hurt emotionally.

As a doctor, Luke had spent his life understanding how humans work so that he could help fix the problems we face. It was important to him, then, to tell us that Jesus was miraculously all God and all human. That means Jesus knows even more about how humans work. He knows how it is to face life as a baby, as a child, as a teenager, as an adult. And He knows how to fix the problems that we face.

Purpose We are to live as Jesus did, showing concern for all.

Theme Jesus the Savior of the World

Date of writing Early 60s A.D

> "For the Son of Man has come to seek and to save that which was lost" (19:10).

Bible Talk

John the Baptist

A lot of times before big concerts, a "front man" will go into a city and get everything ready before the singer shows up. John the Baptist was like Jesus' front man. He prepared the way. He got the place ready.

It was not an easy job. First of all, the people of John's day were not ready to be convinced that Jesus was the Messiah. They wanted a Messiah who would lead an army and overthrow the Roman government. Instead they got a Messiah who let Himself be executed. Once even John himself asked Jesus if He was really *the* One.

But John did the job he came to do. He baptized people into faith in Jesus. He even baptized Jesus. And when it came time, he was more than happy to lose his followers so they could be followers of Christ.

WOMEN IN MINISTRY

The Gospel of Luke mentions women in ministry more than any other Gospel. You might already know that, when Jesus was alive, His culture didn't value women very much. Women were treated like second-class citizens—if they were treated like citizens at all.

Jesus didn't treat women like that, though. He worked side by side with women, as well as with men. There were women who supported His ministry all the way through His death, burial, and the Resurrection.

Jesus came into the world to knock down barriers—including the barriers that say "girls aren't as good as guys."

DEDICATION TO THEOPHILUS

[1]Inasmuch as many have taken in hand to set in order a narrative of those things which have been fulfilled[a] among us, [2]just as those who from the beginning were eyewitnesses and ministers of the word delivered them to us, [3]it seemed good to me also, having had perfect understanding of all things from the very first, to write to you an orderly account, most excellent Theophilus, [4]that you may know the certainty of those things in which you were instructed.

JOHN'S BIRTH ANNOUNCED TO ZACHARIAS

[5]There was in the days of Herod, the king of Judea, a certain priest named Zacharias, of the division of Abijah. His wife *was* of the daughters of Aaron, and her name *was* Elizabeth. [6]And they were both righteous before God, walking in all the commandments and ordinances of the Lord blameless. [7]But they had no child, because Elizabeth was barren, and they were both well advanced in years.

[8]So it was, that while he was serving as priest before God in the order of his division, [9]according to the custom of the priesthood, his lot fell to burn incense when he went into the temple of the Lord. [10]And the whole multitude of the people was praying outside at the hour of incense. [11]Then an angel of the Lord appeared to him, standing on the right side of the altar of incense. [12]And when Zacharias saw *him,* he was troubled, and fear fell upon him.

[13]But the angel said to him, "Do not be afraid, Zacharias, for your prayer is heard; and your wife Elizabeth will bear you a son, and you shall call his name John. [14]And you will have joy and gladness, and many will rejoice at his birth. [15]For he will be great in the sight of the Lord, and shall drink neither wine nor strong drink. He will also be filled with the Holy Spirit, even from his mother's womb. [16]And he will turn many of the children of Israel to the Lord their God. [17]He will also go before Him in the spirit and power of Elijah, '*to turn the hearts of the fathers to the children,*'[a] and the disobedient to the wisdom of the just, to make ready a people prepared for the Lord."

[18]And Zacharias said to the angel, "How shall I know this? For I am an old man, and my wife is well advanced in years."

[19]And the angel answered and said to him, "I am Gabriel, who stands in the presence of God, and was sent to speak to you and bring you these glad tidings. [20]But behold, you will be mute and not able to speak until the day these things take place, because you did not believe my words which will be fulfilled in their own time."

[21]And the people waited for Zacharias, and marveled that he lingered so long in the temple. [22]But when he came out, he could not speak to them; and they perceived that he had seen a vision in the temple, for he beckoned to them and remained speechless.

[23]So it was, as soon as the days of his service were completed, that he departed to his own house. [24]Now after those days his wife Elizabeth conceived; and she hid herself five months, saying, [25]"Thus the Lord has dealt with me, in the days when He looked on *me,* to take away my reproach among people."

CHRIST'S BIRTH ANNOUNCED TO MARY

[26]Now in the sixth month the angel Gabriel was sent by God to a city of Galilee named Nazareth, [27]to a virgin betrothed to a man whose name was Joseph, of the house of David. The virgin's name *was* Mary. [28]And having come in, the angel said to her, "Rejoice, highly favored *one,* the Lord *is* with you; blessed *are* you among women!"[a]

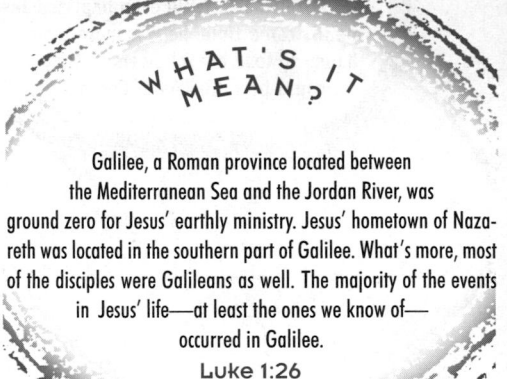

WHAT'S IT MEAN?

Galilee, a Roman province located between the Mediterranean Sea and the Jordan River, was ground zero for Jesus' earthly ministry. Jesus' hometown of Nazareth was located in the southern part of Galilee. What's more, most of the disciples were Galileans as well. The majority of the events in Jesus' life—at least the ones we know of—occurred in Galilee.

Luke 1:26

[29]But when she saw *him,*[a] she was troubled at his saying, and considered what manner of greeting this was. [30]Then the angel said to her, "Do not be afraid, Mary, for you have found favor with God. [31]And behold, you will conceive in your womb and bring forth a Son, and shall call His name JESUS. [32]He will be great, and

will be called the Son of the Highest; and the Lord God will give Him the throne of His father David. ³³And He will reign over the house of Jacob forever, and of His kingdom there will be no end."

³⁴Then Mary said to the angel, "How can this be, since I do not know a man?"

³⁵And the angel answered and said to her, "The Holy Spirit will come upon you, and the power of the Highest will overshadow you; there-fore, also, that Holy One who is to be born will be called the Son of God. ³⁶Now indeed, Elizabeth your rela-tive has also conceived a son in her old age; and this is now the sixth month for her who was called barren. ³⁷For with God nothing will be impossible."

³⁸Then Mary said, "Behold the maidservant of the Lord! Let it be to me according to your word." And the angel departed from her.

> JESUS
> What role does Jesus have in the Trinity? (1:35)

MARY VISITS ELIZABETH

³⁹Now Mary arose in those days and went into the hill country with haste, to a city of Ju-dah, ⁴⁰and entered the house of Zacharias and greeted Elizabeth. ⁴¹And it happened, when Elizabeth heard the greeting of Mary, that the babe leaped in her womb; and Elizabeth was filled with the Holy Spirit. ⁴²Then she spoke out with a loud voice and said, "Blessed *are* you among women, and blessed *is* the fruit of your womb! ⁴³But why *is* this *granted* to me, that the mother of my Lord should come to me? ⁴⁴For indeed, as soon as the voice of your greeting sounded in my ears, the babe leaped in my womb for joy. ⁴⁵Blessed *is* she who believed, for there will be a fulfillment of those things which were told her from the Lord."

THE SONG OF MARY

⁴⁶And Mary said:

"My soul magnifies the Lord,
⁴⁷ And my spirit has rejoiced in God my Savior.
⁴⁸ For He has regarded the lowly state of His maidservant;
For behold, henceforth all generations will call me blessed.
⁴⁹ For He who is mighty has done great things for me,
And holy *is* His name.
⁵⁰ And His mercy *is* on those who fear Him From generation to generation.
⁵¹ He has shown strength with His arm;

He has scattered *the* proud in the imagination of their hearts.
⁵² He has put down the mighty from *their* thrones,
And exalted *the* lowly.
⁵³ He has filled *the* hungry with good things,
And *the* rich He has sent away empty.
⁵⁴ He has helped His servant Israel,
In remembrance of *His* mercy,
⁵⁵ As He spoke to our fathers,
To Abraham and to his seed forever."

⁵⁶And Mary remained with her about three months, and returned to her house.

BIRTH OF JOHN THE BAPTIST

⁵⁷Now Elizabeth's full time came for her to be delivered, and she brought forth a son. ⁵⁸When her neighbors and relatives heard how the Lord had shown great mercy to her, they rejoiced with her.

CIRCUMCISION OF JOHN THE BAPTIST

⁵⁹So it was, on the eighth day, that they came to circumcise the child; and they would have called him by the name of his father, Zacharias. ⁶⁰His mother answered and said, "No; he shall be called John."

⁶¹But they said to her, "There is no one among your relatives who is called by this name." ⁶²So they made signs to his father—what he would have him called.

⁶³And he asked for a writing tablet, and wrote, saying, "His name is John." So they all marveled. ⁶⁴Immediately his mouth was opened and his tongue *loosed,* and he spoke, praising God. ⁶⁵Then fear came on all who dwelt around them; and all these sayings were discussed throughout all the hill country of Judea. ⁶⁶And all those who heard *them* kept *them* in their hearts, saying, "What kind of child will this be?" And the hand of the Lord was with him.

ZACHARIAS'S PROPHECY

⁶⁷Now his father Zacharias was filled with the Holy Spirit, and prophesied, saying:

⁶⁸ "Blessed *is* the Lord God of Israel,
For He has visited and redeemed His people,
⁶⁹ And has raised up a horn of salvation for us
In the house of His servant David,
⁷⁰ As He spoke by the mouth of His holy prophets,
Who *have been* since the world began,

71 That we should be saved from our enemies
   And from the hand of all who hate us,
72 To perform the mercy *promised* to our
   fathers
   And to remember His holy covenant,
73 The oath which He swore to our father
   Abraham:
74 To grant us that we,
   Being delivered from the hand of our
   enemies,
   Might serve Him without fear,
75 In holiness and righteousness before Him
   all the days of our life.

76 "And you, child, will be called the prophet
   of the Highest;
   For you will go before the face of the
   Lord to prepare His ways,
77 To give knowledge of salvation to His
   people
   By the remission of their sins,
78 Through the tender mercy of our God,
   With which the Dayspring from on high
   has visited[a] us;
79 To give light to those who sit in darkness
   and the shadow of death,
   To guide our feet into the way of peace."

⁸⁰So the child grew and became strong in
spirit, and was in the deserts till the day of his
manifestation to Israel.

CHRIST BORN OF MARY

¹And it came to pass in those days *that* a decree went out from Caesar Augustus that all the
world should be registered. ²This census first
took place while Quirinius was governing
Syria. ³So all went to be registered, everyone to
his own city.

⁴Joseph also went up from Galilee, out of the
city of Nazareth, into Judea, to the city of David,
which is called Bethlehem, because he was of
the house and lineage of David, ⁵to be registered
with Mary, his betrothed wife,[a] who was with
child. ⁶So it was, that while they were there, the
days were completed for her to be delivered.
⁷And she brought forth her firstborn Son, and
wrapped Him in swaddling cloths, and laid
Him in a manger, because there was no room
for them in the inn.

GLORY IN THE HIGHEST

⁸Now there were in the same country shepherds living out in the fields, keeping watch

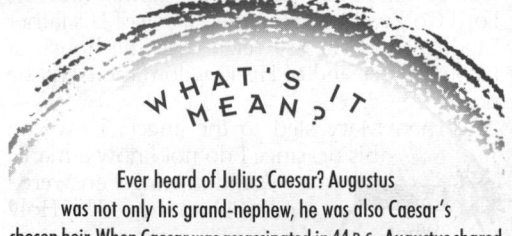

WHAT'S IT MEAN?

Ever heard of Julius Caesar? Augustus
was not only his grand-nephew, he was also Caesar's
chosen heir. When Caesar was assassinated in 44 B.C., Augustus shared
the throne of the Roman Empire with another famous character from
history, Mark Anthony, and a man named Lepidus. By 27 B.C.,
Augustus was the sole ruler of Rome.

Luke 2:1

over their flock by night. ⁹And behold,[a] an angel of the Lord stood before them, and the glory
of the Lord shone around them, and they were
greatly afraid. ¹⁰Then the angel said to them,
"Do not be afraid, for behold, I bring you good
tidings of great joy which will be to all people.
¹¹For there is born to you this day in the city of
David a Savior, who is Christ the Lord. ¹²And
this *will be* the sign to you: You will find a
Babe wrapped in swaddling cloths, lying in a
manger."

¹³And suddenly there was with the angel a
multitude of the heavenly host praising God
and saying:

14 "Glory to God in the highest,
   And on earth peace, goodwill toward
   men!"[a]

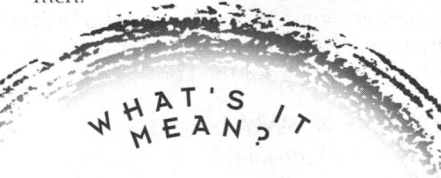

WHAT'S IT MEAN?

Joseph may have been a humble carpenter,
but he had some royal blood in him. He was a direct
descendant of King David, who had been born in Bethlehem and was
a member of the tribe of Judah. The journey from Nazareth to
Bethlehem was about ninety miles—a long
way to go for expectant parents!

Luke 2:4

1:78 [a]NU-Text reads *shall visit.*   **2:5** [a]NU-Text omits *wife.*   **2:9** [a]NU-Text omits *behold.*
2:14 [a]NU-Text reads *toward men of goodwill.*

¹⁵So it was, when the angels had gone away from them into heaven, that the shepherds said to one another, "Let us now go to Bethlehem and see this thing that has come to pass, which the Lord has made known to us." ¹⁶And they came with haste and found Mary and Joseph, and the Babe lying in a manger. ¹⁷Now when they had seen *Him*, they made widely*ª* known the saying which was told them concerning this Child. ¹⁸And all those who heard *it* marveled at those things which were told them by the shepherds. ¹⁹But Mary kept all these things and pondered *them* in her heart. ²⁰Then the shepherds returned, glorifying and praising God for all the things that they had heard and seen, as it was told them.

CIRCUMCISION OF JESUS

²¹And when eight days were completed for the circumcision of the Child,*ª* His name was called JESUS, the name given by the angel before He was conceived in the womb.

JESUS PRESENTED IN THE TEMPLE

²²Now when the days of her purification according to the law of Moses were completed, they brought Him to Jerusalem to present *Him* to the Lord ²³(as it is written in the law of the Lord, "*Every male who opens the womb shall be called holy to the LORD*"),*ª* ²⁴and to offer a sacrifice according to what is said in the law of the Lord, "*A pair of turtledoves or two young pigeons.*"*ª*

SIMEON SEES GOD'S SALVATION

²⁵And behold, there was a man in Jerusalem whose name was Simeon, and this man was just and devout, waiting for the Consolation of Israel, and the Holy Spirit was upon him. ²⁶And it had been revealed to him by the Holy Spirit that he would not see death before he had seen the Lord's Christ. ²⁷So he came by the Spirit into the temple. And when the parents brought in the Child Jesus, to do for Him according to the custom of the law, ²⁸he took Him up in his arms and blessed God and said:

²⁹   "Lord, now You are letting Your servant
        depart in peace,
        According to Your word;
³⁰   For my eyes have seen Your salvation
³¹   Which You have prepared before the face
        of all peoples,

³²   A light to *bring* revelation to the Gentiles,
        And the glory of Your people Israel."

³³And Joseph and His mother*ª* marveled at those things which were spoken of Him. ³⁴Then Simeon blessed them, and said to Mary His mother, "Behold, this *Child* is destined for the fall and rising of many in Israel, and for a sign which will be spoken against ³⁵(yes, a sword will pierce through your own soul also), that the thoughts of many hearts may be revealed."

ANNA BEARS WITNESS TO THE REDEEMER

³⁶Now there was one, Anna, a prophetess, the daughter of Phanuel, of the tribe of Asher. She was of a great age, and had lived with a husband seven years from her virginity; ³⁷and this woman *was* a widow of about eighty-four years,*ª* who did not depart from the temple, but served *God* with fastings and prayers night and day. ³⁸And coming in that instant she gave thanks to the Lord,*ª* and spoke of Him to all those who looked for redemption in Jerusalem.

THE FAMILY RETURNS TO NAZARETH

³⁹So when they had performed all things according to the law of the Lord, they returned to Galilee, to their *own* city, Nazareth. ⁴⁰And the Child grew and became strong in spirit,*ª* filled with wisdom; and the grace of God was upon Him.

THE BOY JESUS AMAZES THE SCHOLARS

⁴¹His parents went to Jerusalem every year at the Feast of the Passover. ⁴²And when He was twelve years old, they went up to Jerusalem according to the custom of the feast. ⁴³When they had finished the days, as they returned, the Boy Jesus lingered behind in Jerusalem. And Joseph and His mother*ª* did not know *it*; ⁴⁴but supposing Him to have been in the company, they went a day's journey, and sought Him among *their* relatives and acquaintances. ⁴⁵So when they did not find Him, they returned to Jerusalem, seeking Him. ⁴⁶Now so it was *that* after three days they found Him in the temple, sitting in the midst of the teachers, both listening to them and asking them questions. ⁴⁷And all who heard Him were astonished at His understanding and answers. ⁴⁸So when they saw Him, they were amazed; and His mother said to Him, "Son, why have You done this to us? Look, Your father and I have sought You anxiously."

2:17 *ª*NU-Text omits *widely.*   2:21 *ª*NU-Text reads *for His circumcision.*   2:23 *ª*Exodus 13:2, 12, 15
2:24 *ª*Leviticus 12:8   2:33 *ª*NU-Text reads *And His father and mother.*   2:37 *ª*NU-Text reads *a widow until she was eighty-four.*   2:38 *ª*NU-Text reads *to God.*   2:40 *ª*NU-Text omits *in spirit.*   2:43 *ª*NU-Text reads *And His parents.*

49And He said to them, "Why did you seek Me? Did you not know that I must be about My Father's business?" 50But they did not understand the statement which He spoke to them.

JESUS ADVANCES IN WISDOM AND FAVOR

51Then He went down with them and came to Nazareth, and was subject to them, but His mother kept all these things in her heart. 52And Jesus increased in wisdom and stature, and in favor with God and men.

JOHN THE BAPTIST PREPARES THE WAY

1Now in the fifteenth year of the reign of Tiberius Caesar, Pontius Pilate being governor of Judea, Herod being tetrarch of Galilee, his brother Philip tetrarch of Iturea and the region of Trachonitis, and Lysanias tetrarch of Abilene, 2while Annas and Caiaphas were high priests,a the word of God came to John the son of Zacharias in the wilderness. 3And he went into all the region around the Jordan, preaching a baptism of repentance for the remission of sins, 4as it is written in the book of the words of Isaiah the prophet, saying:

> "The voice of one crying in the
>   wilderness:
> 'Prepare the way of the LORD;
>   Make His paths straight.
> 5 Every valley shall be filled
>   And every mountain and hill brought
>   low;
>   The crooked places shall be made straight
>   And the rough ways smooth;
> 6 And all flesh shall see the salvation of
>   God.' "a

JOHN PREACHES TO THE PEOPLE

7Then he said to the multitudes that came out to be baptized by him, "Brood of vipers! Who warned you to flee from the wrath to come? 8Therefore bear fruits worthy of repentance, and do not begin to say to yourselves, 'We have Abraham as our father.' For I say to you that God is able to raise up children to

REPENTANCE What effect does repentance have on our relationship with God? (3:7, 8)

Abraham from these stones. 9And even now the ax is laid to the root of the trees. Therefore every tree which does not bear good fruit is cut down and thrown into the fire."

10So the people asked him, saying, "What shall we do then?"

11He answered and said to them, "He who has two tunics, let him give to him who has none; and he who has food, let him do likewise."

12Then tax collectors also came to be baptized, and said to him, "Teacher, what shall we do?"

13And he said to them, "Collect no more than what is appointed for you."

14Likewise the soldiers asked him, saying, "And what shall we do?"

So he said to them, "Do not intimidate anyone or accuse falsely, and be content with your wages."

15Now as the people were in expectation, and all reasoned in their hearts about John, whether he was the Christ or not, 16John answered, saying to all, "I indeed baptize you with water; but One mightier than I is coming, whose sandal strap I am not worthy to loose. He will baptize you with the Holy Spirit and fire. 17His winnowing fan is in His hand, and He will thoroughly clean out His threshing floor, and gather the wheat into His barn; but the chaff He will burn with unquenchable fire."

18And with many other exhortations he preached to the people. 19But Herod the tetrarch, being rebuked by him concerning Herodias, his brother Philip's wife,a and for all the evils which Herod had done, 20also added this, above all, that he shut John up in prison.

JOHN BAPTIZES JESUS

21When all the people were baptized, it came to pass that Jesus also was baptized; and while He prayed, the heaven was opened. 22And the Holy Spirit descended in bodily form like a dove upon Him, and a voice came from heaven which said, "You are My beloved Son; in You I am well pleased."

THE GENEALOGY OF JESUS CHRIST

23Now Jesus Himself began His ministry at about thirty years of age, being (as was supposed) the son of Joseph, the son of Heli, 24the son

> "And Jesus increased in wisdom and stature, and in favor with God and men."
> (Luke 2:52)

3:2 aNU-Text and M-Text read in the high priesthood of Annas and Caiaphas.   3:6 aIsaiah 40:3–5
3:19 aNU-Text reads his brother's wife.

son of Eliezer, *the son* of Jorim, *the son* of Matthat, *the son* of Levi, ³⁰*the son* of Simeon, *the son* of Judah, *the son* of Joseph, *the son* of Jonan, *the son* of Eliakim, ³¹*the son* of Melea, *the son* of Menan, *the son* of Mattathah, *the son* of Nathan, *the son* of David, ³²*the son* of Jesse, *the son* of Obed, *the son* of Boaz, *the son* of Salmon, *the son* of Nahshon, ³³*the son* of Amminadab, *the son* of Ram, *the son* of Hezron, *the son* of Perez, *the son* of Judah, ³⁴*the son* of Jacob, *the son* of Isaac, *the son* of Abraham, *the son* of Terah, *the son* of Nahor, ³⁵*the son* of Serug, *the son* of Reu, *the son* of Peleg, *the son* of Eber, *the son* of Shelah, ³⁶*the son* of Cainan, *the son* of Arphaxad, *the son* of Shem, *the son* of Noah, *the son* of Lamech, ³⁷*the son* of Methuselah, *the son* of Enoch, *the son* of Jared, *the son* of Mahalalel, *the son* of Cainan, ³⁸*the son* of Enosh, *the son* of Seth, *the son* of Adam, *the son* of God.

SATAN TEMPTS JESUS

¹Then Jesus, being filled with the Holy Spirit, returned from the Jordan and was led by the Spirit into* the wilderness, ²being tempted for forty days by the devil. And in those days He ate nothing, and afterward, when they had ended, He was hungry.

³And the devil said to Him, "If You are the Son of God, command this stone to become bread."

⁴But Jesus answered him, saying,* "It is written, 'Man shall not live by bread alone, but by every word of God.' "ᵇ

⁵Then the devil, taking Him up on a high mountain, showed Himᵃ all the kingdoms of the world in a moment of time. ⁶And the devil said to Him, "All this authority I will give You, and their glory; for *this* has been delivered to me, and I give it to whomever I wish. ⁷Therefore, if You will worship before me, all will be Yours."

⁸And Jesus answered and said to him, "Get behind Me, Satan!ᵃ Forᵇ it is written, 'You shall worship the LORD your God, and Him only you shall serve.' "ᶜ

⁹Then he brought Him to Jerusalem, set Him on the pinnacle of the temple, and said to Him, "If You are the Son of God, throw Yourself down from here. ¹⁰For it is written:

'He shall give His angels charge over you,
To keep you,'

On the Edge

John answered, saying to all, "I indeed baptize you with water; but One mightier than I is coming, whose sandal strap I am not worthy to loose. He will baptize you with the Holy Spirit and fire" (Luke 3:16).

Jesus said that in the last days He would pour out His Spirit on all flesh. That means on you and me (see Joel 2:28). Just as He did in the upper room in Acts 2, He wants to baptize you with the Holy Spirit and with fire. This will give you a new power that you've never had before. Acts 1:8 says, "But you shall receive power when the Holy Spirit has come upon you; and you shall be witnesses to Me . . ." The word *power* comes from the Greek word *dunamis,* which is translated as *dynamite!* So the verse actually says that after the Holy Spirit comes upon you, you will receive dynamite power to be witnesses.

This is exactly what happened to Peter. The same Peter who denied Christ three times preached with dynamite power after he received the Holy Spirit and fire in the upper room. In fact, he led 3,000 people to the Lord in one day. Now that's power! That's the same kind of power everyone needs. How do we get it? It's a gift. All we have to do is ask the Lord for it. He wants to baptize us with the Holy Spirit and fire today, so we can receive that dynamite power to be witnesses for Him.

SEE FOR YOURSELF:
Acts 2:1–4, 14–42

of Matthat,ᵃ *the son* of Levi, *the son* of Melchi, *the son* of Janna, *the son* of Joseph, ²⁵*the son* of Mattathiah, *the son* of Amos, *the son* of Nahum, *the son* of Esli, *the son* of Naggai, ²⁶*the son* of Maath, *the son* of Mattathiah, *the son* of Semei, *the son* of Joseph, *the son* of Judah, ²⁷*the son* of Joannas, *the son* of Rhesa, *the son* of Zerubbabel, *the son* of Shealtiel, *the son* of Neri, ²⁸*the son* of Melchi, *the son* of Addi, *the son* of Cosam, *the son* of Elmodam, *the son* of Er, ²⁹*the son* of Jose, the

3:24 ᵃThis and several other names in the genealogy are spelled somewhat differently in the NU-Text. Since the New King James Version uses the Old Testament spelling for persons mentioned in the New Testament, these variations, which come from the Greek, have not been footnoted. **4:1** ᵃNU-Text reads *in.* **4:4** ᵃDeuteronomy 8:3 ᵇNU-Text omits *but by every word of God.* **4:5** ᵃNU-Text reads *And taking Him up, he showed Him.* **4:8** ᵃNU-Text omits *Get behind Me, Satan.* ᵇNU-Text and M-Text omit *For.* ᶜDeuteronomy 6:13

On the Edge

Jesus answered and said to him, "Get behind Me, Satan! For it is written, 'You shall worship the LORD your God, and Him only you shall serve' " (Luke 4:8).

Jesus had been in the desert praying about how to get through to men's hearts. Satan tempted Him to take the easy way out—turn stones into bread instead of fasting; serve him in return for glory and power; or jump off the temple, let the angels miraculously save Him, and immediately be accepted by the people. Jesus knew that the only way to win the souls of men was to suffer and go to the cross. It was the harder way, but it was the only right way. Jesus responded to Satan by telling him that only God was to be worshiped and served.

You are going to face incredible temptation in your life. You must know that Jesus has been there. He knows the battles you face. You've got the same spiritual resources that Jesus had. You have prayer and the love of your heavenly Father. The power of the Holy Spirit was with Jesus (4:1), and the Holy Spirit lives in you. Jesus quoted the Word of God to Satan, and you have the complete Word in your hands. Plus, you now have Jesus in heaven, interceding on your behalf. He has dealt with the devil. And He has completely defeated him.

Satan wants to bring out the worst in us, but God can put the best in us. The next time you are up against the slick devices of Satan, quote a scripture to him and get away from the temptation. Do not play around with Satan. He knows your weakest places, and that's where he'll try to get the best of you. Stay on your toes. Keep alert. Serve God and flee the devil!

SEE FOR YOURSELF:
Deut. 10:20; Ps. 2:10, 11;
Luke 3:22; 4:1;
James 4:7;
1 Pet. 5:8, 9

---

[11]and,

'In their hands they shall bear you up,
Lest you dash your foot against a stone.' "[a]

[12]And Jesus answered and said to him, "It has been said, 'You shall not tempt the LORD your God.' "[a]

[13]Now when the devil had ended every temptation, he departed from Him until an opportune time.

JESUS BEGINS HIS GALILEAN MINISTRY

[14]Then Jesus returned in the power of the Spirit to Galilee, and news of Him went out through all the surrounding region. [15]And He taught in their synagogues, being glorified by all.

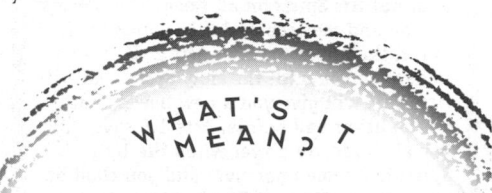

In 1947, an ancient copy of the Book of Isaiah was found among the Dead Sea Scrolls. Experts estimate that the scroll came from the period of 150–50 B.C. It's ten inches high and twenty-four feet long when it's unrolled. Made of thin leather strips sewn together, the scroll is probably very similar to the one Jesus read from.
Luke 4:17

JESUS REJECTED AT NAZARETH

[16]So He came to Nazareth, where He had been brought up. And as His custom was, He went into the synagogue on the Sabbath day, and stood up to read. [17]And He was handed the book of the prophet Isaiah. And when He had opened the book, He found the place where it was written:

[18] "The Spirit of the LORD is upon Me,
Because He has anointed Me
To preach the gospel to the poor;
He has sent Me to heal the brokenhearted,[a]
To proclaim liberty to the captives
And recovery of sight to the blind,
To set at liberty those who are oppressed;
[19] To proclaim the acceptable year of the LORD."[a]

[20]Then He closed the book, and gave it back to the attendant and sat down. And the eyes of all

---

4:11 [a]Psalm 91:11, 12   **4:12** [a]Deuteronomy 6:16   **4:18** [a]NU-Text omits *to heal the brokenhearted.*
4:19 [a]Isaiah 61:1, 2

who were in the synagogue were fixed on Him. ²¹And He began to say to them, "Today this Scripture is fulfilled in your hearing." ²²So all bore witness to Him, and marveled at the gracious words which proceeded out of His mouth. And they said, "Is this not Joseph's son?"

²³He said to them, "You will surely say this proverb to Me, 'Physician, heal yourself! Whatever we have heard done in Capernaum,ᵃ do also here in Your country.'" ²⁴Then He said, "Assuredly, I say to you, no prophet is accepted in his own country. ²⁵But I tell you truly, many widows were in Israel in the days of Elijah, when the heaven was shut up three years and six months, and there was a great famine throughout all the land; ²⁶but to none of them was Elijah sent except to Zarephath,ᵃ in the region of Sidon, to a woman who was a widow. ²⁷And many lepers were in Israel in the time of Elisha the prophet, and none of them was cleansed except Naaman the Syrian."

²⁸So all those in the synagogue, when they heard these things, were filled with wrath, ²⁹and rose up and thrust Him out of the city; and they led Him to the brow of the hill on which their city was built, that they might throw Him down over the cliff. ³⁰Then passing through the midst of them, He went His way.

JESUS CASTS OUT AN UNCLEAN SPIRIT

³¹Then He went down to Capernaum, a city of Galilee, and was teaching them on the Sabbaths. ³²And they were astonished at His teaching, for His word was with authority. ³³Now in the synagogue there was a man who had a spirit of an unclean demon. And he cried out with a loud voice, ³⁴saying, "Let us alone! What have we to do with You, Jesus of Nazareth? Did You come to destroy us? I know who You are— the Holy One of God!"

³⁵But Jesus rebuked him, saying, "Be quiet, and come out of him!" And when the demon had thrown him in their midst, it came out of him and did not hurt him. ³⁶Then they were all amazed and spoke among themselves, saying, "What a word this is! For with authority and power He commands the unclean spirits, and

---

4:23 ᵃHere and elsewhere the NU-Text spelling is *Capharnaum.*   **4:26** ᵃGreek *Sarepta*

Promise   HE PROMISES YOU FREEDOM.

The Spirit of the LORD is upon Me, because He has anointed Me to preach the gospel to the poor; He has sent Me to heal the brokenhearted, to proclaim liberty to the captives and recovery of sight to the blind, to set at liberty those who are oppressed (Luke 4:18).

This is such an exciting verse! Did you know that *you* have been chosen to tell the good news to the poor? The Lord has sent you to announce freedom. But not only have you been sent to announce freedom; you can have freedom as well! There is freedom in Jesus—freedom for everyone who struggles or suffers. What kind of needs do you have? What kind of needs do your friends have? You've been chosen by God, and you've also been equipped with the power of God to get free, stay free, and bring freedom to anyone and everyone who needs it! Now that's power—power over drugs, alcohol, cigarettes, lust, sex, bitterness, or whatever.

There was a movie about a man who gave up his life just to bring freedom to his people. He was beaten, tortured, and put on a chopping block. All he had to do was simply surrender his freedom, and he would live. His people would remain in bondage, but he could live. Instead, he let out a bloodcurdling cry, "Freeeeeedom!" He lost his life, but his people gained their freedom.

There is another story that hits home for all of us. Jesus died a horrible, shameful death on a cross so we could be free from sin, and spend eternity with Him. Don't allow yourself to be in bondage over some stupid sin—a sin that Jesus has already paid the price for. Choose freedom today, and watch God work a miracle in your life and in the lives of your friends! He is the One who sets you free!

SEE FOR YOURSELF:
Matt. 1:21; John 8:36; Rom. 6:14; 2 Cor. 3:17; Gal. 5:1, 13

they come out." ³⁷And the report about Him went out into every place in the surrounding region.

PETER'S MOTHER-IN-LAW HEALED

³⁸Now He arose from the synagogue and entered Simon's house. But Simon's wife's mother was sick with a high fever, and they made request of Him concerning her. ³⁹So He stood over her and rebuked the fever, and it left her. And immediately she arose and served them.

MANY HEALED AFTER SABBATH SUNSET

⁴⁰When the sun was setting, all those who had any that were sick with various diseases brought them to Him; and He laid His hands on every one of them and healed them. ⁴¹And demons also came out of many, crying out and saying, "You are the Christ,^a the Son of God!"

And He, rebuking *them,* did not allow them to speak, for they knew that He was the Christ.

JESUS PREACHES IN GALILEE

⁴²Now when it was day, He departed and went into a deserted place. And the crowd sought Him and came to Him, and tried to keep Him from leaving them; ⁴³but He said to them, "I must preach the kingdom of God to the other cities also, because for this purpose I have been sent." ⁴⁴And He was preaching in the synagogues of Galilee.^a

FOUR FISHERMEN CALLED AS DISCIPLES

¹So it was, as the multitude pressed about Him to hear the word of God, that He stood by the Lake of Gennesaret, ²and saw two boats standing by the lake; but the fishermen had gone from them and were washing *their* nets. ³Then He got into one of the boats, which was Simon's, and asked him to put out a little from the land. And He sat down and taught the multitudes from the boat.

⁴When He had stopped speaking, He said to Simon, "Launch out into the deep and let down your nets for a catch."

⁵But Simon answered and said to Him, "Master, we have toiled all night and caught nothing; nevertheless at Your word I will let down the net." ⁶And when they had done this, they caught a great number of fish, and their net was breaking. ⁷So they signaled to *their* partners in the other boat to come and help them. And they came and filled both the boats, so that they began to sink. ⁸When Simon Peter

saw *it,* he fell down at Jesus' knees, saying, "Depart from me, for I am a sinful man, O Lord!"

⁹For he and all who were with him were astonished at the catch of fish which they had taken; ¹⁰and so also *were* James and John, the sons of Zebedee, who were partners with Simon. And Jesus said to Simon, "Do not be afraid. From now on you will catch men." ¹¹So when they had brought their boats to land, they forsook all and followed Him.

JESUS CLEANSES A LEPER

¹²And it happened when He was in a certain city, that behold, a man who was full of leprosy saw Jesus; and he fell on *his* face and implored Him, saying, "Lord, if You are willing, You can make me clean."

¹³Then He put out *His* hand and touched him, saying, "I am willing; be cleansed." Immediately the leprosy left him. ¹⁴And He charged him to tell no one, "But go and show yourself to the priest, and make an offering for your cleansing, as a testimony to them, just as Moses commanded."

¹⁵However, the report went around concerning Him all the more; and great multitudes came together to hear, and to be healed by Him of their infirmities. ¹⁶So He Himself *often* withdrew into the wilderness and prayed.

WHAT'S IT MEAN?

The Pharisees were obsessive about following the Law of Moses. They lived by a strict code of conduct, going out of their way to make sure that they honored the Sabbath and maintained their purity. They had elaborate rules about what they could and couldn't do—rules that ultimately didn't have much to do with the Spirit of God's Word. The Pharisees also had a tendency to look down on people who seemed to be careless in following the Law of Moses.

Luke 5:17

JESUS FORGIVES AND HEALS A PARALYTIC

¹⁷Now it happened on a certain day, as He was teaching, that there were Pharisees and teachers of the law sitting by, who had come

out of every town of Galilee, Judea, and Jerusalem. And the power of the Lord was *present* to heal them.[a] [18]Then behold, men brought on a bed a man who was paralyzed, whom they sought to bring in and lay before Him. [19]And when they could not find how they might bring him in, because of the crowd, they went up on the housetop and let him down with *his* bed through the tiling into the midst before Jesus. [20]When He saw their faith, He said to him, "Man, your sins are forgiven you."

[21]And the scribes and the Pharisees began to reason, saying, "Who is this who speaks blasphemies? Who can forgive sins but God alone?" [22]But when Jesus perceived their thoughts, He answered and said to them, "Why are you reasoning in your hearts? [23]Which is easier, to say, 'Your sins are forgiven you,' or to say, 'Rise up and walk'? [24]But that you may know that the Son of Man has power on earth to forgive sins"—He said to the man who was paralyzed, "I say to you, arise, take up your bed, and go to your house."

[25]Immediately he rose up before them, took up what he had been lying on, and departed to his own house, glorifying God. [26]And they were all amazed, and they glorified God and were filled with fear, saying, "We have seen strange things today!"

MATTHEW THE TAX COLLECTOR

[27]After these things He went out and saw a tax collector named Levi, sitting at the tax office. And He said to him, "Follow Me." [28]So he left all, rose up, and followed Him.

[29]Then Levi gave Him a great feast in his own house. And there were a great number of tax collectors and others who sat down with them. [30]And their scribes and the Pharisees[a] complained against His disciples, saying, "Why do You eat and drink with tax collectors and sinners?"

[31]Jesus answered and said to them, "Those who are well have no need of a physician, but those who are sick. [32]I have not come to call *the* righteous, but sinners, to repentance."

JESUS IS QUESTIONED ABOUT FASTING

[33]Then they said to Him, "Why do[a] the disciples of John fast often and make prayers, and

5:17 [a]NU-Text reads *present with Him to heal.*   **5:30** [a]NU-Text reads *But the Pharisees and their scribes.*
5:33 [a]NU-Text omits *Why do,* making the verse a statement.

Promise   HE PROMISES TO FORGIVE YOUR SIN.

The Son of Man has power on earth to forgive sins (Luke 5:24).

Some schools have a wall in the school post office where they post the exam grades. Students sometimes affectionately refer to those places as "the wailing walls." One semester, a young man neglected to study for a particular exam and his test grade reflected it! They left the grades of that test up the entire semester. It was a continual reminder to him of how he had messed up. You can imagine what a happy day it was for him when they finally took down the grades at the end of the term. He could have tried covering up that exam with a black marker (which, by the way, he did). But every time he went into the school post office, there was that big black mark reminding him of his failure.

Jesus is the only One who has the right to forgive your sins. John 1:29 says that He takes them away—completely. When He forgives your sins and takes them away, it's like you never sinned at all. What freedom this understanding brings to our lives!

Sin doesn't have any more power over you! You are free from all that junk, so you don't need to let it rule over you. We are no longer required to sin, because we are free from sin. But if we do mess up, if we do fall short, if we do sin, all we have to do is confess our sins and *wham*—they're gone. God wipes them out. They're history!

So if you've been struggling with something, confess your sins to Him right now. Jesus is not only going to forgive you of your sins; He is going to see to it that they are taken away! After all, He is the One who forgives, forgets, and removes!

SEE FOR YOURSELF:
Prov. 24:16; 28:13; Jer. 33:8, 9; John 1:29;
Rom. 8:12–18; 1 John 1:7, 9

likewise those of the Pharisees, but Yours eat and drink?"

³⁴And He said to them, "Can you make the friends of the bridegroom fast while the bridegroom is with them? ³⁵But the days will come when the bridegroom will be taken away from them; then they will fast in those days."

³⁶Then He spoke a parable to them: "No one puts a piece from a new garment on an old one;^a otherwise the new makes a tear, and also the piece that was *taken* out of the new does not match the old. ³⁷And no one puts new wine into old wineskins; or else the new wine will burst the wineskins and be spilled, and the wineskins will be ruined. ³⁸But new wine must be put into new wineskins, and both are preserved.^a ³⁹And no one, having drunk old *wine,* immediately^a desires new; for he says, 'The old is better.' "^b

JESUS IS LORD OF THE SABBATH

¹Now it happened on the second Sabbath after the first^a that He went through the grainfields. And His disciples plucked the heads of grain and ate *them,* rubbing *them* in *their* hands. ²And some of the Pharisees said to them, "Why are you doing what is not lawful to do on the Sabbath?"

³But Jesus answering them said, "Have you not even read this, what David did when he was hungry, he and those who were with him: ⁴how he went into the house of God, took and ate the showbread, and also gave some to those with him, which is not lawful for any but the priests to eat?" ⁵And He said to them, "The Son of Man is also Lord of the Sabbath."

HEALING ON THE SABBATH

⁶Now it happened on another Sabbath, also, that He entered the synagogue and taught. And a man was there whose right hand was withered. ⁷So the scribes and Pharisees watched Him closely, whether He would heal on the Sabbath, that they might find an accusation against Him. ⁸But He knew their thoughts, and said to the man who had the withered hand,

"Arise and stand here." And he arose and stood. ⁹Then Jesus said to them, "I will ask you one thing: Is it lawful on the Sabbath to do good or to do evil, to save life or to destroy?"^a ¹⁰And when He had looked around at them all, He said to the man,^a "Stretch out your hand." And he did so, and his hand was restored as whole as the other.^b ¹¹But they were filled with rage, and discussed with one another what they might do to Jesus.

"But love your enemies, do good, and lend, hoping for nothing in return; and your reward will be great, and you will be sons of the Most High." (Luke 6:35a)

THE TWELVE APOSTLES

¹²Now it came to pass in those days that He went out to the mountain to pray, and continued all night in prayer to God. ¹³And when it was day, He called His disciples to *Himself;* and from them He chose twelve whom He also named apostles: ¹⁴Simon, whom He also named Peter, and Andrew his brother; James and John; Philip and Bartholomew; ¹⁵Matthew and Thomas; James the *son* of Alphaeus, and Simon called the Zealot; ¹⁶Judas the *son* of James, and Judas Iscariot who also became a traitor.

JESUS HEALS A GREAT MULTITUDE

¹⁷And He came down with them and stood on a level place with a crowd of His disciples and a great multitude of people from all Judea and Jerusalem, and from the seacoast of Tyre and Sidon, who came to hear Him and be healed of their diseases, ¹⁸as well as those who were tormented with unclean spirits. And they were healed. ¹⁹And the whole multitude sought to touch Him, for power went out from Him and healed *them* all.

THE BEATITUDES

²⁰Then He lifted up His eyes toward His disciples, and said:

"Blessed *are you* poor,
　　For yours is the kingdom of God.
²¹　Blessed *are you* who hunger now,
　　For you shall be filled.
　Blessed *are you* who weep now,
　　For you shall laugh.
²²　Blessed are you when men hate you,

5:36 ^aNU-Text reads *No one tears a piece from a new garment and puts it on an old one.* **5:38** ^aNU-Text omits *and both are preserved.* **5:39** ^aNU-Text omits *immediately.* ^bNU-Text reads *good.* **6:1** ^aNU-Text reads *on a Sabbath.* **6:9** ^aM-Text reads *to kill.* **6:10** ^aNU-Text and M-Text read *to him.* ^bNU-Text omits *as whole as the other.*

And when they exclude you,
And revile *you*, and cast out your
   name as evil,
For the Son of Man's sake.
23   Rejoice in that day and leap for joy!
For indeed your reward *is* great in
   heaven,
For in like manner their fathers did to
   the prophets.

JESUS PRONOUNCES WOES

24   "But woe to you who are rich,
For you have received your
     consolation.
25   Woe to you who are full,
For you shall hunger.
Woe to you who laugh now,
For you shall mourn and weep.
26   Woe to you*a* when all*b* men speak well of
   you,
For so did their fathers to the false
   prophets.

LOVE YOUR ENEMIES

27"But I say to you who hear: Love your enemies, do good to those who hate you,
28bless those who curse you, and
pray for those who spitefully

CARING

Do we have
to care for
our enemies?
(6:27)

use you. 29To him who strikes
you on the *one* cheek, offer the
other also. And from him who
takes away your cloak, do not
withhold *your* tunic either.
30Give to everyone who asks of you. And from
him who takes away your goods do not ask
them back. 31And just as you want men to do to
you, you also do to them likewise.
32"But if you love those who love you, what
credit is that to you? For even sinners love
those who love them. 33And if you do good to
those who do good to you, what credit is that
to you? For even sinners do the same. 34And if
you lend *to those* from whom you hope to receive back, what credit is that to you? For even
sinners lend to sinners to receive as much back.
35But love your enemies, do good, and lend,
hoping for nothing in return; and your reward
will be great, and you will be sons of the Most
High. For He is kind to the unthankful and evil.
36Therefore be merciful, just as your Father also
is merciful.

DO NOT JUDGE

37"Judge not, and you shall not be judged.
Condemn not, and you shall not be con-

On the Edge

*Bless those who curse you, and
pray for those who spitefully use
you. . . . But love your enemies, do
good, and lend, hoping for nothing in
return; and your reward will be great,
and you will be sons of the Most High.
For He is kind to the unthankful and
evil (Luke 6:28, 35).*

Luke says, "Welcome to the club." People
who love God have been lied about since the
beginning. He also says that God will bless
those who have been mistreated because of
Him. Proverbs 25:18–22 gives us some
wisdom about friends who tell lies about us
or treat us badly. The advice is to do exactly
the opposite of what your friends do. Even
when you're disappointed and angry, you
are supposed to be Christlike. Matthew 5:11
says, "Blessed are you when they revile and
persecute you, and say all kinds of evil
against you falsely" because you love Jesus.
By loving a person who hurts you, "you
will heap coals of fire on his head" (Prov.
25:22).
   Wow—that's pretty tough advice. When
people tell lies or spread rumors about
you, your reputation gets shattered, your pride gets wounded,
and your heart gets broken. And
God wants you to do what? Yep,
He says to love them anyway—
even give food to them if they are hungry
and pray for them, too. By doing so you
prove the strength of your character and
you overcome evil with good. God promises
to reward you for that.

SEE FOR YOURSELF:
   Prov. 25:18–22;
   Matt. 5:11, 12;
   Rom. 12:21

demned. Forgive, and you will be forgiven.
38Give, and it will be given to you: good measure, pressed down, shaken together, and running over will be put into your bosom. For with
the same measure that you use, it will be measured back to you."
39And He spoke a parable to them: "Can the
blind lead the blind? Will they not both fall into
the ditch? 40A disciple is not above his teacher,
but everyone who is perfectly trained will be

6:26 *a*NU-Text and M-Text omit *to you*. *b*M-Text omits *all*.

like his teacher. ⁴¹And why do you look at the speck in your brother's eye, but do not perceive the plank in your own eye? ⁴²Or how can you say to your brother, 'Brother, let me remove the speck that *is* in your eye,' when you yourself do not see the plank that *is* in your own eye? Hypocrite! First remove the plank from your own eye, and then you will see clearly to remove the speck that is in your brother's eye.

On the Edge

Judge not, and you shall not be judged. Condemn not, and you shall not be condemned. Forgive, and you will be forgiven (Luke 6:37).

What do you do when your parents treat your brother better than they treat you? What you may want to do is scream, and pout, and whine. You may even scheme some way to get more attention than your brother gets. If good behavior won't do it, maybe rebellion will. Before you head down that path, look at Luke 6:37. Jesus is laying out some fundamental principles of the universe: Judgment leads to judgment, condemnation leads to condemnation, and forgiveness leads to forgiveness. Forgive your parents and your brother. Don't judge them and try not to be hard on them. Give this to the Lord and allow Him to change your parents' hearts. He can do miracles in places you thought were hopeless. Begin to pray for your parents and forgive them daily. Consider this a challenge that you plus Jesus *can* overcome. Don't give up on them or on the Lord. He wants to restore your family and bring glory to Himself in your home.

SEE FOR YOURSELF:
Prov. 10:12; 27:4;
Matt. 5:14, 15;
2 John 5, 6

A TREE IS KNOWN BY ITS FRUIT

⁴³"For a good tree does not bear bad fruit, nor does a bad tree bear good fruit. ⁴⁴For every tree is known by its own fruit. For *men* do not gather figs from thorns, nor do they gather grapes from a bramble bush. ⁴⁵A good man out of the good treasure of his heart brings forth good; and an evil man out of the evil treasure of his heart^a brings forth evil. For out of the abundance of the heart his mouth speaks.

BUILD ON THE ROCK

⁴⁶"But why do you call Me 'Lord, Lord,' and not do the things which I say? ⁴⁷Whoever comes to Me, and hears My sayings and does them, I will show you whom he is like: ⁴⁸He is like a man building a house, who dug deep and laid the foundation on the rock. And when the flood arose, the stream beat vehemently against that house, and could not shake it, for it was founded on the rock.^a ⁴⁹But he who heard and did nothing is like a man who built a house on the earth without a foundation, against which the stream beat vehemently; and immediately it fell.^a And the ruin of that house was great."

JESUS HEALS A CENTURION'S SERVANT

¹Now when He concluded all His sayings in the hearing of the people, He entered Capernaum. ²And a certain centurion's servant, who was dear to him, was sick and ready to die. ³So when he heard about Jesus, he sent elders of the Jews to Him, pleading with Him to come and heal his servant. ⁴And when they came to Jesus, they begged Him earnestly, saying that the one for whom He should do this was deserving, ⁵"for he loves our nation, and has built us a synagogue."

⁶Then Jesus went with them. And when He was already not far from the house, the centurion sent friends to Him, saying to Him, "Lord, do not trouble Yourself, for I am not worthy that You should enter under my roof. ⁷Therefore I did not even think myself worthy to come to You. But say the word, and my servant will be healed. ⁸For I also am a man placed under authority, having soldiers under me. And I say to one, 'Go,' and he goes; and to another, 'Come,' and he comes; and to my servant, 'Do this,' and he does *it.*"

⁹When Jesus heard these things, He marveled at him, and turned around and said to the crowd that followed Him, "I say to you, I have not found such great faith, not even in Israel!" ¹⁰And those who were sent, returning to the house, found the servant well who had been sick.^a

JESUS RAISES THE SON OF THE WIDOW OF NAIN

¹¹Now it happened, the day after, *that* He went into a city called Nain; and many of His disciples went with Him, and a large crowd.

6:45 ^aNU-Text omits *treasure of his heart.*   **6:48** ^aNU-Text reads *for it was well built.*   **6:49** ^aNU-Text reads *collapsed.*   **7:10** ^aNU-Text omits *who had been sick.*

¹²And when He came near the gate of the city, behold, a dead man was being carried out, the only son of his mother; and she was a widow. And a large crowd from the city was with her. ¹³When the Lord saw her, He had compassion on her and said to her, "Do not weep." ¹⁴Then He came and touched the open coffin, and those who carried *him* stood still. And He said, "Young man, I say to you, arise." ¹⁵So he who was dead sat up and began to speak. And He presented him to his mother.

¹⁶Then fear came upon all, and they glorified God, saying, "A great prophet has risen up among us"; and, "God has visited His people." ¹⁷And this report about Him went throughout all Judea and all the surrounding region.

JOHN THE BAPTIST SENDS MESSENGERS TO JESUS

¹⁸Then the disciples of John reported to him concerning all these things. ¹⁹And John, calling two of his disciples to *him*, sent *them* to Jesus,ᵃ saying, "Are You the Coming One, or do we look for another?"

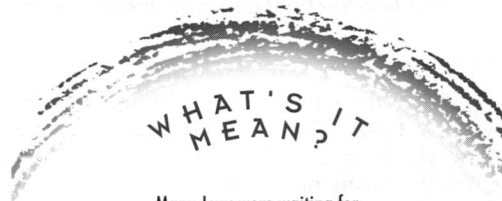

Many Jews were waiting for God to send a special person they called the "Messiah," from a Hebrew word meaning "anointed one." (In case you're wondering, "the Coming One" is another way of saying "the Messiah.") In Old Testament times, kings, priests, and prophets were all anointed—that is, they had oil poured on their heads to show that they were specially chosen by God. The Jews of Jesus' day believed that the Messiah would become their king and free them from the control of the Roman Empire. John's question to Jesus may have been due to the fact that Jesus seemed to show no interest in political things.
Luke 7:18, 19

²⁰When the men had come to Him, they said, "John the Baptist has sent us to You, saying, 'Are You the Coming One, or do we look for another?' " ²¹And that very hour He cured many of infirmities, afflictions, and evil spirits; and to many blind He gave sight.

²²Jesus answered and said to them, "Go and tell John the things you have seen and heard: that *the* blind see, *the* lame walk, *the* lepers are cleansed, *the* deaf hear, *the* dead are raised, *the* poor have the gospel preached to them. ²³And blessed is *he* who is not offended because of Me."

²⁴When the messengers of John had departed, He began to speak to the multitudes concerning John: "What did you go out into the wilderness to see? A reed shaken by the wind? ²⁵But what did you go out to see? A man clothed in soft garments? Indeed those who are gorgeously appareled and live in luxury are in kings' courts. ²⁶But what did you go out to see? A prophet? Yes, I say to you, and more than a prophet. ²⁷This is *he* of whom it is written:

'Behold, I send My messenger before Your face,
    Who will prepare Your way before You.'ᵃ

²⁸For I say to you, among those born of women there is not a greater prophet than John the Baptist;ᵃ but he who is least in the kingdom of God is greater than he."

²⁹And when all the people heard *Him*, even the tax collectors justified God, having been baptized with the baptism of John. ³⁰But the Pharisees and lawyers rejected the will of God for themselves, not having been baptized by him.

³¹And the Lord said,ᵃ "To what then shall I liken the men of this generation, and what are they like? ³²They are like children sitting in the marketplace and calling to one another, saying:

'We played the flute for you,
    And you did not dance;
We mourned to you,
    And you did not weep.'

³³For John the Baptist came neither eating bread nor drinking wine, and you say, 'He has a demon.' ³⁴The Son of Man has come eating and drinking, and you say, 'Look, a glutton and a winebibber, a friend of tax collectors and sinners!' ³⁵But wisdom is justified by all her children."

A SINFUL WOMAN FORGIVEN

³⁶Then one of the Pharisees asked Him to eat with him. And He went to the Pharisee's house, and sat down to eat. ³⁷And behold, a woman in the city who was a sinner, when she knew that

Jesus sat at the table in the Pharisee's house, brought an alabaster flask of fragrant oil, [38]and stood at His feet behind *Him* weeping; and she began to wash His feet with her tears, and wiped *them* with the hair of her head; and she kissed His feet and anointed *them* with the fragrant oil. [39]Now when the Pharisee who had invited Him saw *this*, he spoke to himself, saying, "This Man, if He were a prophet, would know who and what manner of woman *this is* who is touching Him, for she is a sinner."

[40]And Jesus answered and said to him, "Simon, I have something to say to you."

So he said, "Teacher, say it."

[41]"There was a certain creditor who had two debtors. One owed five hundred denarii, and the other fifty. [42]And when they had nothing with which to repay, he freely forgave them both. Tell Me, therefore, which of them will love him more?"

[43]Simon answered and said, "I suppose the *one* whom he forgave more."

And He said to him, "You have rightly judged." [44]Then He turned to the woman and said to Simon, "Do you see this woman? I entered your house; you gave Me no water for My feet, but she has washed My feet with her tears and wiped *them* with the hair of her head. [45]You gave Me no kiss, but this woman has not ceased to kiss My feet since the time I came in. [46]You did not anoint My head with oil, but this woman has anointed My feet with fragrant oil. [47]Therefore I say to you, her sins, *which are* many, are forgiven, for she loved much. But to whom little is forgiven, *the same* loves little."

[48]Then He said to her, "Your sins are forgiven."

[49]And those who sat at the table with Him began to say to themselves, "Who is this who even forgives sins?"

[50]Then He said to the woman, "Your faith has saved you. Go in peace."

MANY WOMEN MINISTER TO JESUS

[1]Now it came to pass, afterward, that He went through every city and village, preaching and bringing the glad tidings of the kingdom of God. And the twelve *were* with Him, [2]and certain women who had been healed of evil spirits and infirmities—Mary called Magdalene, out of whom had come seven demons, [3]and Joanna the wife of Chuza, Herod's steward, and Susanna, and many others who provided for Him[a] from their substance.

THE PARABLE OF THE SOWER

[4]And when a great multitude had gathered, and they had come to Him from every city, He spoke by a parable: [5]"A sower went out to sow his seed. And as he sowed, some fell by the wayside; and it was trampled down, and the birds of the air devoured it. [6]Some fell on rock; and as soon as it sprang up, it withered away because it lacked moisture. [7]And some fell among thorns, and the thorns sprang up with it and choked it. [8]But others fell on good ground, sprang up, and yielded a crop a hundredfold." When He had said these things He cried, "He who has ears to hear, let him hear!"

THE PURPOSE OF PARABLES

[9]Then His disciples asked Him, saying, "What does this parable mean?"

[10]And He said, "To you it has been given to know the mysteries of the kingdom of God, but to the rest *it is given* in parables, that

> 'Seeing they may not see,
> And hearing they may not understand.'[a]

THE PARABLE OF THE SOWER EXPLAINED

[11]"Now the parable is this: The seed is the word of God. [12]Those by the wayside are the ones who hear; then the devil comes and takes away the word out of their hearts, lest they should believe and be saved. [13]But the ones on the rock *are those* who, when they hear, receive the word with joy; and these have no root, who believe for a while and in time of temptation fall away. [14]Now the ones *that* fell among thorns are those who, when they have heard, go out and are choked with cares, riches, and pleasures of life, and bring no fruit to maturity. [15]But the ones *that* fell on the good ground are those who, having heard the word with a noble and good heart, keep *it* and bear fruit with patience.

THE PARABLE OF THE REVEALED LIGHT

[16]"No one, when he has lit a lamp, covers it with a vessel or puts *it* under a bed, but sets *it* on a lampstand, that those who enter may see the light. [17]For nothing is secret that will not be revealed, nor *anything* hidden that will not be known and come to light. [18]Therefore take heed how you hear. For whoever has, to him *more* will be given; and whoever does not have, even what he seems to have will be taken from him."

8:3 [a]NU-Text and M-Text read *them*.   **8:10** [a]Isaiah 6:9

JESUS' MOTHER AND BROTHERS COME TO HIM

¹⁹Then His mother and brothers came to Him, and could not approach Him because of the crowd. ²⁰And it was told Him *by some*, who said, "Your mother and Your brothers are standing outside, desiring to see You."

²¹But He answered and said to them, "My mother and My brothers are these who hear the word of God and do it."

WIND AND WAVE OBEY JESUS

²²Now it happened, on a certain day, that He got into a boat with His disciples. And He said to them, "Let us cross over to the other side of the lake." And they launched out. ²³But as they sailed He fell asleep. And a windstorm came down on the lake, and they were filling *with water*, and were in jeopardy. ²⁴And they came to Him and awoke Him, saying, "Master, Master, we are perishing!"

Then He arose and rebuked the wind and the raging of the water. And they ceased, and there was a calm. ²⁵But He said to them, "Where is your faith?"

And they were afraid, and marveled, saying to one another, "Who can this be? For He commands even the winds and water, and they obey Him!"

WHAT'S IT MEAN?

The physical surroundings of the Sea of Galilee are probably responsible for its dangerous reputation. The lake is surrounded on three sides by cliffs and mountains. The winds rushing down from those mountains can kick up a storm in the wink of an eye.

Luke 8:23

A DEMON-POSSESSED MAN HEALED

²⁶Then they sailed to the country of the Gadarenes,^a which is opposite Galilee. ²⁷And when He stepped out on the land, there met Him a certain man from the city who had demons for a long time. And he wore no clothes,^a nor did he live in a house but in the tombs. ²⁸When he saw Jesus, he cried out, fell down

On the Edge

Who can this be? For He commands even the winds and water, and they obey Him! (Luke 8:25).

Have you ever asked the question, "How can I avoid the storms of life?" Well, the answer is, you can't. Everybody has to go through storms, but the good news is that you don't have to go through them alone.

Jesus—the One who calmed the storms—is with you. So the next time you're experiencing a storm or difficult circumstance, and it looks like there's no way out, remember you are not alone. You can rise above your storm. If the winds and the waves obeyed Jesus, then your storm has to obey His word, too. Victory belongs to you today!

SEE FOR YOURSELF:
Ps. 23; Mark 4:39

before Him, and with a loud voice said, "What have I to do with You, Jesus, Son of the Most High God? I beg You, do not torment me!" ²⁹For He had commanded the unclean spirit to come out of the man. For it had often seized him, and he was kept under guard, bound with chains and shackles; and he broke the bonds and was driven by the demon into the wilderness.

³⁰Jesus asked him, saying, "What is your name?"

And he said, "Legion," because many demons had entered him. ³¹And they begged Him that He would not command them to go out into the abyss.

³²Now a herd of many swine was feeding there on the mountain. So they begged Him that He would permit them to enter them. And He permitted them. ³³Then the demons went out of the man and entered the swine, and the herd ran violently down the steep place into the lake and drowned.

³⁴When those who fed *them* saw what had happened, they fled and told *it* in the city and in the country. ³⁵Then they went out to see what had happened, and came to Jesus, and found the man from whom the demons had departed, sitting at the feet of Jesus, clothed and in his

8:26 ^aNU-Text reads *Gerasenes.* **8:27** ^aNU-Text reads *who had demons and for a long time wore no clothes.*

right mind. And they were afraid. ³⁶They also who had seen *it* told them by what means he who had been demon-possessed was healed. ³⁷Then the whole multitude of the surrounding region of the Gadarenes*ᵃ* asked Him to depart from them, for they were seized with great fear. And He got into the boat and returned.

³⁸Now the man from whom the demons had departed begged Him that he might be with Him. But Jesus sent him away, saying, ³⁹"Return to your own house, and tell what great things God has done for you." And he went his way and proclaimed throughout the whole city what great things Jesus had done for him.

A GIRL RESTORED TO LIFE AND A WOMAN HEALED

⁴⁰So it was, when Jesus returned, that the multitude welcomed Him, for they were all waiting for Him. ⁴¹And behold, there came a man named Jairus, and he was a ruler of the synagogue. And he fell down at Jesus' feet and begged Him to come to his house, ⁴²for he had an only daughter about twelve years of age, and she was dying.

But as He went, the multitudes thronged Him. ⁴³Now a woman, having a flow of blood for twelve years, who had spent all her livelihood on physicians and could not be healed by any, ⁴⁴came from behind and touched the border of His garment. And immediately her flow of blood stopped.

⁴⁵And Jesus said, "Who touched Me?"

When all denied it, Peter and those with him*ᵃ* said, "Master, the multitudes throng and press You, and You say, 'Who touched Me?' "*ᵇ*

⁴⁶But Jesus said, "Somebody touched Me, for I perceived power going out from Me." ⁴⁷Now when the woman saw that she was not hidden, she came trembling; and falling down before Him, she declared to Him in the presence of all the people the reason she had touched Him and how she was healed immediately.

⁴⁸And He said to her, "Daughter, be of good cheer;*ᵃ* your faith has made you well. Go in peace."

⁴⁹While He was still speaking, someone came from the ruler of the synagogue's *house*, saying to him, "Your daughter is dead. Do not trouble the Teacher."*ᵃ*

"For what profit is it to a man if he gains the whole world, and is himself destroyed or lost?"
(Luke 9:25)

⁵⁰But when Jesus heard *it*, He answered him, saying, "Do not be afraid; only believe, and she will be made well." ⁵¹When He came into the house, He permitted no one to go in*ᵃ* except Peter, James, and John,*ᵇ* and the father and mother of the girl. ⁵²Now all wept and mourned for her; but He said, "Do not weep; she is not dead, but sleeping." ⁵³And they ridiculed Him, knowing that she was dead.

⁵⁴But He put them all outside,*ᵃ* took her by the hand and called, saying, "Little girl, arise." ⁵⁵Then her spirit returned, and she arose immediately. And He commanded that she be given *something* to eat. ⁵⁶And her parents were astonished, but He charged them to tell no one what had happened.

SENDING OUT THE TWELVE

¹Then He called His twelve disciples together and gave them power and authority over all demons, and to cure diseases. ²He sent them to preach the kingdom of God and to heal the sick. ³And He said to them, "Take nothing for the journey, neither staffs nor bag nor bread nor money; and do not have two tunics apiece. ⁴"Whatever house you enter, stay there, and from there depart. ⁵And whoever will not receive you, when you go out of that city, shake off the very dust from your feet as a testimony against them."

⁶So they departed and went through the towns, preaching the gospel and healing everywhere.

HEROD SEEKS TO SEE JESUS

⁷Now Herod the tetrarch heard of all that was done by Him; and he was perplexed, because it was said by some that John had risen from the dead, ⁸and by some that Elijah had appeared, and by others that one of the old prophets had risen again. ⁹Herod said, "John I have beheaded, but who is this of whom I hear such things?" So he sought to see Him.

FEEDING THE FIVE THOUSAND

¹⁰And the apostles, when they had returned, told Him all that they had done. Then He took them and went aside privately into a deserted place belonging to the city called Bethsaida.

8:37 *ᵃ*NU-Text reads *Gerasenes*.   **8:45** *ᵃ*NU-Text omits *and those with him*.   *ᵇ*NU-Text omits *and You say, 'Who touched Me?'*   **8:48** *ᵃ*NU-Text omits *be of good cheer*.   **8:49** *ᵃ*NU-Text adds *anymore*.   **8:51** *ᵃ*NU-Text adds *with Him*.   *ᵇ*NU-Text and M-Text read *Peter, John, and James*.   **8:54** *ᵃ*NU-Text omits *put them all outside*.

[11]But when the multitudes knew *it*, they followed Him; and He received them and spoke to them about the kingdom of God, and healed those who had need of healing. [12]When the day began to wear away, the twelve came and said to Him, "Send the multitude away, that they may go into the surrounding towns and country, and lodge and get provisions; for we are in a deserted place here."

[13]But He said to them, "You give them something to eat."

And they said, "We have no more than five loaves and two fish, unless we go and buy food for all these people." [14]For there were about five thousand men.

Then He said to His disciples, "Make them sit down in groups of fifty." [15]And they did so, and made them all sit down.

[16]Then He took the five loaves and the two fish, and looking up to heaven, He blessed and broke *them*, and gave *them* to the disciples to set before the multitude. [17]So they all ate and were filled, and twelve baskets of the leftover fragments were taken up by them.

PETER CONFESSES JESUS AS THE CHRIST

[18]And it happened, as He was alone praying, *that* His disciples joined Him, and He asked them, saying, "Who do the crowds say that I am?"

[19]So they answered and said, "John the Baptist, but some *say* Elijah; and others *say* that one of the old prophets has risen again."

[20]He said to them, "But who do you say that I am?"

Peter answered and said, "The Christ of God."

JESUS PREDICTS HIS DEATH AND RESURRECTION

[21]And He strictly warned and commanded them to tell this to no one, [22]saying, "The Son of Man must suffer many things, and be rejected by the elders and chief priests and scribes, and be killed, and be raised the third day."

TAKE UP THE CROSS AND FOLLOW HIM

[23]Then He said to *them* all, "If anyone desires to come after Me, let him deny himself, and take up his cross daily,[a] and follow Me. [24]For whoever desires to save his life will lose it, but whoever loses his life for My sake will save it. [25]For what profit is it to a man if he gains the whole world, and is himself destroyed or lost? [26]For whoever is ashamed of Me and My words, of him the Son of Man will be ashamed when He comes in His *own* glory, and *in His* Father's, and of the holy angels.

JESUS TRANSFIGURED ON THE MOUNT

[27]But I tell you truly, there are some standing here who shall not taste death till they see the kingdom of God."

On the Edge

Peter and those with him were heavy with sleep; and when they were fully awake, they saw His glory and the two men who stood with Him (Luke 9:32).

Can you imagine waking up and seeing Jesus in His glory? Wow! That would be something—to see the all-powerful and majestic One right there beside you when you wake up!

The fact is, we do serve a glorious God and we have the opportunity to wake up every morning and see "His glory." That's why it's so important to reach over, grab the Word of God, and meditate on it every morning. It gets our thinking headed in the right direction. If we aren't reminded of the glory and power of God every morning, it can be so easy to get caught up in our everyday affairs to the point that we forget that the "all-powerful One" is right beside us!

One thing that will bring us into the presence of His glory is to simply praise the Lord for who He is. He is so awesome, better than anyone or anything you can imagine. Even the heavens shout about His glory. The earth is filled with His glory. In fact, His Word tells us that we are crowned with His glory (see Ps. 8:5; Heb. 2:7).

Take time out right now just to praise God. He's the King of glory. He is the Alpha and Omega—the beginning and the end of everything. He's the lily of the valley, the bright and morning star. He's our safe place and our strong place. He's a tower in which we can hide from our enemy. In Him we are more than winners. He's the glorious God who is more than enough.

Take time to think about the Lord's glory every day. He is the One who is glorious!

SEE FOR YOURSELF:
Ps. 8:5; 19:1; 63:6; 72:19; 92:1, 2

9:23 [a]M-Text omits *daily.*

²⁸Now it came to pass, about eight days after these sayings, that He took Peter, John, and James and went up on the mountain to pray. ²⁹As He prayed, the appearance of His face was altered, and His robe *became* white *and* glistening. ³⁰And behold, two men talked with Him, who were Moses and Elijah, ³¹who appeared in glory and spoke of His decease which He was about to accomplish at Jerusalem. ³²But Peter and those with him were heavy with sleep; and when they were fully awake, they saw His glory and the two men who stood with Him. ³³Then it happened, as they were parting from Him, *that* Peter said to Jesus, "Master, it is good for us to be here; and let us make three tabernacles: one for You, one for Moses, and one for Elijah"—not knowing what he said.

³⁴While he was saying this, a cloud came and overshadowed them; and they were fearful as they entered the cloud. ³⁵And a voice came out of the cloud, saying, "This is My beloved Son.ª Hear Him!" ³⁶When the voice had ceased, Jesus was found alone. But they kept quiet, and told no one in those days any of the things they had seen.

A BOY IS HEALED

³⁷Now it happened on the next day, when they had come down from the mountain, that a great multitude met Him. ³⁸Suddenly a man from the multitude cried out, saying, "Teacher, I implore You, look on my son, for he is my only child. ³⁹And behold, a spirit seizes him, and he suddenly cries out; it convulses him so that he foams *at the mouth;* and it departs from him with great difficulty, bruising him. ⁴⁰So I implored Your disciples to cast it out, but they could not."

⁴¹Then Jesus answered and said, "O faithless and perverse generation, how long shall I be with you and bear with you? Bring your son here." ⁴²And as he was still coming, the demon threw him down and convulsed *him.* Then Jesus rebuked the unclean spirit, healed the child, and gave him back to his father.

JESUS AGAIN PREDICTS HIS DEATH

⁴³And they were all amazed at the majesty of God.

But while everyone marveled at all the things which Jesus did, He said to His disciples, ⁴⁴"Let these words sink down into your ears, for the Son of Man is about to be betrayed into the hands of men." ⁴⁵But they did not understand this saying, and it was hidden from them so that they did not perceive it; and they were afraid to ask Him about this saying.

WHO IS THE GREATEST?

⁴⁶Then a dispute arose among them as to which of them would be greatest. ⁴⁷And Jesus, perceiving the thought of their heart, took a little child and set him by Him, ⁴⁸and said to them, "Whoever receives this little child in My name receives Me; and whoever receives Me receives Him who sent Me. For he who is least among you all will be great."

JESUS FORBIDS SECTARIANISM

⁴⁹Now John answered and said, "Master, we saw someone casting out demons in Your name, and we forbade him because he does not follow with us."

⁵⁰But Jesus said to him, "Do not forbid *him,* for he who is not against usª is on ourᵇ side."

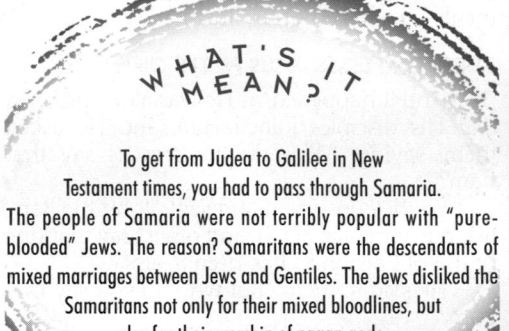

WHAT'S IT MEAN?

To get from Judea to Galilee in New Testament times, you had to pass through Samaria. The people of Samaria were not terribly popular with "pure-blooded" Jews. The reason? Samaritans were the descendants of mixed marriages between Jews and Gentiles. The Jews disliked the Samaritans not only for their mixed bloodlines, but also for their worship of pagan gods.

Luke 9:52

A SAMARITAN VILLAGE REJECTS THE SAVIOR

⁵¹Now it came to pass, when the time had come for Him to be received up, that He steadfastly set His face to go to Jerusalem, ⁵²and sent messengers before His face. And as they went, they entered a village of the Samaritans, to prepare for Him. ⁵³But they did not receive Him, because His face was *set* for the journey to Jerusalem. ⁵⁴And when His disciples James and John saw *this,* they said, "Lord, do You want us to command fire to come down from heaven and consume them, just as Elijah did?"ª

⁵⁵But He turned and rebuked them,ª and

9:35 ªNU-Text reads *This is My Son, the Chosen One.*   **9:50** ªNU-Text reads *you.* ᵇNU-Text reads *your.*
9:54 ªNU-Text omits *just as Elijah did.*   **9:55** ªNU-Text omits the rest of this verse.

said, "You do not know what manner of spirit you are of. [56]For the Son of Man did not come to destroy men's lives but to save *them*."[a] And they went to another village.

THE COST OF DISCIPLESHIP

[57]Now it happened as they journeyed on the road, *that* someone said to Him, "Lord, I will follow You wherever You go."

[58]And Jesus said to him, "Foxes have holes and birds of the air *have* nests, but the Son of Man has nowhere to lay *His* head."

[59]Then He said to another, "Follow Me."

But he said, "Lord, let me first go and bury my father."

[60]Jesus said to him, "Let the dead bury their own dead, but you go and preach the kingdom of God."

[61]And another also said, "Lord, I will follow You, but let me first go *and* bid them farewell who are at my house."

[62]But Jesus said to him, "No one, having put his hand to the plow, and looking back, is fit for the kingdom of God."

THE SEVENTY SENT OUT

[1]After these things the Lord appointed seventy others also,[a] and sent them two by two before His face into every city and place where He Himself was about to go. [2]Then He said to them, "The harvest truly *is* great, but the laborers *are* few; therefore pray the Lord of the harvest to send out laborers into His harvest. [3]Go your way; behold, I send you out as lambs among wolves. [4]Carry neither money bag, knapsack, nor sandals; and greet no one along the road. [5]But whatever house you enter, first say, 'Peace to this house.' [6]And if a son of peace is there, your peace will rest on it; if not, it will return to you. [7]And remain in the same house, eating and drinking such things as they give, for the laborer is worthy of his wages. Do not go from house to house. [8]Whatever city you enter, and they receive you, eat such things as are set before you. [9]And heal the sick there, and say to them, 'The kingdom of God has come near to you.' [10]But whatever city you enter, and they do not receive you, go out into its streets and say, [11]'The very dust of your city which clings to us[a] we wipe off against you. Nevertheless know this, that the kingdom of God has come near you.' [12]But[a] I say to you that it will be more tolerable in that Day for Sodom than for that city.

WOE TO THE IMPENITENT CITIES

[13]"Woe to you, Chorazin! Woe to you, Bethsaida! For if the mighty works which were done in you had been done in Tyre and Sidon, they would have repented long ago, sitting in sackcloth and ashes. [14]But it will be more tolerable for Tyre and Sidon at the judgment than for you. [15]And you, Capernaum, who are exalted to heaven, will be brought down to Hades.[a]

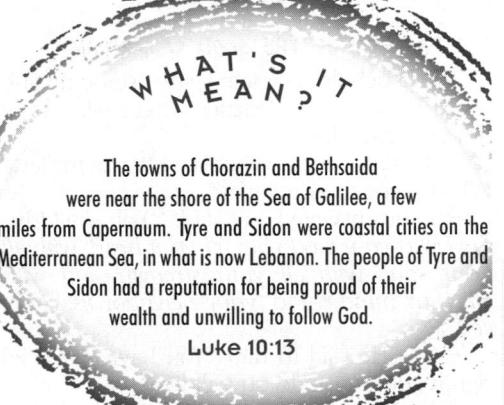

WHAT'S IT MEAN?

The towns of Chorazin and Bethsaida were near the shore of the Sea of Galilee, a few miles from Capernaum. Tyre and Sidon were coastal cities on the Mediterranean Sea, in what is now Lebanon. The people of Tyre and Sidon had a reputation for being proud of their wealth and unwilling to follow God.

Luke 10:13

[16]He who hears you hears Me, he who rejects you rejects Me, and he who rejects Me rejects Him who sent Me."

THE SEVENTY RETURN WITH JOY

[17]Then the seventy[a] returned with joy, saying, "Lord, even the demons are subject to us in Your name."

[18]And He said to them, "I saw Satan fall like lightning from heaven. [19]Behold, I give you the authority to trample on serpents and scorpions, and over all the power of the enemy, and nothing shall by any means hurt you. [20]Nevertheless do not rejoice in this, that the spirits are subject to you, but rather[a] rejoice because your names are written in heaven."

DEMONS
Who do demons submit to? (10:17)

JESUS REJOICES IN THE SPIRIT

[21]In that hour Jesus rejoiced in the Spirit and said, "I thank You, Father, Lord of heaven and earth, that You have hidden these things from *the* wise and prudent and revealed them to babes. Even so, Father, for so it seemed good in

Your sight. ²²All*ᵃ* things have been delivered to Me by My Father, and no one knows who the Son is except the Father, and who the Father is except the Son, and *the one* to whom the Son wills to reveal *Him*."

²³Then He turned to *His* disciples and said privately, "Blessed *are* the eyes which see the things you see; ²⁴for I tell you that many prophets and kings have desired to see what you see, and have not seen *it*, and to hear what you hear, and have not heard *it*."

THE PARABLE OF THE GOOD SAMARITAN

²⁵And behold, a certain lawyer stood up and tested Him, saying, "Teacher, what shall I do to inherit eternal life?"

²⁶He said to him, "What is written in the law? What is your reading *of it?*"

²⁷So he answered and said, " '*You shall love the LORD your God with all your heart, with all your soul, with all your strength, and with all your mind,*'ᵃ and '*your neighbor as yourself.*' "*ᵇ*

²⁸And He said to him, "You have answered rightly; do this and you will live."

²⁹But he, wanting to justify himself, said to Jesus, "And who is my neighbor?"

³⁰Then Jesus answered and said: "A certain *man* went down from Jerusalem to Jericho, and fell among thieves, who stripped him of his clothing, wounded *him*, and departed, leaving *him* half dead. ³¹Now by chance a certain priest came down that road. And when he saw him, he passed by on the other side. ³²Likewise a Levite, when he arrived at the place, came and looked, and passed by on the other side. ³³But a certain Samaritan, as he journeyed, came where he was. And when he saw him, he had compassion. ³⁴So he went to *him* and bandaged his wounds, pouring on oil and wine; and he set him on his own animal, brought him to an inn, and took care of him. ³⁵On the next day, when he departed,ᵃ he took out two denarii, gave *them* to the innkeeper, and said to him, 'Take care of him; and whatever more you spend, when I come again, I will repay you.' ³⁶So which of these three do you think was neighbor to him who fell among the thieves?"

³⁷And he said, "He who showed mercy on him."

Then Jesus said to him, "Go and do likewise."

MARY AND MARTHA WORSHIP AND SERVE

³⁸Now it happened as they went that He entered a certain village; and a certain woman named Martha welcomed Him into her house. ³⁹And she had a sister called Mary, who also sat at Jesus'ᵃ feet and heard His word. ⁴⁰But Martha was distracted with much serving, and she approached Him and said, "Lord, do You not care that my sister has left me to serve alone? Therefore tell her to help me."

⁴¹And Jesusᵃ answered and said to her, "Martha, Martha, you are worried and troubled about many things. ⁴²But one thing is needed, and Mary has chosen that good part, which will not be taken away from her."

THE MODEL PRAYER

¹Now it came to pass, as He was praying in a certain place, when He ceased, *that* one of His disciples said to Him, "Lord, teach us to pray, as John also taught his disciples."

²So He said to them, "When you pray, say:

Our Father in heaven,ᵃ
Hallowed be Your name.
Your kingdom come.*ᵇ*
Your will be done
On earth as *it is* in heaven.
³ Give us day by day our daily bread.
⁴ And forgive us our sins,
For we also forgive everyone who is indebted to us.
And do not lead us into temptation,
But deliver us from the evil one." ᵃ

A FRIEND COMES AT MIDNIGHT

⁵And He said to them, "Which of you shall have a friend, and go to him at midnight and say to him, 'Friend, lend me three loaves; ⁶for a friend of mine has come to me on his journey, and I have nothing to set before him'; ⁷and he will answer from within and say, 'Do not trouble me; the door is now shut, and my children are with me in bed; I cannot rise and give to you'? ⁸I say to you, though he will not rise and give to him because he is his friend, yet because of his persistence he will rise and give him as many as he needs.

KEEP ASKING, SEEKING, KNOCKING

⁹"So I say to you, ask, and it will be given to you; seek, and you will find; knock, and it will

be opened to you. ¹⁰For everyone who asks receives, and he who seeks finds, and to him who knocks it will be opened. ¹¹If a son asks for bread*a* from any father among you, will he give him a stone? Or if *he asks* for a fish, will he give him a serpent instead of a fish? ¹²Or if he asks for an egg, will he offer him a scorpion? ¹³If you then, being evil, know how to give good gifts to your children, how much more will *your* heavenly Father give the Holy Spirit to those who ask Him!"

A HOUSE DIVIDED CANNOT STAND

¹⁴And He was casting out a demon, and it was mute. So it was, when the demon had gone out, that the mute spoke; and the multitudes marveled. ¹⁵But some of them said, "He casts out demons by Beelzebub,*a* the ruler of the demons."

WHAT'S IT MEAN?

Beelzebub was the name of a pagan god that the Jews believed controlled all evil spirits. Jesus linked Beelzebub with Satan.
Luke 11:15

¹⁶Others, testing *Him*, sought from Him a sign from heaven. ¹⁷But He, knowing their thoughts, said to them: "Every kingdom divided against itself is brought to desolation, and a house *divided* against a house falls. ¹⁸If Satan also is divided against himself, how will his kingdom stand? Because you say I cast out demons by Beelzebub. ¹⁹And if I cast out demons by Beelzebub, by whom do your sons cast *them* out? Therefore they will be your judges. ²⁰But if I cast out demons with the finger of God, surely the kingdom of God has come upon you. ²¹When a strong man, fully armed, guards his own palace, his goods are in peace. ²²But when a stronger than he comes upon him and overcomes him, he takes from him all his armor in which he trusted, and divides his spoils. ²³He who is not with Me is against Me, and he who does not gather with Me scatters."

On the Edge

But He said, "More than that, blessed are those who hear the word of God and keep it!" (Luke 11:28).

"Hear and obey God's message." You've probably heard it said before, "To obey is better than sacrifice" (1 Sam. 15:22). And you know what? It's true. When we begin walking in obedience, that's when the blessings of God begin to flow. It's one thing to just hear the Word of God or to read it, but it's something else for us to start obeying it. God's Word says that if we love Him, we will obey Him (see John 14:15; 15:10). That's why when we seek God and His righteousness first, then all these things will be added to us. As we begin to seek righteousness and walk in obedience, blessings will find their way to us. You're going to become a "blessing magnet!"

If you were to go through the entire Bible and read about the men and women who were blessed with riches, fame, wisdom, etc., you'd find that most of them walked in obedience. You have to pay the price to be successful, and part of that price is obeying God's Word—doing what He says to do, and not doing what He says not to do. The choice is up to us: to be blessed or not to be blessed. Choose obedience and get out your bucket; here come the blessings of God! He is the One who blesses!

SEE FOR YOURSELF:
Deut. 5:29; Josh. 1:8;
Matt. 6:33; 7:21;
John 13:17;
James 1:22–25

AN UNCLEAN SPIRIT RETURNS

²⁴"When an unclean spirit goes out of a man, he goes through dry places, seeking rest; and finding none, he says, 'I will return to my house from which I came.' ²⁵And when he comes, he finds *it* swept and put in order. ²⁶Then he goes and takes with *him* seven other spirits more wicked than himself, and they enter and dwell there; and the last *state* of that man is worse than the first."

11:11 *a*NU-Text omits the words from *bread* through *for* in the next sentence. **11:15** *a*NU-Text and M-Text read *Beelzebul*.

KEEPING THE WORD

²⁷And it happened, as He spoke these things, that a certain woman from the crowd raised her voice and said to Him, "Blessed *is* the womb that bore You, and *the* breasts which nursed You!" ²⁸But He said, "More than that, blessed *are* those who hear the word of God and keep it!"

> **OBEDIENCE**
> What will happen to people who obey God's word? (11:28)

SEEKING A SIGN

²⁹And while the crowds were thickly gathered together, He began to say, "This is an evil generation. It seeks a sign, and no sign will be given to it except the sign of Jonah the prophet.ᵃ ³⁰For as Jonah became a sign to the Ninevites, so also the Son of Man will be to this generation. ³¹The queen of the South will rise up in the judgment with the men of this generation and condemn them, for she came from the ends of the earth to hear the wisdom of Solomon; and indeed a greater than Solomon *is* here. ³²The men of Nineveh will rise up in the judgment with this generation and condemn it, for they repented at the preaching of Jonah; and indeed a greater than Jonah *is* here.

THE LAMP OF THE BODY

³³"No one, when he has lit a lamp, puts *it* in a secret place or under a basket, but on a lampstand, that those who come in may see the light. ³⁴The lamp of the body is the eye. Therefore, when your eye is good, your whole body also is full of light. But when *your eye* is bad, your body also *is* full of darkness. ³⁵Therefore take heed that the light which is in you is not darkness. ³⁶If then your whole body *is* full of light, having no part dark, *the* whole *body* will be full of light, as when the bright shining of a lamp gives you light."

WOE TO THE PHARISEES AND LAWYERS

³⁷And as He spoke, a certain Pharisee asked Him to dine with him. So He went in and sat down to eat. ³⁸When the Pharisee saw *it,* he marveled that He had not first washed before dinner.

³⁹Then the Lord said to him, "Now you Pharisees make the outside of the cup and dish clean, but your inward part is full of greed and wickedness. ⁴⁰Foolish ones! Did not He who made the outside make the inside also? ⁴¹But rather give alms of such things as you have; then indeed all things are clean to you.

⁴²"But woe to you Pharisees! For you tithe mint and rue and all manner of herbs, and pass by justice and the love of God. These you ought to have done, without leaving the others undone. ⁴³Woe to you Pharisees! For you love the best seats in the synagogues and greetings in the marketplaces. ⁴⁴Woe to you, scribes and Pharisees, hypocrites!ᵃ For you are like graves which are not seen, and the men who walk over *them* are not aware *of them.*"

⁴⁵Then one of the lawyers answered and said to Him, "Teacher, by saying these things You reproach us also."

⁴⁶And He said, "Woe to you also, lawyers! For you load men with burdens hard to bear, and you yourselves do not touch the burdens with one of your fingers. ⁴⁷Woe to you! For you build the tombs of the prophets, and your fathers killed them. ⁴⁸In fact, you bear witness that you approve the deeds of your fathers; for they indeed killed them, and you build their tombs. ⁴⁹Therefore the wisdom of God also said, 'I will send them prophets and apostles, and *some* of them they will kill and persecute,' ⁵⁰that the blood of all the prophets which was shed from the foundation of the world may be required of this generation, ⁵¹from the blood of Abel to the blood of Zechariah who perished between the altar and the temple. Yes, I say to you, it shall be required of this generation.

⁵²"Woe to you lawyers! For you have taken away the key of knowledge. You did not enter in yourselves, and those who were entering in you hindered."

⁵³And as He said these things to them,ᵃ the scribes and the Pharisees began to assail *Him* vehemently, and to cross-examine Him about many things, ⁵⁴lying in wait for Him, and seeking to catch Him in something He might say, that they might accuse Him.ᵃ

BEWARE OF HYPOCRISY

¹In the meantime, when an innumerable multitude of people had gathered together, so that they trampled one another, He began to say to His disciples first *of all,* "Beware of the leaven of the Pharisees, which is hypocrisy. ²For there is nothing covered that will not be revealed, nor hidden that will not be known. ³Therefore whatever you have spoken in the dark will be heard in the light, and what you

---

11:29 ᵃNU-Text omits *the prophet.*   **11:44** ᵃNU-Text omits *scribes and Pharisees, hypocrites.*   **11:53** ᵃNU-Text reads *And when He left there.*   **11:54** ᵃNU-Text omits *and seeking* and *that they might accuse Him.*

have spoken in the ear in inner rooms will be proclaimed on the housetops.

JESUS TEACHES THE FEAR OF GOD

4"And I say to you, My friends, do not be afraid of those who kill the body, and after that have no more that they can do. 5But I will show you whom you should fear: Fear Him who, after He has killed, has power to cast into hell; yes, I say to you, fear Him! 6"Are not five sparrows sold for two copper coins?[a] And not one of them is forgotten before God. 7But the very hairs of your head are all numbered. Do not fear therefore; you are of more value than many sparrows.

WHAT'S IT MEAN?

Sparrows were what people offered to God when they couldn't afford to sacrifice a goat or a sheep. They were considered a "poor man's sacrifice."

Luke 12:6

CONFESS CHRIST BEFORE MEN

8"Also I say to you, whoever confesses Me before men, him the Son of Man also will confess before the angels of God. 9But he who denies Me before men will be denied before the angels of God.

10"And anyone who speaks a word against the Son of Man, it will be forgiven him; but to him who blasphemes against the Holy Spirit, it will not be forgiven.

11"Now when they bring you to the synagogues and magistrates and authorities, do not worry about how or what you should answer, or what you should say. 12For the Holy Spirit will teach you in that very hour what you ought to say."

THE PARABLE OF THE RICH FOOL

13Then one from the crowd said to Him, "Teacher, tell my brother to divide the inheritance with me."

14But He said to him, "Man, who made Me a judge or an arbitrator over you?" 15And He said to them, "Take heed and beware of covetous-

On the Edge

He said to them, "Take heed and beware of covetousness, for one's life does not consist in the abundance of the things he possesses."

Then He spoke a parable to them, saying, . . . (Luke 12:15–21).

Jesus makes the point in this parable that things aren't "it." Things don't give you a relationship with God. And things don't make your walk with God any deeper. The rich man in this parable thought that he would have an easy life because he had everything he could possibly ever want or need. God called him a fool, because that night when he died, his things could do nothing for him. Where are you spending most of your time? Are you worrying about the next really important "thing" you've got to have and how to get it, or are you thinking about the Lord and how to know and love Him more completely?

Jesus says it's foolish to spend your time accumulating stuff that will only rust and decay in the end. God doesn't give you everything you want because first, you don't need it, and second, those things don't matter anyway. People who always get what they want are commonly known in America as "spoiled brats." They don't have the self-control or discipline it takes to be mature.

God wants you to be mature, to learn what's really valuable and what isn't; to sacrifice for the good of another person, of yourself, or of the kingdom of God. He promises to provide all you need. But His focus is on the eternal—the souls of men and women. That's what really matters to God.

SEE FOR YOURSELF:
Prov. 28:22;
Luke 12:16–21;
1 Tim. 6:6–10;
James 1:10

ness,[a] for one's life does not consist in the abundance of the things he possesses."

16Then He spoke a parable to them, saying: "The ground of a certain rich man yielded plentifully. 17And he thought within himself, saying, 'What shall I do, since I have no room to store my crops?' [18]So he said, 'I will do this: I will pull down my barns and build greater, and there I will store all my crops and my goods. [19]And I will say to my soul, "Soul, you have many goods laid up for many years; take your ease; eat, drink, *and* be merry." ' [20]But God said to him, 'Fool! This night your soul will be required of you; then whose will those things be which you have provided?'

[21]"So *is* he who lays up treasure for himself, and is not rich toward God."

DO NOT WORRY

[22]Then He said to His disciples, "Therefore I say to you, do not worry about your life, what you will eat; nor about the body, what you will put on. [23]Life is more than food, and the body *is more* than clothing. [24]Consider the ravens, for they neither sow nor reap, which have neither storehouse nor barn; and God feeds them. Of how much more value are you than the birds? [25]And which of you by worrying can add one cubit to his stature? [26]If you then are not able to do *the* least, why are you anxious for the rest? [27]Consider the lilies, how they grow: they neither toil nor spin; and yet I say to you, even Solomon in all his glory was not arrayed like one of these. [28]If then God so clothes the grass, which today is in the field and tomorrow is thrown into the oven, how much more *will He clothe* you, O *you* of little faith?

[29]"And do not seek what you should eat or what you should drink, nor have an anxious mind. [30]For all these things the nations of the world seek after, and your Father knows that you need these things. [31]But seek the kingdom of God, and all these things[a] shall be added to you.

[32]"Do not fear, little flock, for it is your Father's good pleasure to give you the kingdom. [33]Sell what you have and give alms; provide yourselves money bags which do not grow old, a treasure in the heavens that does not fail, where no thief approaches nor moth destroys. [34]For where your treasure is, there your heart will be also.

THE FAITHFUL SERVANT AND THE EVIL SERVANT

[35]"Let your waist be girded and *your* lamps burning; [36]and you yourselves be like men who wait for their master, when he will return from the wedding, that when he comes and knocks

they may open to him immediately. [37]Blessed *are* those servants whom the master, when he comes, will find watching. Assuredly, I say to you that he will gird himself and have them sit down *to eat,* and will come and serve them. [38]And if he should come in the second watch, or come in the third watch, and find *them* so, blessed are those servants. [39]But know this, that if the master of the house had known what hour the thief would come, he would have watched and[a] not allowed his house to be broken into. [40]Therefore you also be ready, for the Son of Man is coming at an hour you do not expect."

WHAT'S IT MEAN?

The lamps of New Testament times were made of clay or metal. A wick was placed in a spout or on the rim of the lamp. Olive oil was poured through a hole in the top. Every two to four hours, the wick would need to be trimmed or changed and a fresh supply of oil would need to be added.

Luke 12:35

[41]Then Peter said to Him, "Lord, do You speak this parable *only* to us, or to all *people*?"

[42]And the Lord said, "Who then is that faithful and wise steward, whom *his* master will make ruler over his household, to give *them their* portion of food in due season? [43]Blessed *is* that servant whom his master will find so doing when he comes. [44]Truly, I say to you that he will make him ruler over all that he has. [45]But if that servant says in his heart, 'My master is delaying his coming,' and begins to beat the male and female servants, and to eat and drink and be drunk, [46]the master of that servant will come on a day when he is not looking for *him,* and at an hour when he is not aware, and will cut him in two and appoint *him* his portion with the unbelievers. [47]And that servant who knew his master's will, and did not prepare *himself* or do according to his will, shall be beaten with many *stripes.* [48]But he who did not know, yet committed things deserving of

"For where your treasure is, there your heart will be also." (Luke 12:34)

stripes, shall be beaten with few. For everyone to whom much is given, from him much will be required; and to whom much has been committed, of him they will ask the more.

CHRIST BRINGS DIVISION

⁴⁹"I came to send fire on the earth, and how I wish it were already kindled! ⁵⁰But I have a baptism to be baptized with, and how distressed I am till it is accomplished! ⁵¹Do *you* suppose that I came to give peace on earth? I tell you, not at all, but rather division. ⁵²For from now on five in one house will be divided: three against two, and two against three. ⁵³Father will be divided against son and son against father, mother against daughter and daughter against mother, mother-in-law against her daughter-in-law and daughter-in-law against her mother-in-law."

> **FAMILY**
> Is there anything that is more important than the family? (12:51–53)

DISCERN THE TIME

⁵⁴Then He also said to the multitudes, "Whenever *you see* a cloud rising out of the west, immediately you say, 'A shower is coming'; and so it is. ⁵⁵And when you see the south wind blow, you say, 'There will be hot weather'; and there is. ⁵⁶Hypocrites! You can discern the face of the sky and of the earth, but how *is it* you do not discern this time?

MAKE PEACE WITH YOUR ADVERSARY

⁵⁷"Yes, and why, even of yourselves, do you not judge what is right? ⁵⁸When you go with your adversary to the magistrate, make every effort along the way to settle with him, lest he drag you to the judge, the judge deliver you to the officer, and the officer throw you into prison. ⁵⁹I tell you, you shall not depart from there till you have paid the very last mite."

REPENT OR PERISH

¹There were present at that season some who told Him about the Galileans whose blood Pilate had mingled with their sacrifices. ²And Jesus answered and said to them, "Do you suppose that these Galileans were worse sinners than all *other* Galileans, because they suffered such things? ³I tell you, no; but unless you repent

> **REPENTANCE**
> What would happen to us if we didn't repent of our sin? (13:3–5)

you will all likewise perish. ⁴Or those eighteen on whom the tower in Siloam fell and killed them, do you think that they were worse sinners than all *other* men who dwelt in Jerusalem? ⁵I tell you, no; but unless you repent you will all likewise perish."

THE PARABLE OF THE BARREN FIG TREE

⁶He also spoke this parable: "A certain *man* had a fig tree planted in his vineyard, and he came seeking fruit on it and found none. ⁷Then he said to the keeper of his vineyard, 'Look, for three years I have come seeking fruit on this fig tree and find none. Cut it down; why does it use up the ground?' ⁸But he answered and said to him, 'Sir, let it alone this year also, until I dig around it and fertilize *it*. ⁹And if it bears fruit, *well*. But if not, after that ᵃ you can cut it down.' "

A SPIRIT OF INFIRMITY

¹⁰Now He was teaching in one of the synagogues on the Sabbath. ¹¹And behold, there was a woman who had a spirit of infirmity eighteen years, and was bent over and could in no way raise *herself* up. ¹²But when Jesus saw her, He called *her* to *Him* and said to her, "Woman, you are loosed from your infirmity." ¹³And He laid *His* hands on her, and immediately she was made straight, and glorified God.

¹⁴But the ruler of the synagogue answered with indignation, because Jesus had healed on the Sabbath; and he said to the crowd, "There are six days on which men ought to work; therefore come and be healed on them, and not on the Sabbath day."

¹⁵The Lord then answered him and said, "Hypocrite!ᵃ Does not each one of you on the Sabbath loose his ox or donkey from the stall, and lead *it* away to water it? ¹⁶So ought not this woman, being a daughter of Abraham, whom Satan has bound—think of it—for eighteen years, be loosed from this bond on the Sabbath?" ¹⁷And when He said these things, all His adversaries were put to shame; and all the multitude rejoiced for all the glorious things that were done by Him.

THE PARABLE OF THE MUSTARD SEED

¹⁸Then He said, "What is the kingdom of God like? And to what shall I compare it? ¹⁹It is like a mustard seed, which a man took and put in his garden; and it grew and became a largeᵃ tree, and the birds of the air nested in its branches."

13:9 ᵃNU-Text reads *And if it bears fruit after that, well. But if not, you can cut it down.* **13:15** ᵃNU-Text and M-Text read *Hypocrites.* **13:19** ᵃNU-Text omits *large.*

THE PARABLE OF THE LEAVEN

20And again He said, "To what shall I liken the kingdom of God? 21It is like leaven, which a woman took and hid in three measures*a* of meal till it was all leavened."

THE NARROW WAY

22And He went through the cities and villages, teaching, and journeying toward Jerusalem. 23Then one said to Him, "Lord, are there few who are saved?"

And He said to them, 24"Strive to enter through the narrow gate, for many, I say to you, will seek to enter and will not be able. 25When once the Master of the house has risen up and shut the door, and you begin to stand outside and knock at the door, saying, 'Lord, Lord, open for us,' and He will answer and say to you, 'I do not know you, where you are from,' 26then you will begin to say, 'We ate and drank in Your presence, and You taught in our streets.' 27But He will say, 'I tell you I do not know you, where you are from. Depart from Me, all you workers of iniquity.' 28There will be weeping and gnashing of teeth, when you see Abraham and Isaac and Jacob and all the prophets in the kingdom of God, and yourselves thrust out. 29They will come from the east and the west, from the north and the south, and sit down in the kingdom of God. 30And indeed there are last who will be first, and there are first who will be last."

31On that very day*a* some Pharisees came, saying to Him, "Get out and depart from here, for Herod wants to kill You."

32And He said to them, "Go, tell that fox, 'Behold, I cast out demons and perform cures today and tomorrow, and the third *day* I shall be perfected.' 33Nevertheless I must journey today, tomorrow, and the *day* following; for it cannot be that a prophet should perish outside of Jerusalem.

JESUS LAMENTS OVER JERUSALEM

34"O Jerusalem, Jerusalem, the one who kills the prophets and stones those who are sent to her! How often I wanted to gather your children together, as a hen *gathers* her brood under *her* wings, but you were not willing! 35See! Your house is left to you desolate; and assuredly,*a* I say to you, you shall not see Me until *the time* comes when you say, '*Blessed is He who comes in the name of the LORD!*' "*b*

A MAN WITH DROPSY HEALED ON THE SABBATH

1Now it happened, as He went into the house of one of the rulers of the Pharisees to eat bread on the Sabbath, that they watched Him closely. 2And behold, there was a certain man before Him who had dropsy. 3And Jesus, answering, spoke to the lawyers and Pharisees, saying, "Is it lawful to heal on the Sabbath?"*a*

4But they kept silent. And He took *him* and healed him, and let him go. 5Then He answered them, saying, "Which of you, having a donkey*a* or an ox that has fallen into a pit, will not immediately pull him out on the Sabbath day?" 6And they could not answer Him regarding these things.

TAKE THE LOWLY PLACE

7So He told a parable to those who were invited, when He noted how they chose the best places, saying to them: 8"When you are invited by anyone to a wedding feast, do not sit down in the best place, lest one more honorable than you be invited by him; 9and he who invited you and him come and say to you, 'Give place to this man,' and then you begin with shame to take the lowest place. 10But when you are invited, go and sit down in the lowest place, so that when he who invited you comes he may say to you, 'Friend, go up higher.' Then you will have glory in the presence of those who sit at the table with you. 11For whoever exalts himself will be humbled, and he who humbles himself will be exalted."

12Then He also said to him who invited Him, "When you give a dinner or a supper, do not ask your friends, your brothers, your relatives, nor rich neighbors, lest they also invite you back, and you be repaid. 13But when you give a feast, invite *the* poor, *the* maimed, *the* lame, *the* blind. 14And you will be blessed, because they cannot repay you; for you shall be repaid at the resurrection of the just."

> **CARING**
> Should Christians care for the needy? (14:13, 14)

THE PARABLE OF THE GREAT SUPPER

15Now when one of those who sat at the table with Him heard these things, he said to Him, "Blessed *is* he who shall eat bread*a* in the kingdom of God!"

16Then He said to him, "A certain man gave a great supper and invited many, 17and sent his

---

13:21 *a*Greek *sata*, approximately two pecks in all   **13:31** *a*NU-Text reads *In that very hour.*   **13:35** *a*NU-Text and M-Text omit *assuredly.*   *b*Psalm 118:26   **14:3** *a*NU-Text adds *or not.*   **14:5** *a*NU-Text and M-Text read *son.*   **14:15** *a*M-Text reads *dinner.*

JESUS made a difference

People talk a lot about Jesus the baby and Jesus the man. They don't say much about Jesus the kid. What did the Son of God do when He was your age? His birth, death, and resurrection sure made a big difference—But did Jesus make a difference when He was young? Yes, He did! By the time He was twelve, Jesus knew His Bible. He could talk about it, and He understood that obeying God's Word was the key to life. When He was at church, He listened to adults and asked good questions. He amazed the teachers. He practiced obeying God by obeying His parents. That wasn't easy. He learned that life wasn't just about what He wanted to do. He had to cooperate with His parents. His decision paid off. Think about this summary of Jesus' teenage years:

Cutting Edge

"Jesus increased in wisdom and stature, and in favor with God and men" (Luke 2:52).

YOU can, too!

The best way to shock a teacher is to be interested! Anybody can act bored and disruptive. It takes work to learn—but the benefits are amazing. Asking questions and looking for the truth will make a big difference in at least one life—your own! Practice obeying your parents. They won't know what hit them! The description of Jesus' teenage years really can be the description of your life. It won't be long before you discover that Jesus Himself will help you as you seek to live like He lived.

Want to know more? Read about Jesus and His young life in Luke 2:41–52.

JOHN THE BAPTIST made a difference

People who make a difference are themselves often different. They don't fit. They don't just go along. They stand up and stand out. Some accomplish great good; others create chaos. They are remembered both for what they did and for who they were. John the Baptist was a different person who made a difference in the best way.

God called this John into a life as a messenger, the one who announced the arrival of the Savior Jesus Christ. He understood who he was and was single-minded in pursuing his calling. He removed himself from distractions by living in the wilderness. He wore camel skins and ate desert food. But the only trend he started was a trend of guilt. He pointed out people's sinfulness. He fearlessly called people—the poor, the soldiers, a king—to repentance. He told them to get ready—to prepare a way for the Lord.

What difference did John the Baptist make? Did Jesus get the welcome He deserved? No. But there was a handful prepared for Christ. We know John made a difference because Jesus said so:

" 'Assuredly, I say to you, among those born of women there has not risen one greater than John the Baptist; but he who is least in the kingdom of heaven is greater than he' " (Matt. 11:11).

Cutting Edge

YOU can, too!

John made a difference because he was different, he acted different, and he looked different. Most people get the order exactly reversed and wrong. They focus on looking different and acting different. You can tell who these people are because they often do this in groups. Being different takes more courage. Being different as God instructs and leads takes even more determination.

It's those like John, who set out to be what God has called them to be, who end up making a difference. Have you asked God to make His calling clear to you?

Want to know more? Read about this unique difference-maker in all four Gospels. He is also mentioned several times in Acts.

MARY MAGDALENE made a difference

At least six, maybe seven, distinct Marys are mentioned in the New Testament. Each one made a difference in her own way. We know very little about Mary of Magdala. Mark gives us a summary of what Jesus did for her, and Luke mentions her discipleship. All the Gospels mention her part in the crucifixion and resurrection of Jesus.

We don't know how they met, but Mary Magdalene was possessed by seven demons when Jesus entered her life. Since there was not room for both Jesus and any demons in her life, the demons naturally vacated the premises. In their place we can only imagine the gratitude that flowed from this liberated woman. Jesus transformed her life; He changed her.

Mary joined a group of seldom mentioned women who apparently traveled with Jesus and the disciples. Several of them were wealthy enough to take care of the day-to-day traveling expenses. Luke briefly refers to their role in Luke 8:1–3. Mary's gratitude showed itself in action.

Cutting Edge

Mary's consistent faithfulness put her right in the path of honor. Wanting to anoint Jesus' body after the cross, she was the first to see the living Christ. She became the first eyewitness to the resurrection. Did she make a difference? Her persuasive testimony was the spark that ignited the movement of people who came to be known as Christians.

YOU can, too!

Mary was trying to make a difference in one way: by honoring Jesus' buried body. God had something even greater in mind. She set out to do what was right. That put her right in God's plan and pathway. Obedience has to precede honor and fame. Honor and fame do not necessarily follow obedience, at least on this side of eternity.

This is why it's important not only to live for God, but also to be wherever God is working, like in the church. If you are where God is acting, you may not always get to make a difference, but being there will definitely make a difference for you!

Want to know more? The clearest glimpses of Mary Magdalene can be found in Matthew 27:55—28:11; Mark 15:40—16:11; Luke 8:1–3; 23:55—24:12; John 19:25—20:18.

MARY AND MARTHA made a difference

One of the reasons Mary and Martha of Bethany made a difference comes from the fact that they were different. They were sisters, but clearly not the same. Together, they formed a hospitality team. Each had a unique personality that worked well with the other—most of the time. Mary focused on the guest. She was the conversationalist of the two. Martha busied herself with the details of entertaining. She focused on the guest's needs. Mary and Martha's hospitality was significant because their frequent guest was Jesus.

During one of Jesus' visits, a conflict arose. Martha was upset because Mary was enjoying listening to Jesus while she was having to bustle about to get a meal ready for more than a dozen men. She became flustered and frustrated. Martha finally asked Jesus to order her sister to help. Jesus' answer was an amazing example of tough and tender love: "Martha, Martha, you are worried and troubled about many things. But one thing is needed, and Mary has chosen that good part, which will not be taken away from her" (Luke 10:41, 42). Jesus' point wasn't necessarily that Martha shouldn't have been busy. Rather, His point was that Martha had allowed her busy-ness to make her forget the reason she was busy. Her attention shifted from her guest to herself, which led to resentment toward her sister.

Cutting Edge

Jesus helped them work out their teamwork. The last time the sisters appear in Scripture (John 12:1–3), we see a little change in their approach. Martha is still serving (she can't help it), but there's no hint of sulking. Mary is still focused on Jesus, but she is also acting in service by pouring costly perfume on His feet. Together, each one made a difference for their guest.

YOU can, too! In any situation, you bring something very special to offer—yourself. God's intention in your design is to call you into special service. your ultimate purpose isn't to meet the expectations of anyone other than your Creator. The difference you make in life will really be determined by God. Like Mary, you will accomplish that purpose more effectively if your attention is focused on God rather than on yourself.

Want to know more? Get to know the sisters better as you read

Luke 10:38–42; John 11:1–45; 12:1–3.

servant at supper time to say to those who were invited, 'Come, for all things are now ready.' ¹⁸But they all with one *accord* began to make excuses. The first said to him, 'I have bought a piece of ground, and I must go and see it. I ask you to have me excused.' ¹⁹And another said, 'I have bought five yoke of oxen, and I am going to test them. I ask you to have me excused.' ²⁰Still another said, 'I have married a wife, and therefore I cannot come.' ²¹So that servant came and reported these things to his master. Then the master of the house, being angry, said to his servant, 'Go out quickly into the streets and lanes of the city, and bring in here *the* poor and *the* maimed and *the* lame and *the* blind.' ²²And the servant said, 'Master, it is done as you commanded, and still there is room.' ²³Then the master said to the servant, 'Go out into the highways and hedges, and compel *them* to come in, that my house may be filled. ²⁴For I say to you that none of those men who were invited shall taste my supper.' "

WHAT'S IT MEAN?

Crucifixion was an agonizing process. The person sentenced to die was beaten and then forced to carry the crossbeam to the execution site. There, his arms were fastened to the crossbeam. The crossbeam and the person were then lifted off the ground and attached to an upright wooden stake. After several hours—sometimes several days—of tremendous pain, the person would die, usually either of suffocation or exhaustion.

Luke 14:27

LEAVING ALL TO FOLLOW CHRIST

²⁵Now great multitudes went with Him. And He turned and said to them, ²⁶"If anyone comes to Me and does not hate his father and mother, wife and children, brothers and sisters, yes, and his own life also, he cannot be My disciple. ²⁷And whoever does not bear his cross and come after Me cannot be My disciple. ²⁸For which of you, intending to build a tower, does not sit down first and count the cost, whether he has *enough* to finish *it*— ²⁹lest, after he has laid the foundation, and is not able to finish, all who see *it* begin to mock him, ³⁰saying, 'This man began to build and was not able to finish'.

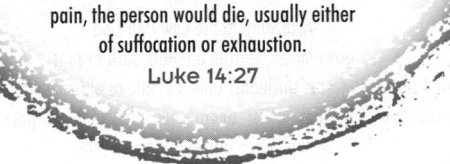

On the Edge

For which of you, intending to build a tower, does not sit down first and count the cost, whether he has enough to finish it—lest, after he has laid the foundation, and is not able to finish, all who see it begin to mock him, saying, "This man began to build and was not able to finish" (Luke 14:28-30).

In this passage Jesus is teaching about the element of planning in regard to discipleship. From His teaching we can apply the principle of financial planning to your goals for college. Like the builders of the tower, you can sit down with your folks and figure out how much it will cost to get through college. Make a plan and work the plan. Apply for scholarships, grants, and work-study programs. Begin planning a few years in advance so summer savings can go toward a college fund. There are also government loans available. Your parents may not be able to afford college, but with good planning, you will be able to get—and finish—a great education.

SEE FOR YOURSELF:
Prov. 2:7; 3:5, 6; 16:3

³¹Or what king, going to make war against another king, does not sit down first and consider whether he is able with ten thousand to meet him who comes against him with twenty thousand? ³²Or else, while the other is still a great way off, he sends a delegation and asks conditions of peace. ³³So likewise, whoever of you does not forsake all that he has cannot be My disciple.

TASTELESS SALT IS WORTHLESS

³⁴"Salt *is* good; but if the salt has lost its flavor, how shall it be seasoned? ³⁵It is neither fit for the land nor for the dunghill, *but* men throw it out. He who has ears to hear, let him hear!"

THE PARABLE OF THE LOST SHEEP

¹Then all the tax collectors and the sinners drew near to Him to hear Him. ²And the Pharisees and scribes complained, saying, "This Man receives sinners and eats with them." ³So He spoke this parable to them, saying:

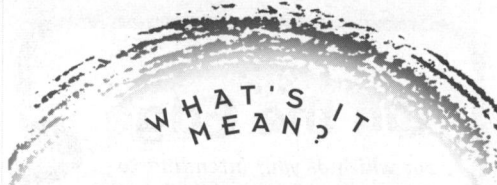

WHAT'S IT MEAN?

Salt was more than just a table flavoring in Jesus' day. Among other things, it was also used to preserve food. Most salt in ancient Palestine came from sea water, specifically water from the Dead Sea, which is nine times saltier than ocean water. It wasn't like the salt we use today, though. Because it was not very pure, salt in New Testament times became stale and disgusting pretty quickly.

Luke 14:34

⁴"What man of you, having a hundred sheep, if he loses one of them, does not leave the ninety-nine in the wilderness, and go after the one which is lost until he finds it? ⁵And when he has found *it*, he lays *it* on his shoulders, rejoicing. ⁶And when he comes home, he calls together *his* friends and neighbors, saying to them, 'Rejoice with me, for I have found my sheep which was lost!' ⁷I say to you that likewise there will be more joy in heaven over one sinner who repents than over ninety-nine just persons who need no repentance.

REPENTANCE
What do the angels do when a sinner repents? (15:7)

THE PARABLE OF THE LOST COIN

⁸"Or what woman, having ten silver coins,ᵃ if she loses one coin, does not light a lamp, sweep the house, and search carefully until she finds *it*? ⁹And when she has found *it*, she calls *her* friends and neighbors together, saying, 'Rejoice with me, for I have found the piece which I lost!' ¹⁰Likewise, I say to you, there is joy in the presence of the angels of God over one sinner who repents."

THE PARABLE OF THE LOST SON

¹¹Then He said: "A certain man had two sons. ¹²And the younger of them said to *his* father, 'Father, give me the portion of goods that falls *to me.*' So he divided to them *his* livelihood. ¹³And not many days after, the younger son gathered all together, journeyed to a far country, and there wasted his possessions with prodigal living. ¹⁴But when he had spent all, there arose a severe famine in that land, and he began to be in want. ¹⁵Then he went and joined himself to a citizen of that country, and he sent him into his fields to feed swine. ¹⁶And he would gladly have filled his stomach with the pods that the swine ate, and no one gave him *anything.*

¹⁷"But when he came to himself, he said, 'How many of my father's hired servants have bread enough and to spare, and I perish with hunger! ¹⁸I will arise and go to my father, and will say to him, "Father, I have sinned against heaven and before you, ¹⁹and I am no longer worthy to be called your son. Make me like one of your hired servants." '

²⁰"And he arose and came to his father. But when he was still a great way off, his father saw him and had compassion, and ran and fell on his neck and kissed him. ²¹And the son said to him, 'Father, I have sinned against heaven and in your sight, and am no longer worthy to be called your son.'

²²"But the father said to his servants, 'Bringᵃ out the best robe and put *it* on him, and put a ring on his hand and sandals on *his* feet. ²³And bring the fatted calf here and kill *it*, and let us eat and be merry; ²⁴for this my son was dead and is alive again; he was lost and is found.' And they began to be merry.

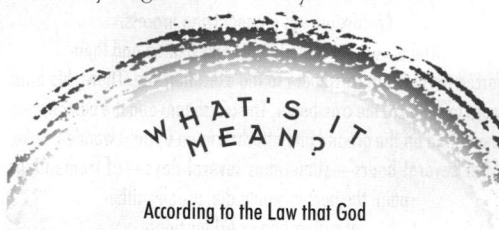

WHAT'S IT MEAN?

According to the Law that God gave Moses, certain animals, such as pigs and shellfish, were "unclean," unacceptable as either food or sacrifices. Not only were Jewish people not allowed to eat pork, they weren't even allowed to touch pigs.

Luke 15:15

²⁵"Now his older son was in the field. And as he came and drew near to the house, he heard music and dancing. ²⁶So he called one of the servants and asked what these things meant. ²⁷And he said to him, 'Your brother has come, and because he has received him safe

---

15:8 ᵃGreek *drachma*, a valuable coin often worn in a ten-piece garland by married women   **15:22** ᵃNU-Text reads *Quickly bring.*

and sound, your father has killed the fatted calf.' ²⁸But he was angry and would not go in. Therefore his father came out and pleaded with him. ²⁹So he answered and said to *his* father, 'Lo, these many years I have been serving you; I never transgressed your commandment at any time; and yet you never gave me a young goat, that I might make merry with my friends. ³⁰But as soon as this son of yours came, who has devoured your livelihood with harlots, you killed the fatted calf for him.'

³¹"And he said to him, 'Son, you are always with me, and all that I have is yours. ³²It was right that we should make merry and be glad, for your brother was dead and is alive again, and was lost and is found.' "

THE PARABLE OF THE UNJUST STEWARD

¹He also said to His disciples: "There was a certain rich man who had a steward, and an accusation was brought to him that this man was wasting his goods. ²So he called him and said to him, 'What is this I hear about you? Give an account of your stewardship, for you can no longer be steward.'

³"Then the steward said within himself, 'What shall I do? For my master is taking the stewardship away from me. I cannot dig; I am ashamed to beg. ⁴I have resolved what to do, that when I am put out of the stewardship, they may receive me into their houses.'

⁵"So he called every one of his master's debtors to *him,* and said to the first, 'How much do you owe my master?' ⁶And he said, 'A hundred measures*ᵃ* of oil.' So he said to him, 'Take your bill, and sit down quickly and write fifty.' ⁷Then he said to another, 'And how much do you owe?' So he said, 'A hundred measures*ᵃ* of wheat.' And he said to him, 'Take your bill, and write eighty.' ⁸So the master commended the unjust steward because he had dealt shrewdly. For the sons of this world are more shrewd in their generation than the sons of light.

⁹"And I say to you, make friends for yourselves by unrighteous mammon, that when you fail,*ᵃ* they may receive you into an everlasting home. ¹⁰He who *is* faithful in *what is* least is faithful also in much; and he who is unjust in *what is* least is unjust also in much. ¹¹Therefore if you have not been faithful in the unrighteous mammon, who will commit to your trust the true *riches*? ¹²And if you have not been faithful in what is another man's, who will give you what is your own?

¹³"No servant can serve two masters; for either he will hate the one and love the other, or else he will be loyal to the one and despise the other. You cannot serve God and mammon."

THE LAW, THE PROPHETS, AND THE KINGDOM

MONEY

Can Christians serve both God and money? (16:13)

¹⁴Now the Pharisees, who were lovers of money, also heard all these things, and they derided Him. ¹⁵And He said to them, "You are those who justify yourselves before men, but God knows your hearts. For what is highly esteemed among men is an abomination in the sight of God.

¹⁶"The law and the prophets *were* until John. Since that time the kingdom of God has been preached, and everyone is pressing into it. ¹⁷And it is easier for heaven and earth to pass away than for one tittle of the law to fail.

¹⁸"Whoever divorces his wife and marries another commits adultery; and whoever marries her who is divorced from *her* husband commits adultery.

THE RICH MAN AND LAZARUS

¹⁹"There was a certain rich man who was clothed in purple and fine linen and fared sumptuously every day. ²⁰But there was a certain beggar named Lazarus, full of sores, who was laid at his gate, ²¹desiring to be fed with the crumbs which fell*ᵃ* from the rich man's table. Moreover the dogs came and licked his sores. ²²So it was that the beggar died, and was carried by the angels to Abraham's bosom. The rich man also died and was buried. ²³And being in torments in Hades, he lifted up his eyes and saw Abraham afar off, and Lazarus in his bosom. ²⁴"Then he cried and said, 'Father Abraham, have mercy on me, and send Lazarus that he may dip the tip of his finger in water and cool my tongue; for I am tormented in this flame.' ²⁵But Abraham said, 'Son, remember that in your lifetime you received your good things, and likewise Lazarus evil things; but now he is comforted and you are tormented. ²⁶And besides all this, between us and you there is a great gulf fixed, so that those who want to pass from here to you cannot, nor can those from there pass to us.'

²⁷"Then he said, 'I beg you therefore, father, that you would send him to my father's house, ²⁸for I have five brothers, that he may testify to

---

16:6 *ᵃ*Greek *batos*, eight or nine gallons each (Old Testament *bath*)   **16:7** *ᵃ*Greek *koros*, ten or twelve bushels each (Old Testament *kor*)   **16:9** *ᵃ*NU-Text reads *it fails.*   **16:21** *ᵃ*NU-Text reads *with what fell.*

them, lest they also come to this place of torment.' [29]Abraham said to him, 'They have Moses and the prophets; let them hear them.' [30]And he said, 'No, father Abraham; but if one goes to them from the dead, they will repent.' [31]But he said to him, 'If they do not hear Moses and the prophets, neither will they be persuaded though one rise from the dead.' "

JESUS WARNS OF OFFENSES

[1]Then He said to the disciples, "It is impossible that no offenses should come, but woe *to him* through whom they do come! [2]It would be better for him if a millstone were hung around his neck, and he were thrown into the sea, than that he should offend one of these little ones. [3]Take heed to yourselves. If your brother sins against you,[a] rebuke him; and if he repents, forgive him. [4]And if he sins against you seven times in a day, and seven times in a day returns to you,[a] saying, 'I repent,' you shall forgive him."

FAITH AND DUTY

[5]And the apostles said to the Lord, "Increase our faith."

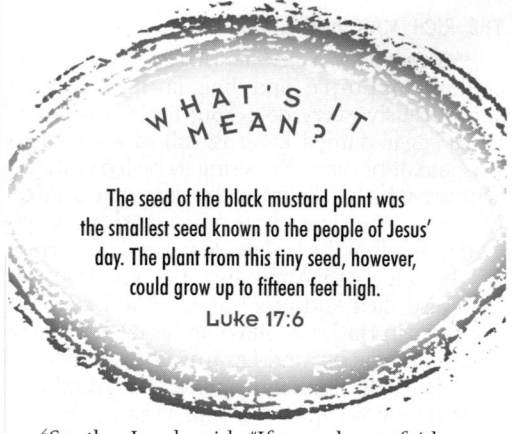

WHAT'S IT MEAN?

The seed of the black mustard plant was the smallest seed known to the people of Jesus' day. The plant from this tiny seed, however, could grow up to fifteen feet high.

Luke 17:6

[6]So the Lord said, "If you have faith as a mustard seed, you can say to this mulberry tree, 'Be pulled up by the roots and be planted in the sea,' and it would obey you.

FAITH

How much faith is needed? (17:6)

[7]And which of you, having a servant plowing or tending sheep, will say to him when he has come in from the field, 'Come at once and sit down to eat'? [8]But will he not rather say to him, 'Prepare something for my supper, and gird yourself and serve me till I have eaten and drunk, and afterward you will eat and drink'? [9]Does he thank that servant because he did the things that were commanded him? I think not.[a] [10]So likewise you, when you have done all those things which you are commanded, say, 'We are unprofitable servants. We have done what was our duty to do.' "

TEN LEPERS CLEANSED

[11]Now it happened as He went to Jerusalem that He passed through the midst of Samaria and Galilee. [12]Then as He entered a certain village, there met Him ten men who were lepers, who stood afar off. [13]And they lifted up *their* voices and said, "Jesus, Master, have mercy on us!"

[14]So when He saw *them*, He said to them, "Go, show yourselves to the priests." And so it was that as they went, they were cleansed.

[15]And one of them, when he saw that he was healed, returned, and with a loud voice glorified God, [16]and fell down on *his* face at His feet, giving Him thanks. And he was a Samaritan.

[17]So Jesus answered and said, "Were there not ten cleansed? But where *are* the nine? [18]Were there not any found who returned to give glory to God except this foreigner?" [19]And He said to him, "Arise, go your way. Your faith has made you well."

THE COMING OF THE KINGDOM

[20]Now when He was asked by the Pharisees when the kingdom of God would come, He answered them and said, "The kingdom of God does not come with observation; [21]nor will they say, 'See here!' or 'See there!'[a] For indeed, the kingdom of God is within you."

[22]Then He said to the disciples, "The days will come when you will desire to see one of the days of the Son of Man, and you will not see *it*. [23]And they will say to you, 'Look here!' or 'Look there!'[a] Do not go after *them* or follow *them*. [24]For as the lightning that flashes out of one *part* under heaven shines to the other *part* under heaven, so also the Son of Man will be in His day. [25]But first He must suffer many things and be rejected by this generation. [26]And as it was in the days of Noah, so it will be also in the days of the Son of Man: [27]They ate, they drank, they married wives, they were given in marriage, until the day that Noah entered the ark, and the flood came and destroyed them all. [28]Likewise as it was also in the days of Lot: They ate, they drank, they bought, they sold, they planted,

17:3 [a]NU-Text omits *against you.*   **17:4** [a]M-Text omits *to you.*   **17:9** [a]NU-Text ends verse with *commanded;* M-Text omits *him.*   **17:21** [a]NU-Text reverses *here* and *there.*   **17:23** [a]NU-Text reverses *here* and *there.*

they built; [29]but on the day that Lot went out of Sodom it rained fire and brimstone from heaven and destroyed *them* all. [30]Even so will it be in the day when the Son of Man is revealed.

[31]"In that day, he who is on the housetop, and his goods *are* in the house, let him not come down to take them away. And likewise the one who is in the field, let him not turn back. [32]Remember Lot's wife. [33]Whoever seeks to save his life will lose it, and whoever loses his life will preserve it. [34]I tell you, in that night there will be two *men* in one bed: the one will be taken and the other will be left. [35]Two *women* will be grinding together: the one will be taken and the other left. [36]Two *men* will be in the field: the one will be taken and the other left."[a]

[37]And they answered and said to Him, "Where, Lord?"

So He said to them, "Wherever the body is, there the eagles will be gathered together."

THE PARABLE OF THE PERSISTENT WIDOW

[1]Then He spoke a parable to them, that men always ought to pray and not lose heart, [2]saying: "There was in a certain city a judge who did not fear God nor regard man. [3]Now there was a widow in that city; and she came to him, saying, 'Get justice for me from my adversary.' [4]And he would not for a while; but afterward he said within himself, 'Though I do not fear God nor regard man, [5]yet because this widow troubles me I will avenge her, lest by her continual coming she weary me.' "

[6]Then the Lord said, "Hear what the unjust judge said. [7]And shall God not avenge His own elect who cry out day and night to Him, though He bears long with them? [8]I tell you that He will avenge them speedily. Nevertheless, when the Son of Man comes, will He really find faith on the earth?"

THE PARABLE OF THE PHARISEE AND THE TAX COLLECTOR

[9]Also He spoke this parable to some who trusted in themselves that they were righteous, and despised others: [10]"Two men went up to the temple to pray, one a Pharisee and the other a tax collector. [11]The Pharisee stood and prayed thus with himself, 'God, I thank You that I am not like other men—extortioners, unjust, adulterers, or even as this tax collector. [12]I fast twice

a week; I give tithes of all that I possess.' [13]And the tax collector, standing afar off, would not so much as raise *his* eyes to heaven, but beat his breast, saying, 'God, be merciful to me a sinner!' [14]I tell you, this man went down to his house justified *rather* than the other; for everyone who exalts himself will be humbled, and he who humbles himself will be exalted."

> **PRAYER**
> What kind of attitude should we pray with? (18:9–14)

> "Whoever seeks to save his life will lose it, and whoever loses his life will preserve it."
> (Luke 17:33)

JESUS BLESSES LITTLE CHILDREN

[15]Then they also brought infants to Him that He might touch them; but when the disciples saw *it*, they rebuked them. [16]But Jesus called them to *Him* and said, "Let the little children come to Me, and do not forbid them; for of such is the kingdom of God. [17]Assuredly, I say to you, whoever does not receive the kingdom of God as a little child will by no means enter it."

JESUS COUNSELS THE RICH YOUNG RULER

[18]Now a certain ruler asked Him, saying, "Good Teacher, what shall I do to inherit eternal life?"

> **WHAT'S IT MEAN?**
> To collect their taxes, the Romans hired local Jewish citizens. These collectors were known for charging their fellow Jews more money than they really owed and keeping the extra cash for themselves. Because of this and because the collectors worked for the hated Roman government, taxmen were usually seen as traitors to their people.
> Luke 18:10

[19]So Jesus said to him, "Why do you call Me good? No one *is* good but One, *that is*, God. [20]You know the commandments: 'Do not commit adultery,' 'Do not murder,' 'Do not steal,' 'Do not bear false witness,' 'Honor your father and your mother.' "[a]

17:36 [a]NU-Text and M-Text omit verse 36.   **18:20** [a]Exodus 20:12–16; Deuteronomy 5:16–20

²¹And he said, "All these things I have kept from my youth."

²²So when Jesus heard these things, He said to him, "You still lack one thing. Sell all that you have and distribute to the poor, and you will have treasure in heaven; and come, follow Me."

²³But when he heard this, he became very sorrowful, for he was very rich.

WITH GOD ALL THINGS ARE POSSIBLE

²⁴And when Jesus saw that he became very sorrowful, He said, "How hard it is for those who have riches to enter the kingdom of God! ²⁵For it is easier for a camel to go through the eye of a needle than for a rich man to enter the kingdom of God."

²⁶And those who heard it said, "Who then can be saved?"

²⁷But He said, "The things which are impossible with men are possible with God."

ASSURANCE

Is false assurance dangerous? (18:18–30)

²⁸Then Peter said, "See, we have left all[a] and followed You."

²⁹So He said to them, "Assuredly, I say to you, there is no one who has left house or parents or brothers or wife or children, for the sake of the kingdom of God, ³⁰who shall not receive many times more in this present time, and in the age to come eternal life."

JESUS A THIRD TIME PREDICTS HIS DEATH AND RESURRECTION

³¹Then He took the twelve aside and said to them, "Behold, we are going up to Jerusalem, and all things that are written by the prophets concerning the Son of Man will be accomplished. ³²For He will be delivered to the Gentiles and will be mocked and insulted and spit upon. ³³They will scourge Him and kill Him. And the third day He will rise again."

³⁴But they understood none of these things; this saying was hidden from them, and they did not know the things which were spoken.

A BLIND MAN RECEIVES HIS SIGHT

³⁵Then it happened, as He was coming near Jericho, that a certain blind man sat by the road begging. ³⁶And hearing a multitude passing by, he asked what it meant. ³⁷So they told him that Jesus of Nazareth was passing by. ³⁸And he cried out, saying, "Jesus, Son of David, have mercy on me!"

³⁹Then those who went before warned him that he should be quiet; but he cried out all the more, "Son of David, have mercy on me!"

⁴⁰So Jesus stood still and commanded him to be brought to Him. And when he had come near, He asked him, ⁴¹saying, "What do you want Me to do for you?"

He said, "Lord, that I may receive my sight."

⁴²Then Jesus said to him, "Receive your sight; your faith has made you well." ⁴³And immediately he received his sight, and followed Him, glorifying God. And all the people, when they saw it, gave praise to God.

JESUS COMES TO ZACCHAEUS' HOUSE

¹Then *Jesus* entered and passed through Jericho. ²Now behold, *there was* a man named Zacchaeus who was a chief tax collector, and he was rich. ³And he sought to see who Jesus was, but could not because of the crowd, for he was of short stature. ⁴So he ran ahead and climbed up into a sycamore tree to see Him, for He was going to pass that *way.* ⁵And when Jesus came to the place, He looked up and saw him,[a] and said to him, "Zacchaeus, make haste and come down, for today I must stay at your house." ⁶So he made haste and came down, and received Him joyfully. ⁷But when they saw *it,* they all complained, saying, "He has gone to be a guest with a man who is a sinner."

⁸Then Zacchaeus stood and said to the Lord, "Look, Lord, I give half of my goods to the poor; and if I have taken anything from anyone by false accusation, I restore fourfold."

⁹And Jesus said to him, "Today salvation has come to this house, because he also is a son of Abraham; ¹⁰for the Son of Man has come to seek and to save that which was lost."

THE PARABLE OF THE MINAS

¹¹Now as they heard these things, He spoke another parable, because He was near Jerusalem and because they thought the kingdom of God would appear immediately. ¹²Therefore He said: "A certain nobleman went into a far country to receive for himself a kingdom and to return. ¹³So he called ten of his servants, delivered to them ten minas,[a] and said to them, 'Do business till I come.' ¹⁴But his citizens hated him, and sent a delegation after him, saying, 'We will not have this *man* to reign over us.'

¹⁵"And so it was that when he returned, having received the kingdom, he then commanded these servants, to whom he had given the money, to be called to him, that he might

---

18:28 [a]NU-Text reads *our own.*   **19:5** [a]NU-Text omits *and saw him.*   **19:13** [a]The *mina* (Greek *mna,* Hebrew *minah*) was worth about three months' salary.

know how much every man had gained by trading. ¹⁶Then came the first, saying, 'Master, your mina has earned ten minas'. ¹⁷And he said to him, 'Well *done*, good servant; because you were faithful in a very little, have authority over ten cities'. ¹⁸And the second came, saying, 'Master, your mina has earned five minas'. ¹⁹Likewise he said to him, 'You also be over five cities'.

²⁰"Then another came, saying, 'Master, here is your mina, which I have kept put away in a handkerchief. ²¹For I feared you, because you are an austere man. You collect what you did not deposit, and reap what you did not sow'. ²²And he said to him, 'Out of your own mouth I will judge you, *you* wicked servant. You knew that I was an austere man, collecting what I did not deposit and reaping what I did not sow. ²³Why then did you not put my money in the bank, that at my coming I might have collected it with interest?'

²⁴"And he said to those who stood by, 'Take the mina from him, and give *it* to him who has ten minas'. ²⁵(But they said to him, 'Master, he has ten minas'.) ²⁶'For I say to you, that to everyone who has will be given; and from him who does not have, even what he has will be taken away from him. ²⁷But bring here those enemies of mine, who did not want me to reign over them, and slay *them* before me'. "

THE TRIUMPHAL ENTRY

²⁸When He had said this, He went on ahead, going up to Jerusalem. ²⁹And it came to pass, when He drew near to Bethphage*ᵃ* and Bethany, at the mountain called Olivet, *that* He sent two of His disciples, ³⁰saying, "Go into the village opposite *you*, where as you enter you will find a colt tied, on which no one has ever sat. Loose it and bring *it* here. ³¹And if anyone asks you, 'Why are you loosing *it*?' thus you shall say to him, 'Because the Lord has need of it'. "

³²So those who were sent went their way and found *it* just as He had said to them. ³³But as they were loosing the colt, the owners of it said to them, "Why are you loosing the colt?"

³⁴And they said, "The Lord has need of him." ³⁵Then they brought him to Jesus. And they threw their own clothes on the colt, and they set Jesus on him. ³⁶And as He went, *many* spread their clothes on the road.

³⁷Then, as He was now drawing near the descent of the Mount of Olives, the whole multitude of the disciples began to rejoice and praise God with a loud voice for all the mighty works they had seen, ³⁸saying:

" 'Blessed is the King who comes in the name of the LORD!'*ᵃ*
Peace in heaven and glory in the highest!"

³⁹And some of the Pharisees called to Him from the crowd, "Teacher, rebuke Your disciples."

⁴⁰But He answered and said to them, "I tell you that if these should keep silent, the stones would immediately cry out."

JESUS WEEPS OVER JERUSALEM

⁴¹Now as He drew near, He saw the city and wept over it, ⁴²saying, "If you had known, even you, especially in this your day, the things *that make* for your peace! But now they are hidden from your eyes. ⁴³For days will come upon you when your enemies will build an embankment around you, surround you and close you in on every side, ⁴⁴and level you, and your children within you, to the ground; and they will not leave in you one stone upon another, because you did not know the time of your visitation."

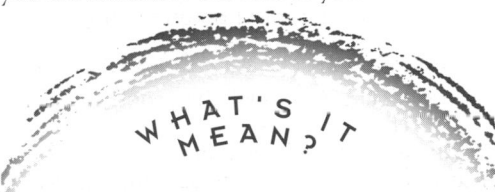

WHAT'S IT MEAN?

This passage predicts the total destruction of Jerusalem—the kind of destruction that occurred in A.D. 70. After the Jews tried to rebel against Rome, the empire retaliated by sending its army, led by a general named Titus, to attack Jerusalem. When the Roman army was done, the temple had been burned to the ground, its sacred furnishings had been taken back to Rome, and the city of Jerusalem had been reduced to rubble. The Jews were no longer permitted any kind of self-rule.

Luke 19:43

JESUS CLEANSES THE TEMPLE

⁴⁵Then He went into the temple and began to drive out those who bought and sold in it,*ᵃ* ⁴⁶saying to them, "It is written, '*My house is*ᵃ a house of prayer*,*'*ᵇ* but you have made it a '*den of thieves*.' "*ᶜ*

19:29 *ᵃ*M-Text reads *Bethphage*.   **19:38** *ᵃ*Psalm 118:26   **19:45** *ᵃ*NU-Text reads *those who were selling*.
19:46 *ᵃ*NU-Text reads *shall be*. *ᵇ*Isaiah 56:7 *ᶜ*Jeremiah 7:11

⁴⁷And He was teaching daily in the temple. But the chief priests, the scribes, and the leaders of the people sought to destroy Him, ⁴⁸and were unable to do anything; for all the people were very attentive to hear Him.

JESUS' AUTHORITY QUESTIONED

¹Now it happened on one of those days, as He taught the people in the temple and preached the gospel, *that* the chief priests and the scribes, together with the elders, confronted Him ²and spoke to Him, saying, "Tell us, by what authority are You doing these things? Or who is he who gave You this authority?"

³But He answered and said to them, "I also will ask you one thing, and answer Me: ⁴The baptism of John—was it from heaven or from men?"

⁵And they reasoned among themselves, saying, "If we say, 'From heaven,' He will say, 'Why then[a] did you not believe him?' ⁶But if we say, 'From men,' all the people will stone us, for they are persuaded that John was a prophet." ⁷So they answered that they did not know where *it was* from.

⁸And Jesus said to them, "Neither will I tell you by what authority I do these things."

THE PARABLE OF THE WICKED VINEDRESSERS

⁹Then He began to tell the people this parable: "A certain man planted a vineyard, leased it to vinedressers, and went into a far country for a long time. ¹⁰Now at vintage-time he sent a servant to the vinedressers, that they might give him some of the fruit of the vineyard. But the vinedressers beat him and sent *him* away empty-handed. ¹¹Again he sent another servant; and they beat him also, treated *him* shamefully, and sent *him* away empty-handed. ¹²And again he sent a third; and they wounded him also and cast *him* out.

¹³"Then the owner of the vineyard said, 'What shall I do? I will send my beloved son. Probably they will respect *him* when they see him.' ¹⁴But when the vinedressers saw him, they reasoned among themselves, saying, 'This is the heir. Come, let us kill him, that the inheritance may be ours.' ¹⁵So they cast him out of the vineyard and killed *him.* Therefore what will the owner of the vineyard do to them? ¹⁶He will come and destroy those vinedressers and give the vineyard to others."

And when they heard *it* they said, "Certainly not!"

¹⁷Then He looked at them and said, "What then is this that is written:

'The stone which the builders rejected
Has become the chief cornerstone'?[a]

¹⁸Whoever falls on that stone will be broken; but on whomever it falls, it will grind him to powder."

¹⁹And the chief priests and the scribes that very hour sought to lay hands on Him, but they feared the people[a]—for they knew He had spoken this parable against them.

THE PHARISEES: IS IT LAWFUL TO PAY TAXES TO CAESAR?

²⁰So they watched *Him,* and sent spies who pretended to be righteous, that they might seize on His words, in order to deliver Him to the power and the authority of the governor. ²¹Then they asked Him, saying, "Teacher, we know that You say and teach rightly, and You do not show personal favoritism, but teach the way of God in truth: ²²Is it lawful for us to pay taxes to Caesar or not?"

²³But He perceived their craftiness, and said to them, "Why do you test Me?[a] ²⁴Show Me a denarius. Whose image and inscription does it have?"

They answered and said, "Caesar's."

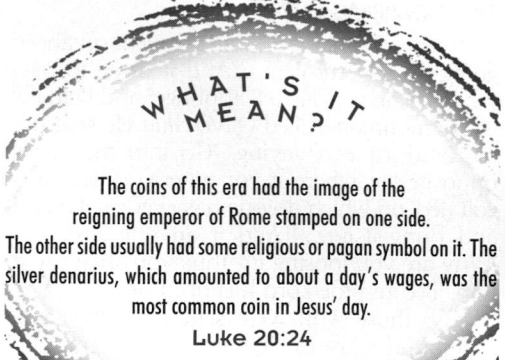

WHAT'S IT MEAN?

The coins of this era had the image of the reigning emperor of Rome stamped on one side. The other side usually had some religious or pagan symbol on it. The silver denarius, which amounted to about a day's wages, was the most common coin in Jesus' day.
Luke 20:24

²⁵And He said to them, "Render therefore to Caesar the things that are Caesar's, and to God the things that are God's."

²⁶But they could not catch Him in His words in the presence of the people. And they marveled at His answer and kept silent.

20:5 [a]NU-Text and M-Text omit *then.* **20:17** [a]Psalm 118:22 **20:19** [a]M-Text reads *but they were afraid.* **20:23** [a]NU-Text omits *Why do you test Me?*

THE SADDUCEES: WHAT ABOUT THE RESURRECTION?

27Then some of the Sadducees, who deny that there is a resurrection, came to *Him* and asked Him, 28saying: "Teacher, Moses wrote to us *that* if a man's brother dies, having a wife, and he dies without children, his brother should take his wife and raise up offspring for his brother. 29Now there were seven brothers. And the first took a wife, and died without children. 30And the second*a* took her as wife, and he died childless. 31Then the third took her, and in like manner the seven also; and they left no children,*a* and died. 32Last of all the woman died also. 33Therefore, in the resurrection, whose wife does she become? For all seven had her as wife."

34Jesus answered and said to them, "The sons of this age marry and are given in marriage. 35But those who are counted worthy to attain that age, and the resurrection from the dead, neither marry nor are given in marriage; 36nor can they die anymore, for they are equal to the angels and are sons of God, being sons of the resurrection. 37But even Moses showed in the *burning* bush *passage* that the dead are raised, when he called the Lord *'the God of Abraham, the God of Isaac, and the God of Jacob.'a* 38For He is not the God of the dead but of the living, for all live to Him."

39Then some of the scribes answered and said, "Teacher, You have spoken well." 40But after that they dared not question Him anymore.

ANGELS
Can angels die? (20:36)

JESUS: HOW CAN DAVID CALL HIS DESCENDANT LORD?

41And He said to them, "How can they say that the Christ is the Son of David? 42Now David himself said in the Book of Psalms:

'The LORD said to my Lord,
"Sit at My right hand,
43   Till I make Your enemies Your
        footstool." ' *a*

44Therefore David calls Him *'Lord'*; how is He then his Son?"

BEWARE OF THE SCRIBES

45Then, in the hearing of all the people, He said to His disciples, 46"Beware of the scribes, who desire to go around in long robes, love greetings in the marketplaces, the best seats in the synagogues, and the best places at feasts, 47who devour widows' houses, and for a pretense make long prayers. These will receive greater condemnation."

On the Edge

Then, in the hearing of all the people, He said to His disciples, "Beware of the scribes, who desire to go around in long robes, love greetings in the marketplaces, the best seats in the synagogues, and the best places at feasts, who devour widows' houses, and for a pretense make long prayers. These will receive greater condemnation" (Luke 20:45–47).

More than anything else, a pastor should be a lover of God and a lover of God's people. A man can be a great fund-raiser or speaker, but if he doesn't truly love the people, everybody suffers. He should know God's Word and be able to teach in a way that is clear to you. He should be teaching truths from the Bible, and not just from his own opinion. A great pastor has compassion for sinners and love for the lost. He has the heart of a servant and the strength of a leader. A man of God listens to God. He does what he hears God tell him to do, and he goes where he senses God leads. A good pastor has honor, integrity, and a passionate devotion to Jesus.

The relationship between a pastor and his congregation can be compared to the relationship between a shepherd and his sheep. When you're looking for a pastor, think of yourself as a sheep and of him as a shepherd. Be wary of flashy and arrogant leaders. A godly pastor can be one of the most important people in your life.

SEE FOR YOURSELF:
Ps. 100:3; Is. 40:11; Jer. 23:4; Ezek. 34:11–16; Matt. 23; John 10:1–16; Acts 20:28; 1 Tim. 3:1–12; Titus 1:5–9

THE WIDOW'S TWO MITES

[1]And He looked up and saw the rich putting their gifts into the treasury, [2]and He saw also a certain poor widow putting in two mites. [3]So He said, "Truly I say to you that this poor widow has put in more than all; [4]for all these out of their abundance have put in offerings for God,[a] but she out of her poverty put in all the livelihood that she had."

JESUS PREDICTS THE DESTRUCTION OF THE TEMPLE

[5]Then, as some spoke of the temple, how it was adorned with beautiful stones and donations, He said, [6]"These things which you see—the days will come in which not one stone shall be left upon another that shall not be thrown down."

WHAT'S IT MEAN?

Construction of the temple in Jerusalem was a pet project of Herod the Great, and it showed. The ornate main building was made of cream-colored stone and gold. Some of the stones used in the construction were almost forty feet long. The main building was completed in 9 B.C. The entire structure wasn't finished until A.D. 64. (Postscript: In A.D. 70, the Romans completely destroyed the temple once again—just six years after the construction had ended.)

Luke 21:5

THE SIGNS OF THE TIMES AND THE END OF THE AGE

[7]So they asked Him, saying, "Teacher, but when will these things be? And what sign will there be when these things are about to take place?"

[8]And He said: "Take heed that you not be deceived. For many will come in My name, saying, 'I am He,' and, 'The time has drawn near.' Therefore[a] do not go after them. [9]But when you hear of wars and commotions, do not be terrified; for these things must come to pass first, but the end will not come immediately."

[10]Then He said to them, "Nation will rise against nation, and kingdom against kingdom. [11]And there will be great earthquakes in various places, and famines and pestilences; and there will be fearful sights and great signs from heaven. [12]But before all these things, they will lay their hands on you and persecute you, delivering you up to the synagogues and prisons. You will be brought before kings and rulers for My name's sake. [13]But it will turn out for you as an occasion for testimony. [14]Therefore settle it in your hearts not to meditate beforehand on what you will answer; [15]for I will give you a mouth and wisdom which all your adversaries will not be able to contradict or resist. [16]You will be betrayed even by parents and brothers, relatives and friends; and they will put some of you to death. [17]And you will be hated by all for My name's sake. [18]But not a hair of your head shall be lost. [19]By your patience possess your souls.

THE DESTRUCTION OF JERUSALEM

[20]"But when you see Jerusalem surrounded by armies, then know that its desolation is near. [21]Then let those who are in Judea flee to the mountains, let those who are in the midst of her depart, and let not those who are in the country enter her. [22]For these are the days of vengeance, that all things which are written may be fulfilled. [23]But woe to those who are pregnant and to those who are nursing babies in those days! For there will be great distress in the land and wrath upon this people. [24]And they will fall by the edge of the sword, and be led away captive into all nations. And Jerusalem will be trampled by Gentiles until the times of the Gentiles are fulfilled.

THE COMING OF THE SON OF MAN

[25]"And there will be signs in the sun, in the moon, and in the stars; and on the earth distress of nations, with perplexity, the sea and the waves roaring; [26]men's hearts failing them from fear and the expectation of those things which are coming on the earth, for the powers of the heavens will be shaken. [27]Then they will see the Son of Man coming in a cloud with power and great glory. [28]Now when these things begin to happen, look up and lift up your heads, because your redemption draws near."

THE PARABLE OF THE FIG TREE

[29]Then He spoke to them a parable: "Look at the fig tree, and all the trees. [30]When they are already budding, you see and know for yourselves that summer is now near. [31]So you also, when you see these things happening, know that the kingdom of God is near. [32]Assuredly, I

say to you, this generation will by no means pass away till all things take place. ³³Heaven and earth will pass away, but My words will by no means pass away.

THE IMPORTANCE OF WATCHING

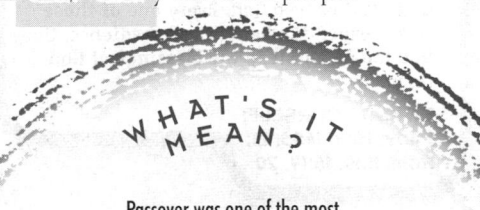

DRINKING

Is becoming drunk dangerous? (21:34)

³⁴"But take heed to yourselves, lest your hearts be weighed down with carousing, drunkenness, and cares of this life, and that Day come on you unexpectedly. ³⁵For it will come as a snare on all those who dwell on the face of the whole earth. ³⁶Watch therefore, and pray always that you may be counted worthy[a] to escape all these things that will come to pass, and to stand before the Son of Man."

³⁷And in the daytime He was teaching in the temple, but at night He went out and stayed on the mountain called Olivet. ³⁸Then early in the morning all the people came to Him in the temple to hear Him.

"Heaven and earth will pass away, but My words will by no means pass away." (Luke 21:33)

THE PLOT TO KILL JESUS

¹Now the Feast of Unleavened Bread drew near, which is called Passover. ²And the chief priests and the scribes sought how they might kill Him, for they feared the people.

WHAT'S IT MEAN?

Passover was one of the most important holidays on the Jewish calendar. It was set aside as a time for recalling how God had rescued the Israelites from slavery in Egypt. To celebrate, the Jewish people ate a meal similar to the one their ancestors had eaten when they prepared to leave Egypt.
Luke 22:1

³Then Satan entered Judas, surnamed Iscariot, who was numbered among the twelve. ⁴So he went his way and conferred with the chief priests and captains, how he might betray Him to them. ⁵And they were glad, and agreed to give him money. ⁶So he promised and sought opportunity to betray Him to them in the absence of the multitude.

JESUS AND HIS DISCIPLES PREPARE THE PASSOVER

⁷Then came the Day of Unleavened Bread, when the Passover must be killed. ⁸And He sent Peter and John, saying, "Go and prepare the Passover for us, that we may eat."

⁹So they said to Him, "Where do You want us to prepare?"

¹⁰And He said to them, "Behold, when you have entered the city, a man will meet you carrying a pitcher of water; follow him into the house which he enters. ¹¹Then you shall say to the master of the house, 'The Teacher says to you, "Where is the guest room where I may eat the Passover with My disciples?"' ¹²Then he will show you a large, furnished upper room; there make ready."

¹³So they went and found it just as He had said to them, and they prepared the Passover.

JESUS INSTITUTES THE LORD'S SUPPER

¹⁴When the hour had come, He sat down, and the twelve[a] apostles with Him. ¹⁵Then He said to them, "With *fervent* desire I have desired to eat this Passover with you before I suffer; ¹⁶for I say to you, I will no longer eat of it until it is fulfilled in the kingdom of God."

¹⁷Then He took the cup, and gave thanks, and said, "Take this and divide *it* among yourselves; ¹⁸for I say to you,[a] I will not drink of the fruit of the vine until the kingdom of God comes."

¹⁹And He took bread, gave thanks and broke *it*, and gave *it* to them, saying, "This is My body which is given for you; do this in remembrance of Me."

²⁰Likewise He also *took* the cup after supper, saying, "This cup *is* the new covenant in My blood, which is shed for you. ²¹But behold, the hand of My betrayer *is* with Me on the table. ²²And truly the Son of Man goes as it has been determined, but woe to that man by whom He is betrayed!"

²³Then they began to question among themselves, which of them it was who would do this thing.

THE DISCIPLES ARGUE ABOUT GREATNESS

24Now there was also a dispute among them, as to which of them should be considered the greatest. 25And He said to them, "The kings of the Gentiles exercise lordship over them, and those who exercise authority over them are called 'benefactors.' 26But not so *among* you; on the contrary, he who is greatest among you, let him be as the younger, and he who governs as he who serves. 27For who *is* greater, he who sits at the table, or he who serves? *Is* it not he who sits at the table? Yet I am among you as the One who serves.

28"But you are those who have continued with Me in My trials. 29And I bestow upon you a kingdom, just as My Father bestowed *one* upon Me, 30that you may eat and drink at My table in My kingdom, and sit on thrones judging the twelve tribes of Israel."

JESUS PREDICTS PETER'S DENIAL

31And the Lord said,[a] "Simon, Simon! Indeed, Satan has asked for you, that he may sift *you* as wheat. 32But I have prayed for you, that your faith should not fail; and when you have returned to *Me*, strengthen your brethren."

33But he said to Him, "Lord, I am ready to go with You, both to prison and to death."

34Then He said, "I tell you, Peter, the rooster shall not crow this day before you will deny three times that you know Me."

SUPPLIES FOR THE ROAD

35And He said to them, "When I sent you without money bag, knapsack, and sandals, did you lack anything?"

So they said, "Nothing."

36Then He said to them, "But now, he who has a money bag, let him take *it*, and likewise a knapsack; and he who has no sword, let him sell his garment and buy one. 37For I say to you that this which is written must still be accomplished in Me: '*And He was numbered with the transgressors.*'[a] For the things concerning Me have an end."

38So they said, "Lord, look, here *are* two swords."

And He said to them, "It is enough."

THE PRAYER IN THE GARDEN

39Coming out, He went to the Mount of Olives, as He was accustomed, and His disciples also followed Him. 40When He came to the place, He said to them, "Pray that you may not enter into temptation."

41And He was withdrawn from them about a stone's throw, and He knelt down and prayed, 42saying, "Father, if it is Your will, take this cup away from Me; nevertheless not My will, but Yours, be done." 43Then an angel appeared to Him from heaven, strengthening Him. 44And being in agony, He prayed more earnestly. Then His sweat became like great drops of blood falling down to the ground.[a]

45When He rose up from prayer, and had come to His disciples, He found them sleeping

---

On the Edge

Father, if it is Your will, take this cup away from Me; nevertheless not My will, but Yours, be done (Luke 22:42).

A lot of people have memorized the Bible verse that tells us to obey our parents in the Lord—to do what they want (Eph. 6:1). Do you ever wonder, "What's the big deal?" The big deal is: God's Word says that "to obey is better than sacrifice" (1 Sam. 15:22). We can spend all of our time in church and put all of our money in the offering, but if we aren't walking the walk, we're missing the point of what God's Word is saying. Remember that obedience is better than a bunch of rituals. In fact, God's Word says that if we truly love Him, we will really do what He says to do (see John 14:15; 15:10). When you obey God, not only does this show the world that you love Him, it shows *Him* that you love Him!

You can study the whole Bible looking at the lives of those who obeyed God and those who didn't. You'll find that the ones who were obedient were the ones who got blessed! Abraham obeyed God. Noah obeyed God. Joseph obeyed God. Daniel obeyed God. Jesus obeyed His Father, God. Paul obeyed God. Every one of those folks reaped the benefits of obedience. Obey God today, and reap the blessings of God tomorrow!

SEE FOR YOURSELF:
Is. 1:19; John 14:15, 21;
Rom. 5:19; 16:19, 20

22:31 [a]NU-Text omits *And the Lord said.*   22:37 [a]Isaiah 53:12   22:44 [a]NU-Text brackets verses 43 and 44 as not in the original text.

from sorrow. ⁴⁶Then He said to them, "Why do you sleep? Rise and pray, lest you enter into temptation."

BETRAYAL AND ARREST IN GETHSEMANE

⁴⁷And while He was still speaking, behold, a multitude; and he who was called Judas, one of the twelve, went before them and drew near to Jesus to kiss Him. ⁴⁸But Jesus said to him, "Judas, are you betraying the Son of Man with a kiss?"

⁴⁹When those around Him saw what was going to happen, they said to Him, "Lord, shall we strike with the sword?" ⁵⁰And one of them struck the servant of the high priest and cut off his right ear.

⁵¹But Jesus answered and said, "Permit even this." And He touched his ear and healed him.

⁵²Then Jesus said to the chief priests, captains of the temple, and the elders who had come to Him, "Have you come out, as against a robber, with swords and clubs? ⁵³When I was with you daily in the temple, you did not try to seize Me. But this is your hour, and the power of darkness."

PETER DENIES JESUS, AND WEEPS BITTERLY

⁵⁴Having arrested Him, they led *Him* and brought Him into the high priest's house. But Peter followed at a distance. ⁵⁵Now when they had kindled a fire in the midst of the courtyard and sat down together, Peter sat among them. ⁵⁶And a certain servant girl, seeing him as he sat by the fire, looked intently at him and said, "This man was also with Him."

⁵⁷But he denied Him,ᵃ saying, "Woman, I do not know Him."

⁵⁸And after a little while another saw him and said, "You also are of them."

But Peter said, "Man, I am not!"

⁵⁹Then after about an hour had passed, another confidently affirmed, saying, "Surely this *fellow* also was with Him, for he is a Galilean."

⁶⁰But Peter said, "Man, I do not know what you are saying!"

Immediately, while he was still speaking, the roosterᵃ crowed. ⁶¹And the Lord turned and looked at Peter. Then Peter remembered the word of the Lord, how He had said to him, "Before the rooster crows,ᵃ you will deny Me three times." ⁶²So Peter went out and wept bitterly.

JESUS MOCKED AND BEATEN

⁶³Now the men who held Jesus mocked Him and beat Him. ⁶⁴And having blindfolded Him, they struck Him on the face and asked Him,ᵃ saying, "Prophesy! Who is the one who struck You?" ⁶⁵And many other things they blasphemously spoke against Him.

JESUS FACES THE SANHEDRIN

⁶⁶As soon as it was day, the elders of the people, both chief priests and scribes, came together and led Him into their council, saying, ⁶⁷"If You are the Christ, tell us."

But He said to them, "If I tell you, you will by no means believe. ⁶⁸And if I also ask *you*, you will by no means answer Me or let *Me* go.ᵃ ⁶⁹Hereafter the Son of Man will sit on the right hand of the power of God."

⁷⁰Then they all said, "Are You then the Son of God?"

So He said to them, "You *rightly* say that I am."

⁷¹And they said, "What further testimony do we need? For we have heard it ourselves from His own mouth."

WHAT'S IT MEAN?

Pilate, the Roman governor of Judea and Samaria, had come to Jerusalem with his troops for the Passover feast. His purpose was to make sure that the thousands of Jews who had traveled to the city for the annual holiday did not attempt to riot or revolt. As the highest authority in the land, Pilate had the power to sentence criminals to death. The Jewish council had the authority to hand down verdicts, but did not have the authority to execute a prisoner without the okay of Roman authorities.

Luke 23:1

JESUS HANDED OVER TO PONTIUS PILATE

¹Then the whole multitude of them arose and led Him to Pilate. ²And they began to accuse Him, saying, "We found this *fellow* perverting theᵃ nation, and forbidding to pay taxes to Caesar, saying that He Himself is Christ, a King."

22:57 ᵃNU-Text reads *denied it*.   **22:60** ᵃNU-Text and M-Text read *a rooster*.   **22:61** ᵃNU-Text adds *today*.
22:64 ᵃNU-Text reads *And having blindfolded Him, they asked Him*.   **22:68** ᵃNU-Text omits *also* and *Me or let Me go*.   **23:2** ᵃNU-Text reads *our*.

³Then Pilate asked Him, saying, "Are You the King of the Jews?"

He answered him and said, "*It is as* you say."

⁴So Pilate said to the chief priests and the crowd, "I find no fault in this Man."

⁵But they were the more fierce, saying, "He stirs up the people, teaching throughout all Judea, beginning from Galilee to this place."

JESUS FACES HEROD

⁶When Pilate heard of Galilee,ᵃ he asked if the Man were a Galilean. ⁷And as soon as he knew that He belonged to Herod's jurisdiction, he sent Him to Herod, who was also in Jerusalem at that time. ⁸Now when Herod saw Jesus, he was exceedingly glad; for he had desired for a long *time* to see Him, because he had heard many things about Him, and he hoped to see some miracle done by Him. ⁹Then he questioned Him with many words, but He answered him nothing. ¹⁰And the chief priests and scribes stood and vehemently accused Him. ¹¹Then Herod, with his men of war, treated Him with contempt and mocked *Him,* arrayed Him in a gorgeous robe, and sent Him back to Pilate. ¹²That very day Pilate and Herod became friends with each other, for previously they had been at enmity with each other.

TAKING THE PLACE OF BARABBAS

¹³Then Pilate, when he had called together the chief priests, the rulers, and the people, ¹⁴said to them, "You have brought this Man to me, as one who misleads the people. And indeed, having examined *Him* in your presence, I have found no fault in this Man concerning those things of which you accuse Him; ¹⁵no, neither did Herod, for I sent you back to him;ᵃ and indeed nothing deserving of death has been done by Him. ¹⁶I will therefore chastise Him and release *Him*" ¹⁷(for it was necessary for him to release one to them at the feast).ᵃ

¹⁸And they all cried out at once, saying, "Away with this *Man*, and release to us Barabbas"— ¹⁹who had been thrown into prison for a certain rebellion made in the city, and for murder.

²⁰Pilate, therefore, wishing to release Jesus, again called out to them. ²¹But they shouted, saying, "Crucify *Him*, crucify Him!"

²²Then he said to them the third time, "Why, what evil has He done? I have found no reason for death in Him. I will therefore chastise Him and let *Him* go."

On the Edge

When they had come to the place called Calvary, there they crucified Him . . . Jesus said, "Father, forgive them, for they do not know what they do" (Luke 23:33, 34).

Jesus says in the Sermon on the Mount (Matt. 5:43–48) that anyone can love someone who treats him or her well. But in order to be like God, we must love our enemies and pray for them. He says, "I say to you, love your enemies, bless those who curse you, do good to those who hate you, and pray for those who spitefully use you and persecute you, that you may be sons of your Father in heaven. . . For if you love those who love you, what reward have you? Do not even the tax collectors do the same? And if you greet your brethren only, what do you do more than others? Do not even the tax collectors do so? Therefore you shall be perfect, just as your Father in heaven is perfect" (Matt. 5:44–48). Like it or not, it's what we've got to do. All throughout the New Testament, the writers emphasize that the goal of our faith, after salvation, is to become more Christlike—to imitate God. We are instructed to love our enemies because that's what God does. Here in Luke 23:33–35, Jesus sets the example for us. He prays for the people who are killing Him, and He asks God to forgive them.

Loving your enemies does not mean that you approve of what they do. It means that you love them *in spite of it*. You can pray for them, yet not participate in what they do. Sometimes you've just got to grit your teeth and determine that you will obey God. Loving when you don't feel like it, but because it's God's command—now that's love. God loves all of us, but hates our sin. Follow His example.

SEE FOR YOURSELF:
  Matt. 5:43–48;
  Mark 11:25, 26;
  Luke 6:27, 35

²³But they were insistent, demanding with loud voices that He be crucified. And the voices of these men and of the chief priests prevailed.ᵃ ²⁴So Pilate gave sentence that it should be as

---

23:6 ᵃNU-Text omits *of Galilee.*   **23:15** ᵃNU-Text reads *for he sent Him back to us.*   **23:17** ᵃNU-Text omits verse 17.   **23:23** ᵃNU-Text omits *and of the chief priests.*

they requested. ²⁵And he released to them*ᵃ* the one they requested, who for rebellion and murder had been thrown into prison; but he delivered Jesus to their will.

THE KING ON A CROSS

²⁶Now as they led Him away, they laid hold of a certain man, Simon a Cyrenian, who was coming from the country, and on him they laid the cross that he might bear *it* after Jesus.

²⁷And a great multitude of the people followed Him, and women who also mourned and lamented Him. ²⁸But Jesus, turning to them, said, "Daughters of Jerusalem, do not weep for Me, but weep for yourselves and for your children. ²⁹For indeed the days are coming in which they will say, 'Blessed *are* the barren, wombs that never bore, and breasts which never nursed!' ³⁰Then they will begin *'to say to the mountains, "Fall on us!" and to the hills, "Cover us!"' ᵃ* ³¹For if they do these things in the green wood, what will be done in the dry?"

³²There were also two others, criminals, led with Him to be put to death. ³³And when they had come to the place called Calvary, there they crucified Him, and the criminals, one on the right hand and the other on the left. ³⁴Then Jesus said, "Father, forgive them, for they do not know what they do."*ᵃ*

And they divided His garments and cast lots. ³⁵And the people stood looking on. But even the rulers with them sneered, saying, "He saved others; let Him save Himself if He is the Christ, the chosen of God."

³⁶The soldiers also mocked Him, coming and offering Him sour wine, ³⁷and saying, "If You are the King of the Jews, save Yourself."

³⁸And an inscription also was written over Him in letters of Greek, Latin, and Hebrew:*ᵃ*

THIS IS THE KING OF THE JEWS.

³⁹Then one of the criminals who were hanged blasphemed Him, saying, "If You are the Christ,*ᵃ* save Yourself and us."

⁴⁰But the other, answering, rebuked him, saying, "Do you not even fear God, seeing you are under the same condemnation? ⁴¹And we indeed justly, for we receive the due reward of our deeds; but this Man has done nothing wrong." ⁴²Then he said to Jesus, "Lord,*ᵃ* remember me when You come into Your kingdom."

⁴³And Jesus said to him, "Assuredly, I say to you, today you will be with Me in Paradise."

JESUS DIES ON THE CROSS

⁴⁴Now it was*ᵃ* about the sixth hour, and there was darkness over all the earth until the ninth hour. ⁴⁵Then the sun was darkened,*ᵃ* and the veil of the temple was torn in two. ⁴⁶And when Jesus had cried out with a loud voice, He said, "Father, *'into Your hands I commit My spirit.'*"*ᵃ* Having said this, He breathed His last.

⁴⁷So when the centurion saw what had happened, he glorified God, saying, "Certainly this was a righteous Man!"

⁴⁸And the whole crowd who came together to that sight, seeing what had been done, beat their breasts and returned. ⁴⁹But all His acquaintances, and the women who followed Him from Galilee, stood at a distance, watching these things.

WHAT'S IT MEAN?

Jesus' tomb was actually a small room carved into a large rock. The heavy stone that was placed in front of the tomb was not intended to keep bodies from coming out, but to keep animals from getting in.
Luke 23:53

JESUS BURIED IN JOSEPH'S TOMB

⁵⁰Now behold, *there was* a man named Joseph, a council member, a good and just man. ⁵¹He had not consented to their decision and deed. *He was* from Arimathea, a city of the Jews, who himself was also waiting*ᵃ* for the kingdom of God. ⁵²This man went to Pilate and asked for the body of Jesus. ⁵³Then he took it down, wrapped it in linen, and laid it in a tomb *that was* hewn out of the rock, where no one had ever lain before. ⁵⁴That day was the Preparation, and the Sabbath drew near.

⁵⁵And the women who had come with Him from Galilee followed after, and they observed

---

23:25 *ᵃ*NU-Text and M-Text omit *to them.*   **23:30** *ᵃ*Hosea 10:8   **23:34** *ᵃ*NU-Text brackets the first sentence as a later addition.   **23:38** *ᵃ*NU-Text omits *written* and *in letters of Greek, Latin, and Hebrew.*   **23:39** *ᵃ*NU-Text reads *Are You not the Christ?*   **23:42** *ᵃ*NU-Text reads *And he said, "Jesus, remember me.*   **23:44** *ᵃ*NU-Text adds *already.*   **23:45** *ᵃ*NU-Text reads *obscured.*   **23:46** *ᵃ*Psalm 31:5   **23:51** *ᵃ*NU-Text reads *who was waiting.*

the tomb and how His body was laid. ⁵⁶Then they returned and prepared spices and fragrant oils. And they rested on the Sabbath according to the commandment.

HE IS RISEN

¹Now on the first *day* of the week, very early in the morning, they, and certain *other women* with them,*ᵃ* came to the tomb bringing the spices which they had prepared. ²But they found the stone rolled away from the tomb. ³Then they went in and did not find the body of the Lord Jesus. ⁴And it happened, as they were greatly*ᵃ* perplexed about this, that behold, two men stood by them in shining garments. ⁵Then, as they were afraid and bowed *their* faces to the earth, they said to them, "Why do you seek the living among the dead? ⁶He is not here, but is risen! Remember how He spoke to you when He was still in Galilee, ⁷saying, 'The Son of Man must be delivered into the hands of sinful men, and be crucified, and the third day rise again.' "

⁸And they remembered His words. ⁹Then they returned from the tomb and told all these things to the eleven and to all the rest. ¹⁰It was Mary Magdalene, Joanna, Mary *the mother* of James, and the other *women* with them, who told these things to the apostles. ¹¹And their words seemed to them like idle tales, and they did not believe them. ¹²But Peter arose and ran to the tomb; and stooping down, he saw the linen cloths lying*ᵃ* by themselves; and he departed, marveling to himself at what had happened.

THE ROAD TO EMMAUS

¹³Now behold, two of them were traveling that same day to a village called Emmaus, which was seven miles*ᵃ* from Jerusalem. ¹⁴And they talked together of all these things which had happened. ¹⁵So it was, while they conversed and reasoned, that Jesus Himself drew near and went with them. ¹⁶But their eyes were restrained, so that they did not know Him.

¹⁷And He said to them, "What kind of conversation *is* this that you have with one another as you walk and are sad?"*ᵃ*

¹⁸Then the one whose name was Cleopas answered and said to Him, "Are You the only stranger in Jerusalem, and have You not known the things which happened there in these days?"

¹⁹And He said to them, "What things?"

So they said to Him, "The things concerning Jesus of Nazareth, who was a Prophet mighty in deed and word before God and all the people, ²⁰and how the chief priests and our rulers delivered Him to be condemned to death, and crucified Him. ²¹But we were hoping that it was He who was going to redeem Israel. Indeed, besides all this, today is the third day since these things happened. ²²Yes, and certain women of our company, who arrived at the tomb early, astonished us. ²³When they did not find His body, they came saying that they had also seen a vision of angels who said He was alive. ²⁴And certain of those *who were* with us went to the tomb and found *it* just as the women had said; but Him they did not see."

²⁵Then He said to them, "O foolish ones, and slow of heart to believe in all that the prophets have spoken! ²⁶Ought not the Christ to have suffered these things and to enter into His glory?" ²⁷And beginning at Moses and all the Prophets, He expounded to them in all the Scriptures the things concerning Himself.

THE DISCIPLES' EYES OPENED

²⁸Then they drew near to the village where they were going, and He indicated that He would have gone farther. ²⁹But they constrained Him, saying, "Abide with us, for it is toward evening, and the day is far spent." And He went in to stay with them.

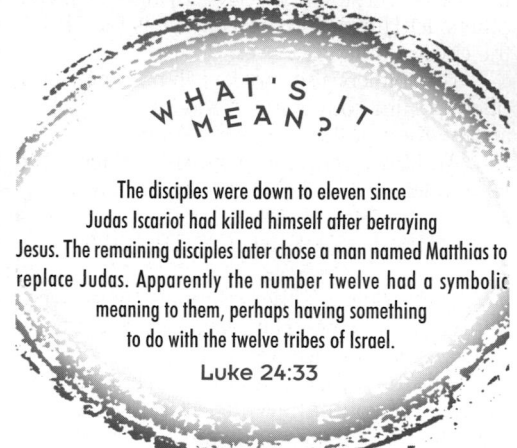

WHAT'S IT MEAN?

The disciples were down to eleven since Judas Iscariot had killed himself after betraying Jesus. The remaining disciples later chose a man named Matthias to replace Judas. Apparently the number twelve had a symbolic meaning to them, perhaps having something to do with the twelve tribes of Israel.
Luke 24:33

³⁰Now it came to pass, as He sat at the table with them, that He took bread, blessed and broke *it*, and gave it to them. ³¹Then their eyes were opened and they knew Him; and He vanished from their sight.

24:1 *ᵃ*NU-Text omits *and certain other women with them.*   **24:4** *ᵃ*NU-Text omits *greatly.*   **24:12** *ᵃ*NU-Text omits *lying.*   **24:13** *ᵃ*Literally *sixty stadia*   **24:17** *ᵃ*NU-Text reads *as you walk? And they stood still, looking sad.*

³²And they said to one another, "Did not our heart burn within us while He talked with us on the road, and while He opened the Scriptures to us?" ³³So they rose up that very hour and returned to Jerusalem, and found the eleven and those *who were* with them gathered together, ³⁴saying, "The Lord is risen indeed, and has appeared to Simon!" ³⁵And they told about the things *that had happened* on the road, and how He was known to them in the breaking of bread.

JESUS APPEARS TO HIS DISCIPLES

³⁶Now as they said these things, Jesus Himself stood in the midst of them, and said to them, "Peace to you." ³⁷But they were terrified and frightened, and supposed they had seen a spirit. ³⁸And He said to them, "Why are you troubled? And why do doubts arise in your hearts? ³⁹Behold My hands and My feet, that it is I Myself. Handle Me and see, for a spirit does not have flesh and bones as you see I have."

⁴⁰When He had said this, He showed them His hands and His feet.ᵃ ⁴¹But while they still did not believe for joy, and marveled, He said to them, "Have you any food here?" ⁴²So they gave Him a piece of a broiled fish and some honeycomb.ᵃ ⁴³And He took *it* and ate in their presence.

THE SCRIPTURES OPENED

⁴⁴Then He said to them, "These *are* the words which I spoke to you while I was still with you, that all things must be fulfilled which were written in the Law of Moses and *the* Prophets and *the* Psalms concerning Me." ⁴⁵And He opened their understanding, that they might comprehend the Scriptures.

⁴⁶Then He said to them, "Thus it is written, and thus it was necessary for the Christ to suffer and to riseᵃ from the dead the third day, ⁴⁷and that repentance and remission of sins should be preached in His name to all nations, beginning at Jerusalem. ⁴⁸And you are witnesses of these things. ⁴⁹Behold, I send the Promise of My Father upon you; but tarry in the city of Jerusalemᵃ until you are endued with power from on high."

GOSPEL

Who is the gospel message for? (24:46, 47)

THE ASCENSION

⁵⁰And He led them out as far as Bethany, and He lifted up His hands and blessed them. ⁵¹Now it came to pass, while He blessed them, that He was parted from them and carried up into heaven. ⁵²And they worshiped Him, and returned to Jerusalem with great joy, ⁵³and were continually in the temple praising andᵃ blessing God. Amen.ᵇ

"And they worshiped Him, and returned to Jerusalem with great joy, and were continually in the temple praising." (Luke 24:52, 53a)

24:40 ᵃSome printed New Testaments omit this verse. It is found in nearly all Greek manuscripts.
24:42 ᵃNU-Text omits *and some honeycomb.*   **24:46** ᵃNU-Text reads *written, that the Christ should suffer and rise.*   **24:49** ᵃNU-Text omits *of Jerusalem.*   **24:53** ᵃNU-Text omits *praising and.*   ᵇNU-Text omits *Amen.*

john

CONTENT The Gospel of John was written by one of Jesus' best friends. It's an inside look by someone who worked right beside Jesus throughout His ministry. John's Gospel isn't so much the story of Jesus' life. Rather, it is more like an overview of why we should believe Jesus was the Son of God.

John wasn't as concerned that we know about what Jesus did (and in what order) as he was that we know Jesus Himself and that we love Him as John did. John wanted us to believe the mystery of Jesus' deity—that while He was a Person, He was really and truly God.

The other Gospels were already written by the time John sat down to have his say. John didn't need to rewrite the same things. So instead of starting with Jesus' birth or even God's promise to Abraham, John started with the creation of the world. Since Jesus was God, Jesus was there when the world was created.

It is a good thing for us that one of Jesus' best friends wrote a Gospel. We need to know what it's like to be a friend of God so that we can learn to be one, too.

Outline

Purpose We can have eternal life by trusting God's Son as our Savior.

Theme Knowing God by Believing in Jesus Christ

Date of writing Late 80s or early 90s A.D.

> "And truly Jesus did many other signs in the presence of His disciples, which are not written in this book; but these are written that you may believe that Jesus is the Christ, the Son of God, and that believing you may have life in His name" (20:30, 31).

Bible Talk

Nicodemus and the Plan of Salvation

One of the most famous verses in the world is in the third chapter of John. You've probably heard John 3:16 many times. It says that God loved the world so much that He sent His only Son, Jesus, so that we could have eternal life by believing in Him. Sound familiar?

Jesus actually said this as a part of a conversation with a man named Nicodemus. Nicodemus was a religious leader. Many of his associates were giving Jesus a hard time. Maybe that's why Nicodemus came to talk to Jesus after it was dark outside. He asked Jesus to explain all this faith and salvation and "born again" stuff to him.

Jesus did that; and, in the process, because of John's Gospel, He explained it to us.

CRUCIFIXION

John was actually there at the cross when Jesus was crucified. It was a gruesome sight. It must have been difficult to watch, but John was there. Jesus even talked to him from the cross. He asked John to take care of Mary, Jesus' mom.

When Jesus died on the cross, it was the single most significant moment the world had ever seen. It was God giving His life for us. It was all of our sins being forgiven in one moment.

And it was one best friend watching another best friend die like a criminal even though He was innocent. What do you think it would have been like to be John standing at the foot of the cross?

THE ETERNAL WORD

¹In the beginning was the Word, and the Word was with God, and the Word was God. ²He was in the beginning with God. ³All things were made through Him, and without Him nothing was made that was made. ⁴In Him was life, and the life was the light of men. ⁵And the light shines in the darkness, and the darkness did not comprehend[a] it.

JESUS

Is Jesus God? (1:1–5)

JOHN'S WITNESS: THE TRUE LIGHT

⁶There was a man sent from God, whose name *was* John. ⁷This man came for a witness, to bear witness of the Light, that all through him might believe. ⁸He was not that Light, but *was sent* to bear witness of that Light. ⁹That was the true Light which gives light to every man coming into the world.[a]

¹⁰He was in the world, and the world was made through Him, and the world did not know Him. ¹¹He came to His own,[a] and His own[b] did not receive Him.

ADOPTION

Who can be called God's children? (1:12)

¹²But as many as received Him, to them He gave the right to become children of God, to those who believe in His name: ¹³who were born, not of blood, nor of the will of the flesh, nor of the will of man, but of God.

THE WORD BECOMES FLESH

¹⁴And the Word became flesh and dwelt among us, and we beheld His glory, the glory as of the only begotten of the Father, full of grace and truth.

¹⁵John bore witness of Him and cried out, saying, "This was He of whom I said, 'He who comes after me is preferred before me, for He was before me.'"

¹⁶And[a] of His fullness we have all received, and grace for grace. ¹⁷For the law was given through Moses, *but* grace and truth came through Jesus Christ. ¹⁸No one has seen God at any time. The only begotten Son,[a] who is in the bosom of the Father, He has declared *Him.*

A VOICE IN THE WILDERNESS

¹⁹Now this is the testimony of John, when the Jews sent priests and Levites from Jerusalem to ask him, "Who are you?"

On the Edge

In the beginning was the Word, and the Word was with God, and the Word was God (John 1:1).

This verse will knock anyone who doesn't believe in the Trinity—that God the Father, God the Son (Jesus), and the Holy Spirit are all three in one—right in the head. Verse 14 says, "The Word became flesh and dwelt among us, and we beheld His glory, the glory as of the only begotten of the Father, full of grace and truth." Jesus is the Word! That's why Hebrews 4:12 says that the Word of God is "living and powerful."

If you want to get closer to God, start by spending time in His Word. Not only will you learn about Him, but you'll hear from Him. Jesus speaks to us through His Word more than any other way. That's why it's so important to read the Bible, study it, and memorize verses.

Did you know that as you spend time in this Book, the Word of God, your faith is being increased? It's vital that you put the Word of God in you when things are going great and you don't think you need it, so it will be there when you do need it. Remember, "Faith comes by hearing, and hearing by the word of God" (Rom. 10:17). That message is in the Word of God. Jesus is the Word!

SEE FOR YOURSELF:
Ps. 138:2; Rom. 10:17; 2 Tim. 2:15

²⁰He confessed, and did not deny, but confessed, "I am not the Christ."

²¹And they asked him, "What then? Are you Elijah?"

He said, "I am not."

"Are you the Prophet?"

And he answered, "No."

²²Then they said to him, "Who are you, that we may give an answer to those who sent us? What do you say about yourself?"

²³He said: "I *am*

1:5 [a]Or *overcome*　**1:9** [a]Or *That was the true Light which, coming into the world, gives light to every man.*　**1:11** [a]That is, His own things or domain　[b]That is, His own people　**1:16** [a]NU-Text reads *For.*　**1:18** [a]NU-Text reads *only begotten God.*

'The voice of one crying in the
wilderness:
"Make straight the way of the LORD," ' [a]

as the prophet Isaiah said."

24Now those who were sent were from the Pharisees. 25And they asked him, saying, "Why then do you baptize if you are not the Christ, nor Elijah, nor the Prophet?"

26John answered them, saying, "I baptize with water, but there stands One among you whom you do not know. 27It is He who, coming after me, is preferred before me, whose sandal strap I am not worthy to loose."

28These things were done in Bethabara [a] beyond the Jordan, where John was baptizing.

THE LAMB OF GOD

29The next day John saw Jesus coming toward him, and said, "Behold! The Lamb of God who takes away the sin of the world! 30This is He of whom I said, 'After me comes a Man who is preferred before me, for He was before me.' 31I did not know Him; but that He should be revealed to Israel, therefore I came baptizing with water."

32And John bore witness, saying, "I saw the Spirit descending from heaven like a dove, and He remained upon Him. 33I did not know Him, but He who sent me to baptize with water said to me, 'Upon whom you see the Spirit descending, and remaining on Him, this is He who baptizes with the Holy Spirit.' 34And I have seen and testified that this is the Son of God."

THE FIRST DISCIPLES

35Again, the next day, John stood with two of his disciples. 36And looking at Jesus as He walked, he said, "Behold the Lamb of God!"

37The two disciples heard him speak, and they followed Jesus. 38Then Jesus turned, and seeing them following, said to them, "What do you seek?"

They said to Him, "Rabbi" (which is to say, when translated, Teacher), "where are You staying?"

39He said to them, "Come and see." They came and saw where He was staying, and remained with Him that day (now it was about the tenth hour).

40One of the two who heard John *speak*, and followed Him, was Andrew, Simon Peter's brother. 41He first found his own brother Simon, and said to him, "We have found the Messiah" (which is translated, the Christ). 42And he brought him to Jesus.

Now when Jesus looked at him, He said, "You are Simon the son of Jonah. [a] You shall be called Cephas" (which is translated, A Stone).

PHILIP AND NATHANAEL

43The following day Jesus wanted to go to Galilee, and He found Philip and said to him, "Follow Me." 44Now Philip was from Bethsaida,

1:23 [a]Isaiah 40:3   **1:28** [a]NU-Text and M-Text read *Bethany.*   **1:42** [a]NU-Text reads *John.*

Promise   HE PROMISES YOU BLESSING.

Of His fullness we have all received, and grace for grace (John 1:16).

Check out what this verse is saying. God has given us "of His fullness . . . and grace for grace." This means He's given us one blessing after another. He is the One who blesses. Notice that the verse doesn't say He *takes* from us.

A lot of people have the idea that God is out to take everything away from them, but that's not true. In fact, His Word says that He has come that we might have abundant life (see John 10:10). *Abundant* means plentiful. God isn't a taker. He's a giver, and He *wants* to give you the desires of your heart (see Ps. 37:4). So what are you going to do? Make God the joy and the delight of your life—and really mean it—and He will bring to pass your heart's desires.

What's your heart's desire? Tell God! He also says that if we will put Him first and do what He wants, He will also add other things to us. What kind of things? Whatever we need. Romans 8:32 sums all of this up: "He who did not spare His own Son, but delivered Him up for us all, how shall He not with Him also freely give us all things?" Don't forget it: He is the One who blesses!

SEE FOR YOURSELF:
Ps. 35:27; 37:4; Matt. 6:33; James 1:17

the city of Andrew and Peter. [45]Philip found Nathanael and said to him, "We have found Him of whom Moses in the law, and also the prophets, wrote—Jesus of Nazareth, the son of Joseph."

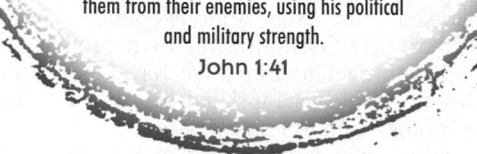

WHAT'S IT MEAN?

Many Jews were waiting for a person called the "Messiah," a name that means "anointed one" in Hebrew. In Old Testament times, kings, priests, and prophets were all anointed, which means they had oil poured on their heads to show that they were specially chosen by God. The Jews of Jesus' day believed that the Messiah was specially chosen by God to rescue them from their enemies, using his political and military strength.

John 1:41

[46]And Nathanael said to him, "Can anything good come out of Nazareth?"

Philip said to him, "Come and see."

[47]Jesus saw Nathanael coming toward Him, and said of him, "Behold, an Israelite indeed, in whom is no deceit!"

[48]Nathanael said to Him, "How do You know me?"

Jesus answered and said to him, "Before Philip called you, when you were under the fig tree, I saw you."

[49]Nathanael answered and said to Him, "Rabbi, You are the Son of God! You are the King of Israel!"

[50]Jesus answered and said to him, "Because I said to you, 'I saw you under the fig tree,' do you believe? You will see greater things than these." [51]And He said to him, "Most assuredly, I say to you, hereafter[a] you shall see heaven open, and the angels of God ascending and descending upon the Son of Man."

WATER TURNED TO WINE

[1]On the third day there was a wedding in Cana of Galilee, and the mother of Jesus was there. [2]Now both Jesus and His disciples were invited to the wedding. [3]And when they ran out of wine, the mother of Jesus said to Him, "They have no wine."

[4]Jesus said to her, "Woman, what does your concern have to do with Me? My hour has not yet come."

[5]His mother said to the servants, "Whatever He says to you, do it."

[6]Now there were set there six waterpots of stone, according to the manner of purification of the Jews, containing twenty or thirty gallons apiece. [7]Jesus said to them, "Fill the waterpots with water." And they filled them up to the brim. [8]And He said to them, "Draw *some* out now, and take *it* to the master of the feast." And they took *it*. [9]When the master of the feast had tasted the water that was made wine, and did not know where it came from (but the servants who had drawn the water knew), the master of the feast called the bridegroom. [10]And he said to him, "Every man at the beginning sets out the good wine, and when the *guests* have well drunk, then the inferior. You have kept the good wine until now!"

WHAT'S IT MEAN?

It wasn't generosity that prompted Herod the Great to renovate the temple in Jerusalem for his Jewish subjects. He wanted to keep the Jews happy with the Roman Empire so that they wouldn't get any ideas about rebelling. Specially trained priests served as advisors for the construction to make sure that the building plans matched the original floor plans that God gave to Moses. Though construction had been going on for decades, the temple was not finished in Jesus' lifetime.

John 2:20

[11]This beginning of signs Jesus did in Cana of Galilee, and manifested His glory; and His disciples believed in Him.

[12]After this He went down to Capernaum, He, His mother, His brothers, and His disciples; and they did not stay there many days.

JESUS CLEANSES THE TEMPLE

[13]Now the Passover of the Jews was at hand, and Jesus went up to Jerusalem. [14]And He found in the temple those who sold oxen and sheep and doves, and the money changers

ANGER

What did Jesus get angry at? (2:13–17)

On the Edge

But Jesus did not commit Himself to them, because He knew all men (John 2:24).

Omniscient? What's that? Is it the science of those little Omni automobiles? No. To be omniscient is to be all-knowing and God is omniscient. In other words, He knows all things! Yep, *everything.* Nobody "taught" God anything. Being omniscient just goes along with being God. There is nothing you can hide from God. Just like in this verse, Jesus knew the people's hearts and knew their thoughts. This is a quality that belongs only to God.

A lot of people con themselves into believing that they are fooling God. You can fool your friends, your family, your youth pastor, and even your closest friend, but you'll never fool God. The good news is that no matter how crummy a day, week, month, or year you're having, God already knows. He knows exactly what you're going through. It doesn't matter if nobody on this earth understands the pain you feel, or even understands you. God does and He's on your side. Going through the tough times is a whole lot easier when you realize that He fully knows and understands what's happening and is right there with you to help. He also knows how everything is going to turn out in the end! When you get to the hard or lonely places in your life, remember—He's omniscient!

SEE FOR YOURSELF:
Ps. 135:15–17; 147:5;
Is. 40:28;
Rom. 11:33

[19]Jesus answered and said to them, "Destroy this temple, and in three days I will raise it up."
[20]Then the Jews said, "It has taken forty-six years to build this temple, and will You raise it up in three days?"
[21]But He was speaking of the temple of His body. [22]Therefore, when He had risen from the dead, His disciples remembered that He had said this to them;[a] and they believed the Scripture and the word which Jesus had said.

THE DISCERNER OF HEARTS

[23]Now when He was in Jerusalem at the Passover, during the feast, many believed in His name when they saw the signs which He did. [24]But Jesus did not commit Himself to them, because He knew all *men,* [25]and had no need that anyone should testify of man, for He knew what was in man.

THE NEW BIRTH

[1]There was a man of the Pharisees named Nicodemus, a ruler of the Jews. [2]This man came to Jesus by night and said to Him, "Rabbi, we know that You are a teacher come from God; for no one can do these signs that You do unless God is with him."

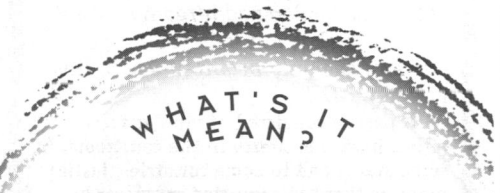

WHAT'S IT MEAN?

The Pharisees were obsessive about following the Law of Moses. They lived by a strict code of conduct and had elaborate rules about what they could and couldn't do—rules that ultimately didn't have much to do with the Spirit of God's Word. The Pharisees were often critical of other Jews and were reluctant to mingle with people whom they believed were not as "pure" as they were.

John 3:1, 2

[3]Jesus answered and said to him, "Most assuredly, I say to you, unless one is born again, he cannot see the kingdom of God."
[4]Nicodemus said to Him, "How can a man be born when he is old? Can he enter a second time into his mother's womb and be born?"
[5]Jesus answered, "Most assuredly, I say to you, unless one is born of water and the Spirit,

doing business. [15]When He had made a whip of cords, He drove them all out of the temple, with the sheep and the oxen, and poured out the changers' money and overturned the tables. [16]And He said to those who sold doves, "Take these things away! Do not make My Father's house a house of merchandise!" [17]Then His disciples remembered that it was written, *"Zeal for Your house has eaten[a] Me up."[b]*

[18]So the Jews answered and said to Him, "What sign do You show to us, since You do these things?"

2:17 [a]NU-Text and M-Text read *will eat.* [b]Psalm 69:9   **2:22** [a]NU-Text and M-Text omit *to them.*

he cannot enter the kingdom of God. [6]That which is born of the flesh is flesh, and that which is born of the Spirit is spirit. [7]Do not marvel that I said to you, 'You must be born again.' [8]The wind blows where it wishes, and you hear the sound of it, but cannot tell where it comes from and where it goes. So is everyone who is born of the Spirit."

[9]Nicodemus answered and said to Him, "How can these things be?"

[10]Jesus answered and said to him, "Are you the teacher of Israel, and do not know these things? [11]Most assuredly, I say to you, We speak what We know and testify what We have seen, and you do not receive Our witness. [12]If I have told you earthly things and you do not believe, how will you believe if I tell you heavenly things? [13]No one has ascended to heaven but He who came down from heaven, *that is*, the Son of Man who is in heaven.[a] [14]And as Moses lifted up the serpent in the wilderness, even so must the Son of Man be lifted up, [15]that whoever believes in Him should not perish but[a] have eternal life. [16]For God so loved the world that He gave His only begotten Son, that whoever believes in Him should not perish but have everlasting life. [17]For God did not send His Son into the world to condemn the world, but that the world through Him might be saved.

[18]"He who believes in Him is not condemned; but he who does not believe is condemned already, because he has not believed in the name of the only begotten Son of God. [19]And this is the condemnation, that the light has come into the world, and men loved darkness rather than light, because their deeds were evil. [20]For everyone practicing evil hates the light and does not come to the light, lest his deeds should be exposed. [21]But he who does the truth comes to the light, that his deeds may be clearly seen, that they have been done in God."

> "For God did not send His Son into the world to condemn the world, but that the world through Him might be saved."
> (John 3:17)

ETERNAL LIFE
What is required for eternal life? (3:15, 16)

JOHN THE BAPTIST EXALTS CHRIST

[22]After these things Jesus and His disciples came into the land of Judea, and there He remained with them and baptized. [23]Now John also was baptizing in Aenon near Salim, because there was much water there. And they came and were baptized. [24]For John had not yet been thrown into prison.

[25]Then there arose a dispute between *some* of John's disciples and the Jews about purification. [26]And they came to John and said to him, "Rabbi, He who was with you beyond the Jordan, to whom you have testified—behold, He is baptizing, and all are coming to Him!"

[27]John answered and said, "A man can receive nothing unless it has been given to him from heaven. [28]You yourselves bear me witness,

---

☙ On the Edge

He who believes in Him is not condemned; but he who does not believe is condemned already, because he has not believed in the name of the only begotten Son of God (John 3:18).

A person convicted of murder faces either justice or mercy in the courtroom. In some states and in some countries, justice requires that the convicted murderer be condemned to death. Yet the judge or the jury can treat the person with mercy if they choose to.

God has chosen mercy. Everyone deserves to be condemned to death—that's the penalty for refusing to obey God. But for those who trust in Jesus, God has set aside the sentence that justice demands. For them there is no punishment (see Rom. 8:1). The punishment for their sins was given to Jesus.

God's mercy is for everyone who has faith in His Son. Faith is not having an intellectual belief in God. It's knowing in your heart that He is real and responding with your life (the things you *do*) to the gift of mercy He gave you through His Son.

SEE FOR YOURSELF:
Neh. 13:22; Ps. 118; John 5:24; Rom. 8:1

3:13 [a]NU-Text omits *who is in heaven.*   **3:15** [a]NU-Text omits *not perish but.*

that I said, 'I am not the Christ', but, 'I have been sent before Him'. ²⁹He who has the bride is the bridegroom; but the friend of the bridegroom, who stands and hears him, rejoices greatly because of the bridegroom's voice. Therefore this joy of mine is fulfilled. ³⁰He must increase, but I *must* decrease. ³¹He who comes from above is above all; he who is of the earth is earthly and speaks of the earth. He who comes from heaven is above all. ³²And what He has seen and heard, that He testifies; and no one receives His testimony. ³³He who has received His testimony has certified that God is true. ³⁴For He whom God has sent speaks the words of God, for God does not give the Spirit by measure. ³⁵The Father loves the Son, and has given all things into His hand. ³⁶He who believes in the Son has everlasting life; and he who does not believe the Son shall not see life, but the wrath of God abides on him."

A SAMARITAN WOMAN MEETS HER MESSIAH

¹Therefore, when the Lord knew that the Pharisees had heard that Jesus made and baptized more disciples than John ²(though Jesus Himself did not baptize, but His disciples), ³He left Judea and departed again to Galilee. ⁴But He needed to go through Samaria.

⁵So He came to a city of Samaria which is called Sychar, near the plot of ground that Jacob gave to his son Joseph. ⁶Now Jacob's well was there. Jesus therefore, being wearied from *His* journey, sat thus by the well. It was about the sixth hour.

⁷A woman of Samaria came to draw water. Jesus said to her, "Give Me a drink." ⁸For His disciples had gone away into the city to buy food.

⁹Then the woman of Samaria said to Him, "How is it that You, being a Jew, ask a drink from me, a Samaritan woman?" For Jews have no dealings with Samaritans.

¹⁰Jesus answered and said to her, "If you knew the gift of God, and who it is who says to you, 'Give Me a drink', you would have asked Him, and He would have given you living water."

¹¹The woman said to Him, "Sir, You have nothing to draw with, and the well is deep. Where then do You get that living water? ¹²Are You greater than our father Jacob, who gave us the well, and drank from it himself, as well as his sons and his livestock?"

¹³Jesus answered and said to her, "Whoever drinks of this water will thirst again, ¹⁴but whoever drinks of the water that I shall give him will never thirst. But the water that I shall give him will become in him a fountain of water springing up into everlasting life."

¹⁵The woman said to Him, "Sir, give me this water, that I may not thirst, nor come here to draw."

WHAT'S IT MEAN?

Samaria was located in what had once been the nation of Israel. When the Assyrians conquered the northern kingdom of Israel in 722 B.C., they took many Israelites away as captives and brought in many foreigners to live in Canaan. It wasn't long before the Israelites who were left behind started getting involved with the new kids in town. Not only did the Israelites begin marrying and having kids with the foreigners, they also adopted their idol worship. This mingling continued generation after generation until the distinction between the Israelites and the foreigners disappeared altogether. The descendants of these mixed marriages were known as Samaritans.

John 4:4

¹⁶Jesus said to her, "Go, call your husband, and come here."

¹⁷The woman answered and said, "I have no husband."

Jesus said to her, "You have well said, 'I have no husband', ¹⁸for you have had five husbands, and the one whom you now have is not your husband; in that you spoke truly."

¹⁹The woman said to Him, "Sir, I perceive that You are a prophet. ²⁰Our fathers worshiped on this mountain, and you *Jews* say that in Jerusalem is the place where one ought to worship."

²¹Jesus said to her, "Woman, believe Me, the hour is coming when you will neither on this mountain, nor in Jerusalem, worship the Father. ²²You worship what you do not know; we know what we worship, for salvation is of the Jews. ²³But the hour is coming, and now is, when the true worshipers will worship the Father in spirit and truth; for the Father is seeking such to worship Him. ²⁴God *is* Spirit, and those who worship Him must worship in spirit and truth."

²⁵The woman said to Him, "I know that Messiah is coming" (who is called Christ). "When He comes, He will tell us all things."

JESUS

Is Jesus the Messiah? (4:21–26)

²⁶Jesus said to her, "I who speak to you am *He.*"

On the Edge

God is Spirit, and those who worship Him must worship in spirit and truth (John 4:24).

Those who worship God must be led by the Spirit. This verse isn't talking about being led by *a* spirit like the ghosts you see floating around old houses on TV. It's talking about being led by the *Holy Spirit.* The Holy Spirit is part of the Trinity: God the Father, God the Son (Jesus), and God the Holy Spirit. The Holy Spirit has been sent to guide you into all truth (see John 16:13). You are free to make your own choices, but if you're going to be successful in life, you must submit to the Holy Spirit and allow Him to guide you.

That's why it's so important to listen to that still, small voice. The next time you're making an important decision or stepping out in a certain direction and you don't feel at peace about it, don't ignore it! That's the Holy Spirit. He wants to lead you. He wants to help you. He wants to see you successful in everything you do. God has given us, as His children, the opportunity and the right to be led by the Holy Spirit. Start being led by the Spirit today, and watch what God will do tomorrow!

SEE FOR YOURSELF:
Ps. 32:8, 9; Prov. 3:5, 6;
Is. 58:11; John 16:13;
Rom. 8:14; Col. 3:15

THE WHITENED HARVEST

²⁷And at this *point* His disciples came, and they marveled that He talked with a woman; yet no one said, "What do You seek?" or, "Why are You talking with her?" ²⁸The woman then left her waterpot, went her way into the city, and said to the men, ²⁹"Come, see a Man who told me all things that I ever did. Could this be the Christ?" ³⁰Then they went out of the city and came to Him.

³¹In the meantime His disciples urged Him, saying, "Rabbi, eat." ³²But He said to them, "I have food to eat of which you do not know." ³³Therefore the disciples said to one another,

"Has anyone brought Him *anything* to eat?" ³⁴Jesus said to them, "My food is to do the will of Him who sent Me, and to finish His work. ³⁵Do you not say, 'There are still four months and *then* comes the harvest'? Behold, I say to you, lift up your eyes and look at the fields, for they are already white for harvest! ³⁶And he who reaps receives wages, and gathers fruit for eternal life, that both he who sows and he who reaps may rejoice together. ³⁷For in this the saying is true: 'One sows and another reaps.' ³⁸I sent you to reap that for which you have not labored; others have labored, and you have entered into their labors."

THE SAVIOR OF THE WORLD

³⁹And many of the Samaritans of that city believed in Him because of the word of the woman who testified, "He told me all that I *ever* did." ⁴⁰So when the Samaritans had come to Him, they urged Him to stay with them; and He stayed there two days. ⁴¹And many more believed because of His own word.

⁴²Then they said to the woman, "Now we believe, not because of what you said, for we ourselves have heard *Him* and we know that this is indeed the Christ,ᵃ the Savior of the world."

WELCOME AT GALILEE

⁴³Now after the two days He departed from there and went to Galilee. ⁴⁴For Jesus Himself testified that a prophet has no honor in his own country. ⁴⁵So when He came to Galilee, the Galileans received Him, having seen all the things He did in Jerusalem at the feast; for they also had gone to the feast.

A NOBLEMAN'S SON HEALED

⁴⁶So Jesus came again to Cana of Galilee where He had made the water wine. And there was a certain nobleman whose son was sick at Capernaum. ⁴⁷When he heard that Jesus had come out of Judea into Galilee, he went to Him and implored Him to come down and heal his son, for he was at the point of death. ⁴⁸Then Jesus said to him, "Unless you *people* see signs and wonders, you will by no means believe." ⁴⁹The nobleman said to Him, "Sir, come down before my child dies!" ⁵⁰Jesus said to him, "Go your way; your son lives." So the man believed the word that Jesus spoke to him, and he went his way. ⁵¹And as he was now going down, his servants met him and told *him,* saying, "Your son lives!"

4:42 ᵃNU-Text omits *the Christ.*

⁵²Then he inquired of them the hour when he got better. And they said to him, "Yesterday at the seventh hour the fever left him." ⁵³So the father knew that *it was* at the same hour in which Jesus said to him, "Your son lives." And he himself believed, and his whole household.

⁵⁴This again *is* the second sign Jesus did when He had come out of Judea into Galilee.

A MAN HEALED AT THE POOL OF BETHESDA

¹After this there was a feast of the Jews, and Jesus went up to Jerusalem. ²Now there is in Jerusalem by the Sheep *Gate* a pool, which is called in Hebrew, Bethesda,ᵃ having five porches. ³In these lay a great multitude of sick people, blind, lame, paralyzed, waiting for the moving of the water. ⁴For an angel went down at a certain time into the pool and stirred up the water; then whoever stepped in first, after the stirring of the water, was made well of whatever disease he had.ᵃ ⁵Now a certain man was there who had an infirmity thirty-eight years. ⁶When Jesus saw him lying there, and knew that he already had been *in that condition* a long time, He said to him, "Do you want to be made well?"

⁷The sick man answered Him, "Sir, I have no man to put me into the pool when the water is stirred up; but while I am coming, another steps down before me."

⁸Jesus said to him, "Rise, take up your bed and walk." ⁹And immediately the man was made well, took up his bed, and walked.

And that day was the Sabbath. ¹⁰The Jews therefore said to him who was cured, "It is the Sabbath; it is not lawful for you to carry your bed."

¹¹He answered them, "He who made me well said to me, 'Take up your bed and walk.' "

¹²Then they asked him, "Who is the Man who said to you, 'Take up your bed and walk'?" ¹³But the one who was healed did not know who it was, for Jesus had withdrawn, a multitude being in *that* place. ¹⁴Afterward Jesus found him in the temple, and said to him, "See, you have been made well. Sin no more, lest a worse thing come upon you."

¹⁵The man departed and told the Jews that it was Jesus who had made him well.

HONOR THE FATHER AND THE SON

¹⁶For this reason the Jews persecuted Jesus, and sought to kill Him,ᵃ because He had done these things on the Sabbath. ¹⁷But Jesus an-

---

On the Edge

He has granted the Son to have life in Himself, and has given Him authority to execute judgment also, because He is the Son of Man (John 5:26, 27).

There was a young man who sat patiently before a judge waiting for his verdict. During the entire trial the young man could not keep his mind on the case, even though the outcome would mean freedom or prison. The only thing he could think about was the fact that the judge looked very familiar. Where had he seen this judge before? *I know I've seen that man before,* thought the young man. Then all of a sudden it hit him! He remembered.

When he was a child, he fell through the ice on a lake he had been playing on. He began to scream for help, and a man who saw him struggling to survive got out of his car, ran to him, and saved his life. That man was the judge! Wow! He couldn't believe it. That must have been close to fifteen years ago. Right as the judge was getting ready to read the verdict, the young man yelled out, "Your Honor! Wait, wait! Remember . . ." The young man told the judge the entire story. The judge remembered saving the boy's life; and he, too, couldn't believe that here was that same frightened boy. "Your Honor," cried the young man, "you saved me then. Won't you please save me now?!"

"I'm so sorry, young man," replied the judge. "Then I was your savior; now I am your judge."

God is a loving God who sent His only Son to die for us, so that we could have new life. Jesus is our Savior; one day He will be our Judge. If you live for Him, He'll give you eternity in heaven!

SEE FOR YOURSELF:
Gal. 6:7, 8; Heb. 12:23;
Rev. 20:11–15

---

swered them, "My Father has been working until now, and I have been working."

¹⁸Therefore the Jews sought all the more to kill Him, because He not only broke the Sabbath, but also said that God was His Father, making Himself equal with God. ¹⁹Then Jesus

---

5:2 ᵃNU-Text reads *Bethzatha.* **5:4** ᵃNU-Text omits *waiting for the moving of the water* at the end of verse 3, and all of verse 4. **5:16** ᵃNU-Text omits *and sought to kill Him.*

answered and said to them, "Most assuredly, I say to you, the Son can do nothing of Himself, but what He sees the Father do; for whatever He does, the Son also does in like manner. ²⁰For the Father loves the Son, and shows Him all things that He Himself does; and He will show Him greater works than these, that you may marvel. ²¹For as the Father raises the dead and gives life to *them,* even so the Son gives life to whom He will. ²²For the Father judges no one, but has committed all judgment to the Son, ²³that all should honor the Son just as they honor the Father. He who does not honor the Son does not honor the Father who sent Him.

LIFE AND JUDGMENT ARE THROUGH THE SON

²⁴"Most assuredly, I say to you, he who hears My word and believes in Him who sent Me has everlasting life, and shall not come into judgment, but has passed from death into life. ²⁵Most assuredly, I say to you, the hour is coming, and now is, when the dead will hear the voice of the Son of God; and those who hear will live. ²⁶For as the Father has life in Himself, so He has granted the Son to have life in Himself, ²⁷and has given Him authority to execute judgment also, because He is the Son of Man. ²⁸Do not marvel at this; for the hour is coming in which all who are in the graves will hear His voice ²⁹and come forth—those who have done good, to the resurrection of life, and those who have done evil, to the resurrection of condemnation. ³⁰I can of Myself do nothing. As I hear, I judge; and My judgment is righteous, because I do not seek My own will but the will of the Father who sent Me.

ASSURANCE
What are Christians assured of? (5:24)

ETERNAL LIFE
Who receives eternal punishment? (5:28, 29)

THE FOURFOLD WITNESS

³¹"If I bear witness of Myself, My witness is not true. ³²There is another who bears witness of Me, and I know that the witness which He witnesses of Me is true. ³³You have sent to John, and he has borne witness to the truth. ³⁴Yet I do not receive testimony from man, but I say these things that you may be saved. ³⁵He was the burning and shining lamp, and you were willing for a time to rejoice in his light. ³⁶But I have a greater witness than John's; for the works which the Father has given Me to finish—the

very works that I do—bear witness of Me, that the Father has sent Me. ³⁷And the Father Himself, who sent Me, has testified of Me. You have neither heard His voice at any time, nor seen His form. ³⁸But you do not have His word abiding in you, because whom He sent, Him you do not believe. ³⁹You search the Scriptures, for in them you think you have eternal life; and these are they which testify of Me. ⁴⁰But you are not willing to come to Me that you may have life.

⁴¹"I do not receive honor from men. ⁴²But I know you, that you do not have the love of God in you. ⁴³I have come in My Father's name, and you do not receive Me; if another comes in his own name, him you will receive. ⁴⁴How can you believe, who receive honor from one another, and do not seek the honor that *comes* from the only God? ⁴⁵Do not think that I shall accuse you to the Father; there is *one* who accuses you—Moses, in whom you trust. ⁴⁶For if you believed Moses, you would believe Me; for he wrote about Me. ⁴⁷But if you do not believe his writings, how will you believe My words?"

FEEDING THE FIVE THOUSAND

¹After these things Jesus went over the Sea of Galilee, which is *the Sea* of Tiberias. ²Then a great multitude followed Him, because they saw His signs which He performed on those who were diseased. ³And Jesus went up on the mountain, and there He sat with His disciples.

⁴Now the Passover, a feast of the Jews, was near. ⁵Then Jesus lifted up *His* eyes, and seeing a great multitude coming toward Him, He said to Philip, "Where shall we buy bread, that these may eat?" ⁶But this He said to test him, for He Himself knew what He would do.

⁷Philip answered Him, "Two hundred denarii worth of bread is not sufficient for them, that every one of them may have a little."

⁸One of His disciples, Andrew, Simon Peter's brother, said to Him, ⁹"There is a lad here who has five barley loaves and two small fish, but what are they among so many?"

¹⁰Then Jesus said, "Make the people sit down." Now there was much grass in the place. So the men sat down, in number about five thousand. ¹¹And Jesus took the loaves, and when He had given thanks He distributed *them* to the disciples, and the disciples*ᵃ* to those sitting down; and likewise of the fish, as much as they wanted. ¹²So when they were filled, He said to His disciples, "Gather up the fragments that remain, so that nothing is lost." ¹³Therefore

---

6:11 *ᵃ*NU-Text omits *to the disciples, and the disciples.*

they gathered *them* up, and filled twelve baskets with the fragments of the five barley loaves which were left over by those who had eaten. [14]Then those men, when they had seen the sign that Jesus did, said, "This is truly the Prophet who is to come into the world."

JESUS WALKS ON THE SEA

[15]Therefore when Jesus perceived that they were about to come and take Him by force to make Him king, He departed again to the mountain by Himself alone.

[16]Now when evening came, His disciples went down to the sea, [17]got into the boat, and went over the sea toward Capernaum. And it was already dark, and Jesus had not come to them. [18]Then the sea arose because a great wind was blowing. [19]So when they had rowed about three or four miles,[a] they saw Jesus walking on the sea and drawing near the boat; and they were afraid. [20]But He said to them, "It is I; do not be afraid." [21]Then they willingly received Him into the boat, and immediately the boat was at the land where they were going.

THE BREAD FROM HEAVEN

[22]On the following day, when the people who were standing on the other side of the sea saw that there was no other boat there, except that one which His disciples had entered,[a] and that Jesus had not entered the boat with His disciples, but His disciples had gone away alone— [23]however, other boats came from Tiberias, near the place where they ate bread after the Lord had given thanks— [24]when the people therefore saw that Jesus was not there, nor His disciples, they also got into boats and came to Capernaum, seeking Jesus. [25]And when they found Him on the other side of the sea, they said to Him, "Rabbi, when did You come here?"

[26]Jesus answered them and said, "Most assuredly, I say to you, you seek Me, not because you saw the signs, but because you ate of the loaves and were filled. [27]Do not labor for the food which perishes, but for the food which endures to everlasting life, which the Son of Man will give you, because God the Father has set His seal on Him."

[28]Then they said to Him, "What shall we do, that we may work the works of God?"

[29]Jesus answered and said to them, "This is the work of God, that you believe in Him whom He sent."

[30]Therefore they said to Him, "What sign will

On the Edge

And Jesus said to them, "I am the bread of life. He who comes to Me shall never hunger, and he who believes in Me shall never thirst" (John 6:35).

"Get a life." Ever heard those words? Ever said those words? Most of the time, when people say that, they mean "Go find something to do."

The life that Jesus gives is more than just enough stuff to do. It's a life beyond a beating heart and a set of breathing lungs. It's something deep that happens in your spirit when Jesus lives inside of you.

Life is living, really experiencing who you are and what happens to you. Jesus came that we might live. We're talking about really living—not just breathing and walking around, not living in a fantasyland, not living with your head in the clouds. We're talking about living to the fullest—having life not just on this earth, but forever, in the presence of God. Jesus is the bread of life. Just like God sent the Israelites manna (life-giving bread) in the wilderness, so He sent Jesus to us as the bread of abundant, eternal life!

Don't settle for second best. Live life to the fullest! That's what the Lord wants for you. That's what Jesus offers you!

SEE FOR YOURSELF:
John 6:48–58;
10:10

You perform then, that we may see it and believe You? What work will You do? [31]Our fathers ate the manna in the desert; as it is written, *'He gave them bread from heaven to eat.'* "[a]

[32]Then Jesus said to them, "Most assuredly, I say to you, Moses did not give you the bread from heaven, but My Father gives you the true bread from heaven. [33]For the bread of God is He who comes down from heaven and gives life to the world."

[34]Then they said to Him, "Lord, give us this bread always."

[35]And Jesus said to them, "I am the bread of life. He who comes to Me shall never hunger,

---

6:19 [a]Literally *twenty-five or thirty stadia*   **6:22** [a]NU-Text omits *that* and *which His disciples had entered.*
6:31 [a]Exodus 16:4; Nehemiah 9:15; Psalm 78:24

and he who believes in Me shall never thirst. ³⁶But I said to you that you have seen Me and yet do not believe. ³⁷All that the Father gives Me will come to Me, and the one who comes to Me I will by no means cast out. ³⁸For I have come down from heaven, not to do My own will, but the will of Him who sent Me. ³⁹This is the will of the Father who sent Me, that of all He has given Me I should lose nothing, but should raise it up at the last day. ⁴⁰And this is the will of Him who sent Me, that everyone who sees the Son and believes in Him may have everlasting life; and I will raise him up at the last day."

RESURRECTION
Who did Jesus promise to raise? (6:38–40)

REJECTED BY HIS OWN

⁴¹The Jews then complained about Him, because He said, "I am the bread which came down from heaven." ⁴²And they said, "Is not this Jesus, the son of Joseph, whose father and mother we know? How is it then that He says, 'I have come down from heaven'?"

⁴³Jesus therefore answered and said to them, "Do not murmur among yourselves. ⁴⁴No one can come to Me unless the Father who sent Me draws him; and I will raise him up at the last day. ⁴⁵It is written in the prophets, 'And they shall all be taught by God.'ᵃ Therefore everyone who has heard and learnedᵇ from the Father comes to Me. ⁴⁶Not that anyone has seen the Father, except He who is from God; He has seen the Father. ⁴⁷Most assuredly, I say to you, he who believes in Meᵃ has everlasting life. ⁴⁸I am the bread of life. ⁴⁹Your fathers ate the manna in the wilderness, and are dead. ⁵⁰This is the bread which comes down from heaven, that one may eat of it and not die. ⁵¹I am the living bread which came down from heaven. If anyone eats of this bread, he will live forever; and the bread that I shall give is My flesh, which I shall give for the life of the world."

⁵²The Jews therefore quarreled among themselves, saying, "How can this Man give us His flesh to eat?"

⁵³Then Jesus said to them, "Most assuredly, I say to you, unless you eat the flesh of the Son of Man and drink His blood, you have no life in you. ⁵⁴Whoever eats My flesh and drinks My blood has eternal life, and I will raise him up at the last day. ⁵⁵For My flesh is food indeed,ᵃ and My blood is drink indeed. ⁵⁶He who eats My flesh and drinks My blood abides in Me, and I in him. ⁵⁷As the living Father sent Me, and I live because of the Father, so he who feeds on Me will live because of Me.

> "Most assuredly, I say to you, he who believes in Me has everlasting life."
> (John 6:47)

6:45 ᵃIsaiah 54:13 ᵇM-Text reads *hears and has learned.* **6:47** ᵃNU-Text omits *in Me.* **6:55** ᵃNU-Text reads *true food* and *true drink.*

Promise   HE PROMISES NOT TO TURN YOU AWAY.

All that the Father gives Me will come to Me, and the one who comes to Me I will by no means cast out (John 6:37).

Some people think that they have to have their lives totally together before they turn to God. They think they need to make themselves worthy of Jesus' friendship. This is a lie that suits Satan's purposes pretty well. The problem is that *nobody* will ever be worthy of what God is offering him or her. That's a part of God's truth that's hard to swallow. And if Satan can keep people believing that they have to somehow earn God's favor—that it's even possible—he can keep them from taking the first step toward God's kingdom.

The truth is that God doesn't ask anyone to be worthy of Him. If you come to Him—without excuses, without trying to justify yourself, just putting your complete trust in Him (like putting all of your weight in a chair)—then Jesus promises not to turn you away. He accepts you because He loves you, not because you've earned His friendship.

SEE FOR YOURSELF:
Matt. 24:24; John 6:45; 10:27, 28

⁵⁸This is the bread which came down from heaven—not as your fathers ate the manna, and are dead. He who eats this bread will live forever."

⁵⁹These things He said in the synagogue as He taught in Capernaum.

MANY DISCIPLES TURN AWAY

⁶⁰Therefore many of His disciples, when they heard *this*, said, "This is a hard saying; who can understand it?"

⁶¹When Jesus knew in Himself that His disciples complained about this, He said to them, "Does this offend you? ⁶²*What* then if you should see the Son of Man ascend where He was before? ⁶³It is the Spirit who gives life; the flesh profits nothing. The words that I speak to you are spirit, and *they* are life. ⁶⁴But there are some of you who do not believe." For Jesus knew from the beginning who they were who did not believe, and who would betray Him. ⁶⁵And He said, "Therefore I have said to you that no one can come to Me unless it has been granted to him by My Father."

⁶⁶From that *time* many of His disciples went back and walked with Him no more. ⁶⁷Then Jesus said to the twelve, "Do you also want to go away?"

⁶⁸But Simon Peter answered Him, "Lord, to whom shall we go? You have the words of eternal life. ⁶⁹Also we have come to believe and know that You are the Christ, the Son of the living God."ᵃ

⁷⁰Jesus answered them, "Did I not choose you, the twelve, and one of you is a devil?" ⁷¹He spoke of Judas Iscariot, *the son* of Simon, for it was he who would betray Him, being one of the twelve.

JESUS' BROTHERS DISBELIEVE

¹After these things Jesus walked in Galilee; for He did not want to walk in Judea, because the Jewsᵃ sought to kill Him. ²Now the Jews' Feast of Tabernacles was at hand. ³His brothers therefore said to Him, "Depart from here and go into Judea, that Your disciples also may see the works that You are doing. ⁴For no one does anything in secret while he himself seeks to be known openly. If You do these things, show Yourself to the world." ⁵For even His brothers did not believe in Him.

⁶Then Jesus said to them, "My time has not yet come, but your time is always ready. ⁷The world cannot hate you, but it hates Me because I testify of it that its works are evil. ⁸You go up to this feast. I am not yetᵃ going up to this feast, for My time has not yet fully come." ⁹When He had said these things to them, He remained in Galilee.

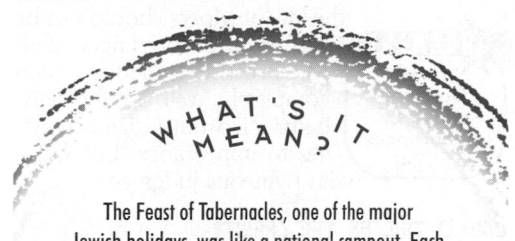

WHAT'S IT MEAN?

The Feast of Tabernacles, one of the major Jewish holidays, was like a national campout. Each year at harvesttime, people made temporary shelters out of tree branches and stayed in those shelters for the entire eight-day holiday. Why, you ask? To remind them of the years their ancestors spent wandering in the desert and living in tents, from the time they left Egypt to the time they entered the Promised Land.
John 7:2

THE HEAVENLY SCHOLAR

¹⁰But when His brothers had gone up, then He also went up to the feast, not openly, but as it were in secret. ¹¹Then the Jews sought Him at the feast, and said, "Where is He?" ¹²And there was much complaining among the people concerning Him. Some said, "He is good"; others said, "No, on the contrary, He deceives the people." ¹³However, no one spoke openly of Him for fear of the Jews.

¹⁴Now about the middle of the feast Jesus went up into the temple and taught. ¹⁵And the Jews marveled, saying, "How does this Man know letters, having never studied?"

¹⁶Jesusᵃ answered them and said, "My doctrine is not Mine, but His who sent Me. ¹⁷If anyone wills to do His will, he shall know concerning the doctrine, whether it is from God or *whether* I speak on My own *authority*. ¹⁸He who speaks from himself seeks his own glory; but He who seeks the glory of the One who sent Him is true, and no unrighteousness is in Him. ¹⁹Did not Moses give you the law, yet none of you keeps the law? Why do you seek to kill Me?"

²⁰The people answered and said, "You have a demon. Who is seeking to kill You?"

²¹Jesus answered and said to them, "I did

6:69 ᵃNU-Text reads *You are the Holy One of God.* **7:1** ᵃThat is, the ruling authorities **7:8** ᵃNU-Text omits *yet.* **7:16** ᵃNU-Text and M-Text read *So Jesus.*

one work, and you all marvel. ²²Moses therefore gave you circumcision (not that it is from Moses, but from the fathers), and you circumcise a man on the Sabbath. ²³If a man receives circumcision on the Sabbath, so that the law of Moses should not be broken, are you angry with Me because I made a man completely well on the Sabbath? ²⁴Do not judge according to appearance, but judge with righteous judgment."

JUDGMENT
Does God ever judge by appearances? (7:24)

COULD THIS BE THE CHRIST?

²⁵Now some of them from Jerusalem said, "Is this not He whom they seek to kill? ²⁶But look! He speaks boldly, and they say nothing to Him. Do the rulers know indeed that this is truly*ᵃ* the Christ? ²⁷However, we know where this Man is from; but when the Christ comes, no one knows where He is from."

²⁸Then Jesus cried out, as He taught in the temple, saying, "You both know Me, and you know where I am from; and I have not come of Myself, but He who sent Me is true, whom you do not know. ²⁹But*ᵃ* I know Him, for I am from Him, and He sent Me."

³⁰Therefore they sought to take Him; but no one laid a hand on Him, because His hour had not yet come. ³¹And many of the people believed in Him, and said, "When the Christ comes, will He do more signs than these which this *Man* has done?"

JESUS AND THE RELIGIOUS LEADERS

³²The Pharisees heard the crowd murmuring these things concerning Him, and the Pharisees and the chief priests sent officers to take Him. ³³Then Jesus said to them,*ᵃ* "I shall be with you a little while longer, and *then* I go to Him who sent Me. ³⁴You will seek Me and not find *Me*, and where I am you cannot come."

³⁵Then the Jews said among themselves, "Where does He intend to go that we shall not find Him? Does He intend to go to the Dispersion among the Greeks and teach the Greeks? ³⁶What is this thing that He said, 'You will seek Me and not find Me, and where I am you cannot come'?"

THE PROMISE OF THE HOLY SPIRIT

³⁷On the last day, that great *day* of the feast, Jesus stood and cried out, saying, "If anyone thirsts, let him come to Me and drink. ³⁸He who believes in Me, as the Scripture has said, out of his heart will flow rivers of living water." ³⁹But this He spoke concerning the Spirit, whom those believing*ᵃ* in Him would receive; for the

---

7:26 *ᵃ*NU-Text omits *truly.*   **7:29** *ᵃ*NU-Text and M-Text omit *But.*   **7:33** *ᵃ*NU-Text and M-Text omit *to them.*
7:39 *ᵃ*NU-Text reads *who believed.*

Promise   HE PROMISES YOU LIVING WATER.

He who believes in Me, as the Scripture has said, out of his heart will flow rivers of living water (John 7:38).

Have you ever been really thirsty—like "walking-across-the-desert-in-search-of-water" thirsty? Then you know that when you get that thirsty, there's nothing better than a nice long, cool glass of refreshing water! That's the kind of water you need. When you gave your heart to Jesus, you received that refreshing, living water. The question is, What are you going to do with that water? Jesus said it flows from you, not just *to* you!

Have you ever been for a ride on a scalding hot summer's day, and thought you saw a shimmering image that looked like water on the street up ahead? This is called a mirage, and it happens all of the time in the desert. We've all seen it on TV—a person in need of water, crawling across the desert spots one. His or her hopes are dashed as he or she realizes what he/she had thought was an oasis is really a mirage. Nothing!

That's the question: Are you going to be a mirage or an oasis of life? You have the living water that this world is searching for. Release it today!

SEE FOR YOURSELF:
Rev. 21:6; 22:17

Holy[b] Spirit was not yet *given*, because Jesus was not yet glorified.

WHO IS HE?

[40]Therefore many[a] from the crowd, when they heard this saying, said, "Truly this is the Prophet." [41]Others said, "This is the Christ."

But some said, "Will the Christ come out of Galilee? [42]Has not the Scripture said that the Christ comes from the seed of David and from the town of Bethlehem, where David was?" [43]So there was a division among the people because of Him. [44]Now some of them wanted to take Him, but no one laid hands on Him.

REJECTED BY THE AUTHORITIES

[45]Then the officers came to the chief priests and Pharisees, who said to them, "Why have you not brought Him?"

[46]The officers answered, "No man ever spoke like this Man!"

[47]Then the Pharisees answered them, "Are you also deceived? [48]Have any of the rulers or the Pharisees believed in Him? [49]But this crowd that does not know the law is accursed."

[50]Nicodemus (he who came to Jesus by night,[a] being one of them) said to them, [51]"Does our law judge a man before it hears him and knows what he is doing?"

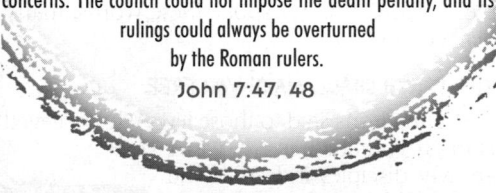

Even though the Romans ultimately controlled the land of Israel, they gave the Jews some say in the way things were run. The Jewish council was a group of seventy-one community leaders who served as a type of "supreme court," making decisions and rulings on legal matters and other special concerns. The council could not impose the death penalty, and its rulings could always be overturned by the Roman rulers.

John 7:47, 48

[52]They answered and said to him, "Are you also from Galilee? Search and look, for no prophet has arisen[a] out of Galilee."

AN ADULTERESS FACES THE LIGHT OF THE WORLD

[53]And everyone went to his *own* house.[a]

[1]But Jesus went to the Mount of Olives. [2]Now early[a] in the morning He came again into the temple, and all the people came to Him; and He sat down and taught them. [3]Then the scribes and Pharisees brought to Him a woman caught in adultery. And when they had set her in the midst, [4]they said to Him, "Teacher, this woman was caught[a] in adultery, in the very act. [5]Now Moses, in the law, commanded[a] us that such should be stoned.[b] But what do You say?"[c] [6]This they said, testing Him, that they might have *something* of which to accuse Him. But Jesus stooped down and wrote on the ground with *His* finger, as though He did not hear.[a] [7]So when they continued asking Him, He raised Himself up[a] and said to them, "He who is without sin among you, let him throw a stone at her first." [8]And again He stooped down and wrote on the ground. [9]Then those who heard *it*, being convicted by *their* conscience,[a] went out one by one, beginning with the oldest *even* to the last. And Jesus was left alone, and the woman standing in the midst. [10]When Jesus had raised Himself up and saw no one but the woman, He said to her,[a] "Woman, where are those accusers of yours?[b] Has no one condemned you?"

[11]She said, "No one, Lord."

And Jesus said to her, "Neither do I condemn you; go and[a] sin no more."

[12]Then Jesus spoke to them again, saying, "I am the light of the world. He who follows Me shall not walk in darkness, but have the light of life."

JESUS DEFENDS HIS SELF-WITNESS

[13]The Pharisees therefore said to Him, "You bear witness of Yourself; Your witness is not true."

[14]Jesus answered and said to them, "Even if I bear witness of Myself, My witness is true, for I know where I came from and where I am

---

7:39 [b]NU-Text omits *Holy*. **7:40** [a]NU-Text reads *some*. **7:50** [a]NU-Text reads *before*. **7:52** [a]NU-Text *is to rise*. **7:53** [a]The words *And everyone* through *sin no more* (8:11) are bracketed by NU-Text as not original. They are present in over 900 manuscripts. **8:2** [a]M-Text reads *very early*. **8:4** [a]M-Text reads *we found this woman*. **8:5** [a]M-Text reads *in our law Moses commanded*. [b]NU-Text and M-Text read *to stone such*. [c]M-Text adds *about her*. **8:6** [a]NU-Text and M-Text omit *as though He did not hear*. **8:7** [a]M-Text reads *He looked up*. **8:9** [a]NU-Text and M-Text omit *being convicted by their conscience*. **8:10** [a]NU-Text omits *and saw no one but the woman*; M-Text reads *He saw her and said*. [b]NU-Text and M-Text omit *of yours*. **8:11** [a]NU-Text and M-Text add *from now on*.

going; but you do not know where I come from and where I am going. ¹⁵You judge according to the flesh; I judge no one. ¹⁶And yet if I do judge, My judgment is true; for I am not alone, but I *am* with the Father who sent Me. ¹⁷It is also written in your law that the testimony of two men is true. ¹⁸I am One who bears witness of Myself, and the Father who sent Me bears witness of Me."

¹⁹Then they said to Him, "Where is Your Father?"

Jesus answered, "You know neither Me nor My Father. If you had known Me, you would have known My Father also."

²⁰These words Jesus spoke in the treasury, as He taught in the temple; and no one laid hands on Him, for His hour had not yet come.

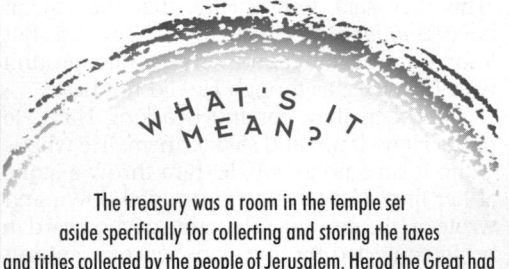

WHAT'S IT MEAN?

The treasury was a room in the temple set aside specifically for collecting and storing the taxes and tithes collected by the people of Jerusalem. Herod the Great had built the temple for the Jewish people, but he expected them to kick in some money every year to help with the cost of maintenance.
John 8:20

On the Edge

And you shall know the truth, and the truth shall make you free (John 8:32).

Jesus makes a big deal about truth because only the truth sets you free. Satan is the father of lies, a master deceiver, and he wants you to believe anything other than the teachings of Jesus. The truth is that believing in Jesus saves you from your sin, and saves you for eternal life. In this verse Jesus says that the truth will set you free because Jesus frees you from your bondage to sin. Satan will whisper lies to you over and over, hoping you'll believe his tricks and get confused. Remember that confusion is not from God (see 1 Cor. 14:33).

When you feel confused or overwhelmed, return to Scripture and read the truth of the words of God. From Him you will find direction and clear guidance. Meditate on those words. Let His truth come alive in your mind and in your heart.

The Bible makes a big deal about truth because lies will lead you astray. Stay focused on the truth of God's Word. Know the truth, follow the truth, tell the truth. It "shall make you free"!

SEE FOR YOURSELF:

Ps. 33:4; John 1:17;
17:17;
Eph. 4:20, 21

JESUS PREDICTS HIS DEPARTURE

²¹Then Jesus said to them again, "I am going away, and you will seek Me, and will die in your sin. Where I go you cannot come."

²²So the Jews said, "Will He kill Himself, because He says, 'Where I go you cannot come'?"

²³And He said to them, "You are from beneath; I am from above. You are of this world; I am not of this world. ²⁴Therefore I said to you that you will die in your sins; for if you do not believe that I am *He*, you will die in your sins."

²⁵Then they said to Him, "Who are You?"

And Jesus said to them, "Just what I have been saying to you from the beginning. ²⁶I have many things to say and to judge concerning you, but He who sent Me is true; and I speak to the world those things which I heard from Him."

²⁷They did not understand that He spoke to them of the Father.

²⁸Then Jesus said to them, "When you lift up the Son of Man, then you will know that I am *He*, and *that* I do nothing of Myself; but as My Father taught Me, I speak these things. ²⁹And He who sent Me is with Me. The Father has not left Me alone, for I always do those things that please Him." ³⁰As He spoke these words, many believed in Him.

THE TRUTH SHALL MAKE YOU FREE

³¹Then Jesus said to those Jews who believed Him, "If you abide in My word, you are My disciples indeed. ³²And you shall know the truth, and the truth shall make you free."

³³They answered Him, "We are Abraham's descendants, and have never been in bondage to anyone. How *can* You say, 'You will be made free'?"

³⁴Jesus answered them, "Most assuredly, I

TRUTH
What does the truth do for us? (8:31, 32)

say to you, whoever commits sin is a slave of sin. ³⁵And a slave does not abide in the house forever, *but* a son abides forever. ³⁶Therefore if the Son makes you free, you shall be free indeed.

ABRAHAM'S SEED AND SATAN'S

³⁷"I know that you are Abraham's descendants, but you seek to kill Me, because My word has no place in you. ³⁸I speak what I have seen with My Father, and you do what you have seen with*ᵃ* your father."

³⁹They answered and said to Him, "Abraham is our father."

Jesus said to them, "If you were Abraham's children, you would do the works of Abraham. ⁴⁰But now you seek to kill Me, a Man who has told you the truth which I heard from God. Abraham did not do this. ⁴¹You do the deeds of your father."

Then they said to Him, "We were not born of fornication; we have one Father—God."

⁴²Jesus said to them, "If God were your Father, you would love Me, for I proceeded forth and came from God; nor have I come of Myself, but He sent Me. ⁴³Why do you not understand My speech? Because you are not able to listen to My word. ⁴⁴You are of your father the devil, and the desires of your father you want to do. He was a murderer from the beginning, and does not stand in the truth, because there is no truth in him. When he speaks a lie, he speaks from his own *resources,* for he is a liar and the father of it. ⁴⁵But because I tell the truth, you do not believe Me. ⁴⁶Which of you convicts Me of sin? And if I tell the truth, why do you not believe Me? ⁴⁷He who is of God hears God's words; therefore you do not hear, because you are not of God."

SATAN

Is Satan completely evil? (8:44)

BEFORE ABRAHAM WAS, I AM

⁴⁸Then the Jews answered and said to Him, "Do we not say rightly that You are a Samaritan and have a demon?"

⁴⁹Jesus answered, "I do not have a demon; but I honor My Father, and you dishonor Me. ⁵⁰And I do not seek My *own* glory; there is One who seeks and judges. ⁵¹Most assuredly, I say to you, if anyone keeps My word he shall never see death."

⁵²Then the Jews said to Him, "Now we know

On the Edge

Jesus said to them, "Most assuredly, I say to you, before Abraham was, I AM" (John 8:58).

Remember when God told Moses to approach Pharaoh and to ask him to let God's people go? How did Moses respond? He asked God, "Indeed, when I come to the children of Israel and say to them, 'The God of your fathers has sent me to you,' and they say to me, 'What is His name?' what shall I say to them?" God simply spoke back, "I AM WHO I AM . . . 'I AM has sent me to you' " (Ex. 3:13–15).

I Am who? God says, "I Am your Savior. I Am your healer. I Am your deliverer. I Am your provider. I Am your help in time of trouble. I Am your friend. I Am your fortress. I Am your joy. I Am your strength. I Am all that you need Me to be!" That's right, God is everything you need Him to be. It doesn't matter what kind of trial you're up against, God is greater.

Just as God had spoken in the Old Testament, Jesus speaks in the New Testament. He, too, is "I Am." Jesus Christ is everything that God is. All of the power of God, all of the love of God, all of the peace of God, and all of the joy of God are in Jesus!

When you find yourself doubting that He exists, remember that He said, "I Am." He wasn't "I Am" for Bible times; He's "I Am" for your life today. He's always existed in power, in glory, and in strength. And He always will.

So the next time you're up against the wall, remember who you are, and who's on your side. He is "I Am"!

SEE FOR YOURSELF:
Ex. 3:13, 14;
14:10–31

that You have a demon! Abraham is dead, and the prophets; and You say, 'If anyone keeps My word he shall never taste death.' ⁵³Are You greater than our father Abraham, who is dead? And the prophets are dead. Who do You make Yourself out to be?"

⁵⁴Jesus answered, "If I honor Myself, My honor is nothing. It is My Father who honors Me, of whom you say that He is your*ᵃ* God.

8:38 *ᵃ*NU-Text reads *heard from.* **8:54** *ᵃ*NU-Text and M-Text read *our.*

⁵⁵Yet you have not known Him, but I know Him. And if I say, 'I do not know Him,' I shall be a liar like you; but I do know Him and keep His word. ⁵⁶Your father Abraham rejoiced to see My day, and he saw *it* and was glad."

⁵⁷Then the Jews said to Him, "You are not yet fifty years old, and have You seen Abraham?"

⁵⁸Jesus said to them, "Most assuredly, I say to you, before Abraham was, I AM."

⁵⁹Then they took up stones to throw at Him; but Jesus hid Himself and went out of the temple,ᵃ going through the midst of them, and so passed by.

A MAN BORN BLIND RECEIVES SIGHT

¹Now as *Jesus* passed by, He saw a man who was blind from birth. ²And His disciples asked Him, saying, "Rabbi, who sinned, this man or his parents, that he was born blind?"

³Jesus answered, "Neither this man nor his parents sinned, but that the works of God should be revealed in him. ⁴Iᵃ must work the works of Him who sent Me while it is day; *the* night is coming when no one can work. ⁵As long as I am in the world, I am the light of the world."

⁶When He had said these things, He spat on the ground and made clay with the saliva; and He anointed the eyes of the blind man with the clay. ⁷And He said to him, "Go, wash in the pool of Siloam" (which is translated, Sent). So he went and washed, and came back seeing.

⁸Therefore the neighbors and those who previously had seen that he was blindᵃ said, "Is not this he who sat and begged?"

⁹Some said, "This is he." Others *said*, "He is like him."ᵃ

He said, "I am *he.*"

¹⁰Therefore they said to him, "How were your eyes opened?"

¹¹He answered and said, "A Man called Jesus made clay and anointed my eyes and said to me, 'Go to the pool ofᵃ Siloam and wash.' So I went and washed, and I received sight."

¹²Then they said to him, "Where is He?"

He said, "I do not know."

THE PHARISEES EXCOMMUNICATE THE HEALED MAN

¹³They brought him who formerly was blind to the Pharisees. ¹⁴Now it was a Sabbath when Jesus made the clay and opened his eyes. ¹⁵Then the Pharisees also asked him again how he had received his sight. He said to them, "He put clay on my eyes, and I washed, and I see."

¹⁶Therefore some of the Pharisees said, "This Man is not from God, because He does not keep the Sabbath."

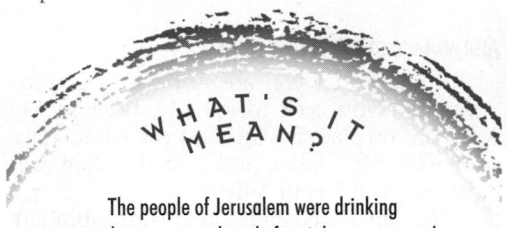

WHAT'S IT MEAN?

The people of Jerusalem were drinking natural spring water long before it became a trendy thing to do. Because there were no rivers close enough to provide water for Jerusalem, the city's water supply came from a spring called Gihon, which was located just outside the city walls. A tunnel brought the water from Gihon Spring into the city, where it was collected in the pool of Siloam.

John 9:7

Others said, "How can a man who is a sinner do such signs?" And there was a division among them.

¹⁷They said to the blind man again, "What do you say about Him because He opened your eyes?"

He said, "He is a prophet."

¹⁸But the Jews did not believe concerning him, that he had been blind and received his sight, until they called the parents of him who had received his sight. ¹⁹And they asked them, saying, "Is this your son, who you say was born blind? How then does he now see?"

²⁰His parents answered them and said, "We know that this is our son, and that he was born blind; ²¹but by what means he now sees we do not know, or who opened his eyes we do not know. He is of age; ask him. He will speak for himself." ²²His parents said these *things* because they feared the Jews, for the Jews had agreed already that if anyone confessed *that* He *was* Christ, he would be put out of the synagogue. ²³Therefore his parents said, "He is of age; ask him."

²⁴So they again called the man who was blind, and said to him, "Give God the glory! We know that this Man is a sinner."

²⁵He answered and said, "Whether He is a sinner *or not* I do not know. One thing I know: that though I was blind, now I see."

[26]Then they said to him again, "What did He do to you? How did He open your eyes?"

[27]He answered them, "I told you already, and you did not listen. Why do you want to hear *it* again? Do you also want to become His disciples?"

[28]Then they reviled him and said, "You are His disciple, but we are Moses' disciples. [29]We know that God spoke to Moses; *as for this fellow,* we do not know where He is from."

[30]The man answered and said to them, "Why, this is a marvelous thing, that you do not know where He is from; yet He has opened my eyes! [31]Now we know that God does not hear sinners; but if anyone is a worshiper of God and does His will, He hears him. [32]Since the world began it has been unheard of that anyone opened the eyes of one who was born blind. [33]If this Man were not from God, He could do nothing."

[34]They answered and said to him, "You were completely born in sins, and are you teaching us?" And they cast him out.

TRUE VISION AND TRUE BLINDNESS

[35]Jesus heard that they had cast him out; and when He had found him, He said to him, "Do you believe in the Son of God?"[a]

[36]He answered and said, "Who is He, Lord, that I may believe in Him?"

[37]And Jesus said to him, "You have both seen Him and it is He who is talking with you."

[38]Then he said, "Lord, I believe!" And he worshiped Him.

[39]And Jesus said, "For judgment I have come into this world, that those who do not see may see, and that those who see may be made blind."

[40]Then *some* of the Pharisees who were with Him heard these words, and said to Him, "Are we blind also?"

[41]Jesus said to them, "If you were blind, you would have no sin; but now you say, 'We see.' Therefore your sin remains.

JESUS THE TRUE SHEPHERD

[1]"Most assuredly, I say to you, he who does not enter the sheepfold by the door, but climbs up some other way, the same is a thief and a robber. [2]But he who enters by the door is the shepherd of the sheep. [3]To him the doorkeeper opens, and the sheep hear his voice; and he calls his own sheep by name and leads them out. [4]And when he brings out his own sheep, he goes before them; and the sheep follow him, for they know his voice. [5]Yet they will by no means follow a stranger, but will flee from him, for they do not know the voice of strangers." [6]Jesus used this illustration, but they did not understand the things which He spoke to them.

JESUS THE GOOD SHEPHERD

[7]Then Jesus said to them again, "Most assuredly, I say to you, I am the door of the sheep. [8]All who *ever* came before Me[a] are thieves and robbers, but the sheep did not hear them. [9]I am the door. If anyone enters by Me, he will be saved, and will go in and out and find pasture. [10]The thief does not come except to steal, and to kill, and to destroy. I have come that they may have life, and that they may have *it* more abundantly.

[11]"I am the good shepherd. The good shepherd gives His life for the sheep. [12]But a hireling, *he who is* not the shepherd, one who does not own the sheep, sees the wolf coming and leaves the sheep and flees; and the wolf catches the sheep and scatters them. [13]The hireling flees because he is a hireling and does not care about the sheep. [14]I am the good shepherd; and I know My *sheep,* and am known by My own. [15]As the Father knows Me, even so I know the Father; and I lay down My life for the sheep. [16]And other sheep I have which are not of this fold; them also I must bring, and they will hear My voice; and there will be one flock *and* one shepherd.

[17]"Therefore My Father loves Me, because I lay down My life that I may take it again. [18]No one takes it from Me, but I lay it down of Myself. I have power to lay it down, and I have power to take it again. This command I have received from My Father."

[19]Therefore there was a division again among the Jews because of these sayings. [20]And

> "The thief does not come except to steal, and to kill, and to destroy. I have come that they may have life, and that they may have it more abundantly."
> (John 10:10)

LIFE
What did Jesus come to give? (10:10)

many of them said, "He has a demon and is mad. Why do you listen to Him?"

²¹Others said, "These are not the words of one who has a demon. Can a demon open the eyes of the blind?"

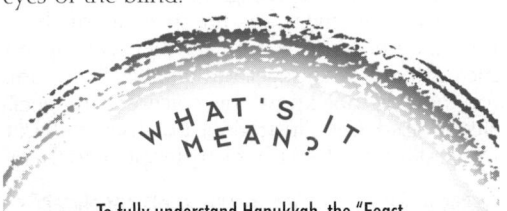

To fully understand Hanukkah, the "Feast of Dedication" mentioned in this verse, you have to know the story of a Syrian king named Antiochus Epiphanes. After the Medes and Persians conquered Babylon, Antiochus Epiphanes took control of the temple in Jerusalem. In a disgusting act of blasphemy, he built an altar to the Greek god Zeus directly over what had been the Jewish altar of burnt offering. As if that weren't bad enough, he then sacrificed a pig on the altar. (Remember, God had declared pigs to be unclean animals.) The one good thing to come from Antiochus Epiphanes' outrageous actions was that the Jews became so enraged they revolted and overthrew the Syrian leaders. In 165 B.C., a group of Jews led by Judas Maccabeus cleansed the temple of its desecration. The eight-day celebration of Hanukkah celebrated that cleansing.

John 10:22

THE SHEPHERD KNOWS HIS SHEEP

²²Now it was the Feast of Dedication in Jerusalem, and it was winter. ²³And Jesus walked in the temple, in Solomon's porch. ²⁴Then the Jews surrounded Him and said to Him, "How long do You keep us in doubt? If You are the Christ, tell us plainly."

²⁵Jesus answered them, "I told you, and you do not believe. The works that I do in My Father's name, they bear witness of Me. ²⁶But you do not believe, because you are not of My sheep, as I said to you.ᵃ ²⁷My sheep hear My voice, and I know them, and they follow Me. ²⁸And I give them eternal life, and they shall never perish; neither shall anyone snatch them out of My hand. ²⁹My Father, who has given *them* to Me, is greater than all; and no one is able to snatch *them* out of My Father's hand. ³⁰I and *My* Father are one."

RENEWED EFFORTS TO STONE JESUS

³¹Then the Jews took up stones again to stone Him. ³²Jesus answered them, "Many good

works I have shown you from My Father. For which of those works do you stone Me?"

³³The Jews answered Him, saying, "For a good work we do not stone You, but for blasphemy, and because You, being a Man, make Yourself God."

³⁴Jesus answered them, "Is it not written in your law, '*I said, "You are gods"* '?ᵃ ³⁵If He called them gods, to whom the word of God came (and the Scripture cannot be broken), ³⁶do you say of Him whom the Father sanctified and sent into the world, 'You are blaspheming,' because I said, 'I am the Son of God'? ³⁷If I do not do the works of My Father, do not believe Me; ³⁸but if I do, though you do not believe Me, believe the works, that you may know and believeᵃ that the Father *is* in Me, and I in Him." ³⁹Therefore they sought again to seize Him, but He escaped out of their hand.

THE BELIEVERS BEYOND JORDAN

⁴⁰And He went away again beyond the Jordan to the place where John was baptizing at first, and there He stayed. ⁴¹Then many came to Him and said, "John performed no sign, but all the things that John spoke about this Man were true." ⁴²And many believed in Him there.

THE DEATH OF LAZARUS

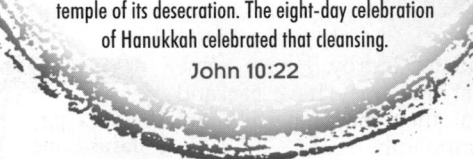¹Now a certain *man* was sick, Lazarus of Bethany, the town of Mary and her sister Martha. ²It was *that* Mary who anointed the Lord with fragrant oil and wiped His feet with her hair, whose brother Lazarus was sick. ³Therefore the sisters sent to Him, saying, "Lord, behold, he whom You love is sick."

⁴When Jesus heard *that,* He said, "This sickness is not unto death, but for the glory of God, that the Son of God may be glorified through it."

⁵Now Jesus loved Martha and her sister and Lazarus. ⁶So, when He heard that he was sick, He stayed two more days in the place where He was. ⁷Then after this He said to *the* disciples, "Let us go to Judea again."

⁸*The* disciples said to Him, "Rabbi, lately the Jews sought to stone You, and are You going there again?"

⁹Jesus answered, "Are there not twelve hours in the day? If anyone walks in the day, he does not stumble, because he sees the light of this world. ¹⁰But if one walks in the night, he stumbles, because the light is not in him." ¹¹These things He said, and after that He said to them, "Our friend Lazarus sleeps, but I go that I may wake him up."

10:26 ᵃNU-Text omits *as I said to you.*   **10:34** ᵃPsalm 82:6   **10:38** ᵃNU-Text reads *understand.*

¹²Then His disciples said, "Lord, if he sleeps he will get well." ¹³However, Jesus spoke of his death, but they thought that He was speaking about taking rest in sleep.

WHAT'S IT MEAN?

In New Testament Israel, you could work eleven hours and still not qualify for overtime. The Jewish work day lasted twelve hours, from sunrise to sunset.

John 11:9

¹⁴Then Jesus said to them plainly, "Lazarus is dead. ¹⁵And I am glad for your sakes that I was not there, that you may believe. Nevertheless let us go to him."

¹⁶Then Thomas, who is called the Twin, said to his fellow disciples, "Let us also go, that we may die with Him."

I AM THE RESURRECTION AND THE LIFE

¹⁷So when Jesus came, He found that he had already been in the tomb four days. ¹⁸Now Bethany was near Jerusalem, about two miles*a* away. ¹⁹And many of the Jews had joined the women around Martha and Mary, to comfort them concerning their brother.

²⁰Now Martha, as soon as she heard that Jesus was coming, went and met Him, but Mary was sitting in the house. ²¹Now Martha said to Jesus, "Lord, if You had been here, my brother would not have died. ²²But even now I know that whatever You ask of God, God will give You."

²³Jesus said to her, "Your brother will rise again."

²⁴Martha said to Him, "I know that he will rise again in the resurrection at the last day."

²⁵Jesus said to her, "I am the resurrection and the life. He who believes in Me, though he may die, he shall live. ²⁶And whoever lives and believes in Me shall never die. Do you believe this?"

ETERNAL LIFE

What does Jesus give? (11:25)

²⁷She said to Him, "Yes, Lord, I believe that

On the Edge

Whoever lives and believes in Me shall never die. Do you believe this? (John 11:26).

"Do you believe this?" Jesus asked. He knew what He said sounded pretty crazy. After all, He had told the disciples that He would be arrested and killed. And the disciples themselves are not still walking around telling their firsthand accounts of Jesus' life.

So what did Jesus mean when He said His followers would never really die? There's a clue in the first part of his statement: "Whoever lives and believes in Me . . ." The life that they had and that you have—and won't ever lose—isn't defined by biological functions. This life comes only from knowing Jesus. And the death that you've escaped is what Paul talked about in Ephesians 2:1: "And you He made alive, who were dead in trespasses and sins." The death you'll never taste is described in Revelation 21:8: "But the cowardly, unbelieving, abominable . . . shall have their part in the lake which burns with fire and brimstone, which is the second death." You have eternal life because of Jesus!

SEE FOR YOURSELF:
John 3:16; Rom. 6:23;
Titus 1:2; 1 John 5:11

You are the Christ, the Son of God, who is to come into the world."

JESUS AND DEATH, THE LAST ENEMY

²⁸And when she had said these things, she went her way and secretly called Mary her sister, saying, "The Teacher has come and is calling for you." ²⁹As soon as she heard *that*, she arose quickly and came to Him. ³⁰Now Jesus had not yet come into the town, but was*a* in the place where Martha met Him. ³¹Then the Jews who were with her in the house, and comforting her, when they saw that Mary rose up quickly and went out, followed her, saying, "She is going to the tomb to weep there."*a*

³²Then, when Mary came where Jesus was, and saw Him, she fell down at His feet, saying

11:18 *a*Literally *fifteen stadia*   **11:30** *a*NU-Text adds *still.* *the tomb to weep there.*   **11:31** *a*NU-Text reads *supposing that she was going to*

to Him, "Lord, if You had been here, my brother would not have died."

[33]Therefore, when Jesus saw her weeping, and the Jews who came with her weeping, He groaned in the spirit and was troubled. [34]And He said, "Where have you laid him?"

They said to Him, "Lord, come and see."

[35]Jesus wept. [36]Then the Jews said, "See how He loved him!"

[37]And some of them said, "Could not this Man, who opened the eyes of the blind, also have kept this man from dying?"

EMOTIONS

Did Jesus experience emotions? (11:35)

LAZARUS RAISED FROM THE DEAD

[38]Then Jesus, again groaning in Himself, came to the tomb. It was a cave, and a stone lay against it. [39]Jesus said, "Take away the stone."

Martha, the sister of him who was dead, said to Him, "Lord, by this time there is a stench, for he has been *dead* four days."

[40]Jesus said to her, "Did I not say to you that if you would believe you would see the glory of God?" [41]Then they took away the stone *from the place* where the dead man was lying.[a] And Jesus lifted up *His* eyes and said, "Father, I thank You that You have heard Me. [42]And I know that You always hear Me, but because of the people who are standing by I said *this*, that they may believe that You sent Me." [43]Now when He had said these things, He cried with a loud voice, "Lazarus, come forth!" [44]And he who had died came out bound hand and foot with graveclothes, and his face was wrapped with a cloth. Jesus said to them, "Loose him, and let him go."

THE PLOT TO KILL JESUS

[45]Then many of the Jews who had come to Mary, and had seen the things Jesus did, believed in Him. [46]But some of them went away to the Pharisees and told them the things Jesus did. [47]Then the chief priests and the Pharisees gathered a council and said, "What shall we do? For this Man works many signs. [48]If we let Him alone like this, everyone will believe in Him, and the Romans will come and take away both our place and nation."

[49]And one of them, Caiaphas, being high priest that year, said to them, "You know nothing at all, [50]nor do you consider that it is expedient for us[a] that one man should die for the people, and not that the whole nation should perish." [51]Now this he did not say on his own *authority*; but being high priest that year he prophesied that Jesus would die for the nation, [52]and not for that nation only, but also that He would gather together in one the children of God who were scattered abroad.

[53]Then, from that day on, they plotted to put Him to death. [54]Therefore Jesus no longer walked openly among the Jews, but went from there into the country near the wilderness, to a city called Ephraim, and there remained with His disciples.

[55]And the Passover of the Jews was near, and many went from the country up to Jerusalem before the Passover, to purify themselves. [56]Then they sought Jesus, and spoke among themselves as they stood in the temple, "What do you think—that He will not come to the feast?" [57]Now both the chief priests and the Pharisees had given a command, that if anyone knew where He was, he should report *it*, that they might seize Him.

THE ANOINTING AT BETHANY

[1]Then, six days before the Passover, Jesus came to Bethany, where Lazarus was who had been dead,[a] whom He had raised from the dead. [2]There they made Him a supper; and Martha served, but Lazarus was one of those who sat at the table with Him. [3]Then Mary took a pound of very costly oil of spikenard, anointed the feet of Jesus, and wiped His feet with her hair. And the house was filled with the fragrance of the oil.

[4]But one of His disciples, Judas Iscariot, Simon's *son*, who would betray Him, said, [5]"Why was this fragrant oil not sold for three hundred denarii[a] and given to the poor?" [6]This he said, not that he cared for the poor, but because he was a thief, and had the money box; and he used to take what was put in it.

[7]But Jesus said, "Let her alone; she has kept[a] this for the day of My burial. [8]For the poor you have with you always, but Me you do not have always."

THE PLOT TO KILL LAZARUS

[9]Now a great many of the Jews knew that He was there; and they came, not for Jesus' sake only, but that they might also see Lazarus, whom He had raised from the dead. [10]But the chief priests plotted to put Lazarus to death

---

11:41 [a]NU-Text omits *from the place where the dead man was lying.*　**11:50** [a]NU-Text reads *you.*　**12:1** [a]NU-Text omits *who had been dead.*　**12:5** [a]About one year's wages for a worker　**12:7** [a]NU-Text reads *that she may keep.*

also, [11]because on account of him many of the Jews went away and believed in Jesus.

THE TRIUMPHAL ENTRY

[12]The next day a great multitude that had come to the feast, when they heard that Jesus was coming to Jerusalem, [13]took branches of palm trees and went out to meet Him, and cried out:

"Hosanna!
'Blessed is He who comes in the name of
   the LORD!'[a]
The King of Israel!"

[14]Then Jesus, when He had found a young donkey, sat on it; as it is written:

[15] "Fear not, daughter of
   Zion;
Behold, your King is
   coming,
Sitting on a donkey's colt."[a]

[16]His disciples did not understand these things at first; but when Jesus was glorified, then they remembered that these things were written about Him and that they had done these things to Him.

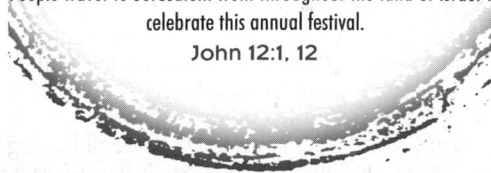

Passover is one of the most important holidays on the Jewish calendar. It was set aside as a time for recalling how God had rescued the Israelites from slavery in Egypt. To celebrate, the Jewish people eat a meal similar to the one their ancestors ate when they prepared to leave Egypt. People travel to Jerusalem from throughout the land of Israel to celebrate this annual festival.
John 12:1, 12

[17]Therefore the people, who were with Him when He called Lazarus out of his tomb and raised him from the dead, bore witness. [18]For this reason the people also met Him, because they heard that He had done this sign. [19]The Pharisees therefore said among themselves, "You see that you are accomplishing nothing. Look, the world has gone after Him!"

THE FRUITFUL GRAIN OF WHEAT

[20]Now there were certain Greeks among those who came up to worship at the feast. [21]Then they came to Philip, who was from Bethsaida of Galilee, and asked him, saying, "Sir, we wish to see Jesus." [22]Philip came and told Andrew, and in turn Andrew and Philip told Jesus.

[23]But Jesus answered them, saying, "The hour has come that the Son of Man should be glorified. [24]Most assuredly, I say to you, unless a grain of wheat falls into the ground and dies, it remains alone; but if it dies, it produces much grain. [25]He who loves his life will lose it, and he who hates his life in this world will keep it for eternal life. [26]If anyone serves Me, let him follow Me; and where I am, there My servant will be also. If anyone serves Me, him My Father will honor.

JESUS PREDICTS HIS DEATH ON THE CROSS

[27]"Now My soul is troubled, and what shall I say? 'Father, save Me from this hour'? But for this purpose I came to this hour. [28]Father, glorify Your name."

Then a voice came from heaven, saying, "I have both glorified it and will glorify it again." [29]Therefore the people who stood by and heard it said that it had thundered. Others said, "An angel has spoken to Him." [30]Jesus answered and said, "This voice did not come because of Me, but for your sake. [31]Now is the judgment of this world; now the ruler of this world will be cast out. [32]And I, if I am lifted up from the earth, will draw all peoples to Myself." [33]This He said, signifying by what death He would die.

[34]The people answered Him, "We have heard from the law that the Christ remains forever; and how can You say, 'The Son of Man must be lifted up'? Who is this Son of Man?" [35]Then Jesus said to them, "A little while longer the light is with you. Walk while you have the light, lest darkness overtake you; he who walks in darkness does not know where he is going. [36]While you have the light, believe

On the Edge

I have come as a light into the world, that whoever believes in Me should not abide in darkness (John 12:46).

The light that gives light! That's what you have—light that will disperse darkness. In other words, you're like a flashlight chasing out the darkness of this world. Don't let your batteries run out, and you'd better check your bulb. The light that Christians give because of Jesus is the only light this world has.

Have you ever been in a room that was pitch black—no light, no windows, totally dark? What happened when you turned on a flashlight or struck a match? The entire room lit up. You couldn't believe how much light that one match or flashlight gave off. That's exactly the kind of effect you can have in your school and everywhere else you go. We live in a dark world, but the good news is that you are the light!

What would you do if you had a friend who was trapped in a cave with a group of people, and they couldn't get out because they couldn't find their way? Let's say that they all died and when their bodies were found, it was discovered that one of the victims had a perfectly good flashlight in his backpack that would have saved all of their lives if it had been used. Wouldn't that upset you?

You know what? You are like that same flashlight that could have saved those lives. Every day you come across the paths of people who desperately need the light of Jesus. Don't hide the light. Use it to impact someone's life forever!

SEE FOR YOURSELF:
Matt. 5:14; John 9:5

> "Lord, who has believed our report?
> And to whom has the arm of the LORD
> been revealed?"[a]

[39]Therefore they could not believe, because Isaiah said again:

[40] "He has blinded their eyes and hardened
> their hearts,
> Lest they should see with their eyes,
> Lest they should understand with their
> hearts and turn,
> So that I should heal them." [a]

[41]These things Isaiah said when[a] he saw His glory and spoke of Him.

WALK IN THE LIGHT

[42]Nevertheless even among the rulers many believed in Him, but because of the Pharisees they did not confess *Him*, lest they should be put out of the synagogue; [43]for they loved the praise of men more than the praise of God.

[44]Then Jesus cried out and said, "He who believes in Me, believes not in Me but in Him who sent Me. [45]And he who sees Me sees Him who sent Me. [46]I have come *as* a light into the world, that whoever believes in Me should not abide in darkness. [47]And if anyone hears My words and does not believe,[a] I do not judge him; for I did not come to judge the world but to save the world. [48]He who rejects Me, and does not receive My words, has that which judges him—the word that I have spoken will judge him in the last day. [49]For I have not spoken on My own *authority*; but the Father who sent Me gave Me a command, what I should say and what I should speak. [50]And I know that His command is everlasting life. Therefore, whatever I speak, just as the Father has told Me, so I speak."

JESUS WASHES THE DISCIPLES' FEET

[1]Now before the Feast of the Passover, when Jesus knew that His hour had come that He should depart from this world to the Father, having loved His own who were in the world, He loved them to the end.

[2]And supper being ended,[a] the devil having already put it into the heart of Judas Iscariot, Simon's *son*, to betray Him, [3]Jesus, knowing that the Father had given all things into His hands, and that He had come from God and was going to God, [4]rose from supper and laid

in the light, that you may become sons of light." These things Jesus spoke, and departed, and was hidden from them.

WHO HAS BELIEVED OUR REPORT?

[37]But although He had done so many signs before them, they did not believe in Him, [38]that the word of Isaiah the prophet might be fulfilled, which he spoke:

12:38 [a]Isaiah 53:1   **12:40** [a]Isaiah 6:10   **12:41** [a]NU-Text reads *because.*   **12:47** [a]NU-Text reads *keep them.*
13:2 [a]NU-Text reads *And during supper.*

aside His garments, took a towel and girded Himself. [5]After that, He poured water into a basin and began to wash the disciples' feet, and to wipe *them* with the towel with which He was girded. [6]Then He came to Simon Peter. And *Peter* said to Him, "Lord, are You washing my feet?"

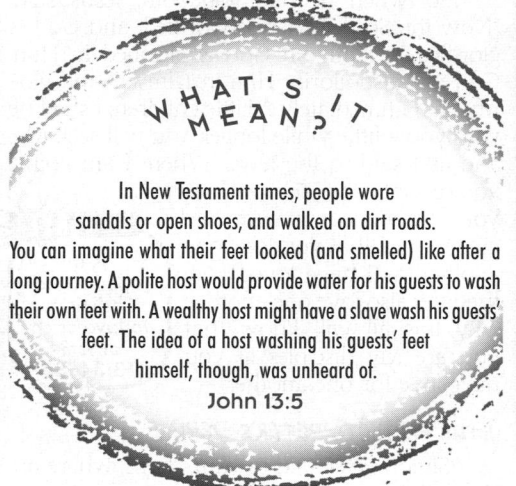

WHAT'S IT MEAN?

In New Testament times, people wore sandals or open shoes, and walked on dirt roads. You can imagine what their feet looked (and smelled) like after a long journey. A polite host would provide water for his guests to wash their own feet with. A wealthy host might have a slave wash his guests' feet. The idea of a host washing his guests' feet himself, though, was unheard of.

John 13:5

[7]Jesus answered and said to him, "What I am doing you do not understand now, but you will know after this."

[8]Peter said to Him, "You shall never wash my feet!"

Jesus answered him, "If I do not wash you, you have no part with Me."

[9]Simon Peter said to Him, "Lord, not my feet only, but also *my* hands and *my* head!"

[10]Jesus said to him, "He who is bathed needs only to wash *his* feet, but is completely clean; and you are clean, but not all of you." [11]For He knew who would betray Him; therefore He said, "You are not all clean."

[12]So when He had washed their feet, taken His garments, and sat down again, He said to them, "Do you know what I have done to you? [13]You call Me Teacher and Lord, and you say well, for *so* I am. [14]If I then, *your* Lord and Teacher, have washed your feet, you also ought to wash one another's feet. [15]For I have given you an example, that you should do as I have done to you. [16]Most assuredly, I say to you, a servant is not greater than his master; nor is he who is sent greater than he who sent him. [17]If you know these things, blessed are you if you do them.

JESUS IDENTIFIES HIS BETRAYER

[18]"I do not speak concerning all of you. I know whom I have chosen; but that the Scrip-

On the Edge

You call Me Teacher and Lord, and you say well, for so I am. If I then, your Lord and Teacher, have washed your feet, you also ought to wash one another's feet. For I have given you an example, that you should do as I have done to you (John 13:13–15).

Jesus gives His disciples a lesson in humility when He washes their feet. He tells them that they are to follow His example. And we, as disciples of Christ, are to do the same. Meeting the needs of other people and sacrificing your own is the example of Jesus, and we are to be like Him. Did you know that when you feel sorry for yourself, one of the best things to help you feel better is to do something good for somebody else? And if you are acting like Jesus, it may cost you something— some time, some energy, some money, maybe even your pride. Sometimes we can serve others secretly, and God gets all of the glory. Jesus came and humbled Himself by being as a servant to others. Being Christlike means that we humble ourselves and do the same. It's the whole point of our time here on earth—following His example, looking more and more like Jesus.

SEE FOR YOURSELF:
  Matt. 16:24–26;
  John 12:26;
  Phil. 3:12–17;
  1 Tim. 4:12; 6:11, 12

ture may be fulfilled, '*He who eats bread with Me[a] has lifted up his heel against Me.*'[b] [19]Now I tell you before it comes, that when it does come to pass, you may believe that I am *He.* [20]Most assuredly, I say to you, he who receives whomever I send receives Me; and he who receives Me receives Him who sent Me."

[21]When Jesus had said these things, He was troubled in spirit, and testified and said, "Most assuredly, I say to you, one of you will betray Me." [22]Then the disciples looked at one another, perplexed about whom He spoke.

[23]Now there was leaning on Jesus' bosom one of His disciples, whom Jesus loved. [24]Simon

13:18 [a]NU-Text reads *My bread.* [b]Psalm 41:9

Peter therefore motioned to him to ask who it was of whom He spoke.

²⁵Then, leaning back*ᵃ* on Jesus' breast, he said to Him, "Lord, who is it?"

WHAT'S IT MEAN?

Bread was a major part of the Jewish diet in New Testament times. A typical meal consisted of bread served with a thin stew or sauce. Several people would share one bowl of sauce, taking turns dipping their bread into it before each bite. Often a host would feed bread to an honored guest as a token of friendship.

John 13:26

²⁶Jesus answered, "It is he to whom I shall give a piece of bread when I have dipped *it*." And having dipped the bread, He gave *it* to Judas Iscariot, *the son* of Simon. ²⁷Now after the piece of bread, Satan entered him. Then Jesus said to him, "What you do, do quickly." ²⁸But no one at the table knew for what reason He said this to him. ²⁹For some thought, because Judas had the money box, that Jesus had said to him,

13:25 *ᵃ*NU-Text and M-Text add *thus*.

"Buy *those things* we need for the feast," or that he should give something to the poor.

³⁰Having received the piece of bread, he then went out immediately. And it was night.

THE NEW COMMANDMENT

³¹So, when he had gone out, Jesus said, "Now the Son of Man is glorified, and God is glorified in Him. ³²If God is glorified in Him, God will also glorify Him in Himself, and glorify Him immediately. ³³Little children, I shall be with you a little while longer. You will seek Me; and as I said to the Jews, 'Where I am going, you cannot come,' so now I say to you. ³⁴A new commandment I give to you, that you love one another; as I have loved you, that you also love one another. ³⁵By this all will know that you are My disciples, if you have love for one another."

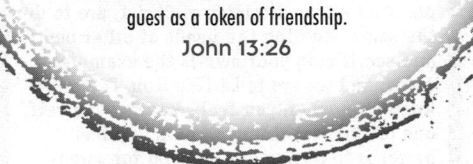

LOVE
Is it important for Christians to love each other? (13:34, 35)

JESUS PREDICTS PETER'S DENIAL

³⁶Simon Peter said to Him, "Lord, where are You going?"

Jesus answered him, "Where I am going you cannot follow Me now, but you shall follow Me afterward."

³⁷Peter said to Him, "Lord, why can I not follow You now? I will lay down my life for Your sake."

³⁸Jesus answered him, "Will you lay down

✦ Promise   HE PROMISES YOU A HOME WITH HIM.

In My Father's house are many mansions; if it were not so, I would have told you. I go to prepare a place for you. And if I go and prepare a place for you, I will come again and receive you to Myself; that where I am, there you may be also. And where I go you know, and the way you know (John 14:2–4).

This is one of the most awesome promises in all of Scripture. Jesus has gone to heaven to prepare our home—our forever home. A room in our Father's house waits for each one of us. And then, when it is time, Jesus will return to take us there. It's the home your heart has been longing for since the day you were born. It's the place where all your wounds will be healed. All your hopes will be fulfilled. Joy will be complete. Laughter will bounce off the walls. Tears will be banned. Worry won't even be a word. Home. Home at last with Jesus. Everything you've ever thought a home should be, and more than you ever dreamed it could be. Not a day too early, but just in time, Jesus will take us home.

SEE FOR YOURSELF:
Deut. 33:27; Matt. 6:19–21; Heb. 12:22–24

your life for My sake? Most assuredly, I say to you, the rooster shall not crow till you have denied Me three times.

THE WAY, THE TRUTH, AND THE LIFE

[1]"Let not your heart be troubled; you believe in God, believe also in Me. [2]In My Father's house are many mansions;[a] if *it were* not so, I would have told you. I go to prepare a place for you.[b] [3]And if I go and prepare a place for you, I will come again and receive you to Myself; that where I am, *there* you may be also. [4]And where I go you know, and the way you know."

[5]Thomas said to Him, "Lord, we do not know where You are going, and how can we know the way?"

[6]Jesus said to him, "I am the way, the truth, and the life. No one comes to the Father except through Me.

ETERNAL LIFE

Where can eternal life be found? (14:6)

THE FATHER REVEALED

[7]"If you had known Me, you would have known My Father also; and from now on you know Him and have seen Him."

[8]Philip said to Him, "Lord, show us the Father, and it is sufficient for us."

[9]Jesus said to him, "Have I been with you so long, and yet you have not known Me, Philip? He who has seen Me has seen the Father; so how can you say, 'Show us the Father'? [10]Do you not believe that I am in the Father, and the Father in Me? The words that I speak to you I do not speak on My own *authority*; but the Father who dwells in Me does the works. [11]Believe Me that I *am* in the Father and the Father in Me, or else believe Me for the sake of the works themselves.

THE ANSWERED PRAYER

[12]"Most assuredly, I say to you, he who believes in Me, the works that I do he will do also; and greater *works* than these he will do, because I go to My Father. [13]And whatever you ask in My name, that I will do, that the Father may be glorified in the Son. [14]If you ask[a] anything in My name, I will do *it.*

JESUS PROMISES ANOTHER HELPER

[15]"If you love Me, keep[a] My commandments. [16]And I will pray the Father, and He will give you another Helper, that He may abide

---

On the Edge

Jesus said to [Thomas], "I am the way, the truth, and the life. No one comes to the Father except through Me" (John 14:6).

If you check the graves of Mohammed or Buddha or any other so-called god, you will find that those graves all have one thing in common: They all have bones in them. There is only one grave that is empty—the grave of our Lord Jesus Christ! He is the only way to get to God, the only way to get to heaven, the only way to have eternal life, the only way to have real life.

A lot of people are out there lost in the world trying to work their way into heaven. Then there are those who think they can buy their way into heaven. There are others who simply believe that as long as you try to be a good person, you'll end up in heaven. And finally there are the kind of people who just don't believe God would send anyone to hell. They believe everyone goes to heaven.

Well, here's some good news and some bad news. There really is a heaven and there really is a hell. It doesn't matter how good you may think you are, how much money you have, or how many times you've been to church. Without Jesus, you can forget it all. He is the only way. He is the only truth. He is the only life.

SEE FOR YOURSELF:
Matt. 10:28;
Rom. 10:13

---

with you forever— [17]the Spirit of truth, whom the world cannot receive, because it neither sees Him nor knows Him; but you know Him, for He dwells with you and will be in you. [18]I will not leave you orphans; I will come to you.

INDWELLING OF THE FATHER AND THE SON

[19]"A little while longer and the world will see Me no more, but you will see Me. Because I live, you will live also. [20]At that day you will

DEATH

Who has power over death? (14:19)

14:2 [a]Literally *dwellings* [b]NU-Text adds a word which would cause the text to read either *if it were not so, would I have told you that I go to prepare a place for you?* or *if it were not so I would have told you; for I go to prepare a place for you.* **14:14** [a]NU-Text adds *Me.* **14:15** [a]NU-Text reads *you will keep.*

know that I *am* in My Father, and you in Me, and I in you. ²¹He who has My commandments and keeps them, it is he who loves Me. And he who loves Me will be loved by My Father, and I will love him and manifest Myself to him."

²²Judas (not Iscariot) said to Him, "Lord, how is it that You will manifest Yourself to us, and not to the world?"

²³Jesus answered and said to him, "If anyone loves Me, he will keep My word; and My Father will love him, and We will come to him and make Our home with him. ²⁴He who does not love Me does not keep My words; and the word which you hear is not Mine but the Father's who sent Me.

THE GIFT OF HIS PEACE

²⁵"These things I have spoken to you while being present with you. ²⁶But the Helper, the Holy Spirit, whom the Father will send in My name, He will teach you all things, and bring to your remembrance all things that I said to you. ²⁷Peace I leave with you, My peace I give to you; not as the world gives do I give to you. Let not your heart be troubled, neither let it be afraid. ²⁸You have heard Me say to you, 'I am going away and coming *back* to you.' If you loved Me, you would rejoice because I said,ᵃ 'I am going to the Father,' for My Father is greater than I.

²⁹"And now I have told you before it comes, that when it does come to pass, you may believe. ³⁰I will no longer talk much with you, for the ruler of this world is coming, and he has nothing in Me. ³¹But that the world may know that I love the Father, and as the Father gave Me commandment, so I do. Arise, let us go from here.

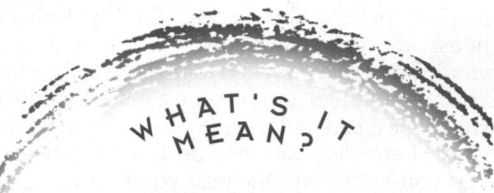

WHAT'S IT MEAN?

Jesus used an image that the Jewish people would have been familiar with. Grape crops were a vital part of the nation's economy. Every year, Jewish farmers pruned their grapevines, removing dead branches and leaves. Only branches with fruit on them were kept, and even those were trimmed back to keep the vine in peak condition. The grapes themselves were either eaten fresh or dried. Their juice was used to make wine and vinegar.

John 15:2

THE TRUE VINE

¹"I am the true vine, and My Father is the vinedresser. ²Every branch in Me that does not bear fruit He takes away;ᵃ and every *branch* that bears fruit He prunes, that it may bear more fruit. ³You are already clean because of the word which I have spoken to you. ⁴Abide in

14:28 ᵃNU-Text omits *I said.*   **15:2** ᵃOr *lifts up*

Promise   HE PROMISES TO HELP YOU BY HIS SPIRIT.

And I will pray the Father, and He will give you another Helper [the Holy Spirit], that He may abide with you forever (John 14:16).

Have you ever needed help? Of course you have. You may need help right now. All of us need help at some time or another. None of us is immune to the storms of life, but the good news is God sent the Holy Spirit to go with us through these storms. Not only did He come to fill us with power, but He was also sent to help us with every trial, every temptation, and every circumstance.

You may be going through something at this very moment, but you know what? The Holy Spirit is there right now ready and willing to help, even as you read this. In fact, if we will become aware of God's presence in us there isn't anything that the devil can throw at us that we can't handle. Jesus, the greater One, lives on the inside! Nothing can stop us now! We have victory! He'll help you!

SEE FOR YOURSELF:

Ps. 33:20; 37:40; Rom. 8:26; 1 John 4:4

On the Edge

I am the true vine, and My Father is the vinedresser (John 15:1).

Let's take a look at this verse. Here are some thoughts that just might jump off this page and be a great encouragement to you. The words "I am" were used in John 6:51. Jesus was talking there about being "living bread"; and in John 1:9, John referred to Him as the "true Light." Both of these relate to the verse here about Jesus being the "true vine." The Greek word for "true vine" lets us know that He was the original vine. Back in Isaiah Jesus was known as the "Root of Jesse"; now that Root is a vine (see Is. 11:10). We are the branches that grow from that vine. In other words, we have life because of Him. The farmer is the one who takes care of the vineyard, and that farmer is God. He's taking care of us so we can produce good fruit. As we allow God to feed us, prune us, and care for us, we will start producing good fruit today. God is the farmer, Jesus is the vine, and you're the branch. God's on your side, and He wants to see you produce good fruit!

SEE FOR YOURSELF:
Prov. 16:3; John 1:9; 6:32, 51

---

have kept My Father's commandments and abide in His love.

¹¹"These things I have spoken to you, that My joy may remain in you, and *that* your joy may be full. ¹²This is My commandment, that you love one another as I have loved you. ¹³Greater love has no one than this, than to lay down one's life for his friends. ¹⁴You are My friends if you do whatever I command you. ¹⁵No longer do I call you servants, for a servant does not know what his master is doing; but I have called you friends, for all things that I heard from My Father I have made known to you. ¹⁶You did not choose Me, but I chose you and appointed you that you should go and bear fruit, and *that* your fruit should remain, that whatever you ask the Father in My name He may give you. ¹⁷These things I command you, that you love one another.

FRIENDSHIP
What is friendship marked by? (15:13–15)

THE WORLD'S HATRED

¹⁸"If the world hates you, you know that it hated Me before *it hated* you. ¹⁹If you were of the world, the world would love its own. Yet because you are not of the world, but I chose you out of the world, therefore the world hates you. ²⁰Remember the word that I said to you, 'A servant is not greater than his master.' If they persecuted Me, they will also persecute you. If they kept My word, they will keep yours also. ²¹But all these things they will do to you for My name's sake, because they do not know Him who sent Me. ²²If I had not come and spoken to them, they would have no sin, but now they have no excuse for their sin. ²³He who hates Me hates My Father also. ²⁴If I had not done among them the works which no one else did, they would have no sin; but now they have seen and also hated both Me and My Father. ²⁵But *this happened* that the word might be fulfilled which is written in their law, '*They hated Me without a cause.*'ᵃ

THE COMING REJECTION

²⁶"But when the Helper comes, whom I shall send to you from the Father, the Spirit of truth who proceeds from the Father, He will testify of Me. ²⁷And you also will bear witness, because you have been with Me from the beginning.

¹"These things I have spoken to you, that you should not be made to stumble. ²They will put you out of the synagogues; yes, the time is

---

Me, and I in you. As the branch cannot bear fruit of itself, unless it abides in the vine, neither can you, unless you abide in Me.

⁵"I am the vine, you *are* the branches. He who abides in Me, and I in him, bears much fruit; for without Me you can do nothing. ⁶If anyone does not abide in Me, he is cast out as a branch and is withered; and they gather them and throw *them* into the fire, and they are burned. ⁷If you abide in Me, and My words abide in you, you willᵃ ask what you desire, and it shall be done for you. ⁸By this My Father is glorified, that you bear much fruit; so you will be My disciples.

LOVE AND JOY PERFECTED

⁹"As the Father loved Me, I also have loved you; abide in My love. ¹⁰If you keep My commandments, you will abide in My love, just as I

15:7 ᵃNU-Text omits *you will*. **15:25** ᵃPsalm 69:4

coming that whoever kills you will think that he offers God service. ³And these things they will do to you[a] because they have not known the Father nor Me. ⁴But these things I have told you, that when the[a] time comes, you may remember that I told you of them.

"And these things I did not say to you at the beginning, because I was with you.

THE WORK OF THE HOLY SPIRIT

⁵"But now I go away to Him who sent Me, and none of you asks Me, 'Where are You going?' ⁶But because I have said these things to you, sorrow has filled your heart. ⁷Nevertheless I tell you the truth. It is to your advantage that I go away; for if I do not go away, the Helper will not come to you; but if I depart, I will send Him to you. ⁸And when He has come, He will convict the world of sin, and of righteousness, and of judgment: ⁹of sin, because they do not believe in Me; ¹⁰of righteousness, because I go to My Father and you see Me no more; ¹¹of judgment, because the ruler of this world is judged.

¹²"I still have many things to say to you, but you cannot bear them now. ¹³However, when He, the Spirit of truth, has come, He will guide you into all truth; for He will not speak on His own *authority*, but whatever He hears He will speak; and He will tell you things to come. ¹⁴He will glorify Me, for He will take of what is Mine and declare *it* to you. ¹⁵All things that the Father has are Mine. Therefore I said that He will take of Mine and declare *it* to you.[a]

SORROW WILL TURN TO JOY

¹⁶"A little while, and you will not see Me; and again a little while, and you will see Me, because I go to the Father."

¹⁷Then *some* of His disciples said among themselves, "What is this that He says to us, 'A little while, and you will not see Me; and again a little while, and you will see Me'; and, 'because I go to the Father'?" ¹⁸They said therefore, "What is this that He says, 'A little while'? We do not know what He is saying."

¹⁹Now Jesus knew that they desired to ask Him, and He said to them, "Are you inquiring among yourselves about what I said, 'A little while, and you will not see Me; and again a little while, and you will see Me'? ²⁰Most assuredly, I say to you that you will weep and

---

16:3 ᵃNU-Text and M-Text omit *to you.*   **16:4** ᵃNU-Text reads *their.*   **16:15** ᵃNU-Text and M-Text read *He takes of Mine and will declare it to you.*

Promise   HE PROMISES TO BE YOUR FRIEND.

You are My friends if you do whatever I command you. No longer do I call you servants, for a servant does not know what his master is doing; but I have called you friends, for all things that I heard from My Father I have made known to you (John 15:14, 15).

Jesus called the disciples His *friends*. That word applies to everyone who would ever become His disciple. In verse 15, Jesus says, "No longer do I call you servants . . . I have called you friends."

You've probably heard a lot about being Jesus' servant. He's done so much for you! Because of Him you're loved more than you can imagine. Because of Him you can be strong and confident. Because of Him you'll spend eternity with God. So a good response to Him is, "Jesus, what can I do for You?" Of course, Jesus wants you to do your best to be a servant who pleases Him. But more than that, He wants you to treat Him like your friend. Jesus is a Person, and like any person, He wants a friend who loves Him more than anyone or anything else. What counts is not wearing yourself out with good deeds, but turning yourself toward Him and loving Him with your whole heart.

Be careful not to take His friendship for granted. He isn't like your friends at school, just as imperfect as you are. He is God. While you're learning to love Him as your best friend, don't ever lose sight of how awesome He is and of all the incredible gifts He gives you. Start to think of yourself as a friend of Jesus.

SEE FOR YOURSELF:

John 14:15, 21; James 2:22, 23

lament, but the world will rejoice; and you will be sorrowful, but your sorrow will be turned into joy. 21A woman, when she is in labor, has sorrow because her hour has come; but as soon as she has given birth to the child, she no longer remembers the anguish, for joy that a human being has been born into the world. 22Therefore you now have sorrow; but I will see you again and your heart will rejoice, and your joy no one will take from you.

23"And in that day you will ask Me nothing. Most assuredly, I say to you, whatever you ask the Father in My name He will give you. 24Until now you have asked nothing in My name. Ask, and you will receive, that your joy may be full.

PRAYER

Whose name should we pray in? (16:23, 24)

JESUS CHRIST HAS OVERCOME THE WORLD

25"These things I have spoken to you in figurative language; but the time is coming when I will no longer speak to you in figurative language, but I will tell you plainly about the Father. 26In that day you will ask in My name, and I do not say to you that I shall pray the Father for you; 27for the Father Himself loves you, because you have loved Me, and have believed that I came forth from God. 28I came forth from the Father and have come into the world. Again, I leave the world and go to the Father."

29His disciples said to Him, "See, now You are speaking plainly, and using no figure of speech! 30Now we are sure that You know all things, and have no need that anyone should question You. By this we believe that You came forth from God."

31Jesus answered them, "Do you now believe? 32Indeed the hour is coming, yes, has now come, that you will be scattered, each to his own, and will leave Me alone. And yet I am not alone, because the Father is with Me. 33These things I have spoken to you, that in Me you may have peace. In the world you willa have tribulation; but be of good cheer, I have overcome the world."

COMFORT

What has Jesus overcome? (16:33)

JESUS PRAYS FOR HIMSELF

1Jesus spoke these words, lifted up His eyes to heaven, and said: "Father, the hour has come. Glorify Your Son, that Your Son also may glorify You, 2as You have given Him authority over all flesh, that He shoulda give eternal life to as

16:33 aNU-Text and M-Text omit will. **17:2** aM-Text reads shall.

Promise HE PROMISES TO SHOW YOU WHAT IS TRUE.

However, when He, the Spirit of truth, has come, He will guide you into all truth; for He will not speak on His own authority, but whatever He hears He will speak; and He will tell you things to come (John 16:13).

Have you ever had a tough time making a decision? Everybody has. Well, the Holy Spirit has been sent to speak to you at those very moments. And this verse assures you that He will not just spout off on His own, but will only say what God says. In other words, when the Holy Spirit speaks to your heart, you can take it to the bank. You'd better go with it! He will speak to you and He's going to show you what is true. That's His job. So make sure you're listening and not ignoring Him.

How do you hear the Holy Spirit speak? Second Timothy 2:15 says, "Be diligent to present yourself approved to God, a worker who does not need to be ashamed, rightly dividing the word of truth." So what do you do? Begin doing your best and studying the Bible—not just reading words, but really getting into the Word of God. Start out by just reviewing a few verses in your mind—over and over. Begin putting the Word of God inside you by memorizing a verse or two. Read Psalm 119:1–24. Notice how the psalmist felt about God's Word. Whenever you read the words *law, statutes, testimonies, commandments,* or *word,* you can think of them as the Bible. As you begin to "feed" yourself the Word of God, you'll begin to notice that you are hearing God speak to you in ways and about things you've never heard before. Start doing it now, and let the Holy Spirit lead you "into all truth"!

SEE FOR YOURSELF:
Ps. 32:8, 9; Prov. 3:5, 6; Is. 58:11; John 4:24

many as You have given Him. ³And this is eternal life, that they may know You, the only true God, and Jesus Christ whom You have sent. ⁴I have glorified You on the earth. I have finished the work which You have given Me to do. ⁵And now, O Father, glorify Me together with Yourself, with the glory which I had with You before the world was.

SALVATION
Does salvation include gaining a relationship with God? (17:1–5)

JESUS PRAYS FOR HIS DISCIPLES

⁶"I have manifested Your name to the men whom You have given Me out of the world. They were Yours, You gave them to Me, and they have kept Your word. ⁷Now they have known that all things which You have given Me are from You. ⁸For I have given to them the words which You have given Me; and they have received *them*, and have known surely that I came forth from You; and they have believed that You sent Me.

⁹"I pray for them. I do not pray for the world but for those whom You have given Me, for they are Yours. ¹⁰And all Mine are Yours, and Yours are Mine, and I am glorified in them. ¹¹Now I am no longer in the world, but these are in the world, and I come to You. Holy Father, keep through Your name those whom You have given Me,ᵃ that they may be one as We *are*. ¹²While I was with them in the world,ᵃ I kept them in Your name. Those whom You gave Me I have kept;ᵇ and none of them is lost except the son of perdition, that the Scripture might be fulfilled. ¹³But now I come to You, and these things I speak in the world, that they may have My joy fulfilled in themselves. ¹⁴I have given them Your word; and the world has hated them because they are not of the world, just as I am not of the world. ¹⁵I do not pray that You should take them out of the world, but that You should keep them from the evil one.

TRUTH
Is God's word truth? (17:17)

¹⁶They are not of the world, just as I am not of the world. ¹⁷Sanctify them by Your truth. Your word is truth. ¹⁸As You sent Me into the world, I also have sent them into the world. ¹⁹And for their sakes I sanctify Myself, that they also may be sanctified by the truth.

JESUS PRAYS FOR ALL BELIEVERS

²⁰"I do not pray for these alone, but also for those who willᵃ believe in Me through their word; ²¹that they all may be one, as You, Father, *are* in Me, and I in You; that they also may be one in Us, that the world may believe that You sent Me. ²²And the glory which You gave Me I have given them, that they may be one just as We are one: ²³I in them, and You in Me; that they may be made perfect in one, and that the world may know that You have sent Me, and have loved them as You have loved Me.

²⁴"Father, I desire that they also whom You gave Me may be with Me where I am, that they may behold My glory which You have given Me; for You loved Me before the foundation of the world. ²⁵O righteous Father! The world has not known You, but I have known You; and these have known that You sent Me. ²⁶And I have declared to them Your name, and will declare *it*, that the love with which You loved Me may be in them, and I in them."

BETRAYAL AND ARREST IN GETHSEMANE

¹When Jesus had spoken these words, He went out with His disciples over the Brook Kidron, where there was a garden, which He and His disciples entered. ²And Judas, who betrayed Him, also knew the place; for Jesus often met there with His disciples. ³Then Judas, having received a detachment *of troops*, and officers from the chief priests and Pharisees, came there with

WHAT'S IT MEAN?

The Brook Kidron began north of Jerusalem and flowed past some of the major sites in New Testament history—the temple of Jerusalem; Calvary, the place of Jesus' crucifixion; the Garden of Gethsemane, where Jesus prayed on the night of His arrest; and the Mount of Olives. During the dry summer months, the brook was nearly nonexistent. During the rainy winter season, it turned into a steadily flowing stream.

John 18:1

17:11 ᵃNU-Text and M-Text read *keep them through Your name which You have given Me.* **17:12** ᵃNU-Text omits *in the world.* ᵇNU-Text reads *in Your name which You gave Me. And I guarded them;* (or *it;*). **17:20** ᵃNU-Text and M-Text omit *will.*

lanterns, torches, and weapons. [4]Jesus therefore, knowing all things that would come upon Him, went forward and said to them, "Whom are you seeking?"

[5]They answered Him, "Jesus of Nazareth."

Jesus said to them, "I am *He.*" And Judas, who betrayed Him, also stood with them. [6]Now when He said to them, "I am *He,*" they drew back and fell to the ground.

[7]Then He asked them again, "Whom are you seeking?"

And they said, "Jesus of Nazareth."

[8]Jesus answered, "I have told you that I am *He.* Therefore, if you seek Me, let these go their way," [9]that the saying might be fulfilled which He spoke, "Of those whom You gave Me I have lost none."

[10]Then Simon Peter, having a sword, drew it and struck the high priest's servant, and cut off his right ear. The servant's name was Malchus.

[11]So Jesus said to Peter, "Put your sword into the sheath. Shall I not drink the cup which My Father has given Me?"

BEFORE THE HIGH PRIEST

[12]Then the detachment *of troops* and the captain and the officers of the Jews arrested Jesus and bound Him. [13]And they led Him away to Annas first, for he was the father-in-law of Caiaphas who was high priest that year. [14]Now it was Caiaphas who advised the Jews that it was expedient that one man should die for the people.

PETER DENIES JESUS

[15]And Simon Peter followed Jesus, and so *did* another[a] disciple. Now that disciple was known to the high priest, and went with Jesus into the courtyard of the high priest. [16]But Peter stood at the door outside. Then the other disciple, who was known to the high priest, went out and spoke to her who kept the door, and brought Peter in. [17]Then the servant girl who kept the door said to Peter, "You are not also *one* of this Man's disciples, are you?"

He said, "I am not."

[18]Now the servants and officers who had made a fire of coals stood there, for it was cold, and they warmed themselves. And Peter stood with them and warmed himself.

JESUS QUESTIONED BY THE HIGH PRIEST

[19]The high priest then asked Jesus about His disciples and His doctrine.

[20]Jesus answered him, "I spoke openly to the world. I always taught in synagogues and in the temple, where the Jews always meet,[a] and in secret I have said nothing. [21]Why do you ask Me? Ask those who have heard Me what I said to them. Indeed they know what I said."

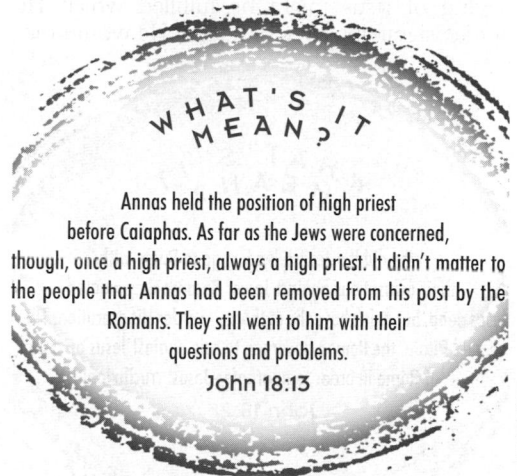

WHAT'S IT MEAN?

Annas held the position of high priest before Caiaphas. As far as the Jews were concerned, though, once a high priest, always a high priest. It didn't matter to the people that Annas had been removed from his post by the Romans. They still went to him with their questions and problems.

John 18:13

[22]And when He had said these things, one of the officers who stood by struck Jesus with the palm of his hand, saying, "Do You answer the high priest like that?"

[23]Jesus answered him, "If I have spoken evil, bear witness of the evil; but if well, why do you strike Me?"

[24]Then Annas sent Him bound to Caiaphas the high priest.

PETER DENIES TWICE MORE

[25]Now Simon Peter stood and warmed himself. Therefore they said to him, "You are not also *one* of His disciples, are you?"

He denied *it* and said, "I am not!"

[26]One of the servants of the high priest, a relative *of him* whose ear Peter cut off, said, "Did I not see you in the garden with Him?" [27]Peter then denied again; and immediately a rooster crowed.

IN PILATE'S COURT

[28]Then they led Jesus from Caiaphas to the Praetorium, and it was early morning. But they themselves did not go into the Praetorium, lest they should be defiled, but that they might eat the Passover. [29]Pilate then went out to them and said, "What accusation do you bring against this Man?"

[30]They answered and said to him, "If He

18:15 [a]M-Text reads *the other.*   18:20 [a]NU-Text reads *where all the Jews meet.*

were not an evildoer, we would not have delivered Him up to you."

[31] Then Pilate said to them, "You take Him and judge Him according to your law."

Therefore the Jews said to him, "It is not lawful for us to put anyone to death," [32] that the saying of Jesus might be fulfilled which He spoke, signifying by what death He would die.

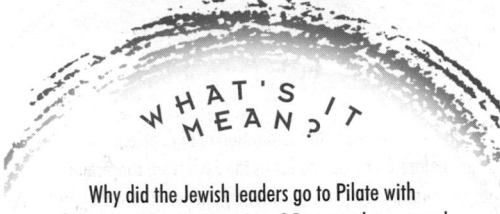

WHAT'S IT MEAN?

Why did the Jewish leaders go to Pilate with their accusations against Jesus? Because they wanted Jesus dead, but didn't have the authority to order His execution. They needed Pilate, the Roman governor, to rule against Jesus on behalf of Rome in order to guarantee Jesus' crucifixion.

John 18:28

[33] Then Pilate entered the Praetorium again, called Jesus, and said to Him, "Are You the King of the Jews?"

[34] Jesus answered him, "Are you speaking for yourself about this, or did others tell you this concerning Me?"

[35] Pilate answered, "Am I a Jew? Your own nation and the chief priests have delivered You to me. What have You done?"

[36] Jesus answered, "My kingdom is not of this world. If My kingdom were of this world, My servants would fight, so that I should not be delivered to the Jews; but now My kingdom is not from here."

[37] Pilate therefore said to Him, "Are You a king then?"

Jesus answered, "You say *rightly* that I am a king. For this cause I was born, and for this cause I have come into the world, that I should bear witness to the truth. Everyone who is of the truth hears My voice."

[38] Pilate said to Him, "What is truth?" And when he had said this, he went out again to the Jews, and said to them, "I find no fault in Him at all.

TAKING THE PLACE OF BARABBAS

[39] "But you have a custom that I should release someone to you at the Passover. Do you

therefore want me to release to you the King of the Jews?"

[40] Then they all cried again, saying, "Not this Man, but Barabbas!" Now Barabbas was a robber.

THE SOLDIERS MOCK JESUS

[1] So then Pilate took Jesus and scourged *Him.* [2] And the soldiers twisted a crown of thorns and put *it* on His head, and they put on Him a purple robe. [3] Then they said,[a] "Hail, King of the Jews!" And they struck Him with their hands.

[4] Pilate then went out again, and said to them, "Behold, I am bringing Him out to you, that you may know that I find no fault in Him."

PILATE'S DECISION

[5] Then Jesus came out, wearing the crown of thorns and the purple robe. And *Pilate* said to them, "Behold the Man!"

[6] Therefore, when the chief priests and officers saw Him, they cried out, saying, "Crucify *Him,* crucify *Him!*"

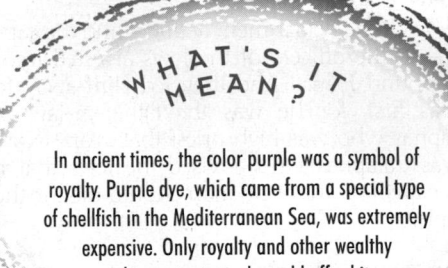

WHAT'S IT MEAN?

In ancient times, the color purple was a symbol of royalty. Purple dye, which came from a special type of shellfish in the Mediterranean Sea, was extremely expensive. Only royalty and other wealthy and important people could afford it.

John 19:2

Pilate said to them, "You take Him and crucify *Him,* for I find no fault in Him."

[7] The Jews answered him, "We have a law, and according to our[a] law He ought to die, because He made Himself the Son of God."

[8] Therefore, when Pilate heard that saying, he was the more afraid, [9] and went again into the Praetorium, and said to Jesus, "Where are You from?" But Jesus gave him no answer.

[10] Then Pilate said to Him, "Are You not speaking to me? Do You not know that I have power to crucify You, and power to release You?"

[11] Jesus answered, "You could have no power at all against Me unless it had been given you

---

19:3 [a]NU-Text reads *And they came up to Him and said.*   **19:7** [a]NU-Text reads *the law.*

from above. Therefore the one who delivered Me to you has the greater sin."

¹²From then on Pilate sought to release Him, but the Jews cried out, saying, "If you let this Man go, you are not Caesar's friend. Whoever makes himself a king speaks against Caesar."

¹³When Pilate therefore heard that saying, he brought Jesus out and sat down in the judgment seat in a place that is called *The* Pavement, but in Hebrew, Gabbatha. ¹⁴Now it was the Preparation Day of the Passover, and about the sixth hour. And he said to the Jews, "Behold your King!"

¹⁵But they cried out, "Away with *Him*, away with *Him!* Crucify Him!"

Pilate said to them, "Shall I crucify your King?"

The chief priests answered, "We have no king but Caesar!"

¹⁶Then he delivered Him to them to be crucified. Then they took Jesus and led *Him* away.[a]

THE KING ON A CROSS

¹⁷And He, bearing His cross, went out to a place called *the Place* of a Skull, which is called in Hebrew, Golgotha, ¹⁸where they crucified Him, and two others with Him, one on either side, and Jesus in the center. ¹⁹Now Pilate wrote a title and put *it* on the cross. And the writing was:

JESUS OF NAZARETH,
THE KING OF THE JEWS.

²⁰Then many of the Jews read this title, for the place where Jesus was crucified was near the city; and it was written in Hebrew, Greek, *and* Latin.

²¹Therefore the chief priests of the Jews said to Pilate, "Do not write, 'The King of the Jews,' but, 'He said, "I am the King of the Jews." ' "

²²Pilate answered, "What I have written, I have written."

²³Then the soldiers, when they had crucified Jesus, took His garments and made four parts, to each soldier a part, and also the tunic. Now the tunic was without seam, woven from the top in one piece. ²⁴They said therefore among themselves, "Let us not tear it, but cast lots for it, whose it shall be," that the Scripture might be fulfilled which says:

"They divided My garments among them,
And for My clothing they cast lots."[a]

Therefore the soldiers did these things.

BEHOLD YOUR MOTHER

²⁵Now there stood by the cross of Jesus His mother, and His mother's sister, Mary the *wife* of Clopas, and Mary Magdalene. ²⁶When Jesus therefore saw His mother, and the disciple whom He loved standing by, He said to His mother, "Woman, behold your son!" ²⁷Then He said to the disciple, "Behold your mother!" And from that hour that disciple took her to his own *home.*

IT IS FINISHED

²⁸After this, Jesus, knowing[a] that all things were now accomplished, that the Scripture might be fulfilled, said, "I thirst!" ²⁹Now a vessel full of sour wine was sitting there; and they filled a sponge with sour wine, put *it* on hyssop, and put *it* to His mouth. ³⁰So when Jesus had received the sour wine, He said, "It is finished!" And bowing His head, He gave up His spirit.

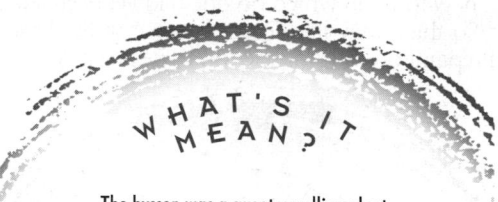

WHAT'S IT MEAN?

The hyssop was a sweet-smelling plant that had been used in religious ceremonies since Old Testament times. Perhaps its most famous appearance in the Bible was as the instrument the Israelites used to mark their doors with blood during the first Passover, when they escaped from Egypt. The angel of death passed over the houses that were marked with blood when he took the lives of all the firstborn sons in Egypt.
John 19:29

JESUS' SIDE IS PIERCED

³¹Therefore, because it was the Preparation *Day,* that the bodies should not remain on the cross on the Sabbath (for that Sabbath was a high day), the Jews asked Pilate that their legs might be broken, and *that* they might be taken away. ³²Then the soldiers came and broke the legs of the first and of the other who was crucified with Him. ³³But when they came to Jesus and saw that He was already dead, they did not break His legs. ³⁴But one of the soldiers pierced His side with a spear, and immediately blood and water came out. ³⁵And he who has seen has testified, and his testimony is true; and he

knows that he is telling the truth, so that you may believe. ³⁶For these things were done that the Scripture should be fulfilled, *"Not one of His bones shall be broken."*ᵃ ³⁷And again another Scripture says, *"They shall look on Him whom they pierced."*ᵃ

JESUS BURIED IN JOSEPH'S TOMB

³⁸After this, Joseph of Arimathea, being a disciple of Jesus, but secretly, for fear of the Jews, asked Pilate that he might take away the body of Jesus; and Pilate gave *him* permission. So he came and took the body of Jesus. ³⁹And Nicodemus, who at first came to Jesus by night, also came, bringing a mixture of myrrh and aloes, about a hundred pounds. ⁴⁰Then they took the body of Jesus, and bound it in strips of linen with the spices, as the custom of the Jews is to bury. ⁴¹Now in the place where He was crucified there was a garden, and in the garden a new tomb in which no one had yet been laid. ⁴²So there they laid Jesus, because of the Jews' Preparation *Day*, for the tomb was nearby.

According to the Law that God gave Moses, touching a dead body made a person unclean, which meant he was considered unfit to take part in any religious ceremonies. Uncleanness wasn't a permanent condition, though. A person was considered clean again after a certain amount of time had passed and certain cleansing rituals had been performed. The Jewish leaders wanted to finish the burial so that they could complete the necessary cleansing rituals before the Sabbath day began.

John 19:42

THE EMPTY TOMB

¹Now the first *day* of the week Mary Magdalene went to the tomb early, while it was still dark, and saw *that* the stone had been taken away from the tomb. ²Then she ran and came to Simon Peter, and to the other disciple, whom Jesus loved, and said to them, "They have taken away the Lord out of the tomb, and we do not know where they have laid Him."

³Peter therefore went out, and the other disciple, and were going to the tomb. ⁴So they both ran together, and the other disciple outran Peter and came to the tomb first. ⁵And he, stooping down and looking in, saw the linen cloths lying *there*; yet he did not go in. ⁶Then Simon Peter came, following him, and went into the tomb; and he saw the linen cloths lying *there*, ⁷and the handkerchief that had been around His head, not lying with the linen cloths, but folded together in a place by itself. ⁸Then the other disciple, who came to the tomb first, went in also; and he saw and believed. ⁹For as yet they did not know the Scripture, that He must rise again from the dead. ¹⁰Then the disciples went away again to their own homes.

MARY MAGDALENE SEES THE RISEN LORD

¹¹But Mary stood outside by the tomb weeping, and as she wept she stooped down *and looked* into the tomb. ¹²And she saw two angels in white sitting, one at the head and the other at the feet, where the body of Jesus had lain. ¹³Then they said to her, "Woman, why are you weeping?"

She said to them, "Because they have taken away my Lord, and I do not know where they have laid Him."

¹⁴Now when she had said this, she turned around and saw Jesus standing *there*, and did not know that it was Jesus. ¹⁵Jesus said to her, "Woman, why are you weeping? Whom are you seeking?"

She, supposing Him to be the gardener, said to Him, "Sir, if You have carried Him away, tell me where You have laid Him, and I will take Him away."

¹⁶Jesus said to her, "Mary!"

She turned and said to Him,ᵃ "Rabboni!" (which is to say, Teacher).

¹⁷Jesus said to her, "Do not cling to Me, for I have not yet ascended to My Father; but go to My brethren and say to them, 'I am ascending to My Father and your Father, and *to* My God and your God.' "

¹⁸Mary Magdalene came and told the disciples that she had seen the Lord,ᵃ and *that* He had spoken these things to her.

THE APOSTLES COMMISSIONED

¹⁹Then, the same day at evening, being the first *day* of the week, when the doors were shut where the disciples were assembled,ᵃ for fear of the Jews, Jesus came and stood in the midst,

19:36 ᵃExodus 12:46; Numbers 9:12; Psalm 34:20   **19:37** ᵃZechariah 12:10   **20:16** ᵃNU-Text adds *in Hebrew.*
20:18 ᵃNU-Text reads *disciples, "I have seen the Lord,"* . . .   **20:19** ᵃNU-Text omits *assembled.*

and said to them, "Peace *be* with you." [20]When He had said this, He showed them *His* hands and His side. Then the disciples were glad when they saw the Lord.

[21]So Jesus said to them again, "Peace to you! As the Father has sent Me, I also send you." [22]And when He had said this, He breathed on *them*, and said to them, "Receive the Holy Spirit. [23]If you forgive the sins of any, they are forgiven them; if you retain the *sins* of any, they are retained."

SEEING AND BELIEVING

[24]Now Thomas, called the Twin, one of the twelve, was not with them when Jesus came. [25]The other disciples therefore said to him, "We have seen the Lord."

So he said to them, "Unless I see in His hands the print of the nails, and put my finger into the print of the nails, and put my hand into His side, I will not believe."

[26]And after eight days His disciples were again inside, and Thomas with them. Jesus came, the doors being shut, and stood in the midst, and said, "Peace to you!" [27]Then He said to Thomas, "Reach your finger here, and look at My hands; and reach your hand *here*, and put *it* into My side. Do not be unbelieving, but believing."

[28]And Thomas answered and said to Him, "My Lord and my God!"

[29]Jesus said to him, "Thomas,[a] because you have seen Me, you have believed. Blessed *are* those who have not seen and *yet* have believed."

THAT YOU MAY BELIEVE

[30]And truly Jesus did many other signs in the presence of His disciples, which are not written in this book; [31]but these are written that you may believe that Jesus is the Christ, the Son of God, and that believing you may have life in His name.

BREAKFAST BY THE SEA

[1]After these things Jesus showed Himself again to the disciples at the Sea of Tiberias, and in this way He showed *Himself:* [2]Simon Peter, Thomas called the Twin, Nathanael of Cana in Galilee, the *sons* of Zebedee, and two others of His disciples were together. [3]Simon Peter said to them, "I am going fishing."

They said to him, "We are going with you also." They went out and immediately[a] got into the boat, and that night they caught nothing. [4]But when the morning had now come, Jesus stood on the shore; yet the disciples did not know that it was Jesus. [5]Then Jesus said to them, "Children, have you any food?"

They answered Him, "No."

[6]And He said to them, "Cast the net on the right side of the boat, and you will find *some*." So they cast, and now they were not able to draw it in because of the multitude of fish.

[7]Therefore that disciple whom Jesus loved said to Peter, "It is the Lord!" Now when Simon Peter heard that it was the Lord, he put on *his* outer garment (for he had removed it), and plunged into the sea. [8]But the other disciples came in the little boat (for they were not far from land, but about two hundred cubits), dragging the net with fish. [9]Then, as soon as they had come to land, they saw a fire of coals there, and fish laid on it, and bread. [10]Jesus said to them, "Bring some of the fish which you have just caught."

> "Jesus said to him, 'Thomas, because you have seen Me, you have believed. Blessed are those who have not seen and yet have believed.'"
> (John 20:29)

WHAT'S IT MEAN?

Not familiar with the Sea of Tiberias? Perhaps you're familiar with another name for it—the Sea of Galilee. Most of Jesus' ministry took place near this sea, which is located about sixty miles north of Jerusalem.

John 21:1

[11]Simon Peter went up and dragged the net to land, full of large fish, one hundred and fifty-three; and although there were so many, the net was not broken. [12]Jesus said to them, "Come and eat breakfast." Yet none of the disciples dared ask Him, "Who are You?"—knowing that it was the Lord. [13]Jesus then came and took the bread and gave it to them, and likewise the fish.

20:29 [a]NU-Text and M-Text omit *Thomas.*　**21:3** [a]NU-Text omits *immediately.*

¹⁴This *is* now the third time Jesus showed Himself to His disciples after He was raised from the dead.

JESUS RESTORES PETER

¹⁵So when they had eaten breakfast, Jesus said to Simon Peter, "Simon, *son* of Jonah,ᵃ do you love Me more than these?"

He said to Him, "Yes, Lord; You know that I love You."

He said to him, "Feed My lambs."

¹⁶He said to him again a second time, "Simon, *son* of Jonah,ᵃ do you love Me?"

He said to Him, "Yes, Lord; You know that I love You."

He said to him, "Tend My sheep."

¹⁷He said to him the third time, "Simon, *son* of Jonah,ᵃ do you love Me?" Peter was grieved because He said to him the third time, "Do you love Me?"

And he said to Him, "Lord, You know all things; You know that I love You."

Jesus said to him, "Feed My sheep. ¹⁸Most assuredly, I say to you, when you were younger, you girded yourself and walked where you wished; but when you are old, you will stretch out your hands, and another will gird you and carry *you* where you do not wish." ¹⁹This He spoke, signifying by what death he would glorify God. And when He had spoken this, He said to him, "Follow Me."

THE BELOVED DISCIPLE AND HIS BOOK

²⁰Then Peter, turning around, saw the disciple whom Jesus loved following, who also had leaned on His breast at the supper, and said, "Lord, who is the one who betrays You?" ²¹Peter, seeing him, said to Jesus, "But Lord, what *about* this man?"

²²Jesus said to him, "If I will that he remain till I come, what *is that* to you? You follow Me."

²³Then this saying went out among the brethren that this disciple would not die. Yet Jesus did not say to him that he would not die, but, "If I will that he remain till I come, what *is that* to you?"

²⁴This is the disciple who testifies of these things, and wrote these things; and we know that his testimony is true.

²⁵And there are also many other things that Jesus did, which if they were written one by one, I suppose that even the world itself could not contain the books that would be written. Amen.

21:15 ᵃNU-Text reads *John.* **21:16** ᵃNU-Text reads *John.* **21:17** ᵃNU-Text reads *John.*

CONTENT

Have you ever watched one of those shows where an actress is supposed to be having a baby? Remember all the pain and the yelling and the not-pushing and then the pushing. Then, there the baby is; and everybody in the room is all smiles and happy tears. That process is called labor and delivery. It's a lot of work on everyone involved.

Reading the Book of Acts is like watching a baby being born. The baby, though, is the church. Before Jesus came and revolutionized the world's thinking, people went to churches called temples. There they learned, worshiped, gave offerings, and offered sacrifices.

With Christ's death and resurrection, though, church meant something different. Church was no longer a place to go to meet with God. Instead, it was the group of people who made up the family of God and the body of Christ.

When Christ was here on earth, He was God in a human body. Then He left; and now we, the church, are God in human bodies. Making that transition was and is a lot of work on everyone involved: apostles, disciples, church members, missionaries, pastors, and so on. Here's how it all began.

Outline

Purpose

The Gospel message is to be carried to the whole world.

Theme

The Work of the Holy Spirit in the Early History of Christianity

Date of writing

Early 60s A.D.

> "But you shall receive power when the Holy Spirit has come upon you; and you shall be witnesses to Me in Jerusalem, and in all Judea and Samaria, and to the end of the earth" (1:8).

Bible Talk

The Early Church: A Commune?

The early church wasn't exactly a commune. They didn't live in the same building or anything. But they did function as a serious community. The people who had money shared with those who didn't. The Bible says there was no poverty in the early church because they took care of each other.

Think of what it was like to walk in their shoes. Jesus had just turned their world upside down. With their very own eyes, they had watched Him go back into heaven. They knew for real that this world was not their home—that heaven was—so they didn't feel ownership over things and money and houses. They shared everything.

How do you think that would work for the church today?

A PERSECUTOR, THEN A MISSIONARY

Paul was one of the most famous people in the New Testament church. Our first glimpse of him is in Acts. His name was Saul, and he was searching out and killing Christians. One day in his travels he was confronted by Jesus, who had already ascended into heaven. "Why are you doing this to Me?" Jesus asked. (The church is considered the body of Christ, so when Saul/Paul destroyed the church, he was destroying Christ's body all over again.) Within a few days, Saul became Paul; and he focused his energy in an entirely different direction. Instead of destroying the church, he became a missionary and started churches in every place that he could. That's how it works when you face Jesus. You can't stay the same.

PROLOGUE

[1]The former account I made, O Theophilus, of all that Jesus began both to do and teach, [2]until the day in which He was taken up, after He through the Holy Spirit had given commandments to the apostles whom He had chosen, [3]to whom He also presented Himself alive after His suffering by many infallible proofs, being seen by them during forty days and speaking of the things pertaining to the kingdom of God.

THE HOLY SPIRIT PROMISED

[4]And being assembled together with *them*, He commanded them not to depart from Jerusalem, but to wait for the Promise of the Father, "which," *He said*, "you have heard from Me; [5]for John truly baptized with water, but you shall be baptized with the Holy Spirit not many days from now." [6]Therefore, when they had come together, they asked Him, saying, "Lord, will You at this time restore the kingdom to Israel?" [7]And He said to them, "It is not for you to know times or seasons which the Father has put in His own authority. [8]But you shall receive power when the Holy Spirit has come upon you; and you shall be witnesses to Me[a] in Jerusalem, and in all Judea and Samaria, and to the end of the earth."

HOLY SPIRIT
What does the Holy Spirit empower us to be? (1:8)

WITNESSING
What are Christians called to do? (1:8)

WHAT'S IT MEAN?

Jesus' followers had expected Him to wrestle control of Israel from the Roman Empire, which had been in charge of the land since 63 B.C.

Acts 1:6

JESUS ASCENDS TO HEAVEN

[9]Now when He had spoken these things, while they watched, He was taken up, and a cloud received Him out of their sight. [10]And

---

On the Edge

"But you shall receive power when the Holy Spirit has come upon you; and you shall be witnesses to Me in Jerusalem, and in all Judea and Samaria, and to the end of the earth."

Now when He [Jesus]had spoken these things, while they watched, He was taken up, and a cloud received Him out of their sight (Acts 1:8, 9).

Just think of it—your favorite teacher calls a class meeting. He or she says, "This is the last time you will ever see me. I'm leaving for heaven in a matter of minutes. Before I go, I have one last thing to say to you." You listen intently. Nothing else matters at this moment. How long will you remember your teacher's last words to you? Probably until the day you die.

That's what's happening here. Jesus leaves His disciples with this final word. He tells them that the Holy Spirit is coming after Him. The Holy Spirit is going to give them power. He'll give them the strength they need to do everything Jesus wants them to do.

As a Christian, you have that same power. The Holy Spirit lives inside of you to give you the power you need to do everything Jesus wants you to do. One thing you know is that He wants you to go out and spread the good news about His love and forgiveness. He's the power for shaky voices, weak knees, butterflies in your stomach. He's the giver of abundant life, the supplier of words, the revealer of truth, and the protector of courageous hearts. He's the One who always loves you and will never leave you. He gives you comfort and good advice. He gives you the power to know what to do in every situation. That's power!

SEE FOR YOURSELF:
Joel 2:28, 29; Luke 9:1, 2; John 14:15–31; Acts 2:38, 39; Rom. 15:13, 19; 1 Cor. 2:4; Eph. 3:7

while they looked steadfastly toward heaven as He went up, behold, two men stood by them in white apparel, [11]who also said, "Men of Galilee, why do you stand gazing up into heaven? This *same* Jesus, who was taken up from you into heaven, will so come in like manner as you saw Him go into heaven."

THE UPPER ROOM PRAYER MEETING

[12]Then they returned to Jerusalem from the mount called Olivet, which is near Jerusalem, a Sabbath day's journey. [13]And when they had entered, they went up into the upper room where they were staying: Peter, James, John, and Andrew; Philip and Thomas; Bartholomew and Matthew; James *the son* of Alphaeus and Simon the Zealot; and Judas *the son* of James. [14]These all continued with one accord in prayer and supplication,[a] with the women and Mary the mother of Jesus, and with His brothers.

MATTHIAS CHOSEN

[15]And in those days Peter stood up in the midst of the disciples[a] (altogether the number of names was about a hundred and twenty), and said, [16]"Men *and* brethren, this Scripture had to be fulfilled, which the Holy Spirit spoke before by the mouth of David concerning Judas, who became a guide to those who arrested Jesus; [17]for he was numbered with us and obtained a part in this ministry."

[18](Now this man purchased a field with the wages of iniquity; and falling headlong, he burst open in the middle and all his entrails gushed out. [19]And it became known to all those dwelling in Jerusalem; so that field is called in their own language, Akel Dama, that is, Field of Blood.)

[20]"For it is written in the Book of Psalms:

'Let his dwelling place be desolate,
And let no one live in it';[a]

and,

'Let[b] another take his office.'[c]

[21]"Therefore, of these men who have accompanied us all the time that the Lord Jesus went in and out among us, [22]beginning from the baptism of John to that day when He was taken up from us, one of these must become a witness with us of His resurrection."

[23]And they proposed two: Joseph called Barsabas, who was surnamed Justus, and Matthias. [24]And they prayed and said, "You, O Lord, who know the hearts of all, show which of these two You have chosen [25]to take part in this ministry and apostleship from which Judas by

On the Edge

Now this man [Judas] purchased a field with the wages of iniquity; and falling headlong, he burst open in the middle and all his entrails gushed out. And it became known to all those dwelling in Jerusalem; so that the field is called in their own language, Akel Dama, that is, Field of Blood (Acts 1:18, 19).

Mike started telling his friends that he didn't have anything to live for. Nothing was fun to him anymore. He wanted to stay in bed all day. He talked a lot about a girl from school who had killed herself. He was so serious all the time. He began to give some of his clothes and stuff away. He withdrew from everybody. He didn't want to go out or to ball games. He seemed depressed. His family thought it was a phase and overlooked it. His friends thought he needed some space and left him alone. He died in his parents' car in their garage one afternoon after school. The note he left said he was just too lonely. Life was too hard. No one seemed to care.

If your friend mentions suicide, talks about not having anything to live for, distances himself/herself from everyone, or shows any other suspicious behavior, take that person seriously. Always take suicide threats seriously. Your friend needs help—quick. Talk to his or her parents, your pastor, a teacher, or counselor until you find someone who cares about your friend and is willing to help. Your job as a friend is to get qualified help. Don't try to handle this one alone. Whatever you do, believe that your friend is hurting, pray for him or her and for wisdom, and get help immediately.

SEE FOR YOURSELF:
Ps. 46:1; Prov. 19:8;
1 Thess. 5:17; Heb. 4:16;
James 1:5

transgression fell, that he might go to his own place." ²⁶And they cast their lots, and the lot fell on Matthias. And he was numbered with the eleven apostles.

COMING OF THE HOLY SPIRIT

¹When the Day of Pentecost had fully come, they were all with one accord[a] in one place. ²And suddenly there came a sound from heaven, as of a rushing mighty wind, and it filled the whole house where they were sitting. ³Then there appeared to them divided tongues, as of fire, and *one* sat upon each of them. ⁴And they were all filled with the Holy Spirit and began to speak with other tongues, as the Spirit gave them utterance.

THE CROWD'S RESPONSE

⁵And there were dwelling in Jerusalem Jews, devout men, from every nation under heaven. ⁶And when this sound occurred, the multitude came together, and were confused, because everyone heard them speak in his own language. ⁷Then they were all amazed and marveled, saying to one another, "Look, are not all these who speak Galileans? ⁸And how *is it that* we hear, each in our own language in which we were born? ⁹Parthians and Medes and Elamites, those dwelling in Mesopotamia, Judea and Cappadocia, Pontus and Asia, ¹⁰Phrygia and Pamphylia, Egypt and the parts of Libya ad-

joining Cyrene, visitors from Rome, both Jews and proselytes, ¹¹Cretans and Arabs—we hear them speaking in our own tongues the wonderful works of God." ¹²So they were all amazed and perplexed, saying to one another, "Whatever could this mean?"

¹³Others mocking said, "They are full of new wine."

WHAT'S IT MEAN?

The countries listed in this passage were all neighbors of Israel. Today, this list would include Iran, Turkey, Egypt, and Saudi Arabia. Cretans were from the island of Crete in the Mediterranean. Many of the Jews who had been deported by the conquering Babylonians and Assyrians in Old Testament times never returned to their homeland. Their descendants did, though—even if it was only to celebrate the Feast of Pentecost. The temple in Jerusalem was the only place Jewish people could participate in the special sacrifices and worship services that went along with the Pentecost celebration.

Acts 2:9–12

2:1 [a]NU-Text reads *together.*

Promise HE PROMISES TO SAVE YOU.

And it shall come to pass that whoever calls on the name of the LORD shall be saved (Acts 2:21).

Salvation is a one-time thing. You make the decision to *become* a Christian one time. You make decisions to *live* like a Christian daily—sometimes even moment by moment. Sometimes people are insecure about their salvation. They keep wondering if they "did it right" the first time. So they wind up raising their hand to accept Christ every time the offer is made.

Jesus promises that when you call out to Him and ask Him to save you, He does. It's that simple. You give your heart to Him, ask Him to forgive your sins, and make Him the Lord and Savior of your life. You are saved from that moment until forever. So nail it down. If you've accepted Jesus Christ as your Savior, then you are saved. It's time to move on and grow up in Christ. If you are still unsure, then turn to Acts 16:30, 31 and find out what you need to do in order to be saved. Salvation isn't a tricky thing. The Lord sees your heart and knows your sincerity. The right attitude is more important than the right words. Jesus' promise is strong—call out to Him, and you will be saved.

SEE FOR YOURSELF:

Mark 16:16; John 10:28; Acts 16:30, 31

PETER'S SERMON

[14]But Peter, standing up with the eleven, raised his voice and said to them, "Men of Judea and all who dwell in Jerusalem, let this be known to you, and heed my words. [15]For these are not drunk, as you suppose, since it is *only* the third hour of the day. [16]But this is what was spoken by the prophet Joel:

[17] 'And it shall come to pass in the last days, says God,
That I will pour out of My Spirit on all flesh;
Your sons and your daughters shall prophesy,
Your young men shall see visions,
Your old men shall dream dreams.

[18] And on My menservants and on My maidservants
I will pour out My Spirit in those days;
And they shall prophesy.

[19] I will show wonders in heaven above
And signs in the earth beneath:
Blood and fire and vapor of smoke.

[20] The sun shall be turned into darkness,
And the moon into blood,
Before the coming of the great and awesome day of the LORD.

[21] And it shall come to pass
That whoever calls on the name of the LORD
Shall be saved.'[a]

[22]"Men of Israel, hear these words: Jesus of Nazareth, a Man attested by God to you by miracles, wonders, and signs which God did through Him in your midst, as you yourselves also know—[23]Him, being delivered by the determined purpose and foreknowledge of God, you have taken[a] by lawless hands, have crucified, and put to death; [24]whom God raised up, having loosed the pains of death, because it was not possible that He should be held by it. [25]For David says concerning Him:

'I foresaw the LORD always before my face,
For He is at my right hand, that I may not be shaken.

[26] Therefore my heart rejoiced, and my tongue was glad;
Moreover my flesh also will rest in hope.

[27] For You will not leave my soul in Hades,

Nor will You allow Your Holy One to see corruption.

[28] You have made known to me the ways of life;
You will make me full of joy in Your presence.'[a]

[29]"Men *and* brethren, let *me* speak freely to you of the patriarch David, that he is both dead and buried, and his tomb is with us to this day. [30]Therefore, being a prophet, and knowing that God had sworn with an oath to him that of the fruit of his body, according to the flesh, He would raise up the Christ to sit on his throne,[a] [31]he, foreseeing this, spoke concerning the resurrection of the Christ, that His soul was not left in Hades, nor did His flesh see corruption. [32]This Jesus God has raised up, of which we are all witnesses. [33]Therefore being exalted to the right hand of God, and having received from the Father the promise of the Holy Spirit, He poured out this which you now see and hear. [34]"For David did not ascend into the heavens, but he says himself:

'The LORD said to my Lord,
"Sit at My right hand,

[35] Till I make Your enemies Your footstool." '[a]

[36]"Therefore let all the house of Israel know assuredly that God has made this Jesus, whom you crucified, both Lord and Christ." [37]Now when they heard *this*, they were cut to the heart, and said to Peter and the rest of the apostles, "Men *and* brethren, what shall we do?" [38]Then Peter said to them, "Repent, and let every one of you be baptized in the name of Jesus Christ for the remission of sins; and you shall receive the gift of the Holy Spirit. [39]For the promise is to you and to your children, and to all who are afar off, as many as the Lord our God will call."

SALVATION
What must we do when we receive salvation? (2:37, 38)

REPENTANCE
Is repentance essential for the Holy Spirit to work? (2:38)

A VITAL CHURCH GROWS

[40]And with many other words he testified and exhorted them, saying, "Be saved from this

2:21 [a]Joel 2:28–32   2:23 [a]NU-Text omits *have taken.*   2:28 [a]Psalm 16:8–11   2:30 [a]NU-Text omits *according to the flesh, He would raise up the Christ* and completes the verse with *He would seat one on his throne.*
2:35 [a]Psalm 110:1

perverse generation." [41]Then those who gladly[a] received his word were baptized; and that day about three thousand souls were added *to them.* [42]And they continued steadfastly in the apostles' doctrine and fellowship, in the breaking of bread, and in prayers. [43]Then fear came upon every soul, and many wonders and signs were done through the apostles. [44]Now all who believed were together, and had all things in common, [45]and sold their possessions and goods, and divided them among all, as anyone had need.

[46]So continuing daily with one accord in the temple, and breaking bread from house to house, they ate their food with gladness and simplicity of heart, [47]praising God and having favor with all the people. And the Lord added to the church[a] daily those who were being saved.

A LAME MAN HEALED

[1]Now Peter and John went up together to the temple at the hour of prayer, the ninth *hour.* [2]And a certain man lame from his mother's womb was carried, whom they laid daily at the gate of the temple which is called Beautiful, to ask alms from those who entered the temple; [3]who, seeing Peter and John about to go into the temple, asked for alms. [4]And fixing his eyes on him, with John, Peter said, "Look at us." [5]So he gave them his attention, expecting to receive something from them. [6]Then Peter said, "Silver and gold I do not have, but what I do have I give you: In the name of Jesus Christ of Nazareth, rise up and walk." [7]And he took him by the right hand and lifted *him* up, and immediately his feet and ankle bones received strength. [8]So he, leaping up, stood and walked and entered the temple with them—walking, leaping, and praising God. [9]And all the people saw him walking and praising God. [10]Then they knew that it was he who sat begging alms at the Beautiful Gate of the temple; and they were

filled with wonder and amazement at what had happened to him.

PREACHING IN SOLOMON'S PORTICO

[11]Now as the lame man who was healed held on to Peter and John, all the people ran together to them in the porch which is called Solomon's, greatly amazed. [12]So when Peter saw *it,* he responded to the people: "Men of Israel, why do you marvel at this? Or why look so intently at us, as though by our own power or godliness we had made this man walk? [13]The God of Abraham, Isaac, and Jacob, the God of our fathers, glorified His Servant Jesus, whom you delivered up and denied in the presence of Pilate, when he was determined to let *Him* go. [14]But you denied the Holy One and the Just, and asked for a murderer to be granted to you, [15]and killed the Prince of life, whom God raised from the dead, of which we are witnesses. [16]And His name, through faith in His name, has made this man strong, whom you see and know. Yes, the faith which *comes* through Him has given him this perfect soundness in the presence of you all.

[17]"Yet now, brethren, I know that you did *it* in ignorance, as *did* also your rulers. [18]But those things which God foretold by the mouth of all His prophets, that the Christ would suffer, He has thus fulfilled. [19]Repent therefore and be converted, that your sins may be blotted out, so that times of refreshing may come from the presence of the Lord, [20]and that He may send Jesus Christ, who was preached to you before,[a] [21]whom heaven must receive until the times of restoration of all things, which God has spoken by the mouth of all His holy prophets since the world began. [22]For Moses truly said to the fathers, *'The LORD your God will raise up for you a Prophet like me from your brethren. Him you shall hear in all things, whatever He says to you.* [23]*And it shall be that every soul who will not hear that Prophet shall be utterly destroyed from among the people.'*[a] [24]Yes, and all the prophets, from Samuel and those who follow,

MONEY
Should we share the resources that God has blessed us with? (2:42–45)

GIVING
What does giving help others to do? (2:44, 45)

JESUS
What is Jesus the Prince of? (3:15)

"Therefore let all the house of Israel know assuredly that God has made this Jesus, whom you crucified, both Lord and Christ." (Acts 2:36)

2:41 [a]NU-Text omits *gladly.*   **2:47** [a]NU-Text omits *to the church.*   **3:20** [a]NU-Text and M-Text read *Christ Jesus, who was ordained for you before.*   **3:23** [a]Deuteronomy 18:15, 18, 19

as many as have spoken, have also foretold[a] these days. 25You are sons of the prophets, and of the covenant which God made with our fathers, saying to Abraham, *'And in your seed all the families of the earth shall be blessed.'*[a] 26To you first, God, having raised up His Servant Jesus, sent Him to bless you, in turning away every one *of you* from your iniquities."

PETER AND JOHN ARRESTED

1Now as they spoke to the people, the priests, the captain of the temple, and the Sadducees came upon them, 2being greatly disturbed that they taught the people and preached in Jesus the resurrection from the dead. 3And they laid hands on them, and put *them* in custody until the next day, for it was already evening. 4However, many of those who heard the word believed; and the number of the men came to be about five thousand.

ADDRESSING THE SANHEDRIN

5And it came to pass, on the next day, that their rulers, elders, and scribes, 6as well as Annas the high priest, Caiaphas, John, and Alexander, and as many as were of the family of the high priest, were gathered together at Jerusalem. 7And when they had set them in the midst, they asked, "By what power or by what name have you done this?"

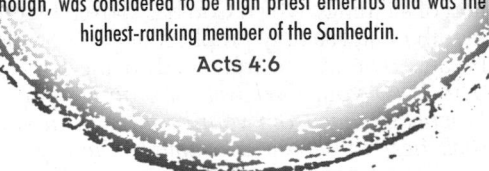

WHAT'S IT MEAN?

The Sanhedrin, a council made up of seventy men plus the high priest, was the highest Jewish court in the land. The council met regularly to settle disputes among the Jewish people. Caiaphas had been selected by the Romans to replace his father-in-law, Annas, as high priest. Annas, though, was considered to be high priest emeritus and was the highest-ranking member of the Sanhedrin.

Acts 4:6

8Then Peter, filled with the Holy Spirit, said to them, "Rulers of the people and elders of Israel: 9If we this day are judged for a good deed done to a helpless man, by what means he has been made well, 10let it be known to you all, and to all the people of Israel, that by the name of Jesus Christ of Nazareth, whom you crucified, whom God raised from the dead, by Him this man stands here before you whole. 11This is the *'stone which was rejected by you builders, which has become the chief cornerstone.'*[a] 12Nor is there salvation in any other, for there is no other name under heaven given among men by which we must be saved."

THE NAME OF JESUS FORBIDDEN

13Now when they saw the boldness of Peter and John, and perceived that they were uneducated and untrained men, they marveled. And they realized that they had been with Jesus. 14And seeing the man who had been healed standing with them, they could say nothing against it. 15But when they had commanded them to go aside out of the council, they conferred among themselves, 16saying, "What shall we do to these men? For, indeed, that a notable miracle has been done through them *is* evident to all who dwell in Jerusalem, and we cannot deny *it.* 17But so that it spreads no further among the people, let us severely threaten them, that from now on they speak to no man in this name." 18So they called them and commanded them not to speak at all nor teach in the name of Jesus. 19But Peter and John answered and said to them, "Whether it is right in the sight of God to listen to you more than to God, you judge. 20For we cannot but speak the things which we have seen and heard." 21So when they had further threatened them, they let them go, finding no way of punishing them, because of the people, since they all glorified God for what had been done. 22For the man was over forty years old on whom this miracle of healing had been performed.

PRAYER FOR BOLDNESS

23And being let go, they went to their own *companions* and reported all that the chief priests and elders had said to them. 24So when they heard that, they raised their voice to God with one accord and said: "Lord, You *are* God, who made heaven and earth and the sea, and all that is in them, 25who by the mouth of Your servant David[a] have said:

3:24 [a]NU-Text and M-Text read *proclaimed.*   **3:25** [a]Genesis 22:18; 26:4; 28:14   **4:11** [a]Psalm 118:22
4:25 [a]NU-Text reads *who through the Holy Spirit, by the mouth of our father, Your servant David.*

'Why did the nations rage,
And the people plot vain things?
26   The kings of the earth took their stand,
And the rulers were gathered together
Against the LORD and against His Christ.'ᵃ

Let's introduce two of the judges in Jesus' trial.
Herod was the ruler of the Jewish people in Galilee
and Perea. Pilate was the Roman governor of Judea and Samaria.
Because Jesus was from Galilee and the charges against Him were
made in Jerusalem, His trial fell under the jurisdiction of both
men. It's interesting to note that neither man found Jesus guilty, yet
both allowed Him to be crucified. You may be wondering what a
Gentile is. Just remember this: If you're not
a Jew, you're a Gentile.

Acts 4:27

²⁷"For truly against Your holy Servant Jesus,
whom You anointed, both Herod and Pontius
Pilate, with the Gentiles and the people of Israel,
were gathered together ²⁸to do whatever Your
hand and Your purpose determined before to
be done. ²⁹Now, Lord, look on their threats, and
grant to Your servants that with all boldness
they may speak Your word, ³⁰by stretching out
Your hand to heal, and that signs and wonders
may be done through the name of Your holy
Servant Jesus."

³¹And when they had prayed, the place
where they were assembled together was shak-
en; and they were all filled with the Holy Spirit,
and they spoke the word of God with boldness.

SHARING IN ALL THINGS

³²Now the multitude of those who believed
were of one heart and one soul; neither did
anyone say that any of the things he possessed
was his own, but they had all things in common. ³³And with great power the apostles gave
witness to the resurrection of the Lord Jesus.
And great grace was upon them all. ³⁴Nor was
there anyone among them who lacked; for all
who were possessors of lands or houses sold
them, and brought the proceeds of the things
that were sold, ³⁵and laid them at the apostles'

feet; and they distributed to each as anyone had
need.

³⁶And Joses,ᵃ who was also named Barnabas
by the apostles (which is translated Son of Encouragement), a Levite of the country of Cyprus, ³⁷having land, sold it, and brought the
money and laid it at the apostles' feet.

LYING TO THE HOLY SPIRIT

¹But a certain man named Ananias, with
Sapphira his wife, sold a possession. ²And he
kept back part of the proceeds, his wife also being aware of it, and brought a certain part and
laid it at the apostles' feet. ³But Peter said, "Ananias, why has Satan filled your heart to lie to
the Holy Spirit and keep back part of the price
of the land for yourself? ⁴While it remained,
was it not your own? And after it was sold, was
it not in your own control? Why have you
conceived this thing in your heart? You have
not lied to men but to God."

⁵Then Ananias, hearing these words, fell
down and breathed his last. So great fear came
upon all those who heard these things. ⁶And
the young men arose and wrapped him up,
carried him out, and buried him.

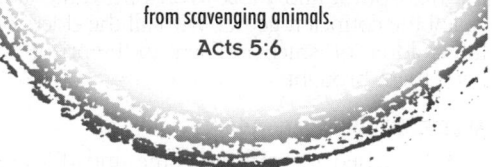

Why were the young men in such a
hurry to bury Ananias? Actually, quick burials
were a necessity in the ancient Middle East. The hot climate caused
the corpses to decay (and stink) pretty quickly. The bodies of wealthy
and powerful people were placed in tombs cut out of rocky hillsides.
A stone was then placed in front of the tomb to protect the body
from scavenging animals.

Acts 5:6

⁷Now it was about three hours later when
his wife came in, not knowing what had happened. ⁸And Peter answered her, "Tell me
whether you sold the land for so much?"

She said, "Yes, for so much."

⁹Then Peter said to her, "How is it that you
have agreed together to test the Spirit of the
Lord? Look, the feet of those who have buried
your husband are at the door, and they will

carry you out." ¹⁰Then immediately she fell down at his feet and breathed her last. And the young men came in and found her dead, and carrying *her* out, buried *her* by her husband. ¹¹So great fear came upon all the church and upon all who heard these things.

CONTINUING POWER IN THE CHURCH

¹²And through the hands of the apostles many signs and wonders were done among the people. And they were all with one accord in Solomon's Porch. ¹³Yet none of the rest dared join them, but the people esteemed them highly. ¹⁴And believers were increasingly added to the Lord, multitudes of both men and women, ¹⁵so that they brought the sick out into the streets and laid *them* on beds and couches, that at least the shadow of Peter passing by might fall on some of them. ¹⁶Also a multitude gathered from the surrounding cities to Jerusalem, bringing sick people and those who were tormented by unclean spirits, and they were all healed.

IMPRISONED APOSTLES FREED

¹⁷Then the high priest rose up, and all those who *were* with him (which is the sect of the Sadducees), and they were filled with indignation, ¹⁸and laid their hands on the apostles and put them in the common prison. ¹⁹But at night an angel of the Lord opened the prison doors and brought them out, and said, ²⁰"Go, stand in the temple and speak to the people all the words of this life."

²¹And when they heard *that*, they entered the temple early in the morning and taught. But the high priest and those with him came and called the council together, with all the elders of the children of Israel, and sent to the prison to have them brought.

APOSTLES ON TRIAL AGAIN

²²But when the officers came and did not find them in the prison, they returned and reported, ²³saying, "Indeed we found the prison shut securely, and the guards standing outside[a] before the doors; but when we opened them, we found no one inside!" ²⁴Now when the high priest,[a] the captain of the temple, and the chief priests heard these things, they wondered what the outcome would be. ²⁵So one came and told

them, saying,[a] "Look, the men whom you put in prison are standing in the temple and teaching the people!"

²⁶Then the captain went with the officers and brought them without violence, for they feared the people, lest they should be stoned. ²⁷And when they had brought them, they set *them* before the council. And the high priest asked them, ²⁸saying, "Did we not strictly command you not to teach in this name? And look, you have filled Jerusalem with your doctrine, and intend to bring this Man's blood on us!"

²⁹But Peter and the *other* apostles answered and said: "We ought to obey God rather than men. ³⁰The God of our fathers raised up Jesus whom you murdered by hanging on a tree. ³¹Him God has exalted to His right hand *to be* Prince and Savior, to give repentance to Israel and forgiveness of sins. ³²And we are His witnesses to these things, and *so* also *is* the Holy Spirit whom God has given to those who obey Him."

> "We ought to obey God rather than men."
> (Acts 5:29)

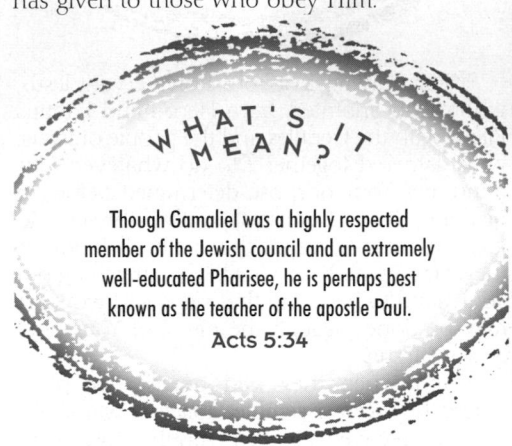

WHAT'S IT MEAN?

Though Gamaliel was a highly respected member of the Jewish council and an extremely well-educated Pharisee, he is perhaps best known as the teacher of the apostle Paul.

Acts 5:34

GAMALIEL'S ADVICE

³³When they heard *this*, they were furious and plotted to kill them. ³⁴Then one in the council stood up, a Pharisee named Gamaliel, a teacher of the law held in respect by all the people, and commanded them to put the apostles outside for a little while. ³⁵And he said to them: "Men of Israel, take heed to yourselves what you intend to do regarding these men. ³⁶For some time ago Theudas rose up, claiming to be somebody. A number of men, about four hundred, joined him. He was slain, and all who

---

5:23 [a]NU-Text and M-Text omit *outside*.   **5:24** [a]NU-Text omits *the high priest*.   **5:25** [a]NU-Text and M-Text omit *saying*.

obeyed him were scattered and came to nothing. [37]After this man, Judas of Galilee rose up in the days of the census, and drew away many people after him. He also perished, and all who obeyed him were dispersed. [38]And now I say to you, keep away from these men and let them alone; for if this plan or this work is of men, it will come to nothing; [39]but if it is of God, you cannot overthrow it—lest you even be found to fight against God."

[40]And they agreed with him, and when they had called for the apostles and beaten *them*, they commanded that they should not speak in the name of Jesus, and let them go. [41]So they departed from the presence of the council, rejoicing that they were counted worthy to suffer shame for His[a] name. [42]And daily in the temple, and in every house, they did not cease teaching and preaching Jesus *as* the Christ.

SEVEN CHOSEN TO SERVE

[1]Now in those days, when *the number of* the disciples was multiplying, there arose a complaint against the Hebrews by the Hellenists,[a] because their widows were neglected in the daily distribution. [2]Then the twelve summoned the multitude of the disciples and said, "It is not desirable that we should leave the word of God and serve tables. [3]Therefore, brethren, seek out from among you seven men of *good* reputation, full of the Holy Spirit and wisdom, whom we may appoint over this business; [4]but we will give ourselves continually to prayer and to the ministry of the word."

[5]And the saying pleased the whole multitude. And they chose Stephen, a man full of faith and the Holy Spirit, and Philip, Prochorus, Nicanor, Timon, Parmenas, and Nicolas, a proselyte from Antioch, [6]whom they set before the apostles; and when they had prayed, they laid hands on them.

[7]Then the word of God spread, and the number of the disciples multiplied greatly in Jerusalem, and a great many of the priests were obedient to the faith.

WHAT'S IT MEAN?

Cyrene, a city in north Africa, and Alexandria, the capital of Egypt (at the time the Book of Acts was written), had one thing in common. Both cities were home to a large number of Jewish people. Cilicia was a region in what is modern-day Turkey.

Acts 6:9

STEPHEN ACCUSED OF BLASPHEMY

[8]And Stephen, full of faith[a] and power, did great wonders and signs among the people. [9]Then there arose some from what is called the Synagogue of the Freedmen (Cyrenians, Alexandrians, and those from Cilicia and Asia), disputing with Stephen. [10]And they were not able to resist the wisdom and the Spirit by which he spoke. [11]Then they secretly induced men to say, "We have heard him speak blasphemous words against Moses and God." [12]And they stirred up the people, the elders, and the scribes; and they came upon *him*, seized him, and brought *him* to the council. [13]They also set up false witnesses who said, "This man does not cease to speak blasphemous[a] words against this holy place and the law; [14]for we have heard him say that this Jesus of Nazareth will destroy this place and change the customs which Moses delivered to us." [15]And all who sat in the council, looking steadfastly at him, saw his face as the face of an angel.

STEPHEN'S ADDRESS: THE CALL OF ABRAHAM

[1]Then the high priest said, "Are these things so?"

WHAT'S IT MEAN?

The Hellenists were people of Jewish descent who were raised in the Greek culture, outside of Israel. Most Hellenists spoke Greek. The Jews who were raised in Israel, and who spoke the native Aramaic language, tended to look down on the Hellenists, believing that they had abandoned their Jewish heritage and culture.

Acts 6:1

5:41 [a]NU-Text reads *the name*; M-Text reads *the name of Jesus.* **6:1** [a]That is, Greek-speaking Jews **6:8** [a]NU-Text reads *grace.* **6:13** [a]NU-Text omits *blasphemous.*

2And he said, "Brethren and fathers, listen: The God of glory appeared to our father Abraham when he was in Mesopotamia, before he dwelt in Haran, 3and said to him, '*Get out of your country and from your relatives, and come to a land that I will show you.'ª* 4Then he came out of the land of the Chaldeans and dwelt in Haran. And from there, when his father was dead, He moved him to this land in which you now dwell. 5And *God* gave him no inheritance in it, not even *enough* to set his foot on. But even when *Abraham* had no child, He promised to give it to him for a possession, and to his descendants after him. 6But God spoke in this way: that his descendants would dwell in a foreign land, and that they would bring them into bondage and oppress *them* four hundred years. 7'*And the nation to whom they will be in bondage I will judge,'ª* said God, '*and after that they shall come out and serve Me in this place.'b* 8Then He gave him the covenant of circumcision; and so *Abraham* begot Isaac and circumcised him on the eighth day; and Isaac *begot* Jacob, and Jacob *begot* the twelve patriarchs.

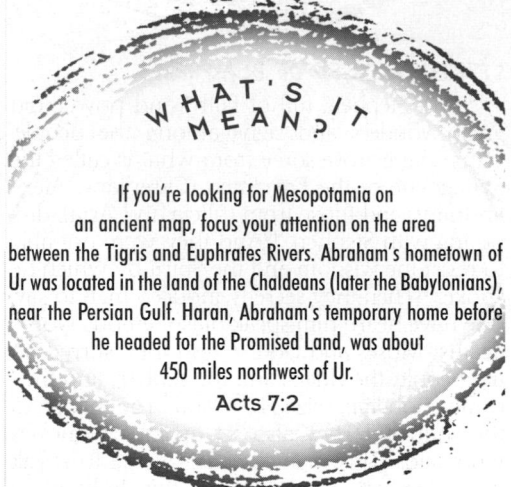

WHAT'S IT MEAN?

If you're looking for Mesopotamia on an ancient map, focus your attention on the area between the Tigris and Euphrates Rivers. Abraham's hometown of Ur was located in the land of the Chaldeans (later the Babylonians), near the Persian Gulf. Haran, Abraham's temporary home before he headed for the Promised Land, was about 450 miles northwest of Ur.

Acts 7:2

THE PATRIARCHS IN EGYPT

9"And the patriarchs, becoming envious, sold Joseph into Egypt. But God was with him 10and delivered him out of all his troubles, and gave him favor and wisdom in the presence of Pharaoh, king of Egypt; and he made him governor over Egypt and all

ENVY
What kind of actions can envy lead to? (7:9)

his house. 11Now a famine and great trouble came over all the land of Egypt and Canaan, and our fathers found no sustenance. 12But when Jacob heard that there was grain in Egypt, he sent out our fathers first. 13And the second *time* Joseph was made known to his brothers, and Joseph's family became known to the Pharaoh.

JEALOUSY
What can jealousy cause? (7:9)

14Then Joseph sent and called his father Jacob and all his relatives to *him*, seventy-fiveª people. 15So Jacob went down to Egypt; and he died, he and our fathers. 16And they were carried back to Shechem and laid in the tomb that Abraham bought for a sum of money from the sons of Hamor, *the father* of Shechem.

GOD DELIVERS ISRAEL BY MOSES

17"But when the time of the promise drew near which God had sworn to Abraham, the people grew and multiplied in Egypt 18till another king arose who did not know Joseph. 19This man dealt treacherously with our people, and oppressed our forefathers, making them expose their babies, so that they might not live. 20At this time Moses was born, and was well pleasing to God; and he was brought up in his father's house for three months. 21But when he was set out, Pharaoh's daughter took him away and brought him up as her own son. 22And Moses was learned in all the wisdom of the Egyptians, and was mighty in words and deeds.

23"Now when he was forty years old, it came into his heart to visit his brethren, the children of Israel. 24And seeing one of *them* suffer wrong, he defended and avenged him who was oppressed, and struck down the Egyptian. 25For he supposed that his brethren would have understood that God would deliver them by his hand, but they did not understand. 26And the next day he appeared to two of them as they were fighting, and *tried to* reconcile them, saying, 'Men, you are brethren; why do you wrong one another?' 27But he who did his neighbor wrong pushed him away, saying, '*Who made you a ruler and a judge over us? 28Do you want to kill me as you did the Egyptian yesterday?'ª* 29Then, at this saying, Moses fled and became a dweller in the land of Midian, where he had two sons.

30"And when forty years had passed, an Angel of the Lordª appeared to him in a flame of fire in a bush, in the wilderness of Mount Sinai.

7:3 ªGenesis 12:1   **7:7** ªGenesis 15:14   bExodus 3:12   **7:14** ªOr *seventy* (compare Exodus 1:5)
7:28 ªExodus 2:14   **7:30** ªNU-Text omits *of the Lord.*

[31]When Moses saw it, he marveled at the sight; and as he drew near to observe, the voice of the Lord came to him, [32]saying, 'I am the God of your fathers—the God of Abraham, the God of Isaac, and the God of Jacob.'[a] And Moses trembled and dared not look. [33]'Then the LORD said to him, "Take your sandals off your feet, for the place where you stand is holy ground. [34]I have surely seen the oppression of My people who are in Egypt; I have heard their groaning and have come down to deliver them. And now come, I will send you to Egypt." '[a]

[35]"This Moses whom they rejected, saying, 'Who made you a ruler and a judge?'[a] is the one God sent to be a ruler and a deliverer by the hand of the Angel who appeared to him in the bush. [36]He brought them out, after he had shown wonders and signs in the land of Egypt, and in the Red Sea, and in the wilderness forty years.

ISRAEL REBELS AGAINST GOD

[37]"This is that Moses who said to the children of Israel,[a] 'The LORD your God will raise up for you a Prophet like me from your brethren. Him you shall hear.'[b]

[38]"This is he who was in the congregation in the wilderness with the Angel who spoke to him on Mount Sinai, and with our fathers, the one who received the living oracles to give to us, [39]whom our fathers would not obey, but rejected. And in their hearts they turned back to Egypt, [40]saying to Aaron, 'Make us gods to go before us; as for this Moses who brought us out of the land of Egypt, we do not know what has become of him.'[a] [41]And they made a calf in those days, offered sacrifices to the idol, and rejoiced in the works of their own hands. [42]Then God turned and gave them up to worship the host of heaven, as it is written in the book of the Prophets:

> 'Did you offer Me slaughtered animals
>   and sacrifices during forty years in the
>   wilderness,
>   O house of Israel?
> [43] You also took up the tabernacle of
>   Moloch,
>   And the star of your god Remphan,
>   Images which you made to worship;
>   And I will carry you away beyond
>   Babylon.'[a]

GOD'S TRUE TABERNACLE

[44]"Our fathers had the tabernacle of witness in the wilderness, as He appointed, instructing Moses to make it according to the pattern that he had seen, [45]which our fathers, having received it in turn, also brought with Joshua into the land possessed by the Gentiles, whom God drove out before the face of our fathers until the days of David, [46]who found favor before God and asked to find a dwelling for the God of Jacob. [47]But Solomon built Him a house.

[48]"However, the Most High does not dwell in temples made with hands, as the prophet says:

> [49] 'Heaven is My throne,
>   And earth is My footstool.
>   What house will you build for Me? says
>   the LORD,
>   Or what is the place of My rest?
> [50] Has My hand not made all these things?'[a]

ISRAEL RESISTS THE HOLY SPIRIT

[51]"You stiff-necked and uncircumcised in heart and ears! You always resist the Holy Spirit; as your fathers did, so do you. [52]Which of the prophets did your fathers not persecute? And they killed those who foretold the coming of the Just One, of whom you now have become the betrayers and murderers, [53]who have received the law by the direction of angels and have not kept it."

STEPHEN THE MARTYR

[54]When they heard these things they were cut to the heart, and they gnashed at him with their teeth. [55]But he, being full of the Holy Spirit, gazed into heaven and saw the glory of God, and Jesus standing at the right hand of God, [56]and said, "Look! I see the heavens opened and the Son of Man standing at the right hand of God!"

[57]Then they cried out with a loud voice, stopped their ears, and ran at him with one accord; [58]and they cast him out of the city and stoned him. And the witnesses laid down their clothes at the feet of a young man named Saul. [59]And they stoned Stephen as he was calling on God and saying, "Lord Jesus, receive my spirit." [60]Then he knelt down and cried out with a loud voice, "Lord, do not charge them with this sin." And when he had said this, he fell asleep.

DEATH

What does the death of Christians bring? (7:59)

7:32 [a]Exodus 3:6, 15   **7:34** [a]Exodus 3:5, 7, 8, 10   **7:35** [a]Exodus 2:14   **7:37** [a]Deuteronomy 18:15   [b]NU-Text and M-Text omit *Him you shall hear.*   **7:40** [a]Exodus 32:1, 23   **7:43** [a]Amos 5:25–27   **7:50** [a]Isaiah 66:1, 2

SAUL PERSECUTES THE CHURCH

[1]Now Saul was consenting to his death.

At that time a great persecution arose against the church which was at Jerusalem; and they were all scattered throughout the regions of Judea and Samaria, except the apostles. [2]And devout men carried Stephen *to his burial,* and made great lamentation over him.

[3]As for Saul, he made havoc of the church, entering every house, and dragging off men and women, committing *them* to prison.

CHRIST IS PREACHED IN SAMARIA

[4]Therefore those who were scattered went everywhere preaching the word. [5]Then Philip went down to the[a] city of Samaria and preached Christ to them. [6]And the multitudes with one accord heeded the things spoken by Philip, hearing and seeing the miracles which he did. [7]For unclean spirits, crying with a loud voice, came out of many who were possessed; and many who were paralyzed and lame were healed. [8]And there was great joy in that city.

THE SORCERER'S PROFESSION OF FAITH

[9]But there was a certain man called Simon, who previously practiced sorcery in the city and astonished the people of Samaria, claiming that he was someone great, [10]to whom they all gave heed, from the least to the greatest, saying, "This man is the great power of God." [11]And they heeded him because he had astonished them with his sorceries for a long time. [12]But when they believed Philip as he preached the things concerning the kingdom of God and the name of Jesus Christ, both men and women were baptized. [13]Then Simon himself also believed; and when he was baptized he continued with Philip, and was amazed, seeing the miracles and signs which were done.

THE SORCERER'S SIN

[14]Now when the apostles who were at Jerusalem heard that Samaria had received the word of God, they sent Peter and John to them, [15]who, when they had come down, prayed for them that they might receive the Holy Spirit. [16]For as yet He had fallen upon none of them. They had only been baptized in the name of the Lord Jesus. [17]Then they laid hands on them, and they received the Holy Spirit.

[18]And when Simon saw that through the laying on of the apostles' hands the Holy Spirit was given, he offered them money, [19]saying, "Give me this power also, that anyone on whom I lay hands may receive the Holy Spirit." [20]But Peter said to him, "Your money perish with you, because you thought that the gift of God could be purchased with money! [21]You have neither part nor portion in this matter, for your heart is not right in the sight of God. [22]Repent therefore of this your wickedness, and pray God if perhaps the thought of your heart may be forgiven you. [23]For I see that you are poisoned by bitterness and bound by iniquity."

[24]Then Simon answered and said, "Pray to the Lord for me, that none of the things which you have spoken may come upon me."

[25]So when they had testified and preached the word of the Lord, they returned to Jerusalem, preaching the gospel in many villages of the Samaritans.

> "And the multitudes with one accord heeded the things spoken by Philip, hearing and seeing the miracles which he did."
> (Acts 8:6)

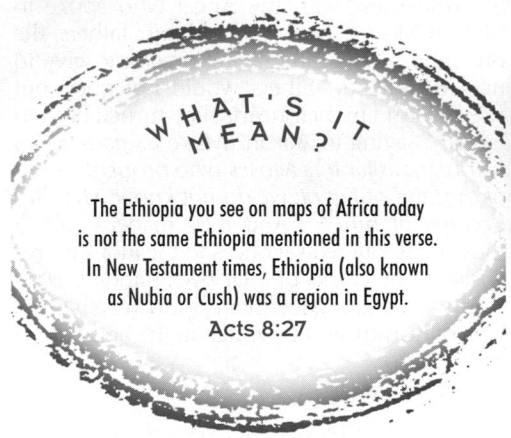

WHAT'S IT MEAN?

The Ethiopia you see on maps of Africa today is not the same Ethiopia mentioned in this verse. In New Testament times, Ethiopia (also known as Nubia or Cush) was a region in Egypt.

Acts 8:27

CHRIST IS PREACHED TO AN ETHIOPIAN

[26]Now an angel of the Lord spoke to Philip, saying, "Arise and go toward the south along the road which goes down from Jerusalem to Gaza." This is desert. [27]So he arose and went. And behold, a man of Ethiopia, a eunuch of great authority under Candace the queen of the Ethiopians, who had charge of all her treasury, and had come to Jerusalem to worship, [28]was

8:5 [a]Or *a*

returning. And sitting in his chariot, he was reading Isaiah the prophet. [29]Then the Spirit said to Philip, "Go near and overtake this chariot."

[30]So Philip ran to him, and heard him reading the prophet Isaiah, and said, "Do you understand what you are reading?"

[31]And he said, "How can I, unless someone guides me?" And he asked Philip to come up and sit with him. [32]The place in the Scripture which he read was this:

> "He was led as a sheep to the
>   slaughter;
> And as a lamb before its shearer is silent,
> So He opened not His mouth.
> [33] In His humiliation His justice was taken
>   away,
> And who will declare His generation?
> For His life is taken from the earth."*a*

[34]So the eunuch answered Philip and said, "I ask you, of whom does the prophet say this, of himself or of some other man?" [35]Then Philip opened his mouth, and beginning at this Scripture, preached Jesus to him. [36]Now as they went down the road, they came to some water. And the eunuch said, "See, *here is* water. What hinders me from being baptized?"

[37]Then Philip said, "If you believe with all your heart, you may."

And he answered and said, "I believe that Jesus Christ is the Son of God."*a*

In the Old Testament, Azotus was known as Ashdod. This coastal city was one of the five capital cities of the Philistines.
Acts 8:40

[38]So he commanded the chariot to stand still. And both Philip and the eunuch went down into the water, and he baptized him. [39]Now when they came up out of the water, the Spirit of the Lord caught Philip away, so that the eunuch saw him no more; and he went on his way rejoicing. [40]But Philip was found at Azotus. And passing through, he preached in all the cities till he came to Caesarea.

THE DAMASCUS ROAD: SAUL CONVERTED

[1]Then Saul, still breathing threats and murder against the disciples of the Lord, went to the high priest [2]and asked letters from him to the synagogues of Damascus, so that if he found any who were of the Way, whether men or women, he might bring them bound to Jerusalem.

Today the city of Damascus is the capital of Syria. In New Testament times, Damascus was a refuge for Jewish Christians. When the persecution of the early church began in Jerusalem, many Christians headed one hundred fifty miles northwest to Damascus to escape danger.
Acts 9:2

[3]As he journeyed he came near Damascus, and suddenly a light shone around him from heaven. [4]Then he fell to the ground, and heard a voice saying to him, "Saul, Saul, why are you persecuting Me?"

[5]And he said, "Who are You, Lord?"

Then the Lord said, "I am Jesus, whom you are persecuting.*a* It *is* hard for you to kick against the goads."

[6]So he, trembling and astonished, said, "Lord, what do You want me to do?"

Then the Lord *said* to him, "Arise and go into the city, and you will be told what you must do."

[7]And the men who journeyed with him stood speechless, hearing a voice but seeing no one. [8]Then Saul arose from the ground, and when his eyes were opened he saw no one. But they led him by the hand and brought *him* into Damascus. [9]And he was three days without sight, and neither ate nor drank.

8:33 *a*Isaiah 53:7, 8   **8:37** *a*NU-Text and M-Text omit this verse. It is found in Western texts, including the Latin tradition.   **9:5** *a*NU-Text and M-Text omit the last sentence of verse 5 and begin verse 6 with *But arise and go.*

ANANIAS BAPTIZES SAUL

¹⁰Now there was a certain disciple at Damascus named Ananias; and to him the Lord said in a vision, "Ananias."

And he said, "Here I am, Lord."

¹¹So the Lord *said* to him, "Arise and go to the street called Straight, and inquire at the house of Judas for *one* called Saul of Tarsus, for behold, he is praying. ¹²And in a vision he has seen a man named Ananias coming in and putting *his* hand on him, so that he might receive his sight."

¹³Then Ananias answered, "Lord, I have heard from many about this man, how much harm he has done to Your saints in Jerusalem. ¹⁴And here he has authority from the chief priests to bind all who call on Your name."

¹⁵But the Lord said to him, "Go, for he is a chosen vessel of Mine to bear My name before Gentiles, kings, and the children of Israel. ¹⁶For I will show him how many things he must suffer for My name's sake."

¹⁷And Ananias went his way and entered the house; and laying his hands on him he said, "Brother Saul, the Lord Jesus,*a* who appeared to you on the road as you came, has sent me that you may receive your sight and be filled with the Holy Spirit." ¹⁸Immediately there fell from his eyes *something* like scales, and he received his sight at once; and he arose and was baptized.

¹⁹So when he had received food, he was strengthened. Then Saul spent some days with the disciples at Damascus.

SAUL PREACHES CHRIST

²⁰Immediately he preached the Christ*a* in the synagogues, that He is the Son of God.

²¹Then all who heard were amazed, and said, "Is this not he who destroyed those who called on this name in Jerusalem, and has come here for that purpose, so that he might bring them bound to the chief priests?"

²²But Saul increased all the more in strength, and confounded the Jews who dwelt in Damascus, proving that this *Jesus* is the Christ.

SAUL ESCAPES DEATH

²³Now after many days were past, the Jews plotted to kill him. ²⁴But their plot became known to Saul. And they watched the gates day and night, to kill him. ²⁵Then the disciples took him by night and let *him* down through the wall in a large basket.

SAUL AT JERUSALEM

²⁶And when Saul had come to Jerusalem, he tried to join the disciples; but they were all afraid of him, and did not believe that he was a disciple. ²⁷But Barnabas took him and brought *him* to the apostles. And he declared to them how he had seen the Lord on the road, and that He had spoken to him, and how he had preached boldly at Damascus in the name of Jesus. ²⁸So he was with them at Jerusalem, coming in and going out. ²⁹And he spoke boldly in the name of the Lord Jesus and disputed against the Hellenists, but they attempted to kill him. ³⁰When the brethren found out, they brought him down to Caesarea and sent him out to Tarsus.

THE CHURCH PROSPERS

³¹Then the churches*a* throughout all Judea, Galilee, and Samaria had peace and were edified. And walking in the fear of the Lord and in the comfort of the Holy Spirit, they were multiplied.

ENCOURAGEMENT

Who is our source of encouragement? (9:31)

AENEAS HEALED

³²Now it came to pass, as Peter went through all *parts of the country*, that he also came down to the saints who dwelt in Lydda. ³³There he found a certain man named Aeneas, who had been bedridden eight years and was paralyzed. ³⁴And Peter said to him, "Aeneas, Jesus the Christ heals you. Arise and make your bed." Then he arose immediately. ³⁵So all who dwelt at Lydda and Sharon saw him and turned to the Lord.

DORCAS RESTORED TO LIFE

³⁶At Joppa there was a certain disciple named Tabitha, which is translated Dorcas. This woman was full of good works and charitable deeds which she did. ³⁷But it happened in those days that she became sick and died. When they had washed her, they laid *her* in an upper room. ³⁸And since Lydda was near Joppa, and the disciples had heard that Peter was there, they sent two men to him, imploring *him* not to delay in coming to them. ³⁹Then Peter arose and went with them. When he had come, they brought *him* to the upper room. And all the widows stood by him weeping, showing the tunics and garments which Dorcas had made while she was with them. ⁴⁰But Peter put them all out, and knelt down and prayed. And turning to the body he said, "Tabitha, arise." And she opened

---

9:17 *a*M-Text omits *Jesus*.   **9:20** *a*NU-Text reads *Jesus*.   **9:31** *a*NU-Text reads *church . . . was edified.*

her eyes, and when she saw Peter she sat up. 41Then he gave her *his* hand and lifted her up; and when he had called the saints and widows, he presented her alive. 42And it became known throughout all Joppa, and many believed on the Lord. 43So it was that he stayed many days in Joppa with Simon, a tanner.

WHAT'S IT MEAN?

Lydda, which was known as Lod in Old Testament times, was only about fifteen miles from Joppa. Today Joppa is called Jaffa and is located near Tel Aviv.

Acts 9:38

CORNELIUS SENDS A DELEGATION

1There was a certain man in Caesarea called Cornelius, a centurion of what was called the Italian Regiment, 2a devout *man* and one who feared God with all his household, who gave alms generously to the people, and prayed to God always. 3About the ninth hour of the day he saw clearly in a vision an angel of God coming in and saying to him, "Cornelius!"

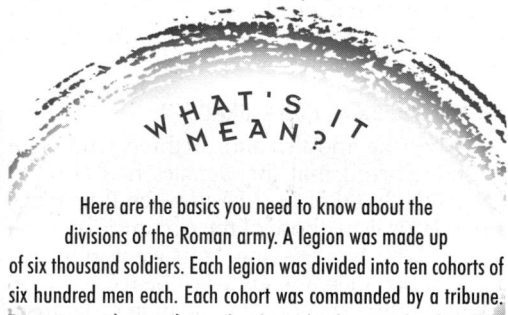

WHAT'S IT MEAN?

Here are the basics you need to know about the divisions of the Roman army. A legion was made up of six thousand soldiers. Each legion was divided into ten cohorts of six hundred men each. Each cohort was commanded by a tribune. Six centurions (captains) served under each tribune, and each captain was in charge of one hundred soldiers.

Acts 10:1

4And when he observed him, he was afraid, and said, "What is it, lord?"

So he said to him, "Your prayers and your alms have come up for a memorial before God. 5Now send men to Joppa, and send for Simon whose surname is Peter. 6He is lodging with Simon, a tanner, whose house is by the sea.*a* He will tell you what you must do." 7And when the angel who spoke to him had departed, Cornelius called two of his household servants and a devout soldier from among those who waited on him continually. 8So when he had explained all *these* things to them, he sent them to Joppa.

PETER'S VISION

9The next day, as they went on their journey and drew near the city, Peter went up on the housetop to pray, about the sixth hour. 10Then he became very hungry and wanted to eat; but while they made ready, he fell into a trance 11and saw heaven opened and an object like a great sheet bound at the four corners, descending to him and let down to the earth. 12In it were all kinds of four-footed animals of the earth, wild beasts, creeping things, and birds of the air. 13And a voice came to him, "Rise, Peter; kill and eat."

14But Peter said, "Not so, Lord! For I have never eaten anything common or unclean."

15And a voice *spoke* to him again the second time, "What God has cleansed you must not call common." 16This was done three times. And the object was taken up into heaven again.

SUMMONED TO CAESAREA

17Now while Peter wondered within himself what this vision which he had seen meant, behold, the men who had been sent from Cornelius had made inquiry for Simon's house, and stood before the gate. 18And they called and asked whether Simon, whose surname was Peter, was lodging there.

19While Peter thought about the vision, the Spirit said to him, "Behold, three men are seeking you. 20Arise therefore, go down and go with them, doubting nothing; for I have sent them."

21Then Peter went down to the men who had been sent to him from Cornelius,*a* and said, "Yes, I am he whom you seek. For what reason have you come?"

22And they said, "Cornelius *the* centurion, a just man, one who fears God and has a good reputation among all the nation of the Jews, was divinely instructed by a holy angel to summon you to his house, and to hear words from you." 23Then he invited them in and lodged *them.*

10:6 *a*NU-Text and M-Text omit the last sentence of this verse.   **10:21** *a*NU-Text and M-Text omit *who had been sent to him from Cornelius.*

On the next day Peter went away with them, and some brethren from Joppa accompanied him.

PETER MEETS CORNELIUS

24And the following day they entered Caesarea. Now Cornelius was waiting for them, and had called together his relatives and close friends. 25As Peter was coming in, Cornelius met him and fell down at his feet and worshiped *him.* 26But Peter lifted him up, saying, "Stand up; I myself am also a man." 27And as he talked with him, he went in and found many who had come together. 28Then he said to them, "You know how unlawful it is for a Jewish man to keep company with or go to one of another nation. But God has shown me that I should not call any man common or unclean. 29Therefore I came without objection as soon as I was sent for. I ask, then, for what reason have you sent for me?"

30So Cornelius said, "Four days ago I was fasting until this hour; and at the ninth hour*a* I prayed in my house, and behold, a man stood before me in bright clothing, 31and said, 'Cornelius, your prayer has been heard, and your alms are remembered in the sight of God. 32Send therefore to Joppa and call Simon here, whose surname is Peter. He is lodging in the house of Simon, a tanner, by the sea.*a* When he comes, he will speak to you.' 33So I sent to you immediately, and you have done well to come. Now therefore, we are all present before God, to hear all the things commanded you by God."

PREACHING TO CORNELIUS' HOUSEHOLD

34Then Peter opened *his* mouth and said: "In truth I perceive that God shows no partiality. 35But in every nation whoever fears Him and works righteousness is accepted by Him. 36The word which *God* sent to the children of Israel, preaching peace through Jesus Christ—He is Lord of all—37that word you know, which was proclaimed throughout all Judea, and began from Galilee after the baptism which John preached: 38how God anointed Jesus of Nazareth with the Holy Spirit and with power, who went about doing good and healing all who were oppressed by the devil, for God was with Him. 39And we are witnesses of all things which He did both in the land of the Jews and in Jerusalem, whom they*a* killed by hanging on a tree. 40Him God raised up on the third day, and showed Him openly, 41not to all the people, but to witnesses chosen before by God, *even* to us who ate and drank with Him after He arose from the dead. 42And He commanded us to preach to the people, and to testify that it is He who was ordained by God *to be* Judge of the living and the dead. 43To Him all the prophets witness that, through His name, whoever believes in Him will receive remission of sins."

> "In truth I perceive that God shows no partiality. But in every nation whoever fears Him and works righteousness is accepted by Him."
> (Acts 10:34b, 35)

THE HOLY SPIRIT FALLS ON THE GENTILES

44While Peter was still speaking these words, the Holy Spirit fell upon all those who heard the word. 45And those of the circumcision who believed were astonished, as many as came with Peter, because the gift of the Holy Spirit had been poured out on the Gentiles also. 46For they heard them speak with tongues and magnify God.

Then Peter answered, 47"Can anyone forbid water, that these should not be baptized who have received the Holy Spirit just as we *have?*" 48And he commanded them to be baptized in the name of the Lord. Then they asked him to stay a few days.

PETER DEFENDS GOD'S GRACE

1Now the apostles and brethren who were in Judea heard that the Gentiles had also received the word of God. 2And when Peter came up to Jerusalem, those of the circumcision contended with him, 3saying, "You went in to uncircumcised men and ate with them!"

4But Peter explained *it* to them in order from the beginning, saying: 5"I was in the city of Joppa praying; and in a trance I saw a vision, an object descending like a great sheet, let down from heaven by four corners; and it came to me. 6When I observed it intently and considered, I saw four-footed animals of the earth, wild beasts, creeping things, and birds of the air. 7And I heard a voice saying to me, 'Rise, Peter; kill and eat.' 8But I said, 'Not so, Lord! For noth-

10:30 *a*NU-Text reads *Four days ago to this hour, at the ninth hour.*   **10:32** *a*NU-Text omits the last sentence of this verse.   **10:39** *a*NU-Text and M-Text add *also.*

ing common or unclean has at any time entered my mouth.' ⁹But the voice answered me again from heaven, 'What God has cleansed you must not call common.' ¹⁰Now this was done three times, and all were drawn up again into heaven. ¹¹At that very moment, three men stood before the house where I was, having been sent to me from Caesarea. ¹²Then the Spirit told me to go with them, doubting nothing. Moreover these six brethren accompanied me, and we entered the man's house. ¹³And he told us how he had seen an angel standing in his house, who said to him, 'Send men to Joppa, and call for Simon whose surname is Peter, ¹⁴who will tell you words by which you and all your household will be saved.' ¹⁵And as I began to speak, the Holy Spirit fell upon them, as upon us at the beginning. ¹⁶Then I remembered the word of the Lord, how He said, 'John indeed baptized with water, but you shall be baptized with the Holy Spirit.' ¹⁷If therefore God gave them the same gift as He *gave* us when we believed on the Lord Jesus Christ, who was I that I could withstand God?"

¹⁸When they heard these things they became silent; and they glorified God, saying, "Then God has also granted to the Gentiles repentance to life."

On the Edge

And when he [Barnabas] had found him [Saul], he brought him to Antioch. So it was that for a whole year they assembled with the church and taught a great many people. And the disciples were first called Christians in Antioch (Acts 11:26).

After Jesus returned to heaven, the disciples and other followers became known as Christians. It literally means "belonging to the party of Jesus." At a restaurant, you may wait with a group until the host calls "table for the Smith party." Everyone who is with your group gets up to be seated. Each one of you is different, but you all belong together. You are recognized as a distinct group. Your party is separate from all the other people in the restaurant. In Antioch, the followers of Christ had become recognized as a separate group of people who belonged together. Followers today are still called Christians, meaning that we belong with all the others who believe in Christ. It is a high privilege to carry the banner of Christ along with those who have gone before us.

SEE FOR YOURSELF:
Acts 26:28;
1 Pet. 4:16

WHAT'S IT MEAN?

With a population of over 100,000, Antioch was the third largest city in the Roman Empire, behind Rome and Alexandria. Roughly three hundred miles north of Jerusalem, the city, now known as Antakya, is located in modern Turkey.

Acts 11:26

BARNABAS AND SAUL AT ANTIOCH

¹⁹Now those who were scattered after the persecution that arose over Stephen traveled as far as Phoenicia, Cyprus, and Antioch, preaching the word to no one but the Jews only. ²⁰But some of them were men from Cyprus and Cyrene, who, when they had come to Antioch, spoke to the Hellenists, preaching the Lord Jesus. ²¹And the hand of the Lord was with them, and a great number believed and turned to the Lord.

²²Then news of these things came to the ears of the church in Jerusalem, and they sent out Barnabas to go as far as Antioch. ²³When he came and had seen the grace of God, he was glad, and encouraged them all that with purpose of heart they should continue with the Lord. ²⁴For he was a good man, full of the Holy Spirit and of faith. And a great many people were added to the Lord.

²⁵Then Barnabas departed for Tarsus to seek Saul. ²⁶And when he had found him, he brought him to Antioch. So it was that for a whole year they assembled with the church and taught a great many people. And the disciples were first called Christians in Antioch.

RELIEF TO JUDEA

²⁷And in these days prophets came from Jerusalem to Antioch. ²⁸Then one of them, named Agabus, stood up and showed by the Spirit that

there was going to be a great famine through-out all the world, which also happened in the days of Claudius Caesar. ²⁹Then the disciples, each according to his ability, determined to send relief to the brethren dwelling in Judea. ³⁰This they also did, and sent it to the elders by the hands of Barnabas and Saul.

HEROD'S VIOLENCE TO THE CHURCH

¹Now about that time Herod the king stretched out *his* hand to harass some from the church. ²Then he killed James the brother of John with the sword. ³And because he saw that it pleased the Jews, he proceeded further to seize Peter also. Now it was *during* the Days of Un-leavened Bread. ⁴So when he had arrested him, he put *him* in prison, and delivered *him* to four squads of soldiers to keep him, intending to bring him before the people after Passover.

PETER FREED FROM PRISON

⁵Peter was therefore kept in prison, but constant^a prayer was offered to God for him by the church. ⁶And when Herod was about to bring him out, that night Peter was sleeping, bound with two chains between two soldiers; and the guards before the door were keeping the prison. ⁷Now behold, an angel of the Lord stood by *him*, and a light shone in the prison; and he struck Peter on the side and raised him up, saying, "Arise quickly!" And his chains fell off *his* hands. ⁸Then the angel said to him, "Gird yourself and tie on your sandals"; and so he did. And he said to him, "Put on your garment and follow me." ⁹So he went out and followed him, and did not know that what was done by the angel was real, but thought he was seeing a vision. ¹⁰When they were past the first and the second guard posts, they came to the iron gate that leads to the city, which opened to them of its own accord; and they went out and went down one street, and immediately the angel de-parted from him.

¹¹And when Peter had come to himself, he said, "Now I know for certain that the Lord has sent His angel, and has delivered me from the hand of Herod and *from* all the expectation of the Jewish people."

¹²So, when he had considered *this*, he came to the house of Mary, the mother of John whose surname was Mark, where many were gathered together praying. ¹³And as Peter knocked at the door of the gate, a girl named Rhoda came to answer. ¹⁴When she recognized Peter's voice, because of *her* gladness she did not open the gate, but ran in and announced that Peter stood before the gate. ¹⁵But they said to her, "You are beside yourself!" Yet she kept insisting that it was so. So they said, "It is his angel."

¹⁶Now Peter continued knocking; and when they opened *the door* and saw him, they were astonished. ¹⁷But motioning to them with his hand to keep silent, he declared to them how the Lord had brought him out of the prison. And he said, "Go, tell these things to James and to the brethren." And he departed and went to another place.

¹⁸Then, as soon as it was day, there was no small stir among the soldiers about what had become of Peter. ¹⁹But when Herod had searched for him and not found him, he exam-ined the guards and commanded that *they* should be put to death.

And he went down from Judea to Caesarea, and stayed *there.*

HEROD'S VIOLENT DEATH

²⁰Now Herod had been very angry with the people of Tyre and Sidon; but they came to him with one accord, and having made Blastus the king's personal aide their friend, they asked for peace, because their country was supplied with food by the king's *country.* ²¹So on a set day Herod, arrayed in royal apparel, sat on his throne and gave an oration to them. ²²And the people kept shouting, "The voice of a god and not of a man!" ²³Then imme-diately an angel of the Lord struck him, because he did not give glory to God. And he was eaten by worms and died.

²⁴But the word of God grew and multiplied.

BARNABAS AND SAUL APPOINTED

²⁵And Barnabas and Saul returned from^a Je-rusalem when they had fulfilled *their* ministry, and they also took with them John whose sur-name was Mark.

¹Now in the church that was at Antioch there were certain prophets and teachers: Bar-nabas, Simeon who was called Niger, Lucius of Cyrene, Manaen who had been brought up with Herod the tetrarch, and Saul. ²As they ministered to the Lord and fasted, the Holy Spirit said, "Now separate to Me Barnabas and Saul for the work to which I have called them." ³Then, having fasted and prayed, and laid hands on them, they sent *them* away.

12:5 ^aNU-Text reads *constantly* (or *earnestly*).   **12:25** ^aNU-Text and M-Text read *to.*

On the Edge

As they ministered to the Lord and fasted, the Holy Spirit said, "Now separate to Me Barnabas and Saul for the work to which I have called them" (Acts 13:2).

In the Book of Acts, we see the disciples looking to the Lord for instruction and guidance. They needed direction about how to spread the message of Christ. In this passage, the Holy Spirit speaks to them about sending out Barnabas and Saul. The Lord still gives clear instruction and direction to believers. The Holy Spirit still guides us through the will of God. The church in Acts worshiped, fasted, and waited for God to give instruction. They actively sought the Lord about what to do. Do you actively seek the Lord about the direction of your life and activities? We must follow the example of the disciples and pursue Him. We hear from God when we listen for Him to speak. If you want God to speak to you, then spend time with Him, worshiping, fasting, and praying. If you will be faithful to listen, then He will speak.

SEE FOR YOURSELF:
Job 37:4, 5;
Ezek. 1:25–28;
Matt. 10:20;
John 10:27; Rev. 3:20

PREACHING IN CYPRUS

[4]So, being sent out by the Holy Spirit, they went down to Seleucia, and from there they sailed to Cyprus. [5]And when they arrived in Salamis, they preached the word of God in the synagogues of the Jews. They also had John as *their* assistant.

[6]Now when they had gone through the island[a] to Paphos, they found a certain sorcerer, a false prophet, a Jew whose name *was* Bar-Jesus, [7]who was with the proconsul, Sergius Paulus, an intelligent man. This man called for Barnabas and Saul and sought to hear the word of God. [8]But Elymas the sorcerer (for so his name is translated) withstood them, seeking to turn the proconsul away from the faith. [9]Then Saul, who also *is called* Paul, filled with the Holy Spirit, looked intently at him [10]and said, "O full

of all deceit and all fraud, *you* son of the devil, *you* enemy of all righteousness, will you not cease perverting the straight ways of the Lord? [11]And now, indeed, the hand of the Lord *is* upon you, and you shall be blind, not seeing the sun for a time."

And immediately a dark mist fell on him, and he went around seeking someone to lead him by the hand. [12]Then the proconsul believed, when he saw what had been done, being astonished at the teaching of the Lord.

AT ANTIOCH IN PISIDIA

[13]Now when Paul and his party set sail from Paphos, they came to Perga in Pamphylia; and John, departing from them, returned to Jerusalem. [14]But when they departed from Perga, they came to Antioch in Pisidia, and went into the synagogue on the Sabbath day and sat down. [15]And after the reading of the Law and the Prophets, the rulers of the synagogue sent to them, saying, "Men *and* brethren, if you have any word of exhortation for the people, say on."

[16]Then Paul stood up, and motioning with *his* hand said, "Men of Israel, and you who fear God, listen: [17]The God of this people Israel[a] chose our fathers, and exalted the people when they dwelt as strangers in the land of Egypt, and with an uplifted arm He brought them out of it. [18]Now for a time of about forty years He put up with their ways in the wilderness. [19]And when He had destroyed seven nations in the land of Canaan, He distributed their land to them by allotment. [20]"After that He gave *them* judges for about

WHAT'S IT MEAN?

If you're confused about the disciple's two names, remember this: Saul was his Jewish name, and Paul was the Greek translation of it. When the disciple was in his Jewish surroundings, he used the name Saul. When he was ministering to the Gentiles, he used the name Paul. Using the Greek version of his name would have helped Paul identify with the people he was teaching about Jesus.

Acts 13:9

13:6 [a]NU-Text reads *the whole island.*   **13:17** [a]M-Text omits *Israel.*

four hundred and fifty years, until Samuel the prophet. [21]And afterward they asked for a king; so God gave them Saul the son of Kish, a man of the tribe of Benjamin, for forty years. [22]And when He had removed him, He raised up for them David as king, to whom also He gave testimony and said, *'I have found David[a] the son of Jesse, a man after My own heart, who will do all My will.'[b]* [23]From this man's seed, according to *the* promise, God raised up for Israel a Savior—Jesus[a]— [24]after John had first preached, before His coming, the baptism of repentance to all the people of Israel. [25]And as John was finishing his course, he said, 'Who do you think I am? I am not *He.* But behold, there comes One after me, the sandals of whose feet I am not worthy to loose.'

[26]"Men *and* brethren, sons of the family of Abraham, and those among you who fear God, to you the word of this salvation has been sent. [27]For those who dwell in Jerusalem, and their rulers, because they did not know Him, nor even the voices of the Prophets which are read every Sabbath, have fulfilled *them* in condemning Him. [28]And though they found no cause for death *in Him,* they asked Pilate that He should be put to death. [29]Now when they had fulfilled all that was written concerning Him, they took *Him* down from the tree and laid *Him* in a tomb. [30]But God raised Him from the dead. [31]He was seen for many days by those who came up with Him from Galilee to Jerusalem, who are His witnesses to the people. [32]And we declare to you glad tidings— that promise which was made to the fathers. [33]God has fulfilled this for us their children, in that He has raised up Jesus. As it is also written in the second Psalm:

'You are My Son,
Today I have begotten You.'[a]

[34]And that He raised Him from the dead, no more to return to corruption, He has spoken thus:

'I will give you the sure mercies of
David.'[a]

[35]Therefore He also says in another *Psalm:*

'You will not allow Your Holy One to see
corruption.'[a]

[36]"For David, after he had served his own generation by the will of God, fell asleep, was buried with his fathers, and saw corruption; [37]but He whom God raised up saw no corruption. [38]Therefore let it be known to you, brethren, that through this Man is preached to you the forgiveness of sins; [39]and by Him everyone who believes is justified from all things from which you could not be justified by the law of Moses. [40]Beware therefore, lest what has been spoken in the prophets come upon you:

FORGIVENESS

Who can receive forgiveness? (13:38, 39)

[41] *'Behold, you despisers,*
Marvel and perish!
For I work a work in your days,
A work which you will by no means
believe,
Though one were to declare it to you.' "[a]

BLESSING AND CONFLICT AT ANTIOCH

[42]So when the Jews went out of the synagogue,[a] the Gentiles begged that these words might be preached to them the next Sabbath. [43]Now when the congregation had broken up, many of the Jews and devout proselytes followed Paul and Barnabas, who, speaking to them, persuaded them to continue in the grace of God.

[44]On the next Sabbath almost the whole city came together to hear the word of God. [45]But when the Jews saw the multitudes, they were filled with envy; and contradicting and blaspheming, they opposed the things spoken by Paul. [46]Then Paul and Barnabas grew bold and said, "It was necessary that the word of God should be spoken to you first; but since you reject it, and judge yourselves unworthy of everlasting life, behold, we turn to the Gentiles. [47]For so the Lord has commanded us:

> "Men and brethren, sons of the family of Abraham, and those among you who fear God, to you the word of this salvation has been sent."
> (Acts 13:26)

13:22 [a]Psalm 89:20 [b]1 Samuel 13:14 **13:23** [a]M-Text reads *for Israel salvation.* **13:33** [a]Psalm 2:7 **13:34** [a]Isaiah 55:3 **13:35** [a]Psalm 16:10 **13:41** [a]Habakkuk 1:5 **13:42** [a]Or *And when they went out of the synagogue of the Jews;* NU-Text reads *And when they went out of the synagogue, they begged.*

'I have set you as a light to the Gentiles,
That you should be for salvation to the
ends of the earth.' "[a]

[48]Now when the Gentiles heard this, they were glad and glorified the word of the Lord. And as many as had been appointed to eternal life believed.

[49]And the word of the Lord was being spread throughout all the region. [50]But the Jews stirred up the devout and prominent women and the chief men of the city, raised up persecution against Paul and Barnabas, and expelled them from their region. [51]But they shook off the dust from their feet against them, and came to Iconium. [52]And the disciples were filled with joy and with the Holy Spirit.

AT ICONIUM

[1]Now it happened in Iconium that they went together to the synagogue of the Jews, and so spoke that a great multitude both of the Jews and of the Greeks believed. [2]But the unbelieving Jews stirred up the Gentiles and poisoned their minds against the brethren. [3]Therefore they stayed there a long time, speaking boldly in the Lord, who was bearing witness to the word of His grace, granting signs and wonders to be done by their hands.

[4]But the multitude of the city was divided: part sided with the Jews, and part with the apostles. [5]And when a violent attempt was made by both the Gentiles and Jews, with their rulers, to abuse and stone them, [6]they became aware of it and fled to Lystra and Derbe, cities of Lycaonia, and to the surrounding region. [7]And they were preaching the gospel there.

IDOLATRY AT LYSTRA

[8]And in Lystra a certain man without strength in his feet was sitting, a cripple from his mother's womb, who had never walked. [9]This man heard Paul speaking. Paul, observing him intently and seeing that he had faith to be healed, [10]said with a loud voice, "Stand up straight on your feet!" And he leaped and walked. [11]Now when the people saw what Paul had done, they raised their voices, saying in the Lycaonian *language,* "The gods have come down to us in the likeness of men!" [12]And Barnabas they called Zeus, and Paul, Hermes, because he was the chief speaker. [13]Then the priest of Zeus, whose temple was in front of their city, brought oxen and garlands to the gates, intending to sacrifice with the multitudes.

[14]But when the apostles Barnabas and Paul heard this, they tore their clothes and ran in among the multitude, crying out [15]and saying, "Men, why are you doing these things? We also are men with the same nature as you, and preach to you that you should turn from these useless things to the living God, who made the heaven, the earth, the sea, and all things that are in them, [16]who in bygone generations allowed all nations to walk in their own ways. [17]Nevertheless He did not leave Himself without witness, in that He did good, gave us rain from heaven and fruitful seasons, filling our hearts with food and gladness." [18]And with these sayings they could scarcely restrain the multitudes from sacrificing to them.

WHAT'S IT MEAN?

If you're not up on your Greek mythology, you should know that Zeus was believed to be the father of gods and the ruler of heaven. Hermes, the Greek god of science and business, was thought to serve as the messenger of the gods.

Acts 14:12

STONING, ESCAPE TO DERBE

[19]Then Jews from Antioch and Iconium came there; and having persuaded the multitudes, they stoned Paul *and* dragged *him* out of the city, supposing him to be dead. [20]However, when the disciples gathered around him, he rose up and went into the city. And the next day he departed with Barnabas to Derbe.

STRENGTHENING THE CONVERTS

[21]And when they had preached the gospel to that city and made many disciples, they returned to Lystra, Iconium, and Antioch, [22]strengthening the souls of the disciples, exhorting *them* to continue in the faith, and *saying,* "We must through many tribulations enter the kingdom of God." [23]So when they had appointed elders in every church, and prayed with fasting, they commended them to the Lord in whom they had believed. [24]And after they had passed through Pisidia, they came to

13:47 [a]Isaiah 49:6

Pamphylia. 25Now when they had preached the word in Perga, they went down to Attalia. 26From there they sailed to Antioch, where they had been commended to the grace of God for the work which they had completed.

WHAT'S IT MEAN?

What do Derbe, Iconium, Lystra, and Antioch have in common? They're all found in modern Turkey.
Acts 14:20, 21

27Now when they had come and gathered the church together, they reported all that God had done with them, and that He had opened the door of faith to the Gentiles. 28So they stayed there a long time with the disciples.

CONFLICT OVER CIRCUMCISION

1And certain *men* came down from Judea and taught the brethren, "Unless you are circumcised according to the custom of Moses, you cannot be saved." 2Therefore, when Paul and Barnabas had no small dissension and dispute with them, they determined that Paul and Barnabas and certain others of them should go up to Jerusalem, to the apostles and elders, about this question.

3So, being sent on their way by the church, they passed through Phoenicia and Samaria, describing the conversion of the Gentiles; and they caused great joy to all the brethren. 4And when they had come to Jerusalem, they were received by the church and the apostles and the elders; and they reported all things that God had done with them. 5But some of the sect of the Pharisees who believed rose up, saying, "It is necessary to circumcise them, and to command *them* to keep the law of Moses."

THE JERUSALEM COUNCIL

6Now the apostles and elders came together to consider this matter. 7And when there had been much dispute, Peter rose up and said to them: "Men and brethren, you know that a good while ago God chose among us, that by my mouth the Gentiles should hear the word of the gospel and believe. 8So God, who knows the heart, acknowledged them by giving them the Holy Spirit, just as *He did* to us, 9and made no distinction between us and them, purifying their hearts by faith. 10Now therefore, why do you test God by putting a yoke on the neck of the disciples which neither our fathers nor we were able to bear? 11But we believe that through the grace of the Lord Jesus Christ[a] we shall be saved in the same manner as they."

WHAT'S IT MEAN?

Circumcision was an important ritual in Jewish tradition. The removal of the foreskin from the male sex organ was a physical sign that the Jews belonged to God. Any male who desired to convert to Judaism had to be circumcised.
Acts 15:5

12Then all the multitude kept silent and listened to Barnabas and Paul declaring how many miracles and wonders God had worked through them among the Gentiles. 13And after they had become silent, James answered, saying, "Men *and* brethren, listen to me: 14Simon has declared how God at the first visited the Gentiles to take out of them a people for His name. 15And with this the words of the prophets agree, just as it is written:

16 'After this I will return
And will rebuild the tabernacle of David,
    which has fallen down;
I will rebuild its ruins,
And I will set it up;
17 So that the rest of mankind may seek the
    LORD,
Even all the Gentiles who are called by
    My name,
Says the LORD who does all these
    things.'[a]

18"Known to God from eternity are all His works.[a] 19Therefore I judge that we should not

---

15:11 [a]NU-Text and M-Text omit *Christ.*   15:17 [a]Amos 9:11, 12   15:18 [a]NU-Text (combining with verse 17) reads *Says the Lord, who makes these things known from eternity (of old).*

trouble those from among the Gentiles who are turning to God, [20]but that we write to them to abstain from things polluted by idols, *from sexual immorality,[a] from* things strangled, and *from* blood. [21]For Moses has had throughout many generations those who preach him in every city, being read in the synagogues every Sabbath."

W H A T ' S
M E A N ? I T

Eating rare meat was a no-no, according to the Law that God gave to Moses. Drinking blood or eating meat before the blood had been drained was forbidden. Why, you ask? Because blood, like sexual orgies, was associated with the worship of idols and pagan gods.

Acts 15:20

THE JERUSALEM DECREE

[22]Then it pleased the apostles and elders, with the whole church, to send chosen men of their own company to Antioch with Paul and Barnabas, *namely,* Judas who was also named Barsabas,[a] and Silas, leading men among the breathren.

[23]They wrote this, *letter* by them:

The apostles, the elders, and the brethren,

To the brethren who are of the Gentiles in Antioch, Syria, and Cilicia:

Greetings.

[24] Since we have heard that some who went out from us have troubled you with words, unsettling your souls, saying, *"You must* be circumcised and keep the law"[a]—to whom we gave no *such* commandment—[25]it seemed good to us, being assembled with one accord, to send chosen men to you with our beloved Barnabas and Paul, [26]men who have risked their lives for the name of our Lord Jesus Christ. [27]We have therefore sent Judas and Silas, who will also report the same things by word of mouth. [28]For it seemed good to the Holy Spirit, and to us, to lay upon you no greater burden than these necessary things: [29]that you abstain from things offered to idols, from blood, from things strangled, and from sexual immorality.[a] If you keep yourselves from these, you will do well.

Farewell.

CONTINUING MINISTRY IN SYRIA

[30]So when they were sent off, they came to Antioch; and when they had gathered the multitude together, they delivered the letter. [31]When they had read it, they rejoiced over its encouragement. [32]Now Judas and Silas, themselves being prophets also, exhorted and strengthened the brethren with many words. [33]And after they had stayed *there* for a time, they were sent back with greetings from the brethren to the apostles.[a]

[34]However, it seemed good to Silas to remain there.[a] [35]Paul and Barnabas also remained in Antioch, teaching and preaching the word of the Lord, with many others also.

DIVISION OVER JOHN MARK

[36]Then after some days Paul said to Barnabas, "Let us now go back and visit our brethren in every city where we have preached the word of the Lord, *and see* how they are doing." [37]Now Barnabas was determined to take with them John called Mark. [38]But Paul insisted that they should not take with them the one who had departed from them in Pamphylia, and had not gone with them to the work. [39]Then the contention became so sharp that they parted from one another. And so Barnabas took Mark and sailed to Cyprus; [40]but Paul chose Silas and departed, being commended by the brethren to the grace of God. [41]And he went through Syria and Cilicia, strengthening the churches.

TIMOTHY JOINS PAUL AND SILAS

[1]Then he came to Derbe and Lystra. And behold, a certain disciple was there, named Timothy, *the* son of a certain Jewish woman who believed, but his father *was* Greek. [2]He was well spoken of by the brethren who were at Lystra and Iconium. [3]Paul wanted to have him go on with him. And he took *him* and circumcised him because of the Jews who were in that region, for they all knew that his father was

---

15:20 [a]Or *fornication*   **15:22** [a]NU-Text and M-Text read *Barsabbas.*   **15:24** [a]NU-Text omits *saying, "You must be circumcised and keep the law."*   **15:29** [a]Or *fornication*   **15:33** [a]NU-Text reads *to those who had sent them.*
15:34 [a]NU-Text and M-Text omit this verse.

Greek. [4]And as they went through the cities, they delivered to them the decrees to keep, which were determined by the apostles and elders at Jerusalem. [5]So the churches were strengthened in the faith, and increased in number daily.

THE MACEDONIAN CALL

[6]Now when they had gone through Phrygia and the region of Galatia, they were forbidden by the Holy Spirit to preach the word in Asia. [7]After they had come to Mysia, they tried to go into Bithynia, but the Spirit[a] did not permit them. [8]So passing by Mysia, they came down to Troas. [9]And a vision appeared to Paul in the night. A man of Macedonia stood and pleaded with him, saying, "Come over to Macedonia and help us." [10]Now after he had seen the vision, immediately we sought to go to Macedonia, concluding that the Lord had called us to preach the gospel to them.

GOD'S WILL
Can we trust God with the events in our lives? (16:6, 7)

LYDIA BAPTIZED AT PHILIPPI

[11]Therefore, sailing from Troas, we ran a straight course to Samothrace, and the next *day* came to Neapolis, [12]and from there to Philippi, which is the foremost city of that part of Macedonia, a colony. And we were staying in that city for some days. [13]And on the Sabbath day we went out of the city to the riverside, where prayer was customarily made; and we sat down and spoke to the women who met *there*. [14]Now a certain woman named Lydia heard *us*. She was a seller of purple from the city of Thyatira, who worshiped God. The Lord opened her heart to heed the things spoken by Paul. [15]And when she and her household were baptized, she begged *us*, saying, "If you have judged me to be faithful to the Lord, come to my house and stay." So she persuaded us.

DEMONS
Who can drive out demons? (16:16–18)

PAUL AND SILAS IMPRISONED

[16]Now it happened, as we went to prayer, that a certain slave girl possessed with a spirit of divination met us, who brought her masters much profit by fortune-telling. [17]This girl followed Paul and us, and cried out, saying, "These men are the servants of the Most High God, who proclaim to us the way of salvation." [18]And this she did for many days.

But Paul, greatly annoyed, turned and said to the spirit, "I command you in the name of Jesus Christ to come out of her." And he came out that very hour. [19]But when her masters saw that their hope of profit was gone, they seized Paul and Silas and dragged *them* into the marketplace to the authorities.

WHAT'S IT MEAN?

In ancient times, the color purple was a symbol of royalty. Purple dye came from a special type of shellfish in the Mediterranean Sea. About two hundred fifty thousand of them were needed to make one ounce of dye. As you may have guessed, the dye, which was used to color clothing, was extremely expensive. Only royalty and other wealthy and important people could afford it.

Acts 16:14

[20]And they brought them to the magistrates, and said, "These men, being Jews, exceedingly trouble our city; [21]and they teach customs which are not lawful for us, being Romans, to receive or observe." [22]Then the multitude rose up together against them; and the magistrates tore off their clothes and commanded *them* to be beaten with rods. [23]And when they had laid many stripes on them, they threw *them* into prison, commanding the jailer to keep them securely. [24]Having received such a charge, he put them into the inner prison and fastened their feet in the stocks.

THE PHILIPPIAN JAILER SAVED

[25]But at midnight Paul and Silas were praying and singing hymns to God, and the prisoners were listening to them. [26]Suddenly there was a great earthquake, so that the foundations of the prison were shaken; and immediately all the doors were opened and everyone's chains were loosed. [27]And the keeper of the prison, awaking from sleep and seeing the prison doors open, supposing the prisoners had fled, drew his sword and was about to kill himself. [28]But Paul called with a loud voice, saying, "Do yourself no harm, for we are all here."

[29]Then he called for a light, ran in, and fell down trembling before Paul and Silas. [30]And he

16:7 [a]NU-Text adds *of Jesus*.

On the Edge

And he brought them out [of jail] and said, "Sirs, what must I do to be saved?" So they said, "Believe on the Lord Jesus Christ, and you will be saved, you and your household" (Acts 16:30, 31).

Tommy thought that since his family went to church every Sunday and he knew the words to the hymns that he must be saved. Alexa goes to a church where they don't talk about being saved. She's heard other people talk about it, but she's confused. Every night she begs God to take her to heaven if she dies in her sleep. Every time she thinks about this "saved" thing, she gets scared. No one has ever explained it to her, and she's too proud to ask. Joey heard from a friend that God loves everybody, and that God would let everyone into heaven. Sounds great.

Tommy, Alexa, and Joey aren't saved. Here's the answer for them and for you: "Believe on the Lord Jesus Christ, and you will be saved." When you decide that you believe in God and in His Son, Jesus, and in the fact that Jesus died on a cross for you, then you are saved from an eternity away from God. That's salvation. Your faith in Jesus saves you. Nothing more. Nothing less. It's a matter of believing so much that you commit your life to Him.

Are you unsure of your salvation? Then nail it down once and for all. Tell the Lord that you love Him, that you believe that Jesus died for you, and that you want Him to be in charge of your life. Ask Him to forgive you of your sins. Ask Him to show you how to live what you have decided to believe. He is waiting to be invited into your life. He is waiting for you to choose Him. Long ago—way before you were born—He chose you. He loves you and wants to spend forever with you.

SEE FOR YOURSELF:
  Mark 16:16;
John 3:16–18; 10:9;
  Acts 2:21;
  Rom. 10:9

brought them out and said, "Sirs, what must I do to be saved?"

[31]So they said, "Believe on the Lord Jesus Christ, and you will be saved, you and your household." [32]Then they spoke the word of the Lord to him and to all who were in his house. [33]And he took them the same hour of the night and washed *their* stripes. And immediately he and all his family were baptized. [34]Now when he had brought them into his house, he set food before them; and he rejoiced, having believed in God with all his household.

PAUL REFUSES TO DEPART SECRETLY

[35]And when it was day, the magistrates sent the officers, saying, "Let those men go."

[36]So the keeper of the prison reported these words to Paul, saying, "The magistrates have sent to let you go. Now therefore depart, and go in peace."

[37]But Paul said to them, "They have beaten us openly, uncondemned Romans, *and* have thrown *us* into prison. And now do they put us out secretly? No indeed! Let them come themselves and get us out."

[38]And the officers told these words to the magistrates, and they were afraid when they heard that they were Romans. [39]Then they came and pleaded with them and brought *them* out, and asked *them* to depart from the city. [40]So they went out of the prison and entered *the house of* Lydia; and when they had seen the brethren, they encouraged them and departed.

PREACHING CHRIST AT THESSALONICA

[1]Now when they had passed through Amphipolis and Apollonia, they came to Thessalonica, where there was a synagogue of the Jews. [2]Then Paul, as his custom was, went in to them, and for three Sabbaths reasoned with them from the Scriptures, [3]explaining and demonstrating that the Christ had to suffer and rise again from the dead, and *saying,* "This Jesus whom I preach to you is the Christ." [4]And some of them were persuaded; and a great multitude of the devout Greeks, and not a few of the leading women, joined Paul and Silas.

ASSAULT ON JASON'S HOUSE

[5]But the Jews who were not persuaded, becoming envious,[a] took some of the evil men from the marketplace, and gathering a mob, set all the city in an uproar and attacked the house of Jason, and sought to bring them out to the people. [6]But when they did not find them, they

17:5 [a]NU-Text omits *who were not persuaded*; M-Text omits *becoming envious.*

dragged Jason and some brethren to the rulers of the city, crying out, "These who have turned the world upside down have come here too. ⁷Jason has harbored them, and these are all acting contrary to the decrees of Caesar, saying there is another king—Jesus." ⁸And they troubled the crowd and the rulers of the city when they heard these things. ⁹So when they had taken security from Jason and the rest, they let them go.

> " 'Sirs, what must I do to be saved?' So they said, 'Believe on the Lord Jesus Christ.' "
>
> (Acts 16:30b, 31a)

MINISTERING AT BEREA

¹⁰Then the brethren immediately sent Paul and Silas away by night to Berea. When they arrived, they went into the synagogue of the Jews. ¹¹These were more fair-minded than those in Thessalonica, in that they received the word with all readiness, and searched the Scriptures daily *to find out* whether these things were so. ¹²Therefore many of them believed, and also not a few of the Greeks, prominent women as well as men. ¹³But when the Jews from Thessalonica learned that the word of God was preached by Paul at Berea, they came there also and stirred up the crowds. ¹⁴Then immediately the brethren sent Paul away, to go to the sea; but both Silas and Timothy remained there. ¹⁵So those who conducted Paul brought him to Athens; and receiving a command for Silas and Timothy to come to him with all speed, they departed.

WHAT'S IT MEAN?

In New Testament times, the city of Athens was known as a center of philosophy and intellectual thought. As Paul discovered, the intellectuals in the city were pretty rough on people who could not express their ideas eloquently.

Acts 17:16

THE PHILOSOPHERS AT ATHENS

¹⁶Now while Paul waited for them at Athens, his spirit was provoked within him when he saw that the city was given over to idols. ¹⁷Therefore he reasoned in the synagogue with the Jews and with the *Gentile* worshipers, and in the marketplace daily with those who happened to be there. ¹⁸Then[a] certain Epicurean and Stoic philosophers encountered him. And some said, "What does this babbler want to say?"

Others said, "He seems to be a proclaimer of foreign gods," because he preached to them Jesus and the resurrection. ¹⁹And they took him and brought him to the Areopagus, saying, "May we know what this new doctrine *is* of which you speak? ²⁰For you are bringing some strange things to our ears. Therefore we want to know what these things mean." ²¹For all the Athenians and the foreigners who were there spent their time in nothing else but either to tell or to hear some new thing.

ADDRESSING THE AREOPAGUS

²²Then Paul stood in the midst of the Areopagus and said, "Men of Athens, I perceive that in all things you are very religious; ²³for as I was passing through and considering the objects of your worship, I even found an altar with this inscription:

TO THE UNKNOWN GOD.

Therefore, the One whom you worship without knowing, Him I proclaim to you: ²⁴God, who made the world and everything in it, since He is Lord of heaven and earth, does not dwell in temples made with hands. ²⁵Nor is He worshiped with men's hands, as though He needed anything, since He gives to all life, breath, and all things. ²⁶And He has made from one blood[a] every nation of men to dwell on all the face of the earth, and has determined their preappointed times and the boundaries of their dwellings, ²⁷so that they should seek the Lord, in the hope that they might grope for Him and find Him, though He is not far from each one of us; ²⁸for in Him we live and move and have our being, as also some of your own poets have said, 'For we are also His offspring.' ²⁹Therefore, since we are the offspring of God, we ought not to think that the Divine Nature is like gold or silver or stone, something shaped by art and

17:18 [a]NU-Text and M-Text add *also.*   **17:26** [a]NU-Text omits *blood.*

man's devising. [30]Truly, these times of ignorance God overlooked, but now commands all men everywhere to repent, [31]because He has appointed a day on which He will judge the world in righteousness by the Man whom He has ordained. He has given assurance of this to all by raising Him from the dead."

[32]And when they heard of the resurrection of the dead, some mocked, while others said, "We will hear you again on this *matter.*" [33]So Paul departed from among them. [34]However, some men joined him and believed, among them Dionysius the Areopagite, a woman named Damaris, and others with them.

MINISTERING AT CORINTH

[1]After these things Paul departed from Athens and went to Corinth. [2]And he found a certain Jew named Aquila, born in Pontus, who had recently come from Italy with his wife Priscilla (because Claudius had commanded all the Jews to depart from Rome); and he came to them. [3]So, because he was of the same trade, he stayed with them and worked; for by occupation they were tentmakers. [4]And he reasoned in the synagogue every Sabbath, and persuaded both Jews and Greeks.

[5]When Silas and Timothy had come from Macedonia, Paul was compelled by the Spirit, and testified to the Jews *that* Jesus *is* the Christ. [6]But when they opposed him and blasphemed,

18:7 [a]NU-Text reads *Titius Justus.*

he shook *his* garments and said to them, "Your blood *be* upon your *own* heads; I *am* clean. From now on I will go to the Gentiles." [7]And he departed from there and entered the house of a certain *man* named Justus,[a] one who worshiped God, whose house was next door to the synagogue. [8]Then Crispus, the ruler of the synagogue, believed on the Lord with all his household. And many of the Corinthians, hearing, believed and were baptized.

[9]Now the Lord spoke to Paul in the night by a vision, "Do not be afraid, but speak, and do

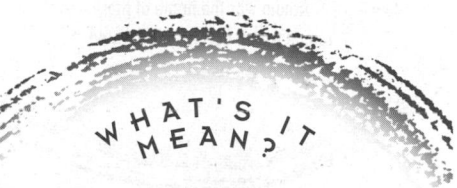

WHAT'S IT MEAN?

Athens was known for its beautiful buildings and schools. Alexandria was known for its library and museum. Corinth, on the other hand, was known for its . . . immorality. Located in southern Greece, about fifty miles from Athens, Corinth was the site of a temple for Aphrodite, the goddess of love. The temple housed one thousand "priestesses," who also worked as prostitutes.

Acts 18:1

Promise   HE PROMISES TO HELP YOU BE WHO YOU ARE.

In Him we live and move and have our being . . . (Acts 17:28).

Ever feel like you're expected to be somebody you're not? Straight-A student? Club president? Perfect little angel? Sure, there are times when you need to venture out of your comfort zone and expect more of yourself than what comes easily for you. And God has given you natural, inborn abilities that (as you begin to spot them) will shape the person you are. He didn't just bundle up a bunch of leftovers and throw them in your direction. He knew what He wanted to do in you, what He wanted you to accomplish, what He wanted you to be good at. And He knew exactly what you'd need in order to pull it off.

He's placed spiritual gifts in you, unique and powerful tools that shape the way you serve Him and relate to others—as a peacemaker, an encourager, a leader.

You're not an afterthought, but a complete package of Christlike potential, waiting to be discovered and put into practice. And you can start living it today. Right where you are. With the people right around you. You'll be miserable being anybody else.

SEE FOR YOURSELF:
Rom. 12:6; 1 Cor. 12:7; Eph. 2:10

not keep silent; [10]for I am with you, and no one will attack you to hurt you; for I have many people in this city." [11]And he continued *there* a year and six months, teaching the word of God among them.

WHAT'S IT MEAN?

Achaia was the name of the region where Corinth was located.

Acts 18:12

[12]When Gallio was proconsul of Achaia, the Jews with one accord rose up against Paul and brought him to the judgment seat, [13]saying, "This *fellow* persuades men to worship God contrary to the law."

[14]And when Paul was about to open *his* mouth, Gallio said to the Jews, "If it were a matter of wrongdoing or wicked crimes, O Jews, there would be reason why I should bear with you. [15]But if it is a question of words and names and your own law, look *to it* yourselves; for I do not want to be a judge of such *matters.*" [16]And he drove them from the judgment seat. [17]Then all the Greeks[a] took Sosthenes, the ruler of the synagogue, and beat *him* before the judgment seat. But Gallio took no notice of these things.

PAUL RETURNS TO ANTIOCH

[18]So Paul still remained a good while. Then he took leave of the brethren and sailed for Syria, and Priscilla and Aquila *were* with him. He had *his* hair cut off at Cenchrea, for he had taken a vow. [19]And he came to Ephesus, and left them there; but he himself entered the synagogue and reasoned with the Jews. [20]When they asked *him* to stay a longer time with them, he did not consent, [21]but took leave of them, saying, "I must by all means keep this coming feast in Jerusalem;[a] but I will return again to you, God willing." And he sailed from Ephesus.

[22]And when he had landed at Caesarea, and gone up and greeted the church, he went down to Antioch. [23]After he had spent some time *there,* he departed and went over the region of Galatia and Phrygia in order, strengthening all the disciples.

MINISTRY OF APOLLOS

[24]Now a certain Jew named Apollos, born at Alexandria, an eloquent man *and* mighty in the Scriptures, came to Ephesus. [25]This man had been instructed in the way of the Lord; and being fervent in spirit, he spoke and taught accurately the things of the Lord, though he knew only the baptism of John. [26]So he began to speak boldly in the synagogue. When Aquila and Priscilla heard him, they took him aside and explained to him the way of God more accurately. [27]And when he desired to cross to Achaia, the brethren wrote, exhorting the disciples to receive him; and when he arrived, he greatly helped those who had believed through grace; [28]for he vigorously refuted the Jews publicly, showing from the Scriptures that Jesus is the Christ.

BIBLE

What does the Bible reveal? (18:28)

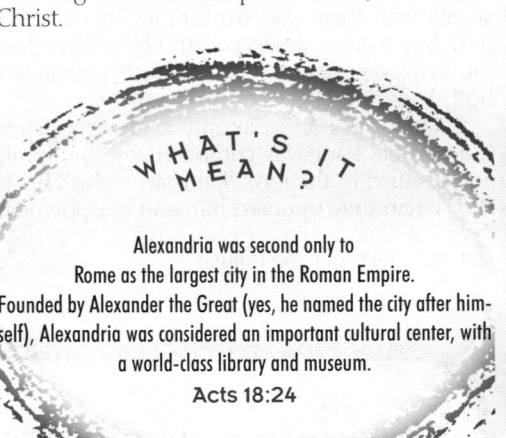

WHAT'S IT MEAN?

Alexandria was second only to Rome as the largest city in the Roman Empire. Founded by Alexander the Great (yes, he named the city after himself), Alexandria was considered an important cultural center, with a world-class library and museum.

Acts 18:24

PAUL AT EPHESUS

[1]And it happened, while Apollos was at Corinth, that Paul, having passed through the upper regions, came to Ephesus. And finding some disciples [2]he said to them, "Did you receive the Holy Spirit when you believed?"

So they said to him, "We have not so much as heard whether there is a Holy Spirit."

[3]And he said to them, "Into what then were you baptized?"

So they said, "Into John's baptism."

[4]Then Paul said, "John indeed baptized with

18:17 [a]NU-Text reads *they all.*   **18:21** [a]NU-Text omits *I must* through *Jerusalem.*

a baptism of repentance, saying to the people that they should believe on Him who would come after him, that is, on Christ Jesus."

⁵When they heard *this*, they were baptized in the name of the Lord Jesus. ⁶And when Paul had laid hands on them, the Holy Spirit came upon them, and they spoke with tongues and prophesied. ⁷Now the men were about twelve in all.

⁸And he went into the synagogue and spoke boldly for three months, reasoning and persuading concerning the things of the kingdom of God. ⁹But when some were hardened and did not believe, but spoke evil of the Way before the multitude, he departed from them and withdrew the disciples, reasoning daily in the school of Tyrannus. ¹⁰And this continued for two years, so that all who dwelt in Asia heard the word of the Lord Jesus, both Jews and Greeks.

MIRACLES GLORIFY CHRIST

¹¹Now God worked unusual miracles by the hands of Paul, ¹²so that even handkerchiefs or aprons were brought from his body to the sick, and the diseases left them and the evil spirits went out of them. ¹³Then some of the itinerant Jewish exorcists took it upon themselves to call the name of the Lord Jesus over those who had evil spirits, saying, "We*ᵃ* exorcise you by the Jesus whom Paul preaches." ¹⁴Also there were seven sons of Sceva, a Jewish chief priest, who did so. ¹⁵And the evil spirit answered and said, "Jesus I know, and Paul I know; but who are you?" ¹⁶Then the man in whom the evil spirit was leaped on them, overpowered*ᵃ* them, and prevailed against them,*ᵇ* so that they fled out of that house naked and wounded. ¹⁷This became known both to all Jews and Greeks dwelling in Ephesus; and fear fell on them all, and the name of the Lord Jesus was magnified. ¹⁸And many who had believed came confessing and telling their deeds. ¹⁹Also, many of those who had practiced magic brought their books together and burned *them* in the sight of all. And they counted up the value of them, and *it* totaled fifty thousand *pieces* of silver. ²⁰So the word of the Lord grew mightily and prevailed.

> "So the word of the Lord grew mightily and prevailed." (Acts 19:20)

DEMONS

Do demons have power? (19:16)

THE RIOT AT EPHESUS

²¹When these things were accomplished, Paul purposed in the Spirit, when he had passed through Macedonia and Achaia, to go to Jerusalem, saying, "After I have been there, I must also see Rome." ²²So he sent into Macedonia two of those who ministered to him, Timothy and Erastus, but he himself stayed in Asia for a time.

²³And about that time there arose a great commotion about the Way. ²⁴For a certain man named Demetrius, a silversmith, who made silver shrines of Diana,*ᵃ* brought no small profit to the craftsmen. ²⁵He called them together with the workers of similar occupation, and said: "Men, you know that we have our prosperity by this trade. ²⁶Moreover you see and hear that not only at Ephesus, but throughout almost all Asia, this Paul has persuaded and turned away many people, saying that they are not gods which are made with hands. ²⁷So not only is this trade of ours in danger of falling into disrepute, but also the temple of the great goddess Diana may be despised and her magnificence destroyed,*ᵃ* whom all Asia and the world worship."

²⁸Now when they heard *this*, they were full of wrath and cried out, saying, "Great *is* Diana of the Ephesians!" ²⁹So the whole city was filled with confusion, and rushed into the theater with one accord, having seized Gaius and Aristarchus, Macedonians, Paul's travel companions. ³⁰And when Paul wanted to go in to the people, the disciples would not allow him. ³¹Then some of the officials of Asia, who were his friends, sent to him pleading that he would not venture into the theater. ³²Some therefore cried one thing and some another, for the assembly was confused, and most of them did not know why they had come together. ³³And they drew Alexander out of the multitude, the Jews putting him forward. And Alexander motioned with his hand, and wanted to make his defense to the people. ³⁴But when they found out that he was a Jew, all with one voice cried out for about two hours, "Great *is* Diana of the Ephesians!"

³⁵And when the city clerk had quieted the crowd, he said: "Men of Ephesus, what man is there who does not know that the city of the

Ephesians is temple guardian of the great goddess Diana, and of the *image* which fell down from Zeus? [36]Therefore, since these things cannot be denied, you ought to be quiet and do nothing rashly. [37]For you have brought these men here who are neither robbers of temples nor blasphemers of your[a] goddess. [38]Therefore, if Demetrius and his fellow craftsmen have a case against anyone, the courts are open and there are proconsuls. Let them bring charges against one another. [39]But if you have any other inquiry to make, it shall be determined in the lawful assembly. [40]For we are in danger of being called in question for today's uproar, there being no reason which we may give to account for this disorderly gathering." [41]And when he had said these things, he dismissed the assembly.

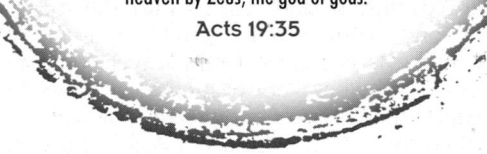

The Greek goddess Artemis had a much more alluring Roman name—Diana. The temple built in her honor in Ephesus was one of the seven wonders of the ancient world. The temple boasted more than one hundred columns, each five stories tall. Inside the temple was an image of Artemis/Diana, carved into a stone that many scholars believe was a meteorite. Worshipers of the goddess claimed that the stone had been sent from heaven by Zeus, the god of gods.

Acts 19:35

JOURNEYS IN GREECE

[1]After the uproar had ceased, Paul called the disciples to *himself*, embraced *them*, and departed to go to Macedonia. [2]Now when he had gone over that region and encouraged them with many words, he came to Greece [3]and stayed three months. And when the Jews plotted against him as he was about to sail to Syria, he decided to return through Macedonia. [4]And Sopater of Berea accompanied him to Asia— also Aristarchus and Secundus of the Thessalonians, and Gaius of Derbe, and Timothy, and Tychicus and Trophimus of Asia. [5]These men, going ahead, waited for us at Troas. [6]But we sailed away from Philippi after the Days of Unleavened Bread, and in five days joined them at Troas, where we stayed seven days.

The Feast of Unleavened Bread was part of the annual Passover celebration. In case you're wondering, unleavened bread does not have yeast in it. Why would people make bread without yeast, the ingredient that makes it rise? When Moses and the Israelites left Egypt, they were in a hurry. There was no time for them to prepare food or to wait for bread to rise. Today unleavened bread is called matzo.

Acts 20:6

MINISTERING AT TROAS

[7]Now on the first *day* of the week, when the disciples came together to break bread, Paul, ready to depart the next day, spoke to them and continued his message until midnight. [8]There were many lamps in the upper room where they[a] were gathered together. [9]And in a window sat a certain young man named Eutychus, who was sinking into a deep sleep. He was overcome by sleep; and as Paul continued speaking, he fell down from the third story and was taken up dead. [10]But Paul went down, fell on him, and embracing *him* said, "Do not trouble yourselves, for his life is in him." [11]Now when he had come up, had broken bread and eaten, and talked a long while, even till daybreak, he departed. [12]And they brought the young man in alive, and they were not a little comforted.

FROM TROAS TO MILETUS

[13]Then we went ahead to the ship and sailed to Assos, there intending to take Paul on board; for so he had given orders, intending himself to go on foot. [14]And when he met us at Assos, we took him on board and came to Mitylene. [15]We sailed from there, and the next *day* came opposite Chios. The following *day* we arrived at Samos and stayed at Trogyllium. The next *day* we came to Miletus. [16]For Paul had decided to sail past Ephesus, so that he would not have to spend time in Asia; for he was hurrying to be at Jerusalem, if possible, on the Day of Pentecost.

19:37 [a]NU-Text reads *our.*   **20:8** [a]NU-Text and M-Text read *we.*

EUTYCHUS made a difference

Eutychus left a mark not so much because of what he did as because of what happened to him. He fell asleep in a meeting. That in itself wasn't that unusual. The meeting was long and late at night. The unusual part of the story turned out to be the location of Eutychus's seat. He was perched on a windowsill in a third-floor room. He had one of those falling dreams, which in his case turned out to be true! He fell out of the window. This might be a good time to point out that Eutychus's name means "Lucky."

There was a doctor in the house—Luke—and he immediately recognized that the fall had been fatal. The apostle Paul offered not so much a second opinion as an alternative treatment. He held the dead boy and prayed. Eutychus lived! The miracle in his life, Luke notes, affected everyone in such a way that

Cutting Edge

"they were not a little comforted" (Acts 20:12). YOU can, too!

In spite of Eutychus's story, falling asleep in church tends to create negative impressions. Perhaps a better lesson to take from Eutychus has to do with the effect changes in a young person's life have on others. Adults tend to have a stereotypical view of youth. They need to receive a good, healthy shock once in a while.

You want to make a difference in your church? Speak up about what God is doing in your life. If God has gotten hold of you, that is no less a miracle than Eutychus being revived on the lawn. But even little lessons will make a difference. Find out how many people know about Eutychus. Tell them the story. You'll be amazed at what a difference it will make to others when they find out God is making a difference in your life.

Want to know more? Luke recorded Eutychus's brief but exciting episode in Acts 20:7–12.

THE EPHESIAN ELDERS EXHORTED

[17]From Miletus he sent to Ephesus and called for the elders of the church. [18]And when they had come to him, he said to them: "You know, from the first day that I came to Asia, in what manner I always lived among you, [19]serving the Lord with all humility, with many tears and trials which happened to me by the plotting of the Jews; [20]how I kept back nothing that was helpful, but proclaimed it to you, and taught you publicly and from house to house, [21]testifying to Jews, and also to Greeks, repentance toward God and faith toward our Lord Jesus Christ. [22]And see, now I go bound in the spirit to Jerusalem, not knowing the things that will happen to me there, [23]except that the Holy Spirit testifies in every city, saying that chains and tribulations await me. [24]But none of these things move me; nor do I count my life dear to myself,[a] so that I may finish my race with joy, and the ministry which I received from the Lord Jesus, to testify to the gospel of the grace of God.

[25]"And indeed, now I know that you all, among whom I have gone preaching the kingdom of God, will see my face no more. [26]Therefore I testify to you this day that I *am* innocent of the blood of all *men*. [27]For I have not shunned to declare to you the whole counsel of God. [28]Therefore take heed to yourselves and to all the flock, among which the Holy Spirit has made you overseers, to shepherd the church of God[a] which He purchased with His own blood. [29]For I know this, that after my departure savage wolves will come in among you, not sparing the flock. [30]Also from among yourselves men will rise up, speaking perverse things, to draw away the disciples after themselves. [31]Therefore watch, and remember that for three years I did not cease to warn everyone night and day with tears.

[32]"So now, brethren, I commend you to God and to the word of His grace, which is able to build you up and give you an inheritance among all those who are sanctified. [33]I have coveted no one's silver or gold or apparel. [34]Yes,[a] you yourselves know that these hands have provided for my necessities, and for those who were with me. [35]I have shown you in every way, by laboring like this, that you must support the weak. And remem-

GIVING

What's better than getting gifts? (20:35)

ber the words of the Lord Jesus, that He said, 'It is more blessed to give than to receive.' "

[36]And when he had said these things, he knelt down and prayed with them all. [37]Then they all wept freely, and fell on Paul's neck and kissed him, [38]sorrowing most of all for the words which he spoke, that they would see his face no more. And they accompanied him to the ship.

WARNINGS ON THE JOURNEY TO JERUSALEM

[1]Now it came to pass, that when we had departed from them and set sail, running a straight course we came to Cos, the following *day* to Rhodes, and from there to Patara. [2]And finding a ship sailing over to Phoenicia, we went aboard and set sail. [3]When we had sighted Cyprus, we passed it on the left, sailed to Syria, and landed at Tyre; for there the ship was to unload her cargo. [4]And finding disciples,[a] we stayed there seven days. They told Paul through the Spirit not to go up to Jerusalem. [5]When we had come to the end of those days, we departed and went on our way; and they all accompanied us, with wives and children, till *we were* out of the city. And we knelt down on the shore and prayed. [6]When we had taken our leave of one another, we boarded the ship, and they returned home.

[7]And when we had finished *our* voyage from Tyre, we came to Ptolemais, greeted the brethren, and stayed with them one day. [8]On the next *day* we who were Paul's companions[a] departed and came to Caesarea, and entered the house of Philip the evangelist, who was *one* of the seven, and stayed with him. [9]Now this man had four virgin daughters who prophesied. [10]And as we stayed many days, a certain prophet named Agabus came down from Judea. [11]When he had come to us, he took Paul's belt, bound his *own* hands and feet, and said, "Thus says the Holy Spirit, 'So shall the Jews at Jerusalem bind the man who owns this belt, and deliver *him* into the hands of the Gentiles.' "

[12]Now when we heard these things, both we and those from that place pleaded with him not to go up to Jerusalem. [13]Then Paul answered, "What do you mean by weeping and breaking my heart? For I am ready not only to be bound, but also to die at Jerusalem for the name of the Lord Jesus."

[14]So when he would not be persuaded, we ceased, saying, "The will of the Lord be done."

20:24 [a]NU-Text reads *But I do not count my life of any value or dear to myself.* **20:28** [a]M-Text reads *of the Lord and God.* **20:34** [a]NU-Text and M-Text omit *Yes.* **21:4** [a]NU-Text reads *the disciples.* **21:8** [a]NU-Text omits *who were Paul's companions.*

PAUL URGED TO MAKE PEACE

¹⁵And after those days we packed and went up to Jerusalem. ¹⁶Also some of the disciples from Caesarea went with us and brought with them a certain Mnason of Cyprus, an early disciple, with whom we were to lodge.

¹⁷And when we had come to Jerusalem, the brethren received us gladly. ¹⁸On the following *day* Paul went in with us to James, and all the elders were present. ¹⁹When he had greeted them, he told in detail those things which God had done among the Gentiles through his ministry. ²⁰And when they heard *it*, they glorified the Lord. And they said to him, "You see, brother, how many myriads of Jews there are who have believed, and they are all zealous for the law; ²¹but they have been informed about you that you teach all the Jews who are among the Gentiles to forsake Moses, saying that they ought not to circumcise *their* children nor to walk according to the customs. ²²What then? The assembly must certainly meet, for they will*ᵃ* hear that you have come. ²³Therefore do what we tell you: We have four men who have taken a vow. ²⁴Take them and be purified with them, and pay their expenses so that they may shave *their* heads, and that all may know that those things of which they were informed concerning you are nothing, but *that* you yourself also walk orderly and keep the law. ²⁵But concerning the Gentiles who believe, we have written *and* decided that they should observe no such thing,*ᵃ* except that they should keep themselves from *things* offered to idols, from blood, from things strangled, and from sexual immorality."

ARRESTED IN THE TEMPLE

²⁶Then Paul took the men, and the next day, having been purified with them, entered the temple to announce the expiration of the days of purification, at which time an offering should be made for each one of them.

²⁷Now when the seven days were almost ended, the Jews from Asia, seeing him in the temple, stirred up the whole crowd and laid hands on him, ²⁸crying out, "Men of Israel, help! This is the man who teaches all *men* everywhere against the people, the law, and this place; and furthermore he also brought Greeks into the temple and has defiled this holy place." ²⁹(For they had previously*ᵃ* seen Trophimus the Ephesian with him in the city, whom they supposed that Paul had brought into the temple.) ³⁰And all the city was disturbed; and the

people ran together, seized Paul, and dragged him out of the temple; and immediately the doors were shut. ³¹Now as they were seeking to kill him, news came to the commander of the garrison that all Jerusalem was in an uproar. ³²He immediately took soldiers and centurions, and ran down to them. And when they saw the commander and the soldiers, they stopped beating Paul. ³³Then the commander came near and took him, and commanded *him* to be bound with two chains; and he asked who he was and what he had done. ³⁴And some among the multitude cried one thing and some another.

WHAT'S IT MEAN?

The temple area in Jerusalem was divided into a series of courts. The outermost court, the Court of the Gentiles, was the only area that non-Jews were allowed to enter.

Acts 21:29

So when he could not ascertain the truth because of the tumult, he commanded him to be taken into the barracks. ³⁵When he reached the stairs, he had to be carried by the soldiers because of the violence of the mob. ³⁶For the multitude of the people followed after, crying out, "Away with him!"

ADDRESSING THE JERUSALEM MOB

³⁷Then as Paul was about to be led into the barracks, he said to the commander, "May I speak to you?"

He replied, "Can you speak Greek? ³⁸Are you not the Egyptian who some time ago stirred up a rebellion and led the four thousand assassins out into the wilderness?"

³⁹But Paul said, "I am a Jew from Tarsus, in Cilicia, a citizen of no mean city; and I implore you, permit me to speak to the people."

⁴⁰So when he had given him permission, Paul stood on the stairs and motioned with his hand to the people. And when there was a great silence, he spoke to *them* in the Hebrew language, saying,

---

21:22 *ᵃ*NU-Text reads *What then is to be done? They will certainly.*   **21:25** *ᵃ*NU-Text omits *that they should observe no such thing, except.*   **21:29** *ᵃ*M-Text omits *previously.*

[1]"Brethren and fathers, hear my defense before you now." [2]And when they heard that he spoke to them in the Hebrew language, they kept all the more silent.

Then he said: [3]"I am indeed a Jew, born in Tarsus of Cilicia, but brought up in this city at the feet of Gamaliel, taught according to the strictness of our fathers' law, and was zealous toward God as you all are today. [4]I persecuted this Way to the death, binding and delivering into prisons both men and women, [5]as also the high priest bears me witness, and all the council of the elders, from whom I also received letters to the brethren, and went to Damascus to bring in chains even those who were there to Jerusalem to be punished.

[6]"Now it happened, as I journeyed and came near Damascus at about noon, suddenly a great light from heaven shone around me. [7]And I fell to the ground and heard a voice saying to me, 'Saul, Saul, why are you persecuting Me?' [8]So I answered, 'Who are You, Lord?' And He said to me, 'I am Jesus of Nazareth, whom you are persecuting.'

[9]"And those who were with me indeed saw the light and were afraid,[a] but they did not hear the voice of Him who spoke to me. [10]So I said, 'What shall I do, Lord?' And the Lord said to me, 'Arise and go into Damascus, and there you will be told all things which are appointed for you to do.' [11]And since I could not see for the glory of that light, being led by the hand of those who were with me, I came into Damascus.

[12]"Then a certain Ananias, a devout man according to the law, having a good testimony with all the Jews who dwelt there, [13]came to me; and he stood and said to me, 'Brother Saul, receive your sight.' And at that same hour I looked up at him. [14]Then he said, 'The God of our fathers has chosen you that you should know His will, and see the Just One, and hear the voice of His mouth. [15]For you will be His witness to all men of what you have seen and heard. [16]And now why are you waiting? Arise and be baptized, and wash away your sins, calling on the name of the Lord.'

[17]"Now it happened, when I returned to Jerusalem and was praying in the temple, that I was in a trance [18]and saw Him saying to me, 'Make haste and get out of Jerusalem quickly, for they will not receive your testimony concerning Me.' [19]So I said, 'Lord, they know that in every synagogue I imprisoned and beat those who believe on You. [20]And when the blood of Your martyr Stephen was shed, I also was standing by consenting to his death,[a] and guarding the clothes of those who were killing him.' [21]Then He said to me, 'Depart, for I will send you far from here to the Gentiles.' "

> " 'Who are You, Lord?'
> And He said to me, 'I am
> Jesus of Nazareth.' "
> (Acts 22:8)

PAUL'S ROMAN CITIZENSHIP

[22]And they listened to him until this word, and then they raised their voices and said, "Away with such a fellow from the earth, for he is not fit to live!" [23]Then, as they cried out and tore off their clothes and threw dust into the air, [24]the commander ordered him to be brought into the barracks, and said that he should be examined under scourging, so that he might know why they shouted so against him. [25]And as they bound him with thongs, Paul said to the centurion who stood by, "Is it lawful for you to scourge a man who is a Roman, and uncondemned?"

[26]When the centurion heard that, he went and told the commander, saying, "Take care what you do, for this man is a Roman."

[27]Then the commander came and said to him, "Tell me, are you a Roman?"

He said, "Yes."

[28]The commander answered, "With a large sum I obtained this citizenship."

And Paul said, "But I was born a citizen."

[29]Then immediately those who were about to examine him withdrew from him; and the commander was also afraid after he found out that he was a Roman, and because he had bound him.

THE SANHEDRIN DIVIDED

[30]The next day, because he wanted to know for certain why he was accused by the Jews, he released him from his bonds, and commanded the chief priests and all their council to appear, and brought Paul down and set him before them.

[1]Then Paul, looking earnestly at the council, said, "Men and brethren, I have lived in all good conscience before God until this day." [2]And the high priest Ananias commanded those who stood by him to strike him on the mouth. [3]Then

22:9 [a]NU-Text omits and were afraid.   22:20 [a]NU-Text omits to his death.

Paul said to him, "God will strike you, *you whitewashed wall!* For you sit to judge me according to the law, and do you command me to be struck contrary to the law?"

⁴And those who stood by said, "Do you revile God's high priest?"

⁵Then Paul said, "I did not know, brethren, that he was the high priest; for it is written, *'You shall not speak evil of a ruler of your people.' "ᵃ*

⁶But when Paul perceived that one part were Sadducees and the other Pharisees, he cried out in the council, "Men *and* brethren, I am a Pharisee, the son of a Pharisee; concerning the hope and resurrection of the dead I am being judged!"

What's the difference between a Pharisee and a Sadducee? Pharisees were ordinary, middle-class people who emphasized the importance of obeying the Law God had given Moses. Sadducees were wealthy and powerful individuals, many of whom served as priests. These two groups of Jewish scholars interpreted Scripture differently and argued over issues, such as the resurrection of the dead and the existence of angels. Because they knew so much about Scripture, members of both groups tended to take pride in themselves and to criticize others. Members of both groups also sat on the Jewish council, the court of law for the Jewish people.

Acts 23:6

⁷And when he had said this, a dissension arose between the Pharisees and the Sadducees; and the assembly was divided. ⁸For Sadducees say that there is no resurrection—and no angel or spirit; but the Pharisees confess both. ⁹Then there arose a loud outcry. And the scribes of the Pharisees' party arose and protested, saying, "We find no evil in this man; but if a spirit or an angel has spoken to him, let us not fight against God."ᵃ

¹⁰Now when there arose a great dissension, the commander, fearing lest Paul might be pulled to pieces by them, commanded the soldiers to go down and take him by force from among them, and bring *him* into the barracks.

THE PLOT AGAINST PAUL

¹¹But the following night the Lord stood by him and said, "Be of good cheer, Paul; for as you have testified for Me in Jerusalem, so you must also bear witness at Rome."

¹²And when it was day, some of the Jews banded together and bound themselves under an oath, saying that they would neither eat nor drink till they had killed Paul. ¹³Now there were more than forty who had formed this conspiracy. ¹⁴They came to the chief priests and elders, and said, "We have bound ourselves under a great oath that we will eat nothing until we have killed Paul. ¹⁵Now you, therefore, together with the council, suggest to the commander that he be brought down to you tomorrow,ᵃ as though you were going to make further inquiries concerning him; but we are ready to kill him before he comes near."

¹⁶So when Paul's sister's son heard of their ambush, he went and entered the barracks and told Paul. ¹⁷Then Paul called one of the centurions to *him* and said, "Take this young man to the commander, for he has something to tell him." ¹⁸So he took him and brought *him* to the commander and said, "Paul the prisoner called me to *him* and asked *me* to bring this young man to you. He has something to say to you."

¹⁹Then the commander took him by the hand, went aside, and asked privately, "What is it that you have to tell me?"

²⁰And he said, "The Jews have agreed to ask that you bring Paul down to the council tomorrow, as though they were going to inquire more fully about him. ²¹But do not yield to them, for more than forty of them lie in wait for him, men who have bound themselves by an oath that they will neither eat nor drink till they have killed him; and now they are ready, waiting for the promise from you."

²²So the commander let the young man depart, and commanded *him*, "Tell no one that you have revealed these things to me."

SENT TO FELIX

²³And he called for two centurions, saying, "Prepare two hundred soldiers, seventy horsemen, and two hundred spearmen to go to Caesarea at the third hour of the night; ²⁴and provide mounts to set Paul on, and bring *him* safely to Felix the governor." ²⁵He wrote a letter in the following manner:

²⁶ Claudius Lysias,

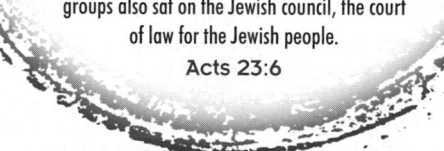

23:5 ᵃExodus 22:28   **23:9** ᵃNU-Text omits last clause and reads *what if a spirit or an angel has spoken to him?*
23:15 ᵃNU-Text omits *tomorrow.*

To the most excellent governor Felix:

Greetings.

27 This man was seized by the Jews and was about to be killed by them. Coming with the troops I rescued him, having learned that he was a Roman. 28And when I wanted to know the reason they accused him, I brought him before their council. 29I found out that he was accused concerning questions of their law, but had nothing charged against him deserving of death or chains. 30And when it was told me that the Jews lay in wait for the man,ᵃ I sent him immediately to you, and also commanded his accusers to state before you the charges against him.

Farewell.

31Then the soldiers, as they were commanded, took Paul and brought *him* by night to Antipatris. 32The next day they left the horsemen to go on with him, and returned to the barracks. 33When they came to Caesarea and had delivered the letter to the governor, they also presented Paul to him. 34And when the governor had read *it*, he asked what province he was from. And when he understood that *he was* from Cilicia, 35he said, "I will hear you when your accusers also have come." And he commanded him to be kept in Herod's Praetorium.

ACCUSED OF SEDITION

1Now after five days Ananias the high priest came down with the elders and a certain orator *named* Tertullus. These gave evidence to the governor against Paul. 2And when he was called upon, Tertullus began his accusation, saying: "Seeing that through you we enjoy great peace, and prosperity is being brought to this nation by your foresight, 3we accept *it* always and in all places, most noble Felix, with all thankfulness. 4Nevertheless, not to be tedious to you any further, I beg you to hear, by your courtesy, a few words from us. 5For we have found this man a plague, a creator of dissension among all the Jews throughout the world, and a ringleader of the sect of the Nazarenes. 6He even tried to profane the temple, and we seized him,ᵃ and wanted to

judge him according to our law. 7But the commander Lysias came by and with great violence took *him* out of our hands, 8commanding his accusers to come to you. By examining him yourself you may ascertain all these things of which we accuse him." 9And the Jews also assented,ᵃ maintaining that these things were so.

THE DEFENSE BEFORE FELIX

10Then Paul, after the governor had nodded to him to speak, answered: "Inasmuch as I know that you have been for many years a judge of this nation, I do the more cheerfully answer for myself, 11because you may ascertain that it is no more than twelve days since I went up to Jerusalem to worship. 12And they neither found me in the temple disputing with anyone nor inciting the crowd, either in the synagogues or in the city. 13Nor can they prove the things of which they now accuse me. 14But this I confess to you, that according to the Way which they call a sect, so I worship the God of my fathers, believing all things which are written in the Law and in the Prophets. 15I have hope in God, which they themselves also accept, that there will be a resurrection of *the* dead,ᵃ both of *the* just and *the* unjust. 16This *being* so, I myself always strive to have a conscience without offense toward God and men.

17"Now after many years I came to bring alms and offerings to my nation, 18in the midst of which some Jews from Asia found me purified in the temple, neither with a mob nor with tumult. 19They ought to have been here before you to object if they had anything against me.

23:30 ᵃNU-Text reads *there would be a plot against the man.* **24:6** ᵃNU-Text ends the sentence here and omits the rest of verse 6, all of verse 7, and the first clause of verse 8. **24:9** ᵃNU-Text and M-Text read *joined the attack.* **24:15** ᵃNU-Text omits *of the dead.*

²⁰Or else let those who are *here* themselves say if they found any wrongdoing*a* in me while I stood before the council, ²¹unless *it is* for this one statement which I cried out, standing among them, 'Concerning the resurrection of the dead I am being judged by you this day.' "

FELIX PROCRASTINATES

²²But when Felix heard these things, having more accurate knowledge of *the* Way, he adjourned the proceedings and said, "When Lysias the commander comes down, I will make a decision on your case." ²³So he commanded the centurion to keep Paul and to let *him* have liberty, and told him not to forbid any of his friends to provide for or visit him.

²⁴And after some days, when Felix came with his wife Drusilla, who was Jewish, he sent for Paul and heard him concerning the faith in Christ. ²⁵Now as he reasoned about righteousness, self-control, and the judgment to come, Felix was afraid and answered, "Go away for now; when I have a convenient time I will call for you." ²⁶Meanwhile he also hoped that money would be given him by Paul, that he might release him.*a* Therefore he sent for him more often and conversed with him.

²⁷But after two years Porcius Festus succeeded Felix; and Felix, wanting to do the Jews a favor, left Paul bound.

PAUL APPEALS TO CAESAR

¹Now when Festus had come to the province, after three days he went up from Caesarea to Jerusalem. ²Then the high priest*a* and the chief men of the Jews informed him against Paul; and they petitioned him, ³asking a favor against him, that he would summon him to Jerusalem—while *they* lay in ambush along the road to kill him. ⁴But Festus answered that Paul should be kept at Caesarea, and that he himself was going *there* shortly. ⁵"Therefore," he said, "let those who have authority among you go down with *me* and accuse this man, to see if there is any fault in him."

⁶And when he had remained among them more than ten days, he went down to Caesarea. And the next day, sitting on the judgment seat, he commanded Paul to be brought. ⁷When he had come, the Jews who had come down from Jerusalem stood about and laid many serious complaints against Paul, which they could not prove, ⁸while he answered for himself, "Neither against the law of the Jews, nor against the temple, nor against Caesar have I offended in anything at all."

⁹But Festus, wanting to do the Jews a favor, answered Paul and said, "Are you willing to go up to Jerusalem and there be judged before me concerning these things?"

¹⁰So Paul said, "I stand at Caesar's judgment seat, where I ought to be judged. To the Jews I have done no wrong, as you very well know. ¹¹For if I am an offender, or have committed anything deserving of death, I do not object to dying; but if there is nothing in these things of which these men accuse me, no one can deliver me to them. I appeal to Caesar."

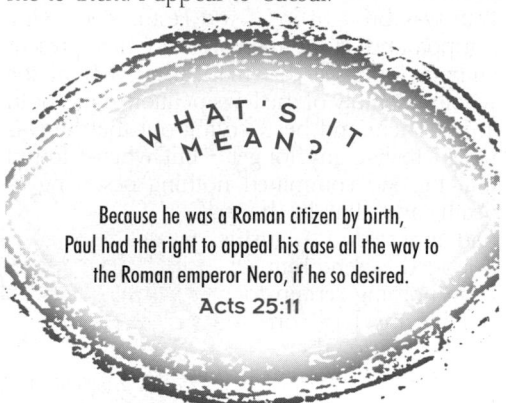

WHAT'S IT MEAN?

Because he was a Roman citizen by birth, Paul had the right to appeal his case all the way to the Roman emperor Nero, if he so desired.

Acts 25:11

¹²Then Festus, when he had conferred with the council, answered, "You have appealed to Caesar? To Caesar you shall go!"

PAUL BEFORE AGRIPPA

¹³And after some days King Agrippa and Bernice came to Caesarea to greet Festus. ¹⁴When they had been there many days, Festus laid Paul's case before the king, saying: "There is a certain man left a prisoner by Felix, ¹⁵about whom the chief priests and the elders of the Jews informed *me*, when I was in Jerusalem, asking for a judgment against him. ¹⁶To them I answered, 'It is not the custom of the Romans to deliver any man to destruction*a* before the accused meets the accusers face to face, and has opportunity to answer for himself concerning the charge against him.' ¹⁷Therefore when they had come together, without any delay, the next day I sat on the judgment seat and commanded the man to be brought in. ¹⁸When the accusers stood up, they brought no accusation against him of such things as I supposed, ¹⁹but had some questions against him about their own religion and about a certain Jesus, who had

---

24:20 *a*NU-Text and M-Text read *say what wrongdoing they found.*　**24:26** *a*NU-Text omits *that he might release him.*　**25:2** *a*NU-Text reads *chief priests.*　**25:16** *a*NU-Text omits *to destruction,* although it is implied.

died, whom Paul affirmed to be alive. [20]And because I was uncertain of such questions, I asked whether he was willing to go to Jerusalem and there be judged concerning these matters. [21]But when Paul appealed to be reserved for the decision of Augustus, I commanded him to be kept till I could send him to Caesar."

[22]Then Agrippa said to Festus, "I also would like to hear the man myself."

"Tomorrow," he said, "you shall hear him."

[23]So the next day, when Agrippa and Bernice had come with great pomp, and had entered the auditorium with the commanders and the prominent men of the city, at Festus' command Paul was brought in. [24]And Festus said: "King Agrippa and all the men who are here present with us, you see this man about whom the whole assembly of the Jews petitioned me, both at Jerusalem and here, crying out that he was not fit to live any longer. [25]But when I found that he had committed nothing deserving of death, and that he himself had appealed to Augustus, I decided to send him. [26]I have nothing certain to write to my lord concerning him. Therefore I have brought him out before you, and especially before you, King Agrippa, so that after the examination has taken place I may have something to write. [27]For it seems to me unreasonable to send a prisoner and not to specify the charges against him."

PAUL'S EARLY LIFE

[1]Then Agrippa said to Paul, "You are permitted to speak for yourself."

So Paul stretched out his hand and answered for himself: [2]"I think myself happy, King Agrippa, because today I shall answer for myself before you concerning all the things of which I am accused by the Jews, [3]especially because you are expert in all customs and questions which have to do with the Jews. Therefore I beg you to hear me patiently.

[4]"My manner of life from my youth, which was spent from the beginning among my own nation at Jerusalem, all the Jews know. [5]They knew me from the first, if they were willing to testify, that according to the strictest sect of our religion I lived a Pharisee. [6]And now I stand and am judged for the hope of the promise made by God to our fathers. [7]To this *promise* our twelve tribes, earnestly serving *God* night and day, hope to attain. For this hope's sake, King Agrippa, I am accused by the Jews. [8]Why should it be thought incredible by you that God raises the dead?

[9]"Indeed, I myself thought I must do many things contrary to the name of Jesus of Nazareth. [10]This I also did in Jerusalem, and many of the saints I shut up in prison, having received authority from the chief priests; and when they were put to death, I cast my vote against *them*. [11]And I punished them often in every synagogue and compelled *them* to blaspheme; and being exceedingly enraged against them, I persecuted *them* even to foreign cities.

PAUL RECOUNTS HIS CONVERSION

[12]"While thus occupied, as I journeyed to Damascus with authority and commission from the chief priests, [13]at midday, O king, along the road I saw a light from heaven, brighter than the sun, shining around me and those who journeyed with me. [14]And when we all had fallen to the ground, I heard a voice speaking to me and saying in the Hebrew language, 'Saul, Saul, why are you persecuting Me? *It is* hard for you to kick against the goads.' [15]So I said, 'Who are You, Lord?' And He said, 'I am Jesus, whom you are persecuting. [16]But rise and stand on your feet; for I have appeared to you for this purpose, to make you a minister and a witness both of the things which you have seen and of the things which I will yet reveal to you. [17]I will deliver you from the *Jewish* people, as well as *from* the Gentiles, to whom I now[a] send you, [18]to open their eyes, *in order* to turn *them* from darkness to light, and *from* the power of Satan to God, that they may receive forgiveness of sins and an inheritance among those who are sanctified by faith in Me.'

PAUL'S POST-CONVERSION LIFE

[19]"Therefore, King Agrippa, I was not disobedient to the heavenly vision, [20]but declared

> "But rise and stand on your feet; for I have appeared to you for this purpose, to make you a minister and a witness both of the things which you have seen and of the things which I will yet reveal to you."
> (Acts 26:16)

26:17 [a]NU-Text and M-Text omit *now*.

first to those in Damascus and in Jerusalem, and throughout all the region of Judea, and *then* to the Gentiles, that they should repent, turn to God, and do works befitting repentance. [21]For these reasons the Jews seized me in the temple and tried to kill *me.* [22]Therefore, having obtained help from God, to this day I stand, witnessing both to small and great, saying no other things than those which the prophets and Moses said would come—[23]that the Christ would suffer, that He would be the first to rise from the dead, and would proclaim light to the *Jewish* people and to the Gentiles."

AGRIPPA PARRIES PAUL'S CHALLENGE

[24]Now as he thus made his defense, Festus said with a loud voice, "Paul, you are beside yourself! Much learning is driving you mad!" [25]But he said, "I am not mad, most noble Festus, but speak the words of truth and reason. [26]For the king, before whom I also speak freely, knows these things; for I am convinced that none of these things escapes his attention, since this thing was not done in a corner. [27]King Agrippa, do you believe the prophets? I know that you do believe." [28]Then Agrippa said to Paul, "You almost persuade me to become a Christian." [29]And Paul said, "I would to God that not only you, but also all who hear me today, might become both almost and altogether such as I am, except for these chains." [30]When he had said these things, the king stood up, as well as the governor and Bernice and those who sat with them; [31]and when they had gone aside, they talked among themselves, saying, "This man is doing nothing deserving of death or chains." [32]Then Agrippa said to Festus, "This man might have been set free if he had not appealed to Caesar."

THE VOYAGE TO ROME BEGINS

[1]And when it was decided that we should sail to Italy, they delivered Paul and some other prisoners to *one* named Julius, a centurion of the Augustan Regiment. [2]So, entering a ship of Adramyttium, we put to sea, meaning to sail along the coasts of Asia. Aristarchus, a Macedonian of Thessalonica, was with us. [3]And the next *day* we landed at Sidon. And Julius treated Paul kindly and gave *him* liberty to go to his friends and receive care. [4]When we had put to sea from there, we sailed under *the shelter of* Cyprus, because the winds were contrary. [5]And when we had sailed over the sea which is off Cilicia and Pamphylia, we came to Myra, *a city* of Lycia. [6]There the centurion found an Alexandrian ship sailing to Italy, and he put us on board.

[7]When we had sailed slowly many days, and arrived with difficulty off Cnidus, the wind not permitting us to proceed, we sailed under *the shelter of* Crete off Salmone. [8]Passing it with difficulty, we came to a place called Fair Havens, near the city *of* Lasea.

PAUL'S WARNING IGNORED

[9]Now when much time had been spent, and sailing was now dangerous because the Fast was already over, Paul advised them, [10]saying, "Men, I perceive that this voyage will end with disaster and much loss, not only of the cargo and ship, but also our lives." [11]Nevertheless the centurion was more persuaded by the helmsman and the owner of the ship than by the things spoken by Paul. [12]And because the harbor was not suitable to winter in, the majority advised to set sail from there also, if by any means they could reach Phoenix, a harbor of Crete opening toward the southwest and northwest, *and* winter *there.*

IN THE TEMPEST

[13]When the south wind blew softly, supposing that they had obtained *their* desire, putting out to sea, they sailed close by Crete. [14]But not long after, a tempestuous head wind arose, called Euroclydon.*[a]* [15]So when the ship was caught, and could not head into the wind, we let *her* drive. [16]And running under *the shelter of* an island called Clauda,*[a]* we secured the skiff with difficulty. [17]When they had taken it on board, they used cables to undergird the ship; and fearing lest they should run aground on the Syrtis*[a] Sands,* they struck sail and so were driven. [18]And because we were exceedingly tempest-tossed, the next *day* they lightened the ship. [19]On the third *day* we threw the ship's tackle overboard with our own hands. [20]Now when neither sun nor stars appeared for many days, and no small tempest beat on *us,* all hope that we would be saved was finally given up.

[21]But after long abstinence from food, then Paul stood in the midst of them and said, "Men, you should have listened to me, and not have sailed from Crete and incurred this disaster and loss. [22]And now I urge you to take heart, for there will be no loss of life among you, but only of the ship. [23]For there stood by me this night

27:14 *[a]*NU-Text reads *Euraquilon.*   27:16 *[a]*NU-Text reads *Cauda.*   27:17 *[a]*M-Text reads *Syrtes.*

an angel of the God to whom I belong and whom I serve, [24]saying, 'Do not be afraid, Paul; you must be brought before Caesar; and indeed God has granted you all those who sail with you.' [25]Therefore take heart, men, for I believe God that it will be just as it was told me. [26]However, we must run aground on a certain island."

[27]Now when the fourteenth night had come, as we were driven up and down in the Adriatic *Sea*, about midnight the sailors sensed that they were drawing near some land. [28]And they took soundings and found *it* to be twenty fathoms; and when they had gone a little farther, they took soundings again and found *it* to be fifteen fathoms. [29]Then, fearing lest we should run aground on the rocks, they dropped four anchors from the stern, and prayed for day to come. [30]And as the sailors were seeking to escape from the ship, when they had let down the skiff into the sea, under pretense of putting out anchors from the prow, [31]Paul said to the centurion and the soldiers, "Unless these men stay in the ship, you cannot be saved." [32]Then the soldiers cut away the ropes of the skiff and let it fall off.

[33]And as day was about to dawn, Paul implored *them* all to take food, saying, "Today is the fourteenth day you have waited and continued without food, and eaten nothing. [34]Therefore I urge you to take nourishment, for this is for your survival, since not a hair will fall from the head of any of you." [35]And when he had said these things, he took bread and gave thanks to God in the presence of them all; and when he had broken *it* he began to eat. [36]Then they were all encouraged, and also took food themselves. [37]And in all we were two hundred and seventy-six persons on the ship. [38]So when they had eaten enough, they lightened the ship and threw out the wheat into the sea.

> **THANKFULNESS**
> Who should we thank for what we have? (27:35)

SHIPWRECKED ON MALTA

[39]When it was day, they did not recognize the land; but they observed a bay with a beach, onto which they planned to run the ship if possible. [40]And they let go the anchors and left *them* in the sea, meanwhile loosing the rudder ropes; and they hoisted the mainsail to the wind and made for shore. [41]But striking a place where two seas met, they ran the ship aground; and the prow stuck fast and remained immovable, but the stern was being broken up by the violence of the waves.

[42]And the soldiers' plan was to kill the prisoners, lest any of them should swim away and escape. [43]But the centurion, wanting to save Paul, kept them from *their* purpose, and commanded that those who could swim should jump *overboard* first and get to land, [44]and the rest, some on boards and some on *parts* of the ship. And so it was that they all escaped safely to land.

PAUL'S MINISTRY ON MALTA

[1]Now when they had escaped, they then found out that the island was called Malta. [2]And the natives showed us unusual kindness; for they kindled a fire and made us all welcome, because of the rain that was falling and because of the cold. [3]But when Paul had gathered a bundle of sticks and laid *them* on the fire, a viper came out because of the heat, and fastened on his hand. [4]So when the natives saw the creature hanging from his hand, they said to one another, "No doubt this man is a murderer, whom, though he has escaped the sea, yet justice does not allow to live." [5]But he shook off the creature into the fire and suffered no harm. [6]However, they were expecting that he would swell up or suddenly fall down dead. But after they had looked for a long time and saw no harm come to him, they changed their minds and said that he was a god.

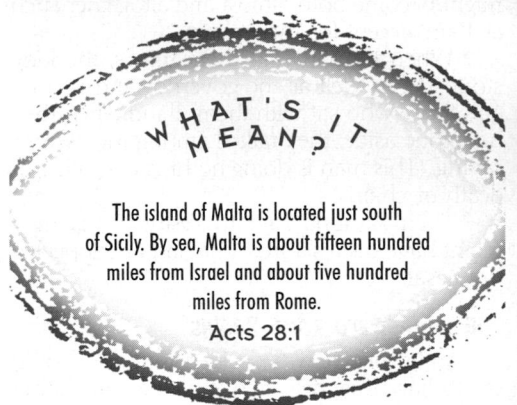

WHAT'S IT MEAN?

The island of Malta is located just south of Sicily. By sea, Malta is about fifteen hundred miles from Israel and about five hundred miles from Rome.
Acts 28:1

[7]In that region there was an estate of the leading citizen of the island, whose name was Publius, who received us and entertained us courteously for three days. [8]And it happened that the father of Publius lay sick of a fever and dysentery. Paul went in to him and prayed, and he laid his hands on him and healed him. [9]So when this was done, the rest of those on the island who

> **GIVING**
> Who should we be mindful to support? (28:10)

had diseases also came and were healed. [10]They also honored us in many ways; and when we departed, they provided such things as were necessary.

ARRIVAL AT ROME

[11]After three months we sailed in an Alexandrian ship whose figurehead was the Twin Brothers, which had wintered at the island. [12]And landing at Syracuse, we stayed three days. [13]From there we circled round and reached Rhegium. And after one day the south wind blew; and the next day we came to Puteoli, [14]where we found brethren, and were invited to stay with them seven days. And so we went toward Rome. [15]And from there, when the brethren heard about us, they came to meet us as far as Appii Forum and Three Inns. When Paul saw them, he thanked God and took courage.

[16]Now when we came to Rome, the centurion delivered the prisoners to the captain of the guard; but Paul was permitted to dwell by himself with the soldier who guarded him.

PAUL'S MINISTRY AT ROME

[17]And it came to pass after three days that Paul called the leaders of the Jews together. So when they had come together, he said to them: "Men *and* brethren, though I have done nothing against our people or the customs of our fathers, yet I was delivered as a prisoner from Jerusalem into the hands of the Romans, [18]who, when they had examined me, wanted to let *me* go, because there was no cause for putting me to death. [19]But when the Jews[a] spoke against *it*, I was compelled to appeal to Caesar, not that I had anything of which to accuse my nation. [20]For this reason therefore I have called for you, to see *you* and speak with *you*, because for the hope of Israel I am bound with this chain."

[21]Then they said to him, "We neither received letters from Judea concerning you, nor have any of the brethren who came reported or spoken any evil of you. [22]But we desire to hear from you what you think; for concerning this sect, we know that it is spoken against everywhere."

[23]So when they had appointed him a day, many came to him at *his* lodging, to whom he explained and solemnly testified of the kingdom of God, persuading them concerning Jesus from both the Law of Moses and the Prophets, from morning till evening. [24]And some were persuaded by the things which were spoken, and some disbelieved. [25]So when they did not agree among themselves, they departed after Paul had said one word: "The Holy Spirit spoke rightly through Isaiah the prophet to our[a] fathers, [26]saying,

'Go to this people and say:
"Hearing you will hear, and shall not
    understand;
And seeing you will see, and not perceive;
For the hearts of this people have grown
    dull.
Their ears are hard of hearing,
And their eyes they have closed,
Lest they should see with their eyes and
    hear with their ears,
Lest they should understand with their
    hearts and turn,
So that I should heal them." '[a]

[28]"Therefore let it be known to you that the salvation of God has been sent to the Gentiles, and they will hear it!" [29]And when he had said these words, the Jews departed and had a great dispute among themselves.[a]

[30]Then Paul dwelt two whole years in his own rented house, and received all who came to him, [31]preaching the kingdom of God and teaching the things which concern the Lord Jesus Christ with all confidence, no one forbidding him.

28:19 [a]That is, the ruling authorities   **28:25** [a]NU-Text reads *your.*   **28:27** [a]Isaiah 6:9, 10   **28:29** [a]NU-Text omits this verse.

romans

CONTENT Do you know what a primer is? It is the most basic handbook you can find. When you learned to read, you probably used a primer of some kind. It is a book that explains a big concept in simple, small pieces. It is an outline of the fundamentals.

The Book of Romans is a kind of primer. It is a primer to the Christian life. Paul wrote it to the Romans so that they would have an introduction to him and to his beliefs before he came to visit them. He wanted to make the most of his trip there, so the more he could explain to them ahead of time, the better. He could answer their questions when he arrived.

The basic message of Romans is this: You are saved by God's grace through faith, not by the good things you do. None of us deserves salvation. It is God's free gift through Jesus.

Life gets complicated sometimes—trying to figure out what to do and what not to do. Romans takes us back to the basics so that we can find our way to God and then figure out life in light of His love.

Outline
1:1–17 .... Paul and His Message of Good News
1:18—3:20 .... Everyone Is Guilty
3:21—4:25 .... Justification by Faith
5:1—8:39 .... A New Life in Christ for God's People
9:1—11:36 .... What About the People of Israel?
12:1—15:13 .... How to Live a Transformed Life of Love
15:14—16:27 ...... Paul's Plans and Personal Greetings

Purpose God declares us righteous and helps us to live righteously.

Theme The Righteousness of God in the Gospel of Christ

Date of writing Spring A.D. 57

> "For I am not ashamed of the gospel of Christ, for it is the power of God to salvation for everyone who believes, for the Jew first and also for the Greek" (1:16).

Bible Talk

Faith: A New Concept?

We are used to talking about faith. It doesn't seem like a difficult concept. We hear songs about it on the radio. We hear the word at least three times every time we go to church. Why does it seem to be such a new thought to the early Christians?

Before Christ's life and death, God was worshiped through sacrifices and rituals. People still had to have faith, but it was faith that *one day* God would send a savior. They still depended on their sacrifices to keep them right with God.

Once Jesus came, He made the one true sacrifice. No one had to do all those rituals to keep themselves right with God anymore. They just had to have faith in Jesus' sacrifice for their sins. In that way, faith was a very new concept.

WANTED: DEAD OR ALIVE

In Paul's letter to the Romans, he makes one bold statement in a lot of different ways: Before we come to believe in Christ and His sacrifice, we are dead in our sins. We are spiritual corpses. Our bodies might be carrying on, but our spirits have no breath in them. We don't function. We can't do the things that we were created to do like spill over with joy and kindness and patience and abundant life.

But when we accept Christ's sacrifice for our sins and put our faith in *His* goodness rather than our own, then we come to life. The Holy Spirit breathes His life into us, and our spirits come alive and dance and sing in the light of God's love.

GREETING

[1]Paul, a bondservant of Jesus Christ, called *to be* an apostle, separated to the gospel of God [2]which He promised before through His prophets in the Holy Scriptures, [3]concerning His Son Jesus Christ our Lord, who was born of the seed of David according to the flesh, [4]*and* declared *to be* the Son of God with power according to the Spirit of holiness, by the resurrection from the dead. [5]Through Him we have received grace and apostleship for obedience to the faith among all nations for His name, [6]among whom you also are the called of Jesus Christ;

[7]To all who are in Rome, beloved of God, called *to be* saints:

Grace to you and peace from God our Father and the Lord Jesus Christ.

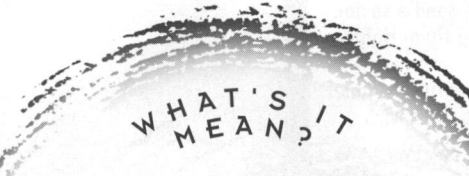

WHAT'S IT MEAN?

As you may have guessed from the name, the capital of the Roman Empire was Rome. Apparently, the city was a pretty good choice for a capital because the country of Italy is using it today. During New Testament times, the population of Rome was about eight hundred thousand, including about ten thousand Jews. One of the most unusual features of the city is that it was built on seven hills. At the time Paul wrote his letter to the church in Rome, Nero was ruling the empire.

Romans 1:7

DESIRE TO VISIT ROME

[8]First, I thank my God through Jesus Christ for you all, that your faith is spoken of throughout the whole world. [9]For God is my witness, whom I serve with my spirit in the gospel of His Son, that without ceasing I make mention of you always in my prayers, [10]making request if, by some means, now at last I may

"First, I thank my God through Jesus Christ for you all, that your faith is spoken of throughout the whole world."
(Romans 1:8)

find a way in the will of God to come to you. [11]For I long to see you, that I may impart to you some spiritual gift, so that you may be established—[12]that is, that I may be encouraged together with you by the mutual faith both of you and me.

[13]Now I do not want you to be unaware, brethren, that I often planned to come to you (but was hindered until now), that I might have some fruit among you also, just as among the other Gentiles. [14]I am a debtor both to Greeks and to barbarians, both to wise and to unwise. [15]So, as much as is in me, *I am* ready to preach the gospel to you who are in Rome also.

THE JUST LIVE BY FAITH

[16]For I am not ashamed of the gospel of Christ,[a] for it is the power of God to salvation for everyone who believes, for the Jew first and also for the Greek. [17]For in it the righteousness of God is revealed from faith to faith; as it is written, *"The just shall live by faith."*[a]

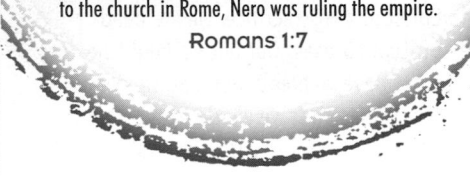

EMBARRASSMENT

Is the gospel a source of embarrassment? (1:16)

GOD'S WRATH ON UNRIGHTEOUSNESS

[18]For the wrath of God is revealed from heaven against all ungodliness and unrighteousness of men, who suppress the truth in unrighteousness, [19]because what may be known of God is manifest in them, for God has shown *it* to them. [20]For since the creation of the world His invisible *attributes* are clearly seen, being understood by the things that are made, *even* His eternal power and Godhead, so that they are without excuse, [21]because, although they knew God, they did not glorify *Him* as God, nor were thankful, but became futile in their thoughts, and their foolish hearts were darkened. [22]Professing to be wise, they became fools, [23]and changed the glory of the incorruptible God into an image made like corruptible man—and birds and four-footed animals and creeping things.

HOMOSEXUALITY

Will homosexuals be held accountable for their actions? (1:18–32)

1:16 [a]NU-Text omits *of Christ.*   **1:17** [a]Habakkuk 2:4

[24]Therefore God also gave them up to uncleanness, in the lusts of their hearts, to dishonor their bodies among themselves, [25]who exchanged the truth of God for the lie, and worshiped and served the creature rather than the Creator, who is blessed forever. Amen.

[26]For this reason God gave them up to vile passions. For even their women exchanged the natural use for what is against nature. [27]Likewise also the men, leaving the natural use of the woman, burned in their lust for one another, men with men committing what is shameful, and receiving in themselves the penalty of their error which was due.

[28]And even as they did not like to retain God in *their* knowledge, God gave them over to a debased mind, to do those things which are not fitting; [29]being filled with all unrighteousness, sexual immorality,[a] wickedness, covetousness, maliciousness; full of envy, murder, strife, deceit, evil-mindedness; *they are* whisperers, [30]backbiters, haters of God, violent, proud, boasters, inventors of evil things, disobedient to parents, [31]undiscerning, untrustworthy, unloving, unforgiving,[a] unmerciful; [32]who, knowing the righteous judgment of God, that those who practice such things are deserving of death, not only do the same but also approve of those who practice them.

GOD'S RIGHTEOUS JUDGMENT

[1]Therefore you are inexcusable, O man, whoever you are who judge, for in whatever you judge another you condemn yourself; for you who judge practice the same things. [2]But we know that the judgment of God is according to truth against those who practice such things. [3]And do you think this, O man, you who judge those practicing such things, and doing the same, that you will escape the judgment of God? [4]Or do you despise the riches of His goodness, forbearance, and longsuffering, not knowing that the goodness of God leads you to repentance? [5]But in accordance with your hardness and your impenitent heart you are treasuring up for yourself wrath in the day of wrath and revelation of the righteous judgment of God, [6]who *will render to each one according to his deeds*:[a] [7]eternal life to those who by patient continuance in doing good seek for glory, honor, and immortality; [8]but to those who are self-seeking and do not obey the truth, but obey unrighteousness—indignation and wrath, [9]tribulation and anguish, on every soul

1:29 [a]NU-Text omits *sexual immorality.* **1:31** [a]NU-Text omits *unforgiving.* **2:6** [a]Psalm 62:12; Proverbs 24:12

Promise HE PROMISES EVERYONE WHO HAS FAITH WILL LIVE.

For in it [the gospel of Christ] the righteousness of God is revealed from faith to faith; as it is written, "The just shall live by faith" (Rom. 1:17).

Most people want to do something so that God will like them. They think that if they're really good, if they do everything—or most things—right, then God will accept them. It makes people feel really good to think there's something so neat about them that they can earn a spot in heaven.

The truth is that no one can be *that* good. There's something special about every single person on earth, but there's some junk in everyone, too. God doesn't accept anyone's goodness as good enough to get into heaven.

But that's not the end of the story. "The righteousness of God is revealed from faith to faith." In other words, God accepts those who come to Him in faith. Now *that's* good news. It's not being good that gets God to accept you; it's having faith in His Son. You don't have to settle for some mealy-mouthed, lip-service faith. You can have a faith so strong, so alive that you can't wait to commit your whole life to Jesus. Then, as Romans 1:17 says, you will live—not just physically, but live with strength and power because you're living in Him.

Keep renewing your mind with God's Word. That's how you build faith. Do your best to live the way God wants you to just because you love Him and you want to please Him. Faith sets you free from the vicious cycle of constantly trying to work your way into God's good graces.

SEE FOR YOURSELF:

Hab. 2:4; Rom. 5:18, 19; Gal. 3:9, 26; Heb. 11

of man who does evil, of the Jew first and also of the Greek; [10]but glory, honor, and peace to everyone who works what is good, to the Jew first and also to the Greek. [11]For there is no partiality with God.

[12]For as many as have sinned without law will also perish without law, and as many as have sinned in the law will be judged by the law [13](for not the hearers of the law *are* just in the sight of God, but the doers of the law will be justified; [14]for when Gentiles, who do not have the law, by nature do the things in the law, these, although not having the law, are a law to themselves, [15]who show the work of the law written in their hearts, their conscience also bearing witness, and between themselves *their* thoughts accusing or else excusing *them*) [16]in the day when God will judge the secrets of men by Jesus Christ, according to my gospel.

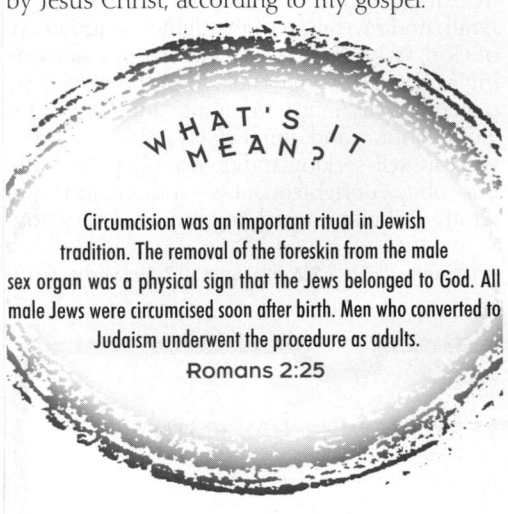

Circumcision was an important ritual in Jewish tradition. The removal of the foreskin from the male sex organ was a physical sign that the Jews belonged to God. All male Jews were circumcised soon after birth. Men who converted to Judaism underwent the procedure as adults.

Romans 2:25

THE JEWS GUILTY AS THE GENTILES

[17]Indeed[a] you are called a Jew, and rest on the law, and make your boast in God, [18]and know *His* will, and approve the things that are excellent, being instructed out of the law, [19]and are confident that you yourself are a guide to the blind, a light to those who are in darkness, [20]an instructor of the foolish, a teacher of babes, having the form of knowledge and truth in the law. [21]You, therefore, who teach another, do you not teach yourself? You who preach that a man should not steal, do you steal? [22]You who say, "Do not commit adultery," do you commit adultery? You who abhor idols, do you rob temples? [23]You who make your boast in the law, do you dishonor God through breaking the law? [24]For *"the name of God is blasphemed*

among the Gentiles because of you,"[a] as it is written.

CIRCUMCISION OF NO AVAIL

[25]For circumcision is indeed profitable if you keep the law; but if you are a breaker of the law, your circumcision has become uncircumcision. [26]Therefore, if an uncircumcised man keeps the righteous requirements of the law, will not his uncircumcision be counted as circumcision? [27]And will not the physically uncircumcised, if he fulfills the law, judge you who, *even* with *your* written *code* and circumcision, *are* a transgressor of the law? [28]For he is not a Jew who is *one* outwardly, nor *is* circumcision that which is outward in the flesh; [29]but *he is* a Jew who is *one* inwardly; and circumcision *is that* of the heart, in the Spirit, not in the letter; whose praise *is* not from men but from God.

GOD'S JUDGMENT DEFENDED

[1]What advantage then has the Jew, or what *is* the profit of circumcision? [2]Much in every way! Chiefly because to them were committed the oracles of God. [3]For what if some did not believe? Will their unbelief make the faithfulness of God without effect? [4]Certainly not! Indeed, let God be true but every man a liar. As it is written:

> *"That You may be justified in Your words,*
> *And may overcome when You are*
> *judged."[a]*

[5]But if our unrighteousness demonstrates the righteousness of God, what shall we say? *Is* God unjust who inflicts wrath? (I speak as a man.) [6]Certainly not! For then how will God judge the world?

[7]For if the truth of God has increased through my lie to His glory, why am I also still judged as a sinner? [8]And *why* not *say*, "Let us do evil that good may come"?—as we are slanderously reported and as some affirm that we say. Their condemnation is just.

ALL HAVE SINNED

[9]What then? Are we better *than they?* Not at all. For we have previously charged both Jews and Greeks that they are all under sin.

[10]As it is written:

GUILT
Are all people guilty of sin? (3:9–12)

> *"There is none righteous, no, not one;*

2:17 [a]NU-Text reads *But if.*　**2:24** [a]Isaiah 52:5; Ezekiel 36:22　**3:4** [a]Psalm 51:4

11 There is none who understands;
There is none who seeks after God.
12 They have all turned aside;
They have together become unprofitable;
There is none who does good, no, not
one."[a]
13 "Their throat is an open tomb;
With their tongues they
have practiced
deceit";[a]
"The poison of asps is
under their lips";[b]
14 "Whose mouth is full
of cursing and
bitterness."[a]
15 "Their feet are swift to
shed blood;
16 Destruction and misery
are in their ways;
17 And the way of peace they
have not known."[a]
18 "There is no fear of God before their
eyes."[a]

19 Now we know that whatever the law says,
it says to those who are under the law, that

every mouth may be stopped, and all the world
may become guilty before God. 20 Therefore by
the deeds of the law no flesh will be justified
in His sight, for by the law is the knowledge
of sin.

GOD'S RIGHTEOUSNESS THROUGH FAITH

21 But now the righteousness of God apart
from the law is revealed,
being witnessed by the Law
and the Prophets, 22 even
the righteousness of God,
through faith in Jesus
Christ, to all and on all[a]
who believe. For there is
no difference; 23 for all have
sinned and fall
short of the
glory of God,
24 being justified
freely by His grace through
the redemption that is in
Christ Jesus, 25 whom God set
forth as a propitiation by His
blood, through faith, to demonstrate His righ-

> "For all have sinned and fall
> short of the glory of God,
> being justified freely by His
> grace through the redemption
> that is in Christ Jesus."
> (Romans 3:23, 24)

SIN

Can God
tolerate sin?
(3:23)

3:12 [a]Psalms 14:1–3; 53:1–3; Ecclesiastes 7:20   3:13 [a]Psalm 5:9 [b]Psalm 140:3   3:14 [a]Psalm 10:7
3:17 [a]Isaiah 59:7, 8   3:18 [a]Psalm 36:1   3:22 [a]NU-Text omits and on all.

Promise   HE PROMISES TO TREAT YOU BETTER THAN YOU DESERVE.

*Being justified freely by His grace through the redemption that is in Christ Jesus
(Rom. 3:24).*

Hate to break it to you this way. You're a pretty good kid and all. But unfortunately, your situation
leaves no other choice. Pockets of sin have been discovered in numerous places on your body—some
leading all the way down to your heart—and your track record certainly bears out the fact that you
do indeed have a serious problem.

So . . . your file's being turned over to the justice department. Been nice knowing you.

However, if it will make you feel better, you should know that you're in good company. In fact, in
all the time that God's been handling this, only one person has ever been cleared of the death
sentence on the first try. Just one. Fellow from Nazareth by the name of Jesus. But ever since
then, before these cases can be properly executed, convicted lawbreakers like you have the right
to pursue one final route of appeal.

It goes something like this. If you'll deliver an honest confession to God that your personal
performance has been a dismal failure, and that you are willing to let Jesus' innocence stand in
the place of all your hard work and effort at passing the grade . . . well, let's just say no one
has ever been turned down yet.

Are you ready to exercise your option? Go for it!

SEE FOR YOURSELF:
Dan. 9:9; Eph. 2:8, 9; Titus 3:4–7

teousness, because in His forbearance God had passed over the sins that were previously committed, [26]to demonstrate at the present time His righteousness, that He might be just and the justifier of the one who has faith in Jesus.

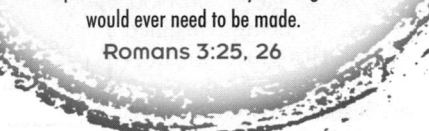

Under the Law that God gave to Moses, whenever a person sinned, an animal had to be sacrificed—meaning, killed on an altar. Usually it was a sheep whose blood was offered as payment for the sin. Jesus put an end to that old system of sacrifice when He became the ultimate sacrifice. Jesus' death paid for the sins of the entire world, once and for all. God accepted His blood as the only offering that would ever need to be made.

Romans 3:25, 26

BOASTING EXCLUDED

[27]Where *is* boasting then? It is excluded. By what law? Of works? No, but by the law of faith. [28]Therefore we conclude that a man is justified by faith apart from the deeds of the law. [29]Or *is He* the God of the Jews only? *Is He* not also the God of the Gentiles? Yes, of the Gentiles also, [30]since *there is* one God who will justify the circumcised by faith and the uncircumcised through faith. [31]Do we then make void the law through faith? Certainly not! On the contrary, we establish the law.

ABRAHAM JUSTIFIED BY FAITH

[1]What then shall we say that Abraham our father has found according to the flesh?[a] [2]For if Abraham was justified by works, he has *something* to boast about, but not before God. [3]For what does the Scripture say? "Abraham believed God, and it was accounted to him for righteousness."[a] [4]Now to him who works, the wages are not counted as grace but as debt.

DAVID CELEBRATES THE SAME TRUTH

[5]But to him who does not work but believes on Him who justifies the ungodly, his faith is accounted for righteousness, [6]just as David also describes the blessedness of the man to whom God imputes righteousness apart from works:

On the Edge

And he [Abraham] received the sign of circumcision, a seal of the righteousness of the faith which he had while still uncircumcised, that he might be the father of all those who believe, though they are uncircumcised, that righteousness might be imputed to them also (Rom. 4:11).

In the Bible, Abraham is famous for his faith. He packed up and left his home when God told him to, even though he had no clue where God was taking him. (Basically, the Lord said, "I'll tell you when you get there.") Later, he obeyed when God told him to sacrifice his only son, Isaac—the one he had waited 100 years to have and the one God had promised him. Abraham's faith in God was so strong that he even raised a knife to kill Isaac as a sacrifice to the Lord. And then an angel of the Lord commanded him to stop. Abraham sinned many times, but his enormous faith made him acceptable to God.

The Jews were so proud of being Abraham's descendants that they went around calling themselves children of Abraham. Everyone wanted to be a child of Abraham because of the great blessings those children were promised. Read about those blessings in Genesis 17. Paul writes that the real children of Abraham are not the people who can write his name at the base of their family tree. The children of Abraham are the people who have the same kind of faith that he had—faith that proves itself by actions.

You are a child of Abraham if you have real, active faith in Jesus. It's your faith that makes you acceptable to God, not your bloodline.

SEE FOR YOURSELF:
  Gen. 17; Matt. 3:9;
  Rom. 4:9–13;
  Gal. 3:7, 29

[7]   "Blessed are those whose lawless deeds are forgiven,
     And whose sins are covered;
[8]   Blessed is the man to whom the LORD shall not impute sin."[a]

4:1 [a]Or *Abraham our (fore)father according to the flesh has found?*   **4:3** [a]Genesis 15:6   **4:8** [a]Psalm 32:1, 2

ABRAHAM JUSTIFIED BEFORE CIRCUMCISION

⁹*Does* this blessedness then *come* upon the circumcised *only*, or upon the uncircumcised also? For we say that faith was accounted to Abraham for righteousness. ¹⁰How then was it accounted? While he was circumcised, or uncircumcised? Not while circumcised, but while uncircumcised. ¹¹And he received the sign of circumcision, a seal of the righteousness of the faith which *he had while still* uncircumcised, that he might be the father of all those who believe, though they are uncircumcised, that righteousness might be imputed to them also, ¹²and the father of circumcision to those who not only *are* of the circumcision, but who also walk in the steps of the faith which our father Abraham *had while still* uncircumcised.

THE PROMISE GRANTED THROUGH FAITH

¹³For the promise that he would be the heir of the world *was* not to Abraham or to his seed through the law, but through the righteousness of faith. ¹⁴For if those who are of the law *are* heirs, faith is made void and the promise made of no effect, ¹⁵because the law brings about wrath; for where there is no law *there is* no transgression.

W H A T' S   I T   M E A N ?

The history of the Jewish people begins with God's promise to Abraham. God appeared to Abraham in Mesopotamia, the land between the Tigris and Euphrates Rivers. The Lord promised Abraham that he would be the father of many nations.

Romans 4:17

¹⁶Therefore *it is* of faith that *it might be* according to grace, so that the promise might be sure to all the seed, not only to those who are of the law, but also to those who are of the faith of Abraham, who is the father of us all ¹⁷(as it is written, *"I have made you a father of many nations"ᵃ*) in the presence of Him whom he believed—God, who gives life to the dead and calls those things which do not exist as though

they did; ¹⁸who, contrary to hope, in hope believed, so that he became the father of many nations, according to what was spoken, *"So shall your descendants be."ᵃ* ¹⁹And not being weak in faith, he did not consider his own body, already dead (since he was about a hundred years old), and the deadness of Sarah's womb. ²⁰He did not waver at the promise of God through unbelief, but was strengthened in faith, giving glory to God, ²¹and being fully convinced that what He had promised He was also able to perform. ²²And therefore *"it was accounted to him for righteousness."ᵃ*

²³Now it was not written for his sake alone that it was imputed to him, ²⁴but also for us. It shall be imputed to us who believe in Him who raised up Jesus our Lord from the dead, ²⁵who was delivered up because of our offenses, and was raised because of our justification.

FAITH TRIUMPHS IN TROUBLE

¹Therefore, having been justified by faith, we haveᵃ peace with God through our Lord Jesus Christ, ²through whom also we have access by faith into this grace in which we stand, and rejoice in hope of the glory of God. ³And not only *that*, but we also glory in tribulations, knowing that tribulation produces perseverance; ⁴and perseverance, character; and character, hope. ⁵Now hope does not disappoint, because the love of God has been poured out in our hearts by the Holy Spirit who was given to us.

CHRIST IN OUR PLACE

⁶For when we were still without strength, in due time Christ died for the ungodly. ⁷For scarcely for a righteous man will one die; yet perhaps for a good man someone would even dare to die. ⁸But God demonstrates His own love toward us, in that while we were still sinners, Christ died for us. ⁹Much more then, having now been justified by His blood, we shall be saved from wrath through Him. ¹⁰For if when we were enemies we were reconciled to God through the death of His Son, much more, having been reconciled, we shall be saved by His life. ¹¹And not only *that*, but we also rejoice in God through our Lord Jesus Christ, through whom we have now received the reconciliation.

DEATH IN ADAM, LIFE IN CHRIST

¹²Therefore, just as through one man sin entered the world, and death through sin, and thus death spread to all men, because all

and of the gift of righteousness will reign in life through the One, Jesus Christ.)

On the Edge

Therefore, having been justified by faith, we have peace with God through our Lord Jesus Christ (Rom. 5:1).

Now that you are a believer, the battle for your spirit is over. You chose the path of victory when you chose Jesus. When you trusted Him, God gave you peace. Are you enjoying the peace you have, or are you trying to fight a battle that's already been won? God wants to come into your life and bring calm to the chaos. He wants to let Him be the light that shatters your darkest storm. A lot of people give their hearts to Jesus and then keep on fighting the same old way they used to. With the peace of God, you can let go of some of your anxiety about grades, college, finances, family, whatever. Do everything you know to do and trust God. You don't have to ma-nipulate decisions and worry about things you can't see. You don't have to go through life by yourself anymore. Rest in the peace God brings. Maybe, if we could hear Him, He would be saying, "Stop fighting that battle. I've already done that for you. Be still. Rest. Open your eyes. My love for you has cast out all fear. Look at what I've done. Stop wringing your hands in worry. I love you. I want you to experience the peace I've given you."

SEE FOR YOURSELF:
John 14:27; Col. 3:15;
   2 Thess. 3:16

WHAT'S IT MEAN?

After God created Adam, He placed him in the Garden of Eden. The place was paradise—literally. The law of the land was pretty simple, too: Eat from any tree in the garden except the tree of the knowledge of good and evil. That's it. That's the only rule Adam had to remember and obey. Guess what? Adam chose to disobey God and eat the fruit from the forbidden tree. Because Adam represented the entire human race, his sin affected all of his descendants.

Romans 5:12

[18]Therefore, as through one man's offense *judgment* came to all men, resulting in condem-nation, even so through one Man's righteous act *the free gift came* to all men, resulting in justi-fication of life. [19]For as by one man's disobedi-ence many were made sinners, so also by one Man's obedience many will be made righteous. [20]Moreover the law entered that the offense might abound. But where sin abounded, grace abounded much more, [21]so that as sin reigned in death, even so grace might reign through righteousness to eternal life through Jesus Christ our Lord.

DEAD TO SIN, ALIVE TO GOD

[1]What shall we say then? Shall we continue in sin that grace may abound? [2]Certainly not! How shall we who died to sin live any longer in it? [3]Or do you not know that as many of us as were baptized into Christ Jesus were baptized into His death? [4]Therefore we were buried with Him through baptism into death, that just as Christ was raised from the dead by the glory of the Father, even so we also should walk in new-ness of life.

[5]For if we have been united together in the likeness of His death, certainly we also shall be *in the likeness* of His resurrection, [6]knowing this, that our old man was crucified with *Him*, that the body of sin might be done away with, that we should no longer be slaves of sin. [7]For he who has died has been freed from sin. [8]Now if we died with Christ, we believe that we shall also live with Him, [9]knowing that Christ, hav-

sinned—[13](For until the law sin was in the world, but sin is not imputed when there is no law. [14]Nevertheless death reigned from Adam to Moses, even over those who had not sinned according to the likeness of the transgression of Adam, who is a type of Him who was to come. [15]But the free gift *is* not like the offense. For if by the one man's offense many died, much more the grace of God and the gift by the grace of the one Man, Jesus Christ, abounded to many. [16]And the gift *is* not like *that which came* through the one who sinned. For the judgment *which came* from one *offense resulted* in condemnation, but the free gift *which came* from many offenses *resulted* in justification. [17]For if by the one man's offense death reigned through the one, much more those who receive abundance of grace ing been raised from the dead, dies no more. Death no longer has dominion over Him. [10]For *the death* that He died, He died to sin once for all; but *the life* that He lives, He lives to God. [11]Likewise you also, reckon yourselves to be dead indeed to sin, but alive to God in Christ Jesus our Lord.

On the Edge

What shall we say then? Shall we continue in sin that grace may abound? Certainly not! How shall we who died to sin live any longer in it? (Rom. 6:1, 2).

Paul went around preaching that people couldn't do anything to earn God's friendship. When he told them that the only way they could know God and go to heaven one day was by having faith and trusting in God's kindness (grace), he probably knew that some people were going to say, "Cool. Then we can do anything we want because it doesn't matter, right?"

Knowing that the question would come up, Paul included something incredible in this letter: "We . . . died to sin." That doesn't sound right. How can Paul say that you're dead to sin when you know that you mess up and sin all the time? Well, Paul wasn't just making that up. He explains it this way: "Therefore we were buried with Him through baptism into death, that just as Christ was raised from the dead by the glory of the Father, even so we also should walk in newness of life" (6:4).

Paul was explaining that because you've put your trust in Jesus, sin only has power over you when you let it. Keep being transformed by God's Word. Keep making the effort to walk in love, forgiveness, and purity before the Lord.

SEE FOR YOURSELF:
Rom. 6; Eph. 2:1–9; Col. 2:11–14

[12]Therefore do not let sin reign in your mortal body, that you should obey it in its lusts. [13]And do not present your members *as* instruments of unrighteousness to sin, but present yourselves to God as being alive from the dead, and your members *as* instruments of righteousness to God. [14]For sin shall not have dominion over you, for you are not under law but under grace.

FROM SLAVES OF SIN TO SLAVES OF GOD

[15]What then? Shall we sin because we are not under law but under grace? Certainly not! [16]Do you not know that to whom you present yourselves slaves to obey, you are that one's slaves whom you obey, whether of sin *leading* to death, or of obedience *leading* to righteousness? [17]But God be thanked that *though* you were slaves of sin, yet you obeyed from the heart that form of doctrine to which you were delivered. [18]And having been set free from sin, you became slaves of righteousness. [19]I speak in human *terms* because of the weakness of your flesh. For just as you presented your members *as* slaves of uncleanness, and of lawlessness *leading* to *more* lawlessness, so now present your members *as* slaves *of* righteousness for holiness.

WHAT'S IT MEAN?

The comparison between sin and slavery probably hit home to many of the people who read Paul's letter. In New Testament times, one out of every four people in the Roman Empire was a slave. People who were captured in battle, whether they were soldiers or civilians, usually became slaves. People who could not afford to pay their debts also became slaves to work off what they owed.

Romans 6:19

[20]For when you were slaves of sin, you were free in regard to righteousness. [21]What fruit did you have then in the things of which you are now ashamed? For the end of those things *is* death. [22]But now having been set free from sin, and having become slaves of God, you have your fruit to holiness, and the end, everlasting life. [23]For the wages of sin *is* death, but the gift of God *is* eternal life in Christ Jesus our Lord.

DEATH
What does sin earn us? (6:23)

FREED FROM THE LAW

[1]Or do you not know, brethren (for I speak to those who know the law), that the law has dominion over a man as long as he lives? [2]For the woman who has a husband is bound by the law to *her* husband as long as he lives. But if

the husband dies, she is released from the law of *her* husband. [3]So then if, while *her* husband lives, she marries another man, she will be called an adulteress; but if her husband dies, she is free from that law, so that she is no adulteress, though she has married another man. [4]Therefore, my brethren, you also have become dead to the law through the body of Christ, that you may be married to another—to Him who was raised from the dead, that we should bear fruit to God. [5]For when we were in the flesh, the sinful passions which were aroused by the law were at work in our members to bear fruit to death. [6]But now we have been delivered from the law, having died to what we were held by, so that we should serve in the newness of the Spirit and not *in* the oldness of the letter.

> "But now having been set free from sin, and having become slaves of God, you have your fruit to holiness, and the end, everlasting life."
> (Romans 6:22)

SIN'S ADVANTAGE IN THE LAW

[7]What shall we say then? *Is* the law sin? Certainly not! On the contrary, I would not have known sin except through the law. For I would not have known covetousness unless the law had said, *"You shall not covet."*[a] [8]But sin, taking opportunity by the commandment, produced in me all *manner of* evil desire. For apart from the law sin *was* dead. [9]I was alive once without the law, but when the commandment came, sin revived and I died. [10]And the commandment, which *was* to *bring* life, I found to *bring* death. [11]For sin, taking occasion by the commandment, deceived me, and by it killed *me.* [12]Therefore the law *is* holy, and the commandment holy and just and good.

LAW CANNOT SAVE FROM SIN

[13]Has then what is good become death to me? Certainly not! But sin, that it might appear sin, was producing death in me through what is good, so that sin through the commandment might become exceedingly sinful. [14]For we know that the law is spiritual, but I am carnal, sold under sin. [15]For what I am doing, I do not understand. For what I will to do, that I do not practice; but what I hate, that I do. [16]If, then, I do what I will not to do, I agree with the law that *it is* good. [17]But now, *it is* no longer I who do it, but sin that dwells in me. [18]For I know that in me (that is, in my flesh) nothing good

dwells; for to will is present with me, but *how* to perform what is good I do not find. [19]For the good that I will *to do,* I do not do; but the evil I will not *to do,* that I practice. [20]Now if I do what I will not *to do,* it is no longer I who do it, but sin that dwells in me.

[21]I find then a law, that evil is present with me, the one who wills to do good. [22]For I delight in the law of God according to the inward man. [23]But I see another law in my members, warring against the law of my mind, and bringing me into captivity to the law of sin which is in my members. [24]O wretched man that I am! Who will deliver me from this body of death? [25]I thank God—through Jesus Christ our Lord!

On the Edge

For as many as are led by the Spirit of God, these are sons of God (Rom. 8:14).

When you put your faith in God's Son, His Spirit became part of your life. God knew that you would need His Spirit to help you live the way He wants you to live. People who haven't trusted Jesus don't have God's Spirit. They have no choice but to live life to please themselves or to get on the good side of other people. But you don't have to live that way. You can let God's Spirit choose the road you're going to take. Living that way pleases God. And it has a fringe benefit for you, too. "To be carnally minded is death, but to be spiritually minded is life and peace" (8:6).

In order for your mind to be ruled by His Spirit, you've got to stay tight with God. Spend time in prayer, in worship, and in His Word. Really work these things into your life—so much that they become a part of you. Then you'll know when the Spirit is leading you, and you'll be able to follow.

SEE FOR YOURSELF:
   Is. 63:11-14;
   Rom. 8:14-17;
2 Cor. 2:14; Gal. 5:16

7:7 [a]Exodus 20:17; Deuteronomy 5:21

So then, with the mind I myself serve the law of God, but with the flesh the law of sin.

FREE FROM INDWELLING SIN

[1]*There is* therefore now no condemnation to those who are in Christ Jesus,[a] who do not walk according to the flesh, but according to the Spirit. [2]For the law of the Spirit of life in Christ Jesus has made me free from the law of sin and death. [3]For what the law could not do in that it was weak through the flesh, God *did* by sending His own Son in the likeness of sinful flesh, on account of sin: He condemned sin in the flesh, [4]that the righteous requirement of the law might be fulfilled in us who do not walk according to the flesh but according to the Spirit. [5]For those who live according to the flesh set their minds on the things of the flesh, but those *who live* according to the Spirit, the things of the Spirit. [6]For to be carnally minded *is* death, but to be spiritually minded *is* life and peace. [7]Because the carnal mind *is* enmity against God; for it is not subject to the law of God, nor indeed can be. [8]So then, those who are in the flesh cannot please God.

[9]But you are not in the flesh but in the Spirit, if indeed the Spirit of God dwells in you. Now if anyone does not have the Spirit of Christ, he is not His. [10]And if Christ *is* in you, the body *is* dead because of sin, but the Spirit *is* life because of righteousness. [11]But if the Spirit of Him who raised Jesus from the dead dwells in you, He who raised Christ from the dead will also give life to your mortal bodies through His Spirit who dwells in you.

SONSHIP THROUGH THE SPIRIT

[12]Therefore, brethren, we are debtors—not to the flesh, to live according to the flesh. [13]For if you live according to the flesh you will die; but if by the Spirit you put to death the deeds of the body, you will live. [14]For as many as are led by the Spirit of God, these are sons of God. [15]For you did not receive the spirit of bondage again to fear, but you received the Spirit of adoption by whom we cry out, "Abba, Father." [16]The Spirit Himself bears witness with our spirit that we are children of God, [17]and if children, then heirs—heirs of God and joint heirs with Christ, if indeed we suffer with *Him,* that we may also be glorified together.

FROM SUFFERING TO GLORY

[18]For I consider that the sufferings of this present time are not worthy *to be compared* with

---

On the Edge

He who did not spare His own Son, but delivered Him up for us all, how shall He not with Him also freely give us all things? (Rom. 8:32).

God is a giver. That's true. A lot of people are under the impression that God is a taker—always wanting something from them—but this is not true. Check out John 10:10, "The thief does not come except to steal, and to kill, and to destroy. I have come that they may have life, and that they may have it more abundantly." God wants you blessed with abundance. Satan is the thief who comes to steal everything you've got.

Not only does God want to meet all of your needs; He also wants to give you the desires of your heart. Psalm 37:4 states, "Delight yourself also in the LORD, and He shall give you the desires of your heart." Does that mean that you can dream up some horrible thing and make it your heart's desire and expect God to let you have it? No! It means that God will put desires in your heart. When you're going after Him with everything you've got, He'll begin to put His desires in your heart. As you begin to understand how good and how right His desires for you are, they'll become your desires, too. It may be your desire to be a lawyer, play pro baseball, go to college, have a car, or simply get a good grade on a test. Do what the Lord wants, and He will give you your heart's desires.

Let the Lord help you identify His desires for you. Let Him help you figure out how your current desires fit into His plan. Let Him know what your desires are, and don't be afraid to ask. He's ready, willing, and able to give you what you need. Just ask Him today.

SEE FOR YOURSELF:
Ps. 2:8; John 14:14

---

the glory which shall be revealed in us. [19]For the earnest expectation of the creation eagerly waits for the revealing of the sons of God. [20]For the creation was subjected to futility, not willingly, but because of Him who subjected *it* in hope; [21]because the creation itself also will be delivered from the bondage of corruption into

---

8:1 [a]NU-Text omits the rest of this verse.

On the Edge

Who shall separate us from the love of Christ? Shall tribulation, or distress, or persecution, or famine, or nakedness, or peril, or sword? As it is written: "For Your sake we are killed all day long; we are accounted as sheep for the slaughter." Yet in all these things we are more than conquerors through Him who loved us. For I am persuaded that neither death nor life, nor angels nor principalities nor powers, nor things present nor things to come, nor height nor depth, nor any other created thing, shall be able to separate us from the love of God which is in Christ Jesus our Lord (Rom. 8:35–39).

Feelings and truth rarely have very much in common. No matter how you feel, the truth is that you are completely loved by God and that nothing can ever separate you from His love. We sometimes compare God's love to the love we know here on earth. The love we know here can be conditional, based on your performance as a friend, a student, or even a child. But God's love has no conditions and nothing you could ever do can remove His constant devotion to you. There is nothing you can do to make God stop loving you. You can't run away from His love. You can't hide from His love. You can only decide to accept or reject it. You are loved perfectly and completely by the Creator of everything. You have His Word on that.

SEE FOR YOURSELF:
Ps. 91:14; 136:1;
139:13, 14; Zeph. 3:17;
Eph. 3:14–19

26Likewise the Spirit also helps in our weaknesses. For we do not know what we should pray for as we ought, but the Spirit Himself makes intercession for us[a] with groanings which cannot be uttered. 27Now He who searches the hearts knows what the mind of the Spirit *is*, because He makes intercession for the saints according to *the will of* God.

28And we know that all things work together for good to those who love God, to those who are the called according to *His* purpose. 29For whom He foreknew, He also predestined *to be* conformed to the image of His Son, that He might be the firstborn among many brethren. 30Moreover whom He predestined, these He also called; whom He called, these He also justified; and whom He justified, these He also glorified.

TRIALS
Does God know what He is doing with our lives? (8:28)

WHAT'S IT MEAN?

If there was one thing the Jewish people knew about, it was sheep. From their earliest days, the Israelites were known as a nation of wandering herdsmen. Throughout the Bible, people are compared to sheep, though usually not in a good way. You see, sheep are pretty helpless creatures. That's why Jesus is often described as the Good Shepherd who protects His flocks from danger.

Romans 8:36

GOD'S EVERLASTING LOVE

31What then shall we say to these things? If God *is* for us, who *can be* against us? 32He who did not spare His own Son, but delivered Him up for us all, how shall He not with Him also freely give us all things? 33Who shall bring a charge against God's elect? *It is* God who justifies. 34Who *is* he who condemns? *It is* Christ who died, and furthermore is also risen, who is even at the right hand of God, who also makes intercession for us. 35Who shall separate us from the love of Christ? *Shall* tribulation, or distress, or persecution, or famine, or nakedness, or peril, or sword? 36As it is written:

the glorious liberty of the children of God. 22For we know that the whole creation groans and labors with birth pangs together until now. 23Not only *that*, but we also who have the firstfruits of the Spirit, even we ourselves groan within ourselves, eagerly waiting for the adoption, the redemption of our body. 24For we were saved in this hope, but hope that is seen is not hope; for why does one still hope for what he sees? 25But if we hope for what we do not see, we eagerly wait for *it* with perseverance.

8:26 [a]NU-Text omits *for us.*

On the Edge

Yet in all these things we are more than conquerors through Him who loved us (Rom. 8:37).

Your team just won the state championship. What a season! You worked hard and it really paid off. The whole city is celebrating. It's so exciting. The great feeling seems like it'll carry you forever. Every time you think about that win you grin from ear to ear. Your team is the best! That feeling does carry you for a while, maybe for the rest of the year, and even on into the next season. But eventually, someone else wins. Your glory fades a little. Every year the light grows a little dimmer. Your trophy gets pushed aside by newer things. Your sweet victory becomes a sweet memory. It doesn't sustain you anymore. It doesn't inspire you to push harder. Now you used to be a winner.

Who says winning is everything? Paul says there's more. He says that being loved by Christ makes you more than a winner. Believers get to share in the victory for eternity. In Christ, victory lasts forever. The celebration never ends. His glory never grows dim. Because of Him, you'll be more than a conqueror, always victorious, with a prize that lasts forever.

SEE FOR YOURSELF:
1 Cor. 15:57;
2 Cor. 2:14

"For Your sake we are killed all day long; We are accounted as sheep for the slaughter."ᵃ

³⁷Yet in all these things we are more than conquerors through Him who loved us. ³⁸For I am persuaded that neither death nor life, nor angels nor principalities nor powers, nor things present nor things to come, ³⁹nor height nor depth, nor any other created thing, shall be able to separate us from the love of God which is in Christ Jesus our Lord.

ISRAEL'S REJECTION OF CHRIST

¹I tell the truth in Christ, I am not lying, my conscience also bearing me witness in the Holy Spirit, ²that I have great sorrow and continual grief in my heart. ³For I could wish that I myself were accursed from Christ for my brethren, my countrymenᵃ according to the flesh, ⁴who are Israelites, to whom *pertain* the adoption, the glory, the covenants, the giving of the law, the service *of God*, and the promises; ⁵of whom *are* the fathers and from whom, according to the flesh, Christ *came*, who is over all, *the* eternally blessed God. Amen.

ISRAEL'S REJECTION AND GOD'S PURPOSE

⁶But it is not that the word of God has taken no effect. For they *are* not all Israel who *are* of Israel, ⁷nor *are they* all children because they are the seed of Abraham; but, *"In Isaac your seed shall be called."ᵃ* ⁸That is, those who *are* the children of the flesh, these *are* not the children of God; but the children of the promise are counted as the seed. ⁹For this *is* the word of promise: *"At this time I will come and Sarah shall have a son."ᵃ*

¹⁰And not only *this*, but when Rebecca also had conceived by one man, *even* by our father Isaac ¹¹(for *the children* not yet being born, nor having done any good or evil, that the purpose of God according to election might stand, not of works but of Him who calls), ¹²it was said to her, *"The older shall serve the younger."ᵃ* ¹³As it is written, *"Jacob I have loved, but Esau I have hated."ᵃ*

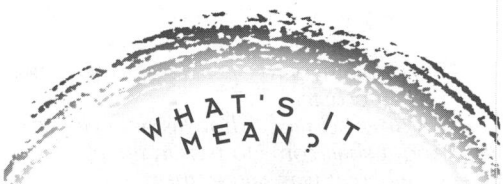

WHAT'S IT MEAN?

In ancient times, the oldest male child in a family received a larger inheritance than the other children. Jacob was a famous exception to that rule. Jacob and his brother Esau were twins, but Esau was born first. God, however, chose to bless Jacob, whom He called Israel. (Sound familiar?) The twelve tribes of Israel were descendants of Jacob's twelve sons.

Romans 9:10–13

ISRAEL'S REJECTION AND GOD'S JUSTICE

¹⁴What shall we say then? *Is there* unrighteousness with God? Certainly not! ¹⁵For He says to Moses, *"I will have mercy on whomever*

I will have mercy, and I will have compassion on whomever I will have compassion."[a] [16]So then *it is* not of him who wills, nor of him who runs, but of God who shows mercy. [17]For the Scripture says to the Pharaoh, *"For this very purpose I have raised you up, that I may show My power in you, and that My name may be declared in all the earth."*[a] [18]Therefore He has mercy on whom He wills, and whom He wills He hardens.

[19]You will say to me then, "Why does He still find fault? For who has resisted His will?" [20]But indeed, O man, who are you to reply against God? Will the thing formed say to him who formed *it,* "Why have you made me like this?" [21]Does not the potter have power over the clay, from the same lump to make one vessel for honor and another for dishonor?

[22]*What* if God, wanting to show *His* wrath and to make His power known, endured with much longsuffering the vessels of wrath prepared for destruction, [23]and that He might make known the riches of His glory on the vessels of mercy, which He had prepared beforehand for glory, [24]*even* us whom He called, not of the Jews only, but also of the Gentiles?

[25]As He says also in Hosea:

> "I will call them My people, who were not My people,
> And her beloved, who was not beloved."[a]
> [26] "And it shall come to pass in the place where it was said to them,
> 'You are not My people,'
> There they shall be called sons of the living God."[a]

[27]Isaiah also cries out concerning Israel:[a]

> "Though the number of the children of Israel be as the sand of the sea,
> The remnant will be saved.
> [28] For He will finish the work and cut it short in righteousness,
> Because the LORD will make a short work upon the earth."[a]

[29]And as Isaiah said before:

> "Unless the LORD of Sabaoth[a] had left us a seed,
> We would have become like Sodom,
> And we would have been made like Gomorrah."[b]

PRESENT CONDITION OF ISRAEL

[30]What shall we say then? That Gentiles, who did not pursue righteousness, have attained to righteousness, even the righteousness of faith; [31]but Israel, pursuing the law of righteousness, has not attained to the law of righteousness.[a] [32]Why? Because *they did* not *seek it* by faith, but as it were, by the works of the law.[a] For they stumbled at that stumbling stone. [33]As it is written:

> "Behold, I lay in Zion a stumbling stone and rock of offense,
> And whoever believes on Him will not be put to shame."[a]

ISRAEL NEEDS THE GOSPEL

[1]Brethren, my heart's desire and prayer to God for Israel[a] is that they may be saved. [2]For I bear them witness that they have a zeal for God, but not according to knowledge. [3]For they being ignorant of God's righteousness, and seeking to establish their own righteousness, have not submitted to the righteousness of God. [4]For Christ *is* the end of the law for righteousness to everyone who believes.

[5]For Moses writes about the righteousness which is of the law, *"The man who does those things shall live by them."*[a] [6]But the righteousness of faith speaks in this way, *"Do not say in your heart, 'Who will ascend into heaven?'"*[a] (that is, to bring Christ down *from above*) [7]or, *"'Who will descend into the abyss?'"*[a] (that is, to bring Christ up from the dead). [8]But what does it say? *"The word is near you, in your mouth and in your heart"*[a] (that is, the word of faith which we preach): [9]that if you confess

"That if you confess with your mouth the Lord Jesus and believe in your heart that God has raised Him from the dead, you will be saved."
(Romans 10:9)

9:15 [a]Exodus 33:19   **9:17** [a]Exodus 9:16   **9:25** [a]Hosea 2:23   **9:26** [a]Hosea 1:10   **9:27** [a]Isaiah 10:22, 23   **9:28** [a]NU-Text reads *For the LORD will finish the work and cut it short upon the earth.*   **9:29** [a]Literally, in Hebrew, Hosts [b]Isaiah 1:9   **9:31** [a]NU-Text omits *of righteousness.*   **9:32** [a]NU-Text reads *by works.*   **9:33** [a]Isaiah 8:14; 28:16   **10:1** [a]NU-Text reads *them.*   **10:5** [a]Leviticus 18:5   **10:6** [a]Deuteronomy 30:12   **10:7** [a]Deuteronomy 30:13   **10:8** [a]Deuteronomy 30:14

with your mouth the Lord Jesus and believe in your heart that God has raised Him from the dead, you will be saved. [10]For with the heart one believes unto righteousness, and with the mouth confession is made unto salvation. [11]For the Scripture says, *"Whoever believes on Him will not be put to shame."*[a] [12]For there is no distinction between Jew and Greek, for the same Lord over all is rich to all who call upon Him. [13]For *"whoever calls on the name of the LORD shall be saved."*[a]

SALVATION

Is our salvation personal?
(10:8–10)

ISRAEL REJECTS THE GOSPEL

[14]How then shall they call on Him in whom they have not believed? And how shall they believe in Him of whom they have not heard? And how shall they hear without a preacher? [15]And how shall they preach unless they are sent? As it is written:

> *"How beautiful are the feet of those who*
> *preach the gospel of peace,*[a]
> *Who bring glad tidings of good things!"*[b]

[16]But they have not all obeyed the gospel. For Isaiah says, *"LORD, who has believed our report?"*[a] [17]So then faith *comes* by hearing, and hearing by the word of God.

[18]But I say, have they not heard? Yes indeed:

> *"Their sound has gone out to all the earth,*
> *And their words to the ends of the*
> *world."*[a]

[19]But I say, did Israel not know? First Moses says:

> *"I will provoke you to jealousy by those*
> *who are not a nation,*
> *I will move you to anger by a foolish*
> *nation."*[a]

[20]But Isaiah is very bold and says:

> *"I was found by those who did not seek*
> *Me;*
> *I was made manifest to those who did*
> *not ask for Me."*[a]

[21]But to Israel he says:

> *"All day long I have stretched out My*
> *hands*
> *To a disobedient and contrary people."*[a]

10:11 [a]Isaiah 28:16 **10:13** [a]Joel 2:32 **10:15** [a]NU-Text omits *preach the gospel of peace, Who.* [b]Isaiah 52:7; Nahum 1:15 **10:16** [a]Isaiah 53:1 **10:18** [a]Psalm 19:4 **10:19** [a]Deuteronomy 32:21 **10:20** [a]Isaiah 65:1 **10:21** [a]Isaiah 65:2

Promise   HE PROMISES THAT ANYONE CAN BE SAVED.

If you confess with your mouth the Lord Jesus and believe in your heart that God has raised Him from the dead, you will be saved. For with the heart one believes unto righteousness, and with the mouth confession is made unto salvation. For the Scripture says "Whoever believes on Him will not be put to shame." For there is no distinction between Jew and Greek, for the same Lord over all is rich to all who call upon Him. For "whoever calls on the name of the LORD shall be saved" (Rom. 10:9–13).

Know any people who think they're too far gone for Jesus? Maybe they think their sins are too big or their lives too ugly. They think God couldn't possibly save them. They think God's probably mad or that He's given up on them by now or that He's too holy to want them around.

Well, this passage is for the hopeless. God delights in saving the unlovable and the lost and the ones who think they could never be saved. To think that God couldn't save you because you're too far gone is to say, "I'm bigger than God. I can do something so evil that He can't forgive me. I have more power than God." The truth is that *everyone* is hopelessly lost without Him and every sin is repulsive to Him. But Jesus died for everybody—no exceptions. Anyone who calls out to Him will be saved.

SEE FOR YOURSELF:
John 3:16–18; Rom. 1:17; Gal. 3:7–9, 26

ISRAEL'S REJECTION NOT TOTAL

[1]I say then, has God cast away His people? Certainly not! For I also am an Israelite, of the seed of Abraham, *of* the tribe of Benjamin. [2]God has not cast away His people whom He foreknew. Or do you not know what the Scripture says of Elijah, how he pleads with God against Israel, saying, [3]*"LORD, they have killed Your prophets and torn down Your altars, and I alone am left, and they seek my life"?*[a] [4]But what does the divine response say to him? *"I have reserved for Myself seven thousand men who have not bowed the knee to Baal."*[a] [5]Even so then, at this present time there is a remnant according to the election of grace. [6]And if by grace, then *it is* no longer of works; otherwise grace is no longer grace.[a] But if *it is* of works, it is no longer grace; otherwise work is no longer work.

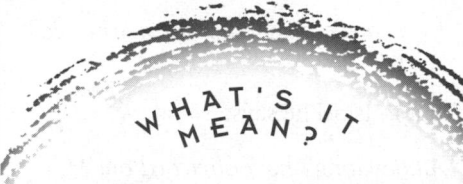

WHAT'S IT MEAN?

In this passage, Paul is referring to an incident in the life of Elijah, the Old Testament prophet. It seems that Ahab, the king of Israel, built a special temple and encouraged the people of his kingdom to worship at it. No problem, right? Wrong. The temple Ahab built was for Baal, a pagan god. Ahab was discouraging the Israelites from worshiping the true God! As prophet, it was Elijah's responsibility to confront the king about his wickedness. When he did, the king's evil wife, Jezebel, threatened to kill the prophet.

Romans 11:2–4

[7]What then? Israel has not obtained what it seeks; but the elect have obtained it, and the rest were blinded. [8]Just as it is written:

> *"God has given them a spirit of stupor,*
> *Eyes that they should not see*
> *And ears that they should not hear,*
> *To this very day."*[a]

[9]And David says:

> *"Let their table become a snare and a trap,*
> *A stumbling block and a recompense to*
> *them.*

[10]*Let their eyes be darkened, so that they*
> *do not see,*
> *And bow down their back always."*[a]

ISRAEL'S REJECTION NOT FINAL

[11]I say then, have they stumbled that they should fall? Certainly not! But through their fall, to provoke them to jealousy, salvation *has come* to the Gentiles. [12]Now if their fall *is* riches for the world, and their failure riches for the Gentiles, how much more their fullness!

[13]For I speak to you Gentiles; inasmuch as I am an apostle to the Gentiles, I magnify my ministry, [14]if by any means I may provoke to jealousy *those who are* my flesh and save some of them. [15]For if their being cast away *is* the reconciling of the world, what *will* their acceptance *be* but life from the dead?

[16]For if the firstfruit *is* holy, the lump *is* also *holy*; and if the root *is* holy, so *are* the branches. [17]And if some of the branches were broken off, and you, being a wild olive tree, were grafted in among them, and with them became a partaker of the root and fatness of the olive tree, [18]do not boast against the branches. But if you do boast, *remember that* you do not support the root, but the root supports you.

[19]You will say then, "Branches were broken off that I might be grafted in." [20]Well *said*. Because of unbelief they were broken off, and you stand by faith. Do not be haughty, but fear. [21]For if God did not spare the natural branches, He may not spare you either. [22]Therefore consider the goodness and severity of God: on those who fell, severity; but toward you, goodness,[a] if you continue in His goodness. Otherwise you also will be cut off. [23]And they also, if they do not continue in unbelief, will be grafted in, for God is able to graft them in again. [24]For if you were cut out of the olive tree which is wild by nature, and were grafted contrary to nature into a cultivated olive tree, how much more will these, who *are* natural *branches*, be grafted into their own olive tree?

[25]For I do not desire, brethren, that you should be ignorant of this mystery, lest you should be wise in your own opinion, that blindness in part has happened to Israel until the fullness of the Gentiles has come in. [26]And so all Israel will be saved,[a] as it is written:

> *"The Deliverer will come out of Zion,*
> *And He will turn away ungodliness from*
> *Jacob;*

27 For this is My covenant with them,
When I take away their sins."[a]

28Concerning the gospel *they are* enemies for your sake, but concerning the election *they are* beloved for the sake of the fathers. 29For the gifts and the calling of God *are* irrevocable. 30For as you were once disobedient to God, yet have now obtained mercy through their disobedience, 31even so these also have now been disobedient, that through the mercy shown you they also may obtain mercy. 32For God has committed them all to disobedience, that He might have mercy on all.

33Oh, the depth of the riches both of the wisdom and knowledge of God! How unsearchable *are* His judgments and His ways past finding out!

34 "For who has known the mind of the
LORD?
Or who has become His counselor?"[a]
35 "Or who has first given to Him
And it shall be repaid to him?"[a]

36For of Him and through Him and to Him *are* all things, to whom *be* glory forever. Amen.

LIVING SACRIFICES TO GOD

1I beseech you therefore, brethren, by the mercies of God, that you present your bodies a living sacrifice, holy, acceptable to God, *which is* your reasonable service. 2And do not be conformed to this world, but be transformed by the renewing of your mind, that you may prove what *is* that good and acceptable and perfect will of God.

MIND

What should a Christian's thoughts be characterized by? (12:2)

SERVE GOD WITH SPIRITUAL GIFTS

3For I say, through the grace given to me, to everyone who is among you, not to think of himself more highly than he ought to think, but to think soberly, as God has dealt to each one a measure of faith. 4For as we have many members in one body, but all the members do not have the same function, 5so we, *being* many, are one body in Christ, and individually members of one another. 6Having then gifts differing according to the grace that is given to us, *let us use them:* if prophecy, *let us prophesy* in proportion to our faith; 7or ministry, *let us use it* in *our* ministering; he who teaches, in teaching; 8he

who exhorts, in exhortation; he who gives, with liberality; he who leads, with diligence; he who shows mercy, with cheerfulness.

BEHAVE LIKE A CHRISTIAN

9Let love *be* without hypocrisy. Abhor what is evil. Cling to what is good. 10*Be* kindly affectionate to one another with brotherly love, in honor giving preference to one another; 11not lagging in diligence, fervent in spirit, serving the Lord; 12rejoicing in hope, patient in tribulation, continuing steadfastly in prayer; 13distributing to the needs of the saints, given to hospitality.

HATRED

What should Christians hate? (12:9)

On the Edge

I beseech you therefore, brethren, by the mercies of God, that you present your bodies a living sacrifice, holy, acceptable to God, which is your reasonable service (Rom. 12:1).

Under the old agreement that God had made with the Jewish people, there were two kinds of sacrifices. One sacrifice was for people's sins; the other sacrifice was an offering of worship. Both sacrifices involved killing an animal, usually a goat or a lamb that didn't have any flaws.

Jesus' death on the cross made a new agreement between God and anyone who has faith in Him. Under that new agreement, Jesus is the once-for-all sacrifice for sin. People don't have to offer lambs or goats to make up for sin. But what do you do about the sacrifice of worship?

Just as *God* chose to make Jesus the sacrifice for sin, *you* choose to make the sacrifice of worship. Instead of offering an animal, you offer your own life to God. You dedicate your life to doing what He wants. That why it's called a *living* sacrifice. Paul says that living a life that's pure and pleasing to God is the best way to serve Him—to worship Him. In other words, living the way God wants you to is your way of saying to Him, "You're awesome and I want everything about me to worship You!"

SEE FOR YOURSELF:
John 12:26; Rom. 1:9;
1 Pet. 2:5

11:27 [a]Isaiah 59:20, 21   **11:34** [a]Isaiah 40:13; Jeremiah 23:18   **11:35** [a]Job 41:11

On the Edge

For as we have many members in one body, but all the members do not have the same function, so we, being many, are one body in Christ, and individually members of one another (Rom. 12:4, 5).

You have a destiny that God has designed for you. He wants you to live in a way that honors Him, to be part of His plan to bring other people to know Him, and eventually to have the same character traits that Jesus has. But part of God's plan is that you wouldn't be able to accomplish any of this by yourself. Of course, you need His Spirit, and He's given you that. But you also need other people.

God wants His people to care about each other and to be able to depend on each other. Your strengths and weaknesses are different from another person's. That person may be able to help you with an area of your life that gives you a lot of trouble. Or you may be able to help someone else see clearly in a situation that is really confusing to him.

Everyone has to trust Jesus as an individual. But once you become a Christian, your life and your relationship with God is connected to other people. You need other Christians! And they need you.

SEE FOR YOURSELF:
Rom. 12:4–8;
1 Cor. 12:12; Col. 1:18

¹⁸If it is possible, as much as depends on you, live peaceably with all men. ¹⁹Beloved, do not avenge yourselves, but *rather* give place to wrath; for it is written, *"Vengeance is Mine, I will repay,"* [a] says the Lord. ²⁰Therefore

> *"If your enemy is hungry, feed him;*
> *If he is thirsty, give him a drink;*
> *For in so doing you will heap coals of fire*
> *on his head."* [a]

²¹Do not be overcome by evil, but overcome evil with good.

SUBMIT TO GOVERNMENT

¹Let every soul be subject to the governing authorities. For there is no authority except from God, and the authorities that exist are appointed by God. ²Therefore whoever resists the authority resists the ordinance of God, and those who resist will bring judgment on themselves. ³For rulers are not a terror to good works, but to evil. Do you want to be unafraid of the authority? Do what is good, and you will have praise from the same. ⁴For he is God's minister to you for good. But if you do evil, be afraid; for he does not bear the sword in vain; for he is God's minister, an avenger to *execute* wrath on him who practices evil. ⁵Therefore *you* must be subject, not only because of wrath but also for conscience' sake. ⁶For because of this you also pay taxes, for they are God's ministers attending continually to this very thing. ⁷Render therefore to all their due: taxes to whom taxes *are due*, customs to whom customs, fear to whom fear, honor to whom honor.

OBEDIENCE

Should Christians obey the government? (13:1–4)

LOVE YOUR NEIGHBOR

⁸Owe no one anything except to love one another, for he who loves another has fulfilled the law. ⁹For the commandments, *"You shall not commit adultery," "You shall not murder," "You shall not steal," "You shall not bear false witness,"* [a] *"You shall not covet,"* [b] and if *there is* any

¹⁴Bless those who persecute you; bless and do not curse. ¹⁵Rejoice with those who rejoice, and weep with those who weep. ¹⁶Be of the same mind toward one another. Do not set your mind on high things, but associate with the humble. Do not be wise in your own opinion.

¹⁷Repay no one evil for evil. Have regard for good things in the sight of all men.

> **"Be kindly affectionate to one another with brotherly love, in honor giving preference to one another; not lagging in diligence, fervent in spirit, serving the Lord." (Romans 12:10, 11)**

12:19 [a]Deuteronomy 32:35   **12:20** [a]Proverbs 25:21, 22   **13:9** [a]NU-Text omits *"You shall not bear false witness."* [b]Exodus 20:13–15, 17; Deuteronomy 5:17–19, 21 lewdness and lust, not in strife and envy. ¹⁴But put on the Lord Jesus Christ, and make no provision for the flesh, to *fulfill its* lusts.

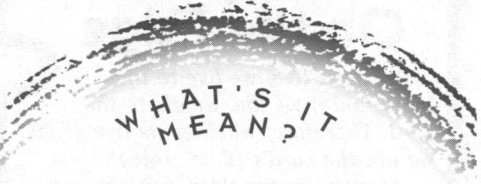

On the Edge

Therefore you must be subject, not only because of wrath but also for conscience' sake. For because of this you also pay taxes, for they are God's ministers attending continually to this very thing. Render therefore to all their due: taxes to whom taxes are due, customs to whom customs, fear to whom fear, honor to whom honor (Rom. 13:5–7).

God is very clear about respecting authority and the rulers who govern us. Even when we disagree with their decisions, we are to obey. God is not surprised by the elections every few years. The laws made by Congress do not upset His plans. He is completely in charge and working through the authority over us to do His will. So, it matters that we drive the speed limit, pay our taxes, and abide by the laws. We obey God when we obey the authority He has allowed to govern us. In the same way, you obey God when you obey the authorities at your school and when you obey your parents. Authority keeps things from going totally out of control. Work with it.

SEE FOR YOURSELF:
Matt. 22:17–21;
Mark 12:14–17;
Luke 20:22–25;
Col. 3:20

WHAT'S IT MEAN?

The Roman government liked to tax its citizens. The Romans taxed everything from property to imported goods to fishing rights. They even collected taxes from the Jews for worshiping at the temple! The Romans claimed that the money was used to pay for the upkeep of the building. Some scholars have estimated that as much as forty percent of the income from an average Jewish household went to taxes.

Romans 13:6

THE LAW OF LIBERTY

¹Receive one who is weak in the faith, *but* not to disputes over doubtful things. ²For one believes he may eat all things, but he who is weak eats *only* vegetables. ³Let not him who eats despise him who does not eat, and let not him who does not eat judge him who eats; for God has received him. ⁴Who are you to judge another's servant? To his own master he stands or falls. Indeed, he will be made to stand, for God is able to make him stand.

⁵One person esteems *one* day above another; another esteems every day *alike.* Let each be fully convinced in his own mind. ⁶He who observes the day, observes *it* to the Lord;ᵃ and he who does not observe the day, to the Lord he does not observe *it.* He who eats, eats to the Lord, for he gives God thanks; and he who does not eat, to the Lord he does not eat, and gives God thanks. ⁷For none of us lives to himself, and no one dies to himself. ⁸For if we live, we live to the Lord; and if we die, we die to the Lord. Therefore, whether we live or die, we are the Lord's. ⁹For to this end Christ died and roseᵃ and lived again, that He might be Lord of both the dead and the living. ¹⁰But why do you judge your brother? Or why do you show contempt for your brother? For we shall all stand before the judgment seat of Christ.ᵃ ¹¹For it is written:

other commandment, are *all* summed up in this saying, namely, *"You shall love your neighbor as yourself."* ᶜ ¹⁰Love does no harm to a neighbor; therefore love *is* the fulfillment of the law.

DRINKING
Is drunkenness appropriate for a Christian? (13:11–14)

PUT ON CHRIST

¹¹And *do* this, knowing the time, that now *it is* high time to awake out of sleep; for now our salvation *is* nearer than when we *first* believed. ¹²The night is far spent, the day is at hand. Therefore let us cast off the works of darkness, and let us put on the armor of light. ¹³Let us walk properly, as in the day, not in revelry and drunkenness, not in

On the Edge

For if we live, we live to the Lord; and if we die, we die to the Lord. Therefore, whether we live or die, we are the Lord's (Rom. 14:8).

As you've gotten older, you've started making choices for yourself rather than letting your parents choose for you. After all, you're an adult now (or almost an adult) and it's your life, not your parents', right?

Well, not exactly. Have you considered the fact that it's not "your life" anymore? It's true that you now have the responsibility of making some decisions that your parents used to make. But since you're a Christian, you belong to the Lord. The decisions you make have to fit in with His plans. You need to be thinking about what He wants, not what you want. Paul says, "So then each of us shall give account of himself to God" (Rom. 14:12). You belong to Him, and He *treasures* you. He values you so much that He went to great lengths to establish a friendship with you. So whatever you do, do it for Him, remembering how much He loves you.

SEE FOR YOURSELF:
Mark 9:41; 1 Cor. 3:23; Gal. 3:26–29

" *As I live, says the* LORD,
Every knee shall bow to Me,
And every tongue shall confess to God." [a]

[12]So then each of us shall give account of himself to God. [13]Therefore let us not judge one another anymore, but rather resolve this, not to put a stumbling block or a cause to fall in *our* brother's way.

THE LAW OF LOVE

[14]I know and am convinced by the Lord Jesus that *there is* nothing unclean of itself; but to him who considers anything to be unclean, to him *it is* unclean. [15]Yet if your brother is grieved because of *your* food, you are no longer walking in love. Do not destroy with your food the one for whom Christ died. [16]Therefore do not let your good be spoken of as evil; [17]for the kingdom of God is not eating and drinking, but righteousness and peace and joy in the Holy Spirit. [18]For he who serves Christ in these things[a] *is* acceptable to God and approved by men.

[19]Therefore let us pursue the things *which make* for peace and the things by which one may edify another. [20]Do not destroy the work of God for the sake of food. All things indeed *are* pure, but *it is* evil for the man who eats with offense. [21]*It is* good neither to eat meat nor drink wine nor *do anything* by which your brother stumbles or is offended or is made weak.[a] [22]Do you have faith?[a] Have *it* to yourself before God. Happy *is* he who does not condemn himself in what he approves. [23]But he who doubts is condemned if he eats, because *he does* not *eat* from faith; for whatever *is* not from faith is sin.[a]

BEARING OTHERS' BURDENS

[1]We then who are strong ought to bear with the scruples of the weak, and not to please ourselves. [2]Let each of us please *his* neighbor for *his* good, leading to edification. [3]For even Christ did not please Himself; but as it is written, *"The reproaches of those who reproached You fell on Me."*[a] [4]For whatever things were written before were written for our learning, that we through the patience and comfort of the Scriptures might have hope. [5]Now may the God of patience and comfort grant you to be likeminded toward one another, according to Christ Jesus, [6]that you may with one mind *and* one mouth glorify the God and Father of our Lord Jesus Christ.

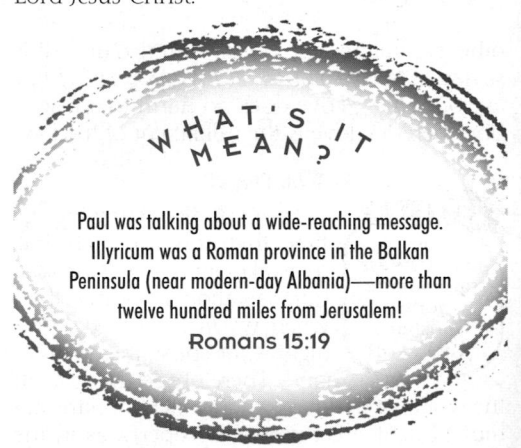

WHAT'S IT MEAN?

Paul was talking about a wide-reaching message. Illyricum was a Roman province in the Balkan Peninsula (near modern-day Albania)—more than twelve hundred miles from Jerusalem!
Romans 15:19

14:11 [a]Isaiah 45:23   **14:18** [a]NU-Text reads *this.*   **14:21** [a]NU-Text omits *or is offended or is made weak.*
14:22 [a]NU-Text reads *The faith which you have—have.*   **14:23** [a]M-Text puts Romans 16:25–27 here.
15:3 [a]Psalm 69:9

GLORIFY GOD TOGETHER

[7]Therefore receive one another, just as Christ also received us,[a] to the glory of God. [8]Now I say that Jesus Christ has become a servant to the circumcision for the truth of God, to confirm the promises *made* to the fathers, [9]and that the Gentiles might glorify God for *His* mercy, as it is written:

> "For this reason I will confess to You
>   among the Gentiles,
>   And sing to Your name."[a]

[10]And again he says:

> "Rejoice, O Gentiles, with His people!"[a]

[11]And again:

> "Praise the LORD, all you Gentiles!
>   Laud Him, all you peoples!"[a]

[12]And again, Isaiah says:

> "There shall be a root of Jesse;
>   And He who shall rise to reign over the
>   Gentiles,
>   In Him the Gentiles shall hope."[a]

[13]Now may the God of hope fill you with all joy and peace in believing, that you may abound in hope by the power of the Holy Spirit.

FROM JERUSALEM TO ILLYRICUM

[14]Now I myself am confident concerning you, my brethren, that you also are full of goodness, filled with all knowledge, able also to admonish one another.[a] [15]Nevertheless, brethren, I have written more boldly to you on *some* points, as reminding you, because of the grace given to me by God, [16]that I might be a minister of Jesus Christ to the Gentiles, ministering the gospel of God, that the offering of the Gentiles might be acceptable, sanctified by the Holy Spirit. [17]Therefore I have reason to glory in Christ Jesus in the things *which pertain* to God. [18]For I will not dare to speak of any of those things which Christ has not accomplished through me, in word and deed, to make the Gentiles obedient—[19]in mighty signs and wonders, by the power of the Spirit of God, so that from Jerusalem and round about to Illyricum I

have fully preached the gospel of Christ. [20]And so I have made it my aim to preach the gospel, not where Christ was named, lest I should build on another man's foundation, [21]but as it is written:

> "To whom He was not announced, they
>   shall see;
> And those who have not heard shall
>   understand."[a]

☼ On the Edge

Now may the God of patience and comfort grant you to be like-minded toward one another, according to Christ Jesus (Rom. 15:5).

Galatians 5:22, 23 lists the fruit or qualities of God's Spirit: love, joy, peace, longsuffering, kindness, goodness, faithfulness, gentleness, self-control. Do you ever look at that list and think, *No way!* Or maybe you think, *Well, three out nine isn't too bad.* Trying to measure up to this list can be kind of intimidating.

But Paul gives you some good news here: "May the God of patience and comfort grant you to be like-minded toward one another." The key to seeing God make things happen in your life is to commit yourself to being open to the changes He wants to make in your heart. Prove your commitment by seriously studying God's Word and putting it into practice. Pray and meditate on Bible verses, especially verses that are relevant to areas you're weak in. God will honor your efforts and make things happen for you.

SEE FOR YOURSELF:
    Gal. 5:22, 23;
    Col. 1:9–12;
    2 Thess. 3:5

PLAN TO VISIT ROME

[22]For this reason I also have been much hindered from coming to you. [23]But now no longer having a place in these parts, and having a great desire these many years to come to you, [24]whenever I journey to Spain, I shall come to you.[a] For I hope to see you on my journey, and to be helped on my way there by you, if first I

15:7 [a]NU-Text and M-Text read *you.*   **15:9** [a]2 Samuel 22:50; Psalm 18:49   **15:10** [a]Deuteronomy 32:43
15:11 [a]Psalm 117:1   **15:12** [a]Isaiah 11:10   **15:14** [a]M-Text reads *others.*   **15:21** [a]Isaiah 52:15   **15:24** [a]NU-Text
omits *I shall come to you* (and joins *Spain* with the next sentence).

may enjoy your *company* for a while. ²⁵But now I am going to Jerusalem to minister to the saints. ²⁶For it pleased those from Macedonia and Achaia to make a certain contribution for the poor among the saints who are in Jerusalem. ²⁷It pleased them indeed, and they are their debtors. For if the Gentiles have been partakers of their spiritual things, their duty is also to minister to them in material things. ²⁸Therefore, when I have performed this and have sealed to them this fruit, I shall go by way of you to Spain. ²⁹But I know that when I come to you, I shall come in the fullness of the blessing of the gospel*ᵃ* of Christ.

³⁰Now I beg you, brethren, through the Lord Jesus Christ, and through the love of the Spirit, that you strive together with me in prayers to God for me, ³¹that I may be delivered from those in Judea who do not believe, and that my service for Jerusalem may be acceptable to the saints, ³²that I may come to you with joy by the will of God, and may be refreshed together with you. ³³Now the God of peace *be* with you all. Amen.

SISTER PHOEBE COMMENDED

¹I commend to you Phoebe our sister, who is a servant of the church in Cenchrea, ²that you may receive her in the Lord in a manner worthy of the saints, and assist her in whatever business she has need of you; for indeed she has been a helper of many and of myself also.

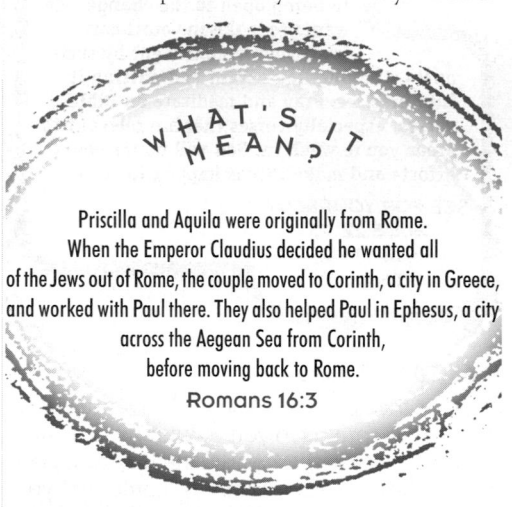

Priscilla and Aquila were originally from Rome. When the Emperor Claudius decided he wanted all of the Jews out of Rome, the couple moved to Corinth, a city in Greece, and worked with Paul there. They also helped Paul in Ephesus, a city across the Aegean Sea from Corinth, before moving back to Rome.
Romans 16:3

GREETING ROMAN SAINTS

³Greet Priscilla and Aquila, my fellow workers in Christ Jesus, ⁴who risked their own necks for my life, to whom not only I give thanks, but also all the churches of the Gentiles. ⁵Likewise *greet* the church that is in their house.

Greet my beloved Epaenetus, who is the firstfruits of Achaia*ᵃ* to Christ. ⁶Greet Mary, who labored much for us. ⁷Greet Andronicus and Junia, my countrymen and my fellow prisoners, who are of note among the apostles, who also were in Christ before me.

Of course you know that Satan is another name for the devil. But did you know that his name means "Accuser" or "Opponent"?
Romans 16:20

⁸Greet Amplias, my beloved in the Lord. ⁹Greet Urbanus, our fellow worker in Christ, and Stachys, my beloved. ¹⁰Greet Apelles, approved in Christ. Greet those who are of the *household* of Aristobulus. ¹¹Greet Herodion, my countryman.*ᵃ* Greet those who are of the *household* of Narcissus who are in the Lord.

¹²Greet Tryphena and Tryphosa, who have labored in the Lord. Greet the beloved Persis, who labored much in the Lord. ¹³Greet Rufus, chosen in the Lord, and his mother and mine. ¹⁴Greet Asyncritus, Phlegon, Hermas, Patrobas, Hermes, and the brethren who are with them. ¹⁵Greet Philologus and Julia, Nereus and his sister, and Olympas, and all the saints who are with them.

¹⁶Greet one another with a holy kiss. The*ᵃ* churches of Christ greet you.

AVOID DIVISIVE PERSONS

¹⁷Now I urge you, brethren, note those who cause divisions and offenses, contrary to the doctrine which you learned, and avoid them. ¹⁸For those who are such do not serve our Lord Jesus*ᵃ* Christ, but their own belly, and by smooth words and flattering speech deceive the hearts of the simple. ¹⁹For your obedience has become known to all. Therefore I am glad on your behalf; but I want you to be wise in what

15:29 *ᵃ*NU-Text omits *of the gospel.*   **16:5** *ᵃ*NU-Text reads *Asia.*   **16:11** *ᵃ*Or *relative*   **16:16** *ᵃ*NU-Text reads *All the churches.*   **16:18** *ᵃ*NU-Text and M-Text omit *Jesus.*

is good, and simple concerning evil. [20]And the God of peace will crush Satan under your feet shortly.

The grace of our Lord Jesus Christ be with you. Amen.

GREETINGS FROM PAUL'S FRIENDS

[21]Timothy, my fellow worker, and Lucius, Jason, and Sosipater, my countrymen, greet you.

[22]I, Tertius, who wrote this epistle, greet you in the Lord.

[23]Gaius, my host and the host of the whole church, greets you. Erastus, the treasurer of the city, greets you, and Quartus, a brother. [24]The grace of our Lord Jesus Christ be with you all. Amen.[a]

"For your obedience has become known to all. Therefore I am glad on your behalf; but I want you to be wise in what is good, and simple concerning evil."
(Romans 16:19)

BENEDICTION

[25]Now to Him who is able to establish you according to my gospel and the preaching of Jesus Christ, according to the revelation of the mystery kept secret since the world began [26]but now made manifest, and by the prophetic Scriptures made known to all nations, according to the commandment of the everlasting God, for obedience to the faith—[27]to God, alone wise, be glory through Jesus Christ forever. Amen.[a]

16:24 [a]NU-Text omits this verse.   **16:27** [a]M-Text puts Romans 16:25–27 after Romans 14:23.

1 Corinthians

CONTENT   Paul helped start the church in Corinth. He loved the people there, and he believed in them. But when he got a letter from one of the church members telling him that everyone was picking on and fighting with each other, he got a little ticked. In fact, when he wrote them the letter that we call First Corinthians, he said he was writing with tears in his eyes. He was disappointed, and he was angry.

But you have to give the Corinthians some credit. They could have read that first letter and ignored Paul's advice. After all, he wasn't even there to check up on them, and who *was* the tattletale anyway?

That's not what they did, though. Instead, they took Paul's words to heart. They changed from nit-picking church members to generous partners in ministry.

Outline   1:1–9 .... Paul's Greeting and Prayer
1:10—4:21 .... A Call for Unity
5:1—7:40 .... Problems in Relationships
8:1—11:1 .... Honoring God Instead of Idols
11:2—14:40 .... Guidance for Worship and Church Life
15:1-58 .... Christ's Victory Over Death
16:1-4 .... An Offering for the Poor
16:5-12 .... Paul's Travel Plans
16:13-24 .... Personal Concerns and Greetings

Purpose   We are to resolve the differences that divide us.

Theme   Resolving Doctrinal and Practical Church Problems and Growth of a Church in Christ

Date of writing   Spring A.D. 56

Bible Talk

Immorality

Corinth was one of the wickedest and wildest cities of its day. Idol worship was everywhere to bizarre extremes. There were actual prostitutes in the temples of the goddess, Venus. If you wanted to do something morally wrong, Corinth was certainly a place that would comply.

Now that you know this, think about what kind of challenges faced the church at Corinth. Somehow they were supposed to stay true to God's commands in a place where no one even pretended to care about God's commands. It's one thing to be tempted in a place where everyone knows sin is wrong. What would it be like to be tempted to sin in a place where no one cared if you did it . . . except God . . . and your friends at church?

IT'S A GIFT!

One of the things that Paul wrote to the Corinthians about was their gifts. He told them that the church is like a body. Everybody has their own job to do. When everyone does their job the body works well. The feet carry it places. The mouth talks on the phone. The hands reach out to give a hug.

Paul tells the Corinthians to find their role and then to be happy in that role instead of wishing they were doing something else.

Paul's words teach us about the church today. We each have a gift to use at church. When we all work together our gifts make us into the body of Christ.

GREETING

[1]Paul, called *to be* an apostle of Jesus Christ through the will of God, and Sosthenes *our* brother,

[2]To the church of God which is at Corinth, to those who are sanctified in Christ Jesus, called *to be* saints, with all who in every place call on the name of Jesus Christ our Lord, both theirs and ours:

[3]Grace to you and peace from God our Father and the Lord Jesus Christ.

WHAT'S IT MEAN?

The word *apostle* means "messenger," but that definition doesn't begin to cover who the apostles of the New Testament were. These were men who had talked with Jesus personally and who had been given—by Him—the responsibility of continuing His ministry of preaching and healing. The original twelve disciples were the first apostles. Others who met with Jesus after He rose from the dead were called apostles as well. Paul's encounter with Jesus, though, was unique. Paul was called to be a messenger when Jesus spoke to him from heaven while Paul was traveling on the road to Damascus.

1 Corinthians 1:1

On the Edge

God is faithful, by whom you were called into the fellowship of His Son, Jesus Christ our Lord (1 Cor. 1:9).

Paul says that God chose you to be Jesus' partner. Being His partner is an honor you don't deserve, but neither does anyone else. But God, because of His kindness and love, chose you for the job even though you aren't qualified for it.

What does it mean to be Jesus' partner? Partners work together toward a common goal. Think about what that goal might be for you and Jesus. Don't just think about your own life—Jesus isn't your genie-in-a-bottle helping you get the things you want. Instead, think about other people. Ask yourself, What does Jesus want to do in my sister's life, my dad's life? What does He want to do for my friends? Ask Jesus those questions, too, and ask Him what you can do to make that happen. He'll answer you.

It's an awesome privilege to be chosen as Jesus' partner, to work with Him to change the lives of people you care about—and maybe even some people you haven't met yet. Make up your mind to be the kind of partner Jesus can be proud of.

SEE FOR YOURSELF:
John 15:4;
Rom. 8:16, 17;
Eph. 2:6; Col. 3:1

SPIRITUAL GIFTS AT CORINTH

[4]I thank my God always concerning you for the grace of God which was given to you by Christ Jesus, [5]that you were enriched in everything by Him in all utterance and all knowledge, [6]even as the testimony of Christ was confirmed in you, [7]so that you come short in no gift, eagerly waiting for the revelation of our Lord Jesus Christ, [8]who will also confirm you to the end, *that you may be* blameless in the day of our Lord Jesus Christ. [9]God *is* faithful, by whom you were called into the fellowship of His Son, Jesus Christ our Lord.

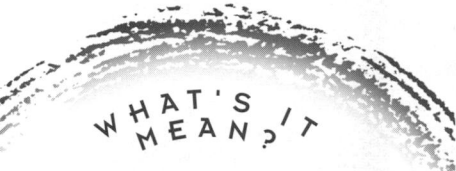

"God is faithful, by whom you were called into the fellowship of His Son, Jesus Christ our Lord." (1 Corinthians 1:9)

SECTARIANISM IS SIN

[10]Now I plead with you, brethren, by the name of our Lord Jesus Christ, that you all speak the same thing, and *that* there be no divisions among you, but *that* you be perfectly joined together in the same mind and in the same judgment. [11]For it has been declared to me concerning you, my brethren, by those of Chloe's *household*, that there are contentions among you. [12]Now I say this, that each of you says, "I am of Paul," or "I am of Apollos," or "I am of Cephas," or "I am of Christ." [13]Is Christ divided? Was Paul crucified for you? Or were you baptized in the name of Paul? [14]I thank God that I baptized none of you except Crispus and Gaius, [15]lest anyone should say that I had baptized in my

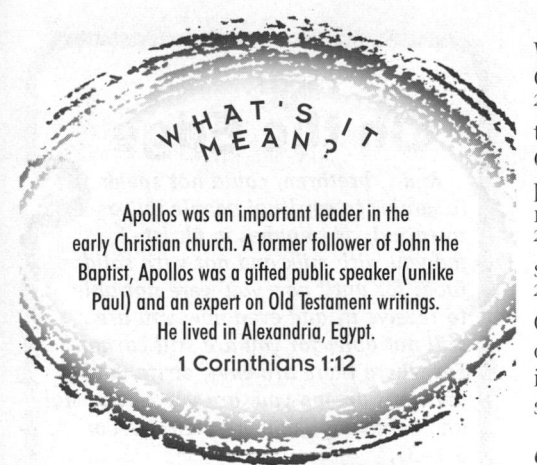

WHAT'S IT MEAN?

Apollos was an important leader in the early Christian church. A former follower of John the Baptist, Apollos was a gifted public speaker (unlike Paul) and an expert on Old Testament writings. He lived in Alexandria, Egypt.

1 Corinthians 1:12

own name. [16]Yes, I also baptized the household of Stephanas. Besides, I do not know whether I baptized any other. [17]For Christ did not send me to baptize, but to preach the gospel, not with wisdom of words, lest the cross of Christ should be made of no effect.

CHRIST THE POWER AND WISDOM OF GOD

[18]For the message of the cross is foolishness to those who are perishing, but to us who are being saved it is the power of God. [19]For it is written:

> "I will destroy the wisdom of the wise,
> And bring to nothing the
>   understanding of the prudent."[a]

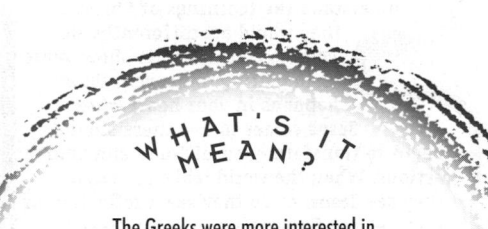

WHAT'S IT MEAN?

The Greeks were more interested in intellectual discussions than in the story of Jesus' death on the cross. Subjects, such as architecture, art, literature, philosophy, politics, and science, were easy for the Greeks to talk about. Something as brutal as a crucifixion would have been a difficult topic for them to understand.

1 Corinthians 1:22

[20]Where *is* the wise? Where *is* the scribe? Where *is* the disputer of this age? Has not God made foolish the wisdom of this world? [21]For since, in the wisdom of God, the world through wisdom did not know God, it pleased God through the foolishness of the message preached to save those who believe. [22]For Jews request a sign, and Greeks seek after wisdom; [23]but we preach Christ crucified, to the Jews a stumbling block and to the Greeks[a] foolishness, [24]but to those who are called, both Jews and Greeks, Christ the power of God and the wisdom of God. [25]Because the foolishness of God is wiser than men, and the weakness of God is stronger than men.

GLORY ONLY IN THE LORD

[26]For you see your calling, brethren, that not many wise according to the flesh, not many mighty, not many noble, *are called*. [27]But God has chosen the foolish things of the world to put to shame the wise, and God has chosen the weak things of the world to put to shame the things which are mighty; [28]and the base things of the world and the things which are despised God has chosen, and the things which are not, to bring to nothing the things that are, [29]that no flesh should glory in His presence. [30]But of Him you are in Christ Jesus, who became for us wisdom from God—and righteousness and sanctification and redemption—[31]that, as it is written, "He who glories, let him glory in the LORD."[a]

CHRIST CRUCIFIED

[1]And I, brethren, when I came to you, did not come with excellence of speech or of wisdom declaring to you the testimony[a] of God. [2]For I determined not to know anything among you except Jesus Christ and Him crucified. [3]I was with you in weakness, in fear, and in much trembling. [4]And my speech and my preaching *were* not with persuasive words of human[a] wisdom, but in demonstration of the Spirit and of power, [5]that your faith should not be in the wisdom of men but in the power of God.

SPIRITUAL WISDOM

[6]However, we speak wisdom among those who are mature, yet not the wisdom of this age, nor of the rulers of this age, who are coming to nothing. [7]But we speak the wisdom of God in a mystery, the hidden

WISDOM

How is God's wisdom different from human wisdom? (2:1–16)

1:19 [a]Isaiah 29:14   1:23 [a]NU-Text reads *Gentiles.*   1:31 [a]Jeremiah 9:24   2:1 [a]NU-Text reads *mystery.*
2:4 [a]NU-Text omits *human.*

wisdom which God ordained before the ages for our glory, [8]which none of the rulers of this age knew; for had they known, they would not have crucified the Lord of glory.

[9]But as it is written:

"*Eye has not seen, nor ear heard,*
   Nor have entered into the heart of man
The things which God has prepared for
   those who love Him."[a]

[10]But God has revealed *them* to us through His Spirit. For the Spirit searches all things, yes, the deep things of God. [11]For what man knows the things of a man except the spirit of the man which is in him? Even so no one knows the things of God except the Spirit of God. [12]Now we have received, not the spirit of the world, but the Spirit who is from God, that we might know the things that have been freely given to us by God.

[13]These things we also speak, not in words which man's wisdom teaches but which the Holy[a] Spirit teaches, comparing spiritual things with spiritual. [14]But the natural man does not receive the things of the Spirit of God, for they are foolishness to him; nor can he know *them*, because they are spiritually discerned. [15]But he who is spiritual judges all things, yet he himself is *rightly* judged by no one. [16]For "*who has known the mind of the LORD that he may instruct Him?*"[a] But we have the mind of Christ.

SECTARIANISM IS CARNAL

[1]And I, brethren, could not speak to you as to spiritual *people* but as to carnal, as to babes in Christ. [2]I fed you with milk and not with solid food; for until now you were not able *to receive it*, and even now you are still not able; [3]for you are still carnal. For where *there are* envy, strife, and divisions among you, are you not carnal and behaving like *mere* men? [4]For when one says, "I am of Paul," and another, "I *am* of Apollos," are you not carnal?

WATERING, WORKING, WARNING

[5]Who then is Paul, and who *is* Apollos, but ministers through whom you believed, as the Lord gave to each one? [6]I planted, Apollos watered, but God gave the increase. [7]So then neither he who plants is anything, nor he who waters, but God who gives the increase. [8]Now he who plants and he who waters are one, and each one will receive his own reward according to his own labor.

WITNESSING
Can Christians make other people's faith grow? (3:5–9)

On the Edge

And I, brethren, could not speak to you as to spiritual people but as to carnal, as to babes in Christ. I fed you with milk and not with solid food; for until now you were not able to receive it, and even now you are still not able; for you are still carnal. For where there are envy, strife, and divisions among you, are you not carnal and behaving like mere men? (1 Cor. 3:1–3).

Little kids fight over a toy because they're little kids. They are babies. Immature. They both think that the world revolves around them. They both think that their pleasure is the most important. Some little kids grow up, become Christians, lay down their toys, and find other things to fight about. The reason is still the same. On the outside they look like adults, but on the inside they're still babies. Still immature. Still believing that their ideas count more and that their pleasure matters most. Paul says in this passage that they are acting like the rest of the world. You can hardly blame the world when they act selfish, because without God, they've only got themselves.

But Christians should know better. Christians who argue and are jealous with each other are babies in their faith. They do not understand the teachings of Christ or they would act differently. Becoming a Christian is about more than getting to heaven. What happens in your heart when Jesus comes to live there should begin to transform your attitude and your actions. When the world looks at you, do they see Jesus, or do they see a reflection of themselves? Growing up in Jesus means looking less like the world and more like Him.

SEE FOR YOURSELF:
   Rom. 12:2;
   Gal. 5:16–18;
   Heb. 5:12, 13

2:9 [a]Isaiah 64:4   **2:13** [a]NU-Text omits *Holy.*   **2:16** [a]Isaiah 40:13

⁹For we are God's fellow workers; you are God's field, *you are* God's building. ¹⁰According to the grace of God which was given to me, as a wise master builder I have laid the foundation, and another builds on it. But let each one take heed how he builds on it. ¹¹For no other foundation can anyone lay than that which is laid, which is Jesus Christ. ¹²Now if anyone builds on this foundation *with* gold, silver, precious stones, wood, hay, straw, ¹³each one's work will become clear; for the Day will declare it, because it will be revealed by fire; and the fire will test each one's work, of what sort it is. ¹⁴If anyone's work which he has built on *it* endures, he will receive a reward. ¹⁵If anyone's work is burned, he will suffer loss; but he himself will be saved, yet so as through fire.

¹⁶Do you not know that you are the temple of God and *that* the Spirit of God dwells in you? ¹⁷If anyone defiles the temple of God, God will destroy him. For the temple of God is holy, which *temple* you are.

AVOID WORLDLY WISDOM

¹⁸Let no one deceive himself. If anyone among you seems to be wise in this age, let him become a fool that he may become wise. ¹⁹For the wisdom of this world is foolishness with God. For it is written, *"He catches the wise in their own craftiness"*;*ᵃ* ²⁰and again, *"The LORD knows the thoughts of the wise, that they are futile."ᵃ* ²¹Therefore let no one boast in men. For all things are yours: ²²whether Paul or Apollos or Cephas, or the world or life or death, or things present or things to come—all are yours. ²³And you *are* Christ's, and Christ *is* God's.

STEWARDS OF THE MYSTERIES OF GOD

¹Let a man so consider us, as servants of Christ and stewards of the mysteries of God. ²Moreover it is required in stewards that one be found faithful. ³But with me it is a very small thing that I should be judged by you or by a human court.*ᵃ* In fact, I do not even judge myself. ⁴For I know of nothing against myself, yet I am not justified by this; but He who judges me is the Lord. ⁵Therefore judge nothing before the time, until the Lord comes, who will both bring to light the hidden things of darkness and reveal the counsels of the hearts. Then each one's praise will come from God.

FOOLS FOR CHRIST'S SAKE

⁶Now these things, brethren, I have figuratively transferred to myself and Apollos for your sakes, that you may learn in us not to think beyond what is written, that none of you may be puffed up on behalf of one against the other. ⁷For who makes you differ *from another?* And what do you have that you did not receive? Now if you did indeed receive *it,* why do you boast as if you had not received *it?*

⁸You are already full! You are already rich! You have reigned as kings without us—and indeed I could wish you did reign, that we also might reign with you! ⁹For I think that God has displayed us, the apostles, last, as men condemned to death; for we have been made a spectacle to the world, both to angels and to men. ¹⁰We *are* fools for Christ's sake, but you *are* wise in Christ! We *are* weak, but you *are* strong! You *are* distinguished, but we *are* dishonored! ¹¹To the present hour we both hunger and thirst, and we are poorly clothed, and beaten, and homeless. ¹²And we labor, working with our own hands. Being reviled, we bless; being persecuted, we endure; ¹³being defamed, we

On the Edge

We are fools for Christ's sake, but you are wise in Christ! We are weak, but you are strong! You are distinguished, but we are dishonored! (1 Cor. 4:10).

Like everybody else, Christians can sometimes act dumb. They come in all shapes and sizes—Bible-thumpers, Scripture-screamers, unforgivers, grace-stealers—the kind of people you wouldn't want to be in a group with because they're ruining it for the rest of us. But there's a whole category of Christians that Paul calls "fools for Christ's sake." The apostles were laughed at and thought of as fools. Their relationship with Christ was so real, but so unusual, that some people laughed at them. Is it possible that some of the "nerds" get ridiculed because they really are trying to live like Jesus—pursuing purity and holiness, giving grace? If that's the case, sign us all up. Let people call you anything as long as God calls you faithful.

SEE FOR YOURSELF:
Job 12:4; Ps. 22:7–10;
Matt. 5:10

3:19 ᵃJob 5:13 **3:20** ᵃPsalm 94:11 **4:3** ᵃLiterally *day*

entreat. We have been made as the filth of the world, the offscouring of all things until now.

PAUL'S PATERNAL CARE

14I do not write these things to shame you, but as my beloved children I warn *you.* 15For though you might have ten thousand instructors in Christ, yet *you do* not *have* many fathers; for in Christ Jesus I have begotten you through the gospel. 16Therefore I urge you, imitate me. 17For this reason I have sent Timothy to you, who is my beloved and faithful son in the Lord, who will remind you of my ways in Christ, as I teach everywhere in every church.

18Now some are puffed up, as though I were not coming to you. 19But I will come to you shortly, if the Lord wills, and I will know, not the word of those who are puffed up, but the power. 20For the kingdom of God *is* not in word but in power. 21What do you want? Shall I come to you with a rod, or in love and a spirit of gentleness?

IMMORALITY DEFILES THE CHURCH

1It is actually reported *that there is* sexual immorality among you, and such sexual immorality as is not even named*a* among the Gentiles—that a man has his father's wife! 2And you are puffed up, and have not rather mourned, that he who has done this deed might be taken away from among you. 3For I indeed, as absent in body but present in spirit, have already judged (as though I were present) him who has so done this deed. 4In the name of our Lord Jesus Christ, when you are gathered together, along with my spirit, with the power of our Lord Jesus Christ, 5deliver such a one to Satan for the destruction of the flesh, that his spirit may be saved in the day of the Lord Jesus.*a*

6Your glorying *is* not good. Do you not know that a little leaven leavens the whole lump? 7Therefore purge out the old leaven, that you may be a new lump, since you truly are unleavened. For indeed Christ, our Passover, was sacrificed for us.*a* 8Therefore let us keep the feast, not with old leaven, nor with the leaven of malice and wickedness, but with the unleavened *bread* of sincerity and truth.

IMMORALITY MUST BE JUDGED

9I wrote to you in my epistle not to keep company with sexually immoral people. 10Yet *I* certainly *did* not *mean* with the sexually immor-

al people of this world, or with the covetous, or extortioners, or idolaters, since then you would need to go out of the world. 11But now I have written to you not to keep company with anyone named a brother, who is sexually immoral, or covetous, or an idolater, or a reviler, or a drunkard, or an extortioner—not even to eat with such a person.

12For what *have* I *to do* with judging those also who are outside? Do you not judge those who are inside? 13But those who are outside God judges. Therefore *"put away from yourselves the evil person."a*

DO NOT SUE THE BRETHREN

1Dare any of you, having a matter against another, go to law before the unrighteous, and not before the saints? 2Do you not know that the saints will judge the world? And if the world will be judged by you, are you unworthy to judge the smallest matters? 3Do you not know that we shall judge angels? How much more, things that pertain to this life? 4If then you have judgments concerning things pertaining to this life, do you appoint those who are least esteemed by the church to judge? 5I say this to your shame. Is it so, that there is not a wise man among you, not even one, who will be able to judge between his brethren? 6But brother goes to law against brother, and that before unbelievers!

7Now therefore, it is already an utter failure for you that you go to law against one another. Why do you not rather accept wrong? Why do you not rather *let yourselves* be cheated? 8No, you yourselves do wrong and cheat, and *you do* these things *to your* brethren! 9Do you not know that the unrighteous will not inherit the kingdom of God? Do not be deceived. Neither fornicators, nor idolaters, nor adulterers, nor homosexuals,*a* nor sodomites, 10nor thieves, nor covetous, nor drunkards, nor revilers, nor extortioners will inherit the kingdom of God. 11And such were some of you. But you were washed, but you were sanctified, but you were justified in the name of the Lord Jesus and by the Spirit of our God.

GLORIFY GOD IN BODY AND SPIRIT

12All things are lawful for me, but all things are not helpful. All things are lawful for me, but I will not be brought under the power of any.

ANGELS

Who will judge the angels? (6:3)

5:1 *a*NU-Text omits *named.*   **5:5** *a*NU-Text omits *Jesus.*   **5:7** *a*NU-Text omits *for us.*   **5:13** *a*Deuteronomy 17:7; 19:19; 22:21, 24; 24:7   **6:9** *a*That is, catamites

¹³Foods for the stomach and the stomach for foods, but God will destroy both it and them. Now the body *is* not for sexual immorality but for the Lord, and the Lord for the body. ¹⁴And God both raised up the Lord and will also raise us up by His power.

SEX

Can sex be casual? (6:13–20)

¹⁵Do you not know that your bodies are members of Christ? Shall I then take the members of Christ and make *them* members of a harlot? Certainly not! ¹⁶Or do you not know that he who is joined to a harlot is one body *with her*? For *"the two,"* He says, *"shall become one flesh."ᵃ* ¹⁷But he who is joined to the Lord is one spirit *with Him.*

On the Edge

Do you not know that your body is the temple of the Holy Spirit who is in you, whom you have from God, and you are not your own? (1 Cor. 6:19).

A temple is a place where God is worshiped. God says that your body is a temple for Him. Think about what you do to your body. If you could see God dwelling inside you, would you treat your body the same? Doing drugs turns the temple into a haunted house. Not only are you tearing down the place God lives, you're making a mockery of His home and His creation. Would you go to an actual temple and mess it all up? No. Neither should you throw trash into your own temple, turn it into a house of prostitution, or cover it with graffiti.

The God who loves you deserves better than a crack house for a temple. He wants to glorify Himself in you. Drugs are stupid and kill. You already know that. But did you know that Satan uses drugs to destroy as many temples as possible? Don't do drugs. Practice self-control and keep your temple pure and holy and healthy. Ask God to dwell richly in you and commit to being a good temple for Him.

SEE FOR YOURSELF:
Rom. 6:12; 1 Cor. 3:16; 2 Cor. 6:16

---

¹⁸Flee sexual immorality. Every sin that a man does is outside the body, but he who commits sexual immorality sins against his own body. ¹⁹Or do you not know that your body is the temple of the Holy Spirit *who is* in you, whom you have from God, and you are not your own? ²⁰For you were bought at a price; therefore glorify God in your bodyᵃ and in your spirit, which are God's.

PRINCIPLES OF MARRIAGE

¹Now concerning the things of which you wrote to me:

It is good for a man not to touch a woman. ²Nevertheless, because of sexual immorality, let each man have his own wife, and let each woman have her own husband. ³Let the husband render to his wife the affection due her, and likewise also the wife to her husband. ⁴The wife does not have authority over her own body, but the husband *does.* And likewise the husband does not have authority over his own body, but the wife *does.* ⁵Do not deprive one another except with consent for a time, that you may give yourselves to fasting and prayer; and come together again so that Satan does not tempt you because of your lack of self-control. ⁶But I say this as a concession, not as a commandment. ⁷For I wish that all men were even as I myself. But each one has his own gift from God, one in this manner and another in that.

⁸But I say to the unmarried and to the widows: It is good for them if they remain even as I am; ⁹but if they cannot exercise self-control, let them marry. For it is better to marry than to burn *with passion.*

KEEP YOUR MARRIAGE VOWS

¹⁰Now to the married I command, *yet* not I but the Lord: A wife is not to depart from *her* husband. ¹¹But even if she does depart, let her remain unmarried or be reconciled to *her* husband. And a husband is not to divorce *his* wife.

¹²But to the rest I, not the Lord, say: If any brother has a wife who does not believe, and she is willing to live with him, let him not divorce her. ¹³And a woman who has a husband who does not believe, if he is willing to live with her, let her not divorce him. ¹⁴For the unbelieving husband is sanctified by the wife, and the unbelieving wife is sanctified by the husband; otherwise your children would be unclean, but now they are holy. ¹⁵But if the unbeliever departs, let him depart; a brother or a sister is

---

6:16 ᵃGenesis 2:24 **6:20** ᵃNU-Text ends the verse at *body.*

not under bondage in such *cases.* But God has called us to peace. [16]For how do you know, O wife, whether you will save *your* husband? Or how do you know, O husband, whether you will save *your* wife?

LIVE AS YOU ARE CALLED

[17]But as God has distributed to each one, as the Lord has called each one, so let him walk. And so I ordain in all the churches. [18]Was anyone called while circumcised? Let him not become uncircumcised. Was anyone called while uncircumcised? Let him not be circumcised. [19]Circumcision is nothing and uncircumcision is nothing, but keeping the commandments of God *is what matters.* [20]Let each one remain in the same calling in which he was called. [21]Were you called *while* a slave? Do not be concerned about it; but if you can be made free, rather use *it.* [22]For he who is called in the Lord *while* a slave is the Lord's freedman. Likewise he who is called *while* free is Christ's slave. [23]You were bought at a price; do not become slaves of men. [24]Brethren, let each one remain with God in that *state* in which he was called.

"You were bought at a price; do not become slaves of men."
(1 Corinthians 7:23)

WHAT'S IT MEAN?

First-century Rome was a dangerous place for Christians. In fact, people throughout the entire Roman Empire were turning against Christians. The emperor Claudius kicked all Jews and Christians out of the city of Rome. Other believers were tortured and killed for their faith in the Lord. Paul knew firsthand about the persecution of Christians. Before he was called to be an apostle of Jesus, Paul himself was a notorious Christian hunter.

1 Corinthians 7:26

TO THE UNMARRIED AND WIDOWS

[25]Now concerning virgins: I have no commandment from the Lord; yet I give judgment as one whom the Lord in His mercy *has made* trustworthy. [26]I suppose therefore that this is good because of the present distress—that *it is* good for a man to remain as he is: [27]Are you bound to a wife? Do not seek to be loosed. Are you loosed from a wife? Do not seek a wife. [28]But even if you do marry, you have not sinned; and if a virgin marries, she has not sinned. Nevertheless such will have trouble in the flesh, but I would spare you.

[29]But this I say, brethren, the time *is* short, so that from now on even those who have wives should be as though they had none, [30]those who weep as though they did not weep, those who rejoice as though they did not rejoice, those who buy as though they did not possess, [31]and those who use this world as not misusing *it.* For the form of this world is passing away.

[32]But I want you to be without care. He who is unmarried cares for the things of the Lord—how he may please the Lord. [33]But he who is married cares about the things of the world—how he may please *his* wife. [34]There is[a] a difference between a wife and a virgin. The unmarried woman cares about the things of the Lord, that she may be holy both in body and in spirit. But she who is married cares about the things of the world—how she may please *her* husband. [35]And this I say for your own profit, not that I may put a leash on you, but for what is proper, and that you may serve the Lord without distraction.

[36]But if any man thinks he is behaving improperly toward his virgin, if she is past the flower of youth, and thus it must be, let him do what he wishes. He does not sin; let them marry. [37]Nevertheless he who stands steadfast in his heart, having no necessity, but has power over his own will, and has so determined in his heart that he will keep his virgin,[a] does well. [38]So then he who gives *her*[a] in marriage does well, but he who does not give *her* in marriage does better.

[39]A wife is bound by law as long as her husband lives; but if her husband dies, she is at liberty to be married to whom she wishes, only in the Lord. [40]But she is happier if she remains as she is, according to my judgment—and I think I also have the Spirit of God.

7:34 [a]M-Text adds *also.*   **7:37** [a]Or *virgin daughter*   **7:38** [a]NU-Text reads *his own virgin.*

BE SENSITIVE TO CONSCIENCE

¹Now concerning things offered to idols: We know that we all have knowledge. Knowledge puffs up, but love edifies. ²And if anyone thinks that he knows anything, he knows nothing yet as he ought to know. ³But if anyone loves God, this one is known by Him.

⁴Therefore concerning the eating of things offered to idols, we know that an idol *is* nothing in the world, and that *there is* no other God but one. ⁵For even if there are so-called gods, whether in heaven or on earth (as there are many gods and many lords), ⁶yet for us *there is* one God, the Father, of whom *are* all things, and we for Him; and one Lord Jesus Christ, through whom *are* all things, and through whom we live.

⁷However, *there is* not in everyone that knowledge; for some, with consciousness of the idol, until now eat *it* as a thing offered to an idol; and their conscience, being weak, is defiled. ⁸But food does not commend us to God; for neither if we eat are we the better, nor if we do not eat are we the worse.

⁹But beware lest somehow this liberty of yours become a stumbling block to those who are weak. ¹⁰For if anyone sees you who have knowledge eating in an idol's temple, will not the conscience of him who is weak be emboldened to eat those things offered to idols? ¹¹And because of your knowledge shall the weak brother perish, for whom Christ died? ¹²But when you thus sin against the brethren, and wound their weak conscience, you sin against Christ. ¹³Therefore, if food makes my brother stumble, I will never again eat meat, lest I make my brother stumble.

A PATTERN OF SELF-DENIAL

¹Am I not an apostle? Am I not free? Have I not seen Jesus Christ our Lord? Are you not my work in the Lord? ²If I am not an apostle to others, yet doubtless I am to you. For you are the seal of my apostleship in the Lord.

³My defense to those who examine me is this: ⁴Do we have no right to eat and drink? ⁵Do we have no right to take along a believing wife, as *do* also the other apostles, the brothers of the Lord, and Cephas? ⁶Or *is it* only Barnabas and I *who* have no right to refrain from working? ⁷Who ever goes to war at his own expense? Who plants a vineyard and does not eat of its fruit? Or who tends a flock and does not drink of the milk of the flock?

⁸Do I say these things as a *mere* man? Or does not the law say the same also? ⁹For it is written in the law of Moses, *"You shall not muzzle an ox while it treads out the grain."*ᵃ Is it oxen God is concerned about? ¹⁰Or does He say *it* altogether for our sakes? For our sakes, no

---

On the Edge

Do you not know that those who run in a race all run, but one receives the prize? Run in such a way that you may obtain it. And everyone who competes for the prize is temperate in all things. Now they do it to obtain a perishable crown, but we for an imperishable crown. Therefore I run thus: not with uncertainty. Thus I fight: not as one who beats the air. But I discipline my body and bring it into subjection, lest, when I have preached to others, I myself should become disqualified (1 Cor. 9:24–27).

In this passage Paul compares life to a race. The goal for believers is to run the whole race and finish well. If life is a race, it is a marathon, not a sprint. An athlete prepares his body for the long distance because he knows it will be grueling at times. The believer has to be prepared as well. You can't wait until you are older to get serious about God for several reasons.

First, you don't know how long your race is. You may already be nearing the end. Second, the blessing is in the race, not back at the concession stand—God gets blessings from a life that honors Him, and He blesses you for a job well done. And third, the race began the minute you arrived. You can jump in now, pace yourself, and finish well, or you can blow it off, hoping your little sprint at the end will count for something. If you choose to wait until later, you can be assured that you will deeply regret all the days you sat and watched everyone else pass you by. God's got a lot for you right now. Don't live another minute without getting serious about Him.

SEE FOR YOURSELF:
Luke 12:35, 36;
Acts 22:16;
Heb. 10:37

9:9 ᵃDeuteronomy 25:4

doubt, *this* is written, that he who plows should plow in hope, and he who threshes in hope should be partaker of his hope. ¹¹If we have sown spiritual things for you, *is it* a great thing if we reap your material things? ¹²If others are partakers of *this* right over you, *are* we not even more?

Nevertheless we have not used this right, but endure all things lest we hinder the gospel of Christ. ¹³Do you not know that those who minister the holy things eat *of the things* of the temple, and those who serve at the altar partake of *the offerings of* the altar? ¹⁴Even so the Lord has commanded that those who preach the gospel should live from the gospel.

¹⁵But I have used none of these things, nor have I written these things that it should be done so to me; for it *would be* better for me to die than that anyone should make my boasting void. ¹⁶For if I preach the gospel, I have nothing to boast of, for necessity is laid upon me; yes, woe is me if I do not preach the gospel! ¹⁷For if I do this willingly, I have a reward; but if against my will, I have been entrusted with a stewardship. ¹⁸What is my reward then? That when I preach the gospel, I may present the gospel of Christ*ᵃ* without charge, that I may not abuse my authority in the gospel.

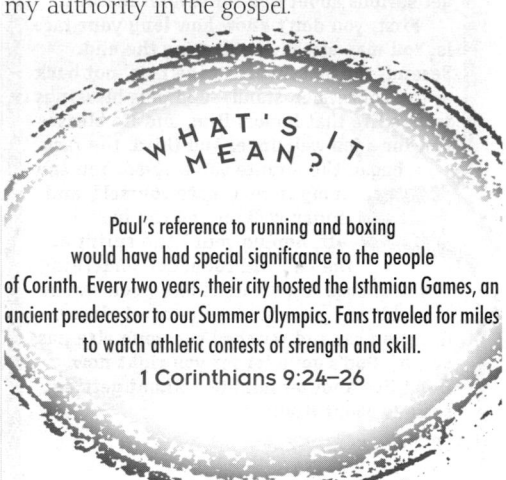

WHAT'S IT MEAN?

Paul's reference to running and boxing would have had special significance to the people of Corinth. Every two years, their city hosted the Isthmian Games, an ancient predecessor to our Summer Olympics. Fans traveled for miles to watch athletic contests of strength and skill.

1 Corinthians 9:24–26

SERVING ALL MEN

¹⁹For though I am free from all *men*, I have made myself a servant to all, that I might win the more; ²⁰and to the Jews I became as a Jew, that I might win Jews; to those *who are* under the law, as under the law,*ᵃ* that I might win those *who are* under the law; ²¹to those *who are* without law, as without law (not being without law toward God,*ᵃ* but under law toward Christ*ᵇ*), that I might win those *who are* without law; ²²to the weak I became as*ᵃ* weak, that I might win the weak. I have become all things to all *men*, that I might by all means save some. ²³Now this I do for the gospel's sake, that I may be partaker of it with *you*.

WHAT'S IT MEAN?

The Israelites didn't pack a chuckwagon when they left Egypt. They weren't carrying a lot of food with them. That didn't matter. God had meals prepared for them. He hand-delivered a special food called manna for them to eat. When the people got thirsty in the desert, God made water flow from rocks.

1 Corinthians 10:3, 4

STRIVING FOR A CROWN

²⁴Do you not know that those who run in a race all run, but one receives the prize? Run in such a way that you may obtain *it*. ²⁵And everyone who competes *for the prize* is temperate in all things. Now they *do it* to obtain a perishable crown, but we *for* an imperishable *crown*. ²⁶Therefore I run thus: not with uncertainty. Thus I fight: not as *one who* beats the air. ²⁷But I discipline my body and bring *it* into subjection, lest, when I have preached to others, I myself should become disqualified.

OLD TESTAMENT EXAMPLES

¹Moreover, brethren, I do not want you to be unaware that all our fathers were under the cloud, all passed through the sea, ²all were baptized into Moses in the cloud and in the sea, ³all ate the same spiritual food, ⁴and all drank the same spiritual drink. For they drank of that spiritual Rock that followed them, and that Rock was Christ. ⁵But with most of them God was not well pleased, for *their bodies* were scattered in the wilderness.

⁶Now these things became our examples, to the intent that we should not lust after evil

9:18 *ᵃ*NU-Text omits *of Christ.*   **9:20** *ᵃ*NU-Text adds *though not being myself under the law.*   **9:21** *ᵃ*NU-Text reads *God's law.* *ᵇ*NU-Text reads *Christ's law.*   **9:22** *ᵃ*NU-Text omits *as.*

things as they also lusted. [7]And do not become idolaters as *were* some of them. As it is written, *"The people sat down to eat and drink, and rose up to play."*[a] [8]Nor let us commit sexual immorality, as some of them did, and in one day twenty-three thousand fell; [9]nor let us tempt Christ, as some of them also tempted, and were destroyed by serpents; [10]nor complain, as some of them also complained, and were destroyed by the destroyer. [11]Now all[a] these things happened to them as examples, and they were written for our admonition, upon whom the ends of the ages have come.

[12]Therefore let him who thinks he stands take heed lest he fall. [13]No temptation has overtaken you except such as is common to man; but God *is* faithful, who will not allow you to be tempted beyond what you are able, but with the temptation will also make the way of escape, that you may be able to bear *it*.

FLEE FROM IDOLATRY

[14]Therefore, my beloved, flee from idolatry. [15]I speak as to wise men; judge for yourselves what I say. [16]The cup of blessing which we bless, is it not the communion of the blood of Christ? The bread which we break, is it not the communion of the body of Christ? [17]For we, *though* many, are one bread *and* one body; for we all partake of that one bread.

[18]Observe Israel after the flesh: Are not those who eat of the sacrifices partakers of the altar?

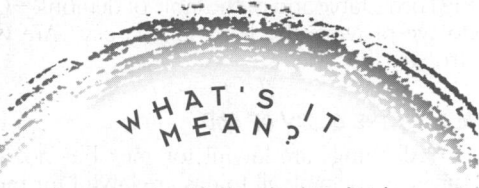

WHAT'S IT MEAN?

Not only was Jesus' final meal with His disciples His "last supper" on earth, it was also a ceremony He wanted His followers to repeat on a regular basis. This ceremony, called the Lord's Supper or Communion, involves eating a piece of bread and drinking wine or grape juice. The bread symbolizes Jesus' body, and the wine or juice symbolizes His blood. Jesus wanted His followers to remember His death on the cross—His sacrifice for them.

1 Corinthians 10:16

[19]What am I saying then? That an idol is anything, or what is offered to idols is anything?

10:7 [a]Exodus 32:6   **10:11** [a]NU-Text omits *all*.

Promise   HE PROMISES NOT TO LET YOU BE TEMPTED MORE THAN YOU CAN HANDLE.

Therefore let him who thinks he stands take heed lest he fall. No temptation has overtaken you except such as is common to man; but God is faithful, who will not allow you to be tempted beyond what you are able, but with the temptation will also make the way of escape, that you may be able to bear it (1 Cor. 10:12, 13).

Before there's heavy breathing and a backseat, there's a door. A way out. Before there's a friend's test paper to cheat off of, there's a window to study by.

Temptations can sometimes get too hot for you to handle on your own, but only because you've passed up a long line of escape hatches along the way—places where God was warning you to turn back, to trust Him, to bail out with His parachute of protection.

If you can learn to avoid temptation when it's just a sprinkle, before it builds into a driving rain that hits you from all sides, you'll find life a lot easier, guilt a lot rarer, and the warm, safe feeling of living under God's umbrella.

He always gives you a way out, over and over again, far in advance of the 40-foot drop-off at the end. And even up there, when you're hanging on by your fingernails—if you'll call on Him to help you and if you'll stop trying to grit your teeth and fight the battle in your own strength, He'll be right there to put you back on solid ground.

SEE FOR YOURSELF:

Matt. 6:13; Heb. 2:18; 2 Pet. 2:9

²⁰Rather, that the things which the Gentiles sacrifice they sacrifice to demons and not to God, and I do not want you to have fellowship with demons. ²¹You cannot drink the cup of the Lord and the cup of demons; you cannot partake of the Lord's table and of the table of demons. ²²Or do we provoke the Lord to jealousy? Are we stronger than He?

ALL TO THE GLORY OF GOD

²³All things are lawful for me,^a but not all things are helpful; all things are lawful for me,^b but not all things edify. ²⁴Let no one seek his own, but each one the other's *well-being.*

²⁵Eat whatever is sold in the meat market, asking no questions for conscience' sake; ²⁶for *"the earth is the LORD's, and all its fullness."*^a

²⁷If any of those who do not believe invites you *to dinner,* and you desire to go, eat whatever is set before you, asking no question for conscience' sake. ²⁸But if anyone says to you, "This was offered to idols," do not eat it for the sake of the one who told you, and for conscience' sake;^a for *"the earth is the LORD's, and all its fullness."*^b ²⁹"Conscience," I say, not your own, but that of the other. For why is my liberty judged by another *man's* conscience? ³⁰But if I partake with thanks, why am I evil spoken of for *the food* over which I give thanks?

³¹Therefore, whether you eat or drink, or whatever you do, do all to the glory of God. ³²Give no offense, either to the Jews or to the Greeks or to the church of God, ³³just as I also please all *men* in all *things,* not seeking my own profit, but the *profit* of many, that they may be saved.

¹Imitate me, just as I also *imitate* Christ.

HEAD COVERINGS

²Now I praise you, brethren, that you remember me in all things and keep the traditions just as I delivered *them* to you. ³But I want you to know that the head of every man is Christ, the head of woman *is* man, and the head of Christ *is* God. ⁴Every man praying or prophesying, having *his* head covered, dishonors his head. ⁵But every woman who prays or prophesies with *her* head uncovered dishonors her head, for that is one and the same as if her head were shaved. ⁶For if a woman is not covered, let her also be shorn. But if it is shameful for a woman to be shorn or shaved, let her be covered. ⁷For a man indeed ought not to cover *his*

head, since he is the image and glory of God; but woman is the glory of man. ⁸For man is not from woman, but woman from man. ⁹Nor was man created for the woman, but woman for the man. ¹⁰For this reason the woman ought to have *a symbol of* authority on *her* head, because of the angels. ¹¹Nevertheless, neither *is* man independent of woman, nor woman independent of man, in the Lord. ¹²For as woman *came* from man, even so man also *comes* through woman; but all things are from God.

¹³Judge among yourselves. Is it proper for a woman to pray to God with her head uncovered? ¹⁴Does not even nature itself teach you that if a man has long hair, it is a dishonor to him? ¹⁵But if a woman has long hair, it is a glory to her; for *her* hair is given to her^a for a covering. ¹⁶But if anyone seems to be contentious, we have no such custom, nor *do* the churches of God.

CONDUCT AT THE LORD'S SUPPER

¹⁷Now in giving these instructions I do not praise *you,* since you come together not for the better but for the worse. ¹⁸For first of all, when you come together as a church, I hear that there are divisions among you, and in part I believe it. ¹⁹For there must also be factions among you, that those who are approved may be recognized among you. ²⁰Therefore when you come together in one place, it is not to eat the Lord's Supper. ²¹For in eating, each one takes his own supper ahead of *others;* and one is hungry and another is drunk. ²²What! Do you not have houses to eat and drink in? Or do you despise the church of God and shame those who have nothing? What shall I say to you? Shall I praise you in this? I do not praise *you.*

INSTITUTION OF THE LORD'S SUPPER

²³For I received from the Lord that which I also delivered to you: that the Lord Jesus on the *same* night in which He was betrayed took bread; ²⁴and when He had given thanks, He broke *it* and said, "Take, eat;^a this is My body which is broken^b for you; do this in remembrance of Me." ²⁵In the same manner *He* also *took* the cup after supper, saying, "This cup is the new covenant in My blood. This do, as often as you drink *it,* in remembrance of Me."

²⁶For as often as you eat this bread and drink this cup, you proclaim the Lord's death till He comes.

10:23 ^aNU-Text omits *for me.* ^bNU-Text omits *for me.* **10:26** ^aPsalm 24:1 **10:28** ^aNU-Text omits the rest of this verse. ^bPsalm 24:1 **11:15** ^aM-Text omits *to her.* **11:24** ^aNU-Text omits *Take, eat.* ^bNU-Text omits *broken.*

EXAMINE YOURSELF

27Therefore whoever eats this bread or drinks *this* cup of the Lord in an unworthy manner will be guilty of the body and blood*a* of the Lord. 28But let a man examine himself, and so let him eat of the bread and drink of the cup. 29For he who eats and drinks in an unworthy manner*a* eats and drinks judgment to himself, not discerning the Lord's*b* body. 30For this reason many *are* weak and sick among you, and many sleep. 31For if we would judge ourselves, we would not be judged. 32But when we are judged, we are chastened by the Lord, that we may not be condemned with the world.

33Therefore, my brethren, when you come together to eat, wait for one another. 34But if anyone is hungry, let him eat at home, lest you come together for judgment. And the rest I will set in order when I come.

SPIRITUAL GIFTS: UNITY IN DIVERSITY

1Now concerning spiritual *gifts*, brethren, I do not want you to be ignorant: 2You know that*a* you were Gentiles, carried away to these dumb idols, however you were led. 3Therefore I make known to you that no one speaking by the Spirit of God calls Jesus accursed, and no one can say that Jesus is Lord except by the Holy Spirit.

> "Therefore whoever eats this bread or drinks this cup of the Lord in an unworthy manner will be guilty of the body and blood of the Lord."
> (1 Corinthians 11:27)

4There are diversities of gifts, but the same Spirit. 5There are differences of ministries, but the same Lord. 6And there are diversities of activities, but it is the same God who works all in all. 7But the manifestation of the Spirit is given to each one for the profit *of all:* 8for to one is given the word of wisdom through the Spirit, to another the word of knowledge through the same Spirit, 9to another faith by the same Spirit, to another gifts of healings by the same*a* Spirit, 10to another the working of miracles, to another prophecy, to another discerning of spirits, to another *different* kinds of tongues, to another the interpretation of tongues. 11But one and the same Spirit works all these things, distributing to each one individually as He wills.

UNITY AND DIVERSITY IN ONE BODY

12For as the body is one and has many members, but all the members of that one body, being many, are one body, so also *is* Christ. 13For by one Spirit we were all baptized into one body—whether Jews or Greeks, whether slaves or free—and have all been made to drink into*a* one Spirit. 14For in fact the body is not one member but many.

15If the foot should say, "Because I am not a hand, I am not of the body," is it therefore not of the body? 16And if the ear should say, "Because I am not an eye, I am not of the body," is it therefore not of the body? 17If the whole body *were* an eye, where *would be* the hearing? If the whole *were* hearing, where *would be* the smelling? 18But now God has set the members, each one of them, in the body just as He pleased. 19And if they *were* all one member, where *would* the body *be?*

20But now indeed *there are* many members, yet one body. 21And the eye cannot say to the hand, "I have no need of you"; nor again the head to the feet, "I have no need of you." 22No, much rather, those members of the body which seem to be weaker are necessary. 23And those *members* of the body which we think to be less honorable, on these we bestow greater honor; and our unpresentable *parts* have greater modesty, 24but our presentable *parts* have no need. But God composed the body, having given

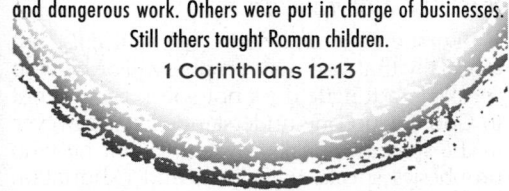

WHAT'S IT MEAN?

The secret to Rome's success was slave labor. A large segment of the Roman population was made up of slaves. What's more, those slaves served a variety of purposes in Roman society. Some were used for extremely difficult and dangerous work. Others were put in charge of businesses. Still others taught Roman children.

1 Corinthians 12:13

11:27 *a*NU-Text and M-Text read *the blood.* **11:29** *a*NU-Text omits *in an unworthy manner.* *b*NU-Text omits *Lord's.* **12:2** *a*NU-Text and M-Text add *when.* **12:9** *a*NU-Text reads *one.* **12:13** *a*NU-Text omits *into.*

greater honor to that *part* which lacks it, ²⁵that there should be no schism in the body, but *that* the members should have the same care for one another. ²⁶And if one member suffers, all the members suffer with *it;* or if one member is honored, all the members rejoice with *it.*

On the Edge

Love suffers long and is kind; love does not envy; love does not parade itself, is not puffed up; does not behave rudely, does not seek its own, is not provoked, thinks no evil (1 Cor. 13:4, 5).

A wise mom once said, "Take it as a compliment that other girls think your guy is great, too." Be secure enough to acknowledge their good taste. If your relationship is about love, then jealousy can't be part of it. Paul spends this whole chapter defining love. He is clear to point out that true love is not jealous. Somehow we've confused this and begun to think that if you love someone, you are supposed to act jealous and possessive. Love is about serving, selflessness, and caring. Arrogance and jealousy are for the insecure. Have faith in Jesus. He will bring the perfect mate for you. Learning to love and trust someone means that you don't worry about who he talks to, or who he's in the same room with. If your guy isn't trustworthy, then he's definitely not the one for you. Don't even start a romantic relationship with him. Start making friendships instead of dating. That way you can spend time with different people until you find the one who lines up with your beliefs and values, the one you have fun with, the one you love, the one you trust completely.

The possibility for boyfriends and girlfriends will come and go. Don't give in to the "gotta have a date" mentality. Commit to having holy courtships and let God bring the one He has chosen for you. When it's really about love, jealousy will lose out and trust will win.

SEE FOR YOURSELF:
2 Cor. 1:12; 2:7, 8;
Eph. 5:2

pointed these in the church: first apostles, second prophets, third teachers, after that miracles, then gifts of healings, helps, administrations, varieties of tongues. ²⁹*Are* all apostles? *Are* all prophets? *Are* all teachers? *Are* all workers of miracles? ³⁰Do all have gifts of healings? Do all speak with tongues? Do all interpret? ³¹But earnestly desire the best*ᵃ* gifts. And yet I show you a more excellent way.

THE GREATEST GIFT

¹Though I speak with the tongues of men and of angels, but have not love, I have become sounding brass or a clanging cymbal. ²And though I have *the gift of* prophecy, and understand all mysteries and all knowledge, and though I have all faith, so that I could remove mountains, but have not love, I am nothing. ³And though I bestow all my goods to feed *the poor,* and though I give my body to be burned,*ᵃ* but have not love, it profits me nothing.

⁴Love suffers long *and* is kind; love does not envy; love does not parade itself, is not puffed up; ⁵does not behave rudely, does not seek its own, is not provoked, thinks no evil; ⁶does not rejoice in iniquity, but rejoices in the truth; ⁷bears all things, believes all things, hopes all things, endures all things.

⁸Love never fails. But whether *there are* prophecies, they will fail; whether *there are* tongues, they will cease; whether *there is* knowledge, it will vanish away. ⁹For we know in part and we prophesy in part. ¹⁰But when that which is perfect has come, then that which is in part will be done away.

¹¹When I was a child, I spoke as a child, I understood as a child, I thought as a child; but when I became a man, I put away childish things. ¹²For now we see in a mirror, dimly, but then face to face. Now I know in part, but then I shall know just as I also am known.

¹³And now abide faith, hope, love, these three; but the greatest of these *is* love.

PROPHECY AND TONGUES

¹Pursue love, and desire spiritual *gifts,* but especially that you may prophesy. ²For he who speaks in a tongue does not speak to men but to God, for no one understands *him;* however, in the spirit he speaks mysteries. ³But he who prophesies speaks edification and exhortation and comfort to men. ⁴He who speaks in a

LOVE
Does true love ever quit? (13:4–8)

²⁷Now you are the body of Christ, and members individually. ²⁸And God has ap-

since you are zealous for spiritual *gifts, let it be* for the edification of the church *that* you seek to excel.

¹³Therefore let him who speaks in a tongue pray that he may interpret. ¹⁴For if I pray in a tongue, my spirit prays, but my understanding is unfruitful. ¹⁵What is *the conclusion* then? I will pray with the spirit, and I will also pray with the understanding. I will sing with the spirit, and I will also sing with the understanding. ¹⁶Otherwise, if you bless with the spirit, how will he who occupies the place of the uninformed say "Amen" at your giving of thanks, since he does not understand what you say? ¹⁷For you indeed give thanks well, but the other is not edified.

¹⁸I thank my God I speak with tongues more than you all; ¹⁹yet in the church I would rather speak five words with my understanding, that I may teach others also, than ten thousand words in a tongue.

TONGUES A SIGN TO UNBELIEVERS

²⁰Brethren, do not be children in understanding; however, in malice be babes, but in understanding be mature. ²¹In the law it is written:

> "With men of other tongues and other lips
> I will speak to this people;
> And yet, for all that, they will not hear
> Me," ᵃ

says the Lord.

²²Therefore tongues are for a sign, not to those who believe but to unbelievers; but

---

On the Edge

For now we see in a mirror, dimly, but then face to face. Now I know in part, but then I shall know just as I also am known (1 Cor. 13:12).

Life seems unfair because we don't see the whole picture. Paul says in this passage that we can only see a dim picture of God. We do not know everything He is doing. We only have earthly eyes that see little parts and earthly minds that understand tiny pieces of God's very big plan. Limited vision requires great faith and trust. The God who created you knows exactly what He is doing. Sometimes we understand later why things happened that at first seemed so unfair. Paul says though, that we won't completely understand everything until we are with God in heaven.

SEE FOR YOURSELF:
Ps. 119:169; Phil. 4:6;
Col. 2:2, 3

---

tongue edifies himself, but he who prophesies edifies the church. ⁵I wish you all spoke with tongues, but even more that you prophesied; forᵃ he who prophesies *is* greater than he who speaks with tongues, unless indeed he interprets, that the church may receive edification.

TONGUES MUST BE INTERPRETED

⁶But now, brethren, if I come to you speaking with tongues, what shall I profit you unless I speak to you either by revelation, by knowledge, by prophesying, or by teaching? ⁷Even things without life, whether flute or harp, when they make a sound, unless they make a distinction in the sounds, how will it be known what is piped or played? ⁸For if the trumpet makes an uncertain sound, who will prepare for battle? ⁹So likewise you, unless you utter by the tongue words easy to understand, how will it be known what is spoken? For you will be speaking into the air. ¹⁰There are, it may be, so many kinds of languages in the world, and none of them *is* without significance. ¹¹Therefore, if I do not know the meaning of the language, I shall be a foreigner to him who speaks, and he who speaks *will be* a foreigner to me. ¹²Even so you,

WHAT'S IT MEAN?

You've probably said it more times than you can count, but do you really know what the word *amen* means? In Hebrew, it means "Yes" or "That's how we want it." Since the earliest days of the church, the word has been used to show agreement with another person's comment or to end a prayer.

1 Corinthians 14:16

14:5 ᵃNU-Text reads *and.*　　**14:21** ᵃIsaiah 28:11, 12

prophesying is not for unbelievers but for those who believe. ²³Therefore if the whole church comes together in one place, and all speak with tongues, and there come in *those who are* uninformed or unbelievers, will they not say that you are out of your mind? ²⁴But if all prophesy, and an unbeliever or an uninformed person comes in, he is convinced by all, he is convicted by all. ²⁵And thus*ᵃ* the secrets of his heart are revealed; and so, falling down on *his* face, he will worship God and report that God is truly among you.

ORDER IN CHURCH MEETINGS

²⁶How is it then, brethren? Whenever you come together, each of you has a psalm, has a teaching, has a tongue, has a revelation, has an interpretation. Let all things be done for edification. ²⁷If anyone speaks in a tongue, *let there be* two or at the most three, *each* in turn, and let one interpret. ²⁸But if there is no interpreter, let him keep silent in church, and let him speak to himself and to God. ²⁹Let two or three prophets speak, and let the others judge. ³⁰But if *anything* is revealed to another who sits by, let the first keep silent. ³¹For you can all prophesy one by one, that all may learn and all may be encouraged. ³²And the spirits of the prophets are subject to the prophets. ³³For God is not *the author* of confusion but of peace, as in all the churches of the saints.

³⁴Let your*ᵃ* women keep silent in the churches, for they are not permitted to speak; but *they are* to be submissive, as the law also says. ³⁵And if they want to learn something, let them ask their own husbands at home; for it is shameful for women to speak in church.

³⁶Or did the word of God come *originally* from you? Or *was it* you only that it reached? ³⁷If anyone thinks himself to be a prophet or spiritual, let him acknowledge that the things which I write to you are the commandments of the Lord. ³⁸But if anyone is ignorant, let him be ignorant.*ᵃ*

³⁹Therefore, brethren, desire earnestly to prophesy, and do not forbid to speak with tongues. ⁴⁰Let all things be done decently and in order.

THE RISEN CHRIST, FAITH'S REALITY

¹Moreover, brethren, I declare to you the gospel which I preached to you, which also you received and in which you stand, ²by which also you are saved, if you hold fast that word which I preached to you—unless you believed in vain.

³For I delivered to you first of all that which I also received: that Christ died for our sins according to the Scriptures, ⁴and that He was buried, and that He rose again the third day according to the Scriptures, ⁵and that He was seen by Cephas, then by the twelve. ⁶After that He was seen by over five hundred brethren at once, of whom the greater part remain to the present, but some have fallen asleep. ⁷After that He was seen by James, then by all the apostles. ⁸Then last of all He was seen by me also, as by one born out of due time.

⁹For I am the least of the apostles, who am not worthy to be called an apostle, because I persecuted the church of God. ¹⁰But by the grace of God I am what I am, and His grace toward me was not in vain; but I labored more abundantly than they all, yet not I, but the grace of God *which was* with me. ¹¹Therefore, whether *it was* I or they, so we preach and so you believed.

THE RISEN CHRIST, OUR HOPE

¹²Now if Christ is preached that He has been raised from the dead, how do some among you say that there is no resurrection of the dead? ¹³But if there is no resurrection of the dead, then Christ is not risen. ¹⁴And if Christ is not risen, then our preaching *is* empty and your faith *is* also empty. ¹⁵Yes, and we are found false witnesses of God, because we have testified of God that He raised up Christ, whom He did not raise up—if in fact the dead do not rise. ¹⁶For if *the* dead do not rise, then Christ is not risen. ¹⁷And if Christ is not risen, your faith *is* futile; you are still in your sins! ¹⁸Then also those who have fallen asleep in Christ have perished. ¹⁹If in this life only we have hope in Christ, we are of all men the most pitiable.

THE LAST ENEMY DESTROYED

²⁰But now Christ is risen from the dead, *and* has become the firstfruits of those who have fallen asleep. ²¹For since by man *came* death, by Man also *came* the resurrection of the dead. ²²For as in Adam all die, even so in Christ all shall be made alive. ²³But each one in his own order: Christ the firstfruits, afterward those *who are* Christ's at His coming. ²⁴Then *comes* the end, when He de-

RESURRECTION
What is the foundation of Christianity? (15:12–21)

14:25 *ᵃ*NU-Text omits *And thus.*   **14:34** *ᵃ*NU-Text omits *your.*   **14:38** *ᵃ*NU-Text reads *if anyone does not recognize this, he is not recognized.*

livers the kingdom to God the Father, when He puts an end to all rule and all authority and power. [25]For He must reign till He has put all enemies under His feet. [26]The last enemy *that* will be destroyed *is* death. [27]For *"He has put all things under His feet."*[a] But when He says "all things are put under *Him*," *it is* evident that He who put all things under Him is excepted. [28]Now when all things are made subject to Him, then the Son Himself will also be subject to Him who put all things under Him, that God may be all in all.

EFFECTS OF DENYING THE RESURRECTION

[29]Otherwise, what will they do who are baptized for the dead, if the dead do not rise at all? Why then are they baptized for the dead? [30]And why do we stand in jeopardy every hour? [31]I affirm, by the boasting in you which I have in Christ Jesus our Lord, I die daily. [32]If, in the manner of men, I have fought with beasts at Ephesus, what advantage *is it* to me? If *the* dead do not rise, *"Let us eat and drink, for tomorrow we die!"*[a]

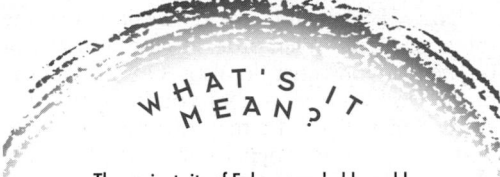

WHAT'S IT MEAN?

The ancient city of Ephesus probably could have supported a professional sports team. After all, it had a twenty-five thousand-seat stadium. Chances are, though, the audience would have been bored by a sporting event. They were used to kill-or-be-killed battles in which slaves fought wild animals or each other. The loser of each contest was put to death in front of the audience.

1 Corinthians 15:32

[33]Do not be deceived: "Evil company corrupts good habits." [34]Awake to righteousness, and do not sin; for some do not have the knowledge of God. I speak *this* to your shame.

A GLORIOUS BODY

[35]But someone will say, "How are the dead raised up? And with what body do they come?" [36]Foolish one, what you sow is not made alive unless it dies. [37]And what you sow, you do not sow that body that shall be, but mere grain— perhaps wheat or some other *grain.* [38]But God

gives it a body as He pleases, and to each seed its own body.

[39]All flesh *is* not the same flesh, but *there is* one *kind of* flesh[a] of men, another flesh of animals, another of fish, *and* another of birds. [40]*There are* also celestial bodies and terrestrial bodies; but the glory of the celestial *is* one, and the *glory* of the terrestrial *is* another. [41]*There is* one glory of the sun, another glory of the moon, and another glory of the stars; for *one* star differs from *another* star in glory.

[42]So also *is* the resurrection of the dead. *The body* is sown in corruption, it is raised in incorruption. [43]It is sown in dishonor, it is raised in glory. It is sown in weakness, it is raised in power. [44]It is sown a natural body, it is raised a spiritual body. There is a natural body, and there is a spiritual body. [45]And so it is written, *"The first man Adam became a living being."*[a] The last Adam *became* a life-giving spirit. [46]However, the spiritual is not first, but the

On the Edge

The first man was of the earth, made of dust; the second Man is the Lord from heaven. As was the man of dust, so also are those who are made of dust; and as is the heavenly Man, so also are those who are heavenly (1 Cor. 15:47, 48).

Call it amazing. God takes a handful of dirt and makes a man. Very humble beginnings for people who think so highly of themselves. Have you felt jealous of anyone lately? Do you think you deserve more than you have? Are you mad at God because your family doesn't have some of the comforts other families do? Maybe it's time to remember where you came from—dust. Yep, you (and all the people you're jealous of) are just a bunch of dust.

Your life is a gift. It's a blessing to be on earth and to be able to enjoy life. You've got the freedom to choose what you're going to do with your life. The point is to make something out of the gifts God has given you. Your body, mind, emotions, and personality are specially crafted by God for His purpose. God wants you to use the time you've got on earth and the gifts you've been given to glorify Him. Your glory comes later. Paul says that everyone in heaven will have a body like the glorified Christ. There's a lot to do between now and the time you get to heaven, so get that old, dusty body in gear. God has great things for you!

SEE FOR YOURSELF:
Gen. 2:7; 3:19;
Is. 40:6

natural, and afterward the spiritual. [47]The first man *was* of the earth, *made* of dust; the second Man *is* the Lord[a] from heaven. [48]As *was* the *man* of dust, so also *are* those *who are made* of dust; and as *is* the heavenly *Man*, so also *are* those *who are* heavenly. [49]And as we have borne the image of the *man* of dust, we shall also bear[a] the image of the heavenly *Man*.

OUR FINAL VICTORY

[50]Now this I say, brethren, that flesh and blood cannot inherit the kingdom of God; nor

does corruption inherit incorruption. [51]Behold, I tell you a mystery: We shall not all sleep, but we shall all be changed—[52]in a moment, in the twinkling of an eye, at the last trumpet. For the trumpet will sound, and the dead will be raised incorruptible, and we shall be changed. [53]For this corruptible must put on incorruption, and this mortal *must* put on immortality. [54]So when this corruptible has put on incorruption, and this mortal has put on immortality, then shall be brought to pass the saying that is written: *"Death is swallowed up in victory."*[a]

[55]   *"O Death, where is your sting?*[a]
      O Hades, where is your victory?"[b]

[56]The sting of death *is* sin, and the strength of sin *is* the law. [57]But thanks *be* to God, who gives us the victory through our Lord Jesus Christ. [58]Therefore, my beloved brethren, be steadfast, immovable, always abounding in the work of the Lord, knowing that your labor is not in vain in the Lord.

COLLECTION FOR THE SAINTS

[1]Now concerning the collection for the saints, as I have given orders to the churches of Galatia, so you must do also: [2]On the first *day* of the week let each one of you lay something aside, storing up as he may prosper, that there be no collections when I come. [3]And when I come, whomever you approve by *your* letters I will send to bear your gift to Jerusalem. [4]But if it is fitting that I go also, they will go with me.

PERSONAL PLANS

[5]Now I will come to you when I pass through Macedonia (for I am passing through Macedonia). [6]And it may be that I will remain, or even spend the winter with you, that you may send me on my journey, wherever I go. [7]For I do not wish to see you now on the way; but I hope to stay a while with you, if the Lord permits.

[8]But I will tarry in Ephesus until Pentecost. [9]For a great and effective door has opened to me, and *there are* many adversaries.

[10]And if Timothy comes, see that he may be with you without fear; for he does the work of the Lord, as I also *do*. [11]Therefore let no one despise him. But send him on his journey in peace, that he may come to me; for I am waiting for him with the brethren.

[12]Now concerning *our* brother Apollos, I

15:47 [a]NU-Text omits *the Lord*.   **15:49** [a]M-Text reads *let us also bear*.   **15:54** [a]Isaiah 25:8   **15:55** [a]Hosea 13:14   [b]NU-Text reads *O Death, where is your victory? O Death, where is your sting?*

strongly urged him to come to you with the brethren, but he was quite unwilling to come at this time; however, he will come when he has a convenient time.

WHAT'S IT MEAN?

Galatia was a Roman province located in what is now Turkey. Paul was familiar with the area because he and Barnabas had started several churches in that region, in cities such as Iconium, Lystra, Derbe, and Pisidian Antioch.

1 Corinthians 16:1

FINAL EXHORTATIONS

[13]Watch, stand fast in the faith, be brave, be strong. [14]Let all *that* you *do* be done with love.

[15]I urge you, brethren—you know the household of Stephanas, that it is the firstfruits of Achaia, and *that* they have devoted themselves to the ministry of the saints—[16]that you also submit to such, and to everyone who works and labors with *us.*

[17]I am glad about the coming of Stephanas, Fortunatus, and Achaicus, for what was lacking on your part they supplied. [18]For they refreshed my spirit and yours. Therefore acknowledge such men.

GREETINGS AND A SOLEMN FAREWELL

[19]The churches of Asia greet you. Aquila and Priscilla greet you heartily in the Lord, with the church that is in their house. [20]All the brethren greet you.

Greet one another with a holy kiss.

[21]The salutation with my own hand—Paul's.

[22]If anyone does not love the Lord Jesus Christ, let him be accursed.[a] O Lord, come![b]

[23]The grace of our Lord Jesus Christ *be* with you. [24]My love *be* with you all in Christ Jesus. Amen.

WHAT'S IT MEAN?

Many people in New Testament times had secretaries who took care of their correspondence and business documents. Some Bible experts believe that Paul needed a secretary to write his letters for him because he had very poor eyesight.

1 Corinthians 16:21

16:22 [a]Greek *anathema* [b]Aramaic *Maranatha*

2 corinthians

CONTENT

You can't really understand how amazing Second Corinthians is without knowing why Paul wrote First Corinthians. When Paul wrote his first letter to the church in Corinth, he was telling them off a little bit. He was setting them straight. He was "letting them have it."

It's difficult enough to do the right thing. It's even harder when you get defensive and hardheaded. That is exactly how the Corinthian church *could* have responded to Paul's correction—but they didn't.

In fact, by the time Paul wrote them the letter that we know as Second Corinthians he was bragging about their giving spirits. He was complimenting them. He was commending them.

As bad as it feels sometimes to be confronted about stuff we do wrong, we are better people if we'll stop and listen. Second Corinthians reminds us of that.

Outline

Purpose

We are to have New Covenant ministries.

Theme

Powerful Ministry Through Weak Vessels

Date of writing

Fall A.D. 56

> "Therefore, if anyone is in Christ, he is a new creation; old things have passed away; behold, all things have become new" (5:17).

Bible Talk

Paul's Thorn in the Flesh

Have you ever heard someone say, "That's my thorn in the flesh"? If you have, you are hearing a reference to Paul's letters to the Corinthians.

We don't know what Paul's "thorn in the flesh" was, but we know from these letters that there was something about Paul that he wanted to change. This thing held him back. It made his life harder, and he thought it made him less effective for Christ.

While we don't know exactly what Paul was talking about, we all know what it is to wish we could change something about ourselves. It's okay to ask God to change that thing. Paul asked God more than once to remove his thorn. But he also didn't let it hold him back from doing what God wanted.

GETTING MAD AT THE TRUTH

We have a lot to learn from the Corinthians about hearing the truth and responding to it. It's so easy to want to be right, whether we really *are* right or not. It's often a matter of pride. When someone tells us something that shows us we are wrong, we want to defend ourselves at all costs.

It's often at church or when we read the Bible that God confronts us about the sin in our lives. When He does, we have to make the choice that the Corinthians had to make with Paul. We can get mad and defensive, or we can listen and let God make us into better people.

It's not worth trying to be right instead of just being humble and letting God make us right.

GREETING

¹Paul, an apostle of Jesus Christ by the will of God, and Timothy *our* brother,

To the church of God which is at Corinth, with all the saints who are in all Achaia:

²Grace to you and peace from God our Father and the Lord Jesus Christ.

COMFORT IN SUFFERING

³Blessed *be* the God and Father of our Lord Jesus Christ, the Father of mercies and God of all comfort, ⁴who comforts us in all our tribulation, that we may be able to comfort those who are in any trouble, with the comfort with which we ourselves are comforted by God. ⁵For as the sufferings of Christ abound in us, so our consolation also abounds through Christ. ⁶Now if we are afflicted, *it is* for your consolation and salvation, which is effective for enduring the same sufferings which we also suffer. Or if we are comforted, *it is* for your consolation and salvation. ⁷And our hope for you *is* steadfast, because we know that as you are partakers of the sufferings, so also *you will partake* of the consolation.

COMFORT
Are hurting people important to God? (1:3–11)

DELIVERED FROM SUFFERING

⁸For we do not want you to be ignorant, brethren, of our trouble which came to us in Asia: that we were burdened beyond measure, above strength, so that we despaired even of life. ⁹Yes, we had the sentence of death in ourselves, that we should not trust in ourselves but in God who raises the dead, ¹⁰who delivered us from so great a death, and does*ᵃ* deliver us; in whom we trust that He will still deliver *us*, ¹¹you also helping together in prayer for us, that thanks may be given by many persons on our*ᵃ* behalf for the gift *granted* to us through many.

PAUL'S SINCERITY

¹²For our boasting is this: the testimony of our conscience that we conducted ourselves in the world in simplicity and godly sincerity, not with fleshly wisdom but by the grace of God, and more abundantly toward you. ¹³For we are not writing any other things to you than what you read or understand. Now I trust you will understand, even to the end ¹⁴(as also you have understood us in part), that we are your boast

1:10 *ᵃ*NU-Text reads *shall.*   **1:11** *ᵃ*M-Text reads *your behalf.*

Promise   HE PROMISES YOU COMFORT.

Blessed be the God and the Father of our Lord Jesus Christ, the Father of mercies and God of all comfort, who comforts us in all our tribulation, that we may be able to comfort those who are in any trouble, with the comfort with which we ourselves are comforted by God (2 Cor. 1:3, 4).

Trouble can come in all sizes. There's the kind you get yourself into, like staying out too late or tossing water balloons at passing cars. There's the kind that other people cause for you, like when somebody tells somebody else something you said when you said something totally different. And there's also the kind that just sort of hits you out of the blue, like when your best friend gets hurt in a car wreck or your grandmother dies on an operating table.

But God's comfort comes in colors to match every problem. It fits every hole left behind by someone you love. It soothes every wound that's opened by the daggers of jealousy and anger. It covers every sin with the hope that Christ's blood can forgive completely—and His discipline can keep you from ever visiting this awful place again.

God's comfort—so real, so refreshing—can appear in a Bible verse, a mom's tender arm around your shoulder, a series of events. But it's always there. And it's always yours. And it's always God.

SEE FOR YOURSELF:
Ps. 23:4; Is. 49:13; 2 Thess. 2:16, 17

as you also *are* ours, in the day of the Lord Jesus.

SPARING THE CHURCH

¹⁵And in this confidence I intended to come to you before, that you might have a second benefit—¹⁶to pass by way of you to Macedonia, to come again from Macedonia to you, and be helped by you on my way to Judea. ¹⁷Therefore, when I was planning this, did I do it lightly? Or the things I plan, do I plan according to the flesh, that with me there should be Yes, Yes, and No, No? ¹⁸But *as* God *is* faithful, our word to you was not Yes and No. ¹⁹For the Son of God, Jesus Christ, who was preached among you by us—by me, Silvanus, and Timothy—was not Yes and No, but in Him was Yes. ²⁰For all the promises of God in Him *are* Yes, and in Him Amen, to the glory of God through us. ²¹Now He who establishes us with you in Christ and has anointed us *is* God, ²²who also has sealed us and given us the Spirit in our hearts as a guarantee.

²³Moreover I call God as witness against my soul, that to spare you I came no more to Corinth. ²⁴Not that we have dominion over your faith, but are fellow workers for your joy; for by faith you stand.

¹But I determined this within myself, that I would not come again to you in sorrow. ²For if I make you sorrowful, then who is he who makes me glad but the one who is made sorrowful by me?

FORGIVE THE OFFENDER

³And I wrote this very thing to you, lest, when I came, I should have sorrow over those from whom I ought to have joy, having confidence in you all that my joy is *the joy* of you all. ⁴For out of much affliction and anguish of heart I wrote to you, with many tears, not that you should be grieved, but that you might know the love which I have so abundantly for you.

⁵But if anyone has caused grief, he has not grieved me, but all of you to some extent—not to be too severe. ⁶This punishment which *was* *inflicted* by the majority *is* sufficient for such a man, ⁷so that, on the contrary, you *ought* rather to forgive and comfort *him*, lest perhaps such a one be swallowed up with too much sorrow. ⁸Therefore I urge you to reaffirm *your* love to him. ⁹For to this end I also wrote, that I might put you to the test, whether you are obedient in all things. ¹⁰Now whom you forgive anything, I also *forgive*. For if indeed I have forgiven any

---

---

thing, I have forgiven that one[a] for your sakes in the presence of Christ, ¹¹lest Satan should take advantage of us; for we are not ignorant of his devices.

TRIUMPH IN CHRIST

¹²Furthermore, when I came to Troas to *preach* Christ's gospel, and a door was opened to me by the Lord, ¹³I had no rest in my spirit, because I did not find Titus my brother; but taking my leave of them, I departed for Macedonia.

¹⁴Now thanks *be* to God who always leads

2:10 [a]NU-Text reads *For indeed, what I have forgiven, if I have forgiven anything, I did it.*

us in triumph in Christ, and through us diffuses the fragrance of His knowledge in every place. [15]For we are to God the fragrance of Christ among those who are being saved and among those who are perishing. [16]To the one *we are* the aroma of death *leading* to death, and to the other the aroma of life *leading* to life. And who *is* sufficient for these things? [17]For we are not, as so many,[a] peddling the word of God; but as of sincerity, but as from God, we speak in the sight of God in Christ.

CHRIST'S EPISTLE

[1]Do we begin again to commend ourselves? Or do we need, as some *others*, epistles of commendation to you or *letters* of commendation from you? [2]You are our epistle written in our hearts, known and read by all men; [3]clearly *you are* an epistle of Christ, ministered by us, written not with ink but by the Spirit of the living God, not on tablets of stone but on tablets of flesh, *that is,* of the heart.

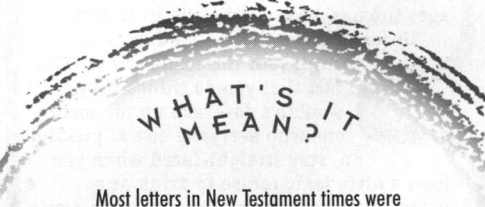

WHAT'S IT MEAN?

Most letters in New Testament times were written on an early form of paper called papyrus. The papyrus plant is a large reed that grows in shallow water. The reed was sliced into very thin, broad strips, which were then pressed together using a muddy, gluelike substance. After being left out in the sun to dry, the sheets were ready to be used.

2 Corinthians 3:3

THE SPIRIT, NOT THE LETTER

[4]And we have such trust through Christ toward God. [5]Not that we are sufficient of ourselves to think of anything as *being* from ourselves, but our sufficiency *is* from God, [6]who also made us sufficient as ministers of the new covenant, not of the letter but of the Spirit;[a] for the letter kills, but the Spirit gives life.

GLORY OF THE NEW COVENANT

[7]But if the ministry of death, written *and* engraved on stones, was glorious, so that the children of Israel could not look steadily at the face

of Moses because of the glory of his countenance, which *glory* was passing away, [8]how will the ministry of the Spirit not be more glorious? [9]For if the ministry of condemnation *had* glory, the ministry of righteousness exceeds much more in glory. [10]For even what was made glorious had no glory in this respect, because of the glory that excels. [11]For if what is passing away *was* glorious, what remains *is* much more glorious.

[12]Therefore, since we have such hope, we use great boldness of speech—[13]unlike Moses, *who* put a veil over his face so that the children of Israel could not look steadily at the end of what was passing away. [14]But their minds were blinded. For until this day the same veil remains unlifted in the reading of the Old Testament, because the *veil* is taken away in Christ. [15]But even

to this day, when Moses is read, a veil lies on their heart. [16]Nevertheless when one turns to the Lord, the veil is taken away. [17]Now the Lord is the Spirit; and where the Spirit of the Lord *is*, there *is* liberty. [18]But we all, with unveiled face, beholding as in a mirror the glory of the Lord, are being transformed into the same image from glory to glory, just as by the Spirit of the Lord.

and not of us. [8]*We are* hard-pressed on every side, yet not crushed; *we are* perplexed, but not in despair; [9]persecuted, but not forsaken; struck down, but not destroyed— [10]always carrying about in the body the dying of the Lord Jesus, that the life of Jesus also may be manifested in our body. [11]For we who live are always delivered to death for Jesus' sake, that the life of Jesus also may be manifested in our mortal flesh. [12]So then death is working in us, but life in you.

[13]And since we have the same spirit of faith,

> **WORRY**
>
> Does God care about our stress?
> (4:8–12)

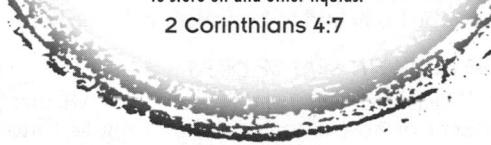

How much do you know about ancient pottery? Maybe it's time you learned a thing or two. "Earthen vessels" is another name for clay jars that were used to hold oil and grain. Before the clay could be shaped by a potter, stones and other large objects had to be removed from it. After the clay was shaped, the potter had two options for drying it: let the sun do it or stick it in a kiln. A sun-dried jar could hold grain, but it would collapse if it were filled with liquid. A jar heated in a kiln—at temperatures above 900 degrees Fahrenheit—became hard and strong and could be used to store oil and other liquids.

2 Corinthians 4:7

THE LIGHT OF CHRIST'S GOSPEL

[1]Therefore, since we have this ministry, as we have received mercy, we do not lose heart. [2]But we have renounced the hidden things of shame, not walking in craftiness nor handling the word of God deceitfully, but by manifestation of the truth commending ourselves to every man's conscience in the sight of God. [3]But even if our gospel is veiled, it is veiled to those who are perishing, [4]whose minds the god of this age has blinded, who do not believe, lest the light of the gospel of the glory of Christ, who is the image of God, should shine on them. [5]For we do not preach ourselves, but Christ Jesus the Lord, and ourselves your bondservants for Jesus' sake. [6]For it is the God who commanded light to shine out of darkness, who has shone in our hearts to *give* the light of the knowledge of the glory of God in the face of Jesus Christ.

CAST DOWN BUT UNCONQUERED

[7]But we have this treasure in earthen vessels, that the excellence of the power may be of God

On the Edge

But we have this treasure in earthen vessels, that the excellence of the power may be of God and not of us (2 Cor. 4:7).

Did you know that God stores His treasure inside of you? That's right! God has given you special qualities that nobody else has. You are God's treasure, filled with unique talents and abilities. It doesn't matter if your parents have referred to you as "mommy's little terror," or if your friends have said you will never amount to anything. It really doesn't matter, because before you were ever born God chose you and formed you and placed His gifts and treasures inside you!

You are special in God's eyes, and somehow or another, He is going to pull that treasure out of you. He's just looking for someone who is willing to be used for His glory. He has great plans for you; He wants to bless you with a future filled with hope—a future of success, not suffering! (Check out Jeremiah 29:11.)

Remember, you are already filled with God's treasure and with His power! They go beyond your own ability and strength. They come from God. Just as if you would bust open a clay pot with a hammer and pull out a treasure, so it is with you and God. He wants to open you up and see you blossom into what He wants you to be. Realize God's treasures are inside of you, and watch what He can do with you.

SEE FOR YOURSELF:
Ps. 37:4; Prov. 16:3;
Jer. 1:5; 29:11

according to what is written, *"I believed and therefore I spoke,"*[a] we also believe and therefore speak, [14]knowing that He who raised up the Lord Jesus will also raise us up with Jesus, and will present *us* with you. [15]For all things *are* for your sakes, that grace, having spread through the many, may cause thanksgiving to abound to the glory of God.

On the Edge

For we know that if our earthly house, this tent, is destroyed, we have a building from God, a house not made with hands, eternal in the heavens. For in this we groan, earnestly desiring to be clothed with our habitation which is from heaven (2 Cor. 5:1, 2).

Your body is just a temporary home. That's right, it's just like a tent—a place for the real you, your spirit, to live. It's important to exercise, eat right, and take care of your body, but someday your tent is going to check out of here. That's just the natural cycle of life. Your body cannot live forever, but, thank God, death is not the end. You're on your way to a much greater place—a place where there's no more sadness, a place we've all heard about, a place called heaven!

Your body may be like a tent down here on earth, but someday you're going to live in a home that God Himself has prepared just for you. Just think—He made the whole world in seven days, but He's still working on your eternal home. Your mind can't even imagine how awesome that place will be! So don't be discouraged with your home here on earth. It won't be long, and you'll be walking those streets of gold!

SEE FOR YOURSELF:
John 14:2; 2 Cor. 4:18; Rev. 21:18–21

SEEING THE INVISIBLE

[16]Therefore we do not lose heart. Even though our outward man is perishing, yet the inward *man* is being renewed day by day. [17]For our light affliction, which is but for a moment, is working for us a far more exceeding *and* eter-nal weight of glory, [18]while we do not look at the things which are seen, but at the things which are not seen. For the things which are seen *are* temporary, but the things which are not seen *are* eternal.

ASSURANCE OF THE RESURRECTION

[1]For we know that if our earthly house, *this* tent, is destroyed, we have a building from God, a house not made with hands, eternal in the heavens. [2]For in this we groan, earnestly desiring to be clothed with our habitation which is from heaven, [3]if indeed, having been clothed, we shall not be found naked. [4]For we who are in *this* tent groan, being burdened, not because we want to be unclothed, but further clothed, that mortality may be swallowed up by life. [5]Now He who has prepared us for this very thing *is* God, who also has given us the Spirit as a guarantee.

[6]So *we are* always confident, knowing that while we are at home in the body we are absent from the Lord. [7]For we walk by faith, not by sight. [8]We are confident, yes, well pleased rather to be absent from the body and to be present with the Lord.

DEATH
Will life in heaven be better than life on earth? (5:6–8)

THE JUDGMENT SEAT OF CHRIST

[9]Therefore we make it our aim, whether present or absent, to be well pleasing to Him. [10]For we must all appear before the judgment seat of Christ, that each one may receive the things *done* in the body, according to what he has done, whether good or bad. [11]Knowing, therefore, the terror of the Lord, we persuade men; but we are well known to God, and I also trust are well known in your consciences.

JUDGMENT
Will Christians be judged for their actions? (5:10)

BE RECONCILED TO GOD

[12]For we do not commend ourselves again to you, but give you opportunity to boast on our behalf, that you may have *an answer* for those who boast in appearance and not in heart. [13]For if we are beside ourselves, *it is* for God; or if we are of sound mind, *it is* for you. [14]For the love of Christ compels us, because we judge thus: that if One died for all, then all died; [15]and He died for all, that those who live should live no longer for themselves, but for Him who died for them and rose again.

4:13 [a]Psalm 116:10

On the Edge

Therefore, if anyone is in Christ, he is a new creation; old things have passed away; behold, all things have become new (2 Cor. 5:17).

The Bible talks a lot about God's power. There are lots of stories about how He wiped out armies, cured diseases, and brought dead people back to life. Here, Paul is talking about one of God's less spectacular miracles. It's an invisible thing, but it's very real. When you let your life belong to Jesus, He makes you a new creation—a new person. What happens is this: Your *spirit*—the real you—is made new. Your mind and body are not. They are your responsibility. Once you make Jesus your Lord, your job is to renew your mind with His Word and to practice purity and self-control in your body. The real you, your spirit, loves God and you tell your mind and body what to do in order to line up with that love.

Here's another miracle: *The past is forgotten.* It's like all the bad things you ever did and all the things that hurt you *never happened.* You don't have to define yourself by things that have happened in the past; instead, you can define yourself by what God says about you. He made you to be happy, confident, and complete. The old junk passes away and you become a brand-new person. He makes you new so that you can live to your fullest potential!

SEE FOR YOURSELF:
Ezek. 36:26; Gal. 6:15; Eph. 4:23, 24

---

passes to them, and has committed to us the word of reconciliation. [20]Now then, we are ambassadors for Christ, as though God were pleading through us: we implore *you* on Christ's behalf, be reconciled to God. [21]For He made Him who knew no sin *to be* sin for us, that we might become the righteousness of God in Him.

MARKS OF THE MINISTRY

[1]We then, *as* workers together *with Him* also plead with *you* not to receive the grace of God in vain. [2]For He says:

> "*In an acceptable time I have heard you,*
> *And in the day of salvation I have helped you.*" [a]

Behold, now *is* the accepted time; behold, now *is* the day of salvation.

[3]We give no offense in anything, that our ministry may not be blamed. [4]But in all *things* we commend ourselves as ministers of God: in much patience, in tribulations, in needs, in distresses, [5]in stripes, in imprisonments, in tumults, in labors, in sleeplessness, in fastings; [6]by purity, by knowledge, by longsuffering, by kindness, by the Holy Spirit, by sincere love, [7]by the word of truth, by the power of God, by the armor of righteousness on the right hand and on the left, [8]by honor and dishonor, by evil report and good report; as deceivers, and *yet* true; [9]as unknown, and *yet* well known; as dying, and behold we live; as chastened, and *yet* not killed; [10]as sorrowful, yet always rejoicing; as poor, yet making many rich; as having nothing, and *yet* possessing all things.

BE HOLY

[11]O Corinthians! We have spoken openly to you, our heart is wide open. [12]You are not restricted by us, but you are restricted by your *own* affections. [13]Now in return for the same (I speak as to children), you also be open.

[14]Do not be unequally yoked together with unbelievers. For what fellowship has righteousness with lawlessness? And what communion has light with darkness? [15]And what accord has Christ with Belial? Or what part has a believer with an unbeliever? [16]And what agreement has the temple of God with idols? For you[a] are the temple of the living God. As God has said:

> "*I will dwell in them*
> *And walk among them.*

---

[16]Therefore, from now on, we regard no one according to the flesh. Even though we have known Christ according to the flesh, yet now we know *Him thus* no longer. [17]Therefore, if anyone *is* in Christ, *he is* a new creation; old things have passed away; behold, all things have become new. [18]Now all things *are* of God, who has reconciled us to Himself through Jesus Christ, and has given us the ministry of reconciliation, [19]that is, that God was in Christ reconciling the world to Himself, not imputing their tres-

WITNESSING
What has God entrusted us with? (5:18–21)

6:2 [a]Isaiah 49:8 **6:16** [a]NU-Text reads *we.*

*I will be their God,
And they shall be My people."* [b]

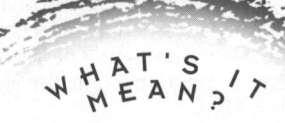

WHAT'S IT MEAN?

Paul was not talking about getting physically dirty in this verse. "Unclean" refers to anything that would make a person unfit to worship or have fellowship with God.

2 Corinthians 6:17

[17]Therefore

*"Come out from among them
And be separate, says the Lord.
Do not touch what is unclean,
And I will receive you."* [a]

[18] *"I will be a Father to you,
And you shall be My sons and daughters,
Says the LORD Almighty."* [a]

6:16 [b]Leviticus 26:12; Jeremiah 32:38; Ezekiel 37:27   **6:17** [a]Isaiah 52:11; Ezekiel 20:34, 41
6:18 [a]2 Samuel 7:14

---

[1]Therefore, having these promises, beloved, let us cleanse ourselves from all filthiness of the flesh and spirit, perfecting holiness in the fear of God.

THE CORINTHIANS' REPENTANCE

[2]Open *your hearts* to us. We have wronged no one, we have corrupted no one, we have cheated no one. [3]I do not say *this* to condemn; for I have said before that you are in our hearts, to die together and to live together. [4]Great *is* my boldness of speech toward you, great *is* my boasting on your behalf. I am filled with comfort. I am exceedingly joyful in all our tribulation.

[5]For indeed, when we came to Macedonia, our bodies had no rest, but we were troubled on every side. Outside *were* conflicts, inside *were* fears. [6]Nevertheless God, who comforts the downcast, comforted us by the coming of Titus, [7]and not only by his coming, but also by the consolation with which he was comforted in you, when he told us of your earnest desire, your mourning, your zeal for me, so that I rejoiced even more.

[8]For even if I made you sorry with my letter, I do not regret it; though I did regret it. For I perceive that the same epistle made you sorry,

---

Promise   HE PROMISES TO COMFORT PEOPLE IN NEED.

Nevertheless God, who comforts the downcast, comforted us by the coming of Titus (2 Cor. 7:6).

Paul is so honest. He wasn't always standing on a spiritual mountaintop, and he doesn't mind admitting it. He spends a lot of time in this book talking about his suffering, worry, tears, and broken heart. He doesn't try to pretend that just because he loves Jesus, nothing hard ever happens. He admits to his struggles and hardships. He talks about the troubles he's faced. He is real and vulnerable.

Somehow over time, Christians have lost sight of Paul's example. Somehow we've replaced honesty with pretending. Too many Christians pretend that their lives are happy and suffer in total silence. They won't admit to their own needs and weaknesses, yet wonder why God doesn't do something. God will bring cheer and comfort to those who are in need. Do you need God to comfort you? Do you need some cheering up? Then talk to the Lord. Be honest with some people who are close to you. Be brave enough to say, "I love God, but life is tough right now." God may use the Holy Spirit, or the body of believers, or the truth of His Word—but He will bring cheer to people in need.

SEE FOR YOURSELF:
Ps. 16:11; John 14:1–24; Acts 3:20

WHAT'S IT MEAN?

Titus was Paul's assistant. (You may recognize his name from the letter Paul wrote to him, a letter that just happens to be the fifty-sixth book of the Bible.) Paul had asked Titus to deliver his first letter to the Corinthians—a letter that had very few good things to say about the Christian church in Corinth. Paul was especially disappointed by the way the Corinthians had ignored the sins of a sexually immoral church member. Paul had expected to meet Titus in Troas to find out how the church responded to the letter, but the two didn't hook up until the apostle got to Macedonia.

2 Corinthians 7:6

EXCEL IN GIVING

¹Moreover, brethren, we make known to you the grace of God bestowed on the churches of Macedonia: ²that in a great trial of affliction the abundance of their joy and their deep poverty abounded in the riches of their liberality. ³For I bear witness that according to *their* ability, yes, and beyond *their* ability, *they were* freely willing, ⁴imploring us with much urgency that we would receive*ᵃ* the gift and the fellowship of the ministering to the saints. ⁵And not *only* as we had hoped, but they first gave themselves to the Lord, and *then* to us by the will of God. ⁶So we urged Titus, that as he had begun, so he would also complete this grace in you as well. ⁷But as you abound in everything—in faith, in

though only for a while. ⁹Now I rejoice, not that you were made sorry, but that your sorrow led to repentance. For you were made sorry in a godly manner, that you might suffer loss from us in nothing. ¹⁰For godly sorrow produces repentance *leading* to salvation, not to be regretted; but the sorrow of the world produces death. ¹¹For observe this very thing, that you sorrowed in a godly manner. What diligence it produced in you, *what* clearing *of yourselves, what* indignation, *what* fear, *what* vehement desire, *what* zeal, *what* vindication! In all *things* you proved yourselves to be clear in this matter. ¹²Therefore, although I wrote to you, *I did* not *do it* for the sake of him who had done the wrong, nor for the sake of him who suffered wrong, but that our care for you in the sight of God might appear to you.

THE JOY OF TITUS

¹³Therefore we have been comforted in your comfort. And we rejoiced exceedingly more for the joy of Titus, because his spirit has been refreshed by you all. ¹⁴For if in anything I have boasted to him about you, I am not ashamed. But as we spoke all things to you in truth, even so our boasting to Titus was found true. ¹⁵And his affections are greater for you as he remembers the obedience of you all, how with fear and trembling you received him. ¹⁶Therefore I rejoice that I have confidence in you in everything.

On the Edge

For you know the grace of our Lord Jesus Christ, that though He was rich, yet for your sakes He became poor, that you through His poverty might become rich (2 Cor. 8:9).

Jesus had it all. In heaven, He had angels singing His praises all day long. He'd been sitting at God's right hand ever since the beginning of time. He ruled the whole universe and walked on streets of gold—comfortable, adored, worshiped. Then, one day, it was decision time. Someone had to go to earth. God loved His people so much that He couldn't stand to watch them suffer and wander. The humans needed someone like them to explain God's plan and purpose. So God sent Jesus to be like the people and to live among them on earth. He poured His glorious body into one like ours, gave up all the magnificence of heaven just to help us learn how to live and be right with God. He became poor so that we could know the riches of heaven—joy in a busted world, love when hearts are broken, peace when chaos is reigning, and other blessings. Jesus said that His riches have become ours by our faith in Him. That's great news—you're rich!

SEE FOR YOURSELF:
Rom. 8:17; 1 Cor. 4:8;
1 Tim. 6:17; James 2:5

8:4 *ᵃ*NU-Text and M-Text omit *that we would receive*, thus changing text to *urgency for the favor and fellowship*....

speech, in knowledge, in all diligence, and in your love for us—*see* that you abound in this grace also.

CHRIST OUR PATTERN

[8]I speak not by commandment, but I am testing the sincerity of your love by the diligence of others. [9]For you know the grace of our Lord Jesus Christ, that though He was rich, yet for your sakes He became poor, that you through His poverty might become rich.

WHAT'S IT MEAN?

The Christians in Jerusalem were experiencing some tough times. They had endured two earthquakes and a severe famine. Christian churches in other cities offered to give their own money to help their brothers and sisters in Christ. Paul and Barnabas were collecting the money and taking it to Jerusalem.

2 Corinthians 8:10, 11

[10]And in this I give advice: It is to your advantage not only to be doing what you began and were desiring to do a year ago; [11]but now you also must complete the doing *of it;* that as *there was* a readiness to desire *it,* so *there* also *may be* a completion out of what you have. [12]For if there is first a willing mind, *it is* accepted according to what one has, *and* not according to what he does not have.

[13]For *I do* not *mean* that others should be eased and you burdened; [14]but by an equality, *that* now at this time your abundance *may supply* their lack, that their abundance also may supply your lack—that there may be equality. [15]As it is written, *"He who gathered much had nothing left over, and he who gathered little had no lack."*[a]

COLLECTION FOR THE JUDEAN SAINTS

[16]But thanks *be* to God who puts[a] the same earnest care for you into the heart of Titus. [17]For he not only accepted the exhortation, but being more diligent, he went to you of his own accord. [18]And we have sent with him the brother

whose praise *is* in the gospel throughout all the churches, [19]and not only *that,* but who was also chosen by the churches to travel with us with this gift, which is administered by us to the glory of the Lord Himself and *to show* your ready mind, [20]avoiding this: that anyone should blame us in this lavish gift which is administered by us—[21]providing honorable things, not only in the sight of the Lord, but also in the sight of men.

[22]And we have sent with them our brother whom we have often proved diligent in many things, but now much more diligent, because of the great confidence which *we have* in you. [23]If *anyone inquires* about Titus, *he is* my partner and fellow worker concerning you. Or if our brethren *are inquired about, they are* messengers of the churches, the glory of Christ. [24]Therefore show to them, and[a] before the churches the proof of your love and of our boasting on your behalf.

ADMINISTERING THE GIFT

[1]Now concerning the ministering to the saints, it is superfluous for me to write to you; [2]for I know your willingness, about which I boast of you to the Macedonians, that Achaia was ready a year ago; and your zeal has stirred up the majority. [3]Yet I have sent the brethren, lest our boasting of you should be in vain in this respect, that, as I said, you may be ready; [4]lest if *some* Macedonians come with me and find you unprepared, we (not to mention you!) should be ashamed of this confident boasting.[a] [5]Therefore I thought it necessary to exhort the brethren to go to you ahead of time, and prepare your generous gift beforehand, which *you* had previously promised, that it may be ready as *a matter of* generosity and not as a grudging obligation.

THE CHEERFUL GIVER

[6]But this *I say:* He who sows sparingly will also reap sparingly, and he who sows bountifully will also reap bountifully. [7]So let each one *give* as he purposes in his heart, not grudgingly or of necessity; for God loves a cheerful giver. [8]And God *is* able to make all grace abound toward you, that you, always having all sufficiency in all *things,* may have an abundance for every good work. [9]As it is written:

> *"He has dispersed abroad,*
> *He has given to the poor;*
> *His righteousness endures forever."*[a]

8:15 [a]Exodus 16:18   **8:16** [a]NU-Text reads *has put.*   **8:24** [a]NU-Text and M-Text omit *and.*   **9:4** [a]NU-Text reads *this confidence.*   **9:9** [a]Psalm 112:9

[10]Now may[a] He who supplies seed to the sower, and bread for food, supply and multiply the seed you have *sown* and increase the fruits of your righteousness, [11]while *you are* enriched in everything for all liberality, which causes thanksgiving through us to God. [12]For the administration of this service not only supplies the needs of the saints, but also is abounding through many thanksgivings to God, [13]while, through the proof of this ministry, they glorify God for the obedience of your confession to the gospel of Christ, and for *your* liberal sharing with them and all *men,* [14]and by their prayer for you, who long for you because of the exceeding grace of God in you. [15]Thanks *be* to God for His indescribable gift!

THE SPIRITUAL WAR

[1]Now I, Paul, myself am pleading with you by the meekness and gentleness of Christ—who in presence *am* lowly among you, but being absent am bold toward you. [2]But I beg *you* that when I am present I may not be bold with that confidence by which I intend to be bold against some, who think of us as if we walked according to the flesh. [3]For though we walk in the flesh, we do not war according to the flesh. [4]For the weapons of our warfare *are* not carnal but mighty in God for pulling down strongholds, [5]casting down arguments and every high thing that exalts itself against the knowledge of God, bringing every thought into captivity to the obedience of Christ, [6]and being ready to punish all disobedience when your obedience is fulfilled.

REALITY OF PAUL'S AUTHORITY

[7]Do you look at things according to the outward appearance? If anyone is convinced in himself that he is Christ's, let him again consider this in himself, that just as he *is* Christ's, even so we *are* Christ's.[a] [8]For even if I should boast somewhat more about our authority, which the Lord gave us[a] for edification and not for your destruction, I shall not be ashamed—[9]lest I seem to terrify you by letters. [10]"For *his* letters," they say, "*are* weighty and powerful, but *his* bodily presence *is* weak, and *his* speech contemptible." [11]Let such a person consider this, that what we are in word by letters when we are absent, such *we will* also *be* in deed when we are present.

On the Edge

Now I, Paul, myself am pleading with you by the meekness and gentleness of Christ—who in presence am lowly among you, but being absent am bold toward you (2 Cor. 10:1).

Paul modeled his ministry after Jesus. Jesus was gentle. The world sometimes mistakes gentleness for weakness; but for Jesus, gentleness was a strength. A gentle spirit comes from loving others more than you love yourself. Jesus was able to calmly handle the wrongs done to Him because He was a gentle Man. He didn't rant and rave, or fuss and fume. He was stronger than that. Paul wanted to be like Him, and so should we. As you grow in maturity, other-centeredness replaces selfish ambitions, short tempers become hearts that are slow to anger, and genuine love replaces jealousy and envy. A gentle spirit is a treasure. When you meet a gentle person, you can know that you have met someone who is strong in heart and in character. You have met someone like Jesus.

SEE FOR YOURSELF:
Ps. 143:10; Is. 42:3;
Matt. 11:29;
John 13:1–17

LIMITS OF PAUL'S AUTHORITY

[12]For we dare not class ourselves or compare ourselves with those who commend themselves. But they, measuring themselves by themselves, and comparing themselves among themselves, are not wise. [13]We, however, will not boast beyond measure, but within the limits of the sphere which God appointed us—a sphere which especially includes you. [14]For we are not overextending ourselves (as though *our authority* did not extend to you), for it was to you that we came with the gospel of Christ; [15]not boasting of things beyond measure, *that is,* in other men's labors, but having hope, *that* as your faith is increased, we shall be greatly enlarged by you in our sphere, [16]to preach the gospel in the *regions* beyond you, *and* not to

9:10 [a]NU-Text reads *Now He who supplies . . . will supply. . . .*   **10:7** [a]NU-Text reads *even as we are.*
10:8 [a]NU-Text omits *us.*

boast in another man's sphere of accomplishment.

17But *"he who glories, let him glory in the Lord."ᵃ* 18For not he who commends himself is approved, but whom the Lord commends.

CONCERN FOR THEIR FAITHFULNESS

1Oh, that you would bear with me in a little folly—and indeed you do bear with me. 2For I am jealous for you with godly jealousy. For I have betrothed you to one husband, that I may present *you as* a chaste virgin to Christ. 3But I fear, lest somehow, as the serpent deceived Eve by his craftiness, so your minds may be corrupted from the simplicityᵃ that is in Christ. 4For if he who comes preaches another Jesus whom we have not preached, or *if* you receive a different spirit which you have not received, or a different gospel which you have not accepted—you may well put up with it!

PAUL AND FALSE APOSTLES

5For I consider that I am not at all inferior to the most eminent apostles. 6Even though *I am* untrained in speech, yet *I am* not in knowledge. But we have been thoroughly manifestedᵃ among you in all things.

7Did I commit sin in humbling myself that you might be exalted, because I preached the gospel of God to you free of charge? 8I robbed other churches, taking wages *from them* to minister to you. 9And when I was present with you, and in need, I was a burden to no one, for what I lacked the brethren who came from Macedonia supplied. And in everything I kept myself from being burdensome to you, and so I will keep *myself.* 10As the truth of Christ is in me, no one shall stop me from this boasting in the regions of Achaia. 11Why? Because I do not love you? God knows!

12But what I do, I will also continue to do, that I may cut off the opportunity from those who desire an opportunity to be regarded just as we are in the things of which they boast. 13For such *are* false apostles, deceitful workers, transforming themselves into apostles of Christ. 14And no wonder! For Satan himself transforms himself into an angel of light. 15Therefore *it is* no great thing if his ministers also transform themselves into ministers of righteousness, whose end will be according to their works.

RELUCTANT BOASTING

16I say again, let no one think me a fool. If otherwise, at least receive me as a fool, that I also may boast a little. 17What I speak, I speak not according to the Lord, but as it were, foolishly, in this confidence of boasting. 18Seeing that many boast according to the flesh, I also will boast. 19For you put up with fools gladly, since you *yourselves* are wise! 20For you put up with it if one brings you into bondage, if one devours *you,* if one takes *from you,* if one exalts himself, if one strikes you on the face. 21To *our* shame I say that we were too weak for that! But in whatever anyone is bold—I speak foolishly—I am bold also.

SUFFERING FOR CHRIST

22Are they Hebrews? So am I. Are they Israelites? So am I. Are they the seed of Abraham? So *am* I. 23Are they ministers of Christ?—I speak as a fool—I *am* more: in labors more abundant, in stripes above measure, in prisons more frequently, in deaths often. 24From the Jews five times I received forty *stripes* minus one. 25Three times I was beaten with rods; once I was stoned; three times I was shipwrecked; a night and a day I have been in the deep; 26in journeys often, *in* perils of waters, *in* perils of robbers, *in* perils of *my own* countrymen, *in* perils of the Gentiles, *in* perils in the city, *in* perils in the wilderness, *in* perils in the sea, *in* perils among false brethren; 27in weariness and toil, in sleeplessness often, in hunger and thirst, in fastings often, in cold and nakedness— 28besides the other things, what comes upon me daily: my deep concern for all the churches. 29Who is weak, and I am not weak? Who is made to stumble, and I do not burn *with indignation?* 30If I must boast, I will boast in the things which concern my infirmity. 31The God and Father of our Lord Jesus Christ, who is blessed forever, knows that I am not lying. 32In Damas-

> "But 'he who glories, let him glory in the Lord.' For not he who commends himself is approved, but whom the Lord commends."
> (2 Corinthians 10:17, 18)

> SATAN
> How does Satan disguise himself?
> (11:14)

10:17 ᵃJeremiah 9:24   **11:3** ᵃNU-Text adds *and purity.*   **11:6** ᵃNU-Text omits *been.*

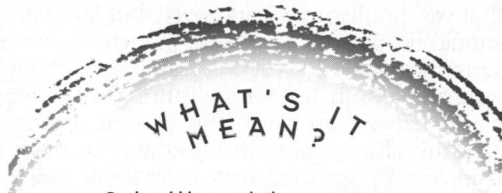

WHAT'S IT MEAN?

Paul could have racked up an impressive number of frequent flier miles if he'd had access to air travel. During his four missionary journeys, the apostle covered thousands of miles on foot. Many of the roads he traveled were more dangerous than you might imagine. Some flooded in the spring when area rivers overflowed their banks. This was especially true of the road between Jerusalem and Antioch. Other roads, such as the one between Perga and Pisidian Antioch, were treacherous because of robbers who preyed on travelers.

2 Corinthians 11:26

cus the governor, under Aretas the king, was guarding the city of the Damascenes with a garrison, desiring to arrest me; ³³but I was let down in a basket through a window in the wall, and escaped from his hands.

THE VISION OF PARADISE

¹It is doubtless*a* not profitable for me to boast. I will come to visions and revelations of the Lord: ²I know a man in Christ who fourteen years ago—whether in the body I do not know, or whether out of the body I do not know, God knows—such a one was caught up to the third heaven. ³And I know such a man—whether in the body or out of the body I do not know, God knows— ⁴how he was caught up into Paradise and heard inexpressible words, which it is not lawful for a man to utter. ⁵Of such a one I will boast; yet of myself I will not boast, except in my infirmities. ⁶For though I might desire to boast, I will not be a fool; for I will speak the truth. But I refrain, lest anyone should think of me above what he sees me *to be* or hears from me.

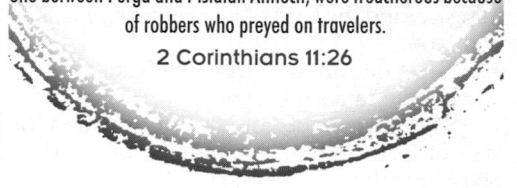

SICKNESS

Who had sickness that God would not heal? (12:7–10)

THE THORN IN THE FLESH

⁷And lest I should be exalted above measure by the abundance of the revelations, a thorn in the flesh was given to me, a messenger of Satan to buffet me, lest I be exalted above measure. ⁸Concerning this thing I pleaded with the Lord three times that it might depart from me. ⁹And He said to me, "My grace is sufficient for you, for My strength is made perfect in weakness." Therefore most gladly I will rather boast in my infirmities, that the power of Christ may rest upon me. ¹⁰Therefore I take pleasure in infirmities, in reproaches, in needs, in persecutions, in distresses, for Christ's sake. For when I am weak, then I am strong.

SIGNS OF AN APOSTLE

¹¹I have become a fool in boasting;*a* you have compelled me. For I ought to have been commended by you; for in nothing was I behind the most eminent apostles, though I am nothing. ¹²Truly the signs of an apostle were accomplished among you with all perseverance, in signs and wonders and mighty deeds. ¹³For what is it in which you were inferior to other churches, except that I myself was not burdensome to you? Forgive me this wrong!

LOVE FOR THE CHURCH

¹⁴Now *for* the third time I am ready to come to you. And I will not be burdensome to you; for I do not seek yours, but you. For the children ought not to lay up for the parents, but the parents for the children. ¹⁵And I will very gladly spend and be spent for your souls; though the more abundantly I love you, the less I am loved.

¹⁶But be that *as it may*, I did not burden you. Nevertheless, being crafty, I caught you by cunning! ¹⁷Did I take advantage of you by any of those whom I sent to you? ¹⁸I urged Titus, and sent our brother with *him*. Did Titus take advantage of you? Did we not walk in the same spirit? Did *we* not *walk* in the same steps?

¹⁹Again, do you think*a* that we excuse ourselves to you? We speak before God in Christ. But *we do* all things, beloved, for your edification. ²⁰For I fear lest, when I come, I shall not find you such as I wish, and *that* I shall be found by you such as you do not wish; lest *there be* contentions, jealousies, outbursts of wrath, selfish ambitions, backbitings, whisperings, conceits, tumults; ²¹lest, when I come again, my God will humble me among you, and I shall mourn for many who have sinned before and have not repented of the uncleanness, fornication, and lewdness which they have practiced.

12:1 *a*NU-Text reads *necessary, though not profitable, to boast.*   **12:11** *a*NU-Text omits *in boasting.*
12:19 *a*NU-Text reads *You have been thinking for a long time . . . .*

COMING WITH AUTHORITY

[1]This *will be* the third *time* I am coming to you. *"By the mouth of two or three witnesses every word shall be established."*[a] [2]I have told you before, and foretell as if I were present the second time, and now being absent I write[a] to those who have sinned before, and to all the rest, that if I come again I will not spare—[3]since you seek a proof of Christ speaking in me, who is not weak toward you, but mighty in you. [4]For though He was crucified in weakness, yet He lives by the power of God. For we also are weak in Him, but we shall live with Him by the power of God toward you.

[5]Examine yourselves *as to* whether you are in the faith. Test yourselves. Do you not know yourselves, that Jesus Christ is in you?—unless indeed you are disqualified. [6]But I trust that you will know that we are not disqualified.

PAUL PREFERS GENTLENESS

[7]Now I[a] pray to God that you do no evil, not that we should appear approved, but that you should do what is honorable, though we may seem disqualified. [8]For we can do nothing against the truth, but for the truth. [9]For we are glad when we are weak and you are strong. And this also we pray, that you may be made complete. [10]Therefore I write these things being absent, lest being present I should use sharpness, according to the authority which the Lord has given me for edification and not for destruction.

GREETINGS AND BENEDICTION

[11]Finally, brethren, farewell. Become complete. Be of good comfort, be of one mind, live in peace; and the God of love and peace will be with you.

[12]Greet one another with a holy kiss.

[13]All the saints greet you.

[14]The grace of the Lord Jesus Christ, and the love of God, and the communion of the Holy Spirit *be* with you all. Amen.

13:1 [a]Deuteronomy 19:15   **13:2** [a]NU-Text omits *I write.*   **13:7** [a]NU-Text reads *we.*

CONTENT

Have you ever tried to explain something to someone over and over and over and just when you think they're about to get it—you realize they don't even know what you are talking about?

That's how Paul felt about the Galatians. Paul had spent time with the churches in Galatia teaching them the basics of Christianity. He thought they had finally gotten the fact that Christ's sacrifice on the cross changed everything. Righteousness was no longer a by-product of rules and regulations followed to a "T". Righteousness now came from faith in Christ's one-time sacrifice of Himself. Compared to the kind of life people had faced under Jewish law, this new understanding of righteousness was pure freedom.

Paul got exasperated with the Galatians because, even though he had taught them this new way of thinking, they had reverted back to trying to earn their righteousness by obeying the Jewish law. Paul was irritated. So he sat down and wrote them a letter to try to get them back on the right track. That is how we got the Book of Galatians in the Bible.

Because of all this, some people call the Book of Galatians the spiritual Declaration of Independence.

Outline

Purpose

We are saved and we live "by faith."

Theme

Justification by Faith Alone

Date of writing

A.D. 48

> "I have been crucified with Christ; it is no longer I who live, but Christ lives in me; and the life which I now live in the flesh I live by faith in the Son of God, who loved me and gave Himself for me" (2:20).

Bible Talk

Judaizers

When the Galatians fell back into legalism (believing you could be righteous by obeying the law) they did it with a little help. There was a group of people called "Judaizers" who came to Galatia and began to influence the church there. The Judaizers believed that anyone who wanted to be a Christian should obey the Jewish customs including circumcision.

Now the Jewish customs were a product of years of traditions passed down from family to family from generation to generation. It would have been a lot for anyone to take, not to mention that Christ had freed the people from those customs. The Judaizers ignored the grace that God offered through Christ. This is why Paul could not ignore their influence.

CHRISTIAN FRUIT

One of the famous passages in Galatians says we should bear fruit. In fact, there are several places in the Bible where Christians are compared to growing things like grapevines and fruit-bearing trees. Do you think being a Christian is like being a tree?

In some ways it is. The purpose of an apple tree is to bear apples. The way you know whether that tree is doing what it is supposed to do is when you pick an apple and take a bite.

That's how we are as Christians. The test of whether we are growing spiritually is the fruit we produce. Galatians says our fruit is love, joy, peace, longsuffering, kindness, goodness, faithfulness, gentleness, and self-control (5:22, 23). What kind of fruit do people pick off your branches?

GREETING

¹Paul, an apostle (not from men nor through man, but through Jesus Christ and God the Father who raised Him from the dead), ²and all the brethren who are with me,

To the churches of Galatia:

³Grace to you and peace from God the Father and our Lord Jesus Christ, ⁴who gave Himself for our sins, that He might deliver us from this present evil age, according to the will of our God and Father, ⁵to whom *be* glory forever and ever. Amen.

ONLY ONE GOSPEL

⁶I marvel that you are turning away so soon from Him who called you in the grace of Christ, to a different gospel, ⁷which is not another; but there are some who trouble you and want to pervert the gospel of Christ. ⁸But even if we, or an angel from heaven, preach any other gospel to you than what we have preached to you, let him be accursed. ⁹As we have said before, so now I say again, if anyone preaches any other gospel to you than what you have received, let him be accursed.

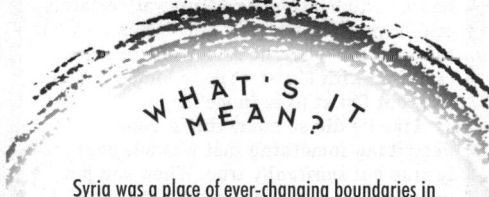

WHAT'S IT MEAN?

Syria was a place of ever-changing boundaries in biblical times. Usually the name was used to describe a general region. At the time of Paul's letter to the Galatians, it was a Roman province that extended northeast from Jerusalem into what is now Turkey. Cilicia was a region in the northern part of Syria, home to such famous cities as Antioch and Tarsus.

Galatians 1:21

¹⁰For do I now persuade men, or God? Or do I seek to please men? For if I still pleased men, I would not be a bondservant of Christ.

CALL TO APOSTLESHIP

¹¹But I make known to you, brethren, that the gospel which was preached by me is not according to man. ¹²For I neither received it from man, nor was I taught *it*, but *it came* through the revelation of Jesus Christ.

¹³For you have heard of my former conduct in Judaism, how I persecuted the church of God beyond measure and *tried to* destroy it. ¹⁴And I advanced in Judaism beyond many of my contemporaries in my own nation, being more exceedingly zealous for the traditions of my fathers. ¹⁵But when it pleased God, who separated me from my mother's womb and called *me* through His grace, ¹⁶to reveal His Son in me, that I might preach Him among the Gentiles, I did not immediately confer with flesh and blood, ¹⁷nor did I go up to Jerusalem to those *who were* apostles before me; but I went to Arabia, and returned again to Damascus.

CONTACTS AT JERUSALEM

¹⁸Then after three years I went up to Jerusalem to see Peter,ᵃ and remained with him fifteen days. ¹⁹But I saw none of the other apostles except James, the Lord's brother. ²⁰(Now *concerning* the things which I write to you, indeed, before God, I do not lie.)

²¹Afterward I went into the regions of Syria and Cilicia. ²²And I was unknown by face to the churches of Judea which *were* in Christ. ²³But they were hearing only, "He who formerly persecuted us now preaches the faith which he once *tried to* destroy." ²⁴And they glorified God in me.

DEFENDING THE GOSPEL

¹Then after fourteen years I went up again to Jerusalem with Barnabas, and also took Titus with *me.* ²And I went up by revelation, and communicated to them that gospel which I preach among the Gentiles, but privately to those who were of reputation, lest by any means I might run, or had run, in vain. ³Yet not even Titus who *was* with me, being a Greek, was compelled to be circumcised. ⁴And *this occurred* because of false brethren secretly brought in (who came in by stealth to spy out our liberty which we have in Christ Jesus, that they might bring us into bondage), ⁵to whom we did not yield submission even for an hour, that the truth of the gospel might continue with you.

⁶But from those who seemed to be something— whatever they were, it makes no difference to me; God shows personal favoritism

JEALOUSY
Is envying other Christians wise?
(2:6)

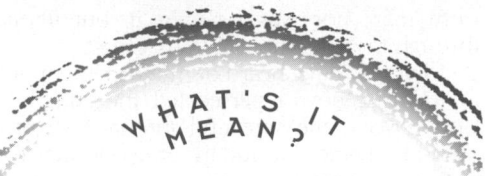

WHAT'S IT MEAN?

Barnabas lived quite an interesting life. Before he became a Christian, he was a wealthy Jew living on the island of Cyprus. After he became a Christian, he sold his property and gave the money to the disciples in Jerusalem. Later, he took on the role of Paul's traveling companion. Titus, who accompanied Paul and Barnabas on their trips, had his own claim to fame. He was one of the first Gentiles (non-Jews) to become a Christian. Titus worked as Paul's assistant, delivering the apostle's messages to various churches in need of guidance and direction.

Galatians 2:1

to no man—for those who seemed *to be something* added nothing to me. [7]But on the contrary, when they saw that the gospel for the uncircumcised had been committed to me, as *the gospel* for the circumcised *was* to Peter [8](for He who worked effectively in Peter for the apostleship to the circumcised also worked effectively in me toward the Gentiles), [9]and when James, Cephas, and John, who seemed to be pillars, perceived the grace that had been given to me, they gave me and Barnabas the right hand of fellowship, that we *should go* to the Gentiles and they to the circumcised. [10]*They desired* only

WHAT'S IT MEAN?

One of the best ways to determine whether a person is a Gentile or not is to ask this question: "Are you a Jew?" If the person says no, he or she is a Gentile. Jewish people in Paul's day set themselves apart from Gentiles by following the customs and rules of the Old Testament, particularly the Law that God gave to Moses.

Galatians 2:8

that we should remember the poor, the very thing which I also was eager to do.

NO RETURN TO THE LAW

[11]Now when Peter[a] had come to Antioch, I withstood him to his face, because he was to be blamed; [12]for before certain men came from James, he would eat with the Gentiles; but when they came, he withdrew and separated himself, fearing those who were of the circumcision. [13]And the rest of the Jews also played the hypocrite with him, so that even Barnabas was carried away with their hypocrisy.

[14]But when I saw that they were not

On the Edge

I have been crucified with Christ; it is no longer I who live, but Christ lives in me; and the life which I now live in the flesh I live by faith in the Son of God, who loved me and gave Himself for me (Gal. 2:20).

Obviously, you're still breathing and your heart's still beating. And Paul was certainly still alive when he wrote this letter. So what did he mean when he said, "I have been crucified with Christ; it is no longer I who live, but Christ lives in me"?

Like he did so many times, Paul was describing something that was not *physically* true but *spiritually* true. When you put your faith in Jesus, something changes inside you. The old you—the old spirit—dies and a new spirit is born in you. You become Christ-centered instead of self-centered. You have a new life in Christ and it's totally different from your old life without Him. You've got a new reason to live.

Before you gave your heart to Jesus, you were on your own. Now you've got the King of Kings with you all the time—loving you, forgiving you, guiding you, inspiring you.

When your old self dies and Christ lives fully in you, all that's left is what God planned for you in the first place. Nothing could be better or more satisfying than that.

SEE FOR YOURSELF:
Ps. 110:1; Col. 3:1

2:11 [a]NU-Text reads *Cephas.*

straightforward about the truth of the gospel, I said to Peter before *them* all, "If you, being a Jew, live in the manner of Gentiles and not as the Jews, why do you[a] compel Gentiles to live as Jews?[b] 15We *who are* Jews by nature, and not sinners of the Gentiles, 16knowing that a man is not justified by the works of the law but by faith in Jesus Christ, even we have believed in Christ Jesus, that we might be justified

> "I have been crucified with Christ; it is no longer I who live, but Christ lives in me."
> (Galatians 2:20a)

by faith in Christ and not by the works of the law; for by the works of the law no flesh shall be justified.

17"But if, while we seek to be justified by Christ, we ourselves also are found sinners, *is* Christ therefore a minister of sin? Certainly not! 18For if I build again those things which I destroyed, I make myself a transgressor. 19For I through the law died to the law that I might live to God. 20I have been crucified with Christ; it is no longer I who live, but Christ lives in me; and the *life* which I now live in the flesh I live by faith in the Son of God, who loved me and gave Himself for me. 21I do not set aside the grace of God; for if righteousness *comes* through the law, then Christ died in vain."

JUSTIFICATION BY FAITH

1O foolish Galatians! Who has bewitched you that you should not obey the truth,[a] before whose eyes Jesus Christ was clearly portrayed among you[b] as crucified? 2This only I want to learn from you: Did you receive the Spirit by the works of the law, or by the hearing of faith? 3Are you so foolish? Having begun in the Spirit, are you now being made perfect by the flesh? 4Have you suffered so many things in vain—if indeed *it was* in vain?

5Therefore He who supplies the Spirit to you and works miracles among you, *does He do it* by the works of the law, or by the hearing of faith?—6just as Abraham *"believed God, and it was accounted to him for righteousness."[a]* 7Therefore know that *only* those who are of faith are sons of Abraham. 8And the Scripture, foreseeing that God would justify the Gentiles by faith, preached the gospel to Abraham beforehand, *saying, "In you all the nations shall be blessed."[a]* 9So then those who *are* of faith are blessed with believing Abraham.

THE LAW BRINGS A CURSE

10For as many as are of the works of the law are under the curse; for it is written, *"Cursed is everyone who does not continue in all things which are written in the book of the law, to do them."[a]* 11But that no one is justified by the law in the sight of God *is* evident, for *"the just shall*

On the Edge

This only I want to learn from you: Did you receive the Spirit by the works of the law, or by the hearing of faith? (Gal. 3:2).

This passage of Scripture shows you that you have God's Spirit by faith in Christ. How did you get saved? It happened by putting your faith in Christ. So how did you receive His Spirit? It was the same way, by putting your faith in Christ. When you received Christ, you received His Spirit.

Paul goes on to say that God will complete the work that He has started in you, and that God gives you His Spirit and works miracles in you (see 3:3–5). Paul was trying to get a point across. He was asking if all these things happen because of obedience to rules, or because of faith in Christ?

After reading this entire passage, you'll see that God's Spirit moves because of faith in Christ. Of course, you have to exercise your faith. Jesus says in Mark 9:23, "If you can believe, all things are possible to him who believes." Hebrews 11:6 tells us that "without faith it is impossible to please Him, . . ." It's faith that saves us, faith that fills us with God's Holy Spirit, faith that heals us. In fact, every promise God has ever given us must be received by faith. Thank God today that you have His Spirit by faith.

SEE FOR YOURSELF:
Mark 9:23; Eph. 1:13;
Heb. 11:6

2:14 [a]NU-Text reads *how can you.* [b]Some interpreters stop the quotation here. **3:1** [a]NU-Text omits *that you should not obey the truth.* [b]NU-Text omits *among you.* **3:6** [a]Genesis 15:6 **3:8** [a]Genesis 12:3; 18:18; 22:18; 26:4; 28:14 **3:10** [a]Deuteronomy 27:26

live by faith." [a] [12]Yet the law is not of faith, but "the man who does them shall live by them." [a]

[13]Christ has redeemed us from the curse of the law, having become a curse for us (for it is written, "Cursed is everyone who hangs on a tree" [a]), [14]that the blessing of Abraham might come upon the Gentiles in Christ Jesus, that we might receive the promise of the Spirit through faith.

THE CHANGELESS PROMISE

[15]Brethren, I speak in the manner of men: Though it is only a man's covenant, yet if it is confirmed, no one annuls or adds to it. [16]Now to Abraham and his Seed were the promises made. He does not say, "And to seeds," as of many, but as of one, "And to your Seed," [a] who is Christ. [17]And this I say, that the law, which was four hundred and thirty years later, cannot annul the covenant that was confirmed before by God in Christ, [a] that it should make the promise of no effect. [18]For if the inheritance is of the law, it is no longer of promise; but God gave it to Abraham by promise.

PURPOSE OF THE LAW

[19]What purpose then does the law serve? It was added because of transgressions, till the Seed should come to whom the promise was made; and it was appointed through angels by the hand of a mediator. [20]Now a mediator does not mediate for one only, but God is one.

[21]Is the law then against the promises of God? Certainly not! For if there had been a law given which could have given life, truly righteousness would have been by the law. [22]But the Scripture has confined all under sin, that the promise by faith in Jesus Christ might be given to those who believe. [23]But before faith came, we were kept under guard by the law, kept for the faith which would afterward be revealed. [24]Therefore the law was our tutor to bring us to Christ, that we might be justified by faith. [25]But after faith has come, we are no longer under a tutor.

SONS AND HEIRS

[26]For you are all sons of God through faith in Christ Jesus. [27]For as many of you as were baptized into Christ have put on Christ. [28]There is nei-ther Jew nor Greek, there is neither slave nor free, there is neither male nor female; for you are all one in Christ Jesus. [29]And if you are Christ's, then you are Abraham's seed, and heirs according to the promise.

HATRED
Is the salvation of all Christians equal? (3:28, 29)

[1]Now I say that the heir, as long as he is a child, does not differ at all from a slave, though

---

3:11 [a]Habakkuk 2:4   **3:12** [a]Leviticus 18:5   **3:13** [a]Deuteronomy 21:23   **3:16** [a]Genesis 12:7; 13:15; 24:7
3:17 [a]NU-Text omits in Christ.

⁖ Promise   HE PROMISES THAT YOU ARE HIS CHILD BY FAITH.

For you are all sons of God through faith in Christ Jesus (Gal. 3:26).

You are God's child, and He is your Father. But how? Because you put your faith in Jesus. What is faith? Belief without proof. Hebrews 11:1 says, "Now faith is the substance of things hoped for, the evidence of things not seen." Even though you've never seen God, you know He exists. Because you know He exists, you put your faith in Him.

God cares for you the same way an earthly father takes care of his children, only better. God is concerned with every detail of your life. He wants to give you good things. He wants to see you grow up and be everything He's designed you to be. He really wants you to know Him—deeply and powerfully. How can you get to know your Father better? By spending time with Him in prayer and by studying His Word.

You're God's child. You're a prince or a princess in His kingdom because the King is your Dad! He loves you so much that He's adopted you as His very own. By faith, take your place as a child of God.

SEE FOR YOURSELF:
Matt. 7:11; John 1:12, 13; Rom. 8:15, 16; 1 John 3:1

he is master of all, [2]but is under guardians and stewards until the time appointed by the father. [3]Even so we, when we were children, were in bondage under the elements of the world. [4]But when the fullness of the time had come, God sent forth His Son, born[a] of a woman, born under the law, [5]to redeem those who were under the law, that we might receive the adoption as sons.

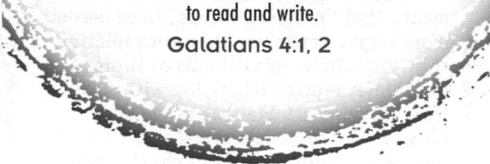

WHAT'S IT MEAN?

Slaves may have been considered second-class citizens in New Testament times, but that didn't stop their masters from entrusting their kids to the slaves' care. Slaves regularly supervised the education of their master's children. According to the custom of the day, most girls received their education at home. Boys, on the other hand, attended school, where they learned to read and write.

Galatians 4:1, 2

[6]And because you are sons, God has sent forth the Spirit of His Son into your hearts, crying out, "Abba, Father!" [7]Therefore you are no longer a slave but a son, and if a son, then an heir of[a] God through Christ.

FEARS FOR THE CHURCH

[8]But then, indeed, when you did not know God, you served those which by nature are not gods. [9]But now after you have known God, or rather are known by God, how is it that you turn again to the weak and beggarly elements, to which you desire again to be in bondage? [10]You observe days and months and seasons and years. [11]I am afraid for you, lest I have labored for you in vain.

[12]Brethren, I urge you to become like me, for I became like you. You have not injured me at all. [13]You know that because of physical infirmity I preached the gospel to you at the first. [14]And my trial which was in my flesh you did not despise or reject, but you received me as an angel of God, even as Christ Jesus. [15]What[a] then was the blessing you enjoyed? For I bear you witness that, if possible, you would have

plucked out your own eyes and given them to me. [16]Have I therefore become your enemy because I tell you the truth?

[17]They zealously court you, but for no good; yes, they want to exclude you, that you may be zealous for them. [18]But it is good to be zealous in a good thing always, and not only when I am present with you. [19]My little children, for whom I labor in birth again until Christ is formed in you, [20]I would like to be present with you now and to change my tone; for I have doubts about you.

TWO COVENANTS

[21]Tell me, you who desire to be under the law, do you not hear the law? [22]For it is written that Abraham had two sons: the one by a bondwoman, the other by a freewoman. [23]But he who was of the bondwoman was born according to the flesh, and he of the freewoman through promise, [24]which things are symbolic. For these are the[a] two covenants: the one from Mount Sinai which gives birth to bondage, which is Hagar—[25]for this Hagar is Mount Sinai in Arabia, and corresponds to Jerusalem which now is, and is in bondage with her children—[26]but the Jerusalem above is free, which is the mother of us all. [27]For it is written:

WHAT'S IT MEAN?

Sarah and Hagar both gave birth to a son of Abraham. The difference between the two women is that Sarah was Abraham's wife and Hagar was Sarah's slave. Before you get the wrong idea about Abraham, you should know that his encounter with Hagar was Sarah's idea. God had promised Abraham and Sarah that they would have a son. Sarah realized that she was too old to have a child, so she thought the next best thing would be for her servant to have Abraham's son. And that's what happened. Hagar gave birth to a son named Ishmael. God, however, made it clear that Ishmael was not the son He had promised. Despite the fact that she was ninety years old, Sarah herself became pregnant and gave birth to a son named Isaac—the one God had promised.

Galatians 4:23

4:4 [a]Or made 4:7 [a]NU-Text reads through God and omits through Christ. 4:15 [a]NU-Text reads Where.
4:24 [a]NU-Text and M-Text omit the.

" *Rejoice, O barren,*
You who do not bear!
Break forth and shout,
You who are not in labor!
For the desolate has many more children
Than she who has a husband." [a]

28Now we, brethren, as Isaac *was,* are children of promise. 29But, as he who was born according to the flesh then persecuted him *who was born* according to the Spirit, even so *it is* now. 30Nevertheless what does the Scripture say? *"Cast out the bondwoman and her son, for the son of the bondwoman shall not be heir with the son of the freewoman."* [a] 31So then, brethren, we are not children of the bondwoman but of the free.

CHRISTIAN LIBERTY

1Stand fast therefore in the liberty by which Christ has made us free,[a] and do not be entangled again with a yoke of bondage. 2Indeed I, Paul, say to you that if you become circumcised, Christ will profit you nothing. 3And I testify again to every man who becomes circumcised that he is a debtor to keep the whole law. 4You have become estranged from Christ, you who *attempt to* be justified by law; you have fallen from grace. 5For we through the Spirit eagerly wait for the hope of righteousness by faith. 6For in Christ Jesus neither circumcision nor uncircumcision avails anything, but faith working through love.

EMOTIONS

Are emotions reliable guides? (5:1–17)

LOVE FULFILLS THE LAW

7You ran well. Who hindered you from obeying the truth? 8This persuasion does not *come* from Him who calls you. 9A little leaven leavens the whole lump. 10I have confidence in you, in the Lord, that you will have no other mind; but he who troubles you shall bear his judgment, whoever he is. 11And I, brethren, if I still preach circumcision, why do I still suffer persecution? Then the offense of the cross has ceased. 12I could wish that those who trouble you would even cut themselves off! 13For you, brethren, have been called to liberty; only do not *use* liberty as an opportunity for the flesh, but through love serve one another. 14For all the law is fulfilled in one word,

even in this: *"You shall love your neighbor as yourself."* [a] 15But if you bite and devour one another, beware lest you be consumed by one another!

WALKING IN THE SPIRIT

16I say then: Walk in the Spirit, and you shall not fulfill the lust of the flesh. 17For the flesh lusts against the Spirit, and the Spirit against the flesh; and these are contrary to one another, so

On the Edge

Stand fast therefore in the liberty by which Christ has made us free, and do not be entangled again with a yoke of bondage (Gal. 5:1).

Being entangled with a yoke of bondage means that "religious things" have become more important to you than your relationship with Christ. What kinds of things sometimes replace fellowship with God? Well, carrying a Bible that rarely gets opened, just so people can see it. Trying to fool people with a bunch of churchy words you don't mean. Showing up for every church service, prayer meeting, concert, or special event just so everyone will think you're so committed.

Those things are bondage. They're about Law and not about Christ. Being involved in Christian activities is not the same as being involved with Jesus. He says you are free. You're free not to pretend anymore; free to say no to sex before marriage; free not to hang out with friends who always get you in trouble; free to —*really* pray—just "real talk" with God; free from sin and sinful habits; free to follow God's leading; free to not care what everyone else thinks; free, free, free!

Worldly success is so temporary. What matters most is that you have a relationship with God and that you do what He tells you to do. The other stuff will burn. Only eternal things matter. And you are free to live for those eternal things. Love God and be free in Him.

SEE FOR YOURSELF:
John 8:32; 2 Cor. 3:17; Gal. 5:13

4:27 [a]Isaiah 54:1   **4:30** [a]Genesis 21:10   **5:1** [a]NU-Text reads *For freedom Christ has made us free; stand fast therefore.*   **5:14** [a]Leviticus 19:18

bitions, dissensions, heresies, [21]envy, murders,[a] drunkenness, revelries, and the like; of which I tell you beforehand, just as I also told *you* in time past, that those who practice such things will not inherit the kingdom of God.

[22]But the fruit of the Spirit is love, joy, peace, longsuffering, kindness, goodness, faithfulness, [23]gentleness, self-control. Against such there is no law. [24]And those *who are* Christ's have crucified the flesh with its passions and desires. [25]If we live in the Spirit, let us also walk in the Spirit. [26]Let us not become conceited, provoking one another, envying one another.

BEAR AND SHARE THE BURDENS

[1]Brethren, if a man is overtaken in any trespass, you who *are* spiritual restore such a one in

---

On the Edge

For the flesh lusts against the Spirit, and the Spirit against the flesh; and these are contrary to one another, so that you do not do the things that you wish (Gal. 5:17).

God's Word tells us to love the Lord with all of our heart, with all of our soul, and with all of our strength (see Deut. 6:4, 5). When you first got saved, you gave your heart to Jesus first. You didn't give Him your soul or your strength first. You gave Him your heart.

Satan will always counterfeit what God does, and do the exact opposite. He'll always go after your mind first, because he knows that if he can get something into your mind and get you to think continually about it, then he can get you to do it. That's why it's so important to realize that you can control your thoughts and desires.

Sin always starts in the mind. It's not sin to have an evil thought—that's temptation; but it is wrong to dwell on and entertain those thoughts. To make it simpler: A bird can lay an egg on your head, but only you can let him build a nest in your hair!

James 1:13–15 reminds us that if we think about sin long enough, we'll desire to sin. If we want to sin, we will eventually sin. After sin is done, it will leave us dead. That's why it's so important to walk in the Spirit and feed your mind with the Word of God.

Paul sums it up in Galatians 5:24, 25: "And those who are Christ's have crucified the flesh with its passions and desires. If we live in the Spirit, let us also walk in the Spirit." His Spirit helps you overcome evil desires!

SEE FOR YOURSELF:
2 Cor. 10:4–6;
James 1:13–15

On the Edge

But the fruit of the Spirit is love, joy, peace, longsuffering, kindness, goodness, faithfulness, gentleness, self-control. Against such there is no law. And those who are Christ's have crucified the flesh with its passions and desires. If we live in the Spirit, let us also walk in the Spirit (Gal. 5:22–25).

The Spirit of God lives in each believer and is the agent of change. He brings power to our lives that we would otherwise be without. Because He is in us, we have the ability to change and become more Christlike. Verses 22 and 23 list some of the areas that the Holy Spirit can change in your life. In which of these areas could you use some help? Find a specific Scripture and use it to renew your mind. Memorize it; meditate on it; say it in your sleep! Then pray for the Holy Spirit to begin working. The most important part is that you cooperate with the Holy Spirit when He reminds you to be gentle instead of whining. It's called obedience. Eventually, little by little, the whining will be replaced and you will have begun to make some changes in your life.

SEE FOR YOURSELF:
Prov. 3:5, 6; 13:10;
Matt. 6:33

---

that you do not do the things that you wish. [18]But if you are led by the Spirit, you are not under the law.

[19]Now the works of the flesh are evident, which are: adultery,[a] fornication, uncleanness, lewdness, [20]idolatry, sorcery, hatred, contentions, jealousies, outbursts of wrath, selfish am-

---

5:19 [a]NU-Text omits *adultery*.   **5:21** [a]NU-Text omits *murders*.

a spirit of gentleness, considering yourself lest you also be tempted. ²Bear one another's burdens, and so fulfill the law of Christ. ³For if anyone thinks himself to be something, when he is nothing, he deceives himself. ⁴But let each one examine his own work, and then he will have rejoicing in himself alone, and not in another. ⁵For each one shall bear his own load.

BE GENEROUS AND DO GOOD

⁶Let him who is taught the word share in all good things with him who teaches.

⁷Do not be deceived, God is not mocked; for whatever a man sows, that he will also reap. ⁸For he who sows to his flesh will of the flesh reap corruption, but he who sows to the Spirit will of the Spirit reap everlasting life. ⁹And let us not grow weary while doing good, for in due season we shall reap if we do not lose heart. ¹⁰Therefore, as we have opportunity, let us do good to all, especially to those who are of the household of faith.

GLORY ONLY IN THE CROSS

¹¹See with what large letters I have written to you with my own hand! ¹²As many as desire to make a good showing in the flesh, these *would* compel you to be circumcised, only that they may not suffer persecution for the cross of Christ. ¹³For not even those who are circumcised keep the law, but they desire to have you circumcised that they may boast in your flesh. ¹⁴But God forbid that I should boast except in

> "And let us not grow weary while doing good, for in due season we shall reap if we do not lose heart."
> (Galatians 6:9)

the cross of our Lord Jesus Christ, by whom[a] the world has been crucified to me, and I to the world. ¹⁵For in Christ Jesus neither circumcision nor uncircumcision avails anything, but a new creation.

BLESSING AND A PLEA

¹⁶And as many as walk according to this rule, peace and mercy *be* upon them, and upon the Israel of God. ¹⁷From now on let no one trouble me, for I bear in my body the marks of the Lord Jesus. ¹⁸Brethren, the grace of our Lord Jesus Christ *be* with your spirit. Amen.

WHAT'S IT MEAN?

Many people in New Testament times used secretaries to write letters for them. Some Bible experts believe that Paul needed a secretary because he had very poor eyesight. Apparently, Paul had dictated his letter to a secretary, but then wrote the last paragraph in his own handwriting, so that the churches in Galatia would know it really came from him.

Galatians 6:11

6:14 [a]Or *by which* (the cross)

CONTENT The Book of Ephesians is a letter of encouragement that Paul wrote from . . . jail? Yes that's right, Paul is sitting in chains and writing letters to churches telling them to be strong and keep the faith. That's commitment, huh?

So what *does* someone write about from prison? What Paul wrote about was God's unending love. Almost half of his letter to the Ephesians is about how much God loves them.

The last half of Paul's letter is about loving each other whether we are family members or church members or work associates. Paul makes the connection between God's love in us pouring out to those around us.

There's a lot of good advice in Paul's letter to the Ephesians. Advice about being patient and loving and forgiving and honest. It's amazing, isn't it, that a prisoner could write a letter to a church in the first century that has so much to do with the life we are living today?

Outline
1:1, 2 .... Greetings
1:3—3:21 .... Christ Gives Spiritual Blessings
4:1—6:20 .... A New Life in Unity with Christ
6:21–24 .... Final Greetings

Purpose Christians are to love and serve one another.

Theme The Glorious Church

Date of writing A.D. 60

"For by grace you have been saved through faith, and that not of yourselves; it is the gift of God, not of works, lest anyone should boast" (2:8, 9).

Bible Talk

Suiting Up for War

If you are going to play football for a team, you suit up. You wear protective gear on every joint and a helmet for your head. If you are going to go scuba diving, you suit up as well. You carry tanks and you wear flippers. For almost anything we do, there are uniforms and some gear attached.

It's no different for the Christian walk. In Ephesians Paul describes how we suit up spiritually and what kind of gear we need to carry. Among other things, he describes our shield of faith and our helmet of salvation (6:11–17). It makes sense, doesn't it, that we would be able to equip ourselves for something so important as the ultimate battle between good and evil?

GIFTS

Do you realize that God has gifted you? Do you realize that He has given you a certain set of skills that allow you to minister to other people? Ephesians 4 gives one of several lists of gifts in the New Testament.

Some people feel like they don't have any gifts at all, but they're wrong. Everyone has a gift from God. Sometimes we get so used to our own gifts that we don't even notice them. We tend to notice the gifts that are different than our own.

If you don't know what your gifts are, start noticing what comes easy to you and what you enjoy the most. Those might be your best clues.

GREETING

[1]Paul, an apostle of Jesus Christ by the will of God,

To the saints who are in Ephesus, and faithful in Christ Jesus:

[2]Grace to you and peace from God our Father and the Lord Jesus Christ.

REDEMPTION IN CHRIST

[3]Blessed *be* the God and Father of our Lord Jesus Christ, who has blessed us with every spiritual blessing in the heavenly *places* in Christ, [4]just as He chose us in Him before the foundation of the world, that we should be holy and without blame before Him in love, [5]having predestined us to adoption as sons by Jesus Christ to Himself, according to the good pleasure of His will, [6]to the praise of the glory of His grace, by which He made us accepted in the Beloved.

[7]In Him we have redemption through His blood, the forgiveness of sins, according to the riches of His grace [8]which He made to abound toward us in all wisdom and prudence, [9]having made known to us the mystery of His will, according to His good pleasure which He purposed in Himself, [10]that in the dispensation of the fullness of the times He might gather together in one all things in Christ, both[a] which are in heaven and which are on earth—in Him. [11]In Him also we have obtained an inheritance, being predestined according to the purpose of Him who works all things according to the counsel of His will, [12]that we who first trusted in Christ should be to the praise of His glory.

[13]In Him you also *trusted*, after you heard the word of truth, the gospel of your salvation; in whom also, having believed, you were sealed with the Holy Spirit of promise, [14]who[a] is the guarantee of our inheritance until the redemption of the purchased possession, to the praise of His glory.

PRAYER FOR SPIRITUAL WISDOM

[15]Therefore I also, after I heard of your faith in the Lord Jesus and your love for all the saints, [16]do not cease to give thanks for you, making mention of you in my prayers: [17]that the God of our Lord Jesus Christ, the Father of glory, may give to you the spirit of wisdom and revelation in the knowledge of Him, [18]the eyes of your understanding[a] being enlightened; that you may know what is the hope of His calling,

what are the riches of the glory of His inheritance in the saints, [19]and what *is* the exceeding greatness of His power toward us who believe, according to the working of His mighty power [20]which He worked in Christ when He raised Him from the dead and seated *Him* at His right hand in the heavenly *places*, [21]far above all principality and power and might and dominion, and every name that is named, not only in this age but also in that which is to come. [22]And He put all *things* under His feet, and gave Him *to be* head over all *things* to the church, [23]which is His body, the fullness of Him who fills all in all.

On the Edge

[The Holy Spirit of promise] is the guarantee of our inheritance until the redemption of the purchased possession, to the praise of His glory (Eph. 1:14).

God is a God of promise. Here, He's promised to pour out everything that He has been saving for you. He wants to bless you with good things! He doesn't want to hold one thing back! As you begin to walk in the Spirit by allowing Him to lead and guide you into God's perfect will, then the blessings of God will start being poured into your lap.

Look at Bartimaeus in Mark 10:46–52. He was a blind beggar who sat outside of God's blessings his entire life. One day, he heard that Jesus was coming down the road. He knew that healing had been stored up for him, so he began crying out, "Jesus, Son of David, have mercy on me!" The crowd told him to knock it off, but he cried out even louder. What happened? He got Jesus' attention! Jesus stopped and called for him. Jesus asked Bartimaeus, "What do you want Me to do for you?" Of course, Bartimaeus wanted his sight and he got it! Healing had been stored up for him, and he was finally set free. God wants to do the same for us. The Holy Spirit "is the guarantee of our inheritance"—the guarantee that God's other promises will happen!

SEE FOR YOURSELF:
Prov. 28:20;
Mark 10:46–52;
2 Cor. 1:20; Eph. 1:3

1:10 [a]NU-Text and M-Text omit *both*.   **1:14** [a]NU-Text reads *which*.   **1:18** [a]NU-Text and M-Text read *hearts*.

BY GRACE THROUGH FAITH

¹And you *He made alive*, who were dead in trespasses and sins, ²in which you once walked according to the course of this world, according to the prince of the power of the air, the spirit who now works in the sons of disobedience, ³among whom also we all once conducted ourselves in the lusts of our flesh, fulfilling the desires of the flesh and of the mind, and were by nature children of wrath, just as the others.

On the Edge

But God . . . made us alive together with Christ (by grace you have been saved), and raised us up together, and made us sit together in the heavenly places in Christ Jesus (Eph. 2:4–6).

A prince is tragically separated from his parents at birth. For years they search for him, sending out soldiers to every region to look for the one who belongs to them. Finally, the boy is found, living in poverty, robbing for food, and acting like a savage. A soldier tells the boy about his father. His father is king of the entire country. In an instant, the beggar child has a new position. He is the son of a king. The one who thought he had no family has become royalty. He has a new life, new power, and a new home. He even has a place to sit beside his father's throne. You, too, are the child of a King. God has been merciful. He knew that you were dead in your sins, ruled by selfish desires, and destined for eternal punishment. He loved you and graciously gave you new life. With your new life has come new power and a new home with Christ in heaven.

SEE FOR YOURSELF:
John 14:1–4;
2 Cor. 5:1, 2; Phil. 3:20

On the Edge

For by grace you have been saved through faith, and that not of yourselves; it is the gift of God (Eph. 2:8).

Being saved means receiving the forgiveness of sins that God offers you because of Jesus' death and resurrection. It takes faith. You have to believe that God loves you. You have to believe that Jesus is God's Son. You have to believe that Jesus' death on the cross made up for everybody's sins. That's why Paul wrote, "by grace you have been saved through faith."

In verse 10 Paul added, "For we are His workmanship, created in Christ Jesus for good works, which God prepared beforehand that we should walk in them." God definitely wants you to do what's right, and the person who has real faith and love will want to do what pleases Him. In fact, your actions say a lot about just how deep your faith goes (read James 2:17). Paul's point is that what you *do* doesn't save you. It's human nature to try to get on God's good side by doing good things, but all the good deeds in the world will not impress Him. The only thing that pleases God is faith.

SEE FOR YOURSELF:
Rom. 10:9; Gal. 3:7, 29;
James 2:17

you have been saved through faith, and that not of yourselves; *it is* the gift of God, ⁹not of works, lest anyone should boast. ¹⁰For we are His workmanship, created in Christ Jesus for good works, which God prepared beforehand that we should walk in them.

WORK
Can eternal life be earned? (2:8, 9)

BROUGHT NEAR BY HIS BLOOD

¹¹Therefore remember that you, once Gentiles in the flesh—who are called Uncircumcision by what is called the Circumcision made in the flesh by hands—¹²that at that time you were without Christ, being aliens from the commonwealth of Israel and strangers from the covenants of promise, having no hope and without God in the world. ¹³But now in Christ Jesus you who once were far off have been brought near by the blood of Christ.

⁴But God, who is rich in mercy, because of His great love with which He loved us, ⁵even when we were dead in trespasses, made us alive together with Christ (by grace you have been saved), ⁶and raised *us* up together, and made *us* sit together in the heavenly *places* in Christ Jesus, ⁷that in the ages to come He might show the exceeding riches of His grace in *His* kindness toward us in Christ Jesus. ⁸For by grace

preached peace to you who were afar off and to those who were near. [18]For through Him we both have access by one Spirit to the Father.

CHRIST OUR CORNERSTONE

[19]Now, therefore, you are no longer strangers and foreigners, but fellow citizens with the saints and members of the household of God, [20]having been built on the foundation of the apostles and prophets, Jesus Christ Himself being the chief cornerstone, [21]in whom the whole building, being fitted together, grows into a holy temple in the Lord, [22]in whom you also are being built together for a dwelling place of God in the Spirit.

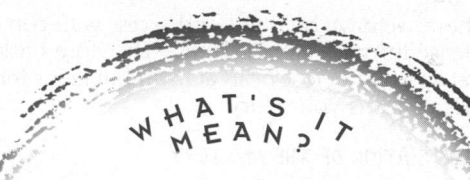

WHAT'S IT MEAN?

If a person is not a Jew, he or she is a Gentile. In New Testament times, if a man was not a Jew, he probably wasn't circumcised. Circumcision was an important ritual in Jewish tradition. The removal of the foreskin from the male sex organ, a surgical procedure usually performed eight days after birth, was a physical sign that the Jews belonged to God. It also set them apart from other people. Many Jews of Paul's time looked down on Gentiles because they weren't circumcised.

Ephesians 2:11

CHRIST OUR PEACE

[14]For He Himself is our peace, who has made both one, and has broken down the middle wall of separation, [15]having abolished in His flesh the enmity, *that is*, the law of commandments *contained* in ordinances, so as to create in Himself one new man *from* the two, *thus* making peace, [16]and that He might reconcile them both to God in one body through the cross, thereby putting to death the enmity. [17]And He came and

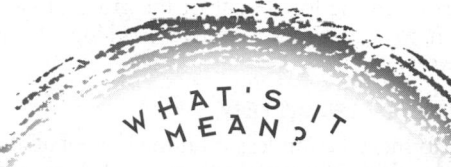

WHAT'S IT MEAN?

The temple area in Jerusalem was divided into a series of courts. The outermost court, which was called the Court of the Gentiles, was the only area of the temple that non-Jews were allowed to enter.

Ephesians 2:14

Promise   HE PROMISES TO HAVE A PLAN FOR YOU.

For we are His workmanship, created in Christ Jesus for good works, which God prepared beforehand that we should walk in them (Eph. 2:10).

Most days just seem to go by like every other day. Same old stuff. Same old everything. Blah blah blah. One day runs into another one. You close your eyes and wake up to do it all over again. Doesn't seem like much of a plan, does it?

Maybe not. But God has an exciting plan for your life—a plan that will give you purpose and fulfillment beyond your wildest dreams. Following God's plan takes commitment from you. You don't just accidentally fulfill what He's planned for you to do. You've got to seek God and ask Him to reveal His plan to you and to give you understanding about how you can fulfill it. Then, you've got to determine to make every day count for Him and for His plan.

Pay attention to every decision you face—even the ones that seem so insignificant. Take seriously every person you meet—even the ones you don't like. Embrace every situation you find yourself in—even the ones that seem to make no sense at all. They're shaping you, molding you, preparing you for the next decision, the next person, the next situation.

Lose yourself in doing what God wants with every aspect of your life. Live your life in light of His plan!

SEE FOR YOURSELF:
Matt. 25:34; John 15:16; Eph. 1:4

THE MYSTERY REVEALED

[1]For this reason I, Paul, the prisoner of Christ Jesus for you Gentiles—[2]if indeed you have heard of the dispensation of the grace of God which was given to me for you, [3]how that by revelation He made known to me the mystery (as I have briefly written already, [4]by which, when you read, you may understand my knowledge in the mystery of Christ), [5]which in other ages was not made known to the sons of men, as it has now been revealed by the Spirit to His holy apostles and prophets: [6]that the Gentiles should be fellow heirs, of the same body, and partakers of His promise in Christ through the gospel, [7]of which I became a minister according to the gift of the grace of God given to me by the effective working of His power.

PURPOSE OF THE MYSTERY

[8]To me, who am less than the least of all the saints, this grace was given, that I should preach among the Gentiles the unsearchable riches of Christ, [9]and to make all see what *is* the fellowship[a] of the mystery, which from the beginning of the ages has been hidden in God who created all things through Jesus Christ;[b] [10]to the intent that now the manifold wisdom of God might be made known by the church to the principalities and powers in the heavenly *places*, [11]according to the eternal purpose which He accomplished in Christ Jesus our Lord, [12]in whom we have boldness and access with confidence through faith in Him. [13]Therefore I ask that you do not lose heart at my tribulations for you, which is your glory.

APPRECIATION OF THE MYSTERY

[14]For this reason I bow my knees to the Father of our Lord Jesus Christ,[a] [15]from whom the whole family in heaven and earth is named, [16]that He would grant you, according to the riches of His glory, to be strengthened with might through His Spirit in the inner man, [17]that Christ may dwell in your hearts through faith; that you, being rooted and grounded in love, [18]may be able to comprehend with all the saints what *is* the width and length and depth and height—[19]to know the love of Christ which passes knowledge; that you may be filled with all the fullness of God.

[20]Now to Him who is able to do exceedingly abundantly above all that we ask or think, according to the power that works in us, [21]to Him *be* glory in the church by Christ Jesus to all generations, forever and ever. Amen.

WALK IN UNITY

[1]I, therefore, the prisoner of the Lord, beseech you to walk worthy of the calling with which you were called, [2]with all lowliness and gentleness, with longsuffering, bearing with one another in love, [3]endeavoring to keep the unity of the Spirit in the bond of peace. [4]*There is one*

3:9 [a]NU-Text and M-Text read *stewardship* (dispensation). [b]NU-Text omits *through Jesus Christ.*
3:14 [a]NU-Text omits *of our Lord Jesus Christ.*

Promise   HE PROMISES YOU BOLDNESS AND CONFIDENCE.

[Christ Jesus our Lord], in whom we have boldness and access with confidence through faith in Him (Eph. 3:12).

Because of the work of Christ, all believers are given the confidence and boldness to come to God. Before you knew Jesus, you were like a stranger to the family of God. You may have even been afraid to talk to God or be in His presence. Through Christ, you have become a member of the family. In a family you can run to your father at anytime. You do not have to beg for his time, or be afraid of his presence. He loves you. He knows you. You are his child. Do not be afraid to run to your heavenly Father. He expects you to come to Him when you have doubts, or questions, or need comfort. You do not have to be timid. You belong to Him, and you can boldly turn to Him with every need.

SEE FOR YOURSELF:
Ps. 119:28; 2 Cor. 3:4; Heb. 4:16; 10:19

body and one Spirit, just as you were called in one hope of your calling; [5]one Lord, one faith, one baptism; [6]one God and Father of all, who *is* above all, and through all, and in you[a] all.

SPIRITUAL GIFTS

[7]But to each one of us grace was given according to the measure of Christ's gift. [8]Therefore He says:

> "When He ascended on high,
> He led captivity captive,
> And gave gifts to men."[a]

[9](Now this, *"He ascended"*—what does it mean but that He also first[a] descended into the lower parts of the earth? [10]He who descended is also the One who ascended far above all the heavens, that He might fill all things.)

[11]And He Himself gave some *to be* apostles, some prophets, some evangelists, and some pastors and teachers, [12]for the equipping of the saints for the work of ministry, for the edifying of the body of Christ, [13]till we all come to the unity of the faith and of the knowledge of the Son of God, to a perfect man, to the measure of the stature of the fullness of Christ; [14]that we should no longer be children, tossed to and fro and carried about with every wind of doctrine, by the trickery of men, in the cunning craftiness of deceitful plotting, [15]but, speaking the truth in love, may grow up in all things into Him who is the head—Christ—[16]from whom the whole body, joined and knit together by what every joint supplies, according to the effective working by which every part does its share, causes growth of the body for the edifying of itself in love.

EDUCATION

When should Christians stop learning about God? (4:14, 15)

THE NEW MAN

[17]This I say, therefore, and testify in the Lord, that you should no longer walk as the rest of[a] the Gentiles walk, in the futility of their mind, [18]having their understanding darkened, being alienated from the life of God, because of the ignorance that is in them, because of the blindness of their heart; [19]who, being past feeling, have given themselves over to lewdness, to work all uncleanness with greediness.

[20]But you have not so learned Christ, [21]if indeed you have heard Him and have been taught by Him, as the truth is in Jesus: [22]that you put off, concerning your former conduct, the old man which grows corrupt according to the deceitful lusts, [23]and be renewed in the spirit of your mind, [24]and that you put on the new man which was created according to God, in true righteousness and holiness.

On the Edge

Let no corrupt word proceed out of your mouth, but what is good for necessary edification, that it may impart grace to the hearers. . . . Let all bitterness, wrath, anger, clamor, and evil speaking be put away from you, with all malice (Eph. 4:29, 31).

These verses aren't just talking about filthy words. They're talking about letting anything corrupt come out of your mouth. Proverbs 18:21 tells us words can bring death or life. You've heard the slogan: "Sticks and stones may break my bones, but words will never hurt me!" This may be true physically, but spiritually, words can be very destructive. Hurtful words can do a lot of damage to people and leave them wounded and bitter. We need to learn to put a guard over our mouths. Our mouths can get us in trouble more than almost anything else. That's why we are commanded to be quick to listen and slow to speak.

We've all had opportunity to get upset and "pop off" at the mouth. When we do, we end up saying things we wish we hadn't, and the worse thing is that we can't take them back. God forgives and forgets, but people usually hang on to those kind of things. So the next time someone rubs you the wrong way, don't rip into that person. Stop and think before you speak. The same is true when we hurt ourselves physically. The next time you hit your thumb with a hammer, or you drop something on your toe, remember . . . don't let anything filthy come out of your mouth! Be clean inside and out. Begin to praise God instead, and watch what God will do.

SEE FOR YOURSELF:
Prov. 12:18; 15:1, 2, 4; 18:21

4:6 [a]NU-Text omits *you*; M-Text reads *us*.   4:8 [a]Psalm 68:18   4:9 [a]NU-Text omits *first*.   4:17 [a]NU-Text omits *the rest of*.

DO NOT GRIEVE THE SPIRIT

[25]Therefore, putting away lying, *"Let each one of you speak truth with his neighbor,"*[a] for we are members of one another. [26]*"Be angry, and do not sin":*[a] do not let the sun go down on your wrath, [27]nor give place to the devil. [28]Let him who stole steal no longer, but rather let him labor, working with *his* hands what is good, that he may have something to give him who has need. [29]Let no corrupt word proceed out of your mouth, but what is good for necessary edification, that it may impart grace to the hearers. [30]And do not grieve the Holy Spirit of God, by whom you were sealed for the day of redemption. [31]Let all bitterness, wrath, anger, clamor, and evil speaking be put away from you, with all malice. [32]And be kind to one another, tenderhearted, forgiving one another, even as God in Christ forgave you.

ANGER

What can anger do? (4:26, 27)

WALK IN LOVE

[1]Therefore be imitators of God as dear children. [2]And walk in love, as Christ also has loved us and given Himself for us, an offering and a sacrifice to God for a sweet-smelling aroma.

[3]But fornication and all uncleanness or covetousness, let it not even be named among you, as is fitting for saints; [4]neither filthiness, nor foolish talking, nor coarse jesting, which are not fitting, but rather giving of thanks. [5]For this you know,[a] that no fornicator, unclean person, nor covetous man, who is an idolater, has any inheritance in the kingdom of Christ and God. [6]Let no one deceive you with empty words, for because of these things the wrath of God comes upon the sons of disobedience. [7]Therefore do not be partakers with them.

SEX

Is sexual immorality improper for Christians? (5:1–3)

WALK IN LIGHT

[8]For you were once darkness, but now *you are* light in the Lord. Walk as children of light [9](for the fruit of the Spirit[a] *is* in all goodness, righteousness, and truth), [10]finding out what is acceptable to the Lord. [11]And have no fellowship with the unfruitful works of darkness, but rather expose *them*. [12]For it is shameful even to speak of those things which are done by them in secret. [13]But all things that are exposed are made manifest by the light, for whatever makes manifest is light. [14]Therefore He says:

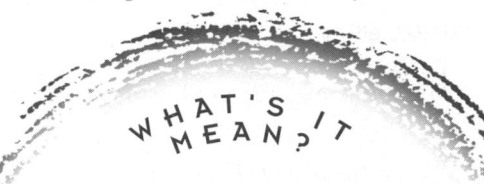

WHAT'S IT MEAN?

Few things are as offensive to God as idol worship. Throughout the Bible, God warned His people not to worship pagan deities. Unfortunately, His people rarely heeded His warnings. The Israelites were always quick to adopt the gods and idols of their pagan neighbors. In Paul's day, however, the word *idol* took on a broader meaning. It came to refer not only to statues and pagan gods, but to anything that was more important than God in a believer's life.

Ephesians 5:5

" Awake, you who sleep,
    Arise from the dead,
    And Christ will give you light."

WALK IN WISDOM

[15]See then that you walk circumspectly, not as fools but as wise, [16]redeeming the time, because the days are evil. [17]Therefore do not be unwise, but understand what the will of the Lord *is*. [18]And do not be drunk with wine, in which is dissipation; but be filled with the Spirit, [19]speaking to one another in psalms and hymns and spiritual songs, singing and making melody in your heart to the Lord, [20]giving thanks always for all things to God the Father in the name of our Lord Jesus Christ, [21]submitting to one another in the fear of God.[a]

DRINKING

What does drunkenness cause? (5:18)

> *"Therefore do not be unwise, but understand what the will of the Lord is."*
> *(Ephesians 5:17)*

MARRIAGE—CHRIST AND THE CHURCH

[22]Wives, submit to your own husbands, as to the Lord. [23]For the husband is head of the

4:25 [a]Zechariah 8:16   **4:26** [a]Psalm 4:4   **5:5** [a]NU-Text reads *For know this.*   **5:9** [a]NU-Text reads *light.*
5:21 [a]NU-Text reads *Christ.*

WHAT'S IT MEAN?

Believe it or not, praise choruses are not a modern church innovation. Music has been a part of worship for a long, long time. Worship services in the original temple in Jerusalem included a four thousand-member choir and an orchestra. The New Testament tells of Christians singing hymns together and even records portions of their songs.

Ephesians 5:19

BONDSERVANTS AND MASTERS

[5]Bondservants, be obedient to those who are your masters according to the flesh, with fear and trembling, in sincerity of heart, as to Christ; [6]not with eyeservice, as men-pleasers, but as bondservants of Christ, doing the will of God from the heart, [7]with goodwill doing service, as to the Lord, and not to men, [8]knowing that whatever good anyone does, he will receive the same from the Lord, whether *he is* a slave or free.

[9]And you, masters, do the same things to them, giving up threatening, knowing that your own Master also[a] is in heaven, and there is no partiality with Him.

wife, as also Christ is head of the church; and He is the Savior of the body. [24]Therefore, just as the church is subject to Christ, so *let* the wives *be* to their own husbands in everything.

[25]Husbands, love your wives, just as Christ also loved the church and gave Himself for her, [26]that He might sanctify and cleanse her with the washing of water by the word, [27]that He might present her to Himself a glorious church, not having spot or wrinkle or any such thing, but that she should be holy and without blemish. [28]So husbands ought to love their own wives as their own bodies; he who loves his wife loves himself. [29]For no one ever hated his own flesh, but nourishes and cherishes it, just as the Lord *does* the church. [30]For we are members of His body,[a] of His flesh and of His bones. [31]*"For this reason a man shall leave his father and mother and be joined to his wife, and the two shall become one flesh."*[a] [32]This is a great mystery, but I speak concerning Christ and the church. [33]Nevertheless let each one of you in particular so love his own wife as himself, and let the wife *see* that she respects *her* husband.

CHILDREN AND PARENTS

[1]Children, obey your parents in the Lord, for this is right. [2]*"Honor your father and mother,"* which is the first commandment with promise: [3]*"that it may be well with you and you may live long on the earth."*[a]

[4]And you, fathers, do not provoke your children to wrath, but bring them up in the training and admonition of the Lord.

On the Edge

For the husband is head of the wife, as also Christ is head of the church; and He is the Savior of the body (Eph. 5:23).

Your brain controls everything that your body does. If you want to walk across the room, your brain tells your feet to go and they go. If your shoulder itches, your brain tells your fingers to scratch, and they do it. If your foot moves when your brain doesn't tell it to, you call that a spasm. If your brain tells your hand to make a fist and your hand lies still, you know you've got a problem—something isn't right. The brain is the boss.

Paul talked a lot about the church—Christians—being the body of Christ. Everyone plays a different part, has a different function. Jesus is the head—the brain. That means that everything you do—as a part of His body—needs to be directed by Jesus. If you do something without Him, it's spastic and useless. And if He tells you to do something and you don't or can't, you know that something in your relationship needs attention.

All the parts functioning independently can turn into chaos (picture a chicken with its head cut off). Jesus brings all the parts together in a way that makes sense.

SEE FOR YOURSELF:
1 Cor. 12:12–31;
Eph. 1:22, 23; Col. 1:18

5:30 [a]NU-Text omits the rest of this verse.   **5:31** [a]Genesis 2:24   **6:3** [a]Deuteronomy 5:16   **6:9** [a]NU-Text reads *He who is both their Master and yours.*

On the Edge

Children, obey your parents in the Lord, for this is right. "Honor your father and mother," which is the first commandment with promise: "that it may be well with you and you may live long on the earth" (Eph. 6:1–3).

God gave you to your parents so that they could raise you. He chose them especially to care for you. The promise in Ephesians 6:3 says that if you obey your father and your mother, "it may be well with you and you may live long on the earth." Also, when you honor the authority that God has put over you, you get His blessing. Kids who choose to rebel and disobey miss the instructions God has for them through their parents. As a result, things go poorly for them. They make bad choices and life becomes difficult. We would be hard pressed to find an adult in a counselor's office boasting, "I rebelled against my parents as a child, disobeyed their every word, and worried them sick. It was the right thing to do. My life is so much better because I always broke their rules." More common are the adults who live in regret under a pile of guilt because they were so ugly to their parents. God is the Master Designer and this is His design: Obedience leads to right choices and a good life, but rebellion leads to regret.

SEE FOR YOURSELF:
Prov. 15:31, 32;
Col. 3:20

that you may be able to withstand in the evil day, and having done all, to stand. [14]Stand therefore, having girded your waist with truth, having put on the breastplate of righteousness, [15]and having shod your feet with the preparation of the gospel of peace; [16]above all, taking the shield of faith with which you will be able to quench all the fiery darts of the wicked one. [17]And take the helmet of salvation, and the sword of the Spirit, which is the word of God; [18]praying always with all prayer and supplication in the Spirit, being watchful to this end with all perseverance and supplication for all the saints—[19]and for me, that utterance may be given to me, that I may open my mouth boldly to make known the mystery of the gospel, [20]for which I am an ambassador in chains; that in it I may speak boldly, as I ought to speak.

WHAT'S IT MEAN?

Paul spent so much time under arrest, chained to soldiers, that he had excellent opportunities to examine their battle dress. Roman foot soldiers wore armor and carried shields for protection. The armor was made of thick leather or of metal. Helmets came in all shapes and sizes. Some covered the entire head with metal, except for a protective screen for the face.

Ephesians 6:11

THE WHOLE ARMOR OF GOD

[10]Finally, my brethren, be strong in the Lord and in the power of His might. [11]Put on the whole armor of God, that you may be able to stand against the wiles of the devil. [12]For we do not wrestle against flesh and blood, but against principalities, against powers, against the rulers of the darkness of this age,[a] against spiritual *hosts* of wickedness in the heavenly *places.* [13]Therefore take up the whole armor of God,

6:12 [a]NU-Text reads *rulers of this darkness.*

A GRACIOUS GREETING

[21]But that you also may know my affairs *and* how I am doing, Tychicus, a beloved brother and faithful minister in the Lord, will make all things known to you; [22]whom I have sent to you for this very purpose, that you may know our affairs, and *that* he may comfort your hearts.

[23]Peace to the brethren, and love with faith, from God the Father and the Lord Jesus Christ. [24]Grace *be* with all those who love our Lord Jesus Christ in sincerity. Amen.

CONTENT

Have you ever written a thank-you note? If you have, someone probably had given you something or had done something nice for you. Then one of your parents probably made you sit down and write a short note saying "thank you."

That is actually part of the reason that Paul wrote the Philippians. He wanted to thank them for supporting his ministry and for their love and friendship.

If there is any word that describes this book, it's "joy." That's a pretty amazing fact since Paul wrote it from jail. But even though he was in jail, he shared his joy about everything from his life in Christ to his friends in Philippi.

There are several keys to being joyful. Paul seemed to understand each one of them. Paul could focus on his blessings even when he had chains on his hands and feet. Somehow he knew that life is more than the difficult moments.

So if you need a pick-me-up, Philippians is the book to read. Maybe we should subtitle it "Philippians: looking up when everything looks down."

Outline

Purpose

Joy is experienced by those who live a truly Christian life.

Theme

Joy in Christ

Date of writing

A.D. 61

> "For to me,
> to live is Christ,
> and to die is gain"
> (1:21).

Bible Talk

An Apostle Jailbird

When you look at all the books of the Bible that Paul wrote while he was in jail, you realize that he was in jail a *lot*. Paul was in and out of jail because he believed that obeying Jesus was the most important thing he could do. That scared the government. If Paul obeyed Jesus instead of the government and got away with it, then *everybody* might start obeying God rather than the government. That didn't feel really good to the authorities, so they kept telling Paul not to preach. Of course, he kept preaching and they kept putting him in jail.

Since Paul was really focused on spreading the Gospel, jail seemed like as good a place as any to do this. Guards and inmates were his "captive" audience.

JOY

There's a big difference between joy and happiness. Happiness is what you feel when circumstances in your life go right. If you make good grades and get what you want for your birthday—those kinds of things make you happy. Because happiness is related to circumstances, it comes and goes with the good times in life.

Joy, on the other hand, is more than an emotion. It is a perspective, a way of looking at life. We have joy when we feel secure inside that, no matter how our circumstances might change, God is still in control. That's why Paul could write a letter about gratitude and joy in a yucky place like prison. He might not have been happy, but in the end he knew that God was in control of his life.

GREETING

¹Paul and Timothy, bondservants of Jesus Christ,

To all the saints in Christ Jesus who are in Philippi, with the bishops*a* and deacons:

²Grace to you and peace from God our Father and the Lord Jesus Christ.

THANKFULNESS AND PRAYER

³I thank my God upon every remembrance of you, ⁴always in every prayer of mine making request for you all with joy, ⁵for your fellowship in the gospel from the first day until now, ⁶being confident of this very thing, that He who has begun a good work in you will complete *it* until the day of Jesus Christ; ⁷just as it is right for me to think this of you all, because I have you in my heart, inasmuch as both in my chains and in the defense and confirmation of the gospel, you all are partakers with me of grace. ⁸For God is my witness, how greatly I long for you all with the affection of Jesus Christ.

⁹And this I pray, that your love may abound still more and more in knowledge and all discernment, ¹⁰that you may approve the things that are excellent, that you may be sincere and without offense till the day of Christ, ¹¹being filled with the fruits of righteousness which *are* by Jesus Christ, to the glory and praise of God.

1:1 *a*Literally *overseers*

WHAT'S IT MEAN?

Talk about a slow judicial system! Paul lived under house arrest in Rome for two years while he waited for Caesar to hear his case. Since electronic monitoring devices weren't available in Paul's day, he had soldiers guarding him day and night. The guards worked four-hour shifts, with at least one person handcuffed to Paul at all times. Even though he was officially a prisoner, Paul was allowed to receive visitors. That gave him an opportunity to share the message of Christ not only with the people who came to see him, but with the soldiers as well.

Philippians 1:7

CHRIST IS PREACHED

¹²But I want you to know, brethren, that the things *which happened* to me have actually turned out for the furtherance of the gospel, ¹³so that it has become evident to the whole palace guard, and to all the rest, that my chains are in Christ; ¹⁴and most of the brethren in the Lord, having become confident by my chains, are much more bold to speak the word without fear.

Promise HE PROMISES TO COMPLETE A GOOD WORK IN YOU.

Being confident of this very thing, that He who has begun a good work in you will complete it until the day of Jesus Christ (Phil. 1:6).

Have you heard? Jesus is coming back again. No, really. It may seem highly unlikely from where you're sitting. But one day, in some heart-pounding way where no one in the world will have to wonder what's happening, He's going to step back in here and finish some business. One of those little unfinished matters . . . is you.

Don't sweat it though. If you're one of His, He won't be coming back to pull the curtain down on your performance, but to raise the blinds and allow you to see what He's been doing in your life. And one day—one great, big, glorious day—He'll let you know what was going on. God finishes what He starts. Give Him permission to get started with you.

SEE FOR YOURSELF:
Ps. 139:16; John 17:24; Acts 20:24

[15]Some indeed preach Christ even from envy and strife, and some also from goodwill: [16]The former[a] preach Christ from selfish ambition, not sincerely, supposing to add affliction to my chains; [17]but the latter out of love, knowing that I am appointed for the defense of the gospel. [18]What then? Only *that* in every way, whether in pretense or in truth, Christ is preached; and in this I rejoice, yes, and will rejoice.

TO LIVE IS CHRIST

[19]For I know that this will turn out for my deliverance through your prayer and the supply of the Spirit of Jesus Christ, [20]according to my earnest expectation and hope that in nothing I shall be ashamed, but with all boldness, as always, so now also Christ will be magnified in my body, whether by life or by death. [21]For to me, to live *is* Christ, and to die *is* gain. [22]But if *I* live on in the flesh, this *will mean* fruit from my labor; yet what I shall choose I cannot tell. [23]For[a] I am hard-pressed between the two, having a desire to depart and be with Christ, which is far better. [24]Nevertheless to remain in the flesh *is* more needful for you. [25]And being confident of this, I know that I shall remain and continue with you all for your progress and joy of faith, [26]that your rejoicing for me may be more abundant in Jesus Christ by my coming to you again.

> **LIFE**
> What is the reason for life? (1:21)

> **HEAVEN**
> Is heaven better than earth? (1:23)

STRIVING AND SUFFERING FOR CHRIST

[27]Only let your conduct be worthy of the gospel of Christ, so that whether I come and see you or am absent, I may hear of your affairs, that you stand fast in one spirit, with one mind striving together for the faith of the gospel, [28]and not in any way terrified by your adversaries, which is to them a proof of perdition, but to you of salvation,[a] and that from God. [29]For to you it has been granted on behalf of Christ, not only to believe in Him, but also to suffer for His sake, [30]having the same conflict which you saw in me and now hear *is* in me.

UNITY THROUGH HUMILITY

[1]Therefore if *there is* any consolation in Christ, if any comfort of love, if any fellowship of the Spirit, if any affection and mercy, [2]fulfill my joy by being like-minded, having the same love, *being* of one accord, of one mind. [3]Let nothing *be done* through selfish ambition or conceit, but in lowliness of mind let each esteem others better than himself. [4]Let each of you look out not only for his own interests, but also for the interests of others.

THE HUMBLED AND EXALTED CHRIST

[5]Let this mind be in you which was also in Christ Jesus, [6]who, being in the form of God,

---

On the Edge

And being found in appearance as a man, He humbled Himself and became obedient to the point of death, even the death of the cross (Phil. 2:8).

For a great story about how humble Jesus was, look at John 13:1–17. It's a fascinating story about humility. Can you imagine sitting in the same room as Jesus only to have Him come up to you and wash your feet? Your feet . . . the ugliest and smelliest part of your body! Wow! Jesus displayed the ultimate act of servanthood in this illustration. We need to serve others in the same way.

What does it really mean to be humble? It means that someone will do anything asked and will do it with a willing heart and a good attitude. It means that you put down the wonderful things about yourself just to love and serve other people. If you know anything about the life and ministry of Jesus, then you know that He was a humble servant. He even said that He didn't come to be served but to serve (see Matt. 20:28). If that was Jesus' attitude, how much more should it be ours? From now on, work on being humble enough to serve others rather than being served yourself. You've heard that pride comes before a fall. If we are humbled before Him as servants, we are imitating Christ—and that's what our Christian walk is all about.

SEE FOR YOURSELF:
Prov. 11:2; Matt. 20:28; 23:12; John 13:3–15

---

did not consider it robbery to be equal with God, [7]but made Himself of no reputation, taking the form of a bondservant, *and* coming in the likeness of men. [8]And being found in appearance as a man, He humbled Himself and became obedient to *the point of* death, even the death of the cross. [9]Therefore God also has highly exalted Him and given Him the name which is above every name, [10]that at the name of Jesus every knee should bow, of those in heaven, and of those on earth, and of those under the earth, [11]and *that* every tongue should confess that Jesus Christ *is* Lord, to the glory of God the Father.

LIGHT BEARERS

[12]Therefore, my beloved, as you have always obeyed, not as in my presence only, but now much more in my absence, work out your own salvation with fear and trembling; [13]for it is God who works in you both to will and to do for *His* good pleasure.

[14]Do all things without complaining and disputing, [15]that you may become blameless and harmless, children of God without fault in the midst of a crooked and perverse generation, among whom you shine as lights in the world, [16]holding fast the word of life, so that I may rejoice in the day of Christ that I have not run in vain or labored in vain.

[17]Yes, and if I am being poured out *as a drink offering* on the sacrifice and service of your faith, I am glad and rejoice with you all. [18]For the same reason you also be glad and rejoice with me.

TIMOTHY COMMENDED

[19]But I trust in the Lord Jesus to send Timothy to you shortly, that I also may be encouraged when I know your state. [20]For I have no one like-minded, who will sincerely care for your state. [21]For all seek their own, not the things which are of Christ Jesus. [22]But you know his proven character, that as a son with *his* father he served with me in the gospel. [23]Therefore I hope to send him at once, as soon as I see how it goes with me. [24]But I trust in the Lord that I myself shall also come shortly.

EPAPHRODITUS PRAISED

[25]Yet I considered it necessary to send to you Epaphroditus, my brother, fellow worker, and fellow soldier, but your messenger and the one who ministered to my need; [26]since he was longing for you all, and was distressed because you had heard that he was sick. [27]For indeed he was sick almost unto death; but God had mercy on him, and not only on him but on me also, lest I should have sorrow upon sorrow. [28]Therefore I sent him the more eagerly, that when you see him again you may rejoice, and I may be less sorrowful. [29]Receive him therefore in the Lord with all gladness, and hold such men in esteem; [30]because for the work of Christ he came close to death, not regarding his life, to supply what was lacking in your service toward me.

ALL FOR CHRIST

[1]Finally, my brethren, rejoice in the Lord. For me to write the same things to you *is* not tedious, but for you *it is* safe.

[2]Beware of dogs, beware of evil workers, beware of the mutilation! [3]For we are the circumcision, who worship God in the Spirit,[a] rejoice in Christ Jesus, and have no confidence in the flesh, [4]though I also might have confidence in the flesh. If anyone else thinks he may have confidence in the flesh, I more so: [5]circumcised the eighth day, of the stock of Israel, *of* the tribe of Benjamin, a Hebrew of the Hebrews; concerning the law, a Pharisee; [6]concerning zeal, persecuting the church; concerning the righteousness which is in the law, blameless.

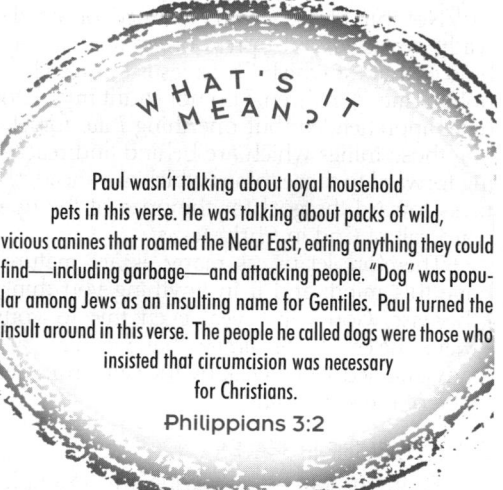

WHAT'S IT MEAN?

Paul wasn't talking about loyal household pets in this verse. He was talking about packs of wild, vicious canines that roamed the Near East, eating anything they could find—including garbage—and attacking people. "Dog" was popular among Jews as an insulting name for Gentiles. Paul turned the insult around in this verse. The people he called dogs were those who insisted that circumcision was necessary for Christians.

Philippians 3:2

[7]But what things were gain to me, these I have counted loss for Christ. [8]Yet indeed I also count all things loss for the excellence of the knowledge of Christ Jesus my Lord, for whom I have suffered the loss of all things, and count them as rubbish, that I may gain Christ [9]and be

3:3 [a]NU-Text and M-Text read *who worship in the Spirit of God.*

found in Him, not having my own righteousness, which *is* from the law, but that which *is* through faith in Christ, the righteousness which is from God by faith; ¹⁰that I may know Him and the power of His resurrection, and the fellowship of His sufferings, being conformed to His death, ¹¹if, by any means, I may attain to the resurrection from the dead.

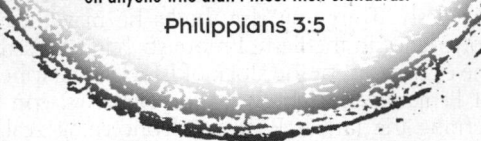

WHAT'S IT MEAN?

The Pharisees were a political and religious group within the Jewish community. They studied the Scriptures constantly and insisted on strict obedience to God's Old Testament laws. Most Jewish people respected the Pharisees' dedication and knowledge. In turn, the Pharisees tended to look down on anyone who didn't meet their standards.

Philippians 3:5

PRESSING TOWARD THE GOAL

¹²Not that I have already attained, or am already perfected; but I press on, that I may lay hold of that for which Christ Jesus has also laid hold of me. ¹³Brethren, I do not count myself to have apprehended; but one thing *I do*, forgetting those things which are behind and reaching forward to those things which are ahead, ¹⁴I press toward the goal for the prize of the upward call of God in Christ Jesus.

¹⁵Therefore let us, as many as are mature, have this mind; and if in anything you think otherwise, God will reveal even this to you. ¹⁶Nevertheless, to *the degree* that we have already attained, let us walk by the same rule,ᵃ let us be of the same mind.

OUR CITIZENSHIP IN HEAVEN

¹⁷Brethren, join in following my example, and note those who so walk, as you have us for a pattern. ¹⁸For many walk, of whom I have told you often, and now tell you even weeping, *that they are* the enemies of the cross of Christ: ¹⁹whose end *is* destruction, whose god *is their* belly, and *whose* glory *is* in their shame—who set their mind on earthly things. ²⁰For our

citizenship is in heaven, from which we also eagerly wait for the Savior, the Lord Jesus Christ, ²¹who will transform our lowly body that it may be conformed to His glorious body, according to the working by which He is able even to subdue all things to Himself.

On the Edge

For our citizenship is in heaven, from which we also eagerly wait for the Savior, the Lord Jesus Christ (Phil. 3:20).

Young women sleep with their boyfriends thinking they will help them feel satisfied. They don't. Maybe having a baby will fill the void? Nope, it's worse than before. Some of us search all our lives for something or someone to fill us up and keep us fulfilled. The truth is that our souls were created to live with God. From time to time you will wrestle with dissatisfaction. Let your feelings remind you that your heart is longing for heaven. Rejoice in knowing that one day you will stand complete and full in the presence of your Savior, never to feel incomplete again.

SEE FOR YOURSELF:
Ps. 91:14; Zeph. 3:17;
Rom. 8:35–39;
Eph. 3:16–19

¹Therefore, my beloved and longed-for brethren, my joy and crown, so stand fast in the Lord, beloved.

BE UNITED, JOYFUL, AND IN PRAYER

²I implore Euodia and I implore Syntyche to be of the same mind in the Lord. ³Andᵃ I urge you also, true companion, help these women who labored with me in the gospel, with Clement also, and the rest of my fellow workers, whose names *are* in the Book of Life.

⁴Rejoice in the Lord always. Again I will say, rejoice!

⁵Let your gentleness be known to all men. The Lord *is* at hand.

WORRY

What can cause worry? (4:4–9)

3:16 ᵃNU-Text omits *rule* and the rest of the verse.   4:3 ᵃNU-Text and M-Text read *Yes.*

⁶Be anxious for nothing, but in everything by prayer and supplication, with thanksgiving, let your requests be made known to God; ⁷and the peace of God, which surpasses all understanding, will guard your hearts and minds through Christ Jesus.

On the Edge

Finally, brethren, whatever things are true, whatever things are noble, whatever things are just, whatever things are pure, whatever things are lovely, whatever things are of good report, if there is any virtue and if there is anything praiseworthy—meditate on these things (Phil. 4:8).

Mom is probably more concerned with the lyrics of the songs than the style of music. So put your CD collection through the Philippians 4:8 test. Do any of the lyrics oppose the teaching of Paul in verse 8? If what you are listening to makes you think about things that are impure, wrong, or immoral, it fails the test. What you put into your mind simmers there and eventually comes back out. So throw out the stuff that's trash and let Mom know that you've cleaned out the music she's been worried about. Wailing guitar riffs may still make Mom's head throb, but a good pair of headphones should bring her some relief. Next time you buy a CD, give it the "4:8" test and ask yourself if God would be pleased.

SEE FOR YOURSELF:
Rom. 12:2;
Eph. 4:20–24;
Col. 3:1, 2

MEDITATE ON THESE THINGS

⁸Finally, brethren, whatever things are true, whatever things *are* noble, whatever things *are* just, whatever things *are* pure, whatever things *are* lovely, whatever things *are* of good report, if *there is* any virtue and if *there is* anything praiseworthy—meditate on these things. ⁹The things which you learned and received and heard and saw in me, these do, and the God of peace will be with you.

PHILIPPIAN GENEROSITY

¹⁰But I rejoiced in the Lord greatly that now at last your care for me has flourished again; though you surely did care, but you lacked opportunity. ¹¹Not that I speak in regard to need, for I have learned in whatever state I am, to be content: ¹²I know how to be abased, and I know how to abound. Everywhere and in all things I have learned both to be full and to be hungry, both to abound and to suffer need. ¹³I can do all things through Christ*ᵃ* who strengthens me.

¹⁴Nevertheless you have done well that you shared in my distress. ¹⁵Now you Philippians

On the Edge

I can do all things through Christ who strengthens me (Phil. 4:13).

Paul had a rough time. He had been thrown in jail, beaten up, and had rocks thrown at him. He'd been robbed, lived through a shipwreck, and gone hungry. At times he barely had enough clothes to keep him warm. So Paul wasn't just blowing smoke when he told the Philippians, "I can do all things through Christ who strengthens me."

You have the same kind of strength in you. It doesn't matter if you can't relate to Paul. It doesn't matter if you aren't an apostle or a missionary living in the jungle. It doesn't matter if you think you'll never have to face the stuff Paul did. The truth is that Paul was strong because Jesus lived inside of him, and the same Jesus lives in you.

That means that, just like Paul, you can face *anything*. You can face a really tough exam. You can face your parents when you need to apologize to them. You can face your friends when doing what God wants isn't cool with them. You can face the future even when you have no idea what's going to happen. Just don't try to do it by yourself. The strength to face all those things comes only from Jesus. He'll make you strong.

SEE FOR YOURSELF:
Ps. 68:35; Jer. 15:20;
Hab. 3:19; Eph. 3:12

4:13 *ᵃ*NU-Text reads *Him who.*

know also that in the beginning of the gospel, when I departed from Macedonia, no church shared with me concerning giving and receiving but you only. ¹⁶For even in Thessalonica you sent *aid* once and again for my necessities. ¹⁷Not that I seek the gift, but I seek the fruit that abounds to your account. ¹⁸Indeed I have all and abound. I am full, having received from Epaphroditus the things *sent* from you, a sweet-smelling aroma, an acceptable sacrifice, well pleasing to God. ¹⁹And my God shall supply all your need according to His riches in glory by Christ Jesus. ²⁰Now to our God and Father *be* glory forever and ever. Amen.

GREETING AND BLESSING

²¹Greet every saint in Christ Jesus. The brethren who are with me greet you. ²²All the saints greet you, but especially those who are of Caesar's household.

4:23 ᵃNU-Text reads *your spirit.*

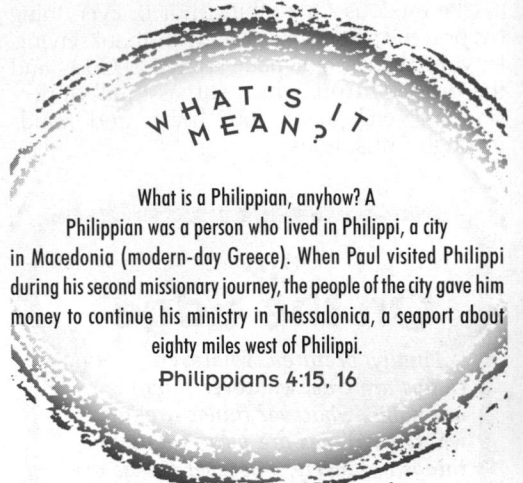

WHAT'S IT MEAN?

What is a Philippian, anyhow? A Philippian was a person who lived in Philippi, a city in Macedonia (modern-day Greece). When Paul visited Philippi during his second missionary journey, the people of the city gave him money to continue his ministry in Thessalonica, a seaport about eighty miles west of Philippi.

Philippians 4:15, 16

²³The grace of our Lord Jesus Christ be with you all.ᵃ Amen.

Colossians

CONTENT Paul wrote to the church at Colosse because they had fallen prey to some heretics (false teachers). There were people in the Colossian church that were teaching that Christianity was just too easy. Righteousness *couldn't* be as simple as faith in Christ. There had to be more to it than that.

Paul wrote to say, "Let's go over it again. There's no more to it. If you add more to it, then you are wrong. Faith in Christ is all there is."

Because of this, Colossians is a good book to read to review the basics of Christianity. At the bottom of it all, the message of Christ is simple and clear. Humans needed to be righteous in order to relate to God. Christ gave His life to provide that righteousness for us. When we put our faith in Christ's sacrifice God sees us through Christ's righteousness.

There is nothing we can do to add to that. If we think we can, then we need to read the Book of Colossians and let Paul set us straight.

Outline

Purpose Faith is to be lived out daily.

Theme The Supremacy and Sufficiency of Christ

Date of writing A.D. 60

> "If then you were raised with Christ, seek those things which are above, where Christ is, sitting at the right hand of God. Set your mind on things above, not on things on the earth" (3:1, 2).

Bible Talk

Do You Have an Apostle Paul in Your Life?

Paul was so important to the early church. He set church members straight when they drifted from the truth. He encouraged them when they were overwhelmed. He was like a big brother and a teacher rolled into one.

Do you have a Paul in your life? If you don't, look around you. Find someone who trusts God and has lived the Christian life for a long time. Find someone you can trust to help you decide what to believe and what to stand against. Find someone who will tell you the truth even when it hurts and even when it may disappoint you.

HOW TO DECIDE IF IT'S HERESY

Several of Paul's letters were written to correct some heresy that had slipped into the church. Do you know when something is heresy and when it is not? Here are some tests . . .

1. Does this way of thinking honor Christ as the one true God?
2. Does this way of thinking require anything more than faith to be righteous?
3. Does this way of thinking help me to be more obedient to God or less?

Be wise and ask questions about what you are taught. Don't let someone fool you into believing a lie.

GREETING

¹Paul, an apostle of Jesus Christ by the will of God, and Timothy our brother,

²To the saints and faithful brethren in Christ *who are* in Colosse:

Grace to you and peace from God our Father and the Lord Jesus Christ.*a*

THEIR FAITH IN CHRIST

³We give thanks to the God and Father of our Lord Jesus Christ, praying always for you, ⁴since we heard of your faith in Christ Jesus and of your love for all the saints; ⁵because of the hope which is laid up for you in heaven, of which you heard before in the word of the truth of the gospel, ⁶which has come to you, as *it has* also in all the world, and is bringing forth fruit,*a* as *it is* also among you since the day you heard and knew the grace of God in truth; ⁷as you also learned from Epaphras, our dear fellow servant, who is a faithful minister of Christ on your behalf, ⁸who also declared to us your love in the Spirit.

WHAT'S IT MEAN?

Epaphras was a Gentile (non-Jew) who became a Christian, probably as a result of Paul's teaching. Epaphras returned to his native city of Colosse to tell others about Jesus and to start a church. During the two years Paul was under house arrest, Epaphras visited him, cheering up the apostle with stories about the good things that were happening in the church at Colosse.

Colossians 1:7

PREEMINENCE OF CHRIST

⁹For this reason we also, since the day we heard it, do not cease to pray for you, and to ask that you may be filled with the knowledge of His will in all wisdom and spiritual understanding; ¹⁰that you may walk worthy of the Lord, fully pleasing *Him*, being fruitful in every good work and increasing in the knowledge of God; ¹¹strengthened with all might, according to His glorious power, for all patience and longsuffering with joy; ¹²giving thanks to the Father who has qualified us to be partakers of the inheritance of the saints in the light. ¹³He has delivered us from the power of darkness

On the Edge

That you may walk worthy of the Lord . . . strengthened with all might, according to His glorious power, for all patience and longsuffering with joy (Col. 1:10, 11).

Remember the story in Luke 8:42–48 about the woman who had been bleeding for twelve years? Talk about enduring. This woman had endured patiently for twelve years trying to get well. Luke reports that she had spent all of her money on doctors. They helped her the best they could, but she still couldn't get well. In fact, she just got worse and worse. Finally, she heard that Jesus was passing by. She knew that if she could just touch Him, that she would be whole. It happened! Do you think she was happy? You bet she was!

The apostle Paul is telling us here that we have been given the power to endure anything. Anything! It doesn't matter what your circumstances look like. As you begin to tap into the power of God, it will produce patience, and that patience will give you the ability to endure anything. And after the storm blows over and you've endured it, the rainbow will come out and there will be joy beyond your wildest thoughts! It's what we do during the storm that will make the difference.

If anyone knew endurance, it was Paul. He was beaten many times, shipwrecked, bitten by a poisonous snake, stoned, and put in jail. That's some rough stuff! But you know what? Paul made it through all of that junk, and if anyone was happy, he was. He's the one who wrote to "rejoice in the Lord always" (Phil. 4:4), and he wrote that while he was stuck in prison! Don't give up. You're going to make it through life's storms. God gives you the power to endure, and He's going to make you truly happy someday!

SEE FOR YOURSELF:
Rom. 5:3, 4;
2 Cor. 6:4, 5

1:2 *a*NU-Text omits *and the Lord Jesus Christ.*   **1:6** *a*NU-Text and M-Text add *and growing.*

and conveyed *us* into the kingdom of the Son of His love, [14]in whom we have redemption through His blood,[a] the forgiveness of sins.

[15]He is the image of the invisible God, the firstborn over all creation. [16]For by Him all things were created that are in heaven and that are on earth, visible and invisible, whether thrones or dominions or principalities or powers. All things were created through Him and for Him. [17]And He is before all things, and in Him all things consist. [18]And He is the head of the body, the church, who is the beginning, the firstborn from the dead, that in all things He may have the preeminence.

JESUS

Did Jesus create the world? (1:15, 16)

RECONCILED IN CHRIST

[19]For it pleased *the Father that* in Him all the fullness should dwell, [20]and by Him to reconcile all things to Himself, by Him, whether things on earth or things in heaven, having made peace through the blood of His cross.

[21]And you, who once were alienated and enemies in your mind by wicked works, yet now He has reconciled [22]in the body of His flesh through death, to present you holy, and blameless, and above reproach in His sight— [23]if indeed you continue in the faith, grounded and steadfast, and are not moved away from the hope of the gospel which you heard, which was preached to every creature under heaven, of which I, Paul, became a minister.

SACRIFICIAL SERVICE FOR CHRIST

[24]I now rejoice in my sufferings for you, and fill up in my flesh what is lacking in the afflictions of Christ, for the sake of His body, which is the church, [25]of which I became a minister according to the stewardship from God which was given to me for you, to fulfill the word of God, [26]the mystery which has been hidden from ages and from generations, but now has been revealed to His saints. [27]To them God willed to make known what are the riches of the glory of this mystery among the Gentiles: which[a] is Christ in you, the hope of glory. [28]Him we preach, warning every man and teaching every man in all wisdom, that we may present every man perfect in Christ Jesus. [29]To this *end* I also labor, striving according to His working which works in me mightily.

1:14 [a]NU-Text and M-Text omit *through His blood.*   **1:27** [a]M-Text reads *who.*

Promise   HE PROMISES TO PRESENT YOU ABOVE REPROACH IN HIS SIGHT.

And you, who once were alienated and enemies in your mind by wicked works, yet now He has reconciled in the body of His flesh through death, to present you holy, and blameless, and above reproach in His sight—if indeed you continue in the faith, grounded and steadfast, and are not moved away from the hope of the gospel which you heard, which was preached to every creature under heaven, of which I, Paul, became a minister (Col. 1:21–23).

It seems like people are always dividing up. Teams, clubs, cliques, or groups. With everyone taking sides, there are a lot of ways you can be left out. Your grades might keep you from the Honor Society or your first-choice college. Lack of skill keeps you off the basketball team. Your friends plan a party and forget to call you. Being left out will happen for all kinds of reasons for the rest of your life. But Jesus promises that, one day in heaven, He will call your name, and you will never be left out again. You won't have to watch while everyone else has all the fun. You won't have to congratulate everyone else on their great accomplishments. Because of Christ, you will be made perfect enough to stand with Him—holy, sinless, and free from the guilt of your sin. You'll be first-team, first-pick, forever included with Jesus and all the saints of heaven.

SEE FOR YOURSELF:
2 Cor. 3:4; Eph. 1:4; Heb. 6:19; 7:25

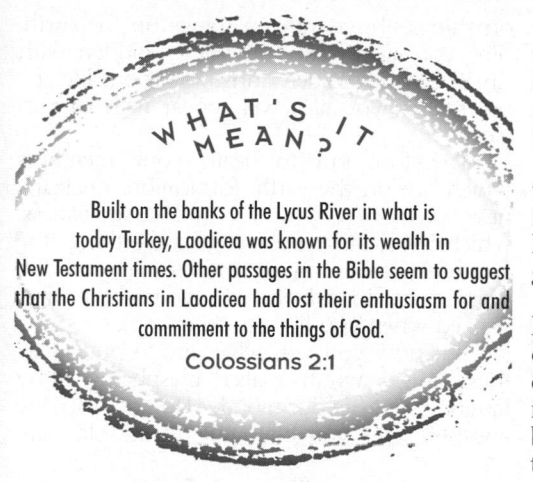

WHAT'S IT MEAN?

Built on the banks of the Lycus River in what is today Turkey, Laodicea was known for its wealth in New Testament times. Other passages in the Bible seem to suggest that the Christians in Laodicea had lost their enthusiasm for and commitment to the things of God.

Colossians 2:1

NOT PHILOSOPHY BUT CHRIST

[1]For I want you to know what a great conflict I have for you and those in Laodicea, and *for* as many as have not seen my face in the flesh, [2]that their hearts may be encouraged, being knit together in love, and *attaining* to all riches of the full assurance of understanding, to the knowledge of the mystery of God, both of the Father and[a] of Christ, [3]in whom are hidden all the treasures of wisdom and knowledge.

[4]Now this I say lest anyone should deceive you with persuasive words. [5]For though I am absent in the flesh, yet I am with you in spirit, rejoicing to see your *good* order and the steadfastness of your faith in Christ.

[6]As you therefore have received Christ Jesus the Lord, so walk in Him, [7]rooted and built up in Him and established in the faith, as you have been taught, abounding in it[a] with thanksgiving.

[8]Beware lest anyone cheat you through philosophy and empty deceit, according to the tradition of men, according to the basic principles of the world, and not according to Christ. [9]For in Him dwells all the fullness of the Godhead bodily; [10]and you are complete in Him, who is the head of all principality and power.

NOT LEGALISM BUT CHRIST

[11]In Him you were also circumcised with the circumcision made without hands, by putting off the body of the sins[a] of the flesh, by the circumcision of Christ, [12]buried with Him in baptism, in which you also were raised with *Him* through faith in the working of God, who raised Him from the dead. [13]And you, being dead in your trespasses and the uncircumcision of your flesh, He has made alive together with

2:2 [a]NU-Text omits *both of the Father and.*   **2:7** [a]NU-Text omits *in it.*   **2:11** [a]NU-Text omits *of the sins.*

Promise   HE PROMISES TO WIPE OUT THE RECORD AGAINST YOU.

And you . . . He has made alive together with Him, having forgiven you all trespasses, having wiped out the handwriting of requirements that was against us, which was contrary to us (Col. 2:13, 14).

We think we're pretty slick with our big-screen TVs and surround-sound systems. But wonder what God's got in store for the day of judgment, when every person who's ever lived has to stand before Him and give account of their lives?

This is just a wild guess—highly unproven—but can't you just imagine some gigantic movie screen, out in the middle of this huge mass of people, playing surveillance camera footage of their secret sins, their bad thoughts, their evil intentions—right there in front of their mamas and everybody?

If that scenario is even remotely true, what do you think would be on your tape? The time you let your sister's pet mouse loose? The day you got mad and told your dad you hated him—and thought something worse?

If you've asked Christ into your heart, your own personal private showing will have been somehow, mysteriously erased . . . deleted from memory by a nail-scarred hand.

SEE FOR YOURSELF:

Ps. 108:12; Is. 43:25; Rom. 3:24

Him, having forgiven you all trespasses, [14]having wiped out the handwriting of requirements that was against us, which was contrary to us. And He has taken it out of the way, having nailed it to the cross. [15]Having disarmed principalities and powers, He made a public spectacle of them, triumphing over them in it.

WHAT'S IT MEAN?

In the days of the Roman Empire, any time a Roman general returned home after a successful military campaign, he was honored with a special ceremony called a triumph. A parade was thrown in his honor, with the general leading the way in his chariot and prisoners of war following along behind it. Those prisoners were then divided into two groups: those who would be executed and those who would become slaves of the Roman Empire.

Colossians 2:15

[16]So let no one judge you in food or in drink, or regarding a festival or a new moon or sabbaths, [17]which are a shadow of things to come, but the substance is of Christ. [18]Let no one cheat you of your reward, taking delight in *false* humility and worship of angels, intruding into those things which he has not[a] seen, vainly puffed up by his fleshly mind, [19]and not holding fast to the Head, from whom all the body, nourished and knit together by joints and ligaments, grows with the increase *that is* from God. [20]Therefore,[a] if you died with Christ from the basic principles of the world, why, as *though* living in the world, do you subject yourselves to regulations—[21]"Do not touch, do not taste, do not handle," [22]which all concern things which perish with the using—according to the commandments and doctrines of men? [23]These things indeed have an appearance of wisdom in self-imposed religion, *false* humility, and neglect of the body, *but are* of no value against the indulgence of the flesh.

NOT CARNALITY BUT CHRIST

[1]If then you were raised with Christ, seek those things which are above, where Christ is, sitting at the right hand of God. [2]Set your mind on things above, not on things on the earth. [3]For you died, and your life is hidden with Christ in God. [4]When Christ *who is* our life appears, then you also will appear with Him in glory.

[5]Therefore put to death your members which are on the earth: fornication, uncleanness, passion, evil desire, and covetousness, which is idolatry. [6]Because of these things the wrath of God is coming upon the sons of disobedience, [7]in which you yourselves once walked when you lived in them.

[8]But now you yourselves are to put off all these: anger, wrath, malice, blasphemy, filthy language out of your mouth. [9]Do not lie to one another, since you have put off the old man

On the Edge

If then you were raised with Christ, seek those things which are above, where Christ is, sitting at the right hand of God (Col. 3:1).

Paul says that because you have a new life in Christ, you are to set your heart and mind on what is in heaven. He isn't saying that you should lose your sense of reality because your head is always somewhere else, but that life in this world will be better if it is lived with the power that comes from heaven. You will handle success, failure, and disappointment with maturity and poise when you have an eternal perspective. An eternal perspective means that you look at today's events in light of eternity.

Does today's "crisis" have any bearing on eternity? Will it matter when you get to heaven? Will it even matter in 100 years? Is it worth all the anxiety, worry, and pain? An eternal perspective lets you give others a lot of grace. You'll be more patient with people and events when you realize that, because of Christ, some things are not a big deal. Since you have been raised to life with Christ, then think about things with a heavenly mind-set. Let the truth of eternity guide your decisions and reactions about the world.

SEE FOR YOURSELF:
Ps. 110:1; Gal. 2:20

2:18 [a]NU-Text omits *not.*   2:20 [a]NU-Text and M-Text omit *Therefore.*

with his deeds, [10]and have put on the new *man* who is renewed in knowledge according to the image of Him who created him, [11]where there is neither Greek nor Jew, circumcised nor uncircumcised, barbarian, Scythian, slave *nor* free, but Christ *is* all and in all.

CHARACTER OF THE NEW MAN

[12]Therefore, as *the* elect of God, holy and beloved, put on tender mercies, kindness, humility, meekness, longsuffering; [13]bearing with one another, and forgiving one another; if anyone has a complaint against another; even as Christ forgave you, so you also *must do.* [14]But above all these things put on love, which is the bond of perfection. [15]And let the peace of God rule in your hearts, to which also you were called in one body; and be thankful. [16]Let the word of Christ dwell in you richly in all wisdom, teaching and admonishing one another in psalms and hymns and spiritual songs, singing with grace in your hearts to the Lord. [17]And *whatever* you do in word or deed, *do* all in the name of the Lord Jesus, giving thanks to God the Father through Him.

MUSIC

Why should we make music? (3:16)

THE CHRISTIAN HOME

[18]Wives, submit to your own husbands, as is fitting in the Lord.

[19]Husbands, love your wives and do not be bitter toward them.

[20]Children, obey your parents in all things, for this is well pleasing to the Lord.

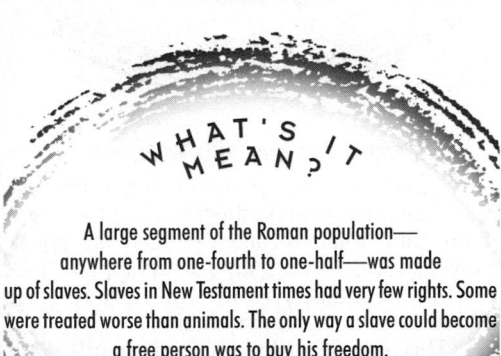

WHAT'S IT MEAN?

A large segment of the Roman population— anywhere from one-fourth to one-half—was made up of slaves. Slaves in New Testament times had very few rights. Some were treated worse than animals. The only way a slave could become a free person was to buy his freedom.

Colossians 3:22

On the Edge

Children, obey your parents in all things, for this is well pleasing to the Lord (Col. 3:20).

In His wisdom, the Lord has put people in places of authority over you. When you are a student, the Lord calls you to obey your parents, your teachers, coaches, and leaders at your church. Even as an adult you will still be under the rule of government, and called to submit to the leadership of church elders. God works out His will in your life through the authority that He has allowed. By obeying your parents or other leaders, you are obeying God. God says that it pleases Him when you obey your parents. So even when you disagree with them, or feel frustrated, remember that obedience to them is a gift that you are giving to God.

SEE FOR YOURSELF:
Prov. 15:21, 31;
Rom. 13:5–7;
Eph. 6:1–13

---

[21]Fathers, do not provoke your children, lest they become discouraged.

[22]Bondservants, obey in all things your masters according to the flesh, not with eyeservice, as men-pleasers, but in sincerity of heart, fearing God. [23]And whatever you do, do it heartily, as to the Lord and not to men, [24]knowing that from the Lord you will receive the reward of the inheritance; for[a] you serve the Lord Christ. [25]But he who does wrong will be repaid for what he has done, and there is no partiality.

[1]Masters, give your bondservants what is just and fair, knowing that you also have a Master in heaven.

CHRISTIAN GRACES

[2]Continue earnestly in prayer, being vigilant in it with thanksgiving; [3]meanwhile praying also for us, that God would open to us a door for the word, to speak the mystery of Christ, for which I am also in chains, [4]that I may make it manifest, as I ought to speak.

[5]Walk in wisdom toward those *who are* outside, redeeming the time. [6]*Let* your speech

---

3:24 [a]NU-Text omits *for.*

On the Edge

Continue earnestly in prayer, being vigilant in it with thanksgiving (Col. 4:2).

What is prayer? Prayer is simply communication with God—just talking and listening to Him. You see, prayer moves the hand of God, and the hand of God moves the world! He wants us to come to Him in prayer. There's not a right or wrong way to pray. All you have to do is talk to God like you would with your best friend.

A lot of people have the idea that prayer is only talking to God. That's only half of it. You really can't communicate with someone without another important activity—listening. Prayer is a two-way street. Not only does God want you to talk to Him; He also wants to talk to you. How can God talk to you? Through His Word.

Try it right now. Whatever need you have, go to God in prayer, and then pick this Bible back up and let God speak to you from His Word. But don't just get in a habit of praying when you're in a bind. God wants you to be in continual prayer, talking to Him throughout the day. Start every day with a quiet time—moments that are reserved for you and God. Prayer can only happen when the two of you are spending time together.

If you were to only talk to a close friend once in a while, what would happen? Your friendship wouldn't be that close. If we expect our relationship with Christ to be strong, we must never stop praying. Kick it up a notch today!

SEE FOR YOURSELF:
Matt. 21:22; 26:41;
John 15:7; Rom. 12:12;
1 Thess. 5:17

vant in the Lord, will tell you all the news about me. [8]I am sending him to you for this very purpose, that he[a] may know your circumstances and comfort your hearts, [9]with Onesimus, a faithful and beloved brother, who is *one* of you. They will make known to you all things which *are happening* here.

[10]Aristarchus my fellow prisoner greets you, with Mark the cousin of Barnabas (about whom you received instructions: if he comes to you, welcome him), [11]and Jesus who is called Justus. These *are my* only fellow workers for the kingdom of God who are of the circumcision; they have proved to be a comfort to me.

[12]Epaphras, who is *one* of you, a bondservant of Christ, greets you, always laboring fervently for you in prayers, that you may stand perfect and complete[a] in all the will of God. [13]For I bear him witness that he has a great zeal[a] for you, and those who are in Laodicea, and those in Hierapolis. [14]Luke the beloved physician and Demas greet you. [15]Greet the brethren who are in Laodicea, and Nymphas and the church that *is* in his[a] house.

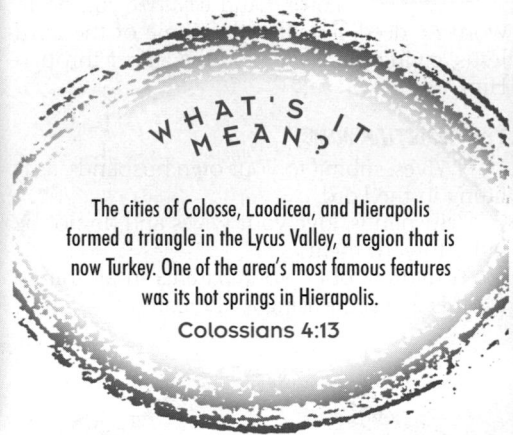

WHAT'S IT MEAN?

The cities of Colosse, Laodicea, and Hierapolis formed a triangle in the Lycus Valley, a region that is now Turkey. One of the area's most famous features was its hot springs in Hierapolis.

Colossians 4:13

CLOSING EXHORTATIONS AND BLESSING

[16]Now when this epistle is read among you, see that it is read also in the church of the Laodiceans, and that you likewise read the epistle from Laodicea. [17]And say to Archippus, "Take heed to the ministry which you have received in the Lord, that you may fulfill it."

[18]This salutation by my own hand—Paul. Remember my chains. Grace *be* with you. Amen.

WITNESSING

What does our speech reflect? (4:6)

always *be* with grace, seasoned with salt, that you may know how you ought to answer each one.

FINAL GREETINGS

[7]Tychicus, a beloved brother, faithful minister, and fellow ser-

4:8 [a]NU-Text reads *you may know our circumstances and he may.*   **4:12** [a]NU-Text reads *fully assured.*
4:13 [a]NU-Text reads *concern.*   **4:15** [a]NU-Text reads *Nympha . . . her house.*

1 Thessalonians

CONTENT

If there's one thing you can say about the church at Thessalonica, it's that they had a lot of questions about Jesus' second coming. For one thing, they wanted to know what would happen to the people who had already died when Christ returns. Paul wrote First Thessalonians, in part, to answer this specific question.

Because the people of Thessalonica had so many questions, we know a lot more about what will happen when Christ returns. Did you know He'll return in the sky? Did you know that the people who have already died will meet Him first? Did you know that there will be a shout and a trumpet?

Some of the most famous verses about Christ's second coming are found in First Thessalonians. It's a message of hope, particularly if you've lost someone you love in death. This book tells us, "Don't worry, death isn't the end of everything. You'll see them again."

Outline

Purpose

Live godly lives while waiting for Jesus to return.

Theme

The Twin Comforts of Past Ministry and the Future Return of the Lord

Date of writing

A.D. 51

> "And may the Lord make you increase and abound in love to one another and to all, just as we do to you, so that He may establish your hearts blameless in holiness before our God and Father at the coming of our Lord Jesus Christ with all His saints" (3:12, 13).

Bible Talk

Waiting and Watching

Jesus really could come back during your lifetime. Many of the prophecies of the Old and New Testament have come true just in the last century. Whether He does or doesn't return while you are alive, live your life so that you are ready to go to heaven at any moment.

It's okay to think that maybe you would like to grow up first or pass some other mile marker in your life. God gave us this life to enjoy. The point is that we keep our lives as clear of sin as possible and continue to grow in our relationship with God. If we do that, then when Christ returns, we will be ready.

JESUS COMES TO EARTH

People have been looking forward to Jesus' coming to earth since the beginning of time. Even in the garden of Eden God promised Someone would come eventually and take care of that evil snake that got Adam and Eve into a pickle. In Old Testament times, people were waiting for Christ's *first* trip to earth.

Since Jesus died and then went to heaven, though, we have been waiting for His next trip to earth. In the first trip, He came as a Servant to die for our sins. At the next trip, He'll come as a triumphant King who will change life as we know it.

We are not a lot different from people back in Bible days. We are still waiting for God's promise to be revealed. Jesus is coming!

GREETING

¹Paul, Silvanus, and Timothy,

To the church of the Thessalonians in God the Father and the Lord Jesus Christ:

Grace to you and peace from God our Father and the Lord Jesus Christ.ᵃ

THEIR GOOD EXAMPLE

²We give thanks to God always for you all, making mention of you in our prayers, ³remembering without ceasing your work of faith, labor of love, and patience of hope in our Lord Jesus Christ in the sight of our God and Father, ⁴knowing, beloved brethren, your election by God. ⁵For our gospel did not come to you in word only, but also in power, and in the Holy Spirit and in much assurance, as you know what kind of men we were among you for your sake.

⁶And you became followers of us and of the Lord, having received the word in much affliction, with joy of the Holy Spirit, ⁷so that you became examples to all in Macedonia and Achaia who believe. ⁸For from you the word of the Lord has sounded forth, not only in Macedonia and Achaia, but also in every place. Your faith toward God has gone out, so that we do not need to say anything. ⁹For they themselves declare concerning us what manner of entry we had to you, and how you turned to God from idols to serve the living and true God, ¹⁰and to wait for His Son from heaven, whom He raised from the dead, *even* Jesus who delivers us from the wrath to come.

> **GOSPEL**
>
> How does believing in the gospel affect a person? (1:4, 5)

WHAT'S IT MEAN?

If you're trying to keep track of Paul's journeys, here's what you need to know. Thessalonica was the capital of Macedonia, a region north of what is now Greece. Speaking of modern-day Greece, in Paul's day it was known as Achaia. The city of Athens was located in Achaia. Paul visited Thessalonica and Athens on his second missionary journey.

1 Thessalonians 1:7

1:1 ᵃNU-Text omits *from God our Father and the Lord Jesus Christ.*

Promise — HE PROMISES TO SAVE US FROM GOD'S WRATH.

For they themselves declare . . . how you turned to God from idols to serve the living and true God, and to wait for His Son from heaven, whom He raised from the dead, even Jesus who delivers us from the wrath to come (1 Thess. 1:9, 10).

The return of Jesus is an incredible source of hope for all believers! We have hope for many reasons, but the one Paul mentions here is that Jesus will save us from God's wrath. God is love and He loves all people and wants them to be saved (see 1 John 4:8–10). But the day will come when God will pour out His wrath on those who have not believed. The great white throne judgment will be a specific time of wrath (Rev. 20:11–15), and the great tribulation (Rev. 6—19) will be another. The anger of God is also poured out on earth, where unbelievers live without the Holy Spirit and without the power and presence of God. Their lives have fallen under the power of Satan.

As a Christian, you can rest in the promise that Jesus saves you from God's anger over sinful human rebellion. You will be kept from it because you are covered with the blood of Jesus. That is, because Jesus is the Lord of your life and you have accepted His work on the cross, God's anger is satisfied. Thank Jesus today for sparing you from God's anger on the day of judgment.

SEE FOR YOURSELF:
John 3:36; Rom. 1:18; 1 John 4:8–10; Rev. 6—19; 20:11–15

PAUL'S CONDUCT

¹For you yourselves know, brethren, that our coming to you was not in vain. ²But even[a] after we had suffered before and were spitefully treated at Philippi, as you know, we were bold in our God to speak to you the gospel of God in much conflict. ³For our exhortation *did* not *come* from error or uncleanness, nor *was it* in deceit.

⁴But as we have been approved by God to be entrusted with the gospel, even so we speak, not as pleasing men, but God who tests our hearts. ⁵For neither at any time did we use flattering words, as you know, nor a cloak for covetousness—God *is* witness. ⁶Nor did we seek glory from men, either from you or from others, when we might have made demands as apostles of Christ. ⁷But we were gentle among you, just as a nursing *mother* cherishes her own children. ⁸So, affectionately longing for you, we were well pleased to impart to you not only the gospel of God, but also our own lives, because you had become dear to us. ⁹For you remember, brethren, our labor and toil; for laboring night and day, that we might not be a burden to any of you, we preached to you the gospel of God.

Rabbis and church leaders in New Testament times often moonlighted at other jobs to support themselves and their families. Paul's second job was making tents, a skill he may have learned as a lad in Cilicia. After all, Cilicia was known for exporting a special kind of cloth made from goat's hair—a cloth that was used to make tents.

1 Thessalonians 2:9

¹⁰You *are* witnesses, and God *also*, how devoutly and justly and blamelessly we behaved ourselves among you who believe; ¹¹as you know how we exhorted, and comforted, and charged[a] every one of you, as a father *does* his own children, ¹²that you would walk worthy of God who calls you into His own kingdom and glory.

THEIR CONVERSION

¹³For this reason we also thank God without ceasing, because when you received the word of God which you heard from us, you welcomed *it* not *as* the word of men, but as it is in truth, the word of God, which also effectively works in you who believe. ¹⁴For you, brethren, became imitators of the churches of God which are in Judea in Christ Jesus. For you also suffered the same things from your own countrymen, just as they *did* from the Judeans, ¹⁵who killed both the Lord Jesus and their own prophets, and have persecuted us; and they do not please God and are contrary to all men, ¹⁶forbidding us to speak to the Gentiles that they may be saved, so as always to fill up *the measure* of their sins; but wrath has come upon them to the uttermost.

The trip from Athens to Thessalonica was about three hundred miles. You might say Athens is still an important city in Greece today. It's the nation's capital.

1 Thessalonians 3:1, 2

LONGING TO SEE THEM

¹⁷But we, brethren, having been taken away from you for a short time in presence, not in heart, endeavored more eagerly to see your face with great desire. ¹⁸Therefore we wanted to come to you—even I, Paul, time and again—but Satan hindered us. ¹⁹For what *is* our hope, or joy, or crown of rejoicing? *Is it* not even you in the presence of our Lord Jesus Christ at His coming? ²⁰For you are our glory and joy.

CONCERN FOR THEIR FAITH

¹Therefore, when we could no longer endure it, we thought it good to be left in Athens alone, ²and sent Timothy, our brother and minister of God, and our fellow laborer in the gospel of Christ, to establish you and encourage you concerning your faith, ³that no one should be shaken by these afflictions; for you yourselves know that we are appointed to this. ⁴For, in fact,

2:2 [a]NU-Text and M-Text omit *even*.   **2:11** [a]NU-Text and M-Text read *implored*.

we told you before when we were with you that we would suffer tribulation, just as it happened, and you know. [5]For this reason, when I could no longer endure it, I sent to know your faith, lest by some means the tempter had tempted you, and our labor might be in vain.

ENCOURAGED BY TIMOTHY

[6]But now that Timothy has come to us from you, and brought us good news of your faith and love, and that you always have good remembrance of us, greatly desiring to see us, as we also to see you—[7]therefore, brethren, in all our affliction and distress we were comforted concerning you by your faith. [8]For now we live, if you stand fast in the Lord.

[9]For what thanks can we render to God for you, for all the joy with which we rejoice for your sake before our God, [10]night and day praying exceedingly that we may see your face and perfect what is lacking in your faith?

PRAYER FOR THE CHURCH

[11]Now may our God and Father Himself, and our Lord Jesus Christ, direct our way to you. [12]And may the Lord make you increase and abound in love to one another and to all, just as we do to you, [13]so that He may establish your hearts blameless in holiness before our God and Father at the coming of our Lord Jesus Christ with all His saints.

WHAT'S IT MEAN?

The Macedonians liked their sexual perversions. The Greek and Roman influences on their culture included pagan worship services that involved all kinds of sexual immorality. God, of course, wanted His followers to have nothing to do with this form of prostitution.

1 Thessalonians 4:3

PLEA FOR PURITY

[1]Finally then, brethren, we urge and exhort in the Lord Jesus that you should abound more and more, just as you received from us how you ought to walk and to please God; [2]for you know what commandments we gave you through the Lord Jesus.

On the Edge

Each of you should know how to possess his own vessel in sanctification and honor, not in passion of lust, like the Gentiles who do not know God (1 Thess. 4:4, 5).

According to the Bible, the requirement for sex is *marriage*, not just love. God gave sex to marriage as a gift. Two people have made a permanent commitment to each other and God gives them the privilege and gift of sex.

If you play the dating game you may love many times and date many people. But those who are wise choose friendships that lead to holy courtships. That kind of relationship reserves sex for the lifelong bond of marriage. Sex outside of marriage can have so many hard consequences. You know what they are—diseases that can kill you, babies you aren't ready to have, stress like you've never known, horrible guilt or shame. The list goes on. Sex as a part of marriage is good and blessed.

Don't have sex with the person you're dating because dating is not marriage. There is no commitment. There is no blessing from God. The consequences could be damaging and even deadly. God's advice is perfect and it's perfectly right and good for you. Take His advice and wait. You'll be so glad you did.

SEE FOR YOURSELF:
1 Cor. 6:18;
1 Thess. 4:3

[3]For this is the will of God, your sanctification: that you should abstain from sexual immorality; [4]that each of you should know how to possess his own vessel in sanctification and honor, [5]not in passion of lust, like the Gentiles who do not know God; [6]that no one should take advantage of and defraud his brother in this matter, because the Lord is the avenger of all such, as we also forewarned you and testified. [7]For God did not call us to uncleanness, but in holiness. [8]Therefore he who rejects this does not reject man, but God, who has also given[a] us His Holy Spirit.

4:8 [a]NU-Text reads *who also gives.*

A BROTHERLY AND ORDERLY LIFE

[9]But concerning brotherly love you have no need that I should write to you, for you yourselves are taught by God to love one another; [10]and indeed you do so toward all the brethren who are in all Macedonia. But we urge you, brethren, that you increase more and more; [11]that you also aspire to lead a quiet life, to mind your own business, and to work with your own hands, as we commanded you, [12]that you may walk properly toward those who are outside, and *that* you may lack nothing.

THE COMFORT OF CHRIST'S COMING

[13]But I do not want you to be ignorant, brethren, concerning those who have fallen asleep, lest you sorrow as others who have no hope. [14]For if we believe that Jesus died and rose again, even so God will bring with Him those who sleep in Jesus.[a]

[15]For this we say to you by the word of the Lord, that we who are alive *and* remain until the coming of the Lord will by no means precede those who are asleep. [16]For the Lord Himself will descend from heaven with a shout, with the voice of an archangel, and with the trumpet of God. And the dead in Christ will rise first. [17]Then we who are alive *and* remain shall be caught up together with them in the clouds to meet the Lord in the air. And thus we shall always be with the Lord. [18]Therefore comfort one another with these words.

PAIN

How should Christians treat each other in times of pain? (4:18)

THE DAY OF THE LORD

[1]But concerning the times and the seasons, brethren, you have no need that I should write to you. [2]For you yourselves know perfectly that the day of the Lord so comes as a thief in the night. [3]For when they say, "Peace and safety!" then sudden destruction comes upon them, as labor pains upon a pregnant woman. And they shall not escape. [4]But you, brethren, are not in darkness, so that this Day should overtake you as a thief. [5]You are all sons of light and sons of the day. We are not of the night nor of darkness. [6]Therefore let us not sleep, as others *do*, but let us watch and be sober. [7]For those who sleep, sleep at night, and those who get drunk are drunk at night. [8]But let us who are of the day be sober, putting on the breastplate of faith and love, and *as* a helmet the hope of salvation. [9]For

On the Edge

You are all sons of light and sons of the day. We are not of the night nor of darkness (1 Thess. 5:5).

Are you more concerned about someone stealing your car or breaking into your house during the day or at night? Something like that can happen anytime, but you're on the lookout for it more at night. People looking to do something illegal are prone to choose night because the darkness hides their actions. In the daytime they're more likely to get caught.

In John 3, Jesus told Nicodemus that some people didn't like the light because they didn't want their evil deeds exposed (see John 3:20). But Paul says because you're a Christian, you can have a different attitude. You belong to the light. You don't mind if people know what's going on with you. Your life can be an open book because your conscience is clean. Even your mistakes and failures don't have to embarrass you because you know that Jesus has taken care of all that. Belonging to the light gives you incredible freedom!

SEE FOR YOURSELF:
Matt. 5:14, 15;
John 12:36; Eph. 5:8

WHAT'S IT MEAN?

The protective gear that Roman soldiers wore wasn't like the suits of armor you see in medieval castles. Roman armor did not cover the soldier's entire body. Instead, the soldier wore pieces of metal or thick leather to protect his most vital organs. Roman helmets came in all shapes. Some covered the entire head, with a screen covering the face that allowed the warrior to breathe and see clearly.

1 Thessalonians 5:8

4:14 [a]Or *those who through Jesus sleep*

God did not appoint us to wrath, but to obtain salvation through our Lord Jesus Christ, [10]who died for us, that whether we wake or sleep, we should live together with Him.

[11]Therefore comfort each other and edify one another, just as you also are doing.

VARIOUS EXHORTATIONS

[12]And we urge you, brethren, to recognize those who labor among you, and are over you in the Lord and admonish you, [13]and to esteem them very highly in love for their work's sake. Be at peace among yourselves.

[14]Now we exhort you, brethren, warn those who are unruly, comfort the fainthearted, uphold the weak, be patient with all. [15]See that no one renders evil for evil to anyone, but always pursue what is good both for yourselves and for all.

[16]Rejoice always, [17]pray without ceasing, [18]in everything give thanks; for this is the will of God in Christ Jesus for you.

[19]Do not quench the Spirit. [20]Do not despise prophecies. [21]Test all things; hold fast what is good. [22]Abstain from every form of evil.

BLESSING AND ADMONITION

[23]Now may the God of peace Himself sanctify you completely; and may your whole spirit, soul, and body be preserved blameless at the coming of our Lord Jesus Christ. [24]He who calls you *is* faithful, who also will do *it*.

[25]Brethren, pray for us.

[26]Greet all the brethren with a holy kiss.

[27]I charge you by the Lord that this epistle be read to all the holy[a] brethren.

[28]The grace of our Lord Jesus Christ *be* with you. Amen.

> "Rejoice always, pray without ceasing, in everything give thanks; for this is the will of God in Christ Jesus for you."
> (1 Thessalonians 5:16-18)

LAZINESS

Who should we encourage to work? (5:12–14)

5:27 [a]NU-Text omits *holy.*

CONTENT

The church at Thessalonica took what Paul said to heart. In fact, some of them maybe took it too much to heart.

In Paul's first letter to this church, he had written that they needed to live their lives in anticipation of Christ's return. Later, he found out that some of them had responded to this by quitting their jobs and literally just *hanging out* waiting for Christ to come back.

These people who were hanging out began to do what anyone does when they hang out too much: they got bored, which led to gossiping, which led to nit-picking, which led to arguing, which led to the same church problems it always leads to.

Paul wrote his second letter to this church to remind them that waiting for Christ's return is a way of living. It *is not* standing in the yard all day and looking at the sky. It *is* living holy lives and connecting with God every day.

Outline

Purpose

Until Jesus does return, live disciplined, godly lives.

Theme

The Return of the Lord—Advance Indicators and Lifestyle in the Meanwhile

Date of writing

A.D. 51

Bible Talk

Gossip in the Church

Gossip can seem very harmless when you are sitting with your friend, laughing at someone else and talking about them. At first, it doesn't seem like it will hurt anyone. Of course, there's always the chance that the person you are gossiping about will hear you or hear about what you said; but if you're careful, that won't happen, will it?

Maybe not, but that's not really the point. When we gossip about each other we disrespect each other. We forget that we are all a part of the body of Christ. When we disrespect someone, we become like a cancer destroying the very body that we are a part of. It is a big deal. That's why Paul made a big deal about it.

ANY EARTHLY GOOD

Have you ever heard that expression about being too heavenly minded to be any earthly good? When someone says that, they are usually talking about someone who has faith, but it's not a practical faith that makes a difference in the everyday details of life. That's also sort of what Paul was writing about in his second letter to the church at Thessalonica.

The people in Thessalonica were doing something that *sounded* good. They were looking for Christ's return. But they forgot that, while Christ's return is important, it isn't the *only* thing God told us to do. He also told us to do good deeds in this life and to be kind to other people. He told us to make a living and to spend time with family.

Be careful whenever you find yourself obeying one of God's commands without thinking about all the other ones.

GREETING

¹Paul, Silvanus, and Timothy,

To the church of the Thessalonians in God our Father and the Lord Jesus Christ:

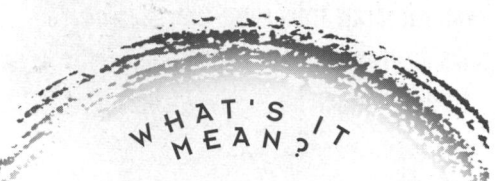

WHAT'S IT MEAN?

Paul was in the middle of a very busy missionary journey when he wrote this second letter to the church in Thessalonica. Apparently, Paul was writing from Corinth, where he was staying after preaching in Athens, Berea, and Thessalonica. Silvanus (better known as Silas) and Timothy are mentioned because they were with Paul when he started the church in Thessalonica.

2 Thessalonians 1:1

²Grace to you and peace from God our Father and the Lord Jesus Christ.

1:10 ^aNU-Text and M-Text read *have believed.*

GOD'S FINAL JUDGMENT AND GLORY

³We are bound to thank God always for you, brethren, as it is fitting, because your faith grows exceedingly, and the love of every one of you all abounds toward each other, ⁴so that we ourselves boast of you among the churches of God for your patience and faith in all your persecutions and tribulations that you endure, ⁵*which is* manifest evidence of the righteous judgment of God, that you may be counted worthy of the kingdom of God, for which you also suffer; ⁶since *it is* a righteous thing with God to repay with tribulation those who trouble you, ⁷and to *give* you who are troubled rest with us when the Lord Jesus is revealed from heaven with His mighty angels, ⁸in flaming fire taking vengeance on those who do not know God, and on those who do not obey the gospel of our Lord Jesus Christ. ⁹These shall be punished with everlasting destruction from the presence of the Lord and from the glory of His power, ¹⁰when He comes, in that Day, to be glorified in His saints and to be admired among all those who believe,^a because our testimony among you was believed.

¹¹Therefore we also pray always for you that our God would count you worthy of *this* calling, and fulfill all the good pleasure of *His* goodness and the work of faith with power, ¹²that the name of our Lord Jesus Christ may be

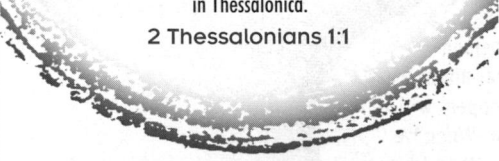

Promise   HE PROMISES TO GIVE YOU REST FROM YOUR TROUBLES.

Since it is a righteous thing with God to repay with tribulation those who trouble you, and to give you who are troubled rest with us when the Lord Jesus is revealed from heaven with His mighty angels, in flaming fire taking vengeance on those who do not know God, and on those who do not obey the gospel of our Lord Jesus Christ (2 Thess. 1:6–8).

Been laughed at lately? Taken any jabs for being a Christian? Been made fun of because you did the right thing? Take heart, because relief is on its way. When Jesus comes, He promises to give you rest from your troubles. You won't have to fight anymore. Jesus will take over with His powerful angels and a flaming fire. He will take care of your enemies and all who would persecute you. Sometimes the battle is bigger than you are. The trouble seems overwhelming. Be courageous enough to know which battles belong to the Lord, and leave them for Him to fight.

SEE FOR YOURSELF:
Jer. 29:11; 31:13; Lam. 3:22, 23; Eph. 3:14–19

glorified in you, and you in Him, according to the grace of our God and the Lord Jesus Christ.

THE GREAT APOSTASY

[1]Now, brethren, concerning the coming of our Lord Jesus Christ and our gathering together to Him, we ask you, [2]not to be soon shaken in mind or troubled, either by spirit or by word or by letter, as if from us, as though the day of Christ[a] had come. [3]Let no one deceive you by any means; for *that Day will not come* unless the falling away comes first, and the man of sin[a] is revealed, the son of perdition, [4]who opposes and exalts himself above all that is called God or that is worshiped, so that he sits as God[a] in the temple of God, showing himself that he is God.

You may know the "man of sin" better as the Antichrist. Led by Satan, this false prophet will claim to be God and will make himself an enemy of all Christians. Who will this man be? Who knows? If you had a nickel for every time someone was accused of being the Antichrist, you'd have a small fortune. One of the few things we know about him is that he will become a world leader.

2 Thessalonians 2:3, 4

[5]Do you not remember that when I was still with you I told you these things? [6]And now you know what is restraining, that he may be revealed in his own time. [7]For the mystery of lawlessness is already at work; only He[a] who now restrains *will do so* until He[b] is taken out of the way. [8]And then the lawless one will be revealed, whom the Lord will consume with the breath of His mouth and destroy with the brightness of His coming. [9]The coming of the *lawless one* is according to the working of Satan, with all power, signs, and lying wonders, [10]and with all unrighteous deception among those who perish, because they did not receive the love of the truth, that they might be saved. [11]And for this reason God will send them strong delusion, that they should believe the lie, [12]that they all may be condemned who did not

On the Edge

But we are bound to give thanks to God always for you, brethren beloved by the Lord, because God from the beginning chose you for salvation through sanctification by the Spirit and belief in the truth (2 Thess. 2:13).

When you gave your heart to Jesus, you became a new person—"a new creation" (see 2 Cor. 5:17). The old you disappeared, and you were transformed from darkness to light—from death to life! Now God wants you to be changed into His likeness, and He has equipped you to do this by His Spirit. The Holy Spirit puts in you the desire not to sin—not just the desire, but also the ability. Sin doesn't have authority over you anymore. You are free! We all need to submit ourselves to God, by remaining set apart for Him. As you begin to do this, it will become easier to walk in His will.

Walking in God's will is nothing more than walking in obedience to Him and to His Word. That's when the true blessings of God will begin to flow in your life. When Paul writes you are chosen "for salvation through sanctification by the Spirit," he is telling you that the Holy Spirit has given you the power to live a holy life. In fact, Titus 2:12 says, "Teaching us that, denying ungodliness and worldly lusts, we should live soberly, righteously, and godly in the present age." You have the power to walk in holiness—not only power to get free, but power to stay free. He is the One who makes you holy!

SEE FOR YOURSELF:
Rom. 12:1, 2;
2 Cor. 5:17

believe the truth but had pleasure in unrighteousness.

STAND FAST

[13]But we are bound to give thanks to God always for you, brethren beloved by the Lord, because God from the beginning chose you for salvation through sanctification by the Spirit and belief in the truth, [14]to which He called you by our gospel, for the obtaining of the glory of our Lord Jesus Christ. [15]Therefore, brethren,

2:2 [a]NU-Text reads *the Lord*.   **2:3** [a]NU-Text reads *lawlessness*.   **2:4** [a]NU-Text omits *as God*.   **2:7** [a]Or *he*
[b]Or *he*

stand fast and hold the traditions which you were taught, whether by word or our epistle.

[16]Now may our Lord Jesus Christ Himself, and our God and Father, who has loved us and given *us* everlasting consolation and good hope by grace, [17]comfort your hearts and establish you in every good word and work.

PRAY FOR US

[1]Finally, brethren, pray for us, that the word of the Lord may run *swiftly* and be glorified, just as *it is* with you, [2]and that we may be delivered from unreasonable and wicked men; for not all have faith.

[3]But the Lord is faithful, who will establish you and guard *you* from the evil one. [4]And we have confidence in the Lord concerning you, both that you do and will do the things we command you.

[5]Now may the Lord direct your hearts into the love of God and into the patience of Christ.

WHAT'S IT MEAN?

Apparently, some impostors had been sending out letters full of false teachings and then signing Paul's name to them. To make sure that the people in Thessalonica knew this was a genuine letter, Paul signed his name to it. You may be wondering why Paul only signed it, as opposed to writing the letter himself. Some Bible experts believe that Paul suffered from an eye disease that made it necessary for him to use a secretary to write the letters he dictated.

2 Thessalonians 3:17

WARNING AGAINST IDLENESS

[6]But we command you, brethren, in the name of our Lord Jesus Christ, that you withdraw from every brother who walks disorderly and not according to the tradition which he[a] received from us. [7]For you yourselves know how you ought to follow us, for we were not disorderly among you; [8]nor did we eat anyone's bread free of charge, but worked with labor and toil night and day, that we might not be a burden to any of you, [9]not because we do not have authority, but to make ourselves an example of how you should follow us.

On the Edge

But as for you, brethren, do not grow weary in doing good (2 Thess. 3:13).

"Surely I have cleansed my heart in vain, and washed my hands in innocence" (Ps. 73:13). Can you relate to this person's frustration? You tell the truth, even when it costs you, because you trust God to reward you for it. You help other people to try to make their lives better. Those are good reasons, but sometimes you just don't see those things happening. It's enough to make you want to give up.

Paul says you *must not* give up. How can you keep from getting tired of doing the right thing when it seems like it's getting you nowhere? Well, it takes some faith. You have to believe that God's going to do what He promised He would—even when His timetable is different from yours (and it usually is). You also have to continually fill up with God's Spirit. If you don't do that, you're like a car that's about to run out of gas. He keeps you going—you can't do it yourself.

Finally, you have to have your priorities straight. Ask yourself: Am I doing this to get results or am I doing it to please God? The answer makes all the difference.

SEE FOR YOURSELF:
Gal. 6:9

[10]For even when we were with you, we commanded you this: If anyone will not work, neither shall he eat. [11]For we hear that there are some who walk among you in a disorderly manner, not working at all, but are busybodies. [12]Now those who are such we command and exhort through our Lord Jesus Christ that they work in quietness and eat their own bread.

[13]But *as for* you, brethren, do not grow weary *in* doing good. [14]And if anyone does not obey our word in this epistle, note that person and do not keep company with him, that he may be ashamed. [15]Yet do not count *him* as an enemy, but admonish *him* as a brother.

LAZINESS
Should lazy people be allowed to take advantage of other people? (3:10)

3:6 [a]NU-Text and M-Text read *they.*

BENEDICTION

¹⁶Now may the Lord of peace Himself give you peace always in every way. The Lord *be* with you all.

¹⁷The salutation of Paul with my own hand, which is a sign in every epistle; so I write.

¹⁸The grace of our Lord Jesus Christ *be* with you all. Amen.

CONTENT   Have you ever gotten a letter or an e-mail from someone older who is really important to you? How do you read it? Do you skip over parts or maybe not even finish? Probably not. Probably you read every word and maybe even read some of them twice.

That might have been how it was for Timothy when he got letters from Paul. Timothy was like a son to Paul. Paul loved him and took him on trips and talked to him about things that mattered. Paul really invested in Timothy's life.

Timothy had a lot to learn. Paul had a lot to teach. We get to read a lot of truth because of that. God used their relationship to teach us about following Christ and being the church.

Outline   1:1, 2 .... Greetings
1:3—3:13 .... Instructions for Church Life
3:14—4:11 .... Be Faithful to Your Calling
4:12—6:21 .... Paul's Advice to Timothy

Purpose   Young adults have a significant role to play in Christ's church.

Themes   Removal of False Doctrine, Preservation of Public Worship, and Proper Leadership in the Church

Date of writing   Fall A.D. 62

Bible Talk

What Kind of Leader Leads a Church?

Paul wrote to Timothy about the kind of people who should be leading the church. We still depend on Paul's requirements for leadership today. It's not that the leaders of the church are any better than anyone else in the church, but they do have more responsibilities than other church members.

Paul said that the leaders of the church should be respected and have self-control. He also said they should be good family members and family leaders. How do you think the leaders in your church measure up? How do you think you'll measure up as a church leader?

WHEN YOU ARE YOUNG

One of the neat things about Paul's letter to Timothy was that Paul was writing to a young person. When you read about the people God used in the Bible, a lot of times those people are old people. Some of them are having babies even when they are too old to have babies. Some of them are teaching and preaching.

Paul's letters to Timothy remind us that God uses people of all ages. He can use us no matter how old or young we are, as long as we are willing to have faith and love others.

GREETING

[1]Paul, an apostle of Jesus Christ, by the commandment of God our Savior and the Lord Jesus Christ, our hope,

MERCY

Is Jesus merciful? (1:2)

[2]To Timothy, a true son in the faith:

Grace, mercy, *and* peace from God our Father and Jesus Christ our Lord.

NO OTHER DOCTRINE

[3]As I urged you when I went into Macedonia—remain in Ephesus that you may charge some that they teach no other doctrine, [4]nor give heed to fables and endless genealogies, which cause disputes rather than godly edification which is in faith. [5]Now the purpose of the commandment is love from a pure heart, *from a* good conscience, and *from* sincere faith, [6]from which some, having strayed, have turned aside to idle talk, [7]desiring to be teachers of the law, understanding neither what they say nor the things which they affirm.

WHAT'S IT MEAN?

How much do you know about your family tree? Do you know the name of your great-grandfather? How about your great-great-grandfather? Do you have any famous ancestors? The Jewish leaders of New Testament times could have answered these questions with no problem. Apparently, they took great pride in being able trace their ancestors all the way back to Abraham. We're talking about genealogies that stretched back over two thousand years!

1 Timothy 1:4

[8]But we know that the law *is* good if one uses it lawfully, [9]knowing this: that the law is not made for a righteous person, but for *the* lawless and insubordinate, for *the* ungodly and for sinners, for *the* unholy and profane, for murderers of fathers and murderers of mothers, for manslayers, [10]for fornicators, for sodomites, for kidnappers, for liars, for perjurers, and if there is any other thing that is contrary to sound doctrine, [11]according to the glorious gospel of the blessed God which was committed to my trust.

On the Edge

I desire therefore that the men pray everywhere, lifting up holy hands, without wrath and doubting (1 Tim. 2:8).

Your best friend tells you she'll call tonight at 8:00. You wait around the house most of the evening, because you care about your friend and you'd love to talk to her. The time goes by so quickly when you two are on the phone. You wait and wait but she never calls. At school, she promises to call again the next night. Still nothing. This goes on for a week and you become incredibly disappointed. You had hoped that your friend would want to spend time with you. She eventually calls a few weeks later, apologizing that she's had too much going on, but really needs you to help her do something. You love your friend so you forgive her and help her out. The Lord is waiting for those who love Him to pray to Him. We shove our time with Him under the pile of everything else, eventually running back when we need Him. He loves us and so He waits, but He hopes for more. He is happy when people pray.

SEE FOR YOURSELF:
Ps. 134; Prov. 15:8; Eph. 6:18

GLORY TO GOD FOR HIS GRACE

[12]And I thank Christ Jesus our Lord who has enabled me, because He counted me faithful, putting *me* into the ministry, [13]although I was formerly a blasphemer, a persecutor, and an insolent man; but I obtained mercy because I did *it* ignorantly in unbelief. [14]And the grace of our Lord was exceedingly abundant, with faith and love which are in Christ Jesus. [15]This *is* a faithful saying and worthy of all acceptance, that Christ Jesus came into the world to save sinners, of whom I am chief. [16]However, for this reason I obtained mercy, that in me first Jesus Christ might show all longsuffering, as a pattern to those who are going to believe on Him for everlasting life. [17]Now to the King eternal, im-

mortal, invisible, to God who alone is wise,[a] be honor and glory forever and ever. Amen.

FIGHT THE GOOD FIGHT

[18]This charge I commit to you, son Timothy, according to the prophecies previously made concerning you, that by them you may wage the good warfare, [19]having faith and a good conscience, which some having rejected, concerning the faith have suffered shipwreck, [20]of whom are Hymenaeus and Alexander, whom I delivered to Satan that they may learn not to blaspheme.

PRAY FOR ALL MEN

[1]Therefore I exhort first of all that supplications, prayers, intercessions, and giving of thanks be made for all men, [2]for kings and all who are in authority, that we may lead a quiet and peaceable life in all godliness and reverence. [3]For this is good and acceptable in the sight of God our Savior, [4]who desires all men to be saved and to come to the knowledge of the truth. [5]For there is one God and one Mediator between God and men, the Man Christ Jesus, [6]who gave Himself a ransom for all, to be testified in due time, [7]for which I was appointed a preacher and an apostle—I am speaking the truth in Christ[a] and not lying—a teacher of the Gentiles in faith and truth.

MEN AND WOMEN IN THE CHURCH

[8]I desire therefore that the men pray everywhere, lifting up holy hands, without wrath and doubting; [9]in like manner also, that the women adorn themselves in modest apparel, with propriety and moderation, not with braided hair or gold or pearls or costly clothing, [10]but, which is proper for women professing godliness, with good works. [11]Let a woman learn in silence with all submission. [12]And I do not permit a woman to teach or to have authority over a man, but to be in silence. [13]For Adam was formed first, then Eve. [14]And Adam was not deceived, but the woman being deceived, fell into transgression. [15]Nevertheless she will be saved in childbearing if they continue in faith, love, and holiness, with self-control.

QUALIFICATIONS OF OVERSEERS

[1]This is a faithful saying: If a man desires the position of a bishop,[a] he desires a good work. [2]A bishop then must be blameless, the husband of one wife, temperate, sober-minded, of good behavior, hospitable, able to teach; [3]not given to wine, not violent, not greedy for money,[a] but gentle, not quarrelsome, not covetous; [4]one who rules his own house well, having his children in submission with all reverence [5](for if a man does not know how to rule his own house, how will he take care of the church of God?); [6]not a novice, lest being puffed up with pride he fall into the same condemnation as the devil. [7]Moreover he must have a good testimony among those who are outside, lest he fall into reproach and the snare of the devil.

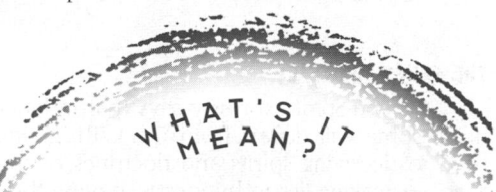

WHAT'S IT MEAN?

It would probably be safe to describe the women of ancient pagan cultures as "high-maintenance." They often spent hours creating elaborate hair arrangements for themselves. They wore fancy clothing and expensive jewelry to attract attention. We should point out, though, that most of the women who fit these descriptions were prostitutes. In Ephesus, the place where Timothy was working, these women could be found at the pagan temple of Diana.
1 Timothy 2:9

QUALIFICATIONS OF DEACONS

[8]Likewise deacons must be reverent, not double-tongued, not given to much wine, not greedy for money, [9]holding the mystery of the faith with a pure conscience. [10]But let these also first be tested; then let them serve as deacons, being found blameless. [11]Likewise, their wives must be reverent, not slanderers, temperate, faithful in all things. [12]Let deacons be the husbands of one wife, ruling their children and their own houses well. [13]For those who have served well as deacons obtain for themselves a good standing and great boldness in the faith which is in Christ Jesus.

THE GREAT MYSTERY

[14]These things I write to you, though I hope to come to you shortly; [15]but if I am delayed, I write so that you may know how you ought to conduct yourself in the house of God, which is

---

1:17 [a]NU-Text reads to the only God.　**2:7** [a]NU-Text omits in Christ.　**3:1** [a]Literally overseer　**3:3** [a]NU-Text omits not greedy for money.

the church of the living God, the pillar and ground of the truth. ¹⁶And without controversy great is the mystery of godliness:

> God*ᵃ* was manifested in the flesh,
> Justified in the Spirit,
> Seen by angels,
> Preached among the Gentiles,
> Believed on in the world,
> Received up in glory.

"God was manifested in the flesh."
(1 Timothy 3:16)

nourished in the words of faith and of the good doctrine which you have carefully followed. ⁷But reject profane and old wives' fables, and exercise yourself toward godliness. ⁸For bodily exercise profits a little, but godliness is profitable for all things, having promise of the life that now is and of that which is to come. ⁹This *is* a faithful saying and worthy of all acceptance. ¹⁰For to this *end* we both labor and suffer reproach,*ᵃ* because we trust in the living God, who is *the* Savior of all men, especially of those who believe. ¹¹These things command and teach.

THE GREAT APOSTASY

¹Now the Spirit expressly says that in latter times some will depart from the faith, giving heed to deceiving spirits and doctrines of demons, ²speaking lies in hypocrisy, having their own conscience seared with a hot iron, ³forbidding to marry, *and commanding* to abstain from foods which God created to be received with thanksgiving by those who believe and know the truth. ⁴For every creature of God *is* good, and nothing is to be refused if it is received with thanksgiving; ⁵for it is sanctified by the word of God and prayer.

SATAN

Who does Satan work through? (4:1)

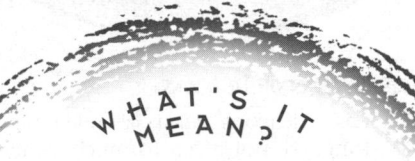

WHAT'S IT MEAN?

Based on Paul's words in this verse, how old do you suppose Timothy was? Obviously, people weren't taking him seriously because they thought he was too young to know anything important. Do you suppose he was twenty-one? Eighteen? Younger? Actually, Timothy would have been between thirty-five and forty years old! In Bible times, people under forty were considered too young to have gained true wisdom.
1 Timothy 4:12

A GOOD SERVANT OF JESUS CHRIST

⁶If you instruct the brethren in these things, you will be a good minister of Jesus Christ,

On the Edge

Let no one despise your youth, but be an example to the believers in word, in conduct, in love, in spirit, in faith, in purity (1 Tim. 4:12).

If you've never given your parents reason to distrust you, they probably trust you more than you know. It's everyone else they worry about. Really. If you've broken your parents' trust and want to restore it, read Proverbs 23:22–25. Look at the things that make parents proud: truth, wisdom, instruction, and understanding. Developing these qualities in your life will help you learn to set a good example—for your parents and for other people. Begin to work on these areas of your life and, though it may take some time, watch your parents' doubt turn to trust. You don't have to transform overnight, just work on one thing at a time. For instance, if you say you'll be home at midnight, be there. Rolling in at 12:10 with a lame excuse doesn't make you trustworthy. After you get the "on-time thing" down, start working on something else.

Even though they're the parents and you're the child, you can still set an example for them. You can still earn their respect. They're watching you more closely than you think!

SEE FOR YOURSELF:
Prov. 23:22–25

TAKE HEED TO YOUR MINISTRY

¹²Let no one despise your youth, but be an example to the believers in word, in conduct, in love, in spirit,ᵃ in faith, in purity. ¹³Till I come, give attention to reading, to exhortation, to doctrine. ¹⁴Do not neglect the gift that is in you, which was given to you by prophecy with the laying on of the hands of the eldership. ¹⁵Meditate on these things; give yourself entirely to them, that your progress may be evident to all. ¹⁶Take heed to yourself and to the doctrine. Continue in them, for in doing this you will save both yourself and those who hear you.

TREATMENT OF CHURCH MEMBERS

¹Do not rebuke an older man, but exhort *him* as a father, younger men as brothers, ²older women as mothers, younger women as sisters, with all purity.

WHAT'S IT MEAN?

If you think it was Paul's idea for Christians to help widows, orphans, and others in need, think again. He was merely repeating the Law that God had given to Moses centuries earlier. A widow usually lived with her husband's family or with one of her children. However, if she had no family to live with, the church was responsible for taking care of her.

1 Timothy 5:3

HONOR TRUE WIDOWS

³Honor widows who are really widows. ⁴But if any widow has children or grandchildren, let them first learn to show piety at home and to repay their parents; for this is good andᵃ acceptable before God. ⁵Now she who is really a widow, and left alone, trusts in God and continues in supplications and prayers night and day. ⁶But she who lives in pleasure is dead while she lives. ⁷And these things command, that they may be blameless. ⁸But if anyone does not provide for his own, and especially for those of his household, he has denied the faith and is worse than an unbeliever.

⁹Do not let a widow under sixty years old be

On the Edge

But if any widow has children or grandchildren, let them first learn to show piety at home and to repay their parents; for this is good and acceptable before God (1 Tim. 5:4).

The most wonderful thing you can give your grandparents is your time. That shows them that they are important to you. They are already so proud of you. They would love to get to know you better, to be seen with you, to be listened to by you. Making time for your grandparents lets them know that you appreciate all the sacrifices they've made and all the love they have shown. One of the best ways you can honor them is to ask questions and learn from them. Senior adults complain that one of the hardest things about growing older is not feeling useful anymore. Let your grandparents know that they are still needed, they are valuable, and they are greatly loved. You hold such a tender place in their hearts— your grandparents will consider their time with you a treasure.

SEE FOR YOURSELF: Lev. 19:32; Prov. 17:6

taken into the number, *and not unless* she has been the wife of one man, ¹⁰well reported for good works: if she has brought up children, if she has lodged strangers, if she has washed the saints' feet, if she has relieved the afflicted, if she has diligently followed every good work.

¹¹But refuse *the* younger widows; for when they have begun to grow wanton against Christ, they desire to marry, ¹²having condemnation because they have cast off their first faith. ¹³And besides they learn *to be* idle, wandering about from house to house, and not only idle but also gossips and busybodies, saying things which they ought not. ¹⁴Therefore I desire that *the* younger *widows* marry, bear children, manage the house, give no opportunity to the adversary to speak reproachfully. ¹⁵For some have already turned aside after Satan. ¹⁶If any believing man orᵃ woman has widows, let them relieve them, and do not let the church be burdened, that it may relieve those who are really widows.

4:12 ᵃNU-Text omits *in spirit*.   **5:4** ᵃNU-Text and M-Text omit *good and*.   **5:16** ᵃNU-Text omits *man or*.

HONOR THE ELDERS

17Let the elders who rule well be counted worthy of double honor, especially those who labor in the word and doctrine. 18For the Scripture says, *"You shall not muzzle an ox while it treads out the grain,"ᵃ* and, *"The laborer is worthy of his wages."ᵇ* 19Do not receive an accusation against an elder except from two or three witnesses. 20Those who are sinning rebuke in the presence of all, that the rest also may fear.

21I charge *you* before God and the Lord Jesus Christ and the elect angels that you observe these things without prejudice, doing nothing with partiality. 22Do not lay hands on anyone hastily, nor share in other people's sins; keep yourself pure.

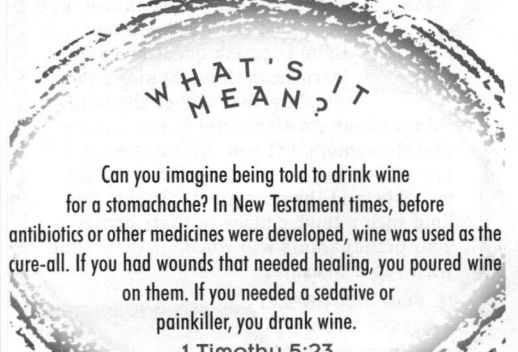

WHAT'S IT MEAN?

Can you imagine being told to drink wine for a stomachache? In New Testament times, before antibiotics or other medicines were developed, wine was used as the cure-all. If you had wounds that needed healing, you poured wine on them. If you needed a sedative or painkiller, you drank wine.

1 Timothy 5:23

23No longer drink only water, but use a little wine for your stomach's sake and your frequent infirmities.

24Some men's sins are clearly evident, preceding *them* to judgment, but those of some *men* follow later. 25Likewise, the good works *of some* are clearly evident, and those that are otherwise cannot be hidden.

HONOR MASTERS

1Let as many bondservants as are under the yoke count their own masters worthy of all honor, so that the name of God and *His* doctrine may not be blasphemed. 2And those who have believing masters, let them not despise *them* because they are brethren, but rather serve *them* because those who are benefited are believers and beloved. Teach and exhort these things.

ERROR AND GREED

3If anyone teaches otherwise and does not consent to wholesome words, *even* the words of our Lord Jesus Christ, and to the doctrine which accords with godliness, 4he is proud, knowing nothing, but is obsessed with disputes and arguments over words, from which come envy, strife, reviling, evil suspicions, 5useless wranglingsᵃ of men of corrupt minds and destitute of the truth, who suppose that godliness is a *means of* gain. From such withdraw yourself.ᵇ

On the Edge

Now godliness with contentment is great gain (1 Tim. 6:6).

Becoming a Christian doesn't mean you have to be poor for the rest of your life. Nor does it mean that the bright red sports car you've been dreaming of will appear in your driveway if you give all your money to the church. Christianity does make you rich, Paul says, by teaching you to look at things in a new way. The reason that a relationship with Jesus makes you content with what you have is that the more you get to know Him, the less your stuff matters. It's fine to enjoy driving a sports car or wearing nice clothes, but what makes you truly, deeply happy is really knowing Jesus and being a part of what He is doing in the world around you. Get preoccupied with His plan for you.

If that isn't you right now, don't give up. Repent. Go after God with everything you've got. Tell Him, "I'm sorry I settled for the stuff of this world and for superficial happiness." Determine to make His work your passion. Use your energy building His kingdom and you won't even notice what kind of stuff you have or don't have because, then, you will be content.

SEE FOR YOURSELF:
Phil. 4:11; Heb. 13:5

6Now godliness with contentment is great gain. 7For we brought nothing into *this* world, *and it is* certainᵃ we can carry nothing out. 8And having food and clothing, with these we shall be content. 9But those who desire to be rich fall into temptation and a snare, and *into* many

---

foolish and harmful lusts which drown men in destruction and perdition. [10]For the love of money is a root of all *kinds of* evil, for which some have strayed from the faith in their greediness, and pierced themselves through with many sorrows.

WHAT'S IT MEAN?

Pontius Pilate was the governor of Judea, the site of Jesus' trial. As the highest authority in the land, Pilate had the power to sentence criminals to death. After questioning Jesus, though, Pilate declared Him innocent of all charges. That didn't sit well with the crowd that had gathered outside. Fearing that the Jewish leaders would incite a revolt, Pilate went along with their plan and allowed Jesus to be executed.

1 Timothy 6:13

THE GOOD CONFESSION

[11]But you, O man of God, flee these things and pursue righteousness, godliness, faith, love, patience, gentleness. [12]Fight the good fight of faith, lay hold on eternal life, to which you were also called and have confessed the good confession in the presence of many witnesses. [13]I urge you in the sight of God who gives life to all things, and *before* Christ Jesus who witnessed the good confession before Pontius Pilate, [14]that you keep *this* commandment without spot, blameless until our Lord Jesus Christ's appearing, [15]which He will manifest in His own time, *He who is* the blessed and only Potentate, the King of kings and Lord of lords, [16]who alone has immortality, dwelling in unapproachable light, whom no man has seen or can see, to whom *be* honor and everlasting power. Amen.

INSTRUCTIONS TO THE RICH

[17]Command those who are rich in this present age not to be haughty, nor to trust in uncertain riches but in the living God, who gives us richly all things to enjoy. [18]*Let them* do good, that they be rich in good works, ready to give, willing to share, [19]storing up for themselves a good foundation for the time to come, that they may lay hold on eternal life.

GUARD THE FAITH

[20]O Timothy! Guard what was committed to your trust, avoiding the profane *and* idle babblings and contradictions of what is falsely called knowledge—[21]by professing it some have strayed concerning the faith.

Grace *be* with you. Amen.

2 timothy

CONTENT   Even as important as Paul was to Timothy on a regular day, this last letter must have been particularly important. Paul was in jail when he wrote. This second letter was the last thing Paul wrote before he died.

Wow. It's pretty amazing that we can read Paul's final words to somebody he loved so much. Remember to hang on every word, just like Timothy probably did when he read this letter the first time. Remember to not just read, but to understand. Remember to ask yourself, *what should I do about this?* And then do it.

That's what Timothy did. He became a leader and put into practice all the things Paul and his mom and his grandmom had taught him. When he did that, he not only pleased God; he also honored the people who taught him about God.

Outline

Purpose   Commitment to Scripture and holy living is essential.

Theme   The Commitment to Ministry

Date of writing   Fall A.D. 67

Bible Talk

Who are your mentors?

Timothy had three important influences in his life (that we know of). One was his grandmother. Her name was Lois. Another was his mom, Eunice. The third was Paul.

As you grow up, it becomes more and more important to be independent and to do things your own way. That doesn't mean you don't need mentors, though. Everyone needs help getting through life. Everyone needs to hear from someone wiser sometimes.

Think about who can be mentors to you. Visit with them. Ask them questions. Trust them to help you make good decisions. Be somebody's Timothy and let somebody be your Paul.

PAUL, AS A JAILBIRD

Paul was in jail several times in his life. He wrote more than one book of the Bible while he was in jail. It seems like Paul would have been discouraged sitting in jail for doing something good: sharing the gospel. Paul had an understanding, though, that helped him not be discouraged.

Paul believed that God was in control of his life. So if he was in jail, he figured that God must need him there. He looked for opportunities to serve God while he was in prison. One of those ways was to write the letters that are now part of the New Testament.

Sort of gives you a new perspective on accepting where you are in life, doesn't it?

GREETING

[1]Paul, an apostle of Jesus Christ[a] by the will of God, according to the promise of life which is in Christ Jesus,

[2]To Timothy, a beloved son:

Grace, mercy, *and* peace from God the Father and Christ Jesus our Lord.

TIMOTHY'S FAITH AND HERITAGE

[3]I thank God, whom I serve with a pure conscience, as *my* forefathers *did*, as without ceasing I remember you in my prayers night and day, [4]greatly desiring to see you, being mindful of your tears, that I may be filled with joy, [5]when I call to remembrance the genuine faith that is in you, which dwelt first in your grandmother Lois and your mother Eunice, and I am persuaded is in you also. [6]Therefore I remind you to stir up the gift of God which is in you through the laying on of my hands. [7]For God has not given us a spirit of fear, but of power and of love and of a sound mind.

NOT ASHAMED OF THE GOSPEL

[8]Therefore do not be ashamed of the testimony of our Lord, nor of me His prisoner, but share with me in the sufferings for the gospel according to the power of God, [9]who has saved us and called *us* with a holy calling, not according to our works, but according to His own purpose and grace which was given to us in Christ Jesus before time began, [10]but has now been revealed by the appearing of our Savior Jesus Christ, *who* has abolished death and brought life and immortality to light through the gospel, [11]to which I was appointed a preacher, an apostle, and a teacher of the Gentiles.[a] [12]For this reason I also suffer these things; nevertheless I am not ashamed, for I know whom I have believed and am persuaded that He is able to keep what I have committed to Him until that Day.

ASSURANCE

Will God ever disappoint His children? (1:12)

BE LOYAL TO THE FAITH

[13]Hold fast the pattern of sound words which you have heard from me, in faith and love which are in Christ Jesus. [14]That good thing which was committed to you, keep by the Holy Spirit who dwells in us.

On the Edge

For God has not given us a spirit of fear, but of power and of love and of a sound mind (2 Tim. 1:7).
The Spirit of God lives in believers. He gives us strength so that we do not have to be afraid anymore. When an adult acts inappropriately toward you, tell the adult, "I am offended by your actions. You have really made me feel uncomfortable and I want you to stop it now!" Then immediately report this person to your parents or to another adult you respect. There are sick adults who choose to mistreat kids because they think kids will be too timid to report them. The Spirit of God gives you power because He lives inside of you. Do not be afraid. Do the right thing and be confident that God will protect you and go before you. Evil must be revealed where you find it or else it will just grow stronger, hurting you and maybe even others.

SEE FOR YOURSELF:
Jer. 15:20; Phil. 4:13

WHAT'S IT MEAN?

Paul wasn't referring to the ancient Chinese or Japanese when he said the people of Asia had rejected him. Asia was the name of a Roman province located in what is now Turkey. At the time Paul wrote this letter, Nero, the Roman emperor, was stepping up his persecution of Christians throughout the empire.
2 Timothy 1:15

[15]This you know, that all those in Asia have turned away from me, among whom are Phygellus and Hermogenes. [16]The Lord grant mercy to the household of Onesiphorus, for he often refreshed me, and was not ashamed of my chain; [17]but when he arrived in Rome, he sought me out very zealously and found *me*.

1:1 [a]NU-Text and M-Text read *Christ Jesus.* **1:11** [a]NU-Text omits *of the Gentiles.*

[18]The Lord grant to him that he may find mercy from the Lord in that Day—and you know very well how many ways he ministered *to me*[a] at Ephesus.

BE STRONG IN GRACE

[1]You therefore, my son, be strong in the grace that is in Christ Jesus. [2]And the things that you have heard from me among many witnesses, commit these to faithful men who will be able to teach others also. [3]You therefore must endure[a] hardship as a good soldier of Jesus Christ. [4]No one engaged in warfare entangles himself with the affairs of *this* life, that he may please him who enlisted him as a soldier. [5]And also if anyone competes in athletics, he is not crowned unless he competes according to the rules. [6]The hardworking farmer must be first to partake of the crops. [7]Consider what I say, and may[a] the Lord give you understanding in all things.

[8]Remember that Jesus Christ, of the seed of David, was raised from the dead according to my gospel, [9]for which I suffer trouble as an evildoer, *even* to the point of chains; but the word of God is not chained. [10]Therefore I endure all things for the sake of the elect, that they also may obtain the salvation which is in Christ Jesus with eternal glory.

[11]*This is* a faithful saying:

For if we died with *Him,*
  We shall also live with *Him.*
[12] If we endure,
  We shall also reign with *Him.*
If we deny *Him,*
  He also will deny us.
[13] If we are faithless,
  He remains faithful;
  He cannot deny Himself.

"For if we died with Him, we shall also live with Him. If we endure, we shall also reign with Him."
(2 Timothy 2:11, 12a)

APPROVED AND DISAPPROVED WORKERS

[14]Remind *them* of these things, charging *them* before the Lord not to strive about words to no profit, to the ruin of the hearers. [15]Be diligent to present yourself approved to God, a worker who does not need to be ashamed, rightly dividing the word of truth. [16]But shun profane *and* idle babblings, for they will increase to more ungodliness. [17]And their message will spread like cancer. Hymenaeus and Philetus are of this sort, [18]who have strayed concerning the truth, saying that the resurrection is already past; and they overthrow the faith of some. [19]Nevertheless the solid foundation of God stands, having this seal: "The Lord knows those who are His," and, "Let everyone who names the name of Christ[a] depart from iniquity."

[20]But in a great house there are not only vessels of gold and silver, but also of wood and clay, some for honor and some for dishonor. [21]Therefore if anyone cleanses himself from the latter, he will be a vessel for honor, sanctified and useful for the Master, prepared for every good work. [22]Flee also youthful lusts; but pursue righteousness, faith, love, peace with those who call on the Lord out of a pure heart. [23]But avoid foolish and ignorant disputes, knowing that they generate strife. [24]And a servant of the Lord must not quarrel but be gentle to all, able to teach, patient, [25]in humility correcting those who are in opposition, if God perhaps will grant them repentance, so that they may know the truth, [26]and *that* they may come to their senses *and escape* the snare of the

WHAT'S IT MEAN?

Many people in Paul's day were sports fans. They would have appreciated and understood his references to athletics. The Isthmian Games, a forerunner to our modern Olympics, were held every two years in the Greek city of Corinth. People came from all around to see these athletic contests.
2 Timothy 2:5

TEMPTATION

What should we do when faced with temptation?
(2:22)

On the Edge

Flee also youthful lusts; but pursue righteousness, faith, love, peace with those who call on the Lord out of a pure heart. But avoid foolish and ignorant disputes, knowing that they generate strife (2 Tim. 2:22, 23).

Run. Mentally run back to the truths of this passage, "Flee also youthful lusts. . . avoid foolish and ignorant disputes." Ask God to give you the courage to stand up to your friends and question their choices. If they still decide to do something you don't feel right about, then leave. Get out of Dodge. Hit the road. Call somebody. Run if you have to, but physically separate yourself from the temptation of your friends' bad decisions. If you hang around, even if you don't participate, you could become a victim of their consequences. God is a just God, and eventually there will be consequences. Sometimes we are more afraid of losing friends than we are of the consequences of our sin. The truth is that doing the right thing takes incredible strength and strong people attract lots of friends—maybe even better ones.

SEE FOR YOURSELF:
Matt. 6:33;
Gal. 5:22–25

WHAT'S IT MEAN?

If you don't recognize the names of Jannes and Jambres, don't be surprised. They're not mentioned in the Old Testament. According to Jewish tradition, Jannes and Jambres were the names of the Pharaoh's court magicians. When Moses was trying to persuade Pharaoh, the king of Egypt, to let the Israelites go, he performed a series of miracles to demonstrate God's power. Believe it or not, Jannes and Jambres were actually able to copy some of the miracles. However, when the time came to reverse them, they couldn't do it.

2 Timothy 3:8

corrupt minds, disapproved concerning the faith; ⁹but they will progress no further, for their folly will be manifest to all, as theirs also was.

THE MAN OF GOD AND THE WORD OF GOD

¹⁰But you have carefully followed my doctrine, manner of life, purpose, faith, long-suffering, love, perseverance, ¹¹persecutions, afflictions, which happened to me at Antioch, at Iconium, at Lystra—what persecutions I endured. And out of *them* all the Lord delivered me. ¹²Yes, and all who desire to live godly in Christ Jesus will suffer persecution. ¹³But evil

WHAT'S IT MEAN?

If you'd like to visit the modern equivalents of Antioch, Iconium, and Lystra, head for Turkey. As far as city authorities were concerned, Paul overstayed his welcome in each city he visited. When people began responding to the message Paul preached in Antioch, city officials ran him out of town. His next stop was Iconium. When the people there started converting to Christianity, Paul was forced to leave out of fear for his life. His next stop was Lystra, Timothy's hometown.

2 Timothy 3:11

devil, having been taken captive by him to *do* his will.

PERILOUS TIMES AND PERILOUS MEN

¹But know this, that in the last days perilous times will come: ²For men will be lovers of themselves, lovers of money, boasters, proud, blasphemers, disobedient to parents, unthankful, unholy, ³unloving, unforgiving, slanderers, without self-control, brutal, despisers of good, ⁴traitors, headstrong, haughty, lovers of pleasure rather than lovers of God, ⁵having a form of godliness but denying its power. And from such people turn away! ⁶For of this sort are those who creep into households and make captives of gullible women loaded down with sins, led away by various lusts, ⁷always learning and never able to come to the knowledge of the truth. ⁸Now as Jannes and Jambres resisted Moses, so do these also resist the truth: men of

men and impostors will grow worse and worse, deceiving and being deceived. [14]But you must continue in the things which you have learned and been assured of, knowing from whom you have learned *them*, [15]and that from childhood you have known the Holy Scriptures, which are able to make you wise for salvation through faith which is in Christ Jesus.

[16]All Scripture *is* given by inspiration of God, and *is* profitable for doctrine, for reproof, for correction, for instruction in righteousness, [17]that the man of God may be complete, thoroughly equipped for every good work.

PREACH THE WORD

[1]I charge *you* therefore before God and the Lord Jesus Christ, who will judge the living and the dead at[a] His appearing and His kingdom: [2]Preach the word! Be ready in season *and* out of season. Convince, rebuke, exhort, with all longsuffering and teaching. [3]For the time will come when they will not endure sound doctrine, but according to their own desires, *because* they have itching ears, they will heap up for themselves teachers; [4]and they will turn *their* ears away from the truth, and be turned aside to fables. [5]But you be watchful in all things, endure afflictions, do the work of an evangelist, fulfill your ministry.

PAUL'S VALEDICTORY

[6]For I am already being poured out as a drink offering, and the time of my departure is at hand. [7]I have fought the good fight, I have finished the race, I have kept the faith. [8]Finally, there is laid up for me the crown of righteousness, which the Lord, the righteous Judge, will give to me on that Day, and not to me only but also to all who have loved His appearing.

THE ABANDONED APOSTLE

[9]Be diligent to come to me quickly; [10]for Demas has forsaken me, having loved this present world, and has departed for Thessalonica—Crescens for Galatia, Titus for Dalmatia. [11]Only Luke is with me. Get Mark and bring him with you, for he is useful to me for ministry. [12]And Tychicus I have sent to Ephesus. [13]Bring the cloak that I left with Carpus at Troas when you come—and the books, especially the parchments.

[14]Alexander the coppersmith did me much harm. May the Lord repay him according to his works. [15]You also must beware of him, for he has greatly resisted our words.

On the Edge

From childhood you have known the Holy Scriptures, which are able to make you wise for salvation through faith which is in Christ Jesus. All Scripture is given by inspiration of God, and is profitable for doctrine, for reproof, for correction, for instruction in righteousness, that the man of God may be complete, thoroughly equipped for every good work (2 Tim. 3:15–17).

The Bible is an awesome book. It's full of answers and advice and wisdom. It's full of war and deceit and natural disasters and family squabbles. It tells you how to live and be successful, and it tells you what to look out for. It's the richest piece of literature ever written.

But beyond all of that, the Bible is the Word of God. It's the letter that God has personally written to you. God's got some things to say and they're all together in this one incredible book. When Jesus lived on earth, He prayed to God one day and said, "Sanctify them by Your truth. Your word is truth" (John 17:17). Are you a follower of Jesus? Then this prayer is for you. Jesus says that God's Word is truth. And what does truth do for you? It makes you free (see John 8:32). The Bible has the power to give you freedom from whatever has got you down—family, school, depression, confusion, guilt, stress, frustration, bad self-image, loneliness, lack of direction, apathy, boredom. You name it. The truth of God's Word can make you free.

The Bible is like a lot of other things. You can't experience it just because it's there. You've got to pick it up and read it. You've got to spend time in it. You've got to get it into your head and into your heart. Of all the stuff you can do in your life, getting serious about God's Word is the very best. Nothing else will make you free.

SEE FOR YOURSELF:
   Ps. 119:11, 105;
   Prov. 30:5;
Is. 40:8; John 1:1–18;
   8:31, 32; 17:17;
   Heb. 4:12;
   1 John 1:1–4

4:1 [a]NU-Text omits *therefore* and reads *and by* for *at*.

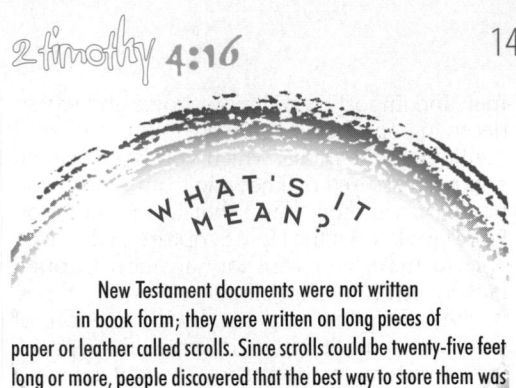

WHAT'S IT MEAN?

New Testament documents were not written in book form; they were written on long pieces of paper or leather called scrolls. Since scrolls could be twenty-five feet long or more, people discovered that the best way to store them was to roll them around a stick (like toilet paper).

2 Timothy 4:13

[16] At my first defense no one stood with me, but all forsook me. May it not be charged against them.

4:22 [a]NU-Text omits *Jesus Christ*.

THE LORD IS FAITHFUL

[17] But the Lord stood with me and strengthened me, so that the message might be preached fully through me, and *that* all the Gentiles might hear. Also I was delivered out of the mouth of the lion. [18] And the Lord will deliver me from every evil work and preserve *me* for His heavenly kingdom. To Him *be* glory forever and ever. Amen!

COME BEFORE WINTER

[19] Greet Prisca and Aquila, and the household of Onesiphorus. [20] Erastus stayed in Corinth, but Trophimus I have left in Miletus sick. [21] Do your utmost to come before winter.

Eubulus greets you, as well as Pudens, Linus, Claudia, and all the brethren.

FAREWELL

[22] The Lord Jesus Christ[a] be with your spirit. Grace be with you. Amen.

TIMOTHY made a difference

What would have happened to Timothy if Paul had never visited Lystra, his hometown? He had been raised in a racially mixed family. His mother, a Jewess, had taught him the Old Testament Scriptures. His father, a Greek, gave him at least a social position that allowed him to move freely in the Roman world.

When Paul came through on his first missionary journey, he used the approach in Lystra that had proven effective elsewhere. He preached the gospel of Jesus Christ to those who already knew God's Word. He challenged them to check out the claims of Jesus against the prophecies and promises of the Old Testament. Timothy took Paul up on the challenge and became convinced Jesus is Lord and Savior. Paul eventually recruited Timothy as a member of his traveling gospel team.

Cutting Edge

Timothy served Paul in various capacities: companion, scribe, and messenger. Although he represented the apostle in places like Thessalonica, Corinth, and Ephesus, he was apparently never comfortable in the spotlight. Paul constantly encouraged Timothy to rely on God for boldness. Paul's other counsel to Timothy indicates that the young disciple struggled with youthful temptations (2 Tim. 2:22) and the tendency to be ashamed of the gospel (2 Tim. 1:8).

Yet, in spite of his youth and weaknesses, Timothy made a difference in Paul's life. Paul wrote of his unique loyalty. He also continues to make a direct difference in lives today as people are influenced by the letters he helped Paul write or find themselves in situations similar to the ones Timothy faced when Paul wrote the two letters to his closest companion. YOU can, too!

Timothy had a powerful model and mentor in his life. Paul may have even been somewhat intimidating to Timothy. You can benefit greatly from the examples and teaching of older Christians. They often know more and they have definitely lived more than you have. your growth can have some definite positive direction under their influence. Ask God to lead you to other believers who can guide and encourage you. Get familiar with Timothy, too.

Want to know more? Timothy enters the Bible in Acts 16.
Several of Paul's letters mention him, and two were addressed to him.

CONTENT Do you know what a "stereotype" is? It is when people in a certain group get a reputation for being a certain way. If you know someone is an athlete, you might assume they'll act like a jock. Or, if you know a girl is a cheerleader, you might assume she'll be really perky.

Titus was the young pastor of the churches on the island of Crete (south of Greece). People from Crete definitely were stereotyped. They were stereotyped as pirates and scoundrels. When most people thought about Crete, they thought of the integrity-challenged. If ever there was a pastor who needed and deserved a letter of instruction from the apostle Paul, it was Titus.

Titus was a Gentile Christian and had been one of Paul's traveling companions. On several occasions he had proven himself to be a good problem solver. Maybe that's why he was given a pastor's job in this particular place.

Understandably, Paul had a lot to say to Titus about the kinds of leadership he should choose for his churches. He also wrote about civil obedience (obeying the law). We might not be as mischievous as Titus's parishioners, but we can still learn a lot from Paul's instructions.

Outline

Purpose Grace creates believers whose good works honor God.

Theme Setting the Church at Crete in Order

Date of writing A.D. 64

GREETING

[1]Paul, a bondservant of God and an apostle of Jesus Christ, according to the faith of God's elect and the acknowledgment of the truth which accords with godliness, [2]in hope of eternal life which God, who cannot lie, promised before time began, [3]but has in due time manifested His word through preaching, which was committed to me according to the commandment of God our Savior;

[4]To Titus, a true son in *our* common faith:

Grace, mercy, *and* peace from God the Father and the Lord Jesus Christ[a] our Savior.

WHAT'S IT MEAN?

Crete is an island in the Mediterranean Sea, southeast of Greece. Paul left Titus behind in Crete to organize the new church that Paul had started on his final missionary journey.

Titus 1:5

QUALIFIED ELDERS

[5]For this reason I left you in Crete, that you should set in order the things that are lacking, and appoint elders in every city as I commanded you— [6]if a man is blameless, the husband of one wife, having faithful children not accused of dissipation or insubordination. [7]For a bishop[a] must be blameless, as a steward of God, not self-willed, not quick-tempered, not given to wine, not violent, not greedy for money, [8]but hospitable, a lover of what is good, sober-minded, just, holy, self-controlled, [9]holding fast the faithful word as he has been taught, that he may be able, by sound doctrine, both to exhort and convict those who contradict.

CHARACTER

What type of people need to be extra careful to be filled with integrity? (1:7)

THE ELDERS' TASK

[10]For there are many insubordinate, both idle talkers and deceivers, especially those of the circumcision, [11]whose mouths must be stopped, who subvert whole households, teaching things which they ought not, for the sake of dishonest gain. [12]One of them, a prophet of their own, said, "Cretans *are* always liars, evil beasts, lazy gluttons." [13]This testimony is true. Therefore rebuke them sharply, that they may be sound in the faith, [14]not giving heed to Jewish fables and commandments of men who turn from the truth. [15]To the pure all things are pure, but to those who are defiled and unbelieving nothing is pure; but even their mind and conscience are defiled. [16]They profess to know God, but in works they deny Him, being abominable, disobedient, and disqualified for every good work.

QUALITIES OF A SOUND CHURCH

[1]But as for you, speak the things which are proper for sound doctrine: [2]that the older men be sober, reverent, temperate, sound in faith, in love, in patience; [3]the older women likewise, that they be reverent in behavior, not slanderers, not given to much wine, teachers of good things— [4]that they admonish the young women to love their husbands, to love their children, [5]to be discreet, chaste, homemakers, good, obedient to their own husbands, that the word of God may not be blasphemed.

[6]Likewise, exhort the young men to be sober-minded, [7]in all things showing yourself *to be* a pattern of good works; in doctrine *showing* integrity, reverence, incorruptibility,[a] [8]sound speech that cannot be condemned, that one who is an opponent may be ashamed, having nothing evil to say of you.[a]

[9]*Exhort* bondservants to be obedient to their own masters, to be well pleasing in all *things*, not answering back, [10]not pilfering, but showing all good fidelity, that they may adorn the doctrine of God our Savior in all things.

TRAINED BY SAVING GRACE

[11]For the grace of God that brings salvation has appeared to all men, [12]teaching us that, denying ungodliness and worldly lusts, we should live soberly, righteously, and godly in the present age, [13]looking for the blessed hope and glorious appearing of our great God and Savior Jesus Christ, [14]who gave Himself for us,

1:4 [a]NU-Text reads *and Christ Jesus.*   **1:7** [a]Literally *overseer*   **2:7** [a]NU-Text omits *incorruptibility.*
2:8 [a]NU-Text and M-Text read *us.*

TITUS made a difference

For one who made such a difference, Titus is, in large part, a mystery to us. He was a Greek believer in Jesus who joined Paul's traveling band of gospel messengers. His effectiveness as a representative of Paul is evident from the way the apostle trusted Titus with difficult and important tasks. Titus served as Paul's example of what God could do in the life of a non-Jewish person. When the Jerusalem church debated whether Gentiles could be called true followers of Jesus without first becoming Jewish converts, Paul presented Titus as proof of Gentile believers.

Titus came from a Greek background, and yet his faith in Jesus was undeniable. His character paved the way for other Gentiles to enter the church. The gospel was emphasized as a universal invitation based partly on people like Titus in the early church. Yes, Titus made a difference.

Cutting Edge

Like Timothy, Titus served Paul in official capacities. He was involved in his most difficult assignment, on the island of Crete, when Paul wrote him the letter that bears his name. Titus reminds us that the gospel and the work of the church must be intentionally passed from one generation to another. The process isn't automatic. It is both spiritual and relational. Those who are further along must take responsibility for those who are coming along. Titus received the torch of the gospel and passed it on faithfully. He made a difference.

YOU can, too! Few believers are too young to begin thinking of those who are younger. Adolescent believers can have a powerful influence on their peers and on younger children. Kids will often listen more attentively to a teenager share his or her faith than they will to an adult. Those who are younger offer you opportunities right now to make a difference for Christ. Have you helped with or led a children's Sunday School class? Explore other possibilities with your pastor.

Want to know more? Outside the letter that bears his name, Titus is mentioned in the following places:

2 Corinthians 2:13; 7:6–16; 8:6, 16–24; 12:18; Galatians 2:1–5; 2 Timothy 4:10.

that He might redeem us from every lawless deed and purify for Himself *His* own special people, zealous for good works. ¹⁵Speak these things, exhort, and rebuke with all authority. Let no one despise you.

GRACES OF THE HEIRS OF GRACE

¹Remind them to be subject to rulers and authorities, to obey, to be ready for every good work, ²to speak evil of no one, to be peaceable, gentle, showing all humility to all men. ³For we ourselves were also once foolish, disobedient, deceived, serving various lusts and pleasures, living in malice and envy, hateful and hating one another. ⁴But when the kindness and the love of God our Savior toward man appeared, ⁵not by works of righteousness which we have done, but according to His mercy He saved us, through the washing of regeneration and renewing of the Holy Spirit, ⁶whom He poured out on us abundantly through Jesus Christ our Savior, ⁷that having been justified by His grace we should become heirs according to the hope of eternal life.

⁸This is a faithful saying, and these things I want you to affirm constantly, that those who have believed in God should be careful to

WHAT'S IT MEAN?

Paul's reference to genealogies has to do with the obsession of certain Jewish leaders with being able to trace their family tree all the way back to Abraham. Apparently, knowing the name of one's great-great-great-great-great-great-great-great-great-grandfather was a big deal to some people in New Testament times.

Titus 3:9

ETERNAL LIFE

What does eternal life give us? (3:7)

maintain good works. These things are good and profitable to men.

AVOID DISSENSION

⁹But avoid foolish disputes, genealogies, contentions, and strivings about the law; for they are unprofitable and useless. ¹⁰Reject a divisive man after the first and second admonition, ¹¹knowing that such a person is warped and sinning, being self-condemned.

Promise HE PROMISES TO PURIFY YOU.

[Jesus Christ] gave Himself for us, that He might redeem us from every lawless deed and purify for Himself His own special people, zealous for good works (Titus 2:14).

Sometimes people think that God's grace is nothing more than the forgiveness of sins. It would be enough if that's all there was to it—just the forgiveness of every sin in your whole life—even the ones you won't commit for another twenty or thirty years.

But God knows you need more than just a clean slate to become all He wants you to be. You also need a heart that's tender toward Him, a mind that can be made to think like His, and a soul that yields its will to the wishes of His Spirit. This verse tells you that He "gave Himself for us, that He might redeem us . . . and purify for Himself His own special people, . . ." You're included.

But gentle and patient to the end, He's also allowed your heart to be tested. He's also given you the power to stand up to temptation. Anything that doesn't agree with God or His Word is temptation. Know His Word so well that you are quick to recognize temptation. When you see it, run.

Your pure heart can feel impure sometimes. If it does, get clean. Ask God's forgiveness and receive it. His forgiveness purifies you.

He's changed your heart forever. Go and live like you believe it.

SEE FOR YOURSELF:
Matt. 5:8; Heb. 9:14; 1 Pet. 1:22

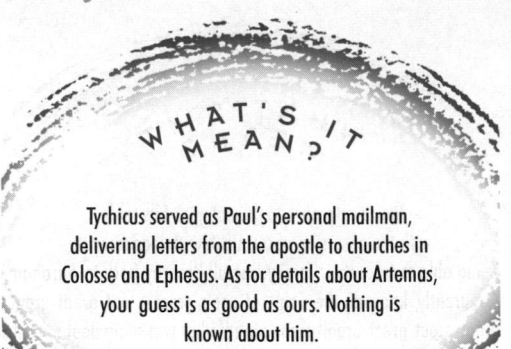

WHAT'S IT MEAN?

Tychicus served as Paul's personal mailman, delivering letters from the apostle to churches in Colosse and Ephesus. As for details about Artemas, your guess is as good as ours. Nothing is known about him.

Titus 3:12

FINAL MESSAGES

¹²When I send Artemas to you, or Tychicus, be diligent to come to me at Nicopolis, for I have decided to spend the winter there. ¹³Send Zenas the lawyer and Apollos on their journey with haste, that they may lack nothing. ¹⁴And let our *people* also learn to maintain good works, to *meet* urgent needs, that they may not be unfruitful.

FAREWELL

¹⁵All who *are* with me greet you. Greet those who love us in the faith.

Grace *be* with you all. Amen.

philemon

CONTENT   If you haven't had to ask for a reference letter yet, you probably will one day. It might be to get a job. It might be to get into a school or an extracurricular program. But somewhere along the way you're going to have to ask someone to vouch for you. If they put that "vouch" in writing, then it's called a reference letter.

Philemon is a reference letter written by Paul for a slave named Onesimus (o-NES-i-muss). In those days, people who were broke or bankrupt had the option of "selling" themselves as servants or slaves. That way they could get work experience and pay off their debts. Usually, at some point in time, they could then choose either to stay servants or move on as free persons.

Onesimus was a slave, but he had run away and so had not kept up his end of the bargain. Then Onesimus met Paul and became a Christian. He needed to go back and make his actions right. In order to pave the way for him, Paul wrote this letter asking Philemon (the owner) to forgive Onesimus and to accept him back into Philemon's home.

Purpose   Coming to know Christ transforms interpersonal relationships.

Theme   Brotherly Love

Date of writing   A.D. 60

Bible Talk

Philemon's Perspective

From Philemon's perspective he had the right to be angry. His servant had run off and had taken money, too. When Paul wrote this letter asking Philemon to forgive, he wasn't just asking Philemon to do what Philemon already knew he should do. No, Paul was asking Philemon to do something that was totally unexpected.

That's hard to take sometimes. When people wrong us or let us down, there's nothing wrong with holding them accountable—but not every time. Sometimes God calls us to lay down our rights, to give them a very undeserved break. Sometimes God calls us to do for them what He has done for us—forgive and let it go.

ONESIMUS'S PERSPECTIVE

How hard do you think it was for Onesimus to return to the scene of his crime? How hard do you think it was for him to face the man he had robbed and abandoned? How much courage do you think it took for him to travel back to the captivity he had known? It probably took a lot out of him, but he did it because his life had changed. He had put his faith in God. He had accepted God's forgiveness. That meant he couldn't live the same as he had before. Things had to change. The first change was facing up to some consequences. That's what happens to us, too, when we receive God's love and forgiveness.

GREETING

[1]Paul, a prisoner of Christ Jesus, and Timothy *our* brother,

To Philemon our beloved *friend* and fellow laborer, [2]to the beloved[a] Apphia, Archippus our fellow soldier, and to the church in your house:

[3]Grace to you and peace from God our Father and the Lord Jesus Christ.

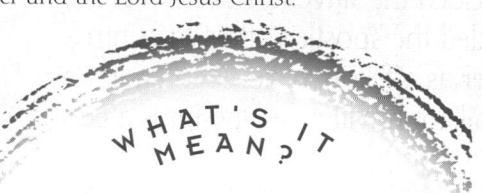

PHILEMON'S LOVE AND FAITH

[4]I thank my God, making mention of you always in my prayers, [5]hearing of your love and faith which you have toward the Lord Jesus and toward all the saints, [6]that the sharing of your faith may become effective by the acknowledgment of every good thing which is in you[a] in Christ Jesus. [7]For we have[a] great joy[b] and consolation in your love, because the hearts of the saints have been refreshed by you, brother.

THE PLEA FOR ONESIMUS

[8]Therefore, though I might be very bold in Christ to command you what is fitting, [9]yet for love's sake I rather appeal *to you*—being such a one as Paul, the aged, and now also a prisoner of Jesus Christ—[10]I appeal to you for my son Onesimus, whom I have begotten *while* in my chains, [11]who once was unprofitable to you, but now is profitable to you and to me. [12]I am sending him back.[a] You therefore receive him, that is, my own heart, [13]whom I wished to keep with me, that on your behalf he might minister to me in my chains for the gospel. [14]But without your consent I wanted to do nothing, that your good deed might not be by compulsion, as it were, but voluntary.

[15]For perhaps he departed for a while for this *purpose*, that you might receive him forever, [16]no longer as a slave but more than a slave—a beloved brother, especially to me but how much more to you, both in the flesh and in the Lord.

PHILEMON'S OBEDIENCE ENCOURAGED

[17]If then you count me as a partner, receive him as *you would* me. [18]But if he has wronged you or owes anything, put that on my account. [19]I, Paul, am writing with my own hand. I will repay—not to mention to you that you owe me even your own self besides. [20]Yes, brother, let me have joy from you in the Lord; refresh my heart in the Lord.

[21]Having confidence in your obedience, I write to you, knowing that you will do even more than I say. [22]But, meanwhile, also prepare a guest room for me, for I trust that through your prayers I shall be granted to you.

FAREWELL

[23]Epaphras, my fellow prisoner in Christ Jesus, greets you, [24]as do Mark, Aristarchus, Demas, Luke, my fellow laborers.

[25]The grace of our Lord Jesus Christ *be* with your spirit. Amen.

2 [a]NU-Text reads *to our sister Apphia.*   **6** [a]NU-Text and M-Text read *us.*   **7** [a]NU-Text reads *had.*   [b]M-Text reads *thanksgiving.*   **12** [a]NU-Text reads *back to you in person, that is, my own heart.*

ONESIMUS made a difference

God often makes a difference through unexpected people. Onesimus was a runaway slave. He and the apostle Paul found each other in Rome. Perhaps they had met previously in the house of Philemon in Colosse when Paul had visited. But this time, Onesimus himself became a believer in Jesus.

Eventually Paul and Onesimus decided the slave must return to the master. Paul's letter to Philemon included the apostle's effort to reintroduce the former runaway to his master as a fellow believer. In an almost humorous way, Paul is certain that Philemon will give Onesimus a good welcome.

Through Onesimus's experience we are reminded that we cannot run away from God. Onesimus's experience also reminds us that when we run away from problems God often works things out so that we have to return to the scene of our departure as part of our training. So Onesimus went home. It is possible that Onesimus eventually became a leader of the church in Colosse. But he didn't make a difference by running away. It wasn't until he met Christ and then returned home that he was in a position to be truly "useful," which is what his name means.

Cutting Edge

YOU can, too!

If one of your problem-solving approaches is to run away, you can learn a lot from Onesimus. His escape was only temporary. In the meantime, God did reach and change him. God can certainly make that kind of difference in your life.

Perhaps you can think of places and people from which you have run. Are there broken relationships and situations that still need to be resolved in your life? God wants to help. Other believers can help, too. Ask God to lead you to a Paul who can give you wisdom and who can run interference during your return.

Want to know more? Onesimus is mentioned briefly in (Colossians 4:9) **and several times in** (Philemon.

CONTENT

Have you ever read Cliffs Notes? These are small paperback books that tell you, in shortened form, the story of famous classics (like Shakespeare's *Romeo and Juliet*). They help you understand the highlights of the plot and the significance of the different story lines. Cliffs Notes were not meant to be substituted for reading the classic; they are meant to supplement it.

Hebrews is like Cliffs Notes for the whole Bible. The writer of Hebrews walked back through the whole history of the Hebrews starting with their earliest and most famous ancestors, Abraham and Moses. The Hebrews were a people with a strong, *strong* sense of tradition. To say that they thought highly of their ancestors is putting it mildly. The whole point for walking back through this history in the Book of Hebrews was to point out that Jesus was greater than any of their ancestors.

Now if you say to a Hebrew that someone is greater than Moses, you are making a bold statement—a statement worth fighting over—so you'd better be sure. The writer of Hebrews was sure. He was trying to convince his Hebrew readers that Jesus was, indeed, the Messiah that all their ancestors had pointed them toward.

Outline

1:1–4 .... The Greatness of God's Son
1:5—2:18 .... Jesus Is Greater Than Angels
3:1—4:13 .... Jesus Is Greater Than Moses and Joshua
4:14—7:28 .... Jesus Is Our Great High Priest
8:1—9:22 .... Jesus Brings a Better Covenant
9:23—10:39 .... Jesus' Sacrifice Is Once and for All
11:1–40 .... Some of God's People Who Had Great Faith
12:1—13:17 .... Follow the Example of Jesus
13:18–25 .... Final Prayers and Greetings

Purpose

Jesus provides all we need for a vital personal relationship with God.

Theme

The Superiority of Jesus Christ Over the Old Covenant

Date of writing

Before A.D. 64

"Therefore we also, since we are surrounded by so great a cloud of witnesses, let us lay aside every weight, and the sin which so easily ensnares us, and let us run with endurance the race that is set before us" (12:1).

Bible Talk

The Law

The writer of Hebrews talks a lot about "the Law." One definition of the law is "the first five books of the Bible" (Genesis, Exodus, Leviticus, Numbers, and Deuteronomy). The Hebrews looked to these books for every law that they needed. Another definition of the law is "all the laws that the Jews had written *based on* the first five books of the Bible." As humans will do, the Hebrews had analyzed the laws until they had expanded them to include every possible scenario. For instance, if the law said that you weren't supposed to work on the Sabbath, the Hebrews wrote laws explaining what "work" actually was, when the "Sabbath" actually was, and how many steps a person had to take before they were actually "working." You can imagine that it got a little confusing.

A BETTER LAW

The revolution of Jesus' life is that the law got simplified. Instead of counting your steps to see if you had broken the Sabbath, Jesus told people that they needed to love God with everything they had and to love each other. Period.

This didn't feel good to the Hebrews. How would they know if they were living a good life if they didn't have the specifics of the law to show them when they messed up? They had put their faith in the law to make them righteous. Now they needed to put their faith in Jesus and *He* would make them righteous. It was a whole new way of thinking for the Hebrews, which is why there is a whole book dedicated to explaining it to them.

GOD'S SUPREME REVELATION

¹God, who at various times and in various ways spoke in time past to the fathers by the prophets, ²has in these last days spoken to us by *His* Son, whom He has appointed heir of all things, through whom also He made the worlds; ³who being the brightness of *His* glory and the express image of His person, and upholding all things by the word of His power, when He had by Himself[a] purged our[b] sins, sat down at the right hand of the Majesty on high, ⁴having become so much better than the angels, as He has by inheritance obtained a more excellent name than they.

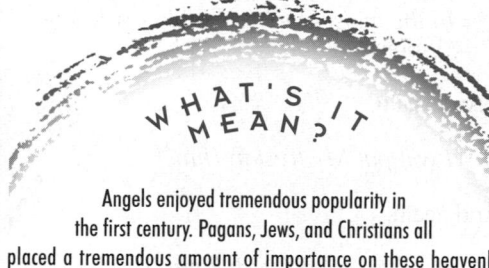

Angels enjoyed tremendous popularity in the first century. Pagans, Jews, and Christians all placed a tremendous amount of importance on these heavenly beings. Some groups may even have gone so far as to worship angels. Others mistakenly believed that Jesus Himself was an angel, because of the miracles He performed.

Hebrews 1:4

THE SON EXALTED ABOVE ANGELS

⁵For to which of the angels did He ever say:

> "You are My Son,
>   Today I have begotten You" ?[a]

And again:

> "I will be to Him a
>   Father,
> And He shall be to
>   Me a Son" ?[b]

⁶But when He again brings the firstborn into the world, He says:

> "Let all the angels of God
>   worship Him." [a]

⁷And of the angels He says:

> "Who makes His angels spirits
>   And His ministers a flame of fire."[a]

⁸But to the Son *He says:*

> "Your throne, O God, is forever and ever;
>   A scepter of righteousness is the scepter of
>   Your kingdom.
> ⁹ You have loved righteousness and hated
>   lawlessness;
>   Therefore God, Your God, has anointed
>   You
>   With the oil of gladness more than Your
>   companions."[a]

¹⁰And:

> "You, LORD, in the beginning laid the
>   foundation of the earth,
>   And the heavens are the work of Your
>   hands.
> ¹¹ They will perish, but You remain;
>   And they will all grow old like a garment;
> ¹² Like a cloak You will fold them up,
>   And they will be changed.
>   But You are the same,
>   And Your years will not fail."[a]

¹³But to which of the angels has He ever said:

> "Sit at My right hand,
>   Till I make Your enemies Your
>   footstool" ?[a]

"You, LORD, in the beginning laid the foundation of the earth, and the heavens are the work of Your hands." (Hebrews 1:10)

¹⁴Are they not all ministering spirits sent forth to minister for those who will inherit salvation?

HELP

How do angels help Christians? (1:14)

DO NOT NEGLECT SALVATION

¹Therefore we must give the more earnest heed to the things we have heard, lest we drift away. ²For if the word spoken through angels proved steadfast, and every transgression and disobedience received a just reward, ³how shall we escape if we neglect

1:3 [a]NU-Text omits *by Himself.* [b]NU-Text omits *our.*   **1:5** [a]Psalm 2:7 [b]2 Samuel 7:14   **1:6** [a]Deuteronomy 32:43 (Septuagint, Dead Sea Scrolls); Psalm 97:7   **1:7** [a]Psalm 104:4   **1:9** [a]Psalm 45:6, 7   **1:12** [a]Psalm 102:25–27   **1:13** [a]Psalm 110:1

so great a salvation, which at the first began to be spoken by the Lord, and was confirmed to us by those who heard *Him,* ⁴God also bearing witness both with signs and wonders, with various miracles, and gifts of the Holy Spirit, according to His own will?

THE SON MADE LOWER THAN ANGELS

⁵For He has not put the world to come, of which we speak, in subjection to angels. ⁶But one testified in a certain place, saying:

> "What is man that You are mindful of
>   him,
> Or the son of man that You take care of
>   him?
> 7   You have made him a little lower than
>   the angels;
> You have crowned him with glory and
>   honor,ᵃ
> And set him over the works of Your
>   hands.
> 8   You have put all things in subjection
>   under his feet."ᵃ

For in that He put all in subjection under him, He left nothing *that is* not put under him. But now we do not yet see all things put under him.

⁹But we see Jesus, who was made a little lower than the angels, for the suffering of death crowned with glory and honor, that He, by the grace of God, might taste death for everyone.

BRINGING MANY SONS TO GLORY

¹⁰For it was fitting for Him, for whom *are* all things and by whom *are* all things, in bringing many sons to glory, to make the captain of their salvation perfect through sufferings. ¹¹For both He who sanctifies and those who are being sanctified *are* all of one, for which reason He is not ashamed to call them brethren, ¹²saying:

> "I will declare Your name to My brethren;
>   In the midst of the assembly I will sing
>   praise to You."ᵃ

¹³And again:

> "I will put My trust in Him."ᵃ

And again:

> "Here am I and the children whom God
>   has given Me."ᵇ

¹⁴Inasmuch then as the children have partaken of flesh and blood, He Himself likewise

2:7 ᵃNU-Text and M-Text omit the rest of verse 7.   **2:8** ᵃPsalm 8:4–6   **2:12** ᵃPsalm 22:22   **2:13** ᵃ2 Samuel 22:3; Isaiah 8:17 ᵇIsaiah 8:18

Promise   HE PROMISES TO AID WHEN YOU ARE TEMPTED.

For in that He Himself has suffered, being tempted, He is able to aid those who are tempted (Heb. 2:18).

It's not unusual to hear somebody excuse personal faults by saying, "Well, that's just the way I am"—as if it would be unfair to expect anything better out of him or her. It's true that everybody has flaws and everyone is susceptible to some temptations. Some people have a hard time being nice when things aren't going well for them; some people are tempted to cheat because they're so driven to make a good grade; some people are sucked in by the buzz they get from drinking or drugs. That's the way they are.

But Jesus never said that it was okay to do wrong because you have a weakness. He told people to do the right thing anyway. He wasn't being heartless. He wasn't looking down from some ivory tower shouting, "You must resist temptation." He was flesh and blood, just like you. He knew what it was like to be tempted. He isn't leaving you to overcome your weaknesses all by yourself. He's right there with you, giving you the strength to make the right choice. He's saying, "You can do it!" He's God. He's given you the strength to overcome and He knows you can!

SEE FOR YOURSELF:
Rom. 8:37; 1 Cor. 10:13; Heb. 4:15, 16; James 1:13–15

shared in the same, that through death He might destroy him who had the power of death, that is, the devil, [15]and release those who through fear of death were all their lifetime subject to bondage. [16]For indeed He does not give aid to angels, but He does give aid to the seed of Abraham. [17]Therefore, in all things He had to be made like *His* brethren, that He might be a merciful and faithful High Priest in things *pertaining* to God, to make propitiation for the sins of the people. [18]For in that He Himself has suffered, being tempted, He is able to aid those who are tempted.

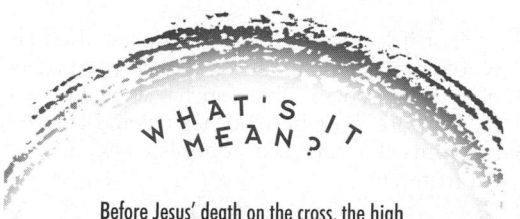

Before Jesus' death on the cross, the high priest was responsible for offering the sacrifice every year that provided forgiveness for the Israelites' sins. The blood of the sacrifice was the payment necessary in God's eyes for all of the sins the people had committed in the previous year.

Hebrews 2:17

THE SON WAS FAITHFUL

[1]Therefore, holy brethren, partakers of the heavenly calling, consider the Apostle and High Priest of our confession, Christ Jesus, [2]who was faithful to Him who appointed Him, as Moses also *was faithful* in all His house. [3]For this One has been counted worthy of more glory than Moses, inasmuch as He who built the house has more honor than the house. [4]For every house is built by someone, but He who built all things *is* God. [5]And Moses indeed *was* faithful in all His house as a servant, for a testimony of those things which would be spoken *afterward,* [6]but Christ as a Son over His own house, whose house we are if we hold fast the confidence and the rejoicing of the hope firm to the end.[a]

BE FAITHFUL

[7]Therefore, as the Holy Spirit says:

> "Today, if you will hear His voice,
> [8] Do not harden your hearts as in the
>   rebellion,

> In the day of trial in the wilderness,
> [9] Where your fathers tested Me, tried Me,
>   And saw My works forty years.
> [10] Therefore I was angry with that
>   generation,
>   And said, 'They always go astray in their
>   heart,
>   And they have not known My ways.'
> [11] So I swore in My wrath,
>   'They shall not enter My rest.' "[a]

[12]Beware, brethren, lest there be in any of you an evil heart of unbelief in departing from the living God; [13]but exhort one another daily, while it is called "*Today*," lest any of you be hardened through the deceitfulness of sin. [14]For we have become partakers of Christ if we hold the beginning of our confidence steadfast to the end, [15]while it is said:

> "Today, if you will hear His voice,
> Do not harden your hearts as in the
>   rebellion."[a]

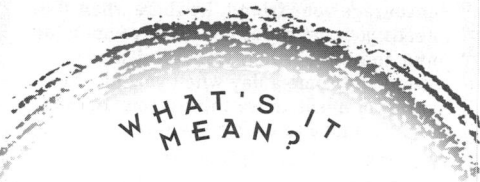

Though there is no address on the letter, the Book of Hebrews apparently was written to Jewish Christians who were being persecuted by the Roman Empire for their beliefs. Here's the problem they faced. As Jews, they had been safe, since Judaism was recognized by the empire as a legitimate religion and was therefore protected under the law. When those Jews became Christians, however, they put themselves in danger. Christianity was not a recognized religion. As a result, new Christians faced harassment not only from Rome, but also from other Jews who were upset with them for leaving the Jewish faith. As you might imagine, some Jewish Christians were seriously considering leaving their Christian faith and going back to Judaism.

Hebrews 3:14

FAILURE OF THE WILDERNESS WANDERERS

[16]For who, having heard, rebelled? Indeed, *was it* not all who came out of Egypt, *led* by Moses? [17]Now with whom was He angry forty years? *Was it* not with those who sinned, whose corpses fell in the wilderness? [18]And to whom

---

3:6 [a]NU-Text omits *firm to the end.*   **3:11** [a]Psalm 95:7–11   **3:15** [a]Psalm 95:7, 8

a certain place of the seventh *day* in this way: "*And God rested on the seventh day from all His works*";[a] [5]and again in this *place*: "*They shall not enter My rest*."[a]

[6]Since therefore it remains that some *must* enter it, and those to whom it was first preached did not enter because of disobedience, [7]again He designates a certain day, saying in David, "*Today*," after such a long time, as it has been said:

> "*Today, if you will hear His voice,*
> *Do not harden your hearts.*"[a]

[8]For if Joshua had given them rest, then He would not afterward have spoken of another day. [9]There remains therefore a rest for the people of God. [10]For he who has entered His rest has himself also ceased from his works as God *did* from His.

On the Edge

But exhort one another daily, while it is called "Today," lest any of you be hardened through the deceitfulness of sin (Heb. 3:13).

Most of us feel insecure when we are in a new place, doing new things, or meeting new people. Somehow we forget everything that is good and strong about ourselves. We can only see our weaknesses and think about our failures. You may have a friend who needs some encouragement in this area.

Verse 13 says she may need it every day. That's what being in the body of Christ is all about. Christians are supposed to encourage one another and remind each other that they are children of a loving God—empowered by His strength and covered by His grace. It's your official job as a Christian to encourage your friend. Be there when she needs you and cheer her on. Give her a big hug and tell her how wonderful she is. There will come a day when you'll be the one who needs those things. Your friend will be happy to return the favor.

SEE FOR YOURSELF:
2 Cor. 1:3, 4;
Gal. 6:9, 10;
1 Thess. 5:14

WHAT'S IT MEAN?

When Moses died, he left some pretty big sandals to fill. After all, he had led the Israelites out of Egypt and through the wilderness for almost forty years. Joshua was the man God chose to succeed Moses. As Israel's spiritual and military leader, Joshua marched the people into the land God had promised them and directed them in the wars they fought against the enemies of God. The Israelites spent years in battle with various tribes throughout the land.

Hebrews 4:8

did He swear that they would not enter His rest, but to those who did not obey? [19]So we see that they could not enter in because of unbelief.

THE PROMISE OF REST

[1]Therefore, since a promise remains of entering His rest, let us fear lest any of you seem to have come short of it. [2]For indeed the gospel was preached to us as well as to them; but the word which they heard did not profit them,[a] not being mixed with faith in those who heard it. [3]For we who have believed do enter that rest, as He has said:

> "*So I swore in My wrath,*
> '*They shall not enter My rest,*' "[a]

although the works were finished from the foundation of the world. [4]For He has spoken in

THE WORD DISCOVERS OUR CONDITION

[11]Let us therefore be diligent to enter that rest, lest anyone fall according to the same example of disobedience. [12]For the word of God *is* living and powerful, and sharper than any two-edged sword, piercing even to the division of soul and spirit, and of joints and marrow, and is a discerner of the thoughts and intents of the heart. [13]And there is no creature hidden from His sight, but all things *are* naked and open to the eyes of Him to whom we *must give* account.

4:2 [a]NU-Text and M-Text read *profit them, since they were not united by faith with those who heeded it.*
4:3 [a]Psalm 95:11   **4:4** [a]Genesis 2:2   **4:5** [a]Psalm 95:11   **4:7** [a]Psalm 95:7, 8

OUR COMPASSIONATE HIGH PRIEST

[14]Seeing then that we have a great High Priest who has passed through the heavens, Jesus the Son of God, let us hold fast *our* confession. [15]For we do not have a High Priest who cannot sympathize with our weaknesses, but was in all *points* tempted as *we are, yet* without sin. [16]Let us therefore come boldly to the throne of grace, that we may obtain mercy and find grace to help in time of need.

JESUS

Has Jesus ever sinned? (4:15)

On the Edge

For we do not have a High Priest who cannot sympathize with our weaknesses, but was in all points tempted as we are, yet without sin (Heb. 4:15).

A weakness is an area of life that's hard to control. It takes concentration and extra effort to avoid a weakness—once you're in the habit of giving in to it. Weaknesses come in all shapes and sizes—jealousy, drugs, alcohol, being irresponsible, manipulation, food, anger, laziness, reckless driving, pornography, or money. You name it, and it's probably a weakness for someone.

When we ask the Lord for strength to overcome a weakness, we can be sure that we are talking to Someone who understands. When Jesus became a man, He took on the weaknesses that people have to deal with. He's walked in your shoes. He's lived on the earth as a boy, a teenager, and a man. He's felt the temptations you feel, but He showed us how to live a life that doesn't give in. His time here made Him sympathetic toward you. He understands the trials you face, and He knows how hard temptation can be.

You can talk to Him and count on Him to provide the strength you need to overcome the things that are hard to control. He's already dealt with the tough places you'll face in life. Determine right now in your heart that you *will not give in*. He's there to help you overcome!

SEE FOR YOURSELF:
Is. 53:3–5; John 14:16; Rom. 8:26; 2 Cor. 5:21

On the Edge

He learned obedience by the things which He suffered. And having been perfected, He became the author of eternal salvation to all who obey Him (Heb. 5:8b, 9).

Flip back a couple of pages and read Hebrews 2:18. You'll see that Jesus experienced suffering and temptation. But how did that make Him perfect? He made the right choices in the midst of His suffering and temptation. Now He is the perfect One to save and strengthen you.

Jesus is perfect, but that does not distance Him from you. He became a man, remained perfect, and died for your sin, so that He could get to know you. He wants a relationship with you. He wants to be there for you in your suffering. He can carry you through it. His strength is perfect when all your strength is gone. His perfection enables Him to minister to you. He can anticipate your needs. And because He is perfect, He knows all the answers. He knows when you're empty. He knows when to send in the troops. You benefit from the perfection of Christ. He is a perfect Savior for the lost, a perfect intercessor for the needy, a perfect friend for everybody.

SEE FOR YOURSELF:
Heb. 2:10; 9:14; 1 Pet. 1:19

QUALIFICATIONS FOR HIGH PRIESTHOOD

[1]For every high priest taken from among men is appointed for men in things *pertaining* to God, that he may offer both gifts and sacrifices for sins. [2]He can have compassion on those who are ignorant and going astray, since he himself is also subject to weakness. [3]Because of this he is required as for the people, so also for himself, to offer *sacrifices* for sins. [4]And no man takes this honor to himself, but he who is called by God, just as Aaron *was*.

A PRIEST FOREVER

[5]So also Christ did not glorify Himself to become High Priest, *but it* was He who said to Him:

*"You are My Son,
Today I have begotten You."* [a]

5:5 [a]Psalm 2:7

⁶As *He* also *says* in another *place:*

"*You are a priest forever*
    According to the order of Melchizedek";ᵃ

⁷who, in the days of His flesh, when He had offered up prayers and supplications, with vehement cries and tears to Him who was able to save Him from death, and was heard because of His godly fear, ⁸though He was a Son, *yet* He learned obedience by the things which He suffered. ⁹And having been perfected, He became the author of eternal salvation to all who obey Him, ¹⁰called by God as High Priest *"according to the order of Melchizedek,"* ¹¹of whom we have much to say, and hard to explain, since you have become dull of hearing.

SPIRITUAL IMMATURITY

¹²For though by this time you ought to be teachers, you need *someone* to teach you again the first principles of the oracles of God; and you have come to need milk and not solid food. ¹³For everyone who partakes *only* of milk *is* unskilled in the word of righteousness, for he is a babe. ¹⁴But solid food belongs to those who are of full age, *that is*, those who by reason of use have their senses exercised to discern both good and evil.

THE PERIL OF NOT PROGRESSING

¹Therefore, leaving the discussion of the elementary *principles* of Christ, let us go on to perfection, not laying again the foundation of repentance from dead works and of faith toward God, ²of the doctrine of baptisms, of laying on of hands, of resurrection of the dead, and of eternal judgment. ³And this we willᵃ do if God permits.

⁴For *it is* impossible for those who were once enlightened, and have tasted the heavenly gift, and have become partakers of the Holy Spirit, ⁵and have tasted the good word of God and the powers of the age to come, ⁶if they fall away,ᵃ to renew them again to repentance, since they crucify again for themselves the Son of God, and put *Him* to an open shame.

⁷For the earth which drinks in the rain that often comes upon it, and bears herbs useful for those by whom it is cultivated, receives blessing from God; ⁸but if it bears thorns and briers, *it is*

5:6 ᵃPsalm 110:4   **6:3** ᵃM-Text reads *let us do.*   **6:6** ᵃOr *and have fallen away*

Promise   HE PROMISES TO TELL THE TRUTH.

Thus God, determining to show more abundantly to the heirs of promise the immutability of His counsel, confirmed it by an oath, that by two immutable things, in which it is impossible for God to lie, we might have strong consolation, who have fled for refuge to lay hold of the hope set before us (Heb. 6:17, 18).

Do you ever doubt God? Maybe you doubt the whole thing—God, the Bible, and all the Jesus stuff. Do you think that everyone who believes must be out to lunch? Maybe you do believe in God, but aren't sure that He's really going to come through for you. Hebrews says that the hope of Christ is right in front of you—"the hope set before us." You are holding a record of the promises God has made to you. He has told the truth. He has kept His promises. His vows have never changed. Be encouraged to run to Him because He never lies. You've got to make up your mind to believe that and you've got to decide that you are going to believe His Word. Until you've made that commitment, you'll constantly struggle with doubt.

The truth of His Word will replace your doubt. John 8:32 says "the truth shall make you free." So immerse yourself in these pages. Commit to do more than just slide your eyes over the words. Really concentrate and study the Bible prayerfully. Read about how God has kept His promises. Read about the incredibly deep and powerful love He has for you. Read about His longing to know you and to be with you forever. Get these words into your heart and into your mind. Pretty soon, all your doubts will be replaced with the absolute certainty of God and of His truth.

SEE FOR YOURSELF:
John 1:14; 8:32; 14:6, 17; 2 Tim. 3:15–17

rejected and near to being cursed, whose end *is* to be burned.

A BETTER ESTIMATE

⁹But, beloved, we are confident of better things concerning you, yes, things that accompany salvation, though we speak in this manner. ¹⁰For God *is* not unjust to forget your work and labor of[a] love which you have shown toward His name, *in that* you have ministered to the saints, and do minister. ¹¹And we desire that each one of you show the same diligence to the full assurance of hope until the end, ¹²that you do not become sluggish, but imitate those who through faith and patience inherit the promises.

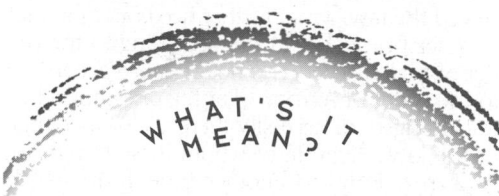

WHAT'S IT MEAN?

In ancient times, six towns in Israel were set aside as "cities of refuge." In order to understand the purpose of cities of refuge, you have to understand the law of the land in Old Testament times. "An eye for an eye" was the rule of the day. If a person killed someone else—even accidentally—legally, he himself could be killed in retaliation. That's why cities of refuge were important. If a person accidentally killed another person, he could run to the nearest city of refuge to escape vengeance-seeking family members of the person he killed. Once the person reached a city of refuge, no one was allowed to harm him until a fair trial could be conducted. If the killing was found to be accidental, the person on trial was allowed to live in the city of refuge with full protection from those who wanted to kill him.

Hebrews 6:18

GOD'S INFALLIBLE PURPOSE IN CHRIST

¹³For when God made a promise to Abraham, because He could swear by no one greater, He swore by Himself, ¹⁴saying, *"Surely blessing I will bless you, and multiplying I will multiply you."*[a] ¹⁵And so, after he had patiently endured, he obtained the promise. ¹⁶For men indeed swear by the greater, and an oath for confirmation *is* for them an end of all dispute. ¹⁷Thus God, determining to show more abundantly to the heirs of promise the immutability of His counsel, confirmed *it* by an oath, ¹⁸that by two immutable things, in which it *is* impos-

sible for God to lie, we might[a] have strong consolation, who have fled for refuge to lay hold of the hope set before *us.* ¹⁹This *hope* we have as an anchor of the soul, both sure and steadfast, and which enters the *Presence* behind the veil, ²⁰where the forerunner has entered for us, *even* Jesus, having become High Priest forever according to the order of Melchizedek.

WHAT'S IT MEAN?

What do we know about Melchizedek? First, we know that in the Book of Genesis, he is described as the king of Salem, a city in Canaan. (Salem may be the city that later became known as Jerusalem.) Second, we know that Melchizedek was a priest of God, as well as a king. Third, we know that Abraham ran into Melchizedek on his way back from rescuing his nephew Lot from the kings who had kidnapped him. Fourth, we know that Abraham recognized something in Melchizedek that caused him to give ten percent of everything he had seized in battle to the king-priest.

Hebrews 7:1

THE KING OF RIGHTEOUSNESS

¹For this Melchizedek, king of Salem, priest of the Most High God, who met Abraham returning from the slaughter of the kings and blessed him, ²to whom also Abraham gave a tenth part of all, first being translated "king of righteousness," and then also king of Salem, meaning "king of peace," ³without father, without mother, without genealogy, having neither beginning of days nor end of life, but made like the Son of God, remains a priest continually.

⁴Now consider how great this man *was,* to whom even the patriarch Abraham gave a tenth of the spoils. ⁵And indeed those who are of the sons of Levi, who receive the priesthood, have a commandment to receive tithes from the people according to the law, that is, from their brethren, though they have come from the loins of Abraham; ⁶but he whose genealogy is not derived from them received tithes from Abraham and blessed him who had the promises. ⁷Now beyond all contradiction the lesser is blessed by the better. ⁸Here mortal men receive

6:10 [a]NU-Text omits *labor of.*   **6:14** [a]Genesis 22:17   **6:18** [a]M-Text omits *might.*

tithes, but there he *receives them*, of whom it is witnessed that he lives. [9]Even Levi, who receives tithes, paid tithes through Abraham, so to speak, [10]for he was still in the loins of his father when Melchizedek met him.

NEED FOR A NEW PRIESTHOOD

[11]Therefore, if perfection were through the Levitical priesthood (for under it the people received the law), what further need *was there* that another priest should rise according to the order of Melchizedek, and not be called according to the order of Aaron? [12]For the priesthood being changed, of necessity there is also a change of the law. [13]For He of whom these things are spoken belongs to another tribe, from which no man has officiated at the altar.

[14]For *it is* evident that our Lord arose from Judah, of which tribe Moses spoke nothing concerning priesthood.[a] [15]And it is yet far more evident if, in the likeness of Melchizedek, there arises another priest [16]who has come, not according to the law of a fleshly commandment, but according to the power of an endless life. [17]For He testifies:[a]

"*You are a priest forever*
According to the order of Melchizedek."[b]

[18]For on the one hand there is an annulling of the former commandment because of its weakness and unprofitableness, [19]for the law made nothing perfect; on the other hand, *there is the* bringing in of a better hope, through which we draw near to God.

GREATNESS OF THE NEW PRIEST

[20]And inasmuch as He was not *made priest* without an oath [21](for they have become priests without an oath, but He with an oath by Him who said to Him:

"*The LORD has sworn*
And will not relent,
'*You are a priest forever*[a]
According to the order of
Melchizedek' "),[b]

[22]by so much more Jesus has become a surety of a better covenant.

[23]Also there were many priests, because they were prevented by death from continuing. [24]But He, because He continues forever, has an unchangeable priesthood. [25]Therefore He is also able to save to the uttermost those who come to God through Him, since He always lives to make intercession for them.

[26]For such a High Priest was fitting for us, *who is* holy, harmless, undefiled, separate from sinners, and has become higher than the heavens; [27]who does not need daily, as those high priests, to offer up sacrifices, first for His own sins and then for the people's, for this He did

On the Edge

For such a High Priest was fitting for us, who is holy, harmless, undefiled, separate from sinners, and has become higher than the heavens (Heb. 7:26).

Jesus, the most honored Person in heaven, sits beside God and tells Him what it's like to be human. He prays the prayers we don't know how to pray. He sympathizes with us. He talks to God for us. He represents us well before the Father. He is honored because of His perfect life, suffering, death, and resurrection. He is honored because He became the sacrifice that saves us forever. He is holy and innocent.

In a time when people are worshiping and honoring angels, the earth, and all kinds of spirits, it's important to remember that Jesus is honored above everything else. All the heavenly beings—saints and angels—are praising and worshiping God, thanking Him for His Son, Jesus. Only Jesus offers salvation. Only Jesus made it possible for people to even get to heaven in the first place. That's why He's honored above heavenly beings. That's why He's higher than the angels. No angel will ever be able to do for you what Jesus Christ can do—and has done.

Does Jesus have a place of honor in your life? Give Him the glory He deserves. Thank Him for the unending mercy and compassion He gives you day after day. Thank Him for giving His life for you. Worship Him with your day. Honor Him with your life.

SEE FOR YOURSELF:
John 3:31; 5:23;
Eph. 1:20; Phil. 2:9;
Heb. 6:20

7:14 [a]NU-Text reads *priests*. **7:17** [a]NU-Text reads *it is testified.* [b]Psalm 110:4 **7:21** [a]NU-Text ends the quotation here. [b]Psalm 110:4

once for all when He offered up Himself. [28]For the law appoints as high priests men who have weakness, but the word of the oath, which came after the law, *appoints* the Son who has been perfected forever.

THE NEW PRIESTLY SERVICE

[1]Now *this is* the main point of the things we are saying: We have such a High Priest, who is seated at the right hand of the throne of the Majesty in the heavens, [2]a Minister of the sanctuary and of the true tabernacle which the Lord erected, and not man.

[3]For every high priest is appointed to offer both gifts and sacrifices. Therefore *it is* necessary that this One also have something to offer. [4]For if He were on earth, He would not be a priest, since there are priests who offer the gifts according to the law; [5]who serve the copy and shadow of the heavenly things, as Moses was divinely instructed when he was about to make the tabernacle. For He said, *"See that you make all things according to the pattern shown you on the mountain."* [a] [6]But now He has obtained a more excellent ministry, inasmuch as He is also Mediator of a better covenant, which was established on better promises.

A NEW COVENANT

[7]For if that first *covenant* had been faultless, then no place would have been sought for a second. [8]Because finding fault with them, He says: *"Behold, the days are coming, says the* LORD, *when I will make a new covenant with the house of Israel and with the house of Judah—* [9]*not according to the covenant that I made with their fathers in the day when I took them by the hand to lead them out of the land of Egypt; because they did not continue in My covenant, and I disregarded them, says the* LORD. [10]*For this is the covenant that I will make with the house of Israel after those days, says the* LORD: *I will put My laws in their mind and write them on their hearts; and I will be their God, and they shall be My people.* [11]*None of them shall teach his neighbor, and none his brother, saying, 'Know the* LORD,' *for all shall know Me, from the least of them to the greatest of them.* [12]*For I will be merciful to their unrighteousness, and their sins and their lawless deeds*[a] *I will remember no more."*[b]

[13]In that He says, *"A new covenant,"* He has made the first obsolete. Now what is becoming obsolete and growing old is ready to vanish away.

8:5 [a]Exodus 25:40 **8:12** [a]NU-Text omits *and their lawless deeds.* [b]Jeremiah 31:31–34

Promise HE PROMISES YOU BETTER THINGS.

But now He has obtained a more excellent ministry, inasmuch as He is also Mediator of a better covenant, which was established on better promises (Heb. 8:6).

Because of Jesus, things are much better for us than they were for our ancestors. We've got a new high priest, a new tent of worship, and a new covenant with God. The priests of our ancestors were sinful and wicked. Their sin kept them from representing the people well before God. Jesus is our new High Priest. His perfection has replaced the old priests, making Him the only way to God the Father.

The old tent of worship is now just a shadow of the real one in heaven. The new tent is where Jesus sits with the Father. Having a new tent of worship means that we can worship God straight out of our own hearts. Our worship isn't dictated by ritual, but by relationship. We worship out of our love for Jesus. The new covenant that God has made through Jesus replaces the one He made with our ancestors. The old covenant didn't work because there was no cure for the people's sinfulness. It promises that, through Jesus Christ, we will belong to the Lord forever and He will belong to us as our God (see Jer. 31:31–34). The new covenant promises to forgive the sins of those who trust in Christ. Because of Christ, we can pray and fellowship directly with the Lord. We can personally ask for the forgiveness of our sins. We can sense His leading and compassion in our lives.

God has promised us better things. He's given us the best gift—a better relationship with Him—through the work of Jesus and the Holy Spirit.

SEE FOR YOURSELF:
Jer. 31:31–34; Heb. 7:22

THE EARTHLY SANCTUARY

[1]Then indeed, even the first *covenant* had ordinances of divine service and the earthly sanctuary. [2]For a tabernacle was prepared: the first *part*, in which *was* the lampstand, the table, and the showbread, which is called the sanctuary; [3]and behind the second veil, the part of the tabernacle which is called the Holiest of All, [4]which had the golden censer and the ark of the covenant overlaid on all sides with gold, in which *were* the golden pot that had the manna, Aaron's rod that budded, and the tablets of the covenant; [5]and above it were the cherubim of glory overshadowing the mercy seat. Of these things we cannot now speak in detail.

LIMITATIONS OF THE EARTHLY SERVICE

[6]Now when these things had been thus prepared, the priests always went into the first part of the tabernacle, performing *the services*. [7]But into the second part the high priest *went* alone once a year, not without blood, which he offered for himself and *for* the people's sins *committed* in ignorance; [8]the Holy Spirit indicating this, that the way into the Holiest of All was not yet made manifest while the first tabernacle was still standing. [9]It *was* symbolic for the present time in which both gifts and sacrifices are offered which cannot make him who performed the service perfect in regard to the conscience—[10]*concerned* only with foods and drinks, various washings, and fleshly ordinances imposed until the time of reformation.

THE HEAVENLY SANCTUARY

[11]But Christ came *as* High Priest of the good things to come,[a] with the greater and more perfect tabernacle not made with hands, that is, not of this creation. [12]Not with the blood of goats and calves, but with His own blood He entered the Most Holy Place once for all, having obtained eternal redemption. [13]For if the blood of bulls and goats and the ashes of a heifer, sprinkling the unclean, sanctifies for the purifying of the flesh, [14]how much more shall the blood of Christ, who through the eternal Spirit offered Himself without spot to God, cleanse your conscience from dead works to serve the living God? [15]And for this reason He is the Mediator of the new covenant, by means of death, for the redemption of the transgressions under the first covenant, that those who are called may receive the promise of the eternal inheritance.

THE MEDIATOR'S DEATH NECESSARY

[16]For where there is a testament, there must also of necessity be the death of the testator. [17]For a testament *is* in force after men are dead, since it has no power at all while the testator lives. [18]Therefore not even the first *covenant* was dedicated without blood. [19]For when Moses had spoken every precept to all the people according to the law, he took the blood of calves and goats, with water, scarlet wool, and hyssop, and sprinkled both the book itself and all the people, [20]saying, *"This is the blood of the covenant which God has commanded you."*[a] [21]Then likewise he sprinkled with blood both the tabernacle and all the vessels of the ministry. [22]And according to the law almost all things are purified with blood, and without shedding of blood there is no remission.

GREATNESS OF CHRIST'S SACRIFICE

[23]Therefore *it was* necessary that the copies of the things in the heavens should be purified with these, but the heavenly things themselves with better sacrifices than these. [24]For Christ has not entered the holy places made with hands, *which are* copies of the true, but into heaven itself, now to appear in the presence of God for us; [25]not that He should offer Himself often, as the high priest enters the Most Holy Place every year with blood of another—[26]He then would have had to suffer often since the foundation of the world; but now, once at the end of the ages, He has appeared to put away sin by the sacrifice of Himself. [27]And as it is appointed for men to die once, but after this the judgment, [28]so Christ was offered once to bear the sins of many. To those who eagerly wait for Him He will appear a second time, apart from sin, for salvation.

DEATH

What should our spiritual life be in preparation of? (9:27, 28)

ANIMAL SACRIFICES INSUFFICIENT

[1]For the law, having a shadow of the good things to come, *and* not the very image of the things, can never with these same sacrifices, which they offer continually year by year, make those who approach perfect. [2]For then would they not have ceased to be offered? For the worshipers, once purified, would have had no more consciousness of sins. [3]But in those *sacrifices there is* a reminder of sins every year. [4]For *it is* not possible that the blood of bulls and goats could take away sins.

9:11 [a]NU-Text reads *that have come.*   **9:20** [a]Exodus 24:8

On the Edge

Therefore, brethren, having boldness to enter the Holiest by the blood of Jesus, by a new and living way which He consecrated for us, through the veil, that is, His flesh (Heb. 10:19, 20).

The temple the Israelites built had a special room called the Most Holy Place (Holiest of All, Heb. 9:8). The door of this room was covered by a thick, heavy curtain because God's presence lived in the room. Because the presence of the Lord is so awesome, the people had to be separated from it. They were sinful and sin cannot stand in the presence of God's love and holiness. Only the high priest could go through the curtain, and he could do it only once a year. At that time, the high priest had to make one sacrifice for sins he and his family had committed and another sacrifice for the sins of the whole nation. The blood of the sacrifice took away the people's sins for the next year (see Lev. 16).

At the moment Jesus died on the cross, the curtain in front of the Most Holy Place was torn from top to bottom (see Matt. 27:51). God's presence was made available to everyone! It's like God had been sitting behind a locked door for years and years; and only the high priest had the key. Then Jesus came along and unlocked that door for everyone. His blood takes away the sins of everyone who trusts in Him. Now He's the High Priest. Because of His death—because the curtain is torn—you can go into the place where God is. You don't need another person as a go-between. You don't have to go to a temple. And you don't have to make another sacrifice next year. Jesus made it possible for you to go into God's presence—personally, freely, as often as you want.

SEE FOR YOURSELF:
Matt. 27:51; 2 Cor. 3:4; Col. 1:21–23; Heb. 6:19

CHRIST'S DEATH FULFILLS GOD'S WILL

[5]Therefore, when He came into the world, He said:

> "Sacrifice and offering You did not desire,
> But a body You have prepared for Me.
> [6] In burnt offerings and sacrifices for sin
> You had no pleasure.
> [7] Then I said, 'Behold, I have come—
> In the volume of the book it is written of Me—
> To do Your will, O God.' "[a]

[8]Previously saying, "Sacrifice and offering, burnt offerings, and offerings for sin You did not desire, nor had pleasure in them" (which are offered according to the law), [9]then He said, "Behold, I have come to do Your will, O God."[a] He takes away the first that He may establish the second. [10]By that will we have been sanctified through the offering of the body of Jesus Christ once for all.

CHRIST'S DEATH PERFECTS THE SANCTIFIED

[11]And every priest stands ministering daily and offering repeatedly the same sacrifices, which can never take away sins. [12]But this Man, after He had offered one sacrifice for sins forever, sat down at the right hand of God, [13]from that time waiting till His enemies are made His footstool. [14]For by one offering He has perfected forever those who are being sanctified.

[15]But the Holy Spirit also witnesses to us; for after He had said before,

[16]"This is the covenant that I will make with them after those days, says the LORD: I will put My laws into their hearts, and in their minds I will write them,"[a] [17]then He adds, "Their sins and their lawless deeds I will remember no more."[a] [18]Now where there is remission of these, there is no longer an offering for sin.

HOLD FAST YOUR CONFESSION

[19]Therefore, brethren, having boldness to enter the Holiest by the blood of Jesus, [20]by a new and living way which He consecrated for us, through the veil, that is, His flesh, [21]and having a High Priest over the house of God, [22]let us draw near with a true heart in full assurance of faith, having our hearts sprinkled from an evil conscience and our bodies washed with pure water. [23]Let us hold fast the confession of our hope without wavering, for He who promised is faithful. [24]And let us consider one another in order to stir up love and good works, [25]not forsaking the assembling of ourselves together, as

10:7 [a]Psalm 40:6–8   10:9 [a]NU-Text and M-Text omit *O God.*   10:16 [a]Jeremiah 31:33
10:17 [a]Jeremiah 31:34

is the manner of some, but exhorting *one another,* and so much the more as you see the Day approaching.

WHAT'S IT MEAN?

The Holiest in the tabernacle, the place only the high priest was allowed to enter, was separated from the rest of the tabernacle by an embroidered curtain or veil.

Hebrews 10:19, 20

THE JUST LIVE BY FAITH

[26]For if we sin willfully after we have received the knowledge of the truth, there no longer remains a sacrifice for sins, [27]but a certain fearful expectation of judgment, and fiery indignation which will devour the adversaries. [28]Anyone who has rejected Moses' law dies without mercy on the testimony of two or three witnesses. [29]Of how much worse punishment, do you suppose, will he be thought worthy who has trampled the Son of God underfoot, counted the blood of the covenant by which he was sanctified a common thing, and insulted the Spirit of grace? [30]For we know Him who said, *"Vengeance is Mine, I will repay,"*[a] says the Lord.[b] And again, *"The* LORD *will judge His people."*[c] [31]It is a fearful thing to fall into the hands of the living God.

[32]But recall the former days in which, after you were illuminated, you endured a great struggle with sufferings: [33]partly while you were made a spectacle both by reproaches and tribulations, and partly while you became companions of those who were so treated; [34]for you had compassion on me[a] in my chains, and joyfully accepted the plundering of your goods, knowing that you have a better and an enduring possession for yourselves in heaven.[b] [35]Therefore do not cast away your confidence, which has great reward. [36]For you have need of endurance, so that after you have done the will of God, you may receive the promise:

[37] *"For yet a little while,*
    And He[a] *who is coming will come and*
        will not tarry.
[38] *Now the*[a] *just shall live by faith;*
    But if anyone draws back,
    My soul has no pleasure in him."[b]

[39]But we are not of those who draw back to perdition, but of those who believe to the saving of the soul.

BY FAITH WE UNDERSTAND

[1]Now faith is the substance of things hoped for, the evidence of things not seen. [2]For by it the elders obtained a *good* testimony.

[3]By faith we understand that the worlds were framed by the word of God, so that the things which are seen were not made of things which are visible.

FAITH

What is the definition of faith? (11:1)

FAITH AT THE DAWN OF HISTORY

[4]By faith Abel offered to God a more excellent sacrifice than Cain, through which he obtained witness that he was righteous, God testifying of his gifts; and through it he being dead still speaks.

[5]By faith Enoch was taken away so that he did not see death, *"and was not found, because God had taken him"*;[a] for before he was taken he had this testimony, that he pleased God. [6]But without faith *it is* impossible to please *Him,* for he who comes to God must believe that He is, and *that* He is a rewarder of those who diligently seek Him.

[7]By faith Noah, being divinely warned of things not yet seen, moved with godly fear, prepared an ark for the saving of his household, by which he condemned the world and became heir of the righteousness which is according to faith.

FAITHFUL ABRAHAM

[8]By faith Abraham obeyed when he was called to go out to the place which he would receive as an inheritance. And he went out, not knowing where he was going. [9]By faith he dwelt in the land of promise as *in* a foreign country, dwelling in tents with Isaac and Jacob, the heirs with him of the same promise; [10]for he waited for the city which has foundations, whose builder and maker *is* God.

10:30 [a]Deuteronomy 32:35 [b]NU-Text omits *says the Lord.* [c]Deuteronomy 32:36 **10:34** [a]NU-Text reads *the prisoners* instead of *me in my chains.* [b]NU-Text omits *in heaven.* **10:37** [a]Or *that which* **10:38** [a]NU-Text reads *My just one.* [b]Habakkuk 2:3, 4 **11:5** [a]Genesis 5:24

were assured of them,[a] embraced *them* and confessed that they were strangers and pilgrims on the earth. [14]For those who say such things declare plainly that they seek a homeland. [15]And truly if they had called to mind that *country from which they had come out*, they would have had opportunity to return. [16]But now they desire a better, that is, a heavenly *country*. Therefore God is not ashamed to be called their God, for He has prepared a city for them.

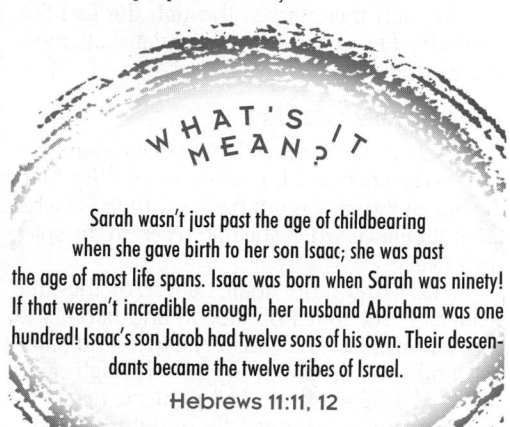

WHAT'S IT MEAN?

Sarah wasn't just past the age of childbearing when she gave birth to her son Isaac; she was past the age of most life spans. Isaac was born when Sarah was ninety! If that weren't incredible enough, her husband Abraham was one hundred! Isaac's son Jacob had twelve sons of his own. Their descendants became the twelve tribes of Israel.

Hebrews 11:11, 12

THE FAITH OF THE PATRIARCHS

[17]By faith Abraham, when he was tested, offered up Isaac, and he who had received the promises offered up his only begotten *son*, [18]of whom it was said, *"In Isaac your seed shall be called,"* [a] [19]concluding that God *was* able to raise *him* up, even from the dead, from which he also received him in a figurative sense.

[20]By faith Isaac blessed Jacob and Esau concerning things to come.

[21]By faith Jacob, when he was dying, blessed each of the sons of Joseph, and worshiped, *leaning* on the top of his staff.

[22]By faith Joseph, when he was dying, made mention of the departure of the children of Israel, and gave instructions concerning his bones.

THE FAITH OF MOSES

[23]By faith Moses, when he was born, was hidden three months by his parents, because they saw *he was* a beautiful child; and they were not afraid of the king's command.

[24]By faith Moses, when he became of age, refused to be called the son of Pharaoh's

---

On the Edge

But without faith it is impossible to please Him, for he who comes to God must believe that He is, and that He is a rewarder of those who diligently seek Him (Heb. 11:6).

The Bible talks a lot about having faith and about people who had faith. In the world, you don't often see much faith. In fact, some people are negative almost all the time. Any time you present them with a big idea, they start rattling off reasons that it won't work. That's not faith.

In order to please God, you've got to have faith. You've got to be sure of "the substance of things hoped for" (see Heb. 11:1) and to believe in what you can't see. God does give people dreams and ideas; and most of the time they'll seem bigger than your abilities and resources. He wants you to be absolutely confident that He can make it happen.

Start by believing the Bible. Faith can really grow as you begin to get confident in His Word. Don't just memorize some verses. Get them into your heart. Try them and let God show you that He means business. He's good for His Word. Believing Him is crucial, and no one else can do it for you. You have to develop your own faith and determine not to be shaken. You'll see it work and God will be pleased.

SEE FOR YOURSELF:
Hab. 2:4; Matt. 9:22; Mark 11:22; Luke 7:50; Rom. 4:9; 12:3; 1 Cor. 16:13; 2 Cor. 5:7; 2 Thess. 1:3; 1 Tim. 6:12; Heb. 11

---

[11]By faith Sarah herself also received strength to conceive seed, and she bore a child[a] when she was past the age, because she judged Him faithful who had promised. [12]Therefore from one man, and him as good as dead, were born *as many* as the stars of the sky in multitude—innumerable as the sand which is by the seashore.

THE HEAVENLY HOPE

[13]These all died in faith, not having received the promises, but having seen them afar off

11:11 [a]NU-Text omits *she bore a child.*   **11:13** [a]NU-Text and M-Text omit *were assured of them.*   **11:18** [a]Genesis 21:12

daughter, ²⁵choosing rather to suffer affliction with the people of God than to enjoy the passing pleasures of sin, ²⁶esteeming the reproach of Christ greater riches than the treasures in^a Egypt; for he looked to the reward.

²⁷By faith he forsook Egypt, not fearing the wrath of the king; for he endured as seeing Him who is invisible. ²⁸By faith he kept the Passover and the sprinkling of blood, lest he who destroyed the firstborn should touch them.

²⁹By faith they passed through the Red Sea as by dry *land, whereas* the Egyptians, attempting *to do* so, were drowned.

BY FAITH THEY OVERCAME

³⁰By faith the walls of Jericho fell down after they were encircled for seven days. ³¹By faith the harlot Rahab did not perish with those who did not believe, when she had received the spies with peace.

³²And what more shall I say? For the time would fail me to tell of Gideon and Barak and Samson and Jephthah, also *of* David and Samuel and the prophets: ³³who through faith subdued kingdoms, worked righteousness, obtained promises, stopped the mouths of lions, ³⁴quenched the violence of fire, escaped the edge of the sword, out of weakness were made strong, became valiant in battle, turned to flight the armies of the aliens. ³⁵Women received their dead raised to life again.

Others were tortured, not accepting deliverance, that they might obtain a better resurrection. ³⁶Still others had trial of mockings and scourgings, yes, and of chains and imprisonment. ³⁷They were stoned, they were sawn in two, were tempted,^a were slain with the sword. They wandered about in sheepskins and goatskins, being destitute, afflicted, tormented—³⁸of whom the world was not worthy. They wandered in deserts and mountains, *in* dens and caves of the earth.

³⁹And all these, having obtained a good testimony through faith, did not receive the promise, ⁴⁰God having provided something better for us, that they should not be made perfect apart from us.

THE RACE OF FAITH

¹Therefore we also, since we are surrounded by so great a cloud of witnesses, let us lay aside every weight, and the sin which so easily ensnares *us,* and let us run with endurance the race that is set before us, ²looking unto Jesus, the author and finisher of *our* faith, who for the

joy that was set before Him endured the cross, despising the shame, and has sat down at the right hand of the throne of God.

On the Edge

For consider Him who endured such hostility from sinners against Himself, lest you become weary and discouraged in your souls (Heb. 12:3).

Life can be tough sometimes—even for a person who has made up his mind to follow Jesus, to be His friend, and to live the way He wants. The person who wrote this letter knew that, and wanted to be sure that these Christians (and you, too) would keep going even when times were tough.

The answer for your hard times is to focus on Jesus. You've got to choose to replace your negative thoughts with thoughts about the hope and grace the Lord has for you. Don't dwell on how awful your life is. That's called self-pity, and it's not good for you. Don't worry about how much harder things might get. Don't waste time being concerned about what other people think of you. Concentrating on these things is just a recipe for depression.

Instead, get your mind on Jesus. He has a solution for you! When other things try to distract you, push your thoughts back to Him. Think about the way He lived—His gentleness, His joy, His mercy, His patience with people who didn't deserve it. Think about the way He died—the incredible sacrifice He made for you. Praise Him for His goodness, His awesomeness. Thank Him for the love He pours out on you. In the face of things like that, it's hard to stay discouraged. He will help you!

SEE FOR YOURSELF:
  Eph. 4:23, 24;
  Phil. 2:5; 4:8

THE DISCIPLINE OF GOD

³For consider Him who endured such hostility from sinners against Himself, lest you become weary and discouraged in your souls. ⁴You have not yet resisted to bloodshed, striving against sin. ⁵And you have forgotten the exhortation which speaks to you as to sons:

11:26 ^aNU-Text and M-Text read *of.*   **11:37** ^aNU-Text omits *were tempted.*

"*My son, do not despise the chastening of
    the LORD,
    Nor be discouraged when you are
        rebuked by Him;*

6   *For whom the LORD loves He chastens,
    And scourges every son whom He
        receives.*"[a]

[7]If[a] you endure chastening, God deals with
you as with sons; for what son is there whom a
father does not chasten? [8]But if you are without
chastening, of which all have become partakers,
then you are illegitimate and not sons. [9]Further-
more, we have had human fathers who corrected *us*, and we paid *them* respect. Shall we
not much more readily be in subjection to the
Father of spirits and live? [10]For they indeed for a
few days chastened *us* as seemed *best* to them,
but He for *our* profit, that *we* may be partakers
of His holiness. [11]Now no chastening seems to
be joyful for the present, but painful; nevertheless, afterward it yields the peaceable fruit of
righteousness to those who have been trained
by it.

RENEW YOUR SPIRITUAL VITALITY

[12]Therefore strengthen the hands which
hang down, and the feeble knees, [13]and make
straight paths for your feet, so that what is lame
may not be *dislocated*, but rather be healed.

[14]Pursue peace with all *people*, and holiness,
without which no one will see the Lord: [15]look-
ing carefully lest anyone fall short of the grace
of God; lest any root of bitterness springing up
cause trouble, and by this many become defiled; [16]lest there *be* any fornicator or profane
person like Esau, who for one morsel of food
sold his birthright. [17]For you know that afterward, when he wanted to inherit the blessing,
he was rejected, for he found no place for repentance, though he sought it diligently with
tears.

THE GLORIOUS COMPANY

[18]For you have not come to the mountain
that[a] may be touched and that burned with fire,
and to blackness and darkness[b] and tempest,
[19]and the sound of a trumpet and the voice of
words, so that those who heard *it* begged that
the word should not be spoken to them anymore. [20](For they could not endure what was
commanded: "*And if so much as a beast
touches the mountain, it shall be stoned*[a] or

shot with an arrow."[b] [21]And so terrifying was
the sight *that* Moses said, "*I am exceedingly
afraid* and trembling."[a])

[22]But you have come to Mount Zion and to
the city of the living God, the heavenly Jerusalem, to an innumerable company of angels, [23]to
the general assembly and church of the firstborn *who are* registered in heaven, to God the
Judge of all, to the spirits of just men made
perfect, [24]to Jesus the Mediator of the new

On the Edge

*Now no chastening seems to be
joyful for the present, but painful;
nevertheless, afterward it yields
the peaceable fruit of righteousness
to those who have been trained by it
(Heb. 12:11).*

God has given every parent the difficult
task of disciplining their children (see Prov.
22:6). For example, it may seem like your
parents are too strict when it comes to
going out. The truth is that the world just
isn't as safe as it once was. Parents have a
good reason to be concerned for your safety.
They're not being jerks; they're looking out
for you. Maybe you think your parents are a
lot tougher on you than your friends' parents are on them. This may be because you
live in a time when a lot of parents have
checked out on raising their children. Kids
get to raise themselves in a lot of homes,
and they aren't doing a very good
job.

While the process may be
frustrating and hard at times, be
thankful that you have parents
who love you and want to do what God has
called them to do. Believe it or not, when
you look back on these years, you will thank
your parents for caring so much about you.
Try to learn from their correction. More
freedom is always given to those who become responsible. Begin to apply these
lessons and see what happens!

SEE FOR YOURSELF:
    Prov. 3:12; 22:6;
    23:13, 14; Eph. 6:4;
    Col. 3:21

12:6 [a]Proverbs 3:11, 12   **12:7** [a]NU-Text and M-Text read *It is for discipline that you endure; God . . . .*
12:18 [a]NU-Text reads *to that which.* [b]NU-Text reads *gloom.*   **12:20** [a]NU-Text and M-Text omit the rest of this
verse. [b]Exodus 19:12, 13   **12:21** [a]Deuteronomy 9:19

covenant, and to the blood of sprinkling that speaks better things than *that of* Abel.

HEAR THE HEAVENLY VOICE

[25]See that you do not refuse Him who speaks. For if they did not escape who refused Him who spoke on earth, much more *shall we not escape* if we turn away from Him who *speaks* from heaven, [26]whose voice then shook the earth; but now He has promised, saying, *"Yet once more I shake[a] not only the earth, but also heaven."[b]* [27]Now this, *"Yet once more,"* indicates the removal of those things that are being shaken, as of things that are made, that the things which cannot be shaken may remain.

[28]Therefore, since we are receiving a kingdom which cannot be shaken, let us have grace, by which we may[a] serve God acceptably with reverence and godly fear. [29]For our God *is* a consuming fire.

CONCLUDING MORAL DIRECTIONS

[1]Let brotherly love continue. [2]Do not forget to entertain strangers, for by so *doing* some have unwittingly entertained angels. [3]Remember the prisoners as if chained with them— those who are mistreated—since you yourselves are in the body also.

[4]Marriage *is* honorable among all, and the bed undefiled; but fornicators and adulterers God will judge.

SEX

When is sex honorable and pure? (13:4)

[5]*Let your* conduct *be* without covetousness; *be* content with such things as you have. For He Himself has said, *"I will never leave you nor forsake you."[a]* [6]So we may boldly say:

> *"The LORD is my helper;
> I will not fear.
> What can man do to me?"[a]*

CONCLUDING RELIGIOUS DIRECTIONS

[7]Remember those who rule over you, who have spoken the word of God to you, whose faith follow, considering the outcome of *their* conduct. [8]Jesus Christ *is* the same yesterday, today, and forever. [9]Do not be carried about[a] with various and strange doctrines. For *it is* good that the heart be established by grace, not with foods which have not profited those who have been occupied with them.

[10]We have an altar from which those who serve the tabernacle have no right to eat. [11]For the bodies of those animals, whose blood is brought into the sanctuary by the high priest for sin, are burned outside the camp. [12]Therefore Jesus also, that He might sanctify the people with His own blood, suffered outside the gate. [13]Therefore let us go forth to Him, outside the camp, bearing His reproach. [14]For here we have no continuing city, but we seek the one to come. [15]Therefore by Him let us continually offer the sacrifice of praise to God, that is, the fruit of *our* lips, giving thanks to His name. [16]But do not forget to do good and to share, for with such sacrifices God is well pleased.

[17]Obey those who rule over you, and be submissive, for they watch out for your souls, as those who must give account. Let them do so with joy and not with grief, for that would be unprofitable for you.

PRAYER REQUESTED

[18]Pray for us; for we are confident that we have a good conscience, in all things desiring to live honorably. [19]But I especially urge *you* to do this, that I may be restored to you the sooner.

BENEDICTION, FINAL EXHORTATION, FAREWELL

[20]Now may the God of peace who brought up our Lord Jesus from the dead, that great Shepherd of the sheep, through the blood of the everlasting covenant, [21]make you complete in every good work to do His will, working in you[a] what is well pleasing in His sight, through Jesus Christ, to whom *be* glory forever and ever. Amen.

[22]And I appeal to you, brethren, bear with the word of exhortation, for I have written to you in few words. [23]Know that *our* brother Timothy has been set free, with whom I shall see you if he comes shortly.

[24]Greet all those who rule over you, and all the saints. Those from Italy greet you.

[25]Grace *be* with you all. Amen.

12:26 [a]NU-Text reads *will shake.* [b]Haggai 2:6   **12:28** [a]M-Text omits *may.*   **13:5** [a]Deuteronomy 31:6, 8; Joshua 1:5   **13:6** [a]Psalm 118:6   **13:9** [a]NU-Text and M-Text read *away.*   **13:21** [a]NU-Text and M-Text read *us.*

CONTENT
Have you ever known anyone who said they wanted to be your friend, but then they didn't act like a friend? Maybe they talked about you behind your back. Maybe they found another friend and left you behind. Whatever they did, their actions didn't match their words. When people's actions don't match their words, which do we usually believe?

Their actions.

The Book of James is about that kind of concept. It's about making the faith that you confess with your words match the way you act. James even goes so far as to say that if your actions don't match your faith, then your faith is worthless.

Whew. That's a little harsh, don't you think? It's the truth, though. What good is it to God or our family or ourselves, or to a world that needs to see a real Christian, if we say a lot of good stuff but don't live according to it?

James is one of those where-the-rubber-meets-the-road kinds of books. It reminds us that we are playing with holy fire when we say we believe. It reminds us that, when we say we believe, we are making a promise that will change everything we do.

Outline

Purpose
Authentic faith produces an authentic Christian lifestyle.

Theme
Faith That Works

Date of writing
Mid-40s A.D.

> "So then, my beloved brethren, let every man be swift to hear, slow to speak, slow to wrath; for the wrath of man does not produce the righteousness of God" (1:19, 20).

Bible Talk

Caution! Caution! Caution!

James is famous for giving us a warning about one of the most dangerous forces known to man. It has the violent nature of a forest fire and a power greater than a wild animal. Know what it is?

The force that James warns about is the human tongue. It's not that the tongue itself has so much power. It's that we use our tongues to speak. When we speak, we use words. When we use words, we hold the power to hurt or to heal, and we are stuck with the outcome. Words are hard to take back.

So when James warns us to learn to control our tongue, he's really saying that we should control our will and our brain and our mouths and all the words that we say.

TEMPTATION

James tells us some very important facts about temptation. He tells us that God will never tempt us with evil. That means when you are wanting to do something you know you shouldn't, God is not testing your will. According to James, more likely that temptation comes from the fact that we humans are evil at best, and we want to do what is wrong.

So when we are tempted, it is not that some force outside of ourselves is trying to get us to sin. We are just getting a snapshot of what is inside of us. That snapshot should send us running to God, the only One who can make us better than we naturally are.

GREETING TO THE TWELVE TRIBES

[1]James, a bondservant of God and of the Lord Jesus Christ,

To the twelve tribes which are scattered abroad:

Greetings.

PROFITING FROM TRIALS

[2]My brethren, count it all joy when you fall into various trials, [3]knowing that the testing of your faith produces patience. [4]But let patience have *its* perfect work, that you may be perfect and complete, lacking nothing. [5]If any of you lacks wisdom, let him ask of God, who gives to all liberally and without reproach, and it will be given to him. [6]But let him ask in faith, with no doubting, for he who doubts is like a wave of the sea driven and tossed by the wind. [7]For let not that man suppose that he will receive anything from the Lord; [8]*he is* a double-minded man, unstable in all his ways.

THE PERSPECTIVE OF RICH AND POOR

[9]Let the lowly brother glory in his exaltation, [10]but the rich in his humiliation, because as a flower of the field he will pass away. [11]For no sooner has the sun risen with a burning heat than it withers the grass; its flower falls, and its beautiful appearance perishes. So the rich man also will fade away in his pursuits.

LOVING GOD UNDER TRIALS

[12]Blessed *is* the man who endures temptation; for when he has been approved, he will receive the crown of life which the Lord has promised to those who love Him. [13]Let no one say when he is tempted, "I am tempted by God"; for God cannot be tempted by evil, nor does He Himself tempt anyone. [14]But each one is tempted when he is drawn away by his own desires and enticed. [15]Then, when desire has conceived, it gives birth to sin; and sin, when it is full-grown, brings forth death.

[16]Do not be deceived, my beloved brethren. [17]Every good gift and every perfect gift is from above, and comes down from the Father of lights, with whom there is no variation or shadow of turning. [18]Of His own will He brought us forth by the word of truth, that we might be a kind of firstfruits of His creatures.

QUALITIES NEEDED IN TRIALS

[19]So then,[a] my beloved brethren, let every man be swift to hear, slow to speak, slow to wrath; [20]for the wrath of man does not produce the righteousness of God.

DOERS—NOT HEARERS ONLY

[21]Therefore lay aside all filthiness and overflow of wickedness, and receive with meekness the implanted word, which is able to save your souls.

[22]But be doers of the word, and not hearers only, deceiving yourselves. [23]For if anyone is a hearer of the word and not a doer, he is like a man observing his natural face in a mirror; [24]for he observes himself, goes away, and immediately forgets what kind of man he was. [25]But he who looks into the perfect law of liberty and continues *in it*, and is not a forgetful hearer but a doer of the work, this one will be blessed in what he does.

BLESSING

What brings us blessing? (1:25)

[26]If anyone among you[a] thinks he is religious, and does not bridle his tongue but deceives his own heart, this one's religion *is* useless. [27]Pure and undefiled religion before God and the Father is this: to visit orphans and widows in their trouble, *and* to keep oneself unspotted from the world.

BEWARE OF PERSONAL FAVORITISM

[1]My brethren, do not hold the faith of our Lord Jesus Christ, *the Lord* of glory, with partiality. [2]For if there should come into your assembly a man with gold rings, in fine apparel, and there should also come in a poor man in filthy clothes, [3]and you pay attention to the one wearing the fine clothes and say to him, "You sit here in a good place," and say to the poor man, "You stand there," or, "Sit here at my footstool," [4]have you not shown partiality among yourselves, and become judges with evil thoughts?

[5]Listen, my beloved brethren: Has God not chosen the poor of this world *to be* rich in faith and heirs of the kingdom which He promised to those who love Him? [6]But you have dishonored the poor man. Do not the rich oppress you and drag you into the courts? [7]Do they not blaspheme that noble name by which you are called?

[8]If you really fulfill *the* royal law according

to the Scripture, *"You shall love your neighbor as yourself,"*[a] you do well; [9]but if you show partiality, you commit sin, and are convicted by the law as transgressors. [10]For whoever shall keep the whole law, and yet stumble in one *point,* he is guilty of all. [11]For He who said, *"Do not commit adultery,"*[a] also said, *"Do not murder."*[b] Now if you do not commit adultery, but you do murder, you have become a transgressor of the law. [12]So speak and so do as those who will be judged by the law of liberty. [13]For judgment is without mercy to the one who has shown no mercy. Mercy triumphs over judgment.

FAITH WITHOUT WORKS IS DEAD

[14]What *does it* profit, my brethren, if someone says he has faith but does not have works? Can faith save him? [15]If a brother or sister is naked and destitute of daily food, [16]and one of you says to them, "Depart in peace, be warmed and filled," but you do not give them the things which are needed for the body, what *does it* profit? [17]Thus also faith by itself, if it does not have works, is dead.

[18]But someone will say, "You have faith, and I have works." Show me your faith without your[a] works, and I will show you my faith by my[b] works. [19]You believe that there is one God.

You do well. Even the demons believe—and tremble! [20]But do you want to know, O foolish man, that faith without works is dead?[a] [21]Was not Abraham our father justified by works when he offered Isaac his son on the altar? [22]Do you see that faith was working together with

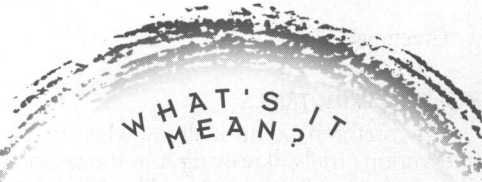

WHAT'S IT MEAN?

It's said that couples who have children later in life appreciate the parenting experience more than young parents do. If that's true, Abraham and Sarah may have been the most appreciative parents in history. When their son Isaac was born, Abraham was one hundred years old and Sarah was ninety. Years later, God tested Abraham's appreciation—and his faith—by asking him to kill Isaac as a sacrifice. Even after waiting a century for the son God had promised him, Abraham didn't hesitate to obey. Just when Abraham was ready to kill Isaac, the Lord stopped him and sent a ram to sacrifice instead.

James 2:21

2:8 [a]Leviticus 19:18   **2:11** [a]Exodus 20:14; Deuteronomy 5:18   [b]Exodus 20:13; Deuteronomy 5:17
2:18 [a]NU-Text omits *your.*   [b]NU-Text omits *my.*   **2:20** [a]NU-Text reads *useless.*

Promise   HE PROMISES THAT YOU WILL INHERIT HIS KINGDOM.

Listen, my beloved brethren: Has God not chosen the poor of this world to be rich in faith and heirs of the kingdom which He promised to those who love Him? (James 2:5).

Maybe you'll find a lot of money, or stumble onto a fortune, or marry into royalty. Most people spend all of their lives trying to build a kingdom or to win one. They haven't heard the news that we're already heirs to a kingdom—the eternal kingdom of God—the one that doesn't rot, or fade away, or go broke.

Where are you spending your time? Building a kingdom on earth, or building the kingdom of heaven. Think for a moment. Do you know your grandmother's name? Easy? How about your great-grandmother's name? Harder, but okay. Now, what's your great-great-grandmother's name? Stumped? It's the sad truth. In about three or four generations, no one will remember your name either. Oh, it'll be written down somewhere, but you'll be long gone. Your earthly kingdom won't matter anymore. If you're a Christian, you'll be with Jesus, sharing in the kingdom He has for you. There, you'll matter forever.

SEE FOR YOURSELF:
Luke 6:20; 2 Thess. 1:5; Heb. 12:28

his works, and by works faith was made perfect? [23]And the Scripture was fulfilled which says, *"Abraham believed God, and it was accounted to him for righteousness."* [a] And he was called the friend of God. [24]You see then that a man is justified by works, and not by faith only.

[25]Likewise, was not Rahab the harlot also justified by works when she received the messengers and sent *them* out another way?

[26]For as the body without the spirit is dead, so faith without works is dead also.

WHAT'S IT MEAN?

Rahab was living proof that it's not what you know; it's who you know. When the Israelites sent spies into Jericho to scope the place out, Rahab, a prostitute in Jericho, helped them get the information they needed and even saved their lives by hiding them from the king's men. Later, when the Israelites returned to conquer Jericho, they destroyed the homes of everyone in the city—except that of Rahab and her family. Rahab had proven herself to be a friend of God's people.

James 2:25

THE UNTAMABLE TONGUE

[1]My brethren, let not many of you become teachers, knowing that we shall receive a stricter judgment. [2]For we all stumble in many things. If anyone does not stumble in word, he *is* a perfect man, able also to bridle the whole body. [3]Indeed,[a] we put bits in horses' mouths that they may obey us, and we turn their whole body. [4]Look also at ships: although they are so large and are driven by fierce winds, they are turned by a very small rudder wherever the pilot desires. [5]Even so the tongue is a little member and boasts great things.

See how great a forest a little fire kindles! [6]And the tongue *is* a fire, a world of iniquity. The tongue is so set among our members that it defiles the whole body, and sets on fire the course of nature; and it is set on fire by hell. [7]For every kind of beast and bird, of reptile and creature of the sea, is tamed and has been tamed by mankind. [8]But no man can tame the tongue. *It is* an unruly evil, full of deadly poison. [9]With it we bless our God and Father, and with it we curse men, who have been made in the similitude of God. [10]Out of the same mouth proceed blessing and cursing. My brethren, these things ought not to be so. [11]Does a spring send forth fresh *water* and bitter from the same opening? [12]Can a fig tree, my brethren, bear

On the Edge

For we all stumble in many things. If anyone does not stumble in word, he is a perfect man, able also to bridle the whole body. . . . Even so the tongue is a little member and boasts great things. See how great a forest a little fire kindles! And the tongue is a fire, a world of iniquity. The tongue is so set among our members that it defiles the whole body, and sets on fire the course of nature; and it is set on fire by hell (James 3:2, 5, 6).

At the time, gossip can seem so harmless—a few words about a friend, information that nobody else knew. You felt big. Everyone paid attention to you and seemed to be impressed. And then, a few days pass. Your friend hears that you told her secrets. You gossiped. She's pretty upset and she's really hurt. You're ashamed, so you try to cover your tracks with lies. But it's too late. She already knows. What a mess.

James says that your tongue gets out of control and causes evil (see v. 8). In other words, your mouth can get you into big trouble. Words are powerful, like "deadly poison" (v. 8). They can ruin somebody's day or somebody's life. They can also save somebody's life. They can hurt or they can heal. Read James 3:10–12. You'll see that blessing and cursing (good words and bad words) can't come out of the same person. So if you want to follow God, you can't gossip. Besides, who wants to be known as the best gossip in town? Watch your words. Use them well. Speak the truth instead of lies. Speak good things instead of bad things.

SEE FOR YOURSELF:
Prov. 11:13; 16:28; 20:19;
Eph. 4:29; 5:4

2:23 [a]Genesis 15:6 **3:3** [a]NU-Text reads *Now if.*

olives, or a grapevine bear figs? Thus no spring yields both salt water and fresh.*

WHAT'S IT MEAN?

You've heard of "hell on earth"? The Hinnom Valley, a deep ravine located south of Jerusalem, was the real thing. The Greek word translated "hell" literally means "Hinnom Valley." The ravine was actually an ancient garbage dump. All kinds of waste material and dead animals were taken to Hinnom Valley to be burned. Eventually, the place came to be used as a symbol of judgment and sorrow.

James 3:6

HEAVENLY VERSUS DEMONIC WISDOM

[13]Who *is* wise and understanding among you? Let him show by good conduct *that* his works *are done* in the meekness of wisdom.

[14]But if you have bitter envy and self-seeking in your hearts, do not boast and lie against the truth. [15]This wisdom does not descend from above, but *is* earthly, sensual, demonic. [16]For where envy and self-seeking *exist,* confusion and every evil thing *are* there. [17]But the wisdom that is from above is first pure, then peaceable, gentle, willing to yield, full of mercy and good fruits, without partiality and without hypocrisy. [18]Now the fruit of righteousness is sown in peace by those who make peace.

PRIDE PROMOTES STRIFE

[1]Where do wars and fights *come* from among you? Do *they* not *come* from your *desires for* pleasure that war in your members? [2]You lust and do not have. You murder and covet and cannot obtain. You fight and war. Yet* you do not have because you do not ask. [3]You ask and do not receive, because you ask amiss, that you may spend *it* on your pleasures. [4]Adulterers and* adulteresses! Do you not know that friendship with the world is enmity with God? Whoever therefore wants to be a friend of the world makes himself an enemy of God. [5]Or do you think that the Scripture says in vain, "The Spirit who dwells in us yearns jealously"?

3:12 *NU-Text reads *Neither can a salty spring produce fresh water.*   **4:2** *NU-Text and M-Text omit *Yet.*
4:4 *NU-Text omits *Adulterers and.*

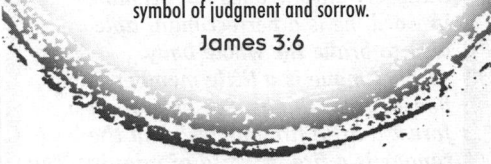

Promise   HE PROMISES TO HONOR HUMBLE PEOPLE.

But He gives more grace. Therefore He says: "God resists the proud, but gives grace to the humble.". . . Humble yourselves in the sight of the Lord, and He will lift you up (James 4:6, 10).

The way up with God, the way toward honor, is to be humble. God is looking for young men and women who will be genuinely humble. He doesn't want a fake humility that says, "I'm really a nothing," but is conceited and arrogant on the inside. Some people think that humility means really believing that you are a nothing. No way. *True humility is knowing and recognizing who God is and who you are.* God says that, through Christ, you can do all things (see Phil. 4:13). He rejoices and sings because of you (see Zeph. 3:17). You are not a nothing!

Being humble does not mean acting like a doormat. It means that you know for certain that you are strong through Jesus Christ. It means that you are secure enough to serve others and not care what people think. You're strong enough to be seen with people who aren't popular. You're secure enough to really care about someone who often gets left out—and you show it.

Pride and arrogance have no place with God. Jesus measures strength not by how cool you act, but by your humility. Look at John 13:3–17. You'll see a great picture of Jesus' humility. Working on humility in your life will help you be more like Him. And that's what it's all about.

SEE FOR YOURSELF:
Ps. 149:4; Prov. 3:34; Dan. 10:12; Matt. 23:12; John 13:3–17; Phil. 2:8

A BOY WITH A LUNCH made a difference

One boy in the Bible lived by a motto that turned out to make quite a difference: Lunch—don't leave home without it. That boy was among the crowd of thousands following Jesus around the Sea of Galilee to hear Him teach. Not knowing how long he would be gone, he had with him a simple meal: five loaves and two fish. That was probably enough for several day snacks for a young boy. When it turned out to be the only food on hand for the huge crowd, it looked pretty insignificant.

But that little lunch was turned over to Jesus. He prayed and multiplied the contents of the meal so that it served everyone, and there were leftovers! The boy himself gave up his meal, but got at least as much in return. Not to mention the thrill of Jesus' miracle. The boy's act of generosity was mentioned by all four Gospel writers.

What seemed to the disciples to be proof of how impossible it was to meet the need Jesus took and used to meet the need. The disciples concluded that they only had five loaves and two fish. They momentarily overlooked the obvious fact that they also had Jesus. He made the difference. Even a little boy's lunch gift was more than enough in Jesus' hands.

YOU can, too!

You may be convinced that you have little to offer Christ. Measured against the needs of the world around you, you may well be right. The choice you must make is between trying to make a difference on your own and placing what little you are and have into God's hands and expecting Him to make a difference in you and through you. What you choose will make a difference!

Want to know more? You can find this story in

Matthew 14:13–21; Mark 6:30–44; Luke 9:10–17; John 6:1–14.

JOHN MARK made a difference

Can someone still make a difference after they have made a big mistake? John Mark may have failed twice before he finally realized what discipleship in Jesus Christ is all about. Actually, that record is probably better than average. John Mark gives us a good example of the fact that people don't make a difference for Christ when they fall, but when they keep getting up by God's grace!

We know John Mark best by his second name, which identifies the Gospel he probably wrote, using Peter as one of his sources. In that Gospel he gives a subtle glimpse of his own uncertain discipleship on the night Jesus was betrayed. He mentions a young disciple who fled in such fear that he ran right out of his clothes (Mark 14:51, 52).

Later, when Paul and Barnabas were setting out on their first missionary journey, they chose John Mark as their traveling assistant. He quit during the adventure. On the next mission, Barnabas wanted to give Mark another try, but Paul refused. The two giants split. Barnabas helped Mark grow up in the faith. Later, Paul realized that Mark had become a real asset to the cause of Christ. It took a while, but Mark made a difference.

Cutting Edge

YOU can, too! Everybody makes mistakes. All of them have consequences—some bad; some good. If and when you decide to follow Jesus, you will find the need to grow through your failures. The journey to maturity—the way to making a difference—takes you right through the middle of mistakes. Remember John Mark; keep getting up by God's grace!

Want to know more? Follow the ups and downs for Mark's journey in these passages: Acts 12:25—13:13; 15:36–40; Colossians 4:10, 11; 2 Timothy 4:11; Philemon 23, 24; 1 Peter 5:13.

RHODA made a difference

People don't find out how much they really believe in prayer until one of God's answers comes knocking at the door! Rhoda was a young believer caught up in exciting days that followed Jesus' resurrection. At first, it may have looked like everyone would turn to the risen Christ. Then came the backlash. Ugly confrontations, imprisonment, and even death were used to resist the wildfire of the gospel message. No one was safe.

Rhoda participated in a fervent prayer meeting, asking God for the safe release of Peter who had been imprisoned. While they were praying, God was working. An angel broke Peter out of his confinement. Once the angel left him on the street, Peter made his way to the house where Rhoda and the others were still in prayer. He knocked on the outer door, and Rhoda went to answer. She recognized Peter's voice and got so excited she rushed back into the house to tell the news. During the next confusing minutes, Peter was left standing out in the street.

Cutting Edge

At first, the others in the house didn't believe Rhoda's report. But someone finally decided that the best way to check her story was to open the door. They found to their surprise and delight that God had answered their prayers. Rhoda had the right attitude; she just forgot an item that would have easily persuaded others—Peter himself. We may chuckle over Rhoda's oversight, but it reminds us how easily we fall into the error of praying for what we don't really expect God to provide. God will not be bound by our prayers, but He often answers them with a precision we miss because we aren't paying close enough attention.

YOU can, too!

We pray to make a difference. We pray to put ourselves in a place where we can see God make a difference. When we pray for rain, we ought to carry our umbrellas with us. Sometimes, when we are surprised by God's answer, we end up giving an unclear report. When God's answers come knocking, open the door. That will make a big difference!

Want to know more? Read about Rhoda's small adventure in

Acts 12:1–17.

JAMES, Jesus' little brother, made a difference

James must have felt that having Jesus as a big brother was a mixed blessing. Did James ever hear his mother say, "Why can't you be more like your big brother?" Now there is an intimidating comparison! James probably had some good reasons to consider his big brother unique and amazing, but the Bible tells us he had a hard time accepting his big brother as his Savior. It took a while. In fact, it took Jesus' death and resurrection to finally convince James that Jesus was much more than his brother. Paul tells us (1 Cor. 15:7) that Jesus paid his little brother a personal visit after His resurrection. That must have been quite a reunion!

James had always watched Jesus. How can you ignore a famous brother? When he finally realized the identity of his brother, James's faith took a great leap forward. Everything he had heard his brother say and had seen his brother do suddenly made sense. All the shapes and colors were there; faith brought the picture into sharp focus. James became a leader in the church almost overnight. He grew up!

Cutting Edge

Even though James was a late bloomer, God used him in several crucial ways. He provided key wisdom in the early days of the church. He also wrote the Book of James, probably the most down-to-earth, practical, how-to manual for the Christian life. Every time someone reads that book, James makes a difference again.

YOU can, too!

Fortunately, you can respond in faith to Jesus at any point in your life. Late bloomer or not, it's never too late to begin applying the lessons James learned and passed on in his book. In fact, one way to think about the Book of James is to describe it as a book written for believers who really want to make a difference for Christ in their lives.

Want to know more? As you read the Gospels, think about what it must have been like as Jesus' little brother to see and hear what Jesus was doing. James is mentioned directly in

John 7:1–5; Acts 15:1–29; 1 Corinthians 15:7; and in his own letter, James.

⁶But He gives more grace. Therefore He says:

"*God resists the proud,*
But gives grace to the humble."ᵃ

HUMILITY CURES WORLDLINESS

⁷Therefore submit to God. Resist the devil and he will flee from you. ⁸Draw near to God and He will draw near to you. Cleanse *your* hands, *you* sinners; and purify *your* hearts, *you* double-minded. ⁹Lament and mourn and weep! Let your laughter be turned to mourning and *your* joy to gloom. ¹⁰Humble yourselves in the sight of the Lord, and He will lift you up.

WORSHIP

When does God draw near to us? (4:8)

DO NOT JUDGE A BROTHER

¹¹Do not speak evil of one another, brethren. He who speaks evil of a brother and judges his brother, speaks evil of the law and judges the law. But if you judge the law, you are not a doer of the law but a judge. ¹²There is one Lawgiver,ᵃ who is able to save and to destroy. Whoᵇ are you to judge another?ᶜ

DO NOT BOAST ABOUT TOMORROW

¹³Come now, you who say, "Today or tomorrow we willᵃ go to such and such a city, spend a year there, buy and sell, and make a profit"; ¹⁴whereas you do not know what *will happen* tomorrow. For what *is* your life? It is even a vapor that appears for a little time and then vanishes away. ¹⁵Instead you *ought* to say, "If the Lord wills, we shall live and do this or that." ¹⁶But now you boast in your arrogance. All such boasting is evil.

¹⁷Therefore, to him who knows to do good and does not do *it*, to him it is sin.

RICH OPPRESSORS WILL BE JUDGED

¹Come now, *you* rich, weep and howl for your miseries that are coming upon *you!* ²Your riches are corrupted, and your garments are moth-eaten. ³Your gold and silver are corroded, and their corrosion will be a witness against you and will eat your flesh like fire. You have heaped up treasure in the last days. ⁴Indeed the wages of the laborers who mowed your fields, which you kept back by fraud, cry out; and the cries of the reapers have reached the ears of the

Lord of Sabaoth.ᵃ ⁵You have lived on the earth in pleasure and luxury; you have fattened your hearts asᵃ in a day of slaughter. ⁶You have condemned, you have murdered the just; he does not resist you.

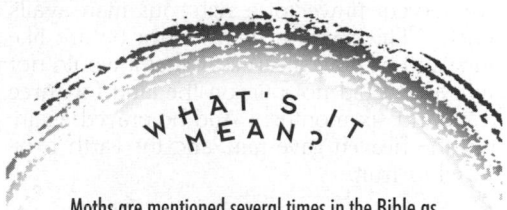

WHAT'S IT MEAN?

Moths are mentioned several times in the Bible as symbols of destruction and the foolishness of putting one's hope in material things. Here's how the little critters are able to do so much damage. Female moths often lay their eggs in clothing. When the eggs hatch, the newborn larvae eat the fibers of the material. Because the larvae chew quietly, the owner of the clothing may not know that damage is being done until it's too late.

James 5:2

BE PATIENT AND PERSEVERING

⁷Therefore be patient, brethren, until the coming of the Lord. See *how* the farmer waits for the precious fruit of the earth, waiting patiently for it until it receives the early and latter rain. ⁸You also be patient. Establish your hearts, for the coming of the Lord is at hand.

⁹Do not grumble against one another, brethren, lest you be condemned.ᵃ Behold, the Judge is standing at the door! ¹⁰My brethren, take the prophets, who spoke in the name of the Lord, as an example of suffering and patience. ¹¹Indeed we count them blessed who endure. You have heard of the perseverance of Job and seen the end *intended by* the Lord—that the Lord is very compassionate and merciful.

¹²But above all, my brethren, do not swear, either by heaven or by earth or with any other oath. But let your "Yes" be "Yes," and *your* "No," "No," lest you fall into judgment.ᵃ

MEETING SPECIFIC NEEDS

¹³Is anyone among you suffering? Let him pray. Is anyone cheerful? Let him sing psalms. ¹⁴Is anyone among you sick? Let him call for the elders of the church, and let them pray over him, anointing him with oil in the name of the

---

4:6 ᵃProverbs 3:34 **4:12** ᵃNU-Text adds *and Judge.* ᵇNU-Text and M-Text read *But who.* ᶜNU-Text reads *a neighbor.* **4:13** ᵃM-Text reads *let us.* **5:4** ᵃLiterally, in Hebrew, *Hosts* **5:5** ᵃNU-Text omits *as.* **5:9** ᵃNU-Text and M-Text read *judged.* **5:12** ᵃM-Text reads *hypocrisy.*

Lord. ¹⁵And the prayer of faith will save the sick, and the Lord will raise him up. And if he has committed sins, he will be forgiven. ¹⁶Confess *your* trespasses[a] to one another, and pray for one another, that you may be healed. The effective, fervent prayer of a righteous man avails much. ¹⁷Elijah was a man with a nature like ours, and he prayed earnestly that it would not rain; and it did not rain on the land for three years and six months. ¹⁸And he prayed again, and the heaven gave rain, and the earth produced its fruit.

BRING BACK THE ERRING ONE

¹⁹Brethren, if anyone among you wanders from the truth, and someone turns him back, ²⁰let him know that he who turns a sinner from the error of his way will save a soul[a] from death and cover a multitude of sins.

On the Edge

Is anyone among you suffering? Let him pray. Is anyone cheerful? Let him sing psalms (James 5:13).

Did you know that grades in school are not very good indicators of how successful a person will be in life? Success comes to people who never quit trying. Failure may shake them up, but it doesn't stop them. You've got to jump right back in and try again when you fail. Don't let a failing grade beat you up. Failing a class doesn't make you a failure in life!

It's important to constantly pursue excellence in every area of your life. But the fact is, you will fall short somewhere along the way. Learn from your mistakes and take all your anxieties to the Lord. One of the cruel things about failure is that it can make you afraid. Some people get so afraid of failing again that they refuse to try. So pray, pray, pray, and ask the Lord for strength to face the challenge again. Ask Him to provide a clear path for you to walk through—removing the obstacles that tripped you up before. Each time you think about your failure, talk to God about it. Give Him the burden of it, thank Him for the great success you are to Him, and listen as He whispers to you, "Never, never give up!"

SEE FOR YOURSELF:
Deut. 28:6; Ps. 103:5;
John 14:16; Heb. 4:16

On the Edge

Confess your trespasses to one another, and pray for one another, that you may be healed. The effective, fervent prayer of a righteous man avails much (James 5:16).

Real accountability keeps you growing and keeps you honest. Meeting regularly with some friends who love you and who love Jesus will strengthen you as a Christian. As you confess your sins to each other, pray together, and grow closer as friends, you'll begin to pull for one another.

Kate and Rachel are accountability partners. Kate is an early bird, but Rachel is a sleepyhead. Kate calls Rachel every morning and they pray together. Kate's had a hard time getting her prayer life going, so her morning prayer time with Rachel not only helps Rachel roll out of bed; it also helps Kate develop her prayer life.

A high-school senior asks his youth pastor to pray with him before he goes on dates. Praying with someone reminds him to commit the date to the Lord, to respect his date, and to honor God with his behavior. He also knows that his youth pastor will ask him later how the time went, and he wants to be able to give a good report.

Accountability can help you conquer areas you've been struggling with. People who have real accountability in their lives seem to grow faster than people who don't. They work as a team and as a family to become more like Jesus. The Lord is pleased with relationships like that.

SEE FOR YOURSELF:
Prov. 27:6, 17;
Rom. 14:12; Heb. 4:13

5:16 [a]NU-Text reads *Therefore confess your sins.*   **5:20** [a]NU-Text reads *his soul.*

1 & 2 peter

CONTENT The letters that Peter wrote to the early church were like survival manuals. These churches faced danger every day. They were written at the time when Nero was actually throwing Christians to the lions. They were written at a time when even admitting what you believed was a dangerous thing. They were written to help people survive both physically and spiritually.

In Peter's first letter, he wrote to the Christians who were being persecuted by people outside of the church. These Christians faced torture and death because of what they believed. Peter wrote to help them gain some perspective in the midst of the struggle to survive. He encouraged their faith even if it endangered their lives. He knew that if their faith stayed strong, they might be in physical danger but their souls would be safe.

In Peter's second letter, he warned the Christians to watch out for traitors *inside* the church. These persecutors took the form of false teachers who taught doctrines that would weaken faith rather than build it up. Paul knew that, for these Christians, even though their bodies weren't in physical danger, their souls were in a precarious position.

Purpose We can triumph over suffering as we follow Jesus.

Theme Suffering as a Christian

Date of writing A.D. 64

Purpose We dare not set our hearts on worldly things.

Theme Remaining True to the Biblical Faith

Date of writing A.D. 65

> "No prophecy of Scripture is of any private interpretation, for prophecy never came by the will of man, but holy men of God spoke as they were moved by the Holy Spirit" (2 Pet. 1:20, 21).

Bible Talk

Why Endure Persecution?

History has taught us that persecution does not deter Christianity. In fact, Christianity has often grown in countries that threatened death to people who declared faith in God. Why do you think that is true?

Part of it is because true faith is true, no matter what. If God is God and if He is active in your life, then that is true, no matter how much people might harass you or intimidate you.

Part of it is because when faith is put to the test, it grows the strongest. Faith in a fire shines the brightest.

And when you think about it, if Christianity is not real, then why should governments and nations and armies go to such great lengths to stamp it out? If Christianity is just an empty custom with no power, what is the big deal after all?

WHAT IS "HERESY" ANYWAY?

Peter warned against false teachers inside of the church. The question is, at what point do you stop saying people have different opinions and start saying they are teaching heresy?

Just about everyone you ask will give you a different answer for that question. We care about our faith, and we work hard to understand it. When someone disagrees with us, it's sometimes hard to feel okay about it.

That doesn't mean that every difference of opinion should result in a disagreement. Real heresy focuses on who Jesus is. If someone is telling you that Jesus is not *really* God in the flesh, then you have some heresy going on. That doesn't mean you have to be angry or even loud-mouthed, but it does mean you have to stand up for the truth.

GREETING TO THE ELECT PILGRIMS

[1]Peter, an apostle of Jesus Christ,

To the pilgrims of the Dispersion in Pontus, Galatia, Cappadocia, Asia, and Bithynia, [2]elect according to the foreknowledge of God the Father, in sanctification of the Spirit, for obedience and sprinkling of the blood of Jesus Christ:

Grace to you and peace be multiplied.

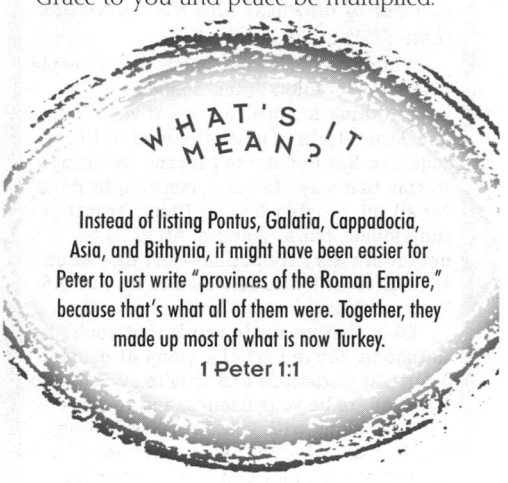

Instead of listing Pontus, Galatia, Cappadocia, Asia, and Bithynia, it might have been easier for Peter to just write "provinces of the Roman Empire," because that's what all of them were. Together, they made up most of what is now Turkey.

1 Peter 1:1

A HEAVENLY INHERITANCE

[3]Blessed *be* the God and Father of our Lord Jesus Christ, who according to His abundant mercy has begotten us again to a living hope through the resurrection of Jesus Christ from the dead, [4]to an inheritance incorruptible and undefiled and that does not fade away, reserved in heaven for you, [5]who are kept by the power of God through faith for salvation ready to be revealed in the last time.

[6]In this you greatly rejoice, though now for a little while, if need be, you have been grieved by various trials, [7]that the genuineness of your faith, *being* much more precious than gold that perishes, though it is tested by fire, may be found to praise, honor, and glory at the revelation of Jesus Christ, [8]whom having not seen[a] you love. Though now you do not see *Him*, yet believing, you rejoice with joy inexpressible and full of glory, [9]receiving the end of your faith—the salvation of *your* souls.

[10]Of this salvation the prophets have inquired and searched carefully, who prophesied of the grace *that would come* to you, [11]searching what, or what manner of time, the Spirit of Christ who was in them was indicating when

He testified beforehand the sufferings of Christ and the glories that would follow. [12]To them it was revealed that, not to themselves, but to us[a] they were ministering the things which now have been reported to you through those who have preached the gospel to you by the Holy Spirit sent from heaven—things which angels desire to look into.

LIVING BEFORE GOD OUR FATHER

[13]Therefore gird up the loins of your mind, be sober, and rest *your* hope fully upon the grace that is to be brought to you at the revelation of Jesus Christ; [14]as obedient children, not conforming yourselves to the former lusts, *as* in your ignorance; [15]but as He who called you *is* holy, you also be holy in all *your* conduct, [16]because it is written, *"Be holy, for I am holy."*[a]

Gold is rarely found by itself. Usually it's mined with many other rocks and substances. So how did ancient miners separate the valuable from the worthless? They put everything into a large container and then set the container over a very hot flame. As the rocks heated, the impurities melted and separated from the gold. As the substance cooled, the impurities formed a crust that could be scraped off. The purifying process greatly increased the value of the gold.

1 Peter 1:7

[17]And if you call on the Father, who without partiality judges according to each one's work, conduct yourselves throughout the time of your stay *here* in fear; [18]knowing that you were not redeemed with corruptible things, *like* silver or gold, from your aimless conduct *received* by tradition from your fathers, [19]but with the precious blood of Christ, as of a lamb without blemish and without spot. [20]He indeed was foreordained before the foundation of the world, but was manifest in these last times for

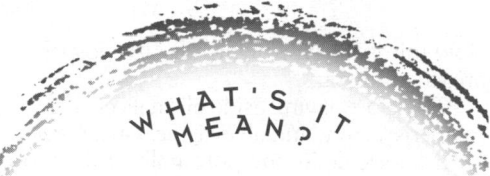

SALVATION
How was our salvation obtained? (1:18, 19)

1:8 [a]M-Text reads *known.*   **1:12** [a]NU-Text and M-Text read *you.*   **1:16** [a]Leviticus 11:44, 45; 19:2; 20:7

you ²¹who through Him believe in God, who raised Him from the dead and gave Him glory, so that your faith and hope are in God.

THE ENDURING WORD

²²Since you have purified your souls in obeying the truth through the Spirit*a* in sincere love of the brethren, love one another fervently with a pure heart, ²³having been born again, not of corruptible seed but incorruptible, through the word of God which lives and abides forever,*a* ²⁴because

" *All flesh is as grass,*
*And all the glory of man*a* as the flower of the grass.*
The grass withers,
And its flower falls away,
²⁵ *But the word of the LORD endures forever."*a*

Now this is the word which by the gospel was preached to you.

¹Therefore, laying aside all malice, all deceit, hypocrisy, envy, and all evil speaking, ²as newborn babes, desire the pure milk of the word, that you may grow thereby,*a* ³if indeed you have tasted that the Lord *is* gracious.

THE CHOSEN STONE AND HIS CHOSEN PEOPLE

⁴Coming to Him *as to* a living stone, rejected indeed by men, but chosen by God *and* precious, ⁵you also, as living stones, are being built up a spiritual house, a holy priesthood, to offer up spiritual sacrifices acceptable to God through Jesus Christ. ⁶Therefore it is also contained in the Scripture,

" *Behold, I lay in Zion*
A chief cornerstone, elect, precious,
*And he who believes on Him will by no means be put to shame."*a*

⁷Therefore, to you who believe, *He is* precious; but to those who are disobedient,*a*

" *The stone which the builders rejected*
*Has become the chief cornerstone,"*b*

⁸and

" *A stone of stumbling*
*And a rock of offense."*a*

On the Edge

But you are a chosen generation, a royal priesthood, a holy nation, His own special people, that you may proclaim the praises of Him who called you out of darkness into His marvelous light (1 Pet. 2:9).

When you don't know many other people who want to follow Jesus, sometimes it's easy to think it's just the two of you—you and Jesus strolling down the road of life together. But God doesn't intend for things to stay that way. He has something in mind for all the people who love Him, not just as individuals, but as a group. All of us together are His holy nation—just like when the nation of Israel belonged to Him in Old Testament times.

What that means to you is that you're not alone. You're part of a group of people known as Christians and they're available to help you, to be your friends, and to serve the Lord along with you. If you're feeling lonely, look for other people your age who really want to know God and do what He says. And don't stop there. God's holy nation is made up of adults and children, too. Find some grown-ups who have won out over some of the challenges you're facing now. Keep an eye out for little kids who might need to know what you had to learn the hard way. Make friends with elderly people whose eyes sparkle with the love of Jesus, and listen to what they have to say.

As a person, you are so incredibly valuable to God. You are also *part* of something valuable to Him—the holy nation that consists of the people who love Him. Let it be important to you, too.

SEE FOR YOURSELF:
Ex. 19:5, 6; Deut. 4:20; 14:2; Is. 43:20, 21; Titus 2:14

They stumble, being disobedient to the word, to which they also were appointed.

⁹But you *are* a chosen generation, a royal priesthood, a holy nation, His own special people, that you may proclaim the praises of Him

1:22 *a*NU-Text omits *through the Spirit.* 1:23 *a*NU-Text omits *forever.* 1:24 *a*NU-Text reads *all its glory.* 1:25 *a*Isaiah 40:6–8 2:2 *a*NU-Text adds *up to salvation.* 2:6 *a*Isaiah 28:16 2:7 *a*NU-Text reads *to those who disbelieve.* *b*Psalm 118:22 2:8 *a*Isaiah 8:14

who called you out of darkness into His marvelous light; ¹⁰who once *were* not a people but *are* now the people of God, who had not obtained mercy but now have obtained mercy.

against you as evildoers, they may, by *your* good works which they observe, glorify God in the day of visitation.

SUBMISSION TO GOVERNMENT

¹³Therefore submit yourselves to every ordinance of man for the Lord's sake, whether to the king as supreme, ¹⁴or to governors, as to those who are sent by him for the punishment of evildoers and *for the* praise of those who do good. ¹⁵For this is the will of God, that by doing good you may put to silence the ignorance of foolish men— ¹⁶as free, yet not using liberty as a cloak for vice, but as bondservants of God. ¹⁷Honor all *people.* Love the brotherhood. Fear God. Honor the king.

On the Edge

Beloved, I beg you as sojourners and pilgrims, abstain from fleshly lusts which war against the soul (1 Pet. 2:11).

Sometimes you can feel like a pilgrim or even an alien on this earth (or in your world) because you love Jesus. That's what a sojourner or a pilgrim is—someone who is just passing through on his way to a better place. A temporary resident. Pilgrims can be rejected because their beliefs are different from those of most people around them. If you're trying to live for Jesus, you may have already felt that way.

Do you pray before your meals in public? If you do, then you know that almost no one else does. Do you tell your friends "no thanks" when they invite you to an out-of-control party? Maybe you don't even get invited anymore because they know it's not your scene. Have you been dumped by someone because you chose not to have sex before marriage? You made the right choice, but it may have made you feel like an alien.

Peter says that a part of being Christlike is continually holding yourself back from the "fleshly lusts"—the sinful pulls of the world. When you hold back or stand apart, then you've become the sojourner or pilgrim Peter is talking about. Take comfort though. Even when you are living here on earth, it is not your home. You have a home in heaven that is so far beyond the beauty and comfort of this world. You'll never feel like a stranger there. You'll be known and loved and respected. You'll be among friends.

SEE FOR YOURSELF:
1 Cor. 2:12; Phil. 3:20; Heb. 11:13

On the Edge

For this is commendable, if because of conscience toward God one endures grief, suffering wrongfully. For what credit is it if, when you are beaten for your faults, you take it patiently? But when you do good and suffer, if you take it patiently, this is commendable before God (1 Pet. 2:19, 20).

Your world can be really cruel sometimes. You do the absolute most right thing, and they laugh, or snicker behind your back, or leave you out. They treat you that way out of their own insecurity. The light of Christ in you shines on their dark lives and they probably feel ashamed. Don't let their attitudes hinder your loyalty to Christ. Keep loving Him visibly.

These verses say that your loyalty to God counts for something with Him. He notices when people make fun of you because of Him. Trust Him and ask Him to make you strong. Keep doing the right thing, and keep the faith that God will bless all your right choices. Maybe your friends will grow up. Maybe they won't. Either way, you must know that God is so proud of you. He commends your actions. He sees the battles you fight because of Him. He will never turn away from you.

SEE FOR YOURSELF:
Ps. 119:157; Matt. 5:10; Rom. 12:14; 2 Tim. 3:12

LIVING BEFORE THE WORLD

¹¹Beloved, I beg *you* as sojourners and pilgrims, abstain from fleshly lusts which war against the soul, ¹²having your conduct honorable among the Gentiles, that when they speak

SUBMISSION TO MASTERS

[18]Servants, *be* submissive to *your* masters with all fear, not only to the good and gentle, but also to the harsh. [19]For this *is* commendable, if because of conscience toward God one endures grief, suffering wrongfully. [20]For what credit *is it* if, when you are beaten for your faults, you take it patiently? But when you do good and suffer, if you take it patiently, this *is* commendable before God. [21]For to this you were called, because Christ also suffered for us,[a] leaving us[b] an example, that you should follow His steps:

> [22] "Who committed no sin,
>   Nor was deceit found in His mouth";[a]

[23]who, when He was reviled, did not revile in return; when He suffered, He did not threaten, but committed *Himself* to Him who judges righteously; [24]who Himself bore our sins in His own body on the tree, that we, having died to sins, might live for righteousness—by whose stripes you were healed. [25]For you were like sheep going astray, but have now returned to the Shepherd and Overseer[a] of your souls.

SUBMISSION TO HUSBANDS

[1]Wives, likewise, *be* submissive to your own husbands, that even if some do not obey the word, they, without a word, may be won by the conduct of their wives, [2]when they observe your chaste conduct *accompanied* by fear. [3]Do not let your adornment be *merely* outward—arranging the hair, wearing gold, or putting on *fine* apparel—[4]rather *let it be* the hidden person of the heart, with the incorruptible *beauty* of a gentle and quiet spirit, which is very precious in the sight of God. [5]For in this manner, in former times, the holy women who trusted in God also adorned themselves, being submissive to their own husbands, [6]as Sarah obeyed Abraham, calling him lord, whose daughters you are if you do good and are not afraid with any terror.

A WORD TO HUSBANDS

[7]Husbands, likewise, dwell with *them* with understanding, giving honor to the wife, as to the weaker vessel, and as *being* heirs together of the grace of life, that your prayers may not be hindered.

CALLED TO BLESSING

[8]Finally, all *of you be* of one mind, having compassion for one another; love as brothers, *be* tenderhearted, *be* courteous;[a] [9]not returning evil for evil or reviling for reviling, but on the contrary blessing, knowing that you were called to this, that you may inherit a blessing. [10]For

---

REVENGE

Whose life should we look to when we are tempted to get revenge on someone? (2:21–23)

On the Edge

Do not let your adornment be merely outward—arranging the hair, wearing gold, or putting on fine apparel—rather let it be the hidden person of the heart, with the incorruptible beauty of a gentle and quiet spirit, which is very precious in the sight of God (1 Pet. 3:3, 4).

Peter says that beauty has more to do with your inside than your outside. God cares about your heart and your attitude more than the shape of your face or the color of your eyes. If you ask Him, God will reveal to you the beauty He created in you. He created you for a purpose. Your life gives Him such pleasure. He thinks you're beautiful. You are precious to Him. Can you see what He sees?

If you feel like God created you for something more than beauty contests, then begin to search and pray for His purpose. Ask Him to show you your strengths and help you use them. The most attractive people in the world are the ones who are confident about their purpose. They know what their life is supposed to be about, and they are hard at work to fulfill God's plan for them.

If you can't stand the way you look, then ask God to show you what He has in mind for you. Ask Him to make you into a person who looks into the mirror and likes the reflection. Focus on the awesome things He built into you. Ask Him to replace your insecurity with His purpose.

SEE FOR YOURSELF:
Is. 43:3, 4; Zeph. 3:17; 1 Tim. 2:8, 9

2:21 [a]NU-Text reads *you.* [b]NU-Text and M-Text read *you.*   **2:22** [a]Isaiah 53:9   **2:25** [a]Greek *Episkopos*
3:8 [a]NU-Text reads *humble.*

> "He who would love life
> And see good days,
> Let him refrain his tongue from evil,
> And his lips from speaking deceit.
> 11 Let him turn away from evil and do good;
> Let him seek peace and pursue it.
> 12 For the eyes of the LORD are on the righteous,
> And His ears are open to their prayers;
> But the face of the LORD is against those who do evil."[a]

SUFFERING FOR RIGHT AND WRONG

13 And who is he who will harm you if you become followers of what is good? 14 But even if you should suffer for righteousness' sake, you are blessed. "And do not be afraid of their threats, nor be troubled."[a] 15 But sanctify the Lord God[a] in your hearts, and always be ready to give a defense to everyone who asks you a reason for the hope that is in you, with meekness and fear; 16 having a good conscience, that when they defame you as evildoers, those who revile your good conduct in Christ may be ashamed. 17 For it is better, if it is the will of God, to suffer for doing good than for doing evil.

CHRIST'S SUFFERING AND OURS

18 For Christ also suffered once for sins, the just for the unjust, that He might bring us[a] to God, being put to death in the flesh but made alive by the Spirit, 19 by whom also He went and preached to the spirits in prison, 20 who formerly were disobedient, when once the Divine longsuffering waited[a] in the days of Noah, while the ark was being prepared, in which a few, that is, eight souls, were saved through water. 21 There is also an antitype which now saves us—baptism (not the removal of the filth of the flesh, but the answer of a good conscience toward God), through the resurrection of Jesus Christ, 22 who has gone into heaven and is at the right hand of God, angels and authorities and powers having been made subject to Him.

1 Therefore, since Christ suffered for us[a] in the flesh, arm yourselves also with the same mind, for he who has suffered in the flesh has ceased from sin, 2 that he no longer should live

3:12 [a]Psalm 34:12–16   **3:14** [a]Isaiah 8:12   **3:15** [a]NU-Text reads *Christ as Lord.*   **3:18** [a]NU-Text and M-Text read *you.*   **3:20** [a]NU-Text and M-Text read *when the longsuffering of God waited patiently.*   **4:1** [a]NU-Text omits *for us.*

Promise   HE PROMISES TO LISTEN TO YOU.

For the eyes of the LORD are on the righteous, and His ears are open to their prayers; but the face of the LORD is against those who do evil" (1 Pet. 3:12).

Maybe you've picked up your Bible today hoping it'll make a little sense out of what you're going through, give you a reason to think God cares whether you live or die.

You've tried praying. But you've wondered if it does any good. You feel like you're just launching words into dead air and thinking they'll magically make a difference.

Why talk when no one's listening?

The guy who wrote this particular book knew the feeling. Rough-and-tumble Peter, sidekick to a mysterious traveling man from Nazareth named Jesus, saw everything he dreamed about blow up in his face as his Lord was led away to die. This is what he gave up a good-paying job for? Ridicule? Embarrassment? Maybe even the end of his life?

"Why me, God?" he must have cried into the heavens. His words seemed to clank against an iron sky and landed back at his feet with an empty thud.

But God *was* listening—and doing something more loving than an easy answer would have done. He was letting Peter do some searching, giving him room to stretch beyond his own strength, to prove to himself that his faith was in God and not in his blessings.

Your ceiling may seem dark and silent. But God *is* watching. And listening. And waiting. And working. And one day, you'll wonder why you thought He wasn't.

SEE FOR YOURSELF:
Ps. 5:3; John 11:42

the rest of *his* time in the flesh for the lusts of men, but for the will of God. ³For we *have spent* enough of our past lifetime*ᵃ* in doing the will of the Gentiles—when we walked in lewdness, lusts, drunkenness, revelries, drinking parties, and abominable idolatries. ⁴In regard to these, they think it strange that you do not run with *them* in the same flood of dissipation, speaking evil of *you.* ⁵They will give an account to Him who is ready to judge the living and the dead. ⁶For this reason the gospel was preached also to those who are dead, that they might be judged according to men in the flesh, but live according to God in the spirit.

SERVING FOR GOD'S GLORY

⁷But the end of all things is at hand; therefore be serious and watchful in your prayers. ⁸And above all things have fervent love for one another, for *"love will cover a multitude of sins."ᵃ* ⁹*Be* hospitable to one another without grumbling. ¹⁰As each one has received a gift, minister it to one another, as good stewards of the manifold grace of God. ¹¹If anyone speaks, *let him speak* as the oracles of God. If anyone ministers, *let him do it* as with the ability which God supplies, that in all things God may be glorified through Jesus Christ, to whom belong the glory and the dominion forever and ever. Amen.

Hospitality was a way of life in biblical times. Throughout the Bible, God's people are commanded to show kindness to visitors. In the early days of Christianity, people were constantly traveling from town to town to share the message about Jesus and to encourage fellow believers. The apostles and preachers of that time depended on the kindness of strangers for food, housing, and even protection from angry mobs who didn't want them teaching about Jesus.
1 Peter 4:9

SUFFERING FOR GOD'S GLORY

¹²Beloved, do not think it strange concerning the fiery trial which is to try you, as though

On the Edge

As each one has received a gift, minister it to one another, as good stewards of the manifold grace of God (1 Pet. 4:10).

Peter says "each one" has something he or she does well—a gift. You might have a hard time believing that. Maybe you think you don't have anything to offer because, as people say, you're "just a teenager." Maybe you think you can't give much because you still have a lot to learn. Maybe self-confidence just isn't your thing. But Peter isn't just telling you what he thinks here; he's telling you what God thinks. So even if you think, *Well, that's not for me,* you can buy it because it's God's Word.

In verse 11, Peter gives two examples of God's gifts. Paul listed others in his letters to various churches (see Rom. 12:6–8; 1 Cor. 12:7–11; Eph. 4:11). It might not be a good idea, though, to comb through the lists to look for a label to pin on yourself. Instead, pay attention to the opportunities God brings your way.

Do everything He wants you to do. Pretty soon you'll discover what gift He's given you. Whatever your gift is, give it all you've got. Don't do it looking for a pat on the back. Peter says to use your gift to "minister it to one another." In other words, do what you do to make life better for other people. Do it because you love God. Do it because—in your heart—you really want to help and serve the people God loves. Be available for Him to love them through you.

SEE FOR YOURSELF:
1 Cor. 12:27–31;
1 Tim. 4:14;
2 Tim. 1:6, 7;
James 1:17

some strange thing happened to you; ¹³but rejoice to the extent that you partake of Christ's sufferings, that when His glory is revealed, you may also be glad with exceeding joy. ¹⁴If you are reproached for the name of Christ, blessed *are you*, for the Spirit of glory and of God rests upon you.*ᵃ* On their part He is blasphemed, but on your part He is glorified. ¹⁵But let none of you suffer as a murderer, a thief, an evildoer, or as a busybody in other people's matters. ¹⁶Yet if

4:3 *ᵃ*NU-Text reads *time.*   **4:8** *ᵃ*Proverbs 10:12   **4:14** *ᵃ*NU-Text omits the rest of this verse.

anyone *suffers* as a Christian, let him not be ashamed, but let him glorify God in this matter.*a*

[17]For the time *has come* for judgment to begin at the house of God; and if *it begins* with us first, what will *be* the end of those who do not obey the gospel of God? [18]Now

> *"If the righteous one is scarcely saved,*
> *Where will the ungodly and the sinner*
> *appear?"* *a*

[19]Therefore let those who suffer according to the will of God commit their souls *to Him* in doing good, as to a faithful Creator.

On the Edge

Casting all your care upon Him,
for He cares for you (1 Pet. 5:7).

Have you ever felt like nobody cared? Maybe you feel like that now. Well, the good news is that Jesus *does* care! It doesn't matter what kind of situation you are going through, or what anyone else says. God is concerned with your problems. Not only that, God is concerned with *everything* about you. He is the One who created you, and He knows what makes you tick better than you do. So let go of your worries by giving them to Him.

Paul tells us in Philippians 4:6, 7 not to worry, but to pray about everything. After you pray, start thanking God for answering those prayers. He goes on to tell us that, after we do this, God will bless us with peace. If you need peace in the midst of a situation, all you need to do is go to Him in prayer.

Look carefully at the last words of 1 Peter 5:7, "for He cares for you." One of the key words here is that little preposition *for*. God cares in your place. He cares so you don't have to. He does it *for* you. So let Him have your concerns. He'll do a better job with them than you will!

SEE FOR YOURSELF:
Ps. 50:15; 118:6;
Matt. 6:31, 32;
Luke 12:25, 26

SHEPHERD THE FLOCK

[1]The elders who are among you I exhort, I who am a fellow elder and a witness of the sufferings of Christ, and also a partaker of the glory that will be revealed: [2]Shepherd the flock of God which is among you, serving as overseers, not by compulsion but willingly,*a* not for dishonest gain but eagerly; [3]nor as being lords over those entrusted to you, but being examples to the flock; [4]and when the Chief Shepherd appears, you will receive the crown of glory that does not fade away.

SUBMIT TO GOD, RESIST THE DEVIL

[5]Likewise you younger people, submit yourselves to *your* elders. Yes, all of *you* be submissive to one another, and be clothed with humility, for

> *"God resists the proud,*
> *But gives grace to the humble."* *a*

[6]Therefore humble yourselves under the mighty hand of God, that He may exalt you in due time, [7]casting all your care upon Him, for He cares for you.

[8]Be sober, be vigilant; because*a* your adversary the devil walks about like a roaring lion, seeking whom he may devour. [9]Resist him, steadfast in the faith, knowing that the same sufferings are experienced by your brotherhood in the world. [10]But may*a* the God of all grace, who called us*b* to His eternal glory by Christ Jesus,

Who are Satan's enemies? (5:8)

after you have suffered a while, perfect, establish, strengthen, and settle *you.* [11]To Him *be* the glory and the dominion forever and ever. Amen.

FAREWELL AND PEACE

[12]By Silvanus, our faithful brother as I consider him, I have written to you briefly, exhorting and testifying that this is the true grace of God in which you stand.

[13]She who is in Babylon, elect together with *you,* greets you; and *so does* Mark my son. [14]Greet one another with a kiss of love.

Peace to you all who are in Christ Jesus. Amen.

4:16 *a*NU-Text reads *name.* **4:18** *a*Proverbs 11:31 **5:2** *a*NU-Text adds *according to God.* **5:5** *a*Proverbs 3:34 **5:8** *a*NU-Text and M-Text omit *because.* **5:10** *a*NU-Text reads *But the God of all grace . . . will perfect, establish, strengthen, and settle you.* *b*NU-Text and M-Text read *you.*

GREETING THE FAITHFUL

[1]Simon Peter, a bondservant and apostle of Jesus Christ,

To those who have obtained like precious faith with us by the righteousness of our God and Savior Jesus Christ:

[2]Grace and peace be multiplied to you in the knowledge of God and of Jesus our Lord, [3]as His divine power has given to us all things that *pertain* to life and godliness, through the knowledge of Him who called us by glory and virtue, [4]by which have been given to us exceedingly great and precious promises, that through these you may be partakers of the divine nature, having escaped the corruption *that is* in the world through lust.

FRUITFUL GROWTH IN THE FAITH

[5]But also for this very reason, giving all diligence, add to your faith virtue, to virtue knowledge, [6]to knowledge self-control, to self-control perseverance, to perseverance godliness, [7]to godliness brotherly kindness, and to brotherly kindness love. [8]For if these things are yours and abound, *you will be* neither barren nor unfruitful in the knowledge of our Lord Jesus Christ. [9]For he who lacks these things is shortsighted, even to blindness, and has forgotten that he was cleansed from his old sins. [10]Therefore, brethren, be even more diligent to make your call and election sure, for if you do these things you will never stumble; [11]for so an entrance will be supplied to you abundantly into the everlasting kingdom of our Lord and Savior Jesus Christ.

PETER'S APPROACHING DEATH

[12]For this reason I will not be negligent to remind you always of these things, though you know and are established in the present truth. [13]Yes, I think it is right, as long as I am in this tent, to stir you up by reminding *you*, [14]knowing that shortly I *must* put off my tent, just as our Lord Jesus Christ showed me. [15]Moreover I will be careful to ensure that you always have a reminder of these things after my decease.

THE TRUSTWORTHY PROPHETIC WORD

[16]For we did not follow cunningly devised fables when we made known to you the power and coming of our Lord Jesus Christ, but were eyewitnesses of His majesty. [17]For He received from God the Father honor and glory when

On the Edge

But also for this very reason, giving all diligence, add to your faith virtue, to virtue knowledge, to knowledge self-control, to self-control perseverance, to perseverance godliness, to godliness brotherly kindness, and to brotherly kindness love. For if these things are yours and abound, you will be neither barren nor unfruitful in the knowledge of our Lord Jesus Christ (2 Pet. 1:5–8).

This passage is talking about improving your faith. When you improve your faith by adding the qualities in these verses, you're developing character. You develop character one step at a time, one day at a time, one decision at a time. It's like building a house by putting one brick on top of another. A lot of Christians are running themselves ragged doing things *for* God, but they may not be doing anything in their walk *with* God. They may not be adding anything to their faith. They just keep doing what they've always done—going to church, reading a devotion, praying before meals.

Peter challenges us to add some things to our faith—things that develop godly character. Faith is great, but it's got to grow. And you've got to add to your faith in order to grow. Part of improving your faith is finding ways to express it. You can do that with virtue, knowledge, self-control, perseverance, godliness, brotherly kindness, and love (vv. 5–7). You won't master these overnight, but you can commit to working on them. Character will develop in you and your faith will grow. You'll have substance and credibility in your life. You'll begin to look more and more like Jesus.

SEE FOR YOURSELF:
  Gal. 5:22, 23;
  Eph. 4:15, 16;
  2 Pet. 1:2; 3:18

such a voice came to Him from the Excellent Glory: "This is My beloved Son, in whom I am well pleased." [18]And we heard this voice which came from heaven when we were with Him on the holy mountain.

[19]And so we have the prophetic word confirmed,[a] which you do well to heed as a

1:19 [a]Or *We also have the more sure prophetic word.*

light that shines in a dark place, until the day dawns and the morning star rises in your hearts; [20]knowing this first, that no prophecy of Scripture is of any private interpretation,[a] [21]for prophecy never came by the will of man, but holy men of God[a] spoke *as they were* moved by the Holy Spirit.

WHAT'S IT MEAN?

Ever heard of the Transfiguration? It's a fancy name for the time Jesus took three of His disciples—Peter (the author of this book), James, and John—to a mountain for a memorable encounter. While the disciples watched, Jesus' appearance began to change. His clothes turned bright white. Then, without warning, Moses and Elijah—two of the most famous men in Jewish history—appeared and began talking with Jesus. To top it all off, a cloud passed overhead and a voice called out from within it, "This is My beloved Son, in whom I am well pleased. Hear Him!" (Matt. 17:5).

2 Peter 1:18

DESTRUCTIVE DOCTRINES

[1]But there were also false prophets among the people, even as there will be false teachers among you, who will secretly bring in destructive heresies, even denying the Lord who bought them, *and* bring on themselves swift destruction. [2]And many will follow their destructive ways, because of whom the way of truth will be blasphemed. [3]By covetousness they will exploit you with deceptive words; for a long time their judgment has not been idle, and their destruction does[a] not slumber.

DOOM OF FALSE TEACHERS

[4]For if God did not spare the angels who sinned, but cast *them* down to hell and delivered *them* into chains of darkness, to be reserved for judgment; [5]and did not spare the ancient world, but saved Noah, *one of* eight *people,* a preacher of righteousness, bringing in the flood on the world of the ungodly; [6]and turning the cit-

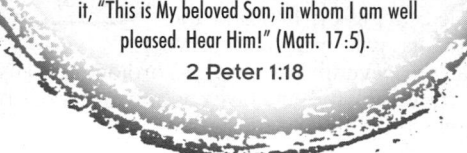

DISOBEDIENCE

What happened to the angels who followed Satan? (2:4)

ies of Sodom and Gomorrah into ashes, condemned *them* to destruction, making *them* an example to those who afterward would live ungodly; [7]and delivered righteous Lot, *who was* oppressed by the filthy conduct of the wicked [8](for that righteous man, dwelling among them, tormented *his* righteous soul from day to day by seeing and hearing *their* lawless deeds)— [9]*then* the Lord knows how to deliver the godly out of temptations and to reserve the unjust under punishment for the day of judgment, [10]and especially those who walk according to the flesh in the lust of uncleanness and despise authority. *They are* presumptuous, self-willed. They are not afraid to speak evil of dignitaries, [11]whereas angels, who are greater in power and might, do not bring a reviling accusation against them before the Lord.

DEPRAVITY OF FALSE TEACHERS

[12]But these, like natural brute beasts made to be caught and destroyed, speak evil of the things they do not understand, and will utterly perish in their own corruption, [13]*and* will receive the wages of unrighteousness, *as* those who count it pleasure to carouse in the daytime. *They are* spots and blemishes, carousing in their own deceptions while they feast with you, [14]having eyes full of adultery and that cannot cease from sin, enticing unstable souls. *They have* a heart trained in covetous practices, *and are* ac cursed children. [15]They have forsaken the right way and gone astray, following the way of Balaam the *son* of Beor, who loved the wages of unrighteousness; [16]but he was rebuked for his iniquity: a dumb donkey speaking with a man's voice restrained the madness of the prophet.

[17]These are wells without water, clouds[a] carried by a tempest, for whom is reserved the blackness of darkness forever.[b]

DECEPTIONS OF FALSE TEACHERS

[18]For when they speak great swelling *words* of emptiness, they allure through the lusts of the flesh, through lewdness, the ones who have actually escaped[a] from those who live in error. [19]While they promise them liberty, they themselves are slaves of corruption; for by whom a person is overcome, by him also he is brought into bondage. [20]For if, after they have escaped the pollutions of the world through the knowledge of the Lord and Savior Jesus Christ, they are again entangled in them and overcome, the latter end is worse for them than the beginning.

1:20 [a]Or *origin* **1:21** [a]NU-Text reads *but men spoke from God.* **2:3** [a]M-Text reads *will not.*
2:17 [a]NU-Text reads *and mists.* [b]NU-Text omits *forever.* **2:18** [a]NU-Text reads *are barely escaping.*

²¹For it would have been better for them not to have known the way of righteousness, than having known *it*, to turn from the holy commandment delivered to them. ²²But it has happened to them according to the true proverb: "*A dog returns to his own vomit*,"ᵃ and, "a sow, having washed, to her wallowing in the mire."

WHAT'S IT MEAN?

You can't imagine how important water was to the people of the ancient Near East. Their entire economy depended on successful crops, which, in turn, depended on sufficient rainfall. During the summer months, rain was virtually nonexistent. People had to rely on well water to nourish their crops. Drought wasn't the only problem ancient farmers faced in the summer, though. Windstorms that produced violent and destructive whirlwinds were also an occupational hazard.

2 Peter 2:17

GOD'S PROMISE IS NOT SLACK

¹Beloved, I now write to you this second epistle (in *both of* which I stir up your pure minds by way of reminder), ²that you may be mindful of the words which were spoken before by the holy prophets, and of the commandment of us,ᵃ the apostles of the Lord and Savior, ³knowing this first: that scoffers will come in the last days, walking according to their own lusts, ⁴and saying, "Where is the promise of His coming? For since the fathers fell asleep, all things continue as *they were* from the beginning of creation." ⁵For this they willfully forget: that by the word of God the heavens were of old, and the earth standing out of water and in the water, ⁶by which the world *that* then existed perished, being flooded with water. ⁷But the heavens and the earth *which* are now preserved by the same word, are reserved for fire

until the day of judgment and perdition of ungodly men.

⁸But, beloved, do not forget this one thing, that with the Lord one day *is* as a thousand years, and a thousand years as one day. ⁹The Lord is not slack concerning *His* promise, as some count slackness, but is longsuffering toward us,ᵃ not willing that any should perish but that all should come to repentance.

THE DAY OF THE LORD

¹⁰But the day of the Lord will come as a thief in the night, in which the heavens will pass away with a great noise, and the elements will melt with fervent heat; both the earth and the works that are in it will be burned up.ᵃ ¹¹Therefore, since all these things will be dissolved, what manner *of persons* ought you to be in holy conduct and godliness, ¹²looking for and hastening the coming of the day of God, because of which the heavens will be dissolved, being on fire, and the elements will melt with fervent heat? ¹³Nevertheless we, according to His promise, look for new heavens and a new earth in which righteousness dwells.

HEAVEN

Where is the home of righteousness? (3:13)

BE STEADFAST

¹⁴Therefore, beloved, looking forward to these things, be diligent to be found by Him in peace, without spot and blameless; ¹⁵and consider *that* the longsuffering of our Lord *is* salvation—as also our beloved brother Paul, according to the wisdom given to him, has written to you, ¹⁶as also in all his epistles, speaking in them of these things, in which are some things hard to understand, which untaught and unstable *people* twist to their own destruction, as *they do* also the rest of the Scriptures.

¹⁷You therefore, beloved, since you know *this* beforehand, beware lest you also fall from your own steadfastness, being led away with the error of the wicked; ¹⁸but grow in the grace and knowledge of our Lord and Savior Jesus Christ.

To Him *be* the glory both now and forever. Amen.

2:22 ᵃProverbs 26:11   **3:2** ᵃNU-Text and M-Text read *commandment of the apostles of your Lord and Savior* or *commandment of your apostles of the Lord and Savior.*   **3:9** ᵃNU-Text reads *you.*   **3:10** ᵃNU-Text reads *laid bare* (literally *found*).

1, 2 & 3 john

CONTENT

You know how sometimes you struggle to learn something, like a math problem or a foreign language? Then, something will "click" and you'll "get it"? It often takes one big concept and then we are on our way to a whole new level of understanding. For the disciple John (who once was called a "Son of Thunder"), that concept was love.

In his Gospel, many believe that John defined himself by the fact that Jesus loved him. It is no surprise that when he wrote to the church, the body of Christ, he most often wrote about love.

We can't really categorize John's letters as "love letters" because when we think of a "love letter" we think of a mushy kind of thing. John's letters weren't mushy. In fact, they were so strong that they have some of the most famous verses in the Bible.

In John's first letter he explores the doctrine of love. He basically expands on John 3:16 (possibly THE most famous verse in the Bible). In his second letter he encourages the church. In his third letter he encourages a friend.

John understood that when Christ came He showed us a whole new way to love God and to love each other. Understanding this kind of love turned John's life inside out. It can do the same for us.

Date of writing

A.D. 90 for 1, 2 and 3 John

Outline

1 John:
1:1–4	The Word of Life
1:5—2:6	God Is Light and Christ Is Our Example
2:7–17	The Old/New Commandment
2:18—3:10	The Enemies of Christ and God's Children
3:11—4:21	God's Love and Our Love
5:1–21	Jesus Overcomes the World

Purpose

To live in fellowship with God, obey His Word, and love His children.

Theme

Jesus Is the Son of God. Those Who Follow Him Must Live Righteously

Outline

2 John:
1–3	Greetings and Prayer
4–11	Walk in Truth and Love
12, 13	Final Greetings

Purpose

Truth is based on the fact that Jesus was both human and divine.

Theme

Warning About False Teachers

Outline

3 John:
1–4	Greetings to Gaius
5–12	The Importance of Working Together
13, 14	Final Greetings

Purpose

Total devotion to the truth of the Gospel is the key to the Christian life.

Theme

Practicing Hospitality Toward Genuine Christian Teachers

Bible Talk

Loving God

John teaches us a lesson. It's something we really should know anyway. We already understand this lesson when we are talking about loving each other. If someone says they love you but they treat you like dirt, you don't really believe they love you, do you? What if they say they love you, but they constantly do things that annoy you and even upset you? Do you really believe they love you?

John teaches us that we show our love for God by our obedience to Him. If we say we love God but we treat Him like He doesn't matter or constantly do things that upset Him, do we really love Him?

That's why obedience matters in love.

LOVING OTHERS

John doesn't just tell us to love people. He tells us why.

He doesn't tell us to love people because they are always lovable. They aren't. He doesn't tell us to love people just because God tells us to. He could have. He doesn't tell us to love people because they love us. Sometimes they don't.

What he tells us to do is to love people because God loved us. He even tells us to love people *the way* God loves us. The message God sent through John is simple: Obeying God means loving people—they go hand in hand.

WHAT WAS HEARD, SEEN, AND TOUCHED

[1]That which was from the beginning, which we have heard, which we have seen with our eyes, which we have looked upon, and our hands have handled, concerning the Word of life—[2]the life was manifested, and we have seen, and bear witness, and declare to you that eternal life which was with the Father and was manifested to us—[3]that which we have seen and heard we declare to you, that you also may have fellowship with us; and truly our fellowship is with the Father and with His Son Jesus Christ. [4]And these things we write to you that your[a] joy may be full.

FELLOWSHIP WITH HIM AND ONE ANOTHER

[5]This is the message which we have heard from Him and declare to you, that God is light and in Him is no darkness at all. [6]If we say that we have fellowship with Him, and walk in darkness, we lie and do not practice the truth. [7]But if we walk in the light as He is in the light, we have fellowship with one another, and the blood of Jesus Christ His Son cleanses us from all sin.

[8]If we say that we have no sin, we deceive ourselves, and the truth is not in us. [9]If we confess our sins, He is faithful and just to forgive us our sins and to cleanse us from all unrighteousness. [10]If we say that we have not sinned, we make Him a liar, and His word is not in us.

[1]My little children, these things I write to you, so that you may not sin. And if anyone sins, we have an Advocate with the Father, Jesus Christ the righteous. [2]And He Himself is the propitiation for our sins, and not for ours only but also for the whole world.

THE TEST OF KNOWING HIM

[3]Now by this we know that we know Him, if we keep His commandments. [4]He who says, "I know Him," and does not keep His commandments, is a liar, and the truth is not in him. [5]But whoever keeps His word, truly the love of God is perfected in him. By this we know that we are in Him. [6]He who says he abides in Him ought himself also to walk just as He walked.

[7]Brethren,[a] I write no new commandment to you, but an old commandment which you have had from the beginning. The old commandment is the word which you heard from the beginning.[b] [8]Again, a new commandment I write to you, which thing is true in Him and in you, because the darkness is passing away, and the true light is already shining.

[9]He who says he is in the light, and hates his brother, is in darkness until now. [10]He who loves his brother abides in the light, and there is no cause for stumbling in him. [11]But he who hates his brother is in darkness and walks in darkness, and does not know where he is going, because the darkness has blinded his eyes.

1:4 [a]NU-Text and M-Text read our.   2:7 [a]NU-Text reads Beloved.   [b]NU-Text omits from the beginning.

Promise — HE PROMISES TO BE YOUR ADVOCATE.

My little children, these things I write to you, so that you may not sin. And if anyone sins, we have an Advocate with the Father, Jesus Christ the righteous (1 John 2:1).

There's a certain sick feeling that comes after you've done something you shouldn't have done. Maybe it's dread or anger or guilt or shame or all of the above—and more—rolled into one big downer of depressing disgust.

But all you want to do is hide from God, to wait until the feeling passes, to go listen to some music or watch some TV and let your mind just go to mush. That's too bad, because Jesus is just waiting for you to call for help. He's waiting to pick you up with one nail-scarred hand, and hold the other one out before His Father—to show that the price has been paid, the debt has been canceled, the way of forgiveness has been paved with cleansing blood.

That's what an Advocate does. He's our counsel for the defense. Call Him up. He's ready and waiting right now.

SEE FOR YOURSELF: Rom. 8:34; Heb. 4:16; 7:25

THEIR SPIRITUAL STATE

12 I write to you, little children,
  Because your sins are forgiven you for
  His name's sake.
13 I write to you, fathers,
  Because you have known Him *who is*
  from the beginning.
  I write to you, young men,
  Because you have
  overcome the
  wicked one.
  I write to you, little
  children,
  Because you have
  known the Father.
14 I have written to you,
  fathers,
  Because you have
  known Him *who is*
  from the beginning.
  I have written to you, young men,
  Because you are strong, and the word
  of God abides in you,
  And you have overcome the wicked
  one.

DO NOT LOVE THE WORLD

15 Do not love the world or the things in the world. If anyone loves the world, the love of the Father is not in him. 16 For all that *is* in the world—the lust of the flesh, the lust of the eyes, and the pride of life—is not of the Father but is of the world. 17 And the world is passing away, and the lust of it; but he who does the will of God abides forever.

DECEPTIONS OF THE LAST HOUR

18 Little children, it is the last hour; and as you have heard that the[a] Antichrist is coming, even now many antichrists have come, by which we know that it is the last hour. 19 They went out from us, but they were not of us; for if they had been of us, they would have continued with us; but *they went out* that they might be made manifest, that none of them were of us. 20 But you have an anointing from the Holy One, and you know all things.[a] 21 I have not written to you because you do not know the truth, but because you know it, and that no lie is of the truth. 22 Who is a liar but he who denies that Jesus is the Christ? He is antichrist who denies the Father and the Son. 23 Whoever denies the Son does not have the Father either; he who acknowledges the Son has the Father also.

LET TRUTH ABIDE IN YOU

24 Therefore let that abide in you which you heard from the beginning. If what you heard

> "Behold what manner of love the Father has bestowed on us, that we should be called children of God!"
> (1 John 3:1a)

2:18 [a]NU-Text omits *the.*   2:20 [a]NU-Text reads *you all know.*

Promise   HE PROMISES THAT YOU WILL HAVE ETERNAL LIFE.

And this is the promise that He has promised us—eternal life (1 John 2:25).

Here is the most awesome promise in all of Scripture. Jesus Christ has promised us eternal life. Could anyone else keep that promise besides the Lord God Himself? Would you believe anyone else if they promised you the same thing? The magnificent truth is that no one else, living or dead, can offer you eternal life. Some other religions claim multiple lives or reincarnation for their followers, but where are their resurrected sons? There are none. The Resurrection of Christ is proof that He holds the power over death. The Resurrection is the basis of our faith and the proof that this promise is real. Only Jesus Christ gives eternal life. Your faith in Him will be rewarded. The reward is all the fellowship, love, and joy of heaven. Commit your heart and life to Christ. Decide that you're going to stick with Him—no matter what. Don't miss out on the best that God has for you. He'll change your life, your stuff, your circumstances; but best of all, He'll change *you* forever.

SEE FOR YOURSELF:
John 3:16; Titus 1:2; 1 John 5:9, 20

from the beginning abides in you, you also will abide in the Son and in the Father. ²⁵And this is the promise that He has promised us—eternal life.

²⁶These things I have written to you concerning those who *try to* deceive you. ²⁷But the anointing which you have received from Him abides in you, and you do not need that anyone teach you; but as the same anointing teaches you concerning all things, and is true, and is not a lie, and just as it has taught you, you will*ᵃ* abide in Him.

THE CHILDREN OF GOD

²⁸And now, little children, abide in Him, that when*ᵃ* He appears, we may have confidence and not be ashamed before Him at His coming. ²⁹If you know that He is righteous, you know that everyone who practices righteousness is born of Him.

¹Behold what manner of love the Father has bestowed on us, that we should be called children of God!*ᵃ* Therefore the world does not know us,*ᵇ* because it did not know Him. ²Beloved, now we are children of God; and it has not yet been revealed what we shall be, but we know that when He is revealed, we shall be like Him, for we shall see Him as He is. ³And everyone who has this hope in Him purifies himself, just as He is pure.

SIN AND THE CHILD OF GOD

⁴Whoever commits sin also commits lawlessness, and sin is lawlessness. ⁵And you know that He was manifested to take away our sins, and in Him there is no sin. ⁶Whoever abides in Him does not sin. Whoever sins has neither seen Him nor known Him.

⁷Little children, let no one deceive you. He who practices righteousness is righteous, just as He is righteous. ⁸He who sins is of the devil, for the devil has sinned from the beginning. For this purpose the Son of God was manifested, that He might destroy the works of the devil. ⁹Whoever has been born of God does not sin, for His seed remains in him; and he cannot sin, because he has been born of God.

SATAN

How did Jesus destroy Satan's work? (3:7, 8)

THE IMPERATIVE OF LOVE

¹⁰In this the children of God and the children of the devil are manifest: Whoever does not practice righteousness is not of God, nor *is* he who does not love his brother. ¹¹For this is the message that you heard from the beginning, that we should love one another, ¹²not as Cain *who* was of the wicked one and murdered his brother. And why did he murder him? Because his works were evil and his brother's righteous.

On the Edge

Behold what manner of love the Father has bestowed on us, that we should be called children of God! Therefore the world does not know us, because it did not know Him (1 John 3:1).

You might hear a preacher tell people they need to "make a decision" for Christ. It almost makes it sound like people can turn themselves into God's children. But John says something different. *God* is the One who makes you His child. He wanted you and chose you—even before you were born.

Now that might have you scratching your head. Didn't you "make a decision" for Christ? Didn't you decide to ask Him to forgive you of your sins and come to live in your heart? Yes, you did. You had to come to the place where you wanted to be a follower of Jesus. But the words you use to express your faith in Jesus and ask for God's forgiveness are not some kind of magic spell and now—poof!—you're a child of God. It isn't a formula you that you repeat three times and then you're saved.

No, there was nothing you did that made you God's child. Instead, when He looked inside your heart and saw real faith, *He* made you His child. He did it because He said He would. He did it because that's what He wanted to do all along.

SEE FOR YOURSELF:
Rom. 8:16; Gal. 4:4, 5; Eph. 1:5

---

¹³Do not marvel, my brethren, if the world hates you. ¹⁴We know that we have passed from death to life, because we love the brethren. He who does not love *his* brother*ᵃ* abides in death. ¹⁵Whoever hates his brother is a murderer,

---

and you know that no murderer has eternal life abiding in him.

THE OUTWORKING OF LOVE

[16]By this we know love, because He laid down His life for us. And we also ought to lay down *our* lives for the brethren. [17]But whoever has this world's goods, and sees his brother in need, and shuts up his heart from him, how does the love of God abide in him?

[18]My little children, let us not love in word or in tongue, but in deed and in truth. [19]And by this we know[a] that we are of the truth, and shall assure our hearts before Him. [20]For if our heart condemns us, God is greater than our heart, and knows all things. [21]Beloved, if our heart does not condemn us, we have confidence toward God. [22]And whatever we ask we receive from Him, because we keep His commandments and do those things that are pleasing in His sight. [23]And this is His commandment: that we should believe on the name of His Son Jesus Christ and love one another, as He gave us[a] commandment.

THE SPIRIT OF TRUTH AND THE SPIRIT OF ERROR

[24]Now he who keeps His commandments abides in Him, and He in him. And by this we know that He abides in us, by the Spirit whom He has given us.

[1]Beloved, do not believe every spirit, but test the spirits, whether they are of God; because many false prophets have gone out into the world. [2]By this you know the Spirit of God: Every spirit that confesses that Jesus Christ has come in the flesh is of God, [3]and every spirit that does not confess that[a] Jesus Christ has come in the flesh is not of God. And this is the *spirit* of the Antichrist, which you have heard was coming, and is now already in the world.

[4]You are of God, little children, and have overcome them, because He who is in you is greater than he who is in the world. [5]They are of the world. Therefore they speak *as* of the world, and the world hears them. [6]We are of God. He who knows God hears us; he who is not of God does not hear us. By this we know the spirit of truth and the spirit of error.

KNOWING GOD THROUGH LOVE

[7]Beloved, let us love one another, for love is of God; and everyone who loves is born of God and knows God. [8]He who does not love does not know God, for God is love. [9]In this the love of God was manifested toward us, that God has sent His only begotten Son into the world, that we might live through Him. [10]In this is love, not that we loved God, but that He loved us and sent His Son *to be* the propitiation for our sins. [11]Beloved, if God so loved us, we also ought to love one another.

SEEING GOD THROUGH LOVE

[12]No one has seen God at any time. If we love one another, God abides in us, and His love has been perfected in us. [13]By this we know that we abide in Him, and He in us, be-

On the Edge

He who does not love does not know God, for God is love (1 John 4:8).

If you say you love your friend, but spread rumors behind her back, then everyone else knows that you didn't really love her. Love is loyal. A dad may tell his kids that he loves them, but divorces their family and moves hundreds of miles away. No one in that family will feel very loved.

Love doesn't run when the going gets hard. You can tell the whole world that you love, but if no one can feel it or see it, then it probably doesn't exist. God is love. If you have a relationship with Him, then you will possess the love of God. Others will know that you are in love with God because His love will flow through you as you grow in Him. You will love others freely. You will forgive with grace. You'll be kind and gentle and merciful. When you have God, you have love because He *is* love. Verses 17 and 18 tell us that there is nothing to be afraid of. You don't have to fear the judgment or punishment of God because you belong to Him. So go for it—love the world like God loves you. There is nothing to lose and everything to gain. Relax and let Him love *you*. Others will trust in Christ and come to know Him because they have seen His love through you.

SEE FOR YOURSELF:
1 Cor. 13; Gal. 5:22, 23; Eph. 2:4–7; 1 John 4:7

3:19 [a]NU-Text reads *we shall know.*   **3:23** [a]M-Text omits *us.*   **4:3** [a]NU-Text omits *that* and *Christ has come in the flesh.*

cause He has given us of His Spirit. ¹⁴And we have seen and testify that the Father has sent the Son *as* Savior of the world. ¹⁵Whoever confesses that Jesus is the Son of God, God abides in him, and he in God. ¹⁶And we have known and believed the love that God has for us. God is love, and he who abides in love abides in God, and God in him.

who fears has not been made perfect in love. ¹⁹We love Him[a] because He first loved us.

OBEDIENCE BY FAITH

²⁰If someone says, "I love God," and hates his brother, he is a liar; for he who does not love his brother whom he has seen, how can[a] he love God whom he has not seen? ²¹And this commandment we have from Him: that he who loves God *must* love his brother also.

¹Whoever believes that Jesus is the Christ is born of God, and everyone who loves Him who begot also loves him who is begotten of Him. ²By this we know that we love the children of God, when we love God and keep His commandments. ³For this is the love of God, that we keep His commandments. And His commandments are not burdensome. ⁴For whatever is born of God overcomes the world. And this is the victory that has overcome the world—our[a] faith. ⁵Who is he who overcomes the world, but he who believes that Jesus is the Son of God?

On the Edge

We love Him because He first loved us. If someone says, "I love God," and hates his brother, he is a liar; for he who does not love his brother whom he has seen, how can he love God whom he has not seen? And this commandment we have from Him: that he who loves God must love his brother also (1 John 4:19–21).

Brothers and sisters can really test your ability to love. They know you so well. They know what makes you cringe and what makes you cry. They can understand you (sometimes) better than anyone else. They can irritate you to no end, but God says that if you love Him you *have* to love them. He says that if you don't, you're a liar. If you don't love the people you can see (the ones who share your bathroom, eat the last of your favorite snacks, and go through your things), then God says you can't possibly love Him, the One you haven't seen. Getting along with your brothers and sisters means you'll get lots of practice at forgiveness. The best thing that could happen is that you'll become really good friends with the people God put right in your home. He can do anything. So love and just watch Him!

SEE FOR YOURSELF:
Lev. 19:18; Matt. 22:39;
Gal. 5:13; Eph. 4:1–3;
1 Pet. 4:8; 2 John 5, 6

WHAT'S IT MEAN?

Christ is not Jesus' last name. It's from the Greek translation of the Hebrew word for "Messiah" or "Anointed One." In Old Testament times, kings, priests, and prophets were all anointed, which means they had olive oil poured on their heads to show that they were specially chosen by God. The Jews of Jesus' day believed that the Messiah would become their king and free them from the control of the Roman Empire. Jesus, however, came as a spiritual leader who freed the world from the effects of sin.

1 John 5:1

THE CERTAINTY OF GOD'S WITNESS

⁶This is He who came by water and blood—Jesus Christ; not only by water, but by water and blood. And it is the Spirit who bears witness, because the Spirit is truth. ⁷For there are three that bear witness in heaven: the Father, the Word, and the Holy Spirit; and these three are one. ⁸And there are three that bear witness

THE CONSUMMATION OF LOVE

¹⁷Love has been perfected among us in this: that we may have boldness in the day of judgment; because as He is, so are we in this world. ¹⁸There is no fear in love; but perfect love casts out fear, because fear involves torment. But he

---

4:19 ᵃNU-Text omits *Him.* **4:20** ᵃNU-Text reads *he cannot.* **5:4** ᵃM-Text reads *your.*

on earth:[a] the Spirit, the water, and the blood; and these three agree as one.

On the Edge

Now this is the confidence that we have in Him, that if we ask anything according to His will, He hears us. And if we know that He hears us, whatever we ask, we know that we have the petitions that we have asked of Him (1 John 5:14, 15).

If your job is getting the best of your homework, and you have to keep your job, then you need a God-solution. It's time to ask God for direction. You can be confident that He will listen. He does care about the details of your life.

In fact, your prayers have already been answered. Begin to pray specifically about what to do. Pray through the different options as they come up. Watch for God's answer. It may be a solution you haven't thought of before. It may require you to be more disciplined or more efficient. It may require more sacrifices. It may just mean you've got to rearrange your time. When you see where God is working, and where He is leading, then follow. Go with Him and praise Him for His interest in your life.

SEE FOR YOURSELF:
Deut. 28:6; Ps. 103:6;
John 14:16; Heb. 4:16

[9]If we receive the witness of men, the witness of God is greater; for this is the witness of God which[a] He has testified of His Son. [10]He who believes in the Son of God has the witness in himself; he who does not believe God has made Him a liar, because he has not believed the testimony that God has given of His Son. [11]And this is the testimony: that God has given us eternal life, and this life is in His Son. [12]He who has the Son has life; he who does not have the Son of God does not have life. [13]These things I have written to you who believe in the name of the Son of God, that you may know that you have eternal life,[a] and that you may *continue to* believe in the name of the Son of God.

CONFIDENCE AND COMPASSION IN PRAYER

[14]Now this is the confidence that we have in Him, that if we ask anything according to His will, He hears us. [15]And if we know that He hears us, whatever we ask, we know that we have the petitions that we have asked of Him.

[16]If anyone sees his brother sinning a sin *which does* not *lead* to death, he will ask, and He will give him life for those who commit sin not *leading* to death. There is sin *leading* to death. I do not say that he should pray about that. [17]All unrighteousness is sin, and there is sin not *leading* to death.

KNOWING THE TRUE—REJECTING THE FALSE

[18]We know that whoever is born of God does not sin; but he who has been born of God keeps himself,[a] and the wicked one does not touch him.

[19]We know that we are of God, and the whole world lies *under the sway of* the wicked one.

[20]And we know that the Son of God has come and has given us an understanding, that we may know Him who is true; and we are in Him who is true, in His Son Jesus Christ. This is the true God and eternal life.

[21]Little children, keep yourselves from idols. Amen.

5:8 [a]NU-Text and M-Text omit the words from *in heaven* (verse 7) through *on earth* (verse 8). Only four or five very late manuscripts contain these words in Greek.   **5:9** [a]NU-Text reads *God, that.*   **5:13** [a]NU-Text omits the rest of this verse.   **5:18** [a]NU-Text reads *him.*

GREETING THE ELECT LADY

The Elder,

[1]To the elect lady and her children, whom I love in truth, and not only I, but also all those who have known the truth, [2]because of the truth which abides in us and will be with us forever:

[3]Grace, mercy, *and* peace will be with you[a] from God the Father and from the Lord Jesus Christ, the Son of the Father, in truth and love.

WALK IN CHRIST'S COMMANDMENTS

[4]I rejoiced greatly that I have found *some* of your children walking in truth, as we received commandment from the Father. [5]And now I plead with you, lady, not as though I wrote a new commandment to you, but that which we have had from the beginning: that we love one another. [6]This is love, that we walk according to His commandments. This is the commandment, that as you have heard from the beginning, you should walk in it.

LOVE

What should Christians be known for? (5)

BEWARE OF ANTICHRIST DECEIVERS

[7]For many deceivers have gone out into the world who do not confess Jesus Christ *as* coming in the flesh. This is a deceiver and an antichrist. [8]Look to yourselves, that we[a] do not lose those things we worked for, but *that* we[b] may receive a full reward.

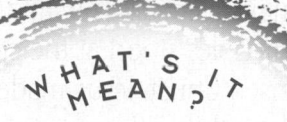

WHAT'S IT MEAN?

The deceivers that John warned about may have been Gnostics, a group of false teachers who plagued the early Christian church. The Gnostics believed that all physical matter was evil, so they refused to accept the fact that Jesus was God in human form.

2 John 7

[9]Whoever transgresses[a] and does not abide in the doctrine of Christ does not have God. He who abides in the doctrine of Christ has both the Father and the Son. [10]If anyone comes to you and does not bring this doctrine, do not receive him into your house nor greet him; [11]for he who greets him shares in his evil deeds.

JOHN'S FAREWELL GREETING

[12]Having many things to write to you, I did not wish *to do so* with paper and ink; but I hope to come to you and speak face to face, that our joy may be full.

[13]The children of your elect sister greet you. Amen.

3 [a]NU-Text and M-Text read *us.*   **8** [a]NU-Text reads *you.*   [b]NU-Text reads *you.*   **9** [a]NU-Text reads *goes ahead.*

JOHN THE APOSTLE made a difference

A fisherman one day, John was called by Jesus to become a fisher of men the next. He walked with and watched Jesus for three years. He alone of the disciples stood at the cross as Jesus died. He was among the first to see the risen Christ. Jesus made a difference in John's life; that's why John made such a difference in so many other lives.

John was probably the youngest of the original Twelve. He lived the longest. We owe him for five New Testament books: John, 1 John, 2 John, 3 John, and Revelation. God chose John to write about the greatest theme of all: God's love. John tells us God is love. He knew God's love firsthand. And the goal of John's writing was to convince readers about Jesus and help them to experience, through Him, God's love. "Behold what manner of love the Father has bestowed on us, that we should be called children of God!" (1 John 3:1a).

Cutting Edge

The love he experienced in Jesus Christ transformed John. It made such a difference in his life that he made a difference in countless others. Think for a moment about how many lives have been changed by these simple words first penned by John: "For God so loved the world that He gave His only begotten Son, that whoever believes in Him should not perish but have everlasting life" (John 3:16).

YOU can, too!

If John could speak to you right now, he would undoubtedly ask if you have ever personalized that verse you just read. Have you ever realized how far God's love went in sending Jesus? Have you believed that gift was for you? Have you accepted forgiveness and eternal life from Him? If you have, the biggest possible difference has begun in your Life. It will last beyond time.

Make sure you offer that difference-making message to others.

Want to know more? Read about John and the Jesus he loved in the Gospel of John as well as in the other Gospels and his other writings.

GREETING TO GAIUS

The Elder,

[1]To the beloved Gaius, whom I love in truth:

[2]Beloved, I pray that you may prosper in all things and be in health, just as your soul prospers. [3]For I rejoiced greatly when brethren came and testified of the truth *that is* in you, just as you walk in the truth. [4]I have no greater joy than to hear that my children walk in truth.[a]

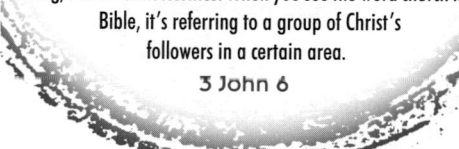

The "church" John describes in this verse is not the same kind of church you're used to. Church buildings as we know them today—places set aside specifically for Christian worship and Bible study—were not common until the third century. Before then, people met together in their homes to study Scripture and pray. Traveling teachers and missionaries moved from city to city, relying on the kindness of local Christians for food, housing, and other necessities. When you see the word *church* in the Bible, it's referring to a group of Christ's followers in a certain area.

3 John 6

GAIUS COMMENDED FOR GENEROSITY

[5]Beloved, you do faithfully whatever you do for the brethren and[a] for strangers, [6]who have borne witness of your love before the church. *If you send them forward on their journey in a manner worthy of God, you will do well,* [7]because they went forth for His name's sake, taking nothing from the Gentiles. [8]We therefore ought to receive[a] such, that we may become fellow workers for the truth.

DIOTREPHES AND DEMETRIUS

[9]I wrote to the church, but Diotrephes, who loves to have the preeminence among them, does not receive us. [10]Therefore, if I come, I will call to mind his deeds which he does, prating against us with malicious words. And not content with that, he himself does not receive the brethren, and forbids those who wish to, putting *them* out of the church.

[11]Beloved, do not imitate what is evil, but what is good. He who does good is of God, but[a] he who does evil has not seen God.

[12]Demetrius has a *good* testimony from all, and from the truth itself. And we also bear witness, and you know that our testimony is true.

FAREWELL GREETING

[13]I had many things to write, but I do not wish to write to you with pen and ink; [14]but I hope to see you shortly, and we shall speak face to face.

Peace to you. Our friends greet you. Greet the friends by name.

4 [a]NU-Text reads *the truth.*   5 [a]NU-Text adds *especially.*   8 [a]NU-Text reads *support.*
11 [a]NU-Text and M-Text omit *but.*

jude

CONTENT

Have you ever read a "letter to the editor" in the newspaper? Sometimes regular, everyday people (which means, not reporters) will write letters to the newspaper. They usually do this when they feel strongly about an issue and they want everyone to know how they feel. The Book of Jude is like one of those letters.

Jude was a man with a mission. Even though Christianity hadn't been around a long time (and maybe *because* of that), there were lots of people twisting and turning the truth of the Gospel to mean something totally different. Some were saying that Christianity was too simple, that there must be more to the Gospel than Jesus' life and death. Others were saying that Christianity was too hard, that with God's grace we didn't really have to worry at all anymore about obeying the law. There were so many fake stories out there that it was difficult to know who was telling the truth.

Jude had no patience for that kind of trickery and lying. He wrote his letter to the church to straighten out these kinds of deceptions and to remind them that what we do matters to God.

Outline

Purpose

Insulate yourselves from false teaching by growing in the faith.

Theme

Contending for the Faith

Date of writing

Early 60s A.D.

GREETING TO THE CALLED

[1]Jude, a bondservant of Jesus Christ, and brother of James,

To those who are called, sanctified[a] by God the Father, and preserved in Jesus Christ:

[2]Mercy, peace, and love be multiplied to you.

CONTEND FOR THE FAITH

[3]Beloved, while I was very diligent to write to you concerning our common salvation, I found it necessary to write to you exhorting you to contend earnestly for the faith which was once for all delivered to the saints. [4]For certain men have crept in unnoticed, who long ago were marked out for this condemnation, ungodly men, who turn the grace of our God into lewdness and deny the only Lord God[a] and our Lord Jesus Christ.

> "I found it necessary to write to you exhorting you to contend earnestly for the faith which was once for all delivered to the saints."
> (Jude 3)

OLD AND NEW APOSTATES

[5]But I want to remind you, though you once knew this, that the Lord, having saved the people out of the land of Egypt, afterward destroyed those who did not believe. [6]And the angels who did not keep their proper domain, but left their own abode, He has reserved in everlasting chains under darkness for the judgment of the great day; [7]as Sodom and Gomorrah, and the cities around them in a similar manner to these, having given themselves over to sexual immorality and gone after strange flesh, are set forth as an example, suffering the vengeance of eternal fire.

[8]Likewise also these dreamers defile the flesh, reject authority, and speak evil of dignitaries. [9]Yet Michael the archangel, in contending with the devil, when he disputed about the body of Moses, dared not bring against him a reviling accusation, but said, "The Lord rebuke you!" [10]But these speak evil of whatever they do not know; and whatever they know naturally, like brute beasts, in these things they corrupt themselves. [11]Woe to them! For they have gone in the way of Cain, have run greedily in the error of Balaam for profit, and perished in the rebellion of Korah.

HELL

What kind of place is hell? (7)

APOSTATES DEPRAVED AND DOOMED

[12]These are spots in your love feasts, while they feast with you without fear, serving only themselves. *They are* clouds without water, carried about[a] by the winds; late autumn trees without fruit, twice dead, pulled up by the roots; [13]raging waves of the sea, foaming up their own shame; wandering stars for whom is reserved the blackness of darkness forever.

[14]Now Enoch, the seventh from Adam, prophesied about these men also, saying, "Behold, the Lord comes with ten thousands of His saints, [15]to execute judgment on all, to convict all who are ungodly among them of all their ungodly deeds which they have committed in an ungodly way, and of all the harsh things which ungodly sinners have spoken against Him."

APOSTATES PREDICTED

[16]These are grumblers, complainers, walking according to their own lusts; and they mouth great swelling *words*, flattering people to gain advantage. [17]But you, beloved, remember the

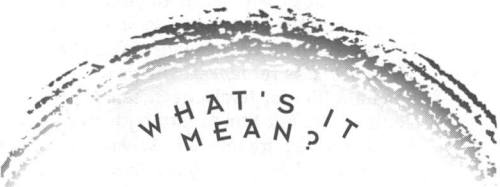

WHAT'S IT MEAN?

What did a person have to do to make this biblical "Hall of Shame"? Cain chose to worship God in his own way, rather than to follow the Lord's instructions. When his brother, Abel, received God's approval for his worship, Cain got jealous and killed Abel. Balaam, who had once been a prophet of God, deliberately led the Israelites into sin. Korah led a rebellion against Moses, God's chosen leader of the Israelites.

Jude 11

---

1 [a]NU-Text reads *beloved*.   **4** [a]NU-Text omits *God*.   **12** [a]NU-Text and M-Text read *along*.

words which were spoken before by the apostles of our Lord Jesus Christ: [18]how they told you that there would be mockers in the last time who would walk according to their own ungodly lusts. [19]These are sensual persons, who cause divisions, not having the Spirit.

MAINTAIN YOUR LIFE WITH GOD

[20]But you, beloved, building yourselves up on your most holy faith, praying in the Holy Spirit, [21]keep yourselves in the love of God, looking for the mercy of our Lord Jesus Christ unto eternal life.

[22]And on some have compassion, making a distinction;[a] [23]but others save with fear, pulling them out of the fire,[a] hating even the garment defiled by the flesh.

GLORY TO GOD

[24] Now to Him who is able to keep you[a]
         from stumbling,
     And to present you faultless
     Before the presence of His glory with
         exceeding joy,
[25] To God our Savior,[a]
     Who alone is wise,[b]
     Be glory and majesty,
     Dominion and power,[c]
     Both now and forever.
     Amen.

22 [a]NU-Text reads who are doubting (or making distinctions).   **23** [a]NU-Text adds and on some have mercy with fear and omits with fear in first clause.   **24** [a]M-Text reads them.   **25** [a]NU-Text reads To the only God our Savior. [b]NU-Text omits Who . . . is wise and adds Through Jesus Christ our Lord. [c]NU-Text adds Before all time.

Promise   HE PROMISES TO HELP YOU PRAY.

But you, beloved, building yourselves up on your most holy faith, praying in the Holy Spirit (Jude 20).

How's your prayer life? Stumbling, fumbling, falling asleep? Don't quite know where to start or how to end? Don't let your lack of practice keep you from spending time with Jesus. The Lord God promises to help you pray through the power of the Holy Spirit.

God is not impressed with big, long prayers or Bible-sounding words. He sees right through all that stuff, clear down to the bottom of your heart. He wants to know how you really feel. You can be totally honest with Him. (He already knows the truth anyway.) He won't be distracted, won't spread rumors, won't act like your stuff is stupid. He loves to hear from you, so speak to Him with reverence, in truth, and according to His will.

Try using the acrostic PRAY to guide your prayer time. *P* stands for *praise*. Spend the first part of your time with the Lord in praise and worship. You may pray through some verses in the Book of Psalms. You might sing some praise choruses. Be creative with your worship. The Holy Spirit will lead you. *R* is for *repent*. The next part of your prayer time is repentance. Tell God about your sin and ask Him for forgiveness. Talk to Him about turning from your sin and the habits you've fallen into. Ask Him for strength and character. Ask Him for the power to overcome temptation. *A* is *ask anything for anybody*. When Jesus prayed for other people, He prayed boldly. You can follow His example and pray boldly for your friends and family. Finally, *Y* is for *yourself*. Bring your concerns and needs to the Lord. Talk through your day and your plans. Ask Him to reveal His will for you today. Ask Him to go before you; then expect Him to be there.

Remember that the acrostic is PRAY, not YARP—the order is important. No matter how you choose to pray, the Holy Spirit promises to help you. Know that your prayers are important, and you will always be heard by the Father.

SEE FOR YOURSELF:
Rom. 8:26, 27; Eph. 6:18; Heb. 7:24, 25

revelation

CONTENT

If we could see the Book of Revelation instead of reading it, it would be a special effects extravaganza. Revelation is a book by John, the disciple, cataloguing a vision he was given of the end of the world. He describes heavenly things in earthly terms. Sometimes it gets pretty bizarre trying to imagine what a whole other dimension of life will look like.

Some of the images in Revelation are a mystery to this day. We won't recognize them until we see them for ourselves in the New Heaven and New Earth. But we do recognize enough of Revelation's message to know this: for now, God gives Satan and human evil some leeway in this world. There will come a day, though, when God will say, "Enough," and we all will be judged according to our faith and our works.

Revelation also teaches us that in the end, those who have their faith in Christ's righteousness will be invited into God's presence forever and Satan will be banished from the kingdom. It's a real and true happily-ever-after kind of story.

Outline

Purpose

God will surely judge sin and provide heaven for believers.

Theme

The Lord Our God the Almighty Reigns

Date of writing

A.D. 96

Bible Talk

The Rapture

The Bible teaches us that, at some point during the last years of the earth, Christ will return and we will be caught up with Him into the heavens. Most people call this the "rapture" even though most Bibles don't use that word.

We don't know exactly how the rapture will happen. Will our clothes be left in a pile on the floor? Will our bodies disappear? Will it be so quick that no one will notice?

The rapture and the other "end times" events can seem frightening sometimes. There is so much we don't know and even the things we do know lead us to more questions.

We have to remember, though, that God will take care of us. When it all happens, it will seem just right to us because God will be handling things.

SHOULD I TRY TO GUESS WHEN JESUS WILL RETURN?

You should be anticipating Christ's return. That means you should live your life so that you are ready to face Him at any moment. But the Bible clearly tells us that there is no way to figure out when Jesus will come back to earth. We may enjoy paying close attention to the prophecies of the Bible and the news headlines to see if we can spot when a prophecy is fulfilled. That's okay as long as we realize that some new information may come along that will force us to rethink the prophecy's meaning and fulfillment.

INTRODUCTION AND BENEDICTION

[1]The Revelation of Jesus Christ, which God gave Him to show His servants—things which must shortly take place. And He sent and signified *it* by His angel to His servant John, [2]who bore witness to the word of God, and to the testimony of Jesus Christ, to all things that he saw. [3]Blessed *is* he who reads and those who hear the words of this prophecy, and keep those things which are written in it; for the time *is* near.

GREETING THE SEVEN CHURCHES

[4]John, to the seven churches which are in Asia:

Grace to you and peace from Him who is and who was and who is to come, and from the seven Spirits who are before His throne, [5]and from Jesus Christ, the faithful witness, the first-born from the dead, and the ruler over the kings of the earth.

To Him who loved us and washed[a] us from our sins in His own blood, [6]and has made us kings[a] and priests to His God and Father, to Him *be* glory and dominion forever and ever. Amen.

[7]Behold, He is coming with clouds, and every eye will see Him, even they who pierced Him. And all the tribes of the earth will mourn because of Him. Even so, Amen.

[8]"I am the Alpha and the Omega, *the* Beginning and *the* End,"[a] says the Lord,[b] "who is and who was and who is to come, the Almighty."

VISION OF THE SON OF MAN

[9]I, John, both[a] your brother and companion in the tribulation and kingdom and patience of Jesus Christ, was on the island that is called Patmos for the word of God and for the testimony of Jesus Christ. [10]I was in the Spirit on the Lord's Day, and I heard behind me a loud voice, as of a trumpet, [11]saying, "I am the Alpha and the Omega, the First and the Last," and,[a] "What you see, write in a book and send *it* to the seven churches which are in Asia:[b] to Ephesus, to Smyrna, to Pergamos, to Thyatira, to Sardis, to Philadelphia, and to Laodicea."

[12]Then I turned to see the voice that spoke with me. And having turned I saw seven golden lampstands, [13]and in the midst of the seven lampstands *One* like the Son of Man, clothed with a garment down to the feet and girded about the chest with a golden band. [14]His head and hair *were* white like wool, as white as snow, and His eyes like a flame of fire; [15]His feet *were* like fine brass, as if refined in a furnace, and His voice as the sound of many waters; [16]He had in His right hand seven stars, out of His mouth went a sharp two-edged sword, and His countenance *was* like the sun shining in its strength. [17]And when I saw Him, I fell at His feet as dead. But He laid His right hand on me, saying to me,[a] "Do not be afraid; I am the First and the Last. [18]I *am* He who lives, and was dead, and behold, I am alive forevermore. Amen. And I have the keys of Hades and of Death. [19]Write[a] the things which you have seen, and the things which are, and the things which will take place after this. [20]The mystery of the seven stars which you saw in My right hand, and the seven golden lampstands: The seven stars are the angels of the seven churches, and the seven lampstands which you saw[a] are the seven churches.

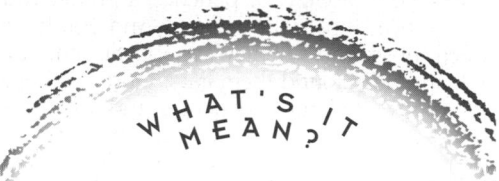

WHAT'S IT MEAN?

The Roman emperor Domitian wasn't exactly what you would call a friend of Christianity. As far as he was concerned, Christianity was an illegal religion, and those who practiced it were asking for persecution. Tradition has it that the apostle John was sentenced to live on the island of Patmos for eighteen months because he refused to stop preaching about Jesus. Don't assume that island life on Patmos was easy, either. People sentenced to the small, rocky island (about thirty-five miles off the coast of what is now Turkey) were forced to work in mines and quarries.

Revelation 1:9

THE LOVELESS CHURCH

[1]"To the angel of the church of Ephesus write,

'These things says He who holds the seven

1:5 [a]NU-Text reads *loves us and freed*; M-Text reads *loves us and washed*. **1:6** [a]NU-Text and M-Text read *a kingdom*. **1:8** [a]NU-Text and M-Text omit *the Beginning and the End*. [b]NU-Text and M-Text add *God*. **1:9** [a]NU-Text and M-Text omit *both*. **1:11** [a]NU-Text and M-Text omit *I am* through third *and*. [b]NU-Text and M-Text omit *which are in Asia*. **1:17** [a]NU-Text and M-Text omit *to me*. **1:19** [a]NU-Text and M-Text read *Therefore, write*. **1:20** [a]NU-Text and M-Text omit *which you saw*.

WHAT'S IT MEAN?

Any list of the major cities of the ancient world would have to include Ephesus. This bustling seaport city boasted a population of two hundred fifty thousand, a thriving business community, and an active religious culture—not to mention one of the seven wonders of the ancient world. The temple dedicated to the Roman goddess Diana was truly an architectural marvel. It also symbolized the pagan worship that went on in the city. The apostle Paul had started a church in Ephesus, and the apostle John had worked in the city for almost thirty years before being shipped off to Patmos.

Revelation 2:1

stars in His right hand, who walks in the midst of the seven golden lampstands: ²"I know your works, your labor, your patience, and that you cannot bear those who are evil. And you have tested those who say they are apostles and are not, and have found them liars; ³and you have persevered and have patience, and have labored for My name's sake and have not become weary. ⁴Nevertheless I have *this* against you, that you have left your first love. ⁵Remember therefore from where you have fallen; repent and do the first works, or else I will come to you quickly and remove your lampstand from its place—unless you repent. ⁶But this you have, that you hate the deeds of the Nicolaitans, which I also hate.

⁷"He who has an ear, let him hear what the Spirit says to the churches. To him who overcomes I will give to eat from the tree of life, which is in the midst of the Paradise of God." '

THE PERSECUTED CHURCH

⁸"And to the angel of the church in Smyrna write,

'These things says the First and the Last, who was dead, and came to life: ⁹I know your works, tribulation, and poverty (but you are rich); and *I know* the blasphemy of those who say they are Jews and are not, but *are* a synagogue of Satan. ¹⁰Do not fear any of those things which you are about to suffer. Indeed, the devil is about to throw *some* of you into prison, that you may be tested, and you will have tribulation ten days. Be faithful until death, and I will give you the crown of life.

¹¹"He who has an ear, let him hear what the Spirit says to the churches. He who overcomes shall not be hurt by the second death." '

On the Edge

And you have persevered and have patience, and have labored for My name's sake and have not become weary. Nevertheless I have this against you, that you have left your first love (Rev. 2:3, 4).

Jesus was talking to some people who had done great things for Him. They had worked hard and persevered; but in all of that, they somehow lost their first love for Him. You probably know people like that. They go to church all the time, wear Christian t-shirts, and scream "Jesus" really loud at concerts. But they're missing a passion for Him.

The Lord wants you to be known as a person who loves Him. He'd rather have you be known as a gentle, humble lover of God than as the most eloquent preacher who just sounds good. All kinds of things will tempt you to love them more than you love Jesus, but don't give in. Hold on tight to your love for Him. When other people walk away from an encounter with you, they should know one thing—that you have a passionate, fervent, fiery love for God that will not quit. You don't want them to know all the great things you've done for God. You want them to know that you know and love Him, that you're connected to Him, that He is number one in your life.

If you've gotten caught up in doing a bunch of stuff in the name of the Lord, slam on the brakes. Run into His presence. Pray and worship Him. Start listening to Him and hearing His voice. Let Him melt your heart again. Ask Him to rekindle your fire for Him. Your service is made great because your love for Him is great. Keep your passion burning for Him!

SEE FOR YOURSELF:
Deut. 6:4–6, 14, 15;
Josh. 23:11;
Matt. 22:36, 37

THE COMPROMISING CHURCH

¹²"And to the angel of the church in Pergamos write,

'These things says He who has the sharp

commit sexual immorality. ¹⁵Thus you also have those who hold the doctrine of the Nicolaitans, which thing I hate.[a] ¹⁶Repent, or else I will come to you quickly and will fight against them with the sword of My mouth.

¹⁷"He who has an ear, let him hear what the Spirit says to the churches. To him who overcomes I will give some of the hidden manna to eat. And I will give him a white stone, and on the stone a new name written which no one knows except him who receives *it*." '

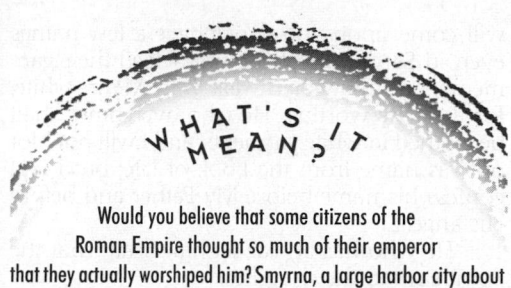

WHAT'S IT MEAN?

Would you believe that some citizens of the Roman Empire thought so much of their emperor that they actually worshiped him? Smyrna, a large harbor city about forty miles north of Ephesus, was the home of a temple built to honor the emperor Tiberius. The city became a center of emperor worship. Christians who chose not to join the pagan worship were severely persecuted. Today the city, which is located in Turkey, is known as Izmir.

Revelation 2:8

two-edged sword: ¹³"I know your works, and where you dwell, where Satan's throne *is*. And you hold fast to My name, and did not deny My faith even in the days in which Antipas *was* My faithful martyr, who was killed among you, where Satan dwells. ¹⁴But I have a few things against you, because you have there those who hold the doctrine of Balaam, who taught Balak to put a stumbling block before the children of Israel, to eat things sacrificed to idols, and to

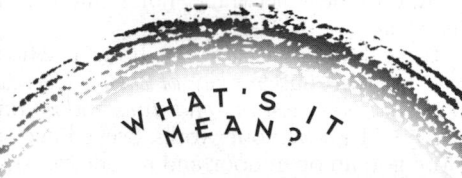

WHAT'S IT MEAN?

Purple was the color of choice for the citizens of Thyatira. The city, located about twenty miles southeast of Pergamos, was famous for the purple dye and cloth that was produced there. Because of Thyatira's focus on business and manufacturing, a number of trade unions were located there. When members of the union weren't discussing business in their meetings, they were usually worshiping pagan gods or committing sexual sins.

Revelation 2:18

THE CORRUPT CHURCH

¹⁸"And to the angel of the church in Thyatira write,

'These things says the Son of God, who has eyes like a flame of fire, and His feet like fine brass: ¹⁹"I know your works, love, service, faith,[a] and your patience; and *as* for your works, the last *are* more than the first. ²⁰Nevertheless I have a few things against you, because you allow[a] that woman[b] Jezebel, who calls herself a prophetess, to teach and seduce[c] My servants to commit sexual immorality and eat things sacrificed to idols. ²¹And I gave her time to repent of her sexual immorality, and she did not repent.[a] ²²Indeed I will cast her into a sickbed, and those who commit adultery with her into great tribulation, unless they repent of their[a] deeds. ²³I will kill her children with death, and all the churches shall know that I am He who searches the minds and hearts. And I will

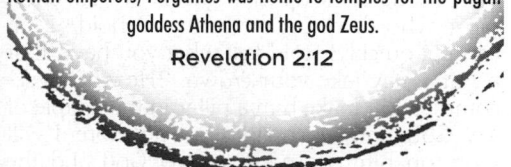

WHAT'S IT MEAN?

Pergamos was the capital of Asia—not the continent of Asia, but the Roman province of the same name. The city, located about fifty miles north of Smyrna, was known for its cultural and scientific communities. Pergamos boasted a library of about two hundred thousand volumes and a famous medical center. The city also offered a wide variety of pagan worship opportunities. In addition to its three temples dedicated to the Roman emperors, Pergamos was home to temples for the pagan goddess Athena and the god Zeus.

Revelation 2:12

2:15 [a]NU-Text and M-Text read *likewise* for *which thing I hate.* **2:19** [a]NU-Text and M-Text read *faith, service.* **2:20** [a]NU-Text and M-Text read *I have against you that you tolerate.* [b]M-Text reads *your wife Jezebel.* [c]NU-Text and M-Text read *and teaches and seduces.* **2:21** [a]NU-Text and M-Text read *time to repent, and she does not want to repent of her sexual immorality.* **2:22** [a]NU-Text and M-Text read *her.*

give to each one of you according to your works.

²⁴"Now to you I say, and* to the rest in Thyatira, as many as do not have this doctrine, who have not known the depths of Satan, as they say, I will* put on you no other burden. ²⁵But hold fast what you have till I come. ²⁶And he who overcomes, and keeps My works until the end, to him I will give power over the nations—

²⁷ 'He shall *rule them with a rod of iron;*
They shall be dashed to pieces like the
*potter's vessels'*ᵃ—

as I also have received from My Father; ²⁸and I will give him the morning star.

²⁹"He who has an ear, let him hear what the Spirit says to the churches." '

Sardis was what you might call a "recovering" city. Located about fifty miles east of Smyrna, the city of Sardis was destroyed by an earthquake in A.D. 17. The Roman emperor Tiberius helped rebuild the city. The citizens were so grateful that they built temples in his honor and made Sardis one of the centers for emperor worship in the Near East.

Revelation 3:1

THE DEAD CHURCH

¹"And to the angel of the church in Sardis write,

'These things says He who has the seven Spirits of God and the seven stars: "I know your works, that you have a name that you are alive, but you are dead. ²Be watchful, and strengthen the things which remain, that are ready to die, for I have not found your works perfect before God.ᵃ ³Remember therefore how you have received and heard; hold fast and repent. Therefore if you will not watch, I will come upon you as a thief, and you will not know what hour I

will come upon you. ⁴Youᵃ have a few names even in Sardis who have not defiled their garments; and they shall walk with Me in white, for they are worthy. ⁵He who overcomes shall be clothed in white garments, and I will not blot out his name from the Book of Life; but I will confess his name before My Father and before His angels.

⁶"He who has an ear, let him hear what the Spirit says to the churches." '

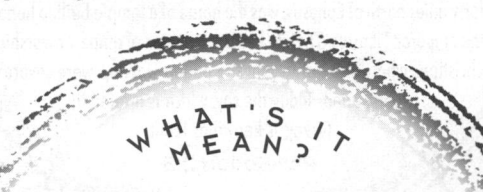

Philadelphia—no, not that Philadelphia—was located about seventy-five miles east of Ephesus. Like Sardis, Philadelphia had been damaged by an earthquake in A.D. 17. Today, the city is known as Allah-shehr, "the city of God." The ruins of many ancient Christian churches have been found there.

Revelation 3:7

THE FAITHFUL CHURCH

⁷"And to the angel of the church in Philadelphia write,

'These things says He who is holy, He who is true, "*He who has the key of David, He who opens and no one shuts, and shuts and no one opens*":ᵃ ⁸"I know your works. See, I have set before you an open door, and no one can shut it;ᵃ for you have a little strength, have kept My word, and have not denied My name. ⁹Indeed I will make *those* of the synagogue of Satan, who say they are Jews and are not, but lie—indeed I will make them come and worship before your feet, and to know that I have loved you. ¹⁰Because you have kept My command to persevere, I also will keep you from the hour of trial which shall come upon the whole world, to test those who dwell on the earth. ¹¹Behold,ᵃ I am coming quickly! Hold fast what you have, that no one may take your crown. ¹²He who overcomes, I will make him a pillar in the temple of My God, and he shall go out no more. I will write on him the name of My God and the name of the city of My God, the New Jerusalem, which comes down out of heaven from My God. And *I will write on him* My new name.

[13]"He who has an ear, let him hear what the Spirit says to the churches." '

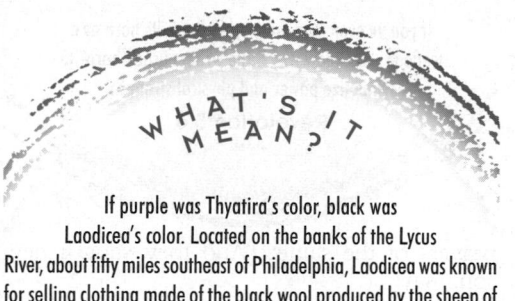

WHAT'S IT MEAN?

If purple was Thyatira's color, black was Laodicea's color. Located on the banks of the Lycus River, about fifty miles southeast of Philadelphia, Laodicea was known for selling clothing made of the black wool produced by the sheep of the region. The city survived until the Middle Ages, when it was destroyed by Muslims during the Crusades.

Revelation 3:14

THE LUKEWARM CHURCH

[14]"And to the angel of the church of the Laodiceans[a] write,

'These things says the Amen, the Faithful and True Witness, the Beginning of the creation of God: [15]"I know your works, that you are neither cold nor hot. I could wish you were cold or hot. [16]So then, because you are lukewarm, and neither cold nor hot,[a] I will vomit you out of My mouth. [17]Because you say, 'I am rich, have become wealthy, and have need of nothing'—and do not know that you are wretched, miserable, poor, blind, and naked—[18]I counsel you to buy from Me gold refined in the fire, that you may be rich; and white garments, that you may be clothed, *that* the shame of your nakedness may not be revealed; and anoint your eyes with eye salve, that you may see. [19]As many as I love, I rebuke and chasten. Therefore be zealous and repent. [20]Behold, I stand at the door and knock. If anyone hears My voice and opens the door, I will come in to him and dine with him, and he with Me. [21]To him who overcomes I will grant to sit with Me on My throne, as I also overcame and sat down with My Father on His throne.

[22]"He who has an ear, let him hear what the Spirit says to the churches." ' "

THE THRONE ROOM OF HEAVEN

[1]After these things I looked, and behold, a door *standing* open in heaven. And the first voice which I heard *was* like a trumpet speaking with me, saying, "Come up here, and I will show you things which must take place after this."

[2]Immediately I was in the Spirit; and behold, a throne set in heaven, and *One* sat on the throne. [3]And He who sat there was[a] like a jasper and a sardius stone in appearance; and *there was* a rainbow around the throne, in appearance like an emerald. [4]Around the throne *were* twenty-four thrones, and on the thrones I saw twenty-four elders sitting, clothed in white robes; and they had crowns[a] of gold on their heads. [5]And from the throne proceeded lightnings, thunderings, and voices.[a] Seven lamps of fire *were* burning before the throne, which are the[b] seven Spirits of God.

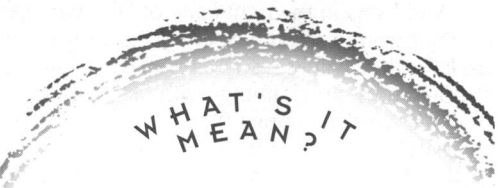

WHAT'S IT MEAN?

This isn't the first time these four bizarre creatures are mentioned in the Bible. The Old Testament prophet Ezekiel saw a very similar vision. Notice that each of the four looks like one of the most powerful creatures on earth—a man, a lion, a bull, and an eagle. Think about it. Human beings rule over every creature on earth. The lion is the king of the jungle. Bulls are the strongest tame animals. Eagles are the fastest, strongest birds.

Revelation 4:7

[6]Before the throne *there was*[a] a sea of glass, like crystal. And in the midst of the throne, and around the throne, *were* four living creatures full of eyes in front and in back. [7]The first living creature *was* like a lion, the second living creature like a calf, the third living creature had a face like a man, and the fourth living creature *was* like a flying eagle. [8]The four living creatures, each having six wings, were full of eyes around

---

3:14 [a]NU-Text and M-Text read *in Laodicea.*   **3:16** [a]NU-Text and M-Text read *hot nor cold.*   **4:3** [a]M-Text omits *And He who sat there was* (which makes the description in verse 3 modify the throne rather than God).
4:4 [a]NU-Text and M-Text read *robes, with crowns.*   **4:5** [a]NU-Text and M-Text read *voices, and thunderings.*
[b]M-Text omits *the.*   **4:6** [a]NU-Text and M-Text add *something like.*

and within. And they do not rest day or night, saying:

"Holy, holy, holy,[a]
Lord God Almighty,
Who was and is and is to come!"

[9]Whenever the living creatures give glory and honor and thanks to Him who sits on the throne, who lives forever and ever, [10]the twenty-four elders fall down before Him who sits on the throne and worship Him who lives forever and ever, and cast their crowns before the throne, saying:

[11] "You are worthy, O Lord,[a]
To receive glory and honor and power;
For You created all things,
And by Your will they exist[b] and were created."

THE LAMB TAKES THE SCROLL

[1]And I saw in the right *hand* of Him who sat on the throne a scroll written inside and on the back, sealed with seven seals. [2]Then I saw a strong angel proclaiming with a loud voice, "Who is worthy to open the scroll and to loose its seals?" [3]And no one in heaven or on the earth or under the earth was able to open the scroll, or to look at it.

[4]So I wept much, because no one was found worthy to open and read[a] the scroll, or to look at it. [5]But one of the elders said to me, "Do not weep. Behold, the Lion of the tribe of Judah, the Root of David, has prevailed to open the scroll and to loose[a] its seven seals."

[6]And I looked, and behold,[a] in the midst of the throne and of the four living creatures, and in the midst of the elders, stood a Lamb as though it had been slain, having seven horns and seven eyes, which are the seven Spirits of God sent out into all the earth. [7]Then He came and took the scroll out of the right hand of Him who sat on the throne.

WORTHY IS THE LAMB

[8]Now when He had taken the scroll, the four living creatures and the twenty-four elders fell down before the Lamb, each having a harp, and golden bowls full of incense, which are the

WHAT'S IT MEAN?

If you've ever seen an ox or bull use its horn as a weapon, you know why Bible writers used "horn" to symbolize power and physical strength.

Revelation 5:6

prayers of the saints. [9]And they sang a new song, saying:

"You are worthy to take the scroll,
And to open its seals;
For You were slain,
And have redeemed us to God by Your blood
Out of every tribe and tongue and people and nation,
[10] And have made us[a] kings[b] and priests to our God;
And we[c] shall reign on the earth."

[11]Then I looked, and I heard the voice of many angels around the throne, the living creatures, and the elders; and the number of them was ten thousand times ten thousand, and thousands of thousands, [12]saying with a loud voice:

"Worthy is the Lamb who was slain
To receive power and riches and wisdom,
And strength and honor and glory and blessing!"

[13]And every creature which is in heaven and on the earth and under the earth and such as are in the sea, and all that are in them, I heard saying:

"Blessing and honor and glory and power
Be to Him who sits on the throne,
And to the Lamb, forever and ever!"[a]

[14]Then the four living creatures said, "Amen!" And the twenty-four[a] elders fell down and worshiped Him who lives forever and ever.[b]

4:8 [a]M-Text has *holy* nine times.   **4:11** [a]NU-Text and M-Text read *our Lord and God.* [b]NU-Text and M-Text read *existed.*   **5:4** [a]NU-Text and M-Text omit *and read.*   **5:5** [a]NU-Text and M-Text omit *to loose.* **5:6** [a]NU-Text and M-Text read *I saw in the midst . . . a Lamb standing.*   **5:10** [a]NU-Text and M-Text read *them.* [b]NU-Text reads *a kingdom.* [c]NU-Text and M-Text read *they.*   **5:13** [a]M-Text adds *Amen.*   **5:14** [a]NU-Text and M-Text omit *twenty-four.* [b]NU-Text and M-Text omit *Him who lives forever and ever.*

FIRST SEAL: THE CONQUEROR

[1]Now I saw when the Lamb opened one of the seals;[a] and I heard one of the four living creatures saying with a voice like thunder, "Come and see." [2]And I looked, and behold, a white horse. He who sat on it had a bow; and a crown was given to him, and he went out conquering and to conquer.

SECOND SEAL: CONFLICT ON EARTH

[3]When He opened the second seal, I heard the second living creature saying, "Come and see."[a] [4]Another horse, fiery red, went out. And it was granted to the one who sat on it to take peace from the earth, and that *people* should kill one another; and there was given to him a great sword.

WHAT'S IT MEAN?

Because bread was served at almost every Jewish meal, wheat was considered a necessity of life. Usually only slaves and poor people ate barley, which was normally used as feed for livestock.

Revelation 6:6

THIRD SEAL: SCARCITY ON EARTH

[5]When He opened the third seal, I heard the third living creature say, "Come and see." So I looked, and behold, a black horse, and he who sat on it had a pair of scales in his hand. [6]And I heard a voice in the midst of the four living creatures saying, "A quart[a] of wheat for a denarius,[b] and three quarts of barley for a denarius; and do not harm the oil and the wine."

FOURTH SEAL: WIDESPREAD DEATH ON EARTH

[7]When He opened the fourth seal, I heard the voice of the fourth living creature saying, "Come and see." [8]So I looked, and behold, a pale horse. And the name of him who sat on it was Death, and Hades followed with him. And power was given to them over a fourth of the earth, to kill with sword, with hunger, with death, and by the beasts of the earth.

FIFTH SEAL: THE CRY OF THE MARTYRS

[9]When He opened the fifth seal, I saw under the altar the souls of those who had been slain for the word of God and for the testimony which they held. [10]And they cried with a loud voice, saying, "How long, O Lord, holy and true, until You judge and avenge our blood on those who dwell on the earth?" [11]Then a white robe was given to each of them; and it was said to them that they should rest a little while longer, until both *the number of* their fellow servants and their brethren, who would be killed as they *were,* was completed.

SIXTH SEAL: COSMIC DISTURBANCES

[12]I looked when He opened the sixth seal, and behold,[a] there was a great earthquake; and the sun became black as sackcloth of hair, and the moon[b] became like blood. [13]And the stars of heaven fell to the earth, as a fig tree drops its late figs when it is shaken by a mighty wind. [14]Then the sky receded as a scroll when it is rolled up, and every mountain and island was moved out of its place. [15]And the kings of the earth, the great men, the rich men, the commanders,[a] the mighty men, every slave and every free man, hid themselves in the caves and in the rocks of the mountains, [16]and said to the mountains and rocks, "Fall on us and hide us from the face of Him who sits on the throne and from the wrath of the Lamb! [17]For the great day of His wrath has come, and who is able to stand?"

THE SEALED OF ISRAEL

[1]After these things I saw four angels standing at the four corners of the earth, holding the four winds of the earth, that the wind should not blow on the earth, on the sea, or on any tree. [2]Then I saw another angel ascending from the east, having the seal of the living God. And he cried with a loud voice to the four angels to whom it was granted to harm the earth and the sea, [3]saying, "Do not harm the earth, the sea, or the trees till we have sealed the servants of our God on their foreheads." [4]And I heard the number of those who were sealed. One hundred *and* forty-four thousand of all the tribes of the children of Israel *were* sealed:

6:1 [a]NU-Text and M-Text read *seven seals.* **6:3** [a]NU-Text and M-Text omit *and see.* **6:6** [a]Greek *choinix;* that is, approximately one quart [b]This was approximately one day's wage for a worker. **6:12** [a]NU-Text and M-Text omit *behold.* [b]NU-Text and M-Text read *the whole moon.* **6:15** [a]NU-Text and M-Text read *the commanders, the rich men.*

5 of the tribe of Judah twelve thousand *were* sealed;[a]
of the tribe of Reuben twelve thousand *were* sealed;
of the tribe of Gad twelve thousand *were* sealed;

6 of the tribe of Asher twelve thousand *were* sealed;
of the tribe of Naphtali twelve thousand *were* sealed;
of the tribe of Manasseh twelve thousand *were* sealed;

7 of the tribe of Simeon twelve thousand *were* sealed;
of the tribe of Levi twelve thousand *were* sealed;
of the tribe of Issachar twelve thousand *were* sealed;

8 of the tribe of Zebulun twelve thousand *were* sealed;
of the tribe of Joseph twelve thousand *were* sealed;
of the tribe of Benjamin twelve thousand *were* sealed.

"Amen! Blessing and glory and wisdom, thanksgiving and honor and power and might, be to our God forever and ever. Amen."
(Revelation 7:12)

WHAT'S IT MEAN?

Palm branches were used as symbols of peace and victory in ancient times. People waved them in parades and celebrations. It must have been an impressive sight, considering the fact that most of the branches were six to eight feet long. The most famous biblical example of palm branch waving occurred when Jesus was greeted by the crowd in Jerusalem when He rode into town the week before His crucifixion.

Revelation 7:9

A MULTITUDE FROM THE GREAT TRIBULATION

9 After these things I looked, and behold, a great multitude which no one could number, of all nations, tribes, peoples, and tongues, stand-ing before the throne and before the Lamb, clothed with white robes, with palm branches in their hands, 10 and crying out with a loud voice, saying, "Salvation *belongs* to our God who sits on the throne, and to the Lamb!" 11 All the angels stood around the throne and the elders and the four living creatures, and fell on their faces before the throne and worshiped God, 12 saying:

> "Amen! Blessing and glory and wisdom,
> Thanksgiving and honor and power and might,
> *Be* to our God forever and ever.
> Amen."

13 Then one of the elders answered, saying to me, "Who are these arrayed in white robes, and where did they come from?"

14 And I said to him, "Sir,[a] you know."

So he said to me, "These are the ones who come out of the great tribulation, and washed their robes and made them white in the blood of the Lamb. 15 Therefore they are before the throne of God, and serve Him day and night in His temple. And He who sits on the throne will dwell among them. 16 They shall neither hunger anymore nor thirst anymore; the sun shall not strike them, nor any heat; 17 for the Lamb who is in the midst of the throne will shepherd them and lead them to living fountains of waters.[a] And God will wipe away every tear from their eyes."

HEAVEN
What will the focus of our attention be in heaven? (7:17)

SEVENTH SEAL: PRELUDE TO THE SEVEN TRUMPETS

1 When He opened the seventh seal, there was silence in heaven for about half an hour. 2 And I saw the seven angels who stand before God, and to them were given seven trumpets. 3 Then another angel, having a golden censer, came and stood at the altar. He was given much incense, that he should offer *it* with the prayers of all the saints upon the golden altar which

---

7:5 [a]In NU-Text and M-Text *were sealed* is stated only in verses 5a and 8c; the words are understood in the remainder of the passage. **7:14** [a]NU-Text and M-Text read *My lord.* **7:17** [a]NU-Text and M-Text read *to fountains of the waters of life.*

was before the throne. [4]And the smoke of the incense, with the prayers of the saints, ascended before God from the angel's hand. [5]Then the angel took the censer, filled it with fire from the altar, and threw *it* to the earth. And there were noises, thunderings, lightnings, and an earthquake.

[6]So the seven angels who had the seven trumpets prepared themselves to sound.

W H A T ' S I T
M E A N ?

Kids in ancient times who wanted to learn to play the trumpet had two choices: metal or bone. One type of trumpet, the shophar, was made of a ram's horn. Its loud blast, which could be heard a great distance away, was used to call soldiers into battle or to alert people of danger.

Revelation 8:6

FIRST TRUMPET: VEGETATION STRUCK

[7]The first angel sounded: And hail and fire followed, mingled with blood, and they were thrown to the earth.[a] And a third of the trees were burned up, and all green grass was burned up.

SECOND TRUMPET: THE SEAS STRUCK

[8]Then the second angel sounded: And *something* like a great mountain burning with fire was thrown into the sea, and a third of the sea became blood. [9]And a third of the living creatures in the sea died, and a third of the ships were destroyed.

THIRD TRUMPET: THE WATERS STRUCK

[10]Then the third angel sounded: And a great star fell from heaven, burning like a torch, and it fell on a third of the rivers and on the springs of water. [11]The name of the star is Wormwood. A third of the waters became wormwood, and many men died from the water, because it was made bitter.

FOURTH TRUMPET: THE HEAVENS STRUCK

[12]Then the fourth angel sounded: And a third of the sun was struck, a third of the moon, and a third of the stars, so that a third of them were darkened. A third of the day did not shine, and likewise the night.

[13]And I looked, and I heard an angel[a] flying through the midst of heaven, saying with a loud voice, "Woe, woe, woe to the inhabitants of the earth, because of the remaining blasts of the trumpet of the three angels who are about to sound!"

FIFTH TRUMPET: THE LOCUSTS FROM THE BOTTOMLESS PIT

[1]Then the fifth angel sounded: And I saw a star fallen from heaven to the earth. To him was given the key to the bottomless pit. [2]And he opened the bottomless pit, and smoke arose out of the pit like the smoke of a great furnace. So the sun and the air were darkened because of the smoke of the pit. [3]Then out of the smoke locusts came upon the earth. And to them was given power, as the scorpions of the earth have power. [4]They were commanded not to harm the grass of the earth, or any green thing, or any tree, but only those men who do not have the seal of God on their foreheads. [5]And they were not given *authority* to kill them, but to torment them *for* five months. Their torment *was* like the torment of a scorpion when it strikes a man. [6]In those days men will seek death and will not find it; they will desire to die, and death will flee from them.

W H A T ' S I T
M E A N ?

At first glance, the locust seems like a pretty unlikely creature of destruction. It looks like a large grasshopper with two sets of wings and a brown-colored body two to three inches long. Nothing to be worried about, right? Wrong. Locusts travel in swarms large enough to blot out the sun in the sky! An average-size swarm of locusts, numbering in the millions, can strip a field completely bare—down to its last leaf—within minutes.

Revelation 9:3

[7]The shape of the locusts was like horses prepared for battle. On their heads were crowns of something like gold, and their faces *were* like the faces of men. [8]They had hair like women's

8:7 [a]NU-Text and M-Text add *and a third of the earth was burned up.*   8:13 [a]NU-Text and M-Text read *eagle.*

hair, and their teeth were like lions' *teeth*. ⁹And they had breastplates like breastplates of iron, and the sound of their wings *was* like the sound of chariots with many horses running into battle. ¹⁰They had tails like scorpions, and there were stings in their tails. Their power *was* to hurt men five months. ¹¹And they had as king over them the angel of the bottomless pit, whose name in Hebrew *is* Abaddon, but in Greek he has the name Apollyon.

¹²One woe is past. Behold, still two more woes are coming after these things.

WHAT'S IT MEAN?

Here are three fast facts about the Euphrates River. One, at eighteen hundred miles, it's the longest river in western Asia. Two, it starts in Armenia (in modern Turkey) and ends at the Persian Gulf. Three, it formed the northern boundary of the land God gave to Israel.

Revelation 9:14

SIXTH TRUMPET: THE ANGELS FROM THE EUPHRATES

¹³Then the sixth angel sounded: And I heard a voice from the four horns of the golden altar which is before God, ¹⁴saying to the sixth angel who had the trumpet, "Release the four angels who are bound at the great river Euphrates." ¹⁵So the four angels, who had been prepared for the hour and day and month and year, were released to kill a third of mankind. ¹⁶Now the number of the army of the horsemen *was* two hundred million; I heard the number of them. ¹⁷And thus I saw the horses in the vision: those who sat on them had breastplates of fiery red, hyacinth blue, and sulfur yellow; and the heads of the horses *were* like the heads of lions; and out of their mouths came fire, smoke, and brimstone. ¹⁸By these three *plagues* a third of mankind was killed—by the fire and the smoke and the brimstone which came out of their mouths. ¹⁹For their power*ᵃ* is in their mouth and in their tails; for their tails *are* like

serpents, having heads; and with them they do harm.

²⁰But the rest of mankind, who were not killed by these plagues, did not repent of the works of their hands, that they should not worship demons, and idols of gold, silver, brass, stone, and wood, which can neither see nor hear nor walk. ²¹And they did not repent of their murders or their sorceries*ᵃ* or their sexual immorality or their thefts.

THE MIGHTY ANGEL WITH THE LITTLE BOOK

¹I saw still another mighty angel coming down from heaven, clothed with a cloud. And a rainbow *was* on his head, his face *was* like the sun, and his feet like pillars of fire. ²He had a little book open in his hand. And he set his right foot on the sea and *his* left *foot* on the land, ³and cried with a loud voice, as *when* a lion roars. When he cried out, seven thunders uttered their voices. ⁴Now when the seven thunders uttered their voices,*ᵃ* I was about to write; but I heard a voice from heaven saying to me,*ᵇ* "Seal up the things which the seven thunders uttered, and do not write them."

⁵The angel whom I saw standing on the sea and on the land raised up his hand*ᵃ* to heaven ⁶and swore by Him who lives forever and ever, who created heaven and the things that are in it, the earth and the things that are in it, and the sea and the things that are in it, that there should be delay no longer, ⁷but in the days of the sounding of the seventh angel, when he is about to sound, the mystery of God would be finished, as He declared to His servants the prophets.

JOHN EATS THE LITTLE BOOK

⁸Then the voice which I heard from heaven spoke to me again and said, "Go, take the little book which is open in the hand of the angel who stands on the sea and on the earth."

⁹So I went to the angel and said to him, "Give me the little book."

And he said to me, "Take and eat it; and it will make your stomach bitter, but it will be as sweet as honey in your mouth."

¹⁰Then I took the little book out of the angel's hand and ate it, and it was as sweet as honey in my mouth. But when I had eaten it, my stomach became bitter. ¹¹And he*ᵃ* said to me, "You must prophesy again about many peoples, nations, tongues, and kings."

9:19 *ᵃ*NU-Text and M-Text read *the power of the horses.*   **9:21** *ᵃ*NU-Text and M-Text read *drugs.* **10:4** *ᵃ*NU-Text and M-Text read *sounded.* *ᵇ*NU-Text and M-Text omit *to me.* **10:5** *ᵃ*NU-Text and M-Text read *right hand.* **10:11** *ᵃ*NU-Text and M-Text read *they.*

THE TWO WITNESSES

¹Then I was given a reed like a measuring rod. And the angel stood,ᵃ saying, "Rise and measure the temple of God, the altar, and those who worship there. ²But leave out the court which is outside the temple, and do not measure it, for it has been given to the Gentiles. And they will tread the holy city underfoot *for* forty-two months. ³And I will give *power* to my two witnesses, and they will prophesy one thousand two hundred and sixty days, clothed in sackcloth."

WHAT'S IT MEAN?

People in ancient times wore sackcloth only in times of great sorrow or distress. If you've ever felt sackcloth, you know why they didn't wear it more often. The cloth was a dark, scratchy material made of goat's hair. The tradition of wearing dark clothing to funerals came from the custom of wearing sackcloth in times of sorrow.

Revelation 11:3

⁴These are the two olive trees and the two lampstands standing before the Godᵃ of the earth. ⁵And if anyone wants to harm them, fire proceeds from their mouth and devours their enemies. And if anyone wants to harm them, he must be killed in this manner. ⁶These have power to shut heaven, so that no rain falls in the days of their prophecy; and they have power over waters to turn them to blood, and to strike the earth with all plagues, as often as they desire.

THE WITNESSES KILLED

⁷When they finish their testimony, the beast that ascends out of the bottomless pit will make war against them, overcome them, and kill them. ⁸And their dead bodies *will lie* in the street of the great city which spiritually is called Sodom and Egypt, where also ourᵃ Lord was crucified. ⁹Then *those* from the peoples, tribes, tongues, and nations will see their dead bodies three-and-a-half days, and not allowᵃ their dead bodies to be put into graves. ¹⁰And those who dwell on the earth will rejoice over them, make merry, and send gifts to one another, because these two prophets tormented those who dwell on the earth.

THE WITNESSES RESURRECTED

¹¹Now after the three-and-a-half days the breath of life from God entered them, and they stood on their feet, and great fear fell on those who saw them. ¹²And theyᵃ heard a loud voice from heaven saying to them, "Come up here." And they ascended to heaven in a cloud, and their enemies saw them. ¹³In the same hour there was a great earthquake, and a tenth of the city fell. In the earthquake seven thousand people were killed, and the rest were afraid and gave glory to the God of heaven.

¹⁴The second woe is past. Behold, the third woe is coming quickly.

SEVENTH TRUMPET: THE KINGDOM PROCLAIMED

¹⁵Then the seventh angel sounded: And there were loud voices in heaven, saying, "The kingdomsᵃ of this world have become *the kingdoms* of our Lord and of His Christ, and He shall reign forever and ever!" ¹⁶And the twenty-four elders who sat before God on their thrones fell on their faces and worshiped God, ¹⁷saying:

"We give You thanks, O Lord God Almighty,

WHAT'S IT MEAN?

The double-barreled reference to Sodom and Egypt says a lot about the "great city." Sodom was one of the cities destroyed by God because of the wickedness of its citizens. Egypt was the place the Israelites were held as slaves until God told Moses to lead them to the land He promised to give them.

Revelation 11:8

11:1 ᵃNU-Text and M-Text omit *And the angel stood.* **11:4** ᵃNU-Text and M-Text read *Lord.* **11:8** ᵃNU-Text and M-Text read *their.* **11:9** ᵃNU-Text and M-Text read *nations see . . . and will not allow.* **11:12** ᵃM-Text reads *I.* **11:15** ᵃNU-Text and M-Text read *kingdom . . . has become.*

The One who is and who was and who
  is to come,[a]
Because You have taken Your great power
  and reigned.
18 The nations were angry, and Your wrath
  has come,
And the time of the dead, that they
  should be judged,
And that You should reward Your
  servants the prophets and the saints,
And those who fear Your name, small
  and great,
And should destroy those who destroy
  the earth."

[19]Then the temple of God was opened in heaven, and the ark of His covenant[a] was seen in His temple. And there were lightnings, noises, thunderings, an earthquake, and great hail.

THE WOMAN, THE CHILD, AND THE DRAGON

[1]Now a great sign appeared in heaven: a woman clothed with the sun, with the moon under her feet, and on her head a garland of twelve stars. [2]Then being with child, she cried out in labor and in pain to give birth.

[3]And another sign appeared in heaven: behold, a great, fiery red dragon having seven heads and ten horns, and seven diadems on his heads. [4]His tail drew a third of the stars of heaven and threw them to the earth. And the dragon stood before the woman who was ready to give birth, to devour her Child as soon as it was born. [5]She bore a male Child who was to rule all nations with a rod of iron. And her Child was caught up to God and His throne. [6]Then the woman fled into the wilderness, where she has a place prepared by God, that they should feed her there one thousand two hundred and sixty days.

SATAN THROWN OUT OF HEAVEN

[7]And war broke out in heaven: Michael and his angels fought with the dragon; and the dragon and his angels fought, [8]but they did not prevail, nor was a place found for them[a] in heaven any longer. [9]So the great dragon was cast out, that serpent of old, called the Devil and Satan, who deceives the whole world; he was cast to the earth, and his angels were cast out with him.

[10]Then I heard a loud voice saying in heaven, "Now salvation, and strength, and the kingdom of our God, and the power of His Christ have come, for the accuser of our brethren, who accused them before our God day and night, has been cast down. [11]And they overcame him by the blood of the Lamb and by the word of their testimony, and they did not love their lives to the death. [12]Therefore rejoice, O heavens, and you who dwell in them! Woe to the inhabitants of the earth and the sea! For the devil has come down to you, having great wrath, because he knows that he has a short time."

THE WOMAN PERSECUTED

[13]Now when the dragon saw that he had been cast to the earth, he persecuted the woman who gave birth to the male *Child*. [14]But the woman was given two wings of a great eagle, that she might fly into the wilderness to her place, where she is nourished for a time and times and half a time, from the presence of the serpent. [15]So the serpent spewed water out of his mouth like a flood after the woman, that he might cause her to be carried away by the flood. [16]But the earth helped the woman, and the earth opened its mouth and swallowed up the flood which the dragon had spewed out of his mouth. [17]And the dragon was enraged with the woman, and he went to make war with the rest of her offspring, who keep the commandments of God and have the testimony of Jesus Christ.[a]

THE BEAST FROM THE SEA

[1]Then I[a] stood on the sand of the sea. And I saw a beast rising up out of the sea, having seven heads and ten horns,[b] and on his horns ten crowns, and on his heads a blasphemous name. [2]Now the beast which I saw was like a leopard, his feet were like *the feet of* a bear, and his mouth like the mouth of a lion. The dragon gave him his power, his throne, and great authority. [3]And *I saw* one of his heads as if it had been mortally wounded, and his deadly wound was healed. And all the world marveled and followed the beast. [4]So they worshiped the dragon who gave authority to the beast; and they worshiped the beast, saying, "Who *is* like the beast? Who is able to make war with him?"

[5]And he was given a mouth speaking great things and blasphemies, and he was given authority to continue[a] for forty-two months. [6]Then he opened his mouth in blasphemy against God, to blaspheme His name, His taber-

---

11:17 [a]NU-Text and M-Text omit *and who is to come*.   **11:19** [a]M-Text reads *the covenant of the Lord*.
12:8 [a]M-Text reads *him*.   **12:17** [a]NU-Text and M-Text omit *Christ*.   **13:1** [a]NU-Text reads *he*.   [b]NU-Text and M-Text read *ten horns and seven heads*.   **13:5** [a]M-Text reads *make war*.

nacle, and those who dwell in heaven. [7]It was granted to him to make war with the saints and to overcome them. And authority was given him over every tribe,[a] tongue, and nation. [8]All who dwell on the earth will worship him, whose names have not been written in the Book of Life of the Lamb slain from the foundation of the world.

[9]If anyone has an ear, let him hear. [10]He who leads into captivity shall go into captivity; he who kills with the sword must be killed with the sword. Here is the patience and the faith of the saints.

THE BEAST FROM THE EARTH

[11]Then I saw another beast coming up out of the earth, and he had two horns like a lamb and spoke like a dragon. [12]And he exercises all the authority of the first beast in his presence, and causes the earth and those who dwell in it to worship the first beast, whose deadly wound was healed. [13]He performs great signs, so that he even makes fire come down from heaven on the earth in the sight of men. [14]And he deceives those[a] who dwell on the earth by those signs which he was granted to do in the sight of the beast, telling those who dwell on the earth to make an image to the beast who was wounded by the sword and lived. [15]He was granted *power* to give breath to the image of the beast, that the image of the beast should both speak and cause as many as would not worship the image of the beast to be killed. [16]He causes all, both small and great, rich and poor, free and slave, to receive a mark on their right hand or on their foreheads, [17]and that no one may buy or sell except one who has the mark or[a] the name of the beast, or the number of his name.

[18]Here is wisdom. Let him who has understanding calculate the number of the beast, for it is the number of a man: His number *is* 666.

THE LAMB AND THE 144,000

[1]Then I looked, and behold, a[a] Lamb standing on Mount Zion, and with Him one hundred *and* forty-four thousand, having[b] His Father's name written on their foreheads. [2]And I heard a voice from heaven, like the voice of many waters, and like the voice of loud thunder. And I heard the sound of harpists playing their harps. [3]They sang as it were a new song before the throne, before the four living creatures, and the elders; and no one could learn that song except the hundred *and* forty-four thousand who were redeemed from the earth. [4]These are the ones who were not defiled with women, for they are virgins. These are the ones who follow the Lamb wherever He goes. These were redeemed[a] from *among* men, *being* firstfruits to God and to the Lamb. [5]And in their mouth was found no deceit,[a] for they are without fault before the throne of God.[b]

THE PROCLAMATIONS OF THREE ANGELS

[6]Then I saw another angel flying in the midst of heaven, having the everlasting gospel to preach to those who dwell on the earth—to every nation, tribe, tongue, and people—[7]saying with a loud voice, "Fear God and give glory to Him, for the hour of His judgment has come; and worship Him who made heaven and earth, the sea and springs of water."

[8]And another angel followed, saying, "Babylon[a] is fallen, is fallen, that great city, because she has made all nations drink of the wine of the wrath of her fornication."

WHAT'S IT MEAN?

Brimstone is another name for sulfur, a fast-burning, disgusting-smelling rock. Ancient armies sometimes used burning sulfur as ammunition in their catapults, launching it over city walls to set buildings on fire inside.

Revelation 14:10

[9]Then a third angel followed them, saying with a loud voice, "If anyone worships the beast and his image, and receives *his* mark on his forehead or on his hand, [10]he himself shall also drink of the wine of the wrath of God, which is poured out full strength into the cup of His indignation. He shall be tormented with fire and brimstone in the presence of the holy

---

13:7 [a]NU-Text and M-Text add *and people*.   **13:14** [a]M-Text reads *my own people*.   **13:17** [a]NU-Text and M-Text omit *or*.   **14:1** [a]NU-Text and M-Text read *the*.   [b]NU-Text and M-Text add *His name and*.   **14:4** [a]M-Text adds *by Jesus*.   **14:5** [a]NU-Text and M-Text read *falsehood*.   [b]NU-Text and M-Text omit *before the throne of God*. **14:8** [a]NU-Text reads *Babylon the great is fallen, is fallen, which has made*; M-Text reads *Babylon the great is fallen. She has made*.

angels and in the presence of the Lamb. [11]And the smoke of their torment ascends forever and ever; and they have no rest day or night, who worship the beast and his image, and whoever receives the mark of his name."

[12]Here is the patience of the saints; here *are* those[a] who keep the commandments of God and the faith of Jesus.

[13]Then I heard a voice from heaven saying to me,[a] "Write: 'Blessed *are* the dead who die in the Lord from now on.'"

"Yes," says the Spirit, "that they may rest from their labors, and their works follow them."

REAPING THE EARTH'S HARVEST

[14]Then I looked, and behold, a white cloud, and on the cloud sat *One* like the Son of Man, having on His head a golden crown, and in His hand a sharp sickle. [15]And another angel came out of the temple, crying with a loud voice to Him who sat on the cloud, "Thrust in Your sickle and reap, for the time has come for You[a] to reap, for the harvest of the earth is ripe." [16]So He who sat on the cloud thrust in His sickle on the earth, and the earth was reaped.

REAPING THE GRAPES OF WRATH

[17]Then another angel came out of the temple which is in heaven, he also having a sharp sickle.

[18]And another angel came out from the altar, who had power over fire, and he cried with a loud cry to him who had the sharp sickle, saying, "Thrust in your sharp sickle and gather the clusters of the vine of the earth, for her grapes are fully ripe." [19]So the angel thrust his sickle into the earth and gathered the vine of the earth, and threw *it* into the great winepress of the wrath of God. [20]And the winepress was trampled outside the city, and blood came out of the winepress, up to the horses' bridles, for one thousand six hundred furlongs.

PRELUDE TO THE BOWL JUDGMENTS

[1]Then I saw another sign in heaven, great and marvelous: seven angels having the seven last plagues, for in them the wrath of God is complete.

[2]And I saw *something* like a sea of glass mingled with fire, and those who have the victory over the beast, over his image and over his mark[a] *and* over the number of his name, standing on the sea of glass, having harps of God. [3]They sing the song of Moses, the servant of God, and the song of the Lamb, saying:

> "Great and marvelous *are* Your works,
> Lord God Almighty!
> Just and true *are* Your ways,
> O King of the saints![a]
> 4 Who shall not fear You, O Lord, and glorify Your name?
> For *You* alone *are* holy.
> For all nations shall come and worship before You,
> For Your judgments have been manifested."

[5]After these things I looked, and behold,[a] the temple of the tabernacle of the testimony in heaven was opened. [6]And out of the temple came the seven angels having the seven plagues, clothed in pure bright linen, and having their chests girded with golden bands. [7]Then one of the four living creatures gave to the seven angels seven golden bowls full of the wrath of God who lives forever and ever. [8]The temple was filled with smoke from the glory of God and from His power, and no one was able to enter the temple till the seven plagues of the seven angels were completed.

[1]Then I heard a loud voice from the temple saying to the seven angels, "Go and pour out the bowls[a] of the wrath of God on the earth."

FIRST BOWL: LOATHSOME SORES

[2]So the first went and poured out his bowl upon the earth, and a foul and loathsome sore came upon the men who had the mark of the beast and those who worshiped his image.

SECOND BOWL: THE SEA TURNS TO BLOOD

[3]Then the second angel poured out his bowl on the sea, and it became blood as of a dead *man*; and every living creature in the sea died.

"Great and marvelous are Your works, Lord God Almighty! Just and true are Your ways, O King of the saints!" (Revelation 15:3b)

14:12 [a]NU-Text and M-Text omit *here are those.*   **14:13** [a]NU-Text and M-Text omit *to me.*   **14:15** [a]NU-Text and M-Text omit *for You.*   **15:2** [a]NU-Text and M-Text omit *over his mark.*   **15:3** [a]NU-Text and M-Text read *nations.*   **15:5** [a]NU-Text and M-Text omit *behold.*   **16:1** [a]NU-Text and M-Text read *seven bowls.*

THIRD BOWL: THE WATERS TURN TO BLOOD

⁴Then the third angel poured out his bowl on the rivers and springs of water, and they became blood. ⁵And I heard the angel of the waters saying:

"You are righteous, O Lord,ᵃ
    The One who is and who was and who
        is to be,ᵇ
    Because You have judged these things.
⁶   For they have shed the blood of saints
        and prophets,
    And You have given them blood to drink.
    Forᵃ it is their just due."

⁷And I heard another fromᵃ the altar saying, "Even so, Lord God Almighty, true and righteous *are* Your judgments."

FOURTH BOWL: MEN ARE SCORCHED

⁸Then the fourth angel poured out his bowl on the sun, and power was given to him to scorch men with fire. ⁹And men were scorched with great heat, and they blasphemed the name of God who has power over these plagues; and they did not repent and give Him glory.

FIFTH BOWL: DARKNESS AND PAIN

¹⁰Then the fifth angel poured out his bowl on the throne of the beast, and his kingdom became full of darkness; and they gnawed their tongues because of the pain. ¹¹They blasphemed the God of heaven because of their pains and their sores, and did not repent of their deeds.

SIXTH BOWL: EUPHRATES DRIED UP

¹²Then the sixth angel poured out his bowl on the great river Euphrates, and its water was dried up, so that the way of the kings from the east might be prepared. ¹³And I saw three unclean spirits like frogs *coming* out of the mouth of the dragon, out of the mouth of the beast, and out of the mouth of the false prophet. ¹⁴For they are spirits of demons, performing signs, *which* go out to the kings of the earth andᵃ of the whole world, to gather them to the battle of that great day of God Almighty.

¹⁵"Behold, I am coming as a thief. Blessed *is* he who watches, and keeps his garments, lest he walk naked and they see his shame."

WHAT'S IT MEAN?

The word *Armageddon* means "hill of Megiddo." In Old Testament times, Megiddo, which was located in the Carmel Mountain range, was a popular spot for military battles.
Revelation 16:16

¹⁶And they gathered them together to the place called in Hebrew, Armageddon.ᵃ

SEVENTH BOWL: THE EARTH UTTERLY SHAKEN

¹⁷Then the seventh angel poured out his bowl into the air, and a loud voice came out of the temple of heaven, from the throne, saying, "It is done!" ¹⁸And there were noises and thunderings and lightnings; and there was a great earthquake, such a mighty and great earthquake as had not occurred since men were on the earth. ¹⁹Now the great city was divided into three parts, and the cities of the nations fell. And great Babylon was remembered before God, to give her the cup of the wine of the fierceness of His wrath. ²⁰Then every island fled away, and the mountains were not found. ²¹And great hail from heaven fell upon men, *each hailstone* about the weight of a talent. Men blasphemed God because of the plague of the hail, since that plague was exceedingly great.

THE SCARLET WOMAN AND THE SCARLET BEAST

¹Then one of the seven angels who had the seven bowls came and talked with me, saying to me,ᵃ "Come, I will show you the judgment of the great harlot who sits on many waters, ²with whom the kings of the earth committed fornication, and the inhabitants of the earth were made drunk with the wine of her fornication."

³So he carried me away in the Spirit into the wilderness. And I saw a woman sitting on a scarlet beast *which was* full of names of blasphemy, having seven heads and ten horns. ⁴The woman was arrayed in purple and scarlet, and adorned with gold and precious stones and

16:5 ᵃNU-Text and M-Text omit *O Lord*. ᵇNU-Text and M-Text read *who was, the Holy One*.
16:6 ᵃNU-Text and M-Text omit *For*.   **16:7** ᵃNU-Text and M-Text omit *another from*.   **16:14** ᵃNU-Text and M-Text omit *of the earth and*.   **16:16** ᵃM-Text reads *Megiddo*.   **17:1** ᵃNU-Text and M-Text omit *to me*.

pearls, having in her hand a golden cup full of abominations and the filthiness of her fornication.[a] 5And on her forehead a name *was* written:

> MYSTERY,
> BABYLON THE GREAT,
> THE MOTHER OF HARLOTS AND OF THE
> ABOMINATIONS OF THE EARTH.

6I saw the woman, drunk with the blood of the saints and with the blood of the martyrs of Jesus. And when I saw her, I marveled with great amazement.

THE MEANING OF THE WOMAN AND THE BEAST

7But the angel said to me, "Why did you marvel? I will tell you the mystery of the woman and of the beast that carries her, which has the seven heads and the ten horns. 8The beast that you saw was, and is not, and will ascend out of the bottomless pit and go to perdition. And those who dwell on the earth will marvel, whose names are not written in the Book of Life from the foundation of the world, when they see the beast that was, and is not, and yet is.[a]

9"Here *is* the mind which has wisdom: The seven heads are seven mountains on which the woman sits. 10There are also seven kings. Five have fallen, one is, *and* the other has not yet come. And when he comes, he must continue a short time. 11The beast that was, and is not, is himself also the eighth, and is of the seven, and is going to perdition.

12"The ten horns which you saw are ten kings who have received no kingdom as yet, but they receive authority for one hour as kings with the beast. 13These are of one mind, and they will give their power and authority to the beast. 14These will make war with the Lamb, and the Lamb will overcome them, for He is Lord of lords and King of kings; and those *who are* with Him *are* called, chosen, and faithful."

15Then he said to me, "The waters which you saw, where the harlot sits, are peoples, multitudes, nations, and tongues. 16And the ten horns which you saw on[a] the beast, these will hate the harlot, make her desolate and naked, eat her flesh and burn her with fire. 17For God has put it into their hearts to fulfill His purpose, to be of one mind, and to give their kingdom to the beast, until the words of God are ful-

filled. 18And the woman whom you saw is that great city which reigns over the kings of the earth."

THE FALL OF BABYLON THE GREAT

1After these things I saw another angel coming down from heaven, having great authority, and the earth was illuminated with his glory. 2And he cried mightily[a] with a loud voice, saying, "Babylon the great is fallen, is fallen, and has become a dwelling place of demons, a prison for every foul spirit, and a cage for every unclean and hated bird! 3For all the nations have drunk of the wine of the wrath of her fornication, the kings of the earth have committed fornication with her, and the merchants of the earth have become rich through the abundance of her luxury."

4And I heard another voice from heaven saying, "Come out of her, my people, lest you share in her sins, and lest you receive of her plagues. 5For her sins have reached[a] to heaven, and God has remembered her iniquities. 6Render to her just as she rendered to you,[a] and repay her double according to her works; in the cup which she has mixed, mix double for her. 7In the measure that she glorified herself and lived luxuriously, in the same measure give her torment and sorrow; for she says in her heart, 'I sit *as* queen, and am no widow, and will not see sorrow.' 8Therefore her plagues will come in one day—death and mourning and famine. And she will be utterly burned with fire, for strong *is* the Lord God who judges[a] her.

THE WORLD MOURNS BABYLON'S FALL

9"The kings of the earth who committed fornication and lived luxuriously with her will weep and lament for her, when they see the smoke of her burning, 10standing at a distance for fear of her torment, saying, 'Alas, alas, that great city Babylon, that mighty city! For in one hour your judgment has come.'

11"And the merchants of the earth will weep and mourn over her, for no one buys their merchandise anymore: 12merchandise of gold and silver, precious stones and pearls, fine linen and purple, silk and scarlet, every kind of citron wood, every kind of object of ivory, every kind of object of most precious wood, bronze, iron, and marble; 13and cinnamon and incense, fragrant oil and frankincense, wine and oil, fine

---

17:4 [a]M-Text reads *the filthiness of the fornication of the earth.*   **17:8** [a]NU-Text and M-Text read *and shall be present.*   **17:16** [a]NU-Text and M-Text read *saw, and the beast.*   **18:2** [a]NU-Text and M-Text omit *mightily.*   **18:5** [a]NU-Text and M-Text read *have been heaped up.*   **18:6** [a]NU-Text and M-Text omit *to you.*   **18:8** [a]NU-Text and M-Text read *has judged.*

flour and wheat, cattle and sheep, horses and chariots, and bodies and souls of men. [14]The fruit that your soul longed for has gone from you, and all the things which are rich and splendid have gone from you,[a] and you shall find them no more at all. [15]The merchants of these things, who became rich by her, will stand at a distance for fear of her torment, weeping and wailing, [16]and saying, 'Alas, alas, that great city that was clothed in fine linen, purple, and scarlet, and adorned with gold and precious stones and pearls! [17]For in one hour such great riches came to nothing.' Every shipmaster, all who travel by ship, sailors, and as many as trade on the sea, stood at a distance [18]and cried out when they saw the smoke of her burning, saying, 'What is like this great city?'

[19]"They threw dust on their heads and cried out, weeping and wailing, and saying, 'Alas, alas, that great city, in which all who had ships on the sea became rich by her wealth! For in one hour she is made desolate.'

[20]"Rejoice over her, O heaven, and you holy apostles[a] and prophets, for God has avenged you on her!"

FINALITY OF BABYLON'S FALL

[21]Then a mighty angel took up a stone like a great millstone and threw it into the sea, saying, "Thus with violence the great city Babylon shall be thrown down, and shall not be found anymore. [22]The sound of harpists, musicians, flutists, and trumpeters shall not be heard in you anymore. No craftsman of any craft shall be found in you anymore, and the sound of a millstone shall not be heard in you anymore. [23]The light of a lamp shall not shine in you anymore, and the voice of bridegroom and bride shall not be heard in you anymore. For your merchants were the great men of the earth, for by your sorcery all the nations were deceived. [24]And in her was found the blood of prophets and saints, and of all who were slain on the earth."

HEAVEN EXULTS OVER BABYLON

[1]After these things I heard[a] a loud voice of a great multitude in heaven, saying, "Alleluia! Salvation and glory and honor and power belong to the Lord[b] our God! [2]For true and righteous are His judgments, because He has judged the great harlot who corrupted the earth with her fornication; and He has avenged on her the blood of His servants shed by her." [3]Again they said, "Alleluia! Her smoke rises up forever and ever!" [4]And the twenty-four elders and the four living creatures fell down and worshiped God who sat on the throne, saying, "Amen! Alleluia!" [5]Then a voice came from the throne, saying, "Praise our God, all you His servants and those who fear Him, both[a] small and great!"

[6]And I heard, as it were, the voice of a great multitude, as the sound of many waters and as the sound of mighty thunderings, saying, "Alleluia! For the[a] Lord God Omnipotent reigns! [7]Let us be glad and rejoice and give Him glory, for the marriage of the Lamb has come, and His wife has made herself ready." [8]And to her it was granted to be arrayed in fine linen, clean and bright, for the fine linen is the righteous acts of the saints.

WHAT'S IT MEAN?

Linen, which was handwoven from the fibers of the hemp plant, was considered to be the highest quality fabric in the ancient world. For the most part, only people of great wealth or power wore linen. Priests and those who served in the temple were the exception. They, too, wore linen. Throughout the Bible, white linen symbolizes purity.

Revelation 19:8

[9]Then he said to me, "Write: 'Blessed are those who are called to the marriage supper of the Lamb!' " And he said to me, "These are the true sayings of God." [10]And I fell at his feet to worship him. But he said to me, "See that you do not do that! I am your fellow servant, and of your brethren who have the testimony of Jesus. Worship God! For the testimony of Jesus is the spirit of prophecy."

CHRIST ON A WHITE HORSE

[11]Now I saw heaven opened, and behold, a white horse. And He who sat on him was called Faithful and True, and in righteousness He judges and makes war. [12]His eyes were like a flame of fire, and on His head were many crowns. He had[a] a name written that no one

---

18:14 [a]NU-Text and M-Text read been lost to you.　**18:20** [a]NU-Text and M-Text read saints and apostles.
19:1 [a]NU-Text and M-Text add something like.　[b]NU-Text and M-Text omit the Lord.　**19:5** [a]NU-Text and M-Text omit both.　**19:6** [a]NU-Text and M-Text read our.　**19:12** [a]M-Text adds names written, and.

knew except Himself. ¹³He *was* clothed with a robe dipped in blood, and His name is called The Word of God. ¹⁴And the armies in heaven, clothed in fine linen, white and clean,*ᵃ* followed Him on white horses. ¹⁵Now out of His mouth goes a sharp*ᵃ* sword, that with it He should strike the nations. And He Himself will rule them with a rod of iron. He Himself treads the winepress of the fierceness and wrath of Almighty God. ¹⁶And He has on *His* robe and on His thigh a name written:

KING OF KINGS
AND LORD OF LORDS.

THE BEAST AND HIS ARMIES DEFEATED

¹⁷Then I saw an angel standing in the sun; and he cried with a loud voice, saying to all the birds that fly in the midst of heaven, "Come and gather together for the supper of the great God,*ᵃ* ¹⁸that you may eat the flesh of kings, the flesh of captains, the flesh of mighty men, the flesh of horses and of those who sit on them, and the flesh of all *people,* free*ᵃ* and slave, both small and great."

¹⁹And I saw the beast, the kings of the earth, and their armies, gathered together to make war against Him who sat on the horse and against His army. ²⁰Then the beast was captured, and with him the false prophet who worked signs in his presence, by which he deceived those who received the mark of the beast and those who worshiped his image. These two were cast alive into the lake of fire burning with brimstone. ²¹And the rest were killed with the sword which proceeded from the mouth of Him who sat on the horse. And all the birds were filled with their flesh.

SATAN BOUND 1000 YEARS

¹Then I saw an angel coming down from heaven, having the key to the bottomless pit and a great chain in his hand. ²He laid hold of the dragon, that serpent of old, who is *the* Devil and Satan, and bound him for a thousand years; ³and he cast him into the bottomless pit, and shut him up, and set a seal on him, so that he should deceive the nations no more till the thousand years were finished. But after these things he must be released for a little while.

THE SAINTS REIGN WITH CHRIST 1000 YEARS

⁴And I saw thrones, and they sat on them, and judgment was committed to them. Then I saw the souls of those who had been beheaded for their witness to Jesus and for the word of God, who had not worshiped the beast or his image, and had not received *his* mark on their foreheads or on their hands. And they lived and reigned with Christ for a*ᵃ* thousand years. ⁵But the rest of the dead did not live again until

On the Edge

And He has on His robe and on His thigh a name written: KING OF KINGS AND LORD OF LORDS (Rev. 19:16).

Wow. Can you imagine seeing Jesus? Can you imagine really, finally coming face-to-face with the One you've been in love with all your life? What would you think when you saw His robe and read the words "KING OF KINGS AND LORD OF LORDS"? A lot of Christians have been tossing that description of Jesus around for ages. But do you get it?

There are kings and lords all over the earth—have been for hundreds of years. You've heard about them in history class—King David, King Saul, King Louis XIV, King Henry VIII. You've heard about them in literature class—Alfred, Lord Tennyson, and George Gordon, Lord Byron.

Kings and lords are known primarily for their power, their wealth, their military might, and their positions as rulers over groups of people. Jesus Christ puts it all to shame. You talk about power. His power can raise the dead. You talk about wealth. His Father owns the cattle on a thousand hills (see Ps. 50:10). You talk about military might. He's raising up an army that will someday defeat the raging forces of Satan. You talk about a ruler. He rules the whole world. Philippians 2:10 says that "every knee should bow, of those in heaven, and of those on earth, and of those under the earth" at just the mention of His name.

He is the King of all the kings who have ever ruled and the Lord of every lord. Go ahead. Enthrone Him in your heart. You'll never find a more loving, merciful, gracious King.

SEE FOR YOURSELF:
1 Tim. 6:15; Rev. 17:14

19:14 *ᵃ*NU-Text and M-Text read *pure white linen.*   **19:15** *ᵃ*M-Text adds *two-edged.*   **19:17** *ᵃ*NU-Text and M-Text read *the great supper of God.*   **19:18** *ᵃ*NU-Text and M-Text read *both free.*   **20:4** *ᵃ*M-Text reads *the.*

the thousand years were finished. This *is* the first resurrection. [6]Blessed and holy *is* he who has part in the first resurrection. Over such the second death has no power, but they shall be priests of God and of Christ, and shall reign with Him a thousand years.

SATANIC REBELLION CRUSHED

[7]Now when the thousand years have expired, Satan will be released from his prison [8]and will go out to deceive the nations which are in the four corners of the earth, Gog and Magog, to gather them together to battle, whose number *is* as the sand of the sea. [9]They went up on the breadth of the earth and surrounded the camp of the saints and the beloved city. And fire came down from God out of heaven and devoured them. [10]The devil, who deceived them, was cast into the lake of fire and brimstone where[a] the beast and the false prophet *are.* And they will be tormented day and night forever and ever.

THE GREAT WHITE THRONE JUDGMENT

[11]Then I saw a great white throne and Him who sat on it, from whose face the earth and the heaven fled away. And there was found no place for them. [12]And I saw the dead, small and great, standing before God,[a] and books were opened. And another book was opened, which is *the Book* of Life. And the dead were judged according to their works, by the things which were written in the books. [13]The sea gave up the dead who were in it, and Death and Hades delivered up the dead who were in them. And they were judged, each one according to his works. [14]Then Death and Hades were cast into the lake of fire. This is the second death.[a] [15]And anyone not found written in the Book of Life was cast into the lake of fire.

ALL THINGS MADE NEW

[1]Now I saw a new heaven and a new earth, for the first heaven and the first earth had passed away. Also there was no more sea. [2]Then I, John,[a] saw the holy city, New Jerusalem, coming down out of heaven from God, prepared as a bride adorned for her husband.

WHAT'S IT MEAN?

Alpha and Omega are the first and last letters of the Greek alphabet. The Greeks learned to use the alphabet from the Phoenicians, a group of sea traders who lived in what is now Lebanon. In turn, the Greeks passed on their alphabet knowledge to the Romans.
Revelation 21:6

[3]And I heard a loud voice from heaven saying, "Behold, the tabernacle of God *is* with men, and He will dwell with them, and they shall be His people. God Himself will be with them *and be* their God. [4]And God will wipe away every tear from their eyes; there shall be no more death, nor sorrow, nor crying. There shall be no more pain, for the former things have passed away."

HEAVEN
Will there be sadness in heaven? (21:4)

[5]Then He who sat on the throne said, "Behold, I make all things new." And He said to me,[a] "Write, for these words are true and faithful."

[6]And He said to me, "It is done![a] I am the Alpha and the Omega, the Beginning and the End. I will give of the fountain of the water of life freely to him who thirsts. [7]He who overcomes shall inherit all things,[a] and I will be his God and he shall be My son. [8]But the cowardly, unbelieving,[a] abominable, murderers, sexually immoral, sorcerers, idolaters, and all liars shall have their part in the lake which burns with fire and brimstone, which is the second death."

"The first earth had passed away. Also there was no more sea." (Revelation 21:1a)

THE NEW JERUSALEM

[9]Then one of the seven angels who had the seven bowls filled with the seven last plagues came to me[a] and talked with me, saying, "Come, I will show you the bride, the Lamb's wife."[b]

20:10 [a]NU-Text and M-Text add *also.* **20:12** [a]NU-Text and M-Text read *the throne.* **20:14** [a]NU-Text and M-Text add *the lake of fire.* **21:2** [a]NU-Text and M-Text omit *John.* **21:5** [a]NU-Text and M-Text omit *to me.* **21:6** [a]M-Text omits *It is done.* **21:7** [a]M-Text reads *overcomes, I shall give him these things.* **21:8** [a]M-Text adds *and sinners.* **21:9** [a]NU-Text and M-Text omit *to me.* [b]M-Text reads *I will show you the woman, the Lamb's bride.*

¹⁰And he carried me away in the Spirit to a great and high mountain, and showed me the great city, the holy*a* Jerusalem, descending out of heaven from God, ¹¹having the glory of God. Her light *was* like a most precious stone, like a jasper stone, clear as crystal. ¹²Also she had a great and high wall with twelve gates, and twelve angels at the gates, and names written on them, which are *the names* of the twelve tribes of the children of Israel: ¹³three gates on the east, three gates on the north, three gates on the south, and three gates on the west.

¹⁴Now the wall of the city had twelve foundations, and on them were the names*a* of the twelve apostles of the Lamb. ¹⁵And he who talked with me had a gold reed to measure the city, its gates, and its wall. ¹⁶The city is laid out as a square; its length is as great as its breadth. And he measured the city with the reed: twelve thousand furlongs. Its length, breadth, and height are equal. ¹⁷Then he measured its wall: one hundred *and* forty-four cubits, *according to* the measure of a man, that is, of an angel. ¹⁸The construction of its wall was *of* jasper; and the city *was* pure gold, like clear glass. ¹⁹The foundations of the wall of the city *were* adorned with all kinds of precious stones: the first foundation *was* jasper, the second sapphire, the third chalcedony, the fourth emerald, ²⁰the fifth sardonyx, the sixth sardius, the seventh chrysolite, the eighth beryl, the ninth topaz, the tenth chrysoprase, the eleventh jacinth, and the twelfth amethyst. ²¹The twelve gates *were* twelve pearls: each individual gate was of one pearl. And the street of the city *was* pure gold, like transparent glass.

THE GLORY OF THE NEW JERUSALEM

²²But I saw no temple in it, for the Lord God Almighty and the Lamb are its temple. ²³The city had no need of the sun or of the moon to shine in it,*a* for the glory*b* of God illuminated it. The Lamb *is* its light. ²⁴And the nations of those who are saved*a* shall walk in its light, and the kings of the earth bring their glory and honor into it.*b* ²⁵Its gates shall not be shut at all by day (there shall be no night there). ²⁶And they shall bring the glory and the honor of the nations into it.*a* ²⁷But there shall by no means enter it anything that defiles, or causes*a* an abomina-

---

21:10 *a*NU-Text and M-Text omit *the great* and read *the holy city, Jerusalem.* **21:14** *a*NU-Text and M-Text read *twelve names.* **21:23** *a*NU-Text and M-Text omit *in it.* *b*M-Text reads *the very glory.* **21:24** *a*NU-Text and M-Text omit *of those who are saved.* *b*M-Text reads *the glory and honor of the nations to Him.* **21:26** *a*M-Text adds *that they may enter in.* **21:27** *a*NU-Text and M-Text read *anything profane, nor one who causes.*

Promise   HE PROMISES TO COME SOON.

He who testifies to these things says, "Surely I am coming quickly." Amen. Even so, come Lord Jesus! (Rev. 22:20).

What if you were God? What if you'd spent years inspiring the Bible, making sure that the people who read it would have access to everything you wanted them to know? What would you tell them at the very end? Would you let your book just fizzle out with some kind of lame ending? Or would you let the whole work build up to one exciting, crucial climax?

God chose to end His Book with a thought that thrills some people and terrifies others. The end of the story is this: Jesus is coming back. And He's coming back soon. Christians should be the ones who are thrilled by this knowledge. It gives you so much hope! It gives you courage to live the challenging days you're living through right now. It gives you powerful motivation to get serious about answering God's call for your life. You want to be ready. You want to have your life right with God when the last trumpet sounds. You can't know the exact moment when He will arrive; you just know it's going to be soon.

Make your prayer the words of Revelation 22:20, "Even so, come Lord Jesus!" Do your part to be ready—be excited about His return. Get your heart tender and right before Him. Share the news with those who don't know. It'll be the most awesome, most glorious moment the world has ever seen.

SEE FOR YOURSELF:
Heb. 10:37; James 5:8; Rev. 1:7; 22:12

tion or a lie, but only those who are written in the Lamb's Book of Life.

THE RIVER OF LIFE

[1]And he showed me a pure[a] river of water of life, clear as crystal, proceeding from the throne of God and of the Lamb. [2]In the middle of its street, and on either side of the river, *was* the tree of life, which bore twelve fruits, each *tree* yielding its fruit every month. The leaves of the tree *were* for the healing of the nations. [3]And there shall be no more curse, but the throne of God and of the Lamb shall be in it, and His servants shall serve Him. [4]They shall see His face, and His name *shall be* on their foreheads. [5]There shall be no night there: They need no lamp nor light of the sun, for the Lord God gives them light. And they shall reign forever and ever.

THE TIME IS NEAR

[6]Then he said to me, "These words *are* faithful and true." And the Lord God of the holy[a] prophets sent His angel to show His servants the things which must shortly take place.

[7]"Behold, I am coming quickly! Blessed *is* he who keeps the words of the prophecy of this book."

[8]Now I, John, saw and heard[a] these things. And when I heard and saw, I fell down to worship before the feet of the angel who showed me these things.

[9]Then he said to me, "See *that you do* not *do that.* For[a] I am your fellow servant, and of your brethren the prophets, and of those who keep the words of this book. Worship God." [10]And he said to me, "Do not seal the words of the prophecy of this book, for the time is at hand. [11]He who is unjust, let him be unjust still; he who is filthy, let him be filthy still; he who is

righteous, let him be righteous[a] still; he who is holy, let him be holy still."

JESUS TESTIFIES TO THE CHURCHES

[12]"And behold, I am coming quickly, and My reward *is* with Me, to give to every one according to his work. [13]I am the Alpha and the Omega, *the* Beginning and *the* End, the First and the Last."[a]

[14]Blessed *are* those who do His commandments,[a] that they may have the right to the tree of life, and may enter through the gates into the city. [15]But[a] outside *are* dogs and sorcerers and sexually immoral and murderers and idolaters, and whoever loves and practices a lie.

[16]"I, Jesus, have sent My angel to testify to you these things in the churches. I am the Root and the Offspring of David, the Bright and Morning Star."

[17]And the Spirit and the bride say, "Come!" And let him who hears say, "Come!" And let him who thirsts come. Whoever desires, let him take the water of life freely.

A WARNING

[18]For[a] I testify to everyone who hears the words of the prophecy of this book: If anyone adds to these things, God will add[b] to him the plagues that are written in this book; [19]and if anyone takes away from the words of the book of this prophecy, God shall take away[a] his part from the Book[b] of Life, from the holy city, and *from* the things which are written in this book.

I AM COMING QUICKLY

[20]He who testifies to these things says, "Surely I am coming quickly."

Amen. Even so, come, Lord Jesus!

[21]The grace of our Lord Jesus Christ *be* with you all.[a] Amen.

22:1 [a]NU-Text and M-Text omit *pure.*   **22:6** [a]NU-Text and M-Text read *spirits of the prophets.*
22:8 [a]NU-Text and M-Text read *am the one who heard and saw.*   **22:9** [a]NU-Text and M-Text omit *For.*
22:11 [a]NU-Text and M-Text read *do right.*   **22:13** [a]NU-Text and M-Text read *the First and the Last, the Beginning and the End.*   **22:14** [a]NU-Text reads *wash their robes.*   **22:15** [a]NU-Text and M-Text omit *But.*
22:18 [a]NU-Text and M-Text omit *For.*   [b]M-Text reads *may God add.*   **22:19** [a]M-Text reads *may God take away.*   [b]NU-Text and M-Text read *tree of life.*   **22:21** [a]NU-Text reads *with all;* M-Text reads *with all the saints.*

Reading Plans

Okay, so you think that reading the Bible is a good idea—but where should you start? The Bible is a BIG book—make that a *library*—of sixty-six books. Should you just start on page 1 and read every page? Sure you could; that's a great way. But there are other ways, too. You might pick a book of the Bible and read it (many people like to start with the Gospel of John). But if you're looking for other options, here are a few ideas for you.

30 DAYS WITH JESUS

Ever ask yourself, *I wonder what Jesus would do?* Here's how you can find out. Take a month and read the story of Jesus.

60 DAYS WITH PAUL

You've probably heard of the apostle Paul. He's the guy who wrote most of the New Testament. After you read Jesus' story, this is a good place to learn what it means to be a disciple of Jesus.

90-DAY OVERVIEW OF THE BIBLE

This plan takes you through the major events of the Bible without your reading the entire book.

365 DAYS THROUGH THE WHOLE BIBLE

Ready for the biggest challenge of all? Why not read through the entire Bible in a year? This plan will take you through every verse of the Bible in one year.

No matter how you decide to read, stick with it. It's normal to skip a day here and there. Don't get discouraged. Just pick up where you left off and read this amazing Book.

30 Days with Jesus

60 Days with Paul

90-Day Overview of the Bible

1. Genesis 1:1—2:3
2. Genesis 3:1—3:24
3. Genesis 6:9—7:24
4. Genesis 8:1—9:17
5. Genesis 17:1-22
6. Genesis 22:1-19
7. Genesis 25:19-34
8. Genesis 27:1—28:9
9. Genesis 37:1-36
10. Genesis 41:1-57
11. Genesis 45:1-28
12. Exodus 1:8—2:15
13. Exodus 3:1—4:17
14. Exodus 5:1—6:13
15. Exodus 12:1-42
16. Exodus 13:17—14:31
17. Exodus 20:1-21
18. Numbers 13:1-33
19. Joshua 2:1-24
20. Joshua 6:1-27
21. Judges 16:4-31
22. 1 Samuel 1:1-28
23. 1 Samuel 3:1-21
24. 1 Samuel 10:1-27
25. 1 Samuel 16:1-13
26. 1 Samuel 17:1-58
27. 1 Samuel 24:1-22
28. 2 Samuel 11:1—12:25
29. 1 Kings 3:1-28
30. 1 Kings 17:8-24
31. 1 Kings 18:1-46
32. 2 Kings 2:1-18
33. 2 Kings 4:8-37
34. 2 Chronicles 35:20—36:23
35. Esther 2:1-23
36. Esther 6:1—8:8
37. Job 1:1—2:13; 42:1-17
38. Psalm 23
39. Psalm 51
40. Psalm 100
41. Psalm 121
42. Psalm 145
43. Proverbs 4:1-27
44. Ecclesiastes 11:9—12:14
45. Isaiah 53:1-12
46. Daniel 1:1-21
47. Daniel 3:1-30
48. Daniel 6:1-28
49. Jonah 1:1—4:11
50. Matthew 1:18—2:23
51. Matthew 5:1-16; 6:1—7:12
52. Matthew 14:13-36
53. Matthew 21:1-17
54. Matthew 26:47-75
55. Matthew 27:15-66
56. Matthew 28:1-20
57. Mark 1:1-20
58. Mark 4:1-20
59. Luke 1:26-56; 2:1-20
60. Luke 10:25-42; 14:25-35
61. Luke 15:1-32
62. Luke 22:1-23
63. Luke 24:13-53
64. John 1:1-18
65. John 3:1-21
66. John 4:1-42
67. John 8:1-11
68. John 11:1-44
69. John 14:1-31
70. Acts 1:1-11
71. Acts 2:1-47
72. Acts 8:26-40
73. Acts 9:1-31
74. Acts 11:1-18
75. Acts 16:11-40
76. Romans 3:1-31
77. Romans 8:1-39
78. Romans 12:1-21
79. 1 Corinthians 13:1-13
80. 1 Corinthians 15:1-58
81. Ephesians 2:1-22; 6:10-20
82. Philippians 3:1—4:9
83. Colossians 3:1—4:1
84. 1 Thessalonians 4:1-18
85. Hebrews 11:1-40
86. James 1:1-27
87. James 3:1-18
88. 1 Peter 1:3-25
89. 1 John 1:1—2:17
90. Revelation 21:1—22:21

365 Days Through the Whole Bible

DATE	REFERENCE	DATE	REFERENCE
January 1	Genesis 1:1—3:24	February 15	Joshua 9:1—12:24
January 2	Genesis 4:1—5:32	February 16	Joshua 13:1—19:51
January 3	Genesis 6:1—8:22	February 17	Joshua 20:1—24:33
January 4	Genesis 9:1—11:32	February 18	Judges 1:1—3:6
January 5	Genesis 12:1—14:24	February 19	Judges 3:7—8:35
January 6	Genesis 15:1—17:27	February 20	Judges 9:1—12:15
January 7	Genesis 18:1—20:18	February 21	Judges 13:1—16:31
January 8	Genesis 21:1—23:20	February 22	Judges 17:1—21:25
January 9	Genesis 24:1—28:9	February 23	Ruth 1:1—4:22
January 10	Genesis 28:10—30:43	February 24	1 Samuel 1:1—3:21
January 11	Genesis 31:1—36:43	February 25	1 Samuel 4:1—7:17
January 12	Genesis 37:1—41:57	February 26	1 Samuel 8:1—12:25
January 13	Genesis 42:1—45:28	February 27	1 Samuel 13:1—15:35
January 14	Genesis 46:1—50:26	February 28	1 Samuel 16:1—17:58
January 15	Exodus 1:1—4:31	March 1	1 Samuel 18:1—20:42
January 16	Exodus 5:1—7:13	March 2	1 Samuel 21:1—26:25
January 17	Exodus 7:14—12:30	March 3	1 Samuel 27:1—31:13
January 18	Exodus 12:31—18:27	March 4	2 Samuel 1:1—4:12
January 19	Exodus 19:1—24:18	March 5	2 Samuel 5:1—7:29
January 20	Exodus 25:1—31:18	March 6	2 Samuel 8:1—10:19
January 21	Exodus 32:1—34:35	March 7	2 Samuel 11:1—12:31
January 22	Exodus 35:1—40:38	March 8	2 Samuel 13:1—14:33
January 23	Leviticus 1:1—7:38	March 9	2 Samuel 15:1—20:26
January 24	Leviticus 8:1—10:20	March 10	2 Samuel 21:1—24:25
January 25	Leviticus 11:1—17:16	March 11	1 Kings 1:1—4:34
January 26	Leviticus 18:1—22:33	March 12	1 Kings 5:1—8:66
January 27	Leviticus 23:1—25:55	March 13	1 Kings 9:1—11:43
January 28	Leviticus 26:1—27:34	March 14	1 Kings 12:1—16:34
January 29	Numbers 1:1—4:49	March 15	1 Kings 17:1—19:21
January 30	Numbers 5:1—10:10	March 16	1 Kings 20:1—22:53
January 31	Numbers 10:11—14:45	March 17	2 Kings 1:1—8:15
February 1	Numbers 15:1—21:35	March 18	2 Kings 8:16—10:36
February 2	Numbers 22:1—25:18	March 19	2 Kings 11:1—13:25
February 3	Numbers 26:1—31:54	March 20	2 Kings 14:1—17:41
February 4	Numbers 32:1—34:29	March 21	2 Kings 18:1—21:26
February 5	Numbers 35:1—36:13	March 22	2 Kings 22:1—25:30
February 6	Deuteronomy 1:1—5:33	March 23	1 Chronicles 1:1—9:44
February 7	Deuteronomy 6:1—11:32	March 24	1 Chronicles 10:1—12:40
February 8	Deuteronomy 12:1—16:17	March 25	1 Chronicles 13:1—17:27
February 9	Deuteronomy 16:18—20:20	March 26	1 Chronicles 18:1—21:30
February 10	Deuteronomy 21:1—26:19	March 27	1 Chronicles 22:1—27:34
February 11	Deuteronomy 27:1—30:20	March 28	1 Chronicles 28:1—29:30
February 12	Deuteronomy 31:1—34:12	March 29	2 Chronicles 1:1—5:1
February 13	Joshua 1:1—5:12	March 30	2 Chronicles 5:2—9:31
February 14	Joshua 5:13—8:35	March 31	2 Chronicles 10:1—14:1

DATE		REFERENCE	DATE		REFERENCE
April 1	. . . . .	2 Chronicles 14:2—16:14	May 27	. . . . .	Psalms 107:1—109:31
April 2	. . . . .	2 Chronicles 17:1—21:3	May 28	. . . . .	Psalms 110:1—112:10
April 3	. . . . .	2 Chronicles 21:4—24:27	May 29	. . . . .	Psalms 113:1—115:18
April 4	. . . . .	2 Chronicles 25:1—28:27	May 30	. . . . .	Psalms 116:1—118:29
April 5	. . . . .	2 Chronicles 29:1—32:33	May 31	. . . . .	Psalm 119:1-176
April 6	. . . . .	2 Chronicles 33:1—35:27	June 1	. . . . .	Psalms 120:1—124:8
April 7	. . . . .	2 Chronicles 36:1-23	June 2	. . . . .	Psalms 125:1—129:8
April 8	. . . . .	Ezra 1:1—2:70	June 3	. . . . .	Psalms 130:1—134:3
April 9	. . . . .	Ezra 3:1—6:22	June 4	. . . . .	Psalms 135:1—137:9
April 10	. . . . .	Ezra 7:1—8:36	June 5	. . . . .	Psalms 138:1—140:13
April 11	. . . . .	Ezra 9:1—10:44	June 6	. . . . .	Psalms 141:1—144:15
April 12	. . . . .	Nehemiah 1:1—2:10	June 7	. . . . .	Psalms 145:1—150:6
April 13	. . . . .	Nehemiah 2:11—3:32	June 8	. . . . .	Proverbs 1:1-33
April 14	. . . . .	Nehemiah 4:1—7:73	June 9	. . . . .	Proverbs 2:1-22
April 15	. . . . .	Nehemiah 8:1—10:39	June 10	. . . . .	Proverbs 3:1-35
April 16	. . . . .	Nehemiah 11:1—13:31	June 11	. . . . .	Proverbs 4:1-27
April 17	. . . . .	Esther 1:1—2:23	June 12	. . . . .	Proverbs 5:1-23
April 18	. . . . .	Esther 3:1—4:17	June 13	. . . . .	Proverbs 6:1-35
April 19	. . . . .	Esther 5:1—10:3	June 14	. . . . .	Proverbs 7:1-27
April 20	. . . . .	Job 1:1—2:13	June 15	. . . . .	Proverbs 8:1-36
April 21	. . . . .	Job 3:1—14:22	June 16	. . . . .	Proverbs 9:1-18
April 22	. . . . .	Job 15:1—21:34	June 17	. . . . .	Proverbs 10:1-32
April 23	. . . . .	Job 22:1—31:40	June 18	. . . . .	Proverbs 11:1-31
April 24	. . . . .	Job 32:1—37:24	June 19	. . . . .	Proverbs 12:1-28
April 25	. . . . .	Job 38:1—41:34	June 20	. . . . .	Proverbs 13:1-25
April 26	. . . . .	Job 42:1-17	June 21	. . . . .	Proverbs 14:1-35
April 27	. . . . .	Psalms 1:1—4:8	June 22	. . . . .	Proverbs 15:1-33
April 28	. . . . .	Psalms 5:1—8:9	June 23	. . . . .	Proverbs 16:1-33
April 29	. . . . .	Psalms 9:1—12:8	June 24	. . . . .	Proverbs 17:1-28
April 30	. . . . .	Psalms 13:1—16:11	June 25	. . . . .	Proverbs 18:1-24
May 1	. . . . .	Psalms 17:1—20:9	June 26	. . . . .	Proverbs 19:1-29
May 2	. . . . .	Psalms 21:1—24:10	June 27	. . . . .	Proverbs 20:1-30
May 3	. . . . .	Psalms 25:1—28:9	June 28	. . . . .	Proverbs 21:1-31
May 4	. . . . .	Psalms 29:1—32:11	June 29	. . . . .	Proverbs 22:1-29
May 5	. . . . .	Psalms 33:1—36:12	June 30	. . . . .	Proverbs 23:1-35
May 6	. . . . .	Psalms 37:1—41:13	July 1	. . . . .	Proverbs 24:1-34
May 7	. . . . .	Psalms 42:1—45:17	July 2	. . . . .	Proverbs 25:1-28
May 8	. . . . .	Psalms 46:1—49:20	July 3	. . . . .	Proverbs 26:1-28
May 9	. . . . .	Psalms 50:1—53:6	July 4	. . . . .	Proverbs 27:1-27
May 10	. . . . .	Psalms 54:1—56:13	July 5	. . . . .	Proverbs 28:1-28
May 11	. . . . .	Psalms 57:1—59:17	July 6	. . . . .	Proverbs 29:1-27
May 12	. . . . .	Psalms 60:1—62:12	July 7	. . . . .	Proverbs 30:1-33
May 13	. . . . .	Psalms 63:1—65:13	July 8	. . . . .	Proverbs 31:1-31
May 14	. . . . .	Psalms 66:1—68:35	July 9	. . . . .	Ecclesiastes 1:1—2:26
May 15	. . . . .	Psalms 69:1—72:20	July 10	. . . . .	Ecclesiastes 3:1—5:20
May 16	. . . . .	Psalms 73:1—75:10	July 11	. . . . .	Ecclesiastes 6:1—8:17
May 17	. . . . .	Psalms 76:1—78:72	July 12	. . . . .	Ecclesiastes 9:1—12:14
May 18	. . . . .	Psalms 79:1—81:16	July 13	. . . . .	Song of Songs 1:1—8:14
May 19	. . . . .	Psalms 82:1—84:12	July 14	. . . . .	Isaiah 1:1—6:13
May 20	. . . . .	Psalms 85:1—89:52	July 15	. . . . .	Isaiah 7:1—12:6
May 21	. . . . .	Psalms 90:1—92:15	July 16	. . . . .	Isaiah 13:1—18:7
May 22	. . . . .	Psalms 93:1—95:11	July 17	. . . . .	Isaiah 19:1—23:18
May 23	. . . . .	Psalms 96:1—98:9	July 18	. . . . .	Isaiah 24:1—27:13
May 24	. . . . .	Psalms 99:1—101:8	July 19	. . . . .	Isaiah 28:1—31:9
May 25	. . . . .	Psalms 102:1—104:35	July 20	. . . . .	Isaiah 32:1—35:10
May 26	. . . . .	Psalms 105:1—106:48	July 21	. . . . .	Isaiah 36:1—39:8

DATE	REFERENCE	DATE	REFERENCE
July 22	Isaiah 40:1—48:22	September 16	Matthew 19:1—20:34
July 23	Isaiah 49:1—52:12	September 17	Matthew 21:1—23:39
July 24	Isaiah 52:13—55:13	September 18	Matthew 24:1—25:46
July 25	Isaiah 56:1—59:21	September 19	Matthew 26:1—28:20
July 26	Isaiah 60:1—66:24	September 20	Mark 1:1—3:35
July 27	Jeremiah 1:1—6:30	September 21	Mark 4:1—7:23
July 28	Jeremiah 7:1—10:25	September 22	Mark 7:24—9:1
July 29	Jeremiah 11:1—15:21	September 23	Mark 9:2—10:52
July 30	Jeremiah 16:1—20:18	September 24	Mark 11:1—12:44
July 31	Jeremiah 21:1—24:10	September 25	Mark 13:1-37
August 1	Jeremiah 25:1—29:32	September 26	Mark 14:1—16:20
August 2	Jeremiah 30:1—33:26	September 27	Luke 1:1—4:13
August 3	Jeremiah 34:1—38:28	September 28	Luke 4:14—6:49
August 4	Jeremiah 39:1—45:5	September 29	Luke 7:1—9:50
August 5	Jeremiah 46:1—52:34	September 30	Luke 9:51—10:42
August 6	Lamentations 1:1—5:22	October 1	Luke 11:1-54
August 7	Ezekiel 1:1—3:27	October 2	Luke 12:1-59
August 8	Ezekiel 4:1—11:25	October 3	Luke 13:1—14:35
August 9	Ezekiel 12:1—17:24	October 4	Luke 15:1—16:31
August 10	Ezekiel 18:1—24:27	October 5	Luke 17:1—19:27
August 11	Ezekiel 25:1—32:32	October 6	Luke 19:28—21:38
August 12	Ezekiel 33:1—39:29	October 7	Luke 22:1-71
August 13	Ezekiel 40:1—48:35	October 8	Luke 23:1-56
August 14	Daniel 1:1—3:30	October 9	Luke 24:1-53
August 15	Daniel 4:1—6:28	October 10	John 1:1—2:12
August 16	Daniel 7:1—12:13	October 11	John 2:13—3:36
August 17	Hosea 1:1—3:5	October 12	John 4:1-45
August 18	Hosea 4:1—5:15	October 13	John 4:46—6:71
August 19	Hosea 6:1—10:15	October 14	John 7:1—10:42
August 20	Hosea 11:1—14:9	October 15	John 11:1—12:50
August 21	Joel 1:1—2:27	October 16	John 13:1—14:31
August 22	Joel 2:28—3:21	October 17	John 15:1—17:26
August 23	Amos 1:1—2:16	October 18	John 18:1—19:42
August 24	Amos 3:1—6:14	October 19	John 20:1—21:25
August 25	Amos 7:1—9:15	October 20	Acts 1:1—4:37
August 26	Obadiah 1-21	October 21	Acts 5:1—7:60
August 27	Jonah 1:1—2:10	October 22	Acts 8:1—12:24
August 28	Jonah 3:1—4:11	October 23	Acts 12:25—15:35
August 29	Micah 1:1—2:13	October 24	Acts 15:36—18:23
August 30	Micah 3:1—5:15	October 25	Acts 18:24—21:16
August 31	Micah 6:1—7:20	October 26	Acts 21:17—28:31
September 1	Nahum 1:1—3:19	October 27	Romans 1:1—3:20
September 2	Habakkuk 1:1—3:19	October 28	Romans 3:21—5:21
September 3	Zephaniah 1:1—3:20	October 29	Romans 6:1—8:39
September 4	Haggai 1:1—2:23	October 30	Romans 9:1—11:36
September 5	Zechariah 1:1—8:23	October 31	Romans 12:1—16:27
September 6	Zechariah 9:1—14:21	November 1	1 Corinthians 1:1—4:21
September 7	Malachi 1:1—4:6	November 2	1 Corinthians 5:1—6:20
September 8	Matthew 1:1—4:25	November 3	1 Corinthians 7:1-40
September 9	Matthew 5:1-48	November 4	1 Corinthians 8:1—11:1
September 10	Matthew 6:1-34	November 5	1 Corinthians 11:2—14:40
September 11	Matthew 7:1-29	November 6	1 Corinthians 15:1—16:24
September 12	Matthew 8:1—10:42	November 7	2 Corinthians 1:1—2:11
September 13	Matthew 11:1—13:52	November 8	2 Corinthians 2:12—7:16
September 14	Matthew 13:53—15:39	November 9	2 Corinthians 8:1—9:15
September 15	Matthew 16:1—18:35	November 10	2 Corinthians 10:1—13:14

A HISTORY OF
THE MACHINE

A HISTORY OF
THE MACHINE

SIGVARD STRANDH

A&W Publishers, Inc., New York

A HISTORY OF THE MACHINE has been designed and produced by AB Nordbok, Gothenburg, Sweden, under the supervision of Einar Engelbrektsson and Turlough Johnston.

Graphical design and colour: Tommy Berglund.

Artwork: Syed Mumtaz Ahmad, Tommy Berglund, Inger Eriksson, Marie Falksten, Ferenc Flamm, Annette Johansson, Lars Jödahl, Hans Linder, Elise Lundqvist, Lennart Molin, Yusuke Nagano, Holger Rosenblad, Ulf Söderqvist, Roland Thorbjörnsson.

Translator: Ann Henning.

Lithographics: Nils Hermansson and Annette Johansson.

Editors: Turlough Johnston, Kerstin Stålbrand.

Assistant editors: Jeremy Franks, Donovan O'Malley.

Nordbok would like to express warm thanks to the following for their advice and assistance: Curt Falkemo, Jan Hult, William T. O'Dea, Holger Rosenblad, and Per Hedelin.

Further, Nordbok would like to thank the following for providing illustration research material or illustration material: Lars Harry Jenneborg, p. 8 ill. 2; Mary Evans Picture Library, p. 9 ill. 9, p. 131 B; P. Haase & Søns Forlag, p. 36 A—C, p. 37 A, B, p. 42 B—D; Derek de Solla Price, p. 46 A; Cambridge University Press, p. 47 C; Almqvist & Wiksell/Focus, p. 51 G; Denny Lorentzen, p. 88 ill. 1, 2; Ronan Picture Library, p. 141 C ill. 3, p. 231 C; Daimler Benz Museum, Stuttgart, p. 146—147 B; Marshall Cavendish, p. 146—147 B, p. 183 D, p. 196 B, p. 211 D, p. 223 D, E, p. 231 E; Teknisk Tidskrift, p. 166 B ill. 1, 2, p. 166 C ill. 1, 2; Chalmers Institution of Information Theory, p. 198; Motor, p. 201 B; P. A. Norstedts förlag, p. 208 A, B; Science Museum, p. 220 B, C, p. 220—221 E; Electrolux, p. 226 C; AEG, p. 232—233 A, C, D, E.

First published in the United States of America in 1979 by
A & W Publishers
95 Madison Avenue
New York, New York 10016
by arrangement with AB Nordbok.

Library of Congress Catalog Card Number: 77-82279
ISBN: 0-89479-025-0

Typeset by Rotogravyr, Solna, Sweden.
Printed in Italy.

CONTENTS

PREFACE

This book is about *machines*, and although this not-easily defined term has been generously interpreted, the machines discussed have been chosen subjectively and arbitrarily. The book is, then, not a comprehensive treatment of the whole field of study, a matter that has anyway become an impossibility. The French encyclopaedists of the latter part of the eighteenth century required thirty-five folio volumes to achieve an essentially complete description of the techniques of contemporary engineering, the natural sciences, and the arts. It is fruitless to speculate about the number of volumes that might be required in order to achieve the same result today.

The book does not, however, concern itself with the evaluation of technology, for all that this is currently in vogue throughout the western world. In my opinion, the writing of history should be clearly distinguished from polemics. Leopold von Ranke commented that the historical method should describe "how things actually occurred"; if this principle be applied in a history of machines, it is possible, by reading the text—and between its lines—to appreciate how technology has dominated the growth of both material well-being and non-material values. Technology has become more and more a carrier of culture and a powerfull instrument in fostering democracy—as it was even before the fall of the Bastille.

Is this to say, then, that the machine is to be regarded as wholly beneficial? Melvin Kranzberg, the American historian of technology, has hit the nail on the head in forming what he calls Kranzberg's First Law: "Technology is neither positive, negative, nor neutral". Professor Kranzberg may be interpreted as wishing to emphasize that while it is intrinsically neither good nor evil, technology is always present, in the midst of things. Since at least the eighteenth century, machine technology has attracted critics who have questioned its development—the first "fire and air" engines provoked reactions in many quarters that resemble the resistance to nuclear energy expressed two hundred years later. At the beginning of the nineteenth century, in England, the Luddites broke up machines that they feared would destroy their livelihood, and a little later, the railway met with scepsis of one sort and another, both in England and elsewhere.

In public debate over the past two centuries, criticism of machines has alternated with an optimistic faith in the machine's future. In the 1960s, the criticism became powerfully adverse, not only in alarm reports, such as Rachel Carson's *Silent Spring* (1961) and Ralph Nader's *Unsafe at Any Speed* (1966), but also in more general works, of which Jacques Ellul's *The Technological Society* is an example. Published in English translation in 1964, its original publication in French in 1954 had attracted practically no attention outside France. Ellul, a lawyer and social scientist, defines technology as not merely machines and techniques, but also all that they have entailed in the way of organization and methods. Having embraced so much in his definition, Ellul condemns this technology for losing control over itself, to the extent of being self-generating to the point where the means of technology have become an end in themselves. Ellul's thesis is that this leads to a condition that is inhuman, because moral values have been eradicated. But is not this appalling perspective already upon us? What if the roles were reversed, so that a technologist, as Ellul would call him, were to attack the judicial apparatus with definitions as all-embracing as Ellul's definition of technology? In countries with high income taxation many regard the politico-administrative rule-by-decree as self-generating and destructive of morals. Both the alarmist and the social philosopher in the spirit of Ellul ignore the fact that machines, in the wider meaning applied in this book, have raised the quality of life, making it easier for us to live in a style that could not have been dreamt of a hundred years ago, even by the most progress-enamoured optimist. This is not to say that I regard "Ellulian" and other criticism of machines as without interest: on the contrary, criticism in its different forms has a vital function in a democratic society, but it can, like the other elements that help to form democracy, lose control over itself. The remedy? One might be to meditate on the talmudic saying, that we do not see things as they are, but as we are.

What is particularly positive today are the powerful movements within the world of technology itself that are striving in a scientific manner towards the goal of "seeing things as they are". This is especially obvious in technology assessment and consequence evaluation of new techniques. The former implies, in fact, that a newly developed technique that is to be launched be first tested by adding to the previously dominating technical-economic parameters others that take account of, for example, repercussions on employment and society at large; in other words, technology is assessed for its effects on the lives of individual people. Consequence evaluation is much the same thing but takes a longer, broader view of inherent risks; much attention has been paid to the function of computer technology, for example in the employment market and in society as a whole, especially taking into account the current, explosive growth of the use of microprocessors. It has become apparent how vital it is to "look before one leaps" when introducing new technology.

Contemporary technology and the natural sciences provide methods and means of correcting development that has run amok. Many examples may be found in environmental engineering, where new processes and routines have rapidly been developed, since it became clear how industrial and urban growth have blighted the natural world. Recent years have seen marked improvements here, both within industry and in matters affecting its contamination of air and water. This book presents some of the techniques that have been used to protect the environment, perhaps primarily to exemplify that concern for the environment was not something brought about by the alarms of the 1960s. Environmental engineering has a history covering several hundred years.

While working on this book, I have greatly enjoyed the help and encouragement given me by many people, who have generously supported me by word and deed. I must thank first my colleagues at the National Museum of Science and Technology, particularly Inga-Britta Sandqvist, archivist. I am particularly grateful, too, to the staffs of the Deutsches Museum in Munich and the Science Museum in London, and to Dr. Brooke Hindle of the Smithsonian Institution in Washington. Dr. Wilhelm Odelberg, Principal Librarian of the Royal Academy of Science, Stockholm, has generously made his wide knowledge of scientific literature available to me. Professor C. G. Nilsson in Luleå has constantly assisted my work by stimulating discussions of problems both large and small. My gratitude extends, naturally, to the members of my family, who have made my work easier in every way. I owe a particular debt to my wife, Eivor, who has, in addition to taking care of the typing, never ceased to encourage me, and Christin and Ricky have helped by their discussion and criticism. Ricky's sketches and drawings—produced with great panache—have been a constant source of inspiration and pleasure, and a couple have inspired illustrations in the book.

Cooperation with Nordbok has been particularly inspiring and congenial during the whole period of production. My warm thanks to all at Nordbok—no one named, no one forgotten!

Sigvard Strandh

CHAPTER 1
WITHOUT TOOLS, NO MACHINES

In one of his many essays the great American statesman-scientist Benjamin Franklin suggested that man is a tool-making animal. It is, he wrote, man's ability to manufacture tools that distinguishes him from the other animals. The study of human culture, both material and spiritual, is a fascinating subject, all the more so if we use as our starting-point the thought-provoking and dynamic combination of Franklin's manufacturing man, *Homo faber*, and Linnaeus's thinking man, *Homo sapiens*, and follow this from the time of man's first appearance, maybe a million years ago.

In the following chapters we shall examine some of the lines of development that have led from that time to the present day, with its host of machines of all kinds. These lines have never been straight and uncomplicated but have often wandered off on perplexing deviations. Our investigation will be further confused by the great number of ideas and inventions which, being born before their time, came to nought.

The origins of the vast multitude of today's machines can be found in the tools and implements fashioned in the dawn of history by *Homo sapiens faber*, our thinking, tool-making ancestor. Of course, it is a matter of definition whether or not the tools made by the early primates can be called machines. The only prime mover (a machine generating or, rather, converting energy) available to early man was his own muscle power. His tools and implements may be regarded as a reinforcement or extension of that power.

The German for "fist" is *Faust*, and in the sixteenth century, German miners used to call a sledge-hammer *Fäustling* (a "fister", as it might be called in English). This combination of arm and sledge-hammer has been called organ projection by the German scholar Ernst Kapp, who is often called the metaphysician of technology. In the hands of the miner, the "fister" was an extension of the muscle power he used to break ore from the bedrock. This combination of hand and "fister" might, perhaps, be regarded as a working machine, i.e., a machine which performs a special type of work.

What, then, is a machine? An oft-quoted definition is that formulated by a German engineer, Franz Reuleaux (1829–1905): "A machine is a combination of solid bodies, so arranged as to compel the mechanical forces of nature to perform work as a result of certain determinative movements."

This technically subtle definition does not really do very much towards clarifying the concept of a machine. It has recurred in many works of reference and has often aroused controversy. For instance, it has been asserted that the phrase "mechanical forces of nature" must exclude the large group of machines which are driven by human and animal muscle power, with the inevitable retort that these creatures must be regarded as part of nature! We, however, can set aside both the definition and the objections to it with an easy conscience and, instead, illustrate in more concrete terms what

A The only prime mover available to early man was his own muscle power. No animals had as yet been domesticated.

B The invention of the wheel—or, rather, the wheel shaft—was one of the great breakthroughs in the history of technology. Shown here is an Etruscan wheel from *c.* 400 BC.

Today, it is generally believed that Earth as a planet has existed for about 4,500 million years. In order to gain perspective on this incomprehensibly long period of time, we can compare it to a flight from New York to London, a distance of almost 3,000 miles (5,000 km). Each mile will then represent a period of about 1.5 million years, while each kilometre will correspond to a period of about a million years.

As the aeroplane takes off from New York's Kennedy Airport, Earth has just come into existence and is still fluid. Only when the aeroplane has covered 900 miles (1,500 km) of its trip (**1**) has the crust solidified to a certain extent, and not until another 300 miles (500 km) have been covered do what are considered to be the first living creatures appear – blue-green algae, which feed on inorganic matter. After 2,400 miles (4,000 km), when

approximately one-fifth of the distance remains (**2**), the first green algae appear. Here, they are represented by *Diplopora phanerospora*; (*a*) section, seen from above, (*b*) side view. The outer lime cover has been removed from the upper part of the alga.

We are now rapidly approaching the destination of our journey, Heathrow Airport in London. When London is 300 miles (500 km) away (**3**), a multitude of invertebrates appears, including *Trilobites*, a large, now extinct group of crustaceans, represented here by *Triarthrus becki* (*a*) and *Acidaspis dufrenoyi* (*b*). At about the same time, cuttlefish (*c*) come into existence, and when a good 150 miles (250 km) remain (**4**), the first bony fishes appear, among them the coelacanth. One coelacanth species, *Latimeria chalumnae* (shown here), was long thought to have been

8

extinct for 65 million years. In 1938, however, the first of several such coelacanths was caught off the coast of southern Africa.

The first species of dinosaur, the order of reptiles which tends to fascinate modern man the most, show up (5) when only 140 miles (250 km) remain of our journey. For the next 60 miles (100 km) or so, more and more species of dinosaur emerge into view and then disappear, and the last of these giant lizards becomes extinct when we are about 40 miles (65 km) from Heathrow. One of the best-known of the herbivorous genera, *Diplodocus*, represents the period of the giant reptiles.

When the sign ''FASTEN SEAT BELTS'' is switched on (6), almost 2 miles (3 km) before landing, the first of the erect apes can be seen, and more than 1.5 miles (2 km) later (7), during the Pleistocene era,

is succeeded by another animal which has given rise to much interest, namely, the mammoth. Its pelt of russet wool and long, almost black bristles well suited it for its life in the cold climate of the Pleistocene era which, after all, we also call the Ice Age.

During the very last part of the flight, we must measure distances in yards or metres instead of miles or kilometres, with 1 yard or 1 metre corresponding to a thousand years. Less than 5 yards (8) before touchdown, we skim over the Egyptian pyramids, while the industrial revolution, here symbolized by the interior of a French steelworks, starts (9) when 6 in (0.2 m) remain of our trip. The passengers in this time-machine in the guise of a jumbo-jet certainly had better keep their eyes open during the last fractions of a second of the flight if they are to see all that went on!

9

The following names sometimes refer to different periods of time depending on the geographical area to which they are applied, but usually, they mean the following:

The Eolithic era (from the Greek *eos*, dawn, and *lithos*, stone). The dawn of the Stone Age.

The Paleolithic era (from the Greek *palaios*, old). Started *c.* 2 million years BC. Itinerant hunters and collectors.

The Mesolithic era (from the Greek *mesos*, middle, intermediate). Started 13000—10000 BC.

The Neolithic era (from the Greek *neos*, new). Started 6000—3000 BC. During this period, the "agrarian revolution" occurs—people once nomadic settle down, build dwellings, and begin to farm and to keep animals. The first cities appear (Jericho, *c.* 6000 BC).

The Aeneolithic era (from the Latin *aenus*, bronze or metal). The Bronze Age, which started 2500—1500 BC. Metals now occur more commonly.

During the Quaternary period, ice ages or glacial eras alternated with relatively warm periods or interglacial eras. In Europe, the main ice ages have been given the names of four Alpine rivers: Würm, Riss, Mindel, and Günz. Similar temperature variations occurred on the other continents as well. The diagram to the right shows the ice ages occurring during the past 600,000 years and gives the names of the glacial and interglacial eras.

Number of years ago	Glacials and interglacials	
10000	Alleröd / Bölling / Lascaux	
20000	Tursac / Paudorf / Arcy	
30000		
40000	Hengelo / Laufen	WÜRM
50000		
60000	Brörup	
70000	Amersfoort	
80000		
90000		
100000	Riss-Würm interglacial	
200000		RISS
300000	Mindel-Riss interglacial	
400000		MINDEL
500000	Günz-Mindel interglacial	
600000		GÜNZ
700000		

machines are and what they could do even in their early, primitive forms.

This is by no means to disparage the work of Franz Reuleaux, which has been of very great significance to generations of engineers during the most expansive period of industrialism. His handbook of engineering was first published in 1861 and was reissued in new, revised editions and translated into many languages way into the twentieth century, becoming a standard work for engineers in every industrialized country in the world. Reuleaux was professor of mechanical engineering at the *Gewerbeakademie* ("Academy of Industry") and later became provost there. In 1875, he published a comprehensive work on the theory of mechanical engineering, *Theoretische Kinematik: Grundzüge einer Theorie des Maschinenwesens*, from which his definition is taken. Reuleaux's main purpose in this book is to determine the various species and types of machines. With genuine Teutonic thoroughness, he defines no less than fourteen species in this massive morphology of the machine.

But, first, let us return to the Palaeolithic period, the Early Stone Age, and consider the tools and implements which the early humans used to improve their lot. The primordial condition—wherever in time one locates it—was certainly no idyll. Without implements of various kinds, man, whatever his environment, was hopelessly inferior to the predatory animals that were once his competitors in the struggle for survival. They were swifter and, in many cases, stronger than him, to whom weapons were vital for defence and for hunting. He needed tools to make clothes for protection against the elements. Mere survival in the struggle to exist was literally a full-time occupation. Primeval man's incentive to improve his lot was, therefore, very strong. Modern man would have an extremely small chance of coping under such conditions.

Archaeological finds during the past thirty or forty years have cast a great deal of light on early primeval cultures and have enabled scientists to date the appearance of man the tool-maker further and further back. The first finds were exciting. During excavations in Sicily, the British palaeontologist Weyland found a number of stone chippings of various sizes among remnants of bones and other traces of human activity. At first, this was thought to be a coincidence, but more stone chippings from the same cultural stratum were soon found on other sites. All these chippings were on some points similar and on others dissimilar. But the important thing about them was that they had been *manufactured*. They had been made by the direct percussion of a stone striker against a stone nodule which was supported on a solid underlay, or anvil. These tools had a sharp cutting edge, but the other edge was comparatively flat and smooth, thus allowing the tool to fit neatly in the hand. The cutting edge was set at different angles on different-sized chippings, although not in a random fashion. This has been interpreted as an indication that toolmaking man had discovered that different materials, such as the various woods, bone, horn, etc., call for different cutting angles in order to achieve the best result. Thousands or tens of thousands of years may have been required to establish this. But early man had plenty of time. The position of the cultural stratum, together with various other factors, enabled Weyland to date finds from various sites to between 100,000 and 250,000 years before our time. Early cultures of this type are known as anvil cultures. Since Weyland's Sicilian excavations, remnants of several such cultures have been unearthed. What they all have in common is the use of an anvil—and a stone striker—in the manufacture of their tools.

The people of the anvil cultures had cutting tools which they used when making other useful implements. For example, they used their "axes" and "knives" to fashion spear shafts, and then they fitted these with pointed heads and used them to kill animals and to cut

A In the earliest cultures, manufactured stone chippings were used for scraping and cutting. These chippings, which modern archaeologists call flakes, are usually two or three times as long as they are wide. Attempts have been made to establish how they were made. It seems likely that the most primitive method was simply to strike a stone nodule (**1**) with a chunk of some hard type of rock. Another early method was pressure-flaking (**2**) of the stone nodule. The next step in human progress was to work the material against a solid underlay, an anvil (**3**).

B How flakes with different cutting angles were produced by indirect percussion, i.e., by holding a "chisel" against a stone nodule and striking the "chisel". Firstly, the top of a suitably shaped flint nodule was detached (*a*). Then chips were struck off, first along one (*b*) and then along the other (*c*) "long side" of the flint nodule—the small illustrations above the main ones show the flint nodule as seen from above. Thereupon, the flakes were detached (*d−h*; the same flake is shown in *d* and *e*), and their sections are shown by the small illustrations below each flake. At *i*, the flint nodule is shown as seen from above. The preliminary chipping has been made, and the parts used for the flakes are indicated.

C A method for working stone through pressure-flaking with a pole made from a hard type of wood. The man uses his feet to keep the nodule firmly in place.

D A great improvement was to provide stone tools with a handle or partly to wrap them in skins, an advance probably made in various different early anvil cultures.

E Compare man's way of holding a stone axe with how he fastened an axe head in a handle: he knew what he was doing.

A1 A2 B1 B2 B3 C2 C3 C1 D E F1 F2 G

A Another important advance was to barb fish-hooks and harpoons. These two bone harpoons were used for catching fish and are 12,000 (**1**) and 25,000 (**2**) years old respectively.
B Fish-hooks made by hand by some present-day peoples. (**1**) Composite wooden hook with bone barb from the Marshall Islands. (**2**) Stone hook from Easter Island. (**3**) Composite Polynesian hook.
C Man started making use of fire at an early stage. In order to start a fire, fire drills were used. In its simplest form (**1**), a fire drill consists of a stick, which is pressed against a wooden block, a "hearth", while being rapidly rotated between the hands. (**2**) The stick can also be equipped with a stone flywheel, its rotary movement being then facilitated by the inertia of the wheel. (**3**) A drill could also be used for making holes, and it became possible to manufacture needles, for instance.
D Oil lamps made from shells or stone have been used for about 15,000 years. The first lamps probably had wicks made from dried plant fibres. Tallow or vegetable oils were used as fuel.
E Neolithic stone axe. The tool has been given an antler sleeve, mounted in a wooden handle.
F Two primitive Egyptian hoes. One (**1**) consists of a forked branch, whereas the other (**2**) consists of a wooden blade attached to a haft.
G Neolithic wooden-hafted hoe.

them up. The hides could then be scraped and used as protection against the wind, for covering huts, and for making clothes. The people of these early cultures knew also how to make fish-hooks and crochet needles.

It is possible that some resourceful primate of an anvil culture may have invented the animal trap, a device which, to some extent at least, fulfils the conditions of Reuleaux's definition of a machine. The pitfall, which can be made with the simplest and most primitive techniques, probably comes from this time, too. The making of a snare or gin trap, both of which have releasing mechanisms, would, however, call for more than a little skill and an even greater measure of constructive thought. If the gin trap was made during Palaeolithic times, and it is highly likely that it was, then it represents the first automatic mechanism. It performs its job—to catch or kill game—without human intervention. At a pinch, the gin may be regarded as the nucleus of the most advanced automatic mechanism of our time, the computer.

Perspective on Our Existence

Despite the creditable efforts of, among others, Reuleaux, it is strange that no one has succeeded in finding a crystal-clear, unambiguous definition of the concept "machine". To try to pinpoint the appearance of the first machine is just as difficult a task, partly due to the vagueness of the definition and partly because this primeval machine—whatever we may understand by the expression—in all probability was invented before the creation of writing, so that no written sources are available. But no matter how primitive this first machine was, it could not have sprung forth, complete, from the brain of its inventor. It had to be manufactured, and the prerequisite for this is, quite simply, our tool-making man; for without tools, there can be no machines.

To attempt to establish when and where the first tool-making man appeared is beyond the scope of this book. But it may not be amiss to try to present a perspective to man's existence on the planet we call Earth, which, it is generally believed, has existed for about 4.5 thousand million years—an inconceivable length of time on man's own time-scale. It is both instructive and entertaining to "translate" this vast expanse of time into the twenty-four hours of the day. The first signs of life appear some time during the afternoon, whereas the first man-like creatures, the hominids, came on stage only a few minutes before midnight. That must, undeniably, give food for thought! Even more drastic results are obtained if we compare the earth's life-span with a flight from New York to London. The hominids entry takes place just before the aeroplane lands at Heathrow!

No certain knowledge of what happened here on earth during its first three or four thousand million years is as yet available, but the considerable progress being made in research in this field makes it probable that the present theories will shortly be replaced by hard facts. Consider, for instance, the recent discovery of the planar structure of the earth's crust. This caused a breakthrough in its field as sensational as the discovery of DNA did in the field of molecular biology.

During the past hundred years or so, archaeologists have been able to form a fairly clear picture of the development that has taken place during the last ten million years, when the prelude to human civilization was first slowly struck up. Interesting climatic changes which have taken place since the arrival of man are shown on the time-scale on page 10. It has been possible to trace about a dozen ice ages during the last 600,000 years. Further, there is reliable evidence to indicate that, even since the last ice age, considerable climatic changes, for better or worse, have taken place. Many scientists maintain that a favourable climate was one of the reasons for the

blossoming of the advanced cultures during antiquity. For instance, they believe that a "pleasant zone" existed in Mesopotamia during the fourth millennium BC, when Ur, Babylon, and Nineveh flourished. A deterioration in the climate, resulting in hotter, drier conditions of the type prevailing in present-day Iran may have contributed to the decline and fall of these cultures. We know for certain that even earlier cultures were swept away by natural disasters. The Bible's Deluge appears in the chronicles of several cultures, with variations in detail but agreement about an all-destroying flood. The Gilgamesh epic gives an exhaustive account of a global cataclysm, as do the Eddic sagas.

During recent years, new finds have been made which originate from cultures existing before the Flood, or whatever one chooses to call the major disaster which befell the earth at the dawn of history. New information is continuously coming to light, and what has just been said of our knowledge of the geological genesis of the earth can also be said about the eras before the appearance of man—the "scientific guesses" we have made so far about these cultures will, in all probability, soon be replaced by well-founded facts. Among other projects that are being worked on is that of the Leakeys in East Africa.

A lot of valuable results were produced by Mary and Louis S. B. Leakey, whose work there started at the beginning of the 1930s. In recent years, their sons Richard and Jonathan have also been working there. The Leakeys' research has brought many fascinating finds to light. For instance, in northern Kenya the remains of human skeletons over two million years old have been found. A partly preserved skull, found by Richard Leakey and numbered 1470, has been identified as belonging to the genus *homo*, and its age has been established at about 2.5 million years. "Tools"—mainly stone chippings—which were used by these ancestors of the human race have also been discovered. Similar finds have been made in other parts of the world, and scientists are now busy tracing the development of these early human beings throughout the past twenty million years.

During the past century, the perspective which we have had on our own existence here on earth has been considerably extended. Even as late as the middle of the nineteenth century, it was the teachings of James Ussher which dominated the ecclesiastical and scientific worlds. Ussher (1581–1656) was Archbishop of Armagh in Ireland. Two years before his death, he published a comprehensive work on biblical chronology, *Annales Veteris et Novi Testamenti*, which created a stir throughout all Christendom. With the help of the genealogical tables in the Old Testament and of datings in the New Testament, Ussher could date the Creation to 4004 BC. His book led to a flood of learned works which went even further in pinpointing the date of the story of creation as recorded in Genesis. A calendar published by St. John's College, Oxford, at the start of the eighteenth century, was able to state that, "In the beginning God created the heaven and the earth" at 9.00 am on March 23, 4004 BC.

Today, we may well smile at this strict dogmatic approach and at the fact that its results were accepted for so long and through centuries which could, after all, boast of considerable progress, not least in the fields of natural science and technology. But then, we must remember that the Church maintained an iron grip on both theological orthodoxy and the secular sciences.

This cocksure dating of the Creation was, however, soon called into question by some remarkable archaeological finds. In the seventeenth century, the remains of long-extinct animals—among them, mammoths—were found in several places in Europe. These remains were discovered in deep earth layers which can only have been formed by deposits left by the Flood or by an even earlier and greater inundation. Supporters of the Bible's chronology countered by explaining that there must have been more than one period of creation!

Several interesting finds of early flint tools were made in the seventeenth and eighteenth centuries. Scientists were perplexed by a well-tooled stone axe, found in c. 1690 during work in a gravel-pit near Gray's Inn Lane in London. It was found in the remains of an elephant's skeleton by an apothecary. Again, the traditionalists had an answer: "It was a weapon used by the courageous Britons in their battles against the elephants of the Roman army during Claudius's invasion of Britain in the fifth decade of our era." Similar finds of tools and weapons were made during the eighteenth and early nineteenth centuries but, with a few exceptions, their origins were explained away and dated in a similar way to that used for the axe found in Gray's Inn Lane.

Today, we know beyond doubt that this axe dates from the Early Stone Age, as do several other tools and implements found during the long period when the scientific world adhered to Archbishop Ussher's dating of the Creation. The breakthrough occurred on the publication, in 1859, of Charles Darwin's theory of evolution in his book *On the Origin of Species . . .*, which immediately caused a violent controversy. While feelings ran at their highest, in 1868, the Cro-Magnon cave was discovered in south-western France, and this discovery was followed, a few years later, by that of the Altamira cave in the Pyrenees. Excavations brought to light skulls, parts of skeletons, and a great number of tools of various kinds, and the famous murals were found in the latter cave. The datings of these finds have long been a matter of dispute, but it was realized from the first that these humans had lived long before the year of Ussher's Creation, 4004 BC. Nowadays, scientists more or less agree that the Cro-Magnon culture goes back to the latest ice age, c. 20,000 years ago, while the Altamira culture is older, being generally considered, at present, to date back to 30,000−40,000 years before our time.

The giant Altamira murals have attracted much attention, and so have the similar paintings in the Lascaux and La Madelaine caves, discovered later. In the present context, we can leave to one side the art experts' interpretation of the significance of the paintings, because of greater interest is the fact that the inhabitants of these cultures could create *the technical prerequisites* of painting−the tools with which to prepare paint and to apply it to the cave wall. The pigments were derived from naturally occurring minerals, for instance, the warm red of iron ochre (the colour of life, probably first used for cult ceremonies), the yellow of manganese oxides, and the blue of cobalt salts. Nature offers a bountiful palette, but most of these minerals are hard and must be pulverized by crushing and grinding, before they can be mixed with a binder and used for painting. The implements used in the preparation of these paints were found in the caves (tools for crushing, grinding, and mixing− processes which are still used in the chemical industry, in the so-called basic unit operations).

A replica of part of the Altamira cave has been built at the Deutsches Museum in Munich. This permanent exhibit, entitled "The Earliest History of Chemical Technology", shows among other things how the paint used in the murals was prepared. The machines now used for these basic unit operations have, without a doubt, a long prehistory!

We can say to sum up that, in a relatively short period of time, our perspective on the existence of our own species on earth has been extended further and further back in history. The arsenal of technical aids at the disposal of the modern archaeologist has helped enormously towards increasing our knowledge of the long prehistory of our time.

The scholars of classical antiquity and the history of art used to be those who worked closely with the archaeologist. Nowadays, his colleagues are more often physicists and technologists, specialists in the Carbon-14 method, pollen analysis, the determination of the age of ceramics by thermoluminescence, and so on. In many cases the archaeologist relies on the computer engineer to process the finds he has made.

A half a million years or so ago, some primate, one of man's precursors, learnt how to master fire. During excavations in China in the 1920s, two Swedish scientists, J. G. Andersson and B. Bohlin, established that the so-called Peking Man, or *Sinanthropus pekingensis* (from *Sin*, "China", and *anthropus*, "human being"), had been acquainted with fire. The dating, three to four hundred thousand years before our time, is a matter of controversy. However, Peking Man was by no means the first to use fire.

In recent years, finds have been made in Central and South Africa of remnants of human skeletons which can be definitely dated earlier than the Peking Man. The scientific names for these hominids (man-like creatures) have since had the element *pithecus* added to them, and this is sometimes combined with *anthropus*. The South African finds showed manifest traces of fire, the earliest yet to have been found−about half a million years old. These primeval masters of fire now go under the name of *Australopithecus prometeus*, *australis* meaning "southern" and the latter part of the name coming from the Titan of Greek mythology, Prometheus, who stole fire from Zeus and gave it to mankind.

And indeed, fire *was* a god-sent gift. It afforded protection against the dark and the cold, and, to a certain extent, against wild animals. But it was also a tool, which could be used to hollow out tree trunks and to shape them into log canoes. Even solid rock was not impervious to the onslaught of fire; alternate heating and drenching will, in the end, crack most rocks. The job can then be finished off with sledge-hammers and pick-axes.

Man also discovered, although much later than the period under discussion, that certain kinds of rock, when heated, start to "bleed" a fluid which rapidly solidifies, and it was thus that metals were discovered. Copper is considered to have been known in Egypt at least 4,500 years before Christ and in the other great river cultures of classical antiquity a millennium or so later. Many finds show that the art of working meteoric iron was known in these cultures, but this, obviously, had no influence on the general development of the art of iron working. The supply of "raw material" was fortuitous and, to say the least, minimal. Its origin was enshrouded in mystery, and anything made from meteoric iron usually became a cult object in religious or magic rites.

The discovery of metal, a new raw material for tools, was not only an important breakthrough in the field of tool development, which was then in its infancy, but also a great step forward for human culture as a whole. Man's ability to shape metals and alloys through casting and forging opened up whole new vistas and led to a wide assortment of new and more effective tools; these, in their turn, made possible the production of many useful everyday articles, as well as−and this is often overlooked−the development of new forms of art. The visual arts are simply inconceivable without the artist's tools and other technical paraphernalia.

Metal Tools

At this very early stage of tool technology, one of the most practical tools to be developed was the scissors. Indeed, the invention of the scissors was a definite step forward, as the technology of the earlier anvil cultures had not been capable of making such a tool. They could make cutting tools, such as knives, axes, and saws, from various types of hard stone, and there still exist some marvellous examples of these well-produced and highly finished tools. However, the introduction of metals made it possible to introduce a new way of working a material—by cutting with scissors. Apart from the purely trivial applications of this new technique—it is hard to imagine how a modern household could function without at least one pair of scissors—the ancient Egyptians began to create works of art with scissors, cutting silhouettes which portrayed their dear ones. This became a high art form, developed to perfection by a much-respected guild of artists and, later, influential in painting, which could begin only when man had mastered the technique of mixing colour pigments with a binding medium and of applying the resulting paint to a surface with a tool, a brush. For thousands of years, the traditional profile view used in the highly developed art of silhouette making came to be used also in portrait painting in that part of the world. During this period, the head was hardly ever painted full face, but in profile, like in a silhouette, but with the almond eyes exquisitely coloured and the lines of forehead, nose, and chin delightfully classic.

But what are almond eyes and portraits in profile doing in a book on the history of the machine? Well, part of the answer is that there is a more concrete connection between pure technical development and the cultivation of the mind—in this case, painting—than is generally supposed. The development of the arts goes hand in hand with advances made in technology. This applies not only to the visual arts, but also to literature—writing materials, the art of printing—and to music, where the instruments can be seen as technical creations.

But let us return to the scissors, which in all their simplicity and functional beauty as the first clipping tool were the first, and thus decisive, application in tool technology of what is called the "simple machine". In classic mechanics, the term "simple machine" covers a handful of fundamental innovations which have contributed in an exceptionally high degree to the progress of human culture. The first of these, the lever, goes back to the earliest anvil cultures. With a lever, it is possible to move heavy objects which could not otherwise be moved by hand. It is, of course, completely futile to speculate on exactly when this technique became manifest to prehistoric man, but it is fairly safe to conjecture that it happened during the Early Stone Age. The same goes for both the inclined plane and the wedge, which are based on the same theory.

The Tools of the Pyramid Builders

The simple machines and the art of working stone are our foremost heritage from prehistoric times, i.e., those before we have access to written sources. In the Nile culture, the art of shaping stone developed very rapidly during the fourth millennium BC. Striking tools were used on chisels of different kinds to form beautifully shaped stone vessels, urns, and vases. The raw material was granite and porphyry, but even rock crystal was used in making ornaments. The Egyptians also developed a special technique for quarrying boulders of considerable size from the bedrock.

It was with this advanced technology, based on purpose-built tools, and with the help of the simple machines known at the time, that the pyramids of Egypt could be built. The first of these, the pyramid of Pharaoh Neter-khet (commonly known as Djoser or Zoser) at Sakkara, rises to a height of about 203 ft (62 m) and was originally covered with polished limestone—a truly remarkable construction, completed around 2,800 BC. Other cultures of very early times had also mastered the technique of erecting monumental structures. Striking examples of this are, for instance, the impressive cult centre at Stonehenge, and the pyramid-like constructions erected by the early mound-building cultures of Mexico and Central America.

In ancient Egypt, shears were used to cut silhouettes (*above*), an art form which was developed to exquisite perfection by an esteemed guild of artists. This tradition later also left its mark on the pictorial art in these parts of the world. For thousands of years, portraits were practically always executed in profile (*below*), as in a silhouette.

A Many scientists nowadays hold the opinion that a "machine tool", a fiddle borer, of the type shown here (**1**) was used during the Stone Age for drilling holes in stone tools. The object to be worked (*a*) was securely anchored beneath a drill (*b*), which was a bone of circular cross-section, perhaps a thigh-bone of some large animal. A flywheel (*c*) facilitated the drill's rotation, which

was imparted by a bowed string (*d*). To bring pressure to bear on the drill, a lever (*e*), equipped with a weight (*f*), was employed. (**2**) Sectional view of how the drill penetrated the stone. Naturally, as the drill material alone—bone—was not hard enough to have any effect on stone, some sort of abrasive (*g*), such as finely ground flintstone, must have been used.

Several scholars who have described the mound cultures of the Neolithic era point out that the archaeological excavations undertaken have given very little information on the tools and implements used when the great structures of classical antiquity, for instance, the pyramids of Egypt, were erected. The Swede Henry Kjellson looks for, among other things, drawing blocks and machines for drawing precious metals and iron into thin, even wires. (Wire was used for a variety of utilitarian and ornamental purposes by the ancient cultures of Sumeria and Egypt.) Axes, chisels, and saws made from hard types of stone can be used to work softer types, but this explains only part of the mystery of how early man in the dawn of history, from the Eolithicum to the Neolithicum, could produce magnificent results in stone, as the many finds from the period testify. The German Albert Neuburger exclaims in his classic *Technik des Altertums* ("The Technology of Antiquity"), "Without mining, no technology!" We can add, "Without metals, no tools to build machines."

As we have said already, man's discovery of metal brought about a definite breakthrough in the art of making tools. In all probability, copper is the earliest known of the metals. From at least 5000 BC, copper ore was mined from opencast and pit mines on Mount Sinai, and we know that rich deposits were being mined in Cyprus a couple of thousand years later. (The Latin for the metal, *cuprum*, is derived from the name of the island.) But copper is a soft metal, and even if the art of alloying it with other metals was known at an early stage— copper alloyed with tin gives bronze, and with zinc gives brass—the tools made from these alloys had little chance of producing good results with hard types of rock, such as granite and porphyry. But these were the very materials used for the artefacts we have mentioned already to demonstrate the advanced stone-working techniques of the Neolithic era.

How, then, was it possible to produce these technically advanced artefacts? There have been no significant finds of any of the tools used. One of the reasons for this may be that, until very recently, archaeologists have concentrated on quite different aspects of the earliest cultures, especially on their religion and art. However, there has been a lot of speculation about the tool technology which made possible these impressive artefacts of hard stone, which we can still examine and admire in museums all over the world. Several scientists have suggested that tools of copper or copper alloy could have been fitted with diamond chips, cast or forged into the metal. This would apply to such stone-working tools as chisels, saws, and drills. On different types of building stones and in quarries, clear indications have been found that show that the tools used penetrated quite deeply into the stone for every revolution or stroke. This further indicates that the tool—a drill or a saw—was the active element in a "machine tool", in which the tool had been exposed by mechanical means to very high pressure. The simple machines, which are our technical heritage from the Palaeolithic era, include the lever and the wedge, and although no finds have been made to verify it, there are good grounds for assuming that both the lever and the wedge were used as construction elements in these early machines.

Numerous artefacts of hard stone, with polished, lustrous surfaces, are known from the earliest of the ancient mound cultures. Also, there is, from the Eolithic and Palaeolithic eras, a multitude of stone striking tools—axes, sledge-hammers, and hammers—in which holes have been drilled to take a shaft. The archaeologists of the nineteenth century and earlier found it almost impossible to explain how these neat holes were made. This is easily understandable, bearing in mind the pitifully poor technical education available to the profession at the time. The reason that these poor humanists were so mystified was that they thought that all of the material in the holes was removed by drilling, an operation which would have taken an unrealistically long time. A drill was, indeed, used, but it was not a solid drill. Many believe that a bone was used as a hollow drill, and a string and bow—a fiddle borer—with a lever and load, converted and increased the power. Naturally, bone is far too soft a material for it alone to have any effect on stone, but with the help of an abrasive material, for instance a powder of a hard rock type, one can work wonders with this simple tool. Many abrasives are naturally available, and the basic unit operations of crushing and grinding were well known. Finely ground flintstone ought to have been effective—and maybe some privileged culture had thought of using crushed diamond chips. In recent times, several attempts have been made to drill holes in stone using these methods. The experiments show that, with a drill of circular section and an abrasive, it is possible to make a tube-shaped cutting in the material, without having to tackle the core of the cutting at all. Several unfinished holes of this sort have been found and dated to the Palaeolithic era. These consist of cylindrical cores left in holes which have been partly drilled with tubular drills; abrasives have clearly been used during the operation.

The sophisticated technique and the highly developed skill used by craftsmen in producing from stone such utility articles as beakers, urns, pots, and vases presuppose the use of specialized tools and some sort of sanding machine and abrasive. Possibly, pulverized flintstone was used as an abrasive, although quartz and basalt could also have been used. But the abrasive which immediately springs to mind is that which occurs so abundantly in that part of the world, namely, the desert sand.

When compared to iron and steel, copper is a soft metal. But when the Mount Sinai copper deposits began to be worked, probably at the beginning of the fifth millennium BC, copper was immediately used to make edged tools, such as axes, chisels, knives, and scissors. Within a millennium, metallurgy had made such purely empirical progress that copper could be made considerably harder by cold-hammering.

In the Brinell scale (B), red copper has a hardness of c. 80−90 B, but cold-hammered copper reaches a degree of 135−145 B. This means that a skilled craftsman could make the edge of a copper stone-cutting chisel as hard as good-quality wrought iron. At the beginning of the third millennium BC, copper mining began in Oman, on the Persian Gulf; the ore there was not as pure as that in the Mount Sinai mines, for it contained nickel, tin, and some other metals. However, these "contaminants" produced an alloy, ready-made by Nature, which was vastly superior to red copper; it had a natural hardness of 140−160 B, and this could be improved to 275 B and over if the metal was skilfully cold-hammered. Thus, an alloy was available that had properties comparable with those of reasonable tool steels in the early 1900s.

At the beginning of the third millennium BC, therefore, everything was poised for a breakthrough in stone-working techniques, above and beyond the technology that had produced the beautiful utility articles already mentioned, for now, man had tools which were capable of working even hard rock. The breakthrough was imminent.

It was at this time that the first *qanaat*s were built. These were conduits for carrying the drinking-water supply to the cities and towns which were springing up during this period; a pre-condition for the formation of any society is the availability of water. When the first *qanaat* was built is not known for sure. In the beginning, *qanaat*s were built of fairly short water pipes with relatively small cross-sections. Later, however, as the Assyrians developed the system, the dimensions of the pipes increased dramatically, and *qanaat*s were

B Levelling instrument used in ancient Egypt. (**1**) Set-square of 90°. (**2**) Instrument used to establish whether a surface was horizontal or not. If it was, the plumb line would hang straight in front of a groove in the middle of the cross-bar. (**3**) Instrument used to establish whether a surface was vertical or not. All these instruments have been found at Thebes and have been dated to c. 1100 BC.

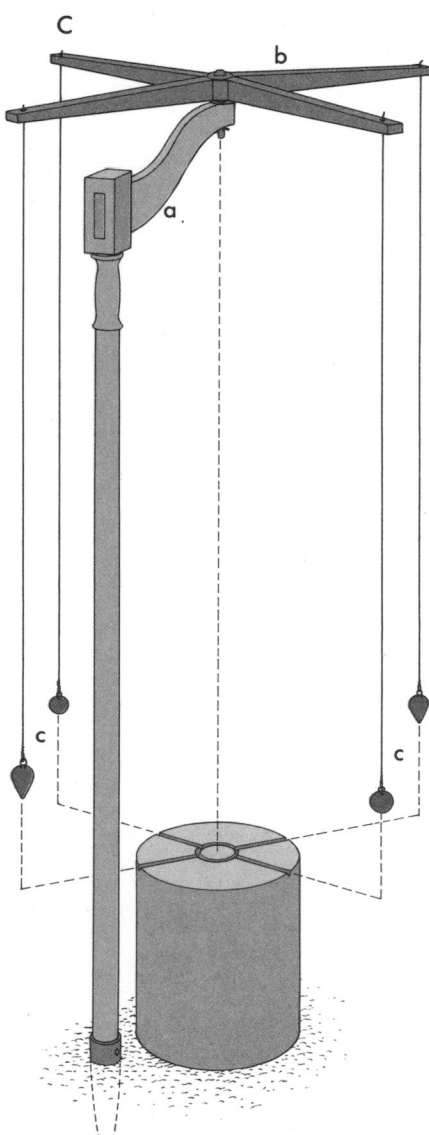

C A *groma*, an instrument used during classical antiquity to set out right angles. It consisted of an arm (*a*), which carried a pivoted, horizontal cross (*b*). A plumb bob (*c*) was suspended from each arm of the cross. One opposing pair of plumb lines was used to align the instrument with a given line, and the other pair was used to lay out a line at right angles to the first. For the instrument to work, it was necessary that the cross was absolutely horizontal, and the weather absolutely calm!

built throughout the countries of classical antiquity—north-east Africa, Iran, and India. In Iran alone, there are today over twenty thousand conduit systems, with an accumulated length of over 168,000 miles (c. 270,000 km), and most of these are still in use, although the majority were built in the third millennium BC.

In order to direct these water tunnels successfully, the difficult art of surveying had been learnt, and the tools necessary for this had been created. The crux was to calculate, and then to drive the tunnels to give, the best inclination for the most effective water-flow. The theory and the technique used in such calculations are fundamentally the same as those used today in laying out safe foundations for large buildings.

The time is a century or so into the third millennium BC. The necessary skills now seem to be well enough developed to explain that great and truly remarkable breakthrough in structural engineering, the building of the pyramids. Posterity has been highly puzzled by the lack of a significant link between the relatively primitive building forms previously in common use and the gigantic pyramids.

True, the earliest Neolithic cultures in various parts of the world had already developed the more relevant constructional principles of structural engineering, but in ancient Egypt, the main building material was *terre pisé*, i.e., clay mixed with straw and baked to form bricks. Simple huts as well as splendid palaces can be built with this material, but it is not very lasting and calls for substantial maintenance. Only fragments of such buildings from this period are still extant.

In any case, a major advance in construction techniques took place, from building in *terre pisé* to building in stone, and the results of this new technique have not been surpassed until very recent times, in terms of volume of material, work effort, precision, and permanence.

How was all this possible five thousand years ago?

The fundamental reasons are three. Firstly, the new tool material, copper alloy, and the metallurgic knowledge of how this material could be tempered by cold-hammering. Secondly, the long tradition of skilled craftsmanship in working hard stone into beautiful utility articles. This tradition also comprises the knowledge, gained by long experience, of tool design and of how it is varied to suit different working materials. Thirdly, a not insignificant knowledge of the mathematical rudiments of engineering, plus the necessary tools, instruments, and implements for surveying and for taking all the measurements required in structural engineering.

A fourth and very significant factor in the construction of the pyramids must be mentioned. This is the ancient Egyptian conception of life after death. If ever there was a state religion, it was the Egyptian during this period. The head of state, the Pharaoh, was the god's representative on earth. As such he was immortal and was an absolute authority, both religious and political, over his subjects. When corporeal death inevitably occurred, the Pharaoh was embalmed—along with his family and servants—so as to be able to live and work in eternity. The art of embalming reached a high level of perfection in this culture and, later, it became a nursery for the young sciences of chemistry and anatomy.

Naturally, the master-builders of the time were fully aware that a palace intended to last forever could not be built of *terre pisé*. The Pharaoh's eternal abode obviously had to be constructed of an everlasting material. The answer to this problem lay in the near-at-hand bedrock, which consisted of granite. If ever there was a lasting material, it was primary rock!

The first engineer whose name is known now enters the arena of history. His name was Imhotep; a polymath, as gifted as he was versatile, and the counsellor of Pharaoh Neter-khet.

The many small Neolithic countries in the Nile valley had been united in the third millennium BC by the legendary Pharaoh Menes, who also founded Memphis, the capital of the Old Kingdom. Memphis had developed into an important cultural centre under several colourful rulers when Pharaoh Neter-khet came into power some time around 2800 BC. His assumption of power, as it happened, took place in extremely unhappy circumstances, which may well have been the decisive factor in triggering off the development of the tooling and machining techniques described below. It was these techniques which made it possible to take the great step of building the pyramids.

When Pharaoh Neter-khet assumed power, the entire Nile valley was stricken by famine, because the otherwise regular flooding of the river had not occurred for several years running. When faced with what he took to be a sinister omen, Neter-khet consulted Imhotep, and they concluded that the divinity of the Nile cataracts—with the African-sounding name of Khnuma—had become incensed with the new Pharaoh. By way of punishment, he had kept back the floods. Imhotep advised Neter-khet to build Khnuma a temple, the like of which the world had never before beheld. This was done under Imhotep's supervision, and the floods returned with their former regularity.

Order was re-established in the country, and Neter-khet could devote himself to planning his eternal abode. The earlier graves in the Old Kingdom consisted of a rectangular sepulchral chamber, sunk into the ground and covered by a couple of more or less crude boulders. Such a grave was called a *mastaba* after the bench which usually stood outside the hut of every Egyptian farmer. Around or on top of the boulders, a wall of mud-brick was built, broad at the base and tapered upwards to counteract the tendency of the material to moulder. It is generally considered that this is the origin of the pyramid shape.

At Sakkara, outside Memphis, Neter-khet ordered a bench grave to be built. However, Imhotep made it square and of stone only. The grave was 230 ft (70 m) square by 29.5 ft (9 m) high—even this was an impressive construction. Obviously, it must have whetted Neter-khet's appetite. Stage by stage, the project assumed gigantic proportions. Firstly, the dimensions of the original mastaba were considerably increased, and then, Imhotep went on building, in several stages, until the first step pyramid, with six steps, was completed in c. 2760 BC. This pyramid was only the start of an even more gigantic structure, with palaces, temples, and other buildings, covering a space of 1,756 × 886 ft (535×270 m), and all surrounded by a 33-ft (10 m) high wall with a total length of 1 mile (1.6 km)—to protect the regal corpse for the course of eternity.

This first edifice of masterfully worked stone was soon followed by several others. Less than a hundred years after this remarkable breakthrough in constructional engineering, the Cheops pyramid, which ranks among the seven wonders of the world, was built. Its foundation is 754.9 ft (230 m) square, and its peak rises almost 490 ft (c. 150 m) above the ground. The Cheops pyramid consists of 2.3 million stone blocks, each weighing around 2.5 tons. These giant blocks were quarried at several places near Aswan, from where they were shipped down the Nile to the building site at Gizeh. They were then hoisted into place after being finely worked with such precision that it is all but impossible to fit a hair between the joints.

Some seventy pyramids of various sizes were built by the Egyptian rulers principally during the Old Kingdom, that is, during the four-hundred-year long period from 2800 BC (a controversial date).

Other Building Aids

We have already mentioned the tools and techniques available to the pyramid builders. But what other aids were at their disposal? Many of those who have speculated over this have started from the Greek historian Herodotus' vivid description of building the pyramids. He mentions, among other things, various mysterious "mechanisms" and cranes which lifted the stone blocks from ledge to ledge. Herodotus also makes several statements about the number of workers employed in the quarries and on the sites; he also tells how long it took to build the pyramids. But we must remember that the erection of the pyramids was as distant in time from Herodotus, the "father of history", as he is from us. When he studied the pyramids on the spot, in the fourth century BC, there were already "tourist guides", who were certainly as accomplished in spinning a yarn as their modern colleagues.

Many riddles concerning the building of the pyramids are as yet unsolved. However, it is generally accepted that working machines for several operations were used at the quarries. This was suggested by Sir W. M. Flinders Petrie (1853–1942), who, in his work *The Pyramid and Temples of Gizeh*, gives detailed descriptions of grooves found in the quarries, on the stone blocks, and on a number of other objects. Unusually enough, this archaeologist had a good enough general technical education to realize that these grooves were marks made by tools with cutting edges of a very hard material, possibly diamond chips embedded in cold-hammered bronze. The great stone sarcophagus found in the sepulchral chamber of the Cheops pyramid has sawn grooves, which suggest not only saws of considerable length (the long side of the groove is 8.2 ft, or 2.5 m), but also the fact that they could stand up to very high loads, judging by the penetration per cut. In theory, such a saw—with a power stroke of at least 10 ft (c. 3 m)—might, of course, have been handled like a modern two-man felling saw—if a dozen men worked each end. Neuburger mentions a quarry in south Germany, worked by the Romans, where monoliths have been found. These obviously have been sawn out of the rock with stone saws, which according to Neuburger must have had a power stroke of at least 15 ft (4.5 m). The same technique, but two thousand years later.

It is, however, also conceivable that some sort of machine tool for sawing stone had been developed, possibly according to the principles illustrated on pages 20–21. The fact that this machine is hypothetical should be stressed, even if it definitely could have been constructed, given the technology of the time. In 1914, an archaeologist in Finland found a saw-toothed knife while excavating a site on the Karelian Isthmus. The find has been dated to about 6000 BC and is made from the shin-bone of a moose. Sharp points of flint have been hammered along the edge of the blade. The knife may have been intended for use as a stabbing weapon, but it could have been used also for sawing wood or similar material.

In Flinders Petrie's opinion, there is proof that the people of the Old Kingdom were familiar with the unsurpassed hardness of diamonds, since he considers it likely that this material was used for engraving hieroglyphics in very hard basalt. On beautifully carved bowls from the fourth dynasty (c. 2700 BC), there are gracefully made inscriptions which, without any doubt, are made "in one stroke", not chiselled or scraped. Several lines lie only about a tenth of a millimetre apart. The engraver must indeed have had splendid eye-sight—the author points out while adjusting his indispensable spectacles—or did he have access to magnifying glasses as well?

Undeniably, it would be tempting to follow that trail, too—so-called reading stones, transparent minerals cut to a planoconvex form, are known since way back in time—but let us return to the quarries of the pyramids!

Through the ages, many theories have been put forward on the methods used to quarry the great monoliths. One explanation com-

A King Neter-khet's step pyramid, the first monumental structure to be built of stone.
B Longitudinal-section of the pyramid, which was originally built as a mastaba (*a*). The burial chamber (*b*) was situated at the foot of a 91-ft (29 m) shaft. However, Imhotep caused the dimensions of the structure to be increased, and the building was given an extra layer of stone all around (*c*). After that, the eastern wall was increased (*d*), and, later, the entire structure was incorporated into the pyramid (*e*). Later still, Imhotep caused further additions (*f*) to be made. (*g*) Tombs for members of the royal family.
C Underneath the pyramid is a maze of galleries and shafts. Certain galleries were intended for use as tombs for members of Neter-khet's family, whereas others were to connect the burial chambers with one another as the pyramid was built. Some of the shafts and galleries may, however, have been made only in order to lead grave-robbers astray. (*a*) The funeral temple.

D Several temples and palaces were erected around the pyramid, and the whole area was surrounded by a high wall.

A

B

A Cracks in the granite were the reason why work on this monolith in one of the Aswan quarries was never completed. It is accepted that dolerite balls were used in cutting the narrow trenches around the block, but how they were used is still a matter of controversy.

B A reconstruction of the almost 8,000-year-old tool found on the Karelian Isthmus. The "knife-blade" is made from the tibia of a moose, and sharp flint chips have been driven into its edge.

monly given is that the pyramids' great stone blocks were broken loose from the bedrock by means of sun-dried wooden plugs, which were driven into bored-out holes in the rock. The force necessary to split the rock was obtained by making the plugs expand by drenching them with water. One would be tempted to accept this explanation, were it not for the fact that drenching a fibrous material such as wood causes it to expand in a way that completely differs from the expansion of metal when heated. When a wooden plug is inserted in a bored hole, a counter-pressure arises, and water poured on it would penetrate into the cavities of the fibres. Several scholars, among them Kjellson, have made experiments which prove that this alleged bursting effect is minute, or even non-existent.

There are many indications that, instead, copper or bronze wedges were used. Neuburger and several other scholars have suggested that the bursting effect of such wedges would have been reinforced by heating after they had been driven in, either by means of boiling water or by covering them with red-hot charcoal.

In one of the Aswan quarries, there is an incompletely quarried monolith, intended as an obelisk which was abandoned apparently because of cracks in the stone. The monolith is *c*. 135 ft (41 m) long, and it has a cross-section of 14.1 ft (4.3 m) at the base and 9.2 ft (2.8 m) at the top. For centuries, the monolith was almost completely covered with sand, but in the early 1920s, the Englishman R. Engelbach dug it out. A narrow trench (*c*. 30 in, or 70 cm) had been cut into the rock on both sides of the monolith. On the sides of these trenches can be seen grooves which are about 10 in (25 cm) wide with rounded cross-sections. Many theories have been put forward about the tools used to make these grooves. Engelbach believes that dolerite balls about 12 in (30 cm) in diameter were struck so hard with sledge-hammers that the granite underneath was ground asunder. When the balls had been worked down a bit into the rock, the stone cutters probably used sturdy wooden poles as links between sledge-hammer and ball.

Others doubt that this was the method employed, although they

C No working machine of the type shown here has been found, but such a machine for sawing stone could have been constructed in ancient Egypt, since all the necessary technical principles were known. (**1**) The saw-blade cuts under the weight of a stone placed in a frame which is pulled to and fro in a trench—part of the trench has not been included here, so that the construction of the machine can be seen clearly. (**2, 3**) The ropes (*a*) attached to either side of the movable frame (*b*) run to two sturdy beams (*c*), which have been pivoted (*d*) in the mountainside and also have been supported (*e*) from above. Draught-animals pull first one beam and then the other away from the machine, and the saw-blade thus cuts through the stone block (*f*).

C₁

C₂

C₃

21

A A shadoof. The man has filled the leather "bucket" with water, and the counterweight (a) now helps him lift it. This application of the lever may have been the prototype of the "building cranes" used when the pyramids were built.
B A reconstruction of a type of

22

building crane which may have been used by the Egyptians. The stone block (a) was lifted when a number of workmen pulled the ends of the ropes (b). The block was then slid into place by means of a ramp (c) and rollers.

C A method for lifting blocks that eliminates the placing of ropes under them. This was described by Hero in his *Mechanica*. A partly wedge-shaped cavity (a) was cut into the top of the block, and a metal wedge (b), a "hanger", with a hole in it, was inserted (c) into the cavity. When the hanger had been fitted into the wedge-shaped part of the cavity (d), a wooden block was inserted in front of it, so that the hanger would be safely secured in the block as it was lifted.

D The muscle power of well-organized masses of workers was used to shift the heavy granite

blocks on land. Log rollers were used to reduce friction along the ground.

E A draught cradle (1), used in ancient Egypt for transporting stone blocks. After a model from the fifteenth century BC, found in Queen Hatshepsut's grave at Deir el-Bahri. It has long been assumed that the blocks were placed on the cradle and dragged along, but a theory which has recently been published suggests instead that cradles might have been fastened round the blocks (2, 3), which were then rolled to their destination.

F As the pyramid rose higher, ramps were built, along which the blocks were transported. The ramps were built of filling material and had a top layer of logs, which prevented the runners of the sledges from digging themselves in.

23

A2

A3

A4

A5

A The culture which erected the famous statues (1) on Easter Island in the southern Pacific Ocean remains a mystery. The six hundred or so statues, which rise between 12 and 33 ft (3.6 and 10 m) above the ground, were probably erected during the Stone Age and were cut out of black volcanic tuff, probably by the sole means of obsidian chisels. Further, each statue has been equipped with "headgear" made of red tuff. One theory of how these monoliths have been erected is illustrated here. (2) The finished statue, transported on rollers or spheres from the quarry to the place where it was to be erected, was tipped into a hole in the ground. (3) In order to get it into an upright position, a rope was slung around its head and connected to a lever, and a mass of workers pulled a rope on the other side of the lever. (4) The statue was then covered with soil, so that the "headgear" could be transported on rollers up a slightly inclined plane. (5). When the red tuff slab was in place, the soil was shovelled away to unearth the statue.

A1

B1

B2

B Wooden poles carved with totem symbols have been erected in various ancient cultures and might perhaps be regarded as counterparts to the Easter Island statues. These two totem poles come from North America (1) and New Zealand (2).

C El Tajin, 6 miles (10 km) west of the Mexican city of Papantla, is the site of the remains of this pyramid-shaped, terraced temple. Its sculptural ornamentation is strangely rich, and 365 square niches line the terraces. The building was erected in the late sixth century AD by the Totonacs, whose Classic Veracruz civilization flourished during the first millennium AD. In this nineteenth-century reconstruction, however, the proportions are completely wrong, for the temple was considerably lower and wider than in this illustration.

D Approximately 3,500 years ago, Stonehenge was erected on a Neolithic graveyard on Salisbury Plain. The theories underlying the monument may derive from the Helladic culture, and the monument is nowadays considered to have had astronomical functions.

C

D

agree that dolerite balls were used, as these have been found on the site. Dolerite is definitely hard enough to crush granite, but as a tool, it could be made more effective if some form of working machine were fitted to it. If the ball was continuously struck and rotated, and if an abrasive powder was used, then the results would have been better. So far, however, no sign of any such machine has been found.

The stones were shipped 620 miles (c. 1,000 km) down the Nile from the Aswan quarries to the construction site at Gizeh. The most difficult part of the operation was moving them to and from the quays. The stone blocks were first placed on rollers and then dragged up slightly inclined ramps by well-organized work gangs. Loading the blocks onto large, specially built barges was quite a story in itself. The barges had a fairly deep draught when fully loaded, so they had to be ballasted with sand to bring their gunwales level with the quay. As loading progressed, the sand was unloaded, so that the barges had safe freeboards.

The first phase in building a pyramid involved levelling the bedrock to an absolutely horizontal square, orientated exactly in the direction of the four cardinal points. As we have already said, the Egyptians had mastered the art of measuring position in relation to a horizontal line or level, and the tools and instruments for such surveying had been developed and refined by the *qanaat* builders.

In the 1920s, an accurate survey using modern geodetic instruments was made of the Cheops pyramid. The results showed that the divergence from the absolute level plane was at its least 0.08 in (2 mm) and at its most 0.43 in (11 mm). Few, if any, great constructions today call for such high precision.

When the foundation had been laid, two methods were used for lifting the stone blocks into place, from the second step upwards. A ramp was built—an inclined plane of soil and sand with an inclination of 1:10 or less. Then the stone blocks were dragged up to their final position, again with organized muscle power.

The second method involved lifting the stone blocks to their correct positions with a "building crane". It is likely that such a crane was also used with a ramp to lift the stone blocks over the last bit. The friction between two even granite surfaces and the weight of the stone block would call for enormous power to move it horizontally. The crane's main constructional element may have been a lever, and its prototype was almost certainly the shadoof, a pole with bucket and counterpoise used mainly in Egypt for raising water and which exists or has existed in many other parts of the world.

The wheel was not known in the Old Kingdom, nor was the pulley, so we can eliminate the possibility of a crane construction which involved a pulley wheel and rope. But cranes of some kind must have been used for hoisting, and the proof of this lies in the longitudinal flanges found on the stone blocks in some of the great pyramids, and in the slits, obviously intended for hoisting-loops, found on other blocks. (The latter arrangement was also used by the builders of the great monuments of Greece and Rome, erected two millennia later.)

The Mighty Five

"The mighty five" is what the philosophers of ancient times called the five simple machines: the inclined plane, the wedge, the screw, the lever, and the wheel. The first three of these are closely interrelated, and so are the wheel and the lever. At least "the mighty four"—the exception being the wheel—were in all probability known by the Palaeolithic age. The lever may well have been one of the very first tools employed by tool-making man. But the wheel has its very special history, which we shall touch upon first.

The wheel can be regarded both as an appliance (for instance, the

A An inclined plane is a flat surface at an angle to the horizontal. To keep an object (a) in place on an inclined plane, a force is required that is equivalent to the proportion of the object's total weight that the inclined plane's height (b) bears to its length (c), if the force is parallel to the inclined plane and directed towards its top, and if friction is ignored. The weight of an object resting on an inclined plane may be divided into two components, one acting at right angles to, and the other acting parallel to the inclined plane; the force needed to move the object up the inclined plane must exceed that of the parallel component, which gets smaller as the length (c) of the inclined plane exceeds its height (b)—with the simple machines, any decrease in force is accompanied by a reciprocal increase in distance.

B The wedge is based on the same principle as the inclined plane. When a wedge of regular section is driven into a piece of wood, for instance by a force acting at right angles to the wedge's base (a), a force acts at right angles to each of the wedge's sides (b). These forces are together greater than the force acting on the wedge's base in the same proportion as the side of the wedge bears to its base.

C Archimedes regarded the screw as the circular analogy of the inclined plane, and his reason for so doing is illustrated here. If a right-angled paper triangle is wound round a cylindrical pencil, starting with one (a) of the two smaller sides running parallel with the pencil, the pitch of the screw's threads will be marked by the hypotenuse (b).

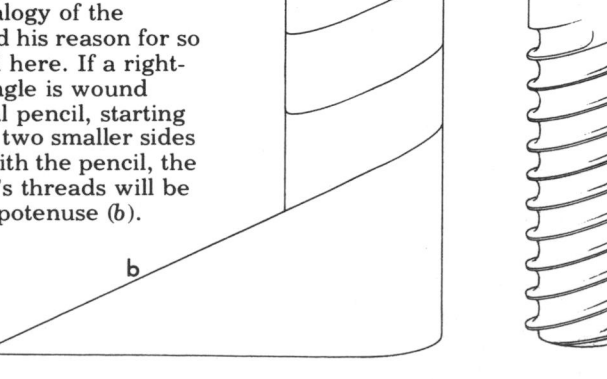

wagon wheel, a means of transportation) and as a mechanical component (at that period, mainly in the form of the cog-wheel). To say that modern civilization would fall apart if these two forms of the wheel did not exist is almost trite. The wheel is what keeps our entire society rolling—literally. True, the wheel can be replaced by other machine elements and components, but the wheel is the lifeblood of the machine age, which is certainly not drawing to a close but will continue for many years yet.

The discovery of a practical use for the wheel was, of course, an enormous step forward for mankind—technically, economically, and socially. But exactly when and where this occurred is unknown. Most historians leave the question more or less open. To date the advent of the wheel from the dating of the first picture of a wagon is, obviously, very questionable. After all, the art of making illustrations in durable materials was not very widespread during the period under discussion, i.e., some time between the fourth and third millennia BC. But as far as is now known, the wheel first appeared in the kingdom of the Sumerians in Mesopotamia. Its several predecessors—the dray, the sledge, and the log roller—can be traced with certainty back to the Palaeolithic era. These are still in use in many developing countries. Charles Singer, the English historian, has pointed out drawings of both a sledge and a four-wheeled wagon which occur in a Sumerian pictograph, found during excavations at Erech, Mesopotamia. This find is generally dated at about 3500 BC. But even if this does not pinpoint the birth of the wheel, it is quite clear that it was in these parts that the first wheel appeared. As further proof, Singer cites an artefact from a grave in Tepe Gawra in the Old Assyrian kingdom. This was a little toy, a covered four-wheeled wagon, from the third millenium BC.

So far, we have been discussing the wagon wheel. But the wheel as a machine element is probably older. Many scholars believe that the throwing wheel, used in pottery, antedates the wheel by about a thousand years. The potter's wheel was in all probability made from wood, and this is why none have survived down the ages. However, Sumerian pottery, obviously made on a throwing wheel, has been found, and Singer dates the oldest example to 3250 BC, give or take 250 years. As is the case with the illustrations, the earliest finds cannot be dated with any certainty. The first use of the throwing wheel may have occurred much earlier; and in all probability, *before* the first practical application of the wagon wheel. One fact which must be considered to be most remarkable is that the Old Kingdom in Egypt, the nearest neighbour to the Sumerian river culture, had no knowledge of the wheel. Only in about 2500 BC did it become known there, probably in the form of a two-wheeled chariot used in battle. During the technologically important era when the great pyramids were built, the wheel was unknown. Instead, the technique of using the sled and log rollers for the transport of heavy loads was developed to near-perfection. Here, one may naturally reflect that it is really rather embarrassing that we have no more exact knowledge of the first appearance of one of the most important constructional elements used by mankind.

Archimedes

The first to systematize the simple machines and propound the theory of their functions was Archimedes of Syracuse (287–212 BC), who was undoubtedly the principal figure in Hellenic cultural circles of his time. It was probably he who invented the compound pulley, a device for increasing traction or lifting power, and it was he who propounded the theory of the lever, both one- and two-armed. Archimedes regarded the wheel as the circular figure described by the rotating one-armed lever, and the screw as the circular analogy of the inclined plane. (The latter is not as difficult as it sounds. Cut a right-angled triangle from a piece of paper and wind it round a cylindrical pencil, so that one arm of the right angle is parallel to the axis. The pitch of the threads will then be marked by the hypotenuse.)

Archimedes was a remarkable man who deserves a somewhat better introduction. He was one of the most distinguished mathematicians and engineers ever. Sarton notes ironically, but rightly, that great engineers of every period have been compared to Archimedes, and considers it foolhardy to compare the achievements of any person to those of the greatest genius of antiquity.

Archimedes was born in Syracuse, Sicily, one of the more important cities in the Hellenistic world, Magna Graecia, as the Romans came to call it. Syracuse had a vast harbour and a highly developed shipbuilding industry, as the economy was based on the export of grain, for which big ships were necessary. Archimedes worked there as technical adviser to his cousin, King Hiero II (and to the latter's son and successor, Gelon II), and he was responsible for the defence of the city. Hiero's great passion was shipbuilding, and he had the *Syrakosia*, the biggest ship of its day, built. Unfortunately, when it was about to be launched, it got stuck and could not be budged. Now Archimedes had become fascinated by the power-amplifying qualities of the simple machines—one of his famous sayings is, "Give me a place to stand, and I will move the earth". Hiero challenged him now not to move the earth, but only the ship.

With the help of compound pulleys coupled to levers at strategic points under the hull, Archimedes was able to give a practical demonstration of the validity of his theories. With an elegant gesture, he offered the end of the main connecting rope to Hiero, who could pull the *Syrakosia* free using only one hand.

But the most interesting of Archimedes' many engineering feats is the construction of the different war engines which he devised to defend his city against the Romans, who had designs on the riches of Syracuse. Tragically, Archimedes himself fell a victim of the Romans during the Second Punic War, in 212 BC, when he was slain by a Roman soldier whom he rebuked for stepping on a diagram he had drawn in the sand while working out a problem.

For a long time, however, Syracuse had been able to withstand the Roman siege, thanks to the monstrous war engines devised by Archimedes. A simply enormous catapult, the construction elements of which were levers and pulleys, hurled giant boulders at the attacking Roman ships. According to the Danish historian A. G. Drachmann, these boulders weighed 550 lb (c. 250 kg), and he quotes Plutarch, who tells that the Romans panicked and fled as soon as a beam of wood or a rope's end became visible on the walls of Syracuse, in the belief that Archimedes had some new diabolical device with which to attack them.

The most gruesome of all the war engines was, however, that intended the last line of defence in the inner basin of Syracuse's harbour. It was a giant claw, which lay hidden under the water. If an enemy ship succeeded in getting that far, the claw was to grab the vessel, lift it high up in the air, turn it over, and shake it until the crew fell out! The existence of such a machine has been doubted, not surprisingly. However, the historian Polybius describes a different version, in which an iron claw, mounted on a tall crane, was to grab the ship, hoist it into the air, and then let go of it, so that it smashed into the water or was dashed against the breakwater.

Of course, it is quite possible that the whole story was pure terror propaganda, invented in order to strike fear into the rank and file of the enemy. There are many examples of this in the history of warfare. Real or not, such a construction is definitely possible, if the principles of the simple machines are applied. This remarkable construction has, apparently, never been depicted, but we have amused

D The characteristics of a lever are that it pivots round a fulcrum and that it moves under the influence of an applied force, or effort, and a load. Two applications of the two-armed lever are shown here: the oar (**1**), whose fulcrum is the rowlock, and the common balance (**2**). The amount of amplification of the effort applied to a lever is known as the mechanical advantage; the effort is increased in the same proportion as the distance between the effort and the fulcrum exceeds the distance between the fulcrum and the weight. The balance here is in a state of equilibrium because although the objects in the scale (*a*) weigh more than the weight on the hook (*c*),

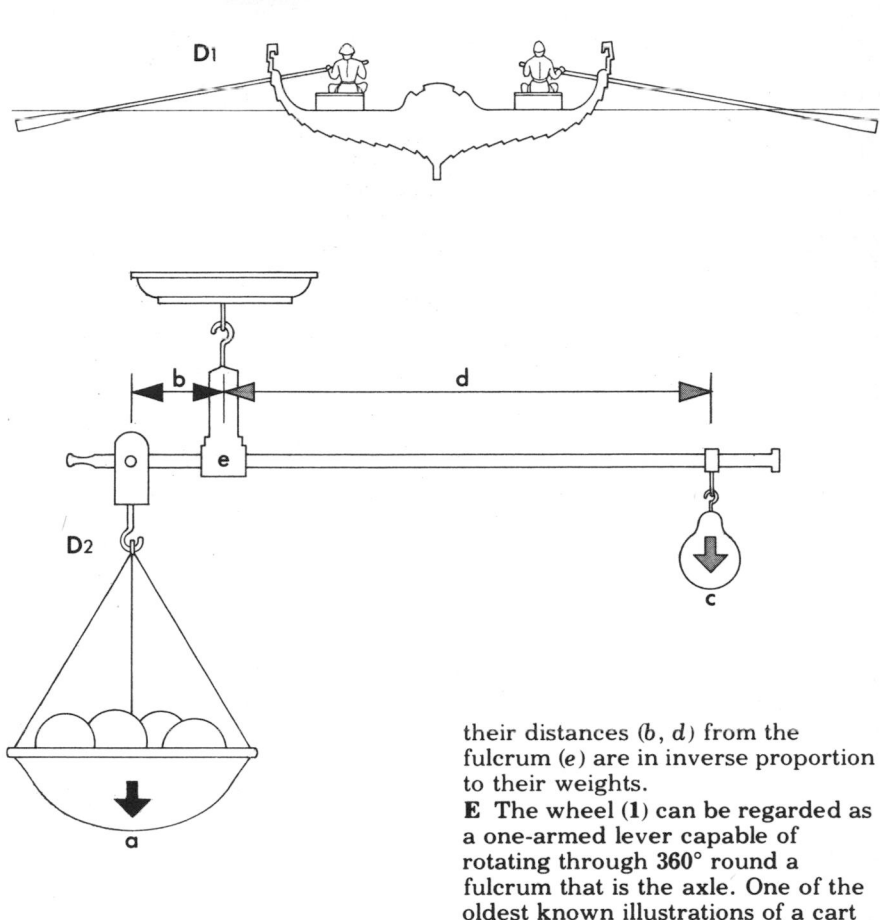

their distances (*b, d*) from the fulcrum (*e*) are in inverse proportion to their weights.

E The wheel (**1**) can be regarded as a one-armed lever capable of rotating through 360° round a fulcrum that is the axle. One of the oldest known illustrations of a cart with wheels (**2**) is part of a Sumerian pictograph, which has been dated to *c*. 3500 BC.

ourselves by illustrating a possible design. Naturally, this reconstruction is based on mere assumption, and it excludes Polybius's version. After all, a tolerably prudent commander would hardly take his ship near such a crane, which, with its giant claw, would be easier to detect than an underwater construction. Even if the latter were visible—for we may assume that the water there was clearer than it is nowadays—it would not have been too difficult to stir up enough mud to cover it, thus allowing its sudden appearance to cause a most horrible shock.

There has been much interest in the burning-mirrors invented by Archimedes to burn the rigs of the attacking Roman vessels. The construction is said to be similar to that of modern sun reflectors, that is to say, it consisted of numerous small, polished metal mirrors on a lattice-work structure of parabolic cross-section, rather like the one at the United States Army Research Station at Matick, Massachusetts. The story of Archimedes' burning-mirror fascinated Leonardo da Vinci (1452–1519), but he doubted if the construction was practicable. True, Archimedes was familiar with mirrors and with geometrical optics, but Leonardo believed that it was impossible to build a great burning-mirror which could be aimed with reasonable accuracy. Leonardo had scrutinized the writings of Archimedes, and he credits him with the much-discussed steam-gun, *architronito*. This consisted of a cylindrical barrel of copper, sealed at one end, that shot a well-fitting, iron cannon-ball. If a little water was poured in between the sealed end and the ball and heated rapidly, enough steam pressure would be created to fire the ball. According to Leonardo's notes, a cannon-ball weighing one talent (17.6 lb or 8 kg) could have been fired a length of six stadia (4,102 ft or c. 1,250 m)—no mean achievement. However, Hart, who is perhaps the foremost of Leonardo's biographers, is of the opinion that the steam-gun was never built. Leonardo is sometimes mentioned as one of the pioneers of steam power, but we must remember that the idea of a steam-gun can, in fact, be traced back to Archimedes.

One of the monstrous engines said to have been constructed by Archimedes was a "ship-shaker" in the form of a giant claw, hidden at the bottom of Syracuse's harbour. It is quite possible to construct such a machine by applying only the principles of the simple machines. It might, for instance, look like the machine to the right—a sturdy platform, carrying a system of levers—which would work as illustrated above. (1) When the enemy ship has managed to enter the harbour, the claws are directed towards it by oxen pulling ropes *a* or *b*, to give the desired direction. These ropes are fastened at the lower part of the claws. (**2**) The sharp points (*c*) between the claws then impale the ship's hull when the oxen pull ropes *d* to provide the lever (*e*) carrying the claws with a pivot. (**3**) The claws grip the hull when the oxen pull the double ropes *f*, which are split at the pulley-blocks (*g*) on the claws. (**4**) The ship is lifted out of the water when the oxen pull ropes *d* further, and when, finally, the oxen alternately pull ropes *a* and *b*, the ship is shaken sideways, so that the crew is thrown out of it!

A A cutler displaying a variety of knives in his shop. The illustration is based on an original found on a Roman tombstone from the time of the birth of Christ.

B From illustrations in the grave of an Egyptian vizier, Rekhmire, in Thebes in the fifteenth century BC. The three men on the left are considered to be goldsmiths, and the one furthest left is hammering gold on an anvil. The man furthest right is using a blowpipe to smelt metal.

C Roman granite mould for embossing gold and silver ornaments.

D Soldering-copper (**1**) and blowpipe (**2**) from ancient Rome, found at Chatelet, France.

E Roman dies, used to punch decorations in metals.

F A blacksmith's workshop. Above the workers, various products from the smithy are shown. From a painting on an Attic vase from the sixth century BC.

G Metal tools forged by the ancient Romans.

Archimedes' achievements as a theorist are in no way overshadowed by his exploits. We will not discuss his extremely subtle and, indeed, brilliant mathematical theories here, although mathematics is one of the more important "tools" of engineering, but we shall give just one example. During his technical calculations, Archimedes was irritated by the prevailing Greek numerical system, in which the numbers 1–9 were simply the first nine letters of the alphabet (alpha to iota), the multiples of ten between 10 and 90 were the following nine letters, and so on. But the alphabet was not long enough to express more than thousands, up to but not including ten thousand. Thus, it was possible to count to 9,999–but that was all. For the number 10,000, the concept of *myria* was introduced, but a word instead of the alphabetical numerals was not very handy when, say, adding. Things were a bit better after the abbreviation M for myriad had been invented; it was then possible to multiply this M with the alphabetical numerals and count all the way to 99,999,999, a number which, nowadays, we can represent, simply, as 10^8-1. Archimedes called the numerical system up to this numeral an octad, i.e., having eight numerals. Here, he must have been fully aware of the mathematical system's tenth power–or, the power series–but he was so

deeply rooted in the Hellenistic way of writing numbers with nine letters that he did not come to think of the decimal system.

Nevertheless, the great mathematician Carl Friedrich Gauss (1777–1855), who was a devotee of Archimedes, could never forgive him for not having taken the radical step of introducing the power series!

Archimedes presented his ideas on high numbers and how to express them in *Arenarius* ("The Sand Counter"), in which he attempted to estimate the number of grains of sand the universe could hold. (It was then the custom, as it was later on, too, to present a theory in the form of a philosophical problem.)

Archimedes continued his numerical system so that it formed finally a myriad octads, that is, a one followed by eight hundred million noughts! His goal had been to expand the Hellenic numerical system so that it could express high numbers. We must agree that he undoubtedly succeeded! Archimedes the sand-counter is still remembered in our language by the word *myriad*, even if its original meaning, "10,000", has been almost lost, and the word now stands for "a very great number".

However, such subtle philosophical problems as this did not occ-

H Reconstruction of a type of tongs used by smiths in ancient Rome.

I Egyptian pottery: the clay is trampled until soft, then kneaded, thrown, and, eventually, fired in ovens of the type in which the material to be fired is fed through the top.
J A cupid sharpening an arrow on a grindstone. Cupids commonly occur in illustrations of trades from the times of classical antiquity.
K This detail (1) from a mural at Thebes shows two men working wood; one uses a mortise-chisel (2) and the other an adze (4). The wooden mallet (3) used with the chisel is of a type which still exists.
L Saws from the times of classical antiquity. (1) Roman saw.
(2) Egyptian compass saw.
(3) A man sawing.

upy Archimedes full-time. His great pioneering contributions to mathematics lie in his elucidation of the mighty five and, above all, in the easily comprehended constructions he created in order to make clear to the engineer the concept of the simple machines as construction elements. Archimedes was both theoretical and practical in his approach.

"Eureka" is a well-known expression all over the world, and for this, too, we can thank Archimedes. He is believed to have shouted this, meaning "I have found it!", when he chanced upon the solution to a problem posed by King Hiero, namely to establish whether or not a crown made for the king by a goldsmith, was of pure gold. Hiero suspected that silver or some other metal had been alloyed with the gold. How could this be proved? Archimedes came upon the answer one day when he was taking a bath, and in his joy, he ran naked through the streets of Syracuse, shouting "Eureka!". He had just discovered what has been known since as Archimedes' principle: that, when a body is immersed in a liquid, its apparent loss of weight is equal to the weight of the liquid it displaces. By working out the specific weights of gold and silver, Archimedes was able to say whether or not the crown was genuine and the goldsmith honest.

History, alas, does not record the outcome of the case, but the principle which Archimedes propounded is still with us and forms the basic theory behind, for instance, the calculation of a ship's stability.

The amplifying power of another of Archimedes' inventions, the compound pulley, fascinated Leonardo da Vinci, who sketched several suggestions for machines in which the compound pulley could be used. In fact, many of Leonardo's ideas for simple machines were based upon the solid theoretical and practical foundation which Archimedes had laid down. Of course, Leonardo's achievements in this and other areas did not benefit technology, as his scientific papers were not published in his time, but lay hidden and forgotten in the archives of several princely houses, and were not scientifically studied or published until the end of the nineteenth century.

The writings of Archimedes, above all those which describe the mighty five, may be regarded as the Genesis of engineering. This statement contains neither blasphemy nor an idolization of the machine, for his writings, and above all the oral tradition of his achievements, became widespread in the classical cultures. The man who contributed the most to spreading the works of Archimedes was the Roman engineer Vitruvius Pollio, who, in his famous book *De architectura*—completed in 37 AD—exhaustively described the simple machines and their technical applications.

Tools and Implements in the Time of Archimedes

What tools and implements did Archimedes and his engineers use to build the great throwing machine or the "ship shaker" in Syracuse harbour? Tools for working iron and wood, and some kind of lifting system, would have been necessary to assemble the various parts. All we know of these tools is that tools and implements used by different trades have changed little from the time of their first recorded appearance. We have already covered the long chain of development that resulted in the tools, implements, and methods used by the pyramid builders. At the time of Christ, tools such as the carpenter's and the mason's were almost identical in form and material to those used fifteen hundred years previously, at the time of the transition from the Old to the New Kingdom in Egypt, and most of them were to remain unchanged for at least another fifteen hundred years.

Naturally, this does not mean that there was no development during this time. New trades came into being as new needs arose. The new methods demanded new tools. Pliny the Elder (23?−79), in his *Naturalis historia*, has covered in detail the methods used by various trades—among them the smith's, the painter's, the carpenter's, and the sculptor's. He leaves the reader with a strong feeling that specialization is an ancient phenomenon, even if seen from Pliny's time perspective!

But even if we do not have very much information about the actual tools used at the time of Archimedes, we do have comprehensive descriptions of the results produced by the skilled craftsmen of the time. In the second century AD, the Greek author Athenaeus of Naucratis wrote an extensive account of the great ship *Syrakosia*, the flagship of Hiero's fleet. This ship is a magnificent example of what could be accomplished with contemporary tools. At the same time, *Syrakosia* is a graphic presentation of a technologically advanced culture.

Athenaeus' account gives no exact dimensions of the ship, but from the freight capacity and all the equipment described, it is clear that they were considerable, even by modern standards. The ship was planned as the first and largest of sixty (!) quadriremes—a ship with four banks of oars—which were to be built for Hiero's fleet. The

A An Archimedean screw. As the handle (a) is turned, a certain amount of water (b) is brought into the helical screw, which then brings the water up to a reservoir or trough.

B Hero's *aelopile*. The lower container (a) was partly filled with water and was heated. The steam that was then produced was led via pipes (b) to a metal sphere (c), which could turn on its axle and had exhaust pipes (d), whose openings were directed at right angles to the axle. As steam escaped into the air, the sphere rotated because of the steam's reaction.

normal warships and merchant ships used by Hiero were triremes or biremes which he caused to be built by his shipbuilder, Archias. For the *Syrakosia*, Archias had to buy timber from the Italian mainland, hemp for the cordage from Spain, and tar from the Rhône valley; he attracted skilled tradesmen from wherever he could get his hands on them. He succeeded in rounding up three hundred specialist tradesmen, "not counting their helpers", to equip and fit out the ship. The hull, which took a year to build, was first covered in canvas saturated with tar. Then it was fitted with lead sheeting, soldered together. Apparently, the shipbuilders had had plenty of experience of the damage that the ship-worm and other marine organisms can cause to wooden hulls.

The ship was heavily armed, as its costly freight would certainly have been an attractive prize for the pirates who roamed the Mediterranean at that time. Sturdy iron bars formed a lattice-work along the bulwarks, and sixty fully armed marines mounted guard there at times of peril. *Syrakosia* was a three-master with eight towers, two each at stern and bow, and four amidships. The towers were equipped with rock-throwing engines, and hoists were installed for raising the projectiles from the deck up to the tower. Deep in the hull was a fresh-water tank, a sea-water well for fish, and space for provision stores, mills for grinding grain, fuel for the galley stoves, and so on. A stable for twenty horses was built on the lower deck, together with quarters for the horsemen (despatch riders on land), their slaves, and the marines. On the middle deck, there were cabins for passengers and the ship's officers. Athenaeus measured these cabins in *clines*, or couches, which at night served as beds. (The Japanese still measure a room by the number of straw mats, also used as beds, which can be fitted into it.) On each side of the ship were thirty cabins, each with four *clines*. The commander's quarters had an area of fifteen *clines*.

Throughout the ship the floor was decorated with mosaics depicting the entire Iliad. The wall and ceiling decorations illustrated the same theme. On the upper deck there was a gymnasium and a garden filled with all kinds of magnificent plants. Vines and ivy were planted along the bulwarks, forming a shaded promenade around the ship. The plants were watered by an ingenious system of pumps and pipes. Also on this deck was a temple to the goddess of fertility, Aphrodite. The floor of the temple was of polished gemstones, the walls were of cypress and cedar, and the doors were inlaid with ivory. The interior was extravagantly decorated with statues, paintings, and magnificent urns. Alongside the temple lay a library filled with books of all kinds, from philosophy to light reading. The interior decoration was of the same high standard as that in the rest of the ship. The roof was vaulted, and in the centre of the library stood a magnificent sun-dial.

The library, too, had a bathroom with three bronze baths and hand-basins of beautiful marble.

Thus far Athenaeus and his description of the *Syrakosia*. We do not need to quote any more to demonstrate that the like of the standard on board Hiero's flagship did not return to the surface of the ocean before the great era of the Atlantic liners in the early twentieth century. A list of all the tradesmen required to build and decorate the *Syrakosia* would make fascinating reading. It would include a strange mixture of types—everything from gardeners and mosaic layers to the builders of war machines. One wonders if the modern shipyards which built the great, but now vanished, Atlantic liners had as many specialized tradesmen!

The Engineers, Machines, and Tools of the Alexandrian School
Alexandria, situated in the western part of the Nile delta, was found-

ed by Alexander the Great (356–323 BC) in 332 BC and quickly grew into a large metropolis, becoming one of the more important scientific and cultural centres of the world. One of the main reasons for this pre-eminence was the excellence of the university, known as the Museum, which was dedicated to the nine muses, the protectresses of science and the fine arts.

Archimedes received his education at the university of Alexandria, where, during the centuries before the birth of Christ, groups of mathematicians and scientists worked, devoting themselves to the construction of numerous fascinating machines, the functions of which were impressive and which were clearly the result of a fine understanding of the principles involved. Best known among the mathematicians is Euclid (fl.c. 300 BC), who, with his *Elements of Geometry*, has been the great master of logic to many generations of students of all kinds from the Middle Ages to the present time.

But the greatest and most colourful of what is known as the Alexandrian school of engineers is undoubtedly Hero, who lived sometime during the second century BC—the exact dates of his life are a matter of dispute. Hero was of a playful turn of mind; therein lay his strength as well as his weakness. His best-known invention is the *aelopile*, the first reaction turbine, which converted heat into mechanical energy through the medium of steam. It never became anything more than an amusing plaything, as it could not be made to function as a working machine, that is, it could not perform useful work. The power which it developed was sufficient to make the ball revolve at a reasonable speed, but in order to produce a power surplus, the speed would have had to be increased to at least a few thousand rpm, and this would have required a very high head of steam, which would have meant a very efficient transfer of heat from the fire to the rotating ball. Another problem was that the centrifugal force, together with the slightest imbalance in the ball, would, at the speed necessary to produce a reasonable effect, have produced great strains on the material. Hero and his assistants probably tried to get the *aelopile* to perform useful work, but they must have been disappointed at the results.

In the 1780s, James Watt had occasion (see page 131) to work out the theoretical operating conditions of a reaction turbine, and his conclusion was that such a turbine could not be built, given the state of contemporary technology.

However, Hero had several other strings to his technical bow. His playful attitude is demonstrated best, perhaps, by the automata he invented. One of the best known and most ingenious of his automatic devices is the one by which the doors of the inner sanctum of a temple were opened by the lighting of a sacrificial fire on a nearby altar. This must have seemed miraculous to the uneducated and illiterate members of the congregation, who undoubtedly believed that this was tangible proof of the almighty power of the gods.

Hero himself would certainly have objected to anyone calling his temple machine "playful" and would have pointed out sharply that very serious thought lay behind both the construction and the function. However, in those of his works that have been preserved, Hero describes many other amusing automatic devices that certainly were designed for amusement and entertainment. Examples of these are the toy birds which were made to sing by a mechanism powered by a water-wheel, and the crown of dancing figurines, rather like a modern angel chimes, which was driven by a heat turbine. These should not be dismissed out of hand just because they were built for pleasure. After all, those principles of natural law that Hero and the other engineers of the Alexandrian school were demonstrating with their automata came to play a significant role in the future development of science and engineering.

The first great engineer of the Alexandrian school was, however, not Hero but Ctesibius, who also lived sometime during the second century BC. He was a most talented mathematician and had certainly become acquainted with Euclid's *Elements* at the Museum. It is a matter of controversy whether he knew the works on the mighty five that had been written by Archimedes and Aristotle. Also a matter of controversy are the exact dates of his life.

Ctesibius, the son of a barber, had in his youth followed his father's footsteps, and it was in the barber's shop that he made his first technical device. It may seem simple to us, but then, of course, it attracted an enormous amount of attention. By suspending a mirror from a rope which ran over concealed rollers, he could raise and lower the mirror due to the fact that it was counterbalanced by a lead cylinder which moved inside a copper tube, built into the wall. Such magic had never been seen before, and it is easy to imagine the astonishment of the clients. This simple device soon had, however, a totally unforeseen technical spin-off.

The counterweight filled the tube so closely that the mirror was difficult to move. Ctesibius must have pondered a great deal on the mystical power that hampered the movement of the counterweight. At length, he concluded quite rightly that the air in the tube was compressed and, consequently, worked as an elastic substance. So he bored a little hole at the bottom of the tube, and this allowed him to raise and lower the mirror without any difficulty, but to the accompaniment of a strange whistling sound. Ctesibius detected the cause of this, too, and this led him to construct the world's first organ.

At this time, very little was known about the properties of air, so we can assume that Ctesibius devoted his time to numerous experiments with pumps and other devices for producing compressed air. He must also have spent time speculating about the fundamental laws of acoustics, for just as little was known about these. He was treading unbroken ground, and the organ he designed had a number of components which can be regarded as basic inventions. Sarton remarks that, if the patent system had existed at the time, there is no doubt that Ctesibius would have been granted a large number of fundamental patents for his organ and his many other inventions.

The literature of the subject quite rightly attributes the water clock to Ctesibius. This device, also called the clepsydra, had certainly been used to measure time in ancient Egypt as early as the second millennium BC, and perhaps even earlier in the Far East. But the early types were not at all accurate. From his work on the pressure of air and of various liquids, Ctesibius realized that the principle of the water clock must be the flow of water at a constant pressure through an unchanging nozzle. Ctesibius made a nozzle out of precious stone and constructed a basin with a spillway which gave a constant pressure, provided that the water flow was constant and slightly excessive.

The works written by Ctesibius himself have been lost, but they were known to some of his successors, and some of their writings have been preserved. Only fragments, sometimes in Arabic translations, remain of many of these original works. Tragically, many priceless and irreplaceable scientific works were lost in 47 BC during Julius Caesar's Egyptian campaign, when he plundered Alexandria and burnt down the Museum. The richly comprehensive library, with its estimated half a million works, was destroyed—a dreadful loss to science, literature, and art.

Ctesibius had many disciples at the Museum, and it is mainly from their writings that we have been able to learn something about the master's work. The more important of these engineers were Philo of Byzantium and Hero of Alexandria.

Philo was active in Alexandria in the latter part of the second century BC. Later, he became a military engineer in the service of

A The water clock, or clepsydra, is considered to have been invented by Ctesibius. His task was made no easier by the fact that the ancient Egyptians divided daylight into twelve hours and the night into twelve watches, so that the length of the hours varied. This reconstruction of Ctesibius's clepsydra works in the following way. Water drops from a container, which must be completely filled to ensure constant pressure, into a funnel (a) and is led into an open cylinder (b), which contains a float (c). Here, the float is adorned by the pointing figure of a man (d). As the water in the cylinder rises, so does the float, and the figure points to the time on the pillar (e). At the same time, the water level in the siphon (f) rises, and when the shorter leg of f is completely filled, the external air pressure forces the water out of the cylinder and into a drum (g) which is divided into compartments. As each compartment becomes full, the drum turns a little. A cog-wheel (h) on the drum shaft then drives three other cog-wheels (i, j, k); k is mounted on the shaft carrying e. The lines showing the time on the pillar are not horizontal, so the length of the hours is varied as the pillar is turned.

B The organ has also been attributed to Ctesibius and has been described by both Hero and Vitruvius. A row of pipes (a) were mounted on a board (b), under which ran a duct (c) for air compressed by a pedal-driven pump (d). To keep the air pressure constant, Ctesibius used a pressure-equalizing tank (e). When air was pumped into the tank, the water inside was forced into the container (f) around it. (1) Under each pipe was a perforated wooden board (g). (2) When one of the sprung keys (h) was pressed, the board protruded, so that its hole connected the pipe to the compressed-air duct; the pipe then emitted a tone.

C This altar has been attributed to Ctesibius's disciple Hero; the fire on it was automatically extinguished when it had burnt for long enough to heat and expand the air inside the metal cylinder (a) enough to force part of the water in the basin (b) up through the pipes (c) inside the statuettes.

D A hot-air version of Hero's aelopile. When the fire is lit, the air inside the altar (a) is heated, expands, and travels through a piping system (b). The figurines are driven round by the heated air, which spurts out through the bent pipe ends (c).

E A jug, designed by Hero, in which a wall (a) separates wine and water. In the upper part of the jug are two holes (b); its top (c) is well sealed. A narrow opening (d) at the bottom is connected to both inner sections of the jug. As long as a finger is held over each of the holes b, nothing can be poured from the jug. When either finger is removed, air can enter into the relevant section(s), and because of the equalization of the pressure, wine, water, or mixture of both pours through d.

F Hero's ingenious device which opened the doors of the temple's inner sanctum. When the sacrificial fire is lighted, the air inside the altar (a) expands, causing the pressure to increase in the sphere (b), which is partly filled with water. The water is forced through a siphon (c) into a basin (d), which then sinks, pulling with it a line (e). This line runs round two trunnions (f) and makes the doors open. When the fire is quenched, the air pressure inside the altar is restored to normal, the water in basin d is sucked back into sphere b, and a counterweight (g) causes the doors to close again.

G Hero combined the simple machines to form many kinds of power-amplifying arrangements, such as this worm-gear.

H A power-amplifying device with multiple blocks, used by Hero to straighten a leaning wall.

I Hero's device for counter-balancing great weights is here used to raise a pillar onto its socle.

J Hero's holy-water slot-machine. When the coin passed through the slot (a), it fell on a lever (b). This opened a valve (c), and a little water could run out before the pressure of the water closed the valve again.

K Cobblestones, bouncing on copper plates of varying thickness and rigidity, caused the rumble in this "thunder machine" designed by Hero.

L Hero's "divine box". When wheel a has been cranked, the bird turns and whistles! On the wheel

shaft is a toothed wheel (b), which meshes with a wheel (c) on whose vertical shaft the bird sits. At the same time, a string is wound onto a drum (d). At the other end of the string, a metal dome (e) hangs over a basin (f), which is partly filled with water. A pipe (g) runs through the roof of the dome and has a whistle at its top. When the crank on wheel a is released, the bird turns the other way, the dome sinks into the water, and the air then forced out of the dome through the pipe causes the whistle to sound.

the rulers of Rhodes, designing all kinds of weapons for attack and defence—ballistas, battering rams, and suchlike. Philo is considered to be the first to have collected and described the age's military engineering technology and its applications. Only a couple of chapters of his comprehensive work, *Mechanice syntaxis*, survive, but one of them, "Pneumatica", on air pumps and compressed air, derives in part from Ctesibius.

The most brilliant engineer of the Alexandrian school was, however, Hero, whom we have already mentioned. His books on mathematics, mechanics, and automata contain descriptions of about seventy mechanical devices, ranging from compound elements, such as gearwheels, to highly complicated automatic devices. Drachmann believes that Hero was aided in his very extensive work by pupils and collaborators. It is probable that he provided the inspiration and ideas for a number of engineers, and that these, in their turn, had skilful craftsmen available to assist them to put their ideas into practice.

A Hero's sand motor for automata theatres, here shown in section from the side (**1**) and from the front (**2**). The tall box contained two compartments, of which the upper was filled with sand, millet, mustard-seed, or something of the same sort. On top of the sand was a weight (*b*), which was connected to the wheel axle (*c*) by a rope (*d*) running over pulleys (*e*). If the theatre was to roll forward onto the stage and then return the way it came, the rope was wound round the axle first in one and then in the other direction; the length of the coil (*f*) then decided for how long the theatre would remain standing on the stage. When the sand was allowed to run out through a small opening in the dividing wall (*h*) into the lower compartment (*g*) of the box, the weight sank and thus pulled the rope, so that the wheel axle was turned and the theatre started to move.

B This combined suction- and force-pump has been described by Hero and was intended for fire-fighting. The contrivance consists of two cylinders with pistons, which are moved up and down by one and the same handle (*a*). The cylinders are connected to each other and to an ascending pipe (*b*), from whose top water is pumped out through an opening (*c*), which can be directed upwards or to either side. When one piston (*d*) is moved upwards, the change in pressure causes a valve (*e*) in the bottom of the cylinder to open, and water comes pouring in. The valve (*f*) which connects the cylinder to the ascending pipe is then closed, for when piston *d* is moved upwards, the other piston (*g*) is lowered, and the water contained in its cylinder is forced through a valve (*h*) into the ascending pipe. The increased pressure of the water then keeps valves *f* and *i* closed.

C Hero's singing birds. Water flows from the lion's head into a covered container (*a*). Air is then forced out of the container through pipes (*b*), leading to whistles inside the birds. When the water level rises above the top of a pipe (*c*) covered by a cope—which lets in water at its lower end and is mounted with its top slightly above the top of the pipe—the pipe and cope together work as a siphon, and the water is emptied from container *a* into another container (*d*). A similar siphon arrangement (*e*) is built into this container, which also contains a float (*f*) to which a rope (*g*) is tied. The rope is wound once round a rotating pillar (*h*) and carries a weight (*i*) at its other end. When the water level—and, thus, the float—rises in container *d*, the pillar with its owl rotates until the water level has risen so high that the siphon starts working, and the container is emptied of water. The float then sinks, and the owl rotates back to its original position.

CHAPTER 2

MACHINE ELEMENTS AND ELEMENTARY MACHINES

Archimedes and, somewhat later, the engineers of the Alexandrian school showed what could be achieved, both in theory and in practice, by the simple machines, "the mighty five". As technical aids in saving power, the balanced lever, the gradient plane, the wedge, the screw, and the wheel added enormously to most areas of human achievement. Each one of the mighty five can rightly be called invaluable, but their combined value is truly infinite. The engineers of the Alexandrian school joined connected levers to cog-wheels, screws, and wedges and thus constructed the first real machines, in the modern sense of the word. Among the first full-scale applications of the newly-defined principles of mechanical engineering were the ingenious stage devices which were used to amaze the audiences in the Greek and Roman amphitheatres. The expression *deus ex machina*, "the god from the machine", derives from these devices. In the ancient theatre, which was often associated with religious festivals, levers, blocks, and ropes would enable, for example, the corpulent Bacchus to be suspended "magically" above the stage. However, the reverse, *machina ex deo*, would be just as appropriate, suggesting that the first real machines originated from the suspended god or similar full-scale applications of the many devices designed in "toy"-scale by Hero and his assistants. This implies that the engineers of the Alexandrian school had fully realized the applicability of the simple machines as machine elements.

The term "machine element" was not introduced until the nineteenth century, when mechanical engineering was first studied seriously from mathematical and kinematic viewpoints by, among others, Reuleaux, who will be dealt with in detail later. However, there is no doubt that, when designing their machines, Hero and his assistants were to a large extent inspired by the immense possibilities that arose when they tried systematically to combine the simple machines in different ways. The first machine elements consisted mainly of combinations of cog-wheels and endless screws, both of which are used in worm gears.

The Gear

The origin of the wheel has been suggested above, where we mentioned the multitude of contradictory and more or less unfounded suppositions that is all we know of the first appearance of this extremely important human invention. We know just as little of its development into a cog-wheel. Very likely, these two phenomena are related—the wheel may have been in use for perhaps a thousand years before it was depicted or mentioned in writing, and this may well be the case with the cog-wheel, too. Very few surviving written sources deal with this branch of engineering. It is probable that there were many early descriptions, but these have since been lost. Moreover, many documents were compiled by disciples of the great men

A One of the gear reduction sets constructed by Hero and intended to lift a weight of a thousand talents with a force of five talents only.

B Hero's *barulkos*, or weight-puller, was a developed version of the gear reduction set shown in illustration **A**. Among other things, an endless screw has been coupled to the last of the cog-wheels.

⟨B⟩

A A reconstruction of Hero's device for cutting female screw threads. (**1**) A round wooden stick, slightly more than twice as long as the screw thread about to be cut, was equipped with a handle (*a*) at one end. A male screw thread (*b*) of the same dimensions as those of the desired female screw thread was cut in the stick. The remaining part (*c*) of the stick was turned on a lathe until its diameter corresponded to that of the male screw's core. This part of the stick was then split lengthwise (**2**), and one lengthwise and one crosswise groove were hollowed out in the part still attached to the stick. An iron cutter (*d*), whose sharp end corresponded to the profile of the desired female screw thread, was fitted into the grooves, and the cut-off part of the stick was replaced. A wedge (*e*) was then forced into the lengthwise groove, so that the cutter was firmly kept in place. A hole, big enough for the male screw to pass through, was drilled in a piece of wood (*f*;

illustration **3** shows a cross-section), and smaller holes were drilled radially against this hole. Small dowels (*g*) of a hard wood were then hammered into the smaller holes, so that the piece of wood worked as a provisional nut when the sharp ends of the dowels guided the female screw thread. Finally, a hole with a diameter corresponding to that of the core of the male screw was drilled in the workpiece (*h*) about to be equipped with a female screw thread, and the piece of wood with the male screw was attached to the workpiece. When the handle (*a*) was then turned, the cutter (*d*) cut female screw threads of the desired dimensions in the workpiece.

of early times; for example, a comprehensive work, *Mechanical Problems*, formerly attributed to Aristotle (384−322 BC), is nowadays generally considered to have been written between 290 and 280 BC. During the years after Aristotle's death, important details may have been lost or neglected. The descriptions of different gear devices in *Mechanical Problems* are considered to be the earliest proof of the existence of cog-wheels and gears, but Drachmann is not convinced that Aristotle actually used cog-wheels, since the text does not mention anything about making them. Aristotle may instead have had plain wheels touching each other, transmitting motion by friction. Still, we shall never know whether the disciple had lost some part of his master's message, when he came to write it down, some forty years after Aristotle's death.

Derek de Solla Price, an American science historian, thinks it probable that Archimedes used the worm gear in one or other of the many war machines he built. It is also possible that the "endless screw" worm was used by Archimedes in the "planetarium" he is believed to have built. We have already mentioned Archimedes' work as well known by Ctesibius and by the other engineers of the Alexandrian school.

Around 60 AD, Hero described several cog-wheels for various uses. One of these he calls *barulkos*, "weight puller", and it is depicted both in Hero's *Mechanics* and in his *Dioptra*, although in slightly different versions. Hero also calculated the number of cogs on the various wheels, that is, the gear ratio of the weight puller, and gives it as 1:200. With a force of five talents, the weight puller should have been able to lift a weight of one thousand talents (about twenty-five tons). The calculation is, of course, purely theoretical−and even somewhat naive, since Hero did not consider the friction, which would be considerable in a case like this−not only between the cogs, but also in the shaft bearings. The cog-wheels are depicted with sawtooth-shaped cogs, and how they meshed is not shown clearly. Drachmann observes that cogs were not shaped like that at the time; but that, usually, they were either shaped as equilateral triangles or given a slightly trapezoid form ("pin-wheels"). The sawtooth shape may have been invented by Hero's draughtsman!

It is quite obvious that the illustrations accompanying Hero's original text have been misunderstood frequently by translators or copyists, both during his lifetime and later. The learned Italian poet Bernardino Baldi (1553−1617) thus mentions in the preface of his translation from the Greek of Hero's *On Automata* that, "ever since ancient times, the illustrations have been distorted by ignorant copiers", and that, for this reason, he has had the illustrations completely redrawn in this Italian edition, which was published in 1589.

One of Hero's illustrations of the weight puller shows a worm working against the last cog-wheel of the gear. The worm, especially the version used for drawing water, is believed to have been invented by Archimedes. The worm gear, that is, a machine element containing an endless screw, should be attributed to Hero, however, for he gave a fairly extensive description of designs for cutting external and internal threads for worm gears. The drawings of worm gears in Hero's book are, however, not easily interpreted, but Drachmann, Beck, and others have made reconstructions based on the text. It is, in other words, a question of the screw in its functions as a fastening (a metal bolt with a nut) and as a machine element. A number of "elementary machines" will be discussed in order to illuminate the development of machine elements over the years.

Hero's Worm Gears and Screw Constructions

Hero designed a great number of machines with the screw as the major machine element. Many of these designs were to remain relatively unchanged up to the days of industrialism.

D A milometer (**1**), built at Augsburg, Germany, at the end of the sixteenth century. The principle for this mechanism is the same as that for Hero's odometer, and many similar meters were built at the time. They were frequently constructed as pedometers for both pedestrians (**2**) and animals (**3**).

B

D1

D2

D3

B Hero's odometer, an instrument for measuring the distance travelled by a vehicle, consisted of four interconnected worm gears and was intended to be fitted (at *a*) to the wheel of a cart. In this version, there was a disc (*b*) with a hole in it on the last axle of the gear. When the hole in the disc had been turned to lie opposite a fixed hole (*c*) in the bottom of a box filled with stone balls, one of the balls fell into a container (*d*). By counting the number of fallen stone balls, the driver of the cart knew the distance covered.

C

C Leonardo da Vinci's distance-recording meter was a developed version of Hero's odometer. Leonardo, too, chose to register the distance covered by means of stone balls, which fell into a box.

B The modern equivalent of the *dioptra* is called a theodolite. In its simplest form, a theodolite consists of a telescope (*a*), equipped with a hairline cross, which can be turned round a horizontal and a vertical axle. Graded circles (*b*) are used for measuring angles in the horizontal and vertical planes.

A Hero's *dioptra*. As is shown by this reconstruction, the instrument consisted of a pillar (*a*) on a foot. On the pillar was a fixed metal disc (*b*) with an endless screw (*c*), which meshed with a turnable cog-wheel (*d*). At the top of the pillar was a fixed axle (*e*), on which either a water-level — used for keeping the instrument exactly vertical — or, as is shown here, a *dioptra* could be placed. Both the water-level and the *dioptra* were equipped with a socket (*f*), from which three pegs protruded. These fitted into holes in the turnable cog-wheel (*d*). The *dioptra* itself consisted of a flat disc (*g*), on which two lines were drawn at right angles to each other. The pivoted arm carried two sights (*h*), and the whole device was mounted on a pivoted, toothed wheel section (*i*), which meshed with an endless screw (*j*).

The odometer, an instrument for measuring the distance travelled by a vehicle, consisted of four worm gears following on each other. It was to be attached to one of the wheels of a cart to measure the distance travelled. Several different versions of the odometer are described in Hero's works. One version was fitted with a disc with holes, similar to a modern telephone dial. This disc was attached to the last axle of the gear, and when the disc had been turned so that one of its holes lay opposite a fixed hole in the bottom of a box filled with stone balls, one of the balls would fall into a container. This version was probably used as a "taximeter" in cabs. Counting a few stone balls was certainly less difficult for a poorly educated driver than reading an instrument. Burstall has called this odometer the first recording instrument. Another version was meant to be a ship's log and had its first gear axle connected to a little paddle-wheel; but it is unlikely that this instrument for measuring the distance sailed would have had a very wide application. Leonardo da Vinci developed Hero's idea of a distance-recording meter, and he drew a design for an instrument which is not unlike those used by surveyors at the end of the nineteenth century.

Milometers first came into use in the sixteenth and seventeenth centuries, when the need for drawn maps was making itself felt in Europe. In the 1640s, the versatile German monk and natural scientist Athanasius Kircher (1602–80) designed milometers for carriages—these instruments were based on Hero's odometer—and pedometers for both horses and pedestrians.

In the previous chapter, we mentioned that the art of surveying by measuring angles and establishing levels in a scientific fashion was well mastered in ancient times. Hero gives a detailed description of a geodetic instrument which he calls *dioptra* (in a paper bearing this

C The German astronomer Johann Hevelius (1611–87) built several instruments for making observations and determining positions with the naked eye. His instruments are characterized by their extreme precision. Shown here are a setting device and dividing scales from Hevelius's *Machina cælestis*.

D A pair of compasses of *c*. 1620, with adjusting screws with right-hand and left-hand threads respectively, so that a uniform motion of the compass legs is ensured.

E Leonardo's screw-cutting machine. When the crank (*a*) was turned, the tool (*b*) cut threads on the workpiece (*c*). The tool was advanced by two lead-screws (*d*, *e*), which were rotated by the gear (*f*) on the crank axle. By varying the ratios of gears *g* and *h*, the pitch of the thread cut on the workpiece could be varied.

F A swivelling crane of c. 1600. When the screw (*a*) is turned in one direction or the other, the load (*b*) is raised or lowered. Since the crane is equipped with a counterweight (*c*), less work is needed to turn the screw.

title); it was intended for measuring angles both vertically and horizontally and was, in other words, based on the same principle as the modern theodolite. Hero here uses the worm to adjust the sight rule in both directions.

When Hero's work was rediscovered during the Renaissance, engineers were inspired to find new applications for the worm gear as well as for the worm. Leonardo da Vinci, among others, used the worm gear for various designs, including a machine for cutting screw threads.

In the ancient cultures, different kinds of presses were used for, among other things, pressing the juice out of grapes and the oil out of olives. In the Old Kingdom of Egypt a version of the press was already known; it can best be described as a wringing machine, in which olives or grapes were placed in a cloth bag, which was then wrung by means of levers and muscle power. The ancient Greeks generally used a press-beam, that is, a single-shank lever, which was pressed against a leather container by weights and muscle power. Wine and olive presses played an important part in the national and domestic economy at that time, and every big household had some such kind of press. Aristotle tells us—with, perhaps, a certain critical irony—a story about the great philosopher and natural scientist Thales of Miletos, who lived in the fifth century BC. One winter, Thales anticipated that the olive harvest would be unusually bountiful and, consequently, bought all the olive presses he could find in the area. When the harvest time approached, he hired them out at prices set by himself. Obviously, neither leasing nor monopoly coups are modern inventions.

Hero built various types of presses, all with the screw as a machine element, and in a couple he also combined the screw with the lever.

A A beam-press, used for olives and grapes. The right-hand end of the beam (a) was placed in a recess in the wall. The fruit was put between planks or in bags, and the whole thing (b) was bound with a rope and placed under the beam, which was loaded with weights (c). The juice was allowed to flow into a vessel (d). Athenian vase decoration, sixth century BC.

B A screw press described by Hero. A sturdy screw (a) was fastened to the beam. A stone weight (b) was attached to a nut (c), which was turned by means of a handle (d). (e) Fruit to be pressed.

C Hero's direct screw press. The screw worked directly on the press lid (a), and the fruit was placed in a box (b) made from interlocked planks between which the juice seeped out.

D A direct double-screw press described by Hero; (1) front view, (2) cross-section. As the screws (a) were turned, the beam (b) bore down on a wooden block (c) on the lid (d) of the press. (e) Fruit container. (f) Box for collecting the juice.

E The first printing presses were simple, wooden screw presses.
F Screw presses were also used for minting, as shown by this copper-plate from 1771.

G A sixteenth-century elbow-joint press is shown here from two sides. It was used to lift and hang large, heavy doors, such as church doors. Usually, two or three presses like this were needed, together with a stable scaffold for horizontal steering, if a heavy door was to be hung on its hinges.
H A press used for minting, from *Encyclopédie Moderne, ou Dictionnaire Abrégé des Sciences, des Lettres, des Arts, etc.*,(Paris, 1863).

In his historical survey of the press, given in *Naturalis historia*, Pliny the Elder regards Hero's designs as new inventions in the development of the press.

Hero's press constructions spread rapidly all over the Mediterranean area, speeded by Pliny's extensive descriptions. These presses can also be said to have become prototypes for later press designs, from the Middle Ages up to modern times. Johann Gutenberg's first printing press, built in the 1430s, was more or less a direct copy of the Hero press with its screw design. The Hero screw was also used in coin-minting machines, where considerable pressure is required. The screw used in Hero's devices, with its pressure and thrust-generating properties, has also been the model for a great number of mechanical devices which came into being around the end of the Middle Ages. One example is the jack.

The Differential

An interesting application of the cog-wheel and the differential is found in what is known as the south-pointing carriage, designed in the third century AD in China. The dating has long been disputed; some sources would date it more than a thousand years earlier, but by relying on archaeological finds as well as on original texts, the English scientist Joseph Needham has been able to clarify the issue.

The carriage had two wheels and carried a wooden sculpture in the shape of a man whose extended arm was supposed to point south, whatever direction the carriage took. During the latter part of the nineteenth century, the first literary evidence of the carriage's actual existence was found. Some fragmentary finds were also made. These were taken as proof that the magnetic compass originated in China. Many writers, including the German historian of technology Franz M. Feldhaus, have depicted the south-pointing carriage with the sculpture mounted on top of a "magic box" between the shafts. The box supposedly contained the magnetic needle, which ensured the constant southerly direction of the pointing arm. This erroneous reconstruction caused some people to speculate that the magnetic compass—in the shape of the south-pointing carriage—had been invented as a result of the competition in the transport of silk and other goods from China to the Mediterranean countries. The caravans crossed the high plateaux of Tibet en route first to Samarkand and then to the commercial towns of the eastern Mediterranean. When the caravans travelled across the plateaux—an obvious short cut—they risked losing their sense of direction, especially in fogs or sand storms, so for safety, they usually skirted the bordering mountains. But time was money, then as now, and there was time to be gained. The solution presented itself in the shape of the south-pointing carriage!

A magnetic compass would certainly have led caravans safely across the high plateaux, a task now considered indisputably beyond the capacity of the south-pointing carriage; in fact, the pointing arm was moved, not by a magnet, but by connected differentials that compensated for the difference of the angle of rotation between the two carriage wheels, that occurred as the carriage turned. The statue was mounted on the outgoing axle of this device and thus pointed constantly south, whatever the direction of the carriage.

This device basically compensated for differences in the angles of rotation; this is quite impressive, for its construction required not only a thorough knowledge of the properties of the differential (which, for example, the almost contemporary Alexandrian school lacked), but also a considerable skill in the art of estimating the gear ratios of composite cog-wheels. The differential mechanism of the south-pointing carriage can hardly have been the result of experiments but must have been based on theoretical calculations.

The American Otto Mayr and several other historians of technology claim that the famous carriage was used as a ''mechanical compass'' by caravans and by travellers, but this appears impossible. Each imperfection in the mechanism and each bump to its wheels due to uneven ground would distort its indication of the direction. Simple mathematics show that a difference of only 1 per cent between the diameters of the two carriage wheels would shift the indicated south by 180° after only about 3 miles (5 km). South and north would then have changed on the compass! The designer was probably quite aware of these deficiencies, and it is likely that the south-pointing carriage was only used by those in power to show the people that their rulers had supernatural powers. One might, therefore, compare its use to Hero's ingenious device, mentioned earlier, which was used to open the doors of the temple's inner sanctum.

A Two-Thousand-Year-Old Calculator

The Antikythera device is a remarkable astronomical calculator dating from the first century BC. Some sponge fishermen found it in 1900 in a wrecked ship near the island of Antikythera, between Crete and the Peloponnesus. The ship lay in more than 130 ft (c. 40 m) of water. On board, there were art treasures and some inconspicuous verdigrised bronze objects, which were later fitted together to form a box of about 12×7×4 in (30×17×10 cm). The art treasures of this first, major marine-archaeological find were immediately examined by experts from the Athens National Museum, but it was not until a couple of years later that someone took an interest in the little box. It turned out that it contained some relatively well preserved cog-wheels and fragments of several others, bearing inscriptions which indicated that they could have been part of an astronomical instrument. The first guess was that the Antikythera device, as the object was soon called, was an astrolabe, but this was immediately contradicted. Over the years, many theories have been aired about the device and its application. Someone even suggested that it had been left behind by astronauts from an alien, advanced civilization visiting Earth, a notion obviously inspired by von Däniken, even if motivated by the very high level of scientific thinking and advanced technology represented in the device; it is unique in the cultural area where it was found and, indeed, elsewhere. Derek de Solla Price comments that the motivation as such may be justified, but that astronauts as a source must be ruled out; instead, we ought to upgrade our estimation of the Hellenic culture's abilities in natural science and technology.

In the early 1950s, Price started to interest himself in the Antikythera device, and in the following two decades, he was given several opportunities to examine its construction. Price is a professor in the history of ideas at Yale University and an internationally acclaimed expert on scientific instruments. Using X-ray, radiography, and other methods, Price succeeded in reconstructing the entire device and in clarifying its function and application. It is an advanced aid for calender calculations, based on such phenomena as the sun's passage through the zodiac and the phases of the moon.

Although the enigma of the function of the Antikythera device has now been largely answered, some questions still remain. Who, for instance, designed and built the instrument? It can hardly have been wholly exceptional, constructed by some Greek Leonardo da Vinci, who had mastered both the necessary theory and the technical problems of construction. The strange mechanism should rather be seen as the unexceptional result of a marriage between a wide-ranging scientific culture and sound craftmanship in precision mechanics.

Price also suggests that the school of Posidonius (135?−51? BC) in Rhodes may have produced this wonder of science and technology, implying that Posidonius had gathered round him natural scientists, technicians, and craftsmen, just as Hero did in Alexandria. Indeed,

A The design of the south-pointing carriage is based on an ingenious use of the properties of the differential. The carriage shown here (**1**) is a reconstruction made at the National Museum of Science and Technology in Stockholm. It was built with standard parts from a mechanical building kit. Illustration **2** is a skeleton drawing of the carriage's construction, whereas illustration **3** shows the carriage as seen in a cutaway view from behind. The rotation of the carriage wheels (a, b) is transferred by gearwheels (c, d) to the differential. This consists of two other gearwheels (e, f) which pivot on the axle g and rotate in opposite directions, meshing with the gears h and i, which pivot on the axle j. This axle is, however, journalled in fixed bearings in the axle g. As long

B

as the carriage wheels rotate at the same speed, axle g does not rotate, since the gears e and f have the same speed and thus rotate the gears h and i round the axle j without the latter (and, consequently, axle g) being rotated. When the carriage turns, however, one of its wheels will rotate slower than the other, and gears e and f, too, will then rotate at different speeds. In order to compensate for this difference in speed, i and h start to rotate about the axle g as well. When the carriage turns in relation to the ground, the south-pointing figure (k) attached to the axle g will turn in relation to the carriage and will stubbornly point towards the south, no matter in which direction the carriage is driven (4).

B The differential is included in most modern cars; fundamentally, it works as is shown here. Engine power is transmitted to the crown wheel (a) by a bevel pinion (not shown here). Bolted to the crown wheel is a differential cage (b), through which the axle shafts (c, d) pass; e and f are axle-shaft gears. As long as the car is driven straight ahead (**1**), the two axle shafts rotate at the same speed, and the differential gears (g, h) rotate together with the crown wheel (a) and the differential cage (b) — without rotating about their own axes. When the car turns (**2**), one axle shaft (c) rotates faster than the other (d), and the differential gears (g, h) will then compensate for the difference in speed by rotating about their own axes.

A1   A2   A3   A4

A5

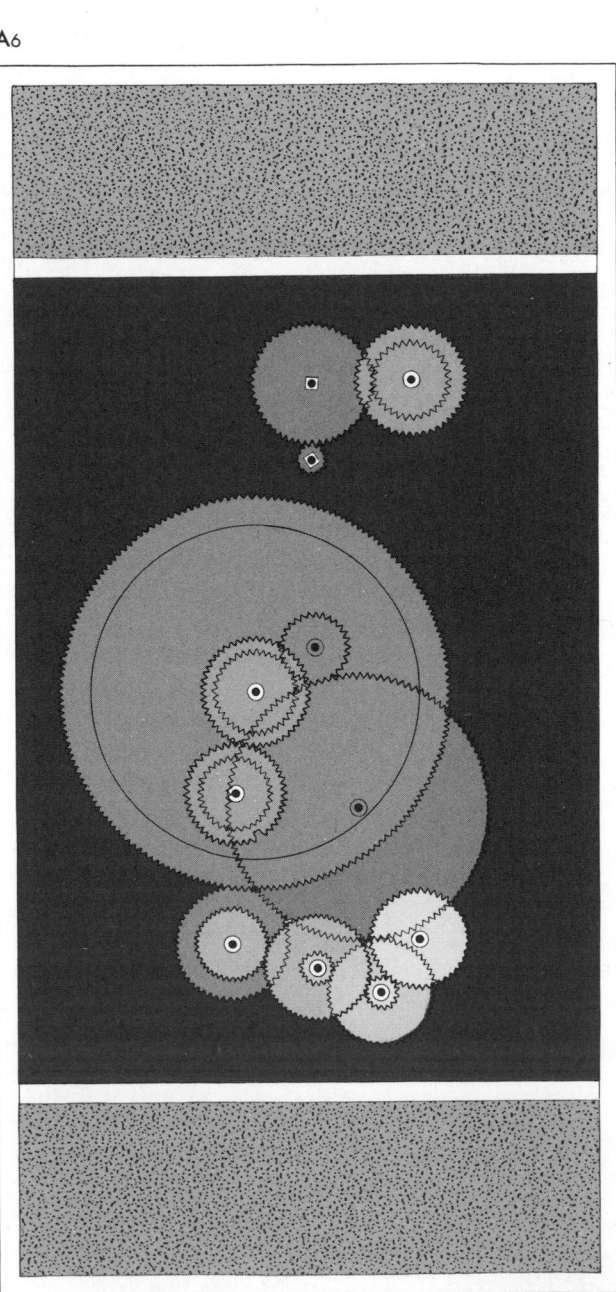

A6

A Four fragments are all that remain of the Antikythera mechanism. It is possible that these were joined when the find was made, but nobody realized then how much wood can distort and split if it is allowed to dry out after being immersed in water for so long. Unfortunately, no photographs were taken of the mechanism when it was retrieved from the almost two-thousand-year-old wreck. Illustrated here is Derek de Solla Price's reconstruction. On the front (**1**) of the mechanism were two circular scales, the outer containing the names of the months, the inner the names of the zodiac. (**2**) A side view of the mechanism: (*a*) front door, (*b*) back door, (*c*) drive axle. (**3**) The back of the mechanism had two sets of circular scales. Both front and back carried inscriptions (**4**). The mechanism itself, here in cross-section, consists of over thirty cog-wheels; (*d*) base plate. (**5**) Cog-wheels for the scales on the front. (**6**) Cog-wheels for the scales on the back of the base plate. Of especial interest is the differential which was used to show how the movements of the sun and moon coincided with the phases of the moon.

the two schools may well have been connected. As mentioned above, Philo of Byzantium found his way from the Alexandrian school to Rhodes, where he designed war machines. But as few texts mention Posidonius of Apamia, as he is usually called, little is known about him, even if some writers, Pliny among them, do refer to him. Sarton remarks that our estimation of Posidonius necessarily must be vague because of this, but that his position could well have been as highly esteemed as that of Aristotle. Perhaps future finds will tell us more about Posidonius and his school.

Water Clocks

Another question in connection with the Antikythera device is whether or not it formed part of another, larger instrument, perhaps something like the famous astronomical clock in the Tower of Winds in Athens. This tower was built in the first century BC and included a water clock, showing by means of cog-wheel mechanisms such astronomical data as the motion of the planets and the moon. Similar water clocks with mechanical "clockworks" existed elsewhere in the ancient cultures, and it is possible that Posidonius's school also designed such a clock, using the Antikythera device as a piece of additional equipment. This, too, can be answered only by new finds.

The Tower of Winds at the Roman *agora* (square) in Athens was built during the Roman period in Greece as a monument to time and space. It is an octagonal marble tower, almost 43 ft (13 m) high, with graceful sundials on the top frieze and a stately weathercock at its very top. The tower is still more or less intact, but the astronomical water clock has not survived. The Romans built many such water-driven ornamental clocks in their huge empire, and the art spread from there to other cultures.

In the fifth century AD, a magnificent ornamental clock was built in Ghaza. This clock was very similar to the mechanical astronomical clocks which became almost status symbols in European cathedrals and town halls from the fourteenth century onwards. Neither the Ghaza clock nor its housing still exist, but the German linguist Hermann Diels has managed to reconstruct them from a comprehensive contemporary description. The works were almost 13 ft (4 m) high and were housed in an open, stylish building with pillars, vaults, and a dome. A statuette depicting the sun god proceeded past twelve doors and pointed to the one corresponding to the hour of the day. Each hour was divided into twelfths, marked by a figure of Hercules successively showing illustrations of his twelve labours. An eagle attached a coronet to Hercules' head for each labour. At night, the doors showing the hours were lit. This ornamental clock not only showed, but also struck, the time: a large statue of Hercules struck a metal cylinder with a hammer on the hour and the half hour.

One can easily see the connection here with the Alexandrian school and its stage devices and theatrical *deus ex machina* effects.

The components of the Ghaza clock were the same as those used by Hero and the unknown designer of the Antikythera device.

The Ghaza clock became very famous and, for centuries, inspired other designers to similar achievements. It was the obvious model for an ornamental clock built in the Large Mosque of Damascus, and which was described in the twelfth century by the oriental explorer al-Kinani. The Damascus clock featured two brass falcons, which dropped brass balls from their beaks into bronze dishes to mark the hours. Above the falcons were twelve doors, which closed automatically along with the passing of the hours, as the brass balls "struck". Eleven men were required to keep this ornamental clock going; apparently, it had not been possible automatically to light and dowse the lanterns which lit the doors that closed automatically at night. Al-Kinani's account spread to China; but Needham says that similar automata had been built there since the eighth century.

B

B A reconstruction of a 6-ft (2 m) high Roman clock.
C A reconstruction of an approximately 40-ft (13 m) high astronomical clocktower, which was built in c. 1090 AD in the Chinese city of Honan by one Su-Sung. The clockwork was driven by a water-wheel (*a*), whose ladles were filled with water from a tub (*b*). An ingenious device prevented the water-wheel from turning while each ladle was being filled. The water-wheel also rotated a bronze planetarium (*c*) and a celestial globe (*d*). A series of automata (*e*) indicated the passage of time by appearing in niches (*f*) and striking bells and gongs.

The water clocks designed in the Middle Ages were not only astronomical. For example, Leonardo da Vinci made a sketch of an alarm clock, but this design was probably more of a joke than a serious proposal. The round dish is held up by a tube which works like a two-armed lever. At the other end of the tube is a flat dish containing water; a rope from this end is fastened by a noose to the sleeper's feet. When the round dish is half filled, it becomes heavier than the flat dish, which swings up, pouring its water through the tube down into the round dish and brutally jerking the rope round the sleeper's ankles.

The Mechanical Clock

It is yet to be established when the first mechanical clock was designed. One of the difficulties in fixing the date is purely linguistic, since the most relevant western languages—Latin, Italian, French, English, and German—use the same word to denote both mechanical and water clocks. In his *Divine Comedy*, Dante Alighieri (1265–1321) mentions (in "Paradiso") a clock, and it has long been disputed whether this was water- or mechanically powered. A. P. Usher, the American historian of technology, feels that Dante's stanzas can be interpreted as describing a mechanical clock, calling upon the Englishman G. H. Baille's work to support this theory. If this is correct, the first "machine of machines" can be dated to the beginning of the fourteenth century.

The distinguishing component of the mechanical clock is the escapement, which controls the constant motion of the hand; the other components, such as cog-wheels with axles and the weight driving the machine, have been known since ancient times. The first escapement is usually attributed to the French architect Villard de Honnecourt, who, in a book of drawings called *Album*, shows one, even if it is rather difficult to interpret. *Album* dates from the late thirteenth century and describes various devices noted by Honnecourt during his travels. It is hardly likely that Honnecourt himself originated this component, but very probably he did see a mechanical clock, for his drawings include a picture of a clock tower, and perhaps the clock he saw may even have been the one mentioned by Dante!

Usher has compiled a list of twenty "clocks" mentioned in literature, inscriptions, and other sources from the period between 1286 and 1335; all of these, according to him, are to be regarded as water clocks. The tower clock of Dover Castle in England was long considered the oldest mechanical clock, being said to have been built in 1348. It was discovered in 1851 in the castle attic, having probably lain there for centuries. It was claimed at the time that "1348" was engraved on its framework, and this date has been given since then. Recently, however, the clock has been restored, but no such inscription has been found. Singer believes that the tower clock was probably made around 1650, whereas Usher dates it at around 1500. The reason the clock was put away seems to be simple enough: it was a very bad timekeeper.

The first sure evidence for the existence of a mechanical clock dates from 1335. It refers to a clock built by Guglielmo Zelandino and mounted in a tower on the San Gottardo chapel in Milan. Similar clocks were made in Modena in 1343, in Padua the following year, and in Monza in 1347. The designer of the Padua clock was Jacopo di Dondi, whose son, Giovanni, made an ingenious astronomical clock which showed the motion of the sun, the moon, and five planets. It also included an eternal calendar of the movable feasts. This clock was completed in 1364, after sixteen years of work, and was placed in the tower of the castle at Pavia. Dondi had obviously looked to the earlier, water-driven, astronomical clocks for several of the design elements of his clock.

At this time, tower clocks, ornamental clocks, and astronomical

A₁   A₂

A₃

A Heinrich von Wiek's ornamental clock of 1354 was a weight-driven clock with a verge escapement. A side view (**1**) and a front view (**2**) of the clockwork are shown here, with an enlarged illustration of the verge escapement (**3**). The weight (*a*) drives a barrel (*b*) with a great wheel (*c*), which meshes with a pinion (*d*) on a spindle. On this spindle is a second wheel (*e*), which transmits the rotary motion by way of a pinion (*f*) to the escape wheel (*g*). This wheel has an odd number of ratchet-shaped teeth, and its rotary motion is constantly impeded by two pallets (*h*), arranged to form an angle with each other on a verge (*i*). When the escape wheel is turned, one of the pallets is pushed aside, causing the verge to turn, and the foliot balance (*j*), a cross-bar with weights, begins turning with increasing velocity until its movement is abrupty checked when the other pallet engages with a tooth on the escape wheel. The verge, and thus the foliot balance, are then turned in the opposite direction until the first pallet again engages with a tooth. The rotary motions are regulated all the time by the foliot balance's inertia, which may be adjusted to some extent by moving the weights. The hand (k) is driven by the weight's (a) influence on the barrel by way of a pinion-and-wheel system (l). (m) Winding pinion and wheel.

B A reconstruction of Giovanni di Dondi's astronomical clock, which was mounted in the castle at Pavia in 1364. Not only the passage of time but also the movements of the planets were indicated by the clock.

C The ornamental clock in the cathedral at Lund, Sweden, in its present state. The clock is surmounted by two knights, and below them is a dial whose hands show local and astronomical time, the sun's passage through the zodiac, and the phases of the moon. At the base of the clock is a calendarium, which completes a 360° clockwise turn per year — every midnight, it moves one step forward. In the middle of the clock, an image of the Virgin Mary is situated; the three wise men and their servants enter through the door on her left.

49

A The mainspring (*a*) in a main-spring-powered watch has its outer end attached to the inside of the rim of the barrel (*b*) and its inner end attached to the arbor (*c*), whose ends pass through the barrel's cover (*d*) and bottom. The spring is wound when either *b* or *c* is turned in relation to the other.

B In order to compensate for the irregularity of the force transmitted by the mainspring – the force is at its greatest when the spring is fully wound and at its least when the spring has almost completely run down – the mainspring barrel can be combined with a fusee. The mainspring arbor (*a*) is then fixed, and the mechanism is wound by turning the fusee's arbor (*b*). A cord (*c*), one end of which is attached to the barrel (*d*), will then be wound onto the fusee's spiral groove (*e*); simultaneously, the barrel will be turned. As the mainspring runs

clocks were built to adorn public buildings and royal palaces all over Europe. In 1354, Strasbourg cathedral was given an ornamental clock with a mechanical cock which crowed and flapped its wings at twelve noon. The German clockmaker Heinrich von Wiek designed several ornamental clocks, the most famous being the one attached to Charles V's palace (now the Palais de Justice) in Paris in 1354.

The astronomical clock in the cathedral at Lund in Sweden – *Horologium Mirabile Lundense* – is considered to date back to the 1380s, but an exact date and information concerning its design, builder, etc., cannot be given. A comparison between the ornamentation and technology of the Lund clock and those of similar ornamental clocks in central Europe confirms this approximate date, although the existence of the clock is not documented in any original text older than 1424. In the 1580s, a comprehensive description of the clock was written by the cathedral's chaplain, Mogens Madsen. Notes from the mid-sixteenth century indicate that, at that time, the clock no longer worked but had fallen into decay. The clockwork was taken out and scrapped in the 1830s, but the front with the faces was kept and set up in the interior wall of the north aisle of the cathedral. Around 1910, a Danish tower clockmaker, Julius Bertram-Larsen, became interested in trying to restore the mediaeval clock. In due course, his work led to a reconstruction of the "wonderful clock in Lund" in all its mediaeval splendour, and it was reinstated in 1923, on the 800th anniversary of the cathedral. During reconstruction, a replica of the clock had been made on a scale of 1:3. This was rotary motion of the escapement wheel (e). One of the twelve pins projecting from the side of the escapement wheel then pushes arm c downwards, so that the pendulum swings outwards. Arm b is then withdrawn from the pallet, which falls down onto the escapement wheel and stops it.

down, the cord is rewound onto the barrel. Thus, when the spring is fully wound, the cord pulls against the smallest part of the fusee, whereas it pulls against the largest spiral when the spring has almost run down. (f) Great wheel.

C The first portable timekeepers usually had a hinged cover over the dial.

D A pendulum clock, constructed according to Galileo's suggestions by his son Vincenzio in 1649. On the pendulum rod (a) are two arms (b, c). As the pendulum swings inwards, arm b lifts a pallet (d), which will then no longer constrain the

E Huygens's pendulum clock (1), a weight-driven clock with a verge escapement. Through his investigations of the theory of the pendulum, Huygens discovered that the pendulum swings with perfect homogeneity of period only if its path is cycloid. A cycloid is a curve which corresponds to the movement of a fixed point on a circle which rolls along a straight line. (2) Huygens solved the problem of how to get the pendulum to swing in this manner by making the top part of the pendulum rod from two silk cords (b), which were suspended from between two cycloid-shaped metal plates (c). (d) Pallets. (e) Crown wheel.

F The anchor escapement was invented in the middle of the eighteenth century. The weight (a) drives the escapement wheel (b) by means of a wheel and pinion. As the pendulum (c) swings to the right, the left-hand pallet of the anchor, which is attached to the pendulum rod, catches a tooth on the escapement wheel and receives an impulse, which makes the pendulum swing to the left. The anchor's right-hand pallet then gets an impulse from the escapement wheel so that the pendulum swings to the right, and so on.

G Mainspring-powered clock with a balance wheel and an anchor escapement. The balance (a) has taken over the pendulum's regulating role. Its movements are limited by the length of the coil-spring (b). (c) Anchor. (d) Escapement wheel. (e) Mainspring barrel. (f) Winder.

given by a patron of the arts to the Stockholm Town Hall, which was opened in 1923, on the 400th anniversary of King Gustavus Vasa's entry into Stockholm. The replica of the Lund clock was displayed in the Town Hall, but for various reasons, it was sold a few years later. After a varied career, it was acquired by the National Museum of Science and Technology in Stockholm in 1966. It is now displayed there after extensive restoration. The clock shows local and astronomical time, the phases of the moon, and the sun's passage through the zodiac. Moreover, it has a calendarium which shows the date and the day of the week. By means of this calendarium, it is also possible to find the day of the week of a given date in any year between 1923 and 2123. It is, however, the automata of the clock that most fascinate onlookers. Two mediaeval knights on the dome of the clock hourly exchange blows to the number of the hour. At twelve o'clock, after the twelfth blow, a hymn resounds from a mechanical trombone, a little door beside an image of the madonna opens, and the three wise kings from the East come out, followed by their servants, and file, bowing, past the Virgin Mary.

The mechanical clock derives technically from the ancient machine elements; but its spiritual roots lie in the regular life led within the walls of the monasteries. The Cistercian monastic rules of about 1260 describe in detail the responsibilities of the bell-minder. When the water clock showed the hour, the bell-minder was to mark this by ringing the monastery bell—hence the synonym "bell" for the word "clock" in some languages. Lewis Mumford comments:

It would not be an exaggeration to say that the monasteries helped to give human enterprises the regular, collective pulse and rhythm of a machine. A clock not only helps to keep track of the hours, but also synchronises the actions of man. . . . The instrument rapidly spread beyond the monastery, and the regular striking gave new regularity to the craftsman's and merchant's lives. The measuring of time turned into time slavery, time estimating and time rationing. When this happened, eternity gradually stopped to be the yardstick and the aim of people's actions. The clock, not the steam engine, is the key machine of the modern industrial age.

Precision Engineering

Up to the middle of the sixteenth century, the progress being made in the development of the clock strongly stimulated the crafts. Many new tools and working methods were developed, and this in turn led to the invention of new machine elements. The escapement was successively refined, and new methods to drive it were invented. The first spring-driven clocks appeared in the early sixteenth century. This invention, and thereby the first pocket-watch, is usually attributed to a Nuremberg locksmith, Peter Henlein (1480–1542), who is believed to have made, around 1510, the first of his *Nürnberger Eierlein*, "Nuremberg eggs", as these clocks came to be called due to their elliptical shape. Usher, however, points out that at least two older spring-driven clocks are known from literature.

The appearance of the pocket-watch challenged craftsmen working in precision mechanics to develop even more precise and still smaller machine elements. The new prime mover, the spring-driven clockwork of the watch, was soon used to power automata of various kinds. For example, mechanical toys of all kinds were spring-driven from the mid-nineteenth century and up to the arrival of the miniature electric motor in the 1950s.

From the late Middle Ages up to the early nineteenth century, the development of the mechanical clock was distinguished by the interaction between science—mainly mathematics and technology—and practical application. Over the years, this process has had a great influence in both directions. The most revolutionary contributions to the techniques of clockmaking were made by the Italian Galileo Galilei (1564–1642) and the Dutchman Christiaen Huygens (1629–95). Even as a student in Pisa in the 1580s, Galileo is believed to have come upon the laws determining the movement of the pendulum. Legend has it that this occurred when he was at mass and saw a chandelier suspended from the ceiling slowly swing back and forth. By counting the beats of his pulse to time the pendulum, Galileo established that all the swings took an equal time. He used a pendulum to measure short intervals of time, but his was a free-swinging pendulum with a manually maintained movement. The problem of mechanically maintaining the swings of the pendulum was solved by Huygens, who, in 1657, patented the first pendulum clock. It was driven by a weight, and the escapement was made up of an escape wheel with sawtooth-shaped cogs, which, with each regular impulse, gave the pendulum a push, making it swing continuously.

Inspired by his success, Huygens tackled the mathematics of time-measuring technology and, in 1673, he published the results of his studies in *Horologium oscillatorium*, which can be considered the first fundamental work on both scientific and practical mechanics. Huygens introduced a great many machine elements, but we shall mention only one here: the coil spring, or fly, which, up to the present, has been the fundamental mechanism in all watches and most clocks.

For obvious reasons, clocks with swinging pendulums are not very suitable for use at sea. In the seventeenth century, the great seafaring nations—England, Holland, and France—tried frantically to produce a precise timepiece so that longitude could be determined at sea. For years, Huygens strove to develop a mechanism as constant as the swinging pendulum but less sensitive to external influence. The breakthrough came in Paris on January 20, 1675, when he could write "Eureka" in his diary next to a sketch of the torsion pendulum. Whether, like Archimedes, he ran naked through the streets on this occasion, crying out his "eureka", is not recorded. Huygens immediately contacted the French Academy of Science and demonstrated his invention. A few days later, he was granted the sole manufacturing rights for it, becoming in due course a rich man. Huygen's contributions to timekeeping technology illustrate one of the many fruitful results of the above-mentioned interaction between theory and practice.

We have touched upon the increased demand for tools and more refined methods of precision working that followed the appearance of the mechanical clock. The demand for high-quality materials also increased sharply, and one of the results of this was crucible steel. The crucible process was discovered by an English clockmaker of German extraction, Benjamin Huntsman, who manufactured clock springs, wheel axles, and other steel parts for his clocks. He had been encountering great difficulty in finding raw material of sufficiently high and uniform quality for his needs, for the commercial steel of the time was, above all, not homogenous, and the clock springs made of it were often of poor quality. In the 1730s, Huntsman began to consider whether melted steel would blend better if it were heated slightly above its melting point. The problem was to achieve the high temperature required. Foundries had never been able to do this. Huntsman, however, managed to build a well-insulated furnace with a high chimney which gave a strong draught. His raw material was powdered blister steel (preferably of Swedish Dannemora iron), which he mixed with crushed glass in a relatively small crucible (about 10 in, or 25 cm, high). The crucible had a stone lid and was embedded in crushed coke. The melting process took three to four hours, and when the steel was sufficiently fluid, it was stirred vigorously before the crucible was taken out of the furnace. Huntsman's crucible steel process, which was successively refined, remained for more than a century the chief method of producing top-quality steel for use in many more areas than the one originally intended. In his search for better material for clock springs, Huntsman thus found a new kind of steel, and this resulted not only in great progress in precision mechanics, but also in new designs in practically all areas of mechanical engineering.

The Machine of Machines

Lewis Mumford calls the mechanical clock "the machine of machines". Nowadays, it is ubiquitous; most of us wear a wrist-watch and have several clocks around us, both at home and at work. The clock made industrialism possible, and more so than the steam-engine and other prime movers, Mumford says, and adds that the clock is the typical symbol of all the development stages of the machine, a statement which holds a great deal of truth—not least from a prophetic point of view, as it was made in the 1930s. Today, in the age of computers, we can observe the marked symbolism of the fact that the mechanics of the clock have given way to electronics, because the electronic oscillating circuit gives far greater accuracy than could be achieved economically by mechanics.

Mumford's symbol of a machine in the form of an innocent watch also plays a key role in a much-reprinted controversial book, first published in 1872, about the machine age. The title of the book is *Erewhon, or Over the Range*, and it was written by Samuel Butler (1835–1902); it has appeared again and again in debates on social matters. It has been interpreted and misinterpreted, and today it is quoted more than ever. In brief, the book is about a sheep-farmer (as a young man, Butler emigrated to New Zealand and for some years had a sheep farm there, before returning to England), who gets lost on unmarked tracks, walks across a mountain range and, to his astonishment, finds an entirely new civilization, called Erewhon, on the other side. Quite inexplicably, he is arrested and put into prison. The language of this country is totally incomprehensible to him, but he eventually learns that the terrible crime he has committed is the possession of a watch. There had been a civil war in Erewhon some five hundred years earlier between the machinists and the anti-machinists, that is, between those who were for and those who were against machines. The anti-machinists had won, and everything in the nature of a machine had been destroyed. Owning a machine in Erewhon was, from that time on, treason of the highest order.

Butler's hero—and *alter ego*—is pardoned in due course, after having learnt the Erewhonian language, and he is taken care of by Mr. Nosnibor (Robinson!), who is a leading merchant in the metropolis. Later on, the sheep-farmer meets venerable professors of the Colleges of Unreason, which is the very telling name of the Erewhonian universities. Butler's sharp satire is positively scathing when he describes these unscientists and their activities. They have long been engaged in, among other things, a careful study of the historical development of mechanical engineering, not with the aim of using such machinery again, but "with the feelings of an English antiquar-

B Ackermann's principle for geometrically correct steering is based upon the theory that the front wheels (*a*) of a vehicle must roll along the peripheries of two different-sized circles, which, however, have a common centre (*b*). This centre must be in line with the rear axle (*c*).

C The position of the wheels (as seen from above) when a car with Ackermann steering is going round a bend (**1**) and when it is being driven straight ahead (**2**). Since the tie rod (*a*) is shorter than the front axle (*b*), the outer wheel is turned less than the inner as the car goes round the bend.

D Independently of Ackermann's patent, the Swedish brothers Birger and Fredrik Ljungström constructed the same steering system in 1894. They used it on the ''rickshaw'' version of their Svea bicycle.

A Watt's three-bar linkage with a pantograph extension; (**1**) as mounted on a steam-engine, (**2**) explanatory sketch. The upper illustration shows the mechanism as seen from the end of the balance beam, from the side, and from above. The piston rod (*a*) was pivoted on the balance beam (*b*) by way of a bar (*c*), which was as long as the middle bar in the three-bar linkage (*d, e, f*). Between the piston rod and the three-bar linkage was another bar (*g*), whose length corresponded to the distance between *c*'s and *e*'s points of attachment to the balance beam, so that a pantograph extension was formed. Yet another piston rod (*h*) was then coupled to the three-bar linkage, so that one more pantograph was formed. Shown at **2** is the curve which would be described by point *i* on *e* if the movement of the three-bar linkage were not limited. Only that part (*j*) of the curve which was a more or less straight line was used for the engine.

ian concerning Druidical monuments or flint arrow-heads". Butler lets a machinist and an anti-machinist explain their views and argue their cases. The standpoint of the machinist is mainly a mixture of the philosophies topical at the time when *Erewhon* was written; in particular, the machinist is impressed by the theories regarding machines as extensions and reinforcements of the human limbs. This idea of "organ projection" had appeared in both Germany and England in the 1860s and was developed with scientific brilliance and thoroughness ten years later by the German Ernst Kapp in his great work, *Grundlinien einer Philosophie der Technik*, which was then very much debated. The idea that a hammer, a spade, or a crowbar externally reinforces the function of the hand and arm needs no further explanation, but Butler's machinist takes the notion even further when he says that a train is "a seven-leagued foot that five hundred people may own at once". The machinist, in other words, has a basically positive attitude to technology. However, the ruling party in Erewhon, the anti-machinists, fear that machines would compensate the weak, thus making equal everybody's ability, so that even those of inferior physique would be able to survive. According to Erewhonian law, illness and weakness are also crimes against the state, and during the centuries of the anti-machinist regime, the rulers had striven to create a physical élite, favouring the strong and tall; all physical frailties were to be abolished. Machines, even of the simplest kind, would enable the weak to assert themselves, and this, according to the anti-machinists, had to be prevented.

For their time, Butler's ideas were not quite so original as is claimed by those who use isolated, out-of-context quotations in today's debate. The key role played by the "machine of machines" at the beginning of the book seems rather anachronistic. The anti-machinists, after many years of fighting and various compromises, had decided to accept any machine older than 271 years, so either Butler or his Erewhonian professors made a mistake over the clock, for the mechanical clock was then far older than that. Still, the ban may have been created according to the rules of the Colleges of Unreason.

Machine Elements of the Steam Era

During the long era when power was produced by harnessing wind and water, wood was the main material used in building machines, and even the machine elements of this era—such as the gearwheel in the power transmission of a windmill—were no exception. Iron fittings were used sparsely up to the beginning of the nineteenth century. Then, when steam power and its associated techniques began their progress, iron became, for various reasons, the predominant building material. Steam generated not only power but also new machine elements, many of which have found additional applications in different technical fields. One example is parallelogram steering, and another is the sun-and-planet drive; both were invented by James Watt.

When designing his steam-engine, Watt encountered the problem of making the piston rod move vertically in a straight line without breaking, although it was connected with the balance beam, the outer end of which oscillated, or moved in a curve. He solved the problem by using two jointed levers to steer the piston rod. His double-acting steam-engine (see also Chapter Five) had a smaller piston pump for the condenser, and this, too, required rectilinear steering of the piston rod. Watt connected the levers of the working piston with the pump piston rod. The connected levers formed a parallelogram, and the levers moved gracefully when the steam-engine was working.

Ever since it was invented, Watt's parallelogram has inspired engineers to many similar designs. A versatile German by the name of Rudolph Ackermann, who lived most of his life in London, took out a patent for the system in 1818, although it had been invented some years earlier by Georg Lankensperger, coachmaker to the king of Bavaria. The system has been used on cars since about 1900. The most common application of the principle today must surely be the tie rod in Ackermann's steering system for cars. The tie rod has an effect, however, contrary to the rectilinear effect intended by Watt; as a car goes round a bend, the inside front wheel, which has a smaller turning circle, gives a larger torsional angle than the outside wheel. The Swedish brothers Birger and Fredrik Ljungström, not being aware of the existence of Ackermann's system, developed the same design for use on the "rickshaw" version of their Svea bicycle, to be described in Chapter Nine.

The sun-and-planet drive is an interesting piece of machinery, which was developed by Watt when he modified his steam-engine to achieve a rotary motion. The background of the design is curious. The obvious way to transform the reciprocating motion of the piston to a rotary motion was to use a crankshaft and connecting rod, for this machine element had been known since the Middle Ages and generally applied in the spinning-wheel, the lathe, and so on. But in 1780, the crank motion with a crank wheel had cleverly been patented by James Pickard, who was apparently tipped off by one of Watt's assistants. Watt, however, never disputed this but decided to get around Pickard's patent. Watt tried a number of designs, but his solution was to attach a cog-wheel to the "connecting rod" and then to marry it to another, usually smaller, cog-wheel, joined to the flywheel. This planetary drive—or sun-and-planet drive, as Watt himself called it—was patented in 1781 and was used extensively in Watt's own steam-engines as well as in several later versions of the steam-engine.

Watt's sun-and-planet drive is a machine element which has been used in widely different contexts and in many forms, for example as a gear box in machine tools. In about 1890, a metal-turning lathe was equipped with such a drive, which made it possible to vary the speed of the lathe spindle over a very large range. Somewhat later, a sun-and-planet motion was introduced on the spindle itself of a different kind of machine tool, in this case, a grinding machine. At the same time as the grinding machine rotated, its centre would move on a circular path. The machine in question was specially developed to make it possible to grind internal holes in workpieces of such a shape that they could not be rotated when they were being machined. Another example of the application of Watt's invention can be found in scales for fine adjustment of measuring instruments, where a sun-and-planet drive—usually made as a friction gear—can give a good gear ratio and great accuracy. These sun-and-planet drives are also common in radio technology, where they are used for fine tuning of tuned circuits in transmitters and receivers.

Machine-made Machine Elements

The machine elements for the clockmaking industry were first made by hand, that is, by manufacture. The clockmaker used simple tools to hand file the teeth of cog-wheels, axles, and other details. One of the first attempts at machine manufacture was made by Christopher Polhem (1661–1751) at the Stjernsund Works in Sweden in the early eighteenth century. The works were founded in 1699 and were mainly intended for the mechanized production of such everyday utility objects as tin mugs, plates, nails, hammer heads, etc. Polhem understood fully the advantages of machines over hands. "Nothing increases the demand as much as a considerable lowering of the price of a product", Polhem wrote, and continued, "That is why we need machines to take over the heavy and time-consuming labour by hand. The result will be a saving of 100–1,000 per cent in costs."

Polhem's machine tools to produce cog-wheels are first mentioned in documents dating from 1708. Very likely, the successful sales of the everyday objects made at the works encouraged Polhem to provide the clockmakers of Sweden with cog-wheel "kits". He believed that it was economically indefensible for craftsmen to waste their skill on so time-consuming a process as making cog-wheels by hand. Therefore, he standardized a number of wheel kits for clocks of different sizes, from wall and table clocks to tower clocks. They were made with the aid of water-wheel-driven machines of different sizes. Six to eight of these machines must have been designed by Polhem and were used at the Stjernsund Works. The largest and probably most automatized was, unfortunately, destroyed in a devastating fire in 1737. Polhem's grandson, Reinhold Rückersköld, who later took over the management of the works, described how:

a machine, driven by water and operated by just one man, simultaneously filed out the teeth in all wheels, both large and small, after the same machine had cut them out of brass to a circular shape with spokes and a centre hub. The machine also cut out the teeth of all gears, which were also provided with axles. These were produced by smoothing and round filing between parallel files.

This machine, so skilfully made and consisting of unlimited connected movements, in eight days produced gearwheels with the accuracy required for clocks, on a scale large enough to supply several clockmakers for a whole year.

The machine described was probably made in 1729. It was not damaged in the fire and was still in use in the 1760s. Today, it is on display in the National Museum of Science and Technology in Stockholm, and it can no doubt be regarded as one of the first automatic machine tools. Another two of Polhem's cutting machines for cog-wheels are preserved at the same museum. One is a robust machine for making cog-wheels for tower clocks, and the other is a model of a manually operated cutting machine.

For various reasons, the mechanized production of cog-wheels at the Stjernsund Works did not turn out to be the success Polhelm had anticipated. One contributory factor was the professional pride of the clockmakers; they felt that a first-class clock should be made completely by hand, and semi-finished products did not appeal to them. Another reason was the difficulty in distributing the goods; Sweden was a sparsely populated country with bad roads and very poor communications. Generally, one could say, with Usher, that the main reason why Polhem's ideas and designs for cog-wheel production were so unappreciated was the fact that here, as in many other areas, Polhem was far ahead of his time.

Mechanized Manufacture of Blocks

The multiple block with the pulley was mentioned above as a machine element in the group of the "mighty five". The block was used at an early stage in the rigging of sailing vessels, and in the great era of sailing, up to 1,000 blocks could be needed to fit out one large ship. In the early nineteenth century, the annual need of the British navy was 130,000 blocks of different sizes. These were manufactured by hand at the Portsmouth Dockyard, where 110 craftsmen were kept busy.

However, the French-born engineer Marc Isambard Brunel (1769–1849) suggested in 1801 that the manufacture of blocks ought to be mechanized. He presented models of a series of block-making machines to the Inspector General of Naval Works, Sir Samuel Bentham, who, a couple of years earlier, had had milling machines installed at the yard, along with saws and other mechanical aids for working wood. Some of these he had designed himself. At this time, a block was almost entirely made of wood; the shell was of oak and

Watt's "sun-and-planet" drive shown here from the front (1) and in cross-section (2). The reciprocating movement of the steam-engine's balance beam (a) was transmitted to a fixed gearwheel (b), the "planet", which meshed with a gearwheel (c), the "sun", on the flywheel axle, making it rotate. An annular guide (d) kept the "planet" in its track round the "sun".

the sheave of lignum vitae, a very hard South American wood. Only the sheave pin was of steel.

At first, Brunel's suggestion met with strong opposition, within the Dockyard as well as from the main supplier of blocks to the navy, but in due course, full-scale machines based on the models were built, and the mechanized production of blocks started in 1803. A total of forty-five machines, driven by two 30-hp steam-engines were in production two years later, and produced blocks of four different size ranges. By adjusting the machines, the dimensions of the blocks could be varied within each size range; in the largest range, for example, the dimensions of the blocks could be varied between 10 and 18 in (25.4 and 45.7 cm). From 1808 on, 10 unskilled workers using Brunel's machines produced as many blocks per unit of time as were previously produced by 110 skilled workers. As a result, the annual production costs were lowered by £17,000 ($85,000).

Brunel's machines contained a number of new construction elements, such as a circular saw, which was used to cut off the material for the block shells. It had a pendulum movement and an interesting type of power transmission by ropes. One machine for mortising the shells employed a cone clutch, a machine part which may have been used for the first time here. Nowadays, the cone clutch is used in all cars which have not been fitted with automatic gear boxes.

Marc Isambard Brunel was born in Normandy and received a technical education at the French marine academy. Among his teachers was the famous mathematician Gaspard Monge (1746–1818). During the French revolution, Brunel fled to the United States, where he continued his technical education, studying civil and mechanical engineering. Eventually, he was appointed chief engineer for the city of New York. In 1798, he went to England to marry Sophia Kingdom, and he then settled in London. An important reason for this was the influential post his brother-in-law held in the navy. From his first years in the United States, Brunel had taken an interest in the mechanical production of blocks and how this could be improved.

The mechanization of block production for the British navy meant a great success for Brunel. Among his later achievements, the greatest was the first tunnel under the Thames in London, a project dramatically begun in 1824 and completed only in 1843. (Non-British literature often confuses Marc Brunel with his son, Isambard Kingdom Brunel (1806–59), who became a celebrated railway engineer who also designed ships and bridges.)

A few decades after Brunel and Bentham had introduced their

B Polhem's water-wheel-powered machine for the manufacture of cogwheels for clocks and watches can be described as one of the first automatic machine tools. It was probably built in 1729 and still survives.

A A manually operated precision cutting machine for the manufacture of gearwheels. The machine is probably the oldest of Polhem's gear-cutting machines, and it is likely that it was built as a simplified model or as a pilot study for the more complicated machine shown at **B**. The large dividing plate (a) was used to line up the gearwheel workpiece (b) at the correct angle for each cog to be cut.

mechanized methods of block-production, the Royal Navy began to go over to steam, and the demand for blocks consequently diminished. At the same time, new block designs were introduced; first, the pulley and the mountings were made of metal, and then the wood was completely replaced by other materials. Nowadays, small blocks are usually made of stainless steel or malleable iron (cast iron processed to a tougher and more ductile form by removing part of the carbon in the material). The pulleys are now usually made of nylon.

Machine Elements in Motion

Leonardo da Vinci was the first to show components separately when he was making drawings of machines. Such drawings are called exploded views and were used by several Renaissance authors; two of these were Agricola and Ramelli, but they did not have access to Leonardo's books as direct examples. Agricola, for example, often described machines by showing detailed drawings of the machine elements which were in reality concealed inside the machine. Christopher Polhem learnt this method during a tour of England and Central Europe in 1694–96. Although very impressed, he could not practise it himself, for the very simple reason that he was totally unable to draw even the easiest of diagrams! His talent was the ability to think in three dimensions and make simple models to express his ideas for designs. After his return from abroad, Polhem designed a number of models of machine elements which he must have seen during his tour or been inspired to invent by the sight of some mechanical device. He often made prototypes of his models himself, and then some skilfull craftsman would take over the final construction.

Polhem considered these working models to be more instructive than illustrations in books, and therefore suitable for teaching mechanical engineering. In an account of his travels, which he gave to the Mines Authority in Stockholm, he suggested that a *laboratorium mechanicum* be established to serve both as a college and as an experimental workshop developing new machinery. What Polhem had in mind was an equivalent of the *laboratorium chymicum* which the great Swedish doctor and natural scientist Urban Hjärne (1641–1724) had opened in 1685 for the production of medicines, for testing medicinal herbs, etc.

In his proposal, Polhem eloquently pleaded the advantages of such a mechanical laboratory, especially when it came to encouraging young, talented people and giving them a thorough education in

C Brunel's mortising machine for medium-sized blocks. The machine could mortise either two blocks or one two-sheaved block at a time. The two chisels (a) were given a working speed of up to 400 strokes a minute by a crank (b) on a rotating shaft (c). Scantlings (d) – cut pieces of wood for the blocks – were placed in a carriage (e), which was slowly brought forwards by a screw (f) as a ratchet-wheel (g) on the screw was turned by one tooth for each revolution of a cam (h) on the shaft. The rotation of the shaft could be interrupted without the flywheel (i) being brought to a halt, since the machine was equipped with a cone clutch (a section of it is shown top left). By means of a lever (j), the conical wheel (k) on the shaft (c) could be brought into contact with either a brake drum (l) or with the driving pulley (m) on the flywheel (i).

D This pendulum saw for cutting logs into scantlings was also constructed by Brunel. The log (a) was drawn forwards to a stop (b) when a handle (c) was rocked. For the transmission of power to the saw blade (d), belts (e) were used. The saw blade could be moved horizontally and vertically since it was mounted on pivoted frames (f, g) which could be adjusted by means of cranks (h, i). When these were turned, the rods j and k were moved by rack-and-pinion devices.

**"LETTERS" IN POLHEM'S
MECHANICAL ALPHABET**

A A mechanism (at **1** as seen from
the side, at **2** as seen from above)
for transforming the movement of
an eccentric disc (*a*) into the reciprocating movement of two rods (*b*).
(*c*) Cylindrical bearings.

B In this mechanism, the rotary
movement of a vertical axle (*a*) is
transformed into the reciprocating
movement of two pairs of parallel
rods (*b*, *c*, *d*, *e*). The disc (*f*) is
toothed along half of its periphery.
As the axle *a* and, thus, the disc *f*
rotate as indicated, the teeth first
engage the drive wheel *g*. The horizontal axle *h* then rotates anticlock-
wise and drives rod *b* downwards,

rod *c* upwards, rod *d* to the left, and
rod *e* to the right. When the teeth on
the disc then engage the drive
wheel *i*, the axle *h* instead rotates
clockwise, and all four rods are then
driven in the opposite direction.

C Here, a rotating disc has been equipped with a track (*a*), in which a peg (*b*) travels. The peg is attached to a bar (*c*), which, consequently, is given a vertically reci-

engineering, using visual aids. He also drew up a magnificent plan for his institution, where some ten instructors and model designers were to be active under his management. The suggestion was submitted in the autumn of 1696, and by the beginning of the following year, a royal decree allowed him to carry out the plans. The Gripenhielm house in Stockholm was bought for the purpose, and the activities of the mechanical laboratory were able to commence the same year. The staff, however, turned out to be not as numerous as Polhem had planned. He had at his disposal two skilled craftsman—a carpenter and a smith—who, aided by two apprentices, made models after his directions. The series of models to be used for teaching was systematized and complemented by Polhem to include all the machine elements known at the time, eighty in all. Several of these had been invented by himself. He called this systematized collection of machine elements "the mechanical alphabet". Polhem believed that, if a poet can produce the finest poetry from simple letters, an engineer, by mastering the mechanical alphabet, should be able to design useful machines. "The mighty five" were the vowels of this alphabet, whereas the other elements were the consonants.

However, Polhem could devote only less than a year to the initial stages of his mechanical laboratory. In the early 1690s, before his travels, he had gained great fame as a designer of remarkable machines, including the *Machina Nova*, an ore-whim installed at the Falu copper mine. On his return from abroad, while he was so preoccupied with his plans for the mechanical laboratory, he was in great demand with several mining companies, who wanted to employ his services. Most of the models of the mechanical alphabet

procating movement. This movement is transferred to arm *d*.

D This mechanism (**1**), too, was used for transforming rotary motion into reciprocating. The square-edged axle (*a*), seen from above at **2** and from the side at **3**, is fitted with four not altogether circular discs (*b*, *c*, *d*, *e*), which are mounted in pairs at two different levels. When the axle (*a*) rotates clockwise, disc *e* strikes the arm *f*, which is mounted on a hinged axle (*g*) and runs in a slot in arm *h*. Arm *f* then pulls *h*,

which is attached to another arm (*i*). As *i* moves to the left, arm *j* whips upwards and arm *k* whips downwards. Immediately after, disc *b* strikes the arm, *l*, which is attached to the hinged axle *m* and runs in a slot in arm *i*. As *i* and *h* thereupon move to the right, arm *k* whips upwards and arm *j* downwards.

59

A

were probably built during the year when Polhem directly supervised the work, but, in the summer of 1698, he left the management to his assistant, Fredrik Buschenfelt, who had been with him on his tour abroad and was conversant with his ideas and objectives.

The main reason, however, why Polhem left his mechanical laboratory to others was the fact that his stay in England had inspired him to set up his own manufacturing company. Preparations for this now claimed all his time, and, in 1699, he founded the Stjernsund Works and equipped it with a large number of newly designed machines which showed in practice how "poetry" could be written with the mechanical alphabet.

Still, Polhem did not completely abandon his mechanical laboratory. In 1706, Buschenfelt died, and the activities of the laboratory ceased for a few years; but in the early 1710s, the institution was re-established at Falun. The various projects Polhem took on during this period included the technical directorship of the Stora Kopparberg mine. His title was *konstmästare*, "art master". King Charles XII of Sweden, whose headquarters were then at Bender in Turkey—where, during his Russian campaign, he had temporarily retired—had received a report of the activities of the laboratory and summoned Polhem to him to discuss the future of the institution. The king had extensive plans for both the Stjernsund Works and the mechanical laboratory. The latter was to be extended into what we would call a research and development laboratory for the works and to be used, at the same time, for education. New products were to be developed there to make Sweden self-sufficient in all kinds of metal goods.

Polhem, however, did not think himself able to undertake the time-consuming and dangerous journey through a turbulent Europe to Turkey, and Charles XII had to be satisfied with providing funds through the Mines Authority to enable Polhem to operate his mechanical laboratory at Stjernsund. How far Polhem followed the wishes of the king is not known, but many young students came to Stjernsund from the German mines, and in return for a handsome fee—Polhem was also a very good businessman—they were boarded there and taught mechanics. In the 1720s, several Swedes also went to Stjernsund as Polhem's pupils and assistants; one of these was Carl Johan Cronstedt (1709–79), who studied mechanics and mechanical engineering with some other young noblemen from 1729 to 1731. Cronstedt later studied architecture under the famous palace architect Carl Hårleman and was to build palaces and machine plants himself; he turned out to be an excellent administrator, however, and crowned his career by becoming the president of the Swedish Crown Lands Judiciary Board.

Cronstedt is of interest here because, in 1729, he systematized and summarized Polhem's mechanical alphabet. His illustrations of these machine elements are preserved in a sketchbook listing no less than 103 "letters"; some twenty elements had been added since Christopher Polhem launched the idea of a mechanical laboratory in 1696, although the basic notion was still the same. Cronstedt wrote in his sketchbook:

It is necessary for a lettered man to keep in mind all the words needed to compose a sentence or an article. In the same way, it is necessary for an engineer to be familiar with all the simple movements. If a writer, when putting the words together, had to find one letter here and one there in hidden or remote places, his writing would become unreadable, full of the most awful trash. In the same way, if an engineer, when compiling machines and inventions, did not know all the simple movements of the *Mechanicus Alphabet* but had to produce them from distant nooks and crannies, that is, in notes, articles, and books, then the work would obviously proceed very slowly. . . . New machines are noth-

A A page from Carl Johan Cronstedt's sketchbook, in which he systematized and summarized Polhem's mechanical alphabet in 1729. **B** Yet another "letter" in the mechanical alphabet. When the crank (*a*) is rotated in a clockwise direction, the rod (*b*) receives a reciprocating motion, due to its being equipped with a cross-bar (*c*).

ing more than words or bodies compiled of letters or limbs, applied to their appropriate places depending on the application of the machine, so that, when finished, they achieve the desired effect.

Cronstedt's neat sketches and drawings of the mechanical alphabet were unfortunately not published. They are now kept in the archives of the National Museum of Science and Technology in Stockholm. Nor did Polhem, incidentally, describe his alphabet in print, and only a few of the designs included in it are mentioned by contemporary text-books, such as *Föreläsningar öfver naturkunnigheten* ("Lectures in Natural Science") by Mårten Triewald, published in two volumes in 1735–36.

The mechanical laboratory operated at Stjernsund with a varying number of pupils up to 1735, when Polhem's wife died. He then moved to his son-in-law, Carl Gripenstierna, of the Kersö estate on the island of Ekerö on Lake Mälar. He brought with him at least a part of his collection of models and went on designing machines. In 1739, he received a special grant to employ three skilled craftsmen, who were to build his "useful" machines, which were intended for use in agriculture and were made both as models and in full scale.

When the old sluice in Stockholm was to be rebuilt in 1746, Polhem was asked to manage and supervise the work on site. He was then eighty-five but just as restlessly active as in previous years. The government now commissioned him to collect all his models, and they were put on public display in a wing of the Royal Palace, called the Royal Model Chamber, where those who were interested could learn a lot about elementary mechanics, even if there was no actual teaching. After Polhem died in 1751, his son Gabriel tried to reorganize a mechanical laboratory along the lines his father had first planned, but engineering was not as popular with the authorities then as it had been in Christopher Polhem's heyday. Gabriel's efforts went unnoticed. Efter varying fortunes, the model collection was taken over by the Technological Institute (later the Royal Institute of Technology) when this was founded in 1827, and, at first, the models were used educationally. In the late 1920s, the model collection was found in the attic of the old Institute building. What had once been national treasures in the Royal Model Chamber were then in a lamentable state; most of the models were simply falling to pieces. The collection was handed over to the National Museum of Science and Technology, where a painstaking job of identifying and restoring it was undertaken by Dr. Torsten Althin; the result was, eventually, a reconstruction of the Royal Model Chamber as a department within the museum.

Kinematics

In his sketchbook, Cronstedt described about a third of the machine elements in Polhem's mechanical alphabet. This description is entitled *De simpla mekaniska rörelser som kunna tjena som ett mechaniskt alphabet* ("The Simple Mechanical Movements which can Serve as a Mechanical Alphabet"). What most fascinated Cronstedt was the fact that relatively simple combinations of "the mighty five" could achieve very advanced – and useful – movements. In his study of the simple machines, Archimedes concentrated mainly on clarifying their power-amplifying properties, which were very important in the development of the first prime movers, the water-wheel and the windmill, and also of the working machines invented in the Middle Ages, during the technical revolution of the Renaissance – whims, ore crushers, forge hammers, and frame-saws. From the beginning of industrialization, in the eighteenth century, these properties became increasingly important in the design of machines. What man had previously done by hand was now executed by machines, of which different elements somehow imitated human movements, as in, for example, the spinning-machine and the mechanical loom.

The designers of these machines (and many other designers during the same era) were talented but pragmatic inventors, who certainly gave little thought to the machines, their laws of motion, and their internal relations. But there were others who did, and they caused mechanics and mechanical engineering to be included in the syllabuses of the technical colleges, both military and civil, which started to emerge at the end of the eighteenth century in the Old World and the New alike, keeping burning, as it were, the light which Polhem first lit.

In 1806, the professor of geometry at the Ecole Polytechnique in Paris, Jean Nicolas Pierre Hachette (1769–1834), gave a course on machine elements while teaching descriptive geometry. Five years later, Hachette published the first text-book on the systematized functions of machine elements. This book set the pattern for at least a hundred years. In it, Hachette defined six "orders" of machine elements, functionally different from each other: *récepteurs* – receiving the motion of a prime mover; *communicateurs* – passing on the motion; *modificateurs* – transforming the motion, for example, from reciprocating to rotary; *supports* – bearings, guides, and so on; *régulateurs* – connecting and disconnecting, speed regulation; and, finally, *opérateurs* – machine elements giving the final effect. It was fashionable to systematize and to clarify, and to introduce definitions tying up conceptions and nomenclature. Hachette's definitions were the beginning of a systematization of mechanical engineering, which can be compared to Carolus Linnaeus's works on flora and fauna, and to Jac Berzelius's work on the standardization of chemical nomenclature.

Among his compatriots, Hachette acquired many followers. The leading name here is André Marie Ampère (1775–1836), a talented mathematician and physicist from Lyons, whose name is best remembered as the unit of electric current. Ampère was professor of theoretical and experimental physics at the Collège de France in Paris, and to equip himself for the task of preparing a syllabus, he took upon himself the enormous job of compiling a survey of all human knowledge! The result was a comprehensive study in two volumes, published in 1829, and in the tradition of the great French encyclopaedists. Unlike d'Alambert and Diderot, however, Ampère devoted plenty of space to the philosophy of natural science, which he regarded as the basis of rational classification. Ampère's classification of mechanics into statics (bodies at rest) and into a new branch, which he called kinematics (bodies in motion), shows the amount of consideration he had given the matter. And his definition of the new science is still valid:

The movements are to be studied as movements, independent of the power creating them, in the same way as we observe the movements of static bodies around us, especially in such combinations as we call machines.

Ampère's definition is just as abstract as is fitting in a philosophical-scientific work. Fundamentally, it implies that the most important thing when designing a machine – say, a mechanical loom – is to establish what movements are required and by what machine elements these can be achieved. Once that is clear, one should calculate the stresses to which the machine elements are to be exposed and adjust their dimensions accordingly.

At this time, two of Ampère's compatriots were particularly active in kinematics – the mathematicians Gustave Gaspard de Coriolis and Charles-Nicolas Peaucellier. Coriolis is mainly known for his discovery of the acceleration power (the Coriolis force), which causes, among other things, the currents of the oceans to move in curved paths. But he also studied machine elements in motion and *en passant* defined the physical notion "work" as the product of the force and the distance.

After Ampère died, the bulk of kinematic study was done in England, which was then very much the homeland of mechanical engineering, where steam power was rapidly developing on land and at sea. In the late 1830s, Robert Willis (1800–75) lectured in Cambridge on the kinematics of machine elements, and in 1841, these lectures were published in book form as *Principles of Mechanism*. Willis was professor of natural and experimental philosophy, a discipline which, today, would hardly be associated with the design of machines. But in England, natural philosophy was the classical name for what would today be called physics and, as such, had been part of the academic world at least since 1662, when the Royal Society was founded. So Willis's subject was theoretical and experimental physics, that is, the subject on which Ampère, too, had lectured.

Willis developed kinematics into a practical science, and his descriptions of machine elements and their functions resulted in mathematical formulae which could be applied directly by a machine designer. Willis's book became one of the first mechanical engineering handbooks and circulated widely.

Willis also introduced the word "kinematics" into the English language. The most important of his pioneering contributions to the subject were his methods of analyzing moving systems, or *pure mechanisms*, as he called them.

Among those who took up Willis's ideas was Ferdinand Redtenbacher, professor of applied mathematics at the Karlsruhe Polytechnic. He made creditable attempts to simplify Willis's methods and to find a practicable system for classifying machine designs, but he was not particularly successful. Instead, it was to be as a talented and inspiring teacher that he was to play an important, albeit indirect, rôle in the development of kinematics. In the early 1850s, Redtenbacher had a young student by the name of Franz Reuleaux, who, guided by his professor, became fascinated by kinematics, realizing their importance to the further progress of mechanical engineering.

Franz Reuleaux, whom we have already met, is worthy of fuller introduction, as he was a leading light not only in the field of kinematics, but also in contemporary cultural circles. His family were Walloons, and he was related in a direct line to the builder who, in the days of Louis XIV, erected the great pumping station at Marly, on the Seine–a gigantic construction which aroused great interest throughout Europe (see page 102). His grandfather was a noted "art master" in Liège, and his father had settled in Eischweiler in the Rhineland, where he had had great success designing and building steam-engines. After leaving school, Franz spent a few years as an apprentice in his father's workshop. In 1850, he began more advanced studies in Karlsruhe. He graduated as an engineer and then continued his schooling at the universities of Berlin and Bonn, studying natural sciences and arts. In 1856, when Reuleaux had just set up an engineering consultancy in Cologne, he was nominated professor of applied mechanics at the Eidgenössische Technische Hochschule in Zürich. He remained there until 1864, when he became a professor at the Gewerbeakademie in Berlin. The following year, he was appointed head of this institution, which later (in 1879) merged with the Berliner Bauakademie, forming the large Technische Hochschule, which was located at Charlottenburg, outside Berlin. Reuleaux was to be head of this school, and a professor there, until he retired in 1896.

For his classes in mechanical engineering, Reuleaux compiled a "mechanical alphabet" of models of different mechanical devices, which eventually numbered almost eight hundred. Just at that time, there was an enormous increase in the number of mechanical devices available for various purposes, so Reuleaux became wholeheartedly involved in systematizing and classifying these. His aim was to achieve the same uncompromisingly logical order in the field of engineering that Linnaeus had established for flora and fauna. In his lectures and papers, Reuleaux referred often to Linnaeus and emphasized the importance of his work in the development of botany and zoology. He and his assistants followed Linnaeus's way of working and attempted to trace every conceivable mechanical construction–no easy task, and the model collection grew and grew.

Reuleaux presented the results of his endeavours to create a "sexual system" of mechanical engineering in a series of elegantly lucid lectures, which soon attained general renown. The audience was treated to practical demonstrations of models from the ever-growing collection, and to theoretical speculation on a high, scientific level of abstraction. In 1875, he published his findings in the great work already mentioned in Chapter One and entitled *Theoretische Kinematik: Grundzüge einer Theorie des Maschinwesens* ("Theoretical Kinematics: Principles of a Theory of Machine Technology"). The book aroused keen interest, not only among engineers and technicians, but also in wider circles. At last, some method and order was to be established also in the ever more complex field of mechanical engineering. The desire to systematize and classify was one of the hall-marks of the optimistic and progressive spirit of the age.

Reuleaux planned this book as the first part of a trilogy, and the other two parts were to follow shortly afterwards. In the event, this was not the case. Twenty-five years were to pass before the second part was published, and the third never got beyond the stage of an incomplete draft.

One of Reuleaux's contemporaries, Alexander B.W. Kennedy, professor of applied mathematics at University College, London, soon translated the book into English, and it was published in England as early as 1876. It was an almost greater success in England, the "workshop of the world", than it was in the Germany of the Second Reich. The Science Museum in London quickly took advantage of this and arranged an exhibition of some of Reuleaux's teaching models. The exhibition, the book, and Reuleaux's scientific work as a whole became the object of great interest and were reviewed and discussed in both the technical and daily press. Technical circles caught something of a "Reuleaux fever", which then spread to other countries.

Reuleaux was not an unknown name internationally. As early as 1861, he had published a handbook on engineering, *Der Konstrukteur* ("The Designer"). This was one of the first books of its kind and was translated into one language after another. Never before 1876, however, had Reuleaux been the object of such enormous interest. His work on kinematics had been translated at just the right psychological moment in the Anglo-Saxon world. In the year that the translation was published, the great Centennial Exposition was opened in Fairmount Park in Philadelphia. This was an international exhibition to commemorate the hundredth anniversary of the signing of the American Declaration of Independence. The exhibition became a monumental manifestation of "pure mechanisms" (in Willis's words) and was an almost stunning expression of confidence in the potential of steam power to solve all the energy and power problems of both society and industry. President Ulysses S. Grant opened the exhibition by starting the huge Corliss steam-engine and, metaphorically speaking, thus released a burning enthusiasm for pure, applied mechanics, a branch of science which would save mankind from the hard, often humiliating, struggle for survival.

Reuleaux was present in Philadelphia as leader of the German delegation, and he gave an account of his impressions in *Briefe aus Philadelphia* ("Letters from Philadelphia"), which was widely read and appreciated in Germany. In it, he eloquently describes the numerous technical wonders demonstrated in Fairmount Park, and he writes that they exceeded everything he had experienced previously. And his statements carried some authority, for he had been on the jury of two earlier world exhibitions, one in Paris in 1867 and another held six years later in Vienna. (Reuleaux also led the German delegations to the world exhibitions in Sydney in 1879 and Melbourne in 1881.) But at Philadelphia there were exhibited not only machines, but also all sorts of products of craft and industry, besides works of art and much else from the whole world. The overall picture of human civilization thus presented made a very strong impression on Reuleaux. He felt that all of it—even the works of art—was, ultimately, the result of technical progress.

In the years following the Philadelphia exhibition, Reuleaux began to develop the relation between technology, culture, and social development. In 1882, he expanded his views of technology as a carrier of culture in a lecture given to an industrial association in Vienna. This lecture, first published in Vienna and in a couple of German journals, was entitled *Kultur und Technik* ("Culture and Technology") and aroused a lively debate which raged for many years. When published in French, Italian, and English journals, it also became the subject of discussion in these countries. As late as 1890, the lecture was printed in the annual report of the Smithsonian Institution, that admirable research institute in Washington, which runs, among other things, the American central museums of technology, natural history, and art.

In his lecture, Reuleaux first gives a brief survey of the world distribution of the civilized peoples, in which he attacks the fairly widespread idea of the time that the races of the world can be divided into active and passive. He then goes on directly to his beloved kinematic fundamentals, ratchet gears, rack gears, and so on. These he generalized and extended to include various other phenomena in technology as well as in society as a whole. For example, he regarded a fire—be it under a steam boiler or a conflagration—as a chemical ratchet, released at the moment the fire started. He also intimated that socio-political events could be seen in a similar manner. This automatically makes one think of the American Norbert Wiener (1894–1964), the man who, seventy-five years later, developed cybernetics, that is, the science of the control and regulation of animals and machines by feed-back circuits—of which more later.

In the 1880s and 1890s, Reuleaux was highly prolific in various fields. The following are a selection of the many articles and books he wrote during this time: *The Machine and the Capacity for Work: Social Contemporary Questions, German Achievements and Future Prospects in Technology and Industry, Indian Miniature Works of Art, On the Importance of Water to Human Welfare, Interpretation of Folk Legends, Oriental Chessmen,* and *Hiawatha,* a German translation of Longfellow's famous poem. From the mid-1870s onwards, Reuleaux became rather unpopular in certain German industrial circles, due to his lectures and articles unceasingly criticizing the low standards and the poor designs of various companies' products. He believed that German goods ran the risk of being considered abroad as *billig und schlecht* ("cheap and bad"). This, too, gave rise to a debate, which in its own way probably had a positive effect on German industrial development.

It is obvious that, in the wide range of interests cultivated by Reuleaux at the height of his powers, kinematics took rather a back seat. His prolific writings and his assumption of the rôle of opinion builder made Reuleaux one of the foremost German cultural figures for at least twenty years.

Reuleaux's pioneering work on theoretical kinematics gave a totally new picture of mechanical engineering in general and of the function of machine elements in particular. The principles he introduced, simplified almost as far as could be, made those designers,

Reuleaux also took an interest in human anatomy. To him, man's limbs and joints were coupled levers, and he tried to apply the methods of kinematics to them in order to find the best possible positions for the human body when it performed different operations. In the illustration of the man at the grindstone (*below*), there is also an indication of how Reuleaux linked one human and one technical system of coupled levers.

Reuleaux's epoch-making studies of composite machine elements and their reciprocal movements turned kinematics into a science.

A Various types of gear-reduction sets were among the machine elements studied by Reuleaux from a kinematic point of view. Shown here is a reduction set with hyperbolic gearwheels. The dashed prolongation line of the smaller cogwheel indicates the shape of the hyperbola.

B This "kinematic linkage with four joints" was used by Reuleaux

to illustrate the thesis that a closed kinematic linkage can be made to move in as many ways as the linkage has bars. The dashed lines show the movements of bars b, c, and d if a is fixed.

C Reciprocally movable machine elements with a continuous engagement between complicated geometric shapes usually led to theoretical calculations of great complexity. Examples of such machine elements are those included in this air-pump.

D This composite machine element was used by Reuleaux as a basis for exercises in which the reciprocal movements of cog-wheels with varying numbers of cogs were calculated.

E Reuleaux considered even the universal joint to be a kinematic chain and stated its theory.

F A kinematic linkage with a cam. The machine elements transformed a rotary to a reciprocating movement.

who were engaged on practical work, stop and think. They now began to strive after the simple rather than the complicated in their designs, for the latter often resulted in poorly functioning machines.

In his analysis of the function of machine elements, Reuleaux distinguished in his first principles between, among other things, "elementary pairs" and "kinematic chains". The first group contained, for example, the nut and bolt, the axle journal and bearing, and a cog-wheel engaging with a rack (rack gearing). The second group included connected and jointed levers, such as the crank, but also combinations, such as Watt's parallel motion linkage, which achieved rectilinear motion. When Reuleaux wrote his book in the 1870s, the kinematics of parallel motion was somewhat in vogue among the great theoreticians, and we shall soon return to that. Reuleaux, however, was totally unconcerned by the sophistry of the great minds and concentrated on the technical realities involved. When analyzing complex constructions, he simplified them quite considerably. For example, he described a number of different designs for rotary steam-engines and stated with obvious delight that they were fundamentally identical; in many cases, he added, the designers had quite needlessly complicated their creations!

In 1900, when at last Reuleaux published the second part of his *Theoretical Kinematics*, his star had started to dwindle. This volume, which deals with the relationship between kinematics and geometry and mechanics, does not have the brilliance and vigour which had distinguished the first, and on the whole it seems to have been little appreciated by those engaged in practical engineering, while the theoreticians gave it scant attention. During the following decades, kinematics and Reuleaux's contributions came to be less esteemed. The principles were certainly considered to be of theoretical interest, but in practice they gave rise to extremely complicated mathematical problems. Reuleaux's *Theoretical Kinematics* was rarely found on the engineer's bookshelf after 1900, although his engineering handbook, *The Designer*, was. However, the latter, too, became the subject of severe criticism when the author's fame was at its lowest. In a commemorative article in 1929, the great mathematician Rudolf von Miese called it a "simple cookery book for engineers". But it was only some ten years later that the tide turned in favour of Reuleaux and kinematics.

"Rectilinear Motion" Leads Kinematics Astray

When James Watt designed his parallel motion linkage, he probably did not realize that he was releasing a flood of solutions—some more imaginative than others—to the problem of achieving rectilinear motion. Watt's linkage solved the particular concrete problem which he had faced in getting his steam-engine to function, and he was very proud of his brilliant invention. He confided to his son, "Though I am not over anxious after fame, yet I am more proud of the parallel motion than of any other mechanical invention I have ever made." But during the next hundred years, a number of geniuses, mainly mathematicians, were to spend their time inventing a number of highly curious devices to give rectilinear motion, despite the fact that Watt had already provided a practicable and satisfactory solution to the problem. And the number of these devices far exceeded the actual need. One of the first came from the English clergyman Edmund Cartwright (1743–1823), to whom the invention of the mechanical loom is usually attributed. In 1800, he took out a patent for a device, as simple as it was ingenious, which converted the reciprocating motion of the steam-engine piston to rotary motion. It consisted of two crank webs, each working on its own cog-wheel, one of which also drove the balance wheel. That which distinguished the device was that the cranks also ensured the rectilinear motion of the piston. However, this invention found very few applications.

G In his essay *Kultur und Technik*, Reuleaux tried to generalize his kinematical theories in order to apply them to phenomena in society. A ratchet gear (**1**), which could be released by pressing the key, would then symbolize, for example, a conflagration or an act of God, whereas a running gear (**2**) symbolized things like international commerce. Since the movement of a ratchet gear was not constant and, further, was different when running forwards and when running backwards, a ratchet gear, according to Reuleaux, differed completely from a running gear.

At about the same time, another Englishman, James White, discovered that the mathematical properties of the hypocycloid (a curve traced by a point on the circumference of a circle rolling along the interior of a larger circle) could be exploited. If the diameter of the inner circle is half that of the outer, a point on the circumference of the inner circle will move back and forth in a straight line. This, White suggested, could be applied to the cog-wheel. He described his device as "pretty" but added that it was not considered generally to be especially good. The motion of this mechanism is certainly pretty—and amusing (it is usually included in most of the mechanical alphabets used in teaching engineering)—but deficiencies in the art of gear cutting at the time caused a number of practical complications, and the invention was, like Cartwright's, little used.

During the following decade, one of the most interesting devices for achieving rectilinear motion was, perhaps, that constructed by the pioneer American steam engineer, Oliver Evans (1755–1819), for his "Columbian Engine", a beam engine with a single-shaft bar. (This type of engine became very popular in England, where it was known as "the grasshopper".) Evans's device produced an almost rectilinear motion. Curiously enough, the design later returned to its country of origin, in a somewhat modified version, on the "Stourbridge Lion", the steam locomotive built by George Stephenson, and the first ever to be used in the United States. The design was used in the coupled levers connecting the driving wheels.

One of the few devices for rectilinear motion which was, like Evans's invention, designed for a definite technical purpose, is usually attributed to the Englishman Richard Roberts (1789–1864). In 1816, he founded a mechanical workshop in Manchester. Some years later, he designed a smooth-planing machine for metal working, in which this "Roberts device" was a machine element. But Eugene Ferguson, the noted American historian of technology who has made a study of kinematics, claims that this device originated in France, where it had been described as early as 1769. Its rectilinear motion was then used for a completely different purpose, namely, to saw off piles under water. But the principle of the device's construction was identical to that of Roberts's.

Various more or less (often more!) bizarre devices for rectilinear motion appeared in the following decades, but these can easily be excluded from this account, as they were of no real importance. However, in the 1860s, things became more interesting in this field. In 1864, the previously mentioned French military engineer Charles-Nicholas Peaucellier wrote a letter to the editor of a mathematical journal, in which he briefly pointed out the possibility of constructing a mechanism with coupled and jointed levers, which could both produce a rectilinear motion and describe a circle of arbitrary radius. But no one, mathematician or otherwise, responded to his suggestion, and the letter was forgotten. In the 1870s, when interest in kinematics began to grow, Peaucellier made a model of such a mechanism, which he called a *compas composé* ("compound compass"). With this he showed that the path followed by a point on, say, a joint can be expressed as an algebraic equation, and that the reverse also applies, that is to say, any curve which can be described in an equation can also be achieved by a kinematic chain. It was "simply" a question of finding the right combination.

The reaction of the experts to Peaucellier's model was immediate. Among them was the Russian mathematician Pafnuti Chebysev (1821–94), who was, at that time, interested in rectilinear motion and had improved upon Watt's design. Chebysev's version achieved considerably greater accuracy but was more complicated. It was used on a steam-engine shown at the world exhibition in Vienna in 1873, but the reaction of the technical press was very negative. The English journal *The Engineer*, for example, pointed out that the design had too many joints and couplings to grease, and too many pins which could break. Reuleaux might have given his Russian colleague a lesson in the complicated art of simplification!

Chebysev is said to have been very impressed by Peaucellier's mechanism, which, according to its originator, gave an exactly straight line. But what Chebysev tried to do was to prove the opposite; he even tried to produce evidence that a kinematic chain, no matter how many links it contains, can never give a mathematically straight line. Throughout the rest of his life, Chebysev attacked this problem with "an interest bordering on obsession", to quote Ferguson, but he never found the solution. The mathematical analysis of kinematic chains leads to extremely complicated equations, which not even a great mathematician like Chebysev could solve.

Chebysev corresponded regularly with the British-American professor of mathematics James Sylvester (1814–97), and in 1873 wrote to urge him to take up kinematics as rewarding and more fruitful than geometry for it would add a fourth dimension to space. Sylvester followed this advice and became almost as obsessed by the subject as his correspondent. Only a year later, he gave a much publicized lecture at the Royal Institution in London, in which he demonstrated Peaucellier's mechanism and developed his own theories on kinematic chains for producing rectilinear motion. The lecture, which was later published, turned out to be an ardent song of praise of Peaucellier's "*compas composé*", which he extolled for its mathematical beauty. Why, Sylvester asked rhetorically, had not

B James White's device for attaining a reciprocating movement. When the small cog-wheel (*a*) rolled along the toothed inside of the periphery of the large wheel (*b*), the pivoted bar (*c*) was given a rectilinear, reciprocating motion. The condition for this was that the diameter of wheel *a* was half the inner diameter of wheel *b*. The weights (*d*) gave the arm-carrying wheel *a* the function of a flywheel.

A Edmund Cartwright's device for transforming the reciprocating movement of the steam-engine piston into a rotary movement. On the piston rod (*a*) was a cross-bar (*b*) with crank webs (*c*) mounted at either end. The crank webs worked two cog-wheels (*d*), of which the one to the left meshed with a smaller cog-wheel (*e*), thus driving the flywheel (*f*). The crank webs also guaranteed the piston's rectilinear movement.

such an apparently simple mechanism been invented much earlier? His answer was that the mechanism, from the mathematical point of view, was so very complicated that it would have been more natural if it had first appeared a good hundred years later!

But the practical use of this simply wonderful mechanism was another of Silvester's questions. One answer lay in the story he told of a well-known London architect who, to a plumber's infinite astonishment, had used the mechanism to guide the piston in a water pump. In the same breath, Sylvester added that this brilliant design ought to be tried out in water closets, where it could replace the flimsy chain!

Today, we may well laugh at such desperate attempts to find practical applications for the *compas composé*, but we must remember that Sylvester was a theoretician and was not particularly interested in the practical uses of the mechanism. It was the mathematical properties of kinematic chains which attracted him, and he designed a number of devices which made it possible to calculate, among other things, square and cube roots and the angle trisector. Sylvester believed that, in this way, the possibilities of constructing mathematical aids were endless.

The chief engineer of the Houses of Parliament, a Mr. Pim, found Sylvester's lectures a source of inspiration, and he installed a "blow-ing engine" in the House of Commons to improve the ventilation there. It was, in actual fact, a large air pump, and Peaucellier's *compas composé* was used to guide the pump rod. The device is said to have worked perfectly, and almost noiselessly.

Sylvester was indefatigable in lecturing on and demonstrating the complex problems of rectilinear motion. This intense and temperamental scientist was also a man of wit and very much enjoyed the society of his fellows. Wherever he came with his message, he was made welcome, even in literary and political circles, where normally the members would not be considered to have too profound an interest in advanced mathematics and engineering. But it was, naturally, in scientific circles that Sylvester had his greatest successes. He has given his own account of his appearance before the Athenaeum Club in London. After the meeting, supper was served, and as they ate their dessert, he passed Peaucellier's *compas composé* around the table. Among the many famous scientists present was the great physicist Sir William Thomson (later Lord Kelvin), who studied the mechanism with great interest. As Sylvester reached out his hand to take back the model, Sir William sharply reproved him and said that he was far from finished with it, stating that it was by far the most beautiful thing he had ever seen!

In the summer of 1876, after spending three years in London as the

C Sylvester's and Kempe's kinematical, translating linkage. The plates (*a*, *b*) can be moved sideways but will remain constantly parallel and equidistant.

D Mr Prim's air-pump, in which he used Peaucellier's *compas composé* to steer the piston (*a*) rectilinearly. The mechanism consisted of four bars (*a*) of uniform length, which were linked together to form a parallelogram. From its opposite corners ran two equally long bars, which were pivoted to a common point of attachment (*d*). When point *e* on the parallelogram was given a circular movement, point *f* moved in a straight line, since the distance between the point of attachment of the bars *c* and the point of attachment of the bar *g*, which ran to a third corner of the parallelogram, was equal to the length of bar *g*.

E A modified version of Evans's mechanism was used for the *Stourbridge Lion*. The piston (*a*) was steered rectilinearly by its being mounted on one end of a beam (*b*), whose other end was attached to a pivoted bar (*c*), and whose movement was limited by a strut (*d*). The other end of the strut was attached to a triangular scaffold (*e*), which was reinforced by rods (*f*). Coupled levers (*g*) connected the driving wheels with one another and with *b*.

great prophet of kinematics, Sylvester left the city to take up the position of professor of mathematics at the highly esteemed John Hopkins University in Baltimore, Maryland. This was the year in which Franz Reuleaux's great work *Theoretical Kinematics* was published in English; it was also the year in which the huge Centennial Exposition took place at Philadelphia. Back in England the cause of kinematics received a new champion in Alfred Kempe, a young lawyer for whom mathematics had long been a hobby. Kempe had closely followed Sylvester's activities. They had become close friends and had started to collaborate; Kempe was obviously as fascinated as Sylvester by the kinematics of rectilinear motion. When Reuleaux's mechanical alphabet was put on display at the Science Museum in London, Kempe gave a series of lectures entitled "How to Draw a Straight Line", which to a large extent contributed to raising the temperature of the Reuleaux and kinematics fever which was then raging in London. Kempe began these lectures, which were published as a book of the same name the following year, 1877, with some almost childishly simple assumptions: a circle can be drawn with a pair of compasses, a straight line can be drawn with a ruler. But why should a ruler give a mathematically defined straight line? Kempe's further thoughts on this are as amusing to read as the title of his book is provocative. However, Kempe was, if possible, even further removed from technical reality than his teacher and mentor, Sylvester. But together they managed to construct some kinematic chains which caught the public eye; one of these was a chain for translatory (reciprocating) rectilinear motion. As far as is known, no practical application has been found for this device, which is one of several models in existence, and it is rather fun to watch it in operation.

"La Belle Epoque" of the Machine

We have already mentioned that Reuleaux and his kinematics went out of fashion during the first decades of the twentieth century. There is indeed a considerable contrast between the enthusiasm for kinematics which in London reached its climax in the events surrounding the exhibition at the Science Museum, and Rudolf von Miese's criticism of *The Designer*, quoted above. There were several reasons for this undeniably remarkable about-face. The last decades of the nineteenth century saw a rapid acceleration in the growth of technology in the industrialized countries and marked a watershed between what was established and what was new in the technical field. Steam power was established; electricity was new and was making great headway. The Centennial Exposition in Philadelphia, in 1876, was one of the last great manifestations of the steam era and of pure mechanics. It was also the beginning of the end both for steam and for machine elements. However, the beautiful designs of both prime movers and working machines still pleased the eye, and the graceful movements of their parts were still a joy to behold. No wonder that young people of today spend so much of their spare time working on the restoration of steam-engines, traction engines, locomotives, and other machines of this period!

What followed were the machines of the electrotechnical age. The first generators and engines were open, exciting constructions, but soon they became enclosed, partly for technical reasons—closed magnetic fields, protection from the dangers of high voltage, etc.—and partly because of new trends in design. And all of a sudden, every single machine was enclosed, and the era of the "grey box" had begun. The colour may have changed, but we are still there.

Another aspect of this development was the increased speed at which machine elements and moving parts generally could be driven. The designer had to consider the dynamic properties of the parts rather than their kinematics, which, according to Ampère's

definition, took into account only the motion as such; forces and strains were disregarded. Thereupon, kinematics had to give way to dynamics.

One lasting effect of the teaching of Reuleaux, Kennedy, and their successors up to the turn of the century, however, was the strong preference which designers were to show for simplicity and efficiency in machine design. It is interesting to follow the development of this trend in the design handbooks which were published from the beginning of the nineteenth century onwards, beginning for instance with the one published by Hachette in 1811. In these books, machine elements for different movements and functions are listed in tabular form. Many of the later books in this genre tried to outdo the others by listing more and more intricate, and often overcomplicated, devices. Technical journals, which had begun to come out during the first part of the nineteenth century, had as a rule a regular feature on new machine elements, including material from newly granted patents as well as articles which were quite simply copied from other journals. *The Scientific American*, first published in 1845 by Rufus Porter, a patent lawyer, had such a feature from its first number onwards. So had *The American Artisan*, the chief editor of which, Henry T. Brown, gathered the most important articles in a book first published in 1867 and entitled *Five Hundred and Seven Mechanical Movements*. It has been reissued many times since then, most recently as late as 1970, when an American machine manufacturer brought out an edition especially for use as a gift book. The heyday of this genre was the period of about twenty years after 1850; in the twentieth century, the number of design handbooks published has diminished considerably. One exception is an American work published in four parts, each containing more than five hundred pages, entitled *Ingenious Mechanisms for Designers and Inventors*. Volume I, published in 1930, and Volume II, published in 1936, were edited by Franklin D. Jones; Volume III, published in 1951, was edited by Holbrook L. Horton; and Volume IV, published in 1967, was edited by Horton and John A. Newell. In this work, each device is described in great detail, and its function, choice of material, and so on are commented on.

There is no doubt that mechanical engineering has been greatly influenced by Reuleaux's wholehearted advocacy of simplicity in the design of machine elements. This applies not only to large machines, such as steam-engines (where the theoretician Chebysev was taught a lesson by the practical engineers), but also to many of the smaller machines which were then appearing on the market and which were intended for daily use in the home, in agriculture, etc. The sewing-machine, the first "domestic appliance", had met with initial resistance when the first types appeared around 1850—their designs were obviously over-complicated, and breakdowns were frequent. When the various components had been simplified and better material introduced, the sewing-machine gradually gained the confidence of housewives. In most industrialized countries, therefore, the sewing-machine did not make its breakthrough until the 1880s or later. The mowing-machine, first mass-produced in 1848, went through a similar process of development. Cyrus McCormick's (1809–84) invention, the "finger-knife", goes back to 1834 but had to be modified considerably before the machine could be mass-produced and marketed. But the mowing-machine, too, had a reputation for needing frequent repairs, and it was simplified further after McCormick's patent had expired. The result of these improvements was that the mowing-machine came to be accepted universally and that designers were encouraged to continue developing agricultural machines. There then followed in rapid succession the reaper, the binder, and the combine harvester—all based on a practically functioning finger knife. The first combines were introduced in the United States in the

1890s. They were impressive machines, pulled by eighteen pairs of horses and operated by a team of twelve to fifteen men.

In March, 1876, the first telephone was patented by the American scientist and inventor Alexander Graham Bell (1847–1922). At the Centennial Exposition in Philadelphia in the same year, Bell was able to demonstrate a working model, which attracted great interest. A speaking telegraph! However, the new invention had not yet found its technical form, but in spite of this, *The Scientific American* published an enthusiastic article (October, 1877) on Bell's telephone, predicting a splendid future for it. A month or so later, the article was read by a Swedish instrument maker, Lars Magnus Ericsson, who became fascinated by the new apparatus. A year previously, he had established a workshop where he and some others repaired telegraphic equipment, fire telegraphs, and other signalling devices used at the time. He had been considering designing and manufacturing telegraphic equipment himself, since working with repairs had given him a good idea of the weaknesses of existing models. He now devoted himself completely to the task of designing a telephone. It was ready by the following year, and the telephone built to that design is considered to be the world's first table telephone. In that year, Ericsson produced twenty telephones, and when the Stockholm Telephone Company was founded some years later, production really got going. The Bell Telephone Company, which Alexander Graham Bell had founded in 1877 and which had opened an office in Stockholm in 1880, was soon ousted from the market by the Stockholm Telephone Company, and by 1885, Stockholm had more telephones than any other capital city in Europe.

Today, we take it for granted that the telephone works properly, but in the early days, it was a highly unreliable appliance. The faults were mainly due to poor design. Lars Magnus Ericsson was determined to produce a telephone in which all the parts exposed to wear and tear would be as robust as possible—and where every single detail had a function. The result was a "telephone that did not look like a telephone", and it later became the company symbol and figured in the trademark for many years. The first model built to this design appeared in 1884 and was soon nicknamed "the dachshund". The magnets in the magneto generator were bent outwards and served also as a stand for the instrument. This version had a fixed microphone and a separate receiver, but as early as 1892, Ericsson launched a model which set the style for future telephones. The "dachshund" was given a hand microphone combined with the receiver—the first of its kind—resting in a cradle. It was both practical and comfortable to use.

Ericsson had studied Reuleaux's work, both *The Designer* and *Theoretical Kinematics*. When designing his table telephone of 1882, he had followed in detail his master's theses on the simplicity and functions of design. The apparatus is a fine example of *la belle époque* of the classical machine.

The Renaissance of Kinematics

By the turn of the century, the great wave of enthusiasm for kinematics, which had been at its height in the latter part of the nineteenth century, had gone into a considerable decline. The exception to this was in Germany, where, all along, kinematics remained on the syllabus of courses in mechanical engineering. Between 1900 and the late 1930s, nothing exciting was written on the subject. Then, however, things began to happen; a German engineer, Robert Kraus, wrote an article on the double-crank mechanism. This was published in the engineering journal *Maschinenbau*. Kraus's article came in for severe criticism from a Russian, Z.S. Bloch, and the ensuing polemics, like most other academic rows, were closely followed by other engineering journals. It is possible that the Second

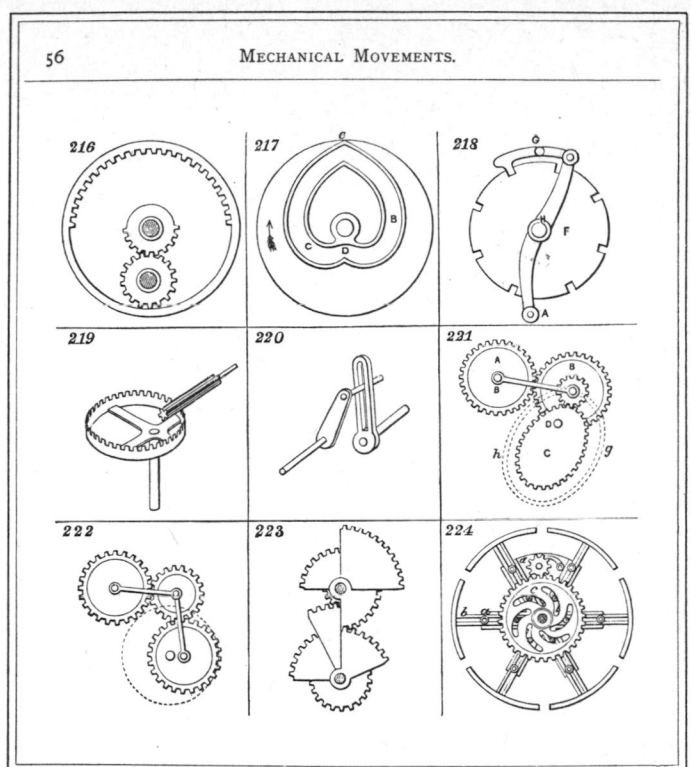

A A page in *Five Hundred and Seven Mechanical Movements*, the book in which Henry T. Brown compiled articles which had earlier been published in *The American Artisan* and dealt with new machine elements.

B This model of L. M. Ericsson's telephone – popularly known as "the dachshund" – was introduced in 1892. Every single part has a function, and the telephone is a good example of *la belle époque* of mechanical engineering – not only with regard to its construction but also to its design.

World War, by then in full progress, was also inspiring machine designers to take up and re-examine long-neglected ideas. Anyhow, the number of publications on kinematics increased considerably at this time. After the War, many important works on kinematics were published both in Europe and in the United States. These dealt with and furthered the thoughts of Reuleaux, Kennedy, and the other great kinematicians and used their terminology and definitions of principles. The old classical kinematical problems were once again the subject of examination and discussion. One work among many in this field deserves special attention, that by the Americans J.A. Hrones and G.L. Nelson, entitled *Analysis of the Four Bar Linkage*. It was published in 1951 and gives a very comprehensive and graphic description of the properties of such mechanisms as Watt's parallel motion . . .

There were several reasons why kinematic chains of this kind—jointed and coupled levers—became topical again. First and foremost is the quite simple fact that, today, we are surrounded by kinematic chains in such profusion that no one in Reuleaux's time could have dreamed of. We use kinematic chains everywhere; normally, of course, we have no reason to reflect on this. The male adult's most popular toy, the motor-car, has, for instance, a great number of kinematic chains. They are found in the mechanisms governing the catching and locking devices of the doors, in the crank mechanisms of the side windows, in the track rod, and in the combination of crankshaft, connecting rod, and piston. Continuing from the car, we find an applied kinematic chain in the upwards-tilting garage door. Coupled levers can be found in most of our domestic appliances, especially in the sewing-machine. No matter how much such an appliance can be controlled electronically, the fact remains that both the needle and the under-thread are moved by combinations of mechanical levers—kinematics of the best kind. Typewriters with type bars are fitted with several coupled levers which perform a number of different functions. Calculators have, or rather, used to have, a number of advanced machine parts with jointed and coupled levers. (Today, the mechanical calculator is almost obsolete, and the electronic calculator is taking over.) Outdoors we can find kinematic chains in such construction machines as bulldozers, excavators, rock drills, and so on; and also in all sorts of means of transport—aeroplanes, locomotives, ships, and not least, the bicycle, which is one of the most highly developed applications of mechanical engineering.

We can also look at our own reflection in a mirror. Man's anatomy and skeletal structure comprise kinematic chains which have been tried and tested over millions of years. Reuleaux had pointed this out and even illustrated it with his models. Today, this is a highly topical subject in ergonomics and the sciences related to work.

So kinematics is well represented in our surroundings. In itself that should be enough to explain why interest in this important branch of mechanical engineering has risen so sharply again, especially in the past few decades. Another factor that has contributed greatly is that, since the 1950s, designers have had access to advanced aids in solving the often extremely difficult mathematical problems that a kinematic analysis can entail. Today, a computer can, easily and elegantly, solve the problems which not even Chebysev and the other great mathematicians of the previous great era of kinematics could get to grips with. Of course, the problem still has to be stated, and this provides the greatest difficulty nowadays, requiring immense theoretical insight before it can be overcome. However, once the problem has been stated, the computer can do the rest in no time at all.

The Eight Saw

There are many examples of problems in technology where inter-

A In the eight saw, a sash of the same type as that of an ordinary frame saw is used. The main difference concerns the suspension and bearing of the sash. In principle, the eight-saw is designed as is shown here. The saw blades (*a*) are braced in a sash which is given a reciprocating movement by a connecting rod (*b*). Blocks (*c*), which are mounted on the frame by spherical bearings, here slide in guides (*d*), which are rotatable round their shafts. The guides are constructed so that the sash describes a curve similar to a figure-of-eight when it is in operation. Thus, "reverse sawing" can be eliminated, and the saw blades are exposed to considerably less wear than were the old frame saw's blades on their way up, fitted, as they were, with fixed guides.

esting and, sometimes, surprising solutions have been arrived at due to the fact that kinematics benefitted from the help of the computer. Most of these problems are very intricate, both from the engineering and the mathematical points of view, but let us look at one example, not only because it is easy to understand, but also because it casts some light on an aspect of the history of technology. From the Middle Ages onwards, the frame-saw was used to saw logs into planks and boards. As such, it played an important rôle in the forestry industry of many countries. The first picture of a frame-saw is considered to be the one found in Villard de Honnecourt's *Album*, which dates back to the late thirteenth century. In Sweden the frame-saw was in common use in the sixteenth century, but in the eighteenth century, it was replaced here and there by the circular saw. Sawn timber was produced mainly for export to England, and it was found that the circular saw gave a smoother surface to the wood. However, the British refused to accept such new-fangled products as smooth-sawn timber. "The surface should be as rough as the fur of a bear", wrote an English importer to his Swedish supplier!

Here we have in a nutshell the main drawback of the frame-saw. The sawn surface of the wood was rough, because the frame-saw's blade saws only when moving downwards. When it moves upwards, however, the timber is still fed forwards, and the saw teeth abrade the surface of the wood. This "back-sawing" was something that, for centuries, just had to be accepted. In the 1950s, however, the band-saw began to replace the frame-saw, and this resulted in an immediate and sharp increase in production at the sawmills. The log could now be fed through more quickly, and the sawing was done continuously. The old frame-saw, with its back sawing and rough planks, was now relegated to the collections in museums of technology.

However, even the band-saw had its drawbacks, for when its speed was increased above a certain limit, the band began to flutter. This resulted in a sawn surface that was corrugated. In the beginning of the 1970s, therefore, a group of engineers at the Convexa laboratory in Stockholm began to analyze the problem of back-sawing from a kinematic point of view. They had access to a computer, which they fed with a number of variations of possible devices. The computer then gave them the solution, which was quite simply to let the blade move in a figure-of-eight. The blade then works continuously, and there is no back-sawing. The older type of frame-saw had, however, another disadvantage, namely that large mass forces were created when the saw frame moved up and down. The base was made very stable, but the vibrations were still considerable. The Convexa team found the solution to this problem as well; they found that the vibrations could be completely eliminated by erecting a pendulum suspension for the frame and by counter-weighting the balance wheels. This rather intricate system was simulated in the computer, which also gave the correct dimensions of the system's components. After extensive prototype tests, the "eight saw" was ready for production in 1977.

New Machine Elements?

In this chapter we have had to go back quite far in time to find the first machine element, and some of the earliest have remained basically unchanged for thousands of years. This may lead one to ask whether or not the field is exhausted. Can we expect new machine elements to be created in the future? This is, naturally, a question of definition, but even if we are fairly restrictive in calling something new, it is clear that new ideas for machines are constantly appearing. One example is the wheel hub without an axle, designed for motor-cars and developed by the SKF European Research Centre in Holland. The idea for this new machine element was introduced in 1972, and the design has now been tested in the field.

B The advantage of the shaftless wheel hub is, among other things, that fewer movable parts are needed for the wheel suspension and that the assembly becomes simpler. Here, we show the inner construction of such a hub (1) as well as a cross-section of the hub as mounted on a car (2). The brake and the wheel are mounted on the flange of the inner ring (a), whereas the suspension is mounted on the outer ring (b). The rings are coupled to each other by a double-row, maintenance-free bearing (c).

A2   A3   A4

A1

B2

A The four non-turnable wheels of a vehicle (**1**) with the ilonator steering system are each equipped with eight slightly spool-shaped rolls, which are mounted at an angle of 45° on a hydraulic-engine-powered rim. Since the rolls run freely, no force can be received in the direction of rolling. In the direction of the shaft, however, a force can be received, and this force can be divided into two components, one which is parallel to the longitudinal axis of the vehicle and one which is perpendicular to it. When the vehicle is driven straight forward (**2**), all the wheels are driven at the same speed and in the same direction. Those force components which are perpendicular to the longitudinal axis of the vehicle then balance each other, and the remaining components drive the vehicle forwards. If the vehicle is to be driven towards one side, for instance to the right (**3**), the two right-hand wheels are driven towards each other at the same speed as the two left-hand wheels are driven away from each other. The force components which are parallel to the vehicle's longitudinal axis then balance each other, and the remaining components drive the vehicle to the right. When the vehicle is to rotate round its own vertical axis (**4**), all four wheels are driven at the same speed in the direction in which the vehicle is to rotate. These three fundamental movements (**2–4**) can be combined with each other in every conceivable way.

B1

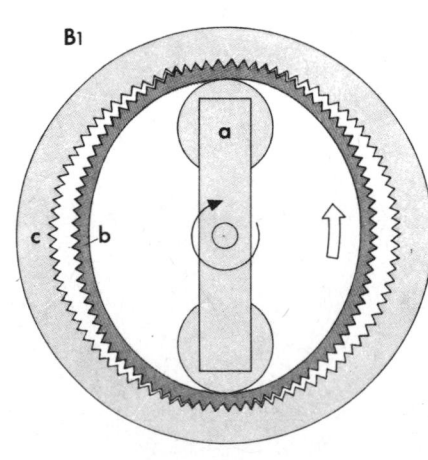

B One of the disadvantages of the conventional planetary gearing is its limited gear ratio. During the 1970s, however, several new planetary-gearing constructions have appeared, and these give a very high gear ratio. One example is the American Harmonic Drive (**1**), which consists of three basic components (**2**): an elliptic "wave generator" (*a*), which has an eccentric ball race, a thin, flexible steel cylinder (*b*), which has cogs on the outside, and a non-flexible steel cylinder (*c*) with internal cogs. When the wave generator rotates, *b* is deformed, and the cogs on those parts of *b* which then protrude mesh with the cogs on the outer steel cylinder. Since the number of cogs on *c* exceeds that of *b* by two, *a*'s rotation causes a relative movement between *b* and *c*. The gear ratio can be from 78:1 to 320:1. If several Harmonic Drive units are coupled to each other, a considerably higher gear ratio is obtained.

CHAPTER 3
FROM HAND TOOL TO INDUSTRIAL ROBOT

After the gradual decline of the Roman Empire and its fall in the fifth century AD, the spiritual development of the West was engulfed in a listless darkness. There was naturally more than one reason for this mental stagnation. Active trade, both within the Empire and with the surrounding countries, collapsed, and this eliminated the economic basis for the growth of science and the arts. The crafts deteriorated, too. The Christian church, growing in strength as fast as the Roman Empire fell apart, more and more dominated intellectual life with its dogmatic message. Charles Singer holds the apostolic father Augustine (354–430) responsible for the stifling effect of this dogmatism on spiritual life. Augustine's leading doctrine was that the individual should turn his gaze in on himself to resist worldly temptations, expressing this metaphorically by saying: "Do not go outside the door, for truth dwells in the heart of Man." Singer adds that, for a thousand years, the thinking man in the Christian West did not venture outside.

Outside Christendom, however, an entirely new cultural sphere was emerging, rapidly and unexpectedly. The Arab world was set in motion in 622, when, on the Mountain of Light, the Prophet Mohammed (570?–632) was called by Allah to preach Islam, the doctrine of submission. Islam then issued forth with irresistible power from the Land of the Twin Rivers over all of North Africa. Within a single century, a spiritual growth blossomed within the borders of Islam, which, in extent and vitality, can be compared to that of ancient Rome.

The Moslems returned to the classics of the ancient Hellenic culture and based their work on the experience of the engineers of the Alexandrian school and of other great engineers and scientists. As mentioned above, many of the classical works in this area are known to us only in Arabic translations and revisions.

Tools, implements, and working methods from the stone construction technology of antiquity were revived by the Arabs, and new masterpieces were built, from Alhambra and Cordoba in the West to Samarkand and Bagdhad in the East—royal palaces, mosques, and minarets. The Moorish palace in Alhambra, with its famous Lion Court, to take only one example, must have needed for its erection and decoration at least those three hundred skilled crafts which King Hiero needed to build his flagship about a thousand years earlier.

The Craft Guilds

Continued specialization by craftsmen in the late Middle Ages resulted in the creation of craft guilds, or more correctly, the re-creation of craft guilds. During the Roman Empire, tradesmen had organized themselves in corporations, which protected their rights, and came to be reckoned as a strong political force. The mediaeval equivalent of these corporations, the guilds, soon became very powerful, both by right of their economical strength and by the effective control exercized by the elders and masters on their colleagues and their work. The guild system naturally had both positive and negative aspects. The strictly prescribed course of training no doubt favoured high standards of work. To learn a craft, a young man had to be accepted as an apprentice of a guild, and a precondition for this was

that the rulers of the guild felt that there was room for a new master once the apprentice had completed his training; in other words, an efficient control of new establishment. After the apprentice had passed his first tests, he had to go out as a journeyman and work with his colleagues, both at home and in foreign countries. In this way, new ideas and methods were spread to an extent which would otherwise have been impossible. The long journey, which often lasted for four or five years, was crowned by a guild entrance test, executed under the strict and critical supervision of the elders.

Technical news could be spread relatively effectively thanks to this journeyman system, but even so, the guild and the strong position of the elders still had a markedly conservative effect on the technical development of the different crafts. How should the journeyman construct the tools for his guild entrance test, and what working methods and practices should he use? This question had mostly a single answer—everything must be precisely as the elders prescribed.

What is known as the Mendel book, from the fifteenth century, is an invaluable source of knowledge of the late mediaeval crafts and tools. The original is in the city library of Nuremberg, but in 1965, this extensive work was published in a magnificent edition of two volumes, in which most illustrations are reproduced full-sized. The Mendel book has an interesting background. The mercantile house of Mendel was active in Nuremberg for several generations, and it flourished in the late 1300s, when three Mendel brothers (Marquart, died 1385, Conrad, died 1414, and Peter, died 1423) ran it. They traded handicrafts from Nuremberg and had agents in places like Rome, Venice, Cologne, and Prague. The city of Nuremberg was, above all, famous for its textiles and leather work, but there were also prominent goldsmiths, pewterers, coppersmiths, and workers in brass. In Nuremberg, however, the guild system lacked the power that it had elsewhere. Merchants dominated the community, which was, very likely, one reason why, in 1388, Conrad Mendel donated money to establish the famous "house of the twelve brethren" to honour the Holy Trinity. In this house, twelve honest craftsmen—the number was in honour of the apostles—were to be given accommodation and a place to work, so far as possible. This "protected workshop" was intended mainly for craftsmen who had been prevented by illness from working or had been worn out prematurely. The house of the twelve brethren existed until the early 1800s.

The rules laid down by Conrad Mendel for his foundation include the stipulation that a "book of thoughts" should be kept, in which both the governors and the brethren should be depicted at work. This stipulation was not given effect, however, until his grandson Marquart became the governor of the Mendel foundation in 1425. He retained this position until his death in 1438. That part of the Mendel book which has been published covers the period to 1539, during which time no less than 355 craftsmen brethren were depicted. Frans M. Feldhaus and many others have wanted to date these frequently reproduced pictures to the late 1300s, but it has now been verified that the paper of the manuscript was made between 1423 and 1429. The paper has water marks which have been identified as coming from the long famous Italian papermill in Fabriano.

New Tools for Precision Mechanics and Heavy Engineering

The appearance of the mechanical clock (see Chapter Two), in the first half of the fourteenth century, opened a new era in tool technology and caused a new branch of technology to be developed—precision mechanics. The clock quickly became a status symbol, and the prominent men of the time were soon vying with each other in installing this novelty on their houses and public buildings. Only half a century after the first mechanical clocks had appeared, very complicated clocks were being built, which testified to both sound craftmanship and a good understanding of astronomical mathematics. Still, the development was not quite as sudden as it seems. At this time—about 1400—there was already a long-established clockmaking tradition, a tradition that had begun with the water clock and which had asserted itself mainly in the cultural circles of Islam. We know very little of the details of the clockmaker's tools. Since ancient times, for example, different types of files had been used to shape and work metals. The ancient Greek word for file, *rine*, also denotes a type of shark, which implies that fish skin with sharp spines had once been used, for example, to smooth a rough surface, but this was probably before tools were commonly made of metal.

Many files have been found from Roman times or later. It has been proved that the files used in the fourteenth and fifteenth centuries were more or less the same types as those used today. They were flat, round, semi-circular, or multi-edged, made in all different sizes, from small tapered files to the large types used for heavy engineering. File cutting at this time was a skilled craft and had certainly been in existence for some time. In the Mendel book, the file cutter is depicted in several illustrations, which also show the methods used to make the file teeth. A hammer shaped like a chisel was employed, and also a separate chisel, which was struck with a mallet. It was natural to mechanize file cutting, if for nothing else than to make the teeth of the files more regular. Leonardo da Vinci made a drawing for such a machine, in which the file being worked was automatically moved forward between each blow. During the following centuries, many file-cutting machines of different designs were built by, among others, Polhem. Various devices to keep the workpiece in place, such as the hand vice, the screw vice, and the carpenter's bench mechanism, all with precedents in ancient cultures, acquired their form in the late Middle Ages.

In precision mechanics, and particularly in the work of the clockmaker and the goldsmith, different methods of joining metals were developed to near perfection at this time. Pliny the Elder describes several different ways to soft- and hard-solder with different fluxes, among them green spar, a basic copper acetate. The Romans also knew how to use a soldering iron, and also, they most probably used a blast pipe to direct a flame at the joint. In the fourteenth and fifteenth centuries, however, the blast pipe was developed into a flexible, all-round tool for joining metals. During this time, the art of the smith was on the upswing. With all the building in the early days of the Renaissance, growing demands were made on blacksmiths to produce both light and heavy products, for example, tools for various purposes, and fittings, cramps, and other objects for churches and other monumental buildings. Increased trade led to a need for forged iron for diverse applications in transport, from iron fittings on barrels and other casks to detailed work and fittings for ships and wagons. The manufacture of arms and armour devoured ever increasing quantities of forged iron and metals, and state controls saw to it that the available metals were directed towards these requirements. At this time, the common man in most European countries, who tilled the land or worked at a craft, was short of iron and copper. Edward III of England (1327–77) introduced a law under which the export, and even the re-export, of iron was prohibited under pain of heavy punishment.

The Technical Revolution of the Renaissance

During the last century of the later Middle Ages, the situation changed radically. The use of water and wind power for purposes other than flour-milling, such as in mining, spread rapidly, reciprocating the emergence of new methods, tools, and implements in heavy engineering. One can with good reason talk about the techni-

A1

A Two illustrations from the Mendel book. Both represent file cutters, but the men use different methods to produce the file teeth. The man in the left-hand picture (**1**) uses a sharp-edged hammer to cut files directly, whereas the man in the right-hand picture (**2**) uses a separate chisel, which he strikes with a mallet. Both men use anvils, which have been spiked to large wooden blocks, as underlays for their work. When the files had been cut, they were tempered by heating and quenching.

A₂

C

B

B A mediaeval vice, in which the upper, movable part (*a*) was brought closer to the lower, fixed part (*b*) when two "nuts" (*c*) were turned. This type of nut was very common until the advent of the hexagonal nut at the beginning of the nineteenth century.

D

C The carpenter's bench, too, attained its form during the late Middle Ages. Just as on a present-day carpenter's bench, the work-piece was braced between a bench clamp (*a*), which was inserted through one of the holes (*b*) in the bench, and a screw (*c*). (*d*) Vice.

D A sketch by Leonardo da Vinci is the basis of this drawing, which shows a file-cutting machine. The file blank (*a*) was braced on a board (*b*), through which a screw (*c*) ran. Before the cutting could start, a rope had to be wound onto a drum (*d*). At the other end of the rope, a weight (*e*) hung, and on the drum shaft, there was a cog-wheel, which meshed with a larger cog-wheel (*g*) mounted on the screw. When the weight was allowed to fall, *g* was rotated, and the board with the file blank was brought towards *g* at an even speed. Another wheel (*h*) on *d*'s shaft was turned at the same time, and its large, sparse teeth in turn brought a lever (*i*) downwards. A sharp-edged hammer (*j*), mounted on the same shaft as *i*, was then lifted, and every time a tooth let go of the lever, the hammer fell against the slowly forward-moving blank.

A One of the oldest known woodcuts. It bears the date 1423 and depicts St. Christopher carrying the Infant Christ on his shoulders. The woodcut was found in a manuscript of 1417 in the middle of the eighteenth century.

B Early woodcuts were made using knives of this type (1). The blade consisted of a piece of clock-spring steel. Later, other special tools, such as this graver (2), were used to hollow out those parts of a block which were to remain white during printing.

C The composing room (1) of an eighteenth-century printer's workshop as depicted by Diderot. The typesetter (*left*) has the copy in front of him. He picks out letters (2) from the typecase and places them in a

composing stick (3). The man in the middle of the picture then puts the completed lines in the galley, a long, narrow tray in which typeset text is stored. When the whole copy has been typeset, the page-maker (*right*) steps in and puts the typeset lines in forms which have the exact width and height of the book's pages. He then sees to it that all types are at the same level by hammering against a flat, wooden board, which is placed over them.

cal revolution of the Renaissance, one that affected almost all ways of life. In many parts of Europe it meant an economic upswing, which stimulated ideas in art, literature, and science. This boom was also one of the reasons why interest was aroused in what lay beyond the horizon; the era of the great geographical discoveries began.

Neither the industrial revolution of the eighteenth century nor this technical revolution was marked by any sudden technical or social upheaval, and in both periods it is more appropiate to talk of an evolution of new practices, tools, implements, and products through internal interaction. The effect of improvements in clockmaking on manufacturing technology during the Renaissance has already been described, as has the way in which a demand for metals affected mining, which in turn stimulated the growth of heavy engineering. Wind and water power were more and more exploited during the fifteenth century, whereas, in the eighteenth century, it was steam power that really got things going. Many useful objects, such as needles, nails, and knives, were manufactured on a "pre-industrial" scale during the fifteenth century. Leonardo da Vinci had many ideas on how needles could be produced in large quantities. He described a machine evidently capable of producing four hundred needles an hour, and he worked out even the profits of such manufacture, provided that prices were the same as those for manually made needles!

In the early sixteenth century, a Dutchman, Walter Vollmar, founded a company for the manufacture of needles on an industrial scale in the Germany city of Aachen. The Mendel book depicts a needle maker who died in 1533. The eye of the needle was then made by hand. The needle was split at one end, and the two parts were then shaped as a loop. The manufacture of needles and pins entirely by machine came relatively late. Pin manufacture was automated first. The so-called rocking machine, which cut off pieces of steel or brass wire and then crushed one end of the piece of wire to form a flat "knob", was invented in Nuremberg in the mid-1680s. The design of the machine was improved in both England and the United States at the beginning of the nineteenth century. In Italy the manufacture of pins with heads of glass in different colours began in 1825.

Even in ancient times, nails were manufactured on a large scale. When some Roman fortifications were excavated in England in the 1950s, the remains of a Roman nail factory were discovered. Packages of nails in "standard" sizes were also found, from nails fit for solid timber to tacks. During the Renaissance, nailsmiths were already recognized as such and established tradesmen, and several nailsmiths are represented in the Mendel book. Nails were formed in moulds, and in the Mendel book one can see how nails of three different sizes could be formed in the same mould. Due to the great demand for nails during the Renaissance, there was a specialization of labour. Apprentices wrought iron into square sections of different sizes, and their masters finished them off. Production could thus be reasonably high.

Knives began to be produced, in principle, in the same way as nails. Apprentices prepared the material for the knife blades, and the master then forged and shaped them. The Mendel book has a picture of a number of knife blades with hafts. It is likely that the hafts were "mass produced" as well.

Art and Literature in Mass Quantities

The tools of precision mechanics were, without doubt, the technical pre-conditions for making wood cuts and for the development of printing. The oldest dated wood engraving is from 1418. It shows fine lines throughout and a richness of detail, which imply that the tools used, the knives, burins, and so on, must have been eminently suitable. At this time, it was only the precision mechanics of clock-making which could achieve the technique required for such tools. A woodcut was produced by transferring a drawing, reversed from left to right, onto a carefully surface-ground "block" of wood, after which the surface wood on either side of each line in the drawing was cut away with a burin of forged steel. The remaining wood on all surfaces which were to be white in the drawing were then cut away with gravers and gouges, so that the lines of the drawing became raised. They were then inked and pressed against paper. The wood-cut method spread rapidly in the late Middle Ages, when pictures were a rarity. At first, skilful craftsmen made the woodcuts, but before long, eminent artists were themselves cutting their own draw-ings in wood. One of the first was the German Albrecht Dürer (1479–1528) who, in 1498, published the famous pictorial series of the Reve-lations of St. John. Graphics had become an independent art form-based on the progress of precision mechanics!

The 1440s saw the first book printed with movable die-cast type. The letter-press printing method used by Johann Gutenberg (1399?–1468) was basically the same as the one used for printing woodcuts, but Gutenberg used cast, movable type instead of cut blocks. The production of dies for the type was made possible by the tools of precision mechanics, too. It does not detract from Gutenberg's con-tribution that printing with movable type had been practised in the Far East, or more specifically Korea, two thousand years prior to this. Several of the techniques described here, which developed so quickly during the technical revolution of the Renaissance, had had predecessors in other parts of the world.

The Art Books of Technology

The technical revolution during the early Renaissance paved the way for the accelerating development which took place during the High Renaissance, when there was progress made in all spheres of human life; in retrospect, this progress must be seen as a sharp contrast to the so-called darkness of the Middle Ages. Enlightened contemporaries were also acutely aware of this. In the sixteenth century, the German humanist Ulrich von Hutten uttered the famous words: " The spirits awaken, and it is a joy to be alive."

During and after the technical revolution of the Renaissance, a whole arsenal of new tools came into being, as well as methods and techniques for using them. The spirits of technology could truly awaken and find joy in designing machines. What are called "art books" first appeared, and they flourished from the sixteenth cen-tury to the middle of the eighteenth. These were magnificent pictor-ial books that contained descriptions of ingenious machines, both real and imaginary. In general, art books were extremely important for the spread of technology in the West, especially for mining, for they illustrated machinery for raising water, and other devices de-scribed by Agricola and Biringuccio, among others. The chief engin-eers, or art masters, of the mines took ideas from the art books, copying the designs or modifying them to suit themselves. This meant that heavy mechanical equipment and the tools used were largely similar in the different European mines, and in the same way, the tools and equipment of all the other crafts soon acquired similar forms all over Europe. Any kind of technical novelty quickly spread via the art books; one example of this is the mangle. The Italian Vittorio Zonca (1580?– ?) gave one of the first descriptions of such a machine in his art book *Novo teatro di machine et edificii*, (Padua, 1607). He even presented two versions of it, one an impres-sive mangle, over 30 ft (c. 9 m) long and driven by two men in a treadmill; the other was driven by a horse capstan. The mangle, one of the first domestic machines, was invented in northern Italy at the end of the sixteenth century, and it was intended for the huge linen-

D1

MANGANO PER MANGANAR ZAMBELOTTI TELE
ET ALTRE GOSE

D2

D One of the earliest known descriptions of a mangle has been found in Vittorio Zonca's art book, from which these illustrations of two such machines have been taken. The upper picture (**1**) depicts a horse-whim-driven mangle, where-as the lower one (**2**) represents a model driven by two men in a treadmill.

In the mid-1650s, Carl Gustaf Wrangel (1613–76), a Swedish military commander in the Thirty Years' War who was exceedingly fond of splendour, decided to have the baroque-style castle of Skokloster erected in the Swedish province of Uppland. Some fifteen years later, the castle was complete, with the exception of a large baronial hall. According to plans, this hall was to be decorated with extravagant architectonic splendour, but the castle had already cost vast sums, and Wrangel had no money left. All the craftsmen who had been engaged to perform the decorative work simply walked out when they were no longer paid for their work. They left their tools and implements behind, and these remained intact until the middle of the 1970s, when restoration of this part of the castle started.

A Some of the master glazier's tools. (**1**) A roller bench, where bars of lead were shaped to profiles of U-section. These were used for leaded window-panes. The rolling machine itself was hand-cranked. (**2**) An anvil used for finishing the U-

section profiles. On the anvil lies a ladle in which lead was smelted when the blanks were to be cast. (**3**) Casting mould for the blanks; the profile was formed when the handle was lowered. In front of the mould is a finished blank.

B Among many other tools in the baronial hall was a large collection of beautifully ornamented planes. (**1, 2**) Finishing planes. (**3**) Profiling plane, used for manufacturing skirtings and suchlike. (**4**) A bench plane, used for working the edges of boards which were to be joined.

C A carpenter's bench, probably built at the beginning of the seventeenth century.

stores of the principal ducal courts. The original meaning of the word "mangle" is "a large machine" and is derived from the Greek word *magganon*, first used to designate large military machines, such as ballistas, but later to cover large, intricate machines in general. Once the mangle had been reduced to easier-to-handle proportions, it spread rapidly all over Europe, and a century later, it formed part of the equipment in almost every large household.

The Tools and Implements of Industrialism

It has already been stressed that the most common hand tools had been realized and had acquired a stable form at a very early stage. Such changes as occurred over the centuries were due to better materials and new occupations that required tools other than those already in existence. From the Middle Ages until the era of industrialism, however, the tools of the carpenter, joiner, and smith remained more or less the same.

The great French encyclopaedia, "*Encyclopédie, ou dictionnaire raisonné des sciences, des arts et des métiers*", edited by Denis Diderot (1713–84) and Jean Lerond d'Alembert (1717–83), and published between 1751 and 1780, is a priceless source of knowledge of the tools, implements, and machines in existence on what was the threshold of industrialism. This bulky work of thirty-five folio-sized volumes describes comprehensively more than eighty trades and illustrates them in a masterly fashion. All tools and implements are depicted in detail, the intention being that any person who was interested and practically inclined could use the encyclopaedia so as to be able to establish himself in one of the trades described. With few exceptions, the tools shown were produced manually, often according to mediaeval principles. (Industrial manufacture of hand tools on anything like a large scale did not occur until the mid-1800s.)

When the last volumes of the encyclopaedia were published at the end of the eighteenth century, an new era—the beginning of industrialism—had started with the appearance of James Watt's steam-engine. Several engineers before Watt had had feasible ideas about exploiting steam power, but the tools and methods to realize their intentions simply did not exist. What we have called heavy engineering was too clumsy, and precision mechanics could be applied only to small items.

Many of the parts and components needed for the exploitation of steam power required new methods and tools, mainly to make pipes, taps, and valves. Even in ancient times, pipes of different materials had been used. In mining, ever since the Middle Ages, pipes had been used for conducting water, but these pipes were hollowed tree-trunks. In the eighteenth century, there was a well-developed technique for the manufacture of such pipes, and in some places it was used even into the nineteenth century. But wooden pipes were not good enough for steam power, which required pipes which were resistant to heat and high pressure.

During the first decades of the steam era, pipes were made manually of iron, copper, and bronze. The process started with sheet metal, which was bent round a steel bar, and the joint or "seam" was then brazed or soldered. The first seamless pipes were cast. In 1790, the Englishman John Wilkinson (1728–1808) patented a method of casting lead pipes in a mould with a steel bar in the middle. Not until the mid-1830s was the same method used for producing pipes of bronze and copper. Steel pipes were not in common use until the 1880s, when the Mannesmann brothers in Germany developed a method of rolling pipes with a mandrel. Similar ideas had cropped up on several previous occasions, for instance, in a British patent granted to G.W. Dyson and H.A. Hall in 1870. In the 1860s, the Mannesmanns' father, Reinhard (1814–94), had already experimented with rolled pipes in his tool factory in Remscheid, which had been

D This water-wheel-driven boring machine was reproduced by Salomon de Caus in his art book, *Les raisons des forces mouvantes*, and was used for boring holes in tree trunks, which were then used as water-pipes. In the foreground, some of the different-sized augers used in the machine can be seen.
E The Mannesmann method for the manufacture of iron tubes was demonstrated at the international exhibition held in Chicago in 1893, and Thomas A. Edison is said to

D

have remarked that this impressed him more than anything else at the whole exhibition. By exposing the surface of a red-hot iron bar to a powerful, stretching machining while the internal parts of the bar were not allowed to partake of the elongation stress, cupping occurred inside the bar. The machining was brought about by two rollers (a) which were mounted at an angle to the bar (b) and rotated, thus forcing the bar towards a mandrel (c).
F Among many other trades described in Diderot's encyclopaedia is that of the goldsmith. The type of lathe shown here was used in the eighteenth century for engraving plates of precious metal. The plate blank (a) was attached to a detachable template (b) on the lathe's turntable (c). The template's edge

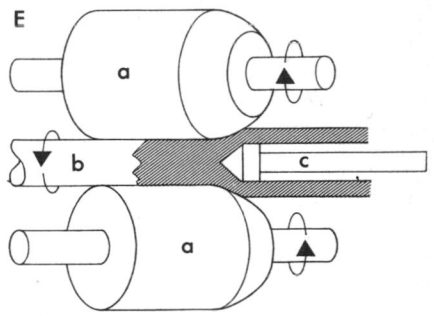

E

was followed by a roller (d) which guided the graver (e) laterally. The plate to which the roller and graver were attached was moved longitudinally along the work table by means of an inner screw device operated by a crank (f).

F

A One of Wilkinson's water-wheel-powered boring mills for producing cylinders. This was erected at the Bersham Ironworks in 1775; (1) outline diagram, (2) a model of the construction, in which two cylinder blanks (one is here shown in section) could be bored simultaneously. The tubular boring bars (*a*) were supported in sturdy bearings and had longitudinal slots. Inside the boring bars were rods which were attached to the cutter heads by lugs running through the slots. The cutter heads could move freely along the boring bars and were automatically moved forwards through the cylinder blanks because the outer ends of the rods (*b*) were jointed to racks (*e*), which meshed with pinions (*f*). On the pinion shafts were weight-loaded levers (*g*), which slowly sank, thus turning the pinions. Cross-bars (*h*) stopped the racks from rotating. (*i*) Water-wheel. (*j*) A lathe, probably used for facing and turning large, disc-shaped objects. (*k*) A simpler lathe.

B When the Soho Foundry was to be closed down at the end of the nineteenth century, a London magazine, *The Engineer*, sent some members of its staff to the foundry. Their task was to depict and describe the foundry's machines before they were dismantled. Among the illustrations later published in *The Engineer* was this one, which shows a large face-plate lathe, built in *c*. 1850.

C Maudslay's screw-cutting lathe, made in *c*. 1797. The bed consisted of two triangular bars (*a*), which were attached to the cast brass feet (*b*). The saddle (*c*)with its cross-slide was driven by a lead-screw (*d*). (*e*) Headstock (one of the parts of a lathe which support the workpiece; through the headstock runs a rotatable shaft, the spindle). (*f*) Tailstock. The workpiece was given the desired length in advance. It was also given centres, into which the points on (*e*) and (*f*) were inserted.

in the family for generations, but it was his sons, Reinhard (1856–1922) and Max (1857–1915), who managed to arrive at a method that was very much in advance of its time, and they patented it in 1885. A few years later, pipes were being made on an industrial scale. The Mannesmann method was shown at the world exhibition in Chicago in 1893. Thomas A. Edison is reputed to have said that this method impressed him more than anything else at the exhibition. The demand for steel pipes increased rapidly and was one reason why the Mannesmann concern developed into one of the largest industrial companies in Germany.

Machine Tools Take Over

A large number of factors contributed to the development of industrialism in the nineteenth century. From the technical point of view, the basic conditions were the constantly improved versions of the old hand tools. These hand tools made it possible to manufacture the new tools required by technical progress, particularly in power engines. Some of these tools and parts have already been mentioned.

"Industrialization" means that manual methods of manufacture are mechanized, that is, taken over by machines. The machine tool is a logical outcome of this process. We have already dealt with many machine tools, such as the potter's wheel and the machines we have suggested were used by the pyramid builders for sawing stone. What we today call machine tools, however, are mainly metal-working machines.

The large French encyclopaedia of the mid-eighteenth century describes a number of lathes for turning wood as well as metal; at that time, the art of turning was quite advanced. One thing shown in the encyclopaedia is an engine lathe, where the material could be formed to a pattern of regularly repeated contours, so-called rose-engine turning (the same name is used for the method of producing on bank-notes and documents, patterns that are hard to forge). Engine turning was a very popular hobby even among princes and statesmen, from the Holy Roman Emperor Maximilian I to Gustavus Adolphus IV of Sweden; wood was the material they worked in, for attempts to use metals were not made until about 1700. The first detailed description of a lathe for turning iron appears in a book by Charles Plumier, *L'art de tourner* ("The Art of Turning"), published in 1701. The lathe must be solidly constructed, Plumier points out, and also must be stiff enough to resist the great forces arising between the tool and the material. Christopher Polhem had at least one iron lathe in operation at the Stjernsund Works at the beginning of the eighteenth century. This lathe was driven by a water wheel, and the tool holder was fed by a lead screw, driven by a gearwheel. In 1760, the Frenchman Jacques de Vaucanson (1709–82), a masterly designer and a man of many talents, built a metal lathe on an iron bed. The whole constructions was braced by a framework, which made it very stable. Vaucanson's lathe is representative of the basic type from which machine tools rapidly developed over the following decades. By the 1830s, machine tools had already assumed the shapes which they have retained up to the present.

We have already pointed out that steam power required a lot of tools and parts (see also Chapter Five). One problem with the manufacture of the earliest steam-engines was to produce good enough cylinders. Attempts were made to cast them, but there was the difficulty of finishing them by chiselling and filing, which left the inside still very rough. In 1774, however, John Wilkinson, a friend and colleague of Matthew Boulton and James Watt, designed a machine intended for machining cylinders that, being very robust, was very accurate. The cylinder material was held firmly in place in a solid bed mounted on a cradle of thick oak beams (Wilkinson was certainly taking Plumier's recommendations seriously!). A strong,

A A lathe of a type common during the latter half of the nineteenth century. (*a*) Bed. (*b*) Headstock in which the cone pulley, gears, and spindle were included. A cone pulley is a belt pulley with several different pulley diameters. Since the lathe was equipped with a cone pulley, various gear ratios could be attained. The spindle was carried in two cradles and was often tubular on this type of lathe. It was then easier to work rod-shaped material, since the blank could simply be inserted into the spindle. (*c*) Movable tailstock. (*d*) Hand wheel for moving *c*. The tailstock was locked in position by means of a lever (*e*). (*f*) Saddle. (*g*) Cross-slide. (*h*) Apron, in which the feed attachments were mounted. (*i*) The lead-screw, a carefully threaded spindle which was used to move the lathe

tool when threads were to be cut. Behind the lead-screw was a rack, which meshed with a pinion. This device was used when one wanted to do other types of turning than threading. When a hand-crank (*j*) was manually rotated, the saddle was rapidly moved sideways without being influenced by the lead-screw.

B In Whitworth's planing machine of 1835, the workpiece was fixed while the slide rest was movable. Shown here is the drawing which accompanied Whitworth's patent application; the machine is seen from its long (**1**) and short (**2**) sides as well as from above (**3**). (*a*) Foot. (*b*) Bed, to which the workpiece was clamped. Two uprights (*c*), each equipped with two wheels (*d*) which were guided along V-slideways (*e*), together carried a cross-slide (*f*), on

patent lock, a delicate construction that required extremely accurate components. Around 1800, Maudslay constructed a lathe primarily intended for cutting threads. The lathe was made entirely of metal and included several new features. The support for the lathe tool, the so-called tool-holder, was carried on a slide-rest driven by a lead-screw along the lathe, while the tool was moved towards the work-piece in a V-slide, by means of a screw fitted with a winch handle. Thanks to the V-slide, the tool could be moved very accurately, and with a considerable saving of labour. The Scots engineer James Nasmyth (1808–90) illustrated this in a drawing showing a lathe of Maudslay's design and an older lathe, in each of which identical workpieces were being turned. The operator of the older lathe was shown using the weight of his whole body to press the tool against the material, while the operator of the Maudslay lathe was keeping it in place by resting one hand on the knob of the support; his other hand rested nonchalantly in his pocket.

Maudslay designed his first machines in 1794, while still working for Bramah, and patented them in 1797, when he opened his own workshop, where he made further improvements to his machines. It was here, about three years later, that the metal lathe found the form it has retained ever since.

Maudslay's work appeared at the right time. The British workshop industry was then beginning to expand rapidly, not least because the patent on Watt's steam-engine expired in 1800. As a result, many engineers introduced new designs exploiting steam power. Maudslay was inundated with orders for his precision lathe, and the first mass production of machine tools started in his workshop during the first decades of the nineteenth century. To be sure, many lathe units were built to order, but they always contained the components patented by Maudslay.

Maudslay's principle, where design was concerned, was precision and more precision. Precision mechanics now started to intrude on areas traditionally occupied by heavy engineering and consequently brought about the technical pre-conditions for both more efficient power engines and an industrial production of machine tools. In England a machine-tool industry came into being and rapidly won world fame.

That striving after precision that was sought and fruitfully attained by Maudslay also influenced the work of Sir Joseph Whitworth (1803–87). In 1835, he patented a face-plate lathe that was so well adapted to its purpose that its success laid the foundations of a machine-tool industry, Whitworth & Company, which was one of the foremost of the time, with an impressively wide range of machines for different purposes. The account of the company's programme which was presented at the world exhibition in London in 1851 became one of the most discussed features of this general demonstration of contemporary technical progress. Accuracy in all kinds of processing became Whitworth's consuming passion and formed the foundation for many of his pioneering contributions. He introduced, for example, a system for indicating measurements in drawings, and he designed an instrument which could measure length to an accuracy of a millionth part of an inch. He also standardized the thread profile and the pitch per unit length, of metal screws and nuts at a time when both wood and metal screws had long been made on an industrial scale, but with threads that varied from factory to factory. Whitworth's system was later named BSW (British Standard Whitworth) and was used alongside threading based on the metric system in most industrial countries, until the Anglo-Saxon countries in the 1970s gradually went over to the metric system.

Great Britain was the leader where machine tools were concerned, but important contributions were made also in other countries. The first milling machine, in the modern sense of the word,

tubular boring bar rotated round the centre-line of the cylinder material and machined the required hole. When Boulton & Watt's workshop had taken delivery of a trial order of Wilkinson's cylinders, they found that the internal diameter of a 50-in (c. 175 cm) cylinder deviated from its proper dimensions by no more than the "thickness of a worn shilling-piece" in any place—a degree of precision that they never had dreamt possible. Wilkinson's machine attracted a great deal of attention, and it set the pattern for at least the next seventy-five years. The design, with slight modifications, was used as late as 1851 to bore cylinders for locomotives! Wilkinson's boring machine is rightly considered the first real machine tool, in the modern sense of the word.

Mainly on the basis of their experience of Wilkinson's machine, Boulton and Watt constructed an improved cylinder-boring machine and a face-plate lathe in the early 1790s. Both machines were pioneering, and similar machines were installed in many mechanical workshops in England and other countries during the following fifty years.

The first modern metal lathe was designed by an Englishman, Henry Maudslay (1771–1831). As a young man, Maudslay had worked for Joseph Bramah (1748–1814), who had invented the first

B

a vice (a) on the work table (b), which had a rack on its underside. The rack meshed with a screw (c). When a hand-crank (d) on the screw's shaft was turned, the workpiece was brought forward. At the same time, a cog-wheel (e) meshed with a worm (f) on whose shaft there was a belt pulley (g). The belt ran over a cone pulley (h) in a headstock, which Whitney had taken from an old lathe. (i) Flywheel. The cutter (j) had hand-filed teeth and was attached to an arbor into which the square-tapered socket of the spindle was inserted. In order to vary the milling machine's cutting depth, packing had to be inserted under the workpiece. Plane surfaces only could be milled.

which the slide rest (g) was mounted. The tool (h) could be rotated through 180° about its axis by means of a cord system (i) and could thus cut both when travelling forwards and backwards. After each stroke, the tool was moved sideways, so that a new shaving was cut next to the previous one. The tool-head assembly was driven by two screws (j), into the flanks of whose threads flanges on small pulleys (k) meshed. The motion of the screws was reversed by means of bevel gears (l) and a simple dog clutch (m).

C Eli Whitney's milling machine of 1818. The workpiece was placed in

was constructed in 1818 by the American Eli Whitney (1765–1825). Whitney was most famous for his cotton *gin*, the cotton-separating machine he had patented in 1794, which made it possible for the Southern states to increase their cotton production considerably. Elisha K. Root (1808–65) also made some pioneering new constructions. He was the chief engineer of the Colt Armory in Hartford, Connecticut, which mass produced the revolver patented in 1835 by Samuel Colt (1814–62). Mass production really is the word, for over 300,000 units of the most popular models were made. Root concentrated on machine tools for precision manufacture. He wanted to use labour-saving machines to eliminate the human factor and to make all the units of a long series identical. He introduced what was later called the American system of interchangeable parts. Appropriately, he and Colt designed the first turret lathe, in the mid-1850s. When metal-working requires several different tools to be used one after the other, much labour is saved when they are mounted on to a revolving drum, called a turret head, and brought into place, step by step, by a spider.

Root and Colt's lathe first appeared in Europe in the mid-1870s, in an improved form that came to be the model on which all further development of this machine tool was based. However, it was not

Root who first came upon the idea of feeding forward tools on a lathe. As early as the 1840s, several companies, among them Silver & Gray, were thinking on these lines, but it was Root and Colt's construction that was to be the model for all further turret-lathe development.

Root's clever system of interchangeable parts soon spread to England and the rest of Europe, although it should be added that this "American system" actually originated in Europe in the late eighteenth century, where hand firearms with interchangeable parts were being manufactured in several countries. From the middle of the nineteenth century, when mass-produced domestic machines began to make their appearance–sewing-machines, typewriters, bicycles, harvesters, etc.–the system of interchangeable parts played a major role.

The Industry of Industry

Mass production of machine tools has been called "the industry of industry", and it became widespread in the 1870s. Industrial manufacture of machine tools had certainly existed in Great Britain since the beginning of the nineteenth century and in the United States since the 1840s, but these machines had been built on only a relatively small scale. The increasing demands for precision in mass production of interchangeable parts called for more and more specialized machine tools, but even so, as late as the latter part of the nineteenth century, it was still quite common for companies to build their own machine tools, at least in smaller factories in the engineering industry. At the world exhibition in Philadelphia in 1876, there was displayed the greatest collection of American and European machine tools that had been seen to date, the many different varieties and novelties making an enormous impression on engineers from both sides of the Atlantic.

The Automats Arrive

In the 1870s, an new kind of machine tool appeared that, fully automatically, made smaller parts according to an adjustable program. After several years' hard work, Christopher M. Spe

(1833–1922), an American, could present the first of these in 1873; in essence it was a turret lathe, in which a camshaft and a camshaft pulley moved levers that fed the workpiece forward and changed the tools.

Spencer built his automat to mass produce parts for a sewing-machine, but it was not long before "Hartford automats" also appeared, Spencer being one of the founders of the Hartford Machine Screw Company. These automats produced screws, nuts, cogwheels, and other things en masse, a fact having an impact on the whole of the engineering workshop industry that can hardly be overrated. Demand was immediately great, and within only some years of Spencer's pioneering contribution, automats had given the "industry of industry" a great boost that would create better resources for the development of new and improved manually operated machine tools.

A The saddle of a turret lathe is equipped with several (usually six) tool holders which, in turn, are brought into working position. The tools are for grinding, threading, cross-cutting, etc.

B A turret lathe, built by Gisholt Machine Co. in the United States. On this machine, the turret head (a) was set at an angle, so the tools would not upset the moving of the machine when large workpieces were being turned. During machining, the workpiece was fitted to a steel mandrel (b). The machine was also equipped with a cross-slide (c), which had holders for lathe tools and could be moved along or across the lathe by means of screws.
C A turret lathe with a vertical turret for six tools. Both this machine and that at **B** were manufactured during the second half of the nineteenth century.

In other words, Spencer's contribution meant an important breakthrough in the development of machine tools. A pioneer in the processing of metals, he had several predecessors in the processing of wood. One was a colourful Englishman, Thomas Blanchard (1788–1864), who, in 1820, designed a lathe to make rifle butts. These had been carved manually ever since hand-held firearms first appeared in the Middle Ages, and the butt makers formed, in due course, a highly esteemed craft guild, taking great pride in making skilfully ornamented rifle butts, a pride reflected, naturally, in high prices. Blanchard's first design could make two rifle butts in an hour, and when this reproducing lathe had been improved, it could make nearly a dozen in the same time. Blanchard built various reproducing lathes to make different objects, including axe handles and shoe lasts. This technology was developed and just about perfected by Holtzappfel & Co., of London, whose reproducing lathes made

D The shaping machine and the slotting machine are both chip-cutting and have short cutter strokes. The slotting machine's cutter (1) makes vertical cuts and the shaping machine's (2) makes horizontal cuts.
E Some simple types of lathe-tool: (a) V-groove steel, (b) groove steel, (c) left-hand corner steel, (d) right-hand roughing steel, (e) internal roughing steel.
F During turning, the workpiece (a) rotates while a lathe tool (b) is fed against it and removes chips (c).
G The purpose of broaching is to enlarge drilled holes. The broach (a) moves downwards while the workpiece (b) is fixed.
H Various methods of machining holes: (a) drilling, (b) broaching, (c) reaming (making the cylindrical surface of the hole even), (d) counter-sinking (bevelling the top of the hole to make room for a screw-head), (e) threading.
I When ordinary milling is performed in a horizontal milling machine, the workpiece (a) is fed in the direction opposite to the rotation of the milling tool (b).
J Three common types of milling tool: (1) face cutter, (2) milling cutter, (3) V-groove cutter.
K In a vertical milling machine, the spindle (a) is mounted vertically. (b) Workpiece.
L Gigantic belt transmissions char-

acterized the mechanical workshops of the early twentieth century.
M Spencer's automatic lathe for screw manufacture; (1) from above (2) from the side. On the bed (a), there were two opposed, belt-driven headstocks (b, c) and the metal rods to be machined were fed through b's spindle. A slowly rotating shaft (d) supported two drums (e, f) with cams in the form of guide rails. These guided the feeding and chucking of the work-pieces as well as their transfer from b to c for the final machining. Cams on f also guided the axial movement of one of the turrets (g), which was attached to a shaft (h) which continuously tried to rotate since a chain (i) connected it to a wheel (j) with a sliding clutch. Shaft h as well as g could, however, not turn when one of the stops (k) on g bore on a fixed abutment (l). Only when a work operation had been concluded had g been pushed far enough sideways to free the stop, so that the next tool could be turned into the working position. When the work-piece had been transferred to c's spindle, the second turret (m) came into use. It was fixed axially but could partake of g's gradual rotation. Mounted on m was, among other tools, a milling cutter (n) for nicking the screw-heads. (o) Cam-shaft pulley, guiding a cross-bar (p) with cross-cutting and other tools.

many different products, mainly mass-produced decorative parts for furniture and other wooden ornaments for interior decoration.

The Machine Tools of the Twentieth Century

Thanks to the rapid expansion of the "industry of industry", engineering workshops at the turn of the century had an abundant supply of both machine tools and automats. There were lathes, drilling machines with multiple spindles, milling machines, shaping machines, and even grinding machines, both for production and for grinding the tools of the machine tools. A typical feature of the engineering workshops of the early twentieth century was the overhead line shafts from which power was transferred to each machine tool by a belt. The shafts were driven by large steam-engines. By the 1890s, small, compact steam-engines had been designed in many parts of the world, and these generated sufficient power to drive individual lathes, drilling machines, and so on. The idea was to distribute steam from a central boiler via pipelines to each machine in the workshop. The advocates of this system maintained that the total efficiency of the system would far exceed that of one employing belt transmission, as the latter suffered a loss of power due to friction. However, at the turn of the twentieth century, steam power was in crisis, as electrical energy was becoming more easily available and offered the possibility of a technically superior method of replacing the old power-consuming belt-transmission system. Machine tools driven individually by electricity began to appear at the end of the 1890s and made their breakthrough in the following decade.

The Development of Cutting Materials

It is obvious that the material of the tools in a machine tool must be harder than the material of the workpiece. In the early machine tools, crucible steel was used to manufacture lathe steel, drills, and so on. Crucible steel for chip removal contained 1–1.4 per cent carbon and was called carbon steel. In the mid-1860s, Robert F. Mushet (1811–91), an Englishman, found that the addition of relatively small amounts of tungsten and manganese to carbon steel gave a tool steel with very good cutting properties. This low alloy steel, Mushet steel, appeared at a time when the machine-tool industry was entering a stage of rapid expansion, and it soon found a wide application.

In 1898, after many years of metallurgical development work, the two Americans Frederick W. Taylor and Mansel White presented a hardening process for low-alloy carbon steel, which made it possible to produce a tool steel with much improved properties. The carbon steel was alloyed with tungsten, chrome, vanadium, and molybdenum, which gave it very high resistance to wear. Taylor steel, which has also been called high-speed steel, initiated a development which became extremely important to the production economy of the workshop industry. The high-speed steel led to an increase of production speed, since workpieces could now be machined many times faster than before.

At a stroke, the new tool steel outdated all the existing machine tools. These were simply too delicate and lacked the dynamic properties required. The driving motors were too weak for the forces and counter forces set up by the tools of the new material. In many places this damaged the reputation of the high-speed steel tools, since they contributed to a premature wearing down of drilling machines and lathes.

The machine-tool manufacturers had to think again. They realized that new designs were necessary, and that these had to be based on the actual performance of the tools. A feature of the continued development was the introduction of new cutting materials which made constantly increasing demands on the machine tools. It be-

came necessary to design motors with more power and constructions with greater stability.

In 1926, this development took an important step forward with the introduction of the first hard metal for cutting material; produced in Germany, it was marketed under the name of Widia. Hard metal is an alloy of chrome, tungsten, and titanium or molybdenum with their carbides (carbon compounds). The alloys can be either cast or sintered, which means that metallic or mineral elements in powder form are heated to the temperature at which one or more of them melt and cement the remainder together. During the next few years, a series of hard metals were introduced, with trade names including, for cast alloys, Celsit, Akrit, Miramant, and Stellit and, for sintered alloys, Carboloy, the name used in the United States for Widia, Ramet, Seco, and Titanit. During the 1970s, the cutting properties and the durability of the hard metals were improved further by new metallurgic processes. Tools made of these metals were also coated with a layer, often no more than a thousandth of a millimetre thick, of titanium carbide and aluminium oxide. This development of cutting materials in the twentieth century has meant a revolution in metal-working technology: machining a 500-mm long steel axle with a diameter of 100 mm required 100 minutes with carbon-steel tools, while the same work can be done in less than a minute by a tool coated with, for example, the hard metal known as Coromant, which was introduced in 1976.

The Automat Becomes an NC-machine

Numerically controlled machine tools (NC-machines) are now making rapid progress in the machine-tool industry, and while it is easy to get the impression that they are quite a new invention that has emerged from computer technology, this is not so. Their development can be traced, logically, from Spencer's pioneering machine-tool automat of the 1870s.

A textbook on machine tools from 1955, for example, describes an automatic lathe from the late nineteenth century as still basically "quite modern". Along with the general technical development in the twentieth century, new components were added to change the position of tools and workpieces—electrical, pneumatic, and hydraulic servo motors—while camshaft pulleys and camshafts were still used to carry out the work program. During the first decades of the twentieth century, the cam gear was added, where the "giving of orders" for the various work stages was released by movable cams on a cylinder. When the new cutting materials started to come into use towards the end of the 1920s, it was possible to increase the speed of the different work operations considerably. A common fault of the machine-tool automats of that time was the omission of one of the work operations. In due course, however, sequence control was introduced, which meant that a new work operation could not be commenced until the preceding operation had finished.

In the 1930s and 1940s, copying control of machine-tool automats was also developed. This type of control was in principle the same as that applied by Blanchard in his first copying lathe, in which a pin followed the contours of a rifle butt, while the pin's vertical and horizontal movements controlled the lathe slide and the tools, enabling the shape of any kind of object to be reproduced.

Copying control had a renaissance with the advent of new methods for sensing, principally the electro-optical methods, in which the sensing system operates by means of a luminous ray and photoelectric cells. These methods were rapidly developed during the Second World War, mainly in the United States. An important step was to develop electro-optical devices capable of reading drawings and using this information to control signals for work operations. A further, decisive step was numerically to transform the data of a drawing into a system of three-dimensional coordinates, the principle being developed at the Massachusetts Institute of Technology, where the first NC-machine was taken into operation in 1952.

NC-machines employ one of two basically different methods: general contour control, and positioning, an intermediate form being called limited contour control. With general contour control, numerical information is fed into the machine to control the tool along a two- or three-dimensional curve; the latter requires numerical data—coordinates—in quantities proportionate to the precision to be achieved and, for this reason, computers were used early on to compute the data needed for a specific level of precision. The data was stored on magnetic tape which could be used as input to the NC-machines.

Positioning is used mainly in drilling machines where the tool is to be brought to a predetermined position. Limited contour control is basically related to positioning and is applied on machines which are controlled in rectilinear movements only. The predominant part of the work operations in the average workshop industry is, however, of this type, and consequently, numerically controlled machine tools with limited contour control have found a wide application.

The first NC-machine from the Massachusetts Institute of Technology was a standard three-geared milling machine with a separate numerical control attachment. By the mid-1950s, when a number of different numerical control attachments had been introduced for standard versions of machine tools, it was becoming obvious that the control devices would have to be fully integrated with the machines, and the first such machine to be mass produced appeared on the market in 1955. It was a milling machine with general contour control, manufactured by an American machine-tool company, Giddings & Lewis. By 1960, however, only about 100 general contour control and about 350 positioning or limited contour control machine tools had found a place in American industry, for their introduction required the routines of an industry to be changed or adjusted, from designs and drawings up to programming. In 1967, within only seven years, half of all newly manufactured machine tools were numerically controlled, and by 1977, more than 30,000 such machines were in operation in the United States, almost 5,000 in West Germany, and over 2,000 in Sweden.

Since the early 1970s, numerical control technology has also been applied to devices other than machine tools, mainly for function tests of different types of electrical and electronic products. In the future, numerical control technology will quite likely be applied in other fields where intricate processes have to be controlled.

The Industrial Robot

No internationally accepted definition yet exists of the somewhat indeterminate concept "industrial robot". At one extreme is the pick-and-place unit intended for moving objects from one place to another, a product derived from automation in the 1950s, while at the other is the radio-controlled robot which, among other things, takes inhuman risks in nuclear industry. We shall, however, mainly take note of production aids marketed as industrial robots.

The Game Becomes Serious

The first industrial robot, the Unimat, was developed in the United States in the early 1960s and stumbled onto the market in 1963. Its design team was less likely to have thought of either Karel Čapek and his robots (see page 202) or the walking tin monsters and other fanciful engineers' toys which were common in the 1930s, than of the numerical control technology that had inspired other designers to automate the industrial handling of materials. Despite all mechanization, workpieces had then, and are still, frequently to be merely

A A three-dimensional curved line can be numerically defined by means of a system of coordinates with three planes which are perpendicular to each other and which cut each other along three axes. The point where the axes x, y, and z meet is called the origin of coordinates. The higher the demanded precision, the shorter must be the distance between those points on the curved line which are defined by coordinates—three for each point (the x, y, and z coordinates. The length of a coordinate is the distance between the origin and the point on one of the planes where an imaginary line drawn at right angles from the point on the curved line crosses the plane. In the curve shown here, the x coordinate of point a is 16 mm, its y coordinate is 13 mm, and its z coordinate 30 mm. The corresponding coordinates for point b are 25, 20, and 55 mm respectively.

B If a detail like this one is to be produced automatically by a turret lathe, the tool (a) must be equipped with general contouring.

C A modern turret lathe, TNC Combi, with general contouring control of twelve tools. The control unit with its operation board is to the left of the illustration. Since the work program can be rapidly changed in numerically controlled machines, these are especially well suited to the manufacture of details in short series.

moved, turned, or twisted by hand between two work operations.

The first industrial robot to appear in Europe was installed in 1964 in a Swedish foundry, being employed to lift castings from moulds and place them on a cooling bed. This was in itself quite a simple operation, but the castings were very hot and of an alloy that gave off a foul, acrid smoke that, despite effective ventilation, was very unpleasant. The company had difficulty finding people willing to work in this section, so the industrial robot was very welcome to the work team! Lifting and moving things is, primarily, the sort of work that has occupied industrial robots, but they are also used for spray painting, arc welding, and other things.

The Anatomy of the Industrial Robot

An industrial robot consists of an arm equipped with a gripping device, a power unit, and a control system. The pattern of movements which a robot can carry out depends on its degrees of freedom, that is, what vertical and horizontal and turning movements it can make. The human hand has 22 degrees of freedom, far more than any industrial robot has yet been equipped with; six degrees of freedom are enough for a robot to move an object from one place to another.

The arm to which the gripping device of the robot is attached is usually made of a set of telescopic steel tubes, so that a driving device can change the length of the arm. It is usually mounted on a column, from which it gets its degrees of freedom in a vertical or horizontal direction. Smaller industrial robots are usually pneumatically driven, whereas the larger ones are hydraulically or electrically driven.

The shape of the gripping device usually attempts to resemble the human hand and it is often "tailored" for specific tasks. The first gripping devices to appear had only two unhinged fingers, but since then, development has been rapid, and modern gripping devices

have several hinged fingers. In recent years, workshop engineers and medical technicians who design artificial hands have cooperated in some very fruitful research in this area. Among other things, they have succeeded in developing a sense of touch in the gripping devices. Although at first there were difficulties because the robots were much too hard-handed—they could handle only robust objects—the matter is now nearly resolved through the use of what are called extension transmitters, applied to the fingers of the gripping device. These feel the objects gripped by the fingers and also register even the minute deformations caused by the force of the grip. These deformations are naturally proportional to the force of the grip, and signals from the extension transmitters then control the servo motor which supplies the force. A demonstration number for this artificial sense of touch is when the robot "eats" a boiled egg, by taking the egg in its "fingers", making a hole in the shell and spooning out the contents without crushing the rest of the shell, a performance possible only if the force of the grip can be moderated within very strict limits. Attempts are also being made to provide the gripping device with "eyesight", or at least an indicator of presence, by equipping it with a mouthpiece, through which air is blown in a fine jet. The pressure of the air is measured in the mouthpiece, and when the pressure changes to indicate an obstacle obstructing the gripping device, the robot receives the information. The gripping device can also be magnetic, for such things as handling steel plate, or pneumatic for handling sheets of metal plate, plastic sheets, plate glass, and so on.

The control system of the industrial robot usually consists of transmitters, which indicate the position, and a programme device. To enable the robot to be controlled in its various degrees of freedom, the position of the gripping device must be known from moment to moment, a job performed by electric potentiometers on the robot.

This pneumatically powered industrial robot (**1**) with six freedom degrees is manufactured by Electrolux in Sweden and is able to move an object to any point within its working area. The robot arm (*a*) can be moved to and fro horizontally and is mounted on a pillar (*b*), by means of which it can be raised and lowered. The arm can also rotate round its shaft (*c*). The grab device (**2**) has two fingers (*d*), which can be moved against, and away from, each other and are mounted on a plate (*e*), which can be moved vertically. The whole grab device can also be rotated round the robot arm.

CHAPTER 4
PRIME MOVERS I
Muscle, Water, Wind

A

The techniques involved in moving the large blocks of stone which were used to build the first pyramids have already been touched upon. The necessary forces were supplied by a well-organized combination of human and animal muscle power. Similar methods were to be used for almost four thousand years, until the invention of other sources of power and means of transport, such as steam, railways, and so on.

In 41 AD, Roman engineers transported an ancient obelisk from Egypt to Rome, where it was erected in Circo di Nero, with the aid of muscle power boosted by levers, blocks, and capstans. Some fifteen hundred years later, in 1586, the obelisk was moved once again, this time merely across Rome to Piazza di San Pietro, under the direction of the military engineer Domenico Fontana: but the means he used were essentially no different from those of his Roman predecessors.

The average man can only develop a power of one seventh of a horsepower, or about one hundred watts. For a short time, he can develop perhaps twice as much. The form of the early European harness prevented the draught animals of ancient times from developing more than perhaps two hundred to four hundred watts; in those days, both horses and oxen were harnessed by a fork-shaped yoke, which was fitted by straps under the animal's neck. If the animal pulled too hard, it choked itself. At the end of the eighth century, the oval horse-collar, which had been in use in China since the third century BC, appeared in the Mediterranean countries and, in the following centuries, spread all over Europe. This collar enables the horse to pull with its shoulders, thus boosting its output at least fourfold. While the horse-collar was spreading across Europe, the iron horseshoe came into use and further increased the horse's output, by giving it a better grip on the ground. Improvements in agriculture and transport were consequences of these developments.

There were very few technical aids which exploited human muscle power in a rational way. Those that did exist were mainly intended to allow as many people as possible to pull or lift simultaneously. The most common aids were rope clusters or ropes with loops for lifting or pulling, and long beams to spread the weight of a heavy object more evenly when it had to be lifted. The combined muscle power could then be boosted by levers or multiple blocks.

"The human use of human beings!", proclaims the mathematician Norbert Wiener (1894–1964) in the title of his book on cybernetics and society (first published in 1951). The diametrical opposite of this would be to use gangs of slaves as prime movers of large ships. Rowing is, of course, almost as old as man himself; the first primates probably paddled themselves along sitting astride a log or in a hol-

A A stone image being moved on a sledge, pulled by a large number of people. Assyrian relief, ninth century BC.

B A simple crane. Several men could lift a heavy load jointly if each pulled at one of the rope ends.

B

C According to a book of travels from the end of the eighteenth century, heavy loads were carried in the manner shown here (1) in China. The weight was distributed on the men by a frame (2).

C2

C1

A In 1586, a 312-ton Egyptian obelisk was moved from Circo di Nero to Piazza di San Pietro in Rome under the direction of Domenico Fontana. Later, Fontana published a detailed account of the work, and it is from this book that the illustrations shown here derive. The obelisk was surrounded by a stout scaffold before it was lifted from its socle (1). For this critical phase of work, Fontana employed 900 men and 75 horses at 37 windlasses (2). Trumpet blasts and bell peals indicated when the windlasses were to be started and stopped. To utter a single word while work was in progress was forbidden on pain of death. In spite of this, a man is reputed to have risked his life by crying "Water on the ropes!" when these threatened to break. He was imprisoned but, later, was rewarded amply. The obelisk was placed on a bed of rollers and transported along a timber-reinforced road to the new site, where it was erected (3). This last phase took thirteen hours and was accomplished by means of blocks.

A3

A2

A1

lowed-out tree-trunk. But it is a long way from that to the vast amount of muscle power which galley-slaves had to produce. Some ancient civilizations—for instance, the Sumerian, the Phoenician, and the Egyptian—had fairly large oar-propelled ships, but it was not until the fourth and third centuries BC that the Hellenic civilization produced the first great galleys. The shipbuilding techniques then used by the Greeks were later adopted by the Romans. Sarton tells of a contemporary description of the flagship of the famous fleet of Ptolemy IV Philopator (244?–203? BC), a ship considered to have been the most magnificent of antiquity, and that is saying a lot when one thinks of the *Syrakosia*, which has been described in Chapter One. Ptolemy's ship was claimed to have been 394 ft (c. 120 m) long and 63 ft (c. 19 m) wide and was manned by 4,000 oarsmen and 400 relief oarsmen, together with 2,850 soldiers for the heavy armament on board. The account omits to say how many banks of oars there were (probably four, which would have made the ship a quadrireme), but it does say that the oars of the upper bank were almost 66 ft (c. 20 m) long. "However", the account continues, "these oars had lead counterweights and thus were very easy to handle." One feels tempted to remark that everything is relative, while recalling Sancho Panza's complaint, when he and Don Quixote ended up in a gallery, that "if this is not hell on earth, then it must be at least purgatory". Sarton doubts the size given for the crew, although all the primary sources give the same figures. But what if the numbers of oarsmen and soldiers are exaggerated?. A tenth of those figures would be impressive enough! (At this time, the Greeks did not use the position system when writing numbers, but used letters instead, and these could be misread easily, especially during translation.)

The Romans developed the galley to as near technical perfection as possible. The trireme, that is, a vessel with three banks of oars, one above the other, was the standard type of the Roman navy. The oars, of considerable length in the upper row, were usually equipped with counterweights, which naturally made rowing less backbreaking, although Sancho Panza's comment still comes to mind. This inhuman exploitation of labour decreased in the Middle Ages, when sail-rigging techniques gradually improved, but a modified form of these ancient galleys survived until steam took over in the nineteenth century. In many countries, the navy used galley slaves to row its ships, although sometimes regular soldiers were told off for this task.

The Capstan and the Treadmill

The simplest and probably the earliest capstan is the vertical winder of the kind used by Fontana in Rome in 1586, but this prime mover, is, very likely, of ancient origin. From the late Middle Ages onwards, there appeared an abundance of imaginative designs for animal-driven capstans and treadmills; many were purely theoretical. For example, Olaus Magnus (1490–1557) mentions in his *History of the Nordic People*, published in 1555, that, in the fifteenth century, a treadmill driven by Nordic brown bears was in use at the Falu copper mine in Sweden, and although the Stora Kopparberg company, which still owns the mine, used advanced techniques even in the Middle Ages, it is probable that Olaus Magnus did not recognize that the story was a joke.

A remarkable warship, propelled by ox-driven paddle-wheels, is described by the author known as Anonymus Byzantinus ("the unknown from Byzantinum"!) in his work *De re bellicis*, which dates from the middle of the sixth century. Byzantinus was a military engineer in the employ of the Byzantine emperor Justinian I (482?–565), who is probably best known as the builder of Hagia Sophia, "the church of divine wisdom", in Constantinople (antiquity's Byzantium). The vessel described was driven by three pairs of paddle-wheels, each being turned by a capstan driven by a pair of oxen.

B The oar arrangement of a trireme. More than one man was needed to handle the upper oars.

C According to the Swedish clergyman Olaus Magnus, bears were used to work treadmills in Scandinavia, but this is highly unlikely. From *Historia de gentibus septentrionalibus* (Rome, 1555).

D This Chinese device for the irrigation of fields was probably invented as early as the second century BC, and it is still being used. From a book of travels, published at the end of the eighteenth century.

A Six oxen turn the capstans on this remarkable paddle-driven ship. From a manuscript of *c.* 1436.
B Giovanni da Fontana's "self-driving" carriage from the beginning of the fifteenth century.
C Francesco di Giorgio Martini's *automobile*. The power transmission from the capstans (*a*) was by worm gears (*b*). (*c*) Steering device.

Byzantinus claims that the mere din of this ox-machine was enough to scare the enemy away! The ship was probably never built, although technically it could have been. Byzantinus really gives free rein to his imagination in *De re bellicis* and suggests other incredible constructions, such as a temporary wartime bridge, which consisted of a gigantic sack of hide. The sack was to be filled with air from two bellows, and the troops were then to march dry-shod across the river!

What is interesting here is that the paddle-wheel was being discussed as a technical possibility in the sixth century AD, although Byzantinus may have based his design on an even older one. This kind of propulsion, in more or less unrealistic designs, also appears here and there in mediaeval literature. A German manuscript from the early fifteenth century illustrates a hand-driven device for powering paddle-wheels on a boat. However, the poor man in the boat looks slightly nonplussed by the impressive cog-wheel! Good advice for him would be to throw the machinery overboard and get himself a pair of oars.

The potential of muscle power boosted by capstans and windlasses inspired many designers to produce curious inventions. From the Middle Ages onwards, many suggestions for self-propelled carriages were put forward. Around 1410, the Italian architect Giovanni Fontana illustrated a hand-driven carriage with an intricate gearing in which the machine elements are very interesting examples of contemporary technology. The driving wheel and the upper "roller" are similar to those used then in windmills, and their configuration is usually known as the "lantern" design, which was used throughout the era of water and wind power. The carriage's large cog-wheel has teeth of a shape similar to those in Hero's writings and in the Antikythera device.

Another remarkable carriage was that designed by the Italian engineer Francesco di Giorgio Martini (1439–1502) in the late fifteenth century. Again, this design probably never left the drawing-board. All four wheels have individual drives powered by winch-type capstans, and power transmission is by worm gears. Unlike most similar designs, this has a steering device. Giorgio Martini called his creation *automobile*, i.e., self-moving, and as far as we know, this is the word's earliest appearance in literature.

The capstan is an example of how a great length of time can elapse between the first and the last applications of an invention. Another example is the treadmill; it was used in the building-crane described by Vitruvius, as well as in the port-and-derrick cranes which were in use in Central Europe as late as the nineteenth century. Many of the latter have been preserved as monuments of the history of technology.

In the latter part of the eighteenth century, many horse-wheels which had been used to power industrial machines, such as machine tools and machines in the textile industry, were replaced. Horse-wheels powered the first spinning-machines in England, among them Sir Richard Arkwright's pioneer machine of 1769, which, in 1771, was adapted to take power from a water-wheel; later, it was converted to steam. The use of the horse-wheel in agriculture, on the other hand, increased in the nineteenth century, and such machines as chaff-cutters, threshing-machines, and hay-hoists were all driven by horse-wheels. From the latter part of the nineteenth century on, horse-wheels were used also to drive milk separators.

Water Power

The origins of the water-wheel and its earliest forms are not yet clear. The first reference to it in Roman literature was around the time of the birth of Christ, but we know that the power of falling water had been exploited in the Far East about six hundred years

D A two-horse-whim, used for raising water from four wells. The illustration is based on an eighteenth-century model in the Museo di Storia della Scienza, Florence.

E A mediaeval, treadmill-powered port crane in the Belgian city of Bruges. The sledge in the foreground was probably used for transporting the casks on land. After a Flemish calendar from the beginning of the sixteenth century.

F A treadmill-powered crane (1) from the eighteenth century. Cranes of this type were used for hundreds of years; a similar device was described by Vitruvius. (2) The treadmill.

B In 1607, the Italian engineer Vittorio Zonca (1580?–?) published his *Novo teatro di machine et edificii* in Padua. It included an illustration of this device, intended to replace the sluice. Horse-whims with high gear ratios were to lift boats onto a wooden platform (*a*), which was then pulled up or down an inclined plane (*b*) from one water level to another.

C This remarkable design for a ship was suggested in 1895 by an American called Chapman. The ship was to be driven by large, flanged cylinders which, in their turn, were "treadmills" for locomotives. Chapman believed that it would take only three days, or less, to cross the Atlantic.

A A sixteenth-century mine hoist. A horse-driven windlass (*a*) hoists ore in an ox-hide bag (*b*) up a mine shaft. The man at the bottom of the picture is operating a braking device, which brings a beam (*c*) into contact with a drum on the drive axle of the hoist. The hook (*e*) can be attached to the chain to keep the bag of ore at any desired level in the shaft. From Agricola's *De re metallica* (1556).

D In 1878, when the Swedish engineer de Laval launched his milk separator, he had also designed a horse-whim to drive it. As can be seen from the illustration, the gear ratio was considerable. The separator worked best at speeds exceeding 7,000 rpm.

E This monumental horse treadmill was intended to power a mine pump and was designed in the early eighteenth century by an Englishman, Walter Churchman. However, it is most unlikely that it ever got beyond the drawing-board.

F An early dredger; (**1**) from the front, (**2**) from above, (**3**) in operation. During the first half of the eighteenth century, many dredgers on pontoons, with outriggers (*a*), were built in France. The construction remained in use until well into the twentieth century. The outriggers were often double and fastened to a small boat (*b*). The dredger shovel (*c*), which was of iron and had a sturdy wooden handle, was hauled in by a windlass (*d*), driven by one or more treadmills (*e*). A barge (*f*) was often moored alongside to take the dredged material.

A The noria, with its jars and paddles, is considered to be the oldest type of water-wheel. Before it came into use, only jars had been mounted on the wheels, which were rotated by muscle power.

C Section of a Norse (also called Greek) mill (**1**). The corn was fed into the hopper (*a*). The water-wheel (*b*) had a vertical shaft and drove the movable millstone (*c*) directly. By pulling beam (*d*) upwards, it was possible to raise the water-wheel from the stream.

B This more developed type of noria is usually attributed to Philo. The rotary movement of the water-driven paddle-wheel (*a*) is transmitted by means of a chain (*b*) to an upper shaft (*c*) on which a triangular drum (*d*) is mounted. When *d* rotates, the water-filled jars are brought up to be emptied in a pipe (*e*).

previously. A. P. Usher believes that three different devices developed independently in different geographical locations. The simplest, and probably the earliest, is thought to have been the paddle-wheel, driven by the current of a river and used to raise water from it. A further extension of the noria, as this device was called in the Mediterranean countries, has been described by Philo of Byzantium, but Drachmann considers that it is likely that, at a later stage, these details were added to Philo's original text during translation. Usher's second device is the horizontal, or Norse, water-wheel, which achieved the first "automation" in household work. The third is the water-wheel often attributed to Vitruvius, which dates back to the first decades after the birth of Christ.

We have already mentioned Hero's use of falling water to drive one of his automata. But the dramatic début of the water-wheel as a prime mover took place in ancient Rome where, within only a few decades, it had quickly become widespread. The first account of a water-wheel in the West is attributed to the Roman engineer Vitruvius, who describes in detail the design and application of this innovation in his book *De architectura*. The first form of this wheel had a vertical shaft and inclined blades, and was used to drive grinding mills. Long previously, grain had been ground in hand-mills; this was a task for the womenfolk that, in large households, often took up most of their day. The water-mill caused, therefore, something of a revolution, and, while poets were loud in praise of this new wonder, they also raised a moral finger of warning at the

D

D This type of mill was once common in the French districts of Provence and Dauphine. The water was led into a chute and drove a vertical-shafted wheel. The lever in the mill window was used to close off the chute.

E This mill with its gearwheels has been described by Vitruvius. On the shaft of the water-wheel (*a*), a toothed wheel (*b*) is mounted. It meshes with another wheel (*c*) which drives the upper, movable millstone. (*d*) Feed hopper.

same time. What, they asked, will the women do now?

This labour-saving device soon spread to other parts of Europe. The Greek poet Antipater of Thessalonica praised the mill in the following lines:

> Stop grinding, ye women who toil at the mill,
> Sleep on, though the crowing cocks announce the break of day.
> Demeter has commanded the water nymphs
> to do the work of your hands.
> Jumping onto the wheel, they turn the axle
> Which drives the gears and the heavy millstones.

In his book *Moving Forward*, Henry Ford writes that the main importance of the machine in the evolution of mankind has been that it has lifted the heavy toil off man's back and placed it on its own shoulders. The same thoughts as Antipater had had two thousand years previously, but now expressed in prose.

Philo's description of the noria dates from the third century BC, the horizontal water-wheel appeared in the first century BC, and the actual water-wheel came some fifty years later. The sharp typological distinction made by Usher between these three designs has a certain appeal nowadays, but in reality these distinctions may not have been so clear-cut. The noria was, apparently, not very widespread in the Mediterranean countries, probably because it requires an abundant supply of swiftly running water. It is rather difficult to dismiss completely the notion that the noria may have belonged to

the same category as the frivolous designs of the Alexandrian school, as Philo's inventions included a whistling water-wheel. This consisted of a paddle-wheel with a horizontal shaft and sealed cavities between the blades. Each cavity had a whistle, which sounded when the water forced the air out. It is not completely unlikely that some practical technician took the joke seriously, eliminated the whistling cavities, and connected the wheel to, say, a mill! After all, the gearing necessary in such a construction was already quite well known.

Between the noria and Vitruvius's water-wheel, there is another form, in which pails are suspended from the blades of a paddle-wheel. This method of drawing water was used in India and Mesopotamia. It was quite a short step for a practical-minded engineer to remove the pails and enlarge the blades. A simple water-wheel of this kind was used to provide motive power for the water-drawing version of the Archimedean screw, which was especially common in Egypt and is still used in many parts of Africa.

The water-mill spread so quickly because its design was simple, and because it afforded relief from the heavy, monotonous toil of grinding grain. As modern advertising would put it, it was "simply indispensable in every household". Still, the water-mill had its limitations. Its output would not now be thought impressive, being only about half a horsepower, or three to four hundred watts; besides, it could not be regulated easily. A horizontal shaft and a reduction gear between the mill and the millstone were obvious steps to take to

A Different types of water-wheels with horizontal shafts. (**1**) Undershot water-wheel. (**2**) Breast-wheel. The flow of water was regulated with a sluice-gate (*a*). (**3**) Overshot water-wheel.

B A reconstruction of a lock system, here seen from the side (**1**) and from above (**2**), which was built during the first half of the nineteenth century in the United States. The arrangement was intended for the transport of barges between two different water levels, and the

transport took place on carriages running on rails. The two parallel locks (*a*, *b*) are here shown during the drained phase of the cycle. A carriage (*c*) with a barge (*d*) has just been pulled up the rails (*e*) in lock *a*, while lock *b* is not being used at the moment. If it were used, the barge using it would reach the lower water level at the same time as *d* reached the upper. (**3**) The carriages in the locks were pulled by a chain (*f*), which was arranged in an M-shaped loop over a sprocket (*g*) and two wheels (*h*), one on each carriage (seen here in one carriage in **1** and **2**). (**4**) The sprocket was driven by a water-wheel (*i*) by way of two gearwheels (*j*, *k*) and a mitre gearing (*l*), whose direction of rotation could be reversed. When the carriages had reached their respective turning-points, the water-wheel (*i*) was stopped, the fore lock gate (*m*) was raised by hand, and, at the same time, a sash gate (*n*) was slid

over the lock's drainage opening (*o*). A smaller water-wheel (*p*) was then started; by way of a gear arrangement (*q*; shown at **5**), *p* opened the rear lock gate (*r*; shown in detail at **6**) by lowering it into a shaft (*s*). Water then rushed into the lock and lifted the barge from its carriage at the same time as the water pressure provided an adequate sealing of *m* and *n*. When the barge had been towed out of the lock chamber and another barge had taken its place, *r* was closed again by the gear arrangement *q*, whose direction of rotation had now been reversed. When *r* had almost reached its topmost position, it automatically slid *n* away by means of a chain (*t*), and the water in the lock chamber ran out through *o*. Lock gate *m* was opened, and the new barge, now placed on carriage *c*, was pulled down the rails. When the barge going upwards weighed (*Continued below, left*)

A1

A2

A3

less than the one going downwards. or when only a downward-going barge was being transported, the water-wheel (*i*) was braked by the arrangement shown at **7**.

C The Roman mill plant (**1**) at Barbegal was erected in the early fourth century AD and no longer exists. It may possibly have looked as shown here. (**2**) Plan of the structure. Water from the aqueduct (*a*) was gathered in a basin (*b*) and directed into two chutes (*c*) over the water-wheels.

C1

C2

D In this seventeenth-century smithy, the same water-wheel is employed to drive the hammer-forge and two bellows. From J. de Strada's *Kunstliche Abriss aller-hand Wasser- Wind- Ross- und Hand Mühlen* (Frankfurt-on-Main, 1617).
E Agricola included this mine-ventilation device in his *De re metallica*, published in 1556. An overshot water-wheel (*a*) rotates a fan (*b*) whose four blades are equipped with long feathers. The fan is enclosed in a drum (*c*), and the air is pumped into the mine through a hollow log (*d*).
F Water-wheel-powered bellows. Protrusions on the shaft of an overshot wheel press first one and then the other of the bellows together. After a manuscript from the fifteenth century.

1

d

c f

e

o m n

j k

l

i

r

s

4

a b

l

j

i

2

p

i

j k

l

b

f f

l

g

q r

n

d

a t

c

f

m

5

7

D

E

b

a

c

F

b

99

A water-wheel-powered mill of the eighteenth century, shown in section from in front (**1**) and from the side (**2**). Based on illustrations in Denis Diderot's *Encyclopédie*, which was published between 1751 and 1780.

improve the design. Quite early on, it must have been necessary to adjust the speed of the wheel, which was largely determined by the speed of the current, to produce optimal milling output.

It should be clear from what has just been said that there does not exist any clear, intrinsic distinction between the different types of water-wheel described above. It is quite likely that they are versions of one and the same phenomenon, the origin of which is still difficult to trace.

During the first centuries AD, the water-mill spread relatively slowly beyond the boundaries of the Roman empire into the north of Europe. However, according to the Danish archaeologist A. Steenberg, the water-mill was known in Denmark at the time of the birth of Christ. In the fourth century AD, the Romans erected a large mill at Barbegal, near Arles, France. Water was supplied from a spring and, via an aqueduct, from the river Arcoule. The aqueduct, which has impressive dimensions−6 ft 7in (2 m) wide and 18 ft 5 in (5.6 m) deep−slopes at an angle of 30° at Barbegal. The eight pairs of overshot wheels have each a diameter of 7 ft 3 in (2.2 m) and a width of 2 ft 4 in (0.7 m), and each wheel drives a pair of millstones. The flour production of the mill, estimated at 2.8 tons a day, would have greatly exceeded the local needs, and most of it was shipped to Rome via the port of Arles. Water-mills are mentioned in an eighth-century Irish law, "Senchus Mor" and are known also to have existed in Central Europe. Further, a document of the period mentions a sawmill driven by a water-wheel.

After the disintegration of the Roman empire, most of the products of its advanced engineering technology fell into disuse−its aqueducts, baths, arenas, and so on−while water-mills actually seem to have been employed more widely and further improved in design. In 1086 in England, the great land census recorded in the Domesday Book that there were more than 5,600 water-mills in the country, which was then relatively sparsely populated. Lewis Mumford has pointed out that this equals one mill per four hundred inhabitants− and this in a country situated "on the outskirts of European civilization".

Already at the time of the Domesday Book, water-wheels drove not only flour-mills, but also ore crushers and forge hammers, and by the end of the Middle Ages, they were used generally in mining to raise ore and to power bellows. Water-wheels drove machines in other processes, too−wire-drawing, leather tanning, cloth fulling, rag-pounding (in paper-making), sawing, crushing minerals for dye-stuffs, to name only some of them.

Floating Mills

An interesting application of the water-wheel occurs in the floating water-mill. Equally interesting is the story of its invention. In 537, when Rome was besieged by the Goths, the eternal city was defended by the Byzantine general Belisarius, who had occupied most of the Roman provinces on the Italian peninsula a year or so earlier. At that time, most of the water-mills in Rome were driven by water from the aqueducts (in actual fact, this is a token of the decline of Roman technology). In an attempt to starve the Romans out, the besieging army cut off the water supply. However, Belisarius found a way out of this dilemma. Possibly inspired by Byzantinus's ox-driven vessel, he caused flour-mills driven by paddle-wheels to be installed in boats that were then moored in the Tiber; Rome's flour supply was thus ensured.

News of this achievement spread far and wide, and within a few centuries, there were floating mills both in Venice and Baghdad. In the twelfth century, three were built under the arches of the Grand Pont in Paris. Towards the end of the Middle Ages, there were many such mills in use on the great rivers of Europe, pumping water or grinding grain; several on the Rhine at Cologne, built in the fifteenth century, were still in use three hundred years later.

The most spectacular installation of this kind was, without a doubt, the pumping station at Marly. Built in the 1680s to supply water to the many fountains of Versailles, the pumping station had 235 pumps, which were driven by thirteen great water-wheels and which pumped water from the river to the reservoirs 525 ft (c.160 m) above. The pumping was carried out in three stages, and the power was transmitted by two rows of oscillating rods and levers. A builder from Liège, Rennequin Sualem, supervised the construction of this enormous plant, which took 1,800 men eight years to complete. The original output was about 125 horsepower, and the capacity was 1.1 million gallons (5 million litres) per day. The plant was difficult to maintain, especially the energy-consuming rod-and-lever transmission. In 1725, the Marly machine was entirely rebuilt, and in the early nineteenth century, a steam-engine of 150 horsepower was installed.

The Ballet-dancing Machine

The Marly pumping station was severely criticized by contemporary engineers, who maintained that the ideas behind the design were erroneous. Undershot water-wheels were very inefficient, and so was the rod-and-lever transmission. The designer defended himself by claiming that there was nothing else available. Maybe he did not know that, more than a century previously, Juanelo Turriano, a talented Spanish engineer of Italian origin in the employ of the emperor, Charles V, had faced the same sort of problem, in Toledo, and solved it successfully. Little is known about his background, but he was over eighty when he died in 1585. He was first employed by the emperor when, as a youth, he managed to repair an ornamental water-clock, which the foremost clockmakers of the day had failed to mend. It is considered to have been of the complicated type described in Chapter Two. Turriano later built a number of other clocks, including a very advanced, mechanical ornamental clock for the emperor. Many of the difficult technical problems of the day were solved by Turriano, one of them being how to provide the city of Toledo with water.

Toledo lies in the centre of a rich mining area and had already grown into a major city, with over 200,000 inhabitants. Its water was carted from the river Tajo, some 1,970 ft (600 m) below the city, in leather bags borne by mules. As the city grew, this means of supplying it with water became inadequate, and German mining engineers were called in to build a pumping station. At first, everything worked satisfactorily; but later the pipes burst.

Some years earlier, the emperor had been residing in the Alcázar in Toledo, and in his entourage was Turriano. When the Germans' installation failed, Turriano was commissioned to do the job, and he could soon demonstrate his solution with a perfect working model, which did not include a single pipe! In the early 1540s, after six years of work, Turriano had the full-scale plant ready.

A combined water-wheel and noria continuously filled a container with water. This was then poured into one end of a "cradle", which was the central element of the whole design. The water-wheel also drove a reciprocating rod-and-lever transmission, which rocked a whole chain of cradles so that each cradle poured its contents into the one above it. The result was a mechanized bucket brigade.

The Toledo waterworks received a great deal of attention all over Europe, and the graceful movements of the transmission system and the cradles, from which not a drop of water spilled, inspired an enthusiastic spectator to describe the plant as "the ballet-dancing machine". In 1645, a ballet, "El Mago", was performed in Madrid, the dancers imitating the movements of Turriano's waterworks,

A The giant Marly machine, which was built on the River Seine in the 1680s. Thirteen water-wheels powered 235 force pumps, which pumped up to 1 million gallons (5,000 m³) of river water into the reservoirs daily. The reservoirs were situated 525 ft (160 m) above the river.

B (**1**) One of the enormous wheels of the Marly machine. On the shaft of the water-wheel was a crank (*a*), whose rotary movement was transformed into a reciprocating movement by a connecting rod (*b*). At the other end of the connecting rod was a rocking arm (*c*), which reciprocated round a fixed shaft (*d*) and was connected to the rocking arm (*e*), which drove the pumps (*f*). (*g*) A device for raising and lowering a sluice (*h*). (*i*) A gate which prevented floating objects from being brought towards the water-wheel by the river water. (**2**) The water-wheels also drove the rows of rocking levers and rods (*j*), which were used to drive the pumps (*m*) in the basins (*n*) at the pumping stations by means of rocking arms (*k*, *l*). (*o*) Detail, showing how the pumps were connected to the water-pipe.

C An eighteenth-century tug, shown here from above (**1**), in cross-section (**2**), and in longitudinal-section (**3**). When the paddle-wheels were rotated by the stream, the tug was pulled upstream by a chain (*a*), one end of which was attached to the

A

C₁

C₂

C₃

D

B1

B2

mooring-place upstream whereas the other end ran round a block at the mooring-place downstream and was attached to the tug. When the tug was to go downstream, gates (b) were lowered in front of the paddle-wheels by means of a crank (c).
D A woodcut of 1531 showing floating mills in the Rhine at Cologne, Germany.
E Section of a floating mill. (a) Water-wheel. (b) The enclosed mill-stones. (c) Feed hopper.

moving with arms crossed as if to transfer water from one to the other in a chain.

Agostino Ramelli, who described the Toledo waterworks in his book *Le diverse et artificiose machine*, published in 1588, states that the capacity of the works equalled that of three hundred mules working day and night, tended by almost as many mule drivers. That capacity is about a fifth of what Louis XIV of France, the Sun King, needed for his fountains in Versailles. Technically, however, it would not have been difficult for Turriano to have built his works on a larger scale or to have doubled or even trebled the number of cradles by using parallel chains.

When the Sun King had his magnificent baroque palace designed, the architects made a serious mistake in not ensuring that the water supply in the area was sufficient. There was, in fact, no water, so enormous sums of money had to be spent building the Marly pumping station, in order that Versailles could be supplied with water.

Tidal Power-stations

The term "lunar power-station", which is sometimes used instead of "tidal power-station", originates in today's France, where a power-station driven by the tide has been built in the tidal estuary of the river Rance in Brittany. The idea of exploiting the tide (and, indirectly, the moon) to produce energy is far from new. As far back as the 1130s, a mill was built near the mouth of the river Adour in France, and a century later, several tide-mills were in operation near Venice. The first tide-mill, however, is believed to have been built in the third century AD in the port of Dover in England. A tide-driven pump was installed on the Thames in 1582 by Peter Morice. This pumped almost 4 million gallons (18 million litres) of water per day up to a tank more than 130 ft (c. 40 m) higher up. However, the design was unsuccessful, and the scheme was soon abandoned.

The Golden Age of Water Power

From the late sixteenth to the late eighteenth century, machines were built to exploit the fall of water with ever-increasing efficiency. Some impressive installations are described by the German Georg Bauer (1494–1555), also called Agricola, in his great work *De re metallica*, published the year after his death. (An English translation was made in the early 1900s by the young mining engineer Herbert C. Hoover, later president of the United States, and his wife.) A clear picture of the progress made during these years in machine construction is provided by the great books on what is now called technology; the best known of these are *Le diverse et artificiose machine* by Agostino Ramelli (Paris, 1588), *Les Raisons des Forces Mouvantes* by Salomon de Caus (Paris, 1615), and *Theatrum machinarum* by Jacob Leupold (Leipzig, 1725). Such books were originally called "art" books, in the sense of human skill rather than nature, while the term "fine arts" was used to designate painting, sculpture, and so on. The word "technology" in its present meaning was not in general use until the early nineteenth century. Until then, for example, the chief engineer of a mine was called the "art master".

Water Turbines

The first turbine is one of the few phenomena in the history of technology that can be dated accurately, as both the machine and its name resulted from a competition held in France, in 1826. La Société d'Encouragement pour l'Industrie Nationale had offered a prize of six thousand francs for the design of a water-wheel for use in industry; one of the conditions was that the water-wheel must work under water without any loss of efficiency. One of the competitors, Claude Burdin (1790–1873), suggested that such a wheel should be called "turbine", from the Latin word *turbo*, a top. Burdin's own

A

B

A Juanelo Turriano's *Artificio*, which provided Toledo with water from the river Tajo. The water-wheel (*a*) continually filled a container (*b*) with water and, at the same time, drove two rows of oscillating rods and levers (*c*) so that ladles (*d*) kept rocking to and fro. The water was thus poured from ladle to ladle all the time. After an illustration in Ramelli's *Le diverse et artificiose machine*, 1588.

B Despite the fact that Christopher Polhem's plans for a new ore-hoisting mechanism at the Swedish Falu mine had been met with the utmost distrust by the "art master" there, Olof Henriksson Trygg, this *Machina Nova* was erected at Blankstöten in 1694. Trygg, however, insisted upon building an ordinary hoisting mechanism beside Polhem's machine, so that the two devices could be compared when hoisting ore from the same depth. It turned out that more than twenty-two barrels of ore could be hoisted in one hour with Polhem's new construction, whereas it was possible to hoist only sixteen with the ordinary mechanism.

The *Machina Nova* was powered by an overshot water-wheel (*a*), on whose shaft a gearwheel (*b*) was mounted. It meshed with another gearwheel (*c*), which had one end of a row of oscillating rods and levers (*d*) attached to its periphery. The other end of *d* was attached to two opposed cross-levers (*e*), to which two pairs of 195-ft (59.4 m) long rods (*f*) were fastened. Each pair was equipped with fifteen pairs of hooks. Each barrel was fastened to a bar which was laid on the pair of hooks at the bottom of the shaft. As the rods were alternately brought upwards and downwards, the bar with its barrel was brought from hook-pair to hook-pair, so that the barrel was hoisted. At ground level, two suspended hooks (*g*) were fastened to the rim of the barrel, and an iron chain (*h*) was hooked to its bottom. The chain was suspended from one of the arms of the cross-lever (*e*), and when it was raised by *d*, the ore was emptied onto the pithead frame (*i*), where it was loaded onto carts. These were driven onto a bridge (*j*), which, too, was raised and lowered by another cross-lever (*k*) on the row of oscillating rods and levers. The ore was then brought into the so-called bucking-house, where it was separated from the barren rock. The empty barrels were attached to an endless chain (*l*) to be brought down again into the mine shaft. The chain was equipped with thirty small, equidistant balls, and its speed was checked by two iron forks, so that the barrels were kept from too rapid a descent.

105

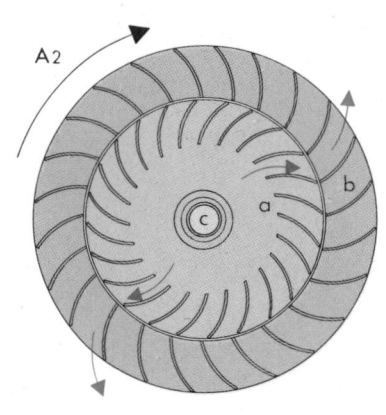

A Like all the early turbines, Fourneyron's (**1**) was a reaction turbine. Water passes under pressure through such a turbine and transmits its energy to the runner by pressure against its blades. Fourneyron's turbine had two concentric, horizontal wheels (**2**); the fixed, inner wheel (*a*) had guide vanes which directed the water through blades set at an angle on the runner (*b*). The shaft (*c*) was vertical. The amount of water passing through the turbine could be regulated by the lowering or raising of a ring which was mounted between the guide vanes and the runner.

entry was not successful, however, as it did not fulfil the necessary conditions; the young engineer Bénoit Fourneyron (1802–67) won with an interesting design featuring two concentric horizontal wheels. The fixed inner wheel had curved guide vanes which directed the water against runner blades on the outer wheel, which is known as the rotor. The efficiency of this outward-flow radial turbine, as the type is called, was as high as eighty to eighty-five per cent, but it had a disadvantage in that turbulence occurred at certain speeds when the water left the guide vanes. However, Fourneyron's technically elegant design set the style for a number of new water turbines which were built during the remainder of the nineteenth century. Later, guide vanes came to be used also in steam turbines. The first Fourneyron turbine was installed between 1835 and 1837 at Saint-Blaise in the Black Forest. This type of turbine spread rapidly all over Europe, often replacing the undershot wheels which were then used where the head of water was small, and which had a very low efficiency—twenty per cent or less.

One of the variations which lay very near Fourneyron's design was a turbine in which the guide vanes were installed above the rotor. This was Karl Anton Henschel's idea, and in 1841, he installed such a turbine in a stone-polishing works in Brunswick, Germany, where a

Frenchman called Jonval saw it and, in 1843, took out a patent for the design.

Another variation of Fourneyron's turbine was arranged with the rotor within the guide vanes, so that the water flowed against the central rotor through an outer circle of fixed guide vanes. First suggested by the Frenchman Jean V. Poncelet in the late 1820s, this idea was patented as the inward-flow radial turbine in the United States by Samuel B. Howd in 1838. Two years later, James B. Francis (1815–92) built such a turbine, under licence from Howd, and achieved very good results with it. Francis later carried out a series of experiments in which he compared the performance of a Fourneyron-type turbine with that of his own, both turbines being installed in a factory in Lowell, north of Boston. The results of these experiments, carried out in the 1850s, were to determine the essential features of the type of turbine which was to become known as the Francis turbine. Considerable improvements, however, were made to this design by the Briton James Thomson (the elder brother of Lord Kelvin), who introduced adjustable guide vanes and curved blades on the rotor. These are still the characteristic features of this type of turbine. Thomson based the shape of the blades on the results of his theoretical studies of the vortices appearing in a centrifugal pump. The rotor is usually called a vortex wheel (from the Latin *vortex*, a whirlpool). In the 1860s, the Francis turbine began to replace the water-wheel and, by the turn of the century, had become the most commonly used turbine in hydroelectric power-stations.

A new type of turbine, whose invention was due to sheer chance, was the Pelton wheel. During the gold rush in California in the 1860s, the most common method of washing for gold was to flush the sand and gravel away with a jet of water under very high pressure. The water was usually led in pipes or hoses to the site from reservoirs higher up the river. About 1870, when the gold ran out, this piped water was often used to drive water-wheels. A mining engineer, Lester A. Pelton (1829–1908), who worked in these parts, had built a water-wheel with curved blades. One day, the water jet happened to strike the outer edges of the blades, and the speed of the wheel increased so much that it flew into pieces.

C

B In Jonval's axial-flow turbine, the guide-vane wheel (*a*) was placed above the runner (*b*), and both wheels had the same diameter. Since the turbine's outlet (*c*) was in the form of a cylindrical draft tube in which suction arose, it was possible to set the turbine wheels well above tail-race level and still make use of the head below the runner.

C An early Francis turbine. Turbines of this type can be mounted both vertically and horizontally and today are usually equipped with a helical flume casing which opens inwards, and with a draft tube. In the turbine shown here, water entered freely through the whole circumference and through the outer ring of guide vanes (*a*), which could be adjusted so that the amount of incoming water could be controlled. The inner runner (*b*) had curved blades, which increased the efficiency of the turbine.

D The Pelton turbine (**1**), an action turbine whose blades consisted of two ladles which were joined to an edge towards which a jet of water was aimed. The jet thus completely changes its direction, as is shown by the explanatory sketch at **2**, and this meant that the force of the water jet was utilized to the full. The nozzle (*a*), through which the water was forced, was improved considerably by a Californian, Abner Doble, who equipped it with a needle (*b*).

D2

D1

E In a tidal power plant, the turbines must have a high efficiency whether the tide is on its way out or in. Consequently, tubular turbine units are used for such power plants. In a tubular turbine unit, a Kaplan turbine (*a*) has its generator enclosed in a streamlined bulb (*b*), which is placed in the waterway. The power plant building (*c*) is erected above the turbine. (*d*) Water storage side. (*e*) Ocean side.

F The Kaplan turbine, a propeller turbine with a – usually – vertical shaft. In the Kaplan turbine, unlike all other propeller turbines, the runner's blades (*a*) were movable. The guide vanes (*b*) could also be turned and were automatically adjusted to an angle suitable to that of the blades by a "combiner", so that the turbine was efficient at different work-loads. A circular stay collar (*c*) absorbed the compressive forces acting on the flume casing (*d*). (*e*) Flume tube. All low-head, high-discharge propeller turbines had to be given amply dimensioned draft tubes (*f*), since the efficiency of the turbines depended on a strong pressure. However, if the height of the draft tube was too great, the water pressure around the runner became so low that cavitation posed a serious problem, and it was therefore sometimes necessary to mount the runner below tail-race level.

E

F

This intrigued Pelton. After long consideration, he realized that the power of the jet was best exploited when its direction was completely reversed by the blade. He changed the blade design to incorporate two buckets, whose edges were joined to form the middle of the blade. This split the jet of water in two, and the shape of the buckets caused both jets to reverse direction. One or more nozzles could be used to supply water to the wheel, which became known as the Pelton wheel or the jet-splitting double-bucket turbine. This type of turbine is especially suitable for large heads of water with a moderate or low rate of flow. Manufacture of the Pelton wheel began on an industrial scale in the 1880s.

A completely new idea in turbine design was put forward in the 1910s by an Austrian, Victor Kaplan (1876–1934). He had been trying to improve the Francis turbine, which, if the head of water is low, has a low effect, when he came upon a better idea and designed a turbine which had a vertical axle and a propeller-like rotor with variable-pitch blades. Kaplan patented his design in 1912 and 1913, and a number of the foremost turbine manufacturers began to produce the turbine under licence. In 1919, the first Kaplan turbine was installed, in a textile mill at Velm in Austria. It had an effect of 25.8 horsepower and a head of 7 ft 6 in (2.3 m). Several others of this size

A In China, this type of vertical-shaft mill is still used in combination with a chain-pump for irrigation and for pumping brine into salines. The sails look very much like the sails on a junk, and it seems probable that the construction used to be built of bamboo poles.

B A type of windmill (**1**) occurring in Poland and, possibly, Portugal in the eighteenth century. The mill had six guide vanes (*a*) and four sails (*b*) which were mounted round a vertical shaft; at **2**, the arrangement is shown as seen from above. A movable screen (*c*) was mounted round part of the circumference of the sails. It was used to adjust the action of the wind on the sails.

were taken into service elsewhere in the following year, and the future seemed bright for the Kaplan turbine. Just then, however, it was discovered that the rotor blades of the Velm turbine had become badly pitted. No reason could be found for this at first, but then Kaplan himself found the cause—cavitation, a phenomenon that occurs when a propeller turns at high speed under water; the flow of water around the propeller creates an area of low pressure on the suction side of the blade, and if the pressure falls enough, bubbles of steam are created. (Water can boil at temperatures way below 100°C—even at 0°C if the pressure is low enough.) When the steam bubbles condense on the blade, they corrode the surface.

This problem caused the manufacturers to have doubts about the Kaplan turbine, and they turned to other designs. At this time, 1920, the Swedish State Power Board was developing the hydroelectric possibilities of the Göta river. A power-station equipped with a Kaplan turbine was planned for Lilla Edet, and the Power Board asked the turbine manufacturer Ignaz Storek, of Kaplan's home town, Brünn, to build it. However, due to the cavitation problem, the project never got beyond the drawing board, so the State Board turned for help to a Swedish company, Karlstads Mekaniska Werkstad, which had built an experimental Kaplan turbine in 1914 and was now working on the cavitation problem. An order for a Kaplan turbine was placed, while a Francis turbine was ordered from another company, in case the Kaplan turbine should fail.

A hectic period of research and development now followed. The company's chief engineer, Olov Englesson (1884–1953), was in almost constant contact with Victor Kaplan. Among other things, the company developed a completely new steering system, in the form of a hydraulic servosystem, for turning the rotor blades. Against all the odds, the turbine was completed and taken into service in 1926, within the contracted time. It had an effect of 10,000 horsepower and a head of 20 ft (6.5 m). The diameter of the rotor was 19 ft (5.8 m). The Francis turbine was never needed, and the company eventually sold it.

Now that the ice was broken, many countries bought Kaplan turbines. Among Karlstads Mekaniska Werkstad's customers was the Soviet Union, which took delivery of eight 28-megawatt Kaplan turbines in 1929 and installed them at a power-station on the river Svir at Lake Ladoga. The Kaplan turbine is specially suited to low heads and large flows, and dominates the market in this field.

During the 1940s, an interesting variation of the Kaplan turbine was developed in Germany. Known as the bulb turbine, it consisted of a Kaplan turbine in which the electric generators were placed in a streamlined case and installed horizontally in the power-station's tunnel. After further development in France, twenty-four 10-megawatt reversible bulb turbines were installed at the Rance tidal power-station. In the Soviet Union in 1968, a small experimental tidal power-station with a bulb turbine was built at Kislogub on the Kola peninsula. The intention is to use the experience gained from this project to design and build very large tidal power-stations elsewhere.

Wind Power

It seems likely that Palaeolithic man used the power of the wind to propel his simple vessels through the water. The sail he used was possibly made of interwoven branches, or even a leafy branch on the tree trunk which formed the actual vessel! The art of cloth-making is ancient, and cloth sails were known to the Sumerians as early as 3,500 BC.

During the last few centuries BC, the art of rigging sails on fairly large ships was well developed in the Mediterranean. Some of the "toy-scale" machines built by the engineers of the Alexandrian school were powered by the wind, and it springs to mind that the sail could have inspired this choice of a power source. An even more direct connection between the sail and the wind motor is the type of windmill which can still be seen on the Greek island of Mykonos in the Cycladic archipelago. During Hellenic times, the inhabitants of this island were great seafarers, who had perfected the art of sailing. It can hardly be a coincidence that the sails on the Mykonos windmills are not made of wood but of sailcloth, which is stretched from a nearly-horizontal "mast" in the hub along wooden "spokes" whose ends are connected by ropes, so that the whole construction forms a wheel. At the beginning of the Christian era, there may have flourished a technically advanced civilization in this area, with Rhodes as its centre. While we know very little about this civilization, Derek de Solla Price believes that it probably produced the Antikythera device. We must hope that new finds will teach us more about this civilization, and thus also cast some light on the earliest uses of wind power in the West.

However, the first windmill is generally considered to have originated in Persia (today's Iran), in the seventh century AD. The exact place of origin is said to be the province of Seistan, which is described as "a country of wind and sand" by an Arabian geographer of the tenth century. He continues: "A characteristic of the area is that the power of the wind is used to drive pumps for watering gardens." It is also generally accepted that the prototype of the Seistan windmill was the wind-driven prayer-wheel, which was common in Central Asia at the time and had been described by Chinese travellers as early as the fifth century. The drive mechanism consisted of a paddle-wheel which rotated round a vertical shaft, not unlike a modern anemometer with cupped or hemispherical blades.

The Seistan windmills also had vertical shafts, which drove the millstones directly, without any form of intermediate gearing. One peculiarity of these windmills was that they were built in two storeys, with the sails on the ground floor and the millstones, one of them fixed, on the upper floor. This design is reminiscent of that of the first water-mills, but it is unlikely that there was any direct connection between the blades of the water-mill and those of the Seistan windmill, even if it is possible that the construction of the millstones in the water-mill may have influenced the design of those of the windmill. Besides, the two constructions appeared in entirely different types of landscape.

Opinions differ about how knowledge of the windmill reached Europe, but it is generally accepted that it travelled along two routes: one followed the spread of Islam through Morocco and Spain, and the other comprised the trade routes from Persia, across the Caspian Sea and along the Russian rivers, to the Baltic countries and northern Europe. Vikings who travelled east may also have contributed to the spread of this knowledge.

The first mention of a windmill in Europe occurs in a Papal Bull of 1105, in which the Abbot of Savigny is granted a concession to build windmills in the dioceses of Bayeux, Coutances, and Evreux. By the early thirteenth century, the windmill had spread throughout most of Europe. It was most popular in Holland, where, from the late thirteenth century, it was used for pumping water and draining land. In 1341, the bishop of Utrecht tried to get a monopoly of all the wind which blew in his diocese! As Lewis Mumford points out, this alone should underline the enormous importance of the windmill at this time in Holland.

Windmills are classified by the way in which their sails are kept constantly facing the wind. One of the two main types is the post-mill, the mill house of which rests on bearings mounted in a fixed foundation of wood or stone. The larger and heavier the mill, the more difficult it is to turn. As a consequence, the second main type,

C Tower-mills with eight to twelve lateen-type sails are still a typical feature of the Aegean landscape. The origins of this type of mill are not known, but it is thought that it was inspired by the tower-mill which came into use in western Europe in the fourteenth century.

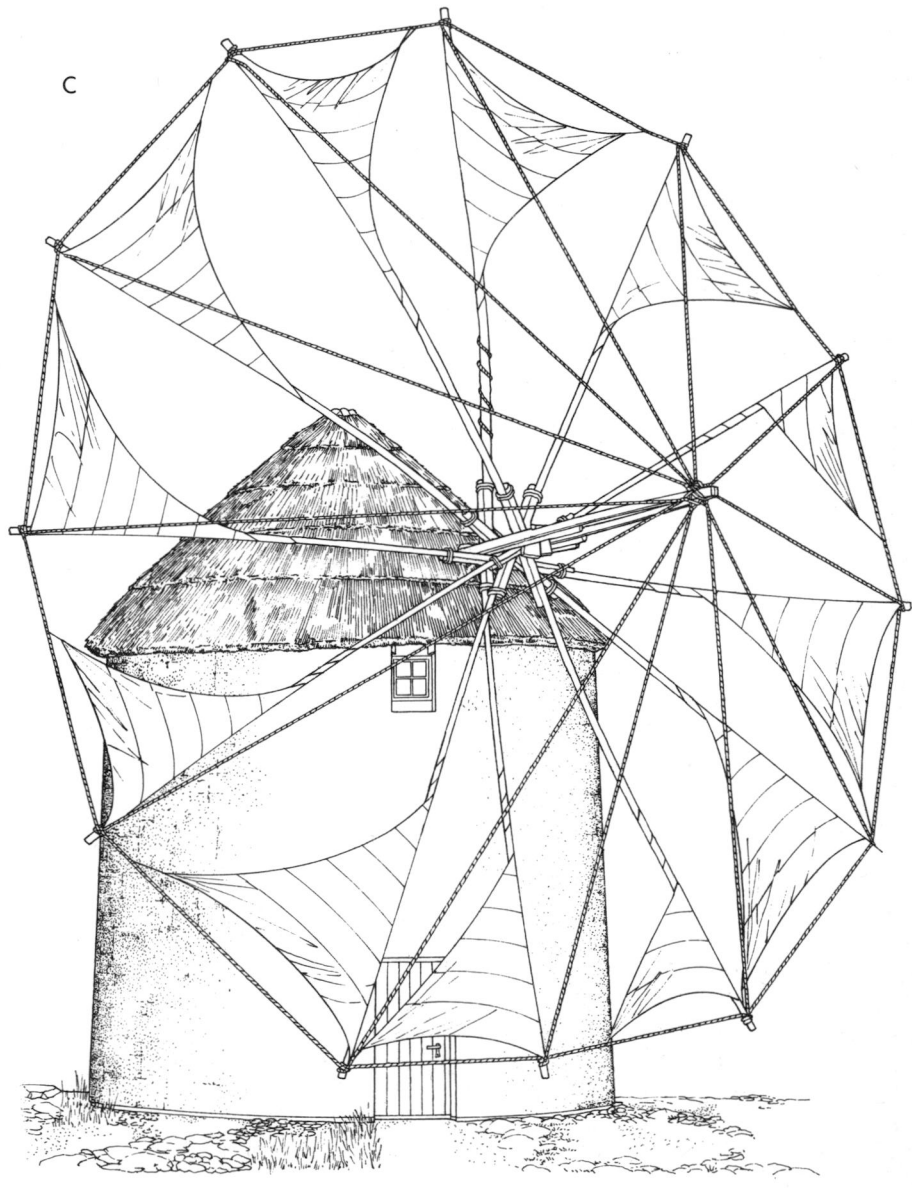

109

A This type of post-mill, which occurs in Denis Diderot's *Encyclopédie*, was common in many parts of eighteenth-century Europe. The entire mill had to be rotated when the wind changed direction.

B The interior of a mill as shown in Diderot's *Encyclopédie*. The miller could control the speed of the millstone by means of a brake (*a*).

C Ramelli was the first to depict windmill interiors. This tower-mill is one of several mill types found in his book of 1588, *Le diverse et artificiose machine*. The system used for rotating the top cap can be clearly seen.

D A Dutch tower-mill of the early eighteenth century. From Peter Linperch's *Architecture mechanica of Moole-Boek van eenige opstallen van Moolens nevens hare Gronden*, published in Amsterdam in 1727.

the tower-mill, was developed. In this, the windshaft of the sails is mounted on bearings in the top cap, the rotatable upper part of the mill house. This type came into use as early as the late fourteenth century.

In the following centuries, wind power was harnessed to perform many other tasks besides grinding grain. In the fifteenth century, wind-driven sawmills were in use, and wind-powered machines were raising and crushing ore at mines.

Just as the water-wheel had done, the windmill fired the imaginations of inventors. An illustrated manuscript of the 1320s, compiled by the monk Walter de Milimete, shows many remarkable uses to which the windmill could be put, one of them being to hurl beehives into besieged castles! (The same manuscript, by the way, contains the first known picture of a cannon.) At the end of the fifteenth century, it was the ambition of several Renaissance engineers, among them Taccola, to build a wind-driven carriage.

An unusual application of wind power was to be found in London of the mid-eighteenth century. A wind engine was erected over the impressive portal of Newgate prison to drive a ventilation system, which had been designed by Dr. Stephen Hale, a biologist. Sanitary conditions, especially ventilation, were then generally very poor in England, due partly to the extraordinary window tax that was levied on residences and prisons alike and charged according to the size of the windows in a building. Hale's ventilation system was installed at Newgate in 1752 and, later, at several other prisons. It was said to have benefited the health of the inmates.

The introduction of windmills and water-mills had a great effect on the science of mechanical engineering and resulted in a number of new trades, from mill building to maintenance, the latter normally being carried out by the miller and his apprentices. These tradesmen were the predecessors of today's mechanical engineers.

For centuries, the work carried out by engineers, *mechanici*, "art masters", or whatever they were called, had been governed by rule of thumb and common sense. It was not until the eighteenth century that attention began to be directed towards the theoretical background of the increasingly impressive machines which were appearing. The works of Isaac Newton (1642–1727) on classical mechanics were by then widespread and contributed to this awakening interest. In the 1690s, Christopher Polhem had built a machine to compare the performances of various types of water-wheels with different blade constructions, etc. He applied his conclusions in practice at the Falu mine and when building the Stjernsund works in 1700. In his descriptions of the results of these experiments, Polhem came very close to defining the unit of power. However, it was James Watt who eventually, in 1783, introduced this unit, the horsepower, which he defined as the work needed to lift 33,000 lb one foot in one minute.

In the 1750s, the Englishman John Smeaton (1724–92) carried out detailed comparative studies of power obtained from water and wind. He tested the results in practice before presenting them to the Royal Society in London in 1759. Smeaton's *Experimental Enquiry Concerning the Natural Power of Water and Wind* came on the eve of the appearance of steam power. Widely read in Europe, it certainly contributed to the fact that wind and water power were used in many places alongside steam until well into the twentieth century.

The role of wind and water power in the early stages of industrialization has often been underrated, for until steam took over, these natural forces provided the power in most factories. Mention has already been made of the fact that Sir Richard Arkwright's famous spinning-machine was driven by a water-wheel; another important machine of this era was driven by a dog-wheel!

E Through the ages, many attempts have been made to use wind power for different purposes. In ancient China, for example, wheelbarrows (1) equipped with sails occurred, and as late as the nineteenth century, a sail-powered cart (2) on rails was constructed. The latter vehicle had, however, little or no success.

F This wind-powered vehicle was constructed during the Renaissance by an Italian engineer called Roberto Valturio (?–1484).

A This device was used by Christopher Polhem at the beginning of the eighteenth century to test the efficiency of, for example, different types of water-wheels. The results of Polhem's experiments were, however, not very reliable, since he failed to realize that the relationship between his results and the results which would be obtained from experiments with full-scale water-wheels and machinery is more complicated than one might be led to believe. The first reliable investigation into the efficiency of different types of water-wheels was carried out by John Smeaton, who published his results in 1757.

B A cross-section of John Smeaton's model of a device with which the power of an undershot water-wheel could be measured. Water was raised into a cistern (a) by means of a plunger-pump (b). The cistern also contained a float with a rod (c) marked in inches. When a sluice (d) was opened, water ran towards the water-wheel (e), round whose shaft a rope (f) was wound. The rope ran over two pulleys (g) and was attached to a beam (h). In one of the pulleys hung a pan loaded with weights. If slightly modified, this device could also be used for experiments with overshot water-wheels.

CHAPTER 5
PRIME MOVERS II:
Steam and Combustion Engines

We have already come across the early attempts to exploit the power of steam—for instance, Hero's *aelopile* and Archimedes' thoughts on a steam cannon, later taken up by Leonardo da Vinci. But what stopped the development? And why did no one take over where Hero and Archimedes left off? (We must disregard Leonardo, as his sketches and notes were hidden in archives until they had lost their novelty.) Some have attempted to answer these questions by saying that there was no need of steam power during antiquity and the Middle Ages, as there was such a good supply of cheap manpower available. If that were the case, could they not just as well have done without wind and water power? Of course not. The powerful princes and feudal lords would have become even more powerful, had they had access to steam-driven prime movers. Their engineers would certainly have designed warships with paddle-wheels driven by steam-power instead of capstans turned by oxen, and assault vehicles driven by steam instead of the wind.

It is nearer the truth to say that, before steam power could be put to use, a knowledge of certain scientific principles was needed, principles which are now considered basic but which were quite obscure until the mid-eighteenth century. For example, well into that century, it was generally believed that water was an element, and what happened when matter burnt was, chemically and physically, a mystery. Did a magical substance, phlogiston, leave a burning object? Fire gave heat, but what was heat, and what happened when water was heated and converted to steam? These questions were first answered in the seventeenth and eighteenth centuries, and it was also then that steam power was born, developed, and attained its majority.

From the days of Leonardo onwards, many people, both scientists and engineers, had been fascinated by the properties of steam. Their imaginations were probably fired by the works of Hero and Archimedes, which had been translated, adapted, and disseminated during the Renaissance. One can discern Hero's *aelopile* behind the imaginative "prime movers" suggested by the Italians Giovanni Battista della Porta (1538–1615), Vannocio Biringuccio (1480–1538?), and Giovanni Branca (1571–1640). In the seventeenth century, the great French engineer Salomon de Caus (1576–1626) experimented with steam pressure in spherical containers and found that, via a pipe into such a container, he could produce a magnificent water jet for his fountains with their dancing and playing statuettes. Caus built full-scale versions of what Hero probably built only on a toy scale.

However, the man who laid the foundations for the breakthrough of steam technology was the versatile mayor of Magdeburg, Otto von Guericke (1602–86). He, too, had been influenced by the engineers of the Alexandrian school and, among other things, considerably improved Ctesibius's air pump, which he later used when experi-

Giovanni Branca's somewhat naive proposal for a steam-turbine-powered stamp-mill, a device which was used to crush ore before it was put into the smelting furnace.

113

A Papin's steam-engine. Steam was fed from the boiler (*a*) to a vessel (*b*) in which there was a float serving as a piston (*c*). Papin planned to fill a container (*d*) in the piston with red-hot scrap-iron in order to superheat the steam, but in reality, this could not be done. When the steam pushed the piston downwards, the clack-valve (*e*) of the container for water to be pumped was closed. Simultaneously, the clack-valve (*f*) of the ascending pipe (*g*) was opened, and the water was pumped into a cistern (*h*), from where it flowed to the fountains. When the piston had reached the bottom of *b*, a tap (*i*) was closed to stop the flow of steam. Simultaneously, a tap (*j*) on *c* was opened, and the steam escaped. Because of the water pressure, *f* was then closed and *e* opened, and more water poured in. (*k*) Safety valve.

menting with vacuums, or the "space devoid of air", his most famous experiment being that with the Magdeburg hemispheres, two large hemispheres of copper; not even four pairs of horses could pull them apart once, having been joined together to form an air-tight sphere, the air had been evacuated from them. Another experiment provided Guericke with dramatic evidence of the pressure of air: his air pump had been connected to a spherical container made of copper plate, and two strong men were working the pump with all their might. A deafening bang—and the sphere crumpled as if made of paper! This, the first known implosion (the opposite of explosion) inspired Guericke to use the vacuum to produce power. He realized immediately that *die Kraft aus dem Nichts* ("power from nothing") could do useful work.

Today, the vacuum and the pressure of air are obvious phenomena, but to the seventeenth-century scholar they were matters for profound philosophical discussion. The philosophers of antiquity designated air as one of the four elements. But what was air? Was it anything at all? In the 1660s, when the English king Charles II and his court visited the Royal Society, they were shown an experiment which attempted to weigh air. The courtiers laughed themselves silly; how could anyone ever think of weighing air? There is nothing in air, anyone can see that!

It is said that Guericke solved one of the mysteries of air by following his nose. One day when he was holding a rose, he noticed that, when he held it a little away from himself, the scent was not so strong. The air diluted the scent, he thought, just as water dilutes a drop of red wine dropped into it. In other words, air must consist of matter! This may be a later rationalization or a poetic improvement of what actually happened, but as the old Italian proverb puts it, *se non è vèro, è ben trovato*, "it may not be true, but it is a good story". In the first experiment with the copper sphere, the sphere was filled with water, so it could be seen that matter was being pumped out. But after learning from the rose, Guericke pumped out only air. That was when the bang came, the starting signal, as it were, for the work which eventually led to the utilization of the "power from nothing".

Guericke has been called the "father of the power machine", and rightly so, although such a sweeping statement should only be accepted with a certain reservation. In the mid-1650s, he published accounts of his experiments with vacuums, and all over Europe the hemisphere experiments were repeated, with spheres both large and small.

Some years later, the pioneering Dutch scientist Christiaen Huygens (1629—95) was living in Paris, where he was assisted by a young French doctor, Denis Papin (1647—1714), in his experiments with high and low pressures. Papin had worked earlier with pressure; in 1681, he published his most famous invention, the "digester", or pressure cooker, for which he had invented the safety valve. Later in the decade, he and Huygens spent some time trying to evacuate the air from a cylinder by igniting gunpowder in it. They soon realized that the pressure in the cylinder did not fall, but rose considerably. They then designed what could be called an internal combustion engine, borrowing the idea of a piston inside a cylinder from Guericke; they intended to use this gunpowder engine to raise water. They offered Louis XIV an improved version of the engine to pump water for the Versailles fountains, but Colbert, the pragmatic minister of finance, declined the offer.

Papin continued his experiments with the vacuum, from 1687 as a professor in Marburg, Germany. He designed a very efficient, double-acting air pump and, according to the German philosopher and mathematician Gottfried Wilhelm von Leibniz (1646–1716), became the first man really to understand what a gas is. Papin now began to study the properties of steam and discovered that what he had been seeking ensued when steam was cooled and condensed. The "power from nothing" had been captured! Papin realized the importance of his discovery, writing triumphantly that what he had tried to achieve with gunpowder could be obtained simply and cheaply by heating water and cooling the steam. With this method, he continued, it would be easy to build machines to drive mills, propel ships against the wind, drive self-propelling carriages . . . In a visionary moment in a letter to the great Leibniz, he enlarged on the blessings the new machines would bring to mankind, when they took over all the heavy work.

Papin was now in the service of the Duke of Hesse, to whom he showed a model of his machine, describing with enthusiasm how it would function as a full-scale machine. There were, however, no ironworks that could produce the large cylinders necessary, nor craftsmen capable of building such a machine. Papin suggested that the duke should finance a factory to manufacture machines, where craftsmen could be trained to assemble and operate them. Despite Papin's assurances of its commercial viability, the duke did not have the money for such an enterprise. Besides, the good duke knew little of natural science and had difficulty in following the scholarly professor's enthusiastic explanations. What he wanted was to improve his gardens in Kassel by installing fountains, like the French king had done at Versailles. Could not Papin design a machine to power fountains?

Of course he could. And that was when his real problems started. After many attempts, he completed a model of a steam pump and delighted the duke with it. He then built it as a full-scale machine and installed it at Kassel in one of the palace towers. Papin had decided to use steam at over atmospheric pressure to drive a piston in a cylinder. The steam boiler was based on Papin's digester with a safety valve, and the plant took a year to build. When the steam pump was tried out, everything went according to plan: the fountains played, the duke was delighted. Then, the ascending pipe to the water tank burst. Another was made—pipes were not kept in stock in those days—but that burst, too. At the height of Papin's troubles, Leibniz wrote to Papin that an Englishman, Thomas Savery, had manufactured a steam pump powered by steam at over atmospheric pressure and by the vacuum obtained when steam condensed.

This was too much for Papin, whose relations with the duke had become somewhat strained. He decided to leave Marburg and settle in London where, in his youth, he had been active in the Royal Society. He planned a memorable return, heading up the Thames in his own paddle-wheeler, which would be driven by steam! Plenty of myths have been woven about this "steamboat", and a statue in Marburg represents Papin holding a model of the boat in his hands. Like so many others in the history of technology, this myth was probably created in retrospect. He certainly arrived in London around 1704 and, in the following year, modified Savery's pump. The only recognition this got, however, was when Jacob Leupold (1674–1727) included it as an interesting machine in his art book *Theatrum machinarum*. Papin lived his final years in poverty and died in 1714.

Thomas Savery (1650–1715) had patented his steam pump in 1698, calling it the "miner's friend", as it was to be used for pumping water from mines. However, it suffered in part from the same deficiencies as had Papin's, for while the demonstration model in his workshop in London worked very well, in practice the ascending pipe caused problems. The steam pressure rose to as much as ten atmospheres, and joints and pipes often burst, or the steam boiler exploded, as there was no safety valve. But Savery must have been a clever businessman, and a number of steam pumps of this design were in use during the first years of the eighteenth century—one of them for powering fountains!

B Savery's steam-engine had neither a piston nor a safety-valve. (**1**) Steam from the boiler was fed into a vessel (*a*), and the water in it was thus forced out through an ascending pipe (*b*) by way of a clack-valve (*c*). When *a* had been emptied, the flow of steam was stopped, and the vessel was cooled by means of cold water, which was sprayed over it from vessel *d*. Since a

vacuum was created when the steam was condensed, water was again sucked into *a* by way of a clack-valve (*e*). While *a* was being cooled, steam was fed into the water-filled vessel *f*, which was emptied, cooled, and refilled with water. (*g*) Water inlet. (**2**) The steam-engine in action in a water-logged mine.

B Newcomen's atmospheric steam-engine worked in the following way. (1) Steam was admitted into the cylinder (*a*) by a tap (*b*); the piston (*c*) was then supposed to be forced up by the pressure of the steam, which was not, however, very great, and the piston was drawn up mainly by the weight of the pump rod (*d*). The power stroke began when the tap (*b*) was closed. (2) At the same time, another tap (*e*) was opened, spurting cold water into the cylinder, thus condensing the steam, turning it into a very small amount of water. The external air pressure then forced the piston down.

If the piston had fitted tightly against the cylinder wall, the cylinder would have been practically

A In 1712, Thomas Newcomen's first atmospheric steam-engine was built at Dudley Castle, near Wolverhampton. This print, published in 1719, was accompanied by a description of the engine. It is interesting to note that, here, the design is called a "steam engine", a name not previously found in print. Newcomen, like Triewald, always used the name "fire and air machine", sometimes abbreviated to "fire machine". This atmospheric steam-engine is estimated to have developed a power just over 5 horsepower, with twelve strokes per minute. About 38.5 gallons (175 l) were pumped up per stroke.

empty of air when the steam condensed. But one of the difficulties with this engine was the roughness of the cylinder wall. The cylinder was cast, since there were then no machines for cutting workpieces internally. The piston was sealed as well as possible by a gasket of leather or rope. To improve the seal, what is known as a water seal was added; water was poured—or dripped, if that was all that was necessary—onto the top of the piston by a tap (f). Due to these imperfections, only about half of the theoretically potential negative pressure in the cylinder is estimated to have been exploited during each power stroke.

"Power from Nothing" Returns

Thomas Newcomen (1663–1729) was a merchant from Dartmouth, England, who traded in mining equipment. In the course of his business, he often visited the mines in Staffordshire, which had great problems with water. Newcomen became interested in the mechanization of mine pumps. This was in the 1690s, at about the same time as Savery was working on his invention. Nevertheless, Newcomen's work was totally independent of Savery's "miner's friend", although he was aware of Papin's ideas for a prime mover based on the creation of a vacuum by the condensation of steam. In 1702, Newcomen wrote for advice to the scientist Robert Hooke (1635–1703) at the Royal Society. Hooke was a man held in high esteem at the time; he confirmed that the principle of Papin's prime mover was correct, but he doubted if it would be possible to produce a piston which could fit tightly in a cylinder. Newcomen, aided by a mechanic called John Calley, continued his experiments, in spite of Hooke's discouragement. In 1712, after many years of experiments, the first "atmospheric" steam-engine was built at Dudley Castle, near Wolverhampton, in Staffordshire.

Thus did Newcomen and Calley become the first to build a practical prime mover in which "power from nothing" performed the work delivered by the machine. Here, the steam was only an intermediary agent, being condensed to create a vacuum. The air pressure was the source of power. The Newcomen engine is, therefore, called the atmospheric steam-engine or, to give it its contemporary name, the fire and air engine, which is a vivid description—the fire gave heat to transform the water to steam, but it was the air which acted.

Newcomen was not a scientist, he was an addicted amateur, and typical of his age. But he knew enough to seek the advice of people with more insight than himself, and he surrounded himself with those who had practical or theoretical qualifications. John Calley was one of the former; Mårten Triewald one of the latter. Triewald (1691–1747) was a very talented Swedish scientist and engineer who, in 1716, left a Sweden badly hit by Charles XII's wars and moved to England, where he received a sound education in natural science at the Royal Society, working as the assistant of John T. Desaguliers. He made friends with the aged Newton and, for some time, worked as Thomas Newcomen's assistant. Triewald helped to build at least one atmospheric steam-engine, and he was the first to give a physically correct description of its *modus operandi*. After his return to Sweden in 1726, Triewald tried to persuade Swedish mining companies to build a Newcomen engine, and the Dannemora mines commissioned one. This engine, to which Triewald had made several useful modifications, was completed in 1728, but it was only six years later that he wrote a comprehensive description of it. His account, "A Description of a Fire and Air Engine at the Dannemora Mines", was, unfortunately, not made available in any internationally useful language until 1928, when an English translation was published by the Newcomen Society, then celebrating the 200th anniversary of the engine. (The Newcomen Society, founded in 1920, is one of the oldest associations of people interested in the history of technology.)

Since Savery's 1698 patent for his steam pump, the "miner's friend", was so comprehensive, Newcomen was unable to patent his atmospheric steam-engine. Into the bargain, Savery had managed to prolong his patent until 1733, so that it greatly exceeded the normal fourteen years. However, Triewald states that, early on, Newcomen bought part of Savery's patent rights from the consortium which administered them after Savery's death in 1715.

After the first atmospheric steam-engine was taken into service in 1712, a few more were built, but the Newcomen design was not made fully practicable until the mid-1720s. Newcomen met the same problems as Denis Papin had before him: a technology much more advanced than that used in the construction of wind and water-mills was required to produce the various parts of his engine, especially its valves, pipes, taps, and joints. The crafts had not yet caught up with theoretical developments. Triewald also had great problems with the Dannemora engine, which started work in June, 1728. Its pump rods and bearings were too weak to stand its characteristically violent jerks, and to start with, the engine was in action for only a couple of days at a time between repairs. One reason the pump rods broke so easily was that the cylinder had a higher effect than was normal with a Newcomen engine. Triewald had achieved this by finishing the inside of the cylinder so well that a tight seal between cylinder and piston resulted. It took two years to pump the mine reasonably dry, and by then, the engine was on its last legs. In 1731, the enraged mine owners sued Triewald, who had to pay heavy damages. This trial, which dragged on in various stages for over ten years, also started a debate about the atmospheric steam-engine. General opinion held the design to be worthless. In his own defence, in 1734, Triewald published the account we have mentioned. This account contained an illustration of the engine.

Triewald was convicted by court of law, and his engine by miners and public opinion. Not until 1768 were the Swedes to try another atmospheric steam-engine, this time at the Persberg mines in Värmland.

Despite the heavy strain of the lengthy court case, Triewald continued his work on the steam-engine. In 1976, some of his papers were discovered, and among them were his drawings for an ingenious arrangement that would change the engine's reciprocating movement to a rotary movement. He intended that the engine be used also for raising ore. For understandable reasons, he never managed to find a backer for this idea.

Newcomen had had great difficulty in sealing the piston in the cylinder. In those days, cylinders with diameters greater than 20–30 in (c. 50–75 cm) could be neither cast nor produced in any other way. The insides of cylinders had to be finished by hand with chisels and files. The top of the piston was usually fitted with a leather washer covered with a thin layer of water to form what was known as a water seal. Due to the inevitably poor fit of the piston, the air pressure on the piston could not be used to its full potential.

The taps and valves on the earliest engines were probably operated by hand, but they were soon mechanized. There are many nice little stories about how this came about, all most probably unfounded. A favourite tells of a shepherd-boy who was given the job of looking after the engine. He got bored with this after a while, so he attached some pieces of string and metal here and there, and the engine functioned automatically. No doubt heart-warming, but very likely just another of the myths we have come across so far.

After Savery's patent had expired in 1733 (Newcomen had died four years earlier), several atmospheric steam-engines were built in England. By the 1760s, more than a hundred were in use, most of them in coal-mines. The engines became bigger and bigger but were still built according to the original design, with few modifications. The atmospheric steam-engine was severely criticized, mainly because of its high fuel consumption and the heavy wear and tear of the material. It was said that an iron-mine was needed to build and maintain one, and a coal-mine to keep one running!

Newcomen's successors in this field were no more than craftsman-mechanics and, as machine designers, had little vision. Oddly enough, none of the great natural scientists, either in England or anywhere else, took any interest in the physical principles of the atmospheric steam-engine. It was left to an engineer whom we have met already, John Smeaton, to do this, and he did it just as meticu-lously as he had conducted his pioneering experiments with prime movers driven by wind and water.

In his youth, Smeaton, who had grown up in a coal-mining area in Yorkshire, had become interested in the Newcomen engine. Later on in life, when several great engineering achievements had brought him fame, he took up this interest again and, in 1767, designed an atmospheric steam-engine for the pumps at the New River waterworks in London, which had previously been powered by a horse-wheel. Although Smeaton's engine probably worked better than the horse-wheel, its efficiency was poor. He therefore built an experimental atmospheric steam-engine in his workshop and tested many different designs and machine elements. He also collected all the information available about the construction and use of more than a hundred Newcomen engines which were active in England at the time. Smeaton then used this information to try to find a connection between different construction data, such as cylinder diameter and length of piston stroke, and the efficiency of the engines. The experience gained by this research he then applied to the experimental engine.

The greatest fault in the machines studied by Smeaton was the one of which Hooke had warned Newcomen and which Papin had also pointed out about a hundred years before, namely, the impossibility of sealing the piston tightly against the wall of the cylinder. As we have pointed out, there was neither the technology nor the craftsmen available to build tightly fitting pistons and cylinders. The craftsmen usually employed to make cylinders were founders of ornaments or bells, used to working in bronze or brass and able to handle the large charges necessary for casting such objects as an equestrian statue or a large church bell. The cylinder for Triewald's Dannemora engine, for example, was cast by the bell-founder Ad. Meijer of Stockholm. But what the founders of the time had no experience of was finishing the surface; indeed, many bell-founders considered a rough surface inside the bell very good for its tone!

The need for a satisfactory internal finish of the cast cylinder led Smeaton to design a machine in which a steel cutting-edge was attached to a rotating axle which was introduced into the centre of the cylinder. The machine worked on the same principle as a modern boring mill, but the idea it embodied appeared in the sixteenth century, when Biringuccio suggested a similar device for boring cannon barrels. Smeaton's design was later improved by the famous machine-tool maker John Wilkinson.

Once Smeaton had produced a cylinder with a really smooth inner surface, he could achieve a better seal than hitherto between the piston and the wall of the cylinder. This meant that his engine could exploit fifty per cent more of the atmospheric pressure than the majority of the engines which he had studied. Further modifications enabled the efficiency to be increased even more, and the engine which Smeaton built in 1772 for the Long Benton coal-mine was two or three times more efficient than the Newcomen engines. But powering even Smeaton's atmospheric steam-engine still required the coal-mine of which Newcomen's critics had spoken; the thermal efficiency of the most successful version was only about one per cent.

Russian Interlude

At about the same time that Smeaton was busy trying to improve Newcomen's engine, a remarkable design was invented in Russia. This was the first continuously operating atmospheric steam-engine, and it was invented by Ivan Polsunov (1728–66). His early death unhappily prevented his technically interesting creation from becoming known, either in Russia or in western Europe, until a hundred years later.

Polsunov, the son of a low-ranking officer, grew up in simple circumstances in Yekaterinburg (now Sverdlovsk). At an early age, he showed signs of great technical talent and, by the age of nineteen, was employed as an engineer at the Altai silver-mines, which were owned by the czar's family and were expanding in the 1740s and 1750s. Polsunov distinguished himself by the great inventiveness of the improvements he introduced to the smelting and mining plants which were then being built. It is probable that he occasionally visited the mines' administrative headquarters at St. Petersburg (now Leningrad), which were situated beside the czar's Summer Gardens, a park built in the French style and based on Louis XIV's gardens at Versailles. With his burning interest in machines, Polsunov would have seized the opportunity of studying the atmospheric steam-engine built there in 1717 by John T. Desaguliers, the friend and teacher of Mårten Triewald. This machine drove the pumps which provided the many fountains in the Gardens with water. Whatever can be said about the Sun King—and a lot has been said—he has certainly had a considerable influence on technical development!

In early 1763, Polsunov had worked out a detailed suggestion for a double-cylindered atmospheric steam-engine, in which the counter-acting pistons achieved a direct rotary motion. The purpose of the design was to create an engine capable of driving any kind of machine found in a mine. While the Altai and other mines in the Urals, unlike those of many parts of England, Sweden, and Central Europe had no problems with water, they still needed power to drive machines for raising and crushing ore and for powering the bellows of the smelting works. As many silver and gold mines can be worked only for a year or so, Polsunov designed his engine so that it could easily be dismantled and moved to another site.

Prospects for Polsunov's engine were, therefore, exceptionally promising. The mines' administration thought so, too, and disregarding all red tape, gave Polsunov a completely free hand to put his ideas into practice. However, when he set to work on his magnificent engine late in 1763, he had the bitter experience of not being able to find craftsmen who were able to build it: the same fate which had befallen Papin, Newcomen, and Smeaton. Assisted only by some apprentice smiths, Polsunov had to build the engine with his own hands. The work must have made great physical demands on Polsunov, for it broke his health. He contracted a deficiency disease, and, in May, 1766, just as his engine was ready to be tested, he died, only thirty-eight years of age. A week after his death, the engine, an impressive structure about 43 ft (13 m) high, was put to work driving four pairs of bellows in the smelting works at the Kolivano-Voskresensky silver-mine. The air was blasted to three smelting furnaces, but the engine was built to supply air to another nine furnaces, which were to be built when the smelting works was expanded; the surplus air was now allowed to escape. The engine was in use until November, 1766, and the fault which then occurred could probably have been repaired easily if the designer had been there. But neither the mining engineers nor the craftsmen who had helped build the engine could get it going again. It was as difficult for them, with the general technical education of the time, to understand the physical principles of the *modus operandi* of the atmospheric steam-engine as it would be for a modern audience of laymen to understand how a nuclear power-station works.

Polsunov's contribution to the development of the atmospheric steam-engine must be seen as a definite breakthrough, mainly due to the fact that rotary motion was produced by the two cylinders, an idea totally unknown to Newcomen, Triewald, and Smeaton. It is unfortunate that death prevented Polsunov from publishing his invention. It remained unknown both in Russia and the rest of the world, despite the great reward given to Polsunov's family by the

Smeaton's first atmospheric steam-engine was put into service in 1772 and worked in essentially the same way as Newcomen's engine. Considerable construction improvements had, however, been made. Smeaton's engine, shown here in section, had a cylinder (a) of considerably greater diameter than that common in Newcomen's engines, and the length of the piston (b) stroke was great — 7 ft (2.13 m). The

two boilers, only one of which (c) can be seen here, were built of rivetted iron plates. Newcomen's boilers were usually manufactured of copper plates combined with lead plates, a construction which was not very durable. In order to lessen the exchange of heat between the piston and the steam, Smeaton provided the under-side of the piston with a layer of wood.

A The first continuously working atmospheric steam-engine was built by Ivan Polsunov and was completed in 1766 in the city of Barnaul. The boiler, which was made from forged copper, had two safety valves (only one of them, *b*, can be seen here) and could be emptied by means of a cock (*c*). Further, there were two pipes with cocks (*d*), with which the water level in the boiler could be checked; if the upper cock was opened, only steam should escape, whereas water should run out when the other cock was opened. Steam from the boiler was admitted through a pipe system (*e*) to the two copper cylinders (*f*). The valves at the bottoms of the cylinders were opened and closed to alternately admit steam in one and cooling water in the other cylinder by a rack-and-pinion device (*g*), powered

by a chain (*h*), and two bars (*i*) which were connected by a chain (*j*). These chains ran over a wheel (*k*) which also carried the chain (*l*) connecting the two piston rods (*m*). The wheel (*k*) was thus rocked to and fro, and this motion was transmitted by way of an endless chain (*n*) to another wheel (*o*), which also carried the chain (*p*) working the two bellows (*q*). These were equipped with weights which squeezed them together after they had been filled with air. A water tank (*r*) supplied cooling water to condense the steam, for use as a water seal, and for the boiler. Condensate and heated cooling water collected in a tank (*t*) and was pumped to *r*.

James Watt

In the 1760s, a young man who was greatly to influence the development of the "fire and air engine" made his entrance on the stage of technology. This was James Watt, who began his career as "Mathematical Instrument Maker to the University" in Glasgow. A model of Newcomen's engine which had been used in the physics department had broken down, and a clockmaker summoned all the way from London could not get it going again. Watt succeeded, but the engine ran out of steam after only five strokes, and it had to "catch its breath" before it could be started again. Watt wondered why the engine needed so much steam. After all, it was the atmospheric pressure which did the work!

He came to the conclusion that the steam kept losing heat when cold water was injected to make the steam condense; this cooled the cylinder, too, which did not improve matters: without actually defining the concept, Watt had discovered latent heat. The potential heat of the steam was wasted by cooling, and this was the main reason for the high fuel consumption.

Watt's remedy was to condense the steam in a separate cylinder, a condenser, which he placed next to the working cylinder. To improve thermal efficiency still more, he fitted a steam jacket round the working cylinder, to keep it as hot as the steam which entered it. Watt made a model of his engine; it worked perfectly. In 1769, he was granted a patent for "A New Method of Lessening the Consumption of Steam and Fuel in Fire Engines"; this is one of the more important patents in the history of technology.

Watt shared his patent with an industrialist, John Roebuck, who financed the construction of a full-scale experimental engine. But Roebuck ran into financial difficulties before the engine could be tested. Watt then got in touch with the great industrialist Matthew Boulton (1728–1809), whose factory lay in Soho, near Birmingham, and who had previously expressed interest in Watt's engine, recognizing its great advantages over Newcomen's engine. Watt then secured an extension of his patent until 1800 (it should have expired in 1783), and in 1775, he and Boulton formed a company, Boulton & Watt, whose factory was the first in the world to manufacture prime movers on an industrial scale.

Matthew Boulton, the son of an art-loving iron merchant, was an experienced man of the world, at his ease in the company of artists and writers. In the 1760s, when Benjamin Franklin spent a few years in London, Boulton contacted him in order to discuss the issues of the day. Franklin had been sent to London by the American colonists to represent them in negotiations with the British government on such issues as the hated stamp duty. The infrequent negotiations gave him plenty of time to devote to his passion, natural science. He and Boulton became good friends and often discussed how they could improve Newcomen's engine. Boulton was worried by a serious problem. He wanted to extend his factory, but the water-wheels which provided the power in it were not able to drive any more machines. On Franklin's advice, Boulton built a model of an improved "fire engine". But Franklin was recalled to his own country, and his place as Boulton's companion in science was taken by James Watt.

Both Boulton and Watt took a great interest in contemporary ideas and were involved with the humanities as well as with the natural sciences. They were founder-members of the famous Lunar Society, a club of artists, writers, scientists, and industrialists which met to discuss the issues of the day. The society met at the home of one of its members every month, on an evening when the moon was full—to allow the members "to enjoy the advantage of a moonlit path homewards". This was before the advent of street lighting, although gas lighting was on the way.

A

As soon as they were put into commission, the first two engines made by Boulton & Watt aroused great public interest. One had a cylinder diameter of 50 in (127 cm) and was installed at a coal-mine in Staffordshire. The other was used to work the bellows of a blast-furnace owned by the John Wilkinson mentioned previously. The fame of these "fire engines", which had a fuel consumption of a third of that of the old coal-eating Newcomen engines, spread rapidly among industrialists in England. The two partners were inundated with orders, especially from the owners of tin-mines in Cornwall, where coal was more expensive than in any other part of the country. Business flourished, and the Soho factories were extended and equipped with the very latest machinery. How Denis Papin would have loved those workshops! His dreams, in which he had tried to interest the Duke of Hesse a hundred years earlier, had been fulfilled by these two men. The Soho workshops attracted many technically talented young men and became a forcing ground for generations of mechanical engineers.

An important factor in Boulton & Watt's success was a clever business idea they had: a form of "leasing". Their engines were not sold outright but were made available to customers on condition that they agreed to pay a fee that equalled the savings they made in fuel cost by using a Boulton & Watt engine instead of a Newcomen engine of similar size.

The instrument maker turned factory-owner was not satisfied with this success but worked tirelessly to improve his engine. In 1781, as we have mentioned, he invented the sun-and-planet drive to solve the problem of converting the piston's reciprocating motion to rotary motion. In the following year, he doubled the engine's output by making it double-acting. As the piston in Watt's double-acting steam-engine worked in both directions, the chains connecting the piston rod and the pump rod to the main beam had to be replaced by rods. That is how parallelogram steering, which Watt later called his masterpiece, was invented. In 1787, the centrifugal governor, which permitted automatic speed regulation, was introduced, and seven years later, a crankshaft came to be used to replace the sun-and-planet drive.

The Century of Steam

The nineteenth century was the great, resplendent era of steam. The effects of steam power were felt not only in the field of technology, but also in most areas of human civilization. During this century, steam was used to power the machines of the rapidly growing industrial sector and to drive the engines of the various means of land and sea transport. All this technical progress caused a great wave of optimism and faith in the future, something which we may find rather difficult to understand today. After centuries in which society more or less stood still, these technical breakthroughs, coming one after the other in quick succession, created an atmosphere in which it was believed that machine technology, aided by steam, was on the brink of rescuing mankind from at least some of the worst of the hard struggle for survival. The Swedish author Harry Martinson (1904–1978), a Nobel laureate in literature, described the railway as the first truly democratic invention and indeed, before the era of steam, travel was not accessible to everyone.

When King George II of England once paid a visit to the Boulton & Watt factory in Soho, near Birmingham, Matthew Boulton assured him: "Your Majesty, I have at my disposal what the whole world demands; something which will uplift civilization more than ever by relieving man of all undignified drudgery. I have *steam power*."

Those words, filled as they are with intimations of power—political as well as industrial—were uttered by a man who knew what he was talking about. More than five hundred of Watt's steam-engines had

B Watt's model of a steam-engine with a separate condenser. Round the cylinder (a) was a jacket (b), into which steam was first admitted (at c). Steam was then let into a through a cock. The air driven out of a was blown through a valve (d) in the condenser (e), which opened into a. When a was completely steam-filled, the cock was shut and a piston in the pump barrel (f) was pulled up by hand. The steam then rushing into e was immediately condensed (both e and f were immersed in cold water) and, since a vacuum was created, the piston (g) was pulled upwards.
C Watt's so-called Cornwall engine with a separate condenser. (a) Pipe from the boiler.

been delivered by Boulton & Watt by the time the patent expired in 1800. The two partners then left the company in the hands of their sons. Watt retired to his country estate and devoted himself to his many other interests. He died in 1819 at the age of eighty-three, one of the great standard-bearers in the history of technology, being not only a pioneer in the field, but also a true humanist. The inscription on his memorial stone in Westminster Abbey is a sublime ode to technology, humanism, and James Watt, benefactor of mankind.

By the time James Watt died, steam had shown that it was a source of energy to be reckoned with. There were, however, negative reactions. One example of these was the riots which broke out in England in the second decade of the nineteenth century, when the Luddites, led by a man who went by the name of Ned Ludd, attacked and destroyed steam-driven spinning machines. They feared that these new machines would cause unemployment. There were similar reactions in most countries. When the designer of the first high-speed press, the German Friedrich König (1774–1833), wanted to install a steam-driven press in the Cotta printing works in Stuttgart, one of the editors declared that he would rather write without a roof over his head than work in the same building as a steam-engine. Modern anxiety about nuclear power springs immediately to mind.

When Boulton & Watt's monopoly of steam-engine construction ended in 1800, the market was open for new designs. Watt's engine had not really been improved since 1785. The company produced a standardized version, and every effort was concentrated on increasing production to meet the growing demand.

Watt's engine was still "atmospheric", that is, the air pressure (the "power from nothing") did all the work. Only a minor improvement was needed to increase the pressure to several atmospheres and thus improve performance. Watt's assistants wanted to make it but Watt refused to listen to them—as a young man, he had seen one of Savery's pumps explode at a London waterworks. He was certainly wise to be so careful; at that time, no one had any experience of designs or materials suitable for the construction of high-pressure steam boilers.

Steam-engines after Watt
During the first half of the nineteenth century, the steam-engine developed along three main lines: higher steam pressure, improved utilization of steam expansion, and new mechanical designs. About the year 1850, however, these trends in development changed course, mainly due to the fact that the theory of heat and how it worked in the steam-engine became better understood.

Two interesting pioneers, one on either side of the Atlantic, Richard Trevithick (1771–1833) in Great Britain and Oliver Evans in the United States, separately improved the steam-engine by increasing the steam pressure, and by trying to develop new design ideas for it.

When Trevithick was growing up in Cornwall, Watt's engines were beginning to appear in the local mining districts. It was only natural that the technically gifted boy should take an interest in these engines and discover their potential—and their weaknesses. Watt's engine, just like Newcomen's, was more or less integrated with a building, its heavy balance beam being supported by a solid pillar, usually of brick. One English mill-owner in the 1790s considered that the steam-engine would never spread if it did not become "as movable as a piece of furniture". Even before Watt's patent expired, Trevithick was experimenting with steam at high pressure. His idea was to build a very compact engine which was to be extremely "movable"—it was intended to propel a vehicle! On Christmas Eve, 1801, he was ready to test his steam-driven carriage. The trial took place outside Camborne, Trevithick's home town, on an uphill (!) slope towards Beacon Hill, a little village on a hilltop. It was not

Between the years 1787 and 1800, quite a large number of double-acting steam-engines of this type were manufactured at the Boulton & Watt workshops. The engine's effect was 10 horsepower, and it worked with twenty-five double strokes a minute. (a) Furnace door. (b) Boiler. (c) A device by means of which the water level in the boiler was controlled. At the bottom end of a string (d), a float was attached. When the float sank too much inside the boiler, a valve (e) was opened and water, hoisted by a feed water pump (f), poured in. When the float had returned to its correct level, the valve was closed again. Steam from the boiler was admitted through a pipe (g) to the cylinder (h) by way of a throttle valve (i), the size of whose aperture was determined by a centrifugal governor (j). By way of a gear train (k) and a belt (l), the governor was powered by the sun (m) of the sun-and-planet drive. The cylinder (h) was closed at both ends, and steam alternately entered it above and below the piston through two valve chests (n), in which the valves were opened and closed by projections (o) on a pump rod. (p) Condenser. (q) Pipe for spraying cold water into the condenser. (r) Manometer. The piston rod's (s) motion was transmitted to the balance (t) by a parallel linkage (u), which was also linked to a pump (v), by means of which condensation water and air were pumped into a cistern (w). (x) Pump, driven by the balance and used to pump cooling water to the cistern in which the condenser and pump v were immersed. The balance's oscillating movement was transformed into a rotary movement by a non-rotating cog-wheel, the planet (z), which meshed with the sun (m) on the flywheel's (y) shaft.

A A reconstruction of Trevithick's steam carriage of 1801 as seen from above (**1**) and from the side (**2**). (*a*) Boiler. (*b*) Furnace with a double right-angled flue duct. This allowed as much heat as possible from the stack gas to be utilized. (*c*) Smoke stack. (*d*) Cocks for control of the water level in *a*. (*e*) Water filler funnel with tap. (*f*) Safety valve. (*g*) Double-acting cylinder. (*h*) Steam distributing cock; a 2×2 plug cock. (*i*) Feed pipe from *a*. (*j*) Exhaust steam pipe. Leads to *c*, where the steam by its blasting action forces the draught. (*k*) Piston. The piston rod's (*l*) extension (*m*) was fork-shaped, in order to give room for the crank web (*n*), and had vertical openings, to give room for the crankshaft (*o*). Because of this arrangement, *o* could be set very close to *g*. (*p*) Connecting rod. (*q*) Guides controlling the fore end of *m*. (*r*) An actuating rod, which was connected to *h* and which, from the driver's

seat, could be made to engage with *l* for an automatic reversal of the distribution of steam to the turning-points of the piston. When disengaged, *r* could probably be used for manual control of *h*. (*s*) Flywheel. (*t*, *u*) Gearwheels for the transmission of power to the wheels. (*v*) Coupling gear, used to disengage either of the wheels when cornering a sharp bend. The front axle (*w*) was turned round a central pivot by means of the handle bar (*x*).

successful. The boiler could not produce enough steam, and the carriage failed to puff up the hill. Three days later, Trevithick tried again, now in the company of some merry friends. This time, the hill was conquered, and they actually reached Beacon Hill, despite damage to the carriage on the frozen, rutted road. Their triumph was celebrated with mulled drinks and stuffed goose at the local inn. The carriage had been parked in a shed—but they had forgotten the fire under the boiler, so when they returned from their hearty repast, all they found was a heap of twisted scrap iron.

This, however, did not daunt Trevithick. By March of the following year, he took out patents for his high-pressure steam-engine and for its use in powering a carriage. These patents represent an essential breakthrough in the history of steam technology. The engine had a cylindrical boiler in which the cylinder was encased, thus avoiding loss of heat. Steam was led to the cylinder via a multiple cock which allowed it to act on either side of the piston in turn. The thought in itself was not new; as early as 1725, Leupold had suggested it in his *Theatrum machinarum*.

Back in the 1780s, the American millwright and engineer Oliver Evans had begun to take an interest in steam as a source of power. He realized its great potential, although in those days in the United States the steam-engine was very rare—in 1800, there were only six in the entire country. Completely independently of Trevithick, Evans built a high-pressure steam-engine. It had a horizontal, cylindrical steam boiler with a three-way cock—driven by the balance wheel—which led steam to a separate vertical cylinder. The steam pressure was about three atmospheres. The engine was built on a wooden base and, like Trevithick's, was movable. In 1804, the engine was ready and was used for various tasks, including driving a marble saw in Philadelphia. Evans's engine was the first movable prime mover.

The multiple cock used by Evans and Trevithick as a valve gear had certain drawbacks. For one thing, it wore out very quickly. In 1799, one of Watt's assistants, the Scotsman William Murdock (1754–1839), took out a patent for what is known as the D-slide valve, which was driven by an excentric disc on the axle of the balance wheel. But Watt was sceptical, and his engines retained the old type of valve gear with levers. Some years later, the slide found its perfect form in the simple flat valve, or valve slide, invented in 1802 by yet another Scotsman, Matthew Murray (1765–1826). This slide, or versions of it, remained in use throughout the steam era.

In a high-pressure steam-engine the steam expands while it works. One of Watt's ideas was to allow the steam to expand in a series of connected cylinders. He had experimented with this idea in 1782, but the steam pressure was too low, and Watt abandoned the scheme. An Englishman, Arthur Woolf, was more successful. He used steam pressure at about four atmospheres and let the steam expand in two cylinders in series, the second cylinder having a larger diameter than the first. Woolf's compound machine, as the invention was called, was made in 1804 and was the first of its kind.

Within only a couple of years of the start of the nineteenth century, the steam-engine had radically changed its appearance. The moment Watt's patent expired, the flood-gates opened, and new ideas flowed out. (This is an example of how the patent system can impede technological development.) But there were other factors contributing to this rapid progress. New machining methods and machines were appearing all the time, and, as the first technical colleges were founded, the engineer who was qualified in both theory and practice came on the scene. These colleges were often military institutions, but later, civilians were admitted to them.

In the following decades, the steam-engine developed at an increasing pace, mainly along the lines indicated above. New designs aimed at raising steam pressure still further and at a better use of the

B Trevithick himself here stands next to his steam-engine of c. 1805. The cylinder (a) was submerged in the boiler (b). The piston rod (c) ended in a cross-bar (d) with two casings which slid along two guides (e). (f) Connecting rods. (g) Crank axle. (h) Inspection cover. (i) Cock for control of the water level in b. (j) Furnace front. (k) Fresh-air intake and ash bin. (l) Safety valve. (m) Connecting link between d and the steam distribution cock.

C Evans's steam-engine of 1813. The fumes from the furnace (a) first flowed round the outside of the boiler (b), then travelled by way of a pipe inside b to the smoke stack (c). (d) Cylinder. (e) Piston rod. (f) Connecting rod. For the power transmission from e to f, a "grasshopper" (g) was used, whose fulcrum (h) was attached in a "floating" fashion to the engine's foundation (i) by two struts (j). A stay (k) between i and g compensated g's tendency to move its free end along an arc.

expansion of steam. One interesting example is the high-pressure steam-engine designed by the German Ernst Alban (1791–1856). This operated in a textile mill in Plau, Mecklenburg (now in East Germany). Alban, originally an oculist, first experimented with pressures of up to fifty atmospheres but decided for practical reasons to settle for about ten atmospheres. The engine had an oscillating cylinder which worked directly on the connecting rod of the balance wheel. It had a centrifugal governor, and the entire engine was built according to a monumental design, with cast-iron pillars in Grecian style supporting a lovely classical pediment. Another of Alban's achievements, produced after much hard work, was a safe and efficient steam boiler suitable for high pressures. He is considered to be the first to design a usable tubular boiler.

As has been mentioned above, new types of steam-engine began to appear about 1850, the main reason being that steam technology was now beginning to get a firmer theoretical ground on which to stand. In the early stages, the exploitation of steam power had been severely hampered by a complete lack of theoretical insight into the real nature of such basic phenomena as air, fire, and water. In 1824, the French engineer and physicist Sadi Carnot (1796–1832) presented the first basic theory of the steam-engine in a pamphlet entitled *Réflexions sur la Puissance Motrice du Feu* ("Reflections on the Driving Power of Fire"). Its subject was all kinds of heat engines, and it was written on a very high level of abstraction, containing a very advanced mathematical presentation of the problems involved. In other words, it was almost completely unintelligible to contemporary practitioners of steam technology and therefore attracted little attention in the engineering journals then beginning to appear. It was not until 1834 that Carnot's compatriot Benoît Clapeyron (1799–1864), a works engineer and a designer of steam-engines, tried to enlarge upon these theories and explain them to those who were working practically in the field. However, he did not have much success either. In 1842, the German scientist J. Robert Mayer (1814—78) introduced his theory of applied thermodynamics, which clarified many concepts. The Englishman James Prescott Joule (1818—89) developed Mayer's ideas in a work published in 1847, and the German Rudolf Clausius (1812—88) did the same in his *Ueber die bewegende Kraft der Wärme)* ("On the Driving Power of Heat"). In the late 1840s, Carnot's book of 1824 found its way into the hands of the great natural scientist William Thomson (later Lord Kelvin), who read it and exclaimed, "Never before in the history of natural science has such a great book been written!"

This may have been a slight exaggeration, but Thomson was the one who was later to sum up all these theories in his formulation of the main laws of thermodynamics, which was first published in 1851. Today, his clearly articulated interpretations of natural laws still form the basis for our attempts to solve the present world energy supply problems.

Pre-eminent among the engineers who broke new ground in steam-engine technology is the American George Henry Corliss

A A steam-engine cylinder with a valve slide. (**1**) The slide (*a*) consisted of a hollowed-out plate. It was moved to and fro on the valve face (*b*), which had two steam passages (*c, d*) leading to the ends of the cylinder, and an outlet (*e*) through which steam left the cylinder. High-pressure steam was let in through an opening (*f*) in the valve chest. (**2**) When *a* was situated in its left-hand position, steam entered from *f* through *c*. The steam which had filled the space to the left of the piston (*g*) simultaneously left the cylinder through *d* and *e*, and the piston was pushed to the left by the pressure of the incoming steam. (**3**) When *a* was positioned in the middle of the valve face, both of the steam passages were blocked. The steam in the cylinder worked through expansion. (**4**) Just before the piston had reached its turning-point, *d* was opened, and steam entered to the left of the piston. At the same time, the steam on the other side of *g* escaped by way of *c* and *e*.

(1817—88). In his twenties, Corliss determined to build a steam-engine in which the vital parts would consist of completely new elements, superior to those already in existence. In 1846, he and two partners founded a mechanical workshop in Providence, Rhode Island, where they manufactured steam-engines. At first, the engines were relatively conventional, but they were successively improved. Corliss first concentrated on the slide mechanism, and he took out a patent for an entirely new idea in 1849—the gear with cylindrical rocking valves, later known internationally as the Corliss slide. Among the foremost of its many advantages was the fact that the slide valve was indirectly controlled by the centrifugal governor so that the amount of steam it admitted depended on the work load of the engine. If the load were heavy, the intake increased, and vice versa. This saved steam and thus improved fuel economy. However, the Corliss slide and Corliss's other important inventions differed so much from those that were established that he could not find customers for them. He solved this problem, however, by lending the engine free of charge—as long as he had his share of the money saved by its lower fuel consumption. His engines came up to expectations, and Corliss was soon the most celebrated engineer in the United States. He reached the zenith of his career as a mechanical engineer when he built the huge engine for the Centennial Exposition in Philadelphia in 1876. This engine became almost a symbol of the Exposition and, indeed, of the whole era of steam. A beam engine with vertical cylinders, Corliss's steam-engine had an effect of 2,500 horsepower and was the largest steam-engine hitherto constructed.

In 1870, when the American Academy of Arts and Sciences awarded Henry Corliss its prestigious Rumford medal, it was tacitly stating that no other inventor since James Watt had meant so much to steam technology. This judgement is indisputable. Corliss's work was of great importance both to steam technology and to the engineering industry in his native country. When his patent expired, his ideas were developed by the principal steam-engine manufacturers in both the United States and Europe.

Several European engineers were inspired by William Thomson's theories of thermodynamics to enter what was to prove a fruitful field of research. In the 1870s, Gustav Adolf Hirn (1815—90), the owner of a textile mill in Alsace, now a part of France, made a comprehensive survey of the steam-engines which drove the spinning-machines in his mill. He wanted to find ways of improving their operating efficiency, and he concentrated especially on the exchange of heat between the steam and the cylinder wall, a phenomenon which is known in steam technology as cylinder condensation, one of the greatest sources of heat loss in the steam-engine. Hirn came to the conclusion that heat loss would be reduced considerably if the steam were superheated. The results of his research were taken up by the Swiss company Gebrüder Sulzer in Winterthur, especially by its chief designer Charles Brown (1827—1905). Brown collaborated with Heinrich Sulzer, the son of one of the brothers who owned the firm, in building the first engine for superheated steam, which was ready in 1866. Both engineers had been very impressed by Corliss's ideas, and among other things, a modified Corliss slide was incorporated in their design. The engine had an effect of 56 horsepower and worked with a steam pressure of five atmospheres. It was shown at the world exhibition in Paris in 1867, together with several engines built by Corliss. The new designs aroused a lot of interest, both at the exhibition itself and in the technical press, and stimulated engineers all over the world to try out new ideas and concepts which would improve the steam-engine. During the following decades, many attempts were made to increase the pressure of the steam in steam-engines. Also the idea of letting steam expand successively in

B The principle of Woolf's compound engine of 1804. (**1**) Steam with a pressure of about four atmospheres entered the high-pressure cylinder through valve *a*. At the same time, valve *b* was opened, so that the expanded steam in the lower part of the high-pressure cylinder could escape inte the low-pressure cylinder for further expan-

sion; also, valve *c* was opened, so that the used steam was let out. Both pistons were thus simultaneously brought downwards. (**2**) Valves *a*, *b*, and *c* were then closed, and high-pressure steam was let in through valve *d* while valves *e* and *f* were opened.

C Ernst Alban's monumental high-pressure steam-engine, which was constructed in 1839 and operated in a textile mill for six decades. The engine's cylinder (*a*) oscillated round a shaft and worked directly on the flyweel's crankshaft (*b*). Thus, no connecting rod was needed for the transmission of power. (*c*) Centrifugal governor.

B Corliss's compound engine with horizontal cylinders (*a*). (*b*) Rocking valve mechanisms. (*c*) Centrifugal governor. (*d*) Flywheel. The engine was intended for belt driving.

C The most famous of all the steam-engines built by Corliss was this one, which he constructed for the Centennial Exposition held in Philadelphia in 1876. The engine weighed 600 tons and was 44 ft 4 in (13.5 m) high. It was the largest steam-engine then built. Properly speaking, it consisted of two separate, single-cylinder beam engines with a common flywheel. The effect was 2,500 horsepower.

A The cylinder with its rocking, cylindrical valves in a Corliss engine; (**1**) longitudinal-section, (**2**) cross-section, (**3**) the valve mechanism on the outside of the cylinder. The cylinder had four valves (*a*, *b*), rocked by means of links (*c*) connected to a wrist plate (*d*), which was given an oscillating movement by a rod (*e*) from an eccentric on the engine shaft. Since the steam entered the cylinder through one opening (*f*) and left through another (*g*), the inlet valves (*a*) were not cooled by the exhaust steam. The movements of the inlet valves were further determined by the position of the centrifugal governor. At a certain point in their movements, the inlet valves were released from the links (*c*) by trip gears, which were controlled by the governor. The valves were then rapidly closed by a heavy weight. Thus, the amount of steam let into the cylinder was automatically varied as the engine's work load varied. (*h*) Piston rod.

a series of two or more cylinders was developed. As early as 1804, Woolf had successfully used two cylinders in his compound engine; seventy years later, Corliss also produced such an engine. Several designers used a series of three cylinders of increasing diameter, which gave a compact engine known as the triple expansion steam-engine, which was particularly suitable for marine propulsion.

During the 1870s and 1880s, several new types of slide mechanism also made their appearance. It was generally considered that the piston steam-engine was now being brought to perfection; its operating efficiency was good and was being constantly bettered as designers began to apply the laws of thermodynamics in their work; and there did not seem to be any limit to the size of the engines that could be built. But then things started to happen. In the late 1870s, the gas engine began to attract more and more attention; within a few years, it was clear that electric power could well become a force to be reckoned with; and in the 1880s, the first petrol engine was invented.

Did these newcomers really threaten the existence of the steam-engine? In England in the early 1880s, there was a heated debate on this subject in industrial and technical circles. It was triggered off by an address given in 1881 to the British Association for the Advancement of Science by Sir W. George Armstrong, a well-known industrialist who was later made a peer. In his speech, which attracted considerable notice, Armstrong severely criticized the piston steam-engine, mainly for its poor operational efficiency. He maintained that entirely new avenues had to be explored in the search for a new prime mover. Sir Frederic Bramwell, who was an authority in the field of technology, agreed with him and added provocatively that there would be no steam-engines in operation fifty years hence—in 1931—they would be museum pieces! In 1888, Sir Frederic repeated this prophecy and also donated a sum of money to the British Association, to be given to anyone who could develop these ideas in an authoritative lecture. Sir Alfred Ewing gave just such a lecture three years later. In the meantime, however, a new prime mover, the steam turbine, had appeared and was showing great promise. Sir Alfred was able to maintain that steam was neither dead nor dying, and that the steam turbine would, very likely, show the world both larger and more efficient machines than Bramwell had ever dreamt of. Today, we know that Sir Alfred Ewing was right.

However, the designers of the steam-engine did not give up so easily. Both in England and on the Continent admirable attempts were made to improve the piston steam-engine. In the early 1890s, the German Wilhelm Schmidt, working along the lines of the Sulzer engine for superheated steam, developed an engine for steam at a temperature of no less than 350°C. In the following decade, another German, Johann Stumpf, developed a simplified piston steam-engine which he called the "uniflow" engine because the steam flowed in one direction only through the cylinder. The uniflow engine enjoyed a certain popularity, especially in Germany, where one of its uses was in locomobiles.

At first, the steam turbine did not appear to be the serious rival to the piston steam-engine that Sir Alfred Ewing had predicted it would be. But around the year 1910, the situation changed, and the turbine gained a great deal of ground. The fate which befell Henry Corliss's engine from the Centennial Exposition in Philadelphia serves to illustrate this. When the engine had been returned to the factory in Providence, George Mortimer Pullman visited Corliss there and bought the engine on the spot. He then used it to drive the machines used in the manufacture of sleeping-cars for the Pullman Palace Car Company until 1910, when it was replaced by a stationary steam turbine.

The Steam Turbine

In the 1770s and 1780s, when Watt's steam-engines were coming into service, the eyes of many engineers were opened to the potential of steam power. But these early engines could only produce a reciprocating motion. If steam could also produce a rotary motion, would it not be of much more general use? Watt himself had raised this question several times. The first occasion was in 1769—the year in which he took out his condenser patent—when he experimented with a ring-shaped "cylinder" in which a piston was to be driven round by steam. However, the device did not work, and he abandoned the scheme. But fifteen years later, he was compelled to reconsider the idea, since the Hungarian Baron Wolfgang von Kempelen (1734–1804) had taken out a patent on a steam turbine. This attracted a great deal of attention in England, not least because von Kempelen claimed that his engine was superior to Watt's and could easily push it off the market. Well, if the good baron was an indefatigable inventor, he was also a great joker. In the history of technology he is best remembered for his chess-playing Turk (see page 178).

The design of von Kempelen's turbine is not unlike that suggested by the Italian Giovanni Branca in 1629. It was known as an action turbine, that is, one in which a jet of steam exerts pressure—"acts"—

A1   A2

A During the last decades of the nineteenth century, tiny steam-engines (1) for household use were marketed. This example was manufactured by Tyson and was considered to be especially well suited for powering sewing-machines (2). In order to regulate the speed of the sewing-machine, a braking device could be attached to the belt pulley. The brake would then be connected to a spring-loaded pedal and a counterweight.

C1

B Steam ploughing in the mid-nineteenth century. A rope was stretched over pulleys round the field. The plough was attached to the rope and was pulled across the field between two of the pulleys when one end of the rope was wound onto a drum and the other end was unwound at the same speed from another drum. The steam-engine alternately drove the drums forwards and backwards, and the pulleys were moved by hand closer and closer to the steam-engine for each furrow to be ploughed.

C₂ C₃

C In 1882, the French company Cie. Générale Transatlantique's British-built Atlantic liner *Normandie* was launched. Part of the ship's machinery is shown here from the side: (**1**) two of the cylinders shown in cross-section, (**2**) from in front. (**3**) The machinery's position and size in relation to the 460-ft (140 m) long ship. The three connected machines were of the compound type and had six cylinders, arranged in pairs one above the other. The effect was 6,600 horsepower, and 110 tons of coal a day were needed to heat the eight boilers.

on the blades of the turbine wheel. But after a thorough examination of such facts as the steam consumption, the speed of rotation, and the output of von Kempelen's engine, Watt concluded that the design was technically impossible. To make the output in any way reasonable, the speed of the turbine wheel would have to be enormous—so enormous that its own centrifugal force would cause it to burst into pieces! At a more normal speed, its steam consumption would be disproportionately high in relation to its output. These calculations were all that Watt needed to calm his partner, Matthew Boulton, who had been quite distressed by the rumours that their steam monopoly was in danger.

During the following decades, several engineers concentrated their efforts on finding a way of producing rotary motion from steam power. In 1797, the versatile English clergyman Edmund Cartwright presented an idea not unlike Watt's but it, too, did not work in practice. In 1799, Watt's assistant William Murdock took out a patent on an interesting device in which two engaged cog-wheels were rotated by a steam jet. The idea was a good one—the same design is still used for things like oil pumps—but in Murdock's day, the necessary precision in manufacturing could not be achieved.

The first person to use steam power to produce rotary motion was Carl Gustaf Patrik de Laval (1845–1913), who developed his first invention, the milk separator, in the 1870s. To achieve the desired result, the container had to be rotated at a very high frequency, 6,000–10,000 rpm. The small hand-cranked units for domestic use employed a gearing to achieve this speed, whereas the larger units were driven by horse-wheels. However, de Laval wanted a prime mover which could be connected directly to the separator without a gear mechanism. He first tried out a simple reaction turbine with an S-shaped rotor; this worked on the same principle as Hero's ball. Twenty years later, de Laval described these experiments:

> Fully convinced that speed is a gift from the gods, I dared, in 1876, to believe in the direct exploitation of steam on a power-generating wheel. It was a bold venture. At that time, only low speeds were employed. The speeds which were considered normal in later separators were never used. In contemporary handbooks they wrote about steam: "Unfortunately, the density of steam is too low to permit any thought of exploiting it in a power-generating wheel." In spite of this I succeeded.

The reason de Laval succeeded was partly his experience of the technical problems which occurred at high speeds, and partly the fact that the turbine gave exactly what he was looking for, namely, high-speed rotation. At the same time that he was working to perfect the separator, which he patented in 1878, de Laval was developing several versions of the S-turbine. He had reached the same conclusion as Watt, that the efficiency of the steam turbine is not satisfactory until it attains 30,000–40,000 rpm. He spent a great amount of time and much effort in trying to solve the very difficult technical problems that occurred at these speeds, for example, how to balance the axle and the S-rotor. The slightest imbalance generated such great forces that they broke even heavy steel axles. It was not until 1883 that de Laval considered that he had mastered these problems, when he took out a patent for his engine for driving milk separators, which was the first steam turbine with a practical application.

Nevertheless, de Laval was not satisfied. He abandoned the reaction turbine and concentrated instead on the action turbine, that is, Branca's model. He tried everything to increase its output while keeping its speed within reasonable limits. "Reasonable" in this context has to be seen from de Laval's point of view. *Gustaf de Laval—Man of High Speeds* is the title of a biography written by Torsten Althin. One version of de Laval's S-turbine was designed for a speed of 42,000 rpm!

While working on his action turbine, de Laval discovered an interesting method of letting the steam jet expand in the nozzle before "acting", thus increasing the exploitation of kinetic energy. The first draft of his design for these nozzles shows that they had "widening outlets" which enabled the steam jet to expand before hitting the blades of the turbine wheel. In 1888, de Laval patented an action turbine with just such a nozzle. Later, the nozzle found many other applications in the field of technology, one being in the rocket engines of spacecraft, where the driving jet of gas expands in Laval nozzles, as they are nowadays called.

De Laval also solved the problem of mass forces. Instead of increasing the diameter and thus the strength of the axle, he made it slimmer and resilient. The turbine-wheel/axle system was so dimensioned that the practically inevitable imbalance produced a resonance in the vibrations at a relatively low speed of rotation (when the turbine was being started or stopped). At the resonance point, the axle could vibrate with an amplitude of about 0.4 in (10 mm) or more. A resilient axle can take this, if it is fitted with bearings which can stand up to such a "whipping" rotary movement. He solved this by fitting the bearing in a spherical segment in which it could follow the motion of the axle. When the resonance point had been passed and the turbine had assumed its running speed, the turbine-wheel/axle system adjusted itself automatically, whereupon the vibrations ceased.

The patent for the nozzle of de Laval's action turbine was taken out in 1888. The combination of expansion nozzle and turbine wheel proved very effective in exploiting steam energy. But the speed was too high and had to be reduced to a level where the turbine could be applied practically.

A lot of dogged research was required to solve this problem. Once de Laval had designed an efficient, slim axle, he tested different gear mechanisms in an effort to find one which could transmit large forces at high speeds. The solution he found was a double helical gear, the so-called fish-bone gear, which was to characterize the de Laval turbines for a long time.

De Laval had many ideas on how his "steam-motor", as he called it, could be put to practical use. For a while, he considered using it to propel ships and, in 1892, had drawings ready for a small turbine-powered vessel. But in the end, he decided to concentrate on producing units for generating electrical energy. These units were built with a capacity ranging from 5 to 500 horsepower.

The turbine had an extremely high operating efficiency. A comparative test made in 1890 between a 6-horsepower steam-engine and a 5-horsepower de Laval steam turbine showed that the steam-engine consumed seventy-five per cent more steam! An important contributory factor to this was a steam boiler with relatively small helical pipes, yet another of de Laval's designs. In this boiler the coils were strongly heated by forced combustion in the furnace, created by automatically controlled electric fans. This produced a huge amount of steam at very high pressure. However, the amount of steam in the helical pipes at any given time was relatively small, so a bursting pipe would cause little damage.

Gustaf de Laval must be considered one of the pioneers of high-pressure steam. At the craft and industry exhibition in Stockholm in 1897, the electric power was supplied by two de Laval units. On one occasion when the Swedish king, Oscar II, the patron of the exhibition, was shown these units, de Laval mentioned that the boiler could produce a pressure of 110 atmospheres; the king instinctively took a step backwards. When they got to the other unit, de Laval informed him that it worked at a pressure of 220 atmospheres; Oscar II rapidly left the exhibition.

By the early 1880s, the idea of a steam turbine was very much in the air. The year after de Laval had taken out a patent for his S-turbine, the Englishman Sir Charles Parsons (1854–1931) set about developing a turbine specifically for driving an electric generator. The year was 1884, and Parsons had to grapple with the technical problems that arose at extremely high speeds, as well as with the problems of bearings and strength—that is to say, with the same problems that were troubling de Laval. Parsons, a brilliant designer and an ingenious inventor, soon overcame these stumbling-blocks. He did not take the usual path via laboratory models and production prototypes but implemented his ideas in a full-scale machine, ready for industrial use. The unit was in operation in the Forth Bank in London until 1900, when it was donated to the Science Museum in the same city.

The basic idea for Parsons's steam turbine was taken from the water turbine as designed by, among others, Fourneyron. Parsons let the steam flow between fixed guide vanes, so that it met the blades of the wheel at right angles. The turbine had fourteen fixed rims with guide vanes, and fourteen rotating blade wheels on a common axle. The steam was admitted at the middle of the axle and flowed parallel to it in both directions, while working and expanding to atmospheric pressure. The steam pressure was 6.5 atmospheres, and the speed of rotation was as high as 18,000 rpm. The electric generator was directly connected to the turbine axle. It must be considered a brilliant achievement of Parsons to have designed a generator that could function at such a high velocity. The electric generators of the time were usually made for 800–1,200 rpm. Parsons's generator gave a voltage of 100V with a maximum load of 75A. The turbine developed about 10 horsepower.

Parsons's axial-flow turbine (with steam working in the direction of the axle) represents an important breakthrough in the history of technology, and it introduced the era of the turbine's spectacular development. While that restless inventor Gustaf de Laval soon left his successful turbine company in other hands and devoted himself to a mass of different projects, Charles Parsons spent the whole of his active life, from 1884 onwards, working on turbines.

By 1889, almost three hundred axial-flow turbines had been produced by the Gateshead-on-Tyne firm of Clarke, Chapman & Co., of which Parsons was a partner. However, due to differences of opinion with his fellow owners, Parsons had to terminate the partnership and give up his turbine and generator patents. This forced him to find fundamentally new designs, if he was to continue in the field. So he formed C. A. Parsons & Co. Ltd., Newcastle-upon-Tyne, later of worldwide renown, and designed a turbine in which steam worked radially, that is, from the centre out towards the periphery. The first Parsons-designed radial turbine was delivered in 1891 to the Cambridge Electric Lighting Co. and was remarkable for the fact that it had an inbuilt condenser in which the steam, after doing its work, was condensed at atmospheric pressure. The spent steam had so far always been exhausted to the outside, but now the condensate could be pumped away. The unit was of 100-kW single-phase alternating current with a frequency of 80 periods per second and a voltage of 2,000 V. The frequency of rotation was only 4,800 rpm, and the operating efficiency was very high.

The Cambridge turbine created a sensation among electrical engineers, both in England and elsewhere. Similar units, but of ever increasing capacity, were soon delivered to different parts of Britain. In 1898, Parsons & Co. built the then largest turbine unit in the world for an electric power-station being built in Elberfeld, Germany. The capacity was 1,000 kW, so high that contemporary engineers felt it to be somewhat risky.

In the 1890s and the early years of the twentieth century, engineers all over the world contributed towards opening up new ground in the field, and by about 1910, the piston steam-engine was totally surpassed by the steam turbine.

In 1895, the American Charles Gordon Curtis (1860–1953) took out a patent for a combination of the principles of the action and reaction turbines. In the Curtis design the steam impinged upon a rotor with fixed guide vanes, like the one used by Parsons in his axial-flow turbine. The guide vanes changed the direction of the steam jet; at the same time, the steam expanded, just as it did in the Laval steam nozzle. Curtis ran a small factory in Brooklyn, New York, in which electrical appliances were manufactured. He contacted the General Electric Co. in Schenectady, in New York State, and offered them the right to develop his invention further. General Electric hesitated for some time before trying out the design in a 500-kW plant which supplied their Schenectady factory with electricity. They were positively surprised by the results, and plans were immediately drawn up for a Curtis turbine of 5,000 kW, which was completed in 1903. It had an interesting design, with a vertical turbine axle necessitating a specially designed axle bearing, which was lubricated with oil under very high pressure. The Curtis GE turbine was later developed under licence by AEG in Germany and by British Thomson-Houston in England.

In France Auguste Rateau (1863–1930) developed what is known as the multi-stage turbine, which he patented in 1896. Rateau divided the expansion of the steam into a number of successive stages, which meant that the fall in steam pressure at each stage was successively smaller. This enabled the turbine wheel to rotate more slowly, yet without any loss of output. As a rule, an electric generator could be connected directly to the turbine axle without the use of an intermediate reduction gear. The first multi-stage turbine designed by Rateau was built in 1898 by Sauter, Harlé & Cie. This type of turbine had its commercial breakthrough at the world exhibition in Paris in 1900. Auguste Rateau was a professor at the Ecole Polytechnique in Paris and was highly thought of both as a research scientist and a designer. Among the companies which manufactured his multi-stage turbine under licence were the well-known engineering company Oerlikon in Switzerland and the Skoda works in Czechoslovakia. The licensees often found ways of improving and developing the turbine.

During the first years of the twentieth century, the Swedish inventors Birger Ljungström (1872–1948) and his brother Fredrik (1875–1964) set about developing a very compact boiler for high pressure steam. Some of the work had been done in England, where, during a visit to Charles Parsons's factory in Newcastle-upon-Tyne, Birger had become fascinated by the potential of the turbine. At the same time as they were working on other projects, the Ljungström brothers began looking for new design principles for turbines. By 1906, after some years' work, they had found a solution that was as original as it was simple, and in which nobody else in Sweden or England believed. They then contacted the leading turbine authority at the time, Professor Aurel Stodola of the Eidgenössische Technische Hochschule in Zürich, Switzerland. Stodola was most positive about their design, but in spite of this, it was very difficult for the brothers to find investors willing to risk their capital in the manufacture of the new turbine. At last, in 1908, a company was founded, and Ljungströms Steam Turbine Co. began its activities.

The principle of the new turbine design was based on making the steam flow radially, from the centre to the periphery, and at the same time, allowing it to expand, while the guide vanes rotated in the opposite direction to the turbine wheel. Actually, the design consisted of two turbine wheels rotating in opposite directions, a blade rim on one wheel acting as a guide vane for a blade rim on the other, and vice versa. In 1910, a full-scale prototype was ready. With

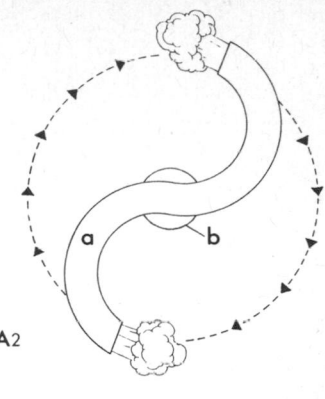

A The simple reaction turbine (1) constructed by de Laval in 1876. The turbine was intended to be connected directly to a separator, and its principle was the same as for Hero's ball. The S-shaped rotor (2, *a*) was set in motion by the reaction pressure occurring when steam escaped through the bent arms of the rotor. The steam was supplied through a pipe (*b*) in the middle of the turbine.

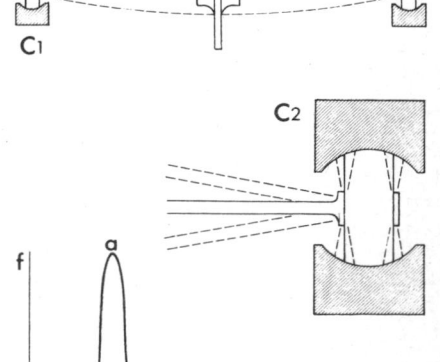

B The principle of de Laval's action turbine. High-pressure steam was blown through nozzles whose inner shape (*a*) allowed the steam to expand to low pressure. Its velocity was then greatly increased, and when the steam jets hit the turbine wheel's bent vanes (*b*), the wheel was set in motion.
C The slim, resilient turbine axle (1) developed by de Laval. The axle bearings were fixed in spherical segments (2) so that the axle could stand up to the "whipping" resonance vibrations. (3) A graphic representation of the size of the resonance vibrations (*f*) in relation to the turbine's speed of rotation (*n*). (*a*) Resonance point. (*b*) The turbine's normal running speed.

C The first man to propose so-called velocity compounding was de Laval, who, in the 1880s, realized the possibility of lessening the peripheral velocity of the wheel in an impulse turbine by letting one after the other of several rows of moving blades absorb the steam's velocity energy. However, he soon gave up his experiments with this type of turbine. Independently of de Laval's work, Curtis started to build impulse turbines according to the velocity-compounding principle in the 1890s. Shown here is an early Curtis steam-turbine generator (**1**) of 12,000 kW. The turbine shaft (*a*) was vertical, and the generator's (*b*)

A Parsons's multi-wheel reaction turbine with axial flow, patented in 1884, is here shown in cross-section (**1**). The steam (*a*) entered at *b* and travelled parallel with the axle through the turbine (*c*) while expanding to atmospheric pressure. Because of the consequent increase of the steam's volume, the lengths of the guide vanes and the moving blades had to be increased more and more the farther from *b* they were positioned. When steam travelled through *c*, it exerted an axial thrust in the direction of the low-pressure part of the turbine. This thrust was counteracted by dummy pistons (*d*), through which steam also travelled. (*e*) Steam outlet. (**2**) In the turbine, the steam travelled between guide vanes (*f*) on fixed wheels, so that it hit the blades (*g*) of the moving wheels at right angles. (**3**) Detail showing the arrangement of guide vanes and blades.

B In a radial-flow turbine (**1**), the steam (*a*) enters at the turbine axle and expands outwards through concentric rings of blades. These rings are alternately attached to one or the other of the outer two discs, and the blades are mounted in such a way that the blades of each ring serve as "guide vanes" for the blades of the next ring while absorbing the energy of the steam. Thus the two discs rotate in opposite directions. (**2**) The arrangement of blades in the radial-flow turbine designed by the Ljungström brothers. The size and shape of the blades as well as their distance from each other varies with their distance from the turbine axle, something which can also be seen in the cross-section of the Ljungström turbine shown here (**3**).

B2   B3

f

e

d

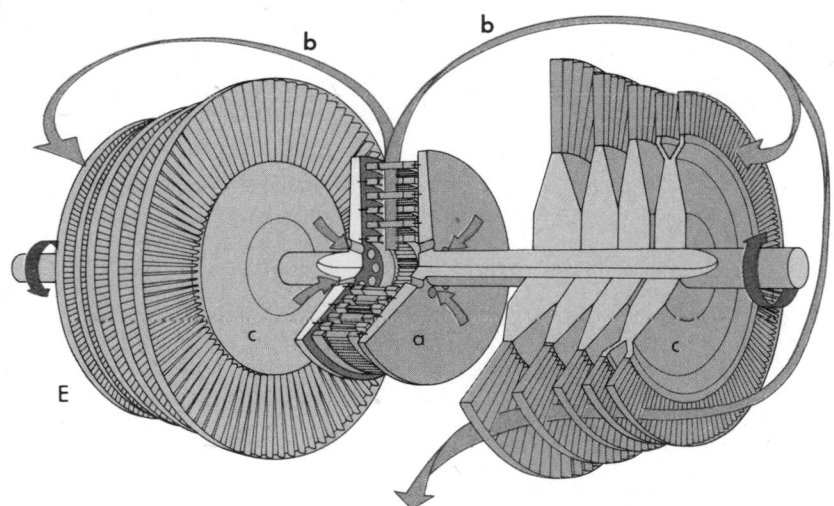

b   b

E

c   a   c

a capacity of 500 horsepower, it was designed for a one hundred per cent overload. Its rate of revolution was 3,000 rpm, and its thermal efficiency about thirty per cent.

The first big order the company received came from Willesden, England. It was for a 1,000-kW unit which was to supply electricity to the town's trams. The unit was delivered in 1912 and remained in operation until 1924. The Ljungström brothers' company was reformed in 1913 to become Svenska Turbinfabriks Aktiebolaget Ljungström (Stal), and from that year onwards, the Ljungström turbines, or the Stal turbines, as they were soon called, were manufactured under licence by the British firm Brush Electrical Engineering Co. in Loughborough.

From the second decade of the twentieth century onwards, the steam turbine became the main source of power used in generating electrical energy, and the demands for greater power per unit kept growing. Designers all over the world searched for new principles upon which they could base further development, but the variations had been more or less exhausted by the work of the above-mentioned pioneers. The 50,000-kW Stal turbine built in 1932 for the Swedish National Power Administration is typical of the development that has taken place since 1930. To enable the unit to achieve the high output required, the turbine was designed for both radial and axial steam flow. The Ljungström brothers had discussed this combination with Stodola as early as 1910, but he had advised them to concentrate on a purely radial turbine—probably a sound piece of advice at that stage. Combining radial with axial flow would, without doubt, have been considered a patent infringement by both Curtis and Parsons.

External Combustion Engines

We have already described the wave of new ideas and designs which appeared when Watt's steam-engine patent expired. At about the same time, people started to speculate about new methods of exploiting heat to produce motion. One possible way was suggested by the colourful and highly talented aviation pioneer, the Englishman Sir George Cayley (1773–1857). He was only twenty when he first began to take an interest in aviation, and in 1799, he outlined the principles of aircraft design, with stiff wings and body, and a stabilizing tail unit with control surfaces. This seems very obvious to us today, but Sir George's contemporaries did not even take him seriously. In 1783, the first balloon ascents had taken place in France (by the Montgolfier brothers in a hot-air balloon and by Professor Jacques Charles in a hydrogen balloon), and these stimulated a lot of ideas about conquering the air with other kinds of craft. Most of these ideas aimed at imitating the flight of birds. At that time, it was more or less axiomatic that this would be the answer. The "flapping-wing flier", or ornithopter, was the aircraft of the future. And from the time of Sir George Cayley until the end of the next century, many inventors tried to design such a machine, but it was not until our own time that a functioning ornithopter has been actually produced—on a toy scale.

Cayley carried out extensive practical experiments, both with scaled-down and full-scale models. His "aeroplanes" (the term had yet to be invented) were based on the principles that he had established. But he needed a prime mover. He discussed this problem in an article in *Nicholson's Journal* in October, 1807, stating that a steam-engine was out of the question, as it was too bulky and heavy. But, he continued, air increases its volume when heated and reduces it when cooled, and these properties can surely be exploited for kinetic energy. He also touched upon the possibility of using a "gunpowder engine", but he went no further than to suggest that a heat engine with air as its medium must be the best means of powering an aircraft. Sir George also made a sketch of this engine, which he

rotor was mounted on the shaft extension. The turbine consisted of five wheels (c), each with two rows of moving blades. The steam entered through nozzles (d) that could be closed automatically and travelled (2) through guide vanes (e), where it expanded, completely or partly, and through moving blades (f), where it parted with velocity energy. It then passed reversing guide vanes (g), where its direction was changed and a possible further expansion took place. The steam's remaining velocity energy was finally absorbed to a large extent by a second row of moving blades (h).
D A Stal turbine from the 1920s with toothed wheel gearing and reversing gear. The machinery was

intended for marine propulsion. Since a steam turbine must revolve very rapidly and a propeller shaft must not be allowed to rotate very fast, some sort of gearing must be employed to connect the two. (a) Turbine. (b) Turbine gear. (c) Reversing gear. (d) Propeller gear. (e) Thrust bearing. (f) Propeller shaft.
E In the 1930s, this type of Stal turbine with both radial and axial flow was developed. The steam first expanded through a radial-flow turbine (a). When the steam's volume was so large that its velocity had almost reached its maximum, the steam jet was split (b) and led to axial-flow turbines (c), where it was allowed to expand further.

A1 A2 A3 A4 A5

called the caloric engine, and of its mode of operation. Although the design never left the drawing-board, we must see Sir George Cayley as the originator of the caloric, or hot-air, engine.

The first practical attempts to realize Sir George's idea were made by the Scottish clergyman Robert Stirling (1790–1879) who began work on his engine in 1816. After extensive experiments in which his brother James helped, Stirling's engine was ready to be patented in 1827. In order to exploit the properties of air, as Cayley had suggested, the Stirling brothers used two cylinders. In one of them, air was heated and cooled alternately. When the air expanded, it effected the power stroke in the other cylinder. The machine is reported to have worked well and efficiently, by the standards of the time. The Stirling brothers built several engines but never mass-produced them. The largest Stirling engine ever built had a power of 21 horsepower; the diameter of the working cylinder was 15.7 in (40 cm), and the piston stroke was 47.2 in (120 cm).

The versatile Swedish inventor John Ericsson (1803–89) was only nineteen when he first took an interest in the ideas that would later lead to the first mass-produced hot-air engine. He reasoned that the heat flow in the steam-engine was an unnecessary detour via water and steam, stating that:

> If the flame itself was alternately admitted to and barred from a chamber corresponding to the cylinder of a steam engine, a kinetic power would result, which would be as useful as that of

A The principle of Stirling's hot-air engine. (**1**) The engine consisted of a cylinder (*a*) which was closed only at its lower end and was connected by way of a pipe to another cylinder (*b*), which was closed at both ends. The piston (*c*) in cylinder *b* was of the usual type. Both pistons were connected to a crank axle. (*e*) Heat source. (*f*) Cooling water. Piston *c* is here in its uppermost and piston *d* in its lowest position. (**2**) As the bottom of cylinder *b* was heated, *c* remained where it was while *d* moved upwards due to the expansion of the air in *b*. (**3**) Piston *d* then remained at its topmost position while piston *c* was lowered. The heated air at the bottom of *b* then travelled through *c* and up to the top of the cylinder, where it was cooled by the water (*f*). While travelling through *c*, the air had also lost a lot of its heat to the iron plates. (**4**) As the air's temperature sank, its pressure fell too, and piston *d* consequently moved downwards. Piston *c* thereupon moved upwards again while piston *d* remained at its lower position. When the cooled air again travelled downwards, it absorbed heat from piston *c* and was further partly heated by *e*.

B Ericsson's first caloric engine employed the same principle as Stirling's engine. The regenerator consisted of a cylindrical vessel (*a*), closed at both ends, through which thin pipes (*b*) ran. These opened towards two domes (*c*, *d*). Metal sheets (*e*) were fitted across the regenerator's inside; they were alternately cut off at the top and at the

bottom, so that air could circulate. Similar metal sheets were fitted inside the thin pipes (*b*) and in pipe *f*, which was surrounded by cooling water. (*g*) Hot-air cylinder. (*h*) Cold-air cylinder. (*i*) Valve chest. (*j*) Furnace.

C Ericsson's caloric engine in its final form. The engine is shown here in longitudinal-section; the drawing was made by the inventor himself.

steam, but would have the advantage of being produced in less time and with less fuel.

Model-scale attempts with this "fire-machine", as Ericsson called it, had encouraging results. Unfortunately, he could not find a partner to help develop his ideas—Sweden at that time was very much of an industrial backwater—so he left for England where, in 1826, he settled. In 1833, after a lot of struggle—both with his "fire-machine" and in the fight to survive—Ericsson completed his caloric engine, which generated 5 horsepower. The engine attracted a lot of attention from industrialists as well as from academics. The principle of the engine was the same as that of the Stirling engine, but the two inventors had arrived independently at their solutions from different starting points. Ericsson, however, had provided his engine with a "regenerator", which he imagined would enable the heat from the furnace to work "over and over again", as he said in his enthusiastic description of the engine in his *The Caloric Engine*, published in London in 1833. The great physicist Michael Faraday (1791–1867) warmly admired Ericsson but had reservations about Ericsson's explanation of the function of the regenerator. It would, he said, almost be a *perpetuum mobile*, if it really worked as Ericsson claimed. The two gentlemen were, however, ignorant of an important detail in the theory of heat—the law of the mechanical equivalence of heat, formulated in 1842 by Robert Mayer.

But John Ericsson had plenty of other interests, one of them being

D How Ericsson's ultimate caloric engine worked. The working piston (*a*) and the feed piston (*b*) worked in the same cylinder. (*c*) Furnace. A crank mechanism (*d*) was necessary in order to make *a* and *b* move in a suitable way. (*e*) Valve regulated by a disc cam on the crank axle and connecting the cylinder space *f* with the outside air. (*g*) Air-pressure-regulated valves. (*h*) Holes connecting cylinder spaces *f* and *i*: uncovered when *b* moved to the right; *e* is closed, holes *h* are uncovered. Since *a* moves faster than *b*, *g* open, and cold air enters the cylinder. (2) Piston *b* turns, *h* are covered, and *e* is opened, so that the air in *f* can escape. (3, 4) Piston *a* turns but moves at a slower speed than *b*, so valves *g* remain open. (5) Piston *b* turns and *e* is closed. The holes (*h*) are uncovered, and when the air enclosed in *i* and *f* is now heated, its pressure increases, and valves *g* close. (6–7) The increasing pressure of the air, which becomes hotter and hotter, forces *a* to the right.

A1

A Rider's closed hot-air engine, which, according to the ads (**1**), was "UNRIVALLED for light or heavy pumping", had an effect of 0.25–1 horsepower. (**2**) Cross-section of the engine. The flywheel (*a*) on the crank axle (*b*) was driven by both plunger pistons (*c, d*) by means of cranks (*e*), which were set almost perpendicularly to each other. The cold-air cylinder (*f*) was surrounded by a jacket (*g*), through which cooling water continually flowed. The engine worked in the following way: first of all, piston *d* compressed the air in *f* to about one-third its normal volume. Simultaneously, piston *c* moved upwards. When *d* had almost completed its down-stroke, the air was transferred – without changing its volume very much – from cylinder *f* to the hot-air cylinder (*h*) by way of a passage (*i*) containing the regenerator. This consisted of small, thin iron plates which gave up their heat to the air as it passed. The air was then further heated since *h* was sunk in the furnace (*j*). The air pressure thus increased considerably and impelled piston *c* upwards. The pressure increase further caused piston *d* to travel upwards and the air rapidly returned to cylinder *f*, giving up its heat to the regenerator when

passing it. In *f*, the air was further cooled by *g*; the air pressure sank to its minimum, and the piston *d* returned downwards.
B In the closed Stirling engine, an inert gas, helium, is used as a working agent. (**1**) The gas in the hot space (*a*) of the cylinder is heated by an external burner (*b*) and expands. The two pistons (*c, d*), which are both connected to a rhombic drive linkage (*e*), are then pushed downwards because of the pressure increase. (**2**) When the gas is almost fully expanded, piston *c* turns, and the hot air starts travelling by way of the regenerator (*f*) and pipes surrounded by cooling water (*g*) down to the cold space (*h*) of the cylinder. During this part of the working cycle, piston *d* is still on its down-stroke. (**3**) As piston *c* approaches the top of its stroke, most of the gas has been transferred to *h*, and, since its pressure is sinking, piston *d* is drawn upwards. The gas is then returned to *a* by way of the regenerator, and the cycle starts anew.

developing the marine propeller. In 1839, he moved to New York, where he continued working on his hot-air engine. In 1851, he had a new and different version ready, and it was shown at the Great Exhibition in London the same year. Initially, Ericsson had imagined that the caloric engine would be most suitable for propelling ships, and, in 1852, he managed to get a couple of investors to finance his project for building a ship in which his engine could demonstrate its real value. A paddle-wheeler was built with a displacement of 2,200 tons; it was almost 295 ft (90 m) long and 46 ft (14 m) wide. The maiden voyage took place at New Year, 1853, and was a complete fiasco. The hot-air engine took up most of the hull space and gave only half the power estimated by Ericsson; the speed was proportionately low. Moreover, the ship was not very seaworthy, and capsized and sank in a storm in the entrance to New York harbour.

John Ericsson, undaunted, set about finding new areas of use for his engine. Only a year or so after the ship failure, he presented yet another version of his engine, this time intended to satisfy the increasing demand for medium-sized sources of power in industry. This engine turned out to be a great success and, in the late 1850s, was manufactured under licence by some ten companies in the United States and in Europe.

In 1862, the American Academy of Arts and Sciences awarded the Rumford medal to Ericsson for his caloric engine. In the same year, Ericsson built a ship—this time with a steam-engine to propel it—which brought him immediate fame. The ship was the *Monitor*, which not only brought about a turning-point in the American Civil War to the advantage of the Northern states, but also introduced a new element into marine warfare.

The caloric engine was enormously popular because it was easy to run and used any kind of fuel. Its successes inspired many inventors to try to produce technically better versions. A weak point in Ericsson's machine was its relatively small furnace, which made constant supervision necessary if it was fired with a quick-burning fuel, such as wood. One inventor who succeeded in improving the hot-air engine was a German, Wilhelm Lehmann, who presented his version in 1868. It worked with a closed system, which further increased fuel economy; it spread not insignificantly in Germany and parts of Central Europe. Among the engineers who produced variations of the hot-air engine in the 1870s and 1880s was the American Alexander K. Rider, who introduced a regenerator in the closed system. Unlike the regenerator tried out by John Ericsson in the 1830s, Rider's design was theoretically sound, due to progress that had been made in thermodynamics since then. Ericsson's caloric engine was manufactured by several companies, among them the DeLamater Iron Works, New York, which employed Rider in 1887. The company had a long-standing connection with Ericsson and had built *Monitor*. Rider and Ericsson soon became partners and formed the Rider-Ericsson Engine Co., which, after Ericsson's death in 1889, bought up the DeLamater Iron Works. Caloric engines of both Rider's and Ericsson's design were produced, and the Rider-Ericsson Engine Co. soon dominated the American market, continuing to produce caloric engines until that type of prime mover was superceded by newer and better types, and the company ceased to operate in the beginning of the 1930s.

Cayley's ideas were, however, tried again in the late 1930s by Philips in Holland. The company was trying to establish new export markets in developing countries for their radio receivers but, in places without electricity, the operating costs of battery-powered radio receivers with current-absorbing electronic tubes became too great. A search began for a power source that would drive a small generator, the hot-air engine was recalled, and engineers led by Dr. Roelof Meijer set about rejuvenating the old ideas. The Second

World War intervened, and when, by the early 1950s, results began to be promising, the original application had been rendered technically redundant by the more economic transistor. Meijer and his research team then sought new applications for what had become known as the Stirling engine. At first, various military applications were suggested, where the silent running of the engine would be an advantage. Another interesting possibility was also tried by running the heat process in the engine backwards, thus creating a cold engine, suitable for powering deep-freezes. Continued development during the 1960s pointed in an entirely different direction, however, for it suggested that the Stirling engine could be used in vehicles, primarily in buses and lorries.

The working medium of the Stirling engine is helium in a closed system, which gives, among other things, minimum mechanical and chemical wear and tear. As a result, lubricating oil consumption is negligible. The external combustion also makes it possible to deliver fuel continuously and to let it mix with air in the proportions that give optimal efficiency and the purest exhaust fumes possible. All this makes the Stirling engine much quieter than other vehicle engines, which "puff" their exhaust fumes out of the cylinders with each exhaust stroke. With suitable fuel, the Stirling engine can be made practically free of harmful exhaust fumes. The connecting rod of the ordinary engine has been replaced in the Stirling engine by what is called rhomboid drive linkage, which all but eliminates vibration. Its efficiency is high, too; in larger units of 300 to 400 horsepower it is nearly twice that of conventional vehicle engines. Even if its power-to-weight ratio cannot yet compete with that of the petrol engine, it certainly can with that of the diesel engine.

Internal Combustion Engines

Time and again, the history of technology records suggestions for burning a high-energy fuel inside a cylinder and for using the combustion gases to do useful work as they expand. We have already mentioned the unsuccessful attempts of Huygens and Papin to build gunpowder engines in the 1680s. In 1684, a French monk, Jean de Hautefeuille, fared no better with various suggestions for a gunpowder-driven fountain.

When different forms of steam-engine started to appear in the eighteenth century, suggestions of how to build "explosion" engines were conspicuously absent, but from about 1800, they were plentiful, and we shall mention a few of them. In 1794, an Englishman, Robert Street, tried to build a cylinder engine in which the piston was to be driven by the combustion of gasified tar or turpentine oil. In 1801, the Frenchman Philippe Lebon came up with a similar idea and tried out a kind of double-acting steam-engine driven by the internal combustion of a mixture of lighting gas and air, ignited electrically. During the 1790s, Lebon had experimented with the preparation from coal and wood of gas for lighting, and, by 1799, he had an apparatus ready for demonstration. Boulton & Watt in England had been thinking along the same lines, and James Watt's son Gregory visited Lebon in Paris. This brought about Boulton & Watt's development, under the supervision of William Murdock, of a commercially viable lighting gas. Lebon, however, took no further part in the development of the engine, for he was assaulted and killed in the Champs Elysées in Paris in 1804.

A report of Lebon's internal combustion engine came to the notice of Sir George Cayley, who was searching indefatigably for a new, compact engine which could help him power a flying machine. In 1809, Sir George described with admirable lucidity how a gas engine ought to work, but, as with the hot-air engine, he did not himself attempt any experiments, although his compatriots William Cecil and Samuel Brown did. In 1817, Cecil, a parson, had made an experimental model of an atmospheric gas engine, which he tried to improve by systematic experiments. The engine is said to have worked very well, but it consumed vast amounts of gas, and Cecil eventually abandoned his efforts. Brown was more successful. He took out a patent for his engine—also of the atmospheric type—in 1823 and subsequently built several engines that were practicable. He attempted to use a two-cylinder version of his design to drive a carriage. It worked well in principle, but he could not possibly think of a way of carrying the gas along with the engine! In 1833, Lemuel Wellman Wright, an Englishman, built an interesting gas engine—the first in which the gas pressure worked directly on the piston. It was much like the high-pressure steam-engines which were then enjoying increasing popularity. Wright's engine, which had a double action and a water-cooled cylinder, was the first to really show the shape of things to come. In 1854, two Italians, Eugène Barsanti and Felix Matteucci, built a gas engine with electrical ignition and a "freely flying" piston. Both of these concepts were to reappear—the latter quite soon.

A remarkable gas engine was invented by a Munich clockmaker called Christian Reithmann (1818–1909). He started his experiments in 1852, and six years later, he was able to demonstrate a gas engine which, today, we would call a two-stroke engine. Reithmann used his engine to drive various machine tools in his workshop. In 1860, he was given a royal Bavarian charter to manufacture his engine, and in due course he founded an engine factory. In 1872 and 1873, he developed the engine into a four-stroke. Later, however, he became involved in serious patent disputes, since several other inventors had thought of the same possibilities.

Etienne Lenoir (1822–1900) was a Frenchman born in Luxemburg. In 1860, he patented a brilliantly thought-out design for a gas engine. He was extremely talented and even as a young man had made some important inventions, including a method of enamelling plate, which had made him financially independent. His first engine employed a horizontal, water-cooled cylinder and generated 4 horsepower. The fuel was lighting gas mixed with air, and the engine had a slide mechanism on either side of the piston. The ignition was electric, current being delivered by two Bunsen elements, and the voltage was stepped up in an induction coil of the Ruhmkorff roll-type with hammer interrupters.

The engine was very well received—at last, an alternative to the steam-engine! Mass production was soon under way, undertaken partly by Marioni & Lefevre (later Société Lenoir) in Paris and

A In 1825, Samuel Brown built this vehicle, which was powered by a two-cylinder atmospheric engine. For a piston, Brown used a float on water. An external gas burner ignited the gas mixture inside the cylinder.
B Between the years 1872 and 1873, Reithmann reconstructed his "two-stroke cycle" engine and turned it

into a four-stroke one, shown here as seen from the side (**1**) and front (**2**). Only a single engine was built. The piston (*a*) moved upwards and sucked in air through a valve (*b*), which was regulated by a cam (*c*) on the steering shaft (*d*). The air travelled from the valve to the compression chamber (*e*) by way of the main slide valve (*f*). When two-thirds of the piston stroke remained, a distributor slide valve (*g*), regulated by a cam (*h*) on *d*, was opened. The air sucked into *e* was then mixed with gas. As the piston (*a*) changed its direction, *b* as well as the upper gas pipe in the slide valve (*g*) were closed. Since the piston was now travelling downwards, the gas mixture in *e* was compressed. It was then ignited and burnt, considerably increasing the pressure. The piston was forced upwards again, and when it had reached its topmost position, a valve (*i*) regulated by a cam (*j*) was opened. The exhaust gas escaped from the compression chamber through *i*, and the piston sank. The lower gas pipe in slide valve *g* was closed as soon as ignition had started. The piston's movement was transmitted to the crankshaft (*k*), on which a flywheel (*l*) and a belt pulley (*m*) were mounted. A cog-wheel (*n*) on the crankshaft meshed with another, larger cogwheel (*o*) on the steering shaft (*d*), which was thus rotating half as fast as *k*. A small pump (*p*), which like the slide valve *f* was powered by a crank (*q*) on *d*, supplied pilot flame *r* with a mixture of gas and air. Pilot flame *s* in the lid of slide valve *f* was connected directly to the gas conduit.

partly by Reading Iron Works Ltd. in England. Lenoir had an eye for publicity and devoted himself to an intense campaign on behalf of his engine, for which he predicted a splendid future. Stationary gas engines of up to 100 horsepower would soon eclipse the steam-engine, he claimed, while others could be used also for locomotives, which would carry gas generators instead of steam boilers. The steam-engine manufacturers gave as good as they got (they had plenty to say about Lenoir's claims), but the Lenoir engine, in spite of—or perhaps because of—the polemics, gained ground in the 1860s. One incontestable point was the fact that its thermal efficiency was higher than that of smaller steam-engines. But there is no evidence that gas engines with a higher output than about 12 horsepower were ever built.

Lenoir's publicity campaign had one effect that he probably had not envisaged: the German merchant Nikolaus August Otto (1832–91) became so interested in the engine that he had a couple of gas engines made under licence by a workshop in Cologne. They did not work very well, however, so Otto, who was convinced of the engine's great potential, sat down and redesigned the whole thing. The new gas engine was patented in England in 1863 and later in France and various other countries. Otto teamed up with an inventive engin-

eer, Eugen Langen (1833–95) and, in 1864, founded N. A. Otto & Co. in Cologne.

The first gas engine built by Otto had several interesting design features. It had a "freely flying" piston, that is, a piston which was driven up quickly, as the gas mixture exploded in the lower part of the cylinder. The piston was fitted with a rack, which, via a ratchet, engaged a cog-wheel on the axle of the balance wheel. As the piston moved up, the rack was disengaged from the balance-wheel axle. After the piston in its extreme top position had been slowed down by a rubber bumper (!), the pressure in the cylinder dropped drastically, the piston was driven down by atmospheric pressure, and at the same time, the ratchet engaged the cog-wheel. During this power stroke, the balance wheel was, in other words, given additional energy. In one of his many books, Franz M. Feldhaus gives a hilarious description of an Otto-Langen engine in operation. He grew up in a German health resort named Godesberg where his father was a director of the company that bottled the spa's mineral water, which an Otto-Langen engine pumped up. Feldhaus describes how, as a little boy, he was scared out of his wits whenever he had to pass the pump house.

The engine was placed in a dark corner, and the piston rose up

C Lenoir's gas engine; (**1**) the construction as seen from above, (**2**) cross-section through the engine, (**3**) an early Lenoir engine as seen from the side. The coal gas entered through two flues (*a*) which were alternately connected to the slide valve flue. From there, the gas was directed through another flue in the slide valve (*c*) and to a mixing chamber (*d*). Air from outside the engine entered *d*, which was connected to the slide valve by a number of small holes (*e*). The gas and air mixture was sucked through these holes and into either end of the cylinder by way of the slide valve (*c*) and one of the cylinder flues (*f*). When the piston (*g*) had travelled less than halfway through the water-cooled cylinder, the gas and air inlets were closed by the slide valve (*c*), and the coal-gas mixture in the cylinder was ignited by an electric spark. The current was delivered by two Bunsen elements (*h*), and the low voltage was transformed into high in an induction coil (*i*). While the combustion gases expanded and forced the piston in front of them, the combustion gases on the other side of the piston left the cylinder through an exhaust slide valve (*j*). (*k*) Centrifugal governor, driven by the crank axle (*l*) by way of a belt (*m*). (*n*) Flywheel. The coal-gas feed could be regulated with taps (*o*).

A Otto's and Langen's gas engine of 1867; (**1**) from above, (**2**) front view, (**3**) side view. Coal gas and air entered the cylinder through a slide valve (**1**) when the piston (**2**) started its upward stroke. The piston was guided by a cross-bar (**3**), fitted on the piston rod (**4**) and glid along two rods (**5**). When the piston had moved a little, the gas and air supplies were closed by the slide valve, and the gas mixture combusted, forcing the piston up until it hit a rubber bumper. Since the gases expanded and transferred heat to the cooling water (**6**), the pressure in the cylinder sank below atmospheric. The piston was forced down, and the piston rod (**4**) with its cogs then drove a cog ring (**7**) on the shaft of the flywheel (**8**). Since the flywheel rotated to the left, the engine had a friction clutch, so that the flywheel shaft was released from the cog ring when the latter was turned to the right (and also when it was turned to the left but ran slower than the flywheel shaft). The clutch is shown here in section. The cog ring (**7**) was attached by four bolts (**9**) to two loose discs, one on either side of a disc (**10**) which was secured to the flywheel axle. The inside of the cog ring was shaped to hold four wedges (**11**) whose wide ends bore against the bolt joints and whose narrow ends had noses. Three small cylinders (**12**) were fitted between each wedge and **7**. When the cog ring rotated to the right and **10** to the left, the wedges stayed in this position and glid against the periphery of the disc. However, when **7** rotated to the left and went faster than **10**, the wedges moved forwards until the cylinders had been clamped against **7**, so that **7** and **10** were engaged. During the last part of the piston's downward stroke, a valve was opened by slide valve **1**, and the combustion gases left the cylinder. The slide valve was controlled by two joined eccentrics (**13, 14**), set at right angles to each other and mounted on shaft **15** without being attached to it. The slide valve was connected by an eccentric rod to the ring on **13**. On **14**, a pawl (**16**) was mounted, which engaged a ratchet wheel (**17**), fixed to shaft **15**, when a lever (**18**) was pushed downwards by a knob (**19**) on **4**. When this happened, the eccentrics rotated with the ratchet wheel. When the piston started upwards again, **18** was lifted by a spring (**20**), **16** was released, and the eccentrics stopped. While the gas mixture entered the cylinder, the piston was raised by a second lever (**21**), whose one end was situated beneath **19** while the other bore against the eccentric band of **14**. When **14** was turned, **21** brought the piston rod upwards. (**22**) Cooling-water inlet. (**23**) Outlet.

B In 1876, "Silent Otto" was developed. Here, its construction can be seen from above (1) and from the side (2); the steering gear (3), the exhaust valve (4), and the slide valve in longitudinal- (5) and cross-section (6) are shown in greater detail. The engine worked according to the four-stroke principle — sucking in of the charge, compression, combustion and expansion, and exhaust of combustion gases took place during four consecutive piston strokes. (1) Piston. (2) Compression chamber. (3) Cooling-water jacket. (4) Cooling-water outlet. (5) Lubricating cup. (6) Exhaust valve for the combustion gases. (7) Cock for control of gas supply. A cog-wheel (8) on the crankshaft meshed with another cog-wheel (9), which had twice as many cogs and was mounted on the camshaft (10). (11) A centrifugal governor which, by way of a gearing, was driven by the camshaft and used a double lever (12) to control the gas supply. When the machine's work load was reduced so that its rpm increased too much, the weights in the governor swung outwards. The governor's casing then rose, and 12 displaced a cam (13) along the camshaft so that another double lever (14) no longer bore against it. This lever opened and closed the gas valve (15) only when it bore against 13. When this was not the case, air only was sucked into the cylinder until the machine's rpm had been reduced. Another cam (16) on 10 controlled the exhaust valve (6) by way of a spring-loaded lever (17). The slide valve (18) was given a reciprocating movement by a crank (19) on 10. (20) Gas pipe for the ignition flame. From the position the slide valve has at 5, it moves left and then back to its original position. Meanwhile, air and gas are sucked into the cylinder; the air enters through duct 21, which is connected to the air outside the engine, travels through the slide-valve duct (22), where it is mixed with gas from duct 23, and eventually enters the cylinder through duct 24. The slide valve also contained a chamber (25) which was connected to a separate gas duct (26) just before ignition was to take place. The chamber was then filled with gas mixed with air, which entered through duct 27. In the slide-valve lid was a continually burning flame which ignited the gas mixture in 25, whereupon the connection between the flame and the chamber was closed; instead, a very narrow duct which connected the chamber with the cylinder's inlet duct (24) was opened. When the pressure in 25 had risen to equal the pressure inside the cylinder, the chamber was connected directly to 24, and the gas combusted.

A The ignition device in combustion engines with a pilot flame was sensitive and not very reliable, and the invention of the controlled hot-tube ignition (**1**) was a great improvement. The tube (*a*) was made of china or nickel and was closed at one end. It was fitted with a flange (*b*), so that it could be attached to the engine. The tube was heated by a gas burner (*c*), and when the gas mixture in the compression chamber (*d*) was to be ignited, a small portion of it was let into the hot tube through a slide-valve flue (*e*) or a valve. In between, the tube was in contact with the outside air, which entered through another flue (*f*). The open hot-tube ignition (**2**) was a later invention used by Daimler and Maybach in the engine they began to construct in 1882. The tube was connected to the compression chamber, and by placing the burner at different distances from the open end of the tube, it was possible to cause earlier or later ignition.

B Daimler's combustion-engine-powered bicycle of 1885 was first tested in November, 1886.

with a terrible crash; with a rattling sound it engaged with the balance wheel, and then descended with an anxious whine. . . . The explosions seemed quite arbitrary, and in between there was only sinister silence. The convulsions of this engine inspired real fear.

The little boy's reaction was quite natural. If an Otto-Langen engine were to be taken into service somewhere in industry today, the union security officer would undoubtedly take immediate action!

At the world exhibition in Paris in 1867, the Otto-Langen engine competed for attention with no less than fourteen Lenoir engines. At first it was marked down, not least because of the awful noise it made, but after Franz Reuleaux, the German representative on the jury, had intervened, the engine was thoroughly tested. It transpired that the operating efficiency of the Otto-Langen engine was much better than that of Lenoir's gas engine, and the gold medal was awarded to Otto and Langen.

This success was incontestable; however, Otto and Langen were aware of the shortcomings of their creation and carried on experimenting. The outcome, in 1876, was a great breakthrough for gas engines: the first four-stroke engine. It was immediately nicknamed "Silent Otto"—a self-explanatory name. The four-stroke engine became a great success. In the first ten years, more than thirty thousand engines were manufactured at the Gasmotorenfabrik Deutz AG, which was the name of Otto and Langen's company after it was reorganized in 1872.

"Silent Otto's" celebrated début on the international market took place at the world exhibition in Paris in 1878. Franz Reuleaux had followed Otto's development work since his first engine had been displayed in 1867, and they had become good friends. Reuleaux now praised "Silent Otto" abundantly. He considered it the greatest step forward in the field of engine technology since James Watt, and this at a time when he had just attacked German industry, accusing it of producing inferior goods—*billig und schlecht*—so this praise was made much of in the papers.

In the following decade, a storm blew up regarding the patent rights of the gas engine. This development could have been anticipated, since several designers had been thinking along the same lines as Nikolaus Otto. In France it was claimed that the principle of the four-stroke engine had been stated as early as 1862 by Alphonse Beau de Rochas (1815–91), although his ideas had never got beyond the drawing-board. The Gasmotorenfabrik Deutz sued Reithmann for patent infringement—his engine worked in the same way as "Silent Otto"—but the case was dismissed, since Reithmann could easily prove that his engine had been in operation since 1873. The clockmaker must have been very bitter to see the Deutz factory expand as rapidly as it did even as early as the 1880s. One might add that this company, which has merged with others and is today called Klöckner-Humboldt-Deutz, has a splendid works museum, containing a fine collection of many of the earliest internal combustion engines, including even Reithmann's engine.

When the great demand for gas engines started in the early 1870s, the Deutz factory took on two engineers, who were later to become very famous. One was Gottlieb Daimler (1834–1900) and the other Wilhelm Maybach (1847–1929). Daimler realized the development potential of the Otto engine and, a few years later, went his own way in order to develop a compact engine capable of a high number of revolutions. In 1882, Daimler set up a little workshop in conjunction with Maybach in Cannstatt outside Stuttgart, where he could try out his ideas in practice. In 1883, he invented hot-tube ignition. He planned to use volatile petroleum derivatives as fuel, and, in the same year, he and Maybach gave their first engine a trial run. The third experimental model was used to drive a bicycle with iron-shod wheels, the engine turning at 900 rpm—the normal rpm of the Otto engine was around 200—and developing 0.5 horsepower. In 1886, this motor vehicle began to roll along the roads, driven by *Benzin*—an almost unknown liquid that, in those days, could be bought in any chemist's shop.

Daimler built his first four-wheel motor vehicle in 1887, but the honour of having designed the first real "motorcar" does not belong to him. The previous year, Karl Benz (1844—1929) had jeopardized the safety of the roads in Mannheim with his three-wheel carriage, driven by an 0.75-horsepower engine. Quite independently of Daimler, Benz had developed an engine with a design almost identical to that of the Daimler engine. In 1871, Benz had started a factory for manufacturing gas engines, Rheinischen Gasmotorenfabrik AG, which he managed successfully. Even as a student at the Polytechnikum in Karlsruhe, he had been toying with the idea of designing an engine-driven vehicle. He worked on the development of this idea parallel with the manufacture of gas engines, and in 1886, his efforts were crowned with success.

The Two-Stroke Engine

Despite the enormous success of the four-stroke engine, it came to be criticized. It was suggested that it was inefficient for the same cylinder to function as a pump on one revolution and as a working cylinder on the next, for its dimensions were adequate for its working function but unneccessarily large for its pumping function. Several designers attacked this problem, and the first to find a successful solution was the Scotsman Sir Dugald Clerk (1854—1932). In 1878, he built a two-stroke engine, in which the fuel was fed in by a special pump cylinder (which Clerk called a "displacer") next to the working cylinder.

Both the four-stroke and the two-stroke engine turned out to be very hard-wearing, and their basic designs have survived until the present day. A number of essential improvements have been added over the years, but in both engines the mode of operation has remained unaltered.

The fascinating story of the development of the automobile has been told in many books. But, here, we shall concentrate on the engine as a prime mover.

Rudolf Diesel and his "Rational Heat Engine"

In December, 1892, Rudolf Diesel (1858—1913) was granted a German patent for the engine which has borne his name ever since. The following year saw the publication of his pioneering work *The Theory and Construction of a Rational Heat Engine*. It attracted a great deal of attention—and considerable criticism. Diesel considered that the cylinder compression should be greatly increased to attain an internal temperature high enough to ignite the fuel that would be injected during the last part of the compression stroke. Diesel based his theory on the fire-piston, which had already been launched in several versions in the early 1800s and was, in a way, a forerunner of the match.

The fuel which Diesel first intended to use in his engine was finely powdered coal, a fuel that many designers were then thinking of using for various kinds of engine. Diesel, however, soon abandoned this idea and instead started to experiment with crude oil. In 1897, after intensive development work which took its toll of his health, Diesel had achieved an engine with an efficiency wholly superior to that of other combustion engines. Before long, the diesel engine had become a concept and had begun its victorious progress round the world. At an early stage, two German companies, Maschinenfabrik Augsburg-Nuremberg (MAN) and the Krupp concern, and the Swiss firm Gebrüder Sulzer had begun to make diesel engines on licence

C A four-stroke Daimler engine of 1897. (a) Adjustable air intake. The carburettor (b) worked by transforming the fuel into a mist. Maybach's carburettor was less sensitive to the degree of volatility than earlier carburettors, and it suppled more fuel in proportion to the amount of air, since the fuel took up less volume when in drop-form than when in gaseous form. The engine lacked a throttle. A certain adjustment could, however, be obtained by varying the amount of air in the fuel/air mixture. The spring-loaded suction valve (c) opened because of the vacuum created in the cylinder (d) at the start of the suction stroke, and it closed again when the piston (e) approached its lowest position. The disadvantage of this was that c always opened too late and closed too early. The exhaust valve (f) was governed by a camshaft (g), which rotated at half the number of engine revolutions. A burner (h) with an "eternal" flame kept the ignition tube (i) glowing. The reason ignition did not take place arbitrarily during the suction and compression strokes was that i's length had been adjusted so that the residue of combusted gases which always remained in the ignition tube stopped the fuel mixture from reaching the glowing part. Only at the very end of the compression stroke had the fuel mixture been pressed far enough into i to be ignited. The engine was switched off when a tap (j) was turned, so that the fuel supply was cut off. (k) The float chamber's overflow. (l) Exhaust pipe. (m) Cooling water inlet. (n) Outlet.

A The front page of Benz & Co.'s 1886 patent for the gas-engine-powered car.
B A motor-car built by Karl Benz in 1888. The carriage (a) was carried by the "chassis" (b) by means of three fully elliptical springs (c), the foremost of which was mounted cross-wise. The rear wheel had iron rims, whereas the front wheel had a massive rubber tyre. On its vertically cradled crankshaft, the one-cylinder, four-stroke engine (d) had a flywheel (e), which ran horizontally, since it was feared that a vertical flywheel would impair manoeuvra-

bility (practical tests, however, allayed these fears). In the evaporation-type carburettor (*f*) the sucked-in air passed over the fuel and became saturated by its vapour. The fuel, petrol, was float-regulated and was kept in a tank underneath the driver's seat. The high-voltage electrical ignition was fed by batteries. The lubricating oil was poured into glass containers (*g*), from which it flowed under its own pressure to the various oiling points. The engine was cooled by simply letting water from a container (*h*) boil away. The power transmission from engine to wheels took place by means of bevel gears (*i*), a belt pulley (*j*), and a belt (*k*), whose forward end ran over one of two parallel belt pulleys, which were situated beneath the driver's seat. One of these belt pulleys ran freely on its shaft, whereas the other was connected to a differential of more or less modern construction. The two separate shafts of the differential (the left-hand one can partly be seen at *l*) drove the rear wheels via sprocket wheels and chains. The chain drive gave a flexible transmission which remained unaffected by the swaying movements of the car; further, the shaft pivots were free from torsion. A crank handle on a lever (*m*) to the left of the driver was used to engage or disengage the gear; when the crank was turned, belt *k* was moved between the above-named parallel belt pulleys. The brakes (*n*) were activated by pulling lever *m* backwards. When a handle (*o*) was reset, a device was actuated which shifted the car's neutral into a crawling forward gear which could be used for climbing steep hills (with an maximum inclination of 1:10). This gear worked by way of an intermediate shaft with chains and sprocket wheels (*p*). However, the car was always set in motion in normal gear; it was only possible to switch from crawling to neutral via normal. The engine's number of revolutions per minute could be varied within certain limits by adjusting the air intake to the carburettor by means of a valve. However, the low cruising speed, about 6 mph (10 km/h)—the maximum speed was about 9 mph (15 km/h)—made engaging, disengaging, and braking unwarranted. (Compare, for instance, how you use the clutch and a constant pressure on the throttle when you reverse a modern car.) The car was steered by means of a lever (*q*) mounted on a vertical shaft which affected the front wheel by way of a pair of racks (*r*). The front end of the steering lever was shaped like an arrow, which indicated the position of the front wheel (not visible from the driver's seat) on a fixed "direction indicator disc" (*s*).

A The principle of Clerk's two-stroke engine. (1) Gas and air was sucked into the pump cylinder (*a*) through a slide valve (*b*) when the pump piston (*c*) travelled to the right. The piston rod was mounted on a crank (*d*) on the drive shaft (*e*), where another crank (*f*) ran 90° after *d* and was connected to the piston (*g*) in the power cylinder (*h*). Thus *g* also travelled to the right during the suction stroke. Cylinder *h* was water-cooled and was connected to *a* by a slide valve (*i*) and a pipe (*j*). Slide valve *i* was closed during the suction stroke. (2) When piston *d* turned, *b* was closed while *i* was opened. The gas mixture in *a* was beginning to be compressed, but by then, piston *g* had moved enough to uncover an opening (*k*). The entering gas mixture then drove out the combustion gases in *h* through *k* and by way of a duct (*l*), which surrounded *h*, to an exhaust duct (*m*). (3) When *g* had turned and once more covered *k*, the compression started – also in *a*. When the gas-mixture transfer from *a* to *h* had ceased and piston *d* had turned, slide valve *i* was closed. (4) When *g* had reached its turning-point, the gas mixture was ignited by a flame in *i*. Piston *g* was forced to the right by the expansion of the gases until *k* was once more uncovered.

B A fire-piston. The principle for this precursor of the match constituted the basis for Diesel's "rational heat engine". (1) The mechanism consisted of a long piston (*a*) with a small piece of tinder (*b*) at its lower end. The piston fitted tightly into a cylinder (*c*). (2) When the piston was rapidly forced into the cylinder, the air pressure increased greatly inside *c*, and the ensuing heat caused the tinder to ignite.

C The working cycle of the diesel engine. (1) When the piston (*a*) moves downwards, air is sucked into the cylinder directly from the atmosphere through a valve (*b*). (2) As the piston turns, valve *b* is

E₁   E₂   E₃

E₄

Left column (bottom)

closed, and the air inside the cylinder is compressed to about 35 atmospheres. Its temperature rapidly increases. (3) Oil is injected under high pressure when the compression has reached its maximum. The oil mist immediately ignites and quietly burns at an almost constant pressure. A governor decides how large an amount of fuel should be injected, so that the charge matches the engine's work load. (4) During the combustion, the piston is forced downwards, and during the last phase (5) of the working cycle, the combustion gases are forced out of the cylinder through a valve (c).
D An early diesel engine; (1) longitudinal-section, (2) cross-section. (a) Cylinder. (b) Cooling-water jacket. (c) Piston. (d) Crankshaft. (e) Air-intake valve. (f) Fuel-injection valve. (g) Exhaust valve. These valves were opened and closed by levers (h), whose movements were controlled by cams (i) on the camshaft (j). A two-stage air compressor (k) with a cooling-water jacket (l) supplied air compressed to 55—60 atmospheres for the fuel injection.
E The Wankel engine consists of an equilateral rotor (a), which turns inside a chamber equipped with a cooling duct (b). The rotor's points run in trochoidal paths along the inside wall of the chamber, where

they form gas-tight seals for three sub-chambers (c, d, e). (f) Drive shaft. (g) Planetary gearing. (1) During the first phase of the working cycle in sub-chamber c, a fuel-and-air mixture is sucked in through a duct (h). At the same time, the fuel mixture in d is compressed, while the combustion gases in e have just reached maximal expansion. (2) The volume of c gets larger and larger because of the rotor's eccentric motion, and fuel mixture is still being sucked into e. The volume of d is decreasing, and when the fuel mixture in it has reached maximal compression, it is ignited by a spark from a spark-plug (i). The combustion gases in e start leaving through the now uncovered exhaust duct (j). (3) The volume of sub-chamber e is now at its largest. The combustion gases in d expand and force the rotor in a clockwise direction; meanwhile, e has almost been emptied of combustion gases. When the rotor has turned a little further, e will start sucking in fuel and air anew. (4) A Wankel engine is often equipped with two rotors to achieve greater efficiency. One is then turned 180° in relation to the other, so that the engine will run as smoothly as possible. In practice, the combustion chambers (k) are partly sunk into the rotors.

Right column (body text)

and also partook in the further development of the engine. In the United States the Diesel Motor Co. of America was founded in St. Louis, Missouri, in 1896, at the instigation of the master brewer Adolphus Busch; the first unit made in the United States was delivered in 1898 and generated 60 horsepower. It was used to power an electric generator. The patent rights for the Swedish market were acquired by the financier Knut Wallenberg, who, in 1899, founded AB Diesels Motorer in Sickla outside Stockholm. Jonas Hesselman was employed there as a designer, and he improved the diesel engine considerably; he also designed the first marine diesel engine, which was ready in 1905.

The Wankel Engine

In the last hundred years, many inventors and technicians have tried to find new ways of developing the combustion engine, but both the four-stroke principle and its technical application in the piston engine have proved extremely long-lasting. The only real newcomer in this area is the Wankel engine, invented by the German engineer Felix Wankel (1902—). This is a four-stroke engine in which the piston and cylinder have been replaced by a rotor, rotating inside a housing. The cross-section of the rotor is shaped like an equilateral triangle with convex sides, and the inside of the rotor housing in cross-section looks like an oval, slightly constricted in the middle. The rotor runs eccentrically on the axle shaft, and the power is transmitted by a sun-and-planet gear. One of the greatest problems in developing this engine was to achieve both a totally tight seal and a minimum of friction between the rotor and the housing. The solution was a sealing strip designed in a way similar to that for the piston rings in a conventional engine. The rotor is oil-cooled, and the housing is normally water-cooled, but air-cooling has also been tried out. After many years of experimental work, Wankel was able to test-drive his first working engine at New Year, 1957. A production prototype was ready as early as 1963, at NSU i Neckarsulm, and the Wankel engine began to be mass produced during the following year. The prototype can now be seen in the Deutsches Museum in Munich.

The advantages of the Wankel engine over the piston engine are its compact structure and the small number of its parts. Vibration is much less due to the fact that it has a rotary motion and not, like the piston engine, a reciprocating motion.

The Gas Turbine

In its design, the gas turbine is the simplest of the combustion engines, but laymen sometimes have difficulty in understanding how it works. In 1897, Nils Gustaf Dalén (1869—1937), a Swedish engineer who won the Nobel prize in physics, wrote a letter to a friend to persuade him to become his partner in the development of a gas turbine engine; he described its principle as follows:

> Imagine a stove! If you blow through the grate, the hot smoke goes out through the chimney. But the clever thing is, if you blow in one cubic metre, two or three will go out. A pump up there, in other words, could drive another pump down there to suck in the air. Now, if we substitute these pumps with turbines. . . .

In his letter, Dalén also made a simple drawing of the process as he imagined it, and the principles expressed in this drawing of his more or less apply also to a modern gas turbine. From the end of the eighteenth century, many designers had devoted themselves to finding a practical application for this simple principle, thus obtaining a heat engine with a technical application. The first to try was, in fact, Leonardo da Vinci, who invented a roasting spit driven by smoke

A The drawing sent by Gustaf Dalén to a friend to whom he wanted
to explain how a gas turbine works.
B The principle of the gas turbine.
Air is sucked into a compressor (*a*)
and is compressed before travelling
on to a combustion chamber (*b*), into
which fuel is sprayed and ignited.
The hot combustion gases expand in
the vanes of a turbine (*c*), where the
heat energy is converted into mechanical energy. Part of this energy
is employed to drive *a*, which is
mounted in the same shaft as *c*.
C Holzwarth's turbine of 1903. (*a*)
Fuel valve. (*b*) Air valve. (*c*) An
electrical ignition device. (*d*) Combustion chamber. (*e*) Nozzle. (*f*)
Valve for *e*. (*g*) Turbine wheel. (*h*)
Turboshaft. (1) Combustion gases in
d expand and travel towards *g* until
the pressure in *d* has sunk to atmospheric pressure. Valve *f* is open; *a*
and *b* are closed. (2) Valve *b* is
opened, and air from a compressor
flows in. The remaining combustion
gases are driven out by the air,
which also cools the vanes on *g*. (3)
Then *f* is closed and *a* is opened, so

that fuel, too, enters *d*. (4) A little
later, *b* is closed while *a* remains
open. (5) Soon, *a* is closed as well,
and the fuel mixture in *d* is ignited
by *c*.
D The combustion chamber of Lemale's and Armengaud's turbine
engine. The fuel was sprayed in at *a*
under a pressure of five atmospheres. At the same time, compressed air entered through *b* and
swept the fuel, now split into very
tiny droplets, along to the chamber
(*c*). The mixture was electrically ignited by a glowing metal wire (*d*),
which had been inserted through an
insulator (*e*). A tube (*f*) was coiled
round the chamber in a double cooling jacket. Water under a pressure

gas. The device worked all right, but it hardly deserves to be called a
gas turbine.

The problems in constructing a gas turbine are many and extremely difficult to solve. The speed of rotation must be very high to give
adequate efficiency, something that Watt stated when von Kempelen
claimed, in 1784, that he had invented a steam turbine; and if this
speed should be achieved, the temperature inside the turbine, and
especially of the turbine blades, would be extremely high so that a
heat-resistant material must be used. Moreover, a gas turbine must
have high efficiency, since no less than two-thirds of the power of the
working turbine are consumed by the compressor that forces air into
the combustion chamber; its total efficiency must exceed fifty-four
per cent if it is to keep going by itself! Not until the end of the
nineteenth century did a constructor of a gas turbine manage to
achieve an efficiency exceeding this magic figure. One of the first
was Egidius Elling (1861–1949), a distinguished Norwegian engineer
and a methodical researcher. He had patented his first gas turbine as
early as 1884, the year Charles A. Parsons was granted a patent for
his steam turbine. But Elling needed another twenty years to modify
this sufficiently to make it efficient; it did not generate surplus energy until 27 June, 1903, and Elling achieved this by cooling the very
hot exhaust fumes from the combustion chamber before they came
in contact with the blades of the working turbine. They were cooled
in the coiled tube of an exhaust-gas boiler, designed like a steam
boiler, and gave off their heat by causing the surrounding water to
boil. The volume of the cooled exhaust gases was augmented by this
steam, and the whole acted on the turbine blades, thus improving
the efficiency of the gas turbine.

Let us return for a moment to Gustaf Dalén, who had had his idea
for a gas turbine while enrolled at the Eidgenössische Technische
Hochschule in Zürich, where he studied under Aurel Stodola. Dalén

managed to persuade a fellow-student, Arthur Hultqvist, to join him
in an attempt to find a practical application for his idea; they rented
some primitive premises in Gothenburg, Sweden, and with the enthusiasm of youth, began their experiments. Just at that time, at the
end of the 1890s, various inventors were attempting to build somewhat fanciful flying machines, and so Dalén and his partner aimed at
producing a light and compact motor to propel these. Their first
experimental engine gave promising results to begin with. Its efficiency was fifty per cent and its turbine wheel achieved 25,000 rpm
but lasted only a short time. They tested another motor with a
redesigned turbine wheel at New Year, 1899; its efficiency was fifty-
eight per cent but even this new turbine wheel could not withstand
the high temperatures. Dalén continued his development work at AB
de Lavals Ångturbin for another couple of years but did not succeed
in solving the problem of materials. The experiments were abandoned in 1902 and Dalén applied himself to other projects. As chief
engineer at AB Gasaccumulator, he had the illuminating idea, to coin
a phrase, of using acetylene gas in the lamps of lighthouses, among
other things. In 1912, he was awarded the Nobel prize in physics for
a number of inventions in this area.

These attempts by Elling and Dalén, at the turn of the century, to
solve the problems of constructing a gas turbine engine illustrate
development up to about 1930. Dalén gave up in the face of the
problem of finding suitable materials. Elling was undoubtedly the
first man to produce a viable gas turbine, elegantly solving the
problem of materials by side-stepping it. But industry in early-
twentieth-century Norway was not highly enough developed to enable any mass production of Elling's turbine.

The Frenchmen Marcel Armengaud and Charles Lemale also experimented with gas turbines in the early twentieth century. Their
first experimental engine, an old rebuilt de Laval turbine, was com-

of five atmospheres entered the coil at *g* and was let into *c* at *h* after the end of the combustion. (*i*) Nozzle for the combustion gases and the steam. (*j*) Turbine vanes.
E The first jet plane to leave the ground, a Heinkel He 178, is here shown from the side (**1**) and from above (**2**). (*a*) The reaction motor's air channel. (*b*) Fuel tank. (*c*) Turbomotor.

E1

E2

F Lysholm's reaction engine of 1933. The engine was intended for aircraft propulsion. (*a*) Compressor. (*b*) Combustion chamber. (*c*) Turbine. (*d*) Exhaust nozzle.
G The Gloster E.28/29, the aeroplane which was equipped with Frank Whittle's first practical reaction motor.
H A cross-section of Whittle's reaction motor. The air entered through *a*, was compressed in a rotary compressor (*b*), and travelled on to the combustion chamber (*c*), into which fuel was sprayed and ignited. The combustion gases expanded in a gas turbine (*d*), mounted on the same shaft (*e*) as the compressor. (*f*) Exhaust nozzle.

pleted in 1905; it was fuelled with paraffin injected into the combustion chamber, into which water was also injected and vaporized, thus cooling the exhaust fumes and so protecting the turbine blades. Its surplus output was only some few per cent, but experiments with it proved the principle to be correct. Armengaud and Lamale founded the Société Anonyme de Turbomoteurs in Paris, and in 1908, they built a larger gas turbine of about 80 horsepower, which, however, also had low efficiency.

In 1903, in Germany, Hans Holzwarth patented a design for a gas turbine based on a partly new principle. This "explosion turbine", as Holzwarth called it, had a combustion chamber with guided admission and exhaust valves, and a spark plug. The first turbine based on this patent was built in Hanover, being completed by 1908. Holzwarth then cooperated with the Mannheim subsidary of the Swiss company Brown Boveri and there designed a gas turbine to generate 1,000 horsepower, although the 1913 prototype managed only 200 horsepower. Brown Boveri continued the development work, however, and the initially simple design became increasingly complicated. Not until 1933, after a 2,000-horsepower gas turbine had been built in 1930, did the company stop development work on the Holzwarth turbine.

So far we have considered only stationary gas turbines, mainly intended for driving generators and producing electrical energy, but it was as a propulsion motor for aeroplanes that the gas turbine came into its own.

In 1929, the Swedish company Bofors decided to develop a gas turbine engine for aeroplanes. The research and development team operated under the direction of Alf Lysholm (1893–1973), a professor of steam technology at Tekniska Högskolan in Stockholm. Bofors had in mind an "aeroplane without a propeller", where the propeller's powerful air stream would be replaced by the gas jet from a steam turbine. After four years of development, Lysholm had an experimental model ready, and, in 1934, he presented two different versions of the propeller-jet turbine (the term "turboprop" had not been invented then), one of them having an output of 1,200 horsepower. Bofors tried to interest the Royal Swedish Air Force in the project, but this happened at a time when the defence budget had been greatly cut, so the scheme was abandoned in 1935.

Many designers in the German aviation industry had been trying since about 1930 to produce a gas turbine which could be used in aeroplanes. A team led by Ernst Heinkel (1888–1958), with Pabst von Ohain as its chief designer, was the first to reach a solution. A few days before the outbreak of the Second World War in 1939, the world's first jet plane, the Heinkel He 178, flew for the first time, at Warnemünde. The air channel ran through the whole body of the jet plane, the exhaust being at the tail. The Junkers works started to develop another gas turbine engine around the New Year of 1940, and the first flights took place two years later with the Jumo 004 engine, designed by Anselm Franz. This later became the first jet engine to be mass produced. A slightly modified version of the Jumo 004 engine was installed in the German twin-engine fighter-bomber aircraft, Messerschmidt Me 262, which began to be produced in 1943.

In England, Frank Whittle (1907–   ) was the chief protagonist for aeroplanes propelled by gas turbine motors. While still a cadet of twenty at the Royal Air Force College in Cranwell, Whittle had been fascinated by the idea of jet propulsion, and he patented a gas turbine in 1930. His superiors in the RAF showed little sympathy for his ideas at first, but in 1936, he was given permission to devote part of his time to experimental work and, together with R. D. Williams, he founded the company Power Jets Ltd. to develop his invention. The following year, Whittle began to test his gas turbine, and at the outbreak of the Second World War, he received an order for one

A In 1950, the British Rover Co. of Birmingham introduced this gas-turbine-powered car. The engine had continuous combustion and was the result of ten years of research work, in which Frank Whittle had also taken part.

B At the end of the 1970s, this advanced gas turbine engine intended for propulsion of road vehicles was built in Sweden under the guidance of Professor Sven-Olof Kronogård. Air is sucked through a dust-collecting filter into the compressor (a), then passes a rotating heat exchanger (b), from which it absorbs heat. The compressed and heated air is then led into the combustion chamber (c), into which fuel is continually sprayed and combusted. The resulting gases first pass through a turbine (d), which drives the compressor, and then through two power turbines (e), one of which powers only the vehicle while the other helps drive the compressor as well. Because of this arrangement, an automatic gearbox can be dispensed with, and the turbine wheels can be given relatively small dimensions. Finally, the combustion gases pass the heat exchanger (b), to which they give off heat before leaving the engine through the exhaust pipe (f). Almost any liquid or gaseous fuel can be utilized to drive the engine.

such motor—given the name W1—while, at the same time, the aeroplane manufacturers Gloster Aircraft Co. Ltd. were given the job of building an experimental aeroplane to fit the motor. This aircraft, the Gloster E.28/39 made its first flight in May, 1941. Further development of Whittle's engine was carried out mainly by British Thomson-Houston Co. Ltd. and by Rolls-Royce.

These startling breakthroughs of gas turbines in aviation opened car manufacturers' eyes to this new power source. In England more than elsewhere, attempts were made to transfer experience of wartime aviation to the car industry. In 1947, Rover began to work intensely on development and started to get results in the early 1950s, when Jet 1, the turbine-driven Rover, became one of the world's most talked-about cars; but, for various reasons, it never went into mass production. In the late 1950s, the French company Renault put a lot of effort into gas turbine propulsion, but the project was abandoned after a few years. In the United States, the Chrysler Corporation was interested early on in jet motors for cars; their first gas-turbine-driven car was completed in 1950, and in 1963, after thoroughgoing improvements, the company took its Chrysler turbine on a European tour which aroused a great deal of interest. Despite the optimism, this motor was never put in production. The turbine motor was too expensive to operate and more expensive to build than a conventional car motor. In the 1970s, trucks and buses with turbine motors have been built, for example, by British Leyland, General Motors, and Ford, but these companies have not had any great success with them. Still, it is not unlikely that various cars in the 1980s will have gas turbine engines. The engines will initially be "hybrids", such as that installed in the Saab Turbo, first mass produced in 1978. Experience based on these designs should make it possible, at a later stage, to go the whole way.

CHAPTER 6
PRIME MOVERS III
Electricity

Electric phenomena of various kinds were already known in antiquity. The word "electricity" derives from the Greek word *elektron*, meaning amber, one of many substances which become electrically charged when rubbed. Over the centuries, many natural scientists had tried to trace the secret of this remarkable natural power, but litte became known until the 1790s, when an Italian physicist, Luigi Aloisio Galvani (1737–98), made his famous experiments on the legs of frogs, after he—or possibly his wife—had noticed that a pair of freshly prepared frogs' legs twitched whenever there was a spark from the conductor of an electric machine, close to which the frogs' legs were suspended on a copper wire. Galvani made a number of experiments and found that the frogs' legs twitched whenever the nerves and muscles were touched at the same time by two different metals which were in contact with each other. His compatriot Allessandro Volta (1745–1827) repeated these experiments and then discovered that electricity was generated when two different metals were in contact with each other. The frogs' legs served merely as evidence of the electrical charge. Later, Volta proved that electricity also appears when a metal is in contact with a fluid. His experiments resulted in the production of the first electric power source, the voltaic pile, which he made public in 1800. The first version consisted of a series of pairs of copper and zinc discs piled one on top of each other (sometimes, silver was used instead of copper). Each disc was separated from the next by a layer of felt or porous board moistened with a solution of sodium chloride. In a later version, the felt or the board was replaced by cups containing sodium chloride solution, in which the zinc and copper discs were immersed (cup elements, or *couronnes de tasses* cells).

Within only a few months of the public showing of the voltaic pile, physicists all over Europe had built their own voltaic piles and attacked this new area of research with great zest. Electricity became the fashion and different colleges competed to build the highest voltaic pile—a competition bringing to mind nuclear research during the 1950s and 1960s, when larger and larger accelerators were built. The largest, most famous voltaic pile was the one installed at the Royal Society in London. With its help, the famous chemist Sir Humphry Davy (1778–1829) made many discoveries and, by electrolysis, isolated several elements that were then unknown, including the metals potassium and sodium. Davy was also able to demonstrate the first electric arc. At the Royal Institution in London the first voltaic pile was successively extended, and in 1819, what was known as the "Great Battery" was put into operation. It consisted of 400 porcelain cups containing 4,000 copper and zinc discs, each with a surface of about 15.5 sq in (*c.* 100 sq cm), and the most popular demonstration of this power source was to cause it to produce its magnificent electric arcs. Even so, in 1819, no one knew

A Galvani's experiments with frogs' legs are shown here in a contemporary illustration. Little hands, wearing neat cuffs and hanging in the air on their own, demonstrate how a metal bar was charged by being held against an electric machine. The bar was then brought into contact with the frogs' legs, which had been arranged in various ways.
B In 1796, Volta constructed the first source of electricity, the voltaic pile (**1**). It consisted of pairs of zinc and silver discs, and between each pair, there was a layer of felt or porous pasteboard, soaked in brine. The pile was supported by four glass bars. If the top disc (which was of zinc) was connected to the bottom disc (which was of silver) by means of a metal wire, an electric current ran through the wire. (**2**) An early voltaic battery.
C In Volta's crown cups, the felt or pasteboard discs had been replaced by cups which contained brine or diluted acid. The zinc (*a*) and silver (*b*) discs were coupled in pairs by metal wires.

A

B

A Örsted demonstrates that an electric current generates a magnetic field, and that a compass needle is thus influenced by a live wire.
B An early galvanic element constructed by the German chemist and physicist Robert W. Bunsen (1811–99). The element consisted of a piece of carbon (a), which was immersed in nitric acid, and a zinc cylinder (b), which was surrounded by diluted sulphuric acid. The liquids were separated by a porous earthen vessel (c), and the element was contained in a glass vessel (d).
C Örsted's great electromagnet consists of a horseshoe magnet which has been wound with insulated wire. He found that if current from eight Bunsen elements, connected in series, was led through the wire, a 32-lb (14.5 kg) iron object, which had been placed between the ends of the magnet, would be held there with a force of about 3,000 lb.
D A model of Ampère's apparatus to demonstrate how electric currents influence each other. It consisted of one fixed (a) and one movable (b) bar; the latter was suspended from pivots hanging in small mercury-filled hollows (mercury is

an excellent electric conductor). If the two bars were connected so that the current flowing through a had the same direction as that in b, the bars attracted one another (**1**), whereas they repelled each other if the current flowing through one of them was reversed (**2**).

C

very much more of the nature of electricity than had Galvani and Volta, and while the first electric power source was indeed a great step forward, its secret still lay concealed.

In 1820, however, hectic activity in the field of electrics was sparked off when the Danish physicist Hans Christian Örsted (1777–1851) discovered, after some simple, methodical experiments, that an electric current can cause a compass needle to change direction. It had long been known that some materials, such as certain ores, had magnetic properties, but the "galvanic" current, on the other hand, was a relatively new discovery. That the two had something to do with each other was a scientific sensation. In July, 1820, Örsted sent a report of his discovery of electromagnetism to European scientists, and later the same year, he published an account of some complementary observations, but after that he left the field open for others. He had unlocked the door to electrical engineering, and all at once, there were many helping to open it. Before the end of 1820, several fundamental components of electrical technology had been arrived at. First, the German physicist Johann Salomo Christoph Schweigger (1779–1857), who was professor at Halle, designed the first electric coil, the solenoid, after observing that a magnetic field was more powerful if the magnetic needle was encircled with more than one turn of wire. Second, the French physicist Dominique François Jean Arago (1786–1853) built a primitive electromagnet, and third, his compatriot Ampère made an important discovery—that electric currents have an effect on each other.

Michael Faraday (1791–1867), Experimentalist at the Royal Institution in London, repeated Örsted's experiments but made up his mind to demonstrate by their means that magnetism could produce electricity, and he succeeded in this in 1831, with the help of his "Faraday's disc". This was a disc of copper, made to rotate between the poles of a horseshoe magnet; on its axis and at its periphery were rubbing contacts, from which electric current could be drawn. Thus, Faraday's disc was the first electric generator!

These discoveries of Faraday's, of electrodynamic and electromagnetic induction, were a great theoretical breakthrough and meant much for the continued practical development of electrical engineering. Faraday realized this but, being primarily a researcher, he left the task of technical application to others. From 1831 until his death, Faraday devoted himself only to experiments and lectures at the Royal Institution, where he had become director in 1825. His discovery was, however, immediately taken up by Ampère in Paris. On Ampère's instructions, Hippolyte Pixii, an instrument maker, built a number of electric machines for experiments and demonstrations, and the first of them was shown in Paris in 1832. This was a hand-driven electromagnetic generator, where the induction affected a number of windings connected in series and gave a higher voltage than Faraday's disc, which had only one induced conductor. Pixii's generator, moreover, was later equipped with a commutator designed by Ampère. This commutator was the first device that could cause the direction of a current in an electric cable to reverse itself, and so, yet another component was added to electromagnetic technology.

The ice was broken as far as electromechanical engineering was concerned, and various engineers all over Europe now entered this new and promising field. They received some quite unexpected assistance. To the public, electricity was something mysterious and exciting which stimulated the imagination. A lot could be read in the papers about its possible uses. Could not this magic "fluid", as the papers called electric current, also have a miraculous effect on man? As early as 1804, the famous Swedish chemist Jac Berzelius (1779–1848) had received a doctor's degree in medicine for his dissertation on the use of galvanic current to cure illnesses. In the 1830s, several

E A drawing by Faraday of his discovery of electromagnetic induction. He had wound five long copper wires, insulated with string and calico, round a ring of soft iron – three on one half, *A*, and two on the other, *B*. The wires on *A* were not in contact with those on *B*. Thereupon, he connected the ends of the wires on *B* two and two with a copper wire and let its coil run over a compass needle, which had been placed about 3 ft (1 m) from the ring. When the ends of the wires on *A* were connected three and three to the poles of a battery, the compass needle flickered – but the deflection did not last, although the wires remained in contact with the battery. However, when the battery was disconnected, the needle flickered again. Thus, it was the

D1

D2

F

variation of the flux in *B*'s magnetic field which caused the induced current impulse.

F Faraday's disc was a copper disc (*a*) on whose shaft there was a crank (*b*). The disc was rotated between the poles of a horseshoe magnet, and a trailing contact (*c*) bore on the shaft of the disc while another (*d*) bore on the disc's periphery between the poles of the magnet. When the disc was rotated, voltage was induced in it at right angles to the flux of the magnetic field and the disc's direction of rotation, and a current could be drawn from the trailing contacts. In the later version of the generator, shown here, Faraday let the disc rotate between the poles of an electromagnet.

G

G A hand-cranked electric generator by Pixii. When the horseshoe magnet (*a*) was rotated, current was induced in two fixed coils (*b*, *c*) which were connected in series. The current in the coils changed direction continuously, since each was alternately exposed to the magnet's south and north poles, and the induced current repeatedly endeavoured to produce a repelling pole at the lower end of each coil. The commutator consisted of a slip ring split in two insulated parts (*d*, *e*). The free ends of the coils were each connected to one part of the commutator by means of trailing contacts (*f*, *g*), while current could be drawn from two other trailing contacts (*h*, *i*). When the commutator rotated, its design caused *h* to bear on *d*

E

B   A

during one half of the revolution; meanwhile, *i* bore on *e*. During the second half of the revolution, *h* instead bore on *e*, while *i* bore on *d*, and since the direction of the current in *b* and *c* alternated, a direct current could be drawn from the generator.

A In the 1850s, several inventors tried to construct electrical engines whose operation corresponded to that of the steam-engine. The American Charles Grafton Page proposed such a "piston" engine, which is shown here at two different stages of its work cycle. Two soft-iron cylinders (*a*, *b*) were, in turn, pulled into solenoids (*c*, *d*) when these, each during one-half of the fly-wheel's (*e*) revolution, were fed with electric current.

B The steam-engine-powered Alliance generator (**1**) was primarily used for lighthouse illumination. (**2**) Explanatory sketch. The machine consisted of a great number (here, twenty-four) of horseshoe magnets (*a*), which were arranged regularly in rows round a drum (*b*). On the drum, twice as many solenoids (*c*) as magnets were symmetrically mounted. (*d*) Belt pulley. The ma-

A

B2

chine was large and heavy, and supplied alternating current; because of the many solenoids, it was difficult to make a useful commutator.

C A generator which was considerably less bulky and heavy than the Alliance generator was constructed in 1866 by Henry Wilde. He had discovered the possibility of replacing the large horseshoe magnets with electromagnets (*a*), which were fed with current from a small generator (*b*). The latter was equipped with an

B1

instrument makers, including E. M. Clarke in London, supplied small hand-driven electric generators, in which the current was conducted to two handles, which the patient grasped firmly to get rid of his ailments. The higher the voltage generated by the device, the better the patient could feel the miraculous effect of the electric current. The manufacturers, consequently, experimented with methods of varying the voltage, their attempts including different ways of winding the coils and a way to short-circuit the magnetic field to a higher or lower degree with a magnetic shunt. The manufacture of these "medicinal" devices was the first large-scale production—although by craftsmen—of electromachines, and as such, had some effect on development. Many such generators also made their way to scientific laboratories. Being simple and straightforward, they certainly contributed to making electricity less dramatic. From 1830 onwards, it attracted the interest of leading physicists. The theories of electricity moved in the high, cool spheres of science, beyond the intellectual reach of the average man. That was at least the common view of electricity in those days, and one can understand the public's attitude by a comparison between electromechanical engineering and steam technology, which was, at this stage, more down-to-earth and accessible. It was typical for the time that Georg Simon Ohm (1787–1854) was excluded from scientific circles and actually had to go underground—he grew a full beard and worked as a livery-man—after propounding his well-known law in 1827, that the current flowing in a metal wire is directly proportional to the voltage between its ends. The relations between current, voltage, and electrical resistance really *could not* be as simple as that! But, before long, Ohm was vindicated.

The first full-scale electromachines were built in the 1840s and 1850s. The magnetic fields of these magneto-electric generators were produced by powerful permanent magnets. The pioneers in this field were principally F. Nollet in France and Frederick Hale Holmes in England. Nollet developed a magnetic-electric generator specially intended for the lamps of lighthouses; it used limelight, with the lime being heated in an electric arc. Nollet, however, died in 1853, but his partner then founded the Compagnie de l'Alliance and summoned Holmes, asking him to continue Nollet's research. Holmes made some important contributions but returned to England after only a few years. The successively improved Alliance generator, with its characteristic appearance, was fairly widespread in the 1860s; it probably the first commercially viable electromachine.

One disadvantage was, however, the dependence on permanent magnets. In generators such as the Alliance, a large array of horseshoe magnets was required to give a reasonably acceptable magnetic field. In the 1850s, many designers tried the logical solution of replacing the permanent magnets by electromagnets. In Britain, Henry Wilde (1833–1919) built a generator in which the magnetic field was created by electromagnets whose current was supplied by an exciter—a smaller magneto-electric generator, connected to the large generator. Several other designers were working on similar solutions, and the next stage of development was not far away—"stealing" part of the generator's working current and feeding it into the field windings. In this way, a self-generating magnetic field could be obtained. This type of machine is called a dynamo, and the dynamo-electric principle was formulated in 1866 by the German industrialist and electrical engineer Werner Siemens (1816–92), who was later ennobled in his home country. At New Year, 1867, Werner's brother William (later Sir William) Siemens showed a demonstration model of the dynamo to the Royal Institution in London. One of the people present was the great electrical engineer Charles Wheatstone (1802–75), who claimed he had reached the same solution. On the same occasion he, too, displayed a similar model!

There was a fierce battle over who was first with the dynamo-electric principle, which was fundamental to all further developments in electrical engineering. Several designers had, no doubt, been pursuing the same idea, but it is quite clear that Siemens was the first to implement it; a dynamo-electric generator made by Siemens was shown at the Paris exhibition in 1867. In his autobiography, *Lebenserinnerungen*, Werner von Siemens refers to this controversy and states—without really taking a stand—firstly that he clearly realized that the dynamo-electric principle immediately made it possible to build generators for practically any voltage and amperage, and secondly that it was he who coined the word dynamo, derived from the Greek word meaning power. Colloquially, it soon became synonymous with "electric generator".

Electric Lighting

During the 1870s, better and better arc-lamps were introduced for lighting, which increased the demand for electric generators. The dynamo underwent considerable improvement, and many companies in both Europe and the United States began manufacturing electromachines. The big breakthrough for electric lighting came, however, when the electric light bulb was introduced. Many people believe that Thomas Alva Edison (1847–1931), "The Wizard of Menlo Park", invented the light bulb. As a matter of fact, he did not—it had been "invented" in different versions before Edison presented his, although his *was* the first practicable light bulb. Edison's great contribution was his creation of a whole system for electric lighting, consisting of a steam-engine-driven electric generator with cables, conductor joints, and other devices for transmitting the current to the consumer. Further, the system included domestic wiring, electric meters, fuses, switches, and fittings for his light bulb, things that, earlier, had not existed. Most components in this system were devised and tested by Edison himself.

Edison's light bulb, the carbon filament lamp, was ready for production in 1879, and in the same year, 115 lamps were installed on board the luxury paddle-steamer *Columbia*, where they lit the velvet-upholstered saloons. The European début of the Edison lamp was at the world exhibition in Paris in 1881, where part of Edison's package solution for electric lighting was also shown. In professional circles Edison's generator attracted a great deal of attention. He himself called it Jumbo (it weighed 27 tons), and it was a further development of European designs. The following year, Edison installed three Jumbo generators, each of 125 horsepower, in Pearl Street, New York, where, in other words, the world's first electric power-station was situated. Via a distribution system, current for 5,000 lamps in 225 houses was delivered. Electricity had become consumer goods, with "free delivery" to the place it was required.

Edison's power-station received full press coverage on both sides of the Atlantic, and soon there were power-stations in other countries. In Sweden the first light bulbs were mounted in Strömparterren at Norrbro in Stockholm. They were lit together with a number of arc-light lamps at the royal palace when, on 16 September, 1881, King Oscar II left Stockholm for Karlsruhe to celebrate the engagement of Crown Prince Gustaf and Princess Victoria of Baden. These light bulbs were not, however, made by Edison but by the Englishman St. George Lane-Fox. In the 1880s, there was a sharp increase in the use of electricity for lighting and other purposes. Electric household appliances soon came into use—cookers, fans, immersion heaters, irons, etc. Electric motors were also taken into operation in workshops and factories. This made great demands on the distribution networks, where Ohm's law quite simply demonstrated that their capacity was limited. Heat losses and voltage drops in cables

iron magnet and was driven by the same steam-engine as was the main engine. (c) Commutator. (d) Belt drive.

D The electrodynamic principle. For the sake of perspicuity, the rotor in this illustration has been

drawn as a single wire coil (a), placed in a magnetic field. When the rotor turns in the direction of the arrow (b), the coil's upper and lower halves cross the magnetic lines of force, and a voltage is induced in the coil. The voltage is proportional to the number of magnetic lines of force passed by the coil per unit of time. Thus, the voltage is at its maximum when the coil is vertical and is equal to zero when the coil is horizontal. As soon as the coil passes the horizontal position, that half of it which was earlier the upper becomes the lower, and vice versa, which means that the polarity of the voltage is reversed. At the same time, however, the two commutator segments (c, d) change places in relation to the brushes (e, f), which means that the segments will keep their polarity. If a light bulb, for instance, is connected to the brushes, an electric current starts passing through the coil because of the voltage. The current generates a magnetic field whose direction is opposite that of the field in which the current moves. This means that the coil now resists being turned round, and the energy needed to turn it is the energy consumed in the connected light bulb (plus the friction loss in the generator).

E Siemens's generator with a drum-wound armature is shown here in section; note how well-enclosed the armature (a) lies in the magnetic field produced by the pole shoes (b, c). This magnetic field is generated by the two "field windings" (d, e), which are fed with current by the generator's armature (self-excitation). This is possible because, in the soft iron, there is from the start a weak, remaining magnetism, which is why the generator always has "something to start with" when it must build up its own magnetic field. In principle, Siemens's construction is still used today.

B The Englishman W. E. Staite (1809–54) experimented with incandescent filaments of platino-iridium alloy, but he did not succeed in making his lamps burn for very long. One reason was that the wire oxidized rather rapidly, since Staite failed to attain a good enough vacuum inside the bulbs; another was that the temperature at which pla-

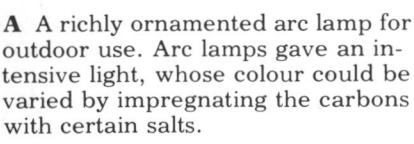

A A richly ornamented arc lamp for outdoor use. Arc lamps gave an intensive light, whose colour could be varied by impregnating the carbons with certain salts.

158

tinum becomes incandescent and that at which the metal starts to melt are too near each other. The light bulb shown here was constructed by Staite in the 1840s.

C The Englishman Warren de la Rue (1815–89), too, had realized the necessity of attaining a vacuum inside the lamps to stop the incandescent wire from oxidizing, but his lamp, which is shown here, did not burn for very long, either.

D An interior of Edison's power-station at Pearl Street. Two years after the power-station had started delivering electric cur-

rent, the number of dynamos had been increased to six, and the current powered over ten thousand light bulbs at 508 subscribers' houses.

E It took two years to lay the 14 miles (22.5 km) of cable needed for Edison's power-station. The cables consisted of double copper wires which had been insulated with impregnated hemp string and had been enclosed in iron tubes. A section of the cable can be seen at the top right of the picture.

F After a great number of experiments, Edison found that the most

made it impossible to extend the distribution networks further than a few miles and limited the power to a few dozen kW. It was suggested that the voltage be increased, so as proportionately to reduce the amperage; the transmitted power would then remain the same, while heat losses and voltage drops would be lessened. But even the voltage employed by Edison at the Pearl Street power station (110 V) was considered by many to be lethal. The distribution systems of those days employed direct current, a property of which is an inability to be transformed to a higher voltage. The solution to this really complicated technical problem came around 1890, from several directions simultaneously. The only choice was obviously—as we may say now—to change over to alternating current, which can easily be transformed. The idea was that if the generator gives a low voltage, this can be stepped up to tens of thoausands of volts for transmission and then be stepped down to a normal consumption voltage. Alternating current as such was already known. Nikola Tesla (1856–1943) in the United States had worked on a polyphase alternating-current system and, in 1888, had patented a polyphase motor. For high voltage transmission, however, an entirely new system was required.

The breakthrough came in 1891, when an international electrical engineering exhibition was held in Frankfurt-on-Main in Germany. The preparations for this were supervised by Oskar von Miller, in many respects a pioneer in electrical engineering. He took the bold step of providing the exhibition with electric power from the waterfalls at Neckar on the river Lauffen, which was over 100 miles (c. 175 km) from the exhibition site. Von Miller put his faith in two inventions made by Michael von Dolovi-Dobrowolsky, chief designer at the Allgemeine Elektrizitäts-Gesellschaft (AEG). These were an alternating-current engine and a system for three-phase alternating current; they had been patented in 1888 and in 1889, respectively. AEG cooperated on the development of transformers and equipment for high-voltage lines with Oerlikon in Switzerland, where Charles Brown was now employed. The power transmission from Lauffen to Frankfurt was energized in August, 1891, and—naturally—became the great sensation of the exhibition. The transmission voltage was 30,000 volts and the output about 175 kW. With this breakthrough, electric power technology came of age. Ever since, there has been rapid and impressive progress, but it is disputable whether we have yet seen the real blossoming of electric power technology.

The question of who was first with the three-phase system has been vehemently debated over the years. In the mid-1950s, the Verein Deutsche Elektrotechniker (VDE) charged an unbiased committee with the task of finding out who was the first to introduce such a system. In 1959, the VDE published an extensive report which stated that von Dolivo-Dobrowolsky and Brown were the first. The report also gave a detailed analysis of the contributions made by a number of other people who had presented similar ideas at the same time.

I

suitable material for incandescent wire was carbon. His first carbon filament lamp, which is shown here, burnt for forty-five hours; the incandescent filament consisted of a piece of carbonized cotton thread which had been fixed between two platinum screw vices. The air inside the bulb was evacuated – this problem had been solved in 1868, when a practicable vacuum pump had been invented in Germany – and the lamp was screwed into a socket. The wires were connected to pole screws on the socket.

G In c. 1880, a Paris department store had these direct-current machines installed. They were used for lighting.

H An electric iron of 1888. In principle, the iron functioned in the same manner as did the light bulb; the current passed through a thread-shaped rheostat, heating it.

I As early as the last decades of the nineteenth century, a great many electrically powered articles, such as these various pots and pans, were manufactured.

Alternative Energy Sources

In 1973, the abstract physical concept of "energy" suddenly hit the headlines all over the world. There was talk of an energy crisis. The reasons for this so-called crisis which, in reality, existed only in the news headlines, will not be enlarged upon here. We shall merely state that it had one important consequence: the public at large became aware of the international energy situation. People began to question if, from a global point of view, we could afford the present intense consumption of energy. The most usual raw materials used for producing energy—coal, oil, natural gas, and uranium — will run out one day. The debate provoked a keen interest in what are called alternative energy sources, such as the wind, the sun, the waves, and the tide.

Before looking more closely at some of these sources of energy, it may be useful to make clear what is meant by the term "energy". First, though, "mechanical work": in physics this is defined as the force multiplied by the distance travelled in the direction in which the motive force is applied, while "power" is "mechanical work" per unit of time. The now obsolescent unit "horsepower" was defined as 550 foot-pounds (75 kilogram metres) per second. By "energy" is meant the capacity to perform "mechanical work", a capacity that is related to some source of energy. "Energy" and "mechanical work" are expressed in the same units, while a principle called in physics "the mechanical heat equivalent" is also relevant here: it states that a given quantity of work or "energy" is the same as a given quantity of heat, meaning that while energy can take different forms, it cannot be created or destroyed.

Let us take a simple example: a tower clock driven by a weight of 8 kg is wound up 1.5 m at the beginning of each week. As the weight slowly sinks, it performs mechanical work. The amount of energy is 8 kg multiplied by 1.5 m, that is 12 kilogram metres (kgm). If this is divided by the number of seconds in one week, 604,800, the result is 0.00002 kilogram metres per second (kgm/s). By winding up the clock, what is called potential energy is transferred to the raised weight, and as it sinks, this potential energy is converted into kinetic energy which, in moving the cog-wheels of the clock, is not consumed except in the sense of once more being converted, this time into heat caused by the friction of the clockwork.

This indestructible quality of energy gave rise to many philosophical speculations when the concept of energy was first being explored, mainly through the thermodynamic studies made in the 1850s by Lord Kelvin. Kelvin talked of the "decadence of energy", meaning that the heat energy comprised in the universe strives towards an equilibrium by becoming more and more uniformly spread.

Generally, energy has to be converted or refined through several stages before it can be used. Electric energy can be seen as a highly refined form of energy. Oil cannot be converted directly into electric energy, but an oil-fired steam boiler can deliver steam to a turbine, which then provides mechanical kinetic energy. This energy can be finally converted in a generator into electric energy.

Wind-Power—in its Second Wind

The keen interest taken today in wind power is widely believed to have originated during the "energy crisis" of 1973. The truth is that this was merely the occasion on which politicians became aware of the energy problem generally and of the potential of wind power in particular. In fact, over the past hundred years or so, very much research and development has gone into attempts to produce better designs than those of the old windmills for exploiting the kinetic energy inherent in the wind.

In the late 1870s in the United States, Stuart Perry designed a

B1

B2

A

b

b

a

A The vanes of the Reinsch wheel were pivoted round their longitudinal axes. Each vane was attached to a rotatable ring (*a*), whose movements were determined by the influence of the centrifugal force on a weight. Propellers (*b*) automatically turned the wheel to face the wind.

B The prototype of all self-regulating wind wheels was the Halladay wheel, seen here in its unfolded (**1**) and folded (**2**) states. The vanes were rotatable and mounted on crossbars, and since their surfaces were greater towards the wheel's periphery than towards its centre in relation to the turning-point, the vanes, under wind pressure, tilted backwards. This movement was opposed by a weight at the back of the wheel. As the wind pressure increased, it outbalanced the weight,

wind turbine of steel, which was based on Daniel Halladay's wooden rotor of 1854 and which later became known as the American fan mill. It immediately became very popular in agricultural areas, where it was used to drive pumps for drainage and irrigation. Unlike the windmills with, typically, four sails, Perry's wind turbine had 100 to 150 small sails on the wind wheel, which had a diameter of 3 to 9 ft (1 to 3 m). These fan mills became quite common also in Europe and, in places, are still a typical feature of the landscape. In the beginning of the 1880s, the market in the United States was supplied with such mills connected to electric generators which, via buffer batteries, delivered power for electric lighting, the great novelty of the time.

During the 1890s, the American fan mill was developed in several countries, mainly Germany, where mills were built with wind wheels measuring up to 30 ft (c 10 m) in diameter. These were equipped with smaller wind wheels, called rosettes, which caused the apparatus automatically to face squarely into the wind. This was an invention taken from the windmills of old. These mills were able to drive many of the machines which were then used in agriculture, such as and the vanes tilted backwards. When only a low output was needed in hard winds, the wheel was kept at a safe speed through the centrifugal force of weights on its periphery causing the vanes to tilt backwards. **C** Sörensen's conical wind wheel is shown here in longitudinal-section (**1**); (**2**) front view. The vanes consisted of small tin plates, each of which was carried on a shaft and could be given a crosswise position when the wheel was to be stopped. The wind wheel's comparatively

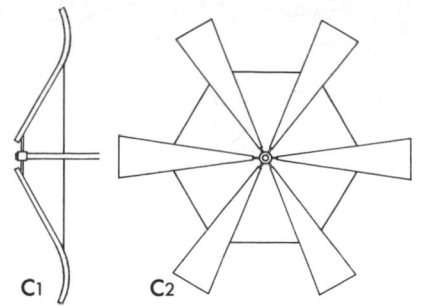

C1 C2

high efficiency was maintained because the vanes were designed to change the direction of the wind which hit them.
D On large farms, wind engines used to be used to power, for example, the chaff cutter (*a*), the grinding machine (*b*), the thresher (*c*), the groats mill (*d*), and the circular saw (*e*). Pumping, irrigation, and draining were other tasks for which wind engines were used.

D

threshing machines, roller-mills, hacking machines, and even circular saws.

During the first decade of the twentieth century, the electrics industry in the United States and Europe spent large amounts of money trying to adapt the American fan mill for the generation of electric power, especially to suit agricultural requirements. In 1900, a Dane, Christian Sörensen, designed a conical wind wheel which had an effect exceeding that of the flat wind wheel by over fifty per cent. Electric power-stations with Sörensen's wind wheel were built by ASEA and others, and the construction had a certain amount of success. Various remedies were tried out in attempts to solve the problem of power regulation. This problem arises from the variation of the wind force and the fact that the power of a fan mill is in proportion to the cube of the wind velocity. In other words, if the wind force is doubled, the capacity will increase by $2^3 = 8$ times. This development work was interrupted when hydroelectric power began to solve the problem of rural electrification.

The first actual research project in the field of wind power was

started in Denmark in 1894. It continued for about ten years and was headed by Poul La Cour (1846–1908), a professor of physics. In an experimental mill built at Askov, La Cour's theoretical calculations were tried out in practice. The main aim of these experiments was to achieve a high output even if the wind velocity was low. The Danish government supported this ambitious project with large sums of money, in the hope that the result would enable them to bring electricity to the countryside. This was of vital importance to the agricultural nation of Denmark, which has no waterfalls of its own; in most other countries, waterfalls provided the power which, in those early days, supplied the farming areas with electricity.

While the admirable experiments carried out by La Cour did not solve the problem of rural electrification, they did set an example for many later Danish experiments with wind power. One of La Cour's successors was Jakob Juul, who, in the mid-1950s, designed a wind turbine with a capacity of 200 kilowatts (kW). It was built at Gedser and began operation in 1957.

During the years between the two world wars, many original wind-power projects were tried out in Europe and the United States. One example is the wind rotor wheel with a vertical axle, which was patented in 1927 by the Frenchman G. J. M. Darrieus. The rotor wheel was about 66 ft (20 m) high and had two blades and a capacity of 10 kW. An experimental model was taken into operation in 1929 and gave very promising results. One advantage of the Darrieus, or arc, rotor wheel is the fact that it works independently of wind direction.

In the 1930s, various German engineers devoted themselves to designing gigantic projects to exploit wind power. Although none of these ever left the drawing-board, they can be said to have paved the way for the designs which are being developed in many places today. Two examples are those suggested by Herman Honeff. One included 1,300-ft (400 m) high towers of framework construction, each having five wind turbines with vertical axles. The towers were to be built in groups of four and give an average power of 50 megawatts (MW). The other project planned by Honeff was to consist of power-stations on pontoons anchored in the turbulent North Sea. The electric power was then to be transferred to land via a sea cable. In the 1950s, Honeff was succeeded by the very able Ulrich Hüttner, who designed a wind power-station of 100 kW. It was completed in 1957 in Stötten in southern Germany and was in operation until 1966.

In the 1930s, the Soviet Union, too, had a wind power-station built near Yalta on the Black Sea. Its output was 100 kW, and it had a rotor wheel with two blades and a diameter of almost 100 ft (30 m).

The largest wind-power project in this period was, however, carried out in the United States. Its originator was a Boston geologist, Palmer C. Putnam. In the late 1930s, a friend of his asked him if he had any idea how to construct a wind generator which could supply electric power to a remote farm. Putnam quickly solved the problem—to his friend's delight—and became fascinated by the potential of wind energy. He attacked the task of designing a wind power-station of 1 megawatt (MW) and, when his project was completed, he showed his plans to Vannevar Bush (1890–1974), the then principal of the Massachusetts Institute of Technology. Bush was impressed by the bold project, managed to find a patron to finance the building of a full-scale prototype, and brought in a number of eminent engineers to solve the various problems involved. In the autumn of 1941, the prototype was put into operation on Grandpa's Knob, a 2,130-ft (650 m) high mountain near Rutland in Vermont. The company financing the wind power-station was S. Morgan Smith & Co., and the power lines were built by the Vermont Public Service Co.

In the past, similar constructions had employed direct-current gen-

A In the 1920s, the Finnish engineer S.J. Savonius constructed this rotor (1) with its vertical shaft. (2) A cross-section of the rotor. The vanes are semi-circular and mounted so that the wind can pass between them, giving the rotor increased torsion.

B Like the Savonius rotor, the Darrieus, or arc, rotor works independently of the wind direction. It consists of two or more vanes (*a*), which are mounted on a vertical shaft.

C This rotor, Giromill, also works independently of the wind's direction. It consists of straight vanes (*a*), whose angle is continually varied during rotation.

D A modern, rapidly rotating two-vane rotor with horizontal shaft. With a rotor like this, up to eighty per cent of the theoretically available wind energy can be transformed into kinetic energy.

E The peripheral speed of a two-vane rotor is high, while the

erators and buffer batteries, but this project, which is now often referred to as the Smith-Putnam project, employed an alternating-current generator. Such a generator can only feed power into an existing distribution network provided it runs synchronously with the grid frequency, and the designers here managed to do this, thus solving the regulation problem of the fan mills. The rotor wheel had two stainless steel blades, about 95 ft (29 m) long, and was mounted on top of a 120-ft (36 m) high tower. The rotor-wheel axle was at an elevation angle of 12.5° and the blades rotated at 28.5 rpm. The rotor wheel drove a synchronous generator via a hydraulic connection, and the generator turned at 600 rpm. The speed was controlled by a centrifugal governor connected to hydraulic servo-motors which affected the rotor blades. In the first three-week period that the power-station was in operation, it supplied 82,000 kW hours (kWh), which considerably exceeded calculations. But after the rotor wheel broke in 1946, the project was abandoned.

During the latter part of the 1970s, many countries initiated sizable projects for exploiting wind energy, most of them based on old ideas and designs which are now being tried again in conjunction with modern technology. In Canada, for example, the Darrieus rotor wheel has been taken up again in a large-scale project. In 1975, the Canadian National Aeronautical Establishment (NAE) gave notice of a competition to design a 1-kW wind generator primarily intended for lighthouses and remote Indian reservations. The competition was won by Dominion Aluminum Ltd. with a 15-ft (4.5 m) high updated version of the Darrieus rotor wheel. This company's next project was a 200-kW wind generator which was 120 ft (36 m) high and had a Darrieus rotor wheel with a diameter of 80 ft (24 m); this power-station was commissioned by the government and built on the windy Magdalen Islands off Nova Scotia. The wind researchers of the NAE are at present at an advanced stage in planning a gigantic 980-ft (300 m) high wind generator with a Darrieus rotor wheel.

In 1974, a then recently formed energy body in the United States, the Energy Research and Development Agency (ERDA), started a research programme to investigate the possibilities of making the nation independent of imported energy by the year 2000. Much of ERDA's programme concentrates on wind energy, and one of the original aims was to have wind power-stations with a total capacity of 100 MW in operation from 1981, with wind power supplying twenty-five per cent of the nation's total energy consumption by the year 2000. As early as the summer of 1975, a 100-kW wind power-station was put into operation at the NASA–Lewis Research Centre in Ohio. The rotor wheel has two blades and a diameter of 123-ft (37.5 m) and is mounted on top of a 100-ft (30 m) high tower. In general terms, this wind power-station has been developed from the previously mentioned construction built by Hütter in Stötten. After a running-in period of about two years and with the necessary modifications made during this period, a small series of similar units were manufactured. These were then offered to the different power companies of the country for further development.

In 1974, in Holland, the promised land of windmills, a development programme for wind energy was initiated. The first project was simply a redesign of a traditional windmill, which was equipped with metal sails and an electric generator of 80 kW. It was built on the island of Texel. But it had an unexpected side effect: the metal sails interfered with the television transmission and gave rise to flickering ghost images on the TV screens. The considerate wind researchers therefore operated the mill only during the day.

The Dutch, incidentally, have always remained faithful to wind power. The traditional windmills are still in operation, and so are thousands of little wind engines which pump water for drainage. At least three Dutch factories currently manufacture wind engines for this purpose. A wind engine is more expensive than an electrically driven pump, but the extra cost is compensated by the fact that no cables have to be drawn across the fields and also by the free supply of energy.

The development work which has been carried out in recent years in the area of wind power has been directed mainly towards the problems of control technology, whereas the basic design ideas have been taken from the past. Several new rotor-wheel designs have been introduced, but the early designs have proved the most reliable.

Solar Energy

Several of the ancient religions worshipped the sun as their supreme god, the god who gave light and heat, life to all that lived. And the sun is in truth a most generous source of energy: it transforms literally astronomical amounts of nuclear energy into radiation. The earth is hit by only about half of one billionth of the total radiation of the sun, but in spite of that, the surface of the earth absorbs an average of 1 kW per 10 sq ft (1 sq m) in clear weather. Some of the incident radiation is consumed in heating the atmosphere—which is one reason why the wind blows, as solar energy is converted into wind power. In the same way, the solar radiation heats oceans and lakes. When heated, these give off vapour which then falls as rain, snow, or hail. In other words, hydroelectric power-stations are ultimately driven by solar energy, as, indeed, are windmills.

The idea of using solar energy has appealed to scientists and engineers ever since antiquity. Euclid, for example, in his work on optics, described the ability of the burning-mirror to concentrate the radiation of the sun and thus achieve a high temperature. Archimedes' feat of using burning-mirrors to set ablaze the rigs of the attacking Roman ships has been mentioned in a previous chapter, although it is unknown whether this is myth or reality. Philo of Byzantium exploited the thermal power of solar energy in a thermoscope, a forerunner of the thermometer: a tube filled with air and sealed at the top had its lower end immersed in water in a container. When the tube was exposed to radiation, the air expanded, and the water in the container rose. The Renaissance engineer Salomon de Caus took up this idea and in his art book of 1615 described two devices in which solar energy was exploited in a similar manner. In one, solar radiation was concentrated through lenses into a sealed container connected to a water tank which was joined to a fountain. As the sun heated the water of the tank, the fountain began to play. The other "sun machine" consisted of the hollow statue of a shepherd. The air inside the statue expanded due to the heat of the sun and was conducted to two organ-pipes which then sounded. These flippant ideas fired the imagination of many natural scientists. Athanasius Kircher, for example, described the "sun machines" in his comprehensive work on light and optics, *Ars magna lucis et umbrae* (1646), without mentioning, however, either Philo or de Caus, as was the custom of the time.

During the seventeenth and eighteenth centuries, various burning-glasses and parabolic burning-mirrors were manufactured in science laboratories. Around 1690, a famous burning-mirror was produced in Dresden by E. W. von Tschirnhausen (1651–1708). It had a diameter of 5 ft 3 in (1.6 m) and was used in experiments with pottery kilns.

number of revolutions per minute is relatively low. The use of a large speed gear is then necessary if the rotor is to drive a generator directly. Another solution is to equip the rotor with brake turbines (*a*), which will achieve a sufficient number of revolutions per minute to drive a generator directly. However, if brake turbines are used, the kinetic energy produced is cut by about one-fourth.
F When the Enfield-Andreau rotor is rotated by the wind, centrifugal force pushes air out through holes in the vane tips. A negative pressure then occurs inside the stand, and air which is sucked in from the outside drives the turbine (*a*).
G Honeff's suggestion for a gigantic wind power-station: 1,300-ft (400 m) high towers, each equipped with five wind turbines, were to be erected in groups of four. According to Honeff, these would produce extremely cheap energy.

But it was not until the latter part of the nineteenth century that any realistic ideas for exploiting solar energy appeared. In the 1860s, the originator of the *Monitor*, John Ericsson, became fascinated by the potential of solar energy, after the crew of the *Monitor* had complained that the sun made the flat deck of the ship so hot that it became almost unbearable in the forecastle. Ericsson enthusiastically attacked the task of designing instruments to measure the energy content of solar radiation—in those days, this was a practically unknown field of research.

Ericsson lived on Beach Street in New York and built a solar research laboratory there on the top floor and the roof. He equipped one of his small caloric engines with a parabolic solar reflector, so that the fuel was replaced by solar energy. The engine drove a meat spit, which was inserted in the focus of another parabolic mirror. Both mirrors were adjusted to start the machinery in time to broil a chicken or steak for lunch. This *rôtissoire solaire* is probably the first example of how solar energy can be applied outside a laboratory.

Ericsson designed in all about fifty measuring instruments for his research in solar energy. In 1868, when he was awarded an honorary doctorate by Lund university in Sweden, he wrote a paper entitled "On the Use of Solar Energy as a Mechanical Driving Power", which was published in the university's periodical, *Acta*. In this paper, Ericsson described his efforts to trace the physical nature of solar radiation. The basic connection between radiation and temperature was, however, not defined until 1884, when an Austrian scientist, Ludwig Boltzmann (1844–1906) managed to deduce theoretically the law which his compatriot Joseph Stefan (1835–93) had stated empirically some years before and which is now called the Stefan-Boltzmann radiation law.

In 1883, when Ericsson was eighty, he designed what was perhaps his most famous solar machine. The mirror was a rectangular trough, 11 ft 6 in (3.5 m) long and 6 ft 6 in (2 m) wide, with a parabolic section. A longitudinal tube with a diameter of 6 in (15 cm) was mounted along the focal line of the mirror and could be used as a boiler for a steam-engine, while the "solar engine", as Ericsson called it, could also drive a caloric engine, if the tube contained air.

At the time when John Ericsson began to take an interest in solar energy, two French engineers, Augustin Mouchot and Abel Pifre, were busy building a solar machine which they demonstrated first in Algeria around 1879 and then in the Tuileries in Paris. The solar collector was a conical mirror with a diameter of 7 ft 3 in (2.2 m) at its base, with a tubular steam boiler at its point. It fed a steam-engine which drove a water pump. Mouchot was something of a missionary for solar energy and often demonstrated his sun machine connected to a small printing press which printed pamphlets about the excellence of solar energy in general and about Mouchot's exploitation of it in particular.

At the beginning of the twentieth century, an Anglo-American consortium took up Ericsson's designs and built a machine which was very much like the one built by Ericsson in 1883, although its dimensions were larger. Experiments were made with this machine at Meadi, near Cairo in Egypt. Once enough experience had been gained, a solar collector was built with a total surface area of 12,900 sq ft (1,200 sq m) which drove a steam-engine of 100 horsepower. The five mirrors, 200 ft (60 m) long and 13 ft (4 m) wide, followed the course of the sun via a system of jointed levers, and the full power of the steam-engine could be achieved for nine hours of the twenty-four. The construction was situated at the edge of the Sahara desert, and the aim of the project was to use an irrigation plant driven by the steam-engine to "make the desert bloom". The mirrors, however, required a lot of space—a surface area of 38,000 sq ft (3,500 sq m)—so that they would not shade each other. Besides, the customers found construction costs too high, and so, the much larger plant planned was never built.

During the first half of the twentieth century, there was little activity in the field of solar energy, one reason for this probably being the fact that the technical applications of solar energy had become closely connected with steam-engines and heat engines generally. When electric power started to triumph, at the beginning of our century, engineers were so much attracted by it that any technology related to steam-engines was considered hopelessly antiquated. When the petrol engine appeared, it meant access to yet another power source which could be moved to where it was needed. It was not until the 1950s that the wind changed for solar power. Several controversial books written then, one of them by the American physicist Harrison Brown, pointed out the limited resources of fuel and minerals on our planet and called for a halt to the ever accelerating increase of energy consumption.

In the United States the Association for Applied Solar Energy was formed in 1954, with its solar research centre situated at Phoenix, Arizona. The association is very active, its activities including the publication of the periodical *The Sun at Work*. During its first decade,

A John Ericsson's solar engine consisted of narrow glass strips which had been silvered on their outer sides and mounted on a stand, bent like a parabolic cylinder. In the focus of the mirror cylinder, a tubular boiler (*a*) was mounted.
B Ericsson's solar engine could also be used to drive a caloric engine.

C Mouchot's and Pifre's solar engine consisted of a wide cone with a 7 ft 3 in (2.2 m) diameter. It was built of copper plates which had been silver-plated on the inside. The tubular boiler was placed in the centre of the mirror and was blackened, to absorb the sun's radiation better. A glass casing prevents heat loss. The steam drove a small, 0.4-horsepower steam-engine which, in turn, drove a printing press.

D The solar furnace at Odeillo. (1) The northern facade of an eleven-storey building faced with a parabolic mirror, which consists of nine thousand smaller mirrors. (2) In the slope in front of the building, eleven thousand movable, flat mirrors (heliostats) are scattered, and these reflect solar radiation towards the parabolic mirror. The solar furnace (*a*) is situated within the parabolic mirror's focus.
E Glaser's suggestion for a solar power-station in space. The power station was to be geostationary, which means that its speed in space would equal the speed of the earth's rotation and it would always appear to be in the same spot in the sky. Since the problems of overcast skies, seasonal variations, and fluctuations between night and day which we have on earth with regard to solar power-stations do not exist

in space, a solar power-station of this type would give a practically constant production of electric current. The conversion from solar radiation to electric direct-current power would take place in photo-cells on the surface of the solar radiation catcher.
F A solar cell has the ability to transform radiation energy into electric energy and consists of semiconductors such as silicon or germanium crystals. These crystals have the ability either to be conductors of electricity or not, depending on the "pollutions" added to them. An atom in a semiconductor crystal easily loses one of its electrons, and the "hole" created will then be filled by an electron from another atom in the crystal. This exchange of electrons goes on continuously, but the crystal still does not become electrically charged, since

the association concentrated on the development of devices which would make it possible to exploit the abundant solar energy available in many developing nations, where there is a shortage of wood; an information campaign was organized to instruct the people in these countries to exploit the heat of the sun, mainly for cooking. One item introduced by the association for this purpose was a handy solar collector, called the "Umbroiler", a compound of "*um*brella" and "*broiler*", the name revealing all about the construction of the device.

In the 1950s, two large solar furnaces were built, one in the United States and one in France; this began a new stage of development. The American solar furnace is situated in Natick in Massachusetts, and its gigantic mirror produces at its focus a temperature of 4,400°C, enough to gasify steel! The large French solar research centre is now at Odeillo in the Pyrenees. The French research board, Centre National de la Récherche Scientifique, initiated research in solar

E

energy as early as 1946, and the first solar furnace in the Pyrennees was built in 1949 at Mont-Louis near Odeillo. It had a capacity of 50 kW and was built under the guidance of Felix Trombe. In the 1960s, a parabolic mirror was built in Odeillo, covering the whole façade of an eleven-storey building. This huge solar collector concentrates solar radiation which is reflected from a large number of small mirrors on the hills in front of the building. The temperature at the point of focus of the solar collector is about 4,000°C, and its effect is 1,000 kW. Extensive development and research work is also carried out at Odeillo to find methods of using solar energy to heat houses and the like.

In the 1950s, the Soviet Union also began to take solar energy seriously, and a trial plant was erected in a desert area in Armenia. Its dimensions were huge—1,300 large mirrors, moving on concentric rails to follow the course of the sun, concentrated the solar radiation towards a steam generator on a 180-ft (55 m) high tower. An electric generator driven by steam turbines then supplied electric power for irrigation, domestic requirements, and other purposes.

Yet another breakthrough in the development of solar energy came during the latter part of the 1950s with the advent of the solar cell, which converts solar radiation directly into electric energy. The first solar cells were built in the United States to supply electric power to space probes and satellites. In very simple terms, one can say that a solar cell works like an inverted transistor; it, too, consists of a coated silicon crystal from which radiation energy displaces electrons which are caught by the coatings. A very large number of such cells are connected in series and in parallel to give the voltage and power required for the electrically powered devices. Solar cells have hitherto been very expensive to produce, but considerable progress has been made in recent years. In the long run, and with a certain optimism, one can look forward to a competitive supply of electricity from solar cells.

In the 1950s, scientists in many parts of the world—for instance in the United States and in Israel—began to take an interest in the use of solar energy for heating houses. The preferred form of solar heater was one for water-borne heat, often connected to a heat pump; this system heated both the central-heating and the hot-water systems. The Royal Swedish Academy of Sciences has a solar research station in Capri, where astrophysical studies of the sun have been carried out for a long time, and in 1960, it installed a solar heating plant there under the supervision of Yngve Öhman. In 1974, the International Energy Agency (IEA) was formed as a sub-division of OECD, the European body for economic cooperation, and this has resulted in widespread international cooperation in the development of possible methods of heating houses by solar energy. At present, domestic heating accounts for more than half of our total energy consumption. Many forecasters believe that, by the turn of the century, solar energy may be responsible for at least fifty per cent of all heating—with variations in both directions, depending on the latitude.

In the 1970s, several projects have been started both in the United States and in Europe for large-scale solar power-stations. In 1975, the American energy body ERDA commissioned plans for a 10-MW solar power-station from the Sandia Laboratories in California. They in turn commissioned four industries to develop the different solutions. All four companies decided to place a steam boiler on top of a tower and arrange thousands of mirrors, or heliostats, to concentrate the solar radiation toward the steam boiler. However, their solutions differ widely when it comes to the construction and control of the heliostats, and the storing of energy, which must be stored so that the power-station can operate continuously, even when the sky is cloudy or after the sun has set. The steam produced by solar energy

F

the total number of electrons in it does not vary. If a small amount of an element whose atoms each have fewer electrons than those of the semiconductor is added to the semiconductor crystal, "holes" are left in the crystal, which will then become positively charged (p-crystal). In the same manner, a semiconductor crystal can become negatively charged (n-crystal) if one adds a small amount of an element whose atoms each have more electrons than have those of the semiconductor. When the sun's rays (a) hit the joint between the solar cell's n-crystal (b) and the surrounding p-crystal, electrons are ejected from the n-crystal, and an electric voltage occurs between the two layers. The conversion efficiency of a solar cell is, however, only about eleven per cent, and such cells are still very expensive to manufacture.

A A wave-powered electric whistle and light buoy from the first decades of the twentieth century. The wave motion was transferred by a jib (a) to the cylindrical buoy, which was then rotated round its longitudinal axis (b). The motion was transmitted to a gear train, which was stopped from turning the wrong way by a pawl (c). As the gearwheels turned, they brought a weight (d) upwards, and when the latter had reached its uppermost position, gravity caused it to fall down on the other side. Since the speed of the gearwheels was then increased, the rotor (e) of a small, electromagnetic engine was rotated fast enough to generate an electric current, which lit up a light bulb (f) and caused a bell (g) to sound.

B A proposal for a wave power-station (1) by Stephen Salter. The floats consist of cams (2) whose front edges are shaped to utilize the available wave energy as much as possible.

C A Swedish proposal for a wave power-station (1). Each buoy (a) is, by way of a spring-loaded hinged rod (b), connected to a float (c) anchored to the sea bed. (d) Electric cable. The transformer (2) contains a bar magnet (e) and an inductor (f) with a spring-loaded suspension (g). (h) Concrete float. (i) Plastic walls. (j) Diode bridge.

is estimated to have a temperature of 500°C and a pressure of about 10 megapascal. In other words, the turbine and the generator part of the solar power-station will be conventional. However, the constructional problems connected with the other parts are rather difficult to solve. One major problem is to build heliostats which can resist strong gusts of wind and yet be easy to orientate towards the sun. ERDA aims to begin operating the first pilot plant in 1980 in Barstow, California.

In Europe, IEA and ERDA are together planning to build a solar power-station of 0.5 MW in the early 1980s, probably in Almeria, Spain. A working party within the European Economic Community also plans a solar power-station, to be built in Italy, but any further details about the plant are, unfortunately, being kept secret.

In the 1970s, moreover, very ambitious plans for solar power-stations have been introduced by American scientists. They want to place solar collectors in space and to transmit the effect to receivers on the earth via microwaves. The first outline for such a power-station was published in 1973, and a more detailed plan was presented in 1977 by Peter E. Glaser, head of the Arthur D. Little Institute in Boston. Glaser suggests that a geo-stationary satellite, at a distance of about 22,500 miles (c. 36,000 km) from the earth, be equipped with a solar collector of about 40 sq miles (c. 100 sq km) (there's plenty of room out there!) which is constantly orientated towards the radiation of the sun. A direct-current power of about 15 GW (gigawatt = 10^9 watt) would be achieved and converted into radio waves for transmittal to earth, where a receiving station with an area of about 20 sq miles (c. 50 sq km) was to be built, consisting of a very large number of dipole antennas, each fitted with a crystal diode to rectify the radio waves. After the whole chain of energy conversions had been completed, about 10 GW would remain of the original 15 GW, which is equal to the estimated total energy demand in Sweden for 1979! The whole development programme for this project has been estimated to cost 60 billion US dollars. In the United States they expect to have some kind of a pilot plant in operation before the turn of the century.

Wave Energy
The energy found in the waves of the oceans and larger lakes is also a form of solar energy. A 10-ft (3 m) high wave contains more than 6 kW per ft (20 kW per metre)! The first patents of devices to exploit the energy of waves did not appear until the 1890s, and they had no practical significance. Not until the 1920s was a device invented which exploited wave energy on a small scale. It has since been used for sound buoys. Such a buoy is anchored to the seabed and contains an air dome where air flows in and out through a turbine driving a generator. Such pneumatic energy converters on a larger scale would be suitable for installation on, for example, oil platforms. A large number of energy converters are at present being studied in different places in the world, and some extensive research and development work is being carried out in Britain, France, the United States, and Scandinavia, with the aim of having wave power-stations in the megawatt class ready for experimental operation in the mid-1980s. Each wave power-station will probably include ten thousand or more converters and will, in other words, take up large areas at sea. Scientists are aware of the negative effect this will have on shipping and fishing, but they believe a positive effect will be a reduction of tidal movement. A wave power-station under favourable conditions could make traffic easier in channels which are normally difficult to navigate, since it would act as a primary breakwater. Cautious forecasters, however, do not expect wave power-stations to make any significant contributions to our energy supply until the year 2000 or so.

CHAPTER 7
THE GENESIS OF CONTROL SYSTEMS

The previous chapters of this book have dealt with some aspects of the technical developments that have led to the multitude of machines and devices which surround us today. If they are to be used as intended, it is often of vital importance that they be properly governed and controlled. The more complicated a machine, the more advanced must be the technique required to govern and control it. It is ultimately a question of man's ability to master technology.

Let us illustrate this with an example: when the bicycle was introduced in the 1860s, it became immediately popular in many places. At last a simple and handy means of transportation! But the first version of the bicycle could be quite lethal in certain situations: it had neither free wheel—that is, the pedals were fixed to the driving wheel—nor braking device. Going downhill, the rider had to keep his feet on the pedals and control his speed as best he could, and were he unsuccessful, he would very likely end up on a wild trip through the scenery. A modern bicycle, however, is equipped with a "control system", i.e., a free-wheel hub and, often, both hand and foot brakes, which together enable it to be controlled fully.

Some Elementary Terms

Modern control systems form one of the most advanced branches of engineering and aim at finding methods of controlling even the most intricate piece of machinery as easily and effectively as one can steer and brake a modern bicycle. A control engineer sees a machine as a system—a word of very general application: it comprehends a bicycle, a washing-machine, a spacecraft, the traffic flowing through a junction, a microwave oven, a nuclear reactor—briefly, any coherent unit which is controllable.

We talk about control *systems*, since the technical devices required nowadays to control plant or machinery have become complicated enough to justify this designation. They may be divided into two groups, those with *open-loop control* and those with *closed-loop*, or *feedback*, *control*. An example of a simple form of an open-loop control system is a light switch, which switches a lamp on and off. Control, or governing, can also be effected in an open system by a programming device which turns the light on or off at certain predetermined times. Such open-loop control systems are to be seen at street junctions, where traffic lights have been programmed for decided, regular intervals, but motorists do not much like such systems for controlling traffic, because queues easily build up on the busier of two roads at a junction. This problem can be solved by implanting vehicle detectors into the road and letting them report to the program device how many cars are approaching the junction. The program device in this case must be equipped with a counter, adjusted to let the traffic lights turn green for the busier road when, say, five cars are reported from one direction and none, or perhaps only one, from the other. Such a control system for traffic surveillance is, to a

A A road junction with an open control system. The automatic controller (*a*) keeps changing the lights so that they are green for the cars on road *b* for as long and as frequently as they are green for the cars on road *c*.

B A road junction with a closed control system. Vehicle detectors (*a*) sunk into the road surfaces report all cars approaching the junction to the automatic controller (*b*). If a single car is reported and the lights are red for traffic on the road in question, the lights will change before the car has reached the junction. However, if the lights are green, the signals will remain unchanged. If a car is approaching on each road, the car first actuating a vehicle detector will be the first to get green, and the lights will change as soon as it has crossed the junction. If a continuous stream of cars is reported from one road (*c*) whereas only one or two cars are reported from the other (*d*), the continuous stream of cars is allowed to cross until a gap occurs; then the signals are changed. If there is heavy, continuous traffic on both roads at the same time, the lights keep changing at regular intervals until a gap occurs in the traffic on either of the roads.

A

B

167

certain extent, responsible for its own actions, due to the feedback given via the vehicle detectors in the road. Consequently, this is called a *closed-loop control* system. An example of a purer feedback control system is the temperature regulation which is used in many buildings, mainly in houses with oil-fired central heating. The terminology used in control technology describes the system like this:

1 The *controlled system* consists of the boiler with its oil burner and the radiators heating the rooms.
2 The thermostat, which is in principle a thermometer, has the function of delivering a continuous *control signal*—a report of the room temperature—to the controlled system.
3 The *desired value* of the control signal is set on the thermostat in each room, indicating the temperature desired in the room.
4 If the desired value for the temperature is 68°F (20°C) and the control signal reports that the room temperature, the actual value, is only 60°F (16°C) an *error signal* is introduced, and the oil burner starts. It remains in operation until the room temperature has gone up to the desired value and eliminated the error. Then it is turned off automatically.
5 A *disturbance* to the system occurs, when, for example, a window is opened and cold air flows into a room.

The distinguishing factor in open-loop as well as closed-loop control systems is that they are automatic. They are therefore called *automatic control systems*.

Simulacra and Automata

Automatic devices appeared at a very early stage in human history. The hunting people of the early Stone Age, for example, probably knew the art of catching or killing wild animals with gin traps. There are many different types of animal trap; one of them, fitted with a "gin", a releasing mechanism, was probably the first automatic device.

An animal trap of interest in this context is the Scandinavian moose spear, an ancient trapping device that was quite common in parts of the region until well into this century. When the moose broke a line with its chest, a spear was released, being propelled by a "spring" formed by a young tree-trunk under tension. This animal trap, and also others of the same sort, in which the gin releases some kind of missile (we do not include things like pitfalls) can be seen as an arrangement whereby man has tried technically to simulate or imitate the way a hunter brings down his quarry, so that these animal traps can be called simulacra. Constructions with the idea of technically imitating human behaviour have been of great importance in the appearance of many tools and aids. The connected levers of a pair of tongs, for example, can be seen as a simulation or imitation of a human hand and its gripping function. This manner of description relates closely to the principle by which a sledge hammer is regarded as an extension of the human arm. We have referred to this principle, called organ projection, earlier; it has made an important contribution to, among other things, ergonomics, or work science, which aims at a better understanding of man's function in different working situations.

The attempt to imitate the behaviour of man or animals in a technical construction has often been the first step of a development in which the next has been an attempt to make this simulation an automatic mechanism—an automaton. When this automaton has achieved a certain degree of technical perfection, the desire has often arisen to try to simulate still more complicated functions. In such a step-by-step chain of development the tension between simulacra and automata emerges as a powerful driving force in furthering technical development in many areas. We shall later give other examples of such chains of development, but let us mention here just

A An example of a feedback control system: thermostat-controlled heating of a house. The controlled system consists of the central-heating boiler (*a*) with its oil burner (*b*) and the radiators (*c*). A thermostat (*d*), which continually delivers information of the prevailing indoor temperature (*e*) is connected to the system. The required value of the control signal (the temperature desired—*f*—in the room) is set on the thermostat. If the actual room temperature sinks below the desired temperature, the oil burner is automatically started and remains in operation until the room temperature is again at the desired level, when *b* is turned off. A disturbance to the system occurs if, for instance, a window is opened and cold air (*g*) flows in.

one, the chain which led to the modern computer. The first mechanical adding machines appeared in the seventeenth century and, in a way, simulated man's habit of counting on his fingers. Then, automatic calculating machines, automata, were produced successively, and after another few development stages, refined electronics managed to simulate man's way of making more complicated calculations. Simply put, this is done by giving the computer a program for calculating. During the course of operation, it can, among other things, store information in and retrieve it from a memory. This is all done automatically, acording to the program it has been fed. In other words, the computer is an automaton. However, methods are at present being developed to make the computer imitate man's ability to receive and interpret verbal instructions. This goal will, most probably, be achieved, and the computer will acquire these simulative functions while also being able to function automatically, that is, it will become a simulacrum as well as an automaton.

Some Early Control Systems

We have suggested that the gin of an animal trap is the earliest automatic mechanism. It is impossible to give the date for its appearance, but it is likely that it occurred while the hunting and gathering people were still nomadic, i.e., perhaps more than ten thousand years ago. The function of the gin has many modern equivalents, such as the limit switch, which releases or interrupts a movement in manufacturing automats, packing machines, etc.

A gin trap can be regarded as an open control system with program control, in which the quarry, in a random manner, supplies the "program". Many of the earliest control systems can be referred to as open systems, and it was not unusual for them to be equipped with some primitive form of programming. One such system is a method of cooking used by the hunting peoples in several of the earliest cultures. The cooking vessel was a leather bag; and heat was obtained from a stone heated in a fire. The stone was selected or brought along because it was just large enough to give the right cooking time for the food to be prepared. The "choice of program", in this case, was the size of the stone. It can be seen, with a little bit of imagination, as an early predecessor of today's electric time-controlled cookers. Almost nine thousand years separate these technically related methods for rationalizing domestic duties. Werner zur Megede, a German historian of technology, reports that North African finds of such cooking equipment have been dated to about 6650 BC.

Continuing our historical review of control systems, we find magnificent examples of programmed control in the huge irrigation systems of the river cultures. When the rivers rose during the rain periods, the water was led off via canals that started a long way upriver from the area that needed irrigation. The water was gathered in large basins well above the high-water level of the river in the area to be irrigated, thus making it possible to irrigate large areas untouched by the flooding. In Mesopotamia, the Land of the Twin Rivers, such irrigation systems, albeit local ones, were built as early as the fourth millennium BC. After the powerful ruler Hammurabi had united the many small kingdoms along the Euphrates and the Tigris in the 1780s BC, he proclaimed a law which aimed at co-ordinating the operation of the many networks of basins and canals which were then in use. Hammurabi's famous law was mainly a handbook for the organization and administration of the irrigation systems. The law laid down the obligation of each citizen to contribute to the maintenance, operation, and extension of the systems. Also, there were detailed paragraphs about the punishment for any neglect of these obligations. The slightest disobedience or negligence in fulfilling the state's severe requirements was seen as a cardinal

B A moose spear is shown here from above (1) and from the side (2). When the moose moved against a line (a), a catch (b) was released. The spear (c), which was mounted on a young tree-trunk under tension, was then flung forwards and buried itself in the moose.

B1

B2

C The ancient Egyptians irrigated areas normally untouched by the Nile's floods by digging feeder canals (a), which started far upstream of the area in question. The water was then allowed to trickle downwards, from basin to basin (b), when dams in the walls between them were opened. Thus, the soil in the basins was thoroughly soaked. Similar irrigation systems occurred in other early river cultures.

crime. It was vital for the whole of society that the irrigation system worked. An enormous labour force was needed to control this huge system during the critical period when the "program device" was released, i.e., when the rivers started to overflow. This did not happen with the precision one should expect from a program device, since both the Euphrates and the Tigris were fairly unpredictable. The very able Sumerian civil engineers were really hard tried, but eventually, they developed an admirably accurate technique for controlling the life-giving water—there was often a difference of only half an inch or so between the successive levels of the irrigation systems. But in the eleventh century BC, when the Euphrates changed course, the surrounding part of the irrigation system became hopelessly confused. This contributed to the disintegration of the society and to the decline of the Sumerian culture.

Irrigation systems similar to the Sumerian were built by other early river cultures—on the Yellow River in China, in the Indus valley, and along the Nile. In ancient Egypt impressive irrigation works were constructed. The Egyptians started somewhat later than the neighbouring Sumerians, but their problem with regulation was much simpler, for the Nile flooded with an unfailing precision that has earned it the epithet, "the gentleman river". Because the program for controlling the irrigation worked perfectly, it was easier to manage the regulation of the water flow, with the result that the long, narrow strips of arable land along the Nile valley could be made wider and wider, thus strengthening the economic foundation of this remarkable, advanced culture.

Early Automata and Closed Systems

The simple water clock, the clepsydra, became common in ancient Greece some time during the sixth or fifth century BC, but had probably come into being in Egypt long before. The oldest document to mention a clepsydra is a record of judicial proceedings where it is named as an aid to ensure that both the prosecutor and the defendant are given the same time for their final pleadings. The simplest form of the clepsydra was a basin with a spillway. Since water was added to the basin continuously, it ran with a reasonably constant flow out of a lower opening and into another, graded vessel. This primitive chronometer was improved and more or less perfected by the engineers of the Alexandrian school, primarily by Ctesibius (see page 33). The clepsydra, in its most refined version, can be regarded as a simulacrum by means of which an imitation is sought of the unfaltering, constant movement of the heavenly bodies, which is the basis of our measuring of time.

The idea of giving the clepsydra an automatic function, however, had already been thought of when this mechanism existed only in its simplest form. No less a person than the great philosopher Plato (427−347 BC) designed such an automaton. The pupils of the academy founded by Plato in Athens in 378 BC had difficulty in waking up in the morning, and it was a problem to gather them for the day's discussions, so Plato built a magnificent "alarm clock", which was placed in the olive grove of the academy. It was a simple clepsydra, in which the usual graded vessel had inside it a bowl which was hinged across its width and contained a number of lead balls. During the night, the vessel filled with water which, as it rose, lifted the bowl, causing, in due time, the lead balls to roll out and fall on a copper plate. The noise ought to have awakened at least the lighter sleepers, who probably then aroused their friends.

Plato's alarm clock, like his academy, attracted a great deal of contemporary attention, and in the following century, many clepsydras with signal devices were designed. One of them used compressed air to achieve a loud, whistling noise. The water of the clepsydra was fed into a container divided into an upper and a

lower compartment; between these ran a pipe which was open at both ends and almost long enough to reach the upper edge of the upper compartment, but not going too far into the lower compartment. A thicker pipe was arched over the first pipe and fixed a small distance above its top. This thicker pipe was closed at the top, and its open end almost reached the dividing wall between the upper and the lower compartments. When the water of the clepsydra had reached the upper edge of the inner pipe, the upper compartment emptied itself relatively quickly, and the water ran into the lower compartment, due to the two pipes working together as a hydrometer. The air in the lower compartment was compressed and pressed out through another pipe in its upper part. This was fitted with a whistle or a flute, which then sounded.

The Alexandrian School

Technology and the natural sciences flourished at that famous seat of learning of antiquity, the Museum of Alexandria, to which we have referred already. A large number of brilliant talents, such as Pythagoras, Ctesibius, Euclid, Hero, and Philo of Byzantium, made their contributions to science there. Archimedes, too, may be reckoned as of the Alexandrian school, although he was active in Syracuse, an important administrative centre within the same cultural sphere. The engineers of the Alexandrian school constructed various simulacra and automata, which have been variously discussed already. One may wonder why these advanced engineers designed things such as singing birds, moving figures for the stage, self-propelled carriages, and automatic devices, some of which, to be sure, had a practical purpose, such as the holy-water dispenser and the odometer-taximeter; but most of them were intended to simulate pure magic, such as the heat machine which automatically opened the doors of the temple's inner sanctum. Why did not the engineers of the Alexandrian school do something useful instead?

The reason is that they regarded themselves as natural philosophers, whose only objective was to explore the laws of nature. This they did by theoretical speculation, calling logics and mathematics to their assistance, when needed. In cases where the theories were suited to experimental trials, devices for practical experiments were built. It is apparent that the natural philosophers had skilful instrument makers and craftsmen available for this work, and that they had a supply of refined equipment and tools. These instrument makers must have had their own internal training system, for which a selected number of apprentices were recruited. The professional skill of the instrument makers was really put to the test when the "professors" ordered the devices they needed to test their theories. Usually, it was a question of designs never tried before, something that must have stimulated thinking along new lines. Many flippant constructions, today attributed to the engineers of the Alexandrian school, were no doubt the result of teamwork between the natural philosophers and their skilful instrument makers.

A rich source of inspiration for the school's ingenious simulacra and automata was the mythology and the whole imaginary world of ancient Greece, which included a comprehensive fauna of artificial birds, walking and talking statues, and skilfully made imitations of divinities as well as servants. Homer's *Iliad* tells about the crafty god Hephaestus, "the engineer of Olympus", who had designed self-propelled carriages. The engineers of the Alexandrian school made this mythological achievement a practical reality (see page 36). Hephaestus surrounded himself with servant girls made of pure gold. According to Homer, these golden girls were both strong and intelligent. They could talk and were assiduous in learning the handicrafts the gods taught them. This is one of the first mentions of artificial human beings, or androids. From the Renaissance onwards, many attempts were made to produce such creatures. We shall come back to this later.

The story about Daedalus, his son Icarus, and their flying adventure is commonly known and, without doubt, belongs to the world of myth. The hellenic fables say that Daedalus served King Minos in Crete and amused himself, and possibly also the king, by designing moving animals, among them a cow. Quite contrary to the story of the flying adventure, there may be a grain of truth in the tradition that Daedalus built moving, walking statues. He is said to have used mercury to change the centre of gravity and so get the arms, legs, and even the eyes of the statues to move. The manner of depicting an "arrested action" in Greek sculpture is attributed to Daedalus (a famous example of arrested action is the discobolus by Myro). The technique of depicting eyes with a hole in the pupil is also attributed to Daedalus.

Many historians and writers of ancient Greece and Rome, including Herodotus of Halicarnassus, Lucian, and Diodorus Siculus, give detailed descriptions of self-propelled mechanisms and androids, and similar accounts occur in other early cultures, especially that of China. What is myth and what reality is often very difficult to determine exactly, but this sphere of thought seems to have excited the imagination everywhere. There is, without doubt, an extremely rich tradition in the history of ideas for the theories of control systems.

The story of Archytas of Tarentum (400?–365? BC) and his famous flying wooden pigeon lies on the borderline between myth and reality. As Archytas was a contemporary and friend of Plato's, and was also a pupil of Pythagoras', he can be considered to belong to the Alexandrian school. Of his work, only fragments remain, among them dissertations on acoustics and musical theory, but there is enough to demonstrate that he was an advanced natural philosopher. What has afforded him his greatest renown is the story about the pigeon; however, this story was first written down several hundred years after his death. In the story, the pigeon has inside its body a magic container, which keeps it soaring in the air. This container was probably no more than a hot-air balloon or kite. The Alexandrian school knew these toys, and the fact that Archytas worked with acoustics makes it likely that he also studied the properties of air. The story about Archytas' flying pigeon has been related by many different chroniclers down the centuries, and each time, it has been expanded in the telling, but the reality behind it may very well be what we have suggested.

One example of the many unsuccessful attempts to solve the problem of flying by simulating the flight of birds occurred in Rome in the middle of the seventeenth century. Members of the learned Roman society, *Accademia dell'Esperienze*, were inspired by the story about Archytas' pigeon to construct a mechanical version driven by springs, but this academic pigeon did not fly. The myth about Daedalus and Icarus, the legend about Archytas' pigeon, and several other stories from antiquity about mechanical birds are probably partly responsible for many inventors, even in the twentieth century, trying to build their flying-machines according to what is called the ornithopter, or flapping, principle, despite Sir George Cayley's statement as early as 1799 that this was not possible.

Back to the Alexandrian school, whose natural philosophers and engineers were certainly unaware of how important their various programmed simulacra and automata would be in the future, or that their devices with feedback, which can now be called the first closed control systems, would be even more important, if that were possible. One of the first was Hero's design for the control of the level of a liquid by means of a floating body which affected the discharge valve, a design whose principle is still used, both in industry and in our immediate surroundings: one variant is to be found in the car

A The simplest type of water clock consisted of a vessel (*a*) with an overflow (*b*). From the lower part of this vessel, water dripped through a tube (*c*) and into another, graded vessel (*d*). Since the water constantly supplied to *a* amounted to a little more than the amount of water dripping out through *c*, the water pressure in *a* was approximately constant.

B Plato's alarm clock was a simple clepsydra, in which a bowl (*a*) containing lead balls had been hinged to the brim of a (usually) graded vessel (*b*). When the water level in *b* had risen enough, the bowl was lifted, and the lead balls were tipped out and fell onto a copper plate (*c*).

C This clepsydra with its signalling device has also been attributed to Plato. The water from the clepsydra was collected in a vessel which was divided into an upper (*a*) and a lower (*b*) compartment. Between these ran a pipe (*c*) which was open at both ends. Vaulted over pipe *c* was a wider pipe (*d*) whose closed upper end was situated a short distance above the top of the inner pipe, whereas its open, lower end had been designed so that water could enter between the two pipes. When the water in *a* had risen above the upper edge of the inner tube (*c*), *a* was fairly rapidly emptied of water, which ran into *b*, since the two pipes together worked as a siphon. The air in *b* was then compressed and forced out through a pipe (*e*), to whose outer end a flute (*f*) was attached.

A In 1863, a Frenchman, J.-J. Bourcart, constructed this pedal-propelled craft with which, in his opinion, one ought to be able to fly. One advantage which he emphasized was that the "pilot" had both hands free.
B This ornithopter model, built in 1870 by the Frenchman Gustave Trouvé, was propelled by gunpowder and could be made to fly all of 77 yds (70 m).
C Accademia dell'Esperienze's clockwork-powered, mechanical pigeon was one of many unsuccessful attempts to simulate the flight of birds.

carburettor and another in the water closet. Several other engineers of the Alexandrian school described different versions of the level control. One of these, a fine example of constructive thinking and usually attributed to Ctesibius, combines the floating body with the valve to form an integral unit, a solution which eliminates the play that can occur in the joints of the levers in Hero's version. Ctesibius's device was intended to meet a demand for precision, namely to achieve a uniform flow of water in a water clock.

Philo of Byzantium, another great thinker of the Alexandrian school, designed a control device adapted to the special requirements of an oil lamp, which does not necessarily need a constant oil level, but whose level must be neither too high nor too low, if the wick is to burn well. Philo's design consisted of a closed oil container with an ascending pipe, open at both ends. The lower end was immersed in the oil bath supplying fuel to the wick. When the level of the oil fell below the lower end of the pipe, air bubbled up through it, allowing oil to run out of two thin pipes at the bottom of the oil container until the level of the oil in the oil bath once again covered the lower end of the ascending pipe, whereupon no more oil ran out of the container because no more air was entering it through the ascending pipe. Philo's control ensured that the level of the oil stayed between a minimum and a maximum level. This closed control system, too, has many successors in modern technology, although it is usual that separate devices assess the upper and lower limits.

Arabic Interlude

We have mentioned briefly that the works of the Alexandrian school became widely spread in the Eastern Roman Empire and in the Arabic cultural sphere after the decline and fall of the Western Empire. A great deal of the literature of antiquity had certainly been lost by the senseless plunderings of the wars of conquest, but a number of classical books had been preserved by scholars and in monasteries. The rapid Islamic conquests in the seventh and eighth centuries AD were followed by a period in which Arabic culture had a magnificent flowering, its main inspiration being the Hellenic heritage, especially as regards the natural sciences. Representative of this cultural revival is the systematic search for the classical works of antiquity, which was instigated by the khalif of Bagdhad, Abdullah-al-Manun (786–833) in the early ninth century. He commissioned three men, the *Banu Musa*, the three sons of his court astrologer, Musa, to go out and buy whatever they could lay their hands on in the way of works by the Greek natural philosophers. One of them travelled extensively in Asia Minor and Greece and tracked down numerous works by the philosophers of the Alexandrian school and by earlier equally distinguished Hellenes. This search laid the foundations of the Bagdhad library, later so renowned. Similar searches resulted in libraries of equivalent standing in Cairo and Cordoba, the other two capitals of the realms of Islam.

Musa's sons translated first and foremost Hero's and Philo's works and also revised them. They described a number of their own designs in the large work *Kitab al-Hiyal* ("The Book of Ingenious Devices"), which became almost a standard work in Arabic culture, judging, at least, by the large number of hand-written copies to be found in libraries and archives in the extensive Islamic dominion. The prototypes of the designs in this work can, however, easily be traced to the Alexandrian school.

The engineers of the Arabic world were no less fascinated by self-propelled devices than their predecessors, but within the Arabic world practical applications were sought for their designs. Many of the Greek prototypes had come about only to illustrate a natural law or a physical principle. In *Kitab al-Hiyal*, the Musa brothers de-

D Philo's oil lamp; (**1**) the lamp, (**2**) cross-section. The middle of the oil container (a) had a riser (b), open at both ends. The riser's lower end opened into the oil bath (c) which provided the wick with fuel. When the level in c sank below the riser's lower end, air could bubble up through b, and oil could flow out through two narrow pipes (d). As soon as the level in c had again risen so that the riser's opening was covered, the oil ceased to flow.

E "The inexhaustible goblet", invented by Hero. Wine was served from a goblet (a) which, by way of a pipe (b), communicated with another vessel (c). Thus, when wine was taken from a, the level of the fluid in c sank as well, as did a float (d). Wine could then flow into c from a large container (e) through a pipe (f). As soon as the wine in a and c was again at its original level, the float once more covered the opening of pipe f, and the wine ceased to flow. The float was kept from moving horizontally by being suspended from a lever (g) with a small counterweight (h).

F This flow-controlling valve was also designed by Hero. It is based on the same principle as "the inexhaustible goblet"—when wine was taken from a goblet (a), the level of the fluid also sank in another vessel (b), connected to a by a pipe (c). A float (d) then pulled a lever (e) downwards, so that the valve (f) of an outlet pipe (g) in a large wine container (h) was opened.

scribed a round one hundred designs and made great efforts to indicate different ways of putting them to practical use. From a modern point of view, many of these constructions may seem slightly far-fetched, but in those days, it may have been enough that on beholding them, "the spectator was petrified", as the writers on a few occasions remarked.

Those who came after the Musa brothers, however, discovered a large and fruitful area in which the designs could be applied, namely clockmaking. From the early Middle Ages onwards, magnificent ornamental clocks were built to adorn the princely houses of the Arabic world. The famous ornamental clock in Ghaza has already been named (see page 47) as an example of advanced manufacturing technology; it had appeared before the spread of Islam and is interesting proof that the heritage of the Alexandrian school was kept alive in this part of the world. Although the details of the design of the clock are unknown, it can be assumed that it was based mainly on the ideas of the Alexandrian engineers.

One of the first important books on clockmaking in the Arabic world is entitled *Work of Archimedes on the Building of Clocks*. The text claims that the book is based on works by Archimedes of Syracuse; in other words, it was a translation and revision of his works, similar to the translations made by the Arabs of Hero, Philo, and other writers. Still, no work on the building of clocks has been found among Archimedes' books, although contemporary writers suggest that he actually did study this branch of technology. It is certainly not unlikely that the great genius of the natural sciences in the ancient

world should have been fascinated by the automata of time-measuring. The Arabic translator may possibly have had a book by Archimedes, which has later been lost. The American historian of technology Otto Mayr cautiously calls the writer of this detailed description of the making of water clocks "Pseudo-Archimedes". It is apparent that the man who wrote the book must have known a great deal about clockmaking and also must have had plenty of practical experience of the existing machine elements. The book, which is thought to have been written in the tenth century AD, was translated into German by Friedrich Hauser and Eilhard Wiedemann in the 1910s. On the basis of the very comprehensive text, they could make a complete reconstruction of this remarkable water clock. It had a square base of 1 ft 8 in (0.5 m) and was more than 19 ft (4 m) high. After each "winding", i.e., filling with water, the clock ran for twelve hours, and the time was marked on a clock face. On the hour, a number of mechanisms were set in motion. A bird's beak dropped stone balls onto a metal gong—as many balls as there were hours to indicate. A snake attacked some birds and the eyes rolled in a representation of a woman's head.

Pseudo-Archimedes' book spread and was widely accepted as a handbook on clockmaking. Several later writers often refer to it, one of them being Ridwan al-Khurasani, the son of a clockmaker who became very famous at the end of the twelfth century for building an intricate ornamental clock at the "Gate of Hours" in the Great Mosque in Damascus. This clock showed the hours of the day with effects rather like those described by Pseudo-Archimedes, but more-

A A water clock, described and illustrated by al-Jazari. The clock was "wound up" when a tank (a) was filled with water. In the tank was a float (b), to which a string was attached. The string ran over pulleys (c), and, as b sank at an even pace, a pointer (d) was pulled by the string along a board (e) with twelve holes, one for each hour. From a, the water ran through a tap (f) into another, smaller vessel (g). The float (h) in this vessel carried on its top a carefully ground stopper, which fitted into the opening of the tap and turned off the flow of water when the float reached its upper level. As soon as it sank again, the water started to run anew. Thus, the water in g flowed under constant pressure through a pipe (i) which was placed near the bottom of g, and into a round vessel (j). In this vessel, there was an overflow (k) through which the water finally left. When k was in its highest position, it was level with the top of vessel g (the proportions in al-Jazari's illustration do not correspond to reality). By turning vessel j, the position of the overflow in relation to vessel g could be altered; thus, the length of the hours could be varied.

B Pseudo-Archimedes described his water clock in such detail that Wiedemann and Hauser, who translated his work to German in the 1910s, could reconstruct practically the whole clock. It is shown here from the front (**1**), in cross-section from one side (**2**), and in semi-cross-section from the rear (**3**). Enough water for twelve hours was poured into a vessel (a) through a funnel (b). Just like al-Jazari's 300-years-earlier construction, Pseudo-Archimedes' clock was driven by a float (c) which sank at an even pace in this vessel, since the outflow of water was governed by a float (d) in a smaller vessel (e), to which a pipe (f) ran. From e, the water flowed through a pipe (g) and out through an overflow (h) whose position could be altered in a vertical direction, since pipe g could be rotated along a scale (i). The length of the hours could thus be varied in this clock as well, since the water's flow could be altered. From h, the water ran into a dipper (j) and on to another, pivoted dipper (k) with a counterweight (l) at one end. When k had been filled, it tipped over and activated the mechanism (m) which made a snake attack birds. Finally, the water was collected in the lower part of the clock, from where it

B1

B2

over, it had a special mechanism to show the time at night. A flame appeared in one after another of the twelve windows. Ridwan al-Khurasani, who is also known in literature as Ibn al-Saati ("the son of the clockmaker"), restored this ornamental clock, which had fallen into decay after the death of his father, and wrote a comprehensive instruction book for its future maintenance.

At the beginning of the thirteenth century, another renowned clockmaker, Ismaeel al-Jazari (1150?–1220?), was active in Amid on the upper reaches of the Tigris. He wrote a large book, *The Science of Ingenious Mechanisms*, in which he described some ten ornamental clocks. His first description is almost identical to Pseudo-Archimedes' design from three hundred years earlier. Apart from different versions of water-clocks, al-Jazari also described a highly original chronometer, which consisted of a wax candle with metal balls held individually in a vertical container. As the candle burnt down, the balls were released and fell onto a metal disc. This was not the first candle with a time-measuring function, but the striking mechanism was probably al-Jazari's invention.

This clockmaker's great fame is evidenced by the fact that he was called to Ghaza to put into working order the renowned ornamental clock, which had by then fallen into almost total decay. He managed to restore it to its past splendour, but the clock only existed for another fifty years or so. Most manifestations of this culture were eradicated when the Mongols attacked the eastern parts of the Arab dominion, Bagdhad falling in 1258.

The Automata of the Renaissance

We have already touched upon the important technical developments which took place in the West during the last few centuries of the Middle Ages. Water and wind power were exploited to a greater and greater extent and for more and more varied purposes. The supply of metals increased and the guilds appeared; one result of this was organized professional training. Many necessities, such as bricks and needles, were manufactured on a semi-industrial scale. Spiritual life also blossomed, with the foundation of universities and the growth of monastic orders. From the end of the thirteenth century onwards, inspiration in all areas was sought in the works of Greek and Roman writers. The culture of classical antiquity was to be reborn! This important phase in the history of technology has been called earlier in this book the "technical revolution of the Renaissance", and this concept is certainly richly emphasized in the field of automata.

Interest in natural science began to stir among the scholars of the time—mainly monks and theologians. It is not surprising that they were particularly interested in the ingenious devices and automata of the Alexandrian school. There is a story, typical for the time, about Thomas Aquinas (1225–74) and his teacher Albertus Magnus (1193?–1280), who was a Dominican friar, Bishop of Regensburg, and one of the great mediaeval polymaths, with extensive scientific interests. Albertus Magnus is said to have constructed a door-keeper of metal, wood, wax, and leather, who greeted visitors by uttering "*Salve*"! and by asking them their business, before admitting them to the great scholar. The young Thomas once became so annoyed with the impertinent questions of the android that he smashed it into pieces. Naturally, Albertus was incensed and admonished his student: "Thomas, Thomas, what have you done? You have smashed the work of thirty years to smithereens!"

This story is obviously a myth, although several versions of it have been repeated in various contexts through the centuries. But it is indicative of its time. People experienced one great change after another, and the technical revolution of the Renaissance often gave them an exaggerated belief in the possibilities of technology to pro-

could be discharged through a cock (*n*). When float *c* sank, it pulled on a string (*o*), which ran round a drum (*p*). Other strings (*q*) on the same drum drove the pointers (*r*) indicating the time on a dial (*s*). The gorgon's (*t*) rolling eyes (*u*) were also driven by a string (*v*) from this drum. Via a gear train (*w*), the drum also drove the mechanism which made a bird's head (*x*) release stone balls onto a metal gong (*y*).

C Al-Jazari's timekeeper in the form of a wax taper with a "striking apparatus". The taper (*a*) was inserted under a bronze disc (*b*) in which there was a hole for the wick. A holder (*c*) underneath the taper was suspended from a string, which ran over a pulley (*d*) and had a lead weight (*e*) at its other end. Thus, the taper was continually pushed upwards as it burned, releasing a metal ball from a small compartment (*f*) once an hour. The ball fell through a tube and out through the beak of a hollow falcon (*g*), landing on a metal plate (*h*). On its way down, the ball hit a mechanism which made the figure of a man swing a sharp sword at the wick, thus snuffing the taper.

A At a very early stage in the history of mechanical clocks, striking devices were constructed. These often took the form of jacquemarts, mechanical watchmen who struck bells with hammers.

B All that remains today of the fourteenth-century clock in the cathedral of Strasbourg is the bellows-powered mechanical cock (**1**), which flapped its wings and crowed at noon. When the mechanism was working, all the lower feathers in the cock's plumage were slanted. The cock, shown in cross-section at **2**, is today exhibited in the museum of Strasbourg.

A

B1   B2

duce "miracles" such as Albertus Magnus's ill-fated talkative doorkeeper.

According to certain historians, the invention of the mechanical clock was a way of solving an irritating problem from which the water clock suffered, namely, that it could work only in temperatures above freezing-point. There is, however, a very obvious common denominator between the more advanced water clocks and the first mechanical clocks. Weights, suspended from a rope over a roller, set various mechanisms working in Pseudo-Archimedes' water clock, and these important components were also used in its many successors. The advanced knowledge and experience of the Arab engineers in the field of self-moving mechanisms could certainly have enabled them to invent a mechanical clock which can be seen as a further development of the weight mechanisms of the water clocks. However, as has already been mentioned, the Mongols prevented this. What the Arab engineers lacked was an efficient "checking mechanism", which could reduce the movement driven by the weight—or rather, by gravity—to a rotation that was constant and slow enough. The escapement in mechanical clocks has this very function. In the mid-thirteenth century, an Arab clockmaker, Taqi al-Din, introduced a device which is extremely interesting in this context, being something of the missing link between the water clock and the mechanical clock. To moderate the movement of a weight-driven mechanism in a water clock, Taqi al-Din built an annular container, partly filled with mercury and contained in the drum round which the rope of the weight was wound. The mercury container was divided radially into sections by walls that had small holes in them; the movement of the drum was regulated by the arrested movement of the mercury through these holes. This device seems to have been unknown in the West at the time of the appearance there of the first mechanical clocks. Taqi al-Din's checking mechanism would probably have been able to provide a more even movement than that given by the first primitive escapements.

During the early Renaissance, the newly awakened interest in the writings of antiquity was undoubtedly a strong force in the development of mechanical clocks. When, in the fourteenth century, the mechanical timekeeper acquired the form of a simulacrum—the constant movement of the universe being simulated by the uniform movement of an axle—its design began to be developed so as to acquire another form of imitation. In the first mechanical clocks, the passage of the hours was indicated on a cylindrical or circular clockface, so that a watchman would know when to sound a horn or ring a bell. The automatic mechanism of the timekeeper was complemented with other mechanisms which copied the tasks of the watchman. These simulacra were the striking mechanisms, and many were built in different versions quite early in the history of mechanical clocks. The most logical thing to do was to make a mechanical copy of a watchman strike a bell. There are many examples of such functional decorations, called clock jacks, on tower clocks from the fourteenth century onwards. (The origin of the word "jack" is unclear, but it is believed that the word comes from the French *jacquemarts*, the *mart* being a corruption of the Latin *martellus*, a hammer.) The striking mechanisms were made as separate devices driven by the clockwork, and this was certainly nothing new. The skilfully made Arabic water clocks often had several separate devices whose functions were released in different ways by the time-measuring escapement. The simplest form of striking mechanism for mechanical clocks was a rudimentary wheel with cams, which enabled the jack to strike a hammer against a bell. The striking mechanism in this context can be seen as an early form of mechanical memory.

In the use of jacks we can trace the strong influence of the theatre automata of the Alexandrian school and of the advanced Arabic art of clockmaking, with its moving figures of gods, people, birds, and other animals. One of the first jacks was not a man with a hammer, but a mechanical cock attached to the tower of the cathedral of Strasbourg about 1350. At twelve o'clock, the cock flapped its wings and crowed. The cock was the symbol of vigilance and, therefore, often appeared—although not usually in its mechanized version—on many European church spires. The mechanical cock in Strasbourg may be regarded as a symbol of the rapid development which was to follow. With water clocks and other designs from antiquity as prototypes, numbers of intricate ornamental clocks were produced which showed the passage of the sun through the zodiac, the phases of the moon, and the movements of the planets. Often, these clocks were additionally equipped with moving figures representing kings, emperors, apostles, warriors, or clowns; these not only marked the passage of time but also performed elegant scenes containing both religious and profane symbolism. The automatic mechanisms must have been made with the same precision and have had the same certainty of motion as the clockwork; this instigated many instances of impressive precision mechanics, which demanded much of the material and of the principles of design, as well as of the craftsmanship. Ornamental clocks have been described from these points of view in Chapter Two.

Life-size Automata

The rapid technical progress that occurred during the Renaissance made it possible for designers to construct life-size automata in a wholly different manner than before—the engineers of the Alexandrian school had built their automatic devices on a scale suitable for playthings. Several revisions of the ancient classics of technology, as well as translations of both Greek and Arabic originals, were published in Europe in the sixteenth and seventeenth centuries. One of these is the extensive work, *Les raisons des forces mouvantes . . .* ("About Violent Forces. A Description of Some Useful and Amusing Devices") by the French engineer Salomon de Caus. This lavishly illustrated artbook was first published in 1615. De Caus was active for a large part of his life in Heidelberg, in the service of the elector, Fredrik V of Pfalz. His book describes many of Hero's automata but develops these construction ideas further, converting them for use in the technology of his own time, a technology embellished with all the colour and panache of the seventeenth century. Unlike many contemporary art books, however, de Caus's work was not merely theoretical: in the garden of the Heidelberg palace, he had built a number of scenes with moving figures, romantically framed by caves. The whole thing was driven by water wheels, and the movements of the figures were released by "programs" consisting of drums with cams. De Caus later built something of the same sort, but on a larger scale, at the Duke of Burgundy's palace, Saint-Germain, outside Paris, which became, because of this, one of the greatest attractions in Europe. Construction of a similar installation began in 1613 at the Hellbrunn Palace at Salzburg, and this also gained a great reputation. It originally consisted of a number of caves with moving mythological figures, dragons, and birds. The installation was enlarged between 1748 and 1752 to comprehend in total 256 figures. The Hellbrunn installation was water-driven, too, and had several gear mechanisms, connected to cylinders with cams, which shifted levers that pulled copper wires to set the figures moving according to a programmed sequence. A hydraulic organ provided effective background music and, moreover, smothered the noise of the driving mechanisms. Salomon de Caus had many successors who copied—as well as they could—his automatic theatre scenes, and for centuries, it remained fashionable to provide stately gardens with caves and moving figures.

Salomon de Caus was the great pioneer of life-size automata construction, an art which flowered at this time. The many royal, imperial, and ducal courts started to employ their own art masters, who made androids and other automata that more or less literally wandered about in the stately salons, showing off their skills. At about the same time, another art emerged and has continued to flourish until our time—the art of producing toy-scale automata, as had been done in classical antiquity. One of the great originators of this art was Juanelo Turriano, the brilliant designer of the "ballet-dancing machine" (see p. 103). This extremely talented engineer served Emperor Charles V, who, forced to abdicate in 1556, retired to the monastery of Geronimo de San Yuste in Estremadura, where he declined in sad meditation of his fate. Turriano tried in every way to cheer up his master by making amusing automata: wooden birds flying round the room, a shepherdess playing the lute, horn blowers and drummers, soldiers fencing with swords, and many other things. Some European museums, including the Kunsthistorisches Museum in Vienna, now have exhibitions of automata attributed to Turriano, but evidently, none of them can be proved to have been made by the clever Cremonese.

Turriano's automata became renowned, as had his great engineering feat of arranging the water supply to the city of Toledo, and the abbot of the monastery of San Yuste contributed a great deal to the fame of the former, although quite unintentionally. He happened to witness a performance of some of Turriano's automata, and the sight of this frivolous spectacle totally convinced the abbot that Turriano was in league with the devil himself. In those days, such an opinion, especially when held by such an important churchman, rapidly spread among the hierarchy and the faithful.

Whether the remarkable Turriano was in league with the devil or not, he certainly became the basis of a large number of myths, and something of a folk hero, especially after providing Toledo with water in such an elegant fashion. A chronicle from the mid-1600s tells how Turriano had designed an android in the form of a valet, who would go out in the streets every day to do the shopping for the household. One might remark that technology seems to have been more advanced at this time than it was when Albertus Magnus was said to have designed a door-keeper! But the myth of Turriano's valet is in the same spirit as that of the door-keeper. Firm belief in the achievements of a recognizedly eminent man formed, in both cases, the basis of the myth. As regards Turriano, the power of legend over thought became so strong that the alley where he lived in Toledo was later given the name *Calle del Hombre del Palo* ("The Alley of the Wooden Man").

There were, however, real equivalents of Turriano's "wooden man". They certainly could not move freely, but they still had an impressive range of skills. A number of goldsmiths and precision mechanics in Nürnberg led the field within this genre, one of the first being the father-in-law of Albrecht Dürer, Hanns Frey, a merchant whose hobby was precision mechanics. Frey built many automata, especially drinking automata, based on Hero's and the Arab masters' designs. His successor, Hanns Bullmann, was more important; he was a goldsmith and a contemporary of Peter Henlein, the locksmith and precision mechanic who designed one of the first spring-driven pocket watches (see page 52). Bullmann was possibly the first designer of automata to use spring-driven clockwork to move his figures; quite probably he was familiar with Henlein's work. A guild chronicle of 1547, *Nachrichten von Künstlern und Werkleute in Nürnberg*, gives a fairly comprehensive description of Bullmann's automata. They consisted of a large number of spring-driven figures of men and women, which could walk back and forth and play different instruments. As a designer of automata, Bullmann later had many automata from this pioneering era. A closer look at the programs and other control devices of the designs reveals that the extremely skilful craftsmen who manufactured them applied many sophisticated techniques which have been reinvented many times since.

When interest in automata became really widespread in the seventeenth century, not only precision engineers but also the great humanists and philosophers began to interest themselves in this technical art. The French philosopher René Descartes (1596–1650), in his pioneering work, *Discourse de la méthode*, published in 1637, deals with, among other things, the relationship between man and animals. They have all been made by God, he writes, but only man has an immortal soul. The animals, however, must be seen as intricate machines, as automata. Descartes goes on to expound his views on *la bête machine* ("the animal as a machine") and maintains that it is quite likely that, one day, man will succeed in designing "soulless machinery", shaped and behaving like animals. He makes his ideas more concrete by comparing the inner organs of man and animals and their hydraulic systems. The heart could be likened to a hydraulic engine (in modern terms), the brain corresponds to a reservoir and the blood system, tendons, and muscles are like the escapement which achieves movement in a clock. It is obvious that Descartes had been inspired both by the automatic devices which were becoming more and more common at this time, and by William Harvey's discovery that the circulation of the blood was like a mechanical pumping procedure. Harvey gave an account of this discovery in a pamphlet published in 1628, which attracted a lot of attention.

Descartes is said to have built a true-to-nature android in the shape of a girl, which he called Francine. He was certainly as advanced a physicist as a religious philosopher, but it is not likely that he would have been able to achieve such a feat in practice. The background of this legend—because it must be considered a legend—is, maybe, the fact that Descartes had a daughter called Francine on the wrong side of the blanket, so that the legendary android Francine could have been a substitute for the girl. The more serious biographers of Descartes neglect this legend, which in one version has a drastic climax: in 1649, Descartes was summoned to the court of Queen Christina of Sweden and set out by boat from Amsterdam to Stockholm, bringing Francine well packed in a seaman's trunk. The captain, however, had heard that this remarkable creation was on board, and when the ship ran into a storm on the North Sea, he blamed Descartes for their troubles, for a man with an android must be in league with the devil! The captain ordered that Francine be thrown overboard, but whether the North Sea grew calmer after that is not revealed.

One might add, by the way, that Descartes's stay in Stockholm had an unfortunate ending. The queen, who was thirsty for knowledge but also very eccentric, received Descartes at five o'clock every morning, in the middle of winter, for lessons in philosophy. The warm-blooded southerner began to teach in the ice-cold halls of the badly heated royal palace but in January, 1650, contracted a heavy cold, and died about a week later.

Descartes's ideas about *la bête machine* were a source of inspiration to future philosophers and theologians. For example, the talented and learned German Jesuit Athanasius Kircher (1602–80), worked with automata, building among other things a talking head, singing birds, and figures playing musical instruments. Kircher also followed Salomon de Caus's line in adopting automatic theatres for gardens. In 1650, he and another Jesuit, Kaspar Schott (1608–66), published a book which describes a number of these.

False Prophets
The great public interest in automata in the eighteenth century also

A One of Salomon de Caus's theatrical sets at Hellbrunn Castle, in which movable figures were placed in mountain caves. Via a gear transmission, a water-wheel (*a*) drove a shaft (*b*) to which both ends of a rope (*c*) were attached. The rope ran over pulleys (*d*) and round a wheel (*e*) at the bottom of a pillar, which carried a mythological figure. Thereupon, the rope ran over more pulleys (*f*) and back to the shaft.

resulted in the appearance of various humbugs. One of the best-known was the Hungarian baron, Wolfgang von Kempelen, who invented the "chess-playing Turk". We have met the imaginative baron before: it was he who introduced a steam turbine which, he claimed, would immediately outdo the existing steam-engine, but on that occasion, James Watt taught the good baron a lesson.

Towards the end of the 1760s, von Kempelen had built an automaton in the form of a male in Turkish dress, which sat beside a sturdy chest, on which was a chessboard. The designer challenged famous chess players to play against the Turk and, for years, he toured Europe and the United States with his show. The android could talk as well, although its vocabulary was limited to "Check!" and "Gardez!". The baron claimed, moreover, that in this android he had managed to copy man's intelligence and ability to combine thoughts. In that case, it would have been a question of a simulacrum rather than an automaton.

After attending a much publicized demonstration of the chess-playing Turk in London, Edgar Allan Poe wrote an essay in which he denounced with sharp logic any suggestion that the device had an ability to think. As a result, the humbug was revealed—von Kempelen had hidden a dwarf, a skilful chess-player, in the chest, and the machinery consisted of mechanisms for moving the chessmen on the board.

Other designers have "succeeded" with different forms of simulacra and automata by hiding individuals within them in one way or another, and in the seventeenth and eighteenth centuries, many news items were written about "self-propelled carriages", based on

B Vaucanson's famous duck (1) had a weight-powered mechanism which consisted of over a thousand movable parts. These were hidden inside the duck and in the foundation upon which the bird stood.

Unfortunately, the duck has now been lost. Some illustrations depicting it survive, however, among them this one (2), showing its innards.

the same secret—sometimes revealed, sometimes not. One example will suffice. In 1793, the French balloon pioneer Jean-Pierre François Blanchard demonstrated a remarkable carriage at an exhibition in Philadelphia, where he also made the first ascent in a balloon in the New World. The balloonist's brother has left an enraptured description of the self-propelled carriage, which could travel faster than a stage-coach and could drive across unbroken ground where no other vehicles could make their way. But nothing is said about the machinery, and there are no accounts of it ever having been disclosed. A modern reader, however, would pity the obviously muscular fellows, who were hard at work inside the carriage . . .

The false prophets with their wishful thinking, however, portended a development which has resulted in the realization of both automotive carriages and chess-playing machines.

A Zenith

The constructions made by the highly talented French engineer Jacques de Vaucanson (1709–82) undoubtedly represent the zenith of the technical genre which produced automata. Even in his youth, in Grenoble, de Vaucanson had worked on various inventions and modifications for machines. In the mid-1730s, he decided to move to Paris and to involve himself with automata, which were all the rage at the time. He approached the subject systematically, beginning with a thorough study of anatomy, as he wanted to use mechanical aids to illustrate an *anatomie mouvante* ("moving anatomy"), which was to present human and animal organs in a three-dimensional atlas, no easy task! Here were Descartes's philosophical ideas, about

to be turned into a technical reality at the hands of the clever de Vaucanson.

After much painstaking work and many failures, de Vaucanson managed to build a life-size flute-playing shepherd. It was not lifelike, the "moving anatomy" being reproduced in the lips, jaws, and tongue. The whole arrangement was controlled by a programming device with a range of twelve tunes, and the air was supplied by three clockwork-driven bellows. The features of the shepherd were copied from a statue by the French sculptor Antoine Coyzevox. De Vaucanson is said to have fallen in love with this statue, which was exhibited in the Tuileries, and he nursed secret hopes of giving it movement and life . . . But even as it was, the flute-player caused a sensation when de Vaucanson showed it to the *Académie des Sciences* in 1738, and this spurred him on to build another automaton, also a shepherd playing the flute, but this time accompanying himself on a tambourine. The flute in this case was a very special instrument, in French called a *galoubet*, which is particularly high-pitched. De Vaucanson was to try out almost three hundred different versions of the design before he was completely satisfied. The musical performances of this automaton have been compared to those of a virtuoso—nothing human could ever have achieved the like.

In pursuit of his ideas about the "moving anatomy", de Vaucanson built yet another automaton, a mechanical duck which could move in the typical, wagging way of a duck, eat and digest fish, and excrete the remains in a "natural" way. The mechanism was driven by a weight and had more than a thousand moving parts, which were concealed, some inside the duck, and some in the base on which the bird stood. The feats performed by the duck were of a similar order to those performed by other automata of the time, but during the course of de Vaucanson's work, his genius for designing gave birth to new ideas, which represent important progress in the development of technology. To produce his mechanisms, which demanded great exactitude, he designed among other things a precision lathe to cut threads. He was also the first to use a rubber hose. In his search for a suitable material for the duck's digestive canal, de Vaucanson came across the reports left by his compatriot Charles Marie de la Condamine about the remarkable material *cautchouc*, which he had discovered on the Amazon River during his expedition to South America in 1731. Vaucanson made hoses of this material and also invented a machine for that purpose.

De Vaucanson became a rich man from exhibiting his automata, and for several years, his mechanical duck was the most talked-about bird in Europe! He was also given public recognition for his work and was elected to the esteemed *Académie des Sciences*. But after touring for only a couple of years, he abandoned the building of automata, which was primarily a hobby, and became the director of the state-owned silk-mills. In his later years, he spent his time collecting interesting machines and pieces of apparatus. These eventually amounted to an impressive collection, which he bequeathed to the *Conservatoire National des Arts et Métiers*, then an institute for technical education, and today a highly thought-of museum.

De Vaucanson's three automata met different fates. The flute- and tambourine-playing shepherd was destroyed in the revolution, while the others were bought by a German collector, Gottfried Christoph Beireis, a judge in Hemstedt. The social circle of this eccentric included Johann Wolfgang Goethe, who in his diary for 1805 described a meeting with de Vaucanson's automata. "They were in the most deplorable condition," the great poet wrote. "The duck was like a skeleton and had digestive problems . . ."

Jacques de Vaucanson initiated a whole new era in the field of self-propelled mechanisms. His automata had an ancient heritage in the history of scientific ideas, but he broke new ground as regards both theory and practice. Much of what he discovered soon found a direct application within the then growing manufacturing industry. It is significant that de Vaucanson, as the director of the silk-mills, renewed their machinery and made considerable improvements to a semi-mechanical loom designed by Basile Bouchon. These improvements later made possible Joseph Marie Jacquard's punch-card programmed, fully automatic loom (see page 195).

Automata had been a technical hobby for a couple of thousand years, but de Vaucanson made it possible to go beyond this and to apply different forms of automata in industry. It was only then that the ideas of the Alexandrian school had matured to a point where an automatic control system could become a reality.

A A description of Bonnemain's temperature governor was published in 1824 by the Société d'encouragement. The governor was then shown mounted in a geyser. (1) The temperature sensor (*a*) was sunk into the water jacket of the furnace. (2) A detail, showing the governor. The temperature sensor (*a*) consisted of a circular iron rod (*b*) whose top end was screwed into a casing (*c*) and which was surrounded by a zinc or lead pipe (*d*). The pipe's lower end ended in a copper plug (*e*) into which *b* had been screwed. At the top of *d* was a copper ring (*f*). Since lead — as well as zinc — expands when heated, more than twice as much as iron, *f* was pushed upwards when the temperature sensor was heated. At a certain temperature, *f* acted on a lever (*g*) which, in its turn, acted on another lever (*h*), equipped with a

counterweight (*i*). The intention behind this arrangement was to multiply *f*'s movement. By way of a rod (*j*), lever *h* was connected to the furnace's damper (*k*), and when the water's temperature sank, the damper's opening was reduced so that there was less draught in the furnace. When the water's temperature sank, the damper's opening was increased. (3) The temperature governor was set at different temperatures when a screw (*l*) was turned. Rod *b* was then raised or lowered, so that the temperature at which ring *f* started to act on the levers was increased or reduced. The desired temperature could be set on a scale (*m*).

Automatic Controls before the Industrial Era

The mythical and real androids and other automata in the sixteenth, seventeenth, and eighteenth centuries were spectacular expressions of the technical heritage of antiquity. But the classical writings also inspired many of the great natural scientists of this era to apply and develop many of the ideas of the Alexandrian school. One of these was the principle of Hero's level control, the first closed control system, which more or less directly became the prototype of early designs of controls for temperature, pressure, and reaction speed, and some examples of these follow.

Temperature Regulators

An obvious similarity can be traced between the ancient level control, as shown in a sixteenth-century translation of Hero's *Pneumatica*, and the first thermostat. Around 1610, the Dutch physicist and chemist Cornelis Drebbel (1572–1634) designed a temperature regulator in two different versions. One was to control the temperature of an oven for chemical experiments, the other to keep the temperature of an incubator constant. Drebbel was a learned natural scientist and had spent most of his working life at the royal court in London. Between 1610 and 1612, however, he visited the court in Prague, where he met, among others, the German astronomer Johannes Kepler. Very little work by Drebbel exists in a published form, but his thermostats have been described in several books by scientists and others who visited him in his laboratory. Drebbel also had active contacts with the scholars of the time, Francis Bacon and Salomon de Caus, for example, and this contributed to the widespread circulation of the knowledge of both the thermostat and of Drebbel's other inventions.

One physicist to develop Drebbel's regulator was the Frenchman René Antoine Ferchault de Réamur (1683–1757), who has lent his name to the temperature scale common in southern Europe. In his old age, Réamur worked on methods to rationalize agriculture, and among other things devoted himself to improving an egg incubator; he equipped this with a simplified version of Drebbel's thermostat. The works published by Réamur about this device came to the attention of a successful poultry breeder in Paris, Bonnemain, a practical man who developed the thermostat into an efficient regulator for incubators. Bonnemain patented his thermostat in 1783, but the details of his construction were not published until 1824.

Pressure Regulators

The first pressure regulator has already been mentioned: the safety valve invented by Denis Papin for his pressure cooker and used for his high-pressure steam-engine (see page 115). When Newcomen's atmospheric steam-engine began to come into more common use, Papin's safety valve was fitted as standard equipment on the boilers. It seems that this simple device worked very satisfactorily, for nothing new in the way of pressure regulators appeared until the end of the eighteenth century, although improvements were made to some of the safety valve's construction details. One factor contributing to the lack of new inventions in this area may, however, have been the fact that the steam pressure used hardly exceeded atmospheric pressure, and it was not until James Watt's patent expired, in 1800, that the field was left free for designers of high-pressure steam-engines.

In 1799, however, two regulator patents came almost simultaneously. One was granted to the Irishman Robert Delap and was for a device in which the supply of steam to a steam-engine was controlled by a cock. The other, invented by the Englishman Matthew Murray, was for a device which worked on a similar principle, but instead controlled the draught in the boiler flue. Four years later, Boulton & Watt patented a pressure regulator which came to be used for several decades, even with high-pressure steam-engines.

A quite different type of pressure regulator became necessary when larger transmission networks for the distribution of town gas came to be built at the beginning of the nineteenth century. The gas pressure was either too low in the outer parts of the network, or too high in the central branches. Samuel Clegg, who had been trained in the workshops of Boulton & Watt, then designed a gas-pressure regulator which was placed at strategic points of the network to give a reasonably uniform pressure in the different branches. He patented his first design in 1815.

Similar problems with pressure were also encountered when the first modern water conduits were extended in the cities. Before it

was realized that the pressure could be moderated by reducing the dimensions of the pipes step-by-step, different kinds of pressure-reducing valves were tried out, including a valve basically like Papin's safety valve. However, by the middle of the nineteenth century, the lever which had been used in the original version was replaced in most cases by a coil spring.

Regulating Windmills

The increasingly advanced technology developed during the Renaissance for improving the exploitation of wind and water has already been discussed, although we would like to repeat for the sake of emphasis that the engineering profession has its roots, to a large

rod's action on e and, thus, f. This arrangement caused f to be turned in proportion to the pressure increase in a.

D Boulton & Watt's pressure regulator of 1803; (**1**) from the side, (**2**) cross-section. Sunk into the boiler (a) was a pipe (b), which was open at both ends and contained a float (c). The float was suspended from a chain which ran over a pulley on a shaft (d). The damper (e) of the furnace also hung on a chain, which ran over another pulley on the same shaft. As soon as the pressure of the steam rose above that of the atmosphere, water was forced into pipe b, and the opening of the damper (e) was reduced in proportion to the

end of the chain hung a weight (l), which was pulled upwards as f was turned, thus producing a torsion, which increased the more the cam was turned and which counteracted the torsion caused by the piston

B Robert Delap's pressure regulator, patented in 1799. Steam from the boiler passed through a pipe (a), in which there was a slide valve (b). As long as the slide valve was sunk into the pipe, steam could pass freely. On the pipe there was also a cylinder (c), open at the top, whose piston was suspended, as was the slide valve, from a pivoted balance beam (d). As soon as the pressure of the steam exceeded that of the atmosphere, the piston was forced upwards, the balance beam was turned, and the slide valve turned off the supply of steam. If steam of a higher or lower pressure than atmospheric was desired, the balance beam was loaded with weights (e) on either side of b's fulcrum.

C In the same year as Delap, Matthew Murray, too, patented a pressure regulator. When the steam pressure in the boiler (a) became too high, a piston (b) was pressed upwards in a cylinder (c). The toothed piston rod (d) then turned a cog-wheel (e) on a shaft (f) on which the damper (g) inside the smoke stack (h) was also mounted. A pointer (i) on f indicated the size of the pressure increase on a scale (j). On shaft f, there was also a cam (k), over which a chain ran. At the other

pressure increase. The water level inside the boiler was controlled by a float (f) suspended from a balance beam (g) at whose other end a counterweight (h) hung. When the water level sank too much, a valve (i) was opened, and more water entered.

E Clegg's pressure regulator consisted of a partly water-filled, cast-iron tank (a), into which a dome (b) was sunk. Gas entered through a pipe (c), which carried a pierced disc (d) on its top. Through the hole in the disc hung a cone (e), the top of which was attached to b. When gas of too high a pressure entered, b was raised, so was e, and the size of the gas inlet was reduced. (f) Gas exit pipe. The size of the inlet could be varied by altering the height of the dome above the water's surface. (g) Counterweight.

A

C Mead's lift-tenter of 1787. The runner stone (*a*) is attached to a shaft (*b*) which runs through the fixed millstone (*c*), the bedder, and rests in a lower bearing (*d*) on a lever (*e*). Between *e* and a roof beam, a chain (*f*) runs and is kept taut like a bow-string by a strut (*g*) because of the weight of a casing (*h*), which can move freely on *b*. The result is that the weight of the runner stone is kept off the bedder for as long as the mill is not in operation. When it is started and the wallower (*i*) begins to rotate, the pendulums (*j*), which are suspended from the wallower, are flung outwards, lifting a bar (*k*) to which they are attached. Since *k*'s central part is ring-shaped, rotatable, and is attached to *h*, the latter is lifted and brings *g*'s end upwards, so that the tension in *f* is reduced. The lever (*e*), the shaft (*b*), and the runner stone (*a*) are then lowered, and the distance between the millstones becomes the correct one for grinding.

D A cutaway of a nineteenth-century windmill which carries the patent sails invented by Cubitt; each

A Oliver Evans's mill at Philadelphia. Since both grain and flour were transported by means of worm conveyors, very few employees were needed to run the mill.

B At an early stage, grain was fed to the millstones by means of a vibrating board (*a*), which was suspended in ropes (*b*, *c*) beneath the feed hopper (*d*) into which the grain was poured. When the upper mill-stone (*e*), the runner stone, rotated, a shoulder on it hit a bar (*f*) on the vibrating board, so that grain was moved forward and fell through the hole in the middle of the runner stone. The amount of grain supplied for each vibration could be adjusted by lengthening or shortening rope *b* to vary the vibrating board's angle of inclination.

wooden shutter on the sails has one edge attached to a long rod pivoted to a cog-wheel, and the rack is in turn mounted on a bell crank whose other end is attached to a rod which runs through the centre of the wind-shaft (*a*). Cogs at the other end of this rod mesh with a cog-wheel, on whose shaft there is another wheel (*b*), which carries a counterweight (*c*) on a rope. By means of (*c*), it was also possible to control the angle of the shutters manually. The drive wheel (*d*) on *a* could be braked by means of a long rod which was used to bring a semi-circular, wooden brake (*e*) to bear against *d*'s periphery. The wallower (*f*), which meshed with *d*, was fixed to the main vertical shaft (*g*) and employed a gear transmission (*h*) to drive two upper stones, which, together with their fixed under stones, were enclosed in cases (*i*) in which the flour was collected. A centrifugal governor (*j*) controlled the gap between the upper and lower millstones. (*k*) Grain bin. A fantail (*l*) worked via a gear transmission (*m*) against a toothed ring (*n*) on the curb. A wind-shift caused the fan to rotate, and the cap to turn until the fan's plane of rotation was again in line with the wind. The cap also could be turned manually by the chain wheel (*o*). The sack hoist (*p*) was driven by *g* via another gear transmission.

B

C

extent, in mill technology. One plant of great interest in this context was built in Philadelphia in the 1780s by Oliver Evans, a man we have already mentioned as a steam-engine pioneer in the United States. The plant, a flour mill requiring a minimum of manpower, can be seen as an early predecessor of the fully-automated factory. It was driven by three water-wheels and had six automatically controlled millstones. Both the grain and the flour were transported by worm conveyors, a word not then invented, the contemporary name being "Archimedean screw". The flour was weighed automatically and moved by an endless-chain conveyor to a worm conveyor, which delivered it directly down into the hold of a ship.

The eighteenth century saw the invention of a number of control devices for windmills, that later became very important to industry; some examples follow.

One problem when grinding is to feed in the grain at the right speed, so as to keep the mill—whether a water- or windmill—from grinding empty; in other words, a flow regulator is required. A primitive version, a hopper of rudimentary design, appeared as early as the Renaissance, and Ramelli describes several versions in his art book. In the first part of the eighteenth century, this regulator acquired the form it was to retain until the end of the windmill era. The grain was fed into a wide funnel, at the bottom of which was a shaking conveyor, vibrated by being struck by projections mounted on one of the millstones. The faster the millstone turned, the more grain was fed to the stones.

Windmills were generally built in places where the wind usually blew from a certain direction, for as soon as the wind shifted, the mill had to be turned so that its sails faced the wind squarely; during the eighteenth century, there were many ideas about how to achieve this automatically. In the 1740s, the Englishman Edmund Lee patented a "Self-Regulating Wind Machine", especially intended for tower mills, that is, windmills with a fixed millhouse and a rotatable upper part, or top cap. Lee arranged a propeller, called a rosette, on a boom so that its plane of rotation was at right angles to that of the sails of the mill; it worked via a gear against a gear rim on the periphery of the top cap. A side wind would cause the propeller, and the top cap, to rotate until the rotation plane of the propeller was once again parallel to, and the windmill's sails were at right angles to, the direction of the wind. Lee's device became very common in England and northern Germany.

Edmund Lee also built a device to control the speed of a mill by varying the size of the surfaces of the sails. This regulator was patented in 1745 but was never tried out, for it soon showed itself to be unworkable. Several inventors attacked the same problem, but a serviceable solution was arrived at only in 1807, when the Englishman William Cubitt patented his method for vaning the hinged, spring-loaded plates, which by now had replaced canvas on the sails of larger mills. Cubitt's "patent sails" became standard for such mills for the remainder of the nineteenth century.

When grain is ground between millstones, the quality of the flour depends largely on two factors: the distance between the fixed and the rotating stone, and the speed of rotation. In the latter part of the eighteenth century, several inventors tried to find ways of varying these factors. In 1787, the Englishman Thomas Mead patented a design which combined the solution of the two problems: the millstones were kept apart when the mill was not working, but when it started, a regulator caused them to press against each other with a force proportional to the speed of rotation. Mead then combined this regulator with another that varied the setting of the sail surfaces, so that the millstone rotated at a controllable speed.

This construction is particularly interesting because Mead used as a sensing device a rotating pendulum, something that later would be

A1

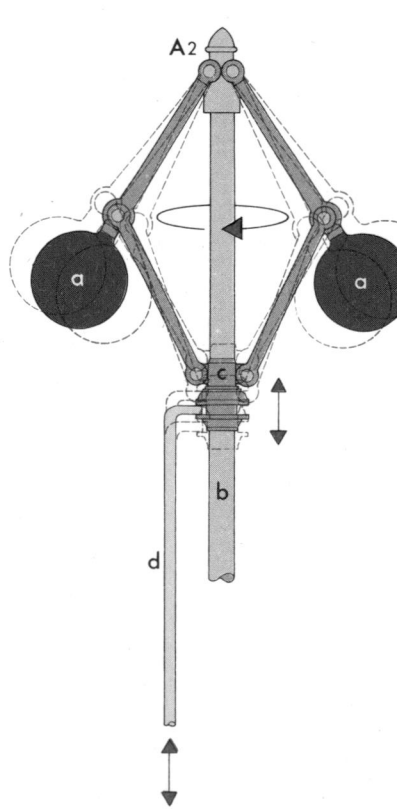

A2

A Watt did not invent the centrifugal governor, but he was the first to use such a construction to automatically regulate a steam-engine. This occurred in 1788, and in November of that year, a drawing (1) of such a governor was entered into Boulton & Watt's "Drawing Day Book", where a running account of the work done in the company's drawing office was kept. Watt's centrifugal governor (2) consisted of two pendulums, equipped with weights (a) and mounted on the output shaft (b) of the steam-engine. The governor's function was based on the fact that the speed of the steam-engine tended to increase when its work load was decreased, whereas the speed decreased when the work load increased. Because of the action of the centrifugal force, the weights swung further and further outwards the faster the regulator revolved. A sliding collar (c) was then brought upwards and pulled with it a rod which, directly or indirectly, regulated the steam supply to the engine.

called a centrifugal regulator. The rotating pendulum was, in fact, not a new machine element, for rotating weights fixed to chains or bars are mentioned in documents dating from the fifteenth century onwards, even if these had the form of a balance wheel or a flywheel mass. Before Mead made his invention, rotating pendulums had been used also in more rudimentary types of regulators, intended to modify the distance between the millstones.

Regulators in Industry

If industrial regulators were to be dealt with here in anything like a comprehensive manner, the result would be a volume of considerably greater bulk than this book, even if we limited ourselves to a mere survey. Therefore, we shall describe here only some of the most important regulators.

The Centrifugal Governor

The first large steam-engine with a rotary motion was installed by Boulton & Watt in 1786 at the Albion Mill in London. The mill machinery had been built by the Scotsman Andrew Meikle (1719–1811), who later installed centrifugal governors for the millstones; it should be noted that the invention of the centrifugal governor is often attributed to Meikle, who was a leading designer of mills, but it is likely that Meikle had based his centrifugal governors on the device that had been patented by Mead in 1787. Be that as it may, in 1788, Boulton reported by letter to Watt that he had visited the Albion Mill and seen the millstone regulators in operation, and also described how they worked. Watt immediately realized the possibility of applying the same principle to controlling the speed of steam-engines, and it is probable that they had tried out such a governor before the end of that year.

Strange as it may seem, Boulton & Watt tried to keep the design of the centrifugal governor secret for as long as possible. However, when Watt's steam-engine patent expired in 1800, centrifugal governors instantly became standard equipment in practically all the steam-engines which then appeared on the market. Few devices in machine technology have taken on so many different shapes as the centrifugal governor during its almost two-hundred-year history. Its heyday as regards the number of varieties in which it existed was, naturally, the era of steam-engines and turbines, but the principle of the centrifugal governor is still applied in a number of different areas.

The theory of the function of the centrifugal governor, the way it reacts to the varying load of the steam-engine and to different kinds of external disturbance, was not worked out fully until the latter part of the nineteenth century, when, in 1868 and 1876 respectively, two great mathematicians, the Scotsman James Clerk Maxwell and the Russian Ivan Vyshnegradsky, presented the general theories of the function of the centrifugal governor. They provided a mathematical basis for the general calculation of automatic control in closed systems. This pattern of development is, by the way, characteristic of all control technology, in that the theoretical analysis usually comes long after the practical introduction of a device.

Electrical Controls

Electric governors of different kinds—and they are now innumerable—are mostly of the same age as that part of electrotechnology to which their function is applied.

The electric relay is a component of control technology, without which today's automatic control systems would be hard put to function. An electric relay usually consists of an electromagnet which breaks or closes another circuit when the circuit of the magnet changes in a certain way. Samuel F. B. Morse (1791–1872) invented the electric telegraph, which is often considered the first technical and commercial application of the electromagnetic principle, which is the basis of the relay. The Englishman Sir Charles Wheatstone, however, had been experimenting with electromagnetic couplings few years prior to this, and it was probably he who introduced the concept of a relay (1839). Wheatstone, too, designed a telegraph, the so-called indicator telegraph, which came into use from the middle of the 1830s in the rapidly expanding British railway network. But his name is better known for Wheatstone's bridge, his design to measure electrical resistance – an electrotechnical equivalent of the balance scale – which he introduced in 1843.

Wheatstone fully realized the potential of using the relay as an electric amplifier. The relatively weak "control current" required by the electromagnet of the relay could be used to close a circuit with a very much more powerful current. This principle found a number of applications during the breakthrough of electric power, some fifty years after Wheatstone had presented his ideas.

However, telecommunications are, without doubt, the largest area of application for the electric relay. Relays have been used in this field from about 1890 onwards, not as amplifiers but as coupling components, particularly in telephone switchboards. The high standards of reliability and safety of operation required by telecommunications have compelled the development of increasingly efficient relays, with important consequences for the application of relays in automatic governing and control of, first and foremost, industrial processes.

Regulating Arc Lamps

The electric arc began to be used for lighting purposes in the 1840s. It gave a very strong light compared to the other light sources of the time: the recently introduced stearin, or tallow, candle and the gas lamp. But the problem was that the arc lamp needed continuous attention, for its carbon rods constantly had to be brought closer together as they burned, lest the arc go out. Even the first arc lamps introduced for general use featured an attempt at controlling automatically the distance between the carbon points. In 1847, the Englishman W. E. Staite (1809–54) designed one of the first devices for this purpose; in it, one carbon rod was moved forward by a clockwork device that was controlled by a copper rod placed close enough to the arc to be affected by its heat. As the distance between the carbon rods increased, the arc became hotter and expanded the copper rod, causing it to lift a catch, thus setting in motion the clockwork which moved the carbon rod far enough forward to reduce the heat, so that the copper rod contracted, lowering the catch and arresting the movement of the carbon rod. More refined versions of this were applied by many arc-lamp manufacturers, among them Edison, as late as the 1870s.

When the arc lamp became more common in the 1860s and 1870s, however, new control methods were invented, which caused the current of the arc and the voltage across it to control the feeding of the carbon rods. Many of the great names of the time in electrical engineering devoted themselves to designing more and more sophisticated governors based on these principles. They included J. B. L. Foucault and V. L. M. Serrin in France, R. E. B. Crompton in England, Werner von Siemens and F. von Hefner-Alteneck in Germany, and C. F. Brush in the United States. Many control principles and couplings that were invented and tried out at this time came to acquire a fundamental importance in controlling current and voltage during the further development of electric power systems.

Synchro Systems

The electric three-phase system came into common use in the 1890s,

B Two connected Morse telegraphs. (**1, 2**) The Morse telegraph consisted of a key (a), which was pressed by a spring (b) against a metal head (c) on the so-called connection block (d). The key handle (e) was made of an insulating material. (**3**) As the telegraphist pushed the handle downwards, the key came into contact with the anvil (f), and an electric circuit was closed from one terminal of the battery (g) to the key anvil and lever (h) and out onto the connecting line (i). The other battery terminal was grounded. (**4**) In the receiving telegraph, the current passed the key's lever (h) and head (c) and continued through the winding of the electromagnet (j) and to the ground. When this occurred, the iron core of the electromagnet became magnetic and attracted a metal armature (k) on a lever, at whose other end was a peg (l), which marked a paper strip (m).

C In Serrin's arc lamp, the upper carbon holder (a) hung from an arm (b), attached to a rod. This ran inside a casing (c) and had at its lower end a weight-loaded rack (d), which meshed with a cog-wheel (e). On e's shaft was a roll (f) to which a chain (g) was attached; this ran over a cylinder (h) and had its other end attached to the lower carbon holder (i). When d sank, g was wound onto f, and the carbons approached. Current entered through the winding of an electromagnet (j), whose core then attracted an armature (k) which pulled a rod (l), attached to (i), downwards with it. Thereupon, e was turned to the right by g, and the carbons were separated to the correct distance for the arc to form. A catch (m) then engaged a cog-wheel (n), connected by other cog-wheels with e. When part of the carbons had been consumed, the resistance increased in the circuit, and the amperage dropped so that j no longer attracted k. The armature was then lifted by a spring (o), and when l and m were lifted at the same time, n was released, so that a and i could again approach each other.

A If two synchronous motors are connected to each other and an alternating-current voltage is applied to the rotor (*a*) of one of them, then the magnetic field of that motor (the transmitter) will be reproduced in the other motor (the receiver). The receiver's rotor (*b*) will then adopt the same angle to stator (*c*) as the transmitter's rotor has to its stator (*d*).

B Farcot's mechanical power amplifier. When the double piston (*a*) in the open control cylinder (*b*) was moved, steam could enter at one or the other side of the piston (*c*) in the working cylinder (*d*) through one of two ducts (*e*), which had earlier been blocked by *c*. At the same time, the space on the other side of *c* was connected to the atmosphere through the other duct. The power amplifier's way of working was based on the principle that if a liquid (or a gas) in a closed vessel is exposed to pressure, then this pres-

sure is propagated equally to all parts of the vessel. Thus, the pressure per square inch was as great on *a* as it was on *c*.

C In aeroplanes, gyroscopes (*a*) were used at an early stage to supervise the yaw (*b*), pitch (*c*), and roll (*d*) controls.

D The gyroscope is based on the principle that a rotating body tends to preserve its plane of rotation. Here, one of Sperry's gyrostatic compasses is shown in vertical section.

not least because of the synchronous motor's great use as a source of motive power. The properties of this motor also resulted in the development of an important component in modern control systems, the torque element. Carl Michalke of Siemens in Germany realized that synchronous motors can be used as transmitters and receivers of position information, that is, the transfer of information primarily about angular torsion. If two synchronous motors be connected and an alternating voltage applied to the rotor of the first, the magnetic field of the first motor will be reproduced in the second, causing its rotor to adopt the same angle to its stator as that between the rotor and the stator of the first. If one rotor be turned, the other will follow it exactly.

To start with, Michalke saw the phenomenon as a curiosity, but nevertheless, he patented his discovery in 1896. Practical application came only after 1910, when torque elements were first used in gunnery control devices in the German navy. The development took off again in the 1930s, when a whole family of governing components, based on Michalke's discovery, was put into use in both military and civil control systems.

Power Amplified Mechanically

The mechanical power amplifier, which in control contexts is usually called the servomotor, is today as indispensable a component in automatic control systems as the electric relay. The servomotor is one of the first examples of a control device invented intrinsically, or within control technology itself, to fulfil one of that technology's own requirements. In the 1860s, the Frenchman M. J. Farcot designed a very sensitive centrifugal governor whose output signal was too weak, however, to affect the steam valve. To make his design work, Farcot had to find a method of amplifying the signal, or, in other words, the controlling power of the rotating pendulum. His solution was a small-diameter control cylinder with a twin piston that directed steam to one or other of the two sides of a piston in a power cylinder of considerably larger diameter. The amplifying factor provided by the device then became proportional to the ratio between the areas of cross-section of the control cylinder and the working cylinder. In his patent specification of 1868, Farcot makes a comparison between his servomotor and the rider of a horse: "The rider can direct the muscular horse with very light movements of his hands; it follows his slightest intention with great force. Only a Frenchman could be so poetic in a patent application; Farcot's was entitled "*Servomoteur, ou moteur asservi*" and is the origin of the word "servomotor".

The Autopilot

One of the first automatic control systems was the autopilot, which came into being comporatively early in aviation. The reason is largely that Orville and Wilbur Wright designed an intentionally unstable aeroplane (the first being completed in 1903) in the firm belief that this would make it easier to manoeuvre. While their first flights confirmed this belief, they showed also that the pilot had to work the controls all the time in order to keep the aeroplane on course and on an even keel. Already at this early stage, they discussed the possibility of transferring at least some of the pilot's work to some kind of automatic device, and about 1910, Elmer Ambrose Sperry (1860–1930), an American engineer, applied himself to this problem. He designed what was later to be called an autopilot; it consisted essentially of gyroscopes functioning as sensing elements, and of servomotors that altered the control surfaces of the aeroplane. A version of this first autopilot was successfully tried out in 1912 in a Curtiss flying-boat.

CHAPTER 8
COMPUTERS

As already mentioned, the interaction of simulacra and automata has been the basis upon which was built the development that has resulted in the computer. In the history of ideas we may locate the roots of the computer's richly branched family tree in the "self-moving" mechanisms of classical antiquity, with its tap root going back to the gin of the late Stone Age animal trap. Other roots show a junction of several development chains, one of which consists of the mechanization of arithmetic and the mathematical principles that have emerged alongside it, mainly in the theory of numbers. Another important root is the continued development that started with the electric relay, whose power-amplifying and connecting functions were soon taken over by electronic components.

Arithmetic Mechanized

Counting on one's fingers can be seen as the imitation of the series of numbers from one to ten, thus making it extremely easy to add or subtract; looked at like this, the use of the fingers as a method of counting can be called a mathematical simulacrum, so that one can continue this line of logic and describe the abacus as a mechanization of counting on the fingers. The abacus can also be seen as a proto- or pre-automaton, that is, the first step towards making arithmetical operations automatic.

The abacus was known in ancient Greece and Rome and was called in some places "Pythagoras' slate". This name gives us a hint of what the original construction was like; stone balls were used and moved on a tablet of stone or marble. The Latin word for a ball of limestone, *calculus*, has given us words like calculate, calculator, etc. The Greeks did not use a tablet but a tray with sand in it, where calculations were made by marking the positions of the balls and notingthe result. "Tray of sand" is called *abax* in Greek; hence the word *abacus*, which in this cultural sphere was the name commonly given to the device. The use of the abacus spread via the Arabic culture to India, the Far East, and Russia. It arrived in China in the twelfth century and was there called a *suan-pan*. About a hundred years later, it was introduced in Japan, where it was called a *soroban*. These countries, mainly Japan and Russia, have developed the art of using this arithmetic instrument to perfection. A skilful person using this technique can achieve a speed of calculation quite on a par with modern desk calculators.

The numbers used in the West are called Arabic numbers and originated in India. It was the Indians who introduced the concept "nought" for an "empty" space on the abacus. This very important step in the development of arithmetic did not reach Europe until the ninth century.

The scientific discoveries of the seventeenth and eighteenth centuries, flourishing trade, and particularly the complications brought about by taxation and its collection were some of the factors which made it necessary to simplify and automate the increasingly time-

A thirteenth-century Chinese *suan-pan*. On an abacus, one indicates a given number by pushing the balls towards the cross-bar. On this abacus, the value of each ball in the various rows underneath the cross-bar is 1 (*a*), 10 (*b*), 100 (*c*), 1,000 (*d*), 10,000 (*e*), and so on, while each ball above the cross-bar corresponds to five balls in the row underneath it. The number indicated on this abacus is thus 965,831.

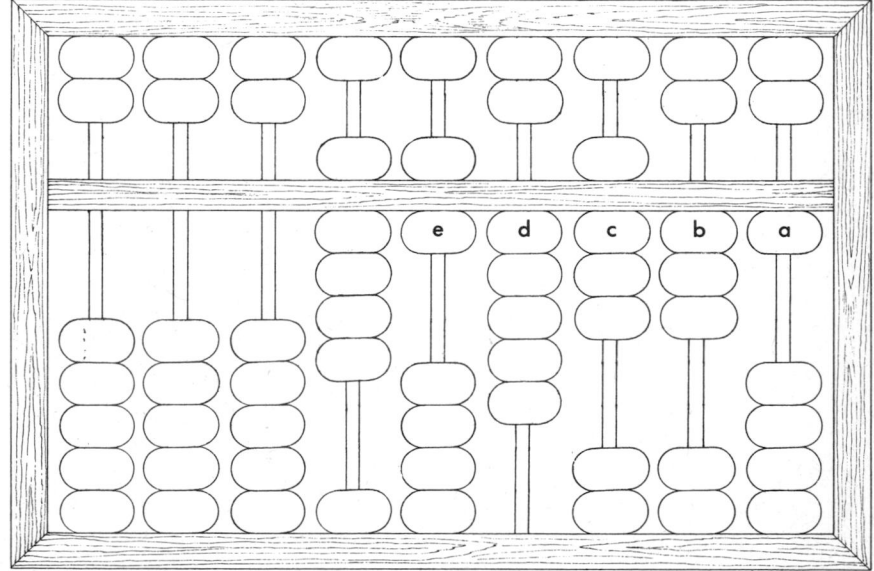

A The young Blaise Pascal seated at the mechanical adding-machine "Pascaline", an invention which brought him great fame. The illustration is based on an engraving in Jean-Gauffin Gallon's *Machines et inventions approuvées par l'Académie Royale des Sciences*, published in Paris in 1735.

B Pascal's machine (**1**) measured only 14.2 × 5.1 × 3.5 in (36 × 13 × 9 cm) and could really only be used for addition and subtraction. It had eight dials, set with a metal stylus. The French monetary unit used in those days, the *livre*, was divided into 12 *deniers*, each subdivided into 20 *sols*; there were dials for *sols*, *deniers*, and up to 999,999 *livres*. The essential part of Pascal's machine was its decimal transfer, that

is, that each toothed wheel was moved on one unit (one-tenth of a revolution on each wheel except those for *deniers* and *sols*) when the previous wheel had completed one revolution. (**2**) Explanatory sketch of the adding-machine's construction. When one wheel (*a*) was moved from 9 to 0, a lever (*c*), which had been lifted by pins (*b*), fell downwards. The lever was coupled to a pawl (*d*) which then brought the next wheel (*e*) one step forward. The numbers on the drums (*f*) could be seen in windows (*g*) on the face of the machine, and by moving a strip (*h*), the complementary number of each number could be seen instead.

C Leibniz realized that a multiplication is really a series of repeated additions. He thus constructed a machine (**1**) in which a set number was automatically repeated each time a crank was turned a full 360°. Leibniz's machine, too, had decimal transfer, but instead of toothed wheels, it had stepped rolls (**2**), that is, cylinders with nine cogs of varying length for the digits 1–9.

D A type of multiplying machine with stepped rolls, shown here with

its lid partly removed. The calculating capacity depended on the number of stepped rolls (here: six). Above each stepped roll (*a*) was a cog-wheel (*b*) moving to and fro on a square shaft (*c*) by means of a setting device (*d*). The latter ran along a scale on which each number corresponded to the number of cogs on the roll with which the cog-wheel (*b*) was going to mesh. The factor to be multiplied (the multiplicand) was set on the scale by means of the setting

devices (*d*) and could then be seen in the windows of the control register (*e*). When a crank (*f*) was turned clockwise once, the set number could be read in the windows of the product register (*g*) at the top of the machine, since dials (*h*) were connected to the crank axle by means of bevel gears (*i*). Each time the crank was turned, the multiplicand was then added to the numeral which could be read in *g*; after seven revolutions, the product of the set number multiplied by seven could be read in the windows of the quotient register (*j*). The machine could be set for division by pushing a lever (*k*) downwards. The stepped rolls then changed their direction of rotation.
E What characterized the Odhner machines (**1**) was that they worked by means of stud wheels (**2**), an eighteenth-century invention which had been considerably improved by, among others, Odhner. (**3**) Explanatory sketch of an Odhner machine. The stud wheel consisted of a disc (*a*) fixed to a crankshaft (*b*), and of a rotatable part (*c*). When one turned *c* by pushing a protrusion (*d*) on it along a scale (*e*) on the top of the machine, cogs ("studs", *f*) protruded along the periphery of the stud wheel. The number of cogs corresponded to the number set on the scale. When a crank (*g*) was then rotated, the cogs meshed with the cogs of a counting apparatus, and the set number could be read in the product register (*h*). (*i*) Quotient register. The calculating capacity of the machine depended on the number of stud wheels, and the crank was turned anti-clockwise when a division was to be made.

consuming calculations required. The first mechanical adding-machine, in the true sense of the word, was designed by the French physicist and mathematician Blaise Pascal (1623–62). His father was a senior inspector of taxes, and even as a young man, Blaise Pascal sought ways to facilitate the hard work involved in tax calculation. In 1645, Pascal's first machine was completed; later, it was improved successively, and a number were made. Descartes brought one with him when he left for the royal court in Stockholm in 1649, and he presented it, and an elevated dedication by Pascal, to Queen Christina. Its fate is unfortunately unknown, although several of Pascal's machines have been preserved, for instance, in the Conservatoire National des Arts et Métiers in Paris, the Science Museum in London, and the Mathematisch-physikalische Salon in Dresden.

Pascal's machine won him great renown throughout Europe, and this inspired several seventeenth-century mathematicians to attempt to produce similar devices. One of them was the polymath Gottfried Wilhelm von Leibniz. In the 1670s, he built a machine which can be called the prototype of our modern mechanical desk calculators, that is, those which have not yet been displaced by electronic ones. The new component introduced by Leibniz was a ratchet wheel for units, tens, hundreds, and so on. The balance wheel of the original version was like a roller with a cam that moved the next roller one step, when number nine on the first had been passed. This principle was developed further by Leibniz, who, in the 1690s, completed a machine which could add, subtract, and multiply by repeated additions. Leibniz also worked out on paper a machine for division and the calculation of square and cube roots, but the precision mechanics of the time were not sophisticated enough to let him realize this in practice. The ratchet wheel has been used as a component in desk calculators far into this century and is still used in simple counters, such as electric kWh meters and milometers.

In the eighteenth century, several attempts were made to produce a handy adding-machine by using the principle of the ratchet wheel, and several variations were developed, the first workable machines coming on the market only at the beginning of the nineteenth century. In 1820, mass production started of the *"Arithomètre"* machine, designed by the Frenchman Charles Xavier Thomas and considered the first commercial adding-machine. Later on, some Swedish designers made pioneering contributions in the area of mechanical adding-machines. They included Willgodt Teophil Odhner, with his well-known whirligig, and Carl Fridén, who designed a number of desk-top calculators and also founded a company in the United States, which is today active in the computer field.

The Computing Machine

The mechanical calculator is a more or less automatic aid in arithmetical calculation, and it relieves the operator of much time-consuming work. Still, the operator has to keep the order of the calculations in mind and constantly provide data for the machine, receive partial results, and generally organize the work. The next link to be forged in the chain of development we have referred to, with its interaction of simulacra and automata should be, logically, the use of a fully developed mechanical calculator to try to simulate the interventions of the operator in the calculation procedure. In this context such a machine could be called a computing machine, a term which implies that the machine takes over even the organization of the mathematical program of the calculations. It might be added that the first computers were actually called "computing machines".

The great pioneer in the area of computing machines was the British mathematician Charles Babbage (1791–1871), a very talented and most eccentric person. Even as a young student in Cambridge, where he studied, among other things, astronomy, Babbage became

A The difference engine for the calculation of logarithmic tables built by Georg and Edvard Scheutz was a simplified version of Babbage's construction.

B Babbage's difference engine had already cost him over £17,000

when work on it was interrupted in 1834. The reasons why the machine was never completed were partly economical difficulties and partly that Babbage's chief instrument maker had resigned after an argument.

obsessed with the great idea of his life: to automate arithmetical calculations completely. He and John F. W. Herschel (1792–1871), the son of the great astronomer Sir F. William Herschel, were together assigned the task of compiling astronomical tables and checking existing tables which had been produced by mechanical calculators. After painstaking figure-work, Herschel and Babbage found many mistakes, due to what is called the human factor. Babbage is said to have remarked that this kind of work ought to be relegated to a "soul-less steam engine".

These were not heedless words spoken by a temperamental twenty-year-old student; they marked the beginning of a remarkable life-long contribution to the task of automating arithmetical calculations. Babbage was wholly familiar with the adding-machines available in 1812, when his idea came to him, but they had not yet achieved the standards he demanded of them. To accomplish this, Babbage was obliged to find new mathematical principles for the function of the machine, for he saw quite clearly that it would not be sufficient merely to improve the design of an existing type. He succeeded in solving this problem by using a principle which meant a considerable short cut in calculation, being moreover particularly suitable for compiling tables. Put very simply, his idea was to base the function of the machine on the constant differences that are obtained between different series of numbers, in contradistinction to counting one by one, as mechanical adding-machines did, and still do. In 1822, Babbage presented these new design principles for a rapid calculating machine in his paper, "On the Theoretical Principles of the Machinery for Calculating Tables", and during the same year, he began to build a machine based on his ideas, calling his creation "Difference Engine No. 1". Here the difficulties cropped up: actually making the machine demanded a degree of precision that no mechanical workshop of the time could provide, not even a clockmaker's. Babbage devoted all his indefatigable energy to solving the technical problems of construction and production, being obliged to invent new tools, no less, to produce the intricate parts for the machine.

Fortunately, Babbage was a man of private means, being the son of a banker who had left him a large fortune. But his work on his difference engine devoured large sums, and in 1829, he applied to the government for financial assistance to complete the project. The Royal Society then appointed a committee to judge Babbage's application, and although the eminent scientists on it reached a very favourable conclusion, no money was forthcoming. By this time, Babbage had been appointed Lucasian Professor of Mathematics at Cambridge University, an honorary title held earlier by Isaac Newton, among others. "The only honour I ever received in my own country", Babbage bitterly remarked in his autobiography.

By the early 1830s, after intensive work, Babbage had completed such parts of the difference engine as could verify the practicability of his principles. By then, he had also compiled over two hundred drawings of the complete machine. A very comprehensive description of it was published in July, 1834, in the *Edinburgh Review* and happened to be seen by an eminent Swedish engineer, Per Georg Scheutz (1785–1873), in Stockholm. Scheutz was, besides, an editor of the *Periodical of the Swedish Association of Industry* and was a well-known journalist who covered technical matters and culture in general. Scheutz, with his all-round technical knowledge and his nose for news, immediately understood the importance of the difference engine, but he realized also, according to his autobiographical notes, "that in spite of all the technical skills in England, no further development can ever be made, as long as these plans are followed". Scheutz, too, tried to build an adding-machine according to Babbage's principles, but he chose a different mechanical construction. His son, Edvard Scheutz (1821–81), who had just commenced his studies at the Teknologiska Institut at the time his father was working on the new version, set about the task of building this simplified difference engine. After much labour and sacrifice, this machine stood ready in 1843 and was demonstrated to the Royal Academy of Sciences. The Scheutzes had plans to go further with the design, thinking to equip it with, among other things, the "output device", to use the modern term for what Babbage had in mind. This was an arrangement whereby the results of the calculation were engraved on a copper plate which was ready to be used to print the calculated tables as soon as the plate was fed out from the machine. But their resources were exhausted, and they turned to the government for financial help. Only after parliamentary bills and extremely favourable statements from the Royal Academy of Sciences, were they granted, in 1854, a small sum to realize their ideas. The following year, the machine was exhibited at the world exhibition in Paris, where it was awarded a Gold Medal. On their way to Paris, Georg and Edvard Scheutz visited London, where they called on Charles Babbage and his son Henry, who gave their Swedish colleagues a very friendly reception. The Scheutz difference engine was also demonstrated to the Royal Society, which treated the two Swedes with distinction.

After the Paris exhibition, the difference engine was sold to the Dudley observatory in Albany, in the state of New York, for the tidy sum of five thousand dollars. The machine was in use there for some decades for astronomical calculations. In the 1930s, it was bought by a private collector in Chicago, and in the early 1960s, the difference engine was acquired by the Smithsonian Institution, being now on display there in the Museum of History and Technology.

The Babbage-Scheutz difference engine represents an advanced automation of arithmetic: it is a automaton, albeit one limited to a single program. But as early as the 1830s, Babbage understood the possibility of going one step further and designing a machine which could make any kind of calculation; in other words, it could organize its own calculations according to given instructions. Consequently, this "analytical engine", as Babbage called it, would be a simulacrum, a technical imitation of a mathematician's way of calculating. Babbage had the idea of grouping auxiliary functions around the difference engine, which would then form an arithmetic unit; one auxiliary unit would then be a mechanical device for feeding calculating instructions, another a unit for storing partial results (a memory), and another a device which could compare the partial results with one another and on that basis make "decisions" regarding the continued course of calculations. A block diagram of these functions would be practically identical to a block diagram of the equivalent functions in a modern computer. For the input and output of data, Babbage thought of using punched cards of the kind that were then being used in Jacquard-type pattern-weaving looms.

Babbage's understanding of the possibilities of the analytical engine was brilliant, even visionary. But this project was even more difficult to realize than his earlier project for the difference engine. Even a simplified version of the analytical engine would have contained over fifty thousand moving parts! Babbage thought of training mechanics to build the machine and employed the most skilful he could find, including Joseph Whitworth, who later became famous for his standardization of thread systems. And for years, Babbage laid seige to the Treasury, pleading for money. The only result of this was that the government caused a fire-proof building to be erected in which Babbage could safely deposit his drawings and calculations.

In 1840, Babbage presented his plans for the analytical engine to a scientific congress in Turin. A good account of it was later published in a Swiss periodical by the Italian military engineer L. F. Mena-

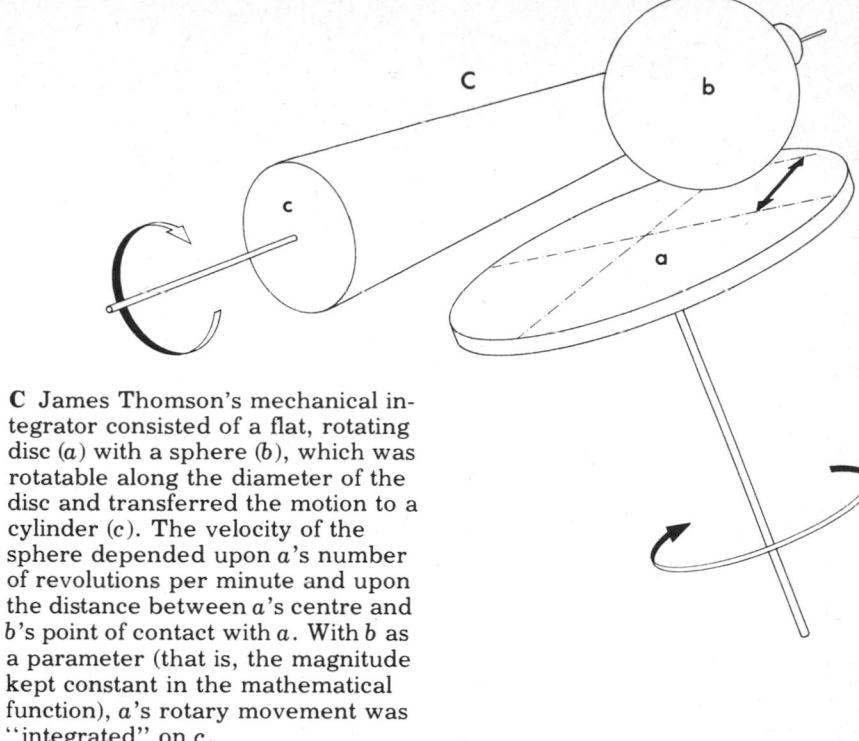

C James Thomson's mechanical integrator consisted of a flat, rotating disc (a) with a sphere (b), which was rotatable along the diameter of the disc and transferred the motion to a cylinder (c). The velocity of the sphere depended upon a's number of revolutions per minute and upon the distance between a's centre and b's point of contact with a. With b as a parameter (that is, the magnitude kept constant in the mathematical function), a's rotary movement was "integrated" on c.

brea; the account was translated into English and commented on by Ada Augusta, Lady Lovelace, Byron's daughter and a mathematician. Both the original account and her comments suggest possible uses for the analytical engine as a scientific instrument, and outline applications which computer technology did not manage to approach until the 1950s. In 1888, Babbage's son Henry published a description of his father's machine, that was mathematically and technically comprehensive. Charles Babbage was far ahead of his time, so much so that there was then no chance of realizing his brilliant ideas for systems to solve the problems of automating mathematical calculations. These ideas had to wait for technical development to catch up.

The Analog Computer

The attention aroused by Babbage's ideas led many mathematicians and physicists in the latter part of the nineteenth century to interest themselves in arithmetic machines. One was William Thomson, later Lord Kelvin, who tried to find a way round the difficulties Babbage had come up against, seeking a solution by abandoning the series of numbers in favour of a machine based on the mechanical analogy to a mathematical function, in this case an integral. In 1876, his brother, James Thomson, had designed a mechanical integrator which consisted of a level, rotating disc along the diameter of which a sphere moved, transferring its motion to a cylinder. Using a system of integrators of this sort, Kelvin built a machine to calculate the motion of the tides, the first analog computer. He designed similar machines for calculations concerning a series of different physical problems, including those leading to differential equations. But Kelvin, too, ran into the problem of insufficiently precise mechanics and did not succeed in achieving the accuracy he desired for his calculations. He was, however, convinced that the analog computer would afford a considerable relief to mathematicians and scientists in their research work, or as he himself put it: "The objective of this machine is to substitute brass for brain in the great mechanical labour of calculating."

During the First World War, some progress in mechanical analog computers was made, and in the late 1920s, Lord Kelvin's ideas were revived, when the American Vannevar Bush (1890–1974), of the Massachusetts Institute of Technology, designed a mechanical differential analysator, based on the principle of integrators. The analysator could carry out a number of different calculating programs. In the 1930s, this analysis engine developed into a quick and reliable computer, its use coming to include the calculation of artillery firing tables.

The Breakthrough

The work of Vannevar Bush, mainly during the 1930s, in developing calculating machines with increased flexibility and capacity has been compared to that of an ice-breaker. In the English-speaking world, great efforts were now devoted to both the physical and theoretical sides of designing calculating machines. In England Alan M. Turing made contributions of lasting value in the theoretical area.

But a technical breakthrough was about to occur, for while purely mechanical components had, in the main, been used in calculating machines, the rapid development of telecommunications in the 1920s had produced a component of great interest in this context—the telephone relay. This had proved its operating reliability in the telephone networks which were becoming more and more automatic. The German Konrad Zuse (1910–   ) was the first to exploit systematically the relay in a calculating machine. In his autobiography, published in 1970, Zuse states that, even as a young student, around 1932, he had thought of building a "universal adding machine . . . so that people with creative talents need not waste their precious time on boring calculations". After graduating as a construction engineer in Berlin in 1935, Zuse worked for about a year with calculations of structural strength, but from 1936 onwards, he worked full-time with his adding machine. An experimental model with mainly mechanical components was complete by 1938, but after that, Zuse designed an arithmetic unit built entirely of electromagnetic relays, and the machine was almost complete at the outbreak of war in 1939. During his military service, Zuse managed to arouse the interest of the German Air Force, which caused the machine to be completed in 1941; it was called Z3 but was, however, destroyed in an air raid. During the final stages of the war, Zuse was active in Göttingen, where he built a full-scale relay machine, Z4, which was put into operation in 1945. It is to be seen today in the Eidgenössische Technische Hochschule in Zürich.

The honour of having designed the first electric arithmetic machine, that is, the first computer in the modern sense of the word, must undoubtedly go to Konrad Zuse, even if his work remained unknown outside the close circle around him, being unpublished until the late 1960s. Therefore, his contributions, although pioneering, never influenced the development of the modern computer.

On the other side of the Atlantic, at Harvard University, work had begun in 1939 on a large relay machine, the Automatic Sequence Controlled Calculator, later called Mark I. The design and construction of the machine was supervised by Professor Howard H. Aiken, and it was built with the assistance of the International Business Machine Corporation (IBM), being completed in 1944. Standard versions of relays had been used for its arithmetic units, but the memory was mechanical, consisting of calculating wheels, whose principle was that of an advanced contemporary office machine. The capacity of its memory was seventy-two "words" of twenty-three figures each—in other words, numbers—and the machine could complete the multiplication of two such numbers in four and a half seconds. A few more machines of the same sort were built, including the Mark II, which was also designed by Aiken. It was ready in 1948 and was used to calculate artillery firing tables.

The great resources devoted to research and technical development in the United States during the Second World War stimulated a demand for larger and quicker computers. Once the theoretical principles of the relay machines had been proved correct, appetites grew for more complicated projects. What people really wanted from computers was higher speeds of calculation and greater memory capacities; relays were soon replaced by electronic tubes, which have the same function as relays but work much faster.

Work on the first electronic computer commenced in 1942 under the supervision of J. G. Brainerd, J. Presper Eckert, and John W. Mauchly at the University of Pennsylvania in Philadelphia. This machine, later to become famous as ENIAC—Electronic Numeral Integrator and Calculator—marks the beginning of the modern computer era. ENIAC was first taken into service at New Year, 1946, and remained in use up to 1955. It was in many ways "first and best". The machine contained eighteen thousand electronic tubes, consumed about 175 kW, and took up a floor space of about 2,150 sq ft (c. 200 sq m). Its calculation speed was a thousand times greater than that of contemporary relay machines. The capacity of the memory was twenty words of ten figure each, and, moreover, the machine could store three hundred words of program instructions.

ENIAC was the definite breakthrough for the automation of arithmetic, and it attracted enormous attention both in scientific circles and among the general public. The press christened ENIAC the "electronic brain", and the British scientific periodical *Nature* introduced it under the headline, "Babbage's Dream Comes True".

The relay and electron-tube computers of the pioneering era of the 1940s and 1950s are usually called first generation computers. Seen from today's point of view, these one-off machines are characterized by a low memory capacity and long access time (the time it takes to gain access to the memory and retrieve data from it).

1 + 1 = 10. True or False?

As the designers of the first computers very likely would not have seen the point of the question: "Is the statement $1 + 1 = 10$ true or false?", any reader who feels confused need not worry. However, this question implies the two main principles of computer theory, both of which were developed intensely from the late 1940s onwards and exemplify once more how control technology has stimulated theoretical considerations. If the apparently simple equation in the question is taken to read "one plus one equals ten", it is, of course, nonsense, but if "ten" is taken as "one-zero", in other words, the binary "ten", then the equation makes complete sense. The binary system of figures, ("binary" deriving from the Latin *bini*, two together), has a base of two and employs two figures only—0 and 1. It was first described by Leibniz in the late seventeenth century. Its properties are simply excellent and fit the components of computer technology like a glove. We shall not enlarge upon the mathematical theories of computers, which belong to the more advanced chapters of modern technology, but the basic principles are surprisingly clear and easy to understand.

What is most unusual about the binary numerical system is the fact that it has a base of two. We have been accustomed since childhood to counting with the decimal system, which has a base of ten, but the two systems are formed in exactly the same way. In the decimal system, the number 365 is equivalent to $3 \times 10 \times 10$ ($3 \times 10^2 = 300$) plus 6×10 ($6 \times 10^1 = 60$) plus 5×1 ($5 \times 10^0 = 5$). If any number is raised to the power of zero, the result is 1. In the binary system, however, the number 365 is equivalent to 1×2^8 ($= 256$) plus 1×2^6 ($= 64$) plus 1×2^5 ($= 32$) plus 1×2^3 ($= 8$) plus 1×2^2 ($= 4$) plus 1×2^0 ($= 1$). Since the series of powers from 2^8 to 2^0 are 2^8, 2^7, 2^6, 2^5, 2^4, 2^3, 2^2, 2^1, and 2^0, the powers 2^7, 2^4, and 2^1 are missing in the number 365. In the binary system, a figure 1 is inserted for the powers included, and a figure 0 for the powers excluded. The number 365 is thus written as 101101101, and the number 2 is written as 10, that is $1 \times 2^1 + 0 \times 2^0$. Therefore, we can say that $1 + 1$ is indeed equal to 10!

If the number of days in a year is thus expressed, the year certainly seems exceptionally long! The binary numbers are altogether unmanageable by people, for whom the decimal system is far superior, but a computer's fundamental components understand the two binary figures 0 and 1 as "yes"–"no", or "either–or", so the computer and the binary system seem made for each other. The mathematicians call these components "bistable elements", meaning that they have only two positions; a current is passed either through the circuit (1, or "yes") or not (0, or "no"), and there is no third choice. Popular scientific books about computers, however, often liken bistable elements to water taps, which can be either off or on. But who does not know that, even in the most costly bathroom or kitchen, a tap has its third position: it drips!

If we recall the title of this section, we can claim to have established that one plus one equals one-zero is "true". The terminology is taken from the other theoretical foundation for computer technology, logical algebra, which was formulated as early as the 1840s by the English logician and mathematician George Boole (1815–64), although it found no practical or theoretical application until the late 1940s, when it was discovered that the Boole algebra's simple means of counting was just what computer technology needed. Its advantage is that it can express in the simplest possible mathematical form, whether combinations "yes–no" and "either–or" are true or false. It is, in other words, very well suited for the binary numerical system: yes = 1, no = 0, either 0 or 1. In its simplest form, Boole's algebra consists of two arithmetic rules. We do not need to go further than this to show the principles.

1 The conjunctive law, $C = A \wedge B$ ($\wedge$ is read as "and"), which says that C is true if A *and* B are true.
2 The disjunctive law, $C = A \vee B$ ($\vee$ is read as "or"), which says that C is true if *either* A or B is true.

Even those who are intimidated by mathematics are bound to agree that Boole's algebra illustrates the logical concepts in a clear and easily understood way.

In 1847, when Boole published his *Mathematical Analysis of Logic*, he was probably totally unaware of the enormous impact his work would have in the future, for at the time, this little book attracted only some casual attention in the world of science, being anyway greatly overshadowed by a more extensive work, *Formal Logic*, published the same year by the English mathematician and philosopher Augustus de Morgan (1806–71). One hundred years later, however, it was discovered that Boole's logical algebra could be extremely useful to computer technology. Those who designed the first computing machines had more or less followed their instincts rather than a particular theory, but in the late 1940s, when several great mathematicians and physicists were devoting themselves to the theoretical principles of the design and function of computers, Boole's little book was rediscovered, reprinted, and discussed. It contained the arithmetic rules that computer technology required!

This was discovered in 1948, the same year that the professor of mathematics at the Massachusetts Institute of Technology, Norbert Wiener, published his pioneering work, *Cybernetics, or Control and Communication in the Animal and the Machine*, in which he presented a general theory for all kinds of automatic control, including the control of computers. This was to be the foundation of a new science, cybernetics, which we shall discuss further on. Although the mathematical descriptions in the book were very complicated, even

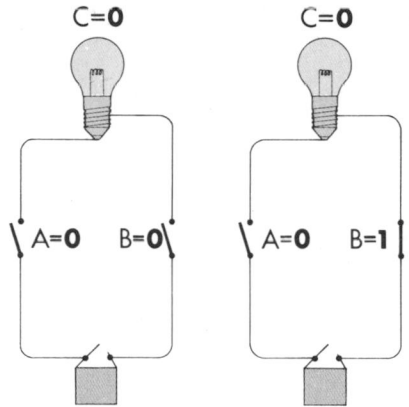

The conjunctive law in Boole's algebra can be illustrated in the following manner: two electric switches, A and B, are connected in series with a light bulb, C, and a battery. If the bulb is to be lit, the circuit must be closed. If A and B are both open (= 0), C will not burn (= 0). If A is open (= 0) and B is closed (= 1), just as if A is closed (= 1) and B is open (= 0), C will still not burn (= 0), but if both A and B are closed (= 1), C will be lit (= 1). The results are entered in a so-called truth table (*left*), from which one can deduce that C is true (= 1) only if A *and* B are true (= 1).

The disjunctive law can be explained in a similar manner. The two switches, A and B, are here connected in parallel to the lightbulb, C, and the battery, which means that the bulb will be lit if either switch is closed. If both A and B are open, C will not burn. If A is open and B is closed, just as if A is closed and B is open, C will burn. If both A and B are closed, C will still burn. From the truth table (*right*) one can deduce that C is true if either A *or* B is true.

for a mathematician, cybernetics became something of a general topic of conversation in wider circles, far beyond those of natural science and technology, for its theory could be applied to practically anything capable of being governed and controlled, from autopilots and computers to socio-economic developments. The debate gained even more momentum the following year when Wiener published a masterly summary of his ideas, which was completely free of reference to mathematics and entitled *The Human Use of Human Beings*.

The same eventful year of 1948 saw further important progress when Claude E. Shannon (1916–   ) published *The Mathematical Theory of Communication*, a work which attracted if possible even more attention than Wiener's book on cybernetics. Shannon was one of Wiener's students and followed in the footsteps of his teacher, giving a mathematical description of his theories. The similarity extended further: Shannon's book, too, became the basis of a new science: information theory. This theory of the transfer of information, which is very general and mathematically very precise, was at first misunderstood and misinterpreted, just as cybernetics was. Several scientists, above all the American mathematician Warren

Weaver, helped, however, to make the ideas accessible to a wider circle. During the Second World War, Weaver had made some pioneering contributions to the automatic control of anti-aircraft guns, and he was well acquainted with the problems of control technology. It was, by the way, Weaver who first thought of using a computer for translating from one language into another.

Further on, we shall give a brief explanation of the practical implications of information theory. But since we are at present discussing the basic technical principles of computers, we shall explain another word, "bit", meaning a unit of information. The word is a contraction of *bi*nary digi*t* and can be seen as a pun: a bit of information. The term was suggested in 1948 by the mathematician John W. Tukey, one of Shannon's colleagues, and was soon accepted internationally. A "bit" is the amount of information represented by a "yes/no" or an "either/or" decision.

Nineteen forty-eight also saw the publication of yet another discovery of great importance to computer technology, one that was to have a fundamental impact on the future of computers. This was the transistor, introduced by the trio John Bardeen, Walter Houser Brattain, and William Shockley of the Bell Telephone Laboratories in the United States. They produced this entirely new electronic component after several years of research. The transistor has been seen, quite rightly, as one of the greatest technological breakthroughs of the twentieth century. The research team shared the 1956 Nobel prize in physics for their discovery.

We shall not enlarge upon the details of the construction and function of the transistor but simply state that it has two important properties: it is a bistable element, and it changes extremely quickly from one state to the other, from conducting to non conducting. The word transistor is a contraction of "*transfer*" and "*resistor*". From the start, the first transistors had very small dimensions, not larger than the head of a match, so that the electrons, that is the electric current, had to move only a very short distance to react. The speed of electric current is about 200,000 miles (300,000 km) per second, in other words, 1 ft (0.3 m) in one thousand millionth of a second (a nano second). One talks about the speed of lightning to describe very quick reactions, but the lightning bolt lasts for at least a few thousandths of a second. So the speed of lightning, compared to the reaction speed of a transistor, is extremely slow: over one million times slower!

The small dimensions and extremely quick reactions of the transistor rekindled the imaginations of mathematicians and researchers. When the sensation surrounding the first computers, and principally ENIAC, had subsided, many mathematicians and others had become sceptical, seeing that the admittedly promising possibilities of the computer were severely restricted by the low capacity of its memory. Should capacity be increased a thousandfold, and this was desirable, the external dimensions of the computer would be extremely unmanageable! ENIAC already required the same amount of floor space as a large ballroom, and besides, it devoured large amounts of energy. With the appearance of the transistor, the limitations of the early computers were suddenly removed, for both memory and computing capacities could now be increased considerably, without making the computer larger than a piece of furniture or any more energy-consuming than a deep freeze!

Many mathematicians all over the world were fascinated by these prospects; one who made essential contributions to the theory and design of the computer was the Hungarian-born American mathematician John von Neumann (1903–57). Very largely, it was he who developed the ideas of Turing and others, while he also adapted Shannon's information theory to the practical reality of the computer. Apart from this, von Neumann's abiding contribution is the

A transistor consists of semi-conductor crystals and is, in its original form (**1**), built like a hamburger in a roll. The hamburger (*a*) is a p-crystal, whereas the roll (*b*, *c*) consists of n-crystals. (**2**) A transistor circuit. If a battery (*d*) is connected to the transistor's base (*a*) and to its emitter (*c*), so that a positive voltage is applied to the base, electrons are brought from the lower n-crystal (*c*) through the p-crystal (*a*) and over to the upper n-crystal (*b*), the collector. A current then flows through the left-hand circuit. However, if a negative voltage is applied to *a*, the current in the outer circuit is stopped.

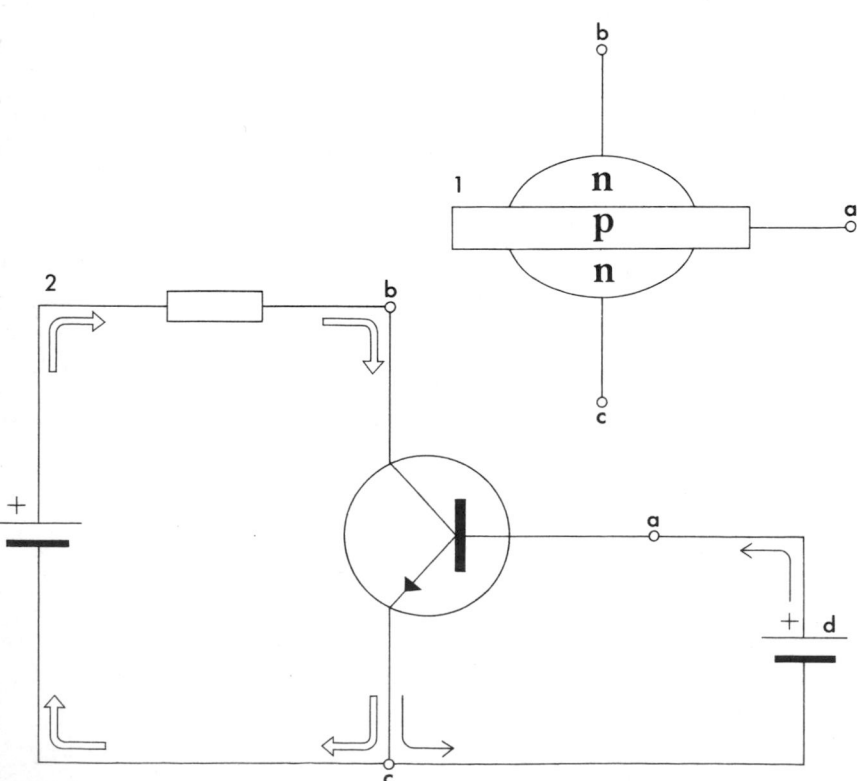

division of the functions of the electronic memory into several specialized units. He introduced a whole hierarchy—this use of the word was coined by him—of memories, each of which had a different task in the handling of data and in making calculations. Von Neumann's principles have guided the internal grouping of the various computer units—the grouping which, later, was to be called the system organization. The first large computer in which von Neumann's ideas were applied was the American UNIVAC (*Universal Automatic Computer*), which came into service in 1951.

The Punched Card and the Punched Tape

The technique used for communicating with UNIVAC was that which Charles Babbage had planned to use for his machine a hundred years earlier, namely the technique of punched cards and punched tape. It had, however, not been invented by Babbage—it is much older than that. We have already come across the talented designer Jacques de Vaucanson, who, after success with his automata, settled in the textile city of Lyons, where he improved the semi-automatic devices for controlling fancy-weaving looms which had been designed by Basile Bouchon (1725) and M. Falcon (1728). In both of these devices, the index fingers (the hooks lifting and lowering the warp threads) were controlled by holes punched in cardboard or an endless paper tape. Each time a new card or a new piece of paper tape was to be fed forward, a manual operation was necessary. Vaucanson then designed such a device which was fully automatic. But since he had plenty of other interests, his device was never commonly known. After his death in 1782, Vaucanson's whole technical estate, including the fancy-weaving device, was transferred to the Conservatoire National des Arts et Métiers, an educational institution in Paris and now a museum of technology.

Joseph Marie Jacquard (1752–1834), who also lived in Lyons, started at an early stage to ponder over a method to mechanize fancy weaving. Both his parents worked in a silk mill, as did Jacquard himself from a very early age. It was quite common that children worked in mills at that time, and the young Jacquard hated this. The children had to sit on top of the looms, looking after the harnesses which made the pattern shafts rise. The work was heavy and monotonous. At the end of the 1790s, Jacquard had completed a design for an automatic harness controlled by punched cards connected in an endless tape. This machine was shown at an industrial exhibition in Paris in 1801, and the following year, Jacquard was granted a patent for his invention. In 1804, Jacquard, thanks to his various designs, which then included a netting machine, was employed by the Conservatoire National in Paris so that he could further develop fully automatic devices for fancy-weaving looms.

In this institution, Jacquard came across Vaucanson's automatic loom, which he had not seen before, although he was familiar with the designs of Bouchon and Falcon. Bouchon was, no doubt, the first to think of using the punched card as a carrier of information. Vaucanson perfected the idea and used it for the automatic control of fancy-weaving looms, and Jacquard combined and developed the previous ideas into an industrially useful design. Jacquard's weaving loom with an automatic harness was completed in 1805 and, as early as 1812, ten thousand Jacquard machines were in operation in France alone.

When Jacquard died, his portrait, about 57 in (1.5 m) square, was woven on a fancy-weaving loom with the aid of twenty-four thousand punched cards. When Charles Babbage saw this extremely detailed portrait, he was convinced that punched cards offered the possibility, as he said, of "weaving algebraic patterns of the same beauty as a Jacquard fabric".

But Babbage was ahead of his time. Not until the end of the

nineteenth century was the idea of using punched cards tried again, when the German-American Hermann Hollerith (1860–1929) was working as a statistician at the United States Census Bureau. According to the American Constitution, a census has to be taken every ten years: the census of 1880 had taken seven years to complete, the population then numbering over 50 million and obviously increasing rapidly. Could the census of 1890 be completed before the next was due? Hollerith's solution was to introduce a rectangular card divided into 240 squares, in each of which a hole could be punched according to a code. Each square corresponded to a question; a punched square represented the answer "yes", an unpunched square a "no". In that way one card could contain information about a person's age, sex, and so on. The punching was done manually, one card per person, but cards were read by a machine; the card was placed on small containers holding mercury, one container for each row of holes, and then a die with electrically conducting pins was brought down upon the card. The holes permitted contact between the pins and the mercury containers, and the coded information was registered by a comptometer. While the population turned out to have grown since 1880 by twenty-five per cent, to 63 million, the result of the 1890 census could be presented after only a little more than two years.

Hollerith developed his methods further and started a company which, in the following decades, was to provide the business world with a whole family of punched-card machines for book-keeping and statistics. It produced punching machines for punching data into the cards, sorting machines, and tabulators for computing operations and for writing out the computed data. Hollerith's company flourished and became one of the corner stones of the International Business Machines Corporation, IBM, which was founded in 1912.

When the computer appeared, there was, in other words, a well-developed technology of information-carrying punched cards and punched tapes. This was very well suited to the "language" of the computer, the binary system of figures, the absence of a hole in a certain place representing 0, and a hole representing 1. In a punched tape with five channels there are $2^5 = 32$ possible combinations in a line, making it possible to include the whole alphabet plus some punctuation marks. With seven channels, $2^7 = 128$ combinations are obtained, which holds the whole alphabet plus all the numbers from 0 to 99.

A magnetic tape stores data similarly, the hole in the punched card becoming a magnetic pulse in a given place in the channels of the tape, and no hole becoming the absence of a magnetic pulse.

Second Generation Computers

In the general enthusiasm following the remarkable breakthroughs in the world of computers in 1948, many people predicted a development at breakneck speed. That never came about for several reasons, but especially because of the extreme difficulty in mastering the mass production of transistors. It took almost ten years from the time when the first laboratory products were tested in 1948 until transistors in large quantities were available on the market. Initially, prices were also relatively high—contrary to early predictions. The first wholly transistorized computer, "Leprechaun", was built at Bell Laboratories and was finished in 1956. A *leprechaun*, one of the little people in Irish mythology, can produce gold and fame with a wave of his hand. The name referred mainly to the speed of the computer—pioneering contributions usually give more fame than gold. Leprechaun soon had successors in both the United States and in Europe, for instance the American IBM 7090 (1958), the British Elliott 803 (1959), and the German ER56 (1959, built by SEL).

During the early 1950s, the large computer companies had been

A Jacquard's automatic draw-loom was invented in 1805. As compared to earlier mechanisms, Jacquard's construction was relatively simple, a fact which contributed to its success.

B A simplified explanatory sketch of Jacquard's automatic draw-loom. The vertical hooks (*a*) ran through eyes in spring-loaded needles (*b*). At the bottom end of the hooks were bunches of strings, which carried the healds (*c*). Through these ran the warp threads (*d*), which were distributed among the needles according to the pattern. The needles bore on a hollowed-out, square-section roller (*e*), over which an endless chain of punched cards (*f*) ran. Every time the weaver pushed a foot-pedal downwards, the roller was rotated one-fourth of a revolution, and a new punched card was pulled forward. At the same time, the griff (*g*) was raised, pulling with it the hooks whose needles had beeen able to enter the roller through the holes in the punched card. All other needles were pulled backwards. (*h*) Pedal rope. The Jacquard looms could have very large numbers of hooks, and at the end of the nineteenth century, looms with four hundred and six hundred hooks were the commonest.

C Hollerith's reading machine for punched cards was originally battery-powered. The cards were hand-fed into the machine, where brush contacts were run across them. Inside the roller were mercury containers, one for each row of holes, and when contact was made, an electric circuit was closed. The circuit either sent impulses to a tabulator's counting device or decided which way the card was to take in order to land in the correct box in a sorting machine. This illustration is based on a drawing in Hollerith's patent application of 1889.

concentrating strongly on computers with miniaturized electron tubes, having more or less given up in the face of the great technical difficulties involved in mass producing transistors, and also of the vast investments required. It was not until the early 1960s that the grand visions of 1948 could be gradually realized. The transistorized computer soon assumed the shape of an acceptable item of furniture and was put into practical use, being used both for scientific calculations and as an aid in administration and management.

The Super Computer which never Arrived

Around 1960, there was a lot of talk in computer circles about a "super computer", a gigantic central computer that was to be the spider in a network of hundreds or thousands of terminals. Large companies as well as small, and even members of the general public, would be able to subscribe to the services of this central computer, which would work as a public utility. The computer intelligence, in other words, like gas, water, and electricity, would be distributed to its consumers.

A series of technical breakthroughs in the latter part of the 1950s had given rise to this idea. The transistor and a number of other technical solutions indicated the possibility of an unlimited extension of the memory capacity of the computer. By greatly increasing speeds of calculation and by organizing systems in a better way, it seemed possible to process several problems simultaneously. On top of all this, drastically simplified methods of instructing and programming were available in the programming languages, principally ALGOL, which appeared in 1958. Instructions about the course of computations, and also other instructions and data, could now be "translated" into a programming language which the computer understood. The word ALGOL is a contraction of *Algo*rithmic *L*anguage, an algorithm being, in computer technology, any partial operation in the computation of a problem. With ALGOL, anyone with a little training could present a problem and then instruct the central computer to solve it. If the central computer had enormous amounts of data stored in its memory, it would not only be capable of working as a calculating machine for research laboratories and of dealing with data processing for companies, but also would be able to help mother to plan next week's menu and father to do the kids' maths homework.

Several companies, such as General Electric in the United States and J. Lyons & Co. in Great Britain, had already installed computers by the beginning of the 1950s to calculate wages and salaries, and these computers had gradually taken over additional tasks, such as inventory control, the issuing of invoices, cost calculations, general book-keeping, and the like. As soon as data could be transferred over great distances, a central computer would be able to serve a whole industrial or business concern, even if offices and other units were geographically far apart. Various such computers, with huge networks of terminals, were actually built in the early 1960s. But all of a sudden, the plans for a gigantic central computer as a public utility were scrapped, the reason being the introduction of a new type of electronic component, and that was the *integrated circuit*.

The second generation computers usually had their electronic circuits built on what were called circuit cards, sheets of insulating material on which were mounted the transistors, resistors, condensors, and other components which formed a connected group of circuits. The connections between the components ended in flat pin plugs which made it easy to extract or exchange the card. In the more advanced integrated circuit, abbreviated here and in computer language to IC, the transistors and other components have been placed on and in a semi-conductor crystal, usually made of silicon. The first mass-produced ICs appeared in 1964 and contained only a few transistors and their associated components. But even at this early stage, it could be seen that development would consist of a drastic miniaturization, and that this would open up entirely new perspectives in computer technology. The transistors with their circuit components on a small silicon chip occupied a surface of only a few square millimetres. As the first computers with ICs became available on the market, only about a year after the introduction of the first ICs, it became clear that the central computer had been technically surpassed.

IC computers are generally called third generation computers, and with them a new era began. The revolution in computer technology can be compared to the revolution that took place in engineering workshops in the early 1900s. Up to then, all machine tools, such as lathes, drills, etc., had been driven by a central steam-engine, with power transmitted by belts, but at the beginning of the century, electric motors were introduced, allowing each machine to be worked individually. In much the same way, the central "steam computers" with their large network of terminals were gradually replaced by smaller computers placed where they were needed, a development that accelerated during the 1970s. It has been made technically possible because of the rapid development of the IC technique. While the first ICs were less than a hundredth the size of the earlier circuit cards, most of their volume consisted of connecting wires; and the solution of this volume problem was found when as many circuits as possible were integrated on one single silicon crystal. *L*arge *S*cale *I*ntegration, LSI, became the motto, but the design and construction of such circuits required a refined technique, a process called *M*etal *O*xide *S*emi-Conductor Technique, MOS, which requires, among other things, that a silicon crystal be oxidized in an oxygen atmosphere and coated with metal in a vacuum. This very sophisticated manufacturing process was introduced in 1967 and, since then, has been refined further. As the properties of a MOS transistor differ slightly from those of the "ordinary" transistor, once-but-now-no-longer common, it became necessary to modify the principles of construction for computer circuits. "If the computer had not been invented by then, we would have found ourselves in a blind alley!" is a remark made by one of the researchers behind the MOS project, and a computer was indeed programmed to design LSI circuits, being fed with the characteristics of the MOS transistors and the properties desired of the circuits. It was programmed further to calculate the shortest possible connections between the components. It produced its results in the form of a neat large-scale constructional drawing of an IC. Through a photographic method, this drawing could be directly used as the basis of production.

A computer designing a computer . . . The popular and daily press made some frightening comments on this in the late 1960s. Was there not a risk that the old legend of the sorcerer's apprentice would become a reality? On the other hand, there is the soothing anecdote of Queen Christina's learned talks with Descartes. When he had made his point about animals being automata, the queen pointed at a clock on the wall and said, "Monsieur Descartes, would you please arrange for that object to have offspring".

In the 1970s, the LSI and MOS techniques with computer-designed computer circuits spectacularly reduced not only the volume of the circuits, but also their price and energy consumption, while at the same time making them more reliable in operation. They have done this to a far greater extent than anyone dared even to suggest during the era of electron tubes, when, after all, the great possibilities of the computer were first suggested.

A Computer in a Nutshell

Larger and larger circuit units were soon produced with the MOS technique, and in 1971, this resulted in an important breakthrough, when the microprocessor was invented, a simplified computer consisting of a small semi-conductor plate, called a chip. The name LSI was now inadequate, so the new term was VLSI (*Very Large Scale Integration*). The microprocessor soon found many areas of application in industrial governing and control systems, being used in industrial robots, among other things. The public at large first met the microprocessor in 1973, when the pocket calculator was introduced and immediately started to spread like wildfire.

The first pocket calculators could calculate the four modes, roots, powers, logarithms, and possibly trigonometric functions. More and more sophisticated calculators followed, however, in rapid succession. These could be programmed over a relatively wide range and had several thousand times the memory capacity that ENIAC once had. One model was able to talk, although with a limited vocabulary. The electronic wrist watch, the quartz watch, became the next triumph for microcircuit technology. The watch was introduced in 1975 and also met with immediate success. Two years later, a quartz watch with a built-in calculator was on sale, and in 1978, an American manufacturer announced the *speaking* quartz clock. The impulses to the figures in this clock—as in the pocket calculator—are transformed to analog speech currents which tell the time via a miniature loudspeaker. A daily paper made this remark: "Let's hope the microelectronics people don't fall asleep now—we're waiting for Dick Tracy's bracelet viewphone."It will probably appear. In 1976, various kinds of television games started to gain popularity, and these entertainment machines are also based on microcircuit technology.

Our closest surroundings will soon see a number of versions of the microprocessor, performing functions which we cannot even imagine today. For example, several automobile manufacturers have equipped their latest models with trip computers which compute information such as the average speed during a certain distance and the distance to, and time of arrival at, the destination. Another gadget also made possible by microprocessors is the talking "traveller's dictionary" of the size of a pocket calculator, which translates some hundred simple phrases and reads them aloud. So far, the translation is word by word, but in most situations, this is sufficient to make oneself understood.

One of the great philosophers has said that all comparisons limp, and the most picturesque fall and break their necks. To get an idea of how quickly computers have changed from ENIAC up to the microprocessor, one can make a comparison with a car, for example, a Volkswagen, the civil version of which appeared in the same year as ENIAC. Had the Volkswagen undergone the same degree of development as computers, it would have a fuel consumption of a few cubic millimetres per mile, cost perhaps a dollar, have a trouble-free working life of about ten thousand years, and have a top speed of over 600,000 mph (c. 1 million km/h). Its fuel consumption is appealing, even if its speed might be a health hazard.

This is merely a somewhat fanciful way of linking the computer and the car in a comparison that, sure enough, stumbles and breaks its neck: our putative Volkswagen would be so small that it would be lost in the dust on the desk at which it has been dreamt up!

Machines Controlling Machines

The technology of the automatic control of industrial procedures emerged from the 1920s onwards, alongside the development described in the previous pages. More and more demands arose for the automatic control of procedures that could no longer be managed manually, since human reactions were insufficient. An example is procedures in the chemical industry, such as the oil refineries which

Microprocessors made their appearance at the beginning of the 1970s. At the foot of this page we illustrate a microprocessor full-size; the outer tab is for its connections. An enlargement of the actual processor unit is shown in the middle of the page. Above, a silicone chip is illustrated in magnification to show the individual transistors.

began to be built in ever-increasing numbers to meet the growing demand for fuel, brought about by the expanding number of motorists.

It was, more than anything else, electrical engineering, with its urgent need for automatic control, that hastened the discovery of new components and principles. Initially, electric power was distributed in relatively small networks with moderate voltages, the current being supplied by a generator driven by a steam-engine or a water turbine. The dominant control component in the driving engine was the centrifugal governor, and the operator had no great difficulty in manually making fine adjustments to the speed—that is, to the frequency in alternating-current networks—or in adjusting the power with a starter rheostat. As the power and load of the networks increased, however, it soon became impossible to intervene only manually, especially when several networks were linked in a grid. It became technically unavoidable that automatic controls would replace man; at first, electromechanical methods were tried out, but it soon became necessary to boost the relatively small output signals which these gave. During the first decades of the twentieth century, Farcot's servomotor was applied in many different ways by those attempting to solve the various problems of electric-power control, and the servomotor was developed along several different lines. Farcot had considered steam to be the most logical driving power, but now, compressed air and oil at pressure—in other words, pneumatics and hydraulics—were tried instead. In due course, several variations on these two themes appeared.

The servomotor, the muscle of control engineering, also turned out to be very useful in other branches of technology, such as the processing industry and the metal-working industry. In the 1920s and 1930s, servomechanics developed into a new branch of engineering, and an industry emerged which manufactured more and more specialized components for automatic control. The "classic" problem of servomechanics is the control of vessels, while in the period between the wars, there was also the problem of aligning anti-aircraft guns. The armaments industries in both Europe and the United States made great efforts to solve the latter, and this work also resulted in the production of a number of control systems which could be applied to civilian industry. At the outbreak of the Second World War, the Massachusetts Institute of Technology set up the Servomechanism Laboratory for research and development in development in control engineering. Pioneering theoretical and practical work was done here by Gordon S. Brown, Donald P. Campbell, N. B. Nichols, and others. They have become famous for their text books, published immediately after the War, which became standard works in this field for a long time afterwards.

Long-Distance Telephones

Let us look now at telecommunications, another branch of electrical engineering which has made some extremely important contributions to modern control technology. We who use the telephone every day sometimes forget that there was a time during the first decades of the telephone age when conversations were limited to an area with a relatively small radius. This was due to the damping of the current on the line. If a normal bare wire was used, this radius was approximately 30 miles (50 km). At the beginning of the century, the damping could be reduced by artificial means—inserting a series of self-induction coils, called coil loading—which extended the radius of the telephone area to about 120 miles (c. 200 km). Experiments were made with a "high-tension microphone", one which could take a very high voltage. The radius could then be extended to about 250 miles (c. 400 km), or the distance between Paris and Berlin. One kilowatt was fed into this monstrous microphone, a normal telephone

microphone needing only about one milliwatt. On top of everything else, as damping is exponential, nearly three hundred gigawatt (300×10^9 W) would be needed to make audible a telephone call through uninsulated wire 620 miles (1,000 km) long, an impossible demand, for this amount of electrical effect was then—about 1910—not even available. Today, this would amount to about half of the total installed capacity in Europe!

Telecommunications had a difficult problem. To make long-distance connections possible, it was necessary to amplify the speech currents at regular intervals along the line and so counteract the damping. The only feasible solution was to use the electron tube, which at that time, however, had hardly left the laboratory stage. The triode, the electronic tube with three electrodes, had been invented in 1906, independently by the German R. von Lieben and by the American Lee de Forest; now, it was a matter of developing it into a safe component in repeaters, and it took over ten years to do this, the First World War both hampering and stimulating the work. Development work was led in the United States by the Western Electric company, and in Europe by several German engineers. One of them, H. Barkhausen, was one of the first people to make use of the word "electronics". The first long-distance cable in Europe was taken into service in 1923: it connected Stockholm and Gothenburg (a distance of about 300 miles, or 500 km) and had been made by Western Electric with triode repeaters.

Long-distance telephony spread very rapidly. Long-distance calls became as easy to make as local calls, and the quality of sound was at least comparable. In a short time, hundreds of thousands of triode repeaters were in operation in the telephone networks—and that was when the deficiencies of this type of repeater were revealed. Slight individual variations in the properties of the triodes, uneven current supply, differences of temperature, and other things could cause a severe disturbance in operation when hundreds of triode repeaters were linked together in a long-distance cable. As so many times before in the history of technology, the solution to one problem had created another.

The attempts to solve this new problem, however, led to a completely new design principle for electron-tube repeaters, namely *negative feedback*, and this had a revolutionary impact, not only on telecommunications. H. S. Black of the Bell Laboratories in the United States first described the negative-feedback repeater in 1923. It played a fundamental role in all telecommunications, which, at the time, was expanding rapidly due to the emergence of broadcasting, and also due to an electrical method, invented in 1925, of recording gramophone records. Feedback gave the repeater or amplifier high stability and made it quite insensitive to external disturbances—properties very well suited to various types of control systems. The word "feedback" became something of a catchword among engineers of the time, and while the feedback repeater was being applied in various control systems, it was also triumphing in the sphere of telecommunications. Still, what had been achieved was merely a technical solution. A more complete description of the theory of the feedback repeater did not appear until the mid-1930s, and then largely thanks to the contributions made by J. Bode and Harry Nyqvist, both of Bell Laboratories. A generalization of this theory also formed the basis of a better understanding of the feedback or closed-control system.

Cybernetics and Information Theory

Very simply put, it may be said that both cybernetics and the information theory are logical extensions of the work done by Black, Bode, Nyqvist, and others in the 1920s and 1930s, for these sciences each include a mathematical and physical extension of the concept of

A

feedback. In the early 1940s, Norbert Wiener became interested as a mathematician in the obvious similarities between technical closed-control systems and various processes in living organisms, especially the transfer of signals in nervous systems. By applying the theories and calculation methods of servomechanisms to experiments on animals, Wiener and his assistant, the neurologist Arturó Rosenbleuth, could predict the contraction and relaxation of a muscle with different loads. These and other experiments gave Wiener the idea of applying the theory of the closed-loop servosystem not only in physiology but also in the behavioural sciences, political economy, and many other areas. Wiener noticed, however, that his "technical" theories and his terminology were accepted only with difficulty within other branches of science, so he then reshaped the whole complex of theories into a new, generalized form. Moreover—and this was, perhaps, the most important thing—he found a new, exciting name for it all: "cybernetics". The name derives from the Greek word for helmsman and, freely translated, means "the science of steerability"; it is interesting to note that Ampère used the same concept in his catalogue of all human knowledge. One of Wiener's colleagues pointed this out to him, and Wiener replied: "Well, that was the only word I came to think of!"

With this new designation, Wiener wanted above all to stress the interdisciplinary character of cybernetics, and he succeeded. Many widely different scientific circles received Wiener's ideas with great enthusiasm—and misunderstood much of them. Even so, he would surely have encountered great resistance, not least among behavioural scientists, had he tried instead to deliver his message as "the theory of the negative-feedback electron tube repeater". Nevertheless, this is the theory on which cybernetics is based, although the form is refined and developed. In economics, for example, a number of feedback processes had been identified as such by the British economist John Maynard Keynes (1883–1946) and others long before Wiener had presented his theory. The ratio between supply and demand is one such process, and another is the increase or decrease in the total consumption of a certain commodity following inversely on a change in its price. A servomechanic block diagram can be drawn up to illustrate such processes, something that can make the concepts clearer and easier to understand. But it is only possible to make a mathematical calculation of a feedback process in economics and to express the results in precise economical terminology, if all the quantities involved are described in the language of mathematical formulae, so that they can be inserted in the equations that express the concept. And this is where the difficulties begin. If the economists could describe the national and global economical processes mathematically with the precision of the astronomers' definitions of the motion of the planets, cybernetics would enable them to calculate very accurately the effects of, say, a devaluation. Today, this is possible neither theoretically nor practically, but the science of cybernetics has to a large extent stimulated economists to try to design mathematical models of economic feedback processes. This has resulted in a new branch of economic sciences, *econometrics*, which has developed methods to define and measure economical changes. The possibility of "simulating" economical reality has also been tried out with the help of computers programmed with econometric mathematical models.

Recently, some historians have launched the term "cliometry" to describe feedback processes in historical studies, Clio being the Greek muse of history. This may for the time being be taken as a joke, for the difficulties of defining the parameters in such a process, with even the slightest mathematical precision, are altogether too great.

The whole technique of cybernetics, however, is still in an early

A Compared to the latest products, early calculators were both uncomplicated and costly. All they could cope with were the four modes: addition, subtraction, division, and multiplication. The model shown here worked off batteries placed in a recess at the back, but it could also be plugged into the mains. (*a*) Plugs for mains connection and for disconnecting the batteries. (*b*) Lead for *a*. (*c*) Diode display of figures, each formed by a number of the seven segments. (*d*) Lead to *c*. (*e*) Transistors activating *c*. (*f*) The calculator unit, which also contains the memory, the whole consisting of many transistors. (*g*) Voltage regulator for mains connection. (*h*) Switch. (*i*) Leads to batteries. (*j*) Button to switch the memory on and off. (*k*) Button for the desired number of decimals.

stage of development, but very likely, the methods will be successively refined, and in the future, cybernetics will be of great practical importance. It will also have a great impact on a number of other sciences, where it has given rise to a fruitful cooperation between different disciplines. One example is the physiological analysis of the human brain, made for the purpose of studying the process of learning, this being one of many cases where cybernetics can be complemented with models of thought from the theory of information.

The scientific theory of information was introduced, as we have mentioned, by Claude E. Shannon, in the eventful year of 1948. It deals with the transfer of information from a "transmitter" via a "channel" to a "receiver", and with what can happen to the information on the way. The transmitter can be a radio transmitter; the information is then telegraphic signals, speech, or music. Those who listen to the short-wave band on the wireless know that there are many sources of interference in the channel—nearby transmitters, electric storms in the atmosphere, the neighbour's electric razor, and so on. Shannon himself has likened the transfer of information to a conveyor belt, loaded at one end with various kinds of wooden goods which are received and sorted at the other end of the belt. During the journey, the pieces of wood (or "bits" of information) can be shaken off, chipped, or in some other way deformed, so that it becomes difficult for the receiver to sort them out. These things happen by chance, just like disturbances to the transfer of information, but statistical methods can give an idea of the damage they cause. Shannon also showed how statistics can help calculate, in "bits", the content of information in a message. The theory of information can thus be seen as an advanced branch of mathematical statistics.

The importance of the information theory for all types of telecommunication is quite clear, but only when it has been applied on an interdisciplinary, general level has the theory of information advanced the frontiers of human knowledge, and this has occurred in many branches of science. For example, when the transmitter is a brain cell of an organism and the receiver a nerve cell in a muscle, the information transmitted can be exposed to interference, caused by disease in the organism. The theory of information has also been successfully applied to everything connected with verbal and other forms of communication between human beings.

The Return of the Androids!

Earlier in this chapter we have come across numbers of actual and imaginary artificial beings. Having been absent from the scene for almost a hundred years, the androids returned in the 1920s. In 1923, the Czech playwright Karel Čapek presented his play *R. U. R.* (Rossum's Universal Robots), and so gave a new name to these walking mechanical monsters. The word robot is derived from the Czech *robota*, compulsory labour, while the word means "to work" in other Slavic languages.

As a contribution to the European social debate, Čapek's play caused a lively discussion, which soon subsided, however. The comic strips, on the other hand, warmly welcomed the robot, but it was mainly films which gave it its great vitality. The first film showing robots was the now classic German *Metropolis*, which was released in 1926, and since then, robots have appeared in a number of different shapes on the screen. In the 1930s, every self-respecting fair or exhibition had its own robot. At the world exhibition in New York in 1939 and 1940, the walking and talking robot "Electro" appeared together with its dog "Sparko", which could run, bark, and sit up and beg at the order of its master.

But the game became serious. It is understandable that many members of the scientific world took it as a bad joke when Norbert

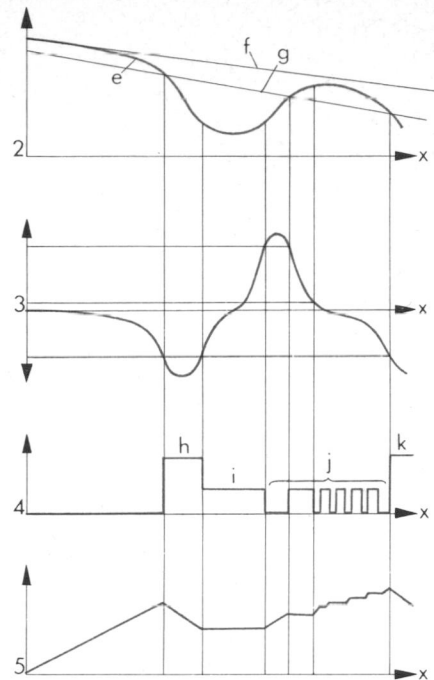

B An anti-locking braking system could not be built until the LSI and MOS techniques had been developed. The German company Bosch launched its **ABS** anti-locking system in 1978 and made it available at first only in Germany and only to order on the more expensive Mercedes and BMWs.

In a car equipped with **ABS** (1) an electromagnetic transmitter (*a*) is mounted in the hub of each front wheel. The transmitter's coil is fitted beside a cog-wheel which rotates with the car's wheel. A similar arrangement (*b*) is mounted on the back axle. The transmitters send continuous electric impulses to a governing device (*c*) as the car's wheels rotate, and if one of them starts to lock, the impulses from it rapidly increase in frequency. The hydraulic unit (*d*), with its electromagnetically controlled valves and pump, then stops the flow of brake fluid to that wheel. If this does not stop the tendency to lock, the pump begins to extract fluid from the relevant braking circuit, so that retardation is reduced. If the electronic governor senses that the transmitter has stopped functioning correctly, it activates the reserve system, and if that fails, the governor cuts out the system's valves and the braking system reverts to a normal, foot-controlled one. (2) Diagrams of one wheel's speed (*e*) in relation to the car's speed (*f*) during sharp braking. The x-coordinate gives the time in each diagram. The bump in *e* indicates that the wheel is about to lock. (*g*) The speed calculated by *c* at which maximum lock-free braking can be achieved. (3) The wheel's change of speed. When the wheel is about to lock—at the bump on the curve—retardation is reduced and the wheel's speed rapidly increases. (4) The governor's instructions upon calculating the changes of speed in **2** and **3**. (*h*) Instructions to the hydraulic valve and pump to reduce pressure in the brake circuit. (*i*) The hydraulic valve is instructed to close, so that the wheel's speed may increase. (*j*) As soon as the wheel has regained enough grip on the road to permit braking, instructions are sent to increase pressure in the brake circuit. (*k*) If the wheel again nearly locks, the instructions in *h* are repeated in a new cycle. (5) The vehicle's changes of speed during braking.

Wiener and his assistant Jerome Wiesner published, in 1950, details of a robot that they called "the moth and the light", an artificial being that could either be attracted by a source of light or, by turning a simple switch, be repelled by it. It was simply a visual demonstration of a cybernetic process. Claude E. Shannon also joined in the serious game and designed a similar robot, which he called "the mouse in the maze". Soon, there was a whole cybernetic menagerie in scientific laboratories all over the world. It was mainly physicists, neurologists, and behavioural scientists who used this "laboratory cybernetics" to enlighten and enrich their sciences, and to study, among other things, the resistance of physiological systems to external disturbances: the automatic maintenance of the stability of such a system is called homeostatis. In the early 1950s, the British neurologist W. Ross Ashby built a very sophisticated robot which he called "homeostat" and which attracted a great deal of attention. Unlike other robots, it consisted of two apparatus boxes with connected magnetic circuits which could internally assume a large number of positions of equilibrium. The system reacted to external disturbance by feeling its way towards a new position of equilibrium. Sometimes, it could be some time before the new position of equilibrium was achieved. Too frequent or too powerful disturbances could bring on a "nervous breakdown" of the homeostat. Several experts in behavioural sciences, among them the Austrian Heinz Zemanek, built similar robots, which they used as aids in the work of exploring the behaviour of man.

In the last years of his life, John von Neumann worked on the theoretical possibilities of constructing an automaton which, unlike Queen Christina's clock, could reproduce itself. It remained a mathematical picture, a blueprint, as von Neumann himself put it. Von Neumann's idea is not totally absurd from a technical point of view, but as far as practice goes, we can relax. Someone must supply such an automation with "food", that is, transistors, connecting wires, and other things, and there must also be someone to program and control it. During the last ten years, various robots have been put to practical use in both industry and research. A number of different types have been produced for handling radioactive material; some are intended for regular work in nuclear power-stations, whereas others are kept prepared for possible emergencies. In the United States the robot "Beetle" has been built for emergencies: it will automatically go to the source of radiation, i.e., the dangerous material, take it, and leave it to be destroyed in the place to which it has been directed.

It is, however, the space researchers who have taken into their service the most sophisticated robots, ranging from moon-vehicles like the unmanned Soviet Lunochod to various kinds of probes which can soft-land on other planets and do as much work as a whole research team on earth, yet another example of a development chain in which automata and simulacra succeed one another.

Automation

Let us return to 1948, that year which was so eventful in terms of the contents of this chapter, when automation, another phenomenon which, a few years later, was to set off a violent debate throughout the western world, lay latent. The word "automation" had been coined in 1947 by Delmar S. Harder of the Ford Motor Co. in Detroit. Harder thought that "automation" ought to be a coordinating concept embracing all designs and devices that attempted to achieve fully automated production. Initially, Harder conducted a campaign for automation within Ford, but rumour of this spread rapidly all over American industry, and a vehement debate was joined about automation. It was felt that its ultimate aim was to rationalize man out of production, and mass unemployment was predicted. There

A

A This modern American robot, Beetle, automatically locates radioactive material and is programmed to bring it out of the danger area and deposit it where it can be neutralized.

B Sabor IV, built in 1938 by the Frenchman Auguste Huber. The robot could both move and speak, its lips moving synchronously with what it said. The legs were moved forwards by little wheels, which were mounted under the soles and were, in turn, rotated and braked.

were similar exaggerations even in the technological/industrial camp, where many people considered automation new and revolutionary. The word "automatology" was coined; automation was to be the science which would start a new era! The same mentality christened automation "the second industrial revolution". At an international seminar on automation in 1957, an American supporter of this attitude painted imaginative futuristic visions of a revolutionary miracle, only to be brought back to earth by an Englishman's levelheaded statement: "Automation is really nothing but a push-button that pushes itself."

The lasting importance of the lively automation debate was in the incipient awareness that all procedures and processes, even those which had previously been reserved for the crafts, could in principle be mechanized and automated. One example of this, which has often been mentioned, is a machine which forms dough into pretzels far faster than the most skilful baker. Another is the "mechanical hand" which rolls cigars more quickly and evenly than any Carmen. The automation debate and the vivid exchange of thoughts between specialists within different branches of industry also resulted in insights about the possibility of generalizing—a system for the automation of a certain procedure can often be modified slightly and used for a different procedure, even though the product may be totally different. For example, automatic systems for making crisp-bread can also be used for producing steam-hardened concrete slabs.

B

Computer Process Control

It has been mentioned already, but bears repeating, that technical solutions in automatic control technology often have preceded theoretical insights. In the wake of the automation debate, bold attempts were made to automate procedures which it had not been possible to master before. Many times, these attempts resulted in bad failures, especially in chemical process technology. In the 1950s, the market began to be offered good-quality components, such as measuring devices, servomotors, and regulators for temperature, pressure, flow, etc. But there was often a lack of knowledge of the dynamic properties of the chemical processes, that is, of how they reacted in operation to various kinds of control intervention. The work of dimensioning the process often resulted in very complicated mathematical expressions. At an early stage, computers had to be used for such computations, and thence it was a short step to letting the computers take over the governing and control of whole processes.

The first computer for process control was designed by the American Ramo-Woolridge Corporation and was called the RW-300. It was first available in 1957 and was soon followed by others. Ten years later, about sixteen hundred process computers were installed in the West and in 1977, the number had risen to about twelve thousand. There are, however, many who believe that this figure will now remain static or at least rise more slowly. Instead, the microprocessor will take over various functions which so far have been directed by the central process computer.

By Rocket to the Planets

By far the most complicated of contemporary processes controlled by computers are space flights—without access to automatic control systems and computers, it would be totally impossible for man to travel into space. The first space pioneers—the Russian Constantin E. Tsiolkovsky (1857–1935), the German Hermann Ganswindt (1856–1934), and others—were criticized by astronomers and mathematicians who believed that it was beyond human ability to correct course and speed with the precision required for space navigation. One of the first to realize the extent of this problem was the German Hermann Oberth (1894–   ), who stressed in his now classical work *Die Rakete zu den Planetenräumen* ("Rockets into Interplanetary Space"), published in 1923, that one precondition for flight in space was access to techniques for automatic governing and control that would have to be far more sophisticated than those then available. In the much extended 1929 edition, *Wege zur Raumschiffahrt* ("Methods for Space Travel"), Oberth quite rightly predicted that the development of rockets with sufficient propulsive force (another essential precondition), would take time and stated that control technology also would have to be improved in that time. The vital necessity for precision in manoeuvring a spaceship is due to the fact that the speeds and distances involved are literally astronomical. On top of this are the complications caused by such phenomena as the motion of the planet systems, and so on.

If the carrier rocket is to place a satellite—a word meaning a companion, and here, a companion to the earth—in an orbit round the earth, it has to achieve a speed of at least 4.911 miles (7.904 km) per second, a velocity called circular, or the first cosmic velocity: it can be rounded off to 5 miles (8 km) per second. Here on earth it is difficult to try to imagine how high this velocity really is. A car driven at 60 mph (100 km/h) needs some five minutes to cover this distance of 5 miles (8 km), so in other words, the rocket must move at a speed three hundred times faster than that of the car! If the velocity of the carrier rocket is increased beyond the first cosmic velocity, the elliptic orbit of the satellite will be larger, since the apogee (the point of orbit furthest removed from the surface of the earth) is then removed

In the early 1960s, AB Wasa Spisbrödsfabrik at Filipstad, Sweden, erected this highly automatized combined mill and bakery for the production of crispbread. (a) At one end of the factory, the raw material, grain, is unloaded from lorries and railway cars. The grain is stored in silos (b) while it is analyzed for, among other things, protein content. When the tests are finished, the grain undergoes preliminary screening (cleaning) (c) and is brought to one of several classification silos (d), depending on its quality. The correct amounts of grain of different qualities for each

even further from the earth. By correcting the velocity of the satellite at suitable points on the orbit, the perigee (the point of orbit closest to the surface of the earth) can be changed until, for example, the orbit alters and becomes more or less circular. If the velocity of the carrier rocket exceeds a certain limit, the satellite will, however, become a spacecraft and travel out into the planetary system. This magic limit is 6.946 miles (11.178 km) per second (about 25,000 mph, or 40,240 km/h), a velocity usually called the velocity of escape, or the second cosmic velocity. It is about forty per cent higher than the first cosmic velocity.

The overriding problem which the early space travel enthusiasts had to combat was how to construct a rocket engine with sufficient propellant force to accelerate a spacecraft to this "astronomical" velocity, which is about twenty times that of a rifle bullet leaving the muzzle. And the only rockets of the 1920s and 1930s were fireworks and the life-saving rockets for shooting lines to ships in distress. If a rocket is to reach out into space, its motor must be able to lift not only its own fuel at the start, but also the oxygen which, later, is needed for combustion. In space, gunpowder rockets are not enough. Pioneering contributions in the area of rocket engines were made primarily by the American Robert H. Goddard (1882–1945), who published his now classic work, *A Method of Reaching Extreme Altitudes*, as early as 1919. In it he describes different liquid-fuelled rockets, and in 1926, he managed to get the first liquid-fuelled rocket to take off, the fuel being hydrocarbons and liquid oxygen.

In 1927, a handful of enthusiasts in Breslau, inspired by Oberth's book mentioned earlier, formed the *Verein für Raumschiffahrt* ("The Society for Space Travel"), and within a year, the society had over five hundred members. The register of members contained not only Germans but also other Europeans and Americans who had been swept up by the huge wave of interest in space travel which was then flooding the world. The leading Soviet rocket experts Nikolaí A. Rynin and Jakov J. Perelman were members, as were the Frenchman Robert Esnault-Pelterie and the Austrian Count Guido von Pirquet. A year after the foundation of the society, Oberth was chairman and Willy Ley vice-chairman. In 1928, the latter presented a masterly book of popular science, *Die Möglichkeit der Weltraumfahrt* ("The Possibility of Space Travel"), to which many theoreticians and scientists had contributed. Space travel now became the object of headlines on the front pages of the daily press, largely helped by the German film of the same year, *Frau im Mond* ("The Girl in the Moon"), directed by the famous Fritz Lang, with Hermann Oberth as scientific advisor.

The time was now ripe—as Willy Ley put it in his book—to transfer the ideas of the theorists to the laboratory and from there to the workshop, where would be made the rocket motors to make space travel possible. The members of the Society for Space Travel put

this into practice in 1930 when, after much hardship, they managed to establish a laboratory for the development of liquid-fuelled rockets in a remote place outside Berlin. The zealots behind this project were Hermann Oberth and his assistants from the work on the film, Rudolph Nebel and Klaus Riedel, together with Willy Ley. They called their eventually well-equipped laboratory *Raketen Flugplatz* ("Rocket Aerodrome"). About a year later, this circle of pioneers was joined by a young engineer called Wernher von Braun (1912–76).

As an eye witness, and to a large extent the stimulus behind the spectacular development of the projects started at the Rocket Aerodrome, Willy Ley wrote a book in which he gives a personal, charming account of the labour pains of modern space adventure. The title of the book is *Raketen und Raumschiffahrt* ("Rockets, Missiles & Space Travel") of which the first edition was published in 1944, in the midst of a raging world war, and since then, over a dozen revised editions and translations have followed.

Robert H. Goddard's contributions in the field of rocket engines should in no way be underrated, but the basic technical progress leading up to the realization, in 1969, of man's immemorial dream to land on the moon was made at the German rocket base Peenemünde on the island of Usedom in the Baltic. Peenemünde was built between 1936 and 1940 and was the joint rocket-base of the army and the air force, rocket research being by this time no longer a private affair. The research and development done at Peenemünde, led mainly by the men who had earlier worked at the Rocket Aerodrome, is one of the most exciting chapters in the history of modern technology. We shall not go into detail here but return to the subject of automatic governing and control.

Willy Ley, like Oberth before him, stressed the fundamental importance of the automatic control of spacecraft. The first units built by the German Air Force, A1 and A2, were mainly intended for testing rocket engines, but it was soon realized that the most serious problem, once a practicable engine had been produced, was to achieve stability. "What was then known about rocket stability could have been written on a postcard, leaving some blank space", Willy Ley wrote in the book we have mentioned. For the third unit, therefore, the A3, the German navy provided an expert who had plenty of experience in stabilizing and aligning gun turrets, the classical problem of servomechanics. But this unit, the A3, was not successful either, because the control mechanism turned out to be inadequate, and after that, in 1942, another, then very advanced, control system was designed, with gyroscopes and accelerometers as the sensor organs and with electric servomotors to move fins which were made of the heat resistant metal molybdenum and placed in the gas jet from the rocket engine. To study the dynamic properties of this system, a mechanical simulator was built, its design being type of bread are then automatically weighed out and mixed in homogenization silos (*e*). (*f*) Preliminary operations control. (*g*) Silos where the various mixtures are stored while awaiting milling. (*h*) Vacuum treatment and conditioning of the grain. (*i*) Screening and sorting.

(*j*) Milling. (*k*) Laboratories. (*l*) Flour silos. Water, yeast, and salt are added to the flour, which is kneaded to a dough and allowed to rise (*m*). (*n*) Dough production control. When the dough has risen, it is formed into large cakes, which are allowed to rise on long conveyor belts (*o*), whereupon the cakes are brought through an oven (*p*). The

baked bread is then dried (*q*) and stored in silos (*r*). (*s*) Screening plant, where defective cakes are removed. (*t*) Sawing and packeting of the crisp-bread. (*u*) A metal detector—a safety measure in case some metal fragment has got into the dough. (*v*) Storage area for ready-packed crisp-bread. (*w*) Delivery department.

based on measurements obtained from a system for radio telemetering from rockets—another pioneering work. By that time, Willy Ley would have needed at least twelve dozen postcards.

This concentration of effort on solving the problems of control and stabilization was to produce A4, the unit which Herr Goebbels later called V2—V for *Vergeltungswaffe* ("retribution weapon"). When the first trial launchings were made with this weapon, it had been provided with extensive radio equipment for telemetering as well as for an attempt at radio control. One such A4 crashed in 1943 on Bornholm, where it was retrieved by Danish intelligence agents who sent photographs and drawings to England via Stockholm. Another went off course and crashed in southern Sweden at midsummer, 1944, and was passed on to the Allies, who in this way were given another warning of what was to come. But it was wrongly concluded that all these rockets were radio controlled. The tests had shown the German researchers that it was impossible to control the rockets with any great accuracy. They were aligned towards the area of destination, first Paris and then London, but once the rocket had been launched, its course could not be affected. The V2 was a mere terror weapon.

During the closing stages of the Second World War, work had been done at Peenemünde on other rocket projects, and engines with greater and greater propulsive power had been designed: the A9 was to be transatlantic. . . Wernher von Braun was arrested by the Gestapo because he talked openly about the possibility of sending objects into space. He was, however, released after the director of the Peenemünde base, General Walter Dornberger, had intervened and explained to the high officials that von Braun's ideas were useful for even more powerful retribution weapons. On the collapse of Germany, in May, 1945, Peenemünde and its whole arsenal of manufactured rockets fell into the hands of the Allies, and by July that year, three hundred freight cars of A4 rockets had arrived at the White Sands Proving Ground in New Mexico. Development work continued here, and the core of the research team was the same as that at the Rocket Aerodrome and Peenemünde.

The difficult of problems of stability and control had already been solved in Peenemünde, and these solutions are still fundamentally valid. Still, the control systems have become more and more sophisticated as further progress has been made in instrument and component technology, and in telecommunications. The simple but useful mechanical simulator built for the A4 has been replaced by computers which handle the navigation and check the function of all systems onboard the rocket.

The demands on course accuracy and velocity control of the first satellites, the Soviet Sputniks 1 and 2 (1957) and the American Explorer (1958), were not as high as they were to become twenty years later. The velocity of their carrier rockets had to exceed the circular

velocity enough to place the perigee at a safe distance from the earth. At this stage, there was no risk that the velocity of escape would be attained, because the rocket engine did not yet have the power necessary for this.

The take-off itself and the first ten seconds of flight are the most critical period when launching a rocket. At the moment of take-off, the stability of the rocket is about that of a pencil balanced on a finger-tip. But after only a few seconds, the rocket reaches a speed at which it can be steered, and its upward course then almost invariably follows that described by Oberth as early as 1929, which he called the synergic (energy saving) curve. Having held a vertical course for about ten seconds, the rocket changes its course gradually, moving on a slight incline towards the horizontal plane. If the rocket is moving east, its speed is accelerated by the rotation of the earth, which gives a certain fuel saving. The rotation speed of the earth at the equator is 1,525 ft (465 m) per second. On the latitudes where the two "satellite states", the Soviet Union and the United States, have their launching sites, this help amounts to about 1,148 ft (350 m) per second.

A rocket flying freely in space has course control and navigation problems of a totally different order. A correction wrong by only a fraction of a degree or one hundredth of a second can have fatal consequences, for all navigation in space must follow the laws of planetary motion which the German astronomer Johannes Kepler established in the seventeenth century. For a rocket, the least energy-consuming course from one planet to another, such as from the earth to Mars, is elliptic. These orbits are called Hohmann ellipses after the German Walter Hohmann, the city architect of Essen, who published calculations of cosmic orbits in Willy Ley's book of 1929.

The real trial of strength concerning the precision of control systems took place in 1964, when the American space probe Mariner 4 was launched to explore the planet Mars. The probe passed Mars at the predetermined distance of about 7,450 miles (c. 12,000 km) and took a great many television pictures of the surface of the planet. A more sophisticated Mariner probe was launched in 1977 to travel round the solar system and, after two years, it passed Jupiter and Saturn. The Americans, within the framework of their Gemini project, have worked to test a system for determining the speed and position of craft in space. By means of what is called the Doppler effect, it was possible, in 1979, to determine the position of a probe far out in interstellar space to within 10 ft (3 m) and its speed to an accuracy of one tenth of a millimetre per second. And remember, the velocity of escape is almost 7 miles (c. 11 km) per second! By choosing this measuring system, the Apollo project could be carried out with the great precision that many of us followed on our television screens.

The first moon landing by man was co-ordinated via radio links (1) to mission control (2) in Houston, Texas, where there was a huge computer staffed by 350 men supervising the whole operation.

The start took place on the morning of 16 July, 1969, at Cape Kennedy, Florida. (3) Apollo 11 on the launch pad during countdown. The cables to the cable tower have been disconnected. (4) The carrier rocket, a Saturn V, takes off with the Command and Service Module "Columbia" and the Lunar Module "Eagle". Three astronauts are on board: Edwin E. Aldrin, Neil A. Armstrong, and Michael Collins. During the first twelve seconds of the flight, the computer steers the craft south-east. (5) Two and a half minutes after blast-off, the first stage has burnt out and is discarded. The second stage is started and, only twelve minutes after takeoff, the craft has entered

the predetermined orbit round the earth. (6) Two and a half hours after blast-off, the third stage is fired, sending Apollo 11 off towards the moon. The moment for firing must be exact to within one hundredth of a second in order to send the rocket into an orbit within which its course can be corrected.

(7) When the last rocket stage has burnt out, "Columbia" is released from Apollo 11 and turns right round to dock with "Eagle", which has been kept in a "garage" in the last stage. The Houston computer directs the burnt-out rocket stage into an orbit round the sun. (8) "Columbia" and "Eagle" now begin their three-day long journey to the moon. During that time, the spacecraft is without any driving power and is only under the influence of universal attraction. When the spacecraft is halfway to the moon, the computer starts "Columbia's" rocket for a few

seconds, thus increasing the speed, which is then increased further when the spacecraft enters the moon's gravitational field.

(9) On the fourth day, the spacecraft enters into holding orbit round the moon. (10) On the thirteenth orbit, it is time for "Eagle", manned by Armstrong and Aldrin, to descend and land on the moon. The moment when "Eagle" is to fly on its own is carefully determined by the Houston computer. (11) On Sunday, 20 July, "Eagle" lands on the moon. The last twenty seconds of the descent are very dramatic, and despite the fact that the action is totally directed by Houston, Armstrong's pulse reaches 156 beats per minute. (12) The same day, Armstrong becomes the first man to set foot on the surface of the moon; Aldrin follows right behind him. In all, "Eagle" spends twenty-four hours on the moon. (13) With the

same precision as before, the computer starts "Eagle's" rockets and, six hours later, brings it to dock (14) with "Columbia", which, with Collins aboard, has stayed in holding orbit round the moon. Now that "Eagle" has finished its job, it is sent by Houston into an orbit round the moon and crashes onto its surface after several orbits.

(15) The rockets start and are driven for a few minutes, this time to send Apollo 11 back towards earth. (16) The Command and Service Module is fired off by its steering rockets a few minutes before the capsule, with the astronauts on board, re-enters the atmosphere. The conic capsule turns so as to be protected by the heat shield during the rapid descent. (17) After releasing a stabilizing parachute, the capsule is slowed down during the last part of its fall by three main parachutes.

A A Hohmann ellipse touches the orbits of both the start (*a*) and the target planet (*b*) and is the least energy-demanding path between two planets. However, it takes a missile longer to follow a Hohmann ellipse than any other ellipse between two planets. (*c*) The sun.
B The initial part of a space missile's synergic orbit. (*a*) During the first few seconds, the missile climbs vertically in order to reach sufficient dynamic stability. (*b*) The missile is then briefly guided in a somewhat smaller angle to the surface of the earth. (*c*) During the next phase, the missile's path is

levelled out, due to gravity.
(*d*) Before the second stage takes over, the missile is aimed upwards to increase the height of orbit.
C In 1842, the Austrian C.J. Doppler (1803–53) discovered that the frequency of a wave motion seems to vary if the wave motion is

emitted from a moving object while the observer is stationary. The radio transmitter of a missile continually emits electromagnetic waves in all directions, but since the missile is moving forwards, the waves do not expand concentrically but are "crowded" in front of it.

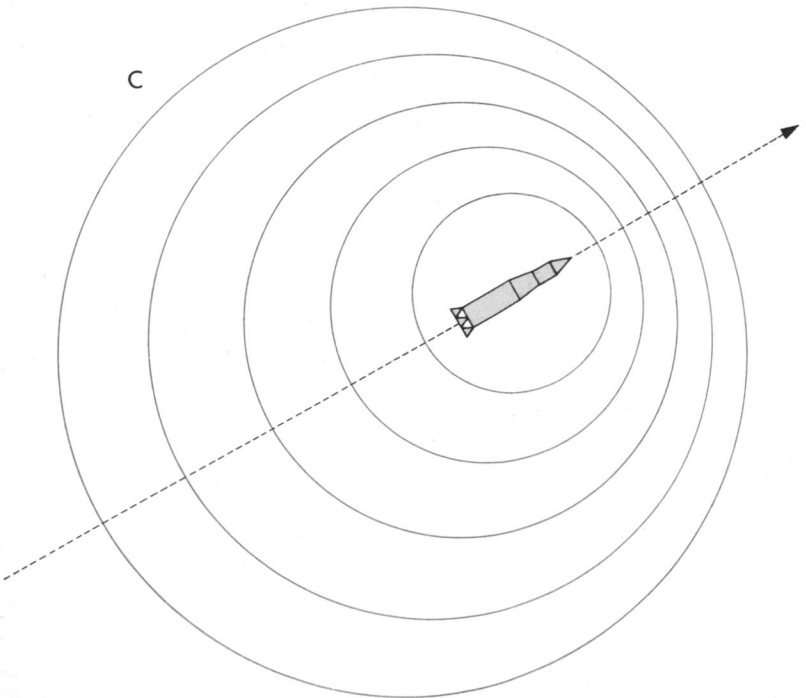

CHAPTER 9

THE MACHINE—
OUR DAILY COMPANION

In daily life, we constantly come across machines, although perhaps indirectly or in shapes we do not recognize; without machines and mechanical aids, we would not have, for example, our daily bread.

Were manual labour, without machines, to take over the whole chain of different procedures preceding the actual baking of the bread—preparation of the land, sowing, harvesting, threshing, and milling—and were the labourers to be paid what is considered a normal wage, the price of bread would far exceed the price of gold. In our industrialized world, such a procedure would be absurd. But that is how it used to be. The exhortation from the Bible, "In the sweat of thy face shalt thou eat bread" was, for many thousands of years, a hard, severe reality for mankind.

Let us look back in time to see what machines have been invented to facilitate the production of our daily bread. For at least the past ten thousand years, bread has been man's staple food, and while its taste and appearance have varied, the difference between the bread we have today and the bread baked by the Sumerians, for example, is not considered very great. Experience taught early man that bread became porous and tastier, if the dough was left to rise before being baked. It was discovered that flour, mixed with tepid water and then left in a warm place for a day, turned into leaven, which could be used to make the bread rise. The fermentation process could also be employed in producing beer from grain, and this art is probably as old as the art of baking bread. Most of the oldest river cultures have closely related words for bread, beer, and fermentation.

During antiquity, enormous numbers of people were required to ensure the supply of daily bread. It was heavy work to till the fields with primitive tools. A simple sickle was used for harvesting, being first made of flint and later of metal. Threshing was done with a flail or some other implement and was also very exhausting, and flour was ground by hand in mortars rather than querns. This process alone kept the women of each household busy for most of the working day. Most cultures seem to have considered it beneath male dignity to undertake this main household chore. In the Odyssey, there is a vivid description of the household at the court of Penelope, Odysseus' beautiful wife, who was considered to be more or less a widow, as her roving husband had been away for so long. She was besieged by suitors who had to be fed and housed while they were courting her! In order to have a sufficient supply of flour for her guests' bread, Penelope had to send messengers to summon all the women in the vicinity.

This was in the eighth century BC, but bread had been made in the same way for many thousands of years and was to continue like that for yet another few hundred years. For the common man—in other words, for nine-tenths of the population—it was hard work just to survive. The biography of one of these people might be summarized briefly like this: "He was born. He worked. He died."

A

A A late nineteenth-century threshing-machine, powered by a traction engine.

B In this double-screening threshing-machine from the start of the twentieth century, the hand-opened sheaves were fed in at *a*. The stalks were pulled onwards and beaten by a threshing drum (*b*) against a concave plate (*c*). Some of the grain and chaff then fell straight down to the riddle plates (*d*), while the straw and the rest of the grain were brought forward to the straw shaker (*e*), through which grain and chaff fell onto a plate (*f*) and slid down to *d*, while the straw was carried forward and was expelled at *g*. The riddle plates (*d*) had a slow, reciprocating movement, and the remaining short pieces of straw (cavings) were expelled at *h*. Grain, chaff, and dust were detached and fell onto plate *i*, whence they were brought into the main riddle (*j*), where air from a fan (*k*) blew away the light chaff and expelled it at *l*, while the heavier, unthreshed ears fell out of the threshing-machine at *m*. The dust was separated and expelled at *n*, while the grain was brought to the elevator (*o*) to be raised to the winnower (*p*). In the winnower, bristle and cusps were rubbed off the ears. The grain then entered another, though smaller, fan-equipped riddle (*q*), where more dust and other foreign particles were separated from it. Finally, small and imperfect grain, weed seeds, etc., were removed by the rotary screen (*r*), whereupon the clean grain fell into a sack (*s*).

As we saw in Chapter Four, milling was not mechanized until the first century BC, when the water-mill appeared and rapidly came into use throughout the Mediterranean world, spreading thence to the rest of Europe. The windmill appeared a little more than a thousand years later, and the first steam-driven mill—the Albion Mill in London—was put into operation in 1786. The women's task had now become big business.

Threshing was originally done by hand, or rather, in the hand, by rubbing the ears to loosen the corn. The first mechanization came with the introduction of the flail, an implement developed many thousands of years ago by several different cultures, which were geographically totally separated, and its form has changed only inessentially since then. Threshing by flail claimed most of the effort of the agricultural labour force, from harvest almost until Christmas. During the eighteenth century, several proposals were made for machines which would make threshing simpler, most of them being mechanical imitations of the flail. One of the many who interested

A

A A harvester, built by McCormick in c. 1880. The cut stalks were bound into sheaves by hand.
B A nineteenth-century mechanical harvester; (**1**) the mechanism as seen from the side, (**2**) the harvester as seen from above, (**3**) detail of the finger-knife. The harvester was pulled by two horses. The fingers (a) on a protruding girder (b) split the stalks into bunches, which were cut by a reciprocating, toothed knife (c). The knife was moved by a crank (d) on a wheel (e), which was driven through two bevel gears (f, g) by a small, toothed wheel engaging the inside of the central

wheel (h), which was driven by being in contact with the ground. A lever (i) could be used to disengage the bevel gears and stop the knife (c). If another lever (j) was depressed, a pawl engaged a ratchet-wheel (k) on g's shaft, and the whole machine came to a standstill. (l) Lever for raising and lowering the cutting mechanism.
C A mechanical harvester at work.
D In this modern Massey Ferguson combine harvester, the cut stalks are pulled towards the cutting table (a) with its knives by a rotating pick-up reel (b). Both a and b are vertically adjustable, as is a rotating

themselves in this was Christopher Polhem, whose threshing-machine was introduced in the 1720s and consisted of a number of vertical thresher bars which were raised and released alternately by a roller with cams. The thresher bars beat the grains out of the ears just like the flail, and some labour was thus saved. In the 1780s, the Scotsman Andrew Meikle introduced an entirely new principle for threshing-machines; in his invention, the corn sheaves were fed, ears first, between two rollers, the grain being extracted from the ear by the action of four thresher bars attached to a rotating horizontal cylinder, called the thresher drum, which worked inside a concave iron covering. The chaff was separated from the grain in a reciprocating shaker, which was placed underneath the cylinder. This design of Meikle's has remained basically unchanged to the present day, although some improvements have been introduced.

Mechanizing the work of harvesting was more difficult, and here as well, attempts were made to design imitative machines. In the 1790s, an Englishman built a harvester employing scythes which rotated beneath a two-wheel carriage and were activated, via a gearing, by the carriage wheels. As a solution, it was, however, rather impractical, if not lethal, and the machine is of little importance in the development of the mechanical harvester. The technical breakthrough did not come until the 1830s, when the young American Cyrus Hall McCormick designed a harvester with finger bars running level with the ground next to a horse-drawn, two-wheel carriage. The use of the machine soon spread in the United States, and in 1851, at the world exhibition in London, it was introduced in Europe. In England, the mowing-machine became common during the following few decades, and it soon spread throughout the rest of Europe as well.

As early as the 1860s, the first so-called distributors were introduced in the United States. These harvesters gathered the cut stalks into suitable bundles, which were then bound into sheaves by hand. But those who bound the sheaves were soon rationalized away, when the first automatic binder, another American invention, was

auger (c) that brings the stalks onto an elevator (d) leading to the threshing unit. Immediately in front of this unit, there is a stone bin (e). The grain is worked by the threshing cylinder (f) with its flails against

the concave arrangement (g), and the rear beater (h) then brings the straw onto the straw walkers (i) which transport the straw to the rear of the harvester, where it is allowed to fall to the ground. The grain passes through a top sieve (j), then slides from the grain delivery pans (k) and down through a sieve cascade (l), where chaff and dust are separated from the grain by blasts of air from a triple fan (m). Finally, the grain is transported by a feed auger to the grain tank, whence it can be loaded directly onto a lorry by means of an unloading auger (n). (o) Engine compartment. (p) Exhaust pipe. (q) Drive wheels. (r) Steering and brake wheels.

introduced in 1875. These developing stages of the harvester, the distributor, and the automatic binder, however, did not achieve very widespread use in Europe until after the First World War.

But what about the combine harvester? The first tentative attempts to design such a device were made in the United States only about ten years after McCormick invented his harvester, but the first machines for combined harvesting and threshing appeared in California in the 1870s. These were veritable technical monsters, drawn by eighteen pairs of horses and operated by a team of five men. These extraordinary combines were gradually improved, and by the 1920s, they had developed into automatic machines which could be operated by one or two men. In Europe, the combine first began to gain ground after the Second World War, but it was not in common use until the 1960s.

The last stage of the long process of obtaining our daily bread is

A A copperplate engraving from an edition of Frontinus's work on the aqueducts of Rome, published in Padua in 1722. The illustration shows the cross-section of an aqueduct with two conduits, and of another with three.
B In the English town of Canterbury, a vast system of water-works and sewers was built in the area around the cathedral in the twelfth century. The water came from a source some 1,300 yds (1,200 m) from the cathedral and passed through several settling-tanks before flowing, in leaden pipes, through the north town wall (a) and into the cathedral area. (b) Reservoirs. Part of the water entering the fish-pond (c) was used to flush the latrines in the grandly dimensioned *necessarium* (d), which had been erected for the employees

in this ecclesiastical centre. The sewer system also drained rainwater from the area. It emptied into the town ditch. The illustration is based on a contemporary drawing, from probably just after the completion of the system in 1153.

today executed in highly automated bakeries which are becoming more and more like chemical process industries, even to the extent of being computer controlled. Still, many people find pleasure and satisfaction in baking their own bread. And this becomes much easier, if they have labour-saving domestic appliances for kneading and thermostat-controlled electric ovens for baking.

Bread production is only one of many examples of the rôle of machines in modern society or—if you will—in the rationalization and automation of agriculture. A hundred years ago, about four-fifths of the population in most of the now industrial countries were employed in agriculture, which was then quite rightly called a "principal occupation", while only one-fifth lived in towns, being employed in trade, administration, and industry. Today, the ratio is the reverse, but the production per capita of those working in agriculture is considerably higher than a hundred years ago.

Another example of the rôle machines play in our daily life is in the production of butter and cheese, which like that of bread, has always played a key rôle in the agricultural household and has its origins in the earliest farming cultures. For thousands of years, butter was made by briskly beating cream in a container until the globules of fat in the cream stuck together to produce lumps which were then kneaded by hand into a mass of butter. The very large quantities of cream required for butter production were obtained by skimming milk which had been left to stand for a day or so in shallow troughs. On larger farms, a lot of people were needed merely to do this, and it was a task which required both routine and skill. Even when the first agricultural machines were introduced, followed by a wave of enthusiasm for the rationalization of agriculture, it was considered impossible to mechanize the skimming of milk. It has been mentioned briefly in Chapter Five that Gustaf de Laval managed to solve this problem. At the time, de Laval was working at the Kloster Iron Foundry Works in Sweden, one of the few small iron works to survive the rationalization which, during some ten years, had reduced the number of iron works from about seven hundred to barely three hundred. The Kloster iron works had managed to survive this painful period by merging with several other small works, each of which had considerable farming and forest lands. The forests supplied the raw materials for the charcoal used in the blast furnaces. After the merger, things went well for the iron works, but the question arose as to how the farms with their great labour forces could be rationalized. The enterprising owner of the works, J. F. Lagergren, presented Gustaf de Laval with this problem, and they decided to see if anything could be done about the skimming of milk, since some new ideas pertaining to this had been circulated recently in the trade journals.

After a long period of extensive experimentation, de Laval had his continuous-process cream separator ready. It exploited centrifugal force to separate the lighter cream from the heavier skimmed milk. In 1878, he took out a patent for the separator, and large-scale manufacture began in the early 1880s. The demand was immediately considerable, not only in Sweden, but also internationally. With the invention of the separator, yet another task of the country household had been taken over by a machine.

For more than fifty years, the separator was indispensable on both large and small farms all over the world. Even after the production of butter and cheese had been taken over by central dairies in the 1920s and 1930s, many farms kept a manual or electric separator for domestic use.

The Invisible Product

The vitally necessary machines which have just been described give highly tangible products. However, like all other industrialized processes in our society, they also produce something else. This product is invisible, or rather, immaterial, although it is indeed noticeable to everyone today: increased leisure time.

Most of us would reject indignantly the statement that we all have slaves who labour and drudge for us. Still, it is true. We have already come across quite a few of these "slaves"—in the shape of machines which, today, do a lot of the work that was really hard labour some generations ago. Most of these machines are electrically powered. In Sweden, each person consumes about 3 kW of electric power daily. A human slave develops a maximum of 100 W, if he works continuously. In other words, each one of us has at his disposal thirty "slaves" working round the clock, performing a number of different tasks. Most of them work, however, behind the scenes. We do not meet them eye to eye, but they are there. For example, when we turn a water tap, several "slaves" are responsible for the cleanliness of the water. Others take care of the waste water.

It might be appropriate to take a brief look at the development of the different techniques for supplying cities with water. The most famous installations of this kind are the Roman aqueducts. During the fourth century BC, Rome developed into a large, unhygienic city; infant mortality was high, and the average life expectancy was only a little over twenty. The eminent statesman Appius Claudius Caecus realized that, first of all, the problem of improving living conditions in Rome had to be solved through an assured supply of food and water; what we would today call the infrastructure. First of all, he caused a road to be built, running south through the agricultural districts to Capua near Naples. This—the *Via Appia*—was finished in 312 BC, and agricultural goods began to flow into the still growing city. A few years later, work was begun on the first large aqueduct, the *Aqua Appia*, which was finished in 305 BC. It was over 10 miles (c. 17 km) long and ran to a large extent underground. The growth of the admirable technology developed by the Romans for building aqueducts dates from this time. The *Aqua Appia* supplied central Rome with water, but as the city kept growing, it became necessary to build another aqueduct some decades later. This was called the *Anio Vetus*, was 41 miles (66 km) long, and diverted water from the river Anio. It was finished about 265 BC, and since its capacity greatly exceeded that of the *Aqua Appia*, the supply of water to the city was assured for the next hundred years. The next aqueduct, the *Aqua Marcia*, was built about 145 BC and was no less than 57 miles (91.7 km) long.

In ancient Rome, arrangements were also made to dispose of sewage. As early as the sixth century BC, work was begun on the large sewer, the *Cloaca Maxima*; it is in part still in use. It had initially been built to drain the marshes where the Forum was later built. The *Cloaca Maxima* was extended bit by bit and given a super-structure of solid stone vaults.

From the beginning of the Christian era, the water supply of the Eternal City was supervised by a water department under the direction of the *curator aquarum*. One holder of this office was an eminent engineer called Sextus Julius Frontinus (30?–104) who devoted much energy to improving and extending the whole system of aqueducts. He summarized his experience in a thick volume, *De aquis urbis Romae*, ("On the Waters of the City of Rome"), completed in 97. This work set the standards for water supply in other cities throughout the Roman Empire. Magnificent ruins of Roman aqueducts are still in existence, for example in Segovia and Tarragona in Spain, and near Nîmes in France. Frontinus's work, however, eventually fell into oblivion but was rediscovered in the eighteenth century, when several annotated editions were published. As late as 1858, a German translation of the book appeared.

The Roman Empire and Roman technology deteriorated together,

and in several places the Church took over responsibility for the water supply and for maintaining the aqueducts. The task was more than it could handle, and after a few hundred years, the aqueducts could no longer serve their purpose. By that time, however, a guild of specialists in water supply had been created under the protection of the Church, and when the monastic orders began to spread over Europe, they took their technique with them. There are many examples of monasteries which had extensive installations for the supply of water. The pipe lines from the source of supply were usually made from hollowed-out logs, connected with cast-iron collars. Indoors, pipes of lead or bronze were used. In ancient Rome, incidentally, all pipes for the detailed distribution of water were of lead (there were about twenty different standard dimensions). But lead is a poisonous metal, and it is to be feared that a common cause of death in Rome was lead poisoning.

C

C Part of the Croton aqueduct.
D The shock siphon for raising water was invented in the eighteenth century. It was mounted so that it was situated a couple of yards below the surface of the water about to be raised. When the shock valve (*a*) was open, water

flowed in through the pipe (*b*) and ran out at *a* until its speed had increased enough for *a* to be lifted by it. Then the water's rapid progress suddenly came to a halt. Because of the ensuing pressure increase, the valves (*c*) of a partly air-filled dome (*d*) were opened, and water was forced through them. The air pressure in *d* then increased, the valves (*c*) were closed once more, and water was forced up through an ascending pipe (*e*). When the rapid flow of water was abruptly stopped, its direction was reversed, and a negative pressure occurred in *b*. A valve (*f*) then opened, and a little air entered. Valve *a*, too, was opened by the pressure decrease, and water could again enter *b*, when *f* was closed.

The monastic methods for providing a water supply were applied in various European cities in the Middle Ages, but the system was difficult to maintain: the wooden pipes rotted easily, and systems often fell into decay. The inhabitants of the cities had then to return to getting their household water from public or private wells.

Whatever arrangements were made for water supply in mediaeval cities, drainage was not too well provided for. The streets were flanked by ditches, only rarely dressed with stone, and people threw rubbish of all sorts into them. It is easy to imagine the situation. Hygienic conditions were appalling, and the population was afflicted with disease and epidemics. The ravages of the Black Death in the 1340s opened the eyes of the surviving administrators in many cities to the sanitary situation. The prosperous trading towns of Flanders were, relatively speaking, spared from the plague, because, in the early fourteenth century, rigorous laws had been introduced prohibiting any kind of contamination of streets and water courses. This legislation set the pattern for an Urban Sanitary Act which came into force in England in 1388 and which prohibited contamination of ditches and water courses under pain of severe penalty.

During the technical revolution of the fifteenth and sixteenth centuries, piston pumps came into use for the draining of mines. This pump technology (hydraulics) developed mainly in southern Germany, whence came the use of pumps to provide cities with water. The water pump is, in fact, the first machine we have come across so far in this short review of water and drainage technology. The Roman aqueducts did not need pumps—gravity did the work.

In the eighteenth century, the development of hydraulics and the rediscovery of Frontinus's work on the Roman aqueducts led to renewed attempts to supply cities with water, steam being used at an early stage to power the pumps. As a rule, however, hollowed-out logs were used for pipes, for at this time, metal pipes were made manually and, anyway, could withstand only very limited pressure. These limitations greatly hampered early attempts to pump water by steam and held back water supply technology in general.

In the nineteenth century, the water systems of most large cities were expanded; new techniques and methods were gradually introduced, steam power came into increasing use, cast-iron and steel pipes came onto the market, and purification plants began to be built. An example of this development is the extension of New York's water-supply system. During the eighteenth century, when New York was becoming more important as a city, its inhabitants had to get water, which was often foul, from public wells, although one of them, the "Tea Water Pump", was famous for its fine, clear water. It was situated on today's Park Row, and water from there was distributed in horse-drawn tank wagons to households, where it was almost a luxury item.

In 1799, the private Manhattan Company was founded, and it built a waterworks system with pipes of hollowed-out logs, establishing wells and reservoirs so that, after some ten years, two thousand households in New York were thus supplied with water. Two 18-horsepower steam-engines were installed to pump water up to reservoirs. In 1800, New York had a population of about sixty thousand, and the city was growing rapidly.

The city authorities of the time realized that they, too, had to contribute, and in 1829, they started to build a waterworks system which was supplied with water from a reservoir of over 175,000 gallons (180,000 US gallons or 800,000 l) situated near Union Square, which was then considered far uptown of lower Manhattan. The main pipes were now of cast iron and had a diameter of 12 in (30 cm), and the water was pumped up from a nearby well to the reservoir by a 12-horsepower steam-engine.

By 1832, the population had increased to two hundred thousand,

and only a few years later, the city fathers realized that they had to look for new sources to ensure an adequate water supply. Their choice fell upon the Croton River, a tributary of the Hudson, which is 42 miles (about 70 km) from New York; a dam was built on the Croton, and from it ran an aqueduct, in places as architecturally resplendent as its Roman predecessors. It took five years to build the aqueduct, which was completed in 1842, and there was a stately inaugural ceremony, also based on the ancient Roman model. During the following decades, new and larger dams were built to increase the supply of water to the Croton aqueduct. The population in New York, however, was soon two million, and by the 1880s, it had become necessary to build yet another Croton aqueduct. This was completed in 1893 after eight years' work and was a mountain tunnel, cut with pneumatic drills and dynamite, and lit by electricity.

By the turn of the century, it once more became obvious that even greater water resources were required, for the population had risen to 3.5 million. Discussion began of a very bold project to supply New York with water from the rivers and lakes of the Catskill Mountains, which lie about 90 miles (150 km) from the city. While many engineers considered this wholly unrealistic, construction work nevertheless began in 1907, after careful planning. Up to seventeen thousand workers were employed on this project, which featured several new construction methods. The aqueduct was taken into service in 1917, and since then the Catskill system has been extended in several stages. Today, New York has aqueducts and water tunnels which in length and capacity greatly surpass their ancient Roman prototypes.

Waterworks in large modern cities are huge plants with technically sophisticated equipment for filtering the water, and treating and controlling it in other ways. In the past few decades, these plants have become more and more like large-scale chemical-process industries. They have been automated to a large extent and, in many cases, are controlled by process computers.

Waste Disposal over the Centuries

We have today a comprehensive technology for the disposal of all the waste our society produces. However, it is instructive to consider how *Homo sapiens* has rid himself of his rubbish throughout the ages, for the modern ecological debate seems often to doubt whether man is rational in this respect.

On excavation, neolithic refuse heaps, or what are called kitchen middens, have yielded much interesting information about, for example, the food that was then eaten. The people of the Stone Age gathered their refuse in one place, not to please archaeologists, but to keep their living quarters tidy, an instinct that, in the early towns, became a necessity. The oldest town-building cultures disposed of their refuse in ways which indicate as highly developed a technology as that required to build *quanaats*, for instance. In the towns of Harappa and Mohenjo-Daro, which came into being during the early culture of the Indus valley in the fourth millennium BC, houses were usually three storeys high and were equipped with chutes, flushed with water supplied through pipes leading from the kitchen and the lavatory. The chutes were used for the immediate disposal of solid and liquid refuse and ran out into an underground tunnel where the refuse was collected in a container, one for each chute. These containers were then transported on ox carts to a place where the refuse was regularly burnt. Most of the transport routes were underground. The first excavation in this part of the Indus valley took place in the 1920s under the supervision of the eminent British archeologist Sir R. E. Mortimer Wheeler, whose work revealed, among other things, this technically very sophisticated refuse-disposal method. Since the mid-1970s, an American research team has been engaged in further excavations that, it is hoped, can answer the question of how the refuse was burnt. It is probable that they used furnaces designed to achieve temperatures high enough to reduce to ashes even the most moist form of refuse. Experience may have taught the engineers of the Indus culture that the temperature is considerably increased if the smoke is allowed to preheat the combustion air, a principle applied in modern reverberatory furnaces.

The technique of refuse combustion spread from the Indus valley via the Sumerian culture of Mesopotamia to the Mediterranean, where it was obviously commonly known and applied during the last millennium BC. We have evidence of this in the biblical simile about the burning Gehenna, which was nothing more than the refuse-disposal unit of Jerusalem. It was equipped with a "reverberatory furnace", in which everything was burnt to ashes at a consuming temperature. If that technique had not been commonly known in this cultural sphere, the Gehenna simile would have been meaningless.

The total combustion of refuse was an important technical advance that, together with many other factors, permitted the formation and continued existence of the early town cultures. When these cultures declined, this form of disposal fell into oblivion. Not until our own century has refuse again been incinerated on a large scale, now in technologically efficients units, in many of which metal can be extracted from the refuse before it is burnt.

Only in the more prosperous parts of medieval Europe were efforts made to solve the problems of refuse disposal. During the Renaissance, sewers were built on the Roman model in the larger cities, and by the middle of the seventeenth century, the system in Paris had grown to comprise over 10 miles (16 km) of sewers. The population of the city was then about 500,000, and it expanded very slowly; about 1800, the population was around 550,000 and the length of the sewers was slightly more than 12 miles (20 km). During the following decades, however, Paris expanded rapidly, and by the early 1830s, the population was nearly 800,000. Neither the water supply nor the sewage system could cope with such a large population, and the city authorities were forced to draw up plans for a large-scale expansion of the system in anticipation of an even more rapid increase of population. Work began in 1833, and several of the most eminent French engineers were employed. The result would show the way for future sewer development. When the project began, Paris had about 24 miles (40 km) of sewers. By 1850, the population exceeded one million, and in the early 1860s, it had increased to 1.7 million. By then, however, the sewage system comprised over 215 miles (350 km) of pipelines and was arranged along radically different principles, being built to cope with the needs of a future population of 2.5 million. In 1951, when Paris celebrated its 2,000th anniversary as a city, its inhabitants numbered 2.8 million.

It was not until the twelfth century that London took on the character of a political capital. In the following centuries, it grew into a typical mediaeval town. To begin with, the river Fleet provided a natural outlet, a "*Cloaca Maxima*", but it became totally silted up in the fourteenth century and was no longer navigable. A drainage system was then gradually built, with the Fleet as the "main pipe". Mediaeval conditions obtained in London until the Great Fire of 1666, when the whole town centre was reduced to ashes and ruins. This devastating catastrophe, however, had one positive effect: the city fathers were entirely free to create a new town plan. When the enormous projects following the fire were being realized, several of London's famous monumental edifices were erected, and the city acquired a completely new and modern look. An organization was set up to dispose of household refuse, which was gathered up in lay-stalls on the street corners and then transported away. Legislation enjoined house owners to keep clean the street in front of their houses, a law that was also applied in many other places.

A cross-section of a street in Paris at the end of the nineteenth century. Directly beneath the paving is the sewage-disposal system with its tunnels and waste pipes. The catacombs are situated considerably further down.

A Sir John Harington's water closet, as presented in his *Metamorphosis of Ajax*, 1596. At the top, the cistern with its overflow (*a*)—and swimming fish—can be seen. In the basin, a pipe (*b*) protrudes from the cistern. The flow of water was stopped by tightening a screw (*c*) with a key *d*. The fortunate owner of this water closet was encouraged to empty the basin twice a day (a long rod was used to unscrew the plug from hole *e*) and to leave fresh water to a depth of half a foot standing in it.

B Joseph Bramah's water closet, patented in 1778. When a handle (*a*) was pulled, a flap valve in the bottom of the basin was opened downwards by a spring-loaded lever (*b*) turning a crank (*c*) on the valve's hinge bolt. At the same time, a two-armed lever (*d*) was turned by *b*. A line attached to the lever's left arm ran to the cistern's spring-loaded flap valve, which was opened so that water could run down through a pipe (*e*) to flush the basin. (*f*) Overflow.

C A complicated nineteenth-century English water closet.

D A water closet from the beginning of the twentieth century. (*a*) Cistern with siphon arrangement. A water-lock (*b*) stopped odours from entering the room from the sewer (*c*). The ventilation pipe (*d*) emerged above the roof of the building.

For centuries, the river Fleet remained the main drain of much of the London sewage system. It had, finally, to be built over, for it stank, and flowed through the most densely populated areas. In the 1830s and 1840s, the riverbed was made into a revetted sewer on top of which a road was built.

This London version of the *Cloaca Maxima*, however, was by no means even an adequate method of disposing all the waste, and the excess—in a mediaeval fashion that persisted into the seventeenth and eighteenth centuries—was thrown into the ditches along the streets or, at best, into the gutters. The turning point for London was the "rediscovery" of the water-closet, a primitive version of which had been designed as early as 1596 by Sir John Harington, although it was not until the end of the eighteenth century that, as the water-supply system was extended, improved versions were actually installed. However, the water-closets could not be connected to the sewage system; instead, each house had a cesspool. The idea was to empty the pools regularly, but this rarely happened, and overflows with the most devastating consequences were quite common. Moreover, the early water-closets had no water seal, which meant that an abominable stench would fill the whole house. In 1782, the water seal was invented by John Gaillait, but not until the first decades of the nineteenth century did it come into common use.

The population in London, and the number of water-closets, increased sharply during the first half of the nineteenth century. The closets were now connected to the sewage system, which became, consequently, greatly overloaded. A number of water courses like the Fleet had been rebuilt into sewage systems, and as they all flowed into the Thames, the river became seriously contaminated. Most of London's supposedly fresh water was taken from the Thames, and the inevitable consequence was serious cholera epidemics, mainly in 1849 and 1853, when almost twenty thousand people died. This prompted the formation of a commission to plan the restructure of the whole drainage system, extending it sufficiently to dispose of the sewage of three to four million inhabitants. Under the guidance of Sir Joseph William Bazalgette (1819–91), a gigantic project was planned and, in 1856, presented. It was to take almost twenty years to complete. The main idea was to build intercepting sewers parallel to the Thames and to let them gather up the contents of the numerous sewers, which up to then had run out into the river. The sewage was then to be conducted to a place about 12 miles (20 km) downstream from London Bridge before being let out there into the Thames.

Work on this project commenced towards the end of the 1850s. The intercepting sewers were built as tunnels whose cross-sections in many cases were larger than the tunnels of the later underground railway. Over 90 miles (150 km) of tunnels were built, and by 1875, Bazalgette's magnificent project was finished. The sewage flowed by gravity through most of the tunnels, but in a couple of places it was necessary to pump, and the machines required to take care of the huge amounts of sewage were gigantic. Each pump station was equipped with eight 140-horsepower steam-engines, each driving two double-acting piston pumps, with cylinders of a diameter of 43.5 in (115 cm). The first of four such pump stations was completed in 1865 and was then described by a London magazine as "perhaps the finest specimen of engineering work in the country".

Towards the end of the nineteenth century, people realized that sewage had to be purified before being released into lakes and rivers. At a very early stage, attempts were made to precipitate the contamination chemically with such precipitants as lime, alum, compounds of iron and aluminium, and iron sulphate. Chemical precipitation is what we today call the "third stage" of sewage treatment. It means that one retrieves the nutritive salts which would otherwise fertilize a choking vegetation in the watercourse into which the purified water is let out. Above all, it is the modern synthetic detergents which are responsible for the high content of nutritive salts in sewage, and in the 1880s, that problem did not exist.

The basis of modern sewage technology must be considered to have been laid in 1895, when the Englishman Cameron took out a patent for the sedimentation, or septic, tank in which the sewage is collected and the organic substances break down as they decompose, a relatively slow process. The sludge has to be removed about once a year—the interval depends on the relative size of the tank. The septic tank soon became very popular and was manufactured in all sizes, from those large enough for a family house to installations adequate for large cities. Over the years, several different versions of Cameron's original design have been invented, but the principle is unchanged in the septic tanks manufactured today.

The disadvantage of the septic tank is that it must be emptied at regular intervals. In the United States, however, a similar but continuous method was tried out in the 1910s, the idea being to lead the sewage relatively slowly through a long, narrow pool, at the bottom of which the sludge gathered. Then the sludge was "activated" by air blown into the pool, thus causing the micro-organisms in the sludge to reproduce themselves rapidly under the stimulation of the increased oxygen supply. They fed on the organic substances in the sewage. The activated sludge was then taken back upstream and mixed with the incoming sewage which, surprisingly soon, became decontaminated. A full-scale plant for the treatment of sewage by the activated-sludge process was built in Milwaukee, Wisconsin, in 1915.

Thereafter, the process was developed mainly in Great Britain, where, since the last decades of the nineteenth century, methods of biological treatment had been tried out under the guidance of the energetic Sir Edward Frankland, who would today be called an ecologist. "Biological beds" of coke or cinders were used to filter the sewage, but the oxygen supply in them was insufficient, however, for the growth of micro-organisms, a problem that was solved by blowing in large quantities of air. From the 1920s onwards, the activated-sludge process became the most important method of sewage treatment, and it has since been improved, mainly in recent times, due to the stimulus derived from the increasing general awareness of the importance of the environment.

The Environment and Technology

The main purpose of the "reverberatory furnace" in Gehenna, of the *Cloaca Maxima*, and of the other installations described here, has been to remove refuse from man's immediate environment. It is true that, in many cases, the more distant environment has suffered because of this. It is easy to imagine the ancient refuse-disposal units, like Gehenna, spreading clouds of belching, stinking smoke. Towards the middle of the last century, however, as refuse disposal became sanitation technology, its goal was the protection of the immediate environment, one example being Sir Joseph Bazalgette's ambitious project to divert London sewage into that part of the Thames that did not flow through the city itself. At the outflow of the intercepting sewers, however, about 12 miles (20 km) downstream from London Bridge, the effect of a rising tide was to prevent the dispersal of the outflowing sewage. Treatment plants were built here after a catastrophe in 1878, when an excursion boat capsized and sank in front of a sewer outlet. Over six hundred people died, and it was found that most of them were not drowned but poisoned.

The treatment plants were enlarged successively during the twentieth century, but many of them were destroyed by bombing during the Second World War. The situation again became precarious, and by the early 1950s, precise continuous analysis of the water in the Thames was begun to determine the measures that should be taken against contamination. It was immediately established that the Thames was a dead river, devoid of fish and all other living creatures. A plan for the total decontamination of the Thames was presented in 1961, an admirable plan with the direct purpose of protecting the environment by technical means.

The cleaning of the Thames took sixteen years and entailed, among other things, the building of several large treatment plants, of which the two largest, at Beckton and Crossness, now take care of sixty per cent of London's sewage and are considered the most sophisticated and automated in Europe. At strategic points along the river, air pumps have been installed to aerate the water, thus helping to increase the chances of survival for living organisms. The whole project cost about £125 million ($250 million) and was completed in 1977. The Thames now supports a rich variety of life and is a fine example of how technology can remedy even the worst environmental problems.

What Can Be Done About Air Pollution?

It is unlikely that anything was done about the belching smoke from Gehenna, but measures to combat air pollution were taken surprisingly early in history. In the thirteenth century, coal was first used for heating in England, but it was bituminous—really more like bitumen than coal—and was gathered on the shores of eastern England, whence it was transported by sea to London. When this sea-coal burnt, it gave off an acrid, thick smoke, especially in rainy and foggy weather, and the contaminated air became difficult to breathe. A decree of 1306 prohibited the use of such coal in London—but only when parliament was in session! The decree was not respected, and capital punishment was introduced for the offence, the first offender being hanged in 1308. It is interesting to note that similar events took place at about the same time in Mexico, where bituminous coal was also used as fuel, and a ban on it was declared and backed up by capital punishment. However, the Mexican authorities were more refined than the British. Their offenders were locked up in a cage—and smoked to death.

In England, and especially in London, frequent measures were taken against air pollution in the fifteenth and sixteenth centuries. In 1661, that chronicler of many talents, John Evelyn (1620–1706), published a thundering polemical pamphlet against the bad air of the capital. It had the title *Fumifugium*, which can be freely translated as, "Get Rid of the Smoke". The measures Evelyn suggested included the planting of trees along all of London's streets. The trees should be "fragrant", although he did not say how he thought that could be arranged. The pamphlet was printed in several editions, one of which was widely read in the last years of the eighteenth century, when the steam-engine was coming into common use, and when many people realized that this was a new source of air pollution. During the first decades of the nineteenth century, when steam had gained considerable ground, the problem became apparent. The growing industrial cities became more and more polluted, and in 1819, parliament felt obliged to appoint a commission to investigate both the damaging effect coal smoke could have on health and the technical means that could be used to reduce or prevent the discharge of smoke. High chimneys and soot traps were suggested, but no legislation was passed on this occasion. When the railway began to spread in Great Britain, however, new commissions were appointed, and these pushed through laws about the control of the discharge of smoke from both locomotives and industry.

When the great breakthrough of industrialism in the United States came in the 1850s, laws were introduced in several states regulating, among other things, the lowest acceptable height of factory smokestacks. In 1864, the first offender against these laws, a factory owner in St. Louis, Missouri, was convicted. In general, a lively and remarkably "modern" ecological debate was carried on in the United States in the latter part of the 1860s. Immigration was on the increase, and many engineers and politicians realized that, even in that vast country, densely populated areas would become established in due course.

By the 1970s, the whole of the industrialized world had become sharply aware of the necessity of protecting the environment against the consequences of industrialization. An entirely new technology began to develop to reduce the pollution of air and water from, for example, the steel and pulp industries. Forced on by increasingly stringent legislation, research and development work in this area managed to find technical solutions to problems which had long been regarded as insoluble. Today, a steelworks can be incomparably cleaner than it was only ten years ago, for the discharge of smoke can be reduced to a fraction of its earlier volume.

From the point of view of the environment, the pulp industry is traditionally the arch-villain. The pulp production process requires large volumes of water which are then badly polluted, and the smoke discharged is both harmful and stinking. At an early stage, the Swedish forestry industry became involved in a large joint research project, the result of legislation—and managed to achieve purification methods which are now being applied in pulp factories in many parts of the world.

But What About the Car?

In most countries, the 1970s have been a turning-point as regards the control of industrial pollution, but much still remains to be done. Ecological technology is advancing rapidly, and the public has been made aware of the values which are at stake. But although the engineers have managed to reduce industrial effluent considerably, there remains one bad source of pollution: the sharply increasing number of cars. The exhaust fumes from cars contain carbon monoxide and poisonous lead compounds. The rubber worn off the tyres of cars is washed away by rain water into natural water-courses and eventually ends up in the water table.

The situation has changed markedly since the first cars appeared in city streets around the turn of the century. "Horseless carriages" were then greeted as liberators from an almost chaotic situation. In New York, for example, the horse-drawn traffic was very lively, and the accident rate was high, due to the human (and also the animal!) factor. Moreover, working horses contributed to the contamination of the streets with large amounts of waste—over 1,000 tons of solid and 60,000 gallons (c. 200 cubic metres) of liquid waste every day! An army of tens of thousands of refuse collectors with horse-drawn carriages was needed to dispose of all this.

The car gave no waste at all, wasn't it wonderful? The little puffs from the exhaust were surely nothing to worry about? Anyway, there were so few cars.

But we know what has happened since. In many cities today, the exhaust fumes from cars are a real plague. There are three ways of reducing the harmful constituents of the exhaust fumes: the level of lead can be reduced, the engine can be equipped with an exhaust emission device, or the petrol engine can be abandoned completely. Some success has been achieved with the first two methods, and in many places, intensive research is going on into entirely new principles of propulsion, both regarding engines and fuels. It is not totally impossible that the steam car may return, perhaps propelled by hydrogen. A wonderful vision—a car running practically without noise, and with exhaust fumes consisting of pure steam!

There is, of course, a fourth way to reduce the damaging effects of

motoring on the environment, and that is to use *bicycles* to a larger extent. In this book we have met many impressive examples of engineering prowess, but the question is whether the bicycle is not the most perfect of all machines, from both the human and the technical point of view. It is also healthy, both for the environment and for the person using it. This wonderful machine has had a great impact on both industrial and cultural development. For this reason, we shall give the bicycle its own section.

The Bicycle—a Technical Beauty

The wheel has existed for at least five thousand years, and it is really quite remarkable that it took so long for someone to think of combining two wheels to make a steerable vehicle. The eminent Roman engineers, for example, had the technical ability to design a bicycle. And the inventive Italian and French engineers of the Renaissance built monstrous versions of four-wheel carriages but never designed a handy two-wheeler! From this point of view alone, the invention of the bicycle must be considered· extremely important. This occurred about 1816, when a German superintendent of forests, Freiherr Karl Friedrich Drais von Sauerbronn (1785–1851) designed his famous "running machine", a steerable bicycle propelled by kicking. The inventive forester became known all over Baden for his wild trips on

A Horse-drawn street-sweepers of this type were used in London and other places during the second half of the nineteenth century. The garbage container was secured with heavy chains (a), and the endless belt with its brushes (b) was driven by the wheel shaft by way of a gear transmission (c). By means of a worm gear (d) to which a chain (e) was attached, the driver could adjust the brush unit's angle to the ground. The gearwheel in d meshed with another gearwheel (f) on a shaft, from which a chain with a counterweight (g) hung over a wheel (h). The brushes brought the garbage up a chute (i) and into the container.
B A horse-drawn street-sprinkler from the end of the nineteenth century; (1) side view, (2) rear view.

Chains (a) ran from two levers (b) at the driver's seat over two blocks (c) each and down to a valve inside the water tank (d). When the driver lowered the levers, the valve was opened, and water could run out through the rear strainer plate.

the running machine, and he is said to have covered the distance between Mannheim and Schwetzingen in only one hour in 1817. It took the mail coach four hours to travel the same distance! It seems that the originator of the steerable bicycle must have had the stamina of a star athlete. Drais was complacently satisfied with his invention, taking out a patent for it in 1818. He would have nothing to do with the various improvements made in the following decades, for instance, the addition of pedals to the front wheel.

However, the first bicycle in the true sense of the word was made in France. Pierre Michaux (1813–83) and his son Ernest (1849–89) built a *vélocipède* for the 1867 world exhibition in Paris. It was modern in appearance. The wooden wheels were iron shod, and it was propelled by pedals which directly drove the front wheel.

In spite of being nicknamed "bone-shaker"—due to the iron-shod wooden wheels—this velocipede soon became popular, and, to meet the demand, the Michauxs were forced to find subcontractors. In 1869, an order for five hundred velocipedes went to a British sewing-machine manufacturer in Coventry, Josiah Turner, who thereupon re-formed his firm, naming it Coventry Machinists Co. But the Franco-Prussian war broke out just as the bicycles were ready for delivery, so Turner had to try to sell the vehicles on the home market. He was successful beyond expectation. The bicycle ap-

peared exactly at the right moment, just as a wave of enthusiasm for physical exercise was sweeping over England.

This was the beginning of an unusual development that resulted not only in the technical perfection of the bicycle, but also in a great boost to the progress of mechanical industry. Moreover, the bicycle literally paved the way for motoring, both from the technical point of view and because of the better roads demanded by cyclists.

In the 1870s, a new bicycle-manufacturing company was founded in Coventry by James Starley (1801–81), formerly a foreman at the Coventry Machinists Co. Together with his partners, William Hillman and B. Smith, Starley made a number of pioneering designs, beginning with the first penny-farthing, which had a large driving wheel with a diameter of 60 in (150 cm) and a smaller rear wheel with a diameter of 20 in (50 cm). The idea of this most extraordinary design had originally come from the Michauxs. The aim was to achieve higher efficiency. For each turn of the pedals, a large driving wheel will take you further than a small one.

It might be added that the penny-farthing, which has many bruised and broken limbs on its metallic conscience, was a mistake in the development of the bicycle. The penny-farthing is sometimes called the "ordinary" bicycle, which is a euphemism, since it is certainly far from ordinary. Still, in spite of its shortcomings, this design persisted for almost twenty years, and it, too, brought development further along, as the radially mounted spokes of the front wheel could not take the great strain, and to remedy this, Starley invented the tangentially spoked wheel, a design he patented in 1874 and still almost invariably applied to bicycle wheels.

The friction in the hubs and handlebars of the bicycles was high, but it could be lessened by the use of ball bearings. The ancient Romans used both ball- and roller-bearings, and the ball-bearing has been rediscovered several times in recent centuries, by, for example, the Englishmen Philip Vaughan (1794) and Louis Thirion (1862) and the Frenchman Jean Suriray (1869). From 1877 onwards, Thirion's bearing was used by Starley, in tricycles, but their price was disproportionately high compared to the price of the other parts. The balls were hand-ground, and this was a slow, laborious method. In 1883, the German Friedrich Fischer designed the first grinding machine for steel balls, and this made the mass production of ball-bearings possible. Friedrich Fischer was the son of Philipp Moritz Fischer, who was a manufacturer of sewing-machines and bicycles, both of which required large numbers of ball-bearings. The factory Friedrich Fischer founded in Schweinfurt for the manufacture of ball-bearings has grown today into a worldwide company.

In 1877, Starley's Coventry factory introduced frames made of steel tubes; this made it possible to produce a light, durable machine, well suited to its purpose. Since then, steel tube designs have found a very wide application in various areas of technology. For one thing, they were used in the first aeroplanes.

In 1879, power transmission by a gear and chain from the bicycle pedals to the rear wheel was introduced. This was a great step forward. The principle of the bicycle chain is included in Leonardo da Vinci's sketch books and had been rediscovered in France in the 1860s. In 1874, an improved version was patented by the Englishman Harry J. Lawson, and he began then to manufacture bicycles with such transmissions. However, the manufacturers found the chain to be a great headache. It may be a very simple construction, but it makes extremely high demands on manufacturing precision and on the durability of the material. Up to about 1900, broken chains were the most common fault with bicycles. The bicycle manufacturers' search for a remedy led them to cooperate with metallurgists in an attempt to produce new materials, new methods for hardening, and so on. They also had to develop machines for the mass production of bicycle chains. By the time mass production of automobiles began, technology had reached a point where the "bicycle" chain could be used in the power transmission of the car, which made even higher demands on the chain than did the bicycle.

From this point of view, the bicycle was the forerunner of the car. Chain drive for cars was, it is true, abandoned after about ten years and replaced by shaft drive, but even today, some car engines have chain drive, for example, to drive the cam shaft from the crank shaft. The "bicycle" chain has become a very useful component in all areas of mechanical engineering and now comes in all dimensions.

The main milestone in the development of the bicycle is the appearance of the Rover Safety Bicycle, manufactured by James Starley's nephew John K. Starley (1854–1901) and introduced on the market in 1885. Both its wheels were the same size, and it had a tubular frame of steel, and pedals with chain drive. The name "sa-

fety bicycle" was, of course, a criticism aimed at the penny-farthing, which was now becoming outdated. The Rover bicycle was an enormous success, and cycling soon had great numbers of devotees in various parts of the world. One important detail, which—if possible—increased the popularity of the bicycle even further, was introduced in 1888. That was the pneumatic rubber tyre, invented by the Scottish veterinary surgeon John B. Dunlop (1840–1921). His son had complained because his fine children's bicycle was so shaky and difficult to ride on uneven surfaces. It occurred to Dunlop that the wheels could be equipped with air-filled inner tubes covered by rubber tyres. The production of tyres and inner tubes soon got under way and greatly contributed to a standardization of bicycle wheels. Also, cycling became more comfortable. Once the safety bicycle with rubber tyres appeared, the modern bicycle had found its form.

A In 1818, Freiherr Drais von Sauerbronn demonstrated his "Draisienne" in Paris. It was propelled, like a scooter, by striking out with the feet. It had wooden wheels and lacked brakes.
B The first proper bicycle is usually

attributed to Pierre and Ernest Michaux, but it is not absolutely clear whether they or a mechanic of their firm, Pierre Lallement, first mounted pedals on the front wheel of a hobby-horse.

C Starley's and Hillman's Ariel bicycle of 1870 was manufactured under licence by Haynes and Jefferies at Coventry. On the front wheel hub was a cross-bar which was connected to the rim by two short, adjustable tie-rods. When the tie-rods were stretched, the rim was turned in relation to the hub, and the spokes were tightened.
D The British Facile bicycle of 1879

had a vertical pedal movement, and the pedals were mounted on levers to bring them closer to the ground.
E John Starley's Rover Safety Bicycle is considered to be the prototype of the modern bicycle. It had pedals with chain transmission, direct steering of the front wheel, an adjustable seat, and tangential spokes.

The bicycle as a machine was perfected in the 1890s, when some important details, such as the free wheel, the brake, and gears were introduced. In 1892, one of the first free wheels was patented by the Swedish inventor Birger Ljungström, who later used it in a bicycle design, the *Svea* velocipede, which he and his brother Fredrik had developed. The project was supported by the "dynamite king", Alfred Nobel. Instead of the normal rotary pedalling movement, the *Svea* bicycle had a vertical pedalling movement. The power was transmitted by a chain from each pedal to eccentric gear wheels on the free wheel of the rear hub. This device made it possible to change gears while the bicycle was moving. Also, the brake could be applied simply by pushing both pedals down at the same time.

In 1896, the *Svea* bicycle was introduced in England, where it gained many supporters, among them the well-known engineer and firearms designer Hiram S. Maxim. The New Cycle Company was

F The Svea bicycle. (*a*) Pedal. (*b*) A "chain", consisting of rope-twisted piano-wire. (*c*) An eccentric cam on the free-wheeling mechanism of the rear hub. The chain ran round a block (*d*) on the brake. When both pedals were pushed downwards simultaneously, the brake was pushed towards the rear wheel.

formed, and the bicycle was made in several different versions, including a bicycle rickshaw. However, in 1898, the English bicycle industry went through a recession, and the company was wound up. Only about a hundred bicycles were made, and these are now much sought-after collectors' pieces. In other words, the Ljungström hub was not the first free-wheel hub to be widely used. This honour instead befell one invented in 1898 by the German Ernst Sachs. He started to manufacture his "Torpedo" hub in Schweinfurt in 1900.

The attentive reader is sure to have noticed that the names of two well-established motor-cars have been mentioned above: Hillman and Rover. The bicycle manufacturer William Hillman went over in due course to manufacturing cars, and the great success Starley had with the Rover bicycle led to a change of the name of the company to The Rover Company. This company produced an electrically driven tricycle in 1889, motor bikes from 1902, and cars from 1904.

The list of bicycle manufacturers who have turned to the motor industry is very long. The many other British car manufacturers who started their careers building bicycles include William Morris and Henry Leyland. In the United States, the first car was built in 1892 by the bicycle manufacturers Charles E. and Frank Duryea. The first petrol-driven "cars" indicate the close relationship with the bicycle: Gottlieb Daimler attached an engine to a Michaux-type velocipede in 1885, and the same year, Karl Benz motorized a tricycle.

The Biggest Industry in the Country

If one speaks of the biggest industry in the country, most people visualize an enormous concern with rows of factories and office blocks. But this industry does not look like that—on the contrary, it is extremely decentralized—for, as regards both production volume and number of employees, domestic households form the biggest industry.

Yet for a long time, this enormous "industry" resisted the mechanization of production that has characterized the industrial unit. The tools and implements used in the home remained largely unchanged until the middle of the nineteenth century, and in many areas until even more recently. Kitchen equipment more than anything else had had the same appearance for generations—in many cases for hundreds or even thousands of years. This applies to the fireplace, for example, which had remained fundamentally unchanged since the early Stone Age. The primitive Stone Age houses probably had a fireplace in the middle, an open hearth bordered by a ring of stones. In the ceiling over the hearth was a hole for the smoke. In ancient Rome, houses were built according to the same principle. The room with the fireplace was placed in the centre of the house; the roof above the fireplace rose in the shape of a pyramid towards a hole through which the smoke escaped. These houses were called *atrium*-houses—atrium is derived from the latin word for "black", for the ceiling and walls of the room with the fireplace were probably covered in soot.

Roman technology and architecture spread all over the Empire, that is, southern Central Europe and England. The design of kitchens assumed many different shapes, as Roman construction technology mingled with local tradition and local culinary customs. In the early Middle Ages, the chimney was added, and the kitchen got the form it then retained almost up until this century.

In large kitchens, the fireplace with its chimney had several different functions. It was formed into a large dome at the point where it joined the chimney, and this became a bearing construction taking the weight of the roof. From the actual hearth, where the food was cooked, one or more vents led to flues which heated up the rooms closest to the kitchen. It was a simple and different type of central heating. In the same way, water could be heated in a large boiler adjoining the hearth. And along the wall above the hearth was often a long, narrow trough for drying malt to brew beer.

A separate oven for baking was usually attached to this central heating plant. The baking oven was often constructed so that it was possible to light a fire inside it, being made of natural stone or brick to enable the maximum amount of heat to be retained. When the temperature of the oven was high enough, the fire was left to burn out, and then the ashes were removed, the oven was brushed clean, and the risen dough was put in. In some places the oven door was sealed or blocked to preserve the heat better. This kind of functional kitchen was mainly found on large farms and estates. The kitchens of the common people had the simplest type of fireplace, even if many of them also had a flue and a boiler.

The first improvement since the Middle Ages to the standard of the kitchen occurred in the eighteenth century with the introduction, in the United States, of the cast-iron stove. Its design was inspired by Benjamin Franklin, and it was consequently called the "Franklin stove". It arrived in Europe some decades later and in places acquired the name "cannon stove", which referred to the large cylindrical mantle characteristic of the design. One practical detail was the round top, which had a small lid and several rings to enable the cook to adapt the size of the hole to the pan in use. This idea turned up later in the kitchen range, which was first manufactured in Central Europe in the 1820s. The practical, efficient kitchen range had been developed gradually. The first version was just a top of cast-iron, equipped with legs or built into the open hearth. On the top there were holes for pans and, often, a grate for grilling. Then the top was given sides, and after that it was a short step to a separate enclosed fire. The first kitchen ranges often had gridirons.

The kitchen range was one of the first products of mechanical engineering to find its way into the kitchen, and in most countries this took place in the middle of the nineteenth century. A few decades earlier, in some places even earlier than that, mass-produced cutlery had become widely available. The most successful products of Christopher Polhem's manufacturing works at Stjernsund in the early eighteenth century were plates and cutlery of tin-plated iron. In France knives and forks were made on a semi-industrial scale around the middle of the same century.

When town gas was introduced around 1800 in France and Great Britain this source of energy was tried both for heating and cooking. Gas networks were developed, mainly in the larger British cities, although gas was mainly intended for lighting large, commercial premises for, in an ordinary home, the dangerous, stinking products of combustion were unbearable. Efficient burners did not come until the 1840s, and it was some time before these were accepted, since people were very sceptical about gas light. It is indicative of the time that the Crystal Palace in London, built for the world exhibition in 1851, did not have gas light. The exhibition, a spectacular monument of contemporary technical progress, closed every day at sunset!

In 1855, the German chemist R. W. Bunsen (1811–99) presented a new burner design, in which the gas was mixed with air before being ignited. This made the flame hotter and burnt the gas completely. The Bunsen burner was originally intended for chemical laboratories (where, ever since its invention, it has formed part of the standard equipment), and it was a long time before the principle of the burner was applied to gas cookers. In Britain, the gas cooker had its breakthrough in the 1870s, and this resulted in a great boom both for the gasworks industry and for the industry that manufactured cookers, lamps, and other equipment. During the following decades, gas technology became one of the most important of British exports. But it did not last very long; gas light was soon overtaken by electric lighting.

The first real machine to enter the home was the sewing-machine. It appeared around 1850 in Britain and the United States, and a few years later in other countries. Wherever it was introduced it was hailed as a sensation, with huge headlines in the newspapers. In the textile industry, a high degree of mechanization had been achieved, while the budding clothing industry occupied large numbers of seamstresses, mainly employed in workshops where large quantities of shirts, blouses, and other garments were made manually.

The first working sewing-machine was patented in 1846 by a Boston instrument maker, Elias Howe (1819–67). In the early 1840s, when Howe was young and newly married, he, like so many other men in the same situation, had problems making ends meet. His pretty young wife had to work at home making dresses to order; this was monotonous, tiring work. In his workshop, Howe heard of sewing-machines and was told that they did not work. He then resolved to build a machine which could sew better and faster than the most skilful seamstress. After a lot of hard work, he finished his machine in 1846 and proudly invited potential manufacturers and financiers to a public showing of the miracle. But those who came were the tailors of Boston, who feared that the sewing-machine would take the bread from their mouths! Howe had to run for safety, and the tailors demolished both his machine and the contents of the room.

In other words, the climate in Boston was not too favourable for sewing-machine manufacture. Howe had the good sense to launch the machine in England instead. His success was beyond his expectations and was the result of some skilful marketing which included competitions to determine whether a whole team of dressmakers or one single person using a sewing-machine could get results faster. This was the right approach in the country which gave the world the concept of "sportsmanship". There was no rebellion, either among tailors or seamstresses. The swift triumph of the sewing-machine in Great Britain was repeated in the United States, as Howe had reckoned, and manufacture soon started on both sides of the Atlantic.

Let us not delve too deeply into the continued development of the sewing-machine for the time being and just state that the sewing-machines of today, with their transistorized automation, are little wonders of technology. Instead, let us refer to the enormous impact the sewing-machine has had on the progress of the light engineering industry. Once the original patents had expired, many people started to manufacture sewing-machines. Competition was extremely sharp, and the manufacturers who survived were those who managed to design and manufacture reliable and durable machines. The sewing-machine, with all its moving parts, could not have come at a better time from the point of view of kinematics, which was the current fashion in design technology, and many eminent engineers were attracted by it. Only a few decades after Howe's breakthrough, the market was able to offer machines that were surprisingly reliable for the time, due mainly to the contribution of the German-American Isaac M. Singer (1811–76).

During the last decades of the nineteenth century, as has been mentioned above, bicycle and sewing-machine manufacturers became by far the largest consumers of ball-bearings, something which meant a lot to the development of the ball-bearing industry. Several leading sewing-machine manufacturers also contributed to the technical development of precision-made interchangeable parts—an area in which the armaments industry is generally considered to have been pioneering. Over the years, several arms companies branched out into sewing-machine manufacture. The sewing-machine industry has also encouraged the production of very durable materials with high resistance to wear and tear; for example, powder metallurgical materials and methods to a large extent have been developed within this industry.

A

B

A Elias Howe's lock-stitch sewing-machine. The cloth was fixed on needles mounted along the edge of the baster plate, a thin metal strip. The plate had a row of holes in which a cog-wheel engaged and moved it forward as each stitch was completed. When a seam as long as the plate had been sewn, the plate had to be moved back to its original position and a new length of cloth attached to it. The machine used a bent needle (a) with the eye at the pointed end. (b) Thread reel. The shuttle (c) was given a reciprocating movement by a picker (d), which—like the needle on its lever and the baster plate—had its movements controlled by cams on a shaft which was rotated manually by means of a crank (e).
B In Singer's first sewing-machine, the cloth was fed by an inter-mittently rotating, serrated wheel.

The presser foot was spring-loaded, and the needle had a rectilinear movement.
C Chain-stitch machine by the American James Perry in 1858.
D A modern sewing-machine; explanatory sketch. (a) Wheel for the belt from the engine. (b) Belt,

C

driving the lower shaft (c). (d) Cams which, via linkages (e), drive the feed dog (f). (g) Shuttle and bobbin. (h) Gear drive for g. (i) Guide for the needle bar (j). (k) Presser foot. (l) Thread take-up lever. (m) Disc for tightening the thread. (n) Linkage to drive j and l.
E Lock-stitch. (**1**) When the needle has pierced the cloth (a), the needle thread forms a loop which is caught by the shuttle's hook (b). (**2**) The loop is pulled down and round the bobbin. (**3, 4**) The hook releases the loop, and the stitch is tightened.

E1   E2   E3   E4

D

A

B

A In this American printing-works, the machines were driven by a central water engine, built by Backus Bros. & Co.
B A cutaway drawing of a water engine. Water entered through a pipe (a), was forced through nozzles (b) towards the buckets (c) of the rotating wheel, and finally left through the bottom of the motor. The motor's effect could be varied by closing one or two of the nozzles by means of plungers (d).
C According to the advertisements, water engines, or motors, were excellent power sources for all sorts of household machinery.

C

The Water Engine

The 1870s saw the introduction of a power source which, today, is entirely forgotten, namely, the water engine. It was connected to the water mains and became widespread, especially in cities and areas with favourable water rates.

At the Centennial Exposition in Philadelphia in 1876, different water engines for powering sewing-machines were shown. Most of these engines were designed basically like the Pelton turbine, but there were other types, too. The manufacturers' catalogues describe how more and more domestic machines driven by water engines appeared during the following decades. Fans were introduced at an early stage, as were cream whippers; washing-machines, clothes wringers, ice-cream machines, and many other machines then followed in rapid succession. Water engines were also used in other areas, for instance, for driving bellows for church organs. Larger models with turbine wheels of diameters up to 50 in (125 cm), were used for driving machines in mechanical workshops, printing works, bakeries, and so on. They were also used for driving hand-rope elevators of a type common in the United States around the turn of the century.

The manufacture of water engines ceased during the First World War. New water rates and the competition provided by small electrical engines contributed to the demise of this episode in the history of power engines—an episode which, nevertheless, lasted for about half a century!

The Electric Era

"Epoch" or "epoch-making" are often abused words, but once the public had gained access to electricity, their living conditions changed radically, and one can really talk about the beginning of a new epoch which saw the transformation of the home and, especially, of the kitchen.

It has often been said that domestic electrical appliances appeared at the same time as the first electric power-station, Edison's "package solution", which came into operation in 1882. But the first patent on an electric cooking utensil was, in fact, taken out as early as 1874 by the Englishman St. George Lane-Fox, who is also one of the many inventors of the light bulb. This might suggest that all kinds of cooking and heating apparatuses got off to a flying start when electric power distribution was introduced. This, however, was not the case, mainly because there were no suitable materials available for the resistor elements which were needed to convert the electric current into heat. In 1890, the Carpenter Company in America introduced an element consisting of fine silver-plated threads embedded in an enamel element, which was at first used in domestic irons, the first electric appliance to break through on a large scale. In 1891, the same company introduced a whole range of electric saucepans, coffee makers, and so on; they were put on display under the slogan "the electric kitchen" at the world exhibition in London the same year. The British firm Crompton & Company became licensees of Carpenter's appliances but then, after about a year, started their own development programme, which made them pioneers in this area.

In 1894, a restaurant with a kitchen that was fully electric opened in New York. It was shown to the guests, which is indicative of the great enthusiasm at this time for electricity as a source of heat: it was clean, hygienic, and efficient. Electricity made it possible to apply heat exactly where it was required and where it would be most useful. And there was no soot.

Enthusiasm was, however, considerably subdued by the fact that, initially, electricity was rather expensive, Edison's first customers having to pay as much as 28 cents per kWh, even if their consumption was low. They had only two kinds of light bulbs to choose between—giving 8 or 16 candlepower—and, so far, there were no electrical appliances to connect. When the first municipal electric power-station was put into operation in Stockholm in 1888, the price of energy was about 18 cents per kWh. In those days, people learnt to have the light on in a room when they were actually in it!

In spite of the price of electrical energy, all the "electric heat appliances" (which was the official term) which we have today existed as early as the mid-1890s. But the resistor elements of the early appliances had several shortcomings. After they had been used for some time, the enamel in them became brittle and broke easily. Some important progress was made in 1907, when a new resistor material was patented in the United States. It was a nickel-chrome alloy, which could be heated up to 1,000°C without oxidizing or deforming, and it opened the possibility of producing all kinds of durable cooking appliances, including good electric toasters. The first one consisted of a horizontal open tray with nickel-chrome wire stretched zigzag under a grille. Around 1910, electric cookers appeared in the United States; the first models could be described as connected hot plates. After the First World War, the electric cooker was introduced in Europe. It had a baking oven and often a warming compartment, too. The first electric baking ovens were not much appreciated, since they needed constant watching. Not until 1930 were the ovens equipped with thermostats, so that the desired temperature could be set beforehand and the oven left to look after itself.

In the early 1930s, yet another resistor material came onto the market. It was called Kanthal and had been developed by the Swedish metallurgist Hans von Kanzow, who patented it in 1926. It consisted of an alloy of iron, chromium, and aluminium and could withstand temperatures of at least 1,400°C. The material soon found a wide application as a resistor material in domestic heat appliances, as did the material which came later, Kanthal Super, which consists of molybdenum silicon compounds and can withstand temperatures of up to 1,700°C. Kanthal Super has also been used for industrial electric furnaces and other industrial heat appliances.

Domestic Appliances of the Electric Era

The sewing-machine was the first domestic appliance of the electric era to be electrified. Singer introduced the first electrically powered sewing-machine in 1889, but it was another twenty years or so before electric power took over completely. Around 1890, the first electrically driven fans appeared on the market. Devices for air conditioning, that is, air cooling, were not produced until the end of the 1930s in the United States.

The vacuum cleaner, one of our most common domestic appliances, took so to speak the long way round before it entered the home. The first practicable vacuum cleaner was designed and patented by the Englishman Hubert Cecil Booth in 1901, but various patents of similar machines had already been granted in, for example, Great Britain, the United States, and France. At the turn of the century, some very bizarre designs appeared for machines which, intended to make house-cleaning easier, could be operated by one person only. The inventors very likely found their inspiration for these in the *fin de siècle* style of interior decoration then so popular among the upper classes, a style that was a dreadful dust-collector. At the time, a reception room was more of a textile-hung cave than a room!

The main problem for the vacuum-cleaner designers was the motor. Electric motors for devices with small energy consumption were still both heavy and bulky, and therefore, it was easier to go the whole way and concentrate on large-scale devices. During the first

D This combination of chandelier and fan derives from the 1890s. According to a contemporary reviewer, the apparatus produced "a current of air, directed downwards, which may well contribute to a pleasant coolness in banqueting halls and suchlike".

E An electric iron from the 1890s; (1) cross-section, (2) side view. The resistor element consisted of argentan wire, embedded in a type of enamel.
F "Electric tea-urns" of this type were manufactured by AEG in Berlin in the 1890s. The resistor element was situated round and beneath the inner water-container.
G Even electric frying-pans were sold in the 1890s to those lucky few who were able to make use of the newfangled source of power.

A About 1900, a French inventor was granted a patent for this dust cleaner. The maid was to be equipped with bellows which were mounted underneath her shoes and which sucked air through a nozzle as she walked about the rooms.

B Hubert Cecil Booth was the first to develop a working vacuum cleaner. It was driven by a 5-horsepower piston engine and contained a powerful pump. Shown here is one of the drawings in Booth's patent application.

C A cutaway drawing of a modern vacuum cleaner for home use. Rotating fans (a) force air towards the rear of the machine and cause a vacuum to form at the front, so that air and dust are sucked into the dust container (b). This container is made usually from paper and is surrounded by a supporting basket (c). (d) Hanging floor. A diffuser filter (e), protected by a grid, stops the exhaust air from whirling up dust. (f) Motor. (g) Sound-insulating casing. (h) Radio and television interference screen. (i) Flex reel. (j) Dust indicator. There are hose connections for both sucking (k) and blowing (l), so that the machine also can be used for spray painting and similar tasks.

C

years of the twentieth century, several companies in Great Britain and Central Europe made some large machines for installation in the basements of blocks of flats and public buildings. The suction was caused by a piston pump, and there were suction hoses built into the walls. Each apartment or group of rooms had one or more connections to the suction system, and the extracted dust was filtered through water-flushed filters at the suction pump.

The first vacuum cleaners designed by Booth were rather heavy and expensive. But Booth was as good at selling as he was at designing, and he gained some royal support. One of his first jobs was to vacuum-clean the carpet used in Westminster Abbey for the coronation of Edward VII. Booth went on to vacuum-clean Buckingham Palace—to the great satisfaction of Queen Alexandra—and continued his triumphant course to Kaiser Wilhelm in Berlin, to Czar Nicolas in St. Petersburg, and to the Turkish Sultan Abdul Hamid II.

Just as the vacuum cleaner had ceased to be a curious novelty and had become a luxury item instead, a young Swedish businessman out walking in Vienna came across one. The year was 1908, the man's name was Axel Wenner-Gren (1881–1961). He bought the vacuum cleaner, which cost £55 ($275) and weighed 88 lb (40 kg), and took it with him back to Stockholm, determined to produce a machine that could be handled easily and marketed at a reasonable price. A few years later, Wenner-Gren and his designers introduced the new vacuum cleaner. It weighed only 13 lb (6 kg), cost £15 ($75), and appeared on the market in 1913. Wenner-Gren was certainly not alone in having this business idea, but his vacuum cleaner had a technically new component, the closed fan, which gave the machine a very powerful suction. Such fans are now used in practically all types of vacuum cleaner.

The problem of storing foodstuffs in such a way that they keep longer has been with mankind ever since the early Stone Age. It was discovered in some of the ancient cultures that food keeps longer in a cool than in a warm place, and a means of making ice was also known. When the cities of the Indus culture were excavated, "ice factories" were found—thousands of moulds with covers, made of unglazed porous stoneware. These moulds were filled with water and covered, sprinkled with water, and fanned by a whole bevy of slaves. The evaporation thus brought about caused the temperature in the moulds to fall below freezing point. Unglazed earthen vessels are still in use in Africa and India to cool drinking water. Alexander the Great had huge ice cellars built to safeguard the food for his troops during the long siege of Petra in 329 BC. In ancient Rome, ice was used to cool both food and drink. The ice was taken in the winter from lakes in the Alps, was packed in straw, and transported to the Eternal City. The Romans also knew the art of making freezing mixtures. If, for example, one portion of salt is mixed with ten portions of crushed ice, the temperature of the mixture will be about −10°C.

During the seventeenth and eighteenth centuries, when the natural sciences had begun to flourish, there were many who attempted to construct freezing machines. Various experiments were made with air pumps, after Otto von Guericke had built a workable pump in about 1650. A bowl of water was placed in a vessel, from which the air was pumped out. The temperature of the water then sank so much that it would even freeze. But no one succeeded in explaining the phenomenon. The theoretical basis of thermodynamics was not formulated in an intelligible manner until the nineteenth century (see page 160).

What the scientists dreamed about was a machine that could make ice, demand for which was constantly increasing. But the only source of ice was in nature, and from the middle of the nineteenth century onwards, and well into the twentieth, ice was an important item of trade. Great Britain imported ice from Norway at an early stage, and by the 1850s, an ice company in London had bought a spring lake with clear and pure water near Dröbak on Oslo Fjord. The trade name of the company's product was "Norwegian Crystal Ice", and it was sold in large quantities for several decades.

The Swedes also exported ice to Great Britain, but their main customers were in the United States, especially in New York and the other East Coast cities. It was mainly fishermen on Lake Väner and Lake Vätter who cut up ice in the winter and transported it down the Göta Canal to Gothenburg, whence it was shipped to New York, where it dominated the market. There were, to be sure, several methods known at the end of the nineteenth century for making ice artificially, but this product was never commercially competitive. However, the winter of 1890–91 was an unusually mild one in Sweden, and the following summer in the United States was unusually long and hot. The outcome was a severe shortage of ice in New York, the artificial-ice manufacturers did good business, and the development of freezing machines was stimulated. After this, the export of ice from Sweden to New York declined to nothing after a few years.

The foundations of modern cooling technology were laid in the 1870s in the brewing industry. In Munich, the Bavarian beer capital, they had great problems keeping the beer from spoiling during the summer months. In 1870, a young professor at the Polytechnicum in Munich, Karl von Linde (1842–1920), started experiments on a cooling process which was based on the main principles of thermodynamics. After three years, he had completed an experimental plant which was installed in the Sedlmayr brewery and gave very promising results. After having added further improvements to the plant, von Linde founded a company for making cooling units, on an industrial scale, based on the compression and expansion of a cooling agent, ammonia.

The 1870s saw the introduction of another important novelty in cooling technology, the first refrigerator ship, the *Frigorifique*, which, in 1877, sailed between Buenos Aires in the Argentine and Rouen in France, loaded with meat. The cooling unit on board had been designed by the French engineer Charles Tellier (1828–1913) and was based on the other main principle for the mechanical production of cold, that is, the absorption principle.

Von Linde's and Tellier's cooling devices were both primarily designed to cool large quantities, and the size of the plants reflected this. Not until well into the twentieth century was it realized that it was possible to build cooling devices on a smaller scale. The first refrigerator with a compressor device was made in Chicago in 1913 and was marketed under the name of Domelse. The cabinet was made of wood and had a compressor unit mounted on top, but it did not find any wide application. Iceboxes were well established, and the distribution of household ice was efficiently organized. Only in the 1920s did the manufacture of refrigerators start on a large scale, first in the United States and then in Europe.

Mild winters in Sweden in the early 1920s led to a severe lack of ice and inspired two engineers at the Tekniska Högskolan in Stockholm to develop a new cooling process based on the absorption principle but working without any moving parts. In simplified terms, when the cooling agent, ammonia, was heated, it evaporated and started to circulate. The next step was to let the ammonia condense and then vaporize again in a hydrogen atmosphere. This drew heat from the air in the refrigerator. The whole unit was hermetically sealed and heated by gas or electricity.

The two designers, Baltzar von Platen and Carl Munters, turned to the then well-established vacuum-cleaner manufacturer Axel Wenner-Gren, who bought the invention. Von Platen and Munters

A

D

E Von Platen's and Munters's absorption refrigerator; (**1**) explanatory sketch, (**2**) the unit as mounted in a cupboard. The machine consisted of a closed tube system without movable parts and worked in the following way: a coiled tube (*a*) was heated electrically or by a gas flame. Ammonia water in the tube then started to boil, and the ammonia evaporated. Water and gaseous ammonia left through the top end of the pipe, and whereas the water dripped into the boiler (*b*), the gaseous ammonia escaped through a pipe (*c*) and into the water-cooled condenser (*d*), where it was condensed to liquid ammonia, which ran into a generator (*e*) inside the cupboard (*f*). Hydrogen, too, was introduced into *e*, and the ammonia thus vaporized at a low temperature. For this process, heat was needed, and it was taken from the inside of the cupboard. The

B1

C

m

B2

A This ice-sawing machine, driven by a steam-engine, was constructed in the early 1880s by an American named Sauncry A. Sager.
B In the nineteenth century, ice was stored in large store-houses (**1**), where the blocks were placed a couple of inches apart (to give room for drainage and ventilation) and were covered with hay. The ice was sometimes brought up to the correct level by horse-powered screw elevators (**2**) The ice blocks were then placed at the bottom of the screw (*a*) behind vertical rods (*b*). When the screw rotated to the left, the blocks slid upwards until they reached a vertically adjustable slide

(*c*), on which they slid into the store-house.
C An ice machine from the middle of the 1870s. It was a compressor-type machine, and it worked according to the same principle as the refrigerating plant shown at **F**.
D An early ice machine for home use. In the container were chemical solutions, and the water to be frozen was poured into a small container which was inserted into the larger one. When the machine was set rocking, a chemical reaction which consumed heat was started, and the necessary heat was taken from the water in the inner container.

mixture of hydrogen and gaseous ammonia then sank, because of its weight, and passed on through a pipe (g) to the absorber (h), in which the ammonia was dissolved in water while the hydrogen passed on through a pipe (i) and back to the generator to be mixed again with ammonia. Since heat was released when the ammonia was absorbed by the water, the absorber was surrounded by a water jacket (j) so that the process would not come to a halt. The ammonia water then passed through a pipe (k), which ran partly inside another pipe (l). The hot water which had given off ammonia in the boiler (b) ran through the latter pipe, and gave off its heat to the ammonia water in k while running towards h to reabsorb ammonia. The ammonia water in k was thus already preheated before entering the coiled tube (a) to be heated. (m) Coolant supply and drainage. Ammonia was used as a cooling medium because it is readily absorbed by water. At average room temperature and normal air pressure, one litre of water can absorb about 660 litres of gaseous ammonia. It is also easy to free the ammonia from the water again by heating the solution. Hydrogen, on the other hand, is not water soluble.

E1

E2

F

F It is possible to produce refrigeration by evaporating liquid ammonia at low pressure. This is the principle of the compressor refrigerator. Here is one from the end of the nineteenth century. A steam-engine (a) drives a pump (b) which sucks in gaseous ammonia from one pipe (c) and delivers it in compressed form into another (d). Via a container (e), the gas is led through a check valve (f) and into pipes (g) in a water chest (h). There, the compressed gas is transformed to a liquid and runs via two containers (i, j) down through a check valve (k) and into the generator (l), where the pressure is low and the liquid ammonia evaporates once more. The heat needed for this process is taken from the chamber (m) which is to be kept cold. The gaseous ammonia then flows through a pipe (c) back to the pump (b), which is lubricated by oil from a tank (n). The oil extracted from the pump by the passing compressed gas is again separated from it in e and runs through a pipe (o) which passes through a water chest (p). Finally, the oil passes through a sieve (q) before returning to the pump.

229

finished an experimental version of their cooling machine in 1923, but the invention was not announced until New Year, 1925. One Stockholm newspaper headlined: "No lack of ice this summer".

In the 1930s, different brands of refrigerator became common in most industrial countries. As a rule, the temperature in a refrigerator is 4–8°C, but as early as the 1920s, several manufacturers started to equip their refrigerators with smaller freezing compartments with a temperature of some degrees below freezing point. These were mainly intended for freezing ice-cubes. Attempts were also made to see whether it was possible to store food for any length of time by cooling it to a temperature which was considerably lower than that of the refrigerator. This freezing technique was developed mainly in the United States during the Second World War. It was discovered that most types of food, after quick freezing to −18° or lower, would keep for at least six months.

Deep-freezing technology had a rapid breakthrough in the United States during the years after the War, and in Europe in the 1950s. It caused major changes within the food industry: modes of production, packing techniques, and distribution systems had to be reorganized, the retail trade had to get deep freezes, and so on. And to domestic households the new technique brought considerable changes. Before the appearance of the deep freeze, most countries had had very few vegetables available all year round. Today, fruit and vegetables are frozen in southern Europe, for example, and transported to the north; or are frozen in Florida and southern California and supplied to the rest of North America and even to Europe. Frozen vegetables are available all year round, often as semi-finished products, so that the cooking takes very little time.

Handling the household laundry used to be a labour consuming task, and attempts to mechanize it were made at an early stage. In Christopher Polhem's model chamber there are a couple of different "mechanical" washing-machines, promoted by Polhem but not too successful on the market. In the middle of the nineteenth century, several models of washing-machine were introduced both in Great Britain and the United States. Large steam-driven laundries also started to appear in Great Britain at that time. These became common in the United States in the early twentieth century, and the technology developed for these became the basis of the domestic washing-machine. As early as the 1920s, the large American laundries were highly automated. The first domestic washing-machines appeared around 1930 and were equipped with a programmer for what is today called semi-automatic drive. Considerable improvements of the programmer were made in the early 1930s by Seeburg & Co. in Chicago, a company which was one of the leading juke-box manufacturers in the United States. The juke box, of course, is also a highly automated machine! The basic product of Seeburg & Co., however, sold badly during the depression of the 1930s, and the company then concentrated on programmers for automatic washing-machines. But it was not until the late 1940s that the washing-machine came into common use.

Along with the new electrically powered domestic machines which became popular in the 1930s and 1940s, a new concept was also created: domestic appliances. Many more of these have appeared since then: different kinds of electric mixers, percolators, liquidizers, dish washers, and can openers, to name but a few. Even the electric coffee-mill made a brief guest appearance on the market.

We have frequently mentioned the increased leisure time which is a result of the appearance of machines. But do we really need machines in our leisure time? It seems like the anticlimax of mechanization, but many people want to use their spare time to produce things, and why should they not take advantage of modern labour-saving equipment—electric drills, hobby lathes, etc.?

A

B

A A wool-washing machine constructed by Polhem in the early eighteenth century. The drum is covered with a net of canvas yarn, so that the wool is pulled from the tub and worked between the drum and the upper roll, which was hand-cranked. It is possible to vary the roll's pressure against the drum by putting weights on the board at the bottom.

B An electric washing-machine of the 1920s, made in Germany. The laundry was placed in a perforated drum (a), and water and detergent were added. Then the lid (b) was put on, and a fire was lit in the furnace (c) underneath the machine. An electric motor (d) was switched on and rotated the drum alternately in one direction or the other. (e) Drainage pump.

C A steam-powered washing-machine which was used in the middle of the nineteenth century at St. Pancras Workhouse in London.

D Around the middle of the nineteenth century, this washing-machine (**1**) was constructed in Germany. It was intended for home use and was—as can be seen—manually operated. On the turnable disc was a number of spring-loaded pegs (**2**) which worked the laundry mechanically when the disc was repeatedly thrust down into the tub.

D1   D2

E Cutaway view of a modern, front-loading, cylinder-type washing-machine. It has a rotating inner drum (*a*), which is perforated so that the detergent solution can pass through it, and a fixed drum (*b*). The inner drum regularly changes its direction of rotation, so that the laundry will not become entangled. The machine can be programmed for different types of washing by means of two controls (*c*). (*d*) Dispensers for detergent and conditioner. The door (*e*) is automatically locked by an electro-magnet when the machine is started. When a button (*f*) is pressed, the electricity is cut off and the lock is released. (*g*) Counterweight to balance (*b*). (*h*) Controls. (*i*) Suspension springs for *b*. (*j*) Support for *a*'s shaft. (*k*) Ball bearings. (*l*) Belt pulley for driving *a*. (*m*) Drive belt. (*n*) Heater. (*o*) Drainage pump. (*p*) Shock absorber. (*q*) Filter. (*r*) Access panel for *q*. (*s*) Thermostat sensor. (*t*) Motor.

In this chapter, we have repeatedly referred to the increased leisure time which is the result of the coming of machines. That we should need machines during our leisure time may give the impression of being the anticlimax of mechanization, but then—why shouldn't we use the existing labour-saving hobby machines? Leisure has become an important industry in itself.

A Self-hammering drill, manufactured by AEG. An electric motor (*a*) drives a ventilation fan (*b*) which ensures that the armature and field do not get overheated. The motor also drives a spindle (*c*) via a speed gear (*d*) with bevelled wheels (the topmost one is seen here in cross-section). At the end of

the spindle there are threads for a drill chuck (*e*). (*f*) Hammering mechanism. (*g*) Milled ring for disconnecting *f*. (*h*) Maintenance-free ball bearings. (*i*) Electric switch. The machine is equipped with a radio and TV disturbance eliminator.

B The hammering mechanism in the drill at **A** works in the following way: (**1, 2**) an axially movable hammer (*a*) is being pressed by five rotating ridges (*b*) against a spring (*c*). (**3**) When the hammer has been pushed all the way back, it is disengaged. The number of blows per minute under full load is 4,500.

C Many electric drills can be converted to grinding machines, lathes, and many other tools by means of various attachments, but in recent years, the number of special tools for the amateur has increased. Shown here is a portable circular saw which can be adjusted to give a cutting depth of up to 3 in (75 mm). A shavings suction set, which is connected to an ordinary home vacuum cleaner, can be mounted on the machine.

D Cross-section of an AEG pendulum compass saw with electronic variable-speed transmission. (*a*) Motor. (*b*) Fan. The saw blade (*c*) is driven by a gear transmission and is guided by a backing roller

E This powerful AEG angle grinding machine can be used not only for grinding things like saws and welding seams but also, for example, the cutting of steel spars.
F A Bosch surface grinder, intended for use on metal, wood, and plastic. The number of grinding movements per minute is 20,000.

G The range of uses for this electric Black & Decker planer includes polishing, planing, chamfering, and rabbeting. The cutting depth of the machine is up to 0.06 in (1.5 mm).
H In this paint spray gun, manufactured by Wagner, a pump sucks up the paint under vacuum and sprays it out under high pressure. (*a*) Intake paint filter. (*b*) Nozzle. (*c*) Pump. (*d*) Electromagnet. (*e*) Control for stepless regulation of the intake speed. (*f*) Electric switch.

(*d*). (*e*) Pendulum control with three positions for different types of material. The foundation plate (*f*) can be swung 45° in either direction for angular sawing. The length of the saw blade's stroke is varied by an electronic control device (*g*), so that the power is constant at any number of strokes per minute.

BIBLIOGRAPHY

General

CHARLES SINGER, (ed.) et al., *A History of Technology*, Vol. I–V. New York, London 1954 ff.

M. DAUMAS, (ed.), *Histoire Générale des Techniques*, Vol. I–IV. Paris 1962 ff.

ARTUR FÜRST, *Das Weltreich der Technik*, Vol. I–V. Berlin 1927 ff.

M. KRANZBERG, C. W. PURSELL JR, *Technology in Western Civilization*, Vol. I–II. New York 1967.

W. STEIN, *Kulturfahrplan*. Munich 1974.

Chapter 1

R. J. FORBES, *Man the Maker*. London 1958.

ALBERT NEUBURGER, *Die Technik des Altertums*. Leipzig 1919.

FRANZ MARIA FELDHAUS, *Die Technik der Antike und des Mittelalters*. Leipzig 1931.

W. FLINDERS PETRIE, *The Arts and Crafts of Ancient Egypt*. London 1910.

AHMED FAKHRY, *The Pyramids*. Chicago 1961.

CURT MERCKEL, *Die Ingenieurtechnik im Alterthum*. Berlin 1899 (facsimile edition: Hildesheim 1969).

A. VARAGNAC, *La Conquête des Energies*. Paris 1972.

KENNETH P. OAKLEY, *Man the Toolmaker*. London 1972.

HENRY KJELLSON, *Forntidens teknik*. Third edition: Uppsala 1973. – *Försvunnen teknik*. Third edition: Uppsala 1973.

Chapter 2

GEORGE SARTON, *A History of Science*, Vol. I–II. Cambridge, Mass., 1959.

ABBOT PAYSON USHER, *A History of Mechanical Inventions*. Fourth edition: London 1970.

A. G. DRACHMANN, *Antikkens teknik*. Copenhagen 1950.

DEREK DE SOLLA PRICE, *Gears from the Greeks; The Antikythera Mechanism – A Calendar Computer from c. 80 B. C.* Philadelphia 1974.

JOSEPH NEEDHAM, *Science and Civilization in China*, Vol. I–IV. Cambridge 1965 ff.

MARSHALL CLAGGETT, *The Science of Mechanics in the Middle Ages*. Madison, Wisc., 1961.

WILLIAM A. JOHNSSON, *Christopher Polhem, The Father of Swedish Technology*. Hartford, Conn., 1963.

SAMUEL BUTLER, *Erewhon, or Over the Range*. London 1872.

JACQUES POLIERI, *Scénographie Nouvelle*. Boulogne 1963.

Chapter 3

LEWIS MUMFORD, *Technics and Civilization*. New York 1934.

FRANZ REULEAUX, *Theoretische Kinematik. Grundzüge einer Theorie des Maschinenwesens*. Braunschweig 1895.

EUGENE S. FERGUSON, *Kinematics since the Time of Watt*. Washington 1962.

WALTHER RATHENAU, *Von kommenden Dingen*. Berlin 1917.

GEORG and PAUL AMBER, *Anatomy of Automation*. Englewood Cliffs 1962.

JOHN DIEBOLD, *Automation. The Advent of the Automatic Factory*. New York 1952.

BERTRAND GILLE, *Les Ingénieurs de la Renaissance*. Paris 1964.

HERMANN HALLENDORFF, *Slagsten och automat*. Stockholm 1967.

Chapter 4

R. S. KIRBY et al, *Engineering in History*. New York 1956.

FRANZ MARIA FELDHAUS, *Die Maschine im Leben der Völker*. Basel 1954.

GÖSTA E. SANDSTRÖM, *Byggarna*. Stockholm 1964.
  – *Sextusen år under jorden*. Stockholm 1964.
  – *The History of Tunneling*. London 1963.

R. KELLERMAN, W. TREUE, *Die Kulturgeschichte der Schraube*. Munich 1962.

Chapter 5

WALTER KIAULEHN, *Die eisernen Engel*. Berlin 1935.

H. W. DICKINSON, *A Short History of the Steam Engine*. Second edition: London 1963.

E. J. HOBSBAWM, *Industry and Empire*. London 1969.

TORSTEN ALTHIN, *Gustaf de Laval – de höga hastigheternas man*. Stockholm 1953.

Chapter 6

JOHN AMBROSE FLEMING, *Fifty Years of Electricity*. London 1921.

P. DUNSHEATH, *A History of Electrical Engineering*. London 1961.

Chapter 7

A. CHAPUIS, E. DROZ, *Les Automates*. Zürich 1949.

HELMUT SVOBODA, *Der künstliche Mensch*. Munich 1967.

WERNER ZUR MEGEDE, *Am Wege zur Automation*. Berlin 1974.

OTTO MAYR, *The Origins of Feedback Control*. London 1970.

Chapter 8

PH. and E. MORRISON (ed.), *Charles Babbage and his Calculating Engines*. New York 1961.

WALTER R. FUCHS, *Knaurs Buch der Denkmaschinen*. 1968.

THOMAS P. HUGHES, *Elmer Ambrose Sperry, Inventor and Engineer*. New York 1970.

WILLY LEY, *Rakete und Raumschiffahrt*. Berlin 1944. (Revised edition: *Vorstoss im Weltall, Rakete und Raumschiffahrt*. Wien 1949.)

Chapter 9

W. H. G. ARMYTAGE, *A Social History of Engineering*. London 1961.

M. KRANZBERG, J. GIES, *By the Sweat of Thy Brow*. New York 1974.

W. T. O'DEA, *The Meaning of Engineering*. London 1961.

VICTOR J. DANILOV (ed.), *The Future of Science and Technology*. Chicago 1976.

STUART CHASE, *Men and Machines*. London 1929.

NIGEL CALDER, *Technopolis*. London 1929.

JACQUES ELLUL, *La Technique ou l'Enjeu du Siècle*. Paris 1954.

INDEX